GATE PREP SERIES

GATE

Graduate Aptitude Test in Engineering

2020

Instrumentation Engineering

G. K. PUBLICATIONS (P) LTD.

CL MEDIA (P) LTD.

Edition : 2020

ISBN : **978-93-89121-80-3**

Typeset by : *CL Media DTP Unit*

Administrative and Production Offices

Published by : **CL Media (P) Ltd.**

A-45, Mohan Cooperative Industrial Area,
Near Mohan Estate Metro Station,
New Delhi - 110044

Marketed by : **G.K. Publications (P) Ltd.**

A-45, Mohan Cooperative Industrial Area,
Near Mohan Estate Metro Station,
New Delhi - 110044

For product information :
Visit ***www.gkpublications.com*** or email to ***gkp@gkpublications.com***

GATE
Instrumentation Engineering

Contents

Part II. Numerical Ability

Engineering Mathematics

Technical Section

Mock Tests and Solved Papers

GATE

Graduate Aptitude Test in Engineering

IIT Institutes

Indian Institute of Technology, Mumbai

Indian Institute of Technology, Kharagpur

GATE 2020 will be conducted by
Indian Institute of Technology, Delhi

GATE 2019 conducted by
Indian Institute of Technology, Chennai

Indian Institute of Technology, Guwahati

Indian Institute of Technology, Roorkee

Indian Institute of Technology, Kanpur

Preface

The Graduate Aptitude Test in Engineering (GATE) is an online exam conducted by the IITs for admissions to PG courses in IITs, IISc Bangalore, NITs and many state run universities as well as private universities. Also there are more than 37 PSUs that use GATE score for recruitments. A large number of corporates are also using GATE score as a tool to screen students for placements.

GK Publications is well known as the "publisher of choice" to students preparing for GATE and other technical test prep examinations in the country. We published first set of books in 1994 when GATE exam, both objective and conventional, was conducted in the paper and pencil environment, and used as a check point for entry to post graduate courses in IITs and IISCs. At that time, students had little access to technology and relied mainly on instructor led learning followed by practice with books available for these examinations.

A lot has changed since then!

Today, GATE is conducted in an online only mode with multiple choice and numerical based questions. The score is valid for three years and is used not only for post graduate courses but is also used by major PSUs for recruitment. Today's students have easy access to technology and the concept of a monologue within the classroom has changed to dialogue where students come prepared with concepts and then discuss topics. They learn a lot of things on the go with their mobile devices and practice for mock tests online.

We, as a leading publisher of GATE books, have also embraced change. Today, our books are no more guides only but come with a fully supported mobile app and a web portal. The mobile App provides access to video lectures, short tests and regular updates about the exam. The web portal in additional to what is available on the App provides full length mock tests to mimic the actual exam and help you gauge your level of preparedness. The combination of practice content in print, video lectures, and short and full length tests on mobile and web makes this product a complete courseware for GATE preparation.

We also know that improvement is a never ending process and hence we welcome your suggestions and feedback or spelling and technical errors if any. Please write to us at gkp@gkpublications.com

We hope that our small effort will help you prepare well for the examination.

We wish you all the best!

GK Publications Pvt. Ltd.

About GATE

The Graduate Aptitude Test in Engineering (GATE) conducted by IISc and IITs has emerged as one of the bench mark tests for engineering and science aptitude in facilitating admissions for higher education (M.Tech./Ph.D.) in IITs, IISc and various other Institutes/Universities/ Laboratories in India. With the standard and high quality of the GATE examination in 23 disciplines of engineering and science subjects, it identifies the candidate's understanding of a subject and aptitude and eligibility for higher studies. During the last few years, GATE score is also being used as one of the criteria for recruitment in Government Organizations such as Cabinet Secretariat, and National/State Public Sector Undertakings in India. Because of the importance of the GATE examination, the number of candidates taking up GATE exams has increased tremendously. GATE exams are conducted by the IITs and IISc as a computer based test having multiple choice questions and numerical answer type questions. The questions are mostly fundamental, concept based and thought provoking. From 2017 onwards GATE Exam is being held in Bangladesh, Ethiopia, Nepal, Singapore, Sri Lanka and United Arab Emirates. An Institute with various nationalities in its campus widens the horizons of an academic environment. A foreign student brings with him/her a great diversity, culture and wisdom to share. Many GATE qualified candidates are paid scholarships/assistantship, especially funded by Ministry of Human Resources Development, Government of India and by other Ministries. Indian Institute of Technology Delhi is the Organizing Institute for GATE 2020.

New in GATE 2019 Onward

A new paper Statistics (ST) is added in GATE 2019

Why GATE?

Admission to Post Graduate and Doctoral Programmes

Admission to postgraduate programmes with MHRD and some other government scholarships/ assistantships in engineering colleges/institutes is open to those who qualify through GATE. GATE qualified candidates with Bachelor's degree in Engineering/Technology/Architecture or Master's degree in any branch of Science/Mathematics/Statistics/Computer Applications are eligible for admission to Master/Doctoral programmes in Engineering/Technology/Architecture as well as for Doctoral programmes in relevant branches of Science with MHRD or other government scholarships/assistantships. Candidates with Master's degree in Engineering/ Technology/Architecture may seek admission to relevant PhD programmes with scholarship/ assistantship without appearing in the GATE examination.

Financial Assistance

A valid GATE score is essential for obtaining financial assistance during Master's programs and direct Doctoral programs in Engineering/Technology/Architecture, and Doctoral programs in relevant branches of Science in Institutes supported by the MHRD or other Government agencies. As per the directives of the MHRD, the following procedure is to be adopted for admission to the post-graduate programs (Master's and Doctoral) with MHRD scholarship/ assistantship. Depending upon the norms adopted by a specific institute or department of the Institute, a candidate may be admitted directly into a course based on his/her performance in GATE only **or** based on his/her performance in GATE **and** an admission test/interview conducted by the department to which he/she has applied **and/or** the candidate's academic record. If the candidate is to be selected through test/interview for post-graduate programs, a minimum of 70% weightage will be given to the performance in GATE and the remaining 30% weightage will be given to the candidate's performance in test/interview and/or academic record, as per MHRD guidelines. The admitting institutes could however prescribe a minimum passing percentage of marks in the test/interview. Some colleges/institutes specify GATE qualification as the mandatory requirement even for admission without MHRD scholarship/assistantship.

To avail of the financial assistance (scholarship), the candidate must first secure admission to a program in these Institutes, by a procedure that could vary from institute to institute. Qualification in GATE is also a minimum requirement to apply for various fellowships awarded by many Government organizations. Candidates are advised to seek complete details of admission procedures and availability of MHRD scholarship/assistantship from the concerned admitting institution. The criteria for postgraduate admission with scholarship/assistantship could be different for different institutions. The management of the post-graduate scholarship/assistantship is also the responsibility of the admitting institution. Similarly, reservation of seats under different categories is as per the policies and norms prevailing at the admitting institution and Government of India rules. *GATE offices will usually not entertain any enquiry about admission, reservation of seats and/or award of scholarship/assistantship.*

PSU Recruitments

As many as 37 PSUs are using GATE score for recruitment. It is likely that more number of PSUs may start doing so by next year. Below is the list of PSUs:

MDL, BPCL, GAIL, NLC LTD, CEL, Indian Oil, HPCL, NBPC, NECC, BHEL, WBSEDCL, NTPC, ONGC, Oil India, Power Grid, Cabinet Secretariat, Govt. of India, BAARC, NFL, IPR, PSPCL, PSTCL, DRDO, OPGC Ltd., THDC India Ltd., BBNL, RITES, IRCON, GHECL, NHAI, KRIBHCO, Mumbai Railway Vikas Corporation Ltd. (MRVC Ltd.), National Textile Corporation, Coal India Ltd., BNPM, AAI, NALCO, EdCIL India.

Important :

1. Admissions in IITs/IISc or other Institutes for M.Tech./Ph.D. through GATE scores shall be advertised separately by the Institutes and GATE does not take the responsibility of admissions.
2. Cabinet Secretariat has decided to recruit officers for the post of Senior Field Officer (Tele) (From GATE papers of EC, CS, PH), Senior Research Officer (Crypto) (From GATE papers of EC, CS, MA), Senior Research Officer (S&T) (From GATE papers EC, CS, CY, PH, AE, BT) in the Telecommunication Cadre, Cryptographic Cadre and Science & Technology Unit respectively of Cabinet Secretariat. The details of the scheme of recruitment shall be published in National Newspaper/Employment News by the concerned authority.
3. Some PSUs in India have expressed their interest to utilize GATE scores for their recruitment purpose. The Organizations who intend to utilize GATE scores shall make separate advertisement for this purpose in Newspapers etc.

Who Can Appear for GATE?

Eligibility for GATE

Before starting the application process, the candidate must ensure that he/she meets the eligibility criteria of GATE given in Table.

Eligibility Criteria for GATE 2020

Qualifying Degree	Qualifying Degree/Examination (Descriptive)	Description of Eligible Candidates	Year of qualification cannot be later than
B.E./B.Tech./ B.Pharm.	Bachelor's degree holders in Engineering/ Technology (4 years after 10+2 or 3 years after B.Sc./Diploma in Engineering/ Technology)	Currently in the final year or already completed	2020
B. Arch.	Bachelor's degree holders of Architecture (Five years course)	Currently in the final year or already completed	2020
B.Sc. (Research)/ B.S.	Bachelor's degree in Science (Post-Diploma/4 years after 10+2)	Currently in the 4th year or already completed	2020
M. Sc./ M.A./MCA or equivalent	Master's degree in any branch of Science/Mathematics / Statistics / Computer Applications or equivalent	Currently in the final year or already completed	2020
Int. M.E. / M.Tech. (Post-B.Sc.)	Integrated Master's degree programs in Engineering / Technology (Four year program)	Currently in the 2nd/3rd/4th year or already completed	2022
Int. M.E./ M.Tech. or Dual Degree(after Diploma or 10+2)	Integrated Master's degree program or Dual Degree program in Engineering / Technology (Five year program)	Currently in the 4th/5th year or already completed	2021
Int. M.Sc./ Int. B.S.-M.S.	Integrated M.Sc. or Five year integrated B.S.-M.S. program	Currently in the final year or already completed	2020
Professional Society Examinations (equivalent to B.E./B.Tech./B.Arch.)	B.E./B.Tech./B.Arch. equivalent examinations, of Professional Societies, recognized by MHRD/UPSC/AICTE (e.g., AMIE by Institution of Engineers-India, AMICE by the Institute of Civil Engineers-India)	Completed section A or equivalent of such professional courses	NA

In case a candidate has passed one of the qualifying examinations as mentioned above in 2019 or earlier, the candidate has to submit the degree certificate / provisional certificate / course completion certificate / professional certificate / membership certificate issued by the society or institute. In case, the candidate is expected to complete one of the qualifying criteria in 2020 or later as mentioned above, he/she has to submit a certificate from Principal or a copy of marks card for section A of AMIE.

Certificate From Principal

Candidates who have to submit a certificate from their college Principal have to obtain one from his/her institution beforehand and upload the same during the online submission of the application form.

Candidates With Backlogs

Candidates, who have appeared in the final semester/year exam in 2020, but with a backlog (arrears/failed subjects) in any of the papers in their qualifying degree should upload a copy of any one of the mark sheets of the final year,

OR

obtain a declaration from their Principal along with the signature and seal beforehand and upload the same during the online submission of the application form.

GATE Structure

Structure of GATE

For the GATE examination, a candidate can apply for only one of the 23 papers listed in Tables below. The syllabus for each of the papers is given separately. Making a choice of the appropriate paper during GATE application is the responsibility of the candidate. Some guidelines in this respect are suggested below.

The candidate is expected to appear in a paper appropriate to the discipline of his/her qualifying degree. However, the candidate can choose any paper according to his/her admission plan, keeping in mind the eligibility criteria of the institutions in which he/she wishes to seek admission. For more details regarding the admission criteria in any particular institute, the candidate is advised to refer to the website of that institute.

List of GATE Papers and Corresponding Codes

Paper	Code	Paper	Code
Aerospace Engineering	AE	Geology and Geophysics	GG
Agricultural Engineering	AG	Instrumentation Engineering	IN
Architecture and Planning	AR	Mathematics	MA
Biotechnology	BT	Mechanical Engineering	ME
Civil Engineering	CE	Mining Engineering	MN
Chemical Engineering	CH	Metallurgical Engineering	MT
Computer Science and Information Technology	CS	Petroleum Engineering	PE
		Physics	PH
Chemistry	CY	Production and Industrial Engineering	PI
		Statistics	ST
Electronics and Communication Engineering	EC	Textile Engineering and Fibre Science	TF
Electrical Engineering	EE	Engineering Sciences	XE*
Ecology and Evolution	EY	Life Sciences	XL**

*XE Paper Sections	Code	**XL Paper Sections	Code
Engineering Mathematics (Compulsory)	A	Chemistry (Compulsory)	P
Fluid Mechanics	B	Biochemistry	Q
Materials Science	C	Botany	R
Solid Mechanics	D	Microbiology	S
Thermodynamics	E	Zoology	T
Polymer Science and Engineering	F	Food Technology	U
Food Technology	G		
Atmospheric and Oceanic Sciences	H		

*XE (Engineering Sciences) and **XL (Life Sciences) papers are of general nature and will comprise of Sections listed in the above table. More detailed explanation is given as following pages.

General Aptitude Questions

All the papers will have a few questions that test the General Aptitude (Language and Analytical Skills), apart from the core subject of the paper.

XE Paper

A candidate appearing in the XE paper has to answer the following

1. Section A – Engineering Mathematics
2. GA – General Aptitude
3. Any two of XE sections B to H

The choice of two sections from B to H can be made during the examination after viewing the questions. Only two optional sections can be answered at a time. A candidate wishing to change midway of the examination to another optional section must first choose to deselect one of the previously chosen optional sections (B to H).

XL Paper

A candidate appearing in the XL paper has to answer the following

1. Section P – Chemistry
2. GA – General Aptitude
3. Any two of XL sections Q to U

The choice of two sections from Q to U can be made during the examination after viewing the questions. Only two optional sections can be answered at a time. A candidate wishing to change midway of the examination to another optional section must first choose to deselect one of the previously chosen optional sections (Q to U).

Duration and Examination Type

The GATE examination consists of a single paper of **3-hour** duration that contains **65** questions carrying a maximum of **100 marks**. The question paper will consist of both multiple choice questions (MCQ) and numerical answer type (NAT) questions. The pattern of question papers is discussed in following paragraphs.

The examination for all the papers will be carried out in an ONLINE Computer Based Test (CBT) mode where the candidates will be shown the questions in a random sequence on a computer screen. The candidates are required to either select the answer (for MCQ type) or enter the answer for numerical answer type question using a mouse on a virtual keyboard (keyboard of the computer will be disabled). Each candidate will be provided with a scribble pad for rough work. The scribble pad has to be returned after the examination. At the end of the 3-hour window, the computer will automatically close the screen from further actions.

Pattern of Question Papers

In all the papers, there will be a total of 65 questions carrying 100 marks, out of which 10 questions carrying a total of 15 marks will be on General Aptitude (GA).

In the papers bearing the codes AE, AG, BT, CE, CH, CS, EC, EE, IN, ME, MN, MT, PE, PI, TF and XE, the Engineering Mathematics will carry around **15% of the total marks**, the General Aptitude section will carry **15% of the total marks** and the **remaining 70% of the total marks** is devoted to the subject of the paper.

In the papers bearing the codes AR, CY, EY, GG, MA, PH and XL, the General Aptitude section will carry **15% of the total marks** and the **remaining 85% of the total marks** is devoted to the subject of the paper.

GATE 2020 would contain questions of two different types in various papers:

> (*i*) **Multiple Choice Questions (MCQ)** carrying 1 or 2 marks each in all papers and sections. These questions are objective in nature, and each will have a choice of four answers, out of which the candidate has to mark the correct answer(s).
>
> (*ii*) **Numerical Answer Questions** of 1 or 2 marks each in all papers and sections. For these questions the answer is a real number, to be entered by the candidate using the virtual keypad. No choices will be shown for this type of questions.

Marking Scheme

For **1-mark** multiple-choice questions, **1/3** mark will be deducted for a wrong answer. Likewise, for **2-mark** multiple-choice questions, **2/3** mark will be deducted for a wrong answer. **There is NO negative marking for numerical answer type questions.**

Consult syllabus before proceeding

General Aptitude (GA) Questions

In all papers, GA questions carry a total of **15 marks**. The GA section includes 5 questions carrying **1-mark** each (sub-total **5 marks**) and 5 questions carrying **2-marks** each (sub-total **10 marks**).

Question Papers other than GG, XE and XL

These papers would contain **25** questions carrying **1-mark** each (sub-total **25 marks**) and **30** questions carrying **2-marks** each (sub-total **60 marks**). The question paper will consist of questions of multiple choice and numerical answer type. For numerical answer questions, choices will not be given. Candidates have to enter the answer (which will be a real number, signed or unsigned, e.g., 25.06, – 25.06, 25, – 25 etc.) using a virtual keypad. An appropriate range will be considered while evaluating the numerical answer type questions so that the candidate is not penalized due to the usual round-off errors.

GG (Geology and Geophysics) Paper

Apart from the General Aptitude (GA) section, the GG question paper consists of two parts: Part A and Part B. Part A is common for all candidates. Part B contains two sections: Section 1 (Geology) and Section 2 (Geo-physics). Candidates will have to attempt questions in Part A and either Section 1 or Section 2 in Part B.

Part A consists of **25** multiple-choice questions carrying **1-mark** each (sub-total **25 marks** and some of these may be numerical answer type questions). Each section in Part B (Section 1 and Section 2) consists of **30** multiple choice questions carrying **2-marks** each (sub-total **60 marks** and some of these may be numerical answer type questions).

XE Paper (Engineering Sciences)

In XE paper, Engineering Mathematics section (Section A) is **compulsory**. This section contains **11** questions carrying a total of **15 marks**: 7 questions carrying **1-mark** each (sub-total **7 marks**), and 4 questions carrying **2-marks** each (sub-total **8 marks**). Some questions may be of numerical answer type questions.

Each of the other sections of the XE paper (Sections B through H) contains 22 questions carrying a total of **35 marks**: 9 questions carrying **1-mark** each (sub-total **9 marks**) and 13 questions carrying **2-marks** each (sub-total **26 marks**). Some questions may be of numerical answer type.

XL Paper (Life Sciences)

In XL paper, Chemistry section (Section P) is **compulsory**. This section contains **15** questions carrying a total of **25 marks**: 5 questions carrying **1-mark** each (sub-total **5 marks**) and 10 questions carrying **2-marks** each (sub-total **20 marks**). Some questions may be of numerical answer type.

Each of the other sections of the XL paper (Sections Q through U) contains 20 questions carrying a total of **30 marks**: 10 questions carrying **1-mark** each (sub-total **10 marks**) and 10 questions carrying **2-marks** each (sub-total **20 marks**). Some questions may be of numerical answer type.

Note on Negative Marking for Wrong Answers

For a wrong answer chosen for the **multiple choice questions** (MCQs), there would be negative marking. For **1-mark** multiple choice questions, **1/3** mark will be deducted for a wrong answer. Likewise, for **2-mark** multiple choice questions, **2/3** mark will be deducted for a wrong answer. However, there is **NO negative marking for a wrong answer in numerical answer type questions**.

GATE Score

After the evaluation of the answers, the raw marks obtained by a candidate will be converted to a normalized GATE Score.

The GATE score will be computed using the formula given below.

Calculation of Normalized Marks for CE, CS, EC, EE and ME papers (multi-session papers)

In GATE, examination for some papers may be conducted in multi-sessions. Hence, for these papers, a suitable normalization is applied to take into account any variation in the difficulty levels of the question papers across different sessions. The normalization is done based on the fundamental assumption that "in all multi-session GATE papers, the distribution of abilities of candidates is the same across all the sessions". This assumption is justified since the number of candidates appearing in multi-session papers in GATE is large and the procedure of allocation of session to candidates is random. Further it is also ensured that for the same multi-session paper, the number of candidates allotted in each session is of the same order of magnitude.

Based on the above, and considering various normalization methods, the committee arrived at the following formula for calculating the normalized marks for the multi-session papers.

Normalization mark of jth candidate in the ith session $\widehat{M_{ij}}$ is given by

$$\widehat{M_{ij}} = \frac{\bar{M}_t^g - M_q^g}{\bar{M}_{ti} - M_{iq}}(M_{ij} - M_{iq}) + M_q^g$$

where

M_{ij} : is the actual marks obtained by the jth candidate in i^{th} session

$\bar{M}_t^g$: is the average marks of the top 0.1% of the candidates considering all sessions

M_q^g : is the sum of mean and standard deviation marks of the candidates in the paper considering all sessions

$\bar{M}_{ti}$: is the average marks of the top 0.1% of the candidates in the ith session

M_{iq} : is the sum of the mean marks and standard deviation of the ith session

After evaluation of the answers, normalized marks based on the above formula will be calculated corresponding to the raw marks obtained by a candidate and the GATE Score will be calculated based on the normalized marks.

For all papers for which there is only one session, actual marks obtained will be used for calculating the GATE Score.

Calculation of GATE Score For All Papers

GATE 2020 score will be calculated using the formula

$$\text{GATE Score} = S_q + (S_t - S_q)\frac{(M - M_q)}{(\bar{M}_t - M_q)}$$

In the above formulae

M : marks obtained by the candidate (actual marks for single session papers and normalized marks for multi-session papers)

M_q : is the qualifying marks for general category candidate in the paper

$\bar{M}_t$: is the mean of marks of top 0.1% or top 10 (whichever is larger) of the candidates who appeared in the paper (in case of multi-session papers including all sessions)

S_q : 350, is the score assigned to M_q

S_t : 900, is the score assigned to $\bar{M}_t$

In the GATE 2020 score formula, M_q is usually 25 marks (out of 100) or + s, whichever is larger. Here μ is the mean and s is the standard deviation of marks of all the candidates who appeared in the paper.

After the declaration of results, GATE Scorecards can be downloaded by

(a) All SC/ST/PwD candidates whose marks are greater than or equal to the qualifying mark of SC/ST/PwD candidates in their respective papers, and

(b) All other candidates whose marks are greater than or equal to the qualifying mark of OBC (NCL) candidates in their respective papers.

There is no provision for the issue of hard copies of the GATE Scorecards

The GATE Committee has the authority to decide the qualifying mark/score for each GATE paper. In case any claim or dispute arises in respect of GATE, the Courts and Tribunals in Bangalore alone shall have the exclusive jurisdiction to entertain and settle any such dispute or claim.

candidates appearing in multi-session papers. In GATE, it is ensured that the procedure of allocation of session to candidates is random. Further, it is also ensured that for the same multi-session paper, the number of candidates allotted in each session is of the same order of magnitude.

Based on the above, and considering various normalization methods, the committee arrived at the following formula for calculating the normalized marks, for the multi-session papers.

Normalization mark of j-th candidate in the i-th session $\hat{M}_{ij}$ is given by

$$\hat{M}_{ij} = \frac{\bar{M}_t^g - M_q^g}{\bar{M}_{ti} - M_{iq}}(M_{ij} - M_{iq}) + M_q^g$$

where,

M_{ij} is the actual marks obtained by the j-th candidate in i-th session

$\bar{M}_t^g$ is the average marks of the top 0.1% of the candidates considering all sessions

M_q^g is the sum of mean and standard deviation marks of the candidates in the paper considering all sessions

$\bar{M}_{ti}$ is the average marks of the top 0.1% of the candidates in the i-th session

M_{iq} is the sum of the mean marks and standard deviation of the i-th session

After evaluation of the answers, normalized marks based on the above formula will be calculated corresponding to the raw marks obtained by a candidate and the GATE Score will be calculated based on the normalized marks.

For all papers for which there is only one session, actual marks obtained will be used for calculating the GATE Score.

Calculation of GATE Score for All Papers

GATE 2020 score will be calculated using the formula

$$\text{GATE Score} = S_q + (S_t - S_q)\frac{(M - M_q)}{(\bar{M}_t - M_q)}$$

In the above formula,

M = marks obtained by the candidate (actual marks for single session papers and normalized marks for multi-session papers)

M_q = is the qualifying marks for general category candidate in the paper

$\bar{M}_t$ = is the mean of marks of top 0.1% or top 10 (whichever is larger) of the candidates who appeared in the paper (in case of multi-session papers including all sessions)

S_q = 350, is the score assigned to M_q

S_t = 900, is the score assigned to $\bar{M}_t$

In the GATE 2020 score formula, M_q is usually 25 marks (out of 100) or $\mu + \sigma$, whichever is larger. Here μ is the mean and σ is the standard deviation of marks of all the candidates who appeared in the paper.

After the declaration of results, GATE Scorecards can be downloaded by

(a) All SC/ST/PwD candidates whose marks are greater than or equal to the qualifying marks of SC/ST/PwD candidates in their respective papers, and

(b) All other candidates whose marks are greater than or equal to the qualifying mark of OBC (NCL) candidates in their respective papers.

There is no provision for the issue of hard copies of the GATE scorecard.

The GATE Committee has the authority to decide the qualifying marks/score for each GATE paper. In case any claim or dispute arises in respect of GATE, the Courts and Tribunals in Bangalore alone shall have the exclusive jurisdiction to entertain and settle any such dispute or claim.

GATE Syllabus

Section 1: Engineering Mathematics

Linear Algebra: Matrix algebra, systems of linear equations, Eigen values and Eigen vectors.

Calculus: Mean value theorems, theorems of integral calculus, partial derivatives, maxima and minima, multiple integrals, Fourier series, vector identities, line, surface and volume integrals, Stokes, Gauss and Green's theorems.

Differential Equations: First order equation (linear and nonlinear), higher order linear differential equations with constant coefficients, method of variation of parameters, Cauchy's and Euler's equations, initial and boundary value problems, solution of partial differential equations: variable separable method.

Analysis of Complex Variables: Analytic functions, Cauchy's integral theorem and integral formula, Taylor's and Laurent's series, residue theorem, solution of integrals.

Probability and Statistics: Sampling theorems, conditional probability, mean, median, mode and standard deviation, random variables, discrete and continuous distributions: normal, Poisson and binomial distributions.

Numerical Methods: Matrix inversion, solutions of non-linear algebraic equations, iterative methods for solving differential equations, numerical integration, regression and correlation analysis.

Section 2: Electrical Circuits

Voltage and current sources: independent, dependent, ideal and practical; v-i relationships of resistor, inductor, mutual inductor and capacitor; transient analysis of RLC circuits with dc excitation.

Kirchoff's laws, mesh and nodal analysis, superposition, Thevenin, Norton, maximum power transfer and reciprocity theorems.

Peak-, average- and rms values of ac quantities; apparent-, active- and reactive powers; phasor analysis, impedance and admittance; series and parallel resonance, locus diagrams, realization of basic filters with R, L and C elements.

One-port and two-port networks, driving point impedance and admittance, open-, and short circuit parameters.

Section 3: Signals and Systems

Periodic, aperiodic and impulse signals; Laplace, Fourier and z-transforms; transfer function, frequency response of first and second order linear time invariant systems, impulse response of systems; convolution, correlation. Discrete time system: impulse response, frequency response, pulse transfer function; DFT and FFT; basics of IIR and FIR filters.

Section 4: Control Systems

Feedback principles, signal flow graphs, transient response, steady-state-errors, Bode plot, phase and gain margins, Routh and Nyquist criteria, root loci, design of lead, lag and lead-lag compensators, state-space representation of systems; time-delay systems; mechanical, hydraulic and pneumatic system components, synchro pair, servo and stepper motors, servo valves; on-off, P, P-I, P-I-D, cascade, feedforward, and ratio controllers.

Section 5: Analog Electronics

Characteristics and applications of diode, Zener diode, BJT and MOSFET; small signal analysis of transistor circuits, feedback amplifiers. Characteristics of operational amplifiers; applications of opamps: difference amplifier, adder, subtractor, integrator, differentiator, instrumentation amplifier, precision rectifier, active filters and other circuits. Oscillators, signal generators, voltage controlled oscillators and phase locked loop.

Section 6: Digital Electronics

Combinational logic circuits, minimization of Boolean functions. IC families: TTL and CMOS. Arithmetic circuits, comparators, Schmitt trigger, multi-vibrators, sequential circuits, flip-flops, shift registers, timers and counters; sample-and-hold circuit, multiplexer, analog-to-digital (successive approximation, integrating, flash and sigma-delta) and digital-to-analog converters (weighted R, R-2R ladder and current steering logic). Characteristics of ADC and DAC (resolution, quantization, significant bits, conversion/settling time); basics of number systems, 8-bit microprocessor and microcontroller: applications, memory and input-output interfacing; basics of data acquisition systems.

Section 7: Measurements

SI units, systematic and random errors in measurement, expression of uncertainty - accuracy and precision index, propagation of errors. PMMC, MI and dynamometer type instruments; dc potentiometer; bridges for measurement of R, L and C, Q-meter. Measurement of voltage, current and power in single and three phase circuits; ac and dc current probes; true rms meters, voltage and current scaling, instrument transformers, timer/counter, time, phase and frequency measurements, digital voltmeter, digital multimeter; oscilloscope, shielding and grounding.

Section 8: Sensors and Industrial Instrumentation

Resistive-, capacitive-, inductive-, piezoelectric-, Hall effect sensors and associated signal conditioning circuits; transducers for industrial instrumentation: displacement (linear and angular), velocity, acceleration, force, torque, vibration, shock, pressure (including low pressure), flow (differential pressure, variable area, electromagnetic, ultrasonic, turbine and open channel flow meters) temperature (thermocouple, bolometer, RTD (3/4 wire), thermistor, pyrometer and semiconductor); liquid level, pH, conductivity and viscosity measurement.

Section 9: Communication and Optical Instrumentation

Amplitude- and frequency modulation and demodulation; Shannon's sampling theorem, pulse code modulation; frequency and time division multiplexing, amplitude-, phase-, frequency-, pulse shift keying for digital modulation; optical sources and detectors: LED, laser, photo-diode, light dependent resistor and their characteristics; interferometer: applications in metrology; basics of fiber optic sensing.

General Aptitude

Part I : Verbal Ability

1 CHAPTER

English Grammar

ERRORS IN USE OF ARTICLES

ARTICLES

Indefinite (A, An)	Definite (The)

Use of 'An'

1. Before words beginning with vowel sounds [a, e, i, o, u are called vowels, others are consonants].
   e.g. an apple, an egg, an owl.
2. Before words beginning with silent 'h' but sounds as vowel.
   e.g. an hour, an honourable man, an heir, an honest man.
3. F, H, L, M, N, R, S, X are letters that are not vowels but begin with vowel sound 'M' has the sound of 'em'. So, 'an' is used before abbreviations beginning with vowels of these letters.
   e.g. an M.L.A., an R.A.F., an N.C.C. officer, an F.I.R., an X-ray, an H.E. school, an S.P.

Use of 'A'

1. In the sense of one.
   e.g. He couldn't speak a word to save himself.
   With 'one' (since 'one' begins with sound of 'w')
   e.g. a one-man show, a one-rupee note.
2. Before words beginning with consonant sound
   e.g. a boy, a box, a dog.
3. With Vowel letters having consonant value.
   e.g. a university, a unique article, a euphenism, a unit, a European language
4. With units and rate (per).
   e.g. He earns rupees five hundred a month.
5. In exclamatory expressions before singular countable nouns.
   *e.g. What **a** pretty girl !*
6. When two subjects or articles are thought of as a single unit.
   *e.g. He was ready with **a** cup and saucer.*
7. With certain expressions of quantity.
   *e.g. **a** lot of , **a** dozen, **a** great deal of, **a** couple.*
8. With a person's name to indicate that the person is perhaps unknown to the person addressed.
   *e.g. **A** Mr. roy is at the door.*
9. With a special meal (to celebrate something or in someone's honour).
   *e.g. I called my friends to **a** lunch to celebrate my success.*
10. To make a common noun of a proper noun.
   *e.g. This man is '**a** second Newton'.*
   (This phrase means 'a philosopher as great as Newton')

Use of 'The'

1. When we speak of a particular person or thing already referred to.
   *e.g. I dislike **the** follow.*
2. When a singular noun represents a whole class.
   e.g. The mango is considered the king among fruits.
3. With name of
   (*i*) gulfs, rivers, oceans, islands and mountains e.g. the Himalayas, the Indian ocean, the Persian Gulf, the Red sea, the Andaman islands, the Brahmaputra river.
   (*ii*) Certain books
   e.g. the Vedas, the Puranas, the Bible, the Ramacharitmanas.
   (*iii*) Musical instruments
   e.g. the flute, the violin, the tabla, the trumpet.
   (*iv*) The inventions
   e.g. I hate the telephone for its constant ringing.
   (*v*) Parts of body
   *e.g. He was wounded in **the** leg.*
   (*vi*) Religious groups
   e.g. the Sikhs, the Hindus, the Parsees.
   (*vii*) Names enforcing law
   e.g. the Police, the Navy, the Air Force.
   (*viii*) Political parties
   e.g. the Congress, the Janata Pary, the B.J.P.
   (*ix*) Aeroplanes, ships, trains etc
   e.g. the Makalu (aeroplane), the Vikrant (Ship), the Rajdhani express (train).
   (*x*) Before names of an empire, dynasty or historical event
   e.g. the Gupta dynastry, the Old Stone Age, the First World War, the American Revolution.
   (*xi*) Clubs, foundations etc.
   e.g. the Lion's Club, the Ford Foundation.
   (*xii*) Before common nouns denoting unique things
   e.g. the sun, the sky, the earth, the worl.
   (*xiii*) With superlatives
   e.g. *He is **the** best boy in the class.*
   (*xiv*) With ordinals
   *e.g. He took **the** first taxi that came his way.*
   (*xv*) Before the comparative degree
   e.g. ***The more*** *they get,* ***the*** *more they want.*
   (*xvi*) Before an adjective when the noun is understood
   *e.g. **The** poor would favour him.*

ERRORS IN USE OF NOUNS

1. Nouns which are used in singular form

(i) Scenery, information, furniture, advice, machinery, stationery, news, poetry, business, mischief, fuel, issue, repair, bedding.

e.g. *The **scenery** of this place is worth seeing.*

(ii) Physics, Mathematics, Economics, Classics, Ethics, Athletics, innings, gallows.

e.g. ***Economics** is a very interesting subject.*

(iii) Brick, bread, fruit, word (as 'promise')

e.g. *Let me buy some **fruit**.*

(iv) Words like dozen, score, hundred, thousand, million when preceded by a numeral.

e.g. *He bought ten **dozen** oranges.*

(v) Expressions as a ten-rupee note, a two-hour journey, a four-mile walk, a Five-year plan, a six-man committee etc.

e.g. *A ten-rupee note is lying there.*

2. Nouns used only in plural form

(i) Cattle, police, poultry, people, gentry, peasantry, artillery.

e.g. *The **police have** caught the thief.*

(ii) Scissors, trousers, stockings, spectacles, shorts, alms, remains, riches, goods, measles.

e.g. *My scissors are very sharp.*

3. Nouns used both as singular and plural in the same form

(i) Dear, sheep, fish, apparatus, wages.

e.g. *The **wages** of sin **is** death.*

*The **wages** of the workers **have** been raised.*

*I saw **a sheep** grazing in the field.*

***Sheep are** sold cheaper than goat.*

(ii) Collective nouns as jury, public, team, audience, committee, government, audience, congregation, orchestra.

e.g. *The **team are** looking quite fit.*

*The **team has** not turned up yet.*

4. Use of Collective Nouns

- **crowd** of people
- **herd** of cattle/cows
- **team** of players
- **flight** of birds
- **bouquet** of flowers
- **Shoal/school** of fish
- **bundle** of sticks
- **army** of soldiers
- **flock** of sheep
- **crew** of sailors
- **swarm** of bees
- **garland** of beads
- **gang** of thieves
- **library** of books
- **mob** of angry people
- **fleet** of ships/cruisers
- **pack** of wolves
- **pack** of cards
- **loaf** of bread
- **heap** of corn
- **stock** of grain
- **class** of pupils
- **bunch** of grapes
- **herd** of lions
- **pile** of books
- **hoarde** of nomads
- **block** of flats
- **file** of papers

5. **One of** or **any of** is followed by plural words.

e.g. *I want **one of** the **books** kept on the table.*

***Any of** these **tools** may serve the purpose.*

6. Plural nouns are used with fractions and decimal over 1.

e.g. *It took us one and a half **hours**.*

ERRORS IN USE OF PRONOUNS

Pronouns are words used to replace nouns or noun groups already mentioned.

Nominative/ Vocative case (comes before verb)	***Accurative/ Objective case (comes after verb)***	***Possessive case***	***Reflexive Pronoun***
I	Me	My	Myself
We	Us	Our	Ourselves
He	Him	His	Himself
She	Her	Her	Herself
They	Them	Their	Themselves
Who	Whom	Whose	—

1. The pronoun '*One*' must be followed by '*one's*'.

e.g. *One must do one's duty to one's country.*

2. When 'one' means 'one in number', the pronoun for it is third person singular pronoun (he, she, it).

e.g. *One of them has given up one's studies.* (×)

One of them has given up his studies. (✓)

3. 'Everyone' or 'Everybody' must be followed by 'his'.

e.g. *Everyone should love his country.*

4. Each, every, anyone, anybody must be followed by the singular pronoun of their person.

e.g. *Anyone can do this if he tries.*

5. 'Let' is followed by pronoun in the objective case.

e.g. *Let him go.*

6. 'But' and 'except' are followed by pronoun in the objective case.

e.g. *Everyone attended the party except him.*

'such as' is followed by pronoun in the subjective case.

e.g. *I have no liking for such a man as he.*

7. Verbs like enjoy, avail, pride, resign, apply, acquit, assert, absent are followed by reflexive pronouns.

e.g. *He absented himself from the class.*

We enjoyed ourselves at the party.

8. Reflexive pronouns are never used with verbs keep, conceal, quality, spread, rest, stay.
   e.g. I stayed away from my class.
   He qualified in the test.
9. When first, second and third person singular pronouns (I, you and He) are used together, they are placed in the order : You, he and I.
   e.g. You he and I are neighbours.
   In case of plural pronouns, 'we' comes first, then 'you' and then 'they'.
   e.g. We, you and they must work together.
   But if we have only two persons including first, then first person pronoun is written first.
   e.g. I and Sanjeev have done this job.
10. 'Who' denotes subject and 'whom' denotes object.
   e.g. Who do you think did the job ?
11. 'Whose' is used for persons and 'which' for lifeless objects.
   e.g. This is the table which I was talking about.
12. 'Which' conveys additional information and 'that' explains a certain thing.
   e.g. *I will tell you the first thing which I remember.*
13. The following expressions usually take 'that' in place of 'who' or 'which'.
   Only, Any, It is, All, Superlatives.
   e.g. He is the only man that can do it.
   Any man that listens to you is a fool.
14. '*Each other*' is used for two; '*one another*' for more than two.
   e.g. Rahul and Renu love each other.
15. The complement of the verb *to be*, when it is expressed by a pronoun, should be in Nominative case.
   e.g. It was he who did it.
16. When the same person is the subject and object, it is necessary to use reflexive pronouns.
   e.g. I cut me shaving this morning. (×)
   I cut myself shaving this morning. (✓)
17. When a pronoun is the object of a verb or preposition it should be in objective case.
   e.g. These books are for you and I. (×)
   These books are for you and me. (✓)
   Between him and me there is an understanding.
18. The Relative Pronoun should be placed as near as possible to the antecedent.
   e.g. I have read Shakespeare's works who was a great dramatist. (×)
   I have read the works of Shakespeare who was a great dramatist.(✓)
19. The case of the pronoun following 'than' and 'as' is decided by mentally supplying the verb and completing the sentence.
   e.g. She is taller than I (am)
   I love more than (I love) him.

ERRORS IN USE OF PREPOSITIONS

A preposition is a word used with a noun or pronoun to show its relation to some other word in a sentence.

PREPOSITIONS OF TIME

1. **At** is used
   (a) with a definite point of time
   e.g. I usually get up at 5 o'clock.
   (b) with festivals
   e.g. He will come at Holi.
2. **In** is used :
   (a) with the parts of the day, (with **noon**, use **at**), months, seasons and years
   e.g. He takes a walk in the afternoon.
   (b) with the future tense referring to the period in which action may take place
   e.g. You must be careful in future.
3. **On** is used : with days and dates
   e.g. My brother will arrive on Monday.
4. **By** refers to the latest time at which an action will be over
   e.g. The examination will be over by 5 p.m.
5. **For** is used with perfect continuous tense showing the duration of action
   e.g. I have been here for three years.
6. **Since** is used with the point of time when action begins and continues :
   e.g. He has been ill since last Tuesday.
7. **From** refers to the starting point of action.
   e.g. This water came from a spring.

PREPOSITIONS OF POSITION

1. **At** refers to an exact point.
   e.g. The tourist stayed at the Tourist Hotel.
   He studied at Oxford.
2. **In** refers to larger areas.
   e.g. He lives in Bombay.
3. **Between** is used for two persons or two things.
   e.g. Share these sweets between him and me.
4. **Among** is used with more than two persons or things but before the word which starts with a consonant letter.
   e.g. Divide the sweets among the three boys.
5. **Amongst** is also used with more than two persons or things but before the word which starts with a vowel letter.
   e.g. Divide the sweets amongst us.
6. **Above** is used for **higher than.**
   e.g. The sun rose above the horizon.
7. **Under** is used for **vertically below.**
   e.g. It is shady under the trees.
8. **Below** is used for **lower than.**
   e.g. When the sun sets it goes below the horizon.
9. **Over** is used for **vertically above.**
   e.g. There is an aircraft coming over.
10. **Beneath** means a lower position.
   e.g. the ground was slippery beneath her.

PREPOSITIONS OF DIRECTION

1. **To** is used to express motion from one place to another.
   e.g. We walked to the river and back.
2. **Towards** refers to direction.
   e.g. He saw me running towards him.
3. **Into** denotes motion towards the inside of something.
   e.g. She fell into a ditch.
4. **At** refers to aim.
   e.g. He aimed at the bird.
5. **For** denotes direction.
   e.g. I will leave for Pune today.
6. **Against** shows pressure.
   e.g. She cleaned the edge of her knife against the plate.
7. **Off** refers to separation.
   e.g. He was wiping sweat off his face.
8. **From** refers to the point of departure.
   e.g. The man parted from his friends.

OTHER USES OF PREPOSITION

1. **About** shows nearness.
   e.g. His father is about to retire.
2. **Along** stands for **in the same line.**
   e.g. She led them along the corridor.
3. **After** refers to sequence.
   e.g. She came after me.
4. **Across** means from one side.
   e.g. He blew a cloud of smoke across the table.
5. **Before** stands for **in front of.**
   e.g. A thief was brought before the judge.
6. **Behind** means **at the back of.**
   e.g. She sat down behind the hedge.
7. **Beyond** means **on the farther side of.**
   e.g. This is beyond his power.
8. **Beside** means **by the side of.**
   e.g. *I sat down beside my wife.*
9. **Besides** means **in addition to.**
   e.g. He is guilty of five killings and more besides.

WORDS FOLLOWED BY PREPOSITIONS

A

- abound with
- abstain from
- according to
- accordance with
- accuse of
- accustomed to
- acquaint with
- acquit of
- adverse to
- affiliate to/with
- afflict with
- afraid of
- agree to/on
- aim at
- allegation
- about
- allude to
- alternate with
- alternative to
- angry with
- apply to (body)
- appreciation of
- apprise of
- approximate of
- arraign against
- arrest in
- arrive at/in
- ashamed of
- aspire to/after/at
- associate with
- assure of
- attribute to

B, C

- beset with
- beware of
- blink at
- boast of
- break off
- bungle over
- careful of
- cause of
- centre on
- charge with
- clamour for
- clamp on
- coerce into
- collide with
- comment on
- compatible with
- complain of
- comply with
- compliment on
- composed of
- concur in
- condole with
- conducive to
- confer on
- confirmation of
- conform to
- congratulate on
- conscious of
- contiguity with
- converge on
- convict of
- co-opt to
- cope with
- correspond with
- converge on
- convict of
- co-opt to
- cope with
- correspond with
- cost of
- credit with
- criticism of
- cure of

D

- decide on
- debar from
- delight in
- deliberate on
- denude of
- depart to
- departure for
- depend on/upon
- deprive of
- derive from
- derogate from
- derogatory to
- desist from
- despair of
- detrimental to
- devoid of
- difficulty in
- diffident of
- disabuse of
- disagree with
- disgusted with
- dispose of
- dissociate from
- divest of
- divide into
- dressed in

E

- effort in (—ing)
- election to
- embroil in
- emphasis on
- employ in
- enamoured of
- encroach on
- endow with
- enlarge on
- engage in
- essential to
- expostulate with
- extend to

F, G, I

- fed up with
- focus on
- forbid to
- fraught with
- fritter in
- full of
- give to
- grapple with
- good at
- identical with
- impose on
- incur on
- indict for
- indifferent to
- indulge in
- infatuate with

- infect with
- infest with
- information on
- insensible to
- insist on
- interest in
- intimate to
- intoxicate with
- intrigue with
- intrude on
- investigation of
- involve in

J, K, L

- jealous of
- jeer at
- jump at
- just to
- knock at
- lash at
- lay siege to
- leave for
- live on (income)
- long for

O, P

- oblivious of
- operate on
- opinion on
- overcome with
- pay a call on
- persevere in
- persist in
- plan for
- plead for
- pleased with
- prefer to
- preference for
- present with
- prevent from
- priority to
- probe into
- prohibit from
- proud of

R, S

- recoil from
- reconcile to
- remand to
- remonstrate with
- repent of
- replete with
- reply to
- research on
- resolve on/to
- sail for
- satiate with
- satisfied with
- sentence to
- sick of
- side with
- sparing
- square with
- stickler for
- subversive of
- succeed in
- sue for
- superior to
- supply with
- sure of
- surprised at
- susceptible to
- suspect of
- sympathy for

T, U, V, W

- testify to
- thank for
- throw at
- tinker at
- tire of
- trace to
- trample on
- translate into
- try to (do)
- unequal to (the task)
- vie with
- vote for (a candidate)
- wait for (or await)
- ways of
- wish for

SOME SPECIAL CASES

- absolve from (blame) / of (sin)
- admit to (hospital, place, class)
- appear for (examination)/at
- begin on (not from Sunday)
- blow down (the roof)/off (steam)/over (pass off)
- buy in (market, store)/at (shop)
- come/go by (bus, train)
- come into (conflict with)
- compare with (one man height with another's)/to (one man's height to a building)
- consist of (to denote the substance)/in (define the subject)
- deal with (somebody)/ in (goods)
- die of (disease)/from (other causes)
- differ from (to be different from)/with (to disagree)
- due to (used after a noun, not after a verb)
- entrust to (somebody a job)
- entrust (somebody) with a job)
- fill with (enthusiasm)/ in (a form)
- fire at (when not hit)/on (when injured to killed)
- glad of (the news)/at (having arrived safe)
- hostility to/in hand (being attended to)/ on hand (in possession of)
- ingratiate (oneself) with
- inquire into (matter) / of (person)/about. often (thing)
- invest with (power/in (blank)
- key of (the door)/to (a problem)
- level (charge) against.
- look at (consider evidence)/to (somebody for aid)
- meeting (called) for (Sunday)
- motive in (doing)/for (an act)
- neglect of (duty)/in (doing a thing)
- nominated to (board)
- noted for (good things)
- owing to (used after a verb, not after a noun)
- part from (people)/with (things)
- preventive for priority
- put out (light)/off (trip)
- Shoot at (when injured)/in (leg, head)
- take up (job)/to (a hobby)
- taste of (sensation)/for (liking)
- tear off (remove)/up (to pieces)
- vest with (The P.M. is vested with power to ...)/ in (Powers are vested in the P.M. to ...)

ERRORS IN USE OF CONJUNCTIONS

1. **Scarcely or hardly** is followed by **when**.
   e.g. *Hardly had I slept when the telephone rang.*
2. **Though** is followed by **yet**.
   e.g. *Though he worked hard yet he failed.*
3. **No sooner** is followed by **than.**
   e.g. *No sooner did we reach there than it began to rain.*
4. **Not only** is followed by **but also.**
   e.g. *Not only did he help her, but also dropped her home safely.*
5. **Lest** is negative and so should not be followed by **not**; it is followed by **should**.
   e.g. *Work hard lest you should fail.*
   If **would or may** is used in place of **should**, then **else** should be used in place of **lest.**
   e.g. *Give him water, else he may die.*
6. **Both** is complemented by **and**, not by **as well as.**
   e.g. *Both Amit and Satish are good at Science.*

7. **So.....as** is used in negative sentences, whereas **as** .....**as** is used in affirmative sentences.

   e.g. He is not so tall as his brother.

8. **Other** is followed by **than**.

   e.g. He has no other claim than his wealth.

9. The word **reason** is not followed by **because,** but by **that.**

   e.g. The reason why he didn't go was that his mother was ill.

10. **Because** denotes reason.

    in order that denotes purpose.

    e.g. He went to the doctor because he was ill.

11. Words such as regard, describe, define, treat, mention, depict, portray are followed by **as**.

    e.g. I regard her as my sister.

12. **As** and **since** are also used to express reason.

    e.g. As he was not there, I spoke to his brother.

13. **Neither** is followed by **nor** and both are followed by same auxiliary verb.

    e.g. Neither Ravi nor Raju was seen.

14. **Either** is followed by **or**.

    e.g. Either you are or he is to blame.

15. **Unless, until, if not, so that** should not be followed by **not.**

    e.g. Wait here until I come.

16. **If** is used in conditional series

    Whether is used in uncertainty.

    e.g. I don't know whether he was present.

17. To express **time before** use **until** or **till** and to express **how long** use **as long as.**

    *e.g. Work **as long as** you live.*

18. **Such** is followed by **as.**

    e.g. We talked about such subjects as the weather.

    Such is followed by **that** if we emphasize degree of something by mentioning the result.

    e.g. The extent of the disaster was such that not a single man could survive.

19. **Like** is followed by pronoun; **as** is followed by a clause.

    e.g. He runs like me.

ERRORS IN SUBJECT–VERB AGREEMENT

1. Singular subject must have singular verb.

   e.g. He writes; I write.

2. Plural subject must have plural verb.

   e.g. They write; We write.

3. Two subjects joined by **and** will always take a plural verb.

   e.g. The doctor and nurse work together.

   The doctor and nurses work together.

   The doctors and nurse work together.

4. Two singular subjects joined by **or** or **nor** will take a singular verb.

   e.g. A doctor or a nurse is working in the hospital.

5. A singular subject and a plural subject joined by **or** or **nor** will take a singular or plural verb depending on which subject is nearer the verb.

   e.g. Neither Deepak nor his friends are joining the tour.

   Neither his friends nor Deepak is joining the tour.

6. If the subject is singular and the predicate is plural, the verb must agree with its subject and not its predicate.

   e.g. Physical conditioning and mental attitude are winning combination.

   The winning combination is physical conditioning and mental attitude.

7. Indefinite pronouns such as

   someone, somebody, each, nobody, anyone, anybody, one, no one, everyone, everybody, either, neither, etc. always take a singular verb.

   e.g. Each of my friends calls me once a month.

8. Indefinite pronouns which indicate more than one (several, few, both, many) always take plural verbs

   e.g. Both of the books required careful reading.

9. Collective nouns (fleet, army, committee, crowd) are singular when the group works together as a unit and hence take singular verbs.

   e.g. The jury has reached its verdict.

10. Collective nouns are plural when the members of the group are acting individually and hence take plural verbs.

    e.g. The jury have argued for five hours.

11. Some words (such as news, measles, mumps etc.) end in —*s* but represent a single thing. These words need singular verbs.

    e.g. The 7 o'clock news is about to begin.

12. Some words (such as scissors, trousers, spectacles, shorts etc.) end in —*s* and seem to represent a single thing, but they are two parts to that single thing. These words take plural verbs.

    e.g. *The scissors are on the table.*

13. Words (such as politics, ethics, athletics etc.) that end in —ies are usually singular and hence take singular verbs.

    e.g. *Mathematics is his favourite subject.*

    But these words are singular when they refer to a study, science or practice. If these words have modifiers with them, they become plural and hence take plural verbs.

    e.g. *His politics are somewhat divided.*

14. Title of the books need singular verbs.

    e.g. *Great Expectations is a good book.*

15. Some nouns in the plural form represent an amount, a fraction, or an element of time. These nouns are considered singular and hence take singular verbs.

    e.g. *Sixty minutes is enough to finish this work.*

16. If two subjects are joined together by **as well as** the verb will act according to the first subject.

    e.g. *Students as well as the teacher are playing.*

17. The subject **Many a .....** is always followed by the singular verb.
   e.g. Many a man was drowned in the sea.
18. If two subjects are joined together by **with** the verb will act according to the subject.
   e.g. The principal together with his students was seeing the final match.
19. If subject is **The number of ...** use a singular verb.
   e.g. The number of books is very small.
20. If the subject begins with **A number of ....** (= many), use a plural verb.
   e.g. A number of books are missing.
21. If two subjects express one idea, use a singular verb.
   e.g. Bread and butter is wholesome food.
22. When adjectives such as **much, less, little** and **more** are used as nouns, they must have a singular verb.
   e.g. A little of good habits makes our life happy.

ERRORS IN THE USE OF TENSES

The changed forms of a verb that indicate time of the action are called **tenses** of the verb.

1. When the verb in the Principal Clause is in the Past tense, the verbs of the Subordinate Clauses should be in the Past tense.
   e.g. He said that he had finished his work.
2. But a past tense in the Principal Clause may or may not be follwoed by the Past tense in the sub-ordinate clause if the latter expresses unviersal or habitual truth.
   e.g. The teacher said that the earth revolves round the sun.
3. Any tense may be used in the sub-ordinate clause if it gives a comparison by using the word **than.**
   e.g. The teacher liked Anil better than he liked me.
4. Any tense can be used when the subordinate clause is in a quotation.
   e.g. I said, "I am going to Delhi today".
5. The Present Perfect Tense (subject + has/have + V_3) cannot be used when an expression of Past time (yesterday, last night, ago etc.) is used.
   e.g. We wrote to you yesterday about his mother.
6. In conditional sentences the subordinate clause, beginning with if, is generally in Present or Past tense but not in future tense.
   e.g. If I go to Delhi, I shall see the Red Fort.
7. With the phrases **as if** and **as though**, Past tense and plural form of the verb should be used.
   e.g. He behaves as if he were a millionaire.
8. Past Perfect tense (subject + had + V_3) is used when a sentence refers to two past actions and one of them occurs earlier than the other.
   e.g. When my uncle came to India I had passed M.A.
9. Words like **usually, generally, often, whenever** etc. are used in Present Indefinite tense.
   e.g. I usually go to play cricket.
10. If the action began in the past and is still continuing in the present, use Present Perfect tense (Subject + has/have + been V_1 + ing).
   e.g. I have been reading in this class for two months.
11. Do not use the Future or the Present tense after such expressions as **suppose that, it is high time, it is time, as if** etc.
   e.g. It is high time that you went home.

GERUND & INFINITIVE

Use of Gerund (V_1 + ing)

1. When an action is being considered in general sense, gerund is used as subject.
   e.g. Swimming is his favourite pastime.
2. Gerund is used as subject in short prohibitions
   e.g. Smoking is prohibited.
3. Verbs such as help, stop, detest, avoid, finish, dread, mind, prevent, dislike, risk, deny, recollect, no good, no use, resent, delay, postpone, defer, enjoy, forgive, pardon, excuse, suggest etc. are followed by the gerund.
   e.g. It is no use saying.
4. A gerund is placed after a preposition :
   e.g. She is tired of walking.
   But the prepositions **except** and **but** are followed by an infinitive.
5. A gerund, showing physical activity, is put after **come** or **go**
   e.g. He is to go shooting.
6. Nouns, followed by a gerund, are put in the possessive case.
   e.g. He hates his brother's drinking everyday.
7. If there is a sense of dislike, hesitation, risk etc. in a sentence, use gerund.
   e.g. I dislike reading cheap novels.
8. Adjective before gerund are put in the possessive case.
   e.g. I do not mind your going away.
9. **With a view to** is always followed by a gerund and not an adjective.
   e.g. We go to school with a view to studying.

INFINITIVE (TO + V_1)

1. Verbs such as learn, remember, promise, swear, consent, neglect, refuse, purpose, try, endeavour, attempt, fail, care, hope, decide, hesitate, prepare, determine, undertake, manage, arrange, seem, forget, agree, regret etc. are followed by infinitive:
   e.g. We endeavour to invite such persons.
   We promise to do this work soon.
2. Verbs such as order, tell, invite, oblige, allow, permit, compel, teach, instruct, advise, tempt, encourage, urge, request, show, remind, forbid, warm etc. are followed by object and infinitive
   e.g. The teacher instructed the students to go.
3. Verbs or expressions like—will, can, do, must, may, let are followed by infinitive without **to**
   e.g. Let him do this work.

4. Expressions like would rather, would sooner, rather than, sooner than, had better are followed by infinitive without **to**

   e.g. You had better tell him.

5. **See** can be used with infinitive or without it

   e.g. Go to see him.

6. The infinitive is used after adjectives like delight, angry, glad, astonished

   e.g. I was astonished to find him.

7. The verb know is never directly followed by the infinitive. It is followed by a conjunction and then the infinitive

   e.g. Do you know to play the harmonium ? (×)

   Do you know how to play the harmonium ?(✓)

8. **...had better** is always followed by the infinitive without to

   e.g. You had better to stop taking the medicine which has harmful side-effects. (×)

   You had better stop taking the medicine which has harmful side-effects.(✓)

9. Infinitive is not used with **to** after verbs of perception like-to see, to hear, to feel, to watch etc.

   e.g. I saw him cross the street.

10. Avoid using split-infinitive :

    e.g. He planned to not go on a vacation this year.(×)

    He planned not to go on a vacation this year.(✓)

AUXILIARY VERBS

These are helping verbs.

1. **May** implies permission, doubt or possibility.

   e.g. It may rain tonight.

2. **Might** is the past form of **may** but it does not necessarily represent past time.

   Often it implies more doubt than **may.**

   e.g. If the clouds are salted, the rains might come.

3. **Can** is used to express ability.

   e.g. He can do this work.

4. **Could** is the past form of **can** but it does not necessarily represent past time. Often it implies a more uncertain condition than **can.**

   e.g. She could refuse, but she never does.

5. **Should** is the past form of **shall**. It is used in sub-ordinate clauses after **in case** and sometimes after **if.**

   e.g. I shall get some money in case brother comes.

   It is also used in past sentences with **so that** and **in order that :**

   e.g. He turned the stereo down very low so that he should not disturb him.

- **Should** can also be used in sub-ordinate clauses when we are expressing the idea that something must be done or is important. The fact is that this happens after verbs like command, order, request, insist, suggest, advise etc. & after adjectives like important, vital, essential, necessary, eager, anxious, concerned etc.

  e.g. I am anxious that nobody should be hurt.

- **Should** is also used in sub-ordinate clauses in sentences where we express personal reactions to events. We express our reactions with words like—amazing, interesting, shocked, sorry, normal, natural, it's a shame etc.

  e.g. I am sorry you should think I did it on purpose.

6. **Must** is followed by the infinitive without **to.**

   e.g. I must get up at five tomorrow.

   Must is used to give strong advice or orders :

   e.g. I really must stop drinking.

   Must is used to say that we are sure about something :

   e.g. I am in love—that must be nice.

   Must is used after a past reporting verb.

   e.g. I felt there must be something wrong.

7. **Should** and **Ought** have similar meanings, but **ought** is followed by **to. Ought to** has a more objective force and is used when we are talking about laws, duties and regulations.

   e.g. We ought to see her tomorrow.

   Should and **ought to** can also be used to talk about strong probability.

   e.g. He has bought thirty pints of whisky—that ought to be enough.

   To talk about things which did not happen, although they were supposed to, we use **should** and **ought to** with the perfect infinitive :

   e.g. The taxi should have arrived at 8.30.

8. **Do** is used to make question and negative forms of ordinary verbs.

   e.g. Do you know Rajat ?

   Do is used in question-tags and short answers

   e.g. Does he know I am here ? —Yes, he does.

   Do is used before an imperative to make the request more persuasive

   e.g. Do accompany us.

   Do is not used in questions which have **who, what or which** as their subject

   e.g. Who said that ?

   What happened ?

   Which one's that ?

   But if **who, what** or **which** is the object of the sentence, **do** is used

   e.g. Who did you see ?

   Which department do you want ?.

   Do is also used with an **—ing** form when we want to talk of activity that takes a certain time or that is repeated. In this case we find determiners like —the, my, some, much, etc.

   e.g. I usually do most of my washing on Sundays.

ERRORS IN USE OF ADJECTIVES

Word qualifying a noun or pronoun is called an **adjective.**

1. The adjectives ending in —ior (prior, junior, senior, superior, inferior, posterior) take 'to' and not 'than' after them.

   e.g. He is senior to me.

2. Some adjectives like unique, ideal, perfect, extreme, complete, universal, infinite, perpetual, chief, entire, round, impossible are not compared.
   e.g. *It is the most unique book.* (×)
   It is a unique book (✓)
3. Comparative degree is used in comparing two things or persons.
   e.g. *It is the better of the two books.*
   Superlative degree is used in comparing more than two things or persons.
   e.g. He *is the best* of the three boys.
4. Double comparatives and double superlatives must not be used.
   e.g. *He is more wiser than his brother.* (×)
   He is wiser than his brother. (✓)
5. When we compare two qualities in the same person or thing, the comparative ending —er is not used.
   e.g. *You are wiser than old.* (×)
   You are more wiser than old. (✓)
6. When two adjectives in superlative or comparative degree are used together, the one formed by adding 'more' or 'most' must follow the other adjective.
   e.g. *He is more intelligent and wiser than his brother.* (×)
   He is *wiser* and *more intelligent* than his brother. (✓)
7. When two adjectives with differing degrees of comparison are used they should be complete in themselves.
   e.g. *He is as wise, if not wiser than his brother.* (×)
   He is as wise as, if not wiser than his brother. (✓)
8. When two changes happen together, comparative degree is used in both.
   e.g. *The higher you go, the cooler you feel.*
9. When comparative degee is used in superlative sense, it is followed by *'any other'*.
   e.g. *Kapil is better than any bowler.* (×)
   Kapil is better than any other bowler. (✓)
10. Compound adjective formed by adding 'worth' is placed after the noun it qualifies.
    e.g. *This is a worth seeing sight.* (×)
    This is a sight worth seeing. (✓)
11. When two or more comparatives are joined by **'and'**, they must be in the same degree.
    e.g. *Russel was one of the wisest and most learned men of the world.*
12. When there are two objects of comparison, then to avoid repetition of noun, 'that' is used for singular noun and 'those' for plural noun.
    e.g. *The climate of Ranchi is better than Gaya.* (×)
    The climate of Ranchi is better than that of Gaya. (✓)
13. If comparison is made by using 'other', 'than' is used instead of 'but'.
    e.g. *He turned out to be no other than my old friend.*
14. **Likely, certain** and **sure** are followed by **'to'**.
    e.g. *He is likely to win.*

CONFUSED ADJECTIVES

1. **Beautiful** is used for woman; **handsome** for man.
   e.g. *He is a handsome youth.*
   She is a beautiful girl.
2. **Less** refers to quantity, **fewer** denotes number.
   e.g. *He takes no less than a litre of milk.*
   They have fewer books than I have.
3. **Last** is the final one; **Latest** is last upto the present.
   e.g. *Z is the last letter of the alphabet.*
   This is the latest edition of the book.
4. **Each** is used for one of two or more things; **every** is used for more than two things, taken as a group.
   e.g. *Each of the two boys was wrong.*
   He read every book I gave him.
5. **Older** refers to persons or things.
   e.g. *This tree is older than that.*
   Elder refers to persons only.
   e.g. He is my elder brother.
6. **Little** means 'not much'.
   A little means 'at least some'.
   e.g. *He slept little.*
   He slept a little.
7. **Farther** means 'more distant'.
   Further means 'additional'.
   e.g. *Mumbai is farther than Delhi.*
   I shall get further information.
8. **Latter** means the second of two things.
   e.g. *Keats and Byron are romantic poets, but I prefer the latter.*
   Later refers to time.
   e.g. *She came to school later than I.*

ERRORS IN USE OF ADVERBS

Adverbs are words that add information about the verb.

1. Adverbs of manner, place and time are usually placed after the verb or object.
   e.g. *He was running slowly.*
   Reena does her work carefully.
2. Adverbs of frequency (e.g. never, often, usually, always, rarely, etc.) and other adverbs (like already, almost, just, quite, nearly, hardly) are normally put between subject and verb. If there is more than one word in the verb, they are put after first word.
   e.g. *He often goes to Delhi.*
   I quite agree with you.
   But if verb is 'am', 'is' and 'are', adverb is placed after the verb.
   e.g. I am *never* late for school.
3. The adverb *enough* is placed after the adjective.
   e.g. *She is cunning enough to tackle him.*
4. 'Ever' is sometimes incorrectly used for 'never'.
   e.g. *He seldom or ever tells a lie.* (×)
   He seldom or never tells a lie. (✓)

5. Adverb 'not' shouldn't be used with words having negative meaning.
   e.g. *The teacher forbade me not to go.* (×)
   The teacher forbade me to go. (✓)
6. The word 'only' should be placed immediately before the word it modifies.
   e.g. *Hari answered only two questions.*
7. An adverb should not be used before an infinitive.
   e.g. *He quickly did the job.* (×)
   He did the job quickly. (✓)
8. The auxiliaries *have to* and *used to* come after the adverb.
   e.g. *He often used to go to cinema.*

SOME MORE TIPS OF USAGE

1. Avoid the use of **lots, a lot** and **a whole lot** in the sense of **much** or **a great deal.**
   e.g. *He expects to earn a lot of money on his sale of farm products.* (×)
   He expects to earn a great deal of money on his sale of farm products. (✓)
2. **Plenty** is a noun and is always followed by **of.**
   e.g. *He has plenty of room in his old house.*
3. **Due to** always modifies a noun and not a verb. Hence, no sentence should begin with **due to,** it must be used only after some form of the verb **to be**.
   e.g. *His death was due to natural causes.*
4. **Alright** is incorrect, use **all right.**
   e.g. *I think it is a quite alright if you stay.* (×)
   I think it is quite all right if you stay. (✓)
5. If the gender is not determined, use the pronoun of the masculine gender.
   e.g. If anybody has got the book let her return it (×)
   If anybody has got the book let him return it (✓)
6. When two nouns are closely connected, apostrophe —'s will be written after second only.
   e.g. *Ravi's and Shikha's mother is ill.* (×)
   Ravi and Shikha's mother is ill. (✓)
7. **Both** and **as well as** cannot be used together in the same sentence because both convey the same sense.
   e.g. *Both Pinki as well as Pooja are beautiful* (×)
   Both Pinki and Pooja are beautiful. (✓)
8. **Supposing** and **if** cannot be used together in the same sentence.
   e.g. *Supposing if he fails, what will he do ?*(×)
   If he fails, what will he do ? (✓)
9. **Endure** suggests **suffering,** usually in silence and **tolerate,** means to allow it with some degree of approval.
   e.g. *He endured the pain without complaint.*
   He will not tolerate laziness.
10. Avoid the use of **had** with **ought.**
   e.g. *You had not ougth to do it.* (×)
   You ought not do it. (✓)
11. **As** is used when one compares things or persons of equal or about equal size or quality, **so** is used when one compares things or persons which are unequal.
   e.g. *He weighs as much as his father.* (×)
   He does not weigh so much as his father. (✓)
12. Avoid using the double comparative and double superlative.
   e.g. *This pen is the most costliest in this store.* (×)
   This pen is the costliest in this store. (✓)
13. **Cent per cent** and **word by word** are wrong uses. The real terms are **hundred percent** and **word for word.**
14. When two comparatives are used in a sentence for proportion, **the** is used before both of them.
   e.g. *The higher we go, the cooler it is.*
15. **Do the needful** is incorrect, write **do what is necessary.**
16. Never say **family members,** say **members of the family.**
   e.g. *His family members have gone to Mumbai.* (×)
   The members of his family have gone to Mumbai (✓)
17. **Else** is always followed by **but** and never by **than.**
   e.g. *It is nothing else but your pride which makes you say such a thing.*
18. **All of** is used in conversation, not in standard written English.
   e.g. *She gave all of her antiques to the museum* (×)
   She gave all her antiques to the museum (✓)
19. **Talking terms** is wrong, use **speaking terms.**
   e.g. *He is not on talking terms with his brother* (×)
   He is not on speaking terms with his brother (✓)
20. Verbs like resemble, recommend, comprise, order, accompany, reach, join, shirk, attack, emphasise, discuss, fear, succeed, resist, request, assist, benefit, afford etc. are not followed by any preposition when used in the active voice.
   e.g. *He emphasised on the need for discipline.* (×)
   He emphasised the need for discipline. (✓)
   She will accompany with you to Chennai. (×)
   She will accompany you to Chennai. (✓)
21. The phrase **type of, sort of** and **kind of** do not follow **a** or **an.**
   e.g. *What kind of a friend are you ?* (×)
   What kind of friend are you ? (✓)
22. A full hour number follows **o'clock,** but in fraction it does not follow.
   e.g. *He left this place by 10.40 o'clock.* (×)
   He left this place by 10.40. (✓)
23. **Yet** means up to the present time something that has not happened.
   e.g. *His brothers are not married even yet.*

EXERCISE – I

MCQ TYPE QUESTIONS

Directions (Q. 1 – 20)

In this section you are required to spot errors in sentences. Read each sentence to find out whether there is any error in any of the parts. Errors, if any, are only in one of the parts. No sentence has more than one error. When you detect an error, in any of the parts of the sentence, choose the corresponding alphabet.

1. (*a*) The scenery here is not good
(*b*) I have lost my furnitures
(*c*) We have received no information
(*d*) He told his mother this news
(*e*) No error.

2. (*a*) Please excuse the trouble
(*b*) He took pains over his work
(*c*) In India there are many poor
(*d*) Scouts wear shorts
(*e*) No error.

3. (*a*) I spent the holidays with my family
(*b*) Gone him some blotting paper
(*c*) Write this in your note book
(*d*) Gone my kind regards to all
(*e*) No error.

4. (*a*) We had a good play of football
(*b*) We saw a play
(*c*) We like acting
(*d*) He is a tall man
(*e*) No error.

5. (*a*) The boy was wearing a new suit
(*b*) He took offence at this
(*c*) Please put your sign here
(*d*) Please put your signature here
(*e*) No error.

6. (*a*) He is my cousin brother
(*b*) We are all brothers
(*c*) I spent the middle of the day working
(*d*) He had a large amount of money
(*e*) No error.

7. (*a*) He got into bad company
(*b*) One of my servant tells me
(*c*) Some of my servants tell me
(*d*) The front of the house
(*e*) No error.

8. (*a*) I had a bathe in the sea
(*b*) I have hurt a toe
(*c*) Each of these days play games
(*d*) None of us went
(*e*) No error.

9. (*a*) A man should work hard
(*b*) A man should not waste his time
(*c*) A boy should not waste his time
(*d*) Here is my cup; please fill it
(*e*) No error.

10. (*a*) Have you a pencil ? I have not got one
(*b*) Is he coming ? Yes I think so
(*c*) He enjoyed during the holidays
(*d*) I asked for my pencil but he did not give it to me
(*e*) No error.

11. (*a*) The boy who does best he will get a prize
(*b*) Whoever does best will get a prize
(*c*) Who did this ? I
(*d*) He and I are brothers
(*e*) No error.

12. (*a*) I went for a walk with some friends
(*b*) He is wiser than I
(*c*) The master tested the boy if he could read English
(*d*) I shall see whether the brakes work well
(*e*) No error.

13. (*a*) Everyone is frightened when he sees a tiger
(*b*) None of us has seen him
(*c*) People strave when they have no money
(*d*) The size of the shoe should be the same as this shoe
(*e*) No error.

14. (*a*) Everyone knows this
(*b*) Every man knows this
(*c*) These all mangoes are ripe
(*d*) He hold the book in both hands
(*e*) No error.

15. (*a*) I have no any friends
(*b*) Neither man has come
(*c*) All idle man should do some work or other
(*d*) Shakespeare is greater than any other poet
(*e*) No error.

16. (*a*) Open your book at page six
(*b*) He is in class ninth
(*c*) This article costs ten rupees
(*d*) He came a second time
(*e*) No error.

17. (*a*) King George VI
(*b*) He is older than I
(*c*) He is better than I
(*d*) Raipur is Hotter thanSimla
(*e*) No error.

18. (*a*) He is worse than I
(*b*) A horse is more useful than a car
(*c*) He gets a small salary
(*d*) I our library the number of books is less
(*e*) No error.

19. (*a*) He is the more clever of the two
(*b*) He is the cleverer of the two
(*c*) From the three he is more clever
(*d*) Of the two plans this is the better
(*e*) No error.

20. (*a*) He is becoming strong
(*b*) There is a very good teacher in that class
(*c*) He will spend the rest of his life here
(*d*) This is a sight worth seeing
(*e*) No error.

Directions (Q. 21 – 30)

Each question below has a sentence, from the choices provided, identify the one which best restates the given sentence and mark its number as the answer.

21. Uneasy lies the head that wears a crown.
(*a*) Uneasily lies the head that wears a crown.
(*b*) Uneasy is the head wearing a crown.
(*c*) The head which wears the crown lies uneasy.
(*d*) The head which is wearing the crown lies uneasy.

22. Had I been a little early, I would not have missed the train.
(*a*) Had I been a little early, I would not have missed the train.
(*b*) Had I been a little early than now, I would not have missed the train.
(*c*) Had I been a little earlier, I would not have missed the train.
(*d*) Had I only been a little early than now, I would not have missed the train.

23. She is as intelligent as her sister if not more.
(*a*) She is more intelligent than her sister.
(*b*) She is as intelligent as her sister if not more intelligent.
(*c*) She and her sister are equally intelligent.
(*d*) She is less intelligent than her sister.

24. You will not succeed unless you are optimistic.
(*a*) You will not be successfull unless you are optimistic.
(*b*) You will not succeed until you are an optimist.
(*c*) You will not succeed unless you don't be optimistic.
(*d*) You will not succeed unless you don't be an optimistic.

25. The students were advised to follow the instructions of the examiner.
(*a*) The instructions of the examiner were followed by the students.
(*b*) The students followed the examiner's instructions.
(*c*) The examiner's instructions were advised to be followed by the students..
(*d*) It has been advised to the students that they should follow the examiner's instructions.

26. Despite being ill, he attended the classes.
(*a*) Despite of being ill, he attended the classes.
(*b*) Despite his illness, he attended the classes.
(*c*) Inspite of his being ill, he attended classes.
(*d*) The classes were attended by him inspite of being ill.

27. That man is aggressive by nature is a hard fact of life and no one can deny it.
(*a*) That man is aggressive by nature is a hard fact of life which none can deny.
(*b*) That man is aggressive by nature is a hard fact of life and no one can deny it.
(*c*) That man is aggressive by nature is a hard fact of life and not one can deny.
(*d*) That man is aggressive by nature is hard for anyone to deny.

28. He is as old as I.
(*a*) He is as old as me.
(*b*) He and I are equally old.
(*c*) He and I are equally older.
(*d*) Both he and I are of the same age.

29. A man becomes wiser with age and experience.
(*a*) A man as he is aged and experienced becomes wiser.
(*b*) A man with age and experience becomes wiser.
(*c*) A man as he is aged and experienced becomes the wiser.
(*d*) With age and experience, a man becomes wiser.

30. Hazards of life cannot be negated but they can be quite effortlessly evaded.
(*a*) Hazards in life can be quite effortlessly evaded and completely nullified.
(*b*) Hazards of lilfe cannot be avoided but they can be made ineffective.
(*c*) To be made ineffective, hazards of life must be avoided.
(*d*) It may not be possible to nullify the hazards of life but they can quite easily be avoided.

Directions(Q. 31 –40)

Each sentence is broken into four parts a, b, c, d. Mark the part which has an error. Ignore errors of punctuation.

31. (*a*) Every man, woman
(*b*) and child
(*c*) in the house on fire
(*d*) have been saved.

32. (*a*) One of the
(*b*) best lawyers in town
(*c*) have been
(*d*) hired.

33. (*a*) I request you (*b*) kindly to
(*c*) come to me (*d*) immediately.

34. (*a*) My friend's mother
(*b*) is the principal
(*c*) of a
(*d*) girl's college.

35. (*a*) To succeed in these tests
(*b*) it is absolutely necessary
(*c*) for us
(*d*) to aim for speed and accuracy.

36. (*a*) The aeroplane is a
(*b*) powerful instrument of war
(*c*) and their peacetime role
(*d*) is just as important.

37. (*a*) The depletion of ozone in the atmosphere
(*b*) is a reminder to all of us
(*c*) both in the developed and developing world
(*d*) that they cannot continue to use contraptions which give out noxious gases.

38. (*a*) Scotsmen are notorious
(*b*) for their thrift
(*c*) and he is the butt
(*d*) of many exaggerated jokes.

39. (*a*) A mixed economy
(*b*) is it in which
(*c*) the public sector
(*d*) and the private sector co - exist.

40. (*a*) Although the beaver's hind feet
(*b*) are webbed for swimming
(*c*) their front feet
(*d*) are small and handlike.

Directions(Q. 41 – 45)

Given below are five sentences, each of which may or may not have errors.
Mark (a), if there is only one error.
Mark (b), if there are two errors.
Mark(c), if there are more than two errors.
Mark (d), if there is no error.

41. "This feels like one big dream," says a weary American woman to her husband, as they sit in a plane flying home.

42. The worst mistake a non - profit organization can make is to take all the money it is given and be beholden to doing things on someone else's terms.

43. Although most hotels in Bhutan has a distinctly local flavour, some pander with the perceived tastes of Western tour groups - and can be rather bland.

44. The crustaceans find sanctuary in the jords, often clinging to the walls in large, gregarious groups.

45. In these tropical lowlands the Maya built an agrarian civilization that eventually supported one of the highest population densities in the pre - industrial America.

Directions (Q. 46–50)

Each of the following questions has two sentences A and B.
Mark (a), if you think sentence A has an error.
Mark (b), if you think sentence B has an error.
Mark (c), if you think both sentences A and B have errors.
Mark (d), if you think neither sentence has an error.

46. A. The boss himself or his secretary answer the phone on Saturday.
B. Neither the quality nor the prices have changed.

47. A. The members re-commended that all delinquents be fined.
B. A stone lying in one position for a long time may gather moss.

48. A. Until I received that letter, I was hoping to have had a visit from Krishnan.
B. Follow the main road for a mile; then you need to take the next road at the left.

49. A. The people to watch closely are the ones ruling behind the political scene.
B. Give the tools to whoever can use them best.

50. A. The magazine has been published continuous since 1951, and it has the funniest cartoons you can possibly imagine.
B. I feel glumly when I read his nightmarish tales.

EXERCISE – II

(QUESTIONS FROM PREVIOUS GATE EXAMS)

MCQ TYPE QUESTIONS

2015

1. Choose the statement where underlined word is used correctly
(*a*) The minister <u>insured</u> the victims that everything would be all right.
(*b*) He <u>ensured</u> that the company will not have to bear any loss.
(*c*) The actor got himself <u>ensured</u> against any accident.
(*d*) The teacher <u>insured</u> students of good results

2. The following question presents a sentence, part of which is underlined. Beneath the sentence you find four ways of phrasing the underline part. Following the requirements of the standard written English, select the answer that produces the most effective sentence.

Tuberculosis, together with its effects, <u>ranks one of the leading causes of death</u> in India.
(*a*) ranks as one of the leading causes of death
(*b*) rank as one of the leading causes of death
(*c*) has the rank of one of the leading causes of death
(*d*) are one of the leading causes of death

3. Choose the statement where underlined word is used correctly.
(*a*) When the teacher eludes to different authors, he is being <u>elusive</u>
(*b*) When the thief keeps eluding the police, he is being <u>elusive</u>
(*c*) Matters that are difficult to understand, identify or remember are <u>allusive</u>
(*d*) Mirages can be <u>allusive</u>, but a better way to express them is illusory

4. Fill in the blank with the correct idiom/phrase.
That boy from the town was a ________ in the sleepy village.
(*a*) Dog out of herd (*b*) Sheep from the heap
(*c*) Fish out of water (*d*) Bird from the flock

5. Select the appropriate option in place of underlined part of the sentence.
<u>Increased productivity necessary</u> reflects greater efforts made by the employees.
(*a*) Increase in productivity necessary
(*b*) Increase productivity is necessary
(*c*) Increase in productivity necessarily
(*d*) No improvement required

6. Ram and Shyam shared a secret and promised to each other that it would remain between them. Ram expressed himself in one of the following ways as given in the choices below. Identify the correct way as per standard English.
(*a*) It would remain between you and me
(*b*) It would remain between me and you
(*c*) It would remain between you and I
(*d*) It would remain with me

7. What is the adverb for the given word below? Misogynous
(*a*) Misogynousness (*b*) Misogynity
(*c*) Misogynously (*d*) Misogynous

8. In the following sentence certain parts are underlined and marked P, Q and R. One of the parts may contain certain error or may not be acceptable in standard written communication. Select the part containing an error. Choose D as your Answer: if there is no error.
The student corrected <u>all the errors</u> (P) that <u>the instructor marked</u> (Q) on the <u>answer book</u> (R)
(*a*) P (*b*) Q
(*c*) R (*d*) No Error

9. Choose the statement where underlined word is used correctly.
(*a*) The industrialist had a <u>personnel</u> jet.
(*b*) I write my experience in my <u>personnel</u> diary.
(*c*) All <u>personnel</u> are being given the day off.
(*d*) Being religious is a <u>personnel</u> aspect.

10. Out of the following four sentences, select the most suitable sentence with respect to grammer and usage:
(*a*) Since the report lacked needed information, it was of no use to them.
(*b*) The report was useless to them because there were no needed information in it.
(*c*) Since the report did not contain the needed information, it was not real useful to them.
(*d*) Since the report lacked needed information, it would not had been useful to them.

11. Select the alternative meaning of the underlined part of the sentence.
The chain snatchers <u>took to their heels</u> when the police party arrived.
(*a*) took shelter in a thick jungle
(*b*) open indiscriminate fire
(*c*) took to flight
(*d*) unconditionally surrendered

2014

12. Which of the following options is the closest in meaning to the word underlined in the sentence below?
In a democracy, everybody has the freedom to <u>disagree</u> with the government.
(*a*) dissent (*b*) descent
(*c*) decent (*d*) decadent

13. 'Advice' is ________.
(*a*) a verb (*b*) a noun
(*c*) an adjective (*d*) both a verb and a noun

14. Which of the options given below best completes the following sentence?
She will feel much better if she ________.
(*a*) will get some rest
(*b*) gets some rest
(*c*) will be getting some rest
(*d*) is getting some rest

15. <u>While trying to collect</u> (I) an envelope <u>from under the table,</u> (II) <u>Mr. X fell down</u> (III) and <u>was losing consciousness.</u> (IV)
Which one of the above underlined parts of the sentence is NOT appropriate?
(*a*) I (*b*) II
(*c*) III (*d*) IV

16. Which of the following options is the closest in meaning to the phrase underlined in the sentence below?
It is fascinating to see life forms <u>cope with</u> varied environmental conditions.
(*a*) Adopt to
(*b*) Adapt to
(*c*) Adept in
(*d*) Accept with

17. In a press meet on the recent scam, the minister said, "The buck stops here". What did the minister convey by the statement?
(*a*) He wants all the money
(*b*) He will return the money
(*c*) He will assume final responsibility
(*d*) He will resist all enquiries

2013

18. The professor (I) ordered to (II) the students to go (III) out of the class. (IV)

Which of the above underlined parts of the sentence is grammatically incorrect?

(a) I (b) II
(c) III (d) IV

19. Choose the grammatically INCORRECT sentence:
(a) He is of Asian origin.
(b) They belonged to Africa.
(c) She is an European.
(d) They migrated from India to Australia.

20. Choose the grammatically CORRECT sentence:
(a) Two and two add four.
(b) Two and two become four.
(c) Two and two are four.
(d) Two and two make four.

21. All engineering students (I) should learn mechanics, (II) mathematics and (III) how to do computation. (IV)

Which of the above underlined parts of the sentence is not appropriate?

(a) I (b) II
(c) III (d) IV

2012

22. Choose the most appropriate alternative from the options given below to complete the following sentence :

Suresh's dog is the one ______ was hurt in the stampede.

(a) that (b) which
(c) who (d) whom

23. Choose the grammatically **INCORRECT** sentence :
(a) They gave us the money back less the service charges of Three Hundred rupees.
(b) This country's expenditure is not less than that of Bangladesh.
(c) The committee initially asked for a funding of Fifty Lakh rupeesr, but later settled for a lesser sum.
(d) This country's expenditure on educational reforms is very less.

24. One of the parts (A, B, C, D) in the sentence given below contains an ERROR. Which one of the following is **INCORRECT** ?

I requested that he should be given the driving test today instead of tomorrow.

(a) requested that
(b) should be given
(c) the driving test
(d) instead of tomorrow

ANSWERS

EXERCISE – I

MCQ Type Questions

1. (b)	**2.** (a)	**3.** (e)	**4.** (a)	**5.** (c)	**6.** (a)	**7.** (b)	**8.** (c)	**9.** (e)	**10.** (c)
11. (a)	**12.** (c)	**13.** (d)	**14.** (c)	**15.** (a)	**16.** (b)	**17.** (d)	**18.** (d)	**19.** (c)	**20.** (a)
21. (c)	**22.** (a)	**23.** (c)	**24.** (a)	**25.** (d)	**26.** (b)	**27.** (a)	**28.** (d)	**29.** (d)	**30.** (d)
31. (d)	**32.** (c)	**33.** (b)	**34.** (d)	**35.** (d)	**36.** (c)	**37.** (d)	**38.** (c)	**39.** (b)	**40.** (c)
41. (a)	**42.** (d)	**43.** (b)	**44.** (d)	**45.** (d)	**46.** (a)	**47.** (d)	**48.** (c)	**49.** (d)	**50.** (c)

EXERCISE – II

MCQ Type Questions

1. (b)	**2.** (a)	**3.** (b)	**4.** (c)	**5.** (c)	**6.** (a)	**7.** (c)	**8.** (b)	**9.** (c)	**10.** (a)
11. (c)	**12.** (a)	**13.** (b)	**14.** (b)	**15.** (d)	**16.** (b)	**17.** (c)	**18.** (b)	**19.** (c)	**20.** (d)
21. (d)	**22.** (a)	**23.** (d)	**24.** (b)						

EXPLANATIONS

EXERCISE – I

MCQ TYPE QUESTIONS

21. Uneasily does not denote a state, which is required in the context. 'Wearing a crown' denotes that the head is doing it, 'is wearing' denotes a continuous action, which is impossible, as the head cannot do it. Hence choice (*c*) restates the given sentence correctly.

22. All the statements have the correct combination of tenses. So, we need not check it. Let us find the errors in other statements. 'Early than now' and 'earlier' suggest that I reached early; in that case, I did not miss the train. So, choices (*b*), (*c*), and (*d*) do not state the same idea as in the question statement. Hence correct choice is (*a*).

23. The given statement states that both she and her sister are equally intelligent. This is given in statement. Hence correct choice is (*c*).

24. 'Unless' denotes condition, 'until' denotes time. Choice (*b*) has adverb clause of time. With unless, another negative is not used. 'Unless ..... don't' is wrong. So, Choices (*c*) and (*d*) are incorrect. Hence correct choice is (*a*).

25. Choices (*a*) and (*b*) state the same idea [(*a*) – passive voice; (*b*) Active voice] that the students followed the instructions, which differs from the question statement. Instructions cannot be advised. So, choice (*c*) is meaningless. Choice (*d*) states the context of the given statement aptly.

26. Despite means inspite of. Despite of is a wrong usage. 'His' need not be used in choice (*c*), as the sentence is about one person. Choice (*d*) means that the classes were ill. Hence correct choice is (*b*).

27. Choice (*a*) best restates the given sentence, though choice (*b*) is the repetition of the given statement. 'Not one can deny' in choice (*c*) and for any one to deny' in choice (*d*) make them incorrect. Hence correct choice is (*a*).

28. In this type of comparison, the pronouns are in subjective case 'Me', which is in objective case is wrongly used in choice (*a*). Equally is not used with 'old'. Of the same age is the correct expression. Hence correct choice is (*d*).

29. Choice (*a*) and (*b*) mean that the prerequisite for wisdom is age and experience, which is incorrect. Just by growing old and working for a long period, a person cannot improve his wisdom. 'The wiser' is used only when we compare wisdom with some other quality. Choice (*d*) is the correct restatement of the given one. Hence correct choice is (*d*).

30. The given statement says that one cannot completely nullify the hazards of life but they can be evaded quite easily. Choice (*a*) which states that hazards cannot be avoided is wrong (*b*) states that hazards can be made ineffective and hence this is also wrong (*c*) does not convey the meaning as stated and hence it too is incorrect. (*d*) correctly restates the idea and is our answer.

31. Every man refers to a singular noun, therefore.... has been saved.

32. has

33. drop 'kindly'

34. Girl's implies possessive noun, whereas the college is meant for girls.

35. aim at, aim for is wrong usage.

36. delete their - add : its

37. delete they - add : we

38. delete he is - add : they are.

39. delete it - add : that

40. delete their - add : its.

41. One sits 'on' a plane.

42. There are no errors.

43. Hotels 'have' and some pander 'to....'

44. There are no errors in this sentence.

45. There are no errors.

48. (A) hoping to have a visit;

(B) .... then take the next road to

50. (A) continuously; (B) glum.

EXERCISE – II

MCQ TYPE QUESTIONS

1. *Insured*–the person, group, or organization whose life or property is covered by an insurance policy.

Ensured–to secure or guarantee

3. Elusive: Difficult to answer.

4. From the statement, it appears that boy found it tough to adapt to a very different situation.

8. The is not required in 'Q'.

22. The correct answer is 'that'. In the given sentence 'was hurt in the stampede' determines which dog belongs to Suresh.

2 CHAPTER Sentence Completion

WHAT ARE SENTENCE COMPLETION PROBLEMS?

Sentence completion problems test your vocabulary skills as well as your reading ability. Unlike the reading comprehension questions, which require you to read long passages, these problems contain a single sentence expressing a complete idea that can be understood without any additional information. Each sentence contains one or two blanks, indicating that one or two words are missing. You are then presented with five words or phrases, or five pairs of words or phrases if there are two blanks in the sentence. From these choices, you need to select the words or phrases that fit into the blanks to best complete the sentence. To make the correct choice, you will need to be able to understand the main idea of the sentence and the logical structure of the sentence. Next, you will need to know the definitions of the words in the answer choices.

BASIC STRATEGIES FOR SENTENCE COMPLETION PROBLEMS

Strategy 1

The first strategy is to break the sentence down into the main clause and introductory clause or phrase in order to identify the relationship it expresses. For example, consider the following:

In a hospital setting, hand washing is primarily a______measure.

(*a*) prophylactic (*b*) pseudocyetic
(*c*) protensive (*d*) propaedeutic

The main clause declares that hand washing is primarily a measure. However, preceding the declaration is a condition or constraint expressed in an introductory phrase, "a hospital setting." This phrase sets the contextual field within which the main clause is to be understood. If you generalize from your knowledge, it would seem that any measure promoted in a hospital should result in good health. Only one of the answers would result in this. That is answer (*a*) in which *prophylactic* means "prevents disease."

Strategy 2

A second strategy is to attend to sets, whether a set of synonyms or antonyms or special word groups. For example, consider the following:

Even when a______ mother was made available to the infant chimpanzee, the infant detected the______and reacted with high anxiety.

(*a*) hedonistic.. contrivance
(*b*) vagrant.. apostasy
(*c*) veteran.. ruse
(*d*) pretender.. interference

Nothing in a common sense association supports the pairing of *hedonistic* and *contrivance, vagrant* and *apostasy, veteran* and *ruse,* or *pretender* and *interference*. The only set of related words is *surrogate* (meaning substitute) and *substitution.*

Strategy 3

Pay attention to the words that control the figurative field of the sentence. Consider the following passage:

In seventeenth-century France, private and public opinion portrayed the physician as a vulture of greed, circling the sick and dying, battening off the suffering of the afflicted, and ______the remains of his prey.

(*a*) spending (*b*) devouring
(*c*) retreating from (*d*) decrying

Clearly the correct answer is (*b*), devouring. The key words that control the figurative field are *vulture, circling,* and *battening.* Read the items carefully and make sure that the completed sentence is meaningful, that it makes sense.

EXERCISE – I

MCQ TYPE QUESTIONS

Directions for Q. 1 to 41 : *In each of the following sentences, a part/parts of the sentence is left unfinished. Beneath each sentence, four different ways of completing the sentence are indicated. Choose the best alternative among the four.*

1. For some of our ruling politicians, social justice has apparently come to mean that __________.
(*a*) they have a right to plunder public money from the treasury
(*b*) they have a right to the plunder of public money from the treasury
(*c*) theirs is the right to plunder public money from the treasury
(*d*) the right is theirs to plunder public money from the treasury

2. Some critics believe that Satyajit Ray never quite came back to the great beginning he made in his path-breaking film Pather Panchali. __________ have endured decades of well-travelled bad prints to become a signpost in cinematic history.
(*a*) The bizarre history of its misty origins
(*b*) Its haunting images
(*c*) Its compelling munificence
(*d*) The breathtaking awe it inspires

3. __________ , the more they remain the same.
(*a*) The less the dynamism
(*b*) The more things change
(*c*) The more pronounced the transformation
(*d*) The more the merrier

4. Revenues are likely to register a dramatic increase if ____________ on the hundred million people who are said to comprise the risingIndian middle class.
(a) a flat tax is collected
(b) a flat tax is placed
(c) taxes at a flat rate are charged
(d) tax is imposed at a flat rate

5. I am an entertainer. ____________ I have to keep smiling because, deep in my heart, laughter and sorrow have an affinity.
(a) Even if I have tears in me
(b) Despite conditions of extreme adversity
(c) Inspite of misery around me
(d) Although I have yet to make it big

6. The stock market is probably ____________ And the way the markets are plunging says a lot about investor confidence.
(a) an ideal indication of the health of public sentiment
(b) the least imperfect mechanism for judging the quantity of the sentiment of the public.
(c) the best indicator of public sentiment
(d) the best barometer to assess the sentiment of the public

7. Home is ____________ one has yet to improve.
(a) a discovery over which
(b) a certain over which
(c) an invention on which
(d) an institution upon which

8. The highest reward for a man's toil is not what he gets for it but what ____________.
(a) he makes out of it.
(b) he gets for others.
(c) he has overcome through it.
(d) he becomes by it.

9. An act of justice closes the book on a misdeed; an act of vengeance ____________.
(a) reopens the first chapter
(b) writes an epoilogue
(c) writes one of its own
(d) opens new books

10. The trail is the thing , not the end of the trail. Travel too fast and you miss ____________.
(a) all you are travelling for.
(b) all the sights you are supposed to see.
(c) the very excitement of your travel.
(d) all the enjoyments of travel.

11. ____________ that in this apparent mess, two things not be interfered with.
(a) It is important.
(b) it is of cardinal important.
(c) It should be urgently under-stood.
(d) It cannot be emphasised.

12. A country's wealth is its people. But instead of drawing out the strengths of the people, instead of drawing out their talent, this use of religion debases, degrades and depresses than ____________.
(a) in greater and greater measure
(b) further
(c) beyond reasonable limit
(d) more and more

13. Wines that yielded a good commercial profit ____________ in the same limited areas of France as of now.
(a) seem to have been produced
(b) appear to have a remarkable semblance
(c) bear a significant similarity in terms of production to those grown
(d) appear to have been similarly produced

14. This is about ____________ a sociological analysis can penetrate.
(a) the other limits that
(b) just how far into the subject that
(c) the relative distance that
(d) as far as

15. The safest general characterisation of the European philosophical tradition as it has developed up to now, with all its diverse proponents, is that it consists of a____________Plato.
(a) series of footnotes to
(b) set of prologues to
(c) collection of chapters on
(d) string of commentatries to

16. The ideas that these companies used seem so simple with ____________ that their competitors will now ____________ themselves for not thinking of them first.
(a) advanced technology, hit
(b) analysis , abuse
(c) passage of time, curse
(d) hindsight, kick

17. No doubt, it was our own government but it was being run on borrowed ideas, using ____________solutions.
(a) worn out
(b) second hand
(c) impractical
(d) appropriate

18. Overall, all the recent policy changes by the government only amount to a ____________ in the sugar industry.
(a) superficial attemp at liberalisation
(b) drop in the ocean
(c) large change
(d) small regulating authority

19. In pusuance of their decision to resist what they saw as anti-labour policies, the company employees, union launched agitation to ________.

(*a*) show their virility
(*b*) reaffirm their commitment to the company.
(*c*) bring down the government
(*d*) demonstrate their strength

20. Scientists have found ________ evidence that Neanderthals, now an extinct species of humans ________ Europe, were cannibals.

(*a*) grisly, living in
(*b*) incontrovertible, a cross
(*c*) chilling inhabiting
(*d*) proper, in

21. The telephone symbolises that awkard ________ in all communication technologies ; while it ________ to bring us together, it keeps us apart.

(*a*) paradox, needs (*b*) irony, intends
(*c*) paradox , tries (*d*) irony wishes

22. The world is fast moving into a period of 'civilisational clash' in which the primary identification of people and countries will not be ________ as during the Cold War, but ________.

(*a*) ideological, technological
(*b*) cultural, ethnic
(*c*) political, economic
(*d*) ideological, cultural

23. In our country, the challenges are to raise ________ incomes to reduce poverty, and to ________ inefficient public sector enterprises.

(*a*) farm, liberalise
(*b*) middle-class, privatise
(*c*) workers, take over
(*d*) rural, restructure

24. The interest generated by the Soccer World Cup is ________ compared to the way cricket ________ the nation.

(*a*) milder, fascinates
(*b*) lukewarm, electrifies
(*c*) tepid, inspires
(*d*) unusual, grips

25. Though one eye is kept firmly on the ________, the company now also promotes ________ contemporary art.

(*a*) present, experimental
(*b*) future, popular
(*c*) present, popular
(*d*) market, popular

26. The law prohibits a person from felling a sandalwood tree, even if it grows on one's own land, without prior permission from the government. As poor people cannot deal with the government, this legal provision leads to a rip-roaring business for ________, who care neither for the ________, nor for the trees.

(*a*) middlemen, rich (*b*) the government, poor
(*c*) touts, rich (*d*) touts, poor

27. It will take some time for many South Koreans to ________ the conflicting images of North Korea, let alone to ________ what to make of their northern cousins.

(*a*) reconcile, decide (*b*) understand, clarify
(*c*) make out, decide (*d*) reconcile, understand

28. In these bleak and depressing times of ________ prices, non-performing governments and ________ crime rates, Sourav Ganguly has given us, Indians, a lot to cheer about.

(*a*) escalating, increasing
(*b*) spiralling, booming
(*c*) spiralling, soaring
(*d*) ascending, debilitating

29. The manners and ________ of the nouveau riche is a recurrent ________ in the literature.

(*a*) style, motif (*b*) morals, story
(*c*) wealth, theme (*d*) morals, theme

30. Many people suggest ________ and still others would like to convince people not to buy pirated cassettes.

(*a*) to bring down audio-cassette prices to reduce the incidence of music piracy, others advocate strong legal action against the offenders,
(*b*) bringing down audio-cassette prices to reduce the incidents of music piracy, others are advocating strong legal action against offenders,
(*c*) bringing down audio-cassette prices to reduce the incidence of music piracy, others advocate strong legal action against offenders,
(*d*) audio-cassette prices to be brought down to reduce incidence of music piracy, others advocate that strong legal action must be taken against offenders,

31. The ancient Egyptians believed ________ so that when these objects were magically reanimated through the correct rituals, they would be able to function effectively.

(*a*) that it was essential that things they portrayed must have every relevant feature shown as clearly as possible
(*b*) it was essential for things they portray to have had every relevant feature shown as clearly as possible,
(*c*) it was essential that the things they portrayed had every relevant feature shown as clearly as possible,
(*d*) that when they portrayed things, it should have every relevant feature shown as clearly as possible

32. Archaeologists believe that the pieces of red-ware pottery excavated recently near Bhavnagar and ______shed light on a hither to dark 600-year period in the Harappan history of Gujarat.

(*a*) estimated with a reasonable certainty as being about 3400 years old,

(*b*) are estimated reasonably certain to be about 3400 years old

(*c*) estimated at about 3400 years old with reasonable certainty,

(*d*) estimated with reasonable certainty to be about 3400 years old,

33. The genocides in Bosnia and Rwanda, apart from being mis-described in the most sinister and ______manner as 'ethnic cleansing', were also blamed, in further hand-washing rhetoric, on something dark and interior to ______ and perpetrators alike.

(*a*) innovative; communicator

(*b*) enchanting; leaders

(*c*) disingenuous; victims

(*d*) exigent; exploiters

34. As navigators, calendar makers, and other ____of the night sky accumulated evidence to the contrary, ancient astronomers were forced to______that certain bodies might move in circles about points, which in turn moved in circles about the earth.

(*a*) scrutinizers; believe

(*b*) observers; agree

(*c*) scrutinizers; suggest

(*d*) observers; concede

35. Every human being, after the first few days of his life, is a product of two factors: on the one hand, there is his ______ endowment; and on the other hand, there is the effect of environment, including ______.

(*a*) constitutional; weather

(*b*) congenital; education

(*c*) personal; climate

(*d*) genetic; pedagogy

36. Exhaustion of natural resources, destruction of individual initiative by governments, control over man's minds by central ______ of education and propaganda are some of the major evils which appear to be on the increase as a result of the impact of science upon minds suited by ______ to an earlier kind of world.

(*a*) tenets; fixation

(*b*) aspects; inhibitions

(*c*) institutions; inhibitions

(*d*) organs; tradition

37. But ______ are now regularly written not just for tools, but well-established practices, organisations and institutions, not all of which seem to be ______ away.

(*a*) reports, withering (*b*) stories, trading

(*c*) books, dying (*d*) obituaries, fading

38. The Darwin who ______ is most remarkable for the way in which he ______ the attributes of the world class thinker and head of the household.

(*a*) comes, figures

(*b*) arises, adds

(*c*) emerges, combines

(*d*) appeared, combines

39. Since her face was free of ______ there was no way to ______ if she appreciated what had happened.

(*a*) make-up, realise

(*b*) expression, ascertain

(*c*) emotion, diagnose

(*d*) scars, understand

40. In this context, the ______ of the British labour movement is particularly ______.

(*a*) affiar, weird

(*b*) activity, moving

(*c*) experience, significant

(*d*) atmosphere, gloomy

41. Indian intellectuals may boast, if they are so inclined, of being ______ to the most elitist among the intellectual ______ of the world.

(*a*) subordinate, traditions

(*b*) heirs, cliques

(*c*) ancestors, societies

(*d*) heir, traditions

Directions for Q. 42 to 47.

Fill the gaps in the passages below with the most appropriate word from the options given for each gap. The right words are the ones used by the author. Be guided by the author's overall style and meaning when you choose the answers.

Von Nuemann and Morgenstern assume a decision framework in which all options are thoroughly considered, each option being independent of others, with a numerical value derived for the utility of each possible outcome (these outcomes reflecting, in turn, all possible combinations of choices). The decision is then made to maximize the expected utility.

(42)_____, such a model reflects major simplifications of the way decisions are made in the real world. Humans are not able to process information as quickly and effectively as the model assumes; they tend not to think (43) _____ as easily as the model calls for; they often deal with a particular option without really assessing its (44) _____, and when they do assess alternatives, they may be extremely nebulous about their criteria of evaluation.

42. (*a*) Regrettably (*b*) Firstly
(*c*) Obviously (*d*) Apparently

43. (*a*) quantitatively (*b*) systematically
(*c*) scientifically (*d*) analytically

44. (*a*) implications (*b*) disadvantages
(*c*) utility (*d*) alternatives

In a large company, (45) _____ people is about as common as using a gun or a switch-blade to (46) _____ an argument. As a result, most managers have little or no experience of firing people, and they find it emotionally traumatic; as result, they often delay the act interminably, much as an unhappy spouse will prolong a bad marriage. And when the firing is done, it's often done clumsily, with far worse side effects than are necessary.

Do the world-class softward organizations have a different way of firing people ? No, but they do the deed swiftly, humanely, and professionally.

The key point here is to view the fired employees as a "failed product" and to ask how the process (47) _____ such a phenomenon in the first place.

45. (*a*) dismissing (*b*) punishing
(*c*) firing (*d*) admonishing

46. (*a*) resolve (*b*) thwart
(*c*) defeat (*d*) close

47. (*a*) derived (*b*) engineered
(*c*) produced (*d*) allowed

Directions for Q. 48 to 57 :

Fill up the blanks, numbered [48], [49]....up to [57], in the two passages below with the most appropriate word from the options given for each blank.

"Between the year 1946 and the year 1955, I did not file any income tax returns." With that [48] statement, Ramesh embarked on an account of his encounter with the Income Tax Department. "I originally owed Rs. 20,000 in unpaid taxes. With [49] and [50], the 20,000 became 60,000. The Income Tax Department then went into action, and I learned first hand just how much power the Tax Department wields. Royalties and trust funds can be [51]; automobiles may be [52], and auctioned off. Nothing belongs to the [53] until the case is settled."

48. (*a*) devious (*b*) blunt
(*c*) tactful (*d*) pretentious

49. (*a*) interest (*b*) taxes
(*c*) principal (*d*) returns

50. (*a*) sanctions (*b*) refunds
(*c*) fees (*d*) fines

51. (*a*) closed (*b*) detached
(*c*) attached (*d*) impounded

52. (*a*) smashed (*b*) seized
(*c*) dismantled (*d*) frozen

53. (*a*) purchaser (*b*) victim
(*c*) investor (*d*) offender

At that time the White House was as serene as a resort hotel out of season. The corridors were [54]. In the various offices, [55] gray men in waistcoats talked to one another in low-pitched voices. The only colour, or choler, curiously enough, was provided by President Eisenhower himself. Apparently, his [56] was easily set off; he scowled when he [57] the corridors.

54. (*a*) striking (*b*) hollow
(*c*) empty (*d*) white

55. (*a*) quiet (*b*) faded
(*c*) loud (*d*) stentorian

56. (*a*) laughter (*b*) curiosity
(*c*) humour (*d*) temper

57. (*a*) paced (*b*) strolled
(*c*) stormed (*d*) prowled.

EXERCISE – II

(QUESTIONS FROM PREVIOUS GATE EXAMS)

MCQ TYPE QUESTIONS

2015

1. Choose the most appropriate word from the options given below to complete the following sentence. The official answered _________ that the complaints of the citizen would be looked into.
(*a*) respectably (*b*) respectfully
(*c*) reputably (*d*) respectively

2. Choose the most appropriate word from the options given below to complete the following sentence.
The principal presented the chief guest with a _________, as token of appreciation.
(*a*) momento (*b*) memento
(*c*) momentum (*d*) moment

3. Choose the appropriate word/phrase, out of the four options given below, to complete the following sentence :
Frogs _________.
(*a*) Croak (*b*) Roar
(*c*) Hiss (*d*) Patter

4. Extreme focus on syllabus and studying for tests has become such a dominant concern of Indian students that they close their minds to anything _________ to the requirements of the exam
(*a*) related
(*b*) extraneous
(*c*) outside
(*d*) useful

5. The Tamil version of _____ John Abraham-starrer Madras café _____ cleared by the Censor Board with no cuts last week but the film's distributors _____ no takers among the exhibitors for a release in Tamil Nadu _____ this Friday.
(*a*) Mr., was, found, on
(*b*) a, was, found, at
(*c*) the, was, found, on
(*d*) a, being, find at

6. Choose the appropriate word/phase, out of the four options given below, to complete the following sentence:
Apparent lifelessness __________ dormant life.
(*a*) harbours (*b*) lead to
(*c*) supports (*d*) affects

7. Choose the correct verb to fill in the blank below:
Let us ____________.
(*a*) Introvert (*b*) Alternate
(*c*) Atheist (*d*) Altruist

8. Choose the most appropriate word from the options given below to complete the following sentence:
If the Athlete had wanted to come first in the race, he __________ several hours everyday
(*a*) should practice
(*b*) should have practiced
(*c*) practiced
(*d*) should be practicing

9. Choose the appropriate word/phrase, out of the four options given below, to complete the following sentence:
Dhoni, as well as the other team members of Indian team, _____ present on the occasion.
(*a*) were (*b*) was
(*c*) has (*d*) have

10. We _______ our friend's birthday and we _______ how to make it up to him.
(*a*) completely forgot — don't just known
(*b*) forget completely — don't just know
(*c*) completely forget —just don't know
(*d*) forgot completely —just don't know

11. Which of the following options is the closest in meaning to the sentence below?
She enjoyed herself immensely at the party.
(*a*) She had a terrible time at the party
(*b*) She had a horrible time at the party
(*c*) She had a terrific time at the party
(*d*) She had a terrifying time at the party

12. Didn't you buy _______ when you went shopping?
(*a*) any paper (*b*) much paper
(*c*) no paper (*d*) a few paper

2014

13. Choose the most appropriate word from the options given below to complete the following sentence:
A person suffering from Alzheimer's disease _________ short-term memory loss.
(*a*) experienced
(*b*) has experienced
(*c*) is experiencing
(*d*) experiences

14. Choose the most appropriate word from the options given below to complete the following sentence:
_________ is the key to their happiness; they are satisfied with what they have.
(*a*) Contentment
(*b*) Ambition
(*c*) Perseverance
(*d*) Hunger

15. Choose the most appropriate word from the options given below to complete the following sentence:
One of his biggest _____ was his ability to forgive.
(*a*) vice (*b*) virtues
(*c*) choices (*d*) strength

16. After the discussion, Tom said to me, 'Please revert!' He expects me to ________.
(*a*) retract (*b*) get back to him
(*c*) move in reverse (*d*) retreat

17. The value of one U.S. Dollar is 65 Indian Rupees today, compared to 60 last year. The Indian Rupee has ________.
(*a*) Depressed (*b*) Depreciated
(*c*) Appreciated (*d*) Stabilized

18. Choose the most appropriate word from the options given below to complete the following sentence:
Communication and interpersonal skills are _________ important in their own ways.
(*a*) each (*b*) both
(*c*) all (*d*) either

19. Choose the most appropriate pair of words from the options given below to complete the following sentence:
She could not ________ the thought of ________ the election to her bitter rival.
(*a*) bear, loosing
(*b*) bare, loosing
(*c*) bear, losing
(*d*) bare, losing

20. Choose the most appropriate phrase from the options given below to complete the following sentence:

The aircraft ________ take off as soon as its flight plan was filed.

(*a*) is allowed to (*b*) will be allowed to
(*c*) was allowed to (*d*) has been allowed to

21. Choose the most appropriate word from the options given below to complete the following sentence:

Many ancient cultures attributed disease to supernatural causes. However, modern science has largely helped ______ such notions.

(*a*) impel (*b*) dispel
(*c*) propel (*d*) repel

22. If she __________ how to calibrate the instrument, she ________ done the experiment.

(*a*) knows, will have
(*b*) knew, had
(*c*) had known, could have
(*d*) should have known, would have

23. Who ___________ was coming to see us this evening ?

(*a*) you said
(*b*) did you say
(*c*) did you say that
(*d*) had you said

24. Choose the most appropriate word from the options given below to complete the following sentence:

He could not understand the judges awarding her the first prize, because he thought that her performance was quite ________________.

(*a*) Superb
(*b*) Medium
(*c*) Mediocre
(*d*) Exhilarating

2013

25. Friendship, no matter how _______ it is, has its limitations.

(*a*) cordial (*b*) intimate
(*c*) secret (*d*) pleasant

26. Were you a bird, you_____ in the sky.

(*a*) would fly (*b*) shall fly
(*c*) should fly (*d*) shall have flown

27. Complete the sentence:

Dare ________ mistakes.

(*a*) commit (*b*) to commit
(*c*) committed (*d*) committing

28. The Headmaster ______ to speak to you.

Which of the following options is incorrect to complete the above sentence?

(*a*) is wanting (*b*) wants
(*c*) want (*d*) was wanting

2012

29. Choose the most appropriate alternative from the options given below to complete the following sentence :

Despite several ______ the mission succeeded in its attempt to resolve the conflict.

(*a*) attempts (*b*) setbacks
(*c*) meetings (*d*) delegations

30. Choose the most appropriate alternative from the options given below to complete the following sentence :

If the tired soldier wanted to lie down, he ___ the mattress out on the balcony.

(*a*) should take
(*b*) shall take
(*c*) should have taken
(*d*) will have taken

31. Choose the most appropriate word from the options given below to complete the following sentence :

Given the seriousness of the situation that he had to face, his ___ was impressive.

(*a*) beggary (*b*) nomenclature
(*c*) jealousy (*d*) nonchalance

2011

32. Choose the most appropriate word from the options given below to complete the following sentence:

If you are trying to make a strong impression on your audience, you cannot do so by being understated, tentative or ______ .

(*a*) hyperbolic
(*b*) restrained
(*c*) argumentative
(*d*) indifferent

33. Choose the most appropriate word(s) from the options given below to complete the following sentence.

I contemplated ______ Singapore for my vacation but decided against it.

(*a*) to visit (*b*) having to visit
(*c*) visiting (*d*) for a visit

34. Choose the most appropriate word from the options given below to complete the following sentence:

Under ethical guidelines recently adopted by the Indian Medical Association, human genes are to be manipulated only to correct diseases for which_______treatments are unsatisfactory.

(*a*) similar (*b*) most
(*c*) uncommon (*d*) available

35. Choose the most appropriate word from the options given below to complete the following sentence:

It was her view that the country's problems had been_________by foreign technocrats, so that to invite them to come back would be counter-productive.

(*a*) identified (*b*) ascertained
(*c*) exacerbated (*d*) analysed

2010

36. Choose the most appropriate word from the options given below to complete the following sentence:

If we manage to ________ our natural resources, we would leave a better planet for our children.

(*a*) uphold
(*b*) restrain
(*c*) cherish
(*d*) conserve

37. Choose the most appropriate word from the options given below to complete the following sentence:

His rather casual remarks on politics _______his lack of seriousness about the subject.

(*a*) masked
(*b*) belied
(*c*) betrayed
(*d*) suppressed

ANSWERS

EXERCISE – I

MCQ Type Questions

1. (1)	**2.** (*b*)	**3.** (*b*)	**4.** (*d*)	**5.** (*b*)	**6.** (*c*)	**7.** (*d*)	**8.** (*d*)	**9.** (*c*)	**10.** (*c*)
11. (*a*)	**12.** (*d*)	**13.** (*a*)	**14.** (*d*)	**15.** (*a*)	**16.** (*d*)	**17.** (*b*)	**18.** (*a*)	**19.** (*d*)	**20.** (*c*)
21. (3)	**22.** (*c*)	**23.** (*d*)	**24.** (*b*)	**25.** (*b*)	**26.** (*d*)	**27.** (*a*)	**28.** (*c*)	**29.** (*d*)	**30.** (*c*)
31. (*c*)	**32.** (*d*)	**33.** (*c*)	**34.** (*d*)	**35.** (*d*)	**36.** (*d*)	**37.** (*d*)	**38.** (*c*)	**39.** (*b*)	**40.** (*c*)
41. (*d*)	**42.** (*d*)	**43.** (*d*)	**44.** (*d*)	**45.** (*c*)	**46.** (*a*)	**47.** (*d*)	**48.** (*b*)	**49.** (*a*)	**50.** (*d*)
51. (*c*)	**52.** (*b*)	**53.** (*d*)	**54.** (*c*)	**55.** (*a*)	**56.** (*d*)	**57.** (*d*)			

EXERCISE – II

MCQ Type Questions

1. (*b*)	**2.** (*b*)	**3.** (*a*)	**4.** (*b*)	**5.** (*c*)	**6.** (*a*)	**7.** (*b*)	**8.** (*b*)	**9.** (*b*)	**10.** (*c*)
11. (*c*)	**12.** (*a*)	**13.** (*d*)	**14.** (*a*)	**15.** (*b*)	**16.** (*b*)	**17.** (*b*)	**18.** (*b*)	**19.** (*c*)	**20.** (*c*)
21. (*b*)	**22.** (*c*)	**23.** (*b*)	**24.** (*c*)	**25.** (*b*)	**26.** (*a*)	**27.** (*b*)	**28.** (*c*)	**29.** (*b*)	**30.** (*a*)
31. (*d*)	**32.** (*b*)	**33.** (*c*)	**34.** (*d*)	**35.** (*c*)	**36.** (*a*)	**37.** (*c*)			

EXPLANATIONS

EXERCISE – I

MCQ TYPE QUESTIONS

1. They in choice (*a*) means 'some of our ruling politicians' (the subject). Also grammatically 'they have a right to plunder ....' is correct wheras'...... right to the punder ......' is incorrect.

2. 'Bizarre' means 'weird'. Hence, choice (*a*) is ruled out. "Its haunting images have endured ' fits syntactically. choice (*c*) can also be ruled out as 'munificence' means generosity and this is not intended in the sentence. Also, the word 'prints' in the given sentence gets with the word 'images' of choice (*b*).

3. 'They' in the part after the comma must refer to somebody or some-thing. Hence, only choice (*b*) will fit as 'they' in that case refers to 'things'.

4. The right word to precede the proposition 'on' is imposed. Tax is not collected on .... people. Tax is not placed on people, Tax is not charged on people. Hence, choices (*a*), (*b*) and (*c*) are not the answers. Tax is imposed ..... on ..... .

5. Choice (*d*) is ruled out as it does not logically fit. Choice (*a*) is also ruled out because of the expression 'tears in me'.

6. The key words are 'plunging' and 'investor confidence'. If markets are plunging, investor confidence is low. This aspect is brought out best by choice (*c*).

7. (*a*) 'Discovery'refers to something that existed previously and came to knowledge later. Home is not a discovery.
   (*b*) Home is not a certain. It is a set up which comes into being as a result of a certain composition of various factors.
   (*c*) Home is not a new invention of anyone at any stage of development.

   So choice (*d*) is the best answer. Home is an institution just like 'marriage. Home is a reality only when its members accept certain principles.

8. (*a*) A man's toil may help to make out wealth, but it is not the ultimate aim.
   (*b*) A man's toil may secure a lot of things for his children or friends . That too is not something great.
   (*c*) A man's toil may help him to overcome many difficulties, but that does not give him much pleasure.

   So, choice (*d*) is the best answer. What one becomes by one's toil is greater than what one gets.

9. (*a*) 'Reopens the first chapter' means begins from the very start.
   (*b*) 'Writes an epilogue' means ends the book.
   (*c*) 'Opens new books' means creates new problems.

   The above three are only partly correct. An act of justice pardons for ever an act of vengeance creates new problems. It is a saying. "An act of justice closes the book on a misdeed; an act of vengeance writes one of its own."

10. Here, the trail is the important thing and hence the excitement of the trail is what you will be looking for.

11. (*b*) The expression must be "it is of cardinal importance".
    (*c*) There is no urgency in understanding, "It should be understood" is enough.
    (*d*) Instead of"it cannot be,' the expression should be it must be'.

    So choice (*a*) is the best, It is important that the two things are not to be interfered with.

13. (*b*) It is not mentioned with what do wines bear semblance.
    (*c*) The 'similarity' is only in terms of production. The similarity in production does not achieve commercial profit.
    (*d*) For the same commercial profit wines need not be produced in the same of similar manner.

    So, choice (*a*) is the best. It does not mention that the wines of similar profit are similarily produced or have semblance with one another.

14. (*a*) A sociological analysis does not stop at the outer limits of the subjects.
    (*b*) No one can indicate how far into the subject can a sociological analysis go.
    (*c*) 'Relative distance' refers to the distance of something else which is not mentioned.

    So, choice (*d*) is the best. This indicates the probable distance to which the sociological analysis can go to.

30. Choices (*a*) and (*d*) are ruled out because 'suggest' does not go with 'to+ verb' form. Choice (2) cannot fit in the blank because of the error in parallelism. The appropriate structure is "Many people suggest.....and others advocate ....".

31. The tense in choices (*a*) and (*b*) is not consistent. Moreover, choice (*a*) uses both 'essential' and 'must'. thus rendering either one of these words redundant. In choice (*d*) 'things' the plural form cannot take it'.

32. Choice (*d*) fits into the blank in choice (*a*) the usage of the indefinite article is erroneous. Choices (*b*) and (*c*) are erroneous due to the incorrect ordering of words.

33. 'Disingenuous' means 'insincere' and this best fits the context as the phrase 'ethnic cleansing' is marked by apostrophes indicating a misrepresentation. Also, the word 'victims' is best in contrast to 'perpetrators'. Hence, option (*c*) is correct.

36. 'Navigators, calendar makers' are best clubbed under the category of 'observers' rather than 'scrutinizers', as the latter term is more used to refer to specialists in a particular field. 'Students' can also fit to a certain extent and this leaves us with options (*b*), (*d*). 'Concede' has more to do with defeat or revision which is more apt in this context than 'agree' or 'conclude'. Hence, option (*c*) is correct.

42. Going by options, 'regrettably' doesn't fit as there is nothing to regret. 'Firstly' is no choice and nothing 'secondly' is mentioned. Paragraph has nothing aggresive tone so 'obviously' does not suit. 'Apparently' is only and most suitable option.

43. All options are suitable for the space but to choose one, the best, is required here 'Analytically' appears to be best. It expresses to analyse something using statistically proven methods to reach a decision.

44. It is a very obvious choice determined from the paragraph giving it an access.

45. 'Firing' comes as best suited option as paragraph explains it as a subject of discussion.

46. An argument is always 'resolved', it is never thwart, defeat or closed.

47. Going by options makes choice easier. Only "how the process allowed......." suits logically.

48. 'Blunt' means `very direct' with respect to a remark. 'Devious' in choice (*d*) means 'dishonest' and is incorrect as the statement is a frank one. For the same reason 'tactful' in choice (*c*) is also not appropriate.

49. 'Interest' is the most appropriate work because the original amout he owed to the department accumulated to the said figure. 'Taxes is redundant while. 'principal' usually refers to a loan (in this case it isn't). 'Returns' is what one gets rather than pays.

50. 'Sanctions is used for an official permission or order that limits trade and is rarely used for an amout. 'Fees' are paid for a service and 'refunds' are what one gets back. 'Fines is the best choice because of the penalty component.

51. 'Attach' is the word used for officially taking something away. 'Impound' means 'confiscate' and is generally used in the context of illegal goods or contraband. Other choices are in no way comparable.

52. 'Smashed in choice (*a*) and 'dismantled' in choice (*c*) are far from being logical. 'Frozen is a wrong choice. 'Frozen is used in the context of making bank accounts inoperable etc. Automobiles are seized.

53. Clearly the topic is about a person who has violated incom tax regulations and he should be called an 'offender' of the law.

55. Choices (*c*) and (*d*) have similar meaning and are misnomers in the given context, as the keywords 'lowpitched voices' require a word that is synonymous with 'quiet' or 'calm'. The usage of the adjective 'faded' in the sentence to describe men is untenable.

56. The given sentence depicts the President as a very angry person as suggested by the keyword 'scowled' Choices (*a*), (*b*) and (*c*) are either positive or neutral and cannot fit in the sentence.

57. 'Paced' in choice (*a*) is not consistent with the mood of the President as depicted in the first part of the sentence. It means 'to walk fast'. 'Strolled' in (*b*) means 'Walk casually' and hence is discarded. 'Stormed' in choice (*c*) refers to 'attack a place suddenly' or 'say something in a loud, angry way'. But here, neither of them fits in. 'Prowled' refers to moving in a restless manner and hence fits.

EXERCISE – II

MCQ TYPE QUESTIONS

2. The principal presented the chief guest with a memento, as token of appreciation.

3. Frogs make 'croak' sound.

4. Extraneous -irrelevant or unrelated to the subject being dealt with.

5. John-Abraham starrer Madras Cafe talks about the movie not the person, so Mr. is ruled out.

'Find no takers' is not the correct phrase. At this Friday is incorrect.

So, option (*c*) is correct.

6. Apparent: looks like

dormant: hidden

Harbour: give shelter

Effect (verb): results in

8. For condition regarding something which already happened, should have practiced is the correct choice.

13. The correct word to fill in the blank is experiences. This is because the sentence is in present tense and the sense is in present indefinite.

14. Contentment is the right word which is appropriate to the meaning of the sentence. Contentment is the sign of true happiness as it gives a sense of fulfillment.

29. The word despite tells us that mission succeeded even though there were problems. Hence the correct answer is Setbacks.

32. Tone of the sentence clearly indicates a word that is similar to understated is needed for the blank. Alternatively, word should be antonym of strong (fail to make strong impression). Therefore, best choice is restrained which means controlled / reserved / timid.

33. Contemplate is a transitive verb and hence is followed by a gerund Hence the correct usage of contemplate is verb + ing form.

34. The context seeks to take a deviation only when existing / present / current / alternative treatments are unsatisfactory. So word for the blank should be a close synonym of existing / present / current / alternative. Available is the closest of all.

35. Clues: foreign technocrats did something negatively to the problems – so it is counter-productive to invite them. All other options are non-negative. Best choice is exacerbated which means aggravated or worsened.

37. Betrayed, **means** 'showed' or revealed.

3 CHAPTER

Synonyms

INTRODUCTION

A Synonym may be defined as a word that has the same meaning or the same general meaning as a particular word in the same Language or is in some applications a more or less satisfactory application of it. Thus the synonym of a word can be an exact equivalent in meaning or should atleast convey its meaning in one way or the other or should show in what sense it can best be used.

SOME IMPORTANT WORDS WITH THEIR SYNONYMS

A

abandon : desert, for sake, jilt, leave, evacuate, quilt, vacate, abdicate, renounce.

abduct : kidnap, run away with, seize, snatch.

abet : aid, assist, back, condone, help, promote, sanction, support, sustain, uphold.

abeyance : adjournment,deferral, discontinuation, inactivity, intermission, postponement, recess.

abide : accept, bear, brook, endure, dwell, linger, live, lodge, reside, sojourn, persist.

ability : adeptness, aptitude, capability, capacity, competence, dexterity, endowment, expertise.

ablaze : afire, aflame, alight, blazing, burning, fiery, flaming, aglow, brilliant, flashing, gleaming, illuminated, radiant, sparkling.

abstain : avoid, decline, deny, desist, renounce, refrain, withhold, forgo.

abundance : affluence, ampleness, bounty, copiousness, exuberance, pro-fusion, fortune, wealth.

abysmal : bottomless, boundless, complete, deep, extreme, incalculable, profound, vast.

accede : accept, admit, agree, comply, concede, concur, consent, endorse, assume, attain.

access : admission, admittance, approach, avenue, course, entering, outburst, paroxysm.

acclaim : applaud, approve, celebrate, eulogize, exalt, hail, praise, salute, clapping.

accompany : attend, chaperon, conduct, convoy, squire, usher, supplement.

accord : agree, assent, concur, conform, harmonize, bestow, concede, endow, render, vouchsafe.

accuse : allege, blame, cite, denounce, impench, incriminate, indict, recriminate.

accustom : acclimatize, acquaint, adapt, descipline, familiarize, habituate, inure.

acquaint : advice, announce, apprise, disclose, enlighten, notify, reveal, tell.

acrid : caustic, harsh, irritating, pungent, stinging, acrimonious, mordant, nasty, sarcastic, trenchant, vitriolic.

acrimony : bitterness, harshness, churlishness, peevishness, rancour, spleen, tartness, virulence.

adamant : determined, firm, immovable, inexorable, intransigent, obdurate, resolute, stubborn, unrelenting, flinty, steely, stony.

adept : adroit, dexterous, masterful, proficient, versed, expert, genius.

adequate : capable, commensurate, competent, requisite, tolerable, sufficient.

adhere : cleave, cling, faster, obey, observe, respect.

adieu : conge, goodbye, valediction.

adjourne : defer, delay, discontinue, prorogue.

admirable : commendable, excellent, exquisite, wonderful, worthy.

admirer : bean, lover, wooer, devotee, enthusiast, votary.

adrift : drifting, unanchored, aimless, amiss, astray.

adroit : clever, cunning, deft, dexterous, ingeneous, nimble, proficient, quick-witted, able.

audacious : courageous, daring, dauntless, intrepid, rash.

austere : exacting, forbidding, grave, grim, harsh, rigorous, severe, solemn, sterr, stringent.

averse : antipathetic, disinclined, hostile, inimical, loath, reluctant, unwilling.

avid : ardent, eager, fanatical, ferrent, passionate, zealous, avaricious,

B

baptism : immersion, purification, sprinkling, debut.

bastion : citadel, defence, fortress, mainstay.

blaspheme : abuse, anathematize, curse, desecrate, execrate, profane, revile, swear.

breach : break, aperture, charm, cleft, fissure, infraction, infringement, estrangement.

broaden : augment, develop, fatten, spread, stretch.

brood : agonize, dwell, mope, ponder, repine, ruminate.

C

catastrophe: affliction, adversity, cataclysm, devastation, disaster, fiasco, culmination.

chaos : anarchy, bedlam, confusion, dis-organization. entropy, tumult, lawlessness,

chastity : celibacy, continence, innocence, modesty, purity.

clan : band, brotherhood, fraternity, gens.

clinch : assure, conclude, confirm, determine, secure.

colloquial : conversational, demotic, everyday, familiar, idiomatic, informal, vernacular.

commotion : ado, agitation, bustle, disorder, disturbance, excitement.

complicate : confuse, entangle, involve, muddle.

contour : curve, figure, lines, profile, relief.

conviction : assurance, certainty, confidence, ferrour.

creditable : admirable, commendable, deserving, estimable, honourable, loudable.

crest : apex, zenith, pinnacle, summit, ridge.

culminate : climax, close, conclude, finish.

cynical : sarcastic, scornful, sneering, distrustful.

D

daunt : dismay, alarm, appal, frighten, intimidate, scare, subdue, terrify.

deed : achievement, act, action, exploit, feat.

deflate : collapse, confract, empty, exhaust, shrink, chasten.

deliberate : cogitate, consult, debate, mediate, ponder, reflect.

diligent : active, attentive, busy, careful, constant.

dire : alarming, appalling, awful, catastrophic, cruel, disastrous.

discreet : careful, cautious, circumspect, diplomatic, judicious, politic, prudent.

dissent : decline, differ, disagree, protest, refuse, disagreement, discord.

ditch : channel, drain, furrow, trench, discord.

dodge : dant, duck, shift, sidestep, avoid, deceive.

dubious : doubtful, hesitant, uncertain, unconvinced, undecided, unsure, ambiguous

dwell : abide, establish, inhabit, settle, sojourn.

E

edgy : anxious, irritable, nervous, touchy.

elusive : difficult to catch, shifty, slippery, tricky, baffling, fleeting, puzzling, subtle.

emblem : badge, gest, device, figure, image, representation.

enchant : beguile, bewitch, captivate, charm, delight, enamour, enrapture, fascinate, hypnotize.

enrage : aggrarate, anger incense, incite, inflame, irritate, provoke.

exalt : advance, dignify, elevate, honour, promote, acclaim, applaud, extol.

exhilarating: breathtaking, cheering, exalting, exciting, vigorating, stimulating.

expedite : accelerate, advance, assist, dispatch, facilitate, hasten, precipitate.

F

fame : celebrity, eminence, glory, honour, prominence, renown, repute, stardom.

famine : scarcity, dearth, destitution, hunger, starvation.

feeble : weak, delicate, etiolated, exhausted, infirm, languid, puny, shilpit.

fierce : barbarous, brutal, cruel, dan-gerous, ferocious, murderous, passionate, savage.

fishy : doubtful, dubious, funny, improbable, suspect, suspicious, deadpan, dull.

flawless : faultless, impeccable, perfect, unblemished.

foresee : anticipate, divine, envisage, forebode, portend, predict, prophesy, presage.

fortress : castle, citadel, fastness, redoubt, stronghold.

fraternity : brotherhood, association, company, comradship.

fretful : captious, complaining, fractions, irritable, peevish, splenetic, touchy.

G

gaiety : animation, blitheness, cheerfulness, elation, exhilaration, glee, humour.

gaudy : bright, brilliant, flashy, florid, garish, glaring, meretricious, showy, vulgar.

gestation : development, evolution, incubation, pregnancy, repening.

gracious : affable, amiable, beneficent, benevolent, cheritable, chivalrous, cordial.

grimace : face, frown, mouth, scowl, sneer.

grubby : dinty, filthy, frowzy, manky, shabby.

H

haggle : bargain, barter, beat down, dicker, higgle, dispute, quarrel, wrangle.

haphazard : accidental, arbitrary, chance, fluky, random, aimless, careless.

hatred : abomination, animosity, animus, antagonism, antipathy, enmity.

hectic : animated, boisterous, chaotic, frantic, furious, turbulent, wild.

hilarious : amusing, comical, convivial, exhilarated, humorous, jolly, jovial, joyful, joyous.

holocaust : annihilation, carnage, destruction, devastation, massacre.

hurricane : cyclone, gale, storm, tempest, tornado, twister.

I

idle : dead, empty, gathering, dust, inactive, jobless, redundant.

immense : enormous, extensive, giant, gigantic, huge, illimitable,

: interminable, jumbo.

implicated : incriminated, involved, suspected, under suspicion.

impudence : assurance, audacity, boldness, bumptiousness, insolence.

incense : anger, enrage, excite, aroma, balm, fragrance, redolence, scent.

indent : order, request, dint, nick, notch.

inept : awkward, bumbling, bungling, clumsy, gauche, inexpert, maladroit, absurd.

insolent : abusive, bold, contemptuous, impertinent, impudent, insulting, rude, saucy.

instigate : actuate, encourage, forment, impel, incite, influence, provoke, persuade.

J, K, L, M

jaunty : airy, breezy, buoyant, carefree, dapper, gay, lively, perky, showy, smart.

jurisdiction : authority, command, control, influence, prerogative, sway.

keepsake : emblem, favour, memento, relic, reminder, souvenir, symbol, token.

latch : bar, bolt, catch, fastening, lock, sneck.

link : component, constituent, division, association, attachment.

meander : ramble, snake, straving, stroll, wander, bend, curve, loop, twist.

melancholy : dejection, depression, despondency, gloom.

N, O, P, Q

nostalgic : homesick, longing, regretful, sentimental, wistful.

obnoxious : abhorrent, abominable, detestable, disagreeable, disgusting, hateable, horrid.

onerous : burdensome, crushing, demanding, difficult, exciting, exhausting, exigent.

paw : grab, handle, roughly, manhandle, maul, molest.

percolate : drain, drip, exude, filter, leache, ooze, penetrate, permeate, pervade.

piety : devotion, dutifulness, faith, grace, piousness, religion, sanctify, veneration.

pudding : dessert, sweet.

quandary : bewilderment, stick, delicate, situation, difficult, dilemma, embarrassment.

quiver : agitate, oscillate, palpitate, pulsate, shudder, tremble, vibrate.

R, S, T

rapt : absorbed, carried away, enthralled, entranced, fascinated, gripped, intent.

reveal : announce, betray, broadcast, communicate, disclose, divulge, impart, proclaim.

rowdy : bristerous, disordely, loutish, noisy, unruly, uproarious, brawler.

sage : acute, canny, intelligent, judicious, polite, prudent, sagacious.

scorn : contempt, despite, disdain, disparagement, slight, sneer, curl, condemn.

shake : fluctuate, bump, joggle, jounce, quake, shiver, shudder, totter, tremble.

sinner : offender, reprobate, trespasser.

snigger : giggle, laugh, smirk, sneer, titter.

stimulus : encouragement, incentive, incitement, inducement, provocation.

tepid : slightly warm, luke warm.

timid : afraid, bashful, cowardly, diffident.

U, V, W, Y, Z

unmask : disclose, discover, expose, reveal, unveil.

urbane : civil, civilized, cosmopolitan, courteous, cultivated, debonair.

vehement : ardent, eager, earnest, emphatic, enthusiastic, fervent, fervid, fierce, forcible.

weired : bizarre, creepy, cerie, freakish, ghostly, mysterious, queer, spooky.

writhe : contont, distant, jerk, struggle, thrash, wiggle, twist, wriggle.

yearn : ache, covet, crave, desire, hanker, hunger, itch, languish.

zenith : acme, apex, apogee, climax, height, meridian, peak, pinnacle, summit, top.

EXERCISE – I

MCQ TYPE QUESTIONS

Directions: Each of the questions below consists of a word followed by four lettered words or phrases. Choose the lettered word or phrase that is most nearly same in meaning to the word.

1. **Abase**
   (*a*) incur (*b*) tax
   (*c*) estimate (*d*) humiliate
2. **Aberration**
   (*a*) deviation (*b*) abhorrence
   (*c*) dislike (*d*) absence
3. **Abet**
   (*a*) conceive (*b*) wager
   (*c*) encourage (*d*) evade
4. **Aabeyance**
   (*a*) obedience (*b*) discussion
   (*c*) excitement (*d*) suspended action
5. **Abjure**
   (*a*) discuss (*b*) renounce
   (*c*) run off secretly (*d*) perjure
6. **Ablution**
   (*a*) censure (*b*) forgiveness
   (*c*) mutiny (*d*) washing
7. **Abnegation**
   (*a*) blackness (*b*) self-denial
   (*c*) selfishness (*d*) cause
8. **Aborigine**
   (*a*) first design
   (*b*) absolution
   (*c*) finale
   (*d*) primitive inhabitant
9. **Abortive**
   (*a*) unsuccessful
   (*b*) consuming
   (*c*) financing
   (*d*) familiar
10. **Abstinence**
    (*a*) restrained (*b*) vulgar display
    (*c*) deportment (*d*) reluctance
11. **Abstruse**
    (*a*) profound (*b*) irrespective
    (*c*) suspended (*d*) protesting
12. **Abut**
    (*a*) stimulate (*b*) grasp
    (*c*) oppose (*d*) adjoin
13. **Abysmal**
    (*a*) bottomless (*b*) eternal
    (*c*) meteric (*d*) diabolic
14. **Accede**
    (*a*) fail (*b*) compromise
    (*c*) correct (*d*) consent
15. **Acclivity**
    (*a*) index
    (*b*) report
    (*c*) upslope of a hill
    (*d*) negotiator
16. **Astute**
    (*a*) sheer (*b*) noisy
    (*c*) astral (*d*) clever
17. **Atrocity**
    (*a*) endurance (*b*) fortitude
    (*c*) session (*d*) heinous act
18. **Atrophy**
    (*a*) capture (*b*) waste away
    (*c*) govern (*d*) award prize
19. **Attenuate**
    (*a*) appear (*b*) be absent
    (*c*) weaken (*d*) testify
20. **Atypical**
    (*a*) superfluous (*b*) fortitude
    (*c*) unusual (*d*) clashing
21. **Audacity**
    (*a*) boldness (*b*) asperity
    (*c*) strength (*d*) stature
22. **Augment**
    (*a*) make noble (*b*) anoint
    (*c*) increase (*d*) harvest
23. **Auxiliary**
    (*a*) righteous (*b*) prospective
    (*c*) assistant (*d*) archaic
24. **Avarice**
    (*a*) easiness (*b*) greed
    (*c*) statement (*d*) invoice

25. Avert
(a) entertain (b) transform
(c) turn away (d) lead toward

26. Awry
(a) recommended
(b) commiserating
(c) started
(d) crooked

27. Baleful
(a) doubtful (b) virtual
(c) deadly (d) conventional

28. Balmy
(a) venturesome (b) dedicated
(c) mild (d) fanatic

29. Banal
(a) philosophical (b) trite
(c) dramatic (d) heedless

30. Baneful
(a) intellectual (b) thankful
(c) decisive (d) poisonous

31. Boisterous
(a) conflicting (b) noisy
(c) testimonial (d) grateful

32. Bombastic
(a) sensitive (b) pompous
(c) rapid (d) sufficient

33. Bouillon
(a) insight
(b) chowder
(c) gold
(d) clear soup

34. Brackish
(a) careful (b) salty
(c) chosen (d) tough

35. Braggadocio
(a) weaponry (b) boasting
(c) skirmish (d) encounter

36. Brazen
(a) shameless (b) quick
(c) modest (d) pleasant

37. Brindled
(a) equine (b) pathetic
(c) hasty (d) spotted

38. Brochure
(a) opening (b) pamphlet
(c) censor (d) bureau

39. bucolic
(a) diseased (b) replusive
(c) rustic (d) twinkling

40. Buxom
(a) voluminous (b) indecisive
(c) convincing (d) plump

41. Cache
(a) lock
(b) hiding place
(c) tide
(d) automobile

42. Cacophony
(a) discord
(b) dance
(c) applause
(d) type of telephone

43. Callow
(a) youthful (b) holy
(c) mild (d) colored

44. Candid
(a) vague (b) outspoken
(c) experienced (d) anxious

45. Chaste
(a) loyal (b) timid
(c) curt (d) pure

46. Chide
(a) unite (b) fear
(c) record (d) scold

47. Chimerical
(a) developing (b) brief
(c) distant (d) fantastic

48. Choleric
(a) musical (b) episodic
(c) hot headed (d) global

49. Churlish
(a) marine (b) economical
(c) impolite (d) compact

50. Ciliated
(a) foolish (b) swift
(c) early (d) hairy

51. Circuitous
(*a*) indirect (*b*) complete
(*c*) obvious (*d*) aware

52. City
(*a*) galvanize (*b*) visualize
(*c*) locate (*d*) quote

53. Clandestine
(*a*) abortive (*b*) secret
(*c*) tangible (*d*) doomed

54. Claustrophobia
(*a*) lack of confidence
(*b*) fear of spiders
(*c*) love of books
(*d*) fear of closed places

55. Cleft
(*a*) split (*b*) waterfall
(*c*) assembly (*d*) adherence

56. Cliche
(*a*) increase (*b*) vehicle
(*c*) morale (*d*) platitude

57. Coerce
(*a*) recover (*b*) begin
(*c*) force (*d*) license

58. Cognizance
(*a*) policy (*b*) knowledge
(*c*) advance (*d*) omission

59. Cohere
(*a*) hold together
(*b*) occur simultaneously
(*c*) recollect
(*d*) materialize

60. Conjecture
(*a*) magic (*b*) guess
(*c*) position (*d*) form

61. Connoisseur
(*a*) gourmand (*b*) lover of art
(*c*) humidor (*d*) delinquent

62. Consanguinity
(*a*) kinship (*b*) friendship
(*c*) bloodletting (*d*) relief

63. Consensus
(*a*) general agreement (*b*) project
(*c*) insignificance (*d*) sheaf

64. Construe
(*a*) explain (*b*) promote
(*c*) reserve (*d*) erect

65. Contaminate
(*a*) arrest (*b*) prepare
(*c*) pollute (*d*) beam

66. Contentious
(*a*) squealing (*b*) surprising
(*c*) quarrelsome (*d*) smug

67. Continence
(*a*) humanity (*b*) research
(*c*) embryology (*d*) self-restraint

68. Contraband
(*a*) purpose (*b*) rogue
(*c*) rascality (*d*) difficulty

69. Contrite
(*a*) smart
(*b*) penitent
(*c*) restful
(*d*) recognized

70. Controvert
(*a*) turnover (*b*) contradict
(*c*) mind (*d*) expolain

71. Convene
(*a*) propose (*b*) restore
(*c*) question (*d*) gather

72. Conversant
(*a*) ignorant
(*b*) speaking
(*c*) incorporated
(*d*) familiar

73. Copious
(*a*) plentiful (*b*) cheating
(*c*) dishonorable (*d*) adventurous

74. Corpulent
(*a*) regenerate (*b*) obese
(*c*) different (*d*) hungry

75. Decimate
(*a*) kill (*b*) disgrace
(*c*) search (*d*) collide

76. Declivite
(*a*) trap (*b*) quadrangle
(*c*) quarter (*d*) downward slope

77. Decollete
(a) flavored (b) demure
(c) flowery (d) low-necked

78. Decorous
(a) momentary (b) emotional
(c) suppressed (d) proper

79. Decrepitude
(a) feebleness (b) disease
(c) coolness (d) melee

80. Default
(a) failure to act
(b) tendency to err
(c) desire to remedy
(d) debt

81. Defection
(a) determination (b) desertion
(c) invitation (d) affection

82. Defile
(a) maincure (b) ride
(c) pollute (d) assemble

83. Degraded
(a) surpprised (b) lowered
(c) ascended (d) learned

84. Deleterious
(a) delaying
(b) experimental
(c) harmful
(d) graduating

85. Deluge
(a) confusion (b) deception
(c) flood (d) mountain

86. Denigrate
(a) refuse (b) blacken
(c) terrify (d) admit

87. Denouement
(a) action (b) scenery
(c) resort (d) solution

88. Depravity
(a) wickedness (b) sadness
(c) heaviness (d) tidiness

89. Deranged
(a) insane (b) systematic
(c) neighborly (d) alphabetical

90. Dwindle
(a) blow (b) inhabit
(c) spin (d) lessen

91. Ecstasy
(a) joy (b) speed
(c) treasure (d) warmth

92. Edify
(a) mystify (b) suffice
(c) improve (d) erect

93. Efface
(a) countenance
(b) encourage
(c) recognize
(d) rub out

94. Effigy
(a) requisition (b) organ
(c) charge (d) dummy

95. Egregious
(a) pious (b) shocking
(c) anxious (d) sociable

96. Egress
(a) entrence (b) bird
(c) exit (d) double

97. Elated
(a) debased
(b) respectful
(c) drooping
(d) gay

98. Elusive
(a) deadly (b) eloping
(c) evasive (d) simple

99. Emaciated
(a) garrulous (b) primeval
(c) vigorous (d) thin

100. Emancipate
(a) set free (b) take back
(c) make worse (d) embolden

101. Embellish
(a) doff (b) don
(c) abscond (d) adon

102. Embroil
(a) cherish (b) overtheat
(c) entangle (d) assure

103. Emendation
(*a*) correction
(*b*) interpretation
(*c*) exhumation
(*d*) inquiry

104. Eminent
(*a*) purposeful (*b*) high
(*c*) delectable (*d*) currious

105. Flored
(*a*) ruddy (*b*) rusty
(*c*) ruined (*d*) patient

106. Foil
(*a*) bury (*b*) frustrate
(*c*) shield (*d*) desire

107. Foment
(*a*) spoil (*b*) instigate
(*c*) interrogate (*d*) spray

108. Foolhardy
(*a*) strong (*b*) unwise
(*c*) brave (*d*) futile

109. Foppish
(*a*) scanty (*b*) radical
(*c*) orthodox (*d*) dandyish

110. Foray
(*a*) exursion (*b*) contest
(*c*) ranger (*d*) intuition

111. Formidable
(*a*) dangerous
(*b*) outlandish
(*c*) grandiloquent
(*d*) impenetrable

112. Foster
(*a*) accelerate (*b*) fondle
(*c*) become infected (*d*) raise

113. Franchise
(*a*) subway (*b*) discount
(*c*) license (*d*) reason

114. Fritter
(*a*) sour (*b*) chafe
(*c*) dissipate (*d*) cancel

115. Frugality
(*a*) foolishness (*b*) extremity
(*c*) indifference (*d*) economy

116. Fulminate
(*a*) fulfill (*b*) contemplate
(*c*) talk nonsense (*d*) protest

117. Furor
(*a*) excitement (*b*) worry
(*c*) flux (*d*) anteroom

118. Furtive
(*a*) underhanded (*b*) coy
(*c*) brilliant (*d*) quick

119. Gadfly
(*a*) humorist
(*b*) nuisance
(*c*) scholar
(*d*) bum

120. Galleon
(*a*) liquid measure (*b*) ship
(*c*) armada (*d*) company

121. Garisth
(*a*) sordid (*b*) flashy
(*c*) prominent (*d*) lusty

122. Garner
(*a*) prevent (*b*) assist
(*c*) collect (*d*) compute

123. Garnish
(*a*) paint (*b*) gamer
(*c*) adorn (*d*) abuse

124. Garrulity
(*a*) credulity
(*b*) senility
(*c*) loquaciousness
(*d*) speciousness

125. Garrulous
(*a*) arid (*b*) hasty
(*c*) sociable (*d*) talkative

126. Gauche
(*a*) rigid (*b*) swift
(*c*) awkward (*d*) taciturn

127. Gaudy
(*a*) holy (*b*) showy
(*c*) sentimental (*d*) mild

128. Gaunt
(*a*) victorious (*b*) tiny
(*c*) stylish (*d*) haggard

129. Genuflect
(*a*) falsify (*b*) trick
(*c*) project (*d*) bend the knee

130. Germane
(*a*) bacteriological
(*b*) middle european
(*c*) prominent
(*d*) relevant

131. Germtinal
(*a*) creative (*b*) excused
(*c*) sterilized (*d*) primitive

132. Gist
(*a*) chaff (*b*) summary
(*c*) expostulation (*d*) expiation

133. Glib
(*a*) slippery (*b*) fashionable
(*c*) antiquated (*d*) articulate

134. Gnome
(*a*) fury (*b*) giant
(*c*) dwarf (*d*) native

135. Inclement
(*a*) unfavorable (*b*) abandoned
(*c*) kindly (*d*) selfish

136. Incompatible
(*a*) capable
(*b*) reasonable
(*c*) faulty
(*d*) alienated

137. Inconsequential
(*a*) disorderly (*b*) insignificant
(*c*) subsequent (*d*) insufficient

138. Incontinent
(*a*) insular (*b*) complaisant
(*c*) crass (*d*) wanton

139. Incorrigible
(*a*) narrow (*b*) straight
(*c*) inconceivable (*d*) unreformable

140. Incriminate
(*a*) exacerbate (*b*) involve
(*c*) intimidate (*d*) lacerate

141. Inculcate
(*a*) exculpate (*b*) educate
(*c*) exonerate (*d*) prepare

142. Indigent
(*a*) lazy (*b*) pusillanimous
(*c*) penurious (*d*) affluent

143. Indigniy
(*a*) pomposity (*b*) bombast
(*c*) obeisance (*d*) insult

144. Indolence
(*a*) sloth (*b*) poverty
(*c*) latitude (*d*) aptitude

145. Indubitably
(*a*) flagrantly (*b*) doubtfully
(*c*) carefully (*d*) cortainly

146. Inebriety
(*a*) revelation (*b*) drunkenness
(*c*) felony (*d*) starvation

147. Inept
(*a*) outward (*b*) spiritual
(*c*) foolish (*d*) clumsy

148. Infallible
(*a*) final
(*b*) unbelievable
(*c*) perfect
(*d*) inaccurate

149. Infirmity
(*a*) disability (*b*) age
(*c*) inoculation (*d*) hospital

150. Ingenuous
(*a*) clever (*b*) stimulating
(*c*) naive (*d*) worried

151. Inimical
(*a*) antagonistic
(*b*) anonymous
(*c*) fanciful
(*d*) accurate

152. Innocuous
(*a*) not capable (*b*) not dangerous
(*c*) not eager (*d*) not frank

153. Insinuate
(*a*) resist (*b*) suggest
(*c*) report (*d*) rectify

154. Insipid
(*a*) witty (*b*) flat
(*c*) wily (*d*) talkative

155. Integrate
(*a*) tolerate (*b*) unite
(*c*) flow (*d*) copy

156. Inter
(*a*) bury (*b*) amuse
(*c*) relate (*d*) frequent

157. Interdict
(*a*) acclain (*b*) dispute
(*c*) prohibit (*d*) decide

158. Intermittent
(*a*) heavy (*b*) fleet
(*c*) occasional (*d*) fearless

159. Intractable
(*a*) culpable (*b*) flexible
(*c*) unruly (*d*) efficient

160. Intransigence
(*a*) lack of training
(*b*) stubbornness
(*c*) novelty
(*d*) timidity

161. Intrepid
(*a*) cold (*b*) hot
(*c*) understood (*d*) courageous

162. Intrinsic
(*a*) extrinsic (*b*) abnormal
(*c*) above (*d*) basic

163. Inundate
(*a*) abuse (*b*) deny
(*c*) swallow (*d*) flood

164. Inveigh
(*a*) speak violently
(*b*) orate
(*c*) disturb
(*d*) apply

165. Lethargy
(*a*) dynamism (*b*) orate
(*c*) disturb (*d*) apply

166. Loquacious
(*a*) verbose (*b*) tacturn
(*c*) rational (*d*) alluring

167. Loath
(*a*) tired (*b*) unwilling
(*c*) sickly (*d*) spirited

168. Mawkish
(*a*) sentimental (*b*) true
(*c*) certain (*d*) devious

169. Mediocre
(*a*) average (*b*) bitter
(*c*) medieval (*d*) industrial

170. Melee
(*a*) heat (*b*) brawl
(*c*) attempt (*d*) weapon

171. Mellifluous
(*a*) porous (*b*) honeycombed
(*c*) strong (*d*) smooth

172. Menial
(*a*) intellectual (*b*) clairvoyant
(*c*) servile (*d*) arrogant

173. Mentor
(*a*) guide (*b*) genius
(*c*) talker (*d*) philosopher

174. Mesmerize
(*a*) remember (*b*) hypnotize
(*c*) delay (*d*) bore

175. Meticulous
(*a*) steadfast (*b*) recent
(*c*) quaint (*d*) painstaking

176. Miasma
(*a*) dream (*b*) noxious fumes
(*c*) scenario (*d*) quantity

177. Militant
(*a*) combative (*b*) dramatic
(*c*) religious (*d*) quaintity

178. Minon
(*a*) monster (*b*) quorum
(*c*) majority (*d*) dependent

179. Mirage
(*a*) dessert (*b*) illusion
(*c*) water (*d*) mirror

180. Misanthrope
(*a*) benefactor
(*b*) philanderer
(*c*) man-hater
(*d*) aesthete

181. Mischance
(*a*) gamble (*b*) ordinance
(*c*) aperture (*d*) anecdote

182. Misdemeanor
(*a*) felony (*b*) peccadillo
(*c*) indignity (*d*) flat

183. Modish
(*a*) sentimental (*b*) stylish
(*c*) vacillating (*d*) contrary

184. Mollify
(*a*) avenge (*b*) attenuate
(*c*) attibute (*d*) appease

185. Monetary
(*a*) boring (*b*) fascinating
(*c*) fiscal (*d*) stationary

186. Moratorium
(*a*) burial (*b*) gathering
(*c*) delay (*d*) refusal

187. Mordant
(*a*) dying (*b*) trenchant
(*c*) fabricating (*d*) controlling

188. Moribund
(*a*) dying (*b*) trenchant
(*c*) fabricating (*d*) controlling

189. Motley
(*a*) active (*b*) disguised
(*c*) variegated (*d*) somber

190. Muggy
(*a*) attacking (*b*) fascinating
(*c*) humid (*d*) characteristic

191. Mulct
(*a*) swindle (*b*) hold
(*c*) record (*d*) pring

192. Multilingual
(*a*) variegated (*b*) polyglot
(*c*) multilateral (*d*) polyandrous

193. Mundane
(*a*) global (*b*) futile
(*c*) spatial (*d*) worldly

194. Munificent
(*a*) grandiose (*b*) puny
(*c*) philanthropic (*d*) poor

195. Musty
(*a*) flat (*b*) necessary
(*c*) indifferent (*d*) nonchalant

196. Myopic
(*a*) visionary (*b*) nearsighted
(*c*) moral (*d*) glassy

197. Nascent
(*a*) incipient (*b*) ignorant
(*c*) loyal (*d*) treacherous

198. Phlegmatic
(*a*) calm (*b*) cryptic
(*c*) practical (*d*) salivary

199. Physiognomy
(*a*) posture (*b*) head
(*c*) physique (*d*) face

200. Piebald
(*a*) motley (*b*) coltish
(*c*) hairless (*d*) thoroughbred

201. Pillage
(*a*) hoard (*b*) plunder
(*c*) versify (*d*) denigrate

202. Pinion
(*a*) express (*b*) report
(*c*) reveal (*d*) restrain

203. Pinnacle
(*a*) foothills (*b*) card game
(*c*) pass (*d*) peak

204. Pious
(*a*) historic (*b*) devout
(*c*) multiple (*d*) fortunate

205. Pique
(*a*) pyramid (*b*) revolt
(*c*) resentment (*d*) struggle

206. Placate
(*a*) determine (*b*) transmit
(*c*) pacify (*d*) allow

207. Plagiarism
(*a*) theft of funds (*b*) theft of ideas
(*c*) belief in god (*d*) arson

208. Plaintive
(*a*) moumful (*b*) senseless
(*c*) persistent (*d*) rural

209. Platitude
(*a*) fatness (*b*) bravery
(*c*) dimension (*d*) trite remark

210. Polemic
(*a*) blackness (*b*) lighting
(*c*) magnetism (*d*) controversy

211. Precarious
(*a*) priceless (*b*) premature
(*c*) primitive (*d*) hazardous

212. Refractory
(*a*) articulate (*b*) sinkable
(*c*) vaunted (*d*) unmanageable

213. Regal
(*a*) oppressive (*b*) royal
(*c*) major (*d*) basic

214. Reiterate
(*a*) gainsay (*b*) revive
(*c*) revenge (*d*) repeat

215. Relish
(*a*) desire (*b*) nibble
(*c*) savor (*d*) violating

216. Remiss
(*a*) lax (*b*) lost
(*c*) foolish (*d*) violating

217. Remonstrate
(*a*) display (*b*) restate
(*c*) protest (*d*) resign

218. Repartee
(*a*) witty retort (*b*) willful departure
(*c*) spectator (*d*) monologue

219. Repllent
(*a*) propulsive (*b*) unattractive
(*c*) porous (*d*) stiff

220. Rpercussion
(*a*) reaction (*b*) restitution
(*c*) resistance (*d*) magnificence

221. Replenish
(*a*) polish (*b*) repeat
(*c*) reinstate (*d*) refill

222. Replica
(*a*) museum piece (*b*) famous site
(*c*) battle emblem (*d*) facsimile

223. Reprisal
(*a*) reevaluation (*b*) assessment
(*c*) loss (*d*) retaliation

224. Reprove
(*a*) prevail (*b*) rebuke
(*c*) ascertain (*d*) prove false

225. Repudiate
(*a*) besmirch (*b*) appropriate
(*c*) annoy (*d*) reject

226. Repugnance
(*a*) belligerence (*b*) tanacity
(*c*) renewal (*d*) loathing

227. Tarry
(*a*) polish (*b*) restrain
(*c*) surpass (*d*) linger

228. Tautology
(*a*) memory (*b*) repetition
(*c*) tension (*d*) smile

229. Tawdry
(*a*) orderly (*b*) meretricious
(*c*) reclaimed (*d*) filtered

230. Temerity
(*a*) timidity (*b*) resourcefulness
(*c*) boldness (*d*) tremulousness

231. Temporal
(*a*) priestly (*b*) scholarly
(*c*) secular (*d*) sleeply

232. Tenacious
(*a*) fast running (*b*) intertional
(*c*) obnoxious (*d*) holding fast

233. Tenacity
(*a*) splendor (*b*) perseverance
(*c*) tendency (*d*) ingratitide

234. Tendentious
(*a*) biased (*b*) likely
(*c*) absurd (*d*) festive

235. Tentative
(*a*) prevalent (*b*) portable
(*c*) mocking (*d*) wry

236. Tenuous
(*a*) vital (*b*) thin
(*c*) careful (*d*) dangerous

237. Tepid
(*a*) boiling (*b*) luckewarm
(*c*) freezing (*d*) gaseous

EXERCISE – II

(QUESTIONS FROM PREVIOUS GATE EXAMS)

MCQ TYPE QUESTIONS

2015

1. The word similar in meaning to 'dreary' is
(*a*) cheerful (*b*) dreamy
(*c*) hard (*d*) dismal

2. Choose the word most similar in meaning to the given word :
Educe
(*a*) Exert (*b*) Educate
(*c*) Extract (*d*) Extend

3. Choose the most suitable one word substitute for the following expression
Connotation of a road or way
(*a*) Pertinacious (*b*) Viaticum
(*c*) Clandestine (*d*) Ravenous

4. Choose the word most similar in meaning to the given word:
Awkward
(*a*) Inept
(*b*) Graceful
(*c*) Suitable
(*d*) Dreadful

5. A generic term that includes various items of clothing such as a skirt, a pair of trousers and a shirt as
(*a*) fabric (*b*) textile
(*c*) fibre (*d*) apparel

6. Which of the following combinations is incorrect?
(*a*) Acquiescence – Submission
(*b*) Wheedle – Roundabout
(*c*) Flippancy – Lightness
(*d*) Profligate – Extravagant

2014

7. A student is required to demonstrate a high level of comprehension of the subject, especially in the social sciences.
The word closest in meaning to comprehension is
(*a*) understanding (*b*) meaning
(*c*) concentration (*d*) stability

8. While receiving the award, the scientist said, "I feel vindicated". Which of the following is closest in meaning to the word 'vindicated'?
(*a*) punished (*b*) substantiated
(*c*) appreciated (*d*) chastened

9. Choose the word that is opposite in meaning to the word "coherent".
(*a*) sticky (*b*) well-connected
(*c*) rambling (*d*) friendly

10. Match the columns:

Column-1	Column-2
1. eradicate	P. misrepresent
2. distort	Q. soak completely
3. saturate	R. use
4. utilize	S. destroy utterly

(*a*) 1 : S, 2 : P, 3 : Q, 4 : R
(*b*) 1 : P, 2 : Q, 3 : R, 4 : S
(*c*) 1 : Q, 2 : R, 3 : S, 4 : P
(*d*) 1 : S, 2 : P, 3 : R, 4 : Q

2013

11. Which of the following options is the closest in meaning to the word given below:
Primeval
(*a*) Modern (*b*) Historic
(*c*) Primitive (*d*) Antique

12. Which one of the following options is the closest in meaning to the word given below?
Nadir
(*a*) Highest (*b*) Lowest
(*c*) Medium (*d*) Integration

13. They were requested not to **quarrel** with others. Which one of the following options is the closest in meaning to the word **quarrel**?
(*a*) make out (*b*) call out
(*c*) dig out (*d*) fall out

2012

14. Which one of the following options is the closest in meaning to the word given below?
Mitigate
(*a*) Diminish (*b*) Divulge
(*c*) Dedicate (*d*) Denote

15. Which one of the following options is the closest in meaning to the word given below ?
Latitude
(*a*) Eligibility (*b*) Freedom
(*c*) Coercion (*d*) Meticulousness

2011

16. Which of the following options is the closest in the meaning to the word below :
Inexplicable
(*a*) Incomprehensible (*b*) Indelible
(*c*) Inextricable (*d*) Infallible

2010

17. Which of the following options is the closest in meaning to the word below:
Circuitous
(*a*) cyclic (*b*) indirect
(*c*) confusing (*d*) crooked

ANSWERS

EXERCISE – I

MCQ Type Questions

1. (*d*) **2.** (*a*) **3.** (*c*) **4.** (*d*) **5.** (*b*) **6.** (*d*) **7.** (*b*) **8.** (*d*) **9.** (*a*) **10.** (*a*)
11. (*a*) **12.** (*d*) **13.** (*a*) **14.** (*d*) **15.** (*d*) **16.** (*d*) **17.** (*d*) **18.** (*b*) **19.** (*c*) **20.** (*c*)
21. (*a*) **22.** (*c*) **23.** (*c*) **24.** (*b*) **25.** (*c*) **26.** (*d*) **27.** (*c*) **28.** (*c*) **29.** (*b*) **30.** (*d*)
31. (*b*) **32.** (*b*) **33.** (*d*) **34.** (*b*) **35.** (*b*) **36.** (*a*) **37.** (*d*) **38.** (*b*) **39.** (*c*) **40.** (*d*)
41. (*b*) **42.** (*a*) **43.** (*a*) **44.** (*c*) **45.** (*d*) **46.** (*d*) **47.** (*d*) **48.** (*c*) **49.** (*c*) **50.** (*d*)
51. (*a*) **52.** (*d*) **53.** (*b*) **54.** (*d*) **55.** (*a*) **56.** (*d*) **57.** (*c*) **58.** (*b*) **59.** (*a*) **60.** (*b*)
61. (*b*) **62.** (*a*) **63.** (*a*) **64.** (*a*) **65.** (*c*) **66.** (*c*) **67.** (*d*) **68.** (*d*) **69.** (*b*) **70.** (*b*)
71. (*d*) **72.** (*d*) **73.** (*a*) **74.** (*b*) **75.** (*a*) **76.** (*d*) **77.** (*d*) **78.** (*d*) **79.** (*a*) **80.** (*a*)
81. (*b*) **82.** (*c*) **83.** (*b*) **84.** (*c*) **85.** (*c*) **86.** (*b*) **87.** (*d*) **88.** (*a*) **89.** (*a*) **90.** (*d*)
91. (*a*) **92.** (*c*) **93.** (*d*) **94.** (*d*) **95.** (*b*) **96.** (*c*) **97.** (*d*) **98.** (*c*) **99.** (*d*) **100.** (*a*)
101. (*d*) **102.** (*c*) **103.** (*a*) **104.** (*b*) **105.** (*a*) **106.** (*b*) **107.** (*b*) **108.** (*b*) **109.** (*d*) **110.** (*a*)
111. (*a*) **112.** (*c*) **113.** (*c*) **114.** (*c*) **115.** (*d*) **116.** (*d*) **117.** (*a*) **118.** (*a*) **119.** (*b*) **120.** (*b*)
121. (*b*) **122.** (*c*) **123.** (*c*) **124.** (*c*) **125.** (*d*) **126.** (*c*) **127.** (*b*) **128.** (*d*) **129.** (*d*) **130.** (*d*)
131. (*a*) **132.** (*b*) **133.** (*d*) **134.** (*c*) **135.** (*a*) **136.** (*d*) **137.** (*b*) **138.** (*d*) **139.** (*d*) **140.** (*b*)
141. (*b*) **142.** (*c*) **143.** (*d*) **144.** (*a*) **145.** (*d*) **146.** (*b*) **147.** (*d*) **148.** (*c*) **149.** (*a*) **150.** (*c*)
151. (*a*) **152.** (*b*) **153.** (*b*) **154.** (*b*) **155.** (*a*) **156.** (*a*) **157.** (*c*) **158.** (*c*) **159.** (*c*) **160.** (*b*)
161. (*d*) **162.** (*d*) **163.** (*d*) **164.** (*a*) **165.** (*b*) **166.** (*a*) **167.** (*b*) **168.** (*d*) **169.** (*a*) **170.** (*b*)
171. (*d*) **172.** (*c*) **173.** (*a*) **174.** (*b*) **175.** (*d*) **176.** (*b*) **177.** (*a*) **178.** (*d*) **179.** (*b*) **180.** (*c*)
181. (*d*) **182.** (*b*) **183.** (*b*) **184.** (*d*) **185.** (*c*) **186.** (*c*) **187.** (*b*) **188.** (*a*) **189.** (*c*) **190.** (*c*)
191. (*a*) **192.** (*b*) **193.** (*d*) **194.** (*c*) **195.** (*a*) **196.** (*b*) **197.** (*a*) **198.** (*a*) **199.** (*d*) **200.** (*a*)
201. (*b*) **202.** (*d*) **203.** (*d*) **204.** (*b*) **205.** (*c*) **206.** (*c*) **207.** (*b*) **208.** (*a*) **209.** (*d*) **210.** (*d*)
211. (*d*) **212.** (*d*) **213.** (*b*) **214.** (*d*) **215.** (*c*) **216.** (*a*) **217.** (*c*) **218.** (*a*) **219.** (*b*) **220.** (*a*)
221. (*d*) **222.** (*d*) **223.** (*d*) **224.** (*b*) **225.** (*d*) **226.** (*d*) **227.** (*d*) **228.** (*b*) **229.** (*b*) **230.** (*c*)
231. (*c*) **232.** (*d*) **233.** (*b*) **234.** (*a*) **235.** (*d*) **236.** (*b*) **237.** (*b*)

EXERCISE – II

MCQ Type Questions

1. (*d*) **2.** (*c*) **3.** (*b*) **4.** (*a*) **5.** (*d*) **6.** (*b*) **7.** (*a*) **8.** (*b*) **9.** (*c*) **10.** (*a*)
11. (*c*) **12.** (*b*) **13.** (*b*) **14.** (*a*) **15.** (*b*) **16.** (*a*) **17.** (*b*)

EXPLANATIONS

EXERCISE – II

MCQ TYPE QUESTIONS

1. *dreary* - depressingly dull and bleak or repetitive.

2. The word similar in meaning to Educe is Extract.

12. Given: A word "Nadir"

To find: Closest meaning word to 'Nadir' in the given options.

Analysis: The dictionary meaning of 'Nadir' is 'Lowest' which is potion (*b*)

Source: Google

Given: A sequence 44, 42, 40,......

To find: Maximum sum of the sequence

Analysis: To find the maximum sum, we have to ignore all the negative terms (they will only decrease the sum). Hence, we terminate the sequence at 0.

Now, the sequence is 44, 42,......,2, 0.

This sequence is an Arithmetic progression with common difference –2. Now, the problem reduces to finding the sum of this A.P.

To find the sum of A.P., we have to find the number of terms in A.P.

Let n be the number of terms

a be the first term

l be the last term

d be the common difference.

$n = ?$

$a = 44, \quad l = 0, \quad d = -2$

Now, $l = a + (n - 1)d$

14. 'Mitigate' means to make something less harmful, serious, intense etc. Hence correct answer is 'Diminis'

16. Inexplicable means not explicable; that cannot be explained, understood, or accounted for. So the best synonym here is incomprehensible.

17. Circuitous means round about or not direct

So circuitous : indirect.

4

CHAPTER

Antonyms

The basic idea of a antonym question is to find an opposite for a word. Antonym items are first and foremost a test of vocabulary.

If you have no idea of the meaning of the given word, there's not much you can do. When you don't know the meaning of an antonym, don't waste a lot of time trying to fiture it out. In other words, once you recognize that you are out of ammunition, just do a random guess, confirm it, and move on the next item.

Each antonym starts with a capitalized word, which is followed by four words of phrases in lowercase letters. The task is to find the word or phrase that is most nearly opposite in meaning to the bold word.

Plan to Answer Antonym Questions

1. Define the capitalized word.
2. Think of a meaning that is opposite to this word.
3. Read all the answer choices. Eliminate those that do not relate to the meaning you thought of. If only one choice remains, mord it and go on.
4. If more than one choice remains, go back and refine your thinking about the bold word.
5. Pick the answer choice that is most nearly opposite to the bold word.

   Tedious

   (*a*) unlimited (*b*) confined

   (*c*) enthralling (*d*) appetizing

   (*i*) The capitalized word means "boring" or "tiresome"

   (*ii*) The opposite of "boring" would be something like *exciting or interesting*.

   (*iii*) Looking at all the answer choices, you can immediately eliminate (*a*), and (*b*) as having nothing to do with excitement. But that leaves (*c*) *enthralling and* (*d*) *apperizing*.

   (*iv*) Of the two remaining choices, *enthralling, which means "captivating"* or fascinating," is more nearly opposite in meaning to *tedious than appetizing*, which means "savory," or "delicious".

   (*v*) Mark (*c*), enthralling, as the correct choice.

   Note :

   (*i*) **Makes sure to read all the answers :** To answer antonym questions you'll sometimes have to distinguish fine shades of meaning. That's why you have to consider very answer choice.

   (*ii*) **Verb or Noun?** If the part of speech of the capitalized word is ambiguous, check the answer choices.

6. Sometimes the test writer selects a word you are likely to be familiar with, but sets up the question to test a meaning you do not ordinarily associate with the word. Here is an example:

   e.g. precipitous

   (*a*) pleasantly sweet

   (*b*) overly ambitious

   (*c*) agreeably situated

   (*d*) gently sloping

   The best choice is (*d*). We most often use the word precipitous to mean rash or foothardy, but its central meaning is related to precipice, a sharp drop-off.

7. **Eleminate non-answers**

   The simple way to eleminate answer choices is to toss out any words that don't have opposite meanings.

8. **Concentrate on answer choices**

   Words can have different meanings based upon their part of speech. If you are uncertain about the part of speech of the bold word, just check the naswer choices. If they're all verbs, for example, so is the bold word.

9. **Play around with the part of speech of a word**

   You can alter the part of speech of the bold word and answer choices in your own mind. Sometimes an antonym will use a word you know but as a part of speech that is unfamiliar to you.

   ***e.g.* sublimity**

   (*a*) erosion (*b*) baseness

   (*c*) conciseness (*d*) insistence

   The best choice is (*b*). You may know the word sublimity better as the adjective sublime, meaning "lofty, high, or noble". So you may find it easire to think about the antonym by changing *sublimity* to the more familiar form *sublime*". As you think about each answer choice, you would then change it in your mind to an adjective *Baseness*, therefore, would become *base*; and *base* is an opposite of *sublime*.

10. **Use word connotations to eliminate answer choices**

    Even if you don't know the exact meaning of a word, you may have a vague recollection of the context in which you first encountered it. So you may know whether the word has positive overtones or negative ones. This recollection may be sufficient to get a correct answer.

***e.g.* raffish**

(*a*) grotesque (*b*) delinquent
(*c*) uncaring (*d*) noble

The correct choice is (*d*). Let's assume that you do not know that is means "low, vulgar, the base. 'Let's further assume, however, that you have a vague knowledge of the word. You've seen it used to describe a character who is dishonest and not trustworthy. So even though you don't know the exact meaning of the word, you know that it has negative overtones. Sine you an looking for the opposite of a word with negative overtones, you would eliminate every answer choice with negative overtones. As it turns out, this strategy workd perfectly with this antonym; only one word is left. *Noble* is the only word with positive overtones.

11. Unlock word meanings by taking the word apart

Even when you encounter a word for the first time, you may be able to ascertain its meaning from its parts.

***e.g.* congnoscitive**

(*a*) courageous (*b*) expensive
(*c*) unconscious (*d*) redundant

The best answer is (*c*). This is very unusual word, but you can probably figure out its meaning by looking at its root cog-. This is the same root found in words such as *cognition and recognize*, and it has to do with knowledge. So we infer that *cognoscitive* has something to do with awareness, and (*c*) looks like a good opposite. A word of caution, however : Don't spend too much time trying to decipher the meaning of a word.

EXERCISE – I

MCQ TYPE QUESTIONS

Directions : *Each question below consists of a word printed in capital lettes, followed by four lettered words of phrases. Choosed the lettered word or phrase that is most nearly opposite in meaning to the word in bold letters.*

1. Abrogate
(*a*) transgress (*b*) signify
(*c*) allevate (*d*) ratify

2. Admonition
(*a*) premonit ion (*b*) hallucination
(*c*) escape (*d*) commendation

3. Adulation
(*a*) youth (*b*) purity
(*c*) brightness (*d*) criticism

4. Advocate
(*a*) define (*b*) oppose
(*c*) remove (*d*) inspect

5. Affable
(*a*) rude (*b*) ruddy
(*c*) needy (*d*) useless

6. Affecfted
(*a*) weary (*b*) unfriendly
(*c*) divine (*d*) unfeigned

7. Affluence
(*a*) poverty (*b*) fear
(*c*) persuasion (*d*) consideration

8. Agility
(*a*) awkwardness (*b*) solidity
(*c*) temper (*d*) harmony

9. Alacrity
(*a*) slowness (*b*) plenty
(*c*) fifth (*d*) courtesy

10. Alleviate
(*a*) endure (*b*) worsen
(*c*) enlighten (*d*) maneuver

11. Allure
(*a*) hinder (*b*) repel
(*c*) ignore (*d*) leave

12. Aloof
(*a*) triangular (*b*) gregarious
(*c*) comparable (*d*) honorable

13. Amalgamate
(*a*) equip (*b*) separate
(*c*) generate (*d*) materialize

14. Ambiguous
(*a*) salvageable (*b*) corresponding
(*c*) responsible (*d*) clear

15. Amble
(*a*) befriend (*b*) hasten
(*c*) steal (*d*) browse

16. Ambulatory
(*a*) convalescent (*b*) valedictory
(*c*) bedridden (*d*) emergency

17. Ameliorate
(*a*) make slow (*b*) make sure
(*c*) make young (*d*) make worse

18. Amicable
(*a*) penetrating (*b*) compensating
(*c*) unfriendly (*d*) zigzag

19. Amoral
(*a*) unusal (*b*) unfriendly
(*c*) ethical (*d*) suave

20. Amorphous
(*a*) nauseous (*b*) obscene
(*c*) providential (*d*) definite

21. Amplify
(*a*) distract (*b*) infer
(*c*) publicize (*d*) decrease

22. Analogous
(*a*) not comparable (*b*) not capable
(*c*) not culpable (*d*) not corporeal

23. Anthematize
(*a*) locate (*b*) deceive
(*c*) regulate (*d*) bless

24. Anemic
(*a*) pailid (*b*) cruel
(*c*) red-blooded (*d*) ventilating

25. Animated
(*a*) worthy (*b*) dull
(*c*) humorous (*d*) lengthy

26. Animus
(*a*) pterodactyl (*b*) bastion
(*c*) giraffe (*d*) favor

27. Anomaly
(*a*) desperation (*b*) requisition
(*c*) registry (*d*) regularity

28. Anonymous
(*a*) desperate (*b*) signed
(*c*) defined (*d*) expert

29. Antediluvian
(*a*) transported (*b*) subtle
(*c*) isolated (*d*) modern

30. Antipathy
(*a*) profundity (*b*) objection
(*c*) willingness (*d*) foundness

31. Antithesis
(*a*) velocity (*b*) maxim
(*c*) similarity (*d*) acceleration

32. Aphasia
(*a*) volubility (*b*) necessity
(*c*) pain (*d*) crack

33. Baroque
(*a*) polished (*b*) constant
(*c*) transformed (*d*) simple

34. Beatific
(*a*) glorius (*b*) dreadful
(*c*) theatrical (*d*) crooked

35. Belittle
(*a*) disobey (*b*) forget
(*c*) magnify (*d*) extol

36. Bellicose
(*a*) peaceful (*b*) naval
(*c*) amusing (*d*) piecemeal

37. Benign
(*a*) tenfold (*b*) peaceful
(*c*) blessed (*d*) malignant

38. Benison
(*a*) curse (*b*) bachelor
(*c*) wedding (*d*) orgy

39. Berate
(*a*) grant (*b*) praise
(*c*) refer (*d*) purchase

40. Bestial
(*a*) animated (*b*) noble
(*c*) zoological (*d*) clear

41. Bigotry
(*a*) arrogance (*b*) approval
(*c*) mourning (*d*) tolerance

42. Bizarre
(*a*) roomy (*b*) veiled
(*c*) subduced (*d*) normal

43. Blanch
(*a*) bleach (*b*) scatter
(*c*) darken (*d*) analyze

44. Bland
(*a*) caustic (*b*) meager
(*c*) soft (*d*) uncooked

45. Blase
(*a*) fiery (*b*) clever
(*c*) intriguing (*d*) ardent

46. Bleak
(*a*) pale (*b*) sudden
(*c*) dry (*d*) cheerful

47. Blithe
(*a*) spiritual (*b*) profuse
(*c*) cheerless (*d*) hybrid

48. Capacious
(*a*) warlike (*b*) cordial
(*c*) curious (*d*) not spacious

49. Capricious
(*a*) satisfied (*b*) insured
(*c*) photographic (*d*) steadfast

50. Captious
(*a*) tolerant (*b*) capable
(*c*) frivolous (*d*) winning

51. Carnal
(*a*) impressive (*b*) minute
(*c*) spiritual (*d*) actual

52. Carnivorous
(*a*) gloomy (*b*) tangential
(*c*) productive (*d*) vegetarian

53. Carping
(*a*) rapid (*b*) uncritical
(*c*) unintellectual (*d*) illegal

54. Castigation
(*a*) commendation (*b*) patience
(*c*) generosity (*d*) understatement

55. Categorical
(*a*) negative (*b*) ironic
(*c*) impartial (*d*) qualified

56. Catholic
(*a*) religious (*b*) pacific
(*c*) narrow (*d*) weighty

57. Celerity
(*a*) assurance (*b*) state
(*c*) acerbity (*d*) delay

58. Celibate
(*a*) investing (*b*) married
(*c*) retired (*d*) commodious

59. Censure
(*a*) process (*b*) enclose
(*c*) interest (*d*) praise

60. Centrifugal
(*a*) centripetal (*b*) ephemeral
(*c*) lasting (*d*) barometric

61. Cessation
(*a*) premium (*b*) gravity
(*c*) beginning (*d*) composition

62. Chaffing
(*a*) achieving (*b*) serious
(*c*) caitalistic (*d*) sneezing

63. Coy
(*a*) weak (*b*) airy
(*c*) brazen (*d*) old

64. Cozen
(*a*) amuse (*b*) treat honestly
(*c*) prate (*d*) shackle

65. Craven
(*a*) desirous (*b*) direct
(*c*) bold (*d*) civilized

66. Crux
(*a*) affiliction (*b*) spark
(*c*) events (*d*) trivial point

67. Cryptic
(*a*) tomblike (*b*) futile
(*c*) famous (*d*) candid

68. Cupidity
(*a*) anxiety (*b*) tragedy
(*c*) generosity (*d*) entertainment

69. Curtail
(*a*) mutter (*b*) lengthen
(*c*) express (*d*) burden

70. Cynical
(*a*) trusting (*b*) effortless
(*c*) conclusive (*d*) gallant

71. Dank
(*a*) dry (*b*) guiltless
(*c*) warm (*d*) babbling

72. Dapper
(*a*) unintelligent (*b*) untidy
(*c*) uncertain (*d*) ungrateful

73. Dauntless
(*a*) stolid (*b*) cowardly
(*c*) irrelevant (*d*) peculiar

74. Dearth
(*a*) life (*b*) abundance
(*c*) brightness (*d*) terror

75. Debacle
(*a*) progress (*b*) refusal
(*c*) masque (*d*) cowardice

76. Debilitate
(*a*) bedevil (*b*) repress
(*c*) strengthen (*d*) animate

77. Debonair
(*a*) awkward (*b*) windy
(*c*) balmy (*d*) strong

78. Derogatory
(*a*) roguish (*b*) immediate
(*c*) openionated (*d*) praising

79. Desecrate
(*a*) desist (*b*) integrate
(*c*) confuse (*d*) consecrate

80. Despicable
(*a*) streeing (*b*) worthy of esteem
(*c*) inevitable (*d*) featureless

81. Destitute
(*a*) affluent (*b*) dazzling
(*c*) stationary (*d*) characteristic

82. Devoid
(*a*) latent (*b*) eschewed
(*c*) full of (*d*) suspecting

83. Devout
(*a*) quiet (*b*) dual
(*c*) impious (*d*) straightforward

84. Diabolical
(*a*) mischievous (*b*) lavish
(*c*) seraphic (*d*) redolent

85. Diatribe
(*a*) mass (*b*) range
(*c*) eulogy (*d*) elegy

86. Diffidence
(*a*) sharapness (*b*) boldness
(*c*) malcontent (*d*) dialogue

87. Dilate
(*a*) procrastinate (*b*) contract
(*c*) conclude (*d*) participate

88. Dilatory
(*a*) narrowing (*b*) prompt
(*c*) enlarging (*d*) portentous

89. Diminution
(*a*) expectation (*b*) context
(*c*) validity (*d*) appreciation

90. Din
(*a*) lightness (*b*) safety
(*c*) silence (*d*) hunger

91. Disabuse
(*a*) crash (*b*) violate
(*c*) renege (*d*) deceive

92. Disconsolate
(*a*) unprejudiced (*b*) thankful
(*c*) threatrical (*d*) joyous

93. Enervate
(*a*) strengthen (*b*) sputter
(*c*) arrange (*d*) scrutinize

94. Enhance
(*a*) degrade (*b*) doubt
(*c*) scuff (*d*) gasp

95. Ennui
(a) hate (b) excitement
(c) seriousness (d) humility

96. Enunciate
(a) pray (b) request
(c) deliver (d) mumble

97. Ephemeral
(a) sensuous (b) passing
(c) popular (d) eternal

98. Equable
(a) flat (b) decisive
(c) stormy (d) dishonest

99. Equanimity
(a) agitation (b) stirring
(c) volume (d) identity

100. Equilibrium
(a) imbalance (b) peace
(c) inequity (d) directness

101. Equitable
(a) able to leave (b) able to learn
(c) unfair (d) preferable

102. Equivocal
(a) mistaken (b) quaint
(c) azure (d) clear

103. Erratic
(a) unromantic (b) free
(c) popular (d) steady

104. Erroneous
(a) accurate (b) dignified
(c) curious (d) abrupt

105. Erudite
(a) professorial (b) stately
(c) short (d) ignorant

106. Ethereal
(a) long-lasting (b) earthy
(c) ill (d) critical

107. Eulogistic
(a) pretty (b) critical
(c) brief (d) stern

108. Euphonious
(a) strident (b) lethargic
(c) literary (d) significant

109. Evasive
(a) frank (b) correct
(c) empty (d) fertile

110. Exasperate
(a) confide (b) formalize
(c) placate (d) betray

111. Excoriate
(a) scandalize (b) encourage
(c) avoid (d) praise

112. Exculpate
(a) blame (b) prevail
(c) acquire (d) ravish

113. Execrable
(a) innumerable (b) philosophic
(c) physical (d) excellent

114. Excrate
(a) decipher (b) sadden
(c) integrate (d) admit

115. Exhume
(a) decipher (b) sadden
(c) integrate (d) inter

116. Exodus
(a) neglect (b) consent
(c) entry (d) gain

117. Exonerate
(a) forge (b) accuse
(c) record (d) doctor

118. Exorbitant
(a) moderate (b) partisan
(c) military (d) barbaric

119. Extemporaneous
(a) rehearsed (b) hybrid
(c) humilating (d) satetesmanlike

120. Extraneous
(a) modern (b) decisive
(c) essential (d) effective

121. Extrinsic
(a) reputable (b) inherent
(c) swift (d) ambitious

122. Extrovert
(a) clown (b) hero
(c) ectomorph (d) introvert

123. Grandiose
(a) false (b) ideal
(c) proud (d) simple

124. Gratuitous
(a) warranted (b) frank
(c) ingenuous (d) frugal

125. Gregarious
(a) antisocial (b) anticipatory
(c) glorious (d) horrendous

126. Grisly
(a) suggestive (b) doubtful
(c) untidy (d) pleasant

127. Gullible
(a) incredulous (b) fickle
(c) tantamount (d) easy

128. Gusto
(a) noise (b) panic
(c) atmosphere (d) distaste

129. Ghusty
(a) clam (b) noisy
(c) fragrant (d) routine

130. Hackneyed
(a) carried (b) original
(c) banned (d) timely

131. Haggard
(*a*) shrewish (*b*) inspired
(*c*) plump (*d*) maidenly

132. Halcyon
(*a*) wasteful (*b*) prior
(*c*) subsequent (*d*) martial

133. Haphazard
(*a*) safe (*b*) indifferent
(*c*) deliberate (*d*) tense

134. Hapless
(*a*) cheerful (*b*) consistent
(*c*) fortunate (*d*) considerate

135. Heed
(*a*) ignore (*b*) hope
(*c*) overtake (*d*) nurture

136. Heretic
(*a*) sophist (*b*) believer
(*c*) interpreter (*d*) pacifist

137. Heterogeneous
(*a*) orthodox (*b*) pagan
(*c*) unlikely (*d*) similar

138. Hibernal
(*a*) musical (*b*) summerlike
(*c*) local (*d*) seasonal

139. Hilarity
(*a*) gloom (*b*) heartiness
(*c*) weakness (*d*) casualty

140. Hirsute
(*a*) scaly (*b*) bald
(*c*) erudite (*d*) quiet

141. Hortatory
(*a*) inquiring (*b*) denying
(*c*) killing (*d*) dissuading

142. Hovr
(*a*) commence (*b*) soothe
(*c*) leave (*d*) transform

143. Hunbbub
(*a*) calm (*b*) fury
(*c*) capital (*d*) axle

144. Hummock
(*a*) ummusical (*b*) scorn
(*c*) wakefulness (*d*) vale

145. Husbandry
(*a*) sportsmanship (*b*) dishonesty
(*c*) wastefulness (*d*) friction

146. Hybrid
(*a*) productive (*b*) special
(*c*) purebred (*d*) oafish

147. Hyperbole
(*a*) velocity (*b*) climax
(*c*) curve (*d*) understatement

148. Hypercritical
(*a*) tolerant (*b*) false
(*c*) extreme (*d*) inarticulate

149. Hypocritical
(*a*) sincere (*b*) narrow-minded
(*c*) shameful (*d*) amiable

150. Hypothetial
(*a*) rational (*b*) fantastic
(*c*) wizened (*d*) axiomatic

151. Ignoble
(*a*) produced by fire (*b*) worthy
(*c*) given to questioning (*d*) huge

152. Illusive
(*a*) not deceptive (*b*) not certain
(*c*) not obvious (*d*) not choherent

153. Irksome
(*a*) interesting (*b*) lazy
(*c*) tireless (*d*) devious

154. Irrelevant
(*a*) lacking piety (*b*) fragile
(*c*) congruent (*d*) pertinent

155. Irreparable
(*a*) legible (*b*) correctable
(*c*) proverbial (*d*) concise

156. Irtreverent
(*a*) related (*b*) mischievous
(*c*) respective (*d*) pious

157. Jaded
(*a*) upright (*b*) stimulated
(*c*) aspiring (*d*) applied

158. Jaundiced
(*a*) whitened (*b*) inflamed
(*c*) quickened (*d*) unbiased

159. Jaunty
(*a*) youthful (*b*) ruddy
(*c*) strong (*d*) sedate

160. Jeopardy
(*a*) patience (*b*) courage
(*c*) safety (*d*) willingness

161. Jettison
(*a*) salvage (*b*) submerge
(*c*) descend (*d*) decelerate

162. Jocular
(*a*) arterial (*b*) bloodless
(*c*) verbose (*d*) serious

163. Judicious
(*a*) punitive (*b*) unwise
(*c*) criminal (*d*) licit

164. Kindle
(*a*) dislike (*b*) quench
(*c*) gather (*d*) sparkle

165. Lachrymose
(*a*) cheering (*b*) smooth
(*c*) passionate (*d*) curt

166. Lackadasical
(*a*) monthly (*b*) possessing time
(*c*) ambitious (*d*) pusillanimous

167. Laconic
(*a*) milky (*b*) verbose
(*c*) wicked (*d*) flagrant

168. Lampoon
(*a*) darken (*b*) praise
(*c*) abandon (*d*) sail

169. Languor
(*a*) vitality (*b*) length
(*c*) embarrassment (*d*) wine

170. Latent
(*a*) trim (*b*) forbidding
(*c*) execrable (*d*) obvious

171. Lavish
(*a*) hostile (*b*) unwashed
(*c*) timely (*d*) frugal

172. Laudatory
(*a*) dritying (*b*) disclaiming
(*c*) defamatory (*d*) inflammatory

173. Lax
(*a*) salty (*b*) strick
(*c*) shrill (*d*) boring

174. Lechery
(*a*) trust (*b*) compulsion
(*c*) zeal (*d*) purity

175. Lethargic
(*a*) convalescent (*b*) beautiful
(*c*) enervating (*d*) invigorating

176. Levite
(*a*) bridge (*b*) dam
(*c*) praise (*d*) solemnity

177. Lilliputian
(*a*) destructive (*b*) proper
(*c*) gigantic (*d*) elegant

178. Limpid
(*a*) erect (*b*) turbid
(*c*) tangential (*d*) timid

179. Lithe
(*a*) stiff (*b*) limpid
(*c*) facetious (*d*) insipid

180. Livid
(*a*) alive (*b*) mundane
(*c*) positive (*d*) undiscolored

181. Loath
(*a*) loose (*b*) evident
(*c*) deliberate (*d*) eager

182. Loquacious
(*a*) taciturn (*b*) sentimental
(*c*) soporific (*d*) soothing

183. Moist
(*a*) crisp (*b*) hard
(*c*) dry (*d*) parched

184. Mask
(*a*) hit (*b*) expose
(*c*) benign (*d*) pompous

185. Moisture
(*a*) dryness (*b*) delegate
(*c*) dampness (*d*) fdefect

186. Magnify
(*a*) produce (*b*) support
(*c*) reduce (*d*) destroy

187. Mendacious
(*a*) broken (*b*) efficacious
(*c*) truthful (*d*) destructive

188. Manumit
(*a*) throw (*b*) lock
(*c*) promise (*d*) enslave

189. Nebulous
(*a*) starry (*b*) clear
(*c*) cold (*d*) fundamental

190. Nefarious
(*a*) various (*b*) lacking
(*c*) benign (*d*) pompous

191. Negation
(*a*) postulation (*b*) hypothecation
(*c*) affirmation (*d*) violation

192. Neophyte
(*a*) veteran (*b*) satellite
(*c*) desperado (*d*) handwriting

193. Niggardly
(*a*) protected (*b*) biased
(*c*) prodigal (*d*) bankrupt

194. Nocturnal
(*a*) harsh (*b*) marauding
(*c*) patrolling (*d*) daily

195. Noisome
(*a*) quiet (*b*) dismayed
(*c*) fragrant (*d*) sleepy

196. Notorious
(*a*) fashionable (*b*) renowned
(*c*) inactive (*d*) interepid

197. Obdurate
(*a*) yielding (*b*) fleeting
(*c*) finite (*d*) fascinating

198. Obese
(*a*) skillful (*b*) cadaverous
(*c*) clever (*d*) unpredictable

199. Objective
(*a*) indecisive (*b*) apathetic
(*c*) markedly inferior (*d*) emotionally involved

200. Obligatory
(*a*) demanding (*b*) optional
(*c*) facile (*d*) friendly

201. Obloquy
(*a*) praise (*b*) rectangle
(*c*) circle (*d*) dialogue

202. Obsequious
(*a*) successful (*b*) democratic
(*c*) supercilious (*d*) ambitious

203. Obsession
(*a*) whim (*b*) loss
(*c*) phobia (*d*) delusion

204. Obsolete
(*a*) heated (*b*) desolate
(*c*) renovated (*d*) frightful

205. Obstreperous
(*a*) turbid (*b*) quiet
(*c*) remote (*d*) lucid

206. Obtuse
(*a*) sheer (*b*) transparent
(*c*) tranquil (*d*) shrewd

207. Odious
(*a*) fragrant (*b*) redolent
(*c*) fetid (*d*) delightful

208. Odium
(*a*) noise (*b*) liking
(*c*) dominant (*d*) hasty

209. Omnipotent
(*a*) weak (*b*) democratic
(*c*) despotic (*d*) passionate

210. Omniscient
(*a*) sophisticated (*b*) ignorant
(*c*) essential (*d*) trivial

211. Opiat
(*a*) distress (*b*) sleep
(*c*) stimulant (*d*) laziness

212. Opportune
(*a*) occasional (*b*) fragrant
(*c*) fragile (*d*) awkward

213. Opportunist
(*a*) man of destiny (*b*) man of principle
(*c*) changeling (*d*) adversary

214. Opporbrium
(*a*) delineation (*b*) aptitude
(*c*) majesty (*d*) praise

215. Optimum
(*a*) pessimistic (*b*) knowledgeable
(*c*) worst (*d*) minimum

216. Opulence
(*a*) pessimism (*b*) patrionsm
(*c*) potency (*d*) poverty

217. Ostentatious
(*a*) inactive (*b*) unassuming
(*c*) impolite (*d*) illicit

218. Overweening
(*a*) humble (*b*) impotent
(*c*) avid (*d*) acrimonious

219. Pejorative
(*a*) positive (*b*) legal
(*c*) determining (*d*) delighting

220. Pellucid
(*a*) logistical (*b*) philandering
(*c*) incomperhensible (*d*) vagrant

221. Penchant
(*a*) distance (*b*) imminence
(*c*) dislike (*d*) attitude

222. Penurious
(*a*) imprisoned (*b*) captivated
(*c*) generous (*d*) vacant

223. Perfunctory
(*a*) official (*b*) through
(*c*) insipid (*d*) vicarious

224. Perigee
(*a*) eclipse (*b*) planet
(*c*) apogee (*d*) refugee

225. Peripatetic
(*a*) wordly (*b*) stationary
(*c*) disarming (*d*) seeking

226. Permeable
(*a*) perishable (*b*) effective
(*c*) plodding (*d*) impenetrable

227. Pernicious
(*a*) practical (*b*) comparative
(*c*) harmless (*d*) tangible

228. Perpetual
(*a*) momentary (*b*) standard
(*c*) serious (*d*) industrial

229. Perspicuity
(*a*) grace (*b*) feature
(*c*) review (*d*) vagueness

230. Pert
(*a*) polite (*b*) perishable
(*c*) moral (*d*) deliberate

231. Pertinacious
(*a*) vengeful (*b*) consumptive
(*c*) superficial (*d*) skilled

232. Pertient
(*a*) understood (*b*) living
(*c*) discontented (*d*) irrelevant

233. Petulant
(*a*) angry (*b*) moral
(*c*) declining (*d*) uncomplaining

234. Precipitate
(*a*) dull (*b*) anticipatory
(*c*) cautious (*d*) considerate

235. Prefatory
(*a*) outstanding (*b*) magnificent
(*c*) conclusive (*d*) intelligent

236. Prelude
(*a*) intermezzo (*b*) diva
(*c*) aria (*d*) aftermath

237. Presumption
(*a*) assertion (*b*) activation
(*c*) motivation (*d*) humility

238. Pretentious
(*a*) ominous (*b*) calm
(*c*) unassuming (*d*) futile

239. Prim
(*a*) informal (*b*) prior
(*c*) exterior (*d*) private

240. Pristine
(*a*) cultivated (*b*) condemned
(*c*) irreligious (*d*) cautious

241. Probity
(*a*) aregert (*b*) assumption
(*c*) corruptibility (*d*) extent

242. Prodigal
(*a*) large (*b*) thrifty
(*c*) consistent (*d*) compatible

243. Prodigious
(*a*) infinitesimal (*b*) indignant
(*c*) indifferent (*d*) indisposed

244. Profane
(*a*) sanctify (*b*) desecrate
(*c*) define (*d*) manifest

245. Prolific
(*a*) unworkable (*b*) backward
(*c*) barren (*d*) controversial

246. Prolix
(*a*) stupid (*b*) indifferent
(*c*) redundant (*d*) pithy

247. Prophylactic
(*a*) causing growth (*b*) causing disease
(*c*) antagonistic (*d*) brushing

248. Propinquity
(*a*) remoteness (*b*) uniqueness
(*c*) health (*d*) virtue

249. Propitious
(*a*) rich (*b*) induced
(*c*) promoted (*d*) unfavorable

250. Prosaic
(*a*) pacified (*b*) reprieved
(*c*) pensive (*d*) imaginative

251. Protean
(*a*) amateur (*b*) catholic
(*c*) unchanging (*d*) rapid

252. Protract
(*a*) make circular (*b*) shorten
(*c*) further (*d*) rectrace

253. Provident
(*a*) unholy (*b*) rash
(*c*) miserable (*d*) disabled

254. Provincial
(*a*) wealthy (*b*) crass
(*c*) literary (*d*) sophisticated

255. Psychotic
(*a*) dangerous (*b*) clairvoyant
(*c*) criminal (*d*) sane

256. Puerile
(*a*) fragrant (*b*) adult
(*c*) lonely (*d*) feminine

257. Pugnacious
(*a*) pacific (*b*) feline
(*c*) mature (*d*) angular

258. Puissant
(*a*) pouring (*b*) fashionable
(*c*) articulate (*d*) weak

259. Pulchritude
(*a*) ugliness (*b*) notoriety
(*c*) bestiality (*d*) masculinity

260. Punctilious
(*a*) happy (*b*) active
(*c*) vivid (*d*) careless

261. Punitive
(*a*) large (*b*) humorous
(*c*) rewarding (*d*) restive

262. Pusillanimous
(*a*) poverty-stricken (*b*) chained
(*c*) posthumous (*d*) courageous

263. Putative
(*a*) colonial (*b*) quarrelsome
(*c*) undisputed (*d*) powerful

264. Resilient
(*a*) pungent (*b*) foolish
(*c*) worthy (*d*) unyielding

265. Restive
(*a*) buoyant (*b*) placid
(*c*) remorseful (*d*) resistant

266. Retentive
(*a*) forgetful (*b*) accepting
(*c*) repetitive (*d*) avoiding

267. Reticence
(*a*) fatigue (*b*) fashion
(*c*) treachery (*d*) loquaciousness

268. Retrograde
(*a*) progressing (*b*) inclining
(*c*) evaluating (*d*) concentrating

269. Revere
(*a*) advance (*b*) dishonor
(*c*) age (*d*) precede

270. Rife
(*a*) direct (*b*) scant
(*c*) peaceful (*d*) grim

271. Robust
(a) weak (b) violent
(c) vicious (d) villainous

272. Rotundity
(a) promenade (b) nave
(c) grotesqueness (d) slimness

273. Rubble
(a) artificial facade (b) unbroken stone
(c) pale complexion (d) strong defense

274. Ruddy
(a) robust (b) witty
(c) wan (d) exotic

275. Rudimentary
(a) pale (b) polite
(c) asinine (d) developed

276. Rueful
(a) trite (b) content
(c) capable (d) capital

277. Rustic
(a) urban (b) slow
(c) corroded (d) mercenary

278. Ruthless
(a) merciful (b) majestic
(c) mighty (d) militant

279. Sadistic
(a) happy (b) quaint
(c) kindhearted (d) vacant

280. Sagacious
(a) foolish (b) bitter
(c) voracious (d) veracious

281. Sallow
(a) salacious (b) ruddy
(c) colorless (d) permitted

282. Salubrious
(a) salty (b) bloody
(c) miasmic (d) maudlin

283. Salvage
(a) remove (b) outfit
(c) burn (d) lose

284. Sanctimonious
(a) hypothetical (b) paltry
(c) mercenary (d) pious

285. Sanguine
(a) choleric (b) sickening
(c) warranted (d) pessimistic

286. Satiety
(a) emptiness (b) warmth
(c) erectness (d) straightness

287. Scanty
(a) collected (b) remote
(c) invisible (d) plentiful

288. Scurrilous
(a) savage (b) scabby
(c) decent (d) volatile

289. Secular
(a) vivid (b) clerical
(c) punitive (d) positive

290. Sedentary
(a) vicarious (b) loyal
(c) accidental (d) active

291. Sedulous
(a) indolent (b) guileless
(c) vindictive (d) upright

292. Senlity
(a) verility (b) loquaciousness
(c) forgetfulness (d) youth

293. Sententious
(a) paragraphed (b) positive
(c) posthumous (d) wordy

294. Tractable
(a) unmanageable (b) irreligious
(c) mortal (d) incapable

295. Traduce
(a) exhume (b) increase
(c) purchase (d) extol

296. Tranquillity
(a) lack of sleep (b) lack of calm
(c) emptiness (d) renewal

297. Transient
(a) carried (b) close
(c) permanent (d) removed

298. Tremulous
(a) steady (b) obese
(c) young (d) healthy

299. Trenchant
(a) lacking bite (b) imperious
(c) inessential (d) unafraid

300. Trepidation
(a) slowness (b) amputation
(c) fearlessness (d) adroitness

301. Trite
(a) correct (b) original
(c) distinguished (d) premature

302. Truculent
(a) juicy (b) overflowing
(c) peaceful (d) determined

303. Tumult
(a) scarcity (b) defeat
(c) cooleness (d) secrenity

304. Turbid
(a) clear (b) improbable
(c) invariable (d) honest

305. Turbulence
(*a*) reaction (*b*) approach
(*c*) impropriety (*d*) calm

306. Turgid
(*a*) rancid (*b*) shrunken
(*c*) cool (*d*) explosive

307. Turpitude
(*a*) amplitude (*b*) heat
(*c*) wealth (*d*) virtue

308. Tyro
(*a*) infant (*b*) rubber
(*c*) personnel (*d*) expert

309. Unearth
(*a*) conceal (*b*) gnaw
(*c*) clean (*d*) fling

310. Unfeigned
(*a*) pretended (*b*) fashionable
(*c*) wary (*d*) switched

311. Ungainly
(*a*) ignorant
(*b*) graceful
(*c*) detailed
(*d*) dancing

312. Unimpeachable
(*a*) fruitful
(*b*) rampaging
(*c*) faulty
(*d*) pensive

313. Unkempt
(*a*) bombed (*b*) washed
(*c*) neat (*d*) tawdry

314. Unruly
(*a*) chatting (*b*) obedient
(*c*) definite (*d*) lined

315. Unseemly
(*a*) effortless (*b*) proper
(*c*) conducive (*d*) pointed

316. Unsullied
(*a*) tranished (*b*) countless
(*c*) soggy (*d*) papered

317. Untenable
(*a*) supportable (*b*) tender
(*c*) sheepish (*d*) tremulous

318. Unwitting
(*a*) clever (*b*) intense
(*c*) sensitive (*d*) intentional

319. Vacillation
(*a*) remorse (*b*) relief
(*c*) respect (*d*) steadfastness

320. Valedictory
(*a*) sad (*b*) collegiate
(*c*) derivative (*d*) salutatory

321. Valor
(*a*) admonition
(*b*) injustice
(*c*) cowardice
(*d*) generosity

322. Vanguard
(*a*) regiment
(*b*) rear
(*c*) echelon
(*d*) protection

323. Vaunted
(*a*) unvanquished
(*b*) fell
(*c*) belittled
(*d*) believed

EXERCISE – II

(QUESTIONS FROM PREVIOUS GATE EXAMS)

MCQ TYPE QUESTIONS

2015

1. Which word is not a synonym for the word *vernacular*?
(*a*) regional (*b*) indigeneous
(*c*) indigent (*d*) colloquial

2011

2. Choose the word from the options given below that is most nearly opposite in meaning to the given word:

Amalgamate
(*a*) merge
(*b*) split
(*c*) collect
(*d*) separate

3. Choose the word from the options given below that is most nearly **opposite** in meaning to the given word :

Frequency
(*a*) periodicity (*b*) rarity
(*c*) gradualness (*d*) persistency

ANSWERS

EXERCISE – I

MCQ Type Questions

1. (*d*) 2. (*b*) 3. (*d*) 4. (*b*) 5. (*a*) 6. (*d*) 7. (*a*) 8. (*a*) 9. (*a*) 10. (*b*)
11. (*b*) 12. (*b*) 13. (*b*) 14. (*d*) 15. (*b*) 16. (*c*) 17. (*d*) 18. (*c*) 19. (*c*) 20. (*d*)
21. (*d*) 22. (*a*) 23. (*d*) 24. (*c*) 25. (*b*) 26. (*d*) 27. (*b*) 28. (*b*) 29. (*d*) 30. (*d*)
31. (*c*) 32. (*a*) 33. (*d*) 34. (*b*) 35. (*d*) 36. (*a*) 37. (*d*) 38. (*a*) 39. (*b*) 40. (*b*)
41. (*d*) 42. (*d*) 43. (*c*) 44. (*a*) 45. (*d*) 46. (*d*) 47. (*c*) 48. (*d*) 49. (*d*) 50. (*a*)
51. (*c*) 52. (*d*) 53. (*b*) 54. (*a*) 55. (*d*) 56. (*c*) 57. (*b*) 58. (*a*) 59. (*b*) 60. (*a*)
61. (*c*) 62. (*b*) 63. (*c*) 64. (*b*) 65. (*c*) 66. (*d*) 67. (*d*) 68. (*c*) 69. (*b*) 70. (*a*)
71. (*a*) 72. (*b*) 73. (*b*) 74. (*b*) 75. (*a*) 76. (*c*) 77. (*a*) 78. (*d*) 79. (*d*) 80. (*b*)
81. (*a*) 82. (*c*) 83. (*c*) 84. (*d*) 85. (*c*) 86. (*b*) 87. (*b*) 88. (*b*) 89. (*d*) 90. (*c*)
91. (*d*) 92. (*d*) 93. (*a*) 94. (*a*) 95. (*b*) 96. (*d*) 97. (*d*) 98. (*c*) 99. (*a*) 100. (*a*)
101. (*c*) 102. (*b*) 103. (*d*) 104. (*a*) 105. (*d*) 106. (*b*) 107. (*b*) 108. (*a*) 109. (*a*) 110. (*c*)
111. (*d*) 112. (*a*) 113. (*d*) 114. (*b*) 115. (*d*) 116. (*c*) 117. (*b*) 118. (*a*) 119. (*b*) 120. (*c*)
121. (*b*) 122. (*d*) 123. (*d*) 124. (*a*) 125. (*a*) 126. (*d*) 127. (*a*) 128. (*d*) 129. (*d*) 130. (*b*)
131. (*c*) 132. (*d*) 133. (*c*) 134. (*c*) 135. (*a*) 136. (*b*) 137. (*d*) 138. (*b*) 139. (*a*) 140. (*b*)
141. (*d*) 142. (*c*) 143. (*a*) 144. (*d*) 145. (*c*) 146. (*c*) 147. (*d*) 148. (*a*) 149. (*a*) 150. (*d*)
151. (*b*) 152. (*a*) 153. (*a*) 154. (*d*) 155. (*b*) 156. (*d*) 157. (*b*) 158. (*d*) 159. (*d*) 160. (*c*)
161. (*a*) 162. (*d*) 163. (*a*) 164. (*b*) 165. (*a*) 166. (*c*) 167. (*d*) 168. (*b*) 169. (*a*) 170. (*d*)
171. (*d*) 172. (*c*) 173. (*b*) 174. (*d*) 175. (*d*) 176. (*d*) 177. (*c*) 178. (*b*) 179. (*a*) 180. (*d*)
181. (*d*) 182. (*a*) 183. (*c*) 184. (*b*) 185. (*a*) 186. (*c*) 187. (*c*) 188. (*d*) 189. (*b*) 190. (*c*)
191. (*c*) 192. (*a*) 193. (*c*) 194. (*d*) 195. (*c*) 196. (*b*) 197. (*d*) 198. (*d*) 199. (*d*) 200. (*b*)
201. (*a*) 202. (*c*) 203. (*a*) 204. (*c*) 205. (*b*) 206. (*d*) 207. (*d*) 208. (*b*) 209. (*a*) 210. (*a*)
211. (*c*) 212. (*d*) 213. (*b*) 214. (*d*) 215. (*c*) 216. (*d*) 217. (*b*) 218. (*a*) 219. (*a*) 220. (*c*)
221. (*c*) 222. (*c*) 223. (*b*) 224. (*c*) 225. (*b*) 226. (*d*) 227. (*c*) 228. (*a*) 229. (*d*) 230. (*a*)
231. (*c*) 232. (*d*) 233. (*d*) 234. (*c*) 235. (*c*) 236. (*d*) 237. (*d*) 238. (*c*) 239. (*a*) 240. (*a*)
241. (*c*) 242. (*b*) 243. (*a*) 244. (*a*) 245. (*c*) 246. (*d*) 247. (*b*) 248. (*a*) 249. (*d*) 250. (*d*)
251. (*c*) 252. (*b*) 253. (*b*) 254. (*d*) 255. (*d*) 256. (*b*) 257. (*a*) 258. (*d*) 259. (*a*) 260. (*b*)
261. (*c*) 262. (*d*) 263. (*c*) 264. (*b*) 265. (*a*) 266. (*d*) 267. (*a*) 268. (*b*) 269. (*b*) 270. (*b*)
271. (*a*) 272. (*d*) 273. (*b*) 274. (*c*) 275. (*d*) 276. (*b*) 277. (*a*) 278. (*a*) 279. (*c*) 280. (*a*)
281. (*b*) 282. (*c*) 283. (*d*) 284. (*d*) 285. (*d*) 286. (*d*) 287. (*d*) 288. (*c*) 289. (*b*) 290. (*d*)
291. (*a*) 292. (*d*) 293. (*d*) 294. (*a*) 295. (*d*) 296. (*b*) 297. (*c*) 298. (*a*) 299. (*a*) 300. (*c*)
301. (*b*) 302. (*c*) 303. (*d*) 304. (*a*) 305. (*d*) 306. (*b*) 307. (*d*) 308. (*d*) 309. (*a*) 310. (*a*)
311. (*b*) 312. (*c*) 313. (*d*) 314. (*b*) 315. (*b*) 316. (*a*) 317. (*a*) 318. (*d*) 319. (*d*) 320. (*d*)
321. (*c*) 322. (*b*) 323. (*d*)

EXERCISE – II

MCQ Type Questions

1. (*c*) 2. (*b*) 3. (*b*)

EXPLANATIONS

EXERCISE – II

MCQ TYPE QUESTIONS

1. *Vernacular* - expressed or written in the native language of a place

   Indigent - deficient in what is requisite

2. Amalgamate means combine or unite to form one organization or structure. So the best option here is split. Separate on the other hand, although a close synonym, it is too general to be the best antonym in the given question while Merge is the synonym; Collect is not related.

3. Best antonym is rarity which means shortage or scarcity.

5
CHAPTER

Reasoning Ability

Reasoning is the process of drawing conclusions from facts. These conclusions must follow inevitably from the facts from which they are drawn. Reasoning is not concerned with some conclusion that has a good chance of being true when facts are true. Indeed, reasoning as used here refers to logical reasoning, not of commonsense reasoning or probabilistic reasoning. The only conclusions that are acceptable are those that follow logically from the supplied facts.

TYPES OF REASONING

Reasoning can be classified in two major parts :

- Verbal Reasoning
- Non-verbal Reasoning

VERBAL REASONING

Verbal reasoning tests words, letters and numbers, and require logical reasoning and a reasonable knowledge of the English Language. It is also necessary to be familiar with simple manipulations with figures, like addition, subtractions division and multiplication. The problems of number in *Test of Reasoning* test how logical we are i.e., how well we reason and think while carrying out simple arithmetic manipulations.

CLASSIFICATION OF VERBAL REASONING

I. SERIES COMPLETION

In verbal series, words, letters or digits are given in a specific sequence/order and we have to find out next word, letter or digit to complete the given series.

Numbers or alphabetical letters, are generally called *terms of the series*. These terms follow a certain pattern throughout. In the questions we have to identify last one or two terms to continue the series or to find a missing term in between given terms to continue the sequence followed in the question. There is no set pattern and each question may follow a different pattern or sequential arrangement of letters or digits, which have to detect using common sense and reasoning ability.

TYPES OF SERIES COMPLETION QUESTIONS

Mainly following four types of question are asked.

1. Alphabet series

In this series, given alphabets follow a particular sequence or order. We have to detect the pattern from the given alphabets and find missing alphabet or the next alphabet to continue the pattern.

- There are no set rules.
- There can be omission of alphabets in an order.
- Alphabets may also be omitted in an increasing/decreasing order, which may be direct increase or decrease.
- There can also be alternate order.
- There may also be alternate sequences
- There may be several other patterns in the letter series.
- To tackle letter series questions, vary position of the alphabet and its position number in both forward and backward sequences.
- To continue the series after Z, we again begin with A. In other words, the sequence is kept in a circular order.
- In solving these questions pattern of the alphabet series should be noted.

Some Skipping Patterns.

(*i*) ***Regular Order :*** Number of alphabets skipped remains the same.

Example. A, D, G, J, ...?

Ans. M

(*ii*) ***Increasing Order :*** Each time the number of alphabets skipped increases in a given pattern.

Example. A C F J O ?

Ans. U

Here, each time number of letters skipped increases by one.

(*iii*) ***Decreasing Order :*** Each time the number of letters skipped decreases in a given pattern.

Example. A G L P S ?

Ans. U

Here number of letters skipped decreases by one each time, *i.e.*, first 5, then 4, then 3, and so on.

(*iv*) ***Interlinked Series*** **:** In this two or more different series are attached together. These different series follow their own different rules.

Example. A D F J M R ?

Ans. V

Here, there are two interlinked series.

2. Letter Series

This type of questions usually consist of a series of small letters which follow a certain pattern.

However, some letters are missing from the series. Then these missing letters are given in a proper sequence as one of the alternatives.

Example. aaa... b...a...

(*a*) baa (*b*) abb (*c*) bab (*d*) aab (*e*) bbb

Ans. (*a*)

Method :

- First blank space should be filled in by 'b', so that we have two a's followed by two b's.
- Second blank space should be filled in either by 'a', so that we have four a's followed by two b's, or by 'b' so that we have three a's followed by three b's.
- Last space must be filled in by 'a'.
- *Thus, we have two possible answers :* 'baa' and 'bba'.

  But, only 'baa' appears in the alternatives. So, the answer is (*a*).

Note : In case, we had both the possible answers in the alternatives, we would have chosen the one that forms a more prominent pattern, which is aabb/ aaabbbaa. Thus, our answer would have been "*bba*".

3. Number series

In the number series, some numbers are arranged in a particular sequence. All the numbers form a series and change in a certain order. Sometimes, one or more numbers are wrongly put in the number series. We are required to observe the trend in which numbers change in the series and find out which number/numbers misfit into the series that number/numbers is *odd number* of the series.

Pure Series.

In this type of number series, the number itself obeys certain order so that the character of the series can be found out.

Number may be Perfect square; Perfect cube; Prime and Combination

Difference Series.

In this type of number series, change in order for the difference between each consecutive number of the series is found out.

Ratio Series.

In this type of number series, change in order for the ratios between each consecutive number of the series is found out.

4. Mixed Series

In this type of number series, numbers obeying various orders of two or more different types of series are arranged alternately in a single number series.

Rules:

1. Difference between consecutive numbers is same.
2. Differences between consecutive numbers are in Arithmetic Progression (A.P.).
3. Difference between consecutive numbers is a perfect square.
4. Differences between consecutive numbers are multiples of a number.
5. Differences between consecutive numbers are prime numbers.
6. Difference between consecutive numbers is a perfect cube.
7. Difference between consecutive numbers are in Geometric Progression (G.P.)
8. Ratio between each consecutive number is the same.
9. Ratio between each consecutive numbers is in Arithmetic Progression (A.P)
10. Ratio between consecutive number is perfect square number.
11. Ratio between consecutive number is the multiple of a number.
12. Ratio between consecutive numbers is a prime number.
13. Ratio between consecutive numbers is a perfect cube number.
14. Ratios between consecutive number are in Geometric Progression (G.P.)

5. Correspondence Series

This type of series consists of three sequences with three different elements (usually capital letters, digits and small letters). On the basis of the similarity in positions in the three sequences, a capital letter is found to correspond with a unique digit and a unique small letter, whenever it occurs. We are required to trace out this correspondence and accordingly choose the elements to be filled in at the desired places.

II. ANALOGY

'*Analogy*' means 'correspondence'.

In questions based on analogy, a particular relationship is given and another similar relationship has to be identified from the given alternatives.

Analogy means similarity or some kind of relationship. Analogy test, therefore tests the ability to see a relationship between two words and to recognize a similar relationship between two other words. It is a test of verbal reasoning ability rather than vocabulary. The key to analogy success is being able to express the relationship between the pair of words.

KINDS OF RELATIONSHIPS WITH EXAMPLES

1. Instrument and Measurement

- Thermometer : Temperature (thermometer is an instrument used to measure temperature).
- Barometer : Pressure
- Anemometer : Wind vane
- Odometer : Speed
- Scale : Length
- Balance : Mass
- Sphygmomanometer: Blood Pressure
- Rain Gauge : Rain
- Hygrometer : Humidity
- Ammeter : Current
- Screw Gauge : Thickness
- Seismograph : Earthquakes
- Taseometer : Strains

2. Quantity and Unit

- Mass : Kilogram (kilogram is the unit of mass)
- Length : Metre
- Force : Newton
- Energy : Joule
- Resistance : Ohm
- Volume : Litre
- Angle : Radians
- Time : Seconds
- Potential : Volt
- Work : Joule
- Current : Ampere
- Luminosity : Candela
- Pressure : Pascal
- Area : Hectare
- Temperature : Degrees
- Power : Watt
- Conductivity : Mho
- Magnetic field : Oersted/Tesla

3. Individual and Group

- Soldiers : Army (group of soldiers is called an army).
- Cattle : Herd
- Flowers : Bouquet
- Grapes : Bunch
- Singer : Chorus
- Artist : Troupe
- Fish : Shoal
- Sheep : Flock
- Riders : Cavalcade
- Bees : Swarm
- Man : Crowd
- Sailors : Crew
- Nomads : Horde

4. Animal and Young one

- Cow : Calf (calf is the young one of cow)
- Horse : Pony
- Cat : Kitten
- Sheep : Lamb
- Butterfly : Caterpillar
- Insect : Larva
- Dog : Puppy
- Cock/Hen : Chicken
- Lion : Cub
- Duck : Duckling
- Man : Child

5. Male and Female

- Horse : Mare (mare is the female horse)
- Dog : Bitch
- Stag : Doe
- Son : Daughter
- Lion : Lioness
- Sorcerer : Sorceress
- Drone : Bee
- Gentleman : Lady
- Nephew : Niece
- Tiger : Tigress

6. Individual and Class

- Monkey : Mammal (monkey belongs to the class of mammal).
- Man : Mammal
- Ostrich : Bird
- Snake : Reptile
- Butterfly : Insect
- Whale : Mammal
- Rat : Rodent
- Lizard : Reptile

7. Individual and Dwelling Place

- Dog : Kennel (dog lives in a kennel)
- Bee : Apiary
- Cattle : Shed
- Lion : Den
- Poultry : Farm
- Monk : Monastery
- Fish : Aquarium
- Birds : Aviary
- Horse : Stable

8. Study and Topic

- Ornithology : Birds (ornithology is the study of birds).
- Seismology : Earthquakes
- Botany : Plants
- Onomatology : Names
- Ethnology : Human Races
- Ontology : Reality
- Herpetology : Amphibians
- Pathology : Diseases
- Astrology : Future
- Anthropology : Man
- Palaeography : Writings
- Ichthyology : Fishes
- Semantics : Language
- Nephrology : Kidney
- Concology : Shells
- Haematology : Blood
- Craniology : Skull
- Mycology : Fungi
- Entomology : Insects
- Zoology : Animals
- Occultism : Supernatural

9. Worker and Tool

- Warrior : Sword (sword is the tool used by a warrior).
- Carpenter : Saw
- Woodcutter : Axe
- Tailor : Needle
- Labourer : Spade
- Soldier : Gun
- Sculptor : Chisel
- Chef : Knife
- Doctor : Stethoscope
- Farmer : Plough
- Author : Pen

10. Tool and Action

- Needle : Sew (needle is used for sewing).
- Knife : Cut
- Sword : Slaughter
- Mattock : Dig
- Filter : Purify
- Steering : Drive
- Pen : Write
- Spanner : Grip
- Spoon : Feed
- Microscope : Magnify
- Gun : Shoot
- Shovel : Scoop
- Chisel : Carve
- Oar : Row
- Axe : Grind
- Auger : Bore
- Spade : Dig

11. Worker and Working Place

- Chef : Kitchen (chef works in a kitchen)

- Farmer : Field
- Warrior : Battlefield
- Engineer : Site
- Sailor : Ship
- Pilot : Cockpit
- Beautician : Parlour
- Artist : Theatre
- Actor : Stage
- Mechanic : Garage
- Lawyer : Court
- Scientist : Laboratory
- Teacher : School
- Doctor : Hospital
- Clerk : Office
- Servant : House
- Driver : Cabin
- Grocer : Shop
- Painter : Gallery
- Waiter : Restaurant
- Worker : Factory
- Umpire : Pitch
- Gambler : Casino

12. Worker and Product

- Mason : Wall (mason builds a wall)
- Farmer : Crop
- Teacher : Education
- Hunter : Prey
- Chef : Food
- Carpenter : Furniture
- Judge : Justice
- Author : Book
- Choreographer : Ballet
- Goldsmith : Ornaments
- Producer : Film
- Butcher : Meat
- Architect : Design
- Cobbler : Shoes
- Tailor : Clothes
- Poet : Poem
- Dramatist : Play

13. Product and Raw Material

- Prism : Glass (prism is made of glass).
- Butter : Milk
- Cloth : Fibre
- Wall : Brick
- Road : Asphalt
- Furniture : Wood
- Book : Paper
- Shoes : Leather
- Sack : Jute
- Pullover : Wool
- Omelette : Egg
- Metal : Ore
- Jewellery : Gold
- Rubber : Latex
- Linen : Flax
- Jaggery : Sugarcane
- Oil : Seed
- Wine : Grapes
- Paper : Pulp
- Fabric : Yarn

14. Part and Whole Relationship

- Pen : Nib (nib is a part of a pen).
- Pencil : Lead
- House : Kitchen
- Fan : Blade
- Class : Student
- Room : Window
- Aeroplane : Cockpit
- Book : Chapter

15. Word and Intensity

- Anger : Rage (rage is of higher intensity than Anger)
- Wish : Desire
- Kindle : Burn
- Sink : Drown
- Quarrel : War
- Error : Blunder
- Famous : Renowned
- Unhappy : Sad
- Refuse : Deny

16. Word and Synonym

- Abode : Dwelling (abode means almost the same as Dwelling)
- Blend : Mix
- Ban : Prohibition
- Assign : Allot
- Vacant : Empty
- Abduct : Kidnap
- Dearth : Scarcity
- Dissipate : Squander
- Sedate : Calm
- Brim : Edge
- House : Home
- Solicit : Request
- Presage : Predict
- Haughty : Proud
- Flaw : Defect
- Fierce : Violent
- Fallacy : Illusion
- Substitute : Replace
- Mend : Repair
- Alight : Descend
- Presume : Assume

17. Word and Antonym

- Attack : Defend (defend means opposite of Attack)
- Advance : Retreat
- Cruel : Kind
- Best : Worst
- Fresh : Stale
- Ignore : Notice
- Initial : Final
- Condense : Expand
- Chaos : Peace
- Create : Destroy
- Gradual : Abrupt
- Sink : Float
- Robust : Weak
- Gentle : Harsh
- Deep : Shallow
- Cordial : Hostile
- Affirm : Deny
- Mourn : Rejoice
- Lethargy : Alertness

18. Part

Gill : Fin (Gill and fin are two parts of a fish)

19. Type

Sword : Weapon(Sword is a type of weapon)

20. Tool & Worker

Paint Brush : Artist (Paintbrush is a tool to artist)

21. Degree

Warm : Hot (Warm is a greater degree of hot)

Fond : Doting (Fond is less extreme than doting)

22. Sign of

Grimace : Pain(Grimace is a sign of pain)

Brush : Discomfiture (A blush signifies discomfiture)

23. A place for

Miner : Quarry (A miner works in a quarry)

24. Sequence relationship

Foreward : Appendix (In a book a foreword precedes the Appendix)

25. Worker and Work

Poet : Sonnet (A sonnet is written by a poet)

Mason : Wall (A mason builds a wall)

26. Cause and Effect

Soporofic : Sleepiness (Soporofic causes sleepiness)

COMMON TYPES OF ANALOGY QUESTIONS

1. Completing Analogous Pair

In this type of questions, given two words are, which related to each other in some way. Another word is also given and we required to find out the relationship between first two words and choose the word from the given alternatives, which bears the same relationship to the third word, as the first two bear.

Example. Doctor : Nurse : : ? : Follower

(*a*) Employer (*b*) Leader (*c*) Worker
(*d*) Manager (*e*) Union

Ans. (*b*)

Just as a nurse follows the Doctor's instructions, so also a follower works as directed by the leader.

2. Choosing Analogous Pair

In this type of questions, a pair of words is given, followed by four pairs of words as alternatives and we are required to choose the pair in which words bear the same relationship to each other as the words of the given pair bear.

Example. Sink : Float : : ?

(*a*) Brim : Edge (*b*) Mend : Repair
(*c*) Gentle : Harsh (*d*) Flow : defect
(*e*) Solicit : Request

Ans. (*b*)

Just as sink is antonym of float, so also gentle is opposite of harsh.

3. Choosing Similar word

In this type of questions, a group of three words is given, followed by four other words as alternatives. The candidate is required to choose the alternative, which is similar to the given three words.

Example. Sitar : Guitar : Tanpura

(*a*) Trumpet (*b*) Violin (*c*) Harmonium
(*d*) Mridanga (*e*) Fluet

Ans. (*b*)

Sitar, Guitar and Tanpura are all string instruments. Violin is also a string instrument.

4. Detecting Analogies

In this type of questions, we are required to trace out hidden analogy or common characteristic among the given words or to choose the word which possesses the same characteristic as the given word.

Example. Judo : Karate : Taekwando

(*a*) They are names of martial arts.
(*b*) They can be performed by obese persons.
(*c*) They are performed on stage.
(*d*) They are important items of Asian Games.
(*e*) They have origin in Kerala

Ans. (*a*)

Judo, Karate and Taekwando are martial arts and (*a*) is most suitable description for all the three.

5. Three word Analogy

In this type of questions, a group of three inter-related words is given and we are required to trace out the relationship among these three words and choose another group with similar analogy, from among the alternatives provided.

Example. Pen : Pencil : Ink

(*a*) Orange : Banana : Juice
(*b*) Table : Chair : Wood
(*c*) Cow : Milk : Curd
(*d*) Fish : Shark : Water
(*e*) Car : Engine : Circle

Ans. (*a*)

Pen contains ink and pencil belongs to the same category as pen i.e. stationery. Similarly, orange contains juice and banana belongs to the same category as orange, *i.e.* fruits.

6. Number Analogy

It includes deals two types of questions :

(*i*) Choosing a similarly related pair as the given number pair on the basis of relation between the numbers in each pair.

Example. 582 : 194 :: 258 : ?

(*a*) 82 (*b*) 86 (*c*) 92 (*d*) 58

Ans. (*b*)

Just as 582 is related to 194 as 582 is 3 times 194, in the same way 258 is 3 times the 86.

(*ii*) Choosing a number similar to a group of numbers on the basis of certain common properties that they possess.

Example. Which number belongs to given set of numbers?

2, 3, 5, 7, 11, 13, 17, 19, 23......

(*a*) 15 (*b*) 9 (*c*) 21 (*d*) 29 (*e*) 27

Ans. (*d*)

Given set of numbers belong to the prime numbers. In the given option, only prime number is 29.

7. Alphabet Analogy

In this type of questions, two groups of alphabets related to each other in same way, are given and we are required to find out this relationship and choose a group of alphabets which is related in the same way to a third group provided in the question.

Example. B C D : P Q R : : X Y Z : ?

(*a*) FGH (*b*) LMN (*c*) RST (*d*) TUV (*e*) STU

Ans. (*b*)

Each letter of the first group is moved fourteen steps forward to obtain the corresponding letter of the second group. A similar relationship will exist between the third and fourth groups.

HOW TO ANSWER ANALOGY QUESTIONS

1. Figure out how the capitalized words are related.
2. Create a sentence that expresses that connection.
3. Test the choices with your sentence and eliminate the ones that don't work.
4. If we are left with more than one answer—or no answer at all—go back and refine your sentence.
5. Choose the best answer. If none of the choices fits exactly, choose the one that works best.

PLAN TO SOLVE ANALOGY QUESTIONS

1. Make your Sentence More Precise

The analogies get more difficult as we work our way through each group. Use the common categories as a starting point, but be prepared to refine the relationship by making your sentence more precise.

Example. Grain : Silo ::

(*a*) Pilot : plane (*b*) judge : courtroom

(*c*) water : reservoir (*d*) clock : time

If we apply the "place where" idea without thinking, here is what happens.

A silo is a place where we would find grain.

(*a*) A *plane* is a place where you would find a *pilot*.

(*b*) A *courtroom* is a place where you would find a *judge*.

(*c*) A *reservoir* is a place where you would find *water*.

(*d*) A *clock* is a place where you would find *time*.

We can eliminate (d), but that still leaves you with four possible answers. Now is express the relationship between silo and grain more precisely?

A silo is a place where grain is stored.

(*a*) A plane is a place where a pilot is stored.

(*b*) A courtroom is a place where a judge is stored.

(*c*) A reservoir is a place where water is stored.

(*d*) A highway is a place where automobiles are stored.

2. Analogies Work only if there's a clear cut connection

An analogy depends upon a necessary connection between pairs of words based on the meaning of the words. This clear connection must exist for both the original capitalized word pair and the correct answer choice, i.e. we can eliminate any answer choice for which we cannot describe a necessary relationship between the words. Use the "clear connection" test to rule out answer choices even when we don't know one of the capitalized words.

Example. Letter : Alphabet : :

(*a*) note : scale

(*b*) ocean : merchandise

(*c*) expert : automobile

(*d*) victory : farmland

We dont't know what the capitalized words are in this analogy, but you can still eliminate choices (*b*), (*c*) and (*d*). There is no clear-cut connection between the words of those choices. The actual analogy above is LETTER : ALPHABET :: note : scale.

3. Some Analogies Work Better by Working Backward

Sometimes the capitalized words fall easily into a sentence that expresses their relationship–and sometimes they don't. If we are having trouble making up a sentence that relates the two words, be prepared to shift gears. Try reversing the order of the original word pair.

Example. *Ice : Glacier ::*

(*a*) train : trestle (*b*) sand : dune

(*c*) path : forest (*d*) feather : bird

If we can't come up with a sentence relating ICE to GLACIER, try relating GLACIER to ICE :

A *glacier* is made of *ice*.

If we reverse the order of the capitalized words, we must also reverse the order of the words in each answer choice.

(*a*) A *trestle* is made up of a *train*.

(*b*) A *dune* is made up of *sand*.

(*c*) A *forest* is made up of a *path*.

(*d*) A *bird* is made up of a *feather*.

Clearly (*b*) exhibits the same relationship as the original pair.

4. Check from the Answer Choices

Many words have different meanings depending upon whether they are used as nouns or verbs or adjectives. If we are not sure how one of the capitalized words is being used, just check the answer choices. In analogies, all the answer choices will have the same grammatical structure as the capitalized words pair. That means if the answer choices are noun : noun, the capitalized pair will be NOUN : NOUN. On the other hand, if the answer choices are adjective : noun, then the capitalized pair will be ADJECTIVE : NOUN.

If we have eliminated all the answer choices with words that we know or sort of know, and we are left with a couple of choices containing words that we have never seen before, just guess and move on.

III. CLASSIFICATION

'Classification' means arrangement of given items on the basis of some common character. In this test, a group of certain items are given, out of which some are similar to in some manner and one is different from the rest. We are required to choose this one item which does not fit into the given group.

TYPES OF CLASSIFICATION QUESTIONS

1. Choosing Odd word

In this type of questions, four (or five) words are given out of which one is dissimilar to the others and students have to find that odd one from the given set.

Example. *Choose the word which is least like the other words in the group.*

(*a*) chair (*b*) cupboard (*c*) Table

(*d*) paper weight (*e*) Bed

Ans. (*d*)

Here, all except paper weight are furnitures.

2. Choosing Odd pair of words

In this type of questions, certain pairs of words are given out of which words in all the pairs except one, bear a certain common relationship. We are required to decipher this relationship and choose the pair in which words are differently related, as the answer.

Example. *Choose the odd pair of words.*

(*a*) Loom : Cloth (*b*) Table : Drawer
(*c*) Book : Page (*d*) Car : Wheel

Ans. (*a*)

In all other pairs, second is part of the first.

3. Choosing Odd numeral

In this type of questions, certain numbers are given, out of which all except one are alike in some manner while one is different and this number is to be chosen as the answer.

Example. *Choose the number which is different from others in the group.*

(*a*) 49 (*b*) 64
(*c*) 121 (*d*) 144
(*e*) 156

Ans. (*e*)

Each of the numbers except 156 is complete square.

4. Choosing the Odd numeral pair/group

In this type of questions, certain pairs/groups of numbers are given out of which all except one are similar in some manner while one is different. The numbers in these similar pairs may have the same property or may be related to each other according to the same rule. We are is required to choose the odd pair/group.

Example. *Choose the numeral pair/group which is different from others.*

(*a*) 83 – 75 (*b*) 58 – 50 (*c*) 49 – 42
(*d*) 25 – 17 (*e*) 131– 123

Ans. (*c*)

In each of the pairs, first number is eight more than the second.

5. Choosing the Odd letter group

In this type of questions, usually four groups of letters are given. Three of them are similar to each other in some manner while one is different and we have to the answer.

Example. *Choose the group of letters which is different from others.*

(*a*) SU (*b*) PN (*c*) IK (*d*) BD

Ans. (*b*)

All other are two alternate letters

IV. CODING-DECODING

A CODE is a '*system of signals*'. Therefore, coding is a method of transmitting a message between the sender and the receiver without a third person knowing it.

Coding and Decoding Test is set up to judge the candidate's ability to decipher the rule that codes a particular word/ message and break the code to decipher the message.

TYPES OF CODING DECODING QUESTIONS

1. Letter Coding

In these questions, real alphabets in a word are replaced by certain other alphabets according to a specific rule to form its code and we are required to detect the common rule and answer the questions accordingly.

Example. If TAP is coded as SZO, then how is FREEZE coded?

(*a*) EQDFYG (*b*) ESDFYF (*c*) GQFDYF
(*d*) EQDDYD (*e*) EPDEZD

Ans. (*d*)

Each letter in the word TAP is moved one step backward to obtain the corresponding letter of the code.

	S	Z	O
–1	↑	↑	↑
	T	A	P

Thus, in FREEZE, F will be coded as E, R as Q, E as D and Z as Y. So, the code becomes EQDDYD.

2. Number Coding

In these questions, either numerical code values are assigned to a word or alphabetical code letters are assigned to the numbers and we are is required to analyse the code as per the directions.

Example. *If CHINA is written as 38126 and NEPAL is 25769, how is PLAINE is coded ?*

Solution : Clearly Alphabets are coded as shown:

C	*H*	*I*	*N*	*A*	*E*	*P*	*L*
3	8	1	2	6	5	7	9

Hence, PLAINE is coded as 796125.

Example. In a certain code '37' means 'which class' and '583' means 'caste and class'. What is the code for 'caste' ?

(*a*) 3 (*b*) 7 (*c*) 8
(*d*) Either 5 or 8

Ans. (*d*)

Given, which class' ≡ '37' ...(*i*)
and'caste and class' ≡ '583' ...(*ii*)

From (*i*) and (*ii*), the common word 'class' is coded as '3'.

From (*ii*), 'caste' is coded as '5' or '8'.

3. Substitution

In this type of questions, some particular objects are assigned code names. Then a question is asked that is to be answered in the code language.

Example. If cook is called *butler*, butler is called manager, manager is called teacher, teacher is called clerk and clerk is called principal, who will teach in a class ?

(*a*) Cook (*b*) Butler (*c*) Manager
(*d*) Teacher (*e*) Clerk

Ans. (*e*)

A 'teacher' teaches in a class and as given 'teacher' is called 'clerk'. So, a 'clerk' will teach in the class.

4. Mixed letter Coding

In this type of questions, three or four complete messages are given in the coded language and the code for a particular word is asked. To analyse such codes, any two messages bearing a common word are picked up. The common code word will mean that word. Proceeding similarly by picking up all possible combinations of two, the entire message can be analysed.

Example. If 'tee see pee' means 'Drink fruit juice'; 'see kee lee'means 'Juice is sweet' and 'fee ree mee' means. "He is intelligent', which word in that language means 'sweet' ?

(*a*) see (*b*) kee (*c*) lee
(*d*) pee (*e*) None of these

Ans. (*b*)

In first and second statements, common word is 'Juice' and common code word is 'see'. So, 'see' means 'Juice'. In second and third statements, common word is 'is' and common code is lee'. So, 'lee' means 'is'. Thus, in second statement, remaining word 'sweet' is coded as 'kee'.

5. Mixed number Coding

In this type of questions, a few groups of numbers each coding a certain short message, are given. Through a comparison of the given coded messages, taking two at a time, the candidate is required to find the number code for each word and then formulate the code for the message given.

Example. In a certain code, '786' means 'study very hard', '958' means 'hard work pays' and '645' means 'study and work'. Which of the following is the code for 'very' ?

(*a*) 8 (*b*) 6 (*c*) 7 (*d*) 5

Ans. (*c*)

In first and second statements, common word is '*hard*'and common code digit is '8'. So, '8' means 'hard'.

In the first and third statements, common word is 'study' and the common code digit is '6'. So, '6' means 'study'.

Thus, in the first statement, '7' means 'very'.

6. Deciphering individual letter codes by analysis

In this type of questions, certain sample words are given along with their codes. The candidate is required to decipher individual codes for different letters by comparing, taking two words at a time, and then answer the given questions accordingly.

V. BLOOD RELATIONS

In these tests, the success of a candidate depends upon the knowledge of the blood relations.

Following Blood relations help solve these Questions :

Mother's or father's son	— Brother
Mother's or father's daughter	— Sister
Mother's or father's brother	— Uncle
Mother's or father's sister	— Aunt
Mother's or father's father	— Grand father
Mother's or father's mother	— Grand mother
Son's wife	— Daughter-in-Law
Daughter's husband	— Son-in-Law
Husband's or wife's sister	— Sister-in-Law
Husband's or wife's brother	— Brother-in-Law
Brother's son	— Nephew
Brother's daughter	— Niece
Uncle or aunt's son or daughter	— Cousin
Sister's husband	— Brother-in-Law
Brother's wife	— Sister-in-Law
Grandson's or Grand daughter's daughter	— Great grand daughter

Types of Blood Relation Questions

(*i*) Deciphering Jumbled up descriptions

In this type of questions, a round-about description is given in the form of certain small relationships and direct relationship between the persons concerned is to be deciphered.

Example. Pointing to a photograph, a man said, *"I have no brother or sister but that man's father is my father's son."* Whose photograph was it ?

(*a*) His own (*b*) His son's
(*c*) His father's (*d*) His nephew's

Ans. (*a*)

Since man has no brother, his father's son is he himself.

(*ii*) Relation Puzzle

In this type, mutual blood relations or other informations of more than two persons are mentioned and information about any two is mentioned.

Example. A and B are brothers. C and D are sisters. A's son is D's brother. How is B related to C.

(*a*) Father (*b*) Brother (*c*) Grandfather
(*d*) Uncle (*e*) None of these

Ans.(*d*)

B is the brother of A; A's son is D's brother. This means D is the daughter of A. Since C and D are sisters, C is also the daughter of A. So, B is the uncle of C.

***(iii)* Coded Relations**

In such questions, relationships are represented by certain codes or symbols such as +, –, ×, ÷,*, Δ etc. Then relationships between certain persons, given in the form of these codes, are to be analysed.

Example. If A + B means A is the sister of B; A – B means A is the brother of B; A × B means A is the daughter of B, which of the following shows the relation that E is the maternal uncle of D?

(*a*) D + F × E (*b*) D – F × E
(*c*) D × F + E (*d*) D × F × E
(*e*) None of these.

Ans.(*c*)

E is the maternal uncle of D means D is the daughter of the sister (say F) of E i.e. D × F + E.

VI. PUZZLE TEST

This type of questions put in the form of puzzles involving certain number or items, be it persons or things and we are required to analyse the given information, condense it in a suitable form and answer the questions asked.

TYPE OF PUZZLE TESTS

1. Classification type Questions

This type consists of questions in which certain items belonging to different groups or possessing different qualities are given along with some clues with the help of which the candidate is required to group and analyse the given items and answer the questions accordingly.

Example. *Read the following information carefully and answer the questions that follow*:

(*i*) Five friends P, Q, R, S and T travelled to five different cities of Chennai, Calcutta, Delhi, Bangalore and Hyderabad by five different modes of transport of Bus, Train, Aeroplane, Car and Boat from Mumbai.

(*ii*) The person who travelled to Delhi did not travel by boat.

(*iii*) R went to Bangalore by car and Q went to Calcutta by aeroplane.

(*iv*) S travelled by boat whereas T travelled by train.

(*v*) Mumbai is not connected by bus to Delhi and Chennai.

1. Which of the following combinations of person and mode is not correct ?
(*a*) P — Bus (*b*) Q — Aeroplane
(*c*) R — Car (*d*) S — Boat
(*e*) T — Aeroplane

2. Which of the following combinations is true for S ?
(*a*) Delhi — Bus (*b*) Chennai — Bus
(*c*) Chennai — Boat (*d*) Data inadequate
(*e*) None of these

3. Which of the following combinations of place and mode is not correct ?
(*a*) Delhi — Bus (*b*) Calcutta — Aeroplane
(*c*) Bangalore — Car (*d*) Chennai — Boat
(*e*) Hyderabad — Bus

4. The person travelling to Delhi went by which of the following modes ?
(*a*) Bus (*b*) Train
(*c*) Aeroplane (*d*) Car
(*e*) Boat

5. Who among the following travelled to Delhi ?
(*a*) R (*b*) S
(*c*) T (*d*) Data inadequate
(*e*) None of these

Ans. *Given information can be analysed as follows :*

Mode of Transport.

R travels by Car, Q by Aeroplane, S by Boat and T by Train.

Now, only P remains. So, P travels by Bus.

Place of Travel.

R goes to Bangalore, Q to Calcutta.

Now, bus transport is not available for Delhi or Chennai. So, P who travels by Bus goes to Hyderabad.

S travels by boat and hence, S did not go to Delhi. So, S goes to Chennai.

Now, only T remains. So, T goes to Delhi.

Person	Place	Mode
P	Hyderabad	Bus
Q	Calcutta	Aeroplane
R	Bangalore	Car
S	Chennai	Boat
T	Delhi	Train

1. (*e*). Incorrect combination is T — Aeroplane
2. (*c*). Correct combination for S is Chennai — Boat
3. (*a*). Incorrect combination is Delhi — Bus
4. (*b*). T travelled to Delhi by Train
5. (*c*). T travelled to Delhi

2. Seating / Placing Arrangements

In this type of questions, some clues regarding seating or placing sequence (linear or circular) of some persons or items is given. The candidate is required to form the proper sequence using these clues and answer the questions accordingly.

Example. Four girls are sitting on a bench to be photographed. Shikha is to the left ofReena. Manju is to the right of Reena. Rita is between Reena and Manju. Who would be second from the left in the photograph ?
(*a*) Reena (*b*) Shikha (*c*) Manju
(*d*) Rita (*e*) Either Shikha or Reena

Ans. (*a*)

Shikha is to the left of Reena and Manju is to her right.

Rita is between Reena and Manju.

Hence order is : Shikha, Reena, Rita, Manju.

In the photograph, Reena will be second from left.

3. Comparison Type Questions

In this type of questions, clues are given regarding comparisons among a set of persons or things with respect to one or more qualities and we are required to analyse the whole information, form a proper ascending/descending sequence and then answer the given questions accordingly.

Example. *Read the information given below and answer the questions that follow :*

(*i*) There is a group of five girls.

(*ii*) Kamini is second in height but younger than Rupa.

(*iii*) Pooja is taller than Monika but younger in age.

(*iv*) Rupa and Monika are of the same age but Rupa is tallest between them,

(*v*) Neelam is taller than Pooja and elder to Rupa.

1. If they are arranged in the ascending order of height, who will be in third position ?

(*a*) Monika
(*b*) Rupa
(*c*) Monika or Rupa
(*d*) Data inadequate
(*e*) None of these

2. If they are arranged in the descending order of their ages, who will be in fourth position ?

(*a*) Monika or Rupa
(*b*) Kamini
(*c*) Monika
(*d*) Data inadequate
(*e*) None of these

3. To answer the question "who is the youngest person in the group", which of the given statements is superfluous ?

(*a*) Only (*i*) (*b*) Only (*ii*) (*c*) Only (*v*)
(*d*) Either (*i*) or (*iv*) (*e*) None of these

Ans. First find sequence of heights

By (*iii*), we have M < P

By (*v*), we have P < N.

Now, Rupa is tallest and Kamini is second in height, hence sequence of heights is :

M < P < N < K < R.

Now, find age sequence :

By (*ii*), we have K < R.

By (*ii*), we have P < M.

By (*iv*), we have R = M.

By (*v*), we have R < N.

Hence sequence of ages is:

P < K < R = M < N or K < P < R = M < N

1. (*e*). In increasing order of height, Neelam is in third position.

2. (*e*). In descending order of ages, Neelam will be in fourth position (because Monika and Rupa both lie at third position).

3. (*a*). Only statement (*i*) is not necessary.

4. Sequential Order of Things

In this type of questions, some clues are given regarding order of occurrence of certain eventsand we are required to analyse the given information, frame the right sequence and then answer the questions accordingly.

Example. *Read the following information carefully and answer the questions given below it :*

(*i*) Eight doctors P, Q, R, S, T, U, V and W visit a charitable dispensary every day except on a holiday i.e. Monday.

(*ii*) Each doctor visits for one hour from Tuesday to Sunday except Saturday. The timings are 9 a.m. to 1 p.m. and 2 p.m. to 6 p.m.; 1 p.m. to 2 p.m. is lunch break.

(*iii*) On Saturday, it is open only in the morning i.e. 9 a.m. to 1 p.m. and each doctor visits for only half an hour.

(*iv*) No other doctor visits the dispensary before doctor Q and after doctor U.

(*v*) Doctor-W comes immediately after lunch break and is followed by R.

(*vi*) S comes in the same order as P in the afternoon session.

1. Doctor P visits in between which of the following pairs of doctors ?

(*a*) S and V (*b*) U and W (*c*) R and W
(*d*) R and U (*e*) None of these

2. At what time the visit of doctor R is over on Sunday?

(*a*) 1 p.m. (*b*) 3 p.m. (*c*) 4p.m.
(*d*) 5p.m. (*e*) None of these

3. At what time the visit of Doctor T would be over on Saturday?

(*a*) 10 a.m.
(*b*) 11 a.m.
(*c*) Either 10 a.m. or 11 a.m.
(*d*) Data inadequate
(*e*) None of these

4. If the lunch break and subsequent visiting hours are reduced by 15 minutes, at what time Doctor U is expected to attend the dispensary ?

(*a*) 3.15 p.m. (*b*) 4 p.m. (*c*) 4.15 p.m.
(*d*) 4.45 p.m. (*e*) None of these

Ans. First form sequence of visit using (*iv*), (*v*) and (*vi*).

From (*iv*),Q visits first and U visits last.

From (*v*),W visits first after break and is followed by R.

From (*vi*), P visits after break.

Hence sequence of visit after break becomes W R P U

Also, S has the same position in morning session as P in afternoon session. Thus, sequence of visit before break is Q, T/V, S, V/T.

1. (*d*). P visits between R and U.

2. (*c*). Time of visit of W is 2 p.m. to 3 p.m., Time of visit of R is 3 p.m. to 4 p.m. So, the visit of doctor R is over at 4 p.m.

3. (*c*). T visits either second or fourth. So, the time of visit on Saturday will be either 9.30 a.m. or 10.30 a.m. Thus, T's visit will be over at either 10 a.m. or 11 a.m.

4. (*b*). As mentioned, lunch break will be over and doctor W will visit at 1.45 p.m., doctor R will visit at 2.30 p.m., doctor P will visit at 3.15 p.m. and U will visit at 4 p.m.

5. Selection based on given conditions

In this type of questions, a few essential criteria for selection of a group of items are given and we have to keep these conditions in mind and make the required selection as per the directions given in each question.

6. Jumbled problems

In this type of questions, some mixed clues regarding three or more qualities of given items or persons is given and we are required to analyse this mixed information with respect to different qualities and classify the items accordingly.

VII. DIRECTION SENSE

In this type of test, the questions consist of a sort of direction puzzle. A successive follow-up of directions is formulated and we are required to ascertain final direction or the distance between two points. The test is meant to judge ability to trace and follow correctly and sense the direction correctly.

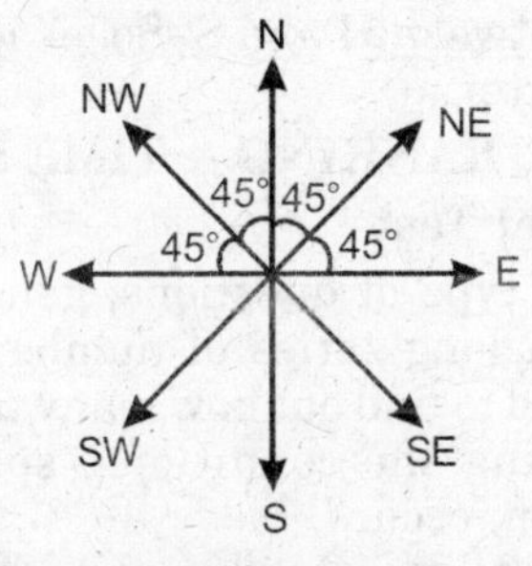

Above figure shows four main directions : North N, South S, East E, West W

Four cardinal directions : North East NE, North West NW, South East SE, South West SW

Pythagoras theorem

The theorem is applicable only in right angle triangles, in which from theorem one angle is of 90°

$$AC^2 = AB^2 + BC^2$$

where, AC is Hypotense
AB is Perpendicular (Height)
BC is Base

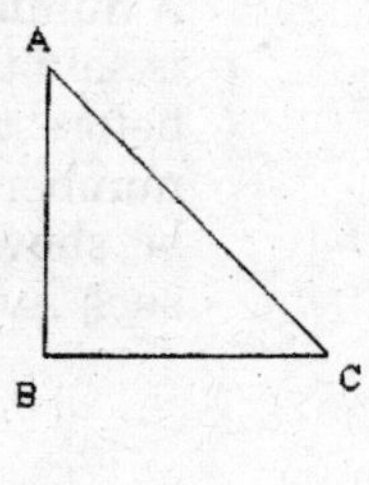

Shortcut method

1. If 2 opposite turns are coming together, they will cancel each other

   Example. left, right and right, left.

2. If similar turns are coming together they will opposite the earlier direction.

   Example. if a person is going in North and taking two left turns it means now person is moving in opposite to North i.e. South.

3. Start from either left side or right side

VIII. LOGICAL VENN DIAGRAMS

This type of questions aim at analysing ability to relate a certain given group of items and illustrate it diagrammatically.

1. LOGICAL DIAGRAMS.

In this type a few types of Venn diagrams with their implications made clear. Let a group of three items are given.

1. If items evidently belong to three different groups, then Venn diagram representing it would be asC shown alongside.

Example. Doctors, Engineers, Lawyers

These three items bear no relationship to each other. So, they are represented by 3 disjoint figures as shown:

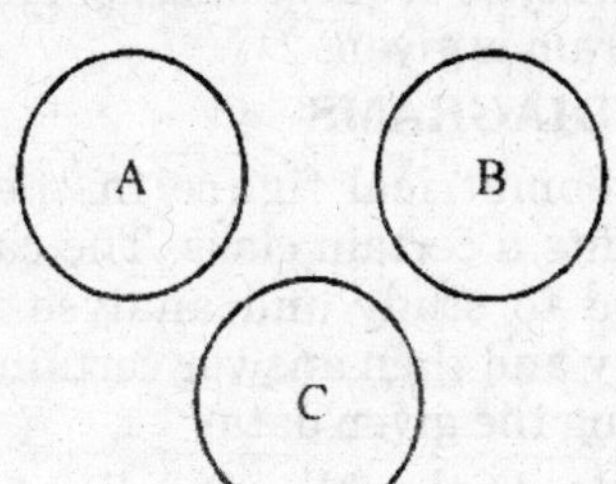

2. If one item belongs to the class of the second and second belongs to the class of third, then representation is in the form of three concentric circles, as shown below:

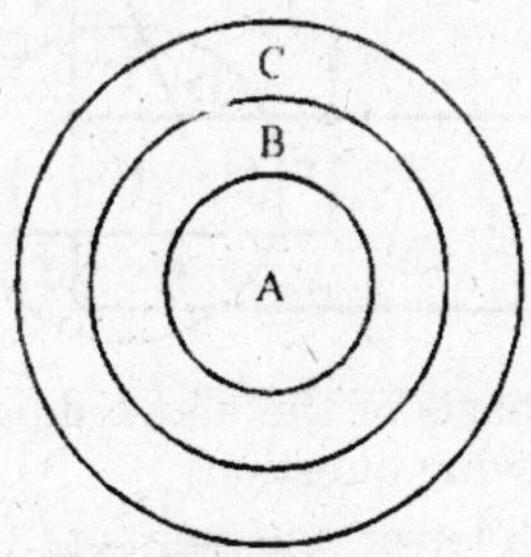

Example. Seconds, Minutes, Hours

Seconds are a part of minutes and minutes are a part of hours. So, Venn diagram would be as shown in the figure with circle A representing Seconds, circle B representing Minutes and circle C representing Hours.

3. If two separate items belong to the class of the third, they are represented by two disjoint circles inside a bigger circle as shown below

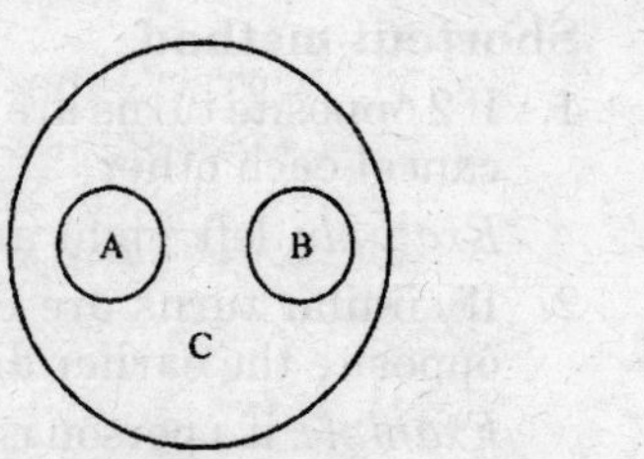

Example. Table, Chair, Furniture

Table and chair are separate items but both are items of furniture. So, they would be represented as in the figure with circle A representing Table, circle B representing Chair and circle C representing Furniture.

4. If two separate things having something common belongs to the class of third, they are represented by two joint figures inside one bigger figure is shown below.

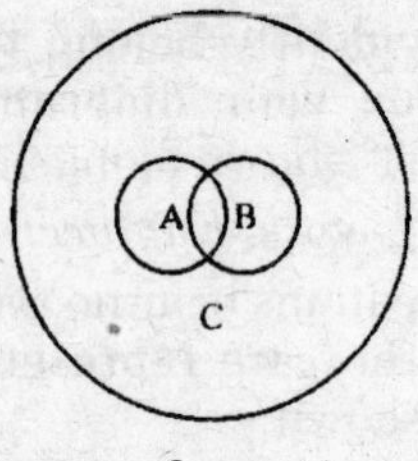

In this type of questions, generally a Venn diagram is given.

2. VENN DIAGRAMS

Each geometrical figure in the diagram represents a certain class. The candidate is required to study and analyse the figure carefully and then answer certain questions regarding the given data.

Example. In the following diagram, square represents girls, the circle represents tall persons, the triangle is for tennis players and the rectangle stands for the swimmers.

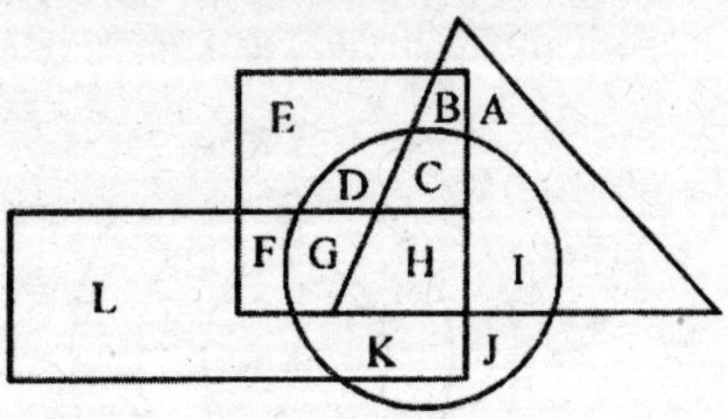

On the basis of the above diagram, answer the following questions :

1. Which letter represents tall girls who are swimmers but don't play tennis ?

(*a*) C (*b*) D (*c*) G (*d*) H (*e*) B

Ans. (*c*)

Tall girls, who are swimmers are represented by the region common to the square, circle and the rectangle i.e., G and H. But, according to the given conditions, the girls shouldn't be tennis players. So, required region should not be a part of the triangle i.e., H should be excluded. Thus, region representing the persons satisfying given conditions is G.

2. Which letter represents girls who are swimmers, play tennis but are not tall?

(*a*) B (*b*) E (*c*) H (*d*) F

(*e*) None of these

Ans. (*e*)

Girls who are swimmers and play tennis are represented by the region common to the square, triangle and rectangle i.e., H. But, it is given that the girls shouldn't be tall. So, required region should not be a part of the circle. Since H is a part of the circle. So none of these is correct

IX. ALPHABETICAL QUIBBLE

In this type of questions, we are given alphabets from A to Z. The position of a letter is given in the form of a puzzle and we are required to find this letter. However, sometimes a random letter series is given and we are required to find out how many times a letter satisfying the conditions specified in the question occurs.

Example. *Following question is based on the following alphabet series.*

ABCDEFGHIJKLMNOPQRSTUVWXYZ

Which letter is exactly midway between H and S in the given alphabet ?

(*a*) L (*b*) M (*c*) N (*d*) O

(*e*) No such letter

Ans. (*e*)

From given series we get that M & N are in midway between H and S. So, exactly midway is no such letter.

X. NUMBER, RANKING & TIME SEQUENCE

1. Number Test

In this type of questions, generally you are given a long series of numbers and we are required to find out how many times a number satisfying the conditions, specified in the question, occurs.

Example. How many 5's are there in the following sequence which are immediately followed by 3 but not immediately preceded by 7 ?

8953253855687335775365335738

(*a*) One (*b*) Two (*c*) Three

(*d*) Four (*e*) More than four

Ans. (*c*)

A number which comes after a given number is said to follow it while the one which comes before the given number precedes it. Thus, numbers satisfying the given conditions, can be shown as follows. Hence there are three such numbers.

2. Ranking Test

In this type of test, generally ranks of a person both from top and bottom are mentioned and total number of persons is asked. However, sometimes this question is put in the form of a puzzle of interchanging seats by two persons.

Example. Anil ranked ninth from the top and thirty eighth from the bottom in a class. How many students are there in the class?

(*a*) 45 (*b*) 46 (*c*) 47

(*d*) 48 (*e*) 49

Ans. (*b*)

Whole class consists of :

(*i*) 8 students who have a rank higher than Anil

(*ii*) Anil; and

(*iii*) 37 students who have rank lower than Anil i.e.,(8 + 1 + 37) = 46 students.

3. Time Sequence Test

Example. Raman remembers that his brother's birthday is after fifteenth but before eighteenth of February whereas his sister Kamla remembers that her brother's birthday is after sixteenth but before nineteenth of February. On which day in February is Raman's brother's birthday ?

(*a*) 16th (*b*) 17th (*c*) 18th

(*d*) 19th (*e*) None of these

Ans. (*b*)

According to Raman, brother's birthday is on one of the days among 16th and 17th February According to Kamla, the brother's birthday is on one of the days among 17th and 18th February. Hence Raman's brother's birthday is on the day common to both the above groups i.e., 17th February.

XI. MATHEMATICAL OPERATIONS

This type questions are based on simple mathematical operations.

Here, four fundamental operations :

Addition, subtraction, multiplication and division *and statements such as*

'less than', 'greater than', 'equal to', 'not equal to', etc.

are represented by symbols, different from the usual ones.

The questions involving these operations are set using artificial symbols. The candidate has to substitute the real signs and solve the questions accordingly, to get the answer.

TYPE OF PROBLEMS.

1. Solving by Substitution

In this type of questions, we are provided with substitutes for various mathematical symbols, followed by a question involving calculation of an expression or choosing the correct/incorrect equation. We are required to put in the real signs in the given equation and then solve the questions as required.

While solving a mathematical expression, proceed according to the rule BODMAS i.e., Brackets, Of, Division, Multiplication, Addition, Subtraction.

2. Deriving appropriate Conclusions

In such questions, the usual algebraic signs and mathematical symbols may be given different meanings or may even be replaced by new symbols. For instance (÷) may denote addition, (×) may denote subtraction (<) may denote division and so on. The simplest way to solve such an equation is to rewrite the problem replacing the given symbols with the signs they are supposed to stand for. For instance, if :

+ means –	÷ means +
'V' means <	– means >
× means =	> means ×
&, < means ÷	

Then equation, 65 < 5 ÷ 2.5 — 15 will be rewritten as 65 ÷ 5 + 2.5 > 15, and problem may be solved.

In yet another type of questions included under this system, even the digits (instead of the symbols)

0, 1, 2, ... 8, 9, may be replaced by alphabets and the candidate may then be asked to perform calculations and solve the given problem. For instance, codes may be used as (a = 1, b = 2, c = 3 etc.) or in reverse (i.e., z = 1, y = 2, x = 3 and so on).

Following question employs such a code.

Q. If y × w = s and u — v = z, what is r/x ?

(*a*) y (*b*) z (*c*) s (*d*) x

Solution : If we count backwards from z, we get y as the 2nd letter, w as the 4th letter, and s as the 8th letter. In this order u is the 6th, v is the 5th and z the 1st letter of the code.

So, 2 × 4 = 8 and 6 – 5 = 1

Hence, r = 9 and x = 3.

So $\frac{r}{x} = \frac{9}{3} = 3$. So the answer is (*d*) x.

In certain cases, arithmetical operations may not be defined. Consider the following question.

Q. If 8 + 12 = 2, and 7 + 13 = 3, then what is the value of 10 + 18 ?

(*a*) 9 (*b*) 6 (*c*) 4 (*d*) 7

Solution : $\frac{12-8}{2} = 2$, and $\frac{13-7}{2} = 3$. So, code employed here is special.

In x + y, '+' stands for $\frac{y-x}{2}$

$\therefore$ 10 + 18 = $\frac{18-10}{2}$ = 4, so the answer is (c).

XII. LOGICAL SEQUENCE OF WORDS

In this type of questions, a group of words is given. The candidate is required to arrange these words in a meaningful order such as the sequence of occurrence of events, sequence from a part to the whole, sequence of increasing/decreasing size, value, intensity etc., and then choose the correct sequence accordingly.

Examples.

1. *Arrange the following in a meaningful sequence :*

1. Consultation 2. Illness
3. Doctor 4. Treatment
5. Recovery

(*a*) 2, 3, 1, 4, 5 (*b*) 2, 3, 4, 1, 5
(*c*) 4, 3, 1, 2, 5 (*d*) 5, 1, 4, 3, 2
(*e*) 2, 3, 4, 5, 1

Ans (*a*)

Illness occurs first. One then goes to the doctor and after consultation with him, undergoes treatment to finally attain recovery. Thus, the correct order is 2, 3, 1, 4, 5.

2. *Arrange the following in a logical order :*

1. Euphoria 2. Happiness
3. Ambivalence 4. Ecstasy
5. Pleasure

(*a*) 4, 1, 3, 2, 5 (*b*) 3, 2, 5, 1, 4
(*c*) 2, 1, 3, 4, 5 (*d*) 1, 4, 2, 5, 3
(*e*) 5, 4, 3, 2, 1

Ans. (*b*)

All the given words stand for 'Joy', but the intensity increases in the order — Ambivalence, Happiness, Pleasure, Euphoria, Ecstasy. Thus, the correct order is 3, 2, 5, 1, 4.

XIII. DECISION MAKING

It with questions in which we have to decide the course of action to be taken upon a candidate who has applied for a vacancy or allotment or membership to an institution, keeping in mind the essential requisites and the data given for the candidate.

TYPE I

In such type of test, a vacancy is declared. The necessary qualifications required in the candidates coming up to fill the vacancy are provided and merits of the candidates mentioned. The decision about each candidate has to be made from amongst the five choices named (*a*), (*b*), (*c*), (*d*), (*e*) which state the courses of action to be taken as per the candidate's potentials.

Example. *Read the following information to answer the given questions*

Following are the criteria for selecting & marketing officer by a company. The candidate must :

(1) be a graduate with at least 50% marks.
(2) have secured at least 40% marks in the written test.
(3) not be less than 24 years and more than 29 years as on 10th October, 2007.
(4) should have work experience of at least two years as an officer. However, if a candidate:
(5) fulfils all other criteria except at (4) above but has a diploma in Marketing Management, his/her case is to be referred to General Manager, Marketing.
(6) fulfils all other criteria except at (3) above but has worked as Marketing Officer at least for three years, his/her case is to be referred to Director, Marketing.

Based on the above criteria and information given in each of the following questions, we have to take the decision in regard to each case. We are not to assume anything. These cases are given as on 10th October, 2007.

Mark answer (*a*) if candidate is to be appointed;

Mark answer (*b*) if the candidate is not to be appointed;

Mark answer (*c*) if the data given are not sufficient to take decision;

Mark answer (*d*) if to be referred to General Manager - Marketing; and

Mark answer (*e*) if to be referred to Director – Marketing.

1. Amit, born on 5th June, 1983, has done his post-graduation in Marketing Management with first class. He has secured 50% marks in the written test. He has been working in an organisation as a Marketing Officer for the last four years.

2. Rohit has been working in an organisation as Officer for the last ten years. His date of birth is 17th February, 1964. He has secured 60% marks in the degree examination and 40% marks in the written test.

3. Manju is a first class graduate and has done a diploma in Marketing Management. She has secured 50% marks in the written test. She was 23 years old as on 5th September, 2006.

4. Nitin was born on 25th August, 1985. He has secured 60% and 50% marks in graduation and in the written test, respectively. He has been working in an organisation as Officer for the last four years.

5 Suman is a graduate with first class and has secured 60% marks in the written test. She has been working as an Officer for the last three years. She was born on 20th May, 1982.

Ans.

1. (*a*). All conditions of eligibility are satisfied.

2. (*e*). Condition (3) is violated but it can be waived by condition (6).

3. (*d*). The candidate satisfies all conditions except (4). But he fulfils condition (5) so that (4) is waived.

4. (*e*). The candidate satisfies condition (2) instead of condition (3).

5. (*a*). All conditions of eligibility are satisfied.

TYPE II. ASSERTION AND REASON

This test is meant to judge the candidate's knowledge and his ability to reason out correctly. In this test, two statements referred to as the Assertion (A) and Reason (R) respectively are provided. Five alternative comments on these are given and the **correct** one is to be chosen.

Example. *For the Assertions (A) and Reasons (R) below, choose the correct alternative from the following*:

(*a*) Both A and R are true and R is the correct explanation of A.

(*b*) **Both A and R are true but R is NOT the correct explanation of A.**

(*c*) **A is true but R is false.**

(*d*) A is false but R is true.

(*e*) Both A and R are false.

1. **Assertion (A) :** Moon cannot be used as a satellite for communication.

   Reason (R) : Moon does not move in the equatorial plane of the earth.

   Ans. (*a*)

   Since R explains A.

2. **Assertion (A) :** Salt is added to cook food at higher altitudes.

   Reason (R): Temperature is lower at higher altitudes.

   Ans. (*b*)

   Since both statements A and R are separately true but R does not explain A.

TYPE III. SITUATION REACTION TEST

In this test, certain situation is described and the candidate is required to choose the most suitable reaction to the given situation from amongst the alternatives provided. This test judges reasoning power of the candidate and his ability to act correctly and promptly to a situation that may arise in emergency.

Example. While travelling in your car, certain persons stop you on the way asking you to take an injured child to the hospital. You would :

(*a*) ask them to leave your way and then drive away.

(*b*) ask them to first call the police.

(*c*) immediately take the child to hospital.

(*d*) get out of the car and ask some other person to help them.

(*e*) None of these

Ans. (*c*)

Situation described above demands that the person should immediately render the help asked for and take the child to the hospital.

Examples

1. While playing cricket in the school, suddenly when you hit the ball, it strikes your classmate on the forehead and blood starts oozing out. You would :

   (*a*) run away from the field.

   (*b*) start fighting with the boy why he came in the way.

   (*c*) blame somebody else for the accident.

   (*d*) take the boy to the first aid room.

   (*e*) None of these

   Ans. (*d*)

   In the above situation, urgent need is to provide first aid to the boy so that the bleeding may stop.

2. You are visiting a place for the first time and are travelling in a bus. Suddenly you realise that the driver is taking the bus to a lonely place with no right intentions. You would :

   (*a*) with the help of some other passengers, try to baffle the driver and take over the bus.

   (*b*) sit and wait to face the repercussions.

   (*c*) jump out of the running bus.

   (*d*) console the worried passengers.

   Ans. (*a*)

   When a wrong doing is expected, immediate action to prevent it is the need.

3. You have gone to enjoy a Diwali Mela organised by a club. Suddenly you come across a lost child crying desperately.

   You would :

   (*a*) neglect and walk away.

   (*b*) ask the child to find his parents.

   (*c*) ask him to stop crying and wait patiently for his parents.

   (*d*) contact with the club authorities and make an announcement for the parents.

   Ans. (*d*)

   Immediate need is to find the child's parents and for this, best way is to announce the child's name and appearance so that his parents might know where the child is.

EXERCISE – I

MCQ TYPE QUESTIONS

1. Given two numbers x and y, define

Addition	A(x, y) = x + y
Subtraction	S (x, y) = x – y
Multiplication	M (x, y) = x, y
Division	D (x, y) = x/y

S[M(D(A(a, b), 2), D(A(a, b), 2)), M(D(S(a, b), 2), D(S(a, b),2))] is equal to

(*a*) $(a - b)^2$ (*b*) ab
(*c*) $(a + b)^2$ (*d*) None of these

Directions Q. 2 – 5 :

Kamal Babu came home just after judging a beauty contest where there were four semi-finalists, Ms. Andhra Pradesh, Ms. Uttar Pradesh, Ms. Maharashtra and Ms. West Bengal. His wife was very keen on knowing who the winner was and Kamal Babu replied immediately that it was the one wearing the yellow saree. When his wife asked for more details, he gave the following information:

* The four girls were wearing sarees of different colours (yellow, red, green, white) and the runner-up was wearing green.
* The four girls were sitting in a row, and Ms. West Bengal was not sitting at either end.
* There was only one runner-up and she was sitting next to Ms. Maharashtra.
* The girls wearing yellow and white sarees occupied the seats at either end.
* Ms. West Bengal was nither the winner nor the runner-up.
* Ms. Maharashtra was wearing white.
* The winner and the runner-up were not sitting next to each other.
* The girl wearing the green saree was not Ms. Andhra Pradesh.

Answer the following questions based on the above information:

2. What was the colour of the saree that Ms. Andhra Pradesh was wearing?
(*a*) White (*b*) Yellow
(*c*) Red (*d*) Cannot be determined

3. Between which two was Ms.West Bengal sitting?
(*a*) Ms. Andhra Pradesh and Ms. Maharashtra
(*b*) Ms. Andhra Pradesh and Ms. Uttar Pradesh
(*c*) Ms. Uttar Pradesh and Maharashtra
(*d*) Cannot be deternmined

4. Who was wearing the red saree?
(*a*) Ms. Andhra Pradesh
(*b*) Ms. Uttar Pardesh
(*c*) Ms. West Bengal
(*d*) Cannot be determined

5. What was the colour of the saree that Ms. Uttar Pradesh was wearing?
(*a*) White (*b*) Green
(*c*) Red (*d*) Yellow

Directions Q. 6 – 7 :

A, B, C, D, E and F are a group of friends from a club. There are two housewives, one lecturer, one architect, one accountant and one lawyer in the group. There are two married couples in the group. The lawyer is married to D who is a housewife. No lady in the group is either an architect or an accountant C. The accountant, is married to F who is a lecturer. A is married to D and E is not a housewife.

6. What is E ?
(*a*) Lawyer (*b*) Architect
(*c*) Lecturer (*d*) Accountant

7. How many members of the group are males?
(*a*) 2 (*b*) 3
(*c*) 4 (*d*) none of these

Directions Q. 8 – 9 :

Seven university cricket players are to be honoured at a special luncheon. the players will be seated on the dais along one side of a single rectangular table.

A and G have to leave for the lunch early and must be seated at the extreme right end of the table which is closest to the exit.

B will receive the Man of the Match award and must be in the center chair.

C and D, who are bitter rivals for the position of wicket keeper, dislike each other and should be seated as far apart as possible.

E and F are best friends and want to sit together.

8. Which of the following may not be seated at either end of the table ?
(*a*) C (*b*) D
(*c*) G (*d*) F

9. Which of the following pairs may not be seated together ?
(*a*) E & A (*b*) B & D
(*c*) C & F (*d*) G & D

Directions Q. 10 –13 :

A study was conducted to ascertain the relative importance that employees in five different countries assigned to five different traits in their Chief Executive Officers. The traits were compassion (C), decisiveness (D), negotiation skills (N), public visibility (P), and vision (V). The level of dissimilarity between two countries is the maximum difference in the ranks allotted by the two countries to any of the five traits. The following table indicates the rank order of the five traits for each country.

	Country				
RANK	INDIA	CHINA	JAPAN	MALAYSIA	THAILAND
1	C	N	D	V	V
2	P	C	N	D	C
3	N	P	C	P	N
4	V	D	V	C	P
5	D	V	P	N	D

10. Which of the following pairs of countries are most dissimilar?

(*a*) China and Japan
(*b*) India and China
(*c*) Malaysia and Japan
(*d*) Thailand and Japan

11. Which of the following countries is least dissimilar to India?

(*a*) China (*b*) Japan
(*c*) Malaysia (*d*) Thailand

12. Which amongst the following countries is most dissimilar to India?

(*a*) China (*b*) Japan
(*c*) Malaysia (*d*) Thailand

13. Three of the following four pairs of countries have identical levels of dissimilarity. Which pair is the odd one out?

(*a*) Malaysia and China
(*b*) China and Thailand
(*c*) Thailand and Japan
(*d*) Japan and Malaysia

Directions Q. 14 – 17 :

Four families decided to attend the marriage ceremony of one of their colleagues. One family has no kids, while others have at least one kid each. Each family with kids has at least one kid attending the marriage.

Given below is some information about the families, and who reached when to attend the marriage.

The family with 2 kids came just before the family with no kids.

Shanthi who does not have any kids reached just before Sridevi's family.

Sunil and his wife reached last with their only kid.

Anil is not the husband of Joya.

Anil and Raj are fathers.

Sridevi's and Anita's daughters go to the same school.

Joya came before Shanthi and met Anita when she reached the venue.

Raman stays the farthest from the venue.

Raj said his son could not come because of his exams.

14. Which woman arrived third ?

(*a*) Shanthi (*b*) Sridevi
(*c*) Anita (*d*) Joya

15. Name the correct pair of husband and wife ?

(*a*) Raj and Shanthi (*b*) Sunil and Sridevi
(*c*) Anil and Sridevi (*d*) Raj and Anita

16. Of the following pairs, whose daughters go to the same school ?

(*a*) Anil and Raman (*b*) Sunil and Raman
(*c*) Sunil and Anil (*d*) Raj and Anil

17. Whose family is known to have more than one kid for certain ?

(*a*) Raman's (*b*) Raj's (*c*) Anil's (*d*) Sunil's

Directions Q. 18 – 20 :

Answer the following questions based on the statements given below:

(*i*) There are three houses on each side of the road.
(*ii*) These six houses are labeled as P, Q, R, S, T and U.
(*iii*) The houses are of different colours, namely, Red, Blue, Green, Orange, Yellow and White.
(*iv*) The houses are of different heights.
(*v*) T, the tallest house, is exactly opposite to the Red coloured house.
(*vi*) The shortest house is exactly opposite to the Green coloured house.
(*vii*) U, the Orange coloured house, is located between P and S.
(*viii*) R, the Yellow coloured house, is exactly opposite to P.
(*ix*) Q, the Green coloured house, is exactly opposite to U.
(*x*) P, the White coloured house, is taller than R, but shorter than S and Q.

18. What is the colour of the house diagonally opposite to the Yellow coloured house?

(*a*) White (*b*) Blue
(*c*) Green (*d*) Red

19. Which is the second tallest house?

(*a*) P (*b*) S
(*c*) Q (*d*) cannot be determined

20. What is the colour of the tallest house?

(*a*) Red (*b*) Blue (*c*) Green (*d*) Yellow

NUMERICAL TYPE QUESTIONS

1. Given two numbers x and y, define

Addition	A(x, y) = x + y
Subtraction	S (x, y) = x – y
Multiplication	M (x, y) = x, y
Division	D (x, y) = x/y

If x = 2, y = 3 and z = 5, then value of M[A(S (x, y), M (y, z)), S (A(x, z), S (z, y))] is ______

Directions Q. 2 – 3 :

These questions are based on the following data

A, B, C, D are standing in a queue. It is known that C and D are not standing adjacent to each other and that B is not in the third place.

2. If A is not in the second place and B is in the first place, then which is the place for D is ______

3. If A is not standing adjacent to B and D is the last in the queue, then the place for C is ______

Directions Q. 4 – 5 :

A boy is asked to put in a basket one mango when ordered 'One', one orange when ordered 'Two', one apple when ordered 'Three' and is asked to take out from the basket one mango and an orange when ordered 'Four'. A sequence of orders is given as

1 2 3 3 2 1 4 2 3 1 4 2 2 3 3 1 4 1 1 3 2 3 4

4. The ______total organges were in the basket at the end of the above sequence.

5. The ______total fruits will be in the basket at the end of the above order sequence.

Directions Q. 6 – 7

Each of the 11 letters A, H, I, M, O, T, U, V, W, X and Z appears same when looked at in a mirror. They are called symmetric letters. Other letters in the alphabet are asymmetric letters.

6. The______ number of four-letter computer passwords can be formed using the symmetric letters (no repetition allowed)

7. The ______ number of three-letter computer passwords can be formed (no repetition allowed) with at least one symmetric letter.

Directions Q. 8 – 9 :

A string of three English letters is formed as per the following rules:

(*a*) The first letter is any vowel

(*b*) The second letter is m, n or p.

(*c*) If the second letter is m then the third letter is any vowel which is different from the first letter

(*d*) If the second letter is n then the third letter is *e* or *u*

(*e*) If the second letter is p then the third letter is the same as the first letter.

8. The ______ strings of letters can possible be formed using the above rules.

9. The ______ strings of letters can possibly be formed using the above rules such that the third letter of the string is e.

EXERCISE – II

(QUESTIONS FROM PREVIOUS GATE EXAMS)

MCQ TYPE QUESTIONS

2015

1. Mr. Vivek walks 6 meters North-East, then turns and walks 6 meters South- East, both at 60 degrees to East. He further moves 2 meters South and 4 meters West. What is the straight distance in meters between the point he started from and the point he finally reached?

(*a*) $2\sqrt{2}$ (*b*) 2

(*c*) $\sqrt{2}$ (*d*) $1/\sqrt{2}$

2. There are 16 teachers who can teach Thermodynamics (TD), 11 who can teach Electrical Sciences (ES), and 5 who can teach both TD and Engineering Mechanics (EM). There are a total of 40 teachers, 6 cannot teach any of the three subjects, i.e. EM, ES or TD. 6 can teach only ES. 4 can teach all three subjects, i.e. EM, ES and TD. 4 can teach ES and TD. How many can teach both ES and EM but not TD?

(*a*) 1 (*b*) 2

(*c*) 3 (*d*) 4

3. The given question is followed by two statements: select the most appropriate option that solves the question

Capacity of a solution tank A is 70% of the capacity of tank B. How many gallons of solution are in tank A and tank B?

Statements:

I. Tank A is 80% full and tank B is 40% full

II. Tank A if full contains 14,000 gallons of solution

(*a*) Statement I alone is sufficient

(*b*) Statement II alone is sufficient

(*c*) Either statement I or II alone is sufficient

(*d*) Both the statements I and II together are sufficient

4. Operators □, ◇ and → are defined by

$$a \,\square\, b = \frac{a-b}{a+b};\ a \Diamond b = \frac{a+b}{a-b};\ a \rightarrow b = ab.$$

Find the value (66□6) →(66◇6)

(*a*) –2 (*b*) –1

(*c*) 1 (*d*) 2

5. Humpty Dumpty sits on a wall every day while having lunch. The wall sometimes breaks. A person sitting on the wall falls if the wall breaks.

Which one of the statements below is logically valid and can be inferred from the above sentences?

(*a*) Humpty Dumpty always falls while having lunch

(*b*) Humpty Dumpty does not fall sometimes while having lunch

(c) Humpty Dumpty never falls during dinner

(d) When Humpty Dumpty does not sit on the wall, the wall does not break

6. If ROAD is written as URDG, then SWAN should be written as :

(a) VXDQ (b) VZDQ

(c) VZDP (d) UXDQ

7. Select the pair that best expresses a relationship similar to that expressed in the pair :

Children : Pediatrician

(a) Adult : Orthopaedist

(b) Females : Gynaecologist

(c) Kidney : Nephrologist

(d) Skin : Dermatologist

8. The head of a newly formed government desires to appoint five of the six selected members P,Q,R,S,T and U to portfolios of Home, Power, Defense, Telecom, and Finance. U does not want any portfolio if S gets one of the five. R wants either Home or Finance or no portfolio. Q says that if S gets either Power or Telecom, then she must get the other one. T insists on a portfolio if P gets one.

Which is the valid distribution of portfolios?

(a) P-Home, Q-Power, R-Defense, S-Telecom, T-Finance

(b) R-Home, S-Power, P-Defense, Q-Telecom, T-Finance

(c) P-Home, Q-Power, T-Defense, S-Telecom, U-Finance

(d) Q-Home, U-Power, T-Defense, R-Telecom, P-Finance

9. Most experts feel that in spite of possessing all the technical skills required to be a batsman of the highest order, he is unlikely to be so due to lack of requisite temperament. He was guilty of throwing away his wicket several times after working hard to lay a strong foundation. His critics pointed out that until he addressed this problem success at the highest level will continue to elude him.

Which of the statement (s) below is/are logically valid and can be inferred from the above passage?

(i) He was already a successful batsman at the highest level

(ii) He has to improve his temperament in order to become a great batsman

(iii) He failed to make many of his good starts count

(iv) Improving his technical skills will guarantee success

(a) (iii) and (iv)

(b) (ii) and (iii)

(c) (i), (ii) and (iii)

(d) (ii) only

10. Alexander turned his attention towards India, since he had conquered Persia.

Which one of the statements below is logically valid and can inferred from the above sentence?

(a) Alexander would not have turned his attention towards India had he not conquered Persia.

(b) Alexander was not ready to rest on his laurels, and wanted to march to India

(c) Alexander was completely in control of his army and could command it to move towards India

(d) Since Alexander's kingdom extended to Indian borders after the conquest of Persia, he was keen to move further

11. Tanya is older than Enc.

Cliff is older than Tanya.

Eric is older than Cliff.

If the first two statements are true, then the third statement is

(a) True (b) False

(c) Uncertain (d) Data insufficient

12. Given below are two statements followed by two conclusions. Assuming these statements to be true, decide which one logically follows:

Statements:

I. No manager is a leader.

II. All leaders are executive.

Conclusions:

I. No manager is a executive.

II. All executive is a manager.

(a) Only conclusion I follows.

(b) Only conclusion II follows.

(c) Neither conclusion I nor II follows.

(d) Both conclusion I and II follow.

13. Find the missing sequence in the letter series below :

A, CD, GHI, _?___, UVWXY

(a) LMN (b) MNO

(c) MNOP (d) NOPQ

14. Ms. X will be in Bagdogra from 1/5/14 to 20/5/14 and from 22/5/14 to 31/5/14. On the morning of 21/5/14, she will reach Kochi via Mumbai.

Which one of the statements below is logically valid and can be inferred from the above sentences?

(*a*) Ms. X will be in Kochi for only one day only in May

(*b*) Ms. X will be in Kochi for only one day in May

(*c*) Ms. X will be only in Kochi for one day in May

(*d*) Only Ms. X will be in Kochi for one day in May

15. Given below are two statements followed by two conclusions. Assuming these statements to be true, decide which one logically follows.

Statement:

I. All film stars are playback singers.

II. All film directors are film stars.

Conclusions:

I. All film directors are playback singers.

II. Some film stars are film directors.

(*a*) Only conclusion I follows

(*b*) Only conclusion II follows

(*c*) Neither conclusion I nor II follows

(*d*) Both conclusions I and II follow

16. Lamenting the gradual sidelining of the arts in school curricula, a group of prominent artists wrote to the Chief Minister last year, asking him to allocate more funds to support arts education in schools. However, no such increase has been announced in this year's Budget. The artists expressed their deep anguish at their request not being approved, but many of them remain optimistic about funding in the future.

Which of the statement(*s*) below is/are logically valid and can be inferred from the above statements?

i. The artists expected funding for the arts to increase this year.

ii. The Chief Minister was receptive to the idea of increasing funding for the arts.

iii. The Chief Minister is a prominent artist.

iv. Schools are giving less importance to arts education nowadays.

(*a*) *iii* and *iv*

(*b*) *i* and *iv*

(*c*) *i*, *ii* and *iv*

(*d*) *i* and *iii*

17. Four branches of a company are located at M, N, O, and P. M is north of N at a distance of 4 km; P is south of O at a distance of 2 km; N is southeast of O by 1 km. What is the distance between M and P in km?

(*a*) 5.34 (*b*) 6.74

(*c*) 28.5 (*d*) 45.49

18. The given statement is followed by some courses of action. Assuming the statement to be true, decide the correct option.

Statement:

There has been a significant drop in the water level in the lakes supplying water to the city.

Course of action:

I. The water supply authority should impose a partial cut in supply to tackle the situation.

II. The government should appeal to all the residents through mass media for minimal use of water.

III. The government should ban the water supply in lower areas.

(*a*) Statements I and II follow.

(*b*) Statements I and III follow.

(*c*) Statements II and III follow.

(*d*) All statements follow.

2014

19. In a group of four children, Som is younger to Riaz. Shiv is elder to Ansu. Ansu is youngest in the group. Which of the following statements is/are required to find the eldest child in the group?

Statements

1. Shiv is younger to Riaz.

2. Shiv is elder to Som.

(*a*) Statement 1 by itself determines the eldest child.

(*b*) Statement 2 by itself determines the eldest child.

(*c*) Statements 1 and 2 are both required to determine the eldest child.

(*d*) Statements 1 and 2 are not sufficient to determine the eldest child.

20. X is 1 km northeast of Y. Y is 1 km southeast of Z. W is 1 km west of Z. P is 1 km south of W. Q is 1 km east of P. What is the distance between X and Q in km?

(*a*) 1 (*b*) $\sqrt{2}$

(*c*) $\sqrt{3}$ (*d*) 2

21. Rajan was not happy that Sajan decided to do the project on his own. On observing his unhappiness, Sajan explained to Rajan that he preferred to work independently.

Which one of the statements below is logically valid and can be inferred from the above sentences?

(*a*) Rajan has decided to work only in a group.

(*b*) Rajan and Sajan were formed into a group against their wishes.

(*c*) Sajan had decided to give in to Rajan's request to work with him.

(*d*) Rajan had believed that Sajan and he would be working together.

22. Find the odd one in the following group: ALRVX, EPVZB, ITZDF, OYEIK

(*a*) ALRVX (*b*) EPVZB

(*c*) ITZDF (*d*) OYEIK

23. Anuj, Bhola, Chandan, Dilip, Eswar and Faisal live on different floors in a six-storeyed building (the ground floor is numbered 1, the floor above it 2, and so on). Anuj lives on an even-numbered floor. Bhola does not live on an odd numbered floor. Chandan does not live on any of the floors below Faisal's floor. Dilip does not live on floor number 2. Eswar does not live on a floor immediately above or immediately below Bhola. Faisal lives three floors above Dilip. Which of the following floor-person combinations is correct?

	Anuj	*Bhola*	*Chandan*	*Dilip*	*Eswar*	*Faisal*
(*a*)	6	2	5	1	3	4
(*b*)	2	6	5	1	3	4
(*c*)	4	2	6	3	1	5
(*d*)	2	4	6	1	3	5

24. Find the next term in the sequence: 13M, 17Q, 19S, ________

(*a*) 21W (*b*) 21V

(*c*) 23W (*d*) 23V

25. If 'KCLFTSB' stands for 'best of luck' and 'SHSWDG' stands for 'good wishes', which of the following indicates 'ace the exam'?

(*a*) MCHTX

(*b*) MXHTC

(*c*) XMHCT

(*d*) XMHTC

26. "India is a country of rich heritage and cultural diversity."

Which one of the following facts best supports the claim made in the above sentence?

(*a*) India is a union of 28 states and 7 union territories.

(*b*) India has a population of over 1.1 billion.

(*c*) India is home to 22 official languages and thousands of dialects.

(*d*) The Indian cricket team draws players from over ten states.

27. In which of the following options will the expression P < M be definitely true?

(*a*) M < R > P > S (*b*) M > S < P < F

(*c*) Q < M < F = P (*d*) P = A < R < M

28. Find the next term in the sequence:

7G, 11K, 13M, ________

(*a*) 15Q (*b*) 17Q

(*c*) 15P (*d*) 17P

29. The multi-level hierarchical pie chart shows the population of animals in a reserve forest. The correct conclusions from this information are:

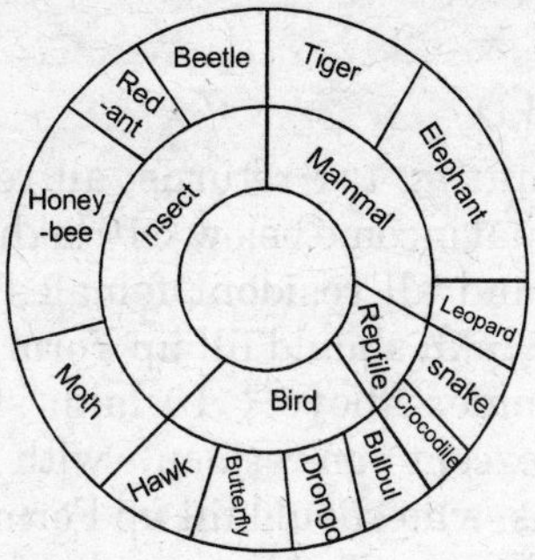

(*i*) Butterflies are birds

(*ii*) There are more tigers in this forest than red ants

(*iii*) All reptiles in this forest are either snakes or crocodiles

(*iv*) Elephants are the largest mammals in this forest

(*a*) (i) and (*ii*) only

(*b*) (*i*), (*ii*), (*iii*) and (*iv*)

(*c*) (*i*), (*iii*) and (*iv*) only

(*d*) (*i*), (*ii*) and (*iii*) only

30. Find the odd one in the following group

Q,W,Z,B B,H,K,M W,C,G,J M,S,V,X

(*a*) Q, W, Z, B (*b*) B, H, K, M

(*c*) W, C, G, J (*d*) M, S, V, X

31. Lights of four colors (red, blue, green, yellow) are hung on a ladder. On every step of the ladder there are two lights. If one of the lights is red, the other light on that step will always be blue. If one of the lights on a step is green, the other light on that step will always be yellow. Which of the following statements is not necessarily correct?

(*a*) The number of red lights is equal to the number of blue lights

(*b*) The number of green lights is equal to the number of yellow lights

(*c*) The sum of the red and green lights is equal to the sum of the yellow and blue lights

(*d*) The sum of the red and blue lights is equal to the sum of the green and yellow lights

32. Read the statements:

All women are entrepreneurs.

Some women are doctors.

Which of the following conclusions can be logically inferred from the above statements?

(*a*) All women are doctors

(*b*) All doctors are entrepreneurs

(*c*) All entrepreneurs are women

(*d*) Some entrepreneurs are doctors

33. Find the odd one from the following group:

(*a*) W,E,K,O

(*b*) I,Q,W,A

(*c*) F,N,T,X,

(*d*) N,V,B,D

34. For submitting tax returns, all resident males with annual income below ₹ 10 lakh should fill up Form P and all resident females with income below ₹ 8 lakh should fill up Form Q. All people with incomes above ₹ 10 lakh should fill up Form R, except non residents with income above ₹ 15 lakhs, who should fill up Form S. All others should fill Form T. An example of a person who should fill Form T is

(*a*) a resident male with annual income ₹ 9 lakh

(*b*) a resident female with annual income ₹ 9 lakh

(*c*) a non-resident male with annual income ₹ 16 lakh

(*d*) a non-resident female with annual income ₹ 16 lakh

35. Which number does not belong in the series below?

2, 5, 10, 17, 26, 37, 50, 64

(*a*) 17 (*b*) 37

(*c*) 64 (*d*) 26

36. A dance programme is scheduled for 10.00 a.m. Some students are participating in the programme and they need to come an hour earlier than the start of the event. These students should be accompanied by a parent. Other students and parents should come in time for the programme. The instruction you think that is appropriate for this is

(*a*) Students should come at 9.00 a.m. and parents should come at 10.00 a.m.

(*b*) Participating students should come at 9.00 a.m. accompanied by a parent, and other parents and students should come by 10.00 a.m.

(*c*) Students who are not participating should come by 10.00 a.m. and they should not bring their parents. Participating students should come at 9.00 a.m.

(*d*) Participating students should come before 9.00 a.m. Parents who accompany them should come at 9.00 a.m. All others should come at 10.00 a.m.

37. The number of people diagnosed with dengue fever (contracted from the bite of a mosquito) in north India is twice the number diagnosed last year. Municipal authorities have concluded that measures to control the mosquito population have failed in this region.

Which one of the following statements, if true, does not contradict this conclusion?

(*a*) A high proportion of the affected population has returned from neighbouring countries where dengue is prevalent

(*b*) More cases of dengue are now reported because of an increase in the Municipal Office's administrative efficiency

(*c*) Many more cases of dengue are being diagnosed this year since the introduction of a new and effective diagnostic test

(*d*) The number of people with malarial fever (also contracted from mosquito bites) has increased this year

38. Geneticists say that they are very close to confirming the genetic roots of psychiatric illnesses such as depression and schizophrenia, and consequently, that doctors will be able to eradicate these diseases through early identification and gene therapy.

On which of the following assumptions does the statement above rely?

(*a*) Strategies are now available for eliminating psychiatric illnesses

(*b*) Certain psychiatric illnesses have a genetic basis

(*c*) All human diseases can be traced back to genes and how they are expressed

(*d*) In the future, genetics will become the only relevant field for identifying psychiatric illnesses

2013

39. Select the pair that best expresses a relationship similar to that expressed in the pair:

Medicine: Health

(*a*) Science : Experiment

(*b*) Wealth : Peace

(*c*) Education : Knowledge

(*d*) Money : Happiness

40. Abhishek is elder to Savar.

Savar is younger to Anshul.

Which of the given conclusions is logically valid and is inferred from the above statements?

(*a*) Abhishek is elder to Anshul

(*b*) Anshul is elder to Abhishek

(*c*) Abhishek and Anshul are of the same age

(*d*) No conclusion follows

41. Complete the sentence:

Universalism is to particularism as diffuseness is to _____

(*a*) specificity (*b*) neutrality
(*c*) generality (*d*) adaptation

42. After several defeats in wars, Robert Bruce went in exile and wanted to commit suicide. Just before committing suicide, he came across a spider attempting tirelessly to have its net. Time and again, the spider failed but that did not deter it to retrain from making attempts. Such attempts by the spider made Bruce curious. Thus, Bruce started observing the near-impossible goal of the spider to have the net. Ultimately, the spider succeeded in having its net despite several failures. Such act of the spider encouraged Bruce not to commit suicide. And then, Bruce went back again and won many a battle, and the rest is history.

Which one of the following assertions is best supported by the above information?

(*a*) Failure is the pillar of success.

(*b*) Honesty is the best policy.

(*c*) Life begins and ends with adventures.

(*d*) No adversity justifies giving up hope.

43. Statement: You can always give me a ring whenever you need.

Which one of the following is the best inference from the above statement?

(*a*) Because I have a nice caller tune.

(*b*) Because I have a better telephone facility.

(*c*) Because a friend in need is a friend indeed.

(*d*) Because you need not pay towards the telephone bills when you give me a ring.

44. Statement: There were different streams of freedom movements in colonial India carried out by the moderates, liberals, radicals, socialists, and so on.

Which one of the following is the best inference from the above statement?

(*a*) The emergence of nationalism in colonial India led to our Independence.

(*b*) Nationalism in India emerged in the context of colonialism.

(*c*) Nationalism in India is homogeneous.

(*d*) Nationalism in India is heterogeneous.

45. Select the pair that best expresses a relationship similar to that expressed in the pair :

water : pipe : :

(*a*) cart : road

(*b*) electricity : wire

(*c*) sea : beach

(*d*) music: instrument

46. All professors are researchers

Some scientists are professors

Which of the given conclusions is logically valid and is inferred from the above arguments :

(*a*) All scientists are researchers

(*b*) All professors are scientists

(*c*) Some researchers are scientists

(*d*) No conclusion follows

2012

47. Wanted Temporary, Part-time persons for the post of Field Interviewer to conduct personal interviews to collect and collate economic data. Requirements: High School-pass, must be available for Day, Evening and Saturday work. Transportation paid, expenses reimbursed.

Which one of the following is the best inference from the above advertisement?

(*a*) Gender-discriminatory

(*b*) Xenophobic

(*c*) Not designed to make the post attractive

(*d*) Not gender-discriminatory

48. Given the sequence of terms, AD CG FK JP, the next term is

(*a*) OV (*b*) OW
(*c*) PV (*d*) PW

2011

49. A transporter receives the same number of orders each day. Currently, he has some pending orders (backlog) to be shipped. If he uses 7 trucks, then at the end of the 4th day he can clear all the orders. Alternatively, if he uses only 3 trucks, then all the orders are cleared at the end of the 10th day. What is the minimum number of trucks required so that there will be no pending order at the end of the 5th day?

(*a*) 4 (*b*) 5
(*c*) 6 (*d*) 7

50. Few school curricula include a unit on how to deal with bereavement and grief, and yet all students at some point in their lives suffer from losses through death and parting.

Based on the above passage which topic would not be included in a unit on bereavement?

(*a*) How to write a letter of condolence

(*b*) What emotional stages are passed through in the healing process

(*c*) What the leading causes of death are

(*d*) How to give support to a grieving friend

51. The question below consists of a pair of related words followed by four pairs of words. Select the pair that best expresses the relation in the original pair :

Gladiator : Arena

(*a*) dancer : stage
(*b*) commuter : train
(*c*) teacher : classroom
(*d*) lawyer : courtroom

52. The horse has played a little known but very important role in the field of medicine. Horses were injected with toxins of diseases until their blood built up immunities. Then a serum was made from their blood. Serums to fight with diphtheria and tetanus were developed this way.

It can be inferred from the passage, that horses were

(*a*) given immunity of diseases
(*b*) generally quite immune to diseases
(*c*) given medicines to fight toxins
(*d*) given diphtheria and tetanus serums

2010

53. The question below consists of a pair of related words followed by four pairs of words. Select the pair that best expresses the relation in the original pair.

Unemployed : Worker

(*a*) fallow : land (*b*) unaware : sleeper
(*c*) wit : jester (*d*) renovated : house

54. Hari (H), Gita (G), Irfan (I) and Saira (S) are siblings (i.e. brothers and sisters). All were born on 1st January. The age difference between any two successive siblings (that is born one after another) is less than 3 years. Given the following facts:

I. Hari's age + Gita age > Irfan's age + Saira's age
II. The age difference between Gita and Saira is 1 year. However, Gita is not the oldest and Saira is not the youngest.
III. There are no twins.

In what order were they born (oldest first)?

(*a*) HSIG (*b*) SGHI
(*c*) IGSH (*d*) IHSG

55. Modern warfare has changed from large scale clashes of armies to suppression of civilian populations. Chemical agents that do their work silently appear to be suited to such warfare; and regretfully, there exist people in military establishments who think that chemical agents are useful tools for their cause.

Which of the following statements best sums up the meaning of the above passage:

(*a*) Modern warfare has resulted in civil strife
(*b*) Chemical agents are useful in modern warfare
(*c*) Use of chemical agents in warfare would be undesirable
(*d*) People in military establishments like to use chemical agents in war

56. If 137 + 276 = 435 how much is 731 + 672?

(*a*) 534
(*b*) 1403
(*c*) 1623
(*d*) 1513

NUMERICAL TYPE QUESTIONS

2015

1. Fill in the missing value

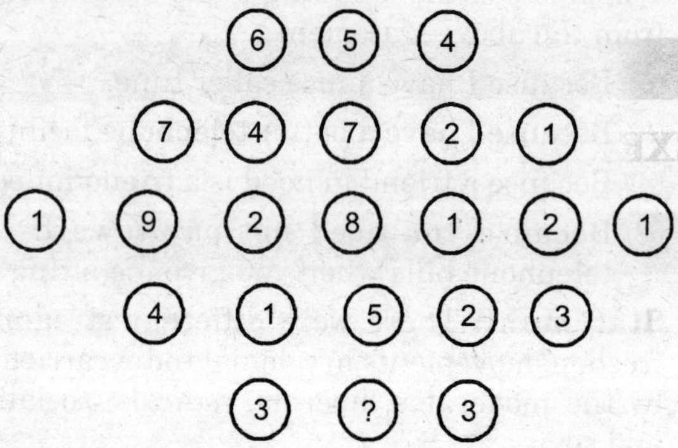

2014

2. The next term in the series 81, 54, 36, 24,.... is ______

3. Fill in the missing number in the series.

2 3 6 15 ___ 157.5 630

4. What is the next number in the series?

12 35 81 173 357 ____

ANSWERS

EXERCISE – I

MCQ Type Questions

1. (*b*) **2.** (*b*) **3.** (*b*) **4.** (*c*) **5.** (*b*) **6.** (*b*) **7.** (*b*) **8.** (*d*) **9.** (*a*) **10.** (*a*)

11. (*b*) **12.** (*d*) **13.** (*d*) **14.** (*a*) **15.** (*b*) **16.** (*c*) **17.** (*b*) **18.** (*d*) **19.** (*d*) **20.** (*b*)

Numerical Type Questions

1. 70 **2.** 105 **3.** 2 **4.** 2 **5.** 11 **6.** 7920 **7.** 12870 **8.** 35 **9.** 10

EXERCISE – II

MCQ Type Questions

1. (*a*) **2.** (*a*) **3.** (*d*) **4.** (*c*) **5.** (*b*) **6.** (*b*) **7.** (*b*) **8.** (*b*) **9.** (*b*) **10.** (*a*)

11. (*b*) **12.** (*c*) **13.** (*c*) **14.** (*b*) **15.** (*d*) **16.** (*b*) **17.** (*a*) **18.** (*a*) **19.** (*a*) **20.** (*c*)

21. (*d*) **22.** (*d*) **23.** (*b*) **24.** (*c*) **25.** (*b*) **26.** (*c*) **27.** (*d*) **28.** (*b*) **29.** (*d*) **30.** (*c*)

31. (*d*) **32.** (*d*) **33.** (*d*) **34.** (*b*) **35.** (*c*) **36.** (*b*) **37.** (*d*) **38.** (*b*) **39.** (*c*) **40.** (*d*)

41. (*a*) **42.** (*d*) **43.** (*c*) **44.** (*d*) **45.** (*b*) **46.** (*c*) **47.** (*d*) **48.** (*a*) **49.** (*c*) **50.** (*c*)

51. (*d*) **52.** (*b*) **53.** (*d*) **54.** (*b*) **55.** (*c*) **56.** (*c*)

Numerical Type Questions

1. (3) **2.** (16) **3.** (45) **4.** (725 to 725)

EXPLANATIONS

EXERCISE – I

MCQ TYPE QUESTIONS

1. S[M(D(A(*a*, *b*)2, D(A(*a*, *b*)2)), M(D(S(*a*,*b*)2)) D(*s*(*a*,*b*)2)]

$$= S\left[\left|M\frac{a+b}{2}, \frac{a+b}{2}\right|\left|M\frac{a-b}{2}; \frac{a-b}{2}\right|\right]$$

$$= \left(\frac{a+b}{2}\right)^2 - \left(\frac{a-b}{2}\right)^2 = ab$$

6 – 7.

A → Lawyer → Male

B → Housewife → Female

C → Accountant → Male

D → Housewife → Female

E → Architect → Male

F → Lecturer → Female

Married Couple : AD & CF

8—9. The seating arrangement is shown below:

Left · Right

7	6	5	4	3	2	1
D/C	E/F	F/E	B	C/D	G/A	A/G

10 – 13.

Level of Dissimilarity is equal to Maximum difference in ranks alloted to any two countries on any of the five traits.

For example, dissimilarity between India and China.

Trait	India'sRank	China's Rank	Difference
C	1	2	1
P	2	3	1
N	3	1	2
V	4	5	1
D	5	4	1

From the above table, maximum difference is 2.

So dissimilarity level between India and China is 2.

10. Calculating the level of dissimilarity for India Vs remaining countries.

China : For the parameter N (3 – 1) = 2

Japan : For the parameter D (5 – 1) = 4

Malaysia : For the parameter C (4 – 1) = 3

Thailand : For the parameter V (4 – 1) = 3

Hence least level of dissimilarity is 2 which is for China.

11. From above calculations, highest level of dissimilarity is 4 which is for Japan.

12. *The level of dissimilarity between*

China and Japan is for the parameter D
$(4 - 1) = 3$

India and China is for the parameter N
$(3 - 1) = 2$

Malaysia and Japan is for the parameter V
$(4 - 1) = 3$

Thailand and Japan is for the parameter D
$(5 - 1) = 4$

13. *The level of dissimilarity between*

Malaysia and China is for the parameter V
$(5 - 1) = 4$

China and Thailand is for the parameter V
$(5 - 1) = 4$

Thailand and Japan is for the parameter D
$(5 - 1) = 4$

Japan and Malaysia is for the parameter V
$(4 - 1) = 3$

14 to 17 :

The given set of questions is based on distribution and sequencing.

Firstly, let us put the names of women and men,

Women : Shanthi, Sridevi, Joya, Anita

Men : Sunil, Anil, Raj, Raman

It is given that(2 kids family) $\xleftarrow{\text{came before}}$ (No kid family)

Also Shanti (0 kids) $\xrightarrow{\text{came before}}$ Sridevi

As Sunil and his wife came with their only kid, hence Sunil cannot be the husband of Shanthi.

As Anil and Raj are fathers, hence neither of them is the husband of Shanthi. Hence Raman is the husband of Shanthi.

Also, Joya came before Shanthi and met Anita on the venue, this gives the following order of their reaching the venue. [Anita, Joya, Shanthi, Sridevi]

As Sunil reached last, Sunil is the husband of Sridevi. This means that Raj is Joya's husband and Anil is Anita's husband.

Following table gives the desired details

Order	Women	Men	No. of Kids
1	Anita	Anil	at least 1
2	Joya	Raj	2
3	Shanthi	Raman	0
4	Sridevi	Sunil	1

14. Shanthi arrived third.

15. Out of the given choices. Sunil and Sridevi is the correct pair.

16. The daughters of Anita and Sridevi go to the same school. Anita's husband is Anil and Sridevi's husband is Sunil. Hence, Sunil and Anil is the correct answer.

17. Raj's family consists of two kids for certain (Anil has at least one kid, hence could be having exactly one kid also).

18 to 20 :

From statements (vii), (viii) and (ix), we get

P	U	S
	Orange	
R	Q	
Yellow	Green	

Then, T is opposite S and the colour of S is red.

From (x), the colour of house P is white, hence the colour of house T is blue.

P	U	S
White	Orange	Red
R	Q	T
Yellow	Green	Blue

Now, from (v) and (x) , we get

$T > S, Q > P > R$

From (vi), U is the shortest.

i.e., the order of houses in the descending order of their heights is T, S/Q, Q/S, P, R, U.

18. R is yellow coloured house and the house diagonally opposite R is S. And the colour of house S is Red.

19. The second tallest house is either S or Q.

20. The tallest house is T and its colour is blue.

NUMERICAL TYPE QUESTIONS

1. $M[A(S(x, y), M(y, z)), S(A(x, z), S(z, y))]$

$= M[A((2 - 3), (3, \times 5)), S((2 + 5), (5 - 3))]$

$= M[A(-1, 15), S(7, 2)]$

$= M[14, 5] = 70.$

2. Since B is in 1, and C and D are not adjacent, the only places possible for them are 2 and 4.

3. Since B is not in the third place and A is not adjacent to B, and D is last in the queue. The position of A will be beside D and B will be at the other corner. C will be between B and A. Hence the positions will be BCAD. Place of C is 2, hence choice (*b*)

The sitting position is as follows.

White	Green	Red	Yellow
Maharashtra	U.P.	West Bengal	A.P.

From the above table,

Ms. Andhra Pradesh $\longrightarrow$ Yellow

4. (1) (2) 3 3 2 1 4 (2) 3 (1) 4 (2) (2) 3 3 (1) 4 1 (1) (3) (2) 3 4

Total no. oranges were in basket = 2

5. Total fruits in the basket = 11

6. Total number of four letter password formed

$$= {}^{11}C_4 \times \angle 4 = 11 \times 10 \times 9 \times 8 = 7920$$

7. Required number of passwords

$$= {}^{26}C_3 \times \angle 3 - {}^{15}C_3 \times \angle 3$$

$$= 26 \times 25 \times 24 - 15 \times 14 \times 13 = 12870$$

8. [ ] [ ] [ ]

1st Letter 2nd letter 3rd letter

There are 5 vowels, $a, e, i, o,, u,$.

hence 1st letter can be any of the 5 vowels ;

$\therefore$ 5 different methods. ...(*i*)

The second letter can be any of the *m, n,* or *p*. But each has its own rule for the third letter. Hence, each case to be considered separately.

[1 Vowel] [m]

In the above case; third letter is one of the remaining 4 vowels

Hence there are 5 × 4 = 20 ways of forming such a string. ...(*ii*)

If the second letter is *n*, the third is either *e* or *u*, *i.e.* 2 different ways.

$\therefore$ total of 5 × 2 ways = 10 ways ...(*iii*)

When 2nd position is filled by P, the third letter is same as the first letter. As the 1st letter is already selected, third can be filled only one way.

Hence, there are 5× 1 = 5 ways ....(*iv*)

From equations (*ii*), (*iii*) and (*iv*),

Total number of strings that can be formed

$$= 20 + 10 + 5 = 35$$

9. Third letter find is '*e*'.

Once again considering each case of the second position being filled by *m, n* or *p,* we have

[1st position] [n] [e]

2nd position 3rd position

The 3rd position shall be different form vowel in first position, *i.e.* vowel for 1st position can be selected out of the vowels *a, i, o, u* only.

Hence 4 different ways ....(*i*)

When 2nd possible is filled by *n*, occupying 2nd position, does not create any restriction on the vowel is position 1.

[e] [n] [ ]

3rd 2nd 1st

Hence, 1st position can be occupied by any of the 5 vowels.

Hence, 5 different ways ....(*ii*)

When 2nd position is filled by *p*,

[e] [p] [ ]

3rd 2nd 1st

In this case, letters in 3rd position out 1st position shall be the same.

Hence, 1st position shall be filled by '*e*'.

i.e. only one way of filling ....(*iii*)

Total number of possible strings = 4 + 5 + 1 = 10

EXERCISE – II

MCQ TYPE QUESTIONS

2.

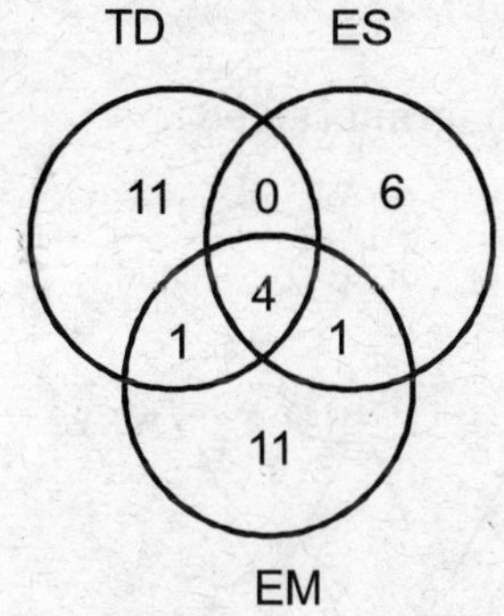

3. Statement-I can be used to solve the question if capacity of both tanks is already known

Statement-II can be used if it is known what quantity of each tank is full/empty.

Therefore, by using both statements

Let capacity of tank B is x

$$\frac{70}{100}x = 14000$$

$$\Rightarrow \quad x = 20000 \text{ gallons}$$

Solution in tank A $= \frac{80}{100} \times 14000 = 11200$ gallons

Solution in tank B $= \frac{40}{100} \times 20000 = 8000$ gallons

$\therefore$ Total solution $= 11200 + 8000 = 19200$ gallons

4. $66\square6 = \frac{66-6}{66+6} = \frac{60}{72} = \frac{5}{6}$

$66\diamond6 = \frac{66+6}{66-6} = \frac{72}{60} = \frac{6}{5}$

$(66\square6) \rightarrow (66\diamond6) = \frac{5}{6} \times \frac{6}{5} = 1$

6. R + 3 = U, O + 3 = R,

A + 3 = D, D + 3 = G;

S + 3 = V, W + 3 = Z,

A + 3 = D, N + 3 = Q

7. Community of people : Doctor

8. Since U does not want any portfolio, (*c*) and (*d*) are ruled out. R wants Home, or Finance or No portfolio, (*a*) is not valid.

Hence option (*b*) is correct.

12. S + 1: S + 2 :

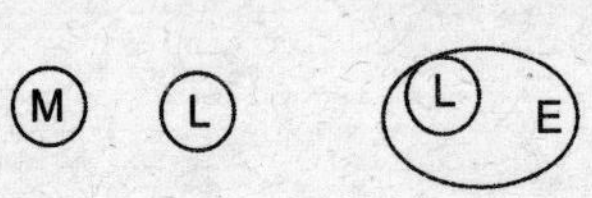

Therefore concluding diagram can be

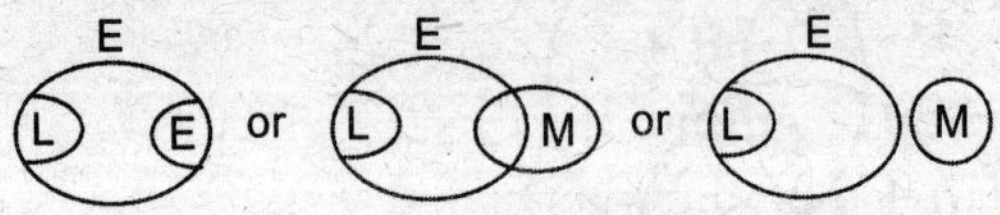

13.

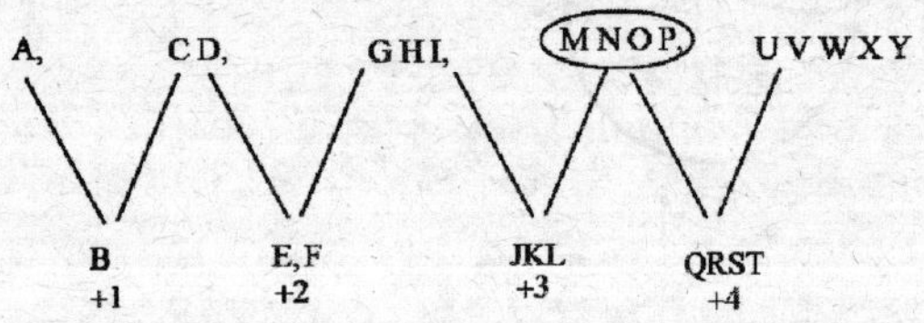

14. Second sentence says that Ms. X reaches Kochi on 21/05/2014. Also she has to be in Bagdogora on 22/05/2014.

$\therefore$ She stays in Kochi for only one day in may.

17.

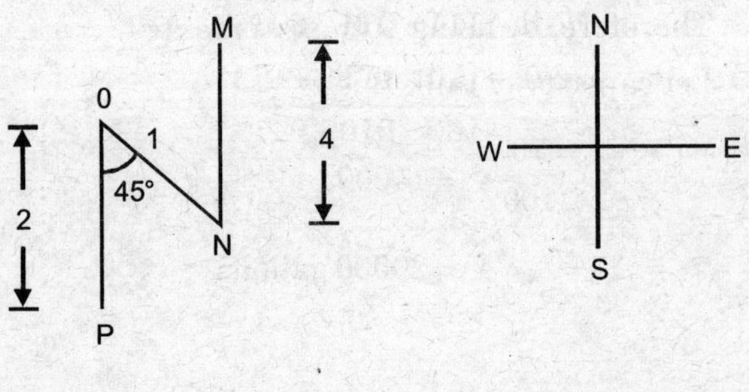

19. Riaz > Som ...(*i*)

Shiv > Ansu ...(*ii*)

Ansu is youngest in the group

$\therefore$ From equations (*i*) and (*ii*)

$\therefore$ Riaz > Som > Shiv > Ansu

20.

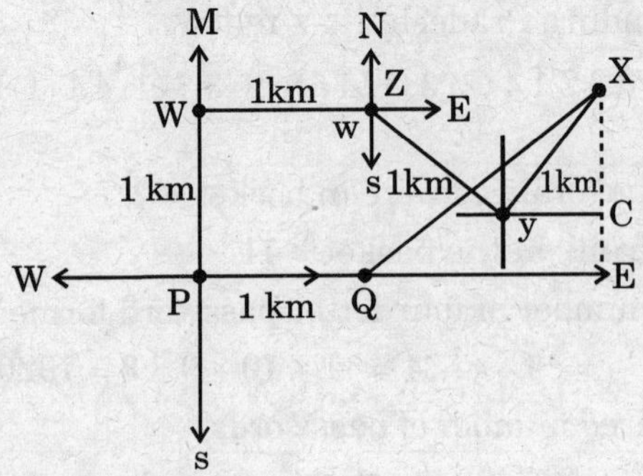

Here XE = 1 km

$$QE = \frac{2}{\sqrt{2}} = \sqrt{2}$$

$\therefore$ using Pythagoras theorem,

$$XQ = \sqrt{(QE)^2 + (XE)^2}$$

$$= \sqrt{2+1} = \sqrt{3} \text{ km}$$

$\therefore$ Statement I itself determines the eldest child which statement 2 is incorrect as Ansu is youngest in the group is not satisfied by statement 2

Hence option (*a*) is correct

22. ALRVX $\rightarrow$ only one vowel

EPVZB $\rightarrow$ only one vowel

ITZDF $\rightarrow$ only one vowel

OYEIK $\rightarrow$ three vowels

23. (*a*) Anuj: Even numbered floor (2, 4, 6)

(*b*) Bhola: Even numbered floor (2, 4, 6)

(*c*) Chandan lives on the floor above that of Faisal.

(*d*) Dilip: not on 2nd floor.

(*e*) Eswar: does not live immediately above or immediately below Bhola

From the options its clear, that only option (*b*) satisfies condition (*e*).

So, correct Ans is (*b*).

25. KCLFTSB: BST-Best, F-Of, LCK-Luck (Reverse order)

SHSWDG: GD-Good, WSHS-Wishes (Reverse order)

Similarly "ace the Exam'- C-Ace, T-The, XM-Exam

26. Diversity is shown in terms of difference language.

29. It is not mentioned that elephant is the largest animal.

30.

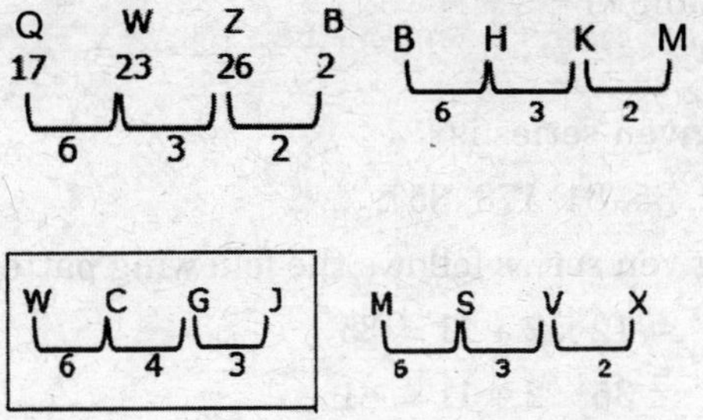

33.

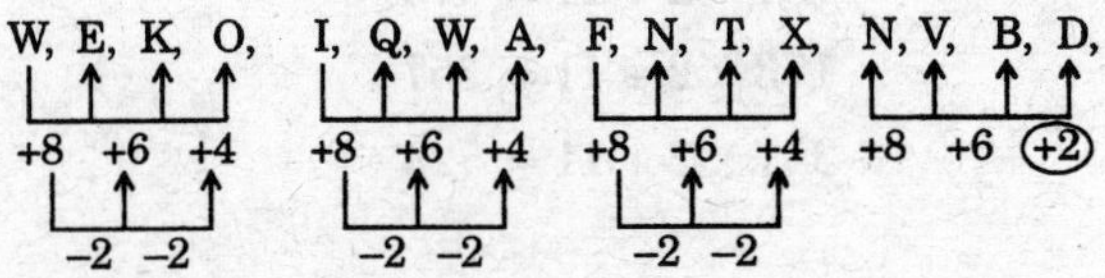

Hence the odd one from the following group is N, V, B, D.

34. By reading the instructions, it is clear that person who fills form T is a resident female with annual income of ₹ 9 Lakh.

37. Among given option, option (*d*) *i.e.* the number of people with malarial fever has increased this year do not contradic the conclusion.

48.

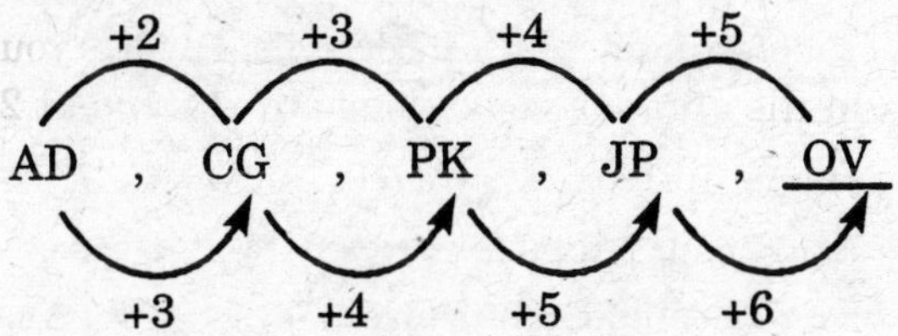

49. Let each truck carry 100 units.

$$2800 = 4n + e$$

where n = normal

$$3000 = 10n + e$$

where e = excess/pending

$$\therefore \quad n = \frac{100}{3}, \quad e = \frac{8000}{3}$$

$$5 \text{ days} \Rightarrow 500x = \frac{5100}{3} + \frac{8000}{3}$$

$$\Rightarrow \quad 500x = \frac{8500}{3} = 17$$

$$\Rightarrow \quad x > 5$$

Minimum possible = 6

50. The given passage clearly deals with how to deal with bereavement and grief and so after the tragedy occurs and not about precautions. Therefore, irrespective of the causes of death, a school student rarely gets into details of causes—which is beyond the scope of the context. Rest all are important in dealing with grief.

51. Given relationship is worker: workplace. A gladiator is

(*i*) a person, usually a professional combatant trained to entertain the public by engaging in mortal combat with another person or a wild.

(*ii*) A person engaged in a controversy or debate, especially in public.

52. From the passage it cannot be inferred that horses are given immunity as in option (*a*), since the aim is to develop medicine and in turn immunize humans. Option (*b*) is correct since it is given that horses develop immunity after some time. Refer "until their blood built up immunities". Even option(*c*) is invalid since medicine is not built till immunity is developed in the horses. Option (*d*) is incorrect since specific examples are cited to illustrate and this cannot capture the essence.

54. $H + G > I + S$ ...(1)

and $G - S = 1$ ...(2)

G is not oldest, S is not youngest

$\therefore$ $H + 1 > I$

Irfan older than Hari

Gita older than Sarita

From given option SGHI

55. Use of chemical agents in warfare would be undesirable

56.

$$\begin{array}{r} 137 - \overline{001}\ \ \overline{011}\ \ \overline{111} \\ +276 - 010\ \ 111\ \ 110 \\ \hline 100\ \ 011\ \ 101 = 435 \end{array}$$

Octal number system

$$\therefore \begin{array}{r} 731 - 111\ \ 011\ \ 001 \\ 672 - 110\ \ 111\ \ 110 \\ \hline \underline{100}\ \ 010\ \ 011 \end{array}$$

Hence 1623

NUMERICAL TYPE QUESTIONS

1. Middle number is the average of number on both sides

$\therefore$ Average of 3 and 3 is $\frac{3+3}{2} = \frac{6}{2} = 3$

2. $81 - 54 = 27; 27 \times \frac{2}{3} = 18$

$54 - 36 = 18; 18 \times \frac{2}{3} = 12$

$36 - 24 = 12; 12 \times \frac{2}{3} = 8$

$\therefore \quad 24 - 8 = 16$

3. 2 3 6 15 **[45]** 157.5 630

1.5 2 2.5 3 3.5 4

$\frac{\text{2nd number}}{\text{1st number}}$ is in increasing order as shown above

4. The given series is

12, 35, 81, 173, 357, ...

The given series follows the following pattern

$12 \times 2 + 11 = 35$

$35 \times 2 + 11 = 81$

$81 \times 2 + 11 = 173$

$173 \times 2 + 11 = 357$

$357 \times 2 + 11 = 725$

■■

General Aptitude

Part II : Numerical Ability

1 CHAPTER

Numbers and Algebra

NUMBERS

Natural Numbers

All positive integers are natural numbers.

e.g. 1, 2, 3, 4, 5,......

There are infinite natural numbers and number 1 is the *least natural number*.

Types of Natural Numbers : *Based on divisibility there are following two types of natural numbers :*

1. *Prime Numbers:*

A natural number larger than unity is a prime number if it does not have other divisors except itself and unity.

Note: Unity *i.e* 1 is not a prime number.

To Check A Number is Prime or not:

(*i*) Take square root of the number.

(*ii*) Round of the square root to the next highest integer and call this number as Z.

(*iii*) Check for divisibility of the number N by all prime numbers below Z. If there is no number below the value of Z which divides N then the number will be prime.

e.g. 241 is prime or not?

$\sqrt{241}$ lies between 15 or 16.Hence take the value of Z =16.

Prime numbers less than 16 are 2, 3, 5, 7, 11 and 13.

241 is not divisible by any of these. Hence we can conclude that 241 is a *prime number.*

2. *Composite Numbers:*

The numbers which are not prime are known as composite numbers.

Note: 1 is neither prime not composite

Co-Primes: Two numbers a and b are said to be co-primes, if their H.C.F is 1.

e.g. (2, 3), (4, 5), (7, 9), (8, 11).....

Tests for Divisibility

A number is divisible by

(1) 2, when its unit's digit is even or 0.

(2) 3, when the sum of its digits is divisible by 3.

(3) 4 when number formed by last two right hand digits is divisible by 4, or if last two digits are 0's.

(4) 5, when its unit's digit is 5 or 0.

(5) 6, when it is divisible by 2 and 3 both.

(6) 8 when number formed by last three right hand digits is divisible by 8, or when last three digit are 0's.

(7) 9, when sum of its digits is divisible by 9.

(8) 10, when its unit's digit is 0.

(9) 11, when difference between sum of the digits in the odd and sum of the digits in the even places is 0 or a multiple of 11.

Note: When any number with an even number of digits is added to its reverse, the sum is always a multiple of 11.

(10) 12, when it is divisible by 3 and 4 both.

HCF AND LCM

Greatest Common Divisor (GCD)

It is the greatest divisor common to two or more given numbers. It is also called HCF (Highest Common Factor).

Method to find HCF of given Numbers.

1. *By method of factorization:*

Express each given number as product of primes. Now take product of common factors, which is HCF.

e.g., Find HCF of 136, 144, 168.

$136 = 2 \times 2 \times 2 \times 17 = 2^3 \times 17$

$144 = 2 \times 2 \times 2 \times 2 \times 3 \times 3 = 2^4 \times 3^2$

$168 = 2 \times 2 \times 2 \times 3 \times 7 = 2^3 \times 3 \times 7$

$\text{HCF} = 2^3 = 8$

2. *By division method:*

Suppose two numbers are given.

Divide greater number by the lesser one; divide lesser by the remainder; divide first remainder by the new remainder, and so on till there is no remainder. Last divisor is the required H.C.F.

e.g., Find H.C.F. of 12 and 15.

```
12)15(1
  -12
  ----
    3)12(4
     -12
     ----
      00
```

$\therefore$ HCF = 3

In case more than two numbers are given, then choose any two of them and find their HCF. HCF of these two and third gives HCF of three numbers and so on.

Note: If 'Z' is HCF of 'X' and 'Y', then Z is also a factor of aX + bY where a, b are integers.

Least Common Multiple (LCM)

LCM of two or more given number is the least number which is exactly divisible by each of the given numbers.

Methods to find LCM of given Numbers.

1. By method of factorization:

Resolve each one of the given numbers into prime factors, then their LCM is product of highest powers of all factors, that occur in these numbers.

e.g., Find LCM of 136, 144, 168

$136 = 2^3 \times 17$

$144 = 2^4 \times 3^2$

$168 = 2^3 \times 3 \times 7$

$LCM = 2^4 \times 3^2 \times 17 \times 7 = 17136$

2. Using the formula:

Product of numbers = HCF × LCM

If two numbers are given, find their HCF.

$$LCM = \frac{\text{Product of two numbers}}{HCF}$$

e.g., Find LCM of 136, 144.

$$LCM = \frac{136 \times 144}{8} = 2448$$

If more than two numbers are given, find LCM of any two of them. Then LCM of this LCM and third number gives LCM of these three numbers and so on.

3. Short cut method using factorization:

e.g. Find LCM of 18, 28, 108, 105.

2	18,	28,	108,	105
2	9,	14,	54,	105
3	9,	7,	27,	105
3	3,	7,	9,	35
3	1,	7,	3,	35
5	1,	7,	1,	35
7	1,	7,	1,	7
	1,	1,	1,	1

$LCM = 2 \times 2 \times 3 \times 3 \times 3 \times 5 \times 7 = 3780$

Alternatively : We can strike out 18 at once, since any multiple of 108 must contain 18 as a factor.

2	28,	108,	105
2	14,	54,	105
3	7,	27,	105
7	7,	9,	35
	1,	9,	5

$LCM = 2 \times 2 \times 3 \times 7 \times 9 \times 5 = 3780$

Note: For any given numbers, HCF is necessarily a factor of their L.C.M.

HCF and LCM of Fractions.

$$\text{HCF of Fractions} = \frac{\text{HCF of Numerators}}{\text{LCM of Denominators}}$$

$$\text{LCM of Fractions} = \frac{\text{LCM of Numerators}}{\text{HCF of Denominators}}$$

e.g. Find HCF and LCM of $\frac{4}{5}, \frac{8}{35}, \frac{2}{15}, \frac{6}{25}$

$$\therefore \quad HCF = \frac{\text{HCF of 4, 8, 2, 6}}{\text{LCM of 5, 35, 15, 25}}$$

$$= \frac{2}{5 \times 7 \times 3 \times 5} = \frac{2}{525}$$

$$LCM = \frac{\text{LCM of 2, 8, 4, 6}}{\text{HCF of 5, 35, 15, 25}} = \frac{24}{5}$$

PROGRESSIONS

Arithmetic Progression (A.P.)

Let 'a' be the first term of an arithmetic progression; 'd' the common difference and 'n' the number of terms in the progression.

$$T_n = n^{th} \text{ term} = a + (n-1)d$$

$$S_n = \text{Sum of n terms} = \frac{n}{2} \times [2a + (n-1)d]$$

Progression can be represented as a, a + d, a + 2d, ..., [a + (n – 1) d]. Here, quantity d is to be added to any chosen term to get next term of the progression. When there are n terms in an arithmetic progression, a is first term and {a + (n – 1) d} is last term.

$$\text{Then} \quad S_n = \frac{n}{2} \times [\text{First Term} + \text{Last Term}]$$

Geometric Progression (G.P.)

Geometric progression can be represented as a, ar, ar^2, ... where a is first term and r is common ratio of the geometric progression.

n^{th} term of the geometric progression = ar^{n-1}.

$$\text{Sum to n terms} = \frac{a(1-r^n)}{1-r} \text{ or } \frac{a(r^n-1)}{r-1}$$

$$= \frac{r \times \text{last term} - \text{First term}}{r-1}$$

Infinite Geometric Progression.

If $-1 < r < +1$ or $|r| < 1$, then sum of a geometric progression does not increase infinitely; it "converges" to a particular value. Such a G.P. is called infinite geometric progression.

Sum of an infinite geometric progression, $S_\infty = \frac{a}{1-r}$

Remember

Sum of first n natural numbers, $= S_n = \sum n = \frac{n(n+1)}{2}$

Sum of squares of first n natural numbers,

$$\sum n^2 = \frac{n(n+1)(2n+1)}{6}$$

Sum of cubes of first n natural numbers,

$$\sum n^3 = \left[\frac{n(n+1)}{6}\right]^2 \frac{n^2(n+1)^2}{4} = \left[\sum n\right]^2$$

AVERAGES, MEAN, MODE and MEDIAN

Averages

A central value around which a group of values shows a tendency to concentrate is called *average*. Thus an average is a single value that is in some way indicative of a group of values.

Measures of Central Tendency

Following are five measures of central tendency :

1. **Mode :** It is the number that occurs most frequently in a given set of numbers.

   e.g., Find mode of the set of numbers 2, 4, 6, 6, 5, 4, 3, 6, 2, 6, 4, 1, 4, 5, 4.

   Since number 4 occurs maximum number of times, hence mode is 4.

   Note : In a given set of data, if two or more values occur the same number of times, then a unique mode does not exist.

2. **Median:** It is the middle value of a group of numbers arranged in an ascending or descending order.

   If number of values (n) in a given set of data is odd, then Median is the $\left(\frac{n+1}{2}\right)^{th}$ value.

   e.g., Find median of the numbers 40, 41, 33, 48, 41, 39 and 38.

   Arrange values in ascending order, i.e. 33, 38, 39, 40, 41, 41, 48.

   Median is the $\left(\frac{7+1}{2}\right)^{th}$ value, 4th value *i.e.,* 40

   If number of values (n) in a given set of data is even, then there will be two middle values say a and b, and hence median is taken as $\frac{a+b}{2}$.

   e.g., Find median of the numbers 16, 15, 13, 14, 23, 44.

   Arrange values in descending order, i.e. 44, 23, 16, 15, 14, 13. Two middle values are 16 and 15.

   $\therefore$ Median $= \frac{16+15}{2} = \frac{31}{2} = 15.5$

MEAN

1. **Arithmetic Mean (A.M.):** The most commonly used average is the arithmetic mean (AM) or simply the average.

   Arithmetic mean of n numbers $x_1, x_2, x_3 \ldots\ldots x_n$ is denoted by $\bar{x}$ and calculated as

   $$x = \frac{x_1 + x_2 + \ldots + x_n}{n} \quad \text{or} \quad x = \frac{\sum_{i=1}^{n} x_i}{n}$$

   where Greek letter Σ(sigma) indicates "*Sum of the terms of the type*". It takes value from 1 to n.

   Arithmetic mean of a and b is $\frac{a+b}{2}$.

   e.g., Find arithmetic mean of 10, 15, 17, 20.

   $$x = \frac{10+15+17+20}{4} = 15.5$$

When large numbers are involved, an Arithmetic Mean is generally assumed to facilitate calculation. If a is assumed Arithmetic mean, then true Arithmetic mean $\bar{x}$ of group of n numbers $x_1, x_2, x_3 \ldots\ldots x_n$ is

$$\bar{x} = a + \frac{\sum_{i=1}^{n} d_i}{n},$$

where $d_i = x_i - a$ is deviation from the assumed mean.

e.g., Find the Arithmetic mean of 42, 46, 48, 50, 55, 60, 70

Let assumed mean be 50

x_i	d_i
42	42 – 50 = – 8
46	46 – 50 = – 4
48	48 – 50 = – 2
50	50 – 50 = 0
55	55 – 50 = 5
60	60 – 50 = 10
70	70 – 50 = 20

$$\therefore \quad \bar{x} = 50 + \frac{\sum_{i=1}^{7} di}{7} = 50 + \frac{21}{7} = 53.$$

Weighted Arithmetic Mean: If values $x_1, x_2, \ldots\ldots x_n$ are assigned weights $w_1, w_2, \ldots\ldots w_n$ respectively, then

$$\text{weighted arithmetic mean , } x_w = \frac{\sum_{i=1}^{n} w_i x_i}{\sum_{i=1}^{n} w_i}$$

The term '*weight*' stands for relative importance that is attached to the different values.

'w' can also be replaced by 'f' in a frequency distribution where 'f' denotes frequency or simply the number of times a particular observation occurs.

e.g.,

x_i	w_i	$w_i x_i$
20	3	60
30	1	30
40	5	200
50	1	50

$\Sigma w_i = 10$; $\Sigma x_i w_i = 340$

$$\therefore \quad \bar{x}_w = \frac{\sum_{i=1}^{4} w_i x_i}{\sum_{i=1}^{4} w_i} = \frac{340}{10} = 34$$

When two or more groups are combined, then combined average of the groups is

$$x_c = \frac{x_1 n_1 + x_2 n_2 + x_3 n_3 + \ldots + x_n n_n}{n_1 + n_2 + n_3 + \ldots + n_n}$$

where x_1, x_2, x_3....x_n individual averages of the groups and n_1, n_2, ..., n_n are number of observations or values in each of the groups.

e.g., Mean marks scored by 50 boys are 70 and those scored by 100 girls are 55. Find average marks scored by this group.

$$x_c = \frac{n_1x_1 + n_2x_2}{n_1 + n_2} = \frac{70 \times 50 + 100 \times 55}{150} = \frac{9000}{150} = 60$$

2. Geometric Mean (G.M.):

G.M. of n numbers x_1, x_2, ... x_n is nth root of their products

i.e., $$\text{G.M.} = \sqrt[n]{x_1 \times x_2 \times x_3 \times \ldots \times x_n}$$

e.g., Geometric mean of 2, 3 and 4 is $\sqrt[3]{2 \times 3 \times 4}$

$$= \sqrt[3]{24} = 2.\sqrt[3]{3}$$

Geometric mean of a and b is $\sqrt{ab}$

e.g., Find Geometric mean of 9 and 4.

$$\text{G.M.} = \sqrt{9 \times 4} = 6$$

Geometric mean is generally used to calculate rate of growth.

If geometric mean of one group of 'a' numbers is 'x' and that of another group of 'b' numbers is 'y', then Geometric mean of the combined groups

$$= (x_a + y_b)\frac{1}{a + b}$$

3. Harmonic Mean (H.M.):

Harmonic mean of n numbers x_1, x_2, ... x_n is calculated as $\dfrac{n}{\sum_{i=1}^{n} \frac{1}{x_i}}$

Harmonic mean of a and b is $\dfrac{2ab}{a + b}$.

e.g., Find Harmonic mean of 1, 0.5, 10.

x_i	$\frac{1}{x_i}$
1	1
0.5	2
10	0.1

$$\sum \frac{1}{x_i} = 3.1$$

$$\text{H.M.} = \frac{3}{3.1} = \frac{30}{31}$$

This is an important result and is generally used to find average speed when equal distances are covered at different speeds. (when different distances are covered in the same time, arithmetic mean is used to determine the average speed).

e.g., A person travels from A to B at 6 kmph and returns at 4 kmph, find his average speed.

Average Speed = Harmonic Mean of 6 and 4

$$= \frac{2 \times 6 \times 4}{6 + 4} = \frac{48}{10} = 4.8 \text{ kmph}$$

Note: This concept will again be covered in time, speed and distance.

Weighted Harmonic Mean: Weighted Harmonic Mean of 3 numbers x_1, x_2 and x_3 with weights w_1, w_2 and w_3 respectively is $\dfrac{\sum_{i=1}^{3} w_i}{\sum_{i=1}^{3} \frac{w_i}{x_i}}$

This is used to calculate average speed when different distances are covered at different speeds.

e.g., A cyclist covers his first 5 km at an average speed of 10 kmph, another 3 km at 8 kmph and last 2 km at 5 kmph. Find his average speed during the journey.

Average Speed = Weighted HM

$$= \frac{5 + 3 + 2}{\frac{5}{10} + \frac{3}{8} + \frac{2}{5}} = 7.84 \text{ kmph}$$

Relation between A.M., G.M. and H.M.

1. Consider two number a and b.

Arithmetic Mean = $\dfrac{a + b}{2}$; Geometric mean = $\sqrt{ab}$

Harmonic mean = $\dfrac{2ab}{a + b}$

$\therefore$ $(GM)^2 = AM \times HM$

e.g., If Arithmetic mean of two numbers is 6.5 and their Geometric mean is 6, what is their Harmonic Mean?

$$HM = \frac{(G.M.)^2}{A.M.} = \frac{6 \times 6}{6.5} = 5.54$$

2. Arithmetic Mean > Geometric Mean > Harmonic Mean

e.g., Arithmetic Mean of 2 and 4 is 3.

Geometric Mean of 2 and 4 is 2.82.

Harmonic Mean of 2 and 4 is 2.66

$\therefore$ $3 > 2.82 > 2.66$

ALGEBRAIC FORMULAE AND THEIR APPLICATION

An equation is a statement that *two algebraic expressions are equal*. If an equation is satisfied by any value of the variable, then equation is said to be an *identity*.

1. $(a + b)^2 = a^2 + 2ab + b^2 = (a - b)^2 + 4ab$
2. $(a - b)^2 = a^2 - 2ab + b^2 = (a + b)^2 - 4ab$
3. $(a + b)^2 + (a - b)^2 = 2(a^2 + b^2)$
4. $(a + b)^2 - (a - b)^2 = 4ab$
5. $(a + b + c)^2 = a^2 + b^2 + c^2 + 2(ab + bc + ca)$
6. $(a + b + c + d)^2 = a^2 + b^2 + c^2 + d^2 + 2a(b + c + d) + 2b(c + d) + 2cd$
7. $(a + b)(a - b) = a^2 - b^2$
8. $(x + a)(x + b) = x^2 + (a + b)x + ab$
9. $(x + a)(x + b)(x + c) = x^3 + (a + b + c)x^2 + (ab + bc + ca)x + abc$
10. $(a + b)^3 = a^3 + 3ab(a + b) + b^3$
11. $(a - b)^3 = a^3 - 3ab(a - b) - b^3$
12. $a^3 + b^3 = (a + b)^3 - 3ab(a + b) = (a + b)(a^2 - ab + b^2)$

13. $a^3 - b^3 = (a-b)^3 + 3ab(a-b) = (a-b)(a^2+ab+b^2)$
14. $a^3+b^3+c^3-3abc = (a+b+c)(a^2+b^2+c^2-ab-ac-bc)$
If $a+b+c=0$ then $a^3+b^3+c^3=3abc$
15. $a^n-b^n=(a-b)(a^{n-1}+a^{n-2}b+a^{n-3}b^2+...+b^{n-1})$ for all n.
16. $a^n+b^n=(a+b)(a^{n-1}-a^{n-2}b+a^{n-3}b^2-...-b^{n-1})$ if n is even
17. $a^n+b^n=(a+b)(a^{n-1}-a^{n-2}b+a^{n-3}b^2+...+b^{n-1})$ if n is odd.
18. $a^4+a^2b^2+b^4=(a^2+ab+b^2)(a^2-ab+b^2)$

POLYNOMIALS

Factors of polynomials: An expression is said to be resolved into factors when expressions of its product are found.

HCF of polynomials: When two or more polynomials are factorized, then product of all the common factors is HCF of the polynomials.

LCM of polynomials: When two or more polynomials are factorized, then product of all the factors with highest power is LCM of the polynomials.

INEQUATIONS

Properties

1. An inequality will still hold after each side has been increased, diminished, multiplied or divided by the same positive quantity.
i.e., if $a > b$ and $c > 0$
$a+c > b+c$
$ac > bc$
$\frac{a}{c} > \frac{b}{c}$
2. In an inequality, any term may be transposed from one side to the other if its sign is changed.
i.e., if $a-c > b$, then $a > b+c$ or $c < a-b$
3. If sides of an inequality be multiplied by same negative quantity, then sign of inequality must be reversed.
i.e., if $a > b$ and $c < 0$, then $ac < bc$
4. If $a > b$, $a, b \geq 0$ then $a^n > b^n$ and $\frac{1}{a^n} < \frac{1}{b^n}$, or $a^{-n} < b^{-n}$; if n is a positive quantity.
5. Square of every real quantity is positive and therefore must be greater than zero
i.e., for $a \neq b$, $(a-b)^2 > 0$; $a^2+b^2 > 2ab$;
Similarly, if $x > 0$, $y > 0$, then
$$\frac{x+y}{2} \geq \sqrt{xy}$$
Hence, Arithmetic mean of two positive quantities is greater than or equal to their Geometric mean.
6. If sum of two positive quantities is given, their product is greatest when they are equal; and if product of two positive quantities is given, their sum is least when they are equal.
7. If a, b, c.... k are n unequal quantities, then
$$\left(\frac{a+b+c+...+k}{n}\right)^n > a \times b \times c \times d ... \times k$$
i.e., $\frac{a+b+c+...+k}{n} > (a \times b \times c \times ... \times k)^{1/n}$
Note: Arithmetic mean of any number of positive quantities is greater than their Geometric mean.
8. If a and b are positive and unequal, then
$\frac{a^m b^m}{2} > \left(\frac{a+b}{2}\right)^m$ except when m is a positiveproper fraction.
If m is a positive integer or any negative quantity, then $\frac{a^m b^m}{2} > \left(\frac{a+b}{2}\right)^m$
If m is positive and less than 1, then $\frac{a^m b^m}{2} < \left(\frac{a+b}{2}\right)^m$
If there are n positive quantities a, b, c ... k, then
$$\left(\frac{a^m+b^m+c^m+...+k^m}{n}\right) > \left(\frac{a+b+c+...+k}{n}\right)^m$$
unless m is a positive proper fraction.
9. If a, b, c are positive and not all equal, then
$(a+b+c)(ab+bc+ca) > 9abc$
and, $(b+c)(c+a)(a+b) > 8abc$.
10. If x is positive and $a < b$, then $\frac{a+x}{b+x} > \frac{a}{b}$
If x is positive and $a > b$, then $\frac{a+x}{b+x} < \frac{a}{b}$
11. If x is positive and $a > b > x$, then $\frac{a-x}{b-x} > \frac{a}{b}$
If x is positive and $x < a < b$, then $\frac{a-x}{b-x} < \frac{a}{b}$
12. $\frac{a+c+e+...}{b+d+f+...}$ is less than greatest and greater than least of the fractions $\frac{a}{b}, \frac{c}{d}, \frac{e}{f}, ...$
13. For positive numbers, if $a > x$, $b > y$, $c > z$, then $a+b+c+... > x+y+z+...$ and $abc ... > xyz ...$
14. $a^2+b^2+c^2 \geq bc+ca+ab$
15. $(n!)^2 > n^n$, for $n > 2$.
16. For any positive integer n, $2 \leq \left(1+\frac{1}{n}\right)^n \leq 3$
17. $a^2b+b^2c+c^2a \geq 3abc$
18. $\frac{a}{b}+\frac{b}{c}+\frac{c}{d}+\frac{d}{a} \geq 4$
19. $a^4+b^4+c^4+d^4 \geq 4abcd$

QUADRATIC EQUATION WITH APPLICATION TO INEQUALITIES

In a quadratic equation $ax^2+bx+c=0$, if $b^2-4ac > 0$, then

$ax^2+bx+c = a(x-\alpha)(x-\beta)$, where α and β are two roots of the equation with $\alpha < \beta$.

$(x-\alpha)(x-\beta)$ is always positive when $x < \alpha$ or $x > \beta$ i.e., x does not lie between α and β.

$(x-\alpha)(x-\beta)$ is always negative when $\alpha < x$ or $x > \beta$ i.e., x lies between α and β.

EXERCISE - I

MCQ TYPE QUESTIONS

1. If $x = b + c$, $y = c - a$, $z = a - b$, then $x^2 + y^2 + z^2 - 2xy - 2xz + 2yz$ is equal to

(a) $a + b + c$ (b) $4b^2$
(c) abc (d) $a^2 + b^2$

2. HCF of $y^3 - 4y$ and $4y(y^3 + 8)$ is

(a) $y(y + 2)$ (b) $y - 2$
(c) $2(y + 2)$ (d) $(y + 2)(y^2 - 2y + 4)$

3. A tiled floor of a room has dimensions m × m sq.m. Dimensions of the tile used are n × n sq.m. All tiles used are green tiles except diagonal tiles which are red. After some years some green tiles are replaced by red tiles to form an alternate red and green tile pattern. How many green tiles are removed?
($m \neq n$ and total number of tiles are odd).

(a) $\dfrac{m^2 - 4mn + 2n^2}{2n^2}$ (b) $\dfrac{(m - 2n)^2 - n^2}{2n^2}$

(c) $\dfrac{m^2 - 4mn - n^2}{2n^2}$ (d) $\dfrac{m^2 - 4mn - 2n^2}{2n^2}$

4. If $\dfrac{x - 4}{-x^2 - 6} \leq \dfrac{2}{-x^2 - 6}$ then

(a) $x \leq 2$ (b) $x \geq 2$
(c) $x \leq 6$ (d) $x \geq 6$

5. Which of the following is true?

(a) $\sqrt{2} + \sqrt{5} = \sqrt{7}$ (b) $\sqrt{2} + \sqrt{5} \leq \sqrt{7}$
(c) $\sqrt{2} + \sqrt{5} < \sqrt{7}$ (d) $\sqrt{2} + \sqrt{5} > \sqrt{7}$

6. If $6 \geq x \geq -2$ and $4 \geq y \geq -4$, then limits for $\dfrac{y}{x}$, where x and y are non zero integers, is

(a) $\dfrac{y}{x} \geq 2, \dfrac{y}{x} \leq \dfrac{2}{3}$ (b) $\dfrac{y}{x} \geq \dfrac{-2}{3}, \dfrac{y}{x} \leq 2$

(c) $\dfrac{y}{x} \geq \dfrac{-2}{3}, \dfrac{y}{x} \leq \dfrac{1}{4}$ (d) $\dfrac{y}{x} \geq -4, \dfrac{y}{x} \leq 4$

7. What are the limits of $\dfrac{2^n(n+1)^n}{n^n}$; where n is a positive integer?

(a) $2 \leq \dfrac{2^n(n+1)^n}{n^n} \leq 3$

(b) $2^{n+1} \leq \dfrac{2^n(n+1)^n}{n^n} \leq 3.2^n$

(c) $2^n \leq \dfrac{2^n(n+1)^n}{n^n} \leq 3.2^n$

(d) None of these

8. If $g = 10^{100}$ and $H = 10^g$, then in which interval does $g! = 1.2.3....10^{100}$ lie?

(a) $10H < g! < H$ (b) $H < g! < 10^H$
(c) $10H < g! < 10^H$ (d) $10^H < g!$

9. Which of the following is true?

(a) Sum of four consecutive even numbers is always divisible by 8.
(b) Sum of four consecutive odd numbers is always divisible by 8.
(c) Product of any n consecutive natural numbers may not be divisible by n!.
(d) Product of 4 consecutive odd numbers is always divisible by 15.

10. If a and b are prime numbers, which of the following is true?

I. a^2 has three positive integer factors.
II. ab has four positive integer factors.
III. a^3 has four positive integer factors.

Codes :

(a) I and II only (b) II and III only
(c) All of these (d) None of these

11. If $7x + 6y = 420$, x and y are natural numbers, then what can be said about x?

(a) x is always odd
(b) x is always even.
(c) x is even only if y is odd.
(d) x is odd if y is even.

12. If a, b, c, d, p and q are non-zero, unequal integers and $\dfrac{a + bi}{c + di} = \dfrac{p}{q}$, then $\dfrac{a^2 + b^2}{c^2 + d^2}$ equals

(a) $\dfrac{p}{q}$ (b) $\dfrac{p^2}{q^2}$
(c) 1 (d) None of these

13. An Egyptian fraction has a numerator equal to 1, and its denominator is a positive integer. What is the maximum number of different Egyptian fraction such that their sum is equal to 1, and their denominators are equal to 10 or less?

(a) 3 (b) 5 (c) 7 (d) 9

14. What is the least number which must be subtracted from 1936 so that the remainder when divided by 9, 10, 15 will leave in each case the same remainder 7?

(a) 32 (b) 53
(c) 46 (d) 39

15. What is the greatest number consisting of six digits which on being divided by 6, 7, 8, 9, 10 leaves 4, 5, 6, 7, 8 as remainders respectively?

(a) 997920 (b) 997918
(c) 999999 (d) 997922

16. What is the least number which on being divided by 5, 6, 8, 9, 12 leaves in each case a remainder 1 but when divided by 13 leaves no remainder?

(a) 2987 (b) 3601
(c) 3600 (d) 2986

17. A group of four numbers has only one prime number amongst them. Which of the following must be true about the group?

I. HCF of the four numbers of the group is either 1 or equal to that prime number.

II. LCM of the four numbers of the group is same as product of the prime number and LCM of the remaining three numbers.

III. Product of four numbers is equal to product of the prime number × HCF of the group × LCM of the group.

(*a*) I only

(*b*) II only

(*c*) I and II only

(*d*) All of these

18. If (a, n)! is defined as product of n consecutive numbers starting from a, where a and n are both natural numbers, and if H is the HCF of (a, n)! and n!, then what can be said about H?

(*a*) H = a! (*b*) H = n!

(*c*) $H \geq n!$ (*d*) $H \geq a \times n$

19. HCF and LCM of two numbers is given. It is possible to find out the two numbers uniquely if

I. either sum or difference between the two numbers is known.

II. HCF of two numbers = LCM of two numbers.

III. $\frac{LCM}{HCF}$ = Prime number.

(*a*) I and II only

(*b*) II only

(*c*) II and III only

(*d*) I, II and III

20. A ball is dropped from a height of 12 m and it rebounds 1/2 of the distance it falls. If it continues to fall and rebound in this way, how far will it travel before coming to rest?

(*a*) 36 m (*b*) 30 m

(*c*) 48 m (*d*) 60 m

21. There are N questions in an exam.
For i = 1, 2, ..., N, there are 2^{N-1} students who answered 1 or more questions wrongly. If total number of wrong answers is 8191, then N will be

(*a*) 12 (*b*) 11 (*c*) 10 (*d*) 13

22. Two new charity organizations C_1 and C_2 were formed, with x members each, on January 1, 2003. On first day of each, subsequent month, in C_1, number of members increases by a certain number a, while in C_2, number of members increases in such a way that ratio of the number of members in a month to the preceding month bear a ratio equal to b. On May 1, 2003, both organizations had the same number of members. If a = 20x, then b will be

(*a*) 2 (*b*) 3 (*c*) 2.5 (*d*) 3.5

23. What is the ratio of common differences d_1 and d_2 of two arithmetic progressions if respective n^{th} terms are in the ratio of 2n + 3 : n – 11?

(*a*) 1 : 2 (*b*) 2 : 3

(*c*) 2 : 1 (*d*) 1 : 3

24. What is the sum upto 20 terms of the series $\frac{2}{3}+\frac{8}{9}+\frac{26}{27}+\frac{80}{81}+......?$

(*a*) $\frac{19.3^{20}+1}{3^{20}}$ (*b*) $\frac{19.3^{20}+1}{2.3^{20}}$

(*c*) $\frac{19.3^{20}-1}{2.3^{20}}$ (*d*) $\frac{39.3^{20}+1}{2.3^{20}}$

25. What is the sum to infinity of the series,
$3 + 6x^2 + 9x^4 + 12x^6 + ...$ given $|x| < 1$?

(*a*) $\frac{3}{(1+x^2)}$ (*b*) $\frac{3}{(1-x^2)^2}$

(*c*) $\frac{3}{(1+x^2)^2}$ (*d*) $\frac{3}{(1-x^2)}$

26. A school has 5 divisions in a class IX having 60, 50, 55, 62 and 58 students. Mean marks obtained in a History test were 56, 64, 72, 63 and 50 by each division respectively. What is overall average of the marks per students?

(*a*) 56.8 (*b*) 58.2

(*c*) 62.4 (*d*) 60.8

27. Average age of a committee of seven trustees is the same as it was five years ago, a younger man having been substituted for one of them. How much younger was he then trustee whose place he took?

(*a*) 32 years (*b*) 35 years

(*c*) 33 years (*d*) 34 years

28. Six men A, B, C, D, E, F agree with a seventh man G to provide a sum of money among them. A, B, C, D, E, F are to subscribe ₹10 each, and G is to pay ₹3 more than the average of the seven. What is the whole sum to be provided?

(*a*) ₹73.50 (*b*) ₹ 74

(*c*) ₹ 73 (*d*) ₹ 72.50

29. Which of the following is/are true?

I. When Arithmetic Mean of a set of values and number of values in the set are known, then Geometric Mean of the set can be found out.

II. When Arithmetic Mean of a set of values and number of values in the set are known, sum of all the elements in the set can be found out.

III. When Geometric Mean of a set of values and number of values in the set are known, then Arithmetic Mean of the set can be found out.

Codes :

(*a*) Only I (*b*) Only II

(*c*) Only I and II (*d*) All except II

30. Which of the following statement/s is/are true?

I. Average of a set of values will always lie between lowest and the largest of these values.

II. If each of the values in a set is increased by a constant k, then new average of the set is increased by k.

III. If each of the values in a set is multiplied by a constant m, then new average will also be 'm' times the old average.

Codes :

(*a*) Only I and II (*b*) Only II and III

(*c*) Only I and III (*d*) I, II and III

31. Three people A, B and C weigh themselves in a particular order. First A, B, C weigh themselves individually and then AB, BC CA and ABC together respectively. Recorded weight for the last measured is 180 kgs. Then average of the 7 measures is

(*a*) 320 kgs (*b*) $\frac{360}{7}$ kgs

(*c*) $\frac{720}{7}$ kgs (*d*) Cannot be determined

32. Average age of a team of 15 employees is 36. Youngest of them is 20 years old and eldest is 36 years old. Two of them with average age 28 leave the team. If one of the two comes back on the condition that he will be made the team leader, then which of the following can possibly be average age of the new team so formed?

(*a*) 35 (*b*) 36 (*c*) 38 (*d*) 39

NUMERICAL TYPE QUESTIONS

1. If $x - y = 1$, then $x^3 - y^3 - 3xy$ equals to ______

2. When $x + y + z = 9$ and $xy + yz + zx = 11$, then $x^3 - y^3 - z^3 - 3xyz$ equals to ______

3. If $x + y + z = 0$, then $\frac{x^2}{yz} + \frac{y^2}{zx} + \frac{z^2}{xy}$ equals to ______

4. In an election for the President, if 261 valid votes are cast, for the 5 contestants then least number of votes a candidate requires to receive to win the election are is ______

5. A number when divided by sum of 555 and 445 gives two times their difference as quotient and 30 as remainder. The number is ______

6. Sum of three prime numbers is 100. If one of them exceeds another by 36, then one of the numbers is ______

7. Sum of all odd numbers up to 100 is______

8. $A = 0.a_1a_1a_1 \ldots$ and $B = 0.a_2a_2a_2$, where a_1 and a_2 are multiples of 3 and also, a_1 and a_2 are distinct integers from 0 to 8. Then value of A + B is ______

9. Anil wants to divide ₹100 into a number of bags so that one can ask for any amount between ₹1 and ₹100, he can give the proper amount by giving certain number of these bags without taking out the amount from them. The minimum number of bags he will require if each bag has whole number of rupees is ______

10. The remainder when $2050 \times 2071 \times 2095$ is divided by 23 is ______

11. The smallest number which when increased by 3 is divisible by 27, 35, 25 and 21 is ______

12. ______is the least number which on being divided by 12, 21 and 35 will leave in each case the same remainder 6

13. A gardener had a number of shrubs to plant in horizontal rows. At first he tried to plant 5 shrubs in each row, then 6, then 8 and then 12, but had always 1 left. On trying 13, in one row he had none left. The smallest number of shrubs that he could have had is ______

14. Sum of an infinite geometric series is 3 and sum of an infinite geometric series formed from squares of the terms of the original series is 6. First term of the first series will be____

15. The maximum sum of the series 60, 58, 56, 54, 52, ... is______

16. On an average my income for 15 days ₹ 7, average for the first 5 days was ₹ 6 and average for the last 9 days was ₹ 8. The income on the sixth day was ______

17. The harmonic mean of two numbers whose geometric mean and arithmetic mean is 8 and 5 respectively is ______

18. Average marks of 15 students in a class is 145, maximum marks being 150. If two lowest scores are removed, the average increases by 5. Also, two lowest scores are consecutive multiples of 9. The lowest score in the class is ______

EXERCISE – II

(QUESTIONS FROM PREVIOUS GATE EXAMS)

MCQ TYPE QUESTIONS

2015

1. Read the following table giving sales data of five types of batteries for years 2006 to 2012

Year	Type I	Type I	Type I	Type I	Type I
2006	75	144	114	102	108
2007	90	126	102	84	126
2008	96	114	75	105	135
2009	105	90	150	90	75
2010	90	75	135	75	90
2011	105	60	165	45	120
2012	115	85	160	100	145

Out of the following, which type of battery achieved highest growth between the years 2006 and 2012?

(*a*) Type V (*b*) Type III
(*c*) Type II (*d*) Type I

2. If $a^2 + b^2 + c^2 = 1$, then $ab + bc + ac$ lies in the interval

(*a*) $\left[1, \frac{2}{3}\right]$ (*b*) $\left[\frac{-1}{2}, 1\right]$
(*c*) $\left[-1, \frac{1}{2}\right]$ (*d*) [2,–4]

3. If the list of letters, P, R, S, T, U is an arithmetic sequence, which of the following are also in arithmetic sequence?

I. 2P, 2R, 2S, 2T, 2U
II. P–3, R–3, S–3, T–3, U–3
III. P^2, R^2, S^2, T^2, U^2

(*a*) I only (*b*) I and II
(*c*) II and III (*d*) I and III

4. The number of students in a class who have answered correctly, wrongly, or not attempted each question in an exam, are listed in the table below. The marks for each question are also listed. There is no negative or partial marking.

Q. No.	Marks	Answered Correctly	Answered Wrongly	Not Attempted
1	2	21	17	6
2	3	15	27	2
3	1	11	29	4
4	2	23	18	3
5	5	31	12	1

What is the average of the marks obtained by the class in the examination?

(*a*) 2.290 (*b*) 2.970
(*c*) 6.795 (*d*) 8.795

2014

5. The monthly rainfall chart on 50 years of rainfall in Agra is shown in the following figure. Which of the following are true? (k percentile is the value such that k percent of the data fall below that value)

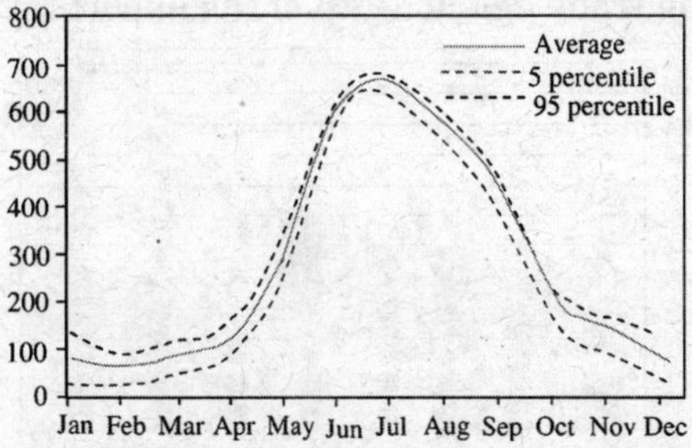

(*i*) On average, it rains more in July than in December
(*ii*) Every year, the amount of rainfall in August is more than that in January
(*iii*) July rainfall can be estimated with better confidence than February rainfall
(*iv*) In August, there is at least 500 mm of rainfall

(*a*) (*i*) and (*ii*) (*b*) (*i*) and (*iii*)
(*c*) (*ii*) and (*iii*) (*d*) (*iii*) and (*iv*)

6. The total exports and revenues from the exports of a country are given in the two charts shown below. The pie chart for exports shows the quantity of each item exported as a percentage of the total quantity of exports. The pie chart for the revenues shows the percentage of the total revenue generated through export of each item. The total quantity of exports of all the items is 500 thousand tonnes and the total revenues are 250 crore rupees. Which item among the following has generated the maximum revenue per kg?

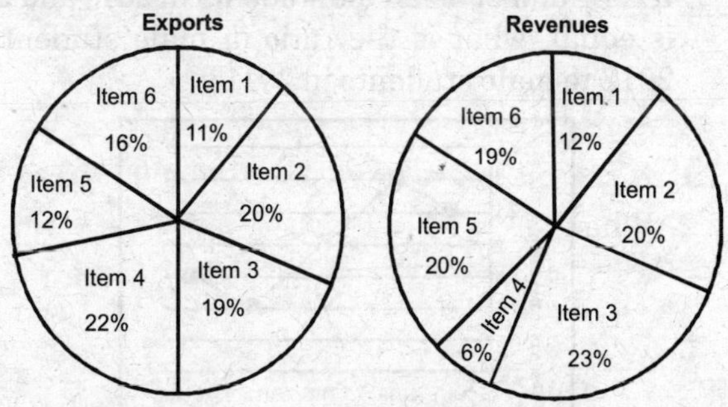

(*a*) Item 2 (*b*) Item 3
(*c*) Item 6 (*d*) Item 5

7. The statistics of runs scored in a series by four batsmen are provided in the following table. Who is the most consistent batsman of these four?

Batsman	Average	Standard deviation
K	31.2	5.21
L	46.0	6.35
M	54.4	6.22
N	17.9	5.90

(*a*) K (*b*) L
(*c*) M (*d*) N

8. The exports and imports (in crores of ₹) of a country from 2000 to 2007 are given in the following bar chart. If the trade deficit is defined as excess of imports over exports, in which year is the trade deficit 1/5th of the exports?

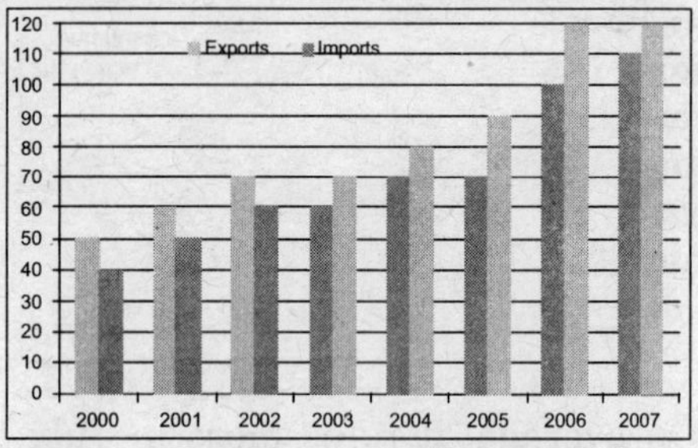

(*a*) 2005 (*b*) 2004
(*c*) 2007 (*d*) 2006

9. The table below has question-wise data on the performance of students in an examination. The marks for each question are also listed. There is no negative or partial marking in the examination.

Q.No.	Marks	Answered Correctly	Answered Wrongly	Not Attempted
1	2	21	17	6
2	3	15	27	2
3	2	23	18	3

What is the average of the marks obtained by the class in the examination?

(*a*) 1.34 (*b*) 1.74
(*c*) 3.02 (*d*) 3.91

10. The ratio of male to female students in a college for five years is plotted in the following line graph. If the number of female students in 2011 and 2012 is equal, what is the ratio of male students in 2012 to male students in 2011?

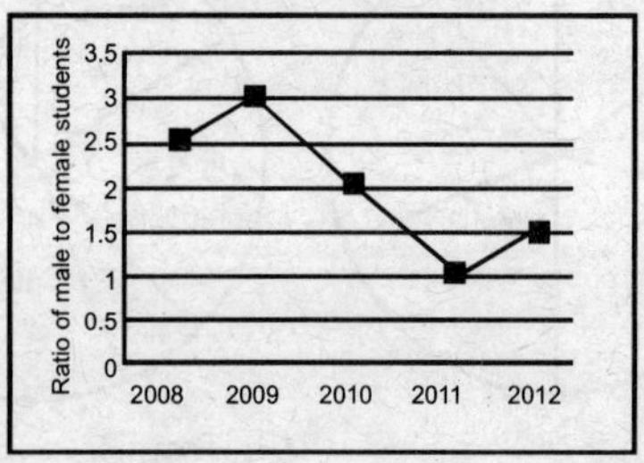

(*a*) 1 : 1 (*b*) 2 : 1
(*c*) 1.5 : 1 (*d*) 2.5 : 1

11. What is the average of all multiples of 10 from 2 to 198?

(*a*) 90 (*b*) 100
(*c*) 110 (*d*) 120

12. The value of $\sqrt{12+\sqrt{12+\sqrt{12+...}}}$ is

(*a*) 3.464 (*b*) 3.932
(*c*) 4.000 (*d*) 4.444

13. If x is real and $|x^2 - 2x + 3| = 11$, then possible values of $|-x^3 + x^2 - x|$ include

(*a*) 2, 4 (*b*) 2, 14
(*c*) 4, 52 (*d*) 14, 52

2013

14. A number is as much greater than 75 as it is smaller than 117. The number is

(*a*) 91 (*b*) 93
(*c*) 89 (*d*) 96

15. Following table provides figures (in rupees) on annual expenditure of a firm for two years - 2010 and 2011.

Category	2010	2011
Raw material	5200	6240
Power & fuel	7000	9450
Salary & wages	9000	12600
Plant & machinery	20000	25000
Advertising	15000	19500
Research & Development	22000	26400

In 2011, which of the following two categories have registered increase by same percentage?

(*a*) Raw material and Salary & wages
(*b*) Salary & wages and Advertising
(*c*) Power & fuel and Advertising
(*d*) Raw material and Research & Development

16. What will be the maximum sum of 44, 42, 40,... ?

(*a*) 502 (*b*) 504
(*c*) 506 (*d*) 500

17. The current erection cost of a structure is ₹ 13,200. If the labour wages per day increase by 1/5 of the current wages and the working hours decrease by 1/24 of the current period, then the new cost of erection in ₹ is

(*a*) 16,500 (*b*) 15,180
(*c*) 11,000 (*d*) 10,120

18. Find the sum of the expression

$$\frac{1}{\sqrt{1}+\sqrt{2}}+\frac{1}{\sqrt{2}+\sqrt{3}}+\frac{1}{\sqrt{3}+\sqrt{4}}+.........+\frac{1}{\sqrt{80}+\sqrt{81}}$$

(*a*) 7 (*b*) 8
(*c*) 9 (*d*) 10

19. In the summer of 2012, in New Delhi, the mean temperature of Monday to Wednesday was 41°C and of Tuesday to Thursday was 43°C. If the temperature on Thursday was 15% higher than that of Monday, then the temperature in °C on Thursday was

(*a*) 40 (*b*) 43
(*c*) 46 (*d*) 49

20. The set of values of p for which the roots of the equation $3x^2 + 2x + p(p - 1) = 0$ are of opposite sign is

(*a*) $(-\infty, 0)$ (*b*) $(0, 1)$
(*c*) $(1, \infty)$ (*d*) $(0, \infty)$

21. Find the sum to n terms of the series 10 + 84 + 734 + ...

(*a*) $\frac{9(9^n+1)}{10}+1$ (*b*) $\frac{9(9^n-1)}{8}+1$

(*c*) $\frac{9(9^n-1)}{8}+n$ (*d*) $\frac{9(9^n-1)}{8}+n^2$

22. If $3 \le X \le 5$ and $8 \le Y \le 11$ then which of the following options is TRUE?

(*a*) $\frac{3}{5} \le \frac{X}{Y} \le \frac{8}{5}$

(*b*) $\frac{3}{11} \le \frac{X}{Y} \le \frac{5}{8}$

(*c*) $\frac{3}{11} \le \frac{X}{Y} \le \frac{8}{5}$

(*d*) $\frac{3}{5} \le \frac{X}{Y} \le \frac{8}{11}$

23. Following table gives data on tourists from different countries visiting India in the year 2011.

Country	Number of Tourists
USA	2000
England	3500
Germany	1200
Italy	1100
Japan	2400
Australia	2300
France	1000

Which two countries contributed to the one third of the total number of tourists who visited India in 2011?

(*a*) USA and Japan
(*b*) USA and Australia
(*c*) England and France
(*d*) Japan and Australia

2012

24. If $(1.001)^{1259} = 3.52$ and $(1.001)^{2062} = 7.85$, then $(1.001)^{3321} =$

(*a*) 2.23 (*b*) 4.33
(*c*) 11.37 (*d*) 27.64

25. Raju has 14 currency notes in his pocket consisting of only ₹ 20 notes and ₹ 10 notes. The total money value of the notes is ₹ 230. The number of ₹ 10 notes that Raju has is

(*a*) 5 (*b*) 6
(*c*) 9 (*d*) 10

26. The data given in the following table summarizes the monthly budget of an average household.

Category	**Amount (Rs.)**
Food	4000
Clothing	1200
Rent	2000
Savings	1500
Other expenses	1800

The approximate percentage of the monthly budget **NOT** spent on savings is

(*a*) 10% (*b*) 14%
(*c*) 81% (*d*) 86%

2011

27. P, Q, R and S are four types of dangerous microbes recently found in a human habitat. The area of each circle with its diameter printed in brackets represents the growth of a single microbe surviving human immunity system within 24 hours of entering the body. The danger to human beings varies proportionately with the toxicity, potency and growth attributed to a microbe shown in the figure below :

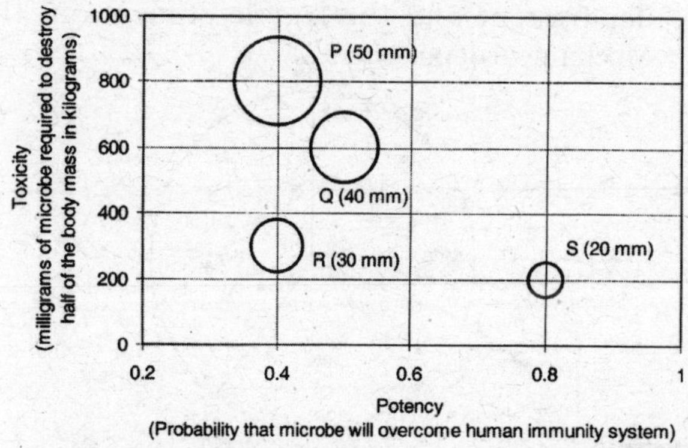

A pharmaceutical company is contemplating the development of a vaccine against the most dangerous microbe. Which microbe should the company target in its first attempt?

(*a*) P (*b*) Q
(*c*) R (*d*) S

28. The sum of n terms of the series 4 + 44 + 444 + ... is

(*a*) (4/81) [$10^{n+1} - 9n - 1$]

(*b*) (4/81) [$10^{n-1} - 9n - 1$]

(*c*) (4/81) [$10^{n+1} - 9n - 10$]

(*d*) (4/81) [$10^{n} - 9n - 10$]

29. Given that $f(y) = |y|/y$, and q is any non-zero real number, the value of $|f(q) - f(-q)|$ is

(*a*) 0 (*b*) –1

(*c*) 1 (*d*) 2

NUMERICAL TYPE QUESTIONS

2015

1. The exports and imports (in crores of Rs.) of a country from the year 2000 to 2007 are given in the following bar chart. In which year is the combined percentage increase in imports and exports the highest ?

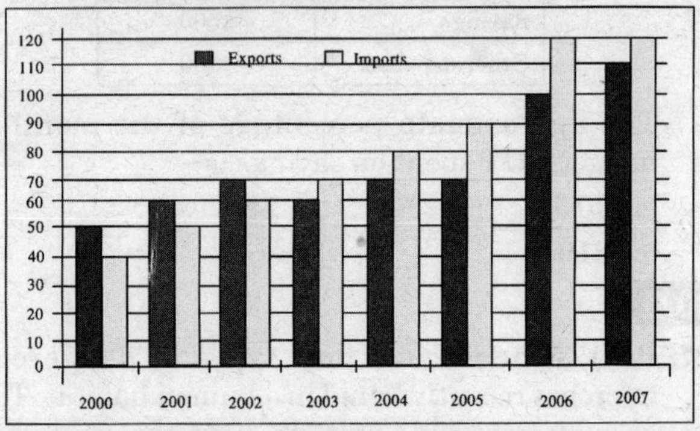

2. The pie chart below has the breakup of the number of students from different departments in an engineering college for the year 2012. The proportion of male to female students in each department is 5 : 4. There are 40 males in Electrical Engineering. What is the difference between numbers of female students in the Civil department and the female students in the Mechanical department?

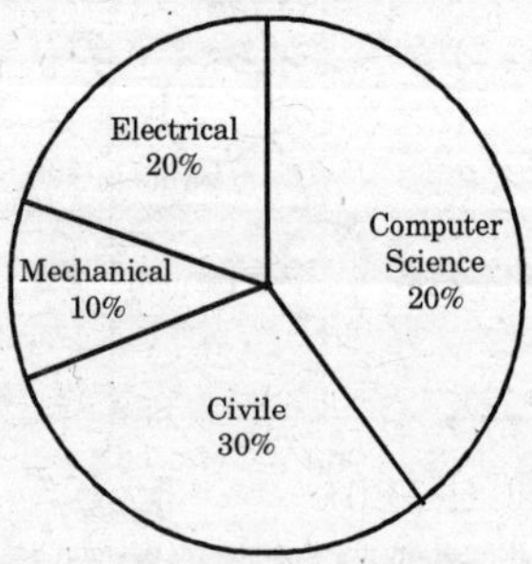

2014

3. A foundry has a fixed daily cost of ₹ 50,000 whenever it operates and variable cost of ₹ 800Q, where Q is the daily production in tonnes. What is the cost of production in ₹ per tonne for a daily production of 100 tonnes?

4. The smallest angle of a triangle is equal to two thirds of the smallest angle of a quadrilateral. The ratio between the angles of the quadrilateral is 3 : 4 : 5 : 6. The largest angle of the triangle is twice its smallest angle. What is the sum, in degrees, of the second largest angle of the triangle and the largest angle of the quadrilateral?

5. In a sequence of 12 consecutive odd numbers, the sum of the first 5 numbers is 425. What is the sum of the last 5 numbers in the sequence?

6. A firm producing air purifiers sold 200 units in 2012. The following pie chart presents the share of raw material, labour, energy, plant & machinery, and transportation costs in the total manufacturing cost of the firm in 2012. The expenditure on labour in 2012 is ₹ 4,50,000. In 2013, the raw material expenses increased by 30% and all other expenses increased by 20%. What is the percentage increase in total cost for the company in 2013?

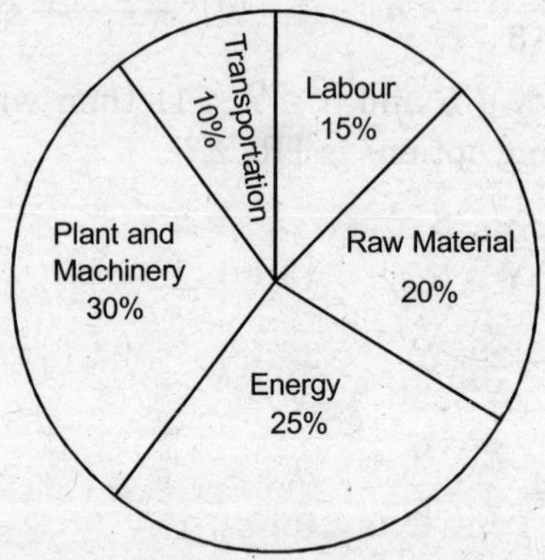

7. A firm producing air purifiers sold 200 units in 2012. The following pie chart presents the share of raw material, labour, energy, plant & machinery, and transportation costs in the total manufacturing cost of the firm in 2012. The expenditure on labour in 2012 is ₹ 4,50,000. In 2013, the raw material expenses increased by 30% and all other expenses increased by 20%. If the company registered a profit of ₹ 10 lakhs in 2012, at what price (in ₹) was each air purifier sold?

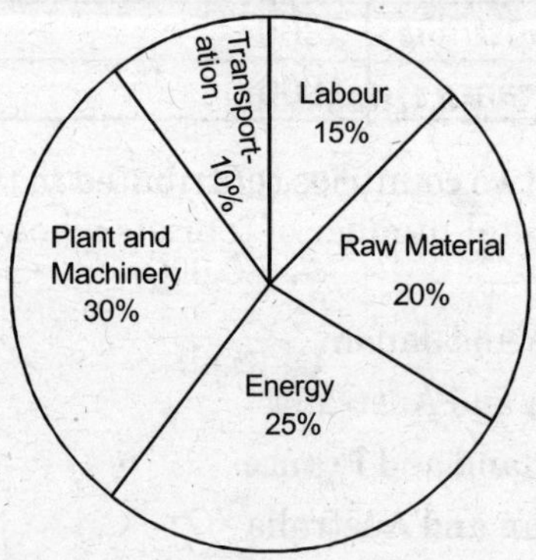

8. The sum of eight consecutive odd numbers is 656. The average of four consecutive even numbers is 87. What is the sum of the smallest odd number and second largest even number?

9. The ratio of male to female students in a college for five years is plotted in the following line graph. If the number of female students doubled in 2009, by what percent did the number of male students increase in 2009?

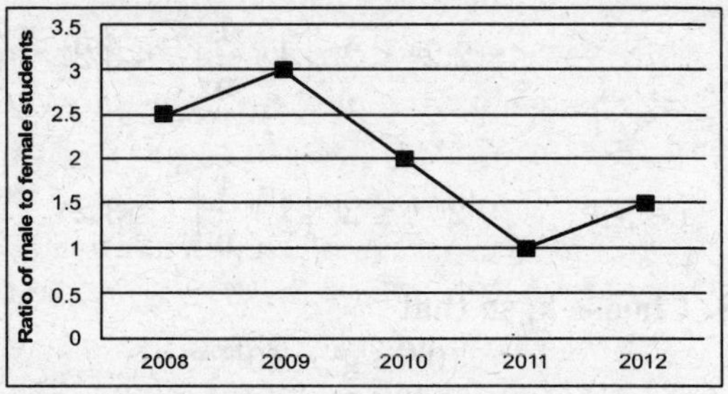

10. If $(z + 1/z)^2 = 98$, compute $(z^2 + 1/z^2)$

11. In a survey, 300 respondents were asked whether they own a vehicle or not. If yes, they were further asked to mention whether they own a car or scooter or both. Their responses are tabulated below. What percent of respondents do not own a scooter?

		Men	Women
Own vehicle	Car	40	34
	Scooter	30	20
	Both	60	46
Do not own vehicle		20	50

12. Round–trip tickets to a tourist destination are eligible for a discount of 10% on the total fare. In addition, groups of 4 or more get a discount of 5% on the total fare. If the one way single person fare is ₹ 100, a group of 5 tourists purchasing round–trip tickets will be charged ₹ ________.

ANSWERS

EXERCISE – I

MCQ Type Questions

1. (*b*)	**2.** (*a*)	**3.** (*b*)	**4.** (*d*)	**5.** (*d*)	**6.** (*d*)	**7.** (*b*)	**8.** (*c*)	**9.** (*b*)	**10.** (*c*)
11. (*b*)	**12.** (*b*)	**13.** (*a*)	**14.** (*d*)	**15.** (*b*)	**16.** (*b*)	**17.** (*a*)	**18.** (*b*)	**19.** (*d*)	**20.** (*a*)
21. (*d*)	**22.** (*b*)	**23.** (*c*)	**24.** (*d*)	**25.** (*b*)	**26.** (*d*)	**27.** (*b*)	**28.** (*a*)	**29.** (*b*)	**30.** (*d*)
31. (*c*)	**32.** (*b*)								

Numerical Type Questions

1. 1	**2.** 432	**3.** 3	**4.** 53	**5.** 220030	**6.** 67	**7.** 2500	**8.** 1	**9.** 7	**10.** 6
11. 4722	**12.** 426	**13.** 481	**14.** 12/5	**15.** 930	**16.** 3	**17.** 12.8	**18.** 108		

EXERCISE – II

MCQ Type Questions

1. (*d*)	**2.** (*b*)	**3.** (*b*)	**4.** (*c*)	**5.** (*b*)	**6.** (*d*)	**7.** (*a*)	**8.** (*d*)	**9.** (*c*)	**10.** (*c*)
11. (*b*)	**12.** (*c*)	**13.** (*d*)	**14.** (*d*)	**15.** (*d*)	**16.** (*c*)	**17.** (*a*)	**18.** (*b*)	**19.** (*c*)	**20.** (*b*)
21. (*d*)	**22.** (*b*)	**23.** (*c*)	**24.** (*d*)	**25.** (*a*)	**26.** (*d*)	**27.** (*d*)	**28.** (*c*)	**29.** (*d*)	

Numerical Type Questions

1. (2006)	**2.** (32)	**3.** (1300 to 1300)	**4.** (180 to 180)	**5.** (495)
6. (22)	**7.** (20,000)	**8.** (163)	**9.** (140 to 140)	**10.** (96)
11. (48)	**12.** (850)			

EXPLANATIONS

EXERCISE – I

MCQ TYPE QUESTIONS

1. $x^2 + y^2 + z^2 - 2xy - 2xz + 2yz = (x - y - z)^2$
$= (b + c - c + a - a + b)^2 = 4b^2$

2.
$$y^3 - 4y = y(y^2 - 4) = y(y - 2)(y + 2)$$
$$4y(y^3 + 8) = 4y(y + 2)(y^2 - 2y + 4)$$
$\therefore$ HCF $= y(y + 2)$.

3. Total red tiles initially $= 2\left(\frac{m}{n}\right) - 1$

Total number of tiles $= \frac{m^2}{n^2}$

As number of red tiles > number of green tiles (since room has odd number of tiles and corner tiles are red)

Hence total red tiles required to form an alternate pattern

$$= \frac{\left(\frac{m}{n}\right)^2 + 1}{2} = \frac{m^2 + n^2}{2n^2}$$

$\therefore$ Number of green tiles removed

$$= \frac{m^2 + n^2}{2n^2} - 2\left(\frac{m}{n}\right) + 1$$

$$= \frac{m^2 + n^2 - 4mn + 2n^2}{2n^2}$$

$$= \frac{(m - 2n)^2 - n^2}{2n^2}$$

4.
$$\frac{x - 4}{-x^2 - 6} \le \frac{2}{-x^2 - 6}$$

i.e. $\frac{x - 4}{-(x^2 + 6)} \le \frac{2}{-(x^2 + 6)}$

i.e. $x - 4 \ge 2$ ...(cancelling a negative term reverses sign of the inequality)

i.e. $x \ge 6$.

5.
$$\left(\sqrt{2} + \sqrt{5}\right)^2 = 2 + 2\sqrt{10} + 5 = 7 + 2\sqrt{10}$$

$\therefore \sqrt{2} + \sqrt{5} > \sqrt{7}$

7.
$$\frac{2^n (n + 1)^n}{n^n} = 2^n\left(\frac{n + 1}{n}\right)^n = 2^n\left(1 + \frac{1}{n}\right)^n$$

Now, $2 \le \left(1 + \frac{1}{n}\right)^n \le 3$

$\therefore$ $2.2^n \le 2^n\left(1 + \frac{1}{n}\right)^n \le 3.2^n$

i.e., $2^{n+1} \le 2^n\left(1 + \frac{1}{n}\right)^n \le 3.2^n$

8. Choose k, so that

$$10^H = g^{\lambda} = 10^{100k},$$

$$k = \frac{H}{100}$$

$\therefore$ $10^H = g^{\frac{H}{100}} > g^g > g!$

On the other hand,

$10H = 10 \times 10^g = 10^{g+1} < g!$

(most factors are much bigger than 10)

$10H < g! < 10^H$

9. (*a*) Four consecutive even numbers can be written as 2n, 2n + 2, 2n + 4 and 2n + 6, where n is any natural number.

$\therefore$ Sum $= 2n + 2n + 2 + 2n + 4 + 2n + 6$
$= 8n + 12$
$= 4(2n + 3)$ not always divisible by 8.

Thus, (*a*) is not true.

(*b*) Four consecutive odd numbers can be written as 2n + 1, 2n + 3, 2n + 5, 2n + 7 where n is a natural number.

Sum $= 2n + 1 + 2n + 3 + 2n + 5 + 2n + 7 = 8n + 16$ divisible by 8

Thus, (*b*) is true

(*c*) In product of n consecutive natural numbers atleast one is divisible by n, atleast one by n – 1 ... till 1.

Thus product is atleast divisible by

$n \times (n - 1) \times (n - 2) \ldots\ldots 1 = n!$.

Thus, (*c*) is not true.

(*d*) Take four consecutive odd numbers as $7 \times 9 \times 11 \times 13$ which is not divisible by 15.

Thus, (*d*) is not true.

10. Factors of a^2 are 1, a and a^2.

Factors of ab are 1, a, b and ab.

Factors of a^3 are 1, a, a^2 and a^3.

11. $7x + 6y = 420$

Equation is of the form:

7x + even number = even number.

∴ 7x has to be even

Hence x has to be even.

12. $$\frac{a+bi}{c+di} = \frac{p}{q}$$

∴ $qa + qbi = pc + pdi$

Equating real and imaginary parts.

$qa = pc$ and $qb = pd$.

$$\Rightarrow \quad a = \frac{p}{q}c \text{ and } b = \frac{p}{q}d$$

$$\therefore \quad \frac{a^2+b^2}{c^2+d^2} = \frac{\frac{p^2}{q^2}c^2 + \frac{p^2}{q^2}d^2}{c^2+d^2} = \frac{p^2}{q^2}$$

13. We ignore $\frac{1}{7}$ and $\frac{1}{9}$ because no sum of other numbers is going to give 7th or 9th in the denominator.

Also, $\frac{1}{5}$ and $\frac{1}{10}$ are not enough to add up to anything $\left(\frac{1}{10}, \frac{2}{10}, \text{ and } \frac{3}{10}\right.$ are going to leave tenths left over no matter what else you add$\left.\right)$.

What's left is $\frac{1}{2}, \frac{1}{3}, \frac{1}{4}, \frac{1}{6}, \frac{1}{8}$.

Sum total of these is $\frac{11}{8}$. So we need all of them except $\frac{1}{8}$, which means $\frac{1}{2} + \frac{1}{3} + \frac{1}{6}$. Which is the only way to do this with egyptian fractions whose denominators are 10 or less. Hence maximum number of Egyptian fractions needed is 3.

14. L.C.M. of 9, 10 and 15 = 90

∴ $1936 = 90 \times 21 + 46$ (Remainder).

But a part of this remainder is 7.

so $46 - 7 = 39$ should be subtracted from 1936.

15. $6 - 4 = 2, 7 - 5 = 2, 8 - 6 = 2, 9 - 7 = 2, 10 - 8 = 2$

L.C.M. of 6, 7, 8, 9, 10 = 2520;

Greatest number of 6 digits = 999999

$2520 \times 396 + 2079 = 999999$

∴ Reminder = 2079.

Subtract 2079 from 999999, then we get

$999999 - 2079 = 997920$.

Subtract 2 from this number to get required number, which is 997918 and which will give the remainders 4, 5, 6, 7, 8 when divided by 5, 6, 7, 8, 9 respectively.

16. L.C.M. of 5, 6, 8, 9 and 12 is 360

Required number = 360 K + 1

$= (13 \times 27 + 9) K + 1$

$= (13 \times 27) K + (9K + 1)$

Now this number must be divisible by 13

∴ K = 10 and required number = 3601.

17. I. In case all the remaining three numbers are multiples of the prime number, HCF of the group is equal to that prime number. otherwise HCF of the group is 1. Thus, I is true.

II. **Case 1:** Let numbers be 2, 4, 6 and 8, where 2 is only prime number, then LCM = 24.

But LCM of 4, 6 and 8 = 24.

LCM = 24 & 2 = 24

Case 2 : Let numbers be 2, 9, 81 and 27 Then LCM = 162 and LCM of 9, 81 and 27 = 81.

Thus, LCM = $81 \times 2 = 162$

Hence II is not always true.

III. Let numbers be 2, 4, 6 and 8

∴ LCM = 24 and HCF = 2

Product of four numbers

$= 2 \times 4 \times 6 \times 8 = 384$

Also, $384 \neq 24 \times 2 \times 2$.

Thus, III is not true.

18. (a. n)! = product of n consecutive natural number starting from 'a' which is atleast divisible by n!.

(n)! = product of n consecutive natural numbers.

For n = 2 :

(a. n)! = a(a + 1) and n! = 2

a(a + 1) is divisible by 2!.

For n = 3 :

(a n)! = a(a + 1)(a + 2) and n! = 6.

One of the factors of a(a + 1)(a + 2) is divisible by 3 and other by 2.

Thus, proceeding in this manner, (a. n)! and n! have HCF = n!

∴ H = n!.

19. Let HCF be h and LCM be l.

I. Let numbers be ah and bh.

Then $abh = l$ and $(a + b)h = m$

$\Rightarrow \quad (a - b)h = n$

Using these ah and bh can be uniquely determined. Thus, I is true

II. If HCF = LCM, then two numbers are equal and same as HCF or LCM.
Thus, II is true.

III. $\frac{LCM}{HCF}$ = a prime i.e., $\frac{\ell}{h} = P$.

Then one of the numbers is equal to h and other is equal to ℓ. Thus, III is true.

20. Total distance travelled by the ball before coming to rest

$$= 12 + 2\,(6 + 3 + 1.5 + ... \text{ to ?})$$

$$= 12 + 2.\left(\frac{6}{1-1/2}\right)$$

$$= 12 + 2(12) = 36m$$

21. Number of students who answered 1 or more questions wrongly = 2^{N-1}.

Number of students who answered 2 or more questions wrongly = 2^{N-2}

Hence number of students who answered 1 question wrongly

$$= 2^{N-1} - 2^{N-2} = 2^{N-2}$$

Similarly it can be shown that number of students who answered 2 questions wrongly

$$= 2^{N-2} - 2^{N-3} = 2^{N-3}$$

Similarly we can find number of students who answered K questions wrongly where K ≥ 3

Hence total number of questions attempted wrongly

$$s = 2^{N-2} + 2(2^{N-3}) + 3(2^{N-4}) + ... + (N-1)(2^{\circ}) + N(1) \quad ...(i)$$

$$\therefore \quad \frac{s}{2} = 2^{N-3} + 2(2^{N-4}) + ... + (N-2)(2^{\circ}) + \frac{N-1}{2} + \frac{N}{2} \quad ...(ii)$$

Substracting equations (*i*) from (*ii*)

$$\frac{s}{2} = 2^{N-2} + 2^{N-3} + ... + 2^{\circ} + \frac{1}{2}$$

$$\Rightarrow \quad s = 2^{N-1} + 2^{N-2} + 2^{N-3} + ... + 1$$

$$= 2^N - 1 = 8191$$

$$\Rightarrow \quad N = 13$$

22. Number of members in C_1 on May 1, 2003 = x + 4a

Number of members in C_2 on May 1, 2003 = xb^4

$$x + 4a = xb^4 \text{ and } a = 20x$$

$$\therefore \quad x(b^4 - 81) = 0$$

As $\quad x \neq 0, \quad b^4 - 81 = 0$

$$\therefore \quad b = 3$$

23. n^{th} terms are in the ratio of $\frac{2n+3}{n-11}$.

If n = 1 in 2n + 3 series, then first term is

$T_1 = 2(1) + 3 = 5$

n = 2, then second term is 2(2) + 3 = 7

$T_2 = 7$

$d = T_2 - T_1 = 7 - 5 = 2$

$\therefore \quad d_1 = 2$

If n = 1 in n − 11series, then first term is 1 − 11 = −10

If n = 2, then second term is 2 − 11 = − 9

$\therefore \quad d_2 = T_2 - T_1 = -9 - (-10) = 1$

$\therefore \quad \frac{d_1}{d_2} = \frac{2}{1}$ or 2 : 1

24. $\frac{2}{3} + \frac{8}{9} + \frac{26}{27} + \frac{80}{81} + ...$ up to 20 terms

$$= \left(1-\frac{1}{3}\right) + \left(1-\frac{1}{9}\right) + \left(1-\frac{1}{27}\right) + \left(1-\frac{1}{81}\right) + \text{ ... up to 20 terms}$$

$$= 20 - \left(\frac{1}{3} + \frac{1}{3^2} + \frac{1}{3^3} + \frac{1}{3^4} + ... + \frac{1}{3^{20}}\right)$$

$$= 20 - \frac{1}{3}\left(\frac{1-\left(\frac{1}{3}\right)^{20}}{1-\frac{1}{3}}\right)$$

$$= 20 - \frac{3^{20} - 1}{2.3^{20}}$$

$$= \frac{40.3^{20} - 3^{20} + 1}{2.3^{20}} = \frac{39.3^{20} + 1}{2.3^{20}}$$

25. Let $\quad s = 3 + 6x^2 + 9x^4 + 12x^6 + ...$

$\therefore \quad x^2 s = 3x^2 + 6x^4 + 9x^6 + 12x^6 + ...$

$\Rightarrow \quad s - x^2 s = 3 + 3x^2 + 3x^4 + 3x^6 + ...$

$\Rightarrow \quad s(1 - x^2) = 3\,[1 + x^2 + x^4 + x^6 + ...]$

$\Rightarrow \quad s(1-x^2) = 3\left[\frac{1}{1-x^2}\right] [\because |x| < 1]$

$$\therefore \quad s = \frac{3}{(1-x^2)^2}$$

26. Average

$$= \frac{60{\times}56 + 50{\times}64 + 55{\times}72 + 62{\times}63 + 58{\times}50}{60+50+55+62+58}$$

$$= \frac{3360 + 3200 + 3960 + 3906 + 2900}{285} = 60.8$$

27. Increase after 5 years should have been

$7 \times 5 = 35$ years.

But since average remains same, difference in their age is 35 years.

28. Let average of the seven men be x.

$$\therefore \quad x = \frac{10 \times 6 + (x+3)}{7}$$

$$\Rightarrow \quad 60 + x + 3 = 7x$$

$$\Rightarrow \quad x = \frac{63}{6} = 10.5$$

$\therefore$ Total amount $= 10.5 \times 7 = 73.5$

29. Consider a set of three numbers a, b and c.

I. $$AM = \frac{a+b+c}{3}$$

Thus, $a + b + c = 3AM$.

But GM $= \sqrt[3]{abc}$ which cannot be found out.

Thus, I is false,

II. $$AM = \frac{a+b+c}{3}$$

$\therefore$ Sum of the numbers $= a + b + c = 3AM$.

Thus, II is true.

III. GM $= \sqrt[3]{abc}$.

But AM $= \frac{a+b+c}{3}$, which cannot be found out.

Thus, III is false.

30. I. Average of a set of numbers is greater than smallest and smaller than the greatest number of the set. Thus, I is true.

II. Consider five numbers a, b, c, d and e whose average is $\frac{a+b+c+d+e}{5}$

Now if each of them is increased by k, then we have average

$$= \frac{a+k+b+k+c+k+d+k+e+k}{5}$$

$$= \frac{a+b+c+d+e}{5} + \frac{5k}{5} = \text{old average} + k.$$

Thus, II is true.

III. Consider three numbers x, y and z whose average is $\frac{x+y+z}{3}$

Now if each of them is multiplied by m then

$$\text{new average} = \frac{xm+ym+zm}{3}$$

$$= m\left(\frac{x+y+z}{3}\right) = m \times \text{odd average}.$$

Thus, III is true.

31. Order of measures is

A, B, C, A + B, B + C, C + A, A + B + C.

Given: A + B + C = 180

Hence, average of the 7 measures

$$= \left[\frac{[(A)+(B)+(C)+(A+B)+(B+C)+(C+A)+(A+B+C)]}{7}\right]$$

$$= \frac{4}{7}(A+B+C) = \frac{4}{7} \times 180 = \frac{720}{7} \text{ kgs.}$$

32. Total age $= 15 \times 36$

After two left, to tal age $= 15 \times 36 - 2 \times 28$

$= 540 - 56$

$= 484$ years.

Let the age of the person who returns be x years.

Then $\quad$ new average $= \frac{484 + x}{14}$

Now x lies between 20 and 36 (both inclusive)

$\therefore$ New average min $= \frac{484+20}{14} = 36$ years

And New average max $= \frac{484+36}{14}$

$= 37.14.$ years.

NUMERICAL TYPE QUESTIONS

1. $x^3 - y^3 - 3xy$

$= x^3 - y^3 - 3xy(x-y)$ ...... as $(x - y) = 1$

$= (x - y)^3 = 1.$

2. $x^3\ \ y^3 - z^3 - 3xyz$

$= (x + y + z)(x^2 + y^2 + z^2 - xy - yz - zx)$

$= 9[(x + y + z)^2 - 3(xy + yz + zx)]$

$= 9(81 - 33) = 432.$

3. $\frac{x^2}{yz} + \frac{y^2}{zx} + \frac{z^2}{xy}$

... (since, $x + y + z = 0$; $x^3 + y^3 + z^3 = 3xyz$)

$$\frac{x^3+y^3+z^3}{xyz} = \frac{3xyz}{xyz} = 3.$$

4. Worst scenario is when other four get equal number of votes.

Let the winning candidate get x votes.

$$\therefore \quad x > \frac{261}{5}$$

$$\Rightarrow \quad x > 52.2$$

$$\therefore \quad x = 53$$

5. Number $= (555+445)\times(555-445)\times 2+30$
$= (555+445)\times 2\times 110+30$
$= 220000+30 = 220030.$

6. $x+(x+36)+y = 100$
$\Rightarrow$ $2x+y = 64$
Therefore y must be even prime which is 2
$2x+2 = 64 \quad \Rightarrow x = 31.$
$\therefore$ Third prime number
$= x+36 = 31+36 = 67.$

7. Given numbers are 1, 3, 5.........99.
This is an A.P with a = 1, d = 2.
Let it contain n terms
$\therefore \quad 1+(n-1)2 = 99 \quad \Rightarrow \quad n = 50$
Hence required sum $= \frac{n}{2}$ (first term +last term)
$= \frac{50}{2}(1+99) = 2500.$

8. $A = 0.a_1a_1a_1\ldots$
$\therefore \quad 10A = a_1.a_1a_1a_1\ldots..$
$\Rightarrow \quad 9A = a_1$
$\Rightarrow \quad A = \frac{a_1}{9}$
Similarly, $B = \frac{a_2}{9}.$
Now, a_1 and a_2 are multiples of 3 and are distinct.
Also, these values are less than 8.
either $a_1 = 3$ and $a_2 = 6$ or $a_1 = 6$ and $a_2 = 3$
$\therefore \quad a_1+a_2 = 9.$
$\therefore \quad A+B = \frac{a_1}{9}+\frac{a_2}{9} = \frac{a_1+a_2}{9} = \frac{9}{9} = 1.$

9. If Anil has to give 1 rupee he needs a bag with ₹1. For 2 rupees he had two bags with ₹1 each or ₹2. bag. To have minimum bags, he has a bag with ₹ 2. Now with the two bags he can give ₹3. So next he will require a bag with ₹4. With these three he can give ₹5. ₹6 and ₹7 and next bag will be one containing ₹8 and so on. Thus he would have bags with ₹1. 2. 4. 8. 16. 32. Sum of which is 63 and remaining 37 can be put in the last bag. So total number of bags is 7.

10. $2050\times 2071\times 2095$
$(23\times 89+3)\times(23\times 90+1)\times(23\times 91+2)$
$= (23[89\times 90+89+90\times 3]+3)\times(23\times 91+2)$
$= (23\times K+3)\times(23\times 91+2)$
$= (23\times[K\times 91+K\times 2+91\times 3]+6)$
$= 23\times L+6$ (where K and L are constants).
Hence remainder is 6.

11. L.C.M. of 27, 35, 25 and 21 = 4725
$\therefore$ Number = 4725 – 3 = 4722.

12. L.C.M. of 12, 21 and 35 = 420
$\therefore$ Number required = 420 + 6 = 426.

13. Number is 120K + 1
$= ((13\times 9+3)K+1)$
$= (13\times 9)K+3K+1,$
which is divisible by 13.
3K + 1 is divisible by 13.
$\therefore$ K = 4. Number = 481.

14. $\frac{a}{1-r} = 3$
$\Rightarrow \quad 3-3r = a$
Also, $\frac{a^2}{1-r^2} = 6$
$\Rightarrow \quad \frac{a}{1-r}.\frac{a}{1+r} = 6$
$\Rightarrow \quad \frac{a}{1+r} = 2$
$\Rightarrow \quad 2+2r = a$
$\therefore \quad 3-3r = 2+2r$
$\Rightarrow \quad r = \frac{1}{5}$
$\therefore \quad a = 3-\frac{3}{5} = \frac{12}{5}$

15. Since d = –2, maximum sum of the series will be sum of all the positive terms.
Least positive term of the series is 2 or 0 (both giving equal sum)
Let, 2 be the nth term
$2 = 60+(n-1)(-2)$
$\Rightarrow \quad n = 30$
$\therefore$ Required sum = 30/2 (60 + 2) = 930

16. Total income for 15 days = 15 × 7 = ₹105
Total income for first 5 days = 5 × 6 = ₹30
Total income for last 9 days = 9 × 8 = ₹72
$\therefore$ Income on sixth day
= 105 – (30 + 72)
= 105 – 102 = ₹3

17. $(GM)^2 = HM\times AM$
$HM = \frac{8\times 8}{5} = \frac{64}{5} = 12.8$

18. Total marks of 15 students = 15 × 145 = 2175.
Average marks of 15 students (excluding two lowest scores) = 13 × (145 + 5) = 1950.
$\therefore$ Total of two lowest scores = 2175 – 1950 = 225
Given that two scores are consecutive multiples of 9
$\therefore \quad 9x+9x+9 = 225$
$\Rightarrow \quad 18x = 216$
$\Rightarrow \quad x = \frac{216}{18}$
$\therefore$ Lowest score $= 9x = \frac{216}{18}\times 9 = 108.$

EXERCISE – II

MCQ TYPE QUESTIONS

1. Type-I achieved a growth of 53% in the period which is higher than any other type of battery

4. Total number of students in class = 44

Average of marks,

$$= \frac{(2\times21)+(3\times15)+(1\times11)+(2\times23)+(5\times31)}{42}$$

$$= \frac{42+45+11+46+155}{44} = \frac{299}{44} = 6.795$$

$\therefore$ Option (*c*) is correct.

5. In the question the monthly average rainfall chart for 50 years has been given.

Let us check the options.

(*i*) On average, it rains more in July than in December $\Rightarrow$ correct.

(*ii*) Every year, the amount of rainfall in August is more than that in January.

$\Rightarrow$ may not be correct because average rainfall is given in the question.

(*iii*) July rainfall can be estimated with better confidence than February rainfall.

$\Rightarrow$ From chart it is clear the gap between 5 percentile and 95 percentile from average is higher in February than that in July $\Rightarrow$ correct.

(*iv*) In August at least 500 mm rainfall

$\Rightarrow$ May not be correct, because its 50 year average.

So correct option (*b*) (*i*) and (*iii*).

6. **Item : 2**

$$\frac{\frac{20}{100}\times250\times10^7}{\frac{20}{100}\times500\times10^3}$$

$0.5\times10^4 = 5\times10^3$ $\boxed{1}$ = Item 2

Item : 3

$$\frac{23\times250\times10^7}{19\times500\times10^3}$$

1.2 = Item 3

Item : 6

$$\frac{19}{16} = 1.18 = \text{Item 6}$$

Item : 5

$$\frac{20}{12} = \frac{5}{3} = 1.6 \Rightarrow \boxed{1.6 = \text{Item 5}}$$

8. **For 2005,**

trade defict = (90 – 70) crores = 20 crores

Now $\frac{1}{5}^{\text{th}}$ of export = $\frac{1}{5}$(70) crores

= 14 crores ≠ 20 crores.

Hence option (*a*) is wrong.

For 2004,

Trade defict =(80 – 70) crores = 10 crores

Now $\frac{1}{5}^{\text{th}}$ of export = $\frac{1}{5}$(70) crores

= 14 crores ≠ 20 crores.

Hence option (*b*) is wrong.

For 2007

Trade defict = (120 – 110) crores

= 10 crores

Now $\frac{1}{5}^{\text{th}}$ of export = $\frac{1}{5}$(110) crores

= 22 crores ≠ 10 crores.

Hence option (*c*) is wrong.

For 2006,

Trade defict = (120 – 100) crores

= 20 crores

Now $\frac{1}{5}^{\text{th}}$ of export = $\frac{1}{5}$(100) crores

= 20 crores = Trade deficts

Hence option (*d*) is correct.

9. Total question

44 × 2 = 88

44 × 3 = 132

$$\frac{144}{132} = \frac{88}{308}$$

Total marks obtained = (21×2) + (15×3) + (23×2)

= 133

Total Number of students = 44

$$\text{Average} = \frac{133}{44} = 3.02$$

10. Take number of female students in 2011 = 100

$\therefore$ Number of male in 2011 = 100

No. of female in 2012 = 100

No. of male in 2012 = 150

$$\text{Ratio} = \frac{150}{100}$$

11. All multiples of 10 from 2 to 198

$= 10, 20, \ldots 190$

Now $a_n = a + (n-1)d$

$190 = 10 + (n-1) \times 10$

$180 = (n-1) \times 10$

$18 = n - 1$

$\therefore \quad n = 19$

Hence total number of multiples are 19.

Now $S_n = \dfrac{n}{2}[2a + (n-1)d]$

$= \dfrac{19}{2}[20 + (18)(10)]$

$= \dfrac{19}{2}[20 + 180] = 1900$

Now average of all multiples of 10 from 2 to198

$= \dfrac{10 + 20 + \ldots + 190}{19}$

$\therefore \quad = \dfrac{1900}{19} = 100$

12. $\sqrt{12 + \sqrt{12 + \sqrt{12 + \ldots}}}$

For a particular type of question

i.e. $\sqrt{a + \sqrt{a + \sqrt{a + \ldots}}}$ we find a two consecutive number whose product is a. The greater number among the two consecutive number is the answer.

Here $a = 12$

i.e. $12 = 3 \times 4$
↓
greater number

Hence $\sqrt{12 + \sqrt{12 + \sqrt{12 + \ldots}}} = 4$

13. Here it is given that x is real

Now $|x^2 - 2x + 3| = 11$

$\Rightarrow \quad x^2 - 2x + 3 = 11$ or $x^2 - 2x + 3 = -11$

For $x^2 - 2x + 3 = 11 \Rightarrow x^2 - 2x - 8 = 0$

$b^2 - 4ac = 4 - 4(1)(-8) = 36 > 0$

Hence roots are real.

and for $x^2 - 2x + 14 = 0$

$b^2 - 4ac = 4 - 4(1)(14) < 0$

Hence roots are imaginary

$\therefore$ The value of x is the root of $x^2 - 2x - 8 = 0$

Now $x = \dfrac{+2 \pm \sqrt{4 - 4(1)(-8)}}{2}$

$= \dfrac{2 \pm \sqrt{36}}{2} = \dfrac{2 \pm 6}{2}$

$\therefore \quad x = 4, -2.$

Now for $x = 4$,

$|-x^3 + x^2 - x| = |-64 + 16 - 4| = 52.$

and for $x = -2$

$|-x^3 + x^2 - x| = |+8 + 4 + 2| = 14$

Hence possible values of $|-x^3 + x^2 - x| = 14, 52$

16. $0 = 44 + (n-1)(-2)$

$n - 1 = 22$

$n = 23$

Sum $= \dfrac{n}{2}(a + l) = \dfrac{23}{2}(44 + 0)$

$= 23 \times 22 = 506$

Hence (*c*) is the answer

17. Let '*d*' be the # of days required

Let '*h*' be the daily working hours.

$\therefore$ *dh* can be taken as a measure of the total work be done in order to erect the structure.

Now working hours per day $h' = \dfrac{23}{24}h$

$\therefore$ # of days $d' = \dfrac{dh}{h'} = \dfrac{dh}{\left(\dfrac{23}{24}h\right)} = \dfrac{24}{23}d$

Let c = daily wages earlier

$\therefore \quad c = \dfrac{13{,}200}{d}$

Now daily wages $c' = \dfrac{6}{5}c$

$\therefore$ Total new cost $= c' \times d'$

$= \dfrac{6}{5} \times \dfrac{13200}{d} \times \dfrac{24}{23}d \approx 16{,}500$

18. Given: The expression

$$S = \frac{1}{\sqrt{1} + \sqrt{2}} + \frac{1}{\sqrt{2} + \sqrt{3}} + \ldots + \frac{1}{\sqrt{80} + \sqrt{81}}$$

To find: Sum of the expression.

Analysis: Each term of the expression is having irrational denominator. One can also see, that both the elements in the denominator of a term differ by only 1.

This gives an idea that on rationalising the denominator, each denominator will become 1, so the sum will be easier than earlier.

Rationalising the denominator,

$$S = \frac{\sqrt{2}-\sqrt{1}}{(\sqrt{2})^2-(\sqrt{1})^2}+\frac{\sqrt{3}-\sqrt{2}}{(\sqrt{3})^2-(\sqrt{2})^2}+...+\frac{\sqrt{81}-\sqrt{80}}{(\sqrt{81})^2-(\sqrt{80})^2}$$

$$= \frac{\sqrt{2}-\sqrt{1}}{1}+\frac{\sqrt{3}-\sqrt{2}}{3-2}+....+\frac{\sqrt{81}-\sqrt{80}}{81-80}$$

$$= \sqrt{2}-\sqrt{1}+\sqrt{3}-\sqrt{2}+....+81-\sqrt{80}$$

Now, one can see that the terms will cancel out. Each term except $\sqrt{1}$ & $\sqrt{81}$

Occurs twice, once as positive and once a negative. So, after cancelling out, we are left with the following:

$$S = \sqrt{81}-\sqrt{1} = 9-1 = 8$$

So, the answer is (*b*).

19. $\frac{\text{Mon + Tues + Wed.}}{3} = 41$

Mon + Tues + Wed. = 123 ...(1)

$\frac{\text{Tues + Wed + Thurs.}}{3} = 43°$

Tue + Wed + Thu. = 129° ...(2)

(2) – (1)

Tues + Wed + Thu – (Mon + Tues. + Wed.)

= 129 – 123 = 6°

Thu. – Mon. = 6° ⇒ $\frac{115x}{100} - x = 6°$

Thus. = Mon × $\frac{115}{100} = \frac{15x}{100} = 6°$

Mon = x $x = 40°$

Thurs = $\frac{115x}{100}$

∴ Thurs = $\frac{115 \times 40}{100} = 46°$

24. Let $1.001 = x$

$x^{1259} = 3.52$, and $x^{2062} = 7.85$

∴ $x^{3321} = x^{1259} . x^{2062}$

$= 3.52 \times 7.85$

$= 27.64$

25. Let number of ₹ 20 notes be x and ₹ 10 notes be y

∴ $20x + 10y = 230$ ...(1)

and $x + y = 14$ ...(2)

Solving equations (1) and (2), we have

$x = 9$ and $y = 5$

Hence numbers of 10 rupee notes are 5.

26. Total budget = 10,500

Expenditure other than savings = 9000

Hence approximate percentage of monthly budget

$$= \frac{9000}{10500} = 86\%$$

27. By observation of the table, we can say S

	P	Q	R	S
Requirement	800	600	300	200
Potency	0.4	0.5	0.4	0.8

28. Let S = 4 (1 + 11 + 111 + ...)

$$= \frac{4}{9}(9 + 99 + 999 + ...)$$

$$= \frac{4}{9}\{(10-1) + (10^2-1) + (10^3-1) + ...\}$$

$$= \frac{4}{9}\{(10 + 10^2 + ...+ 10^n) - n\}$$

$$= \frac{4}{9}\left\{10\frac{(10^n-1)}{9} - n\right\}$$

$$= \frac{4}{81}\{10^{n+1} - 9n - 10\}$$

29. Given : $f(y) = \frac{|y|}{y}$

$$\Rightarrow \quad f(q) = \frac{|q|}{q}$$

$$f(-q) = \frac{|-q|}{-q} = \frac{-|q|}{q}$$

$$|f(q) - f(q)| = \frac{|q|}{q} + \frac{|q|}{q} = \frac{2|q|}{q} = 2$$

NUMERICAL TYPE QUESTIONS

1. Increase in exports in 2006 = $\frac{100-70}{70} = 42.8\%$

Increase in imports in 2006 = $\frac{120-90}{90} = 33.3\%$

which is more than any other year.

2. According to question,

There are 40 males in Electrical Engg.

∴ Total number of females in Electrical Engg.

= 72 – 40 = 32

∴ Total number of students in Electrical Engg. = 72

⇒ 20% = 72

∴ 30% = Total number of students in Civil Engg.

∴ Total number of students in Civil Engg.

$$= \frac{30 \times 72}{20} = 36 \times 3 = 108$$

∴ Number of female students in Civil Engg.

$$= \frac{4 \times 108}{9} = 4 \times 12 = 48$$

Now, total number of students in Mechanical Engg.

$$= \frac{10 \times 72}{20} = 36$$

∴ Number of female students in Mechanical Engg.

$$= \frac{4 \times 36}{9} = 16$$

∴ Difference between female students in Civil and Mechanical departments = 48 – 16 = 32

3. Fixed cost = ₹ 50,000
Variable cost = ₹ 800Q
Q = daily production in tones
For 100 tonnes of production daily, total cost of production = 50,000 + 800 × 100 = 130,000
So, cost of production per tonne of daily production

$$= \frac{130,000}{100} = ₹\ 1300.$$

4. Let the angles of quadrilateral are $3x$, $4x$, $5x$, $6x$
So, $3x + 4x + 5x + 6x = 360$

$$x = 20$$

Smallest angle of quadrilateral = 3 × 20 = 60°

$$\text{Smallest angle of triangle} = \frac{2}{3} \times 60° = 40°$$

Largest angle of triangle = 2 × 40° = 60°
Three angles of triangle are 40°, 60°, 80°
Largest angle of quadrilateral is 120°
Sum (2nd largest angle of triangle + largest angle of quadrilateral) = 60° + 120° = 180°.

5. 8th observation is 7 × 2 = 14 more than 1st observation
9th observation is 14 more than 2nd observation
10th observation is 14 more than 3rd observation
11th observation is 14 more than 4th observation
12th observation is 14 more than 5th observation
Total 14 × 5 = 70
Sum of the first five numbers = 425
Sum of last five numbers = 495

6.

	2012	2013
Transport (10%)	300,000	360,000
Labour (15%)	450,000	540,000
Raw material (20%)	750,000	780,000
Energy (25%)	750,000	900,000
Plant and Machinery (30%)	900,000	1,080,000
Total	**3,000,000**	**3,660,000**

Percentage increase in total cost = 22%

7. $\text{Total expenditure} = \frac{15}{100} x = 4,50,000$

$$x = 3 \times 10^6$$

Profit = 10 lakhs
So, total selling price = 40,00,000 ...(1)
Total purifies = 200 ...(2)
S.P. of each purifier = (1)/(2) = 20,000

8. Eight consecutive odd number = 656
$a - 6, a - 1, a - 2, a, a + 2, a + 4, a + 6$

$$a + 8 = 656$$
$$a = 81$$

Smallest $m = 75$ ...(1)
Average consecutive even numbers

$$\Rightarrow \frac{a-2+a+a+2+a+4}{4} = 87$$

$\Rightarrow a = 86$
Second largest number = 88 ...(2)
Adding equation (1) and (2),

$$75 + 88 = 163$$

9. Ratio of male to female student in 2008 = 5 : 2
In 2009, let the male student be $5x$ and female student be $2x$
Now if number of female students double in 2009
∴ Number of female student = $4x$
∴ Number of male student = $12x$

Gender	2008	2009
Male	$5x$	$12x$
Female	$2x$	$4x$

% of male student increase in 2009

$$= \left[\left(\frac{12x - 5x}{5x}\right) \times 100\right]\%$$

$$= \left[\frac{7}{5} \times 100\right]\%$$

$$= 140\%$$

10. Expanding

$$\left(z + \frac{1}{z}\right)^2 = 98$$

$$\therefore \quad z^2 + \frac{1}{z^2} + 2(z)\left(\frac{1}{z}\right) = 98$$

$$\therefore \quad z^2 + \frac{1}{z^2} = 96$$

11. Total respondents = 300

Now men respondents who do not have scooter

$= 40 + 20 = 60$

And women respondents who do not have scooter

$= 34 + 50 = 84$

$\therefore$ Total respondents who do not have scooter

$= 60 + 84 = 144$

$\therefore$ Required percent $= \left(\frac{144}{300} \times 100\right)\% = 48\%$

12. One way single person fare = ₹ 100

$\therefore$ Two way fare for single person = ₹ 200

$\therefore$ For 5 persons two way fare = ₹ 1000

Now, total discount = (10 + 5)% = 15%

Discount amount = ₹ $\left[\frac{15}{100} \times 1000\right]$ = ₹ 150

Amount to be paid = ₹(1000 – 150) = ₹ 850

■■

2

CHAPTER

Percentage and Its Applications

The term percentage is quite frequently used in our day to day life especially to avoid the fractions less than 1. Instead of treating the complete entity as 1, we treat as 100, and take the ratios accordingly.

PERCENTAGE

Per Cent: This term means for every hundred. A fraction whose denominator is 100 is called *percentage* and numerator of the fraction is called *rate per cent*. It is denoted by the symbol %.

To find % equivalent of a fraction.

Express fraction with the denominator 100 and numerator is the required answer.

e.g., $\frac{11}{24} = \frac{11}{24} \times 100 = 45\frac{5}{6}\%$

To find fraction equivalent of 'a %': Divide 'a' by 100.

e.g., $21\frac{7}{8}\% = \frac{21\frac{7}{8}}{100} = \frac{175}{800} = \frac{7}{32}$

To increase a number by a given %:

Multiply the number by the factor $\frac{100 + \text{rate}}{100}$

e.g., increase 20 by 15%,

i.e $20 \times \left(\frac{100+15}{100}\right) = 20 \times \frac{115}{100} = 23$

or $20 \times 1.15 = 23$

To decrease a number by a given %:

Multiply the number by the factor $\frac{100 - \text{rate}}{100}$

e.g., decrease 30 by 20%, i.e $30 \times \left(\frac{100-20}{100}\right)$

$= 30 \times \frac{80}{100} = 24$

or $30 \times 0.8 = 24$

To find the % increase of a number:

$$\%\text{increase} = \frac{\text{total increase}}{\text{initial value}} \times 100$$

$$= \frac{\text{Final value} - \text{Initial value}}{\text{Initial value}} \times 100$$

e.g., Population of a village in 1980 was 3000 and in 1990 was 3200. Find the % increase.

$$\%\text{ increase} = \frac{3200 - 3000}{3000} \times 100$$

To find % decrease of a number:

$$\%\text{ decrease} = \frac{\text{total decrease}}{\text{Initial value}} \times 100$$

$$= \frac{\text{Initial value} - \text{Final value}}{\text{Initial value}} \times 100$$

e.g., Cost of a bike last year was ₹ 19000. Its cost this year is ₹ 17000. Find the % decrease in its cost.

$$\%\text{ decrease} = \frac{19000 - 17000}{19000} \times 100$$

$$= \frac{2000}{19000} \times 100 = 10.5\%$$

Note:

(1) If price of a commodity increases by r%, then reduction in consumption, so as not to increase expenditure is $\left(\frac{r}{100+r} \times 100\right)\%$

(2) If price of a commodity decrease by r%, then the increase in consumption so as not to decrease expenditure is $\left(\frac{r}{100-r} \times 100\right)\%$

(3) If A's income is r% more than that of B, then B's income is less than that of A by $\left(\frac{r}{100+r} \times 100\right)\%$

(4) If A's income is r% less than that of B, then B's income is more than that of A by $\left(\frac{r}{100-r} \times 100\right)\%$.

SIMPLE INTEREST AND COMPOUND INTEREST

When a sum of money is lent by A to B, A is called *lender* (*creditor*), B the *borrower* (*debtor*).

The sum lent is called *principal* (P).

Interest (I) is the extra money paid by the borrowed to the lender for the use of the money for a specified time.

The time for which the money is borrowed is called *period* (N).

The extra amount paid per 100 rupees in a year is called *rate per cent per annum* (R).

The sum of interest and principal is called *Amount* (A).

$$A = P + I$$

Simple Interest (S.I.)

When interest is paid as it falls due, it is called simple interest i.e., throughout the load period, interest is charged on the original sum (principal) borrowed.

$$\text{S.I.} = \frac{PNR}{100}$$

e.g., Find interest to be paid on ₹ 1500 at 9% per annum for a period of 9 years.

Here P = 1500, R = 9%, N = 3 years

$$\therefore \quad \text{S.I.} = \frac{\text{PNR}}{100} = \frac{1500 \times 3 \times 9}{100} = ₹\ 405$$

Compound Interest (C.I.)

Money is said to be lent at compound interest when at the end of a year or other fixed period, the interest that has become due is not paid to the lender, but is added to the sum lent, and the amount thus obtained becomes the principal for the next year or period. The process is repeated until the amount for the last period has been found. The difference between final amount and the original principal is the *compound interest* (C.I.).

In compound interest, interest is calculated on the accrued interest also.

$$\text{Amount} = \text{P}\left[1 + \frac{\text{R}}{100}\right]^{\text{N}}$$

Compound Interest = Amount – Principal

Note:

(1) The time period after which the interest is added each time to form a new principal is called *conversion period*. It may be annually, semi annually or quarterly.

(2) In case, interest is paid semi annually (half yearly), N is number of half years and R is rate percent per half year *i.e.,*

Number of years × 2 = Number of half years.

Rate percent per annum ÷ 2 = Rate percent per half year.

(3) In case interest is paid quarterly, N is number of quarters and R is rate percent per quarter.

Number of years ÷ 4 = Number of quarters

Rate percent per quarter + 4 = Rate percent per quarter.

(4) When rates are different for different years, say R_1, R_2, R_3 percent of 1st, 2nd and 3rd years respectively then

$$\text{Amount} = \text{P}\left(1 + \frac{R_1}{100}\right)\left(1 + \frac{R_2}{100}\right)\left(1 + \frac{R_3}{100}\right)$$

(5) In case the time is a fraction of a year, say $y\frac{x}{z}$ years, then

$$\text{Amount} = \text{P}\left(1 + \frac{\text{R}}{100}\right)^{y} \times \left(1 + \frac{\frac{x}{z} \times \text{R}}{100}\right)$$

Population Formula: The original population of a town is P and annual increase is r%, then population in n years is $\left(1 + \frac{\text{R}}{100}\right)^{n}$ and if annual decrease is r%, then population in n years is given by a change of sign in the formula

i.e., $\left(1 - \frac{\text{R}}{100}\right)^{n}$

e.g., If annual increase in the population of a town is 4% and present population is 15625, what will be the population in 3 years?

Required population = $15625\,(1.04)^3 = 17576$

Hire Purchase: In a hire purchase plan, a customer can make use of the goods while paying for them. The amount paid at the time of purchase is called *down payment*. The remainder is paid in equal installments and each is the monthly installment. The difference between total amount to be paid and the cash price is called *installment charge*.

Monthly Installment

$$= \frac{\text{Amount to be paid – down payment}}{\text{Number of instalments}}$$

e.g., If a transistor is available at ₹ 400 each or ₹ 100 down payment and ₹ 70 per month for 5 months, find total amount paid for it, and the installment charge

Amount paid = 100 + 70 × 5 = ₹ 450

Installment charge = 450 – 400 = ₹ 50

PROFIT AND LOSS

Cost Price (CP): The price for which an article is bought is called its *cost price*.

Selling Price (SP): The price at which an article is sold is called its *selling price*.

Profit (Gain): The difference between selling price and cost price is called *profit*. For profit, selling price should be greater than cost price.

Loss: The difference between cost price and the selling price is called *loss*. When cost price is greater than the selling price, there is a loss.

Profit and loss is generally represented as a percent of the cost price, unless otherwise stated.

Overhead charges: If an individual has to spend some money on transportation etc., then this extra expenditure is called *overhead charges*.

Marked price (MP): The price on the label is called *marked price* or *list price*.

Discount: The reduction made on the '*marked price*' of an article is called *discount*. When no discount is given, '*selling price*' is the same as '*marked price*'.

List of Formulae

(1) Profit = SP – CP ... (SP > CP)

(2) Loss = CP – SP ... (CP > SP)

(3) $\%\ \text{Profit} = \frac{\text{Profit}}{\text{CP}} \times 100 = \frac{\text{SP} - \text{CP}}{\text{CP}} \times 100$

(4) $\%\ \text{Loss} = \frac{\text{Loss}}{\text{CP}} \times 100 = \frac{\text{CP} - \text{SP}}{\text{CP}} \times 100$

(5) $\text{Profit} = \frac{\text{Profit}\% \times \text{CP}}{100}$

(6) $\text{Loss} = \frac{\text{Loss}\% \times \text{CP}}{100}$

(7) $\text{SP} = \frac{100 + \text{Profit}\%}{100} \times \text{CP}$

(8) $\text{SP} = \frac{100 - \text{Loss}\%}{100} \times \text{CP}$

(9) SP = Marked Price – Discount

(10) $CP = SP \times \left(\frac{100}{100+\text{Profit}\%}\right)$

(11) $CP = SP \times \left(\frac{100}{100-\text{Loss}\%}\right)$

(12) $\text{Discount }\% = \frac{\text{Discount}}{\text{Marked Price}} \times 100$

Some important point:

(1) If two items are sold, each at ₹ X, one at a gain of p% and the other at a loss of p%, there is an overall loss given by $\frac{p^2}{100}\%$. The absolute value of the loss is given by $\frac{2p^2x}{100^2 - p^2}$

(2) If CP of two items is the same and % Loss and % Gain on the two items are equal, then net loss or net profit is zero.

(3) Buy x get y free *i.e.,* if x + y articles are sold at cost price of x articles, then

$$\text{percentage discount} = \frac{x}{x+y} \times 100.$$

(4) By using false weight, if a substance is sold at cost price, then

$$\text{overall gain }\% = \frac{100+\text{Gain}\%}{100} = \frac{\text{True Scale or Weight}}{\text{False Scale or Weight}}$$

(5) In case of successive discount a% and b%, effective discount $= \left(a+b-\frac{ab}{100}\right)\%$.

PARTNERSHIP

It is an association of two or more persons who invest their money in order to carry on a certain business. A partner who manages the business is called *working partner* and the one who simply invests the money is called *sleeping partner*.

If capitals of the partners are invested for the same time, then partnership is called *simple*, and if invested for different periods, the partner is called *compound*.

If period of investment is the same for each partner, then profit or loss is divided in the ratio of their investments.

e.g., (*i*) If A and B are partners in a business, then

$$\frac{\text{Investment of A}}{\text{Investment of B}} = \frac{\text{Profit of A}}{\text{Profit of B}}$$

or

$$\frac{\text{Investment of A}}{\text{Investment of B}} = \frac{\text{Loss of A}}{\text{Loss of B}}$$

(*ii*) If A, B and C are partners in a business, then Investment of A : Investment of B : Investment of C

= Profit of A : Profit of B : Profit of C

OR Loss of A : Loss of B : Loss of C

Monthly Equivalent Investment: It is the product of the capital invested and the period for which it is invested.

If period of investment is different, then profit or loss is divided in the ratio of their Monthly Equivalent Investment.

e.g., If A and B are partners in a business, then,

$$\frac{\text{Monthly Equivalent Investment of A}}{\text{Monthly Equivalent Investment of B}} = \frac{\text{Profit of A}}{\text{Profit of B}} = \frac{\text{Loss of A}}{\text{Loss of B}}$$

i.e.,

$$\frac{\text{Investment of A} \times \text{Period of Investment of A}}{\text{Investment of B} \times \text{Periof of Investment B}} = \frac{\text{Profit of A}}{\text{Profit of B}} = \frac{\text{Loss of A}}{\text{Loss of B}}$$

If A, B and C are partners in a business, then Monthly Equivalent Investment of A

: Monthly Equivalent Investment of B

: Monthly Equivalent Investment of C = Profit of A : Profit of B : Profit of C

or

Monthly Equivalent Investment of A : Monthly Equivalent Investment of B

: Monthly Equivalent Investment of C = Loss of A : Loss of B : Loss of C

STOCKS AND SHARES

Face value: The price of a share is printed on the share certificate is called face value of the share. (Nominal value).

Dividend: Every shareholder of a company is entitled to a proportionate share of the profits of the company. The amount of profits on each share is called *dividend*. Dividend is expressed as a percentage of the face value.

Market Value: In the market, selling price of the share may be different from its face value. Thus, market value of a share is *fluctuable price*.

Shares: *In the market, three types of shares are available*:

(*i*) **Premium share:** If market price of a share is more than nominal value, then it is called *premium share*.

(*ii*) **Par share:** If market price of a share is equal to the nominal value, then it is called *par share*.

(*iii*) **Discount share:** If market price of a share is less than the nominal value, then it is called a *discount share*.

Types of shares: *There are two types of shares:*

(*i*) **Preference shares:** On these shares a fixed rate of dividend is paid to share holders irrespective of whether the company makes any profits or whether it runs into loss. In case the company is not able to pay the agreed dividend to preference shareholders, the dividend on cumulative preference shares goes on accumulating and is paid as and when the company can do so.

(*ii*) **Equity shares:** Profit of the company that is left over after its distribution to the preference shareholders is distributed among the equity share holders. This dividend on equity share may sometimes be more or sometimes less than the dividend on the preference share.

Stock

In order to meet expenses of a certain plan, the Government of India sometimes raises a load from the public at a certain fixed rate of interest. Bonds or promissory notes called *stocks of a fixed value* are used for sale to the public.

Note:

(1) Income per share = Rate of dividend × Nominal value of 1 share.

(2) Annual income = Income per share × Number of shares.

(3) Number of shares

$$= \frac{\text{Nominal value of all the shares}}{\text{Nominal value of one shares}}$$

$$= \frac{\text{Market value of the shares (Investment)}}{\text{Market value of one share}}$$

$$= \frac{\text{Total Dividend}}{\text{Dividend per share}}$$

(4) Rate of interest on the Invest (yield)

$$= \frac{\text{Total income} \times 100}{\text{Total investment}}$$

(5) When stoke/share is purchased, brokerage is added to cost price.

(6) When stock/share is sold, brokerage is subtracted from selling price.

(7) In most problems, face value of a share is taken to be ₹, 100 unless specified.

EXERCISE – I

MCQ TYPE QUESTIONS

1. The Manager (M) of the company along with his Assistant Manager (AM) and a Business Analyst (BA) invest ₹ 55000, ₹ 45000 and ₹ 60000 respectively in a partnership firm for six months. The Manager being the highest authority among the three gets one-tenth of the total profit and Assistant Manager being second highest authority gets $\frac{1}{20}$th of the remaining and the remaining profit is divided among the three in the ratio of their investments. If the total profit was ₹ 40000, who gets the minimum share and how much?

(*a*) BA, ₹ 11400 (*b*) AM, ₹ 11419

(c) AM, ₹ 12500 (*d*) None of these

2. In a business partnership of three people A, B and C, B's share in total profit is ₹ 250 per ₹ 2000. At this profit his return on investment is 15%. If B earns total of ₹ 900. what is the total investment made by A and C in business? Assume that each of A, B and C have invested their money for the entire year and profits are shared in the ratio of their investments.

(*a*) ₹ 48000 (*b*) ₹ 42000

(*c*) ₹ 6000 (*d*) Data insufficient

3. Abhay and Bimal started a business in partnership. Abhay invested a capital of ₹ 50000. Bimal agrees to pay Abhay an interest on half the capital at 8% per annum. Also Bimal receives a salary of ₹ 500 per month for managing the business. After six months Abhay withdraws ₹ 20000 and Bimal pitches in an equal amount. Bimal continues to pay Abhay interest at 8% per annum for the balance amount. At the end of the year they divide the profit equally and found that total earning of Bimal in the year was exactly thrice that of Abhay. The total profit ?

(*a*) ₹ 7200 (*b*) ₹ 6800

(*c*) ₹ 5400 (*d*) ₹ 4800

4. How much stock must be bought in 3 percent $89\frac{1}{8}$ in order that by selling it at $91\frac{3}{8}$ a profit of ₹ 45 may be made?

(*a*) 20 (*b*) 30 (*c*) 40 (*d*) 50

5. Which is the better investment (the security being equal), 3 percents perpetually at par, or 5 percents at 124, the latter stock being redeemable in 20 years at par? (Simple interest to be reckoned).

(*a*) 3% at par

(*b*) 5% at 124

(*c*) Both are same

(*d*) Cannot be determined

6. What rate percent per annum does a man get by buying ₹100 share (₹ 70 paid-up) at ₹ 60 when dividend is 5% per annum?

(*a*) 4.28% (*b*) 7.14%

(*c*) $8\frac{1}{3}$ % (*d*) $5\frac{5}{6}$ %

7. A rejects 0.08% of the meters as defective. How many will he examine to reject 2?

(*a*) 2500 (*b*) 1250

(*c*) 625 (*d*) 5000

8. (a% of b) + (b% of a) is equal to

(*a*) a% of b (*b*) 2% of ab

(*c*) 20% of ab (*d*) 2% of 100 ab

9. Ryan's stock of goods is worth $9462, which is 15% more than Harland's, and 15% less than Lambert's. What is the value of stock carried by Harland and Lambert respectively?

(*a*) $ 8218, $ 10032 (*b*) $ 1419, $ 10881

(*c*) $ 8042, $ 10881 (*d*) $ 8228, $ 11132

10. Numerator of a fraction increases by 25%. What can be said about the resultant fraction?

(*a*) It is 67% less than original.

(*b*) It is equal to the original fraction.

(*c*) It is 67% more than the original fraction.

(*d*) The change cannot be determine.

11. Which of the following statement/s is/are true?

I. If two numbers are such that one is 25% more than the second, then sum of the two numbers is nine times that of the difference of the two numbers.

II. If 56% of a number A is 24% of another number B then 49% of A is 21% of B.

Codes:

(*a*) Only I (*b*) Only II

(*c*) Only I and II (*d*) None of these

12. In the Annual General Meeting of the Rotary club a chairman is to be selected for which A and B is the only two candidates. After the first round, each of them gave a speech on their policy and work plan for the coming year after which another round of election was held. The number of votes not cast for A increased by 25% in the second round over those not cast for him in the first round and A lost second round to B by twice as many votes as that by which he had won in the first round. If total 260 people voted each time what was the percent decrease in votes received by A in the second round assuming that no vote was void in any of the rounds?

(*a*) 18% (*b*) 25% (*c*) 21.43% (*d*) 30%

13. A watermelon weighs 5000 gm. 99% of its weight is water. It is kept in a drying room and after some time it turns out that it is only 98% water by weight. What is its weight now?

(*a*) 2500 gm

(*b*) 4500 gm

(*c*) 4950 gm

(*d*) None of these

14. A sum of ₹ 5000 is divided into two parts A and B such that simple interests at the rate of 20% p.a. on A and B after 2 and 3 years respectively are equal. Which of the following is false about A and B?

(*a*) Ratio of A to B is 2 : 3

(*b*) Ratio of A to B is 3 : 2

(*c*) A exceeds B by ₹ 1000

(*d*) Total interest earned on A and B is ₹ 2400

15. Which amongst the following two offers is the better one? Consider with respect to interest accrued.

I. Investing an amount compounded annually at 1% per annum for 100 years.

II. Investing the amount compounded annually at 100% per annum for 1 year.

Codes:

(*a*) First offer

(*b*) Second offer

(*c*) Both are same

(*d*) Cannot be determined

16. The population of rate in a locality x increases by 20% in one year. Observing this, the pest control committee decided to use a special kind of pesticide 'xyz' which effectively kills 160 rats in 3 months. Just after 2 years, what is the net increase or decrease in the population of rats if, initially the population of rats is 3200 and pesticide is used effectively?

(*a*) Increase of 128 rats.

(*b*) Decrease of 128 rats.

(*c*) Neither an increase nor a decrease in the population.

(*d*) None of these.

17. A man travels from A to B to buy goods which he can get 10% cheaper in B than in A. If expenses of the journey are ₹ 15 and he makes a clear saving of ₹ 10, how much does he pay for the goods?

(*a*) ₹ 225

(*b*) ₹ 200

(*c*) ₹ 150

(*d*) Cannot be determined

18. By selling 5 dozen mangoes for ₹ 156, it was found that $\frac{3}{10}$th of the outlay was gained. What should the retail price per mango be in order to gain 60%?

(*a*) ₹ 4 (*b*) ₹ 2 (*c*) ₹ 3.2 (*d*) ₹ 4.2

19. A man sells sugar to a tradesman at a profit of 20% but the tradesman becoming bankrupt pays only 80 paise in the rupee. How much percentage does the man gain or lose by his sale?

(*a*) 2.5% (*b*) 3% (*c*) 4% (*d*) 5.2%

20. A trader allows a discount of 5 percent to his customers. What price should he mark on a article the cost price of which is ₹ 800 so as to make clear profit of 25 percent on his outlay?

(*a*) ₹ 1000 (*b*) ₹ 1053

(*c*) ₹ 1200 (*d*) ₹ 1123

21. A camera costing ₹550 is marked to be sold at a price, which gives a profit of 30%. What will be its selling price in a sale when 20% is taken off the marked price?

(*a*) ₹ 600 (*b*) ₹ 572

(*c*) ₹ 635 (*d*) ₹ 605

22. Buy two and get one free. Which of the following is true?

(*a*) The person is selling at a loss.

(*b*) The person is selling at a profit.

(*c*) The loss or gain depends on the profit from sale of two articles.

(*d*) The person is selling at the cost price.

Directions (Q.23–25): *Refer to the data below and answer the questions that follow.*

A profit-maximizing producer has the option of discriminating between markets A and B (i.e., charging different prices in markets A and B for the same product) for a product X. Demand for the product in each of the markets A and B is given by

$$Q_A = 42 - 0.2\,P_A$$

$$Q_B = 100 - 0.8\,P_B$$

Total cost in any market is given by

C = 1000 + 5Q, where Q is quantity sold in that market.

Consider two cases:

***Case 1** in which she discriminates between the markets and*

***Case 2** in which she does not discriminate.*

23. What is the approximate ratio of the price in market A to price in market B in Case 1?

(*a*) 1.65 (*b*) 2.00

(*c*) 2.25 (*d*) 2.50

24. What is the ratio of the total quantity of product X sold in Case 1 to the total quantity sold in Case 2?

(*a*) 0.50 (*b*) 1

(*c*) 1.10 (*d*) 1.05

25. What is the difference in total profit in Case 1 and the total profit in Case 2?

(*a*) ₹ 289 (*b*) ₹ 829 (*c*) ₹ – 289 (*d*) ₹ – 829

NUMERICAL TYPE QUESTIONS

1. A and B enter into a partnership. A puts in the whole capital of ₹ 45000 on the condition that the profits will be equally divided after which B will pay A interest on half the capital at 10% p.a. and receive ₹ 60 per month from A for carrying on the concern. The yearly profit in rupees, if B's income is half of A's income is _____

2. A, B and C started a business by investing ₹ 72000, ₹ 27000 and ₹ 81000. It was decided that servant's salary ₹ 2000 per month should be given from the profit. If profit is ₹ 25000 in the first month and ₹ 20000 in the second month and average profit of remaining 10 months is ₹ 21000, then share of C is _____

3. Three friends started a business of renting out air conditioners by investing ₹ 20000, ₹ 24000 and ₹ 16000, respectively. C gets 20% of total profit for repair and maintenance of the air conditioner. If in a particular year, C gets ₹ 487.50 less than total earnings of the other two, then total profit for the year in ₹ is _____

4. A person holds forty ₹ 500 shares in a concern, which pays dividend at the rate of 6 percent per annum. When the shares are at ₹ 675, he sells out and invests half the proceeds in 4 percent stock at 90. With the other half he buys a house. For which he receives an annual rent of ₹ 1440 subject to a deduction of 25P per rupees for repairs and taxes. Alteration in rupees in his annual income will be _____.

5. A person invests ₹ 34539 in three percent at 87. After receiving one year's dividend, he sells out at 89. He then invests the whole in railway stock paying 5 percent at 115. The difference in his income will be_____

6. Difference of two numbers is 1660. If 7.5 % of one number is 12.5% of the other number, then two numbers are_____

7. A school has only three classes which contain 40,50,60 students respectively. The pass percent of these classes are 10, 20 and 10 respectively. Then pass percent in the school will be_____

8. For a sphere of radius 10cm, the numerical value of surface area is_____ percent of the numerical value of its volume.

9. At an election, there are two candidates only, a candidate who gets 43 per cent of the votes is rejected by a majority of 420 votes. Then total number of votes recorded assuming that there was no void vote are_____

10. If price of wheat be raised 30%, then by _____ percent a householder must reduce his consumption of the article so as not to increase his expenditure?

11. A fraction in reduced form is such that when it is squared and then its numerator is reduced by $33\frac{1}{3}\%$ % and denominator is reduced to 20%, its result is twice the original fraction. Sum of the numerator and the denominator is _____

12. A person borrows two equal sums at the same time at 5 and 4 percent respectively and finds that if he repays the former sum with simple interest on certain date 6 months before the latter, he will have to pay in each case the same amount, viz., ₹ 1100. The amount borrowed in rupees is ______

13. Effective annual rate corres-ponding to a nominal rate of 6 percent per annum, payable half-yearly is ______

14. A tradesman puts two prices on his goods, one for ready money and the other for 6 month's credit interest being calculated at $12\frac{1}{2}$% per annum. If credit price on an article be ₹ 26.56, then its cash price in rupees is ______

15. An article costing ₹9000 is sold at a discount which is equal to the simple interest on ₹ 3000 for N months. If rate of discount is same as the rate of interest, the N will be______months

16. A lent B ₹ 900 for a certain time at a certain rate percent per annum, which is equal to the square root of the number of the months of the time. After the time B wanted to return the money, but A, instead of taking the interest which amounted to ₹8 asked for a certain sum of money at the same rate for a certain number of years which is equal to the square root of the rate percent. Sum of money in rupees so that none of them should be the loser will be_______ (Take simple interest)

17. A shopkeeper sells a microwave at a discount on its marked price of ₹ 2500. But in a clearance sale he gives an additional discount of 20% thus selling it at ₹ 1500. Then first discount was_____%

18. A sports goods shop owner has 6 packets of balls each containing the same number of balls. If he sells each ball at ₹ 8 he gains ₹ 96. If there were 1 ball less in each packet and he sells each ball at ₹ 9 then he gains ₹ 90 in the transaction. The cost price of each packet of balls in rupees is ______

19. One merchant correctly calculates his percentage profit on the cost price; another wrongly calculates it on the selling price. The difference in actual profits in rupees if both claim to make $17\frac{1}{2}$% profit on goods sold at ₹ 3760 is______

20. A manufacturer marks his goods in advance at 80 percent more than the cost price, but he allows 15 articles to the dozen and also 10 percent discount for cash. The profit on his outlay does he obtain from a customer who pays cash is _____%

21. A trader buys a certain amount of goods worth ₹ 22520. He decides to make a profit of 5.36% on the sale of goods worth ₹ 5000 and increase the profit percent by 3.14% for sales upto ₹15000 and then increase the profit percent for the sale of remaining lot such that he is able to make a profit of 25% on the sale of the full lot. Then profit in rupees that he makes on the third lot of goods is______

22. Three shepherds A, B and C rented a pasture for a year. A grazed 22 sheeps for 4 months, B grazed 16 sheeps for 8 months and C grazed 32 sheeps for 6 months. If C's share of rent is ₹600, then total rent in rupees for the year was_____

23. Three bachelors, Amar, Akbar and Anthony rented a house for a year. But, Amar left after 4 months, Akbar stayed for 8 months and only Anthony stayed for the entire year. If the annual rent was ₹ 6000, then share of Akbar is______

24. Ram, Shyam and Ghanshyam invest ₹2000, ₹ 10000 and ₹ 5000 to set up a stall. Ram gets 15% of the total profit for running the stall. Ram gets ₹ 500 less than Shyam and Ghanshym together, then total profit of that year is_______

25. x, y and z start a joint venture wherein they make an annual profit of ₹ 3600. x invested one-third of the capital for one-fourth of the time, y invested one-fourth of the capital for one-half of the time, while z invested the remainder of the capital for the entire year. Then share of x in the profit is_____.

EXERCISE – II

(QUESTIONS FROM PREVIOUS GATE EXAMS)

MCQ TYPE QUESTIONS

2014

1. The population of a new city is 5 million and is growing at 20% annually. How many years would it take to double at this growth rate?

(*a*) 3 – 4 years (*b*) 4 – 5 years
(*c*) 5 – 6 years (*d*) 6 – 7 years

2. One percent of the people of country X are taller than 6 ft. Two percent of the people of country Y are taller than 6 ft. There are thrice as many people in country X as in country Y. Taking both countries together, what is the percentage of people taller than 6 ft?

(*a*) 3.0 (*b*) 2.5
(*c*) 1.5 (*d*) 1.25

3. Industrial consumption of power doubled from 2000-2001 to 2010-2011. Find the annual rate of increase in percent assuming it to be uniform over the years.

(*a*) 5.6 (*b*) 7.2
(*c*) 10.0 (*d*) 12.2

4. The Gross Domestic Product (GDP) in Rupees grew at 7% during 2012-2013. For international comparison, the GDP is compared in US Dollars (USD) after conversion based on the market exchange rate. During the period 2012-2013 the exchange rate for the USD increased from ₹ 50/ USD to ₹ 60/ USD. India's GDP in USD during the period 2012-2013

(*a*) increased by 5% (*b*) decreased by 13%
(*c*) decreased by 20% (*d*) decreased by 11%

2013

5. A firm is selling its product at ₹ 60 per unit. The total cost of production is ₹ 100 and firm is earning total profit of ₹ 500. Later, the total cost increased by 30%. By what percentage the price should be increased to maintained the same profit level.

(*a*) 5 (*b*) 10
(*c*) 15 (*d*) 30

2012

6. An automobile plant contracted to buy shock absorbers from two suppliers X and Y. X supplies 60% and Y supplies 40% of the shock absorbers. All shock absorbers are subjected to a quality test. The ones that pass the quality test are considered reliable. Of X's shock absorbers, 96% are reliable. Of Y's shock absorbers, 72% are reliable.

The probability that a randomly chosen shock absorber, which is found to be reliable, is made by Y is

(*a*) 0.288
(*b*) 0.334
(*c*) 0.667
(*d*) 0.720

2011

7. There are two candidates P and Q in an election. During the campaign, 40% of the voters promised to vote for P, and rest for Q. However, on the day of election 15% of the voters went back on their promise to vote for P and instead voted for Q. 25% of the voters went back on their promise to vote for Q and instead voted for P. Suppose, P lost by 2 votes, then what was the total number of voters?

(*a*) 100
(*b*) 110
(*c*) 90
(*d*) 95

NUMERICAL TYPE QUESTION

2015

1. From a circular sheet of paper of radius 30 cm, a sector of 10% area is removed. If the remaining part is used to make a conical surface, then the ratio of the radius and height of the cone is __________.

ANSWERS

EXERCISE – I

MCQ Type Questions

1. (*b*)	**2.** (*b*)	**3.** (*a*)	**4.** (*a*)	**5.** (*b*)	**6.** (*d*)	**7.** (*a*)	**8.** (*b*)	**9.** (*d*)	**10.** (*c*)
11. (*c*)	**12.** (*c*)	**13.** (*a*)	**14.** (*a*)	**15.** (*a*)	**16.** (*c*)	**17.** (*a*)	**18.** (*c*)	**19.** (*c*)	**20.** (*b*)
21. (*b*)	**22.** (*c*)	**23.** (*a*)	**24.** (*b*)	**25.** (*a*)					

Numerical Type Questions

1. 9180	**2.** 103950	**3.** 2812.50	**4.** 480	**5.** 345.2	**6.** (4150, 2490)
7. $13\frac{1}{3}$	**8.** 30	**9.** 3000	**10.** $23\frac{1}{13}$	**11.** 8	**12.** 1000
13. 6.09	**14.** 25	**15.** 4	**16.** 600	**17.** 25	**18.** 48
19. 98	**20.** 29.6	**21.** 4512	**22.** 1275	**23.** 2000	**24.** 1000
25. 480					

EXERCISE – II

MCQ Type Questions

1. (*a*) **2.** (*d*) **3.** (*b*) **4.** (*d*) **5.** (*a*) **6.** (*b*) **7.** (*a*)

Numerical Type Question

1. (2.06)

EXPLANATIONS

EXERCISE – I

MCQ TYPE QUESTIONS

1. The ratio of their investments is 11 : 9 : 12.

So, Manager gets $\frac{1}{10}(40000) = 4000 +$ his share

Remaining amount = 36000.

Asstt.Manager gets $\frac{1}{20}(36000) = 1800 +$ his share

Remaining amount = 36000 – 1800 = 34200

$$\therefore \quad \text{M's share} = \frac{11}{32} \times 34200 + 4000$$
$$= 11756.25 + 4000$$
$$= ₹\,15756.25$$
$$\cong ₹\,15756$$

$$\text{AM's share} = \frac{9}{32} \times 34200 + 1800$$
$$= 9618.75 + 1800$$
$$= ₹\,11418.75$$
$$\approx ₹\,11419$$

$$\text{BA's share} = \frac{12}{32} \times 34200 = ₹\,12825.$$

2. B's share in the profit = 250 per 2000

If B gets ₹ 900, then

$$\text{total profit} = 2000 \times \frac{18}{5} = 7200$$

B's return on investment = 15%

$$\therefore \quad \frac{900}{\text{B's investment}} \times 100 = 15$$

$\therefore$ B's investment = 6000

Hence profits are shared in the ratio of their investments.

$$\text{Total investments} = 6000 \times \frac{7200}{900} = 48000$$

$\therefore$ Investment made by A and C = 48000 – 6000 = 42000.

3. Interest paid by Bimal to Abhay for first six months

$$= \frac{50000}{2} \times \frac{8}{100} \times \frac{1}{2} = ₹\,1000$$

For last six months

$$= \frac{30000 - 20000}{2} \times \frac{8}{100} \times \frac{1}{2}$$
$$= ₹\,200$$

$\therefore$ Total salary paid to Bimal = $12 \times 500 = ₹\, 6000$

Let total profit be ₹ x

$\therefore$ Abhay's earing = $1200 + \dfrac{x - 6000}{2}$

Bimal's earning = $6000 + \dfrac{x - 6000}{2} - 1200$

$\therefore \quad 3\left(1200 + \dfrac{x-6000}{2}\right) = 4800 + \dfrac{x-6000}{2}$

$\Rightarrow \quad 3600 + \dfrac{3x}{2} - 9000 = 4800 + \dfrac{x}{2} - 3000$

$\Rightarrow \quad \dfrac{3x}{2} - \dfrac{x}{2} = 7200;$

$\therefore \quad x = ₹\, 7200$

4. Profit per stocks = $91\frac{3}{8} - 89\frac{1}{8} = ₹\, 2\frac{2}{8}$

$\therefore \quad \dfrac{45}{2\frac{1}{4}} = 20$ stocks

5. Income from a stock at 3% in 20 years at par

$= \dfrac{100}{100} \times 3 \times 20 = 60$

Income from a stock at 5% at 124 in 20 years

$= \dfrac{100}{124} \times 5 \times 20 = 80.64.$

6. He invests ₹ 60 and gets ₹ 100 share

Income = ₹ 5

Required % = $\dfrac{5}{60} \times 100(0.70) = 5.83\% = 5\frac{5}{6}\ \%$

7. Let number of meters to be examined be x.

Then $\quad 0.08\%$ of $x = 2$.

$\Rightarrow \quad \dfrac{0.08}{100} \times x = 2$

$x = \dfrac{2 \times 100}{0.08} = \dfrac{2 \times 100 \times 100}{8} = 2500$

8. $\left(\dfrac{a}{100} \times b\right) + \left(\dfrac{b}{100} \times a\right) = \dfrac{ab}{100} + \dfrac{ab}{100} = \dfrac{2ab}{100}$

$= \dfrac{2}{100} \times ab = 2\%$ of ab.

9. Ryan's stock = $1.15 \times$ Harland's stock

$\therefore$ Harland's stock = $\dfrac{9462}{1.15} = \$8228$

Ryan's stock = $0.85 \times$ Lambert's stock

$\therefore$ Lambert's stock = $\dfrac{9462}{0.85} = \$11132.$

10. Let the fraction be $\dfrac{x}{y}$.

Let $\quad x_1 = x + 0.25x = 1.25x$

$y_1 = y - 0.25x = 0.75x$

$\therefore \quad \dfrac{x_1}{y_1} = \dfrac{1.25x}{0.75x} = \dfrac{5}{3}\dfrac{x}{y}$

$\therefore$ Increase = $\dfrac{\frac{5}{3}\frac{x}{y} - \frac{x}{y}}{\frac{x}{y}} \times 100 = \dfrac{2}{3} \times 100 = 66.67\%$

Thus, resultant fraction is more than the original fraction by 67%. Thus III is true.

11. I. Let first number be x.

$\therefore$ Second number = 1.25x

Sum = x + 1.25x = 2.25x

Difference = 1.25x − x = 0.25x

Also, $\quad 9 \times 0.25x = 2.25x$

Thus I is true.

II. $\dfrac{56}{100} \times A = \dfrac{24}{100} \times B$

Multiplying by $\dfrac{49}{56}$ on both the sides.

$\therefore \quad \dfrac{49}{56} \times \dfrac{56}{100} \times A = \dfrac{49}{56} \times \dfrac{24}{100} \times B$

$\Rightarrow \quad \dfrac{49}{100}A = \dfrac{21}{100}B$

$\Rightarrow$ 49% of A = 21% of B.

Thus, II is true.

12. In the first round, let A get 'a' votes and B get 'b' votes.

Then, $\quad a + b = 260$

i.e., $\quad a = 260 - b \quad \ldots (i)$

In second round, B gets

$b \times \dfrac{125}{100} = \dfrac{5b}{4}$

and A gets $260 - \frac{5b}{4}$

Also, $\frac{5b}{4} - \left(260 - \frac{5b}{4}\right) = 2(a - b)$

$$\frac{10b}{4} - 260 = 2(260 - b - b)$$

$$\frac{10b}{4} - 260 = 520 - 4b$$

$$4b + \frac{10b}{4} = 520 + 260$$

$$b = 120$$

Hence first round, A gets 140 and B gets 120.

In second round A gets 110 and B gets 150.

$\therefore$ % decrease in votes received by A

$$= \frac{140 - 110}{140} \times 100 = 21.43\%$$

13. Non-water matter is 1% of 5000 = 50 gm.
After drying, this matter becomes 2% of the weight of the water-melon. Hence weight of the watermelon now is 2500 gm.

14. Let A = ₹ x and B = ₹ (5000 – x)

Then, $\frac{x \times 2 \times 20}{100} = \frac{(5000 - x) \times 3 \times 20}{100}$

$\Rightarrow$ $2x = 15000 - 3x$

$\Rightarrow$ $5x = 15000$

$\Rightarrow$ $x = 3000$

$A = x = ₹ 3000$

and $B = 5000 - x$

$= 5000 - 3000$

$= ₹ 2000$

$\therefore$ $\frac{A}{B} = \frac{3000}{2000} = \frac{3}{2}$

Thus, (*a*) is not true and (*b*) is true.

$A - B = 3000 - 2000 = ₹ 1000.$

Thus, (*c*) is true.

(*d*) The total interest

$$= \frac{3000 \times 2 \times 20}{100} + \frac{2000 \times 3 \times 20}{100}$$

$= ₹ 2400.$

Thus, (*d*) is true.

15. First investment gives a return

$$P\left(1 + \frac{1}{100}\right)^{100} - P$$

First term is $P\left(1 + \frac{1}{100}\right)^{100} = X,$

such that $2P < X \le 3P$

Hence return X – P lies between P and 2P

i.e., $2P - P < X - P \le 3P - P.$

i.e., $P < X - P \le 2P.$

Whereas second offer.

$$= \text{Return} = P\left(1 + \frac{100}{100}\right)^{1} - P$$

$$= 2P - P = P.$$

Alternatively

Option of investing at 1% for 100 years is obviously better than investing at 100% for 1 year, because total compound interest for 100 years will be atleast 100% of the total amount (1% for each year), plus whatever the compounding effect will have.

16. Growth rate of rat population in 3 months

$$= 20 \times \frac{3}{12} = 5\%.$$

Increase in first 3 months = 3200 × 1.05 = 3360

Also, net decrease in 3 months = 160

$\therefore$ Rat population = 3360 – 160 = 3200

In the same way, after every 3 months, rat population remains the same.

Hence, even after 3 × 8 months i.e., 2 years, the population is maintained

17. Let CP in A be ₹ x

$\therefore$ CP in B = ₹ 0.9x

$\therefore$ $0.9x + 15 + 10 = x$

$\Rightarrow$ $0.1x = 25$

$\Rightarrow$ $x = 250$

$\therefore$ Price in B = 250 × 0.9 = ₹ 225

18. Let CP of 5 dozen mangoes be ₹ x.

SP = ₹ 156 and Gain = 0.3x

$\therefore$ $156 - x = 0.3x$

$\Rightarrow$ $x = 120$

$\therefore$ SP of 60 mangoes = 120 × 1.6 = 192

$\therefore$ SP per mango = ₹ 3.2

19. Let CP be ₹ x ; SP = 1.2x

But he gets only 1.2x × 0.8 = 0.96x

$\therefore$ Loss = 0.04x

$\therefore$ Loss = 4 %

20. Selling price = 800 × 1.25 = ₹ 1000

$\therefore$ Marked price = ₹ $\frac{1000}{0.95}$ = 1053

21. CP = ₹ 550

∴ Marked price = 1.3 × 550 = ₹ 715

∴ Sales price = 0.8 × 715 = ₹ 572.

22. Profit or loss of the sale depends upon how much profit the person is earning on the sale of two articles.

If SP > CP of 1 article, there is a profit.

If SP < CP of 1 article, there is a loss.

If SP = CP of 1 article, there is not profit no loss.

Thus, only (*c*) is true.

23. *Following two key points need to be noted* :

(A) Producer is profit maximizing which implies she will set prices that maximize the profit function.

(B) Quantity demanded in market A is independent of quantity demanded in market B.

CASE 1:

In this case, producer charges different prices in markets A and B. This implies that she will maximize profits individually.

Equations can be re-written as

$$P_A = 210 - 5Q_A$$
$$P_B = 125 - 1.25\ Q_B$$

Profit in Market A = π_A

= Revenue – Cost

$= Q_A \times P_A - C_A$

$= Q_A \times (210 - 5Q_A) - (1000 + 5Q_A)$

At the maximum profit level, differential π_A with respect to Q_A is 0

or

∴ $210 - 10Q_A - 5 = 0$

⇒ $Q_A = 20.5, P_A = 107.5$

and total revenue in market A

= 20.5 × 107.5 = ₹ 2203.75

Similarly

Profit in Market B = π_B

= Revenue Cost

$= Q_B \times P_B - C_B$

$= Q_B \times (125 - 1.25\ Q_B) - (1000 + 5Q_B)$

At maximum profit level, differ-ential of π_B with respect to Q_B is 0

or $125 - 2.5Q_B - 5 = 0$

⇒ $Q_B = 48, P_B = 65$

and total revenue in market B

= 48 × 65 = ₹ 3120

Using the above, we get

$$\frac{P_A}{P_B} = \frac{107.5}{65} \sim 1.65.$$

24. Data for 1 is available above. Consider case 2. In this case, prices across the two markets are the same. Hence, quantity equations can be added to give

$$Q = 142 - P$$

where Q is total quantity and P is price in both markets

⇒ $P = 142 - Q$

∴ $\pi = \text{Profit} = Q \times (142 - Q) - (1000 + 5Q)$

At the maximum profit level, differential of π with respect to Q is 0

∴ Q = 68.5, P = 73.5

and Total Revenue = 5034.75

Given this, we note that quantities sold in both Case 1 and Case 2 are the same. Hence, the ratio is exactly 1.

25. Profit Difference between case 1 and case 2

= Revenue Difference (since quantity sold and hence, cost is the same)

∴ Profit difference = 2203.75 + 3120 – 5034.75

= 289

NUMERICAL TYPE QUESTIONS

1. Interest on ₹ 22500 = 0.1 × 22500 = ₹2250

Charges for managing the concern

= 60 × 12 = ₹ 720

If yearly profit is ₹ x, then

$$\text{B's share} = \frac{\text{A's Share}}{2}$$

∴ $\frac{x}{2} - 2250 + 720 = \frac{1}{2}\left(\frac{x}{2} - 720 + 2250\right)$

⇒ x = ₹ 9180.

2. Total annual profit

= 25000 + 20000 + 21000 × 10

= ₹ 255000

Actual profit

= 255000 – (2000 × 12)

= ₹ 231000

Total investment

= 72000 + 27000 + 81000

= ₹180000

$$\text{A's share} = \frac{72000}{180000} \times 231000$$

= ₹ 92400

$$\text{B's share} = \frac{27000}{180000} \times 231000$$

= ₹ 34650

$$\text{C's share} = \frac{81000}{180000} \times 231000$$
$$= ₹\ 103950.$$

3. 80% of the total profit is divided in the ratio 20000 : 24000 : 16000 = 5 : 6 : 4

80% of total profit = 5x + 6x + 4x = 15x

$$\text{Total profit} = \frac{15x}{80\%} = 18.75x$$

∴ Share of C in profit = 4x + 20% of 18.75

= 4x + 3.75x = 7.75x

Share of A in profit = 5x

Share of B in profit = 6x

∴ (6x + 5x) – 7.75x = 487.50

⇒ 3.25x = 487.50

⇒ x = 150

∴ Total profit = 18.75 × 150 = ₹ 2812.50.

4. Selling price of 40 shares

= 675 ×40 = ₹ 27000

Income from half the proceeds

$$= \frac{13500}{90} \times 4 = ₹\ 600$$

Income from house = 1440 × 0.75 = 1080

Present total income = 1080 + 600 = ₹ 1680

$$\text{Earlier Income} = 40 \times 500 \times \frac{6}{100} = ₹\ 1200$$

Increase in income = ₹480

5. $\text{One years dividend} = \dfrac{34539}{87} \times 3 = ₹\ 1191$

$$\text{Selling Price} = \frac{34539}{87} \times 89 = ₹\ 35333$$

Number of railway stocks bought

$$= \frac{35333}{115} = 307.24$$

Income from railway stocks

= 307.24 × 5 = ₹ 1536.2

Difference in income = 345.2

6. Let two numbers be x and y.

7.5% of x = 12.5% of y

∴ 75x = 125 y

⇒ 3x = 5y

$$\Rightarrow \quad x = \left(\frac{5}{3}\right)y.$$

Now x – y = 1660

$$\Rightarrow \quad \left(\frac{5}{3}\right)y - y = 1660$$

$$\Rightarrow \quad \left(\frac{2}{3}\right)y = 1660$$

⇒ y = 2490

∴ x = 2490 +1660 = 4150.

Hence numbers are 4150, 2490.

7. Number of passed candidates

$$= \frac{10}{100} \times 40 + \frac{20}{100} \times 500 + \frac{10}{100} \times 60$$
$$= 4 + 10 + 6 = 20$$

Total students in school

= 40 + 50 + 60 =150

∴ Required percentage

$$= \frac{20}{150} \times 100 = \frac{40}{3} = 13\frac{1}{3}\%$$

8. $\text{Surface area} = 4 \times \dfrac{22}{7} \times r^2$

$$= \frac{3}{r}\left(\frac{4}{3} \times \frac{22}{7} \times r^3\right) = \frac{3}{r} \times \text{Volume}$$

where r = 10 cm

So we have

$$S = \frac{3}{10}\ V = \frac{3}{10} \times 100\ \%\ \text{of}\ V = 30\ \%\ \text{of}\ V$$

So surface area is 30 % of volume.

9. Difference in % of votes = 57 – 43 = 14%

∴ 14% is represented by 420

$$\therefore \text{Total number of votes} = 420 \times \frac{100}{14} = 3000.$$

10. $\%\ \text{reduction in consumption} = \left(\dfrac{30}{100+30} \times 100\right)\%$

$$= \left(\frac{30}{130} \times 100\right)\% = 23\frac{1}{13}\%$$

11. Let the fraction be $\dfrac{a}{b}$

$$\therefore \quad \frac{a^2}{b^2} \times \frac{\frac{2}{3}}{\frac{1}{5}} = 2\frac{a}{b}\quad \frac{a}{b} \neq 0 \text{ if } a \neq 0,$$

$$\text{then} \quad \frac{a}{b} \times \frac{2}{3/5} = 2$$

$$\Rightarrow \quad \frac{a}{b} = \frac{3}{5}$$

∴ a + b = 8.

12. $$1100 = P + \frac{P \times 5 \times \left(T - \frac{1}{2}\right)}{100}$$

$$1100 = P + \frac{P \times 4 \times T}{100}$$

$$\therefore \quad \frac{P \times 5 \times \left(T - \frac{1}{2}\right)}{100} = \frac{P \times 4 \times T}{100}$$

$$\Rightarrow \quad 5T - \frac{5}{2} = 4T$$

$$\therefore \quad T = \frac{5}{2} \text{ years}$$

$$\therefore \quad 1100 = P\left(1 + \frac{4 \times \frac{5}{2}}{100}\right) = P\left(\frac{110}{100}\right)$$

$$\therefore \quad P = ₹\,1000$$

13. $\left(1 + \frac{3}{100}\right)^2 = 1.0609$

$\therefore$ Effective annual rate = 6.09%

14. Let cash price be ₹P

$$\therefore \quad 26.56 = P + \frac{P \times 12.5 \times 0.5}{100}$$

$$\Rightarrow \quad P \approx ₹\,25.$$

15. Let R be the rate of interest.

$$\text{Discount} = \frac{9000 \times R}{100}$$

$$\text{Interest} = \frac{3000 \times R \times T}{100}$$

By the given information:

$$\frac{9000 \times R}{100} = \frac{3000 \times R \times T}{100}$$

$$\Rightarrow \quad T = \frac{1}{3} \text{ years} = 4 \text{ months.}$$

16. Let N be the number of years

$$\therefore \quad R\% = \sqrt{N \times 12}$$

$$\Rightarrow \quad 48 = \frac{900 \times \sqrt{12N} \times N}{100}$$

Squaring both sides

$$N^2 = \frac{48 \times 48}{9 \times 9 \times 12} = \frac{16 \times 4}{9 \times 3} = \frac{64}{27}$$

$$\therefore \quad R = \sqrt{12 \times \frac{4}{3}} = 4\%$$

$$\therefore \quad 48 = \frac{P \times 4 \times 2}{100}$$

$$\Rightarrow \quad P = ₹\,600$$

17. Let first discount be x%

$$\therefore \quad \frac{(100-20)}{100} \times \frac{100-x}{100} \times 2500 = 1500$$

$$\Rightarrow \quad \frac{80}{100} \times \frac{100-x}{100} \times 2500 = 1500$$

$$\Rightarrow \quad 100 - x = \frac{1500 \times 100 \times 100}{80 \times 2500}$$

$$\Rightarrow \quad 100 - x = 75;$$

$$\Rightarrow \quad x = 25$$

Alternatively,

$$\text{Successive discount} = \left(a + b - \frac{ab}{100}\right)\%$$

$$\therefore \quad \left(\frac{2500-1500}{2500}\right) \times 100 = a + 20 - \frac{20a}{100}$$

$$\Rightarrow \quad \frac{1000}{2500} \times 100 = a + 20 - \frac{a}{5}$$

$$\Rightarrow \quad 40 - 20 = a - 0.2a$$

$$\Rightarrow \quad a = \frac{20}{0.8} = 25\%$$

18. Let there be n number of balls in each packet.

$$\therefore \quad 6n \times 8 = CP + 96$$

$$\Rightarrow \quad 48n = CP + 96 \quad \ldots(i)$$

Also, $6(n-1) \times 9 = CP + 90$

$$\Rightarrow \quad 54n - 54 = CP + 90$$

$$\Rightarrow \quad 54n = CP + 144 \quad \ldots(ii)$$

Solving equations (*i*) and (*ii*), we get,

$$n = 8$$

$$\therefore \quad CP = 48 \times 8 - 96 = 384 - 96 = ₹\,288$$

Each packet cost = ₹48.

19. CP of the merchant who calculates his % profit on

$$CP = \frac{3760}{1.175} = ₹\,3200$$

$$\therefore \quad \text{His profit} = 0.175 \times 3760 = ₹\,560$$

Profit of the merchant who calculates his % profit on SP

$$= 0.175 \times 3760 = ₹\,658$$

$\therefore$ Difference in profit = 658 – 560 = ₹ 98.

20. Let CP be ₹ x

$\therefore$ MP = 1.8x

SP of 15 articles = 12 × 1.8x = 21.6x

$\therefore$ Discount = 0.9 × 21.6x = 19.44x

$\therefore$ Profit on 15 articles = (19.44 – 15)x = 4.44x

$$\therefore \text{ Profit \%} = \frac{4.44x}{15x} \times 100 = 29.6\%.$$

21. C.P. of goods for the trader = ₹ 22520

$$\text{S.P.} = \frac{125 \times 22520}{100} = ₹\ 28150$$

$\therefore$ Profit = ₹ 5630

Now, $5630 = 0.0536 \times 5000 + 0.085 \times 10000 + \frac{x}{100} \times 7520$

$\Rightarrow$ 5630 = 268 + 850 + 75.2x

$\Rightarrow$ 75.2x = ₹ 4512,

Which is nothing but profit from sale of third lot.

22. A's Monthly Equivalent Rent = 22 × 4

B's Monthly Equivalent Rent = 16 × 8

C's Monthly Equivalent Rent = 32 × 6

$$\frac{\text{B's Monthly Equivalent Rent}}{\text{C's Monthly Equivalent Rent}} = \frac{\text{Rent paid by B}}{\text{Rent paid by C}}$$

$$\text{Rent paid by B} = \frac{16 \times 8}{32 \times 6} \times 600 = ₹\ 400$$

Similarly, rent paid by A

$$= \frac{22 \times 4 \times 600}{32 \times 6} = ₹\ 275$$

$\therefore$ Total rent = 400 + 600 + 275 = ₹1275

23. Rate in which the rent is to be divided = 4 : 8 : 12

$\therefore$ Akbar's share of rent

$$= \frac{8}{24} \times 6000$$

= ₹ 2000.

24. 85% of the total profit is divided in the ratio 2 : 10 : 5.

85% of total profit = 2x + 10x + 5x = 17x

$$\text{Total profit} = \frac{17x}{85\%} = 20x$$

$\therefore$ Share of Ram in the profit

= 2x + 15% of 20x

= 2x + 3x = 5x

Share of Shyam in the profit = 10x

Share of Ghanshyam in the profit = 5x

Now, (10x + 5x) – 5x = 500

$\Rightarrow$ 10x = 500

$\Rightarrow$ x = 50

$\therefore$ Total profit = 20 × 50 = ₹ 1000.

25. Let capital invested be C.

Monthly Equivalent Investment of

$$x = \frac{C}{3} \times \frac{T}{4}$$

Monthly Equivalent Investment of

$$y = \frac{C}{4} \times \frac{T}{2}$$

Monthly Equivalent Investment of

$$z = \frac{5C}{12} \times T$$

$\therefore$ Profit is to be shared in the ratio

$$\frac{CT}{12} : \frac{CT}{8} : \frac{5CT}{12}$$

i.e., 2 : 3 : 10

$\therefore$ Share of x in the profit

$$= \frac{2}{15} \times 3600 = ₹\ 480$$

EXERCISE – II

MCQ TYPE QUESTIONS

1. $A = P\left[1 + \frac{r}{100}\right]^t$

$$10 \text{ million} = 5 \text{ million}\left[1 + \frac{20}{100}\right]^t$$

$$2 = \left[1 + \frac{1}{5}\right]^t$$

$$2 = \left(\frac{6}{5}\right)^t = \log 2 = t \log\left(\frac{6}{5}\right)$$

$$0.301 = t\ 0.0791$$

$$t = \frac{0.301}{0.0791} = 3.8 \text{ years}$$

$\therefore$ Hence around 3–4 years would it take to double the growth rate

2. Let number of people in country y = 100

So, number of people in country x = 300

Total number of people taller than 6ft in both the countries $= 300 \times \frac{1}{100} + 100 \times \frac{2}{100} = 5$

% of people taller than 6ft in both the countries

$$= \frac{5}{400} \times 100 = 1.25\%.$$

4. Per ₹ 100 final value ₹ 107

$\Rightarrow$ per $\frac{100}{50}$ Dollars final value $\frac{107}{60}$

for 100 dollars ______?

$$= \frac{100 \times 50}{100} \times \frac{107}{60} = 89.16$$

Descreased by 11%

6.

	X	Y
Supply	60%	40%
Reliable	96%	72%
Overall	0.576	0.288

$$\therefore \quad P(x) = \frac{0.288}{0.576 + 0.288} = 0.334$$

7.

P	Q
40%	60%
–6%	+6%
+15%	–15%
49%	51%

$\therefore \quad 2\% = 2 \quad \Rightarrow \quad 100\% = 100$

NUMERICAL TYPE QUESTION

1. 90% of area of sheet = Cross sectional area of cone

$\Rightarrow 0.9 \times \pi \times 30 \times 30 = \pi \times r_1 \times 30$

($\because$ Slant height of cone (l) = 30)

$\Rightarrow 27 \text{ cm} = r_1$

$\therefore$ Height of the cone = $\sqrt{30^2 - 27^2} = 13.08$ cm

Hence ratio of radius and height is 2.06.

3 CHAPTER

Time and Work

TIME, SPEED AND DISTANCE

Speed.

Speed of a body is defined as the distance covered by it in unit time.

$$\text{Speed} = \frac{\text{Distance}}{\text{Time}}$$

Average Speed: If a body travels $d_1, d_2, d_3 \ldots d_n$ distances, with speeds $s_1, s_2, s_3 \ldots s_n$ in time $t_1, t_2, t_3 \ldots t_n$ respectively, then average speed of the body through the total distance is given by

$$\text{Average Speed} = \frac{\text{Total distance travelled}}{\text{Total time taken}}$$

$$= \frac{d_1 + d_2 + d_3 + \ldots d_n}{t_1 + t_2 + t_3 + \ldots t_n}$$

$$= \frac{s_1t_1 + s_2t_2 + s_3t_3 + \ldots + s_nt_n}{t_1 + t_2 + t_3 + \ldots + t_n}$$

$$= \frac{d_1 + d_2 + d_3 + \ldots + d_n}{\frac{d_1}{s_1} + \frac{d_2}{s_2} + \frac{d_3}{s_3} + \ldots + \frac{d_n}{s_n}}$$

Some Important Points:

(1) If a body covers the distance d_1 and d_2 at a speed of s_1 and s_2 km/hr, respectively, in time t_1 and d_2, then

Total time taken, $\quad T = t_1 + t_2 = \frac{d_1}{s_1} + \frac{d_2}{s_2}$.

Total distance covered, $\quad d = d_1 + d_2 = s_1t_1 + s_2t_2$.

(2) While travelling a certain distance d, if a man changes his speed in the ratio m: n, then ratio of time taken becomes n : m.

(3) If a certain distance (d), say from A to B, is covered at 'a' km/hr and same distance is covered again say from B to A in 'b' km/hr, then average speed during the whole journey is given by

$$\text{Average speed} = \left(\frac{2ab}{a+b}\right)\frac{\text{km}}{\text{hr}} \ldots.$$

(which is harmonic mean of a and b)

Also, if t_1 and t_2 is taken to travel from A to B and B to A respectively, then distance 'd' from A to B is given by

$$d = (t_1 + t_2)\left(\frac{ab}{a+b}\right);\; d = (t_1 - t_2)\left(\frac{ab}{a-b}\right);$$

$$d = (a-b)\left(\frac{t_1t_2}{t_1 - t_2}\right)$$

(4) If a body travels a distance 'd' from A to B with speed 'a' in time t_1 and travels back from B to A i.e., same distance with $\frac{m}{n}$ of the usual speed 'a', then change in time taken to cover the same distance is given by

$$\text{Change in time} = \left(\frac{n}{m} - 1\right) \times t_1;\text{ for } n > m$$

$$= \left(1 - \frac{n}{m}\right) \times t_1;\text{ for } m > n$$

(5) If two persons A and B start at the same time in opposite directions from two points and meet at any point in 'a' and 'b' hr, respectively after having met, then,

$$\frac{\text{A's Speed}}{\text{B's Speed}} = \frac{\sqrt{b}}{\sqrt{a}}$$

Relative speed.

(1) Time taken by a moving object 'x' meters long in passing a stationary object of negligible length from the time they meet is same as the time taken by the moving object to cover 'x' meters with its own speed.

(2) Time taken by a moving object 'x' meters long in passing a stationary object 'y' meters long from the time they meet, is same as the time taken by the moving object to cover 'x + y' meters with its own speed.

(3) If two objects of length 'x' and 'y' meters move in the same direction at 'a' and 'b' m/s, then time taken to cross each other from the time they meet

$$= \frac{\text{Sum of their length}}{\text{Relative speed}}$$

i.e., $\frac{x+y}{a-b}$ if $a > b$ or else, $\frac{x+y}{b-a}$

(4) If two objects of length 'x' and 'y' meters, move in the opposite direction at 'a' and 'b' m/s, then time taken to cross each other from the time they meet

$$= \frac{\text{Sum of their length}}{\text{Relative speed}} = \frac{x+y}{a+b}$$

(5) If speed of a boat in still water is x km/hr and speed of the stream is y km/hr, then

Relative speed while travelling with the stream i.e., speed downstream = (x + y) km/hr.

Relative speed while travelling against the stream i.e., speed upstream = (x – y) km/hr.

(6) Also speed of the boat in still water = $\frac{1}{2}$ (Speed with stream + Speed against stream)

Speed of the river = $\frac{1}{2}$ (Speed with stream – Speed against stream)

RACES

Some Important Points:

(1) 'A gives B a start of x meters', implies that, if distance between starting point and finishing point is L meters, then A covers L meters while B covers L – x metres.

e.g., In a 100 metre race. A gives B a start of 10 metres means, while A runs 100 metres, B runs 100 –10 = 90 metres.

(2) '*A beats B by x metres*', implies that, if distance between starting point and finishing point is L meters, then A wins the race by covering L metres, while B covers L – x metres only.

(3) 'A gives B a start of t seconds', implies that A starts the race t seconds after B starts from the starting point.

(4) '*A beats B by t seconds*', implies that, A and B start together from the starting point, but A reaches the finishing point t seconds before B finishes.

Note: (*iii*) and (*iv*) both imply that B takes t seconds more than A to finish the distance.

(5) A beats B by 'x' metres or 't' seconds means, B runs 'x' metres in 't' seconds.

(6) Winner's distance = Length of the race.

(7) Distance covered by loser = Winner's distance – (Beat distance + Start distance)

(8) Time taken by winner = Time taken by loser – (Beat time + Start time)

(9) $\frac{\text{Winner's Time}}{\text{Loser's Distance}} = \frac{\text{Loser's time}}{\text{Winner's distance}}$

$$= \frac{\text{Beat time + Start time}}{\text{Beat distance + Start distance}}$$

(10) If a race ends in a dead heat, then beat time = 0 and beat distance = 0.

(11) Two persons staring at the same time and from the same point along a circular path will be together again for the first time. When faster gains one complete round over the other, then time taken by faster person to complete one round over the other

$$= \frac{\text{Length of race course}}{\text{Relative Speed}}$$

(12) Two persons, starting at the same time from the same point along a circular path, will be together again for the first time at the same starting point, at a time which is LCM of the time taken by each to complete a round.

(13) Three persons, staring at the same time and from the same point along a circular path, will be together for the first time after the start at a time which is equal to LCM of the time taken by the fastest to gain a complete round over each of the other two.

(14) A overtakes B $\frac{1}{n}$ th of xth round means, when A has completed $\left(x - \frac{1}{n}\right)$ rounds, B has completed $\left[(x-1) - \frac{1}{n}\right]$ round.

Also, $\frac{\text{A's Speed}}{\text{B's Speed}}$

$$= \frac{\text{Rounds completed by A in a given time}}{\text{Rounds completed by B in the same time}}$$

e.g., A overtakes B in the middle of the 4th round implies, when A has completed $3\frac{1}{2}$ rounds, B has completed $2\frac{1}{2}$ rounds. 2 $\frac{\text{A's Speed}}{\text{B's Speed}} = \frac{3\frac{1}{2}}{2\frac{1}{2}}$

WORK

Some Important Points:

(1) If a can do a work in 'a' number of days, then in one day $\frac{1}{a}^{th}$ work is done.

Conversely, if a man does $\frac{1}{a}^{th}$ of a work in 1 day, then he can complete the work in $1 \div \frac{1}{a}$ = a days.

(2) If A is 'x' time as good a workman as B, then he will take $\frac{1}{x}^{th}$ of the time taken by B to do the same work.

(3) If A and B can do a piece of work in 'x' and 'y' days respectively. then working together, they will take $\frac{xy}{x+y}$ days to finish the work and in one day. They finish $\left(\frac{x+y}{xy}\right)^{th}$ part of the work.

(4) To compare the work done by different people, first find the amount of work each can do in the same time.

(5) If number of men to do a job is changed in the ratio a : b, then time required to do the work will be in the ratio b : a, assuming amount of work done by each of them in the given time is the same, or they are identical.

(6) If two men A and B together can finish a job in 'x' days and if A working alone takes 'a' days more than A and B working together and B working alone takes 'b' days more than A and B working together, then $x = \sqrt{ab}$.

(7) To do a piece of work, the number of men employed and the number of days required to do the work are in inverse proportion. Also, the number of men employed and the hours worked per day are in inverse proportion.

PIPES AND CISTERNS

A pipe connected with a cistern is called an *inlet*, if it fills the cistern.

A pipe connected with a cistern is called an *outlet*, if it empties the cistern.

filling or emptying a cistern can be considered as work done.

Some Important Points:

(1) If an inlet pipe fills a cistern in 'a' hours, then $\frac{1}{a}^{th}$ part is emptied in 1 hour.
Similary, if an outlet pipe empties a cistern in 'a' hours, then $\frac{1}{a}^{th}$ part is emptied in 1 hour.

(2) If pipe A is 'x' times bigger than pipe B, then pipe A will take $\frac{1}{x}^{th}$ of the time taken by pipe B to fill the cistern.

(3) If A and B fill a cistern in 'm' and 'n' hours, respectively, then together they will take $\frac{mn}{m+n}$ hours to fill the cistern and in one hour $\frac{m+n}{mn}^{th}$ part of the cistern will be filled.

Similarly, 'A' and 'B' empty a cistern in 'm' and 'n' hours respectively, then, together they will take $\frac{mn}{m+n}^{th}$ hours to empty the cistern and in one hour $\frac{m+n}{mn}^{th}$ part of the cistern will be empty.

(4) If an inlet pipe fills a cistern in 'm' hours and an outlet pipe empties the cistern in 'n' hours, then the net part filled in 1 hour when both the pipes are opened is $\left(\frac{1}{m}-\frac{1}{n}\right)$ i.e., $\frac{n-m}{mn}$ and the cistern will get filled in $\left(\frac{mn}{n-m}\right)$ hours.

For the cistern to get filled, m < n. If m > n, the cistern will never get filled.

In general,

Net part filled of a cistern = (Sum of work done by inlets) – (Sum of work done by outlets)

(5) If an inlet pipe fills a cistern in 'a' minutes, takes 'x' minutes longer to fill the cistern due to a leak in the cistern, then the time in which the leak will empty the cistern is given by $a \times \left(1+\frac{a}{x}\right)$.

(6) If two pipes A and B can fill a cistern in 'x' minutes and if A alone can fill it in 'a' minutes more than 'x' minutes and B alone can fill it in 'b' minutes more than 'x' minutes, then $x = \sqrt{ab}$.

EXERCISE – I

MCQ TYPE QUESTIONS

1. A barrel full of beer has 2 taps, one midway which draws a litre in 6 minutes and the other at the bottom which draws a litre in 4 minutes. The lower tap is normally used after the level of beer in the barrel is lower than midway. The capacity of the barrel is 36 litres. A new assistant opens the lower tap when the barrel is full and draws out some beer. As a result the lower tap has been used 24 minutes before the usual time. For how long was the beer drawn out by the new assistant?
(*a*) 10 mins. (*b*) 8 mins.
(*c*) 16 mins. (*d*) 32 mins.

2. Pipe A can fill a cistern in 36 minutes and B in 48 minutes. If both the pipes are opened together, when should pipe B be closed so that the cistern may be just full in 24 minutes?
(*a*) 8 mins. (*b*) 9 mins.
(*c*) 12 mins. (*d*) 16 mins.

3. Pipes P, Q and R are attached to a tank and each can act as either an inlet or outlet pipe. Pipes P, Q and R respectively take 8, 10 and 12 hours to fill the empty tank or empty the full tank. In the first hour, pipes P and R work as inlet and Q work as outlet. In the second hour, pipes P and Q work as inlet and pipe R as outlet. In the third hour pipes Q and R work as inlet and pipe P as outlet and the process goes on like this. When will the cistern be filled?
(*a*) In the 8th hour. (*b*) In the 9th hour.
(*c*) In the 10th hour. (*d*) In the 11th hour.

4. There are 2 inlet pipes and an outlet pipe. The efficiency of one of the inlet pipes is double than that of the other. Also, the efficiency of the outlet pipe is half that of the lesser efficient inlet pipe. The empty tank gets filled in 16 hours when all the pipes are opened. How many hours will be taken to fill the empty tank when the 'lesser' efficiency inlet pipe is plugged and the rest kept opened?
(*a*) $33\frac{1}{3}$ hours (*b*) $26\frac{2}{3}$ hours
(*c*) 100 hours (*d*) 80 hours

5. A train overtakes 2 persons walking at 2 km/hr and 4 km/hr respectively in the same direction and completely passes them in 9 seconds and 10 seconds. Length of the train and its speed in km/hr respectively are

(*a*) 75 m, 18 km/hr (*b*) 80 m, 21 km/hr
(*c*) 60 m, 20 km/hr (*d*) 50 m, 22 km/hr

6. A policeman goes after a thief who has a 100 m start. The policeman runs 1 km. in 6 mins. and the thief 1 km in 10 mins. How far did the thief go before he was overtaken?

(*a*) 100 m (*b*) 125 m
(*c*) 150 m (*d*) 250 m

7. Everyday Sachin exercises for $2\frac{1}{2}$ hours. He exercises by walking, jogging and running. His speeds while walking, jogging and running in the ratio 1 : 2 : 4. Which of the following statements are true?

I. If he spends equal time on the three activities, then he runs twice the distance that he jogs.

II. If he runs at 8 km per hour and distance covered by running and jogging together is 12 km, then he walks a distance of 1 km in 1 hour.

III. If the time for which he walks, jogs and runs is in the ratio 2 : 2 : 1 and he covers a total distance of 10 km, then his speeds while walking, jogging and running are 2 km/hr, 4 km/hr and 8 km/hr res-pectively.

Codes:

(*a*) I and II (*b*) II and III
(*c*) I and III (*d*) I, II and III

8. A monkey climbing up a greased pole ascends 10 metres and slips down 2 metres in alternate minutes. If the pole is 64 metres high, how long will it take him to reach the top?

(*a*) 16 min
(*b*) 14 min and 48 sec
(*c*) 12 min
(*d*) 14 min

9. A train travelling at 10 m/sec from A to B at 7 a.m. meets a train leaving B at 7:20 a.m. and coming to A at a speed $\frac{1}{3}$ times faster than the first train. If the distance from A to B is 68 km. then, at what distance from A will the two trains meet?

(*a*) 72 km (*b*) 36 km
(*c*) 60 km (*d*) 50 km

10. Two trains A and B start from stations X and Y towards each other. B leaves station Y half an hour after train A leaves station X. Two hours after train A has started, the distance between trains A and B is $\frac{19}{30}$th of the distance between stations X and Y. How much time would it take each train (A and B) to cover the distance X to Y, if train A reaches half an hour later to its destination as compared to B?

(*a*) 8 hrs, 6 hrs (*b*) 5 hrs, 4 hrs
(*c*) 10 hrs, 9 hrs (*d*) 9 hrs, 8 hrs

11. Two men, A and B, run a 4 km race on a circular course of $\frac{1}{4}$ km. If their speeds are in the ratio of 5 : 4, how often does the winner pass the other?

(*a*) Once (*b*) Twice
(*c*) Thrice (*d*) Four times

12. A and B start from the same point to run in opposite directions round a circular path 550 yards in length, A giving B a start of 100 yards. They pass each other when A has run 250 yards. Who will come first to the starting point and at what distance will they be apart?

(*a*) A, 20 yards (*b*) B, 10 yards
(*c*) B, 20 yards (*d*) A, 10 yards

13. Two runners run in the same direction along a circular track 2 km long. The faster runner overtakes the slower one every 30 minutes. What are their speeds, if faster one completes a round one minute sooner than the other?

(*a*) 24 km/hr and 20 km/hr
(*b*) 44 km/hr and 28 km/hr
(*c*) 20 km/hr and 18 km/hr
(*d*) 20 km/hr and 16 km/hr

14. To do certain work alone 'A' takes 4 hrs, 'B' takes 5 hrs and 'C' takes 6 hrs. How long would A and B together take to do a work which C can do in $4\frac{1}{2}$ hrs.?

(*a*) 2 hrs 10 mins. (*b*) 2 hrs 30 mins.
(*c*) 1 hr 20 mins. (*d*) 1 hr 40 mins.

15. A can do piece of work in 8 days which B and C can do in 12 and 16 days respectively. If they work on alternate days, then which of the following is true?

(*a*) If A started the work on the first day followed by B and c, then the work will be finished on the 10th day.

(*b*) If B started the work on the first day followed by C and A, then the work will be finished on the 11th day.

(*c*) If C started the work on the first day followed by A and B, then the work will be finished on the 11th day.

(*d*) None of these

NUMERICAL TYPE QUESTIONS

1. Meera paints walls for a living. She sometimes has Ashok to work with her. Meera takes 2 days to paint a 10 ft by 10 ft wall. Ashok takes 3 days to do the same job. Meera has to pay Ashok for his work on a per day basis, so she'd rather do without him. Meera has recently got a contract to paint the walls and ceiling of a room of dimensions 10 ft by 15 ft and a height of 10 ft. She had promised to do the job within 9 days. The ______ number of days does she need to employ Ashok?

2. 3 pipes can fill a reservoir in 10, 15 and 20 hours respectively. If the three taps are opened one after another in the given order, with a certain fixed time gap between them, the reservoir fills in 5 hours. The time gap will be _____ hr.

3. Two pipes A and B can fill a tank in 8 hours. If only pipe A is open, then it would take 4 hours longer to fill the tank. The_______hours it would take if only pipe B is open.

Directions (Q.4 – 5): *Refer to the data below and answer the questions that follow.*

The boiler tank in a chemical factory holds 10^5 litres. 5 tanks each having one-fifth the capacity of the boiler tank fill in 'hard water' at same rates in the boiler tank in 2 hours. The outlet of the two of smaller tanks work as inlet pipes and other two work as outlet and the fifth tank fill in the main 'boiler' at half its efficiency.

4. The number of hours taken to fill in the main boiler when all the pipes are opened at once is ________

5. Only three pipes are working, two at their full efficiency and the third one with half of its efficiency and all three are acting as an inlet. If all the three are opened alternately with the latter pipe being first to be opened to fill the boiler such that each smaller tank fills 'hard water' in the main boiler for equal time, then number of hours taken to fill the boiler to half its capacity is______

6. A contract is to be completed in 46 days and 117 men were set to work, each working 8 hours a day. After 33 days, 4/7 of the work is completed. The _______ number of additional men may be employed so that the work may be completed in time, each man now working 9 hours a day?

7. A train travelling at 42 km/hr. passes a cyclist going in the same direction in 9 secs.; if cyclist had been going in the opposite direction, the train would have passed him in 5 secs. Length of the train is______ metres

8. A man rows upstream 13 km. and downstream 28 km. taking 5 hrs. each time. Velocity of the current in km/hr_______ is

Directions (Q. 9 – 11): *Refer to the data below and answer the questions that follow.*

The variation in the speed of a car on a particular day at the respective times is shown in the table below:

s(km/hr)	t(hr)
0	11.00 am
40	11.30 am
50	1.00 pm
85	1.30 pm
10	3.30 pm
10	4.30 pm

9. The distance travelled by the car from 11 a.m. to 1 p.m. is _______km

10. If car maintains the speed it has at 4.30 p.m. then at _______ time will the car cover the same distance as it had covered from 11.00 a.m. to 1.00 p.m.?

11. Average speed of the car from 11.00 a.m. to 4.30 p.m. is_______kmph

12. A cheetah chase a deer which is 100 m ahead. The time in which the deer takes 10 leaps the cheetah takes only 6 leaps. In one leap, the deer covers 1 m while the cheetah covers 2 m. In ______ leaps would the cheetah catch up the deer.

13. A hare pursued by a hound who is 50 of her own leaps before him. When the hare takes 4 leaps, the hound takes 3. In one leap, the hare goes $1\frac{3}{4}$ metres and the hound $2\frac{3}{4}$ metres. In how _______ leaps will the hound overtake the hare.

Directions (Q. 14 – 15): *Refer to the graph below and answer the questions that follow.*

The engine of the new car Palio brought by Fiat in the market follows certain mileage characteristics as shown in the diagram below:

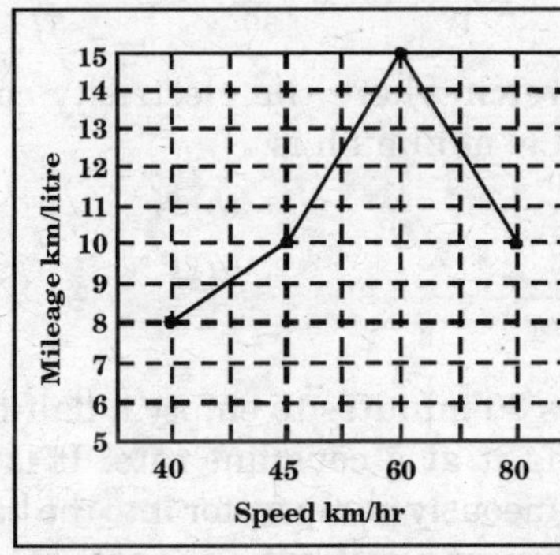

Vijay bought the new car Palio and filled exactly 10 litres in his car. He goes at a speed of 40 km/hr for first 20 km and then at a speed of 60 km/hr for next 60 km and driving at a constant speed reaches his destination which was 115 km away from his starting point.

14. The time in hours taken by Vijay if he reaches his destination in minimum possible time and finishes all the fuel.

15. In the above question, if Vijay had travelled at a constant average speed rather than changing his speed, taking the same minimum time, then the approximate saving in the fuel consumed is ______ litres

16. In a 2 km race on a circular course of $\frac{1}{4}$ of a km. A overlaps B in the middle of his 6th round. Then______ distance (in km) will A win at the same rate of running

17. A runs $1\frac{3}{8}$ times faster than B. A gives B a start of 120 metres. _______ metre must the winning post be so that it may be a dead heat.

18. The work done by a man, a woman and a child is in the ratio of 3 : 2 : 1. There are 20 men, 30 women and 36 children in a factory. Their weekly wages amount of ₹ 780, which is divided in the ratio of work done by the men, women and children. The wages of 15 men, 21 women and 30 children for 2 weeks is ______

19. A can do a work in 6 days and B in 8 days. With the help of a boy, the three complete the work in 3 days and get ₹ 200. The boy's share in rupees, if the money is distributed in the ratio of the work done is ________

20. A can finish a job in 12 days and B when working at twice his efficiency finishes a job in 9 days. The ______ number of days will they take if they work for two days alternately working at their standard rate given that A starts first.

EXERCISE – II

(QUESTIONS FROM PREVIOUS GATE EXAMS)

MCQ TYPE QUESTIONS

2015

1. An electric bus has onboard instruments that report the total electricity consumed since the start of the trip as well as the total distance covered. During a single day of operation, the bus travels on stretches *M, N, O* and *P*, in that order. The cumulative distances travelled and the corresponding electricity consumption are shown in the table below.

Stretch	Comulative distance(km)	Electricity used (kWh)
M	20	12
N	45	25
O	75	45
P	100	57

The stretch where the electricity consumption per km is minimum is

(*a*) M (*b*) N

(*c*) O (*d*) P

2014

2. It takes 30 minutes to empty a half-full tank by draining it at a constant rate. It is decided to simultaneously pump water into the half-full tank while draining it. What is the rate at which water has to be pumped in so that it gets fully filled in 10 minutes?

(*a*) 4 times the draining rate

(*b*) 3 times the draining rate

(*c*) 2.5 times the draining rate

(*d*) 2 times the draining rate

2013

3. A tourist covers half of his journey by train at 60 km/h, half of the remainder by bus at 30 km/h and the rest by cycle at 10 km/h. The average speed of the tourist in km/h during his entire journey is

(*a*) 36

(*b*) 30

(*c*) 24

(*d*) 18

4. A car travels 8 km in the first quarter of an hour, 6 km in the second quarter and 16 km in the third quarter. The average speed of the car in km per hour over the entire journey is

(*a*) 30 (*b*) 36

(*c*) 40 (*d*) 24

2011

5. The fuel consumed by a motorcycle during a journey while traveling at various speeds is indicated in the graph below.

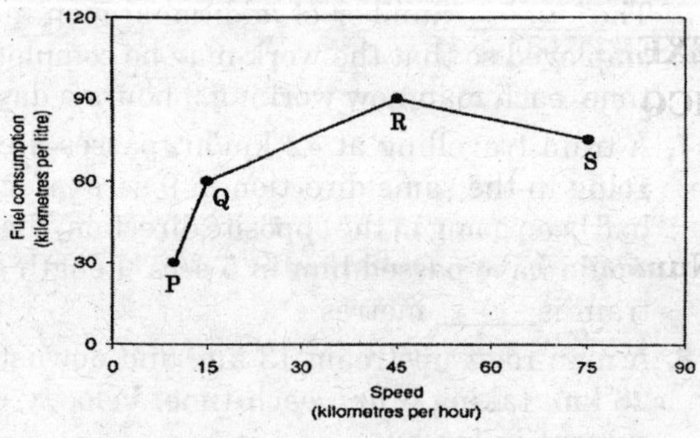

The distances covered during four laps of the journey are listed in the table below

Lap	Distance (kilometers)	Average speed (kilometers per hour)
P	15	15
Q	75	45
R	40	75
S	10	10

From the given data, we can conclude that the fuel consumed per kilometre was least during the lap

(*a*) P (*b*) Q

(*c*) R (*d*) S

2010

6. 5 skilled workers can build a wall in 20 days; 8 semi-skilled workers can build a wall in 25 days; 10 unskilled workers can build a wall in 30 days. If a team has 2 skilled, 6 semi-skilled and 5 unskilled workers, how long will it take to build the wall?

(*a*) 20 days (*b*) 18 days

(*c*) 16 days (*d*) 15 days

NUMERICAL TYPE QUESTIONS

2015

1. A tiger is 50 leaps of its own behind a deer. The tiger takes 5 leaps per minute to the deer's 4. If the tiger and the deer cover 8 metre and 5 metre per leap respectively, what distance in meters will the tiger have a run before it catches the deer?

2014

2. A man can row at 8 km per hour in still water. If it takes him thrice as long to row upstream, as to row downstream, then find the stream velocity in km per hour.

3. A train that is 280 metres long, travelling at a uniform speed, crosses a platform in 60 seconds and passes a man standing on the platform in 20 seconds. What is the length of the platform in metres?

ANSWERS

EXERCISE – I

MCQ Type Questions

1. (*c*) **2.** (*d*) **3.** (*c*) **4.** (*b*) **5.** (*d*) **6.** (*c*) **7.** (*c*) **8.** (*b*) **9.** (*b*) **10.** (*c*)
11. (*c*) **12.** (*d*) **13.** (*a*) **14.** (*d*) **15.** (*c*)

Numerical Type Qucstions

1. 6 **2.** $\frac{1}{2}$ **3.** 16 **4.** 20 **5.** 6 **6.** 81 **7.** 75 **8.** 1.5 **9.** 77.5

10. 12.15 a.m. **11.** 39.3 **12.** 300 **13.** 210 **14.** 2 **15.** $2\frac{1}{3}$ **16.** $\frac{4}{11}$ **17.** 440

18. 1170 **19.** 25 **20.** 14

EXERCISE – II

MCQ Type Questions

1. (*b*) **2.** (*a*) **3.** (*c*) **4.** (*c*) **5.** (*a*) **6.** (*d*)

Numerical Type Questions

1. (800) **2.** (4) **3.** (560 to 560)

EXPLANATIONS

EXERCISE – I

MCQ TYPE QUESTIONS

1. Top tap is operational till 18 litres is drawn out.

$\therefore$ Time after which the lower tap is usually open $= 18 \times 6 = 108$ minutes.

$\therefore$ Time after which it is open now $= 108 - 24 = 84$ minutes.

$\therefore$ Litres drawn $= \frac{84}{6} = 14$ litres

$\therefore$ $18 - 14 = 4$ litres were drawn by the new assistant.

$\therefore$ Time $= 4 \times 4 = 16$ minutes.

Alternatively

Upper tap was not used for 24 minutes.

$\therefore$ Litres drawn $= \frac{24}{6} = 4$ litres.

$\therefore$ Beer was drawn for $4 \times 4 = 16$ minutes.

2. Let pipe B be turned-off after x minutes.

Part filled in x minutes $= x\left(\frac{1}{36}+\frac{1}{48}\right) = \frac{7x}{144}$.

Part filled in 24 – x minutes $= \frac{24-x}{36}$

$$\therefore \quad \frac{7x}{144}+\frac{24-x}{36} = 1$$

$$\Rightarrow \quad \frac{7x+96-4x}{144} = 1$$

$$\Rightarrow \quad x = 16 \text{ minutes}$$

3. In a cycle of 3 hours : pipes P, Q and R are working as inlet pipes for 2 hours each and they are working as outlet pipes for an hour each. So part of tank filled in 3 hours.

$$= 2x\left(\frac{1}{8}+\frac{1}{10}+\frac{1}{12}\right)-\left(\frac{1}{8}+\frac{1}{10}+\frac{1}{12}\right)$$

$$= \frac{1}{8}+\frac{1}{10}+\frac{1}{12} = \frac{15+12+10}{120} = \frac{37}{120}$$

Hence they will take $\frac{120 \times 3}{37} = 9\frac{27}{37}$ hours.

Thus, tank will be filled in 10th hour.

4. Let number of hours taken by the outlet and the 2 inlet pipes be 4x, 2x and x respectively. So in 1 hour the part of empty tank filled is

$$\frac{1}{x}+\frac{1}{2x}-\frac{1}{4x} = \frac{1}{16}$$

$$\frac{5}{4x} = \frac{1}{16}$$

$$\Rightarrow \quad x = 20$$

Hence, inlet pipe with higher efficiency fills the tank in 20 hours.

So in one hour, the desired pipes fill

$$\frac{1}{x}-\frac{1}{4x} = \frac{3}{4x} \text{ th of the tank.}$$

Tank gets filled in

$$\frac{4x}{3} = \frac{80}{3} \text{ hours} = 26\frac{2}{3} \text{ hours.}$$

5. In each case, train has to travel its own length, to pass each man.

If x km/hr is speed of the train, then

$$\text{Length} = \text{Relative speed} \times \text{Time}$$

$$= (x-2) \times \frac{9}{60 \times 60}$$

$$= (x-4) \times \frac{10}{60 \times 60}$$

$$\therefore \quad 9x - 18 = 10x - 40$$

$$\Rightarrow \quad x = 22 \text{ km/hr.}$$

$$\therefore \quad \text{Length} = (22-2) \times \frac{9}{3600}$$

$$= \frac{20 \times 9}{3600} \text{ km} = 50 \text{ m.}$$

6. Policeman gains $= \frac{1}{6}-\frac{1}{10} = \frac{4}{60}$ km/min

$$= 66\frac{2}{3} \text{ m/min.}$$

Hence to gain 100 m, time required

$$= \frac{100}{66\frac{2}{3}} = 1\frac{1}{2} \text{ min.}$$

Hence thief has gone ahead by

$$1\frac{1}{2} \times \frac{1}{10} \times 1000 \text{ metres} = 150 \text{ m.}$$

7. I. Ratio of speed = 1 : 2 : 4

If equal time is spent on each of these, then ratio of distance = 1 : 2 : 4

So, Sachin runs twice the distance that he jogs.

Thus, I is true.

II. He runs at 8 km/hr and therefore walks at 2 km/hr.

Hence II is not true.

III. Ratio of speed = 1 : 2 : 4

Ratio of time = 2 : 2 : 1

Ratio of distance

$= 2 \times 1 : 2 \times 2 : 4 \times 1 = 2 : 4 : 4$

If Sachin covers a total distance of 10 km, then he

Walks for $\frac{2}{2+4+4} \times 10 = 2$ km,

Joggs for $\frac{4}{2+4+4} \times 10 = 4$ km.

Runs for $\frac{4}{2+4+4} \times 10 = 4$ km.

Total time taken is $2\frac{1}{2}$ hours = $\frac{5}{2}$ hours.

Thus, he walks for $\frac{2}{2+2+1} \times \frac{5}{2} = 1$ hour.

jogs for $\frac{2}{2+2+1} \times \frac{5}{2} = 1$ hour.

runs for $\frac{1}{2+2+1} \times \frac{5}{2} = \frac{1}{2}$ hour.

So speed while,

Walking = $\frac{2}{1} = 2$ km/hr

Jogging = $\frac{4}{1} = 4$ km/hr

Running = $\frac{4}{\frac{1}{2}} = 8$ km/hr.

Thus, III is true.

8. In 1 minute, monkey ascends 10 metres but he takes 1 minute to slip down 2 metres. Thus, at the end of 2 minutes, net ascending of the monkey is =10 – 2 = 8 metres.

Thus, to have a net ascending of 8 metres, process of ascending and then slipping happens once. So, to cover 64 metres, above process is repeated $\frac{64}{8}$ or 8 times.

It is clear that in 8 such happenings, the monkey will slip 7 times, because 8th time, he will ascend to the top. Thus, in climbing 7 times and slipping 7 times, he covers (7 × 8) or 56 metres.

Time taken to cover 56 metres

$$= \frac{56 \times 2}{8} = 14 \text{ minutes}$$

Remaining distance = 64 – 56 = 8 metres

Time taken to ascend 8 metres

$$= \frac{8}{10} \text{ min} = \frac{4}{5} \text{ min.}$$

Total time taken = 14 minutes + $\frac{4}{5}$ min

= 14 mins. 48 sec.

9. If they meet t hrs after 7 a.m,

$$10 \times \frac{18}{5} \times t + 10 \times \frac{18}{5} \times \frac{4}{3}\left(t - \frac{1}{3}\right) = 68$$

$$\Rightarrow \quad 36t + 48t - 16 = 68$$

$$\Rightarrow \quad t = 1 \text{ hr.}$$

They meet at a distance of

$$10 \times 60 \times 60 = 36000 \text{ m}$$

i.e., 36 km from A.

10. Two equations are

$$T_1 - T_2 = \frac{1}{2} + \frac{1}{2} = 1 \quad ...(i)$$

where T_1 and T_2 are time taken by trains A and B to cover the whole distance

and $$\frac{2}{T_1} + \frac{1.5}{T_2} = \frac{11}{30} \quad ...(ii)$$

Solving equations (*i*) and (*ii*) ,we get

$T_1 = 10$ hrs. and $T_2 = 9$ hrs.

11. When A runs 5 rounds, B runs 4 rounds (ratio of speeds)

∴ A passes B each time A has run 5 rounds or

$5 \times \frac{1}{4} = \frac{5}{4}$ km. = $1\frac{1}{4}$ km.

$1\frac{1}{4}$ km is contained in 4 km.

3 times.

Hence A passes B thrice.

12. When A has run 250 yards, B should have run

550 – 250 = 300 yards.

∴ B runs 300 – 100 = 200 yards in the same time taken by A to run 250 yards.

∴ Ratio of the speeds of A and B

= 250 : 200 = 5 : 4

If speed of A is 5x yards per minute, then speed at B = 4x yards/min.

Time taken by B to reach the starting point

$$= \frac{450}{4x} = \frac{112.5}{x} \text{ min.}$$

Time taken by A to reach the starting point

$$= \frac{550}{5x} = \frac{110}{x} \text{ min.}$$

∴ A wins by $\frac{2.5}{x}$ min

∴ Distance travelled by B in $\frac{2.5}{x}$ min.

$$= \left(\frac{2.5}{x}\right) \times (4x) = 10 \text{ yards}$$

Hence B is 10 yards behind A.

13. Let n_1 and n_2 be the speeds in km/hr and let n_1 be the greater speed i.e., $n_1 > n_2$.

$$\therefore \quad \frac{2}{n_2} = \frac{2}{n_1} + \frac{1}{60}.$$

$$\Rightarrow \quad n_1 n_2 = 120(n_1 - n_2)$$

Faster runner covers $(n_1 - n_2)$ km. more than the slower runner in 1 hour.
Hence to cover one round of 2 km, he will take $\frac{2}{n_1 - n_2}$ or $\frac{1}{2}$ hour.

$\therefore \quad \frac{2}{n_1 - n_2} = \frac{1}{2}$

$\Rightarrow \quad n_1 - n_2 = 4$

$\Rightarrow \quad n_1 = 4 + n_2$

$\Rightarrow \quad n_2(4 + n_2) = 120 \times 4$

$\Rightarrow \quad n_2^2 + 4n_2 - 480 = 0$

$\Rightarrow \quad n_2 = 20$ or -24 (rejected)

$\therefore \quad n_1 = 4 + n_2 = 24$ km/hr

Hence speeds are 24 km/hr and 20 km/hr

Alternatively

Options may also be substituted to find the result.

14. Work done by A and B in 1 hr

$= \frac{1}{4} + \frac{1}{5} = \frac{9}{20}^{th}$ part.

$\therefore$ Ratio of work done by (A + B)

and $\quad C = \frac{9}{20} : \frac{1}{6}$

$\therefore$ Ratio of time taken

$= \frac{1}{6} : \frac{9}{20} = 10 : 27$

If C takes 27 hrs. (A + B) will take 10 hrs.

If C takes $4\frac{1}{2}$ hrs. (A + B) will take

$\frac{10 \times 9}{2 \times 27} \cong 1$ hr. 40 mins.

15. I. Work done by A, B and C together in 3 days

$\frac{1}{8} + \frac{1}{12} + \frac{1}{16} = \frac{13}{48}$ th of the work.

Thus, in 9 days, total work done will be

$3 \times \frac{13}{48} = \frac{39}{48}$ th of the work

$\therefore$ Work remaining $= 1 - \frac{39}{48} = \frac{9}{48}$ th of the work is left of which A will finish $\frac{6}{48}$ th of work on 10th day and B will finish remaining work on 11th day.

Thus, I is false

II. Work done by A, B, C together in 9 days $= \frac{39}{48}$

Work left $= 1 - \frac{39}{48}$

$= \frac{9}{48}$ th of the whole.

On the 10th day B will finish $\frac{1}{12}$ th of the whole.

$\therefore \quad$ Work left $= \frac{9}{48} - \frac{1}{12}$

$= \frac{5}{48}$ th of the whole.

On 11th day C will finish $\frac{1}{16}$ th of the work

$\therefore \quad$ Work left $= \frac{5}{48} - \frac{1}{16}$

$= \frac{2}{48}$ th of the whole

which will be done by A on the 12th day. Thus, work will be finished on the 12th day. Thus, II is false.

III. Work done by A, B and C in 9 days $= \frac{39}{48}$

Work left after 9 days

$= 1 - \frac{39}{48} = \frac{9}{48}$ th of the whole.

On the tenth day $\frac{1}{16}$ th will be finished by C.

$\therefore \quad$ Work left $= \frac{9}{48} - \frac{1}{16}$

$= \frac{6}{48}$ th of the whole,

which will be finished by A on the eleventh day. Thus, III is true.

NUMERICAL TYPE QUESTIONS

1. Total area to be painted

$= 10 \times 15$ (ceiling) $+ 2 \times 10 \times 10$ (wall) $+ 2 \times 10 \times 15$ (wall)

$= 650$ sq.ft

In one day Meera can paint

$10 \times \frac{10}{2} = 50$ sq.ft

Ashok can paint

$10 \times \frac{10}{3} = \frac{100}{3}$ sq.ft,

So, together they can paint $\frac{250}{3}$ sq.ft per day.

Let number of days Ashok works be x.

Work done in 9 days $= 50(9 - x) + \frac{250}{3}x = 650$

$\therefore \quad 450 - 50x + \frac{250x}{3} = 650$

$\Rightarrow \quad \frac{100}{3}x = 200$

$\Rightarrow \quad x = 6$ days.

2. Let fixed interval be x

$\therefore \quad \frac{5}{10} + \frac{5-x}{15} + \frac{5-2x}{20} = 1$

$\Rightarrow \quad (5)6 + (5-x)4 + (5-2x)3 = 60$

$\Rightarrow \quad 30 + 20 - 4x + 15 - 6x = 60$

$\Rightarrow \quad x = \frac{1}{2}$ hour.

3. Let pipe B alone take b hours longer than if both A and B were open.

$8 = \sqrt{4 \times x}$

$\Rightarrow \quad 64 = 4 \times x$

$\Rightarrow \quad x = 16$ hours.

Alternatively

Part filled if both A and B are open $= \frac{1}{8}$

Part filled if only A is open $= \frac{1}{12}$

$\therefore$ Part filled if only B is open $= \frac{1}{8} - \frac{1}{12} = \frac{1}{24}$

$\therefore$ B alone would take 24 hours, i.e., B alone would take 24 – 8 = 16 hours longer to fill the tank.

4. Since 5 tanks of same efficiency fill the boiler in 2 hours each tank individually takes

$2 \times 5 = 10$ hours to fill it.

Tank with half the efficiency will take

$10 \times 2 = 20$ hours.

In one hour, fraction of boiler getting filled when 4 fully efficient pipes with two as inlet and two as outlet and 5th acts at 50% efficiency as an inlet is

$\frac{1}{10} + \frac{1}{10} + \frac{1}{20} - \frac{1}{10} - \frac{1}{10} = \frac{1}{20}$

Hence it will take 20 hours to fill the boiler tank.

5. Here fraction of tank filled in 1 hour

$\frac{1}{10} + \frac{1}{10} + \frac{1}{20} = \frac{5}{20} = \frac{1}{4}$th

of the tank. If they are opened alternately, then tank gets filled in $4 \times 3 = 12$ hours

Hence half of the tank gets filled in $\frac{12}{2} = 6$ hours.

6. 4/7 of work is completed.

Remaining work $= 1 - \frac{4}{7} = \frac{3}{7}$

Remaining period = 46 – 33 = 13 days

Less work, less men(direct proportion)

Less days, more men(Indirect proportion)

More hours/day, less men(Indirect proportion)

work 4/7 : 3/7

Days 13 : 33 :: 117 : x

hrs/day 9 : 8

$\frac{4}{7} \times 13 \times 9 \times x = \left(\frac{3}{7}\right) 33 \times 8 \times 117$

$x = (3 \times 33 \times 8 \times 117) / (4 \times 13 \times 9)$

$= 198$ men

So, additional men to be employed

$= 198 - 117 = 81$

7. Let L is length of train in km and x is speed of the cyclist, Then

(*i*) $\frac{3600}{9} L = 42 - x = 400L$

(*ii*) $\frac{3600}{5} L = 42 + x = 720 L$

On adding, we get

$1120 L = 84$

$\Rightarrow \quad L = \frac{84 \times 1000}{1120} = 75m$

8. $\frac{13}{\text{Speed upstream}} = 5$

and $\frac{28}{\text{Speed downstream}} = 5$

$\therefore$ Speed upstream $= \frac{13}{5}$ km/hr.

and Speed downstream $= \frac{28}{5}$ km/hr.

$\therefore$ Speed of river $= \frac{1}{2}\left(\frac{28}{5} - \frac{13}{5}\right)$

$= \frac{1}{2} \times \frac{15}{5} = 1.5$ km/hr

9. Graph of speed vs time is plotted as shown. Area under the graph and time axis gives the distance.

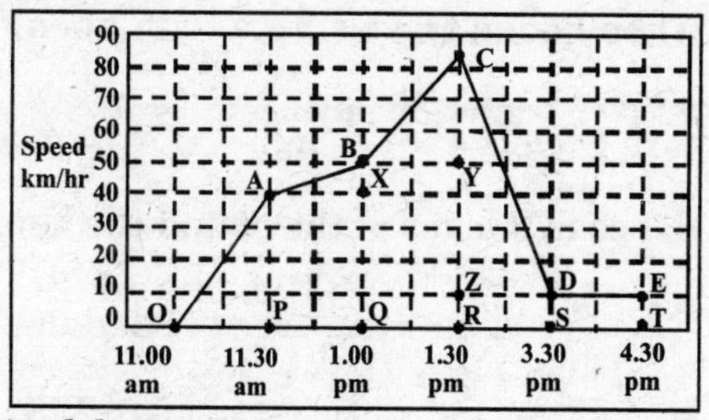

Required distance

$= A(\Delta\, OAP) + A(\Delta\, BXA) + A(\square\, APQX)$

$= \frac{1}{2} \times \left(\frac{1}{2}\right) \times 40 + \frac{1}{2} \times 10 \times \left(\frac{3}{2}\right) + \left(\frac{3}{2}\right) \times 40$

$= 10 + \frac{30}{4} + 60 = 77.5$ km.

10. Distance covered are the same.

Speed in the latter is maintained at 10 kmph.

$\therefore \quad 77.5 = 10 \times x$

$\Rightarrow \quad x = 7.75$ hours.

Hence, clock time will be 4.30 + 7 hours 45 mins

= 12.15 a.m.

11. Average speed = $\dfrac{\text{total distance travelled}}{\text{total time taken}}$

Distance travelled from 1.00 pm to 4.30 p.m.

= A(□BQRY) + A(ΔBYC) + A(ΔCZD) + A(□ZRTE)

$= 50 \times \left(\frac{1}{2}\right) + \left(\frac{1}{2}\right) \times \left(\frac{1}{2}\right) \times 35 + \frac{1}{2} \times (2) \times 75 + 3 \times 10$

$= \frac{50}{2} + \frac{35}{4} + 75 + 30$

= 130 + 8.75

= 138.75 km.

Total distance travelled = 77.5 + 138.75

= 216.25 km.

$\therefore$ Average speed = $\frac{216.25}{5.5}$ = 39.3 kmph.

12. While deer makes 10 leaps, cheetah makes 6 leaps.

$\therefore$ Distance covered in 10 leaps by deer

= 10 × 1 = 10m

Distance covered in 6 leaps by cheetah

= 6 × 2 = 12 m

Hence in six leaps, cheetah gains

12 – 10 = 2 m over the deer.

Cheetah has to gain 100 m over the deer.

So, total leaps required by cheetah

$= \frac{6}{2} \times 100 = 300.$

13. 50 leaps of the hare $50 \times 1\frac{3}{4} = \frac{175}{2} = 87.5$ m.

So, hound should gain $\frac{175}{2}$ m over the hare.

When hound travels $3 \times 2\frac{3}{4}$ m, then

hare travels $4 \times 1\frac{3}{4}$ m.

Hence in 3 leaps of the hound the hound gains

$\frac{33}{4} - \frac{28}{4} = \frac{5}{4}$ metres

$\therefore$ Number of leaps required $= \dfrac{\frac{175}{2}}{\frac{5}{4}} \times 3$

$= \frac{175}{2} \times \frac{4}{5} \times 3 = 210$ leaps.

14. Fuel required for first 20 km = $\frac{20}{8}$ = 2.5 litres.

Fuel required for next 60 km = $\frac{60}{15}$ = 4 litres.

$\therefore$ Petrol left = 10 – 6.5 = 3.5 litres.

Now, he has to travel = 115 – (60 + 20)

= 35 km in 3.5 litres.

So he can go at a speed of either 45 km/hr or 80 km/hr as mileage is 10 km/litre in both cases. But since he reaches in minimum time, he travels at 80 km/hr

$\therefore$ Time taken $= \frac{20}{40} + \frac{60}{60} + \frac{35}{80} = \frac{155}{80}$

$= 1 + \frac{75}{80}$ hours

= 1 hours 56 minutes and 25 seconds.

15. Total distance travelled = 115 km

Total time taken = $\frac{155}{80}$ hours

$\therefore$ Average speed = $\dfrac{115}{\frac{155}{80}}$ = 60 km/hr

$\therefore$ Fuel consumption = $\frac{115}{15} = 7\frac{2}{3}$ litres.

So, fuel saved = $10 - 7\frac{2}{3} = 2\frac{1}{3}$ litres.

16. A overlaps B in the middle of the 6th round

So, when A runs $5\frac{1}{2}$ rounds, B runs only $4\frac{1}{2}$ rounds.

$\therefore \quad \frac{\text{A's Speed}}{\text{B's Speed}} = \frac{5\frac{1}{2}}{4\frac{1}{2}} = \frac{11}{9}$

So when A runs 11 km B runs 9 km.

Thus, when A runs 2 km, B runs $2 \times \frac{9}{11} = \frac{18}{11}$ km.

$\therefore$ A wins by $\left(2 - \frac{18}{11}\right) = \frac{4}{11}$ km.

17. Speeds of A and B are as

$1\frac{3}{8} : 1 = \frac{11}{8} : 1 = 11 : 8$

In a race of 11 metres, A gain

11 – 8 = 3 metres over B.

To gain 120 metres, race must be of

$120 \times \frac{11}{3} = 440$ metres.

18.

	Work	Number
Men	3	20
Women	2	30
Children	1	36

Ratio of wages = (3 × 20) : (2 × 30) : (1 × 36)
= 5 : 5 : 3

Total wages of 20 men = $\frac{5}{13} \times 780 = ₹\ 300$

∴ Wages of a man = ₹ 15.

Similarly, wages of 30 women

$\frac{5}{13} \times 780 = ₹\ 300$

Wages of a woman = ₹ 10

Wages of 36 children $\frac{3}{13} \times 780 = ₹\ 180$

Wages of a child = ₹ 5

∴ Total wages of 15 men, 21 women and 30 children

= 15 × 15 + 21 × 10 + 30 × 5
= ₹ 585

∴ Total wages for 2 weeks = ₹ 1170.

19. Work done by A in 3 days

$= 3 \times \frac{1}{6} = \frac{1}{2}$ of the work.

Work done by B in 3 days

$= 3 \times \frac{1}{8} = \frac{3}{8}$ of the work.

∴ Work done by the boy in 3 days

$= 1 - \left(\frac{1}{2} + \frac{3}{8}\right)$

$= \frac{1}{8}$ of the work.

∴ Ratio of work done

$= \frac{1}{2} : \frac{3}{8} : \frac{1}{8} = 4 : 3 : 1$

∴ Boy's share = $\frac{1}{8} \times ₹\ 200 = ₹\ 25$.

20. A finishes the job at standard rate in 12 days,

So in 1 day, the part of job done by A = $\frac{1}{12}$

Similarly the part of job done by B in 1 day

$= \frac{1}{2 \times 9} = \frac{1}{18}$

If a works for 2 days followed by 2 days of B at standard rate.

Part of work done = $\frac{2}{12} + \frac{2}{18} = \frac{5}{18}$.

So, in (2 alternate days work of 'A' and 'B')

3 × 4 = 12 days

They will finish $3 \times \frac{5}{18} = \frac{15}{18}$th of the work.

Work remaining = $1 - \frac{15}{18} = \frac{3}{18} = \frac{1}{6}$

This is finished by A alone in $\frac{\frac{1}{6}}{12}$ = 2 days.

Hence, total number days = 12 + 2 = 14 days.

EXERCISE – II

MCQ TYPE QUESTIONS

1. For $M \Rightarrow \frac{12}{20} = 0.6$

$N \Rightarrow \frac{25}{45} = 0.55$

$O \Rightarrow \frac{45}{75} = 0.6$

$P \Rightarrow \frac{57}{100} = 0.57$

2. $V_{half} = 30(s)$ drawing rate = s

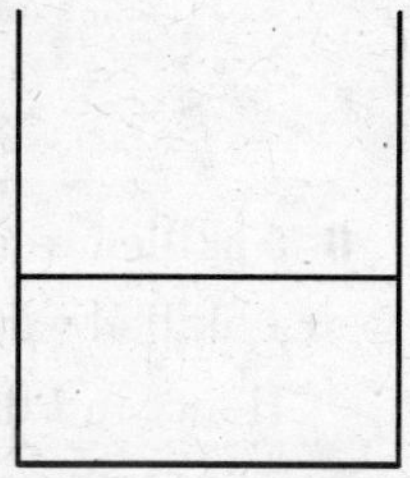

Total volume = 60 S tank

$(s^1)(10) - (s)10 = 30s$

$s^1(s) - s = 3s$

$s1 = 4s$

$s^1 = 4$ drawing rate

3. Given: A tourist covers half the journey at 60 km/h, one fourth at 30 km/h and the remaining one fourth at 10 km/h

To find: Avearge speed of the whole journey.

Analysis: One approach to this is to find individual time consumed in each of the three parts and use that value to get total time, and find average speed.

So,

Lets assume total length of journey = x km

∴ First phase at 60 km/h

Time $t_1 = \frac{\text{Distance}}{\text{Speed}} = \frac{x}{2}\frac{1}{60} = \frac{x}{120} h$

Second phase at 30 km/h

Distance = $\frac{x}{4}$ km

Time $t_2 = \frac{x}{4.30} = \frac{x}{120}$

Third phase at 10 km/h

Distance = $\frac{x}{4}$ km

Time $t_3 = \frac{x}{4.10} = \frac{x}{40} h$

$\therefore$ Total time $= \frac{x}{120}+\frac{x}{120}+\frac{x}{40} = \frac{x}{40}\left(\frac{1}{3}+\frac{1}{3}+1\right)$

$= \frac{x}{40}\frac{(1+1+3)}{3} = \frac{5x}{120}$

$\therefore$ Average speed $= \frac{\text{Total Distance}}{\text{Total time}}$

$= \frac{x \cdot 120}{5x} = 24$ km/h

Hence, the answer is (c)

4. Average Speed $= \frac{\text{Total distance}}{\text{total time taken}}$

Total Distance $= \frac{8+6+16}{15+15+15} = \frac{30 \times 60}{45}$

= 40km/h.

5.

	Fuel consumption	Actual
P	60 km/l	$\frac{15}{60} = \frac{1}{4}l$
Q	90 km/l	$\frac{75}{90} = \frac{5}{6}l$
R	75 km/l	$\frac{40}{75} = \frac{8}{15}l$
S	30 km/l	$\frac{10}{30} = \frac{1}{3}l$

6. 5 skilled workers build wall in 20 days

1 skilled worker build wall in 20 × 5 days

Hence in 1 day, part of work done by skilled work

$= \frac{1}{100}$

Similarly in 1 day part of work done by semi-skilled workers

$= \frac{1}{25 \times 8}$

and in 1 day part of work done by un-skilled worker

$= \frac{1}{30 \times 10}$

So part of work done in 1 day by 2 skilled, 6 semi-skilled and 5 unskilled

$= \frac{2}{100}+\frac{6}{200}+\frac{5}{300} = \frac{1}{15}$

So work done by given workers in days = 15

NUMERICAL TYPE QUESTIONS

1. Tiger – 1 leap ⇒ 8 meter

Speed = 5 leap/hr = 40m/min

Deer → 1 leap = 5 meter

speed = 4hr = 20m/min

Let at time 't' the tiger catches the deer.

$\therefore$ Distance travelled by deer + initial distance between them

50 × 8 ⇒ 400m = distance covered by tiger.

$\Rightarrow 40 \times t = 400 + 20t$

$\Rightarrow t = \frac{400}{200} = 20$ min

⇒ total distance ⇒ 400 + 20 × t = 800 m

2. Speed of man = 8;

Left distance = d

Time taken $= \frac{d}{8}$

Upstream: Speed of stream = s

⇒ speed upstream = S' = (8 – s)

$t' = \left(\frac{d}{8-s}\right)$

Downstream:

Given speed downstream = $t'' = \frac{d}{8+s}$

$\Rightarrow 3t' = t'' \Rightarrow \frac{3d}{8-s} = \frac{d}{8+s}$

$\Rightarrow \frac{3d}{8-s} = \frac{d}{8+s}$

$\Rightarrow$ s = 4 km/hr

3. Let the length of platform = x.m

and train length = 280 m (given)

According to Question

$\frac{x+280}{60} = \frac{280}{20}$

$\therefore$ $x = 560$ m.

4

CHAPTER

Ratio, Proportion and Mixtures

RATIO

Ratio of two terms 'a' and 'b' is denoted by a : b (read as 'a is to b') and is measured by $\frac{a}{b}$.

Numerator 'a' is called *'antecedent'* and denominator 'b' is called 'consequent'.

While comparing two quantities in terms of ratio :

(*i*) Two quantities must be of the same kind.

(*ii*) Units of measurement of the two quantities must be the same.

e.g., if a = ₹ 2 and b = 50 paise,

then a : b = 200 : 50 = 4 : 1.

(*iii*) Ratio is a pure number, i.e., without any unit of measurement as it denotes how many times a given quantity is in comparison to another.

(*iv*) Ratio would stay unaltered even if both antecedent and the consequent are multiplied or divided by the same number.

e.g., $a : b = \frac{a}{b} = \frac{a \times m}{b \times m} = \frac{\frac{a}{m}}{\frac{b}{m}}$.

Properties of Ratios

1. **Invertendo :** If $\frac{a}{b} = \frac{c}{d}$, then $\frac{b}{a} = \frac{d}{c}$ i.e., inverse ratios of two equal ratios are equal.

2. **Alternendo :** If $\frac{a}{b} = \frac{c}{d}$, then $\frac{a}{c} = \frac{b}{d}$ i.e., ratios of antecedents and consequents of two equal ratios are equal.

3. **Componendo :** If $\frac{a}{b} = \frac{c}{d}$, then $\frac{a+b}{b} = \frac{c+d}{d}$ i.e., adding 1 to both sides.

4. **Dividendo :** If $\frac{a}{b} = \frac{c}{d}$, then $\frac{a-b}{b} = \frac{c-d}{d}$ i.e., subtracting 1 from both sides.

5. **Componendo-Dividendo :** If $\frac{a}{b} = \frac{c}{d}$, then $\frac{a+b}{a-b} = \frac{c+d}{c-d}$ i.e., dividing results of componendo by dividend.

Equal Ratio : If $\frac{a}{b} = \frac{c}{d} = \frac{e}{f}$; then each ratio

$$= \frac{\text{Sum of Numerators}}{\text{Sum of Denominators}} = \frac{a+c+e...}{b+d+f...}$$

The principle can also be applied after multiplying Numerator and Denominator of any fraction by the same number.

If $\frac{a}{b} = \frac{c}{d} = \frac{e}{f} = ...$, then each ratio is equal to $\left(\frac{pa^n + qc^n + re^n + ...}{pb^n + qd^n + rf^n + ...}\right)^{1/n}$, where p, q, r, n ... may have any values except that they must not all be zeros.

PROPORTION

When ratio of two terms is equal to the ratio of two other terms, then these four terms are said to be in **proportion,** i.e., if a : b = c : d, then a, b, c and d are in proportion.

a, b, c and d are called first, second, third and fourth proportionals respectively. The terms a and d are called **extremes,** while b and c are called **means.**

If a : b = c : d, then ad = bc i.e., product of extremes is equal to product of means.

Continued Proportion

When $\frac{a}{b} = \frac{b}{c}$, then a, b and c are said to be in continued proportion and b is called *geometric mean* or *mean proportional* between a and c.

Also, $b^2 = a \times c$, $\Rightarrow$ $b = \sqrt{ac}$

If $\frac{a}{b} = \frac{b}{c} = \frac{c}{d} = \frac{d}{e} = ...$, then a, b, c, d, e ... are said to be in continued proportion.

Concept of continued proportion is useful in the following situation.

(*i*) If four quantities a, b, c and d and a : b, b : c and c : d, are know, then we can find a : d as $\frac{a}{d} = \frac{a}{b} \times \frac{b}{c} \times \frac{c}{d}$

(*ii*) If a, b, c and d are four quantities and a : b, b : c, c : d are known, then we can find a : b : c : d.

e.g., If a : b = 2 : 3; b : c = 4 : 5, c : d = 7 : 9, find a : b : c : d.

a : b = 8 : 12, b : c = 12 : 15 (LCM of 3 and 4 is 12)

∴ a : b : c = 8 : 12 : 15

a : b : c = 56 : 84 : 105, c : d = 105 : 135 (LCM of 7 and 15 is 105)

∴ a : b : c : d = 56 : 84 : 105 : 135

MIXTURES AND ALLIGATIONS

Simple Mixture : When two different ingredients are mixed together, it is called *simple mixture.*

Compound Mixture : When two or more simple mixtures are mixed together to form another mixture, it is called compound mixture.

Alligation Rule

Alligation rule states that "When different quantities of the same or different ingredients, of different costs (one cheap and other dear) are mixed together to produce a mixture of a mean cost, then ratio of their quantities is inversely proportional to the difference in their cost from the mean cost."

$$\frac{\text{Quantity of Cheap}}{\text{Quantity of Dear}} = \frac{\text{Price of Dear} - \text{Mean Price}}{\text{Mean Price} - \text{Price of Cheap}}$$

Application of Alligation Rule :

(1) To find mean value of a mixture when prices of two or more ingredients, which are mixed together and the proportion in which they are mixed are given.

(2) To find proportion in which ingredients at given prices must be mixed to produce a mixture at a given price.

Some Important Results :

(1) When x_1 quantity of ingredient A of cost C_1 and x_2 quantity of ingredient B of cost C_2 are mixed, the, cost of the mixture,

$$C_m = \frac{C_1x_1 + C_2x_2}{x_1 + x_2}$$

(2) Similarly, when more than two ingredients are mixed, then $C_m = \dfrac{C_1x_1 + C_2x_2 + C_3x_3 + \ldots C_nx_n}{x_1 + x_2 + x_3 + \ldots x_n}$

(3) When two mixtures M_1 and M_2 each containing ingredient A and B in the ratio a : b and x : y, respectively, are mixed, then proportion of the ingredients A and B i.e., $q_A : q_B$, in the compound mixture is given by.

$$\frac{q_A}{q_B} = \frac{M_1 \times \left(\frac{a}{a+b}\right) + M_2 \times \left(\frac{x}{x+y}\right)}{M_1 \times \left(\frac{b}{a+b}\right) + M_2 \times \left(\frac{y}{x+y}\right)}$$

and, quantity in which M_1 and M_2 is to be mixed when quantity of A and B i.e., q_A and q_B in the compound mixture is known is given by

$$\frac{\text{Quantity of } M_1}{\text{Quantity of } M_2} = \frac{\left(\frac{x}{x+y}\right) - \left(\frac{q_A}{q_A + q_B}\right)}{\left(\frac{q_A}{q_A + q_B}\right) - \left(\frac{a}{a+b}\right)}$$

(4) When a mixture of three ingredients A, B and C is given, take any two ingredients such that cost of the mixture is between costs of the two chosen ones and find the ratio. Once again, take two more ingredients and find their ratio. Then find combined ratio. This will give infinite number of solutions.

(5) If a vessel contains 'a' litres of liquid A, and 'b' litres be withdrawn and replaced by liquid B, then if 'b' litres of mixture be withdrawn and replaced by liquid B, and operation repeated 'n' times in all, then

$$\frac{\text{Liquid A left after } n^{th} \text{ operation}}{\text{Initial quantity of liquid A in vessel}} = \frac{\left(\frac{a-b}{a}\right)^n}{1 - \left(\frac{a-b}{a}\right)^n}$$

$$\frac{\text{Liquid A left after } n^{th} \text{ operation}}{\text{Liquid B left after } n^{th} \text{ operation}} = \frac{\left(\frac{a-b}{a}\right)^n}{1 - \left(\frac{a-b}{a}\right)^n}$$

EXERCISE – I

MCQ TYPE QUESTIONS

1. A cask of wine when fully filled holds 10 litres. 2 litres of wine is removed and filled with water. Then 4 litres in the solution is replaced with water. Then, 6 and 8 litres respectively. At the end of the 4th operation, the ratio of wine to water is

(a) $\frac{4!}{(5)^4}$ (b) $\frac{8!}{(10)^4}$

(c) $\frac{4!}{5^4 - 4!}$ (d) $\frac{8!}{(10)^4 - 8!}$

2. A 20 litre vessel is filled with alcohol. Some of the alcohol is poured out into another vessel of an equal capacity, which is then completely filled by adding water. Then mixture obtained is poured into the first vessel to capacity. Then $6\frac{2}{3}$ litres is poured from the first vessel into second. Both vessels now contain an equal amount of alcohol. How much alcohol was originally poured from the first vessel into the second?

(a) 9 litres

(b) 10 litres

(c) 12 litres

(d) 12.5 litres

3. What is the ratio compounded of $x - y : x + y$ and $y^2 + xy : x^2 - xy$?

(a) $y^2 : x^2$ (b) $xy : 1$

(c) $y : x$ (d) $\sqrt{x} : \sqrt{y}$

4. If ratio of two natural numbers x and y is 'a' and that of y and x is 'b', then value of 'a + b' is

(a) greater than 2

(b) lesser than 1

(c) greater than 1

(d) data insufficient.

5. The charges of a goldsmith is partly fixed and partly variable with the amount in grams of gold. The charge is ₹ 300 for 20 grams of gold and ₹ 550 for 45 grams of gold. Find the charge of work for 100 grams of gold.

(a) ₹ 900

(b) ₹ 1000

(c) ₹ 1100

(d) ₹ 9000

Directions (Q.6–7) : *Refer to the data below and answer the questions that follow.*

The ratio of white collar to blue collar employees in a firm is 8 : 3. Also ratio of male employees to female employees is 7 : 4. It is observed that 60% of the white collar employees are males.

6. What is the ratio of female white collar employees to male blue collar employees?

(a) 16 : 11 (b) 24 : 11

(c) 3 : 1 (d) Data insufficient

7. If there are 48 female blue collar workers, what is the difference between male white collar employees and female blue collar employees?

(a) 288 (b) 240

(c) 220 (d) Data insufficient

8. In a chemical experiment, two NaOH solution bottles are used. Bottle A contains salt and water in the ratio 7 : 3 and bottle B contains salt and water in the ratio 4 : 3. In what proportion should the quantities be taken from A and B to give the 2 : 1 NaOH solution?

(a) 2 : 1 (b) 10 : 7

(c) 20 : 7 (d) 1 : 2

9. A triswitch mixer grinder operates in three stages of speed in revolutions per min i.e., rpm. The speed of the motor with some load in the second stage varies as a square of the speed in stage 1 and that in stage 3 varies as a cube of that in stage 2. If mixer motor makes 50 revolutions in 3 minutes in stage 1, its speed in stage 2 and 3 with the same load is 2500 and 12500 rpm respectively. What will be the speed of motor (in rpm) in stage 3, if at the same load motors speed in rpm is 25 revolutions in 6 minutes in stage 1?

(a) $\frac{3125}{16}$ rpm (b) $\frac{5^5}{2^{10}}$ rpm

(c) $\frac{5^{10}}{2^5}$ rpm (d) None of these

10. Two bags have certain number of mangoes. If half the mangoes from bag 1 are transferred to bag 2, the ratio of mangoes in bag 1 to bag 2 gets reversed. Now one-third and two-third of the mangoes from the first and the second bag are transferred to the second and first bag respectively. The ratio of mangoes in bag 1 to bag 2 now is

(a) 2 : 1 (b) 2 : 2

(c) 4 : 5 (d) 5 : 4

NUMERICAL TYPE QUESTIONS

1. Five litres are drawn from a cask full of wine and it is then filled with water. Five litres of the mixture are drawn and the cask is again filled with water. The quantity of wine now left in the cask to that of the water in it is in the ratio 361 : 39. The cask hold _____ litres.
2. In a mixture of wheat and barley, wheat is 60%. To 400 kg of the mixture a quantity of barley is added and then the wheat is $53\frac{1}{3}\%$. The_____kg of barley are added?
3. Two jars of capacity 3 and 5 litres are filled with mixtures of alcohol and water. In the smaller jar 25% of the mixture is alcohol and in the larger 25% of the mixture is water. The jars are emptied into a 9 litre cask and remaining volume is filled up with water. Then percentage of alcohol in the cask will be _____
4. A man buys milk at ₹ 5 a litre and after adding water, sells it at ₹ 6 a litre, thereby making a profit of $33\frac{1}{3}\%$. The proportion of water to milk in the mixture is_____
5. The percentage of alcohol in two wine tanks is 20 and 40 respectively and rest is grape juice. If a wine glass is filled to its half by the tank 1 and 2 in the ratio 2 : 3 and the rest is filled again by pure alcohol, then the ratio of the grape juice to alcohol in the wine glass is _____
6. In _____ ratio must a grocer mix two varieties of tea worth ₹ 60 a kg and ₹ 65 a kg so that by selling the mixture at ₹ 68.20 a kg he may gain 10%?
7. A container contains 40 lit of milk. From this container 4. lit of milk was taken out and replaced by water. This process was repeated further two times. The _____litres of milk is now contained by the container?
8. A merchant has 1000kg of sugar,part of which he sells at 8% profit and the rest at 18% profit. He gains 14% on the whole. The quantity sold at 18% profit is_____ kg
9. Volumes in the proportion 3 : 4 : 7 of three different substances are mixed together. The densities of equal volume of the substances are in the ratio 5 : 2 : 6 respectively. The weight of the third substance contained in 130 lbs. of the mixture is _____ lbs
10. In a bag, there are 50 paise coins, 25 paise coins and rupee coins, proportional to the numbers 3, 4 and $2\frac{1}{2}$. If they amount to ₹ 210, then number of rupee coins is_____

EXERCISE – II

(QUESTIONS FROM PREVIOUS GATE EXAMS)

MCQ TYPE QUESTIONS

2015

1. A cube of side 3 units is formed using a set of smaller cubes of side 1 unit. Find the proportion of the number of faces of the smaller cubes visible to those which are NOT visible.

   (*a*) 1 : 4

   (*b*) 1 : 3

   (*c*) 1 : 2

   (*d*) 2 : 3

2011

2. A container originally contains 10 litres of pure spirit. From this container 1 litre of spirit is replaced with 1 litre of water. Subsequently, 1 litre of the mixture is again replaced with 1 litre of water and this process is repeated one more time. How much spirit is now left in the container?

   (*a*) 7.58 litres

   (*b*) 7.84 litres

   (*c*) 7 litres

   (*d*) 7.29 litres

ANSWERS

EXERCISE – I

MCQ Type Questions

1. (*c*) **2.** (*b*) **3.** (*c*) **4.** (*c*) **5.** (*c*) **6.** (*a*) **7.** (*b*) **8.** (*c*) **9.** (*b*) **10.** (*a*)

Numerical Type Questions

1. 100 **2.** 50 **3.** 50 **4.** 1 : 9 **5.** 17 : 33 **6.** 3 : 2 **7.** 29.16 **8.** 600 **9.** 84 **10.** 105

EXERCISE – II

MCQ Type Questions

1. (*c*) **2.** (*d*)

EXPLANATIONS

EXERCISE – I

MCQ TYPE QUESTIONS

1.

Stage	$\dfrac{\text{Wine left}}{\text{Original quantity}}$
0	$\dfrac{10}{10}$
1	$\dfrac{8}{10}$
2	$\dfrac{8}{10}\times\dfrac{6}{10}$
3	$\dfrac{8}{10}\times\dfrac{6}{10}\times\dfrac{4}{10}$
4	$\dfrac{8}{10}\times\dfrac{6}{10}\times\dfrac{4}{10}\times\dfrac{2}{10} \Rightarrow \dfrac{4\times3\times2\times1}{5^4} = \dfrac{4!}{5^4}$

$$\therefore \quad \frac{\text{Wine}}{\text{Water}} = \frac{\frac{4!}{5^4}}{1-\frac{4!}{5^4}} = \frac{4!}{5^4-4!}$$

2. 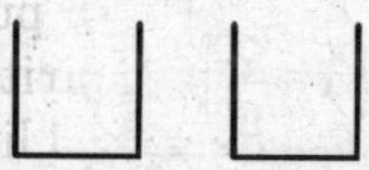

(1) (2)

	C_1	C_2
Operation 1 Operation 2	20 litres alcohol (20 – x) alcohol	Empty x litres alcohol (20 – x) litres water
Operation 3	(20 – x) litres alcohol + xlitres mixture i.e., $\left(\frac{x^2}{20}\right.$ litres alcohol$\left.\right)$	(20 – x) litres mixture

Now $\frac{1}{3}$rd of C_1 poured into C_2

Quantity of alcohol in $C_1 = C_2 = 10$ litres

In C_1 : $\quad \dfrac{2}{3}\left[20 - x + (x)\left(\dfrac{x}{20}\right)\right] = 10$

Solving we get, $\quad x = 10$ litres

Hence10 litres of alcohol was initially poured from C_1 to C_2.

3. Required ratio $= \dfrac{x-y}{x+y}\times\dfrac{y^2+xy}{x^2-xy} = \dfrac{y}{x} = y : x$

4. *Given* : $\dfrac{x}{y} = a$ and $\dfrac{y}{x} = b$

If $\dfrac{x}{y} > 1$, then $\dfrac{y}{x} < 1$,

$\Rightarrow \quad \dfrac{x}{y} + \dfrac{y}{x} > 1$.

Hence option (*c*) is correct.

5. Total charge = fixed + variable

$$T_C = m + kx$$

where m and k are constants.

$\therefore \quad 300 = m + k \times 20$

Also, $\quad 550 = m + k \times 45$

Solving for m and k; we get

$$m = 100;\ k = 10.$$

Hence, for 100 grams,

total charge = 100 + 10 × 100 = ₹ 1100.

Q. 6 and 7.

Using given data, we can draw following table

	Male	Female	
White Collar	4.8x	3.2x	8x
Blue Collar	2.2x	0.8x	3x
	7x	4x	11x

Now, all the questions can be answered.

6. $\frac{\text{Female white collar employess}}{\text{Male blue collar employees}} = \frac{3.2x}{2.2x} = \frac{16}{11}$

7. Since $0.8x = 48$

$\Rightarrow x = 60$

$\therefore$ Required difference $= 4.8x - 0.8x$

$= 4.8 \times 60 - 0.8x = 240$

8. Let 10x be taken from bottle A and 7y be taken from bottle B.

$$\text{Total salt taken} = \left(\frac{7}{10} \times 10x\right) + \left(\frac{4}{7} \times 7y\right)$$

$$= 7x + 4y$$

Total water taken $= 3x + 3y$.

$$\therefore \frac{7x+4y}{3x+3y} = \frac{2}{1}$$

$$\Rightarrow 7x + 4y = 6x + 6y$$

$$\Rightarrow x = 2y$$

$$\therefore \frac{x}{y} = \frac{2}{1}$$

$$\therefore \text{Ratio of quantities} = \frac{10x}{7y}$$

$$= \frac{10}{7} \times \frac{2}{1} = \frac{20}{7}$$

9. Let speed of the motor in stage 1 be x rpm. Then its speed in stage 2 be $(x^2) = ax^2$ (say) and in stage 3 be $(ax^2)^3 = b.a^3x^6$ (say)

Given that $x = \frac{50}{3}$ ...(i)

$ax^2 = 2500$ ...(ii)

$ba^3x^6 = 12500$ ...(iii)

Substituting value of x in (ii), we get

$$a = \frac{2500}{(50)^2} \times 3^2 = 9$$

Again, substituting values of a and x, we get

$$b = \frac{12500}{(2500)^3} = \frac{1}{125} \times 10^{-4}$$

Given : $x = \frac{25}{6}$ rpm

$$\therefore \text{Speed in stage 3} = \frac{10^{-4}}{125} \times (9)^3 \times \left(\frac{25}{6}\right)^6$$

$$= \frac{10^{-4}}{5 \times 25} \times (3)^6 \times \frac{(25 \times 5) \times (5 \times 25^4)}{(2)^6 \cdot (3)^6}$$

$$= \frac{5 \times 25^4}{2^6 \times 10^4} = \frac{5^5}{2^{10}} \text{ rpm}$$

10. Let bag 1 and 2 have

	x mangoes	y mangoes
Step 1	$\frac{x}{2}$	$y + \frac{x}{2}$
But	$\frac{x}{2}$: $y + \frac{x}{2} = y : x$	
Step 2	$\frac{2}{3}y + \frac{2}{3}x$	$\frac{1}{3}y + \frac{1}{3}x$

$$\therefore \text{Required ratio} = \frac{\frac{2}{3}y + \frac{2}{3}x}{\frac{1}{3}y + \frac{1}{3}x} = \frac{2\left(\frac{x+y}{3}\right)}{1\left(\frac{x+y}{3}\right)}$$

$$= 2 : 1$$

NUMERICAL TYPE QUESTIONS

1. Let quantity of wine be a, i.e., capacity of the cask be 'a'

$$\text{i.e.,} \frac{\text{Quantity of wine}}{\text{Quantity of water}} = \frac{\left(1 - \frac{5}{a}\right)^2}{1 - \left(1 - \frac{5}{a}\right)^2}$$

$$\therefore \frac{361}{39} = \frac{\left(1 - \frac{5}{a}\right)^2}{1 - \left(1 - \frac{5}{a}\right)^2}$$

$$\Rightarrow \frac{361}{39} - \frac{361}{39}\left(1 - \frac{5}{a}\right)^2 = \left(1 - \frac{5}{a}\right)^2$$

$\Rightarrow \quad \left(1-\frac{5}{a}\right) = \sqrt{\frac{361}{400}} = \frac{19}{20}$

$\Rightarrow \quad \frac{5}{a} = \frac{1}{20}$

$\therefore \quad a = 100$ litres

2. Quantity of wheat in 400 kg of mixture

$= 0.6 \times 400 = 240$ kg

Quantity of barley = 400 – 240 = 160 kg

Let x kg of barley be added to 400 kg of the mixture

$\therefore \quad \frac{240}{160+x} = \frac{53\frac{1}{3}}{46\frac{2}{3}} = \frac{160}{140} = \frac{8}{7}$

$\Rightarrow \quad 240 \times 7 = 8 \times 160 + 8x$

$\Rightarrow \quad x = 50$ kg

3. Alcohol content in 1st jar = 0.25 × 3 = 0.75 litre

Alcohol content in 2nd jar = 0.75 × 5 = 3.75 litres

$\therefore$ Total alcohol in 9 litre cask = 0.75 + 3.75

= 4.5 litres

$\therefore$ Percentage of alcohol in the cask

$= \frac{4.5}{9} \times 100 = 50\%$

4. Cost price of milk = ₹ 5/litre

Cost price of mixture $= \frac{100}{133\frac{1}{3}} \times 6 =$ ₹ 4.5/litre

$\therefore \quad \frac{\text{Quantity of water}}{\text{Quantity of milk}} = \frac{5-4.5}{4.5-0} = \frac{1}{9}$

i.e.,

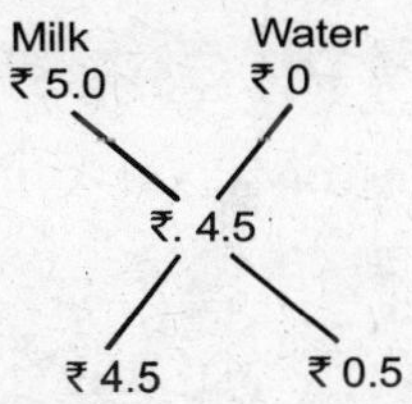

Milk : Water = 9 : 1

5.

	Alcohol	Grape juice	Alcohol : Grape
Tank 1	20%	80%	1 : 4
Tank 2	40%	60%	2 : 3

Ratio of grape juice to alcohol in half filled wine glass

$= \frac{2\times\frac{4}{5}+3\times\frac{3}{5}}{2\times\frac{1}{5}+3\times\frac{2}{5}} = \frac{17}{8}$

So, half capacity of glass = 17 + 8 = 25

So, full capacity = 25 × 2 = 50

Now rest 25 parts has to be filled with alcohol.

So, ratio of the grape juice to alcohol

= 17 : (8 + 25) = 17 : 33.

Alternatively,

As the wine glass is filled to half by taking two parts from tank 1 and three parts from tank 2 and second half is equivalent to five parts which is pure alcohol,

percentage concentration of grape juice

$= \frac{2\times 80+3\times 60+5\times 10}{2+3+5} = 34\%$

Hence ratio of grape juice to alcohol

= 34 : 66 = 17 : 33.

6. S.P of 1 kg of mixture = ₹ 68.20, Gain =10%

S.P of 1 kg of mixture = ₹ $\left(\frac{100}{110}\times 68.2\right)$ = ₹ 62.

Cost of 1 kg tea of 1st kind		Cost of 1 kg tea of 2nd kind
60		65
	Mean Price ₹ 62	
3		2

$\therefore$ Required ratio = 3 : 2.

7. Amount of milk left after 3 operations

$= 40\left(1-\frac{4}{40}\right)^3$

$= 40 \times \frac{9}{10}\times\frac{9}{10}\times\frac{9}{10}$

= 29.16 lit

8.

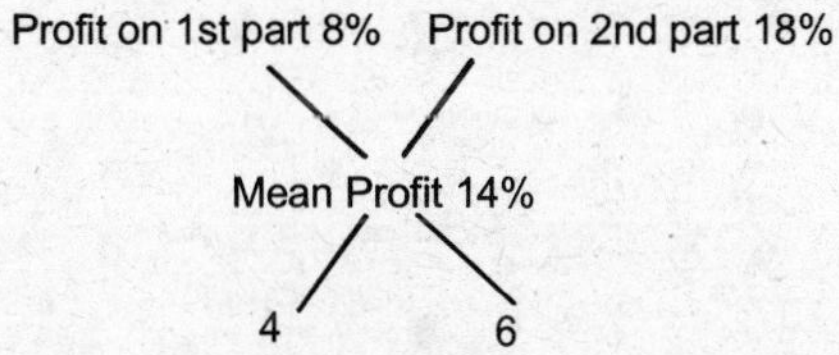

Ratio of 1st and 2nd parts = 4 : 6 = 2 : 3.

Quantity of 2nd part $= \frac{3}{5} \times 1000$ kg = 600 kg.

9. Ratio of volumes $= \frac{3}{14}:\frac{4}{14}:\frac{7}{14}$

Ratio of densities $= \frac{5}{13}:\frac{2}{13}:\frac{6}{13}$

$\therefore$ Ratio of weights $= \frac{3}{14}\times\frac{5}{13}:\frac{4}{14}\times\frac{2}{13}:\frac{7}{14}\times\frac{6}{13}$

= 15 : 8 : 42

... (Mass = Volume × Density)

Weight of the third substance $= \frac{42}{65} \times 130 = 84$ ℓbs.

10. Let number of 50p coins be 3x, number of 25p coins be 4x and number of rupee coins be $2\frac{1}{2}$x.

$$\therefore \quad 2\frac{1}{2}x + \frac{1}{2}\times 3x + \frac{1}{4}\times 4x = 210$$

$$\Rightarrow \quad \frac{5}{2}x + \frac{3}{2}x + x = 210$$

$$\Rightarrow \quad 5x = 210$$

$$\Rightarrow \quad x = 42$$

$\therefore$ Number of rupee coins = $\frac{5}{2}\times 42 = 105.$

EXERCISE – II

MCQ TYPE QUESTIONS

1.

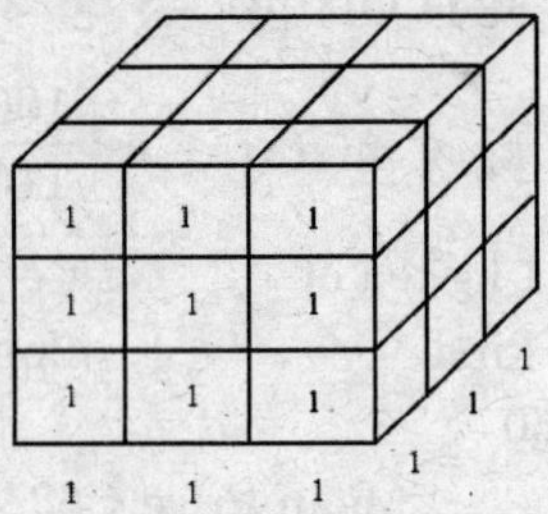

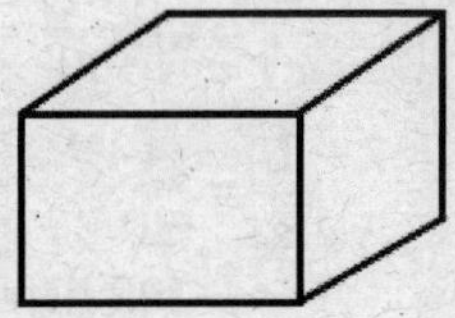

Number of faces per cube = 6

Total number of cubes = 9 × 3 = 27

$\therefore$ Total number of faces = 27 × 6 = 162

$\therefore$ Total number of non visible faces = 162 – 54 = 108

$$\therefore \quad \frac{\text{Number of visible faces}}{\text{Number of non visible faces}} = \frac{54}{108} = \frac{1}{2}$$

2. $10\left(\frac{10-1}{10}\right)^3 = 10\left(\frac{9}{10}\right)^3 = \frac{729}{1000}$

$\therefore \quad \frac{729}{1000}\times 1 = 7.29$ litres

■■

5 CHAPTER Permutations and Combinations & Probability

PERMUTATIONS AND COMBINATION

PERMUTATIONS

Each of the arrangements which can be made by taking some or all of a number of items is called a *Permutation*. Permutation implies *"arrangement"* or that *"order of the items"* is important.

Permutations of three items a, b and c taken two at a time are ab, ba, ac, ca, cb and bc. Since the order in which items are taken is important, ab and ba are counted as two different permutations. The words "permutation" and "arrangement" are synonymous and can be used interchangeably."

Number of permutations of n things taking r at a time is denoted by ^nP_r (and read as "nPr")

COMBINATIONS

Each of the groups or selections which can be made by taking some or all of a number of items is called *Combination*. In combinations, order in which the items are taken is not considered as long as the specific things are included.

Combinations of three items a, b and c taken two at a time are ab, bc and ca. Here, ab and ba are not considered separately because the order in which a and b are taken is not important but it is only required that a combination including a and b is what is to be counted. Words *"combination"* and *"selection"* are synonymous.

Number of combinations of n things taking r at a time is denoted by ^nC_r (and read as "nCr")

$$^nP_r = \frac{n!}{(n-r)!}, \quad ^nC_r = \frac{n!}{r!(n-r)!}$$

Number of ways in which n things may be arranged taking them all at a time, when p of the things are exactly alike of one kind, q of them exactly alike of another kind, r of them exactly alike of a third kind, and the rest all distinct is $\frac{n!}{p!q!r!}$

Number of ways of selecting one or more items from n given items = $2^n - 1$

Number of ways of dividing (p + q) items into two groups of p and q items respectively is $\frac{(p+q)!}{p!q!}$.

Number of ways of dividing 2p items into two equal groups of p each is $\frac{(2p)!}{(p!)^2}$ where two groups have distinct identity.

Number of ways of dividing 2p items into two equal groups of p each is $\frac{(2p)!}{2!(p!)^2}$ where two groups do not have distinct identity.

Number of ways in which (p + q + r) things can be divided into three groups containing p, q and r things respectively is $\frac{(p+q+r)!}{p!q!r!}$

Number of circular arrangements of n distinct items is (n – 1)! If there is a DIFFERENCE between clockwise and anticlockwise arrangements and (n – 1)!/2 if there is NO DIFFERENCE between clockwise and anticlockwise arrangements.

For $x_1 + x_2 + x_3 + \text{-------} + x_n = s$ where $s \geq 0$, number of positive integral solutions (when $s \geq n$) is $^{s-1}C^{n-1}$ and number of non-negative integral solution is $^{n+s-1}C^{n-1}$.

PROBABILITY

If in an experiment there are 'n' occurrences out of which 'm' occurrences are favourable to a particular event E, then probability of the event E [written as P(E)] is defined as P(E) = m/n.

For the event E, non-occurrence of the event is denoted by $\overline{E}$. Out of a total n occurrences, if m occurrences are favourable to the event E, it means that (n – m) occurrences are not favourable to the event $\overline{E}$, i.e. (n - m) occurrences are favourable to the event $\overline{E}$.

Hence, probability of the event $\overline{E}$ will be $P(\overline{E})\ \frac{n-m}{n}$ (complementary event).

We can also see that $P(\overline{E}) + P(E) = 1$.

In some problems when we are asked to find out the probability of an event $\overline{E}$, it becomes easier to calculate probability of E and subtract that probability from 1 to get $P(\overline{E})$.

Note:

(i) Probability [P(E)] of the happening of an event E is called *probability* of success and probability $\left[P(\overline{E})\right]$ of non-happening of the event is called *probability of failure*.

(ii) If P(E) = 1, then event is called a *certain event* and if P(E) = 0, then event is called *impossible event*.

(iii) Instead of saying that the chance of happening of an event is m/n, we can also say that odds in favour of the event are m (to n – m). Similarly, if m/n is probability of the occurrences of an event, since (n – m)/n is probability of non-occurrence of the event, we can also say that the odds against the event are (n – m) to m.

Addition Theorem on Probability

If there are two sets A and B, we know that the number of elements in $A \cup B$ is given by

$$n(A \cup B) = n(A) + n(B) - n(A \cap B).$$

A similar relationship exists in probability theory (called Addition Theorem of Probability) as $P(A \cup B) = P(A) + P(B) - P(A \cap B)$, where A and B are two events.

If A and B are mutually exclusive events (i.e, A and B are disjoint sets), then $P(A \cap B) = 0$

If there are two mutually exclusive events A and B, then $P(A \cup B) = P(A) + P(B)$.

Independent Events

Two events, E_1 and E_2 are said to be independent, if occurrence of the event E_2 is not affected by the occurrence or non-occurrence of the event E_1.

If A and B are two independent events, then

$$P(A \cap B) = P(A) \times P(B)$$

EXERCISE – I

MCQ TYPE QUESTIONS

Directions (Q. 1 – 2) :

If A and B are two possible events of an experiment such that $P(A \cap B) = 0.6$ and $P(A) = 0.3$ then find $P(B)$ given that

1. A and B are mutually exclusive events

(a) $\frac{7}{10}$ (b) $\frac{4}{10}$

(c) $\frac{3}{10}$ (d) $\frac{1}{2}$

2. A and B are independent events

(a) $\frac{4}{7}$ (b) $\frac{9}{10}$ (c) $\frac{3}{10}$ (d) $\frac{3}{7}$

3. Raju throws a fair dice. He is promised an amount (in rupees), which is twice the number showing up if that number is odd and an amount thrice the number showing up, if it is even. What is the maximum amount Raju would be willing to pay each time to throw the dice, if in the long run he wants to make an average profit of ₹ 7 per throw?

(a) ₹ 6 (b) ₹ 7 (c) ₹ 3 (d) ₹ 2

Directions (Q. 4 – 5) :

7 letters are to be placed in seven addressed envelops. If the letters are placed at random into the envelopes, the probability that

4. All of them are placed in the corresponding envelops is

(a) 1

(b) $\frac{1}{6!}$

(c) $\frac{1}{7!}$

(d) None of these

5. Exactly six letters are placed in their corresponding envelopes is

(a) $1-\frac{1}{7!}$ (b) $\frac{1}{7!}$ (c) 1 (d) 0

Directions (Q. 6 – 8) :

If three cards are drawn at random, from a well shuffled pack of cards, then what is the probability that

6. All of them are from the same suit?

(a) $\frac{4\left({}^{13}C_3\right)}{{}^{52}C_3}$ (b) $\frac{\left({}^{13}C_3\right)^3}{{}^{52}C_3}$

(c) $\frac{4\left({}^{13}C_3\right)^2}{{}^{52}C_3}$ (d) $\frac{{}^{13}C_3}{{}^{52}C_3}$

7. All of them are from different suits?

(a) $\frac{13}{{}^{52}C_3}$ (b) $\frac{4(13)^3}{{}^{52}C_3}$

(c) $\frac{{}^{39}C_3}{{}^{52}C_3}$ (d) $\frac{(13)^4}{{}^{52}C_3}$

8. Two of them are number cards from the same suit and the remaining number card is from a different suit?

(a) $\frac{{}^{9}C_2\,{}^{9}C_1}{{}^{52}C_3}$ (b) $\frac{{}^{9}C_2\,{}^{27}C_1}{{}^{52}C_3}$

(c) $\frac{4\left({}^{9}C_2\,{}^{27}C_1\right)}{{}^{52}C_3}$ (d) $\frac{4\left({}^{9}C_2\,{}^{9}C_1\right)}{{}^{52}C_3}$

9. A bag contains 5 white balls and 7 red balls. If 5 balls are drawn at random, then probability that 3 balls are red and the rest are white is

(a) $\frac{175}{198}$ (b) $\frac{175}{396}$

(c) $\frac{38}{132}$ (d) $\frac{221}{396}$

10. A bag contains 6 five rupee coins, 5 two rupee coins and 4 one rupee coins. If 5 coins are selected at random from the bag, then odds in favour of the draw yielding minimum possible amount are

(a) 1:3002 (b) 5:2998

(c) 2:3003 (d) 5:3003

11. In how many ways can 6 girls and 6 boys sit around a circular table so that no two boys sit together?

(a) $(5!)^2$ (b) $(6!)^2$

(c) 5! 6! (d) 11!

12. How many ten-digit numbers can be formed using all the digits of 1324642119 such that the even digits appear only in odd places?

(a) $(5!)^2$ (b) $\frac{(5!)^2}{3!}$

(c) 5! 3! 2! (d) $\frac{(5!)^2}{(2!)^2\,3!}$

Directions (Q. 13 – 14) :

A man has 12 friends whom he wants to invite for lunch. In how many ways can he invite

13. At least one of them?

(a) 4096 (b) 4095

(c) 2047 (d) 2048

14. At least 10 of them?

(a) 66 (b) 140

(c) 153 (d) None of these

15. In how many ways can 6 prizes be distributed among 3 boys, if each boy is eligible to receive one or more prizes?

(a) 3^6 (b) 6^3

(c) ${}^6C_3$ (d) ${}^6P_3$

Directions (Q. 16 – 17) :

Find the number of ways of dividing 16 different books equally

16. Among 4 boys

(a) $\frac{16!}{(4!)^4}$ (b) $\frac{16!}{(4!)^3}$

(c) $\frac{16!}{(4!)^5}$ (d) $(4!)^4$

17. Into 4 parcels (Parcels are not distinct)

(a) $\frac{16!}{(4!)^4}$ (b) $\frac{16!}{(4!)^3}$

(c) $\frac{16!}{(4!)^5}$ (d) $(4!)^4$

18. How many linear arrangements can be made using all the letters of the word ILLUSTRATE which begin with S and end with a vowel?

(a) $\frac{8!}{(2!)^2}$ (b) 8!

(c) $\frac{8!}{2!}$ (d) $\frac{8!}{(2!)^3}$

19. From a group of 10 professors and 6 assistant professors, a management institute desires to send to delegation of 8 persons consisting of 5 professors and 3 assistant professors to the IIMs annual meet. If Prof. Balamurali, a science professor refuses to be in the delegation if assistant Prof. Sheshdari, an arts professor is included in the delegation, then in how many ways can the delegation be formed?

(a) ${}^9C_4\,{}^4C_3$

(b) ${}^9C_5\,{}^4C_2$

(c) ${}^{10}C_5\,{}^6C_3 - {}^9C_4\,{}^5C_2$

(d) ${}^9C_4\,{}^4C_3 + {}^9C_5\,{}^4C_2$

20. Two red pencils, three black pencils and two white pencils are to be arranged in a row such that

1. No two adjacent pencils are of the same colour and
2. Pencils at the two ends of the row are of same colour.

(a) 12 (b) 8 (c) 9 (d) 10

NUMERICAL TYPE QUESTIONS

Directions (Q. 1 – 2) :

The odds against an event are 4 to 5 and the odds in favour of another independent event are 3 to 7. The probability that

1. Exactly one of them will occur is ______

2. Neither of them will occur is ______

Directions (Q. 3 – 5) :

Three persons Shiva, Jagan and Rohit aim at a target. Their respective probabilities of hitting the target are 2/3, 5/7 and 3/8. The probability that

3. None of them hits the target is ______

4. At least two of them hit the target is ______

5. Exactly one of them hits the target si ______

6. If three consecutive letters are selected at random from the English alphabet, then the probability that at least one letter is a vowel is ______

7. Eight unbiased coins are tossed together. The probability that the number of heads is equal to the number of tails is ______

8. In a biased coin, Head occurs three times as frequently as tail occurs. If the coin is tossed 3 times, then the probability of getting two heads is ______

Directions (Q. 9 – 10) :

Two cards are drawn at random from a well shuffled pack of cards. Given that both are black, the probability that the cards have

9. Same honour on them is______
10. Different honours and belong to different suits is ______

Directions (Q. 11 – 13) :

Three mountaineers Akil, Nikil, and Sunil are climbing up a mountain with their respective probability of reaching the summit being $\frac{2}{3}, \frac{5}{8}$ and $\frac{4}{7}$, respectively. The probability that

11. None of them reach the summit is ______
12. Exactly two of them reaches the summit is ______
13. Atleast two of them reach the summit is ______

Directions (Q. 14 – 15) :

There are 12 points in a plane of which 4 are on a straight line and no three of the other points lie on a straight line.

14. The ______number straight lines can be formed by joining these points
15. The ______number of triangles can be formed by joining these points
16. The ______ number of non-negative integral solutions does the equation $x_1 + x_2 + x_3 + x_4 = 10$ have?
17. A certain number of students of a school participated in the chess tournament of their annual sports meet. Each player played 1 game against each of the other player. It was found that in 66 games both the players were girls, and in 240 games one was a girl and the other was a boy. The number of games in which both the players were boys is ______
18. Nine points are marked on a straight line and 10 points are marked on another line which is parallel to the first line. The______ number of triangles can be formed with these points as vertices?
19. The ______ number of positive integers less than 100,000 and divisible by 125 can be formed using the digits 0, 1, 2, 5 and 8, if repetition is allowed?
20. There is an unlimited supply of identical red, blue, and green coloured balls. In ______ number of ways can 12 balls be selected from the supply.
21. Number of positive integral solutions of the equation $a + b + c = 15$ is ______
22. If six unbiased coins are tossed together, then probability that the number of heads exceeds the number of tails is______

EXERCISE – II

(QUESTIONS FROM PREVIOUS GATE EXAMS)

MCQ TYPE QUESTIONS

2015

1. Four cards are randomly selected from a pack of 52 cards. If the first two cards are kings, what is the probability that the third card is a king?

   (*a*) 4/52 (*b*) 2/50
   (*c*) 1/52 × (1/52) (*d*) 1/52 × (1/52) × (1/50)

2. Five teams have to compete in a league, with every team playing every other team exactly once, before going to the next round. How many matches will have to be held complete the league round of matches?

   (*a*) 20 (*b*) 10 (*c*) 8 (*d*) 5

3. Right triangle PQR is to be constructed in the *xy* – plane so that the right angle is at P and line PR is parallel to the-axis. The *x* and *y* coordinates of P, Q, and R are to be integers that satisfy the inequalities: $-4 \le x \le 5$ and $6 \le y \le 16$. How many different triangles could be constructed with these properties?

   (*a*) 110 (*b*) 1,100
   (*c*) 9,900 (*d*) 10,000

4. A coin is tossed thrice. Let X be the event that head occurs in each of the first two tosses. Let Y be the event that a tail occurs on the third toss. Let Z be the event that two tails occurs in three tosses. Based on the above information, which one of the following statements is TRUE?

   (*a*) X and Y are not independent
   (*b*) Y and Z are dependent
   (*c*) Y and Z are independent
   (*d*) X and Z independent

5. Ram and Ramesh appeared in an interview for two vacancies in the same department. The probability of Ram's selection is 1/6 and that of Ramesh is 1/8. What is the probability that only one of them will be selected?

   (*a*) $\frac{47}{48}$ (*b*) $\frac{1}{4}$ (*c*) $\frac{13}{48}$ (*d*) $\frac{35}{48}$

6. Given set A = {2, 3, 4, 5} and Set B = {11, 12, 13, 14, 15}, two numbers are randomly selected, one from each set. What is probability that the sum of the two numbers equals 16 ?

   (*a*) 0.20 (*b*) 0.25
   (*c*) 0.30 (*d*) 0.33

7. The probabilities that a student passes in Mathematics, Physics and Chemistry are m, p and c respectively. Of these subjects, the student has 75% chance of passing in at least one, a 50% chance of passing in at least two and a 40% chance of passing in exactly two. Following relations are drawn in $m, p.c$:

I. $p + m + c = \dfrac{27}{20}$

II. $p + m + c = \dfrac{13}{20}$

III. $(p) \times (m) \times (c) = \dfrac{1}{10}$

(a) Only relation I is true.
(b) Only relation II is true.
(c) Relations II and III are true.
(d) Relations I and III are true.

2014

8. A five digit number is formed using the digits 1,3,5,7 and 9 without repeating any of them. What is the sum of all such possible five digit numbers?

(a) 6666660
(b) 6666600
(c) 6666666
(d) 6666606

9. You are given three coins: one has heads on both faces, the second has tails on both faces, and the third has a head on one face and a tail on the other. You choose a coin at random and toss it, and it comes up heads. The probability that the other face is tails is

(a) 1/4
(b) 1/3
(c) 1/2
(d) 2/3

2013

10. Out of all the 2-digit integers between 1 and 100, a 2-digit number has to be selected at random. What is the probability that the selected number is not divisible by 7?

(a) 13/90
(b) 12/90
(c) 78/90
(d) 77/90

11. What is the chance that a leap year, selected at random, will contain 53 Saturdays?

(a) 2/7 (b) 3/7
(c) 1/7 (d) 5/7

12. In a factory, two machines M1 and M2 manufacture 60% and 40% of the autocomponents respectively. Out of the total production, 2% of M1 and 3% of M2 are found to be defective. If a randomly drawn autocomponent from the combined lot is found defective, what is the probability that it was manufactured by M2?

(a) 0.35 (b) 0.45
(c) 0.5 (d) 0.4

2012

13. A and B are friends. They decide to meet between 1 PM and 2 PM on a given day. There is a condition that whoever arrives first will not wait for the other for more than 15 minutes. The probability that they will meet on that day is

(a) $\dfrac{1}{4}$ (b) $\dfrac{1}{16}$
(c) $\dfrac{7}{16}$ (d) $\dfrac{9}{16}$

2010

14. Given digits 2, 2, 3, 3, 3, 4, 4, 4, 4 how many distinct 4 digit numbers greater than 3000 can be formed?

(a) 50 (b) 51
(c) 52 (d) 54

NUMERICAL TYPE QUESTIONS

2015

1. How many four digit numbers can be formed with the 10 digits 0, 1, 2, ... 9 if no number can start with 0 and if repetitions are not allowed?

2014

2. In any given year, the probability of an earthquake greater than Magnitude 6 occurring in the Garhwal Himalayas is 0.04. The average time between successive occurrences of such earthquakes is _____ years.

3. 10% of the population in a town is HIV^+. A new diagnostic kit for HIV detection is available; this kit correctly identifies HIV^+ individuals 95% of the time, and HIV^- individuals 89% of the time. A particular patient is tested using this kit and is found to be positive. The probability that the individual is actually positive is ______

4. A batch of one hundred bulbs is inspected by testing four randomly chosen bulbs. The batch is rejected if even one of the bulbs is defective. A batch typically has five defective bulbs. The probability that the current batch is accepted is ________

ANSWERS

EXERCISE – I

MCQ Type Questions

1. (c)	**2.** (d)	**3.** (d)	**4.** (c)	**5.** (d)	**6.** (a)	**7.** (b)	**8.** (c)	**9.** (b)	**10.** (b)
11. (c)	**12.** (d)	**13.** (b)	**14.** (d)	**15.** (a)	**16.** (a)	**17.** (c)	**18.** (b)	**19.** (c)	**20.** (d)

Numerical Type Questions

1. $\frac{47}{90}$	**2.** $\frac{14}{45}$	**3.** $\frac{5}{84}$	**4.** $\frac{107}{168}$	**5.** $\frac{17}{56}$	**6.** $\frac{13}{24}$	**7.** $\frac{35}{128}$	**8.** $\frac{27}{64}$	**9.** $\frac{4}{325}$	**10.** $\frac{12}{325}$
11. $\frac{3}{56}$	**12.** $\frac{37}{84}$	**13.** $\frac{19}{28}$	**14.** 61	**15.** 216	**16.** 286	**17.** 190	**18.** 765	**19.** 99	**20.** 91
21. 91	**22.** $\frac{57}{64}$								

EXERCISE – II

MCQ Type Questions

1. (b)	**2.** (b)	**3.** (c)	**4.** (d)	**5.** (b)	**6.** (a)	**7.** (d)	**8.** (b)	**9.** (b)	**10.** (d)
11. (a)	**12.** (c)	**13.** (c)	**14.** (b)						

Numerical Type Questions

1. 4536 **2.** (25 to 25) **3.** (0.47 to 0.48) **4.** (0.8145)

EXPLANATIONS

EXERCISE – I

MCQ TYPE QUESTIONS

1 and 2

Given : $P(A \cup B) = 0.6$

and $P(A) = 0.3$

1. If A and B are mutually exclusive events, then

$$P(A \cap B) = 0$$

$$\therefore \quad P(A \cup B) = P(A) + P(B)$$

$$0.6 = 0.3 + P(B)$$

$$\Rightarrow \quad 0.3 = P(B)$$

Hence $\quad P(B) = 0.3$

2. If A and B are independent events, then

$$P(A \cap B) = P(A).P(B)$$

$$\therefore \quad P(A \cup B) = P(A) + P(B) - P(A \cap B)$$

$$= P(A) + P(B) - P(A).\ P(B)$$

$$P(A \cap B) = P(A) + P(B)\,[1 - P(A)]$$

$$\Rightarrow \quad 0.6 = 0.3 + P(B)\,(1 - 0.3)$$

$$0.3 = P(B)(0.7)$$

$$\Rightarrow \quad \frac{0.3}{0.7} = P(B)$$

$$\therefore \quad P(B) = \frac{3}{7}$$

3. When a die is rolled, for each number the probability of getting it is $\frac{1}{6}$.

When number on the dice is 1, 3 or 5 Raju receives ₹ 2, ₹ 6 and ₹10 respectively.

When the number on the die is 2, 4 or 6, then Raju receives ₹ 6, ₹ 12 and ₹ 18 respectively.

$\therefore$ Expected value= $\frac{1}{6}$ [2 + 6 + 10 + 6 + 12 + 18]

$= \frac{54}{6} =$ ₹ 9

Hence to make an average profit of ₹ 7 per throw, Raju must pay ₹ 2 (9 – 7) for each time to throw the die.

4. 7 letters can be arranged in 7 addressed envelopes in 7! ways.

$\therefore \quad n(S) = 7!$

We can arrange 7 letters into corresponding 7 addressed envelopes in only one way.

$\therefore$ Required probability = $\frac{1}{7!}$.

5. If six letters can be placed in their corresponding addressed envelopes, then seventh letter is also in the correct envelope.

Hence required probability is 0.

6, 7 and 8.

Three cards can be drawn from 52 cards in $^{52}C_3$ ways

$n(S) = 52c_3$

6. Since we have 4 suits i.e., Diamonds, Spades, Clubs and Hearts and each suit contains 13 cards. Three cards can be selected from 13 cards in $^{13}C_3$ ways.

$\therefore$ Number of favorable outcomes = 4. $^{13}C_3$

Required probability = $4.\frac{^{13}C_3}{^{52}C_3}$

7. From four suits we can select 3 suits in $^4C_3$ ways. One card can be selected from each suit in $^{13}C_1.\ ^{13}C_1.\ ^{13}C_1$

$\therefore$ Number of favorable outcomes

$= {}^4C_3.\ ^{13}C_1.\ ^{13}C_1.\ ^{13}C1$

$\therefore$ Required probability = $\frac{4(13)^3}{^{52}C_3}$

8. Each suit contains 9 number cards. 2 number cards can be drawn from 9 cards in $^9C_2$ ways.. Third card can be selected from the remaining 27 number cards in $^{27}C_1$ ways.

Hence total number of favorable outcomes is $4(^9C_2)(^{27}C_1)$

Required probability = $\frac{4\left(^9C_2\right)\left(^{27}C_1\right)}{^{52}C_3}$

9. Total number of balls in the bag = 5 + 7 = 12.

5 balls can be drawn from 12 balls in $^{12}C_5$ ways

Number of ways of drawing 3 red balls and 2 white balls from 5 white balls and 7 red balls is $^5C_2.\ ^7C_3$

$\therefore$ Required probability = $\frac{^5C_2.\ ^7C_3}{^{12}C_5}$

$= \frac{10\times35}{792} = \frac{175}{396}$

10. Total number of coins in bag = 6 + 5 + 4 = 15.

5 coins can be drawn from 15 coins in $^{15}C_5$ ways.

When 4 coins are one rupee coins and fifth coin is a two rupee coin the amount will be minimum.

$\therefore$ Number of favourable cases = $^4C_4.\ ^{45}C_1 = 5$

Probability that the amount will be minimum is

$P(E) = \frac{5}{^{15}C_5} = \frac{5}{3003}$

$\therefore \quad P(\bar{E}) = 1 - P(E) = 1 - \frac{5}{3003} = \frac{2998}{3003}$

$\therefore$ Odds in favour of the required event = 5: 2998

11.

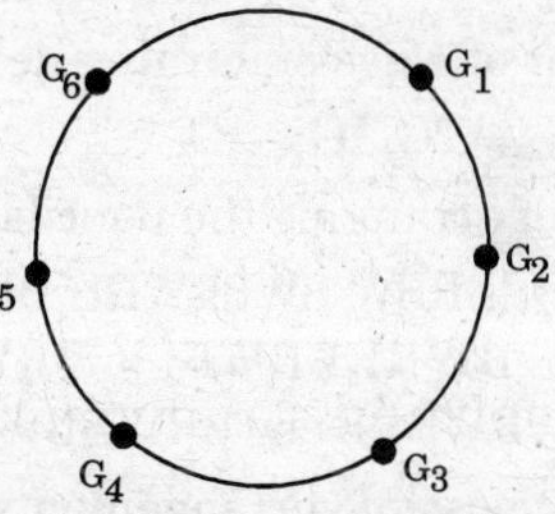

Six girls can be arranged around a circle in 5! ways.

Now, the six boys can be arranged in the six places in between the girls in 6! ways.

Hence, required number of ways = 5 ! 6!

12. Of the 10 places available, there are 5 even places. Digits 2, 4, 6, 4 and 2 can be placed in these 5 even places in $\frac{5!}{2!2!}$ ways.

Remaining digits 1, 3, 1, 1 and 9 can be placed in the remaining 5 places in $\frac{5!}{3!}$ ways.

Hence, required number of ways

$= \frac{5!}{2!2!}\frac{5!}{3!} = \frac{(5!)^2}{(2!)^2\ 3!}$

13. Number of ways of inviting at least one friend is

$$2^{12} - 1 = 4095$$

14. Number of ways of inviting at least 10 friends

$$= {}^{12}C_{10} + {}^{12}C_{11} + {}^{12}C_{12}$$
$$= 66 + 12 + 1 = 79$$

15. Each prize can be distributed in 3 ways, so, 6 prizes can be distributed in 3^6 ways.

16. Number of ways of dividing 16 books equally among 4 boys

$$= \frac{16!}{4!4!4!4!} = \frac{16!}{(4!)^4}$$

17. Number of ways of dividing 16 books equally into 4 parcels

$$= \frac{16!}{4!(4!)^4} = \frac{16!}{(4!)^5}$$

18. There are four vowels viz., U, A, I, E in the word "ILLUSTRATE".

First letter must be S and the last letter can be any one of the vowels U, A, I and E.

Remaining 8 places can be filled with the remaining 8 letters in $\frac{8!}{2!2!}$ ways.

Hence, required number of arrangements is

$$= 4 \times \frac{8!}{2!2!} = 8!$$

19. Prof. Balamurali and Asst. B of Sheshadri cannot be included together in the delegation.

Hence, number of ways of forming delegation

$$= {}^{10}C_5\,{}^6C_3 - {}^9C_4\,{}^5C_2$$

20. Possible ways of arranging the pencils are:

RBWBWBR, WBRBRBW, BWBRWRB, BRBWRWB, BWRBWRB, BWRRBRWB, BRWBRWB, BRWBWRB, BWRWBRB and BRWBBWB

i.e. a total of 10 possible arrangements.

NUMERICAL TYPE QUESTIONS

1 and 2 :

Let A and B be the two events.

Given: $P(\bar{A}) : P(A) = 4 : 5$

$$\Rightarrow \quad P(\bar{A}) = \frac{4}{9};\ P(A) = \frac{5}{9}$$

Also, $P(B) : P(\bar{B}) = 3 : 7$

$$\Rightarrow \quad P(B) = \frac{3}{10} \text{ and } P(\bar{B}) = \frac{7}{10}$$

1. $A \cap \bar{B}$ and $\bar{A} \cap B$ denote events that exactly one of them will occur.

$$P(A \cap \bar{B}) = P(A)\,P(\bar{B}) = \frac{5}{9}\cdot\frac{7}{10} = \frac{7}{18}$$

$$= P(\bar{A} \cap B) = P(\bar{A}).P(B)$$

$$= \frac{4}{9}\cdot\frac{3}{10} = \frac{2}{15}$$

Required probability is

$$= \frac{7}{18} + \frac{2}{15} = \frac{35+12}{90} = \frac{47}{90}$$

2. P (neither of them occurs)

$$= P(\bar{A} \cap \bar{B}) = P(\bar{A}).P(\bar{B}) = \frac{7}{10}\left(\frac{4}{9}\right) = \frac{14}{45}$$

3, 4 and 5.

Let A, B and C be the events that Shiva, Jagan and Rohit hit the target respectively.

$$\therefore \quad P(A) = \frac{2}{3}; \qquad P(\bar{A}) = \frac{1}{3}$$

$$P(B) = \frac{5}{7}; \qquad P(\bar{B}) = \frac{2}{7}$$

$$P(C) = \frac{3}{8}; \qquad P(\bar{C}) = \frac{5}{8}$$

3. P (None of them hit the target)

$$= P(\bar{A} \cap \bar{B} \cap \bar{C}) = P(\bar{A}).P(\bar{B}).P(\bar{C})$$

$$= \left(\frac{1}{3}\right)\cdot\left(\frac{2}{7}\right)\cdot\left(\frac{5}{8}\right) = \frac{5}{84}$$

4. Event $(A \cap B \cap \bar{C}) \cup (A \cap \bar{B} \cap C) \cup (\bar{A} \cap B \cap C)$ denotes that exactly two persons hit the target, and $A \cap B \cap C$ is the event that all the three persons hit the target.

$$P(A \cap B \cap \bar{C}) = P(A)\,P(B)\,P(\bar{C})$$

$$= \frac{2}{3}\cdot\left(\frac{5}{7}\right)\cdot\left(\frac{5}{8}\right) = \frac{25}{84}$$

$$P(A \cap \bar{B} \cap C) = P(A)\,P(\bar{B})\,P(C)$$

$$= \frac{2}{3}\cdot\left(\frac{2}{7}\right)\cdot\left(\frac{3}{8}\right) = \frac{1}{14}$$

$$P(\bar{A} \cap B \cap C) = P(\bar{A})\,P(B)\,P(C)$$

$$= \frac{1}{3}\cdot\left(\frac{5}{7}\right)\cdot\left(\frac{3}{8}\right) = \frac{5}{56}$$

$$P(A \cap B \cap C) = P(A)\,P(B)\,P(C)$$

$$= \frac{2}{3}\cdot\left(\frac{5}{7}\right)\cdot\left(\frac{3}{8}\right) = \frac{5}{28}$$

Hence required probability

$$= P\left(A \cap B \cap \bar{C}\right) + P\left(A \cap \bar{B} \cap C\right) + P\left(\bar{A} \cap B \cap C\right) + P\left(A \cap B \cap C\right)$$

$$= \frac{25}{84} + \frac{1}{14} + \frac{5}{56} + \frac{5}{28} = \frac{50+12+15+30}{168} = \frac{107}{168}$$

5. Exactly one of them hits the target

$\left(A \cap \bar{B} \cap \bar{C}\right) \cup \left(\bar{A} \cap B \cap \bar{C}\right) + \left(\bar{A} \cap \bar{B} \cap C\right)$

denotes that exactly one of them hits the target.

$$P\left(A \cap \bar{B} \cap \bar{C}\right) = P(A) \,.\, P(\bar{B}) \,.\, P(\bar{C})$$

$$= \frac{2}{3} \times \frac{2}{7} \times \left(\frac{5}{8}\right) = \frac{5}{42}$$

$$P\left(\bar{A} \cap B \cap \bar{C}\right) = P\left(\bar{A}\right).P(B).P\left(\bar{C}\right) = \frac{1}{3}.\frac{2}{7}.\frac{3}{8} = \frac{1}{28}$$

$$P\left(\bar{A} \cap \bar{B} \cap C\right) = P(\bar{A}).P(\bar{B})P(C) = \frac{1}{3}.\frac{5}{7}.\frac{5}{8} = \frac{25}{168}$$

Hence required probability is

$$= P\left(A \cap \bar{B} \cap \bar{C}\right) + P\left(\bar{A} \cap B \cap \bar{C}\right) + P\left(\bar{A} \cap \bar{B} \cap C\right)$$

$$= \frac{5}{42} + \frac{25}{168} + \frac{1}{28} = \frac{20+25+26}{168} = \frac{51}{168} = \frac{17}{56}$$

6. Three consecutive letters can be selected from English alphabet in 24 ways.

$\therefore \quad n(S) = 24$

Since, no two consecutive letters are vowels, the number of ways that among three letters one letter is vowel is 13.

$\therefore$ Required probability $= \frac{13}{24}$

7. Eight coins are tossed, so $n(S) = 2^8$

Let E be the favorable event. It is required to get 4 heads and 4 tails which is possible in the favorable out come HHHHTTTT.

This can be arranged in $\frac{8!}{4!4!}$ ways.

$$n(E) = \frac{8 \times 7 \times 6 \times 5 \times 4!}{4 \times 3 \times 2 \times 1 \times 4!} = 70$$

$\therefore$ Required probability $= \frac{n(E)}{n(S)} = \frac{70}{2^8} = \frac{35}{128}$

8. *Given* : $P(H) = 3P(T)$

We know

$$P(H) + P(T) = 1$$
$$3P(T) + P(T) = 1$$
$$P(T) = \frac{1}{4}$$
$$P(H) = \frac{3}{4}$$

Since the coin is tossed 3 times, two heads may occur in 1st and 2nd trial, 2nd and 3rd trial or 1st and 3rd trial.

$\therefore$ Required probability

$$= \frac{3}{4} \times \frac{3}{4} \times \frac{1}{4} + \frac{1}{4} \times \frac{3}{4} + \frac{3}{4} \times \frac{1}{4} \times \frac{3}{4}$$

$$= \frac{9}{64} + \frac{9}{64} + \frac{9}{64} = \frac{27}{64}$$

9. Two black cards can be selected in $26c_2$ ways.

A pack contain 8 black honours.

Hence number ways of selecting two same honours is 4.

$\therefore$ Required probability $= \frac{4}{26c_2} = \frac{4}{325}$

10. Let one card is king, then second card can be any of the other 3 cards from the other suit and it can be selected in $4 \times 3 = 12$ ways. Since there are four honour cards, hence

$\therefore$ Required probability $= \frac{12}{325}$

11, 12 and 13

Probability that Akil reach the summit

$= P(A) = 2/3$

$\therefore \quad P\left(\bar{A}\right) = 1/3$

Probability that Nikil reach the summit is

$P(N) = 5/8$

$\therefore \quad P\left(\bar{N}\right) = 3/8$

Probability that Sunil reach the summit

$$P(S) = \frac{4}{7}$$

$\therefore \quad P\left(\bar{S}\right) = \frac{3}{7}$

11. Probability that none of them reaches the summit

$$= P\left(\bar{A} \cap \bar{N} \cap \bar{S}\right) = P\left(\bar{A}\right)P\left(\bar{N}\right)P\left(\bar{S}\right)$$

$$= \frac{1}{3} \times \frac{3}{8} \times \frac{3}{7} = \frac{3}{56}$$

12. Probability that exactly two of them reaches the summit

$$= P(A \cap S \cap \bar{N}) + P(A \cap N \cap \bar{S}) + P(\bar{A} \cap N \cap S)$$

$$= P(A)P(S)P(\bar{N}) + P(A)P(N)P(\bar{S}) + P(N)P(S)P(\bar{A})$$

$$= \frac{2}{3}.\frac{4}{7}.\frac{3}{8} + \frac{2}{3}.\frac{5}{8}.\frac{3}{7} + \frac{1}{3}.\frac{5}{8}.\frac{4}{7} = \frac{37}{84}$$

13. Probability that atleast two of them reaches the summit

= Exactly two of them reach summit

+ three of them reach the summit

$$= \frac{37}{84} + \frac{5}{21} = \frac{57}{84} = \frac{19}{28}$$

14. 2 points determine a line.

Hence12 points can form $^{12}C_2$ straight lines.

But 4 points are collinear, i.e they give only one line.

Number of straight lines that can be formed

$$= {}^{12}C_2 - {}^{4}C_2 + 1 = 66 - 6 + 1 = 61$$

15. Three points determine a triangle.

∴ 12 non-collinear points can give $^{12}C_3$ triangles.

But 4 points are collinear, so, these 4 points do not give any triangles.

Hence, number of triangles = $^{12}C_3 - {}^{4}C_3 = 216$

16. Number of non-negative integral solutions of the equation

$$x_1 + x_2 + ... + x_k = n \text{ is } {}^{(n+k-1)}C_{k-1}.$$

Hence number of non-negative integral solutions of

$$x_1 + x_2 + x_3 + x_4 = 10 \text{ is } {}^{13}C_3 = 286.$$

17. Let m, n be the number of girls and the number of boys respectively. Then

$$^{m}C_2 = 66$$

$$\Rightarrow \quad \frac{m(m-1)}{2!} = 66 \quad \Rightarrow \quad m = 12$$

Also, $\quad {}^{m}C_1 \times {}^{n}C_1 = 240 \Rightarrow n = 20$

Hence, number of games in which both the players were boys = $^{20}C_2 = \dfrac{20(19)}{2} = 190$

18. Points lying on a straight line do not form triangles. Hence, number of triangles that can be formed by using the given points

$$= {}^{19}C_3 - ({}^{9}C_3 + {}^{10}C_3) = 765$$

19. A number is divisible by 125 if and only if number formed by its last three digits is divisible by 125.

So, possible combinations for last three digits are: 000, 125, 250 and 500.

Now, number of three-digit number divisible by 125 is 3.

Number of four-digit numbers divisible by 125

= 4 (4) = 16.

Number of five-digit numbers divisible by 125

= 4 (4) (5) = 80.

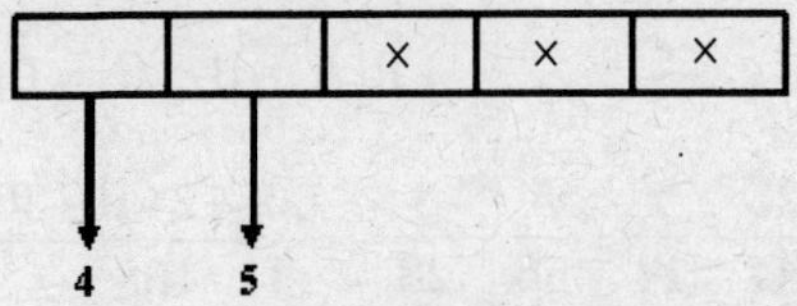

Hence, required number of numbers

= 3 + 16 + 80 = 99.

20. Let the number of red, blue and green balls selected from the supply be x_1, x_2 and x_3 respectively.

Then, $x_1 + x_2 + x_3 = 12$.

Number of non-negative integral solutions of the above equation

$$= {}^{(n+k-1)}C_{k-1} = {}^{14}C_2 = 91.$$

21. Number of positive integral solutions of equation

$$x_1 + x_2 + ... + x_k = n \text{ is } {}^{n-1}C_{k-1}.$$

Number of positive integral solutions of the equation

Hence $\quad a + b + c = 15$

$$^{15-1}C_{3-1} = {}^{14}C_2 = 91$$

22. When 'n' coins are tossed together, then probability of getting exactly 'r' tails = $\dfrac{^{n}C_r}{2^n}$

Hence probability of getting atleast two tails

= 1 – (probability of getting no tail

+ probability of getting exactly one tail)

$$= 1 - \left\{\frac{^{6}C_0}{64} + \frac{^{6}C_1}{64}\right\} = 1 - \frac{7}{64} = \frac{57}{64}$$

EXERCISE – II

MCQ TYPE QUESTIONS

1. There are 4 kings in a pack of 52 cards.

If 2 cards are selected and both are kings, remaining cards will be 50 out of which 2 will be kings.

2. For a match to be played, we need 2 teams

No. of matches = No. of ways of selections 2 teams out of 5

$$= {}^{5}C_2 = 10$$

4. $\quad x$ = {HHT, HHH}

y depends on x

z = {TTH, TTT}

∴ '*d*' is the correct choice.

5. P (Ram) = 1/6; p(Ramesh) = 1/8

p(only at) = p (Ram) × p (not ramesh) + p(Ramesh) × p(n_0 × R_{am})

$$= \frac{1}{6} + \frac{7}{8} + \frac{1}{8} \times \frac{5}{6}$$

$$\Rightarrow \frac{12}{40} = \frac{1}{4}$$

6. Here the given sets are

A = {2, 3, 4, 5}

and B = {11, 12, 13, 14, 15}

desired outcome = {(2, 14), (3, 13), (4, 12), (5, 11)}

∴ n(E) = 4

and total outcome = 4 × 5 = 20

∴ $n(s)$ = 20

∴ Probability of an event

$$= \frac{n(E)}{n(s)} = \frac{4}{20} = \frac{1}{5} = 0.2$$

8. The digit in unit place is selected in 4! Ways

The digit in tens place is selected in 4! Ways

The digit in hundreds place is selected in 4! Ways

The digit in thousands place is selected in 4! Ways

The digit in ten thousands place is selected in 4! Ways

Sum of all values for 1

$4! \times 1 \times (10^0 + 10^1 + 10^2 + 10^3 + 10^4)$

= 4! × 11111 × 1

Similarly for '3' 4! × (11111) × 3

Similarly for '5' 4! × (11111) × 5

Similarly for '7' 4! × (11111) × 7

Similarly for '9' 4! × (11111) × 9

∴ sum of all such numbers

4! ×(11111)× (1+ 3 + 5 + 7 + 9)

= 24 × (11111) × 25

= 6666600

9. The probability that the other face is tail is $\frac{1}{3}$.

10. Given: All the 2-digit numbers

To find: Probability of selecting a number at random not divisible by 7

Analysis: Total number of 2-digit numbers

10, 11, ..., 99 → 90 numbers

Unfavourable numbers *i.e.* numbers divisible by

7 : 14, 21, ..., 98

Number of unfavourable numbers = 13

This can be hand counted or we can use the following properties:

Last term = First time + (no. – 1) Diff

98 = 14 + (no. – 1) 7

⇒ no. = 13

$$\Rightarrow \text{Probability} = \frac{\text{Total} - \text{unfavourable}}{\text{Total}}$$

$$= \frac{90-13}{90} = 77/90$$

Hence, the solution is (d)

11. at a leap year

52 weeks, and 2 extra day they are (Mon, Tues) (Tues, Wed) (Wed Thu.) (Thus. Fri) (Fri. Sat) (Sat. Sun) (Sun Mond.)

$n(s)$ = 7

n(E) = 2 P(E) = $\frac{2}{7}$

13.

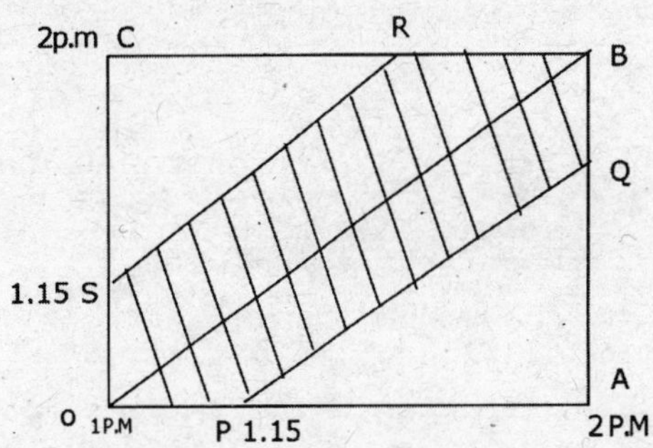

OB is the line when both A and B arrive at same time.

Total sample sapce = 60 × 60 = 3600

Favourable cases = Area of OABC – 2(Area of SRC)

$$= 3600 - 2 \times \left(\frac{1}{2} \times 45 \times 45\right)$$

= 1575

$$\therefore \text{ Required probability } = \frac{1575}{3600} = \frac{7}{16}$$

14. 2, 2, 3, 3, 4, 4, 4 $x > 3000$

322 — 3, 4	344 — 2, 3, 4
323 — 2, 3, 4	422 — 3, 4
324 — 2, 3, 4	423 — 2, 3, 4
332 — 2, 3, 4	424 — 2, 3, 4
333 — 2, 4	432 — 2, 3, 4
334 — 2, 3, 4	433 — 2, 3, 4
342 — 2, 3, 4	434 — 2, 3, 4
343 — 2, 3, 4	442 — 2, 3, 4
	443 — 2, 3, 4
	444 — 2, 3, 4

NUMERICAL TYPE QUESTIONS

1. In thousands place, 9 digits except 0 can be placed

   In hundreds place, 9 digits can be placed (including 0, excluding the one used in thousands place)

   In tens place, 8 digits can be placed (excluding the ones used in thousands and hundreds place)

   In ones place, 7 digits can be placed (excluding the one used in thousands, hundreds and tens place)

   Total number of combinations

   $$= 9 \times 9 \times 8 \times 7 = 4536$$

2. Given, in one year, probability of an earthquake > 6 magnitude = 0.04

   So, average time between successive earthquakes = 1/0.04 = 25 years

3. Given, 10% of the population is HIV^+, so probability = 0.1 for HIV^+ and 0.9 for HIV^-

   The diagnostic kit identifies $\rightarrow$ 0.95 HIV^+ and 0.89 HIV^- correctly

   So, the required probability that the person is actually HIV^+ = 0.95/2 = 0.475

4. Probability for one bulb to be non-defective is

   $$\frac{95}{100}$$

   $\therefore$ Probabilities that none of the bulbs is defectives $\left(\frac{95}{100}\right)^4 = 0.8145$

■■

6

CHAPTER

Miscellaneous

EXERCISE – I

MCQ TYPE QUESTIONS

1. If one root of a quadratic equation is $3 + \sqrt{2}$, then quadratic equation is
   (a) $x^2 - 6x - 7 = 0$ (b) $x^2 + 6x + 7 = 0$
   (c) $x^2 + 6x - 7 = 0$ (d) $x^2 - 6x + 7 = 0$
2. Three consecutive positive integers such that square of their sum exceeds the sum of their squares by 214, are
   (a) 5, 6, 7 (b) 10, 11, 12
   (c) 9, 10, 11 (d) 7, 8, 9
3. A and B attempt to solve a quadratic equation of the form $ax^2 + bx + c = 0$. A starts with a wrong value of b and gets the roots as –3 and –5. B starts with a wrong value of C and gets the roots as 6 and 2. The correct roots are
   (a) 3, 4 (b) 3, 5
   (c) 4, 6 (d) 2, 3
4. What is the value of

$$\frac{1}{5+\dfrac{1}{5+\dfrac{1}{5+.....}}}?$$

   (a) $\frac{5+\sqrt{29}}{2}$ (b) $\frac{5-\sqrt{29}}{2}$
   (c) $\frac{5\pm\sqrt{29}}{2}$ (d) 7
5. A man buys two horses for ₹ 86. By selling one for three – quarters of its cost price, and the other for four-thirds of its cost price, he makes a profit of ₹ 3 on the whole transaction. The cost price (in rupees) of each horse is
   (a) ₹ 39, ₹ 47 (b) ₹ 34, ₹ 52
   (c) ₹ 48, ₹ 38 (d) ₹ 44, ₹ 42
6. What is the number of triplets (a, b, c) where a, b, c are positive integers, which satisfy the simultaneous equations ?
   (i) ab + bc = 44
   (ii) ac + bc = 23 is/are
   (a) 1
   (b) 2
   (c) 4
   (d) Indefinitely many
7. A man sitting beside me at a hotel ate idlis one after the other by ordering plate by plate. He said to me after drinking some water the last one I ate was my hundredth idli in last five days. Each day I ate 6 more than the previous day. How many he ate yesterday?
   (a) 26 (b) 24 (c) 22 (d) 20
8. A man, who went out between five and six o'clock and returned between six and seven o'clock, found that the hands of the watch had exchanged places. When did he go out?
   (a) $32\frac{4}{13}$ minutes past 5 o'clock.
   (b) $27\frac{2}{13}$ minutes past 5 o'clock.
   (c) $37\frac{3}{13}$ minutes past 5 o'clock.
   (d) $31\frac{5}{13}$ minutes past 5 o'clock.
9. What is the time between 7 a.m. and 8 a.m. when hands of a clock will be in the same straight line but not coincide?
   (a) 7 hours $5\frac{5}{11}$ min
   (b) 7 hours $3\frac{5}{11}$ min
   (c) 7 hours $7\frac{3}{11}$ min
   (d) 7 hours $7\frac{7}{11}$ min

NUMERICAL TYPE QUESTIONS

1. When $x^5 + x^4 + 5x^2 - 3$ is divided by (x + 2), the remainder will be_______
2. Pressure of a gas is inversely proportional to the volume. If pressure of oxygen is 84 atm when the volume is 1000 cm^3, then volume when the pressure is 28 atm will be_______ cm^3
3. The value of 'a' will make $x^2 - ax + 25$ a perfect square is _______

4. The value of $\alpha^3 + \beta^3$ if α and β are roots of the equation : $2x^2 - 7x - 4 = 0$ is ______

5. Sum of Anita's and Sunita's age is 43 years. 11 years hence, Anita's age will be $\frac{7}{6}$ times Sunita's age then. Sunita's present age is___ years

6. In a school trip, the students were accommodated in two rooms A and B. If 5 students are shifted from room A to room B then there will be equal number of students in both the rooms. But if 5 students from room B is shifted to room A, then the resulting number of students in room A is double the number of students left in room B. Total number of students are ______

7. A band of workers unloaded a certain number of boxes from their ship. The number of workers were between 50 and 60 (both inclusive). Each worker handled exactly 11 boxes, and each box was handled by exactly 7 workers. Exactly______number of boxes were there?

8. If ax = b,by = c ,cz = a, then value of xyz is______

9. The value of

$$\frac{1}{\left(1+\frac{xb}{xa}+\frac{xc}{xa}\right)}+\frac{1}{\left(1+\frac{xa}{xb}+\frac{xc}{xb}\right)}+\frac{1}{\left(1+\frac{xb}{xc}+\frac{xa}{xc}\right)}$$

is ______

10. A palm tree was 90 cm high, when it was planted. It grows by an equal number of cm each year, and at the end of the seventh year it was one ninth taller than at the end of the sixth year. The height of tree in cm at the end of the twelfth year is ______

11. A bottle and its cork together cost ₹ 1.10, and the bottle costs ₹ 1.00 more than its cork. The price of the bottle is ______

12. The value of is (100 – 1) (100 – 2) (100 – 3) .... (100 + 1) (100 + 2) (100 + 3) is ______

13. The value of $\dfrac{2+\cfrac{1}{3+\cfrac{4}{5}}}{2+\cfrac{1}{3+\cfrac{1}{1+\cfrac{1}{4}}}}$ is ______

14. Three integers, a, b and c, are such that $\frac{b}{c} = 3$. The fraction $\frac{b}{a}$ is in its lowest form. The______ is the possible value of a.

EXERCISE – II

(QUESTIONS FROM PREVIOUS GATE EXAMS)

MCQ TYPE QUESTIONS

2015

1. If $\log_x\left(\frac{5}{7}\right) = -\frac{1}{3}$, then the value of x is

(a) $\frac{343}{125}$ (b) $\frac{125}{343}$

(c) $-\frac{25}{49}$ (d) $-\frac{49}{25}$

2. A function $f(x)$ is linear and has a value of 29 at $x = -2$ and 39 at $x = 3$. Find its value at $x = 5$.

(a) 59 (b) 45

(c) 43 (d) 35

3. If $x > y > 1$, which of the following must be true?

(i) $\ln x > \ln y$ (ii) $e^x > e^y$

(iii) $y^x > x^y$ (iv) $\cos x > \cos y$

(a) i and ii (b) i and iii

(c) iii and iv (d) ii and iv

4. log tan1° + log tan2° +------+ log tan89° is ____.

(a) 1 (b) $1/\sqrt{2}$

(c) 0 (d) –1

5. Based on the given statements, select the most appropriate option to solve the given question. What will be the total weight of 10 poles each of same weight?

Statements:

(I) One fourth of the weight of a pole is 5 kg

(II) The total weight of these poles is 160 kg more than the total weight of two poles.

(a) Statement II alone is not sufficient

(b) Statement II alone is not sufficient

(c) Either I or II alone is sufficient

(d) Both statements I and II together are not sufficient.

6. Consider a function $f(x) = 1 - |x|$ on $-1 \le x \le 1$. The value of x at which the function attains a maximum, and the maximum value of function are:

(a) 0, –1

(b) –1, 0

(c) 0, 1

(d) –1, 2

7. In a triangle PQR, PS is the angle bisector of ∠QPR and ∠QPS = 60°. What is the length of PS?

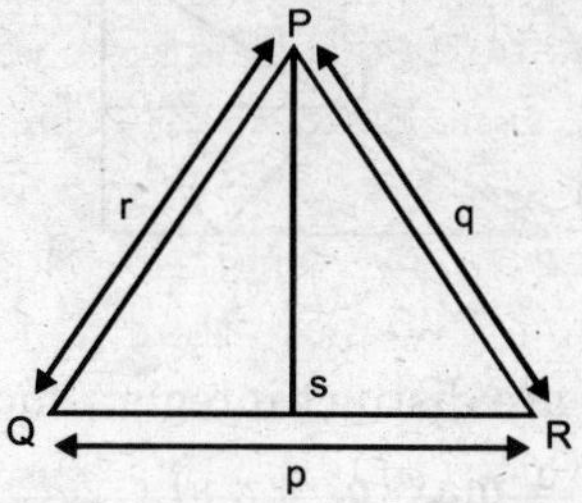

(*a*) $\frac{(q+r)}{qr}$ (*b*) $\frac{qr}{(q+r)}$

(*c*) $\sqrt{(q^2+r^2)}$ (*d*) $\frac{(q+r)^2}{qr}$

8. Based on the given statements, select the most appropriate option to solve the given question.

If two floors in a certain building are 9 feet apart, how many steps are there in a set of stairs that extends from the first floor to the second floor of the building?

Statements:

I. Each step is ¾ foot high.

II. Each step is 1 foot wide.

(*a*) Statement I alone is sufficient, but statement II alone is not sufficient.

(*b*) Statement II alone is sufficient, but statementI alone is not sufficient.

(*c*) Both statements together are sufficient, but neither statement alone is sufficient.

(*d*) Statement I and II together are not sufficient.

2014

9. If $y = 5x^2 + 3$, then the tangent at $x = 0, y = 3$

(*a*) passes through $x = 0, y = 0$

(*b*) has a slope of +1

(*c*) is parallel to the x-axis

(*d*) has a slope of –1

10. Let $f(x, y) = x^n y^m = P$. If x is doubled and y is halved, the new value of f is

(*a*) 2^{n-m} P (*b*) 2^{m-n} P

(*c*) $2(n - m)$ P (*d*) $2(m - n)$ P

11. A regular die has six sides with numbers 1 to 6 marked on its sides. If a very large number of throws show the following frequencies of occurrence: 1 → 0.167; 2 → 0.167; 3 → 0.152; 4 → 0.166; 5 → 0.168; 6 → 0.180. We call this die

(*a*) irregular (*b*) biased

(*c*) Gaussian (*d*) insufficient

12. Consider the equation : $(7526)_8 - (Y)_8 = (4364)_8$, where $(X)_N$ stands for X to the base N. Find Y.

(*a*) 1634 (*b*) 1737

(*c*) 3142 (*d*) 3162

13. At what time between 6 *a.m.* and 7 *a.m.* will the minute hand and hour hand of a clock make an angle closest to 60°?

(*a*) 6 : 22 *a.m.* (*b*) 6 : 27 *a.m.*

(*c*) 6 : 38 *a.m.* (*d*) 6 : 45 *a.m.*

14. The roots of $ax^2 + bx + c = 0$ are real and positive a, b and c are real. Then $ax^2 + b|x| + c = 0$ has

(*a*) No roots (*b*) 2 real roots

(*c*) 3 real roots (*d*) 4 real roots

2012

15. The cost function for a product in a firm is given by $5q^2$, where q is the amount of production. The firm can sell the product at a market price of ₹ 50 per unit. The number of units to be produced by the firm such that the profit is maximized is

(*a*) 5 (*b*) 10

(*c*) 15 (*d*) 25

16. Which of the following assertions are **CORRECT ?**

P : Adding 7 to each entry in a list adds 7 to the mean of the list

Q : Adding 7 to each entry in a list adds 7 to the standard deviation of the list

R : Doubling each entry in a list doubles the mean of the list

S : Doubling each entry in a list leaves the standard deviation of the list unchanged

(*a*) P, Q (*b*) Q, R

(*c*) P, R (*d*) R, S

17. A political party orders an arch for the entrance to the ground in which the annual convention is being held. The profile of the arch follows the equation $y = 2x - 0.1x^2$ where y is the height of the arch in meters. The maximum possible height of the arch is

(*a*) 8 meters (*b*) 10 meters

(*c*) 12 meters (*d*) 14 meters

18. There are eight bags of rice looking alike, seven of which have equal weight and one is slightly heavier. The weighing balance is of unlimited capacity. Using this balance, the minimum number of weighings required to identify the heavier bag is

(*a*) 2 (*b*) 3

(*c*) 4 (*d*) 8

2011

19. If log (P) = (1/2) Log (Q) = (1/3) Log (R), then which of the following options is TRUE?

(*a*) $P^2 = Q^3 R^2$ (*b*) $Q^2 = PR$

(*c*) $Q^2 = R^3 P$ (*d*) $R = P^2 Q^2$

20. The variable cost (V) of manufacturing a product varies according to the equation V = 4q, where q is the quanity produced. The fixed cost (F) of production of same product reduces with q according to the equation $F = 100/q$. How many units should be produced to minimize the total cost (V + F)?

(*a*) 5 (*b*) 4
(*c*) 7 (*d*) 6

21. Three friends R, S and T shared toffee from a bowl. R took 1/3rd of the toffees, but returned four to the bowl. S took 1/4th of what was left but returned three toffees to the bowl. T took half of the remainder but returned two back into the bowl. If the bowl had 17 toffees left, how many toffees were originally there in the bowl?

(*a*) 38 (*b*) 31
(*c*) 48 (*d*) 41

NUMERICAL TYPE QUESTIONS

2015

1. In the given figure angle Q is a right angle, PS : QS = 3:1, RT : QT = 5:2 and PU : UR = 1:1. If area of triangle QTS is 20 cm², then the area of triangle PQR in cm² is ______.

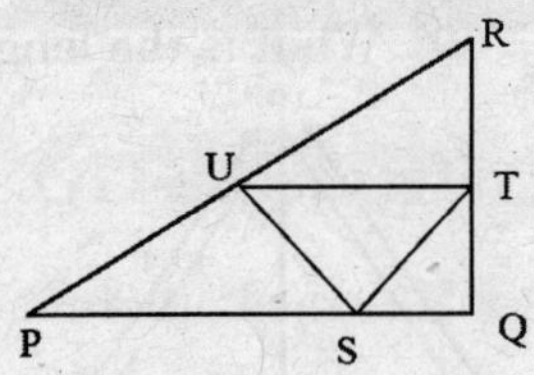

2. If p, q, r, s are distinct integers such that:

$f(p, q, r, s) = \max(p, q, r, s)$

$g(p, q, r, s) = \min(p, q, r, s)$

$h(p, q, r, s)$ = remainder of $(p \times q)/(r \times s)$ if $(p \times q) > (r \times s)$ or remainder of $(r \times s)/(p \times q)$ if $(r \times s) > (p \times q)$

Also a function $fgh(p, q, r, s) = f(p, q, r, s) \times g(p, q, r, s) \times h(p, q, r, s)$

Also the same operations are valid with two variable function of the form $f(p, q)$.

What is the value of $fg(h(2, 5, 7, 3), 4, 6, 8$

2014

3. When a point inside of a tetrahedron (a solid with four triangular surfaces) is connected by straight lines to its corners, how many (new) internal planes are created with these lines? ________.

ANSWERS

EXERCISE – I

MCQ Type Questions

1. (*d*) **2.** (*a*) **3.** (*b*) **4.** (*a*) **5.** (*d*) **6.** (*b*) **7.** (*a*) **8.** (*a*) **9.** (*a*)

Numerical Type Questions

1. 1 **2.** 3000 **3.** 10 **4.** $\frac{511}{8}$ **5.** 19 **6.** 60 **7.** 88 **8.** 1 **9.** 1

10. 450 **11.** 1.05 **12.** 0 **13.** 1 **14.** 104

EXERCISE – II

MCQ Type Questions

1. (*a*) **2.** (*c*) **3.** (*a*) **4.** (*c*) **5.** (*c*) **6.** (*c*) **7.** (*b*) **8.** (*a*) **9.** (*c*) **10.** (*a*)

11. (*b*) **12.** (*c*) **13.** (*a*) **14.** (*d*) **15.** (*a*) **16.** (*c*) **17.** (*b*) **18.** (*a*) **19.** (*b*) **20.** (*a*)

21. (*c*)

Numerical Type Questions

1. 280 **2.** (8) **3.** (6)

EXPLANATIONS

EXERCISE – I

MCQ TYPE QUESTIONS

1. If one root = $3 + \sqrt{2}$, then other root = $3 - \sqrt{2}$

$\therefore$ Sum of roots = $3 + \sqrt{2} + 3 - \sqrt{2} = 6$

$\therefore$ Product of roots

$= (3 + \sqrt{2})(3 - \sqrt{2}) = 9 - 2 = 7$

Quadratic equation is

x^2 – (Sum of roots) x + Product of roots = 0

i.e., $x^2 - 6x + 7 = 0$

2. Let consecutive positive integers be $x - 1$, x and $x + 1$

$\therefore [x - 1 + x + x + 1]^2$

$= (x - 1)^2 + x^2 + (x + 1)^2 + 214$

$(3x)^2 = x^2 + 1 - 2x + x^2 + x^2 + 2x + 1 + 214$

$9x^2 = 3x^2 + 216$

$6x^2 = 216$

$x^2 = 36 ; x = \pm 6$

But x is a positive integer, hence x = 6

So, numbers are 5, 6, and 7.

3. Equation formed by A with the roots –3 and –5 is

$x^2 - (-8x) + 15 = 0$

i.e., $x^2 + 8x + 15 = 0$

But value of B is wrong.

Hence coefficient of x is wrong.

Equation formed by B with roots 6 and 2 is

$x^2 - 8x + 12 = 0$

But the value of C is wrong.

hence constant term is wrong.

So, correct equation is

$x^2 - 8x + 15 = 0.$

Hence, real roots are 3 and 5.

4. Let

$$x = 5 + \cfrac{1}{\left[5 + \cfrac{1}{5 + \cfrac{1}{5 + \ldots}}\right]}$$

i.e., $x = 5 + \frac{1}{x} = \frac{5x + 1}{x}$

$\Rightarrow x^2 = 5x + 1$

$\Rightarrow x^2 - 5x - 1 = 0$

$\Rightarrow x = \frac{5 \pm \sqrt{(-5)^2 - 4(-1)(1)}}{2}$

$= \frac{5 \pm \sqrt{25 + 4}}{2} = \frac{5 \pm \sqrt{29}}{2}$

Since, all the terms are positive. The answer has to be $\frac{5 + \sqrt{29}}{2}$.

5. Let cost price of horses by ₹ x and ₹ y.

$\therefore \quad x + y = 86 \quad \ldots(1)$

and $\quad \frac{3x}{4} + \frac{4y}{3} = 89$

$\Rightarrow \quad 9x + 16y = 1068 \quad \ldots(2)$

Multiplying (1) by 9, $\quad 9x + 9y = 774 \quad \ldots(3)$

Subtracting (3) from (2),

$7y = 294$

$\Rightarrow \quad y = 42$

Substituting value of 'y' in equation (1),

$x + 42 = 86$

$\Rightarrow \quad x = 44.$

6. Equation (ii) is $c(a + b) = 23$, a prime number.

So, 2 factors must be 1, 23.

Since a, b are positive, therefore $a + b > 1$

$\Rightarrow c = 1; a + b = 23$

Put $c = 1; b = 23 - a$ in (i)

$\Rightarrow a^2 - 22a + 21 = 0$

$\Rightarrow a = 1$ or 21

$\Rightarrow b = 22$ or 2

$\therefore$ Solution sets are (1, 22, 1); (21, 2, 1).

7. First day the number of idlis he ate be x

Second day the count is (x+6)

Third day --------------------- (x+12)

Fourth day -------------------(x+18)

Fifth day ----------------------(x+24)

Total is5x + 6(1+2+3+4) =100

5x + 60 =100

x = 8

Day	Idlis
1	8
2	14
3	20
4	26
5	32

So, on fourth day, number of idlis the man ate were 26.

8.

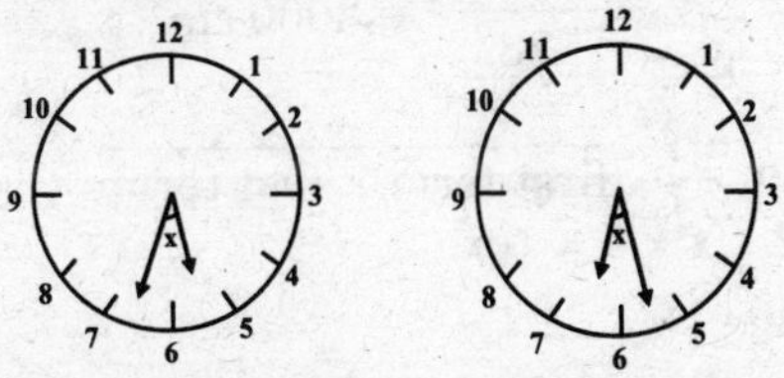

When hour hand moves 1 minute space, then minute hand moves 12 minute spaces.

Hence when hour hand moves x minutes, then minute hand moves 12x minutes.

$\therefore \quad 12x = 60 - x$

$\Rightarrow \quad x = \frac{60}{13}$

Interchangeable positions occur when original interval between the hands is $4\frac{8}{13}$ minute spaces or a multiple of this.

Hour hand moves through $\frac{60}{13}$ minute spaces.

At 5 O'clock, minute hand is 25 minutes behind time.

It has to gain $25\frac{60}{13} = \frac{385}{13}$ minutes.

$\frac{385}{13}$ minutes will be gained in

$$\frac{385}{13} \times \frac{60}{55} = \frac{420}{13} = 32\frac{4}{13} \text{ minutes.}$$

Hence man went out at $32\frac{4}{13}$ minutes past 5 O'clock.

9. When they are in the same straight line, in opposite direction. Minute hand and hour hand are 30 minute spaces apart.

At 7 p.m. they are 25 minute spaces apart.

So, minute hand has to gain only (30 – 25) = 5 minute spaces.

i.e., $\frac{60}{55} \times 5 = \frac{60}{11} = 5.\frac{5}{11}$ minutes.

Hence hands are in the same straight line at $5\frac{5}{11}$ minutes past 7.

NUMERICAL TYPE QUESTIONS

1. $p(x) = x^5 + x^4 + 5x^2 - 3$

$= (-2)^5 + (-2)^4 + 5(-2)^2 - 3$

$= (-32) + 16 + 5 \times 4 - 3 = 1$

2. $p \propto \frac{1}{v}$

$\therefore \quad p = \frac{k}{v}$

where, $k = 84 \times 1000$

$\therefore \quad v = \frac{k}{p} = \frac{84 \times 1000}{28} = 3000 \text{ cm}^3$

3. Middle term = $2\sqrt{\text{first term} \times \text{last term}}$

$ax = 2 \times x \times 5 = 10x$

$\therefore \quad a = 10$

4. $\alpha + \beta = \frac{7}{2}$

$\alpha\beta = -\frac{4}{2} = -2$

$(\alpha + \beta)^3 = \alpha^3 + \beta^3 + 3\alpha\beta(\alpha + \beta)$

$\left(\frac{7}{2}\right)^3 = \alpha^3 + \beta^3 + 3(-2)\left(\frac{7}{2}\right)$

$\frac{343}{8} = \alpha^3 + \beta^3 - 21$

$\frac{343}{8} + 21 = \alpha^3 + \beta^3$

$\therefore \quad \frac{511}{8} = \alpha^3 + \beta^3$

5. Let Anita's present age be 'x' years and that of Sunita by 'y' years.

$\therefore \quad x + y = 43$ ...(1)

and $(x + 11) = \frac{7}{6}(y + 11)$

$\Rightarrow \quad 6x + 66 = 7y + 77$

$\Rightarrow \quad 6x - 7y = 11$ ...(2)

Multiplying (1) by 6.

$6x + 6y = 258$ ...(3)

Subtracting (3) from (2),

$-13y = -247$

$\therefore \quad y = 19$ years.

6. Let the number of students in room A be x and number of students in room B be y.

$\therefore \quad x - 5 = y + 5$

$x - y = 10$ ...(1)

Also, $x + 5 = 2(y - 5)$

$\Rightarrow \quad x - 2y = -15$ ...(2)

Solving (1) and (2) we get,

$x = 35$ and $y = 25$

$\therefore \quad x + y = 60$

7. Let P be the number of workers, and let C be the number of boxes. Then, by counting the number of boxes handling in 2 different ways yields 11P = 7C.

Since P and C are integers, it follows that P must be divisible by 7.

Since $50 \le P \le 60$,

P must equal 56

$\therefore \quad C = 11 \times \frac{56}{7} = 88$

8. $ax = b$

$\Rightarrow$ (cz) x = b ....[since cz = a]

$\Rightarrow$ (by) xz = b ....[since by = c]

$\Rightarrow$ xyz = 1

9. $$\frac{1}{\left(1 + \frac{xb}{xa} + \frac{xc}{xa}\right)} + \frac{1}{\left(1 + \frac{xa}{xb} + \frac{xc}{xb}\right)} + \frac{1}{\left(1 + \frac{xb}{xc} + \frac{xa}{xc}\right)}$$

$$= \frac{xa}{(xa + xb + xc)} + \frac{xb}{(xa + xb + xc)} + \frac{xc}{(xa + xb + xc)}$$

$$= \frac{(xa + xb + xc)}{xa + xb + xc} = 1$$

10. Let tree grows x cm each year

Height of the tree at the end of the sixth year

$= (90 + 6x)$ cm

Growth in seventh year,

$$x = \frac{1}{9}(90 + 6x) \text{ cm}$$

$$x = 10 + \frac{2x}{3} \qquad \therefore \quad x = 30$$

Hence height of tree at the end of the twelfth year $= (90+12 \times 30) = 450$cm.

11. Let B = price of the bottle

C = price of the cork

Given : B + C = ₹ 1.10 ...(1)

and B – C = ₹ 1.00 ...(2)

From equations (1) and (2)

B = ₹ 1.05

C = ₹ 0.05.

12. (100 – 1) (100 – 2) (100 – 3)......... (100 – 100) (100+1) (100+2) (100+3)

$\Rightarrow$ (100 – 1)(100 – 2)(100 – 3)......... (0) (100 + 1) (100 + 2) (100 + 3) = 0.

13. $$\frac{2+\frac{1}{19}}{2+\frac{5}{3+\frac{4}{5}}} = \frac{2+\frac{5}{19}}{2+\frac{5}{19}} = 1$$

14. $\frac{b}{c} = 3 \Rightarrow b = 3c$, i.e., b is divisible by 3.

Also, $\frac{b}{c}$ cannot be reduced,

i.e., a is not divisible by 3.

EXERCISE – II

MCQ TYPE QUESTIONS

1. $\frac{5}{7} = x^{-1/3} \Rightarrow \frac{7}{5} = x^{1/3} \Rightarrow \left(\frac{7}{5}\right)^3 = x \Rightarrow x = \frac{343}{125}$

2. $f(x) = 2x + 33 = 2(5) + 33 = 43$

3. For whole numbers, greater the value greater will be its log.

Same logic for power of *e*.

4. $\log \tan 1° + \log \tan 89° = \log(\tan 1° \times \tan 89°)$

$= \log(\tan 1° \times \cot 1°)$

$= \log 1 = 0$

Using the same logic total sum is '0'.

6. The given function is

$$f(x) = 1 - |x| \text{ on } -1 \le x \le 1$$

In order to find maximum and minimum value of function in interval [–1, 1]

At $x = -1$, $f(-1) = 1 - |-1| = 1 - 1 = 0$

At $x = -0.5$, $f(-0.5) = 1 - |-0.5| = 1 - 0.5 = 0.5$

At $x = 0$, $f(0) = 1 - |0| = 1$

At $x = 0.5$, $f(0.5) = 1 - |0.5| = 0.5$

At $x = 1$, $f(1) = 1 - |1| = 1 - 1 = 0$

$\therefore$ Hence, maximum value occurs at $x = 0$ and its maximum value is 1.

$\therefore$ Option (*c*) is correct.

9. $y = 5x^2 + 3, \quad \frac{dy}{dx} = 10x$

Slope of tangent $= \left(\frac{dy}{dx}\right)_{x=0,y=3} = 10 \times 0 = 0$

Slope $= 0 \Rightarrow$ tangent is parallel to *x*-axis.

10. $P' = 2^n X^n \left(\frac{1}{2}\right)^m y^m = 2^{n-m} X^n Y^m = 2^{n-m} P$

11. For a very large number of throws, the frequency should be same for unbiased throw. As it not same, then the die is baised.

12. $(7526)_8 - (y)_8 = (4364)_8$

$\Rightarrow y_8 = (7526)_8 - (4364)_8$

$$\begin{array}{cccc} & 4 & (8+2=10) & \\ 7 & \not{5} & 2 & 6 \\ 4 & 3 & 6 & 4 \\ \hline 3 & 1 & 4 & 2 \end{array}$$

When we have base 8, we borrow 8 instead of 10 as done in normal subtraction.

13.

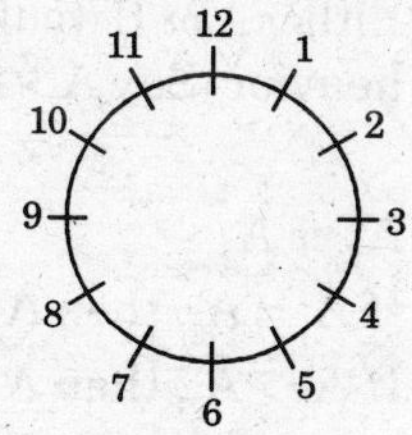

From option

At 6 a.m.

Both hand – 180° aparts,

At 6 : 20 a.m. – both hand apart

$\Rightarrow \quad 180° + 10° - 120° = 70°$

At 6 : 22 a.m. – both hand apart

$\Rightarrow \quad 180° + 12° - 132° = 60°$ (closest)

14. $ax^2 + bx + c = 0$

Roots are real and positive

$\therefore \quad b^2 - 4ac > 0$

By the above condition we get two positive real roots

Now, $ax^2 + b|x| + c = 0$

This can be written as;

$ax^2 + bx + c$

$\Delta = b^2 - 4ac > 0$

Now for $ax^2 - bx + c$

$(-b)^2 - 4ac \Rightarrow b^2 - 4ac$

Again $b^2 - 4ac > 0$

So again we get real roots

Thus we have 4 real roots of $ax^2 + b|x| + c = 0$

15. $P = 50q - 5q^2$

$\frac{dp}{dq} = 50 - 10q; \frac{d^2p}{dq^2} < 0$

$\therefore$ p is maximum at $50 - 10q = 0$ or, $q = 5$

Else check with options

16. P and R always holds true

Else consider a sample set {1, 2, 3, 4} and check accordingly

17. $y = 2x - 0.1x^2$

$\frac{dy}{dx} = 2 - 0.2x$

$\frac{d^2y}{dx^2} < 0$

$\therefore$ y maximises at $2 - 0.2x = 0$

$\Rightarrow x = 10$

$\therefore$ $y = 20 - 10 = 10$m

18. Let us categorize bags in three groups as

$A_1 A_2 A_3$ $B_1 B_2 B_3$ $C_1 C_2$

1st weighing A vs B

Case-1	**Case-2**
$A_1 A_2 A_3 = B_1 B_2 B_3$	$A_1 A_2 A_3 \neq B_1 B_2 B_3$
Then either C_1 or C_2 is heavier	Either A or B would be heavier (Say A > B)
2nd weighing	
C_1 vs C_2	A_1 vs A_2
If $C_1 > C_2$, then C_1	If $A_1 = A_2$, then A_3
If $C_1 < C_2$, then C_2	If $A_1 > A_2$, then A_1
If $A_1 < A_2$, then A_2	

19. $\log P = \frac{1}{2} \log Q = \frac{1}{3} \log (R) = k$

$\therefore$ $P = b^k, Q = b^{2k}, R = b^{3k}$

Hence, $Q^2 = b^{4k} = b^{3k} b^k = PR$

20. Checking with all options in formula: (4q+100/q) i.e. (V+F). Option (*a*) gives the minimum cost.

21. Let total number of toffees in bowl be x

R took $\frac{1}{3}$ of toffees and returned 4 to the bowl

$\therefore$ Number of toffees with R = $\frac{1}{3}x - 4$

Remaining of toffees in bowl = $\frac{2}{3}x + 4$

Number of toffees with S = $\frac{1}{4}\left(\frac{2}{3}x+4\right) - 3$

Remaining toffees in bowl = $\frac{3}{4}\left(\frac{2}{3}x+4\right)+4$

Number of toffees with T = $\frac{1}{2}\left(\frac{3}{4}\left(\frac{2}{3}x+4\right)+4\right)+2$

Remaining toffees in bowl

$$= \frac{1}{2}\left[\frac{3}{4}\left(\frac{2}{3}x+4\right)+4\right]+2$$

Given : $\frac{1}{2}\left[\frac{3}{4}\left(\frac{2}{3}x+4\right)+4\right]+2 = 17$

$\Rightarrow \frac{3}{4}\left(\frac{2}{3}x+4\right) = 27$

$\Rightarrow x = 48$

NUMERICAL TYPE QUESTIONS

1. Let area of triangle PQR be 'A'

$$\frac{SQ}{PQ} = \frac{1}{1+3} = \frac{1}{4}$$

$$\frac{QT}{QR} = \frac{2}{2+5} = \frac{2}{7}$$

$\therefore$ Area of $\Delta QTS = \frac{1}{2} \times SQ \times QT$

$$= \frac{1}{2} \times \left(\frac{1}{4}PQ\right) \times \left(\frac{2}{7}QR\right)$$

$$= \frac{1}{4} \times \frac{2}{7} \times \left(\frac{1}{2} \times PQ \times QR\right)$$

$$= \frac{1}{14} \times \text{Area of } \Delta PQR$$

Given 20 cm^2 = $\frac{1}{14} \times A$

$\therefore$ $A = 14 \times 20 = 280$ cm^2

2. $fg(h(2, 5, 7, 3), 4, 6, 8) = fg(1, 4, 6, 8)$

$= f(1, 4, 6, 8) \times g(1, 4, 6, 8)$

$= 8 \times 1 = 8$

Engineering Mathematics

1 CHAPTER Linear Algebra

DETERMINANTS

A determinant of order n has n rows and n columns. It has $n \times n$ elements.

$$\Delta = \begin{vmatrix} a_{11} & a_{12} & a_{13} & \dots & a_{1n} \\ a_{21} & a_{22} & a_{23} & \dots & a_{2n} \\ \dots & \dots & \dots & \dots & \dots \\ \dots & \dots & \dots & \dots & \dots \\ a_{n1} & a_{n2} & a_{n3} & \dots & a_{nn} \end{vmatrix}$$

MINOR

If a_{ij} is an element which is in the ith row and j^{th} column of a squre matrix A, then determinant of the matrix obtained by deleting i^{th} row and j^{th} column of A is called minor of a_{ij} and is denoted by M_{ij}

e.g. If $A = \begin{vmatrix} a_{11} & a_{12} & a_{13} \\ a_{21} & a_{22} & a_{23} \\ a_{31} & a_{32} & a_{33} \end{vmatrix}$, then

$$M_{11} = \text{minor of } a_{11} = \begin{vmatrix} a_{22} & a_{23} \\ a_{32} & a_{33} \end{vmatrix} = a_{22}\, a_{33} - a_{32}\, a_{23}$$

$$M_{12} = \text{minor of } a_{12} = \begin{vmatrix} a_{21} & a_{23} \\ a_{31} & a_{33} \end{vmatrix}$$

$$= a_{21}\, a_{33} - a_{31}\, a_{23} \text{ and so on.}$$

9 minors can be obtained corresponding to 9 elements of Δ.

e.g. Minor of the element

$$a_{11} = \begin{vmatrix} a_{22} & a_{23} \\ a_{32} & a_{33} \end{vmatrix} = M_{11}$$

$$a_{12} = \begin{vmatrix} a_{21} & a_{23} \\ a_{31} & a_{33} \end{vmatrix} = M_{12} \text{ and so on.}$$

Determinant of a Square Matrix

Only square matrix can have determinants because in a determinant, number of rows is equal to number of columns.

Let $A = [a_{ij}]_{max}$ be a square matrix of order n.

Then $$|A| = \begin{vmatrix} a_{11} & a_{12} & a_{13} & \dots & a_{1n} \\ a_{21} & a_{22} & a_{23} & \dots & a_{2n} \\ \dots & \dots & \dots & \dots & \dots \\ a_{n1} & a_{n2} & a_{n3} & \dots & a_{nn} \end{vmatrix}$$

is called *determinant of matrix A.*

Properties of Determinants

(*i*) If all the elements of one column or one row of a determinant are multiplied by the same number "C", then value of the new determinant is "C" times the value of the given determinant.

(*ii*) Value of a determinant does not change when rows and columns are interchanged.

(*iii*) If any two columns or two rows of a determinant are interchanged, then value of the determinant is multiplied by – 1.

(*iv*) In a determinant, sum of the products of the element of any column (or row) with the cofactors of the corresponding elements of any other column (or row) is zero.

(*v*) If two columns (or two rows) of a determinant are identical, then value of the determinant is zero.

(*vi*) If in a determinant each element in any column (or row) consists of sum of two terms, then determinant can be expressed as the sum of two determinants of the same order.

(*vii*) If the elements of a column (or row) of a determinant are added K times the corresponding elements of another column (or row), then value of the determinant obtained is equal to value of the original determinant.

CO-FACTOR

If a_{ij} is an element which is in the ith row and j^{th} column of a square matrix A, then product of $(-1)^{i+j}$ and minor of a_{ij} is called cofactor of a_{ij} and is denoted by A_{ij}.

e.g. If $A = \begin{bmatrix} a_{11} & a_{12} & a_{13} \\ a_{21} & a_{22} & a_{23} \\ a_{31} & a_{32} & a_{33} \end{bmatrix}$, then

$$A_{11} = \text{cofactor of } a_{11} = (-1)^{1+1} M_{11}$$

$$= +1 \begin{vmatrix} a_{22} & a_{23} \\ a_{32} & a_{33} \end{vmatrix} = a_{22}\, a_{33} - a_{32}\, a_{23}$$

$$A_{12} = \text{cofactor of } a_{12} = (-1)^{1+2} M_{11}$$

$$= -1 \begin{vmatrix} a_{21} & a_{23} \\ a_{31} & a_{33} \end{vmatrix} = (a_{31}\, a_{23} - a_{21}\, a_{33})$$

and so on.

and if $A = \begin{bmatrix} a_1 & b_1 & c_1 \\ a_2 & b_2 & c_2 \\ a_3 & b_3 & c_3 \end{bmatrix}$, then

$$A_1 = \text{cofactor of } a_1 = (-1)^{1+1}\begin{vmatrix} b_2 & c_2 \\ b_3 & c_3 \end{vmatrix} = b_2c_3 - b_3c_2$$

$$B_1 = \text{cofactor of } b_1 = (-1)^{1+2}\begin{vmatrix} a_2 & c_2 \\ a_3 & c_3 \end{vmatrix} = -(a_2c_3 - a_3c_2) = a_3c_2 - a_2c_3$$

C_1 = cofactor of c_1

$$= (-1)^{1+3}\begin{vmatrix} a_2 & b_2 \\ a_3 & b_3 \end{vmatrix} = a_2b_3 - a_3b_2 \text{ and so on.}$$

Example. If $A = \begin{bmatrix} 1 & 2 & 3 \\ 4 & 5 & 6 \\ 7 & 8 & 9 \end{bmatrix}$, then find all cofactors of element of A.

Solution. $A_{11} = (-1)^{1+1}\begin{vmatrix} 5 & 6 \\ 8 & 9 \end{vmatrix} = +(45-48) = -3$

$$A_{12} = (-1)^{1+2}\begin{vmatrix} 4 & 6 \\ 7 & 9 \end{vmatrix} = -(36-42) = 6$$

$$A_{13} = (-1)^{1+3}\begin{vmatrix} 4 & 5 \\ 7 & 8 \end{vmatrix} = +(32-35) = -3$$

$$A_{21} = (-1)^{2+1}\begin{vmatrix} 2 & 3 \\ 8 & 9 \end{vmatrix} = -(18-24) = 6$$

$$A_{22} = (-1)^{2+2}\begin{vmatrix} 1 & 3 \\ 7 & 9 \end{vmatrix} = +(9-21) = -12$$

$$A_{23} = (-1)^{2+3}\begin{vmatrix} 1 & 2 \\ 7 & 8 \end{vmatrix} = -(8-14) = 6$$

$$A_{31} = (-1)^{3+1}\begin{vmatrix} 2 & 3 \\ 5 & 6 \end{vmatrix} = +(12-15) = -3$$

$$A_{32} = (-1)^{3+2}\begin{vmatrix} 1 & 3 \\ 4 & 6 \end{vmatrix} = -(6-12) = 6$$

$$A_{33} = (-1)^{3+3}\begin{vmatrix} 1 & 2 \\ 4 & 5 \end{vmatrix} = +(5-8) = -3$$

ALGEBRA OF MATRICES

Matrix

A set of m,n numbers (real or complex) arranged in the form of a rectangular may have m rows and n columns is called an *$m \times n$ matrix.*

An $m \times n$ matrix is written as

$$A = \begin{bmatrix} a_{11} & a_{12} & a_{13} & \dots & a_{1n} \\ a_{21} & a_{22} & a_{23} & \dots & a_{2n} \\ \dots & \dots & \dots & \dots & \dots \\ a_{m1} & a_{m2} & a_{m3} & \dots & a_{mn} \end{bmatrix}$$

Element a_{ij} belongs to i^{th} row and j^{th} column and is sometimes called as $(i, j)^{th}$ element of the matrix.

Note: In a matrix, number of rows and columns need not be equal.

Types of matrix

1. Square matrix

In this matrix, the number of rows is equal to the number of columns.

e.g. $\begin{bmatrix} 1 & 2 \\ 3 & 4 \end{bmatrix}_{2\times2}$ and $\begin{bmatrix} 1 & 1 & 2 \\ 0 & 1 & 2 \\ 1 & 0 & 3 \end{bmatrix}_{3\times3}$

In these square matrices, $m = n$

Elements a_{ij} of a square matrix $A = [a_{ij}]_{n\times n}$ for which $i = j$ are called *diagonal elements* and line along which they lie is called *principal diagonal* of the matrix.

2. Null matrix or Zero matrix

The $m \times n$ matrix whose all elements are 0 is called *null matrix* (or zero matrix) of the type $m \times n$. It is denoted by 0.

e.g. $\begin{bmatrix} 0 & 0 & 0 & 0 \\ 0 & 0 & 0 & 0 \\ 0 & 0 & 0 & 0 \end{bmatrix}_{3\times4}$ is zero matrix of type 3×4

Above matrix can be written as

$$A = [a_{11}\, a_{22}\, a_{33}\, a_{44}]$$

3. Diagonal matrix

In this matrix, elements above and below the principal diagonal are all zero.

e.g. $A = \begin{bmatrix} a_{11} & 0 & 0 & 0 \\ 0 & a_{22} & 0 & 0 \\ 0 & 0 & a_{33} & 0 \\ 0 & 0 & 0 & a_{44} \end{bmatrix}$

4. Scalar matrix

In this matrix, all diagonal elements are equal.

e.g. $A = \begin{bmatrix} C & 0 & 0 \\ 0 & C & 0 \\ 0 & 0 & C \end{bmatrix}$

- If A be a matrix and $A^2 = A$, then A is called *idempotent*.

  If $AB = A$ and $BA = B$, then A and B are called *idempotent*.
- If A be a matrix and satisfies $A^2 = I$, then A is called *invalutory*.

5. Rectangular matrix

A matrix of order $m \times n$ is called a *rectangular matrix* if $m \neq n$

e.g. $\begin{bmatrix} 1 & 2 & 3 \\ 4 & 0 & 1 \end{bmatrix}_{2\times3}$, $\begin{bmatrix} 1 & 0 \\ 0 & 2 \\ 1 & 2 \end{bmatrix}_{3\times2}$, $\begin{bmatrix} 1 & 2 & 5 & 7 \\ 2 & 4 & 6 & 8 \end{bmatrix}_{2\times4}$

6. Unit matrix or Identity matrix

A square matrix each of whose diagonal elements is 1 and each of whose non-diagonal elements is equal to zero is called a *unit matrix or an identity matrix*. It is denoted by I_n when n is order of the matrix.

e.g. $I_2 = \begin{bmatrix} 1 & 0 \\ 0 & 1 \end{bmatrix}, I_3 = \begin{bmatrix} 1 & 0 & 0 \\ 0 & 1 & 0 \\ 0 & 0 & 1 \end{bmatrix}, I_4 = \begin{bmatrix} 1 & 0 & 0 & 0 \\ 0 & 1 & 0 & 0 \\ 0 & 0 & 1 & 0 \\ 0 & 0 & 0 & 1 \end{bmatrix}$

are unit matrices of order 2, 3, 4, respectively.

7. Column matrix

Any $m \times 1$ matrix which has m rows and only one column is a column matrix or a column vector.

Row matrix

Any $1 \times n$ matrix which has only one row and n columns is called a row matrix or as row vector.

e.g. $X_1 = [1\ 2\ 3\ 4\ 5\ 6]_{1 \times 6}$ is a row matrix of the type 1×6

$X_2 = \begin{bmatrix} 1 \\ 2 \\ 3 \\ 4 \end{bmatrix}_{4\times1}$ is a column matrix of type 4×1

8. Triangular matrix

It is of two types

(*i*) **Lower triangular matrix.** In this matrix, all the elements above the principal diagonal are zero.

e.g. $\begin{bmatrix} a_{11} & 0 & 0 \\ a_{21} & a_{22} & 0 \\ a_{31} & a_{32} & a_{33} \end{bmatrix}_{3\times3}$

The diagonal and lower triangular elements may or may not be zero.

(*ii*) **Upper triangular matrix.** In this matrix, all the elements below the principal diagonal are zero.

e.g. $\begin{bmatrix} a_{11} & a_{12} & a_{13} & a_{14} \\ 0 & a_{22} & a_{23} & a_{24} \\ 0 & 0 & a_{33} & a_{34} \\ 0 & 0 & 0 & a_{44} \end{bmatrix}_{4\times4}$

The diagonal and upper triangular elements may or may not be zero.

Types of Square Matrices

(*i*) **Nilpotent matrix**

A square matrix A is called a *nilpotent matrix* if there exists a positive integer n such that $A^n = 0$ and $A^{x-1} \neq 0$

If n is least positive integer such that $A^n = 0$, then n is called *index of the nilpotent* matrix A.

(*ii*) **Symmetrical matrix**

It is a square matrix in which $a_{ij} = a_{ji}$ for all i, j. A symmetric matrix is necessarily a square one.

If A is symmetric, **then** $A^T = A$

e.g. $\begin{bmatrix} a & h & g \\ h & b & f \\ g & f & c \end{bmatrix}$

(*a*) A A^T is always symmetric matrix.

(*b*) $\dfrac{A+A^T}{2}$ is always symmetric matrix.

(c) If A and B are symmetric then A + B and A – B also symmetric AB, BA may or May not by symmetric.

(*iii*) **Skew-symmetrical matrix**

It is a square matrix in which $a_{ij} = -a_{ji}$ for all i and j.

In a skew symmetrical matrix, all elements along the diagonal are zero.

e.g. $\begin{bmatrix} 0 & h & g \\ h & 0 & f \\ g & f & 0 \end{bmatrix}$

For any matrix A, the matrix $\dfrac{A-A^T}{2}$ is always skew symmetric.

Theorem:

Every square matrix can be uniquely expressed as a sum of a symmetric matrix and a skew symmetric matrix.

(*iv*) **Hermitian matrix**

It is a square matrix A in which $(i,j)^{th}$ element is equal to conjugate complex of the $(j, i)^{th}$ element. i.e. $a_{ij} = \bar{a}_{ji}$ for all i and j

e.g. $\begin{bmatrix} x & 3-4i & 1+2i \\ 3+4i & 0 & 5-4i \\ 1-2i & 5+4i & 1 \end{bmatrix}$

A necessary and sufficient condition for a matrix A to be hermitian is that

$$A = A^\theta$$

where A^θ is transposed conjugates of A.

(*v*) **Skew-Hermitian matrix**

It is a square matrix $A = [a_{ij}]$ in which $a_{ij} = -\bar{a}_{ji}$ for all i and j.

The diagonal elements of a skew-Hermitian matrix must be pure imaginary numbers or zero.

A necessary and sufficient condition for a matrix A to be skew-Hermitian is that

$$A^\theta = -A$$

(vi) Orthogonal matrix

A square matrix A is called *orthogonal matrix if*

$$AA^T = A^TA = I$$

e.g. If $A = \begin{bmatrix} \cos\theta & -\sin\theta \\ \sin\theta & \cos\theta \end{bmatrix}$ and

$$A^T = \begin{bmatrix} \cos\theta & \sin\theta \\ -\sin\theta & \cos\theta \end{bmatrix}$$

then $AA^T = \begin{bmatrix} \cos\theta & -\sin\theta \\ \sin\theta & \cos\theta \end{bmatrix}\begin{bmatrix} \cos\theta & \sin\theta \\ -\sin\theta & \cos\theta \end{bmatrix}$

$$= \begin{bmatrix} \cos^2\theta + \sin^2\theta & 0 \\ 0 & \sin^2\theta + \cos^2\theta \end{bmatrix}$$

$$= \begin{bmatrix} 1 & 0 \\ 0 & 1 \end{bmatrix} = I$$

(vii) Adjoint matrix

Let A be the square matrix given by

$$A = \begin{bmatrix} a_{11} & a_{12} & a_{13} & \dots & a_{1n} \\ a_{21} & a_{22} & a_{23} & \dots & a_{2n} \\ \dots & \dots & \dots & \dots & \dots \\ a_{n1} & a_{n2} & a_{n3} & \dots & a_{nn} \end{bmatrix}$$

Let A_{ij} be the cofactor a_{ij} then transpose of the matrix $[A_{ij}]$ is called *adjoint of the matrix A.*

$$\text{Adjoint } A = \begin{bmatrix} A_{11} & A_{21} & \dots & \dots & A_{n1} \\ A_{12} & A_{22} & \dots & \dots & A_{n2} \\ \dots & \dots & \dots & \dots & \dots \\ A_{1n} & A_{2n} & \dots & \dots & A_{nn} \end{bmatrix}$$

If A be an n-rowed square matrix, then $(\text{Adj } A)\, A = A\, (\text{Adj } A) = |A|\, I_n$

where I_n is the $n \times n$ identity matrix.

Sub-matrix

Any matrix obtained by omitting some rows and columns from a given $(m \times n)$ matrix B is called *submatrix of B*.

The matrix B itself is a sub-matrix of B as it can be obtained from B by omitting no rows or columns.

Principal Sub-matrix

A square sub-matrix of a square matrix B whose diagonal elements are also diagonal elements of matrix B is called *principal sub-matrix*.

Addition of Matrices

Let A and B be two matrices of the same type $m \times n$.

If $A = [a_{ij}]_{m \times n}$, $B = [b_{ij}]_{m \times n}$, then

$$A + B = [a_{ij} + b_{ij}]_{m \times n}$$

e.g. If $A = \begin{bmatrix} a_{11} & a_{12} & a_{13} & \dots & a_{1n} \\ a_{21} & a_{22} & a_{23} & \dots & a_{2n} \\ \dots & \dots & \dots & \dots & \dots \\ a_{m1} & a_{m2} & a_{m3} & \dots & a_{mn} \end{bmatrix}$

and $B = \begin{bmatrix} b_{11} & b_{12} & b_{13} & \dots & b_{1n} \\ b_{21} & b_{22} & b_{23} & \dots & b_{2n} \\ \dots & \dots & \dots & \dots & \dots \\ b_{m1} & b_{m2} & b_{m3} & \dots & b_{mn} \end{bmatrix}$

then, $A + B = \begin{bmatrix} a_{11}+b_{11} & a_{12}+b_{12} & a_{13}+b_{13} & \dots\dots & a_{1n}+b_{1n} \\ a_{21}+b_{21} & a_{22}+b_{22} & a_{23}+b_{23} & \dots\dots & a_{2n}+b_{2n} \\ \dots\dots & & \dots\dots & \dots\dots & \\ a_{m1}+b_{m1} & a_{m2}+b_{m2} & a_{m3}+b_{m3} & \dots\dots & a_{mn}+b_{mn} \end{bmatrix}$

Properties of Matrix Addition

(i) **Matrix addition is Commulative**

If A and B be two $m \times n$ matrices, then

$$A + B = B + A$$

(ii) **Matrix addition is Associative**

If A, B, C be three matrices each of type $m \times n$, then

$$(A + B) + C = A + (B + C)$$

(iii) **Existence of Additive identity**

If 0 be the $m \times n$ matrix each of whose element is zero, then $A + 0 = A = 0 + A$

where A is a $m \times n$ matrix

(iv) **Existence of additive inverse**

If $B = [b_{ij}]_{m \times n}$, then negative of matrix B is defined as he matrix $[-b_{ij}]_{m\times n}$ and is denoted by $-B$.

$$-B + B = 0 = B + (-B)$$

0 is null matrix of order $m \times n$

(v) **Cancellation Law**

If A, B, C are three main matrices, then

$B + A = C + A$

$\Rightarrow$ $B = C$ (right cancellation law)

$A + B = A + C$

$\Rightarrow$ $B = C$ (left cancellation law)

These cancellation laws hold good in the case of addition of matrices.

(vi) The equation $B + X = 0$ has a unique solution in the set of all $m \times n$ matrices.

EQUALITY OF TWO MATRICES

Two matrices $A = [a_{ij}]$ and $B = [b_{ij}]$ are said to be equal if

(*i*) both are the same size, and

(*ii*) $a_{ij} = b_{ij}$ for each pair of subscripts i and j.

If two matrices A and B are equal, then we write

$$A = B$$

Multiplication of a Matrix

1. By a scalar

Let C any real number called scaler and B be any $m \times n$ matrix, then

$$CB = BC = [cb_{ij}]_{m \times n}$$

where, $[b_{ij}]_{m \times n} = B$

Properties

(*i*) If p and q are two scalars and B is any $m \times n$ matrix, then

$$p(qB) = (pq)B$$

(*ii*) $(p + q)B = pB + qB$

(*iii*) If A and B are two matrices each of the type $m \times n$, then

$$p(A + B) = p(A) + p(B)$$

where p is any scalar.

(*iv*) If B be any $m \times n$ matrix, then

$$(-p)B = (-pB) = p(-B)$$

(*a*) $1B = B$

(*b*) $(-1)B = -B$

2. By a matrix

Let $A = [a_{ij}]_{l \times m}$ and $B = [b_{jk}]_{m \times n}$ be two matrices such that number of columns in A is equal to number of rows in B. Then in $l \times n$ matrix

$$C = [C_{ik}]_{l \times n} \text{ such that } C_{ik} = \sum_{j=1}^{n} a_{ij}\, b_{jk}$$

is called *product of the matrices A and B*.

We can write $C = AB$

Properties

(*i*) **Associative laws**

If A, B, C are $l \times m$, $m \times n$ and $n \times p$ matrices respectively, then

$$A(BC) = (AB)C$$

(*ii*) **Distributive laws**

$$A(B + C) = AB + AC$$

where A, B, C are any three $l \times m$, $m \times n$ and $n \times p$ matrices respectively.

(*iii*) **Commutative**

Multiplication of matrices is not always commutative.

For commutative $AB = BA$

For anti commutative $AB = -BA$

(*iv*) Product of two matrices can be zero matrix while neither of them is a zero matrix.

(*v*) If A be an $l \times m$ matrix. and I_m denotes m rowed unit matrix, then

$$AI_m = A = I_l A$$

TRANSPOSE OF A MATRIX

If row and column are interchanged in a matrix A, then matrix obtained is called *transpose matrix A* and is denoted by A^T.

- If $A = \begin{bmatrix} a_{11} & a_{12} & a_{13} \\ a_{21} & a_{22} & a_{23} \\ a_{31} & a_{32} & a_{33} \end{bmatrix}$, then $A^T = \begin{bmatrix} a_{11} & a_{21} & a_{31} \\ a_{12} & a_{22} & a_{32} \\ a_{13} & a_{23} & a_{33} \end{bmatrix}$
- If $A = [a_{ij}]$, then $A^T = [a_{ji}]$
- If A is a square matrix, then $|A| = |A^T|$

Properties of transpose

Theorem 1

If A is any matrix, then $(A^T)^T = A$.

Theorem 2

If A and B are two matrices of same type, then

$$(A + B)^T = A^T + B^T.$$

Note : If A is any matrix and k is any complex number, then $(kA)^T = kA^T$.

Theorem 3

If A and B are two matrices for which conformability for multiplication is assured, then

$$(AB)^T = B^T A^T.$$

Corollary 1 : If $A_1, A_2, \ldots\ldots A_n$ are n matrices which are conformable for multiplication, then

$$(A_1, A_2, \ldots.. A_n)^T = A_n^T A_{n-1}^T \ldots\ldots\ldots\ldots A_1^T.$$

Note : If A is any matrix, then AA^T and A^TA are defined. They are square matrices but their order may be different.

e.g. If $A = \begin{bmatrix} 1 & 2 & 0 \\ -2 & 0 & 3 \end{bmatrix}$ then $A^T = \begin{bmatrix} 1 & -2 \\ 2 & 0 \\ 0 & 3 \end{bmatrix}$

and $AA^T = \begin{bmatrix} 5 & -2 \\ -2 & 13 \end{bmatrix}$

$$A^TA = \begin{bmatrix} 5 & 2 & -6 \\ 2 & 4 & 0 \\ -6 & 0 & 9 \end{bmatrix}$$

Inverse of Matrix

Let A and B are two square matrices of the same order, such that AB = BA = I

then B is called *inverse of* A and is denoted by A^{-1}.

$$A^{-1} = \frac{(adjA)}{|A|}$$

Properties

(i) A^{-1} exists only when A is non singular, i.e. $|A| \neq 0$

(ii) The inverse of a matrix is unique.

(iii) $(AB)^{-1} = B^{-1} A^{-1}$

(iv) $(A^T)^{-1} = (A^{-1})^T$

(v) $(A^{-1})^{\theta} = (A^{\theta})^{-1}$

Inverse of a Square Matrix

A square matrix A is said to be an invertible matrix if there exists a square matrix B such that

AB = BA = I, then matrix B is called inverse of A.

- A rectangular matrix can not be invertible.
- Every square matrix need not be invertible.

Theorem 1

An invertible matrix has unique inverse.

If A is an invertible matrix, then its inverse is denoted by A^{-1}

Hence $AA^{-1} = A^{-1}A = I.$

Theorem 2

If A is an invertible matrix, and A^{-1} is also invertible then $(A^{-1})^{-1} = A$

Theorem 3

If A and B are two invertible matrices of same type, then AB is also invertible and $(AB)^{-1} = B^{-1} A^{-1}$.

Corollary 1: If $A_1, A_2, \ldots A_n$ are invertible matrices of same type, then $A_1A_2 \ldots A_n$ is also invertible and

$$(A_1 A_2 \ldots A_n)^{-1} = A_n^{-1} A_{n-1}^{-1} \ldots A_1^{-1}$$

If A is an invertible matrix and k is a non zero complex number, then kA is invertible and

$$(kA)^{-1} = k^{-1} A^{-1}$$

Theorem 4

If A is an invertible matrix, then A^T is also invertible and $(A^T)^{-1} = (A^{-1})^T$

Theorem 5

If A is a non singular matrix, then A is invertible and

$$A^{-1} = \frac{\text{Adj A}}{\det A}$$

If A is a square matrix, then

$$A\,(\text{Adj A}) = (\det A)\, I$$

Theorem 6

If A is an invertible matrix, then A is non singular.

If A is an invertible matrix, then

$$\det(A^{-1}) = \frac{1}{\det A}$$

Theorem 7

A square matrix A is non singular if A is invertible.

Corollary 2 : If $A = \begin{bmatrix} a & b \\ c & d \end{bmatrix}$ and $ad \neq bc$, then

$$A^{-1} = \frac{1}{ad - bc}\begin{bmatrix} d & b \\ c & a \end{bmatrix}$$

ORTHOGONAL MATRIX

An invertible square matrix is called orthogonal, if

$$A^T = A^{-1}$$

$\therefore$ $AA^T = I$

$\Rightarrow$ $|A| = |A^T|$

$\Rightarrow$ $|A| = \pm 1$

Example. If $A = \begin{bmatrix} 2 & 3 \\ 5 & 7 \end{bmatrix}$, then find A^{-1}.

Solution. $A^{-1} = \frac{1}{14-15}\begin{bmatrix} 7 & -3 \\ -5 & 2 \end{bmatrix}$

$$= -1\begin{bmatrix} 7 & -3 \\ -5 & 2 \end{bmatrix} = \begin{bmatrix} 7 & -3 \\ -5 & 2 \end{bmatrix}$$

Theorem 8

Let A, B, C be three square matrices of same type and A be a non-singular matrix. Then

AB = AC $\Rightarrow$ B = C

and BA = CA $\Rightarrow$ B = C.

Theorem 9

If A and B are non singular matrices of same type, then

$$\text{Adj}(AB) = (\text{Adj B})(\text{Adj A})$$

Theorem 10

If A is a square matrix of type n, then

$\det(\text{Adj A}) = (\det A)^{n-1}$

Example. If A is a square matrix of type 3 and det A = 10, then find (Adj A).

Solution. $\det(\text{Adj A}) = (\det A)^{3-1} = 10^2 = 100$

RANK OF A MATRIX

If A is not a null matrix; then rank of the matrix A is positive integer, if it possesses following two properties

(i) Each minor of order $n + 1$ of the matrix A vanishes (i.e. is zero).

(ii) There exists at least one minor of order n of the matrix A which is not zero.

If A is a null matrix, then rank of A is defined as *zero.* A need not be square matrix.

Properties

- Rank of A is denoted by $p(A)$ and is UNIQUE.
- Every matrix will have a rank.
- If A is a matrix of order $m \times n$, then
  $p(A) \leq m$ and n (smaller of the two).
- If $P(A) = n$, then every minor of order $n + 1$, $n + 2$, etc. is zero.
- If A is a matrix of order $n \times n$, then
  A is non-singular $\Leftrightarrow p(A) = n$.
- Rank of $I_n = n$.
- A is a matrix of order $m \times n$. If every kth order minor ($k < m$, $k < n$) is zero, then
  $$P(A) < k$$
- A is a matrix of order $m \times n$. If there is a minor of order $k (k < m, k < n)$ which is not zero, then
  $$p(A) \geq k$$
- Rank of a zero matrix is defined to be zero. The rank of a unit matrix is defined to be one.
- If x is a non-zero column matrix and y is a non-zero row matrix, then $p(x\,y) = 1$
- Rank of a matrix is greater than or equal to (not less than) rank of every sub-matrix thereof.
- If A is any n-rowed square matrix of rank, $n - 1$, then adj A $\neq 0$.
- Rank of the transpose of a matrix is equal to rank of the original matrix.
- Rank of a matrix does not change by pre-multiplication or post-multiplication with a non-singular matrix.
- If A ~ B, then $p(A) = p(B)$.
- Rank of a product of two matrices cannot exceed rank of either matrix.
- Rank of the sum of two matrices cannot exceed sum of their ranks.
- Elementary transformations do not change the rank of a matrix.

Echelon form of a Matrix

Let A be the given matrix of order m × n, then it can be reduced to Echelon form by row tranformation.

If we can make all the entries equal to zero, then

R (A) = Number of none zero rows

Consistency and Solution of Algebraic equations

In argument matrix A*, we reduce echelon form.

(*i*) If Rank of A* = Rank of A,
then equation are consistent.

(*ii*) If Rank of A* ≠ Rank of A,
then system is inconsistent (i.e. no solution)

Homogenous system of equations AX = 0

(*i*) If rank = number of unknowns,
then it has zero solution.

(*ii*) If rank < number of unknowns,
then it has infinitely may solution.

Elementary Transformation of a Matrix

Following operations on a matrix are called *elementary transformations*.

(*i*) Interchange of any two rows (or columns).

(*ii*) Multiplication of elements of any row (or column) by any non-zero number.

(*iii*) Addition to elements of any other row (or column) the corresponding elements of any other row (or column) multiplied by any number.

Solution of Simultaneous Linear Equations by Matrix

Simultaneous linear equations of two or three variables are solved by using matrices.

1. Homogeneous linear equations

Let system of m homogeneous equations in n unknown $x_1, x_2, \ldots, x_n$ be

$$\left.\begin{aligned} a_{11}x_1 + a_{12}x_2 + a_{13}x_3 + \ldots + a_{1n}x_n &= 0 \\ a_{21}x_1 + a_{22}x_2 + a_{23}x_3 + \ldots + a_{2n}x_n &= 0 \\ \ldots\ldots\ldots\ldots\ldots\ldots\ldots\ldots\ldots\ldots \\ a_{m1}x_1 + a_{m2}x_2 + a_{m3}x_3 + \ldots + a_{mn}x_n &= 0 \end{aligned}\right\} \quad \ldots(i)$$

$$\text{Let } A = \begin{bmatrix} a_{11} & a_{12} & \ldots & a_{1n} \\ a_{21} & a_{22} & \ldots & a_{2n} \\ \ldots & \ldots & \ldots & \ldots \\ \ldots & \ldots & \ldots & \ldots \\ a_{m1} & a_{m2} & \ldots & a_{mn} \end{bmatrix}_{m \times n}$$

$$X = \begin{bmatrix} x_1 \\ x_2 \\ x_3 \\ \ldots \\ \ldots \\ \ldots \\ x_n \end{bmatrix}_{n \times 1} ; B = \begin{bmatrix} 0 \\ 0 \\ 0 \\ \ldots \\ \ldots \\ 0 \end{bmatrix}_{m \times 1}$$

where A, X and B are $m \times n$, $n \times 1$ and $m \times 1$ matrices respectively.

Equation (*i*) can be written in the form of a single matrix equation

$$AX = B \quad \ldots(ii)$$

The matrix A is called *coefficient matrix* of the system of equation (*i*)

Solutions of equation AX = B

Working Rule

Reduce the coefficient matrix A to Echelon form by applying elementary row transformations only.

From this we know rank of the matrix A.

Let matrix A is of the type $m \times n$ and its rank is r.

- If $r < m$, then $(m - n)$ equations will be eliminated. Thus given system of m equations will be replaced by an equivalent system of r equations. Solving these r equations we can express values of some unknown in terms of remaining $n - r$ unknowns. These $n - r$ unknown can be given any arbitrarily chosen values.
- If $r = n$, then zero solution (trivial solution) will be the only solution.
- If $r < n$, there will be an infinity of solutions.

2. Linear non-homogeneous equations

Let system of m simultaneous equations in n unknowns $x_1, x_2, \ldots, x_n$ be

$$a_{11}x_1 + a_{12}x_2 + a_{13}x_3 + \ldots + a_{1n}x_n = K_1$$
$$a_{21}x_1 + a_{22}x_2 + a_{23}x_3 + \ldots + a_{2n}x_n = K_2$$
$$a_{m1}x_1 + a_{m2}x_2 + a_{m3}x_3 + \ldots + a_{mn}x_n = K_m$$

Let $A = \begin{bmatrix} a_{11} & a_{12} & \ldots & a_{1n} \\ a_{21} & a_{22} & \ldots & a_{2n} \\ \ldots & \ldots & \ldots & \ldots \\ a_{m1} & a_{m2} & \ldots & a_{mn} \end{bmatrix}$, $X = \begin{bmatrix} x_1 \\ x_2 \\ \ldots \\ \ldots \\ x_n \end{bmatrix}_{n \times 1}$,

$K = \begin{bmatrix} K_1 \\ K_2 \\ \ldots \\ \ldots \\ K_m \end{bmatrix}_{m \times 1}$

where A, X, K are $m \times n$, $n \times 1$ and $m \times 1$ matrices respectively.

Above equations can be written in the form of a single matrix equation AX = K

Consistent and Inconsistent equations

If above system has a solution, then equations are *consistent* otherwise equations are *called inconsistent equations*.

- The system of equation AX = K is consistent, i.e. possesses a solution, if and only if coefficient matrix A and augmented matrix [A K] are of the same rank.
- If A be an n-rowed non-singular matrix, X be an $n \times 1$ matrix, K be an $m \times 1$ matrix, then system of equation AX = K has a unique solution.

Solution of equation AX = K

Working rule

Let coefficient matrix A is of the type $m \times n$.

Write augmented matrix [A K] and reduce it to a Echelon form by applying only elementary row transformation on it. This Echelon form will give ranks of the augmented matrix [A K] and coefficient matrix A.

Different cases

Case I : *Rank A < Rank [A K]*

In this case, equation AX = K are inconsistent, i.e. they have no solution.

Case II : *Rank A = Rank [A K] = r (suppose)*

In this case, equation AX = K are consistent.

- If $r < m$, then in the process of reducing the matrix [A K] to Echelon form, $(m - r)$ equations will be eliminated. Then given system of m equations will be replaced by an equivalent system of r equations. From these r equations we shall be able to express the values of some r unknowns in terms of the remaining $n - r$ unknowns which can be given any arbitrary chosen values.
- If $r = n$, there will be a unique solution.
- If $r < n$, then $n-r$ variables can be assigned arbitrary values. So there will be an infinite number of solutions. Only $n - r + 1$ solutions will be linearly independent and rest of the solutions will be linear combinations of them.
- If $m < n$, then $r \le m < n$.
  Thus $n - r > 0$.

Therefore when number of equations is less than the number of unknowns, equations will always have an infinite number of solutions, provided they are consistent.

Matrix Inversion Method

Theorem 1

If A is a non singular matrix, then $A^{-1}B$ is a solution AX = B.

Proof : A is non singular

$\Rightarrow$ A^{-1} exists and $AA^{-1} = A^{-1}A = I$

$\Rightarrow$ $A(A^{-1}B) = (AA^{-1})B = IB = B$

$\therefore$ $X = A^{-1}B$ is a solution of AX = B.

Theorem 2

If A is a non singular matrix, then AX = B has a unique solution.

Proof : A is non singular

$\Rightarrow$ A^{-1} exists and $AA^{-1} = A^{-1}A = I$

By theorem 1, $X = A^{-1}B$ is a solution of AX = B

Let $X = X_1$, $X = X_2$ be two solutions of AX = B.

$\therefore$ $AX_1 = B, AX_2 = B$

$\Rightarrow$ $AX_1 = AX_2$

$\Rightarrow \quad A^{-1}(AX_1) = A^{-1}(AX_2)$

$\Rightarrow \quad (A^{-1}A)X_1 = (A^{-1}A)X_2$

$\Rightarrow \quad IX_1 = IX_2$

$\Rightarrow \quad X_1 = X_2$

Hence AX = B has a *unique solution.*

Theorem 3

If A is a non singular matrix, then $X = A^{-1}B$ is the unique solution of AX = B.

Method of finding solution $X = A^{-1}B$ of AX = B is called **matrix inversion method**

Example. Solve following equations by matrix inversion method

$$x + y + z = 6$$
$$2x - y + z = 3$$
$$x + 2y - z = 2.$$

Solution

Let $A = \begin{bmatrix} 1 & 1 & 1 \\ 2 & -1 & 1 \\ 1 & 2 & -1 \end{bmatrix}, X = \begin{bmatrix} x \\ y \\ z \end{bmatrix}, B = \begin{bmatrix} 6 \\ 3 \\ 2 \end{bmatrix}$

Given equations can be written as

$$AX = B$$

By matrix inversion method solution is,

$$X = A^{-1}B$$

$$\det A = 1(1-2) - 1(-2-1) + 1(4+1)$$
$$= -1 + 3 + 5 = 7.$$

Cofactors of elements of A are

$$A_{11} = +(1-2) = -1$$
$$A_{12} = -(-2-1) = 3$$
$$A_{13} = +(4+1) = 5$$
$$A_{21} = -(-1-2) = 3$$
$$A_{22} = +(-1-1) = -2$$
$$A_{23} = -(2-1) = -1$$
$$A_{31} = +(1+1) = 2$$
$$A_{32} = -(1-2) = 1$$
$$A_{33} = +(-1-2) = -3$$

$$\therefore \quad \text{Adj } A = \begin{bmatrix} A_{11} & A_{21} & A_{31} \\ A_{12} & A_{22} & A_{32} \\ A_{13} & A_{23} & A_{33} \end{bmatrix} = \begin{bmatrix} -1 & 3 & 2 \\ 3 & -2 & 1 \\ 5 & -1 & -3 \end{bmatrix}$$

$$A^{-1} = \frac{\text{Adj } A}{\det A} = \frac{1}{7}\begin{bmatrix} -1 & 3 & 2 \\ 3 & -2 & 1 \\ 5 & -1 & -3 \end{bmatrix}$$

$$X = A^{-1}B = \frac{1}{7}\begin{bmatrix} -1 & 3 & 2 \\ 3 & -2 & 1 \\ 5 & -1 & -3 \end{bmatrix}\begin{bmatrix} 6 \\ 3 \\ 2 \end{bmatrix}$$

$$= \frac{1}{7}\begin{bmatrix} -6 & +9 & +4 \\ 18 & -6 & +2 \\ 30 & -3 & -6 \end{bmatrix} = \frac{1}{7}\begin{bmatrix} 7 \\ 14 \\ 21 \end{bmatrix} = \begin{bmatrix} 1 \\ 2 \\ 3 \end{bmatrix}$$

$\therefore \quad x = 1, y = 2, z = 3$ is the solution.

CRAMER'S RULE

Theorem 4

Let
$$a_1x + b_1y + c_1z = d_1$$
$$a_2x + b_2y + c_2z = d_2 \qquad \ldots(i)$$
$$a_3x + b_3y + c_3z = d_3$$

be a system of linear equations.

If $\Delta = \begin{vmatrix} a_1 & b_1 & c_1 \\ a_2 & b_2 & c_2 \\ a_3 & b_3 & c_3 \end{vmatrix} \neq 0, \Delta_1 = \begin{vmatrix} d_1 & b_1 & c_1 \\ d_2 & b_2 & c_2 \\ d_3 & b_3 & c_3 \end{vmatrix},$

$$\Delta_2 = \begin{vmatrix} a_1 & d_1 & c_1 \\ a_2 & d_2 & c_2 \\ a_3 & d_3 & c_3 \end{vmatrix}, \Delta_3 = \begin{vmatrix} a_1 & b_1 & d_1 \\ a_2 & b_2 & d_2 \\ a_3 & b_3 & d_3 \end{vmatrix}.$$

then solution of equation, (*i*) is

$$x = \frac{\Delta_1}{\Delta}, y = \frac{\Delta_2}{\Delta}, z = \frac{\Delta_3}{\Delta} \text{ is}$$

Proof : Let $A = \begin{bmatrix} a_1 & b_1 & c_1 \\ a_2 & b_2 & c_2 \\ a_3 & b_3 & c_3 \end{bmatrix}, X = \begin{bmatrix} x \\ y \\ z \end{bmatrix}, B = \begin{bmatrix} d_1 \\ d_2 \\ d_3 \end{bmatrix}.$

Then $\det A = \Delta \neq 0$

$\therefore \quad AX = B$ has unique solution

Hence equation (*i*) has unique solution.

Let, A_1, A_2, A_3 be the cofactors of a_1, a_2, a_3 respectively. Thus

$$(a_1x + b_1y + c_1z)A_1 + (a_2x + b_2y + c_2z)A_2 + (a_3x + b_3y + c_3z)A_3$$
$$= d_1A_1 + d_2A_2 + d_3A_3$$

$$\Rightarrow \quad x[a_1A_1 + a_2A_2 + a_3A_3] + y[b_1A_1 + b_2A_2 + b_3A_3] + z[c_1A_1 + c_2A_2 + c_3A_3] = \Delta_1$$

$$\Rightarrow \quad x\Delta + y0 + z0 = x = \Delta_1$$

$$\Rightarrow \quad x = \frac{\Delta_1}{\Delta}$$

Similarly, $y = \frac{\Delta_2}{\Delta}$, and $z = \frac{\Delta_3}{\Delta}$

Hence solution of (*i*) is $x = \frac{\Delta_1}{\Delta}, y = \frac{\Delta_2}{\Delta}, z = \frac{\Delta_3}{\Delta}$

- $\Delta_1, \Delta_2, \Delta_3$ are also denoted as $\Delta_x, \Delta_y, \Delta_z$ respectively.
- $\frac{x}{\Delta_1} = \frac{y}{\Delta_2} = \frac{z}{\Delta_3} = \frac{1}{\Delta}$

Example. Solve following equations by Cramer's rule.

$$x + y + z = 6$$
$$2x - y + z = 3$$
$$x + 2y - z = 2.$$

Solution $\Delta = \begin{vmatrix} 1 & 1 & 1 \\ 2 & -1 & 1 \\ 1 & 2 & -1 \end{vmatrix}$

$= 1(1-2) - 1(-2-1) + 1(4+1)$

$= -1 + 3 + 5 = 7$

$\Delta_1 = \begin{vmatrix} 6 & 1 & 1 \\ 3 & -1 & 1 \\ 2 & 2 & -1 \end{vmatrix}$

$= 6(1-2) - 1(-3-2) + 1(6+2)$

$= -6 + 5 + 8 = 7$

$\Delta_2 = \begin{vmatrix} 1 & 6 & 1 \\ 2 & 3 & 1 \\ 1 & 2 & -1 \end{vmatrix}$

$= 1(-3-2) - 6(-2-1) + 1(4-3)$

$= -5 + 18 + 1 = 14$

$\Delta_3 = \begin{vmatrix} 1 & 1 & 6 \\ 2 & -1 & 3 \\ 1 & 2 & 2 \end{vmatrix}$

$= 1(-2-6) - 1(4-3) + 6(4+1)$

$= -8 - 1 + 30 = 21$

By Cramer's rule,

$$\frac{x}{\Delta_1} = \frac{y}{\Delta_2} = \frac{z}{\Delta_3} = \frac{1}{\Delta}$$

$$\therefore \quad \frac{x}{7} = \frac{y}{14} = \frac{z}{21} = \frac{1}{7}$$

Hence solution is, $x = 1, y = 2, z = 3$

Coefficient and Augmented matrix

Let $a_1x + b_1y + c_1z = d_1$

$a_2x + b_2y + c_2z = d_2$ ... (*i*)

$a_3x + b_3y + c_3z = d_3$

be a system of linear equations.

Then matrix, $A = \begin{bmatrix} a_1 & b_1 & c_1 \\ a_2 & b_2 & c_2 \\ a_3 & b_3 & c_3 \end{bmatrix}$ is called **Coefficient matrix.**

and matrix $K = \begin{bmatrix} a_1 & b_1 & c_1 & d_1 \\ a_2 & b_2 & c_2 & d_2 \\ a_3 & b_3 & c_3 & d_3 \end{bmatrix}$ is called **Augmented matrix.**

EIGEN VALUES AND EIGEN VECTORS

Let $A = [a_{ij}]$ be an $n \times n$ matrix.

- Matrix $A - \lambda I$ is called *characteristic matrix* of A, where I is identity matrix.
- Determinant $|A - \lambda I|$ is called *characteristic polynomial of A.*
- Equation $|A - \lambda I| = 0$ is called *characteristic equation* of A and its roots are called *eigen values.*
- Problem of finding the eigen values of a matrix is called *eigen-value problem.*
- If λ is a characteristic root or eigen values of an $n \times n$ matrix A, then a non-zero vector X such that $AX = \lambda X$ is called *characteristic vector* or *eigen vector of* A corresponding to the characteristic root λ.

  The set of eigen values of A is called the spectrum of A.

Relations between Eigen values and Eigen vectors

- λ is a eigen values of a matrix A if and only if there exists a non-zero vector X such that

$$AX = \lambda X$$

- If X is a characteristic vector of a matrix A corresponding to the characteristic value λ, then KX is also a characteristic vector of A corresponding to the same characteristic value λ. Here K is any non-zero scalar.
- If X is a eigen vector of a matrix A, then X cannot correspond to more than one eigen value of A.
- Eigen vectors corresponding to distinct characteristic roots of a matrix are linearly independent.

Properties of Eigen values

(*i*) Sum of all the eigen values of a matrix is equal to sum of the elements of the principal diagonal.

(*ii*) Product of the eigen values of a matrix is equal to its determinant.

(*iii*) If λ is an eigen value of a matrix A, then $\frac{1}{\lambda}$ is the eigen value of A^{-1}.

(*iv*) If λ is an eigen value of an orthogonal matrix, then $\frac{1}{\lambda}$ is also its eigen value.

(*v*) If $\lambda_1, \lambda_2 \ldots\ldots\ldots\ldots \lambda_m$ are the eigen values of a matrix A, then A^n has the eigen values $\lambda_1^n, \lambda_2^n \ldots\ldots\ldots\ldots \lambda_m^n$.

(*vi*) Eigen value of A = Eigen value of A^T

(*vii*) Maximum number of distinct eigen values = size of A

(*viii*) In a triangular and diagonal matrix, Eigen values are diagonal elements themselves.

(*ix*) If A and B are two matrices of same order then the matrix AB and BA will have same characteristic roots.

Cayley-Hamilton theorem.

Every square matrix satisfies its characteristic equation, i.e. if for a square matrix A of order n

$$|A - \lambda I| = (-1)^n [\lambda^n + a_1\lambda^{n-1} + a_2\lambda^{n-2} + \ldots\ldots + a_n]$$

then matrix equation

$$X^n + a_1 X^{n-1} + a_2 X^{n-2} + a_3 X^{n-3} + \ldots\ldots + a_n I = 0$$

is satisfied by X = A

i.e., $A^n + a_1 A^{n-1} + a_2 A^{n-2} + \ldots\ldots + a_n I = 0$

SOLVED PROBLEMS

1. Find inverse of $\begin{bmatrix} 1 & 1 & 3 \\ 1 & 3 & -3 \\ -2 & -4 & -4 \end{bmatrix}$

Solution

Determinant of given matrix A is

$$\Delta = \begin{bmatrix} 1 & 1 & 3 \\ 1 & 3 & -3 \\ -2 & -4 & -4 \end{bmatrix} = \begin{bmatrix} a_1 & b_1 & c_1 \\ a_2 & b_2 & c_2 \\ a_3 & b_3 & c_3 \end{bmatrix}$$

If A_1, A_2 ... be the co-factors of a_1, a_2... in Δ, then

$$A_1 = -24, \quad A_2 = -8, \quad A_3 = -12,$$
$$B_1 = 10, \quad B_2 = 2, \quad B_3 = 6,$$
$$C_1 = 2, \quad C_2 = 2, \quad C_3 = 2$$

Thus, $D = a_1A_1 + a_2A_2 + a_3A_3 = -8$

$$\therefore \text{ Adj. A} = \begin{bmatrix} A_1 & A_2 & A_3 \\ B_1 & B_2 & B_3 \\ C_1 & C_2 & C_3 \end{bmatrix} = \begin{bmatrix} -24 & -8 & -12 \\ 10 & 2 & 6 \\ 2 & 2 & 2 \end{bmatrix}$$

Hence inverse of matrix A

$$= \frac{\text{adj.A}}{\Delta} = \frac{1}{-8}\begin{bmatrix} -24 & -8 & -12 \\ 10 & 2 & 6 \\ 2 & 2 & 2 \end{bmatrix}$$

$$A^{-1} = \begin{bmatrix} 3 & 1 & \frac{3}{2} \\ -\frac{5}{4} & -\frac{1}{4} & -\frac{3}{4} \\ -\frac{1}{4} & -\frac{1}{4} & -\frac{1}{4} \end{bmatrix}$$

2. Determine rank of the matrix $\begin{bmatrix} 1 & 2 & 3 \\ 1 & 4 & 2 \\ 2 & 6 & 5 \end{bmatrix}$

Solution

Operate $R_2 - R_1$ and $R_3 - 2R_1$, therefore

$$\sim \begin{bmatrix} 1 & 2 & 3 \\ 0 & 2 & -1 \\ 0 & 2 & -1 \end{bmatrix} = \text{A (say)}$$

Obviously, 3rd oder minor of A vanishes. All its second order minors formed by 2nd and 3rd rows are zero.

But another minor

$$\begin{bmatrix} 1 & 3 \\ 0 & -1 \end{bmatrix} = -1 \neq 0$$

Hence rank of A is 2

3. Investigate value of λ and μ, so that the equations

$$2x + 3y + 5z = 9$$
$$7x + 3y - 2z = 8$$
$$2x + 3y + \lambda z = \mu$$

have

(*i*) no solution,

(*ii*) a unique solution, and

(*iii*) an infinite number of solutions

Solution

We have $\begin{bmatrix} 2 & 3 & 5 \\ 7 & 3 & -2 \\ 2 & 3 & \lambda \end{bmatrix}\begin{bmatrix} x \\ y \\ z \end{bmatrix} = \begin{bmatrix} 9 \\ 8 \\ \mu \end{bmatrix}$

The system admits of unique solution if, and only if, coefficent matrix is of rank 3. This requires in

$$\begin{vmatrix} 2 & 3 & 5 \\ 7 & 3 & -2 \\ 2 & 3 & \lambda \end{vmatrix} = 15\,(5 - \lambda) \neq 0$$

Thus for a unique solution $\lambda \neq 5$ and m may have any value.

If $\lambda = 5$, the system wil have no solution for those values of μ for which the matrices

$$A = \begin{bmatrix} 2 & 3 & 5 \\ 7 & 3 & -2 \\ 2 & 3 & \lambda \end{bmatrix}$$

and $$K = \begin{bmatrix} 2 & 3 & 5 & 9 \\ 7 & 3 & -2 & 8 \\ 2 & 3 & 5 & \mu \end{bmatrix}$$

are not of the same rank. But A is of rank 2 and K is not of rank 2 unless $\mu = 9$.

Thus if $\lambda = 5$ and $\mu \neq 9$, the system will have no solution.

If $\lambda = 5$ and $\mu = 9$, the system will have an infinite number of solutions.

4. Find eigen values and eigen vectors of the matrix.

$$A = \begin{bmatrix} 8 & -6 & 2 \\ -6 & 7 & -4 \\ 2 & -4 & 3 \end{bmatrix}$$

Solution

Characteristic equation is

$$|A - \lambda I| = \begin{bmatrix} 8-\lambda & -6 & 2 \\ -6 & 7-\lambda & 4 \\ 2 & -4 & 3-\lambda \end{bmatrix}$$

$$= \lambda^3 + 18\lambda^3 - 45\lambda = 0$$

$$\Rightarrow \quad \lambda(\lambda - 3)(\lambda - 15) = 0$$

$$\therefore \quad \lambda = 0, 3, 15$$

Thus eigen values of A are 0, 3, 15.

If x, y, z be the component of an eigen vectors corresponding to the eigen value λ, then

$$[A-\lambda I]X = \begin{bmatrix} 8-\lambda & -6 & 2 \\ -6 & 7-\lambda & -4 \\ 2 & -4 & 3-\lambda \end{bmatrix}\begin{bmatrix} x \\ y \\ z \end{bmatrix} = 0$$

Putting $\lambda = 0$, we have

$$8x - 6y + 2z = 0,$$
$$-6x + 7y + 4z = 0,$$
$$2x - 4y + 3z = 0$$

These equations determine a single linearly independent solution which may be takne as (1, 2, 2), so that every non-zero multiple of this vector is an eigen vector corresponding to $\lambda = 0$.

Similarly, eigen vectors corresponding to $\lambda = 3$ and $\lambda = 15$ are arbitrary non-zero multiples of the vectors (2, 1, –2) and (2, –2, 1) which are obtained from above equation.

Hence three vectors may be taken as (1, 2, 2), (2, 1, – 2), (2, –2, 1)

5. If $A\begin{bmatrix} -2 & 1 \\ 3 & 5 \end{bmatrix} = \begin{bmatrix} -1 & 7 \\ -1 & 20 \end{bmatrix}$, find matrix A

Solution

$$A = \begin{bmatrix} -1 & 7 \\ -1 & 20 \end{bmatrix}\begin{bmatrix} -2 & 1 \\ 3 & 5 \end{bmatrix}^{-1}$$

$$= \begin{bmatrix} -1 & 7 \\ -1 & 20 \end{bmatrix}\frac{1}{-10-3}\begin{bmatrix} 5 & -1 \\ -3 & -2 \end{bmatrix}$$

$$= \frac{-1}{13}\begin{bmatrix} -1 & 7 \\ -1 & 20 \end{bmatrix}\begin{bmatrix} 5 & -1 \\ -3 & -2 \end{bmatrix}$$

$$= \frac{-1}{13}\begin{bmatrix} -26 & -13 \\ -65 & -39 \end{bmatrix} = \begin{bmatrix} 2 & 1 \\ 5 & 3 \end{bmatrix}$$

6. If ω is cube root of –1, then find vlaue of

$$\begin{vmatrix} 1 & -\omega & \omega^2 \\ -\omega & \omega^2 & 1 \\ \omega^2 & 1 & -\omega \end{vmatrix}$$

Solution

Since ω is cube root of –1, therefore

$$\omega^3 = -1$$

i.e., $\omega^3 + 1 = 0$

$\Rightarrow$ $(\omega + 1)(\omega^2 - \omega + 1) = 0$

Hence either $\omega = -1$ or $\omega^2 - \omega + 1 = 0$

Let $A = \begin{vmatrix} 1 & -\omega & \omega^2 \\ -\omega & \omega^2 & 1 \\ \omega^2 & 1 & -\omega \end{vmatrix}$

$$C_1 \rightarrow C_1 + C_2 + C_3$$

$$A = \begin{vmatrix} 1-\omega+\omega^2 & -\omega & \omega^2 \\ -\omega+\omega^2+1 & \omega^2 & 1 \\ \omega^2+1-\omega & 1 & -\omega \end{vmatrix} = \begin{vmatrix} 0 & -\omega & \omega^2 \\ 0 & \omega^2 & 1 \\ 0 & 1 & -\omega \end{vmatrix}$$

$= 0$ (since $1 - \omega + \omega^2 = 0$)

7. If $A = \begin{bmatrix} -3 & 5 \\ 2 & 1 \end{bmatrix}$, find $|A^{-1}|$.

Solution

$$A = \begin{bmatrix} -3 & 5 \\ 2 & 1 \end{bmatrix}$$

$\therefore$ $|A| = -3 - 10 = -13 \neq 0$

and $$A^{-1} = \frac{A/dj\,A}{|A|} = \frac{\begin{bmatrix} 1 & -5 \\ -2 & -3 \end{bmatrix}}{-13}$$

$$|A^{-1}| = \frac{-1}{13}(-3-10) = 1$$

8. If α, β are roots of the equation $\begin{vmatrix} 2x+3 & 1 \\ x & x+2 \end{vmatrix} = 0$, then find $\frac{1}{\alpha} + \frac{1}{\beta}$.

Solution

Given: $\begin{vmatrix} 2x+3 & 1 \\ x & x+2 \end{vmatrix} = 0$

$\therefore$ $(2x + 3)(x + 2) - x = 0$

$\Rightarrow$ $2x^2 + 6x + 6 = 0$

$\Rightarrow$ $x^2 + 3x + 3 = 0$

Since α, β are roots of this equation, therefore

$$\alpha + \beta = -3, \quad \alpha\beta = 3$$

$\therefore$ $$\frac{1}{\alpha} + \frac{1}{\beta} = \frac{\alpha+\beta}{\alpha\beta} = \frac{-3}{3} = -1$$

EXERCISE

MCQ TYPE QUESTIONS

1. Eigen values of the matrix $\begin{bmatrix} 3 & -1 & -1 \\ -1 & 3 & -1 \\ -1 & -1 & 3 \end{bmatrix}$ are

(a) 1, 1, 1 (b) 1, 1, 2 (c) 1, 4, 4 (d) 1, 2, 4

2. Rank of the following $(n+1)\times(n+1)$ matrix, where a is a real number, is

$$\begin{bmatrix} 1 & a & a^2 & . & . & . & a^n \\ a & a & a^2 & . & . & . & a^n \\ . & . & . & . & . & . & . \\ . & . & . & . & . & . & . \\ . & . & . & . & . & . & . \\ 1 & a & a^2 & . & . & . & a^n \end{bmatrix}$$

(a) 1
(b) 2
(c) n
(d) dependent upon the value of A

3. Matrices $\begin{bmatrix} \cos\theta & -\sin\theta \\ \sin\theta & \cos\theta \end{bmatrix}$ and $\begin{bmatrix} a & 0 \\ 0 & b \end{bmatrix}$ commute under multiplication

(a) if $a = b$ or $\theta = n\pi$, where n is an integer
(b) always
(c) never
(d) if $a \cos\theta \neq b \sin\theta$

4. If $A = \begin{bmatrix} 0 & 2 & 3 \\ -2 & 0 & 5 \\ -3 & -5 & 0 \end{bmatrix}$, then

(a) $A' = -A$ (b) $A' = A$
(c) $A' = -\dfrac{1}{A}$ (d) none of these

5. Eigen values of the system represented by

$$\dot{X} = \begin{bmatrix} 0 & 1 & 0 & 0 \\ 0 & 0 & 1 & 0 \\ 0 & 0 & 0 & 1 \\ 0 & 0 & 0 & 1 \end{bmatrix} X \text{ are}$$

(a) 0, 0, 0, 0 (b) 1, 1, 1, 1
(c) 0, 0, 0, –1 (d) 1, 0, 0, 0

6. Matrix, $A = \begin{bmatrix} \cos\theta & \sin\theta & 0 \\ \sin\theta & \cos\theta & 0 \\ 0 & 0 & 1 \end{bmatrix}$ is not

(a) orthogonal (b) non–singular
(c) singular (d) have A^{-1} exists

7. In the matrix equation $Px = q$, which of the following is a necessary condition for the existence of at least one solution for the unknown vector x?

(a) Augmented matrix [Pq] must have the same rank as matrix P
(b) Vector q must have only non-zero elements
(c) Matrix P must be singular
(d) Matrix P must be square

8. Eigen vectors of a real symmetric matrix corresponding to different eigen values are

(a) orthogonal (b) singular
(c) non-singular (d) none of these

9. An arbitrary vector X is an eigen vector of the matrix $A = \begin{bmatrix} 1 & 0 & 0 \\ 0 & a & 0 \\ 0 & 0 & b \end{bmatrix}$, if (a, b) =

(a) (0, 0) (b) (1, 1) (c) (0, 1) (d) (1, 2)

10. For which value of k, following system is consistent?

$$2x - 5ky + 6z = 0$$
$$kx + 2y - 2z = 0$$
$$2x + 2y - kz = 0$$

(a) 1 (b) 2 (c) 3 (d) 5

11. The system of equations

$$a_1x + a_2y = 0$$
$$b_1x + b_2y = 0$$

where a_1, a_2, b_1, b_2, are real numbers, has a non-trivial solution if

(a) $a_1b_1 = a_2b_2$ (b) $a_1b_2 = b_1a_2$
(c) $a_1a_2 = b_1b_2$ (d) none of these

12. Solution of the given matrix equation is

$$\begin{bmatrix} 2 & 2 & 2 \\ 1 & 5 & -3 \\ -1 & -3 & 1 \end{bmatrix} \begin{bmatrix} x_1 \\ x_2 \\ x_3 \end{bmatrix} = \begin{bmatrix} 0 \\ 0 \\ 0 \end{bmatrix}$$

(a) $x_1 = 0, x_2 = 0, x_3 = 0$
(b) $x_1 = 1, x_2 = 1, x_3 = 0$
(c) $x_1 = 0, x_2 = 1, x_3 = 1$
(d) $x_1 = 2, x_2 = -5, x_4 = -1$

13. If product of matrix

$$A = \begin{bmatrix} \cos^2\theta & \cos\theta\sin\theta \\ \cos\theta\sin\theta & \sin^2\theta \end{bmatrix} \text{ and}$$

$$B = \begin{bmatrix} \cos^2\phi & \cos\phi\sin\phi \\ \cos\phi\sin\phi & \sin^2\phi \end{bmatrix}$$

is a null matrix, then θ and ϕ differ by an

(a) odd multiple of π (b) even multiple of π
(c) odd multiple of $\pi/2$ (d) even multiple of $\pi/2$

14. Inverse of the matrix $\begin{Bmatrix} ab & 0 \\ 0 & 1 \end{Bmatrix}$ is

(a) $\begin{Bmatrix} a & 0 \\ 0 & a \end{Bmatrix}$ (b) $\begin{Bmatrix} b & 0 \\ a & b \end{Bmatrix}$

(c) $\begin{pmatrix} 1/a & 0 \\ 0 & 1/b \end{pmatrix}$ (d) $\begin{Bmatrix} a & 0 \\ 0 & 1/b \end{Bmatrix}$

15. The system of equations

$$2x + 4y = 10,$$
$$5x + 10y = 25$$

has

(a) no unique solution (b) only one solution
(c) only two solutions (d) infinite solutions

16. Sum of the eigen values of the matrix $\begin{pmatrix} 3 & 4 \\ x & 1 \end{pmatrix}$ for real and negative values of x is

(a) greater than zero
(b) less than zero
(c) zero
(d) dependent on the value of x

17. The system of equations

$$4x + 6y + 8z = 0$$
$$7x + 8y + 9z = 0$$
$$3x + 2y + z = 0$$

has

(a) no solution
(b) only one solution
(c) two solutions
(d) infinite number of solutions

18. Eigen values of $\begin{bmatrix} 1 & 1 & 1 \\ 1 & 1 & 1 \\ 1 & 1 & 1 \end{bmatrix}$ are

(a) 0, 0 0 (b) 0, 0 1 (c) 0, 0, 3 (d) 1, 1, 1

19. For following set of simulataneous equations

$$1.5x - 0.5y = 2$$
$$4x + 2y + 3z = 9$$
$$7x + y + 5z = 10$$

(a) solution is unique
(b) infinitely many solutions exist
(c) equations are incompatible
(d) finite number of multiple solutions exist

20. If $R = \begin{bmatrix} 1 & 0 & -1 \\ 2 & 1 & -1 \\ 2 & 3 & 2 \end{bmatrix}$, then top row of R^{-1} is

(a) [5 6 4] (b) [5 −3 1]
(c) [2 0 −1] (d) [2 −1 1/2]

21. The system of simultaneous equations

$$x + 2y + z = 6$$
$$2x + y + 2z = 6$$
$$x + y + z = 5$$

has

(a) unique solution
(b) infinite number of solutions
(c) no solution
(d) exactly two solutions

22. For which value of x, will the matrix $\begin{bmatrix} 8 & x & 0 \\ 4 & 0 & 2 \\ 12 & 6 & 0 \end{bmatrix}$ become singular?

23. Eigen vectors of the matrix $\begin{bmatrix} 1 & -1 \\ -1 & 1 \end{bmatrix}$ is (are)

(a) (1, 0) (b) (0, 1) (c) (1, 1) (d) (1, −1)

24. Inverse of the matrix $\begin{bmatrix} -3 & 5 \\ 2 & 1 \end{bmatrix}$ is

(a) $\begin{bmatrix} \frac{5}{13} & \frac{-1}{13} \\ \frac{2}{13} & \frac{3}{13} \end{bmatrix}$ (b) $\begin{bmatrix} \frac{2}{13} & \frac{5}{13} \\ \frac{-1}{13} & \frac{3}{13} \end{bmatrix}$

(c) $\begin{bmatrix} \frac{-1}{13} & \frac{5}{13} \\ \frac{2}{13} & \frac{3}{13} \end{bmatrix}$ (d) $\begin{bmatrix} \frac{1}{13} & \frac{-5}{13} \\ \frac{2}{13} & \frac{3}{13} \end{bmatrix}$

25. If A and B are square matrices of size n × n, then which of the following statement is not true ?

(a) det (AB) = det (A) det (B)
(b) det (kA) = k^n det (A)
(c) det (A + B) = det (A) + det (B)
(d) det (A^T) = 1/det (A^{-1})

26. If matrix A is m × n and B is n× p, then number of multiplication operations and addition operations needed to calculate the matrix AB, respectively are

(a) mn^2p, mpn (b) mpn, $(n - 1)$
(c) mpn, mpn (d) $mn^2 p$, $(m + p) n$

27. If A be an invertible matrix and inverse of 7A is $\begin{bmatrix} -1 & 2 \\ 4 & -7 \end{bmatrix}$, then matrix A is

(a) $\begin{bmatrix} 1 & 2/7 \\ 4/7 & 1/7 \end{bmatrix}$ (b) $\begin{bmatrix} 7 & 2 \\ 4 & 1 \end{bmatrix}$

(c) $\begin{bmatrix} 1 & -4/7 \\ -2/7 & 1/7 \end{bmatrix}$ (d) $\begin{bmatrix} 7 & 4 \\ 2 & 1 \end{bmatrix}$

28. Solution(s) to the equations

$$2x + 3y = 1$$
$$x - y = 4$$
$$4x - y = a$$

will exist if a is equal to

(a) − 33 (b) 0 (c) 9 (d) 12

29. Matrix $B = A^T$, where A is any matrix is

(a) skew symmetric
(b) symmetric about the secondary diagonal
(c) always symmetric
(d) another general matrix

30. If $A^T = A^{-1}$, where A is a real matrix, then A is

(a) normal (b) symmetric
(c) Hermitian (d) orthogonal

31. If A and B are non-zero squarematrices, then AB = I implies
(*a*) A and B are orthogonal
(*b*) A and B are singular
(*c*) B is singular
(*d*) A is singular

32. Eigen values of a square symmetric matrix are always
(*a*) positive (*b*) real and imaginary
(*c*) negative (*d*) real

33. If $A = \begin{bmatrix} 1 & 0 \\ 0 & 1 \end{bmatrix}$, then state transition matrix e^{At} is

(*a*) $\begin{bmatrix} 0 & e^{-t} \\ e^{-t} & 0 \end{bmatrix}$ (*b*) $\begin{bmatrix} e^{t} & 0 \\ 0 & e^{t} \end{bmatrix}$

(*c*) $\begin{bmatrix} e^{-t} & 0 \\ 0 & e^{-t} \end{bmatrix}$ (*d*) $\begin{bmatrix} 0 & e^{t} \\ e^{t} & 0 \end{bmatrix}$

34. For matrix $p = \begin{bmatrix} 3 & -2 & 2 \\ 0 & -2 & 1 \\ 0 & 0 & 1 \end{bmatrix}$, if one of the eigen values is equal to –2, then which of the following is an eigen vector ?

(*a*) $\begin{bmatrix} 3 \\ -2 \\ 1 \end{bmatrix}$ (*b*) $\begin{bmatrix} -3 \\ 2 \\ -1 \end{bmatrix}$

(*c*) $\begin{bmatrix} 1 \\ -2 \\ 3 \end{bmatrix}$ (*d*) $\begin{bmatrix} 5 \\ 2 \\ 0 \end{bmatrix}$

35. Eigen values and corresponding eigen vectors of a 2 × 2 matrix are given by

Eigenvalue	Eigenvector
$\lambda_1 = 4$	$v_1 = \begin{bmatrix} 1 \\ 1 \end{bmatrix}$
$\lambda_2 = 8$	$v_2 = \begin{bmatrix} 1 \\ -1 \end{bmatrix}$

The matrix is

(*a*) $\begin{bmatrix} 6 & 2 \\ 2 & 6 \end{bmatrix}$ (*b*) $\begin{bmatrix} 4 & 6 \\ 6 & 4 \end{bmatrix}$ (*c*) $\begin{bmatrix} 2 & 4 \\ 4 & 2 \end{bmatrix}$ (*d*) $\begin{bmatrix} 4 & 8 \\ 8 & 4 \end{bmatrix}$

36. A second order system starts with an initial condition of $\begin{bmatrix} 2 \\ 3 \end{bmatrix}$ without any external input. The state transition matrix for the system is given by $\begin{bmatrix} e^{-2t} & 0 \\ 0 & e^{-t} \end{bmatrix}$. The state of the system at the end of 1 second is given by

(*a*) $\begin{bmatrix} 0.271 \\ 1.100 \end{bmatrix}$ (*b*) $\begin{bmatrix} 0.135 \\ 0.368 \end{bmatrix}$

(*c*) $\begin{bmatrix} 0.271 \\ 0.736 \end{bmatrix}$ (*d*) $\begin{bmatrix} 0.135 \\ 1.100 \end{bmatrix}$

NUMERICAL TYPE QUESTIONS

1. Rank of the matrix $A = \begin{bmatrix} 0 & 0 & 0 & 0 \\ 4 & 2 & 3 & 0 \\ 1 & 0 & 0 & 0 \\ 4 & 0 & 3 & 0 \end{bmatrix}$ is______

2. Rank of the diagonal matrix 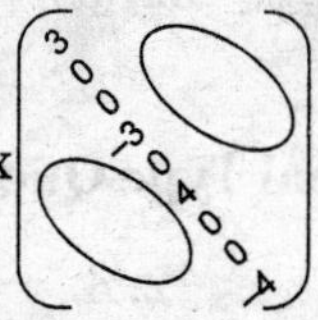

is______

3. Rank of the matrix $A = \begin{bmatrix} 1 & 3 & 5 & 1 \\ 2 & 4 & 8 & 0 \\ 3 & 1 & 7 & 5 \end{bmatrix}$ is______

4. Rank of the matrix $\begin{bmatrix} 1 & 1 \\ 0 & 0 \end{bmatrix}$ is______

5. The value of λ for which the equations

$$2x + y + 2z = 0$$
$$x + y + 3z = 0$$
$$4x + y + \lambda z = 0$$

have a non-zero solution, is______

6. The system of linear equations

$$(4d - 1)\, x + y + z = 0$$
$$-y + z = 0$$
$$(4d - 1)\, z = 0$$

has a non-trivial solution, if d equals ______

7. Rank of a 3 × 3 matrix C (= AB), found by multiplying a non-zero column matrix A of size 3 × 1 and a non-zero row matrix B of size 1 × 3, is______

8. Sum of eigen values of the matrix $\begin{bmatrix} 1 & 1 & 3 \\ 1 & 5 & 1 \\ 3 & 1 & 1 \end{bmatrix}$ is______

9. Rank of the matrix, $A = \begin{bmatrix} 1 & -2 & -1 \\ -3 & 3 & 0 \\ 2 & 2 & 4 \end{bmatrix}$ is______

10. If $A = \begin{bmatrix} 2 & -0.1 \\ 0 & 3 \end{bmatrix}$ and $A^{-1} = \begin{bmatrix} \frac{1}{2} & a \\ 0 & b \end{bmatrix}$, then (a + b) equals ______

11. For matrix $\begin{bmatrix} 4 & 2 \\ 2 & 4 \end{bmatrix}$, eigen value corresponding to the eigen vector $\begin{bmatrix} 101 \\ 101 \end{bmatrix}$ is______

ANSWERS

EXERCISE

MCQ Type Questions

1. (*c*)	**2.** (*a*)	**3.** (*a*)	**4.** (*a*)	**5.** (*d*)	**6.** (*b,d*)	**7.** (*a*)	**8.** (*a*)	**9.** (*b*)	**10.** (*b*)
11. (*b*)	**12.** (*a*)	**13.** (*c*)	**14.** (*c*)	**15.** (*d*)	**16.** (*a*)	**17.** (*b*)	**18.** (*c*)	**19.** (*c*)	**20.** (*b*)
21. (*c*)	**22.** (*a*)	**23.** (*c,d*)	**24.** (*c*)	**25.** (*c*)	**26.** (*b*)	**27.** (*a*)	**28.** (*d*)	**29.** (*c*)	**30.** (*d*)
31. (*a*)	**32.** (*d*)	**33.** (*b*)	**34.** (*d*)	**35.** (*a*)	**36.** (*a*)				

Numerical Type Questions

1. 3	**2.** 4	**3.** 3	**4.** 1	**5.** 8	**6.** $\frac{1}{4}$	**7.** 1	**8.** 7	**9.** 2
10. $\frac{7}{20}$	**11.** 6							

EXPLANATIONS

MCQ TYPE QUESTIONS

1. Characteristic equation is

$$[A - \lambda I] = 0$$

$$\Rightarrow \begin{bmatrix} 3-\lambda & -1 & -1 \\ -1 & 3-\lambda & -1 \\ -1 & -1 & 3-\lambda \end{bmatrix} = 0$$

$$\Rightarrow (3-\lambda)\{(3-\lambda)^2-1\} - 1(3-\lambda)+1\} - 1\{(3-\lambda)+1\} = 0$$

$$\Rightarrow \{(3-\lambda)+1\}\{(3-\lambda)(3-\lambda-1)\}-2\} = 0$$

$$\lambda = 1, 4, 4$$

$\therefore$ λ = **1, 4, 4** are eigen values.

4. $A' = \begin{bmatrix} 0 & -2 & -3 \\ 2 & 0 & -5 \\ 3 & 5 & 0 \end{bmatrix} = -\begin{bmatrix} 0 & 2 & 3 \\ -2 & 0 & 5 \\ -3 & -5 & 0 \end{bmatrix} = -A.$

This is a skew-symmetric matrix.

6. Determinant A = 1 ($\cos^2\theta - \sin^2\theta$)

Hence A is non-singular and A^{-1} exists.

7. According to *Rouche's theorem,* the system is consistent if and only if coefficient matrix and augmented matrix K are of the same rank, otherwise the system is inconsistent.

8. Let A be a real symmetric matrix, therefore

$$A^T = A$$

Let α_1 and α_2 be different eigen values of the matrix A, and X_1 and X_2 be the corresponding vectors, then

$$AX_1 = \alpha_1 X_1 \quad \text{and} \quad AX_2 = \alpha_2 X_2$$

Taking transpose of the second equation

$$(AX_2)^T = (\alpha_2 X_2)^T$$

$$\Rightarrow \quad X_2^T A^T = \alpha_2 . X_2^T$$

But $\quad A^T = A,$

$$\therefore \quad X_2^T A = \alpha_2 . X_2^T$$

Post multiply by X_1, we get

$$X^T{}_2 AX_1 = \alpha_2 X_2^T X_1$$

But $\quad AX_1 = \alpha_1 X_1$

$$\therefore \quad X^T{}_2 \alpha_1 X_1 = \alpha_2 X_2^T X_1$$

$$\Rightarrow \quad (\alpha_1 - \alpha_2) X_2^T X_1 = 0$$

Since $\alpha_1 \neq \alpha_2$, $\alpha_1 - \alpha_2 \neq 0$

$$\therefore \quad X_2^T X_1 = 0$$

i.e. X_2 and X_1 are orthogonal.

9. Since matrix is triangular, hence eigen values are α, *a*, *b*.

If (X_1, X_2, X_3) is an arbitrary eigen vector, say corresponding to 1, then

$$\begin{bmatrix} 1 & 0 & 0 \\ 0 & a & 0 \\ 0 & 0 & b \end{bmatrix} \begin{bmatrix} X_1 \\ X_2 \\ X_3 \end{bmatrix} = 1 \begin{bmatrix} X_1 \\ X_2 \\ X_3 \end{bmatrix}$$

X_2, X_3 being not zero, we have

$$X_1 = X_1;\ aX_2 = X_2$$

which gives $a = 1$

and $bX = X_3$

$\Rightarrow$ $b = 1$

$\therefore$ $(a, b) = (1, 1).$

10. $$A = \begin{bmatrix} 2 & -5k & 6 \\ k & 2 & -2 \\ 2 & 2 & -k \end{bmatrix}$$

Equations are consistent, if rank of A and that of k are equal. But in this case it is always true. Hence equations will have a trivial solution if $|A| \neq 0$ Therefore only non-trivial solution will exist if $|A| = 0$

i.e. $$\begin{vmatrix} 2 & -5k & 6 \\ k & 2 & -2 \\ 2 & 2 & -k \end{vmatrix} = 0$$

$\Rightarrow$ $2(-2k+4) + 5k(-k^2+4) + 6(2k-4)$

$\Rightarrow$ $-5k^3 + 20k - 4k + 8 + 12k - 24 = 0$

$\Rightarrow$ $5k^3 - 28k + 16 = 0$

$\Rightarrow$ $5k^3 - 10k^2 + 10k^2 - 20k - 8k + 16 = 0$

$\Rightarrow$ $(5k^2 + 10k - 8)(k - 2) = 0$

$$k = \frac{-10 \pm \sqrt{100+160}}{2} \text{ or } 2$$

$$= -1 \pm \sqrt{13/5} \text{ or } 2$$

11. $\frac{x}{y} = -\frac{a_2}{a_1}$ and $\frac{x}{y} = -\frac{b_2}{b_1}$

Equations are consistent only if

$$-\frac{a_2}{a_1} = -\frac{b_2}{b_1} \Rightarrow a_1b_2 = b_1a_2$$

12. Let matrics, $A = \begin{bmatrix} 2 & 2 & 2 \\ 1 & 5 & -3 \\ -1 & -3 & 1 \end{bmatrix}$

$$X = \begin{bmatrix} x_1 \\ x_2 \\ x_3 \end{bmatrix} \text{ and } B_1 = \begin{bmatrix} 0 \\ 0 \\ 0 \end{bmatrix}$$

$\therefore$ $AX = B$

Multiplying both sides by A^{-1},

$$X = A^{-1}B$$

But as $B = 0$; therefore $X = 0$

Hence $\begin{bmatrix} x_1 \\ x_2 \\ x_3 \end{bmatrix} = \begin{bmatrix} 0 \\ 0 \\ 0 \end{bmatrix}$

$\therefore$ $x_1 = 0,\quad x_2 = 0,\quad x_3 = 0.$

13. AB

$$= \begin{bmatrix} \cos\theta.\cos\phi\cos(\theta-\phi) & \cos\theta.\sin\phi.\cos(\theta-\phi) \\ \cos\phi\sin\theta.\cos(\theta-\phi) & \sin\theta.\sin\phi\cos(\theta-\phi) \end{bmatrix}$$

= A null matrix, when $\cos(\theta - \phi) = 0$

i.e. if $(\theta - \phi)$ is an odd multiple of $\left(\frac{\pi}{2}\right)$.

16. Eigen values are given by the solution of equation,

$$\begin{vmatrix} 3-\lambda & 4 \\ x & 1-\lambda \end{vmatrix} = 0$$

Since x is real and negative, put $x = -k$, where k is positive constant

$\therefore$ $(3-\lambda)(1-\lambda) + 4k = 0$

$\Rightarrow$ $\lambda^2 - 4\lambda + 3 + 4k = 0$

If λ_1 and λ_2 be the solutions of above equation, then λ_1 and λ_2 are eigen values.

Now, Sum of eigen values

= Sum of roots of above equation

i.e. $\lambda_1 + \lambda_2 = \frac{-(-4)}{1} = 4 (> 0)$

17. For given system of equations,

$$\Delta = \begin{vmatrix} 4 & 6 & 8 \\ 7 & 8 & 9 \\ 3 & 2 & 1 \end{vmatrix} = 4(8-18) - 6(7-27) + 8(14-24)$$

$$= -40 + 120 - 80 = 0$$

Since $\Delta = 0$, hence given system of equations has unique solution, *i.e.* only one solution.

18. Given matrix is $\begin{bmatrix} 1 & 1 & 1 \\ 1 & 1 & 1 \\ 1 & 1 & 1 \end{bmatrix}$

Now $\begin{bmatrix} (1-\lambda) & 1 & 1 \\ 1 & (1-\lambda) & 1 \\ 1 & 1 & (1-\lambda) \end{bmatrix} = 0$

$R_1 \rightarrow R_1 + R_2 + R_3$

$$\Rightarrow \begin{bmatrix} (3-\lambda) & (3-\lambda) & (3-\lambda) \\ 1 & (1-\lambda) & 1 \\ 1 & 1 & (1-\lambda) \end{bmatrix} = 0$$

$$\Rightarrow (3-\lambda)\begin{vmatrix} 1 & 1 & 1 \\ 1 & (1-\lambda) & 1 \\ 1 & 1 & (1-\lambda) \end{vmatrix} = 0$$

$C_2 \rightarrow C_2 - C_1$

$C_3 \rightarrow C_3 - C_1$

$$\Rightarrow (3-\lambda)\begin{vmatrix} 1 & 0 & 0 \\ 1 & -\lambda & 1 \\ 1 & 0 & -\lambda \end{vmatrix} = 0$$

Hence eigen values are 0, 0, 3

20. $\text{Adj } R = \begin{bmatrix} 5 & -6 & 4 \\ -3 & 4 & -3 \\ 1 & -1 & 1 \end{bmatrix}^T = \begin{bmatrix} 5 & -3 & 1 \\ -6 & 4 & -1 \\ 4 & -3 & 1 \end{bmatrix}$

Since, $|R| = 1$, therefore top row $\rightarrow$ [5 −3 1]

21. Given equations are :

$$x + 2y + z = 6$$
$$2x + y + 2z = 6$$
$$x + y + z = 5$$

Given system can be written as

$$\begin{bmatrix} 1 & 2 & 1 \\ 2 & 1 & 2 \\ 1 & 1 & 1 \end{bmatrix} . \begin{bmatrix} x \\ y \\ z \end{bmatrix} = \begin{bmatrix} 6 \\ 6 \\ 5 \end{bmatrix}$$

Applying row operation

$R_2 = R_2 - 2R_1$, $R_3 = R_3 - R_1$, we get

$$\begin{bmatrix} 1 & 2 & 1 \\ 0 & -3 & 0 \\ 0 & -1 & 0 \end{bmatrix} . \begin{bmatrix} x \\ y \\ z \end{bmatrix} = \begin{bmatrix} 6 \\ -6 \\ -1 \end{bmatrix}$$

Applying $R_3 = 3R_3 - R_2$, we get

$$\begin{bmatrix} 1 & 2 & 1 \\ 0 & -3 & 0 \\ 0 & 0 & 0 \end{bmatrix} . \begin{bmatrix} x \\ y \\ z \end{bmatrix} = \begin{bmatrix} 6 \\ -6 \\ 3 \end{bmatrix}$$

Since rank of co-efficient matrix is 2 and rank of argument matrix is 3, which is not equal. Hence system has no solution.

22. For singular matrix,

$$\begin{vmatrix} 8 & x & 0 \\ 4 & 0 & 2 \\ 12 & 6 & 0 \end{vmatrix} = 0$$

$\Rightarrow \quad 8[0 - 12] - x[0 - 2 \times 12] = 0$

$\Rightarrow \quad -96 + 24x = 0$

$\Rightarrow \quad x = 4$

23. Eigen value are roots of the equation

$$\begin{bmatrix} 1-\alpha & -1 \\ -1 & 1-\alpha \end{bmatrix} = 0$$

i.e. $\quad (1 - \alpha)^2 - 1 = 0$

$\Rightarrow \quad \alpha^2 - 2\alpha = 0$

$\Rightarrow \quad \alpha = 0 \text{ or } \alpha = 2$

When $\alpha = 0$, $\begin{bmatrix} 1 & -1 \\ -1 & 1 \end{bmatrix} \begin{bmatrix} x \\ y \end{bmatrix} = 0$

$\Rightarrow \quad \begin{bmatrix} x \\ y \end{bmatrix} = \begin{bmatrix} 0 \\ 0 \end{bmatrix}$

This gives, $\quad x = y$

When $\alpha = 2$, $\begin{bmatrix} 1 & -1 \\ -1 & 1 \end{bmatrix} \begin{bmatrix} x \\ y \end{bmatrix} = 2$

$\Rightarrow \quad \begin{bmatrix} x \\ y \end{bmatrix} = \begin{bmatrix} 2x \\ 2y \end{bmatrix}.$

This gives, $\quad x = -y$

Hence, eigen vectors corresponding to 0 and 2 are $\begin{bmatrix} x \\ x \end{bmatrix}$ and $\begin{bmatrix} x \\ -x \end{bmatrix}$, or $\begin{bmatrix} 1 \\ 1 \end{bmatrix}$ and $\begin{bmatrix} 1 \\ -1 \end{bmatrix}$

24. For matrix $\quad A = \begin{bmatrix} -3 & 5 \\ 2 & 1 \end{bmatrix}$

cofactors are :

$$a_{11} = 1, a_{21} = -5, \; a_{12} = -2, a_{22} = -3$$

$\therefore$ Matrix by cofactors $= \begin{bmatrix} 1 & -2 \\ -5 & -3 \end{bmatrix}$

$$\text{Adjoint } A = \begin{bmatrix} 1 & -5 \\ -2 & -3 \end{bmatrix}$$

$$|A| = -3(1) - 5(2)$$
$$= -3 - 10 = -13$$

$\therefore \quad A^{-1} = \dfrac{\text{Adjoint } A}{|A|} \begin{bmatrix} -\dfrac{1}{13} & \dfrac{5}{13} \\ \dfrac{2}{13} & \dfrac{3}{13} \end{bmatrix}.$

27. Inverse of $7A = \begin{bmatrix} -1 & 2 \\ 4 & -7 \end{bmatrix}$

$\det |\Delta| = \begin{vmatrix} -1 & 2 \\ 4 & -7 \end{vmatrix} = 7 - 8 = -1$

$\therefore$ Matrices of cofactor $= \begin{bmatrix} -7 & -4 \\ -2 & -1 \end{bmatrix}$,

and it's transpose, $\quad A^T = \begin{bmatrix} -7 & -2 \\ -4 & -1 \end{bmatrix}$

$\therefore \quad \text{Inverse} = \dfrac{A^T}{|\Delta|} = \begin{bmatrix} 7 & 2 \\ 4 & 1 \end{bmatrix}$

$\therefore \quad A = \dfrac{1}{7}\left[\dfrac{A^T}{|\Delta|}\right] = \begin{bmatrix} 1 & \dfrac{2}{7} \\ \dfrac{4}{7} & \dfrac{1}{7} \end{bmatrix}$

28. Equations are consistent when

$$\begin{vmatrix} 2 & 3 & -1 \\ 1 & -1 & -4 \\ 4 & -1 & -a \end{vmatrix} = 0$$

$\Rightarrow \quad 2(a-4) - 3(-a+16) - 1(-1+4) = 0$

$5a - 8 - 48 - 3 = 0$

$5a = 59$

$$a = \frac{59}{5} \approx 12$$

33. Here $\quad [s\,I - A]^{-1} = \begin{bmatrix} s-1 & 0 \\ 0 & s-1 \end{bmatrix}^{-1}$

Then, $\quad 2^{-1}[sI - A]^{-1} = 2^{-1}\left\{\begin{bmatrix} \frac{1}{s-1} & 0 \\ 0 & \frac{1}{s-1} \end{bmatrix}\right\}$

$$= \begin{bmatrix} e^t & 0 \\ 0 & e^t \end{bmatrix}$$

34. $|P - \lambda I| = \begin{vmatrix} 3-\lambda & -2 & 2 \\ 0 & -2-\lambda & 1 \\ 0 & 0 & 1-\lambda \end{vmatrix} = 0$

$\therefore \quad \lambda = -2, 3, 1$

Putting $\lambda = -2$, we get

$5x - 2y + 2z = 0$

$z = 0$

So. $\quad 5x = 2y$ eigen vector $= \begin{bmatrix} 5 \\ 2 \\ 0 \end{bmatrix}$

35. Given matrix : $\quad A = \begin{bmatrix} 6 & 2 \\ 2 & 6 \end{bmatrix}$

We know $\quad |\lambda I - A| = 0$

$\Rightarrow \quad \begin{vmatrix} \lambda-6 & -2 \\ -2 & \lambda-6 \end{vmatrix} = 0$

$\Rightarrow \quad \lambda^2 - 12\lambda + 32 = 0$

$\Rightarrow \quad \lambda = 4, 8$ (eigen values)

For $\lambda_1 = 4$,

$$(\lambda_1 I - A) = \begin{bmatrix} -2 & -2 \\ -2 & -2 \end{bmatrix}, \; v_1 = \begin{bmatrix} 1 \\ 1 \end{bmatrix}$$

For $\lambda_1 = 8$,

$$(\lambda_2 I - A) = \begin{bmatrix} 2 & -6 \\ -6 & 2 \end{bmatrix}, \; v_2 = \begin{bmatrix} 1 \\ -1 \end{bmatrix}$$

36. State of the system at time t is,

$$X(t) = [sI - A]^{-1}X(0) = \phi(t)X(0)$$

$$= \begin{bmatrix} e^{-2t} & 0 \\ 0 & e^{-t} \end{bmatrix}\begin{bmatrix} 2 \\ 3 \end{bmatrix} = \begin{bmatrix} 2e^{-2t} \\ 3e^{-t} \end{bmatrix}$$

At $\quad t = 1, \quad X(1) = \begin{bmatrix} 2e^{-2} \\ 3e^{-1} \end{bmatrix} = \begin{bmatrix} 0.271 \\ 1.100 \end{bmatrix}$

NUMERICAL TYPE QUESTIONS

1. Determinant A = 0

$\Rightarrow \quad \begin{vmatrix} 4 & 2 & 3 \\ 1 & 0 & 0 \\ 4 & 0 & 3 \end{vmatrix} = (-1) \times 6 = -6 \neq 0$

Hence rank of A = 3

2. Since the number of non-zero elements on this diagonal matrix is four, hence the rank is four.

3. Given matrix A possesses a minor of order 3

viz. $\quad \begin{vmatrix} 1 & 3 & 1 \\ 2 & 4 & 0 \\ 3 & 1 & 5 \end{vmatrix} = \begin{vmatrix} 0 & 0 & 1 \\ 2 & 4 & 0 \\ -2 & -14 & 5 \end{vmatrix}$

Replacing C_1 and C_2 by $C_1 - C_3$ and $C_2 - 3C_3$.

$= \begin{vmatrix} 2 & 4 \\ -2 & -14 \end{vmatrix}$ expanding with respect to R_1

$= 2(-14) - (4)(-2) = -28 + 8 \neq 0$

$\therefore \quad p(A) \geq 3 \qquad$ ... (*i*)

Also A does not possess any minor of order 4, *i.e.* 3 + 1

$\therefore \quad p(A) \leq 3 \qquad$ ... (*ii*)

From equations (*i*) and (*ii*), we get

$p(A) = 3$ *i.e.* rank of A is 3.

5. Equivalent matrix equation is

$$\begin{bmatrix} 2 & 1 & 2 \\ 1 & 1 & 3 \\ 4 & 3 & \lambda \end{bmatrix}\begin{bmatrix} x \\ y \\ z \end{bmatrix} = 0$$

In order that given system of equations may have non-zero solution, rank of A should be less than 3. This requires that

$$\begin{bmatrix} 2 & 1 & 2 \\ 1 & 1 & 3 \\ 4 & 3 & \lambda \end{bmatrix} = 0$$

Interchanging R_1 and R_2,

$$\begin{bmatrix} 1 & 1 & 3 \\ 2 & 1 & 2 \\ 4 & 3 & \lambda \end{bmatrix} = 0$$

By $(R_2 - 2R_1)$ and $(R_3 - 4R_1)$,

$$\begin{bmatrix} 1 & 1 & 3 \\ 1 & -1 & -4 \\ 0 & -1 & \lambda-12 \end{bmatrix} = 0$$

$\Rightarrow \quad \begin{bmatrix} -1 & -4 \\ -1 & \lambda-12 \end{bmatrix} \Rightarrow -1(\lambda - 12) - (-1)(4) = 0$

$\Rightarrow \quad \lambda = 8$

6. The system of homogeneous linear equations has a non-trivial solution if

$$\begin{bmatrix} 4d-1 & 1 & 1 \\ 0 & -1 & 1 \\ 0 & 0 & 4d-1 \end{bmatrix} = 0$$

$\Rightarrow -(4d-1)^2 = 0 \qquad \Rightarrow d = \dfrac{1}{4}$

7. Let $A = \begin{bmatrix} a_1 \\ b_1 \\ c_1 \end{bmatrix}$; $B = [a_2\ b_2\ c_2]$

$$\therefore \quad C = \begin{bmatrix} a_1a_2 & a_1b_2 & a_1c_2 \\ b_1a_2 & b_1b_2 & b_1c_2 \\ c_1a_2 & c_2b_2 & c_1c_2 \end{bmatrix}$$

$$= a_1\, a_2\, [b_1\, b_2\, c_1\, c_2 - b_1 b_2\, c_1 c_2] = 0$$

$$\text{Cofactor} = \begin{vmatrix} a_1a_2 & a_1b_2 \\ b_1a_2 & b_1a_b \end{vmatrix} = 0$$

So rank = 1

8. Sum of eigen values of given matrix
= Sum of element of diagonal of given matrix
= 1 + 5 + 1 = 7

9. Since, $\det A = \begin{vmatrix} 1 & -2 & -1 \\ -3 & 3 & 0 \\ 2 & 2 & 4 \end{vmatrix} = 12 - 24 + 12 = 0$

and $M_{11} = 12 \neq 0$. Hence rank is 2.

11. Given : Matrix $M = \begin{bmatrix} 4 & 2 \\ 2 & 4 \end{bmatrix}$

$$\therefore \quad M - \lambda I = \begin{bmatrix} 4-\lambda & 2 \\ 2 & 4-\lambda \end{bmatrix}$$

For the eigen vector $\begin{bmatrix} 101 \\ 101 \end{bmatrix}$

$$(4 - \lambda)(101) + 2(101) = 0$$

$$\Rightarrow \quad 4 - \lambda + 2 = 0 \quad \Rightarrow \quad \lambda = 6 \text{ (eigen value)}$$

■■

2

CHAPTER

Calculus

FUNCTIONS OF SINGLE VARIABLE

LIMITS

By limit we are able to find out behaviour of a function $f(x)$ near a point c, when distance between x and c is very small i.e. $|x-c|$ is small.

Specifically, we would like to know whether there is some real number k such that $f(x)$ approaches k as x approaches c.

We write as $\lim_{x \to c} f(x) = k$

Right hand and Left hand limits

Left-hand limit: $\lim_{x \to c^-} f(x) = k$

Right-hand limit: $\lim_{x \to c^+} f(x) = k$

If $\lim_{x \to c^-} f(x) = \lim_{x \to c^+} f(x)$, then limit of $f(x)$ as $x \to c$ exists and is written as $\lim_{x \to c} f(x)$.

The limit of a function f(x) may not exist in any of the following situations :

(*i*) $\lim_{x \to c^-} f(x)$ does not exist

(*ii*) $\lim_{x \to c^+} f(x)$ does not exist

(*iii*) Both $\lim_{x \to c^-} f(x)$, and $\lim_{x \to c^+} f(x)$ exist but are unequal

Theorems on Limits

If $\lim_{x \to c} f(x)$ and $\lim_{x \to c} g(x)$ exist, then

(1) $\lim_{x \to c} (f(x) \pm g(x)) = \lim_{x \to c} f(x) \pm \lim_{x \to c} g(x)$

(2) $\lim_{x \to c} (f(x).g(x)) = \lim_{x \to c} f(x).\lim_{x \to c} g(x)$

(3) $\lim_{x \to c} \dfrac{f(x)}{g(x)} = \dfrac{\lim_{x \to c} f(x)}{\lim_{x \to c} g(x)}$ where $\left(\lim_{x \to c} g(x) \neq 0\right)$

Some useful Limits

(1) $\lim_{x \to 0} \dfrac{\sin x}{x} = 1 = \lim_{x \to 0} \cos x = \lim_{x \to 0} \dfrac{\tan x}{x}$

(2) $\lim_{x \to 0} (1+x)^{\frac{1}{x}} = e = \lim_{x \to \infty} \left(1+\dfrac{1}{x}\right)^x$

(3) $\lim_{x \to 0} \dfrac{\log_a(1+x)}{x} = \log_a e \quad (a > 0, a \neq 0)$

(4) $\lim_{x \to 0} \dfrac{\log(1+x)}{x} = 1$

(5) $\lim_{x \to 0} \dfrac{a^x - 1}{x} = \log a \quad (a > 0)$

(6) $\lim_{x \to 0} \dfrac{(1+x)^m - 1}{x} = m$

(7) $\lim_{x \to \infty} \dfrac{\log x}{x^m} = 0 \quad (m > 0)$

(8) $\lim_{x \to 0} \dfrac{x^n - a^n}{x - a} = na^{n-1}$

L' HOSPITAL'S RULE

It states that for functions f and g if

$$\lim_{x \to c} f(x) = \lim_{x \to c} g(x) = 0$$

or $\lim_{x \to c} g(x) = \pm \infty$

(condition that $\lim_{x \to c} f(x) = \pm \infty$ is not necessary)

and if $\lim_{x \to c} \dfrac{f'(x)}{g'(x)}$ exists then

$$\lim_{x \to c} \frac{f(x)}{g(x)} = \lim_{x \to c} \frac{f'(x)}{g'(x)}$$

Note : If f' and g' again satisfy above conditions of f and g, then

$$\lim_{x \to c} \frac{f(x)}{g(x)} = \lim_{x \to c} \frac{f''(x)}{g''(x)} \text{ and so on}$$

e.g. $\lim_{x \to 0} \dfrac{\sin x}{x} = \dfrac{0}{0}$

By L' Hospital Rule

$$\lim_{x \to 0} \frac{\sin x}{x} = \lim_{x \to 0} \frac{\cos x}{x} = \frac{1}{1} = 1$$

e.g. $\lim_{x \to 0} \dfrac{x^2 + x - \sin x}{x^2} = \dfrac{0}{0}$

By L' Hospital Rule

$$\Rightarrow \lim_{x \to 0} \frac{x^2 + x - \sin x}{x^2} = \lim_{x \to 0} \frac{2x + 1 - \cos x}{2x} = \frac{0}{0}$$

$$\Rightarrow \lim_{x\to 0} \frac{x^2+x-\sin x}{x^2} = \lim_{x\to 0} \frac{2+\sin x}{2} = 1$$

e.g. $\lim_{x\to 0} \frac{x^n}{x^m} = \frac{0}{0}$

By L' Hospital Rule

$$\lim_{x\to 0} \frac{x^n}{x^m} = \frac{nx^{n-1}}{mx^{m-1}} = \frac{0}{0}$$

$$\Rightarrow \lim_{x\to 0} \frac{x^n}{x^m} = \frac{n(n-1)x^{n-2}}{m(m-1)x^{m-2}} = \frac{0}{0}$$

$$\lim_{x\to 0} \frac{x^n}{x^m} = \frac{n(n-1).......1}{m(m-1).....1} = \frac{n!}{m!}$$

so on

CONTINUITY AND DISCONTINUITY

Continuity

- The function f is said to be *continuous* at $x = c$ if $\lim_{x\to c} f(x) = f(c)$
- The function f is said to be continuous on an open interval (a, b) if it is continuous at each point of (a,b)
- The function is said to be continuous on a closed interval $[a, b]$ if
  (*i*) f is continuous at each point of (a, b)
  (*ii*) $\lim_{x\to a^+} f(x) = f(a)$
  (*iii*) $\lim_{x\to b^-} f(x) = f(b)$

Note : Graphically, $f(x)$ is continuous if its graph can be drawn on paper without raising the pencil.

Discontinuity

A function f is said to be discontinuous at c if it is not continuous at that point. A function f is said to be discontinuous on an interval if it is discontinuous at least one point of the interval.

A function is discontinuous at c under any of the following circumstances:

(*i*) f is not defined at c

(*ii*) $\lim_{x\to c} f(x)$ does not exist

(*iii*) f is defined at c and $\lim_{x\to c} f(x)$ exists but $\lim_{x\to c} f(x) \neq f(c)$

Note : If f and g are continuous at $x = c$, then $f + g$, $f.g$, αf, and $\frac{f}{g}$ is also continuous at $x = c$ $(g(c) \neq 0)$

DIFFERENTIABILITY

A function $f(x)$ is said to be differentiable at $x = a$ if

both $\lim_{h\to 0} \frac{f(a+h)-f(a)}{h}$, $h > 0$

and $\lim_{h\to 0} \frac{f(a-h)-f(a)}{-h}$, $h > 0$

exist and have common value (finite). This common value is called *derivative of* $f(x)$ at the point $x = a$ and is denoted by $f'(a)$.

FUNCTIONS OF TWO VARIABLES

Let $f(x,y)$ be any function of two independent varibles x and y.

Limit

A function f tends to a limit l, when (x, y) tends to (a, b)

$$\lim_{(x,y)\to(a,b)} f(x,y) = l$$

Note : If $\lim_{(x,y)\to(a,b)} f(x,y) = l$ and if $y = \phi(x)$ is any function such that $\phi(x) \to b$ when $x \to a$, then $\lim_{(x,y)\to(a,b)} f(x,\phi(x))$ must exist and be equal to l.

Repeated Limits

If a function f is defined in some neigbourhood of (a, b), then limit $\lim_{y\to b} f(x,y)$ if exists, is a function of x, say $\phi(x)$.

If limit $\lim_{x\to a} \phi(x)$ exists and is equal to K, we write

$$\lim_{x\to a}\lim_{y\to b} f(x,y) = \text{K}$$

Here K is repeated limits of f as $y \to b$, $x \to a$

If we change order of taking the limit, we get other repeated limit.

$$\lim_{y\to b}\lim_{x\to a} f(x,y) = \text{K}'$$

when first $x \to a$ and then $y - b$

These two limits may or may not be equal.

Note :

(*i*) If repeated limits are not equal, then simultaneous limits cannot exist.

(*ii*) In case simultaneous limit exists, these two repeated limits if they exist are necessarily equal but the converse is not true.

Continuity

A function f is said to be *continuous* at a point (a,b) of its domain to definition if

$$\lim_{(x,y)\to(a,b)} f(x,y) = f(a,b)$$

Computing the Derivative

Rules of Differentiation

$(f+g)' = f' + g'$ → Sum Rule

$(f-g)' = f' - g'$ → Difference Rule

$(f.g)' = fg' + gf'$ → Product Rule

$\left(\frac{f}{g}\right)' = \frac{gf' - fg'}{g^2}$ → Quotient Rule

$\frac{1}{dx}(f(g(x))) = \frac{df}{dg}.\frac{dg}{dx}$ → Chain Rule

Some Standard Derivative

$f(x)$	$f'(x)$	$f(x)$	$f'(x)$
x^n	nx^{n-1}	$\sin h\, x$	$\cos h\, x$
$ln\, x$	$1/x$	$\cos h\, x$	$\sin h\, x$
$log_a\, x$	$log_a e.\frac{1}{x}$	$\sin^{-1} x$	$\frac{1}{\sqrt{1-x^2}}$
e^x	e^x	$\cos^{-1} x$	$\frac{-1}{\sqrt{1-x^2}}$
a^x	$a^x \log_a e$	$\tan^{-1} x$	$\frac{1}{1+x^2}$
$\sin x$	$\cos x$	$\text{cosec}^{-1} x$	$\frac{-1}{x^2\sqrt{x^2-1}}$
$\cos x$	$\sin x$		
$\tan x$	$\sec^2 x$	$\sec^{-1} x$	$\frac{1}{x\sqrt{x^2-1}}$
$\sec x$	$\sec x \tan x$	$\cot^{-1} x$	$\frac{1}{1+x^2}$
$\text{cosec}\, x$	$-\text{cosec}\, x \tan x$	$\lvert x\rvert$	$\frac{x}{\lvert x\rvert}$
$\cot x = -\text{cosec}^2 x$			$(x \neq 0)$

DIFFERENTIATION BY SUBSTITUTION

If a function contain as expression of the form

(1) $a^2 - x^2$; put $x = a \sin t$ or $x = a \cos t$

(2) $a^2 + x^2$; put $x = a \tan t$ or $x = a \cot t$

(3) $x^2 - a^2$; put $x = a \sec t$ or $x = a\, \text{cosec}\, t$

(4) $\sqrt{\frac{a-x}{a+x}}$ or $\sqrt{\frac{a+x}{a-x}}$; put $x = a \cos t$

(5) $a \cos x \pm b \sin x$; put $a = r \cos \theta$, and $b = r \sin\theta, r > 0$

Partial Derivatives

The partial differential coefficient of $z = f(x, y)$ with respect to x is defined as

$$\underset{\delta x \to 0}{\text{Lt}} \frac{f(x+\delta x, y) - f(x, y)}{\delta x}$$

provided this limit exists and is denoted by

$$\frac{\partial f}{\partial x} \text{ or } \frac{\partial z}{\partial x} \text{ or } f_x \text{ or } z_x$$

Similarly, partial derivatives of $f(x, y)$ with respect to y is defined as

$$\underset{\delta y \to 0}{\text{Lt}} \frac{f(x, y+\delta y) - f(x, y)}{\delta y}$$

provided this limit exists and is denoted by

$$\frac{\partial f}{\partial y} \text{ or } \frac{\partial z}{\partial y} \text{ or } f_y \text{ or } z_y$$

$\frac{\partial z}{\partial x}$ and $\frac{\partial z}{\partial y}$ are called *first order partial derivatives of z.*

- *The partial derivation of f(x, y) with respect to y is the ordinary derivative of f(x, y) when x is regarded as constant.*

Example. If $z = \log (x^2 + y^2)$, find $x\frac{\partial z}{\partial x} + y\frac{\partial z}{\partial y}$

Solution

Given : $z = \log (x^2 + y^2)$

$$\therefore \quad \frac{\partial z}{\partial x} = \frac{2x}{x^2 + y^2}$$

$$\Rightarrow \quad x\frac{\partial z}{\partial x} = \frac{2x^2}{x^2 + y^2}$$

$$\frac{\partial z}{\partial y} = \frac{2y}{x^2 + y^2}$$

$$\Rightarrow \quad y\frac{\partial z}{\partial y} = \frac{2y^2}{x^2 + y^2}$$

$$\therefore \quad x\frac{\partial z}{\partial x} + y\frac{\partial z}{\partial y} = \frac{2(x^2+y^2)}{(x^2+y^2)} = 2$$

Partial Derivatives of Higher Order

Since f_x and f_y are also functions of x and y and so we can further differentiate f_x and f_y partially with respect to x or y. The further partial derivatives of f_x or f_y are called *partial derivatives f higher order of u.*

- Partial derivatives of $\frac{\partial u}{\partial x}$ with respect to x and y are $\frac{\partial^2 u}{\partial^2 x}$ or $\frac{\partial^2 u}{\partial y\, \partial x}$ respectively.

- Partial derivatives $\frac{\partial^2 u}{\partial^2 x^2}, \frac{\partial^2 u}{\partial y\, \partial x}, \frac{\partial^2 u}{\partial xy}, \frac{\partial^2 u}{\partial y^2}$ are also denoted by $f_{xx}, f_{yx}, f_{xy}, f_{yy}$ respectively.

Example. If $u = e^{xyz}$, then find $\frac{\partial^3 u}{\partial x \partial y \partial z}$.

Solution

Given : $u = e^{xyz}$

$\therefore \quad \dfrac{\partial u}{\partial z} = e^{xyz}\, xy = uxy, \quad \dfrac{\partial u}{\partial y} = uxz$

and $\dfrac{\partial u}{\partial x} = uyz$

Now, $\dfrac{\partial^2 u}{\partial y \partial z} = ux + xy$

$\dfrac{\partial u}{\partial y} = ux + (xy)(uxz) = ux + ux^2 yz$

$$\therefore \quad \frac{\partial^3 u}{\partial x \partial y \partial z} = u + x\frac{\partial u}{\partial x} + 2u\, xyz + x^2 yz\frac{\partial u}{\partial x}$$

$$= u + x(uyz) + 2uxyz + x^2yz\,(uyz)$$

$$= e^{xyz}(1 + 3xyz + x^2 y^2 z^2)$$

MAXIMA AND MINIMA OF FUNCTIONS OF TWO VARIABLES

A function $f(x, y)$ is said to have a maximum or minimum at $x = a, y = b$, according as $f(a + h, b + k)$ is less or greater than $f(a, b)$ for all positive or negative small values of h and k.

In other words, if $\Delta = f(a + h, b + k) - f(a, b)$ is of the same sign for all small values of h, k and if this sign is negative, then $f(a, b)$ is a maximum. If this sign is positive, then $f(a, b)$ is a minimum.

A maximum or minimum value of a function is called its *extreme value*.

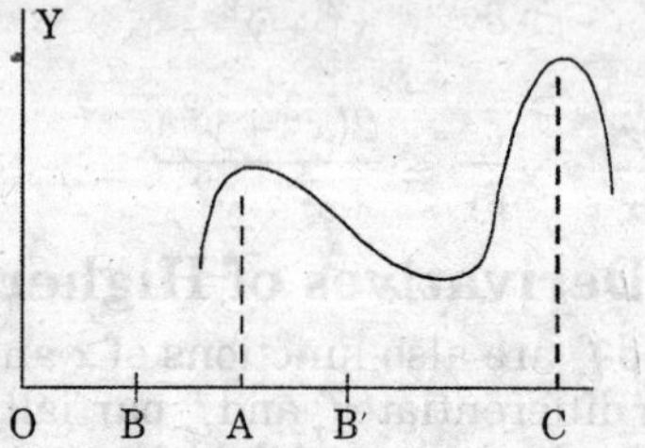

Above figure shows a graph of the function $f(x)$ and $OA = a$, *i.e.*, $f(x)$ has a maximum value for $x = a$ because $f(a)$ has a value more than the values of $f(x)$ for every value of x between B and B′. $f(x)$ is said to be a *maximum* at $x = a$, even though value of $f(x)$ at $x = a$ should be greater than all other values of $f(x)$ in some small neighbourhood. Thus a maximum value of $f(x)$ is not necessarily the greatest value of $f(x)$. In fact, a curve might have several maxima (and minima).

Condition for Maxima and Minima

Necessary conditions for existence of a maximum or a minimum of $f(x)$ at $x = a, y = b$ is

$$\left(\frac{\partial f}{\partial x}\right)_{\substack{x=a\\y=b}} = 0; \text{ and } \left(\frac{\partial f}{\partial y}\right)_{\substack{x=a\\y=b}} = 0$$

Sufficient condition for Maxima and Minima

Let $r = \left(\dfrac{\partial^2 f}{\partial x^2}\right)_{\substack{x=a\\y=b}}, \; s = \left(\dfrac{\partial^2 f}{\partial x \partial y}\right)_{\substack{x=a\\y=b}}$

and $t = \left(\dfrac{\partial^2 f}{\partial y^2}\right)_{\substack{x=a\\y=b}}$

Case I: $rt - s^2 > 0$

$f(x, y)$ will have maximum or a minimum of $x = a, y = b$.

Again, $f(x, y)$ is a maximum or a minimum according as r is negative or positive

Case II: $rt - s^2 < 0$

$f(x,y)$ will have neither a maximum nor a minimum at $x = a, y = b$.

Case III: $rt - s^2 = 0$

This case is doubtful and further investigation is needed to determine whether

(x, y) is maximum or a minimum at $x = a, y = b$ or not.

Finding Absolute Maxima and Minima Values

Working rules

If f is a differentiable function in $[a\ b]$ except at finitely many points, then to find absolute maximum and absolute minimum values, adopt following procedure :

(*i*) Evaluate $f(x)$ at the points, where $f'(x) = 0$.

(*ii*) Evaluated $f(a)$ and $f(b)$.

Then maximum of these values is the **absolute maxima** and minimum of these values is called **absolute minima.**

Finding Local Maxima and Local Minima

Working rules

Condition for maxima

- Function $f(x)$ has a maximum value $f(a)$ if $f'(a) = 0$ and $f'(x)$ changes sign from +ve to –ve as x passes through 'a' from left to right.
- In general, for any even number n, $f'(a) = f''(a) = f'''(a) \;\ldots = f^{n-1}(a) = 0$ and $f^n(a) < 0$, then $f(a)$ is a maximum value of $f(x)$.
- In particular, if $n = 2$, then $f'(a) = 0$ and $f''(a) < (o)$, and the function is maximum at $x = a$.

Condition for minima :

- Function $f(x)$ has a minimum value $f(a)$ if $f'(a) = 0$ and $f'(x)$ changes sign from –ve to +ve as x passes through $x = a$ from left to right.
- In general, for any even number n, if $f'(a) = f''(a) = f'''(a) = \;\ldots f^{n-1}(a) = 0$, and $f^n(a) > 0$, then $f(a)$ is minimum value of $f(x)$
- In particular, if $n = 2$, then $f'(a) = 0$ and $f''(a) > 0$, the function is minimum at $x = a$.

Note : If n is a even number such that

$$f'(a) = f''(a) = \ldots f^n(a) = 0, f^{n+1}(a) \neq 0,$$

then $f(a)$ is neither maximum nor minimum of the function $f(x)$.

In particular if $n = 2$ and $f'(a) = f''(a) = 0$. $f'''(a) \neq 0$, then $f(a)$ is neither maximum nor minimum values of $f(x)$. Then the point $x = a$ is called **point of inflexion.**

Extreme value

Either a maximum value or minimum value $f(a)$ of the function $f(x)$ is called *extreme value.*

Stationary value

If $f'(a) = 0$, then $f(a)$ is called *stationary value.*

Every extreme value is stationary but every stationary value of the function need not to be extreme value

Example. Find the extreme value of

$$f(x) = x^5 - 5x^4 + 5x^3 - 1$$

Solution

$$f'(x) = 5x^4 - 20x^3 + 15x^2$$

and $\quad f'(0) = 0$

Hence, $f(0)$ is stationary value but $f(0)$ is not an extreme value because $f''(0) = 0$ but $f'''(0) \neq 0$.

Greatest Value

The greatest value of the function in an interval (a, b) is either a maximum value in an interval or end value (i.e. at $x = a$ or $x = b$) of $f(x)$ whichever is greater.

Least Values

The least value of $f(x)$ in an interval (a, b) is either a minimum value of $f(x)$ at a point inside the interval or an end value (i.e. at $x = a$ or $x = b$) of $f(x)$ whichever is less.

Example. Find greatest and least value of the function $2x^2 - 9x - 1$, in the internal [2, 5]

Solution

Let $\quad f(x) = 2x^2 - 9x - 1$

$\Rightarrow \quad f'(x) = 4x - 9$

At $x = \frac{9}{4} \quad f'(x) = 0$

$\therefore \quad f''(x) = 4 > 0$

$\therefore \quad f\left(\frac{9}{4}\right) = -\frac{89}{8}$ is a minimum value.

Also, $\quad f(2) = -11, f(5) = 4$

$\therefore$ Greatest value = 4, and least value $= -\frac{89}{8}$

SOME STANDARD INTEGRATIONS

1. $\int x^n = \frac{x^{n+1}}{n+1}, (n \neq -1)$

2. $\int \frac{1}{x} dx = \log x$

3. $\int e^x dx = e^x$

4. $\int a^x dx = \frac{a^x}{\log a}$

5. $\int \sin x \, dx = -\cos x$

6. $\int \cos x \, dx = \sin x$

7. $\int \sec^2 x \, dx = \tan x,$

8. $\int \text{cosec}^2 dx = -\cot x$

9. $\int \sec x \tan x \, dx = \sec x$

10. $\int \text{cosec}\, x \cot x \, dx = -\text{cosec}\, x$

11. $\int \tan x \, dx = \log \sec x = -\log \cos x$

12. $\int \cot x \, dx = \log \sin x$

13. $\int \sec x \, dx = \log (\sec x + \tan x)$

14. $\int \text{cosec}\, x \, dx = -\log (\text{cosec}\, x + \cot x) = \log \tan \frac{x}{2}$

15. $\int \frac{1}{\sqrt{1-x^2}} dx = \sin^{-1} x$ or $-\cos^{-1} x$

16. $\int \frac{1}{\sqrt{1+x^2}} dx = \sin h^{-1} x$

17. $\int \frac{1}{a^2+x^2} dx = \frac{1}{a} \tan^{-1}\left(\frac{x}{a}\right)$

18. $\int \frac{1}{x\sqrt{x^2-1}} dx = \sec^{-1} x = \cos^{-1} \frac{1}{x}$

19. $\int \sin hx \, dx = \cos hx$

20. $\int \cos hx \, dx = \sin hx$

21. $\int \frac{1}{\sqrt{x^2-a^2}} dx = \log\left(x + \sqrt{x^2 - a^2}\right) = \cos h^{-1} \frac{x}{a}$

22. $\int \frac{1}{\sqrt{a^2+x^2}} dx = \log\left(x + \sqrt{a^2 + x^2}\right)$

23. $\int \frac{1}{\sqrt{a^2+x^2}} dx = \sin h^{-1}\left(\frac{x}{a}\right)$

24. $\int \frac{dx}{x\sqrt{x^2-a^2}} = \frac{1}{a} \sec^{-1} \frac{x}{a} = \frac{1}{a} \cos$

25. $\int \frac{dx}{x^2+a^2} = \frac{1}{a} \tan^{-1}\left(\frac{x}{a}\right)$

26. $\int \frac{dx}{x^2-a^2} = \frac{1}{2a} \log\left(\frac{x-a}{x+a}\right)$ if $x > a$

27. $\int \frac{dx}{a^2 - x^2} = \frac{1}{2a}\log\left(\frac{a+x}{a-x}\right)$ if $x < a$

28. $\int u \cdot v\, dx = u \int v\, dx - \int\left[\left(\frac{du}{dx}\right)\left(\int v dx\right)\right] dx$

where u and v are the function of x. u is a first function and v as a second function.

29. $\int e^x[f(x) + f'(x)]\, dx = e^x f(x) + c$

30. $\int \frac{f'(x)}{f(x)} \mathbf{dx} = \log f(x) + C$

Note : ILATE

I → Inverse

L → Logarithmic function

A → Algebraic

T → Trigonometric

E → Exponential

Example. Calculate $\int \frac{e^{\tan^{-1} x}}{1+x^2} dx$

Solution

Let $\tan^{-1}x = y \Rightarrow \frac{1}{1+x^2} dx = dy$

then $\int \frac{e^{\tan^{-1} x}}{1+x^2} dx = \int e^y dy = e^y + C = e^{\tan^{-1} x} + C$

Example. Calculate $\int 1. \sin^{-1}x\, dx$

Solution

Take $u = \sin^{-1} x$ and $v = 1$

Then $\int \sin^{-1}x dx = \sin^{-1} x \int dx - \int\left[\frac{d(\sin^{-1}x)}{dx}\int dx\right] dx$

$= x \sin^{-1} x - \int \frac{x}{\sqrt{1-x^2}} x\, dx$

$= x \sin^{-1} x - \int \frac{x}{\sqrt{1-x^2}} dx$

$= x \sin^{-1} x + \sqrt{1-x^2} + C$

Example. Calculate $\int \frac{e^x + e^{-x}}{e^x - e^{-x}} dx$

Solution

Let $y = e^x - e^{-x} \Rightarrow dy = (e^x + e^{-x})\, dx$

$\therefore \int \frac{(e^x + e^{-x})}{e^x - e^{-x}} = \int \frac{dy}{y} = \log y + C = \log(e^x + e^{-x}) + C$

DEFINITE INTEGRAL

If a function is defined in the interval $[a, b]$, then definite integral of $f(x)$ is

$$\int_a^b f(x)\, dx = [F(x)]_a^b = F(b) - F(a)$$

where F(x) is an integral of $f(x)$

$f(b)$ is the value of $f(x)$ at $x = b$, and

$f(a)$ is the value of $f(x)$ at $x = a$.

a and b are called *lower upper limit respectively.*

Geometrically, definite integral represents the area bounded by curve $y = f(x)$, x-axis and the lines $x = a$ and $x = b$.

Properties of Definite Integrals

Let $\int f(x)\, dx = F(x)$. Then

1. $\int_a^b f(x)\, dx = \int_a^b f(y)\, dy$

i.e. in definite integral the variable of integration is dummy.

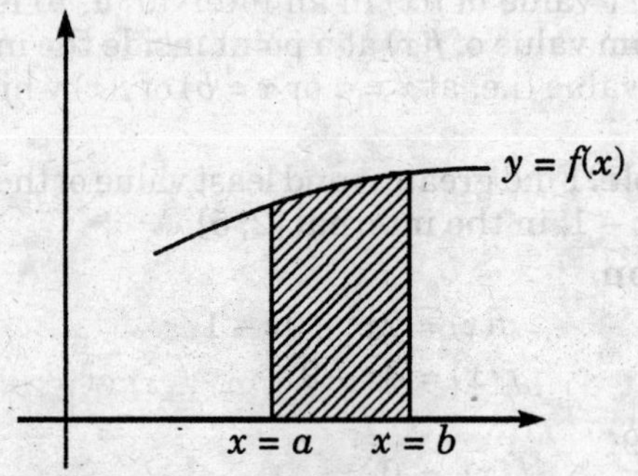

2. $\int_a^b f(x)\, dx = -\int_b^a f(x)\, dx$

3. $\int_a^b f(x)\, dx = \int_a^c f(x)\, dx + \int_c^b f(x)\, dx$

where c is a point lies between the interval $[a, b]$. and $f(x)$ integrable over $[a, c]$ and $[c, b]$.

4. $\int_0^a f(x)\, dx = \int_0^a f(a-x)\, dx$

5. $\int_{-a}^a f(x)\, dx = \int_0^a f(x)\, dx + \int_0^a f(-x)\, dx$

If function is even, i.e. $f(-x) = f(x)$, then

$$\int_{-a}^a f(x)\, dx = 2\int_0^a f(x)\, dx$$

If function is odd, i.e. $f(-x) = -f(x)$, then

$$\int_{-a}^a f(x)\, dx = 0$$

6. $\int_0^{2a} f(x)\,dx = \int_0^{a} f(x)\,dx + \int_0^{a} f(2a-x)\,dx$

If $f(x) = f(2a-x)$, then

$$\int_0^{2a} f(x)\,dx = 2\int_0^{a} f(x)\,dx$$

and if $f(x) = -f(2a-x)$, then

$$\int_0^{2a} f(x)\,dx = 0$$

Definite Integral as Limit of sum

If a function $f(x)$ is either increasing or decreasing on $[a, b]$, then

$$\int_a^b f(x)\,dx = \operatorname*{Lt}_{h\to 0} h[f(a)+f(a+h)+\ldots+f(a+(n-1)h]$$

$$= \operatorname*{Lt}_{h\to 0} h\,[f(a+h)+f(a+2h)+\ldots+f(a+nh)]$$

where, $h = \dfrac{b-a}{n}$

Example. From definition of a definite integral as the limit of a sum, evaluate $\int_1^2 (x+x^2)\,dx$.

Solution

$$\int_1^2 (x+x^2)\,dx$$

$$= \operatorname*{Lt}_{h\to 0} \sum_{i=1}^{n} h\,[(1+ih)+(1+ih)^2 \ldots..] \text{ where}\left(h=\frac{1}{n}\right)$$

$$= \operatorname*{Lt}_{h\to 0} h \sum_{i=1}^{n} [1+ih+1+2\,ih+i^2h^2]$$

$$= \operatorname*{Lt}_{h\to 0} h \sum_{i=1}^{n} (2+3hi)+i^2h^2$$

$$= \operatorname*{Lt}_{h\to 0} \left[2h\sum_{i=1}^{n}1 + 3h^2\sum_{i=1}^{n} i + h^3\sum_{i=1}^{n} i^2\right]$$

$$= \operatorname*{Lt}_{h\to 0} \left[2nh + \frac{3}{2}h^2 n\,(n+1) + \frac{1}{6}h^3 n\,(n+1)(2n+1)\right]$$

$$= \operatorname*{Lt}_{h\to 0} \left[2+\frac{3}{2}(1+h)+\frac{1}{6}(1+h)(2+h)\right] \quad \text{...since } nh = 1$$

$$= 2+\frac{3}{2}+\frac{1}{3} = \mathbf{\frac{23}{6}}$$

Improper Integral

Definite intgral $\int_0^a f(x)\,dx$ is *called improper integral* if

(*i*) range of integration is infinite and integrand is bounded.

(*ii*) range of integration is definite and integrand is unbounded.

(*iii*) neither range of integration is finite nor integrand is bounded over it.

MULTIPLE INTEGRALS

Let a single-valued and bounded function $f(x,y)$ of two independent variables x,y be defined in a closed region R of the xy-plane. Divide the region R into sub-regions by drawing lines parallel to co-ordinate axes. Number the rectangles which lie entirely inside the region R from 1 to n.

Let (x_r, y_r) be any point inside the rth rectangle whose area is δA_r

$$f(x_1,y_1)\,\delta A_1 + f(x_2,y_2)\,\delta A_2 + \ldots . f(x_n,y_n)\,\delta A_n$$

$$= \sum_{r=1}^{n} f(x_r,y_r)\delta A_r \quad \text{.... (i)}$$

Let number of these sub-regions increases indefinitely such that the largest linear dimension (i.e.diagonal) of δA_r approaches zero. The limit of the sum(*i*), if it exists, irrespective of the mode of sub-division, is called *double integral of f(x,y)* over the region R and is denoted by $\iint_R f(x,y)\,dA$.

In other words, $\operatorname*{Lt}_{\substack{n\to\infty\\ \delta A_r\to 0}} \sum_{r=1}^{n} f(x_r,y_r)\,\delta A_r = \iint_R f(x,y)\,dA$

which is also expressed as $\iint_R f(x,y)\,dxdy$

or $\iint_R f(x,y)\,dy\,dx$

Let the region R be bounded by the curves

$x = x_1$ *and* $y = y_2$

$x = x_2$ *and* $y = y_2$

Properties of a Double Integral

(i) When x_1, x_2 are functions of y and y_1, y_2 are constants.

Let AB and CD be the curves $x_1=\phi_1(y)$ and $x_2=\phi_2(y)$. Then

$$\iint_R f(x,y)\,dxdy = \int_{y_1}^{y_2}\int_{x_1=\phi_1(y)}^{x_2=\phi_2(y)} f(x,y)\,dx\;dy$$

(ii) When y_1, y_2 are functions of x and x_1, x_2 are constants.

Let AB and CD be the curves $y_1 = \phi_1(x)$ and $y_2=\phi_2(x)$. Then

$$\iint_R f(x,y)\,dx\,dy = \int_{x_1}^{x_2}\int_{y_1=\phi_1(x)}^{y_2=\phi_2(x)} f(x,y)\,dy\;dx$$

***(iii)* When $x_1, x_2, y_1 y_2$ are constants.**

Here the region of integration R is the rectangle. Therefore

$$\iint_R f(x,y)\,dxdy = \int_{y_1}^{y_2}\int_{x_1}^{x_2} f(x,y)\,dx\,dy$$

$$= \int_{x_1}^{x_2}\int_{y_1}^{y_2} f(x,y)\,dy\,dx$$

(*i*) If region R is partitioned into two parts, say R_1 and R_2, then

$$\iint_R f(x,y)\,dx\,dy = \iint_{R1} f(x,y)\,dx\,dy + \iint_{R2} f(x,y)\,dx\,dy$$

(*ii*) Double integral of the algebraic sum of a fixed number of functions is equal to algebraic sum of the double integrals taken far each term. Thus

$$\iint_R [f_1(x,y) + f_2(x,y) + f_3(x,y) + ...]\,dx\,dy$$

$$= \iint_R f_1(x,y)\,dx\,dy + \iint_R f_2(x,y)\,dx\,dy + \iint_R f_3(x,y)\,dx\,dy + ...$$

(*iii*) A constant factor may be taken outside the integral sign. Thus

$$\iint_R K\,f(x,y)\,dx\,dy = K\iint_R f(x,y)\,dx\,dy$$

where K is constant

Evaluation of Double Integrals

During evaluating double intergrals, first integrate with respect to the variable limits, treating other varibles as constant, and then integrate with respect to the variable with constant limit.

CHANGE OF ORDER OF INTEGRATION

In a double integral, if limits of integration are constant, then order of integration is immaterial, provided limits of integration are changed accordingly. Thus

$$\int_c^d \int_a^b f(x,y)\,dx\,dy = \int_a^b \int_c^d f(x,y)\,dy\,dx$$

But if limits of integration are variable, a change in the order of integration changes in the limits of integration.

TRIPLE INTEGRALS

Consider a function $f(x,y,z)$ which is continuous at every point of the 3-dimensional finite region V.

Divide V into n elementary volumes $\delta V_1, \delta V_2, ... \delta V_n$.

Let (x_r, y_r, z_r) be any point within rth sub-division δV_r.

Consider the sum $\sum_{r=1}^{\infty} f(x_r, y_r, z_r)\,\delta V_r$

The limit of this sum, if it exists, as $n \to \infty$ and $\delta V_r \to 0$ is called *triple integral* of $f(x,y,z)$ over the region V and is denoted by $\iiint f(x,y,z)\,dV$

It can also be expressed as the repeated integral

$$\int_{x_1}^{x_2}\int_{y_1}^{y_2}\int_{z_1}^{z_2} f(x,y,z)\,dx\,dy\,dz.$$

FOURIER SERIES

If numbers $a_0, a_1, ..., a_n, ..., b_1, b_2, ..., b_n, ...$ are derived from a function f by means of Euler-Fourier formulas

$$a_n = \frac{1}{\pi}\int_{-\pi}^{\pi} f(x)\cos nx\,dx \qquad (n = 0,1,2,...)$$

$$b_n = \frac{1}{\pi}\int_{-\pi}^{\pi} f(x)\sin nx\,dx \qquad (n = 1,2,...)$$

then series $a_0 + \sum_{n=1}^{\infty} (a_n \cos nx + b_n \sin nx)$ is called *Fourier series.*

Dirichlet's Condition

Assumptions for expansion in a Fourier's series :

(*i*) Given function $f(x)$ is assumed to be defined and single valued in the given range $(-l, l)$.

(*ii*) $f(x)$ is periodic outside $(-l, l)$ with period $2l$.

(*iii*) Series $a_0 + \sum_{n=1}^{\infty} (a_n \cos nx + b_n \sin nx)$ is uniformly convergent, so that term by term integration of the series is possible.

Even and Odd function of x (sine series and cosine series)

Case I: *When f(x) is an even function*

$$f(x) = a_0 + \sum_{n=1}^{\infty} a_n \cos nx$$

where,

$$a_0 = \frac{1}{\pi}\int_0^{\pi} f(x)\,dx$$

$$a_n = \frac{2}{\pi}\int_0^{\pi} f(x)\cos nx\,dx$$

$$b_n = 0$$

Case II: *When f(x) is an odd function*

$$f(x) = \sum_{n=1}^{\infty} (b_n \sin nx)$$

where,

$$b_n = \frac{2}{\pi}\int_0^{\pi} f(x)\sin nx\,dx$$

$$a_0 = 0$$

$$a_n = 0$$

Half Range Expansions

A series which contains only sine terms or cosine terms is called *half range Fourier sine or cosine series* respectively.

In this case, function $f(x)$ is generally defined in the interval $(0, l)$.

Now if $f(x)$ is an even function, then Fourier cosine series is

$$f(x) = a_0 + \sum_{n=1}^{\infty} a_n \cos \frac{nx\pi}{l}$$

where $a_0 = \frac{1}{l}\int_0^l f(x)\, dx$;

$$a_n = \frac{2}{l}\int_0^l f(x) \cos \frac{n\pi x}{l} dx$$

If $f(x)$ is an odd function of x, then Fourier sine series is

$$f(x) = \sum_{n=1}^{\infty} b_n \sin \frac{nx\pi}{l}$$

where, $a_0 = 0$ $b_n = \frac{2}{l}\int_0^l f(x) \sin \frac{n\pi x}{l} dx$

Fouriers series in the interval (a, b)

If function $f(x)$ satisfies Dirichlet's conditions in the interval (a, b), then

$$f(x) = a_0 + \sum_{n=1}^{\infty}\left(a_n \cos \frac{2n\pi x}{b-a} + b_n \sin \frac{2n\pi x}{b-a}\right)$$

where, $a_0 = \frac{1}{b-a}\int_a^b f(x)\, dx$

$$a_n = \frac{2}{b-a}\int_a^b f(x) \cos \frac{2n\pi x}{b-a} dx$$

$$b_n = \frac{2}{b-a}\int_a^b f(x) \sin \frac{2n\pi x}{b-a} dx$$

CONVERGENCE SERIES

SEQUENCE

A set of numbers $u_1, u_2 .... u_n .....$ formed according to some definite rule is called a *sequence*. A sequence is generally denoted by $\{u_n\}$.

Finite Sequence

A sequence is called a *finite sequence* if it has a finite number of terms.

Infinite Sequence

If sequene has infinite number of terms, then it is called an *infinite sequence*.

Positive Term Sequence

A series $u_1 + u_2 + u_3.....$ is called *positive term series*, if $u_n > 0\ \forall\ n$.

SERIES

Sum of the corresponding terms of the sequence $u_1, u_2, u_3 .....$, *i.e.*, $u_1 + u_2 + u_3.....$ is called *series*.

A series is called a *finite* or *infinite* according as the corresponding sequence is *finite* or *infinite*.

Infinites series $u_1 + u_2 + u_3 + ... + u_n + ...$ is denoted by $\sum u_n$ and sum of the first n terms series is denoted by S_n.

$\therefore \qquad S_n = u_1 + u_2 + u_3 + ... + u_n$

Alternating series

A series $u_1 - u_2 + u_3.....$ is called *alternating series*, if $u_n > 0\ \forall\ n$.

Nature of Series

(1) Convergent

Infinite series $u_1 + u_2 + u_3 + ...$ is said to be convergent, if

$\lim_{n\to\infty} S_n = \lim_{n\to\infty}(u_1 + u_2 + ... + u_n)$is finite.

(2) Divergent

Infinite series $u_1 + u_2 + u_3 + ...$ is said to be divergent, if

$\lim_{n\to\infty} S_n = \lim_{n\to\infty} (u_1 + u_2 + ...u_n)$
$= + \infty$ or $- \infty$

(3) Oscillatory

Infinite series $u_1 + u_2 + u_3 + ...$ is said to be an oscillatory series, if

$\lim_{n\to\infty} S_n = \lim_{n\to\infty} (u_1 + u_2 + ...u_n)$

is not defined or oscillates between two limites.

Properties of Convergent and Divergent Series

(*i*) Nature of an infinite series remains unaltered by adding or removing a finite number of terms.

(*ii*) Nature of an inifinite series remains unaltered by multiplying or dividing the terms by some fixed non zero constant.

(*iii*) If $\sum u_n$ and $\sum v_n$ are two series such that $0 \le u_n \le v_n$ for all n and $\sum v_n$ is convergent, then $\sum u_n$ is also convergent.

(*iv*) If $\sum u_n$ and $\sum v_n$ are two series such that $u_n \ge v_n \ge 0$ for all n and $\sum v_n$ is divergent, then $\sum u_n$ is also divergent.

(*v*) If infinite series $\sum u_n$ and $\sum v_n$ both are convergent, then $\sum(u_n + v_n)$, $\sum(u_n - v_n)$ and $\sum(\lambda u_n + \lambda v_n)$ are also convergent.

(*vi*) If series $\sum u_n$ of positive terms is convergent, then $\lim_{n\to\infty} u_n = 0$ (only necessary not sufficient).

(*vii*) The series $\sum u_n$ is not convergent, $\lim_{n\to\infty} u \ne 0$

Absolutely Convergent Series

Series $\sum u_n$ is called *absolutely convergent* if series $\sum |u_n|$ is convergent.

Conditionally (or semi) Convergent series

A convergent series Σu_n is called conditionlly convergent series, if $\sum |u_n|$ is divergent.

Series Tests

1. Leibnitz's test (Alternating series test)

Infinite series $u_1 - u_2 + u_3 - u_4 + \ldots$ is convergent, if

(i) $u_1 > u_2 > u_3 > u_4 + \ldots\ldots$, and

(ii) $u_n \to 0$ as $n \to \infty$

2. Geomteric Series test

Geometric series $a + ar + ar^2 + \ldots$ is

(i) convergent, if $|r| < 1$

(ii) divergent, if $r \geq 1$

(iii) osillatory, when $r \leq -1$

3. Hyperharmonic or *p*-Series test

Inifinite series $\sum \frac{1}{n^p} = \frac{1}{1^p} + \frac{1}{2^p} + \frac{1}{3^p} + \ldots$ is

(i) convergent if $p > 1$

(ii) divergent if $p \leq 1$

4. Comparison test

If $\sum u_n$ and $\sum v_n$ are two series of positive terms such that $\lim_{n\to\infty} \frac{u_n}{v_n}$ is finite ($\neq 0$), then $\sum u_n$ and $\sum v_n$ behave alike.

Note : Test series $\sum v_n$ of the comparison test is called *auxiliary series* and

$$v_n = \frac{\text{highest power term in numerator of } u_n}{\text{highest power term in denominator in } u_n}$$

5. D' Alembert's ratio test

If $\sum u_n$ is a series of positive terms and, if

$$\lim_{n\to\infty} \frac{u_n}{u_{n+1}} = \text{L},$$

then the series is

(i) convergent, if L > 1

(ii) divergent if, L < 1

(iii) the test fails, if L = 1

Note:

I. If $\lim_{n\to\infty} \frac{u_n}{u_{n+1}} = 1$ and $\frac{u_n}{u_{n+1}}$ contains e, then Logarithmic test is used.

II. If $\lim_{n\to\infty} \frac{u_n}{u_{n+1}} = 1$ and $\frac{u_n}{u_{n+1}}$ does not contains e, then either Raabe's test of Gauss's test is used.

6. Raabe's test

$\sum u_n$ is a series of positive terms and, if

$\lim_{n\to\infty} n\left(\frac{u_n}{u_{n+1}} - 1\right)$ = L, then the series is

(i) convergent, if L > 1

(ii) divergent, if L < 1

(iii) The test fails, if L = 1

7. Gauss's test

If $\sum u_n$ is a series of positive terms and if ratio $\frac{u_n}{u_{n+1}}$ is expressed in the form

$$\frac{u_n}{u_{n+1}} = 1 + \frac{\lambda}{n} + \frac{\mu}{n^2} + \frac{\alpha}{n^3} + \ldots$$

then the series is

(i) convergent, if $\lambda > 1$

(ii) divergent if $\lambda \leq 1$

8. Logrithmic test

If $\sum u_n$ is series of positive terms and if

$\lim_{n\to\infty}\left(n \log \frac{u_n}{u_{n+1}}\right)$ = L, then the series is

(i) convergent, if L > 1

(ii) divergent, if L < 1

(iii) the test fails, if L = 1

9. De Morgan and Bertrand's test

If $\sum u_n$ is series of positive terms and if

$$\lim_{n\to\infty}\left[\left\{n\left(\log \frac{u_n}{u_{n+1}} - 1\right) - 1\right\}\log n\right] = \text{L},$$

then the series is

(i) convergent, if L > 1

(ii) divergent if, L < 1

(iii) the test fails, if L = 1

10. Higher Logarithmic test

If $\sum u_n$ is series of positive terms and if

$$\lim_{n\to\infty}\left\{\left(n \log \frac{u_n}{u_{n+1}} - 1\right)\log n\right\} = \text{L},$$

then the series is

(i) convergent, if L > 1

(ii) divergent, if L < 1

(iii) the test fails, if L = 1

11. Cauchy's Root test

If $\sum u_n$ is a series of positive terms and if $\lim_{n\to\infty}(u_n)^{1/n}$ = L, then the series is

(i) convergent, if L < 1

(ii) divergent, if L > 1

(iii) the test fails, if L = 1

12. Cauchy's Condensation test

If $\sum u_n$ is series of positive terms and if $u_{n+1} < u_n$ then series $\sum u_n$ and $\sum a^n u_n$ (a > 1 any integer) behave alike.

13. Cauchy's Integral test

If $\sum u_n$ is series of positive terms and $f(x)$ be a continuous positive decreasing function of $(x > 0)$, then $\sum u_n$ and $\int_1^\infty f(x)\,dx$ behave alike.

14. Kummer's test

Let a divergent series of positive terms $\sum (d_n)^{-1}$ is given, and let a terms of a series of positive terms $\sum u_n$ be such that

$$\lim_{n\to\infty}\left(d_n \frac{u_n}{u_{n+1}} - d_n + 1\right) = L,$$

then the series is

(*i*) convergent, if L > 0

(*ii*) divergent, if L < 0

(*iii*) the test fails, if L = 1

VECTOR

Vector is completely specified by its magnitude and direction.

Vector is represented by a directed line segment. Thus $\overline{PQ}$ represents a vector where magnitude is the length PQ and direction is form P (starting point) to Q (end point)

Unit Vector

A vector of unit magnitude is called *unit vector.* Unit vector corresponding to vector A is written as $\bar{A}$.

Null Vector

A vector of zero magnitude, which can have no direction associated with it is called *zero (or null) vector* and is denoted by O-a thick zero.

PRODUCT OF TWO VECTORS

1. Scalar or Dot Product

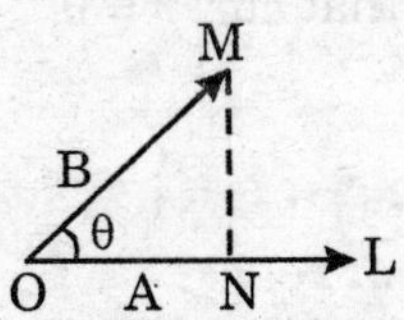

Scalar or dot product of two vectors A and B is defined as scalar ab cos θ, where θ is angle between A and B.

Mathematically, $A.B = ab \cos\theta$

Properties

(*i*) For two vectors to be perpendicular, their scalar product should be zero, i.e.

$$A.\,B = ab \cos 90° \quad ...[\theta = 90°]$$

$$\Rightarrow \quad A.\,B = 0$$

(*ii*) Mutually perpendicular unit vectors i, j, k, are have relation

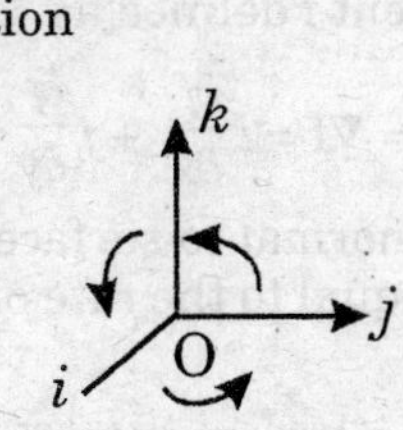

$$i.j = j.k = k.i = 0 \quad ...(i = 0)$$

and $\quad i^2 = j^2 = k^2 = 1$

2. Vector or Cross Product

Vector or cross product of two vectors A and B is defined as a vector ab sin θ, where θ is angle between A and B.

Mathematically, $A \times B = ab \sin\theta\, N$

N is unit vector normal to the plane A and B.

Properties

(*i*) For two non zero vectors to be parallel, their vector product should be zero.

$$\theta = 0° \text{ or } 180°$$

$$\therefore \quad A \times B = \sin 0° \text{ or } \sin 180°$$

$$\Rightarrow \quad A \times B = 0$$

(*ii*) For the orthonormal vectors i, j and k, we have the relation

$$i \times i = j \times j = k \times k = 0,$$
$$i \times j = k,\ j \times i = -k$$
$$j \times k = i,\ k \times j = -i$$
$$k \times i = j,\ i \times k = -j$$

Differentiation of Vector

If a vector R varies continuously as a scalar variable t changes, then R is said to be function of t and is written as R = f(t)

In scalar calculus, we define derivative of vector function R = f(t) as

$$\underset{\delta t\to 0}{\text{lt}} = F\frac{(t + dt) - F(t)}{dt}$$

and it is written as $\frac{dR}{dt}$ or $\frac{df}{dt}$ or $F'(t)$

- If F(t) has constant magnitude, then $F.\frac{df}{dt} = 0$

For $\quad F(t).\,F(t) = [F(t)]^2 = \text{constant}$

$$F.\frac{dF}{dt} = 0, \text{ i.e. } \frac{dF}{dt} \text{ is perpendicular to } F$$

- If F(t) has constant or fixed direction, then

$$F \times \frac{dF}{dt} = 0$$

VECTOR CALCULUS

Consider a vector operator ∇ (del) defined by

$$\nabla = i\frac{\partial}{\partial x} + j\frac{\partial}{\partial y} + k\frac{\partial}{\partial z}$$

Gradient

Del (∇) applied to vector function ∇f is defined as the gradient of the scalar point function f and written as grad f. Thus gradient f defined as

$$\text{Grad } f = \nabla f = i\frac{\partial f}{\partial x} + j\frac{\partial f}{\partial y} + k\frac{\partial f}{\partial z}$$

Grad f is a vector normal to surface f = constant, and has a magnitude equal to the rate of change of f along this normal.

DIRECTIONAL DERIVATIVE

If δr denotes the length PP′ and N′ is a unit vector in the direction PP′, then limiting value of $\frac{\delta f}{\delta r}$ as $\delta r \to 0$ is called *directional derivative of f* at P along the direction PP′.

Since $\delta r = \frac{\delta N}{\cos\alpha} = \frac{\delta N}{N} . N'$

$$\therefore \quad \frac{\partial f}{\partial r} = \underset{\delta r \to 0}{\text{Lt}} \left[N.N\frac{\partial f}{\partial n} \right] = \vec{N} \frac{\partial f}{\partial n} \vec{N} = N' \nabla f$$

Thus directional derivative of f in the direction of N′ is the resolved part of ∇f in the direction of N′

Since $\nabla f N' = |\nabla f| \cos\alpha \le |\nabla f|$.

therefore ∇f gives the maximum rate of change of f.

Vector Identities

1. grad (U + V) = grad U + grad V,
   i.e. $\nabla(U + V) = \nabla U + \nabla V$
2. $\text{div}\left(\vec{A} + \vec{B}\right) = \text{div } A + \text{div } B$,
   i.e. $\nabla . A + \nabla . B$
3. $\text{Curl}\left(\vec{A} + \vec{B}\right) = \text{Curl } A + \text{Curl } B$,
   i.e. $\nabla \times (A + B) = \nabla \times A + \nabla \times B$
4. $\nabla . \left(U\vec{A}\right) = (\nabla U) . A + U(\nabla . A)$
5. $\nabla \times \left(U\vec{A}\right) = (\nabla U) \times A + U(\nabla \times A)$
6. $\nabla . \left(\vec{A} \times \vec{B}\right) = B(\nabla \times A) - A . (\nabla \times B)$
7. $\nabla \times \left(\vec{A} \times \vec{B}\right) = (B.\nabla)A - B(\nabla.A) - (A.\nabla)B + A(\nabla.B)$
8. $\nabla(A.B) = (B.\nabla)A + (A.\nabla)B + B \times (\nabla \times A) + A \times (\nabla \times B)$
9. $\nabla . (\nabla U) = \nabla^2 U$
10. $\nabla \times (\nabla U) = 0$, i.e. curl of grad of U = 0
11. $\nabla(\nabla \times A) = 0$, i.e. div of the curl A = 0
12. $\nabla \times (\nabla \times A) = \nabla(\nabla . A) - \nabla^2 A$

Note : (*i*) $\nabla\left(\frac{f}{g}\right) = \frac{g\nabla f - f\nabla g}{g^2}$; $\nabla(f.g) = f\nabla g - g\nabla f$

(*ii*) $\text{div}\left(\vec{r} \times \vec{a}\right) = 0$, if $\vec{a}$ is a constant vector

(*iii*) $\text{curl}\left(\vec{r} \times \vec{a}\right) = -2\vec{a}$, if $\vec{a}$ is a constant vector

(*iv*) If div $f = 0$, then f is called **solenoidal.**

Example. Find the unit vector normal to the surface $xy^3z^2 = 4$ at the point (–1, –1, 2).

Solution

A vector normal to the surface is given by

$$\nabla(xy^3z^2) = i\frac{\partial}{\partial x}(xy^3z^2) + j\frac{\partial}{\partial y}(xy^3z^2) + \hat{k}\frac{\partial}{\partial z}(xy^3z^2)$$

$$= i(y^3z^2) + j(3xy^2z^2) + \hat{k}(2xy^3z)$$

$$= -4i - 12j + 4\hat{k} \text{ at } (-1, -1, 2)$$

Hence desired unit normal to the surface

$$= \frac{-4i - 12j + 4k}{\sqrt{(-4)^2 + (-12)^3 + 4^2}} = -\frac{1}{\sqrt{11}}(i + 3j - k)$$

Example. Find the directional derivative of $f(x, y, z) = xy^2 + yz^3$ at the point (2, –1, 1) in the direction of vector $i + 2j + 2k$.

Solution $\nabla f = y^2 i + (2xy + z^3)j + (3yz^2)\hat{k}$
$= i - 3j - 3k$ at (2, –1, 1)

Hence, directional derivative of f in the direction $i + 2j + 2k$

$$= (i - 3j - 3k) . \frac{(i + 2j + 2k)}{\sqrt{1^2 + 2^2 + 2^2}} = \frac{(1 - 6 - 6)}{3} = \frac{11}{3}$$

Example. Prove that curl $r = 0$

Solution

$$\text{Curl } \vec{r} = \nabla \times \vec{r}$$

$$= \left(i\frac{\partial}{\partial x} + j\frac{\partial}{\partial y} + k\frac{\partial}{\partial z}\right) \times \left(xi + yj + z\hat{k}\right)$$

$$= i \times i + j \times j + k \times k = 0 + 0 + 0 = 0$$

DIVERGENCE

The divergence of a continuously differentiable vector point function F is denoted by divergence F and is define by the equation

$$\text{div } F = \nabla F = i.\frac{\partial F}{\partial x} + j\frac{\partial F}{\partial y} + k.\frac{\partial F}{\partial z}$$

If $F = fi + \phi j + \psi k$, then

$$\text{div } F = \nabla.F = \left(i.\frac{\partial}{\partial x} + j\frac{\partial}{\partial y} + k.\frac{\partial}{\partial z}\right)(fi + \phi j + \psi k)$$

$$\text{div } F = \left(i.\frac{\partial f}{\partial x} + j\frac{\partial \phi}{\partial y} + k.\frac{\partial \psi}{\partial z}\right)$$

CURL

The curl of a continuously differentiable vector point function F is defined by the equation

$$\text{Curl } F = \nabla \times F = i \times \frac{\partial F}{\partial x} + j \times \frac{\partial F}{\partial y} + k \times \frac{\partial F}{\partial x}$$

If $F = f\,i + \phi\,j + \psi\,k$, then $F = \nabla \times F$

$$= \left(i.\frac{\partial}{\partial x} + j\frac{\partial}{\partial y} + k.\frac{\partial}{\partial z}\right) \times (fi + \phi j + \psi k)$$

$$= \begin{vmatrix} i & j & k \\ \frac{\partial}{\partial x} & \frac{\partial}{\partial y} & \frac{\partial}{\partial z} \\ f & \phi & \psi \end{vmatrix}$$

$$= i\left(\frac{\partial \psi}{\partial y} - \frac{\partial \phi}{\partial z}\right) + j\left(\frac{\partial \psi}{\partial y} - \frac{\partial f}{\partial z}\right) + k\left(\frac{\partial \phi}{\partial x} - \frac{\partial f}{\partial y}\right)$$

Del (∇) Applied Twice to Point Function

- Div grad $f = \nabla.\nabla f = \nabla^2 f = \frac{\partial^2 f}{\partial x^2} + \frac{\partial^2 f}{\partial y^2} + \frac{\partial^2 f}{\partial z^2}$
- Curl grad $f = \nabla \times \nabla f = 0$
- Div curl $F = \nabla.\nabla \times F = 0$
- Curl Curl F = grad div $F - \nabla^2 f$

  i.e. $\nabla \times (\nabla \times F) = \nabla(\nabla.f) - \nabla^2 f$
- Grad div F = curl Curl $F + \nabla^2 F$

  i.e. $\nabla(\nabla.F) = \nabla \times (\nabla \times F) + \nabla^2 F$

Del(∇) Applied to Product of Point Functions

- $\nabla(fg) = f\nabla g + g\nabla f$
- $\nabla.(fG) = \nabla f.G + f\nabla.G$
- $\nabla \times (fG) = \nabla f \times G + f\nabla \times G$
- $\nabla(F.G) = (F.\nabla)G + (G.\nabla)F + F \times (\nabla \times G) + G \times (\nabla \times F)$
- $\nabla.(F \times G) = G.(\nabla \times F) - F.(\nabla \times F)$
- $\nabla \times (F \times G) = F(\nabla.G) - G(\nabla.F) + G.\nabla F - F.\nabla G$

EXERCISE

MCQ TYPE QUESTIONS

1. $\lim_{x\to\infty} x^n e^{-x}$ is equal to

(a) ∞ (b) 1 (c) $\lfloor n$ (d) 0

2. $\lim_{n\to 0} e^{\left(\frac{1}{n\log n}\right)}$ is

(a) 1 (b) 0
(c) ∞ (d) does not exist

3. If $|x|$ denotes the greatest integer not greater than 2, then $\lim_{x\to 2}[x]$ is

(a) 0 (b) 1
(c) 2 (d) does not exist

4. If two functions $f(x) = \begin{cases} x\sin\frac{1}{x} & , x\neq 0 \\ 0 & , x\neq 0 \end{cases}$ $g(x) = |x|$

are given, then at $x = 0$

(a) both f and g continuous
(b) f is continuous and g is discontinuous
(c) f is discontinuous and g is continuous
(d) both f and g are discontinuous

5. If $f(x) = |x|$, then $f(x)$ is

(a) discontinuous at $x = 0$
(b) continuous only at $x = 0$
(c) continuous at all values of x
(d) discontinuous at $x = 1$

6. The function $f(x) = \begin{cases} ax^2 + b & if \quad x > 2 \\ 2 & if \quad x = 2 \\ 2ax - b & if \quad x < 2 \end{cases}$

is continuous at $x = 2$, if

(a) $a = 0, b = \frac{1}{2}$ (b) $a = \frac{1}{2}, b = 0$

(c) $a = -\frac{1}{2}, b = 0$ (d) $a = 0, b = -\frac{1}{2}$

7. If $f(x) = x - [x]$, then $f(x)$ is discontinuous

(a) $\forall x \in Z$
(b) $\forall x \in Q$
(c) $\forall x \in R$
(d) at very real number except integers

8. Maxima and Minima occur

(a) simultaneously (b) once
(c) alternately (d) rarely

9. If $x + y = k, x > 0, y > 0$, then xy is the maximum when

(a) $x = ky$ (b) $kx = y$
(c) $x = y$ (d) none of these

10. The triangle of maximum area inscribed in a circle of radius r is

(a) a right angled triangle with hypotenuse measuring $2r$
(b) an equilateral triangle
(c) an isosceles triangle of height r
(d) does not exist

11. Sum of the perimeters of a circle and a square is l. If the sum of area is least, then

(a) side of the square is double the radius of the circle
(b) side of the square is half of the radius of the circle
(c) side of the square is equal to radius of the circle
(d) none of these

12. Which of the following is false?

(a) $f(a)$ is an extreme value of $f(x)$ if $f'(a) = 0$
(b) If $f(a)$ is an extreme value of $f(x)$, then $f'(a) = 0$
(c) If $f'(a) = 0$, then f(a) is an extreme value of $f(x)$
(d) None of these

13. Let $f(x) = |x|$, then

(a) $f'(0) = 0$
(b) $f(x)$ is maximum at $x = 0$
(c) $f(x)$ is minimum at $x = 0$
(d) none of these

14. The greatest and the least value of $f(x) = x^4 - 8x^3 + 22x^2 - 24x + 1$ in [0, 2] are

(a) 0, 8 (b) 0, – 8 (c) 1, 8 (d) 1, – 8

15. The function $f(x) = x^5 - 5x^4 + 5x^3 - 1$ has

(a) one minima and two maxima
(b) two minima and one maxima
(c) two minima and two maxima
(d) one minima and one maxima

16. The maximum value of $\frac{\log x}{x}$ in $(0, \infty)$ is

(a) e (b) $\frac{1}{e}$
(c) 1 (d) none of these

17. Maximum volume of a cylinder in a cone with semi vertical angle 'α' and height 'b' is

(a) $\frac{4}{27}\pi b^3 \tan^2\alpha$ (b) $\frac{4}{27}\pi b^2 \tan\alpha$

(c) $\frac{4}{27}\pi b \tan^3\alpha$ (d) none of these

18. The maximum point on the curve $x = e^x y$ is

(a) $(1, e)$ (b) $(1, e^{-1})$

(c) $(e, 1)$ (d) $(e^{-1}, 1)$

19. The value of function $f(x) = x + \frac{1}{x}$ at the points of minimum and maximum are respectively

(a) -2 and 2 (b) 2 and -2

(c) -1 and 1 (d) 1 and -1

20. The series $1 - \frac{1}{2} + 1 - \frac{3}{4} + 1 - \frac{7}{8} + \ldots$ is

(a) convergent

(b) conditionally convergent

(c) absolutely convergent

(d) oscillatory

21. The series $1 + 2x + 3x^2 + 4x^3 + \ldots$ where $0 < x < 1$, is

(a) convergent

(b) divergent

(c) oscillatory

(d) semi-convergent

22. For geometric series $1 - k + k^2 - k^3 + \ldots$ which of the following is false?

(a) The series is convergent if $k = -\frac{1}{3}$

(b) The series is divergent if $k = -3$

(c) The series is oscillatory if $k = -1$

(d) The series is divergent if $k = -2$

23. The series $\frac{1}{1.2.3} + \frac{3}{2.3.4} + \frac{5}{3.4.5} + \ldots$ is

(a) convergent (b) divergent

(c) oscillatory (d) none of these

24. The series $\frac{2}{1^P} + \frac{3}{2^P} + \frac{4}{3^P} + \ldots$ is

(a) convergent if $p \geq 2$ and divergent if $p < 2$

(b) convergent if $p > 2$ and divergent if $p \leq 2$

(c) convergent if $p \leq 2$ and divergent if $p > 2$

(d) convergent if $p < 2$ and divergent if $p \geq 2$

25. The series $\sum \frac{\sqrt{n}}{\sqrt{n^2+1}} x^n$ is

(a) convergent if $x < 1$ and divergent if $x \geq 1$

(b) convergent if $x \leq 1$ and divergent if $x > 1$

(c) convergent if $x > 1$ and divergent if $x \leq 1$

(d) convergent if $x \geq 1$ and divergent if $x < 1$

26. The series $\frac{x}{1} + \frac{1}{2} \cdot \frac{x^3}{3} + \frac{1.3}{2.4} \cdot \frac{x^5}{5} + \frac{1.3.5}{2.4.6} \cdot \frac{x^7}{7} + \ldots$ is

(a) convergent if $x^2 > 1$ and divergent is $x^2 \leq 1$

(b) convergent if $x^2 \geq 1$ and divergent if $x^2 < 1$

(c) convergent if $x^2 < 1$ and divergent if $x^2 \geq 1$

(d) convergent if $x^2 \leq 1$ and divergent is $x^2 > 1$

27. Sum of the alternating harmonic series

$$1 - \frac{1}{2} + \frac{1}{3} - \frac{1}{4} + \ldots \text{ is}$$

(a) zero

(b) infinite

(c) log 2

(d) not defined as the series is not convergent

28. The series $x + \frac{2^2 x^2}{\lfloor 2} + \frac{3^3 x^3}{\lfloor 3} + \frac{4^4 x^4}{\lfloor 4} + \ldots$ is convergent if

(a) $0 < x < \frac{1}{e}$ (b) $x > \frac{1}{e}$

(c) $\frac{2}{e} < x < \frac{3}{e}$ (d) $\frac{3}{e} < x < \frac{4}{e}$

29. The alternating series $u_1 - u_2 + u_3 - u_4 + \ldots (0 < u_n < n)$ is convergent if

(a) $u_n < u_{n+1}$ and $u_n \to 0$ as $n \to \infty$

(b) $u_n < u_{n+1}$ and $u_n \to \infty$ as $n \to \infty$

(c) $u_n > u_{n+1}$ and $u_n \to 0$ as $n \to \infty$

(d) $u_n > u_{n+1}$ or $u_n \to \infty$ as $n \to \infty$.

30. The series $\frac{a}{b} + \frac{a(a+1)}{b(b+1)} + \frac{a(a+1)(a+2)}{b(b+1)(b+2)} + \ldots$ is

(a) convergent if $b - a < 1$ and divergent if $b - a \geq 1$

(b) convergent if $b \leq 1 + a$ and divergent if $b > 1 + a$

(c) convergent if $b > 1 + a$ and divergent if $b \leq 1 + a$

(d) convergent if $b \geq 1 + a$ and divergent if $b < 1 + a$

31. The series $x + x^{1+1/2} + x^{1+1/2+1/3} + x^{1+1/2+1/3+1/4} + \ldots$ is

(a) convergent if $x \geq \frac{1}{e}$

(b) divergent if $x \geq \frac{1}{e}$

(c) convergent if $x > \frac{1}{e}$

(d) divergent if $x \leq \frac{1}{e}$

32. The series $\frac{1}{n(\log n)^p}$ is divergent if

(a) $p > 1$ (b) $p \geq 1$ (c) $p < 1$ (d) $p \leq 1$

33. Let Σu_n be a series of positive terms and let $\sum \frac{1}{d^n}$ be a divergent series of positive terms such that $\lim_{n\to\infty}\left(d_n \frac{u_n}{u_{n+1}} - d_{n+1}\right) = k$, then the series is

(a) convergent if $k > 0$
(b) divergent if $k \geq 0$
(c) divergent if $k < 0$
(d) both (a) and (c)

34. The series $\sum_{n=3}^{\infty} \frac{1}{n \log n (\log \log n)^p}, p > 0$ is

(a) convergent if $p < 1$ and divergent if $p \geq 1$
(b) convergent if $p \leq 1$ and divergent if $p > 1$
(c) convergent if $p > 1$ and divergent if $p \leq 1$
(d) convergent if $p \geq 1$ and divergent if $p < 1$

35. The series $x + \frac{x(x+1)}{\lfloor 2} + \frac{x(x+1)(x+2)}{\lfloor 3} + \ldots$ is

(a) convergent if $x > 0$ (b) divergent if $x > 0$
(c) convergent if $x > 1$ (d) divergent if $-1 < x < 0$

36. Which of the following series is convergent?

(a) $\sum \sin \frac{1}{n}$
(b) $\sum \cos \frac{1}{n}$
(c) $\sum \frac{1}{n} \sin \frac{1}{n}$
(d) $\sum \sqrt{n^2+1} - \sqrt{n^2}$

37. The series $\sum \frac{\lfloor n . 2^n}{n^n}$ is

(a) convergent
(b) divergent
(c) conditionally convergent
(d) none of these

38. The series $\sum \frac{4.7\ldots(3n+1)}{1.2\ldots n} x^n$ is convergent, if

(a) $|x| < 1$ (b) $|x| < \frac{1}{3}$
(c) $|x| < \frac{1}{4}$ (d) $|x| < \frac{1}{2}$

39. The series $\frac{2}{1^2} - \frac{3}{2^2} + \frac{4}{3^2} - \frac{5}{4^2} + \ldots$ is

(a) conditionally convergent
(b) absolutely convergent
(c) divergent
(d) none of these

40. The sequence $\left(\frac{n}{e^n}\right)_{n=1}^{\infty}$ is

(a) divergent
(b) convergent
(c) monotonic increasing
(d) oscillating

41. Which of the following series is divergent?

(a) $1 + \frac{2.1}{3.4} + \frac{2.4.1}{3.5.6} + \frac{2.4.6.1}{3.5.7.8} + \ldots$
(b) $\sum \frac{n^3 + a}{2^n + a}$
(c) $\sum \frac{n^2}{\lfloor n}$
(d) $\sum \frac{\sqrt{n}}{n + \sqrt{n}}$

42. The series $\sum_{n=1}^{\infty} \sin \frac{\pi}{n^p}$ is

(a) convergent for all value of p
(b) convergent for $p \leq 1$ and divergent for $p > 1$
(c) convergent for $p > 1$ and divergent for $p \leq 1$
(d) divergent for all values of p

43. The series $\sum \cos\left(\frac{1}{n}\right)$ is

(a) convergent (b) divergent
(c) oscillatory (d) none of these

44. The series $x \log x + x^2 \log 2x + \ldots + x^n \log nx + ..$ is convergent if

(a) $x < 1$
(b) $x \leq 1$
(c) $x \geq 1$
(d) none of these

45. If p and q are positive real numbers, then the series $\frac{2^p}{1^q} + \frac{3^p}{2^q} + \frac{4^p}{3^q} + \ldots$ *ad inf*, is converges for

(a) $p < q - 1$ (b) $p < q + 1$
(c) $p \geq q - 1$ (d) $p \geq q + 1$

NUMERICAL TYPE QUESTIONS

1. $\lim_{x\to 0}\frac{e^x-1}{x}$ is equal to ______

2. If $\lim_{x\to 1}\frac{f(x)-2}{f(x)+2}=0$, then $\lim_{x\to 1}f(x)$ is equal to______

3. $\lim_{x\to 0}\frac{1-\cos x}{2}$ is equal to______

4. $\lim_{x\to 1}\frac{\sqrt{1+x}-\sqrt{1-x}}{x}$ is given by______

5. $\lim_{x\to\infty}x\sin\frac{1}{x}$ is______

6. $\lim_{x\to\infty}\left[\frac{1}{n^2}+\frac{2}{n^2}+\frac{3}{n^2}+\ldots+\frac{1}{n}\right]$ is______

7. The minimum value of $|x^2-5x+2|$ is ______

8. The maximum value of $\frac{1}{\sqrt{2}}(\sin x-\cos x)$ is______

9. Maximum slope of the curve $-x^3+6x^2+2x+1$ is ______

10. A rectangular box with square base in open at the top. The maximum volume of the box made from 300 m³ wood is ______

11. A series $\sum_1^\infty u_n$ of positive terms is convergent, if $\lim_{n\to\infty}\frac{u_n}{u_{n+1}}=l$ and l is greater than ______

ANSWERS

MCQ Type Questions

1. (d)	2. (b)	3. (d)	4. (a)	5. (c)	6. (b)	7. (d)	8. (c)	9. (d)	10. (b)
11. (a)	12. (d)	13. (c)	14. (d)	15. (d)	16. (b)	17. (a)	18. (b)	19. (d)	20. (a)
21. (a)	22. (c)	23. (a)	24. (b)	25. (a)	26. (c)	27. (c)	28. (a)	29. (a)	30. (c)
31. (b)	32. (d)	33. (d)	34. (c)	35. (b)	36. (c)	37. (a)	38. (b)	39. (a)	40. (b)
41. (d)	42. (c)	43. (b)	44. (a)	45. (a)					

Numerical Type Questions

1. 1	2. 2	3. 0	4. 1	5. 0	6. $\frac{1}{2}$	7. 0	8. 1
9. 14	10. 500	11. 1					

EXPLANATIONS

MCQ TYPE QUESTIONS

1. $\lim_{x\to\infty} x^n e^{-x} = \lim_{x\to\infty} \frac{x^n}{e^x}$ $\left[\text{form}\frac{\infty}{\infty}\right]$

By L'Hospital Rule Differentiating denominator and numerator n times, we get

$$\lim_{x\to\infty}\frac{x^n}{e^x} = \lim_{x\to\infty}\frac{\lfloor n}{e^x} = 0$$

2. Let $A = \lim_{n\to 0} e^{\frac{1}{n\log n}}$

$\therefore \log_e A = \lim_{n\to 0}\frac{1}{n\log n}$

$\Rightarrow \log_e A = \lim_{n\to 0}\frac{1/n}{\log n}$ $\left[\text{form}\frac{\infty}{\infty}\right]$

$$= \lim_{n\to 0}\frac{-1/n^2}{1/n} = \lim_{n\to 0} -\frac{1}{n}$$

$\log_e A = -\infty$

$A = e^{-\infty} = 0$

4. L. $\lim_{x\to 0} f(x) = \lim_{h\to 0} f(0-h) = \lim_{h\to 0} -h\sin\left(-\frac{1}{h}\right)$

$= \lim_{h\to 0} +h\sin\frac{1}{h} = 0$

R. $\lim_{x\to 0} f(x) = \lim_{h\to 0} f(0+h)$

$= \lim_{h\to 0} -h\sin\left(\frac{1}{h}\right) = 0$

Also $f(0) = 0$

Since L. $\lim_{x\to 0} f(x) =$ R. $\lim_{x\to 0} f(x) = f(0) = 0$

Hence $f(x)$ is continuous at $x = 0$

Now, L. $\lim_{x\to 0} g(x) = \lim_{h\to 0} g(0-h)$

$= \lim_{h\to 0}|-h| = \lim_{h\to 0} h = 0$

R. $\lim_{x\to 0} g(x) = \lim_{h\to 0} g(0+h)$

$= \lim_{h\to 0}|h| = \lim_{h\to 0} h = 0$

$g(0) = |0| = 0$

$\therefore$ L. $\lim_{x\to 0} g(x) =$ R. $\lim_{x\to 0} g(x) = g(0) = 0$

Hence $g(x)$ is also continuous at $x = 0$

5. Let $a \in$ R (real numbers)

L. $\lim_{x\to a} f(x) = \lim_{h\to 0}|a-h| = \lim_{h\to 0}(a-h) = a$

R. $\lim_{x\to a} f(x) = \lim_{h\to 0}|a+h| = \lim_{h\to 0} a+h = a$

and $f(a) = |a| = a$

$\therefore \lim_{x\to a}|x| = a = f(a)$

Hence $\lim_{x\to a}|x|$ continuous for all values of x.

6. L. $\lim_{x\to 2} f(x) = \lim_{h\to 0} 2a(2-h) - b = 4a - b$

R. $\lim_{x\to 2} f(x) = \lim_{h\to 0} a(2+h)^2 + b = 4a + b$

The function will be continuous if

L. $\lim_{x\to 2} f(x) =$ R. $\lim_{x\to 2} f(x) = f(2)$

$\therefore$ $4a - b = 2$

$4a + b = 2$

Solving we get, $a = \frac{1}{2}$, $b = 0$

7. Given function is, $f(x) = x - [x]$

Let a is a real number except integer and h be a very small real number, then

$[a-h] = b$ (an integer less than to a)

$[a+h] = b$ (an integer greater than to a)

Also $[a] = b$

$\therefore$ L. $\lim_{x\to 0} f(x) = \lim_{h\to 0}(a-h) - [a-h]$

$= \lim_{h\to 0}(a-h) - b = a - b$

Also $f(a) = (a) - [a] = a - b$

$\therefore$ L. $\lim_{x\to a} f(x) =$ R. $\lim_{x\to a} f(x) = f(a) = a - b$

$\therefore$ $f(x) = x - [x]$

is continuous all real except integers.

10. Let ABC be a triangle inscribed in the circle with centre O and radius r.

If area of this triangle is maximum, then vertex C should be at a maximum distance from the base AB i.e., CD must be perpendicular to AB. Hence ABC is an isosceles triangle.

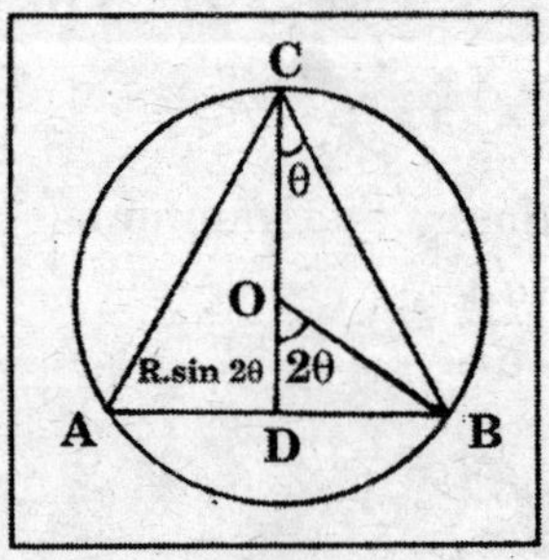

If $\angle BCD = \theta$,

where D is the mid-point of AB, then

$\angle BOD = 2\theta$

$\therefore$ $AB = 2BD = 2r \sin 2\theta$

$CD = CO + OD = r + r \cos 2\theta$

If S be the area of the triangle ABC, then

$$S = \frac{1}{2} AB \times CD = \frac{1}{2} \times 2r \sin 2\theta \,(r + r\cos 2\theta)$$

$$\therefore \quad \frac{ds}{d\theta} = r^2[\sin 2\theta\,(-2\sin 2\theta] + (1 + \cos 2\theta)(2\cos 2\theta)]$$

For maximum and minimum,

$$\frac{dS}{d\theta} = 0$$

$\therefore$ $\cos 4\theta + \cos 2\theta = 0$

$\Rightarrow$ $2\cos 3\theta \cos\theta = 0$

Hence either $\cos 3\theta = 0$, or $\cos\theta = 0$

If $\cos\theta = 0$, then $\theta = \frac{\pi}{2}$

If $\cos 3\theta = 0$, then $3\theta = \frac{\pi}{2}$

$\Rightarrow$ $\theta = \frac{\pi}{6}$

$\left(\frac{d^2S}{d\theta^2}\right)_{\theta=\pi/6}$ is negative.

Hence S is maximum for $\theta = \frac{1}{6}\pi$

$$\angle ACB = 2\theta = 2\left(\frac{\pi}{6}\right) = \frac{\pi}{3}$$

$$= \angle ABC = \angle BAC$$

Hence ΔABC is an equalateral triangle.

11. Let radius of circle is r and side of a sqaure is x.

$\therefore$ Perimeter $= 2\pi r + 4x = l$ ...(*i*)

Let area be A

$\therefore$ $A = \pi r^2 + x^2$

$$= \pi r^2 + \left(\frac{l - 2\pi r}{4}\right)^2 \quad \text{[from equation (i)]}$$

$$\frac{dA}{dr} = 2\pi r + \frac{2}{16}(1 - 2\pi r).(-2\pi)$$

and $\frac{d^2A}{dr^2} = 2\pi + \frac{\pi^2}{2}$

For maximum and minimum,

$$\frac{dA}{dr} = 0$$

$\Rightarrow$ $2\pi r - \frac{\pi}{4}(l - 2\pi r) = 0$

$\Rightarrow$ $l = 8r + 2\pi r$ ...(*ii*)

$\frac{d^2A}{dr^2} > 0$, hence area is least

From equations (*i*) and (*ii*),

$$2\pi r + 4x = 8r + 2\pi r$$

$\Rightarrow$ $4x = 8r$ $\Rightarrow$ $x = 2r$

Hence side of a square is double the radius of circle.

12. Since statements (*a*), (*b*), (*c*) are all correct, hence the statement (*d*) is false.

14. $f(x) = x^4 - 8x^3 + 22x^2 - 24x + 1$

$f(0) = 1$

$f(2) = 2^4 - 8.2^3 + 22.2^2 - 24.2 + 1 = -7$

Now $f'(x) = 4x^3 - 24x^2 + 44x - 24$

For maximum and minimum,

$f'(x) = 0$

$\Rightarrow$ $4x^3 - 24x^2 + 44x - 24 = 0$

$\Rightarrow$ $4(x-1)(x-2)(x-3) = 0$

$\therefore$ $x = 1, 2, 3$

Since $x = 3$ does not lie in [0, 2]

Hence, consider only $x = 1$ and $x = 2$.

We have

$f(1) = 1^4 - 8.1^3 + 22.1^2 - 24.1 + 1 = -8$

Greatest of $f(x)$ = largest of $\{1, -7, -8\} = 1$

Least of $f(x)$ = smallest of $\{1, -7, -8\} = -8$

15. $f(x) = x^5 - 5x^4 + 5x^3 - 1$

$f'(x) = 5x^4 - 20x^3 + 15x^2$

$f''(x) = 20x^3 - 60x^2 + 30x$

$f'''(x) = 60x^2 - 120x + 30$

For maximum and minimum

$f'(x) = 0$

$\therefore$ $x^4 - 4x^3 + 3x^2 = 0$

$\Rightarrow$ $x^2(x-1)(x-3) = 0$

$\therefore$ $x = 0, 1, 3$

$f''(0) = 0$

$f'''(0) = 30 \neq 0$

$\therefore f(x)$ is neither maximum nor minimum at $x = 0$

$f''(1) = 20 - 60 + 30 = -10 < 0$

$\therefore f(x)$ is maximum at $x = 1$

$f''(3) = 540 - 540 + 90 = 90 > 0$

$\therefore f(x)$ is maximum at $x = 3$

Hence there is one maximum and one minimum for $f(x)$.

16. Given function is

$$f(x) = \frac{\log x}{x}$$

$$\therefore \quad f'(x) = \frac{x.\frac{1}{x} - \log x.1}{x^2} = \frac{1 - \log x}{x^2}$$

and $$f''(x) = \frac{x^2.\left(-\frac{1}{x}\right) - (1 - \log x).2x}{x^4}$$

$$= \frac{2\log x - 3}{x^3}$$

For maximum and minimum of $f(x)$,

$f'(x) = 0 \Rightarrow 1 - \log x = 0 \quad \Rightarrow \quad x = e$

$\therefore \quad f''(e) = \frac{2-3}{e^3} = -\frac{1}{e^3} < 0$

Hence $f(x)$ is maximum at $x = e$

$\therefore$ Maximum value, $f(e) = \frac{\log e}{e} = \frac{1}{e}$

NUMERICAL TYPE QUESTIONS

1. $\lim_{x\to 0}\frac{e^x - 1}{x} = \lim_{x\to 0}\frac{\left(1+x+\frac{x^2}{\lfloor 2}+\frac{x^3}{\lfloor 3}+\ldots\right)-1}{x}$

$= \lim_{x\to 0}\left(1+\frac{x}{\lfloor 2}+\frac{x^2}{\lfloor 3}+\ldots\right) = 1$

By L' Hospital's Rule

$\lim_{x\to 0}\frac{e^x-1}{x}\left[\text{form}\frac{0}{0}\right] = \lim_{x\to 0}\frac{e^x}{1} = 1$

4. $\lim_{x\to 0}\frac{\sqrt{1+x}-\sqrt{1-x}}{x}$

$= \lim_{x\to 0}\frac{\sqrt{1+x}-\sqrt{1-x}}{x}\times\left(\frac{\sqrt{1+x}+\sqrt{1-x}}{\sqrt{1+x}+\sqrt{1-x}}\right)$

$= \lim_{x\to 0}\frac{1+x-1+x}{x(\sqrt{1+x}+\sqrt{1+x})}$

$= \lim_{x\to 0}\frac{2x}{x(\sqrt{1+x}+\sqrt{1-x})}$

$= \frac{2}{\sqrt{1+0}+\sqrt{1-0}} = \frac{2}{1+1} = 1$

5. $\lim_{x\to\infty} x\sin\frac{1}{x}$ = Let $\frac{1}{x} = n$

So, $\quad x \to \infty,\ n \to 0$

$\lim_{n\to 0}\frac{\sin n}{n} = 1$

6. $\lim_{n\to\infty}\left[\frac{1}{n^2}+\frac{2}{n^2}+\frac{3}{n^2}+\ldots+\frac{1}{n}\right]$

$= \lim_{n\to\infty}\left[\frac{1+2+3+\ldots+n}{n^2}\right] = \lim_{n\to\infty}\frac{n(n+1)/2}{n^2}$

$= \lim_{n\to\infty}\frac{1}{2}\left(1+\frac{1}{n}\right) = \frac{1}{2}(1+0) = \frac{1}{2}$

7. Value of a mod function cannot be less than zero, therefore

$f(x) = |x^2 - 5x + 2|$ is zero.

8. Let $\quad f(x) = \frac{1}{\sqrt{2}}(\sin x - \cos x)$

$= \sin x \cos\frac{\pi}{4} - \cos x \sin\frac{\pi}{4} = \sin\left(x - \frac{\pi}{4}\right)$

Since maximum value of $\sin\theta$ is 1, hence maximum value of $f(x) = 1$

9. Let $\quad f(x) = -x^3 + 6x^2 + 2x + 1$

Slope of the function is,

$f'(x) = -3x^2 + 12x + 2 = F(x)$ (say)

Now to find minimum or maximum of $F(x)$.

$\therefore \quad F'(x) = -6x + 12$

and $\quad F''(x) = -6$

For maxima and minima

$F'(x) = 0$

$\Rightarrow \quad x = 2$

$\therefore \quad F''(2) = -6 < 0$

Hence $F(x)$ (slope) is maximum at $x = 2$

$\therefore$ Maximum slope $= F(2) = -3(2)^2 + 12(2) + 2 = 14$

10. Volume is maximum at $x = 10$

At $x = 10$, $\quad y = \frac{300-100}{40} = 5$

$\therefore \quad$ Maximum volume $= x^2y = (10)^2 \times 5 = 500$

■■

3 CHAPTER Differential Equations

An equation which contains independent variable, dependent variables and their derivatives with respect to independent variables, is called *differential equation.*

I. ORDINARY DIFFERENTIAL EQUATION

A differential equation which involves only one independent variables is called *ordinary differential equation.*

e.g. $$\frac{dy}{dx} + xy = 0$$

and $$x\left(\frac{dy}{dx}\right)^2 - y\frac{dy}{dx} + 1 = 0$$

Order of Differential equation

It is the order of the highest derivative involving in the equation.

Degree of Differential equation

It is the degree of the highest order derivative involving in the equation, when the equation is free from radicals and fractional powers.

e.g. $$\frac{dy}{dx} + xy = 0$$

is equation of first order and first degree.

$$\frac{d^2y}{dx^2} + x\frac{dy}{dx} = 2$$

is equation of second order and first degree.

$$\frac{d^2y}{dx^2} = \left[1+\left(\frac{dy}{dx}\right)\right]^{1/3}$$

is equation of second order and third degree.

Solution of a Differential equation

It is any relation between variables involved which satisfies the differential equation.

General or Complete Solution of a Differential equation

Solution of a differential equation in which number of arbitrary constant is equal to order of the differential equation is called *general solution.*

Variable Separables

$$f_1(x)\,dx = f_2(y)\,dy$$

It's solution is

$$\int f_1(x) = \int f_2(y)\,dy + c$$

Homogeneous equation

$$\frac{dy}{dx} = \frac{\phi_1(x,y)}{\phi_2(x,y)}$$

where, ϕ_1, ϕ_2 are of same degree

$$\frac{dy}{dx} = f\left(\frac{y}{x}\right)$$

Put $\frac{y}{x} = v$; $\frac{dy}{dx} = v + x\frac{dv}{dx}$

$$\therefore \quad \frac{dv}{f(v)-v} = \frac{dx}{x}, \Rightarrow \int\frac{dv}{f(v)-v} = \log x + c$$

Equation Reducible to Homogeneous Equation

$$\frac{dy}{dx} = \frac{ax+by+c}{a'x+b'y+c'}$$

$$a : b \neq a' : b'$$

Putting $x = x + h$, $y = y + k$

$$\frac{dy}{dx} = \frac{ax+by+ah+bk+c}{a'x+b'y+a'h+b'k+c'}$$

Choosing h, k such that

$$ah + bk + c = a'h + b'k + c'$$

$$\frac{dy}{dx} = \frac{ax+by}{a'x+b'y} = \frac{y}{x} = v$$

Special Case

When $a : b = a' : b'$

then $ax + by = v$

Linear Differential Equation

$$\frac{dy}{dx} + py = \mathrm{Q}$$

where P and Q are functions of x only.

Integrating factor I.F. $= e^{\int pdx}$

$$y.\,e^{\int pdx} = \int \mathrm{Q}.\,e^{\int pdx}dxt + \mathrm{C}$$

Equations Reducible to Linear Form

$$\frac{dy}{dx} + Py = Qy^n$$

Extended form of linear equation are Bernoulli's equation

$$\frac{1}{y^n}\frac{dy}{dx} + \frac{P}{y^{n-1}} = Q$$

Put $y^{1-n} = t$

$$\Rightarrow \quad dt = (1-n)\, y^{-n} dy \quad \Rightarrow \quad \frac{dy}{y^n} = \frac{1}{(1-n)} dt$$

$$\therefore \quad \frac{dt}{dx} + P(1-n)t = Q(1-n)$$

$$\frac{dy}{dx} + y\frac{d\phi}{dx} = \phi(x)\frac{d\phi}{dx}$$

$$\Rightarrow \quad \frac{\frac{dy}{dx} + y\frac{d\phi}{dx} = \phi(x)\frac{d\phi}{dx}}{\left(\frac{d\phi}{dx}\right)}$$

$$\Rightarrow \quad \frac{dy}{d\phi} + y = \phi(x)$$

$$ye^x = \int \phi(x)e^x dx + C$$

Exact Differential Equation

$$Mdx + Ndy = 0$$

$$\frac{\partial M}{\partial Y} = \frac{\partial N}{\partial X}$$

(a) Integrate M with respect to x regarding Y as a constant.

(b) Integrate N with respect to Y and then retain only that term which have not been already obtained by integrating M, *i.e.* in (a) above.

(c) Add the two expression obtained in (a) and (b) above and equate the result to an arbitrary constant which gives the required solution.

Differential Equations of First Order and First Degree

Type I : Variable Separation Form

The equation of this type can be put in the form,

$$f(x)\, dx + g(y) dy = 0$$

Now, $\int f(x)\, dx + \int g(y)\, dy = C$

Example. Solve $(e^y + 1)\, dx + xe^y\, dy = 0$

Solution

Given equation can be written as

$$e^y\, dx + xe^y\, dy + dx = 0 \quad \Rightarrow \quad d\left(xe^y\right) + dx = 0$$

Integrating $\int d\left(xe^y\right) + \int dx = \int 0 \Rightarrow xe^y + x = C$

Type II : Linear Differential Equations

A linear equations is called linear if the dependent variable and its derivative occuring in it are of the first degree and are not multiplied together.

Linear differential equation is of the form

$$\frac{dy}{dx} + Py = Q,$$

where P and Q are functions of x only.

Solution of the linear differential equations is

$$y \cdot e^{\int pdx} = \int\left(Q \cdot e^{\int pdx}\right) dx + C$$

where, $e^{\int pdx}$ is called I.F

Example. Solve $(x + 2y^3)\, dy = ydx$

Solution

Given equation can be written as

$$y\frac{dx}{dy} = x + 2y^3 \quad \Rightarrow \quad \frac{dx}{dy} - \frac{1}{y}x = 2y^2$$

Here, $P = -\frac{1}{y}$ and $Q = 2y^2$

$$\therefore \quad I.F. = e^{\int -\frac{1}{y}dy} = e^{-\log y} = e^{\log(1/y)} = \frac{1}{y}$$

Solution of the equation is,

$$x(IF) = \int (Q \cdot IF \cdot dy)$$

$$\therefore \quad x\left(\frac{1}{y}\right) = \int 2y^2 \frac{1}{y} dy$$

$$\Rightarrow \quad \frac{x}{y} = y^2 + C \quad \Rightarrow \quad x = y\,(C + y^2)$$

Type III : Homogeneous Differential Equations

This equation is of the form, $\dfrac{dy}{dx} = \dfrac{f(x, y)}{\phi(x, y)}$

where $f(x, y)$ and $\phi(x, y)$ are homogeneous functions of same degree.

This can be solved by putting $y = vx$

$$\therefore \quad \frac{dy}{dx} = v + x\frac{dy}{dx}$$

Substitute the value of y and then solve by variable-separable method.

Example. Solve $x^2dy + y\,(x + y)\, dx = 0$

Solution

Here $\dfrac{dy}{dx} = -\dfrac{y(x+y)}{x^2}$

Let $y = vx,$

$\Rightarrow \quad \dfrac{dy}{dx} = v + x\dfrac{dv}{dx}$

Now $\quad v + x\dfrac{dv}{dx} = -\dfrac{x(vx) + v^2x^2}{x^2} = -(v^2 + v)$

$\Rightarrow \quad x\dfrac{dv}{dx} = -(v^2 + 2v)$

Integrating $\quad \displaystyle\int \frac{dv}{v^2 + 2v} = -\int \frac{dx}{x}$

$\Rightarrow \quad \displaystyle\int \frac{dv}{v(v+2)} = -\int \frac{dx}{x}$

$\Rightarrow \quad \displaystyle\int \frac{1}{2}\left(\frac{1}{v} - \frac{1}{v+2}\right) dv = -\int \frac{dx}{x}$

$\Rightarrow \quad \dfrac{1}{2}\ln v - \dfrac{1}{2}\ln(v+2) = -\ln x + C$

$\Rightarrow \quad \dfrac{1}{2}\log\dfrac{v}{v+2} = -\log x + C$

$\Rightarrow \quad \dfrac{1}{2}\log\dfrac{(y/x)}{(y/x)+2} = -\log x + C$

$\Rightarrow \quad \log\dfrac{y}{2x+y} = \ln\dfrac{1}{x^2} + C$

$\Rightarrow \quad \dfrac{y}{2x+y} = \dfrac{C'}{x^2}$

$\Rightarrow \quad x^2y = K'(2x + y)$

Type IV : Exact Differential Equations

A differential equation is said to be exact if it can be derived from its primitive by direct differentiation without any further transformation such as elimination, etc.

e.g. $\quad (x^2 - ay)\,dx + (y^2 - ax)\,dy = 0$

is exact in as much as it can be derived from its primitive

$x^3 - 3ayx + y^3 = C$ by direct differentiation.

Theorem : The necessary and sufficient condition for the differential equation,

$$M + N\frac{dy}{dx} = 0$$

$\Rightarrow \quad Mdx + Ndy = 0$

to be exact is that $\quad \dfrac{\partial M}{\partial y} = \dfrac{\partial N}{\partial x}$

If equation $Mdx + Ndy = 0$ is exact, then it can be integrated as follows :

(*i*) Firstly integrate M with respect to x regarding y as a constant.

(*ii*) Then integrate with respect to y those of the terms in N which do not involve x.

(*iii*) Sum of the two expressions thus obtained equated to a constant is the required solution.

i.e. $\quad \displaystyle\int Mdx + \int Ndy = C$

$\therefore$ y = constant terms contain $x = 0$

Example. Show that

$$(x^4 - 2xy^2 + y^4)\,dx - (2x^2y - 4xy^3 + \sin y)\,dy = 0$$

is exact and also solve it.

Solution

Here, $M = x^4 - 2xy^2 + y^4$

and $\quad N = -(2x^2y - 4xy^3 + \sin y)$

$\therefore \quad \dfrac{\partial M}{\partial y} = -4xy + 4y^3$

and $\dfrac{\partial N}{\partial x} = -4xy + 4y^3 \Rightarrow \dfrac{\partial M}{\partial y} = \dfrac{\partial N}{\partial x}.$

Thus the given equation is exact.

Now, $\displaystyle\int (x^4 - 2xy^2 + y^4)\,dx$

$$-\int (2x^2y - 4xy^3 + \sin y)\,dy = C$$

(since terms contains $x = 0$)

$\Rightarrow \quad \dfrac{1}{5}x^5 - x^2y^2 + xy^4 + \cos y = C$

Integrating Factors (I.F.)

Sometimes an equation which is not exact may become so on multiplication by some suitable function known as an *integrating factor.*

Consider an equation $xdy - ydx = 0$, which is not exact

It will become exact on multiplication by $\dfrac{1}{y^2}$. Then

$$\frac{x}{y^2}dy - \frac{1}{y}dx = 0$$

Hence solution is, $\quad \displaystyle -\int \frac{1}{y}dx + \int \frac{x}{y^2}dy = C$

$\Rightarrow \quad -\dfrac{x}{y} + 0 = C \quad \Rightarrow \quad \dfrac{x}{y} = C$

Rule 1 : If equation $Mdx + Ndy = 0$ is homogeneous and $Mx + Ny \neq 0$, then

$$\text{I.F.} = \frac{1}{Mx + Ny}$$

Rule 2 : If equation is of the form

$$f_1(x, y)\,ydx + f_2(x, y)\,xdy = 0$$

and $\quad Mx - Ny \neq 0$, then

$$\text{I.F.} = \frac{1}{Mx + Ny}$$

Rule 3 : If equation $Mdx + Ndy = 0$

and $\frac{1}{N}\left(\frac{\partial M}{\partial y} - \frac{\partial N}{\partial x}\right) = f(x)$, is a function of x, then

$$\text{I.F.} = e^{\int f(x)dx}$$

Rule 4 : If equation $Mdx + Ndy = 0$ and

$$\frac{1}{M}\left(\frac{\partial N}{\partial x} - \frac{\partial M}{\partial y}\right) = f(y), \text{ then}$$

$$\text{I.F.} = e^{\int f(y)dy}$$

Integrating Factors

- $d\left(\frac{y}{x}\right) = \frac{xdy - ydx}{x^2}$
- $d\left(\frac{x}{y}\right) = \frac{ydx - xdy}{y^2}$
- $d(xy) = xdy + ydx$
- $d\left(\frac{x^2}{y}\right) = \frac{2yxdx - x^2dy}{y^2}$
- $d\left(\frac{y^2}{x^2}\right) = \frac{2.y.x^2dy - 2xy^2dx}{x^4}$
- $d\left(\tan^{-1}\frac{x}{y}\right) = \frac{ydx - xdy}{x^2 + y^2}$
- $d\left(\tan^{-1}\left(\frac{y}{x}\right)\right) = \frac{xdy - ydx}{x^2 + y^2}$
- $d\left(\frac{1}{2}\log(x^2 + y^2)\right) = \frac{xdx + ydy}{x^2 + y^2}$
- $d\left(-\frac{1}{xy}\right) = \frac{xdy + ydx}{x^2y^2}$
- $d\log\left(\frac{x}{y}\right) = \frac{ydx - xdy}{xy}$
- $d\log\left(\frac{y}{x}\right) = \frac{xdy - ydx}{xy}$
- $d\left(\frac{e^x}{y}\right) = \frac{ye^xdx - e^xdy}{y^2}$

Example. Solve $(x^2 + y^2 + 2x)\,dx + 2ydy = 0$.

Solution

Here, $M = x^2 + y^2 + 2x$

$\Rightarrow$ $\frac{\partial M}{\partial y} = 2y$ and, $N = 2y$; $\frac{\partial N}{\partial x} = 0$

$\therefore$ $\frac{1}{N}\left(\frac{\partial M}{\partial y} - \frac{\partial N}{\partial x}\right) = 1$ which is function of x

Now $\quad \text{I.F.} = e^{\int 1.dx} = e^x$

Multiplying by I.F, we get

$$e^x(x^2 + y^2 + 2x)\,dx + 2ye^x\,dy = 0$$

which is exact equation.

Hence the solution is,

$$\int_{y=\text{const}} e^x\left(x^2 + y^2 + 2x\right)dx + \int_{f(x)} 2ye^x dy = C$$

$$\Rightarrow \quad e^x(x^2 + y^2) = C$$

Example. Solve $\cos^2 x\left(\frac{dy}{dx}\right) + y = \tan x$ ...(i)

Solution

Given equation can be written as

$$\frac{dy}{dx} + \sec^2 xy = \sec^2 x \tan x$$

It is linear equation in y.

Here $P = \sec^2 x$

$\therefore$ $\text{I.F.} = e^{\int pdx} = e^{\int \sec^2 xdx} = e^{\tan x}$

Multiplying equation (ii) by I.F., we get

$$\left(\frac{dy}{dx} + y\sec^2 x\right)e^{\tan x} = \tan x \sec^2 x\, e^{\tan x}$$

Integrating, we get

$$y.\,e^{\tan x} = C + \int \tan x \sec^2 x.\, e^{\tan x}\, dx$$

where C is an arbitrary constant

Putting $t = \tan x$

$$dt = \sec^2 xdt$$

$\therefore$ $y\,e^{\tan x} = C + \int t\,e^t\,dt$

Integration by parts

$y\,e^{\tan x} = C + (te^t - e^t) \quad \Rightarrow \; y\,e^{\tan x} = C + e^{\tan x}(\tan x - 1)$

Clairaut's Equation

Equation of the form $y = Px + f(P)$ is called *Clairaut's equation.*

Here $\quad P = \frac{dy}{dx}$

Solution of the equation is,

$$y = cx + f(c)$$

Example. Solve $P = \tan(Px - y)$

Solution

$Px - y = \tan^{-1} P \quad \Rightarrow \quad y = Px - \tan^{-1} P$

Hence general solution of the equation is

$$y = cx - \tan^{-1} C$$

Singular Solution

Let $f(x, y, p) = 0$ be a given differential equation and its general solution is $\phi(x, y, c) = 0$.

Envelope of the family of curves $\phi(x, y, c) = 0$ is contained in the locus obtained by eliminating c between $\phi(x, y, c) = 0$ and $\frac{\partial}{\partial c}\phi(x, y, c) = 0$.

Example. Find singular solution of the differential equation,

$$P^3 + Px - y = 0$$

Solution

Given equation is, $y = Px + P^3$

Hence, general solution is,

$$y = cx + c^3$$

Let $\phi(x, y, c) = cx + c^3 - y = 0$ ...(i)

$\therefore$ $\frac{\partial}{\partial c}\phi(x, y, c) = x + 3c^2 = 0$ ...(ii)

Eliminating c between equations (i) and (ii), we get

$$y^2 = c^2(x + c^2)^2$$

$$\Rightarrow \quad y^2 = -\frac{x}{3}\left(x - \frac{x}{3}\right)^2 \quad \Rightarrow \quad 27y^2 + 4x^3 = 0$$

Linear Differential Equation with of nth Order (Higher Order)

Linear equations are the equations in which the dependent variable and its derivatives appear only in the first degree and are not multiplied together.

$$\frac{d^n y}{dx^n} + P_1\frac{d^{n-1}}{dx^{n-1}} + P_2\frac{d^{n-2}}{dx^{n-2}} + ... + P_n y = X$$

where $P_1, P_2, ... P_n$ are functions of x only.

The operator $\frac{d}{dx}$ is denoted by D.

$\therefore$ $D^n y + P_1 D^{n-1}y + ... + P_n y = X$

$\Rightarrow$ $f(D)y = X$

where, $f(D) = D^n + P_1 D^{n-1} + ... + P_n = 0$

Case I : *When A.E. has Distinct and real roots, i.e.*

$$m_1 \neq m_2 \neq m_3 ....$$

$$y = c_1 e^{m_1 x} + c_2 e^{m_2 x} + c_3 e^{m_3 x} + ...$$

Case II : *When A.E. has real and some equal roots.*

If $m_1 = m_2 \neq m_3 \neq m_4$ .....

then $y = (c_1 + c_2 x)\, e^{m1x} + c_3 e^{m3x} + ...,$

If $m_1 = m_2 = m_3 \neq m_4 \neq m_5$ .....

then $y = (c_1 + c_2 x + c_3 x^2)\, e^{m1x} + c_4 e^{m4x} + ...$

Case III : *When A. E. has complex roots,*

i.e. $m_1, m_2 = \alpha \pm i\beta,\ m_3, m_4$ ......

$y = (A\cos\beta x + B\sin\beta x)\, e^{\alpha x} + C_3 e^{m3x} + C_4 e^{m4x} + ...$

If complex roots are equal, then

$$y = [(A_1 + A_2 x)\cos\beta x + (B_1 + B_2 x)\sin\beta x]\, e^{\alpha x} + c_5 e^{m5x} + ...$$

Example. Solve $\frac{d^2y}{dx^2} - 5\frac{dy}{dx} + 6y = 0$

Solution

A.E. is, $D^2 - 5D + 6 = 0$

$\therefore$ $D = 3, 2$

Hence solution is, $y = c_1 e^{3x} + c_2 e^{2x}$

PARTICULAR INTEGRAL

When the equation is, $f(D)\, y = X$

then general solution is, $y = (C.F.) + (P.I.)$

A particular integral is given by $\frac{1}{f(D)}X$

I. When $X = e^{ax}$, then

$$P.I. = \frac{1}{f(D)}e^{ax} = \frac{1}{f(a)}e^{ax}, \text{ if } f(a) \neq 0$$

II. When $f(a) = 0$, then

$$P.I. = \frac{1}{f(D)}e^{ax}$$

$$= \frac{x}{f'(a)}e^{ax}, \text{ if } f'(a) \neq 0$$

III. If $f'(a) = 0$, then

$$P.I. = \frac{1}{f(D)}e^{ax} = \frac{x^2}{f''(a)}e^{ax} \text{ if } f''(a) \neq 0$$

Example. Find P.I. when $(D^2 + 4)\, y = \sin 2x + \cos 3x$

Solution

$$P.I. = \frac{1}{D^2+4}\sin 2x + \frac{1}{D^2+4}\cos 3x$$

$$= \frac{x}{2D}\sin 2x + \frac{1}{-3^2+4}\cos 3x = \frac{x}{2D^2}D\sin 2x - \frac{1}{5}\cos 3x$$

$$= \frac{2x}{-8}\cos 2x - \frac{1}{5}\cos 3x = -\frac{x}{4}\cos 2x - \frac{1}{5}\cos 3x$$

Example. Find general solution of the equation

$$(D^2 + D - 2)\, y = e^x$$

Solution

A.E. is, $D^2 + D - 2 = 0$

$\Rightarrow$ $D = -1, 2$

$C.F. = C_1 e^{-x} + C_2 e^{2x}$

Now $P.I. = \frac{1}{D^2 + D - 2}e^x = x\frac{1}{2D+1}e^x$

Hence general solution is,

$$y = c_1 e^{-x} + c_2 e^{2x} + \frac{x}{3} e^x$$

IV. $\text{P.I.} = \frac{1}{F(D^2)}.\sin ax$

$$= \frac{1}{F(-a^2)} \sin ax, \quad \text{if } F(-a^2) \neq 0$$

V. $\text{P.I.} = \frac{1}{F(D^2)} \cos ax$

$$= \frac{1}{F(-a^2)} \cos ax \quad \text{if } F(-a^2) \neq 0$$

VI. $\text{P.I.} = \frac{1}{F(D)} x^m$

Expansion is to be carried upto the term D^m, since $D^{m+1} x^m = 0, D^{m+2} x^m = 0,$

VII. When $X = e^{ax} v(x)$, then

$$\text{P.I.} = \frac{1}{f(D)} e^{ax} v(x) = e^{ax} \frac{1}{f(D+a)} v(x)$$

Example. Solve $(D^2 - 4D + 1) y = e^{2x} \sin 2x$

Solution

A.E. is $m^2 - 4m + 1 = 0$

$\therefore \quad m = 2 \pm \sqrt{3}$

$$\therefore \quad \text{C.F.} = c_1 e^{(2+\sqrt{3})x} + c_2 e^{(2-\sqrt{3})x}$$

$$= e^{2x} \left[c_1 e^{\sqrt{3}x} + c_2 e^{-\sqrt{3}x} \right]$$

Now, $\text{P.I.} = \frac{1}{D^2 - 4D + 1} e^{2x} \sin 2x$

$$= e^{2x} \frac{1}{(D+2)^2 - 4(D+2) + 1} \sin 2x$$

$$= e^{2x} \frac{1}{D^2 + 4D + 4 - 4D - 8 + 1} \sin 2x$$

$$= e^{2x} \frac{1}{D^2 - 3} \sin 2x = e^{2x} \frac{1}{-4-3} \sin 2x$$

$$= \frac{-1}{7} e^{2x} \sin 2x$$

Hence general solution is

$$y = \left(c_1 e^{\sqrt{3}x} + c_2 e^{-\sqrt{3}x} \right) e^{2x} - \frac{1}{7} e^{2x} \sin 2x$$

VIII. When $X = x\, v(x)$, then

$$\text{P.I.} = \frac{1}{f(D)} xv(x) = \left[x - \frac{f'(D)}{f(D)} \right] \frac{1}{f(D)} v(x)$$

Example. Find PI of $(D^2 - 1) y = x \sin x$

Solution

$$\text{P.I.} = \frac{1}{D^2 - 1} x \sin x$$

$$= \left[x - \frac{2D}{D^2 - 1} \right] \frac{1}{D^2 - 1} \sin x$$

$$= \left(x - \frac{2D}{D^2 - 1} \right) \frac{\sin x}{-2}$$

$$= -\frac{1}{2} \left[x \sin x - \frac{2D \sin x}{-2} \right]$$

$$= -\frac{1}{2} [x \sin x + \cos x]$$

IX. $Q = e^{ax}$ and $F(a) = 0$

$$\text{P.I.} = \frac{1}{\phi(a)} e^{ax} . \frac{x^n}{n} = \frac{e^{ax}}{(D+a)}$$

X. To find P.I., when Q is of the form xV, where V is any function of x.

By Leibnitz's theorem,

$$\frac{1}{F(D)}(x.V) = x \frac{1}{F(D)} V - \frac{F'(D)}{\{F(D)\}^2}$$

XI. To find P.I. when Q is of the form x^m. V where V is any function of x.

(*i*) If $V = x^n$, then $x^m . x^n = x^{m+n}$

(*ii*) If $V = e^{ax}$, then $x^{mv} = x^m e^{ax}$ [evaluate as (X)]

(*iii*) If $V = \cos ax$, then $x^{mv} = x^m \cos ax$

$$\text{P.I.} = \frac{1}{F(D)} x^m \cos ax = \frac{1}{F(D)} (\text{Real part of } x^m e^{iax})$$

$$= \text{Real part of } \frac{1}{F(D)} x^m e^{iax}$$

If $V = \sin ax$, then

$$\text{P.I.} = \text{I.P. of } \frac{1}{F(D)} x^m e^{iax}$$

and calculate as above.

XII. $\frac{1}{D-a} Q = e^{ax} \int Q e^{-ax} dx$

XIII. $\frac{1}{(D^2 - a^2)} = \text{cosec } ax \frac{1}{2ia} \left[\left(\frac{1}{D - ia} \right) - \left(\frac{1}{D + ia} \right) \right]$

Method of Variation of Parameters

Finding Particular Integral

Consider linear differential equation

$$a\frac{d^2y}{dx^2}+b\frac{dy}{dx}+cy=X$$

Complementary function $= C_1y_1 + C_2y_2$

and Particular integral $= uy_1 + vy_2$

where $u = \int \frac{-y_2X}{y_1y_2' - y_1'y_2}\,dx$

and $v = \int \frac{y_1X}{y_1y_2' - y_1'y_2}\,dx$

Complete solution = Complementary function + Particular integral.

Method of Undetermined Coefficients to Find Particular Integral

Consider a linear differential equation

$$D^ny + p_1D^{n-1}y + \ldots + p_ny = X$$

For particular integral, assume a trial solution containing unknown constants which are determined by substitution in the given equation. The trial solution to be assumed in each case, depends on the form of X. Thus

(1) When $X = 2e^{3x}$

Trial solution $= ae^{3x}$

(2) When $X = 3\sin 2x$

Trial solution $= a_1\sin 2x + a_2\cos 2x$

(3) When $X = 2x^3$

Trial solution $= a_1x^3 + a_2x^2 + a_3x + a_4$

However when $X = \tan x$ or $\sec x$, this method fails, since number of terms obtained by differentiating $X = \tan x$ or $\sec x$ is infinite.

This method holds as long as no term in the trial solution appears in the C.F.

If any term of the trial solution appears in the C.F., multiply this trial solution by the lowest positive integral power of x which is large enough so that none of the terms which are then present, appear in the C.F.

Example : Solve $\left(\frac{d^4y}{dx^4}+m^4\right)y=0$

Solution

Given equation can be written as

$(D^4 + m^4)y = 0$

here, $D = \frac{d}{dx}$

Its auxiliary equation is

$$M^4 + m^4 = 0$$

$$\Rightarrow (M^2+m^2)^2 - 2M^2m^2 = 0$$

$$\Rightarrow (M^2+m^2)^2 - \left(\sqrt{2}Mm\right)^2 = 0$$

$$\Rightarrow (M^2+m^2+\sqrt{2}Mm)(M^2+m^2-\sqrt{2}Mm) = 0$$

$$M = \frac{-\sqrt{2}m \pm \sqrt{2m^2-4m^2}}{2};\ \frac{\sqrt{2}m \pm \sqrt{2m^2-4m^2}}{2}$$

$$= \frac{-\sqrt{2}m \pm \sqrt{2}mi}{2};\ \frac{\sqrt{2}m \pm \sqrt{2}mi}{2}$$

$$= \frac{-m}{\sqrt{2}} \pm \frac{m}{\sqrt{2}}i;\ \frac{m}{\sqrt{2}} \pm \frac{m}{\sqrt{2}}i$$

Hence required solution,

$$e^{-mx/\sqrt{2}}\{C_1\cos(mx/\sqrt{2}) + C_2\sin(mx/\sqrt{2})\} + e^{mx/\sqrt{2}}\{C_3\cos(mx/\sqrt{2}) + C_4\sin(mx/\sqrt{2})\}$$

where C_1, C_2, C_3, C_4 are arbitrary constants.

Example : Solve $(D^2 - 2D + 5)y = e^{-x}$

Solution

Given equation is $(D^2 - 2D + 5)y = e^{-x}$

Auxiliary equation is $m^2 - 2m + 5 = 0$,

where roots are $m = -1 \pm 2i$

Complementary Function,

$$C.F. = e^{-x}(C_1\cos 2x + C_2\sin 2x)$$

where C_1 and C_2 are arbitrary constants.

$$\text{and P.I.} = \frac{1}{D^2-2D+5}e^{-x} = \frac{e^{-x_1}}{(-1)^2-2(-1)+5}$$

$$= \frac{e^{-x}}{1+2+5} = \frac{e^{-x}}{8}$$

Hence required solution is

$$y = C.F. + P.I$$

$$= e^{-x}(C_1\cos 2x + C_2\sin 2x) + \frac{e^{-x}}{8}$$

First Order Equations (Linear and Non-Linear)

Order of a differential equation means order of the highest differential coefficient which appears in it.

Linear Differential Equations

$$\frac{dy}{dx} + Py = Q$$

where P and Q are constant or functions of x alone.

This equation is called *linear differential* of the first order in y.

It's integrating factor is, I.F. $= e^{\int pdx}$

Multiplying both sides by I.F., we get

$$\left(\frac{dy}{dx}+Py\right)e^{\int pdx} = Q\,e^{\int pdx} \qquad ...(i)$$

Now, $$\frac{d}{dx}(ye^{\int pdx}) = y.\frac{d}{dx}\left[e^{\int pdx}\right]+e^{\int pdx}.\frac{dy}{dx}$$

$$= y.e^{\int pdx}.P+e^{\int pdx}.\frac{dy}{dx}$$

$$\frac{d}{dx}(ye^{\int pdx}) = \left(Py+\frac{dy}{dx}\right)e^{\int pdx}$$

From equation (i), $$\frac{d}{dx}\left[ye^{\int pdx}\right] = Q\,e^{\int pdx}$$

Integrating both sides with respect to x, we get

$$y.e^{\int pdx} = C+\int Q.e^{\int pdx}dx$$

where, C is a integration constant.

This equation is complete solution.

Cauchy's Homogeneous Linear Equation

$$x^n\frac{d^ny}{dx^n}+a_1x^{n-1}\frac{d^{n-1}y}{dx^{n-1}}+a_2x^{n-2}\frac{d^{n-2}y}{dx^{n-2}}+....+a_ny=X(x)$$

where $a_1, a_2, ..., a_n$ are constants and X is a function of x. This can be reduced to linear differential equation with constant co-efficients by the substitution

$$x = e^t \quad\Rightarrow\quad \log x = t$$

which can be solved by above methods.

Legendre's Homogeneous Linear Equation

$$(ax+b)^n\frac{d^ny}{dx^n}+a_1(ax+b)^{n-1}\frac{d^{n-1}y}{dx^{n-1}}$$
$$+a_2(ax+b)^{n-2}\frac{d^{n-2}y}{dx^{n-2}}+....+a_ny = X$$

where $a_1, a_2, ... a_n$ are constants and X is a function of x. If we substitute $ax+b=t$, then above equation will reduce to the Cauchy's form and then a further substitution $t = e^z$ reduces it to the linear differential equation with constant co-efficients. A single substitution $ax+b=e^z$ will reduce the above equation to the linear differential equation with constant coefficients.

Example. Solve by the method of variation of parameters : $\frac{d^2y}{dx^2}+y = \text{cosec } x$.

Solution

Its A.E. is $D^2+1=0 \Rightarrow D=\pm i$

$\therefore$ C.F. $=C_1\cos x+C_2\sin x = C_1F_1+C_2F_2$ (say)

where, $F_1 = \cos x$ and $F_2 = \sin x$

Now P.I. $= PF_1+QF_2$

where, $$P = -\int\frac{F_2X}{F_1F_2'-F_2F_1'}dx$$

and, $$Q = \int\frac{F_1X}{F_1F_2'-F_2F_1'}dx$$

$F_1 = \cos x \Rightarrow F'_1 = -\sin x$

and $F_2 = \sin x \Rightarrow F'_2 = \cos x$

$$\therefore\ F_1F'_2-F_2F'_1 = \cos^2x-(\sin x)(-\sin x)$$
$$= \cos^2x+\sin^2x = 1$$

$$\therefore\ P = -\int\frac{\sin x\,\text{cosec}\,x}{1}dx = -x$$

Similarly, $$Q = \int\frac{F_1X}{F_1F_1'-F_2F_1'}dx$$

$$= \int\frac{\cos x}{1}\text{cosec}\,x\,dx = \int\frac{\cos x}{\sin x}dx$$

$$= \int\cot x\,dx = \log\sin x.$$

$$\therefore\ \text{P.I.} = PF_1+QF_2$$
$$= -x\cos x+\log(\sin x).\sin x$$
$$= -x\cos x+\sin x\log(\sin x)$$

Hence complete solution is,

$$y = C_1\cos x+C_2\sin x-x\cos x+\sin x.\log(\sin x).$$

Euler-Cauchy Equations

Homogeneous

If the ODE is of the form

$$ax^2y''+bxy''+cy = 0, \qquad ...(1)$$

where a, b and c are constants; then (1) is called homogeneous Euler-Cauchy equation. Two linearly independent solutions (i.e. basis) depend on the quadratic equation

$$am^2+(b-a)m+c = 0. \qquad ...(2)$$

Equation (2) is called *characteristic equation* for (1). The ODE (1) is singular at $x = 0$. Hence, we solve (1) for $x \neq 0$. We consider the case when $x > 0$.

Theorem

(i) If the roots of (2) are real and distinct, say m_1 and m_2, then two linearly independent (LI) solutions of (1) are x^{m1} and x^{m2}. Thus, the general solution to (1) is

$$y = C_1x^{m1}+C_2x^{m2}.$$

(ii) If the roots of (2) are real and equal, say $m_1 = m_2 = m$, then two LI solutions of (1) are x^m and $x^m \ln x$. Thus, the general solution to (1) is

$$y = (C_1 + C_2 \ln x)x^m.$$

(iii) If the roots of (2) are complex conjugate, say $m_1 = \alpha + i\beta$ and $m_2 = \alpha - i\beta$, then two real LI solutions of (1) are $x^\alpha \cos(\beta \ln x)$ and $x^\alpha \sin(\beta \ln x)$. Thus, the general solution to (1) is

$$y = x^\alpha (C_1 \cos(\beta \ln x) + C_2 \sin(\beta \ln x)).$$

Example. *Solve* $x^2y'' - xy' - 3y = 0$

Solution

The characteristic equation is $m^2 - 2m - 3 = 0$

$\Rightarrow m = -1, 3$. The general solution is $y = C_1/x + C_2x^3$

(ii) If $p(m) = 0$ has real equal roots $m_1 = m_2 = m$, then x^m is a solution of (1). To find the other solution, note that if m is repeated root, then $p(m) = p'(m) = 0$. This suggests differentiating (3) w.r.t. m. Since L consists of differentiation w.r.t. x only,

$$\frac{\partial}{\partial m}(L(x^m)) = L\left(\frac{\partial}{\partial m}x^m\right)$$

$$= L(x^m \ln x).$$

Now $\quad L(x^m \ln x) = (p'(m) + p(m)\ln x)x^m$

where $'$ represents the derivative. Since, m is a repeated root, the RHS is zero. Thus, $x^m \ln x$ is also a solution to (1) and it is independent of x^m. Hence, the general solution to (1) is

$$y = (C_1 + C_2 \ln x)x^m.$$

Example. *Solve* $x^2y'' - 3xy' + 4y = 0$

Solution

The characteristic equation is $m^2 - 4m + 4 = 0$

$\Rightarrow m = 2, 2.$

The general solution is $y = (C_1 + C_2 \ln x)x^2$.

(iii) If $p(m) = 0$ has complex conjugate roots, say $m_1 = \alpha + i\beta$ and $m_2 = \alpha - i\beta$, then two LI solutions are

$$Y_1 = x^{(\alpha+i\beta)} = x^\alpha e^{i\beta \ln x},$$

and

$$Y_2 = x^\alpha e^{-i\beta \ln x}.$$

But these are complex valued. Note that if Y_1, Y_2 are LI, then so are $y_1 = (Y_1 + Y_2)/2$ and $y_2 = (Y_1 - Y_2)/2i$. Hence, two real LI solutions of (1) are $y_1 = x^\alpha \cos(\beta \ln x)$ and $y_2 = x^\alpha \sin(\beta \ln x)$. Thus, the general solution to (1) is

$$y = x^\alpha(C_1\cos(\beta \ln x) + C_2\sin(\beta \ln x).$$

Nonhomogeneous

If the ODE is of the form

$$ax^2y'' + bxy'' + cy = \tilde{r}(x), \qquad \text{...(4)}$$

where a, b and c are constants; then (4) is called nonhomogeneous Euler-Cauchy equation. We can use the method of variation of parameters as follows. First divide (4) by ax^2 so that the coefficient of y'' becomes unity:

$$y'' + \frac{b}{ax}y'' + \frac{c}{ax^2}y = r(x) \qquad \text{...(5)}$$

where $r(x) = \tilde{r}(x)/ax^2$. Now we already know two LI solutions y_1, y_2, of the homogeneous part. Hence, the particular solution to (4) is given by

$$y_p(x) = -y_1(x)\int\frac{y_2(x)r(x)}{W(y_1,y_2)}dx + y_2(x)\int\frac{y_1(x)r(x)}{W(y_1,y_2)}dx.$$

Thus, the general solution to (4) is

$$y(x) = C_1y_1(x) + C_2y_2(x) + y_p(x).$$

Example. *Consider*

$$x^2y'' - xy' - 3y = \frac{\ln x}{x}, \; x > 0.$$

The characteristic equation is $m^2 - 2m - 3 = 0$

$\Rightarrow m = -1, 3.$

Hence $y_1 = 1/x$ and $y_2 = x^3$. Hence,

$$y_p(x) = y_1(x)u(x) + y_2(x)v(x)$$

where

$$u(x) = -\int\frac{y_2(x)r(x)}{W(y_1,y_2)}dx$$

$$v(x) = \int\frac{y_1(x)r(x)}{W(y_1,y_2)}dx.$$

Now $W(y_1,y_2) = 4x$ and $\boxed{r(x) = \ln x/x^3}$! Hence,

$$u(x) = -\int\frac{\ln x}{4x}dx$$

$$= -\frac{(\ln x)^2}{8}$$

$$v(x) = \int\frac{\ln x}{4x^5}dx$$

$$= -\frac{\ln x}{16x^4} - \frac{1}{16x^4}$$

Hence, $\quad y_p(x) = -\frac{(\ln x)^2}{8x} - \frac{\ln x}{16x} - \frac{1}{64x}$

Hence the general solution is $y = c_1y_1 + c_2y_2 + y_p$, i.e.

$$y(x) = \frac{A}{x} + Bx^3 - \frac{(\ln x)^2}{8x} - \frac{\ln x}{16x}.$$

Note that last term of y_p is absorbed with y_1.

Aliter: Let us make the transformation $t = \ln x$. Then the given transformed to

$$\ddot{y} - 2\dot{y} - 3y = te^{-t},$$

where $\dot{} = d/dt$. This is the same problem we have solved in lecture 9 using method of undetermined coefficients.

The solution is (see lecture 9)

$$y(t) = C_1 e^{-t} + C_2 e^{3t} - \frac{te^{-1}}{16}(2t+1).$$

which in terms of original x variable becomes

$$y(x) = \frac{C_1}{x} + C_2 x^3 - \frac{\ln x}{16x}(2\ln x + 1),$$

Solutions to Differential Equations Using Laplace Transformation

As promised, we can now solve differential equations using Laplace Transforms. What we do is transform the differential equation into an algebraic relation using Lapalce Transforms, solve for the Laplace Transform of the solution, then use inverse Laplace Transforms to bring the solution back into the time domain. The most important property of the Laplace transform in this case is the differentiation property:

$$\mathcal{L}\left\{\frac{d}{dt}f(t)\right\} = sF(s) - f(0^-),$$

$$\mathcal{L}\left\{\frac{d^2}{dt^2}f(t)\right\} = s\mathcal{L}\left\{\frac{d}{dt}f(t)\right\} - \frac{df}{dt}(0^-)$$

$$= s^2F(s) - sf(0^-) - \frac{dt}{dt}(0^-)$$

$$\mathcal{L}\left\{\frac{d^n}{dt^n}f(t)\right\} = s^nF(s) - s^{n-1}f(0^-) -$$

$$\ldots - s^n f^{(n-2)}(0^-) - f^{n-1}(0^-).$$

A good starting point to remember this is: if the initial conditions are zero, we can replace n^{th} order differentiation with s^n. Note that because we have defined the Laplace Transform with the lower limit of integration zero, we must always take the starting time as 0, which is no problem for linear constant coefficient differential equations.

Example. Here is a simple differential equation:

$$\frac{dx}{dt} = 1 \quad t \geq 0.$$

Since the functions are equal on the left and right, the Laplace Transforms will be equal:

$$sX(s) - x(0^-) = \frac{1}{s}.$$

Solve for $X(s)$:

$$X(s) = \frac{1}{s^2} + \frac{x(0^-)}{s}$$

We recognize the Laplace Transforms on the right hand side, resulting in the solution

$$x(t) = t + x(0^-) \quad t \geq 0.$$

A. Initial Value Problems

- These are the types of problems we have been solving with RK methods

$$\frac{dy_1}{dt} = f_1(t, y_1, y_2)$$

$$\frac{dy_2}{dt} = f_2(t, y_1, y_2)$$

Subject to :

$t = 0$

$y_1(t = 0) = Y_1$

$y_2(t = 0) = Y_2$

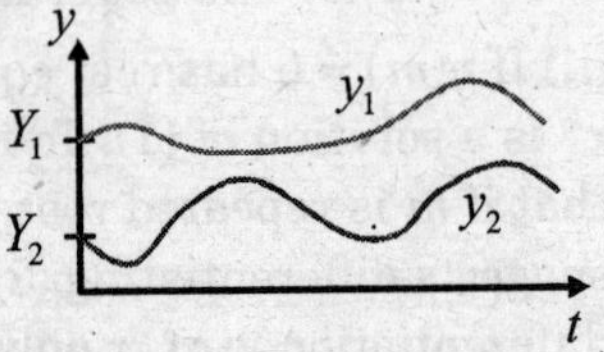

- These are the types of problems we have been solving with RK methods

$$\frac{dy_1}{dt} = f_1(t, y_1, y_2)$$

$$\frac{dy_2}{dt} = f_2(t, y_1, y_2)$$

All conditions are specified at the same value of the independent variable!

Subject to :

$t = 0$

$y_1(t = 0) = Y_1$

$y_2(t = 0) = Y_2$

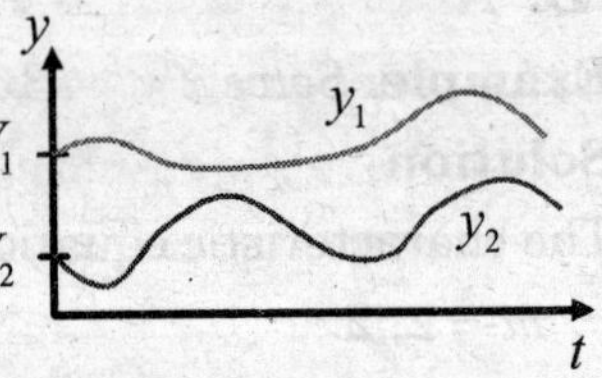

B. Boundary Value Problems

- Auxiliary conditions are specified at the boundaries (not just a one point like in initial value problems)

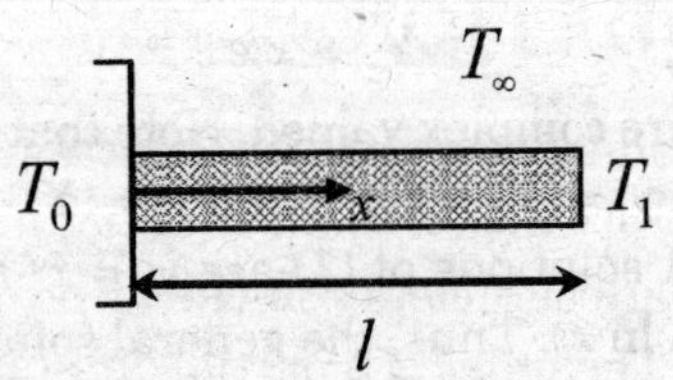

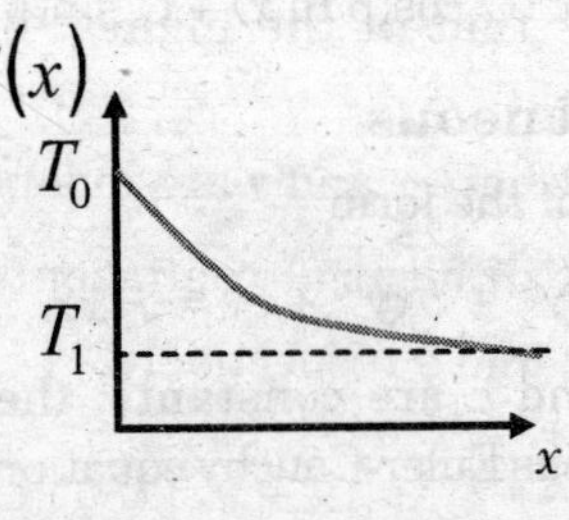

Two Methods: Shooting Method Finite Difference Method

- Auxiliary conditions are specified at the boundaries (not just a one point like in initial value problems)

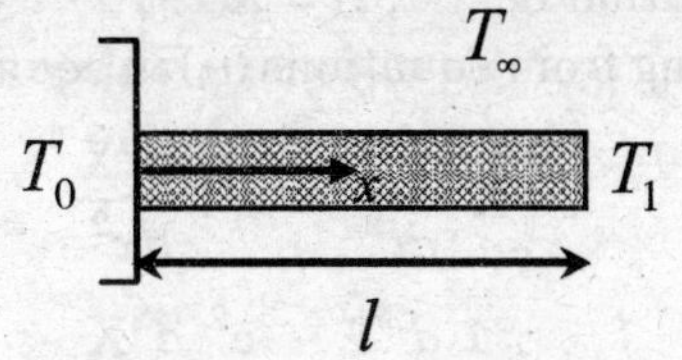

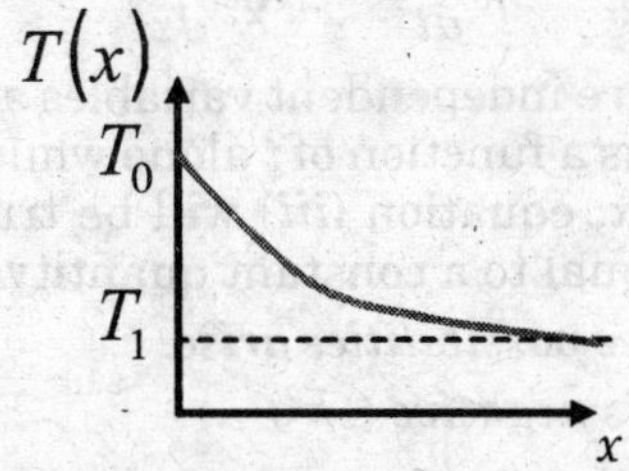

Conditions are specified at different values of the independent variable!

Two Methods: Shooting Method Finite Difference Method

C. Shooting Method

- Applicable to both linear & non-linear Boundary Value (BV) problems.
- Easy to implement
- No guarantee of convergence

D. Approach

- Convert a BV problem into an initial value problem
- Solve the resulting problem iteratively (trial & error)
- Linear ODEs allow a quick linear interpolation
- Non-linear ODEs will require an iterative approach similar to our root finding techniques.

II. PARTIAL DIFFERENTIAL EQUATIONS

If a dependent variable is a function of two or more independent variables, an equation involving partial differential coefficients is called *partial differential equation.* The order of a partial differential equation is the same as that of the highest order differential coefficient in it.

If $z = f(x, y)$ where x and y are independent variables, then partial differntial coefficients $\frac{\partial z}{\partial x}, \frac{\partial z}{\partial y}$ will be denoted by p and q respectively.

Formation of Partial Differential Equation

The partial differential equations can be formed either by elimination of arbitrary constants from a relation between x, y, z or by the elimination of arbitrary functions of these variables.

Solutions of Partial Differential Equations

- The solution $f(x, y, z, a, b) = 0$ of a first order partial differential equation, which contains two orbitrary constants is called *complete solution* or *complete integral.*
- If in this solution, we put $b = \phi(a)$ and find evnelope of the family of surfaces $f(x, y, z, a, \phi(a)) = 0$, we get a solution involving an arbitrary function ϕ. This is called *general solution* or *general integral.*
- A solution obtained from the complete integral by giving particular values to the arbitrary constant is called *particular solution* or *particular integral.*

Equations Solved by Direct Integration

Those equations which contain **only one** partial derivative can be solved by direct integration. However, in place of the constants of integration, we must use arbitrary functions of the variable kept constant.

Linear Partial Differential Equations of First Order

A differential equation involving first order partial derivatives p and q only is called *paritial diferential equation* of the first order. If p and q both occur in the first degree only and are not multiplied together, then it is called a *linear partial differential equation of the first order.*

Lagrange's Linear Equation

Partial differential equation of the form $Pp + Qq = R$, where P, Q and R are functions of x, y, z is the standard form of a linear partial differential equation of the first order and is called *Lagrange's linear equation.*

WORKING PROCEDURE TO SOLVE $P_p + Q_q = R$

(*i*) Form Auxiliary equations $\frac{dx}{P} = \frac{dy}{Q} = \frac{dz}{R}$

(*ii*) Find two independent solutions of the auxiliary equations.

Let $u = c_1$ and $v = c_2$ be two solutions of these equations. Then $f(u, v) = 0$ or $u = f(v)$ is solution of the given equation.

Example. The equation of any sphere of radius r having its centre in the XOY plane is

$$(x-a)^2+(y-b)^2+z^2=r^2$$

Form a partial differential equation by eliminating the constants a, b.

Solution

Given : $(x-a)^2+(y-b)^2+z^2=r^2$

Differentiating with respect to x and y, we get

$$2(x-a)+2z\frac{\partial z}{\partial x}=0 \quad \Rightarrow \quad x-a=-z.\frac{\partial z}{\partial x}$$

and $2(y-b)+2z\dfrac{\partial z}{\partial y}=0 \Rightarrow y-b=-z.\dfrac{\partial z}{\partial y}$

Substituting values, we get

$$z^2\left[\left(\frac{\partial z}{\partial x}\right)^2+\left(\frac{\partial z}{\partial y}\right)^2+1\right]=r^2$$

Applications of Partial Differential Equations

Method of Separation of Variables (Product Method)

This method describes a solution which breaks up into a product of functions each of which depends only on one variable.

i.e. if u is a dependent variable and depends on two independent variables x and t, *i.e.* $u(x, t)$, then we assume solution of the equation in the form

$$u=X(x)\,T(t)$$

where X is a function of x alone and T is a function of t alone.

Substitution for u from above equation in the given differential equation reduces to ordinary differential equations which can be conveniently studied.

Wave Equations

(*i*) One dimensional wave equation or equation of the vibration of a string.

$$\frac{\partial^2 u}{\partial t^2}=c^2\frac{\partial^2 u}{\partial x^2}$$

(*ii*) Two dimensional wave equation or equation of the vibration of a rectangular membrance.

$$\frac{\partial^2 u}{\partial t^2}=c^2\left(\frac{\partial^2 u}{\partial x^2}+\frac{\partial^2 u}{\partial y^2}\right)$$

(*iii*) Three dimensional wave equation is

$$\frac{\partial^2 u}{\partial t^2}=c^2\left(\frac{\partial^2 u}{\partial x^2}+\frac{\partial^2 u}{\partial y^2}+\frac{\partial^2 u}{\partial z^2}\right)$$

Solution of Wave Equation by Separation of Variables

Wave equation is, $\dfrac{\partial^2 y}{\partial t^2}=c^2\dfrac{\partial^2 y}{\partial x^2}$ ...(*i*)

Let its solution be, $y(x, t)=X(x)\,T(t)$ ...(*ii*)

Substituting from equations (*ii*) in equation (*i*), we get

$$X\frac{d^2T}{dt^2}=c^2T\frac{d^2X}{dx^2}$$

$$\Rightarrow \quad \frac{1}{T}\frac{d^2T}{dt^2}=\frac{c^2}{X}\frac{d^2X}{dx^2} \quad ...(iii)$$

Since x and t are independent variables and left side of equation (*iii*) is a function of t alone while right side is a function of x; equation (*iii*) will be true only when each side is equal to a constant quantity.

Following three possibilities arise:

(*i*) *Constant is negative* ($-k^2$).

General solution is,

$$y(x,t)=(A\cos kt+B\sin k)\left(C\cos\frac{k}{c}x+D\sin\frac{k}{c}x\right)$$

(*ii*) *Constant is zero.*

General solution is,

$$y(x,t)=(At+B)(Cx+D)$$

(*iii*) *Constant is positive* (k^2).

General solution is

$$y(x,t)=(Ae^{kt}+Be^{-kt})(Ce^{(k/c)x}+De^{-(k/c)x})$$

Example. Solve by method of separation of variables the equation

$$\frac{\partial^2 u}{\partial t^2}-2\frac{\partial u}{\partial t}+\frac{\partial u}{\partial x}=0.$$

Solution

Let $u=XT$ ...(*i*)

$$\therefore \quad X\frac{d^2T}{dt^2}-2X\frac{dT}{dt}+T\frac{dX}{dx}=0$$

$$\Rightarrow \quad \frac{1}{T}\left(\frac{d^2T}{dt^2}-2\frac{dT}{dt}\right)=-\frac{1}{X}\frac{dX}{dx}=k\text{ (say)}$$

[since x and t are independent of each other]

$$\frac{d^2T}{dt^2}-2\frac{dT}{dt}-kT=0 \quad ...(ii)$$

and $\dfrac{dX}{dx}+kX=0$ ...(*iii*)

Solutions of equations (*ii*) and (*iii*) are

$$T=A\,e^{\{1+\sqrt{(1+k)}\}t}+B\,e^{\{1-\sqrt{(1+k)}\}t} \quad \text{and} \quad X=C\,e^{-kx}$$

Substituting for X and T in equation (*i*), we get

$$u=\left[A'\,e^{\{1+\sqrt{(1+k)}\}t}+B'\,e^{\{1-\sqrt{(1+k)}\}t}\right]e^{-kx}$$

where $A'=AC$ and $B'=BC$.

EXERCISE

MCQ TYPE QUESTIONS

1. The solution for the differential equation

$$\frac{d^2y}{dx^2} + 5\frac{dy}{dx} + 6y = 0 \text{ is}$$

(a) $C_1 e^{-2t} + C_2 e^{3t}$ (b) $C_1 \sin 2t + C_2 \cos 2t$
(c) $C_1 e^{2t} + C_2 e^{-2t}$ (d) $C_1 e^{-2t} + C_2 e^{-3}$

2. Integrating factor for the differential equation

$$\left(\cos^2 x\right)\frac{dy}{dx} + y = \tan x, \text{ is}$$

(a) $e^{\tan x}$ (b) $\cos 2x$
(c) $e^{-\tan x}$ (d) $\sin 2x$

3. Find range of values for a constant K to yield a stable system in the following set of time dependent differential equations

$$\frac{dy_1}{dt} = -5\,y_2 + (4 - K)\,y_2;\quad \frac{dy_2}{dt} = y_1 - 2y_2$$

(a) $0 < K < 7$ (b) $6.25 < K < 10$
(c) $-6 < K \le 6.25$ (d) $0 \le K \le 7$

4. Differential equation,

$$\frac{d^2x}{dt^2} + 10\frac{dx}{dt} + 25x = 0$$

will have a solution of the form

(a) $(C_1 + C_2 t)\,e^{-5t}$ (b) $C_1 e^{-2t}$
(c) $C_1 e^{-5t} + C_2 e^{5t}$ (d) $C_1 e^{-5t} + C_2 e^{2t}$

where C_1 and C_2 are constants.

5. Differential equation for the variation of the amount of salt x in a tank with time t is given by

$$\frac{dx}{dt} + \frac{x}{20} = 10$$

where x is in kg and t is in minutes.

Assuming that there is no salt in the tank initially, the time (in min.) at which the amount of salt increases to 100 kg is

(a) 10 ln 2 (b) 20 ln 2
(c) 50 ln 2 (d) 100 ln 2

6. Solve the differential equation

$$xdx + ydy + 2(x^2 + y^2)\,dx = 0$$

(a) $x^2 - y^2 = ce^{-4x}$
(b) $x^2 + y^2 = ce^{+4x}$
(c) $x^2 + y^2 = ce^{-4x}$
(d) $x^2 - y^2 = ce^{4x}$

7. The differential equation

$$\frac{d^2y}{dx^2} + \sin x\,\frac{dy}{dx} + ye^{x} = \sinh x$$

is

(a) first order and linear
(b) first order and non-linear
(c) second order and linear
(d) second order and non-linear

8. For the differential equation $\frac{dy}{dt} + 5y = 0$ with $y(0) = 1$, the general solution is

(a) e^{5t} (b) e^{-5t}
(c) $5e^{-5t}$ (d) $e^{\sqrt{-5t}}$

9. The necessary and sufficient for the differential equation of the from

$$M(x, y)\,dx + N(x, y)\,dy = 0$$

to be exact is

(a) $M = N$ (b) $\frac{\partial M}{\partial x} = \frac{\partial N}{\partial y}$
(c) $\frac{\partial M}{\partial y} = \frac{\partial N}{\partial x}$ (d) $\frac{\partial^2 M}{\partial x^2} = \frac{\partial^2 N}{\partial y^2}$

10. The differential equation

$$y'' + (s^3 \sin x)^5\,y' + y = \cos x^3 \text{ is}$$

(a) homogeneous
(b) nonlinear
(c) second order linear
(d) non-homogeneous with constant coefficients

11. For the differential equation,

$$f(x, y)\frac{dy}{dx} + g(x, y) = 0$$

to be exact

(a) $\frac{\partial f}{\partial y} = \frac{\partial g}{\partial x}$ (b) $\frac{\partial f}{\partial x} = \frac{\partial g}{\partial y}$
(c) $f = g$ (d) $\frac{\partial^2 f}{\partial x^2} = \frac{\partial^2 g}{\partial y^2}$

12. If $f(D)\,y = 0$ be a linear differential equation with constant coefficients, then its auxiliary equation is

(a) $f(m^3) = 0$
(b) $f(m) = 0$
(c) $f(D - m) = 0$
(d) $f(x) = 0$

13. The general solution of the linear differential equation $(D^4 - 81)y = 0$ is given by

(a) $(C_1 + C_2x)\,e^{3x} + (C_3 + C_4x)\sin 3x$

(b) $(C_1 + C_2x)\,e^{3x} + (C_3 + C_4x)\,e^{-3x} + (C_5 + C_6x)\cos 3x + (C_7 + C_8x)\sin 3x$

(c) $C_1e^{3x} + C_2e^{-3x} + C_3\cos 3x + C_4\sin 3x$

(d) $C_1e^{3x} + C_2e^{-3x} + e^{3x}(C_3\cos x + C_4\sin x)$

14. $\dfrac{1}{D-\alpha}Q(x)$ is equal to

(a) $e^{\alpha x}\int Q(x)dx$ (b) $e^{-\alpha x}\int e^{\alpha x}Q(x)dx$

(c) $e^{-\alpha x}\int Q(x)dx$ (d) $e^{\alpha x}\int e^{-\alpha x}Q(x)dx$

15. P.I. of $(D^2 - 2D)\,y = e^x \sin x$ is

(a) $-\dfrac{1}{2}e^x \sin x$ (b) $e^x \cos x$

(c) $-\dfrac{1}{2}e^x \cos x$ (d) none of these

16. General solution of the differential equation $(D^2 - m^2)\,y = 0$ is

(a) $y = (C_1 + C_2x)e^{mx}$

(b) $y = C_1 \sin x + C_2 \cos x$

(c) $y = C_1 \cosh x + C_2 \sinh x$

(d) none of these

17. $\dfrac{1}{\phi(D)(D-a)^n}e^{ax}$ is equal to

(a) $\dfrac{x^n e^{ax}}{\phi(a)}$ (b) $\dfrac{x^n e^{ax}}{n!\phi(a)}$

(c) $\dfrac{x^n e^{ax}}{\phi(a)}, \phi(a) \neq 0$ (d) $\dfrac{x^n e^{ax}}{n!\phi(a)}, \phi(a) \neq 0$

18. If V be any function of x, then $\dfrac{1}{f(D)}xV$ is equal to

(a) $\left[x + \dfrac{f(D)}{f'(D)}\right]f'(D).V$

(b) $\left[x - \dfrac{f'(D)}{f(D)}\right]f(D).V$

(c) $\left[x - \dfrac{f'(D)}{f(D)}\right]\dfrac{1}{f'(D)}.V$

(d) $\left[x - \dfrac{f'(D)}{f(D)}\right]\dfrac{1}{f(D)}.V$

19. If $y = 1 + \cos x$ and $y = 1 + \sin x$ solutions of the differential equation $\dfrac{d^2y}{dx^2} + y = 1$, then its solution will be also

(a) $y = 2(1 + \cos x)$

(b) $y = 2 + \cos x + \sin x$

(c) $y = \cos x - \sin x$

(d) $y = 1 + \cos x + \sin x$

20. Solution of the differential equation

$$\frac{d^2y}{dx^2} - \frac{dy}{dx} - 2y = 3e^{2x},$$

where $y(0) = 0$ and $y'(0) = -2$ is

(a) $y = e^{-x} - e^{2x} + xe^{2x}$ (b) $y = e^{x} - e^{-2x} - xe^{2x}$

(c) $y = e^{-x} + e^{2x} + \dfrac{x}{2}e^{2x}$ (d) $y = e^{x} - e^{-2x} - \dfrac{x}{2}e^{2x}$

21. The general solution of the differential equation $\dfrac{d^2y}{dx^2} + n^2y = 0$ is

(a) $c_1\sqrt{\cos nx} + c_2\sqrt{\sin nx}$

(b) $c_1 \cos nx + c_2 \sin nx$

(c) $c_1 \cos^2 nx + c_2 \sin^2 nx$

(d) $c_1 \cos^3 nx + c_2 \sin^3 nx$

22. The particular integral for the differential equation $\dfrac{d^2y}{dx^2} - 5\dfrac{dy}{dx} + 6y = e^{3x}$ is

(a) xe^{-x} (b) x^2e^{-x}

(c) $(x - 1)e^{3x}$ (d) $(x - 2)e^{4x}$

23. Solution of the differential equation $\dfrac{d^2y}{dx^2} = x$ is

(a) $y = \dfrac{x^3}{6} + c_1x^2 + c_2$

(b) $y = \dfrac{x^3}{6} + c_1x + c_2$

(c) $y = \dfrac{x^2}{6} + c_1x + c_2$

(d) $y = -\dfrac{x^2}{6} + c_1x + c_2$

24. Particular integral of $\dfrac{d^2y}{dx^2} + \dfrac{dy}{dx} = x^2 + 2x + 4$ is

(a) $\dfrac{x^2}{3} + 4x$ (b) $\dfrac{x^3}{3} + 4x$

(c) $\dfrac{x^3}{3} + 4$ (d) $\dfrac{x^3}{3} + 4x^2$

NUMERICAL TYPE QUESTIONS

1. The value of y as $t \to \infty$ for an initial value of $y(1) = 0$, for the differential equation

$$\left(4t^2 + 1\right)\frac{dy}{dt} + 8yt - t = 0 \text{ is } \_\_\_$$

2. The number of boundary conditions required to solve the following differential equation $\dfrac{\partial^2\phi}{\partial x^2} + \dfrac{\partial^2\phi}{\partial y^2} = 0$ is/are ___

ANSWERS

MCQ Type Questions

1. (*d*) **2.** (*c*) **3.** (*c*) **4.** (*a*) **5.** (*b*) **6.** (*c*) **7.** (*d*) **8.** (*b*) **9.** (*c*) **10.** (*c*)

11. (*b*) **12.** (*b*) **13.** (*c*) **14.** (*d*) **15.** (*a*) **16.** (*c*) **17.** (*d*) **18.** (*d*) **19.** (*d*) **20.** (*a*)

21. (*b*) **22.** (*c*) **23.** (*b*) **24.** (*b*)

Numerical Type Questions

1. (1/8) **2.** (2)

EXPLANATIONS

MCQ TYPE QUESTIONS

3. Given : $\frac{dy_1}{dt} = -5y_2 + (4-k)\ y_2$ ...(*i*)

and $\frac{dy_2}{dt} = y_1 - 2y_2$ ...(*ii*)

Putting $\frac{d}{dt} = D$, we have from equation (*i*),

$$Dy_1 + 5y_2 - (4-K)\,y_2 = 0$$

$$\Rightarrow (D+5)y_1 - (4-K)\,y_2 = 0 \quad \text{...(iii)}$$

From equation (*ii*)

$$Dy_2 = y_1 - 2y_2$$

$$\Rightarrow (D+2)y_2 - y_1 = 0 \quad \text{...(iv)}$$

$$\Rightarrow y_1 = (D+2)\,y_2$$

Putting in equation (*iii*), we get

$$(D+5)(D+2)y_2 - (4-K)y_2 = 0$$

$$\Rightarrow [D^2 + 7D + (6+K)]y_2 = 0$$

$$\Rightarrow D^2 + 7D + 6K = 0$$

$$\Rightarrow D = \frac{-7 \pm \sqrt{49 - 4(6+K)}}{2\times 2}$$

For real value of D,

$$49 - 4(6+K) \geq 0$$

$$\Rightarrow 49 - 24 - 4K \geq 0$$

$$\Rightarrow 4K \leq 25$$

$$\Rightarrow K \leq \frac{25}{4} \Rightarrow K \leq 6.25$$

4. $\frac{d^2x}{dt^2} + 10\frac{dx}{dt} + 25x = 0$

$\Rightarrow (D^2+10D+25)\,x = 0 \quad \Rightarrow (D+5)^2 = 0$

$\Rightarrow D = -5, -5$

Hence soloution is $(C_1 + C_2t)\,e^{-5t}$

5. Given differential equation is,

$$\frac{dx}{dt} + \frac{x}{20} = 10$$

$$\Rightarrow \frac{dx}{dt} = 10 - \frac{x}{20} = \frac{200-x}{20}$$

Integrating,

$$20\int_0^{100} \frac{dx}{200-x} = \int_0^t dt$$

$$\therefore \quad t = 20\left[\ln\frac{1}{200-x}\right]_0^{100} = 20 \ln$$

7. Given: $\frac{d^2y}{dx^2} + \sin x\frac{dy}{dx} + ye^x = \sinh x$

The above equation is second order and non linear.

8. Given : $\frac{dy}{dt} + 5y = 0$

$$\Rightarrow \frac{dy}{y} = -5\,dt$$

Integrating, we get $\log_e y = c - 5t$

When $t = 0$, $y = 1$.

$$\therefore \log_e 1 = c - 5\times 0$$

$$\Rightarrow c = 0$$

$$\therefore \log_e y = -5t$$

$$\Rightarrow y = e^{-5t}$$

10. y'' indicates that it is of second order. Degree of y'', y' and y is one. Hence given differential equation is second order linear equation.

11. For the differential equation $Mdx + Ndy = 0$, to be exact, $\dfrac{\partial M}{\partial y} = \dfrac{\partial N}{\partial x}$

Hence for the differential equation

$$f(x, y)\frac{dy}{dx} + g(x, y) = 0 \text{ to be exact } \frac{\partial f}{\partial x} = \frac{\partial g}{\partial y}$$

13. $(D^4 - 81)y = 0$

Auxiliary equation is

$m^4 - 81 = 0 \Rightarrow (m + 3)(m - 3)(m + 3i)(m - 3i) = 0$

Hence Solution is

$$y = C_1e^{3x} + C_2e^{-3x} + C_3 \cos 3x + C_4 \sin 3x$$

15. $$\text{P.I.} = \frac{1}{D^2 - 2D}e^x \sin x = e^x \frac{1}{(D+1)^2 - 2(D+1)} \sin x$$

$$= e^x \frac{1}{D^2 - 1}\sin x = e^x \frac{1}{(-1^2) - 1}\sin x$$

$$= -\frac{1}{2}e^x \sin x$$

16. Auxiliary equation of the given equation is,

$D^2 - m^2 = 0 \qquad \Rightarrow D = \pm m$

Hence C.F. is $y = C_1e^x + C_2e^{-x}$

$= C_1 \cosh x + C_2 \sinh x$

17. $$\frac{1}{\phi(D)(D-a)^n}e^{ax} = \frac{1}{\phi(a)}.\frac{1}{(D-a)^n}e^{ax}$$

$$= \frac{1}{\phi(a)}x.\frac{1}{\frac{d}{dD}(D-a)^n}e^{ax} \, (\because f(a) = 0)$$

$$= \frac{1}{\phi(a)}x.\frac{1}{n(D-a)^{n-1}}e^{ax}$$

$$= \frac{1}{\phi(a)}x^2.\frac{1}{n\frac{d}{dD}(D-a)^{n-1}}e^{ax} \quad (\because f'(a) = 0)$$

$$= \frac{1}{\phi(a)}x^2.\frac{1}{n(n-1)(D-a)^{n-2}}e^{ax}$$

$$= \frac{1}{\phi(a)}x^n.\frac{1}{n(n-1)(n-2)...2.1}e^{ax}$$

$$= \frac{1}{\phi(a)}.\frac{x^n e^{ax}}{n!}$$

19. $y = 1 + \cos x + \sin x$

$$\therefore \frac{dy}{dx} = -\sin x + \cos x \text{ and } \frac{d^2y}{dx^2} = -\cos x - \sin x$$

$$\therefore \quad y + \frac{d^2y}{dx^2} = 1$$

Hence $y = 1 + \cos x + \sin x$ is solution of, $\dfrac{d^2y}{dx^2} + y = 1$

20. Auxiliary equation is,

$m^2 - m - 2 = 0$

$\therefore m = -1, 2$

$\text{CF} = c_1e^{-x} + c_2e^{2x}$

$$\text{P.I.} = \frac{1}{D^2 - D - 2}.3.e^{2x} = 3.\frac{1}{D^2 - D - 2}e^{2x}$$

$$= 3x\frac{1}{2D - 1}e^{2x} = 3x\frac{1}{3}.e^{2x} = xe^{2x}$$

$\therefore y = c_1e^{-x} + c_2e^{2x} + xe^{2x}$

$$\frac{dy}{dx} = -c_1e^{-x} + c_2e^{2x} + 2xe^{2x} + e^{2x}$$

$y(0) = c_1 + c_2 = 0$ (given)

$y'(0) = -c_2 + 2c_2 + 1 = -2$ (given)

$\therefore c_1 + c_2 = 0$ ...(*i*)

$c_1 - 2c_2 = 3$ ...(*ii*)

Solving equations (*i*) and (*ii*), we get

$c_1 = 1, c_2 = -1$

Hence required solution is

$$y = e^{-x} - e^{2x} + xe^{2x}$$

22. Given equation is,

$(D^2 - 5D + 6) = e^{3x}$

$$\therefore \quad \text{P.I.} = \frac{1}{D^2 - 5D + 6}e^{3x} = \frac{1}{(D-3)(D-2)}e^{3x}$$

$$= \frac{1}{D-3}e^{3x} - \frac{1}{D-2}e^{3x}$$

$$= x.e^{3x} - \frac{1}{3-2}e^{3x} = (x - 1)e^{3x}$$

24. Given differential equation is, $D^2 + D = x^2 + 2x + 4$

$$\therefore \quad \text{P.I.} = \frac{1}{D(D+1)}(x^2 + 2x + 4)$$

$$= \frac{1}{D}(D+1)^{-1}(x^2 + 2x + 4)$$

$$= \frac{1}{D}(1 - D + D^2)(x^2 + 2x + 4)$$

$$= \frac{1}{D}(x^2 + 2x + 4 - 2x - 2 + 2) = \frac{x^3}{3} + 4x$$

NUMERICAL TYPE QUESTION

1. Given: $(4t^2 + 1)\frac{dy}{dt} + 8yt - t = 0$

$$\Rightarrow \quad \frac{dy}{dt} + \frac{8t}{4t^2+1}y = \frac{t}{4t^2+1} \quad \text{...}(i)$$

$$\therefore \quad \text{I.F.} = e^{\int .8t/(4t^2+1)} = (4t^2 + 1)$$

Hence solution of equation (i) is

$$y\,(4t^2 + 1) = \int \frac{t}{(4t^2+1)}.(4t^2+1)\,dt + C = \frac{t^2}{2} + C$$

$$\Rightarrow \quad y = \frac{t^2}{2(4t^2+1)} + \frac{C}{(4t^2+1)} \quad \text{...}(ii)$$

But $\quad y(1) = 0,$

$$\therefore \quad 0 = \frac{1}{10} + \frac{C}{5} \quad \Rightarrow \quad C = -\frac{1}{2}$$

From equation (ii), we have

$$y = \frac{t^2}{2(4t^2+1)} - \frac{1}{2(4t^2+1)}$$

$$\therefore \quad y\big|_{t\to\infty} = \underset{t\to\infty}{\text{Lt}} \frac{1}{2(4+1/t^2)} - \frac{1}{2(4t^2+1)}$$

$$= \frac{1}{2(4+0)} - 0 = \frac{1}{8}$$

4 CHAPTER Probability and Statistics

PROBABILITY

It is a concept of mathematics which measures the degree of certainty or uncertainty of the occurrence of events.

- If any event can happen in m ways and fails in n ways and each of the $(m+n)$ ways are equally likely to occur, then probability of the happening of the events is defined as the ratio, $\frac{m}{m+n}$ and that of its failing as $\frac{n}{m+n}$.

  If probability of the happening is denoted by p and not happening by q, then $p+q=1$.
- If event is certain to happen, its probability is unity.
- If happening is impossible, then its probability is zero.

SAMPLING

A small section selected from the population is called a *sample* and the process of drawing a sample is called *sampling*.

Random Sampling

It is essential that the sample must be a random selection so that each member of the population has the same chance of being included in the sample. Thus the fundamental assumption underlying theory of sampling is *random sampling*

Simple Sampling

A special case of random sampling in which each event has the same probability p of success and the chance of success of different events are independent whether previous trials have been made or not, is called *simple sampling*.

Parameters

The statistical constants of the population such as mean (μ), standard deviation (σ) etc. are called *parameters*.

Statistics

Constants for the sample drawn from the given population, i.e. mean ($\bar{x}$), standard deviation (S) etc. are called *statistic*. The population parameters are in general, not known and their estimates given by the corresponding sample statistic are used. Greek letters are used to denoted population parameters and Roman letters for sample statistic.

Objectives of Sampling

Sampling aims at gathering the maximum information about the population with the minimum effort, cost and time. The object of sampling studies is to obtain the best possible value of the parameters under specific conditions. Sampling determines reliability of these estimates. The logic of the sampling theory is the logic of induction in which we pass from a particular (sample) to general (population). Such a generalization from sample to population is called *statistical inference*.

Sampling Distribution

Consider all possible sample of size n which can be drawn from a given population at random. For each sample, mean can be computed. The mean of the samples will not be identical. If these different means are grouped according of their frequencies, the frequency distribution so formed is called *sampling distribution of the mean*. Similarly sampling distribution of the standard deviation etc, can be obtained.

When drawing each sample, the previous sample is put back so that the parent population remains the same. This is called *sampling with replacement* and all subsequent formulae will pertain to sampling with replacements.

Standard Error

It is used to assess the difference between expected and observed values. Standard deviation of the sampling distribution is called *standard error* **(S.E.)**. Thus standard error of the sampling distribution of means is called *standard error of means*. The reciprocal of the standard error is called *precision*.

If $n \geq 30$, a sample is called **large** otherwise **small**. The sampling distribution of large samples is assumed to be normal.

Population

Collection of all possible samples is population. It is impractical to collect data on each sample of a population. Statistics helps to determine best estimate of the population parameter from randomly selected samples. Because random erros are involved in determination of parameters, the estimate will represent a parameter with a given probability only.

Given an event B such that $P(B)>0$ and any other event A, we define conditional probability of A given by

$$P(A|B)=\frac{P(A\cap B)}{P(B)}$$

Simple Multiplication Rule

$$P(A\cap B)=P(B)P(A|B)=P(A)P(B|A)$$

Example. Let a balanced die is tossed once. Use the definition to find the probability of getting 1, given that an odd number was obtained.

Solution.

Probability of A given that the event B has occurred,

$$P(A|B)=\frac{P(A\cap B)}{P(B)} \quad \text{But} \quad P(B)=\frac{1}{2},$$

$$\therefore \quad P(A|B) = \frac{P(A\cap B)}{P(B)} = \frac{\frac{1}{6}}{\frac{1}{2}} = \frac{1}{3}$$

CONDITIONAL PROBABILITY

Consistency of the definition with the relative frequency concept of probability can be obtained from the following construction.

Let an experiment is repeated a large number, of times, N resulting in

both A and B, $A\cap B$, n_{11} times;

A, not B, $A\cap \bar{B}$, n_{21} times;

B, not A, $\bar{A}\cap B$, n_{12} times;

and neither A nor B, $\bar{A}\cap \bar{B}$, n_{22} times.

These results are:

	A	$\bar{A}$	
B	n_{11}	n_{12}	$n_{11}+n_{12}$
$\bar{B}$	n_{21}	n_{22}	$n_{21}+n_{22}$
	$n_{11}+n_{21}$	$n_{12}+n_{22}$	N

$n_{11}+n_{12}+n_{21}+n_{22} = N.$

Then it follows that with large N

$$P(A) \approx \frac{n_{11}+n_{21}}{N},\ P(B) \approx \frac{n_{11}+n_{12}}{N},$$

$$P(A\cup B) \approx \frac{n_{11}+n_{12}+n_{21}}{N}$$

and conditional probabilities

$$P(B|A) \approx \frac{n_{11}}{n_{11}+n_{21}} \quad \text{and} \quad P(A\cap B) \approx \frac{n_{11}}{N}$$

$$P(A/B) \approx \frac{n_{11}}{n_{11}+n_{12}}$$

Here definitions of P(B | A) and P(A | B) is verified.

Example. Let a box contains r red balls labeled 1, 2, 3, ..., r and b black balls labeled 1, 2, 3, ..., b. Assume that the probability of drawing any particular ball is $\frac{1}{b+r}$

If a ball from the box is known to be red, what is the probability it is the red ball labeled 1?

Solution.

First find probability that it is red (event A).

$$P(A) = \frac{r}{b+r}$$

Then compute probability that the ball is the red ball with the number 1 on it.

$$P(A\cap B) = \frac{1}{b+r}$$

where B is the event that the ball has a 1 on it. Then probability that the ball is red and labeled 1 given that it is red is given by

$$P(B|A) = \frac{P(A\cap B)}{P(A)} = \frac{\frac{1}{b+r}}{\frac{r}{b+r}} = \frac{1}{r}$$

This differs from the unconditional probability of B, which is given by

$$P(B) = \frac{2}{b+r}$$

Summation Rule

Let $B_1, B_2, ..., B_n$ be (pairwise) disjoint events of positive probability whose union is $\cap$.

Then $\quad A = \bigcup_{j=1}^{n}(A\cap B_j)$

Using multiplication rule, we have

$$P(A) = P\left(\bigcup_{j=1}^{n}(A\cap B_j)\right) = \sum_{j=1}^{n} P(A\cap B_j)$$

$$= \sum_{j=1}^{n} P(A|B_j)P(B_j)$$

e.g. Consider rolling a die. Let the sample space be given by $\Omega = \{1, 2, 3, 4, 5, 6\}$

Now consider a partition B_1, B_2, B_3, given by

$B_1 = \{1, 2\}$

$B_2 = \{3, 4\}$

$B_3 = \{5, 6\}$

Let A be the event that the number on the die is equal to one or greater than or equal to four. This gives

A = {1, 4, 5, 6}

$$P(A) = \frac{4}{6} = \frac{2}{3}.$$

This can also be computed using the formula as follows :

$$P(A) = P(A|B_1)P(B_1) + P(A|B_2)P(B_2) + P(A|B_3)P(B_3)$$

$$= \left(\frac{1}{2}\right)\left(\frac{1}{3}\right) + \left(\frac{1}{2}\right)\left(\frac{1}{3}\right) + (1)\left(\frac{1}{3}\right)$$

$$= \frac{1}{6} + \frac{1}{6} + \frac{1}{3} = \frac{2}{3}$$

Bayes Rule

$$P(B_i|A) = \frac{P(A|B_i)P(B_i)}{P(A)}$$

Now, if $B_1, B_2, ..., B_n$ are disjoint events of positive probability whose union is Ω, then

$$P(B_i|A) = \frac{P(A|B_i)P(B_i)}{\sum_{j=1}^{n} P(A|B_j)P(B_j)}$$

Consider same example as before.

Probability for B_1,

$$P(B_1|A) = \frac{P(A|B_1)P(B_1)}{P(A)} = \frac{\left(\frac{1}{2}\right)\left(\frac{1}{3}\right)}{\frac{2}{3}} = \frac{\frac{1}{6}}{\frac{2}{3}} = \frac{1}{4}$$

Probability for B_2,

$$P(B_2|A) = \frac{P(A|B_2)P(B_2)}{P(A)} = \frac{\left(\frac{1}{2}\right)\left(\frac{1}{3}\right)}{\frac{2}{3}} = \frac{\frac{1}{6}}{\frac{2}{3}} = \frac{1}{4}$$

Probability for B_3,

$$P(B_3|A) = \frac{P(A|B_3)P(B_3)}{P(A)} = \frac{(1)\left(\frac{1}{3}\right)}{\frac{2}{3}} = \frac{\frac{1}{3}}{\frac{2}{3}} = \frac{1}{2}$$

Conditional Probability for given Multiple events

Conditional probability of A given $B_1, B_2, ...B_n$, is written $P(A|B_1, B_2, ..., B_n)$ and is defined as

$$P(A|B_1, B_2, ..., B_n) = P(A|B_1 \cap B_2 \cap ... \cap B_n)$$

for any events A, $B_1, B_2, ..., B_n$ such that

$$P(B_1 \cap B_2 \cap ... \cap B_n) > 0$$

More Complex Multiplication Rule

$$P(B_1 \cap B_2 \cap B_3 ... \cap B_n)$$

$$= P(B_1)P(B_2 | B_1)P(B_3 | B_1B_2)...P(B_n | B_1, B_2, ...B_{n-1})$$

ELEMENTS OF PROBABILITY

1. Experiment

It is a process in which a certain work is repeated under the same conditions, the outcomes (or results) of which need not be the same.

e.g. tossing a coin or rolling a dic are experiments

2. Sample space

The set S of all possible outcomes of a given experiment is called *sample space* for the experiment. An outcome an element of S, is called a *sample point*.

e.g. for experiment of tossing a fair (or unbiased) coin

sample space S = (H, T)

where H, T refer to head, tail respectively.

3. Event

A subset of the sample space S is called an *event*. The set (a) consisting of a single sample point a in S is called *elementary event*.

Since empty set ϕ and S are always subsets of S, they are also events ϕ is called *impossible event* or *null event*, and S is called *sure* or *certain event*.

Given two events A, B. form New events can be formed using the set operations of union, intersection and complementation.

(*i*) $A \cup B$ is the event that occurs if and only if A occurs or B occurs (or both).

(*ii*) $A \cap B$ is the event that occurs if and only if both A and B occurs.

(*iii*) A^c or $\overline{A}$, the complement of A, is the event that occurs if and only if A does not occur.

Mutually exclusive events

Two events A and B are said to be mutually exclusive if and only if they cannot occur simultaneously, i.e. if $A \cap B = \phi$.

Three or more events are called *mutually exclusive*, if every two of them are mutually exclusive.

Example. Find total number of possible events that can occur for an experiment.

Solution

Let sample space S consist of n sample points. Then total number of possible events

= total number of subsets of S

= $|p(S)|$

where $p(S)$ is power set of $S = 2^n$.

Example. In an experiment, a fair coin is tossed 4 times. Describe the sample

Solution

The sample space S consists of 16 (= 2^4) sample points.

S = [HHHH, HHHT, HHTH, HTHH, THHH, HHTT, HTTH, TTHH, THTH, HTHT, THHT, HTTT, THTT, TTHT, TTTH, TTTT]

Finite Sample Space

A sample space S is said to be a finite sample space, if S is a finite set.

Finite Probability Space

Let S = $(a_1, a_2 ...., a_n)$ be a finite sample space. S is said to be a finite probability space or probability model, if each sample point a_i in S we can assign a real number p_i, called probability of a_i such that

(*i*) $p_i \geq 0$, for each i

(*ii*) $p_1 + p_2 + ... + p_n = 1$

If A is an event, then probability of A, denoted by P(A) is sum of the probabilities of the sample points in A. For the elementary event $\{a_i\}$ we write $P(a_i)$ instead of $P(a_i)$.

Equiprobable Space

A finite probability space S in which each sample point has the same probability is called an *equiprobable space*. If E is an event, then

$$P(E) = \frac{\text{number of elements in E}}{\text{number of elements in S}} = \frac{|E|}{|S|}$$

$$= \frac{\text{number of outcomes favourable to E}}{\text{total number of possible outcomes}}$$

- The word *"at random"* is used only when dealing with a equiprobable space. By the statement, *"a ball is drawn at random from a bag condisining 10 balls"* we mean that each ball in the bag has the same probability of being chosen.

- If p = probability of happening of an event E = P(E),

  q = probability of not happening of event E = $P(\overline{E})$

  then $q = P(\overline{E}) = \frac{|\overline{E}|}{|S|} = \frac{|S|-|E|}{|S|} = 1 - \frac{|E|}{|S|} = 1 - p$

  $\Rightarrow \quad p + q = 1$

DEPENDENT EVENTS

Events A and B in the space S are said to be independent if occurence of one of them does not influence the occurence of the other

i.e. B is dependent of A if P(B/A) = P(B).

Now, $P(A \cap B) = P(A).\, P(B\,|\,A) = P(A)\, P(B)$

Thus events A and B are independent, if

$$P(A \cap B) = P(A).P(B)$$

Mutual Independence

Let (E_k : k is a positive integer) be a collection of events. These events are said to be mutually independent if for each finite non-empty subset $\{E_1, E_2, ...E_n\}$

$$P(E_1 \cap E_2 \cap .... \cap E_n) = P(E_1).\, P(E_2) .... P(E_n)$$

Pairwise Independence

Let $\{E_k$: k is a positive integer) be a collection of events. These events are said to be pairwise independent if

$$P(E_i \cap E_j) = P(E_i).\, P(E_j) \text{ for all } i \neq j.$$

Possible event

An event E is said to be a possible event, if P (E) > 0.

- Possible independent events are not mutually exclusive.
- Possible mutually exclusive events are not independent.

Example. Let p be the probability that a man aged y years will meet with an accident in a year. What is the probability that a man among n men all aged y years will meet with an accident first ?

Solution

Probability that a man aged y years will not meet with an accident = $1 - p$

P (none meets with an accident)

$= (1-p)(1-p)......(1-p)$ (n times) $= (1-p)^n$

$\therefore$ P (atleast one man meets with an accident)

$= 1-(1-p)^n$

So, P (atleast one man meets with anaccident

[a person is chosen) $= \frac{1}{n} \times [1-(1-p)^n]$

Example. A box contains 4 white, 3 blue and 5 green balls. Four balls are chosen. What is the probability that all three colours are represented ?

Solution

Total number of balls in the box is 12.

Hence total number of ways in which 4 balls can be chosen

$$= {}^{12}C_4 = \frac{12 \times 11 \times 10 \times 9}{4 \times 3 \times 2 \times 1} = 495$$

Each colour will be represented in the following mutually exclusive ways :

	White	Blue	Green
(i)	2	1	1
(ii)	1	2	1
(iii)	1	1	2

Hence number of ways of drawing four balls in the above fashion

$= {}^4C_2 \times {}^3C_1 \times {}^5C_1 + {}^4C_1 \times {}^3C_2 \times {}^5C_1 + {}^4C_1 \times {}^3C_1 \times {}^5C_2$

$= 90 + 60 + 120 = 270$

$\therefore$ Required probability $= \frac{270}{495}$.

LAW OF TOTAL PROBABILITY

Let B_1 B_2, ... B_n be mutually exclusive and let an event A occur only if anyone of B_i occurs. Then

$$P(A) = \sum_{i=1}^{n} P(A / B_i) P(B_i)$$

Baye's Theorm

Let E_1, E_2, ... E_n be mutually exclusive events such that $P(E_i) > 0$ for each i.

Then for any event $A \subseteq \bigcup_1^n E_i$ such that P(A) > 0, we have

$$P(E_i/A) = \frac{P(A / E_i)P(E_i)}{\sum_{i=1}^{n} P(A / E_i)P(E_i)}, \; i = 1, 2, .., n$$

Example. Three urns A, B and C have 1 white , 2 black, 3 red balls, 2 white 1 black, 1 red balls and 4 white, 5 black, 3 red balls respectively. One urn is chosen at random and two balls are drawn. They happen to be white and red balls. What is the probability that they came from urn B ?

Solution

Let E_1, E_2 and E_3 be the events of choosing urns A, B and C respectively.

Then $P(E_1) = P(E_2) = P(E_3) = \frac{1}{3}$ ... (i)

Let X be the event of choosing two balls, white and red. To find $P(E_2/X)$.

By Baye's theorem, (E_2/X)

$$= \frac{P(X / E_2)P(E_2)}{P(X / E_1)P(E_1) + P(X / E_2)P(E_2) + P(X / E_3)P(E_3)}$$

$$= \frac{P(X / E_2)}{P(X / E_1) + P(X / E_2) + P(X / E_3)} \quad \{\text{from } (i)\}$$

Now, $P(X/E_1) = \frac{{}^1C_1 \times {}^3C_1}{{}^6C_2} = \frac{1}{5}$;

$P(X/E_2) = \frac{{}^2C_1 \times {}^1C_1}{{}^4C_2} = \frac{1}{3}$ and $P(X/E_3)$

$= \frac{{}^4C_1 \times {}^3C_1}{{}^{12}C_2} = \frac{2}{11}$

From *(ii)*, $P(E_2/X) = \frac{\frac{1}{3}}{\frac{1}{5}+\frac{1}{3}+\frac{2}{11}} = \frac{55}{118}$

MEASURES OF CENTRAL TENDENCY

1. **Mean** (Arithmetic Mean A.M. or the average),
2. **Median** (positional average)
3. **Mode** (value of the variable which occurs most, frequently)
4. **Geometric Mean** (G.M. used extensively in finding the rate of population growth)
5. **Harmonic Mean** (H. M.)

1. Arithmetic mean ($\bar{x}$)

Let $x_1, x_2, \ldots\ldots\ldots\ldots x_n$ be the observed values and let f_i be the frequency of x_i (t_i) value of x_i repeated f_i times.

i.e., if the data is 3, 1, 3, 3, 2, 1, 3, 2, 2, then $x_1 = 1, x_2 = 2$ and $x_3 = 3$, and $f_1 = f_2 = 3$ and $f_3 = 4$.

$$\bar{x} = \frac{1}{n}(x_1 + x_2 + \ldots. + x_n) = \frac{1}{n}\sum_{i=1}^{n} x_i$$

and for frequency distribution

$$\bar{x} = \frac{1}{N}(f_1x_1 + f_2x_2 + \ldots. + f_nx_n)$$

$$\bar{x} = \frac{1}{N}\sum_{i=1}^{n} f_i x_i \text{ where } N = \sum_{i=1}^{n} f_i$$

2. Median

Median is the middle score. If number of events are even then average of the two middles are taken. The median is better for describing the typical value.

Example. At a ski rental shop, data was collected on number of rentals on each of ten consecutive Saturdays:

44, 50, 38, 96, 42, 47, 40, 39, 46, 50.

To find sample mean, add them and divide by 10:

$$\frac{44+50+38+96+42+47+40+39+46+50}{10} = 49.2$$

Note: Mean value is not a value of the sample.

To find the median, first sort the data:

38, 39, 40, 42, 44, 46, 47, 50, 50, 96

There are two middle numbers 44 and 46. To find the median, we take average of the two.

$$\text{Median} = \frac{44+46}{2} = 45$$

Also mean is larger than all but three of the data points. The mean is influenced by outliers while the median is robust.

$$\text{Median} = L + \left(\frac{\frac{N}{2} - F_{i-1}}{f_m}\right)h$$

where, L = lower limited of Median class
N = Total Number of data items
h = width of Median class
f_m = frequency of Median class.

3. Mode

Mode is the value which occurs most frequently.

$$\text{Mode} = a + \frac{C(f_i - f_{i-1})}{2f_i - f_{i-1} - f_{i+1}}$$

where a = modal class
f_i = maximum frequency
C = constant difference for each class.

Example. Find median of the following data.

Cost	10–20	20–30	30–40	40–50	50–60
Items in a group	4	5	3	6	3

Solution

Cost	Number of items in the group	Cumulative frequency
10 – 20	4	4
20 – 30	5	9
30– 40	3	12
40 – 50	6	18
50 – 60	3	21

Here, $N = 21.$

$\therefore \quad \frac{N}{2} = 10.5$

The median class is 30 – 40.

$$\text{From formula, Median} = 30 + \frac{10}{12}(10.5 - 9) = 30 + 1.25 = \mathbf{31.25}$$

Example. Find mode for the following distribution:

Class interval	0 – 10	10 – 20	20 – 30	30 – 40	40 – 50	50 – 60	60 – 70	70 – 80
Frequency	5	9	8	12	28	20	12	11

Solution

Maximum frequency = 28

$\therefore$ Modal class = 40 – 50

$$\text{Mode} = a + \frac{C(f_i - f_{i-1})}{2f_i - f_{i-1} - f_{i+1}} = 40 + \frac{10(28-12)}{(2 \times 28) - 12 - 20} = 40 + 6.666 = \mathbf{46.67}$$

Example. The expenditure of 100 families is given in the following frequency table.

Monthly Expenditure (in hundreds of rupees)	0 – 10	10 – 20	20 – 30	30 – 40	40 – 50
Number of families	14	?	27	?	15

If mode for the distribution is 24, calculate the missing frequencies.

Solution

Let missing frequencies for the classes 10 – 20 and 30 – 40 be f_1 and f_2 respectively.

Expenditure	**Number of families**	**Cumulative frequency**
0 – 10	14	14
10 – 20	f_1	$14 + f_1$
20 – 30	27	$41 + f_1$
30 – 40	f_2	$41 + f_1 + f_2$
40 – 50	15	$56 + f_1 + f_2$

$$N = 100 = 56 + f_1 + f_2$$

$\Rightarrow \quad f_1 + f_2 = 100 - 56 = 44 \quad \ldots\ldots(i)$

Mode is given to be 24, which lies in the class 20 – 30. So 20 – 30 is the modal class.

$$\text{Mode} = a + \frac{C(f_i - f_{i-1})}{2f_i - f_{i-1} - f_{i+1}}$$

$$\therefore \quad 24 = 20 + \frac{10(27 - f_1)}{(2 \times 27) - f_1 - f_2}$$

$$\Rightarrow \quad 24 - 20 = \frac{270 - 10f_1}{54 - f_1 - f_2} = \frac{270 - 10f_1}{54 - 44} \quad (\because f_1 + f_2 = 44)$$

$\therefore \quad f_1 = 23$

Substituting in (i), we get $f_2 = 21.$

Relation between Mean, Mode and Median

For a symmetrical distribution

Mean = Median = Mode

For a moderately asymmetrical distribution

Mean – Mode = 3 (Mean – Median)

4. Geometric mean (G)

$$G = \sqrt[n]{x_1 x_2 \ldots\ldots x_n} = (x_1 x_2 \ldots\ldots\ldots x_n)^{1/n}$$

For a frequency distribution,

$$G = \left(x_1^{f_1} x_2^{f_2} \ldots\ldots x_n^{f_n}\right)^{1/N}, \quad \text{where } N = \sum_{i=1}^{n} f_i$$

For both cases, taking log

$$\log G = \frac{1}{n}\sum_{i=1}^{n} \log(x_i)$$

For a frequency distribution

$$\log G = \frac{1}{N}\sum_{i=1}^{n} f_i \log(x_i)$$

- If n_1 and n_2 are sizes and G_1 and G_2 are geometric means of two series, then geometric mean of the combined series is given by

$$\log G = \frac{n_1 \log G_1 + n_2 \log G_2}{n_1 + n_2}$$

- Geometric mean is used to find the rate of population growth and the rate of interest and it is also used in the construction of index numbers.

5. Harmonic mean

It is the reciprocal of mean of reciprocals, i.e.

$$H = \frac{1}{\left(\frac{1}{n}\sum_{i=1}^{n}(1/x_i)\right)}$$

For a frequency distribution,

$$H = \frac{1}{\left(\frac{1}{N}\sum_{i=1}^{n}(f_i/x_i)\right)}; \text{ where } N = \sum_{i=1}^{n} f_i$$

Skewness

It is defined as lack of symmetry.

$$\text{Coefficient of skewness} = \frac{\text{Mean} - \text{Mode}}{\text{Standard deviation}}$$

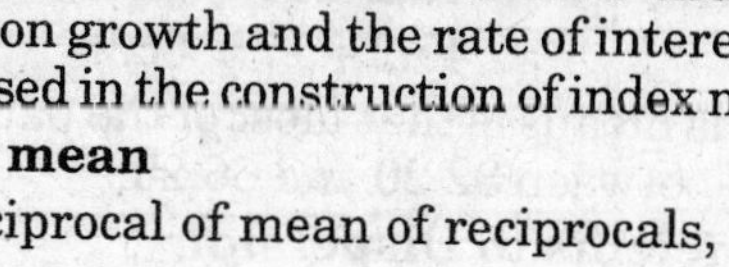

Negatively skewed   Positively skewed

MEASURES OF DISPERSION

The set of constant which would in a concise way explain the "*variability*" or "*spread*" in a data is called *measures of dispersion or variability.*

The average for two groups of the same number of measurements may be equal, but one group may be more variable than the other.

e.g. set of five values 5, 6, 7, 8, 9 has the mean as 7; while another set of five values 1, 6, 4, 10, 14 also has the same mean 7. The second set has, obviously more variability than the first.

Usually four measures of dispersion or variability are defined:

1. Range

This is the difference between two extreme observations in the data given.

In a frequency distribution ,

R = (largest x value) – (smallest x value).

Obviously, this is not a very satisfactory measure except in cases where the number of observations are small and a quick calculation for the scatter is needed. It is used in statistical quality control studies rather widely.

2. Quartile deviation (Q.D.)

Median bisects the distribution. If distribution divided into four parts, *quartiles* are obtained. *First quartile*, Q_1, would have 25 percent of the values below it and the rest above it;

Third quartile, Q_3 would have 75 percent of values below it and the rest above it. The method of calculation of quartiles is similar to that of the median with slight variations.

$$Q_1 = l + \frac{\frac{N}{4} - f_{Q_1}}{f} \times C; \quad Q_3 = l + \frac{\frac{3N}{4} - f_{Q_3}}{f} \times C$$

where we locate Q_1 – class and Q_3 – class properly

l = lower limit of the quartile class

C = common factor

Quartile deviation is defined as

$$\text{Q.D.} = \frac{1}{2}(Q_3 - Q_1)$$

3. Average deviation (A)

If average chosen is A (say), then average deviation about A is average deviation

$$\text{A. D. (A)} = \frac{1}{n}\sum |(x_i - A)| \text{ for discrete data}$$

$$= \frac{1}{n}\sum f_i |x_i - A| \text{ for a frequency distribution.}$$

Usually, either median or the mean are takes as the average.

4. Standard deviation (Root mean square deviation)

Standard deviation,

$$\sigma = \sqrt{\frac{1}{n}\Sigma(x_i - \bar{x})^2} \qquad \text{for discrete data}$$

$$= \sqrt{\frac{1}{N}\Sigma f_i(x_i - \bar{x})^2} \text{ for frequency distribution.}$$

Square of the standard deviation , σ^2 is defined as the *variance* (V).

$$\therefore \quad V = \sigma^2 = \frac{1}{N}\Sigma f_i(x_i - \bar{x})^2$$

Out of these measures, σ is widely used as a companion to $\bar{x}$ on which is based, when dealing with dispersion or scatter.

Calculation of V or σ

$$V = \left[\frac{\Sigma f_i d_1^2}{N} - \frac{(\Sigma f_i d_1^2)^2}{N}\right] \times C^2$$

Some important results

- Average deviation is least when taken from the median.
- Standarsd deviation is not less than the average deviation from the mean.
- For raw data $x_1, x_2, ...x_n$,

$$V = \frac{\Sigma x^2}{N} - \left(\frac{\Sigma x}{N}\right)^2 \quad \text{or} \quad V = \frac{\Sigma x^2}{n} - (\bar{x})^2$$

If n_1, n_2 are sizes of two groups, $\bar{x}_1$, $\bar{x}_2$ their means; σ_1, σ_2 their standard deviations, then standard deviation of the combined group is determined from

$$(n_1 + n_2)\,\sigma_2 = n_1\left(\sigma_1^2 + d_1^2\right) + n_2\left(\sigma_2^2 + d_2^2\right)$$

where, $d_1 = \bar{x} - \bar{x}_1$ and $d_2 = \bar{x} - \bar{x}_2$,

$\bar{x}$ being the combined mean.. This result can be extended to more than two groups.

Determination of Variance and Standard Deviation

Steps

1. Calculate the mean, $\bar{x}$.
2. Write a table that subtracts the mean from each observed value.
3. Square each of the differences.
4. Add this column.
5. Divide by $n - 1$, where n is number of items in the sample This is the *variance*.
6. To get the *standard deviation,* take square root of the variance.

Example. The owner of a restaurant is interested in how much people spend at the restaurant. He examines 10 randomly selected receipts for parties of four and writes down the following data :

44, 50, 38, 96, 42, 47, 40, 39, 46, 50

Find mean, standard deviation and variance.

Solution

Mean is calculated by adding and dividing by 10

Mean, $\bar{x}$ = 49.2

Following table is used for getting standard deviation :

p	*x*–49.2	(*x*–49.2)^2
44	–5.2	27.04
50	0.8	0.64
38	11.2	125.44
96	46.8	2190.24
42	–7.2	51.84
47	–2.2	4.84
40	–9.2	84.64
39	–10.2	104.04
46	–3.2	10.24
50	0.8	0.64
Total		**2600.4**

$$\text{Now } V = \left(\frac{2600.1}{10-1}\right) = 288.7 \approx 289$$

Hence variance is 289 and standard deviation is square root of 289 = 17.

Since standard deviation can be thought of measuring how far the data values lie from the mean, we take mean and move one standard deviation in either direction. The mean for this example was about 49.2 and the standard deviation was 17.

We have, 49.2 – 17 = 32.2

and 49.2 + 17 = 66.2

What is means is that most of the patrons probably spend between 32.20 and 66.20.

Coefficients to Dispersion

When two series of measurements have to be compared, then averages may be different and the units which the measurements are recorded may also be different. Hence, coefficients of dispersion are provided as

- $\frac{\text{Range}}{A + B}$, *where A is largest and B is smallest of the values.*
- $\frac{Q_3 - Q_1}{Q_3 + Q_1}$
- $\frac{\text{Average deviation about} A}{A}$
- *Each of these is free from units of measurement* and is a pure number.

$$\text{Coefficient of variation (C.V.)} = \frac{\sigma}{x} \times 100$$

Thus coefficient of variation is a percentage.

RANDOM VARIABLE

Many variables of interest in a system are not expressible on explicit function of time, all such variable on explicit function of time, all such variable are classified as random variable. These are implying uncertainty about their exact nature.

Random Variable

Discrete — Continuous

Random variable deal with probability theory

Discrete Probability Theory — Continuous Probability Theory

Let X be a random variable.

- Function $F(x) = P(X \le x)$ is called *distribution function of X.*
- Mean or Expectation of $X = \mu = E(X)$

$$= X(a_1)P(a_1) + \ldots\ldots\ldots\ldots + X(a_n)P(a_n)$$

$$= \sum_{i=1}^{n} X(a_i)P(a_i),$$

where S is probability space $(a_1, a_2, \ldots\ldots a_n)$

- Variance of $X = \text{Var}(X) = \sigma^2 = E(X^2) - [E(X)]^2$

Standard deviation of $X = \sigma$

Example. Find expectation of the number of points when a fair die is rolled.

Solution

Let X be the random variable showing number of points.

Then $X = 1, 2, 3, 4, 5, 6$

a_i	$P(X = a_i) = P(a_i)$	Product
1	$\frac{1}{6}$	$\frac{1}{6}$
2	$\frac{1}{6}$	$\frac{2}{6}$
3	$\frac{1}{6}$	$\frac{3}{6}$
4	$\frac{1}{6}$	$\frac{4}{6}$
5	$\frac{1}{6}$	$\frac{5}{6}$
6	$\frac{1}{6}$	$\frac{6}{6}$
	E(X) =	$\frac{21}{6} = \frac{7}{2}$

$\therefore$ Expectation $= \frac{7}{2}$.

Example. What is the expectation of the number of failure preceding the first success in an infinite series of independent trials with constant probability of success p in each trial ?

Solution

Let p = probability of succes

$\therefore \quad q$ = probability of failure $= 1 - p$

Let X be the random variable representing the number of failure preceding the first success.

Since an infinite series of independent trials are conducted, $X = 0, 1, 2$

$P(X = x)$ = probability that there are x failures preceding the first success.

$$= q \times q \times \ldots\ldots\times q \times p = q^x p$$

$$\therefore \quad E(X) = \sum_{x=0}^{\infty} xp(X = x) = \sum_{x=0}^{\infty} xq^x p$$

$$= 1\,qp + 2q^2p + 3q^3p + \ldots\ldots$$

$$= qp\,(1 + 2q + 3q^2 + \ldots\ldots)$$

$$= qp\,(1-q)^{-2} \ [\because (1-q)^{-2} \text{by Binomial theroem}]$$

$$= \frac{qp}{(1-q)^2} = \frac{qp}{p^2} = \frac{q}{p}$$

Example. The Bernouilli probability law with parameter p in which $0 \le P \le 1$ is defined by a random variable X taking the value 1 with probability P and the value 0 with probability q. Find the mean and variance of X.

Solution

a_i	$P(a_i)$	Product
1	p	p
0	q	0
		$E(X) = p$

$\therefore$ Mean $= E(X) = p$.

Now to find Var (X) :

a_i	a_i^2	$P(a_i)$	Product $[a_i^2 \times P(a_i)]$
1	1	p	p
0	0	q	0
			$E(X^2) = p$

$$\therefore \quad \text{Var}(X) = E(X^2) - [E(X)]^2 = p - p^2 = (1-p)\,p = pq$$

Absolute Frequency

Let a value x_i is repeated f_i times, then f_i is called *frequency or absolute frequency.*

Let N = sum of all frequencies f_i, then

$\frac{f_i}{N}$ is called *relative frequency*, $i = 1, 2 \ldots\ldots\ldots n$.

Sum of all relative frequencies

$$= \frac{f_1}{N} + \frac{f_2}{N} + \ldots\ldots\ldots\ldots + \frac{f_n}{N}$$

$$= \frac{f_1 + f_2 + \ldots\ldots\ldots\ldots + f_n}{N} = \frac{N}{N} = 1.$$

PROBABILITY DISTRIBUTION

Let a random experiment is repeated n times. If an event A occurs n_A times, then its probability is defined as

$$p(A) = p(x_k) = \lim_{n\to\infty} \frac{n_A}{n}$$

$$= \text{Probability of outcome A.}$$

where, n_A = times occur A

n = total time experiment

- This limit may not exist.
- This definition presumes that all outcomes are equally likely to occur.

$$p(A + B) = p(A) + p(B) - p(AB)$$

Here, p(AB) = joint probability.

Type of Probability Distribution

The are of two types :

1. Discrete Distribution

It is of two types.

(*i*) Binomial Distribution

It is concerned with trials of a repetitive nature in which only the occurrence or non-occurrence, success or failure, acceptance or erejection, yes or no of a particular event is of interest.

If a series of independent trials are perfomed such that for each trial, *p* is the probability of success and q that of a failure, then probability of r successes in a series of n trials is given by $^nC_rp^rq^{n-r}$, where r takes any integral value from 0 to n.

The probabilities of 0, 1, 2,......r,.....,n successes are therefore, given by

$$q^n, {}^nC_1 pq^{n-1}, {}^nC_2 p^2q^{n-2},....{}^nC_rp^rq^{n-r},......,p^n$$

Probability of the number of successes so obtained is called **binomial distribution** because probabilities are successive terms in the expansion of the binominal $(q + p)^n$.

Hence sum of the probabilities

$$= q^n + {}^nC_1 pq^{n-1} + {}^nC_2 p^2q^{n-2} +....+ p^n$$
$$= (q + p)^n = 1$$

Constants of Binomial Distribution

Moment generating function about the origin,

$$M_o(t) = E(e^{tx}) = \sum {}^nC_1 p^xq^{n-x} e^{tx}$$
$$= \sum^n C_x (pe^t)^x q^{n-x} = (q + pe^t)^n$$

Differentiating with respect to t and putting $t = 0$, we get mean given by

$$M_m(t) = e^{-npt} (q + pe^t)^n = (qe^{-pt} + pe^{qt})^n$$

$$= 1 + pq\frac{t^2}{2!} + pq(q^2 - p^2)\frac{t^3}{3!}$$

$$+ pq(q^3 + p^3)\frac{t^4}{4!} + ...$$

$$\Rightarrow 1 + \mu_1 t + \mu_2\frac{t^2}{2!} + \mu_3\frac{t^3}{3!} + \mu_4\frac{t^4}{4!} +.....$$

$$= 1 + npq\frac{t^2}{2!} + npq(q - p)\frac{t^3}{3!}$$

$$+npq\,[1 + 3(n - 2)\,pq]\frac{t^4}{4!} +....$$

Equating coefficients of like power of t on either side, we have

$$\mu_2 = npq,\ \mu_3 = npq(q-p),\ \mu_4 = npq\,[1+ 3(n - 2)pq]$$

Also, $$\beta_1 = \frac{\mu_3^2}{\mu_2^3} = \frac{(q-p)^2}{npq} = \frac{(1-2p)^2}{npq}$$

$$\beta_1 = \frac{\mu_4}{\mu_2^2} = 3 + \frac{1-6pq}{npq}$$

$\therefore$ Mean = np

Standard deviation = $\sqrt{(npq)}$

$$\text{Skewness} = \frac{1-2p}{\sqrt{npq}}$$

Kurtosis = β_2

Obs. Skewness is

positive for $p < \left(\frac{1}{2}\right)$

negative for $p > \left(\frac{1}{2}\right)$

zero for $p = \left(\frac{1}{2}\right)$, i.e. when probability curve of binomial distribution will be symmetrical (bell-shaped)

As number of trials *n* increase indefinitely $\beta_1 \to 0$ and $\beta_2 \to 3$

Binomial Frequency Distribution

If n independent trials constitute one experiment and this experiment be repeated N times, then frequency of r successes = $N^n\, C_r\, p^r\, q^{n-r}$.

The possible number of successes together with these expected frequencies constitute binomial frequency distribution.

Applications of Binomial Distribution

This distribution is applied to problems concerning

(*a*) number of defectives in a sample from production line.

(*b*) estimation of reliability of system.

(*c*) number of rounds fired from a gun hitting a target.

(*d*) rader detection.

Bernouilli Trials

Independent repeated trials of an experiment with two outcomes only are called *Bernouilli trials,* call One of the outcomes is called *success* and the other outcome is called *failure*.

Let p = probability of success in a Bernouilli trial
q = probability of failure = $1 - p$.

A binomial experiment consisting of a fixed number n of trials is denoted by B (n, p).

Probability of r success in the experiment B (n, p) is given by

$$P(r) = {}^nC_r\, p^r q^{n-r}$$

The function P(r) for r = 0 , 1, 2 ...., n for B (n, p) is called **binomial distribution.**

Example. If four coins are tossed , find the chance that there should be two heads and two tails.

Solution.

$$p = \text{probability of a head} = \frac{1}{2}$$

$$q = \text{probability of a tail} = 1 - p = \frac{1}{2}$$

Hence probability of getting 2 heads (and 2 tails) when four coins are tossed

$$= P(2) = {}^4C_2\, p^2 q^{4-2}$$

$$= 6 \times \left(\frac{1}{2}\right)^2 \times \left(\frac{1}{2}\right)^2 = \frac{3}{8}$$

***(ii)* Poisson Distribution**

It is a distribution related to the probabilities of events which are extremely rare, but which have a large number of independent opportunities for occurrence.

e.g. number of persons born blind per year in a large city is the phenomena, in which this law is followed.

This distribution can be derived as limiting case of the binomial distribution by making n very large and p very small keeping np fixed (= m, say)

The probability of r successes in a binomial distribution

$$P(r) = {}^nC_r p^r q^{n-r}$$

$$= \frac{n(n-1)(n-2)\ldots(n-r+1)\, p^r q^{n-r}}{r!}$$

$$= \frac{np(np-p)(np-2p)..(np-r-1p)(1-p)^{n-r}}{r!}$$

As $n \to \infty$, $p \to 0$ (np = m),

$$p(r) = \frac{m^r}{r!} \underset{n\to\infty}{Lt} \frac{(1-m/n)^2}{(1-m/n)^r} = \frac{m^r}{r!} e^{-m}$$

so that probabilities of 0, 1, 2, ..., r,...... success in poisson distributio is given by

$$e^{-m},\ me^{-m},\ \frac{m^2 e^{-m}}{2!}, \ldots\ \frac{m^r . e^{-m}}{r!}, \ldots$$

Sum of these probabilities is unity as it should be.

2. Continuous Probability Distribution

When a variate X takes every value in an interval, it gives rise to continuous distribution of X. e.g. distributions defined by the variates like heights or weights are continuous distributions.

A major conceptual difference, however, exists between discrete and continuous probabilities. When thinking in discreate terms, the probability associated with an event is meaningful. With continuous event, however, where number of events is infinitely large, the probability that a specific event will occur is practically zero. For this reason, continuous probability statements must be worded somewhat, differently from discrete ones. Instead of finding the probability that z equals some value, we find the probability of x falling in a small interval.

Thus probability distribution of a continuous variate x is defined by a function f(x) such that probability of the variate x falling in the small interval

$$[x - \frac{1}{2} dx] \text{ to } [x + \frac{1}{2} dx] \text{ is } f(x)\, dx.$$

Let X be a continuous random variable. If $f(x)$ is probability density functions of X, then

- $P(X \le a) = \int_{-\infty}^{a} f(x)dx$
- $P(a \le X \le b) = \int_{a}^{b} f(x)dx$
- Expectation of X = E (X) = Mean = $\int_{-\infty}^{\infty} xf(x)dx$
- Variance of X = y (X) = $\int_{-\infty}^{b} [x - E(x)^2 f(x)dx]$
- $\int_{-\infty}^{\infty} f(x)dx = 1$

Types of Continuous Probability Distribution

(i) Uniform Distribution

A continuous random variable X is said to follow uniform distribution or rectangular distribution if its probability density function is given by

$$f(x) = \frac{1}{b-a},\ a \le x \le b = 0, \text{ otherwise}$$

The uniform distribution generally arises in the study of round off errors where measurements are recorded upto a certain level of accuracy.

Cumulative distribution function of X is given by

$$f(x) = p(X \le x).$$

$$= \int_{-\infty}^{x} f(x)dx = \begin{cases} 0 & if\ x \le a \\ \frac{x-a}{b-a}, & if\ a \le x \le b \\ 1 & if\ x > b \end{cases}$$

$$\text{Mean} = \frac{a+b}{2}, \text{ and Variance} = \frac{(b-a)^2}{12}$$

Example. The melting point X of a certain specimen be assumed to be a continuous random variable which is uniformly distributed over the interval [110, 120]. Find density function of X, mean of X, variance of X and P $(112 \le x \le 115.)$.

Solution

Here, a = 100, b = 120

$$\therefore \quad f(x) = \begin{cases} \dfrac{1}{120-110} & 110 \le x \le 120 \\ 0, & \text{otherwise} \end{cases}$$

$$= \begin{cases} \dfrac{1}{10} & 110 \le x \le 120 \\ 0, & \text{otherwise} \end{cases}$$

$$\text{Mean of X} = \frac{a+b}{2} = \frac{110+120}{2} = 115$$

$$\text{Variance of X} = \frac{(b-a)^2}{12} = \frac{(120-110)^2}{12} = \frac{25}{3}$$

$$P(112 \le x \le 115) = \int_{112}^{115} f(x)dx = \int_{112}^{115} \frac{1}{10}dx = \frac{3}{10}$$

(ii) Exponential Distribution

A continuous random variable X is said to have the exponential distribution if its probability density function is given by

$$f(x) = \begin{cases} ae^{-ax}, & x > 0 \\ 0, & \text{otherwise} \end{cases}$$

a being some positive number, called its *parameter*

This distribution arises in the study of life-length of electronic components.

Also the inter-arrival time and service time in queuing theory have exponential distributions.

$$\text{Mean} = \frac{1}{a}, \text{ Variance} = \frac{1}{a^2}$$

Example. The sales tax return of a salesman is exponentially distributed with parameter $\frac{1}{4}$. What is the probability that his sale will exceed ₹ 10,000 assuming that sales tax is charged at the rate of 5% on the sales ?

Solution

$$\text{Here,} \quad f(x) = \begin{cases} \frac{1}{4}e^{-\frac{x}{4}}, & x > 0 \\ 0 \quad , & \text{otherwise} \end{cases}$$

Sales tax for the sale of ₹ 10,000

$$= 10000 \times \frac{5}{100} = ₹\,500$$

Now, P $(x > 500)$ = 1 P $(x \le 500)$

$$= 1 - \int_0^{500} f(x)dx = 1 - \frac{1}{4}\int_0^{500} e^{-x/4}dx$$

$$= 1 + \left(e^{-x/4}\right)_0^{500} = e^{-125}$$

(iii) Normal Distribution

A continuous random variable X is said to follow normal distribution if its probability density function is

$$f(x) = \frac{1}{\sigma\sqrt{2\pi}} e^{-\frac{(x-\mu)^2}{2\sigma^2}}$$

$$-\infty \le x \le \infty, \sigma > 0, -\infty < \mu < \infty$$

In such a situation, write X – N (μ, σ^2)

The distribution involves two parameters μ and σ.

Properties.

(*a*) Distribution is symmetrical.

(*b*) Mean = μ, Variance = σ^2.

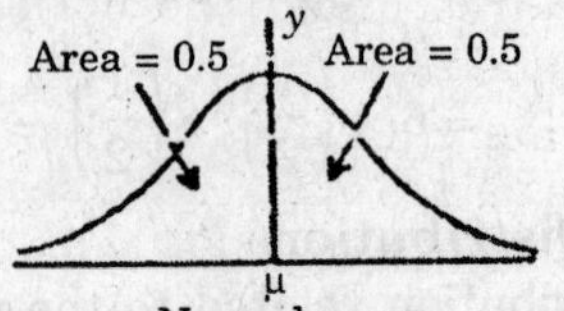

Normal curve

(*c*) Mean, median and mode coincide.

(*d*) $f(x) \ge 0$ for all x.

(*e*) $\int_{-\infty}^{\infty} f(x)dx = 1$, *i.e.* total area under the curve $y = f(x)$ bounded by the axis of x is 1.

Note:

Curve $y = f(x)$, called *normal curve* is a *bell-shaped curve*. It is symmetrical about $x = \mu$. The two tails on the left and right sides of the mean extend to infinity.

Put $z = \dfrac{x-\mu}{\sigma}$. Then z is called a standard *normal variate* and its probability density function is given by

$$p(z) = \frac{1}{\sqrt{2\pi}} e^{-\frac{z^2}{2}}, -\infty \le z \le \infty .$$

Mean of the standard normal distribution is 0 and variance is 1. Write Z – N (0, 1).

Area under the standard normal curve

(*a*) Between $z = -1$ and $z = 1$ is 0.6827 (since total area under standard normal curve is 1)

i.e. $p(-1 < z < 1) = 0.6827$

(*b*) Between $z = -2$ and $z = 2$ is 0.9545

i.e., $p(-2 < z < 2) = 0.9545$

(*c*) Between $z = -3$ and $z = 3$ is 0.9973

i.e., $p(-3 < z < 3) = 0.9973$

In other words,

$p(\mu-\sigma < x < \mu+\sigma) = 0.6827$
$p(\mu-2\sigma < x < \mu+2\sigma) = 0.9545$
$p(\mu-3\sigma < x < \mu+3\sigma) = 0.9973$
$p(\mu-1.96\,\sigma < x < \mu+1.96\sigma) = 0.95$
$p(\mu-2.58\sigma < x < \mu+2.58\,\sigma) = 0.99$

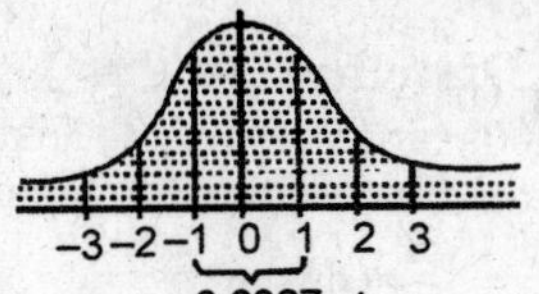

Since distribution is symmetric, we consider only positive values of z.

Then $\phi(z) = \frac{1}{\sqrt{2\pi}}\int_0^z e^{-\frac{z^2}{2}}\,dz$

gives area under the normal curve between $z = 0$ and $z = z$.

For different values of z, $\phi(z)$ can be calculated. These values of $\phi(z)$ have been tabulated. There is another table called *table of ordinates*. We read

$$p(z) = \frac{1}{\sqrt{2\pi}}e^{-\frac{z^2}{2}}$$

corresponding to a value of z from this table. Many distributions tend to a normal distribution in the limit.

When a variable is not normal, it can be made normal using some suitable transformation.

When the sample size is large, distributions of the sample mean, sample variance etc. approach normality. Thus distribution forms a basis for tests of significance.

Normal distribution is also called *distribution of errors*.

Normalized Gaussian random variable

It mean of the standard normal distribution is 0 and variance is 1, write $Z - N(0, 1)$.

The distribution function of X are plotted respectively. Mean and variance of X are

$$\mu_x = E[X] = \mu$$
$$\sigma_x^2 = E[(X-\mu_x)^2] = \sigma^2$$

Notation $N(\mu\,;\sigma^2)$ are used to denote that X is normal (or Gaussian) with mean m and variance σ^2.

In particular, $X = N(0\,;1)$, i.e. X with zero mean and unit variance is defined as a *normalized Gaussian random variable*.

Central Unit Theorem

Normal (or Gaussian) distribution has played a significant role in the study of random phenomena in nature. Many naturally occurring random phenomena are approximately normal. *Central–limit theore* states that *sum of a large number of independent random variables, under certain conditions can be approximated by a normal distribution.*

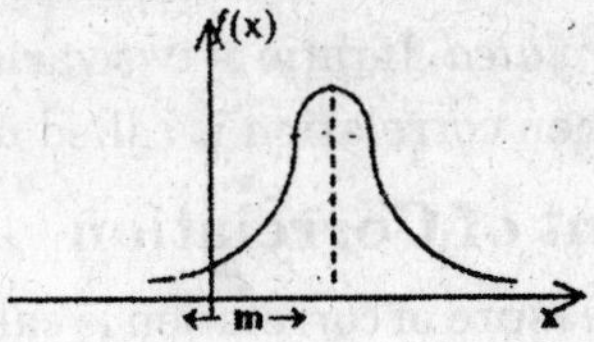

$$f(x) = \frac{1}{\sigma\sqrt{2\pi}}\exp - \frac{(x-\mu)^2}{2\sigma^2}$$

If mean = 0, i.e. $\mu = 0$,

then $$f(x) = \frac{1}{\sigma\sqrt{2\pi}}\exp - \frac{(x)^2}{2\sigma^2}$$

Gaussian Process

$$f(y) = \frac{1}{\sqrt{(2\pi\sigma_y^2)}}\exp\frac{[-(y-\mu_y)^2}{2\sigma_y^2}$$

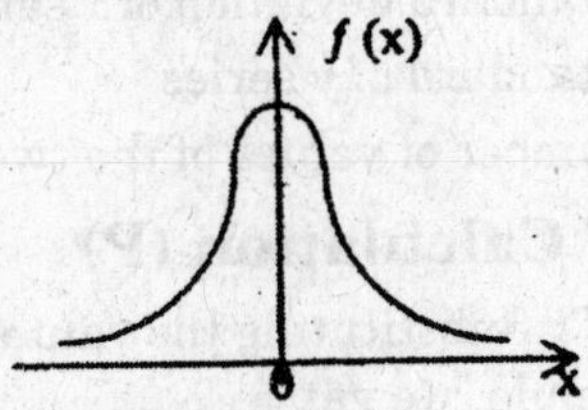

A Gaussian Pulse

where, μ_y = mean
σ_y^2 = variance

Properties of Gaussian process

(*i*) If a Gaussian process x(t) is applied to a stable linear filter, then random process y(t) developed. The output of the filter is also Gaussian.

(*ii*) Consider the set of random variables or samples $x(t_1), x(t_2), x(t_3)$ ----- obtained by observing a random process x(t) at time t_1, t_2, -----.

Second moment or Mean square value

Consider random variable X which assume the possible value x_1, x_2, x_3 ----- x_m. In a sequence of n experiment, let event x_1 occur n_1 time, x_2 occur n_2 times etc.

Arithmetic average or mean of x_k is

$$X_{avg} = \frac{n_1x_1 + n_2x_2 + ----- + x_m\,n_m}{n} = \frac{1}{n}\sum_{k=1}^{m} x_k n_k$$

If $n \to \infty$, then $\frac{n_1}{n} \to p(x_1)$

$$\therefore \quad X_{avg} = p_1x_1 + p_2x_2 + ---- p_m\,x_m = \sum_{k=1}^{m} p_k\,x_k$$

and $$X^2_{avg} = \frac{n_1x_1^2 + n_2\,x_2^2 + ----}{N}$$

CORRELATION

In a divariate distribution, if the classes in one variable are associated by clases in the other, then variables are called *correlated*. If ratio of two variable deviations is constant, then correlation is called *perfect*.

Co-efficient of Correlation

Numerical measure of correlation is called *co-efficient of correlation* and is defined as

$$r = \frac{\Sigma XY}{n\sigma_x\sigma_y}$$

$$= \frac{\Sigma XY}{\sqrt{\Sigma X^2 \Sigma Y^2}} \quad .... \left[\because \sigma_x^2 = \frac{\Sigma x^2}{n}; \sigma_y^2 = \frac{\Sigma y^2}{n}\right]$$

where, X = deviation from mean, $= x - \bar{x}$

Y = deviation from mean, $= y - y$

σ_x = standard deviation of x series

σ_y = standard of y series

n = number of values of the two variables

Method of Calculation (P)

Direct method : Substituting the value of σ_x and σ_y in the above formula, we get

$$r = \frac{\Sigma XY}{\sqrt{\Sigma X^2 \Sigma Y^2}},$$

or

$$\frac{n\sum XY}{\sqrt{\left[n\sum x^2 - \left(\sum x\right)^2 \times \left\{n\sum y^2 - \sum x^2\right\}\right]}}$$

Rank Correlation

A group of n individuals may be arranged in order of merit respect to some characteristic. The same group would give different order for different characteristics. Consider order corresponding to two characteristic A and B. The correlation between these n pairs of ranks is called *rank correlation* in the *characteristics A and B* for that group of individuals.

Let x_i, y_i be the ranks of the ith individuals in A and B respectively. Assuming that no two individuals are bracketed equal in either case, each of the variables taking the values 1, 2, 3,....., n, we have

$$\bar{x} = \bar{y} = \frac{1+2+3+...+n}{n} = \frac{n(n+1)}{2n} = \frac{n+1}{2}$$

If X, Y be the deviation of x, y from their mean, then

$$\Sigma X_i^2 = \Sigma(x_i - \bar{x})^2$$

$$= \Sigma x_i^2 + n(\bar{x})^2 - 2\bar{x}\,\Sigma x_i$$

$$= \Sigma n^2 + \frac{n(n+1)^2}{4} - 2\frac{n+1}{2}.\Sigma n$$

$$= \frac{n(n+1)(2n+1)}{4} + \frac{n(n+1)^2}{4} - \frac{n(n+1)^2}{2}$$

$$= \frac{1}{12}(n^3 - n)$$

Similarly $\Sigma Y_i^2 = \dfrac{1}{12}(n^3 - n)$

Now let $d_i = x_i - y_i$

$\therefore$ $d_i = (x_i - \bar{x}) - (y_i - \bar{y}) = X_i - Y_i$

$$\Sigma d_i^2 = \Sigma X_i^2 + \Sigma Y^2 - 2\,\Sigma X_i Y_i$$

$$\Sigma X_i Y_i = \frac{1}{2}(\Sigma X_i^2 + \Sigma Y_i^2 - \Sigma d_i^2)$$

$$= \frac{1}{12}(n^3 - n) - \frac{1}{2}\Sigma d_i^2$$

Hence correlation coefficient between these variables

$$\rho = \frac{\sum X_i Y_i}{\sqrt{\sum X_i^2 \sum Y_i^2}}$$

$$= \frac{\left(\frac{1}{12}\right)(n^3 - n) - \left(\frac{1}{2}\right)\sum d_i^2}{[1/12](n^3 - n)}$$

$$= 1 - \frac{6\sum d_i^2}{n^3 - n}$$

This is called *rank correlation coefficient.*

Line of Regression

If dots of scatter diagram generally, tend to cluster along a well defined direction which suggests a linear relationship between variables x and y, such a line of best – fit for the given distribution of dots is called *line of regression*.

There are two such lines, one giving the best possible mean values of y for each specified value of x and the other giving the best possible mean values for x for given values of y. The former is called the *line for regression of y on x* and the later is called the *line of regression of x on y*.

First consider the line of regression of y on x.

Let straight line satisfying the general trend of n dots in a scatter diagram be

$$y = a + bx \quad ...(i)$$

We have to determine the constants a and b so that equation (*i*) gives for each value of x, the best estimate for the average value of y in accordance with the principle of least squares. Thus normal equations for a and b are

$$\Sigma y = na + b\Sigma x \quad ...(ii)$$
$$\Sigma xy = a\Sigma x + b\Sigma x^2$$

Equation (*ii*) gives $\frac{1}{n}\Sigma y = a + b.\frac{1}{n}\Sigma x$

i.e. $\bar{y} = a + b\bar{x}$

This shows that ($\bar{x}$, $\bar{y}$), i.e. means of x and y lie on (*i*)

Shifting the origin to ($\bar{x}$, $\bar{y}$), equation (*iii*) takes the form

$$\Sigma(x - \bar{x})(y - \bar{y}) = a\Sigma(x - \bar{x} + b\Sigma(x - \bar{x})^2$$

But $\Sigma(x - \bar{x}) = 0$

$$\therefore \quad b = \frac{\Sigma(x-\bar{x})(y-\bar{y})}{\Sigma(x-\bar{x})^2} = \frac{\Sigma XY}{\Sigma X^2} = \frac{\Sigma XY}{n\sigma_x^2}$$

$$= r\frac{\sigma_y}{\sigma_x} \quad ...\left(\because r = \frac{\Sigma XY}{n\sigma_x\sigma_y}\right)$$

Thus line of best fit becomes

$$(y - \bar{y}) = r\frac{\sigma_y}{\sigma_x}(x - \bar{x})$$

which is equation of the *line of regression of y on x*. Its slope is called *regression co-efficient of y on x*

Interchanging x and y, the line of regression of x on y is

$$(x - \bar{x}) = r\frac{\sigma_x}{\sigma_y}(y - \bar{y})$$

Thus regression co-efficient of y on $x = r\frac{\sigma_y}{\sigma_x}$

and regression co-efficient of x on $y = r\frac{\sigma_x}{\sigma_y}$

Cor. Correlation co-efficient is the geometric mean between the two regression cofficients

$$r\frac{\sigma_y}{\sigma_x} \times r\frac{\sigma_x}{\sigma_y} = r^2$$

Regression co-efficient

It is defined as the hope of lines of regression,

i.e. regression coefficient of line *x* on $y = r\frac{\sigma_x}{\sigma_y}$

SOLVED EXAMPLES

1. A bag contains 8 white and 6 red balls. Find the probability of drawing two balls of the same colour.

Solution

Two balls out of 14 can be drawn in $^{14}C_2$ ways which is total number of outcomes.

Two white balls out of 8 can be drawn in $^8C_2$ ways.

Thus probability of drawing 2 white balls

$$= \frac{^8C_2}{^{14}C_2} = \frac{28}{91}$$

Similarly 2 red balls out of 6 can be drawn in $^6C_2$ ways.

Thus probability of drawing 2 red balls

$$= \frac{^6C_2}{^{14}C_2} = \frac{15}{91}$$

Hence probability of drawing 2 balls of the same colour (either both white or both red)

$$= \frac{28}{91} + \frac{15}{91} = \frac{43}{91}$$

2. Find probability of drawing an ace or a spade or both from a deck of cards?

Solution.

Probability of drawing an ace from a deck of 52 cards $= \frac{4}{52}$

Similarly probability of drawing a card of spades

$$= \frac{13}{52}$$

and probability of drawing an ace of spades $= \frac{1}{52}$.

Since two events (i.e., a card being an ace and a card being of spades) are not mutually exclusive. Hence probability of drawing an ace or a spade

$$= \frac{4}{52} + \frac{13}{52} - \frac{1}{52} = \frac{4}{13}.$$

3. A pair of dice is tossed twice. Find the probability of scoring 7 points

(*a*) once (*b*) at least once (*c*) twice.

Solution

In a single toss of two dice, the sum 7 can be obtained as (1, 6), (2, 5), (3, 4), (4, 3), (5, 2), (6, 1) i.e., in 6 ways

Hence probability of getting 7 $= \frac{6}{36} = \frac{1}{6}$.

Thus, probability of not getting 7 $= 1 - \frac{1}{6} = \frac{5}{6}$.

(*a*) Probability of getting 7 in the first toss and getting 7 in the second toss

$$= \frac{1}{6} \times \frac{5}{6} = \frac{5}{36}.$$

Similarly, probability of not getting 7 in the first toss and getting 7 in the second toss

$$= \frac{5}{6} \times \frac{1}{6} = \frac{5}{36}.$$

Since these are mutually exclusive events, addition law of probability applies.

$$\therefore \text{ Required probability} = \frac{5}{36} + \frac{5}{36} = \frac{5}{18}$$

(*b*) Probability of not getting 7 in either toss

$$= \frac{5}{6} \times \frac{5}{6} = \frac{25}{36}$$

Hence probability of getting 7 at least once

$$= 1 - \frac{25}{36} = \frac{11}{36}.$$

(*c*) Probability of getting 7 twice

$$= \frac{1}{6} \times \frac{1}{6} = \frac{1}{36}.$$

4. There are two groups of subjects; one of which consists of 5 science and 3 engineering subjects, and the other consists of 3 science and 5 engineering subjects. An unbiased die is cast. If the number 3 or number 5 turns up, a subject is selected at randam from the first group, otherwise the subject is selected at randam from the second group. Find probability that an engineering subject is selected ultimately.

Solution

Probability of turning up 3 or 5 $= \frac{2}{6} = \frac{1}{3}$.

Probability of selecting an engineering subject from first group $= \frac{3}{8}$

Hence probability of selecting an engineering subject from first group on turning up 3 or 5

$$= \frac{1}{3} \times \frac{3}{8} = \frac{1}{8}$$

Now probability of not turning 3 or 5

$$= 1 - \frac{1}{3} = \frac{2}{3}$$

Probability of selecting an engineering subject from second group $= \frac{5}{8}$

Hence probability of selecting an engineering subject from second group on turning up 3 or 5

$$= \frac{2}{3} \times \frac{5}{8} = \frac{5}{12}.$$

Thus probability of selecting an engineering subject

$$= \frac{1}{8} + \frac{5}{12} = \frac{13}{24}$$

5. A box A contains 2 white and 4 black balls. Another box B contains 4 white and 7 black balls. A ball is transferred from the box A to the box B. Then a ball is drawn from the box B. Find the probability that it is white.

Solution

Probability of drawing a white ball from box B will depend on whether the transferred ball is black or white.

If a black ball is transferred, its probability is $\frac{4}{6}$.

There are now 5 white and 8 black balls in the box B. Then probability of drawing white ball from box B is $\frac{5}{13}$.

Thus probability of drawing a white ball from urn B, if transferred ball is black $= \frac{4}{6} \times \frac{5}{13} = \frac{10}{39}$.

Similarly the probability of drawing a white ball from urn B, if transferred ball is white

$$= \frac{2}{6} \times \frac{6}{13} = \frac{2}{13}.$$

$$\therefore \text{ Required probability} = \frac{10}{39} + \frac{2}{13} = \frac{16}{39}.$$

6. Two persons A and B toss an unbiased coin alternately on the understanding that the first who gets the head wins. If A starts the game, find their respective chances of winning.

Solution

Probability of getting a head $= \frac{1}{2}$.

Then A can win in 1st, 3rd, 5th, ... throws. Hence chances of A's winning

$$= \frac{1}{2} + \left(\frac{1}{2}\right)^2 \frac{1}{2} + \left(\frac{1}{2}\right)^4 \frac{1}{2} + \left(\frac{1}{2}\right)^6 \frac{1}{2} + \ldots..$$

$$= \frac{\frac{1}{2}}{1 - \left(\frac{1}{2}\right)^2} = \frac{1}{2} \cdot \frac{4}{3} = \frac{2}{3} \ldots..$$

Hence chance of B's winning $= 1 - \frac{2}{3} = \frac{1}{3}$.

7. (*i*) Is the function defined as follows a density function?

$$f(x) = e^{-x}, x \geq 0 = 0, \quad x < 0$$

(*ii*) If so, determine probability that the variate having this density will fall in the interval (1, 2) ?

(*iii*) Also find cumulative probability function F(2)?

Solution

(*i*) $f(x)$ is clearly ≥ 0 for every x in (1, 2) and

$$\int_{-\infty}^{\infty} f(x)dx = \int_{-\infty}^{0} 0.dx + \int_{0}^{\infty} e^{-x}dx = 1$$

Hence function $f(x)$ satisfies the requirements for a density function.

(*ii*) Required probability = P $(1 \leq x \leq 2)$

$$= \int_{1}^{2} e^{-x}dx = e^{-1} - e^{-2}$$

$$= 0.368 - 0.135 = 0.233.$$

This probability is equal to the shaded area in Fig. (*a*).

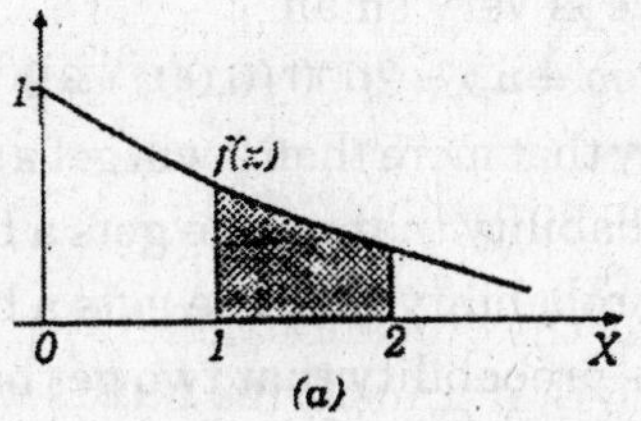

(*a*)

(*iii*) Cumulative probability function F(2)

$$\int_{-\infty}^{2} f(x)dx = \int_{-\infty}^{0} 0.dx + \int_{0}^{2} e^{-x}dx$$

$$= 1 - e^{-2} = 1 - 0.135 = 0.865$$

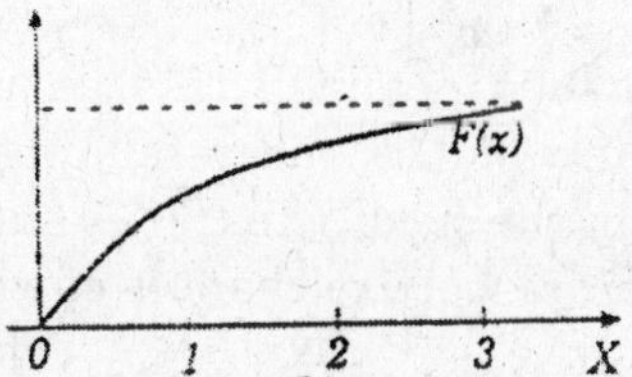

(*b*)

which is shown in Fig.(*b*).

8. X is a continuous random variable with probability density function given by

$$f(x) = kx\ (0 \leq x < 2) = 2k\ (2 \leq x < 4)$$

$$= -kx + 6k\ (4 \leq x < 6)$$

Find k and mean value of X.

Solution.

Since total probability is unity

$$\therefore \quad \int_{0}^{6} f(x)dx = 1$$

i.e., $\int_{0}^{2} kx\,dx + \int_{2}^{4} 2k\,dx + \int_{4}^{6} (-kx + 6k)dx = 1$

$$\Rightarrow k\left|\frac{x^2}{2}\right|_0^2 + 2k|x|_2^4 + \left(-k\frac{x^2}{2} + 6kx\right)_4^6 = 1$$

$$\Rightarrow 2k + 4k + (-10k + 12k) = 1 \Rightarrow k = \frac{1}{8}.$$

Mean of X

$$= \int_{0}^{6} xf(x)dx$$

$$= \int_{0}^{2} kx^2dx + \int_{2}^{4} 2kx\,dx + \int_{4}^{6} x(-kx + 6k)dx$$

$$= k\left|\frac{x^3}{3}\right|_0^2 + 2k\left|\frac{x^2}{2}\right|_2^4 + \left(-k\left|\frac{x^3}{3}\right|_4^6 + 6k\left|\frac{x^2}{2}\right|_4^6\right)$$

$$= k\left(\frac{8}{3}\right) + k(12) - k\left(\frac{152}{3}\right) + 3k(20) = \frac{1}{8}(24) = 3$$

9. The frequency distribution of a measurable characteristic varying between 0 and 2 is as under

$$f(x) = x^3, 0 \leq x \leq 1 = (2 - x)^3, 1 \leq x \leq 2.$$

Calculate standard deviation and also mean deviation about the mean.

Solution

$$\text{Total frequency, N} = \int_{0}^{1} x^3\,dx + \int_{1}^{2} (2-x)^3\,dx$$

$$= \frac{1}{4} + \frac{1}{4} = \frac{1}{2}$$

$\therefore$ μ_1' (about the origin)

$$= \frac{1}{N}\left[\int_{0}^{1} x.x^3\,dx + \int_{1}^{2} x(2-x)^3\,dx\right]$$

$$= 2\left\{\left|\frac{x^5}{5}\right|_0^1 + \left|-x.\frac{(2-x)^4}{4}\right|_1^2 - \left|\frac{(2-x)^5}{20}\right|_1^2\right\}$$

$$= 2\left(\frac{1}{5} + \frac{1}{4} + \frac{1}{20}\right) = 1$$

μ_2' (about the origin)

$$= \frac{1}{N}\left[\int_{0}^{1} x^2.x^3dx + \int_{1}^{2} x^2(2-x)^3\,dx\right]$$

$$= 2\left\{\left|\frac{x^6}{6}\right|_0^1 + \left|-x^2\frac{(2-x)^4}{4}\right|_1^2 + \frac{1}{2}\int_{1}^{2} x(2-x^4)dx\right\}$$

$$= 2\left\{\frac{1}{6} + \frac{1}{4} + \frac{1}{2}\left[\frac{1}{5} + \frac{1}{30}\right]\right\} = \frac{16}{15}$$

$$\therefore \quad \sigma^2 = \mu_2 = \mu_2' - (\mu_1')^2 = \frac{1}{15}$$

i.e., standard deviation $\sigma = \frac{1}{\sqrt{15}}$

Mean deviation about the mean

$$= \frac{1}{N}\left\{\int_0^1 |x-1| x^3 dx + \int_1^2 |x-1|(2-x)^3 dx\right\}$$

$$= 2\left\{\int_0^1 (1-x)x^3 dx + \int_1^2 (x-1)(2-x)^3 dx\right\}$$

$$= 2\left\{\left(\frac{1}{4}-\frac{1}{5}\right)+\left(0+\frac{1}{20}\right)\right\} = \frac{1}{5}$$

10. The probability that a pen manufactured by a company will be defective is $\frac{1}{10}$. If 12 such pens are manufactured, find the probability that

(*a*) exactly two will be defective.

(*b*) at least two will be defective.

(*c*) none will be defective

Solution

Probability of a defective pen = $\frac{1}{10}$ = 0.1

Hence probability of a non-defective pen

$1 - 0.1 = 0.9$

(*a*) Probability that exactly two will be defective

$= {}^{12}C_2\,(0.1)^2\,(0.9)^{10} = 0.2301.$

(*b*) Probability that at least two will be defective

= 1 – (probability that either none or one is non-defective)

$= 1 - [{}^{12}C_0(0.9)^{12} + {}^{12}C_1(0.1)(0.9)^{11}] = 0.3412.$

(*c*) Probability that none will be defective

$= {}^{12}C_{12}\,(0.9)^{12} = 0.2833$

11. In 256 sets of 12 tosses of a coin, in how many cases one can expect 8 heads and 4 tails.

Solution

$$P(\text{head}) = \frac{1}{2} \text{ and } P(\text{tail}) = \frac{1}{2}$$

By Binomial distribution, probability of 8 heads and 4 tails in 12 trials,

$$P(X=8) = {}^{12}C_8\left(\frac{1}{2}\right)^8\left(\frac{1}{2}\right)^4 = \frac{12!}{8!4!}\cdot\frac{1}{2^{12}} = \frac{495}{4096}$$

$\therefore$ Expected number of such cases in 256 sets

$$= 256 \times P(X=8) = 256\,\frac{495}{4096} = 30.9 \approx 31$$

12. If probability of a bad reaction from a certain injection is 0.001, determine the chance that out of 2,000 individuals more than two will get a bad reaction.

Solution

It follows a Poisson distribution as probability of occurrence is very small.

Mean, $m = np = 2000\,(0.001) = 2$

Probability that more than 2 will get a bad reaction

= 1 – [probability that no one gets a bad reaction

+ probability that one gets a bad reaction

+ probability that two get bad reaction]

$$= 1 - \left[e^{-m} + \frac{m^1 e^{-m}}{1!} + \frac{m^2 e^{-m}}{2!}\right]$$

$$= 1 - \left[\frac{1}{e^2} + \frac{2}{e^2} + \frac{2}{e^2}\right] \quad \ldots[\because m = 2]$$

$$= 1 - \frac{5}{e^2}$$

$$= 0.32 \quad [\because e = 2.718]$$

EXERCISE

MCQ TYPE QUESTIONS

1. If A, B, C are three events, then $P[A \cap (B \cup C)] =$

(a) $P(A) + P(B) + P(C) - P(A \cap B) - P(A \cap C)$

(b) $P(A) + P(B) + P(C) - P(B)\,P(C)$

(c) $P(A \cap B) + P(A \cap C) - P(A \cap B \cap C)$

(d) $P(B \cap C) + P(A \cap B) - P(A \cap B \cap C)$

2. If A and B are two arbitrary events, then $P(A \cap B)$ cannot be

(a) less than $P(A) + P(B) - 1$

(b) greater than $P(A) + P(B)$

(c) equal to $P(A) + P(B) - P(A \cup B)$

(d) equal to $P(A) + P(B) + P(A \cup B)$

3. If M and N are two events, then probability that exactly one of them occurs is not equal to

(a) $P(M) + P(N) - 2P(M \cap N)$

(b) $P(M) + P(N) - P(M \cap N)$

(c) $P(\overline{M}) + P(\overline{N}) - 2P(\overline{M} \cap \overline{N})$

(d) $P(M \cap \overline{N}) + P(\overline{M} \cap N)$

4. If A and B are any two events then which one of the following pairs of events are mutually exclusive ?

(a) $A \cup B$ and $A \cap \overline{B}$

(b) $A \cup B$ and $\overline{A} \cap B$

(c) $A \cup B$ and $\overline{A} \cap \overline{B}$

(d) $A \cup B$ and $A \cap B$

5. There are three events A, B, C one of which must, and only one can happen, the odds are 8 to 3 against A, 5 to 2 against B. The odds against C are

(a) 43 to 34 (b) 32 to 23

(c) 34 to 13 (d) none of these

6. A has one share in a lottery in which there is 1 prize and 2 blanks; B has three shares in a lottery in which there are 3 prizes and 6 blanks; compare the probability of A's success to that of B's success is

(a) 7 : 16 (b) 16 : 7 (c) 6 : 14 (d) 14 : 6.

7. If A and B are independent, then A and $\overline{B}$ are also

(a) independent (b) dependent

(c) both (a) and (b) (d) none of these

8. Let $S = \left\{1, \frac{1}{2}, \left(\frac{1}{2}\right)^2, ..., \left(\frac{1}{2}\right)^n\right\}$.

Let A and B be two events defined as $A = \left\{1, \frac{1}{2}\right\}$ and $B = \left\{\left(\frac{1}{2}\right)^2, \left(\frac{1}{2}\right)^4, ...\right\}$.

Then $P(A \cap B)$ will be

(a) 0 (b) 1

(c) ∞ (d) none of these

9. If $E_1, E_2, ..., E_n$ are n mutually exclusive events, then the probability of the happening of any one of them is equal to the sum of the probabilities of the happening of separate events.

i.e., $P(E_1 \cup E_2 \cup E_3 .....\cup E_n)$

$= P(E_1) + P(E_2) + ... + P(E_n)$.

This is

(a) Law of total probability

(b) Law of probability

(c) Both (a) and (b)

(d) None of these

10. What is the probability of correctly choosing an unknown integer between 0 to 9 within three chances ?

(a) $\frac{963}{1000}$ (b) $\frac{973}{1000}$

(c) $\frac{983}{1000}$ (d) None of these

11. If $P(A/C) \geq P(B/C)$ and $P(A/\overline{C_1}) \geq P(B/\overline{C_1})$, then

(a) $P(A) \geq P(B)$ (b) $P(A) \leq P(B)$

(c) $P(A) < P(B)$ (d) $P(A) > P(B)$

12. If A and B are independent and $P(C) = 0$, then A, B and C are independent.

(a) True (b) False

13. Six dice are thrown simultaneously. The probability that all will show different faces is

(a) $\frac{5!}{6^5}$ (b) $\frac{5!}{6^4}$

(c) $\frac{5!}{6^3}$ (d) none of these

14. Given two events A and B and $P(A) = \frac{1}{4}$, $P(B/A) = \frac{1}{2}$ and $P(A/B) = \frac{1}{4}$.

State that following is true?

(a) A is sub-event of B

(b) $P(A/B) = \frac{3}{4}$

(c) $P(A/B) + P(A/\overline{B}) = 1$

(d) None of these

15. If P (A) = 0, then $P(A \cap B) = ?$
(a) 0 (b) 1
(a) ∞ (b) none of these

16. Which of the following is correct?
(a) If P (A) > 0, P (B) > 0 and P (A/B) = P (B/A), then
P (A) = P (B).
(b) If A and B mutually exclusive, then
$P(A/\bar{B}) = P(A)/(1 - P(B))$.
(c) If A and B are independent, then
$P(A \cup B) = 1 - P(\bar{A}) . P(\bar{B})$
(d) All of these

17. If $P(A) = \frac{3}{4}$ and $P(B) = \frac{5}{8}$, then
(a) $P(A \cup B) \geq \frac{3}{4}$ (b) $\frac{3}{8} < P(A \cap B) \leq \frac{5}{8}$
(c) $\frac{1}{8} \leq P(A \cap \bar{B}) \leq \frac{3}{8}$ (d) All of these

18. Three machines M_1, M_2 and M_3 produce identical items. Of their respective output 5%, 4% and 3% of items are faulty. On a certain day, M_1 has produced 25% of the total output, M_2 has produced 30% and M_3 the remainder. An item selected at random is found to be faulty. What are the chances that it was produced by the machine with the highest output?
(a) 0.155 (b) 0.255 (c) 0.355 (d) 0.455

19. In an experiment a coin is tossed 4 times. What is the size of the sample space?
(a) 12 (b) 14 (c) 16 (d) 20

20. For any two events A and B
(a) $P(\bar{A} \cap B) = P(B) - P(A \cap B)$
(b) $P(A \cup B) = P(A) + P(B) - P(A \cap B)$
(c) $P(A/B) \leq P(A)$.
(d) All of these

21. Which of the following is correct?
(a) $P(A \cup B/C) = P(A/C) + P(B/C) - P(A \cap B/C)$
(b) $P(A \cap B/C) + P(A \cap B/C) = P(A/C)$
(c) If A and B are independent, then A and $\bar{B}$ are also independent.
(d) All of these

22. Which of the following is correct?
(a) If A, B and C are mutually independent, then $A \cup B$ and C are also independent.
(b) The events $E_1, E_2, ..., E_n$ are mutually exclusive. Let $E = \bigcup_{i=1}^{n} E_1$.
If $P(A/E_i) = P(B/E_i)$, i = 1, 2, ..., n, then
P (A/E) = P (B/E).
(c) Both (a) and (b)
(d) None of these

23. Let p be the probability that a man aged y will get into an accident in a year. What is the probability that a man among n men of all aged y will get into an accident first ?
(a) $\frac{1}{n}\left(1-(1+p)^n\right)$ (b) $\frac{1}{n}\left(1-(1+p)^n\right)$
(c) $n\left(1-(1+p)^n\right)$ (d) None of these

24. What would be the expectation of the number of failures preceding the first success in an infinite series of independent trials with the constant probability of success p ?
(a) $\frac{1}{p}$ (b) $\frac{1}{q}$
(c) $\frac{q}{p}$ (d) None of these

25. A restaurant serves two special dishes A and B to its customers consisting of 60% men and 40% women. 80% of men order dish A and the rest B and 70% women order dish A and the rest B. In what ratio of A to B should the restaurant prepare the dishes?
(a) 19 : 6 (b) 6 : 9 (c) 16 : 7 (d) 7 : 16

26. If A and B are mutually exclusive and $P(A \cup B) = P(A) + P(B)$, then $P(A/A \cup B) =$
(a) $\frac{P(A)}{P(A)+P(B)}$ (b) $\frac{P(A)}{P(A)-P(B)}$
(c) $\frac{P(B)}{P(A)+P(B)}$ (d) None of these

27. If $P(A) = P(\bar{B})$, then
(a) $A = \bar{B}$ (b) B = 0
(c) $A \neq B$ (d) None of these

28. If P (A) = 0, then
(a) $A = \phi$ (b) A = 0
(c) $A = \infty$ (d) none of these

29. The mean of a set of number is $\bar{x}$. If each number is increased by λ, then mean of the new set is
(a) $\bar{x}$ (b) $\bar{x} + \lambda$
(c) $\lambda\bar{x}$ (d) none of these

30. If each observation of raw data whose variance is σ^2, is increased by λ, then variance of the new set is
(a) σ^2 (b) $\lambda^2\sigma^2$
(c) $\lambda + \sigma^2$ (d) $\lambda^2 + \sigma^2$

31. If μ is mean of distribution, then $\sum f_i(\gamma_i - \mu)$ is equal to
(a) M.D (b) stamdard deviation
(c) 0 (d) none of these

32. $b_{xy} \times b_{yx}$ is equal to

(a) $\rho(X, Y)$ (b) cov (x, y)

(c) $\{\rho(x, y)\}^2$ (d) None of these

33. If cov (X, Y) = 0, then which of the following is negative?

(a) b_{yx} (b) b_{xy}

(c) ρ (X, Y) (d) none of these

34. The mean of a set of observations is $\bar{x}$. If each observation is divided by α, $\alpha \neq 0$ and then is increased by 10, then the mean of new set is

(a) $\frac{\bar{x}}{\alpha}$ (b) $\frac{\bar{x}+10}{\alpha}$

(c) $\frac{\bar{x}+10\alpha}{\alpha}$ (d) $\alpha\bar{x}+10$

35. S.D. of n observation $a_1, a_2, a_3, \ldots\ldots\ldots a_n$ is σ, then If S.D. of the observations $\lambda a_1, \lambda a_2, \lambda a_3, \ldots\ldots \lambda a_n$ is

(a) $\lambda\sigma$ (b) $-\lambda\sigma$

(c) $|\lambda|\sigma$ (d) σ

36. If two lines of regression are Y = $3x - 5$ and Y = $2x - 4$, then ρ(X, Y) is equal to

(a) $\sqrt{\frac{2}{3}}$ (b) $\sqrt{\frac{1}{6}}$

(c) $\sqrt{\frac{3}{2}}$ (d) none of these

37. If two lines regression are $3x - y - 5 = 0$ and $2x - y - 4 = 0$, then $\bar{x}$ and $\bar{y}$ are respectively

(a) 1 and –2 (b) –1 and 2

(c) 2 and –1 (d) –2 and –1

38. If regression equation of Y on X is Y = $\lambda x + 4$ and that of X on Y be $4x$ = Y – 5, then

(a) $0 < 4\lambda \leq 1$ (b) $0 \leq \lambda \leq 1$

(c) $0 \leq \lambda \leq 4$ (d) none of these

39. If cov (X,Y) = 0, then two lines of the regression are

(a) parallel (b) concident

(c) at right angles (d) none of these

40. If in a regression analysis problem, $b_{yx} = -0.9$ and $b_{xy} = 0.4$, then $\rho(x, y)$ is

(a) 0.6 (b) –0.6

(c) 0 (d) none of these

41. It b_{xy} and b_{yx} be the two regression coefficients, then coefficient of correlation ρ is given by

(a) $\rho = \sqrt{b_{xy}b_{yx}}$

(b) $\rho = -\sqrt{b_{yx}b_{yx}}$

(c) $\rho = \left(S_{gn}\, b_{yx}\right)\sqrt{b_{xy}b_{yx}}$

(d) none of these

42. It standard deviation for two variables X and Y are 3 and 4 respectively and their covariance is 8, then correlation coefficient between them is

(a) $\frac{2}{3}$ (b) $\frac{8}{3\sqrt{2}}$ (c) $\frac{9}{8\sqrt{2}}$ (d) $\frac{2}{9}$

43. Mean deviation of the data $a, a+d, a+2d, \ldots a+2nd$ from the mean is equal to

(a) $\frac{n(n+1)|d|}{2n+1}$ (b) $\frac{n(n+1)d}{2n+1}$

(c) $\frac{(n+1)|d|}{2n}$ (d) none of these

44. If two variables X and Y have a perfect correlation (direct or indirect), then they may be connected by a relation of the type

(a) $xy = a^2$ (b) $\frac{a}{x}+\frac{b}{y}=1$

(c) $\frac{x}{a}+\frac{y}{b}=1$ (d) none of these

45. If $\rho > 0$ and $m = \frac{b_{yx}+b_{xy}}{2}$, then

(a) $m \geq \rho$ (b) $m = \rho$

(c) $m \leq \rho$ (d) none of these

46. If two lines of regression are $x + 2y = 7$ and $2x + y = 7$, then regression equation of Y and X is

(a) $2x + y = 7$ (b) $x + 2y = 7$

(c) $x + 2y = 0$ (d) $2x + y = 0$

47. Two variables X and Y are connected by the relation $ax + by + c = 0$ where $ab < 0$, then $\rho(x, y)$ is equal to

(a) $\frac{a}{b}$ (b) $\frac{b}{a}$ (c) –1 (d) 1

48. Mean of the numbers 0, 1, 2, 3, ...n with respective weight $^nC_0$, $^nC_1$, $^nC_2$,......, ^nC_n is

(a) $\frac{2^n}{n+1}$ (b) $\frac{2^{n+1}}{n+1}$

(c) $\frac{n}{2}$ (d) none of these

NUMERICAL TYPE QUESTIONS

1. A card is taken out of a pack of 52 cards numbered 2 to 53. The probability that the numbers on the card is a prime number less than 20 is _______
2. The probability of getting a number between 1 and 100. Which is divisible by one and itself only is _______
3. If A and B are two elements such that $P(A) = \frac{2}{3}$, $P(B) = \frac{3}{4}$, $P(A \cap B) = \frac{1}{2}$, then $P(A \cup B)$ is _______

4. If A and B are two events such that $P(A \cup B) = 0.65$, $P(A \cap B) = 0.15$, then $P(\bar{A}) + P(\bar{B})$ is ________

5. There are two bags one of which contains 3 black and 4 white balls while other contains 4 black and 3 white balls. A die is cast, if the face 1 or 3 turns up, a ball is taken from first bag and if any other face turns up, a ball is chosen from second bag. The probability of choosing of black ball is________

6. An urn contains 5 red and 10 black balls. Eight of them are placed in another urn. The chance that the latter then contains 2 red and 6 black balls is________

7. The chance that a leap year selected at random will contain 53 Sundays is ________

8. A five figure number is formed by the digits 0, 1, 2, 3, 4 without repetition. Then the probability that the number formed is divisible by 4 is____

9. A man alternately tosses a coin and throws a dice, beginning with the coin. Then the probability that he will get a head before he gets a 5 or 6 on dice is________

10. A box A contains 2 white and 4 black balls. Another box B contains 5 white and 7 black balls. A ball is transferred from the box A to the box B. Then a ball is drawn from the box B. The probability that it is white is________

11. A problem in mechanics is given to three students A, B and C whose chances of slogging it are $\frac{1}{2}$, $\frac{1}{3}$ and $\frac{1}{4}$ respectively. Then probability that the problem will be solved is______

12. A and B throw alternately with a pair of dice. A wins if he throws 6 before B throws 7 and B wins if he throws 7 before A throws 6. If A begins, then his chance of winning is ________

13. If mode of a data is 18 and mean is 24, then median is ________

14. Regression equation of Y on X is

$$8x - 10y + 66 = 0 \text{ and } \sigma_x = 3$$

Hence cov (X, Y) is equal to ________

15. Coefficient of correlation between two variates X and Y is ________

X	1	2	3	4	5
Y	5	4	3	2	1

16. If mean = (3 median – mode) x, then value of x is________

17. If median = (mode + 2 mean) μ, then μ is equal to________

18. If two lines of regression are at right angles, then ρ (X, Y) is equal to ________

19. Given : $n = 10$, $\Sigma x = 4$, $\Sigma y = 3$, $\Sigma x^2 = 8$, $\Sigma y^2 = 9$ and $\Sigma xy = 3$, then coefficient of correlation is ______

20. 25% of the items of data are less than 35 and 25% of the items are more than 75. Q.D of the data is________

21. If X and Y are two independent variables such that $\bar{x} = 5$, $\bar{y} = 10$ $\sigma_x^2 = 4$ $\sigma_y^2 = 9$ and if $u = 3x + 4y$, $v = 3x - y$, then $\rho(u, v)$ is equal to ________

ANSWERS

MCQ Type Questions

1. (c)	2. (c)	3. (b)	4. (c)	5. (a)	6. (a)	7. (a)	8. (a)	9. (a)	10. (b)
11. (a)	12. (a)	13. (b)	14. (d)	15. (a)	16. (a)	17. (d)	18. (c)	19. (c)	20. (d)
21. (a)	22. (a)	23. (a)	24. (c)	25. (a)	26. (a)	27. (a)	28. (a)	29. (b)	30. (b)
31. (c)	32. (c)	33. (d)	34. (c)	35. (c)	36. (a)	37. (a)	38. (c)	39. (c)	40. (d)
41. (c)	42. (a)	43. (a)	44. (c)	45. (a)	46. (b)	47. (d)	48. (c)		

Numerical Type Questions

1. $\frac{2}{13}$	2. $\frac{25}{98}$	3. $\frac{11}{12}$	4. 1.2	5. $\frac{11}{21}$	6. $\frac{140}{429}$	7. $\frac{2}{7}$	8. $\frac{5}{16}$	9. $\frac{3}{4}$
10. $\frac{16}{39}$	11. $\frac{3}{4}$	12. $\frac{30}{61}$	13. 22	14. 7.2	15. –1	16. $\frac{1}{2}$	17. $\frac{1}{3}$	18. 0
19. $\frac{1}{4}$	20. 50	21. 0						

EXPLANATIONS

MCQ TYPE QUESTIONS

5. Since odds are 8 to 3 against A

$\therefore \quad P(A) = \frac{3}{11}; \quad (P(B) = \frac{2}{7})$

since odds are 5 to 2 aganist B

and $\quad P(A) + P(B) + P(C) = 1$

$\therefore \quad P(C) = \frac{1}{1} - \frac{3}{11} - \frac{2}{7} = \frac{34}{77}$

Hence odds against C are 43 to 34.

6. A can draw a ticket in ${}^3C_1 = 3$ ways.
Number of cases in which A can get a prize is clearly 1.

$\therefore \quad$ Probability of A's success $= \frac{1}{3}$.

Again B can draw a ticket in ${}^9C_3 = \frac{9\times8\times7}{3\times2\times1}$
$= 84$ way.

Number of ways in which B gets all blanks

$= {}^6C_3 = \frac{6\times5\times4}{3\times2\times1} = 20.$

$\therefore \quad$ Number of ways of getting a prize
$= 84 - 20 = 64$

Thus, probability of B's success $= \frac{64}{84} = \frac{16}{21}$

$\therefore \quad$ A's probability of success : B's probability of success

$= \frac{1}{3} : \frac{16}{21} = 7 : 16$

7. $P(A\cap\overline{B}) = P(A) - P(A\cap B)$
$= P(A) - P(A)\,P(B)$
$= P(A)\,(1 - P(B)) = P(A)\,P(\overline{B})$

Hence, A and $\overline{B}$ are independent.

8. $A\cap B = \phi$

$\therefore \quad P(A\cap B) = 0$

10. $S = \{0, 1, 2, ..., 9\}$

Suppose we want a particular integer "3" to be chosen.

Probability of not choosing "3" is $\frac{9}{10}$ (in one chance)

Probability of not choosing 3 in all the three chances

$= \frac{9}{10}\times\frac{9}{10}\times\frac{9}{10}$

Hence probability of choosing it in at least one of the three chances

$= 1 - \frac{27}{1000} = \frac{973}{1000}$

11. $\frac{P(A\cap C)}{P(C)} > \frac{P(B\cap C)}{P(C)}$

$\Rightarrow \quad P(A\cap C) > P(B\cap C)$

and $\quad \frac{P(A\cap\overline{C})}{P(\overline{C})} > \frac{P(B\cap\overline{C})}{P(\overline{C})}$

$\Rightarrow \quad P(A\cap\overline{C}) > P(B\cap\overline{C})$

Adding

$P(A\cap C) + P(A\cap\overline{C}) > P(B\cap C) + P(B\cap\overline{C})$

$P(A) > P(B)$ since $(A\cap C)$ and $A\cap\overline{C}$ are disjoint.

12. $P(C) = 0$

$\Rightarrow \quad C = \phi$

$P(A\cap B\cap C) = P(A\cap B\cap\phi)$
$= P(\phi) = 0$

$P(A)\times P(B)\times P(C) = 0 \quad$ ... since $P(C) = 0$

$\therefore \quad P(A\cap B\cap C) = P(A) - P(B) - P(C)$

Hence A, B, C are independent.

13. Number of ways different numbers can occur on six dice = 6!

Total number of ways of occurrence $= 6^5$

$\therefore \quad$ Required probability, $\quad P = \frac{6!}{6^5} = \frac{5!}{6^4}$

14. $P(A) = \frac{1}{4}$

and $\quad P(B/A) = \frac{P(B\cap A)}{P(A)} = \frac{1}{2}$

$\Rightarrow \quad P(A\cap B) = \frac{1}{8},\ P(A/B) = \frac{1}{4}$

$\Rightarrow \quad \frac{P(A\cap B)}{P(B)} = \frac{1}{4} \Rightarrow P(B) = \frac{1}{2}$

(a) If A is a sub-event of B, $A\subset B$, then $A\cap B = A$
$\therefore$ $P(A\cap B)$ should be equal to $P(A)$. This is false.

(b) $\quad P(A/B) = \frac{3}{4}$ is false.

(c) $P(A\cap\overline{B}) = P(A) - P(A\cap B) = \frac{1}{4} - \frac{1}{8} = \frac{1}{8}$

$\therefore \quad P(A/\overline{B}) = \frac{P(A\cap\overline{B})}{P(\overline{B})} = \frac{\frac{1}{8}}{1-\frac{1}{2}} = \frac{1}{4}$

$\therefore \quad P(A/B) + P(A/\overline{B}) = \frac{1}{4} + \frac{1}{4} = \frac{1}{2}$

Hence given statement is false.

15. $P(A) = 0$

$\Rightarrow$ $A = \phi$

$\therefore$ $A \cap B = \phi$

$\therefore$ $P(A \cap B) = P(\phi) = 0$

17. $(A \cup B) \supset A$

(*a*) $P(A \cup B) \geq P(A) = \dfrac{3}{4}$

(*b*) $A \cap B \subset B$

$\therefore$ $P(A \cap B) \leq P(B) = \dfrac{5}{8}$

Also $P(A \cap B) = 1 - P(A \cap B)^c$
$= 1 - P(A^c \cup B^c)$
$> 1 - \{P(A^c) + P(B^c)\}$
$= 1 - \left\{\dfrac{1}{4} + \dfrac{3}{8}\right\} = \dfrac{3}{8}$

(*c*) $A \cap \overline{B} \subset \overline{B}$

$\therefore P(A \cap \overline{B}) \leq P(\overline{B}) = \dfrac{3}{8}$

Also $A \cap \overline{B} = (\overline{\overline{A} \cup B})$

$\therefore P(A \cap \overline{B}) = 1 - P(\overline{A} \cup B) \geq 1 - \{P(\overline{A}) + P(B)\}$

$= 1 - \left\{\dfrac{1}{4} + \dfrac{5}{8}\right\} = \dfrac{1}{8}$

18. Let the event of drawing a faulty item from any of the machines be A, and the event that an item drawn at random was produced by M_i be B_i. To $P(B_i/A)$ proceed as follows :

	M_1	M_2	M_3	Remarks
$P(B_i)$	0.25	0.30	0.45	$\because$ sum = 1
$P(A/B_i)$	0.05	0.04	0.03	
$P(B_i)P(A/B_i)$	0.0125	0.012	0.0135	sum = 0.38
$P(B_i/A)$	$\dfrac{0.0125}{0.038}$	$\dfrac{0.0125}{0.038}$	$\dfrac{0.0135}{0.038}$	By Baye's theorem

The highest output being from M_3, required probability $= \dfrac{0\cdot0135}{0\cdot038} = 0.355$.

19. Sample space, $S = \{HHHH, HHHT, HHTH, HHTT, \ldots, TTTT\}$

Clearly, $|S| = 2^4 = 16.$

20. (*a*) $B = (A \cap B) \cup (\overline{A} \cap B)$

$\Rightarrow$ $P(B) = P(A \cap B) + P(\overline{A} \cap B)$ as $A \cap B$ and $\overline{A} \cap B$ are mutually exclusive.

$\Rightarrow$ $P(\overline{A} \cap B) = P(B) - P(A \cap B)$.

(*b*) $P(A \cup B) = P[A \cup (\overline{A} \cap B)]$
$= P(A) + P(\overline{A} \cap B)$
$= P(A) + P(B) - P(A \cap B)$

(*c*) $P(A/B) = P(A)\,P(B/A)$
$\leq P(A)$ as $P(B/A) \leq 1$.

21. (*a*) $P(A \cup B) = P(A) + P(B) - P(A \cap B)$

$\therefore$ $P((A \cap C) \cup (B \cap C)) = P(A \cap C) + P(B \cap C) - P(A \cap C \cap B \cap C)$

and $P((A \cup B) \cap C) = P(A \cap C) + P(B \cap C) - P(A \cap B \cap C)$

$\Rightarrow$ $\dfrac{P((A \cup B) \cap C)}{P(C)} = \dfrac{P(A \cap C)}{P(C)} + \dfrac{P(B \cap C)}{P(C)} \;\; \dfrac{P(A \cap B \cap C)}{P(C)}$

$\Rightarrow P(A \cup B/C) = P(A/C) + P(B/C) - P(A \cap B/C)$

(*b*) $P\left(A \cap \overline{B}/C\right) + P(A \cap B/C)$

$= \dfrac{P(A \cap \overline{B} \cap C)}{P(C)} + \dfrac{P(A \cap B \cap C)}{P(C)}$

$= \dfrac{P(A \cap \overline{B} \cap C) + P(A \cap B \cap C)}{P(C)}$

$= \dfrac{P(A \cap \overline{B} \cap C) \cup (A \cap B \cap C)}{P(C)}$

$= \dfrac{P(A \cap C)}{P(C)} = \mathbf{P(A/C)}$

(*c*) $P(A \cap \overline{B})$
$= P(A) - P(A \cap B) = P(A) - P(A)\,P(B)$
$= P(A)(1 - P(B)) = P(A)\,P(\overline{B})$

Hence A and $\overline{B}$ are independent.

22. (*a*) $P((A \cup B) \cap C) = P((A \cap C) \cup (B \cap C))$
$= P(A \cap C) + P(B \cap C) - P(A \cap B \cap C)$
$= P(A)\,P(C) + P(B)\,P(C) - P(A)\,P(B)\,P(C)$
$= P(C)\,(P(A) + P(B) - P(A \cap B))$
$= P(C)\,P(A \cup B)$

(*b*) $P(A/E) = P(B/E)$

$\dfrac{P(A \cap E)}{P(E)} = \dfrac{P(B \cap E)}{P(E)}$

if $P(A \cap E) = P(B \cap E)$

if $P\left(A \cap \bigcup_{i=1}^{n} E_i\right) = P\left(B \cap \bigcup_{i=1}^{n} E_i\right)$

if $P \bigcup_{i=1}^{n} (A \cap E_i) = P\left(\bigcup_{i=1}^{n} (B \cap E_i)\right)$

$\sum_{i=1}^{n} P(A \cap E_i) = \sum_{i=1}^{n} P(B \cap E_i)$

This is true since $P(A \cap E_i) = P(B \cap E_i)$ for each i.

23. Let E_i be the event of a person to get into an accident. Then

$$P(E_i) = p \ \forall \ i$$

P (at least one man meet with an accident)

$$= P(E_1 \cup E_2 \cup \ldots \cup E_n)$$
$$= 1 - P(\overline{E}_1 \cup \overline{E}_2 \cup \ldots \cup \overline{E}_n)$$
$$= 1 - P(\overline{E}_1 \cap \overline{E}_2 \cap \ldots \cap \overline{E}_n)$$
$$= 1 - P(\overline{E}_1)\,P(\overline{E}_2) \ldots P(\overline{E}_n)$$
$$= 1 - (1-p)(1-p) \ldots (1-p)$$
$$= 1 - (1-p)^n$$

Hence P (at least one man meets with an accident/a person is chosen) $= \frac{1}{n}(1-(1-p)^n)$.

24. Expectation of X = E(X) = average = mean

$$= \frac{1}{n}\sum_{i=1}^{n} X_i$$

$$= \sum_{i=1}^{n} p_i x_i$$

where p_i denote probability of occurrence of x_i.

Let $q = 1 - p$.

Then probabilities of success in 1st, 2nd, 3rd trials are

$$p, qp, q^2p, \ldots..$$

$$\therefore \quad E(X) = (0)\cdot p + (1)\cdot qp + (2)\cdot q^2 p + \ldots$$
$$= qp\,(1 + 2q + 3q^2 + \ldots + nq^{\,n+1} + \ldots)$$
$$= \frac{qp}{(1-q)^2} = \frac{qp}{p^2} = \frac{q}{p}$$

25. Ratio of A and B

$$= 60 \times 80 + 40 \times 70 : 60 \times 20 + 40 \times 30$$
$$= 76 : 24 = \mathbf{19 : 6}$$

26. $$P(A/A \cup B) = \frac{P(A \cap (A \cup B))}{P(A \cup B)}$$
$$= \frac{P(A)}{P(A \cup B)} = \frac{P(A)}{P(A) + P(B)}$$

27. $$P(A) = P(\overline{B})$$

$\Rightarrow \quad P(A) = 1 - P(B) \quad \Rightarrow \quad P(A) + P(B) = 1$

$\Rightarrow \quad P(A \cup B) - P(A \cap B) = 1 = P(S)$

Hence $\quad A \cup B = S$ only if $A \cap B = \phi$

i.e. $\quad A = \overline{B}$ only if $A \cap B = \phi$

28. $$P(A) = 0$$

$$\Rightarrow P\left(\frac{A}{S}\right) = 0 \Rightarrow \frac{n(A)}{n(S)} = 0 \Rightarrow n(A) = 0$$

$\Rightarrow \quad A = \phi$

29. When each item is increased by λ, the mean is also increased by λ.

30. When each item is increased by λ, the S.D. is multiplied by $|\lambda|$ and variance is multiplied by λ^2.

31. $\Sigma f_i\,(y_i - \mu) = f_i\,y_i - M\,\Sigma f_i = \Sigma f_i\,y_i - \Sigma f_i\,Y_i = 0$

32. $$b_{yx}\,b_{xy} = \frac{\text{cov}(X,Y)}{\sigma_x^{\,2}}\,\frac{\text{cov}(X,Y)}{\sigma_y^{\,2}}$$

$$= \left\{\frac{\text{cov}(X,Y)}{\sigma_x \sigma_y}\right\}^2 = \{\rho\,X, Y\}^2$$

33. Cov (X, Y), b_{xy}, b_{xy} and ρ(X, Y) all are either positive, or 0 or negative simultaneously.

34. When each item is divided by α, *i.e.* it becomes $\frac{-}{\alpha}$

When each item is increased by 10, mean also increased by 10.

$$\therefore \quad \text{New mean} = \frac{-}{\alpha} + u = \frac{\ \ +10\alpha}{\alpha}$$

35. Standard Deviation of new data

$$= \sqrt{\frac{\Sigma(\lambda a_1)^2}{n} - \left(\frac{\Sigma \lambda a_i}{n}\right)^2} = \sqrt{\lambda^2}\,\sqrt{\frac{\Sigma\,a_1^{\,2}}{n} - \left(\frac{\Sigma a_i}{n}\right)^2} = |\lambda|\sigma$$

36. If we take $y = 3x - 5$ as regression equation of Y on X and $Y = 2x - 4$ as that of X on Y, then

$$b_{yx} = 3\,b_{xy} = \frac{1}{2}$$

$$\Rightarrow \ b_{yx}\,b_{xy} = \frac{3}{2}, \text{ which is not possible.}$$

Hence, equation $y = 3x - 5$, *i.e.* $x = \frac{1}{3}y + \frac{5}{3}$ is the regression equation of X on Y and equation, $\quad Y = 2x - 4$ is that Y on X.

Then $\quad b_{yx} = 2$ and $b_{xy} = \frac{1}{3}$

$$\Rightarrow \ b_{xy}\,b_{xy} = \frac{3}{2}$$

$$\Rightarrow \ \{\rho\,(X, Y)\}^2 = \frac{3}{2}$$

$$\Rightarrow \rho(XY) = \sqrt{\frac{2}{3}}$$

37. Solving equations

$3x - y - 5 = 0$ and $2x - y - 4 = 0$,

we get $\quad x = 1$ and $y = -2$.

38. Here $b_{yx} = \lambda$ and $b_{xy} = \frac{1}{4}$.

Since $0 \le b_{yx}\,b_{xy} \le 1$, therefore we must have

$$0 \le \lambda\left(\frac{1}{4}\right) \le 1 \quad \Rightarrow \quad 0 \le \lambda \le 4$$

As $\ b_{xy} \ne 0, \quad \therefore \ b_{yx} \ne 0 \quad \Rightarrow \lambda \ne 0.$

Hence, we must have $\ 0 < \lambda \le 4$.

39. $\text{Cov}(X, Y) = 0 \Rightarrow b_{yx} = b_{xy} = 0$

So, two lines of regression are $y - \bar{y} = 0$ and $x - \bar{x} = 0$, which are at right angles.

40. Given : $b_{yx} = -0.9$ is negative and $b_{xy} = 0.4$ is positive which is not possible as b_{yx} and b_{xy} are always of same sign. Hence given data is inconsistent.

41. We know $b_{yx}\, b_{xy} = \rho^2 \Rightarrow \rho = \pm\sqrt{b_{yx}\, b_{xy}}$

But b_{yx} and b_{xy} ρ and cov (X, Y) are all of the same sign

$$\therefore \quad \rho = (\text{sgn}\, b_{yx})\sqrt{b_{yx}\, b_{xy}}$$

42. $\rho(X, Y) = \dfrac{\text{cov}(X, Y)}{\sigma_x \sigma_y} = \dfrac{8}{3 \times 4} = \dfrac{2}{3}$

43. Mean, $\bar{x} = \dfrac{a + (a + d) + (a + 2d) + ... + (a + 2nd)}{2n + 1}$

$$= \frac{2n+1}{2}\{a + (a + (a + 2nd))\} = a + nd$$

Sum of numerical deviations from the mean

$$= \sum_{i=1}^{2n+1} |\{a + (i-1)d\} - \{a + nd\}|$$

$$= |a - a - nd| + |a + d - a - nd| + ... + |a + nd - a - nd| + |a + (n + 1)\, d - a - nd| + ... + |a + 2nd - a - nd|$$

$$= |d|\{n + (n - 1) + (n - 2) + ... + 1 + 0 + 1 + 2 + ... + n\}$$

$$= |d| \times 2\{1 + 2 + 3 + ... + n\} = n(n + 1)|d|$$

$$\therefore \quad \text{M.D. (about mean)} = \frac{n(n+1)|d|}{2n+1}$$

44. If two variables X and Y are in perfect correlation (direct or indirect), then there is a linear relationship between the two variables.

45. Since $\rho > 0$, therefore b_{yx} and b_{xy} are also positive

Hence $\dfrac{b_{yx} + b_{xy}}{2} \geq \sqrt{b_{yx}\, b_{xy}}$

$$\Rightarrow \frac{b_{yx} + b_{xy}}{2} \geq \sqrt{\rho^2}$$

$$\Rightarrow \frac{b_{yx} + b_{xy}}{2} \geq \rho \Rightarrow m \geq \rho$$

46. If first time $x + 2y = 7$ is taken as regression equation of Y on X, then we write it as

$$y = -\frac{1}{2}x + \frac{7}{2} \Rightarrow b_{yx} = -\frac{1}{2}$$

Also the second equation (which will be regression equation X on Y) can be written as

$$x = -\frac{1}{2}y + \frac{7}{2} \Rightarrow b_{xy} = -\frac{1}{2}$$

$$\therefore \quad b_{yx}\, b_{xy} = \left(\frac{-1}{2}\right)\left(\frac{-1}{2}\right) = \frac{1}{4} \leq 1$$

Hence regression equation of Y on X is

$$x + 2y = 7$$

47. Since X and Y connected by linear relationship, therefore they are in perfect correlation.

Also $ab < 0$

$$\frac{a}{b} < 0.$$

$\therefore\ y = \left(-\dfrac{a}{b}\right)x - \dfrac{c}{b}$ shows that when x increases, y also increases; so X and Y are in perfect direct correlation

$$\Rightarrow \quad \rho(X, Y) = 1.$$

48. Required mean

$$= \frac{0^n C_0 + 1^n C_1 + 2^n C_2 + ... + n^n C_n}{{}^n C_0 + {}^n C_1 + {}^n C_2 + ... + {}^n C_n} = \frac{n 2^{n-1}}{2^n}$$

$$= \frac{n}{2} \quad (\because C_1 + 2C_2 + 3C_3 + ... nC_n = n2^{n-1})$$

NUMERICAL TYPE QUESTIONS

5. Let E_1 be the event that a ball is drawn from first bag, E_2 the event that a ball is drawn from second bag and E the event a black ball is chosen, therefore

$$P(E) = P(E_1)\, P\left(\frac{E}{E_1}\right) + P(E_2)\, P\left(\frac{E}{E_2}\right)$$

$$= \frac{2}{6} \times \frac{3}{7} + \frac{4}{6} \times \frac{4}{7} = \frac{11}{21}$$

6. Number of ways in which 8 balls can be drawn out of 15 is ${}^{15}C_8$.

Number of ways of drawing 2 red balls is ${}^5C_2$ and corresponding to each of these ${}^5C_2$ ways of drawing a red ball, there are ${}^{10}C_6$ ways of drawing 6 black balls.

Hence total number of ways in which 2 red and 6 black balls can be drawn $= {}^5C_2 \times {}^{10}C_6$.

$$\therefore \quad \text{Required probability} = \frac{{}^5C_2 \times {}^{10}C_6}{{}^{15}C_8}$$

$$= \frac{140}{429}$$

7. A leap year consists of 366 days, so that there are 52 full weeks (and hence 52 Sundays) and two extra days. These two days can be

(i) Monday, Tuesday
(ii) Tuesday, Wednesday,
(iii) Wednesday, Thursday
(iv) Thursday, Friday
(v) Friday, Saturday

(vi) Saturday, Sunday
(vii) Sunday, Monday
Of these 7 cases, the last two are favourable

$\therefore$ Required probability $= \frac{2}{7}$.

8. The five digits can be arranged in 5! ways, out of which 4! will begin with zero.

$\therefore$ Total number of 5-figure numbers formed $= 5! - 4! = 96$.

Those numbers formed will be divisible by 4 which will have two extreme right digits divisible by 4,

i.e., numbers ending in 04, 12, 20, 24, 32, 40.

Now, numbers ending in 04 = 3! = 6,
numbers ending in 12 = 3! – 2! = 4,
numbers ending in 20 = 3! = 6,
numbers ending in 24 = 3! – 2! = 4,
numbers ending in 32 = 3! – 2! = 4,
andnumbers ending in 40 = 3! = 6.

[Numbers having 12, 24, 32 in the extreme right are (3! – 2!), since the numbers having zero on the extreme left are to excluded.]

$\therefore$ Total number of favourable ways $= 6 + 4 + 6 + 4 + 4 + 6 = 30$

Hence, required probability $= \frac{30}{96} = \frac{5}{16}$.

9. $P(H) = \frac{1}{2}$, $P(T) = \frac{1}{2}$

Let A be the event of getting 5 or 6.

$\therefore$ $P(A) = \frac{1}{3}$ and B be the event of getting 1, 2, 3, 4;

$\therefore$ $P(B) = \frac{2}{3}$

In order to get a 'Head' before "5 or 6", the following events have to occur:

H, TBH, TBTBH, TBTBTBH, ...

$$\therefore \quad P = \frac{1}{2}+\frac{1}{2}\times\frac{2}{3}\times\frac{1}{2}+\left(\frac{1}{3}\right)^2\cdot\frac{1}{2}+\left(\frac{1}{3}\right)^3\cdot\frac{1}{2}$$

$$= \frac{\frac{1}{2}}{1-\frac{1}{3}} = \frac{3}{4}$$

10. Probability of drawing a white ball from box B will depend on whether transferred ball is black or white.

If a black ball is transferred, then its probability is $\frac{4}{6}$.

There are now 5 white and 8 black balls in the box B. Then probability of drawing white ball from box $B = \frac{5}{13}$

Hence probability of drawing a white ball from urn B, if the transferred ball is black

$$= \frac{4}{6}\times\frac{5}{13} = \frac{10}{39}$$

Similarly, probability of drawing a white ball from urn B, if transferred ball is white

$$= \frac{2}{6}\times\frac{6}{13} = \frac{2}{13}.$$

$$\therefore \quad \text{Required probability} = \frac{10}{39}+\frac{2}{13} = \frac{16}{39}$$

12. The sum 6 can be obtained as follows :
(1, 5), (2, 4), (3, 3), (4, 2), (5, 1), *i.e.* in 5 ways.

Probability of A's throwing 6 with 2 dice $= \frac{5}{36}$

$\therefore$ Probability of A's not throwing 6 $= \frac{31}{36}$

Similarly, probability of B's throwing 7 $= \frac{6}{36}$, i.e. $\frac{1}{6}$

$\therefore$ Probability of B's not throwing 7 $= \frac{5}{6}$

Now A can win, if he throws 6 in the first, third, fifth, seventh etc. throws.

$\therefore$ Chance of A's winning

$$= \frac{5}{36}+\frac{31}{36}\times\frac{5}{6}\times\frac{5}{36}+\frac{31}{36}\times\frac{5}{6}\times\frac{31}{36}\times\frac{5}{6}\times\frac{5}{36}+\ldots$$

$$= \frac{5}{36}\times\left[1+\left(\frac{31}{36}\times\frac{5}{6}\right)+\left(\frac{31}{36}\times\frac{5}{6}\right)^2+\left(\frac{31}{36}\times\frac{5}{6}\right)^3+\ldots\right]$$

$$= \frac{5}{36}\times\frac{1}{1-(31/36)\times(5/6)} = \frac{5}{36}\times\frac{36\times6}{61} = \frac{30}{61}$$

13. $18 = 3$ Median -2×24

14. Given regression limit is

$$8x - 10y + 66 = 0$$

$$\Rightarrow \quad y = \frac{8}{10}x+\frac{66}{10} = \frac{4}{5}x+\frac{33}{5}$$

Hence $\quad b_{yx} = \frac{4}{5}$

$$\Rightarrow \quad \frac{\text{cov}(X,Y)}{\sigma_x^2} = \frac{4}{5}$$

$$\Rightarrow \quad \text{cov}(X, Y) = \frac{9\times4}{5}$$

15. Since, $x + y = 6$ for all the pairs of observations,

$$\therefore \quad b_{xy} = b_{yx} = -1$$

$$\Rightarrow \quad \rho(X, Y) = -1$$

16. Mode = 3 Median – 2 Mean

$$\Rightarrow \quad \text{Mean} = \frac{3}{2}\text{Median}-\frac{1}{2}\text{Mode}$$

$$= \frac{1}{2}(3\,\text{Median}-\text{Mode})$$

17. Mode= 3 Median – 2 Mean

$\Rightarrow$ 3 Median= Mode + 2 Mean

$\Rightarrow$ Median= $\frac{1}{3}$ (Mode + 2 Mean)

$\Rightarrow$ M = $\frac{1}{3}$

18. The two lines of regression are at right angles only when

$$b_{yx}\left(\frac{1}{b_{xy}}\right) = -1 \Rightarrow b_{yx} = -b_{xy}$$

But both b_{yx} and b_{xy} are of same sign, therefore we must have

$$b_{yx} = b_{xy} = 0 \Rightarrow \rho(X, Y) = 0$$

19.
$$\rho(X, Y) = \frac{\Sigma xy - \frac{1}{n}\Sigma x \Sigma y}{\sqrt{\Sigma x^2 - \frac{1}{n}(\Sigma x)^2}\sqrt{\Sigma y^2 - \frac{1}{n}(\Sigma y)^2}}$$

$$= \frac{3 - \frac{1}{10}\times 4\times 3}{\sqrt{\left\{8 - \frac{1}{10}(4)^2\right\}\times\left\{9 - \frac{1}{10}(3)^2\right\}}} = \frac{1}{4}$$

20. Given : Lower quartile, $Q_1 = 35$

Upper quartile $Q_3 = 75$.

$\therefore$ Quartile deviation $= \frac{Q_3 - Q_1}{2} = \frac{75 - 35}{2} = 20$

21. Here, $\bar{u} = 3\bar{x} + 4\bar{y}$ and $\bar{v} = 3\bar{x} - \bar{y}$

$$u - \bar{u} = 3(x - \bar{x}) + 4(y - \bar{y})$$
$$v - \bar{v} = 3(x - \bar{x}) - (y - \bar{y})$$

$$\Rightarrow \text{cov}(u, v) = \frac{1}{n}\Sigma(u - \bar{u})(v - \bar{v})$$

$$= \frac{1}{n}\Sigma\{9(x - \bar{x})^2 - 4(y - \bar{y})^2 + 9(x - \bar{x})(y - \bar{y})\}$$

$$= 9\left(\frac{\Sigma(x - \bar{x})^2}{n}\right) - 4\left(\frac{\Sigma(y - \bar{y})^2}{n}\right) + 9\left(\frac{\Sigma(x - \bar{x})(y - \bar{y})}{n}\right)$$

$$= 9\,\sigma_x^2 - 4\,\sigma_y^2 + 9\ \text{cov.}\ (x, y)$$
$$= 9 \times 4 - 4 \times 9 + 9(0) = 0$$

{since X, Y are independent, therefore cov (X, Y) = 0}

$$\Rightarrow \rho(u, v) = \frac{\text{cov}(u, v)}{\sigma_u \sigma_v} = 0$$

■■

5

CHAPTER

Numerical Methods

ALGEBRAIC EQUATIONS

An equation of type $y = f(x)$ is said to be algebraic if it can be expressed in the form

$$f_n y_n + f_{n-1} y_{n-1} + \dots + f_1 y_1 + f_0 = 0$$

where f_1 is an ith order polynomial in x.

This equation can be thought of as having a general form

$$f(x, y) = 0$$

This implies that above equation portrays a dependence between the variables x and y.

e.g. $3x + 5y - 21 = 0$ (linear)

$2x + 3xy - 25 = 0$ (non-linear)

$x^3 - xy - 3y^3 = 0$ (non-linear)

These equations have an infinite number of pairs of values of x and y which satisfy them.

POLYNOMIAL EQUATIONS

Polynomial equations are a simple class of algebraic equations that are represented as follows:

$$a_n x^n + a_{n-1} x^{n-1} + \dots + a_1 x + a_0 = 0$$

This is called ***n*th degree polynomial** and has n roots. The roots may be

(*i*) real and different

(*ii*) real and repeated

(*iii*) complex numbers

Since complex roots appear in pairs, if n is odd, then polynomial has at least one real root.

e.g. a cubic equation of the type $a_3x^3 + a_2x^2 + a_1x + a_0 = 0$ will have at least one real root and the remaining two may be real or complex roots.

Specific examples of polynomial equations:

(*i*) $5x^5 - x^3 + 3x^2 = 0$

(*ii*) $x^3 - 4x^2 + x + 6 = 0$

(*iii*) $x^2 - 4x + 4 = 0$

TRANSCENDENTAL EQUATIONS

A non-algebraic equation is called *transcendental equation.* These include trigonometric, exponential and logarithmic functions.

e.g. $2 \sin x - x = 0,\ e^x \sin x - \frac{1}{2x} = 0, \log x^2 - 1 = 0,\ x - e^{1/x} = 0$

A transcendental equation may have finite or infinite number of real roots or may not have real root at all.

METHODS OF SOLVING NON-LINEAR EQUATIONS

(1) Direct Analytical Methods

In certain cases, roots can be found by using direct analytical methods.

e.g. consider a quadratic equation $ax^2 + bx + c = 0$

Solution of this equation is

$$x = \frac{-b \pm \sqrt{b^2 - 4ac}}{2a} \text{ (x: gives roots of equation)}$$

This equation gives the two roots of quadratic equation. However, there are equations that cannot be solved by analytical methods.

e.g. simple transcendental equation

$$2 \sin x - x = 0$$

cannot be solved analytically. Direct methods for solving non-linear equations do not exist except for certain simple cases.

(2) Graphical Methods

These are useful when we are satisfied with approximate solution for a problem. This method involves plotting the given function and determining the points where it crosses the x-axis. These points represent approximate values of the roots of the function.

(3) Trial and Error Methods

This method involves a series of guesses for x, each time evaluating the function to see whether it is close to zero. The value of x that causes the function value closer to zero is one of the approximate roots of the equation.

Although graphical and trial and error methods provide satisfactory approximations for many problem situations, they become cumbersome and time consuming. Moreover, accuracy of the results are inadequate for the requirements of many engineering and scientific problems.

(4) Iterative Methods

It usually begins with an approximate value of the root called *initial guess*, which is then successively corrected iteration by iteration. The process of iteration stops when desired level of accuracy is obtained. Since iterative methods involve a large number of iterations and arithmetic operations to reach a solution, the use of computers has become inevitable to make the task simple and efficient.

Before initiating an iterative process, we have to determine either an approximate value of root or a *search interval* that contains a root.

One simple method of guessing starting points is to plot the curve of $f(x)$ and to identify a search interval near the root of interest. Graphical representation of a function cannot only provide rough estimates of the roots, but also help in understanding the properties of the function, thereby identifying possible problems in numerical computing.

A plot of $f(x) = x^3 - x - 1$ is shown in the figure.

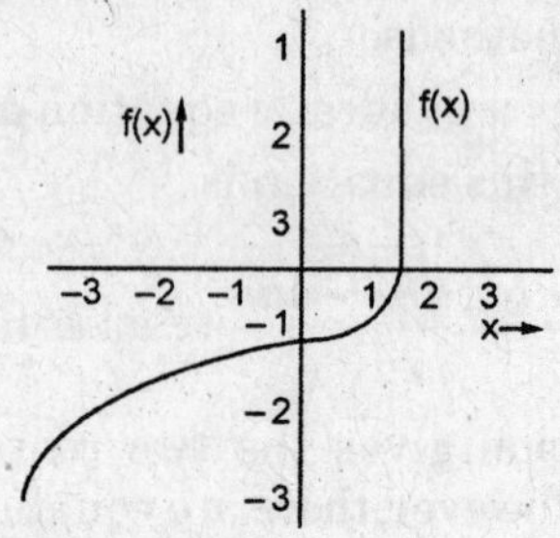

Fig. Plot of $f(x) = x^3 - x - 1$

Although $f(x)$ is a cubic function, it intersects x-axis at only one point. This suggests that remaining two roots are imaginary ones.

In the case of polynomials, many theoretical relation-ships between roots and coefficients are available.

Relation Used for Making Initial Guesses.

For a polynomial represented by

$$f(x) = a_n x^n + a_{n-1} x^{n-1} + \dots a_1 x \; a_0$$

the *largest possible* root is given by $f(x_1) = \dfrac{a_{n-1}}{a_n}$

This value is taken as the initial approximation when no other value is suggested by the knowledge of the problem at hand.

Types of Iterative Methods

There are a number of iterative methods that have been tried and used successfully in various problem situations. All these methods typically generate a sequence of estimates of the solution which is expected to converge to the true solution.

All iterative methods begin their process of solution with one or more guesses at the solution being sought.

Types of iterative methods based on number of guesses they use are

***(i)* Bracketing methods**

These are also called *interpolation methods.* It start with two initial guesses that 'bracket' the root and then systematically reduce the width of bracket until the solution is reached.

Types of Braketing methods:

(*a*) Bisection method

(*b*) False position method

These methods are based on the assumption that the function changes sign in the vicinity of a root.

***(ii)* Open end methods**

These are also called *extrapolation methods.* It uses a single starting value or two values that do not necessarily bracket the root.

Types of open end methods:

(*a*) Newton-Raphson method

(*b*) Secant method

(*c*) Muller's method

(*d*) Fixed-point method

(*e*) Bairstow's method

Note : Bracketing methods require to find sign changes in the function during every iteration. Open end methods do not require this.

NEWTON-RAPHSON METHOD

If point x_0 is close to the root α, then tangent line to the graph of $f(x)$ at x_0 is a good approximation to $f(x)$ near α. So, root of the tangent line, where line cuts the x-axis ; x_1 is a better approximation to α than x_0 is.

$$\text{Slope of the tangent} = \frac{f(x_0)}{x_0 - x_1} = f'(x_0)$$

$$\therefore \quad x_0 - x_1 = \frac{f(x_0)}{f'(x_0)}$$

$$\Rightarrow \quad x_1 = x_0 - \frac{f(x_0)}{f'(x_0)}$$

Repeating process, we obtain a better approximation

$$x_2 = x_1 - \frac{f(x_1)}{f'(x_1)}$$

and, in general, for $n = 0, 1, 2, \dots,$

$$x_{n+1} = x_n - \frac{f(x_n)}{f'(x_n)}$$

If x_0 is sufficiently close to α, $x_n \to \alpha$ as $n \to \infty$.

Order of Convergence

Let $x_0, x_1, x_2, \dots, x_n, \dots$ be a sequence of approximations to a root α produced by a numerical method, where $\lim_{n\to\infty} x_n = \alpha$.

Let $\varepsilon_n = \alpha - x_n$

If $\lim_{n\to\infty} \frac{|\varepsilon_{n+1}|}{|\varepsilon_n|^p} = C$, for some p and some *non-zero* constant C, then method has *order of convergence* p, and C is asymptotic error constant (bigger p is, faster the convergence).

Now consider Newton Raphson method, where $f(x)$ is assumed to be twice differentiable, and α is a simple root.

Then $f(\alpha) = f(x_n) + (\alpha - x_n)f'(x_n) + \frac{(\alpha - x_n)^2}{2} f''(\xi) = 0$

where ξ is an unknown point between x_n and α;

$$i.e.\quad \alpha - x_n + \frac{f(x_n)}{f'(x_n)} = \frac{-(\alpha - x_n)^2 f''(\xi)}{2f'(x_n)}$$

$$\Rightarrow \quad \alpha - x_{n+1} = \frac{-(\alpha - x_n)^2 f''(\xi)}{2f'(x_n)}$$

$$\Rightarrow \quad \frac{|\varepsilon_{n+1}|}{|\varepsilon_n|^2} = \frac{|f''(\xi)|}{2|f'(x_n)|}$$

$$\Rightarrow \quad \lim_{n\to\infty} \frac{|\varepsilon_{n+1}|}{|\varepsilon_n|^2} = \frac{|f''(\alpha)|}{2|f'(\alpha)|} \text{ if } x_n \to \alpha \text{ as } n \to \infty$$

Thus, in case of a simple root α, Newton's method has second order quadratic—convergence, with asymptotic error constant $\frac{|f''(\alpha)|}{2|f'(\alpha)|}$

Note. If α is a root of multiplicity m, then

$$f(x) = (x - \alpha)^m g(x)$$

$$\Rightarrow \quad f_0'(x) = (x - \alpha)^m g'(x) + m(x - \alpha)^{m-1} g(x)$$

$$= (x - \alpha)^{m-1}[(x - \alpha)g'(x) + mg(x)]$$

So, $\quad f'(\alpha) = 0$ unless $m = 1$,

in which case $f'(\alpha) = g(\alpha) \neq 0$.

Hence requirement that α be simple for the method to be quadratically convergent.

Otherwise, if α is not simple,

$$x_{n+1} - \alpha = x_n - \alpha - \frac{f(x_n)}{f'(x_n)}$$

$$= x_n - \alpha - \frac{(x_n - \alpha)g(x_n)}{(x_n - \alpha)g'(x_n) + mg(x_n)}$$

So, dividing across by $x_n - \alpha$ and taking absolute values of both sides, we have

$$\frac{|x_{n+1} - \alpha|}{|x_n - \alpha|} = \left|1 - \frac{g(x_n)}{(x_n - \alpha)g'(x_n) + mg(x_n)}\right|$$

$$\therefore \lim_{n\to\infty} \frac{|\varepsilon_{n+1}|}{|\varepsilon_n|} = \left|1 - \frac{g(\alpha)}{mg(\alpha)}\right|$$

$$= 1 - \frac{1}{m} = \frac{m-1}{m}; m \geq 2$$

assuming $\lim_{n\to\infty} x_n = \alpha$.

So, order of convergence for multiple roots is only 1—linear and as m, multiplicity of the root gets bigger, convergence slows down since asymptotic error constant $\frac{m-1}{m} \to 1$.

However, function $q(x) = \frac{f(x)}{f'(x)}$ always has simple roots :

$$q(x) = \frac{(x-\alpha)g(x)}{(x-\alpha)g'(x) + mg(x)}$$

So $\quad q(\alpha) = 0$

$$\therefore q'(x) = \frac{[(x-\alpha)g'(x) + mg(x)][(x-\alpha)g'(x) + g(x)] - (x-\alpha)g(x)[(x-\alpha)g''(x) + (m+1)g'(x)]}{[(x-\alpha)g'(x) + mg(x)]^2}$$

$$\text{Hence,}\quad q'(\alpha) = \frac{mg(\alpha)^2}{m^2 g(\alpha)^2} = \frac{1}{m} \neq 0$$

Hence, Newton's method applied to $q(x)$ will be quadratically convergent:

$$x_{n+1} = x_n - \frac{q(x_n)}{q'(x_n)}$$

$$q'(x) = \frac{f'(x)^2 - f(x)f''(x)}{f'(x)^2}$$

$$\Rightarrow \quad \frac{q(x)}{q'(x)} = \frac{f(x)f'(x)}{f'(x)^2 - f(x)f''(x)}$$

Thus, we have *modified Newton method:*

$$x_{n+1} = x_n - \frac{f(x_n)f'(x_n)}{f'(x_n)^2 - f(x_n)f''(x_n)}$$

which will be quadratically convergent to a root of any multiplicity; it is more unwieldy than Newton's method and requires calculation of $f''(x_n)$.

Alternatively

If $f(x) = k(x - \alpha)^m$ for some constant k, then

$$f'(x) = km(x - \alpha)^{m-1}$$

$$\therefore \quad \frac{f(x)}{f'(x)} = \frac{(x-\alpha)}{m}$$

So, $\quad \alpha = x - m\frac{f(x)}{f'(x)}$ for any x.

In general case of a multiple root, this becomes an approximation rather than an equality, and we have another modified Newton method:

$$x_{n+1} = x_n - m\frac{f(x_n)}{f'(x_n)}$$

This method does not require calculation of $f''(x_n)$;

but it does require calculation of the multiplicity m from

$$\frac{|\varepsilon_{n+1}|}{|\varepsilon_n|} \approx \frac{m-1}{m}$$

where ε_n and ε_{n+1} are errors in Newton's method.

Example. $f(x) = x - \cos x$ ($\alpha = 0.739085$)

$f'(x) = 1 + \sin x$

$$x_{n+1} = x_n - \frac{x_n - \cos x_n}{1 + \sin x_n}$$

$$= \frac{x_n \sin x_n + \cos x_n}{1 + \sin x_n}$$

n	x_n	$\varepsilon_n = \alpha - x_n$	$x_{n+1} - x_n$
0	0	0.739085	1
1	1	−0.260915	−0.249636
2	0.750364	−0.011279	−0.011251
3	0.739113	−0.000028	−0.000028
4	0.739085	0	0
5	0.739085	0	

In this case, $\frac{|\varepsilon_1|}{|\varepsilon_0|^2} = 0.47765$; $\frac{|\varepsilon_2|}{|\varepsilon_1|^2} = 0.165681$;

$$\frac{|\varepsilon_3|}{|\varepsilon_2|^2} = 0.220098$$

Note : $x_{n+1} - x_n$ is a good approximation for $\alpha - x_n$ as x_n approaches α.

Example : $f(x) = x^2 - 4x + 4 = 0$;

$\alpha = 2$ $m = 2$

$f'(x) = 2x - 4$

From Newton's method :

$$x_{n+1} = x_n - \frac{x_n^2 - 4x_n + 4}{2x_n - 4} = \frac{x_n^2 - 4}{2x_n - 4} = \frac{x_n + 2}{2}$$

n	x_n	$\varepsilon_n = \alpha - x_n$	$x_{n+1} - x_n$
0	1	1	0.5
1	1.5	0.5	0.25
2	1.75	0.25	0.125
3	1.875	0.125	0.0625
4	1.9375	0.0625	

Here,

$$\frac{|\varepsilon_{n+1}|}{|\varepsilon_n|} = \frac{|\alpha - x_{n+1}|}{|\alpha - x_n|} = \frac{1}{2} = \frac{|x_{n+1} - x_n|}{|x_n - x_{n+1}|} \text{ for all } n.$$

Thus convergence is only linear :

$$\frac{m-1}{m} = \frac{1}{2}$$

$\Rightarrow$ $2m - 2 = m$

$\Rightarrow$ $m = 2$

So an alternative method should be used.

Using first modified method :

$$f(x) = x^2 - 4x + 4$$

$\Rightarrow$ $f'(x) = 2(x - 2)$

$\Rightarrow$ $f''(x) = 2$

$$\therefore \quad x_{n+1} = x_n - \frac{2(x_n - 2)^3}{4(x_n - 2)^2 - 2(x_n - 2)^2}$$

$$= x_n - (x_n - 2) = 2$$

Using second method :

$$x_{n+1} = x_n - 2\frac{f(x_n)}{f'(x_n)}$$

$$\Rightarrow \quad x_{n+1} = x_n - \frac{2(x_n - 2)^3}{2(x_n - 2)} = 2$$

Example. $f(x) = x^4 - 2x^3 + 2x - 1 = 0$; & $\alpha = 1$ $f'(x) = 4x^3 - 6x^2 + 2$

Using Newton's method,

$$x_{n+1} = x_n - \frac{x_n^4 - 2x_n^3 + 2x_n - 1}{4x_n^3 - 6x_n^2 + 2} = \frac{3x_n^4 - 4x_n^3 + 1}{4x_n^3 - 6x_n^2 + 2}$$

n	x_n	$\varepsilon_n = \alpha - x_n$	$x_{n+1} - x_n$	$\frac{\lvert\alpha - x_{n+1}\rvert}{\lvert\alpha - x_n\rvert}$	$\frac{\lvert x_{n+2} - x_{n+1}\rvert}{\lvert x_{n+1} - x_n\rvert}$
0	0	1	0.5	0.5	0.375
1	0.5	0.5	0.1875	0.625	0.59227
2	0.6875	0.3125	0.11102	0.64474	0.62836
3	0.79852	0.20148	0.06976	0.65376	0.64464
4	0.86828	0.13172	0.04497	0.65859	0.65288
5	0.91325	0.08675	0.02936	0.66156	
6	0.94261	0.05739			

Here $\frac{m-1}{m} \approx \frac{2}{3}$ $\Rightarrow$ $3m - 3 = 2m$ $\Rightarrow$ $m = 3$

Since root is multiplicity 3, we use modified method.

$$x_{n+1} = x_n - 3\frac{f(x_n)}{f'(x_n)}$$

$$= x_n - \frac{3(x_n^4 - 2x_n^3 + 2x_n - 1)}{4x_n^3 - 6x_n^2 + 2}$$

$$= \frac{x_n^4 - 4x_n^3 + 3}{4x_n^3 - 6x_n^2 + 2}$$

Using this method, we have

n	x_n
0	0
1	1.5
2	1.03125
3	1.00016
4	0.99993
5	0.99961
6	1.00006
7	1.00000

So, there is a root of multiplicity 3 at $x = 1$.

In practice, Newton's method would be terminated if $\frac{|x_{n+2} - x_{n+1}|}{|x_{n+1} - x_n|}$ approached a non-zero limit after a preset number of steps and whatever the most recent value of x_n was would be used as an initial guess for the modified method.

Limitations of Newton-Raphson Method

This method fails in the following situations :

(*i*) Division by zero may occur if $f'(x_i)$ is zero or very close to zero.

(*ii*) If initial guess is too far away from the required root, the process may converge to some other root.

(*iii*) A particular value in the iteration sequence may repeat, resulting in an infinite loop. This occurs when to the curve $f(x)$ at $x = x_{i+1}$ cuts the x-axis again at $x = x_i$.

Example. Find by Newton Raphson's method, real root of equation $xe^x - 2 = 0$ correct to three decimal places.

Solution :

Let $f(x) = xe^x - 2$ ...(*i*)

Then $f(0) = -2$ and $f(1) = e - 2 = 0.7183$

So a root of (*i*) lies between 0 and 1 and nearer to 1.

Let us take $x_0 = 1$.

Also, $f'(x) = xe^x + e^x$

and $f'(1) = e + e = 5.4366$

By Newton's rule,

first appoximation, $x_1 = x_0 - \frac{f(x_0)}{f'(x_0)}$

$$= 1 - \frac{0.7183}{5.4366} = 0.8679$$

$\therefore$ $f(x_1) = 0.0672$,

and $f'(x_1) = 4.4491$

second approximation,

$$x_2 = x_1 - \frac{f(x_1)}{f'(x_1)} = 0.8679 - \frac{0.0672}{4.4491} = 0.8528$$

Thus, required root is 0.0853 correct to 3 decimal places.

SECANT METHOD

This method may be regarded as an approximation to Newton's method where, instead of $f'(x_n)$, the quotient $\frac{f(x_n) - f(x_{n-1})}{x_n - x_{n-1}}$ is used; *i.e.* instead of tangent to the graph of $f(x)$ at x_n, we use *secant joining* the points $(x_{n-1}, f(x_{n-1}))$ and $(x_n, f(x_n))$.

Equating two expressions for the slope of the secant, we have

$$\frac{f(x_n)}{x_n - x_{n+1}} = \frac{f(x_n) - f(x_{n-1})}{x_n - x_{n-1}}$$

$$\Rightarrow \quad x_{n+1} = x_n - \frac{(x_n - x_{n-1})f(x_n)}{f(x_n) - f(x_{n-1})}$$

Convergence rate of the secant method is 1.618, *i.e. almost quadratic,* if α is a simple root.

Advantage

$f'(x)$ need not be evaluated; so the number of function evaluations is half that of Newton's method. However, its convergence rate is slightly less than Newton and it requires two initial guesses x_0 and x_1.

In common with Newton's method, its convergence rate deteriorates for multiple roots, and if m can be estimated, the modification

$$x_{n+1} = x_n - m\frac{(x_n - x_{n-1})f(x_n)}{f(x_n) - f(x_{n-1})}$$ should be used.

Also in common with Newton's method, convergence is not guaranteed at all unless x_0 and in case of secant method x_1 also is a sufficiently good initial guess. For this reason a starting method such as Bisection method or *Regula Falsi* is used where applicable for a few iterations to obtain a good initial guess for one of the more accurate methods.

SOLUTION OF NON-LINEAR SIMULTANEOUS EQUATIONS

1. Newton-Raphson Method

Consider equations, $f(x, y) = 0$ and $g(x, y) = 0$

If an initial approximation (x_0, y_0) to a solution has been found by graphical method or otherwise, then a better approximation (x_1, y_1) can be obtained as follows :

Let $\quad x_1 = x_0 + h \quad$ and $\quad y_1 = y_0 + k$

$\therefore \quad f(x_0 + h, y_0 + k) = 0; \; g(x_0 + h, y_0 + k) = 0$

Expanding each of the functions by Taylor's series to first degree terms, we get approximately

$$f_0 + h\frac{\partial f}{\partial x_0} + k\frac{\partial f}{\partial y_0} = 0$$

$$g_0 + h\frac{\partial g}{\partial x_0} + k\frac{\partial g}{\partial y_0} = 0$$

where, $f_0 = f(x_0\, y_0)$, $\dfrac{\partial f}{\partial x_0} = \left(\dfrac{\partial f}{\partial x}\right)_{x_0, y_0}$ etc.

Solving above equations for h and k, we get a new approximation to the root as

$$x_1 = x_0 + h, \; y_1 = y_0 + k$$

This process is repeated till we get the values to the desire accuracy.

Example. Solve the system of non-linear equations

$$x^2 + y = 11$$
$$y^2 + x = 7$$

Solution

An initial approximation to the solution is obtained from a rough graph of above equations, as

$$x_0 = 3.5 \text{ and } y_0 = -1.8$$

We have, $\quad f = x^2 + y - 11$

and $\quad g = y^2 + x - 7$

$\therefore \quad \dfrac{\partial f}{\partial x} = 2x, \dfrac{\partial f}{\partial y} = 1$

and $\quad \dfrac{\partial g}{\partial x} = 1, \dfrac{\partial g}{\partial y} = 2y$

Newton-Raphson's equations above will be

$$7h + k = 0.55$$

and $\quad h - 3.6k = 0.26$

Solving these, we get

$$h = 0.0855$$

Repeating the above process, replacing (x_0, y_0) by (x_1, y_1), we get

$$x_2 = 3.5844,$$
$$y_2 = -1.8482$$

2. Bisection Method

It is one of the simplest and most reliable of iterative methods for the solution of nonlinear equations. This method, also called *binary chopping or half-interval method,* relies on the fact that if $f(x)$ is real and continuous in the interval $a < x < b$, and $f(a)$ and $f(b)$ are of opposite signs, i.e.

$$f(a) f(b) < 0$$

then there is at least one real root in the interval between a and b (there may be more than one root in the interval).

Let $x_1 = a$ and $x_2 = b$.

Let us also define another point x_0 to be the midpoint between a and b, i.e.

$$x_0 = \frac{x_1 + x_2}{2}$$

Now, there exists following three conditions:

(i) If $f(x_0) = 0$, we have a root at x_0.

(ii) If $f(x_0) f(x_1) < 0$, there is a root between x_0 and x_1.

(iii) If $f(x_0) f(x_2) < 0$, there is a root between x_0 and x_2.

It follows that by testing sign of the function at midpoint, we can deduce which part of the interval contains the root.

Figure shows that, since $f(x_0)$ and $f(x_2)$ are of opposite signs, a root lies between x_0 and x_2.

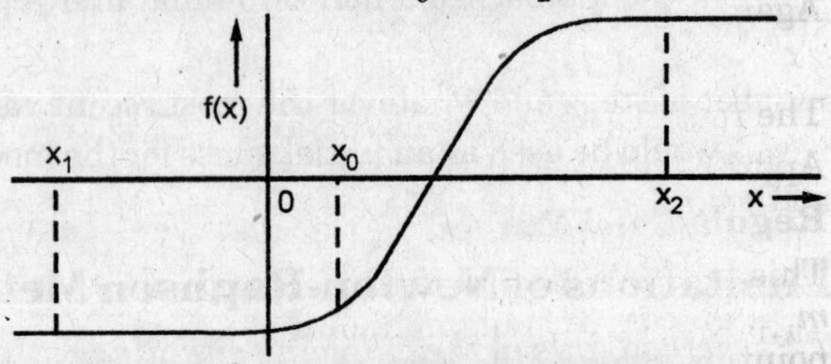

This subinterval can be further divided into two halves to locate a new sub-interval containing the root. This process can be repeated until interval containing the root is as small as needed.

Example. Find a root of the equation,

$$x^2 - 4x - 10 = 0 \text{ using bisection method.}$$

Solution

First step is to guess two initial values that would bracket a root.

Using equation

$$\left|x^*_{\max}\right| = \sqrt{\left(\frac{a_n - 1}{a_n}\right)^2 - 2\left(\frac{a_n - 2}{a_n}\right)}$$

maximum absolute of the solution can be decided.

Thus $\quad x_{\max} = \sqrt{\left(\dfrac{-4}{1}\right)^2 - 2\left(\dfrac{-10}{1}\right)} = 6$

Therefore, both the roots in the interval (– 6, 6). The table below gives values of $f(x)$ between –6 and 6 and shows that there is a root in the interval (– 2, – 1) and another in (5, 6).

x	–6	–5	–4	–3	–2	–1	0	1	2	3	4	5	6
f(x)	50	35	22	11	2	–4	–10	–13	–14	–13	–10	–5	2

Now, take $x_1 = -2$ and $x_2 = -1$

Then $x_0 = \frac{-2-1}{2} = -1.5$

$f(-2) = 2$ and $f(-1.5) = -1.75$

Since $f(-2)\, f(-1.5) < 0$

the root must be in the interval (– 2, – 1.5).

The next step begins.

$x_1 = -1, x_2 = -1.5$ and $x_0 = -1.75$

$f(-1.75) = 0.0625$

Since $f(-1.75)$ and $f(-1.5)$ are of opposite sign, the root lies in the interval (– 1.75, – 1.5), another iteration begins.

$x_1 = -1.75, x_2 = -1.5$ and $x_0 = -1.625$

$f(-1.625) = -0.859$

Now, root lies in the interval (– 1.75, – 1.625)

$\therefore \quad x_0 = -1.6875$

$f(-1.6875) = -0.40$

Again $x_0 = -\frac{1.75+1.6875}{2} = -1.72$

$f(-1.72) = -0.1616$

Again, $x_0 = -\frac{1.75+1.72}{2} = -1.735$

$f(-1.735) = -0.05$

Again, $x_0 = 1.7425$

$f(-1.7425) = +0.0063$

The root lies between – 1.735 and – 1.7425.

Approximate root is – 1.7416.

3. Regula Falsi Method

This is a variation of the bisection method, where m_{k+1}, instead of being midpoint of $I_k = (a_k, b_k)$ is the point of intersection with the x-axis of the secant joining $(a_k, f(a_k))$ and $(b_k, f(b_k))$.

$$m_{k+1} = \frac{a_k f(b_k) - b_k f(a_k)}{f(b_k) - f(a_k)}$$

Like bisection method, it only work for odd roots, and has linear convergence rate.

Advantages

(*i*) It always converges to odd roots.

(*ii*) Error bounds are easily obtained.

(*iii*) Convergence is unaffected by the multiplicity of the root.

Disadvantages

(*i*) Slow to converge.

(*ii*) Skips even roots.

NUMERICAL INTERGRATION

The process of evaluating a definite integral from a set of tabulated values of the integrand $f(x)$ is called *numerical integration.* This process when applied to a function of a single variable is called *quadrature.*

1. Newton-Cote's quadrature formula

Let $\quad I = \int_a^b f(x)\,dx$

where $f(x)$ takes the values $y_0, y_1, y_2, \ldots\ldots, y_n,$

For $x = x_0, x_1, x_2 \ldots x_n$ divide the interval (a, b) into n sub-intervals of width h, so that

$x_0 = a, x_1 = x_0 + h, x_2 = x_0 + 2h, \ldots\ldots, x_n = x_0 + nh = b.$

Then $\quad I = \int_{x_0}^{x_0+nh} f(x)\,dx$

Putting $\quad x = x_0 + rh$

$\Rightarrow \quad dx = h\,dr$

$\therefore \quad I = h\int_0^n f(x_0 + rh)\,dr$

By Newton's forward interpolation formula

$$I = h\int_0^n \left[y_0 + r\Delta y_0 + \frac{r(r-1)}{2!}\Delta^2 y_0 + \frac{r(r-1)(r-2)}{3!}\Delta^3 y_0 + \ldots \right] dr$$

Integrating term by term, we get

$$\int_{x_0}^{x_0+nh} f(x)\,dx = nh\left[y_0 + \frac{n}{2}\Delta y_0 + \frac{n(2n-3)}{12}\Delta^2 y + \frac{n(n-2)^2}{24}\Delta^3 y + \ldots \right] \quad \ldots (i)$$

2. Trapezoidal rule

For definite integrals such as

$$\int_0^1 \sqrt{1-x^3}\,dx \quad \text{or} \quad \int_0^1 e^{-x^2}\,dx$$

fundamental theorem of calculus cannot be used to evaluate them since there are no elementary functions that are antiderivatives of $\sqrt{1-x^3}$ or e^{-x^2}. *Approximation methods are used for such integrals.*

Trapezoidal rule is a numerical method that approximates value of a definite integral.

Consider the definite integral $\int_a^b f(x)\,dx$.

Assume that $f(x)$ is continuous on $[a, b]$ and divide $[a, b]$ into n subintervals of equal length

$$\Delta x = \frac{b-a}{n}$$

using $n + 1$ points $x_0 = a, x_1 = a + \Delta x, x_2 = a + 2\Delta x, \ldots,$ $x_n = a + n\Delta x = b.$

Compute value of $f(x)$ at these points.

$$y_0 = f(x_0), y_1 = f(x_1), y_2 = f(x_2), \ldots, y_n = f(x_n)$$

Approximate integral by using n trapezoids formed

by using straight line segments between points (x_{i-1}, y_{i-1}) and (x_i, y_i) for $1 \le i \le n$ as shown in the figure below.

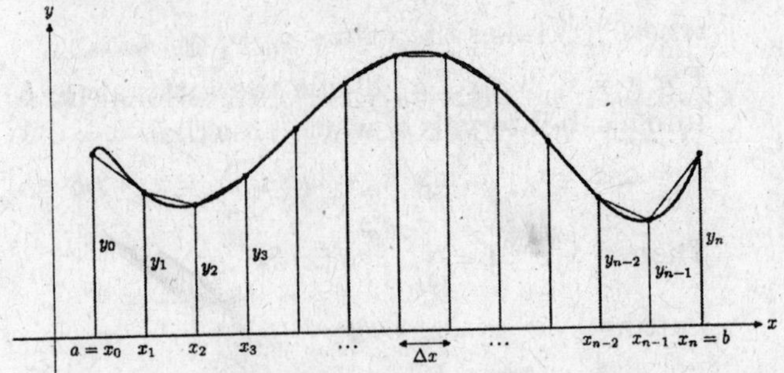

Area of a trapezoid is obtained by adding areas of a rectangle and triangle.

$$A = y_0\,\Delta x + \frac{1}{2}(y_1 - y_0)\Delta x = \frac{(y_0 + y_1)\Delta x}{2}$$

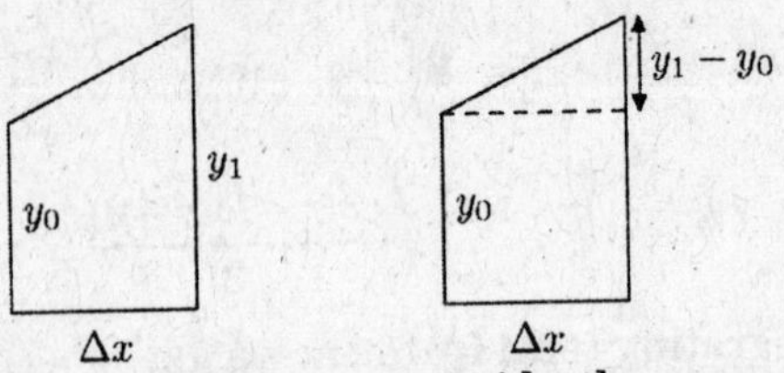

Adding area of the n trapezoids, the approximation obtained is

$$\int_a^b f(x)\,dx \approx \frac{(y_0 + y_1)\Delta x}{2} + \frac{(y_1 + y_2)\Delta x}{2} + \frac{(y_2 + y_3)\Delta x}{2} + \cdots + \frac{(y_{n-1} + y_n)\Delta x}{2}$$

which simplifies to the trapezoidal rule formula.

$$\int_a^b f(x)dx \approx \frac{\Delta x}{2}\left(y_0 + 2y_1 + 2y_2 + \ldots + 2y_{n-1} + y_n\right)$$

Example 1. Use trapezoidal rule with $n = 8$ to estimate $\int_1^5 \sqrt{1+x^2}\,dx$.

Solution For $n = 8$, $\quad \Delta x = \dfrac{5-1}{8} = 0.5.$

Compute the values of $y_0, y_1, y_2, \ldots, y_8$.

x	1	1.5	2	2.5	3	3.5	4	4.5	5
$y = \sqrt{1+x^2}$	$\sqrt{2}$	$\sqrt{3.25}$	$\sqrt{5}$	$\sqrt{7.25}$	$\sqrt{10}$	$\sqrt{13.25}$	$\sqrt{17}$	$\sqrt{21.25}$	$\sqrt{26}$

Therefore,

$$\int_1^5 \sqrt{1+x^2}\,dx \approx \frac{0.5}{2}\left(\sqrt{2} + 2\sqrt{3.25} + 2\sqrt{5} + 2\sqrt{7.25} + 2\sqrt{10} + 2\sqrt{13.25} + 2\sqrt{17} + 2\sqrt{21.25} + \sqrt{26}\right)$$

$$\approx 12.76$$

Example 2. Following points were found empirically.

x	2.1	2.4	2.7	3.0	3.3	3.6
y	3.2	2.7	2.9	3.5	4.1	5.2

Use the trapezoidal rule to estimate $\int_{2.1}^{3.6} y\,dx$.

Solution

By inspection, $\quad \Delta x = 0.3$

$$\therefore \quad \int_{2.1}^{3.6} y\,dx \approx \frac{0.3}{2}(3.2 + 2(2.7) + 2(2.9) + 2(3.5) + 2(4.1) + 5.2)$$

$$\approx 5.22$$

3. Simpson's one-third rule

Putting $n = 2$ in equation (i) above and taking the curve through (z_0, z_0) (z_1, y_1) and (z_2, y_2) as a parabola, *i.e.* a polynomial of second order so that differences of order higher than second vanish, we get

$$\int_{x_0}^{x_0+2h} f(x)dx = 2h\left(y_0 + \Delta y_0 + \frac{1}{6}\Delta^2 y_0\right)$$

$$= \frac{h}{3}(y_0 + 4y_1 + y_2)$$

Similarly, $$\int_{x_0+2h}^{x_0+4h} f(x)dx = \frac{h}{3}(y_2 + 4y_3 + y_4)$$

$$\int_{x_{0(n-2)h}}^{x_0+nh} f(x)dx = \frac{h}{3}(y_{n-2} + 4y_{n-1} + y_n)$$

n being even.

Adding all these integrals, when n is even,

$$\int_{x_0}^{x_0+nh} f(x)dx = \frac{h}{3}\,[(y_0 + y_n) + 4(y_1 + y_3 + \ldots + y_{n-1}) + 2(y_2 + y_4 + \ldots + y_{n-2})]$$

4. Simpson's three-eighth rule

Putting $n = 3$ in equation (i) above and taking the curve through (x_i, y_i) $i = 0, 1, 2, 3$ as a polynomial of third order so that differences above the third order vanish, we get

$$\int_{x_0}^{x_0+3h} f(x)dx = 3h\left(y_0 + \frac{3}{2}\Delta y_0 + \frac{3}{4}\Delta^2 y_0 + \frac{1}{8}\Delta^3 y_0\right)$$

$$= \frac{3h}{8}(y_0 + 3y_1 + 3y_2 + y_3)$$

Similarly, $$\int_{x_0+3h}^{x_0+6h} f(x)dx = \frac{3h}{8}\,(y_3 + 3y_4 + 3y_5 + y_6)$$

Adding all such expressions from x_0 to $x_0 + nh$, where n is a multiple of 3, we get

$$\int_{x_0}^{x_0+nh} f(x)dx = \frac{3h}{8}\,[(y_0 + y_n) + 3(y_1 + y_2 + y_4 + y_5 + \ldots + y_{n-1}) + 2(y_3 + y_6 + y_{n-3})]$$

Example. Evaluate $\int_0^6 \dfrac{dx}{1+x^2}$ by using Trapezoidal rule, Simpson's $\dfrac{1}{3}$ rule, and Simpson's $\dfrac{3}{8}$ rule,

Solution

Divide the interval (0, 6) into six parts each of width $h = 1$.

The values of $f(x) = \dfrac{1}{1+x^2}$ are given below :

x	0	1	2	3	4	5	6
$f(x)$	1	0.5	0.2	0.1	0.0588	0.0385	0.027
	y_0	y_1	y_2	y_3	y_4	y_5	y_6

(*i*) By Trapezoidal rule,

$$\int_0^6 \frac{dx}{1+x^2} = \frac{h}{2}[(y_0+y_6)+2(y_1+y_2+y_3+y_4+y_5)]$$

$$= \frac{1}{2}[(1+.027)+2(.5+.2+.1+0588+.0385)]$$

$$= \mathbf{1.4108}$$

(*ii*) By Simpson's $\frac{1}{3}$ rule

$$\int_0^6 \frac{dx}{1+x^2} = \frac{h}{3}[(y_0+y_6)+4(y_1+y_3+y_5)+2(y_2+y_4)]$$

$$= \frac{1}{3}[(1+.027)+4(0.5+0.1+0.0385)+2(0.2+0.0588)]$$

$$= \mathbf{1.3662}$$

(*iii*) By Simpson's $\frac{3}{8}$ rule,

$$\int_0^6 \frac{dx}{1+x^2} = \frac{3h}{8}[(y_0+y_6)+3(y_1+y_2+y_4+y_5)+2y_3]$$

$$= \frac{1}{8}[(1+0.027)+3(0.5+0.2+0.0588+0.0385+2(0.1)]$$

$$= \mathbf{1.3571}$$

NUMERICAL SOLUTION OF ORDINARY DIFFERENTIAL EQUATIONS

1. Runge-Kutta Method

This methods do not require calculations of higher order derivatives. These methods agree with Taylor's series solution upto the terms in h^r, where r differs from method to method and is called *order of that method.* Euler's method, Modified Euler's method and Runge's method are Runge-Kutta methods of the first, second and third order respectively.

The fourth-order Runge-Kutta method is most commonly used and is often referred to as 'Runge-Kutta method only'.

Working rule for finding increment k of y corresponding to an increment h of x by Runge-Kutta method from, $\frac{dy}{dx} = f(x, y), y(x_0) = y_0$, is as follows :

Calculate successively,

$$k_1 = hf(x_0, y_0)$$

$$k_2 = hf\left(x_0 + \frac{1}{2}h, y_0 + \frac{1}{2}k_1\right)$$

$$k_3 = hf\left(x_0 + h, y_0 + \frac{1}{2}k_2\right)$$

$$k_4 = hf(x_0 + h, y_0 + k_3)$$

and finally compute,

$$k = \frac{1}{6}(k_1 + 2k_2 + 2k_3 + k_4)$$

which gives required approximate value

$$y_1 = y_0 + k.$$

(*Note : k is weighted mean of k_1, k_2, k_3 and k_4*)

Example. Apply Runge-Kutta fourth order method, to find an approximate value of y when $h = 0.2$. Given: $\frac{dy}{dx} = x + y$ and $y = 1$, when $x = 0$.

Solution

$$x_0 = 0,\quad y_0 = 1,\quad h = 0.2,\quad f(x_0, y_0) = 1$$

$$\therefore \quad k_1 = hf(x_0, y_0) = 0.2 \times 1 = 0.2$$

$$k_2 = hf\left(x_0 + \frac{1}{2}h, y_0 + \frac{1}{2}k_1\right)$$

$$= 0.2 \times f(0.1, 1.1) = 0.2400$$

$$k_3 = hf\left(x_0 + \frac{1}{2}h, y_0 + \frac{1}{2}k_2\right)$$

$$= 0.2 \times f(0.1, 1.12) = 0.2440$$

and $\quad k_4 = hf(x_0 + h, y_0 + k_3)$

$$= 0.2 \times f(0.2, 1.244) = 0.2888$$

$$\therefore \quad k = \frac{1}{6}(k_1 + 2k_2 + 2k_3 + k_4)$$

$$= \frac{1}{6}(0.2000 + 0.4880 + 0.2888) = \mathbf{0.2428}$$

Hence, required approximate value of

$$Y_1 = Y_0 + K$$

$$= 1 + 0.2428 = 1.2428$$

2. Taylor's Series Method

Given initial value problem

$$y' = \frac{dy}{dx} = f(x, y), \text{ with } y(x_0) = y_0 \quad ...(i)$$

Then $\quad y'' = \frac{d^2y}{dx^2} = f_x + f_y y' = f_x + f_y f$

$$y''' = \frac{d^3y}{dx^3} = f_{xx} + 2f_{xy}f + f_{yy}f^2 + f_x f_y + f_y{}^2 f \quad ...(ii)$$

By Taylor's theorem, series about a point $x = x_0$

$$y = y_0 + (x - x_0)(y')_0 + \frac{(x - x_0)^2}{2!}(y'')_0 + \frac{(x - x_0)^3}{3!}(y''')_0 + \ldots \quad ...(iii)$$

From equation (*iii*) we can find the value y_1 of y for $x = x_1$ and $y', y'', y''', ...$ can be found at $x = x_1$ with equations (*i*) and (*ii*) and so on.

3. Euler's Method

Given initial value problem

$$y' = \frac{dy}{dx} = f(x, y), \text{ with } y(x_0) = y_0$$

By Taylor series, for $h \to 0$,

$$y(x + h) = y(x) + hy'(x) = y(x) + hf(x, y)$$

This gives, $\quad y_{n+1} = y_n + hf(x_n, y_n)$

where $\quad h = \frac{x_n - x_0}{n}$ (*i.e.*, $x_n = x_0 + nh$)

EXERCISE

MCQ TYPE QUESTIONS

1. The order of error is the Simpson's rule for numerical integration with a step size h is

(a) h (b) h^2

(c) h^3 (d) h^4

2. Four arbitrary points (x_1, y_1), (x_2, y_2), (x_3, y_3), (x_4, y_4) are given in the x, y-plane. Using the method of least squares, if regressing y upon x gives the fitted line $y = ax + b$; and regressing x upon y gives the fitted line $x = cy + d$, then

(a) two fitted lines must coincide

(b) two fitted lines need not coincide

(c) it is possible that $ac = 0$

(d) a must be $1/c$

3. The accuracy of Simpson's rule quadrature for a step size h is

(a) $O(h^2)$ (b) $O(h^3)$

(c) $O(h^4)$ (d) $O(h^5)$

4. The Newton's-Raphson iterative formula for finding $f(x) = x^2 - 1$, is

(a) $x_{i+1} = \dfrac{x_i^2 - 1}{2x_i}$ (b) $x_{i+1} = \dfrac{x_i^2 + 1}{2x_i}$

(c) $x_{i+1} = \dfrac{2x_i^2 + 1}{2x_i}$ (d) $x_{i+1} = \dfrac{2x_i}{2x_i^2 + 1}$

5. The convergence of which of the following method is sensitive to starting value?

(a) False position

(b) Gauss seidal method

(c) Newton-Raphson method

(d) All of these

6. Newton-Raphson method of solution of numerical equation is not preferred when

(a) graph of A(B) is vertical

(b) graph of $x(y)$ is not parallel

(c) graph of $f(x)$ is nearly horizontal where it crosses the x-axis.

(d) none of these

7. In which of the following methods, proper choice of initial value is very important ?

(a) Bisection method

(b) False position

(c) Newton-Raphson

(d) Bairsto method

8. Newton-Raphson method is applicable to the solution of

(a) both algebraic and trans-cendental equations

(b) both algebraic and trans-cendental and also used when the roots are complex

(c) algebraic equations only

(d) transcendental equations only

9. The root of $x^3 - 2x - 5 = 0$ correct to three decimal places by using Newton-Raphson method is

(a) 2.0946 (b) 1.0404

(c) 1.7321 (d) 0.7011

10. Using Newton-Raphson method, a root correct to three decimal places of the equation $e^x = 1 + 2x$ is

(a) 1.256 (b) 1.255

(c) 1.286 (d) none of these

11. A real root of equation $x^3 + x^2 - 1 = 0$ by iteration (method of successive approximation) method is

(a) 0.7548765 (b) 0.7548756

(c) 0.7548776 (d) 0.7548764

12. A real root of equation $\cos x = 3x - 1$ correct to seven decimal places by the method of successive approximation is

(a) 0.6071016 (b) 0.6071015

(c) 0.60711516 (d) none of these

13. From certain experiment following data has been obtained:

x	1	3	4
y	4	12	19

Using Langrange's inverse formula, the value of x for which y = 7, will be

(a) 2.124 (b) 1.857

(c) 2.429 (d) 1.946

14. The Lagrange interpolating polynomial of degree 2 approximating the function y = ln x defined by the following table of values. The value of ln 2.7 will be

x	2	2.5	3.0
y = ln x	0.69315	0.91629	1.09861

(a) 0.9941162 (b) 0.9941164

(c) 0.9941165 (d) 0.9941166

15. The function y = sin x is tabulated below

x	0	π/4	π/2
y = sin x	0	0.70711	1.0

Using Lagrange's interpolation formula, the value of sin (π/6) will be

(a) 0.52743 (b) 0.52742

(c) 0.51743 (d) none of these

NUMERICAL TYPE QUESTIONS

1. Solving $x^2 - 2 = 0$ by Newton Raphson technique, when initial guess $x_0 = 1.0$, then subsequent estimate of x (*i.e.* x_1) will be________

2. Following are the values of a function

$y(x) : y(-1) = 5, y(0), y(1) = 8$

$\frac{dy}{dx}$ at x = 0 as per Newton's central difference scheme is _______

3. Using Newton-Raphson method, a root correct to three decimal places of the equation $x^3 - 3x - 5 = 0$ is______

4. Using Newton-Raphson method, a root correct to three decimal places of the equation sin x = 1 – x is______

5. A root of the equation $x^3 - x - 11 = 0$ correct to four decimals using bisection method, is_______

6. Using Bisection method, the negative of $x^3 - x + 11 = 0$ is

7. A real root of the equation $x^3 - 2x - 5 = 0$ by the method of false position correct to three decimal places is _______

8. Using Bisection method, the negative root of $x^3 - 4x + 9 = 0$ correct to three decimal places is_____

9. A real root of the equation x – cos x = 0 by the method of false position correct to four decimal places is

10. The double (repeated) root of $4x^3 - 8x^2 - 3x + 9 = 0$ by Newton-raphson method will be

11. Using trapezoidal rule, and the table given below, $\int_4^{5.2} \ln x \, dx$ will be

x :	4	4.2	4.4	4.6	4.8	5	5.2
In x:	1.39	1.44	1.48	1.53	1.57	1.61	1.65

12. Using trapezoidal rule, taking 10 equal interval $\int_0^{\pi} \sin x \, dx$ will be_______

13. If $y_1 = 4$, $y_3 = 12$, $y_4 = 19$ and $y_x = 7$, then x will be _______

ANSWERS

MCQ Type Questions

1. (*b*) **2.** (*d*) **3.** (*d*) **4.** (*b*) **5.** (*c*) **6.** (*c*) **7.** (*c*) **8.** (*a*) **9.** (*a*) **10.**(*a*)
11. (*c*) **12.** (*a*) **13.** (*b*) **14.** (*b*) **15.** (*c*)

Numerical Type Questions

1. 1.5 **2.** 1.5 **3.** 2.279 **4.** 0.511 **5.** 2.3736 **6.** – 2.3736
7. 2.0944 **8.** – 2.506 **9.** 0.7391 **10.** 1.5 **11.** 1.8277 **12.** 1.984
13. 1.86

EXPLANATIONS

MCQ TYPE QUESTIONS

2.
$$y = ax + b \quad ....(i)$$
$$x = cy + d$$
$$\Rightarrow \quad x - d = cy$$
$$\Rightarrow \quad y = \frac{1}{c}x - d$$

From equatons (*i*),

$$a = \frac{1}{c} \text{ and } b = -d$$

14.
$$L_0(x) = \frac{(x-2.5)(x-3.0)}{(-0.5)(-1.0)}$$
$$= 2x^2 - 11x + 15$$

Similarly,

$$L_1(x) = -(4x^2 - 20x + 24)$$
$$L_2(x) = 2x^2 - 9x + 10$$
$$\therefore \quad L_2(x) = (2x^2 - 11x + 15)(0.69315) - (4x^2 - 20x + 24)(0.091629) + (2x^2 - 9x + 10)(1.09861)$$
$$= -0.08164x^2 + 0.81366x - 0.60761$$

which is the required quadratic polynomial.

Putting $x = 2.7$ in the above polynomial, we get

$$\ln 2.7 \approx L_2(2.7)$$
$$= -0.08164\,(2.7)^3 + 0.81366\,(2.7) - 0.60761$$
$$= 0.9941164$$

15. $$\sin\frac{\pi}{6} \approx \frac{\left(\frac{\pi}{6}-0\right)\left(\frac{\pi}{6}-\frac{\pi}{2}\right)}{\left(\frac{\pi}{4}-0\right)\left(\frac{\pi}{4}-\frac{\pi}{2}\right)}(0.70711) + \frac{\left(\frac{\pi}{6}-0\right)\left(\frac{\pi}{6}-\frac{\pi}{4}\right)}{\left(\frac{\pi}{2}-0\right)\left(\frac{\pi}{2}-\frac{\pi}{4}\right)}(1)$$

$$= \frac{8}{9}(0.70711) - \frac{1}{9}$$

$$= \mathbf{0.51743}$$

NUMERICAL TYPE QUESTIONS

1. $x^2 - 2 = 0$

$$x_1 = x_0 - \frac{f(x_0)}{f'(x_0)}$$

$$= 1 + \frac{1}{2} = 1.5$$

$$f(x_0) = 1^2 - 2 = -1$$
$$f(x_0) = 2x$$
$$f(x_0) = 2x_0 = 2(1) = 2$$

2. $$\left(\frac{dy}{dx}\right)_{at\ x=0} = \frac{y_2 - y_1}{x_2 - x_1}$$

$$= \frac{y(1) - y(-1)}{1-(-1)}$$

$$= \frac{8-5}{2} = 1.5$$

13. $$x = \frac{(-5)(-12)}{(-8)(-15)}(1) + \frac{(3)(-12)}{(8)(-7)}(3) + \frac{(3)(-5)}{(15)(7)}(4)$$

$$= \frac{1}{2} + \frac{27}{14} - \frac{4}{7} = \mathbf{1.86}$$

■■

6 CHAPTER Complex Variables

LIMIT OF A COMPLEX FUNCTION

Let f be a complex valued function of the complex variable z defined on a set E_2 (where E_2 is a two dimensional euclidean space) and be single valued for all values of z in the neighbourhood of $z = z_0$ with the possible exception of $z = z_0$ itself.

Then number l is limit of $f(z)$ as z approaches z_0 and write

$\lim_{Z \to Z_0} f(z) = l$ if for any positive number $\in$, however small, some positive number δ (usually depending on $\in$) can be found such that

$$|f(z) - l| < \in \text{ whenever } 0 < |z - z_0| < \delta.$$

Note that limit is independent of the manner in which $z \to z_0$.

CONTINUITY OF A COMPLEX FUNCTION

Let f be defined and single valued on a set in E_2 for all values of a complex variable z in a neighbourhood of $z = z_0$ as well as at $z = z_0$.

The function $f(z)$ is said to be continuous at the point z_0 provided that

$$\lim_{z \to z_0} f(z) = f(z_0)$$

Note :

- If a function $f(z)$ is continuous in a region, then real and imaginary parts of the function $f(z)$ are also continuous in that region.
- If function $f(z)$ is continuous in a closed region is bounded in that region, i.e. there exists a constant M such that $|f(z)| < M$ for all points in z of the region.

DERIVATIVES OF A COMPLEX FUNCTION.

- If $f(z)$ is a complex single-valued function in some region R of the z-plane, then derivative of $f(z)$ is defined as

$$f'(z) = \lim_{\delta z \to 0} \frac{f(z+\delta z) - f(z)}{\delta z}$$

provided that this limit exists and independent of the manner in which $\delta z \to 0$.

- If f is a complex valued function defined on an open set $S \in E_2$ and it is assumed that $z_0 \in S$, then f is said to have a derivative $f'(z_0)$ at z_0 if the limit

$$\lim_{\delta z \to z_0} \frac{f(z) - f(z_0)}{\delta z} = f'(z_0) \text{ exists.}$$

Note : If a function $f(z)$ is differentiable at any point z_0, then it is not enough that

$$\lim_{\delta z \to z_0} \frac{f(z) - f(z_0)}{z - z_0}$$

exists, but it is also required to prove that this limit must be unique, i.e. it must have the same value along whatever path z approaches z_0.

ANALYTIC FUNCTIONS

A function f(z) which is single-valued and possesses a unique derivative with respect to z at all points of regions R, is called *analytic* or *regular function* of z in that region.

A point at which an analytic function cease to possess a derivative is called *singular point of the function*. Thus if u and v are real single – valued functions of x and y such that $\left[\frac{\partial u}{\partial x}\right], \left[\frac{\partial u}{\partial y}\right], \left[\frac{\partial v}{\partial x}\right]\left[\frac{\partial v}{\partial x}\right]$ are continuous thoughtout a region R, then Cauchy-Riemann equation

$$\frac{\partial u}{\partial x} = \frac{\partial v}{\partial y}; \quad \frac{\partial u}{\partial y} = \frac{-\partial v}{\partial x}$$

are both necessary and sufficient conditions for the function $f(z) = u + iv$ to be analytic in R.

The real and imaginary parts of an analytic function are called *conjugate functions*. The relation between two conjugate functions is given by C-R equation.

- Analytic function is called *regular function* or holomorphic function.
- A point at which an analytic function ceases to possesses a derivative is called *singular point of the function*.

Cauchy's Theorem

If f(z) is an analytic function and f(z) is continuous at each point within or on a closed curve C, then

$$\int_C f(z)\, dz = 0$$

Writing f(z) = u(x, y) + iv(x, y) and noting that dz = dx + idy

$\int_C f(z) = dz \int_C = (udx - vdy) + i\int_C (vdx + udy)$ ...(i)

Since f′(z) is continuous, therefore

$$\frac{\partial u}{\partial x}, \frac{\partial u}{\partial y}, \frac{\partial v}{\partial x}, \frac{\partial v}{\partial y}$$

are also continuous in the region D enclosed by C. Hence Green's theorem can be applied to integral (i), giving

$$\int_C f(z)\,dz = -\iint_D \left(\frac{\partial v}{\partial x} + \frac{\partial u}{\partial y}\right) dx\,dy$$

$$+ i\iint_D \left(\frac{\partial u}{\partial x} - \frac{\partial v}{\partial y}\right) dx\,dy \quad ...(ii)$$

Now f(z) being analytic, u and v necessarily satisfy the Cauchy-Riemann equation and thus the integrands of the two double integrals in integral (ii) vanish identically

Hence $\int_C f(z)\,dz = 0$

Obs.1. Cauchy-Riemann equations are precisely the conditions for the two real integrals in integral (i) to be independent of the path. Hence line integral of a function f(z) which is analytic in the region D, is independent of the path joining any two points of D.

Obs. 2. Extension of Cauchy's Theorem. If f(z) is analytic in the region D between two simple closed curves C and C_1, then

$$\int_C f(z)\,dz = \int_{C_1} f(z)\,dz + \int_{BA} f(z)dz = 0$$

To prove this, we need to introduce the cross-cut AB. Then $\int f(z)\,dz = 0$

where path is as indicated by arrows in Fig. (a), i.e. along AB-along C_1 in clock-wise sense and along BA–along C_1 in anti-clockwise sense

i.e. $\int_{AB} f(z)\,dz + \int_{C_1} f(z)\,dz + \int_C f(z)\,dz \int_{BA} f(z)dz = 0$

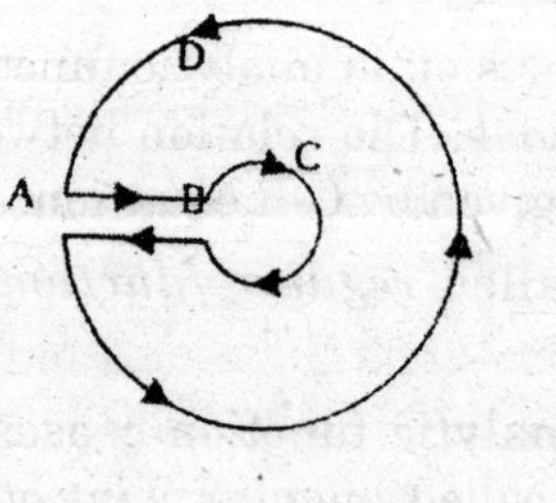

Fig. (a)

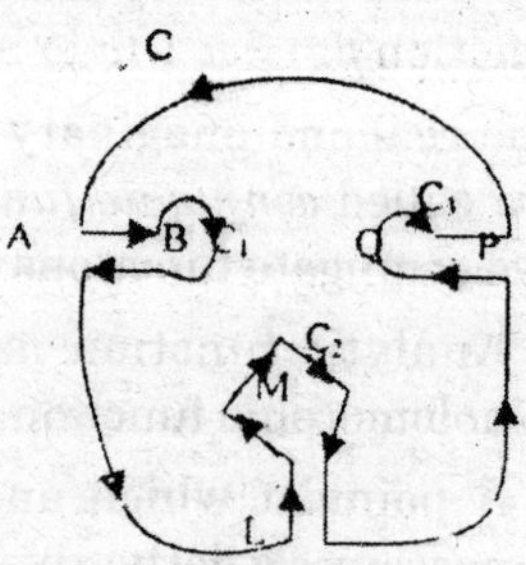

Fig. (b)

But, since integrals along AB and BA cancel,

$$\int_C f(z)\,dz + \int_{C_1} f(z)\,dz = 0$$

Reversing the direction or integral around C_1 and transposing, we get

$$\int_C f(z)\,dz = \int_{C_1} f(z)\,dz$$

Each integration being taken in the anti-clockwise sense.

If C_1, C_2, C_3 .... be any number of closed curves with C in Fig. (b), then

$$\int_C f(z)\,dz = \int_{C_1} f(z)\,dz + \int_{C_2} f(z)\,dz + \int_{C_3} f(z)\,dz$$

Cauchy's Integral Formula

If f(z) is analytic within and on a closed curve and if a is any point with C, then

$$f(a) = \frac{1}{2\pi i}\int_C \frac{f(z)dz}{z-a}$$

Consider the function $\frac{f(z)}{(z-a)}$ which is analytic at all points within C except at z = a. With the point 'a' as center and radius r, draw a small circle C_1 lying entirely within C.

Now $\frac{f(z)}{(z-a)}$ being analytic in the region enclosed by C and C_1, we have by Cauchy's therorem

$$\int_C \frac{f(z)}{z-a}dz = \int_{C_1} \frac{f(z)}{z-a}dz$$

For any point on C_1,

$$z - a = re^{i\theta} \quad \Rightarrow \quad dz = ire^{i\theta}\,d\theta$$

$$\therefore \quad = \int_{C1} \frac{f(a + re^{i\theta})}{re^{i\theta}} . ire^{i\theta}\,d\theta = i\int_{C1} f(a + re^{i\theta})\,d\theta \quad ...(i)$$

In the limiting form, as the circle C_1 shrinks to the point 'a', i.e. as r→0, the integral (i) will approach to

$$i\int_{C1} f(a)\,d\theta = if(a)\int_0^{2\pi} d\theta = 2\pi i f(a)$$

$$\therefore \quad \int_C \frac{f(z)}{z-a}dz = 2\pi i f(a)$$

$$\Rightarrow \quad f(a) = \frac{1}{2\pi i}\int_C \frac{f(z)}{z-a}dz \quad ...(ii)$$

which is desired Cauchy's integral formula.

Cor. Differentiation both sides of equation (ii) with respect to a, we get

$$f'(a) = \frac{1}{2\pi i}\int_C \frac{\partial}{\partial a}\left(\frac{f(z)}{z-a}\right)dz = \frac{1}{2\pi i}\int_C \frac{f(z)}{(z-a)^2}dz \quad ...(iii)$$

Similarly, $$f''(a) = \frac{2!}{2\pi i}\int_C \frac{f(z)}{(z-a)^3}dz \quad ...(iv)$$

and in general, $f^n(a) = \frac{n!}{2\pi i}\int_c \frac{f(z)}{(z-a)^{n+1}}dz$ ...(v)

Thus from results (ii) to (v) if a function f(z) is known to be analytic on the simple closed curve C, then values of the functions and all its derivative can be found at any point of C. Thus *an analytic function possesses derivative of all orders and these are themselves all analytic.*

Residue Theorem

If f(z) is analytic in a closed curve C except at a finite number of singular point within C, then

$\int_C f(z)\,dz = 2\pi i \times$ (sum of residues at the singular points within C

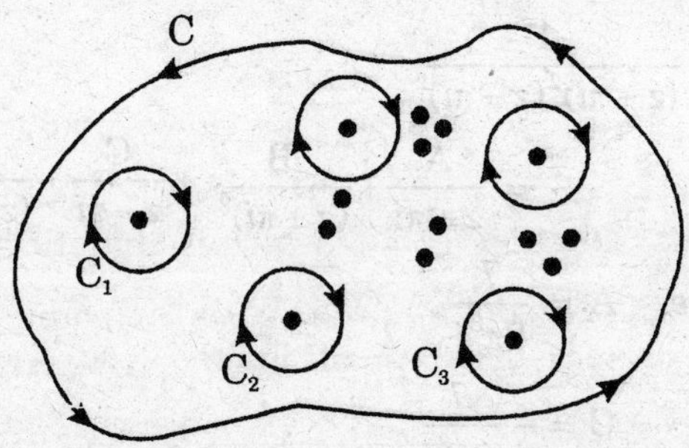

Let us surround each of the singular points $a_1, a_2, \ldots a_n$ by a small circle such that it encloses no other singular point. Then these circles $C_1, C_2, \ldots, C_n$ together with C form a multiply connected region in which f(z) is analytic.

Applying Cauchy's theorem, we have

$$\int_C f(z)\,dz = \int_{C_1} f(z)dz + \int_{C_2} f(z)\,dz + \text{-----} + \int_{C_n} f(z)\,dz$$

$$= 2\pi i\,[\text{Res } f(a_1) + \text{Res } f(a_2) + \ldots.. + \text{Res } f(a_n)]$$

Taylor's Series

If f(z) is analytic inside a circle C with center at 'a', then for z inside C

$$f(z) = f(a) + f'(a)(z-a) + \frac{f''(a)}{2!}(z-a)^2$$

$$+ \ldots\ldots \frac{f^n(a)}{n!}(z-a)^n + \ldots.. \quad \ldots(i)$$

Obs. Complex analytic functions can always represented by power series of the form (i).

Laurent's Series

If f(z) is analytic in the ring-shaped region R bounded by two concentric circles C and C_1 of radii r and r_1 $(r > r_1)$ and with centre at 'a', then for all z in R

$$f(z) = a_0 + a_1(z-a) + a_2(z-a)^2 + \ldots..$$
$$+ a_{-1}(z-1)^{-1} + a_{-2}(z-a)^{-2} + \ldots..$$

where, $a_n = \frac{1}{2\pi i}\int_r \frac{f(t)}{(t-a)^{n+1}}dt$

r being any curve is R, encircling C_1

Obs. Laurent series of a given analytic function f(z) in its annulus of convergence is unique. There may be different Laurent series of f(z) in two annuli with the same center.

SOLVED EXAMPLES

Example. Evaluate $\int_C \frac{z^2-z+1}{z-1}dx$,

where C is the circle

(i) $|z| = 1$,

(ii) $|z| = \frac{1}{2}$

Solution :

(i) Here $f(z) = z^2 - z + 1$ and $a = 1$.

Since $f(z)$ is analytic within and on circle C : $|z| = 1$ and $a = 1$ lies on C.

By Cauchy's integral formula

$$\frac{1}{2\pi i}\int_C \frac{f(z)}{z-a} = f(a) = 1 \text{ i.e. } \int_C \frac{z^2-z+1}{z-1}dz = 2\pi i.$$

(ii) Here, $a = 1$ lies outside the circle

$$C : |z| = \frac{1}{2}.$$

So $(z^2 - z + 1)(z - 1)$ is analytic everywhere within C.

By Cauchy's theorem,

$$\int_C \frac{z^2-z+1}{z-1}dx = 0$$

Example. Evaluate, using Cauchy's integral formula:

(i) $\int_C \frac{e^{2z}dz}{(z-1)(z-2)}$, where C is the circle $|z| = 3$.

(ii) $\int_C \frac{\cos \pi z}{z^2-1}dz$ around a rectangle with vertices $2 \pm i, -2 \pm i$.

Solution :

(i) $f(z) = e^{2z}$ is analytic within the circle C : $|z| = 3$ and two singular points $a = 1$ and $a = 2$ lie inside C.

$$\therefore \int_C \frac{e^{2z}}{(z-1)(z-2)}dz = \int_C e^{2z}\left(\frac{1}{z-2} - \frac{1}{z-1}\right)dz$$

$$= \int_C \frac{e^{2z}}{z-2}dz - \int_C \frac{e^{2z}}{z-1}dz = 2\pi i e^4 - 2\pi i e^2$$

$= 2\pi i\,(e^4 - e^2)$ [By Cauchy's integral formula]

(ii) $f(z) = \cos \pi z$ is analytic in the region bounded by given rectangle and two singular points $a = 1$ and $a = -1$ lie inside this rectangle.

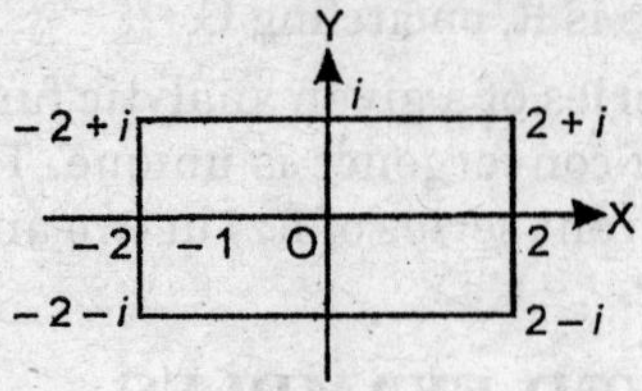

$$\therefore \quad \int_C \frac{\cos \pi z}{z^2 - 1} dz = \frac{1}{2} \int_C \left(\frac{1}{z-1} - \frac{1}{z+1} \right) \cos \pi z \, dz$$

$$= \frac{1}{2} \int_C \frac{\cos \pi z}{z-1} dz - \int_C \frac{\cos \pi z}{z+1} dz$$

$$= \frac{1}{2} \{2\pi i \cos \pi(1)\} - \frac{1}{2} \{2\pi i \cos \pi(-1)\}$$

$$= 0$$

[By Cauchy's integral formula]

Example. Evaluate

(i) $\int_C \frac{\sin^2 z}{(z - \pi/6)^3} dz$, where C is the circle $|z| = 1$.

(ii) $\int_C \frac{e^{2z}}{(z+1)^4} dz$, where C is the circle $|z| = 2$.

(iii) $\int_C \frac{e^z}{(z^2 + \pi^2)^2} dz$ where C is $|z| = 4$.

Solution :

(i) $f(z) = \sin^2 z$ is analytic inside the circle C : $|z| = 1$ and point $a = \frac{\pi}{6}$ (≈ 0.5) lies within C.

By Cauchy's integral formula

$$f''(a) = \frac{2!}{2\pi i} \int_C \frac{f(z)}{(z-a)^3} dz,$$

$$\therefore \int_C \frac{\sin^2 z}{(z - \pi/6)^3} dz = \pi i \left[\frac{d^2}{dz^2} (\sin^2 z) \right]_{z = \pi/6}$$

$$= \pi i (2 \cos 2z)_{z = \pi/6}$$

$$= 2\pi i \cos \pi/3 = \pi i$$

(ii) $f(z) = e^{2z}$ is analytic within the circle C : $|z| = 2$.

Also $(a) = -1$ lies inside C.

By Cauchy's integral formula,

$$f'''(a) = \frac{3!}{2\pi i} \int_C \frac{f(z) dz}{(z-a)^4}$$

$$\therefore \quad \int_C \frac{e^{2z}}{(z+1)^4} dz = \frac{2\pi i}{6} \left| \frac{d^3 (e^{2z})}{dz^3} \right|_{z=-1}$$

$$= \frac{\pi i}{3} \left[8e^{2z} \right]_{z=-1}$$

$$= \frac{8\pi i}{3} e^{-2}.$$

(iii) $\frac{e^z}{(z^2 + \pi^2)^2} = \frac{e^z}{(z + \pi i)^2 (z - \pi i)^2}$ is not analytic at $z = \pm \pi i$.

However both $z = \pm \pi i$ lie within the circle $|z| = 4$.

Now $\frac{1}{(z + \pi i)^2 (z - \pi i)^2}$

$$= \frac{A}{z + \pi i} + \frac{B}{(z + \pi i)^2} + \frac{C}{z - \pi i} + \frac{D}{(z - \pi i)^2}$$

where, $A = \frac{7}{2\pi^3 i}$,

$C = -\frac{7}{2\pi^3 i}$,

$B = D = -\frac{1}{4\pi^2}$

$$\therefore \int_C \frac{e^z}{(z^2 + \pi^2)^2} dz$$

$$= \frac{7}{2\pi^3 i} \left\{ \int_C \frac{e^z}{z + \pi i} dz - \int_C \frac{e^z}{z - \pi i} dz \right\}$$

$$- \frac{1}{4\pi^2} \left\{ \int_C \frac{e^z}{(z + \pi i)^2} dz + \int_C \frac{e^z}{(z - \pi i)^2} dz \right\}$$

$$= \frac{7}{2\pi^3 i} [2\pi i f(-\pi i) - 2\pi i f(\pi i)]$$

$$- \frac{1}{4\pi^2} [2\pi i f'(-\pi i) + 2\pi i f'(\pi i)]; \text{ where } f(z) = e^z$$

$$= \frac{7}{\pi^2} (e^{-\pi i} - e^{\pi i}) - \frac{i}{2\pi} (e^{-\pi i} + e^{\pi i})$$

$$= -\frac{14i}{\pi^2} \left(\frac{e^{\pi i} - e^{-\pi i}}{2i} \right) - \frac{i}{\pi} \left(\frac{e^{\pi i} + e^{-\pi i}}{2} \right)$$

$$= -\frac{14i}{\pi^2} \sin \pi - \frac{i}{\pi} \cos \pi = \frac{i}{\pi}.$$

Example. Expand $f(z) = \frac{1}{[(z-1)(z-2)]}$ in the region:

(a) $|z| < 1$,

(b) $1 < |z| < 2$,

(c) $|z| > 2$,

(d) $0 < |z - 1| < 1$.

Solution :

(*a*) By partial fractions

$$\frac{1}{(z-1)(z-2)}=\frac{1}{z-2}-\frac{1}{z-1} \quad ...(i)$$

$$=-\frac{1}{2}\left(1-\frac{z}{2}\right)^{-1}+(1-z)^{-1} \quad ...(ii)$$

For $|z|<1$, both $\left|\frac{z}{2}\right|$ and $|z|$ are less than 1.

Hence gives on expansion

$$f(z)=-\frac{1}{2}\left(1+\frac{z}{2}+\frac{z^2}{4}+\frac{z^3}{8}+...\right)$$
$$+(1+z^2+z^2+z^3+...)$$
$$=\frac{1}{2}+\frac{3}{4}z+\frac{7}{8}z^2+\frac{15}{16}z^3+...$$

which is a *Taylor's series*.

(*b*) For $1<|z|<2$, write (*i*) as

$$f(z)=-\frac{1}{2}\frac{1}{(1-z/2)}-\frac{1}{z(1-z^{-1})} \quad ...(iii)$$

and both $\left|\frac{z}{2}\right|$ and $|z^{-1}|$ are less than 1, hence (*iii*) on expansion gives

$$f(z)=-\frac{1}{2}\left(1+\frac{z}{2}+\frac{z^2}{4}+\frac{z^3}{8}+...\right)$$
$$-\frac{1}{z}(1+z^{-1}+z^{-2}+z^{-3}+...)$$
$$=...-z^{-4}-z^{-3}-z^{-2}-z^{-1}-\frac{1}{2}-\frac{1}{4}z$$
$$-\frac{1}{8}z^2-\frac{1}{16}z^3-...$$

which is a *Laurent's series*.

(*c*) For $|z|>2$, write (*i*) as

$$f(z)=\frac{1}{z(1-2z^{-1})}-\frac{1}{z(1-z^{-1})}$$
$$=z^{-1}(1-2z^{-1}+4z^{-2}+8z^{-3}+...)$$
$$-z^{-1}(1+z^{-1}+z^{-2}+z^{-3}+...)$$
$$=...+7z^{-4}+3z^{-3}+z^{-2}+...$$

(*d*) For $0<|z-1|<1$, write (*i*) as

$$f(z)=\frac{1}{(z-1)-1},-\frac{1}{z-1}$$
$$=-(z-1)^{-1}-[1-(z-1)]^{-1}$$
$$=-(z-1)^{-1}-[1+(z-1)+(z-1)^2+(z-1)^3+...]$$

Example. Find sum of the residues of $f(z)=\dfrac{\sin z}{z\cos z}$ at its poles inside the circle $|z|=2$.

Solution :

$f(z)$ has simple poles at $z=0,\pm\frac{\pi}{2},\pm 3\frac{\pi}{2},-...$

Only poles $z=0$ and $z=\pm\frac{\pi}{2}$ lies inside $|z|=2$.

$$\therefore \quad \text{Res} f(0)=\underset{z\to 0}{\text{Lt}}[z.f(z)]$$
$$=\underset{z\to 0}{\text{Lt}}\left(\frac{\sin z}{\cos z}\right)=0$$

$$\text{Res} f\left(\frac{\pi}{2}\right)=\underset{z\to\pi/2}{\text{Lt}}\left[\left(z-\frac{\pi}{2}\right)f(z)\right]$$
$$=\underset{z\to\pi/2}{\text{Lt}}\left\{\frac{(z-\pi/2)\sin z}{z\cos z}\right\}$$
$$=\underset{z\to\pi/2}{\text{Lt}}\frac{(z-\pi/2)\cos z+\sin z}{\cos z-z\sin z} \quad \left[\text{being } \frac{0}{0} \text{ form}\right]$$
$$=\frac{1}{-\pi/2}$$
$$=-\frac{2}{\pi}$$

and
$$\text{Res} f(-\pi/2)=\underset{z\to-\pi/2}{\text{Lt}}\left\{\frac{(z+\pi/2)\sin z}{z\cos z}\right\}$$
$$=\underset{z\to-\pi/2}{\text{Lt}}\frac{(z+\pi/2)\cos z+\sin z}{\cos z-z\sin z}$$
$$=\frac{-1}{-\pi/2}$$
$$=\frac{2}{\pi}$$

Hence sum of residues $=0-\frac{2}{\pi}+\frac{2}{\pi}=0.$

Example. Evaluate $\int_C \frac{z-3}{z^2+2z+5}dz$, where C is the circle

(*i*) $|z|=1$

(*ii*) $|z+1-i|=2$

(*iii*) $|z+1+i|=2$

Solution :

Poles of $f(z)=\dfrac{z-3}{z^2+2z+5}$ are given by

$$z^2+2z+5=0$$

i.e.
$$z=\frac{-2\pm\sqrt{(4-20)}}{2}=-1\pm 2i.$$

(*i*) Both poles $z = -1 + 2i$ and $z = -1 - 2i$ lie outside the circle $|z| = 1$. Therefore, $f(z)$ is analytic everywhere within C.

Hence by Cauchy's theorem,

$$\int_C \frac{z-3}{z^2+2z+5}dz = 0.$$

(*ii*) Here only one pole $z = -1 + 2i$ lies inside the circle $C : |z+1-i| = 2$.

Therefore, $f(z)$ is analytic within C except at this pole.

$$\therefore \text{ Res } f(-1+2i) = \underset{z \to -1+2i}{\text{Lt}} [\{z-(-1+2i)\}f(z)]$$

$$= \underset{z \to -1+2i}{\text{Lt}} \frac{(z+1-2i)(z-3)}{z^2+2z+5}$$

$$= \underset{z \to -1+2i}{\text{Lt}} \frac{z-3}{z+1+2i}$$

$$= \frac{-4+2i}{4i}$$

$$= i + \frac{1}{2}$$

Hence by residue theorem

$$\int_C f(z)dz = 2\pi i \text{ Res } f(-1+2i)$$

$$= 2\pi i(i + 1/2)$$

$$= \pi(i-2).$$

(*iii*) Here only pole $z = -1 - 2i$ lies inside the circle $C : |z + 1 + i| = 2$.

Therefore, $f(z)$ is analytic within C except at this pole.

$$\therefore \text{ Res } f(-1-2i) = \underset{z \to -1-2i}{\text{Lt}} \frac{(z+1+2i)(z-3)}{z^2+2z+5}$$

$$= \underset{z \to -1-2i}{\text{Lt}} \frac{z-3}{z+1-2i}$$

$$= \frac{-4-2i}{-4i}$$

$$= \frac{1}{2} - i$$

Hence by residue theorem,

$$\int_C f(z)dz = 2\pi i \text{ Res } f(-1-2i)$$

$$= 2\pi i\left(\frac{1}{2} - i\right) = \pi(2+i)$$

Example. Evaluate $\oint_C \frac{e^z}{\cos \pi z} dz$, where C is the unit circle $|z| = 1$.

Solution :

$f(z) = \dfrac{e^z}{\cos \pi z}$ has simple poles at

$$z = \pm \frac{1}{2}, \pm\frac{3}{2}, \pm \frac{5}{2}, \ldots$$

Out of these only poles at $z = 1/2$ and $z = -\dfrac{1}{2}$ lie inside the given circle $|z| = 1$.

$$\therefore \quad \text{Res } f(1/2) = \underset{z \to 1/2}{\text{Lt}} \left[\left(z - \frac{1}{2}\right)f(z)\right]$$

$$= \underset{z \to 1/2}{\text{Lt}} \left\{\frac{\left(z-\frac{1}{2}\right)e^z}{\cos \pi z}\right\} \quad \left[\frac{0}{0}\text{form}\right]$$

$$= \underset{z \to 1/2}{\text{Lt}} \frac{e^z + \left(z - \frac{1}{2}\right)e^z}{-\pi \sin \pi z}$$

$$= \frac{e^{1/2}}{-\pi}$$

and

$$\text{Res } f(-1/2) = \underset{z \to -1/2}{\text{Lt}} \left\{\frac{\left(z-\frac{1}{2}\right)e^z}{\cos \pi z}\right\} \quad \left[\frac{0}{0}\text{form}\right]$$

$$= \underset{z \to -1/2}{\text{Lt}} \frac{e^z + \left(z - \frac{1}{2}\right)e^z}{-\pi \sin \pi z}$$

$$= \frac{e^{-1/2}}{\pi}$$

Hence

$$\oint_C \frac{e^z}{\cos \pi z}dz = 2\pi i\left\{\text{Res } f\left(\frac{1}{2}\right) + \text{Res } f\left(-\frac{1}{2}\right)\right\}$$

$$= 2\pi i\left(-\frac{e^{1/2}}{\pi} + \frac{e^{-1/2}}{\pi}\right)$$

$$= -4i\left(\frac{e^{1/2} - e^{-1/2}}{2}\right)$$

$$= -4i \sinh \frac{1}{2}.$$

Example. Evaluate $\int_C \tan z\, dz$

where C is the circle $|z| = 2$

Solution :

Poles of $f(z) = \sin z/\cos z$ are given by $\cos z = 0$

$$i.e.\ z = \pm\frac{\pi}{2}, \pm\frac{3\pi}{2}, \pm\frac{5\pi}{2}$$

Of these poles, $z = \frac{\pi}{2}$, and $-\frac{\pi}{2}$ only are within the given circle.

$$\therefore \quad \text{Res } f(\pi/2) = \underset{z\to\pi/2}{\text{Lt}} \frac{\sin z}{\frac{d}{dz}(\cos z)}$$

$$= \underset{z\to\pi/2}{\text{Lt}} \left(\frac{\sin z}{-\sin z}\right) = -1$$

$$\text{Similarly Res } f(-\pi/2) = \underset{z\to-\pi/2}{\text{Lt}} \frac{\sin z}{\frac{d}{dz}(\cos z)} = -1.$$

Hence by residue theorem,

$$\int_C f(z)\,dz = 2\pi i\,\{\text{Res } f(\pi/2) + \text{Res } f(-\pi/2)\}$$

$$= 2\pi i\,(-1-1) = 4\pi i.$$

EXERCISE

MCQ TYPE QUESTIONS

1. Taylor series expansion of the function,

$$F(x) = \frac{x}{1+x} \text{ around } x = 0 \text{ is}$$

(a) $x + x^2 + x^3 + x^4$............

(b) $1 = x + x^2 + x^3 + x^4$..............

(c) $2x + 4x^2 + 8x^3 + 16x^4$.............

(d) $x - x^2 + x^3 - x^4$..............

2. If $u = x^3 - 3xy^2 + 3x^2 - 3y^2 + 1$, then analytic function $f(z) = u(x, y) + iv(x, y)$ is

(a) $3xy - y^3 + 6xy^2 + C$

(b) $3x^2y - y^3 + 6xy + C$

(c) $3x^2y^2 - y^3 + 6xy + C$

(d) $3x^2y - y^3 + 6xy^2 + C$

3. The function $f(z) = \frac{xy^2(x+iy)}{x^2+y^4}$, $z \neq 0$

and $f(0) = 0$

(a) is not analytic at the origin

(b) is analytic at the origin

(c) can't be said

(d) none of these

4. $\oint_C \frac{\sin \pi z^2 + \cos \pi z^2}{(z-1)(z-2)}$, where C is the circle and $|z| = 3$, is equal to

(a) $2\pi i$ (b) $3\pi i$

(c) $4\pi i$ (d) $5\pi i$

5. The residue of $f(z) = \frac{z^2-2z}{(z+1)^2(z^2+4)}$ is

(a) $\frac{1\pm i}{25}$ (b) $\frac{3\pm i}{25}$

(c) $\frac{5\pm i}{25}$ (d) $\frac{7\pm i}{25}$

6. For $|z| = 1$, $\int_C \frac{z-3}{z^2+2z+5}\,dz$, where C is the circle, is

(a) 0 (b) 1

(c) 2 (d) none of these

7. For $|z+1-i| = 2$, $\int_C \frac{z-3}{z^2+2z+5}\,dz$, where C is the circle, is

(a) $\pi(i-2)$ (b) $\pi(i-3)$

(c) $\pi(i-4)$ (d) $\pi(i-5)$

8. Expansion of sin z about $z = \frac{\pi}{2}$ is

(a) $1 + 0 - \frac{\left(z-\frac{\pi}{2}\right)^2}{2!} + \frac{\left(z-\frac{\pi}{2}\right)^4}{4!} + \ldots$

(b) $1 + 0 + \frac{\left(z-\frac{\pi}{2}\right)^2}{2!} + \frac{\left(z-\frac{\pi}{2}\right)^4}{4!} + \ldots$

(c) $1 - 0 + \frac{\left(z-\frac{\pi}{2}\right)^3}{2!} + \frac{\left(z-\frac{\pi}{2}\right)^3}{3!} + \ldots$

(d) $1 - \frac{(z-\pi)^2}{2!} + \frac{(z-\pi)^3}{3!} + \ldots$

9. The most general complex analytical function

$f(z) = u(x, y) + iv(x, y)$ for $u = x^2 - y^2$ is

(a) z (b) $2z$

(c) z^3 (d) $1/z^2$

10. If $f(z) = u + iv$, then solution for $f'(z)$ is

(a) $\frac{\partial u}{\partial x} - i\frac{\partial u}{\partial x}$

(b) $\frac{\partial v}{\partial y} - i\frac{\partial u}{\partial x}$

(c) $\frac{\partial u}{\partial x} - i\frac{\partial v}{\partial x}$

(d) both (a) and (b)

11. If $v = 2xy$, then analytic function $f(z) = u + iv$ is

(a) $z^2 + c$ (b) $z^{-2} + c$

(c) $z^3 + c$ (d) $z^{-3} + c$

12. If $v = \frac{x - y}{x^2 + y^2}$, then analytic function $f(z) = u + iv$ is

(a) $z + c$ (b) $z^{-1} + c$

(c) $(1 - i)\frac{1}{z} + c$ (d) $(1 + i)\frac{1}{z} + c$

13. If $u = \frac{\sin 2x}{\cosh 2y - \cos 2x}$, then analytic function $f(z) = u + iv$ is

(a) $\cot z + ic$

(b) $\operatorname{cosec} z + ic$

(c) $\sinh z + ic$

(d) $\cosh z + ic$

14. If C is the circle $|z| = 3$, then $\int_C \frac{\cos \pi z}{z - 1} dz$ equals

(a) $i2\pi$ (b) $-i2\pi$

(c) $i6\pi^2$ (d) $-i6\pi^2$

15. Laurent's series of $f(z) = \frac{z}{(z+1)(z^2+4)}$ is, where $|z| < 1$

(a) $\frac{1}{4}z - \frac{5}{16}z^3 + \frac{21}{64}z^5 \ldots\ldots\ldots$

(b) $\frac{1}{2} + \frac{1}{4}z^2 + \frac{5}{16}z^4 + \frac{21}{64}z^6 \ldots\ldots\ldots$

(c) $\frac{1}{2}z - \frac{3}{4}z^3 + \frac{15}{8}z^5 \ldots\ldots\ldots$

(d) $\frac{1}{2} + \frac{1}{2}z^2 + \frac{3}{4}z^4 + \frac{15}{8}z^6 \ldots\ldots\ldots$

16. If C is $|z - 1| = 1$, then $\int_C z^2 e^{\frac{1}{z}} dz$ is

(a) $i3\pi$ (b) $-i3\pi$

(c) $\frac{i\pi}{3}$ (d) none of these

NUMERICAL TYPE QUESTIONS

1. Residue of the function $\frac{1 - e^{2z}}{z^4}$ at its pole is_____.

2. Residue of $z \cos\frac{1}{z}$ at $z = 0$ is_____.

ANSWERS

MCQ Type Questions

1. (d)	**2.** (b)	**3.** (a)	**4.** (c)	**5.** (d)	**6.** (a)	**7.** (a)	**8.** (a)	**9.** (b)	**10.** (d)
11. (a)	**12.** (d)	**13.** (a)	**14.** (b)	**15.** (a)	**16.** (c)				

Numerical Type Questions

1. $\frac{-4}{3}$ **2.** $\frac{-1}{2}$

EXPLANATIONS

MCQ TYPE QUESTIONS

1. $f(x) = \frac{x}{1+x}$

$f(x) = f(0) + f'(0)(x-0) + \frac{f''(0)}{\lfloor 2}(x-a)^2 + \frac{f'''(0)}{\lfloor 3}x^3 + ...$

$= 0 + x + (-x^2) + x^3 + ...$

$= x - x^2 + x^3 + ...$

2. Given: $u = x^3 - 3xy^2 + 3x^2 - 3y^2 + 1$

$\therefore \quad \frac{\partial u}{\partial x} = 3x^2 - 3y^2 + 6x$

and $\quad \frac{\partial u}{\partial y} = -6xy - 6y$

By C.R. equations,

$\frac{\partial u}{\partial x} = 3x^2 - 3y^2 + 6x$

$\therefore \quad V = 3x^2y - y^3 + 6xy + \phi(x) + C \quad ...(i)$

$\frac{\partial u}{\partial x} = -\frac{\partial v}{\partial x} = -6xy - 6y$

$\Rightarrow \quad \frac{\partial v}{\partial x} = 6xy + 6y$

$\therefore \quad V = 3x^2y + 6xy + \phi(y) + C \quad ...(ii)$

From equations (*i*) and (*ii*), we get

$3x^2y - y^3 + 6xy + \phi(x) + C = 3x^2y + 6xy + \phi(y) + C.$

$\Rightarrow \quad \phi(x) - \phi(y) = y^3$

$\therefore \quad \phi(x) = 0, \quad$ and $\quad \phi(y) = -y^3.$

$\therefore \quad V = 3x^2y - y^3 + 6xy + C.$

3. We know that given function is not analytic at (0, 0) if derivative $f'(z)$ does not exists at (0, 0)

Now, $\quad f'(z) = \lim_{z\to 0}\frac{f(z)-f(0)}{z-0}$

$= \lim_{z\to 0}\frac{f(z)}{z} = \lim_{\substack{x\to 0\\ y\to 0}}\left[\frac{xy^2}{x^2+y^4}\right]$

provided this limit exists independent of the manner in which $z \to 0$.

Consider two ways in which $z \to 0$.

Case I : $x = 0, y \to 0$

Then $\lim_{x\to 0}\frac{0}{0+y^4} = 0$

Case II : $x = y^2, x \to 0$

Then $\lim_{x\to 0}\frac{x.x}{x^2+x^2} \lim_{x\to 0}\frac{x^2}{2x^2} = \frac{1}{2}$

This shows that above limit is not unique, i.e. it depends on the manner in which $z \to 0$. So derivative $f'(z)$ does not exists at (0, 0) and hence given function $f(z)$ is not analytic at (0, 0).

4. Since $\frac{1}{(z-1)(z-2)} = \frac{1}{z-2} - \frac{1}{z-1}, ...$

$\therefore \quad \oint \frac{\sin \pi z^2 + \cos \pi z^2}{(z-1)(z-2)}$

$= +\int_c \frac{\sin \pi z^2 + \cos \pi z^2}{z-2} dz$

$- \int_c \frac{\sin \pi z^2 + \cos \pi z^2}{z-1} dz$

By Cauchy integral formula.

$\int_c \frac{\sin \pi z^2 + \cos \pi z^2}{z-2} dz = 2\pi i[\sin \pi (2)^2 + \cos \pi (2)^2]$

$= 2\pi i\,[0 + 1]$

$= 2\pi i$

and $\int_c \frac{\sin \pi z^2 + \cos \pi z^2}{z-1} dz$

$= 2\pi i\,[\sin \pi + \cos \pi]$

$= -2\pi i$

$\therefore$ Required integral $= 2\pi i - (-2\pi i) = 4\pi i$

5. $f(z)$ has a double pole at $z = -1$ and simple poles at $z = \pm 2i$

$\text{Res}(-1) = \lim_{z\to(-1)} \frac{1}{1!}\frac{d}{dz}\left\{(z+1)^2 \frac{z^2-2z}{(z+1)^2(z^2+4)}\right\}$

$= \lim_{z\to -1} \frac{(z^2+4)(2z-2)-(z^2-2z)(2z)}{(z^2+4)^2}$

$= \frac{14}{25}$

$$\text{Res}(2i) = \lim_{z\to -2}\frac{(z+2i)(z^2-2z)}{(z^2+4)(z+1)^2}$$

$$= \frac{z^2-2z}{(z+2i)(z+1^2)}$$

$$= \frac{(2i)^2-4i}{4i(2i+1)^2}$$

$$= \frac{7+i}{25}$$

$$\text{Res}(-2i) = \lim_{z\to -2}\frac{(z+2i)(z^2-2z)}{(z^2+4)(z+1)^2}$$

$$= \frac{(-2i)^2+2(2i)}{(-2i-2i)(-2i+1)^2}$$

$$= \frac{7-i}{25}$$

6. Poles of $f(z) = \dfrac{z-3}{z^2+2z+5}$ are given by

$z^2 + 2z + 5 = 0$

$$\therefore \quad z = \frac{-2\pm 4i}{2} = -1 \pm 2i$$

Since, both the poles lie outside the circle $|z| = 1$, therefore $f(z)$ is analytic inside the circle

$$\therefore \quad \oint \frac{z-3}{z^2+2z+5}dz = 0$$

7. When $z = -1 - 2i$,

$|-1-2i+1-1| = |-3i| = 3 > 2.$

When $z = -1 + 2i$,

$|-1+2i+1-i| = |i| = 1 < 2.$

Therefore only $-1 + 2i$ lie inside the closed curve.

Res at $(-1 + 2i)$

$$= \lim_{x\to -1+2i}[z-(-1+2i)]\frac{z-3}{z^2+2z+5}$$

$$= \lim_{x\to 1+2i}\frac{z-3}{(z+1+2i)}$$

$$= \frac{-1+2i-3}{-1+2i+1+2i}$$

$$= \frac{-4+2i}{4i}$$

$$= \left(i+\frac{1}{2}\right)$$

Hence by residue theorem,

$$\oint_c \frac{z-3}{z^2+2z+5}dz = 2\pi i\left(i+\frac{1}{2}\right) = \pi(i-2)$$

8. Here $a = \pi/2$

$$f(z) = \sin z,\ f\left(\frac{\pi}{2}\right) = 1$$

$$f'(z) = \cos z,\ f'\left(\frac{\pi}{2}\right) = 0$$

$$f''(z) = -\sin z,\ f''\left(\frac{\pi}{2}\right) = -1$$

$$f'''(z) = -\cos z,\ f'''\left(\frac{\pi}{2}\right) = 0$$

$$\therefore \quad f(z) = f(a) + f'(a)(z-a) + \frac{f''(a)}{2i}(z-a)^2 + \ldots.$$

$$= 1 + 0 - \frac{\left(z-\frac{\pi}{2}\right)^2}{2i} + \frac{\left(z-\frac{\pi}{2}\right)^4}{4i} + - \ldots.$$

9. Here, $f(z) = u(x, y) + iv(x, y)$ and $u = x^2 - y^2$

From Cauchy-Riemann equation

$$\frac{\partial u}{\partial x} = \frac{\partial v}{\partial y} = 2y$$

$$\Rightarrow \quad \frac{\partial u}{\partial y} = -\frac{\partial v}{\partial x} = -2y$$

$$\text{Now,}\quad \frac{df(z)}{dz} = \frac{\partial u}{\partial x} + i\frac{\partial v}{\partial y} = 2x + i2y = 2(x+iy) = 2z$$

10.

$$f'(z) = \frac{df}{dz} = \lim_{\Delta z\to 0}\frac{\Delta f}{\Delta z}$$

$$\Rightarrow \quad f'(z) = \lim_{\Delta z\to 0}\frac{\Delta u + i\Delta v}{\Delta x + i\Delta y} \qquad \ldots(i)$$

Now, derivative $f'(z)$ exits of the limit in equation (i) is unique, i.e. it does not depends on the path along which $\Delta z \to 0$.

Let $\Delta z \to 0$ along a path parallel to real axis

$\Rightarrow \quad \Delta y \to 0$

$\therefore \quad \Delta z \to 0$

$\Rightarrow \quad \Delta x \to 0$

From equation (i)

$$f'(z) = \lim_{\Delta x \to 0} \frac{\Delta u + i\Delta v}{\Delta x}$$

$$= \lim_{\Delta x \to 0} \frac{\Delta v}{\Delta x} + i \lim_{\Delta x \to 0} \frac{\Delta v}{\Delta x}$$

$$\Rightarrow \quad f'(z) = \frac{\partial u}{\partial x} + i\frac{\partial v}{\partial x} \quad ...(ii)$$

Again, let $\Delta z \to 0$ along a path parallel to imaginary axis, then

$\Delta x \to 0$, $\Delta z \to 0 \Rightarrow \Delta y \to 0$

From equation (i)

$$\phi'(z) = \lim_{\Delta y \to 0} \frac{\Delta z + i\Delta v}{i\Delta y}$$

$$= \lim_{\Delta y \to 0} \frac{\Delta u}{i\Delta y} + i \lim_{\Delta y \to 0} \frac{\Delta v}{i\Delta z}$$

$$= \frac{\partial u}{i\partial y} + \frac{\partial v}{\partial y}$$

$$\therefore \quad f'(z) = \frac{-i\partial u}{\partial y} + \frac{\partial v}{\partial y} \quad ...(iii)$$

For existence of $f'(z)$ R.H.S. of equations (ii) and (iii) must be same i.e.,

$$\frac{\partial u}{\partial x} + i\frac{\partial v}{\partial x} = \frac{\partial v}{\partial y} - i\frac{\partial u}{\partial y}$$

$$\frac{\partial u}{\partial x} = \frac{\partial v}{\partial y} \text{ and } \frac{\partial v}{\partial x} = -\frac{\partial u}{\partial y}$$

$$\therefore \quad f'(z) = \frac{\partial u}{\partial x} - i\frac{\partial u}{\partial y}$$

$$= \frac{\partial v}{\partial y} + i\frac{\partial u}{\partial x}$$

11. $\frac{\partial v}{\partial x} = 2y = h(x,y)$,

$$\frac{\partial v}{\partial y} = 2x = g(x,y)$$

By Milne's method

$$f'(z) = g(z,0) + ih(z,0)$$

$$= 2z + i0 = 2z$$

Integrating, we get

$$f'(z) = z^2 + c$$

12. $$\frac{\partial v}{\partial y} = \frac{-(x^2+y^2)-(x-y)2y}{(x^2+y^2)^2}$$

$$= \frac{y^2-x^2-2xy}{(x^2+y^2)^2} = g(x,y)$$

and $$\frac{\partial v}{\partial x} = \frac{(x^2+y^2)-(x-y)2x}{(x^2+y^2)^2}$$

$$= \frac{y^2-x^2+2xy}{(x^2+y^2)^2} = h(x,y)$$

By Milne's method

$$f'(z) = g(z,0) + ih(z,0)$$

$$= -\frac{1}{z^2} + i\left(-\frac{1}{z^2}\right) = -(1+i)\frac{1}{z^2}$$

Integrating, we get

$$f'(z) = -(1+i)\int \frac{1}{z^2} dz + c = (1+i)\frac{1}{z} + c$$

13. $$\frac{\partial u}{\partial x} = \frac{2\cos 2x(\cosh 2y - \cos 2x) - 2\sin^2 2x}{(\cosh 2y - \cos 2x)^2}$$

$$= \frac{2\cos 2x \cosh 2y - 2}{(\cosh 2y - \cos 2x)^2} = \phi(x,y)$$

$$\frac{\partial u}{\partial x} = \frac{2\sin 2x \sinh 2y}{(\cosh 2y - \cos 2x)^2} = \psi(x,y)$$

By Milne's method

$$f'(z) = \phi(z,0) - i\psi(z,0)$$

$$= \frac{2\cos 2z - 2}{(1-\cos 2z)^2} - i(0)$$

$$= \frac{-2}{1-\cos 2z} = -\text{cosec}^2 z$$

Integrating, we get

$$f'(z) = -\int \text{cosec}^2 z\, dz + ic = \cot z + ic$$

14. Let $f(z) = \cos \pi z$

Then $f(z)$ is analytic within and on $|z| = 3$

By Cauchy's integral formula

$$f(z_0) = \frac{1}{2\pi i}\int_c \frac{f(z)}{z-z_0} dz \Rightarrow \int_c \frac{f(z)dz}{z-z_0} = 2\pi i f(z_0)$$

Taking $f(z) = \cos \pi z$ and $z_0 = 1$, we have

$$\int_{|z|=3} \frac{\cos \pi z}{z-1} dz = 2\pi i f(1) = 2\pi i \cos \pi = -2\pi i$$

15. $f(z) = \dfrac{z}{(z^2+1)(z^2+4)}$

$$= \frac{z}{3(z^2+1)} - \frac{z}{3(z^2+4)}, |z|<1 \Rightarrow |z^2|<1$$

$$f(z) = \frac{z}{3}(1+z^2)^{-1} - \frac{z}{12}\left(1+\frac{z^2}{4}\right)^{-1}$$

$$= \frac{z}{3}(1-z^2+z^4-...)^{-1} - \frac{z}{12}\left(1-\frac{z^2}{4}+\frac{z^4}{16}-...\right)$$

$$= \frac{1}{4}z - \frac{5}{16}z^3 + \frac{21}{64}z^5.....$$

16. $f(z) = z^2 e^{\frac{1}{z}}$

$$= z^2\left(1+\frac{1}{z}+\frac{1}{2!z^2}+\frac{1}{3!z^3}+.....\right)$$

$$= z^2 + z + \frac{1}{2} + \frac{1}{6z} + ...$$

The only pole of $f(z)$ is at $z = 0$, which lies within the circle $|z| = 1$

$$\int_c f(z)dz = 2\pi i \text{ (residue at z = 0)}$$

Residuce of $f(z)$ at $z = 0$ is coefficient of $\frac{1}{z}$ i.e., $\frac{1}{6}$

$$\therefore \quad \int_c f(z)dz = 2\pi i \times \frac{1}{6} = \frac{1}{3}\pi i$$

NUMERICAL TYPE QUESTIONS

1. Let $f(z) = \dfrac{1-e^{2z}}{z^4}$

then $f(z)$ has a pole at $z = 0$ of order 4.

Residue of $f(z)$ at $z = 0$

$$= \frac{1}{3!}\lim_{z\to z_0}\frac{d^3}{dz^3}(1-e^{2z})$$

$$= \frac{1}{(m-1)!}\lim_{z\to z_0}\frac{d^{m-1}}{dz^{m-1}}(z-z_0)^m f(z)$$

$$= \frac{1}{(4-1)!}\lim_{z\to z_0}\frac{d^3}{dz^3}\left[z^4.\left(\frac{1-e^{2z}}{z^4}\right)\right]$$

$$= \frac{-1}{3!}\lim_{z\to z_0} 8e^{2z}$$

$$= \frac{-8}{6}(e^0)$$

$$= \frac{-8}{6} = \frac{-4}{3}$$

2. Putting $z = 0 + t$ we have

$$f(z) = z\cos\frac{1}{z}$$

$$= t\cos\frac{1}{t}$$

$$= t\left(1-\frac{1}{2!}\frac{1}{t^2}+\frac{1}{4!}\frac{1}{t^4}.....\right)$$

$$= t - \frac{1}{2t} + \frac{1}{24t^3} - .....$$

Residue of $f(z)$ at $z = 0$ is coefficient of $\frac{1}{t}$ i.e. $-\frac{1}{2}$

TECHNICAL SECTION

BASICS OF CIRCUITS AND MEASUREMENT SYSTEMS | 1

1.1 KIRCHOFF'S LAW

1.1.1. Kirchoff's Current Law (KCL).

In any network, the algebraic sum of currents meeting at a point is always zero. Thus, total current leaving a junction is equal to the total current entering that junction.

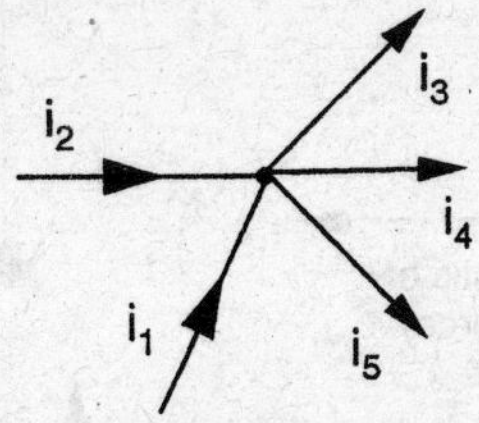

Fig. 1.1

$$\Sigma I_{(at\ node)} = 0$$
$$\Sigma I = +i_1 + i_2 - i_3 - i_4 - i_5 = 0$$

i.e. $i_1 + i_2 = i_3 + i_4 + i_5$

1.1.2. Kirchoff's Voltage Law (KVL).

In any network the algebraic sum of the voltage drops across the circuit elements of any closed path is equal to algebraic sum of the *e.m.f.* in the path.

Thus algebraic sum of all the branch voltages, around any closed path or closed loop is always zero.

Around a closed path $\Sigma V = 0$

1.1.3. Source Transformation.

A real physical source is represented by

(i) a resistance in series with an ideal voltage source.

(ii) a resistance in parallel with an ideal current source.

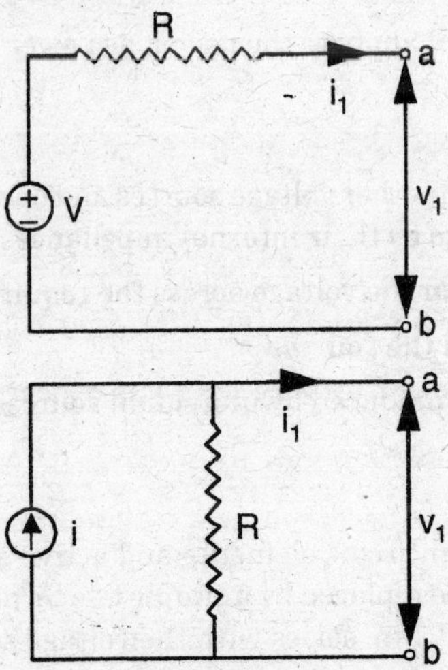

Fig. 1.2

Hence, To convert a voltage source V in series with an internal resistance R into an equivalent current source, replace the voltage source with a current source of value (V/R) placed in parallel with a resistance R as shown in the Fig. 1.2.

If a current source I in parallel with a resistance R is to be converted into a voltage source, it is achieved by substituting a voltage source (IR) in series with a resistance R.

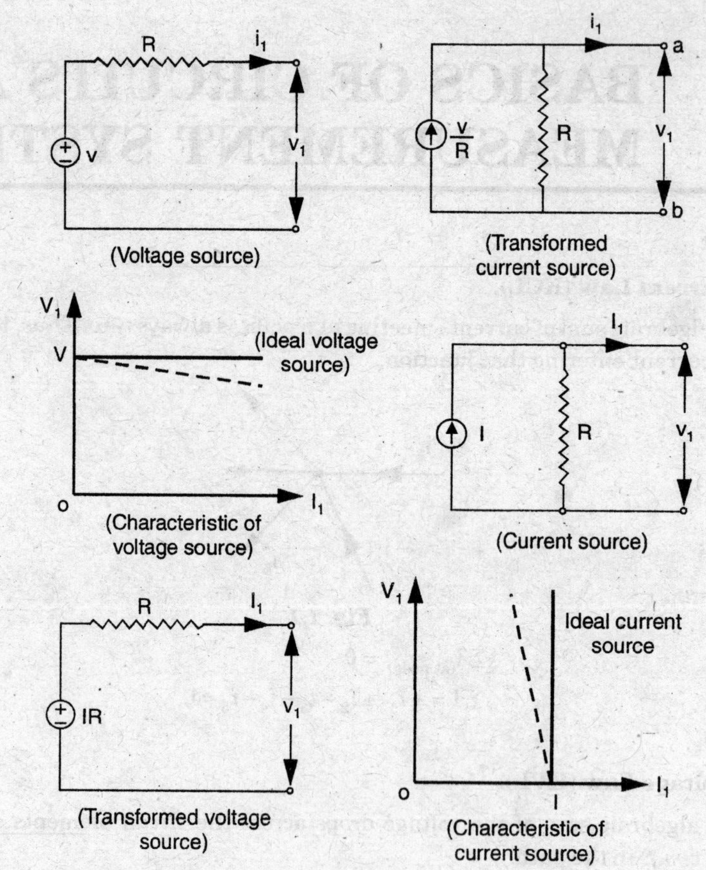

Fig. 1.3

For Ideal voltage source internal resistance = 0

For Ideal current source internal resistance = ∞

1.2 NETWORK THEOREMS

1.2.1. Superposition Theorem.

The response in any element of LTI network linear, bilateral network containing more than one sources is the sum of the responses produced by the sources each acting independently.

The superposition theorem does not apply to the power, as power is proportional to square of the current which is not a linear function.

Steps :

(i) Select a single source. Short the other voltage sources and open the current sources, if internal impedances are not known. If known, replace them by their internal impedances.

(ii) Find out the current through or the voltage across the required element, due to the source under consideration.

(iii) Repeat the above steps for all the sources

(iv) Add all the individual effects produced by individual sources to obtain the total current in or voltage across the element.

1.2.2. Thevenin's Theorem.

Any combination of linear bilateral circuit elements and active sources, regardless of the connection or complexity, connected to a given load Z_L, may be replaced by a simple two terminal network consisting of a single voltage source of V_{TH} volts and a single impedance Z_{eq} in series with the voltage source, across the two terminals of the load Z_L.

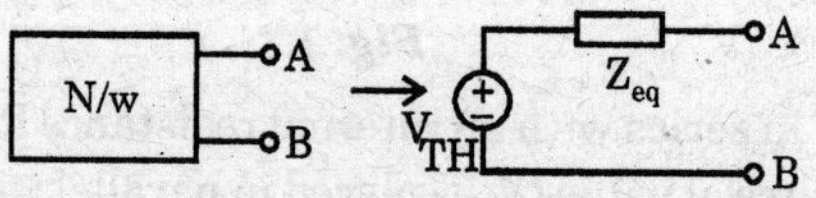

Steps :

(i) Remove branch impedance, through which current is required to calculate.

(ii) Calculate voltage across the open circuited terminals. This voltage is Thevenin's equivalent voltage V_{TH}

(iii) Calculate equivalent impedance Z_{eq} as viewed through two terminals of the branch from which current is to be calculated by removing that branch impedance and replacing all the independent sources by their internal impedance.

(iv) Required current through the branch is given by,

$$I = \frac{V_{TH}}{Z_L + Z_{eq}}$$

1.2.3. Norton's Theorem

Any combination of linear bilateral circuit elements and active sources regardless of the connection or complexity, connected to a given load Z_L can be replaced by a simple two terminal network consisting of a single current source of I_N and a single impedance Z_{eq} in parallel with it, across the two terminals of the load Z_L.

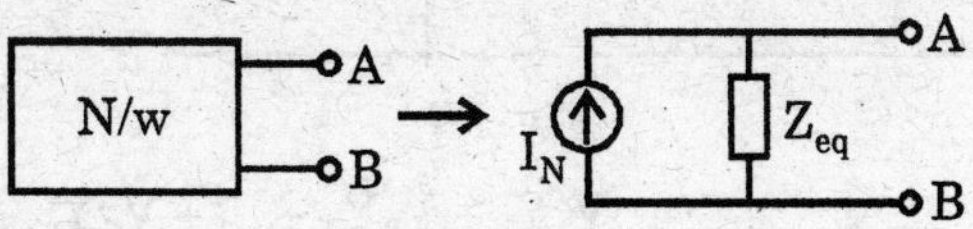

Steps :

(i) Short the branch through which the current is to be calculated.

(ii) Find out the current through this short circuited branch. This current is nothing but Norton's current I_N.

(iii) Calculate equivalent impedance Z_{eq} as viewed through the two terminals of interest by removing the branch impedance and making all the independent sources inactive.

(iv) Current through the branch of interest is given by,

$$I = I_N \times \frac{Z_{eq}}{Z_{eq} + Z_L}$$

$$Z_{eq} = \frac{V_{th}}{I_N}$$

1.2.4. Maximum Power Transfer Theorems.

In an active network, maximum power transfer to the load takes place when the load impedance is complex conjugate of an equivalent impedance of the network as viewed from the terminals of the load.

i.e. $Z_0 = Z_i$

Let the load $Z_l = R_l + jX_l$

and $Z_i = R_i + jX_i$

Power transfered from source to the load

Case 1

if $Z_i = R_i + jX_i$

$Z_L = R_L + jX_L$

then $Z_L = Z_i$

$R_i = R_L ; X_L = -X_i$

Case 2

If $Z_L = R_L$

then $R_L = \sqrt{R_i^2 + X_i^2}$

Case 3

If $Z_L = R_L$

$Z_i = R_i$

$R_L = R_i$

The maximum power transfer to the load from the source is only 50% of the total power generated by the source.

1.2.5. Millman's Theorem.

If n voltage sources $V_1, V_2, ..V_n$ having internal impedances (or series impedances) $Z_1, Z_2, .Z_n$ respectively in series then these sources may be replaced by a single voltage source of voltage V_M having a series impedance Z_M, where V_M and Z_M are given by

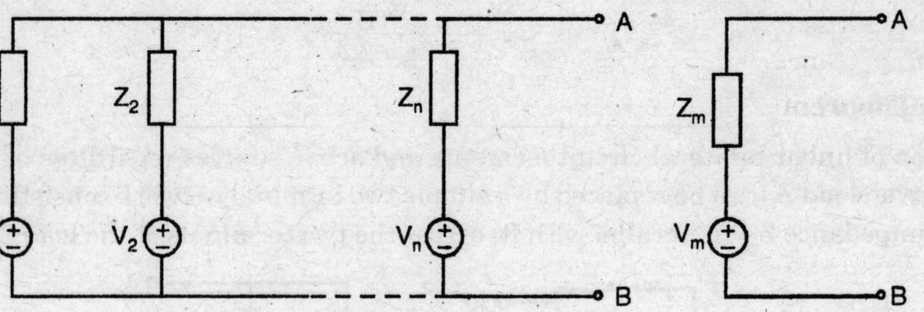

Fig. 1.4

$$V_M = \frac{V_1Y_1 + V_2Y_2 + \ldots + V_nY_n}{Y_1 + Y_2 + \ldots + Y_n}$$

$$Z_M = \frac{1}{Y_1 + Y_2 + \ldots + Y_n}$$

1.2.6. Reciprocity Theorem.

In any linear network consisting of linear and bilateral impedances and active sources, the ratio of voltage V introduced in one loop to the current I in other loop is same as the ratio obtained if positions of V and I are interchanged in the network.

1.2.7. Tellegan's Theorem.

In an arbitrary lumped network, algebraic sum of the instantaneous powers in all the branches, at any instant is zero.

Mathematically, $$\sum_{K=1}^{b} v_K i_K = 0$$

$\therefore$ $$P = I^2R$$

where R = resistive part of the equivalent impedance of the circuit.

1.3 SOLUTION METHODS

1.3.1. Loop or Mesh Analysis.

Mesh analysis is specially useful for the circuits that have many nodes and loops.

In the network shown, there are two loops. So, assuming two loop currents as I_1 and I_2, while assuming loop currents, consider the loops such that each element of the network will be included atleast once in any of the loops.

No. of Loops or Mesh = $b - (n - 1)$

where b = no. of branches

n = no. of nodes

Thus, writing loop equations for the network.

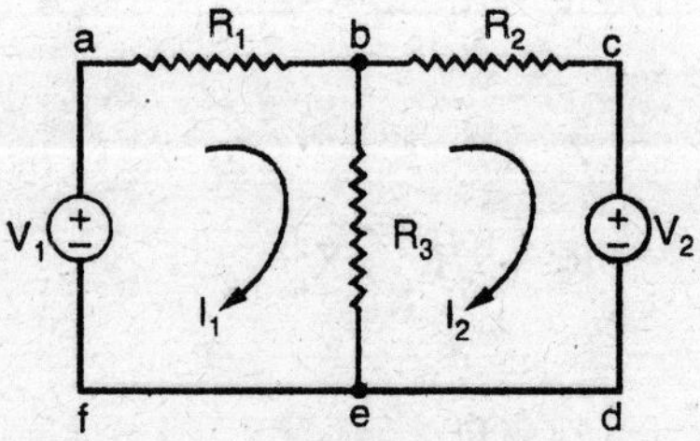

Fig. 1.5

For loop $a - b - e - f - a$,

$$-I_1R_1 - (I_1 - I_2)R_3 + V_1 = 0$$

For loop $b - c - d - e - b$,

$$-R_2I_2 - (I_2 - I_1)R_3 + V_2 = 0$$

- While assuming loop currents make sure that atleast one loop current links with every element.
- No two loops should be identical.
- Choose minimum number of loop currents.
- Convert current sources if present into their equivalent voltage sources for loop analysis whenever possible.
- If current in a particular branch is required, then try to choose loop current in such a way that only one loop current links with that branch.

1.3.2. Node Analysis.

Node analysis is mainly based on Kirchoff's Current Law (KCL). This method uses the analysis of different nodes of the network. In nodal analysis, one of the nodes is assumed as reference node whose potential is assumed to be zero. Other voltages at different nodes are to be measured with respect to this reference node. The reference node should be given a number zero and then equations are to be written for all other nodes by applying KCL.

No. of KCL equation = $n - 1$

where n = no. of Nodes.

Node 1 :

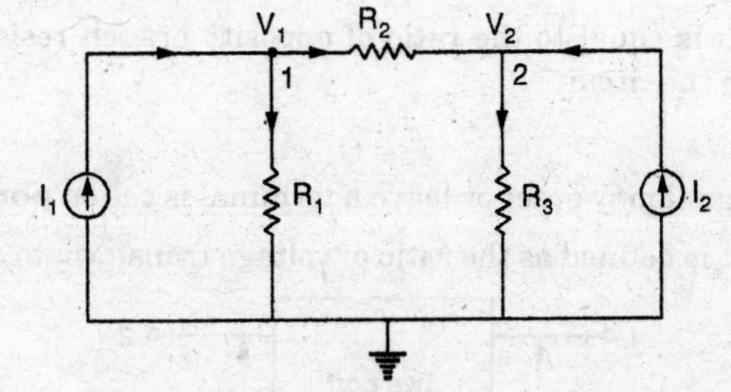

Fig. 1.6

$$I_1 - \frac{V_1}{R_1} - \frac{(V_1 - V_2)}{R_2} = 0 \quad \text{... (1)}$$

Node 2 :

$$\frac{(V_1 - V_2)}{R_2} - \frac{V_2}{R_3} + I_2 = 0 \quad \text{... (2)}$$

Rearranging equations (1) and (2), we get

$$V_1\left[\frac{1}{R_1} + \frac{1}{R_2}\right] - V_2\left[\frac{1}{R_2}\right] = I_1$$

and

$$-V_1\left[\frac{1}{R_2}\right] + V_2 \cdot \left[\frac{1}{R_2} + \frac{1}{R_3}\right] = I_2$$

Above equations can be solved simultaneously to get the unknown node voltages from which any branch current can be calculated.

- While assuming branch currents, make sure that each unknown branch current is considered atleast once.
- Convert voltage source present into their equivalent current sources for node analysis wherever possible.
- Follow the same sign convention, currents entering at node are to be considered positive, while currents leaving the node are to be considered as negative.

1.3.3. Voltage Division and Current Division.

Voltage division in series circuit :

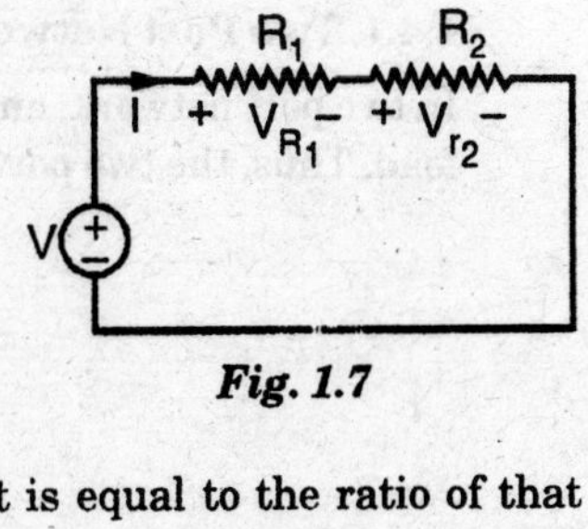

Fig. 1.7

$$V_{R_1} = \left[\frac{R_1}{R_1 + R_2}\right] V$$

$$V_{R_2} = \left[\frac{R_2}{R_1 + R_2}\right] V$$

Thus, voltage drop across any resistor or combination of resistors, in a series circuit is equal to the ratio of that resistance value to the total resistance, multiplied by the source voltage.

Current division in parallel circuit:

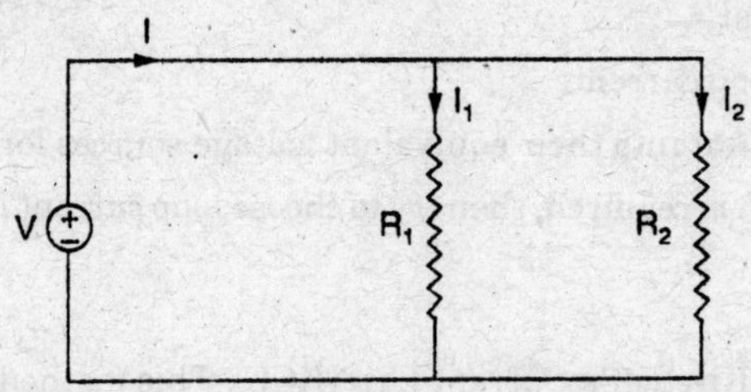

Fig. 1.8

$$I_1 = \left[\frac{R_2}{R_1 + R_2}\right] I$$

$$I_2 = \left[\frac{R_1}{R_1 + R_2}\right] I$$

Thus, the current in any branch is equal to the ratio of opposite branch resistance to the total resistance value, multiplied by the total current in the circuit.

1.4 TWO PORT NETWORK

A pair of terminals at which a signal may enter or leave a terminal is called **port**.

The transfer impedance at a port is defined as the ratio of voltage transform to current transform of a network.

Fig. 1.9

$$Z(s) = \frac{V(s)}{I(s)}$$

Similarly, Transfer admittance Y(*s*) is defined as

$$Y(s) = \frac{I(s)}{Z(s)}$$

The impedance or admittance found at a given port is called *driving point impedance or admittance function.*

$$\text{Voltage transform function} = G_{12}(s) = \frac{V_1(s)}{V_2(s)}\ ;\ G_{12}(s) = \frac{V_2(s)}{V_1(s)}$$

$$\text{Current transform function} = \alpha_{12}(s) = \frac{I_1(s)}{I_2(s)}\ ;\ \alpha_{21}(s) = \frac{I_2(s)}{I_1(s)}$$

$$\text{Transfer impedance function} = Z_{12}(s) = \frac{V_1(s)}{I_2(s)}\ ;\ Z_{21}(s) = \frac{V_2(s)}{I_1(s)}$$

$$\text{Transfer admittance function} = Y_{12}(s) = \frac{I_1(s)}{V_2(s)}\ ;\ Y_{21}(s) = \frac{I_2(s)}{V_1(s)}$$

1.4.1. Two Port Network Parameters.

In two port network, one port is used as input for connecting energy source and other is used as output for connecting load. Thus, the two port network has two pairs of voltage and current.

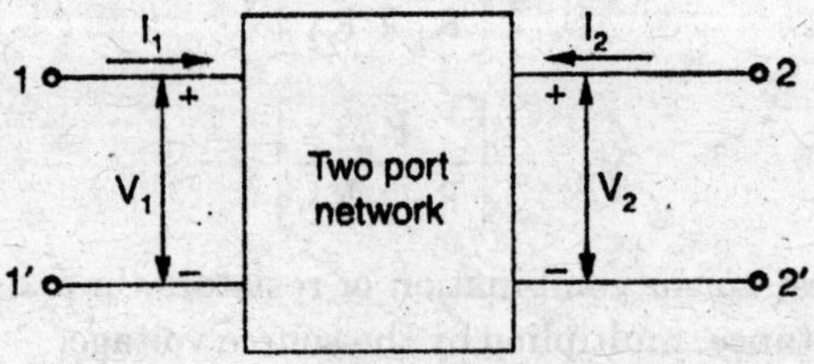

Fig. 1.10

Z-parameters :

These are also called *impedance parameters.*

$$V_1 = f_1(I_1, I_2)$$
$$V_2 = f_2(I_1, I_2)$$

In equation form,

$$V_1 = Z_{11}I_1 + Z_{12}I_2$$
$$V_2 = Z_{21}I_1 + Z_{22}I_2$$

Z_{11} = with output port open circuit input driving point impedance = $\left.\frac{V_1}{I_1}\right|_{I_2=0}$

Z_{22} = with input port open circuit output driving point impedance = $\left.\frac{V_2}{I_2}\right|_{I_1=0}$

Z_{12} = with input port open circuit forward transfer impedance = $\left.\frac{V_1}{I_2}\right|_{I_1=0}$

Z_{21} = with output port open circuit reverse transfer impedance = $\left.\frac{V_2}{I_1}\right|_{I_2=0}$

***h*-parameters :**

These are also called *hybrid parameters.*

$$V_1 = f_1(I_1, V_2)$$
$$I_2 = f_2(I_1, V_2)$$

In equation form,

$$V_1 = h_{11}I_1 + h_{12}V_2$$
$$I_2 = h_{21}I_1 + h_{22}V_2$$

Short circuit input impedance $= h_{11} = \left.\frac{V_1}{I_1}\right|_{V_2=0} = h_i$

Forward short circuit current gain $= h_{21} = \left.\frac{I_2}{I_1}\right|_{V_2=0} = h_f$

Reverse open circuit voltage gain $= h_{12} = \left.\frac{V_1}{V_2}\right|_{I_1=0} = h_r$

Open circuit output admittance $= h_{22} = \left.\frac{I_2}{V_2}\right|_{I_1=0} = h_o$

ABCD parameters :

These are also called *transmission parameters.*

$$V_1 = f_1(V_2, -I_2)$$
$$I_2 = f_2(V_2, -I_2)$$

In equation form,

$$V_1 = AV_2 + B(-I_2)$$
$$I_1 = CV_2 + D(-I_2)$$

Open circuit reverse voltage gain $= A = \left.\dfrac{V_1}{I_1}\right|_{I_2=0}$

Open circuit transfer admittance $= C = \left.\dfrac{I_1}{V_2}\right|_{I_2=0}$

Short circuit transfer impedance $= B = \left.\dfrac{V_1}{-I_2}\right|_{V_2=0}$

Short circuit reverse current gain $= D = \left.\dfrac{I_1}{\pm I_2}\right|_{V_2=0}$

Table : Condition for symmetry and reciprocity of network.

Parameter	*Condition for Reciprocity of Network*	*Condition for symmetry of Network*
Z	$Z_{12} = Z_{21}$	$Z_{11} = Z_{22}$
Y	$Y_{12} = Y_{21}$	$Y_{11} = Y_{22}$
h	$h_{12} = -h_{21}$	$h_{11} h_{22} - h_{12} h_{21} = 1$
T	$AD - BC = 1$	$A = D$

1.5 FOURIER SERIES

Fourier series can be represented in the form of infinite trigonometric series or infinite exponential series. Fourier series consists *dc* terms as well as *ac* terms of all harmonics.

1.5.1 Trigonometric Fourier Series.

If any function f(t) is periodic, it satisfies the Dirichlet conditions as follows :

(i) It has at most a finite number of discontinuities in the period T.

(ii) It has at most a finite number of maxima and minima in the period T.

(iii) If it has a finite average value, *i.e* the integral $\int_{-T/2}^{T/2} |f(t)|\, dt$ is finite, then the periodic function $f(t)$ can be expanded into an infinite trigonometric Fourier series as

$$f(t) = a_0 + a_1 \cos \omega t + a_2 \cos 2\omega t + ..+ a_n \cos n\omega t + \ldots + b_1 \sin \omega t + b_2 \sin 2\omega t + ..+ b_n \sin n\omega t$$

$$= a_0 + \sum_{n=1}^{\infty} (a_n \cos n\omega t + b_n \sin n\omega t)$$

where coefficients a_n and b_n are given by

$$a_n = \frac{2}{T} \int_0^T f(t) \cos n\omega t \, dt$$

$$a_0 = \frac{1}{T} \int_0^T f(t)\, dt$$

$$b_n = \frac{2}{T} \int_0^T f(t) \sin n\omega t \, dt$$

1.5.2 Existence of the Fourier Series : Dirichlet Conditions.

(i) For the series to exist, the coefficients a_0, a_n and b_n must be finite. Existence of these coefficients is guaranteed if $f(t)$ is absolutely integrable over one period

$$\int_0^T |f(t)\, dt| < \infty$$

This is called *weak Dirichlet condition*. If a function $f(t)$ satisfies the weak Dirichlet condition, the existence of a Fourier series is guaranteed, but the series may not converge at every point.

(*ii*) The function $f(t)$ have only a finite number of maxima and minima in one period and it may have only a finite number of finite discontinuities in one period.

These two conditions are *called strong Dirichlet conditions*.

1.5.3 Exponential Fourier Series.

A signal $f(t)$ can be expressed over an interval of duration T_0 seconds as an expontial Fourier series

$$f(t) = \sum_{n=-\infty}^{\infty} D_n e^{jn\omega_0 t} dt$$

where
$$D_n = \frac{1}{T_0}\int_0^{T_0} f(t)\, e^{-jn\omega_0 t}\, dt$$

The exponential Fourier series is basically another form of the trigonometric Fourier series.

The compact trigonometric Fourier series of a periodic signal $f(t)$ is given by

$$f(t) = C_0 + \sum_{n=1}^{\infty} C_n \cos(n\omega_0 t + \theta_n)$$

where
$$C_n = \sqrt{a_n^2 + b_n^2}$$

From this
$$f(t) = D_0 + \sum_{n=1}^{\infty} D_n e^{jn\omega_0 t} + D_{-n} e^{-jn\omega_0 t} = D_0 + \sum_{n=-\infty (n\neq 0)}^{\infty} D_n e^{jn\omega_0 t}$$

where
$$D_n = \frac{1}{2} C_n e^{j\theta_n}$$

and
$$D_{-n} = \frac{1}{2} C_n e^{-j\theta_n}$$

$$D_n = \frac{a_n - jbn}{2}$$

$$D_{-n} = \frac{a_n + jbn}{2}$$

1.5.4 Parseval's Theorem.

The power P_f of $f(t)$ is equal to the power of its Fourier series. Because Fourier series consists of terms that are mutually orthogonal over one period, the power of Fourier series is equal to sum of the powers of its Fourier components.

$$f(t) = C_0 + \sum_{n=1}^{\infty} C_n \cos(n\omega_0 t + \theta_n)$$

$$P_f = C_0^2 + \frac{1}{2}\sum_{n=1}^{\infty} C_n^2$$

For exponential Fourier series,

$$f(t) = D_0 + \sum_{\substack{n=-\infty \\ (n\neq 0)}}^{\infty} D_n e^{jn\omega_0 t}$$

$$P_f = \sum_{n=-\infty}^{\infty} |D_n|^2$$

$$P_f = D_0^2 + 2\sum_{n=1}^{\infty} |D_n|^2$$

1.6 DUAL NETWORKS

The two networks are said to be dual networks of each other if mesh (loop) equations of given network are node equations of other network.

Dual networks are based on Kirchhoff's voltage and Kirchoff's current laws.

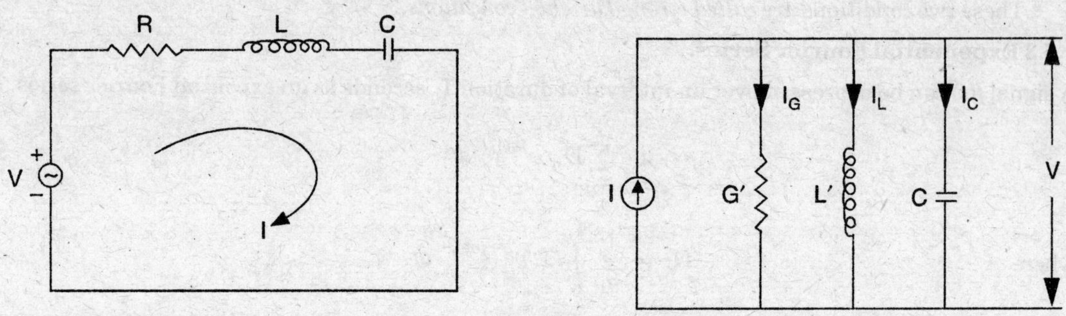

Fig. 1.11

Dual networks are not equivalent networks of each other. Principle of duality only implies that circuit equations are of the same mathematical form and the dual networks behave similarly but with interchanged variables.

1.6.1. Requirement for the dual networks.

(i) The number of meshes in given network must be equal to the numbers of nodes of a dual network

(ii) The total impedance of a given network must be equal to the total admittance of a dual network

(iii) The impedance of a branch common to two meshes must be equal to the admittance between two nodes in the dual network

(iv) Voltage source common to both the loops must be represented as a current source between two nodes.

(v) The switch opening at $t = 0$ in the given network must be shown as a switch closing at $t = 0$ in the dual network.

1.6.2. Type of Networks.

Network.

An electric network is interconnection of electric circuit elements or branches.

Network element.

Any individual circuit element with two terminals which can be connected to other circuit element.

Linear Network.

A circuit containing all linear elements is called *linear network.*

Linear element is the element which is having linear relationship between voltage applied and current flowing through it.

Bilateral Network.

A circuit whose characteristics are same irrespective of direction of current is known as *bilateral network.* Network consisting resistances is the example of bilateral netowrk.

Unilateral Network.

A circuit whose characteristics are dependent on the direction of operation is known as *unilateral network.* Network consisting diodes are example of unilateral network.

Active Network.

A network which contains active source (Ex. V, I) along with other network elements is known as *active network.*

Passive Network.

A network which contains only passive elements (Ex. R, L, C) and not the active source is known as *passive network* Mostly passive network is used as a load.

Lumped Network.

A network in which all the elements are physically separable is known as *lumped network.*

Active Source

Sources which deliver some power to external element are called active source. Ex. Voltage, current source.

Passive Source

Sources which consume some power or absorb some power are called passive source. Ex. R, L, C sources.

1.6.3. Energy Sources.

There are basically two types of energy sources :

(i) **Voltage source :** Ideal voltage source is defined as the energy source which gives constant voltage across its terminals irrespective of the current drawn through its terminals.

But practically, every voltage source has small internal resistance.

(ii) **Current source :** I deal current source is the source which gives constant current at its terminal irrespective of the voltage appearing across its terminals.

But practically every current source has high internal resistance.

Dependent Sources.

Dependent sources are those whose value of source depends on voltage or current in the circuit.

(i) **Voltage Dependent Voltage Source (VDVS) :**

It produces a voltage as a function of voltages else where in the given circuit.

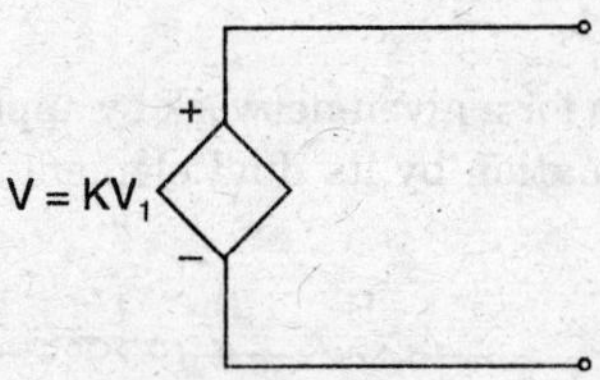

Fig. 1.12

(ii) **Current Dependent Current Source (CDCS) :**

It provides a current as a function of currents else where in a given circuit.

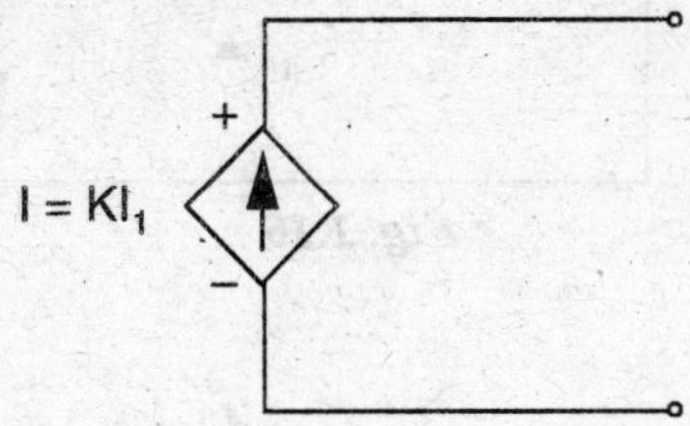

Fig. 1.13

(iii) **Current Dependent Voltage Source : (CDVS) :**

It produces a voltage as a function of current elsewhere in a given circuit.

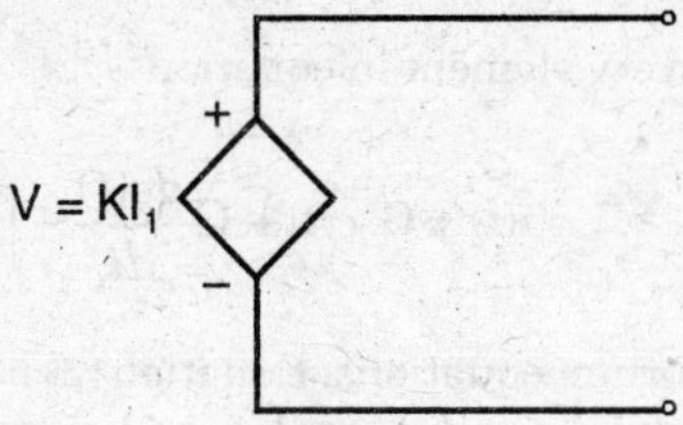

Fig. 1.14

(iv) **Voltage Dependent Current Source : (VDCS) :**

It produces a current as a function of voltage elsewhere in a given circuit.

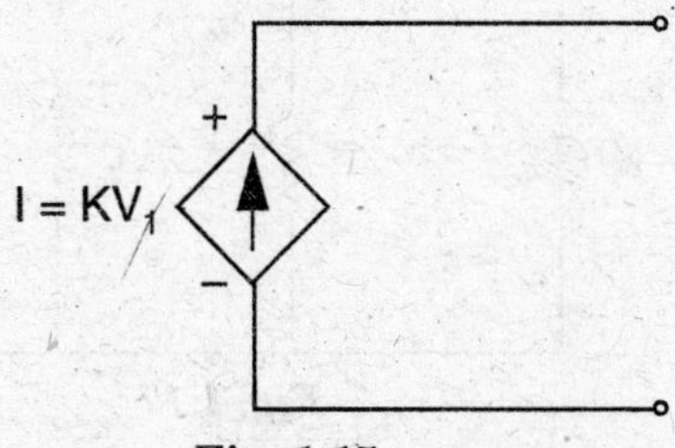

Fig. 1.15

S.N.	Element	Dual Element
1.	Resistance	Conductance
2.	Capacitance	Inductance
3.	Inductance	Capacitance
4.	Series Branch	Parallel Branch
5.	Voltage Source	Current Source
6.	Current Source	Voltage Source
7.	Switch closed (at t = 0)	Switch opened (at t = 0)
8.	Charge	Flux linkage
9.	Mesh	Node
10.	Link	Twig

1.6.4 Construction of a dual Network.

First find out the equilibrium equation for a given network by applying Kirchoff's basic laws. Then replace each and every element in that equilibrium equation by its dual element so that new equation will represent equilibrium equation of a dual network.

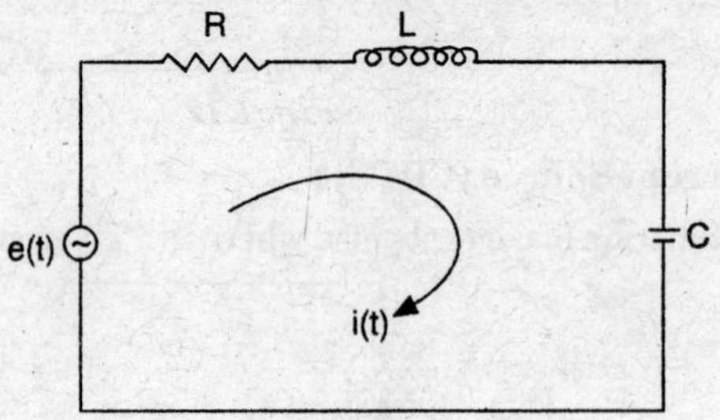

Fig. 1.16

Applying KVL to the above circuit.

$$e(t) = i(t)\,R + L\frac{di(t)}{dt} + \frac{1}{C}\int i(t)\,dt \qquad ....(1)$$

Now above equation is equilibrium equation of a given network. Now replace each and every element by its dual element.

Writing dual elements for each and every element in equation

$$i(t) = G.\,e(t) + C\frac{de(t)}{dt} + \left(\frac{1}{L}\right)\int e(t)\,dt \qquad ....(2)$$

Thus equations (1) and (2) are equilibrium equations. Equation (2) has all terms as current and they are adding each other *i.e.* it is based on KCL and currents in each branch is added at particular node as the branches are in parallel.

Thus the dual network constructed from equation (2).

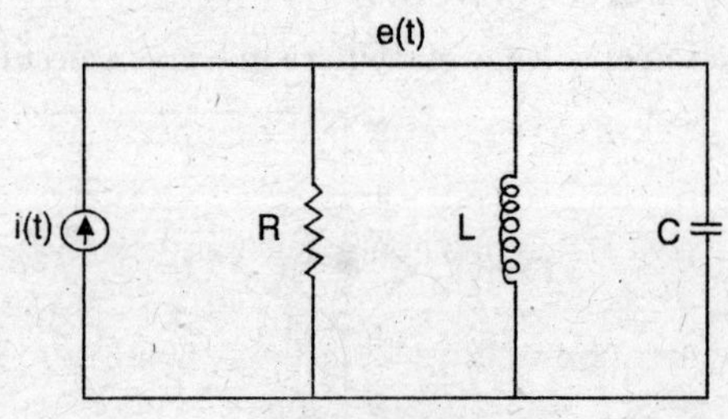

Fig. 1.17

1.7 MEASUREMENT SYSTEM PERFORMANCE

The treatment of instrument and measurement system characteristic can be divided into two distinct categories

(1) Static characteristics.

Static characteristic of a measurement system are in general, those must be considered when the system or instrument is used to a condition not varying with time.

Main static characteristics are :

(*i*) Accuracy

(*ii*) Sensitivity

(*iii*) Reproducibility

(*iv*) Drift

(*v*) Static error

(*vi*) Dead zone

(2) Dynamic characteristics.

Many measurements are concerned with rapidly varying quantities and therefore for such cases we must examine the dynamic relation which exist between output and the input. Performance criteria based upon dynamic relations constitute dynamic characteristics.

1.8 ERRORS IN MEASUREMENT

The degree to which a measurement nears the true value is expressed in terms of the error of measurement. Error is defined as the deviation of true value from the desired value. It is expressed either as absolute or as a percentage of error.

Absolute error is defined as the difference between true value of the variable and the measured value of the variable, i.e.

$$\varepsilon_o = Y_n - X_n$$

where ε_0 = absolute error

Y_n = true value

X_n = measured value

Hence

$$\% \text{ Error} = \frac{\text{Absolute Error}}{\text{True value}} \times 100 = \frac{\varepsilon_o}{Y_n} \times 100$$

$$\% \text{ Error} = \left(\frac{Y_n - X_n}{Y_n}\right) \times 100$$

Accuracy.

It is the closeness with which an instrument reading approaches the true value of the quantity being measured. It is specified in terms of limits of errors and is expressed as either percentage of scale or range of percentage of true value.

Precision.

It is a measure of the reproducibility of the measurements, *i.e.* for a fixed value of a quantity, precision is a measure of the degree of agreement within a group of measurements. An indication of the precision of the measurement is obtained from the number of significant figures in which it is expressed. The more the significant figures, the greater the precision of measurement. The high precision does not mean high accuracy. A high precisely instrument can be inaccurate.

1.8.1. Types of Errors.

Static error.

It is the numerical difference between true value of a quantity and its value as obtained by measurement. *These are sub-divided into three types*

(*i*) Gross errors.

These errors are due to human mistakes in reading or in using instruments or errors in recording observations.

(*ii*) Systematic errors.

These errors occur due to shortcomings of the instrument such as defective or worn parts or ageing or effects of the environment on the instrument or the user.

(*a*) Instrumental errors : These are inherent in measuring instruments, because of their mechanical structure. These can be avoided by selecting a suitable instrument for the particular measurement application or by applying correction factors after determining the amount of instrumental error of calibrating the instrument against a standard.

(*b*) **Environment errors :** These are due to conditions external to the measuring device including conditions in the area surrounding the instrument such as effects of changes in temperature, humidity, barometric pressure or effect of magnetic or electrostatic fields.

(*c*) **Observational errors :** These are errors introduced by the observer. The most common is the parallax error introduced in reading a meter scale and the error of estimation.

(*iii*) Random errors.

These are due to unknown causes and are normally small and follow the low of probability. These are treated mathematically.

1.8.2. Sources of Errors.

(*i*) Insufficient knowledge of process parameters and design conditions.

(*ii*) Poor maintenance.

(*iii*) Change in process parameters irregularities, upsets etc.

(*iv*) Poor design.

(*v*) Design limitations.

(*vi*) Due to person operating the instrument.

When two or more quantities, each of which is subjected to error, are combined. Following rules will apply

(1) Sum of two or more quantities.

Suppose the final result y is sum of measured quantities u, v and z, each of which is subjected to possible systematic error $\pm\,\delta u$, $\pm\,\delta v$, $\pm\,\delta z$ respectively.

Nominal result is
$$y = u + v + z$$

$$\frac{dy}{y} = \frac{d\,(u+v+z)}{y} = \frac{du}{y} + \frac{dv}{y} + \frac{dz}{y}$$

Expressing in terms of relative increments

$$\frac{dy}{y} = \frac{u}{y}\frac{du}{u} + \frac{v}{y}\frac{dv}{v} + \frac{z}{y}\frac{dz}{z}$$

Relative limiting error
$$\frac{\delta y}{y} = \pm\left(\frac{u}{y}\cdot\frac{\delta u}{u} + \frac{v}{y}\cdot\frac{\delta v}{v} + \frac{z}{y}\cdot\frac{\delta z}{z}\right)$$

Hence resultant systematic error is equal to sum of the products formed by multiplying individual systematic errors by the ratio of each terms to the function.

(2) Difference of two quantities.

Let
$$y = u - v$$

$$\therefore \quad \frac{dy}{y} = \frac{du}{y} - \frac{dv}{y}$$

$$\Rightarrow \quad \frac{dy}{y} = \frac{u}{y}\cdot\frac{du}{u} - \frac{v}{y}\cdot\frac{dv}{v}$$

Relative limiting error δy in y is
$$\frac{\delta y}{y} = \pm\left(\frac{u}{y}\cdot\frac{\delta u}{u} + \frac{v}{y}\cdot\frac{\delta v}{v}\right)$$

(3) Product of two or more quantities.

Let
$$y = u\,v\,z$$

Taking logarithm of both sides, we get
$$\log_e y = \log_e u + \log_e v + \log_e z$$

Differentiating with respect to y, we get
$$\frac{1}{y} = \frac{1}{u}\cdot\frac{du}{dy} + \frac{1}{v}\cdot\frac{dv}{dy} + \frac{1}{z}\cdot\frac{dz}{dy}$$

or
$$\frac{dy}{y} = \frac{du}{u} + \frac{dv}{v} + \frac{dz}{z}$$

$\therefore$ Relative limiting error is,
$$\frac{\delta y}{y} = \pm\left(\frac{\delta u}{u} + \frac{\delta v}{v} + \frac{\delta z}{z}\right)$$

Relative limiting error of the product of the terms is equal to the sum of the relative errors of the terms.

(4) Quotient of two quantities.

Let $$y = \frac{u}{v}$$

Taking logarithm of both sides,

$$\log_e y = \log_e u - \log_e v$$

Differentiating with respect to y, we get

$$\frac{1}{y} = \frac{1}{u}\frac{du}{dy} - \frac{1}{v}\frac{dv}{dy}$$

or $$\frac{dy}{y} = \frac{du}{u} - \frac{dv}{v}$$

∴ Relative limiting error, $$\frac{\delta y}{y} = \pm\frac{\delta u}{u} \mp \frac{\delta v}{v}$$

The maximum possible error occurs when $\frac{\delta u}{u}$ is positive and $\frac{\delta v}{v}$ is negative or vice versa.

$$\frac{\delta y}{y} = \pm\left(\frac{\delta u}{u} + \frac{\delta v}{v}\right)$$

(5) Power of a factor.

Let $$y = u^u$$

where n may be positive or negative, integral or fractional

Taking logarithm of both sides, we get

$$\log_e y = n \log_e u$$

Differentiating with respect to y, we get

$$\frac{1}{y} = n\frac{1}{u}\frac{du}{dy}$$

or $$\frac{dy}{y} = n\frac{du}{u}$$

∴ Relative limiting error is,

$$\frac{\delta y}{y} = \pm\, n\frac{\delta u}{u}$$

(6) Composite factors.

Let $$y = u^n v^m$$

Taking logarithm of both sides, we get

$$\log_e y = n \log_e u + m \log_e v$$

Differentiating with respect to y, we get

$$\frac{1}{y} = \frac{n}{u}\frac{du}{dy} + \frac{m}{v}\frac{du}{dy}$$

or $$\frac{dy}{y} = n\frac{du}{u} + m\frac{dv}{v}$$

∴ Relative limiting error of y is,

$$\frac{\delta y}{y} = \pm\left(n\frac{\delta u}{u} + m\frac{\delta v}{v}\right)$$

Example. *The solution for the unknown resistance for a wheatstone bridge is*

$$R_x = \frac{R_2 R_3}{R_1}$$

where $R_1 = 100 \pm 0.5\%\ \Omega$

$R_2 = 1000 \pm 0.5\%\ \Omega$

$R_3 = 842 \pm 0.5\%\ \Omega$

Determine magnitude of the unknown resistance and limiting error in percent and in ohm for the unknown resistance R_x,

Solution :

Unknown resistance, $$R_x = \frac{R_2 R_3}{R_1} = \frac{1000 \times 842}{100} = \mathbf{8420\ \Omega}$$

Relative limiting error of R_x is,

$$\frac{\delta R_x}{R_x} = \pm\left(\frac{\delta R_2}{R_2} + \frac{\delta R_3}{R_3} + \frac{\delta R_1}{R_1}\right) = \pm(0.5 + 0.5 + 0.5) = \pm\mathbf{1.5\%}$$

$$\text{Limiting error in ohm} = \pm\frac{1.5}{100} \times 8420 = \pm\mathbf{126.3\ \Omega}$$

∴ Guaranteed values of resistance are between :

$$8420 - 126.3 = \mathbf{8293.7\ \Omega}$$

and $$8420 + 126.3 = \mathbf{8546.3\ \Omega}$$

1.8.3 Statistical Analysis.

(*i*) Arithmetic mean

$$\overline{X} = \frac{X_1 + X_2 + X_3 + \ldots + X_n}{n} = \frac{\Sigma X}{n}$$

where $\overline{X}$ = arithmetic mean,

$X_1, X_2, X_3 \ldots\ldots X_n$ = readings taken,

n = number of readings taken.

(*ii*) Deviation from means

$$\text{Deviation of } X_1 = d_1 = X_1 - \overline{X}$$

$$\text{Deviation of } X_2 = d_2 = X_2 - \overline{X}$$

(*iii*) Average deviation

$$D = \frac{|d_1| + |d_2| + |d_3| + \ldots |d_n|}{n} = \frac{\Sigma|d|}{n}$$

(*iv*) Standard deviation

$$\sigma = \sqrt{\frac{d_1^2 + d_2^2 + d_3^3 + \ldots d_n^2}{n}} = \sqrt{\frac{\Sigma d^2}{n}}$$

(*v*) Variance

$$\text{Variance} = \text{Mean square deviation} = \sigma^2$$

(*vi*) Probable error of one reading

$$r_1 = 0.6745\sqrt{\frac{\Sigma|d|^2}{n}} = 0.6745\,\sigma$$

(*vii*) Probable error of mean.

$$r_m = \frac{r_1}{\sqrt{n-1}}$$

Example. *A set of independent ten measurements were made to determine the weight of a lead shot. The weights in gram were 1.570, 1.597, 1.591, 1.562, 1.577, 1.580, 1.564, 1.586, 1.550, 1.575.*

Determine

(*i*) *arithmetic mean*

(*ii*) *average deviation*

(*iii*) *standard deviation*

(*iv*) *varianc*

(*v*) *probable error of one reading*

(*vi*) *probable error of the mean.*

Solution.

Observations can be tabulated as under :

X	d	d^2
1.570	– 0.0052	0.0000274
1.597	+ 0.0218	0.00047524
1.591	+ 0.0158	0.00024964
1.562	– 0.0132	0.00017424
1.577	– 0.0018	0.00000324
1.580	+ 0.0048	0.00002304
1.564	– 0.0112	0.00012544
1.586	+ 0.0108	0.00011664
1.550	– 0.0252	0.00063504
1.575	– 0.0002	0.0000004
Σx = 15.752	**Σ|d| = 0.11**	**Σd² = 0.00183**

(i) Mean weight = Arithmetic mean = $\bar{X} = \frac{\Sigma X}{n} = \frac{15.752}{10} = \mathbf{1.5752\,g}$

(ii) Standard deviation for a finite number of readings.

$$\sigma = \sqrt{\frac{\Sigma d^2}{n}} = \sqrt{\frac{0.00183}{10}} = \mathbf{0.01352\ g}$$

(iii) Average deviation $= \frac{\Sigma|d|}{n} = \frac{0.11}{10} = \mathbf{0.011}$

(iv) Variance $= \sigma^2 = (0.01352)^2 = \mathbf{0.000183\ g^2}$

(v) Probable error of one reading, $r_1 = 0.6745\,\sigma$

$$r_1 = 0.6745 \times 0.01352 = \mathbf{0.009119\ g}$$

(vi) Probable error of the mean, $r_m = \frac{r_1}{\sqrt{n-1}}$

$$r_m = \frac{0.009119}{\sqrt{10-1}} = 0.003039\ g$$

1.8.4 Unccrtainity Analysis.

Many times a data available is a single sample data and therefore statistical methods cannot be applied directly. On account of single sample nature of the data, it is not possible to observe their scatter by plotting a frequency distribution curve. Hence, it becames essential to modify our approach.

Klline and Mcclintock have proposed a method based upon probability and statistics which analyzes the data employing uncertainity distribution rather than frequency distribution.

They suggested that a single sample result may be expressed in terms of a mean value and an uncertainity interval based upon stated odds.

The result may be written as :

$$X = \bar{X} \pm \omega \text{ (b to 1)}$$

where $\bar{X}$ = value of only one reading is available on the arithmetic mean of several readings

ω = uncertainity interval

b = odds or the chance that the true value lies within stated range, based upon opinion of the experimeter.

The concept of uncertainity may be explained as

$$T = 100°C \pm 1°C \text{ (20 to 1)}$$

The result expressed in the above form is that there is an uncertainity of ± 1°C and experiment is willing to be between 20 to 1 odds.

OBJECTIVE TYPE QUESTIONS

NETWORK ELEMENT

1. All resistance in the circuit in the figure are at R ohms each. The switch is initially open. What happens to the lamps intensity when the switch is closed?

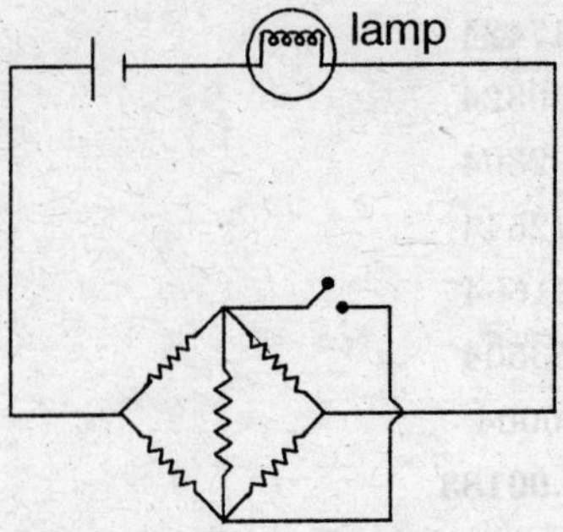

(a) increases

(b) decreases

(c) remain same

(d) answer depends on the value at R

2. The time constant of the network shown in the figure is

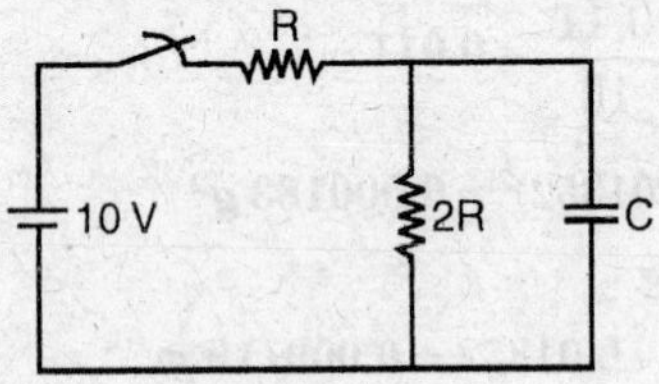

(a) 2 RC

(b) 3 RC

(c) $\frac{RC}{2}$

(d) $\frac{2\ RC}{3}$

3. When all the resistances in the circuit are at one ohm each, the equivalent resistance across the point A and B will be

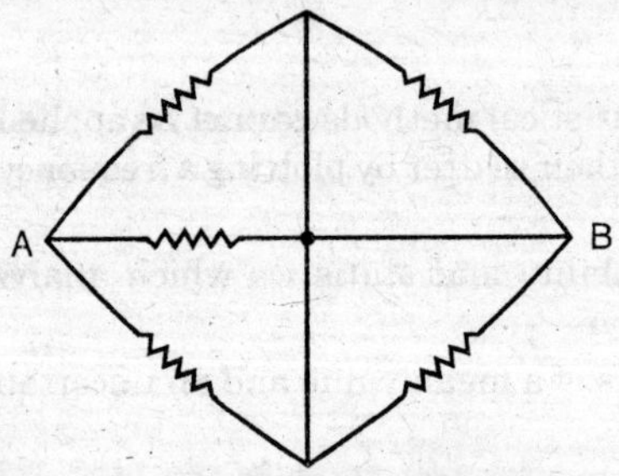

(a) 1 Ω (b) 0.5 Ω

(c) 2 Ω (d) 1.5 Ω

4. A 35 V source is connected to a series circuit at 600 ohms and R as shown. If a voltmeter at internal resistance 1.2 kilo ohms is connected across 600 ohm resistor it reads 5 V. The value of R is

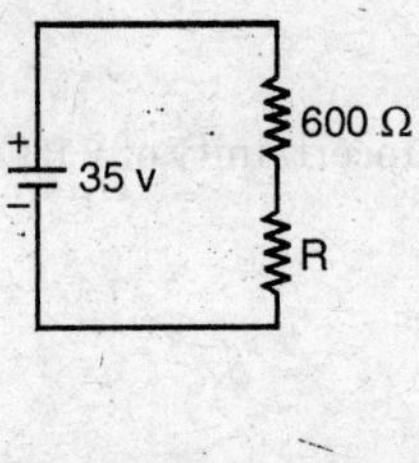

(a) 1.2 kΩ

(b) 2.4 kΩ

(c) 3.6 kΩ

(d) 7.2 kΩ

5. The energy stored in the magnetic field at a solenoid 30 cm long and 3 cm diameter wound with 1000 turns of wire carrying a current at 10 A, is

(a) 0.015 Joule (b) 0.15 Joule

(c) 0.5 Joule (d) 1.15 Joule

6. Two coils having equal resistance but different inductances are connected in series. the time constant of the series combination is the

(a) sum of the time constants of the individual coils

(b) average of the time constants of individual coils

(c) geometric mean of the time constants of the individual coils

(d) product of the time constants of the individual coils

7. At a certain current, the energy stored in iron cored coil is 1000 J and its copper loss is 2000 W. The time constant (in seconds) of the coil is

(a) 0.25 (b) 0.5

(c) 1.0 (d) 2.0

8. The current waveform in a pure resistor at 10Ω is shown in the given figure. power dissipated in the resistor is

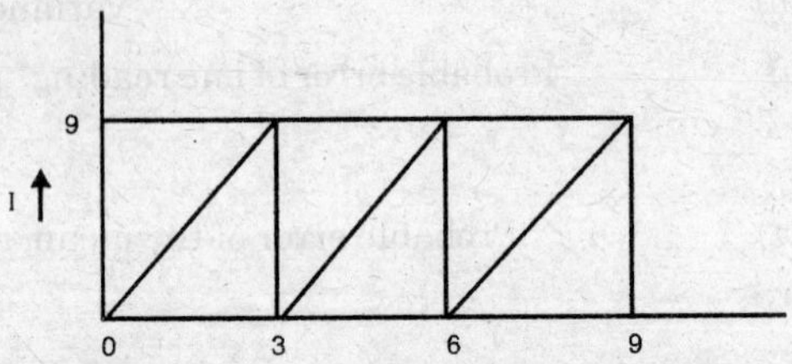

(a) 7.29 W (b) 52.4 W

(c) 135 W (d) 270 W

9. The effective inductance of the circuit across the terminal AB in the figure shown below, is

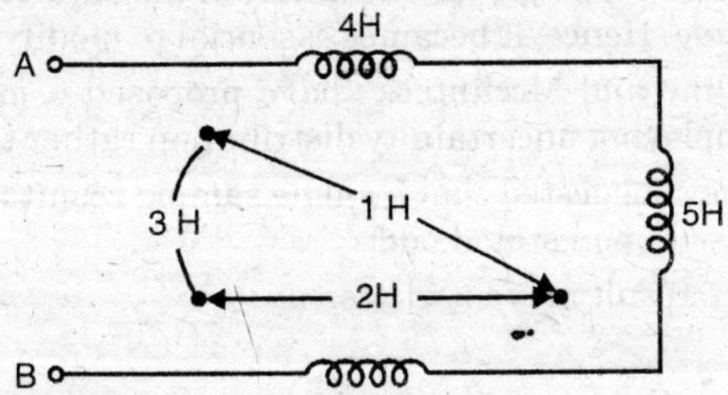

(a) 9 H (b) 21 H

(c) 11 H (d) 6 H

10. A series RLC circuit consisting of R = 10 ohms, X_L = 20 ohms and X_c = 20 ohms is connected across an ac supply of 100 V (rms). The magnitude and phase angle (with reference to supply voltage) of the voltage across the inductive coil are respectively

(a) 100 V, 90° (b) 100 V, – 90°

(c) 200 V, – 90° (d) 200 V, 90°

11. A coil with large distributed capacitance has a

(*a*) high Q

(*b*) low Q

(*c*) low resonant frequency

(*d*) high resonant frequency

12. When a unit impulse voltage is applied to an inductor of 1 H, the energy supplied by the source is

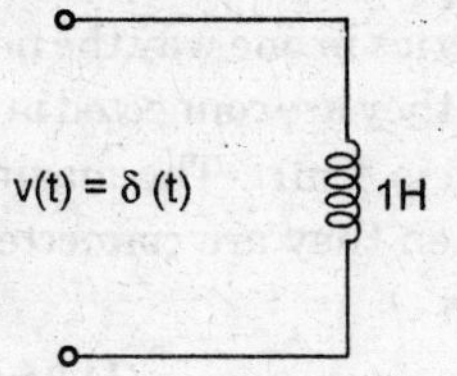

(*a*) ∞ (*b*) 1 J

(*c*) $\frac{1}{2}$ J (*d*) 0.

13. In the figure below, the current of 1 ampere flows through the resistance of

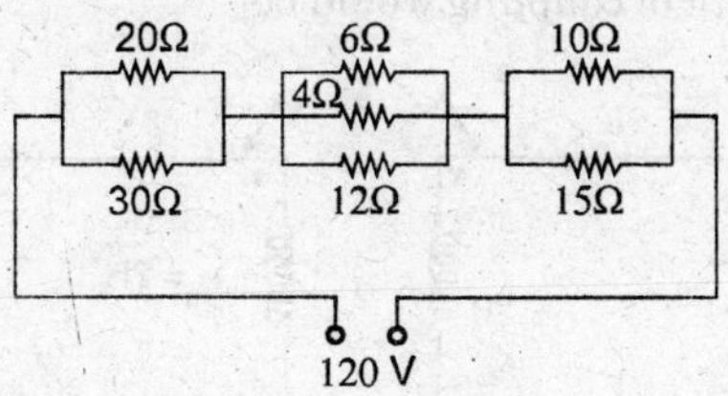

(*a*) 4 ohms (*b*) 20 ohms

(*c*) 30 ohms (*d*) 12 ohms

14. Two coils in differential connection have self inductance of 2 mH and 4 mH and a mutual inductance of 0.15 mH. The equivalent inductance of the combination is

(*a*) 5.7 mH (*b*) 5.85 mH.

(*c*) 6 mH (*d*) 6.15 mH.

15. In the network shown in the figure, the effective resistance faced by the voltage source is

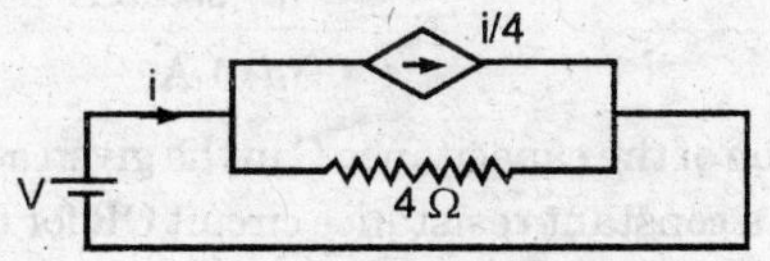

(*a*) 4 Ω (*b*) 3 Ω

(*c*) 2 Ω (*d*) 1 Ω

16. The current through an electrical conductor is 1 ampere when the temperature of the conductor is 0° C and 0.7 ampere when the temperature is 100°C. The current when the temperature of the conductor is 1200° C must be

(*a*) 0.08 A

(*b*) 0.16 A

(*c*) 0.32 A

(*d*) 0.64 A

17. In the circuit shown in figure, $I_B = 10$ micro-amperes, the value of resistance R_{in} is

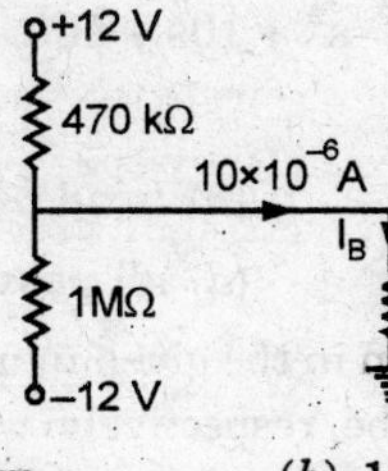

(*a*) 1 kilo-ohm (*b*) 10 kilo-ohm

(*c*) 100 kilo-ohm (*d*) 1 Mega-ohm

18. The circuit shown has i (t) = 10 sin (120 π t). The power (time average power) dissipated in R is

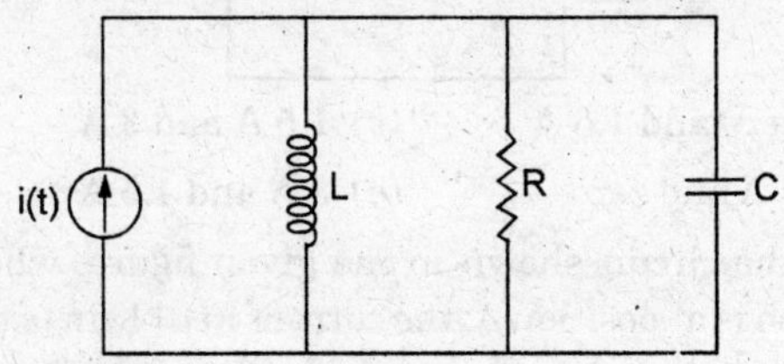

$R = 1\,\Omega$ $C = \frac{1}{60}\pi H$

$L = \frac{1}{120}\pi H$ $R = 1\,\text{ohm}.$

(*a*) 25 watts (*b*) 100 watts

(*c*) $\frac{10}{\sqrt{2}}$ watts (*d*) 50 watts

19. In the circuit shown in the figure below, the effective resistance faced by the voltage source is

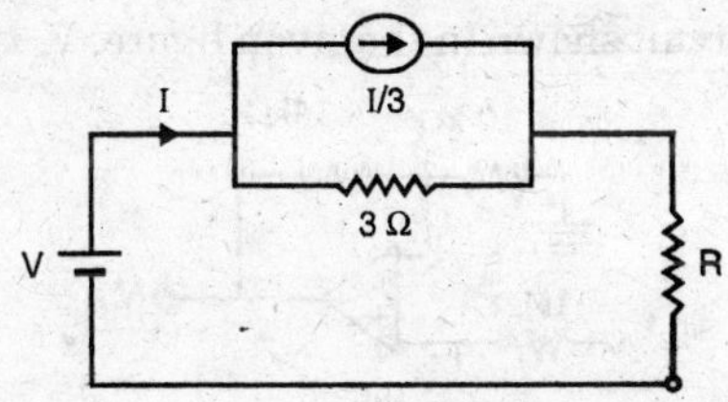

(*a*) 1Ω (*b*) 3Ω

(*c*) 2Ω (*d*) 3.3Ω

20. In the circuit shown in the figure, what value of C will cause a unity power factor at the ac source ?

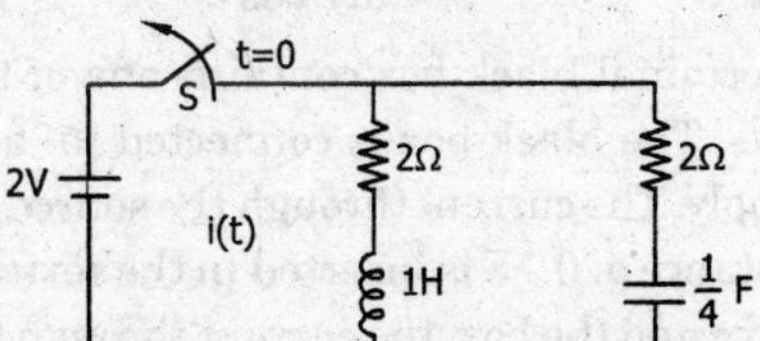

(*a*) 68.1 μF

(*b*) 165 μF

(*c*) 0.681 μF

(*d*) 6.81 μF

21. The transfer function

$$\frac{V_2(s)}{V_1(s)} = \frac{10.\ S}{s^2 + 10s + 100}$$

is for an active

(*a*) low pass filter (*b*) band pass filter

(*c*) high pass filter (*d*) all pass filter

22. In the circuit shown in the given figure, the values of $I(0^+)$ adn $I(\infty)$, will be, respectively

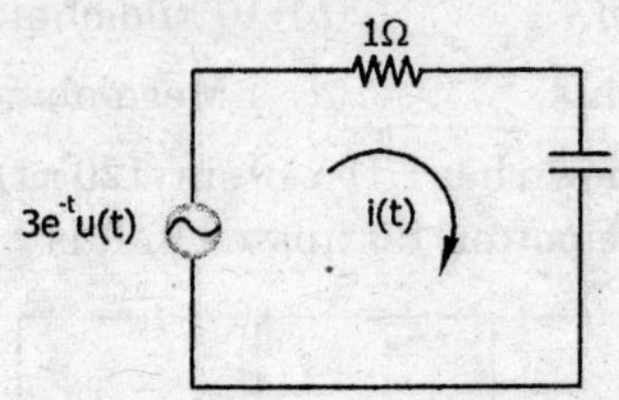

(*a*) zero and 1.5 A (*b*) 1.5 A and 3 A

(*c*) 3 A and zero (*d*) 3 A and 1.5 A

23. For the circuit shown in the given figure, when the switch is at position A, the current $i(t) = I \sin(\omega t + 30°)$ A. When switch is moved to position B at time t = 0, the power dissipated at the switching instant in the resistor R remains unchanged The value of I and the element X would respectively, be

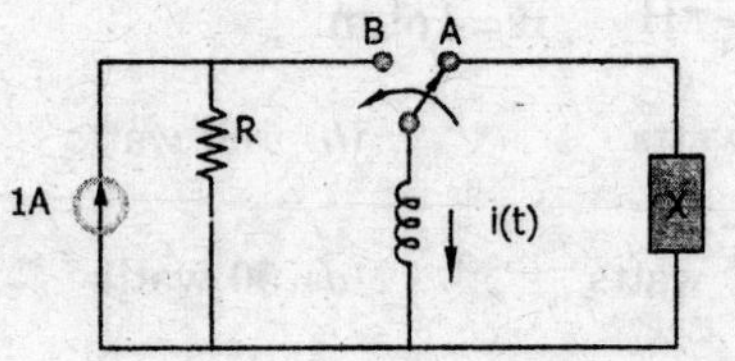

(*a*) 1 A and resistor (*b*) 2 A and capacitor

(*c*) 3 A and resistor (*d*) 4 A and capacitor

24. In the circuit shown in the given figure, V_0 is given by

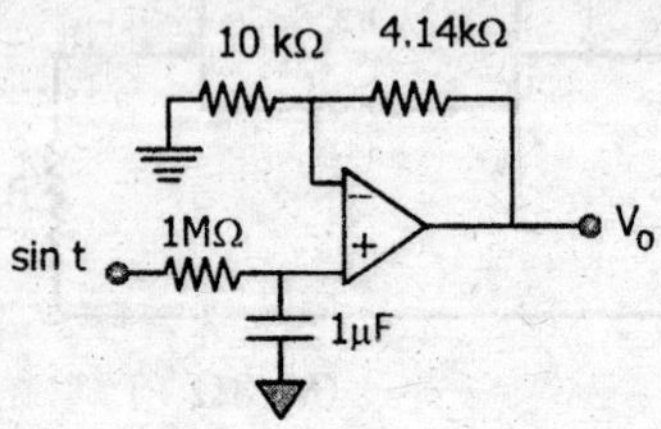

(*a*) $\sin\left(t - \frac{\pi}{4}\right)$ (*b*) $\sin\left(t + \frac{\pi}{4}\right)$

(*c*) $\sin t$ (*d*) $\cos t$

25. A two terminal black box contains one of the R.L.C. elements. The black box is connected to a 220 volts A.C. supply. The current through the source is I. When a capacitance of 0.1F is inserted in the series between the source and the box, the current through the source is 2I. The element is

(*a*) a resistance

(*b*) an inductance

(*c*) a capacitance of 0.5F

(*d*) it is not possible to determine the element.

26. A resistance 'R' Ω and inductance of 'L' H are connected across 240 V, 50 Hz supply. Power dissipated in the circuit is 300 W and the voltage across R is 100 V. In order to improve the power factor to unity, the capacitor that is to be connected in series should have a value of

(*a*) 43.7 μF (*b*) 4.37 μF

(*c*) 437 μF (*d*) 4.37 μF

27. When two coupled coils of equal self-inductance are connected in series in one way the net inductance is 12 mH, and when they are connected in the other way, the net inductance is 4 mH. The maximum value of net inductance when they are connected in parallel in a suitable way is

(*a*) 2 mH (*b*) 3 mH

(*c*) 4 mH (*d*) 6 mH

28. In the transformer shown in the given figure, the inductance measured across the terminal 1 and 2 was 4 H with open terminals 3 and 4. It was 3 H when the terminal 3 and 4 are were short circuited. The coefficient of coupling would be

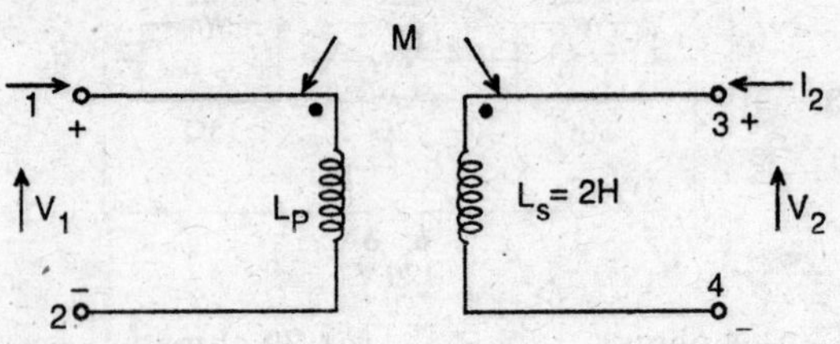

(*a*) 1

(*b*) 0.707

(*c*) 0.5

(*d*) indeterminate due to insufficient data

29. Five cells are connected in series in a row and then four such rows are connected in parallel to feed the current to a resistive load of 1.25 Ω. Each cell has emf of 1.5 V with internal resistance of 0.2 Ω. Th current through the load will be

(*a*) 3.33 A (*b*) 23.33 A

(*c*) 5 A (*d*) 1 A

30. The value of the capacitance C in the given ac circuit to make it a constant resistance circuit OR for the supply current to be independent of its frequency is

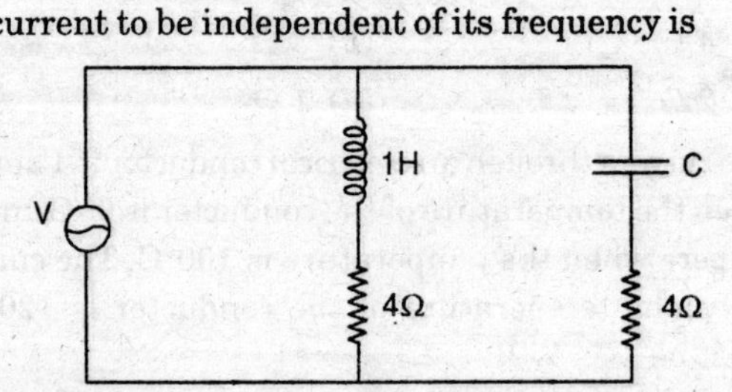

(*a*) $\frac{1}{16}$F (*b*) $\frac{1}{12}$F

(*c*) $\frac{1}{8}$F (*d*) $\frac{1}{4}$F

31. The resonant frequency of the given series circuit is

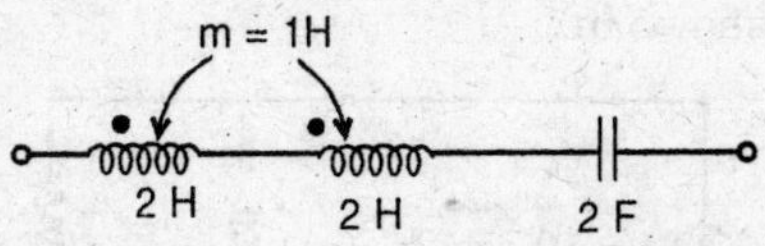

(a) $\frac{1\text{Hz}}{2\pi\sqrt{3}}$ (b) $\frac{1\text{Hz}}{4\pi\sqrt{3}}$

(c) $\frac{1\text{Hz}}{4\pi\sqrt{2}}$ (d) $\frac{1\text{Hz}}{\pi\sqrt{2}}$

32. In the circuit shown in the given figure, S is open for a long time and steady state is reached. S is closed at t = 0. The current I at t = 0^+ is

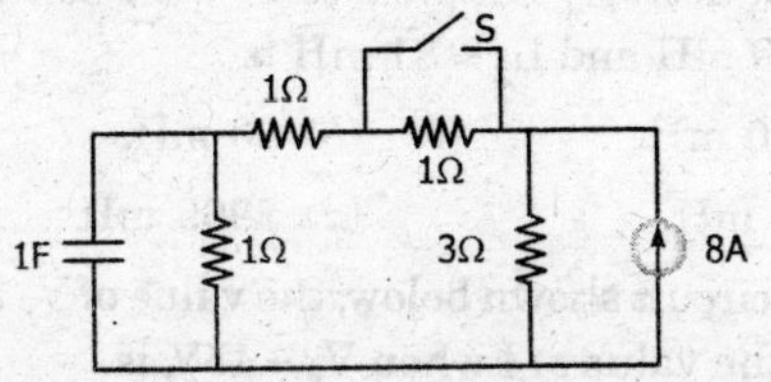

(a) 4 A (b) 3 A

(c) 2 A (d) 1 A

33. In the circuit shown in the given figure, the current supplied by the sinusoidal current source I is

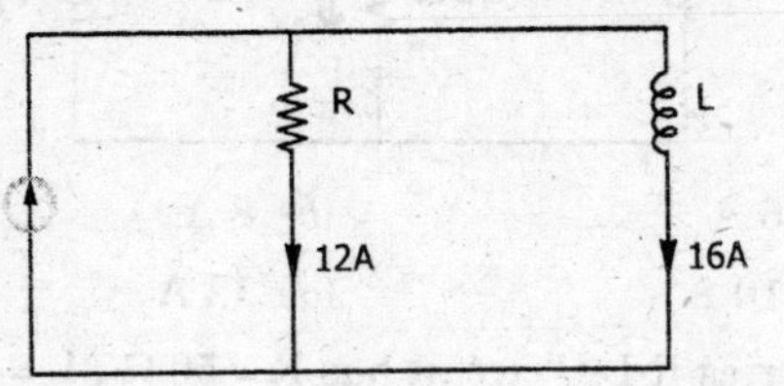

(a) 28 A

(b) 4 A

(c) 20 A

(d) not determinable from the data given

34. A network contains linear resistors and ideal voltage sources. If values of all the resistors are doubled, then the voltage across each resistor is

(a) halved

(b) doubled

(c) increased by four times

(d) not changed

35. The impedance seen by the source in the circuit in the figure is given by

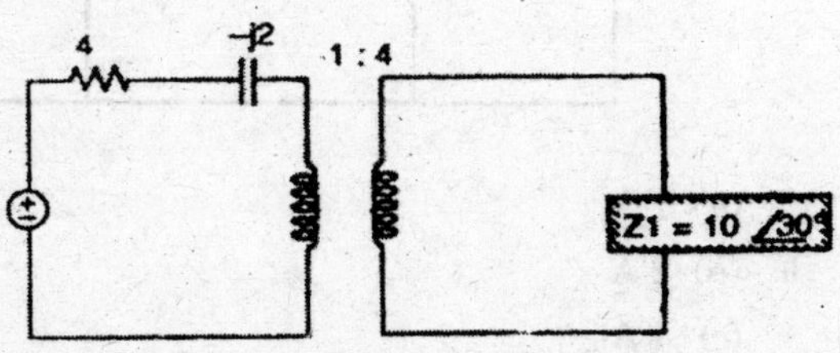

(a) $(0.54 + j0.313)$ ohms (b) $(4 - j2)$ ohms

(c) $(4.54 - j1.69)$ ohms (d) $(4 + j2)$ ohms

36. When a resistor R is connected to a current source, it consumes a power of 18 W. When the same R is connected to a voltage source having the same magnitude as the current source, the power absorbed by R is 4.5 W. The magnitude of the current source and the value of R are

(a) $\sqrt{18}$ A and 1 Ω (b) 3A and 2 Ω

(c) 1A and 18 Ω (d) 6 A and 0.5 Ω

37. Current I_1, I_2 and I_3 meet at a junction (node) in a circuit. All currents are marked as entering the node. If $I_1 = -6\sin(\omega t)$ mA and $I_2 = 8\cos(\omega t)$ mA, then I_3 will be

(a) $10\cos(\omega t + 36.87)$ mA

(b) $14\cos(\omega t + 36.87)$ mA

(c) $-14\sin(\omega t + 36.87)$ mA

(d) $-10\cos(\omega t + 36.87)$ mA

38. The voltage phasor of a circuit is $10\angle 15°$ V and current phasor is $2\angle -45°$ A. The active and the reactive powers in the circuit are

(a) 10 W and 17.32 VAr.

(b) 5 W and 8.66 VAr.

(c) 20 W and 60 VAr.

(d) $20\sqrt{2}$ W and $10\sqrt{2}$ VAr.

39. The current in the circuit shown in the given figure is

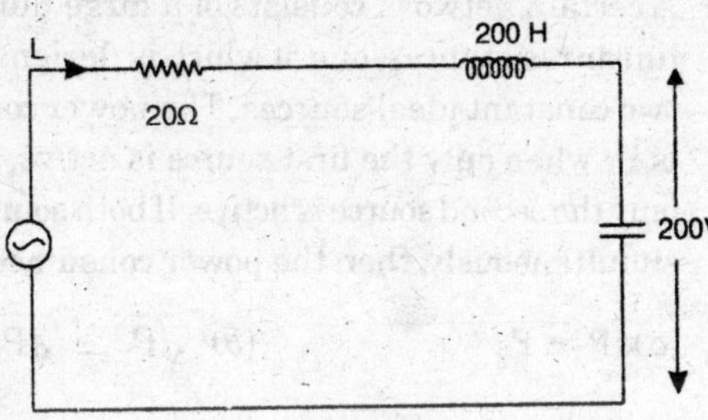

(a) 5 A. (b) 10 A.

(c) 15 A. (d) 25 A.

40. Two incandescent light bulbs of 40 W and 60W rating are connected in series across the mains. Then

(a) the bulbs together consume 100 W

(b) the bulbs together consume 50 W

(c) the 60 W bulb glows brighter

(d) the 40 bulb glows brighter

41. Given two coupled inductors L_1 and L_2, their mutual inductance M satisfies

(a) $M = \sqrt{L_1^2 + L_2^2}$

(b) $M > \frac{(L_1 + L_2)}{2}$

(c) $M > \sqrt{L_1 L_2}$

(d) $M \le \sqrt{L_1 L_2}$

42. Figure shows the waveform of the current passing through an inductor of resistance 1 Ω and inductance 2 H. The energy absorbed by the inductor in the first four seconds is

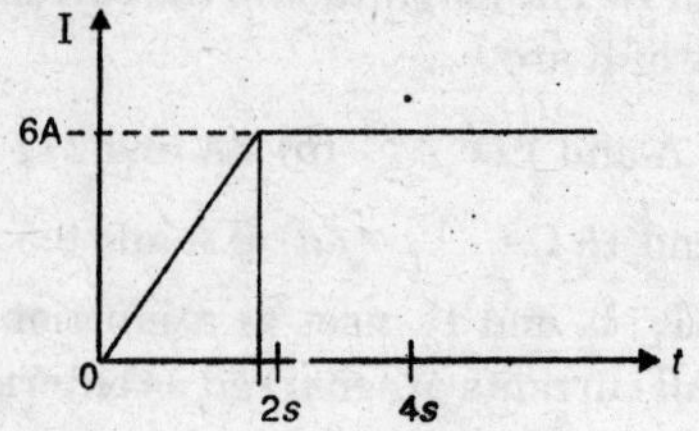

(*a*) 144 J (*b*) 98 J
(*c*) 132 J (*d*) 168 J

43. In the circuit of the given figure, the magnitudes of V_L and V_C are twice that of V_R. The inductance of the coil is

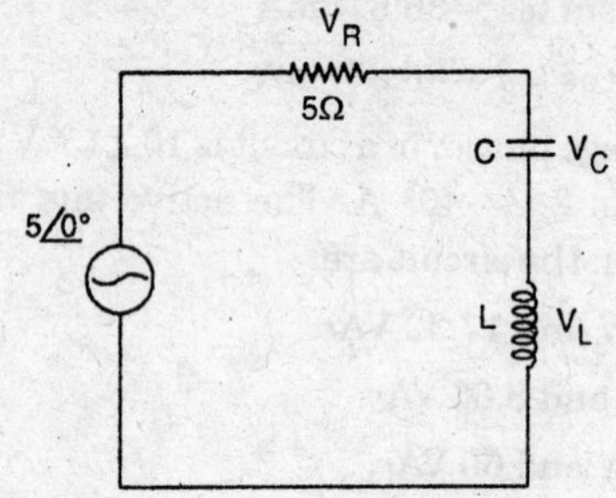

(*a*) 2.14 mH (*b*) 5.30 H
(*c*) 31.8 mH (*d*) 1.32 H

44. A certain network consists of a large number of ideal linear resistances, one of which is designated as R and two constant ideal sources. The power consumed by R is P_1 when only the first source is active, and P_2 when only the second source is active. If both sources are active simultaneously, then the power consumed by R is

(*a*) $P_1 \pm P_2$ (*b*) $\sqrt{P_1} \pm \sqrt{P_1}$
(*c*) $\left(\sqrt{P_1} \pm \sqrt{P_2}\right)^2$ (*d*) $(P_1 \pm P_2)^2$

45. An initially relaxed RC- series network with R = 2 MΩ and C = 1μ F is switched on to a 10 V step input. The voltage across the capacitor after 2 seconds will be

(*a*) zero (*b*) 3.68 V
(*c*) 6.32 V (*d*) 10 V

46. The block box as shown in the circuit above contains resistors and independent sources for R = 0 and 2 ; the value of current I is 3 and 1.5, respectively. The value of I for R = 1 will be

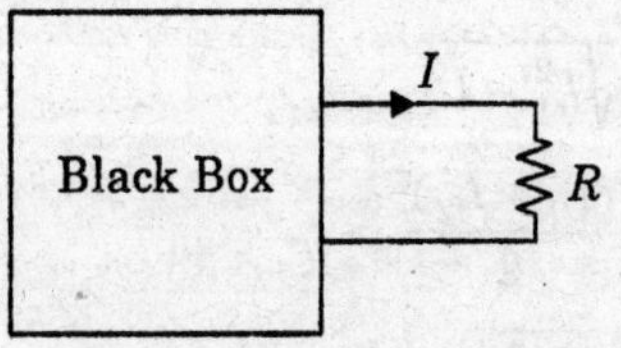

(*a*) 0.5 (*b*) 1.5
(*c*) 12.0 (*d*) 13.0

47. The phasor current through the inductance in the given circuit shown in

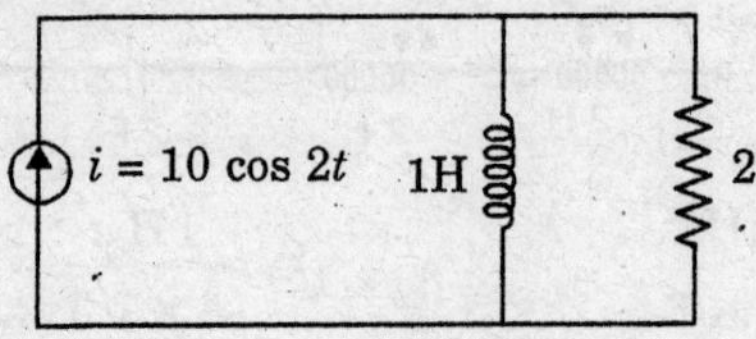

(*a*) $\left(\frac{10}{\sqrt{2}}\right)\angle -45°$ (*b*) $\left(\frac{10}{\sqrt{2}}\right)\angle 45°$
(*c*) $5\angle 45°$ (*d*) $5\angle -45°$

48. The maximum value of mutual inductance of two inductively coupled coils with selfinductance, L_1 = 49 mH and L_2 = 81 mH is

(*a*) 130 mH (*b*) 63 mH
(*c*) 32 mH (*d*) 3969 mH

49. In the circuit shown below, the value of V_s is 0, when I = 4A. the value of I when V_s = 15V, is

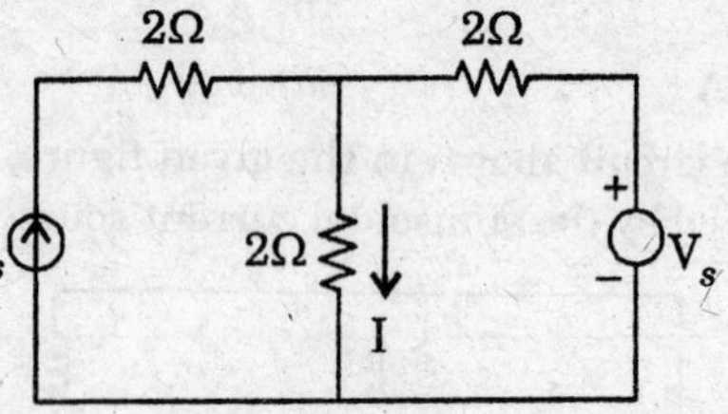

(*a*) 6 A (*b*) 8 A
(*c*) 10 A (*d*) 12 A

50. A series R-L-C circuit has R = 50 Ω , L = 100 μF and C = 1 μF. The lower half power frequency of the circuit is

(*a*) 30.55 kHz
(*b*) 51.92 kHz
(*c*) 3.055 kHz
(*d*) 1.92 kHz

NETWORK ANALYSIS

51. In the circuit shown, the value at I is

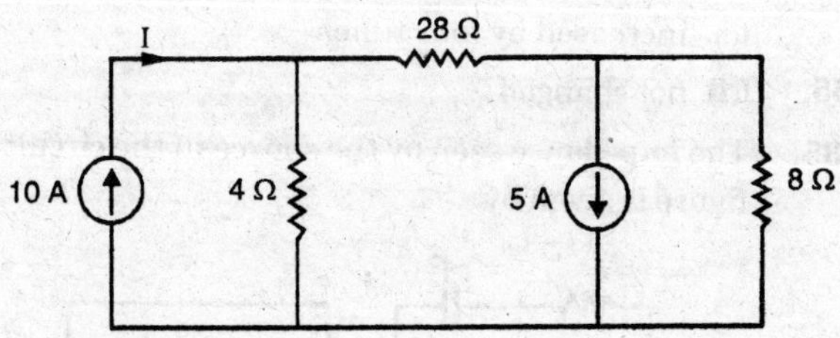

(*a*) 1 A
(*b*) 2 A
(*c*) 4 A
(*d*) 8 A

52. In the circuit shown in the figure, X is an element which always absorbs power during a particular operation it sets up a current of 1 amp in the direction shown and absorbs a power P_x. It is possible that X can absorb the same power P_x for another current I. the value of this current is

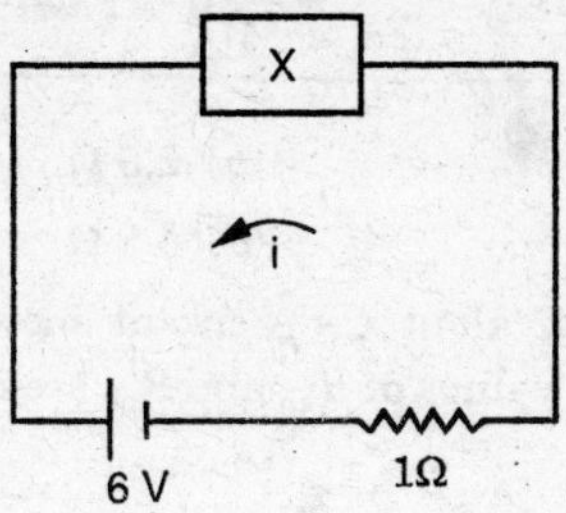

(*a*) $(3 - \sqrt{14})$ amps (*b*) $(3 + \sqrt{14})$ amps

(*c*) 5 amps (*d*) none of the above

53. The value of R required for maximum power transfer in the network shown below is

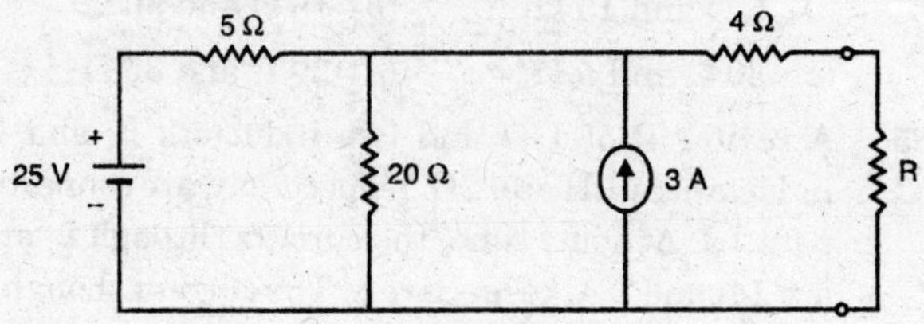

(*a*) 2 (*b*) 4

(*c*) 8 (*d*) 16

54. In the network shown in the given figure, for the current to be zero in R_L, the value of R should be adjusted to

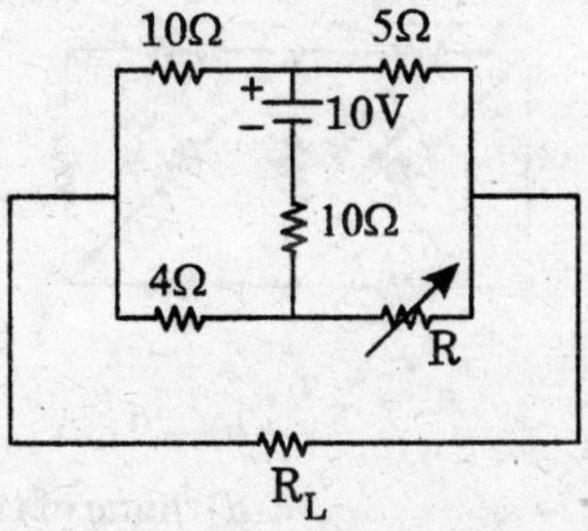

(*a*) 1Ω (*b*) 2Ω

(*c*) 5Ω (*d*) 10Ω

55. The voltage across the 1 kΩ resistor between the nodes A and B of the network shown in the given figure is

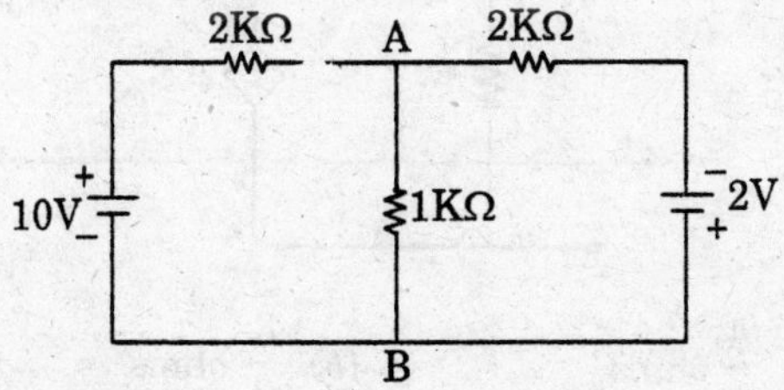

(*a*) 2 V (*b*) 3 V

(*c*) 4 V (*d*) 8 V

56. A resistor R is connected to a voltage source V_s having an internal resistance R_s. A voltmeter of resistance R_m is connected across the termionals of the resistor R. The voltmeter will read a voltage of

(*a*) $\dfrac{V_s R_s R_m}{R_s R_m + R_s R + R R_m}$

(*b*) $\dfrac{V_s R}{R + R_s}$

(*c*) $\dfrac{V_s R_m}{R R_s + R_m}$

(*d*) $\dfrac{V_s R R_m}{R_s R + R_s R_m + R R_m}$

57. Consider the two circuits I and II shown in the following figures

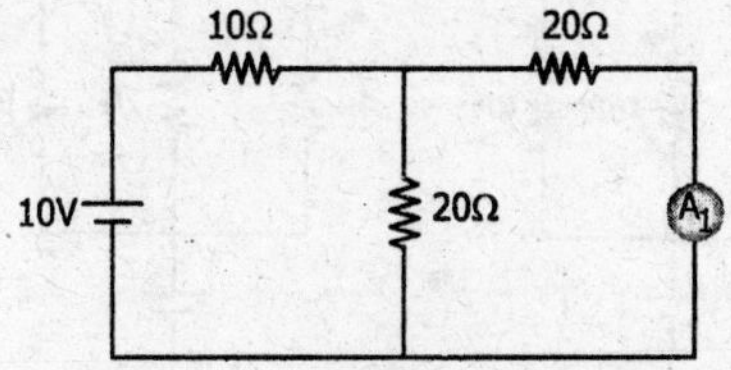

Circuit-I

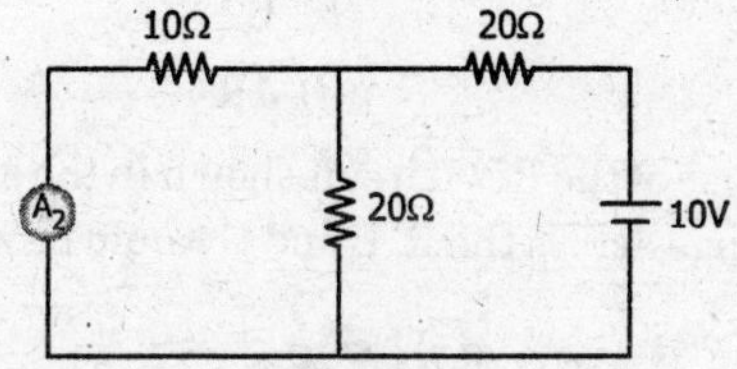

Circuit-II

Which one of the following statements regarding the current flowing through the ammeters A_1 and A_2 is correct

(*a*) The currents in A_1 and A_2 are the same value of equal 0.25 A

(*b*) The currents in A_1 and A_2 are respectively 0.25 A and 2.5 A

(*c*) The currents in both the ammeters is of the same value of equals 2.5 A

(*d*) The currents in A_1 and A_2 are respectively 2.5 A and 0.25 A

58. A battery charger can drive a current of 5A into a 1ohm resistance connected at its output teminals. If it is able to charge an ideal 2 V battery at 7 A rate, then its Thevenin's equivalent will be

(*a*) 7.5 V in series with 0.5 ohm

(*b*) 12.5 V in series with 1.5 ohms

(*c*) 7.5 V in parallel with 0.5 ohm

(*d*) 1.25 V in parallel with 1.5 ohms

59. The resistance R looking into the terminals AB in the circuit shown in the figure will be

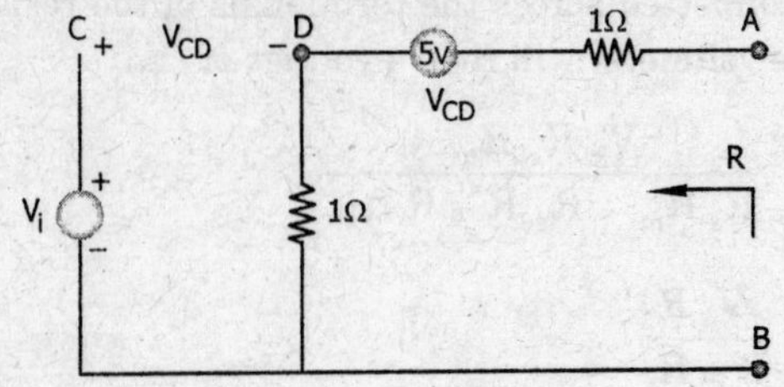

(*a*) 0.5 Ω (*b*) 2 Ω

(*c*) 3 Ω (*d*) 7 Ω

60. The circuit shown in Fig-I is replaced by that in Fig-II. If current I remains the same, then R_0 will be

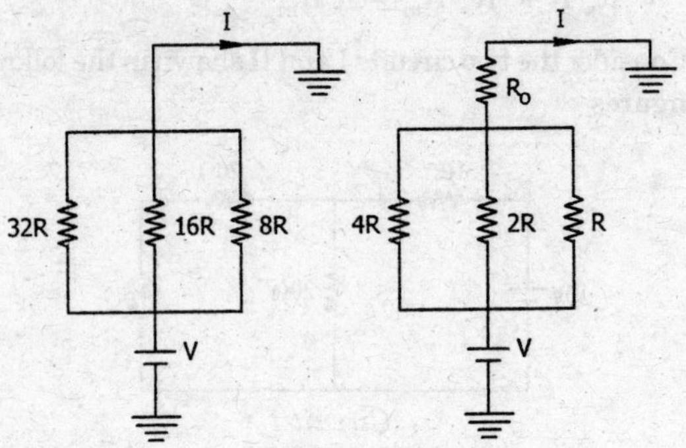

(*a*) zero (*b*) R

(*c*) 2R (*d*) 4R

61. In the case of the RLC circuit shown in the given figure, the voltage across the R, L and C would be respectively

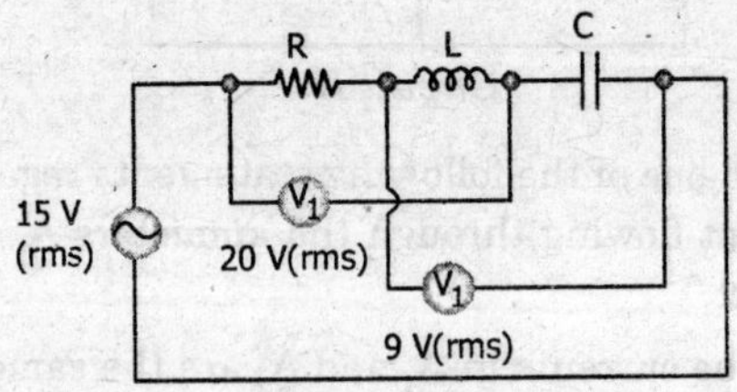

(*a*) 12 V, 16 V and 7 V or 25 V

(*b*) 16 V, 12 V and 7 V or 25 V

(*c*) 7 V, 16 V and 12 V

(*d*) 16 V, 12 V and 25 V

62. The current in the given circuit with a dependent voltage source is

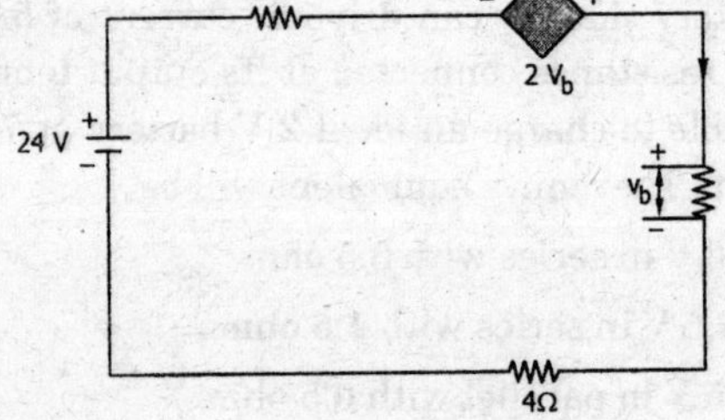

(*a*) 10 A (*b*) 12 A

(*c*) 14 A (*d*) 16 A

63. The value of resistance R shown in the given figure is

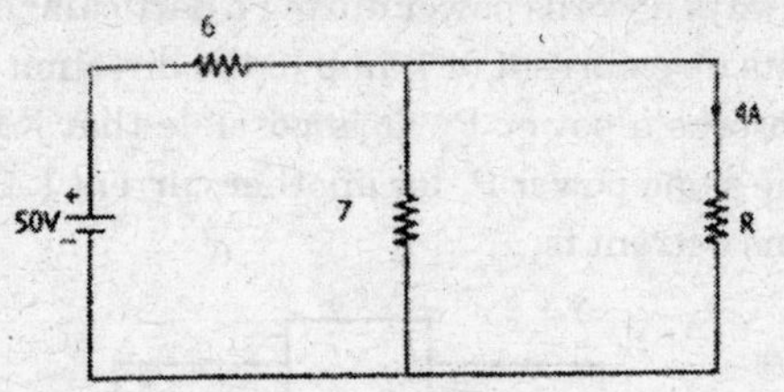

(*a*) 3.5 Ω (*b*) 2.5 Ω

(*c*) 1 Ω (*d*) 4.5 Ω

64. For the equivalent λ ≡ Δ circuit shown in the given firgure, the values of R_{AB} and R_{BC} are respectively

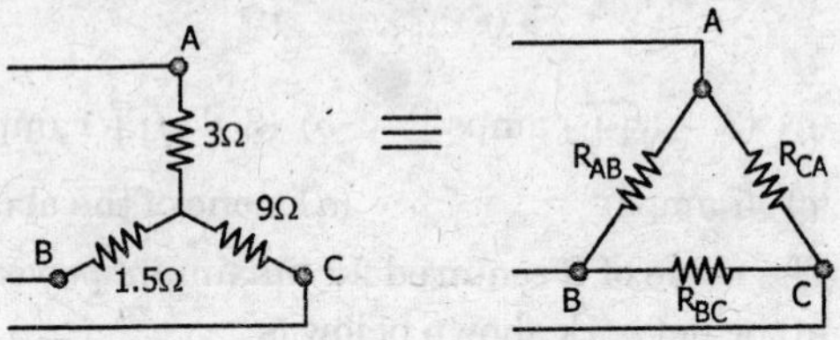

(*a*) 5 Ω and 15 Ω (*b*) 15 Ω and 30 Ω

(*c*) 30 Ω and 5 Ω (*d*) 20 Ω and 35 Ω

65. A resitor R of 1 Ω and two inductors L_1 and L_2 of inductances 1 H and 2H, respectively, are connected in parallel. At some time, the curents through L_1 and L_2 are 1 A and 2 A, respectively. The current though R at time t = ∞ will be

(*a*) zero (*b*) 1 A

(*c*) 2 A (*d*) 3 A

66. The current i_4 in the circuit of given figure is equal to

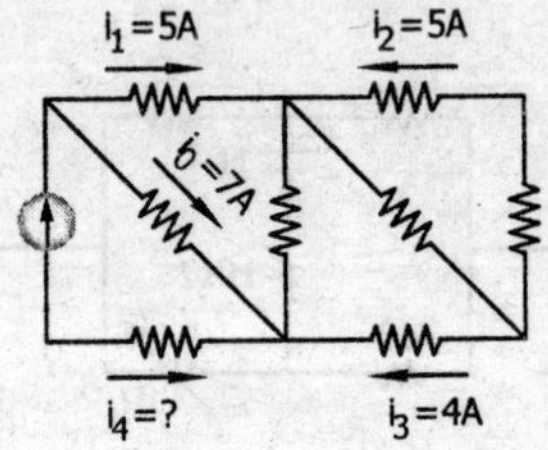

(*a*) 12 A (*b*) – 12 A

(*c*) 4 A (*d*) none of these

67. The circuit shown in the given figure is equivalent to a load of

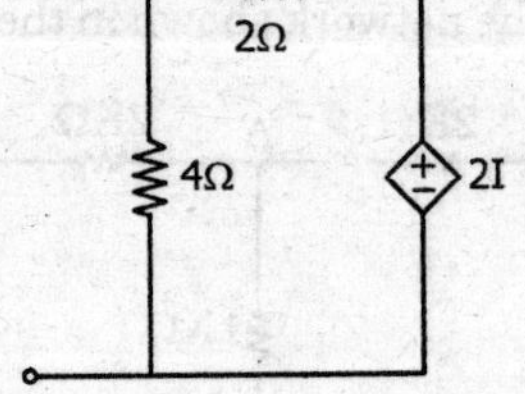

(*a*) $\frac{4}{3}$ ohms (*b*) $\frac{8}{3}$ ohms

(*c*) 4 ohms (*d*) 2 ohms

68. Consider the star network shown in the given figure. The resistance between terminals A and B with C open is 6 Ω, between terminals B and C with A open is 11 Ω, and between terminals C and A with B open is 9 Ω. Then

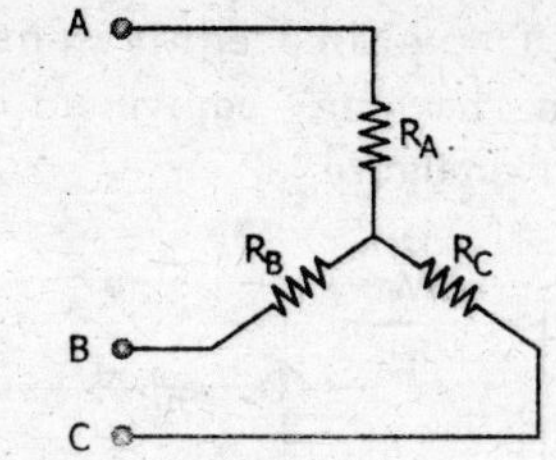

(*a*) $R_A = 4\Omega, R_B = 2\Omega, R_C = 5\Omega$
(*b*) $R_A = 2\Omega, R_B = 4\Omega, R_C = 7\Omega$
(*c*) $R_A = 3\Omega, R_B = 3\Omega, R_C = 4\Omega$
(*d*) $R_A = 5\Omega, R_B = 1\Omega, R_C = 10\Omega$

69. The voltage V in the given figure is

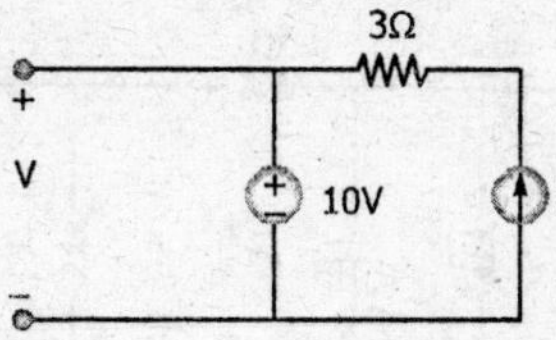

(*a*) 10V (*b*) 15V
(*c*) 5V (*d*) none of these

70. The value of the resistance R, connected across the terminals A and B, (see given figure), which will absorb the maximum power, is

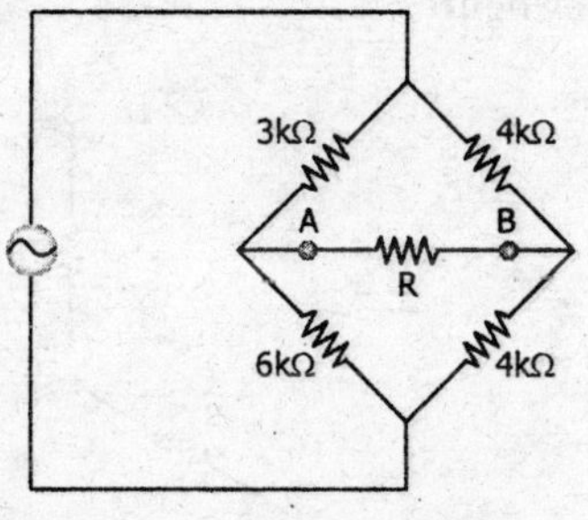

(*a*) 4.00 kΩ (*b*) 4.11 kΩ
(*c*) 8.00 kΩ (*d*) 9.00 kΩ

71. Viewed from the terminal AB, the following circuit shown in the figure can be reduced to an equivalent circuit of a signle voltage source in series with a single resistor with which of the following parameters ?

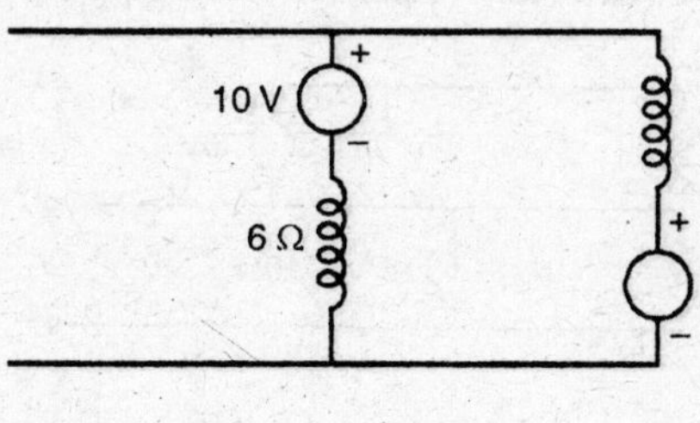

(*a*) 4 volts source in series with 10 Ω resistor
(*b*) 1 volt source in series with 2.4 Ω resistor
(*c*) 15 volts source in series with 2.4 Ω resistor
(*d*) 1 volt source in series with 10 Ω resistor

NETWORK THROREM (SOLUTION METHOD)

72. In the delta equivalent of the given star connected circuit, $\overline{Z}_{QR}$ is equal to

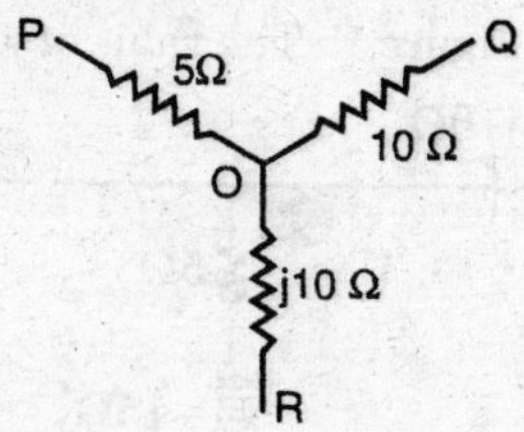

(*a*) 40 Ω (*b*) (20 + j10) Ω
(*c*) $(5 + j\frac{10}{3})$ Ω (*d*) (10 + j30) Ω

73. The thevenin equivalent of a network is as shown in the given figure. For maximum power transfer to the variable and purely resistive load R_L its resistance should be

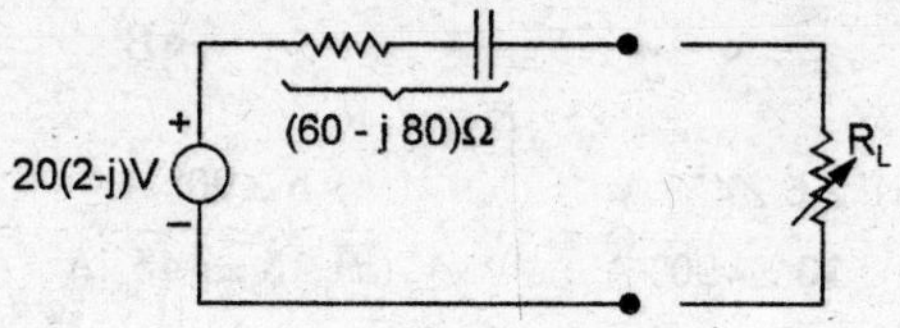

(*a*) 60 Ω (*b*) 80 Ω
(*c*) 100 Ω (*d*) infinity

74. A delta connected network with Y-equivalent is shown below.

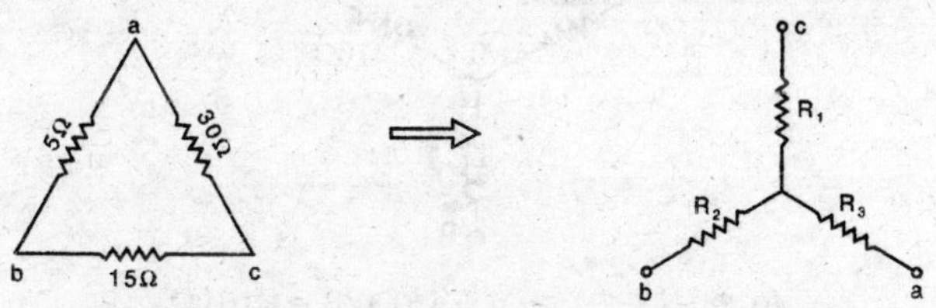

The resistances R_1, R_2, R_3 (in ohms) are respectively
(*a*) 1.5, 3 and 9 (*b*) 3, 9 and 1.5
(*c*) 9, 3 and 1.5 (*d*) 2, 1.5 and 9 (*b*) low

75. Thevenin's equivalent resistance R_{th} for the network shown in the given figure is known to be 2Ω. The value of R in ohms is

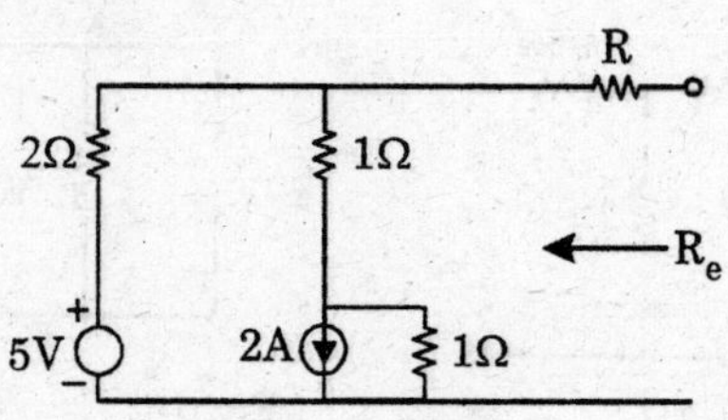

(*a*) 1 (*b*) 2
(*c*) 3 (*d*) 4

76. The Thevenin resistance of the network comprising of a resistor of 1Ω in series with a parallel combination of a current source of 2I amperes and a resistor of 1Ω through which 1 impere of current flows is

(*a*) 2 (*b*) 0.5

(*c*) $\frac{4}{3}$ (*d*) 1

77. The circuit shown in Figure-I replaced by its Norton's equivalent in Figure-II. The value of will be

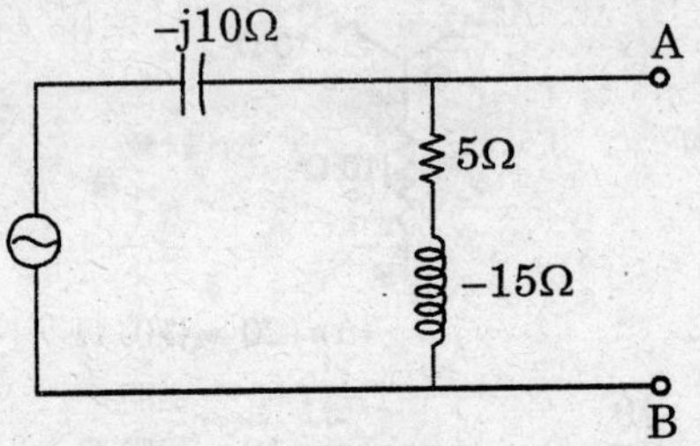

Figure-I

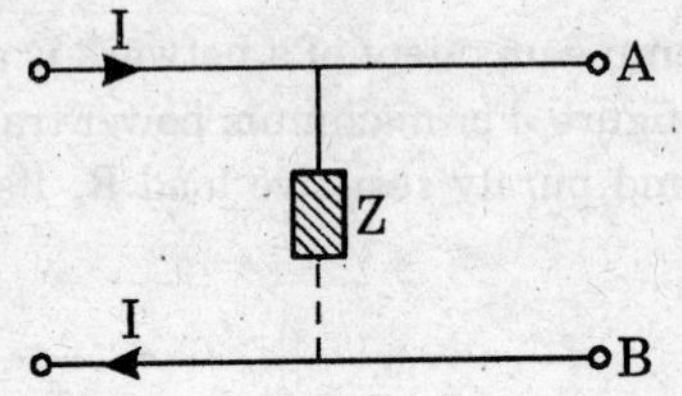

Figure- II

(*a*) 2.5 ∠45° A (*b*) 5 ∠90° A

(*c*) 10 ∠–90° A (*d*) 15 ∠–45° A

78. In the delta equivalent of the given star-connected circuit $\overline{Z}_{QR}$ is equal to

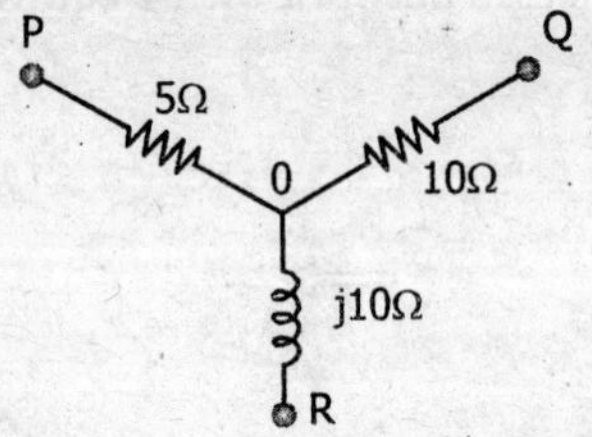

(*a*) 40 Ω (*b*) (20 + j 10) Ω

(*c*) $5 + j\left(\frac{10}{3}\right)$ Ω (*d*) (10 + *j* 30) Ω

79. The Norton's equivalent of circuit shown in Figure I is drawn in the circuit shown in Figure II. The values of I_{SC} and R_{eg} in Figure II are respectively

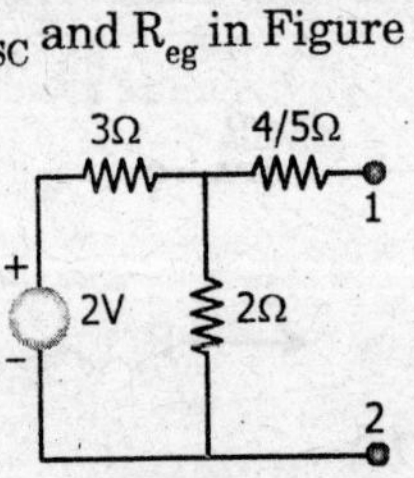

Fig. I

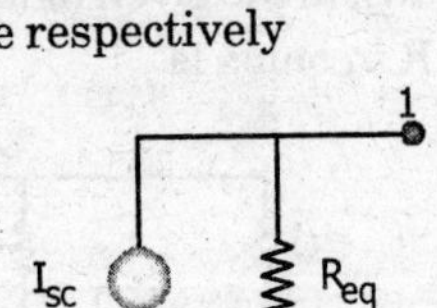

Fig. II

(*a*) $\frac{5}{2}$ A *and* 2 Ω (*b*) $\frac{2}{5}$ A *and* 2 Ω

(*c*) $\frac{4}{5}$ A *and* $\frac{12}{5}$ Ω (*d*) $\frac{2}{5}$ A *and* 2 Ω

80. Which one of the following combinations of open circuit voltage and Thevenin's equivalent resistance represents the Thevenin's equivalent of the circuit shown in the given figure ?

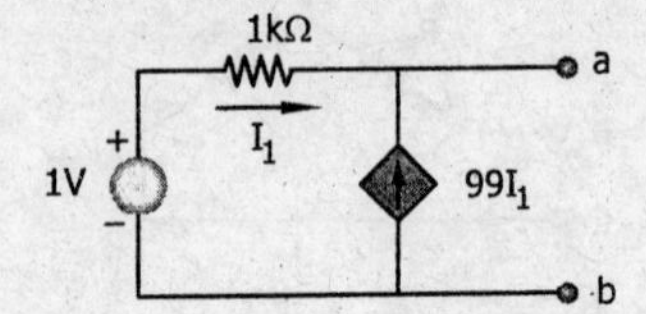

(*a*) 1 *v*, 10 Ω (*b*) 1 *v*, 1*k* Ω

(*c*) 1 *mv*, 1*k* Ω (*d*) 1 *mv*, 10 Ω

81. The Thevenin equivalent voltage V_{TH} appearing between the terminals A and B of the network shown in the figure is given by

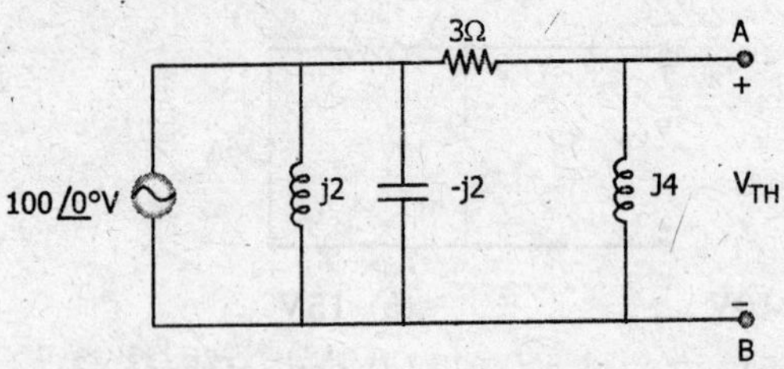

(*a*) *j*16(3 – *j*4) (*b*) *j*16(3 + *j*4)

(*c*) 16(3 + *j*4) (*d*) 16(3 – *j*4)

82. A Delta-connected network with its Wye-equivalent is shown in the figure.

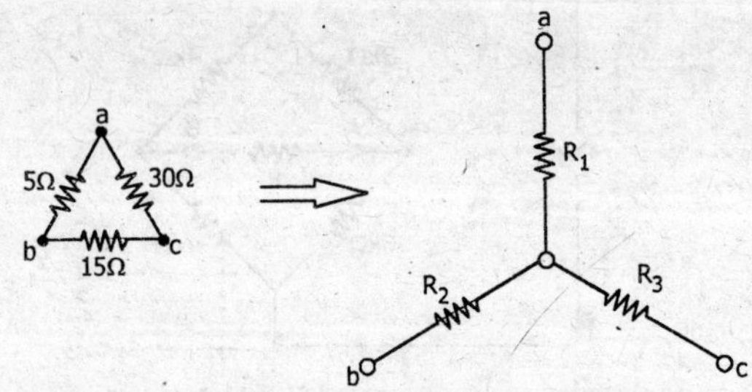

The resistances R_1, R_2 and R_3 (in ohms) are respectively

(*a*) 1.5, 3 and 9

(*b*) 3, 9 and 1.5

(*c*) 9, 3 and 1.5

(*d*) 3, 1.5 and 9

83. For the circuit shown, the Thevenin equivalent is

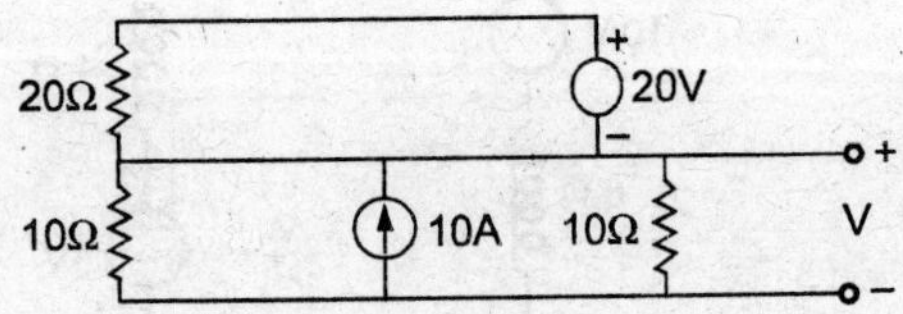

(a) 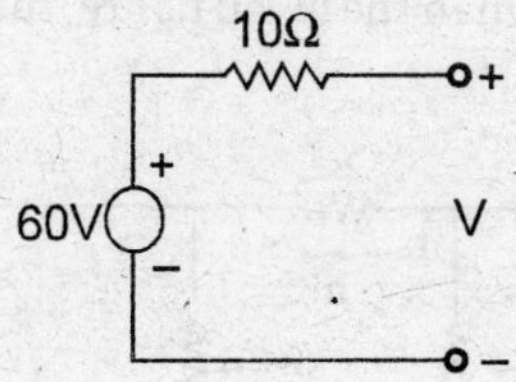

(b) 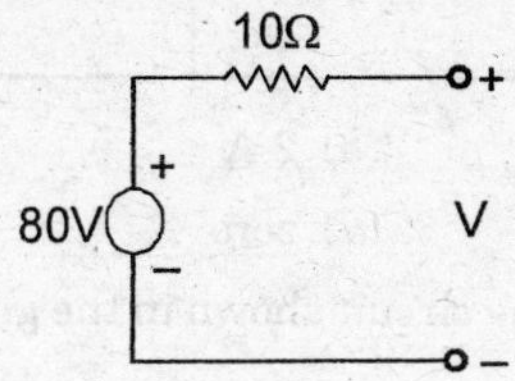

(c) 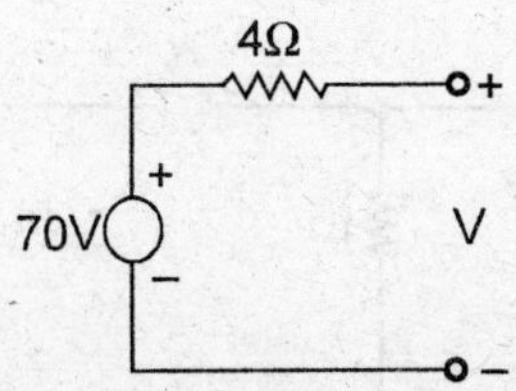

(d) 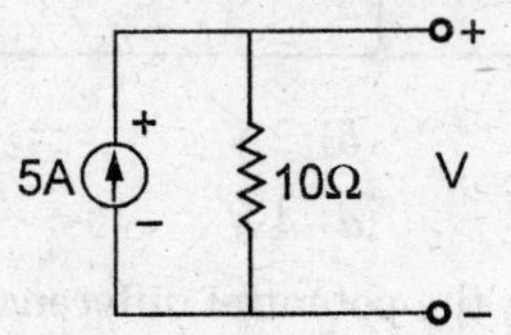

84. The Thevenin equivalent of the network shown in Fig. (a) is 10 V in series with a resistance of 2Ω. If now, a resistance of 3Ω is connected across AB as shown in Fig. (b), the Thevenin equivalent of the modified network across AB will be

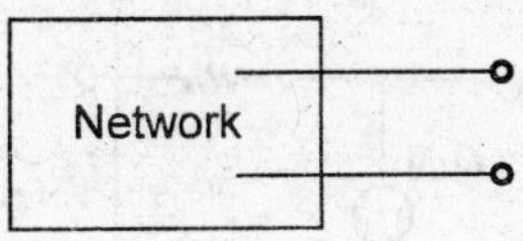

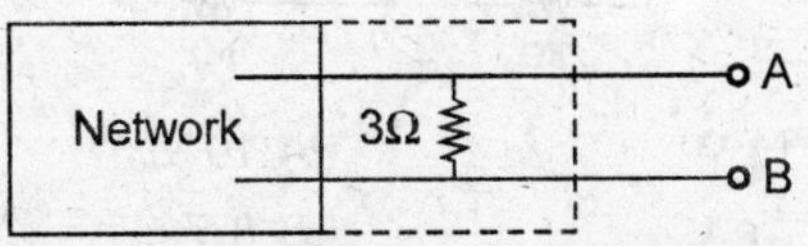

(a) 10 V in series with 1.2 Ω resistance

(b) 6 V in series with 1.2 Ω resistance

(c) 10 V in series with 5 Ω resistance

(d) 6 V in series with 5 Ω resistance

85. A network is shown in the given figure. Which one of the following equations would represent the equation for loop 3 ?

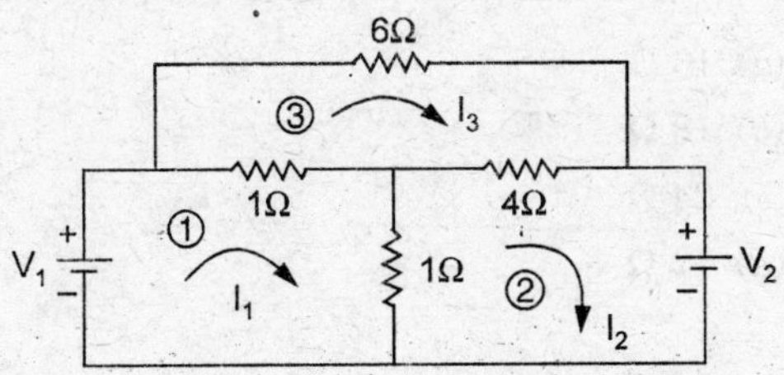

(a) $-I_1 + 4I_2 + 11I_3 = 0$

(b) $I_1 + 4I_2 + 11I_3 = 0$

(c) $-I_1 - 4I_2 + 11I_3 = 0$

(d) $I_1 + 4I_2 + 6I_3 = 0$

86. For the network shown in the given figure, the voltage V_B will be

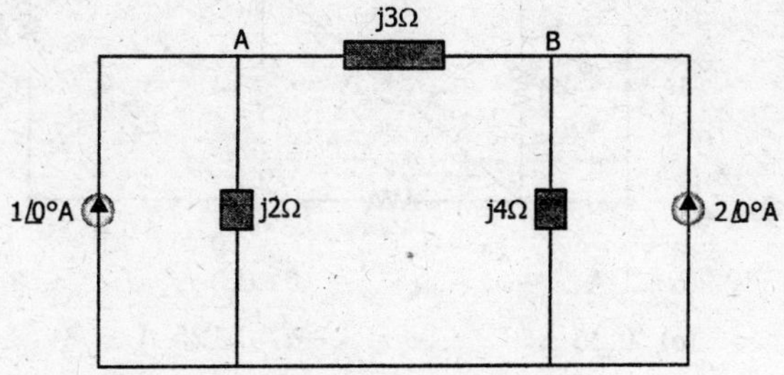

(a) (j 5.33) V (b) (5.33) V

(c) (–j 5.33) V (d) (j 3.33) V

87. In the circuit shown in the given figure, if $I_1 = 1.5$ A, then I_2 will be

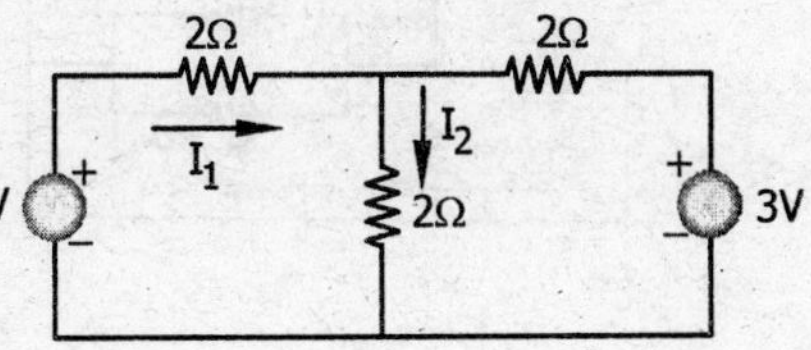

(a) 0.5 A

(b) 1.0 A

(c) 1.5 A

(d) 3.0 A

88. In the given circuit, $V_1 = 40$ V when R is 10 Ω. When R is zero, the value of V_2 will be

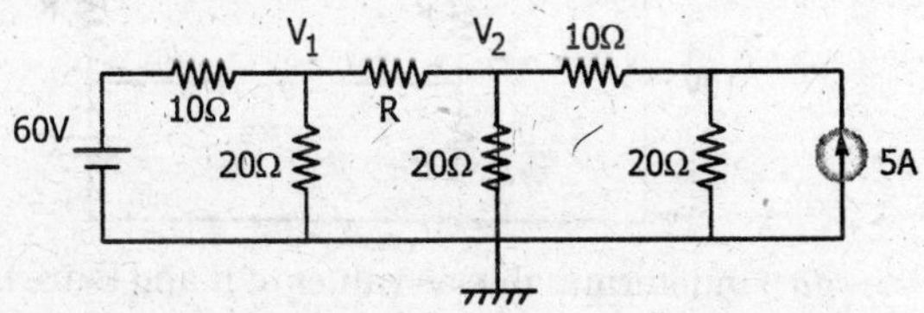

(a) 40 V

(b) 30 V

(c) 20 V

(d) 10 V

89. A network contains only independent current sources and resistors. If the values of all resistors are doubled, the vlaues of the node voltages

(a) will become half

(b) will remain unchanged

(c) will become double

(d) cannot be determined unless the circuit configuration and the values of the resistors are known

90. If a resistance R of 1 Ω is connected across the terminals AB as shown in the given figure, then the current flowing through R will be

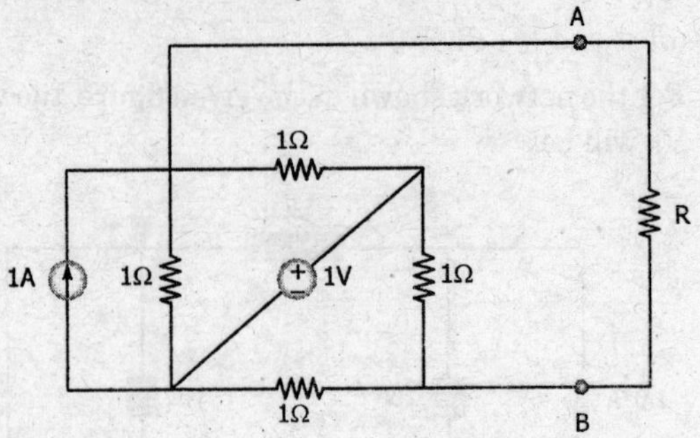

(*a*) 1 A (*b*) 0.5 A
(*c*) 0.25 A (*d*) 0.125 A

91. For the circuit shown in the figure, the current I is

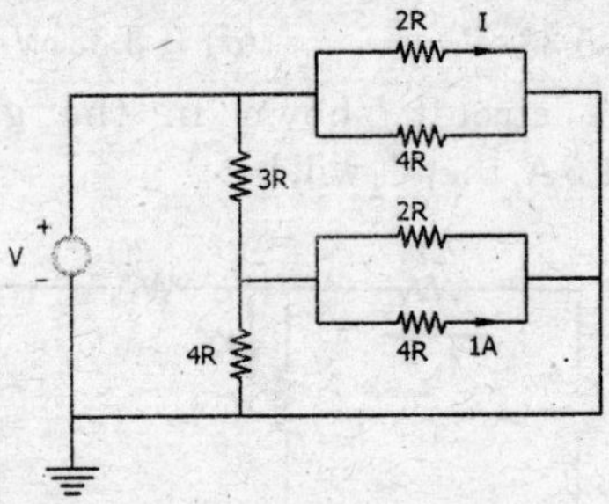

(*a*) indeterminable due to inadequate data
(*b*) zero
(*c*) 4 A
(*d*) 8 A

92. In the circuit shown in the figure, output $|V_0(j\omega)|$ is

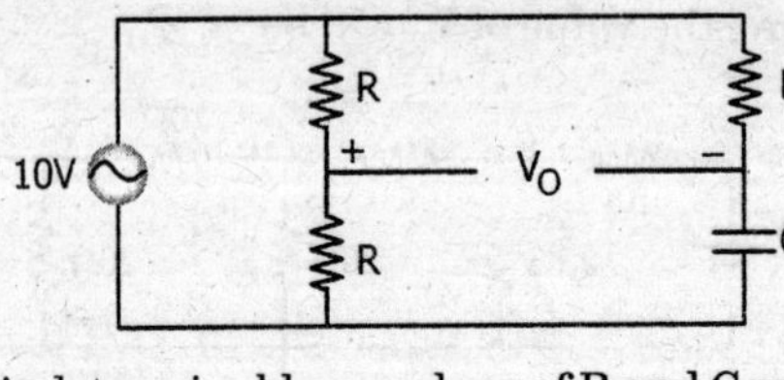

(*a*) indeterminable as values of R and C are not given
(*b*) 2.5 V
(*c*) $5\sqrt{2}$ V
(*d*) 5 V

93. For the circuit shown in the given figure, the voltage V_{AB} is

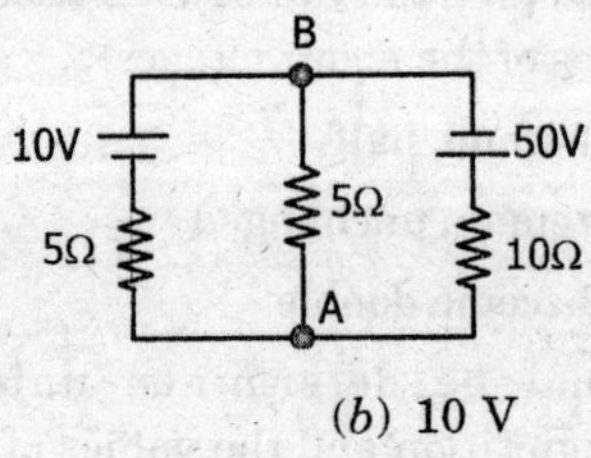

(*a*) 6 V (*b*) 10 V
(*c*) 25 V (*d*) 40 V

94. For the circuit shown in the given figure, the current I is given by

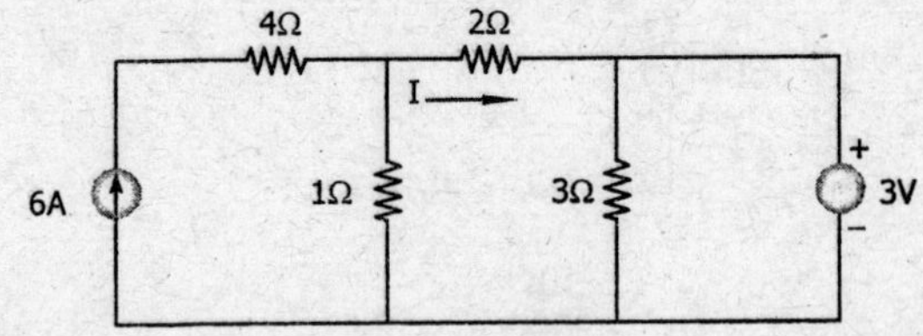

(*a*) 3 A (*b*) 2 A
(*c*) 1 A (*d*) zero

95. The value of V in the circuit shown in the given figure is

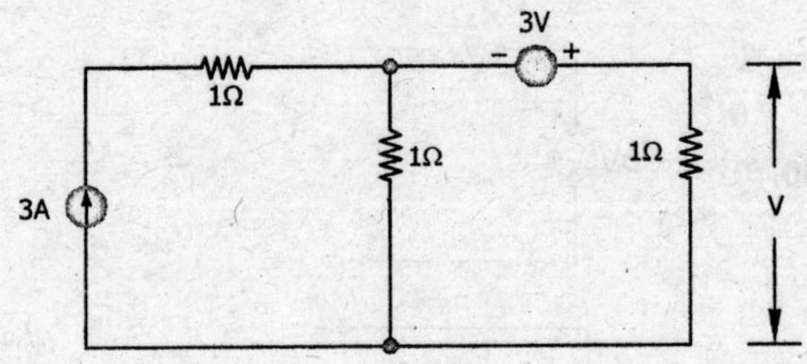

(*a*) 1 V (*b*) 2 V
(*c*) 3 V (*d*) 4 V

96. In the given figure, the potential difference between points P and Q is

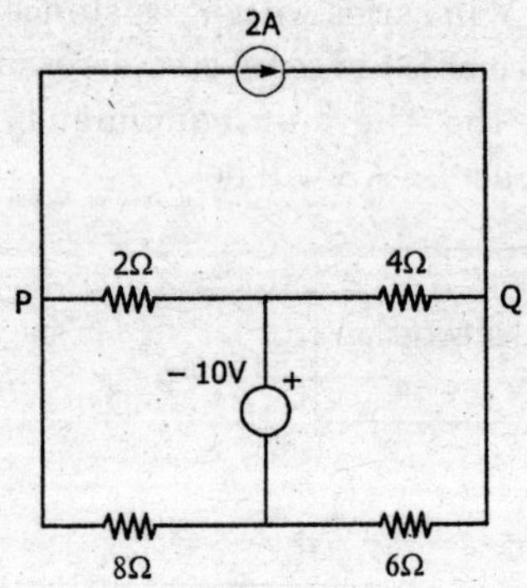

(*a*) 12 V (*b*) 10 V
(*c*) – 6 V (*d*) 8 V

97. In the given figure, the value of R is

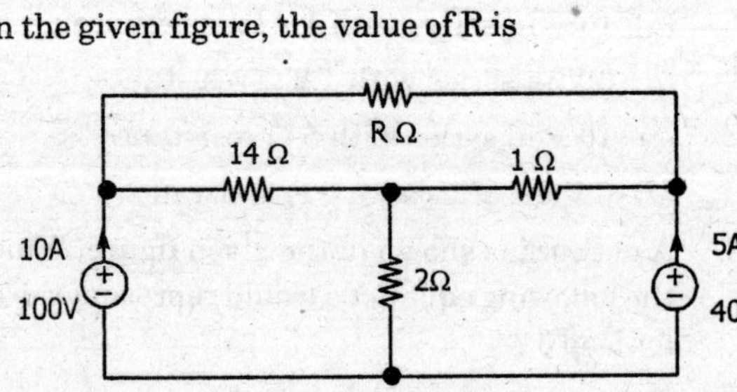

(*a*) 10 Ω
(*b*) 18 Ω
(*c*) 24 Ω
(*d*) 12 Ω

98. The voltage V in the given figure is equal to

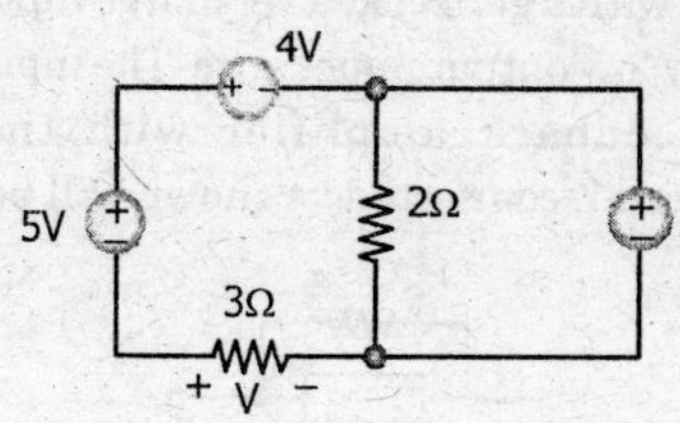

(a) 3V (b) – 3V

(c) 5V (d) none of these

99. The nodal method of circuit analysis is based on

(a) KVL and Ohm's law

(b) KCL and Ohm's law

(c) KCL and KVL

(d) KCL, KVL and Ohm's law

100. The voltage e_0 in the given figure is

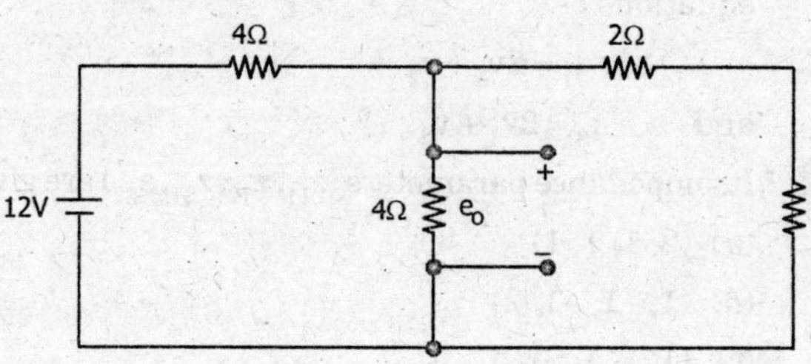

(a) 2 V (b) $\frac{4}{3}$ V

(c) 4 V (d) 8 V

101. In the circuit of given figure, the voltage v(t) is

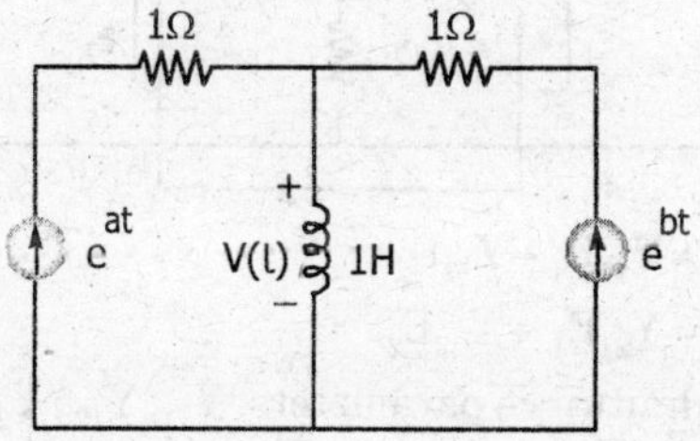

(a) $e^{at} - e^{bt}$ (b) $e^{at} + e^{bt}$

(c) $ae^{at} - be^{bt}$ (d) $ae^{at} + be^{bt}$

102. For the circuit in the given figure, the voltage v_0 is

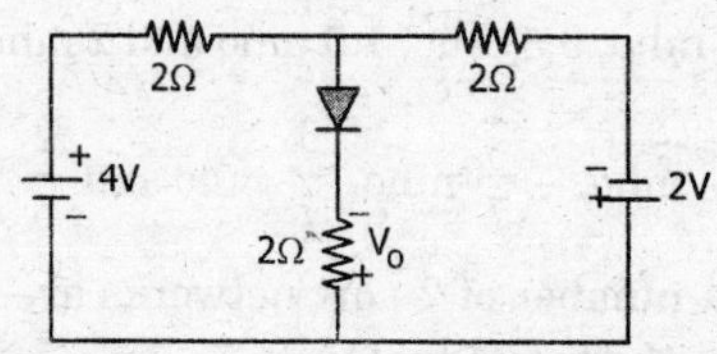

(a) 2V

(b) 1V

(c) – 1V

(d) none of these

TWO-PORT NETWORK

103. The figure shows two different sets of input and output variables for the same two-port resistive network. I_x is

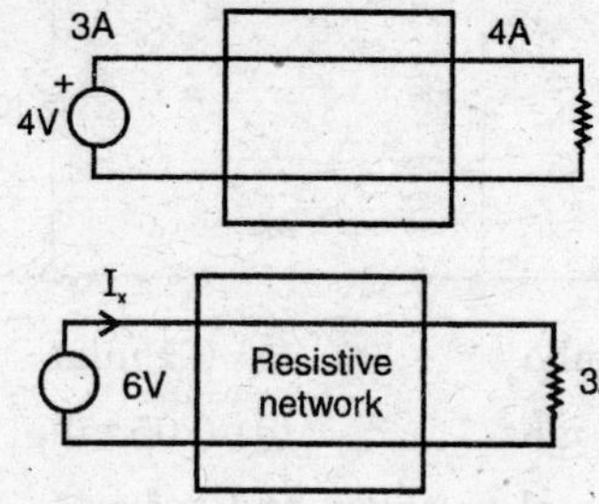

(a) –12 A (b) – 8 A

(c) – 9 A (d) $-\frac{3}{2}$ A

104. A 2-port network is shown in the figure. The parameter h_{21} for this network can be given by

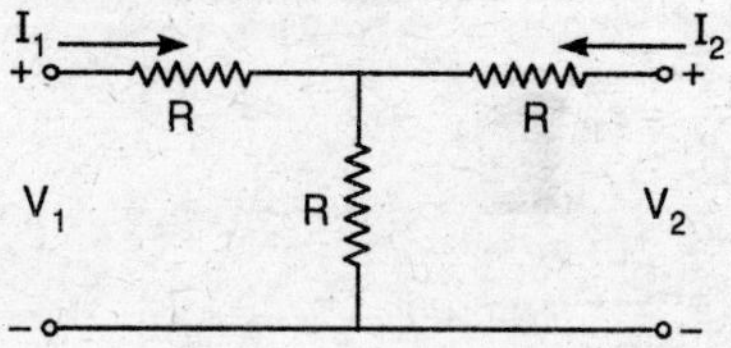

(a) $-\frac{1}{2}$ (b) $+\frac{1}{2}$

(c) $-\frac{3}{2}$ (d) $+\frac{3}{2}$

105. Two two-port networks are connected in cascade. The combination is to be represented as a single two-port network. The parameters of the network are obtained by multiplying the individual

(a) z-parameter matrix

(b) *h*-parameter matrix

(c) *y*-paramter matrix

(d) ABCD parameter matrix

106. The open circuit impedance matrix of the 2 port network shown in the figure is

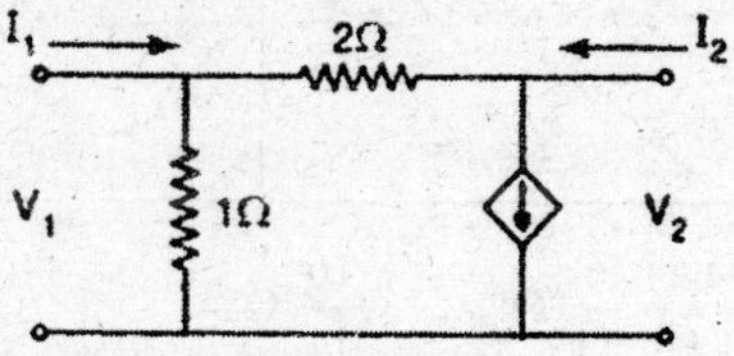

(a) $\begin{bmatrix} -2 & 1 \\ -8 & 3 \end{bmatrix}$ (b) $\begin{bmatrix} -2 & -8 \\ 1 & 3 \end{bmatrix}$

(c) $\begin{bmatrix} 0 & 1 \\ 1 & 0 \end{bmatrix}$ (d) $\begin{bmatrix} 2 & -1 \\ -1 & 3 \end{bmatrix}$

107. The admittance parameter Y_{12} in the 2-port network in the given figure is

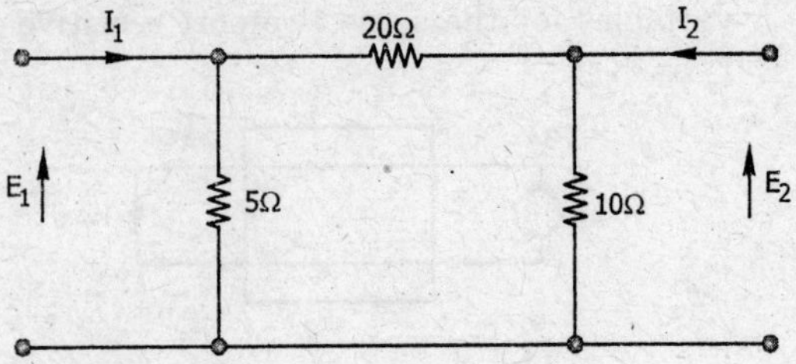

(a) – 0.2 mho (b) 0.1 mho

(c) – 0.05 mho (d) 0.05 mho

108. The terminal voltages and currents of a two-port network are indicated on the given figure. If the two-port network is reciprocal, then

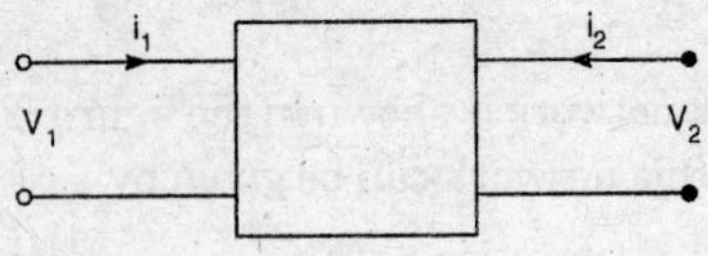

(a) $\frac{z_{12}}{y_{12}} = z_{12}^2 - z_{11} \cdot z_{22}$

(b) $z_{12} = \frac{1}{y_{22}}$

(c) $h_{12} = -h_{21}$

(d) AD – BC = 0

109. A passive 2-port network is in a steady-state. Compared to its input, the steady state output can never offer

(a) higher voltage

(b) lower impedance

(c) greater power

(d) better regulation

110. The z parameters z_{11} and z_{21} for the 2-port network shown in the given figure respectively are

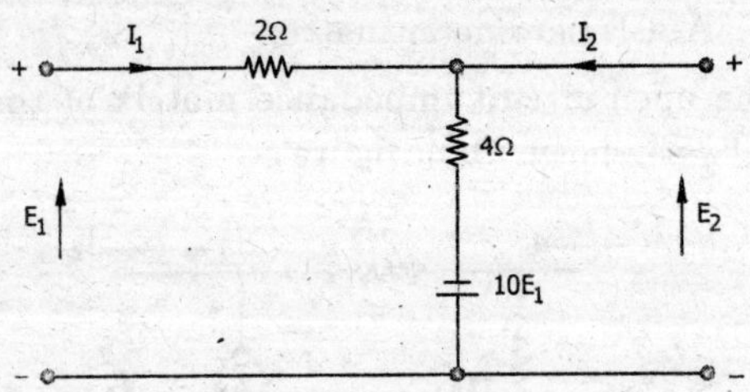

(a) $z_{11} = -\frac{6}{11}\ \Omega;\ z_{21} = \frac{16}{11}\ \Omega$

(b) $z_{11} = \frac{6}{11}\ \Omega;\ z_{21} = \frac{4}{11}\ \Omega$

(c) $z_{11} = \frac{6}{11}\ \Omega;\ z_{21} = -\frac{16}{11}\ \Omega$

(d) $z_{11} = \frac{4}{11}\ \Omega;\ z_{21} = \frac{4}{11}\ \Omega$

111. In the circuit shown in the figure, N is a finite gain amplifier with a gain of k, a very large input impedance and a very low output impedance. The input impedance of the feedback amplifier with the feedback impedanced Z connected as shown will be

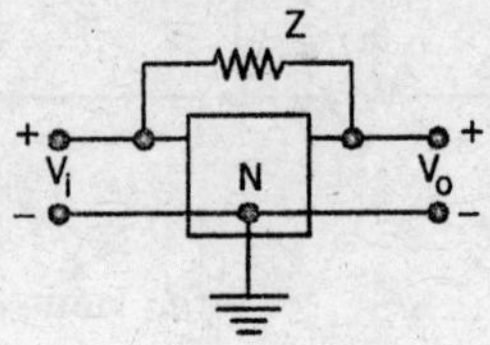

(a) $Z\left(1 - \frac{1}{k}\right)$ (b) $Z(1 - k)$

(c) $\frac{Z}{(k-1)}$ (d) $\frac{Z}{(1-k)}$

112. A two-port device is defined by the following pair of equations :

$$i_1 = 2v_1 + v_2$$

and $i_2 = 2v_1 + v_2$.

Its impedance parameters ($z_{11}, z_{12}, z_{21}, z_{22}$) are given by

(a) (2, 1, 1, 1)

(b) (1, –1, –1, 2)

(c) (1, 1, 1, 2)

(d) (2, –1, –1, 1)

113. A twoport network, shown in the figure is described by the following equations

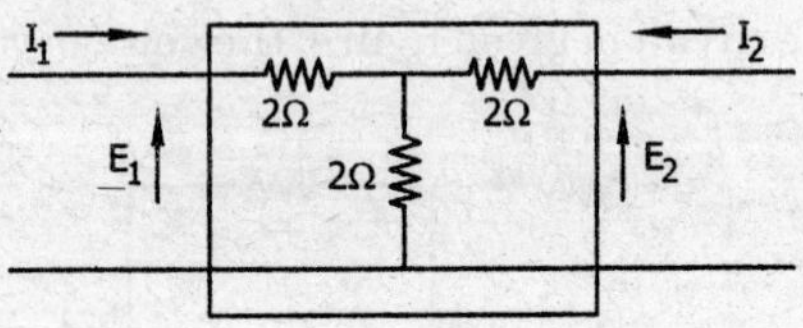

$$I_1 = Y_{11}E_1 + Y_{12}E_2$$
$$I_2 = Y_{21}E_1 + Y_{22}E_2$$

The admittance parameters, Y_{11}, Y_{12}, Y_{21} and Y_{22} for the network shown are respectively

(a) 0.5 mho, 1 mho, 2 mho and 1 mho

(b) $\frac{1}{3}$ mho, $-\frac{1}{6}$ mho, $-\frac{1}{6}$ mho and $\frac{1}{3}$ mho

(c) 0.5 mho, 0.5 mho, 1.5 mho and 2 mho

(d) $-\frac{2}{5}$ mho, $-\frac{3}{7}$ mho, $\frac{3}{7}$ mho and $\frac{2}{5}$ mho

114. When a number of 2 port networks are connected in cascade, the individual

(a) Z_{OC} matrices are added

(b) V_{SC} matrices are added

(c) Chain matrices are multiplied

(d) H-matrices are multiplied

115. The z and h parameter at the network shown in the given figure will be

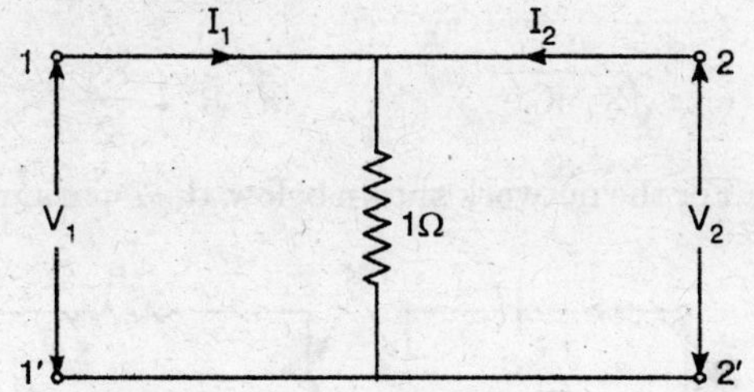

(a) $z = \begin{bmatrix} 0 & 1 \\ -1 & 1 \end{bmatrix}$, $h = \begin{bmatrix} 1 & 1 \\ 1 & 1 \end{bmatrix}$

(b) $z = \begin{bmatrix} 1 & 1 \\ 1 & 1 \end{bmatrix}$, $h = \begin{bmatrix} 0 & 1 \\ -1 & 1 \end{bmatrix}$

(c) $z = \begin{bmatrix} 1 & 0 \\ -1 & 1 \end{bmatrix}$, $h = \begin{bmatrix} -1 & 1 \\ 1 & 1 \end{bmatrix}$

(d) $z = \begin{bmatrix} 0 & 1 \\ 1 & 0 \end{bmatrix}$, $h = \begin{bmatrix} 0 & -1 \\ 2 & ½ \end{bmatrix}$

116. The circuit shown in the given figure is in the steady state with the switch S closed

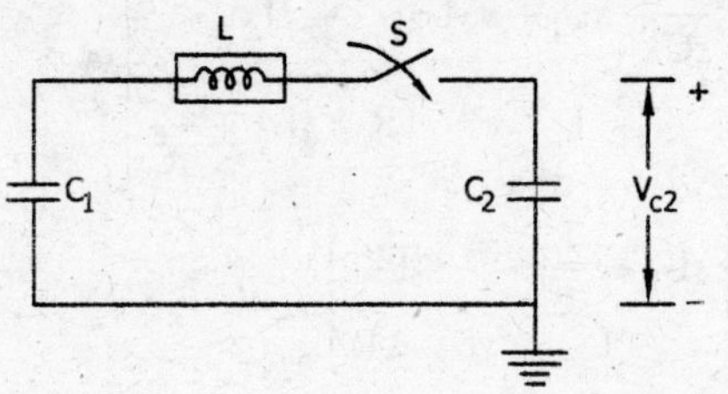

The current i(t) after S is opened at t' = 0 is

(a) a decreasing exponential

(b) an increasing exponential

(c) a damped sinusoid

(d) oscillatory

117. The sinusoidal steady-state voltage gain of the network shown in the given figure will have magnitude equal to 0.707 at an angular frequency of

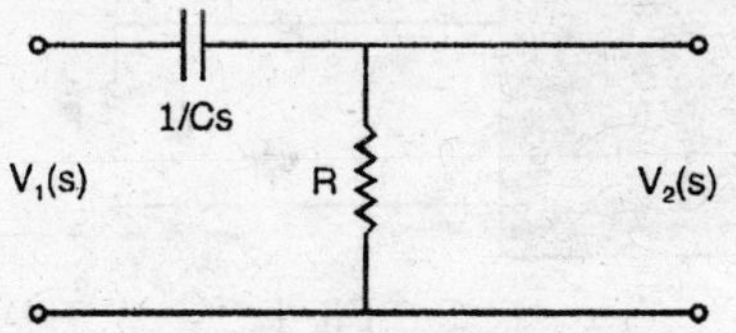

(a) zero (b) RC rad/s

(c) $\frac{1}{RC}$ rad/s (d) 1 rad/s

118. The input impedance at port-2 of the network of above is

(a) $\frac{A}{C}$ (b) $\frac{AD}{BC}$

(c) $\frac{AB}{DC}$ (d) $\frac{D}{C}$

119. The impedance Z (s) of the one-port network shown in the figure is given by

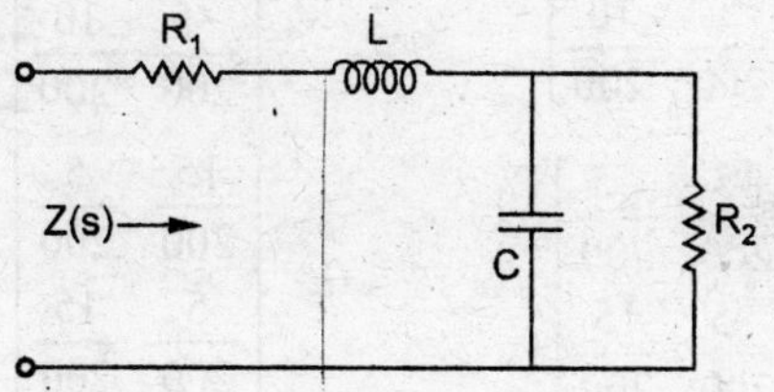

(a) $\frac{s^2 + s(L/C) + (R_1/LC)}{s + (1/LC)}$

(b) $L\frac{s^2 + s(L+R_1R_2C/R_2LC) + (R_1+R_2)/R_2CL}{s + (1/R_2C)}$

(c) $L\frac{s^2 + s(L+C)/R_2 + (R_1/LC)}{s + (1/R_2C)}$

(d) $\frac{s^2 + s(L+R_2C)/R_1LC) + (R_1+R_2)/R_1LC}{s + (1/R_1C)}$

120. For the circuit shown in the given figure, if the input impedance Z_1 at port 1 is given by

$$Z_1 = K_1\frac{(s+2)}{s+5}$$

then the input impedance Z_2 at port 2 will be

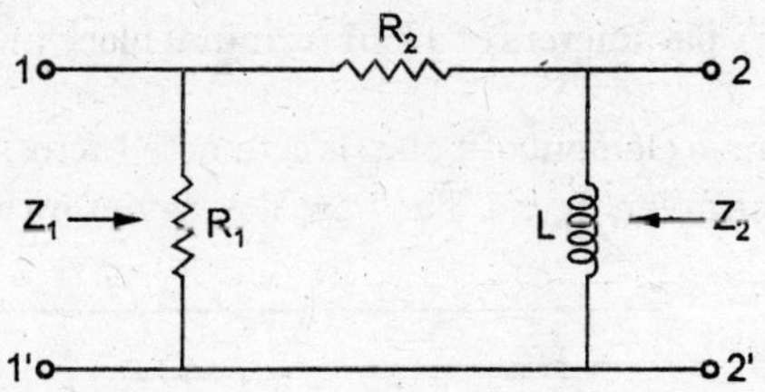

(a) $\frac{K_2(s+3)}{s+5}$ (b) $\frac{K_2(s+2)}{s+3}$

(c) $\frac{K_2 s}{s+5}$ (d) $\frac{K_2 s}{s+2}$

121. The driving-point impedance of a one-port reactive network is given by

(a) $\frac{(s^2+1)(s^2+2)}{s(s^2+3)(s^2+4)}$ (b) $\frac{(s^2+1)(s^2+3)}{s(s^2+2)(s^2+4)}$

(c) $\frac{s^2(s^2+1)}{(s^2+2)(s^2+3)}$ (d) $\frac{1}{s+1}$

122. A T-network is shown in the given figure. Its Y matrix will be (units in siemens)

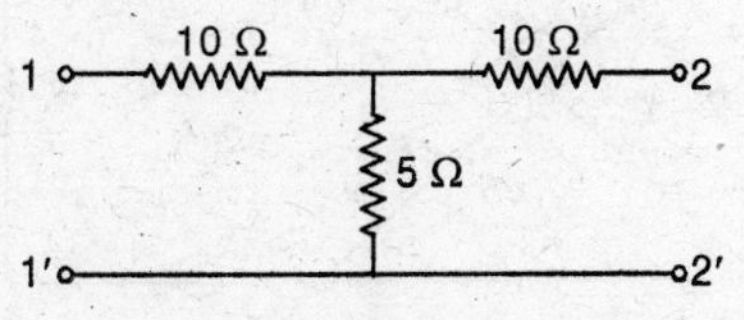

(a) $\begin{bmatrix} \frac{10}{200} & \frac{5}{200} \\ \frac{5}{200} & \frac{10}{200} \end{bmatrix}$ (b) $\begin{bmatrix} \frac{10}{200} & \frac{-5}{200} \\ \frac{-5}{200} & \frac{10}{200} \end{bmatrix}$

(c) $\begin{bmatrix} \frac{15}{200} & \frac{-5}{200} \\ \frac{-5}{200} & \frac{15}{200} \end{bmatrix}$ (d) $\begin{bmatrix} \frac{15}{200} & \frac{5}{200} \\ \frac{5}{200} & \frac{15}{200} \end{bmatrix}$

123. In a two-port network containing linear bilateral passive circuit elements, which one of the following conditions for z-parameters would hold ?

(a) $z_{11} = z_{22}$ (b) $z_{12}z_{21} = z_{11}z_{22}$

(c) $z_{11}z_{12} = z_{22}z_{21}$ (d) $z_{12} = z_{21}$

124. The two electric sub-networks N_1 and N_2 are connected through three resistors as shown in the figure below. The voltage across 5Ω resistor and 1Ω resistor are given to be 10V and 5V respectively. Then voltage across 15Ω resistor is

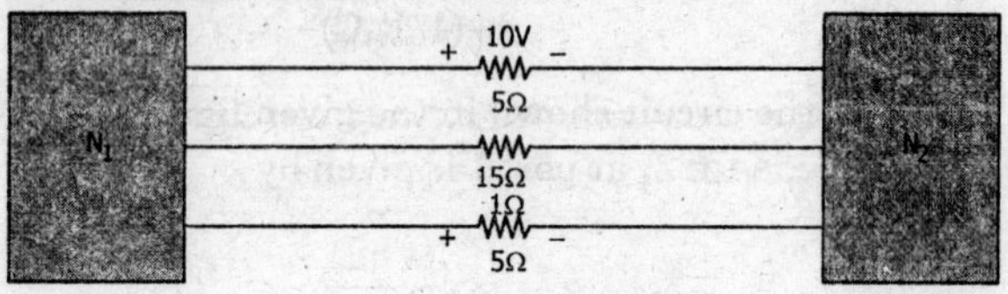

(a) –105 V (b) + 105 V

(c) –15 V (d) + 15 V

125. The Y parameters of a four terminal block are $\begin{bmatrix} 4 & 2 \\ 1 & 1 \end{bmatrix}$.

A single element of 1 ohm is connected across as shown in the given figure. The new Y parameters will be

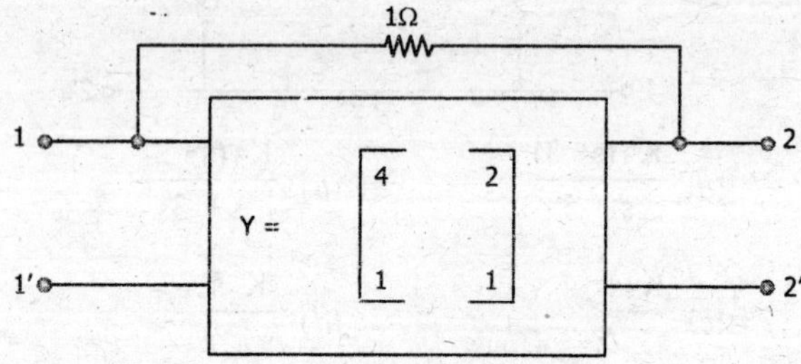

(a) $\begin{bmatrix} 5 & 1 \\ 0 & 2 \end{bmatrix}$ (b) $\begin{bmatrix} 4 & 3 \\ 2 & 2 \end{bmatrix}$

(c) $\begin{bmatrix} 3 & 2 \\ 1 & 1 \end{bmatrix}$ (d) $\begin{bmatrix} 4 & 2 \\ 1 & 1 \end{bmatrix}$

126. For latice type attenuator shown in the given figure, the characteristic impedance R_0 is

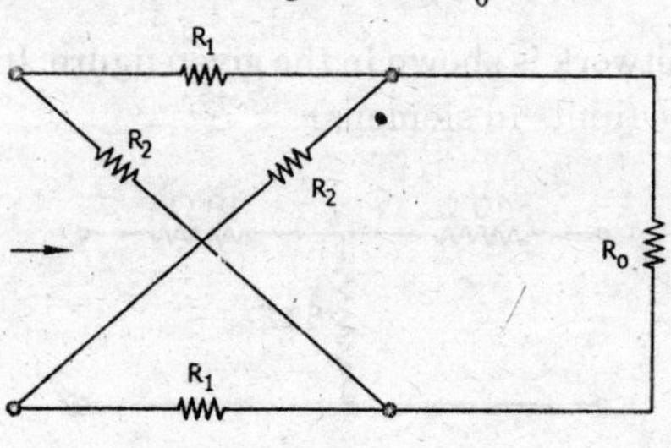

(a) $\dfrac{R_1 + R_2}{2}$ (b) $\dfrac{2R_1 + R_2}{R_1 + R_2}$

(c) $\sqrt{R_1 R_2}$ (d) $R_1 + \dfrac{R_2}{2}$

127. For the network shown below, the Z-parameter will be

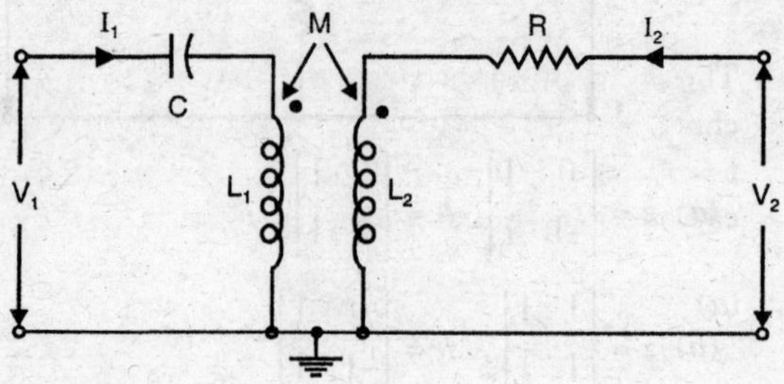

(a) $\begin{bmatrix} \frac{1}{sC} + sL_1 & sM \\ sM & R + sL_2 \end{bmatrix}$

(b) $\begin{bmatrix} \frac{1}{sC} + sL_1 & -sM \\ -sM & R + sL_2 \end{bmatrix}$

(c) $\begin{bmatrix} \frac{1}{sC} + sL_1 + sM & 1 \\ 1 & R + sL_2 + \frac{1}{sC} \end{bmatrix}$

(d) $\begin{bmatrix} sL_1 + \frac{1}{sC} & -1 \\ -1 & sL_2 + R \end{bmatrix}$

128. A two-part network is reciprocal if and only if

(a) $Z_{11} = Z_{22}$ (b) BC – AD = – 1

(c) $Y_{12} = -Y_{21}$ (d) $h_{12} = h_{21}$

129. A certain network N feeds a load resistance R as shown in Fig-I. It consumes a power of P W. If an identical network is added as shown in Fig-II, the power consumed by R will be

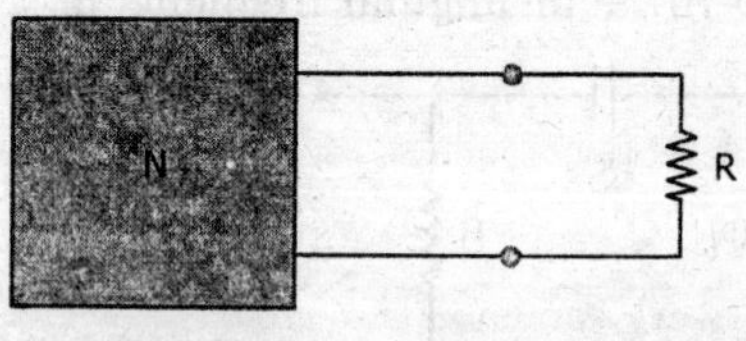

Fig-I

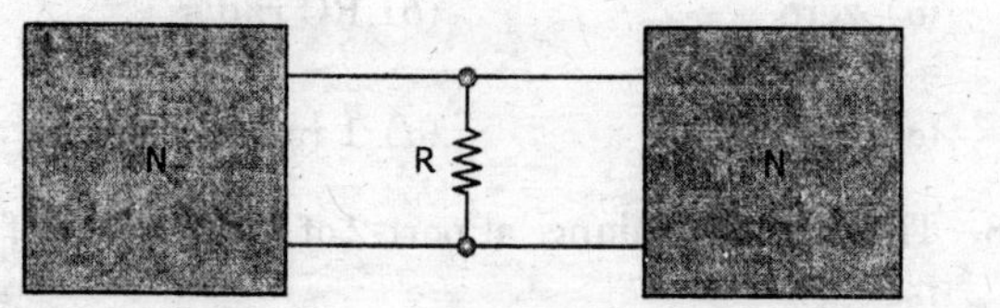

Fig-II

(a) less than P (b) equal to P

(c) between P and 4P (d) more than 4P

130. 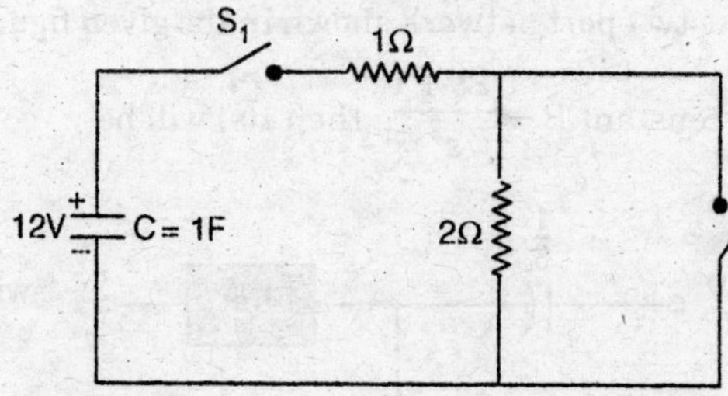

The capacitor in the circuit as shown above is initially charged to 12 V with S_1 and S_2 open. S_1 is closed at t = 0 while S_2 is closed at t = 3. The wavefrom of the capacitor current is represented by

(*a*) 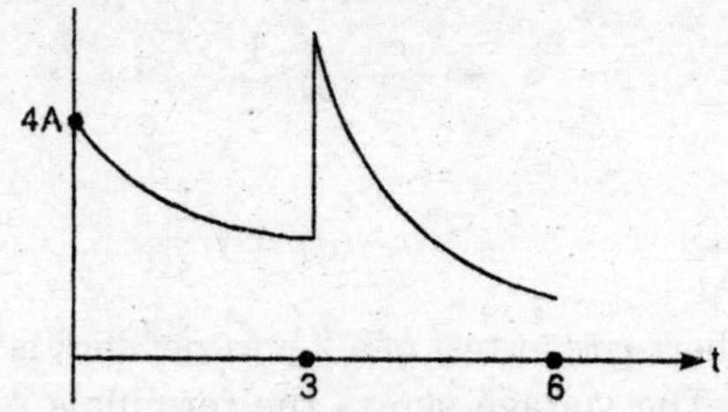

(*b*) 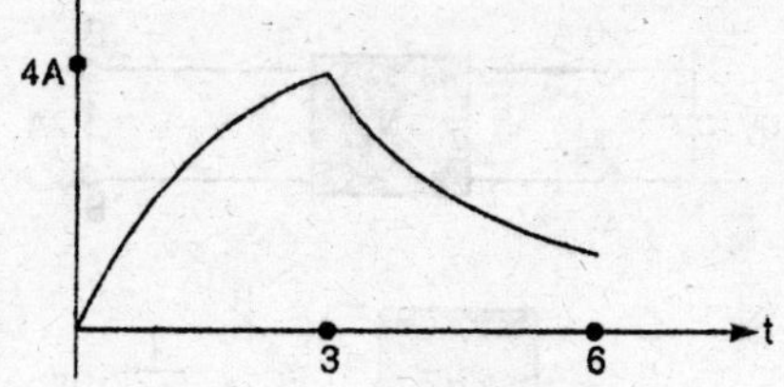

(*c*) 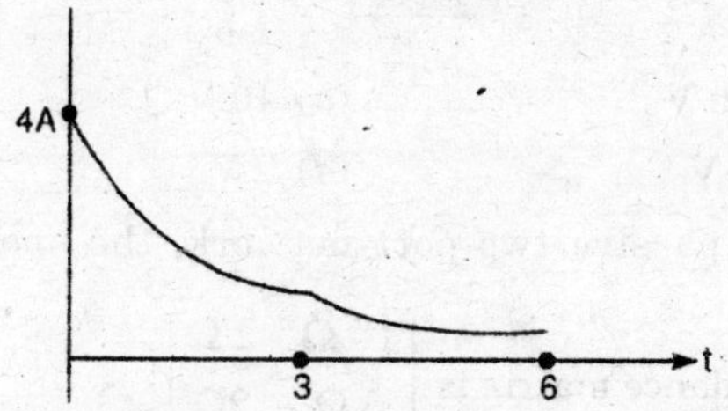

(*d*) 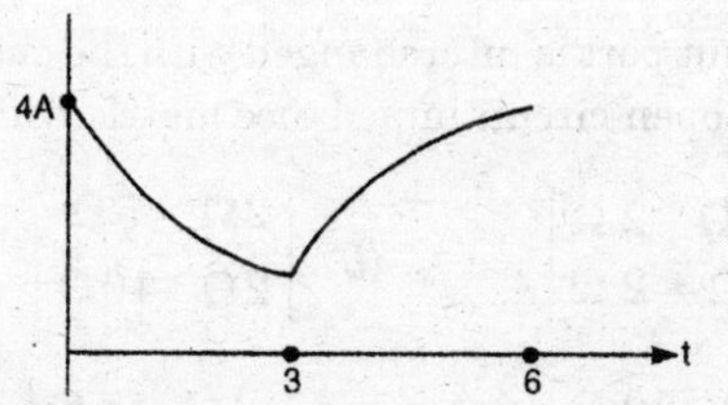

131. An impedance match is desired at the 1 – 1 port of the two-port network shown in the given figure. The match will be obtained when z_g equals

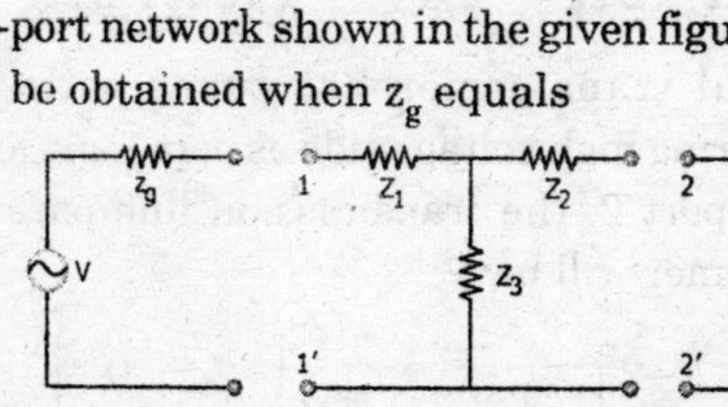

(*a*) $z_1 + z_3$

(*b*) $z_1 + \dfrac{z_3\,(z_2 + z_L)}{z_2 + z_3 + z_L}$

(*c*) $\dfrac{z_1\,(z_2 + z_3)}{z_1 + z_2 + z_3}$

(*d*) z_{1321}.

132. Initially, the circuit shown in the given figure was relaxed. If the switch is closed at t= 0, the values of $i_R(0^+)$, $\dfrac{di}{dt}(0^+)$ and $\dfrac{d^2i}{dt^2}(0^+)$ will respectively be

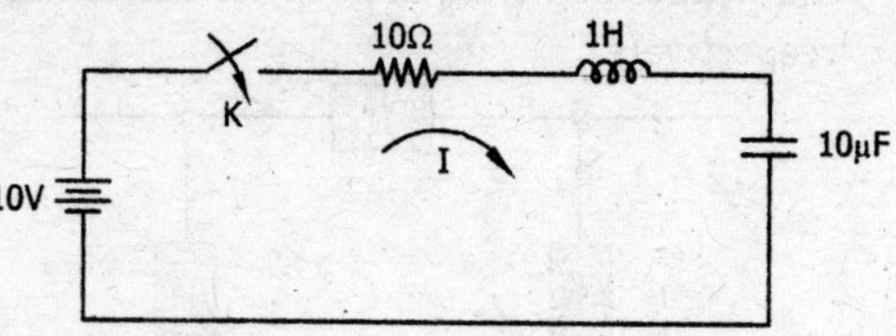

(*a*) 0, 10 and –100 (*b*) 0, 10 and 100

(*c*) 10, 100 and 0 (*d*) 100, 0 and 10

133. The Y_{21} parameter of the network shown in the given figure will be

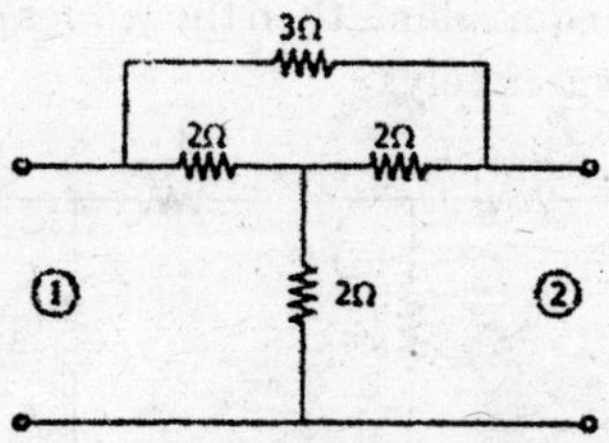

(*a*) $\dfrac{1}{6}\,\Omega$ (*b*) $-\dfrac{1}{6}\,\Omega$

(*c*) $\dfrac{1}{3}\,\Omega$ (*d*) $-\dfrac{1}{3}\,\Omega$

134. The V-I relation for the network shown in the given box is :

$$V = 4I - 9$$

If now a resistor R = 2 Ω is connected across it, then the value of I will be

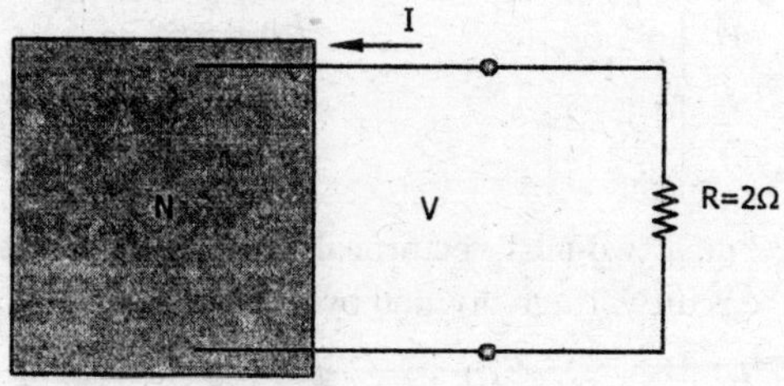

(*a*) – 4.5 A

(*b*) – 1.5 A

(*c*) 1.5 A

(*d*) 4.5 A

135. When a number of 2-port networks are connected in cascade, the individual

(*a*) z_{∞} matrices are added

(*b*) z_{∞}-matrices are added

(*c*) chain matrices are multiplied

(*d*) *h*-matrices are multiplied

136. In respect of the 2-port network shown in the figure, the admittance parameters are :

$Y_{11} = 8$ mho, $Y_{12} = Y_{21} = -6$ mho and $Y_{22} = 6$ mho.

The values of Y_A, Y_B and Y_C (in units of mho) will be respectively

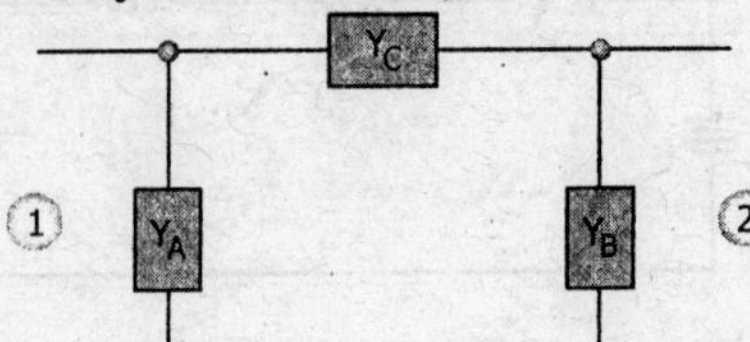

(*a*) 2, 6 and – 6 (*b*) 2, 6 and 0

(*c*) 2, 0 and 6 (*d*) 2, 6 and 8

137. If the p-network of Fig-I and T-network of Fig-II are equivalent, then the values of R_1, R_2 and R_3 will be respectively

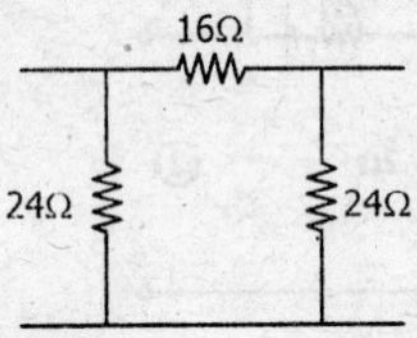

Fig. I

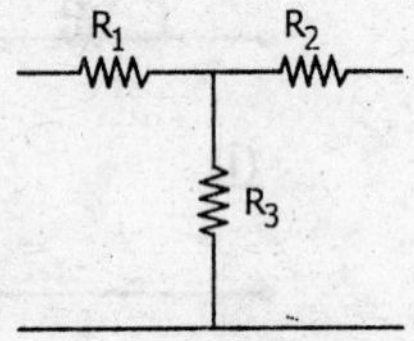

Fig. II

(*a*) 6 Ω, 6 Ω and 6 Ω (*b*) 6 Ω, 6 Ω and 9 Ω

(*c*) 9 Ω, 6 Ω and 9 Ω (*d*) 6 Ω, 9 Ω and 6 Ω

138. The impedance matrices of two, two-port networks are given by

$$\begin{bmatrix} 3 & 2 \\ 2 & 3 \end{bmatrix} \text{ and } \begin{bmatrix} 15 & 5 \\ 5 & 25 \end{bmatrix}$$

If these two networks are connected in series, the impedance matrix of the resulting two-port network will be

(*a*) $\begin{bmatrix} 3 & 5 \\ 2 & 25 \end{bmatrix}$ (*b*) $\begin{bmatrix} 18 & 7 \\ 7 & 28 \end{bmatrix}$

(*c*) $\begin{bmatrix} 15 & 2 \\ 5 & 3 \end{bmatrix}$ (*d*) indeterminate

139. For a two-port reciprocal network, the output open-circuit voltage divided by the input current equal to

(*a*) B (*b*) z_{12}

(*c*) $\dfrac{1}{y_{12}}$ (*d*) h_{12}

140. In the circuit shown in the figure, for R = 20 Ω the current I is 2 A. When R is 10 Ω the current I would be

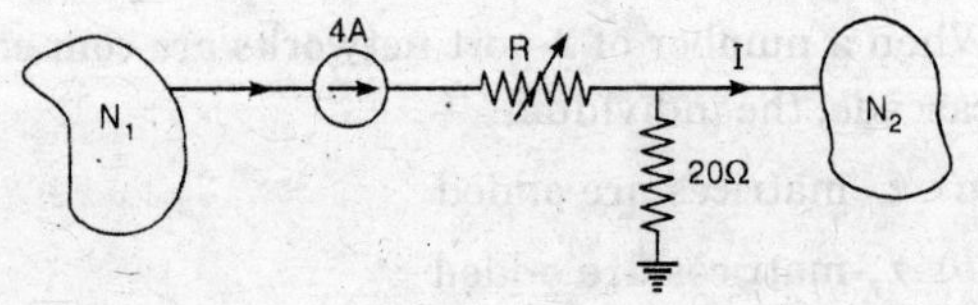

(*a*) 1 A (*b*) 2 A

(*c*) 2.5 A (*d*) 3 A

141. If the two-port network shown in the given figure has the constant B = $\dfrac{2s+1}{s^2}$, then z(s) will be

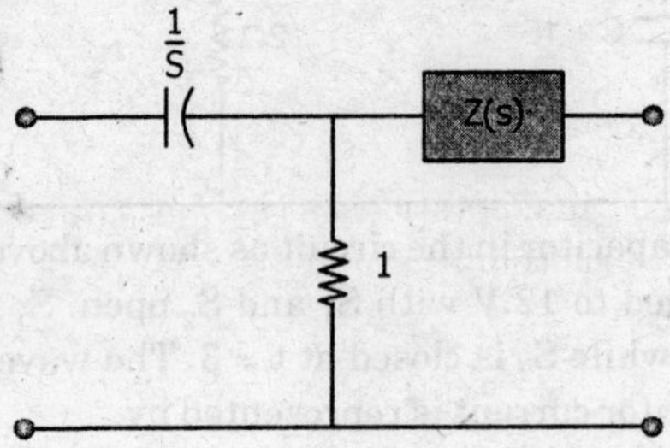

(*a*) s (*b*) $\dfrac{1}{s}$

(*c*) s + 1 (*d*) $1+\dfrac{1}{s}$

142. The short-circuit test of a 2-port network is shown in Fig-I. The voltage across the terminals AA' in the network shown in Fig-II will be

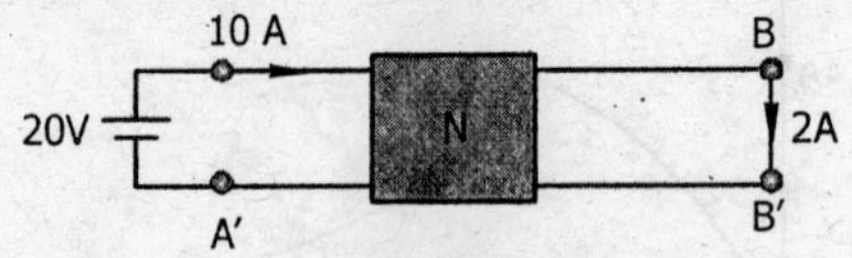

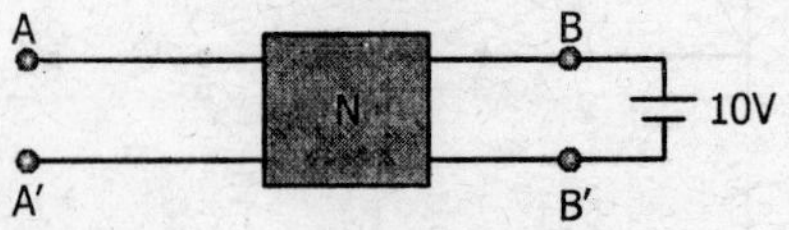

(*a*) 20 V (*b*) 10 V

(*c*) 5 V (*d*) 2 V

143. In a passive two-port network, the open-circuit impedance matrix is $\begin{bmatrix} 10\,\Omega & 2\,\Omega \\ 5\,\Omega & 2\Omega \end{bmatrix}$

If the input port is interchanged with the output port, then the open-circuit impedance matrix will be

(*a*) $\begin{bmatrix} 10\,\Omega & 2\,\Omega \\ 5\,\Omega & 2\,\Omega \end{bmatrix}$ (*b*) $\begin{bmatrix} 2\Omega & 5\Omega \\ 2\Omega & 10\Omega \end{bmatrix}$

(*c*) $\begin{bmatrix} 5\,\Omega & 10\,\Omega \\ 2\,\Omega & 2\,\Omega \end{bmatrix}$ (*d*) $\begin{bmatrix} 2\,\Omega & 5\,\Omega \\ 10\,\Omega & 2\,\Omega \end{bmatrix}$

144. An ideal transformer has turns ratio of 2 : 1. Considering high voltage side as port 1 and low voltage side as port 2, the transmission line parameters of transformer will be

(*a*) $\begin{bmatrix} 0 & -2 \\ 0.5 & 0 \end{bmatrix}$ (*b*) $\begin{bmatrix} -2 & 0 \\ 0 & -0.5 \end{bmatrix}$

(*c*) $\begin{bmatrix} 2 & 0 \\ 0 & -0.5 \end{bmatrix}$ (*d*) $\begin{bmatrix} 0.5 & 0 \\ 0 & 2 \end{bmatrix}$

145. A two-port network is defined by the relations $I_1 = 2V_1 + V_2$, $I_2 = 2V_1 + 3V_2$ Then z_{12} is

(a) $-2\ \Omega$ (b) $-1\ \Omega$

(c) $-\frac{1}{2}\Omega$ (d) $-\frac{1}{4}\Omega$

146. With the usual notations, a two-port resistive network satisfies the condition

$$A = D = \frac{3}{2}B = \frac{4}{3}C$$

The z_{11} of the network is

(a) $\frac{5}{3}$ (b) $\frac{4}{3}$

(c) $\frac{4}{3}$ (d) $\frac{1}{3}$

147. The driving point impedance of the infinite ladder network shown in the figure is (Given : $R_1 = 2\ \Omega$ and $R_2 = 1.5\ \Omega$)

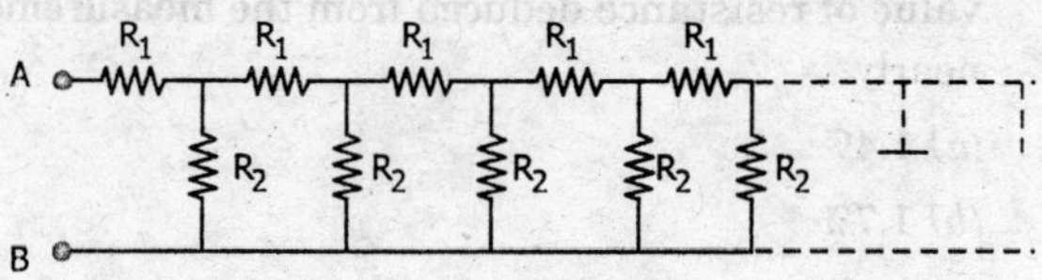

(a) $3\ \Omega$ (b) $3.5\ \Omega$

(c) $\frac{3}{3.5}\Omega$ (d) $1_n\left(1+\frac{3}{3.5}\right)\Omega$

148. The driving point function of the circuit shown in the given figure where $s \to 0$ and $s \to \infty$, (the elements are normalised) will respectively be

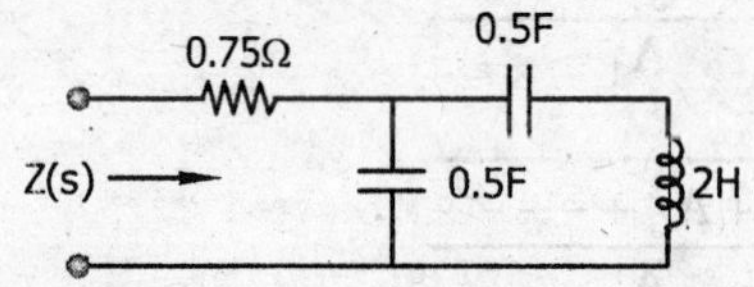

(a) $\frac{1}{s}$ and $\frac{2}{s}$ (b) $\frac{1}{s}$ and 0.75

(c) 0.75 and $\frac{2}{s}$ (d) $\frac{2}{s}$ and 0.75

149. For a two-port symmetrical bilateral network, if A = 3 and B = 1 Ω, the value of parameter C will be

(a) 4 *s* (b) 6 *s*

(c) 8 *s* (d) 16 *s*

150. For the given driving point impedance function

$$Z(s) = \frac{4s^4 + 7s^2 + 1}{s(2s^2 + 3)}$$, the circuit realization is shown in the given figure. Then the values of L and C are respectively

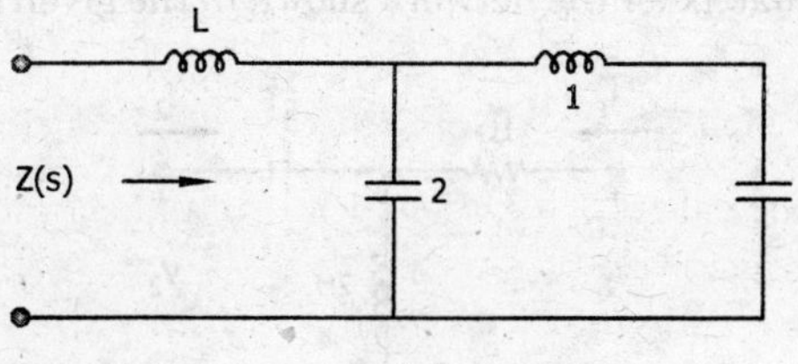

(a) 0.5 and 3 (b) 2 and 1

(c) 4 and 1 (d) 4 and 3

151. The h parameters h_{11} and h_{22} are related to z any y parameters as

(a) $h_{11} = z_{11}$ and $h_{22} = \frac{1}{z_{22}}$

(b) $h_{11} = z_{11}$ and $h_{22} = y_{22}$

(c) $h_{11} = \frac{1}{y_{11}}$ and $h_{22} = \frac{1}{z_{22}}$

(d) $h_{11} = \frac{1}{y_{11}}$ and $h_{22} = y_{22}$

152. The driving point impedance $Z(s) = \frac{s+3}{s+2}$. The system is initially at rest. For a voltage signal of unit step, the current i(t) through the impedance Z is given by

(a) $2 - e^{-t}$ (b) $\frac{3}{2} - \frac{1}{2}e^{-3t}$

(c) $\frac{3}{2} - \frac{1}{2}e^{-2t}$ (d) $3 - 2e^{-2t}$

153. For the circuit shown in the given figure, when the voltage E is 10 V, the current i is 1 A. If the applied voltage across terminal C-D is 100 V, the short circuit current flowing through the terminal A-B will be

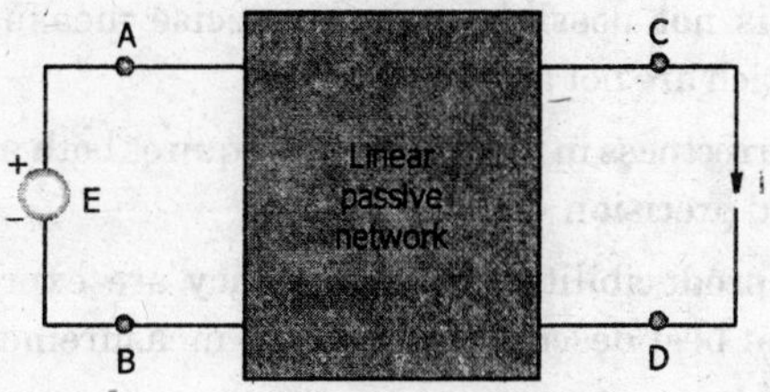

(a) 0.1 A (b) 1 A

(c) 10 A (d) 100 A

154. Which one of the following parameters does not exist for the two-port network shown in the given figure ?

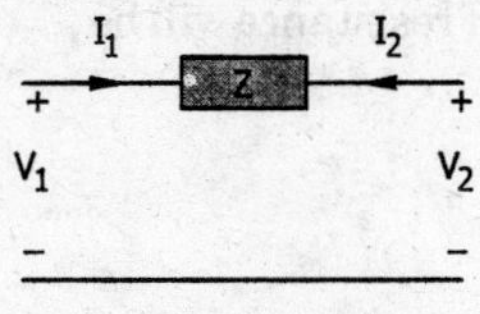

(a) ABCD (b) *y*

(c) *h* (d) *z*

155. z-matrix for the network shown in the given figure is

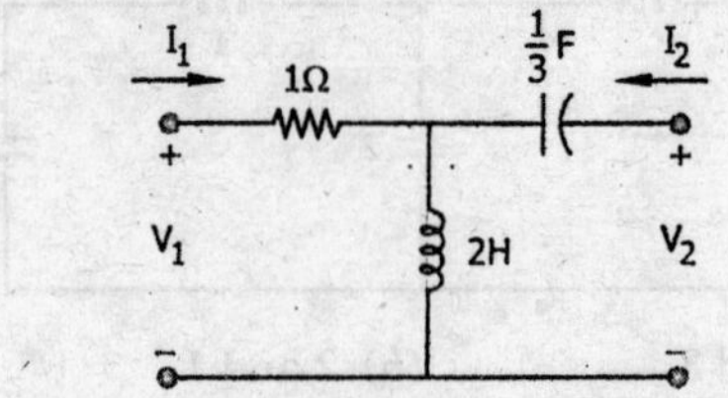

(a) $\begin{bmatrix} 2s+1 & 2s \\ 2s & 2s+\frac{3}{s} \end{bmatrix}$ (b) $\begin{bmatrix} 2s+1 & -2s \\ -2s & 2s+\frac{3}{s} \end{bmatrix}$

(c) $\begin{bmatrix} 2s+1 & +2s \\ -2s & 2s+\frac{3}{s} \end{bmatrix}$ (d) $\begin{bmatrix} 2s+\frac{3}{2} & -2s \\ 2s & 2s+\frac{3}{s} \end{bmatrix}$

ERROR ANYLYSIS

156. Four ammeter M_1, M_2, M_3 and M_4 with the following specifications are available :

Instrument Type	Full scale value (A)	Accuracy % of FS
M_1 3½ digit dual scope	20	± 0.10
M_2 PMMC	10	± .20
M_3 Electro-dynamic	5	± 0.50
M_4 Moving iron	1	± 1.00

A current of 1 A is to be measured. To obtain minimum error in the reading, one should select meter

(a) M_1 (b) M_2
(c) M_3 (d) M_4

157. Which one of the following statement is not correct ?

(a) It is not possible to have precise measurement which are not accurate

(b) Correctness in measurement requires both accuracy and precision

(c) Reproducibility and consistency are expressions that best describe precision in measurements

(d) An instrument with 2% accuracy is better than another with 5% accuracy

158. The limiting error of measurement of power consumed by and the current passing through a resistance are ± 1.5% and ±1% respectively. Then the limiting error of measurement of resistance will be

(a) ± 0.5 %

(b) ± 1 0%

(c) ± 2.5%

(d) ± 3.5%

159. A resistor of 10k-ohm with 5% tolerance is connected in series with a 5k-ohms resistor at 10% tolerance. The tolerance limit of the series Network will be

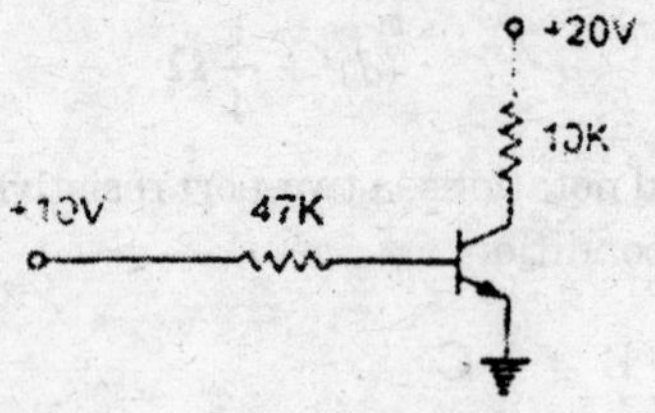

(a) 5% (b) 6.67%

(c) 10% (d) 8.38%

160. A resistance is measured by the voltmeterammeter method employing d.c. excitation and a voltmeter of very high resistance connected directly across the unknown resistance. If the voltmeter and ammeter readings are subject to maximum possible errors of ± 2.4% and ± 1.0% respectively, then the magnitude of maximum possible percentage error in the value of resistance deduced from the measurement is nearly

(a) 1.4%

(b) 1.7%

(c) 2.4%

(d) 3.4%

161. A distorted sinusoid has the Amplitudes A_1, A_2, A_3, ... of the fundamental second harmonic third harmonic, ... respectively. The total harmonic distortion is

(a) $\sqrt{\dfrac{A_2^2 + A_3^2 + ----}{A_1}}$

(b) $\sqrt{\dfrac{A_2^2 + A_3^2 + ----}{A_1}}$

(c) $\sqrt{\dfrac{A_2^2 + A_3^2 + ----}{A_1^2 + A_2^2 + A_3^2 + ----}}$

(d) $\sqrt{\dfrac{A_2^2 + A_3^2 + ----}{A_1}}$

162. A 150 V moving iron voltmeter of accuracy class 1-0 reads 75V when used in a circuit under standard conditions. The maximum possible percentage error in the reading is

(a) 0.5

(b) 1.0

(c) 2.0

(d) 4.0

163. In the circuit given in the figure, the limiting error in the power dissipation 'I^2R' in the resistor R is

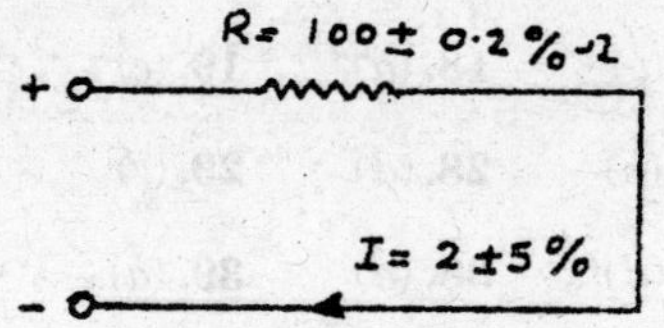

(a) 1.2% (b) 5.2%

(c) 10.2% (d) 25.2%

164. Two resistance 100 Ω ± 5 Ω and 150 Ω ± 15Ω are connected in series. If the errors are specified as standard deviations, the resultant error will be

(a) ± 10 Ω (b) ± 10.6 Ω

(c) ± 15.8 Ω (d) ± 20 Ω

165. A zero to 300 V voltmeter has guaranteed accuracy of 1% full scale reading. The voltage measured by the instrument is 83V. The percent limiting error is

(a) 0.95 (b) 1.81

(c) 3.62 (d) 4.85

166. The power in a 3-phase, 3-wire load is measured using two 100W full-scale wattmeters W_1 and W_2. W_1 is of a accuracy class ±1% and reads 100 W. W_2 is of accuracy class ± 0.5% and reads –50 W. Then uncertainty in the computation of total power is

(a) ± 1.5% (b) ±0.5%

(c) ±4% (d) ±3%

167. A d.c. circuit can be represented by a voltage source of 10 V in series with an output resistance of 1 kΩ. An ammeter of 50 Ω resistance is connected to the source terminals for measurement of current. The accuracy of measurement is neary

(a) – 4.8% (b) +4.8%

(c) 99% (d) 95.2%

168. An 0 – 10 A ammeter has guaranteed accuracy of 1 percent of full scale deflection. The limiting error while reading 2.5 is

(a) 1% (b) 2%

(c) 4% (d) none of these

169. A 0 – 300 V voltmeter has an error of ±2% of full scale deflection. If true voltage is 30 V, then range of readings will be

(a) 24 V – 36 V (b) 29.4 V – 30.6 V

(c) 20 V to 40 V (d) none of these

170. A wattmeter has a full scale range of 2500 W. It has an error ±1% of true value. It true power is 1250 W, range of reading will be

(a) 1225 W – 1275 W (b) 1245 W – 1255 W

(c) 1200 W – 1300 W (d) 1237.5 W –1262.5 W

171. Power in a d.c. circuit is measured by measuring the voltage across and current through the circuit. The voltage and current measurement are made to an accuracy of ±2% and ±3% respectively. The errors are limiting errors. The error in measurement of power is

(a) ± 2% (b) ±3%

(c) ±6% (d) ±5%

172. Power in a d.c. circuit is measured by measuring a current through a resistor. The current is measured with an accuracy of ±1.5% and the tolerance band of the resistor ±0.5%. The errors are limiting or Guarantee errors. The accuracy with which power is measured is

(a) ± 1.125%

(b) ±3.5%

(c) ±2%

(d) ±2.5%

173. The voltage of a circuit is measured by a voltmeter having an input impedence comparable with the output impedance of the circuit thereby causing error in voltage measurement. This error may be called

(a) Gross error

(b) Random error

(c) Error caused by misue of instrument

(d) Error caused by loading effect

174. The units whose sizes cannot be choosen independently are called

(a) Derived units

(b) Fundamental units

(c) Absolute units

(d) Auxiliary fundamental units

175. The power factor in a single phase circuit is cos ϕ = P/VI where is the power read by an wattmeter, V is the voltage read by a voltmeter and I is the current read by an ammeter. All the three instruments have a limiting error of ±1%. The power factor of the circuits can be known if only one meter i.e. an electrodynamometers type power factor having an limiting error ±1% used. The preferred method is to use a single instrument like a power factor meter rather than using 2 instruments because the error with using wattmeter, voltmeter and ammeter is

(a) ± 2%

(b) ± 3%

(c) ±1%

(d) –1%

ANSWERS

1. (*c*)	2. (*d*)	3. (*a*)	4. (*b*)	5. (*b*)	6. (*b*)	7. (*c*)	8. (*d*)	9. (*c*)	10. (*d*)
11. (*a,c*)	12. (*c*)	13. (*d*)	14. (*a*)	15. (*b*)	16. (*b*)	17. (*c*)	18. (*a*)	19. (*c*)	20. (*a*)
21. (*b*)	22. (*c*)	23. (*d*)	24. (*a*)	25. (*b*)	26. (*a*)	27. (*b*)	28. (*d*)	29. (*c*)	30. (*a*)
31. (*b*)	32. (*a*)	33. (*c*)	34. (*d*)	35. (*c*)	36. (*b*)	37. (*d*)	38. (*a*)	39. (*a*)	40. (*d*)
41. (*d*)	42. (*a*)	43. (*c*)	44. (*c*)	45. (*c*)	46. (*c*)	47. (*c*)	48. (*b*)	49. (*d*)	50. (*c*)
51. (*b*)	52. (*d*)	53. (*c*)	54. (*b*)	55. (*a*)	56. (*d*)	57. (*a*)	58. (*b*)	59. (*b*)	60. (*d*)
61. (*a*)	62. (*b*)	63. (*a*)	64. (*a*)	65. (*a*)	66. (*b*)	67. (*b*)	68. (*b*)	69. (*a*)	70. (*a*)
71. (*b*)	72. (*d*)	73. (*c*)	74. (*c*)	75. (*a*)	76. (*c*)	77. (*a*)	78. (*d*)	79. (*d*)	80. (*b*)
81. (*d*)	82. (*d*)	83. (*c*)	84. (*b*)	85. (*c*)	86. (*a*)	87. (*c*)	88. (*a*)	89. (*d*)	90. (*b*)
91. (*d*)	92. (*d*)	93. (*a*)	94. (*c*)	95. (*c*)	96. (*c*)	97. (*d*)	98. (*a*)	99. (*b*)	100. (*c*)
101. (*d*)	102. (*d*)	103. (*b*)	104. (*a*)	105. (*d*)	106. (*a*)	107. (*c*)	108. (*c*)	109. (*c*)	110. (*c*)
111. (*d*)	112. (*b*)	113. (*b*)	114. (*c*)	115. (*b*)	116. (*b*)	117. (*c*)	118. (*d*)	119. (*b*)	120. (*c*)
121. (*b*)	122. (*c*)	123. (*a*)	124. (*a*)	125. (*a*)	126. (*c*)	127. (*a*)	128. (*b*)	129. (*c*)	130. (*a*)
131. (*b*)	132. (*a*)	133. (*b*)	134. (*c*)	135. (*c*)	136. (*c*)	137. (*b*)	138. (*b*)	139. (*b*)	140. (*b*)
141. (*b*)	142. (*d*)	143. (*b*)	144. (*c*)	145. (*)	146. (*b*)	147. (*a*)	148. (*b*)	149. (*c*)	150. (*b*)
151. (*c*)	152. (*c*)	153. (*c*)	154. (*c*)	155. (*d*)	156. (*d*)	157. (*a*)	158. (*d*)	159. (*c*)	160. (*a*)
161. (*b*)	162. (*c*)	163. (*c*)	164. (*c*)	165. (*c*)	166. (*d*)	167. (*d*)	168. (*c*)	169. (*a*)	170. (*d*)
171. (*d*)	172. (*b*)	173. (*d*)	174. (*a*)	175. (*b*)					

EXPLANATIONS

2.

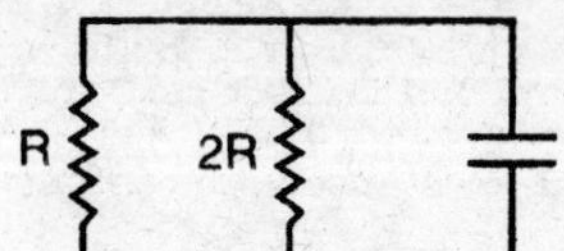

$$R_{eq} = \frac{R \times 2R}{3R} = \frac{2R}{3}$$

$$\tau = R_{eq} \times C = \frac{2}{3} R \times C = \frac{2}{3} RC$$

3. It is a balance bridge network with the addition of a resistor across AB. Thus total resistance as measured between A and B shall be 1 ohm.

4. When the voltmeter of 1.2 kΩ meter resistance is connected across 600 Ω, the net resistance becomes

$$\frac{600 \times 1200}{600 + 1200} = 400\ \Omega$$

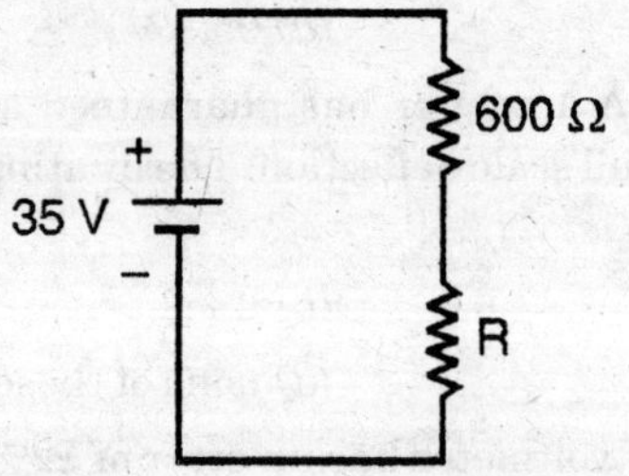

Voltage across this is 5 V and therefore voltage across R is

$$35 - 5 = 30\ \text{V}$$

current will be same $\frac{V}{400} = \frac{V_R}{R}$

$$\frac{5}{400} = \frac{30}{12}$$

or $\quad$ $R = 2.4\ \text{k}\Omega$

5.
$$L = \frac{N^2\mu_0 A}{l}\ A$$
$$= \pi r^2$$
$$= \frac{10^6 \times 4\pi \times 10^{-7} \times \frac{\pi}{4} \times (9\times 10^{-4})}{0.3}$$
$$= \frac{9\pi^2 \times 10^{-5}}{0.3}$$
$$= 2.96 \times 10^{-3}$$
$$\therefore \quad \text{Energy} = \frac{1}{2}LI^2$$
$$= \mathbf{0.148 \text{ or } 0.15 \text{ Joules}}$$

6.
$$T = \frac{L_1 + L_2}{R_1 + R_2}$$
$$= \frac{L_1 + L_2}{2R}$$
$$= \frac{1}{2}\left[\frac{L_1}{R} + \frac{L_2}{R}\right]$$

Thus the time constant is the average of the time constant of individual coils.

7. Time constant, $\left(\frac{1}{2}LI^2 = 1000\right)$
$$T = \frac{L}{R}$$
$$= \frac{I^2 L}{I^2 R}$$
$$= \frac{2 \times 1000}{2000}$$
$$= 1$$

8.
$$I^2_{rms} = \frac{1}{3}\int_0^3 \left(\frac{9}{3}t\right)^2 \cdot dt$$
$$= \frac{9}{3}\left[\frac{t^3}{3}\right]_0^3$$
$$= 27A$$
$$\text{Power} = I^2R$$
$$= 27 \times 10$$
$$= \mathbf{270\ W}$$

9. Effective inductance across AB terminals
$$= L_1 + L_2 + L_3 - 2M_{12} - 2M_{13} + 2M_{23}$$
$$= 4 + 5 + 6 - 2\times 1 - 2\times 3 + 2\times 2$$
$$= \mathbf{11\ H}$$

10. Since the reactance are cancelling each other, the circuit is purely resistive and the current is in phase with the applied voltage. The voltage across the inductor leads the current through it by 90°

Since $\bar{I} = 100\angle 0° / \{10 + j(20 - 20)\}$
$$= 10\angle 0°$$
$$\bar{V}_L = jx_L \bar{I}$$
$$= 20 \times 10 \angle 90$$
$$= \mathbf{200\angle 90°}$$

12. Current that flows is given by,
$$V(s) = sL\,I(s)$$
$$1 = s\,I(S)$$
$$I(s) = 1/s$$
$$I = u(t) = 1\text{ A}$$
$$\text{Energy supplied} = \frac{1}{2}LI^2$$
$$= \frac{1}{2} \times 1 \times 1$$
$$= \mathbf{\frac{1}{2}\ J.}$$

13. There are three parallel banks which are in turn connected in series

Equivalent resistance of 20 ohm and 30 ohm parallel resistors
$$= \frac{20\times 30}{20+30}$$
$$= 12 \text{ ohms.}$$

Equivalent resistance of 6 ohm, 4 ohm and 12 ohm bank = 2 ohms.

Total resistance of the circuit
$$= 12 + 2 + 6$$
$$= 20 \text{ ohms}$$

∴ Current drawn from supply
$$= \frac{V}{I}$$
$$= \frac{120}{20}$$
$$= 6A$$

Current through 20 ohms resistor
$$= 6 \times \frac{30}{20+30}$$
$$= 3.6A$$

Current through 30 ohms resistor
$$= 6 - 3.6$$
$$= 2.4\text{ A}$$

Equivalent resistance of 6 ohm, 4 ohm and 12 ohm bank = 2 ohm,

Voltage drop = 6 × 2 = 12 V.

∴ Current through 6 ohm resistor

$$= \frac{12}{6} = 2A$$

Current through 4 ohm resistor

$$= \frac{12}{4} = 3A$$

Current throughn 12 ohm resistor

$$= \frac{12}{12} = 1A$$

14. When two inductors are connected in series, the effective inductance

$$L_{eff} = L_1 + L_2 \pm 2M$$

In this case, $L_{eff} = L_1 + L_2 - 2M$

$$= 2 + 4 - 2 \times 0.15$$

$$= \mathbf{5.7\ mH.}$$

15. Current through the 4-ohm resistor $= i - \frac{i}{4} = \frac{3i}{4}$.

Therefore, the voltage drop across it

$$= \left(\frac{3i}{4}\right) \times 4 = 3i \text{ which must equal V.}$$

Thus effective resistance faced by the voltage source is 3 Ω.

16. Let α be the temperature coefficient, then

$$R_t = R_0 (1 + \alpha t)$$

where R_t is resistance at t^0 C and R_0 is resistance at 0° C.

Assuming that for a given potential difference,

$$I \propto \frac{1}{R}$$

$$\therefore \quad \frac{1\text{amp}}{0.7\text{amp}} = \frac{R_0(1+\alpha t)}{R_0}$$

$$= 1 + \alpha . 100$$

$$\therefore \quad \alpha = 0.0043 \text{ per °C}$$

Current, I at 1200°C is given by

$$\frac{1}{I} = \frac{R_0(1+\alpha.1200)}{R_0}$$

$$= 1 + \alpha.1200$$

$$= 1 + 0.0043 \times 1200$$

$$= 6.16$$

$$\therefore \quad I = \left(\frac{1}{6.16}\right)$$

$$= \mathbf{0.16\ amp.}$$

17. Let the current I_{B1}, flow through resistance R_{in} when – 12 V battery is removed.

$$\therefore \quad I_{B1} = \frac{12}{470 \times 1000 + R_{in}}$$

Similarly current I_{B2} flows in resistance R_{in} when + 12V battery is removed.

$$\therefore \quad I_{B1} = \frac{12}{1000 \times 1000 + R_{in}}$$

Since the two voltages are in opposite directions, their currents will subtract. Hence,

$$I_B - I_{B2} = 10 \times 10^{-6}$$

$$10{\times}10 - 6 = \frac{12}{470 \times 1000 + R_{in}} - \frac{12}{1000 \times 1000 + R_{in}}$$

$$= [12\,(1000 \times 100 + R_{in}) - 12\,(470 \times 1000 + R_{in})]$$

$$= 10 \times 10^{-6}\,(1000{\times}1000 + R_{in}) \times (470 \times 1000 + R_{in})$$

or $R_{in}^{\ 2} + 1470 \times 1000\,R_{in} - 16.6 \times 10^8 = 0$

Solving for R_{in}, we have

$$R_{in} = \frac{-1470 \times \pm\sqrt{(1470 \times 1000)^2 + 66.4 \times 10^8}}{2}$$

$$= \mathbf{100{,}000\ ohms}$$

(rejecting the negative value)

18. Using the addition of admittances in parallel,

$$Y = Y_L + Y_R + Y_C$$

$$= R + \frac{1}{j\omega L} + j\omega C$$

$$= 1 + j$$

The phasor voltage becomes

$$V = \frac{I}{Y}$$

Using phasors in polar format,

$$I = 10\,e^{-j3\pi/4}$$

$$Y = \sqrt{2}\ e^{-j\pi/4}$$

The power (time average power) dissipated in R,

$$P = \frac{1}{2}\ \text{Re}\ \frac{(VV^*)}{R}$$

$$v(t) = \frac{10}{\sqrt{2}} \cos\left(\omega t - \frac{3\pi}{4}\right)$$

from which, $P = \frac{1}{2}\frac{(v)^2(t)}{R}$

$$= \mathbf{25\ watts.}$$

19. $$V = \frac{2I}{3} \cdot 3$$

or $$R_{eff} = \frac{V}{I} = 2\Omega$$

20. At u.p.f. operation admittance of both branches

$$Y = j\omega C + \frac{1}{30\angle 40}$$

$$= j\omega C + \frac{1}{30(0.76 + 0.64j)}$$

Equalizing imaginary part, we get

$$C = \mathbf{68.1\ \mu F.}$$

22. $$I(s) = \frac{3}{(s+1)\left(1+\dfrac{1}{2s}\right)}$$

$$= \frac{3s}{(s+0.5)(s+1)}$$

$$= \frac{-3}{(s+0.5)} + \frac{6}{s+1}$$

or $$i(t) = L^{-1}(I(s))$$

$$= 6e^{-t} - 3e^{-0.5t}$$

At $t = 0, i(0^+) = 3A$,

and at $t = \infty, i(\infty) = 0$

24. $$V_+ = \frac{\sin t}{1+j} = V_-$$

and $$V_0 = V_-\left(1 + \frac{4.14}{10}\right)$$

$$= \sqrt{2}\, V_-$$

$$= \sqrt{2}\, \frac{\sin t}{1+j}$$

or $$V_0 = \sin\left(t - \frac{\pi}{4}\right)$$

25. Initially, $$I = \frac{V}{R + jX}$$

When capacitance inserted,

$$2I = \frac{V}{R + jX + \dfrac{1}{jwC}}$$

or $$\frac{2}{R+jX} = \frac{1}{R + jX - \dfrac{j}{\omega C}}$$

or $$2R + 2jX - \frac{2j}{\omega C} = R + jX$$

or $$R + jX = \frac{2j}{\omega C}$$

$$X = \frac{2}{\omega C}$$

Here '+' ve sign element is inductance

26.

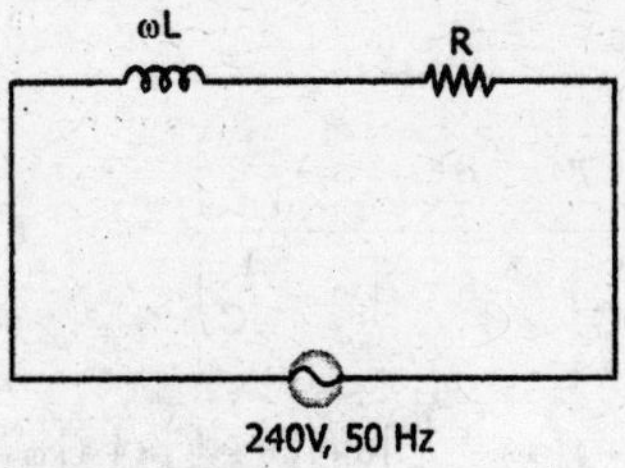

Power dissipated

$$\frac{V^2}{R} = 300$$

or $$R = \frac{100^2}{300} = \frac{100}{3}\,\Omega$$

and $$IR = V$$

$$= 100\ V$$

or $$I = \frac{100}{\left(\dfrac{100}{3}\right)}$$

$$= 3\ \text{amp.}$$

For the p.f. to be equal to unity,

$$I(\omega L) = I\left(\frac{1}{\omega C}\right)$$

$$= V_L$$

or $$\frac{1}{\omega C} = \sqrt{240^2 - 100^2}$$

$$= 218.17\ \text{Volt}$$

or $$C = \frac{3}{2\pi \times 50 \times 218.17}$$

$$= 43.7 \times 10^{-6} = 43.7\ \mu F.$$

27. As, $2L + 2M = 12$

$2L - 2M = 4$

Then, $L = 4, \Rightarrow M = 2,$

To get maximum value in parallel connection,

$$L_{max} = \frac{(L+M)(L+M)}{2L + 2M}$$

$$= 3\ \text{mH.}$$

29. $$R_{eq} = \frac{5 \times 0.2}{4} = 0.25$$

$$I = \frac{5.E}{R_L + R_{eg}} = \frac{5 \times 1.5}{1.25 + 0.25} = 5A.$$

30. $$Z_{eq} = \frac{\left(4+\frac{1}{j\omega C}\right)(4+j\omega)}{8+j\left(\omega-\frac{1}{\omega C}\right)} \times \frac{8-j\left(\omega-\frac{1}{\omega C}\right)}{8-j\left(\omega-\frac{1}{\omega C}\right)}$$

$$= \frac{-j\left(16+\frac{1}{C}\right)\left(\omega-\frac{1}{\omega C}\right)+j\left(4\omega-\frac{4}{\omega C}\right)8+\left(16+\frac{1}{C}\right)8+4\left(\omega-\frac{1}{\omega C}\right)^2}{64+\left(\omega-\frac{1}{\omega C}\right)^2}$$

For constant resistance, equating imaginary term to zero,

$$\therefore \left(16+\frac{1}{C}\right)\left(\omega-\frac{1}{\omega C}\right) = 32\left(\omega-\frac{1}{\omega C}\right)$$

$$\therefore \quad C = \frac{1}{16}F$$

31. $$L_{eq} = L_1 + L_2 + 2M = 6\text{ H}$$

At resonance, $$\omega = \frac{1}{\sqrt{L_{eq} \cdot C}} = \frac{1}{\sqrt{12}}$$

$$f = \frac{1}{4\pi\sqrt{3}}\text{Hz.}$$

33. $$I = \sqrt{I_R^2 + I_L^2}$$

(both I_R and I_L in quadrature)

$$= \sqrt{12^2 + 16^2} = 20\text{ A.}$$

34. **First Method :**

$\frac{V}{I}$ ratio is a constant R. If R is doubled current will become half.

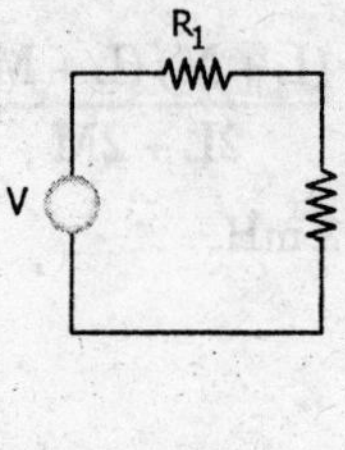

$$\therefore \quad V = 2R\frac{I}{2} = RI.$$

Second Method :

$$V_{R_1} = \frac{V}{R_1 + R_2} \times R_1$$

and $$V_{R_2} = \frac{V}{R_1 + R_2} \times R_2$$

If R_1 and R_2 are doubled, then

$$V'_{R_1} = \frac{V \times 2R_1}{2(R_1 + R_2)} = V_{R1}$$

and $$V'_{R_2} = \frac{V \times 2R_1}{2(R_1 + R_2)} = V_{R2}$$

35. $$Z'_L = 10 \angle 30° \left(\frac{1}{4}\right)^2 = (0.54 + j0.31)\Omega$$

Total impedance = $(4.54 - j1.69)\ \Omega$

43. Since $V_L = V_C$, then circuit is in resonance and

current, $I = \frac{5}{R} = \frac{5}{5} = 1A$

Now voltage,

$$V_L = 2V_R = 10$$

or $$\omega L = 10$$

$$\therefore \quad L = \frac{10}{\omega} = \frac{10}{2\pi F} = \frac{10}{2\pi \times 50}$$

$$= \mathbf{31.8\ mH.}$$

44. $$i_1 = \sqrt{\frac{P_1}{R}}$$

and $$i_2 = \sqrt{\frac{P_2}{R}}$$

When both source are active, then

$$i = i_1 \pm i_2 = \sqrt{\frac{P_1}{R}} \pm \sqrt{\frac{P_2}{R}}$$

$\therefore$ Total power consumed = i^2 R

$$= \left(\sqrt{\frac{P_1}{R}} \pm \sqrt{\frac{P_2}{R}}\right)^2 R = \left(\sqrt{P_1} \pm \sqrt{P_2}\right)^2$$

47. $$i_L(t) = \frac{10\cos 2t}{2+j\omega L}.2$$
$$= \frac{20\cos 2t}{2+j2}$$
$$= \frac{10\cos 2t}{1+j}$$
$$= \frac{10}{\sqrt{2}}\cos(2t-45°)$$
or $$i_L(t) = \frac{10}{\sqrt{2}}\angle -45°$$

48. $$M < k\sqrt{L_1L_2}$$
or $$M_{max} = k\sqrt{L_1L_2}$$
$$= \sqrt{L_1L_2}$$
$$= \sqrt{40\times 81}$$
$$= \mathbf{63\ mH.}$$

50. For series RLC circuit, at lower half power frequency
$$\omega_1 L - \frac{1}{\omega_1 C} = -R$$
or $$2\pi f_1 \times 100\times 10^{-6} - \frac{1}{2\pi f_1\times 1\times 10^{-6}} = -50$$
$$f_1 = \mathbf{3.055\ kHz.}$$

51. Converting current source into voltage source

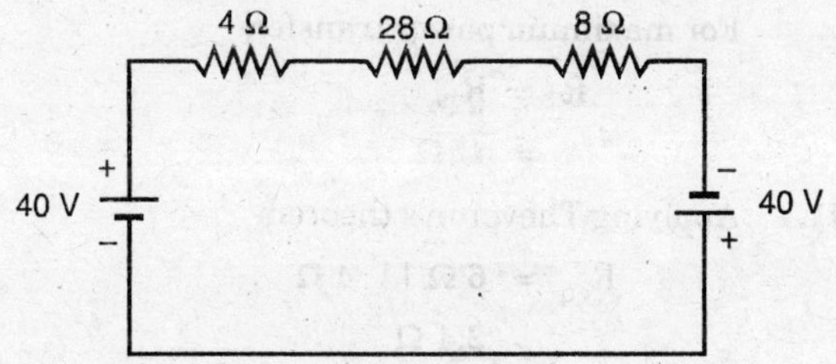

$$I = \frac{80}{40} = 2A$$

52. As the element absorbs power, let it be R_x
$$i = 1$$
$$= \frac{6}{R_x+1}$$
⇒ $$R_x = 5\ \Omega$$
$$P = \left(\frac{6}{6}\right)^2\times 5 = 5W$$
For 5A, $$P = 5^2\times 5$$
$$= 125\ W$$

For $3+\sqrt{14}$, $P = 227$ W

For $3-\sqrt{14}$, $P = 2.75$ W

Hence none of the above is correct.

54. As, $$V_A = V_B$$
then $$10I_1 + 5I_2 = 0$$
and $$4I_1 + RI_2 = 0$$
These gives, $R = 2\Omega$.

For balance bridge
$$10\ R = 5\times 4$$
$$R = 2\ \Omega$$

55. By Superposition theorem,

Current across 1 kΩ resistor
$$= \frac{10}{\left(\frac{8}{3}\right)}\times\frac{2}{3} - \frac{2}{\left(\frac{8}{3}\right)}\cdot\frac{2}{3}$$
$$= 2\text{ amp}$$
∴ Voltage across 1 kΩ resistor
$$= 2\times 1$$
$$= 2\text{ volts}$$

58.

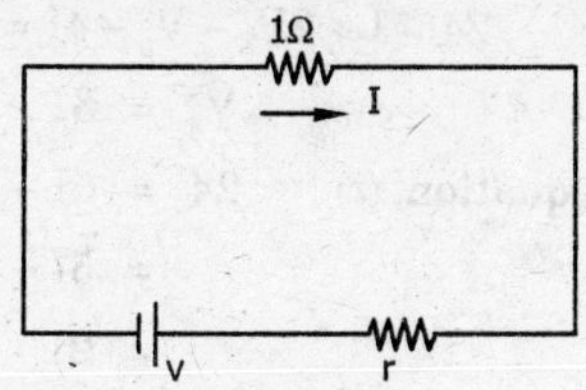

fig. (a)

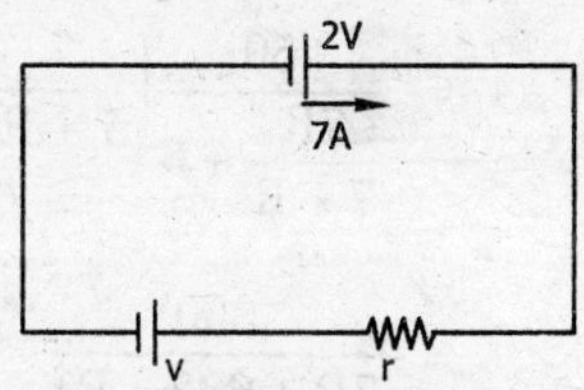

fig. (b)

From Fig. (*a*) $$V = I(1+r) \quad ...(i)$$
$$V = 5(1+r) \quad ...(ii)$$
From Fig. (*b*), $$V-2 = 7r$$
From equations (*i*), add (*ii*), we get
$$V = 12.5\text{volts and, } r = 1.5\ \Omega$$

60. In figure I,
$$I = \frac{V}{32R}+\frac{V}{16R}+\frac{V}{8R} = \frac{7V}{32R}$$
In figure-II
$$I = (V - IR_0)\left(\frac{1}{4R}+\frac{1}{2R}+\frac{1}{R}\right)$$
$$= \frac{7(V-IR_0)}{4R}$$

Since current remains same

$$\therefore \quad \frac{7(V - IR_0)}{4R} = \frac{7V}{32R}$$

$$\text{or} \quad (V - IR_0) = \frac{V}{8}$$

$$\text{or} \quad IR_0 = \frac{7V}{8}$$

$$= 4R.I$$

$$\text{or} \quad R_0 = 4R$$

61. From the circuit,

$$20 = \sqrt{V_R^2 + V_L^2} \quad \ldots (i)$$

$$9 = \pm (V_L - V_C) \quad \ldots (ii)$$

$$\text{and} \quad 15 = \sqrt{V_R^2 + (V_L - V_C)^2} \quad \ldots (iii)$$

From equations (*i*), (*ii*) and (*iii*), we get

$$V_R = 12 \text{ volt},$$

$$V_L = 16 \text{ V},$$

$$V_C = 7\text{V or } 25 \text{ V}.$$

62. KVL through the loop gives,

$$24 - I + 2V_b - V_b - 4I = 0 \quad (i)$$

$$\text{and,} \quad V_b = 3I$$

From equation, (*i*)

$$24 = 5I - V_b$$

$$= 5I - 3I$$

$$= 2I$$

$$\text{or} \quad I = 12 \text{ amp.}$$

63.

$$4 = \frac{50}{\dfrac{7R}{7+R} + 6}\left(\frac{7}{7+R}\right)$$

$$= \frac{350}{7R + 6(7+R)}$$

$$\text{or} \quad R = 3.5\,\Omega.$$

64.

$$R_{AB} = \frac{R_A \cdot R_B + R_C \cdot R_B + R_C \cdot R_A}{R_C}$$

$$= \frac{4.5 + 13.5 + 27}{9}$$

$$= \frac{45}{9} = 5\,\Omega$$

$$\text{and} \quad R_{BC} = \frac{R_A R_B + R_C R_B + R_C R_A}{R_A}$$

$$= \frac{45}{3}$$

=15 W.

67. Applying KCL

$$\frac{V}{4} + \frac{V - 2I}{2} = I$$

$$\Rightarrow \quad \frac{V}{I} = \frac{8}{3}\Omega.$$

68. Given,

$$R_A + R_B = 6 \quad \text{with C open}$$

$$R_B + R_C = 11 \quad \text{with A open}$$

$$R_C + R_A = 9$$

then, $R_A + R_B + R_C = 13$

By Solving $R_A = 2\,\Omega.$

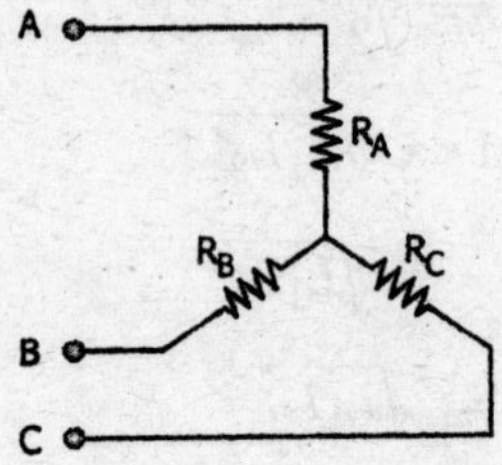

70. The circuit is drawn below by shorting the voltage source.

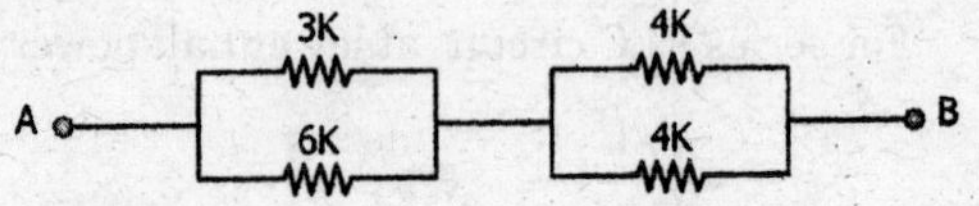

Taking the Thevenin's equivalent between points A, B, we have

$$R_{Th} = \left(\frac{6 \times 3}{6+3} + \frac{4 \times 4}{4+4}\right) k\Omega$$

$$= 4\,k\Omega$$

For maximum power transfer,

$$R = R_{Th}$$

$$= 4k\Omega$$

71. Applying Thevenin's theorem

$$R_{eq} = 6\,\Omega \,||\, 4\,\Omega$$

$$= 2.4\,\Omega$$

$$V_{ab} = 10 - 6\left(\frac{15}{10}\right)$$

$$= 1\,\text{V}$$

72.

$$Z_{QR} = \frac{5 \times 10 + 10 \times j10 + j10 \times 5}{5}$$

$$= (10 + j30)\,\Omega$$

73. For maximum power transfer to the variable load resistance R_L, R_L should have a value equal to the magnitude of impedance of rest of the circuit.

$$R_L = \sqrt{60^2 + 80^2}$$

$$= 100\,\Omega$$

74.

$$R_1 = \frac{R_{ab}\, R_{ac}}{R_{ab} + R_{ac} + R_{bc}}$$

$$= \frac{150}{50} = 3$$

$$R_2 = \frac{R_{ab}\ R_{ac}}{R_{ab} + R_{ac} + R_{bc}}$$

$$= \frac{5 \times 25}{50} = 1.5$$

$$R_3 = \frac{30 \times 15}{50} = 9$$

75. Drawing equivalent of the given circuit,

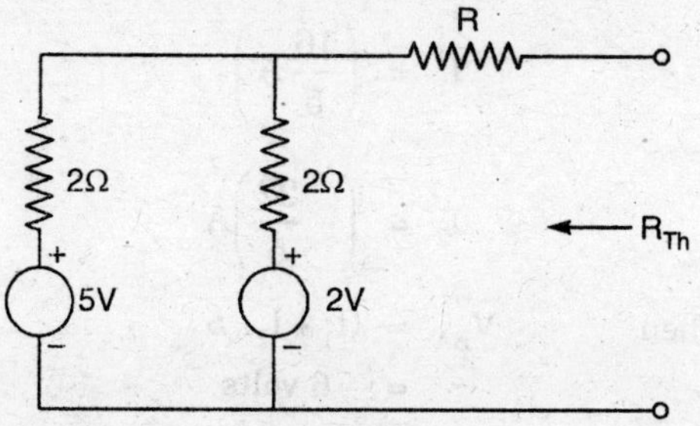

$$R_{TH} = (2 \parallel 2)\Omega = 1\Omega$$

77. $$I = \frac{25}{5 - j10 + j5}$$

$$= \frac{25}{5 - 5j}$$

$$= 2.5\angle 45°\text{A}.$$

78. $$Z_{QR} = \frac{Z_{OP}Z_{OQ} + Z_{OP}Z_{QR} + Z_{OR}Z_{OQ}}{Z_{OP}}$$

$$= \frac{50 + 50j + 100j}{5}$$

$$= 10 + 30\,j$$

82. $$R_1 = \frac{R_{ab}R_{ac}}{R_{ab} + R_{ac} + R_{bc}}$$

$$= \frac{5 \times 30}{50} = 3$$

$$R_2 = \frac{R_{ab}R_{ac}}{R_{ab} + R_{ac} + R_{bc}}$$

$$= \frac{5 \times 25}{50}$$

$$= \frac{3}{2} = 1.5$$

$$R_3 = \frac{R_{ac}R_{ac}}{R_{ab} + R_{ac} + R_{bc}}$$

$$= \frac{30 \times 15}{50} = 9.$$

83. The Thevenin equivalent is given by a single voltage source (open circuit voltage) in series with a single equivalent resistor

$[R = -V\,(i = 0) / i\,(V = 0)]$.

Note that the 20 ohm resistor in parallel with the 20 V source does not contribute to the current or voltage at the terminals.

84. $$R_{eq} = \frac{2 \times 3}{2+3} = \mathbf{1.2\ \Omega}$$

$$V_{oc} = \frac{10 \times 3}{3+2} = \mathbf{6V.}$$

85. Loop equation,

$$(I_3 - I_1)\,1 + 6\,I_3 + (I_3 - I_2)\,.\,4 = 0$$

or $$-I_1 - 4\,I_2 + 11\,I_3 = 0$$

86. Drawing equivalent circuit, we have

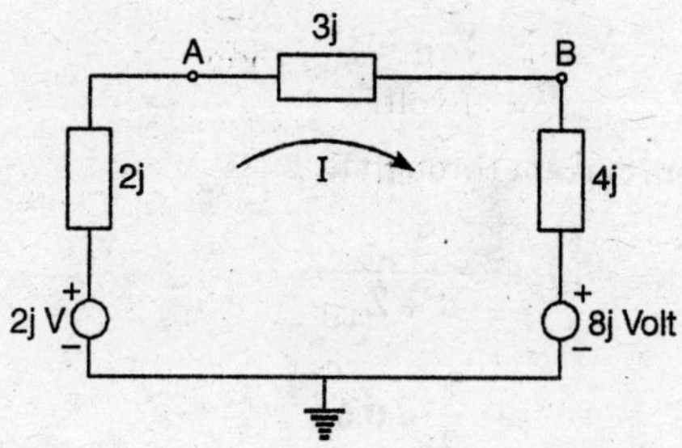

Cureent, $$I = \frac{-8j + 2j}{9j}$$

$$= \left(-\frac{2}{3}\right) \text{amp}$$

Then, $$V_B = 8j + 4j.I$$

$$= 8j - \frac{8j}{3}$$

$$= \frac{16j}{3}$$

$$= \mathbf{5.33\,jV}$$

87. From the circuit, we have

$$6 = 2I_1 + 2I_2$$

or $$I_2 = 1.5\text{A}$$

88. Applying KCL at node (1), we have

$$\frac{V_1 - 60}{10} + \frac{V_1}{20} + \frac{V_1 - V_2}{R} = 0$$

or $$\left(\frac{V_1 - 60}{10} + \frac{V_1}{20} + \frac{V_1}{R}\right) = \frac{V_2}{R}$$

or $$V_2 = \left(\frac{V_1 - 60}{10} + \frac{V_1}{20}\right)R + V_1$$

$R = 0$ gives, $V_2 = V_1$

Also, $\frac{V_1 - 60}{10} + \frac{V_1}{20} = 0$

or, $V_1 = 40$ volts

Thus, $V_2 = 0$ V

90. Shorting the voltage source and opening current source, we have $Z_{TH} = 1\Omega$ looking left into terminal AB.

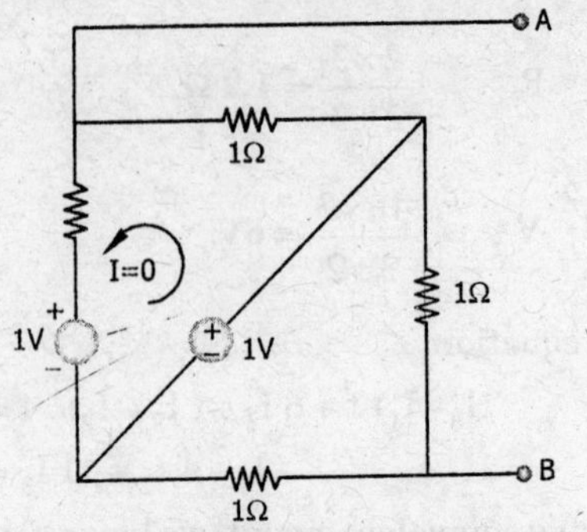

Now, for V_{TH}, from the circuit, we have

$$V_{AB} = V_{TH} = 1 \text{ volt.}$$

Then, current through R

$$= \frac{V_{AB}}{R + Z_{TH}} = \frac{1}{2} = \mathbf{0.54}$$

91. Redrawing the circuit, we have

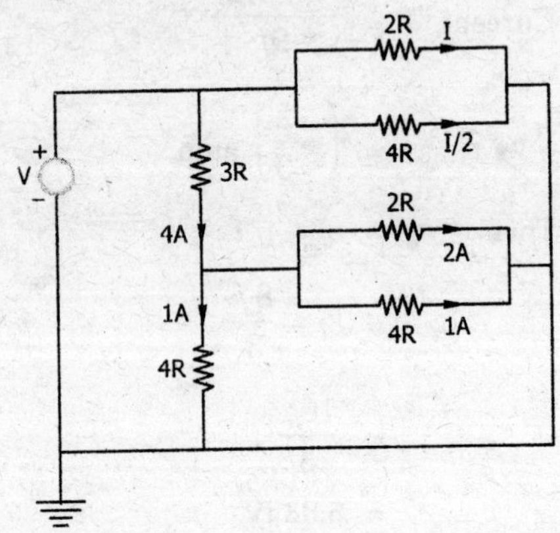

From the circuit,

$$V = 2RI \qquad \text{....}(i)$$

and, $V = (3R)4 + (4R) \,.\, 1$

$$= 16 \text{ R} \qquad \text{....}(ii)$$

From equations (*i*) and (*ii*), we get

$$I = 8A$$

92.

$$V_0 = \frac{10}{2} - \frac{10 \,.\, \frac{1}{j\omega C}}{R + \frac{1}{j\omega C}}$$

$$V_0(jw) = 5\left(\frac{j\omega RC - 1}{j\omega RC + 1}\right)$$

and $|V_0(j\omega)| = 5$ volts.

93. From the circuit,

$$10 = 10\,I_1 + 5\,I_2 \qquad \text{...}(i)$$

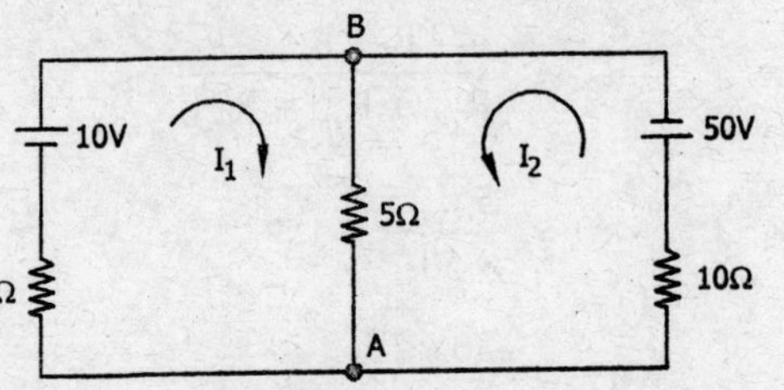

and $-50 = 15\,I_2 + 5\,I_1 \qquad \text{...}(ii)$

From equations (*i*) *and* (*ii*)

$$I_1 = \left(\frac{16}{5}A\right)$$

$$I_2 = \left(-\frac{22}{5}\right)A$$

Then, $V_{BA} = (I_1 + I_2).\,5$

$$= -6 \text{ volts}$$

$$V_{AB} = 6 \text{ volts.}$$

94. Shorting 3V source, current through 2Ω,

$$I_1 = 6 \times \frac{1}{3} = 2A$$

Now, opening 6A source,

$$I_2 = -\frac{3}{3} = -1A$$

Then, $I = I_1 + I_2 = 2 - 1 = 1$ amp.

96. In open-circuiting current source, the circuit will be as

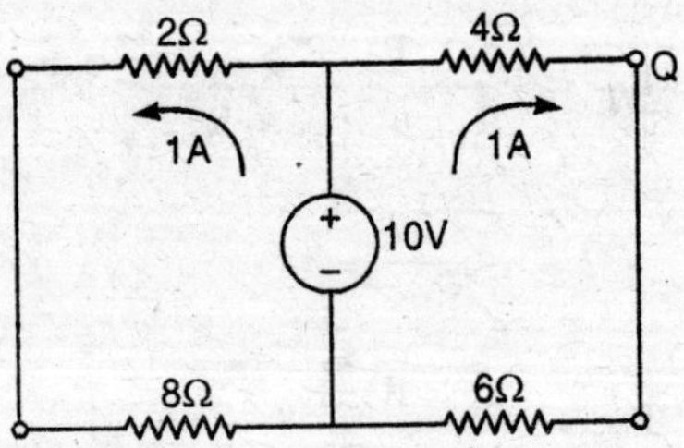

Short-circuiting the voltage source, the circuit will be as

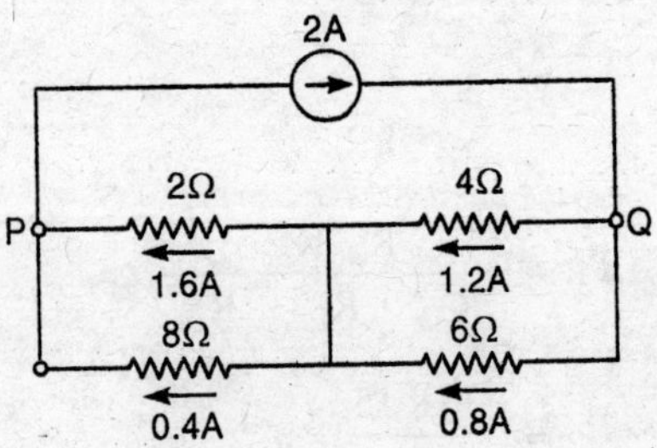

$$\therefore \quad -V_{PQ} = V_{PQ1} + V_{PQ2}$$
$$= (1.6 \times 2 + 1.2 \times 4) + (2 \times 1 - 4 \times 1)$$
$$= 6 \text{ volts}$$

or $\quad V_{PQ} = -6$ volts

97.

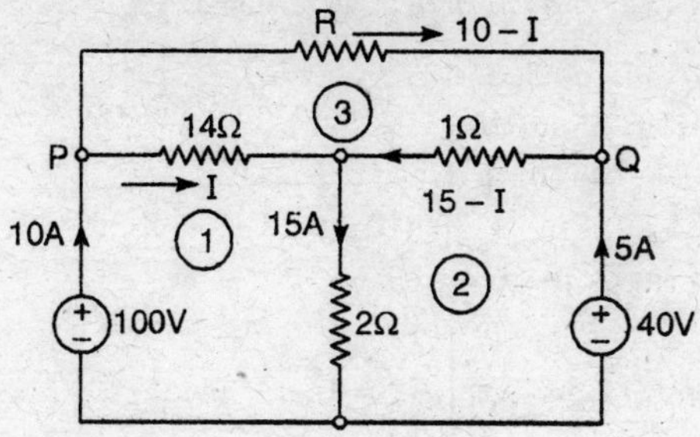

Using KVL in loop 1

$$100 - 14I - 30 = 0$$

or $\quad I = \dfrac{70}{4} = 5A$

then, $\quad V_P - V_Q = 14I - (15 - I).1$
$$= 70 - 10$$
$$= 60 \text{ volts}$$

Thus, $\quad$ value of $R = \dfrac{V_{PQ}}{10 - I}$
$$= \frac{60}{10-5}$$
$$= 12\ \Omega$$

99. The nodal method of circuit analysis is based on KCL and Ohm's law.

101. $\quad V(t) = \dfrac{Ldi}{dt}$
$$= \frac{d}{dt}(e^{at} + e^{bt})$$
$$= ae^{at} + be^{bt}$$

103. Since output port voltage = 4 × 1 = 4V and input voltage is also 4V, the network N consists of merely a shunt element

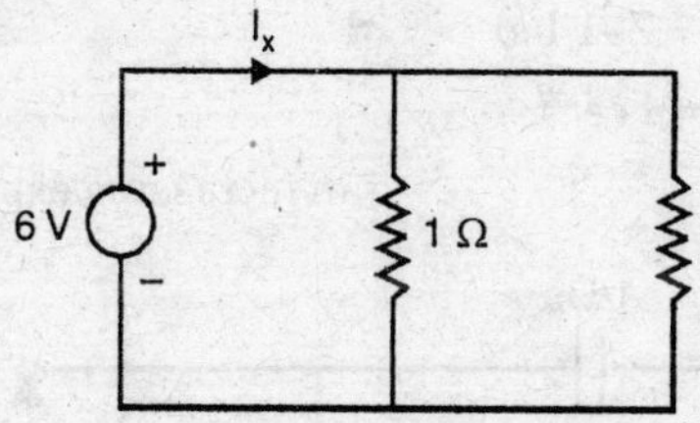

$$I_x = -\frac{6}{\dfrac{3 \times 1}{3+1}}$$
$$= -\frac{6 \times 4}{3} = -8A$$

104. Set $\quad V_2 = 0$, then
$$R(I_1 + I_2) + RI_2 = 0$$

or $\quad RI_1 + 2RI_2 = 0$

Hence $\quad h_{21} = \dfrac{I_2}{I_1} = -\dfrac{1}{2}$

106.

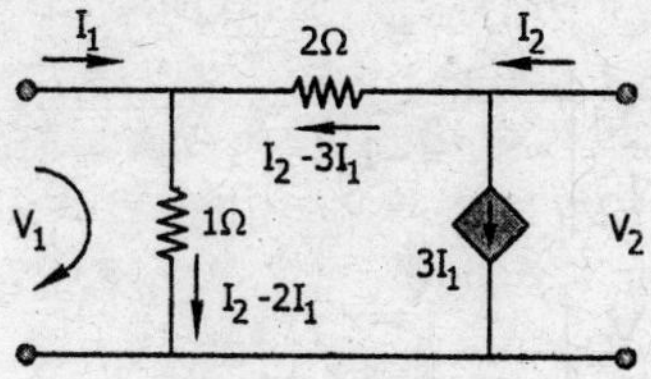

$$V_1 = -2I_1 + I_2$$
$$V_2 = 2I_2 - 6I_1 - V_1$$
$$= 2I_2 - 6I_1 + I_2 - 2I_1$$
$$= -8I_1 + 3I_2$$
$$\begin{bmatrix} V_1 \\ V_2 \end{bmatrix} = \begin{bmatrix} -2 & 1 \\ -8 & 3 \end{bmatrix} \begin{bmatrix} I_1 \\ I_2 \end{bmatrix}$$

110. Apply Loop law's to both loops,
$$11E_1 = 6I_1 + 4I_2 \quad \text{....}(i)$$
$$E_2 = (I_1 + I_2)4 - 10\,E_1 \quad \text{....}(ii)$$

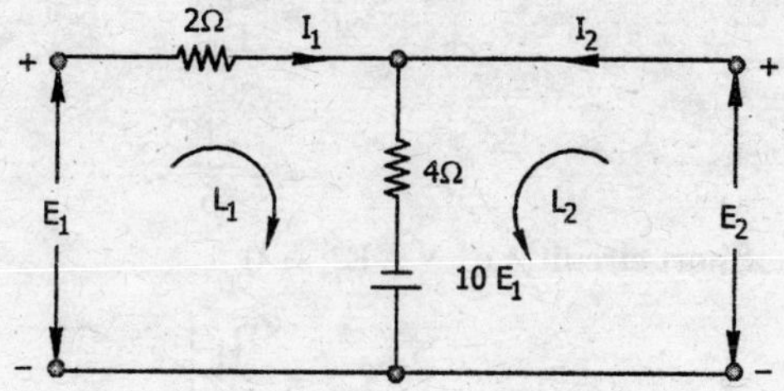

Putting the expression for E_1 from equation (*i*) in equation (*ii*), we get
$$E_2 = (I_1 + I_2)4 - \frac{10[6I_1 + 4I_2]}{11}$$
$$= I_1\left[4 - \frac{60}{11}\right] + I_2\left(4 - \frac{40}{11}\right)$$

Putting $I_2 = 0$ and as $z_{21} = \left.\dfrac{E_2}{I_1}\right|_{I_2=0}$, therefore
$$E_2 = I_1\left[\frac{44-60}{11}\right] = -\frac{16}{11}I_1$$

From equation (*i*), we get
$$z_{11} = \left.\frac{E_1}{I_1}\right|_{I_2=0}$$
$$= \frac{6}{11}\ \Omega.$$

112. $z_{11} = \left.\dfrac{V_1}{I_1}\right|_{I_2=0} = 1$

$\Rightarrow \quad z_{22} = \left.\dfrac{V_2}{I_2}\right|_{I_1=0} = 2$

$\Rightarrow \quad z_{12} = \left.\dfrac{V_1}{I_2}\right|_{I_2=0} = -1$

$\Rightarrow \quad z_{21} = \left.\dfrac{V_2}{I_1}\right|_{I_2=0} = -1$

113.

$$I_1 = Y_{11}E_1 + Y_{12}E_2$$
$$I_2 = Y_{21}E_1 + Y_{22}E_2$$

Short circuit, i.e. $E_2 = 0$

$$Y_{11} = \left.\frac{I_1}{E_1}\right|_{E_2=0} = \frac{1}{3}$$

$$Y_{21} = \left.\frac{I_2}{E_1}\right|_{E_2=0} = -\frac{1}{6}$$

Short circuit, i.e. $E_1 = 0$

$$\Rightarrow \quad Y_{12} = \left.\frac{I_1}{E_2}\right|_{E_1=0} = -\frac{1}{6}$$

$$Y_{22} = \left.\frac{I_2}{E_2}\right|_{E_1=0} = \frac{1}{3}$$

115. The defining equations are

$$V_1 = Z_{11}I_1 + Z_{12}I_2$$
$$V_2 = Z_{21}I_1 + Z_{22}I_2$$

and

$$V_1 = h_{11}I_1 + h_{12}V_2$$
$$I_2 = h_{21}I_1 + h_{22}V_2$$

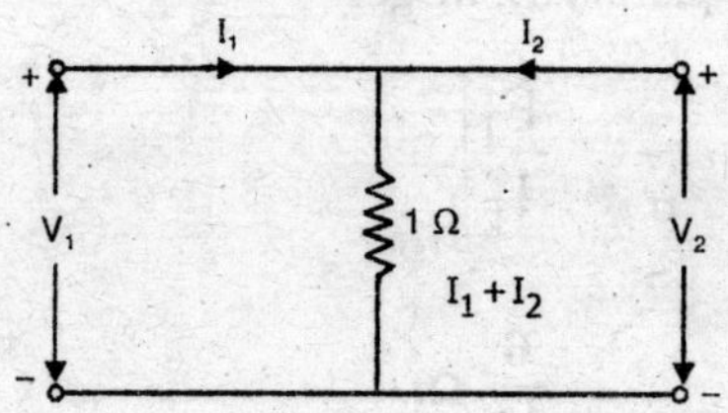

$$Z_{11} = \left.\frac{V_1}{I_1}\right|_{I_2=0}$$

$$= 1, \quad Z_{12} = \left.\frac{V_1}{I_2}\right|_{I_1=0} = 1$$

$$Z_{21} = \left.\frac{V_2}{I_1}\right|_{I_2=0}$$

$$= 1, Z_{22}$$

$$= \left.\frac{V_2}{I_2}\right|_{I_1=0} = 1$$

and $h_{11} = \left.\dfrac{V_1}{I_1}\right|_{V_2=0}$

$$= 0, h_{12} = \left.\frac{V_1}{V_2}\right|_{I_1=0}$$

$$= 1\, h_{21} = \left.\frac{I_2}{I_1}\right|_{V_2=0}$$

$$= -1, h_{22}$$

$$= \left.\frac{I_2}{V_2}\right|_{I_1=0} = 1$$

116. After $t > 0$,

$$I(s) = \frac{4}{s\left(2 + s + \dfrac{4}{s}\right)} \quad \left[\begin{array}{l} As,\ i(0^+) = 2 \text{ amp} \\ \text{and, } V(0^+) = 4 \text{ volt} \end{array}\right]$$

$$= \frac{4}{s^2 + 4s + 4}$$

$$= \frac{4}{(s+2)^2}$$

Then, $i\,(t) = Z{-}1\ I(s)$

$$= 4\,t\,e^{-2t}$$

[an increasing exponential.]

117.

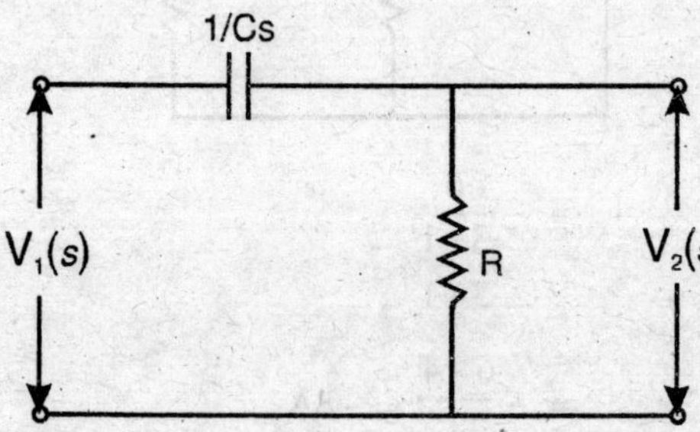

$$\frac{V_2(s)}{V_1(s)} = \frac{R}{R+\frac{1}{Cs}}$$

$$= \frac{s}{s+\frac{1}{RC}}$$

$$M(j\omega) = \frac{V_2(j\omega)}{V_1(j\omega)}$$

$$= \frac{\omega}{\sqrt{\omega^2+\left(\frac{1}{RC}\right)^2}} \text{ with } \omega$$

$$= \frac{1}{RC}$$

118.

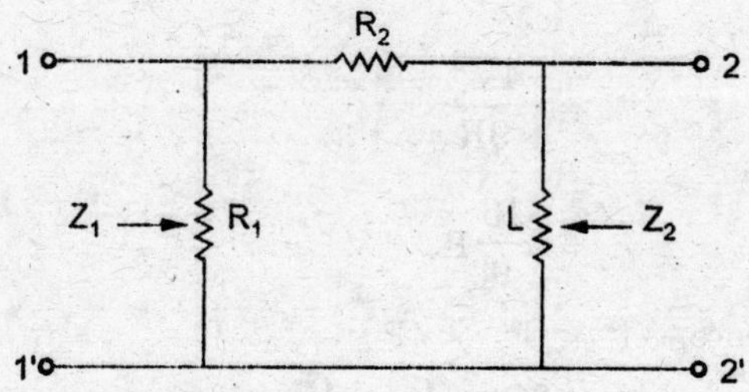

Input impedance is,

$$\left.\frac{V_1}{I_1}\right|_{I_2=0} = 0$$

$$\therefore \quad 0 = V_2 - DI_2$$

$$\text{or} \quad \frac{V_2}{I_2} = \frac{\mathbf{D}}{\mathbf{C}}.$$

119.

$$Z(s) = R_1 + Ls + \frac{R_2 \cdot \frac{1}{Cs}}{R_2+\frac{1}{Cs}}$$

$$= R_1 + Ls + \frac{R_2}{1+R_2Cs}$$

$$= \frac{R_1 + R_1 + R_2Cs + Ls + R_2CLs^2 + R_2}{1+R_2Cs}$$

120.

$$Z_1 = K_1\frac{(s+2)}{s+5}$$

$$Z_1 = \frac{R_1\left(s+\frac{R_2}{L}\right)}{\left(\frac{R_1+R_2}{L}+s\right)}$$

We see that

$$Z_1 = \frac{R_1(R_2+Ls)}{R_1+R_2+Ls}$$

$$Z_1 = \frac{K_1(s+2)}{s+5}$$

$$\therefore \quad R_1 = K_1$$

$$\frac{R_2}{L} = 2$$

$$\frac{R_1+R_2}{L} = 5$$

$$\text{Again,} \quad R_2 = \frac{2}{3}K_1$$

$$L = \frac{K_1}{3}$$

$$\therefore \quad Z_2 = \frac{Ls(R_1+R_2)}{Ls+R_1+R_2}$$

$$L = \frac{K_1}{3}$$

$$R_1+R_2 = \frac{5K_1}{3}$$

$$Z_2 = \left(\frac{\frac{sK_1}{3}\cdot\frac{5K_1}{3}}{s}\right) \Bigg/ \left(\frac{sK_1}{3}+\frac{5K_1}{3}\right)$$

$$= \left(\frac{5s}{s+5}\right)$$

$$= \frac{K_2 s}{s+5}$$

121. For an L–C network the driving-point impedance function poles and zeros should alternate. This is satisfied by the function at (*b*) alone.

124. By KCL, if we take a cutset along all three branches, then total current at the junction is zero

$$\text{Then} \quad I_1 + I_2 + I_3 = 0$$

$$\text{or} \quad \frac{10}{5} + I_2 + \frac{5}{1} = 0$$

$$\text{or} \quad I_2 = 7A$$

$$\text{and} \quad V = -105 \text{ V.}$$

125. The Y parameter of two networks in parallel are the sums of the corresponding Y-parameters,

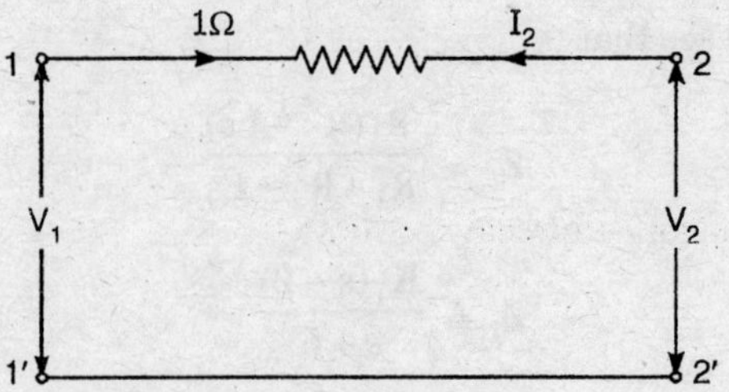

As $Y_1 = \begin{bmatrix} 1 & -1 \\ -1 & 1 \end{bmatrix}$

$$Y_2 = \begin{bmatrix} 4 & 2 \\ 1 & 1 \end{bmatrix}.$$

$$\therefore \quad Y = Y_1 + Y_2$$

$$= \begin{bmatrix} 5 & 1 \\ 0 & 2 \end{bmatrix}$$

126. Characteristic impedance,

$$R_0 = \sqrt{R_{sc} R_{oc}}$$

Since $R_{sc} = 2\dfrac{R_1 R_2}{R_1 + R_2}$

$$R_{oc} = \frac{R_1 + R_2}{2}$$

therefore, $R_0 = \sqrt{R_1 R_2}$

127. Using KVL,

$$V_1(s) = \left(\frac{1}{sC} + sL_1\right) I_1(s) + sM.\, I_2(s)$$

and $V_2(s) = (R + SL_2)\, I_2(s) + sM\, I_1(s)$

then $Z_{ij}(s) = \left.\dfrac{V_i(s)}{I_j(s)}\right|_{I_k(s)=0}$; $k \neq j$

or $Z(s) = \begin{bmatrix} \dfrac{1}{sC} + sL_1 & sM \\ sM & R + sL_2 \end{bmatrix}$

128. If the network is reciprocal, then ratio of the response transform to the excitation transform would not vary after interchanging the position of the excitation.

129. Let, newtwork N contains a resistance R and voltage V, then, Fig-I is redrawn as

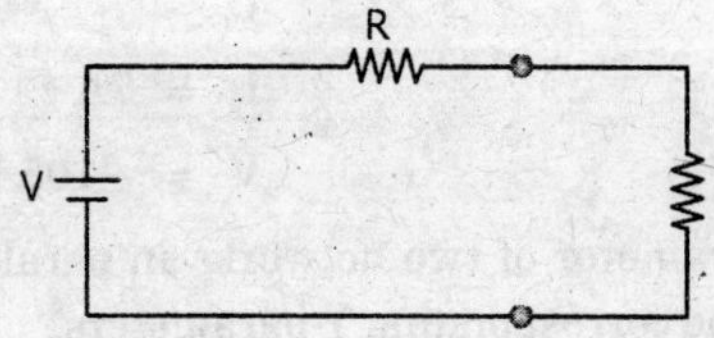

and $P = \left(\dfrac{V}{2R}\right)^2 R$

$$= \frac{V^2}{4R}$$

Now, redrawing Fig II, we have power dissipated in

$$R = P$$

$$= V\,(2I)^2 R$$

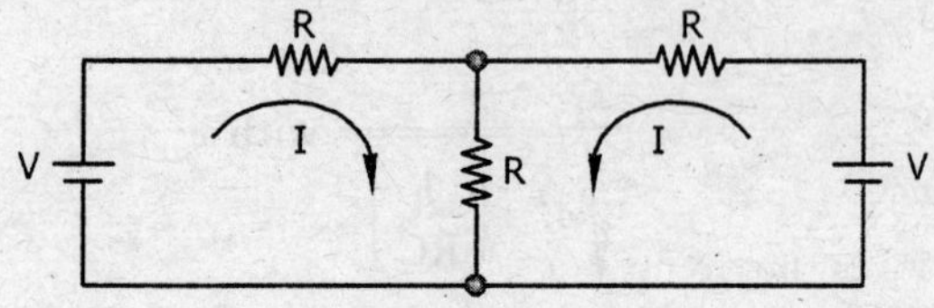

$$P' = \left(\frac{2V}{3R}\right)^2 R$$

$$= \frac{4V^2}{9R}$$

$$= \frac{16}{9} P$$

Hence, $P < P' < 4P$

130. At $t = 3$, since 2Ω is shorted, I_c jumps to a new value and then decreases with reduced time constant

131. The equivalent resistance looking right through terminal 11′, is

$$Z_{eq} = \frac{(Z_2 + Z_L)Z_3}{Z_2 + Z_3 + Z_L} + Z_1$$

For impedance matching,

$$Z_{eq} = Z_g$$

132. By KVL equation

$$10 = iR + \frac{Ldi}{dt} + V_c \quad \text{... }(i)$$

At $t = 0^+$, $t = 0$ and $V_c = 0$ (short-circuited)

Then, $10 = \dfrac{Ldi}{dt}$

or $\left.\dfrac{di}{dt}\right|_{t=0^+} = 10$

Differentiating equation (*i*), we have

$$\frac{di}{dt}R + \frac{Ld^2i}{dt^2} + \frac{dv_c}{dt}$$

or $\dfrac{Ld^2i}{dt^2} = -\dfrac{di}{dt}R$ .... $\left[\text{as } \dfrac{dV_c}{dt} = \dfrac{i}{C} = 0\right]$

or $\frac{d^2i}{dt^2} = -10 \times 10$

$= -10$

133. $Y_{21} = \left.\frac{I_2}{V_1}\right|_{V_2=0}$

134. $V = 4I - 9$

$= -IR$

or $4I - 9 = -2I$

or $I = 1.5\text{ A}$

136. From the circuit,

$I_1 = (V_1 - V_2)\,Y_C + V_1.Y_A$

$= V_1\,(Y_A + Y_C) - V_2.\,Y_C$ ....(*i*)

$I_2 = V_1Y_C + V_2\,(Y_B + Y_C)$ ...(*ii*)

$Y_A + Y_C = Y_{11}$

$= 8\Omega$

$Y_C = Y_{12}$

$= -Y_{21}$

$= 6\Omega$

$Y_B + Y_C = Y_{22}$

$= 6\Omega$

then, $Y_A = 2$

$Y_B = 0$

$Y_C = 6\Omega$

137. $R_1 = \frac{24 \times 16}{24 + 16 + 24}$

$= 6\Omega$

$R_2 = \frac{24 \times 16}{24 + 16 + 24}$

$= 6\Omega$

$R_3 = \frac{24 \times 24}{24 + 16 + 24}$

$= 9\Omega$

138. $Z_{eq} = \begin{bmatrix} 3 & 2 \\ 2 & 3 \end{bmatrix} + \begin{bmatrix} 15 & 5 \\ 5 & 25 \end{bmatrix}$

$= \begin{bmatrix} 18 & 7 \\ 7 & 28 \end{bmatrix}$

139. $Z_{21} = \left.\frac{V_2}{I_1}\right|_{I_2=0}$

and for reciprocal network,

$Z_{21} = Z_{12}.$

140. When $I = 2$ amp,

$V_{N2} = 20\,(4 - I)$

$= 40$ volts.

Now, when $R = 10\,\Omega$,

then VN_2 remains unchanged.

and $I = 4 - \left(\frac{V_{N2}}{20}\right)$

$= 4 - 2$

$= 2$ amp.

141. $B = \left.\frac{V_1}{I_2}\right|_{V_2=0}$

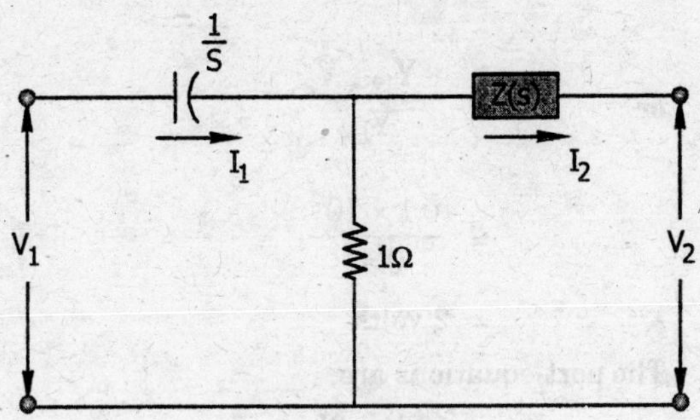

If $V_2 = 0$, then

$I_1(s) = \frac{V_1(s)}{\frac{Z(s)}{Z(s)+1} + \frac{1}{s}}$

and $I_2(s) = I_1 \times \frac{1}{Z(s)+1}$

$= \frac{V_1(s).s}{sZ(s) + [1 + Z(s)]}$

Given, $B = \frac{2s+1}{s^2}$

$\therefore \frac{V_1(s)}{I_2(s)} = \frac{sZ(s) + (1 + Z(s))}{s}$

$= \frac{2}{s} + \frac{1}{s^2}$

or, $$\frac{(s+1)\,z(s)}{s} = \frac{(s+1)}{s^2}$$

or $$Z(s) = \frac{1}{s}.$$

142. $$Y_{11} = \left.\frac{I_1}{V_1}\right|_{V_2=0}$$

$$= 0.5$$

$$Y_{21} = \left.\frac{I_2}{V_1}\right|_{V_2=0}$$

$$= \frac{-2}{20}$$

$$= -0.1$$

$$= Y_{12}$$

Now, in Fig.-II,

$$I_1 = Y_{11}V_1 + Y_{12}\,.\,V_2$$

$$= 0$$

or $$V_1 = \frac{-Y_{12}\,.\,V_2}{Y_{11}}$$

$$= \frac{0.1 \times 10}{0.5}$$

$$= 2 \text{ volts}$$

143. The port-equations are,

$$V_1 = 10\,I_1 + 2I_2 \quad ....(i)$$

$$V_2 = 5I_1 + 2\,I_2 \quad ....(ii)$$

Rewriting equations (*i*) and (*ii*) as

$$V_1 = 5\,I_2 + 2I_1 \quad ....(iii)$$

$$V_2 = 10\,I_2 + 2\,I_1 \quad ....(iv)$$

Writing in matrix form,

$$\begin{bmatrix} V_2 \\ V_1 \end{bmatrix} = \begin{bmatrix} 5 & 2 \\ 2 & 10 \end{bmatrix}\begin{bmatrix} I_2 \\ I_1 \end{bmatrix}$$

$$\begin{bmatrix} \frac{V_1}{V_2} \end{bmatrix} = \begin{bmatrix} 2 & 5 \\ 2 & 10 \end{bmatrix}\begin{bmatrix} I_1 \\ I_2 \end{bmatrix}$$

144. $$\frac{V_1}{V_2} = \frac{I_2}{I_1}$$

$$= \frac{N_1}{N_2}$$

$$= \frac{2}{1}$$

or $$V_1 = 2V_2$$

$$I_1 = 0.5\,I_2$$

In matrix form,

$$\begin{bmatrix} V_1 \\ I_1 \end{bmatrix} = \begin{bmatrix} 2 & 0 \\ 0 & 0.5 \end{bmatrix}\begin{bmatrix} V_2 \\ I_2 \end{bmatrix}$$

145. From the equations,

$$I_1 = 2V_1 + \frac{(I_2 - 2V_1)}{3}$$

or $$V_1 = 3I_1 - \frac{I_2}{4}$$

Thus, $$Z_{12} = \frac{1}{4}\Omega$$

146. $$Z_{11} = \frac{A}{C}$$

$$= \frac{4}{3}$$

147. $$R_{eq} = R_1 + \frac{R_2R_{eq}}{R_2 + R_{eq}}$$

$$R_{eq} = \frac{R_1R_2 + R_{eq}^2 + R_2R_{eq}}{R_2R_{eq}}$$

or $$R_{eq}\,.\,R_1 + R_{eq}\,.\,R_2 + R_{eq}^2$$

$$= R_1^2 + R_1R_2 + R_{eq}R_1 + R_1R_2 + R_{eq}\,.\,R_2$$

or $$R_{eq} = \sqrt{R_1^2 + 2R_1R_2}$$

$$= \sqrt{4 + 2.2.15}$$

$$= \sqrt{10}$$

$$= 3.5\Omega$$

$$R_{eq} = 3$$

149. Condition for symmetry is,

$$A = D$$

then, $$D = 3$$

and, network is summetrical, then

$$AD - BC = 1$$

or $C = \frac{AD - 1}{B}$

$= \frac{9-1}{1}$

$= 8$

150. $Z(s) = Ls + \frac{\left(s + \frac{1}{Cs}\right)\frac{1}{2s}}{s + \frac{1}{Cs} + \frac{1}{2s}}$

$= Ls + \frac{(Cs^2 + 1)}{s\,(2Cs^2 + 2 + C)}$

$= \frac{2LCs^4 + (2 + C)\,Ls^2 + Cs^2 + 1}{s\,(Cs^2 + 2 + s)}$

Comparing from the given one, we have

$C = 2F$

and $2LC = 4$

or $L = 1H$

152. $I(s) = \frac{(s+3)}{s\,(s+2)}$

$= \frac{3}{2s} - \frac{1}{2}\cdot\frac{1}{s+2}$

or $i(t) = \frac{3}{2} - \frac{1}{2}e^{-2t}$

153. Using Y-parameter,

$I_2 = Y_{21}\,.\,V_{AB} + Y_{22}\,.\,V_{CD}$

When $V_{AB} = E = 10_V$

$I_2 = 1_A$

and $V_{CD} = 0$

then $Y_{21} = 0.1$

When port 1 becomes port 2 and vice-versa,

then $I_2 = Y_{21}\,.\,V_{CD} + Y_{22}\,.\,V_{AB}$

and $V_{AB} = 0$

$V_{CD} = 100$

then $I_2 = 0.1 \times 100$

$= 10_A$

154. Y-parameter $= \frac{1}{Z}\begin{bmatrix} 1 & -1 \\ -1 & 1 \end{bmatrix}$

and $\Delta_y = 0$

Then, Z-parameter can not exist.

155. From the circuit,

$V_1 = I_1 + (I_1 + I_2)\,.\,2s$

$= (2s + 1)\,I_1 + I_2\,.\,2s$

and $V_2 = \frac{3I_2}{s} + (I_1 + I_2)\,2s$

$= 2\,sI_1 + I_2\left(2s + \frac{3}{s}\right)$

Then, Z-matrix will be $\begin{bmatrix} 2s+1 & 2s \\ 2s & 2s + \frac{3}{s} \end{bmatrix}$

156. $M_1 = 20 \times 0.001$

$= 0.02$

Relative error at 1 A $= \frac{0.02}{1}$

$= 2\%$

$M_2 = 10 \times 0.002$

$= 0.02$

Relative error $= \frac{0.02}{1}$

$= 2\%$

$M_3 = 5 \times 0.005$

$= 0.025$

Relative error $= \frac{0.025}{1}$

$= 2.5\%$

$M_4 = 1 \times 0.01$

$= 0.01$

Relative error $= \frac{0.01}{1}$

$= 1\%$

158. If $W = U^a/V^b$, then

Limiting error (in W)

= a × limiting error in U + b × limiting error in V

$R = \frac{P}{I^2}$

∴ Limiting error in the measurement of resistance R = limiting error in the measurement of power + 2 × limiting error in the measurement of current

$= \pm\,(1.5 + 2 \times 1) = \mathbf{\pm\,3.5\%}$

160. Ammeter error, $\Delta = \pm\,2.4\%$

Voltmeter error, $\Delta V = \pm\,2.4\%$

Resistance to be measured, R = V/1

In case, error in resistance measurement is $\pm \Delta R$, then the maximum possible error will be

$$R + \Delta R = V + \Delta V/1 - \Delta|$$

or $$R| + |\Delta R–R\,\Delta|\Delta R = V + \Delta V$$

Neglecting $\Delta|\Delta R$ being small and substituting V

= R| we have

$$V+|\Delta R–R\,\Delta|\Delta R = V + \Delta V$$

or $$|\Delta R–R\,\Delta = \Delta V$$

Dividing by $|R\Delta R / R - \Delta|/| = \Delta V/|R = \Delta V/V$

or $$\Delta R/R = \Delta V/V + \Delta|/1$$

$\therefore$ Maximum percentage error = 2.4 % + 1% = 3.4%

162. The error specified is always with respect to full scale reading and this is the maximum error that may be present at any deflection

$$\therefore \quad \%\text{ error} = \frac{1.0}{100} \times 150 \times \frac{1}{75} \times 100$$

$$= \mathbf{2.0}$$

163. $$P = I^2R$$

$$\frac{dP}{P} = \frac{2dI}{I} + \frac{dR}{R}$$

$\therefore$ Limiting error in the power

$$= 2 \times 0.05 + 0.002$$

$$= 0.102$$

$$= \mathbf{10.2\%}$$

164. Here, $R_1 = 100$ ohm $\pm$ 5 ohm.

$R_2 = 150$ ohm $\pm$ 15 ohm.

$$R = R_1 + R_2$$

The errors are specified at standard deviations or are probable errors in this case.

$$R = \pm\sqrt{R_1^{\,2} + R_2^{\,2}}$$

$$= \pm\sqrt{5^2 + 15^2}$$

$$= \pm\sqrt{250}$$

$$= \mathbf{\pm\, 15.8\ ohms.}$$

165. 1% accuracy means that a maximum possible error of $\frac{300 \times 1}{100}$ = 3 may be present in any reading. Since the deflection is 83V so percent limiting error

$$= \frac{3}{83} \times 100 = \mathbf{3.62.}$$

166. Here, $W_1 = 100W + 1W$

$$W_2 = -50 + 0.5W$$

$$\therefore \quad W_1 + W_2 = 50 \pm \frac{1.5}{50} \times 100$$

$$= \mathbf{\pm\, 3\%}$$

■■

METROLOGY, MECHANICAL MEASUREMENTS AND INDUSTRIAL INSTRUMENTATION

2

2.1 FLATNESS

A flat surface is one of the fundamentals of workshop engineering.

Fig. 2.1. Surface plate

The methods which are most convenient for verifying flatness are either to test the surface against the another surface which is known to be flat or test with a straight edge. A surface plate has a surface of proved flatness, and when testing, the top of the plate should first be rubbed with a thin smear of a paste made up of lead and oil. The surface to be tested should be wiped clean, and then placed in contact with the surface plate and moved about. If it is reasonably flat, upon examination after this treatement, spots of the real lead will be visible all over it.

A straight edge may be in the form of steel strip or a stiff casting with the edge straight, as a the figure 2.2. For length greater than 300 mm the ribbed cast-iron pattern is to be recommended. The surface to be tested should be compared with the straight edge in several directions.

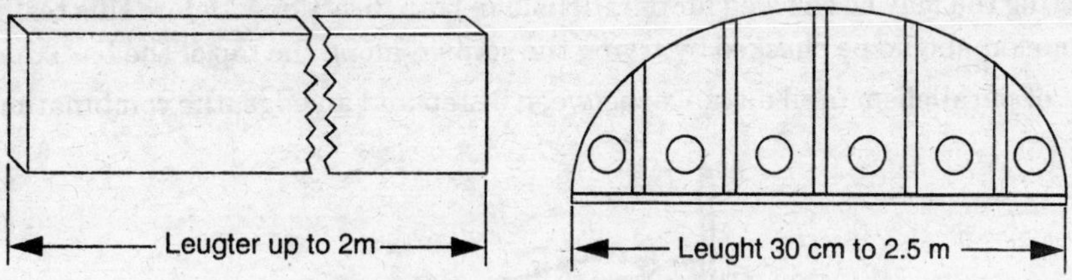

Fig. 2.2. Cast iron straightedge

If an edge is placed against a surface and then held up to the light any small discrepancy can be detected by the appearance of the light between the two, and our eyes are so sensitive that a gap of $\frac{1}{200}$ of a millimeter can be seen. If we can guarantee air straight edge, this method then gives us a good test for flatness.

2.2 ROUNDNESS

The easiest and most obvious way to verify roundness is to be use a micrometer or calipers and test the diameter of the part in several different positions in the same plane. If these dimensions vary, the part is not round, if the test shows diameter to be the same at every position, the part can be assumed to be round.

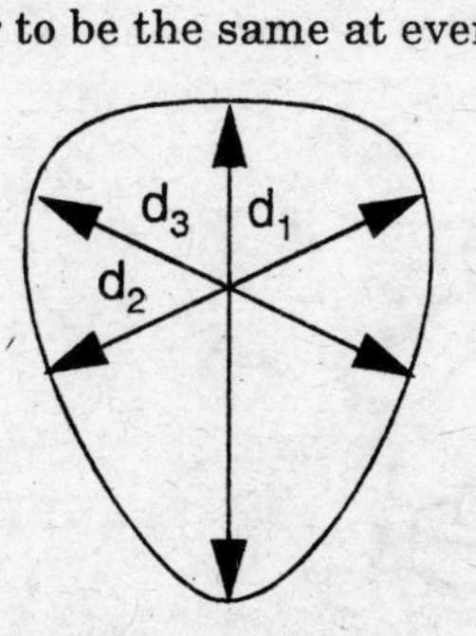

(a) Constant Diameter

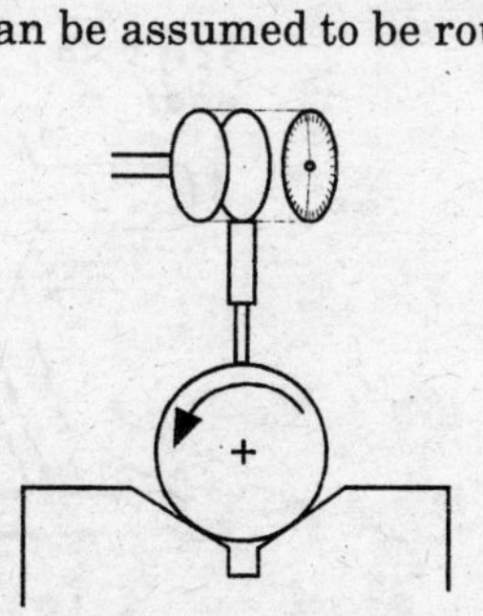

(b) V-block and clock indicator

Fig. 2.3

2.3 ANGULAR MEASUREMENT

When two surfaces are at any angle other than 90°, the angle between them must be measured by some form of protector, instrument for this purpose may have a scale of degrees, enabling the angle to be read off or they may consist of gauge which must be set to the angle before use.

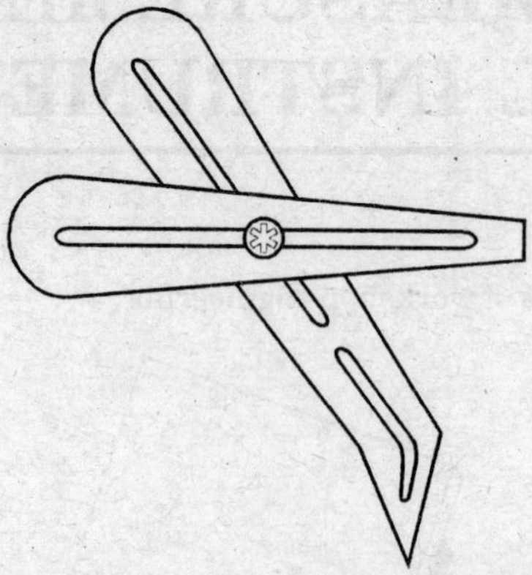

Fig. 2.4 Bevel

Accurate angular measurement should be carried out with the vernier protector. The main scale on the protector is divided up into degree from a 90° each way. The vernier scale is divided up so that 12 of its division occupy the same space as 23° on the main scale, so that one vernier division = $\frac{23}{12} = 1\frac{11°}{12}$ *i.e.* $\frac{1}{12}$ degree or 5 minutes less than 2°.

2.4 PARALLELISM

In this method there is testing of parallelism of two surfaces. For the flatness of surface measurement surface gauge or scribing black is used. The scriber of the surface gauge has one end bent at right-angles and this may be used as shown in fig. 2.5 *(a)* when the hole being checked as shown at Fig. 2.5 *(b)*. The longer the bar that is put through the hole, the more accurate will be the test, but the bar itself must be parallel. Shown in the fig. 2.5 *(c)* below, how the ends of a motor engine connecting rod may be checked for parallelism in both directions. Before this test is made, the Vee Block supporting the bottom bar should be checked by trying the scriber along the top of the bar supported in them.

To the measurement of parallelism (and distance) between a step and an edge, the combination square may be used.

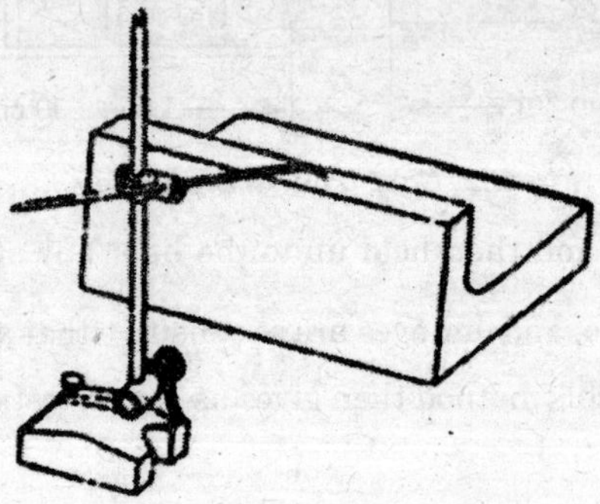

(a) Parallelism of casting surface

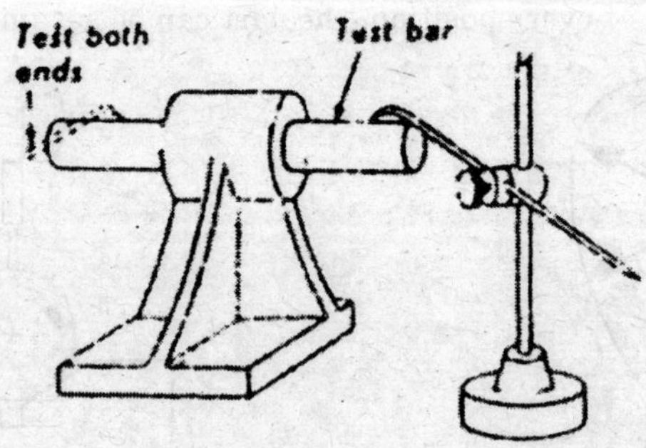

(b) Test for bore of bracket being parallel with base

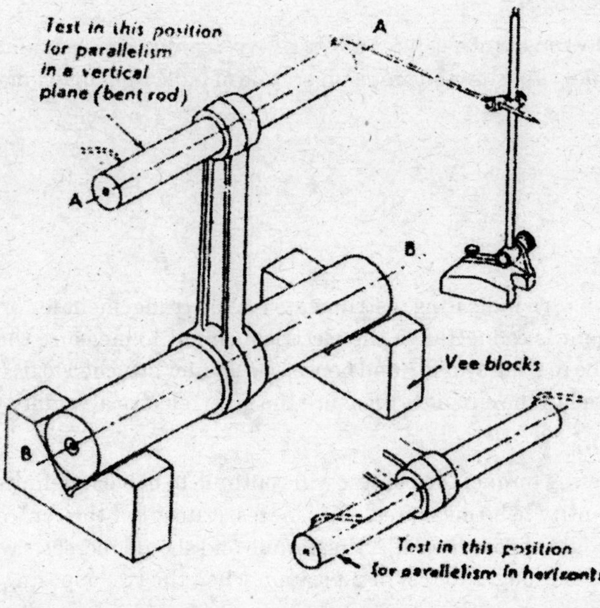

(c)

Fig. 2.5 Test with scribing block

2.5 CALIBERATION STANDARDS

International standard calibration is standarised by international agreement which is closest to the accuracy possible. This is checked by international standard which is absolute measurements.

Primary standard. It is maintained by the national level standard laboratories in the different parts of the world. *i.e.* HPL in Britain and SI-Standard in India.

Secondary standard. This is used in the industrial measurement laboratories. It is checked locally against the other reference standards.

Mass standard. One pound = 0.45359237 kg

Meter. 1650.763.73 wave lengths of the orange-red radiations *i.e.* distance traveled by light in a vacuum is $\frac{1}{299.792458}$ sec = 1 meter.

Temperature standard. Temperature SI unit is Kelvin. It is defined at the tripple point of water at exactly 273.16 K.

$$t\,(°C) = T(K) - T_0$$

These instruments measured and register by a set of dials and pointers, either the total quantity of electricity (in amp-hours) or the total amount of electrical energy (in watt-hours or kWh) supplied to a circuit in a given time. The summation gives the product of time and the electrical quantity but gives no direct indication as to the rate at which the quantity or energy is being supplied because their registrations are independent of this rate provided the current flowing through the instrument is sufficient to operate it. Ampere-hour and watt-hours meters fall in this class.

2.6 INSTRUMENTS

Instruments can be classified as

(*a*) Absolute

(*b*) Secondary Instruments

(*a*) Absolute instruments : These are those which give the value of quantity to be measured in terms of the constants of the instrument and deflection only. No previous calibration or comparison is necessary in their case.

(*b*) Secondary instruments : These are those in which value of physical quantity to be measured can be determined from the deflection of the instrument only when they have been pre-calibrated by comparison with an absolute instrument

Secondary instrument can be classified as :

(*i*) Indicating instrument

(*ii*) Recording instrument

(*iii*) Integrating instrument

2.6.1. INDICATING INSTRUMENTS

All such instruments essentially consist of a pointer moving over a calibrated scale and attached to the moving system pivoted in jewel bearings. In order to ensure the proper operation of indicating instruments, the following three torques are needed.

(*i*) Deflecting torque

(*ii*) Controlling torque

(*iii*) Damping torque

(*i*) Deflecting Torque (T_d).

One important requirement in a indicating instruments is the arrangement for producing deflecting or operating torque when the instrument is connected in the electrical circuit to measure the given electrical quantity. The deflecting torque caused the moving system (and hence, the pointer attached to it) to move from zero position when the instrument is connected in the circuit to measure the given electrical quantity.

(*ii*) Controlling Torque (T_c).

Under the action of deflecting torque, the pointer will continue to move indefinitely and shall be independent of the value of electrical quantity to be measured. This necessitates that the controlling torque must be provided. This controlling torque should oppose the deflecting torque and should increase with the deflection of the moving system so that the pointer is brought to rest at a position when the two opposing torques are equal.

The controlling torque performs the following two functions.

(*a*) It opposes the deflecting torque and increases with the deflection of the moving system. It thus, limits the movement of the pointer so that the magnitude of deflection is always the same for the given value of electrical quantity to be measured.

(*b*) It brings the pointer back to zero position when the deflecting torque is removed. If it were not provided, the pointer once deflected would not return to zero position on removing the deflecting torque.

The controlling or restoring or balancing torque is provided either by a spring or by gravity. A hair spring usually of phosphor-bronze is attached to the moving system of the instrument. With the movement of pointer, the spring is twisted in opposite direction. The twist in spring produces restoring torque. Gravity control is obtained by attaching a small adjustable weight to the moving system. Such that the two exert torques in opposite directions.

(*iii*) Damping torque.

If the moving system is acted upon by deflecting and controlling torques alone, then the pointer due to its inertia will oscillate about final position before coming to rest. These oscillations are undesirable and must be prevented. In order to avoid these oscillations of the pointer and to bring it quickly to its deflected position, damping torque is provided which opposes the movement (backward or forward) of the pointer and operates only when the system is moving.

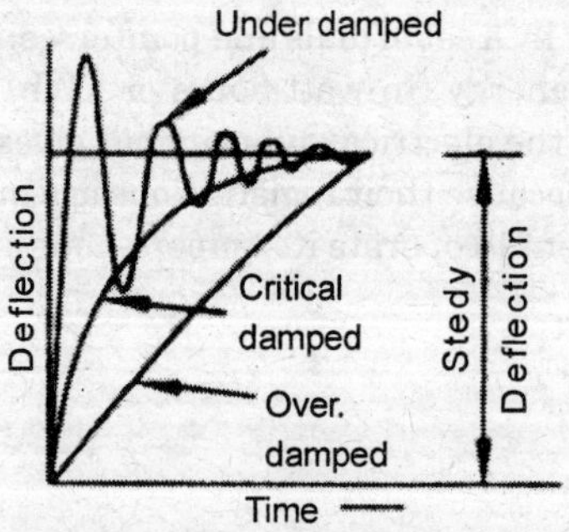

Graph for Damping

It is worthwhile to mention here that damping torque acts only when the pointer is in motion. When the pointer is in a particular final position, though deflecting and controlling torques are acting on the moving system but the damping torque is zero because the pointer is steady there is no movement of the moving system.

The degree of damping decides the behaviour of the moving system. If the instrument is under damped, the pointer will oscillate about the final position and take some time to come to rest. On the other hand, if the instrument is overdamped, the pointer will become slow and lithargic. However, if the degree of damping is adjusted to such a value that the pointer moves and quickly comes to its final position, the instrument is said to be dead beat. Fig.2.6 shows the graph for under- damping, over-damping and critical damping (dead beat).

Damping force can be produced by *air friction, eddy currents and fluid friction.*

In air- friction damping an aluminium piston attached to the moving system is aranged to travel in a fixed air chamber closed at one end. The necessary damping effect is produced by movement of piston in the chamber. Fluid friction is similar in action to the air friction. Damping is produced by movement of piston is oil.

The most efficient type of damping is obtained by eddy-current damping . A non-magnetic metallic disc, attached to the moving system, cuts the magnetic flux. Hence, eddy currents are produced in the disc which produce a damping force in such a direction to oppose the cause producing them, i.e. the motion of moving system.

Types of Indicating Instruments :

(i) Moving iron instruments
(ii) Moving coil instuments
(iii) Induction type instruments
(iv) Hot wire instruments
(v) Electrostatic instruments

(*i*) Moving Iron Instruments.

Moving iron instruments are of two types:

(*a*) Attraction type
(*b*) Repulsion type

(*a*)Attraction Type Moving Iron Instruments :

Principle. These instruments are based on the principle that when an unmagnetised soft iron piece is placed in the magnetic field of a coil, then the piece is attracted towards the coil. The moving system of the instrument is attached to the soft iron piece and the operaing current is passed through a coil placed near it. The operating current sets up magnetic field which attracts the iron piece and thus moves the pointer over the scale.

Construction. It consists of a hollow cylindrical coil or solenoid which is kept fixed as shown in Fig. 2.7. An oval shaped soft iron pieces is attached to the spindle so that it is deflected with the motion of the soft iron piece. The controlling torque on the moving system is provided by spring control method while damping is provided by air friction.

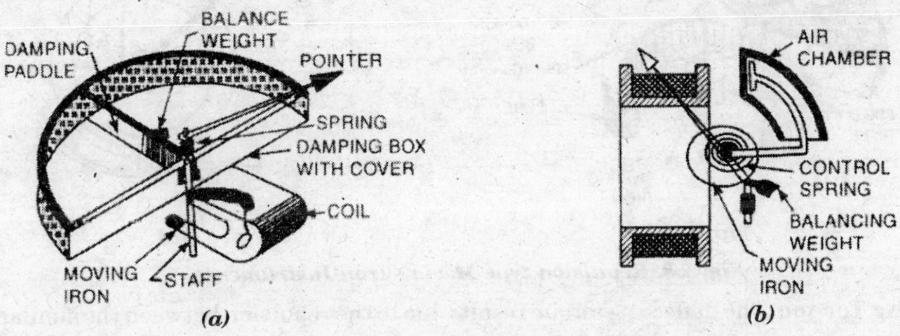

Fig. 2.7. Attraction type Moving Iron Instruments

Working. When the instrument is connected in the circuit, the operating current flows through the coil. The current sets up magnetic field in the coil. In other words, the coil behaves like a magnet and, therefore, it attracts the soft iron piece towards it. The result is that the pointer attached to the moving system moves from zero position.

If current in the coil is reversed, the direction of magnetic field also reverses and so does the magnetism produced in soft iron piece. Therefore, the direction of deflection torque remains unchanged. It follows, therefore, that such instruments can be used for both D.C. as well As A.C. work.

Deflecting torque. The force F pulling the soft iron piece towards the coil depends upon :

(*i*) Field strength H produced by the coil.

(*ii*) Pole strength *m* developed by the piece

$$F \propto mH$$

$$F \propto H^2 \quad ..(\because m \propto H)$$

$$\therefore \quad \text{Deflecting torque, } T_d \propto F \propto H^2$$

If premeability of iron is assumed constant then

$$H \propto I$$

$$\therefore \quad T_d \propto I^2$$

If the controlling torque is provided by the springs,

$$T_c \propto \theta \text{ (deflection)}$$

In the steady position of deflection,

$$T_d = T_c$$

$$\theta \propto I^2 \quad \text{.... (for d.c.)}$$

$$\propto I_{rms} \quad \text{... (for a.c.)}$$

Since deflection $\theta \propto I^2$, therefore, scale of such instruments is non-uniform, being crowded in the beginning. In order to make the scale of such instruments uniform, suitably shaped (tongue shaped) iron piece is used

(b) Repulsion Type Moving Iron Instruments :

Principle. These instruments are based on the principle of repulsion between the two iron pieces similarly magnetized.

Construction. It consists of a fixed cylindrical hollow coil which carries operating current (Fig. 2.8). Inside the coil, there are two soft iron pieces or vanes, one of which is fixed and other is movable. The fixed iron piece is attached to the coil whereas the movable iron piece is attached to the pointer shaft. Under the action of deflecting torque, the pointer attached to the moving system moves over the scale. The conrolling torque is produced by spring control method and damping torque is provided by air friction damping.

Working. When the instrument is connected in the circuit, current flows through the coil. This current sets up magnetic field in the coil. The magnetic field magnetizes both iron pieces in the same direction i.e. both pieces become similar magnets and hence they repel each other. Due to this force of repulsion only movable iron piece moves as the other piece is fixed and cannot move. The result is that the pointer attached to the moving system moves from zero position.

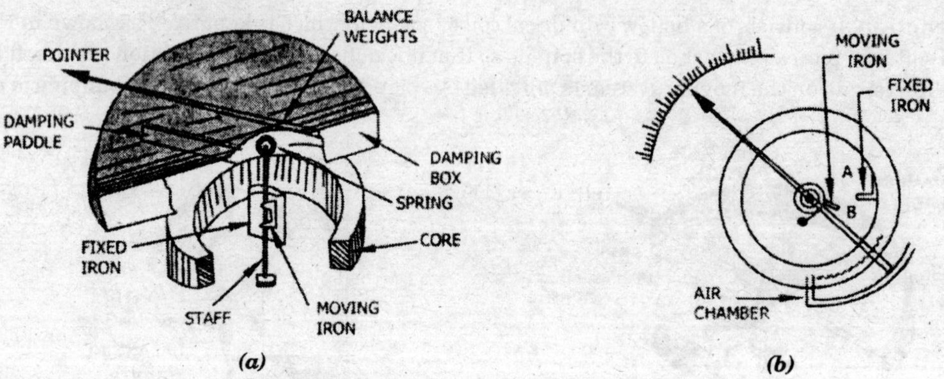

Fig. 2.8. Repulsion type Moving Iron Instruments

Deflecting Torque. The deflecting torque results due to the repulsion between the similarly magnetized iron pieces. If two pieces develop pole strengths m_1 and m_2 respectively, then,

Instantaneous deflecting torque $\propto$ repulsive force

$$\propto m_1, m_2$$

Since pole strength developed are proportional to H, therefore

Instantaneous deflecting torque, $T_d \propto H^2$

Assuming constant permeability, H$\propto$ current i through the coil

$\therefore$ Deflecting torque, $T_d \propto i^2$

Controlling torque provided by springs, $T_c \propto \theta$

In the steady position of deflection,

$$T_d = T_c$$

$$\theta \propto i^2$$

$$\propto I^2 \quad \text{... (for d.c.)}$$

$$\propto I_{r.m.s} \quad \text{... (for a.c.)}$$

Since deflection θ is proportional to square of current through the coil, therefore, scale of such instruments is non-uniform being crowd in the beginning. However, scale of such instruments can be made uniform by using tongue shaped iron pieces.

Advantage and Disadvantages of Moving Iron Instruments

Advantages.

1. These are cheap, robust and simple in construction
2. The instruments can be used for both A.C. as well as D.C. circuits
3. These instruments have high operating torque
4. These instruments are reasonable accurate.

Disadvantages.

1. Such instruments have non-uniform scale
2. These instruments are not very sensitive
3. Errors are introduced due to changes in frequency in case of a.c. measurements.
4. Higher power consumption.

(*ii*) Moving Coil Instruments

Moving coil instruments are of two types :

(*a*) Permanent magnet type (for d.c. work only)

(*b*) Dynamo meter type (for both a.c. and d.c. works)

(*a*) Permanent Magnet Moving Coil Instruments. These instruments are employed either as ammeters or voltmeters and can be used for d.c. work only.

Principle. This type of instrument is based on the principle that when a current carrying conductor is placed in a magnetic field, mechanical force acts on the conductor. The coil placed in magnetic field and carrying operating current is attached to the moving system. With the movement of the coil the pointer moves over the scale.

Construction. It consists of a powerful permanent magnet with soft iron pieces and light rectangular coil of many turns of fine wire wound on aluminium former inside which is an iron core as shown in Fig. 2.9. The purpose of coil is to make the field uniform. The coil is mounted on the spindle and acts as the moving element. The current is led into and out of the coil by means of the two control hair springs, one above and the other below the coil. The springs also provides the controlling torque. Eddy current damping is provided by aluminium former.

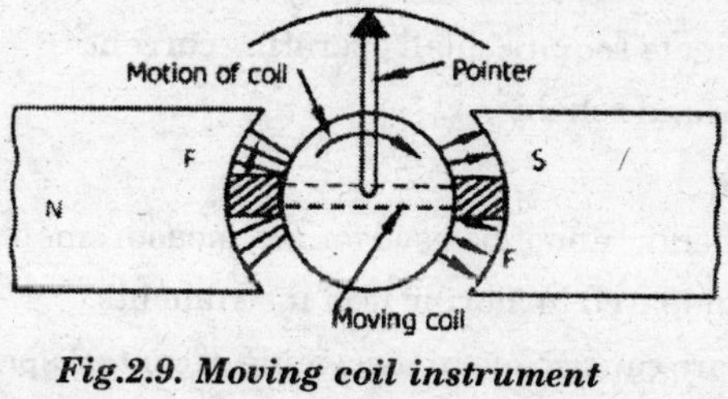

Fig.2.9. Moving coil instrument

Working. When the instrument is connected in the circuit, operating current flows through the coil. This current carrying coil is placed in the magnetic field produced by the permanent magnet and therefore, mechanical force acts on the coil. As the coil attached to the moving system, the pointer moves over the scale.

It may be noted here that if current direction is reversed, the torque will also be reversed since the direction of the field of permanent magnet is same. Hence, the pointer will move in the opposite direction, i.e. it will go on the wrong side of zero (below zero). In other words, these instruments work only when current in the circuit is passed in a definite direction i.e., for d.c. circuit only.

It is worthwhile to mention here that such instruments are called permanent magnet moving coil instruments because a coil moves in the field of a permanent magnet.

Deflecting Torque. When current is passed through the coil, a deflection torque is produced due to the reaction between permanent magnet field and the magnetic field of the coil as shown Fig. 2.9.

Let B = flux density in wb/m^2 in the air gap between the magnetic poles and iron core

l = active length of the coil side in meters

N = number of turns of coil

If a current of I amperes flows in the coil in the direction shown, then force F acting on each coil side is given by

$$F = BI/N \text{ newtons}$$

$\therefore$ Deflecting torque,

$$T_d\,\omega = \text{Force} \times \text{perpendicular distance}$$
$$= F.\,2r \text{ newton-meters}$$

where r is the distance of coil side from the axis of rotation in meters

$$T_d = NBIl.\,2r \text{ newton-meters}$$

If A $(= l.2\,r)$ is the surface area of the coil, then

$$T_d = NBIA \text{ newton-meter}$$

i.e. Deflection torque = Ampere turns on coil (NI). Area of coil (A). flux density B

Since N, B and A are constant, therefore,

$$T_d \propto I \qquad ...(i)$$

Since the control is by springs, therefore controlling torque is proportional to the angle of deflection i.e.

$$T_c \propto I \qquad ...(ii)$$

The pointer will come to rest at a position when,

$$T_d = T_c$$

From equation (i) and (ii) we get

$$\theta \propto I$$

Thus, the deflection θ is directly proportional to the operating current. Therefore, such instruments have uniform scale

Advantages

1. Uniform scale.
2. Very effective eddy current damping.
3. Power consumption is low.
4. No hysteresis loss.
5. As working field is very strong, therefore, such instruments are not affected stray fields.
6. Such instruments require small operating current.
7. Very accurate and reliable.

Disadvantages

1. Such instruments cannot be used for a.c. measurements.
2. Costlier as compared to moving iron instruments.
3. Some errors are caused due to the ageing of control springs and the permanent magnet.

(*b*) Dynamometer Type Instruments.

These instruments are the modified form of permanent magnet type. Here operating field is produced not by a permanent but by another fixed coil. The moving system and the control system are similar to those of permanent magnet type. Such instruments can be used for both a.c. and d.c. circuits. They can be used as ammeters and voltmeters but are generally used as wattmeters.

Principle. These instruments are based on that principle the mechanical force exists between the current carrying conductors.

Construction. A dynamometer type instrument as shown in Fig.2.10 esseentially consists of a fixed coil and a moving coil. The fixed coil is split into two equal parts which are placed closed together and parallel to each other. The moving coil is pivoted in between the two fixed coils. The fixed and moving coils may be excited separately or they may be connected in series depending upon the use to which the measurement is put. The moving coil is attached to the moving system so that under the action of deflecting torque, the pointer moves over the scale.

The controlling torque is provided by two springs which also serve the additional purpose of leading the current into and out of the moving coil. Air friction damping is provided in such instruments.

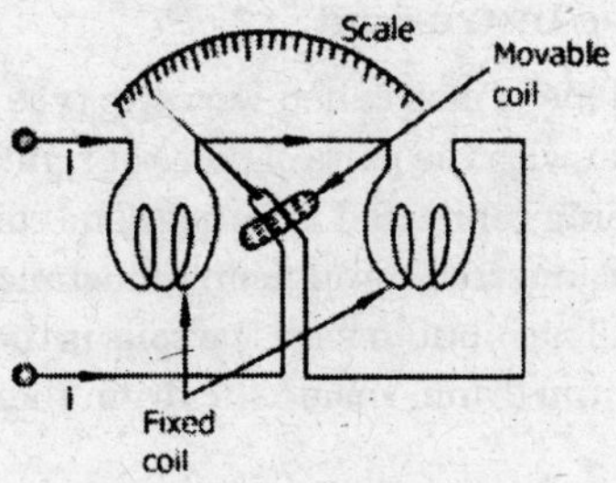

Fig. 2.10

Working. When instrument is connected in the circuit, operating currents flow through the coils. Due to this, mechanical force exists between the coils. The result is that the moving coil (which is capable of moving) moves the pointer over the scale. The pointer comes to rest at a position where deflecting torque is equal to the controlling torque.

By reversing the current, the field due to fixed coils is reversed as well as the current in the moving coil, so that direction of deflecting torque remains unchanged. Therefore, such instruments can be used for both d.c. and a.c. measurements.

Deflecting Torque

Let I_f = current through fixed coil

I_m = current through moving coil

$\therefore \quad T_d \propto I_f I_m$

Since, $I_f = I_m$, because the fixed and coils are in series,

$$\therefore \quad T_d \propto I^2 \qquad ...(i)$$

Since the control is by springs, therefore, controlling torque is proportional to the angle of deflection θ, i.e.

$$T_c \propto \theta \qquad ....(ii)$$

The pointer will come to rest at a position when $T_d = T_c$

From equations (*i*) and (*ii*), we get

$$\theta \propto I^2$$

It is clear that deflection of the pointer is directly proportional to the square of the operating current. Hence, the scales of these instruments is non-uniform being crowded in their lower parts and spread out at the top.

Advantages.

1. These instruments can be used for both a.c. and d.c. measurements.
2. Such instruments are free from hysteresis and eddy current errors.

Disadvantages.

1. Since torque/weight ratio is small, therefore, such instruments have frictional errors which reduce sensitivity.
2. Scale is not uniform (in case of ammeters and voltmeters).
3. A good amount of screning of the instruments is required to avoid the effect of stray fields.
4. These instruments are costlier than types and, therefore, they are rarely used as ammeters or voltmeters.

(*iii*) Induction Type Instruments

These instruments are based on the principle of induction motor.

Principle. When a drum or disc of a non-magnetic conducting material is placed in a rotating magnetic field, eddy currents are induced in it. The reaction between the rotating flux and the eddy current produced by it creates a torque which rotates the disc or drum. The rotating flux is produced by the current or voltage to be measured. The eddy current again is proportional to the flux.

$$\therefore \quad T \propto \phi i \propto i^2$$

The single phase supply is converted into two phases in the instrument, this is done by split phase or shaded pole arrangement.

Accordingly induction instruments are classified as

(*a*) Split phase type (*b*) Shaded pole type

(a) Split Phase Type Instrument

Construction. This is also called Ferraris type instrument and is shown in Fig.2.11. It consists of a laminated magnet with the pairs of poles at right angles to each other. Coils are wound on the poles, the opposite poles being connected in series. The coils on the two pairs of poles are connected in parallel. One set of coil is connected through an inductance and another with a high resistance to create a phase difference of 90°. The input to both the coils is the current to be measured. In the centre of the yoke and coil is an aluminium drum. Inside the drum there is cylindrical laminated iron core to strengthen the magnetic field.

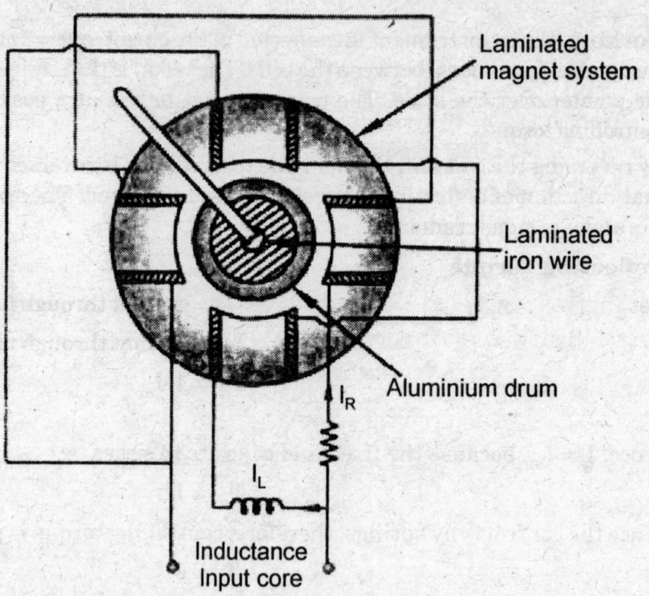

Fig.2.11. Split phase type induction instrument

Working. When the instrument is connected in the circuit current flows through the coils. A rotating magnetic field is produced. This field induces eddy currents in the drum and a torque is produced by the reaction of magnetic field and current. This torque deflects the pointer attached to the drum. Controlling torque is produced by spring.

Deflecting torque. Deflecting torque produced, is given by

$$T \propto \frac{I_R I_L f}{Z} \cos\theta \sin\alpha$$

For an ammeter,

$$T \propto \frac{I2}{Z} \cos\theta \sin\alpha$$

For a voltmeter,

$$T \propto \frac{V^2}{Z} \cos\theta \sin\alpha$$

where, I_R = current through resistor

I_L = current through inductor

f = supply frequency

Z = impedance of eddy current path

θ = phase angle between voltage and current in resistor

α = phase angle between currents in resistor and inductor

θ is almost zero and R is very much larger than reactive part of eddy paths. Hence

$$T \propto \frac{I^2}{R} \sin\alpha$$

Obviously α should be as high as possible for high torque

(b) Shaded Pole Type Instrument

Construction. Shaded pole type instrument is shown in Fig.2.12. A band of copper is placed in pole faces, this makes the two fluxes of shaded and unshaded portions of differ in phase by 90°. A metallic disc rotates between the pole faces. The damping is provided by another magnet as shown in Fig.2.12.

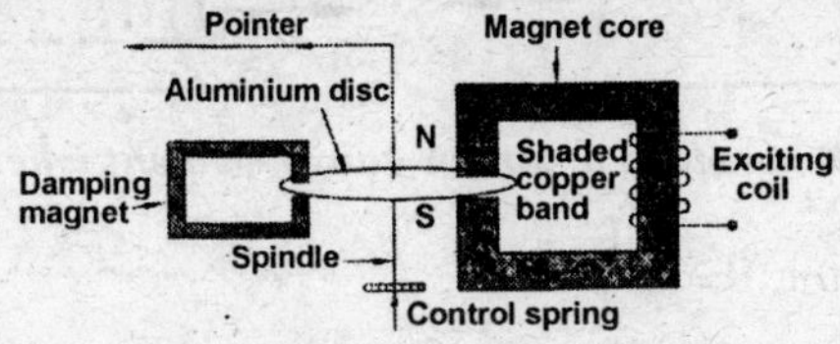

Fig. 2.12. Shaded pole type Induction Instrument

Working. The current flowing through the exciting coil sets up flux. Eddy currents are induced in the Cu band. Flux of the eddy current opposes the flux in the magnetic core and a two phase flux same as Ferraris type instrument.

2.7 TRANSDUCERS

These are the devices which convert energy from one form to another. Most of the quantities to be measured are non-electrical, e.g. temperature, pressure displacement etc. Since these quantities can not be measured directly, these are required to be sensed and changed into some other form.

Various electrical phenomena employed in transduction elements of transducers are

1. Resistive
2. Capacitive
3. Inductive
4. Electromagnetic
5. Piezo-electric
6. Ionization
7. Photo-electric
8. Photo conductive
9. Photo-voltaic
10. Thermo-electric
11. Potentiometric
12. Frequency generating

2.7.1 MEASUREMENT OF STRAIN

Strain Gauge

The strain gauges are used for measurement of strain and associated stress and these can be used as secondary transducers in many applications. These are based on the principle that, "*if a metal conductor is stretched or compressed, its resistance changes on account of change in length and diameter of conductor, also there is change in resistivity of conductor, due to strain.*" Some strain gauges are shown in figures.

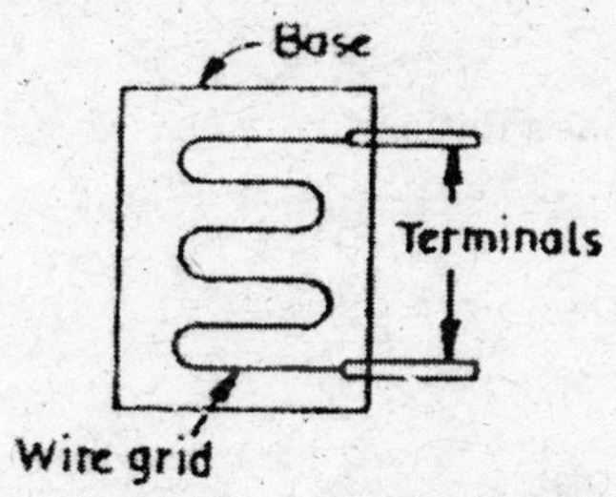

Fig. 2.13 Resistance wire strain gauge

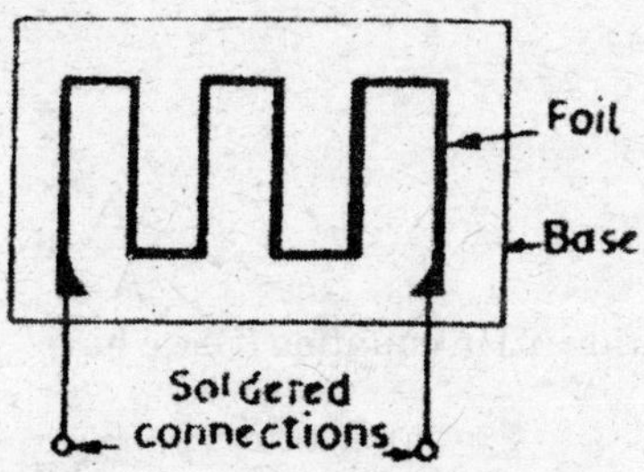

Fig. 2.14. Bonded metal foil gauge

Theory of Strain Gauge

Consider a strain gauge made of circuit wire. The wire has dimensions:

length = L, area = A, diameter = D before being strained.

The material of wire has resistivity.

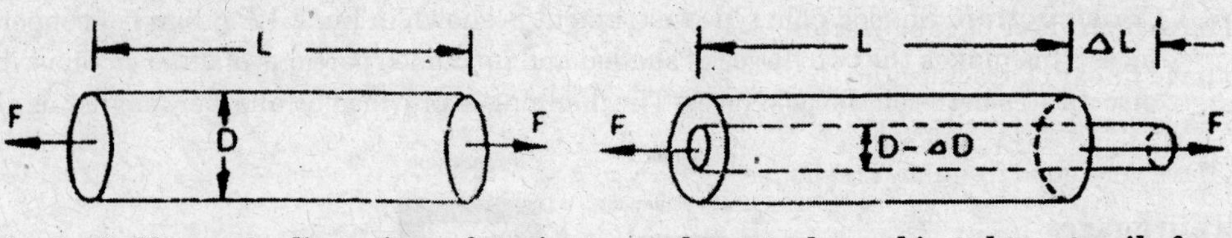

Fig. 2. 15. Change in dimensions of strain gauge element when subjected to a tensile force.

Resistance of unstrained conductor, $R = \rho \dfrac{L}{A}$

On the application of stress, resistance changes by ΔR due to change in length ΔL and change in cross-section by ΔA.

$$\frac{dR}{ds} = \frac{d}{ds}\left(\rho \frac{L}{A}\right) = \frac{\rho}{A}\cdot\frac{dL}{ds} - \frac{\rho L}{A^2}\frac{dA}{ds} + \frac{L}{A}\frac{d\rho}{ds}$$

$$\frac{1}{R}\frac{dR}{ds} = \frac{1}{L}\frac{dL}{ds} - \frac{1}{A}\frac{dA}{ds} + \frac{1}{\rho}\frac{d\rho}{ds}$$

or
$$\frac{\Delta R}{R} = \frac{\Delta L}{L} - \frac{\Delta A}{A} + \frac{\Delta \rho}{\rho} \qquad \text{....}(i)$$

Under strained conditions

$$\text{Area, } A = \frac{\pi}{4}D^2$$

or
$$\frac{\partial A}{\partial s} = 2 \times \frac{\pi}{4} D \frac{\partial D}{\partial s}$$

Dividing both sides by A, we get

$$\frac{1}{A}\cdot\frac{\partial A}{\partial s} = \frac{2\frac{\pi}{4}D}{\frac{\pi}{4}D^2}\frac{\partial D}{\partial s}$$

For small variations

$$\frac{\partial A}{A} = \frac{2\partial D}{D}$$

Now change in diameter of wire is related with change in length as

$$\frac{\Delta D}{D} = \nu \frac{\Delta L}{L}$$

where,
$$\upsilon = \frac{\text{Lateral strain}}{\text{Longitudinal strain}}$$

$$= \frac{\partial D / D}{\partial L / L} = \text{Poissons's Ratio}$$

$$\frac{\Delta A}{A} = -2\,\upsilon \frac{\Delta L}{L} \qquad \text{...}(ii)$$

Substituting equation (*ii*) in equation (*i*), we have

$$\frac{\Delta R}{R} = \frac{\Delta L}{L} + 2\,\upsilon \frac{\Delta L}{L} + \frac{\Delta \rho}{\rho}$$

or
$$\frac{\Delta R / R}{\Delta L / L} = 1 + 2 + \frac{\Delta \rho / \rho}{\Delta l / l} = G$$

The gauge factor G indicates the strain sensitivity of the gauge in resistance per unit strain. Neglecting change in resistivity of the material under strained condition, the gauge factor will be

$$G = 1 + 2\upsilon$$

Characteristics of Strain Gauges

(*i*) Element should be of low resistance temperature coefficient

(*ii*) Should have high value of gauge factor

(*iii*) Should have linear characteristics

(*iv*) Should have very high resistance

(*v*) Should have very good frequency response.

Types of Strain guages

These are mainly of 3 types

(*i*) Wire strain gauge

(*ii*) Foil strain gauge

(*iii*) Semiconductor gauge

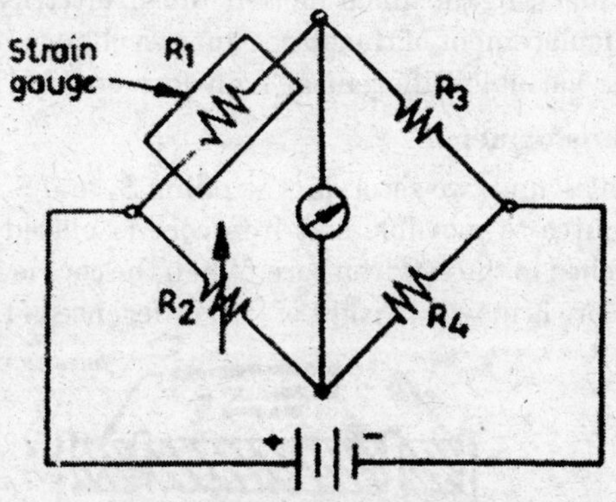

Fig 2.16 Wheatstone bridge

Since under strained contition, the resistance gets changed, this change in resistance is measured by precise measurement of low resistance, e.g. Wheatstone bridge method.

Let the initial resistance of strain guage under normal (unstrained) condition be R_1. All resistance R_1, R_2, R_3 and R_4 are taken equal.

Now let under strained condition change in resistance of strain gauge be ΔR_1

Now $$\text{gauge factor, } G = \frac{\Delta R_1 / R_1}{\varepsilon}$$

or, $$\text{Strain } \varepsilon = \frac{\Delta R_1 / R_1}{G} \quad \text{...}(i)$$

For balancing the bridge resistance R_2 is changed. Let this change be ΔR_2 which will be equal to change in resistance of strain gauge i.e. ΔR_1.

Substituting $\Delta R_1 = \Delta R_2$ in equation (i) we, get

$$\text{Strain, } \varepsilon = \frac{\Delta R_2 / R_1}{G}$$

i.e. ΔR_2 gives direct measurement of strain ε.

Example. *A strain gauge is bonded to a steel beam 0.1m long and has a cross-sectional area 4 cm². Young's modulus for steel is 207 GN/m². The strain gauge has an unstrained resistance of 240 Ω and a gauge factor of 2.2. When a load is applied, the resistance of gauge changes by 0.013 ohm. Calculate force applied to the beam.*

Solution:

$$\text{Gauge factor, } G = 2.2$$

$$\text{Young's modulus, } E = \frac{\text{Stress}}{\text{strain}} = \frac{s}{\varepsilon} = 207 \text{ GN/m}^2$$

$$\text{Area of cross-section, } A = 4 \times 10^{-4} \text{m}^2$$

$$\text{Resistance of gauge, } R = 240\Omega$$

$$\text{Change in resistance, } \Delta R = 0.013 \text{ W}$$

Length of unstrained gauge, $L = 0.1\ m$

$$\text{Gauge factor}, G = \frac{\Delta R/R}{\Delta L/L}$$

$$\therefore \quad \text{Change in length}, \Delta L = \frac{\Delta R.L}{RG} = \frac{0.013 \times 0.1}{240 \times 2.2}$$

$$\text{Stress}, s = \varepsilon E = \frac{207 \times 10^{9} \times 2.46 \times 10^{-6}}{0.1} = 5.092\ x\ 106\ N/m^2$$

Force, $\quad F = sA = 5.092 \,.\, 106 \,.\, 4 \,.\, 10^{-4} = 2.037 \,.\, 103\ N$

2.7.2 MEASUREMENT OF DISPLACEMENT.

Here an inductive transducer for translating the linear motion into an electrical signal is used. A plate is placed at right angles to the axis of the coil. The displacement of the plate causes a change in the inductance of the coil. Most widely used inductive transducer is Linear Variable Differential Transformer (LVDT).

Linear Variable Differential Transformer.

It consists of single primary winding P and two secondary winding S_1 and S_2 wound on a cylindrical former. Primary winding is connected to an a.c. source. A movable soft iron core is placed inside former. The displacement to be measured is applied to an arm attached to the soft iron core. When the core is in null position, equal voltages are in the two secondary winding. When the core is moved to right of left, difference of the two voltages is produced.

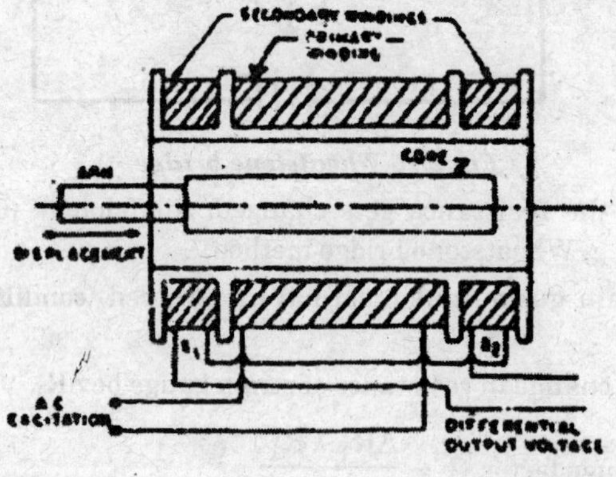

Fig. 2.17 Linear Variable Differential Transformer

In null position $\quad E_{s1} = E_{s2}$

$\therefore \quad E_0 = 0$

When the core is moved to left $F_{s1} > E_{s2}$

$\therefore \quad E_0 = E_{s1} - E_{s1}$

When the core is moved to right,

$E_0 = E_{s2} - E_{s1}$

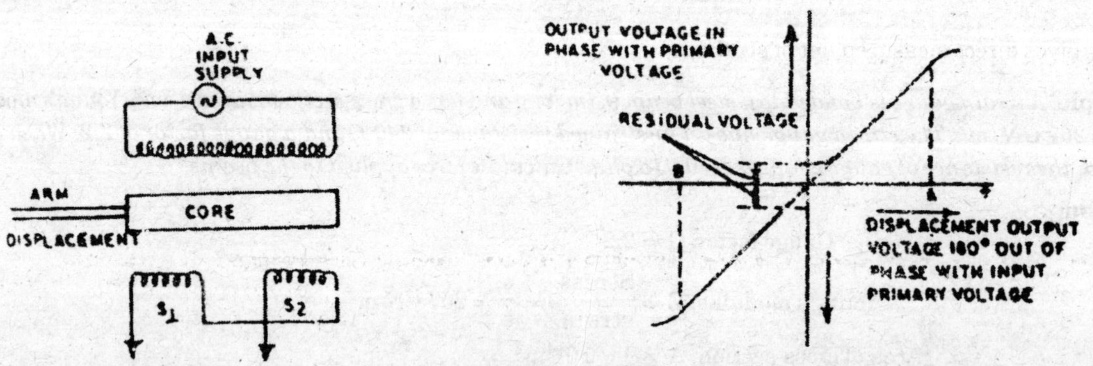

(a) Circuit *(b) Variation of Differential Output Voltage With Displacement of LVDT*

Fig. 2.18. LVDT

Hence, the difference of output voltages of secondary windings gives the amount of displacement.

Advantages

(*i*) Almost linear characteristics

(*ii*) Infinite resolution

(*iii*) Low power consumption

(*iv*) Output impedance is constant.

Disadvantages

(*i*) Affected by vibrations

(*ii*) Sensitive to stray magnetic fields

(*iii*) Performance affected by temperature

(*iv*) Larger displacements necessary for appreciable differential output.

2.7.3 Measurement of Force or Pressure

The measurement of force or pressure is done by changing the applied force/pressure into displacement.

The sensors used for measurements of pressure/force are:

1. **Bellows.** These are corrugated shaped having thin walled tube. These provide high force and wide pressure range.

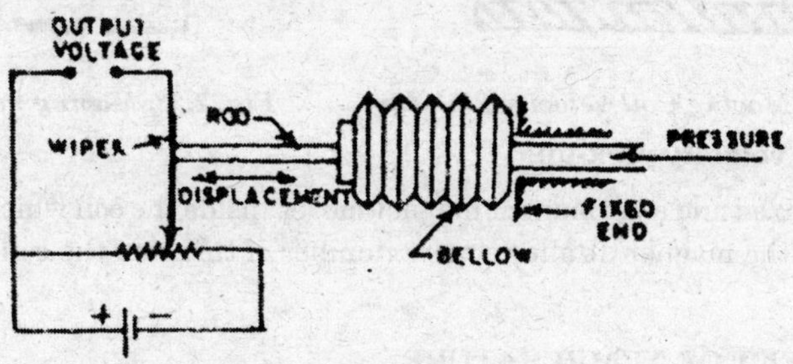

Fig. 2.19. Measurement of Pressure using Bellow and Potentiometer

2. **Diaphragms.** These are made of metal alloys such as bronze, phosphor bronze, beryllium, copper, stainless steel. ferrous nickel alloy etc. These have a high accuracy and good response.

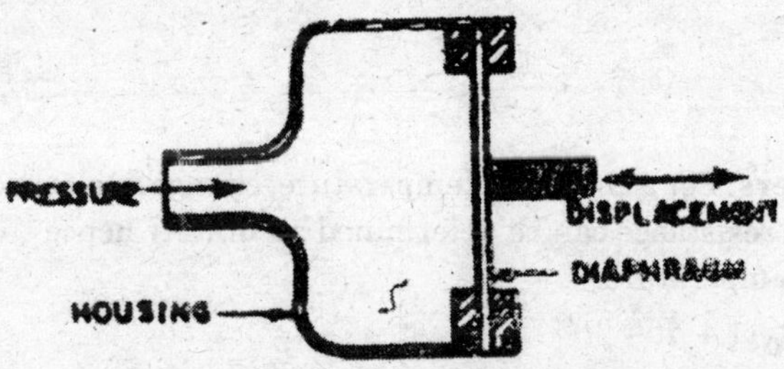

Fig 2.20 Diaphragm

3. **Bourden Tube.** These are curved or twisted metallic tube having elliptical cross-section and is made of a long thin walled cylinder.

(a) C-Shapted Bourden *(b) Twisted Bourden* *(c) Helical Bourden*

Fig 2.21

2.7.4 MEASUREMENT OF VELOCITY.

1. **Moving coil velocity pick-up**

EMF induced in a coil is given by

$$E = B\,l\,v \sin\theta \text{ volts}$$

where B = flux density of the magnetic field in Tesla

l = length of moving conductor in meters

v = velocity of conductor in the magnetic field in m/s

θ = angle of conductor with the direction of field

Since B, l and θ are constant, induced emf is a function of its velocity.

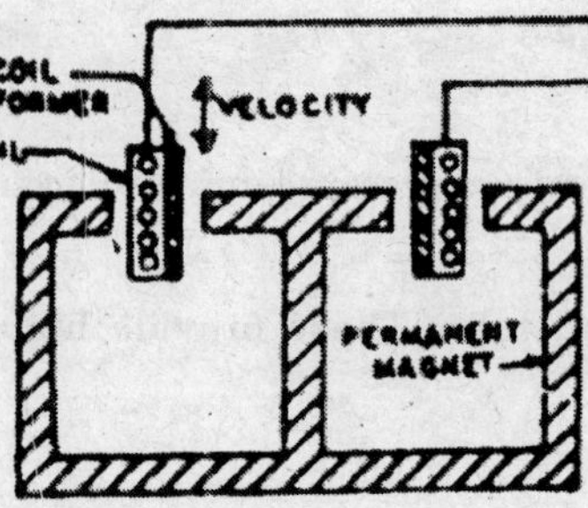

Fig. 2.22. Moving Coil Velocity Pick-Up

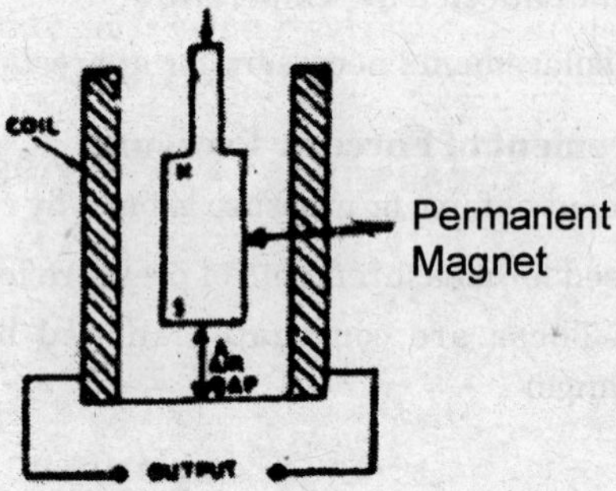

Fig. 2.23. Moving magnet Velocity Pick-Up

2. **Moving magnet velocity pick-up**

Here coil is kept fixed and a permanent magnet moves inside the coil which induces an emf in the coil proportional to the velocity of the magnet. It allows more number of turns on the coil which ensures a sufficient high output voltage.

2.7.5 MEASUREMENT OF TEMPERATURE

Following devices are used of temperature measure-ment.

1. Resistance Thermometers
2. Thermistors
3. Radiation Pyrometers
4. Optical Pyrometers
5. Thermo Couples

1. **Resistance Thermometers.** For a change in temperature, change in electrical resistance is constant for a given conductor. Since electrical resistance can be determined accurately hence the temperature. Platinum is mostly used for measurement of temperature.

$$R_t = R_0 (1 + \alpha t - \beta t^2)$$

where R_t = resistance of resistor at t°C

R_0 = resistance of resistor at 0°C

α and β are constants

For Platinum $\alpha = 0.0037$

$\beta = 0.00000057$

For small changes in temperature

$$R_t = R_0 (1 + kt)$$

where k = fundamental constant $= \dfrac{R_{100} - R_0}{100 R_0}$

$$\therefore \quad R_t = R_0\left[1 + \frac{R_{100} - R_0}{100R_0} t\right] = R_0 + \frac{R_{100} - R_0}{100} t$$

Advantages :

(*i*) Wide temperature range.

(*ii*) Good stability accuracy

(*iii*) Fast response

Disadvantages :

(*i*) Expensive

(*ii*) Large in size

(*iii*) Required power supply and bridge circuit sets.

2. **Thermistors.** These are semiconductor devices which have a negative temperature coefficient of resistance. These are widely used in the low temperature range applications (–100°C to 300°C).

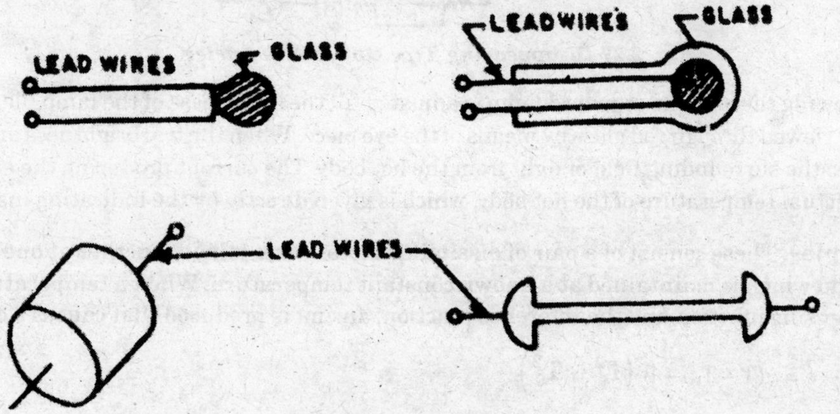

Fig. 2.24. Thermistors

The non- linear resistance temperature relation is given by

$$R_1 = R_0\left[\beta\left(\frac{1}{T_1} - \frac{1}{T_0}\right)\right]$$

where R_1 = Resistance at temperature T_1

R_0 = Resistance at temperature T_0

β = characteristic constant of material

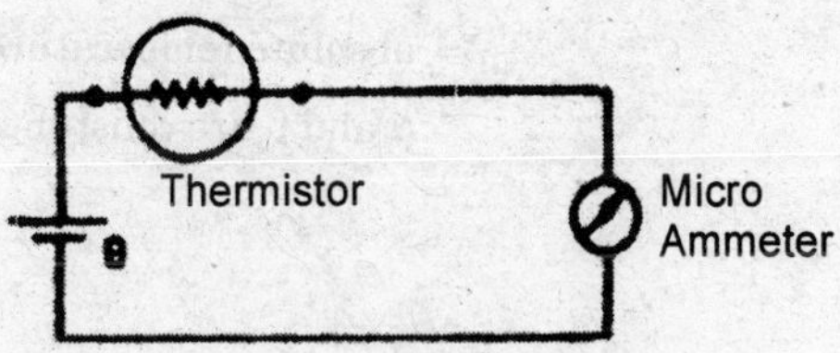

Fig. 2.25. Thermistors connection

Temperature in measured by connecting a thermistor in series with a battery and a micro ammeter. The micro-ammeter is calibrated to read temperature directly in case of using constant emf battery and limited current.

Pyrometers. These are used for measurement of high temperatures of the order of thousand.

3. **Radiation Pyrometers.** These operate on the basis of Stefan-Bolt law of radiation which states that the energy radiated by a noted black body (i.e. a body for which the radiated energy for a given temperature is maximum) is proportional to the fourth power of its absolute temperature

$$W = K\left(T_2^4 - T_1^4\right)$$

where W = energy per square metre/second need by the cool body

K = constant = 1.279×10^{-8}*gm* calories/second/sq meter

T_1 = absolute temperature of a colder body near it

T_2 = absolute temperature of a hot body near it

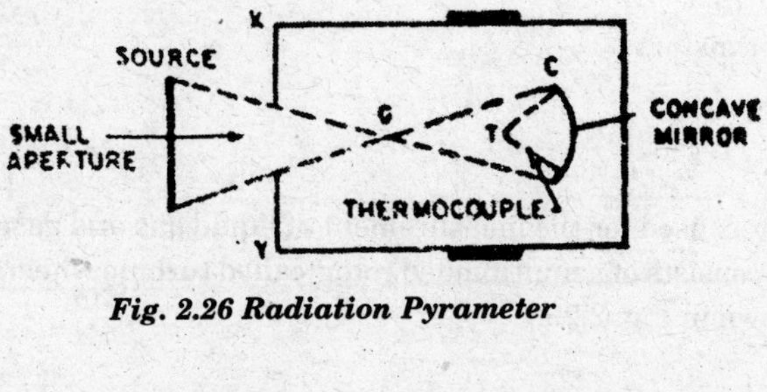

Fig. 2.26 Radiation Pyrameter

4. **Optical Pyrometers.** It consists of a standard lamp fed from source of variable voltage, galvanometer calibrated to read temperature directly by measurement of current flowing through the lamp and lens which is used to focus the light radiated from the hot body upon the plane containing the lamp filament. The light from the hot body and that from the lamp are viewed though an eye piece. A red glass is used to made the light monochromatic, which is very helpful in comparing brightness.

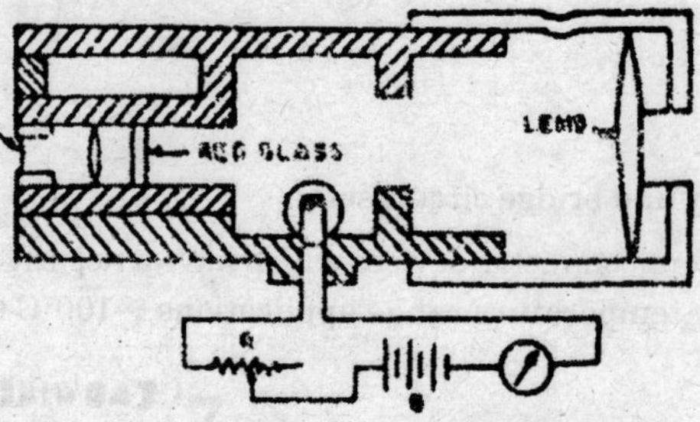

Fig. 2.27 Disappearing Type Optical Pyrometer

The current flowing through the standard lamp is adjusted till the brightness of the lamp filament is equal to that of the hot body viewed through red glass by means of the eye piece. When the two brightness are equal, the filament disappears into the surrounding field of light from the hot body. The current producing the equality of brightness indicates the actual temperature of the hot body, which is given directly by the indicating instrument.

5. **Thermo Couples.** These consist of a pair of dissimilar metal wires joined together at one end and terminated at the other end which is maintained at a known constant temperature. When a temperature difference exists between the sensing junction and the reference junction, an emf is produced that causes a current in the circuit

$$e = \alpha(T - T_0) + \beta\left(T^2 - T_0^2\right)$$

where e = thermo-electric emf in volts

T = absolute temperature of hot junction

T_0 = absolute temperature of cold junction

α and β are constants

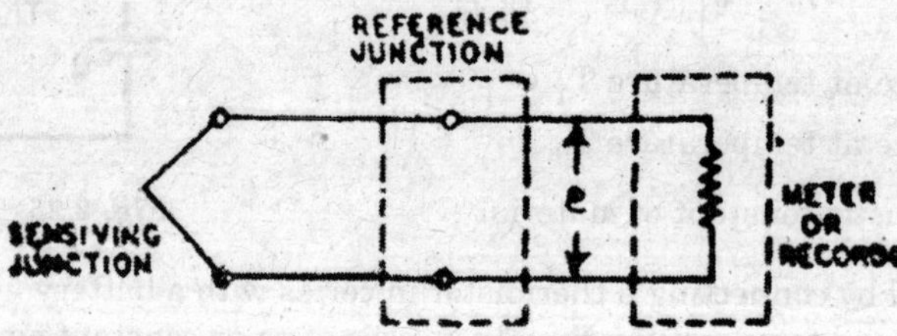

Fig. 2.28. Basic Thermocouple circuit

2.7.6 MEASUREMENT OF FLOW.

There are a number of devices sensing the rate of fluid flow. These operate on the principle of placing an obstruction in the path of fluid causing a change in fluid pressure which is dependent upon the rate of flow. By measuring the difference in pressure before and after the obstruction by means of differential pressure senson, the rate of flow may be determined.

Some flow meters are used for measuring the fluid flow :

(1) Turbine Flow Meter

(2) Hot Wire Anemometer

(3) Magnetic Flow Meter

(4) Flow Meter Using Thermistors

(5) Nucleonic Flow Meters.

1. **Turbine Flow Meter.**

The turbine flow meter is used for the measurement of liquid gas and gases of very low flow rate. It works on the principle of turbine. It consists of a multibladed rotor (called turbine wheel) which is mounted 90° to the axis of the following liquid as shown in Fig. 2.29.

The rotor is supported by the ball or sleeve bearing on a shaft which is retained in the flow meter housing by shaft support section. The rotor is free to rotate about its axis. The following liquid strikes the turbine blades (rotor) imparting a force to the blade surface which causes the rotation of the rotor. At a steady rotational speed, the speed of the rotor is proportional to the fluid velocity and hence to the volumetric flow rate. The speed of rotation is monitored by magnetic pick-up which is fitted to the outside of the meter housing. The magnetic pick-up coil consists of permanent magnet with coil winding which is mounted near rotor into fluid channel. A voltage pulse is generated as each blade passes the magnetic pick-up coil. Total number of pulses give a measure of the flow. The K factor is given as number of pulses generated per gallon flow.

$$K = \frac{T_K f}{Q}$$

where K = pulses per unit volume

T_k = time constant in minutes

f = frequency in Hz

Q = volumetric flow rate in gmp

2. **Magnetic flow Meters.** These meters work on the principle of Faraday's law of electromagnetic induction, which states that whenever a conductor moves through a magnetic field of given field strength, a voltage is induced in the conductor proportional to the relative velocity between the conductor and the magnetic field. This concept is used in electric generators. In case of flowmeter, electrically conductive flowing liquids work as the conductor. The induced voltage is given by the equation.

$$E = C . B . L . V$$

where E = induced voltage in volts

C = dimensional constants

B = magnetic flux in WB/m^2

L = length of the conductor (fluid) in m

V = velocity of the conductor (fluid) in m/s.

The equation to convert a velocity measurement to volumetric flow rate is

$$Q = V . A$$

where Q = volumetric flow rate

V = fluid velocity

A = cross-sectional area of the flowmeter

Since $$V = \frac{E}{CBL}$$

Therefore $$Q = \frac{EA}{CBL}$$

For a given flow meter, A, C, B, L are constants.

Therefore $$Q = K . E$$

where $$K = \frac{A}{C\,BL}$$

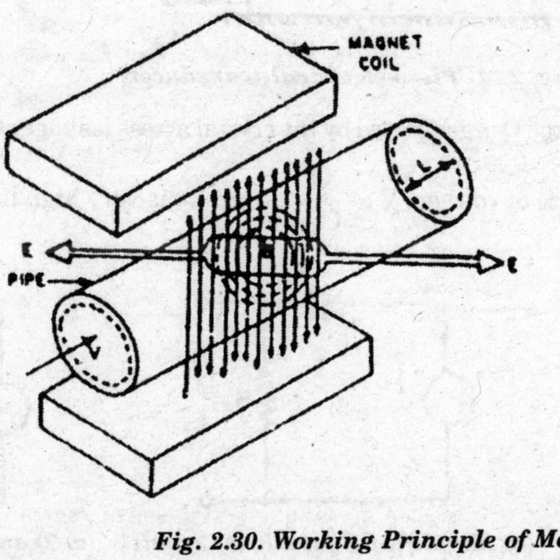

Fig. 2.30. Working Principle of Magnetic Flowmeter

Therefore the induced voltage is linear and directly proportional to the volumetric flow rate.

Construction. The magnetic flow meter consists of an electrically insulated or non-conducting pipe, such as fibre glass, with pair of electrodes mounted opposite each other and flush with the inside walls of the pipe and with the magnetic coil mounted around the pipe so that a magnetic field is generated in a plane mutually perpendicular to the axis of the flow meter body and to the plane of the electrodes. If a metal pipe is used, an electrically insulating linear is provided on the inside of the pipe. The basic operating principle of a magnetic flowmeter in which the flowing liquid acts as a conductor is shown in Fig. 2.30.

The length L is the distance between the electrodes and equals the pipe diameter. As liquid passes through the pipe section, it also passes through the magnetic field set up by the magnet coils thus inducing a voltage in the liquid, which is detected by a pair of electrodes mounted on the pipe wall. The amplitude of the induced voltage is proportional to the velocity of the flowing liquid.

Advantages of Magnetic Flowmeter

(*i*) It can handle slurries and greasy materials.

(*ii*) It can handle corrosive fluids.

(*iii*) It has very low pressure drop.

(*iv*) It is totally obstructionless.

(*v*) It is available in large pipe sizes and capacity as well as in several construction materials.

(*vi*) It is capable of handling low volume flows (with minimum size, less than 3.175 mm inside diameter) and very high volume flow rate (with sizes as large as 3.04m).

(*vii*) It can be used as bi-directional meter.

Disadvantages of Magnetic Flowmeter

(*i*) It is relatively expensive.

(*ii*) It is relatively heavy, especially in large sizes.

(*iii*) It must be full at all times.

(*iv*) It must be explosion proof when installed in hazardous electrical areas.

2.7.7 PIEZO-ELECTRIC TRANSDUCER

These are used for measurement of force and pressure. Materials used are quartz, crystal, rochelle salt etc. When mechanical force is applied on to it, then due to dimensional changes, a potential difference appears across the opposite faces of the materials.

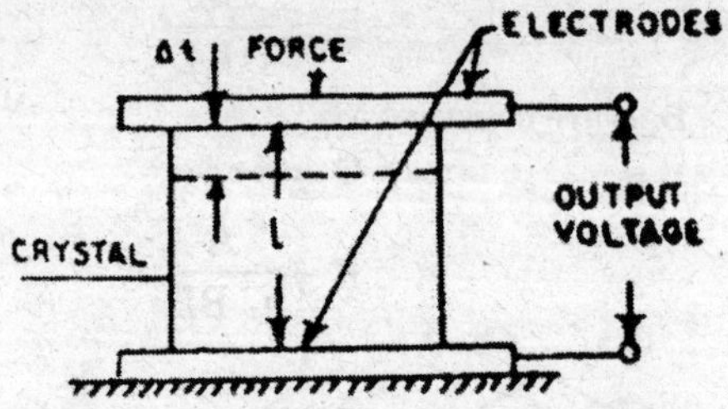

Fig. 2.31. Piezo-electrical transducer

Equivalent Circuit. In Fig.2.32 (*a*), charge Q is generated by the crystal across leakage resistance R_C and capacitance C_C. This is equivalent to a voltage source of voltage, $V = \dfrac{Q}{C_C}$, since R_C is very high it is omitted in Fig. 2.32 (*c*)

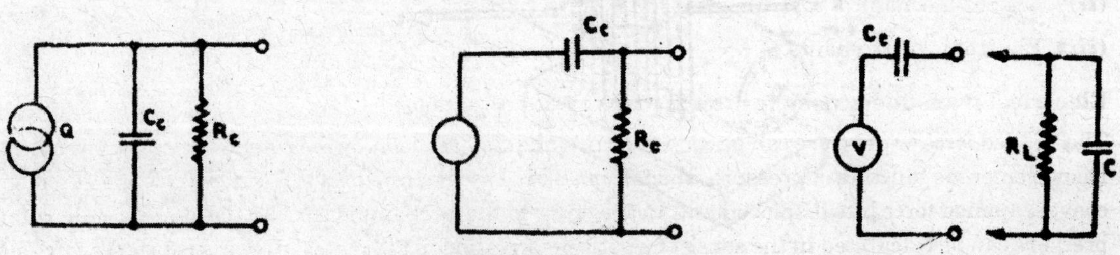

(a) Equivalent Circuit *(b) Simplified Equivalent Circuit* *(c) Tranducer with Electrical Load*

Fig. 2.32. Equivalent Circuits

Total impedance offered to voltage source

$$Zs = \frac{1}{j\omega C_C} + \frac{R_L}{1 + j\omega C_L R_L}$$

$$= \frac{1 + j\omega R_L (C_C + C_L)}{j\omega C_C (1 + j\omega C_L R_L)}$$

$$V_{out} = \frac{Z_L}{Z_s} = \left[\frac{R_L}{1 + j\omega C_L R_L} \cdot \frac{j\omega C_C (1 + j\omega C_L R_L)}{1 + jwR_L (C_C + C_L)}\right] V$$

$$= \frac{j\omega C_C R_L}{1 + j\omega R_L (C_C + C_L)} V$$

and

$$V = \frac{Q}{C_C} = \frac{dF}{C_C}$$

Putting this value of voltage V in above expression

$$V_{out} = \left[\frac{j\omega R_L C_C}{1 + j\omega R_L (C_C + C_L)}\right] \frac{dF}{C_C} = \left[\frac{j\omega R_L}{1 + j\omega R_L (C_C + C_L)}\right] dF$$

This relates the output voltage, V_{out} of transducer with applied force F.

2.7.8 PRESSURE MEASUREMENT

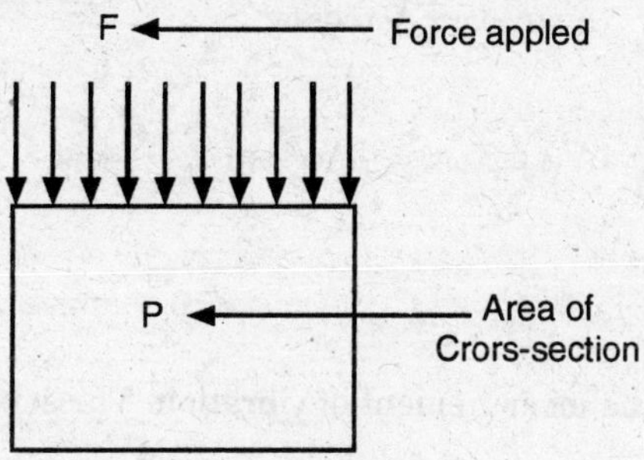

Fig. 2. 33

Pressure is represented by p and it equal to force per unit area.

i.e.

$$p = \frac{F}{A}$$

where, F = force applied

and A = Area of cross-section

The same principle is use for the measurement of temperature, flow and liquid level.

Device which is used for the measurement of pressure

(*i*) Mechanical Instruments.

(*ii*) Electro-mechanical instruments, and

(*iii*) Electronic instruments.

Electrical transducer used for the measurement of pressure

The applied force or pressure can be converted into the displacement by the elastic device which is primary transducer. Displacement is function of pressure which is measured by the transducer. The mechanical method have been used to convert applied force into displacement. In this process the force applied on the object and equilibrium is reached, the pressure can be calculated in the sense of elastic deformation in the material. For this process force summing method is used.

2.7.9 MEASUREMENT OF VIBRATION

The vibration monitoring has impotance in machines as power station turbine and generation to give an easly warning of impending conditions which may develop and lead to complete failure and destruction of equipment.

Calculation of Vibration

Shown in the figure. 2.34

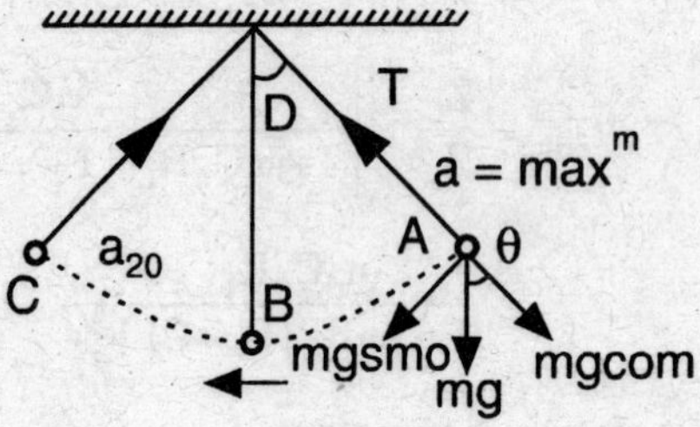

Fig. 2. 34

At a point A having velocity $v = 0$ and acceleration is maximum at A and minimum at B.

Velocity is maximum at B and zero at A = 0.

Consider the sinusoidal vibration,

the displacement, $x = \text{A} \sin \omega t$

where A = amplitude

ω = angular frequency

$$\text{Velocity } \frac{dx}{dt} = v = \frac{d}{dt}(\text{A} \sin \omega t) = \text{A}\omega \cos \omega t$$

$$\text{Acceleration, } \frac{dv}{dt} = \frac{d}{dt}(\text{A}\,\omega \cos \omega t) = -\text{A}\omega^2 \sin \omega t = -\omega^2 x$$

Maximum acceleration, $a_0 = -\omega^2 x$

Seismic Transducer

The seismic transducer is used for the measurement of vibration. The seismic transducer may be used in following ways :

(*i*) Displacement mode, and

(*ii*) Acceleration mode

The mass, spring and damper combinations is shown in the figure.

Input, $x_1 = x_{m1} \cos \omega t$

The equation of motion is,

$$\frac{\text{M}\, d^2 x}{dt^2} + \frac{\text{B}\, dx}{dt} + \text{K} x_2 = \text{B} x_1 + \text{K} x_1$$

The relative displacement, $x_0 = (x_1 - x_2)$

$$\therefore \quad \frac{d^2 x}{dt^2} + \frac{\text{D}}{\text{M}} \frac{dx_2}{dt} + \frac{\text{K}}{\text{M}} x_2 = x_0 \left[\left(\frac{\text{K}}{\text{M}}\right) \cos \omega_1 t - \left(\frac{\text{D}}{\text{M}}\right) \omega_1 \sin \omega_1 t\right]$$

The steady state response,

$$x_0 = x_2 - x_1$$

$$= \frac{\text{M}\, x_{ml}\, \omega_1^2 \cos(\omega_1 t - \phi)}{\left[(\text{K} - \text{M}\,\omega_1^2)^2 + \text{D}^2\, \omega_1^2\right]^{1/2}}$$

Amplitude of relative displacement,

$$(x_0)_0 = (x_2 - x_1)_0$$

$$= \frac{x_{m1}(\omega_1/\omega_n)^2}{\left[\left\{(1-(\omega_1/\omega_n)^2\right\}^2 + \left\{2a(\omega_1/\omega_n)\right\}^2\right]^{1/2}}$$

Let

$$u = \frac{\omega_1}{\omega_n}$$

$$= \frac{x_{m1}\, u^2}{[(1-u^2)^2 + (2a\,u)^2]^{1/2}}$$

$$\phi = \tan^{-1}\left(\frac{2\,a\,u}{1+u^2}\right)$$

Acceleration amplitude of vibration

$$a_0 = \frac{d^2x}{dt^2} = \omega_1^2\, x_{m1}$$

2.7.10 HUMIDITY MEASUREMENT

The Humidity is a measure of how much water vapour is present in unit volume of gass and it has absolute humidity, relative humidity, or dew point temperature.

Hygrometer

Hygrometer measures the relative humidity which is present in air.

Capacitive Hygrometer

The hygroscopic materials shows change in dielectric constant with change in humidity. The presence of water vapoure in air changes so that dielectric constant is also changes. So that change in capacitance can be measured with the change in dielectric constant. It also involve the frequency response.

2.7.11 VISCOSITY

The property of a fluid due to which it opposses the relative motion between its different layers is called viscosity (fluid friction or internal friction) and the force between the layers opposing the relative motion is viscous force.

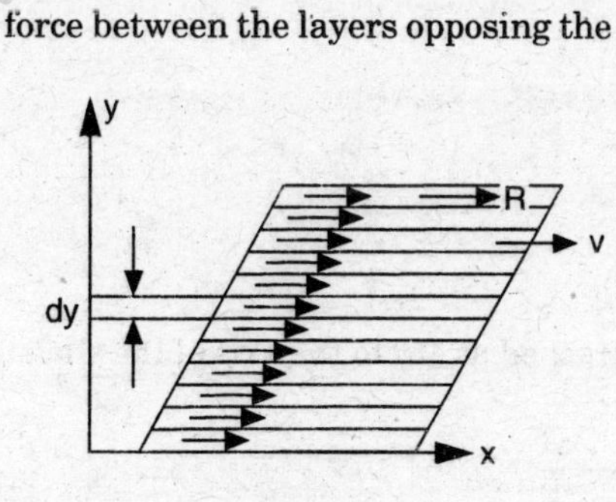

Fig. 2.35

The force between the different layer is directly propor-tional to the area (A) and velocity gradiant $\left(\frac{dv}{dy}\right)$.

i.e.

$$F \propto A\frac{dv}{dy}$$

i.e.

$$F = \eta\, A\frac{dv}{dy}$$

where η is a constant is called coefficient of viscosity.

Force, $F = \sigma \pi \eta r v_T$

where, v_T = terminal velocity = $\dfrac{2g(\rho - \sigma) r^2}{9 \eta}$

σ = density of liquid

ρ = density of solid body

r = radius

g = 9.8 m/sec^2

2.7.12 TORQUE TRANSDUCER

In this method torque is transmitted by a rotating shaft is based upon the angular displacement. The strain in sensed by transducer and is measured. There are number of device which is used for the measurement of relative angular displacement-strain by piezo-resistive variable inductance.

Strain gauge torque meter

Both the strain gauges are attached to the shaft at an angle of 45° to each other.

The figure 2.36 is shown below :

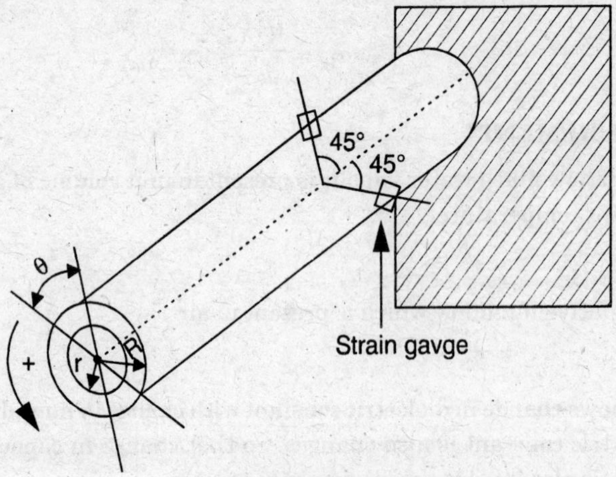

Fig. 2.36

$$\text{Torque,} \quad T = \frac{\pi G (R^2 - r^4)}{2L} \theta \text{ Nm}$$

where r = smaller shaft radius

R = outer radius

G = modulus of rigidity

L = length of shaft

θ = angular deflection of shaft.

Strain indicate when strain gauges attached at 45° to the axis of the shaft.

$$\epsilon_{45^\circ} = \pm \frac{TR}{\pi G (R^4 - r^4)}$$

2.7.13 OSCILLATION TRANSDUCERS

Oscillation transducers uses a force summing member to changes the inductance (L) or capacitance (C) of an LC oscillating circuit. The output frequency of oscillating circuit is depends on the value of L and C. When we change in L and C, output frequency should be changes and the changes in inductance (L) due to force summing member acting upon an inductive device and its output is modulated output can be demodulated and calibrated in terms of pressure or force applied.

Advantages.

(*i*) This measures dynamtic and static phenomena.

(*ii*) It is very useful in telemetry applications.

Disadvantages

(*i*) It has limited temperature and poor thermal stability.

(*ii*) It has low accuracy.

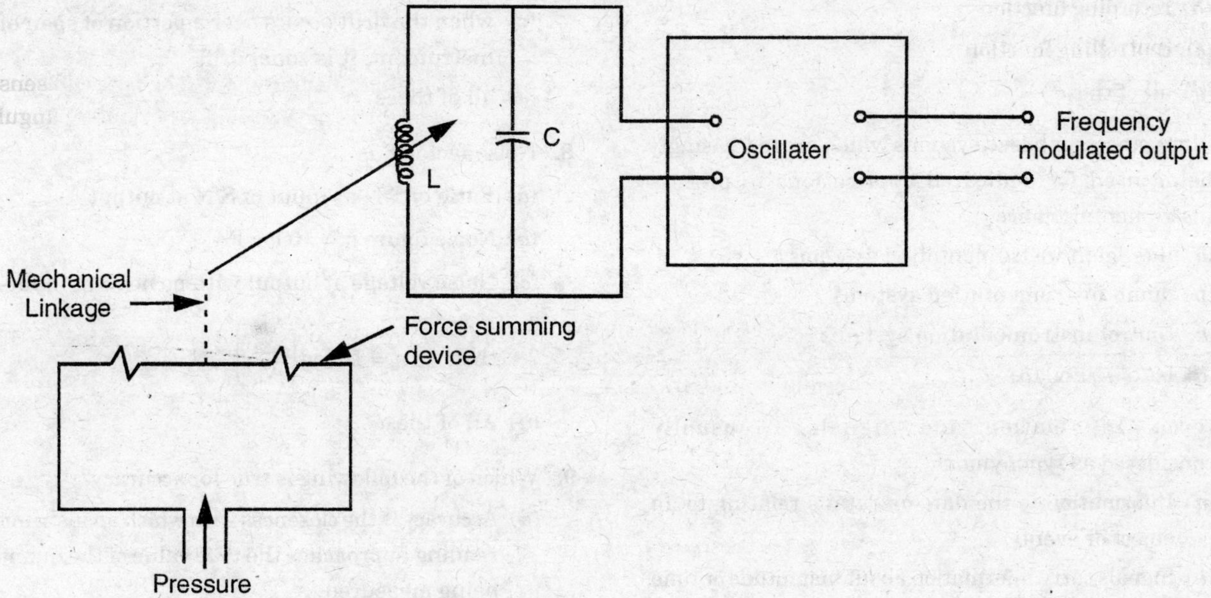

Fig. 2.37. Oscillation transducer

2.7.14 MEASUREMENT OF pH-VALUE

Many industrial processor require that the acidity and alkalinity of solutions be measured and controlled. The degree of acidity or alkalinity of aqueous solution is determined by the relative concentration of hydrogen and hydroxyl ions in the solution.

Hydrogen ion concentration is measured on a scale called **pH scale**.

pH value of a solution is defined as the negative logarithm of the Hydrogen ion concentration

or $$pH = -\log_{10} (H^+)$$

This scale ranges from 0 to 14

The measurement of pH value is obtained by immersing a pair of electrodes into the solution to be measured and measuring the voltage developed across them. In the pH cell, one of the electrodes, called the reference electrode is at a constant potential regardless of the pH value of the solution under test. The potential on the other electrode, called the measuring electrode is determined by the pH value of the solution. Thus the potential difference between the two electrodes depends upon the pH value of the solution.

OBJECTIVE TYPE QUESTIONS

1. Mechanical measurements are classified into
   (*a*) Mechanics type (*b*) Power type
   (*c*) Both (*a*) and (*b*) (*d*) None of these

2. Function of measurement systems is/are
   (*a*) indicating function
   (*b*) recording function
   (*c*) controlling function
   (*d*) all of these

3. Microprocessor based systems which are increasingly being used for dedicated applications in process instrumentation are
   (*a*) inteligent instrumentation systems
   (*b*) dumb instrumentation systems
   (*c*) control instrumentation systems
   (*d*) both (*a*) and (*b*)

4. terms "Information" and "Signals" are usually considered as synonymous
   (*a*) Information is the data or details relating to an object or event
   (*b*) Signals carry information about magnitude or time relating to an object or event i.e., a physical quantity
   (*c*) Both (*a*) and (*b*)
   (*d*) None of these

5. In the figure the circut RC is a

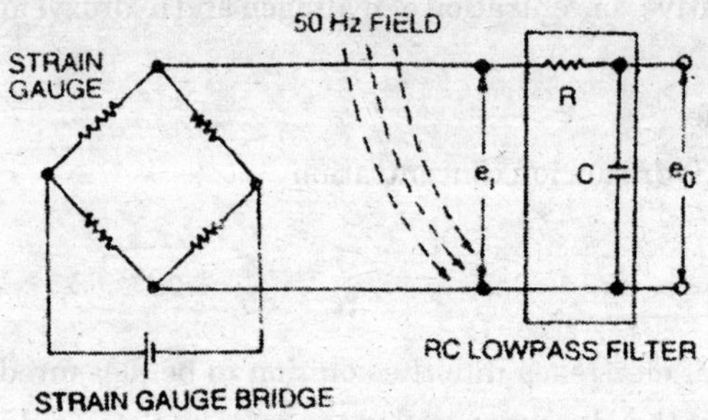

   (*a*) low pass filter (*b*) band pass filter
   (*c*) high pass filter (*d*) all pass filter

6. Repeatability
   (*a*) describes the closeness of the output readings, when the same input is applied repetitively over a short period under same conditions of environments
   (*b*) describes the closeness of output readings for the same input when there are changes in method of measurement under same conditions of environments
   (*c*) both (*a*) and (*b*) are true
   (*d*) none of these

7. In drift
   (*a*) when calibration gradually shifts due to slippage, permanent set, zero drift sets in
   (*b*) when there is proportional change in the indication all along the upward scale, the drift is called span drift or sensitivity drift
   (*c*) when the drift occurs over a portion of span of an instrument, it is zonal drift
   (*d*) all of these

8. Noise factor F is
   (*a*) Ratio of S/N at input of S/N at output
   (*b*) Noise figure $\eta_f = 10 \log F$
   (*c*) Noise voltage at output with no noise at input-V_n, then $\eta_f = 10 \log\left(\frac{V_n}{V_0}\right)^2$
   (*d*) All of these

9. Which of the following is true for accuracy?
   (*a*) Accuracy is the closeness with which an instrument reading approaches the true value of the quantity being measured
   (*b*) Point accuracy is the accuracy of the instrument only at one point on its scale
   (*c*) When an instrument has uniform scale, its accuracy may be expressed in terms of scale range
   (*d*) All of these

10. Accuracy is specified as ± 0.5% of true value. At 5% of full scale, error of the instrument will be
   (*a*) (±) 0.025% (*b*) (±) 0.5%
   (*c*) (±) 2.5% (*d*) (±) 25%

11. A known length of 100 mm, measured with a meter rod indicates values as 104, 103, 105, 103 and 105 mm
   (*a*) The meter rod connot be depended on for an accuracy better than 5%
   (*b*) It indicates a precision of (±) 1%
   (*c*) The instrument can be calibrated to read ± 1 mm dependable
   (*d*) All of these

12. Largest deviation from the mean is
   (*a*) range of doubt
   (*b*) possible error
   (*c*) either (*a*) or (*b*)
   (*d*) standard deviation

13. If maximum deviation of output from the idealized straight line is D_{MAX}, then

(*a*) Non-linearity

$$= \left(\frac{D_{MAX}}{\text{Actual reading}}\right) \times 100$$

(*b*) Non-linearity

$$= \left(\frac{D_{MAX}}{\text{Full scale deflection}}\right) \times 100$$

(*c*) Both (*a*) and (*b*)

(*d*) None of these

14. Match list I with list II and select the correct answer from the codes given below the lists.

List -I	List-II
A. A device whose output is enlarged version of output	1. Calibration
B. The act or process of making adjustments or makings on scale so that the instruments readings conform to accepted standards	2. Signal
C. Measures and generates an opposing effect to maintain zero deflection	3. Amplifier
D. An action to convey information	4. Null type detector.

Codes :

	A	B	C	D
(*a*)	3	1	4	2
(*b*)	2	1	4	3
(*c*)	3	4	1	2
(*d*)	3	2	4	1

15. The noise figure of an amplifier is 30 dB. If its input SNR is 100, then output SNR will be

(*a*) 0.1 (*b*) 1

(*c*) 10 (*d*) 100

16. A noise voltage of 10% of the signal voltage is applied at the input of the amplifier. If noise voltage at the output of the amplifier is 20% of the signal voltage, then noise figure of the amplifier will be

(*a*) $\frac{1}{2}$ dB (*b*) 2 dB

(*c*) 3.01 dB (*d*) 6.02 dB

17. A recording instrument requires 0.05 A to overcome initial friction and produce motion of the movement. The effect is

(*a*) hysteresis of 0.05 A

(*b*) dead zone of 0.05 A

(*c*) hysteresis and dead zone each of 0.1 A

(*d*) none of these

18. A self balancing potentiometer is connected to a spatial encoder, required to read 2000. linearity is 0.05%, then accuracy of the readout will be 1 part in

(*a*) 500

(*b*) 1000

(*c*) 2000

(*d*) 4000

19. In modern measurement systems, undesirable static characteristics are

(*a*) dead zone

(*b*) drift

(*c*) static error and non-linearity

(*d*) all of these

20. The output of a voltmeter under a set of environment is represented by $V_0 = a + b\,V_i$, where V_i is the input voltage, a and b are constant with $b \neq 1$. The theoretical input output relationship is represented by a straight line passing through zero. This is the case of

(*a*) zero drift only

(*b*) sensitivity drift only

(*c*) both (*a*) and (*b*) together

(*d*) none of these

21. Zero centre analog ammeter has a range of (–) 10 A to (+) 10 A. There is a detectable change of the pointer from either side of the scale, only if the current reaches a value of 1 A. The ammeter has a

(*a*) resolution of 1 A

(*b*) dead zone of 1 A

(*c*) resolution of 2 A

(*d*) dead zone of 2 A

22. In AC circuits, the connection of measuring instruments causes loading errors which may affect the measurand's

(*a*) magnitude

(*b*) phase

(*c*) waveform

(*d*) all of these

23. Johnson noise is caused by

(*a*) thermal agitation of free electrons carrying current thereby modulating the current

(*b*) vibrations into circuit through conductors

(*c*) randon emission of electrons across PN junction

(*d*) electromagnetic radiation into the circuit

24. The values of static stiffness and compliance in a measurement system determine the amount of

(*a*) current drain from a system

(*b*) potential drain from a system

(*c*) power drain from a system

(*d*) energy drain from a system

25. Backlash is

(*a*) unwanted signal tending to obscure the transducer signal

(*b*) maximum angle or distance through which any part of mechanical system may be moved in one direction without causing motion of the next part

(*c*) departure of instrument output from its calibrated value

(*d*) all of these

26. A pressure gage 0— 100 Pa has a guaranteed accuracy of 1% of full scale deflection. The limiting error while reading 25 Pa will be

(*a*) 1% (*b*) 2%

(*c*) 2.5% (*d*) 4%

27. In a PMMC ammeter, the deflection of the pointer is proportional to the product of flux density of the magnetic field produced by the permanent magnet and the current in the moving coil (B × I). When the strength of the permanent magnet becomes 90% of the original value, the meter gives erroneous reading resulting into error. The error is called

(*a*) Gross error

(*b*) Random error

(*c*) Systematic error

(*d*) Combination of these

28. When the mean value is $\overline{X}$ and standard deviation is σ, then measured value $\overline{X} \pm 3\sigma$ means

(*a*) approximately 99% of the readings lie within (±) 3 σ limits

(*b*) 26 readings out of 1000 will be outside (±) 3 σ limits

(*c*) odds for any reading to lie within (±) 3 σ limits are 256 to 1

(*d*) all of these

29. Uncertainty distribution is used to analyse

(*a*) single sample data

(*b*) multi sample data

(*c*) both (*a*) and (b)

(*d*) none of these

30. According to Chauvenet's criterion, a reading out of a set of n readings should be rejected, when the probability of obtaining the particular deviation from mean is

(*a*) less than $\frac{n}{\sqrt{2}}$

(*b*) less than $\frac{1}{n}$

(*c*) less than $\frac{1}{2n}$

(*d*) greater than $\frac{1}{2n}$

31. Dynamic response of a system consists of

(*a*) steady state response only

(*b*) transient state response only

(*c*) both (*a*) and (*b*)

(*d*) none of these

32. Desirable dynamic characteristics of a measurement system are

(*a*) fast response and fidelity

(*b*) fast response and dynamic error

(*c*) fidelity and measuring lag

(*d*) none of these

33. The time constant of a first order system is 20s. It is subjected to a step input. The settling time of the output is the time to reach (±) 5% of the final steady state value. The settling time of the system is

(*a*) 20s

(*b*) 40s

(*c*) 60s

(*d*) 95s

34. The steady state error of a second order system is 0.02. If both viscous friction constant and spring constant are doubled, then steady state error will become

(*a*) 0.0025

(*b*) 0.01

(*c*) 0.02

(*d*) 0.04

35. The first order thermometer used has a time constant of 50s. If it is subjected to a sinusoidal input at cycling of 0.002 Hz, Then time lag produced in the instrument will be

(*a*) 0.02s

(*b*) 22.3s

(*c*) 44.6s

(*d*) 50s

36. A second order underdamped system has a damping factor of 0.8. If a sinusoidal input of unit amplitude is applied to it, the resonant peak of the output will be

(*a*) 25%

(*b*) 91%

(*c*) 110%

(*d*) none of these

37. An inverse transducer is

(*a*) Potentiometer

(*b*) LVDT

(*c*) Piezoelectric crystals

(*d*) All of these

38. Active transducer is

(*a*) Photo emissive cell

(*b*) Photo voltaic cell

(*c*) Selsyn

(*d*) All of these

39. The lower limit of useful working range of a transducer is determined by its

(*a*) error

(*b*) noise

(*c*) both (*a*) and (*b*)

(*d*) none of these

40. A resistance potentiometer is a zero order instrument with increase of load to potentiometer resistance, its non-linearity

(*a*) decreases

(*b*) increases

(*c*) increase as square root of the resistance

(*d*) remains constant

41. Unbonded strain gages are

(*a*) exclusively used for transducer applications

(*b*) exclusively used for stress analysis

(*c*) used for unbonded strains only

(*d*) none of these

42. Metal foil type of strain gages are superior to wire wound metal strain gages because, they

(*a*) have a higher rate of heat dissipation capacity

(*b*) have a larger surface area which makes the bonding easier

(*c*) can be fabricated economically as a microelectronic circuitry

(*d*) all of these

43. Desirable property of a conductor material used in RTD is/are

(*a*) change in resistance per unit change in temperature should be as large as possible

(*b*) change of resistance with temperature should be a linear function

(*c*) resistance of the material should have continuous and stable relationship with temperature

(*d*) all of these

44. The resistance of thermistor at 300°K is 5000Ω. Its resistance temperature co-efficient is 0.04/°C. A measurement with a lead resistance of 10 Ω will cause an error of

(*a*) 0.025°C (*b*) 0.05°C

(*c*) 0.075°C (*d*) 0.10°C

45. Inductive transducers are used in differential configuration, because it gives output not influenced by

(*a*) external magnetic fields

(*b*) variations in supply voltage and frequency

(*c*) changes in temperature

(*d*) all of these

46. A LVDT has linearity of 0.05%. It is linear upto a displacement of (±) 5 mm. It has

(*a*) an infinite resolution and high sensitivity of the order of 40 V/mm

(*b*) good frequency response

(*c*) no effect due to stray magnetic fields

(*d*) a zero voltage at null point even if the supply voltage has harmonics and unsymmetrical configuration of the secondary windings

47. A capacitive transducer is working on the principle of change of capacitance with displacement. It exhibits non-linear characteristics. To make it linear, which of the following is used ?

(*a*) Differential connection

(*b*) Measure very small displacement

(*c*) OPAMP

(*d*) All of these

48. Piezoelectric transducers are active transducers and they use Quartz and Rochelle salt, because they

(*a*) are polycrystalline in nature

(*b*) are basically made of barium titanate

(*c*) do not have piezo electric properties in their original state but these properties are created by special polarization on them

(*d*) all of these

49. Moire fringes are used to measure rotary displacement alongwith

(*a*) contact type encoders only

(*b*) optical encoders only

(*c*) both (*a*) and (*b*)

(*d*) none of these

50. CMMR of a differential amplifier is 10,000. If it has a difference mode gain of 100, then common mode gain will be

(*a*) 0.001 (*b*) 0.01

(*c*) 0.1 (*d*) 1

51. Range of an analog transducer is 0 — 10 V. For a resolution of 5 mV, the bits of ADC will be

(*a*) 8 (*b*) 9

(*c*) 10 (*d*) 11

52. The measurement of a quantity or a variable is an act of comparison of an unknown quantity

(*a*) or a variable with a predefined acceptable standard which is accurately known

(*b*) or a variable with another quantity or variable

(*c*) with a known quantity whose accuracy may be known or may not be known

(*d*) none of these

53. Measurement finds application in

(*a*) automatic control of processes and operations

(*b*) engineering experimental analysis

(*c*) monitoring of processes and operations

(*d*) all of these

54. The desirable static characteristics in the measurement systems is/are

(*a*) sensitivity

(*b*) reproducibility

(*c*) accuracy

(*d*) all of these

55. Multimeters are provided with separate scale for low a.c. voltages to

(*a*) have high accuracy

(*b*) improve readability of the scale

(*c*) both (*a*) and (*b*)

(*d*) none of these

56. A voltmeter with a broadband width has

(*a*) high noise level and high sensitivity

(*b*) low noise level and low sensitivity

(*c*) low noise level and high sensitivity

(*d*) high noise level and low sensitivity

57. Q-factor of Q-meter is

(*a*) $\frac{\omega_0 R}{L}$

(*b*) $\frac{LR}{\omega_0}$

(*c*) $\frac{\omega_0 L}{R}$

(*d*) none of these

58. In a digital frequency meter, the schmitt trigger is used for

(*a*) scaling of sinuosidal waveforms

(*b*) providing time base

(*c*) coverting sinusoidal wavforms into rectangular pulses

(*d*) none of these

59. In a digital frequency meter the multi period average mode of operation, the main gate is held open for more than one period of the unknown signal so that

(*a*) resolution is increased

(*b*) range of the instrument is extended

(*c*) errors on account of dead time are eliminated

(*d*) period is extended in order that counters show more digits thereby an increased accuracy is obtained

60. A very accurate voltmeter gives an accurate reading when used for measuring voltage across a low resistance because

(*a*) meter sensitivity is too low

(*b*) meter senitivity is too high

(*c*) voltmeter is taking too low current

(*d*) higher scale has been selected

61. Which of the material is used for the swamping resistance that is connected in series with the working coil of a voltmeter ?

(*a*) Constantan

(*b*) Manganin

(*c*) Eureka

(*d*) Nichrome

62. A moving iron voltmeter coil has large number of turns of their wire in order to have

(*a*) high resistance and draw a current as small as possible

(*b*) high sensitivity

(*c*) effective damping

(*d*) large scale

63. Dynamometer type moving coil instruments are provided with

(*a*) eddy current damping

(*b*) pneumatic damping

(*c*) fluid friction damping

(*d*) electrostatic damping

64. Voltmeter is a galvanometer with.

(*a*) high resistance

(*b*) low resistance

(*c*) both (*a*) and (*b*)

(*d*) uncertain

65. The maching interpretable outputs for an analog transducer can be had from

(*a*) teletypewriter

(*b*) punched cards and tapes

(*c*) magnetic tapes

(*d*) all of these

66. If an information is required to be stored over a short interval of time, which of the following is used ?

(*a*) CRO with photographic equipment

(*b*) Storage type oscilloscope

(*c*) Single number devices

(*d*) Direct writing recorder or a magnetic tape recorder

67. Law of intermediate metals in thermocouples allows them to

(*a*) use meters for measurement without disturbing the circuit conditions

(*b*) use reference junction compensation

(*c*) both (*a*) and (*b*)

(*d*) none of these

68. When measuring strain, ballast circuits use a capacitor to act as high pass filter. This is done when

(*a*) both static and dynamic strains are being measured

(*b*) dynamic strains are being measured

(*c*) static strains are being measured

(*d*) none of these

69. Strain gauge rosettes are used when the direction of

(*a*) hoop stress is not known

(*b*) principal stress is not known

(*c*) prinicipal stress is known

(*d*) longitudinal stress is not known.

70. Output signal of LVDT for sinusoidal displacement of its core is a/an

(*a*) d.c. voltage

(*b*) frequency modulated voltage

(*c*) suppressed-carrier double-side band voltage

(*d*) amplitude modulated voltage with degree of modulation less than 100%

71. The pressure at a remote point is measured by an instrumentation system comprising a transmitter [specified accuracy (SA) within ± 0.3%], a relay (SA within ± 1.1%) and a receiver element (SA with ± 0.6%). The maximum possible error of the measurement system will be

(*a*) ± 1.1%

(*b*) ± 1.4%

(*c*) ± 2.0%

(*d*) ± 2.2%

72. A force digital transducers measures the pressure in the range of 0–200 N with a resolution of 0.1% of full scale. The smallest charge it can measure is

(*a*) 0.2 N

(*b*) 0.4 N

(*c*) 0.5 N

(*d*) 1.000 N

73. A thermocouple system has a time constant of 8 s. It is used to measure temperature of a surface varying sinusoidally between 400°C and 450°C with a periodic time of 60 s. The thermocouple will indicate the maximum temperature of

(*a*) 405.8°C

(*b*) 425°C

(*c*) 444.20°C

(*d*) 450°C

74. In a liquid level measuring system is shown in the figure, one leg of the U-type is calibrated. The measured liquid has a density of 900 kg/m². The relative density of mercury is 13.6. The sensitivity of the measuring system will be

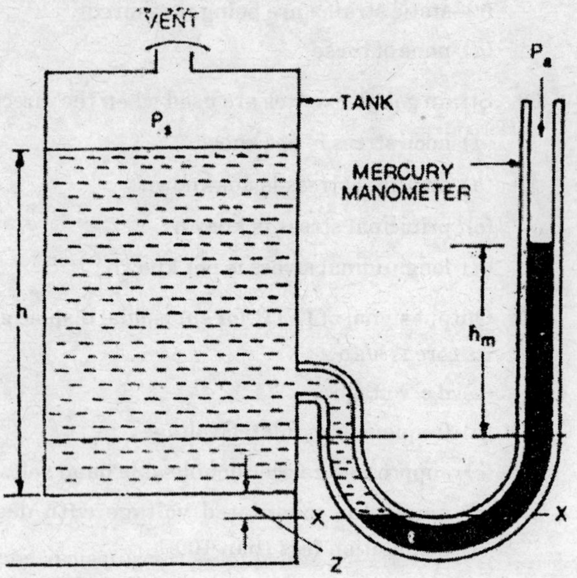

(*a*) 0.0342

(*b*) 0.0513

(*c*) 0.0756

(*d*) 0.0866

75. In a platinum resistance thermometer which is used to measure temperature, if the resistance temperature co-efficient of Platinum is 0.00392/°C, then its sensitivity at room temperature will be

(*a*) $\frac{0.00392}{20}$ Ω/°C

(*b*) $\frac{0.00392}{2}$ Ω/°C

(*c*) 0.00392 Ω/°C

(*d*) 0.00784 Ω/°C

76. A copper constant, thermocouple with reference junction temperature of 20°C is used to measure an unknown temperature. $(E_2 - E_0) = 0.7936$ mV. The reading of potentiometer is 2.877 mV. The slope of the curve is 0.04 mV/°C. The unknown temperature will be

(*a*) 46°C

(*b*) 70.7°C

(*c*) 86.6°C

(*d*) 92°C

77. A rotameter is calibrated to measure a liquid of density 1000 kg/m³. It has a scale range of 1 to 100 litre per minute. It measures the flow of gas of density 1.25 kg/m³ with a flow range of 20 to 2000 litre per minute. If value density of original one is 2000 kg/m³, then volume density of new float will be

(*a*) 200 kg/m³

(*b*) 250 kg/m³

(*c*) 500 kg/m³

(*d*) 6400 kg/m³

78. A venturi flume is built in a rectangular channel 1 m wide. It has a throat width of 400 mm. The upstream head is 570 mm, and measured head in throat is 500 mm. The discharge through the venturi flume will be

(*a*) 0.11 m³/s

(*b*) 0.22 m³/s

(*c*) 0.33 m³/s

(*d*) 0.414 m³/s

79. Water is flowing with a depth of 0.9 m over a rectangular notch 1.2 wide. In the right angled notch, height of the water will be

(*a*) 0.9 m (*b*) 1.0 m

(*c*) 1.1 m (*d*) 1.2 m

80. An aircraft is travelling at a speed of 800 km relative to air. If atmospheric pressure is 92.5 kN/m², temperature is 268°K and Gas constant is 287 J/kg K, then stagnation pressure will be

(*a*) 111 kN/m²

(*b*) 122 kN/m²

(*c*) 133 kN/m²

(*d*) 144 kN/m²

81. Natural frequency of a Seismic instrument is 4 Hz. If damping ratio is 0.66, excited frequency is 6 Hz, then due to proximity the error will be

(*a*) (–) 3.9% (*b*) (–) 1.95%

(*c*) (+) 1.95% (*d*) (+) 3%

82. A stroboscope is directed at a rotating disc having five equispaced radial lines on it. The highest flashing frequency at which a true pattern is observed is 2000 flashes per minute. A 5 line pattern will be produced at flashing frequency in flashes per minute are

(*a*) 400 or 500 (*b*) 666.7 or 1000

(*c*) 2000 (*d*) All of these

83. A variable reluctance type tachometer has 60 rotor slots. If counter records 3600 counts per second, then the speed is

(*a*) 60 rpm

(*b*) 360 rpm

(*c*) 1800 rpm

(*d*) 3600 rpm

84. A digital timer is used to determine the torque in a rotating shaft using single toothed flanges and inductive pick-ups. An applied torque of 1 kN produces a twist of an angle of one degree. When the shaft rotates at 500 rpm, the timer reading is 1200 Nm. If the timer displays a final unit of 10^{-5} s with accuracy of 0.05% of reading ± 1 in the final digit, then maximum probable error will be

(*a*) ± 0.1% (*b*) 1.1%

(*c*) 1.414% (*d*) 2.55%

85. A hydraulic testing machine is to apply a maximum force of 300 kN/m². The diameter of ram is 130 mm. For an arc of 270°, the pressure will be

(*a*) 22.6 N/m²

(*b*) 22.6 N/m²

(*c*) 22.6 MN/m²

(*d*) 22.6 GN/m²

86. A transducer measures forces in the range of 5 to 40 N. It consists of 4 strain gauge mounted on a cantilever 2 on top and 2 on bottom at a distance of 100 mm and 50 mm from the free end of the cantilever where force is applied. If maximum stress on the cross section at strain gauge is 75 MN/m², then thickness of cantilever will be

(*a*) 2 mm

(*b*) 4 mm

(*c*) 8 mm

(*d*) 12 mm

87. A balance is constructed as weight of beam is 50 g, distance of centre of gravity from fulcrum is 3 mm, length of each arm of balance is 200 mm and distance of Pulcrum from line joining the knife edge s is 0.1 mm. The uncertainty to measure a mass of 1 kg will be

(*a*) 0.01 g

(*b*) 10^{-5}

(*c*) 1 Part in 100,000

(*d*) all of these

88. A rectangular rosette is mounted on a steel plate having E as 200 GN/m², and Poisson ratio, v is 0.3. If measured strains are $\varepsilon_1 = +500 \times 10^{-6}$ and $\varepsilon_2 = +400 \times 10^{-6}$ and $\varepsilon_3 = \varepsilon_3 = -100 \times 10^{-6}$, then value of maximum principle strain will be

(*a*) (–) 161 × 10^{-6}

(*b*) (–) 100 × 10^{-6}

(*c*) 500 × 10^{-6}

(*d*) 561 × 10^{-6}

89. A Wheatstone bridge has $R_3 = R_4 = 100\Omega$. Galvanometer resistance = 50 Ω, Strain gauge $R_1 = 120\ \Omega$, The value of R_2 is adjusted for zero strain, $G_f = 2$. Battery voltage is 4 V. For a strain of 400 microstrain, galvanometer current will be

(*a*) 5 μA

(*b*) 10 μA

(*c*) 15 μA

(*d*) 20 μA

90. A micrometer screw gave the physical lengths as follows :

Length, x mm	Deviation, $\delta = x - \overline{x}$	δ^2
1.41	– 0.121	0.0146
1.45	– 0.081	0.00656
1.63	0.099	0.9098
1.54	0.009	0.000081
1.49	– 0.041	0.00168
1.51	– 0.021	0.000441
1.6	0.069	0.00476
1.55	0.019	0.000361
1.47	– 0.061	0.00372
1.66	0.129	0.01664
Sum 15.31	0.65	0.0586

Match the values :

List-I	List-II
A. Arithmetic mean	1. 0.065 mm
B. Average deviation	2. ±0.0516 mm
C. Variance	3. 0.0765 mm
D. Standard deviation	4. 1.531 mm
E. Probable error	5. 0.00586 mm²

Codes.

	A	B	C	D	E
(*a*)	4	1	5	3	2
(*b*)	4	1	3	5	2
(*c*)	4	5	1	3	2
(*d*)	4	3	5	1	2

91. A voltmeter is used to measure a voltage of 75 V. If 40% of readings are within 0.8 V of true value, then its standard deviation will be [P(0.5025) = 0.2]

(*a*) 0.4 (*b*) 0.75
(*c*) 0.8 (*d*) 1.592

92. If spring of a transducer deflects 0.04 m when subjected to a force of 8 kN, then the spring sensitivity will be

(*a*) $\frac{4}{8}$ m/kN
(*b*) 0.5 m/kN
(*c*) 0.05 m/kN
(*d*) 0.005 m/kN

93. Let discharge co-efficient,

$$C_d = \frac{m}{t \rho A \sqrt{2gh}}.$$

For m = (400 ± 0.25) kg, t = (600 ± 2) s, h = (3.65 ± 0.003) m, g = (9.807 ± 0.1%) m/s², ρ = (100 ± 0.1%) kg/m³, A = (1.23 × 10^{-4} ± 0.4%) m², the relative error in discharge co-efficient is

(*a*) ± 0.00987
(*b*) ± 0.01037
(*c*) ± 0.01237
(*d*) ± 0.01287

94. A McLeod gage has volume of bulbs and measuring capillary, V = 100 × 10^{-6} m³ and diameter of measuring capillary is 1 mm. For the reading of 60 mm, the pressure will be

(*a*) 14 μm (*b*) 28 μm
(*c*) 42 μm (*d*) 56 μm

95. An industrial mercury manometer consists of a well on the LHS and a circular tube on RHS. A float is placed in the well. EM transducer is used to measure the displacement of the fluid. When a pressure of 100 kN/m² is applied the float moves through a distance of 10 mm. Density of mercury is 13.6 × 10³ kg/m³. If diameter of float in the well is 40 mm, then diameter of float will be

(*a*) 2.33 mm
(*b*) 3.33 mm
(*c*) 4.66 mm
(*d*) 6.66 mm

96. A manometer uses transformer oil (sp. gr. = 0.864) as measuring fluid. The scale is graduated in mm of water. The well has a bore of 20 mm and tube of bore 2 mm. When a pressure of 1 mm head of water (9.81 Pa) is applied to give an inclined deflection of 4 mm, the angle of inclination is

(*a*) 8.33°
(*b*) 16.66°
(*c*) $\frac{\pi}{8}$ rad
(*d*) $\frac{\pi}{6}$ rad

97. A thermistor has resistance of 1 kΩ. Its temperature co-efficient is 4.5%/°K. Around 300°K, it has an internal temperature rise of 0.2°K/mW. It is included in a d.c. bridge with 3 fixed resistances, each having a value of 1 kΩ. If the rise of internal temperature is limited to 0.1°K, the value of its maximum voltage sensitivity will be

(*a*) 0.159 mV/°K
(*b*) 1.159 mV/°K
(*c*) 15.9 mV/°K
(*d*) 159 mV/°K

98. A piezoelectirc transducer has a capacitance of 1000 pF and a charge sensitivity of 40 × 10^{-3} C/m. The capacitance of connecting cable is 300 pF and that if oscilloscope for readout is 50 pF parallel with a resistance of 1 MΩ. The sensitivity of transducer alone is

(*a*) 10 × 10^{6} V/m
(*b*) 20 × 10^{6} V/m
(*c*) 30 × 10^{6} V/m
(*d*) 40 × 10^{6} V/m

99. A torsion bar of radius 15 mm is used to measure a torque of 120 Nm. If shear modulus of mild steel is 80 GN/m², the angle of twist will be

(*a*) 0.2832 degree
(*b*) 0.2832 rad
(*c*) 0.02832 rad
(*d*) 0.2832 × 10^{-3} rad

100. A batch of capacitors have a mean value of 100.00 pF and a standard deviation, σ of 0.2 pF. If probability corresponding to 2σ is 0.9546, then value of odds that randomly selected capacitor will lie within (100.00 ± 0.40) pF will be

(*a*) 1 to 1

(*b*) 2 to 1

(*c*) 21 to 1

(*d*) 99 to 1

ANSWERS

1. (*c*)	**2.** (*d*)	**3.** (*c*)	**4.** (*c*)	**5.** (*a*)	**6.** (*a*)	**7.** (*d*)	**8.** (*d*)	**9.** (*d*)	**10.** (*a*)
11. (*d*)	**12.** (*c*)	**13.** (*c*)	**14.** (*a*)	**15.** (*a*)	**16.** (*d*)	**17.** (*b*)	**18.** (*c*)	**19.** (*d*)	**20.** (*c*)
21. (*d*)	**22.** (*d*)	**23.** (*a*)	**24.** (*d*)	**25.** (*b*)	**26.** (*d*)	**27.** (*c*)	**28.** (*d*)	**29.** (*c*)	**30.** (*c*)
31. (*c*)	**32.** (*a*)	**33.** (*c*)	**34.** (*c*)	**35.** (*c*)	**36.** (*d*)	**37.** (*c*)	**38.** (*b*)	**39.** (*c*)	**40.** (*a*)
41. (*a*)	**42.** (*d*)	**43.** (*d*)	**44.** (*b*)	**45.** (*d*)	**46.** (*a*)	**47.** (*d*)	**48.** (*d*)	**49.** (*b*)	**50.** (*b*)
51. (*d*)	**52.** (*a*)	**53.** (*d*)	**54.** (*d*)	**55.** (*d*)	**56.** (*d*)	**57.** (*c*)	**58.** (*c*)	**59.** (*d*)	**60.** (*a*)
61. (*b*)	**62.** (*a*)	**63.** (*b*)	**64.** (*a*)	**65.** (*d*)	**66.** (*b*)	**67.** (*c*)	**68.** (*b*)	**69.** (*b*)	**70.** (*)
71. (*c*)	**72.** (*a*)	**73.** (*c*)	**74.** (*a*)	**75.** (*c*)	**76.** (*d*)	**77.** (*c*)	**78.** (*b*)	**79.** (*c*)	**80.** (*b*)
81. (*a*)	**82.** (*d*)	**83.** (*d*)	**84.** (*d*)	**85.** (*c*)	**86.** (*b*)	**87.** (*d*)	**88.** (*d*)	**89.** (*a*)	**90.** (*a*)
91. (*d*)	**92.** (*d*)	**93.** (*a*)	**94.** (*b*)	**95.** (*c*)	**96.** (*b*)	**97.** (*c*)	**98.** (*d*)	**99.** (*d*)	**100.** (*c*)

EXPLANATIONS

3. Intelligent instrumentation. It means use of an instrumentation system to evaluate a physical variable employing a digital computer to perform all or nearly all signal and information processing. In this system, after a measurement has been made of the variable, further processing whether in digital or analog form is carried out to refine the data to present it to an observer or other computer.

Dumb instrumentation. In this system once the measurement is made, the data must be processed by the observer.

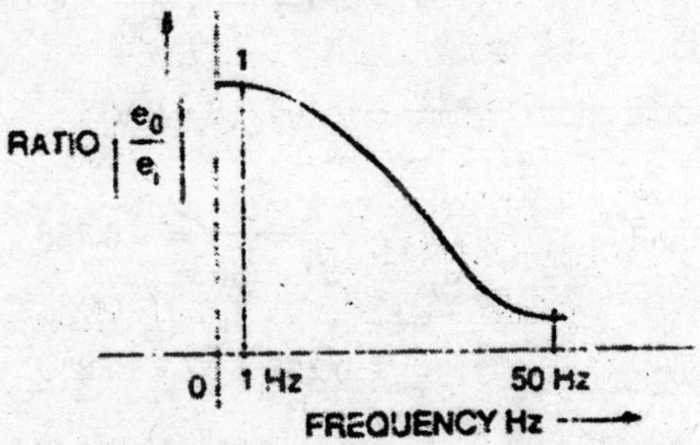

low-pass filter characteristics

5.

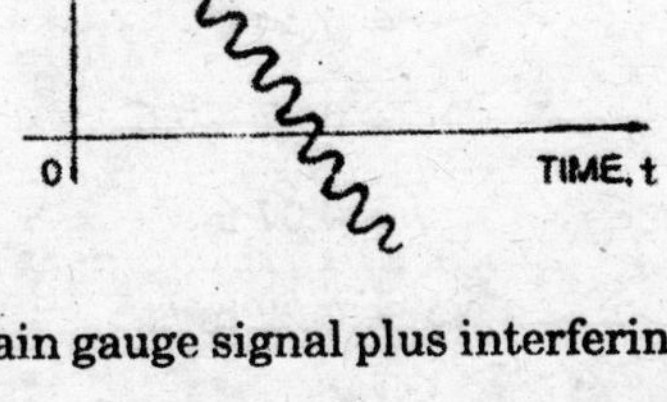

strain gauge signal plus interfering signal

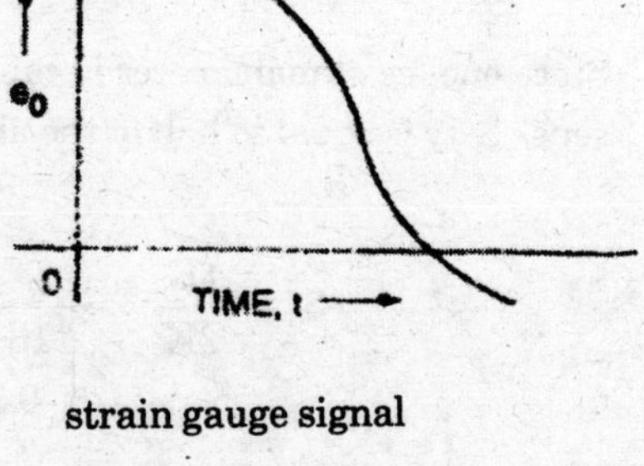

strain gauge signal

10. Error = $\frac{5}{100} \times \pm 0.5 = (\pm)\ 0.025\%$.

15. $n_f = 10 \log F = 30.;\ F = \frac{j/p\ S/N}{o/p\ S/N}$

16. $n_f = 10 \log F = 10 \log\left(\frac{10}{20}\right)^2 = 6.02.$

21. Dead zone = 2 × 1 = 2 A.

26. Error = 1 Pa. % = $\frac{1}{25} \times 100 = 4\%$

33. 3T = 3 × 20 = 60s.

37. When voltage is applied to the crystal, pressure is obtained as an output.

38. Photo voltaic cell produces voltage on incident sun rays.

71. $\pm(\alpha_1 + \alpha_2 + \alpha_3 +) = \pm 2\%.\ \pm(1.1 + 0.3 + 0.6) = \pm 2\%$

72. Resolution = 0.1% = $\frac{0.1}{100} \times 200 = 0.2$N.

73. The temperature oscillate between 400°C and 450°C with a mean value of 425°C. Amplitude is 25°C.

∴ Frequency of oscillation,

$$\omega = 2\pi f = \frac{2\pi}{t} = \frac{2\pi}{60} = 0.104 \text{ rad/s}$$

∴ $$\omega\tau = 0.104 \times 8 = 0.832$$

and $$\frac{\theta_0}{\theta_i} = \frac{1}{\sqrt{1 + (\omega\tau)^2}} = 0.768$$

or $$\theta_0 = 0.768 \times 25 = 19.2°\text{C}$$

Maximum temperature = 425 + 19.2 = 444.2°C.

74. We know $h = khm$,

∴ Sensitivity $s = \frac{hm}{h} = \frac{1}{k}$

Since one leg of manometer is calibrated, therefore, sensitivity is equal to half of the above value, i.e.

$$S = \frac{1K}{2K} = \frac{1}{2\left(\frac{13.6}{0.9} - \frac{1}{2}\right)} = 0.0342.$$

75. $S = \alpha R_0 = \frac{dR}{dT} = 0.00392\ \Omega/°\text{C}.$

76. $$(E_i - E_0) = (E_1 - E_2) + (E_2 - E_0)$$
$$= 2.877 + 0.7936 = 3.68 \text{ mV}$$

∴ $$T = \frac{3.68}{0.04} = 92°\text{C}.$$

77. $$Q = C$$

$$Q = C_d \frac{(A_t - A_f)}{\sqrt{1 - \left(\frac{A_t - A_f}{A_t}\right)^2}\sqrt{2g\frac{V_f}{A_f}\left(\frac{\rho_f - P}{\rho}\right)}}$$

Since, C_d, A_t, A_f and V_f are constant for same dimension, therefore

for liquid flow, $Q_1 = K\sqrt{\frac{(\rho_{f1} - \rho_1)}{\rho_1}}$ for liquid flow

and for gas flow, $Q_1 = k\sqrt{\frac{(\rho_{f2} - \rho_2)}{\rho_2}}$ for gas flow

$$\text{Scale ratio} = \frac{20}{1} = \frac{2000}{100} = 20 = \frac{Q_2}{Q_1}$$

$$= \left[\left(\frac{\rho_{f2} - \rho_2}{\rho_{f1} - \rho_1}\right)\left(\frac{\rho_1}{\rho_2}\right)\right]^{1/2} = (20)^2$$

$$= \frac{(\rho_{f2} - 1.25) \times 1000}{(2000 - 1000) \times 1.25}$$

So, $$\rho_{f2} = 500 \text{ kg/m}^3.$$

78. We know $$Q = \frac{C_{A2}}{\sqrt{1 + \left(\frac{A_2}{A_1}\right)^2}}\sqrt{2gh}$$

Here, $$A_1 = 1 \times 0.57$$
$$= 0.57 \text{ m}^2$$
$$A_2 = 0.4 \times 0.5$$
$$= 0.2 \text{ m}^2$$
$$h = 0.57 - 0.5$$
$$= 0.07 \text{ m.}$$

∴ $$Q = 0.22 \text{ m}^3/\text{s}.$$

79. For rectangular notch, $Q = \frac{2}{3} C_d L \sqrt{2g}\ H^{1.5}$

$$= 3.02\ C_d$$

For V notch, $Q = \frac{8}{15} C_d L \sqrt{2g}\ H^{2.5} \tan\frac{\theta}{2}$

$$\therefore \quad 3.02\ C_d = \frac{8}{15} C_d \sqrt{2 \times 9.81} \times H^{2.5} \times 1$$

or $H = 1.1$ m.

80.
$$\rho = \frac{P_a}{R_T} = \frac{92.5 \times 10^3}{287 \times 268}$$

$$= 1.2\ \text{kg/m}^3$$

$$V_{mean} = \sqrt{\frac{2}{\rho}(P - P_0)} = \frac{800 \times 1000}{3600}$$

or $P - P_0 = 29.6$ kN/m

$\therefore$ $P = 29.6 + 92.5 = 122.1$ kN/m².

81.
$$\frac{(x_2 - x_1)\,m}{x_{m1}} = \frac{\mu^2}{(1-\mu^2)^2 + (2r\,\mu)^2} = 0.961$$

$\therefore$ Error = (–) 3.9%.

82. The highest flashing frequency to give a 5 line pattern is 2000/minute. Others that give a 5 line pattern are a submultiple of the highest frequencies

i.e., $\frac{2000}{2} = 1000$, $\frac{2000}{3} = 666.7$, $\frac{2000}{4} = 500$

$\frac{2000}{5} = 400$.

83. $\frac{3600}{60}$ rps $= \frac{3600}{60} \times 60$ rpm $= 3600$ rpm.

84. $1° = 1000$ N

$\therefore$ Angular speed $= 360 \times \frac{500}{60} = 3000°/s$

or $1s = 3000° = 3000 \times 1000 = 30{,}00{,}000$ N–m

Final digit of timer represents

$$10^{-5}\ s = 10^{-5} \times 30{,}00{,}000 = 30\ N$$

$$\text{Error} = \frac{0.05}{100} \times 1200 = 0.6\ \text{N–m}$$

Total = 30+0.6 = 30.6 N–m

$$\text{Percentage error} = \frac{30.6}{1200} \times 100 = 2.55\%.$$

85.
$$A = \frac{\pi}{4}(130)^2 \times 10^{-6} = 0.1327\ \text{m}^2$$

$$\therefore \quad P = \frac{F}{A} = \frac{300 \times 1000}{0.1327}$$

$$= 22.6\ \text{MN/m}^2.$$

86.
$$s_{max} = \frac{6Fl}{bt^2}$$

Here, $t = 4$ mm.

87.
$$S = \frac{\theta}{\Delta W} = 0.571$$

Uncertainty, $W_0 = 0.25 = \frac{0.25\,\pi}{180}$ rad

In weight measurement,

$$\frac{W_\theta}{S} = \frac{0.25\,\pi}{180 \times 0.571} = 0.00764\ g$$

Counting other uncertainties,

Total uncertainty = 0.01 g = $\frac{0.01}{1000}$

$= 10^{-5}$ or 1 part in 100,000.

88.
$$\varepsilon_{max}, \varepsilon_{min} = \frac{\varepsilon_1 + \varepsilon_3}{2} \pm \frac{1}{\sqrt{2}}\,[(\varepsilon_1 - \varepsilon_2)^2 + (\varepsilon_2 - \varepsilon_3)^2]^{1/2}$$

$$= \frac{500 - 100}{2} \pm \frac{1}{\sqrt{2}}[(500 - 400)^2 + (400 + 100)^2]^{1/2}$$

$$= 561 \times 10^{-6},\ (-)\ 161 \times 10^{-6}.$$

89. Denominator,

$$C = R_1 R_3(R_2 + R_4) + R_2 R_4(R_1 + R_3) + R_m(R_1 + R_3)(R_2 + R_4)$$

$$= 7.7 \times 10^6\ \Omega$$

$$I_m = \frac{R_1 R_4}{C} G_f \varepsilon e_i$$

$$= \frac{120 \times 100}{7.7 \times 10^6} \times 2 \times 400 \times 10^{-6} \times 4$$

$$= 5\mu A.$$

90. A. Average mean = $\frac{15.31}{10} = 1.531$ ...(4)

B. Average deviation, $D = \frac{\Sigma(\delta)}{n} = \frac{0.65}{10} = 0.065$ ...(1)

C. Variance = $\sigma^2 = (0.0765)^2 = 0.00586 \text{ mm}^2$ ...(5)

D. Standard deviation, $\sigma = \sqrt{\frac{\sum \delta^2}{n}} = 0.0765$ ...(3)

E. Probable error = $\pm$ 0.6745 σ = $\pm$ 0.0516. ...(2)

91. Consider a normal distribution curve of 20% of the readings have a positive error and 20% have a negative error.

For P(z) = 0.2, z = 0.5025

$$\therefore \quad \frac{x - \bar{x}}{\sigma} = 0.5025 = \frac{0.8}{6}$$

or $\sigma = 1.592.$

92. $K = \frac{\text{Output}}{\text{Input}} = \frac{0.04\text{m}}{8 \text{ kN}} = 0.005 \text{ m/kN}.$

93. $$\frac{\partial C_d}{C_d} = \pm\left[\frac{\delta m}{m} + \frac{\delta t}{t} + \frac{\partial \rho}{\rho} + \frac{\partial A}{A} + \frac{\partial g}{2g} + \frac{\partial h}{2h}\right]$$

$$= \pm\left[0.000625 + 0.0033 + 0.001 + 0.004 + \frac{0.001}{2} + \frac{0.000822}{2}\right]$$

$= \pm$ 0.00987.

94. $$P = \frac{A_t h^2}{V} = \frac{\frac{\pi}{4} \times \left(10^{-6}\right)^2 (60 \times 10^{-3})^2}{100 \times 10^{-6}}$$

$= 28.24$ µm.

95. $P = \rho_m gh$

$dA = (h - d)a$

Now, $P \doteq P_m gd\left(1 + \frac{A}{a}\right)$

$$\therefore \quad 100 \times 1000 = 13.6 \times 1000 \times 9.81 \times \frac{10}{1000}\left(1 + \frac{A}{a}\right)$$

or $\left(1 + \frac{A}{a}\right) = 75$

or $\frac{a}{A} = \frac{13.5}{1000}$

So, diameter of RHS tube, $d = \sqrt{\frac{135}{1000} \times 40 \times 40}$

$= 4.66$ mm.

96. We know $P = g\rho_m R \sin\theta\left(1 + \frac{A}{a}\right)$

$$\therefore \quad 9.81 = 9.81 \times 0.864 \times 10^3 \times 10 \times 10^{-3} \sin\theta\left(1 + \frac{4}{400}\right)$$

or $\theta = 16.66°.$

97. Power dissipation due to change of 0.1°K = $\frac{0.1}{0.2}$

$= 0.5 \text{ mW} = \left(\frac{e_{im}}{2}\right)^2 \times \frac{1}{R} = P$

or $e_{im} = 2\sqrt{PR} = 1.41$ V

$\Delta R_1 = \alpha \Delta\theta R = \frac{4.5}{100} \times 0.1 \times 1000 = 4.5\Omega$

$\Delta e_0 = \frac{\Delta R_1 / R}{4} e_i$

Maximum output voltage = $\frac{4.5}{1000 \times 4} \times 1.41 = 1.59$ mV

Maximum bridge sensitivity = $\frac{\Delta e_0}{\Delta\theta} = 15.9$ mV/°K.

98. $K = \frac{K_q}{C_p} = \frac{40 \times 10^{-3}}{1000 \times 10^{-12}} = 40 \times 10^6$ V/m.

99. $\theta = \frac{16T}{\pi G_D^3} = 0.2832 \times 10^{-3}$ rad.

ANALOG CIRCUITS 3

3.1 ENERGY BANDS

Atoms together form a molecule, which exerts an influence on one another; as a result allowed energy level split into closely spaced levels. Similarly, when many atoms come together to form a solid, then splitted energy levels form continuous band of allowed energy level.

Any solid has many bands but according to electrical properties following two upperbands are important :

(1) Conduction band

(2) Valence band

Types of Solids

According to the energy band diagram (electrical property), solids are of following three types:

1. **Insulator.**

   It offers a very low level of conductivity under pressure from an applied voltage source. In insulators conduction and valence band are widely separated approximately by 15 eV.

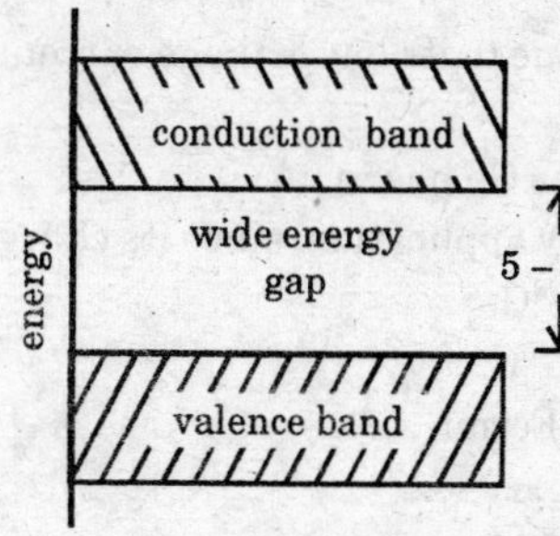

Fig. 3.1

   These requires very high electric field for transformation of any electron from valence to conduction band. Conductivity of insulator lies in the range 10^{-12} to10^{-20} $(\Omega - m)^{-1}$

2. **Conductor.**

   It support a generous flow of charge when a voltage source of limited magnitude is applied across its terminals. Conductors have overlapped conduction and valence band.

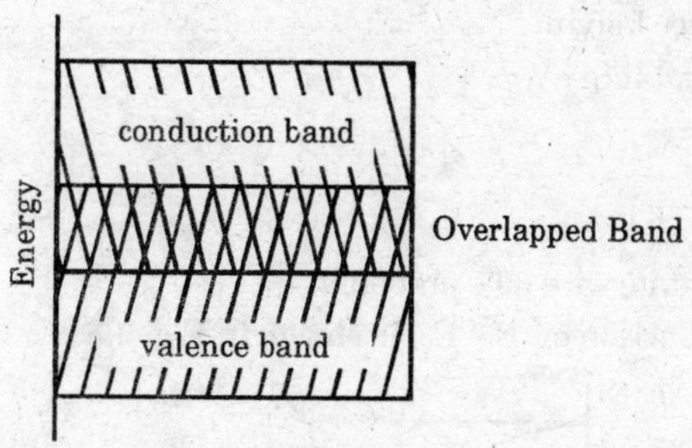

Fig. 3.2

   These have positive temperature coefficient and its conductivity lies in the range of 10^5 to 10^8 $(\Omega - m)^{-1}$. The overlapping in conduction and valence band in the metal provides lots of free electrons for conduction. Therefore a small electric field start conduction very heavily. When electron achieves its maximum velocity, it is called *drift velocity*.

   In metal or conductor, $V_d \propto E$

   $\Rightarrow$ $$V_d = \mu_e E$$

   where, μ_e = mobility of electron (m^2/V.sec)

   Current density of a conductor, $J = \frac{1}{A} = \sigma E$

This is called point form of *Ohm's law.*

$\Rightarrow \quad J = ne\,V_d = ne\mu_e\,E$

where, $ne = \rho_v$ = volume charge density

From above relation, conductivity, $\sigma = ne\mu_e$

Power density = J.E = σE^2

Conductivity of materials :

Material	Conductivity
Conductor	$10^5 - 10^8\ (\Omega m)^{-1}$
Semiconductor	$10^{-7} - 10^4\ (\Omega m)^{-1}$
Insulator	$10^{-12} - 10^{-20}\ (\Omega m)^{-1}$

Energy gap of materials :

Material	Energy gap
Conductor	0 eV
Semiconductor	1 – 2 eV
Insulator	5 – 8 eV

- Silicon is used in high power application due to its high temperature range, i.e. 200°C whereas Ge has a temperature range of 80°C.
- In low power application, Si is used due to its low leakage current.
  $\therefore$ Low power losses $P = I^2R$
  Leakage current of Si is in nA whereas Ge has in μA.
- Ge finds application in high frequency application, since its charge carriers are more mobile than Si.
- Conductivity of Si is increased by 8%/°C.
- Conductivity of Ge is increased by 6%/°C.
- Radius of an electron, $r = 10^{-15}$ m = 1 Fermi.
- Mass of an electron, $m = 9.1 \times 10^{-31}$ kg.
- Radius of an atom, $r = 10^{-10}$ m = 1Å.

Energy distribution of electrons in metals :

Probability of electron lying in the energy state E is given by Fermi Dirac function

$$f(E) = \frac{1}{1 + e^{\left(\frac{E-E_F}{K_T}\right)}}$$

where, K = Boltzmann constant (1.38×10^{-23} J/°K)

T = temperature in degree kelvin

E_F = fermi level of the crystal in eV.

Fermi level (E_F) :

When $E = E_F$ then $\quad f(E) = \frac{1}{2}$

i.e. Fermi level represent energy state with 50% probability.

Fermi Dirac function $f(E)$ as a function of $(E - E_F)$ is shown in Fig. 3.3.

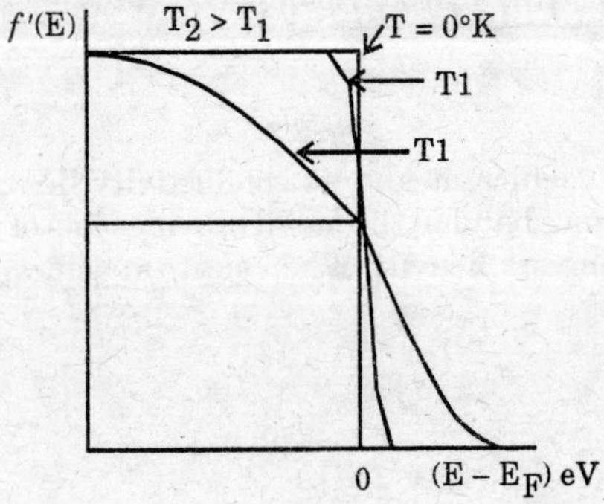

Fig. 3.3

- *When temperature, $T = 0° K$ and $E > E_F$*

  $f(E)$ is zero, *i.e.*, at absolute 0°K probability of electrons occupying energy level $E > E_F$ is zero.
- *When temperature, $T = 0° K$ and $E < E_F$:*

  $f(E)$ is one *i.e.*, probability of electron occupying energy level less than E_F is one.

  Fermi level, $E_F = 3.64 \times 10^{-19}\ n^{\frac{2}{3}}$

  where, n = density of metal.

3. **Semiconductor.**

   It has a conductivity level somewhere between extremes of an insulator and a conductor. It has almost filled valence band and nearly empty conduction band with very small energy gap ($E_g \cong 1$ eV) separating the two. These have negative temperature coefficient of resistance.

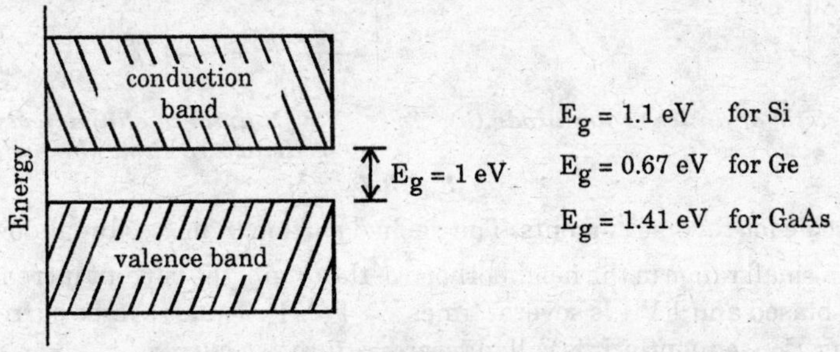

Fig. 3.4

When a suitable metallic impurity is added to a semiconductor, its current conducting properties changes appreciably. Hence, semiconductor is most important in electronic circuits.

3.2 DIODES

3.2.1. OPERATION

(*i*) Reverse Biased. A battery shown in Fig. 3.5 is connected across the terminals of a *p-n* junction in such a way that both the holes in the *p* type and the electron in the *n* type move away from the junction. The applied voltage increases the barrier potential to $V + V_B$, thereby blocking the flow of majority carrier. Although, in this case, there is practically no current flow due to majority charge carriers, yet there is a small current (a few μA) due to the flow of minority carriers.

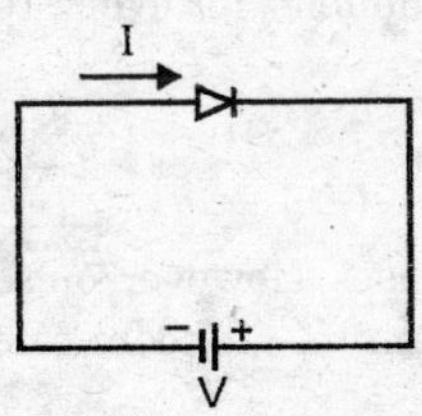

Fig. 3.5. p-n junction biased in the reverse direction

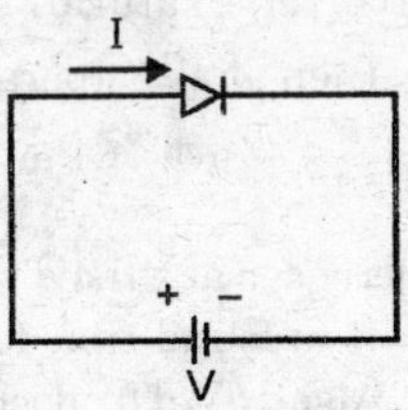

Fig. 3.6. p-n junction biased in forward direction

(*ii*) Forward Biased. When an external voltage applied with the polarity shown in Fig. 3.6, diode is called *forward biased*. In this case height of the potential barrier at the junction will be lowered by the applied forward voltage V. The equilibrium initially established between forces tending to produce diffusion of majority carriers and restraining influence of the potential-energy barrier at the junction will be disturbed. Hence, for a forward bias, holes cross the junction from *p*-type into the *n*-type region, where they constitute an injected minority current. Similarly, electrons cross the junction in the reverse direction and become a minority current injected into the *p* side. Holes travelling from left to right constitute a current in the same direction as electron moving from right to left. Hence resultant current crossing the junction is sum of the hole and electron minority currents.

3.2.2. VOLT-AMPERE CHARACTERISTIC

For a *p-n* junction, current I is related to the voltage V by the equation

$$I = I_o \left(\varepsilon^{\frac{V}{\eta V_T}} - 1 \right) \qquad \text{...(3.1)}$$

At rated current, $\eta = 1$; Ge, $\eta = 2$; Si

Symbol V_T stands for volt equivalent of temperature, and is given by

$$V_T \equiv \frac{T}{11,600} \qquad \text{...(3.2)}$$

At room temperature (T = 300°K), $V_T = 0.026$ V = 26 *m*V.

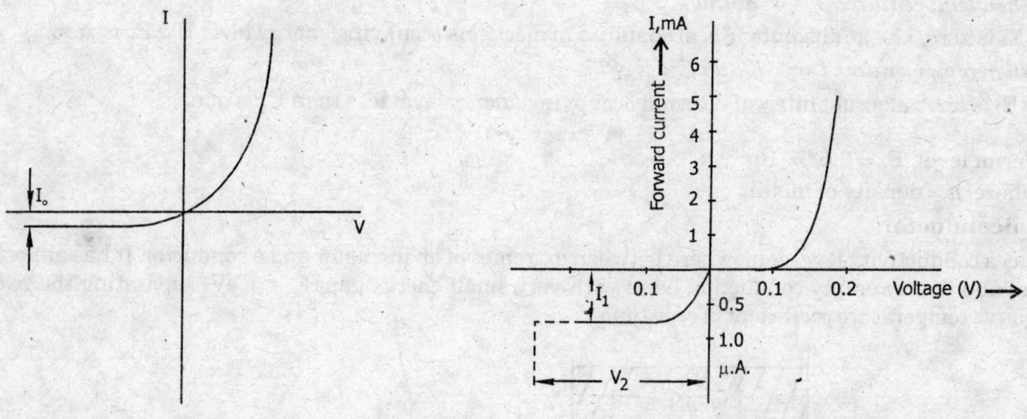

(a) Volt-ampere characteristic of an ideal p-n diode.(b) *Volt-ampere characteristic for a germanium diode redrawn to show the order of magnitude of currents.*

Fig. 3.7

Note : The expanded scale for reverse currents. The dashed portion indicates breakdown at V_Z.

Accordingly, except for a small range in the neighborhood of the origin, the current increases exponentially with voltage. When diode is reverse-biased and $|V|$ is several times V_T, $I \approx -I_o$. Thus, reverse current is constant, independent of the applied reverse bias. Consequently, I_o is called *reverse saturation current.*

Ordinarily, range of forward currents over which a diode is operated in many orders of magnitude larger than the reverse saturation current. To display forward and reverse characteristics conveniently, it is necessary, as in Fig. 3.7 (*b*), to use two different current scales. The volt-ampere characteristic shown in Fig. 3.7 (*b*) has a forward-current scale in milliamperes and a reverse scale in microamperes. The dashed portion of the curve of shows that, at a reverse-biasing voltage V_Z, diode characteristic exhibits an abrupt and marked departure from equation (3.1). At this critical voltage, a large reverse current flows, and diode is said to be in the *breakdown region.*

The volt-ampere relationship given by equation (3.1) contains temperature implicitly in the two symbols V_T and I_o. It is shown that theoretical variation of I_e with T is 8 percent/°C for silicon and 11 percent/°C for germanium. From experimental data, reverse saturation current increases approximately 7 percent/°C for both silicon and germanium. Since $(1.07)^{10} \approx 2.0$, reverse saturation current approximately doubles for every 10°C rise in temperature.

If $I_o = I_{o1}$ at $T = T_1$, then at a temperature T, I_o is given by

$$I_o(T) = I_{o1} \times 2^{(T - T_1)/10}$$

If temperature is increased at a fixed voltage, then current increases. However, on reducing V, I may be brought back to its previous value. It is found that for either silicon or germanium (at room temperature) in order to maintain a constant value of I. Also $|dV/dT|$ decreases with increasing T.

$$\frac{dV}{dT} = -2.5\ mV/°C$$

3.2.3. TEMPERATURE CHARACTERISTICS

Temperature coefficient of a diode is given as the percentage change in reference voltage per centigrade degree change in diode temperature. The coefficient may be either positive or negative and will normally be in the range ± 0.1 percent/°C. If then reference voltage is above 6 V, where physical mechanism involved is avalanche multiplication, then temperature coefficient is positive. However, below 6 V, where true Zener breakdown is involved, temperature coefficient is negative.

A qualitative explanation of sign (positive or negative) of the temperature coefficient of V_Z is now given. A junction having a narrow depletion-layer width, and hence high field intensity will break down by the Zener mechanism. An increase in temperature increases energies of the valence electrons, and hence makes it easier for these electrons to escape from the covalent bonds. Thus, less applied voltage is required to pull these electrons from their positions in the crystal lattice and convert them into conduction electrons. Therefore Zener-breakdown voltage decreases with temperature.

A junction with a broad depletion layer, and therefore a low field intensity, will break down by the avalanche mechanism. In this case, intrinsic carriers are relied upon to collide with valence electrons and create avalanche multiplication. As temperature increases, vibrational displacement of atoms in the crystal grows. This vibration increases probability of collisions with the lattice atoms of the intrinsic particles as they cross depletion width. Thus intrinsic holes and electrons have less of an opportunity to gain sufficient energy between collisions to start the avalanche process. Therefore value of the avalanche voltage must increase with increased temperature.

3.2.4. RESISTANCE OF DIODE

Since operating point of a diode moves from one region to another, hence resistance of the diode also change due to non-linear shape of the characteristic.

Types of Diode Resistance

On the basis of input signal, diode resistances are of following types:

(1) Static or d.c. resistance (R_{dc}).

If d.c. signal is applied to a semiconductor diode, then operating point of the characteristic curve will not change with time. Therefore, Q point will not move.

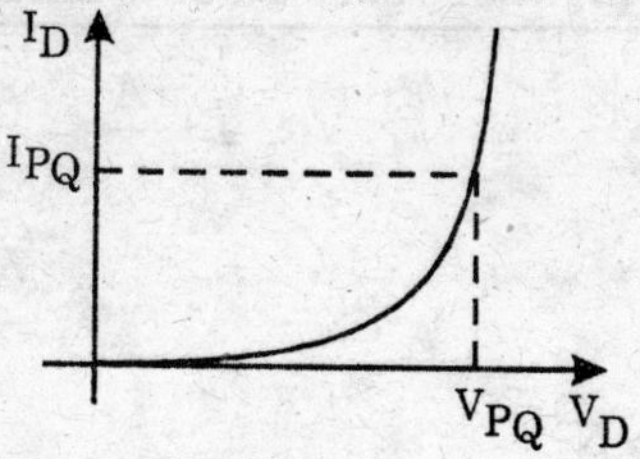

Fig. 3.8

From the above curve, static resistance, $R_{dc} = \dfrac{V_{DQ}}{I_{DQ}}$

(2) A.C. or Dynamic resistance (r_d).

It is a small amplitude a.c. signal at input vary the Q point and resistance offered to small signal

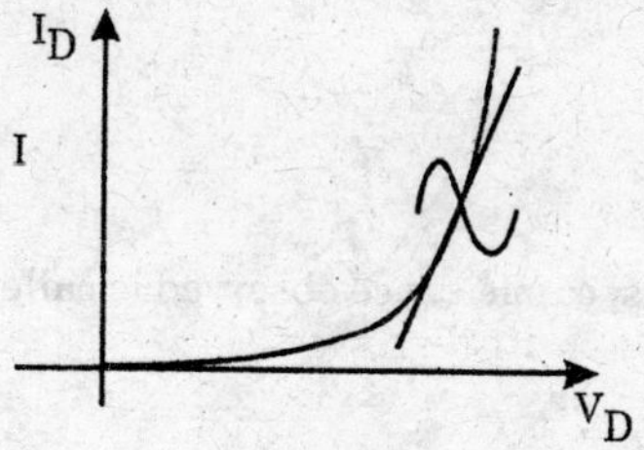

Fig. 3.9

$$r_d = \frac{1}{\text{slope of tangent}} = \frac{dV_D}{dI_D}$$

We know,

$$I_D = I_0\left(e^{\frac{V_D}{\eta V_r}} - 1\right)$$

$\therefore$

$$\frac{dI_D}{dV_D} = \frac{1}{\eta}\left(e^{\frac{V_D}{\eta V_r}}\right) = \frac{I_D + I_0}{\eta V_r} = \frac{I}{r_a}\ \frac{I_D}{\eta V_r} \qquad \text{.......(since } I_D >> I_0)$$

$\Rightarrow$

$$r_d = \frac{\eta V_r}{I_D}$$

where, r_d = temperature dependent.

(3) Average a.c. resistance or Large signal or Point to point resistance (r_{av}).

A large ammplitude signal at input, generate very broad swing in the Q point.

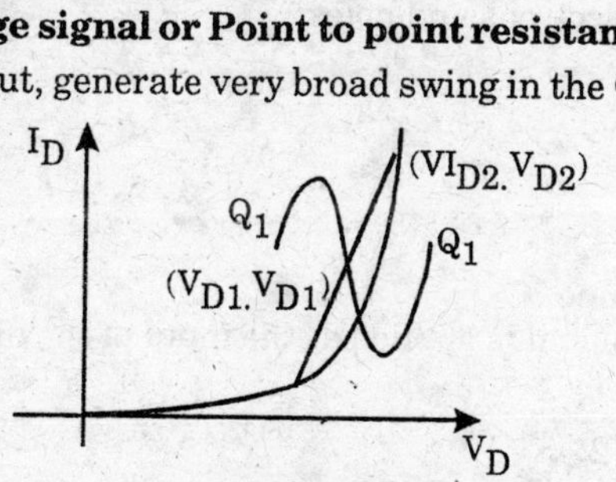

Fig. 3.10

$$\text{Average a.c. resistance, } r_{av} = \frac{1}{\text{slope of line } Q_1, Q_2} = \frac{V_{D2} - V_{D1}}{I_{D2} - I_{D1}}$$

3.2.5. CAPACITANCE OF DIODE

Space charge or Transition capacitance (C_T)

In reverse bias region, $C_T = \left|\frac{dQ}{dV}\right|$

where, dQ = increase in charge caused by a change dV in voltage.

- Thickness of space charge layer at the junction increases with reverse voltage.
- Capacitance C_T depend on magnitude of the reverse voltage.
- Transition capacitance dominant in reverse bias, is due to uncovered charge ions.

$$C_T = \frac{\varepsilon A}{w}$$

where, ε = permittivity
A = area
w = width of depletion layer.

For step or abrupt junction, when $N_D >> N_A$

Junction voltage under reverse bias, $V_j = \frac{q.N_A w^2}{2\varepsilon}$

For linearly graded junction, $V_j = \frac{q.N_A w_1^3}{2\varepsilon}$

where, w = width of the depletion layer., ε = permittivity of the depletion layer

Hence for step graded, $C_r \propto V_j^{-1/2}$ V1

For linearly graded, $C_r \propto V_j^{-1/3}$

Diffusion Capacitance

When diode is connected in forward bias, capacitance observed is called *diffusion capacitance.*

Types of Diffusion capacitance.

(1) Static Diffusion capacitance: C_S

It is the diffusion capacitance when diode is connected with d.c. voltage and it is due to storage of charge in the junction under forward bias.

Static diffusion capacitance, $C_S = \frac{dQ}{dV}$

$$= \tau.\frac{dI}{dV} = \tau.g = \frac{\tau}{r_d} \quad \text{..(since, } g = \frac{1}{r_d}\text{)}$$

$$\Rightarrow \quad C_D \propto \text{current} \propto \frac{1}{\text{temperature}}$$

Heve, $r_d = \frac{\eta V_r}{I}$ and $\tau = \frac{L^2}{D}$

where, L = diffusion length
D = diffusion constant
τ = mean lifetime of electrons and holes.

$$\therefore \quad C_D = \frac{\tau}{\eta r_d}$$

where, r_d diode resistance = $\frac{V_D}{I_D}$

(2) Dynamic Diffusion capacitance (C_D) :

It is the capacitance when a.c. signal is applied at the input of the diode.

For sinusoidal input, $C_D = \frac{1}{2}.\tau.g$;

if $\omega\tau << 1$ for small frequency.

and $C_D = \left(\frac{\tau}{2\omega}\right)^{1/2}$;

if $\omega\tau >> 1$ for higher frequency.

3.2.6. ANALYSIS OF NETWORKS EMPLOYING ZENER DIODES

Zener model to be employed for the "ON" state is shown in Fig. 3.11 (*a*) For "OFF" state as defined by a voltage less than V_Z but greater than 0 V with the polarity shown in Fig. 3.11 (*b*), Zener equivalent is the open circuit that also appears.

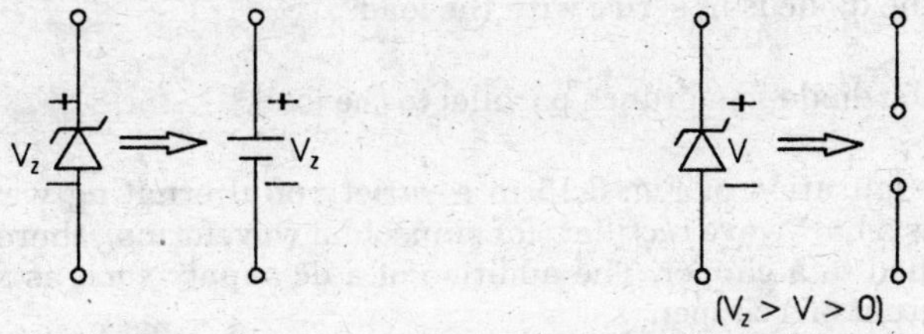

(*a*) *"on" state* (*b*) *"off" state*

Fig. 3.11 Zener diode equivalents for the "ON" and "OFF" states

V_i and R Fixed

The simplest of Zener diode networks is shown in Fig. 3.5. The applied dc voltage is fixed, as is the load resistor. *Fundamentally analysis can be split down into two steps.*

(1) *Determine state of the Zener diode by removing it from the network and calculating voltage across the resulting open circuit.*

Applying step 1 to the network of Fig. 3.12, we will get in the network of Fig. 3.13, where an application of the voltage divider rule will give

$$V = V_L = \frac{R_L V_i}{R + R_L}$$

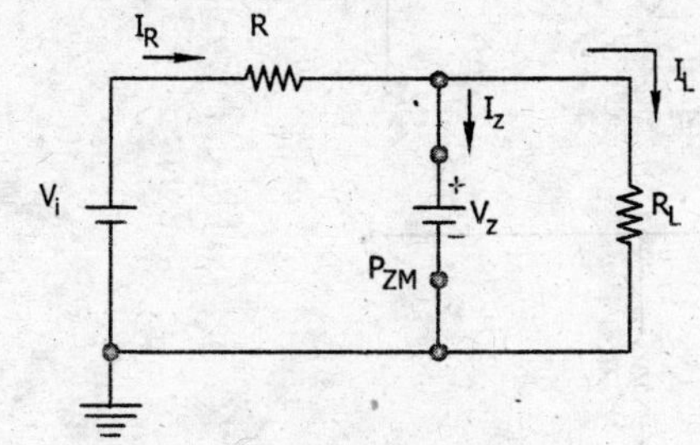

Fig. 3.12 Basic Zener regulator

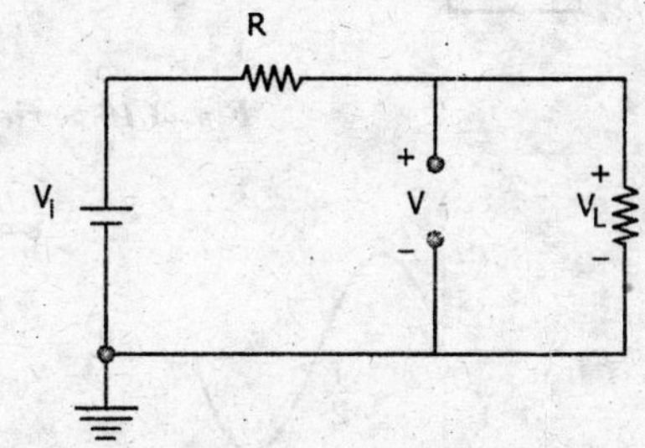

Fig. 3.13 Determining state of the Zener diode

If $V \geq V_Z$, then Zener diode is "ON" and equivalent model of Fig. 3.11 (*a*) can be substitued.

If $V < V_Z$, then diode is "OFF" and open-circuit equivalence of Fig. 3.11 (*b*) substituted.

(2) *Substitute appropriate equivalent circuit and solve for the desired unknowns.*

For the network of Fig. 3.11, the "ON" state will result in the equivalent network of Fig. 3.14. Since voltages across parallel elements must be the same, we get following figure.

$$V_L = V_Z$$

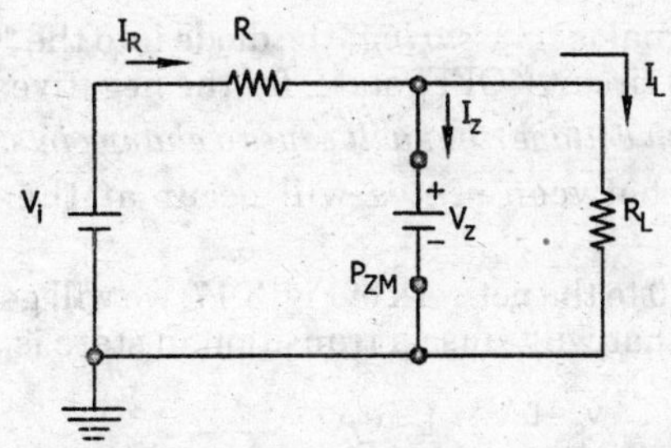

Fig. 3.14 Substituting Zener equivalent for "ON" situation

Zener diode current must be determined by an application of Kirchhoff's current law.

i.e., $I_R = I_Z + I_L$

and $I_Z = I_R - I_L$

where, $I_L = \dfrac{V_L}{R}$ and $I_R = \dfrac{V_R}{R} = \dfrac{V_i - V_L}{R}$

Power dissipated by the Zener diode is determined by

$$P_Z = V_Z I_Z$$

which must be less than the P_{ZM} specified for the device.

3.3 DIODE CIRCUITS

3.3.1. CLIPPERS

There are two general categories of clippers :

(1) The series configuration

It is defined as one where the diode is in series with the load.

(2) Parallel configuration

It is defined as one where the diode in a branch parallel to the load.

Series configuration

Response of the series configuration of Fig. 3.15 to a variety of alternating waveforms is given in Fig. 3.16. Although first introduced as a half-wave rectifier (for sinusoidal waveforms), there are no boundaries on the type of signals that can be applied to a clipper. The addition of a dc supply such as shown in Fig. 3.17 can have a pronounced effect on the output of a clipper.

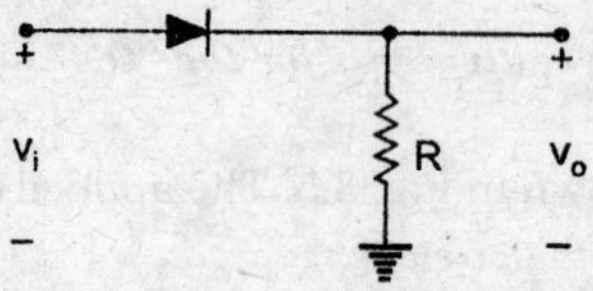

Fig 3.15 Series Clipper circuit

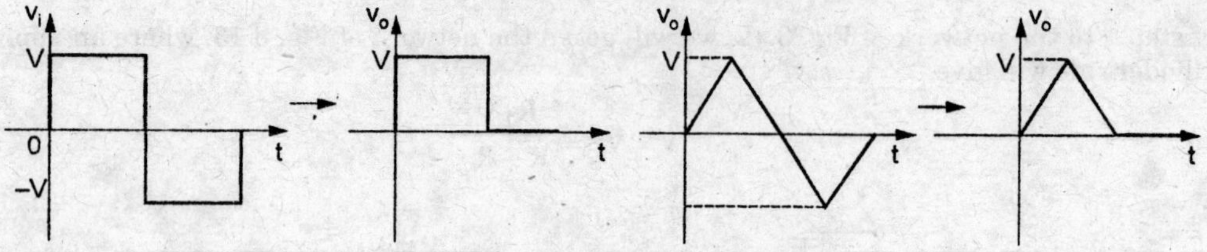

Fig. 3.16 Series clipper response

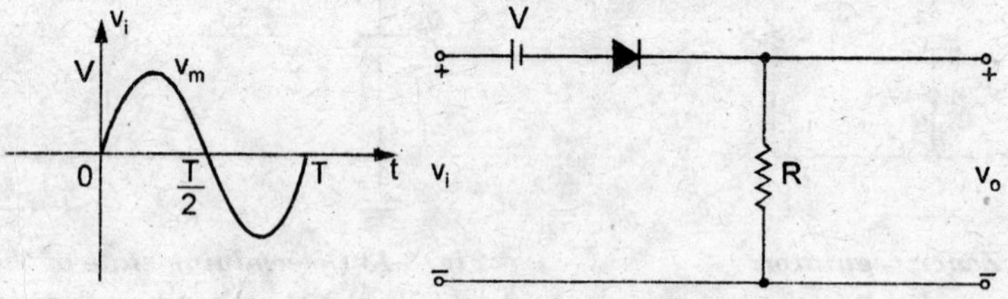

Fig. 3.17 Series clipper with dc supply

There is no general procedure for analyzing networks such as shown in Fig. 3.17, but following points should be considered to get a solution.

(i) *Make a mental sketch of the response of the network based on direction of the diode and applied voltage levels.*

For the network of Fig. 3.17, direction of the diode suggests that signal v_i must be positive to turn it ON. The dc supply further requires that the voltage v_i be greater than V volts to turn the diode ON.

The negative region of the input signal is "*pressuring*" the diode into the "OFF" state, supported further by the dc supply. In general, diode is an open circuit ("OFF" state) for the negative region of the input signal.

(ii) *Determine applied voltage (transition voltage) that will cause a change in state for the diode.*

For ideal diode, the transition between states will occur at the point on the characteristics where $v_d = 0$ V and $i_d = 0$ A.

Applying the condition $i_d = 0$ at $v_d = 0$ to the network of Fig. 3.17, we will get in the configuration of Fig. 3.17, where it is recognized that the level of v_i that will cause a transition in state is, $v_i = V$.

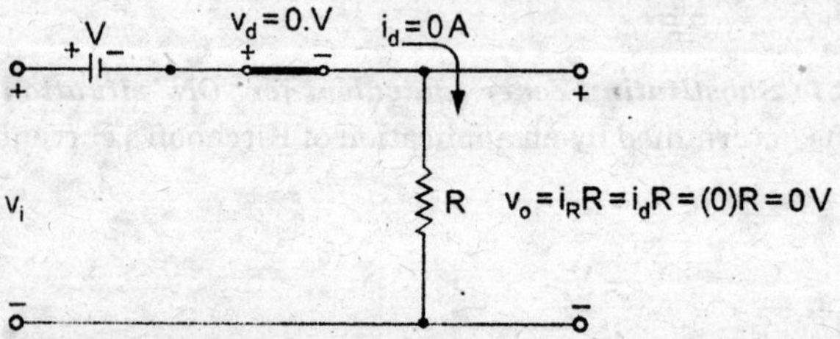

Fig. 3.18 Determining transition level for the circuit of Fig. 3.15

For an input voltage greater than V volts, diode is in the short-circuit state, while for input voltages less than V volts, diode is in the open-circuit or "off" state.

(iii) *Be continually aware of the defined terminals and polarity of v_o.*

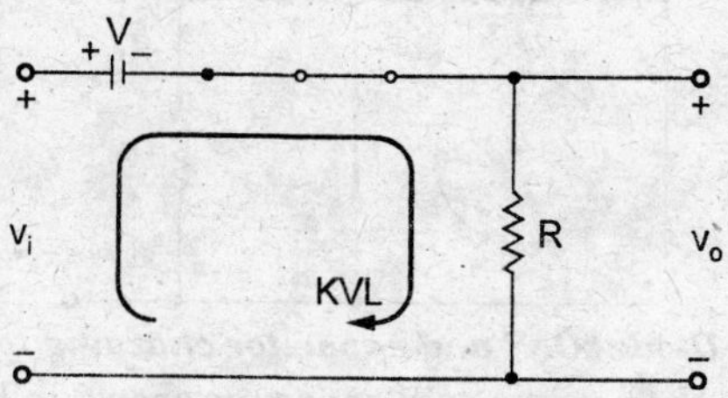

Fig. 3.19 Determining v_o

When diode is in the short-circuit state, as shown in Fig. 3.19, then output voltage v_o can be determined by applying Kirchhoff's voltage law in the clockwise direction

$v_i - V - v_o = 0$ (clockwise direction)

and $v_o = v_i - V$

(iv) *It can be helpful to draw input signal above the output and determine output at instantaneous values of the input.*

For $V_m > V$, the diode is in the short-circuit state and $v_0 = V_m - V$, as shown in Fig. 3.20.

At $v_i = V$, the diodes changes state and at $v_i = -V_m$, $v_o = 0$ V,

Complete curve for v_o can be drawn as shown in Fig. 3.20.

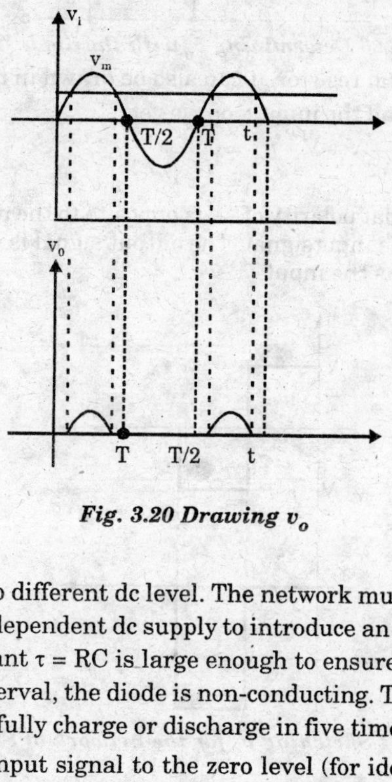

Fig. 3.20 Drawing v_o

3.3.2. CLAMPERS

Clamping network "*clamp*" a singal to different dc level. The network must have a capacitor, a diode, and a resistive element, but it can also employ an independent dc supply to introduce an additional shift. The magnitude of R and C must be chosen such that time constant $\tau = RC$ is large enough to ensure that volatge across the capacitor does not discharge significantly during the interval, the diode is non-conducting. Throughout the analysis assume that for all practical purposes, the capacitor will fully charge or discharge in five time constants.

The network of Fig. 3.21 clamp the input signal to the zero level (for ideal diodes). The resistor R can be the load resistor or a parallel combination of the load resistor and a resistor designed to provide desired level of R.

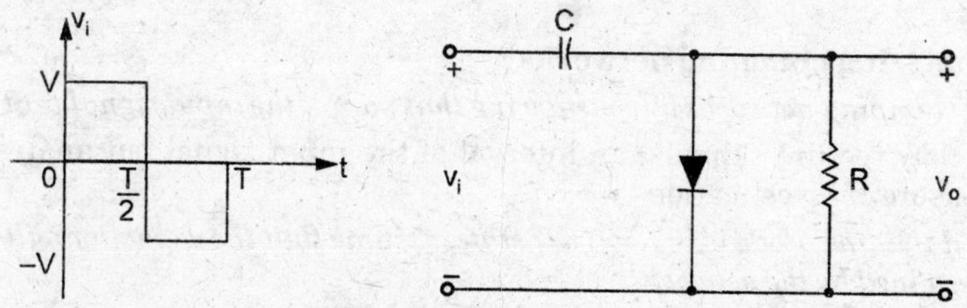

Fig. 3.21 Clamper

During the interval $0 \rightarrow T/2$, the network will appear as shown in Fig. 3.22, with the diode in the "ON" state effectively "*shorting out*" the effect of the resistor R. The resulting RC time constant is so small (R determined by inherent resistance of the network) that the capcitor will charge to V volts very quickly. During this interval, output voltage is directly across the short circuit and $v_o = 0$ V.

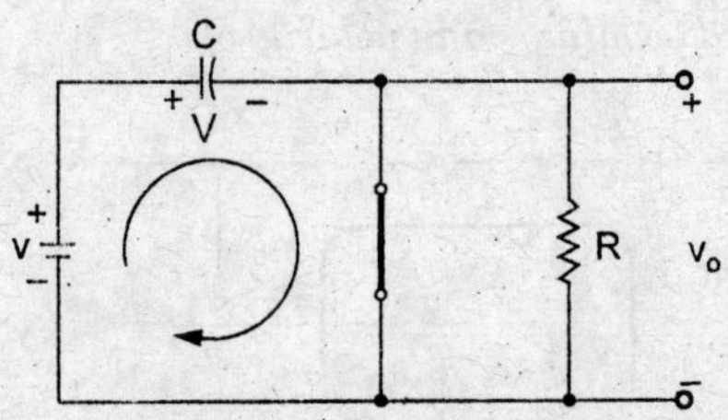

Fig. 3.22 Diode "ON" and capacitor charging to V volts

When input switches to the - V state, the network will appear as shown in Fig. 3.23, with the open-circuit equivalent for the diode determined by the applied signal and stored voltage across the capacitor — both *"pressuring"* current through the diode from the cathode to anode. Now R is back in the network the time constant determined by the RC product is sufficiently large to establish a discharge period 5τ much greater than the period T/2 → T and it can be assumed on an approximate basis that the capacitor holds onto all its charge and therefore voltage (since V = Q/C) during this period.

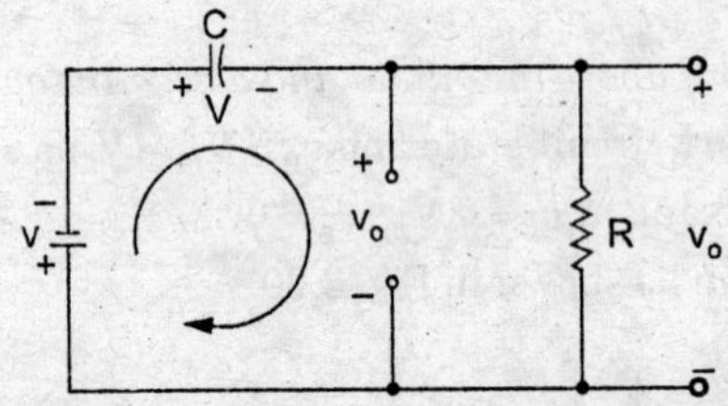

Fig. 3.23 Determining v_o with the diode "off"

Since v_o is in parallel with the diode and resistor, it can also be drawn in the alternative position shown in Fig. 3.23. Applying Kirchhoff's voltage law around the input loop,we get

$$-V - V - v_o = 0$$

and

$$v_o = -2\,V$$

negative sign resulting from the fact that polarity of 2V is opposite to the polarity defined for v_o. The resulting output waveform appears in Fig. 3.24 with the inputsignal. The output signal is clamped to 0 V for the interval 0 to T/2 but maintains the same total swing (2V) as the input.

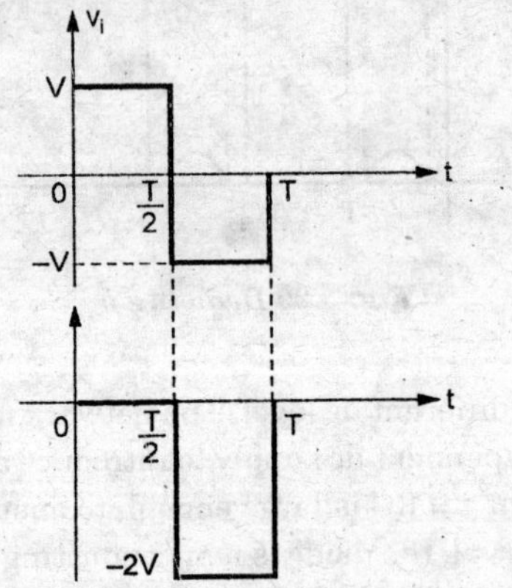

Fig. 3.24 Sketching v_o for the network of Fig 3.16

Clamping network

The total swing of the output is equal to the total swing of the input signal. This fact is an excellent checking tool for the result obtained.

Steps helpful in analyzing clamping networks :

(1) *Start analysis of clamping networks by considering that part of the input signal that will forward bias the diode.*

This statement may require skipping an interval of the input signal but analysis will not be extended by an unnecessary measure of investigation.

(2) *During the period that the diode is in the "ON" state, assume that the capacitor will charge up instantaneously to a voltage level determined by the network.*

(3) *Assume that during the period when diode is in the "OFF" state, the capacitor will hold on to its established voltage level.*

(4) *Throughout the analysis, maintain a continual awareness of the location and reference polarity for v_o to ensure that the proper levels for v_o are obtained.*

(5) *Remember general rule that, total swing of the total output must match swing of the input signal.*

3.3.3. VOLTAGE MULTIPLIERS

These circuits are used to find multiple of magnitude of input sine wave.

Types of voltage multiplier Circuits

(1) Half wave voltage doubler.

During positive half cycle at input diode D1 in the secondary winding of transformer conducts and capacitor is charged upto V_m and diode D2 is OFF.

During negative half cycle D1 is OFF and diode D2 conducts and capacitor C2 is charged by $2V_m$.

The output is taken across C2, i.e. $2V_m$.

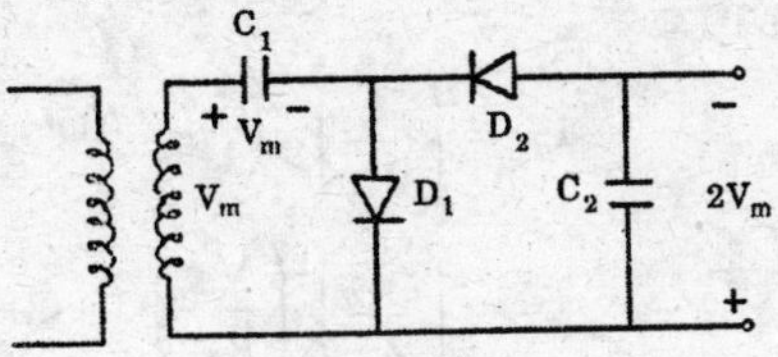

Fig. 3.25

(2) Full wave voltage multiplier.

In this, voltage across different capacitor have different multiple of the magnitude of input voltage.

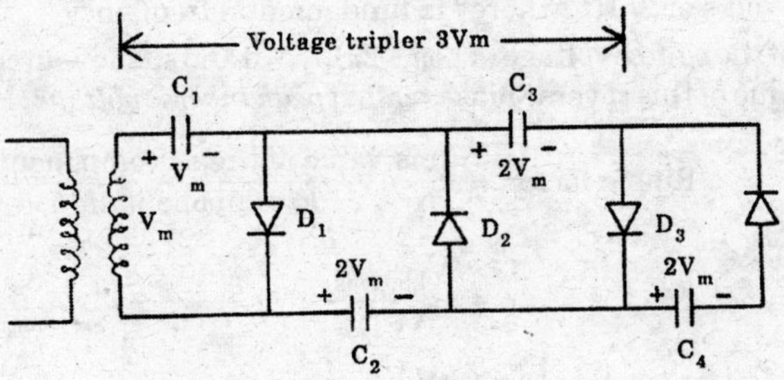

Fig. 3.26

3.3.4. RECTIFIER

It is a device which convert alternating voltage or current into direct voltage or current due to a certain type of non-lenearity of its charteristics.

Type of rectifiers

(1) Half-wave rectifier

Fig. 3.27 (*a*) shows the circuit of a half -wave rectifier (single diode between load and source).

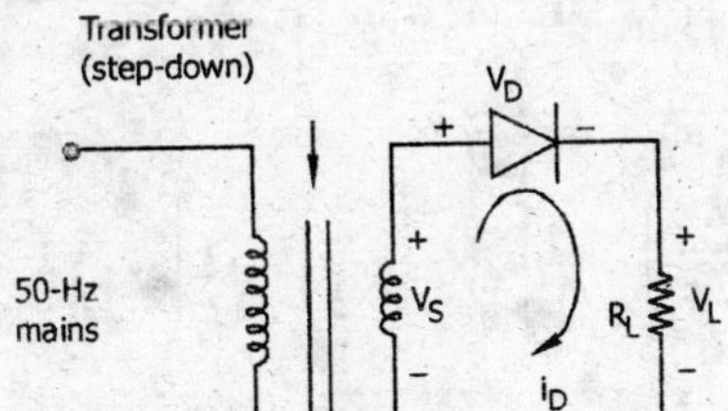

(*a*) ***Half-wave rectifier***

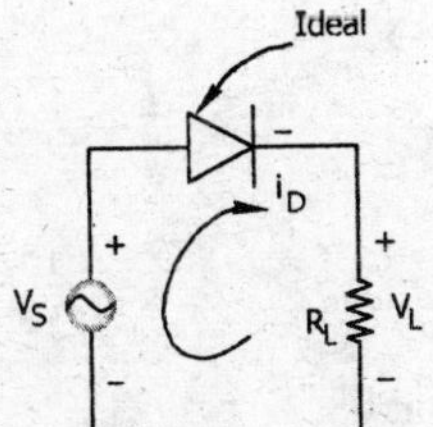

(*b*) ***Circuit model***

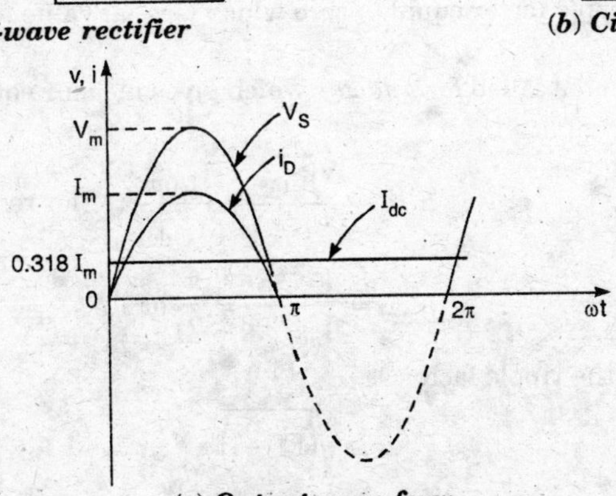

(*c*) ***Output wave form***

Fig. 3.27

Now, assuming the diode to be an ideal switch, the circuit model of rectifier of Fig. 3.27 (*a*) with a resistive load R_L is drawn in Fig. 3.27 (*b*). The ideal diode conducts during the positive half cycles of the voltage. The voltage and current wave shapes along with the dc (average) current are drawn in Fig. 3.27 (*c*).

Let $$v_S = V_m \sin \omega t$$

Then $$i_D = (V_m/R_L) \sin \omega t; \quad 0 \le \omega t \le \pi$$
$$= I_m \sin \omega t; \qquad I_m = V_m/R_L = 0; \quad \pi \le \omega t \le 2\pi$$

Also, voltage drop across load,

$$v_L = V_m \sin \omega t; \quad 0 \le \omega t \le \pi; \; v_D = 0 = 0; \; \pi \le \omega t \le 2\pi$$

dc(average) value of the load current

$$I_{dc} = \left(\frac{1}{2\pi}\right)\int_0^{2\pi} i_D \, d(\omega t) = \left(\frac{1}{2\pi}\right)\int_0^{\pi} \frac{V_m}{R_L}\sin(\omega t)\, d(\omega t)$$

$$= \left(\frac{1}{2\pi}\right)\left(\frac{V_m}{R_L}\right)\left[-\cos\omega t\right]_0^{\pi} = \frac{(V_m/\pi)}{R_L} = \frac{I_m}{\pi} = 0.318\, I_m$$

Then, $$V_{dc} = \frac{V_m}{\pi}, \; I_{dc} = \frac{V_{dc}}{R_L}$$

The ripple frequency is 2 ω rad/s or 2*f* Hz, where *f* is fundamental frequency.

During negative half cycle of the source voltage ($\pi \le \omega t \le 2\pi$), $i_D = 0$ and so the source voltage appears across the diode in reverse bias. The peak value of this reverse bias is called *peak inverse voltage* (PIV) and is equal to V_m.

Now, $$\text{Ripple factor} = \frac{\text{rms value of the ac component of load voltage}}{\text{dc component of load voltage}}$$

$$\gamma = \frac{V_{Lac\,rms}}{V_{Ldc}} \qquad \text{...(3.3)}$$

But, as $$V^2_{Lrms} = (V_{L\,ac\,rms})^2 + (V_{L\,dc})^2$$

$$\gamma = \left[\left(\frac{V_{L\,rms}}{V_{L\,dc}}\right)^2 - 1\right]^{1/2} = \left[\left(\frac{I_{L\,rms}}{I_{L\,dc}}\right)^2 - 1\right]^{1/2}; \text{ load being resistive}$$

Now, $$I_{L\,rms} = \left[\left(\frac{1}{2\pi}\right)\int_0^{2\pi} i_D^2 \, d(\omega t)\right]^{1/2}$$

$$= \left[\left(\frac{1}{2\pi}\right)\int_0^{\pi} I_m^2 \sin^2 \omega t \, d(\omega t)\right]^{1/2} = \frac{I_m}{2}$$

Hence, $$\text{Ripple factor, } \gamma = \left[\left(\frac{I_m/2}{I_m/\pi}\right)^2 - 1\right]^{1/2} = \left[\left(\frac{\pi}{2}\right)^2 - 1\right]^{1/2} = 1.21$$

For a dc wave form, $$V_{L\,rms} = V_{L\,dc}$$

Hence equation (3.3) gives ripple factor equal to zero which is ideal value to be achieved as close as possible in a rectifier circuit.

Also, there is another parameter called *form factor* which gives measure of the ac content of the output voltage, defined by,

Form factor, $$F = \frac{V_{L\,rms}}{V_{L\,dc}} = \frac{I_{L\,rms}}{I_{L\,dc}}; \quad \text{(for resistive load)}$$

$$= \frac{I_m/2}{I_m/\pi} = \frac{\pi}{2} \text{ or } 1.57$$

The form factor is related to the ripple factor as

$$\gamma = \sqrt{(F^2 - 1)}$$

Power conversion efficiency :

$$\text{Power conversion efficiency, } \eta = \frac{\text{dc power output}}{\text{input power}} \times 100$$

$$\text{dc output power, } P_d = I^2_{dc} R_L$$

$$\text{input power, } P_{in} = \left(\frac{\pi}{2}\right)\int_0^{2\pi} v_S i_D \, d(\omega t) = I^2_{rms} (R_S + R_F + R_L)$$

$$\eta = \frac{I^2_{dc} R_L}{I^2_{rms} (R_S + R_F + R_L)} \times 100$$

But,

$$\frac{I_{dc}}{I_{rms}} = \frac{I_m / \pi}{I_m / 2} = \frac{2}{\pi}$$

$\therefore$

$$\eta = \frac{(2/\pi)^2}{1 + \dfrac{(R_S + R_F)}{R_L}} = \frac{40.5}{1 + \dfrac{(R_S + R_F)}{R_L}} \%$$

Voltage regulation :

$$\% \text{ Regulation} = \frac{V_{\text{no-load}} - V_{\text{full-load}}}{V_{\text{full-load}}} \times 100$$

Substituting the values, we have

$$\% \text{ Regulation} = \frac{\dfrac{V_m}{\pi} - \left[\dfrac{V_m}{\pi} - I_{dc}(R_S + R_F)\right]}{\dfrac{V_m}{\pi} - I_{dc}(R_S + R_F)} \times 100$$

But

$$I_{dc} = \frac{(V_m / \pi)}{(R_S + R_F + R_L)}$$

$$\% \text{ Regulation} = \left(\frac{R_S + R_F}{R_L}\right) \times 100$$

(2) Full-wave rectifier.

The circuit of a full-wave rectifier of Fig. 3.28 (*a*) is drawn in Fig. 3.28 (*b*) wherein $v_{S1} = v_{an}$, 180° out of phase with $v_{S2} = v_{bn}$. The load voltage and current wave forms are drawn in Fig. 3.28 (*c*).

Diode D_1 conducts for $0 \le \omega t \le \pi$, when v_{S1} is positive, while diodeD_2 conducts for $\pi \le \omega t \le 2\pi$ when v_{s2} is positive; the current through the load being unidirectional as shown in Fig. 3.28 (*b*). The average or dc current through the load is also shown in Fig. 3.28 (*c*).

From the figure,

$$V_{dc} = \left(\frac{2V_m}{\pi}\right) - I_{dc} (R_S + R_F)$$

and

$$I_{dc} = avg. < i_{D_1} > + avg. < i_{D_2} > = \frac{2I_m}{\pi} = \frac{2V_m}{\pi(R_S + R_F + R_L)}$$

where V_m= peak *ac* voltage of one half of the transformer secondary and *av* indicates average value.

Now,

$$\% \text{ Regulation} = \frac{R_S + R_F}{R_L} \times 100; \text{ (no change)}$$

$$I_{L\ rms} = \frac{I_m}{\sqrt{2}}$$

and

$$\text{Ripple factor, } \gamma = \left[\left(\frac{I_{L\,rms}}{I_{L\,dc}}\right)^2 - 1\right]^{1/2} = \left[\left(\frac{\pi}{(2\sqrt{2})^2}\right) - 1\right]^{1/2}$$

$$= 0.482 \text{ (compare with half-wave rectifier)}$$

$$\text{From factor, F} = \frac{I_{L\,rms}}{I_{L\,dc}} = \frac{\pi}{(2\sqrt{2})} = 1.11$$

$$\text{Power conversion efficiency, } \eta = \frac{81.2}{1 + \dfrac{(R_S + R_F)}{R_L}} \%$$

It is double that of half-wave rectifier.

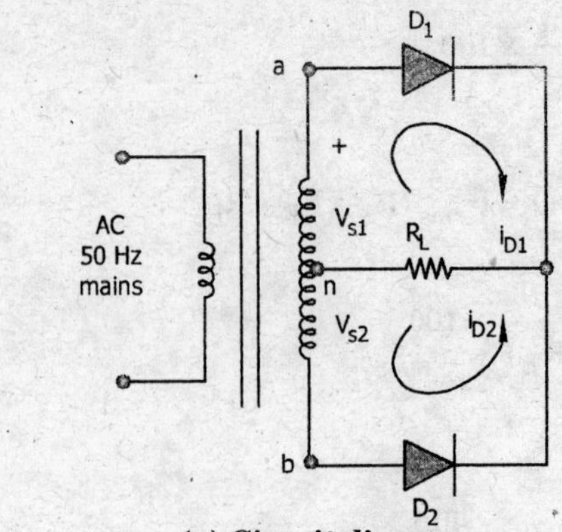

(a) Circuit diagram

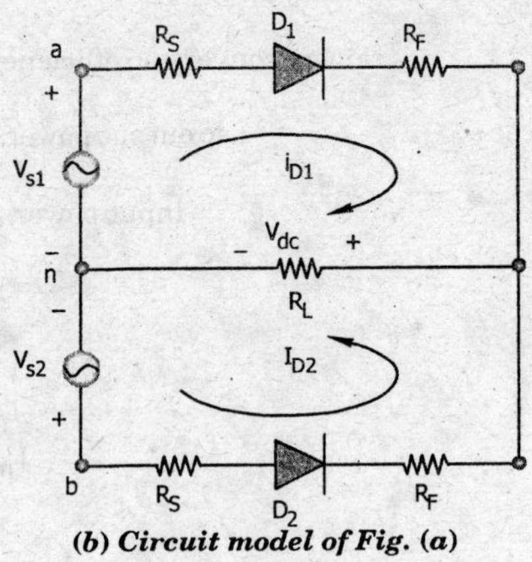

(b) Circuit model of Fig. (a)

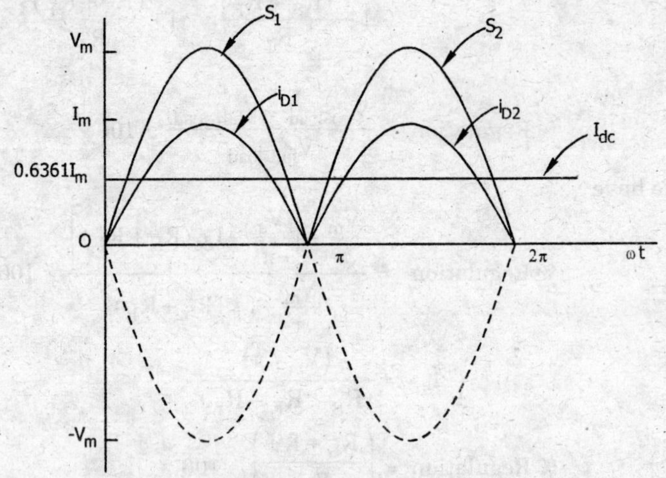

(c) Input/output wave form

Fig. 3.28 Full-wave rectifier with phase inverter

Peak inverse voltage (PIV) can be found by applying KVL to the outer loop of Fig. 3.28(*b*) and neglecting the voltage drops in R_S and R_F. Hence, across nonconducting diode(say D_1), we have

$$\begin{aligned} \text{PIV} &= v_{S1} - v_{S2} \\ &= V_m - (-V_m) = 2\,V_m \\ &= \text{peak voltage of the full secondary voltage.} \end{aligned}$$

(3) Bridge rectifier.

This type of rectifier employs a bridge of four diodes for full-wave rectification as shown in Fig. 3.29 (*a*). The bridge is fed at its opposite edges from the secondary of a transformer which does not require centre tapping.

In the circuit of Fig. 3.29 (*a*), during positive half of the supply voltage ($0 \le \omega t \le \pi$) diodes D_2, D_3 conduct through the load resistance, while during the negative half of the supply voltage ($\pi \le \omega t \le 2\pi$) diodes D_4, D_1 conduct as shown in Fig. 3.29 (*b*). This results in full-wave rectification.

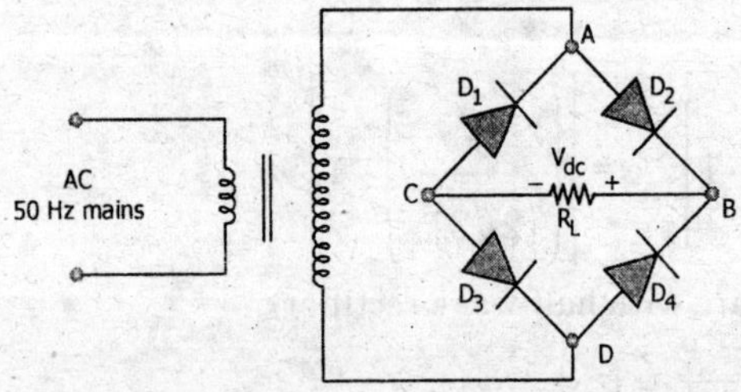

(a) Bridge Rectifier circuit

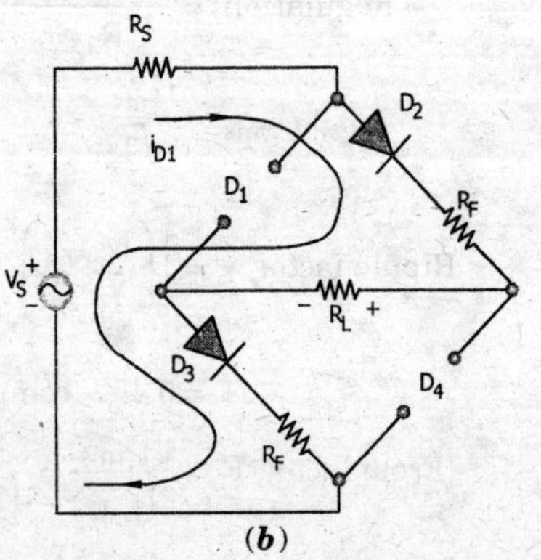

(*b*)

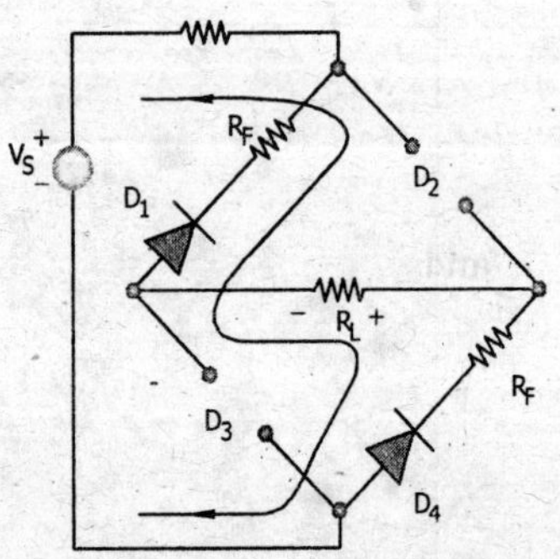

(*c*)

(b) and (c) Conduction path during positive and negative halves of supply voltage

Fig. 3.29

Let peak voltage (V_m) of the transformer secondary to be much larger than the diode threshold L voltage ($2\ V_T$).

Then $$V_{dc} \approx 2\left(\frac{V_m}{\pi}\right) - I_{dc}\ (R_S + 2\ R_F)$$

$$I_{dc} = \frac{2V_m}{\pi(R_S + 2R_F + R_L)}$$

where R_S = transformer resistance seen on secondary side

V_m = peak voltage of secondary voltage.

and $$\text{Percentage regulation} = \frac{R_S + 2R_F}{R_L} \times 100$$

The ripple factor, form factor and conversion efficiency expressions remain the same as for the full-wave rectifier.

Referring Figs. 3.29 (*b*) and (*c*) as one diode pair conducts, the other pair appears in parallel across the source in reverse bias. Assuming R_S and R_F to be small for each of the four diodes, the peak inverse voltage is PIV V_m

3.3.5. CHARACTERISTIC OF DIODES

Device	Principal	Biasing	Application
Zener diode	Operates in breakdown region	Reverse bias	Voltage regulator
LED	Emits non coherent light	Forward bias	DC or AC indicators
Photodiode	Light produces minority carriers	Reverse bias	Light detectors
Optocoupler	Combines LED and photodiode	-	input/output isolators
Laser diode	Emits Coherent light		CD players, broadband communication
Schottky diode	Has no charge storage	Forward bias	High-frequency rectifiers (300 MHz)
Varactor diode	Acts like variable capacitance	Reverse bias	TV and receiver tuners
Varistor	Breaks down both ways	-	Line spike protectors
Step recovery diode	Snaps off during reverse conduction	-	Frequency multiplier
Back diode	Conducts better in reverse	-	Weak signal rectifiers
Tunnel diode	Has a negative resistance region	Forward bias	High frequency oscillators

3.3.6. COMPARISION BETWEEN RECTIFIERS

Particulars	Half wave	Center tap	Bridge type
Number of diodes	1	2	4
Maximum Efficiency	40.6%	81.2%	81.2%
Average value of current	$\frac{I_m}{\pi}$	$\frac{2I_m}{\pi}$	$\frac{2I_m}{\pi}$
rms value of current	$\frac{I_m}{2}$	$\frac{I_m}{\sqrt{2}}$	$\frac{I_m}{\sqrt{2}}$
Form-Factor	1.57	1.11	1.11
Ripple Factor	1.21	0.481	0.481
PIV rating	V_m	$2V_m$	V_m
Transformer Utilization factor (TUF)	0.287	0.693	0.81
Output frequency	f_{in}	$2f_{in}$	$2f_{in}$

3.3.7. FILTERS

Even though the ripple factor of a full wave rectifier is much lower than of a half-wave rectifier, the current wave form is still unsatisfactory for most electronic circuits. It is therefore necessary to filter out harmonics of the rectifier reducing ripple content of the output wave form; these circuits should be so devised as not to reduce level of the dc voltage. Effective filtering is done by means of series L or shunt C. Series L reduces ac voltage at output but does not affect the dc voltage (L is short circuit for dc) and shunt C filters out harmonics in current by offering a low impedance (I/Cω) path, so these currents do not flow through the load. Series L is employed where large output currents are involved. A simple capacitor filter is quite effective for electronic circuits with low currents. Also, R and L of the transformer provide additional series filtering effect.

Capacitor Filter

A simple capacitor filter for a half-wave rectifier circuit as shown in Fig. 3.30 (*a*) having capacitor in shunt across the load resistance. Capacitor causes smoothening of the output voltage waveform by absorbing current when voltage rises and feeding current to the load when voltage begins to drop. The wave forms of v_S, v_L and i_D shown in Fig. 3.30 (*b*) assuming that steady state conditions have been reached in the circuit.

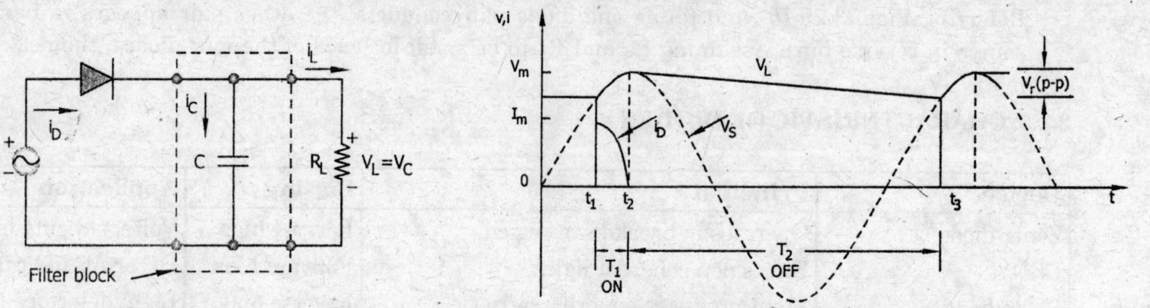

(*a*) *Circuit* (*b*) *Voltage and current wave forms*

Fig. 3.30 Half-wave rectifier with filter

At $t = t_1$, the source voltage v_S begins to rise above the load voltage and diode begins to conduct so that $v_L = v_S$ (diode assumed ideal); capacitor begins getting charged ($i_C = C\, dv_L/dt$).

At $t = t_2$, v_S falls below v_L and capacitor begins discharging into load (according to time constant R_LC).

Hence during charging period $t_1 < t < t_2$, we have

$$v_L = v_S = V_m \sin \omega t$$

and, during discharging period, $t_2 < t < t_3$

$$v_L = e^{\frac{-(t-t_2)}{R_LC}}$$

The charging and discharging cycle repeats from t_3. From wave form of v_L, magnitude of ripple voltage (peak-to-peak) is

$V_r(p-p) << V_m$ (which is ripple voltage without the filter)

With a large filter capacitor, the discharging circuit time constant is large enough for the slow exponential decay to be approximated as linear (Fig. 3.30 (*b*)). Hence, charge that passes through the load is given by

$$Q \approx I_{dc} T_2 = C\, \Delta v_C = C\, V_r\, (p-p) \text{ (peak-to-peak)}$$

where $T_2 = t_3 - t_2$ = diode OFF period.

For better filtering action, ON period of diode, $T_1 = (t_2 - t_1)$ is to be made as small as possible and so T_2 becomes almost equal to one period of ac wave.

$$\therefore \qquad T_2 \approx (T_1 + T_2) = \frac{1}{f}$$

where f = fundamental frequency

Now,
$$V_r\,(p-p) = \frac{I_{dc} T_2}{C} = \frac{I_{dc}}{fC} = \frac{V_{dc}}{fC\,R_L}$$

Also, during OFF period,
$$I_{dc} = \frac{V_{dc}}{R_L}$$

The average output voltage (filtered) can be approximated as

$$V_{dc} = V_m - V_r\,(p-p)/2 = V_m - I_{dc}/(2fC)$$

3.4 BIPOLAR JUNCTION TRANSISTOR (BJT)

A bipolar juction transistor is a three-layer device (*npn* or *pnp*) with two junctions and can provide circuit properties of both a current-controlled source (employed for signal amplification) and a switch (employed for digital signal processing). Figs. 3.31 *(a)* and *(b)* also depict the circuit symbols of *pnp* and *npn* BJTs. The direction of the arrow on E-terminal indicates the direction of conventional current flow.

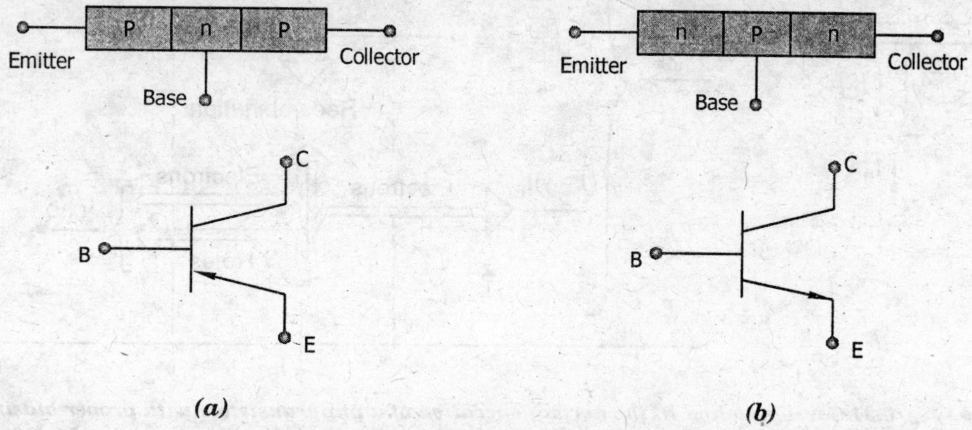

Fig 3.31 BJT schematics and circuit symbols.

3.4.1. OPERATION

It is easier to describe the operation of a BJT using *pnp* configuration. Then operation of the *npn* configuration immediately follows by imagining interchange of the roles played by electrons and holes.

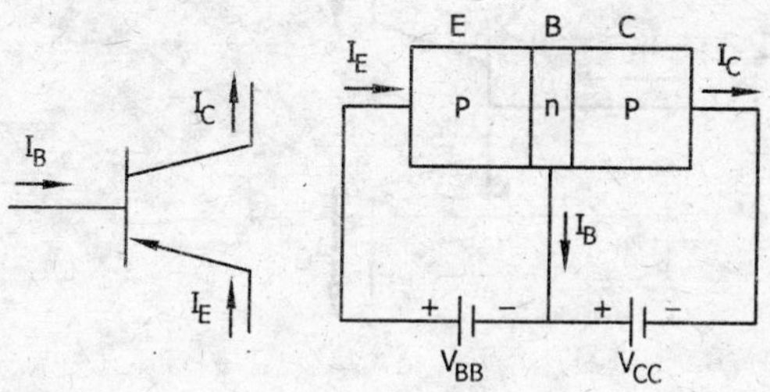

Fig. 3.32 Biased pnp transistor

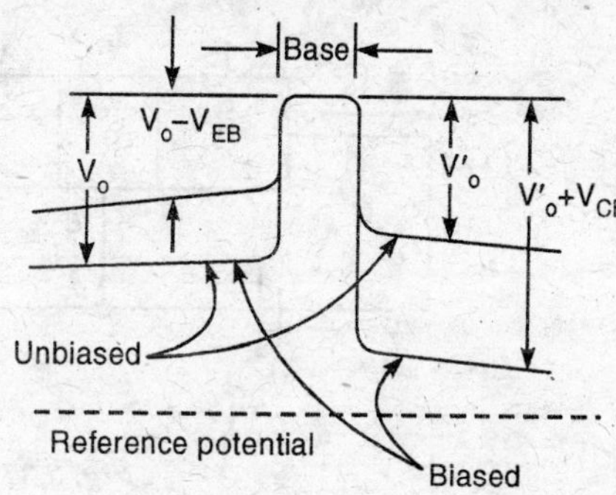

Fig.3.33 Potential distribution of pnp transistor

The operation of a *pnp* transistor (biased as in Fig. 3.32 will now be explained with the help of the enlarged diagram of Fig. 3.34. Because of forward biasing the emitter injects a large number of holes into the base region, where these become '*minority carriers*'. In the base region, holes diffuse towards the collector-base junction and are swept into the collector because of the high field intensity associated with reverse bias. Thus emitter current injected into the base increases minority carrier density in the base on which depends value of the reverse minority collector current. So input emitter current controls the output collector current making BJT act as a current controlled current source. However, a fraction of the holes injected into the base recombine with the electrons (which are the majority carriers in the base). To replenish this loss of electrons due to recombination, an electron current flows into the base from the base terminal.

Besides the holes injected from the emitter, thermally generated holes in the base and electrons in the collector also cross the collector-base junction contributing to the collector current.

Thus the collector current consists of two components :

(*i*) due to injected holes at the emitter base junction

(*ii*) attributed to thermally generated carriers (which constitute reverse saturation current) crossing the collector base junction.

Since both holes and electrons contribute to the device current, hence device is called *bipolar*. Also, assume that potential is constant within each region and no conduction (drift) currents exist. Hence all the currents in the transistor are diffusion currents.

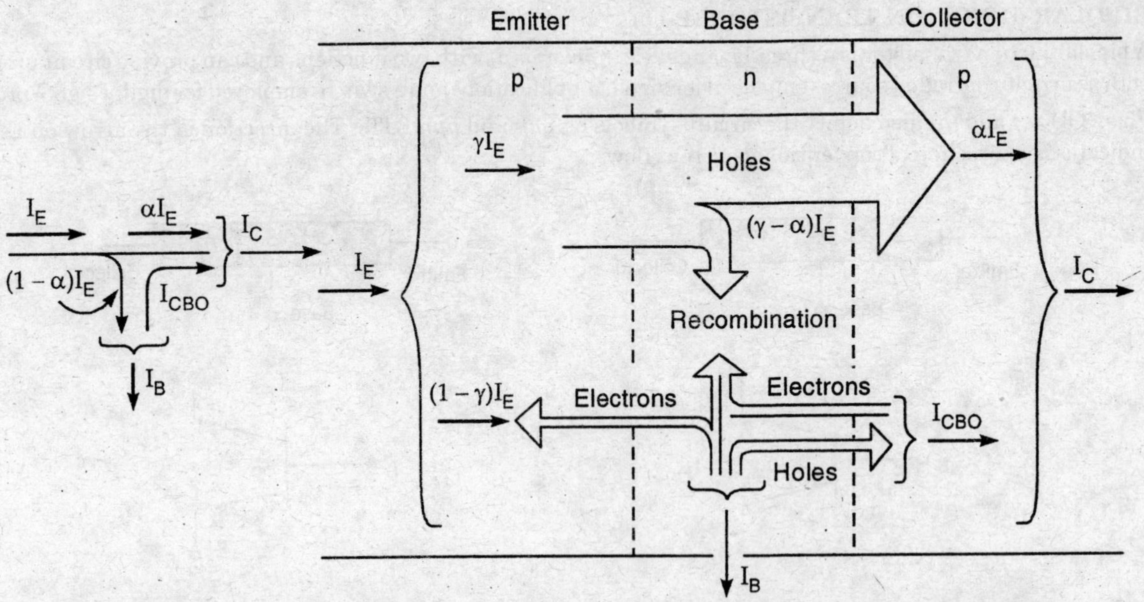

Fig. 3.34 Carrier motion in the normal operation of a pnp transistor (with proper biasing)

The correspondence between conventional current directions of Fig. 3.34 and 3.36 now becomes obvious. Fig. 3.35 shows a similarly biased *npn* transistor. Electrons now flow into emitter and out of collector and also a hole current flows into base to provide for recombination in the base. Reverse saturation current is contributed by minority electrons crossing from base to collector and minority holes from collector to base.

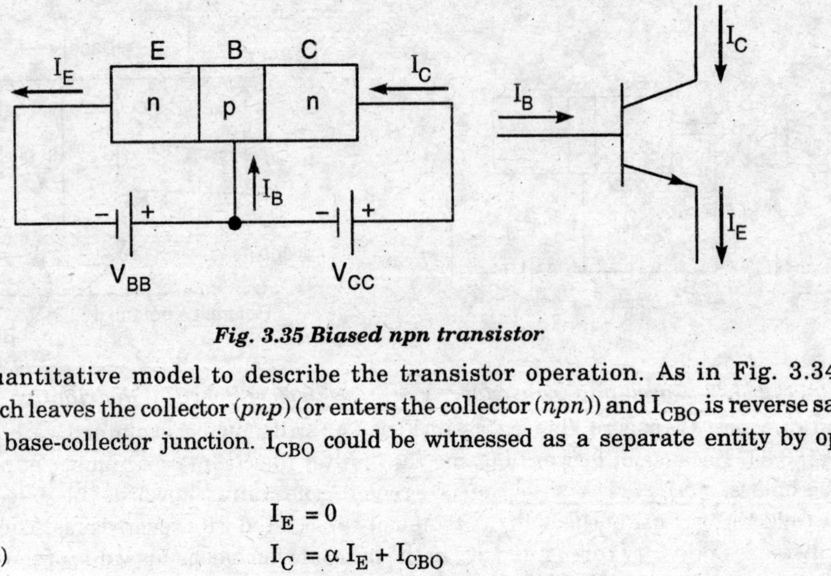

Fig. 3.35 Biased npn transistor

Now develop a quantitative model to describe the transistor operation. As in Fig. 3.34, α is fraction of emitter current which leaves the collector (*pnp*) (or enters the collector (*npn*)) and I_{CBO} is reverse saturation current in the reverse biased base-collector junction. I_{CBO} could be witnessed as a separate entity by opening the emitter connection,

i.e. $I_E = 0$

From Fig. 3.34 (left) $I_C = \alpha\, I_E + I_{CBO}$ ...(3.4)

and $I_B = (1-\alpha)\, I_E - I_{CBO}$ ...(3.5)

Adding equations (3.4) and (3.5), we get

$$I_C + I_B = I_E \quad ...(3.6)$$

Substituting value of I_E from Equation (3.6) in Equation (3.7), we get

$$I_C = \left(\frac{\alpha}{1-\alpha}\right) I_B + \left(\frac{1}{1-\alpha}\right) I_{CBO} \quad ...(3.7)$$

Equations (3.4), (3.5) and (3.6) are fundamental BJT transistor relations and apply for both *pnp* and *npn* transistors with the conventional current directions as indicated respectively in Fig. 3.32 and Fig. 3.35.

As carriers injected into the base (thin slice) stay there for very short duration before being swept off to the collector region, recombination current is very small and the ratio α is as high as 0.98-0.998.

3.4.2. COMMON EMITTER (CE) CONFIGURATION

When a large current gain is required, the BJT is used with the base as the input electrode and the emitter as the common node between the input and output circuits as shown in Fig. 3.36.

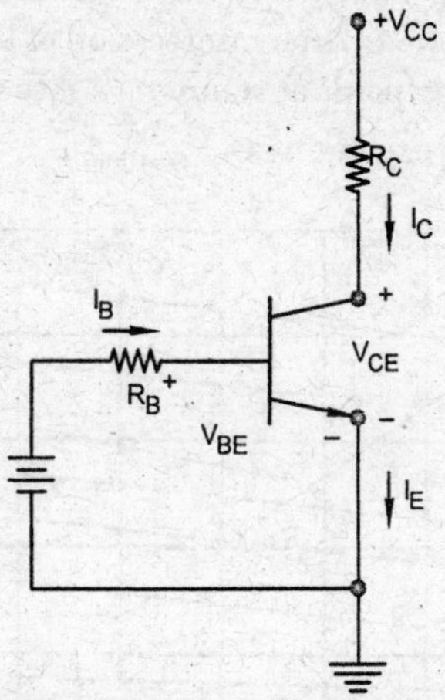

Fig. 3.36 CE configuration

Such a configuration is called *common emitter (CE) configuration*. This is most important and frequently encountered transistor configuration because it is desirable to use small base current rather than large emitter current as the control quantity. In the CE configuration, I_B, the input current and V_{CE}, the output voltage are *independent variables* whereas input voltage V_{BE} and output current I_C are *dependent variables*.

From equation (3.7),
$$I_C = \left(\frac{\alpha}{1-\alpha}\right) I_B + \frac{I_{CBO}}{1-\alpha}$$

We define $\beta = \dfrac{\alpha}{1-\alpha}$ as common emitter dc forward current gain of the transistor.

Then collector current,
$$I_C = \beta I_B + (1+\beta) I_{CBO} \qquad \text{...(3.8)}$$

As reverse saturation current I_{CBO} is of negligible order, therefore
$$I_C \approx \beta I_B \quad \text{or} \quad \beta \approx \frac{I_C}{I_B}$$

Also, if $I_B = 0$, then
$$I_{CEO} = \frac{I_{CBO}}{1-\alpha} = (1+\beta)\, I_{CBO}$$

where, I_{CEO} = emitter collector current with the base open circuited (collector cut-off current (CE configuration)).

Equation (3.18) can then be written as $I_C = \beta I_B + I_{CEO}$

I_{CEO} is of negligible order

The common emitter output characteristic is the family of curves shown in Fig. 3.37 in which I_C vs V_{CE} is plotted for varying values of I_B (Fig. 3.37 *(b)*), while I_B vs V_{BE} Fig. 3.37 *(a)* is the typical forward biased diode characteristic.

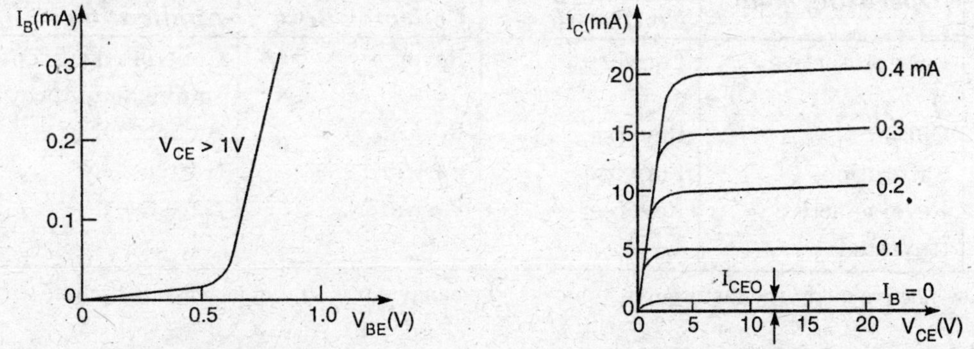

(a) Base characteristics *(b) Collector characteristics*

Fig. 3.37 Common-emitter characteristics of an npn transistor

Applying KVL to the loop of Fig. 3.36

$$V_{CC} = R_C I_C + V_{CE} \quad ...(3.9)$$

Equation (3.9) defines a straight line which intercepts V_{CC} and V_{CC}/R_C on the V_{CE} and I_C axes respectively. This is called the *dc load line* and is shown in Fig. 3.38 (V_{CC} = 10 V,R_C = 250 Ω). At the operating point equation (3.9) as well as transistor characteristic must be satisfied. Thus intersection of the load line and the characteristic corresponding to a given base current gives the operating point at that value of the base current.

In Fig. 3.38, Q is the Operating point corresponding to $I_{B = 100\,\mu A}$.

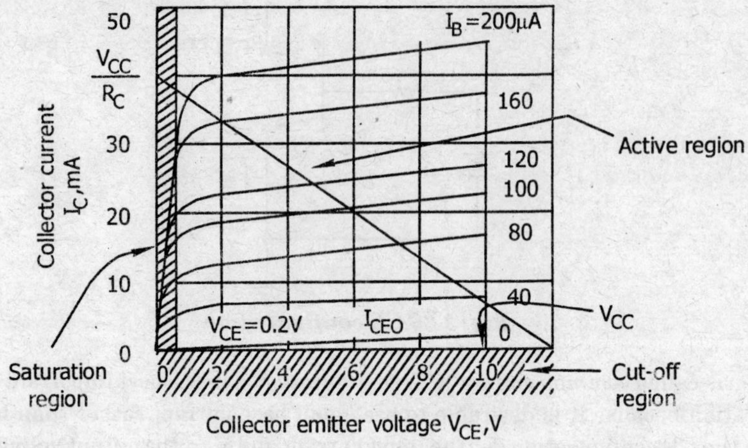

Fig. 3.38 Common-emitter output characteristics of a npn silicon transistor

BJT can also be used in common base and in common collector (CC) configuration, but common collector configuration is not commonly used.

3.4.3. OPERATING MODES

BJT can operate in cut-off, active and saturation modes (Fig. 3.38) If both collector and the emitter junctions are reverse biased, the transistor is in the cut-off mode. If collector-base junction is reverse biased and the emitter-base junction forward biased, then transistor is operating in the active region. For this region, the mathematical relationship is derived. If both the junctions are forward biased, the transistor is said to be in *saturation*. To understand how the collector base junction gets forward biased, observe that.

$$V_{CB} = V_{CE} - V_{BE}$$

As V_{CE} decreases, voltage across the collector-base junction becomes successively less reverse biased till it reaches cut-in voltage of the *pn*-junction. This occurs for

$$V_{CE} \approx 0.2\text{ V},$$

when V_{CB} = 0.2 – 0.7 = – 0.5 V (= cut-in voltage of *pn* junction)

In this region I_B no longer 'controls' I_C, so that mathematical relationships derived for the active region are no longer valid.

Table 3.1. Operating Modes of a BJT

Operating mode	**Junction bias**		
	Emitter-Base	***Collector-Base***	***Application***
Forward-active	Forward	Reverse	Controlled current source; amplification
Cut-off	Reverse	Reverse	Switch "OFF"
Saturation	Forward	Forward	Switch "ON"
Reverse-active (Inverted)	Reverse	Forward	Rare use

In reverse-active mode, the last item in Table 3.1, the behaviour is that of a controlled source with

$$I_E = \beta_R I_B$$

where β_R = reverse current gain.

As $\beta_R << \beta$ (forward current gain), this mode is unsuitable in general except for certain special applications in digital circuits.

3.5. FIELD-EFFECT TRANSISTORS

3.5.1. JUNCTION FIELD-EFFECT TRANSISTOR

The structure of an n-channel field-effect transistor is shown in Fig. 3.39. and 3.40 Ohmic contacts are made to the two ends of a semiconductor bar of n-type material (if p-type silicon is used, the device is referred to as a p-channel FET). Current is caused to flow along the length of the bar because of the voltage supply connected between the ends. The symbol of a p-channel and n-channel FET is shown in Fig. 3.41.

Standard FET notations.

Source : The source S is the terminal through which the majority carriers enter the bar.

Drain : The drain D is the terminal through which the majority carriers leave the bar. The drain-to-source voltage is called V_{DS}, and is positive if D is more positive than S.

From Fig. 3.40, $V_{DS} = V_{DD}$ = drain supply voltage.

Gate : On both sides of the n-type bar of Fig. 3.31, heavily doped (p+) regions of acceptor impurities have been formed by alloying, by diffusion, or by any other procedure available for creating p-n junctions.

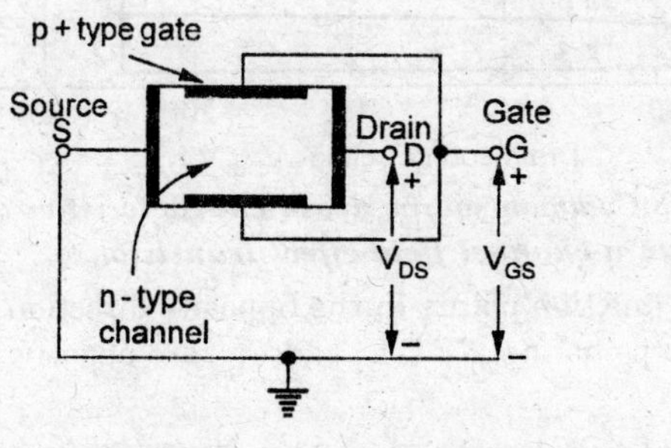

Fig 3.39 Simplified view of n-channel FET

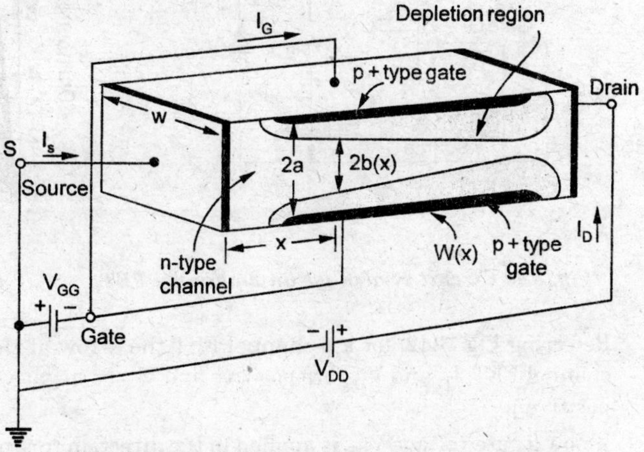

Fig 3.40 Detailed drawing of n-channel FET

(a) p-channel FET *(b) n-channel FET*

Fig 3.41 FET symbol

The normal polarities of the drain-to-source (V_{DD}) and gate-to-source (V_{GG}) supply voltages are shown. In a p-channel FET the voltages would be reversed.

These impurity regions are called the gate G. Between the gate and the source a voltage, $V_{GS} = -V_{GG}$ is applied in the direction to reverse-bias the p-n junction. Conventional current entering the bar at G is designated I_G.

Channel : The region in Fig. 3.39 and 3.40 of n-type material between the two gate regions is the channel through which the majority carriers move from source to drain.

FET Operation : As the reverse bias across the junction increases, so also does the thickness of the region of immobile uncovered charges. The conductivity of this region is normally zero because of the unavailability of current carriers. Hence the effective width of the channel in Fig. 3.39 and 3.40 will become progressively decreased with increasing reverse bias. Accordingly, for a fixed drain-to-source voltage, the drain current will be a function of the reverse-biasing voltage across the gate junction. The term field effect is used to describe this device because the mechanism of current control is the effect of the extension, with increasing reverse bias, of the field associated with the region of uncovered charges.

FET Static Characteristics : The circuit for an FET is shown in Fig. 3.42. The direction of the arrow at the gate of the junction FET in Fig. 3.39 and 3.48 indicates the direction in which gate current would flow if the gate junction were forward-biased. The common-source drain characteristic for a typical n-channel FET shown in Fig. 3.48 give I_D against V_{DS}, with V_{GS} as a parameter. To see qualitatively why the characteristics have the form shown, consider, the case for which $V_{GS} = 0$.

For $I_D = 0$, the channel between the gate junctions is entirely open. In response to a small applied voltage V_{DS}, the *n*-type bar acts as a simple semiconductor resistor, and the current I_D increases linearly with V_{DS}. With increasing current, the ohmic voltage drop between source and the channel region reverse-biases the junction, and conducting portion of the channel begins to construct. Because of the ohmic drop along the length of thechannel itself, the constriction is not uniform, but is more pronounced at distances farther from the source, as shown in Fig. 3.40. Eventually, a voltage V_{DS} is reached at which the channel is "*pinched off.*" This is the voltage, not too sharply defined in Fig. 3.43, where the current I_D begin to level off and approach a constant value. It is in principle not possible for the channel to close completely and thereby reduce the current I_D to zero. In such a case, the ohmic drop required to provide the necessary back bias would itself be lacking.

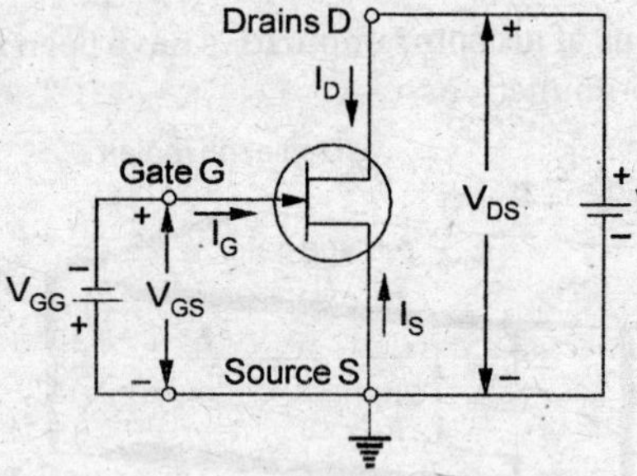

Fig. 3.42 Circuit symbol for an n-channel FET.

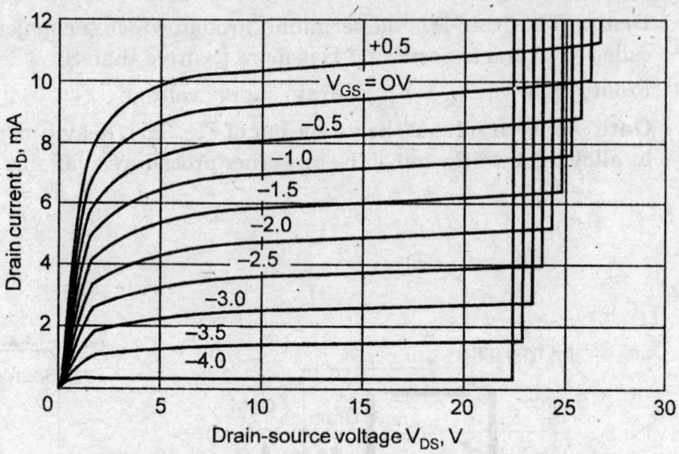

Fig. 3.43 Common-source drain characteristics of an n-channel field-effect transistor.

Referring Fig. 3.42, for a p-channel FET the arrow at the gate junction points in the opposite direction.) For an n-channel FET, I_D and V_{DS} are positive and V_{GS} is negative. For a p-channel FET, I_D and V_{DS} are negative and V_{GS} is positive.

If now a gate voltage V_{GS} is applied in the direction to provide additional reverse bias, pinch-off will occur for smaller values of $|V_{DS}|$, and the maximum drain current will be smaller.

The maximum voltage that can be applied between any two terminals of the FET is the lowest voltage that will cause Avalanche breakdown across the gate junction. From Fig. 3.43 Avalanche occurs at a lower value of $|V_{DS}|$ when the gate is reverse-biased than for $V_{GS} = 0$. This is caused by the fact that the reverse-bias gate voltage adds to the drain voltage, and hence increases the effective voltage across the gate junction.

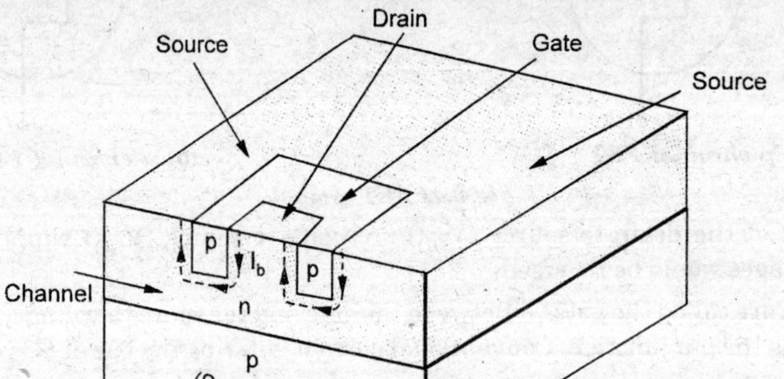

Fig. 3.44 Single-ended-geometry junction FET

The pinch-off voltage V_p is the diode reverse voltage that removes all free charge from the channel. It is given by

$$|V_p| = \frac{qN_D}{2\varepsilon} a^2 \qquad \text{...(3.10)}$$

$$V_{GS} = \left(1 - \frac{b}{a}\right)^2 V_p \qquad \text{...(3.11)}$$

Voltage V_{GS} represents the reverse bias across the gate junction and is independent of distance along the channel if $I_D = 0$.

3.5.2. JFET VOLT-AMPERE CHARACTERISTICS

At first, assume that a small voltage V_{DS} is applied between drain and source. The resulting small drain current I_D will then have no appreciable effect on the channel profile. Under these conditions, the effective channel cross section A to be constant throughout its length.

Hence
$$A = 2bw \quad \text{...(3.12)}$$

where $2b$ = channel width corresponding to zero drain current as given by equation (3.11) for a specified V_{GS}, and

w = channel dimension perpendicular to the b direction, as shown in Fig. 3.41 and 3.42.

Since no current flows in the depletion region, then drain current,

$$I_D = AqN_D\mu_n\varepsilon = 2bwqN_D\mu_n\frac{V_{DS}}{L} \quad \text{...(3.13)}$$

where L = length of the channel.

Substituting b from equation (3.12) in equation (3.13), we have for small I_D,

$$I_D = \frac{2awqN_D\mu_n}{L}\left[1-\left(\frac{V_{GS}}{V_P}\right)^{\frac{1}{2}}\right]V_{DS} \quad \text{...(3.14)}$$

ON Resistance $r_{d,\,ON}$: Equation (3.14) describes the volt-ampere characteristics of Fig. 3.43 for very small V_{DS}, and it suggests that under these conditions the FET behaves like an ohmic resistance whose value is determined by V_{GS}. The ratio V_{DS}/I_D at the origin is called the ON drain resistance $r_{d\,ON}$.

For a JFET from Equation (3.14), with $V_{GS} = 0$,

$$r_{d,\,ON} = \frac{L}{2awqN_D\mu_n} \quad \text{...(3.15)}$$

Pinch-off Region: If a substantial drain current I_D flows, drain end of the gate is more reverse-biased than the source end, and hence boundaries of the depletion region are not parallel to the longitudinal axis of the channel, but converge as shown in Fig. 3.40. If convergence of the depletion region is gradual, the previous one-dimensional analysis is valid in a thin slice of the channel of thickness Δx and at a distance x from the source. Subjects to this condition of the *"gradual" channel*, the current may be written by referring Fig. 3.40 as

$$I_D = 2b(x)wqN_D\mu_n\varepsilon_x \quad \text{...(3.16)}$$

As V_{DS} increases, ε_x and I_D increase, whereas $b(x)$ decrease because the channel narrows, and hence current density $J = I_D/2b(x)w$ increases. Complete pinch-off ($b = 0$) cannot take place because, if it did, J would become infinite, which is a physically impossible condition. If J were to increase without limit, then, from equation (3.16), so also would ε_x, provided that μ_n remains constant.

Region before Pinch-off : FET behaves as an ohmic resistance for small V_{DS} and as a constant-current device for large V_{DS}. In this region the mobility is at first independent of electric field and then μ varies with $\varepsilon_x^{-\frac{1}{2}}$ for larger values of ε_x (before pinch-off). Taking this relationship into account, it is possible to obtain an expression for I_D as a function of V_{DS} and V_{GS} which agrees quite well with experimentally determined curves.

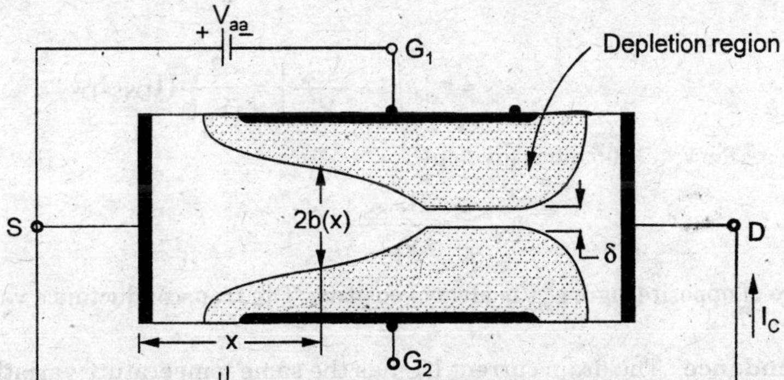

Fig. 3.45 After pinch-off, as V_{DS} is increased, then L′ increases but δ and I_D remain essentially constant. (G_1 and G_2 are tied together.)

Transfer Characteristic : In amplifier applications the FET is almost always used in the region beyond pinch-off (also called the constant-current, pentode, or current-saturation region). Let the saturation drain current be designed by I_{DS}, and its value with the gate shorted to the source ($V_{GS} = 0$) by I_{DSS}.

The relationship between I_{DS} and V_{GS} is given by

$$I_{DS} = I_{DSS}\left(1-\frac{V_{GS}}{V_P}\right)^2 \quad ...(3.17)$$

Cut-off : Consider an FET operating at a fixed value of V_{DS} in the constant-current region. As V_{GS} is increased in the direction to reverse-bias the gate junction, the conducting channel will narrow.

When $V_{GS} = V_P$, the channel width is reduced to zero, and $I_{DS} = 0$.

But some leakage current $I_{D,\ OFF}$ still flows even under the cut-off condition

$$|V_{GS}| > |V_P|.$$

3.5.3. FET SMALL-SIGNAL MODEL

Transconductance g_m and Drain Resistance r_d

If both the gate and drain voltages are varied, the change in drain current is given by

$$\Delta i_D = \left.\frac{\partial i_D}{\partial v_{GS}}\right|_{V_{DS}} \Delta v_{GS} + \left.\frac{\partial i_D}{\partial v_{DS}}\right|_{V_{GS}} \Delta v_{DS}$$

Here, $\quad \Delta i_D = i_d,\ \Delta v_{GS} = v_{gs},\ \text{and}\ \Delta v_{DS} = v_{ds}$

$$\therefore \quad i_d = g_m v_{gs} + \frac{1}{r_d} v_{ds} \quad ...(3.18)$$

where

$$g_m \equiv \left.\frac{\partial i_D}{\partial v_{GS}}\right|_{V_{DS}} \approx \left.\frac{\Delta i_D}{\Delta v_{GS}}\right|_{V_{DS}} = \left.\frac{i_d}{v_{gs}}\right|_{V_{DS}} \quad ...(3.19)$$

is the *mutual conductance*, or *transconductance*. It is also designated by y_{fs} or g_{fs} and called (common source) forward *transadmittance*.

The second parameter r_d in equation (3.18) is the drain (or output) resistance, and is defined by

$$r_d \equiv \left.\frac{\partial v_{DS}}{\partial i_D}\right|_{V_{GS}} \approx \left.\frac{\delta v_{DS}}{\Delta i_D}\right|_{V_{GS}} = \left.\frac{v_{ds}}{i_d}\right|_{V_{GS}}$$

The reciprocal of r_d is *drain conductance*, g_d. It is also designated by y_{os} and g_{os} and called (common-source) *output conductance*.

An amplification factor μ for an FET is defined by

$$\mu \equiv -\left.\frac{\partial v_{DS}}{\partial v_{GS}}\right|_{I_D} = -\left.\frac{\Delta v_{DS}}{\Delta v_{GS}}\right|_{I_D} = -\left.\frac{v_{ds}}{v_{gs}}\right|_{i_d=0}$$

But μ, r_d, and g_m are related by $\quad \mu = r_d g_m$

By setting $i_d = 0$ in equation (3.18), an expression for g_m is obtained by applying the definition of equation (3.19) to equation (3.17)

$$g_m = g_{mo}\left(1-\frac{V_{GS}}{V_P}\right) = \frac{2}{|V_P|}\left(I_{DSS}I_{DS}\right)^{\frac{1}{2}}$$

where g_{mo} is value of g_m for $V_{GS} = 0$, and is given by

$$g_{mo} = \frac{-2I_{DSS}}{V_P}$$

Since I_{DSS} and V_P are of opposite sign, g_{mo} is always positive. The transconductance varies as the square root of the drain current.

Temperature Dependence : The drain current I_{DS} has the same temperature variation as does g_m. The principal reason for the negative temperature coefficient of I_{DS} is that the mobility decreases with increasing temperature. Since this majority-carrier current decreases with temperature (unlike the bipolar transistor whose minority-carrier current decreases with temperature), the troublesome phenomenon of thermal runaway is not encountered with field-effect transistors.

FET Model : A circuit which satisfies equation (3.18) is indicated in Fig. 3.46 (*a*). The input resistance between gate and source is infinite, since it is assumed that the reverse-biased gate takes no current.

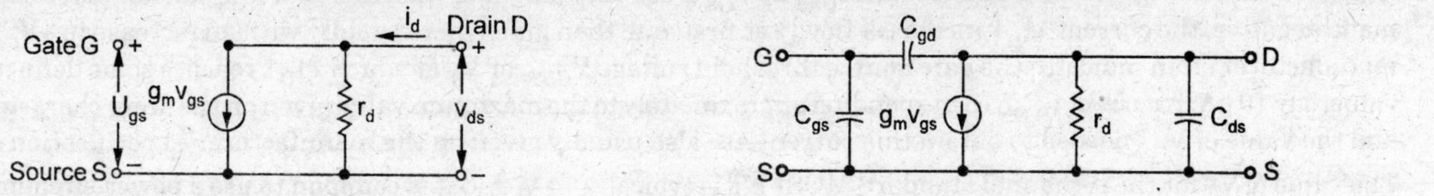

(a) low-frequency small-signal FET model. *(b) high-frequency model, taking node capacitors into account.*

Fig. 3.46

Due to same reason the resistance between gate and drain is assumed to be infinite.

The FET model of Fig. 3.46 (*a*) should be compared with the *h*-parameter model of the bipolar junction transistor of Fig. 3.46. The latter also has a Norton's output circuit, but the current generated depends upon the input current, whereas in the FET model the generator current depends upon the input voltage. There is no feedback at low frequencies from output to input in the FET, whereas such feedback exists in the bipolar transistor through the parameter h_{re}. Finally, the high (almost infinite) input resistance of the FET is replaced by an input resistance of about 1 K for a CE amplifier. The field-effect transistor is a much more ideal amplifier than the conventional transistor at low frequencies. But this is not true beyond the audio range.

Table 3.2. Range of parameter values for an FET

Parameter	*JFET*	*MOSFET*
g_m	0.1 – 10 *mA/V*	0.1 – 20 *mA/V* or more
r_d	0.1 – 1 M	1 – 50 K
C_{ds}	0.1 – 1 *pF*	0.1 – 1 *pF*
C_{gs}, C_{gd}	1 – 10 *pF*	1 – 10 *pF*
r_{gs}	$> 10^8\ \Omega$	$> 10^{10}\ \Omega$
r_{gd}	$> 10^8\ \Omega$	$> 10^{14}\ \Omega$

3.6 METAL-OXIDE-SEMICONDUCTOR FET (MOSFET)

The *p*-channel MOSFET consists of a lightly doped *n*-type substrate into which two highly doped p^+ regions are diffused. The chip area of a MOSFET is 3 square mils or less, which is only about 5-percent of that required by a bipolar junction transistor.

The metal area of the gate, in conjunction with the insulating dielectric oxide layer and the semiconductor channel, form a parallel-plate capacitor. Because of insulating layer of silicon dioxide, this device is called the *insulated-gate field-effect transistor*.

3.6.1. ENHANCEMENT MOSFET

Apply negative voltage at the gate, an electric field will be directed perpendicularly through the oxide. This field will end on "induced" positive charges on the semiconductor site, as shown in Fig. 3.47. The positive charges, which are minority carriers in the *n*-type substrate, form an "*inversion layer.*" As the magnitude of the negative voltage on the gate increases, the induced positive charge in the semiconductor increases. The region beneath the oxide now has *p*-type carriers, the conductivity increases, and current flows from source to drain through the induced channel. Thus drain current is "*enhanced*" by the negative gate voltage, and such a device is called *enhancement-type MOS*.

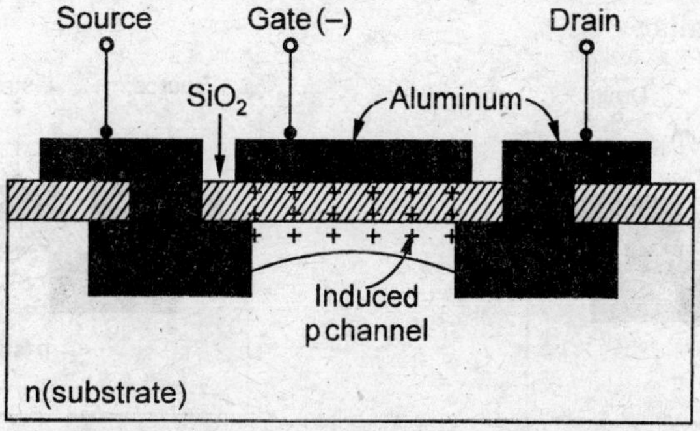

Fig. 3.47 Enhancement in a p-channel MOSFET

Threshold voltage

The volt-ampere drain characteristics of a *p*-channel enhancement-mode MOSFET are given in Fig. 3.48 (*a*) and its transfer curve in Fig. 3.48 (*b*). The current I_{DSS} at $V_{GS} \geq 0$ is very small, of the order of a few nanoamperes. As V_{GS} is made negative, the current $|I_D|$ increases slowly at first, and then much more rapidly with an increase in $|V_{GS}|$. The manufacturer often indicates the gate-source threshold voltage V_{GST}, or V_T at which $|I_D|$ reaches some defined small value, say 10 μA. A current $I_{D,ON}$ corresponding approximately to the maximum value given on the drain characteristics, and the value of V_{GS} needed to obtain this current are also usually given on the manufacturer's specification sheets. The value of V_T for the *p*-channel standard MOSFET is typically - 4 V, and it is common to use a power-supply voltage of – 12 V for the drain supply.

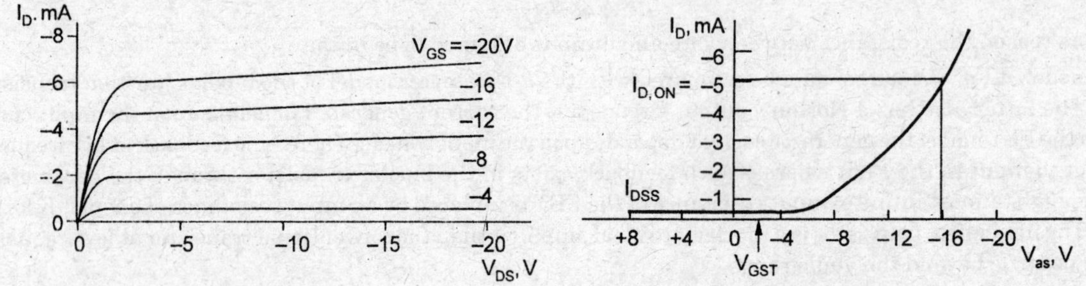

(*a*) *Drain characteristics*

(*b*) *Transfer curve (for V_{DS} = 10 V) of a p-channel enhancement-type MOSFET*

Fig. 3.48

Power Supply Requirements :

Table 3.3 gives voltage customarily used with high-threshold and low-threshold *p*-channel MOSFETs. V_{SS} refers to the source, V_{DD} to the drain, and V_{GG} to the gate supply voltages. The subscript 1 denotes that the source is grounded and the subscript 2 designates that the drain is at ground potential.

The low-threshold MOS circuit require lower power supply voltages and this means less expensive system power supplies. In addition, the input voltage swing for turning the device ON and OFF is smaller for the lower-threshold voltage, and this means faster operation. Another feature of low-threshold MOS circuits is that they are directly compatible with bipolar ICs. They require and produce essentially the same input and output signal swings and the system deginer has the flexibility of using MOS and bipolar circuits in the same system.

Table 3.3. Power supply voltages for *p*-channel MOSFETs, in volts

	V_{SS1}	$-V_{DD1}$	$-V_{GG1}$	V_{SS2}	V_{DD2}	$-V_{GG2}$
High-threshold	0	– 12	– 24	+ 12	0	– 12
Low-threshold	0	– 5	– 17	+ 5	0	– 12

3.6.2. DEPLETION MOSFET

Consider an *n*-channel structure, shown in Fig. 3.49 (*a*). With this device an appreciable drain current I_{DSS} flows for zero gate-to-source voltage V_{GS} = 0. If the gate voltage is made negative, positive charges are induced in the channel through the SiO_2 of the gate capacitor. Since the current in an FET is due to majority carriers (electrons for an *n*-type material), the induced positive charges make the channel less conductive, and drain current drops as V_{GS} is made more negative. The redistribution of charge in the channel causes an effective depletion of majority carriers, which accounts for the designation depletion MOSFET. In Fig. 3.49 (*b*) because of the voltage drop due to the drain current, the channel region nearest the drain is more depleted than is the volume near the source like that of pinch-off occurring in a JFET at the drain end of the channel. As a matter of fact, the volt-ampere characteristics of the depletion-mode MOS and the JFET are quite similar.

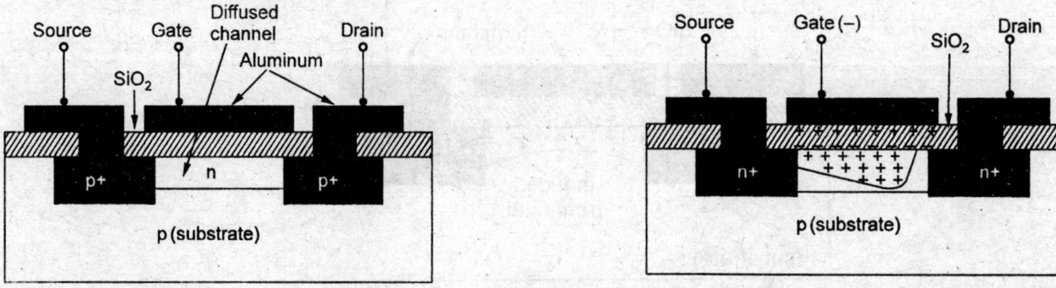

(*a*) *n-channel depletion-type MOSFET*

(*b*) ***Channel depletion with the application of a negative gate voltage***

Fig. 3.49

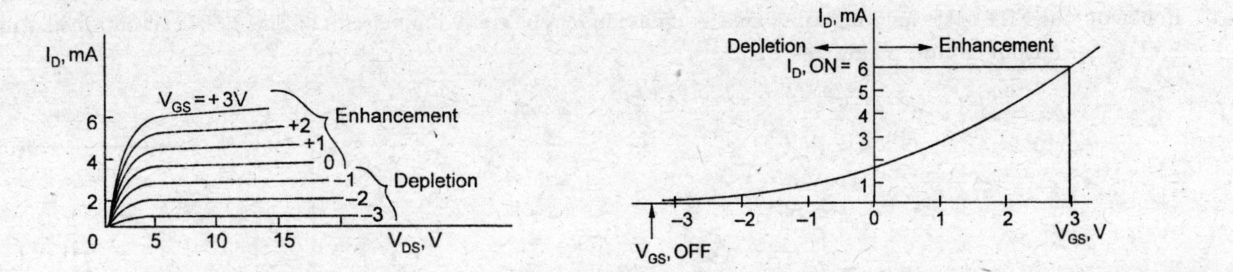

(a) Drain characteristics ***(b) Transfer curve (for V_{DS} = 10 V) for an n-channel MOSFET***

Fig. 3.50

A MOSFET of the depletion type may also be operated in an enhancement mode. It is only necessary to apply a positive gate voltage so that negative charges are induced into the *n*-type channel. In this manner, conductivity of the channel increases and current rises above I_{DSS}. The volt-ampere characteristics of this device are indicated in Fig. 3.50 (*a*) and the transfer curve is given in Fig. 3.50 (*b*).

3.6.3. MOSFET GATE PROTECTION

Since the SiO_2 layer of the gate is extremely thin, it may easily be damaged by excessive voltage. An accumulation of charge on an open-circuited gate may result in a large enough field to punch through the dielectric. To prevent this damage some MOS devices are fabricated with a Zener diode between gate and substrate. In normal operation this diode is open and has no effect upon the circuit. However, if voltage at the gate becomes excessive, then diode breaks down and the gate potential is limited to a maximum value equal to the Zener voltage.

3.6.4. CIRCUIT SYMBOLS

Most MOSFETs, are triodes, with the substrate internally connected to the source. The circuit symbols are indicated in Fig. 3.51. Often the substrate lead is omitted from the symbol as in Fig. 3.51 (*a*), and is then understood to be connected to the source internally.

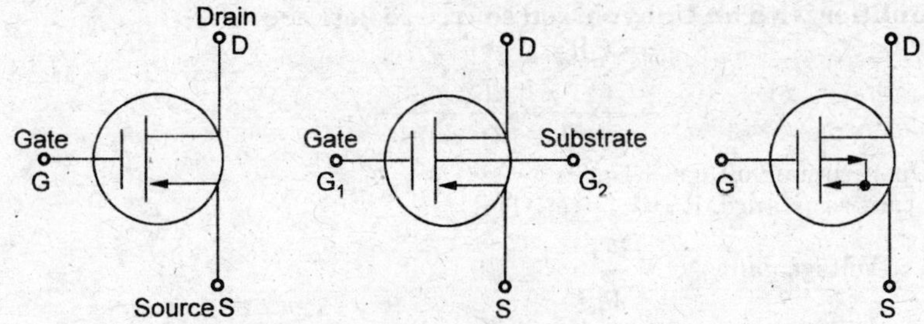

(a) ***(b)*** ***(c)***

Fig. 3.51 Three circuit symbols for a p-channel MOSFET

Referring Fig. 3.51 (*a*) and (*b*) can be either depletion or enhancement types, whereas Fig. 3.51 (*c*) represents specifically an enhancement device. In Fig. 3.51 (*a*), the substrate is understood to be connected internally to the source. For an n-channel MOSFET the direction of the arrow is reversed.

3.6.5. DIGITAL MOSFET CIRCUITS

The most common applications of MOS devices are digital, such a logic gates and registers, or memory arrays. Because of the gate-to-drain and gate-to-source and substrate parasitic capacitances, MOSFET circuits are slower than corresponding bipolar circuits. The lower power dissipation and higher density of fabrication make MOS devices attractive and economical for many low-speed applications.

3.6.6. LOW-FREQUENCY COMMON-SOURCE AND COMMON-DRAIN AMPLIFIERS

The common-source (CS) stage indicated in Fig. 3.52 (*a*) and the common-drain (CD) configuration in Fig. 3.52 (*b*) are analogous to the bipolar transisitor CE amplifier, and to the CC stage respectively. For the CS stage, the ouput is v_{o1} taken at the drain and $R_s = 0$. For the CD stage, the output in v_{o2} taken at the source and $R_d = 0$. Signal-source resitance is unimportant since it is in series with the gate, which draws negligible current.

(a) CS ***(b) CD configurations***

Fig. 3.52

Replacing the FET by its low-frequency small-signal model, the equivalent circuit of Fig. 3.53 (*a*) is obtained. Applying KVL to the output circuit, we get

$$i_d R_d + (i_d - g_m v_{os})\, r_d + i_d R_s = 0 \qquad \text{...(3.20)}$$

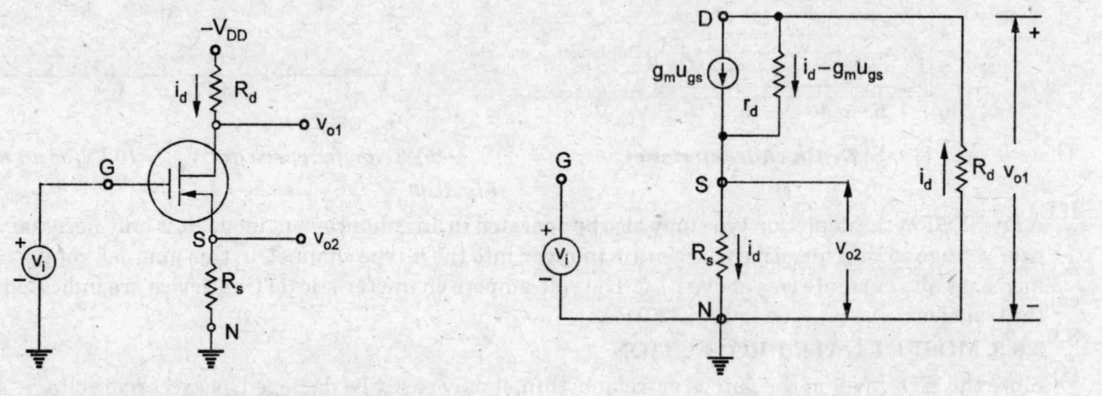

(a) Generalized FET amplifier configuration ***(b) Small-signal equivalent circuit***

Fig. 3.53

From Fig. 3.53 (*b*), voltage from G to S is given by

$$v_{os} = v_i - i_d R_s \qquad \text{...(3.21)}$$

Combining equations (3.20) and (3.21) and using $\mu = r_d g_m$

we get
$$i_d = \frac{\mu v_i}{r_d + R_d + (\mu + 1) R_s}$$

Common-source Amplifier with an Unbypassed source resistance

Since
$$v_{o1} = -i_d R_d$$

then
$$v_{o1} = \frac{-\mu v_i R_d}{r_d + R_d + (\mu + 1) R_s} \qquad \text{...(3.22)}$$

and
$$\text{Open-circuit voltage} = -\mu v_i$$
$$\text{output resistance, } R_o = r_d + (\mu + 1) R_s.$$
$$\text{Voltage gain, } A_v = \frac{v_{o1}}{v_i}.$$

minus sign in equation (3.22) indicates that output is 180° out of phase with the input. If R_s is bypassed with a large capacitance or if the source is grounded, the above equations are valid with $R_s = 0$, then

$$A_v = \frac{v_{o1}}{v_i} = \frac{-\mu R_d}{r_d + R_d} = -g_m R'_d \qquad \text{...(3.23)}$$

where
$$\mu = r_d g_m$$
and
$$R'_d = R_d \,||\, r_d.$$

Common-drain Amplifier with a Drain resistance

Since $v_{o2} = i_d R_s$, then from equation (3.22)

$$v_{o2} = \frac{-\mu v_i R_s}{r_d + R_d + (\mu + 1) R_s} = \frac{\left[\dfrac{\mu v_i}{(\mu + 1)}\right] R_s}{\dfrac{(r_d + R_d)}{(\mu + 1)} + R_s} \qquad \text{...(3.24)}$$

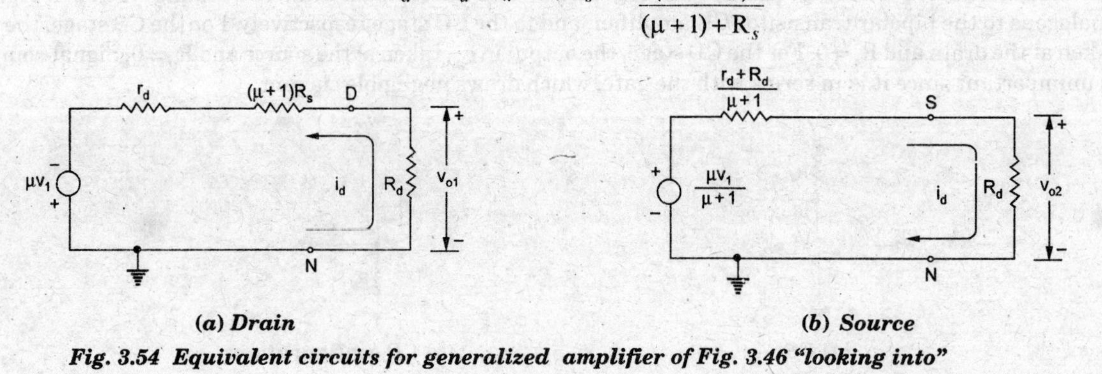

(a) Drain ***(b) Source***

Fig. 3.54 Equivalent circuits for generalized amplifier of Fig. 3.46 "looking into"

From equation (3.24), we get Thevenin's equivalent circuit of Fig. 3.54 (*b*) "looking into" the source node (to ground).

$$\text{Open-circuit voltage} = \frac{\mu v_i}{(\mu+1)}$$

$$\text{Output resistance, } R_o = \frac{\mu v_i}{(\mu+1)}.$$

$$\text{Voltage gain, } A_v = \frac{v_{o2}}{v_i}.$$

There is no phase shift between input and output.

If $R_d = 0$ and if $(\mu + 1) R_s >> r_d$, then $A_v \approx \frac{\mu}{(\mu+1)} \approx 1$ for $\mu >> 1$.

A voltage gain of unity means that the output (at the source) follows the input (at the gate). Hence CD configuration is called *source follower* (analogous to the emitter follower for a bipolar junction transistor).

3.6.7. BIASING THE FET

(*i*) Source Self-bias

The configurtion shown in Fig. 3.55 can be used to bias junction FET devices or depletion-mode MOS transistors. For a specified drain current I_D, the corresponding gate-to-source voltage V_{GS} can be obtained applying either Equation (3.17) or the plotted drain or transfer characteristics. Since the gate current (and, hence, the voltage drop across R_g) is negligible, the source resistance R_s can be found as the ratio of V_{GS} to the desired I_D.

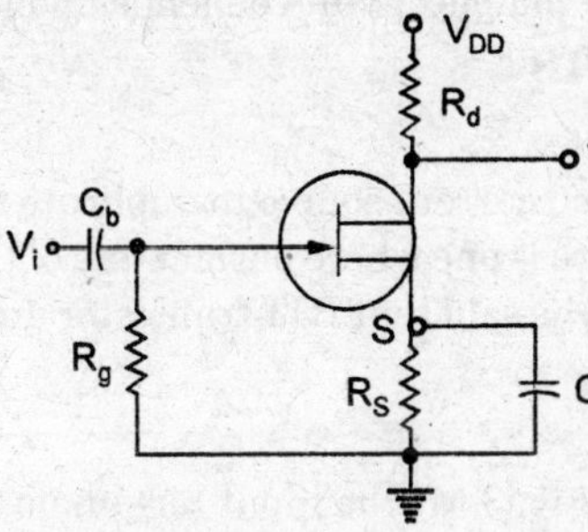

Fig. 3.55 Source self-bias circuit.

(*ii*) Biasing against Device variation

The transfer characteristics for a given type of *n*-channel FET may appear as in Fig. 3.56 (*a*), where top and bottom curves are for extreme values of temperature and device variation. It is necessary to bias the device at a drain current which will not drift out of $I_D = I_A$ and $I_D = I_B$. Then bias line $V_{GS} = -I_D R_s$ must intersect the transfer characteristic between the points A nd B, as indicated in Fig. 3.56 (*a*). The slope of this bias line is determined by the source resistance R_s. For any transfer characteristic between two extremes indicated that, current I_Q is such that $I_A < I_Q < I_B$, as desired.

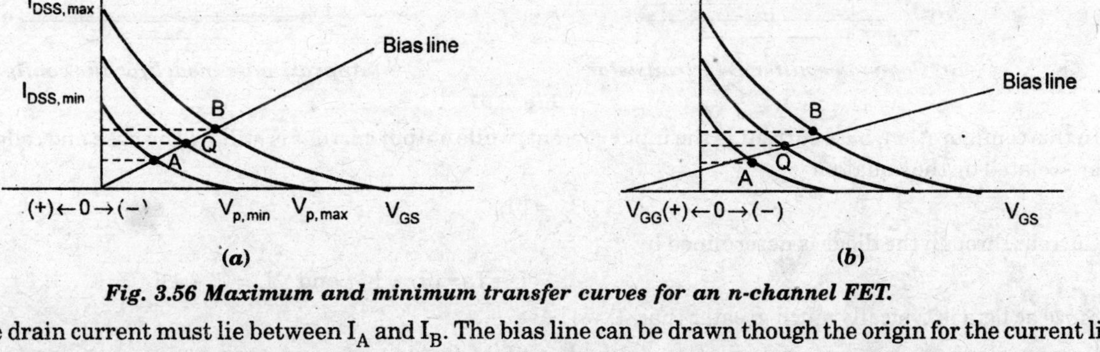

Fig. 3.56 Maximum and minimum transfer curves for an n-channel FET.

The drain current must lie between I_A and I_B. The bias line can be drawn though the origin for the current limits indicated in Fig. 3.56 (*a*), but this is not possible for the currents specified in Fig. 3.56 (*b*). Consider the situation indicated in Fig. 3.56 (*b*), where a line drawn to pass between points A and B does not pass through the origin. This bias line satisfies the equation

$$V_{GS} = V_{GG} - I_D R_s$$

3.6.8. CIRCUIT DISTORTION

A circuit distortion that may arise, either from inherent nonlinearity in the characteristics of the transistors or FETs or from the influence of the associated circuit.

Types of distortions

These exist either separately or simultaneously.

(*i*) Non-linear Distortion.

This type of distortion results from production of new frequencies in the output which are not present in the input signal. These new frequencies, or harmonics, result from the existence of a nonlinear dynamic curve for the active device. This distortion is sometimes called *amplitude distortion.*

(*ii*) Frequency Distortion.

This type of distortion exists when signal components of different frequencies are amplified differently. In a transistor or a FET, this distortion is caused by the internal device capacitances, or arises because associated circuit is reactive. Under these circumstances, gain A is the complex number whose magnitude and phase angle depend upon frequency of the impressed signal. A plot of gain (magnitude) vs frequency of an amplifier is called *amplitude frequency-response characteristic.* If frequency-response characteristic is not a horizontal straight line over the range of frequencies under consideration, the circuit is said to exhibit frequency distortion over this range.

(*iii*) Decay or Phase-shift Distortion.

Phase-shift distortion results from unequal phase shifts of signals of different frequencies. This distortion is due to the fact that the phase angle of the complex gain A depends upon the frequency.

3.7 TRANSISTOR EQUIVALENT CIRCUITS

3.7.1. r_e TRANSISTOR MODEL

The r_e model employs a diode and controlled current source to duplicate the behaviour of a transistor in the region of interest. A current-controlled current source is one where parameters of the current source are controlled by a current elsewhere in the network. Generally it can be said that BJT transistor amplifiers are referred to as *current-controlled devices.*

Common Emitter configuration

For the common-emitter configuration of Fig. 3.57, the input terminals are the base and emitter treminals, but the output set is now the collector and emitter terminals. In addition, the emitter terminal is now common between the input and output ports of the amplifier. Substituting r_e equivalent circuit for the *npn* transistor will result in the configuration of Fig. 3.57 (*b*). The controlled-current source is still connected between collector and base terminals and the diode between base and emitter terminals.

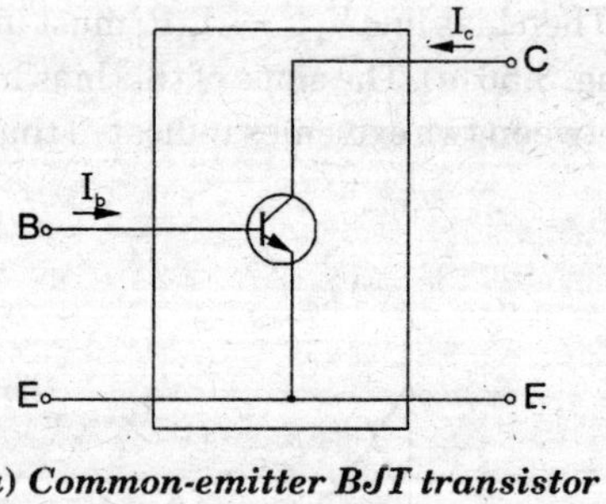

(*a*) Common-emitter BJT transistor

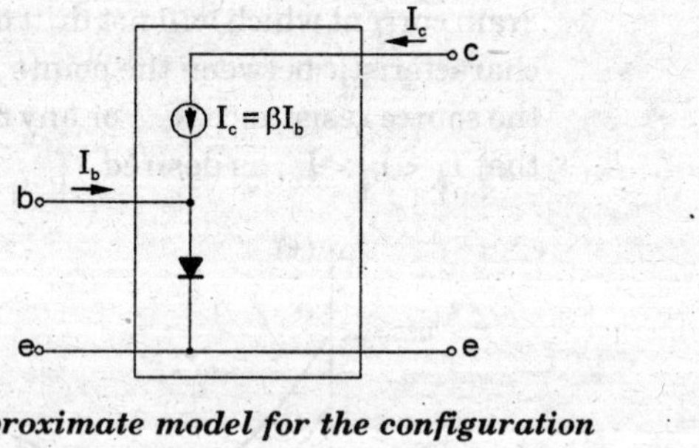

(*b*) Approximate model for the configuration

Fig. 3.57

In this configuration, base current is the input current, while output current is still I_c. The base and collector currents are related by the equation

$$I_c = \beta I_b$$

Current through the diode is determined by

$$I_e = I_c + I_b = \beta I_b + I_b \quad \text{and} \quad I_e = (\beta + 1)I_b$$

Since ac beta is typically much greater than 1, we have

$$I_e \cong \beta I_b$$

$$\text{Input impedance, } Z_i = \frac{V_i}{I_i} = \frac{V_{be}}{I_b}$$

Voltage V_{be} is across the diode resistance as shown in Fig. 3.58. The level of r_e is still determined by the dc current I_E.

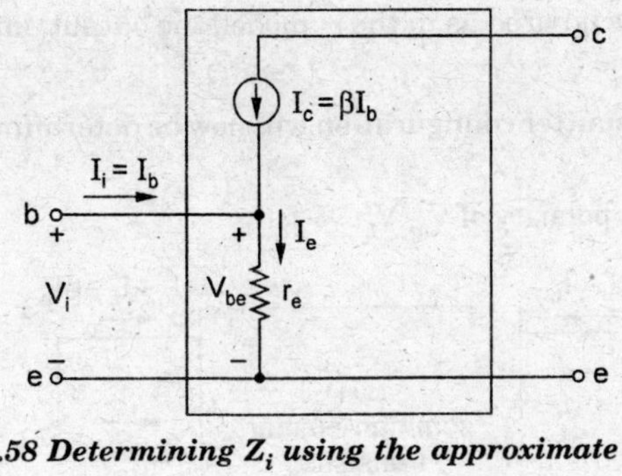

Fig. 3.58 Determining Z_i using the approximate model

Using Ohm's law, we have

$$V_i = V_{be} = I_e r_e \cong \beta\, I_b r_e$$

Substituting, we get

$$Z_i = \frac{V_{be}}{I_b} \cong \frac{\beta I_b r_e}{I_b}$$

and

$$Z_i \cong \beta\, r_e \;\; \text{CE}$$

This equation states that the input impedance for a situation such as shown in Fig. 3.59 is beta times the value of r_e. In other words, a resistive element in the emitter leg is reflected into the input circuit by a multiplying factor β.

For the common-emitter configuration, typical values of Z_i defined by $\beta\, r_e$ range from a few hundred ohms to the kilohm range with maximum of about 6–7 kilohms.

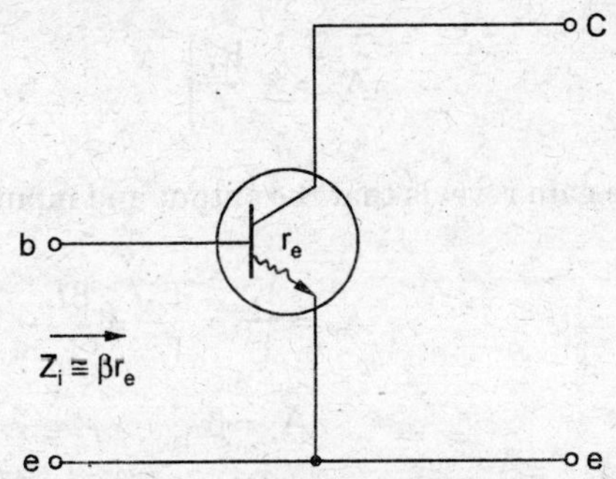

Fig. 3.59 Impact of r_e on input impedance

For the output impedance the characteristics of interest are the output set of Fig. 3.60. Slope of the curves increases with increse in collector current. The steeper the slope, the less the level of output impedance (Z_o).

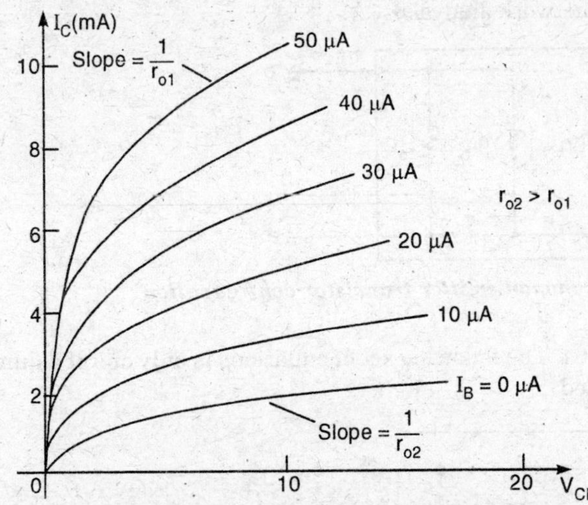

Fig. 3.60 Defining r_o for the common-emitter configuration

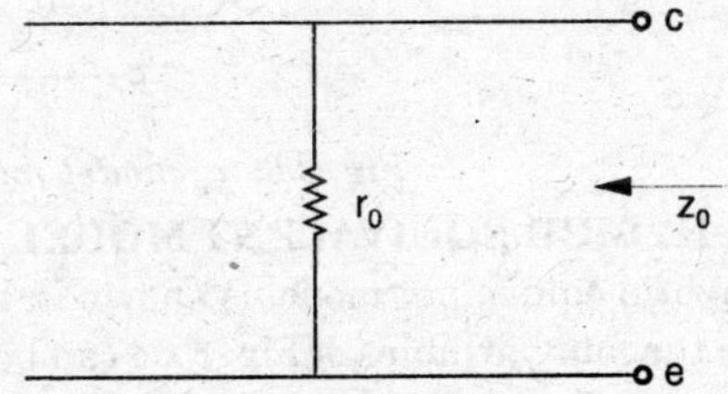

Fig. 3.61 Including r_o in the transistor equivalent circuit.

For the common-emitter configuration, typical values of Z_o are in the range of 40 to 50 kΩ.

For the model of Fig. 3.61, if applied signal is set to zero, the current I_c is 0 A and the output impedance is

$$Z_o = r_o \;\; \text{CE}$$

But, if the contribution due to r_o is ignored as in the r_e model, the output impedance is defined by

$$Z_o = \infty\,\Omega.$$

The voltage gain for the common-emitter configuration will now be determined for the configuration of Fig. 3.62 using the assumption that $Z_o = \infty\,\Omega$.

For the defined direction of I_o and polarity of V_o, $V_o = -I_oR_L$

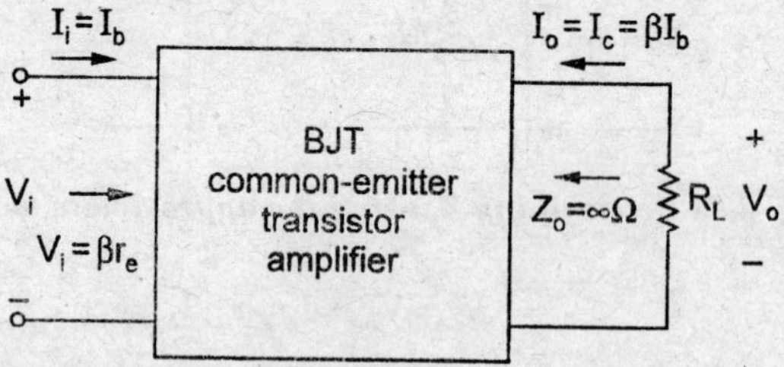

Fig. 3.62 Determining the voltage and current gain for the common-emitter transistor amplifier

The minus sign simply reflects the fact that the direction of I_o in Fig. 3.62 would establish a voltage V_o with the opposite polarity. Continuing gives

$$V_o = -I_oR_L = -I_cR_L = -\beta I_bR_L$$

and $$V_i = I_iZ_i = I_b\beta r_e$$

∴ $$A_v = \frac{V_o}{V_i} = \frac{\beta I_bR_L}{I_b\beta r_e}$$

and $$A_v = -\frac{R_L}{r_e}\Bigg|_{CE,\, r_o = \infty\Omega}$$

Resulting minus sign for the voltage gain reveals that the output and input voltages are 180º out of phase.

For the configuration of Fig. 3.62,

Current gain, $$A_i = \frac{I_o}{I_i} = \frac{I_c}{I_b} = \frac{\beta I_b}{I_b}$$

and $$A_i = \beta \quad_{CE,}\quad r_o = \infty\,\Omega$$

Using the facts that the input impedance is βr_e, the collector current is βI_b, and the output impedance is r_o, the equivalent model of Fig. 3.63 can be an effective tool in the analysis to follow. Common-emitter configuration can be considered as one that has a moderate level of input impedance, a high voltage and current gain, and an output impedance that may have to be included in the network analysis.

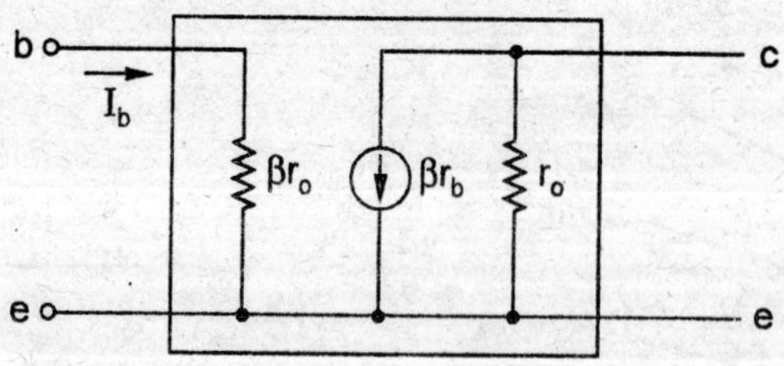

Fig. 3.63 r_e model for the common-emitter transistor configuration

3.7.2. HYBRID EQUIVALENT MODEL

The hybrid equivalent model is shown in Fig. 3.64. The following set of equations is only one of a number of ways in which the four variables of Fig. 3.64 can be related.

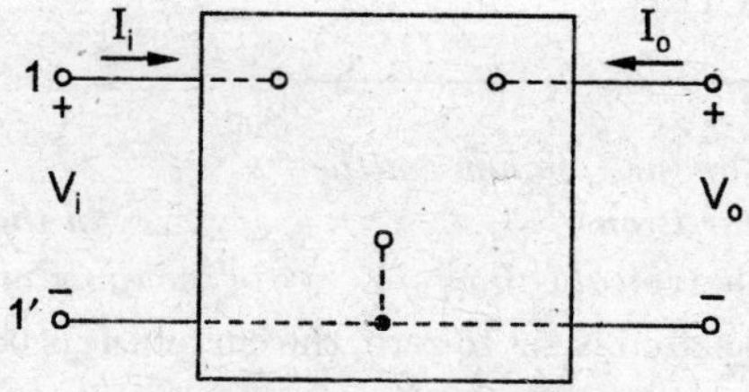

Fig. 3.64 Two-port system

$$V_i = h_{11}I_i + h_{12}V_o \quad ...(3.25)$$

$$I_o = h_{21}I_i + h_{22}V_o \quad ...(3.26)$$

The parameters relating the four variables are called *h-parameters* from the word "hybrid." The term "hybrid" was chosen because the mixture of variables (V and I) in each equation results in a "hybrid" set of units of measurement for the h-parameters.

If we set $V_o = 0$ (short circuit the output terminals), and solve for h_{11} in equation (3.25), we get

$$h_{11} = \left.\frac{V_i}{V_o}\right|_{V_o=0} \quad \text{ohms}$$

The ratio indicates that, parameters h_{11} is an impendance parameter with the units of ohms. Since it is the ratio of the input voltage to the input current with the output terminals shorted, it is called *short-circuit input-impedance parameter*. The subscript 11 of h_{11} defines the fact that the parameter is determined by a ratio of quantities measured at the input terminals.

If I_i is set equal to zero by opening the input leads, the following will results for h_{12}.

$$h_{12} = \left.\frac{V_i}{V_o}\right|_{I_i=0} \quad \text{unitless}$$

The parameter h_{12}, therefore is the ratio of the input voltage to the output voltage with the input current equal to zero. It has no units since it is a ratio of voltage levels and is called the open-circuit reverse transfer voltage ratio parameter. The subscript 12 of h_{12} reveals that the parameter is a transfer quantity determined by a ratio of input to output measurements. The first integer of the subscript defines the measured quantity to appear in the numerator; the second integer defines the source of the quantity to appear in the denominator. The term reverse is included because the ratio is an input voltage over an output voltage rather than the reverse ratio which is the matter of interest.

Now, if in equation (3.26), V_o is equal to zero by again shorting the output terminals, the following will result for h_{21}.

$$h_{21} = \left.\frac{I_i}{I_o}\right|_{V_o=0} \quad \text{unitless}$$

Now we have the ratio of an output quantity to an input quantity. The term forward will now be used rather than reverse as indicated for h_{12}. The parameter h_{21} is the ratio of the output current to the input current with the output terminals shorted. This parameter, like h_{12}, has no units since it is the ratio of current levels. It is formally called *short-circuit forward transfer current ratio parameter*. The subscript 21 again indicates that it is a transfer parameter with the output quantity in the numerator and the input quantity in the denominator.

The last parameter, h_{22}, can be found by again opening the input leads to set $I_1 = 0$ and solving for h_{22} in equation (3.26) :

$$h_{22} = \left.\frac{I_i}{V_o}\right|_{I_i=0} \quad \text{siemens}$$

Since it is the ratio of the output current to the output voltage, it is the output conductance parameter and is measured in siemens (S). It is called the open-circuit output admittance parameter. The subscript 22 reveals that it is determined by a ratio of output quantities.

Since each term of equation (3.25) has the unit volt, apply Kirchhoff's voltage law "in reverse" to find a circuit "fits" the equation. Performing this operation will result in the circuit of Fig. 3.65. Since the parameter h_{11} has the unit ohm, it is represented by a resistor in Fig. 3.65. The quantity h_{12} is dimentionless and therefore simply appears as a multiplying factor of the "feedback" term in the input circuit.

Since each term of equation (3.26) has the units of current, now apply Kirchhoff's current law "in reverse" to obtain the circuit of Fig. 3.66. Since h_{22} has the units of admittance, which for the transistor model is conductance, it is represented by the resistor symbol. Remember that the resistance in ohms of this resistor is equal to the reciprocal of conductance ($1/h_{22}$).

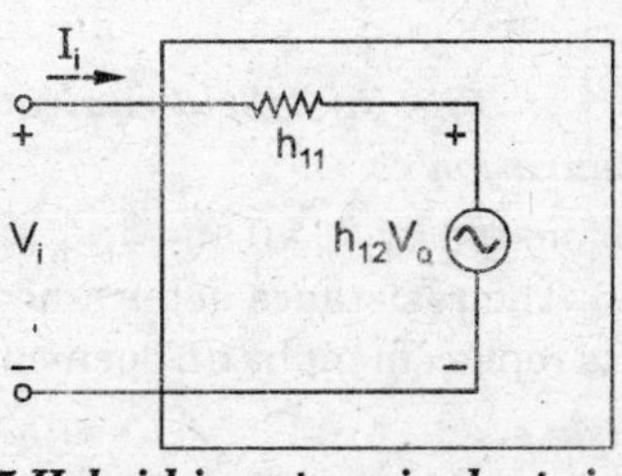

Fig. 3.65 Hybrid input equivalent circuit

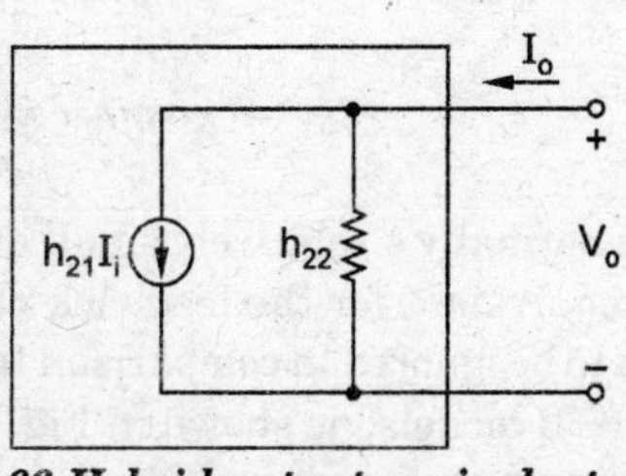

Fig. 3.66 Hybrid output equivalent circuit

The complete "ac" equivalent circuit for the basic three-terminal linear device is indicated in Fig. 3.67. with a new set of subscripts for the h-parameters.

The h-parameters are

$h_{11} \rightarrow$ input resistance $\rightarrow h_i$

$h_{12} \rightarrow$ reverse transfer voltage ratio $\rightarrow h_r$

$h_{21} \rightarrow$ forward transfer current ratio $\rightarrow h_f$

$h_{22} \rightarrow$ output conductance $\rightarrow h_o$

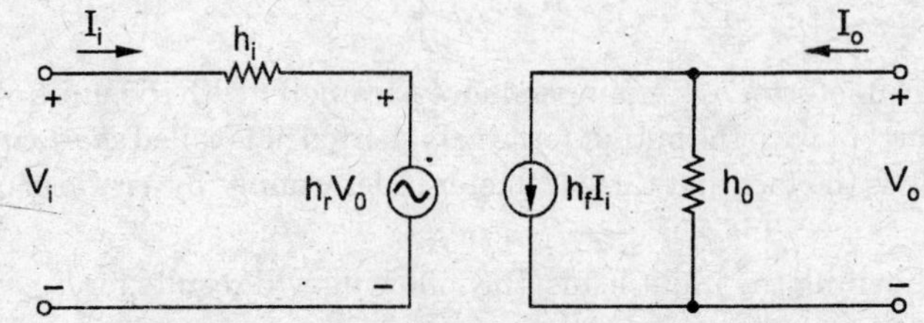

Fig. 3.67 Complete hybrid equivalent circuit

The circuit given in Fig. 3.67 is applicable to any linear three-terminal electronic device or system with no internal independent sources. The input and output sections of the network of Fig. 3.67 can be connected as shown in Fig. 3.68, since the potential level is the same. Essentially, therefore, the transistor model is a three-terminal two-port system. The h-parameters, however, will change with each configuration. To distinguish which parameter has been used or which is available, a second subscript has been added to the h-parameter notation. For the common-base configuration, the lowercase letters b was added, while for the common-emitter and common-collector configurations the letter e and c were added, respectively. The hybrid equivalent network for the common-emitter configuration appears with standard notation is in shown in Fig. 3.68.

Here $\quad I_i = I_b, I_o = I_c$

and by Kirchhoff's current law $\quad I_e = I_b + I_c.$

The input voltage is now V_{be} with the output voltage V_{ce}.

For the common-base configuration of Fig. 3.69,

$$I_i = I_e, I_o = I_c$$

with $\quad V_{eb} = V_i$ and $V_{cb} = V_o$

The networks of Figs. 3.68 and 3.69 are applicable for *pnp* or *npn* transistors.

Fig. (a) Graphic symbol *Fig. (b) Hybrid equivalent circuit*

Fig. 3.68 Common-emitter configuration

Fig. (a) graphic symbol *Fig. (b) hybrid equivalent circuit*

Fig. 3.69 Common-base configuration

As h_r is normally a relatively small quantity, its removal is approximated by $h_r \cong 0$ and $h_rV_o = 0$, resulting in a short-circuit equivalent for the feedback element as shown in Fig. 3.70. The resistance determined by $1/h_o$ is often large enough to be ignored in comparison to a parallel load permitting its replacement by an open-circuit equivalent for the CE and CB models, as shown in Fig. 3.70.

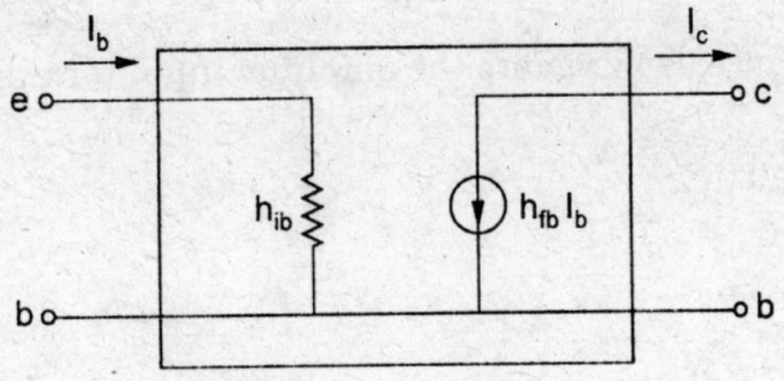

Fig.3.70 *Effect of removing h_{re} and h_{oe} from the hybrid equivalent circuit*

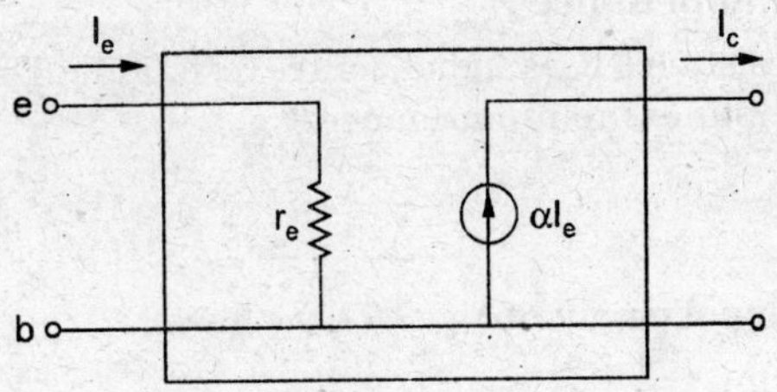

Fig. 3.71 Approximate hybrid equivalent model

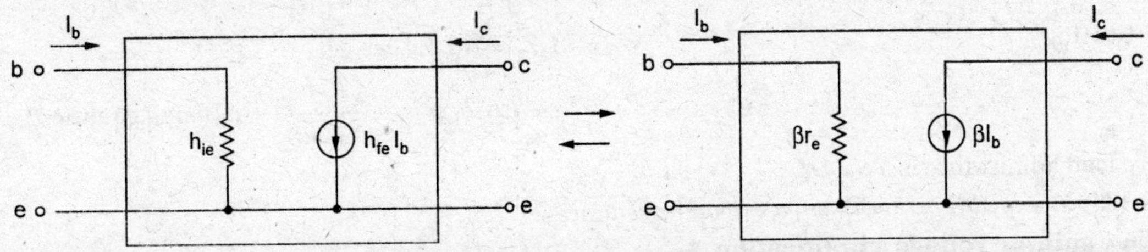

(a) Common-emmitter configuration

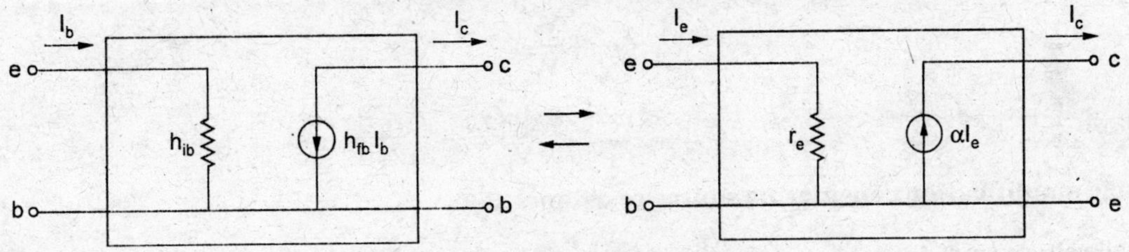

(b) Common-base configuration

Fig. 3.72 Hybrid versus r_e model

The resulting equivalent of Fig. 3.71 is quite similar to the general structure of the common-base and common-emitter equivalent circuits obtained with the r_e model. Infact, the hybrid equivalent and the r_e model for each configuration have been repeated in Fig. 3.72 for comparison. It should be reasonably clear from Fig. 3.72 (*a*) that

$$h_{ie} = \beta r_e, \text{ and } h_{fe} = \beta_{ac},$$

From Fig. 3.72 (*b*), $\quad h_{ib} = r_e$, and $h_{fb} = -\alpha \cong -1$

minus sign in the equation accounts for the fact that the current source of the standard hybrid equivalent circuit is pointing down rather than in the actual direction as shown in the r_e model of Fig. 3.72 (*b*).

3.7.3. ANALYSIS OF A TRANSISTOR AMPLIFIER CIRCUIT USING *h*-PARAMETERS

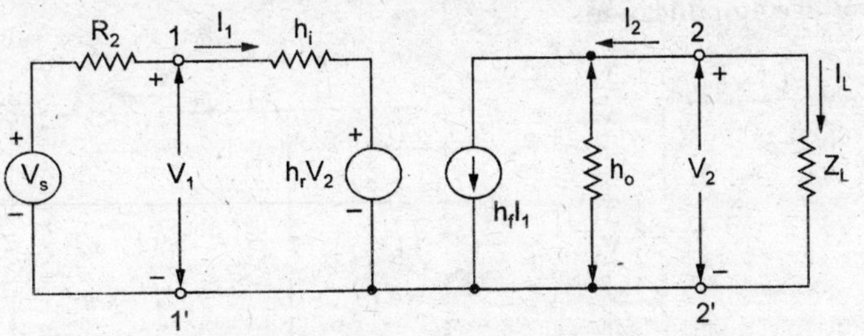

Fig. 3.73 Transistor is replaced by its h-parameter model.

Assuming sinusoidally varying voltages and currents, analysis of the circuit of Fig. 3.73 is carried out, using the phasor (sinor) notation to represent following sinusoidally varying quantities :

(*i*) Current gain, or Current amplification, A_I

It is defined as the ratio of output to input currents, or

$$A_I \equiv \frac{I_L}{I_1} = -\frac{I_2}{I_1}$$

From the circuit of Fig. 3.73, we have $\quad I_2 = h_f I_1 + h_o V_2$

Substituting $V_2 = -I_2 Z_L$, we get $\quad A_I = -\frac{I_2}{I_1} = -\frac{h_f}{1 + h_o Z_L}$

(ii) Input impedance Z_i

The resistance R_s is signal-source resistance. The impedance, looking into the amplifier input terminals (1, 1′) is the amplifier input impedance Z_i,

$$Z_i \equiv \frac{V_1}{I_1}$$

From input circuit of Fig. 3.73, we have

$$V_1 = h_i I_1 + h_r V_2$$

Then,

$$Z_i = \frac{h_f I_1 + h_r V_2}{I_1} = h_i + h_r \frac{V_2}{I_1}$$

Substituting,

$$V_2 = -I_2 Z_L = A_I I_1 Z_L, \text{ we get}$$

$$Z_i = h_i + h_r A_I Z_L = h_i - \frac{h_f h_r}{Y_L + h_o} \quad \text{...[using equation]}$$

where load admittance is $Y_L \equiv 1/Z_L$.

Note : *Input impedance is a function of load impedance.*

(iii) Voltage gain, or Voltage amplification, A_V

The ratio of output voltage V_2 to input voltage V_1 gives voltage gain of the transistor

$$A_V \equiv \frac{V_2}{V_1}$$

We have,

$$A_V = \frac{A_I I_1 Z_L}{V_1} = \frac{A_I Z_L}{Z_i}$$

Voltage amplification considering source resistance R_s :

Overall voltage gain,
$$A_{Vs} \equiv \frac{V_2}{V_s} = \frac{V_2}{V_1}\frac{V_1}{V_s} = A_V \frac{V_1}{V_s}$$

From equivalent input circuit of the amplifier, shown in Fig. 3.74 (*a*),

$$V_1 = \frac{V_s Z_i}{Z_i + R_s}$$

Then

$$A_{Vs} = \frac{A_V Z_i}{Z_i + R_s} = \frac{A_I Z_L}{Z_i + R_s}$$

If $R_s = 0$, then $A_{Vs} = A_V$.

Hence *A_V is the voltage gain for an ideal voltage source* (one with zero internal resistance).

In practice, the quantity A_{Vs} is more meaningful than A_V since, usually, source resistance has an appreciable effect on the overall voltage amplification.

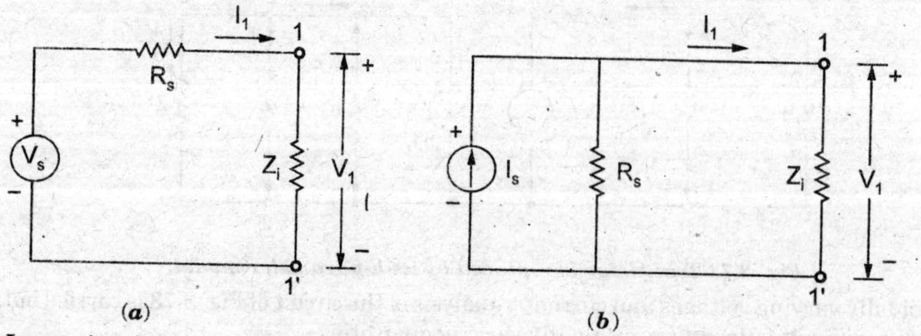

Fig. 3.74 Input circuit of a transistor amplifier using (a) Thevenin's equivalent for the source and (b) a Norton's equivalent for the source.

Current amplification, A_{Is}, taking into account the source resistance R_s :

If input source is a current generator I_s in parallel with a resistance R_s, as shown in Fig. 3.74 (*b*), then

overall current gain ,
$$A_{Is} \equiv \frac{-I_2}{I_s} = \frac{-I_2}{I_1}\frac{I_1}{I_s} = A_I \frac{I_1}{I_s}$$

From Fig. 3.74 (*b*),

$$I_1 = \frac{I_s R_s}{Z_i + R_s}$$

$$\therefore \qquad A_{Is} = \frac{A_I R_s}{Z_i + R_s}$$

If $R_s = \infty$, then $\qquad A_{Is} = A_I$.

Hence A_I *is the current gain for an ideal current source* (one with infinite source resistance).

Independent of the transistor characteristic, the voltage and current gains, taking source impedance into account, are related by

$$A_{Vs} = A_{Is} \frac{Z_L}{R_s}$$

This relationship is valid if the current and voltage generators have the same source resistance R_s.

(iv) Output Admittance

By definition, output impedance, $Z_o = 1/Y_o$ is obtained by setting the source voltage V_s to zero and the load impedance Z_L to infinity and by driving the output terminals from a generator V_2.

If current drawn from V_2 is I_2, then

$$Y_o \equiv \frac{I_2}{V_2} \text{ with } V_s = 0 \text{ and } R_L = \infty$$

Also,

$$Y_o = h_f \frac{I_1}{V_2} + h_o$$

From Fig. 3.74, with $V_s = 0$

$$R_s I_1 + h_i I_1 + h_r V_2 = 0$$

or

$$\frac{I_1}{V_2} = -\frac{h_r}{h_i + R_s}$$

$$\therefore \qquad Y_o = h_o - \frac{h_f h_r}{h_i + R_s}$$

The output admittance is a fucntion of the source resistance. If source impedance is resistive, as we have assumed, then Y_o is real (a conductance).

The important formulas derived above are summarized in Table 3.4. The expressions for A_V, A_{Vs}, and A_{Is} are without reference to the hybrid parameters, and hence are valid regradless of what equivalent circuit we use for the transistor. In particular, these expressions are valid at high frequencies, where the h parameters are functions of frequency or where we may prefer to use another model for the transistor.

Table 3.4. Small-signal analysis of a transistor amplifier

$A_I = -\dfrac{h_f}{1 + h_o Z_L}$	$Y_o = h_o - \dfrac{h_f h_r}{h_i + R_s} = \dfrac{1}{Z_o}$
$Z_i = h_i + h_r A_I Z_L$	$A_{Vs} = \dfrac{A_V Z_i}{Z_i + R_s} = \dfrac{A_I Z_L}{Z_i + R_s}$
$A_V = \dfrac{A_I Z_L}{Z_i}$	$A_{Is} = \dfrac{A_I R_s}{Z_i + R_s} = A_{Vs} \dfrac{R_s}{Z_L}$

Approximate Equivalent Circuit

Table : 3.5. Typical *h*-parameter values for a transistor (at I_E = 1.3 mA) :

Parameter	CE	CC	CB
$h_{11} = h_i$	1.1K	1.1K	21.6Ω
$h_{12} = h_r$	2.5×10^{-4}	~ 1	2.9×10^{-4}
$h_{21} = h_f$	50	–51	–0.98
$h_{22} = h_o$	24μ A/V	25μ A/V	0.49μ A/V
$\dfrac{1}{h_o}$	40 K	40 K	40 K

From Table 3.5, $h_{re} V_{ce}$ is small, hence almost short circuit and $\dfrac{1}{h_{ce}}$ is large, thus equivalent to open circuit.

3.7.4. EMITTER FOLLOWER

The circuit for the emitter follower is shown in Fig. 3.75. Since, voltage gain for this configuration is close to unity, and hence a change in base voltage appears as an equal change across the load at the emitter, it is called *emitter follower*. The most common use of it is as a buffer stage which performs the function of resistance transformation (from hign to low resistance) over a wide range of frequencies, with voltage gain close to unity. In addition, the emitter follower increases the power level of the signal.

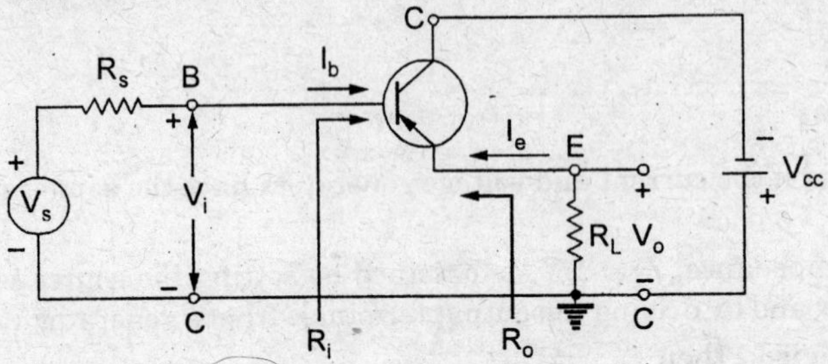

Fig. 3.75 Common-collector, or emitter-follower, configuration

Expressions for current gain, input resistance, voltage gain, and output resistance are given as

$$A_I = \frac{-I_e}{I_b} = \frac{-h_{fc}}{1+h_{oc}R_L} = \frac{1+h_{fe}}{1+h_{oc}R_L}$$

$$R_i = \frac{V_i}{I_b} = h_{ic} + h_{rc}A_I R_L = h_{ie} + A_I R_L$$

$$A_V = \frac{V_o}{V_i} = \frac{A_I R_L}{R_i} = \frac{R_i - h_{ie}}{R_i} = 1 - \frac{h_{ie}}{R_i}$$

$$Y_o = h_{oc} - \frac{h_{fc}h_{rc}}{h_{ic}+R_s} = h_{oc} + \frac{1+h_{fe}}{h_{ie}+R_s}$$

3.7.5. SIMPLIFIED COMMON-EMITTER HYBRID MODEL

Consider a common-emitter configuration with the condition that

$$h_{oe}R_L < 0.1$$

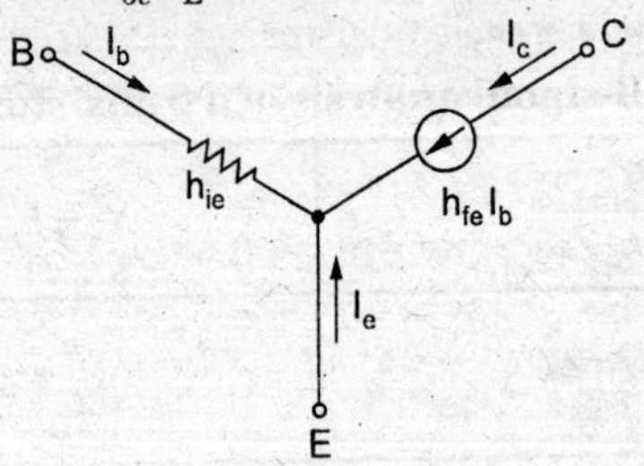

Fig. 3.76 Approximate hybrid model which may be used for all three configurations CE, CC, and CB

CE stage with the transistor replaced by the approximate model of Fig. 3.76.

Now compare the exact results with those obtained from the simplified analysis.

Current gain :

CE current gain i, $$A_r = \frac{-h_{fe}}{1+h_{oe}R_L}$$

After approximation Fig. 3.77, we have $A_r \approx -h_{fe}$

overestimates the magnitude of the current gain by less than 10 percent if $h_{oe}R_L < 0.1$.

Input Impedance :

Input resistance, $$R_i = h_{ie} + h_{re}A_I R_L$$

which may be put in the form

$$R_i = h_{ie}\left(1 - \frac{h_{re}h_{fe}}{h_{ie}h_{oe}}\frac{|A_I|}{h_{fe}}h_{oe}R_L\right)$$

Using the h-parameter values, $$\frac{h_{re}\,h_{fe}}{h_{ie}\,h_{oe}} \approx 0.5.$$

Also, $$|A_I| < h_{fe}.$$

Hence, if $h_{oe}R_L < 0.1$, it follows from that the approximation obtained from Fig. 3.77

$$R_i = \frac{V_b}{I_b} \approx h_{ie}$$

overestimates input resistance by less than 5 percent.

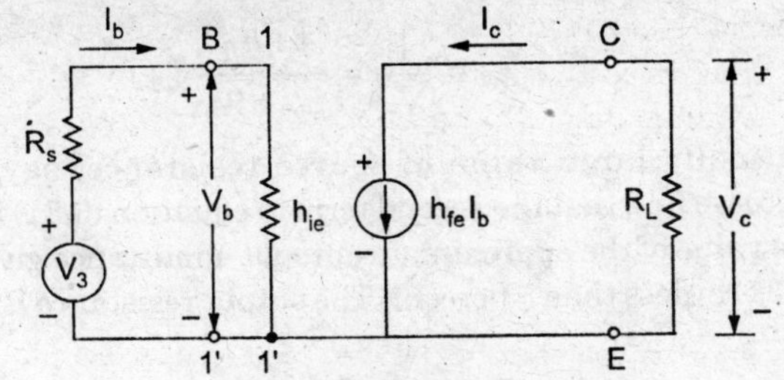

Fig. 3.77 Approximate CE model

Voltage gain :

voltage gain, $$A_V = A_I\frac{R_L}{R_i} = -\frac{h_{fe}R_L}{h_{ie}}$$

Taking logarithm of this equation and differentiating, we get

$$\frac{dA_V}{A_V} = \frac{dA_I}{A_I} - \frac{dR_i}{R_i} \quad ...(3.27)$$

Maximum errors for $h_{oe}R_L < 0.1$ are

$$\frac{dA_I}{A_I} = +0.1, \quad \text{and} \quad \frac{dR_i}{R_i} = +0.05$$

Hence maximum error in voltage gain is 5 percent, and magnitude of A_v is overestimated by this amount.

3.7.6. SIMPLIFIED CALCULATION FOR THE COMMON-COLLECTOR CONFIGURATION

Current Gain :

From Fig. 3.78, $$A_I = -\frac{I_e}{I_b} = 1 + h_{fe} \quad ...(3.28)$$

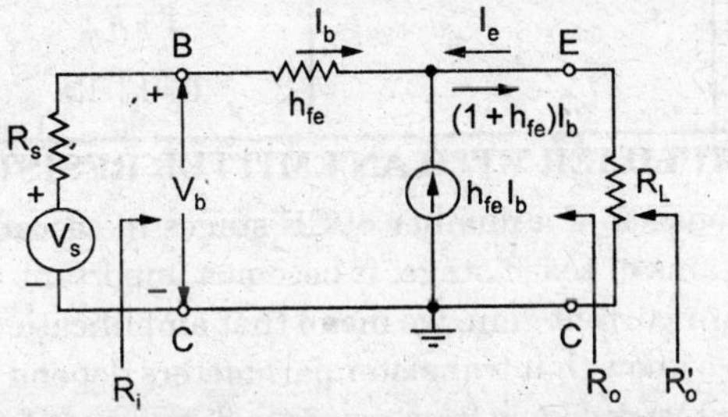

Fig 3.78 Simplified hybrid model for the CC circuit.

Comparing this equation with the exact expression, It can be concluded that when simplified equivalent circuit of Fig. 3.78 is used, the current gain is overestimated by less than 10 percent if

$$h_{oe}R_L < 0.1.$$

Input resistance :

From Fig. 3.78, $$R_i = \frac{V_b}{I_b} = h_{ie} + (1 + h_{fe})R_L \quad ...(3.29)$$

$R_i >> h_{ie} \approx 1$ K even if R_L is as small as 0.5 K, because $h_{fe} >> 1$. However, it is just concluded that equation (3.28) gives too high a value of A_I by at most 10 percent. Hence it follows that R_i, as calculated from equation (3.29) or Fig. 3.78, is also overestimated by less than 10 percent.

Voltage gain : If equation (3.27) is used for the voltage gain, it follows from the same arguments as used in the CE case that there will be very little error in the value of A_V. The voltage gain of the emitter follower is close to unity,

or $$1 - A_V = h_{ie}/R_i$$

If, however, an approximate value of R_i is used, which is 10 percent too high, then

$$\frac{h_{ie}}{R_i} = \frac{1}{11} = 0.99 \quad \text{and} \quad A_V = 0.91$$

Hence approximate calculation for A_V gives a value which is only 1 percent too high.

Output impedance : In Fig. 3.78, open-circuit output voltage is V_s and short-circuit output current is

$$I = (1 + h_{fe})\, I_b = \frac{(1+h_{fe})V_s}{h_{ie} + R_s} \quad ...(3.30)$$

Hence ouput admittance of the transistor alone is,

$$Y_o = \frac{I}{V_s} = \frac{1+h_{fe}}{h_{ie} + R_s} \quad ...(3.31)$$

Even if we choose an abnormally large value of source resistance, say, R_s = 100 K, then (using typical h-parameter values in Table 3.5) we find that the second term in equation (3.31) is large (500 μA/V) compared with the first term (25 μA/V). Hence the value of the approximate outoput admittance given by equation (3.30) is smaller than the value given by equation (3.31) by less than 5 percent. The output resistance R_o of the transistor, calculated from the simplified model,

$$R_o = \frac{h_{ie} + R_s}{1+h_{fe}}$$

is an overestimation by less than 5 percent. The output resistance R'_s of the stage, taking the load into account, is R_o inparallel with R_L.

Table 3.6. Summary of Approximate equation equations for h_{oe} (R_e + R_L) ≤ 0.1

	CE	CE with R_e	CC	CB
A_I	$-h_{fe}$	$-h_{fe}$	$1 + h_{fe}$	$-h_{fb} = \frac{h_{fe}}{1+h_{fe}}$
R_i	h_{ie}	$h_{ie} + (1 + h_{fe}) R_e$	$h_{ie} + (1 + h_{fe}) R_L$	$h_{ib} = \frac{h_{ie}}{1+h_{fe}}$
A_V	$-\frac{h_{fe} R_L}{h_{ie}}$	$-\frac{h_{fe} R_L}{R_i}$	$1 - \frac{h_{ie}}{R_i}$	$\frac{R_L}{h_{fe}\ h_{ie}}$
R_o	∞	∞	$\frac{R_s + h_{ie}}{1+h_{fe}}$	∞
R'_o	R_L	R_L	$R_o \parallel R_L$	R_L

3.7.7 COMMON-EMITTER AMPLIFIER WITH AN EMITTER RESISTANCE

Usually a transistor amplifier consists of a number of CE stages in cascade. Since voltage gain of the amplifier is equal to product of the voltage gains of reach stage, it becomes important to stabilize voltage amplification of each stage. By stabilization of voltage or current gain, we mean that amplification becomes essentially independent of the h parameters of the transistor. We know that transistor parameters depend on temperature, aging and the operating point. Moreover, these parameters vary widely from device to device even for the same type of transistor.

The necessity for voltage stabilization is seen from the following example :

Two commercially built six-stage amplifiers are to be compared. If each stage of the first has a gain which is only 10 percent below that of the second, the overall amplification of the latter is $(0.9)^6$ = 0.53 (or about one-half that of the former).And this value may be below the required specification. A simple and effective way to obtain voltage-gain stabilization is to add an emitter resistor R_c to a CE stage, as indicated in the circuit of Fig. 3.79. This stabilization is a result of the feedback provided by the emitter resistor.

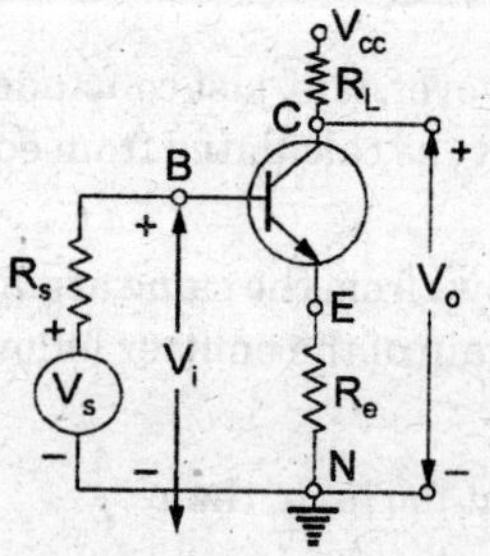

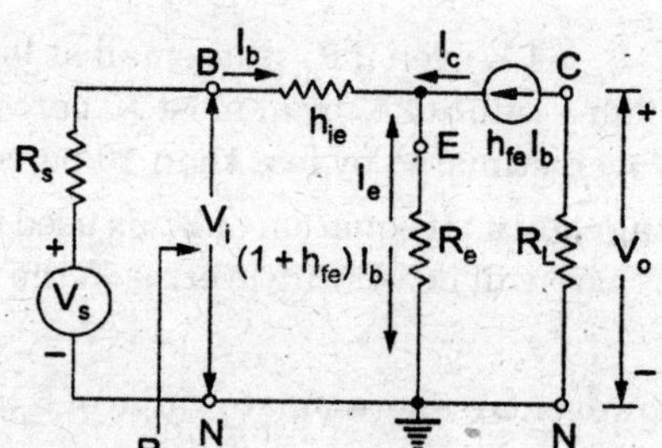

(a) Common-emitter amplifier with an emitter resistor (b) Approximate small-signal equivalent circuit

Fig. 3.79

Approximate solution

An approximate analysis of the circuit of Fig. 3.79 (*a*) shown in Fig. 3.79 (*b*).

From Fig. 3.79 (*b*), Current gain

$$A_I = \frac{-I_c}{I_b} = \frac{-h_{fe}I_b}{I_b} = -h_{fe}$$

The current gain equals the short-circuit value, and is unaffected by the addition of R_c.

From inspection of Fig. 3.79 (*b*), input resistance,

$$R_i = \frac{V_i}{I_b} = h_{ie} + (1 + h_{fe})\, R_c$$

The input resistance is augmented by $(1 + h_{fe})R_c$, and may be very much larger than h_{ie}. Hence an emitter resistance greatly increases the input resistance. The voltage gain is

$$A_V = \frac{A_I R_L}{R_i} = \frac{-h_{fe}R_L}{h_{ie} + (1 + h_{fe})R_e}$$

Clearly, addition of an emitter resitance greatly reduces the voltage amplification.

If $(1 + h_{fe})\, R_e >> h_{ie}$, and since $h_{fe} >> 1$, therefore

$$A_V \approx \frac{-h_{fe}}{1 + h_{fe}} \frac{R_L}{R_e} \approx \frac{-R_L}{R_e}$$

Here, A_V is completely stable (if stable resistances are used for R_L and R_e), since it is independent of all transistor parameters.

The output resistance of the transistor alone (with R_L considered external) is infinite for the approximate circuit of Fig. 3.79. Hence output impedance of the stage, including the load, is R_L.

3.7.8. HIGH-INPUT-RESISTANCE TRANSISTOR CIRCUITS

To achieve larger input impedances, the circuit shown in Fig. 3.80 (*a*), called *Darlington connection*, is used.

Two transistors form a composite pair :

(*i*) input resistance of the second transistor form a composite pair,

(*ii*) Input resistance of the second transistor constituting the emitter load for the first.

More specifically, the Darlington circuit consists of two cascaded emitter followers with infinite emitter resistance in the first stage, as shown in Fig. 3.80 (*b*).

The Darlington composite emitter follower will be analyzed by referring to Fig. 3.81.

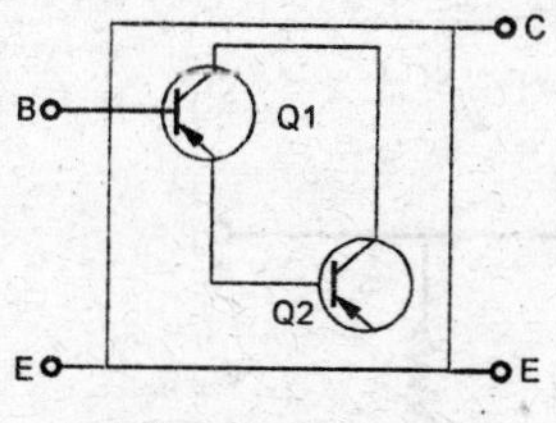

(a) Darlington pair

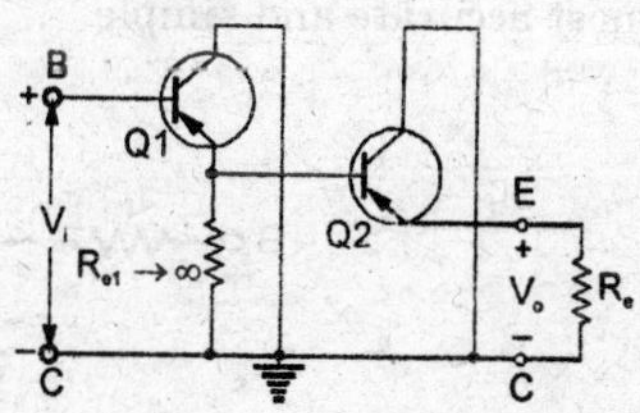

(b) Darlington circuit drawn as two cascaded CC stages

Fig. 3.80

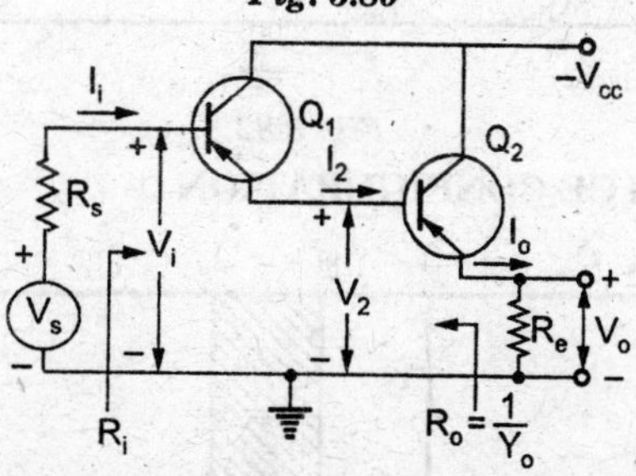

Fig. 3.81 Darlington emitter follower.

Assuming that $h_{oe}R_e \leq 0.1$ and $h_{fe}R_e >> h_{ie}$, current gain and input impedance of the second stage are given as

$$A_{I2} = \frac{I_o}{I_2} \approx 1 + h_{fe} \qquad R_{i2} \approx (1 + h_{fe})\, R_e$$

Since effective load for transistor Q1 is R_{i2}, which usually does not meet the requirement $h_{oe}R_{i2} \leq 0.1$, exact expression is used for current gain of the first transistor :

$$A_{I1} = \frac{I_2}{I_i} = \frac{1+h_{fe}}{1+h_{oe}(1+h_{fe})R_e}$$

and since $h_{oe}R_e \le 0.1$, we have

$$A_{I1} \approx \frac{1+h_{fe}}{1+h_{oe}h_{fe}R_e}$$

Overall current gain,
$$A_I = \frac{I_o}{I_i} = \frac{I_o}{I_2}\frac{I_2}{I_i} = A_{I2}A_{I1}$$

or
$$A_{I1} \approx \frac{(1+h_{fe})^2}{1+h_{oe}h_{fe}R_e}$$

Similarly, input resistance of Q1 is,

$$R_{i1} = h_{ie} + A_{I2}R_{i2} \approx \frac{(1+h_{fe})^2 R_e}{1+h_{oe}h_{fe}R_e}$$

This equation for the input resistance of the Darling circuit is valid for $h_{oe}R_{i2} \le 0.1$

Voltage gain of the Darlington emitter follower is,

$$A_V \approx 1 - \frac{h_{ie2}}{R_{i2}}(2 + h_{oe}h_{fe}R_e)$$

and, output impedance, $$R_o \approx \frac{R_s}{(1+h_{fe})^2} + \frac{2h_{ie2}}{1+h_{fe}}$$

Hence Darlington emitter follower has a high input impedance and voltage gain close to unity.

3.7.9. TRANSISTORS AT HIGH FREQUENCIES

At low frequencies, it is assumed that transistor responds instantly to changes of input voltage or current but actually, such is not the case, because mechanism of transport of charge carries from emitter to collector is essentially one of diffusion. To find transistor behaviour at high frequencies, a hybrid-μ model has been developed to make high frequency analysis almost accurate and simple.

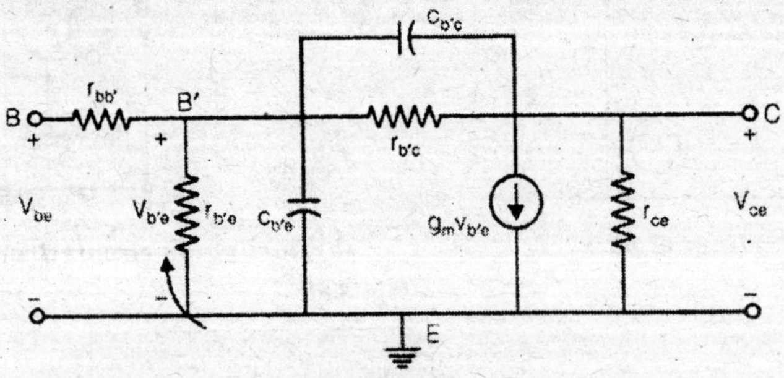

Fig. 3.82

3.7.10. π-EQUIVALENT OF BJT IN CE CONFIGURATION

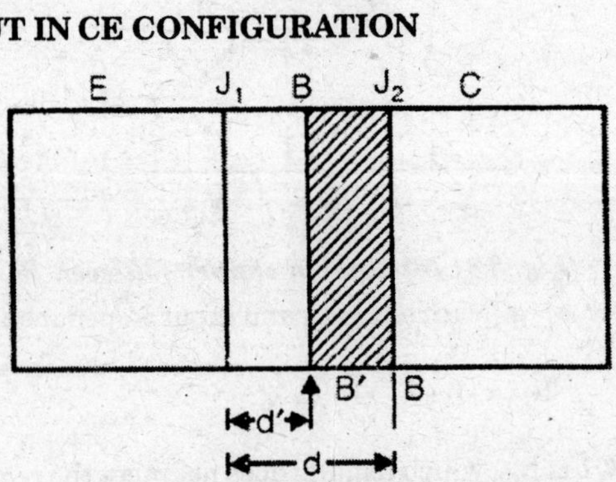

Fig. 3.83 Circuit components

Origination of terminal B′

Junction J_1 is forward biased and J_2 is reverse biased

Let d' = efffective base width under RB condition

d = physical width (RB = 0)

As reverse bias increases, depletion layer width increases and effective base width decreases. This terminal B′ exists due to R.B applied.

Base spreading resistance ($r_{bb'}$).

It represents effective resistance of the base region when reverse bias has been applied. Since doping of the base region is very low, this resistance has very low value of the order of 80 Ωs.

$r_{b'e}$.

It represents resistance of the forward biased junction J_1 and has a relatively low value of the order of 1 kΩ.

$r_{b'c}$.

It represents resistance of the reverse bias junction J_2 and have a very high value of the order of 4 mega ohms.

r_{bc}.

It represents total resistance of the combined forward biased junction J_1 and reverse biased junction J_2. It has relatively high value of the order of 100 k.

Transconductance (g_m).

It's value is 200 ms.

$g_m V_{b'e}$.

It represents a current source which accounts for voltage gain of the CE amplifier at high frequenceis.

$C_{b'e}$.

It represents junction capacitance of the forward biased junction J_1. Since width of the depletion layer is very small at J_1, this capacitance has relatively a high value of the order of 100 picofaread.

$C_{b'c}$.

It represents junction capacitance of the reverse bias junction J_2. Since width of depletion layer is large, this capacitance has a low value of the order of 3 picofarad.

Relation between High frequency and Low frequency parameters

$$g_m = \frac{|I_C|}{V_T} \qquad V_T = \frac{T}{11600}$$

$$r_{b'e} = \frac{h_{fe}}{g_m}$$

$$r_{bb'} = h_{ie} - r_{b'e}$$

$$r_{b'c} = \frac{r_{b'e}}{h_{re}}$$

$$r_{ce} = \left(h_{re} = \frac{1+h_{fe}}{r_{b'e}}\right)^{-1}$$

$$c_{b'e} = \frac{g_m}{2\pi f_T}$$

$$c_{b'c} = kV_{CE}^{-n}$$

where, f_T = frequency at which short-circuit current gain of CE amplifier at high frquency becomes unity

k = constant

$n = \frac{1}{2}$ ... for abrupt or step junction

$= \frac{1}{3}$ ... for linearly graded junction.

Short-circuit Current gain, f_T, f_β and Current gain bandwidth Product

Consider a common emitter amplifier at high frequency and its equivalent π model.

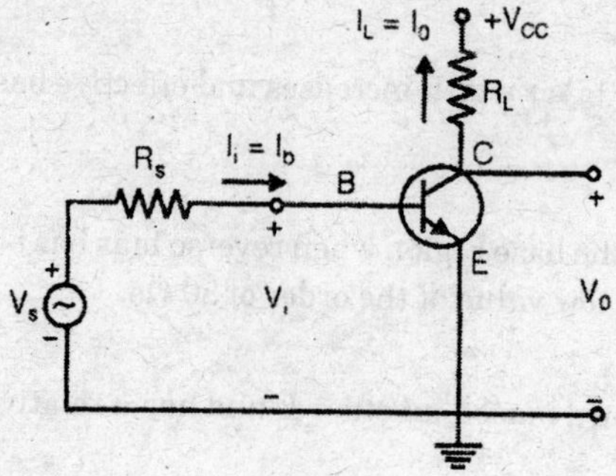

Fig. 3.84

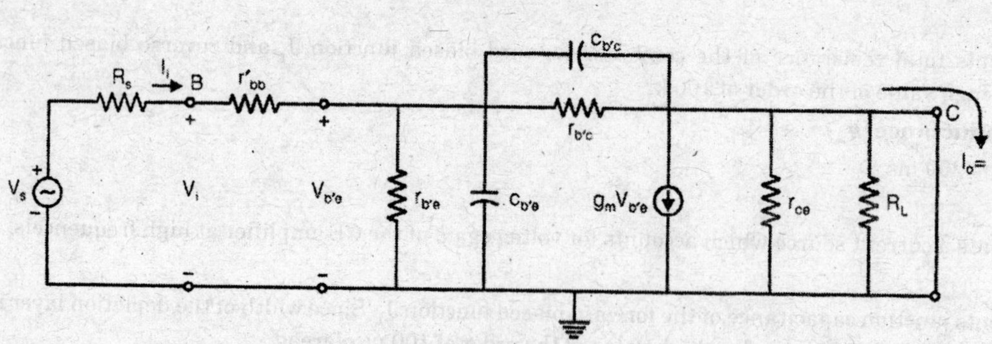

Fig. 3.85

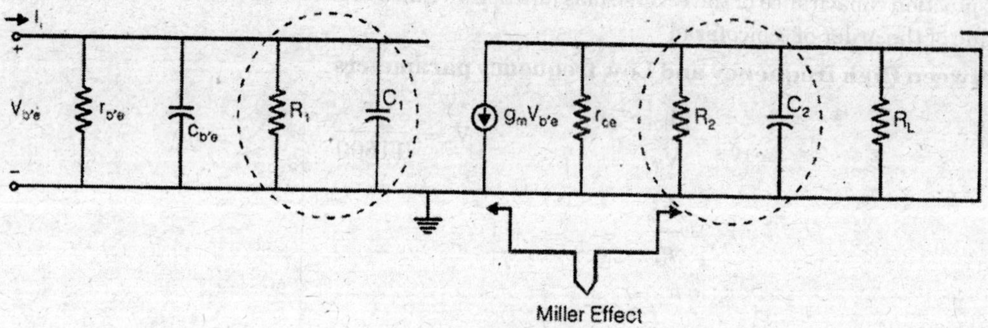

Fig. 3.86

$$R_1 = \frac{r_{b'c}}{1 - A_V}$$

As output is short circuited,

$$A_V = \frac{V_O}{V_i} = 0$$

$\therefore$

$$R_1 = r_{b'c} \quad \text{...(3.32)}$$

$$R = r_{b'c} \parallel R_1 = r_{b'c} \parallel r_{b'c}$$

$$Z_1 = \frac{Z}{1 - A_V} \quad A_V = 0$$

$$\frac{1}{j\omega C_1} = \frac{1}{j\omega C_{b'c}}$$

$\therefore$

$$C_1 = C_{b'c}$$

$$C = C_{b'c} + C_1 = C_{b'c} + C_{b'c} + C_{b'c} \approx C_{b'c} \quad \text{...(3.33)}$$

Hence equations (3.32) and (3.33) takes the form as :

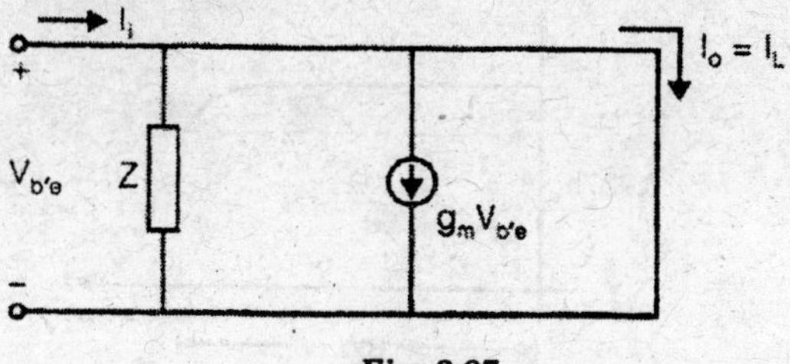

Fig. 3.87

$$Z = R\,||\,\frac{1}{j\omega C} = r_{b'e}\,||\,\frac{1}{j\omega C_{b'e}}$$

$$= \frac{r_{b'e} \times \frac{1}{j\omega C_{b'e}}}{r_{b'e} + \frac{1}{j\omega C_{b'e}}} = \frac{r_{b'e}}{1 + j\omega C_{b'e} r_{b'e}}$$

$$Z \approx \frac{r_{b'e}}{1 + j\left(\frac{\omega}{\omega_\beta}\right)} = \frac{r_b{}'_e}{1 + j\left(\frac{f}{f_\beta}\right)}$$

$$f_\beta = \frac{1}{2\pi r_{b'e} C_{b'e}}$$

$$V_{b'e} = I_i Z$$

$$I_O = -g_m V_{b'e}$$

$$\therefore \quad I_O = -g_m zI_i$$

$$\frac{I_O}{I_i} = A_i = -g_m z = \frac{-g_m r_{b'e}}{1 + j(f/f_\beta)} \equiv \frac{-h_{fe}}{1 + j(f/f_\beta)}$$

Short circuit current gain,

$$A_i = \frac{I_O}{I_i} = \frac{-h_{fe}}{\sqrt{1 + (f/f_\beta)^2}}$$

$$\Rightarrow \quad A_i = \frac{-h_{fe}}{\sqrt{1 + (f/f_\beta)^2}}$$

$$\phi = 180° - \tan^{-1} \frac{f}{f_\beta}$$

where,

$$f_\beta = \frac{1}{2\pi r_{b'e} C_{b'e}}$$

Thus, at high frequency, current gain for the common emitter amplifier is complex and is frequency dependent. As frequency of operation increases, the current gain decreases. The phase between input and output currents is other than 180° and is frequency dependent as frequency of the operation increases, its phase shift with reference to 180° increases.

Now $C_{b'e} \equiv C_\pi$, $\quad r_{b'e} = r_\pi$

$C_{b'e} \equiv C_\mu$, $\quad r_{b'c} = r_\mu$

Bandwidth of the amplifier,

$$f_\beta = \frac{1}{2\pi r_{b'e} C_{b'e}} = \frac{1}{2\pi r_\pi C_\pi}$$

$$|A_i| = \frac{h_{fe}}{\sqrt{1 + (f/f_\beta)^2}} \qquad ...(3.34)$$

Case 1 : When $f << f_\beta$, then $\quad |A_i| \approx h_{fe}$

Case 2 : When $f = f_\beta$, then $\quad |A_i| = \frac{1}{\sqrt{2}} = 0.707$

Case 3 : When $f >> f_\beta$, then $\quad |A_i| = \frac{h_{fe} \cdot f_\beta}{f}$

Equation (3.34) can be drawn as shown in Fig. 3.88.

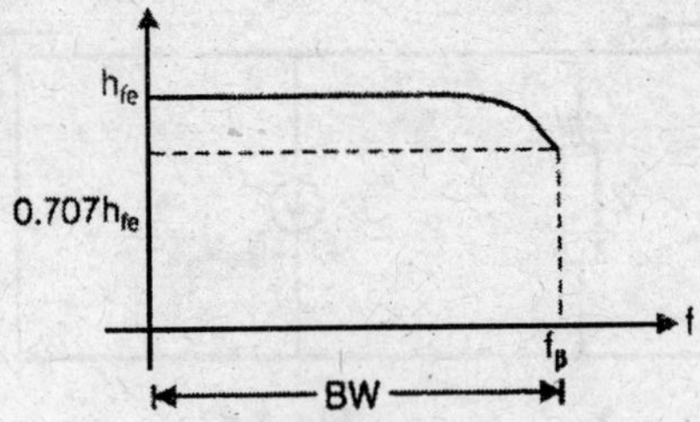

Fig. 3.88

Bandwidth of the amplifier represents total range of frequency of operation where current gain is almost constant or at the point where it falls to 0.707 of maximum current gain.

Frequency f_T at which short circuit gain of CE amgplifier at high frequency becomes unity.

$$|A_i| = \frac{h_{fe}}{\sqrt{1+\left(\frac{f}{f_\beta}\right)^2}}$$

But at $f = f_T$,

$$|A_i| = 1$$

$\therefore$

$$\frac{h_{fe}}{\sqrt{1+\left(\frac{f}{f_\beta}\right)^2}} = 1$$

$\Rightarrow$

$$h_{fe}^2 = 1 + \left(\frac{f_T}{f_\beta}\right)^2$$

$\Rightarrow$

$$\left(\frac{f_T}{f_\beta}\right)^2 = h_{fe}^2 - 1 \approx h_{fe}^2$$

Hence current gain bandwidth product,

$$f_T \equiv h_{fe} f_\beta = h_{fe} \frac{1}{2\pi\, r_{b'e} C_{b'e}}$$

But

$$\frac{h_{fe}}{r_{b'e}} = g_m$$

$\therefore$

$$f_T = \frac{g_m}{2\pi\, C_{b'e}} = \text{constant}$$

$\Rightarrow$

$$C_{b'e} = \frac{g_m}{2\pi\, f_T}$$

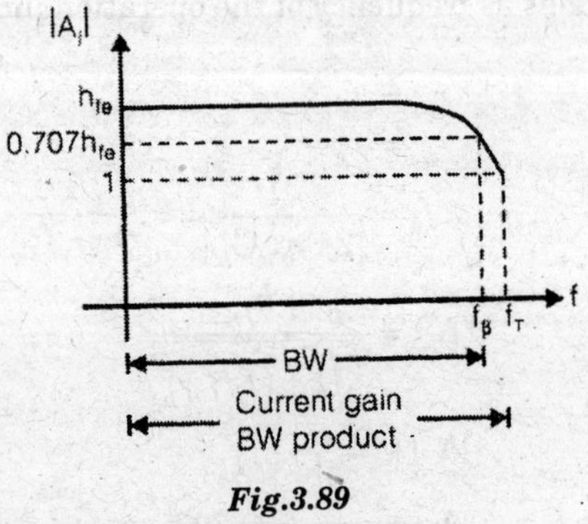

Fig.3.89

In logarithmatic terms, 0.707 h_{fe} amounts to – 3dB points from h_{fe}.

f_β is called *bandwidth of amp/cut* off frequency/3dB frequency/half power frequency

f_T is current gain-band width product/figure of merit.

3.8 RC-COUPLED AMPLIFIER

A cascaded arrangement of common-emitter (CE) transistor stages is shown in Fig. 3.90 (*a*), and of the common-source (CS) FET stages is shown in Fig. 3.90 (*b*).

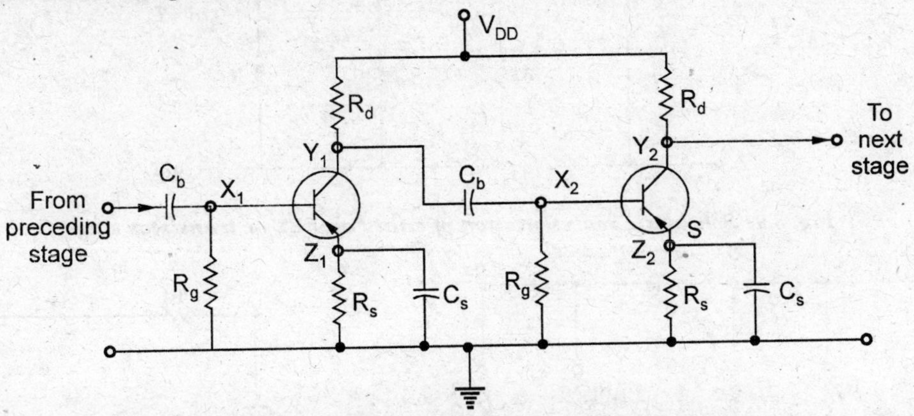

(a) A cascade of common-emitter (CE) transistor stages

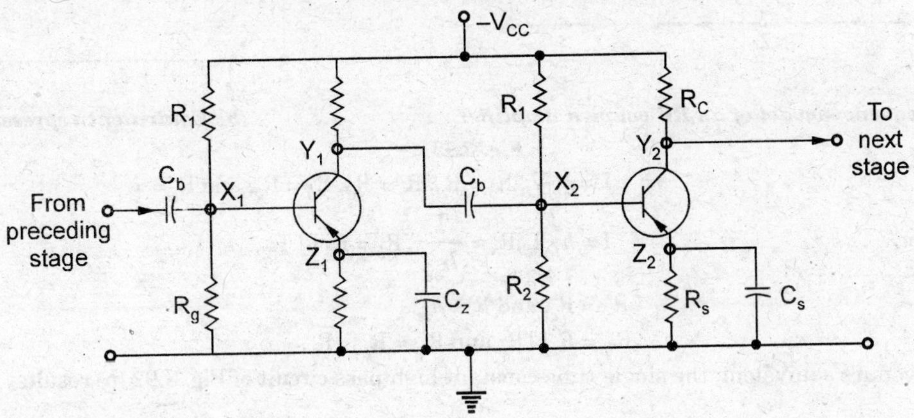

(b) A cascade common-source (CS) depletion-type, or JFET stages

Fig.3.90

The ouput Y_1 of one stage is coupled to the input X_2 of the next stage via a blocking capacitor C_b which is used to keep the dc component of the output voltage at Y_1 from reaching the input X_2. Resistor R_g is from gate to ground, and the collector (drain) circuit resistor is $R_c(R_d)$. The source resistor R_s, the emitter resistor R_e, and the resistors R_1 and R_2 are used to establish the bias. The bypass capacitors, used to prevent loss of amplification due to negative feedback are C_z in the emitter circuit and C_s in the source circuit. Also present are junction capacitances, to be taken into account when we consider the high-frequency response, which is limited by their presence.

3.8.1. LOW-FREQUENCY RESPONSE OF AN RC-COUPLED STAGE

Assume that C_z and C_s capacitances are arbitrarily large and act as ac (incremental) short circuits across R_e and R_s, respectively. A single intermediate stage of any of the cascade in Fig. 3.90 may be represented schematically as in Fig. 3.91. The resistor r_b represents the gate resistor R_g for an FET and equals R_1 in parallel with R_2 if a transistor stage is under consideration. The resistor R_y represents R_c for transistor, or R_d for an FET, and R_i represents the input resistance of the following stage.

The low-frequency equivalent circuit is obtained by neglecting all shunting capacitances and all junction capacitances by replacing amplifier A_1 by its Norton's equivalent Fig. 3.92 (*a*).

For a field-effect transistor, $R_i = \infty$

Output impedance, $R_o = r_d$ (the drain resistance),

and $I = g_m V_i$ (transconductance times gate signal voltage).

For a transistor these quantities may be expressed in terms of the CE hybrid parameters

$$R_i \approx h_{ie} \text{ (for small values of } R_c)$$

$$R_o = 1/h_{oe} \text{ (for a current drive)}$$

and $$I = h_{fe} I_b$$

where I_b = base signal current.

Let R'_o represent R_o in parallel with R_y, and let R'_i be R_i in parallel with R_b.

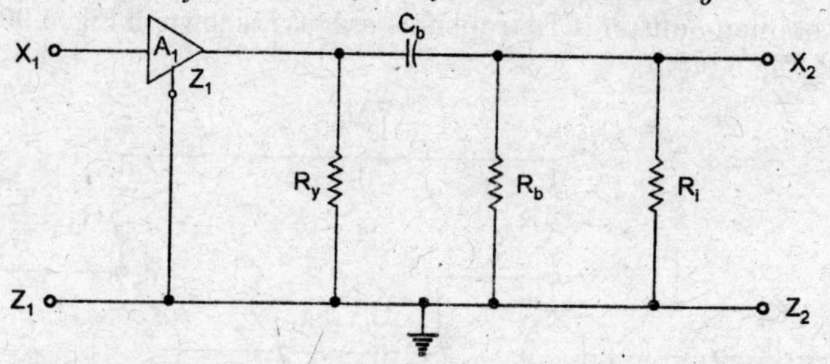

Fig. 3.91 Schematic representation of either an FET or transistor stage.

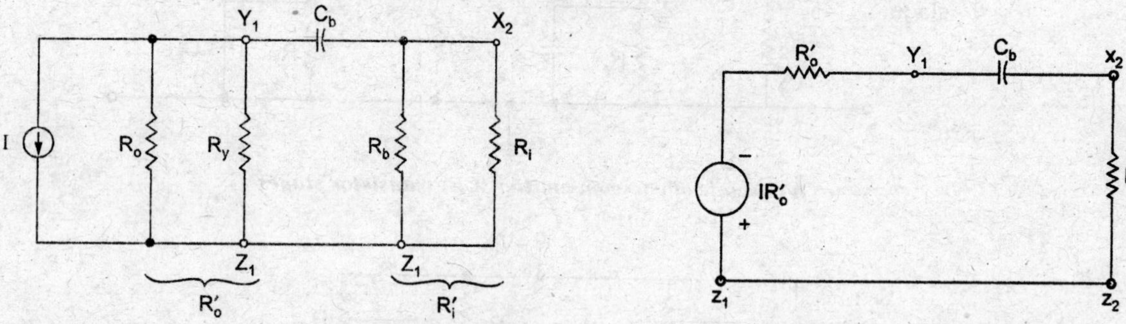

(a) Low-frequency model of an RC-coupled amplifier *(b) Equivalent representation*

Fig. 3.92

For an FET, $I = g_m V_i$, $R_o = R_d$, $R_y = R_d$, $R_b = R_g$, and $R_i = \infty$.

For a transistor, $I = h_{fe} I_b$, $R_o \approx \dfrac{1}{h_{oe}}$, $R_b = R_1 \,||\, R_2$,

$R_y = R_c$, and $R_i \approx h_{ie}$.

Also, $R'_i = R_i \,||\, R_b$ and $R'_o = R_o \,||\, R_y$.

R'_o by the Thevenin's equivalent, the single-time-constant high-pass circuit of Fig. 3.92 (*b*) results.

∴ Low 3-dB frequency,

$$f_L = \frac{1}{2\pi\left(R'_o + R'_i\right) C_b}$$

For an FET amplifier, $R'_i = R_g >> R_d$.

Since $R'_o < R_d$ because R'_o is R_d in parallel with R_o, then

$$R'_i = R_g >> R'_o \text{ and } f_L \approx \frac{1}{2\pi C_b R_g}.$$

3.8.2. EFFECT OF AN EMITTER BYPASS CAPACITOR ON LOW-FREQUENCY RESPONSE

If an emitter resistor R_e is used for self-bias in an amplifier and if it is desired to avoid the degeneration, and hence the loss of gain due to R_e, we might attempt to bypass this resitors with avery large capacitance C_z. The circuit is indicated in Fig. 3.93 (*a*).

Consider the single stage of Fig. 3.93 (*a*). To simplify the analysis we assume that $R_1 \,||\, R_2 >> R_s$ and that the load R_c is small. The equivalent circuit subject to these assumptions is shown in Fig. 3.93 (*b*).

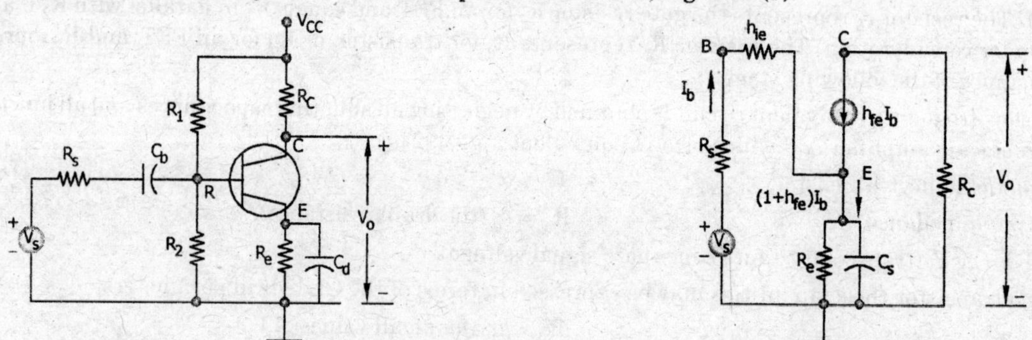

(a) An amplifier with a bypassed emitter resistor; *(b) Low-frequency simplified h-parameter model of the circuit in (a).*

Fig. 3.93

Output voltage, $$V_o = -I_b h_{fe} R_c = -\frac{V_s h_{fe} R_c}{R_s + h_{ie} + Z'_e} \quad ...(3.35)$$

where $$Z'_e \approx (1 + h_{fe}) \frac{R_e}{1 + j\omega C_z R_e} \quad ...(3.36)$$

Substituting equation (3.36) in equation (3.35) and solving, we get

$$A_v = \frac{V_o}{V_s} = -\frac{h_{fe} R_c}{R + R'} \frac{1 + j\omega C_z R_e}{1 + j\omega C_z \left[\frac{R_e R}{R + R'}\right]} \quad ...(3.37)$$

where $R \approx R_s + h_{ie}$

and $R' \equiv (1 + h_{fe}) R_e$

The midband gain A_o is obtained as $\omega \to \infty$, or

$$A_o = -\frac{h_{fe} R_c}{R} = \frac{-h_{fe} R_c}{R_s + h_{ie}}$$

Hence $$\frac{A_v}{A_o} = \frac{1}{1 + \frac{R'}{R}} \frac{1 + jf/f_o}{1 + jf/f_p} \quad ...(3.38)$$

where $$f_o \equiv \frac{1}{2\pi C_z R_e}$$

$$f_p \equiv \frac{1 + R'/R}{2\pi C_z R_e} \quad ...(3.39)$$

f_c determines zero and f_p determines pole of the gain $\frac{A_v}{A_o}$.

Since usually, $\frac{R'}{R} >> 1$, then $f_p >> f_o$, so that the pole and zero are widely separated.

The magnitude of $|A_v/A_o|$ in decibels is given by

$$20 \log \left|\frac{A_v}{A_o}\right| = -20 \log \left(1 + \frac{R'}{R}\right) + 20 \log \sqrt{1 + \left(\frac{f}{f_o}\right)^2} - 20 \log \sqrt{1 + \left(\frac{f^2}{f_p}\right)}$$

The first term represents a horizontal line, the second term has an asymptote passing through $f = f_o$ with a positive slope of 6 dB per octave, and the third term has an asymptote passing through $f = f_p$, with a negative slope of the same magnitude. These lines are shown dashed in Fig. 3.94 and the idealized Bode plot is obtained by adding three asymptotes together to form the shaded broken-line- continuous curve.

For $f \geq f_p$, result of adding a gain which increases 6 dB per octave to a gain which decreases 6 dB per octave gives a constant gain.

For $f >> f_p$, gain must approach its midband value A_o, and hence horizontal line for $f > f_p$ occurs at $20 \log |A_v/A_o| = 0$ dB, as shown.

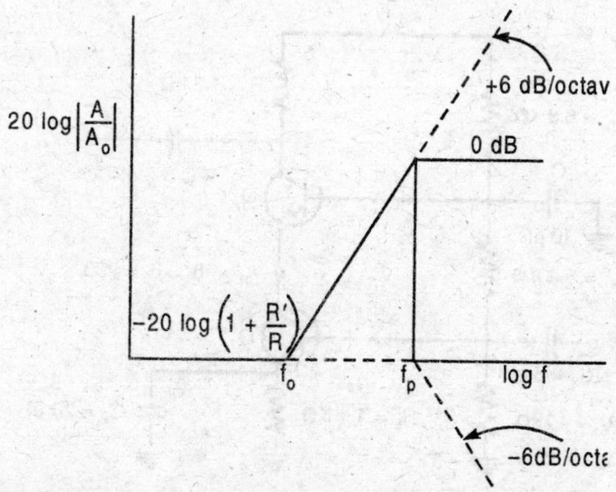

Fig.3.94 Idealized Bode amplitude plot for a transfer function with one zero $f = f_o$ and one pole $f = f_p$. The individual asymptotes are shown dashed, and the resultant is drawn as a shaded continuous broken-line plot.

The frequency response for an amplifier with a bypassed emitter resistor shown in Fig. 3.95.

From $f_p >> f_o$ and using equations (3.37) and (3.38), for $f = f_p$,

$$\left|\frac{A_v}{A_o}\right| = \frac{1}{1+\frac{R'}{R}} \frac{f_p/f_o}{\sqrt{1+1}} = \frac{1}{\sqrt{2}}$$

Hence $f = f_p$ is that frequency at which the gain has dropped 3 dB. Thus the low 3-dB frequency f_L is approximately equal to f_p. If condition $f_p >> f_o$ is not satisfied, then $f_L \neq f_p$ a 3-dB frequency may not exist.

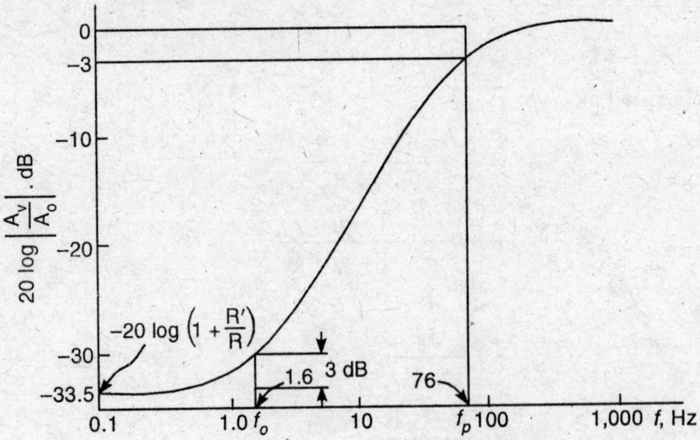

Fig. 3.95 Frequency response of an amplifier with a bypassed emitter resistor. **Square-wave response**

If $f_p >> f_o$, the network in Fig. 3.93 behaves like a single-time-constant circuit and the percentage tilt to a square wave is given by,

$$P = \frac{\pi f_p}{f} \times 100 = \frac{1+\frac{R'}{R}}{2fC_zR_e} \times 100\%$$

$$\text{As } \frac{R'}{R} >> 1, P \approx \frac{R'\times 100}{2fC_zRR_e} = \frac{1+h_{fe}}{2fC_z(R_e+h_{ie})} \times 100\%$$

3.9 COMPOUND CONFIGURATION

It include connection which provides stages in series, cascode connection places one transistor on top of another. Darlington connection and the feedback pair connection provide multiple transistors connected for operation as a single transistor for improved performance, usully with much larger current gain. The CMOS connection uses both p-type enhancement and n-type enhancement MOSFET transistors in a very low power operating circuit and also they allow very high packing density in integrated circuits.

Cascode connection

It has one transistor on top of another.

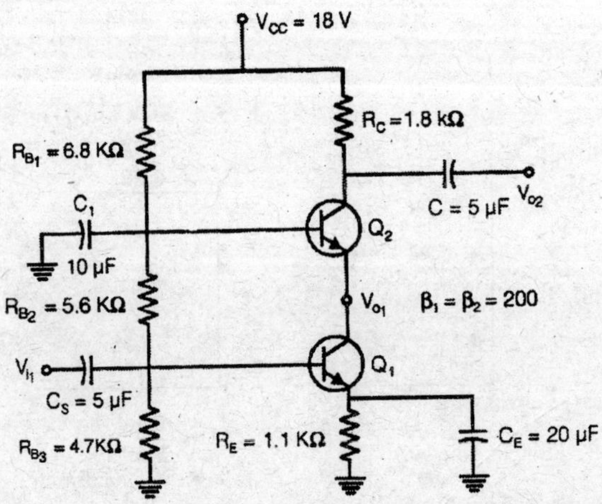

Fig. 3.96. Practical version of BJT in cascode configuration (CE-CB connection).

Using DC bias analysis

$$V_{B1} = \left[\frac{4.7}{4.7+5.6+6.8}\right] \times 18 = 4.9\text{ V}$$

$$V_{B2} = \left[\frac{5.6}{4.7+5.6+6.8}\right] \times 18 = 10.8\text{ V}$$

$$I_{B1} = \frac{V_{B_1} - V_{BE}}{R_{th} + (\beta+1)R_E}$$

$$= \frac{4.2}{0.274 + (201)(1.1\text{ k}\Omega)} = 0.0189\text{ mA}$$

$$I_{C1} = I_{C2} = \beta I_{\beta 1} = 3.8\text{ mA}$$

$\therefore$ Dynamic resistance of each transistor, $r_e = \dfrac{26}{I_E} = \dfrac{26}{3.8} = 6.8\ \Omega$

For first stage CE, voltage gain, $A_{V1} \approx \dfrac{-R_C}{r_e} = \dfrac{-r_e}{r_e} = -1$

For second stage CB, $A_{V2} = \dfrac{R_e}{r_e} = \dfrac{1.8\text{k}\Omega}{6.8\Omega} = 265$

Overall cascode amplifier gain, $A_V = A_{V1}\,A_{V2} = (-1)(265) = -265$

CE stage with a gain of –1 provides higher input impedance of a CE stage (over that of a CD stage). With a voltage gain of only – 1, the Miller input capacitance is kept quite small. Then a large voltage gain is provided by the CB stage, resulting in a large overall gain ($A_V = -265$)

Darlington circuit

It is also called *superbeta transistors*

$\beta_D = \beta_1\,\beta_2$

= Product of current gain of individual transistors

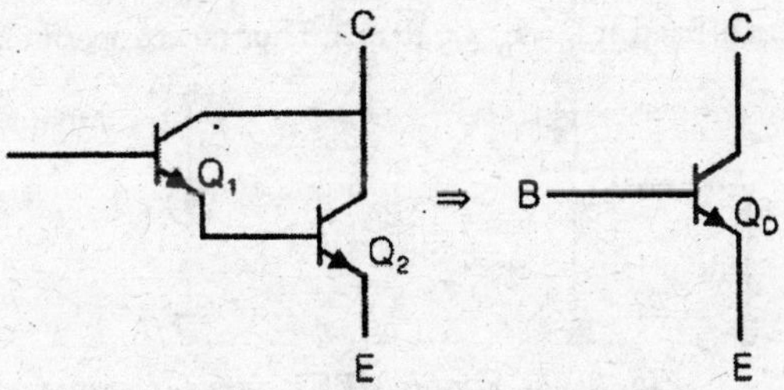

Fig. 3.97

Practical feedback pair connection

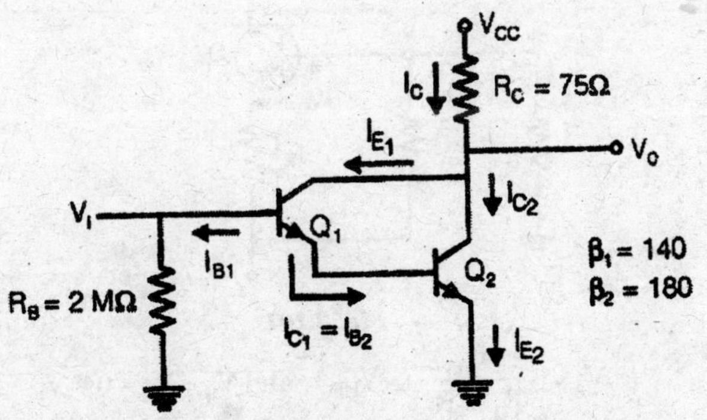

Fig. 3.98 Practical feedback pair connection

It is a two-transistor circuit that operates like Darlington circuit. It uses a pnp transistor driving an npn transistor, the two devices acting effectively much like one pnp transistor.

From transistor Q, base-emitter loop,

$$V_{CC} - I_C R_C - V_{EB1} - I_{B1} R_B = 0$$

$$V_{CC} - \beta_1 \beta_2 I_{B_1} R_C - V_{EB_1} - I_{B_1} R_B = 0$$

$\therefore$ Base current, $I_{B_1} = \dfrac{V_{CC} - V_{EB_1}}{R_B + \beta_1 \beta_2 R_C}$

Collector current of Q_1, $I_{C_1} = \beta_1 I_{B_1} = I_{B_2}$

which is also the base Q_2 current.

Transistor Q_2 collector current, $I_{C_2} = \beta_2 I_{B_2} \approx I_{E_2}$

Hence current through R_C is, $I_C = I_{E_1} + I_{C_2} \approx I_{C_1} + I_{C_2} \approx I_{C_2}$

CMOS or Complementary MOSFET circuit

It uses opposite (n-channel and p-channel enhancement type) transistors. The input Vi is applied to both gates with the output taken from the connected drains.

3.9.1. CURRENT SOURCE CIRCUITS

***(i)* An ideal current source**

It has R = ∞, while a practical source includes some very large resistance

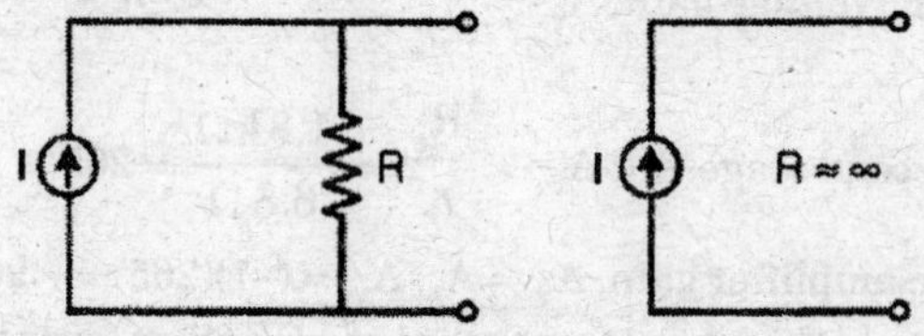

Fig. 3.99

Anb ideal current source provides a constant current regardless of the load connected to it. There are many uses in electronics for a circuit providing a constant current at a very high impedance. Constant current circuits can be built using FET devices, bipolar devices and a combination of these components. There are circuits used in discrete form and others more suitable for operation in ICs.

***(ii)* JFET current source**

With V_{GS} set to 0 V, drain current is fixed at $I_D = I_{DSS} = 10$ mA. Thus device operates like a current source of 10 mA.

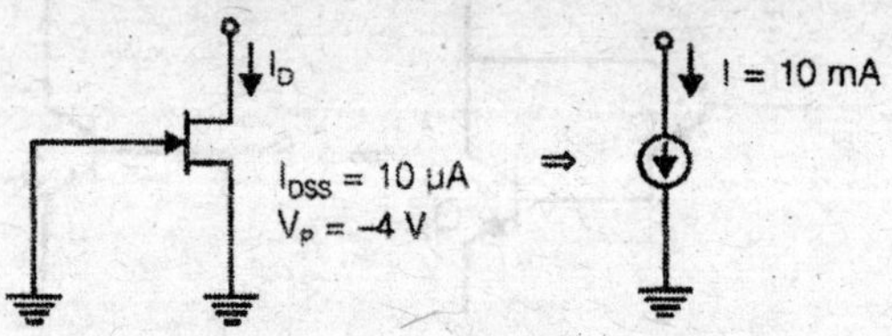

Fig. 3.100. simple JFET current shource

***(iii)* Bipolar transistor constant-current source**

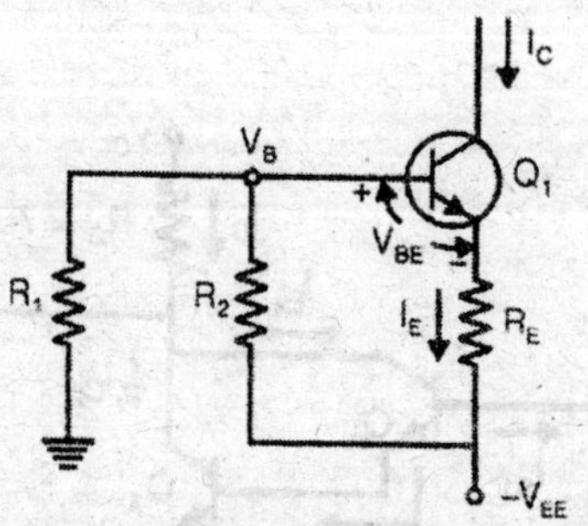

Fig. 3.101

$$V_B = \frac{R_1}{R_1 + R_2}(-V_{EE}), \text{ and } V_E = V_B - 0.7 \text{ V}$$

with $I_E = \dfrac{V_E - (-V_{EE})}{R_E} \approx I_C$

where I_C = constant current provided by above circuit

(iv) Transistor/Zener Constant-current source

In Fig.3.101, if we replace R_2 with a zener diode as shown in the figure below, it provides an improved constant-current source over that of Fig. 3.101. The zener diode results in a constant current calculated using base-emitter KVL equation. Value of I can be calculated using

$$I \approx I_E = \frac{V_Z - V_{BE}}{R_E}$$

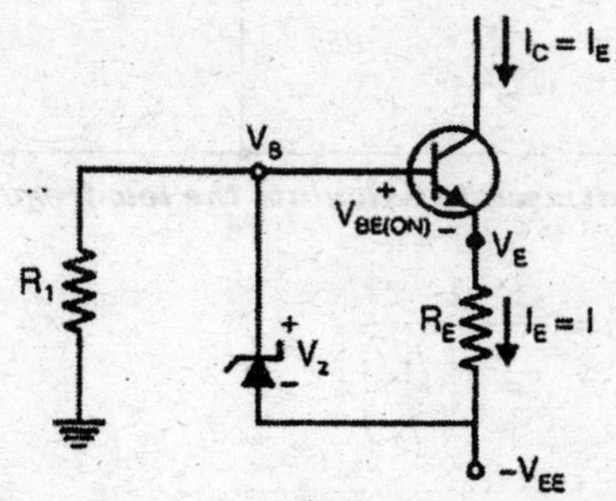

Fig. 3.102

Constant current depends on zener diode voltage, which remains quite constant and emitter resistor R_E. The voltage supply V_{EE} has no effect on the value of I.

3.9.2. CURRENT MIRROR CIRCUITS

It provides a constant current and is used primarily in integrated circuits. The constant current is obtained from an output current, which is reflection or mirror of a constant current developed on one side of the circuit. The circuit is particularly suited to IC manufacture since circuit requires that the transistors used have identical base-emitter voltage drops and identical values of beta-results best achieved when transistors are formed at the same time in IC manufacture shown in Fig. 3.103.

Assuming I_E for Q_1, Q_2, same, we have

$$I_B = \frac{I_E}{\beta+1} \approx \frac{I_E}{\beta}$$

$\therefore$ Collector current of each transistor, $I_C \approx I_E$

Thus, current through resistor R_X,

$$I_X = I_E + \frac{2I_E}{\beta} = \frac{\beta I_E + 2I_E}{\beta} = \frac{\beta+2}{\beta}\, I_E \approx I_E$$

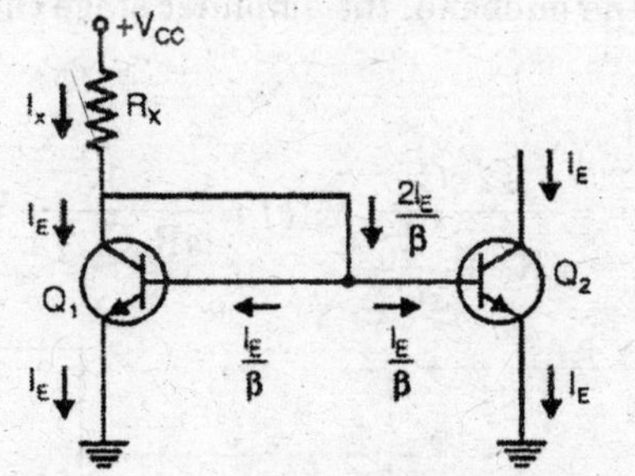

Fig. 3.103

Hence constant current is provided at the collector of Q_2 mirrors that of Q_1

Since
$$I_X = \frac{V_{CC} + V_{BE}}{R_X}$$

therefore current I_X set V_{CC} and R_X is mirrored in the current into the collector of Q_2.

3.10 FREQUENCY RESPONSE OF AN AMPLIFIER

3.10.1. LOW-FREQUENCY RESPONSE

From the circuit of Fig. 3.104, we get

$$V_o(s) = V_i(s)\, \frac{R_1}{R_1 + \dfrac{1}{sC_1}} = \frac{sR_1C_1}{sR_1C_1 + 1} V_i \qquad \text{...(3.40)}$$

Thus voltage transfer function at low frequencies, $A_L(s) \equiv \dfrac{V_o(s)}{V_i(s)}$, has one zero at $s = 0$ and one pole at $s = \dfrac{1}{R_1C_1}$.

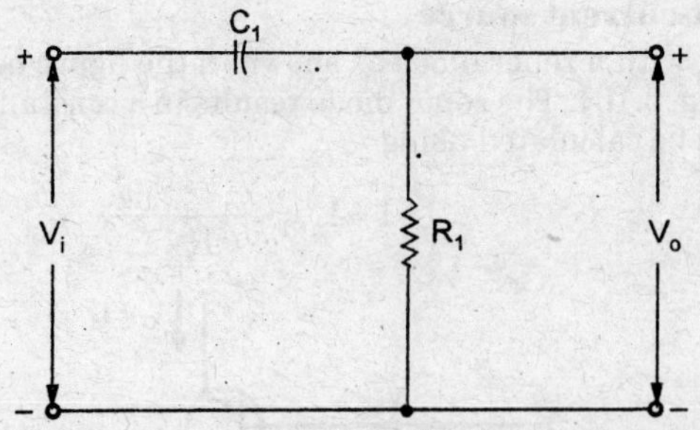

Fig. 3.104. High-pass RC circuit used to calculate the low-frequency response of an amplifier

For real frequencies, $s = j\omega = j2\pi f$,

Hence equation (3.40) becomes $A_L(jf) = \dfrac{1}{1 - j\left(\dfrac{f_L}{f}\right)}$

where, $f_L \equiv \dfrac{1}{2\pi R_1 C_1}$

The magnitude $|A_L|$ and phase lead θ_L of the gain are given by

$$|A_L(jf)| = \frac{1}{\sqrt{1+\left(\dfrac{f_L}{f}\right)^2}}, \qquad \theta_L = \arctan \frac{f_L}{f}$$

At the frequency $f = f_L$, $A_L = \dfrac{1}{\sqrt{2}} = 0.707$

whereas in the midband region ($f >> f_L$), $A_L \to 1$. Hence, f_L is that frequency at which the gain has fallen to 0.707 times its midband value A_o. This drop in signal level corresponds to a decibel reduction of 20 log $\left(\dfrac{1}{\sqrt{2}}\right)$, or 3 dB. Accordingly, f_L is referred to as the lower 3-dB frequency. f_L is that frequency for which the resistance R_1 equals the capacitive reactance $\dfrac{1}{2\pi f_L C_1}$.

High-frequency response

In the high-frequency region, above the midband, the amplifier stage can often be approximated by the simple low-pass circuit of Fig. 3.105.

In terms of complex variable s, we get

$$V_o(s) = \frac{1/sC_2}{R_2 + \dfrac{1}{sC_2}} V_i(s) = \frac{1}{sR_2C_2 + 1} V_i(s)$$

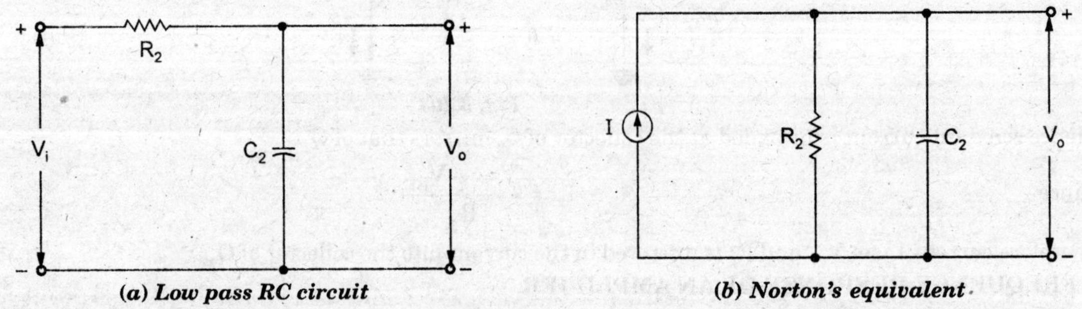

(a) Low pass RC circuit ***(b) Norton's equivalent***

Fig 3.105

A low-pass RC circuit used to calculate high-frequency response of an amplifier is shown in Fig. 3.105 (*a*)

Here $I = \dfrac{V_i}{R_2}$

Transfer function in this region has a single pole of

$$s = -\frac{1}{R_2C_2}.$$

For real frequencies, $s = j\omega = j2\pi f$

$$|A_H(jf)| = |V_o(s)/V_i(s)|_{s=j2\pi f}$$

and for phase lead angle θ_H of the gain in the high-frequency region,

$$|A_H(jf)| = \frac{1}{\sqrt{1+\left(\frac{f}{f_H}\right)^2}}$$

$$\theta_H = -\arctan\frac{f}{f_H}$$

where, $$f_H = \frac{1}{2\pi R_2 C_2}$$

Since at $f = f_H$, gain is reduced to $\frac{1}{\sqrt{2}}$ times its midband value, then f_H is called *upper 3-dB frequency*.

It also represents that frequency at which resistance R_2 equals the capacitive reactance $\frac{1}{2\pi f_H C_2}$. In the above expression θ_L and θ_H represent the angle by which the output leads the input, neglecting the initial 180° phase shift through the amplifier. The frequency dependence of the gains in the high-and low-frequency range is to be seen in Fig. 3.106.

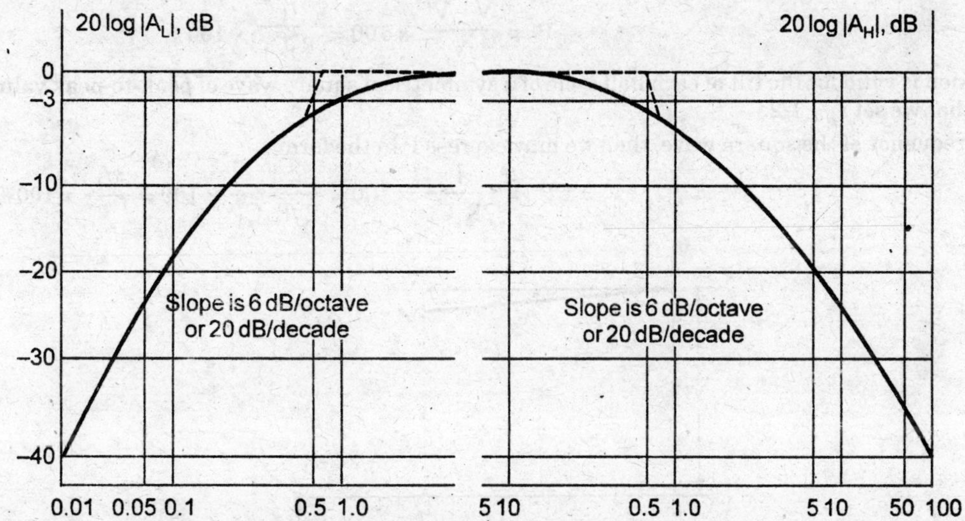

Fig 3.106 Semi-log plot of the amplitude frequency-response (Bode) characteristic of an RC-coupled amplifier. The dashed curve is the idealized Bode plot.

3.10.2. STEP RESPONSE OF AN AMPLIFIER

Rise time

The response of the low-pass circuit to a step input of amplitude V is exponential with a time constant R_2C_2. Since the capacitor voltage cannot change instantaneously, the output starts from zero and rises towards the steady-state value V, as shown in Fig. 3.107

$$v_o = V\left(1 - e^{-\frac{t}{R_2C_2}}\right)$$

The time required for v_o to reach one-tenth of its final value is readily found to be 0.1 R_2C_2, and the time to reach nine-tenths its final value is 2.3 R_2C_2. The difference between these two values is called the rise time t_r of the circuit and is shown in Fig. 3.107. The time t_r is an indication of how fast the amplifier can respond to a discontinuity in the input voltage.

We have, $$t_r = 2.2\, R_2C_2 = \frac{2.2}{2\pi f_H} = \frac{0.35}{f_H}$$

The rise time is inversely proportional to the upper 3-dB frequency.

For an amplifier with 1 MHz bandpass, $t_r = 0.35\ \mu s$.

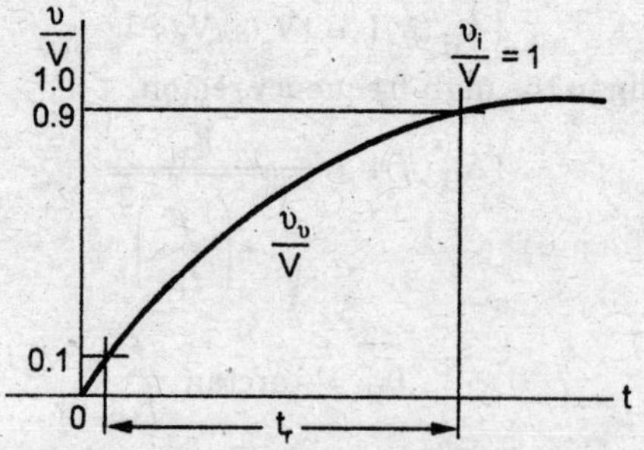

Fig. 3.107. Step-voltage response of the low-pass RC circuit

Tilt or Sag

If a step of amplitude V is impressed on the high-pass circuit, then output is

$$v_o = V e^{-\frac{t}{R_2C_2}}$$

For time t which are small compared with the time constant R_1C_1, the response is given by

$$v_o \approx V\left(1 - \frac{t}{R_1C_1}\right)$$

From Fig. 3.108, the percent tilt, or sag, in time t_1 is given by

$$P \equiv \frac{V - V'}{V} \times 100 = \frac{t_1}{R_1C_1} \times 100\%$$

This expression is valid for the tilt of each half cycle of a symmetrical square wave of peak-to-peak value V and period T provided that we set $t_1 = T/2$.

If $f = 1/T$ is frequency of the square wave, then we may express P in the form

$$P = \frac{T}{2R_1C_1} \times 100 = \frac{1}{2fR_1C_1} \times 100 = \frac{\pi f_L}{f} \times 100\%$$

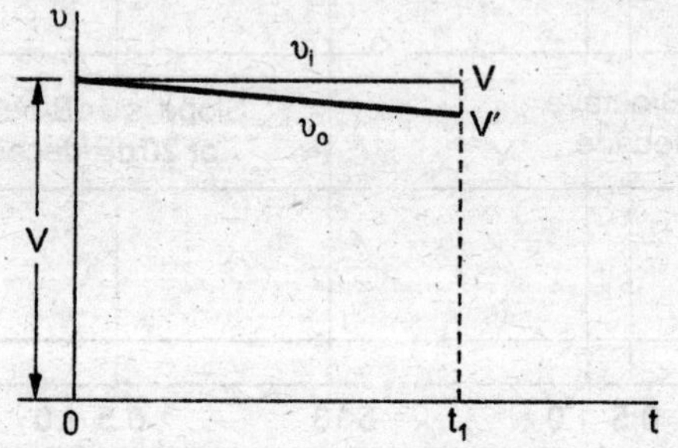

Fig. 3.108. Response u_o when a step v_i is applied to a high-pass RC circuit, exhibits a tilt

The tilt is directly proportional to the lower 3-dB frequency. If it is required to pass a 50-Hz square wave with less than 10 percent sag, then f_L must not exceed 1.6 Hz.

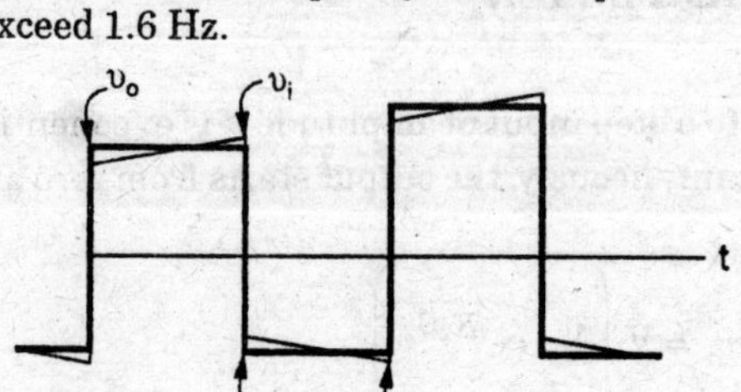

Fig. 3.109. Square-wave (shaded) input signal is distorted by an amplifier with a lower 3-db frequency f_L. The output (solid) wave form shows a tilt where the input is horizontal.

3.10.5. BANDPASS OF CASCADED STAGES

The high 3-dB frequancy for n cascaded stages is f^*_H and equals the frequency for which the overall voltage gain falls 3-dB to $\frac{1}{\sqrt{2}}$ of its midband value to obtain overall transfer function of noninteracting stages, the transfer gains of the individual stages are multiplied together. Hence, if each stage has a dominant pole and if the high 3-dB frequency of the ith stage is f_{Hi}, where $i = 1, 2, ..n$, then f^*_H can be calculated from the product

$$\frac{1}{\sqrt{1+\left(\frac{f_H^*}{f_{H1}}\right)^2}}\cdots\frac{1}{\sqrt{1+\left(\frac{f_H^*}{f_{Hi}}\right)^2}}\cdots\frac{1}{\sqrt{1+\left(\frac{f_H^*}{f_{Hn}}\right)^2}}=\frac{1}{\sqrt{2}}$$

For n stages with identical upper 3-dB frequencies, we have

$$f_{H1}=f_{H2}=\ldots=f_{Hi}=\ldots=f_{Hn}=f_H$$

Thus f^*_H is calculated from $\left[\frac{1}{\sqrt{1+\left(\frac{f_H^*}{f_H}\right)^2}}\right]^n=\frac{1}{\sqrt{2}}$ to be

$$\frac{f_H^*}{f_H}=\sqrt{2^{\frac{1}{n}}-1}$$

If low 3-dB frequency for n identical non-interacting cascaded stages if f^*_L, then corresponding to above equation, we get

$$\frac{f_L^*}{f_L}=\frac{1}{\sqrt{2^{\frac{1}{n}}-1}}$$

Thus a cascade of stages has a lower f_H and a higher f_L than a single stage, resulting in a shrinkage in bandwidth.

3.11 AMPLIFIER BIASING

3.11.1. FIXED-BIAS CIRCUIT

For the dc analysis, the network can be isolated from the indicated ac levels by replacing capacitors with an open-circuit equivalent. In addition, the dc supply V_{CC} can be separated into two supplies (for analysis purpose only) as shown in Fig. 3.110.

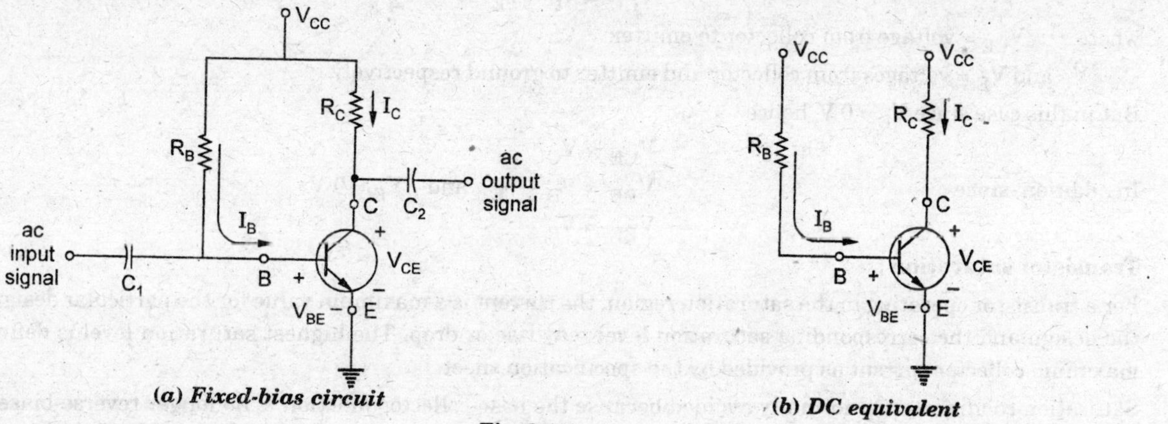

(a) Fixed-bias circuit ***(b) DC equivalent***

Fig. 3.110

Forward Bias of Base-Emitter

Consider first the base-emitter circuit loop of Fig. 3.111.

Writing Kirchhoff's voltage equation in the clockwise direction for the loop, we have, $+V_{CC}-I_BR_B-V_{BE}=0$

Solving equation for the current I_B, we get

$$I_B=\frac{V_{CC}-V_{BE}}{R_B}$$

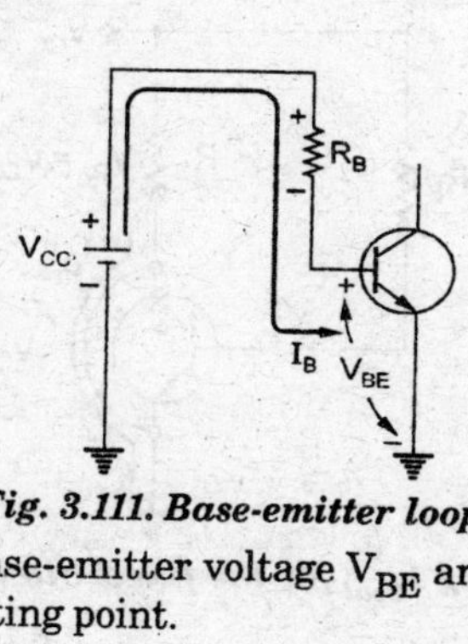

Fig. 3.111. Base-emitter loop

Here, since supply voltage V_{CC} and the base-emitter voltage V_{BE} are constants, the selection of a base resistor, R_B, sets the level of base current for the operating point.

Collector-Emitter Loop

The collector-emitter section of the network appears in Fig. 3.112 with the indicated direction of current I_C and the resulting polarity across R_C.

Collecter current, $I_C = \beta I_B$

Since base current is controlled by the level of R_1 and I_C is related to I_B by a constant β, magnitude of I_C is not function of the resistance R_C. Change R_C to any level and it will not affect the level of I_B or I_C as long as we remain in the active region of the device. But, level of R_C will determine the magnitude of V_{CE}.

Applying Kirchhoff's voltage law in Fig. 3.112, we have

$$V_{CE} + I_C R_C - V_{CC} = 0$$

$$V_{CE} = V_{CC} - I_C R_C$$

which states that voltage across the collector-emitter region of a transistor in the fixed-bias configuration is supply voltage less the drop across R_C.

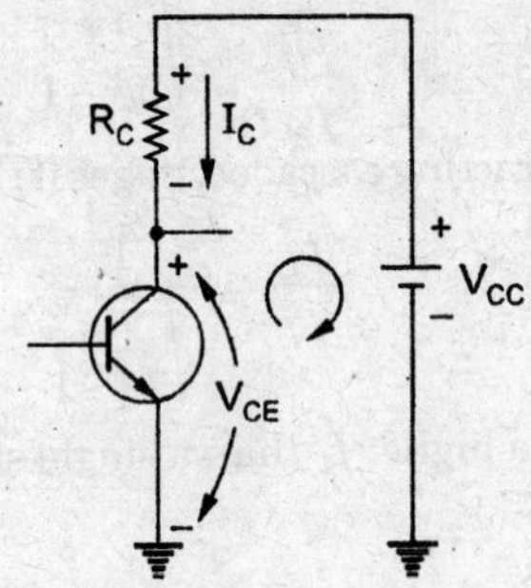

Fig. 3.112 Collector-emitter loop

The single and double-subscript notation recall that

$$V_{CE} = V_C - V_E$$

where, V_{CE} = voltage from collector to emitter

V_C and V_E = voltages from collector and emitter to ground respectively.

But in this case since $V_E = 0$ V, hence

$$V_{CE} = V_C$$

In addition, since $V_{BE} = V_B - V_E$ and $V_E = 0$ V

$\therefore$ $V_{BE} = V_B$

Transistor saturation :

For a transistor operating in the saturation region, the current is a maximum value for the particular design. Change the design and the corresponding saturation level may rise or drop. The highest saturation level is defined by the maximum collector current as provided by the specification sheet.

Saturation conditions are normally avoided because the base-collector junction is no longer reverse-biased and the output amplified signal will be distorted. In an operating region the characteristic curves join and the collector-to-emitter voltage is at or below V_{CEsat}. In addition, the collector current is relatively high on the characteristics.

If it is required to know the approximate maximum collector current (saturation level) for a particular design, simply insert a short-circuit equivalent between collector and emitter of the transistor and calculate the resulting collector current. In short, set $V_{CE} = 0$ V. For the fixed-bias configuration of Fig. 3.113, the short circuit has been applied, causing the voltage across R_C to be the applied voltage V_{CC}. The resulting saturation current for the fixed-bias configuration is

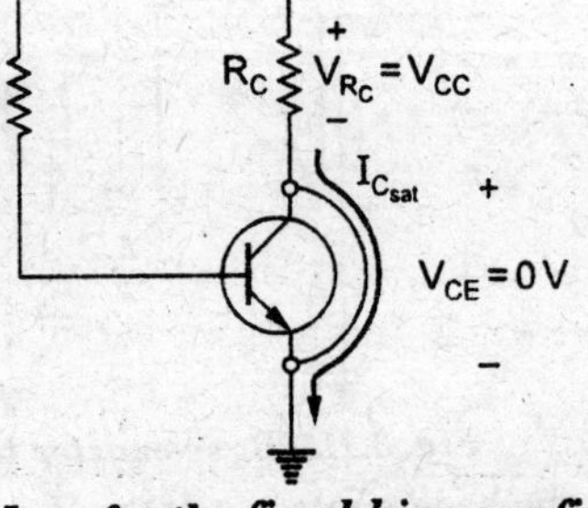

Fig. 3.113. Determining I_{Csat} for the fixed bias configuration

$$I_{Csat} = \frac{V_{CC}}{R_C}$$

Hence, if I_{Csat} is known we have some idea of the maximum possible collector current for the chosen design and the level to stay below if linear amplification is expected.

Load-Line Analysis

In the Fig. 3.114, the equation relating the variables I_C and V_{CE} is given as,

$$V_{CE} = V_{CC} - I_C R_C.$$

The output characteristics of the transistor relate the two variables I_C and V_{CE} as shown in Fig. 3.90. Therefore, we have a network equation and a set of characteristics that employ the same variables. The common solution of the two occurs where the constraints established by each are satisfied simultaneously.

The device characteristics of I_C versus V_{CE} are given in Fig. 3.115. Now, superimpose the straight line on the characteristics. The fact that a straight line is defined by two points.

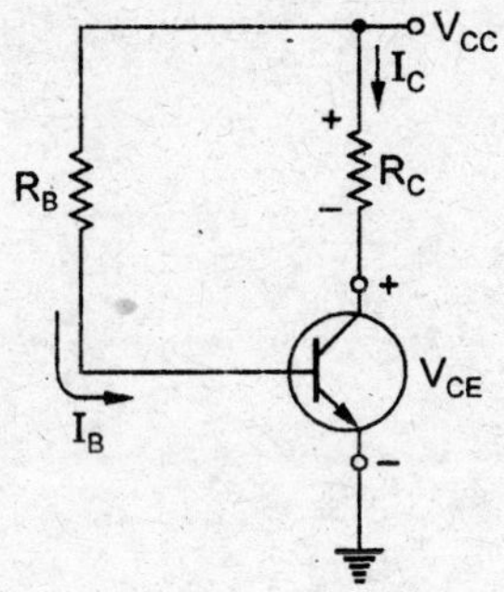

Fig. 3.114. The network

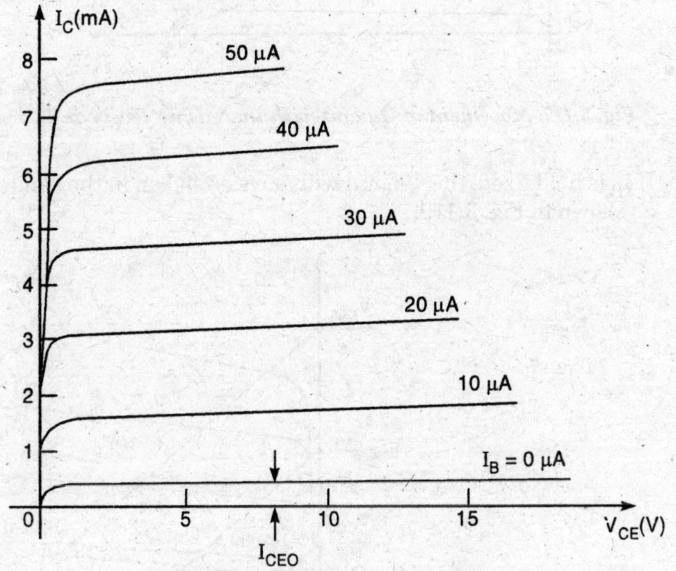

Fig. 3.115. Device characteristicxs

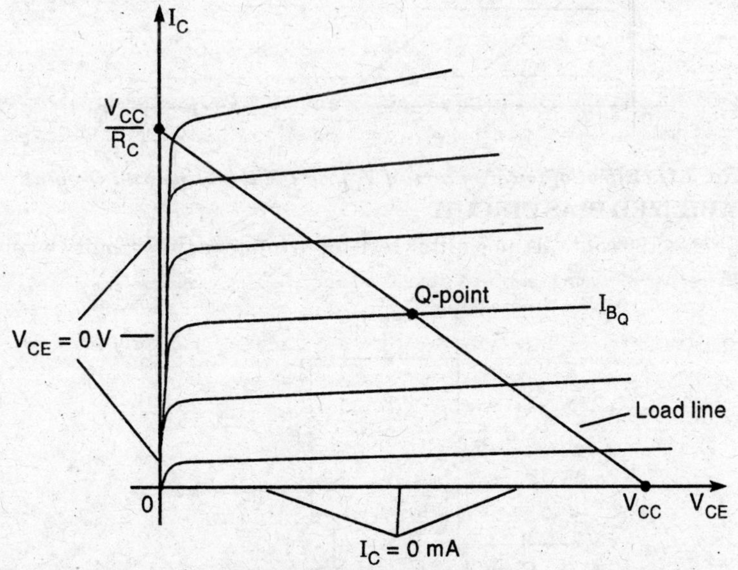

Fig. 3.116. Fixed-bias load line

The resulting line on the graph of Fig. 3.116 is called *load line* since it is defined by the load resistor R_C. By solving for the resulting level of I_B the actual Q-point can be established as shown in Fig. 3.116.

If level of I_B is changed by varying the value of R_B, the Q-point moves up or down the load line as shown in Fig. 3.117. If V_{CC} is held fixed and R_C changed, the load line will shift as shown in Fig. 3.118.

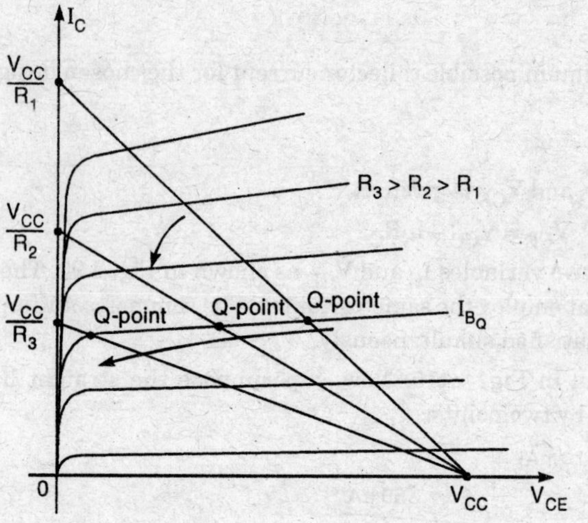

Fig. 3.117. Movement of Q-point with increasing levels on I_B

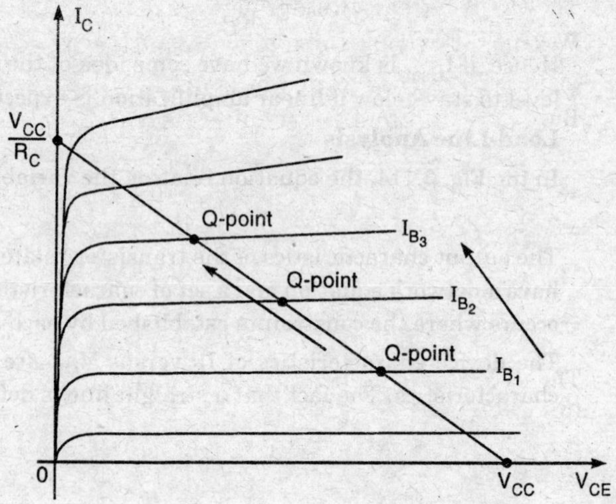

Fig. 3.118. Effect of increasing levels of R_c on the load line and Q-point

If I_B is held fixed, the Q-point will move as shown in the same figure. If R_C is fixed and V_{CC} varied, the load line shifts as shown in Fig. 3.119.

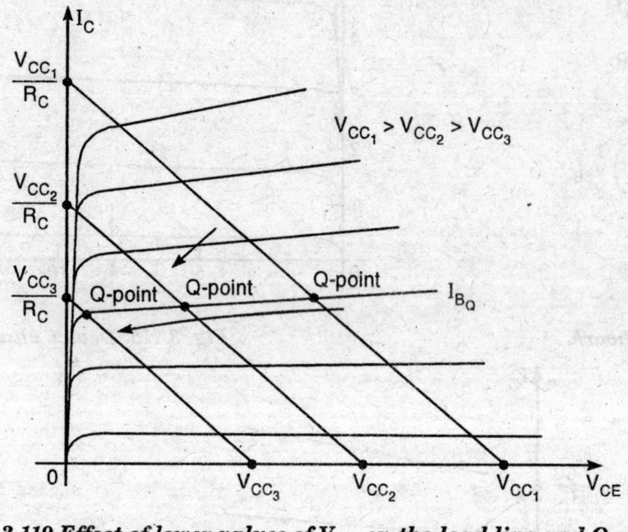

Fig. 3.119 Effect of lower values of V_{CC} on the load line and Q-point.

3.11.2. EMITTER-STABILIZED BIAS CIRCUIT

The dc bias network of Fig. 3.120 contains an emitter resistor to improve the stability level over that of the fixed-bias configuration.

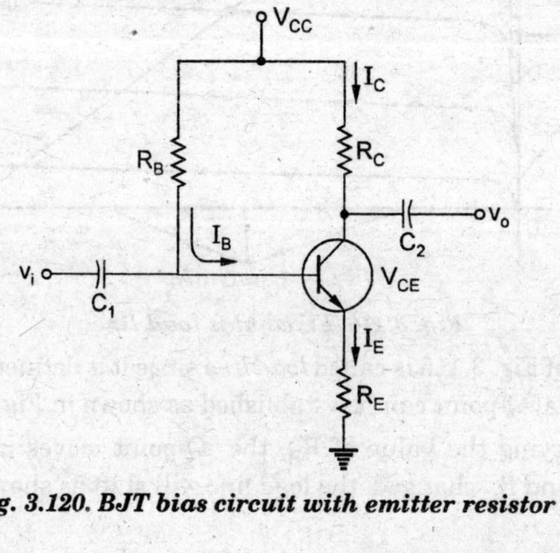

Fig. 3.120. BJT bias circuit with emitter resistor

Base-Emitter Loop :

The base-emitter loop of the network of Fig. 3.120 can be redrawn as shown in Fig. 3.121.

Writting Kirchhoff's voltage law around the indicated loop in the clockwise direction, we get

$$+V_{CC} - I_B R_B - V_{BE} - I_E R_E = 0$$

But Emitter current, $I_E = (\beta + 1) I_B$

$\therefore$ $V_{CC} - I_B R_B - V_{BE} - (\beta + 1) I_B R_E = 0$

$\Rightarrow$ $-I_B (R_B + (\beta + 1) R_E) + V_{CC} - V_{BE} = 0$

$\Rightarrow$ $I_B (R_B + (\beta + 1) R_E) - V_{CC} + V_{BE} = 0$

$\Rightarrow$ $I_B (R_B + (\beta + 1) R_E) = V_{CC} - V_{BE}$

$\Rightarrow$ $$I_B = \frac{V_{CC} - V_{BE}}{R_B + (\beta + 1) R_E}$$

The only difference between this equation for I_B and that obtained for the fixed-bias configuration is the term $(\beta + 1) R_E$.

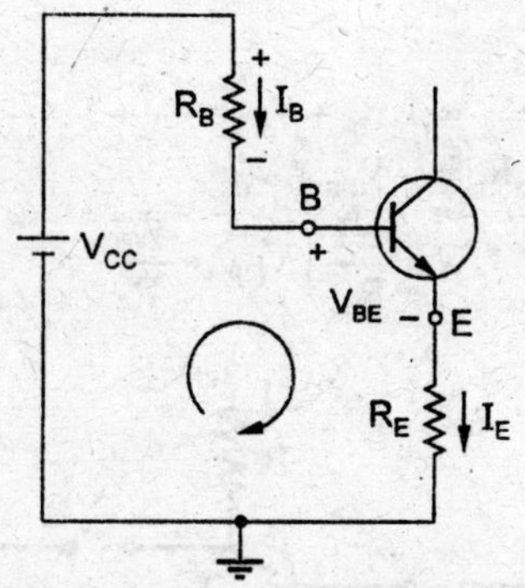

Fig. 3.121. Base-emitter loop

Collector-Emitter loop

The collector-emitter loop is redrawn in Fig. 3.122

Writing Kirchhoff's voltage law for the indicated loop,we have

$$+I_E R_E + V_{CE} + I_C R_C - V_{CC} = 0$$

Substituting $I_E \cong I_C$, we get

$$V_{CE} - V_{CC} + I_C (R_C + R_E) = 0$$

$\Rightarrow$ $V_{CE} = V_{CC} - I_C (R_C + R_E)$

As, $V_E = I_E R_E$

Voltage from collector to ground can be determined from

$$V_{CE} = V_C - V_E$$

and $V_C = V_{CE} + V_E$

or $V_C = V_{CC} - I_C R_C$

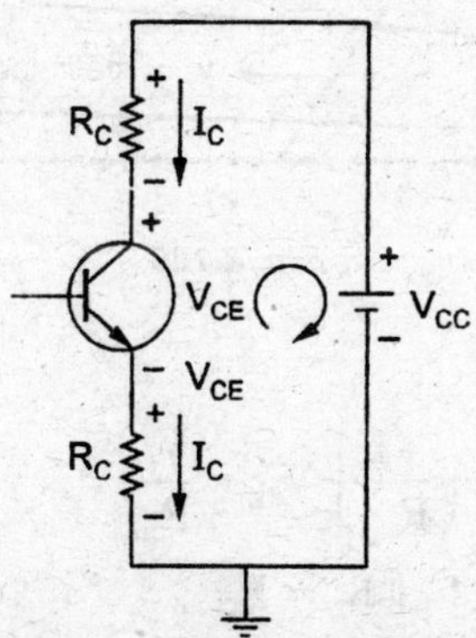

Fig. 3.122. Collector-emitter loop

The voltage at the base with respect to ground can be determined from

$$V_B = V_{CC} - I_B R_B$$

or $V_B = V_{BE} + V_E$

3.11.3. CONCEPT OF Q POINT, AC AND DC OR DYNAMIC AND STATIC LOAD LINES

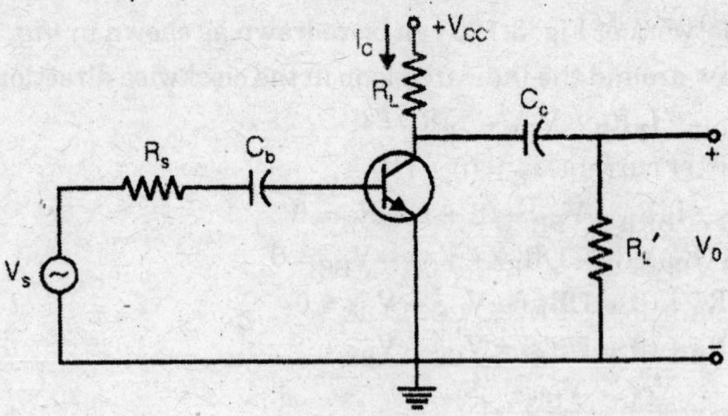

Fig. 3.123

Case 1: *Zero signal (dc) analysis*

C_b and C_c open

Applying KVL, we have

$$V_{CC} = I_C R_L + V_{CE}$$

$$\Rightarrow \quad I_C R_L = -V_{CE} + V_{CC}$$

$$\Rightarrow \quad I_C = \left(\frac{-1}{R_L}\right) V_{CE} + \frac{V_{CC}}{R_L}$$

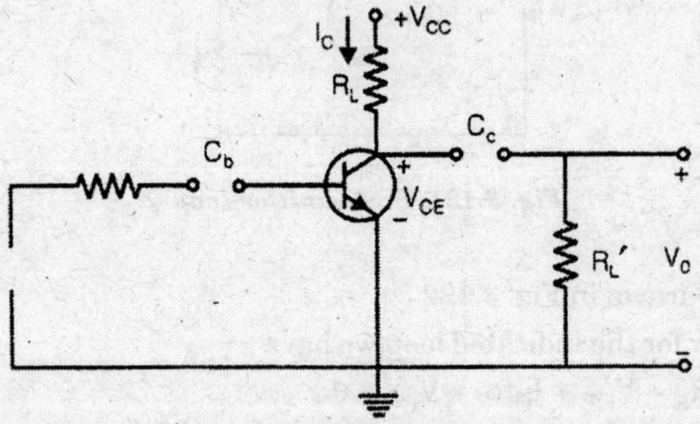

Fig. 3.124

According to this equation, draw I_C *vs* V_{CE} which is called *load line characterstric.*

Here, Q = Quiescent point or operating point.

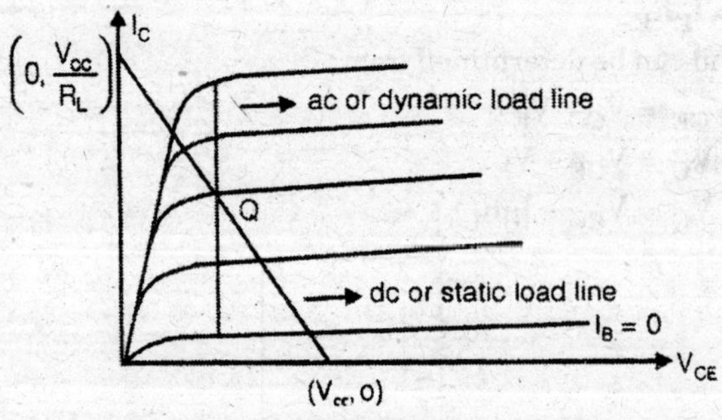

Fig. 3.125

Case 2 : *Small signal anlysis*

C_b and C_c short circuit

$$I_C = \left(\frac{-1}{R_{ac}}\right) V_{CE} + \frac{V_{cc}}{R_{ac}}$$

where, $R_{ac} = R_L \parallel R_L' < R_L$

Slope of ac load line > Slope of dc load line

Hence Q point is adjusted almost in the middle portion of the output characteriistic of the transistor, so that when ac voltage is superimposed on it, its positive half and negative half of the ac voltage must remain in the linear or active region of the characteristic.

This Q point is fixed by the variation of the power supply V_{CC} and load resistor R_L.s

3.11.4. COLLECTOR BASE BIASING

Applying, we have

$$V_{CC} = (I_B + I_C)R_C + I_B R_b + V_{BE}$$

$$\Rightarrow \quad I_B(R_b + R_c) + I_C R_C = V_{CC} - V_{BE}$$

$$\therefore \quad \frac{\partial I_B}{\partial I_C} = \frac{-R_C}{R_b + R_C}$$

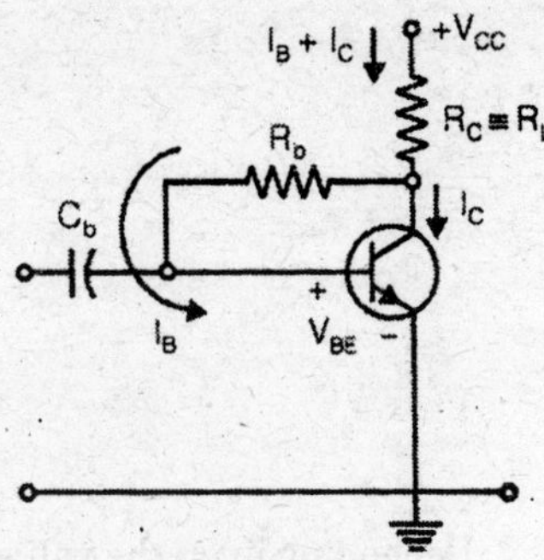

Fig. 3.126

By definition,

$$S = \frac{1+\beta}{1-\beta\dfrac{\partial I_B}{\partial I_C}}$$

$$\Rightarrow \quad S = \frac{1+\beta}{1+x}$$

where, $x = \dfrac{\beta R_C}{R_b + R_C}$

$$S < 1 + \beta$$

Thus thermal stability has become slightly better.

Potential Divider biasing or Self-biasing

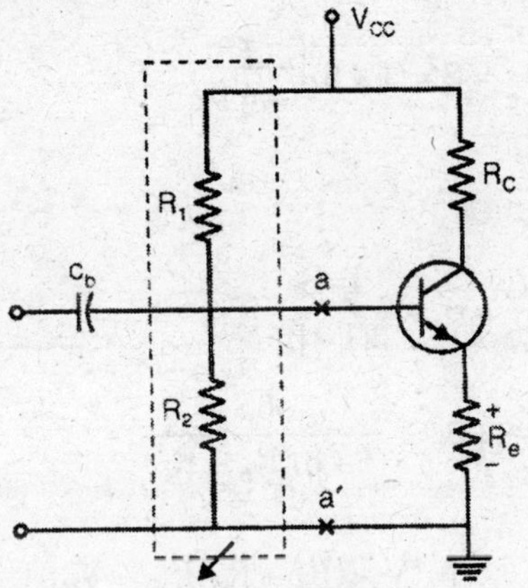

Fig. 3.127

aa' = Thevenin equivalent model.

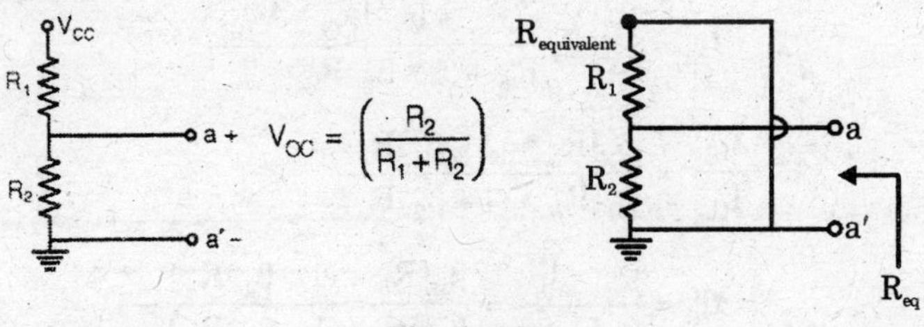

Fig. 3.128

Thevenin equivalent circuit for Fig. 3.128 is shown in Fig. 3.129

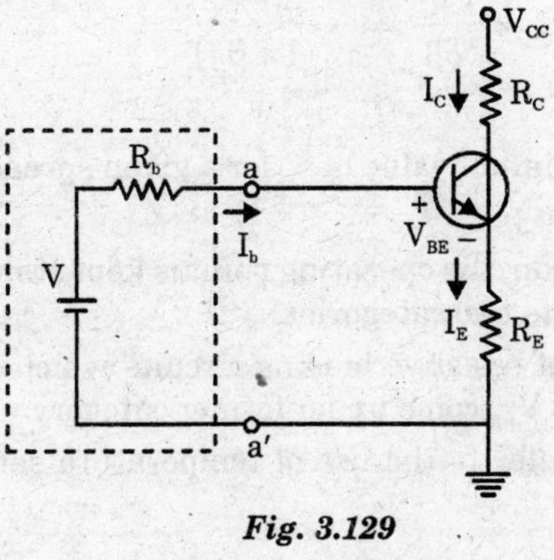

Fig. 3.129

Applying KVL, we have $$V = I_B R_b + V_{BE} + (I_B + I_C)R_e$$

$\Rightarrow$ $$I_B (R_L + R_e) + I_C R_e = V - V_{BE}$$

$\therefore$ $$\frac{\partial I_B}{\partial I_C}(R_b + R_e) + R_e = 0$$

$\Rightarrow$ $$\frac{\partial I_B}{\partial I_C} = \frac{-R_e}{R_b + R_e}$$

$\therefore$ $$S = \frac{1+\beta}{1-\beta\frac{\partial I_B}{\partial I_C}} = \left[\frac{1+\beta}{1+\beta\frac{R_e}{R_b+R_e}}\right]$$

Depending upon the values of R_b, R_e, this circuit has lowest value of the stability factor 'S'. Thus this circuit has best thermal stability among the three biasing circuits.

Determination of S, S_β and S_V

$$I_B(R_b + R_e) + I_C R_e = V - V_{BE}$$

Relation between I_B and I_C for the specified circuits.

$$I_C = \beta I_B + (1 + B)I_{CO}$$

This is general equation and is (valid for tall circuits)

Eliminate I_B, we get $$I_C = \frac{\beta[V + (R_b + R_e)I_{CO} - V_{BE}]}{R_b + (1+\beta)R_e}$$

$\therefore$ $$\frac{\partial I_C}{\partial I_{C_0}} = S = (1+\beta)\left(\frac{x}{x+\beta}\right)$$

where $x = 1 + \frac{R_b}{R_e}$, $R_b = R_1 \| R_2$

$$\frac{\partial I_C}{\partial V_\beta} = S_\beta = \frac{I_C S}{\beta(1+\beta)}$$

$$\frac{\partial I_C}{\partial V_{BE}} = S_V = \frac{-\beta S}{(1+\beta)(R_b + R_e)}$$

Determining Modified value of S_β

$$I_{C1} = \frac{\beta_1[V + (R_b + R_c)I_{CO} - V_{BE}]}{R_b + (1+\beta_1)R_e}$$

and $$I_{C2} = \frac{\beta_2[V + (R_b + R_c)I_{CO} - V_{BE}]}{R_b + (1+\beta_2)R_e}$$

$\therefore$ $$\frac{I_{C_2}}{I_{C_1}} = \frac{\beta_2[R_b + (1+\beta_1)R_e]}{\beta_1[R_b + (1+\beta_2)R_e]}$$

and $$\Delta I_C = \frac{I_{C_2} - I_{C_1}}{I_{C_1}} = \frac{\beta_2[R_b + (1+\beta_1)R_e]}{\beta_1[R_b + (1+\beta_2)R_e]} - 1$$

$$S_\beta = \frac{\partial I_C}{\partial \beta} = \frac{I_{C_1} S_2}{\beta_1(1+\beta_2)}$$

where, $S_2 = S|_{\beta = \beta_2}$

This equation allows to determine maximum value of S_β for a given spread in β and a given I_{C1}. This variation in β.

Bias Compensation

In biasing a transistor in the active region, the operating point is kept stable by keeping I_C and V_{CE} constant. But to do this, techniques have been classified into two categories.

(*i*) **Stabilization techniques :** Use of resistive biasing circuits which allow I_B to vary so as to keep I_C relatively constant, with variations in I_{CD}, β & V_{BE} come under former category.

(*ii*) **Compensation techniques :** It refer to the use of temperature sensitive devices such as diodes, transistors, thermistors etc.

Diode Compensation

Case 1 : For V_{BE}

By KVL around the base cirucit, we have

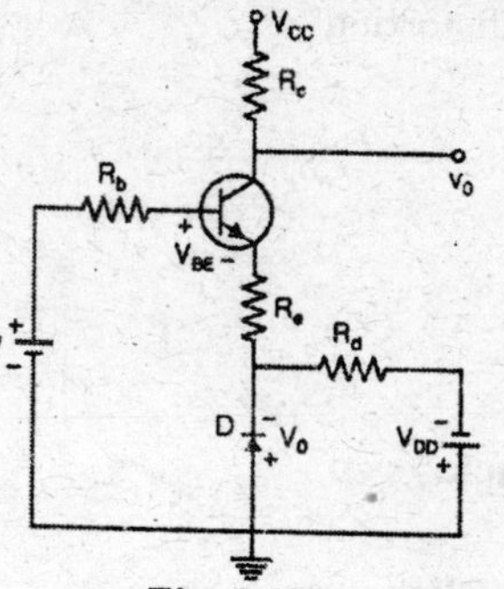

Fig. 3.130

$$I_C = \frac{\beta[V-(V_{BE}-V_0)]+(R_b+R_e)(\beta+1)I_{CO}}{R_b+R_e(1+\beta)}$$

Since in this equation, V_{BE} tracks V_0 with respect to temperature, I_C will be insensitive to variations in V_E.

Case 2 : For I_{CD}

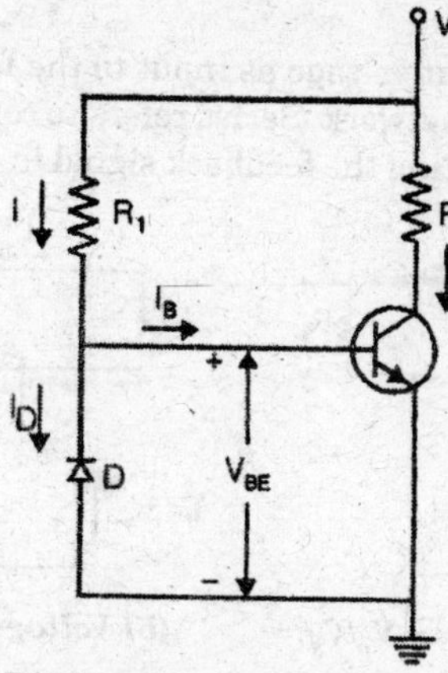

Fig. 3.131. Diode compensation for a Ge transistor

If diode and transistor are of the same type and material, then reverse saturation current I_0 of the diode will increase with temperature at the same rate as the transistor collector saturation current I_{CO}. For Ge transistors, change in I_{CD} with temperature play the more important role in collector current stability. The diode compensation circuit offers stabilization against variations in I_{CO}, and is therefore useful for stabilizing germanium transistors.

$$I = \frac{V_{CC}-V_{BE}}{R_1} = \frac{V_{CC}}{R_1} = \text{constant}$$

Base current, $I_B = I - I_o$

$\therefore$ $I_C = \beta I - \beta I_0 + (1-\beta)I_{CO}$

If $\beta >> 1$ and if I_0 of D and I_{CO} of Q track each other over the desired temperature range, then I_C remain essentially constant.

3.12 FEEDBACK AMPLIFIERS

FEEDBACK

It is a process of injecting some energy from output to input depending on the phase of input signal.

Classification of Feedback

Feedback can be divided into two categories :

(1) Positive feedback.

If feedback signal is applied in phase with the input signal, then feedback is called *regenerative feedback*. It increases gain but because of excessive distortion it is seldom used. Positive feedback used in oscillators.

(2) Negative feedback.

If feedback signal is applied out of phase with input signal, then feedback is called *negative feedback*. It is also called *degenerative feedback*.

Advantages of Negative feedback:

(*i*) Increased stability

(*ii*) Increased bandwidth

(*iii*) Less amplitude and harmonic distortion

(*iv*) Decreased noise

(*v*) Less frequency distortion

(*vi*) Less phase distortion

(*vii*) Higher input impedance

(*viii*) Lower output impedance

(*ix*) Improved frequency response

Disadvantage of Negative feedback:

Reduction in gain.

3.12.1. FEEDBACK CONNECTION TYPES

There are four basic ways of connecting the feedback signal. Both voltage and current can be feedback to the input either in series or parallel.

1. Voltage-series feedback [Fig. 3.132 (*a*)]
2. Voltage-shunt feedback [Fig. 3.132 (*b*)]
3. Current-series feedback [Fig. 3.132 (*c*)]
4. Current-shunt feedback [Fig. 3.132 (*d*)]

Here, voltage refers to connecting the output voltage as input to the feedback network; current refers to tapping off some output current through the feedback network. Series refers to connecting the feedback signal in series with the input signal voltage; shunt refers to connecting the feedback signal in shunt (parallel) with an input current source.

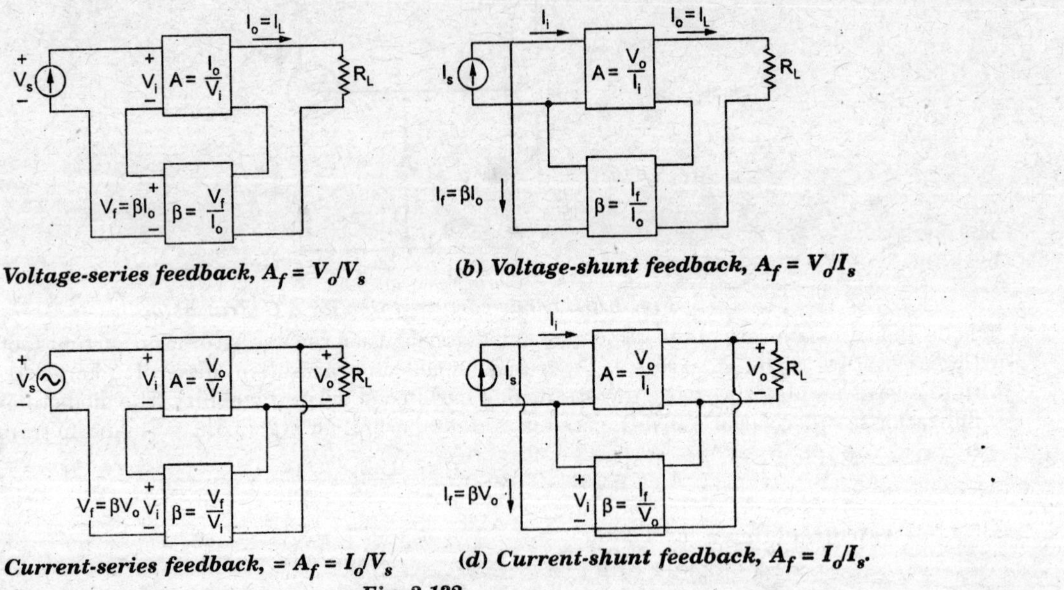

(a) Voltage-series feedback, $A_f = V_o/V_s$ *(b) Voltage-shunt feedback,* $A_f = V_o/I_s$

(c) Current-series feedback, $= A_f = I_o/V_s$ *(d) Current-shunt feedback,* $A_f = I_o/I_s$.

Fig. 3.132

Gain with Feedback

Here we examine gain of each of the feedback circuit connections of Figures 3.132 (*a*) to 3.132 (*d*). The gain without feedback, A, is that of the amplifier stage. With feedback, β, the overall gain of the circuit is reduced by a factor (1 + βA).

Table 3.7. Gain, Feedback, and Gain with Feedback From Fig. 3.132 (*a*) to (*d*)

	Voltage-Series	Voltage-Shunt	Current-Series	Current-Shunt	
Gain without feedback	A	$\frac{V_o}{V_i}$	$\frac{V_o}{I_i}$	$\frac{I_o}{V_i}$	$\frac{I_o}{I_i}$
Feedback	β	$\frac{V_f}{V_o}$	$\frac{i_f}{V_o}$	$\frac{V_f}{I_o}$	$\frac{I_f}{I_o}$
Gain with feedback	A_f	$\frac{V_o}{V_s}$	$\frac{V_o}{I_s}$	$\frac{I_o}{V_s}$	$\frac{I_o}{I_s}$

Voltage-Series Feedback

Fig. 3.132 (*a*) shows the voltage-series feedback connection with a part of the output voltage feedback in series with the input signal, resulting in an overall gain reduction.

If there is no feedback ($V_f = 0$), then voltage gain of the amplifier stage is

$$A = \frac{V_o}{V_s} = \frac{V_o}{V_i}$$

If a feedback signal, V_f, is connected in series with the input, then

$$V_i = V_s - V_f$$

Since $\quad V_o = AV_i = A(V_s - V_f) = AV_s - AV_f = AV_s - A(\beta V_o)$

then $\quad (1 + \beta A)V_o = AV_s$

Hence overall voltage gain with feedback is

$$A_f = \frac{V_o}{V_s} = \frac{A}{1+\beta A} \qquad ...(3.41)$$

This equation shows that the gain with feedback is the amplifier gain reduced by the factor (1 + βA).

Voltage-Shunt Feedback

The gain with feedback for the network of Fig. 3.132 (*b*) is

$$A_f = \frac{V_o}{I_s} = \frac{AI_i}{I_i+I_f} = \frac{AI_i}{I_i+\beta V_o} = \frac{AI_i}{I_i+\beta AI_i} = \frac{A}{1+\beta A}$$

INPUT IMPEDANCE WITH FEEDBACK.

Voltage-Series Feedback

A more detailed voltage-series feedback connection is shown in Fig. 3.133. The input impedance can be determined as follows :

$$I_i = \frac{V_i}{Z_i} = \frac{V_s - V_f}{Z_i} = \frac{V_s - \beta V_o}{Z_i} = \frac{V_s - \beta AV_i}{Z_i}$$

$$I_i Z_i = V_s - \beta AV_i$$

$$V_s = I_i Z_i + \beta AV_i = I_i Z_i + \beta AI_i Z_i$$

$$Z_{if} = \frac{V_s}{I_i} = Z_i + (\beta A) Z_i = Z_i (1 + \beta A)$$

The input impedance with series feeback is seen to be the value of the input impedance without feedback multiplied by the factor (1 + βA) and applied to both voltage-series [Fig. 3.132 (*a*)] and current-series [Fig. 3.132 (*c*)] configurations.

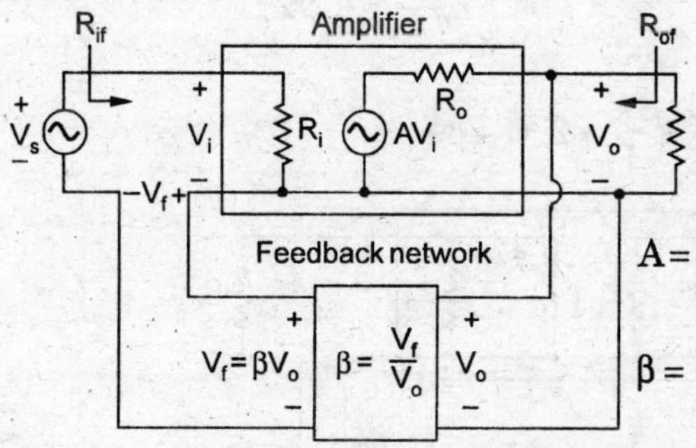

$$\left.\begin{aligned} A &= \frac{V_o}{V_i} \\ \beta &= \frac{V_f}{V_o} \end{aligned}\right\} A_f = \frac{V_o}{V_s} = \frac{A}{1+bA}$$

Fig. 3.133 Voltage-series feedback connection

Voltage-Shunt Feedback

A more detailed voltage-shunt feedback connection is shown in Fig. 3.132. The input impedance can be determined to be

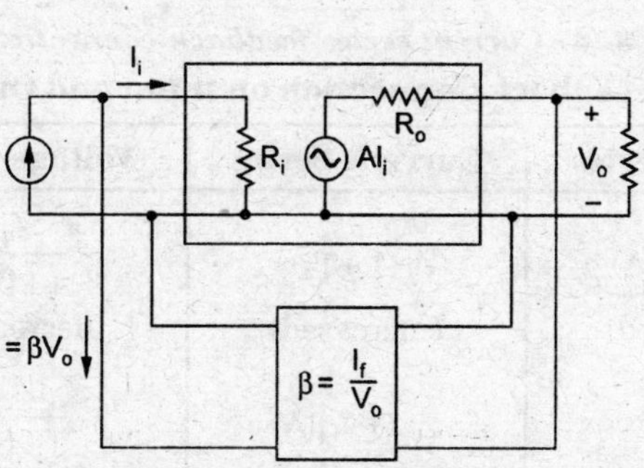

Fig. 3.134 Voltage-shunt feedback connection

$$Z_{if} = \frac{V_i}{I_s} = \frac{V_i}{I_i + I_f} = \frac{V_i}{I_i + \beta V_o} = \frac{V_i / I_i}{\frac{I_i}{I_i} + \frac{\beta V_o}{I_i}}$$

or
$$Z_{if} = \frac{Z_i}{1 + \beta A}$$

This reduced input impedance applies to the voltage-series connection of Fig. 3.132 (*a*) and the voltage-shunt connection of Fig. 3.132 (*b*).

Output Impedance with Feedback

The output impedance for the connections of Fig. 3.132 (*a*) to Fig. 3.132 (*d*) are dependent on the use of voltage or current feedback. For voltage feedback, the output impedance is decreased, while current feedback increases the output impedance.

Voltage-Series Feedback

The voltage-series feedback circuit of Fig. 3.133 provides sufficient circuit detail to determine the output impedance with feedback. The output impedance is determined by applying a voltage, V, resulting in a current, I, with V_s shorted out ($V_s = 0$). Then

$$\text{Voltage, } V = IZ_o + AV_i$$

For $V_s = 0$,
$$V_i = -V_f$$

$\therefore$
$$V = IZ_o - AV_f = IZ_o - A(\beta V)$$

Rewriting the equation as
$$V + \beta AV = IZ_o$$

allows solving for the output resistance with feedback :

$$Z_{of} = \frac{V}{I} = \frac{Z_o}{1 + \beta A}$$

This equation shows that with voltage-series feedback, the output impedance is reduced from that without feedback by the factor $(1 + \beta A)$.

Current-Series Feedback

The output impedance with current-series feedback can be determined by applying a signal V to the output with V_s shorted out, resulting in a current I, the ratio of V to I being the output impedance. Figure 3.135 shows a more detailed connection with current-series feedback. For the output part of a current-series feedback connection shown in Fig. 3.135, the resulting output impedance is determined as follows.

With $V_s = 0$,
$$V_i = V_f$$

$$I = \frac{V}{Z_o} - AV_i = \frac{V}{Z_o} - AV_f = \frac{V}{Z_o} - A\beta I$$

$$Z_o(1 + \beta A)\, I = V$$

$$Z_{of} = \frac{V}{I} = Z_o(1 + \beta A)$$

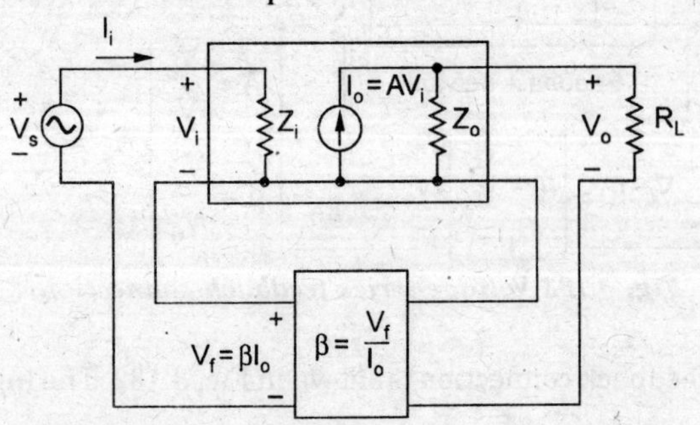

Fig. 3.135 Current-series feedback connection

Table 3.8. Effect of Feedback Connection on Input and Output Impedance

	Voltage-Series	Current-Series	Voltage-Shunt	Current-Shunt
Z_{if}	$Z_i(1 + \beta A)$ (increased)	$Z_i(1 + \beta A)$ (increased)	$\frac{Z_i}{1+\beta A}$ (decreased)	$\frac{Z_i}{1+\beta A}$ (decreased)
Z_{of}	$\frac{Z_o}{1+\beta A}$ (decreased)	$Z_o(1 + \beta A)$ (increased)	$\frac{Z_o}{1+\beta A}$ (decreased)	$Z_o(1 + \beta A)$ (increased)

3.12.2. CHARACTERISTICS OF FEEDBACK

(i) Reduction in Frequency Distortion

For a negative-feedback amplifier having $\beta A >> 1$, the gain with feedback is $A_f \cong 1/\beta$.

It follows that if feedback network is purely resistive, the gain with feedback is not dependent on frequency even though the basic amplifier gain is frequency dependent. Practically, the frequency distortion arising because of varying amplifier gain with gain frequency is considerably reduced in a negative-voltage feedback amplifier circuit.

(ii) Reduction in noise and Nonlinear distortion

Signal feedback tends to hold down the amount of noise signal (such as power-supply hum) and non-linear distortion. The factor $(1 + \beta A)$ reduces both input noise and resulting non-linear distortion for considerable improvement. However, there is a reduction in overall gain (the price required for the improvement in circuit performance). If additional stages are used to bring the overall gain up to the level without feedback, the extra stage(s) might introduce as much noise back into the system as that reduced by the feedback amplifier. This problem can be somewhat alleviated by readjusting the gain of the feedback-amplifier circuit to obtain higher gain while also providing reduced noise signal.

(iii) Effect of negative feedback on Gain and Bandwidth

In Table (3.7) the overall gain with negative feedback is

$$A_f = \frac{A}{1+\beta A} \cong \frac{A}{\beta A} = \frac{1}{\beta} \qquad \text{for } \beta A >> 1$$

As long as $\beta A >> 1$, the overall gain $\approx 1/\beta$.

For a practical amplifier (for single low-and high-frequency breakpoints) the open-loop gain drops off at high frequencies due to the active device and circuit capacitances. Gain may also drop off at low frequencies for capacitively coupled amplifier stages. Once the open-loop gain A drops low enough and the factor βA is no longer much larger than 1, $A_f \cong 1/\beta$ no longer holds true.

Fig. 3.136 shows that the amplifier with negative feedback has more bandwidth (B_f) than the amplifier without feedback (B). The feedback amplifier has a higher upper 3-dB frequency and smaller lower 3-dB frequency.

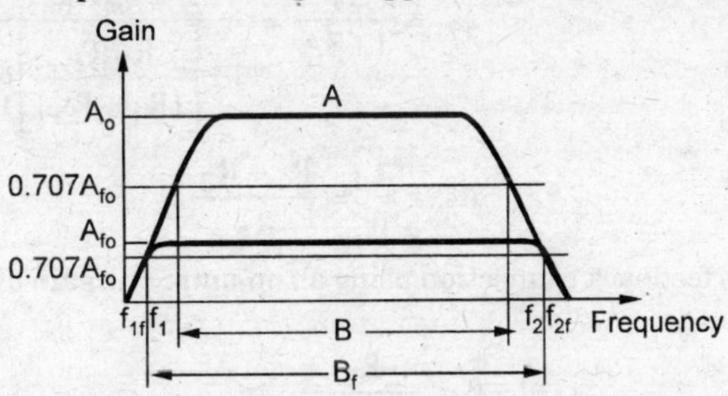

Fig. 3.136 Effect of negative feedback on gain and bandwidth

The use of feedback, while resulting in a lowering of voltage gain, has provided an increase in B and in the upper 3-dB frequency, particularly. In fact, the product of gain and frequency remains the same so that the gain–bandwidth product of the basic amplifier is the same value for the feedback amplifier. However, since the feedback amplifier has lower gain, the net operation was to trade gain for bandwidth (we use bandwidth for the upper 3-dB frequency since typically $f_2 >> f_1$).

Gain Stability with Feedback

The fractional change in amplification with feedback divided by the fractional change without feedback is called *sensitivity of the transfer gain*.

Differentiating equation 3.41, we have

$$\left|\frac{dA_f}{A_f}\right| = \frac{1}{|1+\beta A|}\left|\frac{dA}{A}\right|$$

For $\beta A >> 1$,

$$\left|\frac{dA_f}{A_f}\right| = \left|\frac{1}{\beta A}\right|\left|\frac{dA}{A}\right|$$

This shows that magnitude of the relative change in gain $\left|\frac{dA_f}{A_f}\right|$ is reduced by the factor $|\beta A|$ compared to that without feedback $\left(\left|\frac{dA}{A}\right|\right)$.

$\therefore$
$$\text{Sensitivity} = \frac{1}{\beta A} \qquad \text{for } \beta A >> 1.$$

3.12.3. PRACTICAL FEEDBACK CIRCUITS

(1) Voltage-Series Feedback

Figure 3.137 shows an FET amplifier stage with voltage-series feedback. A part of the output signal (V_o) is obtained using a feedback network of resistor R_1 and R_2. The feedback voltage V_f is connected in series with the source signal V_s, their difference being the input signal V_i.

Prior to feedback, amplifier gain, $$A = \frac{V_o}{V_i} = -g_m R_L$$

where R_L = parallel combination of resistors

$$R_L = R_D \,||\, R_o \,||\, (R_1 + R_2)$$

$$\text{Feedback factor, } \beta = \frac{V_f}{V_o} = \frac{-R_2}{R_1 + R_2}$$

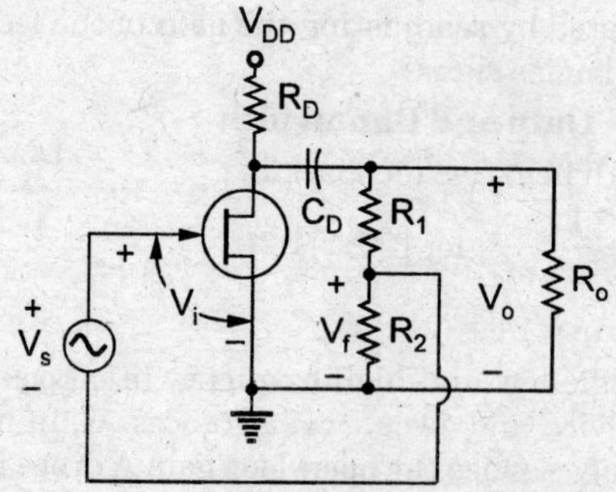

Fig. 3.137 FET amplifier stage with voltage-series feedback

Using the values of A and β above in equation (3.41), we get the gain with negative feedback as

$$A_f = \frac{A}{1+\beta A} = \frac{-g_m R_L}{1 + \left[\dfrac{R_2 R_L}{(R_1 + R_2)}\right] g_m}$$

If βV >> 1, we have $$A_f \cong \frac{1}{\beta} = \frac{R_1 + R_2}{R_2}$$

Fig. 3.138 shows a voltage-series feedback connection using an op-amp. The gain of theop-amp, A, without feedback, is reduced by the feedback factor.

$$\beta = \frac{R_2}{R_1 + R_2}$$

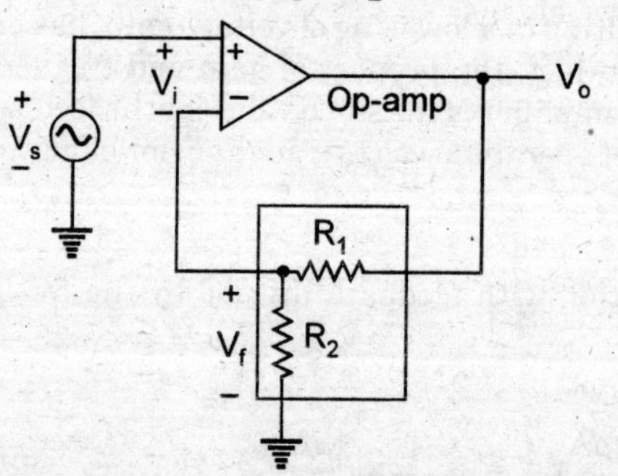

Fig. 3.138 Voltage-series feedback in an op-amp connection

The emitter-follower circuit of Fig. 3.139 provides voltage-series feedback. The signal voltage, V_s, is the input voltage, V_i. The output voltage, V_o, is also the feedback voltage in series with the input voltage. The amplifier, as shown in Fig. 3.108 provides the operation *with* feedback. The operation of the circuit without feedback provides $V_f = 0$, therefore

$$A = \frac{V_o}{V_s} = \frac{h_{fe} I_b R_E}{V_s} = \frac{h_{fe} R_E \left(\dfrac{V_s}{h_{ie}}\right)}{V_s} = \frac{h_{fe} R_E}{h_{ie}}$$

and $$\beta = \frac{V_f}{V_o} = 1$$

The operation with feedback then provides that

$$A_f = \frac{V_o}{V_s} = \frac{A}{1+\beta A} = \frac{h_{fe}R_E/h_{ie}}{1+(1)\left(\frac{h_{fe}R_E}{h_{ie}}\right)} = \frac{h_{fe}R_E}{h_{ie}+h_{fe}R_E}$$

For $h_{fe}R_E >> h_{ie}$, $A_f \cong 1$

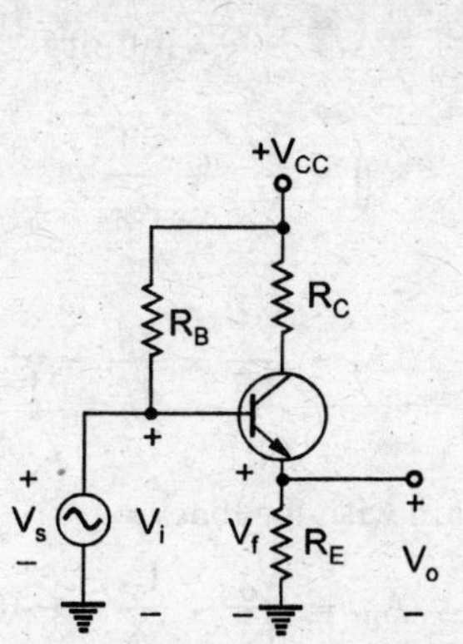

Fig. 3.139 Voltage-series feedback circuit (emitter-follower)

(2) Current-Series Feedback

Fig. 3.140 shows a single transistor amplifier stage. Since the emitter of this stage has an unbypassed emitter, it effectively has current-series feedback. The current through resistor R_E results in a feedback voltage that opposes the source signal applied so that the output voltage V_o is reduced. To remove the current-series feedback the emitter resistor must be either removed or bypassed by a capacitor.

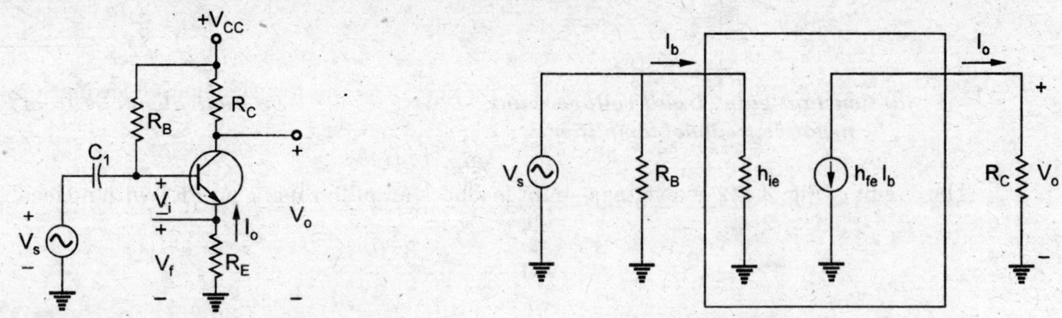

(a) Transistor amplifier with unbypassed emitter resistor (R_E) for current-series feedback.

(b) ac equivalent circuit without feedback of Fig. (a)

Fig. 3.140

Without Feedback :

Referring to the Fig. 3.132 (*a*), we have

$$A = \frac{I_o}{V_i} = \frac{-I_b h_{fe}}{I_b h_{ie}+R_E} = \frac{-h_{fe}}{h_{ie}+R_E}$$

$$\beta = \frac{V_f}{I_o} = \frac{-I_o R_E}{I_o} = -R_E$$

The input and output impedances are,

$$Z_i = R_B \,||\, (h_{ie}+R_E) \cong h_{ie}+R_E$$
$$Z_i = R_C$$

With feedback :

$$A_f = \frac{I_o}{V_s} = \frac{A}{1+\beta A} = \frac{-h_{fe}/h_{ie}}{1+(-R_E)\left(\frac{-h_{fe}}{h_{ie}+R_E}\right)} \cong \frac{-h_{fe}}{h_{ie}+h_{fe}R_E}$$

Input and output impedance is calculated as,

$$Z_{if} = Z_i(1+\beta A) \cong h_{ie}\left(1+\frac{h_{fe}R_E}{h_{ie}}\right) = h_{ie}+h_{fe}R_E$$

$$Z_{of} = Z_o(1+\beta A) = R_C\left(1+\frac{h_{fe}R_E}{h_{ie}}\right)$$

Voltage gain (A) with feedback is, $$A_{vf} = \frac{V_o}{V_s} = \frac{I_o R_C}{V_s} = \left(\frac{I_o}{V_s}\right)R_C = A_f R_C \cong \frac{-h_{fe}R_C}{h_{ie}+h_{fe}R_E}$$

(3) Voltage-Shunt Feedback :

The constant-gain op-amp circuit of Fig. 3.141 (*a*) provides voltage-shunt feedback. Referring Fig. 3.141 (*b*) and op-amp ideal characteristics $I_i = 0$, $V_i = 0$, and voltage gain of infinity; we have

$$A = \frac{V_o}{I_i} = \text{infinity}$$

$$\beta = \frac{I_f}{V_o} = \frac{-1}{R_o}$$

Then gain with feedback is

$$A_f = \frac{V_o}{I_s} = \frac{V_o}{I_i} = \frac{A}{1+\beta A} = \frac{1}{\beta} = -R_o$$

This is a *transfer resistance gain*.

The more usual gain is the voltage gain with feedback,

$$A_{vf} = \frac{V_o}{I_s} - \frac{I_s}{V_1} = (-R_o)\frac{1}{R_1} = \frac{-R_o}{R_1}$$

(a) Transistor amplifier with unbypassed ***(b) a***

(a) Constant gain circuit voltage-shunt negative feedback amplifier ***(b) Equivalent circuit of Fig. 3.142(b)***

Fig. 3.141

The circuit of Fig. 3.142 is a voltage-shunt feedback amplifier using an FET with no feedback, $V_f = 0$.

$$A = \frac{V_o}{I_i} \cong -g_m R_D R_S$$

$$\text{Feedback, } \beta = \frac{I_f}{V_o} = \frac{-1}{R_F}$$

With feedback, gain of the circuit is

$$A_f = \frac{V_o}{I_s} = \frac{A}{1+\beta A} = \frac{-g_m R_D R_S}{1+(-1/R_F)(-g_m R_D R_S)} = \frac{-g_m R_D R_S R_F}{R_F + g_m R_D R_S}$$

Then voltage gain of the circuit with feedback is

$$A_{vf} = \frac{V_o}{I_s}\frac{I_s}{V_s} = \frac{-g_m R_D R_S R_F}{R_F + g_m R_D R_S}\left(\frac{1}{R_S}\right) = \frac{-g_m R_D R_F}{R_F + g_m R_D R_S}$$

$$= (-g_m R_D)\frac{R_F}{R_F + g_m R_D R_S}$$

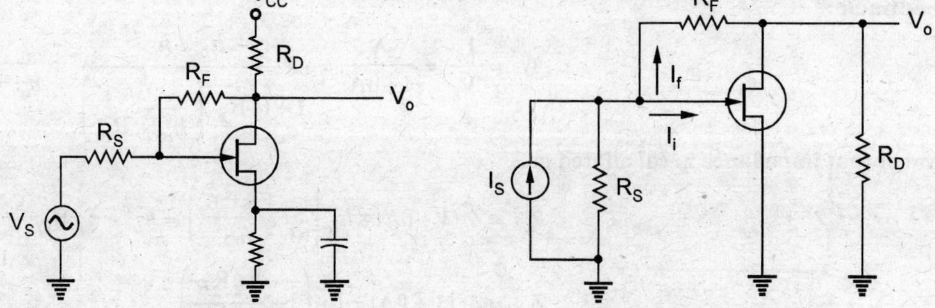

(a) Circuit ***(b) Equivalent circuit***

Fig. 3.142 Voltage-shunt feedback amplifier using an FET

3.13 FET AMPLIFIER

Just like in BJT, FETs have two popular categories of amplifiers :

(1) Common-source amplifier

(2) Common drai amplifier.

Equivalent circuits of FET at LOW frequecies

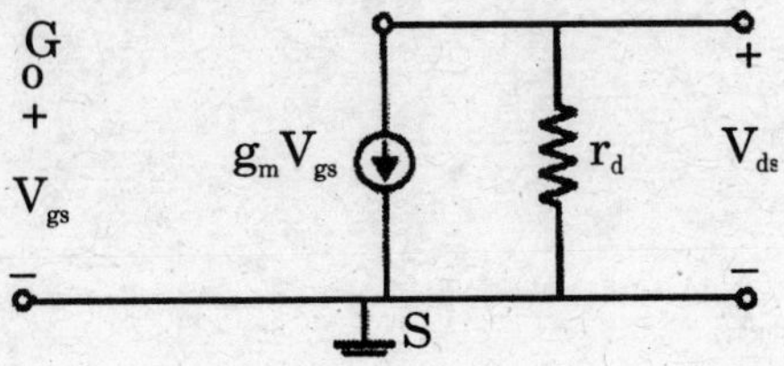

(a) Circuit

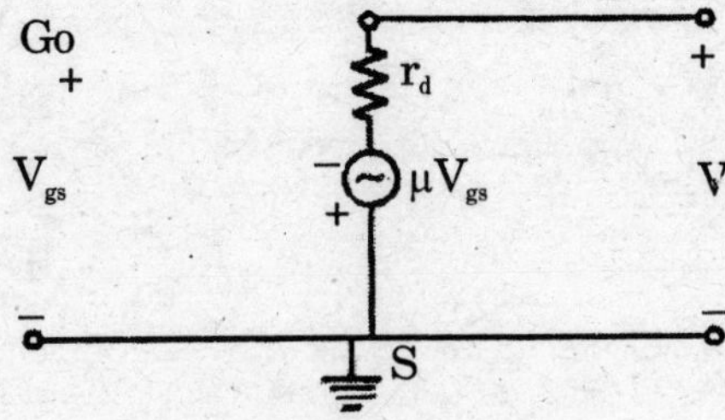

(b) Equivalent circuit

$$\mu = g_m r_d$$

At high frequencies,
$$Z = \frac{1}{j\omega C}$$

and therefore ω increases means impedance decreases and ω decreases means impedance increases. Interelectrode capacitance draw some current at high frequncies, hence cannot be neglected and therefore Fig. 3.143 shows high frequency equivalent.

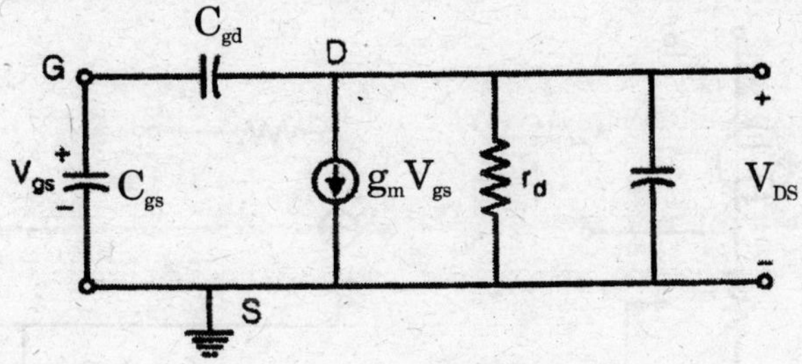

(a) Circuit

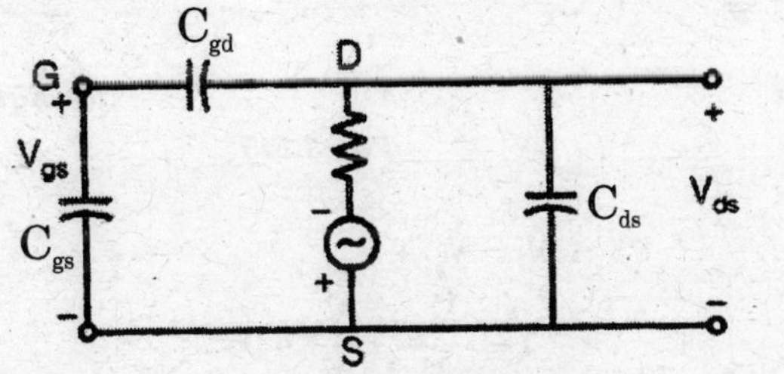

(b) Equivalent circuit

Fig. 3.143

3.13.1. COMMON-SOURCE AMPLIFIER.

(1) FET amplifier at low frequncy in common source mode

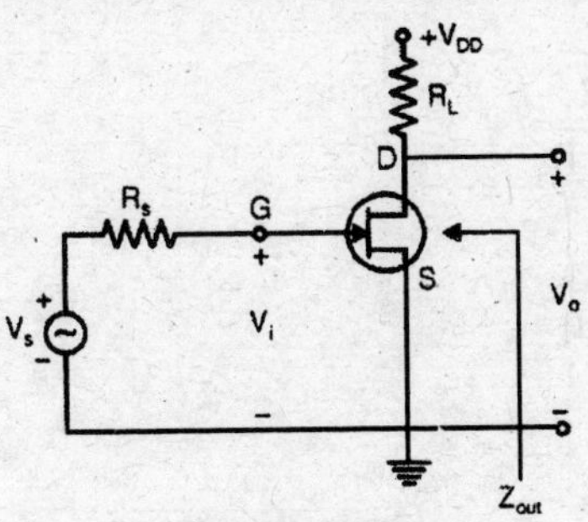

(a) Circuit

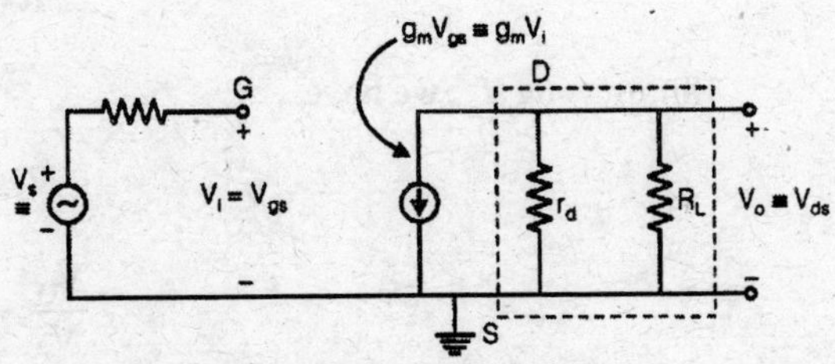

(b) Equivalent circuit

Fig. 3.144

Voltage gain, A_v

$$V_O = -g_m V_i R$$

where,
$$R = R_L \parallel r_d = \frac{r_d R_L}{r_d + R_L}$$

$$\frac{V_O}{V_i} = A_v = -g_m R = \frac{-g_m R_L r_d}{R_L + r_d}$$

$$A_V = \frac{-\mu R_L}{r_d + R_L}$$

$$\therefore \quad |A_V| = \frac{\mu R_L}{r_d + R_L}$$

$$\phi = 180°, A_{VS} = A_V$$

Output impedance,
$$Z_{out} = r_d \parallel R_L = \frac{r_d R_L}{r_d + R_L}$$

Characteristics :

(*i*) High voltage gain

(*ii*) Input and output voltages are out of phase by 180°.

(*iii*) Almost infinite input impedance

(*iv*) Relatively low output impedance

(*v*) Since voltage gain is high, it can be used as a voltage amplifier.

(2) Common-drain FET amplifier or Source follower

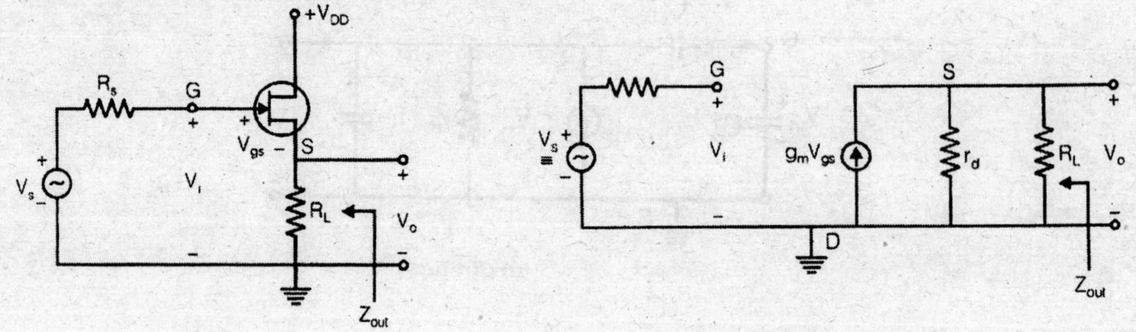

(*a*) *Circuit* **(*b*) *Equivalent circuit***

Fig. 3.145

Applying KVL, we have

$$V_i = V_{gs} + V_C$$

$$\therefore \quad 1 = \frac{V_{gs}}{V_i} + \frac{V_0}{V_i} s$$

$$\therefore \quad A_V = 1 - \frac{V_{gs}}{V_i} < 1$$

$$V_O = g_m V_{gs} R$$

$$V_i = V_{gs} + g_m V_{gs} R$$

$$R = r_d \parallel RL = \frac{r_d R_L}{r_d + R_L}$$

Eliminating V_{gs}, we have

$$V_i = \frac{V_O}{g_m R}\{1 + g_m R\}$$

$$\frac{V_O}{V_i} = \frac{g_m R}{1 + g_m R}$$

$$A_V = 1$$

$$A_V = \frac{g_m\left(\frac{r_d R_L}{r_d+R_L}\right)}{1-g_m\left[\frac{r_d R_L}{r_d+R_L}\right]}$$

$$= \frac{\mu R_L}{r_d + R_L(1+\mu)} = \frac{+\mu R_L}{r_d+(1+\mu)R_L}$$

Output impendance, $$Z_{out} = r_d \parallel R_L = \frac{r_d R_L}{r_d+R_L}$$

Characteristics :

(*i*) Voltage gain always less than one.

(*ii*) Input and output voltages are in phase.

(*iii*) Since voltage gain is less than one, it cannot be used as a voltage amplifier and hence its basic application is impedance matching.

(*iv*) Output voltage or the source terminal follows the input voltage and hence called *source follower.*

(3) Common source FET amplifier at High frequencies

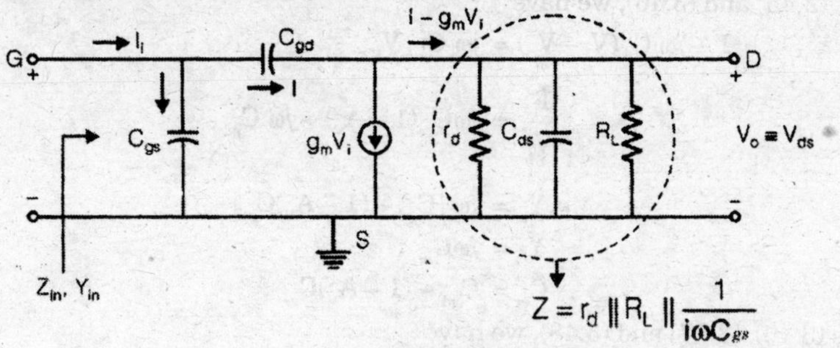

Fig. 3.146

$$I_i - I = (j\omega\, C_{gs})\, V_i \quad ...(3.42)$$

$$I = j\omega(C_{gd})(V_i - V_O) \quad ...(3.43)$$

$$V_O = (I - g_m V_i)Z$$

From equations (3.42) and (3.43), we have

$$I_i - j\omega G_{gd}\,(V_i - V_O) = j\omega C_{gs}\, V_i \quad ...(3.44)$$

$$\frac{I_i}{V_i} = j\omega\, C_{gd}\left(1-\frac{V_O}{V_i}\right) + j\omega C_{gs}$$

$$Y_{in} = j\omega[C_{gs} + (1-A_V)C_{gd}]$$

$$Y_{in} = j\omega\, C_{in}$$

$$\therefore \quad C_{in} = C_{gs} + (1-A_V)\, C_{gd}$$

From equations (3.43) and (3.44), we have

$$V_O = j\omega\, C_{gd}(V_i - V_O)\, Z - g_m V_i Z$$

$$V_O[1 + j\omega C_{gd}\, Z] = V_i\, \{j\omega C_{gd}\, Z - g_m Z\}$$

$$\therefore \quad \frac{I_O}{V_i} = A_V = \frac{(j\omega C_{gd} - g_m)Z}{(1 + j\omega C_{gd} Z)}$$

Characteristics :

(*i*) Voltage gain is frequency dependent and is always complex in nature.

(*ii*) Input impendance is always finite and is frequency dependent.

(*iii*) At high frequency, input impedance or input admittance is always capactive in nature.

(*iv*) Load impedance for the amplifier at high frequencies is always complex.

(*v*) At high frequencies, voltage gain decreases due to presence of interelectrode capacitances.

(4) Common Drain FET amplifier at High frequencies

It is also called *source follower* at high frequencies

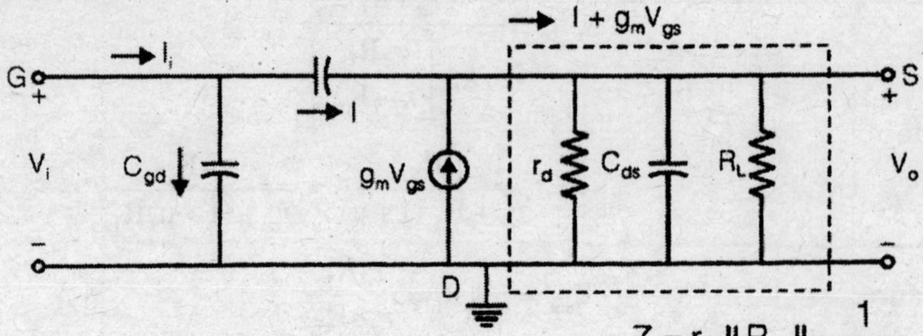

$$Z = r_d \parallel R_L \parallel \frac{1}{j\omega C_{ds}}$$

Fig. 3.147

$$I_i - I = j\omega C_{gd} V_i \quad \text{...(3.45)}$$

$$I = j\omega\, C_{gs}(V_i - V_O) \quad \text{...(3.46)}$$

$$V_O = (I + g_m\, V_S) \quad \text{...(3.47)}$$

$$V_{gs} = V_i - V_O \quad \text{...(3.48)}$$

From equations (3.45) and (3.46), we have

$$I_i - j\omega\, C_{gs}(V_i - V_O) = j\omega\, C_{gd}\, V_i$$

$$\frac{I_i}{V_i} = j\omega C_{gs}(1 - A_V) + j\omega\, C_{gd}$$

$$Y_{in} = j\omega\,[C_{gd} + (1 - A_V)C_{gs}]$$

$$Y_{in} = j\omega C_{in}$$

$$C_{in} = C_{gd} + (1 - A_V)C_{gs}$$

From equations (3.46), (3.47) and (3.48), we have

$$V_O = j\omega\, C_{gs}(V_i - V_O)\, Z + g_m\, Z(V_i - V_O)$$

$$\therefore \quad V_O[1 + (j\omega C_{gs} + g_m)Z] = (j\omega\, C_{gs} + g_m)V_i Z$$

$$\therefore \quad A_v = \frac{V_O}{V_i} = \frac{(j\omega C_{gd} - g_m)Z}{1 + (j\omega C_{gd} - g_m)Z}$$

Characteristics :

(*i*) Voltage gain has a magnitude always less than one and it depends upon frequency of operation.

(*ii*) Voltage gain is frequency dependent and is always complex.

(*iii*) Input admittance is purely capacitive in nature and is frequency dependent.

(*iv*) Input and output voltages are always in phase but this phase may change slightly depending upon the frequency of operation.

3.13.2. FET BIAS CONFIGURATIONS

Type	*Configuration*	*Equations*	*Graph*
JEET Fixed-bias	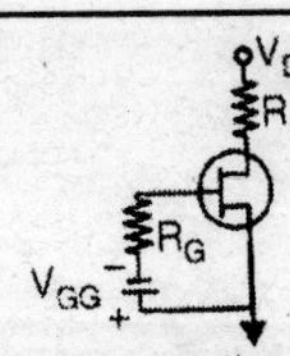	$V_{GS_Q} = V_{GG}$ $V_{DS} = V_{DD} - I_D R_S$	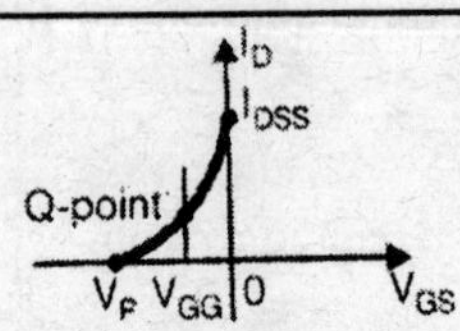
JEET Self-bias	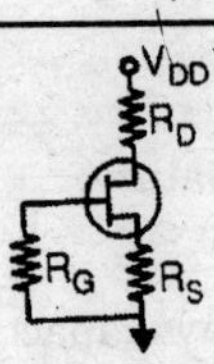	$V_{GS} = -I_D R_S$ $V_{DS} = V_{DD} - I_D (R_D + R_S)$	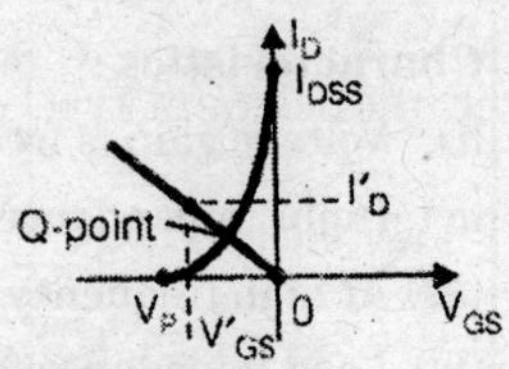

Type	*Configuration*	*Equations*	*Graph*
JEET Votage-divider bias	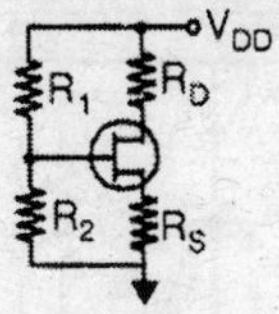	$V_G = \frac{R_2 V_{DD}}{R_1 + R_2}$ $V_{GS} = V_G - I_D R_S$ $V_{DS} = V_{DD} - I_D(R_D + R_S)$	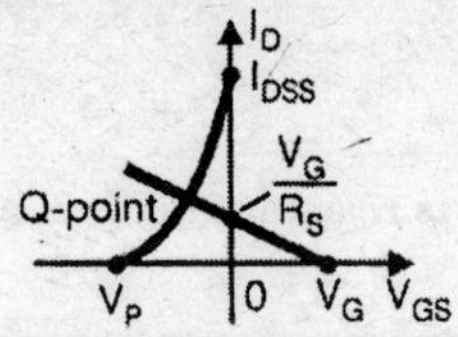
JEET Common-gate	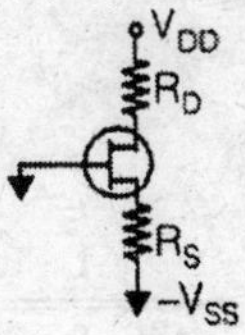	$V_{GS} = V_{SS} - I_D R_S$ $V_{DS} + V_{DD} + V_{SS} + I_D(R_D + R_S)$	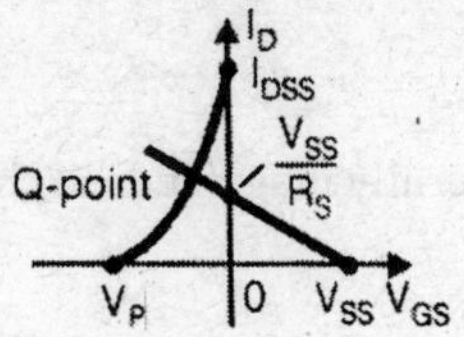
JEET ($V_{GS_0} = 0V$)	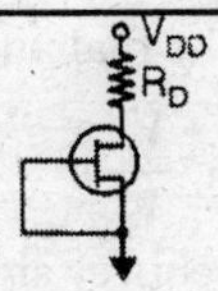	$V_{GS_0} = 0V$ $I_{D_Q} = I_{DSS}$	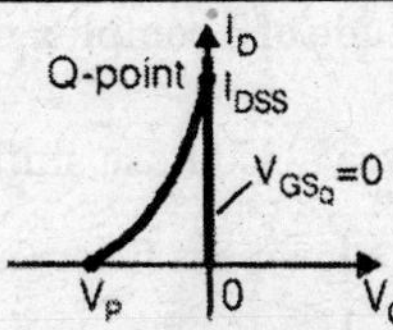
JEET ($R_D = 0\Omega$)	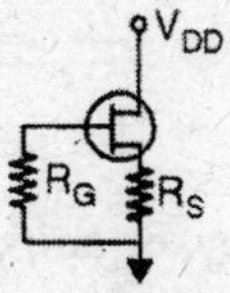	$V_{GS} = I_D R_S$ $V_D = V_{DD}$ $V_S = I_D R_S$ $V_{DS} = V_{DD} - I_D R_S$	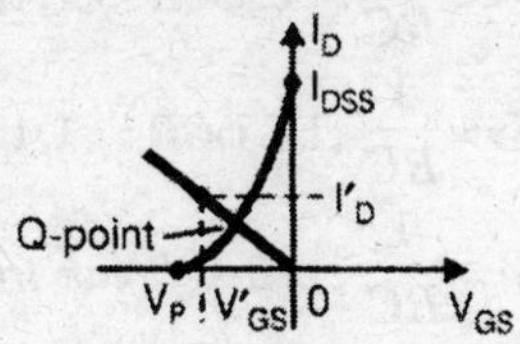
Depletion-type MOSFET Fixed-bias	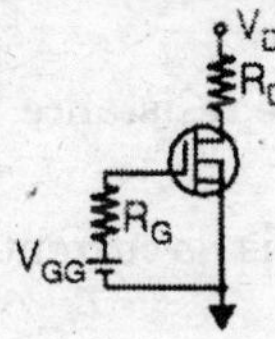	$V_{GS} = I_D R_S$ $VD = V_{DD}$ $V_S = I_D R_S$ $V_{DS} = V_{DD} = I_D R_S$	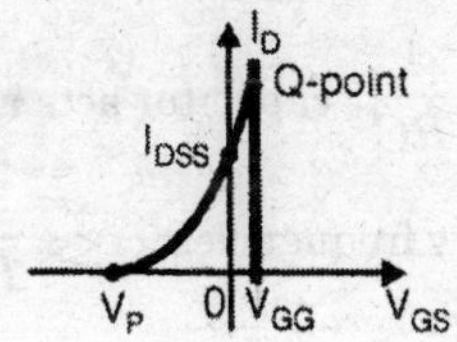
Depletion-type MOSFET Voltage-divider bias	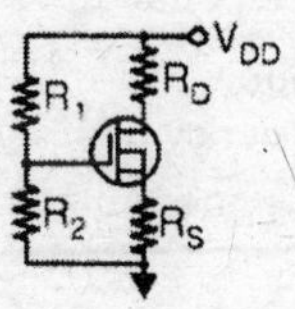	$V_{GS_Q} = + V_{GG}$ $V_{DS} = V_{DD} - I_D R_S$	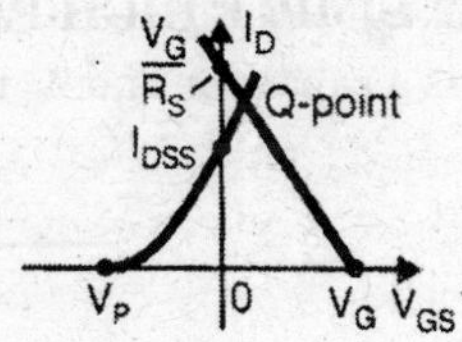
Enhancement type MOSFET Feedback configuration	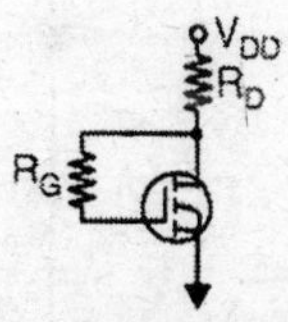	$V_G = \frac{R_2 V_{DD}}{R_1 + R_2}$ $V_{GS} = V_G - I_S R_S$ $V_{DS} = V_{DD} - I_D(R_D + R_S)$	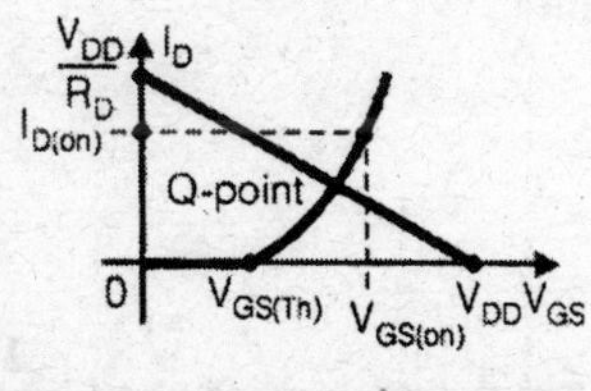
Enhancement type MOSFET Voltage-divider bias	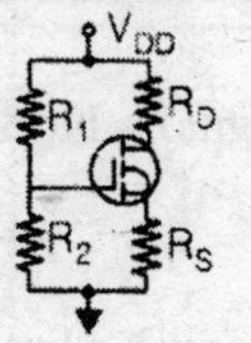	$V_{GS} = V_{DS}$ $V_{GS} = V_{DD} - I_D R_S$	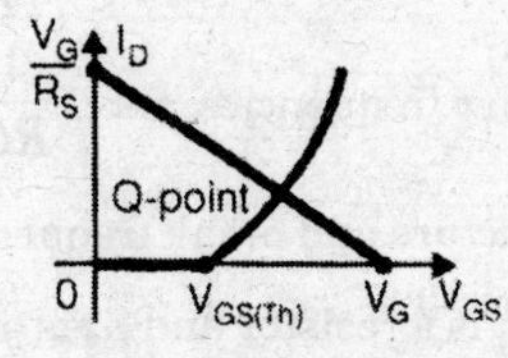

3.14 FILTERS

3.14.1. SIMPLE LOW-PASS CIRCUIT

Consider simple case of voltage divider to see the use of complex inpedances.

$$\frac{V_n}{V_i} = \frac{Z_2}{Z_1 + Z_2}$$

If Z_1 is resistor and Z_2 is a capacitor, then

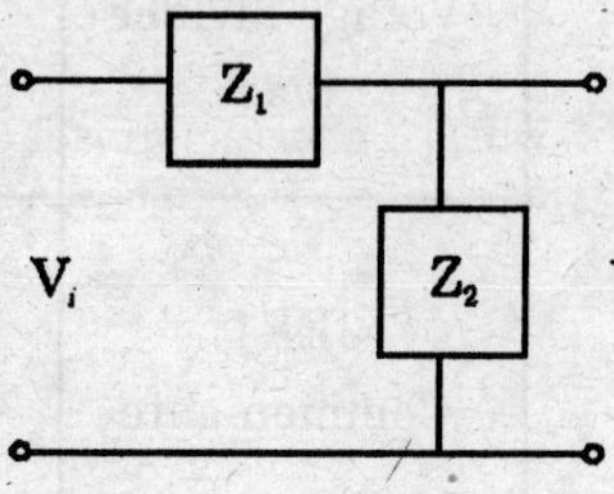

Fig. 3.148

$$\frac{V_0}{V_i} = \frac{\frac{1}{sC}}{\frac{1}{sC} + R} = \frac{1}{1 + sCR}$$

Generally magnitude of the response is given by

$$\left|\frac{V_0}{V_i}\right| = \left|\frac{1}{1 + sCR}\right| = \left|\frac{1}{1 + j\omega CR}\right| = \frac{1}{\sqrt{1^2 + (\omega CR)}}$$

Magnitude of a complex number is square root of the sum of squares of the real and imaginary parts.

There are also phase shifts associated with the transfer function (or gain, $\frac{V_o}{V_i}$).

This is a low pass filter (i.e. low frequency signals are passed and high frequecy signals are blocked).

If $\omega << \frac{1}{RC}$, i.e. ωCR <<1, then magnitude of the gain approximately unity, and output equals the input.

If $\omega >> \frac{1}{RC}$, i.e. ωCR >>1, then gain goes to zero, as does the output.

At $\omega = \frac{1}{RC}$, called *break frequency* (or *cutoff frequency*, or *3dB frequency*, or *half-power frequency*, or *bandwidth*), magnitude of the gain is $\frac{1}{\sqrt{2}}$ = 0.7. In this case (and all first order RC circuit) high frequency is defined as $\omega >> \frac{1}{RC}$; capacitor acts as a short circuit and all the voltage is zcross the resistance.

At low frequencies, $\omega << \frac{1}{RC}$, capacitor acts as an open circuit and there is no current (so voltage across the resistor is near zero).

If Z_1 is an inductor and Z_2 is a resistor, anther low pass structure results with a break frequency of R/L.

3.14.2. SIMPLE HIGH-PASS CIRCUIT

If Z_1 is a capacitor and Z_2 is a resistor, then we can repeat the calculation.

$$\frac{V_0}{V_i} = \frac{R}{\frac{1}{sC} + R} = \frac{sCR}{1 + sCR},$$

and

$$\left|\frac{V_0}{V_i}\right| = \left|\frac{sCR}{1 + sCR}\right|$$

$$= \left|\frac{j\omega CR}{1 + j\omega CR}\right| = \frac{\omega CR}{\sqrt{1^2 + (\omega CR)^2}}$$

At high frequencies, $\omega >> \frac{1}{RC}$, capacitor acts as a short and the gain is 1 (signal is passed).

At low frequencies, $\omega << \frac{1}{RC}$, capacitor is an open and output is zero (signal is blocked). This is obviously a high pass structure and break frequency is again $\frac{1}{RC}$

If Z_1 is a resistor and Z_2 is an inductor, then resulting circuit is high pass with a break frequency of R/L. This concept of a complex impedence is extremely powerful and can be used when analyzing operational amplifier circuits.

3.14.3. ACTIVE FILTERS

Low-Pass filters (intergrator reconsidered)

Transfer function for the circuit shown in Fig. 3.149 will be

$$\frac{V_0}{V_i} = \frac{H_0\omega_0}{S+\omega_0} \text{ or } \left|\frac{V_0}{V_i}\right| = |H_0| \frac{\omega_0}{\sqrt{\omega^2+\omega_0^2}}$$

which is general form for first-order (one reactive element) low-pass filters. At high frequencies ($\omega>>\omega_0$), capacitor acts as a short, so gain of the amplifier goes to zero.

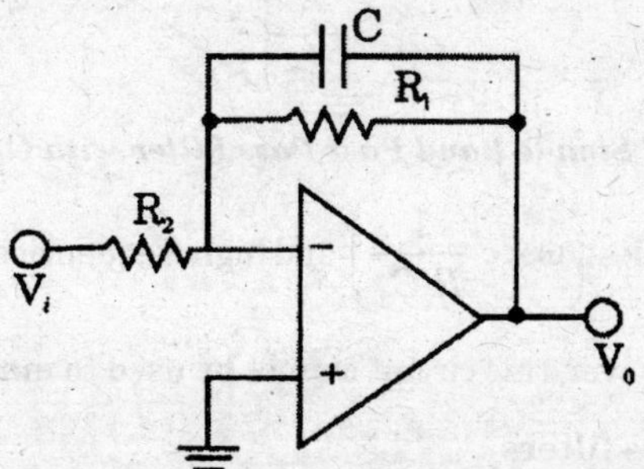

Fig 3.149 First Order Low Pass Filter with Op-Amp

At very low frequencies ($\omega<<\omega_0$), capacitor is an open and gain of the circuit is H_o.

The frequency can be considered to be high when large majority of current goes through the capacitor *i.e.,* when magnitude of the capacitor impedance is much less than that of R_i.

In other words, we have high frequency when $\frac{1}{\omega C} << R_i$, or $\omega >> \frac{1}{R_1 C} = \omega_o$. Since R_1 now has little effect on the circuit, it should act as an integrator.

Similarly low frequency occurs when $\omega << \frac{1}{R_1 C}$, and the circuit will act as an implifier with gain $-\frac{R_1}{R_2} = H_0$.

High-Pass filters differentiator reconsidered)

The circuit shown in Fig.3.150 is a modified differentiator, and acts as a high pass filter. Using analysing techniques similar to those used for the flow pass filter, we have

$$\frac{V_0}{V_i} = H_0 \frac{S}{S+\omega_0}$$

$$\Rightarrow \quad \left|\frac{V_0}{V_i}\right| = |H_0| \frac{\omega_0}{\sqrt{\omega^2+\omega_0^2}}$$

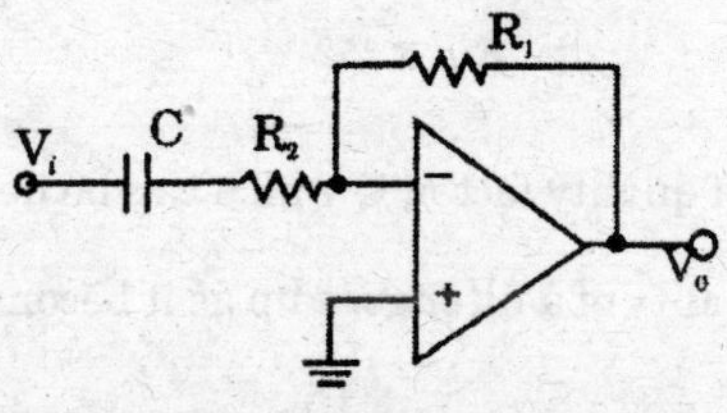

Fig 3.150 First order Highpass Filter with Op amp

which is general form for first-order (one reactive element) low-pass filters.

At high frequencies ($\omega>>\omega_0$), capacitor acts as a short, so gain of the amplifier goes to $H_0 = -\frac{R_1}{R_2}$

At very low frequencies ($\omega<<\omega_o$), capacitor is an open and gain of the circuit is H_o.

For this circuit $\omega_0 = \frac{1}{R_2 C}$. Therefore this circuit is a high-pass filter, it passes high frequency signals, and blocks low frequency signals.

3.14.4. BAND-PASS CIRCUITS

Other common types are band-reject (blocks certain signals) and band-pass (rejects high and low frequencies, passing only signals around some intermediate frequency).

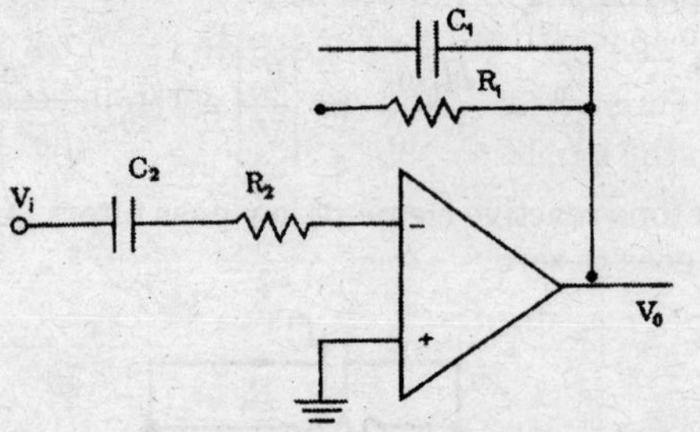

Fig 3.151 Simple Band Pass Pass Filter with Op-Amp

This circuit will alternate low frequencies $\left(\omega << \frac{1}{R_2C_2}\right)$ and high frequencies $\left(\omega >> \frac{1}{R_1C_1}\right)$, but will pass intermediate frequencies with a gain of $-\frac{R_1}{R_2}$. However, this circuit cannot be used to make a fitler with a very narrow band.

High Q (Low bandwidth) bandpass filters

For second-order band-pass filter, transfer function is given by

$$H(s) = \frac{V_0}{V_i} = \frac{H_0\beta s}{s^2 + \beta s + \omega_0^2}$$

where, ω_0 = center frequency

β = bandwidth

Ho = maximum amplitude of the filter.

These quantities are shown in the figure. The quantities in parentheses are in radian frequencies, and other quantities are in Hertz

(i.e. $f_o = \frac{\omega_0}{2\pi}$, $B = \frac{\beta}{2\pi}$).

In equation or the figure, as ω–>0 and ω–>infinity that $|H(s = j\omega)|$–>0.

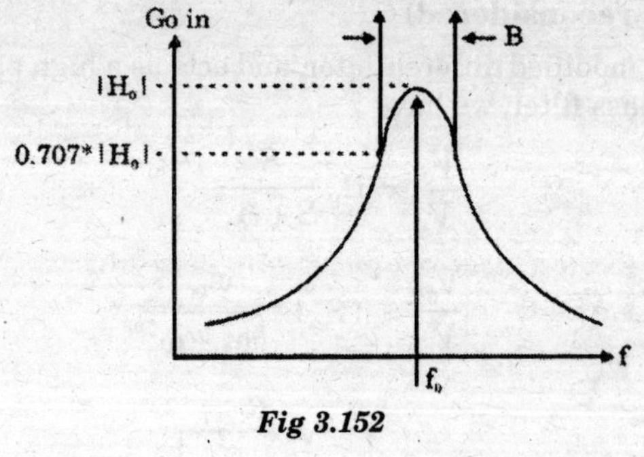

Fig 3.152

At $\omega = \omega_0$, $|S(s = j\omega_0)| = H_0$.

Often above equation written in terms of quality factor, Q which can be defined in terms of bandwidth, β, and center frequency, ω_0, as $Q = \frac{\omega_o}{\beta}$. Thus Q, or quality of a filter goes up as it becomes narrower and its bandwidth decreases.

3.15 OSCILLATORS

In general, input and output signals (sinusoidal) are phasors, and gains are complex numbers. The overall gain expressed as

$$\frac{\overline{V_o}}{\overline{V_s}} = \frac{\overline{A}}{1+\overline{\beta A}}$$

At a particular frequency the phase shift of $\overline{\beta A}$ becomes 180°, reversing the polarity of the feedback voltage $\overline{V_f}$. So the feedback is now positive and the overall gain is,

$$\frac{\overline{V_o}}{\overline{V_s}} = \frac{\overline{A}}{1-|\overline{\beta A}|}$$

For $|\overline{\beta A}| = 1$, and $< |\overline{BA}| = 180°$; the gain becomes infinite, i.e. the input $\overline{V_s}$ needed to produce any output $\overline{V_o}$ is zero. With the signal $\overline{V_s}$ removed, the circuit still oscillates at a frequency at which $< \overline{\beta A} = 180°$.

Barkhausen condition for oscillation.

Condition combined for oscillation, $\overline{\beta A} = -1$

In basic oscillator scheme of Fig. 3.153, as the switch included in the circuit is closed, the amplifier amplifies the internal noise which is fed round the loop positively and the signal builds up.

Theoretically in a negative feedback circuit with $\overline{\beta A} = -1$, the output would become infinite. But, the signal amplitude is limited by setting in of saturation in the amplifier.

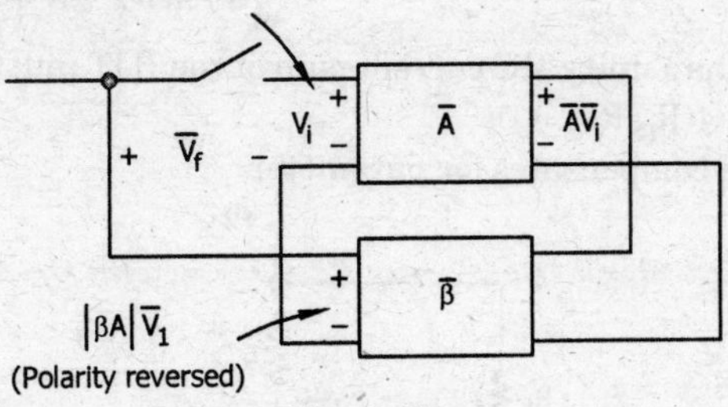

Fig. 3.153

3.15.1. PHASE SHIFT OSCILLATOR

To build an oscillator circuit, phase shift in feedback path of an amplifier can be an RC network as shown in Fig. 3.154. This network has a phase shift of 180° at a frequency of

$$f = \frac{1}{2\pi RC\sqrt{6}}$$

Corresponding feedback gain, $\beta = \dfrac{1}{29}$

So the circuit will oscillate if A > 29.

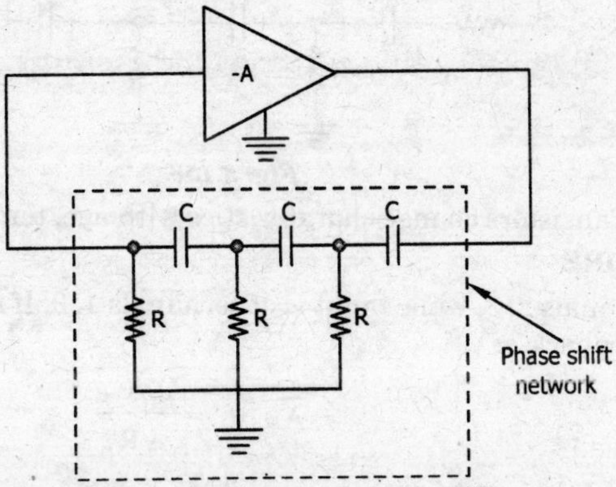

Fig. 3.154 Idealized phase shift oscillator

3.15.2. FET PHASE SHIFT OSCILLATOR

The circuit of FET phase oscillator is shown in Fig. 3.155.

Load resistance, $R_L = R_D \,||\, r_d$

and, amplifier gain, $A = -g_m R_L$

negative in the amplifier gain cause the feedback to be negative. The network phase shift of 180° causes this feedback round the loop to become positive.

At high frequencies the input capacitance of the FET contributes loading effect, and oscillation condition would need larger sufficiently gain at low frequencies.

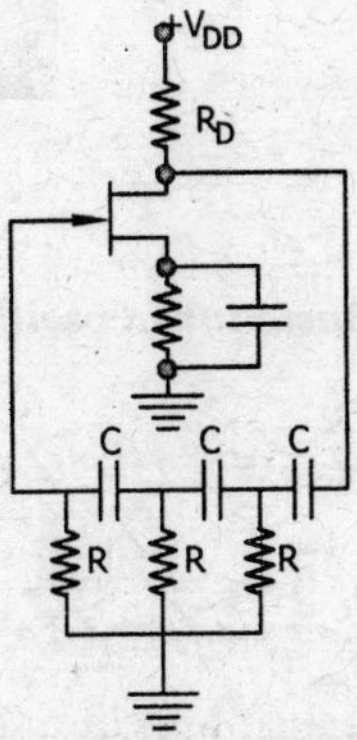

Fig. 3.155

3.15.3. BJT PHASE SHIFT OSCILLATOR

In this case the input resistance r_π of the BJT will load the output so it may be better to use two transistors with the second one in emitter follower connection. However, in case of a single transistor as in Fig. 3.156, voltage shunt feedback is preferred.

Analysing the circuit, we have

$$f = \frac{1}{2\pi RC} \frac{1}{\sqrt{[6+4(R_C/R)]}}$$

For the loop gain to be greater than unity, the current gain of the BJT must meet the condition

β (or h_{fe}) $\geq 23 + 29\,(R/R_C) + 4(R_C/R)$

sign *'more than'* in this equation compensates for parameter

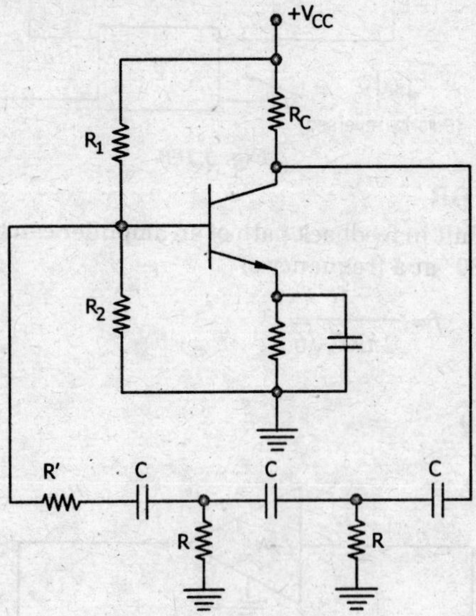

Fig. 3.156

changes in the amplifier. As transistors change charateristics with age, temperature, voltage, etc.

3.15.4. TUNED OSCILLATORS

The output is taken from terminals 2, 3, while input is at terminals 1, 3. If A is the open-circuit gain of the amplifier, gain with load but without feedback, is

$$\bar{A}_L = \frac{\bar{Z}_L A}{\bar{Z}_L + R_o}$$

where, R_o = output resistance of the amplifier.

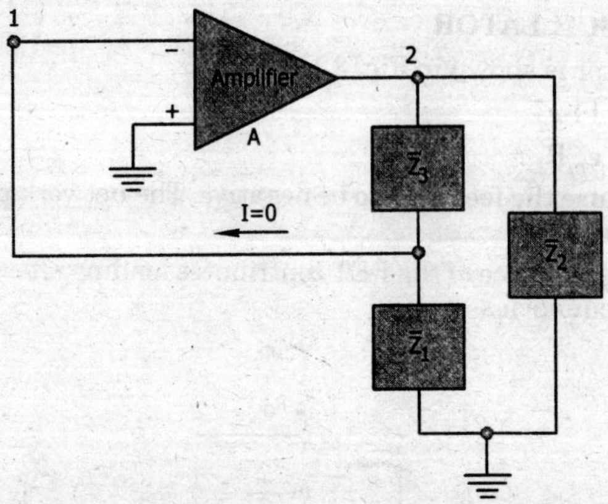

Fig. 3.157 Basic tuned oscillator circuit

In Fig. 3.157

load impedance, $\bar{Z}_L = \bar{Z}_2 \parallel (\bar{Z}_2 + \bar{Z}_3)$

and

feedback factor is, $\bar{\beta} = \frac{\bar{Z}_1}{\bar{Z}_1 + \bar{Z}_3}$

$$\text{Loop gain, } -\bar{\beta}\bar{A}_L = \frac{-A\bar{Z}_1\bar{Z}_2}{R_o(\bar{Z}_1+\bar{Z}_2+\bar{Z}_3)+\bar{Z}_2(\bar{Z}_1+\bar{Z}_3)}$$

For the oscillation to occur we need to set $-\overline{\beta A}_L = 1$.

If we select, $\bar{Z}_1 = jX_1$, $\bar{Z}_2 = jX_2$ and $\bar{Z}_3 = jX_3$; purely reactive, then

$$-\overline{\beta A}_L = \frac{AX_1X_2}{jR_o(X_1+X_2+X_3)-X_2(X_1+X_3)}$$

Loop gain in this equation can be made real by setting

$$X_1 + X_2 + X_3 = 0$$

This is also the condition for the circuit to oscillate at the resonance frequency of the series combination of X_1, X_2 and X_3. Above equation then simplifies to

$$-\beta A_L = \frac{-AX_1}{X_1+X_3} = \frac{AX_1}{X_2}$$

For this circuit to oscillate, it requires $BA_L = -1$ in above equation, which means that X_1 and X_2 must be both inductive or both capacitive.

The choice of X_1, X_2 and X_3 gives the three oscillator types as shown in Table 3.8

Table 3.9

Oscillator type	*Reactive elements*		
	X_1	X_2	X_3
Colpitts	C	C	L
Hartley	L	L	C
Tuned input, tuned output	LC	LC	

3.15.5. WEIN BRIDGE OSCILLATOR

A practical oscillator circuit shown in Fig. 3.119 uses an OPAMP and RC bridge circuit, with the oscillator frequency set by R and C components. Resistors R_1, R_2 and capacitor C_1, C_2 form the frequency adjustement elements, while R_3, R_4 form part of the feedback path.

The condition of oscillation is

$$\frac{R_3}{R_4} = \frac{R_1}{R_2} + \frac{C_2}{C_1}$$

and the frequency of oscillation as

$$f_o = \frac{1}{2\pi} \cdot \frac{1}{\sqrt{(R_1R_2C_1C_2)}}$$

If we choose $R_1 = R_2 = R$,

and $C_1 = C_2 = C$,

then, resulting oscillation frequency, $f_o = \dfrac{1}{2\pi(RC)}$

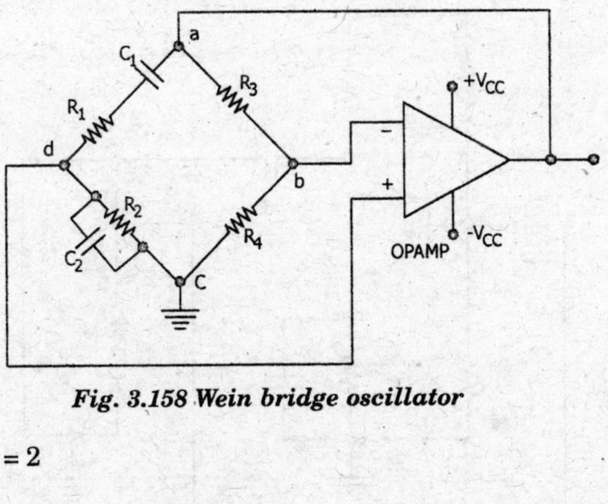

Fig. 3.158 Wein bridge oscillator

and condition of oscillation, $\dfrac{R_3}{R_4} = 2$

Hence, condition for the circuit to oscillate is, $\left(\dfrac{R_3}{R_4}\right) > 2$

3.15.6. TRANSISTOR COLPITTS OSCILLATOR

Here

$$X_1 = -1/\omega C_1$$
$$X_2 = -1/\omega C_2$$
$$X_3 = \omega L$$

It satisfies the condition that X_1 and X_2 are both reactive.

The output frequency of the circuit is then given as

$$\frac{1}{\omega_o C_1} + \frac{1}{\omega_o C_2} = \omega_o L$$

which gives $f_o = \dfrac{1}{2\pi\sqrt{(LC_{eq})}}$; $C_{eq} = \dfrac{C_1\,C_2}{C_1 + C_2}$

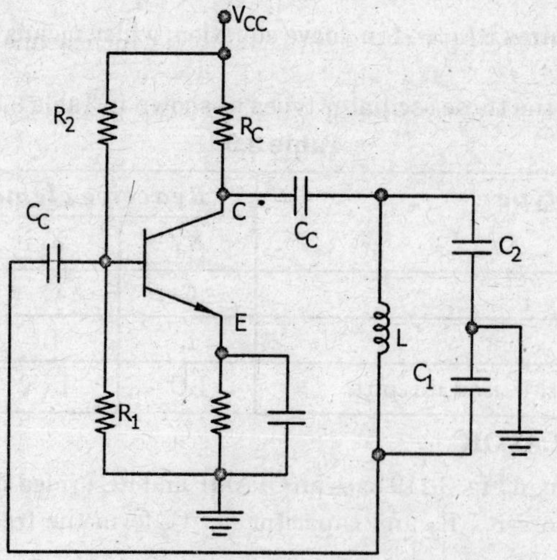

Fig. 3.159 Transistor Colpitts oscillator

3.15.7. TRANSISTOR HARTLEY OSCILLATOR

Here,

$$X_1 = \omega (L_1 + M)$$
$$X_2 = \omega (L_2 + M)$$
$$X_3 = -1/\omega C$$

With unity loop gain, the oscillator frequency is

$$f_o = \frac{1}{2\pi\sqrt{(LC_{eq})}},\ L_{eq} = L_1 + L_2 + 2M$$

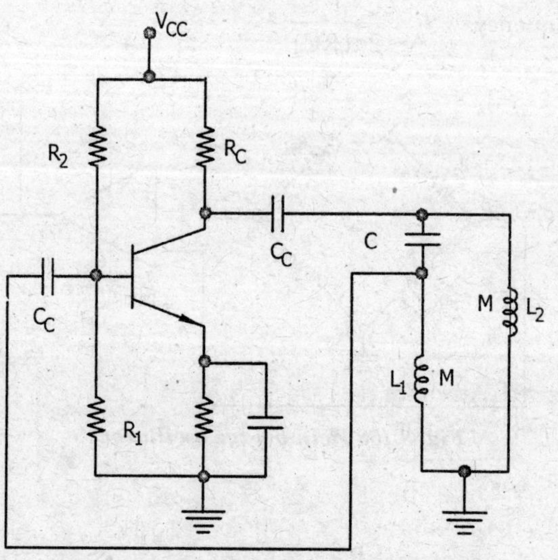

Fig. 3.160 Transistor Hartley oscillator.

3.15.8. CRYSTAL OSCILLATOR

If piezoelectric crystal, usually quartz, has electrodes plated on its opposite faces and a potential is applied across these, the electric field so set up exerts forces on bound charges within the crystal. As a result the crystal responds electromechanically, i.e. it vibrates. The crystal's resonant frequency and its Q (quality factor) depends upon its dimensions, orientation of its surfaces with respect to its axis and the mechanical mounting. Crystals are available with a wide range of frequencies from a few kHz to 100 MHz and with Q factors from a few thousand to several hundred thousands. The resonant frequency of these crystals is extremely stable with respect to temperature changes and aging.

The symbol for a crystal is given in Fig. 3.161 (*a*) and its electric analog is drawn in Fig. 3.161 (*b*)

where, L = mass of crystal (inductance)

C = compliance (reciprocal of spring constant)

R = viscous damping capacitance between the electrodes

C′ = electrostatic capacitance between the electrodes; C′>> C

Typical parameters of a 90 kHz crystal are :

L = 137 H, C = 035 *p*F, R = 15 kΩ, Q = 5500, C′ = 3.5 *p*F

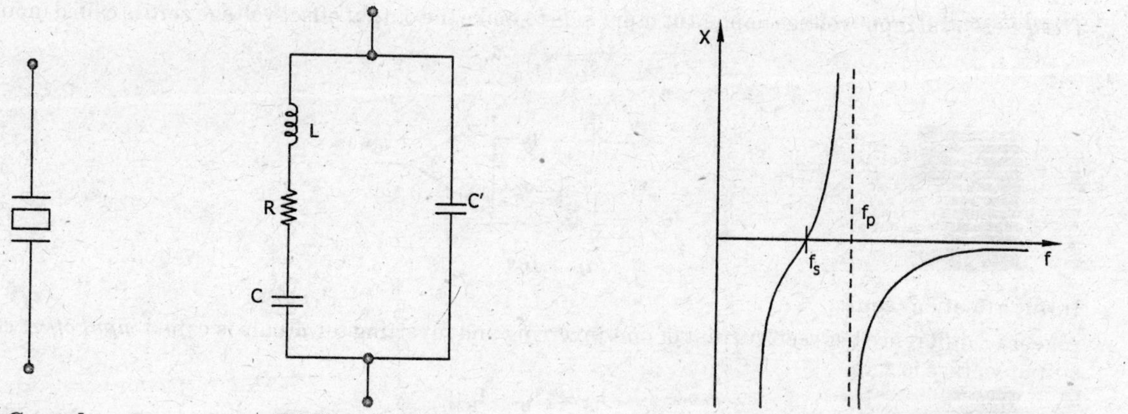

(*a*) *Crystal* (*b*) *Circuit model* (*c*) *Reactance (X) vs frequency assuming R = 0*

Fig. 3.161

The crystal oscillator exhibits following two resonant frequencies.

Series resonant frequency, $$f_s = \frac{1}{2\pi\sqrt{(LC)}}$$

Parallel resonant frequency, $$f_p = \frac{1}{2\pi\sqrt{(LC_{eq})}}$$

where, $$C_{eq} = \left(\frac{1}{C} + \frac{1}{C'}\right)$$

As C′ >> C, $$f_p = \frac{1}{2\pi\sqrt{(LC)}}$$

∴ $$f_p \approx f_s$$

but $$f_p > f_s$$

as shown in Fig. 3.161 (*c*) whereas X = 0 at f_s and X = ∞ at f_p.

3.16 OPERATIONAL AMPLIFIER

It is basically a direct coupled amplifier.

3.16.1. STAGES IN OP-AMP

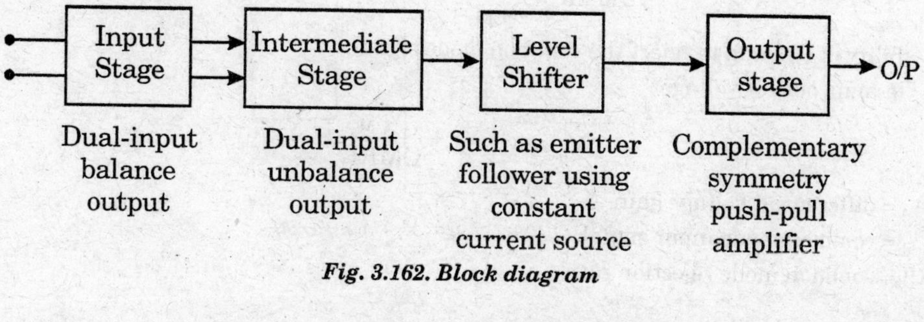

Fig. 3.162. Block diagram

(i) Input stage

It provides almost all the voltage gain of Op-amp and also establish the input impedance of Op-amp.

(ii) Intermediate stage

It provides remaining gain of OP-amp.

(iii) Level shifting

Because of the direct coupling d.c. voltage at output is well above the ground level in order to get back the d.c. level to ground potential. Thus, variation in output is only because of input signal we use level shifting.

(iv) Output stage

It raises the current supplying capability and increases the output voltage swing and this stages proper design will provides the low output resistance.

3.16.2. DEFINITIONS

Output offset voltage.

When both the input are grounded output voltage is called *output offset voltage*. It should be zero for ideal voltage.

Input offset voltage.

The differential input voltage applied at input side to make the output offset voltage zero is called input offset voltage.

$$V_0 = V_{s1} - V_{s2}$$

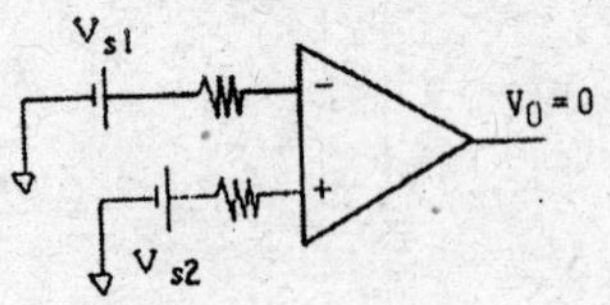

Fig. 3.163

Input offset current.

Algebraic difference between current of non-inverting and inverting terminals is called *input offset current* provided output voltage is zero.

$$I_{i0} = |I_{B1} - I_{B2}|$$

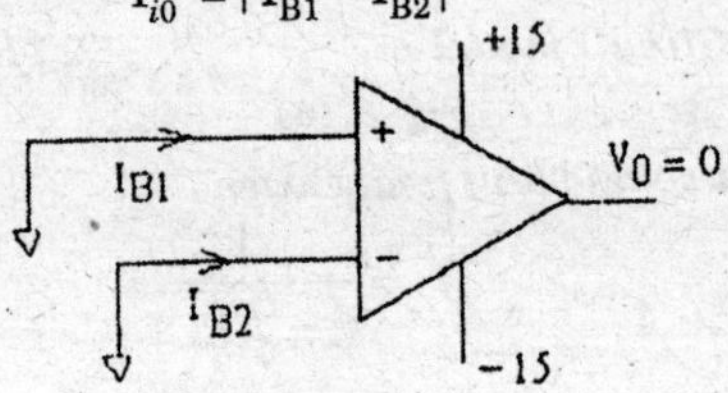

Fig. 3.164

Input bias current.

Average of two current that flow through inverting and non-inverting terminal is called *input bias current* provided output voltage is zero.

$$I_B = \frac{I_{B1} + I_{B2}}{2}$$

Power supply rejection ratio.

Change in input offset voltage with power supply variation is called *power supply rejection ratio*.

$$\text{SVVR} = \frac{\Delta V_{i0}}{\Delta V_{ii}}$$

Common Mode Rejection Ratio (CMRR).

It is the most important characteristic of Op-amp. It is defined as the ratio of differential gain to common mode gain.

$$\text{CMRR} = \frac{A_d}{A_{CM}}$$

It represents ability of Op-amp to reject the common mode signal.

For practical Op-amp, output voltage

$$V_0 = A_d\left(V_d + \frac{V_{CM}}{\text{CMRR}}\right)$$

where, A_d = differential voltage gain

V_{CM} = common mode input signal

CMRR = common mode rejection ratio

In order to avoid any common mode amplification CMRR should be infinite which can be achieved by increasing R_E because

$$\text{CMRR} = \frac{A_d}{A_{CM}}$$

and,
$$A_{CM} = \frac{R_C}{2R_E}$$

An operational amplifier (Op amp) is basically a multistage high gain ($A_v > 10^5$), direct coupled amplifier with two differential inputs and a single ended output and uses feedback to control the overall response characteristics.

3.16.3. IDEAL OP-AMPS

An op-amp amplifies the difference $v_d \equiv v_1 - v_2$ between two input signals, exhibiting the open-loop voltage gain

$$A_{OL} \equiv \frac{v_o}{v_d}$$

In Fig. 3.165, terminal 1 is inverting input (labelled with a minus sign on the actual amplifier); signal v_1 is amplified in magnitude and appears phase-inverted at the output. Terminal 2 is noninverting input (labelled with a plus sign); output due to v_2 is phase-reserved.

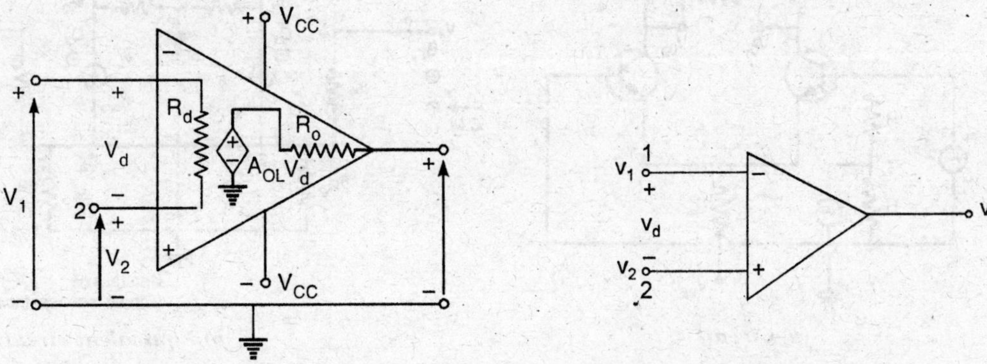

(a) *Complete representation* (b) *Simplified representation*

Fig. 3.165 Operational amplifier

In magnitude, open-loop voltage gain in op amps ranges from 10^4 to 10^7. The maximum magnitude of the output voltage from an op-amp is called its *saturation voltage*; this voltage is approximately 2 V smaller than the power-supply voltage.

In other words, the amplifier is linear over the range

$$-(V_{CC} - 2) < v_o < V_{CC} - 2\text{ V}$$

Characteristics of ideal op-amp.

It has three essentail characteristics which serve as standards for assessing the goodness of a practical op-amp :

(*i*) The open-loop voltage gain A_{OL} is negatively infinite.

(*ii*) The input impedance R_d between terminals 1 and 2 is infinitely large; thus, the input current is zero.

(*iii*) The output impedance R_o is zero; consequently, the output voltage is independent of the load.

3.16.4. OPERATING MODES

Operation can be in the following modes :

(*i*) **Differential mode.**

Here, two voltages V_1 and V_2 are equal and opposite in phase

Input voltage, $V_{id} = V_1 - V_2$

Output voltage, $A_d = A_{Vd} = \dfrac{V_{od}}{V_{id}} = \dfrac{V_{od}}{V_1 - V_2}$

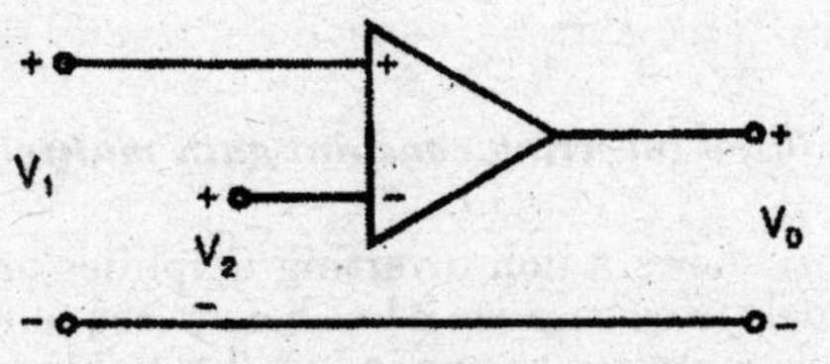

Fig. 3.166

(ii) Common mode.

Here two voltages V_1 and V_2 are almost equal in magnitude and are in phase

$$\text{Input voltage, } V_{ic} = \frac{V_1 - V_2}{2}$$

$$\text{Voltage gain, AC} = \frac{V_{oc}}{V_{ic}} = \frac{V_{oc}}{\frac{1}{2}(V_1 - V_2)}$$

where, V_{oc} output voltage.

$$\text{Common-mode rejection ration (CMRR)} = \left|\frac{A_d}{A_c}\right|$$

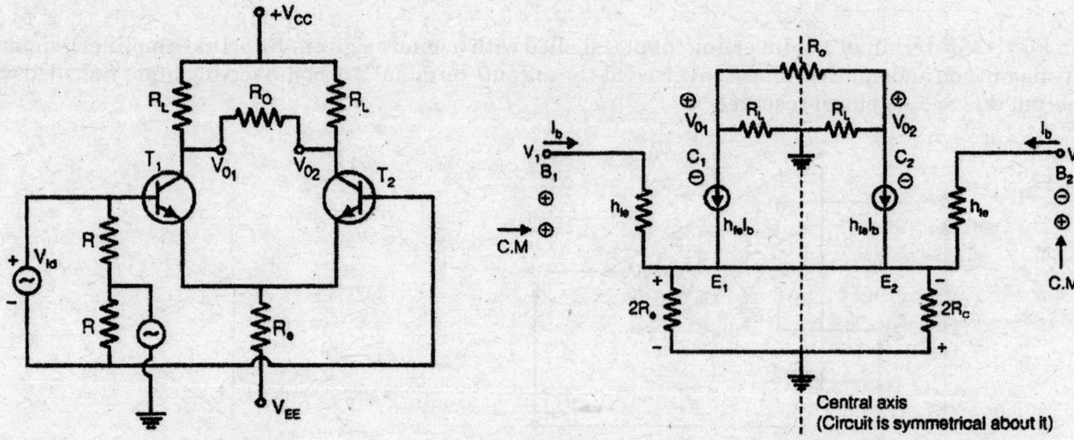

(a) Circuit *(b) Equivalent circuit*

Fig. 3.167

Assumptions :

(i) The two transistors are identical so that they have identical parameters.

(ii) h_{ce} $R_L \leq 0.1$, so that the approximate analysis holds good for the amplifier.

(iii) Parameter h_{fc} is large.

(iv) R_0 respresents the impedance of measuring device and is large so that

$$R_0 >> R_L$$

3.16.5. PRACTICAL OP-AMPS CIRCUITS

(1) Inverting Amplifier

This is the most widely used constant-gain amplifier circuit, shown in Fig. 3.168. The output is obtained by multiplying the input by a fixed or constant gain, set by the input resistor (R_1) and feedback resistor (R_f). This output also being inverted from the input and given as,

$$V_o = -\frac{R_f}{R_1} V_1$$

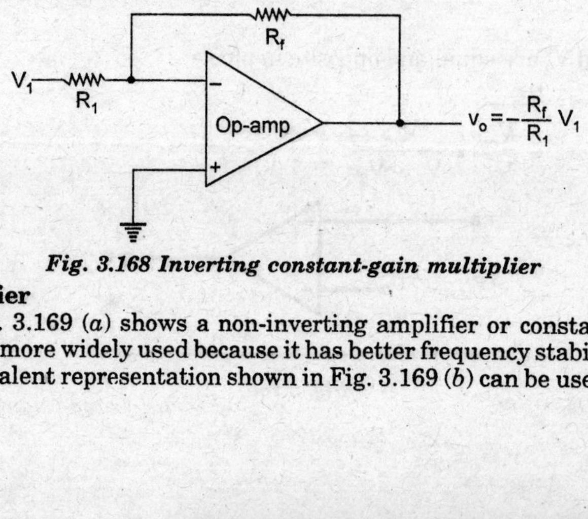

Fig. 3.168 Inverting constant-gain multiplier

(2) Noninverting Amplifier

This connection of Fig. 3.169 (a) shows a non-inverting amplifier or constant-gain multiplier. The inverting amplifier connection is more widely used because it has better frequency stability. To determine the voltage gain of the circuit, the equivalent representation shown in Fig. 3.169 (b) can be used.

Since $V_1 \approx 0$ V, we have $$V_1 = \frac{R_1}{R_1 + R_f} V_o$$

which gives $$\frac{V_o}{V_1} = \frac{R_1 + R_f}{R_1} = 1 + \frac{R_f}{R_1}$$

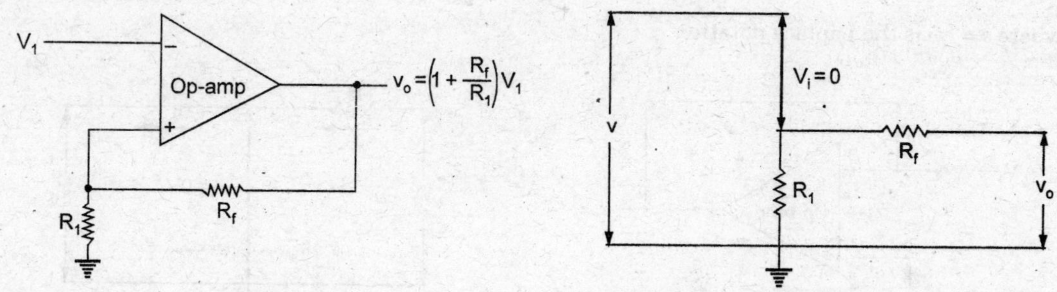

(a) *(b)*

Fig. 3.169 Noninverting constant-gain multiplier

(3) Unity Follower

This unity-follower circuit, shown in Fig. 3.170 (*a*), provides a gain of unity(1) with no polarity or phase reversal. From equivalent circuit, we have $V_o = V_1$

and that the output is the same polarity and magnitude as the input. The circuit operates like an emitter- or source-follower circuit except that the gain is exactly unity.

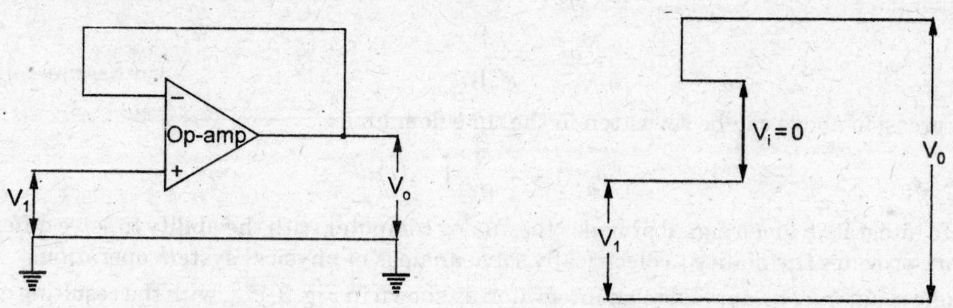

(a) Unity follower ***(b) Virtual-ground equivalent circuit***

Fig. 3.170

(4) Summing Amplifier

The circuit of summing amplifier is shown in Fig. 3.171 (*a*). The circuit shows a three-input summing amplifier circuit which provides a means of algebracially summing (adding) three voltages, each multiplied by a constant-gain factor. Using equivalent representation shown in Fig. 3.171 (*b*), output voltage can be expressed in terms of the inputs as

$$V_o = -\left(\frac{R_f}{R_1} V_1 + \frac{R_f}{R_2} V_2 + \frac{R_f}{R_3} V_3\right)$$

Thus, each input adds a voltage to the output multiplied by its separate constant-gain multiplier. If more inputs are used, they each add an additional component to the output. It is probably most used among the OP-AMP circuits.

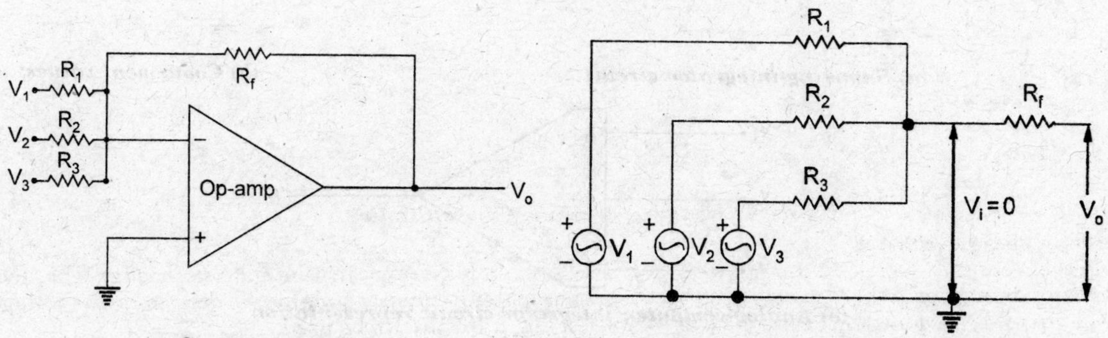

(a) Summing amplifier ***(b) Virtual-ground equivalent circuit***

Fig. 3.171

(5) Integrator

If feedback component used is a capacitor, as shown in Fig. 3.172 (*a*), the resulting connection is called *intergrator*. The virtual-ground equivalent circuit Fig. 3.172 (*b*) shows that an expression for the voltage between input and output can be derived in terms of current I, from input to output.

Capacitive impedance, $$X_C = \frac{1}{j\omega C} = \frac{1}{sC}$$

where $s = j\,\omega$ is the Laplace notation.

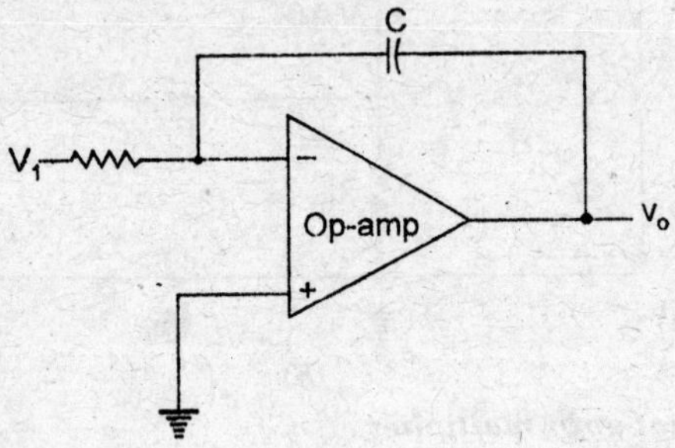

(*a*)

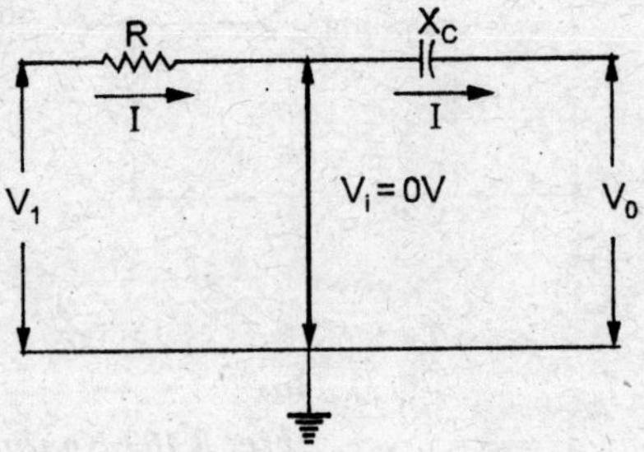

(*b*)

Fig. 3.172 Integrator

Now, solving for V_o/V_1, we have

$$I = \frac{V_1}{R} = -\frac{V_o}{X_C} = \frac{-V_o}{\frac{1}{sC}} = -s\,CV_o$$

$$\frac{V_o}{V_1} = \frac{-1}{sCR}$$

Now, the expression above can be rewritten in the time domain as

$$v_o(t) = -\frac{1}{RC}\int v_1(t)\,dt$$

The ability to integrate a given signal provides the analog computer with the ability to solve differential equations and therefore provides the ability to electrically solve analogs of physical system operation.

More than one input may be applied to an integrator, as shown in Fig. 3.173, with the resulting operation given by

$$v_o(t) = -\left[\frac{1}{R_1C}\int v_1(t)\,dt + \frac{1}{R_2C}\int v_2(t)\,dt + \frac{1}{R_3C}\int v_3(t)\,dt\right]$$

As example of a summing integrator as used in an analog computer is given in Fig. 3.173. The actual circuit is shown with input resistors and feedback capacitor, whereas the analog-computer representation indicates only the scale factor for each input.

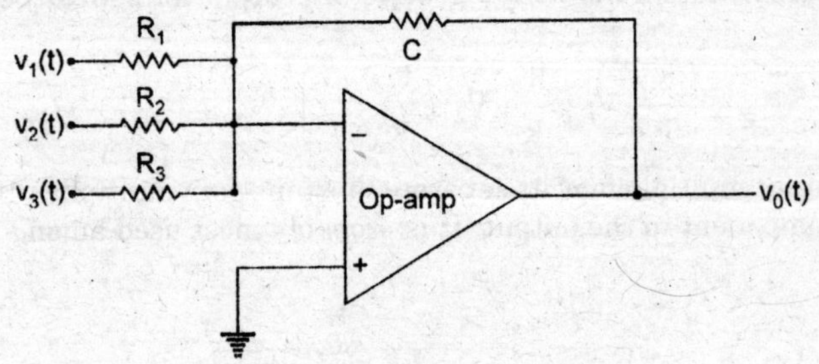

(a) Summing-integrator circuit

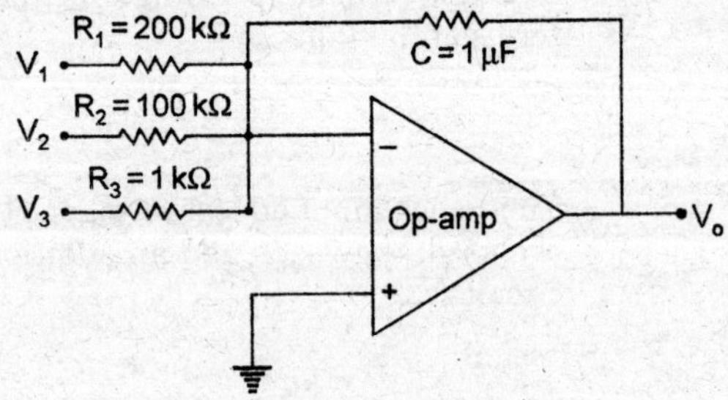

(b) Component values;

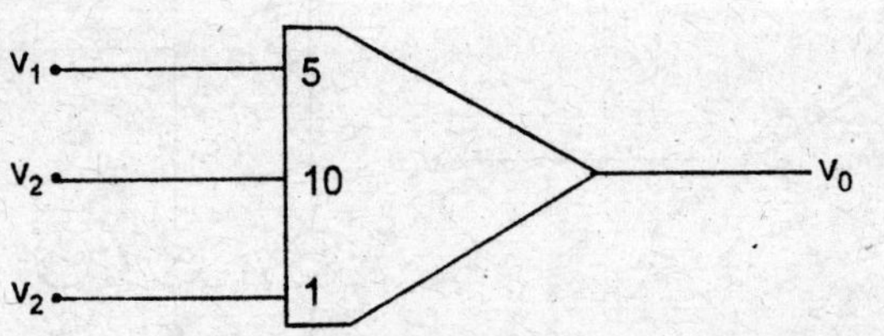

(c) Analog-computer, integrator-circuit representation

Fig. 3.173

(6) Differentiator:

A differentiator circuit shown in Fig. 3.174. While not as useful as the circuit forms covered above, the differentiator does provide a useful operation, the resulting relation for the circuit being

$$v_o(t) = -RC\frac{dv_1(t)}{dt}$$

where, $-RC$ = scale factor

If input, $v_1(t) = \sin \omega t$

then, $v_o(t) = -RC\,\omega \cos \omega t$

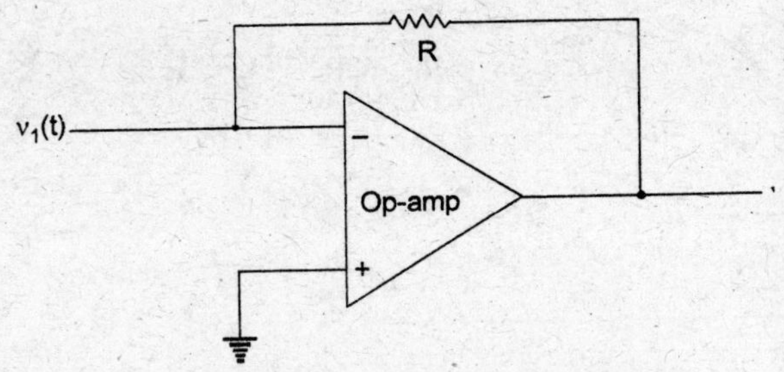

Fig. 3.174 Differentiator Circuit

Here, magnitude of the output increases linearly with increasing frequency and the differentiator circuit has high gain at high frequencies. This results, amplification of high components of the amplifier noise and the noise output can observe the differentiated signal completely.

3.16.6. SOME OTHER IMPORTANT LINEAR OP-AMP CIRCUITS

(1) Double Integrator

$$V_0 = \frac{-4}{(RC)^2}\iint V_i\,dt\,dt$$

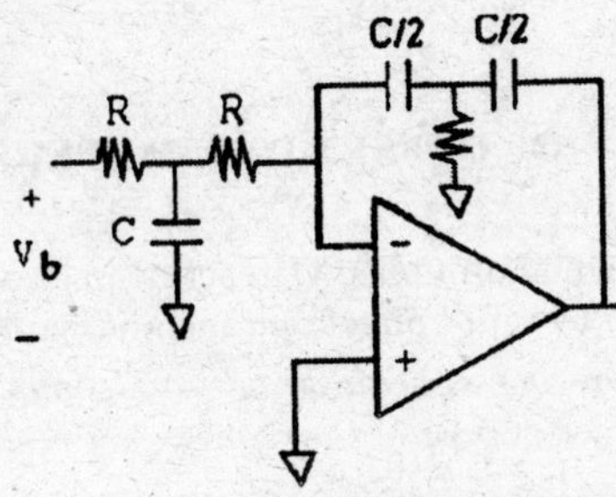

Fig. 3.175

(2) Current amplifier

$$\frac{I_0}{I} = -\left(\frac{R_1}{R_2}+1\right)$$

Current I_0 is independent of R_L.

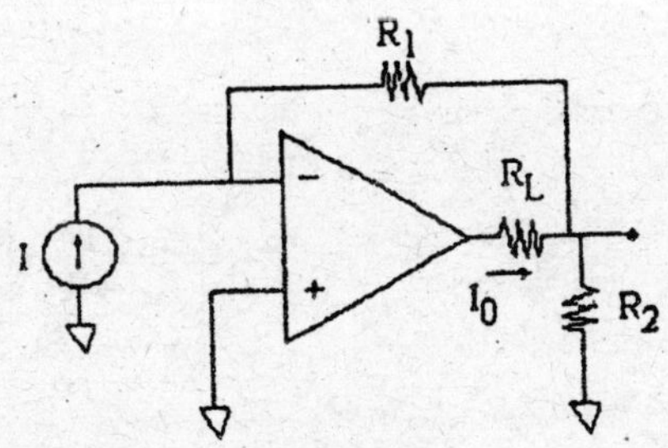

Fig. 3.176

(3) Floating load voltage to current convertor

$$I_L = \frac{V_s}{R_1}$$

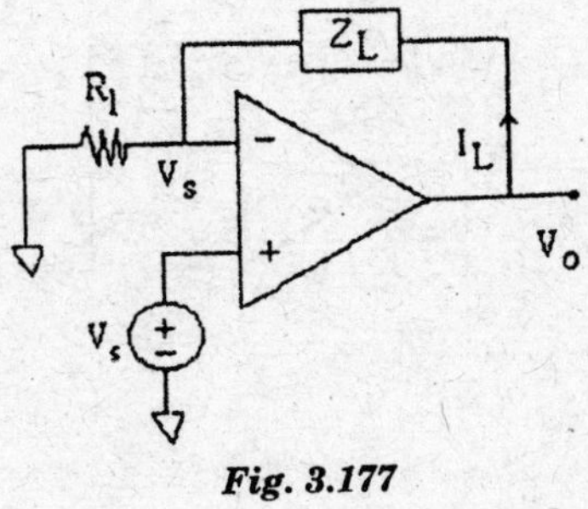

Fig. 3.177

(4) Grounded load voltage to current convertor

When $\frac{R_S}{R_2} = \frac{R'}{R_1}$, $I_L = -\frac{V_S}{R_2}$

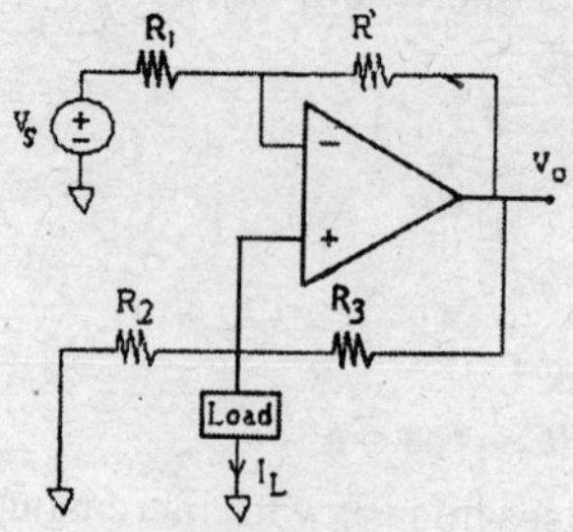

Fig. 3.178

(5) Current to voltage convertor

$$V_0 = -I_S R_F$$

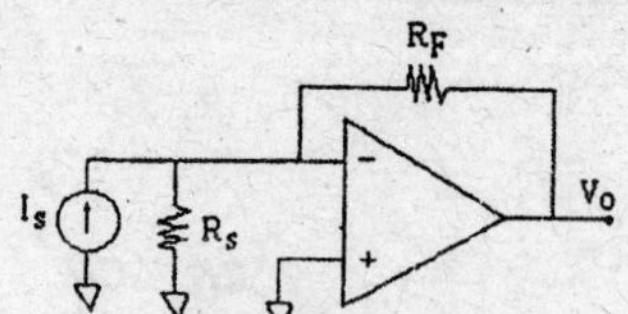

Fig. 3.179

3.16.7. OP-AMP SPECIFICATIONS — DC OFFSET PARAMETERS

(1) Offset currents and voltages

While op-amp output should be 0 V when input is 0 V, in actual operation there is some offset voltage at the output. Output offset voltage is determined by input offset voltage and gain of the amplifier.

Output offset voltage is also affected by two separate circuit conditions :

(i) Input offset voltage, V_{IO}

(ii) Offset current due to the difference in currents resulting at the plus (+) and minus (–) inputs.

(2) Input offset voltages, V_{IO}

To determine effect of this input voltage on the output, consider connection shown in Fig. 3.182.

Using $V_o = AV_i$, we can write

$$V_o = AV_i = A\left(V_{IO} - V_o \frac{R_1}{R_1 + R_f}\right)$$

Solving for V_o, we get

$$V_o = V_{IO} \frac{A}{1 + A\left[\frac{R_1}{R_1 + R_f}\right]}$$

$$\approx V_{IO} \frac{A}{A\left[\frac{R_1}{(R_1 + R_f)}\right]}$$

$$\therefore \quad V_o\text{ (offset)} = V_{IO} \frac{R_1 + R_f}{R_1}$$

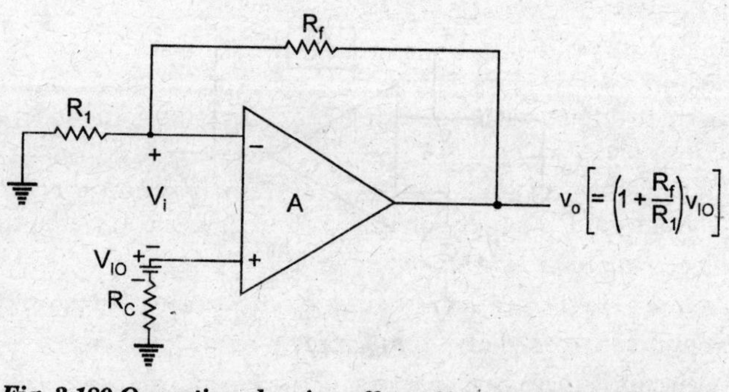

Fig. 3.180 Operation showing effect of input offset voltage V_{IO}

(3) Output offset voltage due to Input offset current, I_{IO}

An output offset voltage will also result due to any difference in dc bias currents at both inputs. Since two input transistors are never exactly matched, each will operate at a slightly different current. For a typical op-amp connection, such as that shown in Fig. 3.181 (*a*), an output offset voltage can be determined as follows. Replacing bias currents through the input resistors by the voltage drop that each develops, as shown in Fig. 3.181 (*b*).

Now, using superposition, output voltage due to input bias current I^+_{IB} denoted by V^+_o, is

$$V^+_o = I^+_{IB} R_C \left(1 + \frac{R_f}{R_1}\right)$$

while the output voltage due to only I^-_{IB}, denoted by V^-_o, is 1

$$V^-_o = I^-_{IB} R_1 \left(-\frac{R_f}{R_1}\right)$$

for a total output offset voltage of

$$V_o \text{ (offset due to } I^+_{IB} \text{ and } I^-_{IB}) = I^+_{IB} R_C \left(1 + \frac{R_f}{R_1}\right) - I^-_{IB} R_1 \frac{R_f}{R_1} \quad \text{...(3.49)}$$

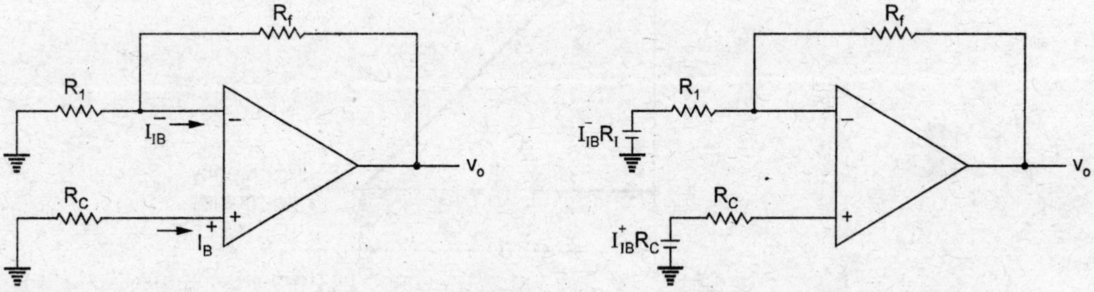

(a) OP-amp connection showing input bias currents *(b) Redrawn circuit of Fig. (a)*

Fig. 3.181

Since main consideration is the difference between input bias currents rather than each value, define offset current I_{IO} by

$$I_{IO} = I^+_{IB} - I^-_{IB}$$

Since compensating resistance R_C is usually approximately equal to the value of R_1, using $R_C = R_1$ in equation (3.49), we have

$$\begin{aligned} V_o \text{ (offset)} &= I^+_{IB} (R_1 + R_f) - I^-_{IB} R_f \\ &= I^+_{IB} R_1 - I^-_{IB} \\ &= R_f (I^+_{IB} - I^-_{IB}) \end{aligned}$$

which gives, V_o (offset due to I_{IO}) $= I_{IO} R_f$

(4) Input bias current, I_{IB}

A parameter related to I_{IO} and separate input bias currents I^+_{IB} and I^-_{IB} is the average bias current defined as

$$I_{IB} = \frac{I^+_{IB} + I^-_{IB}}{2}$$

It is possible to determine separate input bias current using specified values I_{IO} and I_{IB}.

But for $I^+_{IB} > I^-_{IB}$

$$I^+_{IB} = I_{IB} + \frac{I_{IO}}{2}, \text{ and } I^-_{IB} = I_{IB} - \frac{I_{IO}}{2}$$

3.16.8. OP-AMP SPECIFICATIONS – FREQUENCY PARAMETERS

An op-amp is designed to be a high-gain, wide-bandwidth amplifier. This operation tends to be unstable (oscillate) due to positive feedback. To ensure stable operation, op-amps are built with internal compensation circuitry, which also causes the very high open-loop gain to dimish with increasing frequency. This gain reduction is referred to as roll-off. In most op-amps roll-off occurs at a rate of 20 dB per decade (– 20 dB/decade) or 6 dB per octave (– 6 dB/octave).

While op-amp specfications list an open-loop voltage gain (A_{VD}), the user typically connects the op-amp using feedback resistors to reduce the circuit voltage gain to a much smaller value (closed-loop voltage gain, A_{CL}).

From this gain reduction following circuit improvments occur :

(*i*) Amplifier voltage gain is a more stable, precise value set by the external resistors;

(*ii*) Input impedance of the circuit is increased over that of the op-amp alone; and

(*iii*) Frequency response of the circuit is increased over that of the op-amp alone.

Specification

(1) Gain–Bandwidth.

Because of the internal compensation circuitry included in an op-amp, the voltage gain drops off as frequency increases. Op-amp specifications provide a descriptions of the gain versus bandwidth. Figure 3.182 provides a plot of gain versus frequency for a typical op-amp. At low frequency down to dc operation, the gain is that value listed by the manufacturer's specification A_{VD} (voltage differential gain) and is typically a very large value. As the frequency of the input signal increases the open-loop gain drops off until it finally reaches the value of 1 (unity). The frequency at this gain value is specified by the manufacturer as the unity-gain bandwidth, B_1. While this value is a frequency (see Fig. 3.182) at which the gain becomes 1, it can be considered a bandwidth, since the frequency band from 0 Hz to the unity-gain frequency is also a bandwidth. One could therefore refer to the point at which the gain reduces to 1 as the unity-gain frequency (f_1) or unity-gain bandwidth (B_1).

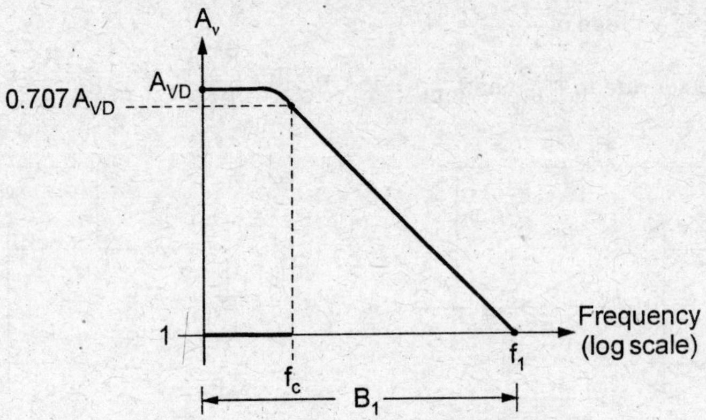

Fig. 3.182 Gain versus frequency plot.

Another frequency of interest is that shown in figure, at which the gain drop by 3 dB (or to 0.707 the dc gain, A_{VD}), this being the cutoff frequency of the op-amp, f_C. In fact, the unity-gain frequency and cut-off frequency are related by

$$f_1 = A_{VD} f_C$$

This equation shows that the unity-gain frequency may also be called the gain-bandwidth product of the op-amp.

(2) Slew Rate, SR.

The slew rate reflect the op-amp's ability to handle varying signals.

Slew rate = maximum rate at which amplifier output can change in volts per microsecond (V/μs)

$$SR = \frac{\Delta V_o}{\Delta t} = V/\mu s \text{ with } t \text{ in } \mu s$$

The slew rate provides a parameter specifying the maximum rate of change of the output voltage when driven by a large step-input signal. If the output at a rate of voltage changes greater than the slew rate, the output would not be able to change fast enough and would not vary over the full range expected, resulting in signal clipping or distortion. In any case the output would not be an amplified duplicate of the input signal if the op-amp slew rate is exceeded.

(3) Maximum signal frequency.

The maximum frequency that an op-amp may operate at depends on both the band-width (BW) and slew rate (SR) parameters of the op-amp.

For a sinusoidal signal of general form $v_o = K \sin(2\pi f t)$

Maximum voltage rate of change can be shown to be

signal maximum rate of change = $2\pi f K$ V/s

It should be noted that, to prevent distortion at the output the rate of change must also be less than the slew rate, *i.e.*

$$2\pi f K \le SR$$

$$\omega K \le SR$$

$$\therefore \quad f \leqq \frac{SR}{2\pi K} \text{ Hz}$$

$$\omega \leqq \frac{SR}{K} \text{ rad/s}$$

Also, the maximum frequency, f, in the above equation, is also limited by the unity-gain bandwidth.

3.17 555 TIMER

The circuit symbol for a 555 is a box with the pins arranged to suit the circuit diagram e.g. 555 pin 8 at the top for the $+V_s$ supply, 555 pin 3 output on the right. Usually pin numbers are used and they are to labelled with their function.

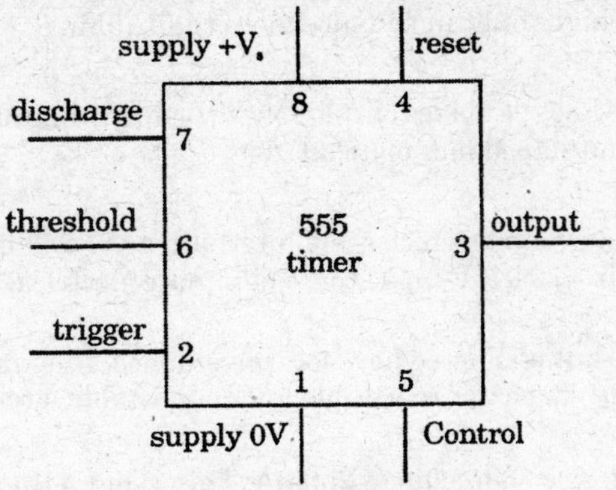

Fig. 3.183. Circuit symbol

555 can be used with a supply voltage (Vs) in the range 4.5 to 15V (18 V absolute maximum).

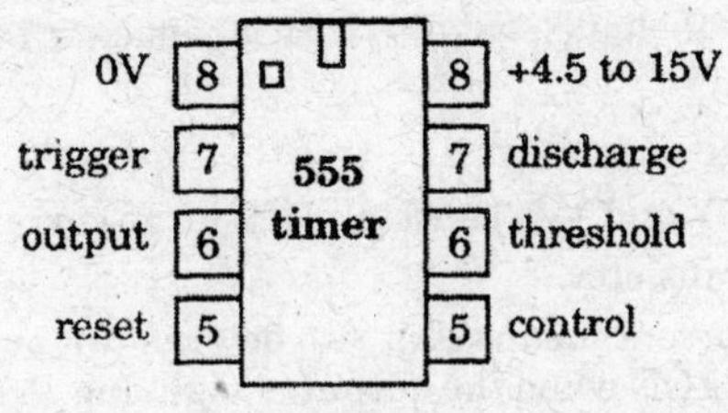

Fig.3.184

Standard 555 ICs create a significant 'glitch on the supply when their output changes state. This is rarely a problem in simple circuits with no other ICs, but in more complex circuits a smoothing capacitor (e.g. 100μ.F) should be connected across the $+V_s$ and OV supply near the 555.

Input and Output pin functions

- *Astable :* producing a square wave
- *Bistable :* simple memory which can be set and reset
- *Monostable :* producing a single pulse when triggered
- *Buffer :* inverting buffer (Schmitt trigger)

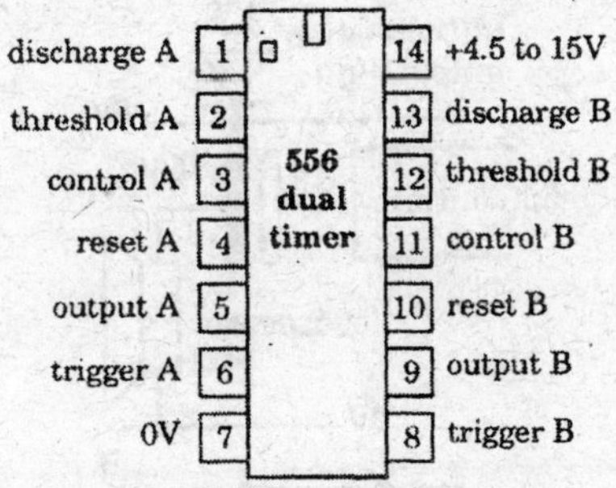

Fig.3.185. Actual pin arrangements

Trigger input.

When input $< \frac{1}{3} V_s$ ('active low'), it makes the output high ($+V_s$).

It monitors discharging of the timing capacitor in an astable circuit. It has a high input impedance than 2MΩ.

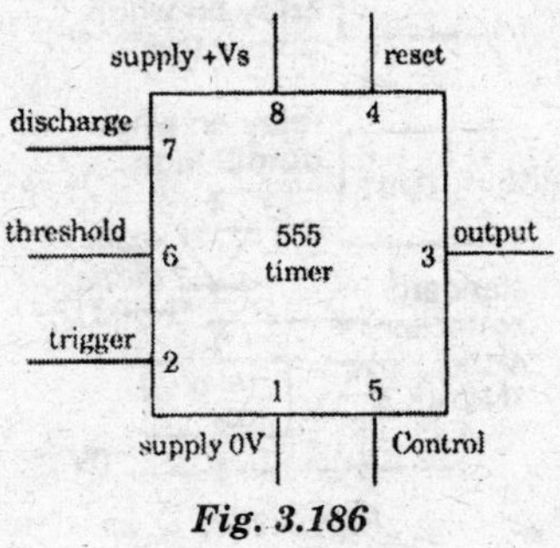

Fig. 3.186

Threshold input

When > $\frac{2}{3}V_s$ ('active high'), it makes output low (0V) providing trigger input > $\frac{1}{3}V_s$, otherwise trigger input will override threshold input and hold output high ($+V_s$) It monitors charging of the timing capacitor in astable and monostable circuits. It has a high input impedance more than 10M.

Reset input.

When less than about 0.7V ('active low'), it makes output low (0V), overriding other inputs. When not required it should be connected to $+V_s$. It has an input impedance of about 10k.

Control input

This can be used to adjust threshold voltage which is set internally to be 2/3. Usually this function is not required and control input is connected to 0V with a 0.01μF capacitor to eliminate electrical noise. It can be left unconnected if noise is not a problem.

The discharge pin is not an input, but it is listed here for convenience. It is connected to 0V when timer output is low and is used to discharge the timing capacitor in astable and monostable circuits.

Output of 555

Output of a standard 555 can sink and source up to 200mA. This is more than most ICs and it is sufficient to supply many output transducers directly, including

- LEDs (with a resistor in series)
- low current lamps, piezo transducers, loudspeakers (with a capacitor in series)
- relay coils (with diode protection)
- some motors (with diode protection).

Output voltage does not quite reach 0V and $+V_s$, especially if a large current is flowing.

To switch larger currents connect a transistor.

The ability to both sink and source current means that two devices can be connected to the output so that one is ON when the output is low and the other is ON when the output is high. Fig. 3.187 shows two LEDs connected in this way. This arrangement is used in the *Level Crossing project* to make the red LEDs flash alternately.

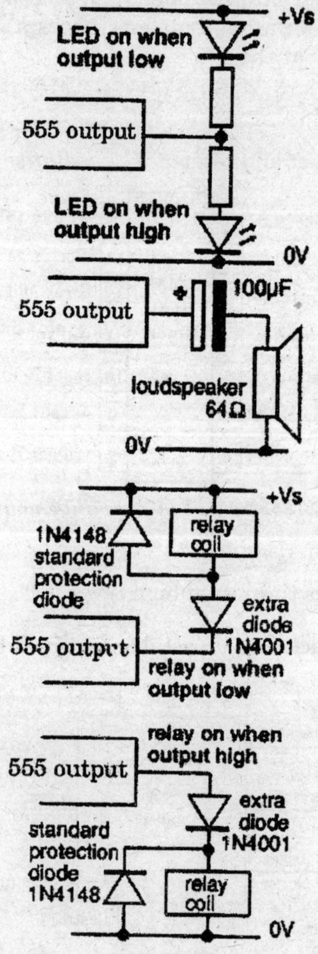

Fig. 3.187

Loudspeakers

Loudspeaker (minimum resistance 64) may be connected to the output of a 555 astable circuit but a capacitor (about 100μF) must be connected in series. The output is equivalent to a steady DC of about $\frac{1}{2}$Vs combined with a square wave AC (audio) signal. The capacitor blocks the DC, but allows the AC to pass as explained in capacitor coupling. Piezo transducers may be connected directly to the output and do not require a capacitor in series.

Relay coils and other inductive loads

Like all ICs, 555 must be protected from the brief high voltage *spike* produced when an inductive load such as a relay coil is switched OFF. The standard protection diode must be connected *backwards* across the the relay coil as shown in Fig.3.187.

However, 555 **require an extra diode** connected in series with the coil to ensure that a small *glitch* cannot be fed back into the IC. Without this extra diode, monostable circuits may re-trigger themselves as the coil is switched OFF! The coil current passes through the extra diode, so it must be a IN4001 or similar rectifier diode capable of passing the current, a signal diode such as a IN4148 is usually not suitable.

555 Astable Multivibrator

An astable circuit produces a '*square wave*'; this is a digital waveform with sharp transitions between low (0V) and high (+V_s). The durations of low and high states may be different. The circuit is called *astable* because it is not stable in any state; the output is continually changing between '*low*' and '*high*'.

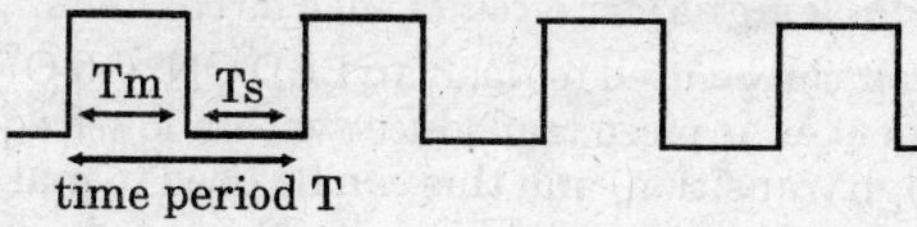

Fig. 3.188. 555 astable output (square wave) (T_m and T_s may be different)

Time period (T) of the square wave is the time for one complete cycle, but it is usually better to consider frequency (f) which is the number of cycles per second.

$$T = 0.7 \times (R_1 + 2R_2) \times C_I$$

and

$$f = \frac{1}{T}$$

where, T = time period in seconds (s)

f = frequency in hertz (Hz)

R_1 = resistance in ohms (Ω)

R_2 = resistance in ohms (Ω)

C_1 = capacitance in farads (F)

Time period can be split into two parts:

$$T = T + T$$

where T_m = mark time (output high) = $0.7 \times (R_1 + R_2) \times C_1$

T_s = space time (output low) = $0.7 \times R \times C$

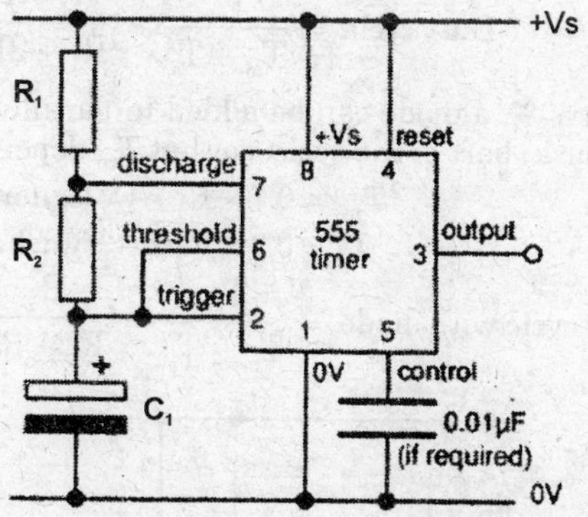

Fig. 3.189. 555 astable circuit

Many circuits require T_m and T_s to be almost equal, this is achieved if R_2 is much larger than R_1.

For a standard astable circuit, T_m cannot be less than R_s, but this is not too restricting because output can both sink and source current.

e.g. LED can be made to flash briefly with long gaps by connecting it (with its resistor) between +V_s and the output. This way LED is ON during T_s, so brief flashes are achieved with R_1 larger than R_2, making T_s short and T_m long.

Astable operation:

With output ($+V_s$), capacitor C_1 is charged by current flowing through R_1 and R_2. The threshold and trigger inputs monitor the capacitor voltage and when it reaches $\frac{2}{3}$ (threshold voltage), output becomes low and discharge pin is connected to 0V.

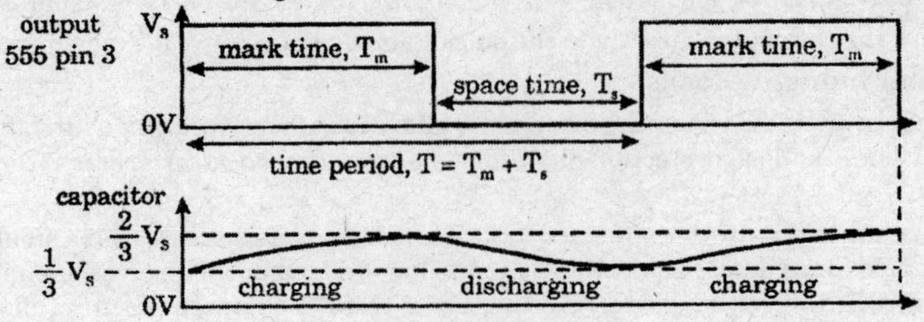

Fig. 3.190

Now the capacitor discharges with current flowing through R_2 into the discharge pin. When voltage falls to $\frac{1}{3}V_s$ (trigger voltage), output becomes high again and discharge pin is disconnected, allowing the capacitor to start charging again. This cycle repeats continuously unless the reset input is connected to 0V which forces output low while reset is 0V.

An astable can be used to provide **clock signal** for circuits such as *counters*.

Low frequency astable (<10Hz): It can be used to flash an LED ON and OFF, higher frequency flashes are too fast to be seen clearly. Driving a loudspeaker or piezo transducer with a low frequency of less than 20Hz will produce a series of '*clicks*' (one for each low/high transition) and this can be used to make a simple metronome.

Audio frequency astable (20Hz to 20kHz): It can be used to produce a sound from a loudspeaker or piezo transducer. The sound is suitable for buzzes and beeps. The natural (resonant) frequency of most piezo transducers is about 3kHz and this will make them produce a particularly loud sound.

Duty cycle:

Duty cycle of an astable circuit is the proportion of complete cycle for which the output is high (mark time). It is usually given as a percentage.

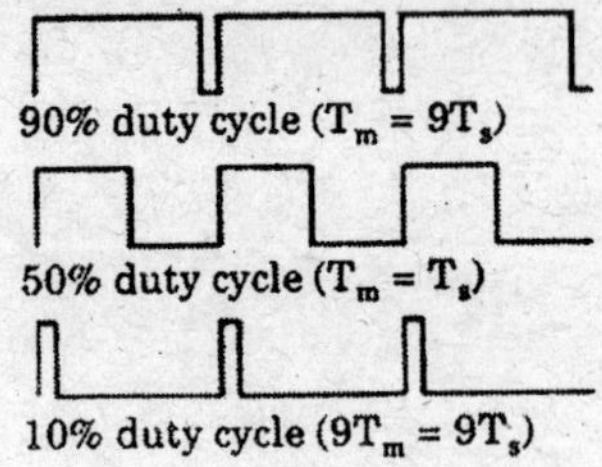

Fig. 3.191

For a standard 555, astable circuit mark time (T) must be greater than the space time (T), so duty cycle must be at least 50%.

$$\text{Duty cycle} = \frac{T_m}{T_m + T_s} = \frac{R_1 + R_2}{R_1 + 2R_2}$$

To achieve a duty cycle of less than 50%, a diode can be added in parallel with R_2 as shown in the Fig. 3.192. This bypasses R_2 during the charging (mark) part of the cycle, so that T_m depends only on R_1 and C_1:

$$T_m = 0.7 \times R_1 \times C_1 \text{ (ignoring 0.7V across diode)}$$

$$T_s = 0.7 \times R_2 \times C_1 \text{ (unchanged)}$$

$$\text{Duty cycle with diode} = \frac{T_m}{T_m + T_s} = \frac{R_1}{R_1 + R_2}$$

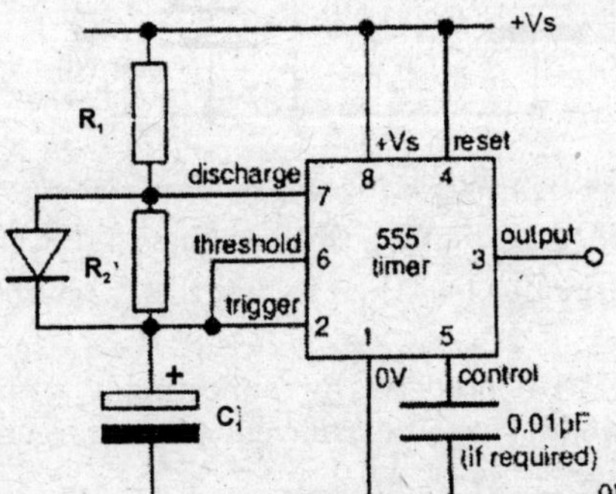

Fig. 3.192. A 555 astable circuit with diode across R_2

555 Monostable Multivibrator

A monostable circuit produces a single output pulse when triggered. It is called monostable because it is stable in just one state, *'output low'*. The *'output high'* state is temporary.

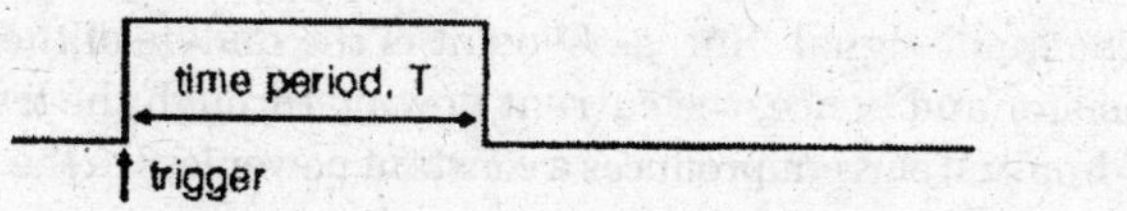

Fig. 3.193. 555 monostable output, a signal pulse

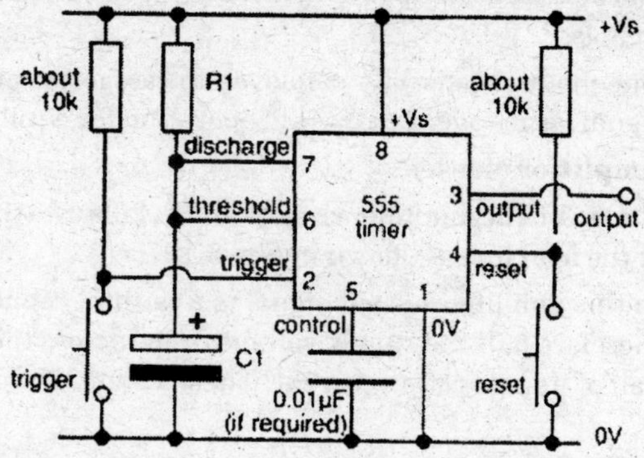

Fig. 3.194. 555 monostable circuit with manual trigger

Duration of the pulse is called **time period** (T) and this is determined by resistor R_1 and capacitor C_1:

$$\text{Time period, } T = 1.1 \times R_1 \times C_1$$

where, T = time period in seconds (s)

R_1 = resistance in ohms

C_1 = capacitance in farads (F)

Monostable operation

Timing period is triggered (started) when trigger input (555 pin 2) is less than $\frac{1}{3}$ Vs, this makes output high V_s) and the capacitor C_1 starts to charge through resistor R_1.

Once the time period has started further, trigger pulses are ignored. **Threshold** input (555 pin 6) monitors the voltage across C_1 and when this reaches $\frac{2}{3}V_s$, the time period is over and the output becomes low. At the same time, discharge (555 pin 7) is connected to 0V, discharging the capacitor ready for the next trigger.

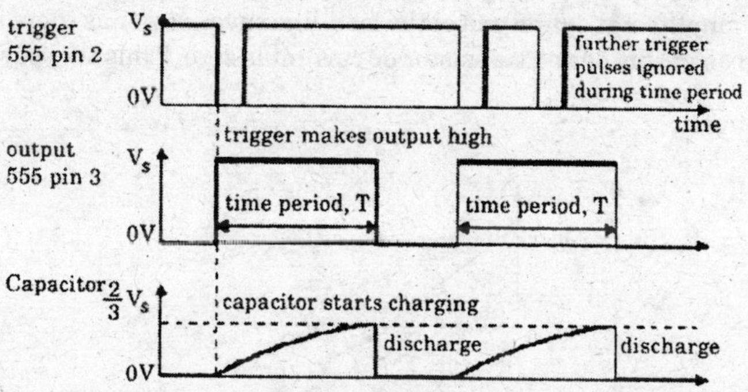

Fig. 3.195

Reset input (555 pin 4) overrides all other inputs and the timing may be cancelled at any time by connecting reset to 0V, this instantly makes the output low and discharges the capacitor. If reset function is not required, reset pin should be connected to $+V_S$.

3.18 POWER AMPLIFIER

Power amplifiers or large-signal amplifiers provide sufficient power to an output load to drive a speaker or other power device, typically a few watts to tens of watts.

Main features of a large-signal amplifier are

(i) Circuits power efficiency

(ii) Maximum amount of power that the circuit is capable of handling

(iii) Impedance matching to the output device.

A block diagram of a simple audio amplifier shown below in Fig. 3.199, which shows amplification close by small-signal amplifier and power-amplifier.

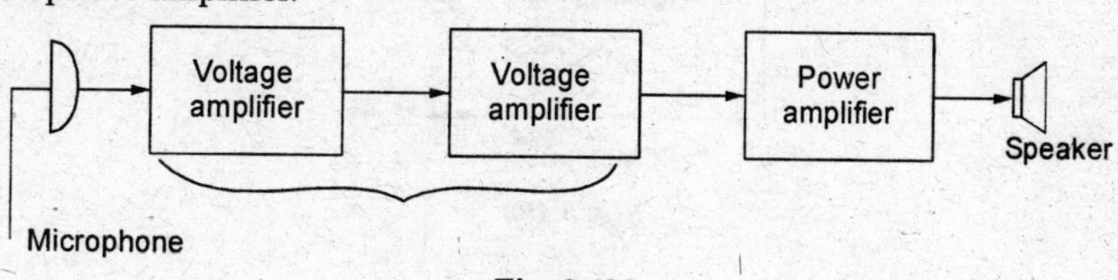

Fig. 3.196

In Fig. 3.196, microphone produces a very small signal. The first two stages amplify this audio signal and it becomes larger in voltage level but current level remains low, thus low power level. The last stage produces a much larger signal and also sufficient power to drive the loud speaker coil. Thus a power amplifier has to handle large voltage and current swings.

One method generally employed to categorize amplifier is by class which basically represent the amount of output signal varies over one cycle of operation for a full cycle of input signal.

Amplifier classes

Class A : The amplifier circuits which falls into this category are linear as these operate in a small region in the middle of the load line as shown in Fig. 3.197.

In this amplifier output signal is a faithful replica of the input signal. But, as Q-point is the middle of the load line, therefore half the supply voltage drops across the transistor and hence, the current flowing through the transistor is half of its saturation current. These values of voltage drop and current produces a constant power loss in the transistor.

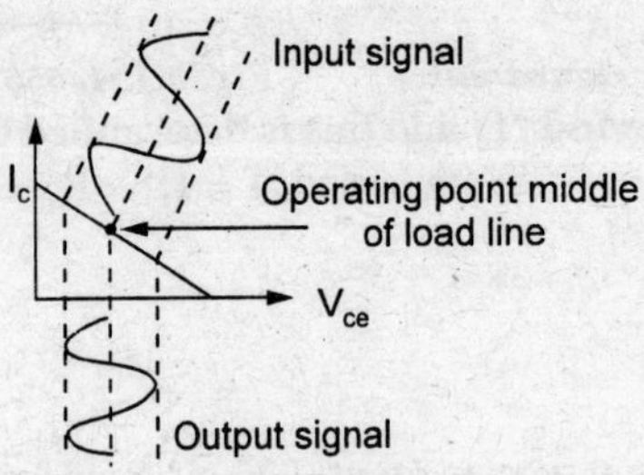

Fig. 3.197

Even there is a power loss in class-A amplifier when there is no signal is being amplified.

Class B : This amplifier circuit provides an output signal varying over one-half the input signal cycle as shown in Fig. 3.198.

Class B operation creates a very distorted output as reproduction of the input takes place for only 180° of the output signal swing. Biasing this amplifier at cut-off end of the load-line saves power as there is no drain in the supply during the non-conduction period as in this period transistor dc current is zero. Thus the, power efficiency of class-B is more than that of Class-A.

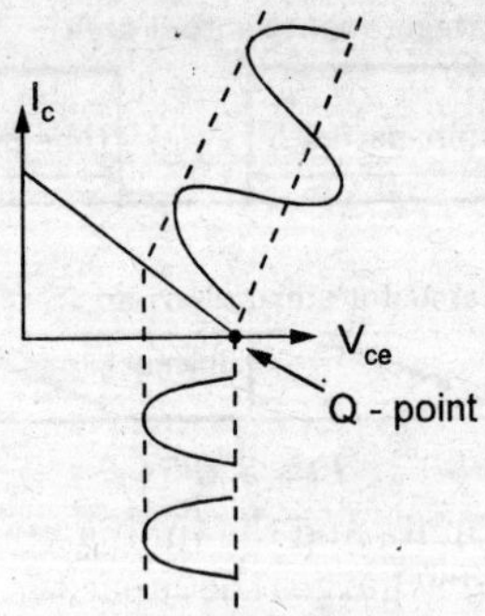

Fig. 3.198

Class AB : This amplifier is biased at a dc level above the zero base current level of class B and above one-half supply voltage level of class A. For class AB operation, the output signal during occurs between 180° to 360° and is neither class A nor class B operation as shown in Fig. 3.199.

Class C : The output of class C amplifier is biased for operation at less than 180° of the cycle and will operate only with a tuned circuit which provides a full cycle of operation for the tuned frequency.

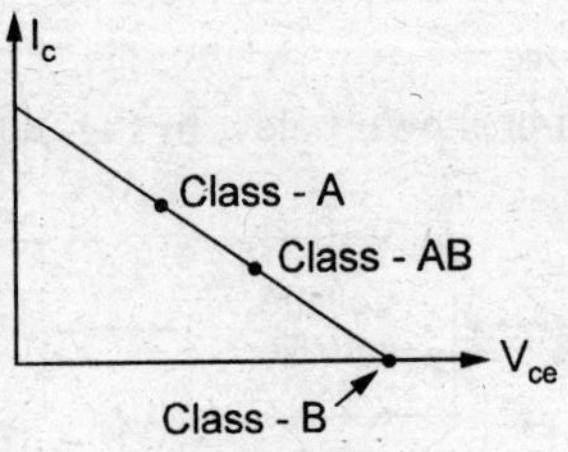

Fig. 3.199

Class D : In this amplifier circuit, amplification is done with pulse signals which are ON for a short interval and OFF for a longer interval, which causes for its high efficiency.

Power consideration

Power into an amplifier provided by supply, $P_i(dc) = V_{CC}I_{CQ}$

where, I_{CQ} = current drawn with no input signal.

Note : Even with an *ac* signal supplied, the average power drawn from the supply remain the same.

Output power

The *ac* power delivered to the load R_C can be expressed as,

$$P_O(ac) = V_{CE}(\text{rms})\, I_C(\text{rms}) = I_C^2(\text{rms})\, R_C = \frac{V_C^2(\text{rms})}{R_C}$$

Using peak signals $$P_O(ac) = \frac{V_{CE}(p)I_C(p)}{2} = \frac{I_C^2(p)}{2}.R_C = \frac{V_{CE}^2(p)}{2R_C}$$

Using peak-to-peak signals $$P_O(ac) = \frac{V_{CE}^2(p-p)\cdot I_C(p-p)}{8}$$

$$= \frac{I_C^2(p-p)}{8}R_C = \frac{V_{CE}^2(p-p)}{8R_C}.$$

Efficiency

Efficiency of an amplifier represent the amount of *ac* power delivered from the *dc* source and can be calculated as

$$\% \eta = \frac{P_O(ac)}{P_i(dc)} \times 100\%$$

3.18.1. CLASS-A POWER AMPLIFIERS

There are two configuration of class-A power amplifier:

(1) Series-fed class-A Amplifier

The circuit connection for this amplifier is shown in Fig. 3.200 :

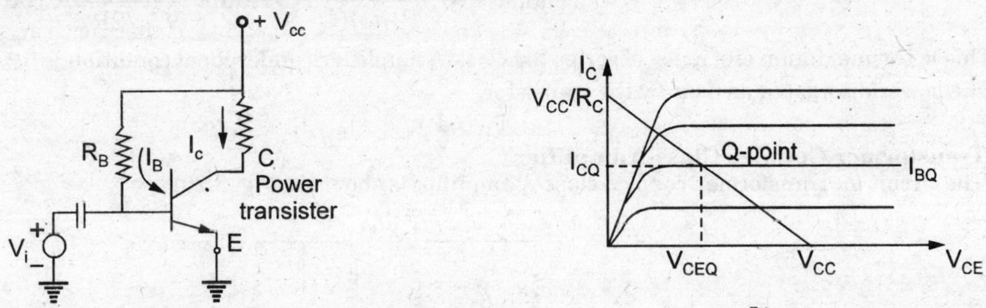

(a) Circuit *(b)*

Fig. 3.200

In this biasing, the Q-point is fixed by V_{CC} and R_B,

i.e., $$I_C = \beta I_B = \frac{\beta(V_{CC} - V_{BE})}{R_B}$$

and, collector-emitter voltage,

$$V_{CE} = V_{CC} - I_C R_C$$

In the load-line drawn in Fig. 3.157 above, the Q-point is located. If this point is set half way between 0 and V_{CC}/R_C, then the largest collector current sewing will be possible.

Input power from the voltage supply,

$$P_i(dc) = V_{CC}I_{CQ}$$

Fig. 3.201 shows the waveforms of I_C and V_{CC} (*ac* component) for the input base current I_b.

From the Fig. 3.201, we have

$$i_c(\text{peak}) = \frac{V_{CC}}{2R_C}, \quad V_{ce}(\text{peak}) = \frac{V_{CC}}{2}.$$

then, power delivered to the load by the transistor,

$$P_O(ac) = I_c(\text{rms}) \cdot V_{ce}(\text{rms}) = \frac{i_c(p-p)}{2\sqrt{2}} \cdot \frac{V_{cc}(p-p)}{2\sqrt{2}} = \frac{i_c(p-p)\cdot V_{ce}(p-p)}{8}$$

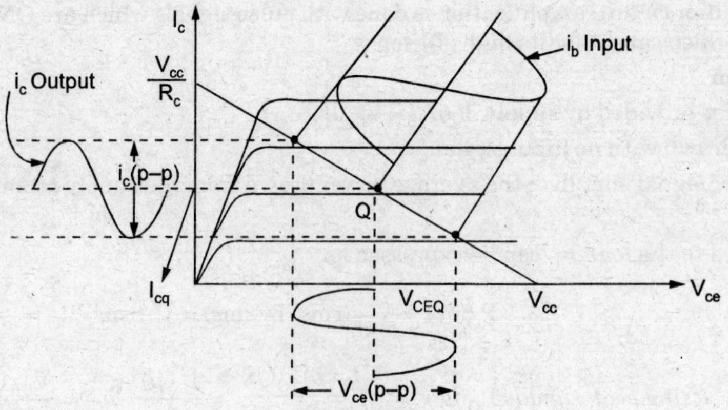

Fig. 3.201

∴ Efficiency of the amplifier,
$$\eta = \frac{P_o(ac)}{P_i(dc)} \times 100$$

Now, Maximum output power,
$$P_o(ac)\,(\max) = \frac{\max i_e(p-p) \cdot \max v_{ce}(p-p)}{8} = \frac{V_{CC}^2}{8R_C}$$

If the Q-point is at the middle of load line, then
$$I_{CQ} = \frac{V_{CC}/R_C}{2}$$

and,
$$P_i(dc)(Q) = V_{CC}^2 I_{CQ} = \frac{V_{CC}^2}{2R_C}$$

Hence, maximum efficiency,
$$\eta(\max) = \frac{P_o(ac)(\max)}{P_i(dc)(Q)} \times 100 = \frac{V_{CC}^2/8R_C}{V_{CC}^2/2R_C} \times 100 = 25\%$$

This is the maximum efficiency of series-fed class-A amplifiers under ideal condition.

The power dissipated as heat by the transistor,
$$P_D = P_i(dc) - I_{CQ}{}^2R_C - P_O(ac)$$

(2) Transformer-Coupled Class-A amplifier

The circuit for transformer-coupled class-A amplifier is shown in Fig. 3.202.

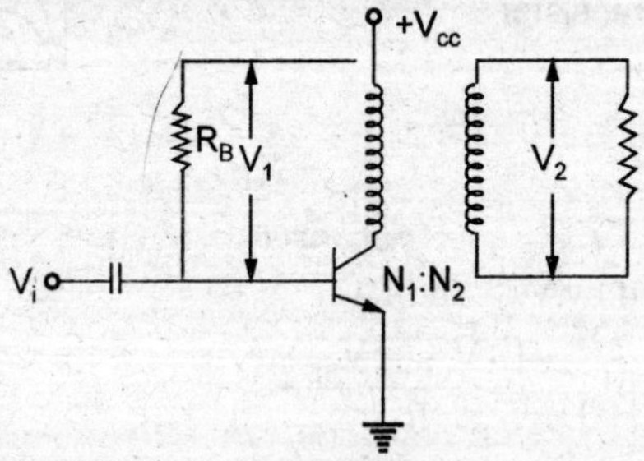

Fig. 3.202

Under *dc* conditions, the *dc* resistance seen on the primary side is quite low and it is indeed the resistance of the primary winding (under *dc* conditions load resistance is not seen on the primary side). It implies that almost all the supply voltage will drop across the transistor at the operating point. Hence, as shown in Fig. 3.203, *dc* load line is almost vertical.

It should be kept in mind that due to series resistance corresponding to the battery resistance and the transformer primary resistance, the *dc* load line will not be vertical, but quite steep.

Now, for the *ac* signal the load resistance seen on the primary side of the transformer is,
$$R'_L = \left(\frac{N_1}{N_2}\right)^2 \cdot R_L$$

The *ac* load line is drawn in Fig. 3.203. The value of $2V_{CC}$ on the V_{CC}-axis of the *ac* load line can be explained by the fact that transformer is an inductive circuit element so as the current I_C collapses (hence core flux also), a voltage is induced in the transformer primary in the direction to aid the supply voltage (Lenz's law), so that V_{CC} becomes $2V_{CC}$.

Now, $$P_o(ac)(\max) = \frac{(2V_{CC}/R'_L)\cdot 2V_{CC}}{8} = \frac{V_{CC}^2}{2R'_L}$$

and, $$P_i(dc)(Q) = V_{CC}\, I_{CQ} = V_{CC}\left(\frac{V_{CC}}{R'_L}\right) = \frac{V_{CC}^2}{R'_L}$$

Therefore, $$\eta(\max) = \left(\frac{V_{CC}^2}{2R'_L}\right)\Big/\left(\frac{V_{CC}^2}{R'_L}\right) = 0{\cdot}5 = 50\%.$$

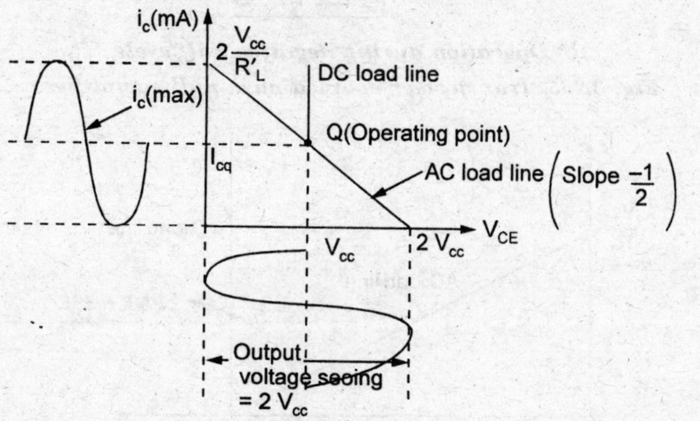

Fig. 3.203

Here, transformer coupling raises the maximum possible efficiency of the amplifier circuit to 50%.

3.18.2. CLASS-B POWER AMPLIFIER

The transistor shown in Fig. 3.204 is biased at cut-off, *i.e.*, $I_B = 0$, $V_{CE} = V_{CC}$ and so transistor in cut-off state during half cycle of the signal and goes into conduction state during state positive half cycle of the signal. Hence, highly distorted output results. To overcome from this problem, a second device operation in class-B is added in such a way that one transistor conducts only for the negative half cycles. This mode of operation is called **push-pull operation.**

Consider transformer coupled push-pull amplifier shown in Fig. 3.205.

When $V_S = 0$, T_1 and T_2 are both at cut-off.

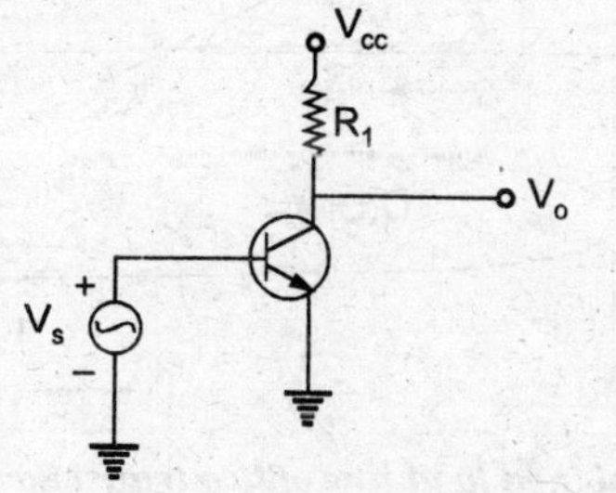

Fig. 3.204

When V_S is in its positive cycle, T_1 goes ON and a circuit current i, flows in the direction as shown in Fig. 3.208 (*a*).

Load resistance, $R'_L = R_L\left(\frac{N_1/2}{N_2}\right)^2 = \left(\frac{R_L}{4}\right)\left(\frac{N_1}{N_2}\right)^2$

When v_S is in its negative cycle, T_2 goes ON and a current i_2 flows in the direction as shown in Fig. 3.205 (*b*).

Now, drawing the load lines for the circuit given in Fig. 3.162 and when $v_S = 0$, V_{CC} appears across both the transistors. Since *dc* resistance of transformer winding being negligible, the *dc* load line is almost vertical.

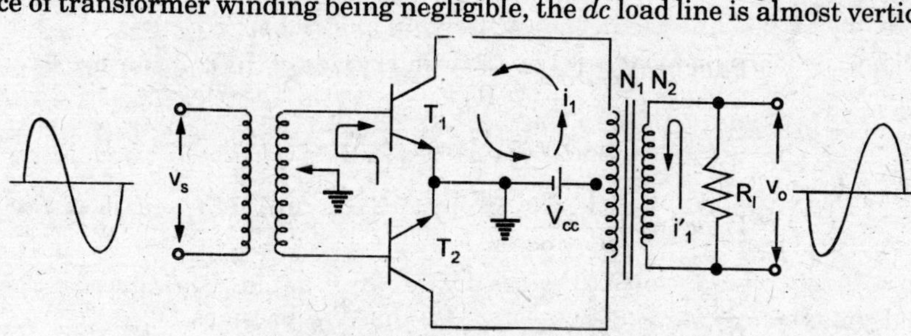

(a) Operation during positive half cycle

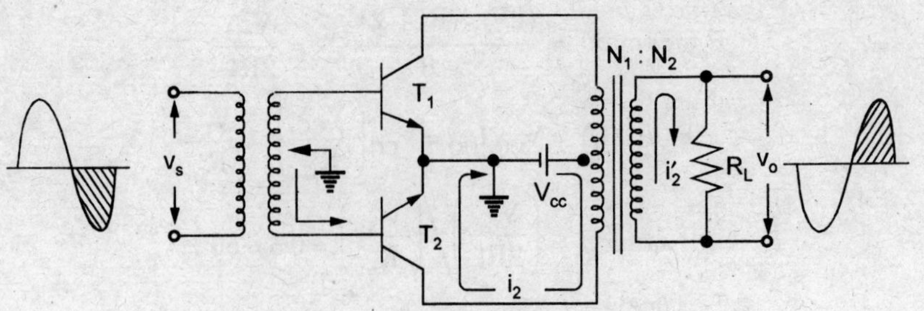

(b) Operation during negative half cycle

Fig. 3.205. Transformer coupled push-pull complifier

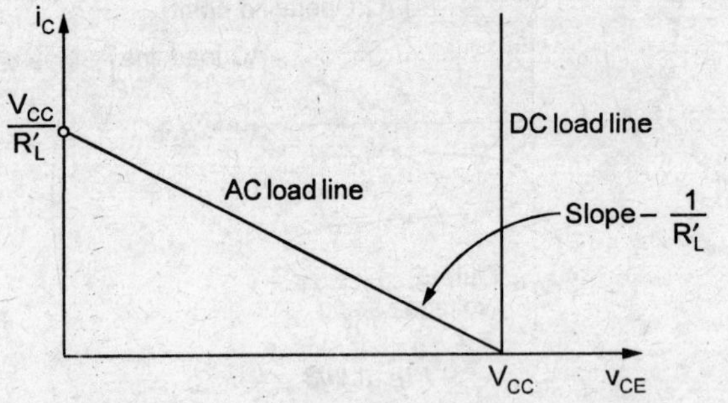

Fig. 3.206. Load line for push-pull complifier

When v_S is non-zero, resistance R'_L is presented to i_1 to i_2. The current i_1 in Fig. 3.205 (a) is taken as +ve and anticlockwise current i_2 in Fig. 3.208 (b) is then –ve. The combination of two half cycles shown in Fig. 3.207.

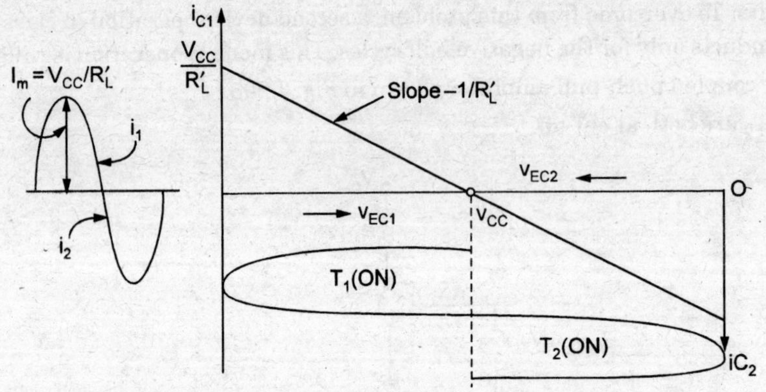

Fig. 3.207. Combined load line of two transistor in push-pull

Now, direct current supplied by the battery

$$I_{dc} = i_1(dc) + i_2(dc) = \frac{2I_m}{\pi}$$

$$\therefore \quad P_i(dc) = \frac{2V_{CC}\, I_m}{\pi}$$

where I_m = peak value of half cycle of i_c (conducted by T_1 or T_2)

AC output power

$$P_o(ac) = V_{rms} I_{rms} = \frac{I_{rms}^2}{R'_L}$$

$$I_{rms} = i_c(p-p)/(2\sqrt{2}) = I_m/\sqrt{2}$$

$$\therefore \quad P_o(ac) = \frac{I_m^2}{(R'_L/2)}$$

Now from Fig. 3.207, $I_m(\max) = \dfrac{V_{CC}}{R'_L}$

$$\therefore \qquad P_i(dc)(\max) = \frac{2V_{CC}^2}{\pi R_L'}$$

$$P_o(ac)(\max) = \frac{V_{CC}^2}{2R_L'}$$

$$\therefore \qquad \text{Efficiency, } \eta = \frac{P_o(ac)}{P_i(dc)} = \frac{I_m^2 R_L'/2}{2V_{CC}I_m/\pi} = \frac{\pi I_m R_L'}{4V_{CC}}$$

or,

$$\eta(\max) = \frac{P_o(ac)(\max)}{P_i(dc)(\max)} = \frac{\pi I_m(\max) R_L'}{4V_{CC}} = \pi/4 \text{ or } 78{\cdot}54\%.$$

3.18.3. CLASS-AB AMPLIFIERS

In this amplifiers, the Q-point (operating point) of the transistors lies between that for class-A and class-B type amplifiers. A complementary-symmetry class-B amplifier shown in Fig. 3.208 can be made as class-AB by choosing R_1 and R_2 such that the V_{BE} of both T_1 and T_2 places each transistor away from the cut-off point *i.e.*, $V_{BE} > 0{\cdot}6V$.

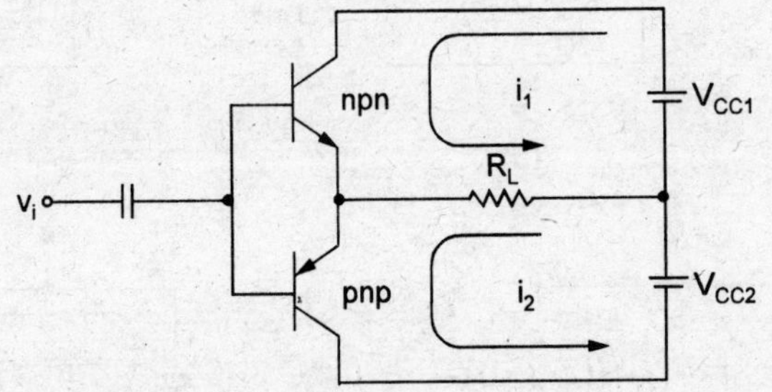

Fig. 3.208. Complementary-symmetry circuit

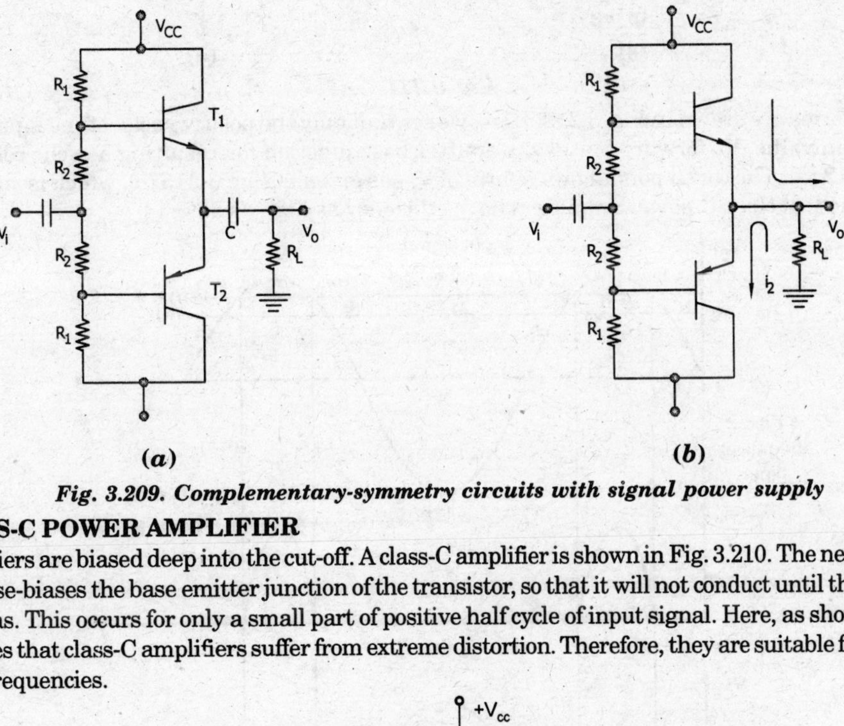

Fig. 3.209. Complementary-symmetry circuits with signal power supply

3.18.4. CLASS-C POWER AMPLIFIER

Class-C amplifiers are biased deep into the cut-off. A class-C amplifier is shown in Fig. 3.210. The negative voltage at the base terminal reverse-biases the base emitter junction of the transistor, so that it will not conduct until the input signal overcomes this reverse bias. This occurs for only a small part of positive half cycle of input signal. Here, as shown above i_c is in the form of pulses implies that class-C amplifiers suffer from extreme distortion. Therefore, they are suitable for the audio work and are used at radio frequencies.

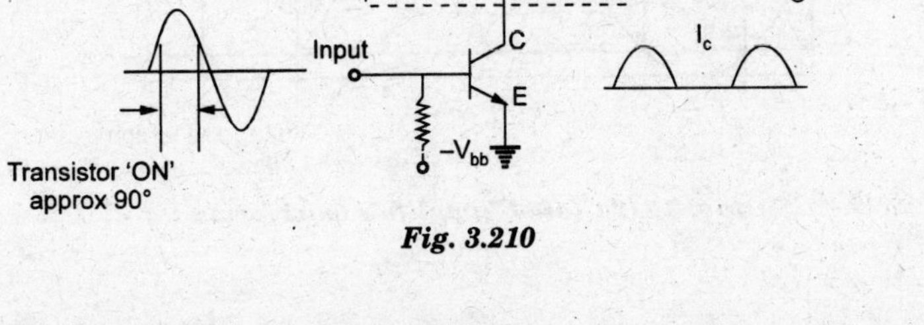

Fig. 3.210

In Fig. 3.210 a tank circuit in the collector circuit of the class-C amplifier, which restores the sine wave form of the input signal at the output. But there is problem with it is that, it can not restore rectangular waveform or complex audio wave forms.

The tank circuit shown is a parallel LC oscillating circuit and is excited by collector current pulse, which sets the circuit into self oscillations. In this circuit, the energy transfers back and fourth between the capacitor and inductor, thus producing a sinusoidal waveform. Because of the small effective resistance of the tank circuit, the energy loss occurs which is being maintained by cyclic pulses of the tank. This is accomplished in class-C amplifier by the collector current pulse recharging the capacitor every cycle. Frequency of oscillation of the tank circuit is,

$$f = \frac{1}{2\pi\sqrt{LC}}$$

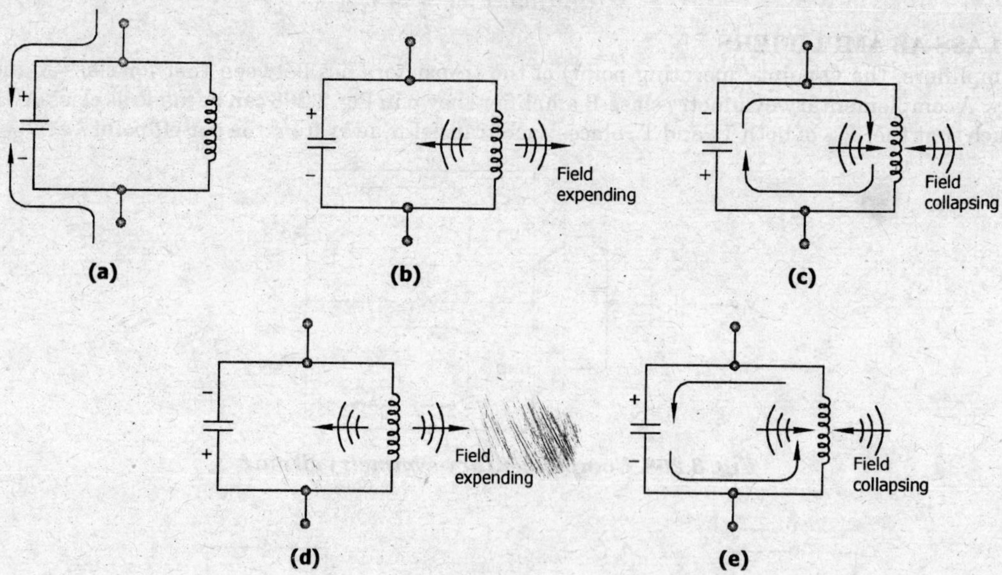

Fig. 3.211

The class-C waveforms are drawn in Fig. 3.212. Here, we see that only the positive peak of the input signal in Fig. 3.212 (*a*) above the cut-in value. V_Y forward biases the emitter-base junction for resulting a cyclic collector current pulse shown in Fig. 3.212 (*b*). The corresponding waveform of V_{CE} is given in Fig. 3.215 (*c*), which is sinusoidal due to tank circuit action. Practical class-C power amplifiers have efficiency as high as 85%.

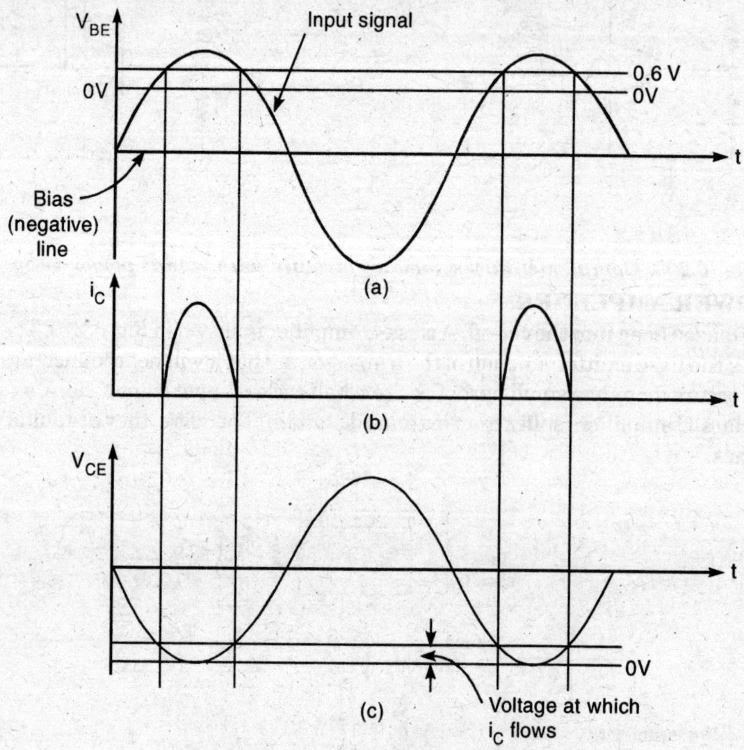

Fig. 3.212 Class-C amplifier waveforms

3.18.5. DISTORTION IN AMPLIFIERS

In power amplifiers, the signals are large in amplitude and so the operating region extends to nonlinear portions of the transistor characteristics. The nonlinearity arises as the static output characteristics are not equidistant straight lines for constant increments of input excitation. Consequently, operating region enters into the portions of the dynamic characteristic where it significantly deviates from a straight line. As the signal excursion enters in the nonlinear region because of large amplitude of the signal, this kind of distortion is also called **amplitude distortion.**

Harmonic Distortion

When a sinusoidal excitation is applied to a transistor, the nonlinear characteristic causes the position half of the signal to be amplified more than its negative half. The result is that the output signal contains a *dc* component (average of positive and negative halves of the output current/voltage being nonzero). Moreover, frequencies which are integral multiples of the input signal frequency (fundamental frequency) called harmonics are present in the output, hence, called *harmonic distortion.* Thus, this type of distortion has to be analysed using Fourier series.

For exact application of Fourier series for assessment of harmonic distortion the output wave form needs to be constructed graphically. However, to proceed analytically it is fairly accurate to approximate the dynamic characteristic to be a parabola. Thus for a BJT

$$i_c = K_1 i_b + K_2 i_b^2 \quad \text{...(3.50)}$$

where K_1 and K_2 are constants.

Let the input signal be $i_b = I_{bm} \cos \omega t$ ...(3.51)

$$\therefore \quad i_c = K_1 I_{bm} \cos \omega t + K_2 I_{bm}^2 \cos^2 \omega t$$

which can be written in the form

$$i_c = \frac{1}{2} K_2 I_{bm}^2 + K_1 I_{bm} \cos \omega t + \frac{1}{2} K_2 I_{bm}^2 \cos 2\omega t$$

$$= B_0 + B_1 \cos \omega t + B_2 \cos 2\omega t$$

Hence presence of the *dc* component and second harmonic, both of which were not present in the input (Eq. 3.51).

$$\therefore \quad \text{Total collector current, } i_C = I_C + i_c$$

$$= I_C + B_0 + B_1 \cos \omega t + B_2 \cos 2\omega t \quad \text{...(3.52)}$$

The magnitude of B_0, B_1 and B_2 can be read from the static characteristics and load line

Choose $\omega t = 0$ when $i_C = I_{max}$

then $\omega t = \frac{\pi}{2}$ $i_C = I_C$; suffic Q is dropped

and at $\omega t = \pi$ $i_C = I_{min}$

Substituting these values in equation (3.52), we get

$$I_{max} = I_C + B_0 + B_1 + B_2$$

$$I_C = I_C + B_0 - B_2 \quad \text{...(3.53)}$$

$$I_{min} = I_C + B_0 - B_1 + B_2$$

Solving we get

$$B_1 = \frac{I_{max} - I_{min}}{2}$$

$$B_0 = B_2 = \frac{I_{max} - I_{min} - 2I_C}{4}$$

We define the second-harmonic distortion as

$$D_2 = \left|\frac{B_2}{B_1}\right|$$

The three LHS values in equation (3.53) are read from the static transistor characteristic and the load line.

When the input has large swings, the parabolic approximation is not valid and higher harmonics will be appearing whose amplitudes have to be evaluated by graphic-numerical calculation. We can thus write

$$i_C = I_C + B_0 + B_1 \cos \omega t + B_2 \cos 2\,\omega t + B_2 \cos 3\,\omega t + \ldots$$

Higher order harmonic distortion are then defined as

$$D_2 = \left|\frac{B_2}{B_1}\right|, D_3 = \left|\frac{B_3}{B_1}\right|$$

Total harmonic distortion factor, $D = \sqrt{[D_2^2 + D_3^2 + \ldots]}$

Power output

Power delivered at fundamental frequency, $$P_1 = \frac{B_1^2 R_L}{2}$$

Total power delivered, $$P = (B_1^2 + B_2^2 + B_3^2 \ldots)\frac{R_L}{2} = (1 + D_2^2 + D_3^2 + \ldots)P_1 = (1 + D^2)\,P_1$$

If distortion factor is 10%, then $$P = [1 + (0{\cdot}1)^2]P_1 = 1{\cdot}01\ P_1$$

And so we find that only 1% of fundamental power is contained in higher harmonics.

Distortion in Class-AB and Class-B

As the conduction in these amplifiers is 180° (class-B) and a little more than 180° (class-AB), distortion as such particularly of the second harmonic kind would be very high. But in the push-pull circuits used for these amplifiers, this distortion is all but eliminated. This is analytically proved below.

If the input signal to an amplifier is $X_{in} \cos \omega t$ the output signal has its Fourier representation of the form

$$I_{0Q} + B_0 + B_1 \cos \omega t + B_2 \cos \omega t + \ldots$$

where B_0 is the *dc* component of the output signal and other B's are the various Fourier coefficients.

Now mathematically verify that class-B amplifies in push-pull configuration eliminate second harmonic distortion.

Consider the push-pull amplifier in Fig. 3.204 (*a*) and (*b*).

In this circuit i_1 and i_2 can be expressed as

$$i_1 = I_{0Q} + B_0 + B_1 \cos \omega t + B_2 \cos 2\omega t + B_3 \cos 3\omega t + \ldots$$

and $$i_2 = I_{0Q} + B_0 + B_1 \cos (\omega t + \pi) + B_2 \cos 2(\omega t + \pi) + B_3 \cos 3(\omega t + \pi) + \ldots$$

where it is observed that i_1 and i_2 are out of phase. The expression for i_2 may be written as

$$i_2 = I_{0Q} + B_0 - B_1 \cos \omega t + B_2 \cos 2\omega t - B_3 \cos 3\omega t + \ldots$$

The load current is proportional to $(i_1 - i_2)$ which is given as

$$i_1 - i_2 = 2B_1 \cos \omega t + 2B_3 \cos 3\omega t + \ldots$$

Hence there are no even harmonics present at the output.

Crossover Distortion

In the push-pull operation of class-B amplifiers discussed earlier, the output wave form is not a perfect sinusoid as presented earlier. Instead, the wave form is something like the one shown in Fig. 3.213. The encircled region shows a marked deviation from sinusoidal behaviour. $i_B - v_{BE}$ characteristic of each transistor is similar to that of a diode and has nonlinear region below cut-in voltage $V_\gamma = 0{\cdot}6 - 0{\cdot}7$ V where the base current drawn is almost zero. Consequently as shown in Fig. 3.213, while the input voltage is sinusoidal the current i_B is nonsinusoidal near the zero crossing region, where its value is almost zero. This type of distortion in i_B appears in complementary-symmetry circuits. The wave form of i_B is replicated in i_C and so the output voltage v_a has crossover distortion.

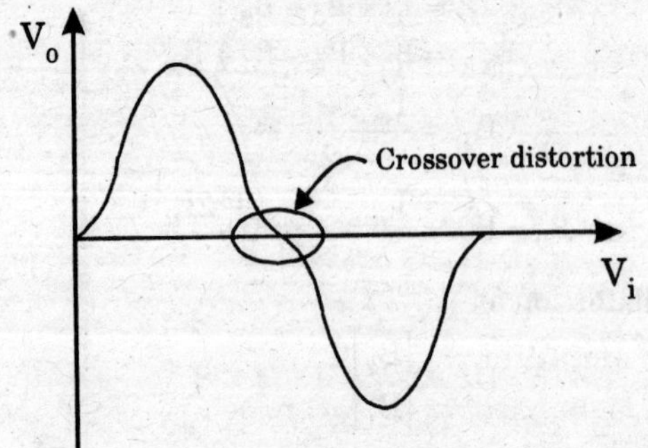

Fig. 3.213

The solution for the problem of crossover distortion is to provide some forward bias to the transistors which is just sufficient to prevent them from operating in the nonlinear portion of $i_B - v_{BE}$ characteristic. In a BJT with characteristic as in Fig. 3.213. This means that v_{BE} should not be allowed to reduce below 0·6 V. By not operating in the nonlinear portion of the characteristic. The problem of crossover distortion is eliminated.

At the extreme high-frequency end of the spectrum distortion is caused by noise *i.e.*, random signal unrelated to the input. When the input signal is weak, the output mainly consists of noise and the input signal is submerged in it. This phenomenon is easily observed as "snow" on the television screen when the signal is weak or is disconnected. One important source of noise is the random thermal motion of electrons in the amplifier circuit. Another source of noise is the *shot effect* of individual electrons crossing a junction. Noise introduced at the initial stages of an amplifier is most troublesome as at these stages the signal level is low and the noise would get amplified in later stages by as much as the signal itself producing an output with unfavourable signal/noise ratio. The two limits of the dynamic range of an amplifier are : the high level at which the signal is obscured by noise and the low level at which the amplitude distortion becomes excessive.

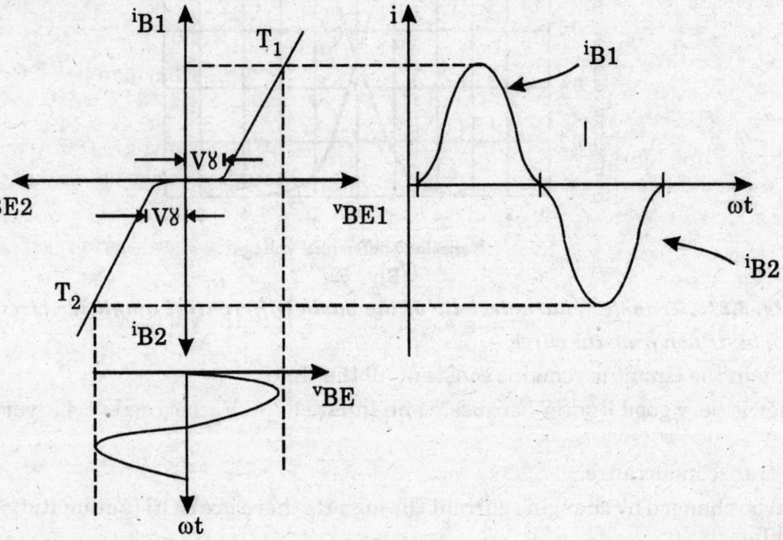

Fig. 3.214

3.19 DIFFERENTIAL AMPLIFIER

It is most widely used circuit building block in analog integrated circuit. BJT differential amplifier is also a basis for high speed logic family (ECL). It also has application as a comparators.

Differential amplifier consist of two identical emitter coupled transistor as shown in Fig. 3.215:

Differential amplifier amplifies the difference of two input signal, $V_0 = A(V_{in1} - V_{in2})$

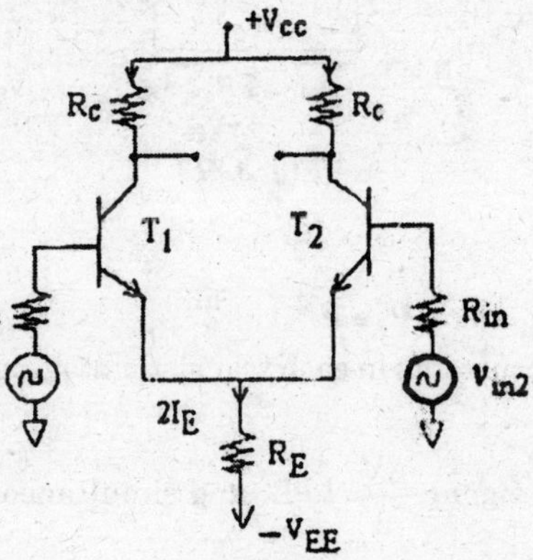

Fig. 3.215

Configurations of Differential amplifier

Differential amplifier can work in four different configurations:

(1) Dual Input balance output

(2) Dual input unbalance output

(3) Single input balance output

(4) Single input unbalance output

Transfer characteristic of Differential amplifier

From Fig. 3.216, when V_{B2} is greater than V_{B1} most of the current flow through T_2 as V_{B1} increases the current is switched from T_2 to T_1. Now with $V_{B1} > V_{B2}$, most of the current flows through T_1.

Curve follows the exponential relation because for any transistor I_E and V_{BE} are related exponentially by

$$I_E = I_s e^{V/V_{BE}}$$

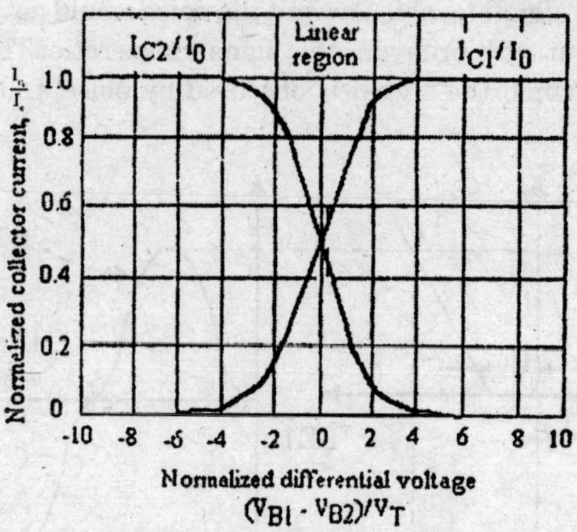

Fig. 3.216. Transfer characteristic of the basic Differential amplifier circuit

Following conclusion can be drawn from the curve.

(1) Overall current through the circuit is remains constant all the time.

(2) Differential amplifier is very good limiter because when input ($V_{B1} - V_{B2}$) exceeds ± 4T, very little further increase in output is possible.

(3) Slope of curve gives transconductance.

(4) Differential gain can be changed by changing current through R_E therefore AGC (automatic gain control) is also possible in differential amplifier.

Fig. 3.218 shown below a BJT version of a differential amplifier and if the emitter resistance R_C is large then its performance will be much better.

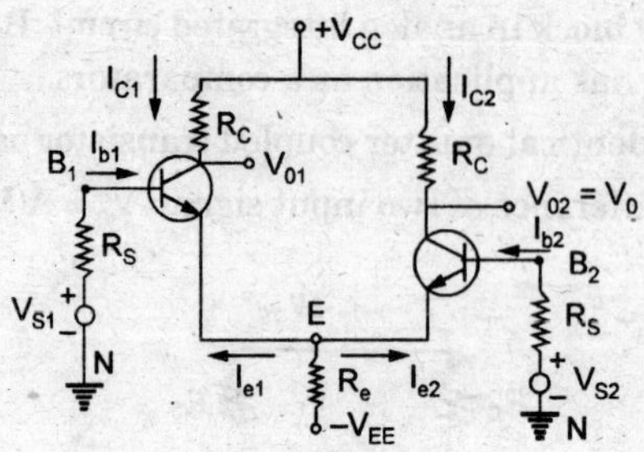

Fig. 3.217

Circuit has two special modes

(1) Differential Mode

If $V_{S1} = V_{S2} = V_S$, then $V_d = V_1 - V_2 = 0$.

In this case, collector and emitter currents in each transistor stage are equal. But due to symmetrical circuit, there is negligible current in Re.

Now, if we apply an incremental signal $\frac{\Delta V}{2}$ to B_1 and simultaneously apply $-\frac{\Delta V}{2}$ to B_2 such that differential voltage, $V_d = V_1 - V_2 = \Delta V$.

Assuming linearity, it can be said that I_{C1} increases by ΔI_C and I_{C2} decreases by ΔI_C. Consequently, the current in R_E remains unchanged. Thus, V_E remains unchanged and for such incremental change $\left(\frac{+\Delta V}{2}, \frac{-\Delta V}{2}\right)$, emitter can be assumed as being grounded.

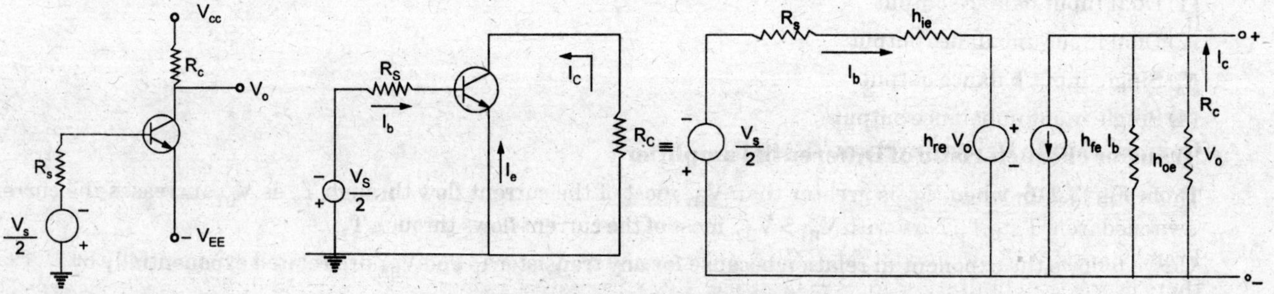

(a) Differential mode ***(b) Equivalent circuit of Fig. (a)***

Fig. 3.218

From the equivalent circuit, we have

$$A_I = \frac{-h_{fe}}{(1+h_{oe}R_c)}$$

and, $R_i = h_{ie} + h_{re}A_IR_C$

then, $$A'_V = -\frac{V_0}{V_S/2} = -2A_d = \frac{A_IR_C}{R_i + R_s}$$

or $$-2A_d = \frac{-h_{fe}R_C}{1+h_{oe}R_C} \Bigg/ \left(R_S + h_{ie} - \frac{h_{re}h_{fe}R_C}{1+h_{oe}R_C}\right) = \frac{-h_{fe}R_C}{(1+h_{oe}R_C)(R_S+h_{ie})}$$ [Here, $h_{re}h_{fe}R_C << (h_{ie}+R_S)$]

Now, if $h_{oe}R_C << 1$,

then $$A_d = \frac{1}{2}\cdot\frac{h_{fe}R_C}{h_{ie}+R_S} \quad ...(3.54)$$

(2) Common mode.

Consider both V_{S1} and V_{S2} increase by $\Delta V/2$ and difference V_d remains zero. Because of R_E, both I_{C1} and I_{C2} will exhibit a small increase in ΔI_C. Changes in I_C appear at the emitter and the current in R_E increases by $2\Delta I_C$. This situation is shown in the Fig. 3.219 (*a*). It is being equivalent to a common emitter stage with an emitter resistance of $2R_E$.

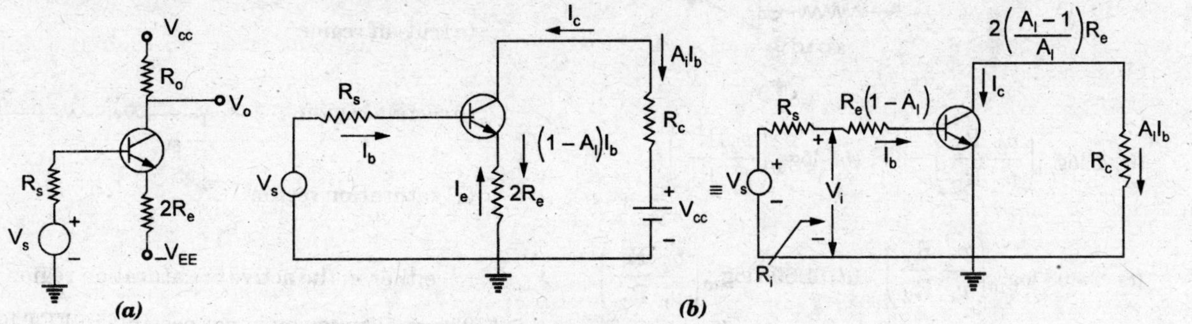

Fig. 3.219

Using Miller's theorem, current gain, $$A_I = \frac{-h_{fe}}{1+h_{oe}R'_L}$$

or $$A_I = \frac{-h_{fe}}{1+h_{oe}\left[R_C + 2\left(\frac{A_I-1}{A_I}\right)R_e\right]}$$

or $$A_I = \frac{h_{oe}R_C - h_{fe}}{1+h_{oe}(R_C+2R_e)}$$

and $R_i = (1-A_I)(2R_e) + h_{ie} + h_{re}A_I(R_C+2R_e)$

Voltage gain, $$A_V = \frac{A_IR_L}{R_i+R_s}$$

or $$A_v = \frac{(2h_{oe}R_e - h_{fe})R_C/[1+h_{oe}(R_C+2R_e)]}{R_S + \frac{2h_{oe}R_e - h_{fe}}{1+h_{oe}(R_C+2R_e)}[h_{re}(R_C+2R_e) - 2R_e] + 2R_e + h_{ie}}$$

If $h_{re}(R_C+2R_e) << 2R_e$ and $h_{oe}R_c << 1$

then, $$A_v = \frac{(2h_{oe}R_C - h_{fe})R_C}{2R_e(1+h_{fe}) + (R_S+h_{ie})(2h_{oe}R_e+1)} \quad ...(3.55)$$

Common Mode Rejection Ratio (CMRR).

This ratio is defined as, $$CMRR = \frac{A_d}{A_c}$$

From equations (3.54) and (3.55), CMRR ratio increases with R_e. But, as quiescent *dc* voltage drop across the R_e, there is practical limitation on its magnitude. Therefore, if R_e is increased, then V_{EE} should be much larger in order to maintain the quiescent current at its proper value. If the operating currents of the transistor are allowed to decrease, this will lead to higher h_{ie} value and lower values of h_{fe}.

OBJECTIVE TYPE QUESTIONS

DIODES, BJT & FET

1. In an FET as V_{GS} is changed from zero to increasing reverse bias, the value of g_m

(*a*) increased (*b*) decreased

(*c*) remains constant (*d*) falls suddenly to zero

2. In the circuit given in the figure, if both transistor Q_1 and Q_2 are identical, then output voltage at T = 300 K is

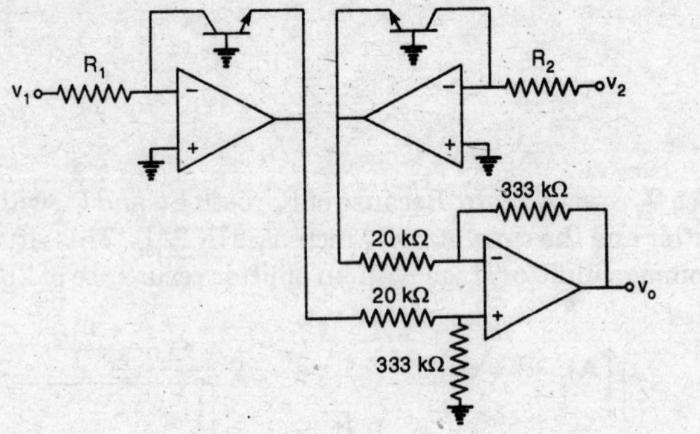

(*a*) $2\log_{10}\left(\frac{v_2}{v_1}\frac{R_1}{R_2}\right)$ (*b*) $\log_{10}\left(\frac{v_2}{v_1}\frac{R_1}{R_2}\right)$

(*c*) $2.303\log_{10}\left(\frac{v_2}{v_1}\frac{R_1}{R_2}\right)$ (*d*) $4.605\log_{10}\left(\frac{v_2}{v_1}\frac{R_1}{R_2}\right)$

3. For the clamping network shown below, resulting output for the applied input will be

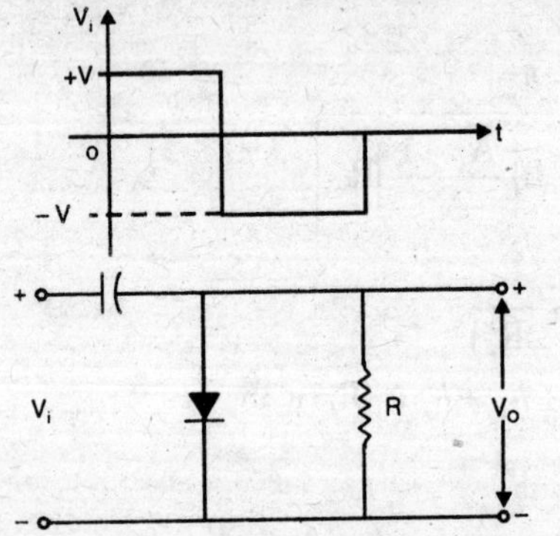

(*a*)

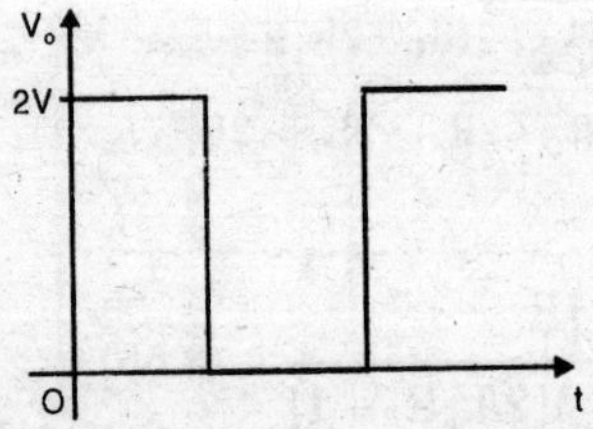

(*b*)

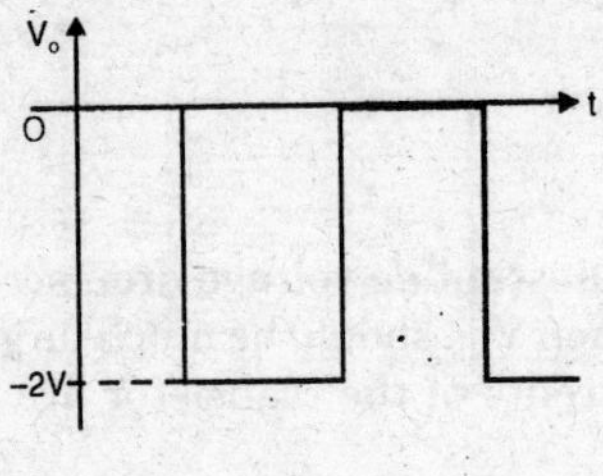

(*c*)

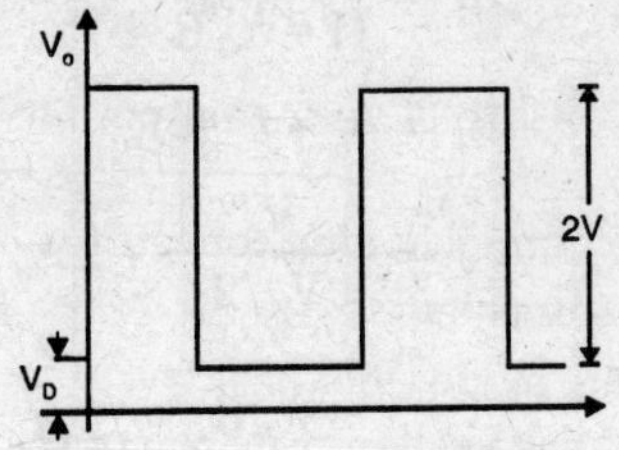

(*d*)

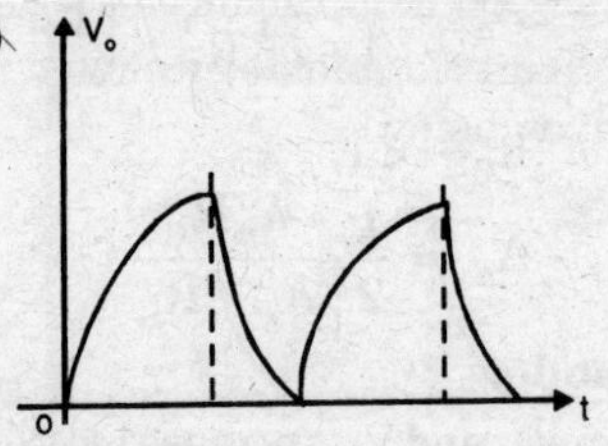

4. The transistor in the circuit shown is operating in

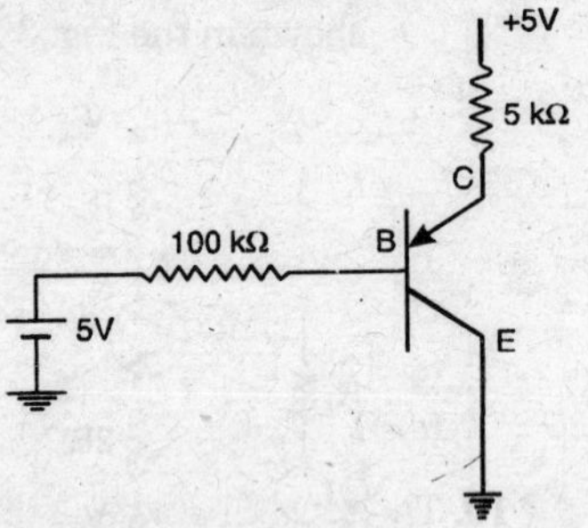

(*a*) cut-off region

(*b*) active region

(*c*) saturation region

(*d*) either in the active or saturation region

5. Thermal runaway is not possible in FET because as the temperature of FET increases

(*a*) mobility decreases

(*b*) transconductance increases

(*c*) drain current increases

(*d*) none of these

COMMON DATA Q. 6 - 7

All transistors in the circuit in the figure have parameter V_{TN} = 1V and $\lambda = 0$

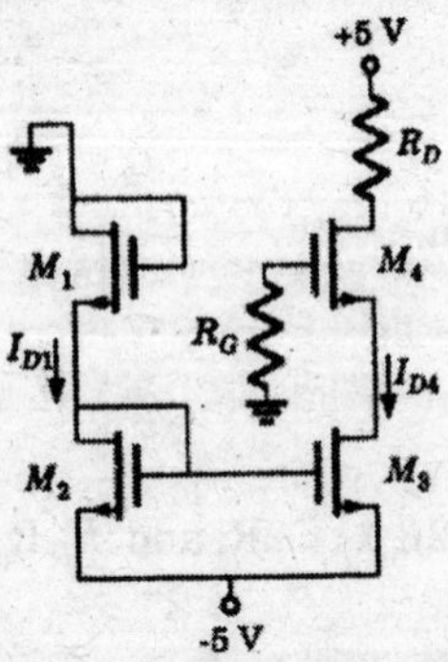

The conduction parameter are as follows:

$K_{n1} = 400\ \mu A/V^2$ $K_{n2} = 200\ \mu A/V^2$

$K_{n3} = 100\ \mu A/V^2$ $K_{n4} = 80\ \mu A/V^2$

6. I_{D1} = ?

(*a*) 0.23 mA (*b*) 0.62 mA

(*c*) 0.46 mA (*d*) 0.31 mA

7. I_{D4} = ?

(*a*) 0.62 mA (*b*) 0.31 mA

(*c*) 0.46 mA (*d*) 0.92 mA

8. The threshold voltage of an n-channel MOSFET can be increased by

(*a*) increasing channel doping concentration

(*b*) reducing channel length

(*c*) reducing gate oxide thickness

(*d*) decreasing channel doping concentration

9. Three different circuits for biasing junction transistor amplifiers are given below

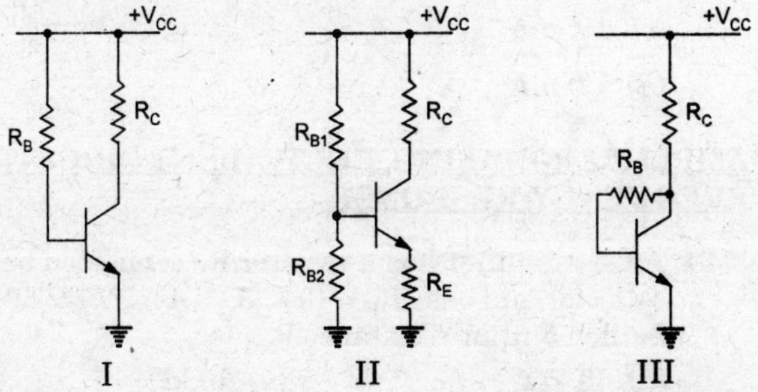

The correct decreasing order of preference of these circuits from the point of view of bias stabilisation is

(*a*) I, II, III (*b*) III, II, I

(*c*) II, III, I (*d*) I, III, II

10. The MOSFET switch in its on-state may be considered equivalent to

(*a*) resistor (*b*) inductor

(*c*) capacitor (*d*) battery

11. In the transistor circuit shown in the figure, collector-to-ground voltage is +20 V. Which of the following is the probable error ?

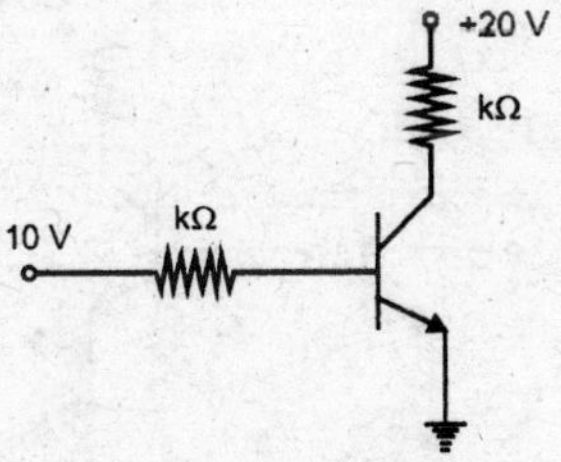

(*a*) Collector-emitter terminals shorted

(*b*) Emitter to ground connection open

(*c*) 10 kΩ resistor open

(*d*) Collector-base terminal shorted

12. The centre tap full-wave single-phase rectifier circuit uses 2 diodes as shown in the given figure. The rms voltage across each diode is

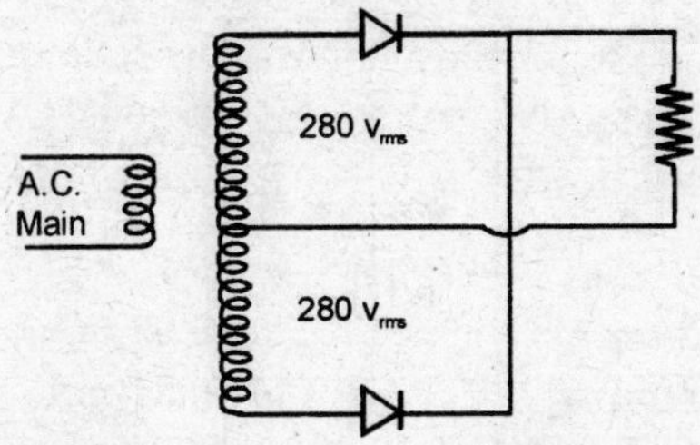

(*a*) 790.7 V (*b*) 395.3 V

(*c*) 280 V (*d*) 201.3 V

13. In the circuit shown in the given figure, transistor is in the active mode. V_{BE} = 0.7 volt. The best approximation without knowing h_{fe} for V_C as shown in the figure is

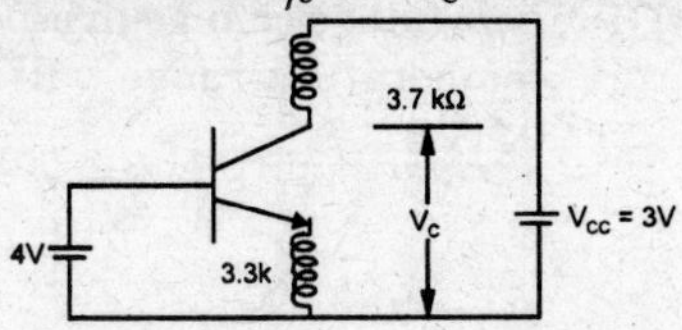

(*a*) 1.0 V

(*b*) 3.3 V

(*c*) 4.3 V

(*d*) 4.7 V

14. A voltage source V_{AB} = 4 sinωt is applied to the terminals A and B of the circuit shown in the given figure. The diodes are assumed to be ideal. The impedance by the circuit across the terminals A and B is

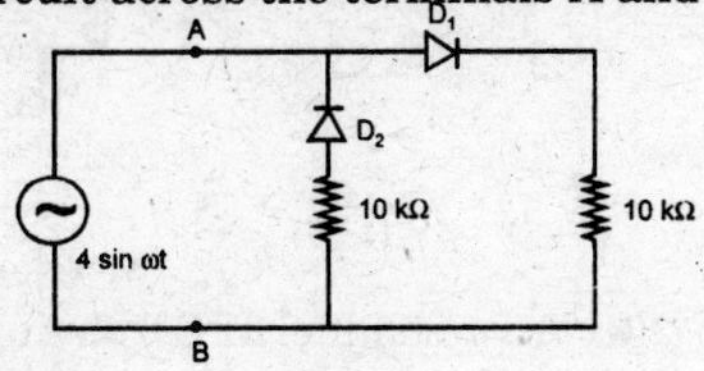

(*a*) 5 kΩ

(*b*) 10 kΩ

(*c*) 15 kΩ

(*d*) 20 kΩ

15. If α = 0.98, I_{CO} = 6 μA and I_β = 100μA for a transistor, then value of I_C will be

(*a*) 2.3 mA (*b*) 3.1 mA

(*c*) 4.6 mA (*d*) 5.2 mA

16. For the given input, output waveform across the diode shown in the figure will be

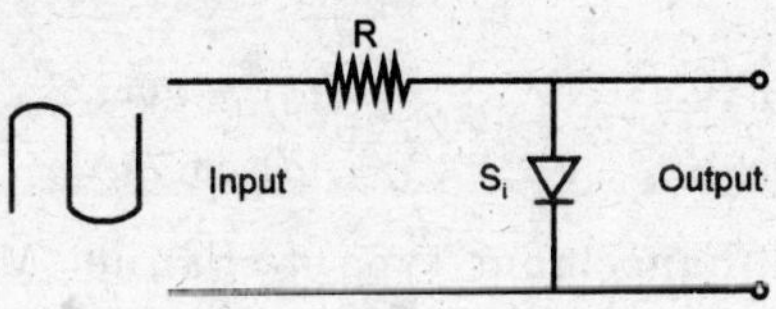

(*a*)

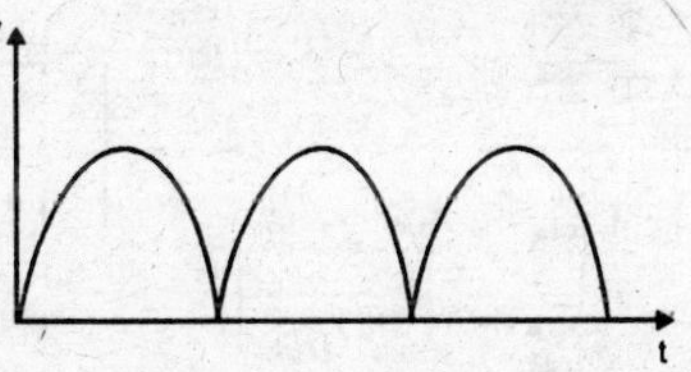

(*b*)

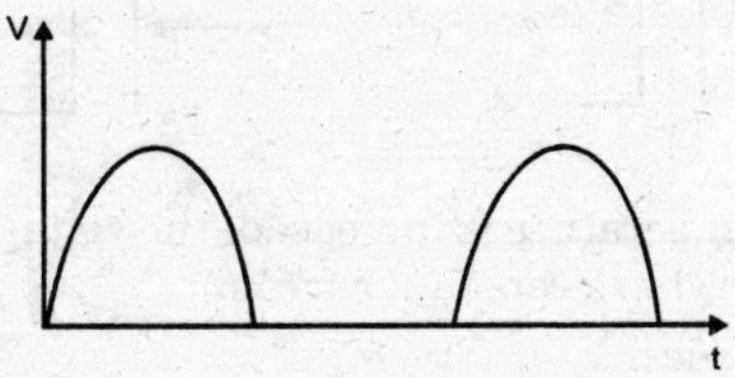

(*c*)

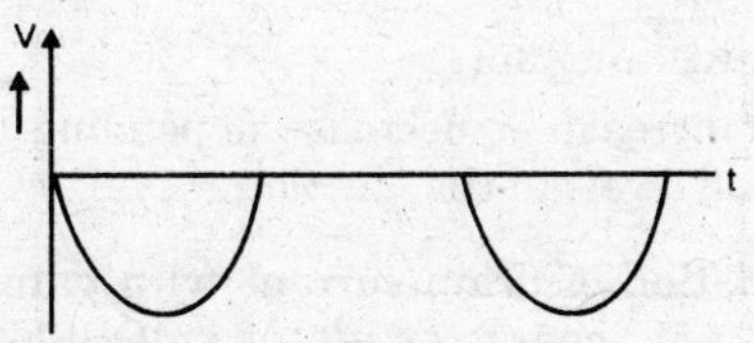

(*d*)

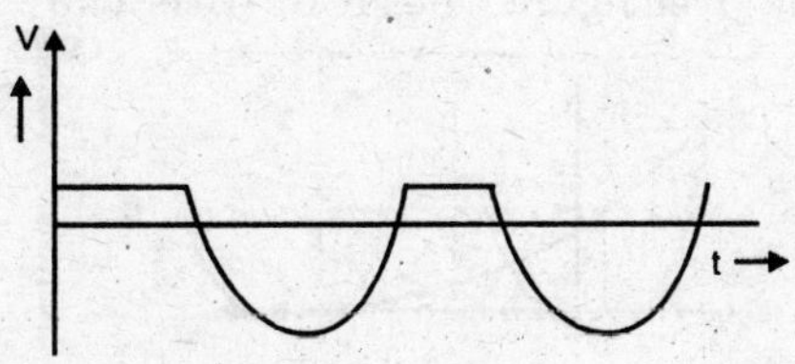

17. The base-biased transistor circuit of figure is subjected to increase in junction temperature from 25°C to 75°. If β increases from 100 to 150 with rising temperature, percentage change in a-point value (I_C, V_{CE}) over the temperature range will be (assume V_{BE} reacts at 0.7 V)

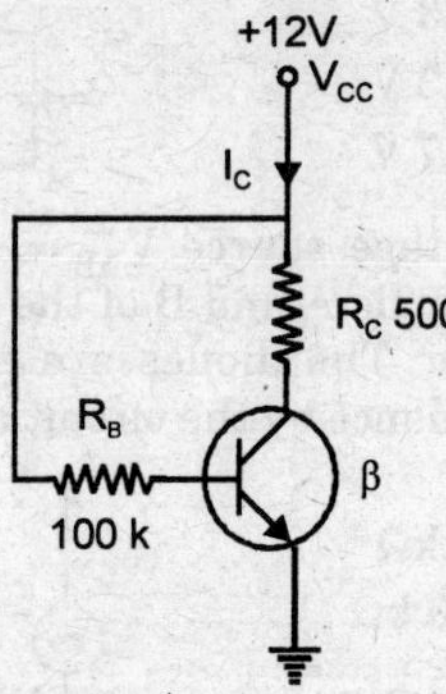

(*a*) – 40 %

(*b*) – 44.57 %

(*c*) – 46.57%

(*d*) –48.0 %

18. An *n*-channel JFET having a pinch-off voltage (V_P) of –5V shows a transconductance (g_m) of 1 mA/V, when applied gate-to-source voltage (V_{GS}) is –3V. Its maximum transconductance (in mA/V) will be **GATE**

(*a*) 1.5 (*b*) 2.0

(*c*) 2.5 (*d*) 3.0

19. mobility of an electron in a conductor is expressed in terms of **GATE**

(*a*) $cm^2/V\text{-}s$ (*b*) cm/V-s

(*c*) cm^2/V (*d*) cm^2/s

20. An enhancement type *n*-channel MOSFET is represented by the symbol **GATE**

(*a*)

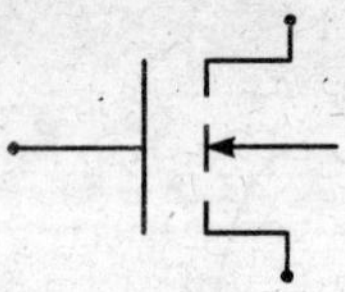

(*b*)

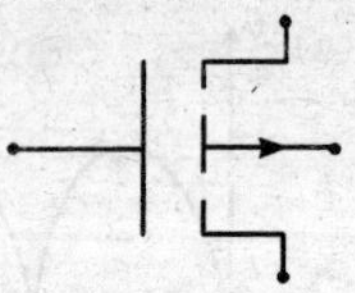

(*c*)

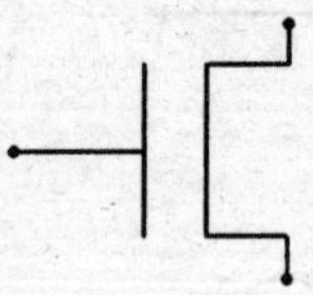

(*d*)

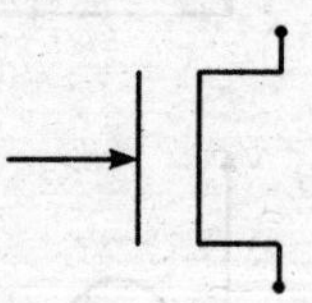

21. As the temperature is increased, the voltage across a diode carrying a constant current **GATE**

(*a*) increases

(*b*) decreases

(*c*) remains constant

(*d*) may increase or decrease depending upoon the doping levels in the junction

22. The variation of drain current with gate-to-source voltage (I_D-V_{GS} characteristic) of a MOSFET is shown in the given figure. The MOSFET is a/an

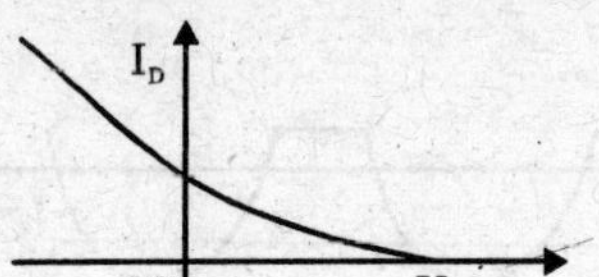

GATE

(*a*) *n*-channel depletion mode device

(*b*) *n*-channel enhancement mode device

(*c*) *p*-channel depletion mode device

(*d*) *p*-channel enhancement mode device

23. For the *n*-channel enhancement MOSFET shown in the given figure, threshold voltage V_{tn} = 2V. The drain current I_D of the MOSFET is 4 mA when drain resistance R_D is 1 kΩ. If value of R_D is increased to 4 kΩ, then drain current I_D will become

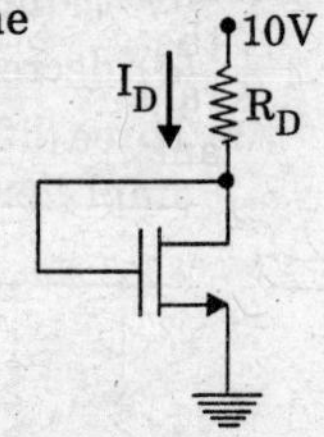

(*a*) 2.8 mA

(*b*) 2.0 mA

(*c*) 1.4 mA

(*d*) 1.0 mA

AMPLIFIER-BIASING, EQUIVALENT CIRCUIT AND FREQUENCY RESPONSE

24. A CE amplifier has a resistor R_F connected between collector and base R_F = 40 k. R_C = 4*k*. If h_{fe} = 50, r_π = 1 *k*, then output resistance R_0 is

(*a*) 40 kΩ (*b*) 20 kΩ

(*c*) 4 kΩ (*d*) 0.66 kΩ

25. The gain bandwidth product of a two stage CE amplifier is

(*a*) same as that of one stage

(*b*) greater than that of one stage

(*c*) less than that of one stage

(*d*) product of the two gain bandwidth products of each stage

26. In the transistor circuit shown below, the collector to ground voltage is + 20 V.

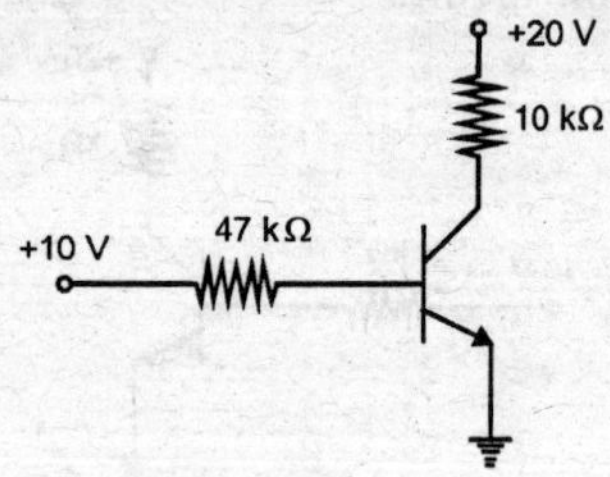

The possible condition is

(*a*) collector-emitter terminals shorted

(*b*) emitter to ground connection open

(*c*) 10 kilo-ohms resistor open

(*d*) collector-base terminals shorted

27. In the following two non-linear transistor biasing circuits, the resistors

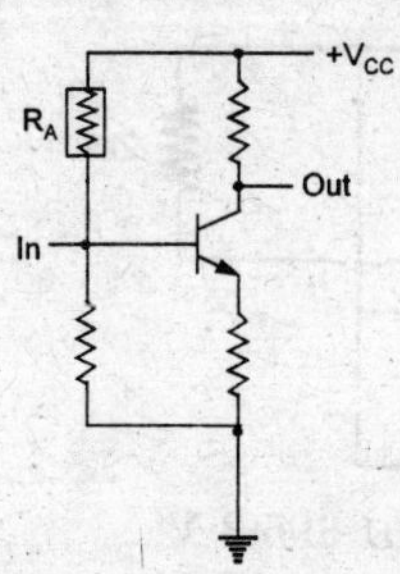

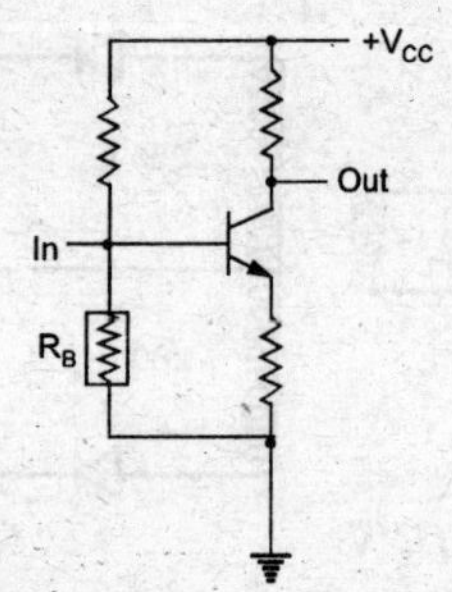

(*a*) R_A and R_B, both have negative temperature coefficient.

(*b*) R_A and R_B, both have positive temperature coefficient.

(*c*) R_A has negative temperature coefficient and R_B has positive temperature coefficient.

(*d*) R_A has positive temperature coefficient and R_B has negative temperature coefficient.

28. In the circuit shown in the given figure, assuming that the capacitor C is almost shorted for the frequency range of interest of the input signal, voltage gain of the amplifier will be approximately

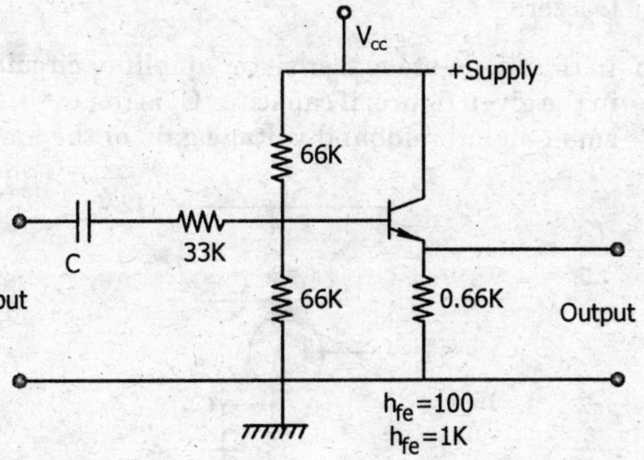

(*a*) 0.33 (*b*) 0.5

(*c*) 0.66 (*d*) 1

29. What will be the input independence Z_i for the network shown below ?

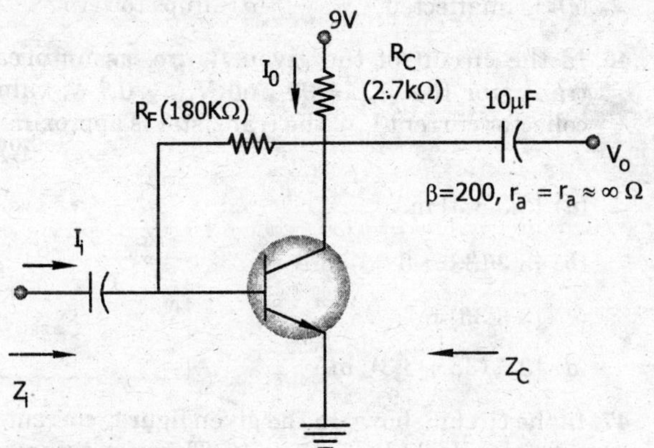

(*a*) 560.5 Ω (*b*) 56.05 Ω

(*c*) 937 Ω (*d*) 617.7 Ω

30. If an npn transistor has a beta cut-off frequency f_B of 1MHz, and emitter short circuit low-frequency current gain β_0 of 200, then unity gain frequency f_T and alpha cut off frequency f_α respectively are

(*a*) 200 MHz, 201 MHz

(*b*) 200 MHz, 199 MHz

(*c*) 199 MHz, 200 MHz

(*d*) 201 MHz, 200 MHz

31. If an *npn* transistor (with C = 0.3 pF) has a unity gain cut-off frequency f_T of 400 MHz at a d.c. bias current I_c = 1mA, then value of its C_μ is approximately (V_T = 26 mV)

(*a*) 15 (*b*) 30

(*c*) 50 (*d*) 96

32. The voltage V_{CB} and current I_B for the CB-configuration of the figure shown below will be

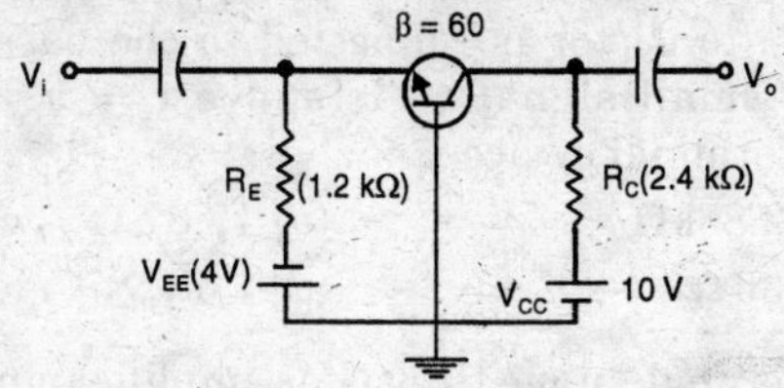

(*a*) 3.4 V and 45.8 μA (*b*) 6V, and 2.75 mA

(*c*) 34 V and 4.5 mA (*d*) None of these

33. Mirror current I of the given circuit is

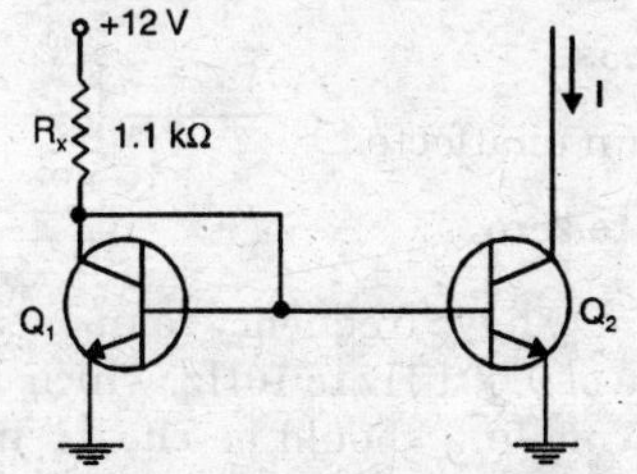

(*a*) 10.27 mA (*b*) 12.53 mA

(*c*) 0.636 mA (*d*) 10.90 mA

34. Current I for the circuit shown will be

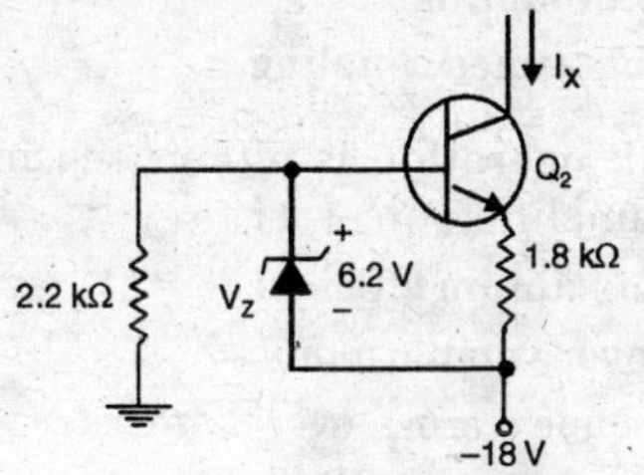

(*a*) 3 mA (*b*) 2.81 mA

(*c*) 6.16 mA (*d*) 10 mA

35. For a class B amplifier providing a 20 V peak signal to 16Ω load and a power supply of V_{cc} = 30 V, efficiency will be

(*a*) 52.3 % (*b*) 25.65%

(*c*) 75% (*d*) 78.6%

36. A multistage amplifier has a low-pass response with three real poles at $s = -\omega_1$, $s = -\omega_2$ and $s = -\omega_3$. The approximate overall bandwidth B of the amplifier is given by

(*a*) $B = \omega_1 + \omega_2 + \omega_3$

(*b*) $\frac{1}{B} = \frac{1}{\omega_1} + \frac{1}{\omega_2} + \frac{1}{\omega_3}$

(*c*) $B = (\omega_1 \omega_2 \omega_3)^{1/3}$

(*d*) $B = \sqrt{\omega_1^2 + \omega_2^2 + \omega_3^2}$

37. If a two-stage amplifier is required to have an upper cut-off frequency of 2 MHz and a lower cut-off frequency of 30 Hz then upper and lower cut-off frequencies of individual stage are respectively

(*a*) 4 MHz, 60 Hz (*b*) 3 MHz, 20 Hz

(*c*) 3 MHz, 60 Hz (*d*) 4 MHz, 20 Hz

38. For a transistor, parameters are β = 180 and V_A = 150V, and it is biassed at I_{CQ} = 2m A. If collector of the tansistor is connected to the base terminal, then small signal resistaance $r_e = v_{ce}/i_c$ of this two-terminal device is

(a) 12.88kΩ (b) 12.87 Ω

(c) 2.33 Ω (d) 1.53 Ω

39. In the single stage transistor amplifier circuit shown in the figure, if capacitor C_E is removed, then ac small signal midband voltage gain of the amplifier will

(a) increase

(b) decrease

(c) remain unaffected

(d) drop to zero

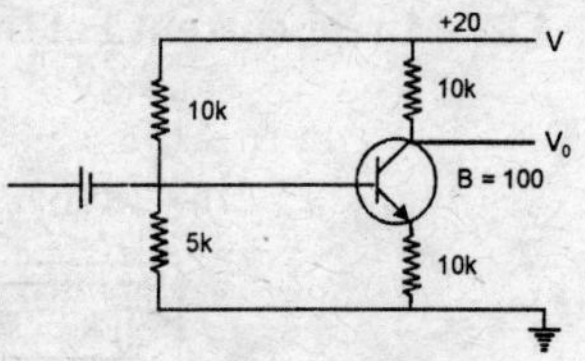

40. A signal may have frequency components which lie in the range of 0.001 Hz to 10Hz. which of the following types of coupling should be chosen in a multistage amplifier designed to amplify this signal ?

(a) RC coupling

(b) Transformer coupling

(c) Direct coupling

(d) Double-tuned coupling

41. Class AB operation is often used in power (large signal) amplifiers in order to

(a) get maximum efficiency

(b) remove even harmonics

(c) overcome a cross-over distortion

(d) reduce collector dissipation

42. Consider self biased circuit given in the figure. If driven by a current source

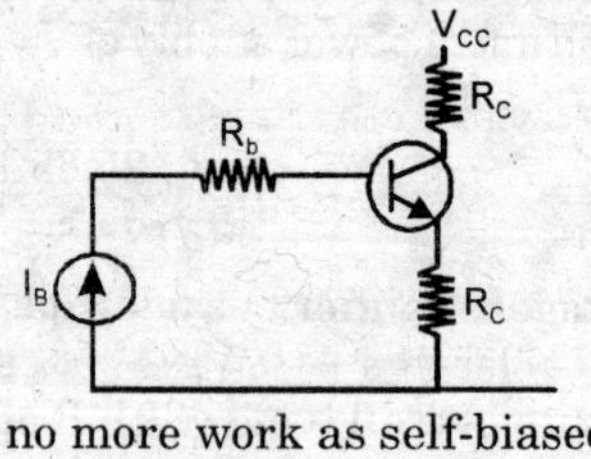

(a) it will no more work as self-biased circuit

(b) circuit would stabilize operating point as in the case when driven by voltage source

(c) stability can be increased with small value of R_e

(d) stability can be increased with increase of α of the transistor

43. A junction transistor operating at room temperature with I_C = 2 mA, where $\frac{kT}{q}$ = 20 mV and β = 100. The values of parameter g_m in mhos and r_π in ohm respectively are

(a) 0.04 and 2500

(b) 0.08 and 1250

(c) 0.5 and 800

(d) 0.08 and 5000

44. If an input signal with non-zero dc component is applied to a low pass RC network, then dc component in the output will be

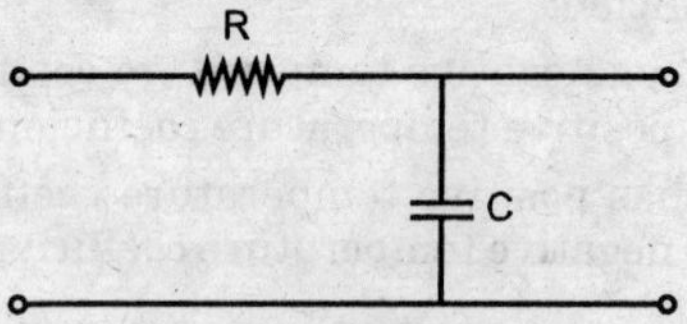

(a) same as that in the input

(b) less than that in the input

(c) more than that in the input

(d) zero

45. In the single-stage transistor amplifier circuit shown in the given figure, if capacitor C_E is removed, then, ac small-signal midband voltage gain of the amplifier

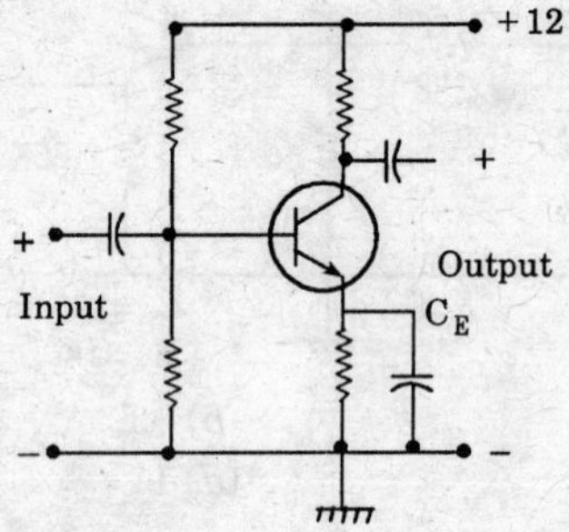

(a) increases (b) decreases

(c) is unaffected (d) drops to zero

46. In the circuit of the given figure, assuming that transistor has h_{FE} = 99 and V_{BE} = 0.7 V, value of collector current I_C of the transistor is approximately **GATE**

(a) [3.3/3.3] mA

(b) [3.3/(3.3 + 0.33)] mA

(c) [3.3/33] mA

(d) [3.3/(33 + 3.3)] mA

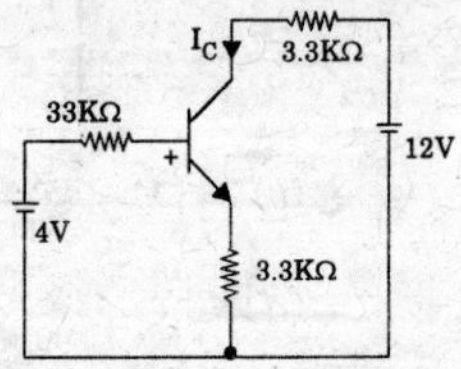

47. In the circuit shown in the given figure, current gain (b) of the ideal transistor is 10. The operating point of the transistor (V_{ce}, I_c) is **GATE**

(a) (40V, 4A)

(b) (40V, 5A)

(c) (0V, 4A)

(d) (15V, 4A)

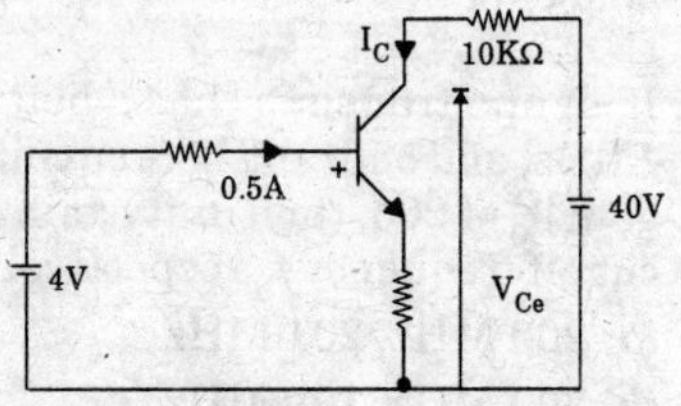

OSCILLATOR AND FEEDBACK AMPLIFIER

48. If an amplifier with gain of –1000 and feedback of b = –0.1 had a gain change of 20% due to temperature, then change in gain of the feedback amplifier would be

(a) 10% (b) 5 %

(c) 0.2 % (d) 0.01 %

49. A constant current signal across a parallel RLC circuit gives an output of 1.4 volts at the signal frequency of 3.89 kHz and 4.1 kHz. At frequency of 4kHz, output voltage will be

(*a*) 1 volt (*b*) 2 volts
(*c*) 1.4 volts (*d*) 2.8 volts

50. In the circuit shown in the given figure, the type of feedback used is

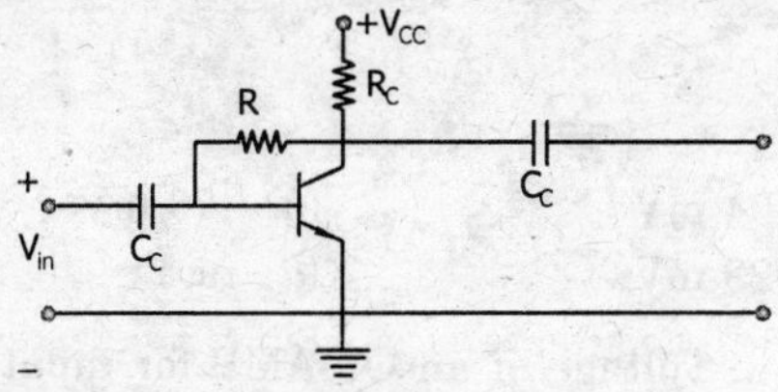

(*a*) voltage series feedback
(*b*) voltage shunt feedback
(*c*) current series feedback
(*d*) current shunt feedback

51. An amplifier has an open loop gain of 100, an input impedance of 1kΩ , and an output impedance of 100 Ω . If a feedback network with a feedback factor of 0.99 is connected in a voltage series feedback mode then new input and output impedances are

(*a*) 10 Ω and 1 Ω (*b*) 10 Ω and 10 kΩ
(*c*) 100 k Ω and 1Ω (*d*) 100 kΩ 10 kΩ

52. The resonant frequency of the Wein bridge oscillator of given in figure, is

(*a*) 19597 Hz

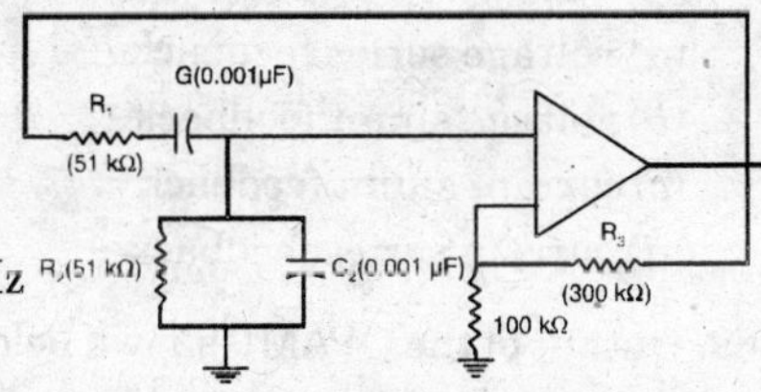

(*b*) 1592.35 Hz

(*c*) 3120.7 Hz

(*d*) 4777 Hz

53. RC network shown in the given figure can provide maximum theoretical phase shift of

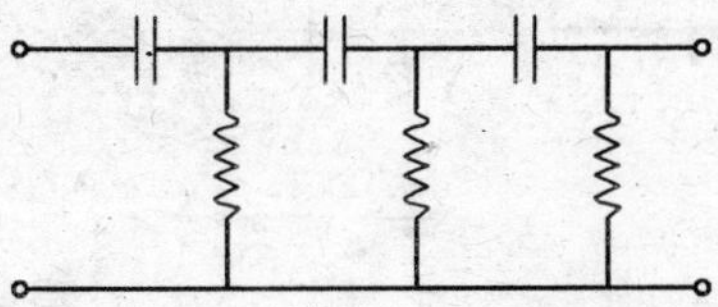

(*a*) 90° (*b*) 180°
(*c*) 270° (*d*) 360°

54. If an amplifier with resistive negative feedback has two left half planes poles in its open-loop transfer function then amplifier

(*a*) will always be unstable at high frequencies.
(*b*) will be stable for all frequncies.
(*c*) may be unstable, depending upon the feedback factor.
(*d*) will oscillate at low frequencies.

55. A high Q-quartz crystal exhibits series resonance at the frequency ω_s and parallel resournce at ω_p. Then

(*a*) ω_s is very close but less than ω_p
(*b*) $\omega_s << \omega_p$
(*c*) ω_s is very close, but greater than ω_p
(*d*) $\omega_s >> \omega_p$

56. In a common emitter amplifier, the unbypassed emitter resistance provides

(*a*) voltage-shunt feedback
(*b*) current-series feedback
(*c*) negative-voltage feedback
(*d*) positive-current feedback

57. Given figure represents ac equivalent circuit of a parallel voltage feedback amplifier stage. If h_{fe} , h_{fc} are h parameters in common emitter and common collector operations respectively at Q, then current gain (I_o/I_t) of this stage is

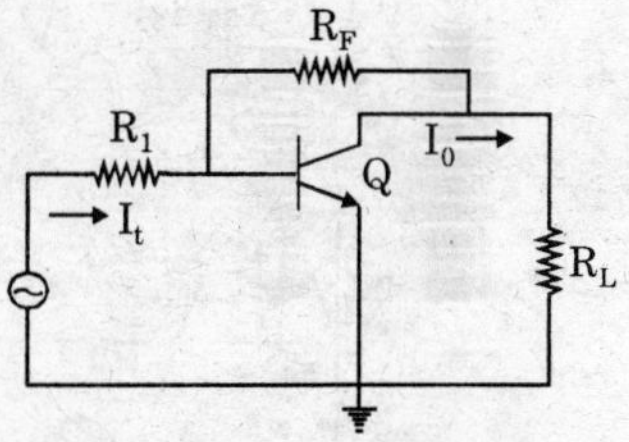

(*a*) $\frac{R_F}{R_L}$
(*b*) h_{fe}
(*c*) $\frac{R_L}{R_F}$
(*d*) h_{fc}

58. An amplifier with mid-band gain |A| = 500 has negative feedback $\beta = \frac{1}{100}$. If upper cut-off without feedback were at 60 Hz, then with feedback it would become

(*a*) 10 kHz (*b*) 12 kHz
(*c*) 300 kHz (*d*) 360 kHz

59. Feedback factor for the circuit shown in the given figure is

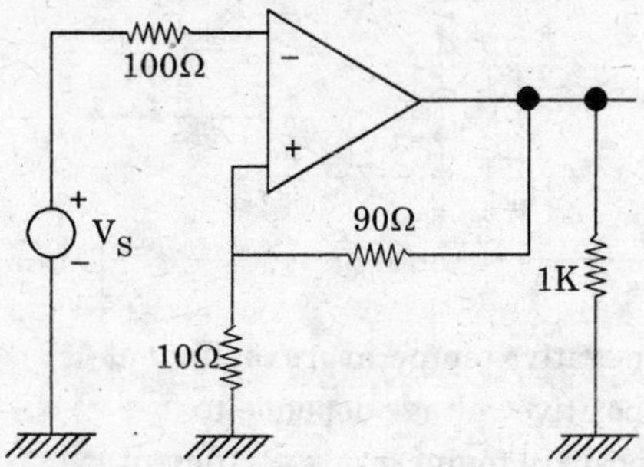

(*a*) 9/100 (*b*) 9/10
(*c*) 1/9 (*d*) 1/100

OPERATIONAL AMPLIFIER

60. If differential amplifier has a differential gain of 20,000. CMRR = 80 dB, then common mode gain is

(*a*) 2
(*b*) 1
(*c*) 1/2
(*d*) 0

61. In the OP-AMP circuit shown in the given figurs V_0 is given by

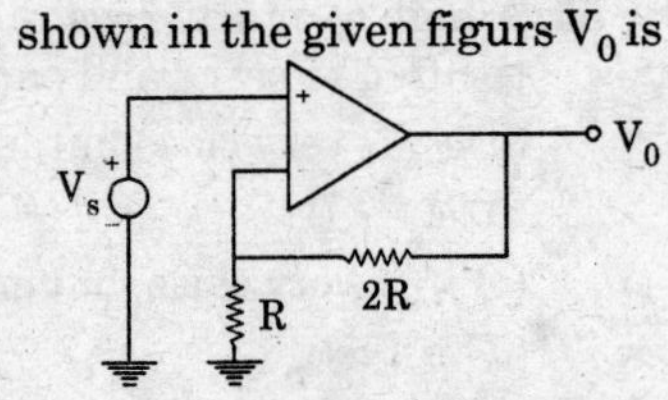

(*a*) $2V_s$
(*b*) $-2V_s$
(*c*) $3V_s$
(*d*) $-3V_s$

62. OPAMP used as a tuned amplifier has the tuned circuit connected

(*a*) across input
(*b*) across series impedance at the input
(*c*) across feedback impedance Z_f
(*d*) across output

63. For the circuit shown in the given figure, assuming ideal diodes, output waveform V_0 will be

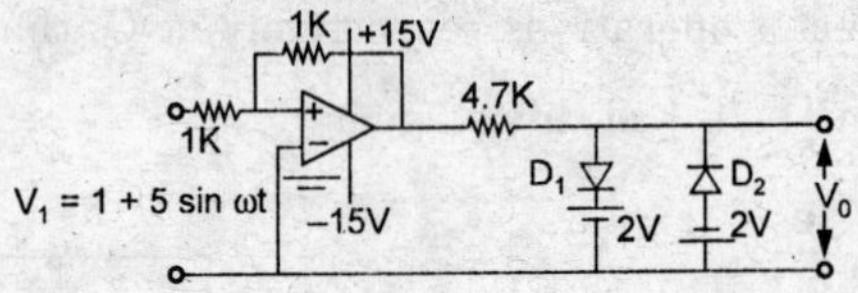

(*a*)

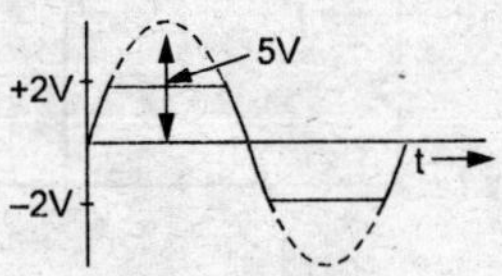

(*b*)

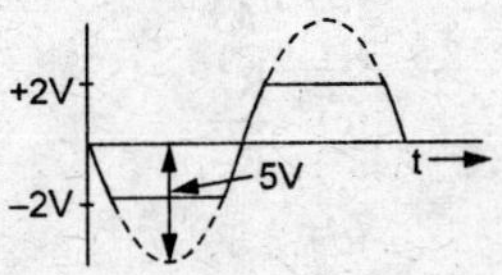

(*c*)

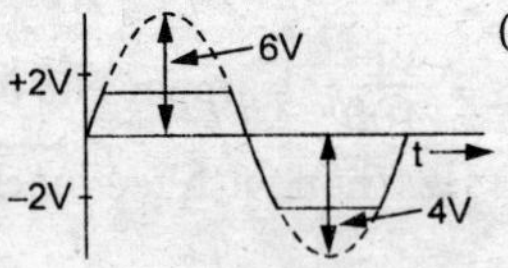

(*d*)

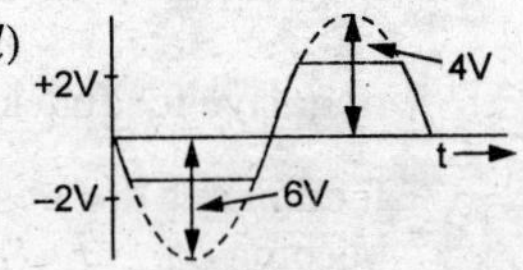

64. In the OP-AMP based Wein bridge RC Oscillator shown in the given figure, R_2 is invariably a resistor having

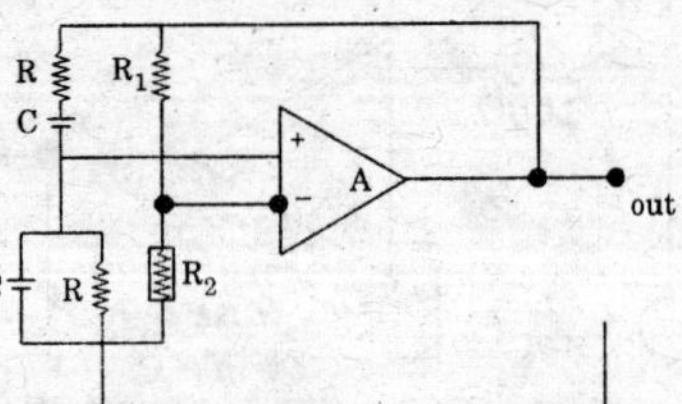

(*a*) negative temperature coefficient
(*b*) positive voltage dependence
(*c*) positive temperature coefficient
(*d*) negative voltage dependence

65. An OP-AMP has a slew rate of 5 V/μs. The largest sinewave output voltage possible at a frequency of 1 MHz is

(*a*) 10 π volts
(*b*) 5 volts
(*c*) $\frac{5}{\pi}$ volts
(*d*) $\frac{5}{2\pi}$ volts

66. Total offset voltage for the circuit shown below with given input offset voltageV_{IO} = 4 mV, and input offset current I_{10} = 150 mA will be

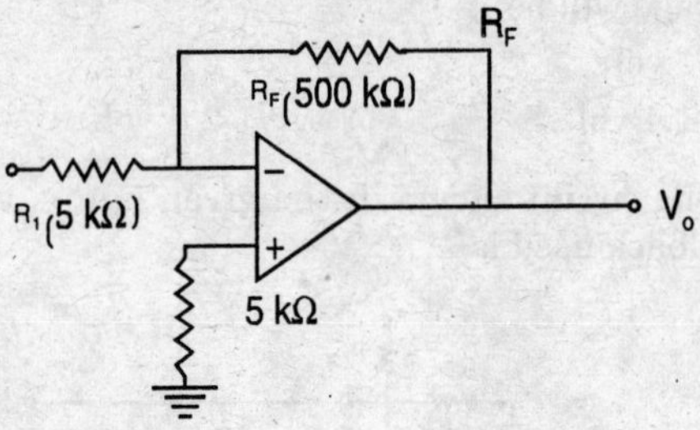

(*a*) 404 mV (*b*) 479 mV
(*c*) 329 mV (*d*) zero

67. Output voltage of an OP-AMP for input voltage of V_{i1} = 150 μV, V_{i2} = 140 μV if amplifier has a differential gain of A_d = 4000 and value of CMRR is 100, is

(*a*) 45.8 mV (*b*) 40.006 mV
(*c*) 10 μV (*d*) 145μV

68. A circuit using an OPAMP shown below, has

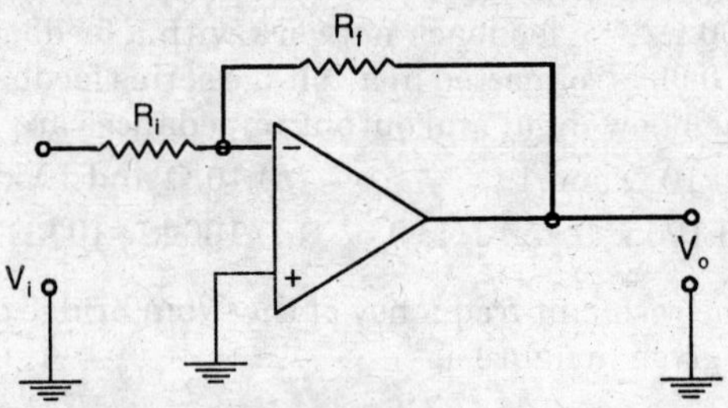

(*a*) voltage series feedback
(*b*) voltage shunt feedback
(*c*) current shunt feedback
(*d*) current series feedback

69. Output of the OPAMP shown below will be (assuming it to be ideal)

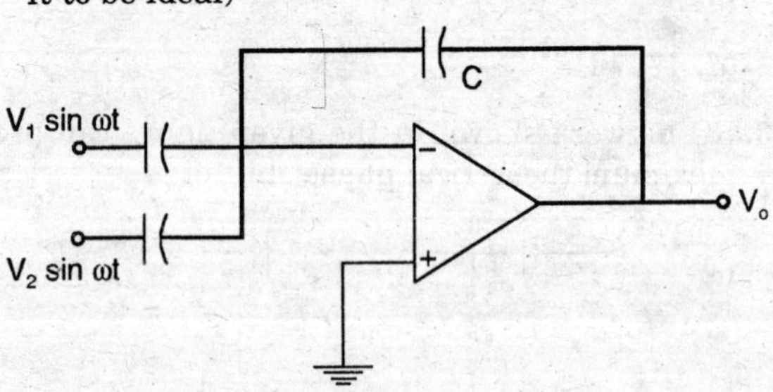

(*a*) zero
(*b*) $-(V_1-V_2)$ sin ωt
(*c*) $+(V_1+V_2)$ sin ωt
(*d*) $-(V_1+V_2)$ sin ωt

70. Given circuit shows is an OP-AMP based. The ratio V_{out}/V_{in} is equal to

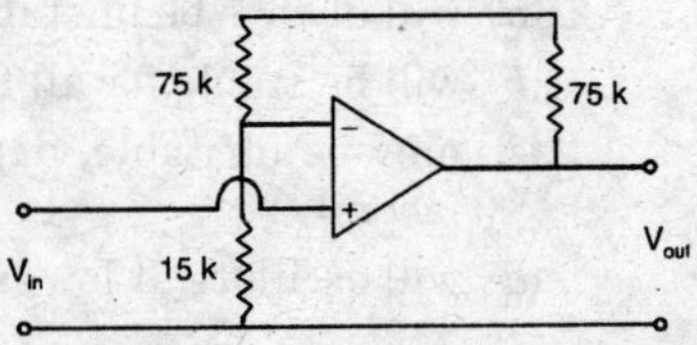

(*a*) 9
(*b*) 11
(*c*) 10
(*d*) 21

71. In the circuit shown in the figure, if CMRR of the OP-AMP is 60dB, then magnitude of the v_o is

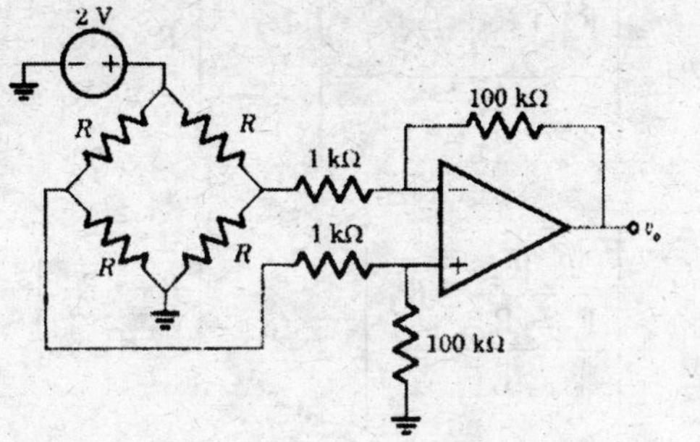

(*a*) 1 mV (*b*) 2 mV
(*c*) 100 mV (*d*) 200 mV

72. In the given circuit, V_{in} = 10 mV dc maximum, maximum possible output offset voltage V_{oo} caused by the input voltage V_{io} with respect to ground is

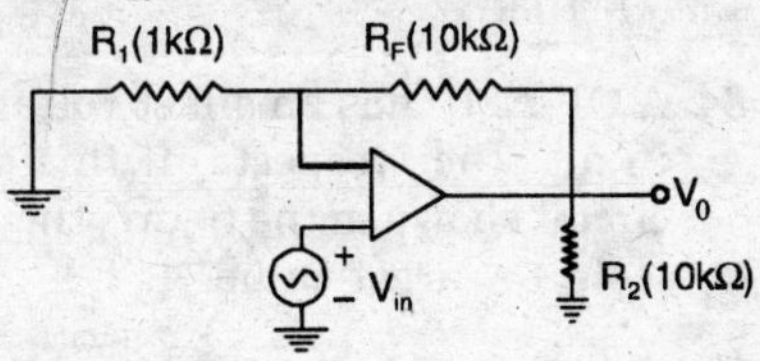

(*a*) 60 mV dc
(*b*) 110 mV dc
(*c*) 130 mV dc
(*d*) 150 mV dc

73. If I.C. amplifier shown in the figure has an input voltage V_i = 0.1 cos (2π × 100t) volts, then waveform of the output voltage V_0 is

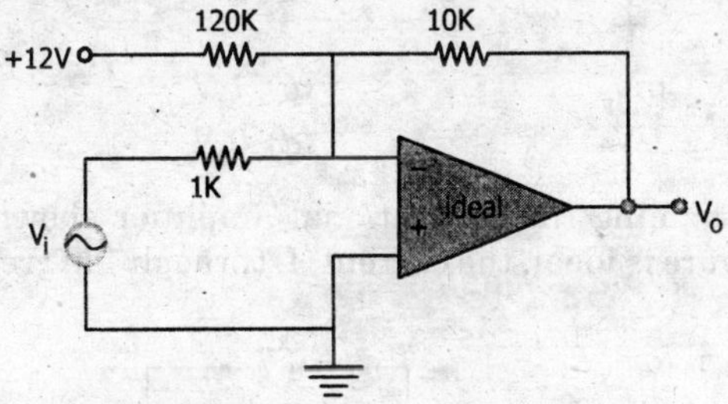

(*a*)
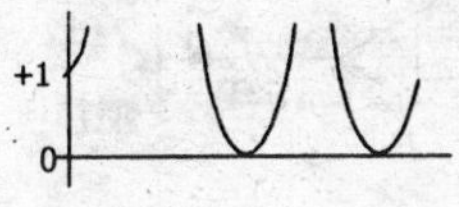
(*b*)
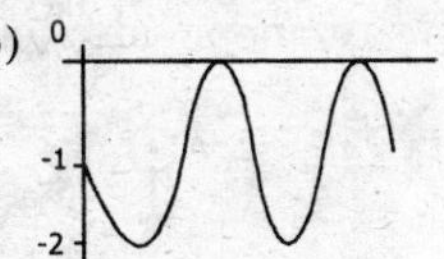
(*c*)
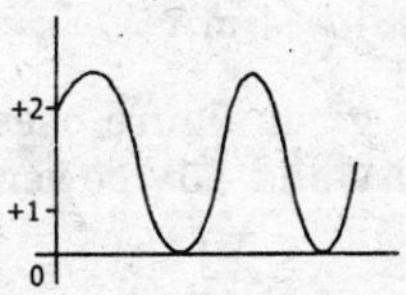
(*d*)
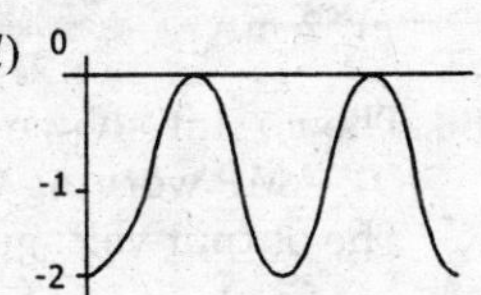

74. Magnitude of the gain in the inverting op-amp amplifier circuit shown in the figure be x with switch S_1 open. When switch S_1 is closed, then magnitude of gain becomes

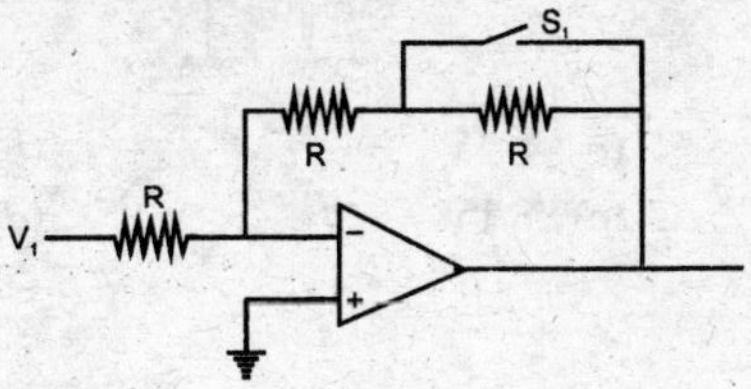

(*a*) $\frac{x}{2}$
(*b*) $-x$
(*c*) $2x$
(*d*) $-2x$

75. In an non-inverting OP-AMP summer is shown in the figure, output voltage V_o will be

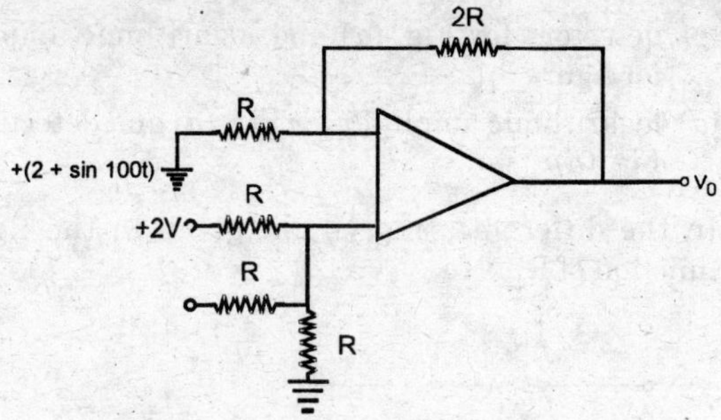

(*a*) $\left(\frac{3}{2}\right)$ sin (100t) (*b*) 3 sin (100t)
(*c*) sin (100 t) (*d*) 2 sin (100 t)

76. The common mode voltage is completely alternated at the output of the differential amplifier shown in the figure, if

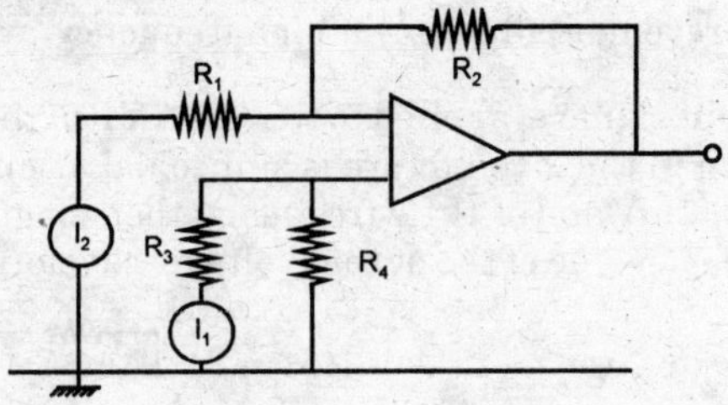

(*a*) $R_1 + R_2 = R_3 + R_4$ (*b*) $R_1 - R_2 = R_3 - R_4$

(*c*) $\frac{R_1}{R_2} = \frac{R_3}{R_4}$ (*d*) $\frac{R_2}{R_1} = \frac{R_3}{R_4}$

77. Output voltage V_o in the given amplifier circuit is

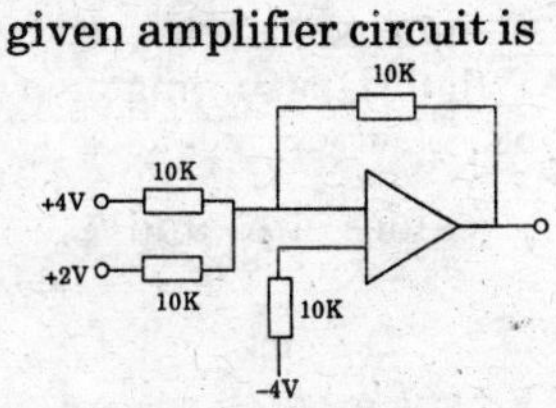

(*a*) 4 V
(*b*) 6 V
(*c*) 8 V
(*d*) 10 V

78. The circuit connection of OP-AMP given in the Fig. (*a*) and Fig. (*b*) represent

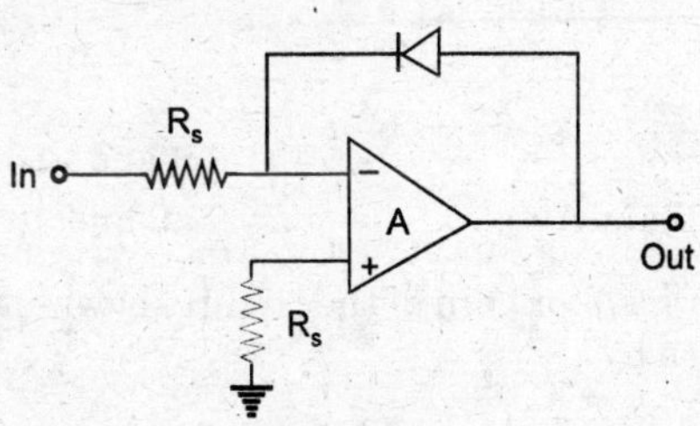

Fig. (*a*)

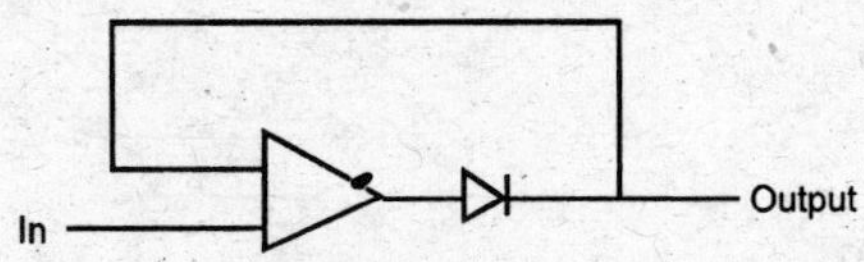

Fig. (*b*)

(*a*) logarithmic amplifiers for both Fig. (*a*) and (*b*)

(*b*) detectors for both Fig. (*a*) and (*b*)

(*c*) detectors for Fig. (*a*) and logarithmic amplifier for figure (b)

(*d*) logarithmic amplifier for Fig. (*a*) and detector for Fig. (*b*)

79. In the differentiating circuit given in the figure, function of R_1 is to

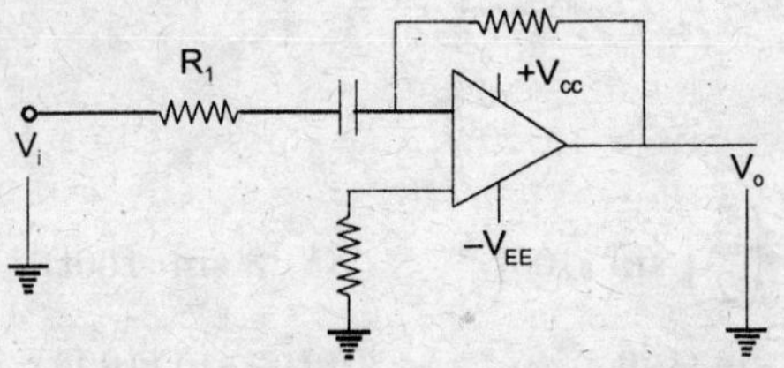

(*a*) enable circuit to approach ideal differentiator

(*b*) maintain high input impedance

(*c*) eliminate high frequency noise spikes

(*d*) prevent oscillations at high frequency

80. If input signal e_i applied to the OP-AMP of the circuit shown in the given figure is sinusoidal at maximum value 1 mV and of 1kHz frequency, then magnitude of the peak value of the output voltage waveform would be

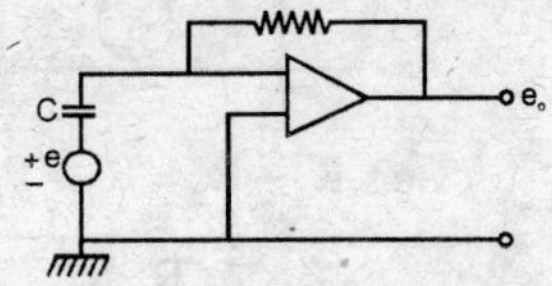

(*a*) 1.59 mV

(*b*) 6.28 mV

(*c*) 159 mV

(*d*) 628 mV

81. Expression for the output voltage V_o in terms of the input voltage V_1 and V_2 in the circuit shown in the figure, assuming operational amplifier to be ideal is

$$V_o = A_1V_1 + A_2V_2$$

Values of A_1 and A_2 would be respectively

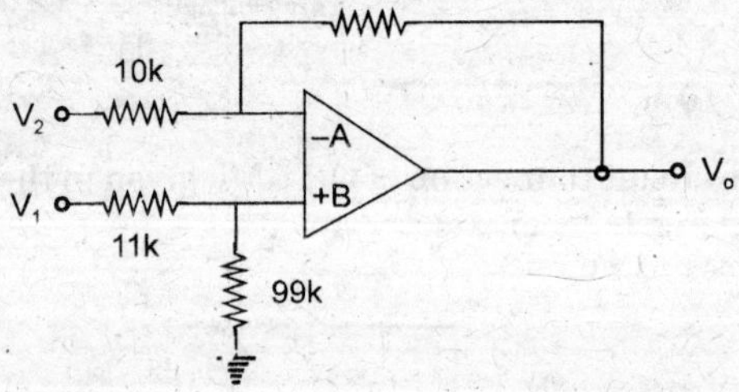

(*a*) 9 and – 10 (*b*) 9.9 and –10

(*c*) – 9 and 10 (*d*) –9.9 and 10

82. The transistor gain of the circuit shown in the figure is given by

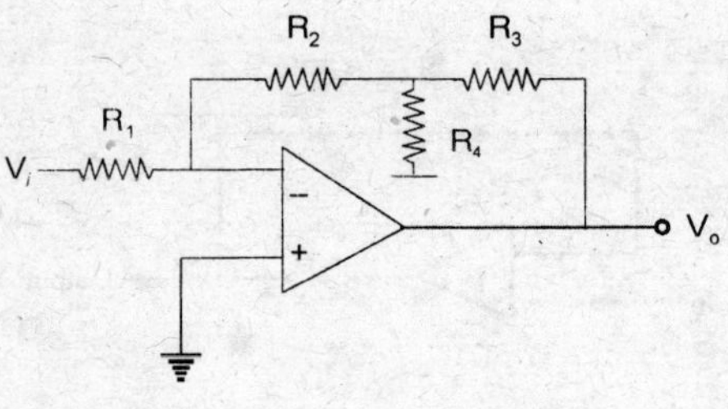

(*a*) $-\left[\dfrac{R_2 + R_3 + \dfrac{R_2R_3}{R_4}}{R_1}\right]$ (*b*) $-\left[\dfrac{\dfrac{R_3R_4}{R_3+R_4} + R_2}{R_1}\right]$

(*c*) $-\left[\dfrac{\dfrac{R_2R_4}{R_2+R_4} + R_3}{R_1}\right]$ (*d*) $-\left[\dfrac{R_2 + R_3}{R_1}\right]$

83. An op-amp is open-loop gain of 10^5 and open-loop upper cut-off frequency of 10 Hz. If this OP-AMP is connected as an amplifier with a closed-loop gain at 100, then new uper cut-off frequency will be

(*a*) 10 Hz (*b*) 100 Hz

(*c*) 10 kHz (*d*) 100 kHz

84. A OP-AMP has an offset voltage of 1m V and is ideal in all other respects. If this op-amp is used in the circuit shown in the figure, then output voltage will be (select nearest value)

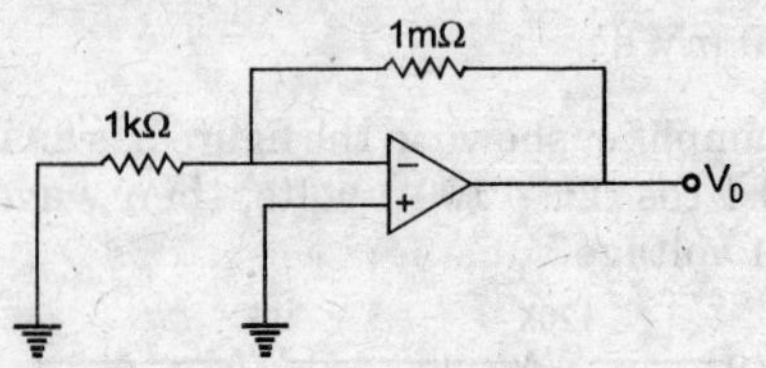

(*a*) 1 mV (*b*) 1 V

(*c*) ± 1 V (*d*) 0 V

85. Assuming that operational amplifier shown in the figure is ideal, the current, I, through 1 kΩ resistor is

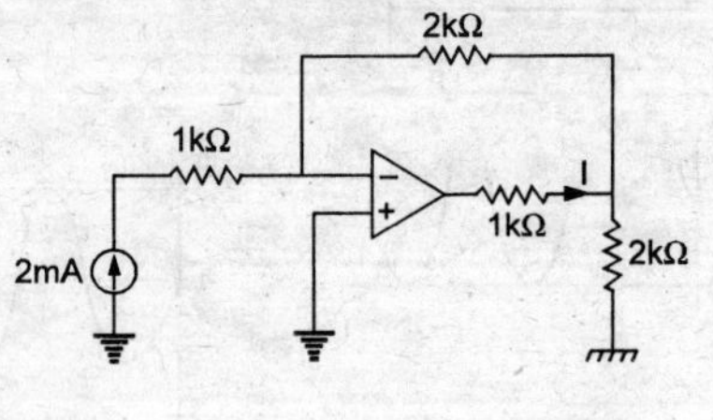

(*a*) – 4 mA (*b*) – 2 mA

(*c*) 2 mA (*d*) 4 mA

86. The circuit shown in the given figure uses an ideal OP-AMP working with +5V and – 5V power supplies. The output voltage V_0 is

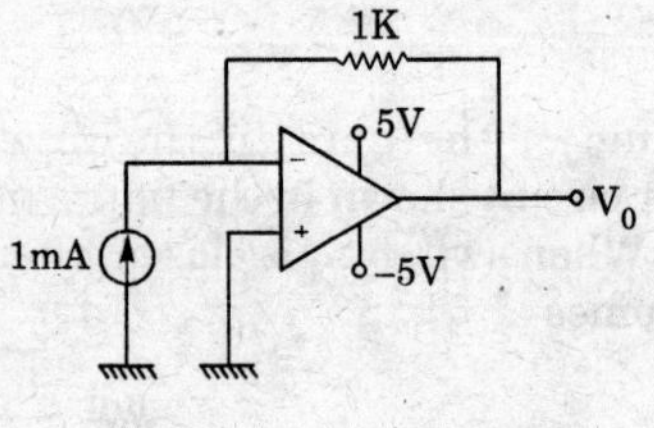

(*a*) + 5V (*b*) – 5V

(*c*) + 1V (*d*) – 1V

87. In the circuit of shown in the figure, LED will be ON if v_i is

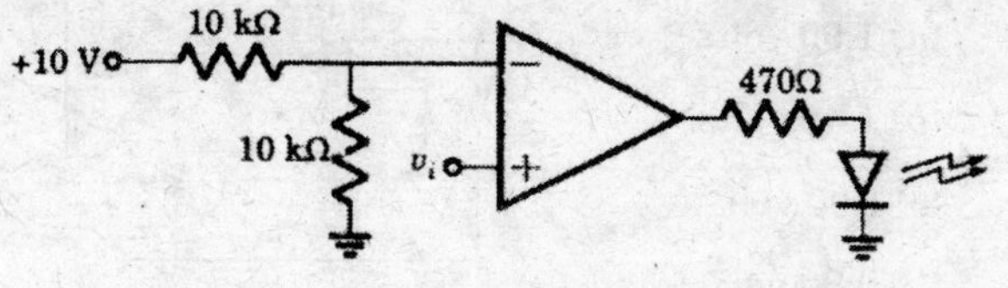

(*a*) > 10 V (*b*) < 10 V

(*c*) > 5 V (*d*) < 5 V

88. An op-amp, having a slew rate of 62.8 V/msec, is connected in a voltage follower configuration. If maximum amplitude of the input sinusoid is 10 V, then minimum frequency at which slew rate limited distortion would set in at the output is

(*a*) 1.0 MHz (*b*) 6.28 MHz

(*c*) 10.0 MHz (*d*) 62.8 MHz

89. For the circuit of the given figure with an ideal operational amplifier, maximum phase shift of the output V_{out} with reference to the input V_{in} is

(*a*) 0° (*b*) – 90°

(*c*) + 90° (*d*) + 180°

90. Assuming operational amplifier to be ideal, gain V_{out}/V_{in} for the circuit shown in the given figure is

(*a*) – 1

(*b*) – 20

(*c*) – 100

(*d*) – 120

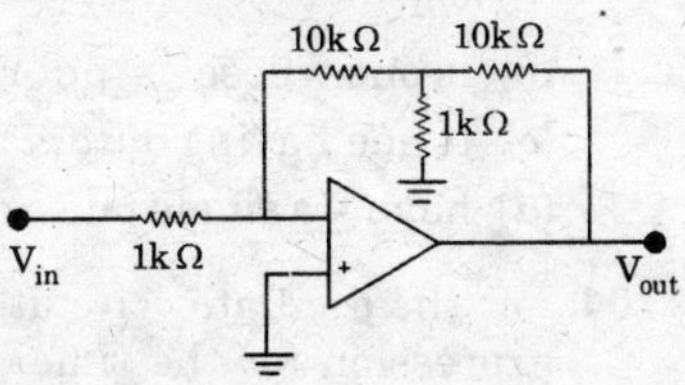

91. In circuit shown in the figure if input voltage v_i is 0.2 V, then output voltage v_0 is

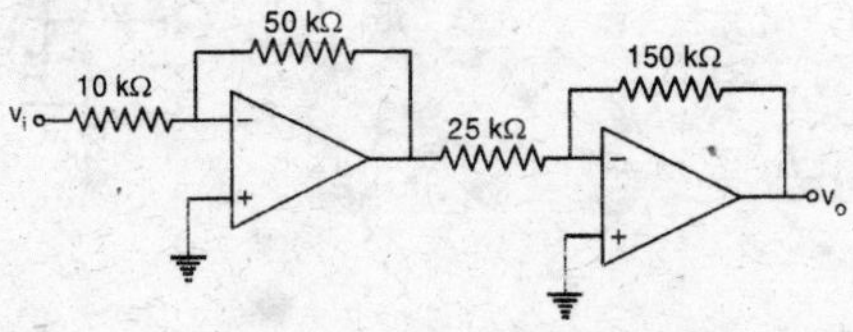

(*a*) 6 V (*b*) – 6 V

(*c*) 8 V (*d*) – 8 V

92. For the op-amp circuit shown in figure, the voltage gain $A_v = v_0/v_i$ is

(*a*) – 8

(*b*) 8

(*c*) – 10

(*d*) 10

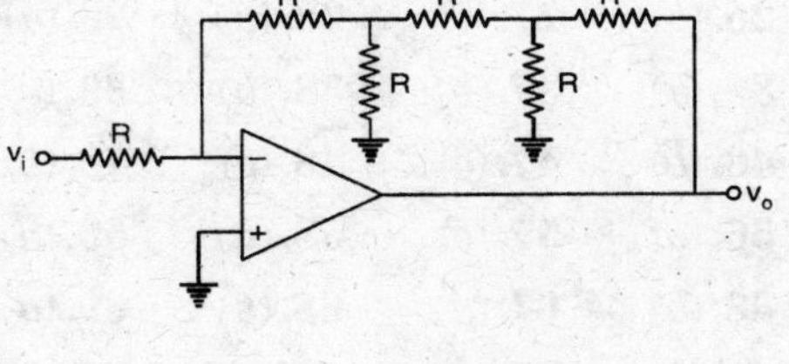

93. For the circuit shown in figure, true relation is

(*a*) $v_{o1} = v_{o2}$

(*b*) $v_{o1} = -v_{o2}$

(*c*) $v_o = 2v_{o2}$

(*d*) $2v_{o1} = v_{o2}$

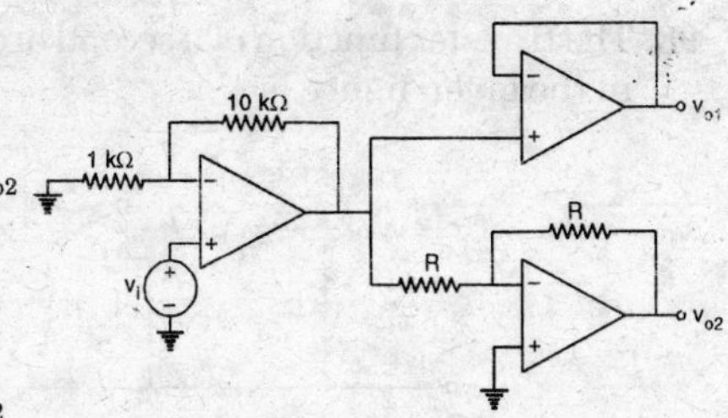

94. In the circuit given in figure, op-amp slew rate is SR = 0.5 V/μs. If amplitude of input signal is 0.02 V, then maximum frequency that may be used is

(*a*) 0.55×10^6 rad/s

(*b*) 0.55 rad/s

(*c*) 1.1×10^6 rad/s

(*d*) 1.1 rad/s

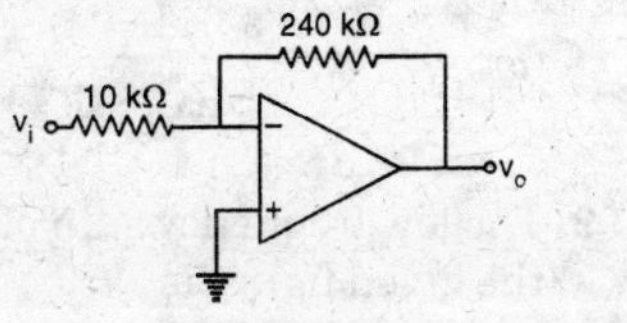

95. If phase shift oscillator shown in the given figure operte at f = 80 kHz, value of resistance R_F is

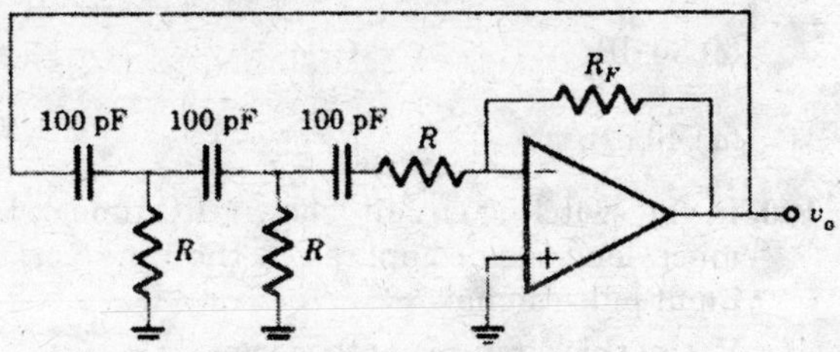

(*a*) 236 kΩ (*b*) 148 kΩ

(*c*) 438 kΩ (*d*) None of these

96. For the circuit in the figure output voltage is $v_0 = 2.5$ V in response to input voltage $v_i = 5$ V. Finite open-loop differential gain of the OP-AMP is

(*a*) 5×10^4

(*b*) 250.5

(*c*) 2×10^4

(*d*) 501

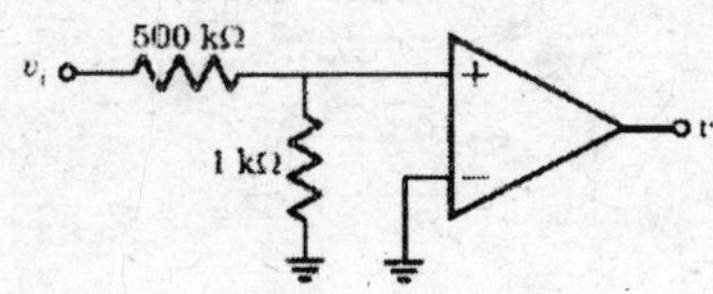

97. In the circuit shown in the given figure, OP-AMP is ideal. If $\beta_F = 60$, then total current supplied by the 15 V source is

(*a*) 123. 1 mA

(*b*) 98.3 mA

(*c*) 49.4 mA

(*d*) 168 mA

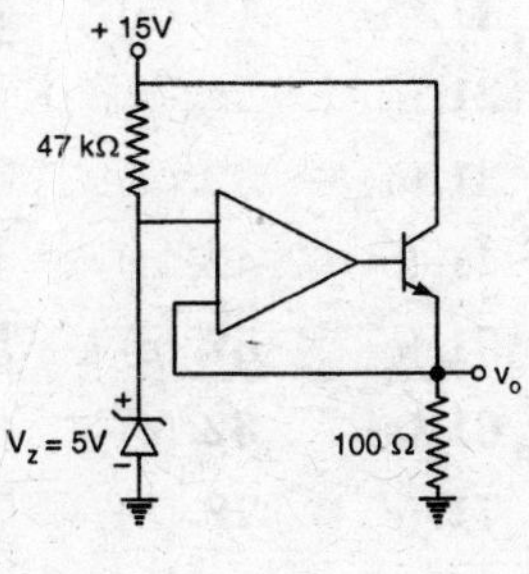

FILTERS

98. The transfer function of a second order LP filter shown in the given figure is

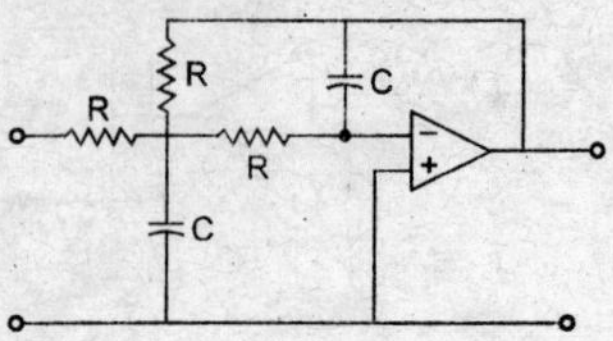

(a) $\frac{1}{R^2C^2s^2+3RCs+1}$ (b) $\frac{RCs}{R^2C^2s^2+3RCs+1}$

(c) $\frac{R^2C^2s^2+1}{R^2C^2s^2+3RCs+1}$ (d) $\frac{R^2C^2s^2}{R^2C^2s^2+3RCs+1}$

99. The low frequency gain of the low pass filter shown in the given figure is

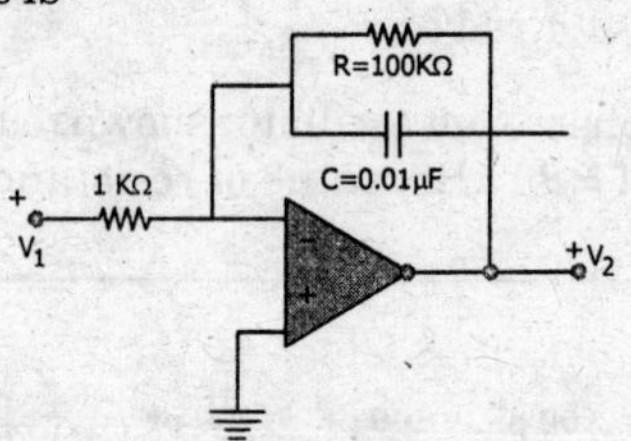

(a) 10 dB

(b) 20 dB

(c) 30 dB

(d) 40 dB

100. In the switcling circuit shown, RC time constant is much longer as compared to the time period of its input pulse signal.

V_{out} of this circuit is of the form

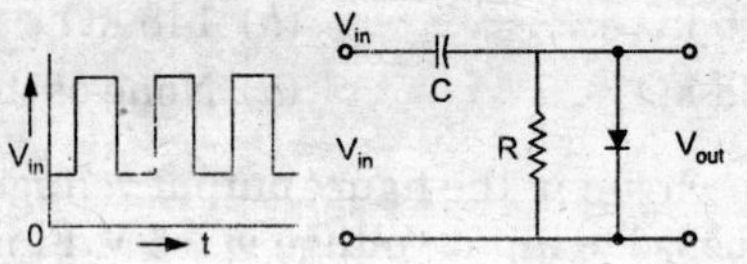

(a) 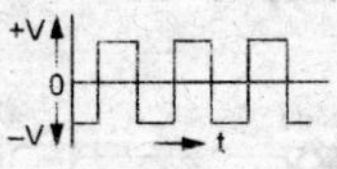 (b) 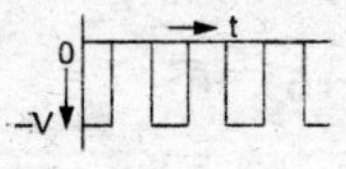

(c) 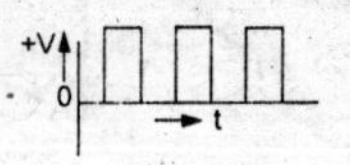 (d) 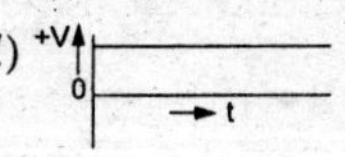

101. What is the hysterisis voltage of the submitt trigger shown if $V_{sat} = \pm 10V$?

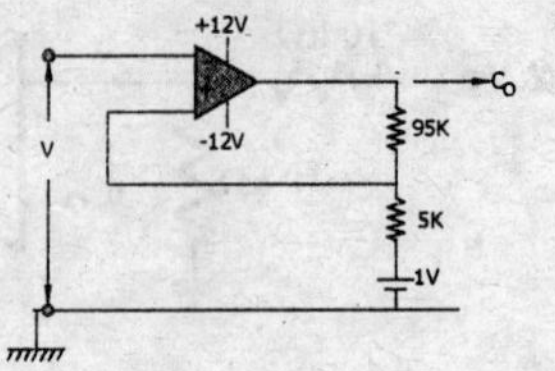

(a) 1.90 volts

(b) 1.45 volts

(c) 1.00 volt

(d) 0.90 volt

102. The period of the output waveform for the circuit of figure shown, when triggered by a negative pulse is

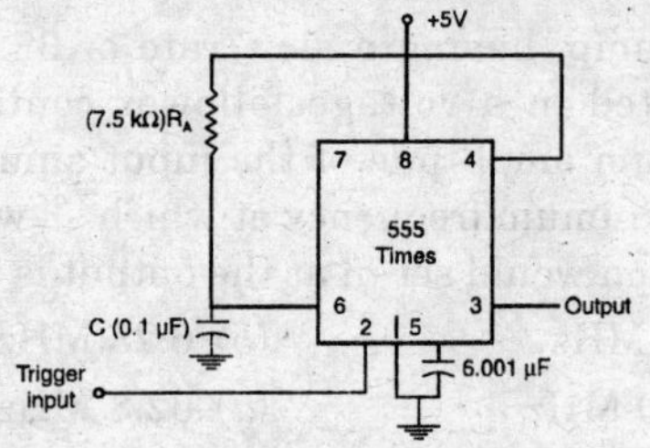

(a) 0.75 ms (b) 0.825 ms

(c) 0.525 ms (d) 1.5 ms

103. The circuit shown in the figure

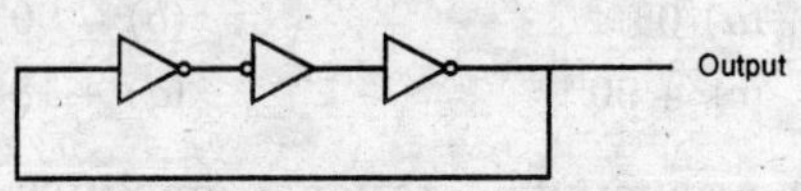

(a) is an oscillating circuit and its output is a square wave

(b) is one whose output remains stable in '1' state

(c) is one having output semains stable in '0' state

(d) having a single pulse of 3 times propagation delay.

104. For the oscillator circuit shown in the given figure, expression for the time period of oscillation can be given by (where t = RC)

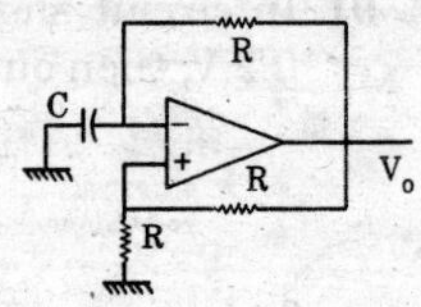

(a) $\tau \ln 3$

(b) $2\tau \ln 3$

(c) $\tau \ln 2$

(d) $2\tau \ln 2$

ANSWERS

1. (b)	2. (b)	3. (b)	4. (c)	5. (a)	6. (b)	7. (b)	8. (b)	9. (c)	10. (c)
11. (b)	12. (b)	13. (c)	14. (b)	15. (d)	16. (d)	17. (b)	18. (c)	19. (a)	20. (a)
21. (a)	22. (d)	23. (a)	24. (d)	25. (a)	26. (b)	27. (c)	28. (d)	29. (a)	30. (a)
31. (a)	32. (a)	33. (a)	34. (a)	35. (a)	36. (a)	37. (b)	38. (b)	39. (b)	40. (c)
41. (c)	42. (a)	43. (b)	44. (a)	45. (b)	46. (b)	47. (c)	48. (c)	49. (b)	50. (b)
51. (c)	52. (c)	53. (b)	54. (b)	55. (a)	56. (c)	57. (c)	58. (d)	59. (d)	60. (a)
61. (c)	62. (c)	63. (d)	64. (c)	65. (d)	66. (b)	67. (a)	68. (b)	69. (d)	70. (b)
71. (c)	72. (b)	73. (d)	74. (a)	75. (b)	76. (b)	77. (d)	78. (d)	79. (b)	80. (d)
81. (b)	82. (a)	83. (c)	84. (c)	85. (a)	86. (d)	87. (c)	88. (a)	89. (d)	90. (d)
91. (a)	92. (a)	93. (b)	94. (c)	95. (a)	96. (b)	97. (c)	98. (a)	99. (d)	100. (b)
101. (c)	102. (b)	103. (a)	104. (b)						

EXPLANATIONS

2. $v_0 = \dfrac{333}{20}(v_{01} - v_{02})$

$v_{01} = -v_{BE1} - V_t \ln\left(\dfrac{i_{c1}}{i_s}\right),$

$v_{02} = -v_{BE2} - V_t \ln\left(\dfrac{i_{c2}}{i_s}\right)$

$v_{01} - v_{02} = -V_t \ln\left(\dfrac{i_{c1}}{i_{c2}}\right) = V_t \ln\left(\dfrac{i_{c2}}{i_{c1}}\right)$

$i_{c1} = \dfrac{v_1}{R_1}, \quad i_{c2} = \dfrac{v_2}{R_2}$

$v_{01} - v_{02} = V_t \ln\left(\dfrac{v_2}{R_2}\dfrac{R_1}{v_1}\right), \quad V_t = 0.0259\text{ V}$

$v_0 = \dfrac{333}{20}(v_{01} - v_{02})$

$= \dfrac{333}{20}(0.0259)\ln\left(\dfrac{v_2}{v_1}\dfrac{R_1}{R_2}\right) = 0.4329 \ln\left(\dfrac{v_2}{v_1}\dfrac{R_1}{R_2}\right)$

$= 0.4329\,(2.3026)\log_{10}\left(\dfrac{v_2}{v_1}\dfrac{R_1}{R_2}\right) = \log_{10}\left(\dfrac{v_2}{v_1}\dfrac{R_1}{R_2}\right)$

4. From the figure,

$I_B = \dfrac{5 - V_{BE}}{100K} = \dfrac{4.2}{100K} = 4.2\text{ mA}$

$I_c = \dfrac{4.8}{5}\text{ mA}$

Since $(I_B)_{min} = \dfrac{I_C}{h_{FE}} \le I_B,$

hence the transistor will operate in saturation region.

6. $I_{D1} = K_{n1}(V_{GS1} - V_{TN})^2 = K_{n2}(V_{GS2} - V_{TN})^2$

$V_{GS1} = 5 - V_{GS2}$

$\Rightarrow \quad (5 - V_{GS2} = -1)^2 = 200(V_{GS2} - 1)^2$

$\Rightarrow \quad V_{GS2} = 2.76\text{ V},\ V_{GS1}\ 2.24\text{ V}$

$I_{D1} = 400 \times 10^{-6}(2.24 - 1)^2 = 0.62\text{ mA}$

7. $V_{GS2} = V_{GS3} = 2.76\text{ V}$

$I_{D4} = K_{n4}(V_{GS4} - V_{TN})^2 = K_{n3}(V_{GS3} - V_{TN})^2$

$= 100 \times 10^{-6}(2.76 - 1)^2 = 0.31\text{ mA}$

10. MOSFET switch in ON state is equivalent to a capacitor.

11. For collector to ground which is the same as emitter terminal to read full supply voltage at 20 V, no current should be drawn and this can happen if emitter to ground connection is open as then there will be neither I_H or I_C.

12. PIV across each diode = $2 \times 280\sqrt{2}$ volts.

When diode is conducting (during half cycle) voltage across the diode is zero.

Hence rms value of the voltage across the diode

$= \dfrac{PIV}{2} = 280\sqrt{2} = $ **395.3 V**

13. $I_C \simeq I_E = \dfrac{(4 - 0.7)}{3.3\text{ k}\Omega}$ volt = 1 mA

$\therefore \quad V_C = 8 - 3.7 \times 1 = $ **4.3 volts**

14. Diode D_1 conducts through 10 kΩ on the extreme right and diode D_2 is blocked. Diode D_2 conducts through 10kΩ in the middle branch and diode D_1 is blocked. Thus source always sees a resistance of 10 kΩ.

15. $I_C = \dfrac{I_{CO}}{1-\alpha} + \dfrac{\alpha}{1-\alpha}I_B = \dfrac{6}{1-0.98} + \dfrac{0.98}{1-0.98} \times 100$

= **5.2 mA**

16. The diode will not conduct in the negative half of the wave and while it conducts, there will be a small voltage drop across it, shown as 0.06 V on (*d*)

17. $I_B = \dfrac{V_{CC} - V_{BE}}{R_B} = \dfrac{12 - 0.7}{100 \times 10^3} = 0.113\text{ mA}$

$I_C = \beta I_B = 100 \times 0.113 = 11.3\text{ mA}$

$V_{CE} = V_{CC} - I_C R_C$

$= 12 - (11.3 \times 10^{-3} \times 500) = 5.35\text{ V}$

At 75° C $\quad I_B = 0.113\text{ mA}$

$I_C = \beta I_B = 150 \times 0.113 = 16.95\text{ mA}$

$V_{CE} = 12 - (16.95 \times 10^{-3} \times 500)$

$= 3.32\text{ V}$

$\therefore \quad \Delta I_C = \dfrac{16.75 - 11.3}{11.3} \times 100 = 50\,\%$ (increased)

and $\quad \Delta V_{CE} = \dfrac{3.52 - 6.35}{6.35} \times 100$

= **– 44.57% (decreased)**

18. $g_m = g_{mo}\left(1 - \dfrac{V_{GS}}{V_P}\right)$

where g_{mo} is maximum transconductance

$\therefore \quad 1.0 \times 10^{-3} = g_{mo}\left(1 - \left(\dfrac{-3}{-5}\right)\right) = g_{mo}\left(\dfrac{2}{5}\right)$

$\Rightarrow \quad g_{mo} = \dfrac{5.0 \times 10^3}{2} = $ **2.5 mA/V**

23. $I_D = K(V_{GS} - V_{E(TH)})^2$

$\Rightarrow \quad 4mA = K(V_{GS} - 2)^2$

Here, $V_{GS} = 10 - 4 \times 1 = 6$

$\therefore \quad 4 = K(6 - 2)^2$

$\Rightarrow \quad K = \dfrac{4}{16} = \dfrac{1}{4}$

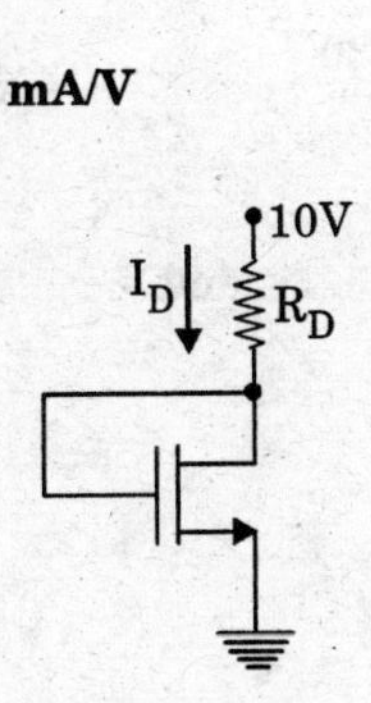

When R_D is increased to 4kΩ,

$$V_{GS} = 10 - 4I_D$$

Now $I_D = \frac{4}{16}(10 - 4I_D - 2)^2$

$\Rightarrow$ $4I_D = (8 - 4I_D)^2 = 64 + 16I_D^2 - 64I_D$

$\Rightarrow$ $16I_D^2 - 68I_D + 64 = 0$

$\Rightarrow$ $4I_D^2 - 17I_D + 16 = 0$

$\Rightarrow$ $I_D = \mathbf{2.8\ mA}$

24. $R_0 = R_L' = R_c \parallel R_p = \frac{4 \times 40}{44} = 3.64\,k\Omega$

$$1 + \beta = \frac{\beta R_C}{R_F + R_C} = 50 \times \frac{4K}{44K} = \frac{50}{11}$$

$$1 + \beta A = D = \frac{61}{11}$$

$$R_{of} = \frac{R_0}{D} = \frac{116}{44} \times \frac{11}{61} = \mathbf{0.66\ k\Omega}$$

28. $A_V = \frac{A_I R_L}{R_i} = \frac{(1 + h_{fe}) R_L}{R_i}$

$$= \frac{(1 + h_{fe}) R_L}{h_{ie}} = \frac{100 \times 0.66K}{1K} = 66$$

$$A_{vs} = \frac{A_V . R_i}{R_i + R_S} = 66 \times \frac{1}{66 + 1} = 0.985 \approx \mathbf{1}$$

29. $I_B = \frac{V_{CC} - V_{BE}}{R_F + \beta R_C}$

$$= \frac{9 - 0.7}{180\,k\Omega + 200 \times 2.7\,k\Omega} = 11.53\,\mu A$$

$I_E = (\beta + 1) I_B$
$= 201 \times 11.53\mu A = 2.32$ mA

$$r_e = \frac{26mV}{I_E} = \frac{26mV}{2.32\,mA} = 11.21\Omega$$

$$\therefore \quad Z_i = \frac{r_e}{\frac{1}{\beta} + \frac{R_C}{R_F}} = \frac{11.21}{0.005 + 0.015} = \mathbf{560.5\ \Omega}$$

30. $f_T = \beta_0 \times f_\beta$
$= (200) \times 1$ MHz $= \mathbf{200\ MHz}$

and $f_\alpha = \frac{f_\beta}{1 - \alpha} = \frac{f_\beta}{1 - \frac{\beta}{1+\beta}}$

$= f_\beta(\beta + 1)$
$= 10^6 (200 + 1) 10^6 \times 201$
$= \mathbf{201\ MHz}$

31. Given : C = 0.3 pF

$$\therefore \quad g_m = \frac{|I_C|(mA)}{26\,mV} = \frac{1}{26}\ A/V.$$

$$\Rightarrow \quad C_\mu = \frac{g_m}{2\pi f_T} = \frac{1/26}{2\pi \times 4 \times 10^8} = \mathbf{15\ pF}$$

32. $I_E = \frac{V_{EE} - V_{BE}}{R_E} = \frac{4 - 0.7}{1.2K} = 2.75$ mA

and $V_{CB} = V_{CC} - I_C R_C$ ..... (assuming $I_C \approx I_E$)
$= 10 - (2.75) \times 2.4 = \mathbf{3.4\ V}$

$$\therefore \quad I_B = \frac{I_C}{\beta} = \frac{2.75}{60} = \mathbf{45.8\ \mu A}$$

33. $I = I_x = \frac{V_{CC} - V_{BE}}{R_x} = \frac{12 - 0.7}{1.1\,k\Omega} = \mathbf{10.27\ mA}$

34. $I = \frac{V_Z - V_{BE}}{R_E} = \frac{6.2 - 0.7}{1.8\,k} = \mathbf{3.06\ mA}$

35. $I_{dc} = \frac{2}{\pi} \times I_L = \frac{2}{\pi} \times \frac{V_L}{R_L} = \frac{2}{\pi} \times \left(\frac{20}{10}\right)$

$$= 1.25\ A \times \frac{2}{\pi} = 0.796\ A$$

$P_{dc} = V_{CC} \times I_{dc} = (30) \times (0.796) = 23.9W$

Power delivered to the load,

$$P_0 = \frac{V_L^2}{2R_L} = \frac{(20)^2}{2 \times 16} = 12.5W$$

$$\%\ \text{efficiency},\ \eta = \frac{P_0}{P_{dc}} \times 100 = \frac{12.5}{23.9} \times 100 = \mathbf{52.3\ \%}$$

36. Cascading amplifier results in higher low–3dB frequency and higher 3–dB frequency.

37. $f_L^* = \frac{f_L}{\sqrt{2^{1/n} - 1}}$

and $f_H^* = f_H \sqrt{2^{1/n} - 1}$

Putting $n = 2$, we have

$f_H \approx$ **3.1 MHz** and $f_L \approx$ **19.3 MHz ≈ 20 Hz**

38. Since B–C junction is not reverse biased, therefore transistor continues to operate in the forward-active-mode.

$$r = \frac{v_{ce}}{g_m V_{ce}} = \frac{1}{g_m}$$

$$\therefore \quad r_\pi = \left(\frac{1}{g_m}\right) \Big\| \, r_0$$

$$r_\pi = \frac{(100)(0.0259)}{2m} = 2.33k\Omega$$

$$\delta_m = \frac{|I_{CQ}|}{V_T} mA/mV = \frac{2m}{0.259} = 77.2\,mA/V$$

$$\Rightarrow \quad \frac{1}{g_m} = 12.95$$

$$r_o = \frac{V_A}{I_{CQ}} = \frac{150}{2m} = 75\,k\Omega$$

$$\therefore \quad r_e = (2.33k)\,||\,(12.95)\,||\,(75k) = 12.87\,\Omega$$

42. Since I_B is constant, hence self-bias is not operative

43. $$g_m = \frac{I_C}{V_T} = \frac{2}{25} = \mathbf{0.08}$$

$$r_\pi = \frac{\beta}{g_m} = \frac{100}{0.8} = \mathbf{1250}$$

45.

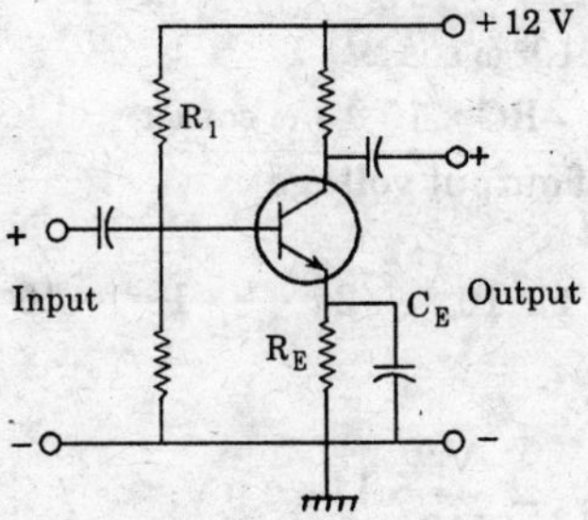

With C_E, voltage gain

$$A_v = \frac{-h_{fe}\,R_L}{h_{ie} + (1+h_{fe})\,R_E}$$

If R_E by passed with capacitor C_E, A_V will increase Hence, after removing C_E mid band voltage gain decreases.

46.

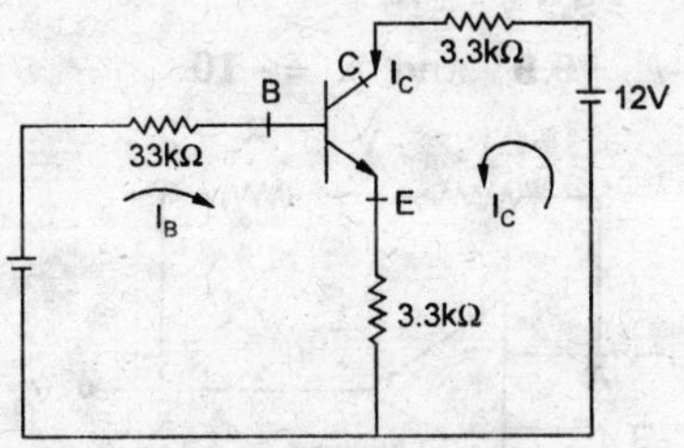

Using KVL in B – E loop, we get

$$4 - 33I_B - V_{BE} - 3.3\,I_E = 0$$

$$\Rightarrow \quad \frac{3.3}{33 + 3.3\,(\beta+1)} = I_B \quad [\text{since } I_E = (\beta + 1)\,I_B]$$

$$\rightarrow \quad I_B = \frac{3.3}{33+330}\,mA$$

and $\quad I_C = \beta\,I_B$

$$= \frac{99\,(3.3)}{33+330}\,mA \approx \frac{3.3}{3.3+0.33}\,mA$$

47.

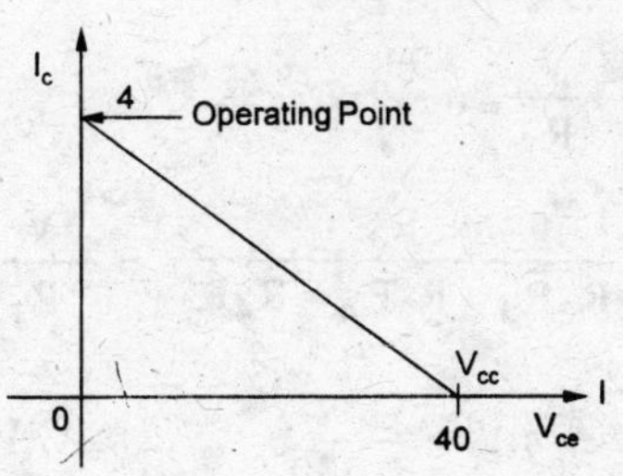

$$V_{ce} = V_{cc} - I_c\,R_c$$

$$= 40 - \beta\,I_\beta \times R_c = -10$$

Since for $I_c = 5$ mA, V_{ce} goes negative, then we take operating point as (0V, 4A), i.e. at the I_c - axis.

48. $$A_f = \frac{A}{1+\beta A}$$

$$\therefore \quad \frac{\partial A_f}{\partial A} = \frac{1+\beta A - \beta A}{(1+\beta A)^2}$$

$$\Rightarrow \quad \partial A_f = \frac{\partial A}{(1+\beta A)^2}$$

$$\therefore \quad \frac{\partial A_f}{A_f} = \frac{\partial A / A}{1+A\beta}$$

$$\Rightarrow \quad \frac{\partial A_f \times 100}{A_f} = \frac{20}{1+100} = \frac{20}{100}\ \mathbf{0.2\%}$$

51. $Z_{if} = Z_i\,(1 + \beta A) = 1\,k\,(1 + 100 \times 0.99) = \mathbf{100\,k\Omega}$

$$Z_{of} = \frac{Z_0}{1+\beta A} = \frac{100}{100} = \mathbf{1\Omega.}$$

52. $$f = \frac{1}{2\pi RC} = \frac{1}{2\pi\,(51\times10^3)\,(0.001\times10^{-6})}$$

$$= \mathbf{3120.7\,Hz}$$

53. Each section having phase shift of 60°, adding up to 180°

59. Feed back factor $= \dfrac{10}{1000} = \dfrac{1}{100}$

60. $$20\log\frac{A_d}{A_c} = 80$$

$$\Rightarrow \quad \frac{A_d}{A_c} = 10^4$$

$$\Rightarrow \quad \frac{A_d}{10^4} = A_c$$

$$\Rightarrow \quad A_c = \frac{2\times10^4}{10^4} = 2$$

61. $$\frac{V_0}{V_s} = \frac{3R}{R} = 3$$

$$\Rightarrow \quad V_0 = 3V_s$$

63. Voltage at OP-AMP output

$$V_1 = -1 - 5\sin\omega t$$

At $\omega t = \dfrac{\pi}{2}$, $\quad V_0 = -6$ volts

At $\omega t = \dfrac{3\pi}{2}$, $\quad V_0 = 4$ volts

During '–' ve cycle of the waveform, when $V_I < -2V$, diode D_2 conducts and $V_0 = -2V$

During '+' ve cycle, when $V_1 > 2V$, D_1 conducts and $V_0 = 2V$.

65. $V = V_m \sin \omega t$

$\therefore \quad \dfrac{dV}{dt} = V_m \,\omega \cos \omega t$

$\Rightarrow \quad \left|\dfrac{dV}{dt}\right|_{max} = V_m\,\omega = 5 \times 10^6$

$\Rightarrow \quad V_m = \dfrac{5 \times 10^6}{2\pi \times 10^6} = \dfrac{5}{2\pi}$ **volts**

66. Offset due to $V_{IO} = V_{IO}\dfrac{R_1 + R_F}{R_1} = (4\text{ mV}).\dfrac{5+500}{5}$

$= \mathbf{404\ mV}$

Offset due to $I_{IO} = I_{IO} \times R_F$

$= (150 \times 10^{-9}) \times 500\text{ k}\Omega = \mathbf{75\ mV}$

$\therefore$ Total offset $= 404 + 75 = \mathbf{479\ mV}$

67. $V_0 = A_d V_d \left(1 + \dfrac{1}{CMRR}.\dfrac{V_c}{V_d}\right)$

$= (400)(10\mu V)\left(1 + \dfrac{1}{100}.\dfrac{145\mu V}{10\mu V}\right) = \mathbf{45.8\ mV}$

68. $I_f = \dfrac{V_i - V_o}{R_f} \approx -\dfrac{V_o}{R_f} = \beta V_o \left[\beta = -\dfrac{1}{R_f}\right]$

As feedback current is proportional to output voltage, it is a voltage-shunt feedback amplifier.

70. $\dfrac{V_o}{V_i} = \dfrac{75+75+15}{15} = \mathbf{11.}$

71. $v_- = (2)\dfrac{R}{2R} = 1V, v_d = 0$

$V_{CM} = \dfrac{v_+ + v_-}{2} = 1$

$v_o = \dfrac{R_F}{1}\dfrac{V_{CM}}{CMRR}$

Here, CMRR = 60 dB = 10^3

$\therefore \quad v_o = \dfrac{100}{1}\dfrac{1}{10^3} = 100\text{ mV}$

72. Applying KVL at the inverting node, we have

$\dfrac{V_{in} - 0}{R_1} + \dfrac{V_{in} - V_0}{R_F} = 0$

$\Rightarrow \quad V_0 = \left(\dfrac{1}{R_1} + \dfrac{1}{R_F}\right)R_F = \mathbf{110\ mV}$

74. $\dfrac{V_o}{V_i} = A = \dfrac{-2R}{R} = -2 = x$

When switch S_1 is closed ,

$A = \dfrac{-R}{R} = -1 = \dfrac{x}{2}$

75. $V_0 = -2\left(1 + \dfrac{2R}{R}\right) + (2 + \sin 100\,t)\left(1 + \dfrac{2R}{R}\right)$

$= -6 + 6 + 3\sin 100\,t = \mathbf{3\sin 100\,t}$

77. $I = \dfrac{4-(-2)}{10}\text{ mA} = 0.6\text{ mA}$

$\therefore \quad V_0 = 4 + 10 \times 0.6 = \mathbf{10\ V}$

80. $\dfrac{0 - e_i}{1/j\omega C} = \dfrac{e_0 - 0}{R}$

$\therefore \quad e_0 = -j\omega RCe_i = -RC\dfrac{de_i}{dt}$

Input voltage, $e_i = 10^3\,\omega \cos \omega t$

$\therefore \quad e_0 = -RC \times 10^{-3} \times \omega \cos \omega t$

Maximum value of output voltage

$= RC\,\omega \times 10^{-3}$

$= 100 \times 10^3 \times 1 \times 10^{-3} \times (2\pi \times 1 \times 10^3) \times 10^{-3}$

$= \mathbf{628\ mV.}$

81. $V_B = V_1 - \dfrac{V_1}{110} \times 11 = 0.9\,V_1$

$V_A = V_B = 0.9\,V_1$

Again $\dfrac{V_0 - V_A}{100K} = \dfrac{V_A - V_2}{10K}$

$\Rightarrow \quad \dfrac{V_0 - 0.9V_1}{100} = \dfrac{0.9V_1 - V_2}{10}$

$\Rightarrow \quad V_0 = 9.9\,V_1 - 10\,V_2$

$\therefore \quad A_1 = \mathbf{9.9}$ and $A_2 = \mathbf{-10}$

82.

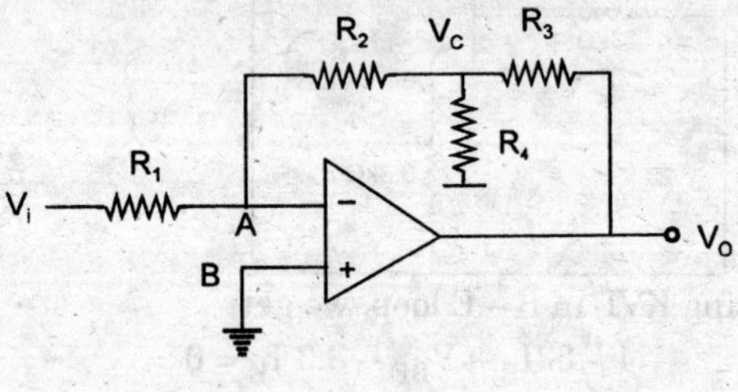

$\dfrac{V_O - V_C}{R_3} = \dfrac{V_C}{R_4} + \dfrac{V_C}{R_2}$

(A and B can be measured to be the same potential)

$V_C = \dfrac{V_O}{R_3}\dfrac{R_2R_3R_4}{R_2R_3 + R_3R_4 + R_4R_2}$

$= V_O\dfrac{R_2R_4}{R_2R_3 + R_3R_4 + R_4R_2}$

Then $\dfrac{V_C}{R_2} + \dfrac{V_i}{R_1} = 0$

$\therefore \quad V_O \cdot \dfrac{R_4}{R_2R_3 + R_3R_4 + R_4R_2} = -\dfrac{V_i}{R_1}$

$\therefore$ Transfer gain,

$$\frac{V_O}{V_i} = -\frac{1}{R_1}\left(\frac{R_2R_3 + R_3R_4 + R_4R_2}{R_4}\right)$$

$$= -\frac{1}{R_1}\left(R_2 + R_3 + \frac{R_2R_3}{R_4}\right)$$

83. Upper cut-off frequency at closed loop gain $= f_o \times (1 + \beta A) = 10 \times 100 =$ **10 kHz**

84. For the given op-amp, we have

$$V_0 = V_{os} \times \text{gain} = \frac{1 \times 10^{-3} \times 10^6}{10^3} = 1\text{ V}$$

It can be either positive or negative i.e. **± 1V.**
voltage follower

85. In this case, $V_0 = 4V$

$$I_s = -\frac{4}{2} = -2\text{ mA}$$

But $I_s = I + 2$

$\therefore$ **I = – 4 mA.**

87. $v_- = \dfrac{(10)(10k)}{10k + 10k} = 5V$

When $v_+ > 5$ V, output will be positive and LED will be ON Hence (c) is correct answer.

88.

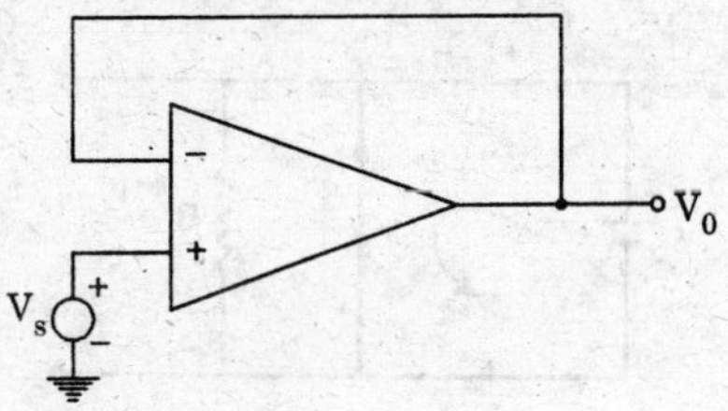

Input, $V_s = V_m \sin \omega t$

Here, $V_m = 10V$

In a voltage follower,

output voltage, $V_0 = V_s$ (input voltage)

$\therefore$ $V_0 = V_m \sin \omega t$

$$\text{Slew rate} = \frac{ds}{dt} = \omega V_m \cos \omega t$$

$$\text{Maximum } \frac{dV_0}{dt} = \omega Vm \geq s \text{ [gain]}$$

$\Rightarrow$ $2\pi f V_m \geq s$

$$\Rightarrow f \geq \frac{s}{2\pi V_m} \geq \frac{62.8}{10^{-6} \times 6.28 \times 10} \geq 10^6 \text{ MHz}$$

$$f_{min} = 1 \text{ MHz}$$

89. From the circuit,

$$V_+ = \frac{V_{in}}{1 + j\omega RC}$$

and $V_- = V_+$ (Ideal OPAMP)

$$\text{Now } \frac{V_{in} - V_-}{R_1} = \frac{V_- - V_0}{R_1}$$

$\Rightarrow$ $V_0 = 2V_- - V_{in} = 2V_+ - V_{in}$

$$= \left[\frac{2}{1 + j\omega RC} - 1\right]V_{in} = \frac{1 - j\omega RC}{1 + j\omega RC} V_0$$

$\therefore$ $\angle(V_0/V_i) = -2\tan^{-1}\omega RC$

For $-90° \leq \theta \leq 90°$

Phase-shift $\angle(V_0/V_i) = \pm 180°$

90.

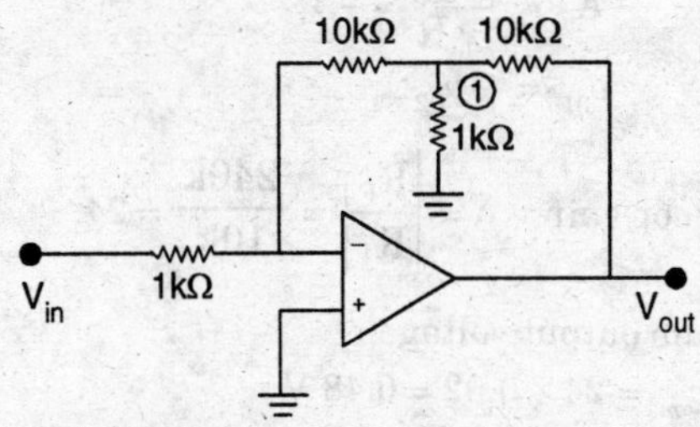

Using KCL at the node 1 we have

$$\frac{V - 0}{10} + \frac{V}{1} + \frac{V - V_{out}}{10} = 0$$

$\Rightarrow$ $12V = V_{out}$ ...(*i*)

Also, using KCL at inverting node, we get

$$\frac{V_{in} - 0}{1} = \frac{0 - V}{10}$$

$\Rightarrow$ $V = -V_{in} . 10$ ...(*ii*)

From equations (*i*) and (*ii*), we get

$$\frac{V_{out}}{V_{in}} = -\mathbf{120}$$

91. Gain of first stage, $A_{v1} = -\dfrac{50}{10} = -5$

Gain of second stage, $A_{v2} = -\dfrac{150}{25} = -6$

Total gain $A_v = A_{v1}A_{v2} = 30$

$v_0 = 30 \times 0.2 = 6$ V

92. $\dfrac{0 - v_i}{R} + \dfrac{0 - v_1}{R} = 0$

$\Rightarrow$ $v_1 = -v_i$

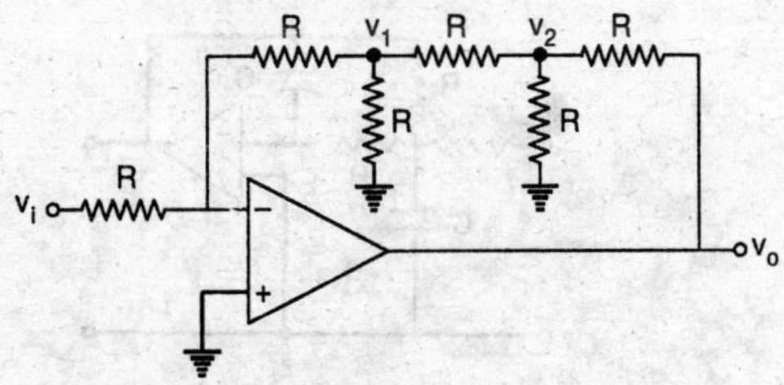

$$\text{Now } \frac{v_1 - 0}{R} + \frac{v_1 - v_2}{R} + \frac{v_1}{R} = 0$$

$\Rightarrow$ $3v_1 = v_2$

$\therefore$ $v_2 = -3v_i$

$$\therefore \frac{v_2 - v_1}{R} + \frac{v_2}{R} + \frac{v_2 - v_0}{R} = 0$$

$$\Rightarrow \quad -3v_i + v_i - 3v_i - 3v_i = v_0$$

$$\Rightarrow \quad \frac{v_0}{v_i} = -8$$

93. At second stage input to both op-amp circuit is same.
Upper op-amp circuit is buffer having gain, $A_V = 1$.
Lower op-amp circuit is inverting amplifier having gain

$$A_v = -\frac{R}{R} = -1.$$

$$\therefore \quad v_{01} = -v_{02}$$

94. Closed loop gain, $A = \left|\frac{R_F}{R_1}\right| = \frac{240k}{10k} = 24$

Maximum output voltage,

$$v_{om} = 24 \times 0.02 = 0.48 \text{ V}$$

$$\omega \le \frac{SR}{v_{om}} = \frac{0.5/\mu}{0.48} = 1.1 \times 10^6 \text{ rad/s}$$

95. Oscillation frequency

$$f = \frac{1}{2\pi\sqrt{6}RC}$$

$$\Rightarrow \quad 80k = \frac{1}{2\pi\sqrt{6}R(100\pi)}$$

$$= \frac{1}{(80k)(2\pi\sqrt{6})(100\pi)} = 8.12\Omega$$

And, $\frac{R_F}{R} = 29$

$$\Rightarrow \quad R_F = (8.12k)(29) = 236 \text{ k}\Omega$$

96. $v_+ = \frac{v_i}{500+1}, v_0 = \frac{A_{od}\, v_i}{501}$

$\therefore$ $(2.5)(501) = A_{od}(5)$

$\Rightarrow$ $A_{od} = 250.5$

97. $v_+ = 5V = v_- = v_E$,

Input current to the op-amp is zero.

$$I = i_Z + i_C = i_Z + \alpha_F i_E$$

$$= \frac{15-5}{47k} + \frac{60}{61}\left(\frac{5}{100}\right) = 49.4 \text{ mA}$$

98.

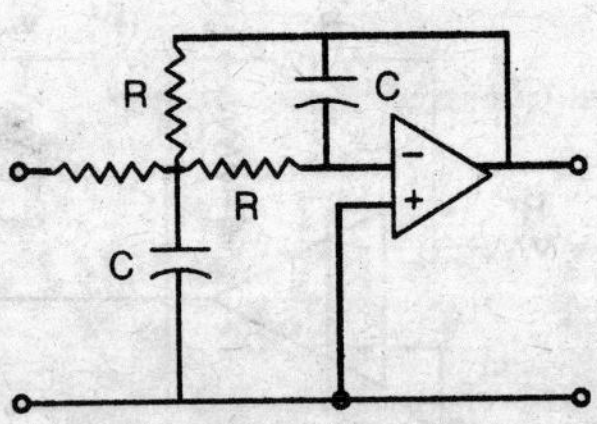

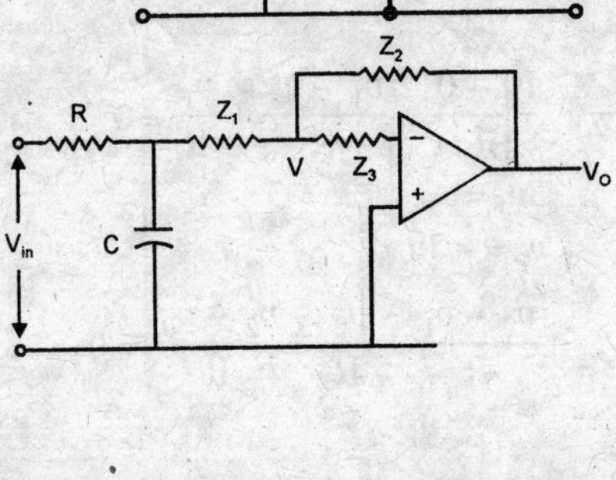

Using $\Delta - Y$ conversion,

$$Z_1 = \frac{R^2Cs}{2RCs+1}$$

$$Z_2 = \frac{R}{2RCs+1}$$

$$Z_3 = \frac{R}{2RCs+1}$$

From the figure, using KCL, we have

$$\frac{V_0}{V_{in}} = \frac{1}{R^2C^2s^2 + 3RCs + 1}$$

99.

$$\left|\frac{V_2}{V_1}\right| = \frac{R}{R_1} \cdot \frac{1}{RCs+1}$$

$$= 100\, \frac{1}{10^{-3}j+1} \approx 100$$

$$\therefore \quad 20 \log \left|\frac{V_2}{V_1}\right| = \mathbf{40\ dB.}$$

100. During '+' ve cycle, diode turns ON and $V_0 = 0V$.
Between positive peaks, diode is OFF and $V_0 = 2V_{in}$

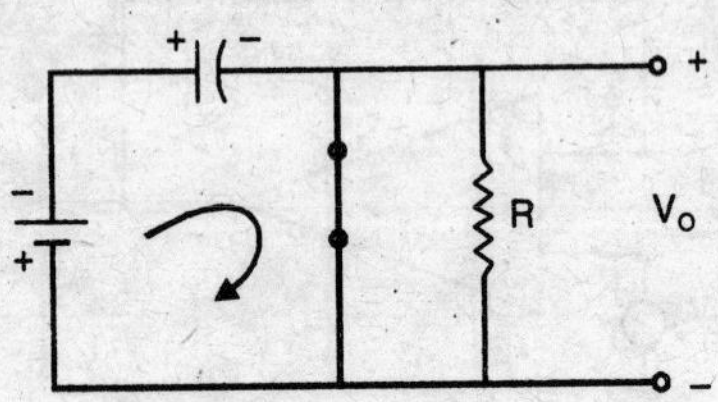

Fig. (a) Diode is ON

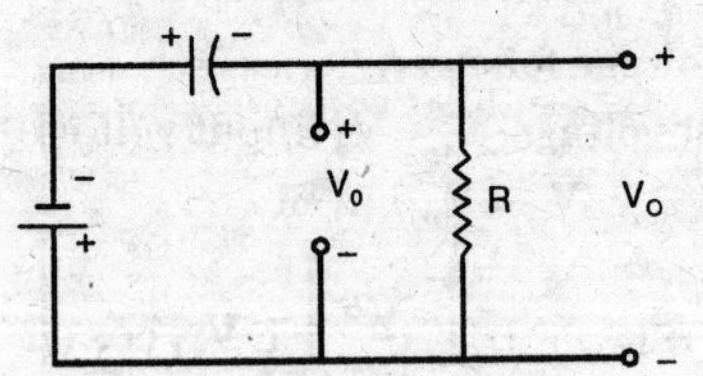

Fig. (b) Diode is OFF

101. Hysterisis voltage,

$$V_H = \frac{2R_2 V_0}{R_1 + R_2} = \frac{2 \times 5 \times 10}{100} = \mathbf{1\ volt.}$$

102.

$$T = (1.1)\, R_A C$$

$$= 1.1(7.5 \times 10^3)\ (0.1 \times 10^{-6})$$

$$= \mathbf{0.825\ ms.}$$

104.

$$T = 2RC\, ln\, \frac{1+\beta}{1-\beta}$$

Here, $\beta = \frac{1}{2} = \frac{R}{R+R}$.

$$\therefore \quad T = 2\,RC\, ln\, 3 = 2\,\tau ln\, 3$$

PRACTICE QUESTIONS

1. In the level shifter circuit shown in the figure, what is the value of R for V_0 to become zero? Assume $V_D = V_{BE} = -0.7$ V and h_{FE} is very large.

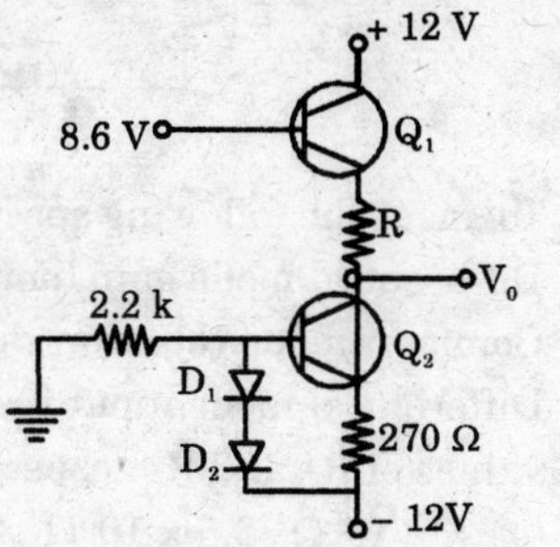

(a) 2.06 kΩ

(b) 2.56 kΩ

(c) 3.06 kΩ

(d) 3.56 kΩ

2. For the circuit shown in the figure given below, what is the magnitude of transfer function is V_o/V_i?

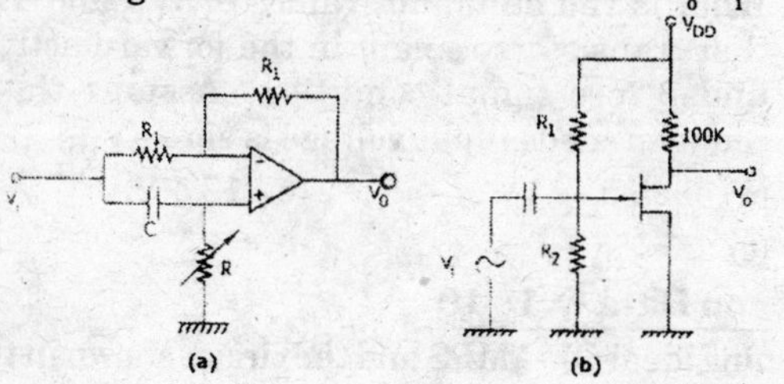

(a) 0 (b) 1

(c) 2 (d) 4

3. For the JEET amplifier shown in the given figure, $\mu = 100$ and $r_d = 50$ kΩ. What is the voltage gain of the amplifier ?

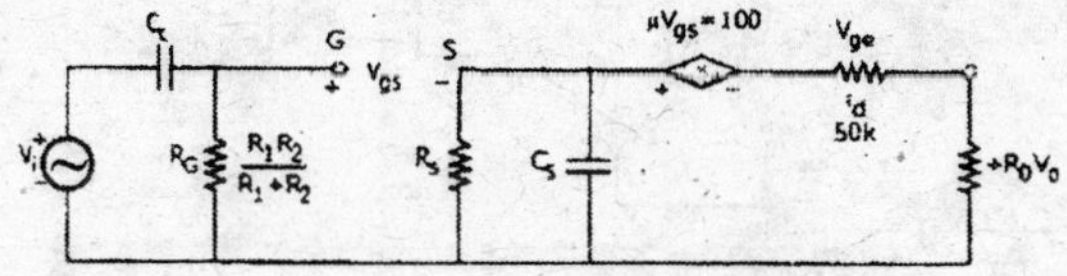

(a) – 33.33 (b) – 66.670

(c) – 99.99 (d) None of these

4. What is the output voltage, V_o of the following circuit shown in the figure below ? (assume ideal op-amp behaviour)

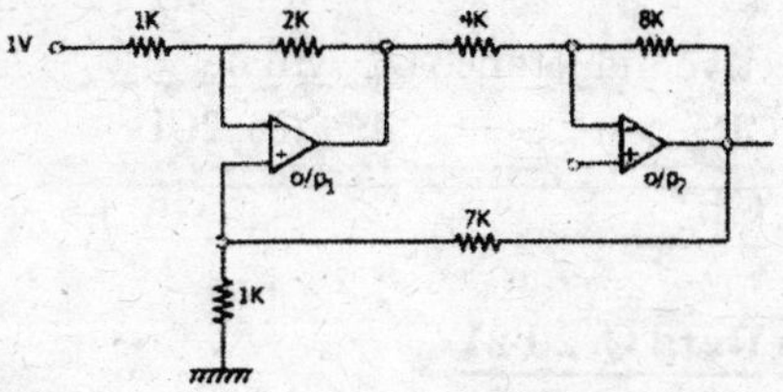

(a) 2 V (b) 4 V

(c) 6 V (d) 8 V

Common Data Q. 5-6

In the transistor circuit shown below, $I_{CBO} = 2\mu$ A at 25° C and doubles for every 10° C increase in temperature.

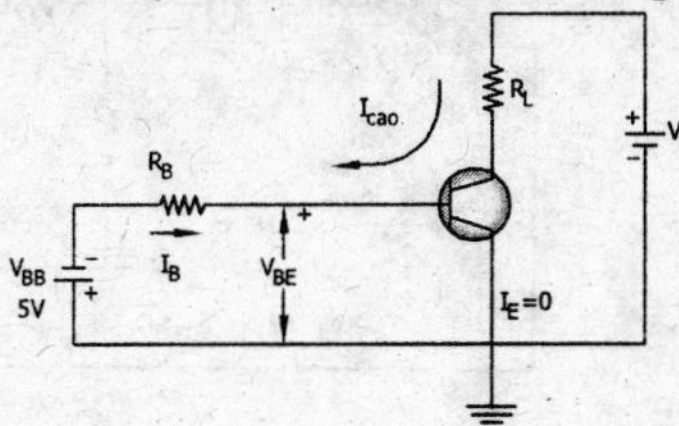

5. What is the maximum allowable value of R_B if the transistor is to remain cut-off at 75° C? Assume V_{BE}(cut-off) = – 0.1 V.

(a) 56.5 V (b) 66.5 V

(c) 76.5 V (d) 96.5 V

6. If V_{BB} = 1.0 V and R_B = 50 k Ω, how high may the temperature increase before the transistor comes out of cut-off ?

(a) 36°C (b) 46°C

(c) 56°C (d) 66°C

LINKED ANSWER Q. 7-8

A currrent amplifier has an input resistance of 10Ω, an output resistance of 10kΩ and a current gain of 1000. It is feed by a current source having a sorce resistance of 10kΩ and its output is connected to a 10Ω load resistance.

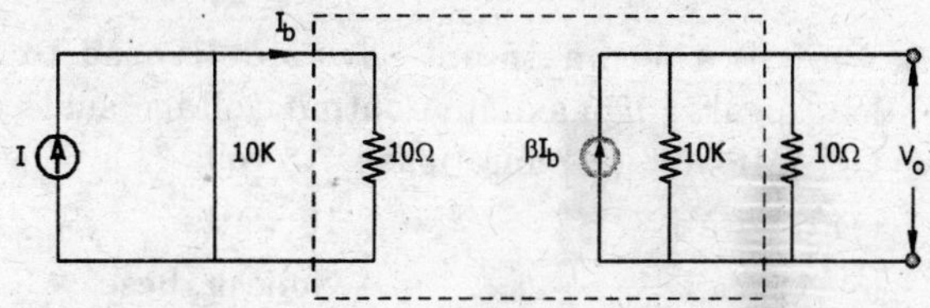

7. Voltage gain will be

(a) 997 (b) 998

(c) 999 (d) none of these

8. Power gain will be

(a) 997×10^3

(b) 998×10^3

(c) 999×10^3

(d) none of these

Linked Answer Q. 9-11

An active filter consisting of an op-amp, resistors R_1, R_2, R_3 and two capacitors of value C each, has a transfer function

$$T(s) = \frac{\dfrac{-s}{(R_1C)}}{s^2 + \dfrac{2s}{(R_3C)} + \dfrac{1}{(RR_3C^2)}}$$

where $R = R_1 \| R_2$, $R_1 = 2k\Omega$, $R_2 = 2/3\ k\Omega$, R_3 200 kΩ and C = 0.1 μF

9. Gain A_F of the filter will be

(a) 80 (b) 100

(c) 200 (d) 240

10. Q of the filter will be

(a) 10.18 (b) 11.18

(c) 111.8 (d) 100.8

11. Centre frequency, ω_o will be

(a) 1008 rad/sec

(b) 1108 rad/sec

(c) 1118 rad/sec

(d) 1018 rad/sec

Common Data Q. 12-13

A pick-up signal N_{10} is power-amplified using a complementary symmetry pushpull amplifier and fed to a 5-ohm loudspeaker as shown in the figure. Specifications of the power transistor are :

(*i*) $I_c|_{max}$ = maximum collector current = 2 amps.

(*ii*) $I_c|_{max}$ = maximum Power disipassion = 1 watt.

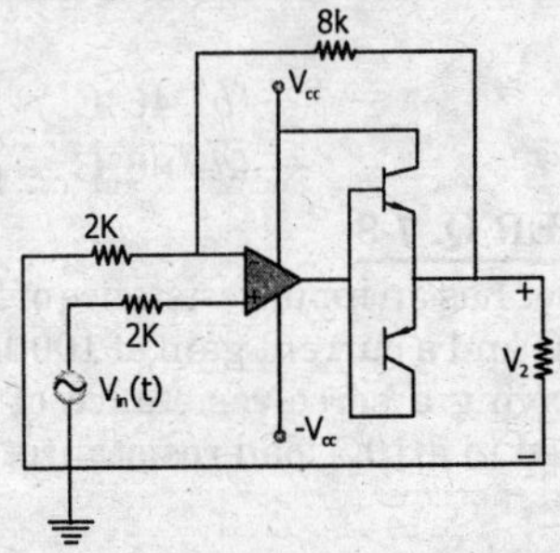

12. What is the maximum power delivered to the loudspeaker if maximum output voltage subject to OP-AMP voltage limitations is 15 volts ?

(*a*) 0.1 watt (*b*) 10 watts

(*c*) 11 watt (*d*) None of these

13. If transistors are mounted on a heat sink so that P_{cmax} changes to 3 watts, what will be the new value of the maximum power delivered ?

(*a*) 0.1 watt (*b*) 0.13 watt

(*c*) 1.13 watt (*d*) 11 watt

Common Data Q. 14-15

The circuit shown in the figure below uses an ideal operational amplifier. Assume that the impedances at nodes A and B do not load the preceding bridge circuit.

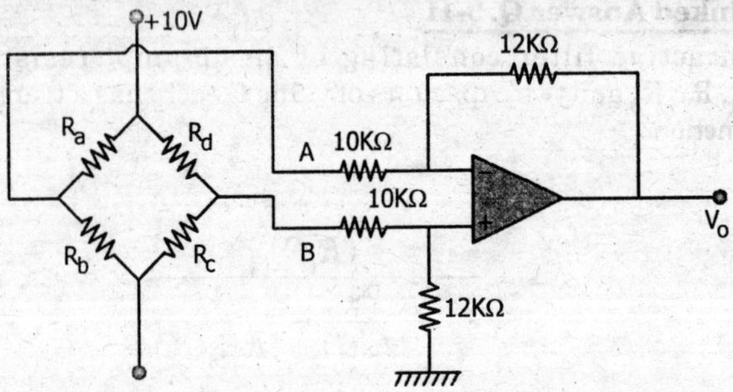

14. When $R_a = R_b = R_d$ = 100 ohms, output voltage V_0 will be

(*a*) 0 (*b*) 10

(*c*) 100 (*d*) 120

15. When $R_a = R_b = R_c$ = 100 ohms and R_d = 120 ohms, output voltage V_0 will be

(*a*) – 0.345 V (*b*) – 0.445 V

(*c*) – 0.545 V (*d*) – 0.645 V

Linked Answer Q. 16-17

A resistively loaded and resistively biased differential amplifier circuit is shown in the figure below Neglect base current and assume matched transistors with

$V_A \to \infty$ and $\beta = 100$

Use V_T = 26 mV, V_{BE} (on) = 0.7 V and V_{CE} (sat) = 0.1 V

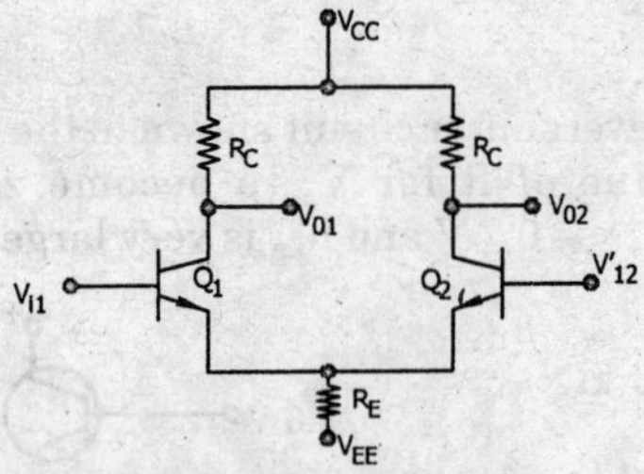

16. To meet the following specifications :

Differential mode gain (double ended) = – 500

Common-mode rejection ratio = 500

Differential mode input resistance = 2 MΩ

values of R_C and R_E respectively are

(*a*) $5 \times 10^6\Omega$, $3.5 \times 10^6\Omega$ (*b*) $4 \times 10^6\Omega$, $2.5 \times 10^6\Omega$

(*c*) $5 \times 10^6\Omega$, $2.5 \times 10^6\Omega$ (d) $4 \times 10^6\Omega$, $3.5 \times 10^6\Omega$

17. What is the minimum values of V_{CC} and V_{EE} such that transistors remain in the forward active region under zero-signal condition? Assume tha ^e dc common-mode input voltage is zero.

(*a*) 6.25 V (*b*) 12.5 V

(*c*) 25 V (*d*) 48 V

Common Data Q. 18-19

Assuming ideal OP-AMPS and the circuit shown in the figure below, simulates an inductor.

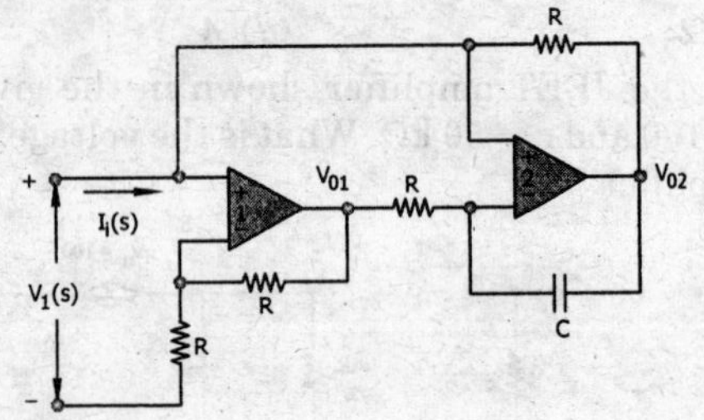

18. $\dfrac{V_i(s)}{I_i(s)}$ will be equal to

(*a*) sL (*b*) $\dfrac{s}{L}$

(*c*) $\dfrac{L}{s}$ (*d*) $\dfrac{1}{sL}$

19. Effective inductance L_{eff} will be

(*a*) CR^2 (*b*) $2CD^2$

(*c*) $\dfrac{CR^2}{2}$ (*d*) $\dfrac{CR}{2}$

Common Data Q. 20-21

The circuit of given figure is used for generating sinusoidal oscillations.

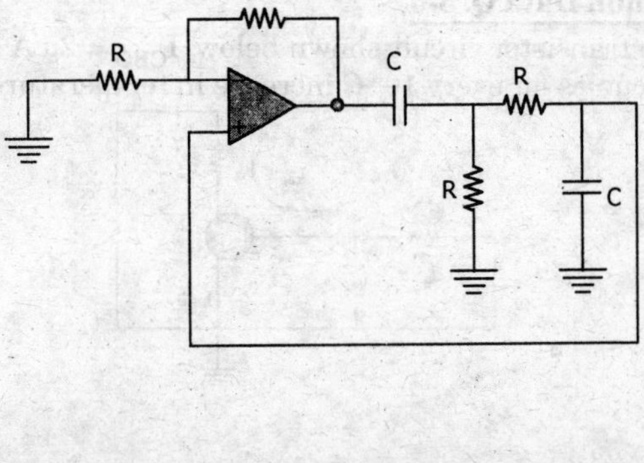

20. What is the frequency of oscillations ?

(*a*) CR (*b*) $\frac{C}{R}$

(*c*) $\frac{1}{CR}$ (*d*) $\frac{R}{C}$

21. What is the value of R′?

(*a*) R′ = R (*b*) R′ = 2R

(*c*) R′ = R/2 (*d*) R′ = R/4

Common Data Q. 22-23

A JFET having $\mu = 50$ and $r_d = 10\ k\Omega$ is used in a common-source configuration as shown in the figure below. The JFET capacitances are :

$$C_{gs} = 5\ pF, C_{gd} = 2\ pF, \text{and } C_{ds} = 2\ pF$$

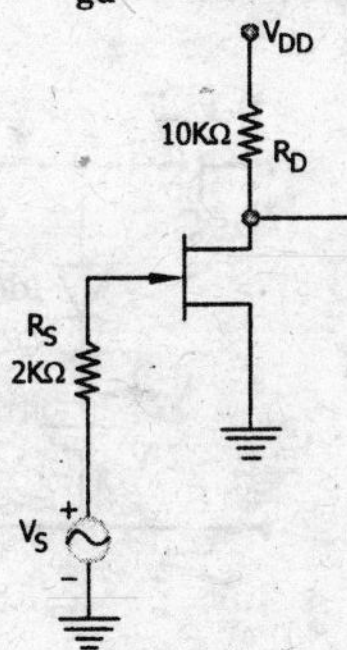

22. ac small-signal midband voltage gain (V_o/V_s) will be

(*a*) – 15 (*b*) – 20

(*c*) – 25 (*d*) – 30

23. Upper 3 dB frequency of the circuit will be

(*a*) 12.9 MHz (*b*) 13.9 MHz

(*c*) 14.9 MHz (*d*) 15.9 MHz

24. Consider the above circuit, for $V_i = V_m \sin \omega t$, the output voltage V_o for $R_L \to \infty$ will be

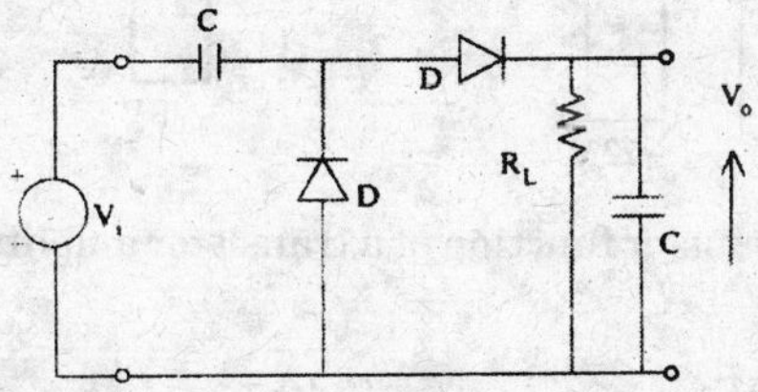

(*a*) zero (*b*) V_m

(*c*) 2 V_m (*d*) $-V_m$

25.

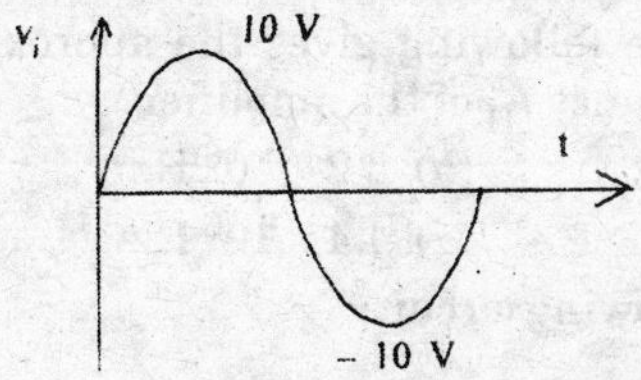

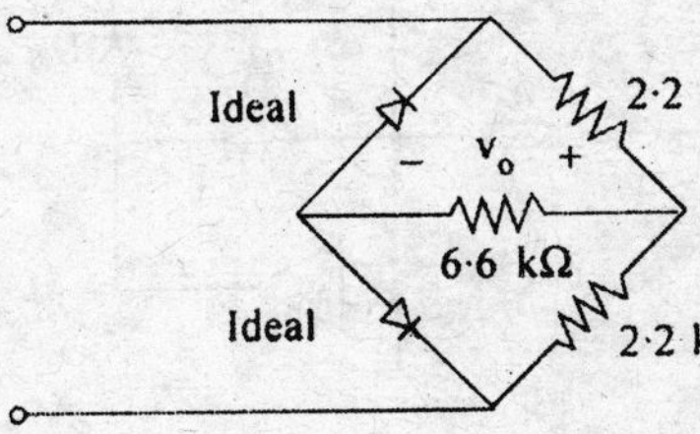

The correct waveform for output (V_o) for the above network is

(*a*)

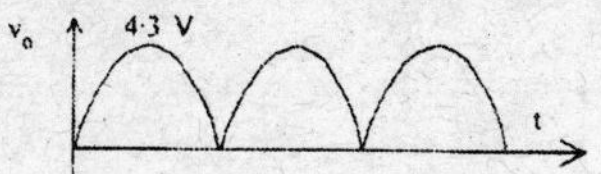

(*b*)

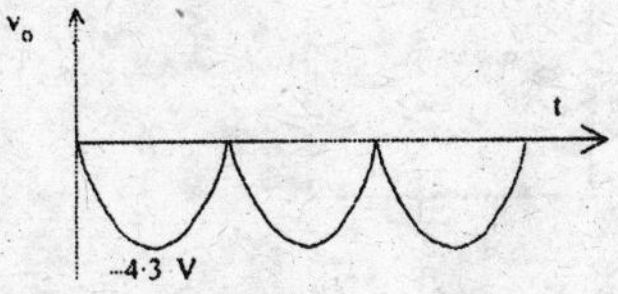

(*c*)

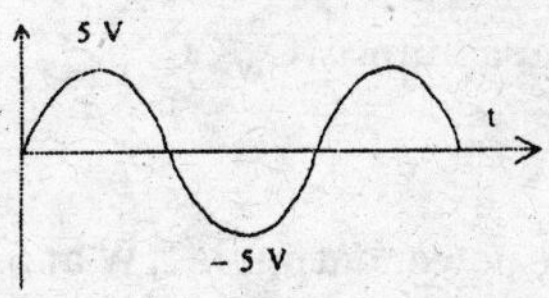

(*d*)

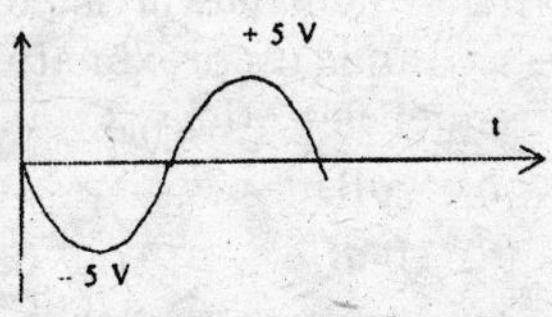

26. The output V_{dc} from the above circuit is

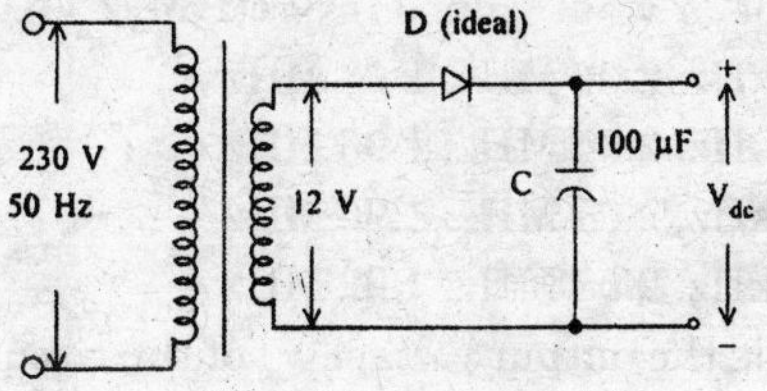

(*a*) $12\sqrt{2}$ (*b*) $12/\pi$

(*c*) $24/\pi$ (*d*) $12/\sqrt{2}$

27. The figure given below shows the transfer characteristics of

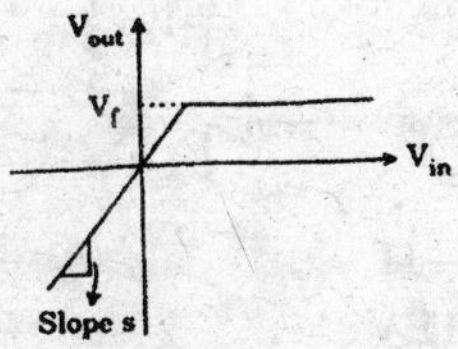

(*a*) Peak clipper

(*b*) Bottom clipper

(*c*) Clamper

(*d*) Two level clipper

28. The figure shown below is a circuit of

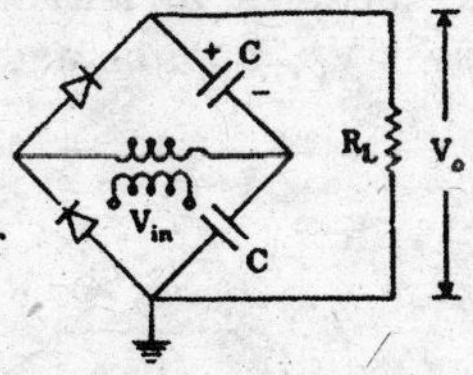

(*a*) Bridge rectifier

(*b*) Voltage doubler

(*c*) Rectifier with filter

(*d*) Comparator

29. An amplifier has gain A = 100 ∠ 180°, upper cut-off frequency of 100 kHz and lower cut off frequency of 1 kHz. A negative feedback of $\beta = 0.1$ is added. Which one of the following is not correct ?

(*a*) Gain becomes 100/11

(*b*) Lower cut off frequency becomes (1000/11) Hz

(*c*) Upper cut off frequency becomes 1.1 MHz

(*d*) dB of feedback is 20 $\log_{10}$ 11

30. For the amplifier shown in the figure given below, the lower cut-off frequency depends on

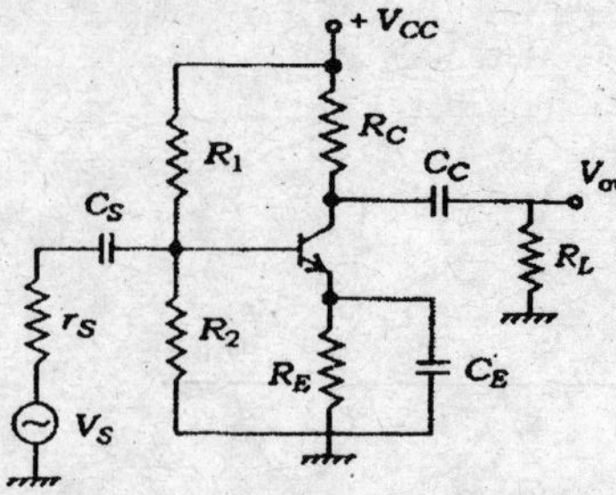

(*a*) C_S, C_E, internal junction capacitances of transistor
(*b*) Strong wiring capacitance (C_W), C_C
(*c*) C_S, C_E, C_C
(*d*) C_S, C_E only

31. In an amplifier, the power output is 2 W at 5 kHz, and 0.5 W at 50 Hz. If the input power is constant at 10 mW, what is the variation (approximate) of power gain in dB at two frequencies ? ($\log_{10}2 \approx 0.30$)

(*a*) 6 dB (*b*) 8 dB
(*c*) 3 dB (*d*) 16 dB

32. A tuned amplifier has peak output at 2 MHz and quality factor 50. The bandwidth and 3-dB frequencies shall be at what values respectively?

(*a*) 40 kHz, 2.02 MHz, 1.98 MHz
(*b*) 40 kHz, 2.04 MHz, 1.96 MHz
(*c*) 80 kHz, 2.04 MHz, 1.96 MHz
(*d*) 80 kHz, 2.08 MHz, 1.92 MHz

33. What is the output voltage V_o of the circuit below?

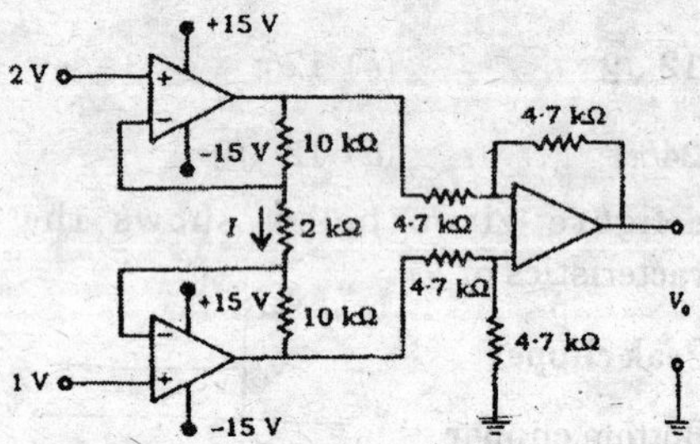

(*a*) – 11 V (*b*) 6 V
(*c*) 11 V (*d*) – 6 V

34. The transistor circuit shown in the figure given below is to function as an amplifier. If I_C = 3 mA, what is the value of V_{CC} approximate?

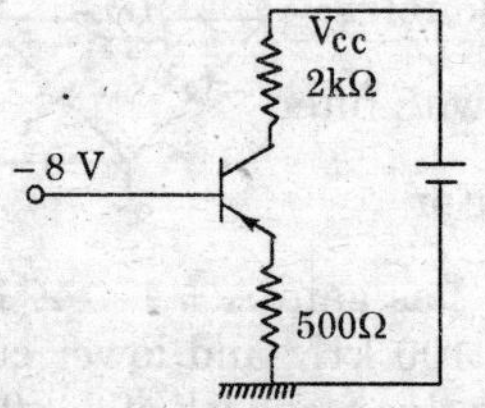

(*a*) 15V
(*b*) –15V
(*c*) –10 V
(*d*) –13.5 V

35. An amplifier has an open loop gain of 1000 ± 10. Negative feedback is provided such that the gain variation remains within 0.1%. What is the amount of feedback b_F?

(*a*) 1/10 (*b*) 1/9
(*c*) 9/100 (*d*) 9/1000

36. The two stages of a cascade amplifier have individual upper cut-off frequencies f_1 = 5 MHz and f_2 = 3.33 MHz. What is the best approximation for the upper cut-off frequency of the cascade combination?

(*a*) 4.16 MHz (*b*) 3.33 MHz
(*c*) 2.5 MHz (*d*) 5.00 MHz

37. Select the correct output (v_o) wave-shape for a given input (v_i) in the clamping network given below :

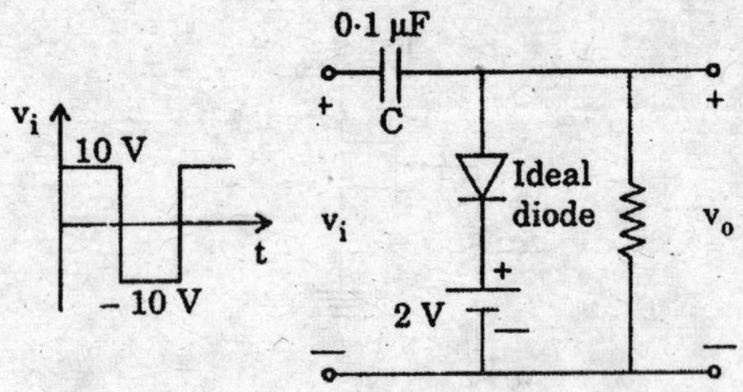

(*a*)
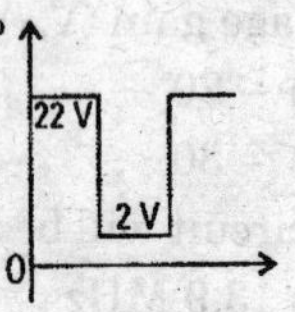

(*b*)
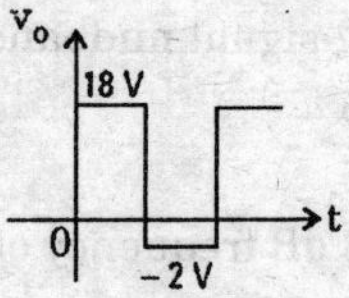

(*c*)
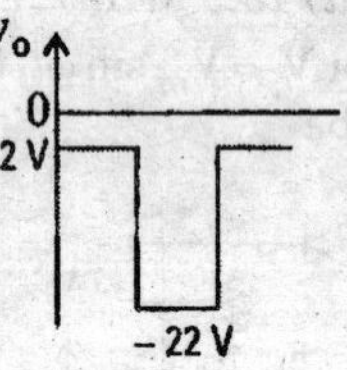

(*d*)
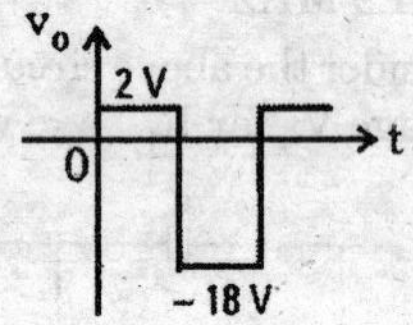

38. The transfer function of a transistor amplifier is given by

$$A_V = \frac{V_0}{V_s} = \frac{4240}{\left(1 + j\dfrac{f}{4 \times 10^5}\right)\left(1 + j\dfrac{f}{4 \times 10^6}\right)}$$

Which one of the following gives the approximate upper 3-dB frequency f_H of the amplifier?

(*a*) 4×10^5 Hz (*b*) 2.2×10^6 Hz
(*c*) 4×10^6 Hz (*d*) 4.4×10^6 Hz

39. Consider the following circuit:

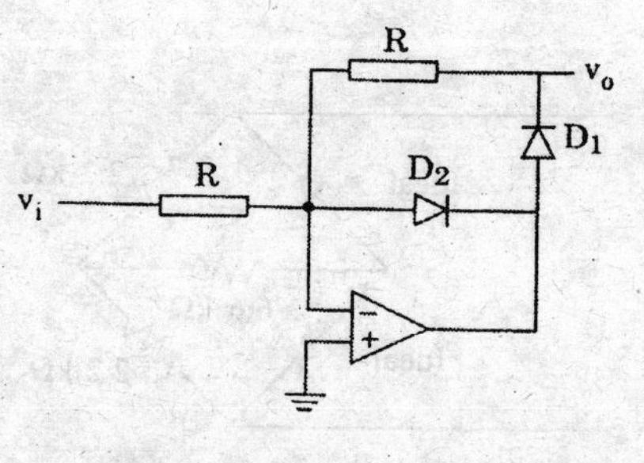

What is the function of diode D_2 in the above circuit?

(*a*) To avoid saturation of the Op-Amp

(*b*) To provide negative feedback when the input is negative

(*c*) To reduce reverse breakdown voltage of D_1

(*d*) As a buffer

40. Consider the following circuit:

What is the value of R_4 in the circuit, if the voltage V_- and V_+ are to be amplified by the same amplification factor?

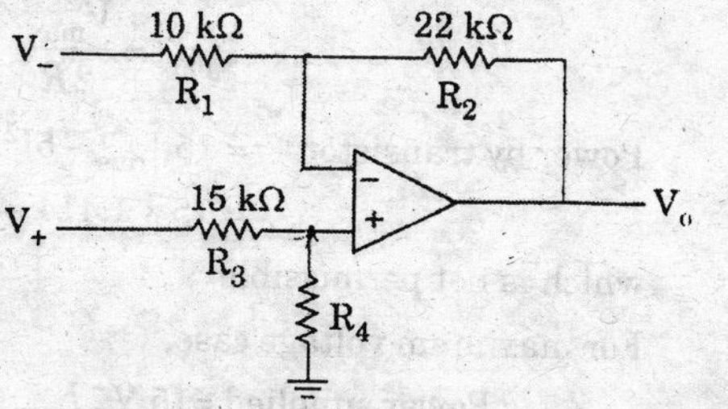

(*a*) 7 kΩ

(*b*) 22 kΩ

(*c*) 33 kΩ

(*d*) 35 kΩ

41. In the circuit shown below, the transformers are centre tapped and the diodes are connected as shown in a bridge. Between the terminals 1 and 2 an a.c. voltage source of frequency 400 Hz is connected. Another a.c. voltage of 1.0 MHz is connected between 3 and 4. The output between 5 and 6 contains components at

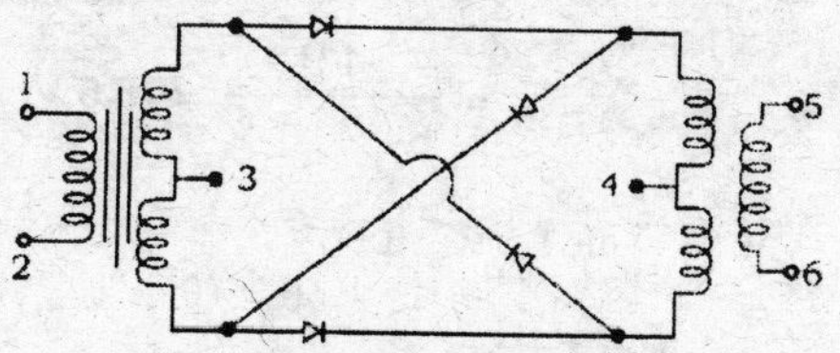

(*a*) 400 Hz, 1.0 MHz, 1000.4 kHz, 999.6 kHz

(*b*) 400 Hz, 1000.4 kHz, 999.6 kHz

(*c*) 1 MHz, 1000.4 kHz, 999.6 kHz

(*d*) 1000.4 kHz, 999.6 kHz

ANSWERS

1. (*c*)	**2.** (*b*)	**3.** (*b*)	**4.** (*b*)	**5.** (*c*)	**6.** (*c*)	**7.** (*c*)	**8.** (*a*)	**9.** (*b*)	**10.** (*b*)
11. (*c*)	**12.** (*a*)	**13.** (*b*)	**14.** (*a*)	**15.** (*c*)	**16.** (*c*)	**17.** (*b*)	**18.** (*a*)	**19.** (*c*)	**20.** (*c*)
21. (*b*)	**22.** (*c*)	**23.** (*d*)	**24.** (*c*)	**25.** (*a*)	**26.** (*b*)	**27.** (*a*)	**28.** (*b*)	**29.** (*d*)	**30.** (*c*)
31. (*a*)	**32.** (*b*)	**33.** (*a*)	**34.** (*b*)	**35.** (*d*)	**36.** (*d*)	**37.** (*d*)	**38.** (*a*)	**39.** (*a*)	**40.** (*b*)
41. (*d*)									

EXPLANATIONS

1. In upper transistor circuit

$8.6 - 0.7 - I_R.R = V_0$

$\Rightarrow$ $I_R.R = 7.9$ V (since $V_0 = 0$, required) ...(*i*)

In lower circuit,

$2.2\, I_1 + 1.4 = 12$

$$\Rightarrow \quad I_1 = \frac{10.6}{2.2}$$

$= 4.82$ mA

and $2.2 \times 4.82 - 0.7 - 0.270\, I_R = 12$

$\Rightarrow$ $I_R = 2.578$ mA ...(*ii*)

From equations (i) and (ii), we get

$$R = \frac{7.9}{2.578}$$

$= 3.06$ kΩ

2.

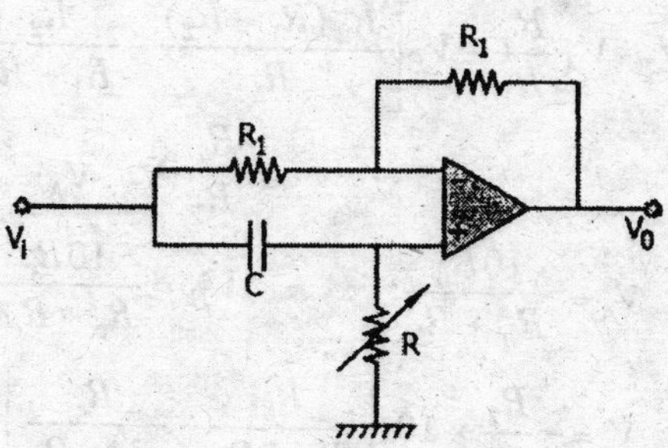

Applying superposition theorem

$$V_o(-) = V_i\left(-\frac{R_1}{R_1}\right) = -V_i$$

$$V_o(+) = V_i(+)\left(1+\frac{R_1}{R_1}\right) = 2V_i(+)$$

$$V_i(+) = V_i\frac{R}{R+\frac{1}{j\omega C}} = V_i\frac{j\omega CR}{1+j\omega CR}$$

Vo (total) = $V_o(-) + V_o(+)$

$$= \frac{2V_i j\omega CR}{1+j\omega CR} - V_i = V_i\left(\frac{2j\omega CR - 1 - jwCR}{1+jwCR}\right)$$

$$\text{Transfer function} = \frac{V_o}{V_i} = \frac{-1+j\omega CR}{1+j\omega CR}$$

$$\text{Magnitude, M} = \sqrt{\frac{(-1)^2+(\omega CR)^2}{(\omega CR)^2}} = 1$$

3. Since other values are not given, therefore

$$\text{Voltage gain, } A_v = -\mu\frac{R_D}{r_d + R_D}$$

$$= -100\frac{100}{50+100} = -66.67$$

here negative sign indicates phase inversion.

5. Given : $I_{CBO} = 2\mu A$ at 25° C and doubles for every 10° C increase in temperature.

At 75°C, $I_{CBO} = 2 \times 2 \times 2 \times 2 \times 2 \times 2 = 64\ \mu A$

At cut-off $I_B = I_{CBO}$ and $V_B = -0.1$ V

$\therefore$ $V_{BE} = -V_{BB} + R_B I_{CBO} \leq 0.1$ V

$\Rightarrow$ $-0.1V = -5 + R_B \times 64 \times 10^{-6}$

$$\Rightarrow \quad R_B = \frac{4.9}{64 \times 10^{-6}} = \mathbf{76.5\ V}$$

6. $V_{BE} = -V_{BB} + R_B \times I_{CBO}$

$\therefore$ $-0.1 = -1 + 50 \times 10^3 \times I_{CBO}$

$\Rightarrow$ $0.9 = 50 \times 10^3 \times I_{CBO}$

$$\Rightarrow \quad I_{CBO} = \frac{0.9}{50 \times 10^3} = 1.8 \times 10^{-5} = 18\ \mu A$$

For temperature rise, we have

$$18 = 2 \times 2^{(T-25)/10}$$

$$\Rightarrow \quad \frac{T-25}{20} = \log_2 9 \approx 3.1$$

$\Rightarrow$ T = 56°C

7. $V_i = I_b R_i = 10\, I_b\ V$

$$V_0 = \frac{\beta I_b R_0 R_L}{(R_0 + R_L)}$$

$$= \frac{1000 \times 10 \times 10^3 \times 10}{(10 \times 10^3 + 10)} = 999\, I_b\ V$$

$$A_v = \frac{V_0}{V_i} = 999$$

$$A_I = 998$$

8. Power gain $= A_v \times A_I = 997 \times 10^3$

9.
$$R_1 = \frac{Q}{2\pi f_C C A_F} \quad \ldots(i)$$

$$R_2 = \frac{Q}{2\pi f_C C\,(2Q^2 - A_F)} \quad \ldots(ii)$$

$$R_3 = \frac{Q}{\pi f_C\, C} \quad \ldots(iii)$$

$$A_F = \frac{R_3}{2R_1} = \frac{200}{2} = 100$$

10. From equations (*ii*) and (*iii*), we get

$$2Q^2 = \frac{R_3}{2R_2} + A_F$$

$$= \frac{200 \times 3}{2 \times 2} + 100 = 250$$

or $Q = 11.18$

11. From equation (*iii*),

$$f_C = \frac{Q}{R_3 \pi C}$$

$$= \frac{11.18}{200 \times 10^3 \times 3.14 \times 0.1 \times 10^{-6}}$$

$$= 177.94 \text{ Hz}$$

$$\therefore \quad \omega_0 = 2\pi f_C = 1118 \text{ rad/sec}$$

12. *Complementary sysmmetry push pull*

$I_c = 2A$, $p_c = 1$ watt, $V_{o,\,max} = 15$ V, $I_{max} = 2A$

$$\frac{V_{in}}{2} + \frac{V_{in} - V_{o\,max}}{8} = 0$$

$$\Rightarrow \quad 5V_{in} = V_{omax}$$

$$\text{Now,} \quad 2 = \frac{V_{o\,max}}{5} + \frac{V_{o\,max} - V_{in}}{8k}$$

$$\Rightarrow \quad 2 = \frac{V_{o\,max}}{5}$$

$$\Rightarrow \quad V_{o,max} = 10V$$

$$\therefore \quad P_{max} = \frac{V_{max}^2}{2R} = 10 \text{ W}$$

Power by transistor $= 15\, I_{rms} - 5I^2_{rms}$

$= 15 \times 1.414 - 10 = 11$ W

which is not permissible

For maximum voltage case,

Power supplied $= 15\ V \cdot I_{rms}$

Power in load $= 5\, I^2_{rms}$

$\therefore$ $15\, I_{rms} = 5\, I^2_{rms} + 2$

$\Rightarrow$ $5\, I^2_{rms} - 15\, I_{rms} + 2 = 0$

$$\therefore \quad I_{rms} = \frac{15 \pm \sqrt{225 - 40}}{10} = 0.14 \text{ A}$$

Since peak current is 2 A, this is not permissible

$\therefore$ $P = I^2 R = 0.1$ watt $(I_{rms} = 14)$

which is possible

13. *After heat sink,*

$$P_{cmax} = 3 \text{ Watt}$$

$\therefore$ $5\, I_{rms} = 5\, I^2_{rms} + 6$

$$\Rightarrow \quad I_{rms} = \frac{+15 \pm \sqrt{225 - 120}}{10}$$

$$= \frac{15 \pm 10.25}{10} = 2.5,\ 0.475$$

$$\therefore \quad P = I^2_{rms} R = 1.13 \text{ watt}$$

14.
$$V_c = \frac{V_B . R_2}{R_1 + R_2}$$

$$\frac{V_o - \dfrac{V_B . R_2}{R_1 + R_2}}{R_2} + \frac{V_A - \dfrac{V_B}{R_1 + R_2}}{R_1} = 0$$

$$\therefore \quad V_o - V_A \frac{R_2}{R_1} - V_B \left[\frac{R_2^2 (R_1 + R_2)}{R_1} - \frac{R_2}{R_1 + R_2} \right]$$

$$= \frac{R_2}{R_1}(V_B - V_A)$$

$$\text{But} \quad V_A = \frac{10R_b}{R_a + R_b}; \qquad V_B = \frac{10R_c}{R_c + R_d}$$

$$\therefore \quad V_o = -\frac{R_2}{R_1} \times 10 \left[\frac{R_b}{R_a + R_b} - \frac{R_c}{R_c + R_d} \right]$$

But $R_a = R_b = R_c = R_d = 100\ \Omega$

$$\therefore \quad V_o = -\frac{12}{10}\left[\frac{100}{200} - \frac{100}{200}\right] \times 10 = 0$$

15. $R_a = R_b = R_c = R_d = 100\ \Omega;\quad R_d = 120\ \Omega$

$$\therefore \quad V_o = -\frac{12}{10} \times 10\left[\frac{100}{200} - \frac{100}{200}\right] = -0.545\text{V}$$

16. $A_{DM} = -g_m R_C,\quad A_{CM} = \dfrac{-R_L}{2R_E}$

$$R_{i1} = R_{i2} = 2h_{ie}$$

$$\therefore \quad 2h_{ie} = 2 \times 10^6\ \Omega$$

$$\Rightarrow \quad h_{ie} = 1 \times 10^6\ \Omega$$

$$A_{DM} = \frac{-h_{fe}\ R_C}{h_{ie}} = -\frac{100 \times R_C}{10^6} = -500$$

$$R_C = \frac{500 \times 10^6}{100} = 5 \times 10^6\ \Omega$$

$$CMRR = \frac{A_{DM}}{A_{CM}} = 2g_m R_E$$

$$= 2 \times \frac{h_{fe}}{h_{ie}} \times R_E = 500$$

$$\therefore \quad 2 \times \frac{100}{10^6} \times R_E = 500$$

$$\Rightarrow \quad R_E = \frac{500 \times 10^6}{200} = 2.5 \times 10^6\ \Omega$$

17. For one transistor,

$$h_{ie} = \frac{V_T(\beta + 1)}{I_E}$$

$$I_E = \frac{0.026 \times 101}{1 \times 10^6} = 2.626 \times 10^{-6} A$$

Again, $2I_E = \dfrac{V_{EE} - V_{BE}}{R_E}$

$$\therefore \quad V_{EE} = 2I_E \times R_E \times V_{BE}$$

$$= 2 \times 2.626 \times 10^{-6} \times 2.5 \times 10^6 \times 0.7$$

$$= 13.83\ \text{V}$$

Now $\quad -V_{CC} + I_C R_C + V_{CE} + 2I_E R_E - V_{EE} = 0$

$$\Rightarrow \quad V_{CC} = -V_{EE} + 13.13 + 0.2 + I_C \times 10^6$$

and $\quad I_B + (100 \times I_B) = 2.626 \times 10^{-6}$

$$\Rightarrow \quad I_B = \frac{2.626 \times 10^{-6}}{101} = 0.026 \times 10^{-6}$$

$$I_C = 100 \times 0.026 \times 10^{-6} = 2.6 \times 10^{-6} A$$

$$V_{CC} = -13.83 + 13.13 + 0.2 + (2.6 \times 10^{-6} \times 5 \times 10^6)$$

$$= 12.5\ \text{V.}$$

18. $V_{02} = V_{01} \times \dfrac{1}{sCR}$

$$V_{01} = V_i(s)\left(1 + \frac{R}{R}\right) = 2\,V_i(s)$$

$$V_{02} = -\frac{2V_i(s)}{sCR}$$

$$V_{02} = -I_i(s)\,R$$

Equating, we get

$$\frac{-2V_i(s)}{sCR} = -I_i(s)\,R$$

$$\Rightarrow \quad \frac{V_i(s)}{I_i(s)} = \frac{sCR^2}{2} = sL$$

19. $L_{eff} = \dfrac{CR^2}{2}$

20-21.

At node a : $\dfrac{V_a}{R} + \dfrac{V_a - V_c}{R} = 0$

$$\therefore \quad V_c = V_a\left(1 + \frac{R'}{R}\right) \quad .....(i)$$

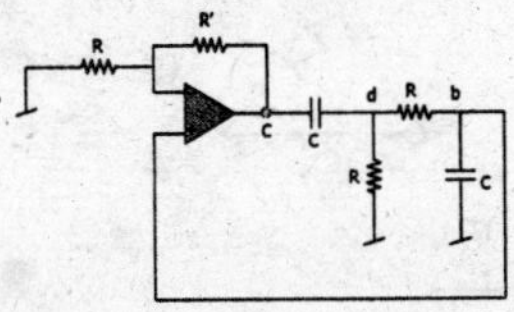

At node b : $V_a = V_b$

$$\therefore \quad V_c = V_b\left(1 + \frac{R'}{R}\right) \quad ...(ii)$$

$$\Rightarrow \quad 0 + (V_b)\,sC + V_c\,\frac{V_b - V_d}{R} = 0$$

$$\Rightarrow \quad V_b\,(1 + sCR) = V_d \quad ...(iii)$$

At node d :

$$(V_d - V_c)\,sC + \frac{V_d}{R} + \frac{V_d - V_b}{R} = 0$$

$$\Rightarrow \quad V_d\,(2 + sCR) = V_c\,(sCR) + V_b \quad ...(iv)$$

From equations (*ii*), (*iii*) and (*iv*), we have

$$V_d\,(1 + sCR)\,(2 + sCR) = V_b\left(1 + \frac{R'}{R}\right)(sCR) + V_b$$

$$\Rightarrow \quad 2 + 3\,sCR + s^2C^2R^2 - \left(1 + \frac{R'}{R}\right) sCR - 1 = 0$$

$$\Rightarrow \quad 2 + s^2C^2R^2 + \left(2 - \frac{R'}{R}\right) sCR = 0$$

For oscillation $R' = 2R$ and $\omega = \dfrac{1}{CR}$

22. JFET is common source configuration

Given : $\mu = 50,\ r_d = 10\ \text{k}\Omega$

$$g_m = \frac{\mu}{r_d} = \frac{50}{10 \times 10^3} = 5 \times 10^{-3}$$

Voltage gain, $\dfrac{V_o}{V_s} = -g_m\,\dfrac{r_d R_D}{r_d + R_D} = -\dfrac{\mu\,R_D}{r_d + R_D}$

$$= \frac{50 \times 10 \times 10^3}{10 \times 10^3 + 10 \times 10^3} = -25$$

23. In mid frequency range, all interelectrode capacitors C_{gs}, C_{gd} and C_{ds} behave as open circuit and only resistive compounds are present.

Upper 3 db frequency,

$$f_2 = \frac{1}{2\pi C_o R_{eq}}$$

$$= \frac{1}{2\pi \times 2 \times 10^{-12} \times 5 \times 10^3} = 15.9 \text{ MHz}$$

where, $C_o = C_{gd}(1 + g_m) = 2 \text{ pF}$

$R_{eq} = r_d \,||\, R_D = 5 \text{ K}$

24 Given : $V_i = V_m \sin \omega t$

It is voltage doubler circuit so,

output, $V_0 = 2 V_m$

when $R_L \to \infty$

25.

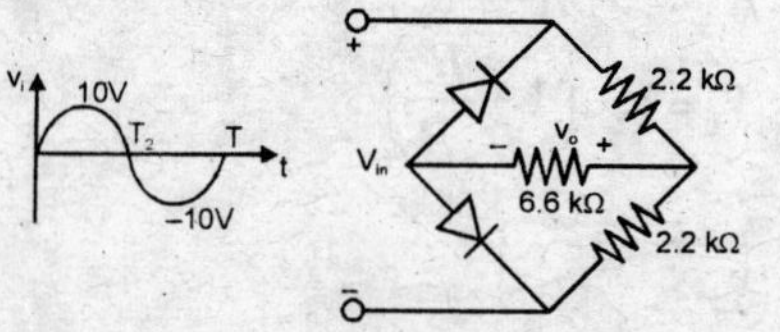

For +ve half input

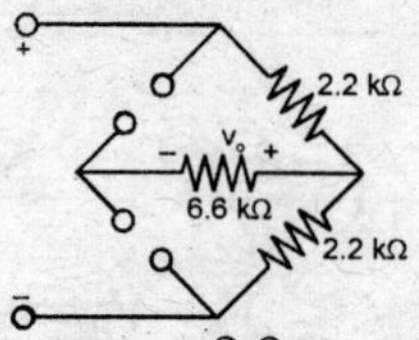

$$V_o = \frac{\frac{3.3}{2}}{2.2 + \frac{3.3}{2}} \times V_{in}$$

$$= \frac{3.3}{7.7} \times V_{in} = \frac{3}{7} \times 10 \sin \omega t$$

$$= 4.2857 \sin \omega t$$

For $0 < t < T$ $\sin \omega t > 0$

For $-ve$ half cycle

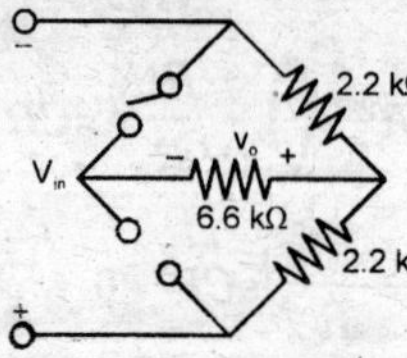

$$V_o = -\frac{3}{7} \times V_{in} = -\frac{3}{7}(-10 \sin \omega t)$$

$$= +4.2857 \sin \omega t$$

31. Variation,$= 10 \log \frac{Po_1}{Po_2}$

$$= 10 \log \frac{2}{0.5} = 6 \text{ dB.}$$

33.

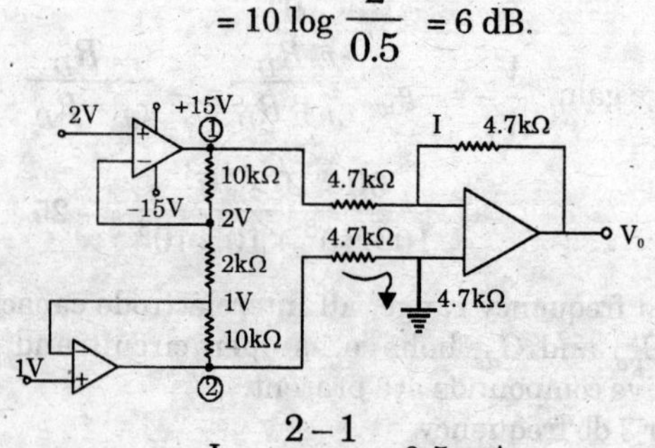

$$I = \frac{2-1}{2} = 0.5 \text{ mA}$$

$$V_1 - V_2 = 22 \times 0.5 = 11 \text{ volt}$$

$$V_+ = \frac{V_2 \times 4.7}{4.7 + 4.7} = \frac{V_2}{2}$$

and, $\frac{V_0 - V_-}{4.7} = \frac{V_- - V_1}{4.7}$

$\Rightarrow V_0 + V_1 = 2V_-$

$\Rightarrow V_- = \frac{V_0 + V_1}{2}$

As $V_+ = V_-$

$\therefore \frac{V_2}{2} = \frac{V_0 + V_1}{2}$

$\Rightarrow V_0 = V_2 - V_1 = -11 \text{volt.}$

34. From the circuit

$$V_{CC} - I_{CQ} \cdot R_C - V_{CE} - (I_{CQ} + I_{BQ}) \cdot R_E = 0$$

and, $-8 - V_{BE} - I_{EQ}(.500) = 0$

$\Rightarrow I_{EQ} = -\frac{8.7}{0.5} = -17.4 \text{ mA}$

$\Rightarrow V_{CC} \cong I_{CQ}(R_C) + R_E I_{EQ} + V_{CE}$

$\cong -3 \times 2 + (-17.4) \times 0.5 + (-0.2)$

$\cong -14.9$ volts

35. $A_f = \frac{A}{1 + \beta A}$

$\Rightarrow \left|\frac{dA_f}{A_f}\right| = \left|\frac{1}{1 + \beta A}\right| \cdot \frac{dA}{A}$

$\therefore 0.001 = \left|\frac{1}{1 + \beta A}\right| \cdot \frac{10}{1000}$

$\Rightarrow \beta A = 9$

$\Rightarrow \beta = \frac{9}{1000}$

36. $\frac{1}{f_H} = 1.1 \sqrt{\frac{1}{f_1^2} + \frac{1}{f_2^2}} = 1.1 \sqrt{\frac{1}{5^2} + \frac{1}{3.33^2}}$

$f_H = 2.5 \text{ MHz}$

37. $10 - V_c - 2 = 0$

$\Rightarrow V_c = 8V$

$\Rightarrow V_0 = 2V$

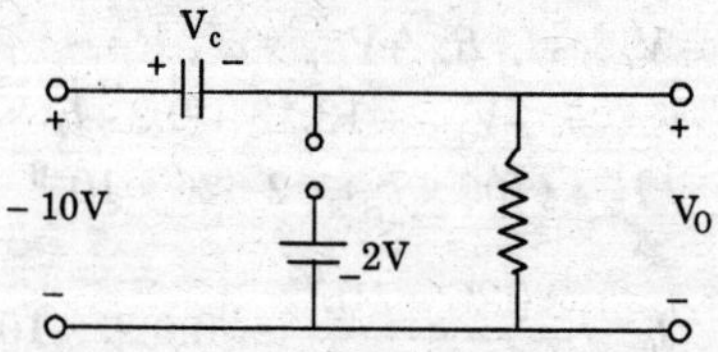

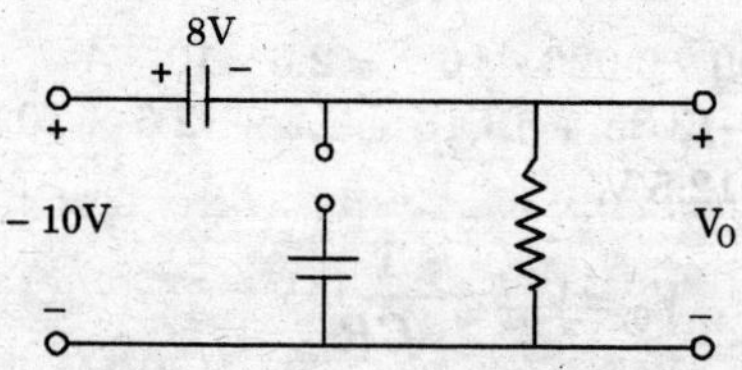

$V_0 = -18 \text{ V}$

41. Only two side will be present and carrier is cancelled.

DIGITAL CIRCUITS 4

4.1 NUMBER SYSTEM

Many physical quantities which are analog in nature, are often the inputs and outputs that are being monitored, operated on, and controlled by a system.

e.g. temperature, pressure, position, velocity, liquid level, flow rate etc.

Digitization

It is the process of converting continuous analog signal into a finite number of discrete states, to the extent that the states are sufficiently well separated so that noise does create errors.

The resulting digital signals allow following advantages :

(*i*) They are generally easier to design

(*ii*) Information storage is easy

(*iii*) Accuracy and precision are more

(*iv*) Operation can be programmed

(*v*) Digital circuits are less affected by noise

(*vi*) More digital circuitry can be fabricated on IC chips

Some information is intrinsically digital, so it is natural to process and manipulate it using purely digital techniques.

e.g. numbers and words.

Drawback of Digitization

Digital signal needs many discrete states or bits, in order to give a satisfactory reproduction.

e.g., it requires a minimum of 10 bits to determine 'a voltage at any given time to an accuracy of ≈ 0.1%. For transmission, one now requires 10 lines instead of the one original analog line.

The developments in digital techniques and technology has been made possible by incredible increase in the density of digital circuitry, its robust performance, its relatively low cost, and its speed. The requirement of using many bits in reproduction is better.

The circuitry is based upon the transistor, which can be operated as a switch with two states. Hence, digital information is intrinsically binary. So in practice, the terms digital and binary are used interchangeably.

TYPES OF NUMBER SYSTEMS.

There are four types of number systems of arithmetic.

1. Decimal Number System

It contains 10 unique symbols : 0, 1, 2, 3, 4, 5, 6, 7, 8 and 9.

Because it has 10 symbols its base used is 10.

e.g. $325.75_{10} = 3 \times 10^{Z} + 2 \times 10^{1} + 5 \times 10^{0} + 7 \times 10^{-1} + 5 \times 10^{-2}$

2. Binary Number system

This system uses only two digits 0 and 1. The base for this system is 2 and position to left and right of the binary points carry weights increasing or decreasing in powers of 2.

e.g. $101011\,.\,1101 = 1 \times 2^5 + 0 \times 2^4 + 1 \times 2^3 + 0 \times 2^2 + 1 \times 2^1 + 1 \times 2^0 + 1 \times 2^{-1} + 1 \times 2^{-2} + 0 \times 2^{-3} + 1 \times 2^{-4}$

$= 43.\,812_{10}$

3. Hexadecimal Number System

It is commonly used in computers. This system is formed from a binary number (word) by grouping bits in a group of four bits each, starting at binary points. In a group of 4 bits, the decimal numbers 0-15 can be represented as given below. For this system base (radix) is 16.

Table 4.1 Number System

Binary		Hexadecimal		Decimal		Octal
0000	⟶	0	⟶	0	⟶	0
0001	⟶	1	⟶	1	⟶	1
0010	⟶	2	⟶	2	⟶	2
0011	⟶	3	⟶	3	⟶	3
0100	⟶	4	⟶	4	⟶	4
0101	⟶	5	⟶	5	⟶	5
0110	⟶	6	⟶	6	⟶	6
0111	⟶	7	⟶	7	⟶	7
1000	⟶	8	⟶	8	⟶	10
1001	⟶	9	⟶	9	⟶	11
1010	⟶	A	⟶	10	⟶	12
1011	⟶	B	⟶	11	⟶	13
1100	⟶	C	⟶	12	⟶	14
1101	⟶	D	⟶	13	⟶	15
1110	⟶	E	⟶	14	⟶	16
1111	⟶	F	⟶	15	⟶	17

e.g. (*i*) *Hexa to binary conversion:*

A B 2

$AB2 = 1010 \quad 1011 \quad 0010_2$

(*ii*) *Binary to Hexa:*

$$11010010 = \underbrace{1101}_{D}\ \underbrace{0010}_{2}$$

$$= D2$$

(*iii*) *Hexadecimal to Decimal:*

$$ED2 = 14 \times 16^2 + 13 \times 16^1 + 2 \times 16^0$$

$$= 3794_{10}$$

(here in decimal system E = 14, D = 13)

(*iv*) *Decimal to Hexadecimal:*

72905_{10} ⟶		Remainder ⇔	Hexa notation
	16) 72905		
	16) 4556	------ 9	9
	16) 284	------ 12	C
	16) 17	------ 12	C
	16) 1	------ 1	1
	16) 0	------ 1	1

$\therefore \quad 72905_{10} = 11CC9_{16}$

4. Octal Number System

This system is formed by grouping bits in group of 3, starting at binary point. The highest digit in octal system is 7. Its base (radix) is 8.

e.g. (*i*) *Binary to Octal conversion*

$$11011\ 101_2 = \underbrace{011}\ \underbrace{011}\ \underbrace{101} = 335_8$$

(*ii*) *Octal to Binary conversion:*

$$4372_8 = \overset{4}{100}\ \overset{3}{011}\ \overset{7}{111}\ \overset{2}{010} = 100011111010_2$$

(*iii*) *Decimal to Octal conversion:* 56

$$
\begin{array}{r|l}
8 & 56 \\
8 & 7 \longrightarrow 0 \uparrow \\
8 & 0 \longrightarrow 7 \\
\end{array}
$$

$56_{10} = 70_8$

4.1.1. NUMBER CONVERSION

Binary-to-decimal conversion.

To convert a binary number to its decimal equivalent, add the decimal equivalent of each position occupied by a 1.

e.g. $(111001.01)_2 = 1 \times 2^5 + 1 \times 2^4 + 1 \times 2^3 + 0 \times 2^2 + 0 \times 2^1 + 1 \times 2^0 + 0 \times 2^{-1} + 1 \times 2^{-2}$

$= 2^5 + 2^4 + 2^3 + 0 + 0 + 1 + 0 + 0.25$

$= 32 + 16 + 8 + 1 + 0.25 = (57.25)_{10}$

The subscript 2 and 10 respectively identify the base of binary and decimal number systems.

Decimal-to-Binary Conversion.

A decimal number can be converted to its equivalent binary form by *double dabble* method. It can be summarized as:

To convert a decimal number to its binary equivalent, progressively divide the decimal number by 2, noting the remainders; the remainders taken in reverse order form the binary equivalent.

To convert a decimal fraction to its binary equivalent, progressively multiply the fraction by 2, removing and noting the carries; the carries taken in forward order form the binary equivalent.

Example : *Convert the decimal number 25.375 to its binary equivalent.*

Solution. Using double-dabble method on the integer part,

$$
\begin{array}{r|l}
2 & 25 \quad 1 \uparrow \\
2 & 12 \quad 0 \\
2 & 6 \quad 0 \\
2 & 3 \quad 1 \\
 & 1
\end{array}
$$

remainders-read up

Therefore, the binary equivalent of 25 is 11001. Now consider the fraction,

0.375×2	$= 0.75$	0	
0.75×2	$= 1.5$	1	carries–read down
0.5×2	$= 1.0$	1	
0.0×2	$= 0$	0	

The binary equivalent of 0.375 is 0110 = 011. Therefore, the binary equivalent of 25.375 is 11001.011.

4.1.2. BINARY ARITHMETIC

Rules of Binary Addition and Subtraction

1. *Rules of binary addition :*

A	B	SUM	CARRY
0	0	0	0
0	1	1	0
1	0	1	0
1	1	0	1

2. *Rules of binary subtraction :*

A	B	SUB	BORROW
0	0	0	0
0	1	1	1
1	0	1	0
1	1	0	0

In subtraction, subtract column by column, borrowing wherever necessary from higher position.

SIGNED NUMBERS.

There are three binary signed number systems in decimal number system :

(*i*) Sign-magnitude Representation.

In this representation, MSB is used to represent sign (0 for positive and 1 for negative) and remaining bits are used to repersent magnitude of the number.

e.g., binary 6–bit number 011010 represents a positive number and its value is 26, whereas 111010 represents a negative number written as – 26.

In general, maximum positive number that can be represented using sign-magnitude form is $+(2^{n-1}-1)$ *and maximum negative number that can be represented is* $-(2^{n-1}-1)$, *where n is number of bits.*

(*ii*) One's Complement Notation.

In a binary number, if we replace each 0 by 1 and each 1 by 0, we obtain another binary number which is one's complement of the first binary number.

e.g. while $(0111)_2$ represents $(+7)_{10}$, $(1000)_2$ represents $(-7)_{10}$.

In general, maximum positive and negative number that can be represented are $(2^{n-1}-1)$ and $-(2^{n-1}-1)$ respectively.

(*iii*) Two's Complement Notation.

By adding 1 to the one's complement of a binary number we get two's complement of that binary number. This can also be used for representing negative numbers.

e.g. 0101 represents + 5, whereas its 2's complement, 1011 (1's complement + 1) represents – 5.

Here, for an *n*-bit number, maximum positive number that can be represented is $+(2^{n-1}-1)$ and maximum negative number that can be represented is $-(2^{n-1})$.

Binary Subtraction Using Two's Complement

Two's complement representation is usually preferred over other representations because of the ease in binary subtraction.

e.g., in evaluating (A – B) (A and B are binary numbers) we subtract B from A, adding 2's complement of B to A. If a final carry is generated, it is discarded and answer is given by the remaining bits which is positive (A is greater than B). If final carry is 0, then answer is negative (B is greater than A) and is in the 2's complement form.

Example. *Represent* $(-22)_{10}$ *in 8–bit 2's complement notation.*

Solution : By adding 1 to the one's complement, we get

$$-22 \longrightarrow -10110 \longrightarrow -00010110$$

$$\longrightarrow 11101001 + 1 \longrightarrow 11101010$$

The 11101010 is 2's complement representation of – 22.

Rule of finding 2's complement of a Binary number :

Scan the number from LSB to MSB and write bits as they are upto and including occurrence of the first 1 and complement all other bits.

Binary Multiplication

Binary multiplication is similar to decimal multiplication. In binary multiplication, say A × B, each partial product is either 0 or A itself (*i.e.* multiplicand) as multiplication is either by 0 or by 1 respectively.

Example : *Multiply 1101 by 1010*

Solution.

```
       1101       Multiplicand
     × 1010
     ------
       0000  ⎫
      1101   ⎪    Partial products
     0000    ⎬
    1101     ⎪
   --------  ⎪
   10000010  ⎭    Product
```

Binary Division

Binary division is again performed in a similar way to decimal division.

Example : *Divide 1011011 by 111*

Solution.

```
111)1011011(1101
    0111
    ----
     1000
     0111
     ------
     000111
        111
        ---
          0
```

4.1.3 OCTAL NUMBER SYSTEM

It is one of the popular number system. There are $8(2^3)$ combinations of 3-bit binary numbers. Therefore, sets of 3-bit binary numbers can be conveniently represented by octal numbers with base 8.

These numbers are 0, 1, 2, 3, 4, 5, 6 and 7.

e.g., $(1062.403)_8$ is an octal number and can be written as

$$(1062.403)_8 = 1\times 8^3 + 0\times 8^2 + 6\times 8^1 + 2\times 8^0 + 4\times 8^{-1} + 0\times 8^{-2} + 3\times 8^{-3}$$

$$= 512 + 48 + 2 + \frac{4}{8} + \frac{3}{512}$$

$$= (562.50586)_{10}$$

This procedure gives the decimal equivalent of an octal number.

Octal-to-Binary and Binary-to-Octal Conversion

Octal numbers can be converted to equivalent binary numbers by replacing each digit by its 3-bit binary equivalent.

e.g. $(642.71)_8 = (110100010.111001)_2$

Similarly, binary numbers can be converted into equivalent octal numbers by making groups of 3-bits starting from LSB and moving towards MSB for integer part.

e.g. $(101110011)_2 = 101\ 110\ 011 = (563)_8$

For fractional parts, we start grouping from the bit next to the binary point and move towards right.

e.g. $(0.10110110)_2 = 0.101\ 101\ 100 = (0.554)_8$

In forming the 3-bit groupings, sometimes we may have to add 0's to complete the MSD group in the integer part and the LSD group in the fractional part.

Table 4.2. Binary and Octal equivalents of decimal numbers 0–7

Decimal	*Binary*	*Octal*
0	000	0
1	001	1
2	010	2
3	011	3
4	100	4
5	101	5
6	110	6
7	111	7

4.1.4 HEXADECIMAL NUMBER SYSTEM

Hexadecimal numbers are extensively used in association with microprocessors. Hexadecimal means 16. There are 16 combinations of 4-bit binary numbers and sets of 4-bit binary numbers can be entered in the microprocessor in the form of hexadecimal digits. The base (or radix) of hexadecimal number is 16. This means that it uses 16 symbols to represent all numbers. These are

0, 1, 2, 3, 4, 5, 6, 7, 8, 9, A, B, C, D, E, F.

Since both numbers as well as alphabets are used to represent the digits in hexadecimal number system, it is also called as *alphanumeric number system.*

Table. Binary and Hexadecimal equivalences of decimal numbers

Decimal	*Binary*	*Hexadecimal*
0	0000	0
1	0001	1
2	0010	2
3	0011	3
4	0100	4
5	0101	5
6	0110	6
7	0111	7
8	1000	8
9	1001	9
10	1010	A
11	1011	B
12	1100	C
13	1101	D
14	1110	E
15	1111	F

Since 16 digits are used, the weights are in powers of 16. The decimal equivalent of a hexadecimal string equals sum of all hexadecimal digits multiplied by their weights.

e.g.
$$\begin{aligned}(\text{F8E. 2B})_{16} &= \text{F} \times 16^2 + 8 \times 16^1 + \text{E} \times 16^0 + 2 \times 16^{-1} + \text{B} \times 16^{-2} \\ &= 15 \times 16^2 + 8 \times 16^1 + 14 \times 16^0 + 2 \times 16^{-1} + 11 \times 16^{-2} \\ &= 3840 + 128 + 14 + \frac{2}{16} + \frac{11}{256} \\ &= (3982.16796875)_{10}\end{aligned}$$

Conversion from decimal to hexadecimal is similar to the procedure used in binary and octal conversion except that here, 16 is used in dividing for integer part and multiplying for fractional part.

Hexadecimal-to-Binary and Binary-to-Hexadecimal Conversions

Hexadecimal numbers can be converted into equivalent binary by replacing each hexadecimal digit by its equivalent 4–bit binary number.

e.g. $(\text{20E.CA})_{16} = (0010\ 0000\ 1110.1100\ 1010)_2 = (001000001110.11001010)_2$

Binary numbers can also be converted into hexadecimal numbers by making groups of four bits starting from LSB and moving towards MSB, for integers, and then replacing each group of four bits by its hexadecimal equivalents. Sometimes, in forming 4-bit groupings, 0's may be required to complete the most significant digit group in the integer part.

e.g., $(1\,0\,1\,0\,0\,1\,1\,0\,1\,1\,1\,1\,1\,1\,0)_2 = (0010\ 1001\ 1011\ 1110)_2 = (\text{29BE})_{16}.$

For fractional part, the above procedure is repeated starting from the bit next to the hexadecimal point and moving towards the right. Here again, in forming 4-bit groupings 0's may be required to complete the least significant digit group.

e.g. $(0.00111110111101)_2 = (0.0011\ 1110\ 1111\ 0100)_2 = (0.\text{3EF4})_{16}$

4.1.5. CODES

Table 4.3. Some commonly used binary codes

Decimal Number	*Binary*	*BCD*	*Excess-3*	*Gray*
0	0000	0000	0011	0000
1	0001	0001	0100	0001
2	0010	0010	0101	0011
3	0011	0011	0110	0010
4	0100	0100	0111	0110
5	0101	0101	1000	0111
6	0110	0110	1001	0101
7	0111	0111	1010	0100
8	1000	1000	1011	1100
9	1001	1001	1100	1101
10	1010			1111
11	1011			1110
12	1100			1010
13	1101			1011
14	1110			1001
15	1111			1000

Binary Code

This is obtained by converting decimal numbers to their binary equivalents. The CPUs of computers process only binary numbers.

BCD Code

This is a binary code in which decimal digits 0 to 9 are represented by their binary equivalents using four bits. As the weights in BCD code are 8, 4, 2, 1, it is also known as 8421 code. *e.g.*, decimal 257 converts to BCD as follows

$$\begin{array}{ccc} 2 & 5 & 7 \\ \downarrow & \downarrow & \downarrow \\ 0010 & 0101 & 0111 \end{array}$$

Therefore, 0010 0101 0111 is the BCD equivalent of $(257)_{10}$. The reverse conversion is similar. *e.g.*,

$$(986)_{10} = 1001\ \ 1000\ \ 0110$$

BCD numbers are very useful for input and output operations in digital circuits. It is used to represent decimal digits in systems like digital calculators, digital voltmeters, digital clocks, electronic counters etc.

Excess–3 Code

This code is derived from natural binary code by adding 3 to each number to be coded. For example, 7 in Excess-3 is represented as 1010. It is quite useful because the nines complement of the decimal digit represented by this code can be easily obtained by simply complementing each bit.

e.g., 5 in excess-3 is 1000 and its 9's complement is 0111 in excess-3 code. Therefore, it can be used for performing subtraction operation in digital computers.

Gray Code

In Gray code, representation of successive numbers differs only by one bit and is therefore often used in digital systems.

e.g. 0100 represents 7 and 1100 represents 8 in Gray code.

A four-bit Gray code is obtained from the binary code in the following way :

$$G_3 = B_3$$

$$G_2 = B_3 \oplus B_2$$

$$G_1 = B_2 \oplus B_1$$

$$G_0 = B_1 \oplus B_0$$

For example, the binary number 1101 in Gray code becomes 1011. To generalize, MSB of Gray code and binary code are the same. Subsequent Gray code bits are obtained by EX-Oring that bit of the binary code with its immediate higher bit.

4.1.6. BOOLEAN RELATIONS

Some basic Logic gate Relations, Operations

(*i*) OR operation.

$A + 0 = A, \quad A + 1 = 1$

$A + A = A, \quad A + \overline{A} = 1$

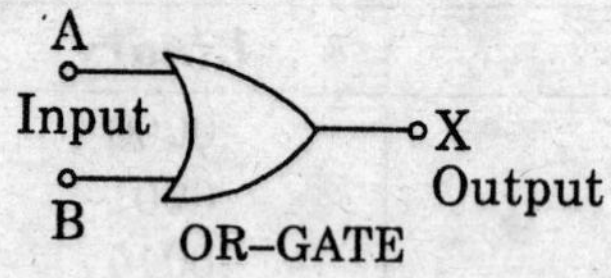

(*ii*) AND operation.

$A . 0 = 0, \quad A . 1 = A$

$A . A = A, \quad A . \overline{A} = 0$

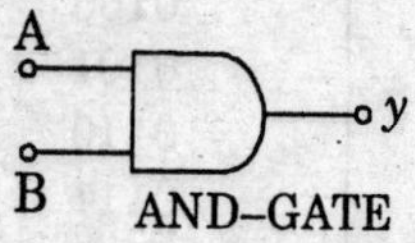

(*iii*) NOT operation.

A(input); $\overline{A}$ (output)

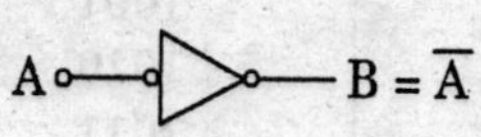

Some laws related to Logic Gates

(*i*) Commutative law.

$$A + B = B + A$$

(*ii*) Associative law.

$$A + (B + C) = (A + B) + C$$

(*iii*) Distributive law.

$$A . (B + C) = A . B + A . C$$

(*iv*) $A + (B . C) = (A + B) . (A + C)$

(*v*) $A = \overline{\overline{A}}$

De Morgan's Theorem

(*i*) $\overline{A + B} = \overline{A} . \overline{B}$

(*ii*) $\overline{A . B} = \overline{A} + \overline{B}$

To obtain the inverse of any Boolean function, invert all variable and replace all OR's by AND's and vice versa.

Table 4.4. Truth Table to Prove De Morgan's Theorem

A	B	$\overline{A}$	$\overline{B}$	$\overline{A.B}$	$\overline{A} + \overline{B}$	$\overline{A + B}$	$\overline{A} . \overline{B}$
0	0	1	1	1	1	1	1
0	1	1	0	1	1	0	0
1	0	0	1	1	1	0	0
1	1	0	0	0	0	0	0

Duality Theorem

Starting with a Boolean relation, we can derive another Boolean relation, called its *dual* by the following steps :

(*i*) Changing each OR sign to an AND sign

(*ii*) Changing each AND sign to an OR sign

(*iii*) Complementing all 0's and 1's

e.g., dual of A . 0 = 0 is written as A + 1 = 1.

Applying duality theorem to A . (B + C) = A . B + A . C

by relationship *(iv)* above, we get

$$A + (B . C) = (A + B) . (A + C),$$

Table 4.5. Boolean Algebraic Theorems/Laws/Expressions

S. No.	Theorems
1	$A + 0 = A$
2	$A.1 = A$
3	$A + 1 = 1$
4	$A.0 = 0$
5	$A + A = A$
6	$A.A = A$
7	$A + \overline{A} = 1$
8	$A.\overline{A} = 0$
9	$A.(B + C) = A.B + A.C$
10	$A + (B.C) = (A + B).(A + C)$
11	$A + (A.B) = A$
12	$A.(A + B) = A$
13	$A + \overline{A}B = A + B$
14	$A.(\overline{A} + B) = A.B$
15	$A.B + A.\overline{B} = A$
16	$(A + B).(A + \overline{B}) = A$
	De Morgan's Law
17	$\overline{A.B.C...} = \overline{A} + \overline{B} + \overline{C} + ...$
18	$\overline{A + B + C + ...} = \overline{A}.\overline{B}.\overline{C}.....$
	Expressions
19	$A.B + \overline{A}.C = (A + C).(\overline{A} + B)$
20	$(A + B).(\overline{A} + C) = (A.C) + (\overline{A}.B)$
21	$(A.B) + (\overline{A}.C) + (B.C) = (A.B) + (\overline{A}.C)$
22	$(A + B).(\overline{A} + C).(B + C) = (A + B).(\overline{A} + C)$

Proofs of Some Theorems/Expressions

12.
$$\begin{aligned} A.(A + B) &= A.A + A.B \\ &= A + A.B \\ &= A.(1 + B) = A \end{aligned}$$

13.
$$\begin{aligned} A + \overline{A}.B &= (A + \overline{A}).(A + B) && \text{...(Theorem 10)} \\ &= A + B \end{aligned}$$

19.
$$\begin{aligned} A.B + \overline{A}.C &= AB(C + \overline{C}) + \overline{A}C(B + \overline{B}) \\ &= ABC + AB\overline{C} + \overline{A}BC + \overline{A}\overline{B}C \\ &= BC(A + \overline{A}) + AB\overline{C} + \overline{A}\overline{B}C \\ &= BC + AB\overline{C} + \overline{A}\overline{B}C \\ &= C(B + \overline{A}\overline{B}) + AB\overline{C} \\ &= C(B + \overline{A}) + AB\overline{C} && \text{...(By Theorem 13)} \\ &= CB + C\overline{A} + AB\overline{C} \\ &= B(C + A\overline{C}) + \overline{A}C \\ &= B(C + A) + \overline{A}C && \text{...(By Theorem 13)} \\ & BC + AB + \overline{A}C + A\overline{A} \\ &= C(\overline{A} + B) + A(\overline{A} + B) \\ &= (A + C)(\overline{A} + B) \end{aligned}$$

22. $(A + B) \cdot (\bar{A} + C) \cdot (B + C) = (B + A)(B + C)(\bar{A} + C)$ ...(rearranging)

$= (B + AC)(\bar{A} + C)$ ...(By Theorem 10)

$= B(\bar{A} + C) + AC(\bar{A} + C)$

$= \bar{A}B + BC + AC$

$= \bar{A}B + BC + AC + A\bar{A}$

$= A(\bar{A} + C) + B(\bar{A} + C)$

$= (A + B)(\bar{A} + C)$

4.1.7. DIGITAL LOGIC GATE

Boolean two variables true or false may be represented by ON or OFF states of electronic switching circuits. On account of such functioning of switching circuits, Boolean algebra becomes of practical significance and is implemented through these switches that act as electronic logic circuits called *logic gates*.

Graphic symbol, Algebraic function and Truth Table for various Logic gates :

Logic gate	Graphic symbol	Algebraic function	Truth table x	y	F
AND		$F = xy$	0 0 1 1	0 1 0 1	0 0 0 1
OR		$F = x+y$	0 0 1 1	0 1 0 1	0 1 1 1
Inverter		$F = \bar{x}$	0 1		1 0
Buffer		$F = x$	0 1		0 1
NAND		$F = \overline{xy}$	0 0 1 1	0 1 0 1	1 1 1 0
NOR		$F = \overline{(x+y)}$	0 0 1 1	0 1 0 1	1 0 0 0
Exclusive-OR (XOR)		$F = x\bar{y} + \bar{x}y = x \oplus y$	0 0 1 1	0 1 0 1	0 1 1 0
Exclusive-NOR or equivalence		$F = xy + \bar{x}\bar{y} = x \odot y$	0 0 1 1	0 1 0 1	1 0 0 1

4.1.8. SUM-OR-PRODUCTS/PRODUCT-OF-SUMS METHOD

Switching function (Boolean function) implied by a truth table may be stated as Sum-OF-Products (SOP) or a Product-Of-Sums (POS).

e.g., for an X-OR truth table

Output $= \bar{A}B + A\bar{B}$; (SOP form)

and Output $= (A + B)(\bar{A} + \bar{B})$ (POS form)

Here each term contains all the inputs, *i.e.* individual Boolean variables in complemented or uncomplemented form called *literals*. This is *canonical* or *standard form*. Each term in standard SOP form is called a **minterm** and that each term in standard POS form is called a **maxterm.** For n inputs there are 2^n maxterms. Two logically different functions do not contain same set of minterms (maxterms).

Table 4.6. Truth Table

A	B	Y	Minterm	Maxterm
0	0	0	$\bar{A}\bar{B}$	$A+B$
0	1	1	$\bar{A}B$	$A+\bar{B}$
1	0	1	$A\bar{B}$	$\bar{A}+B$
1	1	1	AB	$\bar{A}+\bar{B}$

Output is given by sum of minterm corresponding to 1 output.

$Y = \bar{A}B + A\bar{B} + AB$; (SOP form)

Output can be written as product of those maxterms which correspond to 0 output, *i.e.*

$Y = A + B$; (POS form)

Equivalence of these expression is established below :

$$Y = \bar{A}B + A\bar{B} + AB$$

$$= \bar{A}B + A(\bar{B} + B)$$

$$= \bar{A}B + A = A + \bar{A}B$$

$$= (A + \bar{A})(A + B) \quad \text{(Distributive law)}$$

$$= (A + B)$$

Example. *Obtain SOP and POS expressions for the truth table of Table given below.*

A	B	C	Y	Minterm	Maxterm
0	0	0	0	$\bar{A}\bar{B}\bar{C}$	$A+B+C$
0	0	1	1	$\bar{A}\bar{B}C$	$A+B+\bar{C}$
0	1	0	0	$\bar{A}B\bar{C}$	$A+\bar{B}+C$
0	1	1	1	$\bar{A}BC$	$A+\bar{B}+\bar{C}$
1	0	0	0	$A\bar{B}\bar{C}$	$\bar{A}+B+C$
1	0	1	1	$A\bar{B}C$	$\bar{A}+B+\bar{C}$
1	1	0	0	$AB\bar{C}$	$\bar{A}+\bar{B}+C$
1	1	1	1	ABC	$\bar{A}+\bar{B}+\bar{C}$

Solution :

From given table, choosing minterms corresponding to Y = 1 in the truth table, we can write

$$Y = \bar{A}\,\bar{B}C + \bar{A}BC + A\bar{B}C + ABC \text{ ; SOP form}$$

In term of maxterms which correspond to Y = 0, we can write

$$Y = (A+B+C)(A+\bar{B}+C)(\bar{A}+B+C)(\bar{A}+\bar{B}+C)\text{; POS form}$$

But $\quad Y + \bar{Y} = 1$

so while minterms which correspond to 1 outputs constitute SOP, the complimentary minterms which correspond to 0 outputs, their SOP would then constitute $\bar{Y}$,

i.e.
$$\bar{Y} = \bar{A}\bar{B}\,\bar{C} + \bar{A}B\,\bar{C} + A\bar{B}\bar{C} + AB\bar{C}$$

Similarly for maxterms, outputs corresponding to 1 outputs would constitute $\bar{Y}$,

i.e.
$$\bar{Y} = (A+B+\bar{C})(A+\bar{B}+\bar{C})(\bar{A}+B+\bar{C})(\bar{A}+\bar{B}+\bar{C})$$

As per SOP expression of Truth Table, combinational circuit is drawn below :

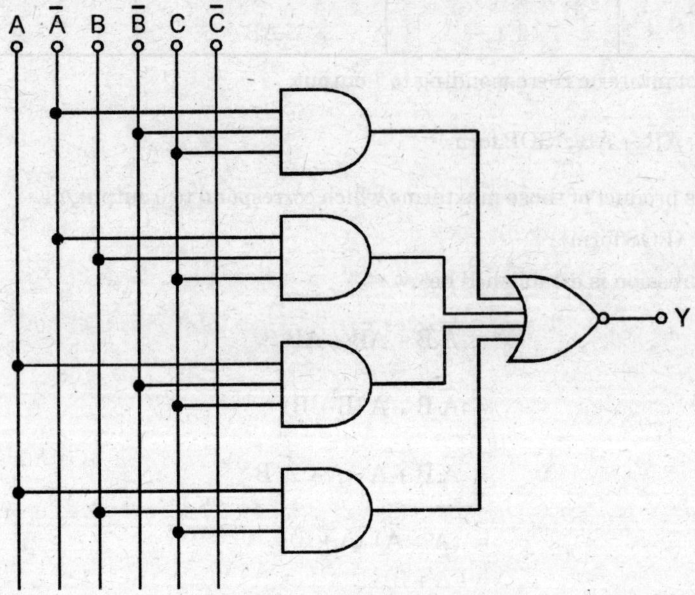

Fig. Sum of products circuit

Example : *Factorize following Boolean equations*

(i) $Y = A\bar{B} + AB$

(ii) $Y = AB + AC + BD + CD$

(iii) $Y = (B + CA)(C + \bar{A}B)$

(iv) $Y = \bar{A}\,\bar{B}\,\bar{C}\,\bar{D} + \bar{A}\,\bar{B}\,\bar{C}D + A\,\bar{B}\,\bar{C}\,\bar{D} + A\,\bar{B}\,\bar{C}\,D$

Solution.

(i) $\quad Y = A\bar{B} + AB = A(\bar{B} + B) = A \,.\, 1 = A$

(ii) $\quad Y = AB + AC + BD + CD$

$\quad = A(B + C) + D(B + C)$

$\quad = (A + D)(B + C)$

(iii) $Y = (B + CA)(C + \bar{A}B)$

$= B(C + \bar{A}B) + CA(C + \bar{A}B)$

$= BC + B\bar{A}B + CAC + CA\bar{A}B;$

$= BC + \bar{A}B + AC$

(iv) $Y = \bar{A}\bar{B}\bar{C}\bar{D} + \bar{A}\bar{B}\bar{C}D + A\bar{B}\bar{C}\bar{D} + A\bar{B}\bar{C}D$

$= \bar{B}\,\bar{C}(\bar{A}\,\bar{D} + \bar{A}D + A\bar{D} + AD)$

$= \bar{B}\bar{C}[\bar{A}(\bar{D} + D) + A(\bar{D} + D)]$

$= \bar{B}\,\bar{C}(\bar{A} + A)$

$= \bar{B}\,\bar{C}\,.1 = \bar{B}\,\bar{C}$

Example. *Compare AND / OR gate realization of the Boolean function of previous example part (ii) and its reduced form.*

Solution. From Figs. (*a*) and (*b*), realization of the original function needs 5 gates (4 AND's and 1 OR), while simplified function needs only 3 gates (1 AND and 2 OR's). There is a considerable saving in realization by carrying out simplification of the original function.

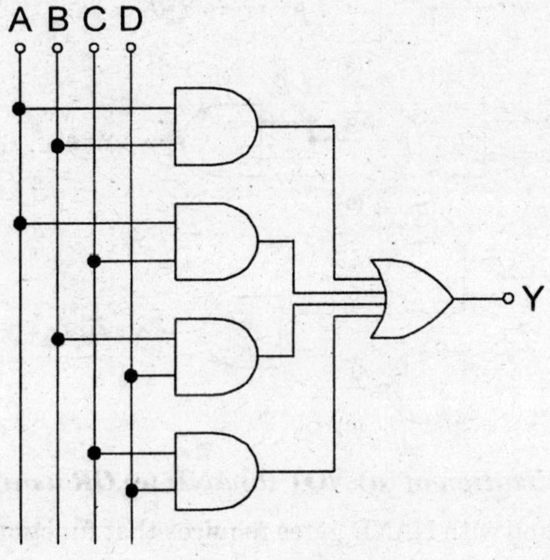

(a)

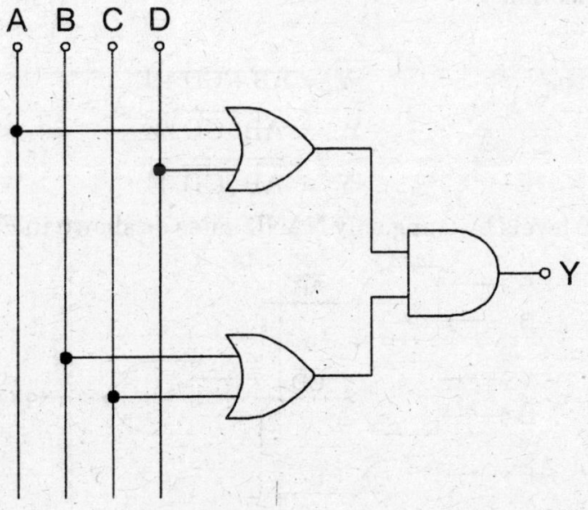

(b)

Fig. Logic circuits

Example. *Analyze logic circuit of figure given below and show that it can be replaced by a single NAND gate.*

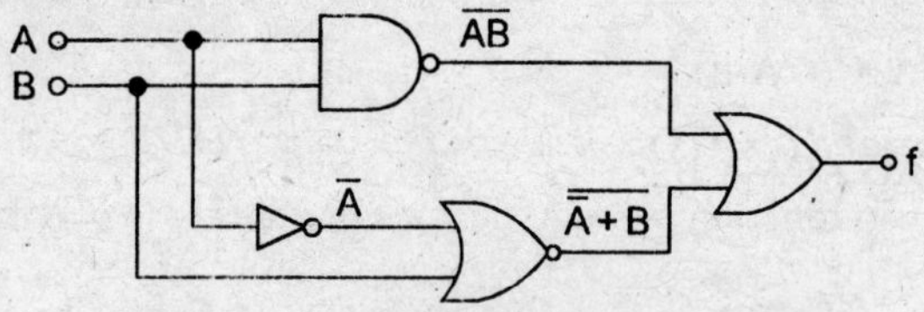

Solution. Suboutputs are given in the figure. Simplification of the function is

$$f = \overline{AB} + \overline{\overline{A}+B}$$

$$= \overline{(A\,B).(\overline{A}+B)} \quad \text{...(De Morgan's law)}$$

$$= \overline{AB\overline{A} + ABB} \quad (\because A\overline{A} = 0.\ BB = B)$$

$$= \overline{AB}$$

Thus, above circuit is simply equivalent to a NAND gate.

4.1.9 NAND AND NOR IMPLEMENTATION

It is an attractive preposition to realize combinational circuits using NAND/NOR gates (universal gates) as only one type of gates are required.

NAND Implementation

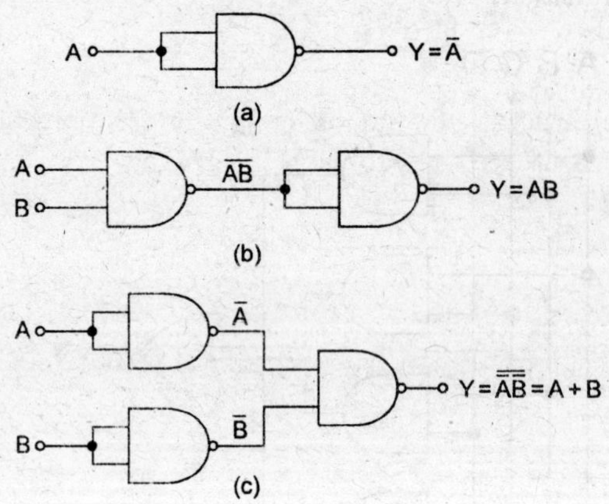

Fig. 4.1 Realization of (a) NOT (b) AND (c) OR using NAND gates.

Implementation of a Boolean function with NAND gates requires that function be simplified in the sum-or-products form.

Now we apply De Morgan's theorem.

e.g., consider function

$$Y = AB + CD + E$$

$$\overline{Y} = \overline{AB}.\overline{CD}.\overline{E}$$

$$\Rightarrow \qquad Y = \overline{\overline{AB}.\overline{CD}.\overline{E}}$$

This can be implemented in 2 levels by using only NAND gates as shown in Fig. 4.2.

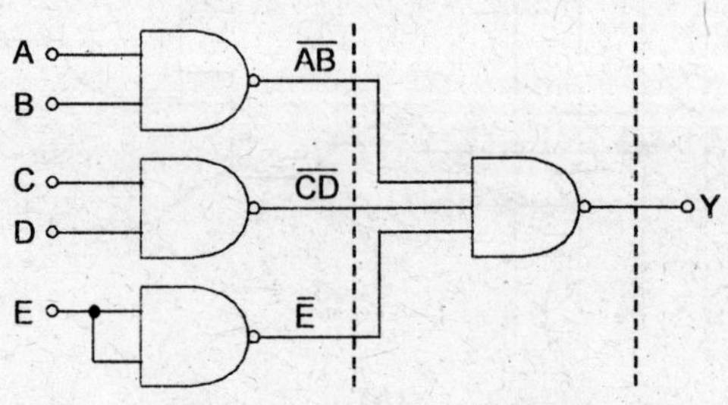

Fig. 4.2 Realization of Y = AB + CD + E.

Example : *Given the Boolean function*

$$F = (A+\overline{B})(CD+E)$$

Obtain AND-OR implementation and also its implementation using NAND gates only.

Solution. The realization of given function using AND and OR gates is shown in the figure below.

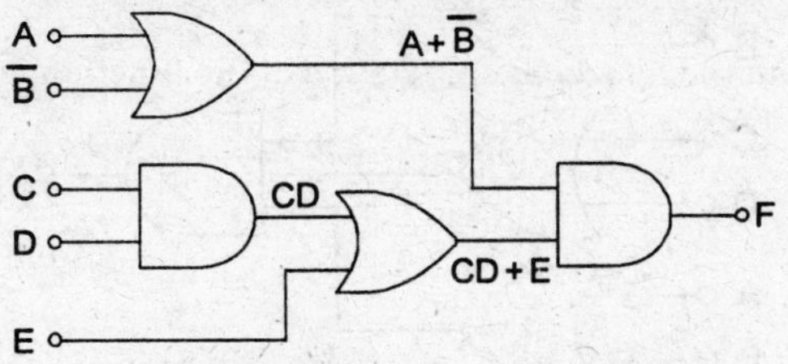

Fig. AND/OR implementation

Consider again, the function

$$F = (A+\overline{B})(CD+E)$$

We can write $A+\overline{B} = \overline{\overline{A}.B}$

and similarly, $CD+E = \overline{\overline{CD}.\overline{E}}$

Therefore, $F = \overline{\overline{A}.B}.\overline{\overline{CD}.\overline{E}}$

NAND realization of the above equation is shown in the figure below. Output of NAND gate is $\overline{F}$. So to obtain F, invert output of gate 4 by using an inverter NAND gate (5).

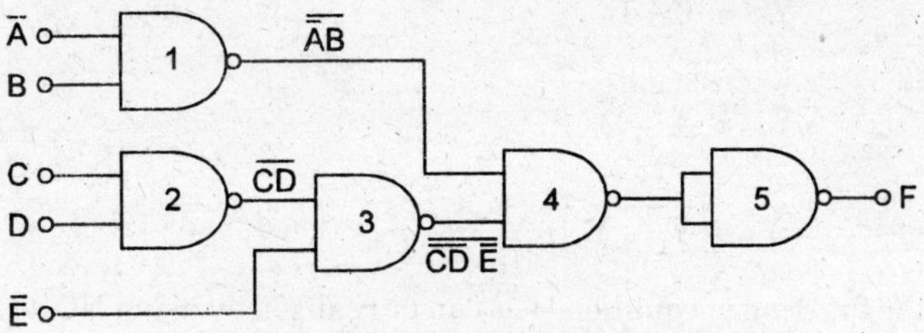

Fig. NAND implementation

NOR Implementation

NOR function is the dual of NAND function. Hence, all the procedures and rules for NOR logic are the dual of corresponding procedures and rules of NAND logic.

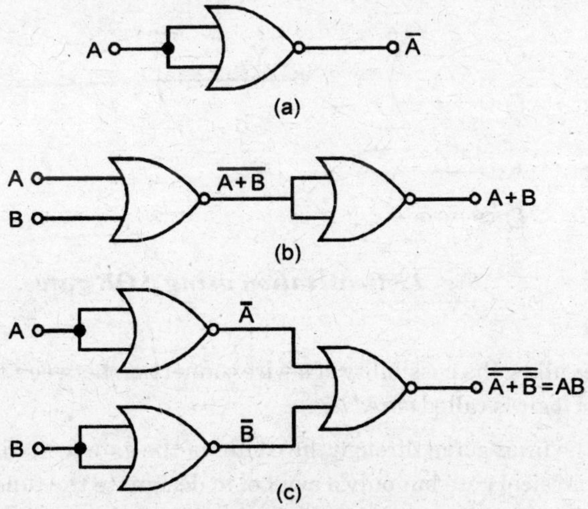

Fig. 4.3 Implementation of (a) NOT (b) OR (c) AND using NOR gates.

Example. $Y = (A + B)(C + D)(A + \overline{D})$ ...(4.1)

Obtain AND-OR implementation and also its implementation using NOR gates only.

Solution. Y is in product-of-sums form. This can be realized using OR-AND gates as shown in Fig. 4.4.

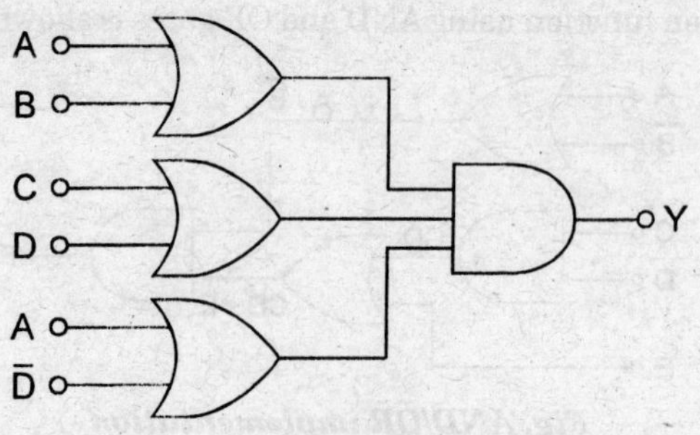

Fig. 4.4 Realization using OR-AND gates.

Using De Morgan's theorem we can write above equation as

$$\overline{Y} = \overline{(A + B)(C + D)(A + \overline{D})} \quad ...(4.2)$$

$$\overline{Y} = \overline{(A + B)} + \overline{(C + D)} + \overline{(A + \overline{D})}$$

$$\overline{Y} = Y_1 + Y_2 + Y_3 \quad ...(4.3)$$

where $Y_1 = \overline{A + B}$

$$Y_2 = \overline{C + D}$$

$$Y_3 = \overline{A + \overline{D}}$$

$\therefore$ $$Y = \overline{Y_1 + Y_2 + Y_3} \quad ...(4.4)$$

Using equation (4.4), the function of equation (4.1) can be realized by using NOR gates only as shown in Fig. 4.5. Thus by expressing a Boolean function in product-of-sums form and applying De Morgan's theorem, it can always be realized by only NOR gates.

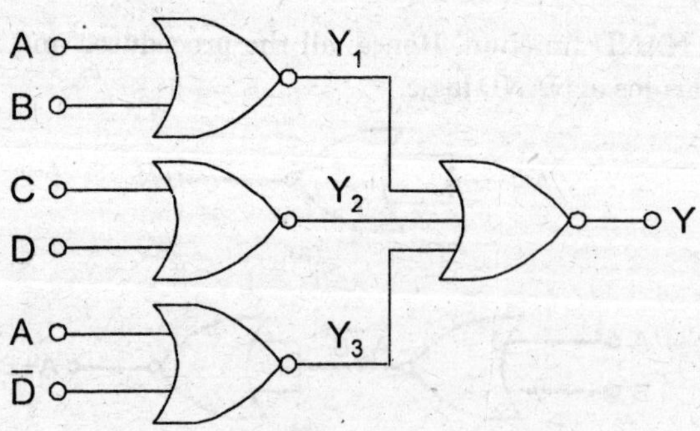

Fig. 4.5 Realization using NOR gates.

Phantom or Wired logic

Some NAND or NOR gates allow the possibility of a wire connection between outputs of two gates to provide a specific logic function. This type of logic is called *wired logic.*

AND gate is drawn with the lines going through the center of the gate to distinguish it from a conventional gate. The wired AND gate is not a physical gate but only a symbol to designate the function obtained from the indicated wired connection. The logic function implemented by the circuit shown below is given by

$$F = \overline{(A.B)}.\overline{(C.D)} = \overline{(AB + CD)}$$

and is called AND-OR-INVERT function. The wired logic can be physically implemented by connecting the collector of two TTL NAND gates. The parallel connection of collector of TTL–NAND gates reduces the resistance which in turn, increases power dissipation in ON-state. In order to avoid high power dissipation, open collector TTL-NAND gates are used for Phantom Logic.

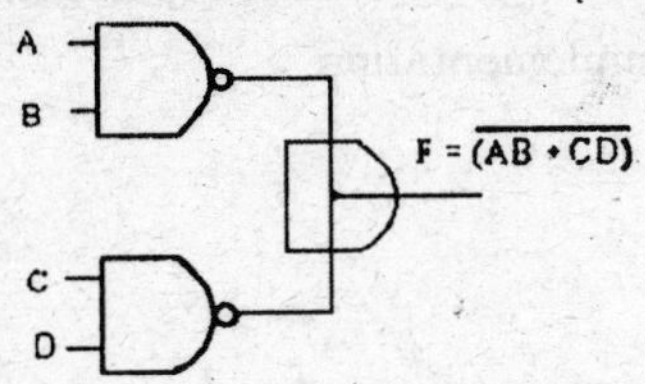

Fig. 4.6 Wired AND (AND-OR-INVERT)

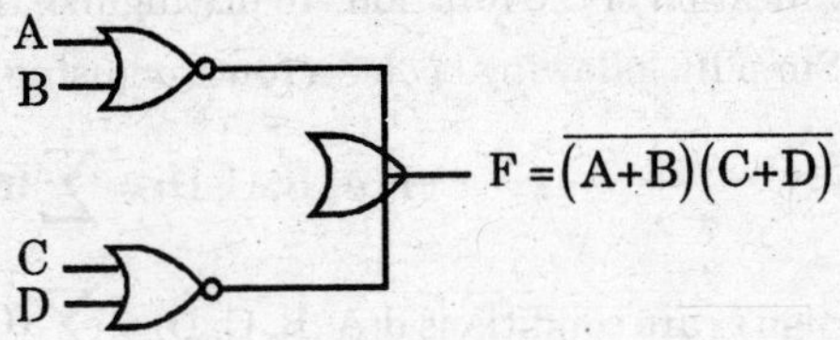

Fig. 4.7 Wired OR (OR-AND-INVERT)

Similarly, NOR output can be tied together to perform a wired-OR function.

The logic function implemented by above circuit is

$$F = \overline{(A + B)} + \overline{(C + D)} = \overline{(A+B)(C+D)}$$

and is called OR-AND-INVERT function. Wired-OR function can be implemented by connecting NOR output of two ECL gates together.

4.1.10. KARNAUGH MAP SIMPLIFICATION

Tabulation Method

Karnaugh map method is convenient as long as the number of variables are limited to five or six; but as the variables increases, excessive number of squares prevents the selection of adjacent groups. This method is called *Quine Ms Clusky method.*

The tabulation method overcomes this difficulty. It is a specific step by step procedure that is guaranteed to product a simplified standard form expression for a function.

Tabular method of simplification consists of two parts.

First part determines all the prime implicants of a given function.

Second part determines a set of essential prime implicants by making prime implicant chart *then* minimal cover for remaining minterms is found.

SOP Form Simplification Using K-Map

To get simplified expression in SOP form (AND-OR configutation), corresponding to each minterm in the given function, '1' is entered in the corresponding cell of the K map.

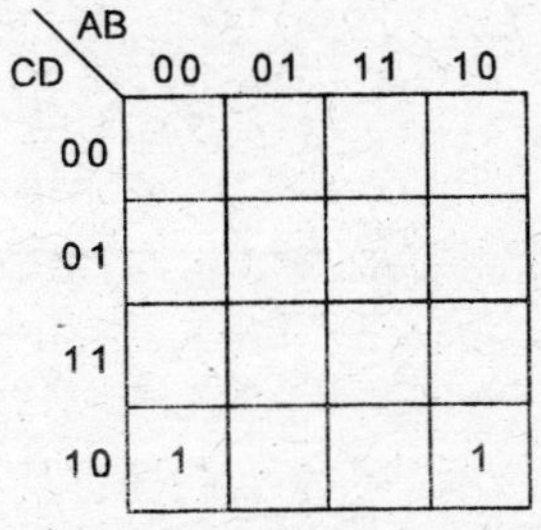

Fig. 4.8 Karnaugh Map

Consider the term $\overline{B}\,C\,\overline{D}$. Enter 1 in the two cells with B = 0, C = 1 and D = 0 but A can be either 0 or 1. These entries are indicated in Fig. 4.8. Such entries are made for all terms of a sum-of-products expression.

Simplification proceeds by combining 1's of adjacent cells.

Two cells are said to be adjacent if

(*i*) these are vertically above each other or are in the top and bottom cells of a column and

(*ii*) these are horizontally side by side or in left and right most cells of a row.

In combining adjacent cells it is to be noted that these differ in one variable only because of the use of Gray code.

1's of the K-map are combined in groups of 2^i where $i = 1, 2, \ldots, n$; n being number of variables.

Don't Care Conditions

In some cases, certain input combinations never occur.

e.g. In BCD system, 1010 to 1111 are never used and are *don't care terms.* We don't care what the function output is to be because they are guaranted never to occur. These don't care condition can be used on a map to provide further simplification of the function. To distinguish the don't care from 1's and 0's an X will be used to represent.

e.g. Simplify following boolean function using K-map and obtain AND-OR implementation

$$F(A, B, C, D) = \sum m(1,3,7,11,19)$$

and don't care conditions $d(A, B, C, D) = \sum (0,2,5)$

TYPES OF COMBINATIONS FOR SIMPLIFICATION

Pair

The sum-of-products terms corresponding to a pair of adjacent 1's can be combined to **eliminate** variable, which appears in complemented form in these terms; this results from the use of Gray code.

Thus in Fig. 4.9, for the pair of 1's

CD \ AB	00	01	11	10
00	0	0	0	0
01	0	1	1	0
11	0	0	0	0
10	0	0	0	0

Fig 4.9 Pair on a K-map.

$$Y = \bar{A}B\bar{C}D + AB\bar{C}D$$
$$= B\bar{C}D(\bar{A}+A)$$
$$= B\bar{C}D; \quad \text{A is eliminated.}$$

Quad

It is a group of four adjacent 1's in a K-map. It can appear in various ways as shown in Fig. 4.10. This group is called a **quad** which leads to the elimination of two variables. Thus Y's corresponding to the four quads of Fig. 4.10 are given as

CD \ AB	00	01	11	10
00				
01	1	1	1	1
11				
10				

(a) $Y = \bar{C}D$

CD \ AB	00	01	11	10
00				
01				
11			1	1
10			1	1

(b) $Y = AC$

CD \ AB	00	01	11	10
00		1	1	
01				
11				
10		1	1	

(c) $Y = B\bar{D}$

CD \ AB	00	01	11	10
00	1			1
01				
11				
10	1			1

(d) $Y = \overline{BD}$

Fig. 4.10 Quads in K-map

Octet

It is a group of eight adjacent 1's as shown in Fig. 4.11. It leads to elimination of three variables.

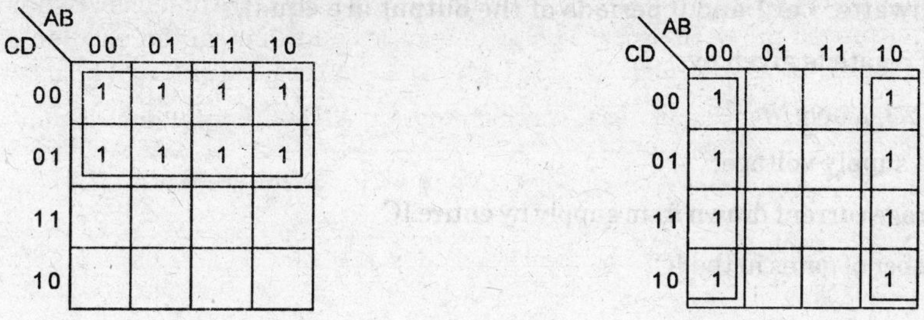

(a) $Y = \overline{C}$ *(b)* $Y = \overline{B}$

Fig. 4.11 Octet in K-maps.

In a K-map there may be more than one pair or a quad or an octet. Because of simplification afforded identification must proceed first as octet, followed by quads and then pairs. The 1's which cannot be grouped must also be encircled. Then Boolean equation is obtained by ORing the products corresponding to the encircled groups.

While forming groups, it is to be noted that

overlapping of groups is allowed, *i.e.* two groups can have one or more 1's in common.

and redundancy is not allowed, *i.e.* a group whose all 1's are overlapped by other groups.

Both these grouping are shown in Fig. 4.12.

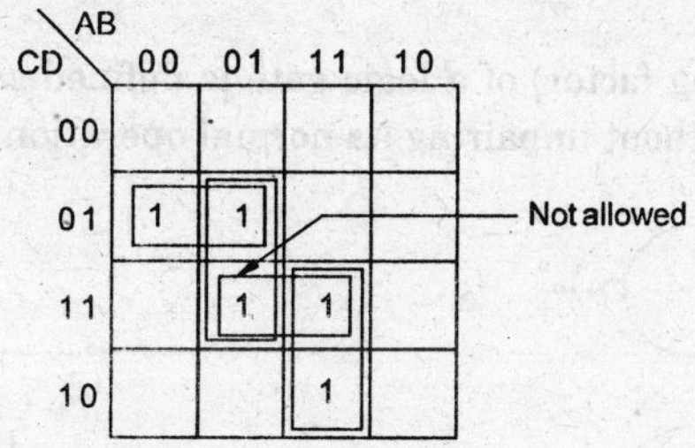

Fig. 4.12 Redundant group not allowed

4.2 DIGITAL IC FAMILIES

4.2.1. IC SPECIFICATION TERMINOLOGY

(1) Propogation Delay

It is the amount of time lapse during propagation of pulse through a gate from input to output. It is the average transition delay time expressed by

$$t_{pd} = \frac{t_{PLH} + t_{PHL}}{2}$$

where,

t_{PLH} = signal delay time when output goes form a logic 0 to a logic 1 state, and

t_{PHL} = signal delay time when output goes from a logic 1 to a logic 0 state.

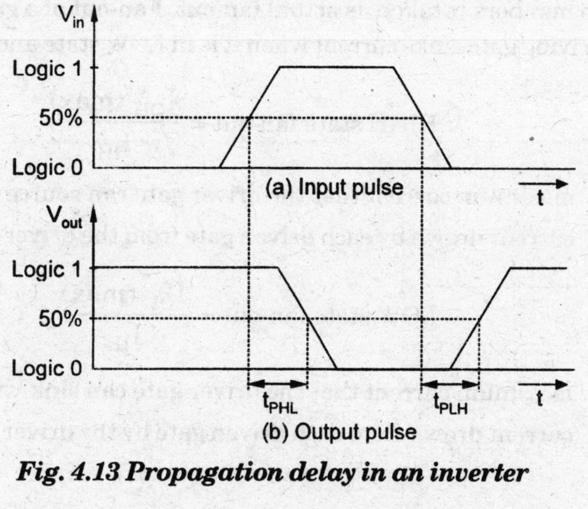

Fig. 4.13 Propagation delay in an inverter

(2) Power Dissipation (P_D)

P_D of a logic gate is the power required by the gate to operate with 50% duty cycle at a specified frequency and is expressed in milliwatts, i.e. 1 and 0 periods of the output are equal.

Power dissipation of a gate is given by

$$P_D = V_{CC} \times I_{CC}(avg)/n$$

where, V_{CC} = gate supply voltage,

I_{CC} (avg) = average current drawn from supply by entire IC

n = number of gates in the IC.

$$\text{Now, } I_{CC}(avg) = \frac{I_{CCH} + I_{CCL}}{2}$$

where, I_{CCH} = current drawn by the IC when all gates in the IC are in HIGH state,

I_{CCL} = current drawn by the IC when all gates in the IC are in LOW state.

Total power consumed by an IC is equal to product of the power dissipated by each gate and number of gates in that IC.

(3) Fan-In

The fan-in of a logic gate is defined as the number of inputs that the gate is designed to handle.

(4) Fan-Out

The fan-out (also called loading factor) of a logic gate is defined as maximum number of standard loads that output of the gate can drive without impairing its normal operation.

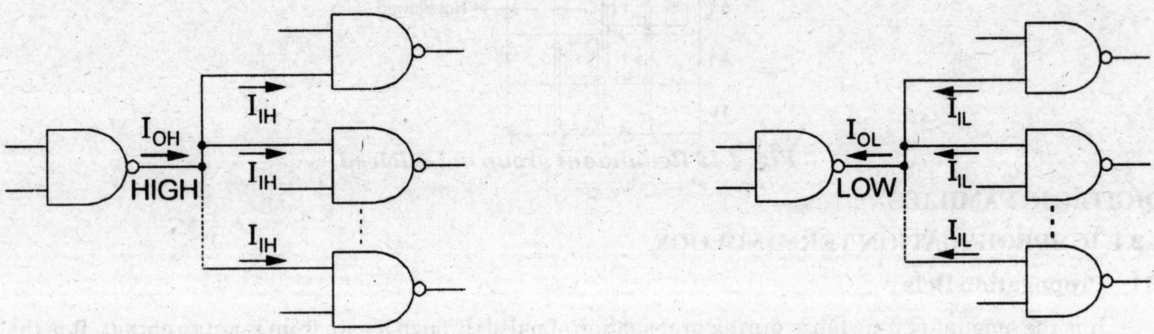

(a) Current sourcing in HIGH state ***(b) Current sinking in LOW state***

Fig. 4.14 High state and Low state fan-outs

Fan-out may be HIGH state fan-out or LOW state fan-out.

HIGH state fan-out, *i.e.* fan-out of the gate when its output is at logic 1,

LOW state fan-output, *i.e.* fan-out of the gate when its output is at logic 0.

Smaller of these two numbers is taken as actual fan-out. Fan-out of a gate affects propagation delay time as well as saturation. The driving gate sinks current when it is in LOW state and sources current when it is in HIGH state.

$$\text{HIGH state fan-out} = \frac{I_{OH}(max)}{I_{IH}}$$

where I_{OH} (max) = maximum current that the driver gate can source when it is in a 1 state, and

I_{IH} = current drawn by each driven gate from the driver gate.

$$\text{LOW state fan-out} = \frac{I_{OL}(max)}{I_{IL}}$$

where I_{OL} (max) = maximum current that the driver gate can sink when its output is a logic 0 and

I_{IL} = current drawn from each driven gate by the driver gate.

(5) Voltage and Current Parameters

V_{IH} (min) (HIGH level input voltage).

It is the minimum voltage level required at the input of a gate for that input to be treated as a logic 1. Any voltage below this level will not be accepted as a logic 1 input by the logic circuit.

V_{OH}(min) (HIGH level output voltage).

It is the minimum voltage level required at the output of a gate for that output to be treated as a logic 1. Any voltage below this level will not be accepted as a logic 1 output.

V_{IL} (max) (LOW level input voltage).

It is the maximum voltage level that can be treated as a logic 0 at the input of the gate. Any voltage above this level will not be treated as a logic 0 input by the logic gate.

V_{OL} (max) (LOW level output voltage).

It is the maximum voltage level that can be treated as a logic 0 at the output of the gate. Any voltage above this level will not be treated as a logic 0 output.

I_{IH} (HIGH level input current).

The current that flows into an input when a specified HIGH level voltage is applied to that input.

I_{IL} (LOW level input current).

It is the current that flows into an input when a specified LOW level voltage is applied to that input.

I_{OH} (HIGH level output current).

It is the current that flows from an output in a logic 1 state under specified load conditions.

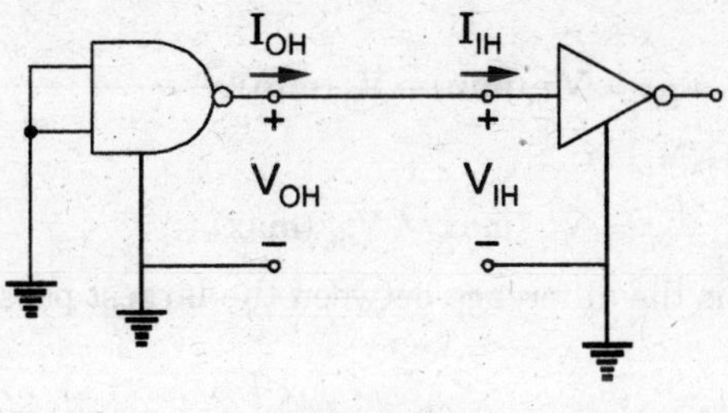

(a) HIGH state

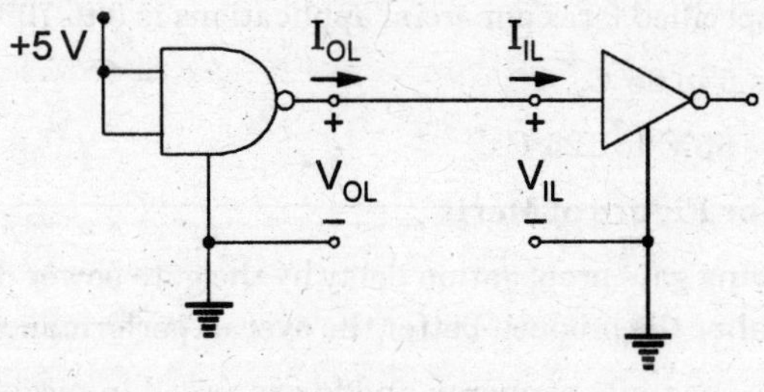

(b) LOW state

Fig. 4.15 Currents and voltages in the HIGH and LOW states

(6) Noise Margin

Noise immunity of a logic circuit refers to the circuits ability to tolerate noise voltages at its inputs. A quantitative measure of noise immunity is called **noise margin**. Unwanted spurious signals are called **noise**.

Noise may be ac noise or dc noise. A drift in the voltage levels of signals is called dc noise. The ac noise is a random pulse caused by other switching signals. Noise margin is expressed in volts and represents maximum noise signal that can be added to the input signal of a digital circuit without causing an undersirable change in the circuit output.

Fig. 4.16 (*a*) shows range of output voltages that can occur in a logic circuit. Voltages greater than V_{OH} (min) are considered as a logic 1 and voltages lower than V_{OL} (max) are considered as a logic 0. Voltages in the disallowed range should not appear at a logic circuit output under conditions. Fig. 4.16 (*b*) shows input voltage requirements of a logic circuit. The logic circuit will respond to any input greater than V_{IH} (min) as a logic 1 and to any input lower than V_{IL} (max) as a logic 0. Voltages in the indeterminate range will produce an unpredictable response and should not be used.

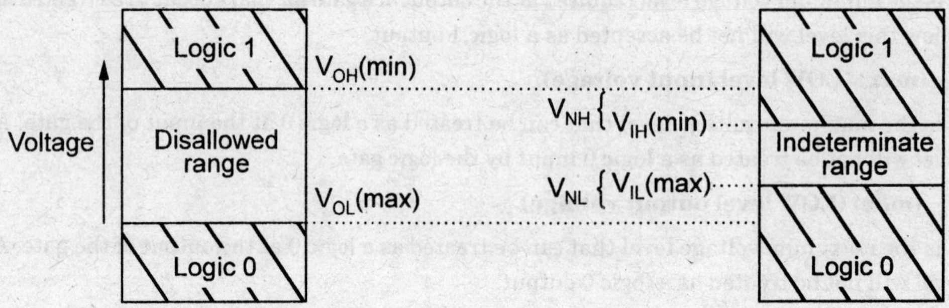

(a) Output voltage ranges ***(b) Input voltage ranges***

Fig. 4.16 DC noise margins.

Types of Noise Margin.

Noise margin may be of following two types :

(*i*) High state noise margin (NM_H) is :

High state noise margin is the difference between lowest possible high output and minimum input voltage required for a HIGH.

$$V_{NH} = V_{OH}(\text{min}) - V_{IH}(\text{min})$$

(*ii*) Low state noise margin (NM_L) is :

$$V_{NL} = V_{IL}\,(\text{max}) - V_{OL}\,(\text{max})$$

Low state noise margin is the difference between the largest possible low output and the maximum input voltage for a LOW.

Overall noise margin = $[V_{NH}, V_{NL}]_{min}$

(7) Operating Temperatures

For IC gates, the range specified for commercial applications is 0 to 70°C,

industrial applications is 0 to 85°C,

military applications is – 55°C to 125°C.

(8) Speed Power Product or Figure of Merit

It is obtained by multiplying gate propagation delay by the gate power dissipation. A low value of speed power product is desirable. Smaller the product, better the overall performance.

Speed power product has the units of energy and is expressed in picojoules. It is the figure of merit of an IC family.

Let an IC family has an average propagation delay of 10 ns and an average power dissipation of 5 mW.

Then Speed power product = 10 ns × 5 mW

= 50×10^{-12} watt-seconds

= 50 picojoulses (pJ)

4.2.2. IC FAMILIES

(1) Resistor-Transistor Logic (RTL)

It was most popular form of logic in common use before development of ICs. It consist of resistors and transistors and was the earliest logic family to be integrated. The basic RTL gate is a NOR gate as shown in Fig. 4.17. For the sake of simplicity, a two-input NOR gate driving N similar gates is shown in the figure, which can be extended to accommodate a larger number of inputs.

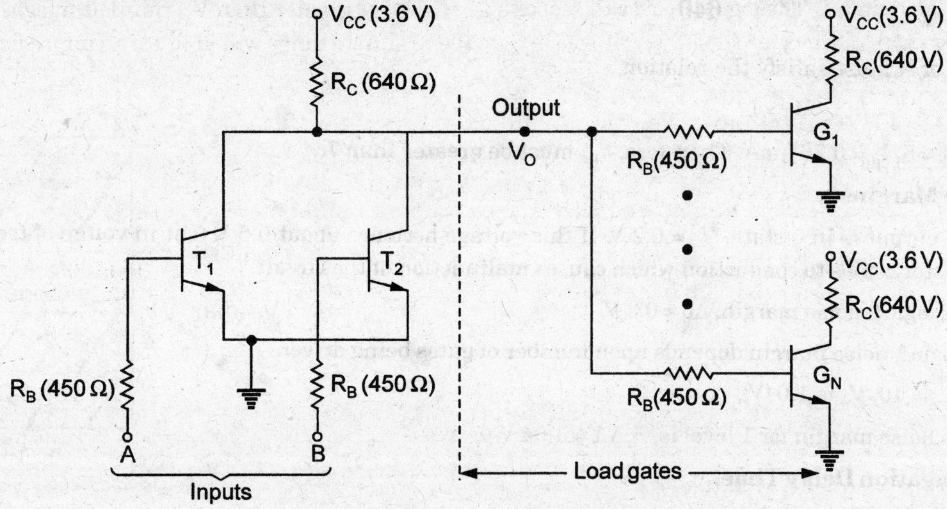

Fig. 4.17 A 2-input RTL NOR gate driving N similar gates.

Logic Operation.

Inputs representing logic levels are applied at A and B terminals. Voltage corresponding to LOW level should be low enough to drive corresponding transistor to cut-off. Similarly, input voltage corresponding to HIGH level should be high enough to drive corresponding transistor to saturation.

If both the inputs are LOW, transistors T_1 and T_2 are cut-off and output is High. A High level on any input will drive corresponding transistor to saturation causing the output to go Low. Low (0) level output voltage is $V_{CE,sat}$ of a transistor (~ 0.2 V) and High (1) level output voltage depends on the number of gates connected to the output. This causes output voltage to be variable and is a deciding factor for the fan-out of the gate.

When N similar gates are being driven, then load will be equivalent to a resistor of value 450/N ohms in series with a voltage source of 0.8 V (being the voltage between base and emitter of a transistor in saturation). The relevant portion of the circuit is shown in Fig. 4.18.

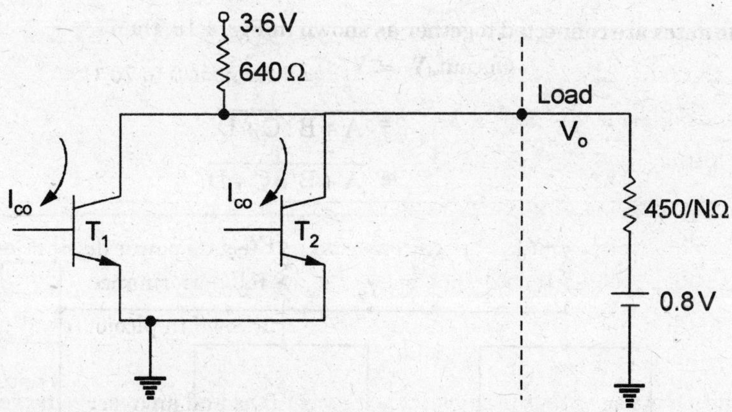

Fig. 4.18 Circuit showing equivalent circuit at the input of load gates

For each load transistor,

$$\text{Base current, } I_B = \left(\frac{3.6 - 0.8}{640 + \frac{450}{N}}\right) \cdot \frac{1}{N} = \frac{2.8}{640\,N + 450}$$

For load transistor in saturation,

$$\text{Collector current, } I_{C,sat} = \frac{3.6 - 0.2}{640} = 5.31 \text{ mA}$$

Value of N must satisfy the relation,

$$h_{FE} \cdot I_B > I_{C,sat}$$

For N = 5, $I_B = 0.767$ mA. Therefore, h_{FE} must be greater than 7.

Noise Margins.

When output is in 0 state, $V_0 = 0.2$ V. If this voltage becomes about 0.5 V (cut-in voltge of transistor), the load transistor comes to conduction which causes malfunction of the circuit.

Hence logic 0 noise margin, $\Delta 0 \approx 0.3$ V.

The logic 1 noise margin depends upon number of gates being driven.

For $h_{FE} = 10$, V_0 is 1.04V

Hence noise margin for 1 level is, $\Delta 1 = 1.04$ V.

Propagation Delay Time.

It is also affected by the number of gates it drives.

When output of the gate is in Low state, all the load transistors are cut-off and base–emitter junction of each of these transistors appears to be a capacitor, C.

When output has to change from Low to High level due to changes at the input, it will do so with a time constant given by

$$\left(640 + \frac{450}{N}\right) N.C = (640\,N + 450)\,C$$

Current Source Logic.

The gate supplies current to the load transistors when in 1 level, whereas leakage-current (reverse-saturation base current) of load transistors flow through T_1 or T_2 in 0 level. Since source current is much greater than the sink current, it is called **current source logic**.

Wired-Logic.

If outputs of the gates are connected together as shown in Fig. 4.19, then

$$\text{Output, } Y = Y_1 . Y_2$$

$$= \overline{A+B} . \overline{C+D} \qquad \left(\text{using } \bar{x}.\bar{y} = \overline{x+y}\right)$$

$$= \overline{A+B+C+D}$$

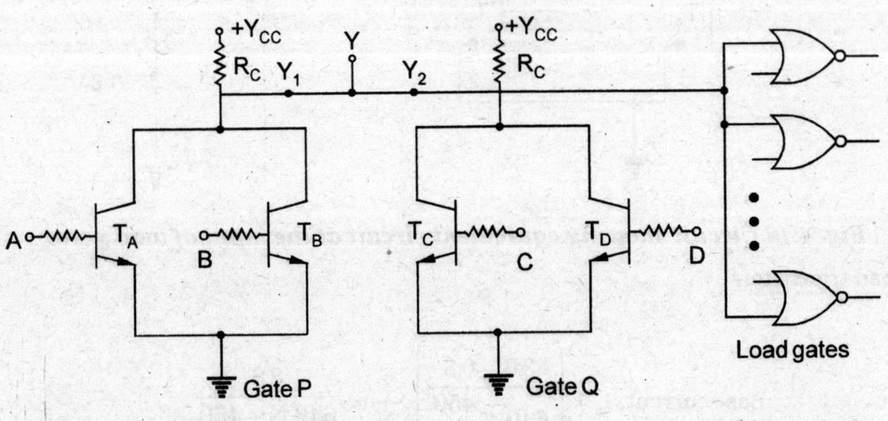

Fig. 4.19 Wired-AND connection of RTL gates driving similar gates

This shows that fan-in can be increased by this connection which is called wired-AND or implied-AND.

(2) Diode–Transistor Logic (DTL)

It is more complex than RTL but because of its greater fan-out and improved noise margins has replaced RTL. Its main disadvantage is slower speed and because of this it was modified and emerged as transistor–transistor logic (TTL) which is most popular logic family today.

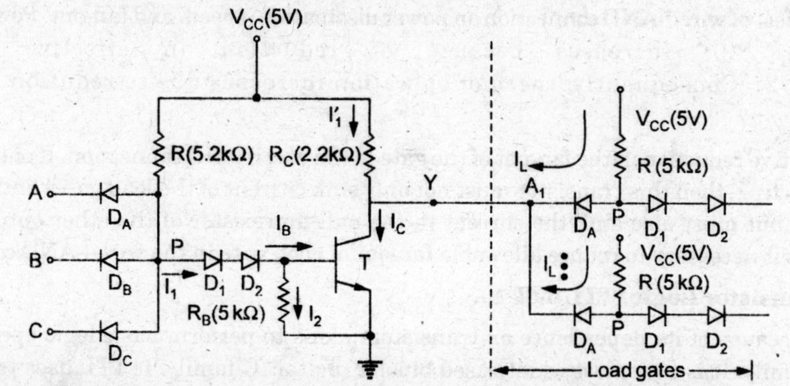

Fig. 4.20 3-input DTL NAND gate driving N similar gates.

Operation of DTL NAND Gate.

Basic DTL gate is a NAND gate. A 3-input NAND gate driving N similar gates is shown in Fig. 4.20. The input diodes D_A, D_B, and D_C conduct through the resistor R, if corresponding input is in the LOW state, while corresponding to HIGH state, the diode is nonconducting. Therefore, if atleast one of the inputs in LOW state, the diode connected to this input conducts and voltage V_P at point P is one diode drop above the low level voltage at the input. The voltage V_P should be such as to keep T in cut-off. Therefore, output of T is V_{CC} and, if all the three inputs are in HIGH state, then input diodes are cut-off and consequently current flowing from V_{CC} through R should be sufficient to drive T in saturation. Therefore, output of T is $V_{CE,sat}$.

If we consider voltages corresponding to logic 1 and 0 as V_{CC} and $V_{CE,sat}$ respectively, this circuit performs NAND operation.

Propagation Delays.

Delays are associated with the turning-on (turn-on delay) and turning-off (turn off delay) of the output transistor. Turn-off delay is considerably larger than the turn-on delay, often by a factor of 2 or 3. The propagation delay time of commercially available DTL gates are of the order of 30 to 80 ns.

Current Sink Logic.

This gate supplies reverse-saturation current of input diodes of the load gates in 1 state and sinks current flowing through the forward-biased input diodes of the load gates in the output transistor of the gate in 0 state. Since sink current is much greater than the source current, this is called *current sink logic*.

Wired-Logic.

If outputs of gates are connected together as shown in Fig. 4.21, additional logic is performed without additional hardware. This type of connection is called *wired-logic, wired-AND, or implied-AND.*

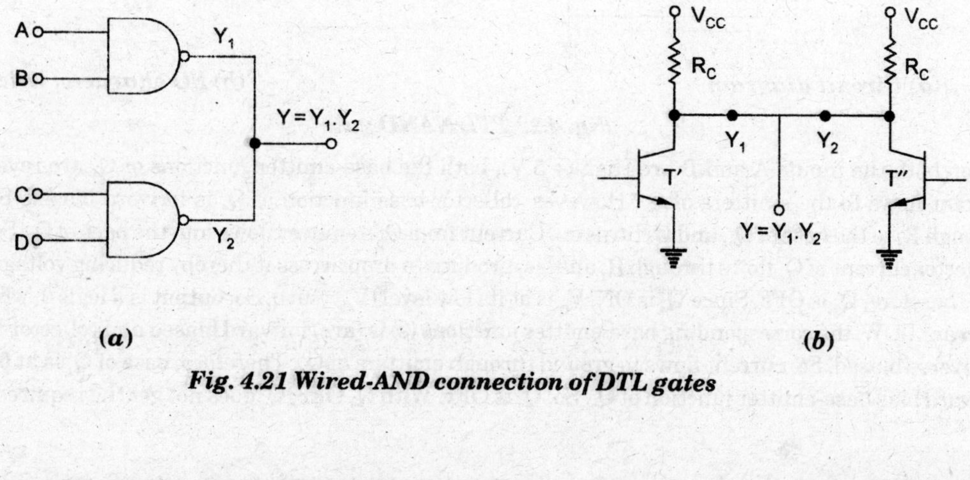

Fig. 4.21 Wired-AND connection of DTL gates

If $Y_1 = Y_2 = 1$, then $Y = 1$,

But if any one (Y_1 or Y_2) or both are 0, then Y = 0.

Output, $Y = Y_1$ $\quad Y_2 = \overline{(AB)}.\overline{(CD)} = \overline{AB + CD}$

Now consider effect of wired-AND connection on power dissipation, speed, and fan-out. Power dissipation in LOW output state P(0) increases because of reduction in effective collector resistor ($R_C \,||\, R_C = R_C/2$). Consequently, speed of operation increases due to redution in charging resistor ($R_C/2$).

There is an effective reduction in the fan-out of the gate in the wired-AND connection. If only one output transistor (say T') is conducting, then this transistor must not only sink current of the load gates and current due to its own pull-up resistor but must also sink the current in the pull-up resistor of the other output transistor T". This situation makes it necessary to reduce allowable fan-out of each gate in the wired-AND connection.

(3) Transistor Transistor Logic (TTL or T²L).

It is so called because of its dependence on transistors alone to perform basic logic operations. It is the most popular logic family. It is also most widely used bipolar digital IC family. It TTL uses transistors operating in saturated mode. It is fastest of the saturated logic families. The basic TTL logic circuit is the NAND ga

Advantages :

Good speed, low manufacturing cost, wide range of circuits, and the availability in SSI and MSI

Disadvantages :

Tight V_{CC} tolerance, relatively high power consumption, moderate packing density, generation of noise spikes and susceptibility to power transients.

Two-Input TTL NAND Gate.

In the circuit of two-input TTL NAND gate shown in Fig. 4.22, input transistor Q_1 is a multiple emitter transistor. Transistor Q_2 is called **phase splitter**. Transistor Q_3 'sits above' Q_4 and, therefore, Q_3 and Q_4 make a totem pole arrangement at any time only one of them will conduct. Diodes D_1 and D_2 protect Q_1 from being damaged by negative spikes of voltages at the inputs. When negative apikes appear at the input terminals, then diodes conduct simultaneously. Transistor Q_3 acts as an emitter follower.

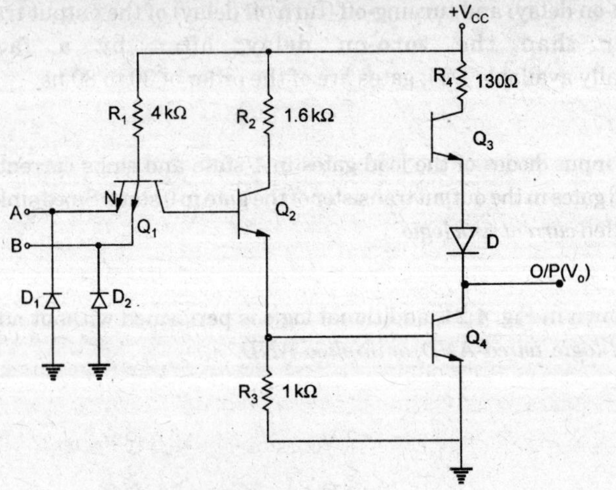

(a) Circuit diagram

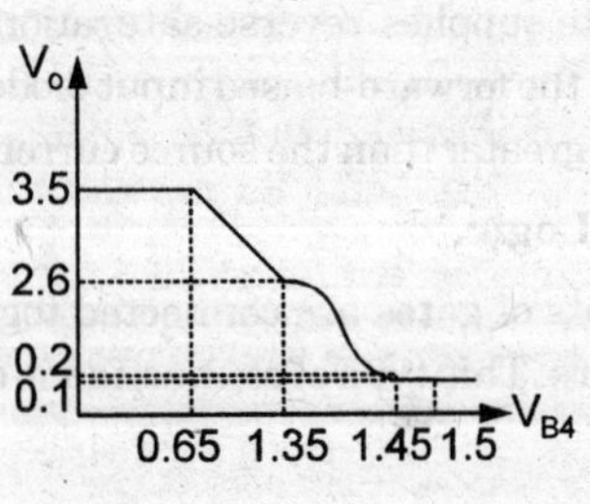

(b) I/O characteristics

Fig. 4.22 TTL NAND gate

When both the inputs A and B are High (+ 5 V), both the base-emitter junctions of Q_1 are reverse biased. So, no current flows to the emitters of Q_1. However, collector-base junction of Q_1 is forward biased. So, a current flows through R_1 to the base of Q_2, and Q_2 turns on. Current from Q_2's emitter flows into the base of Q_4. So, Q_4 is turned ON. Collector current of Q_2 flows through R_2 and, so, produces a drop across it thereby reducing voltage at the collector of Q_2. Therefore, Q_3 is OFF. Since Q_4 is ON, V_O is at its low level (V_{CE} (sat)). So, output is a logic 0, when either A or B or both are LOW, the corresponding base-emitter junctions (s) is (are) forward biased and collector-base junction of Q_1 is reverse biased. So, current flows to ground through emitters of Q_1. Therefore, base of Q_1 is at 0.7 V, which cannot forward bias base-emitter junction of Q_2. So, Q_2 is OFF. With Q_2 OFF, Q_4 does not get the required base drive. So, Q_4

is also OFF. Transistor Q_3 gets enough base drive because Q_2 is OFF, *i.e.* since no current flows into the collector of Q_2, all the current flows into the base of Q_3, and therefore, Q_3 is ON.

$$\text{Output voltage, } V_O = V_{CC} - V_{R2} - V_{BE3} - V_D$$
$$\approx 3.4 - 3.8 \text{ V.}$$

which is a logic HIGH level. So, circuit acts as a two-input NAND gate. When Q_4 is OFF, no current flows through it, but stray and output capacitances between output terminal, i.e. collector of Q_4, and ground get charged to this voltage of 3.4–3.8 V.

I/O characteristics of a TTL NAND gate are shown in Fig. 4.22 *(b)*.

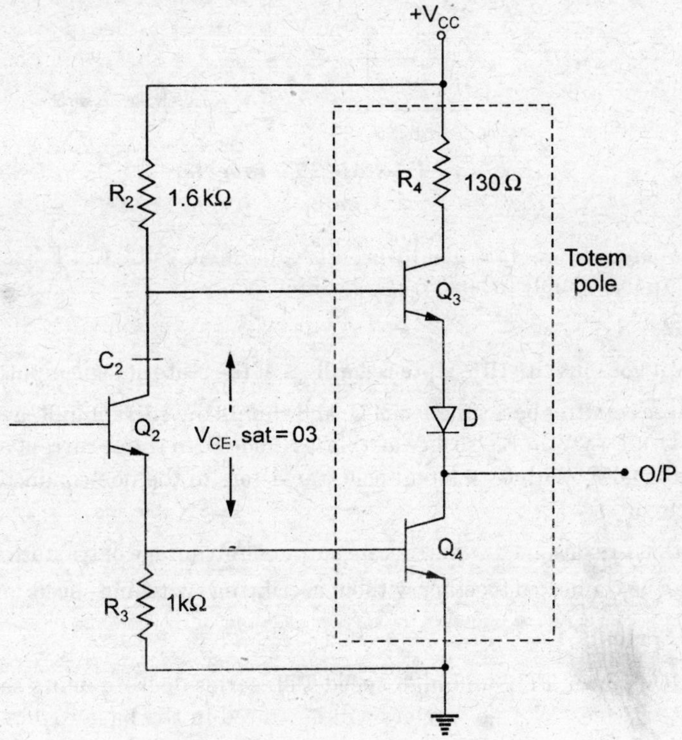

Fig. 4.23 Totem-pole output

Advantage of Totem-Pole.

In the output HIGH state, Q_3 acts as an emitter follower with its associated low output impedance. This low output impedance provides a small time constant for charging up any capacitive load on the output. This action is commonly called *active pull-up* and it provides very fast rise time waveforms at TTL output.

Disadvantages of Totem-Pole.

(*i*) During transition of the output from LOW to HIGH, Q_4 turns off more slowly than Q_3 and Q_4 are conducting and, therefore, relatively large currents will be drawn from the supply. So, TTL circuits suffer from internally generated current transients or current spikes because of the totem-pole connection.

(*ii*) Totem-pole outputs cannot be wire AND ed, i.e. outputs of a number of gates cannot be tied together to obtain AND operation of those outputs.

Tri-State (3–State) TTL

Tri-state configuration utilizes advantage of high speed of operation of the totem-pole configuration and wire ANDing of the open-collector configuration. It is called tri-state TTL, because it allows three possible output states :

HIGH, LOW, and HIGH impedance (Hi-Z).

In the Hi-Z state, both transistors in the totem-pole arrangements are turned OFF, so that output terminal is a HIGH impedance to ground or V_{CC}. In fact, output is an open or floating terminal, i.e. neither a LOW nor a HIGH. In practice output terminal is not an exact open circuit, but has a resistance of several Mega ohms or more relative to ground and V_{CC}.

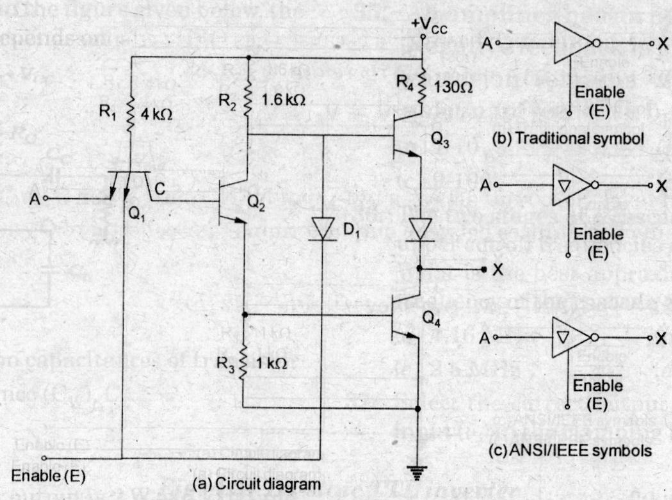

Fig. 4.24 Tri-state TTL inverter

Enabled State.

With E = 1, the circuit operates as a normal inverter because high voltage at E has no effect on Q_1 or Q_2. In this enabled condition, output is simply inversion of logic input A.

Disabled State (Hi-Z)

When E = 0, the circuit goes into its Hi-Z state regardless of the state of logic input A.

LOW at E forward biases emitter base junction of Q_1 and shunts the current in R_1 away from Q_2, so that, Q_2 turns OFF, which in turns Q_4 off. LOW at E also forward biases diode D_1 to shunt current away from the base of Q_3, and therefore, Q_3 also turns OFF. With both totem-pole transistors in the non-conducting state, output terminal is essentially an open circuit.

There are many ICs that are designed with tri-state outputs. Advantage of tri-state configuration is that outputs of the tri-state ICs can be connected together without sacrificing switching speed.

Schottky TTL, 74S Series

The standard TTL, low power TTL, and high speed TTL series operate using saturated switching. When a transistor is saturated, excess charge carriers will be stored in the base region and they must be removed before the transistor can be turned OFF. So, owing to storage time delay, the speed is reduced. Schottky TTL 74S series reduces this storage time delay by not allowing the transistor to go into full saturation. This is accomplished by using a *Schottky Barrier Diode* (SBD) between base and collector of each transistor. Virtually, all modern TTL devices incorporate this so-called *Schottky clamp*. SBD has a forward voltage of only 0.25 V. The circuits in the 74S series also use smaller resistance values to improve speed of operation. Speed of the 74S series is twice that of the 74H series. Schottky TTL has more than three times the switching speed of standard TTL, at the expense of approximately doubling the power consumption.

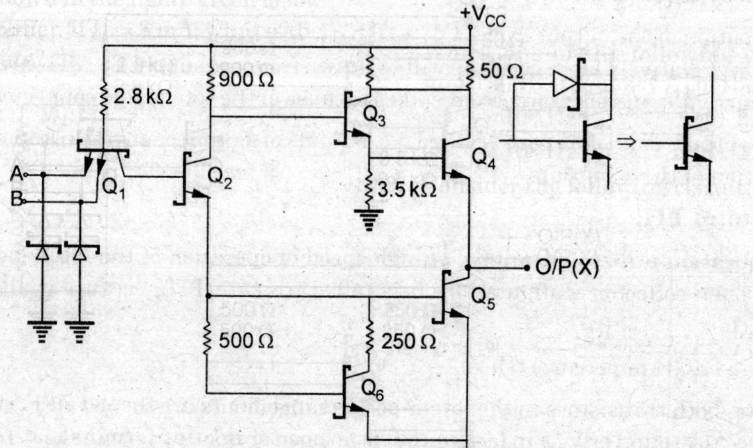

Fig. 4.25 Circuit diagram of a two-input Schottky TTL NAND gate

(4) Emitter-Coupled Logic (ECL).

It is, also called current-mode logic or *current-steering logic.*

It is the fastest of all logic families because of following reasons :

(*i*) It is a non-saturated logic, in the sense that transistors are not allowed to go into saturation. So, storage time delays are eliminated and, therefore speed of operation is increased.

(*ii*) Currents are kept high, and the output impedance is so low that circuit and stray capacitances can be quickly charged and discharged.

(*iii*) Of the limited voltage swing.

It is called ECL because of its use of BJTs that are coupled (joined) at their emitters. In ECL, transistors are prevented from going into saturation when input changes from LOW to HIGH, by choosing logic levels very close to each other.

One disadvantage of having logic levels close to each other is that, it is difficult to achieve good noise immunity. Also, power consumption is increased since transistors are not saturated. But advantage is that current drawn from the supply is more steady and ECL gates do not experience large switching transients. ECL family has considerably greater power consumption compared to other families.

ECL operates on the principle of current switching, whereby a fixed bias current less than I_C(sat) is switched from one transistor's collector to another. Because of this current mode operation, this form is also called *Current-Mode Logic* (CML). It is also called *Current-Steering Logic* (CSL), because current is steered from one device to another. ECL family is not as popular and widely used as TTL and MOS, except in very high frequency applications where its speed is superior.

Characteristics of ECL gates :

(*i*) Transistors never saturate ; so, speed is high with t_{pd} = 1 ns.

(*ii*) Logic levels are negative, – 0.9 V for a logic 1 and – 1.7 V for a logic 0.

(*iii*) Noise margin is less, about 250 mV. This makes ECL unreliable for use in heavy industrial environment.

(*iv*) ECL circuits produce the output and its complement, and therefore, eliminate the need for inverters.

(*v*) Fan-out is large because the output impedance is low. It is about 25.

(*vi*) Power dissipation per gate is large, P_D = 40 mW.

(*vii*) Total current flow in ECL is more or less constant. So, no noise spikes will be internally generated.

ECL OR/NOR Gate

Figure 4.26 (*a*) shows two-input ECL OR/NOR gate and Fig. 4.26 (*b*) shows its I/O characteristics. It has two outputs which are complements of each other. Transistors Q_2 and Q_{IA} form a differential amplifier. Transistors Q_{IA} and Q_{IB} are in parallel. Transistors Q_3 and Q_4 are emitter followers whose emitter voltages are same as the base voltages (less than 0.8 V base to emitter drops). Inputs are applied to Q_{IA} and Q_{IB}, and Q_2 is supplied with constant – 1.3 V.

When inputs A and B are both LOW, *i.e.* – 1.7 V, Q_2 is more forward biased than Q_{IA} and Q_{IB}, and so, Q_2 is ON and Q_{IA} and Q_{IB} are OFF. The value of R_2 is such that current flowing through Q_2 puts the collector at about – 0.9 V. Therefore, emitter of Q_4 is at, – 0.9 – 0.8 = – 1.7 V, and so, OR output is LOW. The base current of Q3 passing through R_1 is very small. The value of R_1 is such that this current puts collectors of Q_{IA} and Q_{IB} at about – 0.1 V. So, smitter of Q_3 is at, – 0.1 – 0.8 = – 0.9 V, i.e. NOR output is HIGH.

When A is HIGH, or B is HIGH, or both A and B are HIGH, then corresponding transistors are ON, because they ae more forward biased than Q_2, and Q_2 is OFF. So, collectors of Q_{IA} and Q_{IB} are at – 0.9 V, which makes NOR output = – 0.9 – 0.8 = – 1.7 V, *i.e.* a logic 0. Only small base current of Q_4 flows through R_2. So, collector of Q_2 is approximately at – 0.1 V, and therefore, OR output is, – 0.1 – 0.8 = – 0.9 V, *i.e.* a logic 1. This shows that above circuit works as a OR/NOR gate. Fig. 4.26 (*c*) shows the logic symbol a two-input ECL OR/NOR gate.

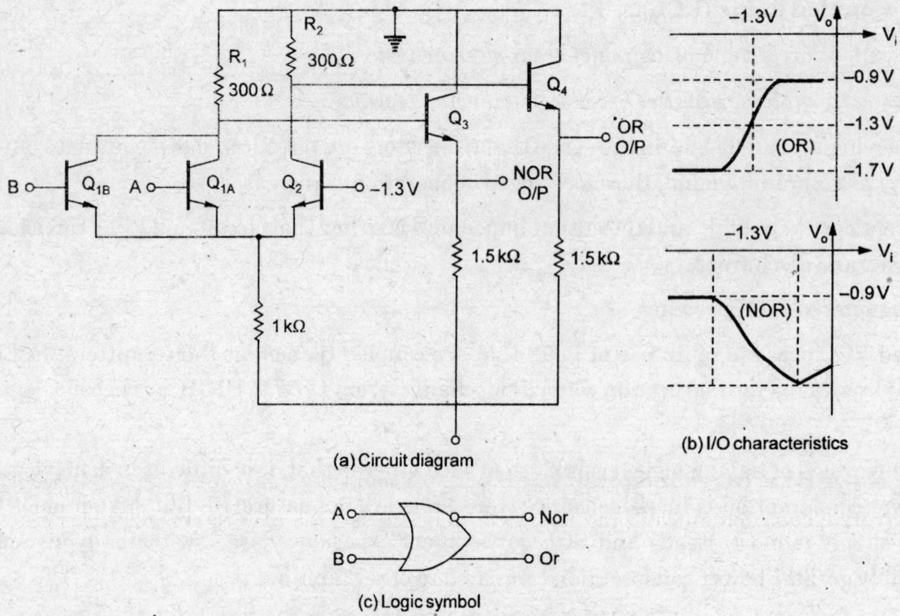

(a) Circuit diagram

(b) I/O characteristics

(c) Logic symbol

Fig. 4.26 Two-input ECL OR/NOR gate

Interfacing ECL Gates

Since ECL logic levels are so different from those of TTL and CMOS circuits, interfacing ECL gates with other logic families requires special level shifter circuits called **level translators.** Level translators are available in various ECL series to facilitate interfacing of ECL with other families.

(5) Complementary Metal Oxide Semiconductor (CMOS) Logic

CMOS logic family uses both P and N channel MOSFETs in the same circuit to realize several advantages over PMOS and NMOS families. CMOS family is faster and consumes less power than the other MOS families. These advantages are offset somewhat by the increased complexity of the IC fabrication process and a lower packing density. CMOS can be operated at higher voltages resulting in improved noise immunity. It is widely used for general purpose logic circuitry. CMOS technology has been used to construct small, medium and large scale ICs for a wide variety of applications ranging from general purpose logic to microprocessors. Because of its extremely small power consumption, it is useful for applications in watches and calculators. However, CMOS cannot yet compete with MOS in applications requiring the atmost in LSI. CMOS has very high input resistance. Thus, it draws almost zero current from the driving gate, and therefore, its fan-out is very high. Its output resistance is small (1 kΩ) compared to that of NMOS (100 kΩ). Hence, it is faster than NMOS. The speed of CMOS decreases with inrease in load. In CMOS, there is always a very high resistance between the V_{DD} terminal and ground, because of the MOSFET in the current path. Hence, its power consumption is very low. Noise margin of CMOS is the same in both the LOW and HIGH states and it is 30% of V_{DD}, indicating that noise margin increases with an increase in power supply voltage. So in noisy environments, CMOS with large V_{DD} is preferred. However, an increase in V_{DD} results in the corresponding increase in P_D. CMOS loses some of its advantages at high frequencies.

4.3 COMBINATIONAL CIRCUIT

4.3.1. ADDERS AND SUBTRACTORS

XOR gate

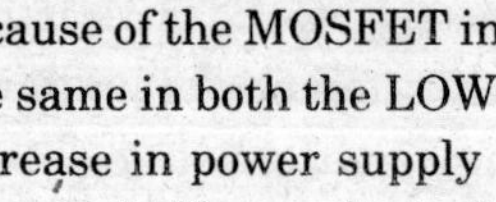

(a) Symbol

A	B	A ⊕ B
0	0	0
0	1	1
1	0	1
1	1	0

(b) Truth table

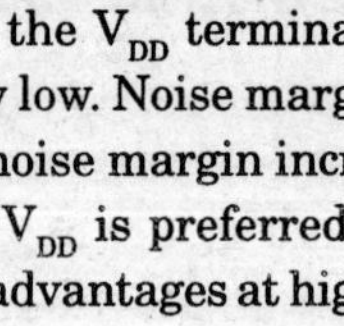

(c) K-map

Fig. 4.27 XOR gate

$$A \oplus B = \overline{A}B + A\overline{B}$$
$$= \overline{A}B + A\overline{A} + A\overline{B} + B\overline{B}$$
$$= \overline{A}(A+B) + \overline{B}(A+B)$$
$$= (A+B)(\overline{A} + \overline{B})$$
$$= (A+B)(\overline{AB})$$

XOR implementation via function of of above equation is shown in Fig. 4.28.

It needs three gates :

(1) OR

(2) NAND

(3) AND.

Function $(\overline{A}B + A\overline{B})$ is called **inequality comparator,** because it provides an output 1 only if A and B are not equal. The inverse (complement) of inequality comparator is an equality comparator.

It is functionally manipulated as

$$\overline{\overline{A}B + A\overline{B}} = (A+\overline{B})(\overline{A}+B) = AB + \overline{A}\overline{B}$$

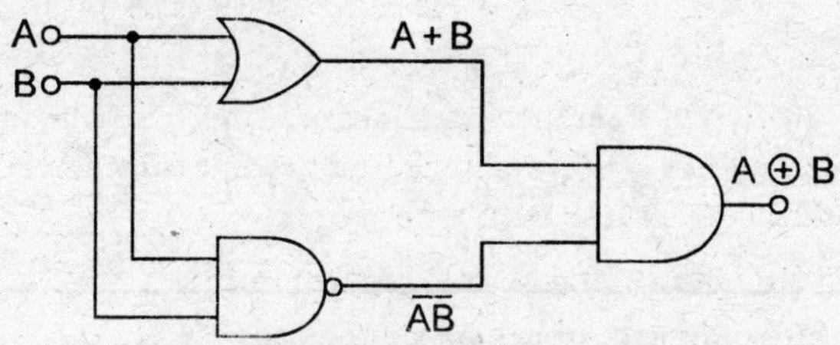

Fig. 4.28 Implementation of XOR gate

4.3.2. HALF ADDER (HA)

This circuit adds two binary variables, yields a carry but does not accept carry from another circuit (adder). The truth table of half adder is given in Fig. 4.29 *(a)* from which we can write

$$S = \overline{A}B + A\overline{B} = A \oplus B$$
$$C = AB$$

A	B	S	C
0	0	0	0
0	1	1	0
1	0	1	0
1	1	0	1

(a) Truth Table

S = Sum; C = Carry

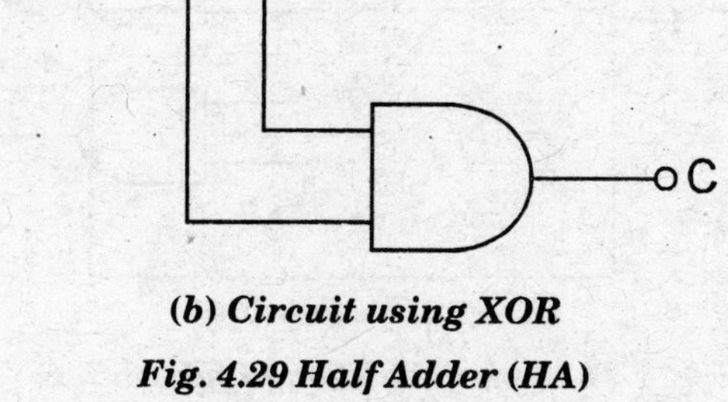

(b) Circuit using XOR

Fig. 4.29 Half Adder (HA)

4.3.3. FULL ADDER

This circuit can add two binary numbers, accept a carry and yield a carry. Such a circuit can easily be visualized by means of two half adders (HA) and OR as shown in Fig. 4.30

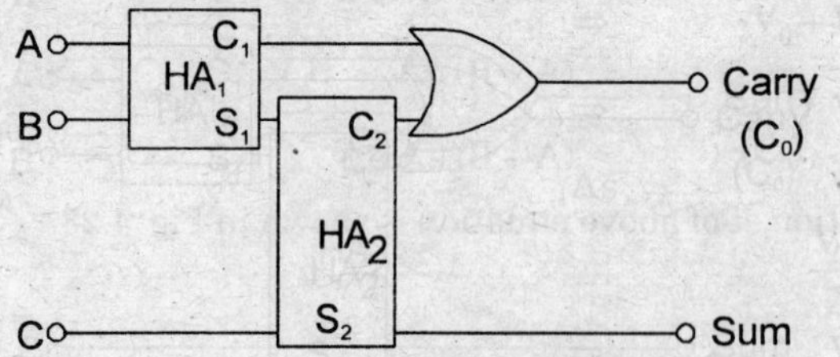

Fig. 4.30. Full adder using two half adders

Truth-table for Full Adder

A	B	C_i	S	C_0
0	0	0	0	0
0	0	1	1	0
0	1	0	1	0
0	1	1	0	1
1	0	0	1	0
1	0	1	0	1
1	1	0	0	1
1	1	1	1	1

From truth-table given above, full-adder circuit can be synthesize.

It can concluded from the table that,

$$S = \overline{A}\,\overline{B}\,C + \overline{A}\,B\,\overline{C} + A\,\overline{B}\,\overline{C} + ABC$$

and $$C_0 = \overline{A}\,B\,C + A\,\overline{B}\,C + AB\,\overline{C} + ABC$$

Since, Y + Y + ... + Y = Y and adding ABC, twice to right hand side of above equation, we can write

$C_0 = (\overline{A}B\,C + ABC) + (A\overline{B}C + ABC) + (AB\overline{C} + ABC)$

Observing that $Y + \overline{Y} = 1$, we get

$$C_0 = BC + AC + AB$$

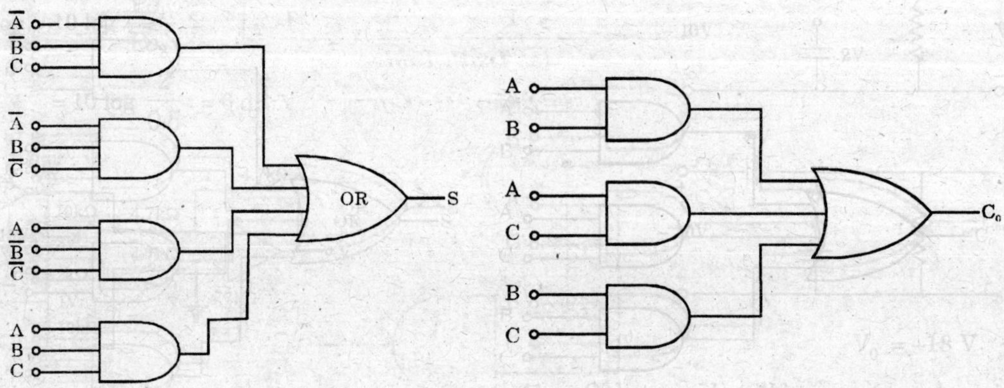

Fig. 4.31 Implementation of full adder

4.3.4. SERIAL ADDER

Parallel adder performs addition of two binary numbers at a relatively faster rate. The disadvantage of the parallel addition is that, it requires a large amount of logic circuitry. This increases in direct proportion with the number of bits in the numbers being added.

In *serial addition,* addition operation is carried out bit-by-bit. Therefore, serial adder requires simpler circuitry than a parallel adder but results in a low speed of operation.

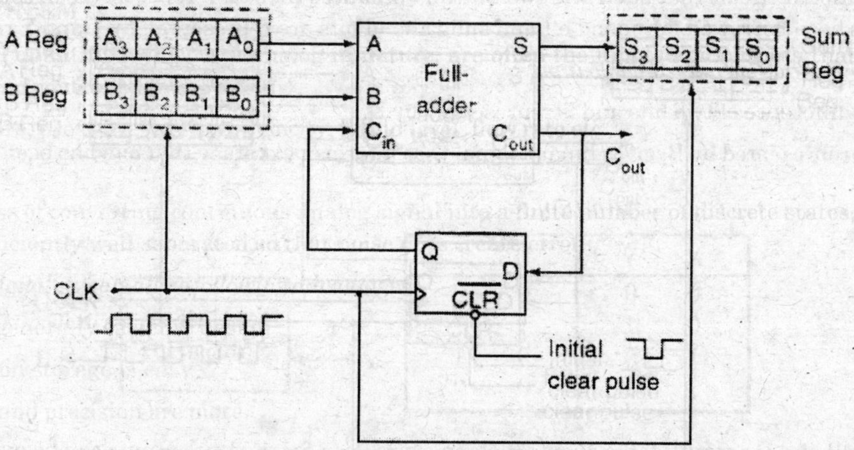

Fig. 4.32 4-bit serial adder

Two shift registers A and B are used to store numbers to be added serially. A single full-adder is used to add one pair of bit at a time along with the carry. D flip-flop, i.e. carry flip-flop, is used to store carry output of the full-adder, so that it can be added to the next significant position of the numbers in the registers. Contents of the shift registers shift from left to right and their outputs starting from A_0 and B_0 are fed into a single full-adder along with the output of the carry flip-flop upon application of each clock pulse.

The sum output of the full-adder is fed to the Most Significant Bit (S_3) of the sum register. For each succeeding clock pulse, contents of both the shift registers are shifted once to the right, and new sum bit and new carry bit are transferred to sum register and carry flip-flop respectively. This process continues until all pairs of bits are added.

Operation of a serial adder :

Let augend ($A_3 A_2 A_1 A_0$) be 0111 and addend ($B_3 B_2 B_1 B_0$) be 0010, stored in shift registers A and B respectively. Also, carry flip-flop has been initially cleared to the 0 state, so that $C_{in} = 0$.

First Clock pulse.

Before first clock pulse occurs, as inputs to the full-adder are $A_0 = 1$, $B_0 = 0$ and $C_{in} = 0$, full-adder outputs will be $S = 1$ and $C_{out} = 0$.

When first clock pulse occurs, value in the A and B registers shift from left to right by one bit. In addition, sum (S) is transferred to S_3 of sum register, and C_{out} is transferred to the carry flip-flop, whose output becomes 0, which is carry input of the full-adder.

Second Clock pulse.

Now, $A_0 = 1$, $B_0 = 1$ and $C_{in} = 0$, at the full-adder input. Therefore, $S = 0$ and $C_{out} = 1$.

When second clock pulse occurs, A, B and sum registers again shift right; $S = 0$ is transferred to S_3 and $C_{out} = 1$ is transferred to the input of the flip-flop.

Third Clock pulse.

Values of A_0 and B_0 are now 1 and 0 respectively, and C_{in} is 1. These values produce $S = 0$ and $C_{out} = 1$ at the full-adder outputs. On the occurrence of third pulse, A, B and sum registers shift right, sum = 0 goes to S_3, and $C_{out} = 1$ goes to the carry flip-flop.

Fourth Clock pulse.

Both A_0 and B_0 are now zero, and $C_{in} = 1$. Therefore full-adder produces $S = 1$ and $C_{in} = 0$. Fourth clock pulse transfers $S = 1$ to initiates all the other transfers. At the end of this fourth clock pulse, sum (1001) will be available in the sum register, and C_{out} is 0.

4.3.5. SUBTRACTORS

Subtractors of two binary numbers can be obtained by taking complement of the subtrahend and adding it to the minuend.

By this method, each subtrahend bit of number is subtracted from its corresponding significant minuend bit to form a difference bit. If minuend bit is smaller than the subtrahend bit, a 1 is borrowed from next significant position.

Half Subtractor

It is a combinational circuit that subtracts two bits and produces their difference at the output. It has an output to specify if 1 has been borrowed. Minuend bit and subtrahend bits are represented by X and Y respectively.

Half subtractor has two outputs and two inputs

First output is difference of two bits and is represented by D.

Second output represented by B, gives binary signal that informs next stage that one has been borrowed.

Truth table

X	Y	B	D
0	0	0	0
0	1	1	1
1	0	0	1
1	1	0	0

Block diagram

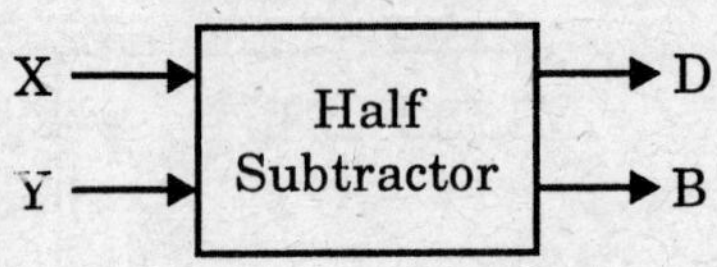

By minimizing B and D or truth table above, boolean expression for the two outputs can be written as

$$D = X \oplus Y = \overline{X}Y + X\overline{Y}$$

$$B = \overline{X}Y$$

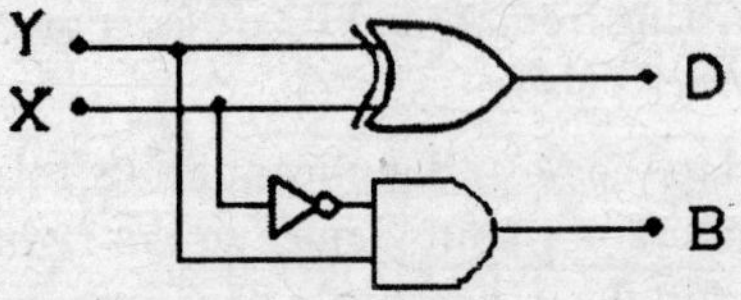

From the above expression, logic for D is same as the logic for output S in a half adder.

Full Subtractor

It is a circuit which performs a subtraction between two bits taking into account that a 1 may have been borrowed by a lower significant stage. A full subtractor has three inputs X, Y and Z are minuend, subtrahend and previous borrow respectively. Two outputs D and B are difference and output borrow respectively.

Truth table

X	Y	Z	B	D
0	0	0	0	0
0	0	1	1	1
0	1	0	1	1
0	1	1	1	0
1	0	0	0	1
1	0	1	0	0
1	1	0	0	0
1	1	1	1	1

Boolean expression for two outputs of the full subtractor is simplified using K-map

$$D = \overline{X}\overline{Y}Z + \overline{X}Y\overline{Z} + X\overline{Y}\overline{Z} + XYZ$$

$$B = \overline{X}Y + \overline{X}Z + YZ$$

Full subtractor can be realized using two half subtractors shown in the figure below :

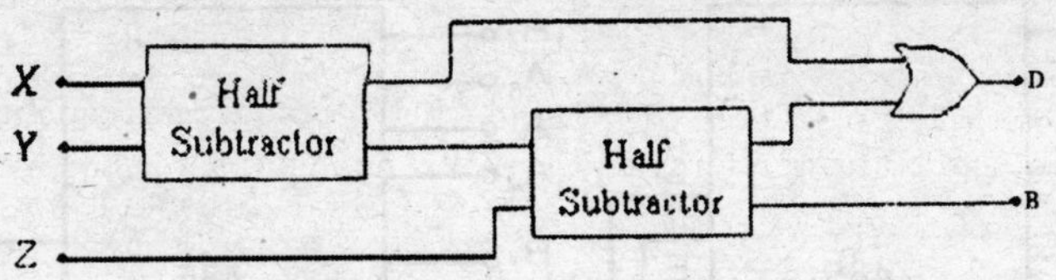

Logic function for output D in the full subtractor is exactly same as the output S obtained for full adder.

4.3.6 DIGITAL COMPARATOR

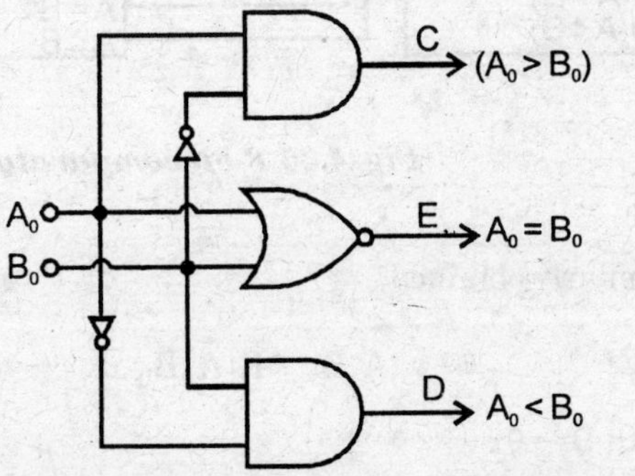

Fig. 4.33 Single bit magnitude comparator

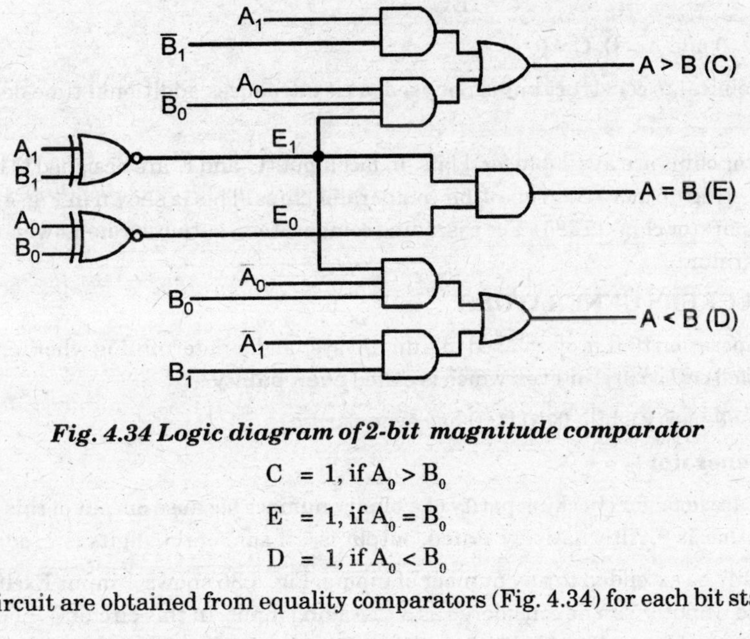

Fig. 4.34 Logic diagram of 2-bit magnitude comparator

$$C = 1, \text{ if } A_0 > B_0$$

$$E = 1, \text{ if } A_0 = B_0$$

$$D = 1, \text{ if } A_0 < B_0$$

E inputs for this circuit are obtained from equality comparators (Fig. 4.34) for each bit stage (E = 1 if corresponding bits are equal).

For A = B, all corresponding bits are equal, *i.e.* $A_0 = B_0$, $A_1 = B_1$

Output of E-gate (AND gate) is given by, $E = E_1E_0$

At input of E gate, E is set HIGH (=1), and so for A = B, E = 1 and A ≠ B, E = 0.

If A > B, any one of the following conditions must be met :

$$A_1 > B_1 \text{ (MSB)}$$

or $$A_1 = B_1$$

and $$A_0 > B_0$$

These conditions are written in form of the Boolean equation as

$$C = A_1\overline{B}_1 + E_1A_0\overline{B}_0$$

This Boolean equation is realized by AND-OR circuit shown in Fig. 4.35.

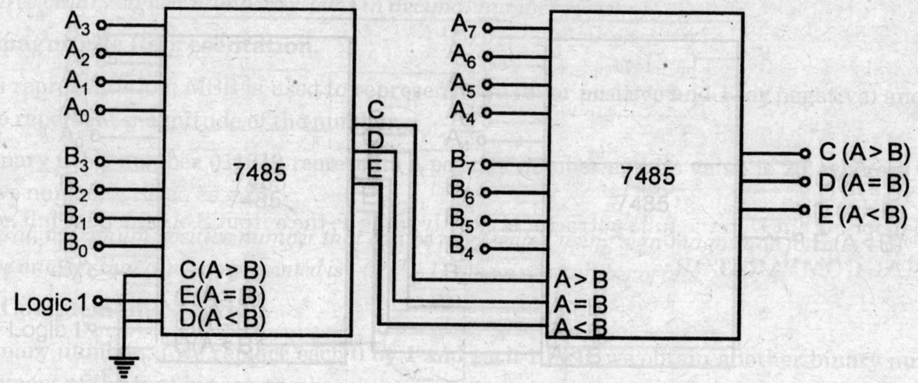

Fig. 4.35 8-bit comparator

When C = 1. A > B (with C' = 0).

The condition for A < B, is similarly obtained

$$E = \overline{A}_1B_1 + E_1\overline{A}_0B_0$$

which is satisfied if D = 1 (with D' = 0).

The condition A > B could also be obtained by

$$D = \overline{EC}$$

because if A ≠ B, E = 0 and A > B, C = 0.

This would be economical to construct but is not used, as it introduces additional time delay of an AND gate and an inverter.

Standard comparator chips are available for 4 bits. In fact inputs C' and E' are designed to build a comparator of more than 4 bits by connecting up more than one 4-bit comparator chips. This is shown in Fig. 4.35 for an 8-bit comparator using two 4-bit comparator chips (7485). For cascading comparators, outputs from Lower order comparator are fed to Higher order comparator.

4.3.7 PARITY CHECKERS/GENERATORS

It is an arithmetic operation that is often used in a digital system for determining whether number of 1 in binary bits are odd which is called *odd parity*, or even which is called **even parity**.

e.g., 11000010 has odd parity while 01011100 has even parity.

Parity Checker/Generator

Exclusive OR gates are ideal for checking parity of a binary number because output of this gate is 1, if and only if, one input is 1 and the other is 0. Alternatively stated, output is 1 if sum of the digits is 1, odd parity.

The concept can easily be extended to any number of inputs. Fig. 4.36 shows 4-input Exclusive-OR tree for checking parity of a 4-bit word. Input P' can be considered as a cascading input. In this circuit Z = 1 or Y = 0, if sum of the input bits A, B, C and D is odd. Hence, if input P' is grounded (P' = 0), then P = 0 for odd parity and P = 1 for even parity.

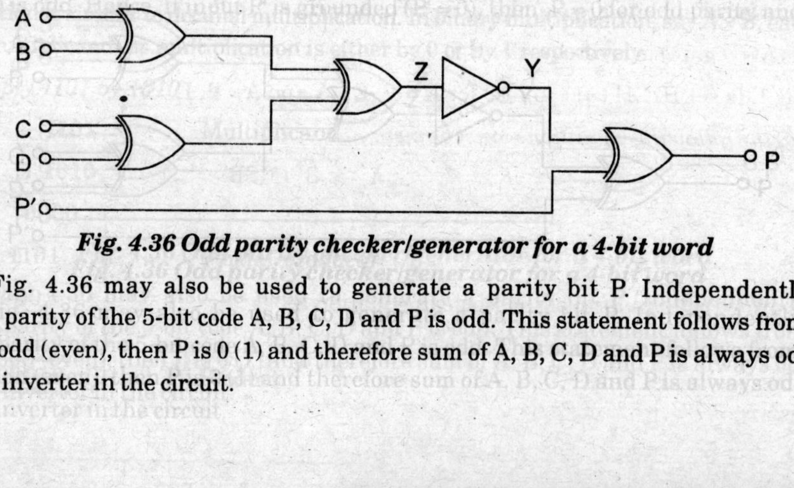

Fig. 4.36 Odd parity checker/generator for a 4-bit word

The circuit of Fig. 4.36 may also be used to generate a parity bit P. Independently of the parity of the 4-bit input word, parity of the 5-bit code A, B, C, D and P is odd. This statement follows from the fact that, if sum of A, B, C, and D is odd (even), then P is 0 (1) and therefore sum of A, B, C, D and P is always odd. To get an even parity generator, delete inverter in the circuit.

4.3.8. MULTIPLEXERS

It is a logic circuit that receives binary information from several inputs and transmits information to a single output. The input selected is controlled by a set of selected inputs. In order to select one out of n input lines for connection to the output, the number of select lines required is m such that $2^m = n$. So, one input line being selected is determined by bit combination of m select lines. *e.g.*, logic diagram of Fig. 4.37 (*a*) and block diagram of Fig. 4.37 (*b*) are of a 4 : 1 multiplexer with its truth-table given in Table 4.7.

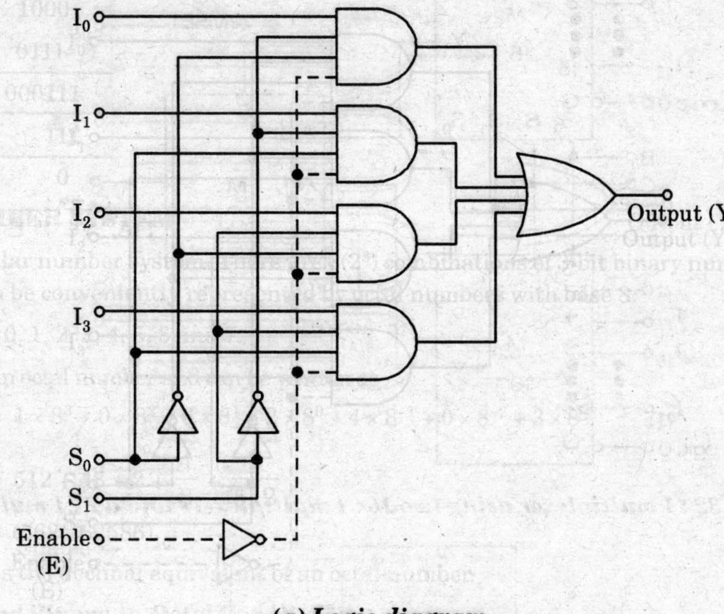

(a) Logic diagram

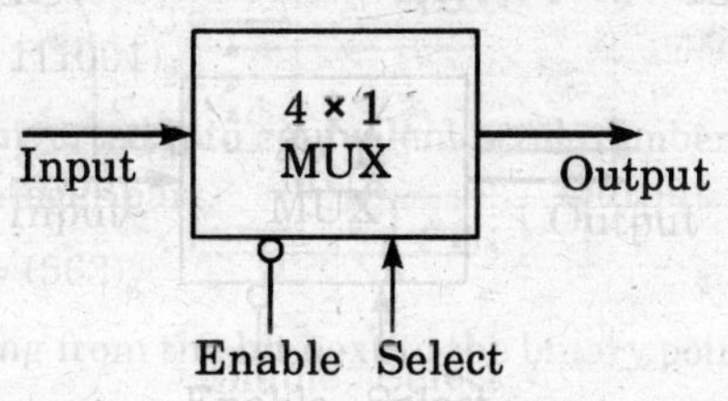

(b) block diagram

Fig. 4.37. 4 : 1 multiplexer

Table 4.7. Truth-table of 4 : 1 multiplexer

Select inputs		Output
S_1	S_0	Y
0	0	I_0
0	1	I_1
1	0	I_2
1	1	I_3

From Table 4.7, output,

$$Y = \overline{S}_1\overline{S}_0 I_0 + \overline{S}_1 S_0 I_1 + S_1\overline{S}_0 I_2 + S_1 S_0 I_3$$

Realization of the above expression using AND and OR gates is multiplexer of Fig. 4.37 (*a*).

E = 0 at the enable provides a 1 input to all the AND gates, which then are controlled by the select inputs as explained abve.

E = 1 input at the enable, disables multiplexer producing Y = 0 independent of the select inputs.

4.3.9. DEMULTIPLEXERS/DECODERS

It performs reverse operation of a multiplexer. It is a digital function that receives information on a single line and transmits this information to one of the 2^n possible output lines. The output line being selected is determined by bit combination of the select lines.

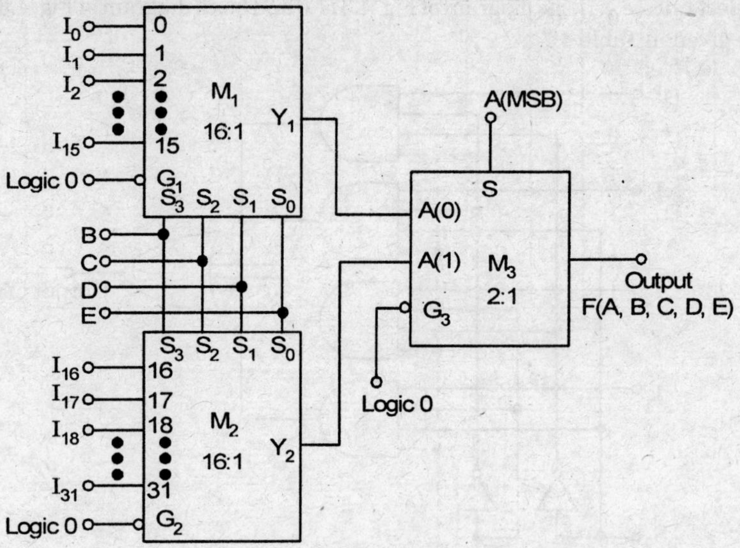

Fig. 4.38. 32 : 1 multiplexer using two 16 : 1 multiplexers and a 2 : 1 multiplexer.

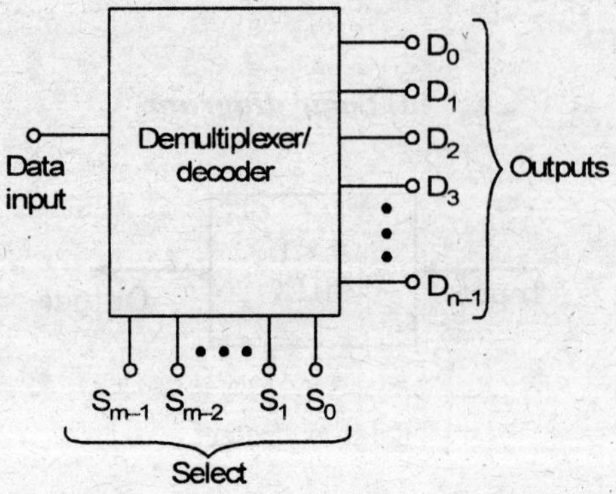

Fig. 4.39. Block diagram of a demultiplexer

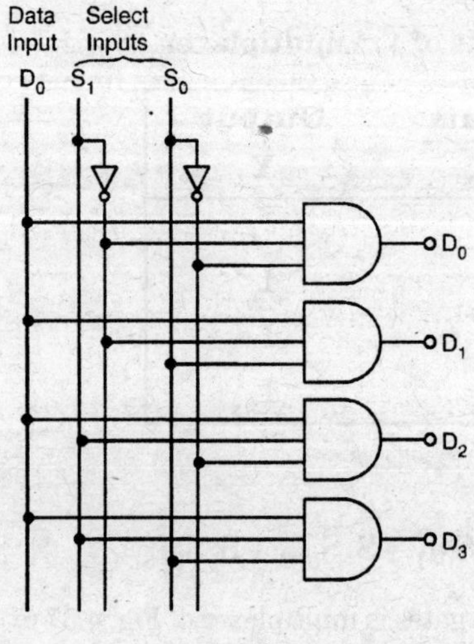

(a) Logic diagram

Input	Select S_1 S_0	Output D_3 D_2 D_1 D_0
1	0 0	0 0 0 1
1	0 1	0 0 1 0
1	1 0	0 1 0 0
1	1 1	1 0 0 0

(b) Truth table

Fig. 4.40. 1 : 4 demultiplexer.

The multiplexer 8 : 1 is connected accordingly in Fig. 4.41.

Data Input	Select Input			Outputs							
D	S_2	S_1	S_0	D_7	D_6	D_5	D_4	D_3	D_2	D_1	D_0
D	0	0	0	0	0	0	0	0	0	0	D
D	0	0	1	0	0	0	0	0	0	D	0
D	0	1	0	0	0	0	0	0	D	0	0
D	0	1	1	0	0	0	0	D	0	0	0
D	1	0	0	0	0	0	D	0	0	0	0
D	1	0	1	0	0	D	0	0	0	0	0
D	1	1	0	0	D	0	0	0	0	0	0
D	1	1	1	D	0	0	0	0	0	0	0

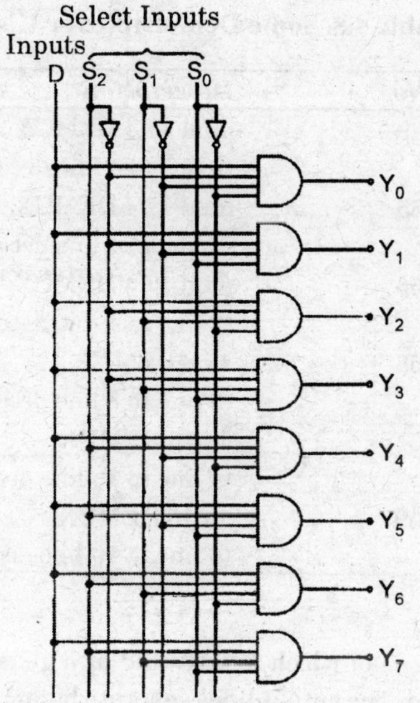

Fig. 4.41 Realization of Table using 8 : 1 multiplexer.

PAL (Programmable Array Logic)

It is a programme logic device with fixed OR array and programmable AND array.

Since only AND gates are programmable, PAL is easier to programe but is less flexible compared to PLA.

PLA (Programmable Array Logic)

Where number of don't care conditions are large, it is more economical to use PLA which is an L.S.I. component.

PLA is similar to PROM, but PLA does not provide full decoding of the variables and does not generate all the minterms.

In PLA, decoder is replaced by a group of AND gates each of which can be programmed to generate a product term of the input variables.

Specific boolean functions are implemented in the SOP form by opening appropriate links and leaving desired connections.

For PLAs,

(*i*) Number of inputs = Number of buffer-inverter gates = n

(*ii*) Number of product terms = Number of AND gates = k

(*iii*) Number of outputs = Number of OR gates = Number of EX-OR gates = m

(*iv*) Number of connections between input and AND arrays = $2n \times k$

(*v*) Number of connections between AND, OR gates = $k \times m$

(*vi*) Number of connections associated with EX-OR gates = 'm'

4.3.10 MULTIPLEXER TREE

Since largest available multiplxer IC is the 16 : 1, the problem of multiplexing larger inputs occurs. This can be actually overcome with the help of enable (or strobe) inputs and thus larger multiplexer trees can be designed. The realization of 32 : 1 multiplexer using two 16 : 1 multiplexer and one 2 : 1 multiplexer is shown in Fig. 4.38. This method can be employed for multiplexing any number of inputs without any difficulty.

The circuitry of Fig. 4.40 *(a)* can also be used as binary-to-decimal decoder, if binary input is applied at the select lines and output is obtained on the corresponding line. The data input line is used as an enable pin and is connected to logic 1 for chip operation. Thus, circuit of Fig. 4.40 *(a)* can be considered as a 2-line-to-4-line decoder. As per the truth-table of Fig. 4.40 *(b)*, l's at D_0, D_1, D_2, D_3 represent decimal digit 0, 1, 2, 3 corresponding to binary inputs 00, 01, 10, 11 respectively. Because of the similarity of decoders and demultiplexer, these circuits are usually called *demultiplexer / decoder circuits.*

Decoder ICs are very useful in the design of multiple output combinational circuits as these require minimum package count. Some of the decoders available as standard ICs are given in Table 4.8.

Output of these devices are active low and an active low enable pin is also available.

Table 4.8. Some Demultiplexer ICs

IC No.	*Description*
74139	dual 1 : 4 DEMUX (2 line to 4 line decoder)
74155	dual 1 : 4 DEMUX (2 line to 4 line decoder)
74156	dual 1 : 4 DEMUX (2 line to 4 line decoder)
74158	1 : 8 DEMUX (3 line to 8 line decoder)
74154	1 : 16 DEMUX (4 line to 16 line decoder)
74159	1 : 16 DEMUX (4 line to 16 line decoder)

4.3.11. ENCODER

An encoder has 2^n input lines, only one of which is activated at a given time and produces an n-bit output code, depending on which input is activated. The output lines generate binary code for the 2^n variables.

Octal to Binary Encoder

This encoder converts octal numbers to binary. It has eight input lines and three output lines, all of which are normally at low states. The circuit allows only one of the input lines to be activated at any given time, so there are only eight possible input combinations. It is designed so that it generates 3 bit binary code that corresponds to the input line that is activated.

Truth table and Logic circuit of octal to binary encoder is shown below :

Inputs								Outputs		
I_0	I_1	I_2	I_3	I_4	I_5	I_6	I_7	C	B	A
1	0	0	0	0	0	0	0	0	0	0
0	1	0	0	0	0	0	0	0	0	1
0	0	1	0	0	0	0	0	0	1	0
0	0	0	1	0	0	0	0	0	1	1
0	0	0	0	1	0	0	0	1	0	0
0	0	0	0	0	1	0	0	1	0	1
0	0	0	0	0	0	1	0	1	1	0
0	0	0	0	0	0	0	1	1	1	1

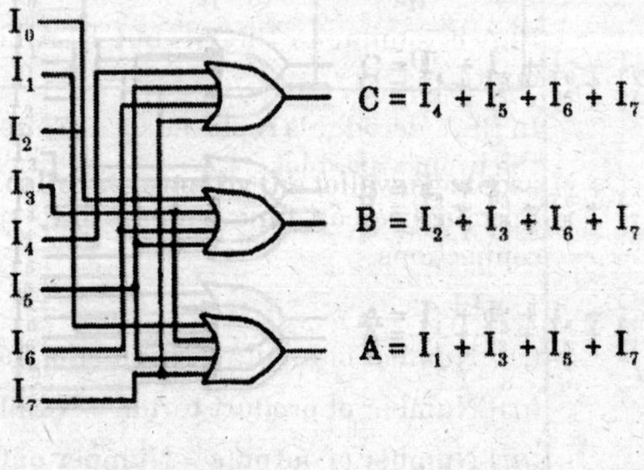

Fig. 4.42

If more than one input line is activated at one time in this basic circuit, then outputs will be garbled.

4.3.12. DECODERS

It is a combinational circuit that converts binary information from n input lines to a maximum of 2^n unique output lines. If unit decoded information has unused or don't care combinations, then decoder output will have less than the outputs. Decoders are used whenever an output or group of outputs is to be activated only on occurrence of specific input combination. Decoders are widely used in the memory system of computer.

3 to 8 line Decoder

In this, three input lines are decoded into eight output lines. It is also called *binary to octal converter* or *decoder* as it takes three binary input code and activates one of them corresponding to that code. As shown in Fig. 4.43(*a*), three inverters provide complement of the inputs and each one of the eight AND gates generates one of the minterms.

Some decoders have one or more enable inputs to control operation of the decoder. This input allows decoder to be casceadable. This also allows decoder to act as demultiplexer.

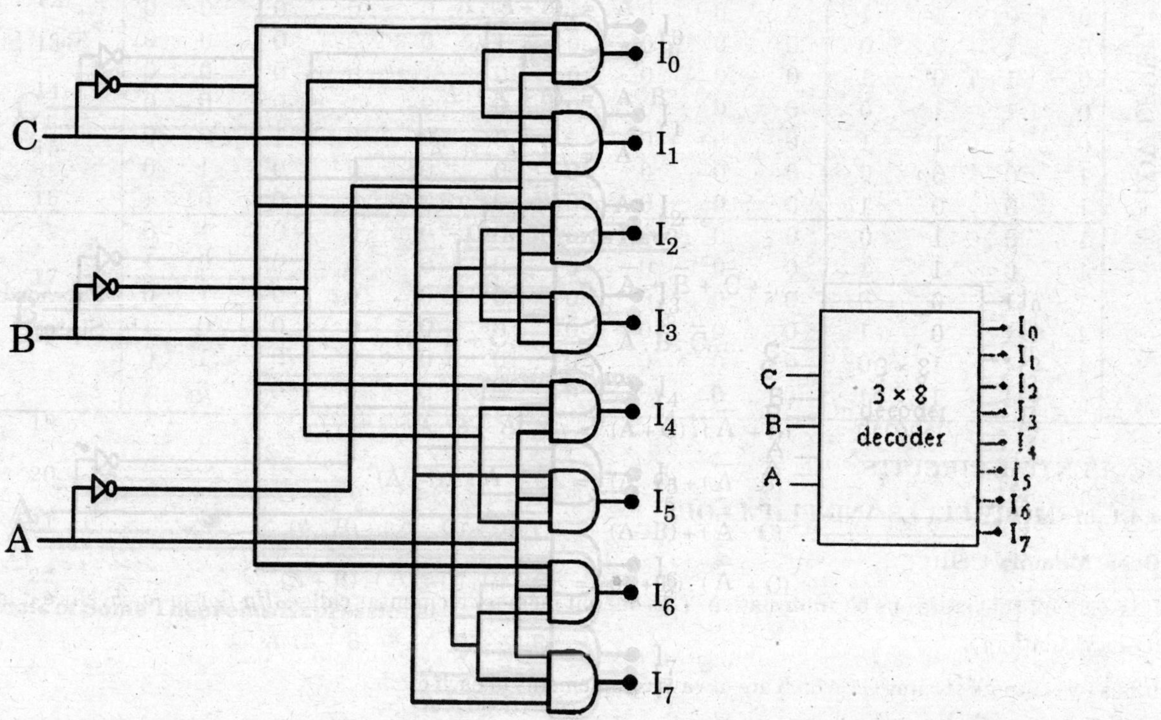

(a) Logic circuit *(b) Block diagram*

Fig. 4.43

Truth table of 3 to 8 line Decoder :

Inputs			Outputs							
A	B	C	I_0	I_1	I_2	I_3	I_4	I_5	I_6	I_7
0	0	0	1	0	0	0	0	0	0	0
0	0	1	0	1	0	0	0	0	0	0
0	1	0	0	0	1	0	0	0	0	0
0	1	1	0	0	0	1	0	0	0	0
1	0	0	0	0	0	0	1	0	0	0
1	0	1	0	0	0	0	0	1	0	0
1	1	0	0	0	0	0	0	0	1	0
1	1	1	0	0	0	0	0	0	0	1

Decoders can be used to generate minterms and external OR gate to form the sum. Therefore any combination circuit can be implemented with *n* inputs and *m* outputs. This can be realised using with *n* to 2^n line decoder and *m* OR gates.

BCD to Decimal Decoder

This decoder is used to obtain a decimal equivalent of a BCD code. This decoder has four intputs and ten outputs that correspond to the ten BCD code groups. This decoder does not utilize all the combinations of four inputs bits. This type of decoders are designed such that if any of invalid code group is applied to input, none of the output is activated. This decoder is also called *1 to 10 decoder* or *4 to 10 decoder*.

Truth table of BCD to decimal decoder

	Inputs				Outputs										
	D	C	B	A	I_0	I_1	I_2	I_3	I_4	I_5	I_6	I_7	I_8	I_9	
1 = HIGH LEVEL 0 = LOW LEVEL	0	0	0	0	1	0	0	0	0	0	0	0	0	0	
	0	0	0	1	0	1	0	0	0	0	0	0	0	0	
	0	0	1	0	0	0	1	0	0	0	0	0	0	0	
	0	0	1	1	0	0	0	1	0	0	0	0	0	0	
	0	1	0	0	0	0	0	0	1	0	0	0	0	0	BCD States
	0	1	0	1	0	0	0	0	0	1	0	0	0	0	
	0	1	1	0	0	0	0	0	0	0	1	0	0	0	
	0	1	1	1	0	0	0	0	0	0	0	1	0	0	
	1	0	0	0	0	0	0	0	0	0	0	0	1	0	
	1	0	0	1	0	0	0	0	0	0	0	0	0	1	
	1	0	1	0	0	0	0	0	0	0	0	0	1	0	
	1	0	1	1	0	0	0	0	0	0	0	0	0	1	
	1	1	0	0	0	0	0	0	0	0	0	0	1	0	Extraordinary States
	1	1	0	1	0	0	0	0	0	0	0	0	0	1	
	1	1	1	0	0	0	0	0	0	0	0	0	1	0	
	1	1	1	1	0	0	0	0	0	0	0	0	0	1	

4.4 SEQUENTIAL CIRCUITS

4.4.1. MEMORY CELLS AND FLIP-FLOPS

Basic Memory Cell

It is a circuit that store one bit information. This one-bit memory element is called *flip-flop* or *latch*, since it latches (or locks) data in it.

It has two outputs ; Q and $\overline{Q}$, which are always complements of each other.

In set state, Q is HIGH (logic 1) and $\overline{Q}$ is LOW (logic 0) ;

In reset state, $\overline{Q}$ is HIGH (logic 1) and Q is LOW (logic 0) ;

For a flip-flop to act as a memory device, it should retain information stored in it. Thus, if it is set state, it should remain set and if it is in reset state, it should remain reset.

This function can be realized by using two NAND or NOR inverters connected in a feedback loop as shown in Fig. 4.45.

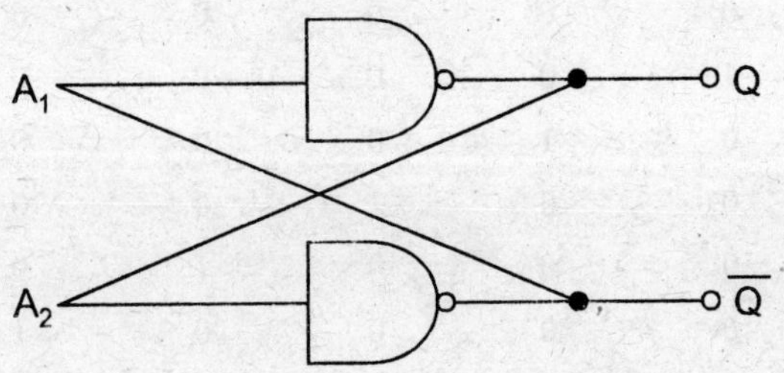

$Q = \overline{A}_1 = A_2$

$\overline{Q} = \overline{A}_2 = A_1$

QA_2	$\overline{Q}$	A_1	
1	1	0	0
0	0	1	1

Fig. 4.44 Basic memory cell

4.4.2. SR FLIP-FLOP

To store desired bits in the flip-flops, two-input NAND or NOR gates are used as shown in Fig. 4.45.

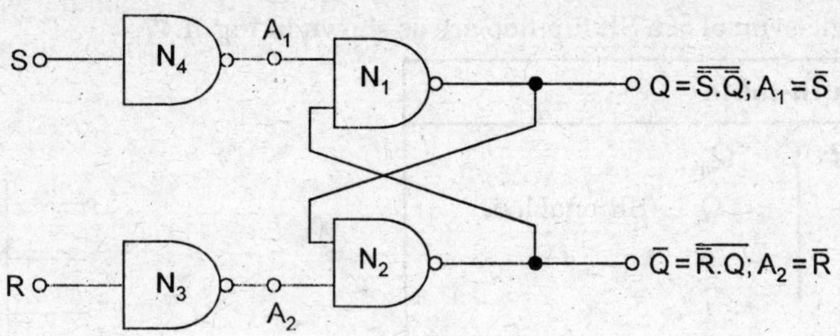

Fig. 4.45 SR flip-flop

Truth-table				
S	**R**	**A_1**	**A_2**	**State**
0	0	1	1	No change
0	1	1	0	Reset
1	0	0	1	Set
1	1	0	0	Race

Following observations are made from this figure and the truth-table :

Set State : When S = 1 and R = 0, A_1 becomes 0, making Q = 1. So, $\overline{Q} = \overline{1.1} = 0$. This input condition sets the flip-flop (Q = 1, $\overline{Q}$ = 0) ; so it is called **set state.**

Reset State : When S = 0 and R = 1, A_2 becomes 0, making $\overline{Q}$ = 1 and Q = $\overline{1.1}$ = 0. This input condition resets the flip-flop (Q = 0, $\overline{Q}$ = 1); so it is called **reset state.**

No Change : When S = R = 0, Q = $\overline{1.\overline{Q}}$ = Q and $\overline{Q} = \overline{1.\overline{Q}} = \overline{Q}$. The flip-flop remains in whatever state it is in, the function is that of a basic memory cell discussed earlier.

Race : When S = R = 1, A_1 and A_2 both become 0. So Q = $\overline{Q}$ = 1. This is an undesired output state because if S and R now change to 0, A_1 and A_2 will be 1, both Q and $\overline{Q}$ will try to become 0.

The actual state of flip-flop depends on relative delays of the two gates.

If N_2 is faster, $\overline{Q}$ will become $\overline{1.1}$ = 0 first and will make Q = 1.

If N_1 is faster, Q will become 0 first and will make $\overline{Q}$ = 1.

This is called *race condition*. Here state of the flip-flop is uncertain, so this condition is not allowed. This circuit is called SR *flip-flop*. It is an asynchronous circuit because output changes with changes as and when S,R inputs change.

4.4.3. CLOCKED SR FLIP-FLOP

SR flip-flop modified to include clock (CLK) pulses is shown in Fig. 4.46.

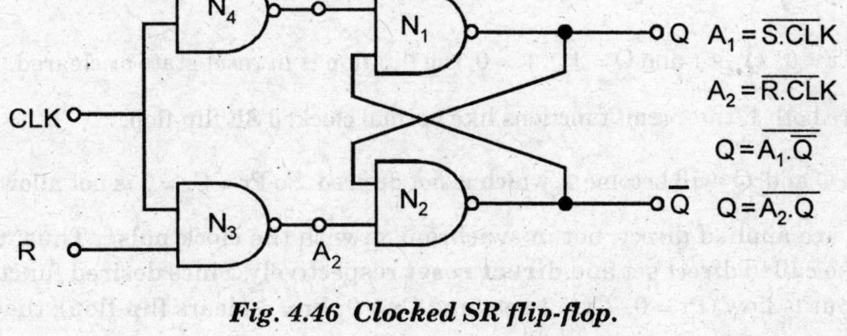

Fig. 4.46 Clocked SR flip-flop.

When CLK = 1, $A_1 = \overline{S}$ and $A_2 = \overline{R}$, the circuit functions like SR flip-flop.

When CLK = 0, $A_1 = A_2 = 1$, the circuit reduces to that of a basic memory cell and outputs remain unchanged (latched).

Here N_1, and N_2 form basic latch, whereas N_3 and N_4 control state of the flip-flop.

The truth-table and logic-symbol of a SR flip-flop are as shown in Fig. 4.47.

Truth-table

CLK	*S*	*R*	Q_{n+1}
1	0	0	Q_n (SR enabled)
1	0	1	0
1	1	0	1
1	1	1	Not allowed
0	×	×	Q_n (SR disabled)

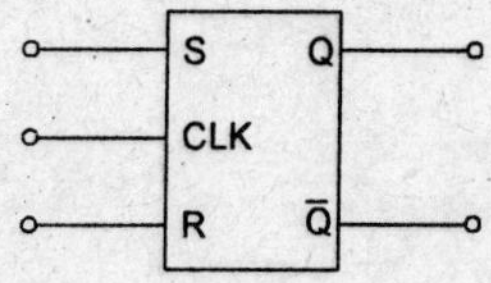

Fig. 4.47 Symbol clocked SR.

4.4.4. TRIGGERING

In *level triggering*, output changes only when clock is in HIGH or LOW level.

In the clocked SR flip-flop, the output changes according to the input condition as long as clock is HIGH. This is called *positive level triggering.*

If clock pulse is inverted before applying it at the input, then output will change only when clock is LOW.

This is called *negative level triggering*. In *edge triggering*, the output changes only when clock pulse makes a transition (from LOW to HIGH or from HIGH to LOW).

4.4.5. PRESET AND CLEAR

When power is turned ON, flip-flop assumes a random state depending upon time delay of the gates. It is often desirable to predefine starting state (sets or reset) of the flip-flop. This is achieved by two inputs called *preset* and *clear* as shown in Fig. 4.48. These inputs are applied in the interval between two clock pulses.

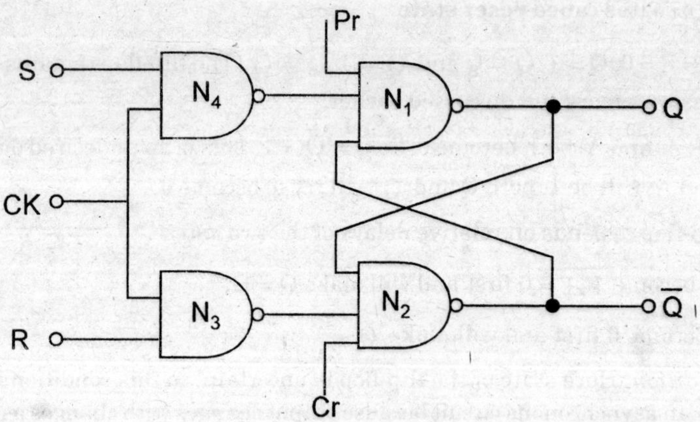

Fig. 4.48

Assume CLK = 0.

When P*r* = 0 and Cr = 1, Q is 1, so $\overline{Q} = \overline{1.1.1} = 0$; the flip-flop is set.

When Pr = 1 and Cr = 0, $\overline{Q}$ is 1 and $Q = \overline{1.1.1} = 0$; the flip-flop is in reset state or cleared.

When Pr and Cr are both 1, the circuit functions like normal clocked SR flip-flop.

If Pr = Cr = 0, both Q and $\overline{Q}$ will become 1, which is not desired. So Pr = Cr = 0 is not allowed.

Pr and Cr inputs are applied direct, not in synchronism with the clock pulse. Thus, they are asynchronous inputs and are also called direct set and **direct reset** respectively. Since desired function is performed when corresponding input is Low (Pr = 0, Cr = 1 sets and Cr = 0, Pr = 1 clears flip-flop); they are active low inputs (indicated by placing a bubble at these inputs). The symbol of a clocked SR flip-flop and its truth-table with active low preset and clear is shown in Fig. 4.49.

Truth-table

CLK	*Pr*	*Cr*	*S*	*R*	Q_{n+1}
1	1	1	0	0	Q_n
			0	1	0
			1	0	1
			1	1	Not allowed
0	0	1	×	×	1 (Set)
0	1	0	×	×	0 (Reset)

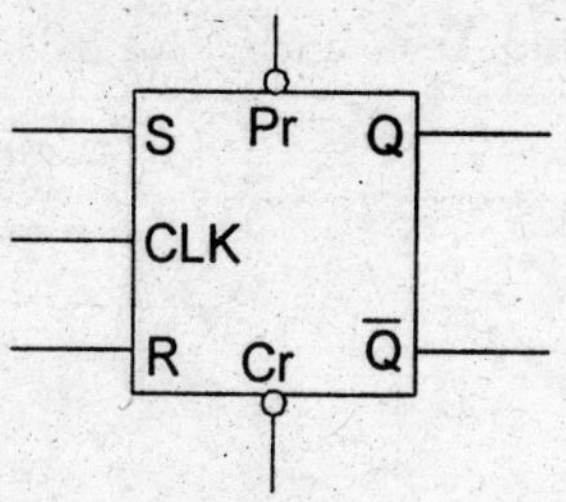

Fig. 4.49 Symbol clocked SR with preset and clear

4.4.6. JK FLIP-FLOP

In an SR flip-flop, the input combination S = R = 1 is not allowed because its output is uncertain.

This is called *JK flip-flop* with inputs J and K. Also, Table 4.9 gives combined of SR/JK flip-flops.

Table 4.9. Truth-table SR/JK Flip-flops

J	K	Q_n	Q_{n+1}	S	R	
0	0	0	0	0	0/1	Inactive
0	0	1	1	1/0	0	$Q_{n+1} = Q_n$
0	1	0	0	0	0/1	Reset state
0	1	1	0	0	1	$Q_{n+1} = 0$
1	0	0	1	1	0	Set state
1	0	1	1	1/0	0	$Q_{n+1} = 1$
1	1	0	1	1	0	Toggle state
1	1	1	0	0	1	$Q_{n+1} = \overline{Q}_n$

K-maps with S and R as outputs, and taking J, K and Q_n as inputs, are shown in Fig. 4.50.

Fig. 4.50

Based on K-map JK–FF has been designed as shown in Fig. 4.51 and its qualified circuit diagram in Fig. 4.52.

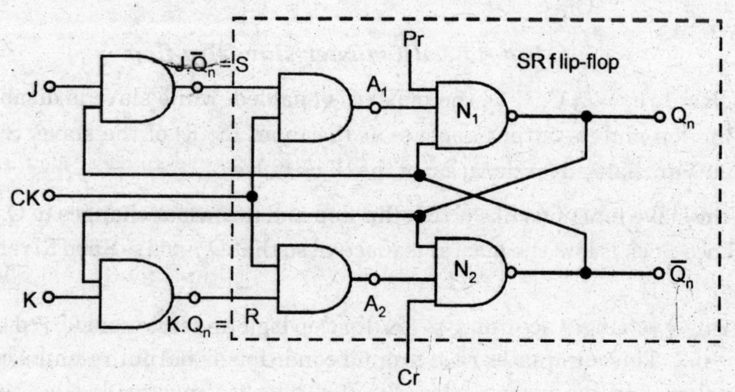

Fig. 4.51

Table 4.10. Truth-table JK Flip-flop

J	*K*	Q_{n+1}
0	0	Q_n
0	1	0
1	0	1
1	1	$\overline{Q}_n$

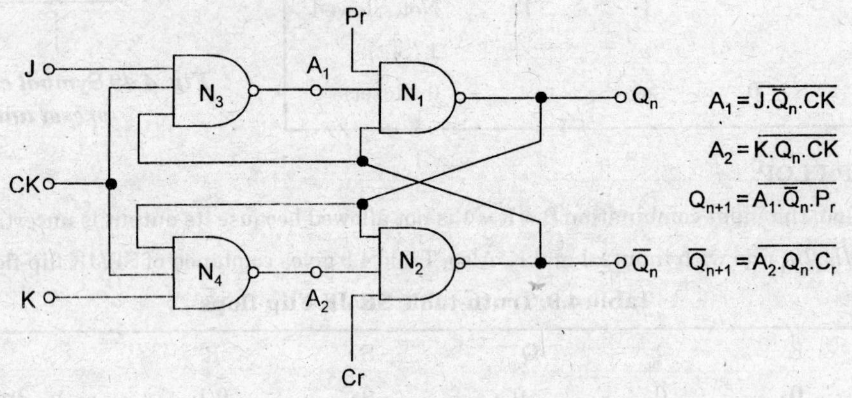

Fig. 4.52

4.4.7. JK MASTER-SLAVE FLIP-FLOP

This flip-flop is made of two SR flip-flops. Output of the first, called *master flip-flop*, is given to the inputs of the second, called *slave flip-flop*. Output of the slave is fedback to the inputs of the master. The master is triggered by a positive clock pulse and slave is triggered by a negative clock pulse, obtained by inverting clock pulse applied to the master. The circuit of a MS flip-flop is shown in Fig. 4.53.

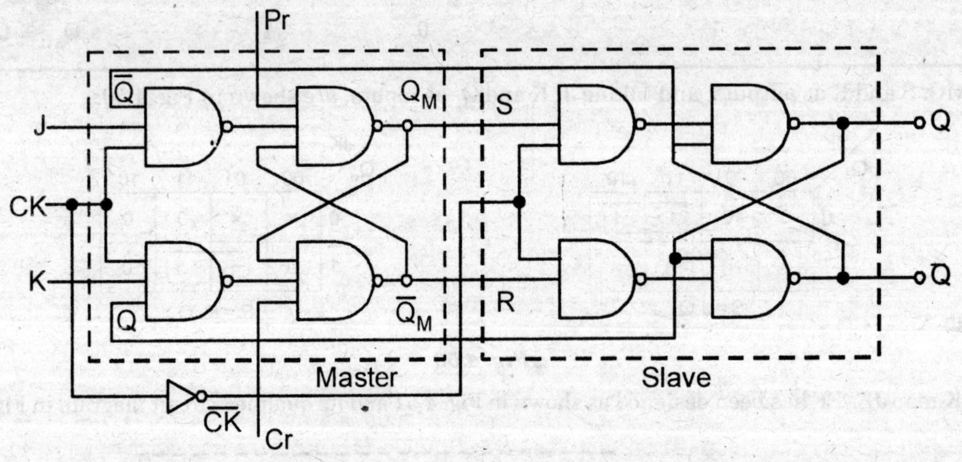

Fig. 4.53. JK master-slave flip-flop

When clock is high (CK = 1, Pr = 1, Cr = 1), the master is enabled, while slave is disabled as $\overline{CK} = 0$. So, master functions like a JK flip-flop and its output appears at the input (S, R) of the slave. Since CK is low, the slave is inactive. Thus Q remains unchanged for duration of the clock pulse t_p.

When clock goes low, the slave functions like an SR flip-flop and its output changes to Q_M, which also appears at the input of the master. Since clock is low, the master is inactive so that Q_M (and so S and R) remains unchanged as long as the clock remains low.

Thus, when clock is high, Q_M changes according to JK flip-flop logic and it is transferred to Q when the clock goes low (negative edge transition). This eliminates race-around condition as output remains constant for duration of one clock pulse. This flip-flop is called *master slave flip-flop* because master decides the output, which is simply latched out by the slave. The truth-table of this flip-flop is shown in Table 4.11.

Table 4.11. Truth-table for MS JK Flip-flop

Pr	Cr	CK	J	K	Q_{n+1}	States
0	0	×	×	×	?	Not desired
0	1	×	×	×	1	Preset
1	0	×	×	×	0	Clear
1	1	×	0	0	Q_n	Inactive
1	1	⎍	0	1	0	Zero
1	1	⎍	1	0	1	One
1	1	⎍	1	1	$\overline{Q}_n$	Toggle

4.4.8. D FLIP-FLOP

In a D flip-flop, output follows the input whenever flip-flop is triggered. This can be realized by means of a JK/SR flip-flop. The JK/SR inputs needs to achieve D logic are given in the truth table of Table 4.12.

Table 4.12. Truth-table JKSR Flip-flop

D	Q_n	Q_{n+1}	*J*	*K*	*S*	*R*
0	0	0	0	0/1	0	0/1
0	1	0	0/1	1	0	1
1	0	1	1	0/1	1	0
1	1	1	0/1	0	0/1	0

K-maps for J, K, S, R are given in Fig. 4.54, from which it follows that

$$D = J = \overline{K}$$

Also

$$D = S = \overline{R}$$

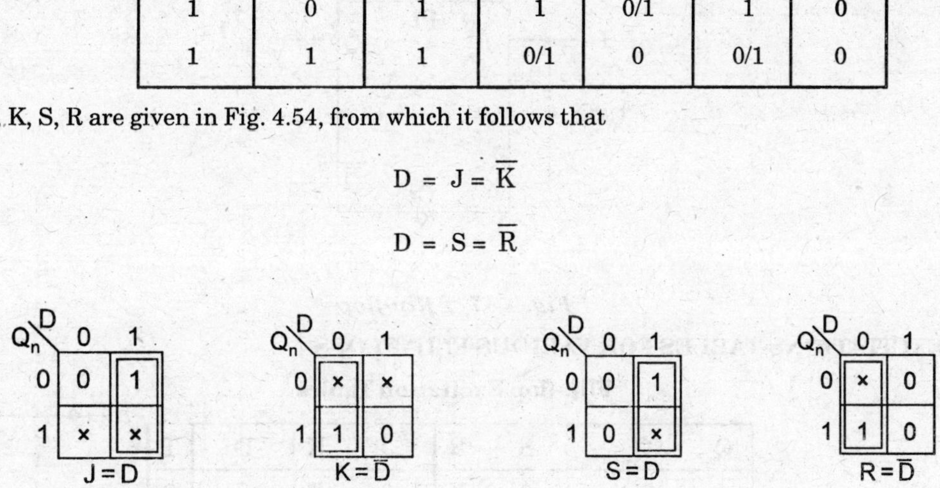

Fig. 4.54

Using these equations, design of a D flip-flop using JK flip-flop/SR flip-flop along with its truth-table is as given in Figs. 4.55 (*a*), (*b*) and (*c*) respectively. Here output follows the input, when flip-flop is triggered. If flip-flop is edge triggered, then output is same as the input, but is delayed by one clock pulse. Due to this property, D flip-flop is used as a delay device. From Fig. 4.56, short duration spurious pulses in the datas (D) (called **glitches**) are eliminated in the output (Q).

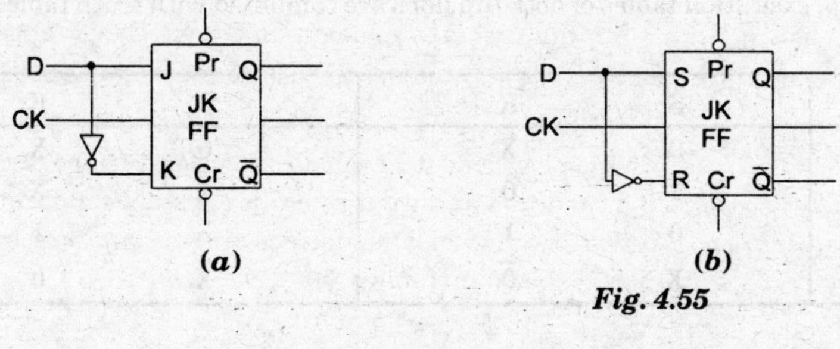

Truth-table

D	Q_{n+1}
0	0
1	1

(*a*) (*b*) (*c*)

Fig. 4.55

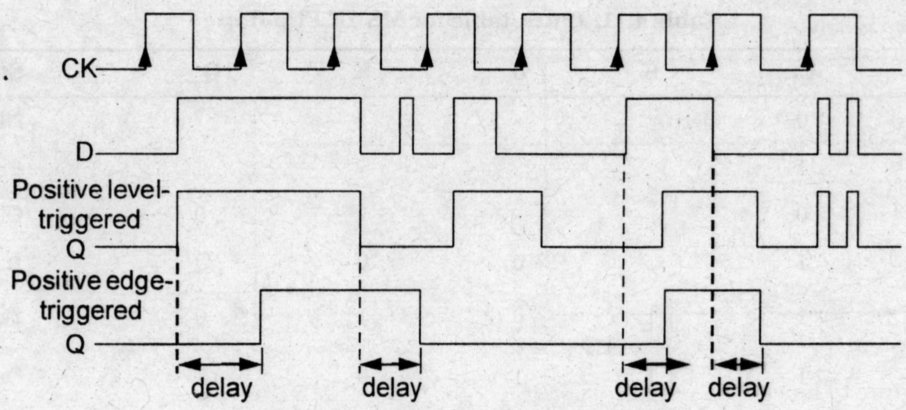

Fig. 4.56 Wave form of a D flip-flop

4.4.9. T FLIP-FLOP

Two combinations of J and K inputs of a JK flip-flop are used to make a D flip-flop. These were J = 0, K = 1 and J = 1, K = 0.

The remaining two combinations can be used to make a T flip-flop. These combinations are J = K = 0 and J = K = 1.

As J = K for both the inputs, this is equivalent to a single input T (0/1) connected to both J and K as shown in Fig. 4.57 along with its truth-table. This configuration is called **T flip-flop**.

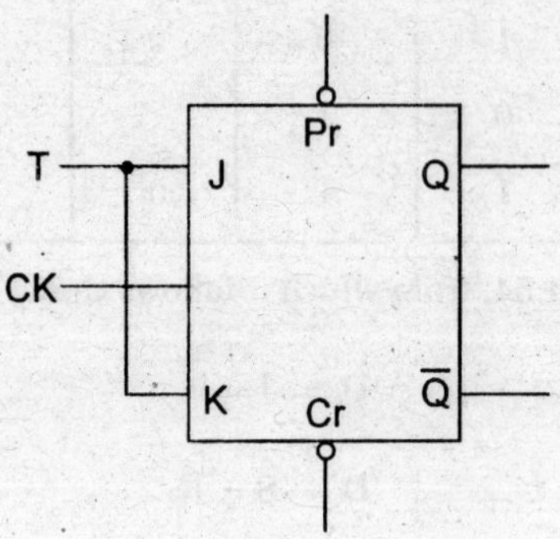

Fig. 4.57 T flip-flop

4.4.10. EXCITATIONS-TABLES FOR VARIOUS FLIP-FLOPS

Flip-flop Excitation Tables

Q_n	Q_{n+1}	S	R	J	K	D	T
0	0	0	X	0	X	0	0
0	1	1	0	1	X	1	1
1	0	0	1	X	1	0	1
1	1	X	0	X	0	1	0

CONVERSION OF FLIP FLOP.

(1) RS to JK Flip Flop

To convert RS flip flop into JK flip flop, excitation tables of both flip flops are combined with truth table as given below:

Q(n)	Q(n + 1)	S	R	J	K
0	0	0	X	0	X
0	1	1	0	1	X
1	0	0	1	X	1
1	1	X	0	X	0

Now, K map is solved for input R, S and Q(n) and J and K as output

Input			Output	
J	K	Q(*n*)	S	R
0	x	0	0	x
1	x	0	1	0
x	1	1	0	1
x	0	1	x	0

Solving for K map, we get R = KQ and S = $J\overline{Q}$.

Block diagram to convert RS to JK flip flop is

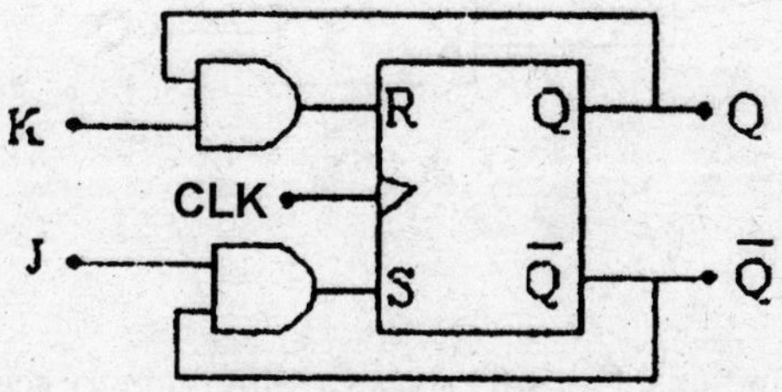

Fig. 4.58

(2) D to T Flip Flop

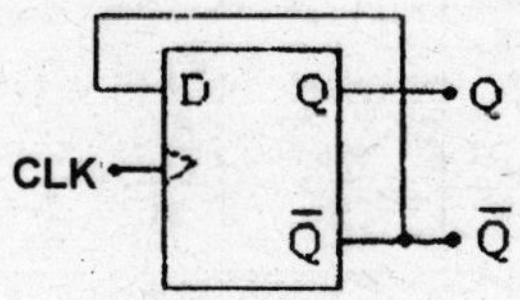

(a) Toggle only

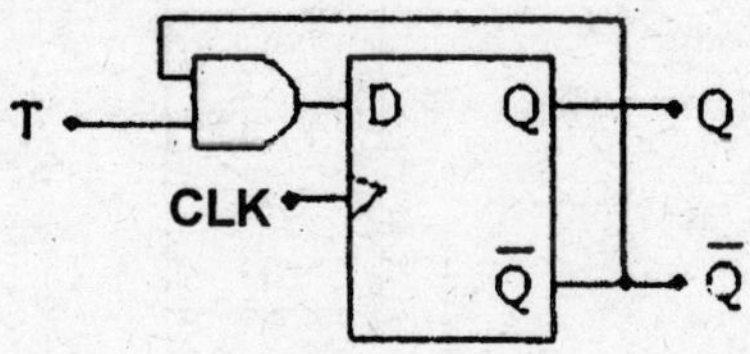

(b) With T data input

Fig. 4.59

(3) RS to D Flip Flop

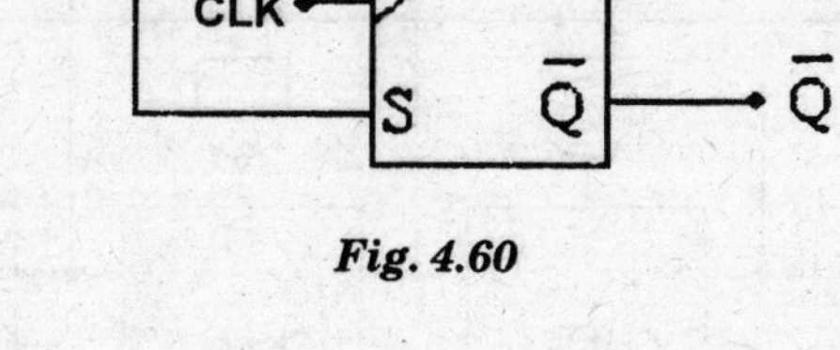

Fig. 4.60

(4) RS to T Flip Flop

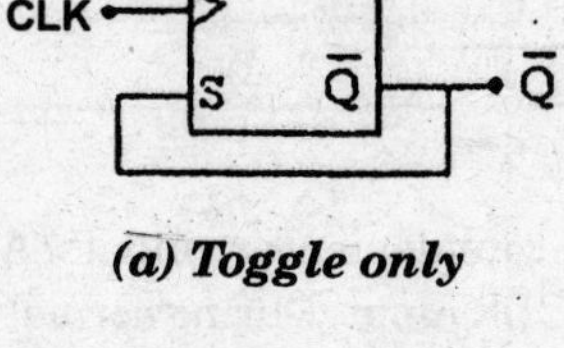

(a) Toggle only

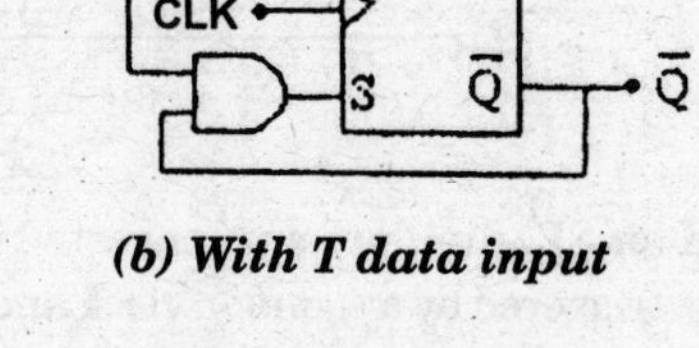

(b) With T data input

Fig. 4.61

(5) JK to D Flip Flop

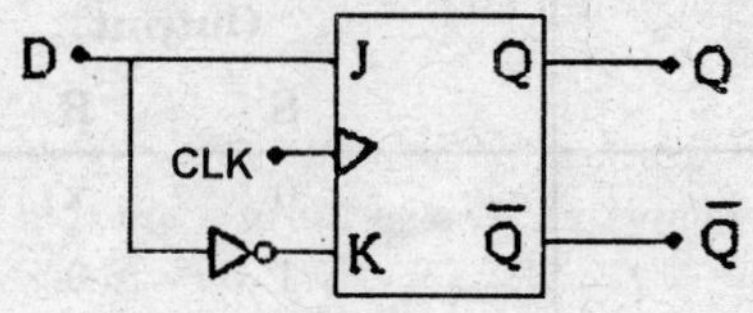

Fig. 4.62

(6) JK to T Flip Flop

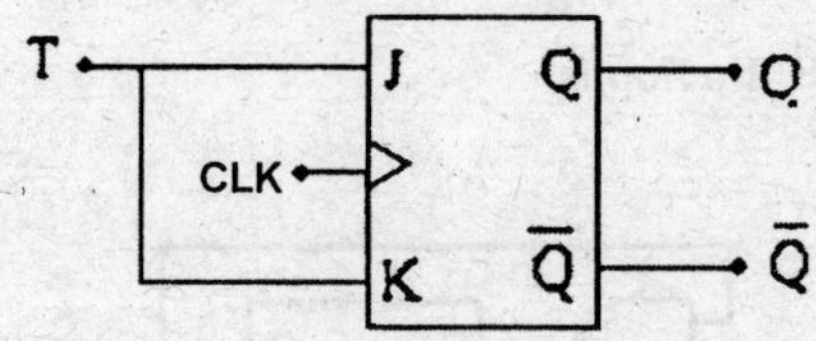

Fig. 4.63

4.4.11. REGISTERS

Memory Registers

These store n bits of data using n flip-flops. Fig. 4.64 shows a 4-bit memory register (or buffer) composed of four D flip-flops which are triggered by a common clock. All the four flip-flops can be cleaved by giving a 0 at the CLR input. Data input (4–bits).

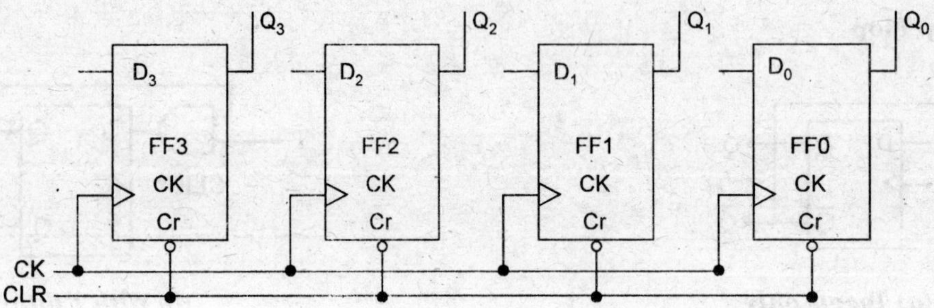

Fig. 4.64 4-bit memory register

Shift Registers

Shift registers store as well as manipulate data.

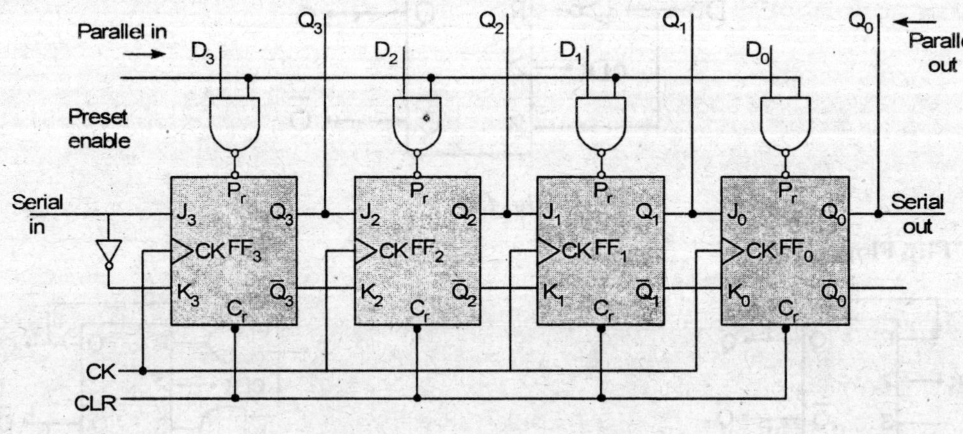

Fig. 4.65 4-bit shift register.

Four JK (or SR) flip-flops are converted into D flip-flops by giving mutually complementary inputs. All the four flip-flops are triggered by a common clock and can be cleared by giving a 0 at the CLR input. During normal operation, this input is held at 1.

Serial-In Serial-Out Shift register (SISO)

In Fig. 4.65, after initially clearing the flip-flops, CLR input is held at 1 and Preset enable input is held at 0, which keeps Pr inputs of the flip-flops at 1.

Data bits are entered serially, LSB first and MSB last. This form of data, in which bits are separated in time, is called **temporal code**. Input data is given at the serial-in input. Let word 0101 is to be entered. LSB 1, is given at the serial-in input, which is transferred to Q_3 when first clock pulse occurs. By similar D flip-flop logic, this 1 gets transferred to Q_2 and next bit (0 here) appears at Q_3 after second clock pulse.

Thus, after fourth clock pulse, all the four bits are entered into the register and stored till the next clock pulse appears. Data can be read serially at the serial-out output. LSB first and MSB last, by giving three clock pulses. After fourth clock pulse, all the four flip-flops get reset to 0.

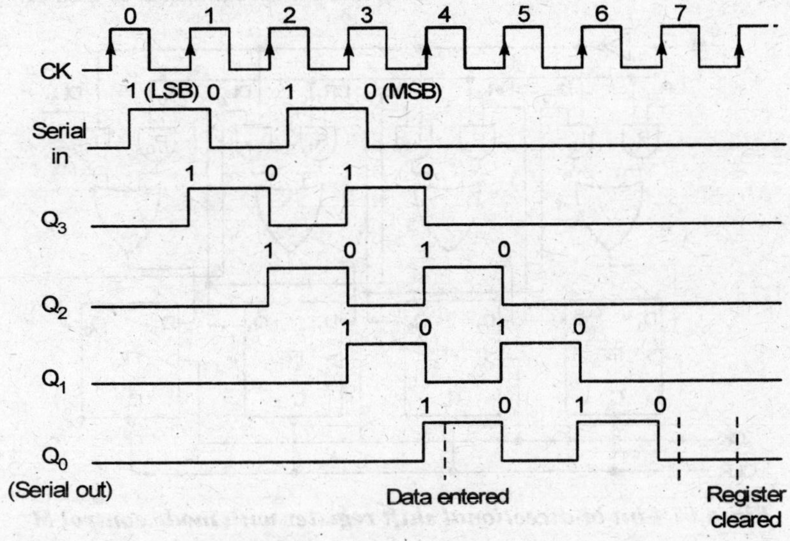

Fig. 4.66 Wave forms in 4-bit shift register–SISO

Table 4.13

Clock pulse	*Serial in*	Q_3	Q_2	Q_1	*Serial out* Q_0
0	1 (LSB)	0	0	0	0
1	0	1	0	0	0
2	1	0	1	0	0
3	0 (MSB)	1	0	1	0
4	0	0	1	0	1 Data entered
5	0	0	0	1	0
6	0	0	0	0	1
7	0	0	0	0	0
8	0	0	0	0	0 Register is cleared

Serial-In Parallel-Out Shift register (SIPO)

In this, input data is a temporal code and output is a special code, in which all bits of a data word are read at the same time. Data is entered serially. For an *n*-bit register, all the *n*-bits are entered into the *n* flip-flops at the end of *n*th clock pulse.

Parallel-In Parallel-Out Shift register (PIPO)

In this, input and output data are in the form of special code. Input data bits are applied at the parallel in inputs (D_3, D_2, D_1, D_0) and are read at the parallel-out outputs (Q_3, Q_2, Q_1 Q_0).

Application : PIPO registers can be used as Read/Write memory registers.

Parallel-In Serial-Out Shift registers (PISO)

In Fig. 4.65, input data is in the form of special code, whereas output data is in the form of temporal code.

Input data bits are applied at the parallel-in inputs and Preset enable input is held at 1. Thus, input word is written into the register.

Now, Preset enable is held at 0 and clock pulses are applied. The data bits can be read at the serial-out output as explained under SISO.

Application : In digital transmission, n-bit data words can be converted into a serial code by using a PISO register and then can be transmitted along a single transmission line.

Bi-Directional Shift register

SISO and PISO registers shift n-bit data word to right by one place at the occurrence of a clock pulse. This results in a binary number which is the previous number divided by two, given that 1 is not shifted out of the LSB.

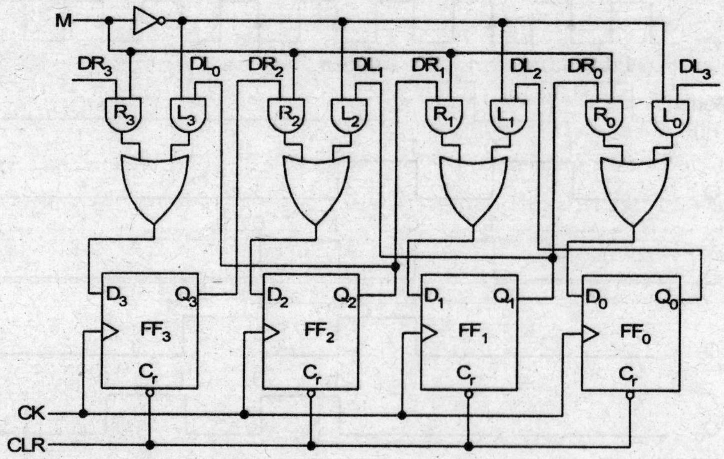

Fig. 4.67 4-bit bi-directional shift register with mode control M

If instead of giving outputs of FF_3 to the inputs of FF_2 and so on, we give outputs of FF_0 to the inputs of FF_1. FF_1 to FF_2, and FF_2 to FF_3 we can shift the data word to left by one bit by giving a clock pulse. This results in a binary number which is the previous number multiplied by two given that 1 is not shifted out of the MSB.

When M is 1, the AND gates labeled as R_3, R_2, R_1, R_0 are enabled and register functions as a shift right register.

When M is 0, AND gates labeled as R_i are disabled and ones labeled as L_3, L_2, L_1, L_0 are enabled. This makes the register function as a *left shift register*. The data for shift right operation is entered at the Shift Right Serial-In input (DR_3). The data for shift left register is entered at the Shift Left Serial-In input (DL_3).

4.4.12. COUNTERS

Binary counters are most important and widely used digital circuits. Counter is a circuit which counts number of occurrences of an input (in terms of positive or negative edge transitions in the case of a binary input). Each count, a binary number, is called a *state of the counter*. Hence, a counter counting in terms of n-bits has 2^n different states. The number of different states of a counter is also called *modulus of the counter*. Thus an n-bit counter is a modulo 2^n. counter.

Counter circuits are primarily constituted of flip-flops which alongwith combinational elements are used for the generation of control signals.

Depending on the manner in which flip-flops are triggered, counters can be divided into two major categories :

1. Asynchronous Counter (ripple counter)
2. Synchronous Counter

In case of an asynchoronous counter, all the flip-flops are not clocked simultaneously, where as in a synchronous counter all the flip-flops are clocked simultaneously.

UP/DOWN Counters

If counter counts in such a way that decimal equivalent of the output increases with successive clock pulses. It is called *UP counter*. If it decreases it is called *DOWN counter*. An UP/DOWN counter can also be designed which can count in any direction depending upon the control input.

Decoding circuit can be connected to the output of a counter in such a way that output of the cirtuit goes high (or low) only when counter contents are equal to a given state.

4.4.13. ASYNCHRONOUS COUNTERS

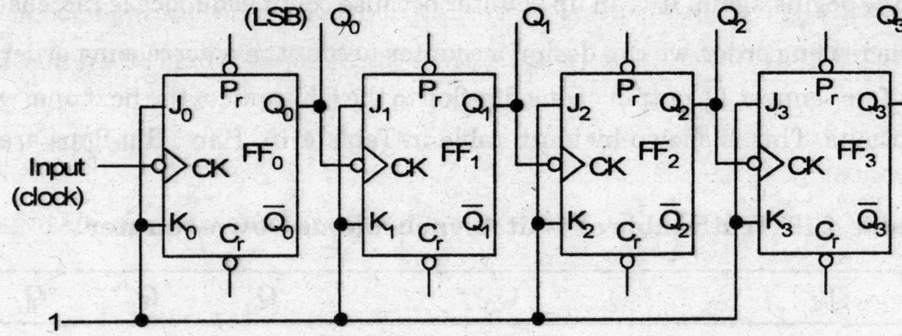

Fig. 4.68. 4-bit (modulo-16) asynchronous counter

Four negative edge triggered JK flip flops are converted into T flip-flops by making J = K = 1 for all four of them. The Q output of one flip-flop is fed to the CK input of the next one.

From Fig. 4.68, it can be seen that for every negative edge transition (1 to 0) of the input pulse, output of FF_0, *i.e.* Q_0 toggles. Similarly for every negative transition of Q_0, Q_1 toggles and so on for Q_2 and Q_3. This is shown in terms of truth-table (Table 4.14) and wave forms of Fig. 4.69; assuming that all the flip-flops were reset to '0' at the beginning of the input pulse. Also, it is assumed that flip-flops change state without any delays.

Table 4.14. Truth-table of 4-bit Asynchronous Counter (Up-counter)

Input pulse number	Q_3	Q_2	Q_1	Q_0	
0	0	0	0	0	
1	0	0	0	1	– ve edge
2	0	0	1	0	
3	0	0	1	1	
4	0	1	0	0	
5	0	1	0	1	
6	0	1	1	0	
7	0	1	1	1	
8	1	0	0	0	
9	1	0	0	1	
10	1	0	1	0	
11	1	0	1	1	
12	1	1	0	0	
13	1	1	0	1	
14	1	1	1	0	
15	1	1	1	1	
0	0	0	0	0	

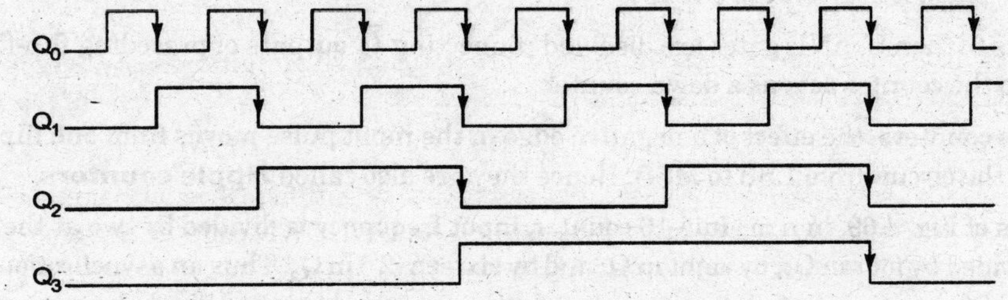

Fig. 4.69. Waveforms of 4-bit asynchronous counter

Thus outputs Q_3, Q_2, Q_1, Q_0 change in increasing sequence from 0000 through 1111. After 15th pulse, they are reset back to 0000 and counting begins again. It is an up-counter because count sequence is increasing in order.

Instead of counting in increasing order, we can design a counter to count in a decreasing order. This is called **down-counter.** In table 4.15, if we connect $\overline{Q}$ output of one flip-flop to the CK input of the next one, we can get a decreasing count sequence at Q outputs. This is shown by truth-table in Table 4.15. Here, flip-flops are set to '1' state in the beginning.

Table 4.15. Truth-table of 4-bit Asynchronous Down-counter

Input pulse	$\overline{Q_3}$	$\overline{Q_2}$	$\overline{Q_1}$	$\overline{Q_0}$	Q_3	Q_2	Q_1	Q_0
0	0	0	0	0	1	1	1	1
1	0	0	0	1	1	1	1	0
2	0	0	1	0	1	1	0	1
3	0	0	1	1	1	1	0	0
4	0	1	0	0	1	0	1	1
5	0	1	0	1	1	0	1	0
6	0	1	1	0	1	0	0	1
7	0	1	1	1	1	0	0	0
8	1	0	0	0	0	1	1	1
9	1	0	0	1	0	1	1	0
10	1	0	1	0	0	1	0	1
11	1	0	1	1	0	1	0	0
12	1	1	0	0	0	0	1	1
13	1	1	0	1	0	0	1	0
14	1	1	1	0	0	0	0	1
15	1	1	1	1	0	0	0	0
0	0	0	0	0	1	1	1	1

An up/down counter with a control signal controlling increasing/decreasing order of counting is shown in Fig. 4.70.

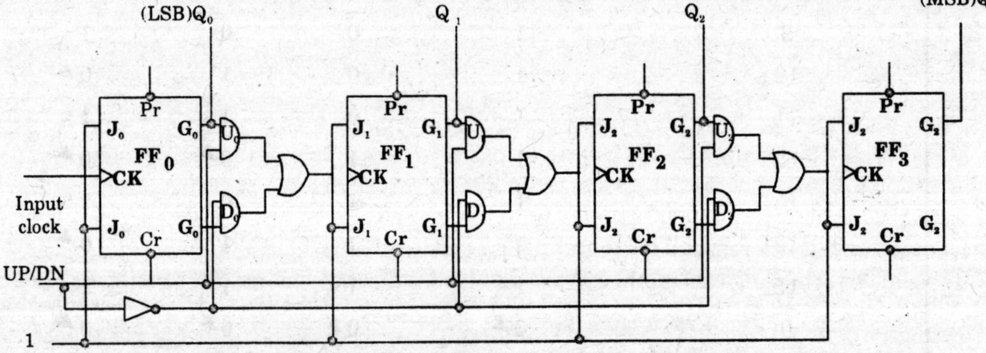

Fig. 4.70 4-bit a sychfronous up/down counter

When up/down (UP/$\overline{\text{DN}}$) is 1, then D_i AND gates are disabled and Q outputs of preceding flip-flops goes to CK inputs of the next ones. Thus, it acts as a up enter.

When UP/$\overline{\text{DN}}$ is 0, then U_i AND gates are disabled connecting $\overline{Q}$ outputs of preceding flip-flops to CK inputs of the next ones and so the counter acts as a down counter.

In asynchronous counters, the effect of a negative edge in the input pulse moves from one flip-flop to the next one, or ripples through the circuit from LSB to MSB. Hence they are also called **ripple counters**.

From waveforms of Fig. 4.69, in a modulo-16 counter, input frequency is divided by two at the output of FF_0 (Q_0 wave form). This is divided by four in Q_1, by eight in Q_2 and by sixteen (2^4) in Q_3. Thus an asynchronous counter can be used to generate various frequencies. A modulo-*n* asynchronous counter is also called divide-by *n* (power of 2) counter because input frequency gets divided by *n* at the output of the last flip-flop (MSB).

Nonbinary Counters

With n flip-flops, we can generate 2^n different states using a modulo 2^n counter. For the numbers that are not powers of 2, some simple combinational logic can be used to generate a modulo m counter for any m. This is shown by flollowing modulo 12 counter.

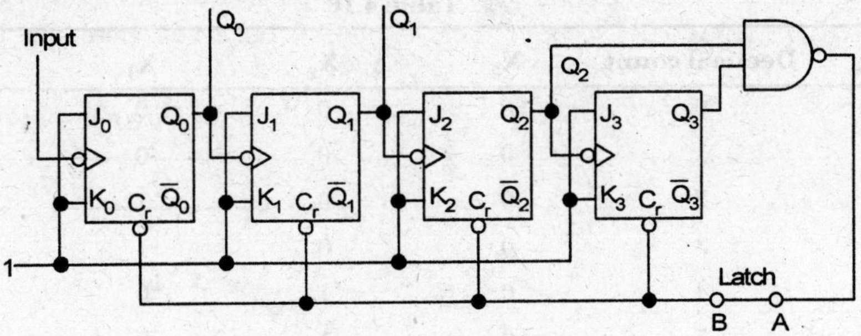

Fig. 4.71 Modulo 12 counter

Since $2^3 < 12 < 2^4$, we will required atleast four flip-flops for a modulo 12 counter. With four flip-flops, counter must be reinitialized when count reaches 12 $(1100)_2$ *i.e.*, flip-flops must be reset to count again from 0000 to 1011. Fig. 4.71 shows the circuit for this.

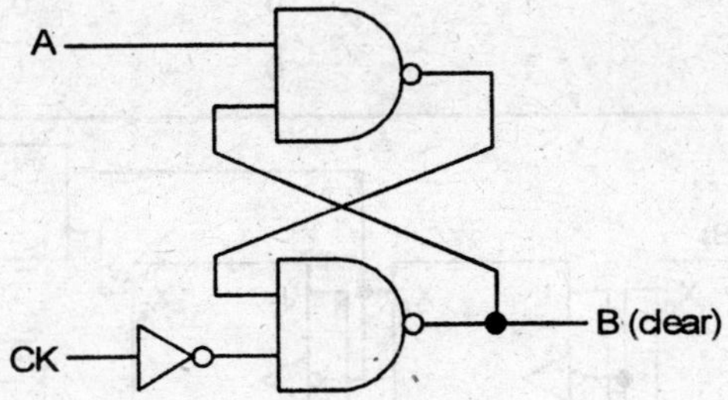

(a) Latch

A	CK	B	
1	1	0	
1	0	1	(after A = 1; CK = 1)
0	0	0	
1	0	0	(after A = 0; CK = 0)
0	1	1	

(b) Truth table of latch

Fig. 4.72

Since $Q_2 = Q_3 = 1$ is not true for $(0000)_2$ to $(1011)_2$ and is true for $(1100)_2$, the NAND gate will give a 0 at its output when count reaches 12. This will reset all the four flip-flops and hence count will start again. We can design a counter for any desired modulo by following this method of providing a feedback circuit for clearing the flip-flops.

In modulo–12 counter of Fig. 4.71, a latch shown in Fig. 4.72 (*a*), is connected between AB to keep clear line at 0 till both flip-flops are cleared. The truth table of the latch is given in Fig. 4.72 (*b*).

Asynchronous counters are quite easy to design, but they have one drawback. Due to the fact that one flip-flop can change its state only after the preceding one changes, propagation delays are cumulative. If output response time delay of each flip-flop is T_r, then Q_3 (MSB) output for modulo–16 counter will be delayed by $4T_r$. If modulo is large, there will be a large number of flip-flops in series and time delay of the MSB can become larger than the time between two input pulses, making it impossible to read correct value of the count between pulses.

BCD (or Decade) Counters

It is a nonbinary counter which counts normally until it reaches 1001 (*i.e.* decimal 9) and then reset itself, while generating a carry, which will be used for the BCD count of next decimal digit. A typical BCD counter (using 4 flip-flops) is shown in Fig. 4.73 (*a*). The output states of the flip-flop (till the state 1001) are indicated in Table 4.16 when next negative going edge occurs at the input, the BCD counter returns to all 0's. At the same time (*i.e.*, during the interval when the counter goes from 9 to 0), a negative-going signal edge occurs at the CARRY output. This CARRY output can be connected to the input of another BCD counter, which will be stepped by 1 when first BCD stage goes from 9 to 0. This is shown in Fig. 4.73 (*b*), where several four flip-flop BCD stages are combined to make a large counter.

Table 4.16

Decimal count	X_3	X_2	X_1	X_0
0	0	0	0	0
1	0	0	0	1
2	0	0	1	0
3	0	0	1	1
4	0	1	0	0
5	0	1	0	1
6	0	1	1	0
7	0	1	1	1
8	1	0	0	0
9	1	0	0	1
10	1	0	1	0

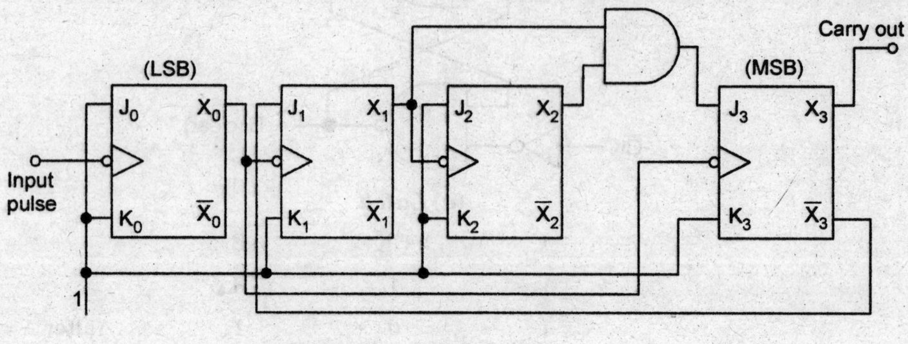

(a) Decade or BCD counter

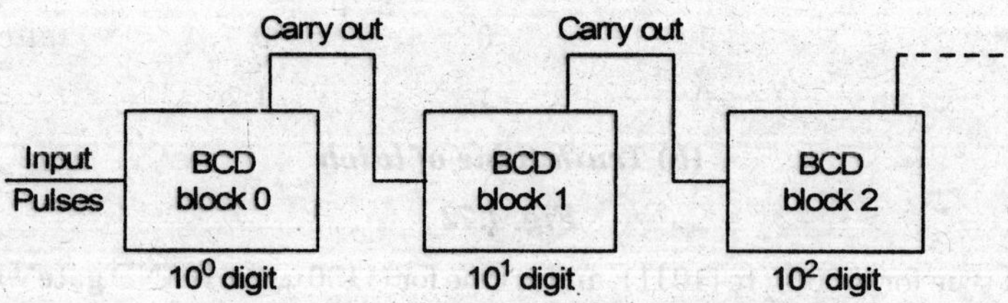

(b) Cascading BCD counter Fig. 4.73

With reference to Fig. 4.73 (*a*) and Table 4.16 from 0 to count 6, we have $X_3 = 0$, $\overline{X_3} = 1$, which keeps J of FF1 at 1. Therefore, it works as a T-FF and the count ripples through up to 4.

- *At count 6* : $X_0 = 0$, $X_1 = X_2 = 1$, AND gate output makes J = 1 at FF_3 which becomes T-FF.
- *At count 7* : $X_0 = 1$, no other change.
- *At count 8* : $X_0 = 0$ which ripples through and so $X_1 = X_2 = 0$. and $X_3 = 1$, $\overline{X_3} = 0$.

  So J = 0. K = 1 at FF_1, ready for clearing. Also AND gate output changes to 0 and so J = 0, K = 1 at FF_3. Thus FF_3 is also ready for clearing.
- *At count 9* : $X_0 = 1$, no other change.
- *At count 10* : $X_0 = 0$, $X_1 = 1$, $X_2 = 0$ and FF_3 clears to $X_3 = 0$, $\overline{X_3} = 1$. Carry out is generated. The cycle is ready for "repeat".

Let states on the block 0 and block 1 of Fig. 4.73 (*b*) are respectively 0001 and 0010. This corresponds to a count of 21.

4.4.14. SYNCHRONOUS COUNTERS

In a synchronous counter all the flip-flops are triggered by a common clock pulse. Thus, maximum propagation delay is equal to that of one flip-flop and any additional combinational circuitry required.

To design a modulo-16 synchronous counter, following steps should be covered. This is a typical example of synchronous counter design but a counter with any desired modulus can be designed by following steps :

(i) $16 = 2^4$, so 4 flip-flops are required. We use T flip-flops.

(ii) Truth-table for desired output sequence of Q_3, Q_2, Q_1, Q_0 is given in Table 4.17

In the truth-table, T-inputs are required to be 1 for the states for which corresponding Q outputs toggle and T-inputs are to be 0 for the states for which the corresponding Q outputs remain unchanged in the next state. A truth-table which gives excitations of flip-flops to produce a desired output is called *state table*.

Table 4.17

Input (Clock)	Q_3	Q_2	Q_1	Q_0	T_3	T_2	T_1	T_0
0	0	0	0	0	0	0	0	1
1	0	0	0	1	0	0	1	1
2	0	0	1	0	0	0	0	1
3	0	0	1	1	0	1	1	1
4	0	1	0	0	0	0	1	1
5	0	1	0	1	0	0	1	1
6	0	1	1	0	0	0	0	1
7	0	1	1	1	1	1	1	1
8	1	0	0	0	0	0	0	1
9	1	0	0	1	0	0	1	1
10	1	0	1	0	0	0	0	1
11	1	0	1	1	0	1	1	1
12	1	1	0	0	0	0	0	1
13	1	1	0	1	0	0	1	1
14	1	1	1	0	0	0	0	1
15	1	1	1	1	1	1	1	1
0	0	0	0	0				

(iii) Here, $T_0 = 1, T_1 = Q_0$

$$T_2 = Q_1Q_0\,(\overline{Q}_3\overline{Q}_2 + \overline{Q}_3Q_2 + Q_3\overline{Q}_2 + Q_3Q_2) = Q_1Q_0$$

$$T_3 = \overline{Q}_3Q_2Q_1Q_0 + Q_3Q_2Q_1Q_0 = Q_2\,Q_1\,Q_0$$

(iv) Hence, circuit of a modulo-16 synchronous counter is as shown in Fig. 4.74.

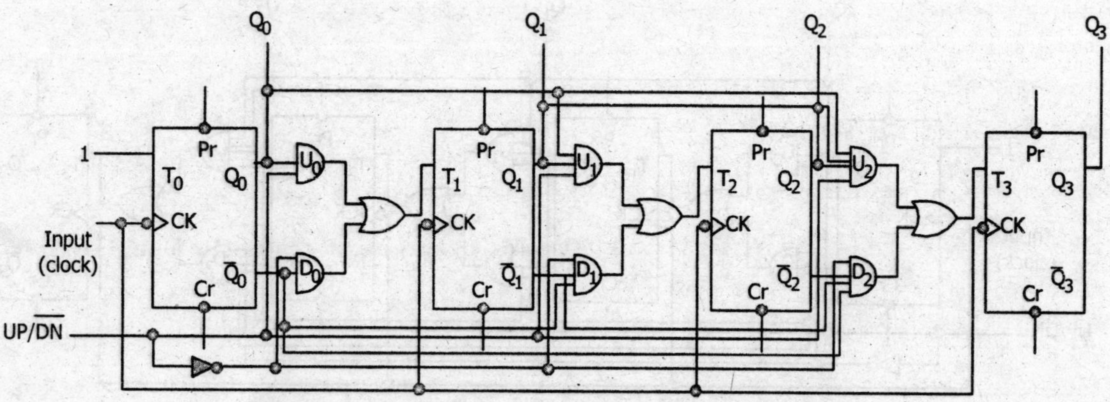

Fig. 4.74 Modulo-16 synchronous counter (serial carry).

Similar to the case of asynchronous counters, a down counter can be generated by inverting the flip-flop inputs in an up-counter. Table 4.18 shows required T-inputs for the generation of count down sequence.

Table 4.18

Clock	Q_3	Q_2	Q_1	Q_0	T_3	T_2	T_1	T_0
0	1	1	1	1	0	0	0	1
1	1	1	1	0	0	0	1	1
2	1	1	0	1	0	0	0	1
3	1	1	0	0	0	1	1	1
4	1	0	1	1	0	0	0	1
5	1	0	1	0	0	0	1	1
6	1	0	0	1	0	0	0	1
7	1	0	0	0	1	1	1	1
8	0	1	1	1	0	0	0	1
9	0	1	1	0	0	0	1	1
10	0	1	0	1	0	0	0	1
11	0	1	0	0	0	1	1	1
12	0	0	1	1	0	0	0	1
13	0	0	1	0	0	0	1	1
14	0	0	0	1	0	0	0	1
15	0	0	0	0	1	1	1	1
0	1	1	1	1				

Here $T_0 = 1, T_1 = \overline{Q}_0$

$$T_2 = Q_3Q_2\overline{Q}_1\overline{Q}_0 + Q_3\overline{Q}_2\overline{Q}_1\overline{Q}_0 + \overline{Q}_3Q_2\overline{Q}_1\overline{Q}_0 + \overline{Q}_3\overline{Q}_2\overline{Q}_1\overline{Q}_0$$

$$= \overline{Q}_1\overline{Q}_0$$

$$T_3 = Q_3\overline{Q}_2\overline{Q}_1\overline{Q}_0 + \overline{Q}_3\overline{Q}_2\overline{Q}_1\overline{Q}_0 = \overline{Q}_2\overline{Q}_1\overline{Q}_0$$

Using these expressions for the T-inputs, a modulo-16 synchronous down counter can be designed.

To design an up/down counter with a control signal, we can combine two sets of expressions to get circuit of Fig. 4.75 for a modulo-16 up/down synchronous counter.

For UP/$\overline{\text{DN}}$ = 1, the U_i gates are enabled generating an increasing count sequence.

For UP/$\overline{\text{DN}}$ = 0, the D_i gates are enabled generating a decreasing count sequence.

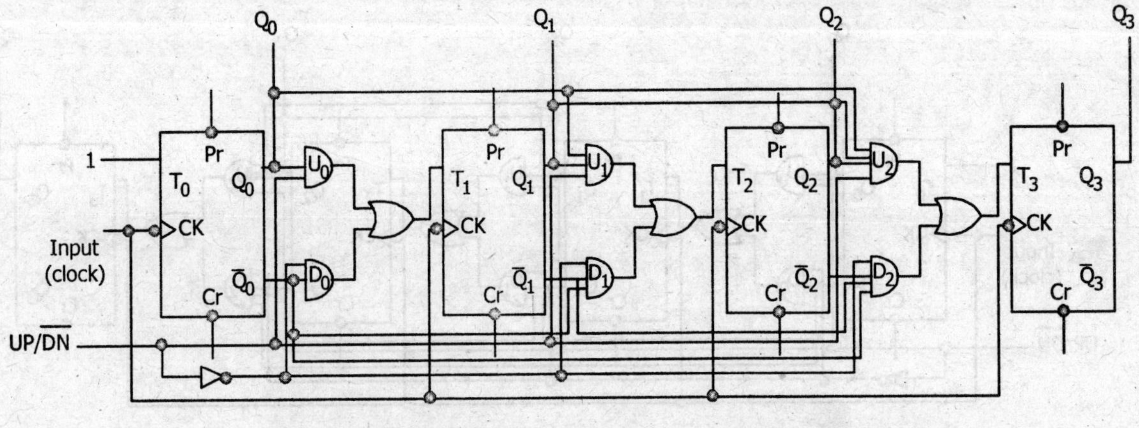

Fig. 4.75 Up/down synchronous counter (parallel carry)

Synchronous Up/Down Counter

A synchronous counter can count in upward as well as downward direction. A parallel up counter can be converted into a down counter by connecting $\overline{A}$, $\overline{B}$ and $\overline{C}$ outputs in place of A, B and C respectively. Then count of the counter proceed 1111 to 0000, i.e. in reverse order.

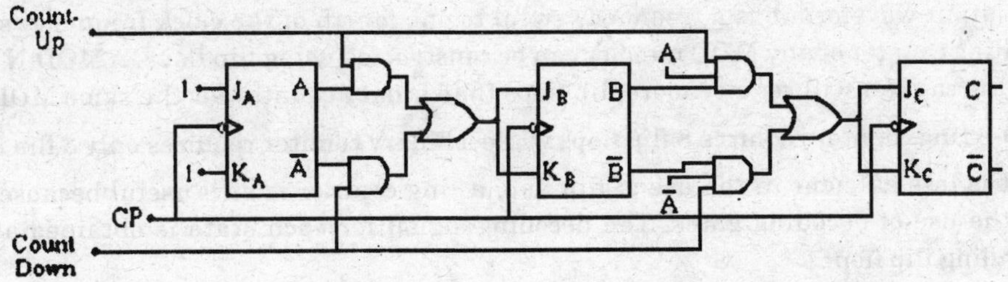

Fig. 4.76 MOD-8 up down counter.

From updown counter, control inputs Count-up and Count-down are used to control whether normal flip flop outputs or inverted outputs are fed to the J and K inputs.

When *Count up control* is 1, then MOD-8 counter will count from 000 to 111.

When *Count-down control* input is 1, then counter counts from 111 to 000.

HIGH input on the Count-up line and a LOW on Count-down enables AND gates 1 and 2 and disables 3 and 4. This allows A and B outputs are applied to J and K inputs and counter count up when pulses are applied. The counter will work as count-down when HIGH input is applied at Count-down and a LOW input is applied at Count up.

Shift Register Counter

It can be arranged to form different types of counters. Shift register counters use feed-back, which means output of the last flip flop in the register is connected back to the first flip flop in some way.

Commonly used Shift register Counters.

1. **Ring counter.**

Simple shift register counter is a circulating shift register connected, so that output of last flip flop shifts its value into the first flip flop. Such arrangement using D flip flop is shown below :

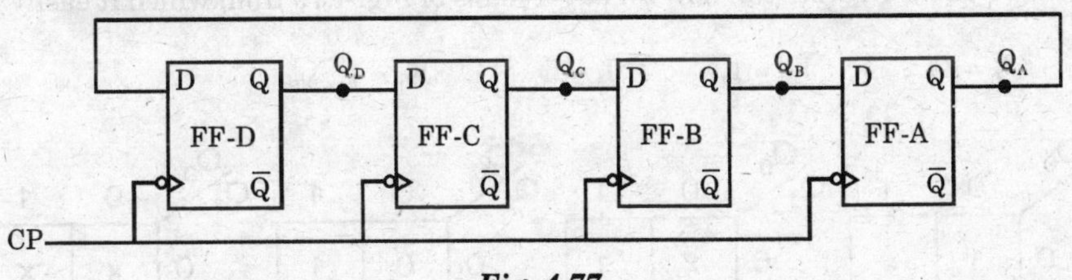

Fig. 4.77

Flip flops are connected, so that information shifts from left to right and back around from Q_A to Q_B. In most instances, only a single 1 is in the register and it is made to circulate around the register as long as clock pulses are applied. Therefore it is called *ring counter*.

Truth table

Q_D	Q_C	Q_B	Q_A	Clock
1	0	0	0	0
0	1	0	0	1
0	0	1	0	2
0	0	0	1	3
1	0	0	0	4 and so on

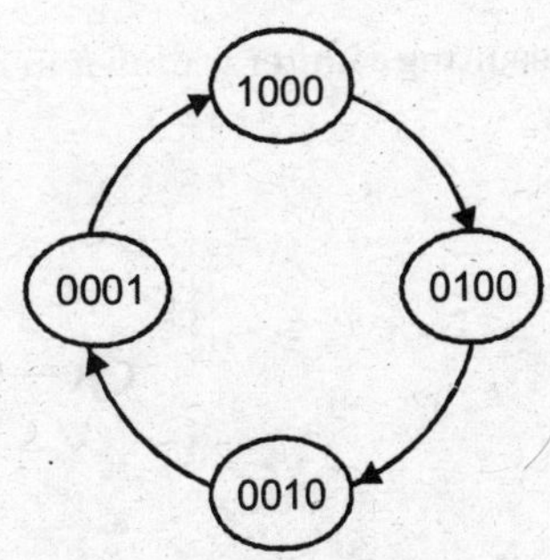

Fig. 4.78 State diagram

From the above table, assume a starting state of $Q_D = 1$ and $Q_C = Q_B = Q_A = 0$ which is necessary preset condition of ring shift counter. After first clock pulse 1 is shifted from Q_D to Q_C and counter is in 0100 state, second clock pulse produces 0010 state and third clock pulse produces 0001 state. On application of fourth pulse, 1 from Q_A is transferred to Q_D resulting 1000 state which is initial state. Fourth clock pulses cause the sequence to repeat.

Since it has four-distinct states before the sequence repeats, this counter is called *MOD-4 counter*. Each flip flop output waveform has a frequency equal to one fourth of the clock frequency since it is a MOD-4 counter. Ring counter of any MOD number can be constructed using flip flops. A MOD-N flip flop uses N flip flops. A ring counter will require more flip flops than binary counter for the same MOD number.

e.g. MOD-8 ring counter requires 8 flip flops while a binary counter requires only 3 flip flops.

Even if it is less efficient in the use of flip flop, a ring counter is still useful because it can be decoded without the use of decoding gates. The decoding signal for each state is obtained at the output of its corresponding flip flop.

2. Nonbinary Counters.

There are too many ways in which a nonbinary counter can be designed to make it practical or even worthwhile to develop general procedures for designing nonbinary counters.

Now design a mod-3 counter.

A mod-3 counter requires two flip-flops and would go through three states specified in Table 4.19 below. Table 4.20 gives excitation table for JK flip-flop, using which we can fill out the states of FFO (J_0, K_0) and FF1 (J_1, K_0) in Table 4.19. Observe that a ripple counter is not possible in the present case, so a synchronous counter will be designed.

Table 4.19

Counter states	Q_1	Q_0	J_0	K_0	J_1	K_1
0	0	0	1	×	0	×
1	0	1	×	1	1	×
2	1	0	0	×	×	1
0	0	0				

Table 4.20

Q_n	Q_{n+1}	J	K
0	0	0	×
0	1	1	×
1	0	×	1
1	1	×	0

With reference to Table 4.19, we can now fill out K-maps of Fig. 4.79 from which it easily follows that

$$J_0 = \overline{Q}_1, \quad K_0 = 1, \quad J_1 = Q_0, \quad K_1 = 1$$

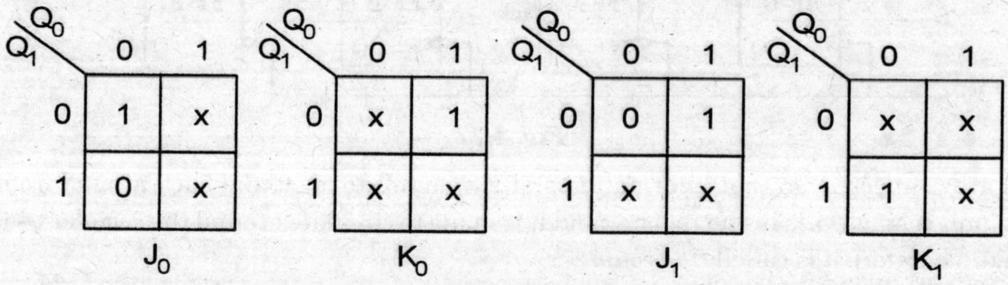

Fig. 4.79

Resulting counter is drawn in Fig. 4.80.

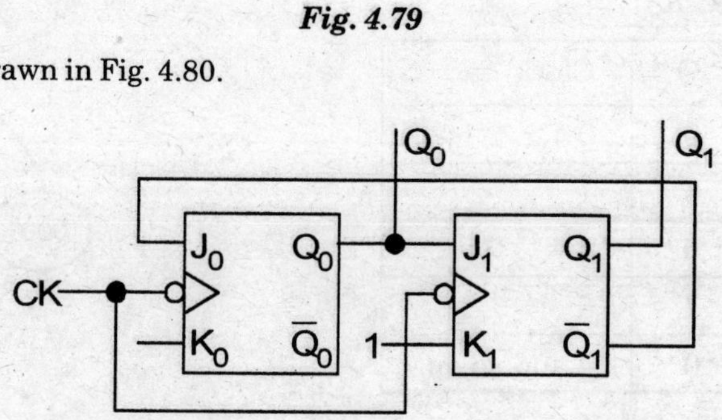

Fig. 4.80. Mod-3 counter (synchronous)

Consider a 4-bit shift register. If serial output Q_0 is connected back to the serial input as in Fig. 4.81, then injected pulse will keep circulating. This circuit is called *ring counter*.

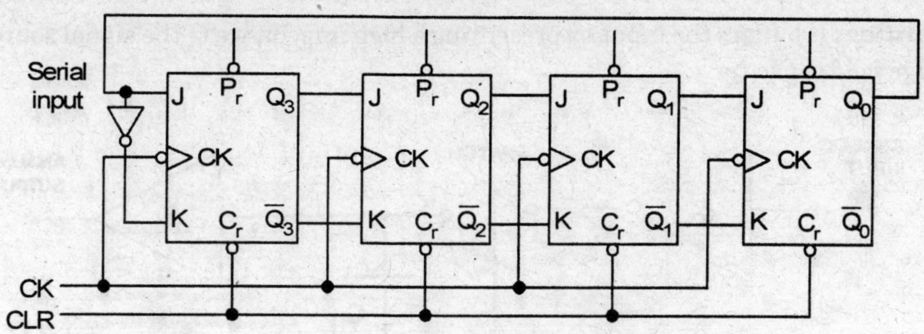

Fig. 4.81. A 4-bit ring counter

Waveforms at the output are of a ring counter are shown in Fig. 4.82.

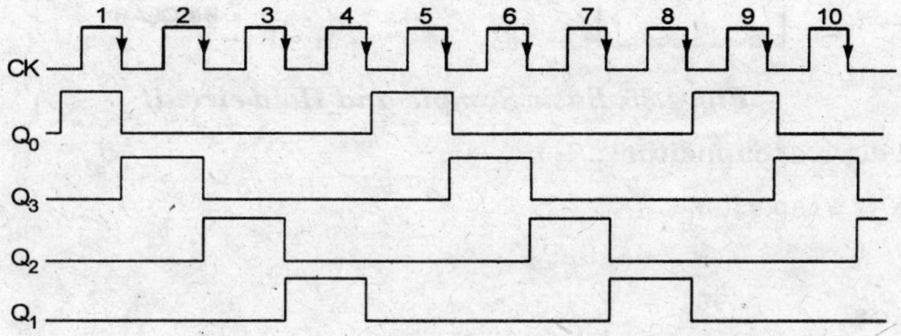

Fig. 4.82. Output waveforms of ring counter

The outputs are sequential non-overlapping pulses, which are useful for control state counters. and for stepper motors which require sequential pulses to rotate these from one position to the next. etc. This counter can also be used to count number of pulses. These can be read by noting which flip-flop is in 1 state. No decoding circuitry is required.

If in the 4-bit shift register of Q_0 is connected to the serial input, the resulting circuitry is called *twisted ring counter*. If clock pulses are applied after clearing all flip flops, square waveform is obtained at the Q output as shown in Fig. 4.83.

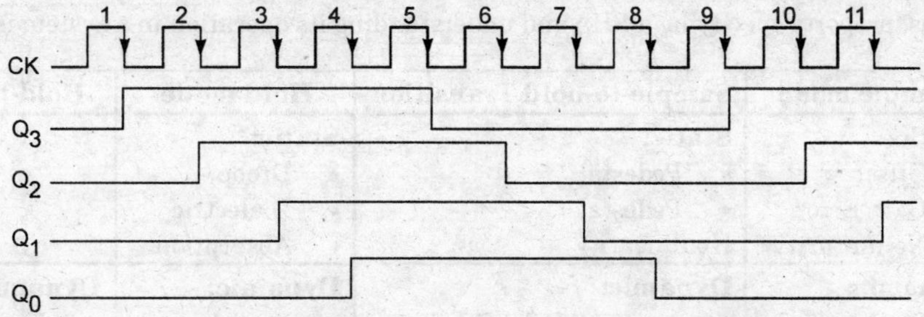

Fig. 4.83. Output wave forms of twisted-ring counter

Advantages of Synchronous Counters

Synchronous counters offer reduced time delays as compared to asynchronous counters, hence offering higher frequencies. Moreover, since all the flip-flops simultaneously change their states, there doesn't arise a danger of false reading at any instant in the counting sequence.

4.4.15 SAMPLE AND HOLD

The purchase of sample and hold circuitry is to take a snapshot of the sensor signal and hold the value ADC must have a stable signal in order to accurately perform a conversion. An equivalent circuit for the sample and hold is shown in Fig. 4.84. The switch connects capacitor to the signal conditioning circuit once every sample period. The capacitor holds voltage value measured until a new sample is acquired. Many times, sample and hold circuitry is incorporated into the same integrated circuit package.

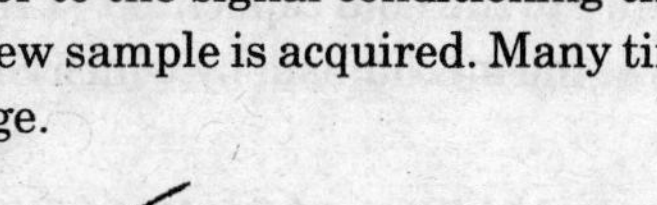

Fig. 4.84 Equivalent circuit for a sample and Hold

Basic Operation

Regardless of the circuit details or type of SHA, all such devices have four major components:

(1) **Input Amplifier :** It buffers the input by presenting a high impedance to the signal source and providing current gain to charge hold capacitor.

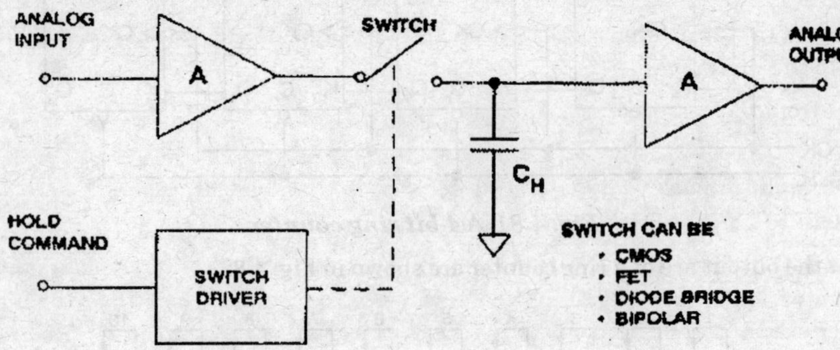

Fig. 4.85. Basic Sample-and-Hold circuit

(2) **Energy storage device (capacitor) :**

Heart of the SHA, is a capacitor.

(3) **Output buffer**

(4) **Switching circuits**

Sample and Hold Specification

(1) Track mode

(2) Track-to-hold transition

(3) Hold mode

(4) Hold-to-track transition.

These specifications are given in the table below. Because there are both dc and ac performance implications for each of the four modes, property specifying a SHA and understanding its operation in a system is a complex matter.

Sample mode	Sample-to-hold Transition	Hold mode	Hold-to-sample
Static: • Offset • Gain Error • Nonlinearity	**Static:** • Pedestal • Pedestal Nonlinearity	**Static:** • Droop • Dielectric • Absorption	
Dynamic: • Settling Time • Bandwidth • Slew Rate • Distortion • Nouise	**Dynamic:** • Aperture Delay Time • Aperture Jitter • Switching Transient • Settling Time	**Dynamic:** • Feedthrough • Distortion • Nouise	**Dynamic:** • Acqisition Time • Switching • Transient

Track mode voltage on the hyold capacitor follows (or tracks) the input signal (with some delay and bandwidth limiting).

Hold mode switch is opened, and capacitor retains the voltage present before it was disconnected from the input buffer.

The output buffer offers a high impedance to the hold capacitor to keep hold voltage from discharging prematurely. The switching circuit and its driver form the mechanism by which SHA is alternately switched between track and hold.

4.4.16 CONVERTERS [Analog to Digital (A/D) And Digital to Analog (D/A)]

Most physical variables are analog in nature and can take any value within a continuous range of values.

e.g. temperature, pressure, light intensity rotational speed etc.

Digital systems perform all their internal operation using digital circuitry. Any information that has to be inputted to a digital system therefore it is necessary to convert these quantities from analog to digital and vice versa.

Hence, ADC and DAC functions as an interface between a completely digital system like a computer and the analog world.

1. Digital to Anlog Converter (DAC)

It is the process of taking a value represented in digital code and converting it to a voltage or current which is proportional to the digital value.

Digital output from the computer is connected to a DAC, which converts it to a proportional analog voltage or current.

e.g., computer might produce a digital output ranging from 00000000, 11111111 which the DAC converts to a voltage from 0 to 10V. Fig. 4.86 (*b*) shows a 4-bit D A converter.

Digital inputs D, C, B and A are usually derived from output register of the digital system. From the table , for each input number, D/A converter output voltage is a unique value. The analog input V_{out} is equal in volts to binary number or some other proportionality factor.

D	C	B	A	V_{out} (in volts)
0	0	0	0	0
0	0	0	1	1
0	0	1	0	2
0	0	1	1	3
0	1	0	0	4
0	1	0	1	5
0	1	1	0	6
0	1	1	1	7
1	0	0	0	8
1	0	0	1	9
1	0	1	0	10
1	0	1	1	11
1	1	0	0	12
1	1	0	1	13
1	1	1	0	14
1	1	1	1	15

(a) Input Output Table

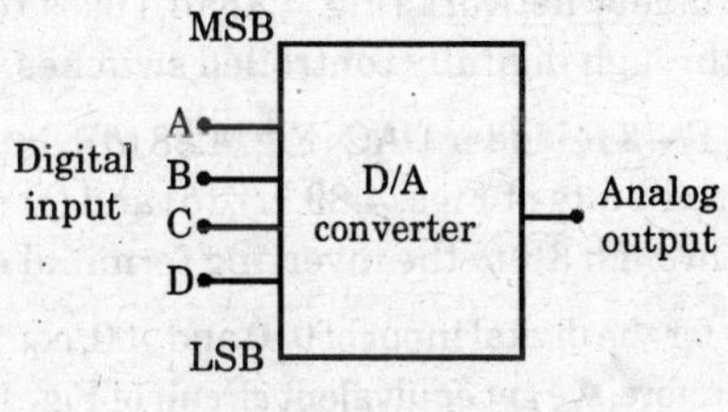

(b) Block diagram

Fig. 4.86

In general, Analog output = K × Digital input in decimal where K is proportionality factor and is a constant value for a given DAC.

Analog output may be a voltage or current.

Analog output voltage V_A of an N-bit straight binary DAC converter is related to the digital equation

$$V_A = K(2^{N-1} b_{N-1} + 2^{N-2} b_{N-2} + \dots + 2b_1 + b_0)$$

where, K = proportionality factor

$$b_j = \begin{cases} +1 \text{ if } j\text{th bit of input } 1 \\ 0 \text{ if } j\text{th bit of input is } 0 \end{cases} \quad j = 0 \text{ to } (N-1)$$

Weighted Resistor DAC.

As conversion D/A involves a weighted sum corresponding to the input to the converter, the summing circuit of Fig. 4.87 can be used as a DAC.

In this circuit,

$$I_i = I_{N-1} + I_{N-2} + \dots + I_1 + I_0$$

These currents can be expressed in terms of voltages as

$$I_{N-1} = V_{N-1}/R$$

$$I_{N-2} = V_{N-2}/2R$$

$$I_0 = V_0/2^{N-1} R$$

Let $V(0) = 0$

$V(1) = -V_R$

Then $V_N = -b_n V_R$

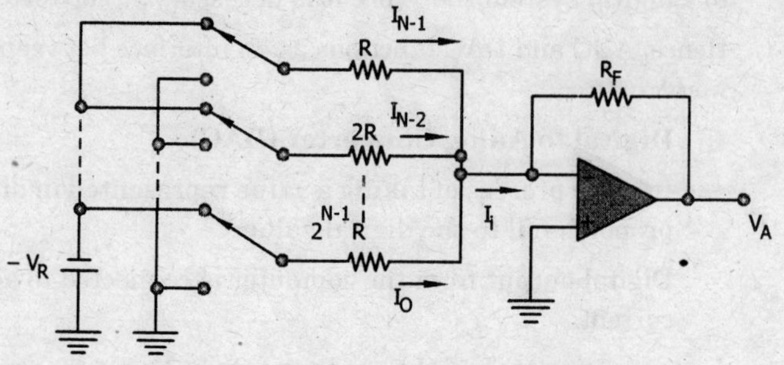

Fig. 4.87. Weighted resistor DAC.

Switches in the circuit are digitally controlled causing b_n to acquire values 0 or 1.

Now,

$$I_i = -V_R\left[\frac{1}{R}b_{N-1} + \frac{1}{2R}b_{N-2} + \ldots + \frac{1}{2^{N-1}R}b_0\right]$$

Analog output of the circuit is given by

$$V_A = -R_F I_i$$

$$V_A = V_R\left[\frac{R_F}{R}b_{N-1} + \frac{R_F}{2R}b_{N-2} + \ldots + \frac{R_F}{2^{N-1}R}b_0\right]$$

$$= K[2^{N-1} b_{N-1} + 2^{N-1} b_{N-2} + \ldots + 2^1 b_1 + 2^0 b_0]$$

where,

$$K = \frac{R_F}{2^{N-1}R}$$

Hence circuit is a DAC.

R-2R Ladder Network.

An R-2R ladder network [Fig. 4.88 (*a*)] uses resistors of only two values R and 2R. Inputs to the resistor network is applied through digitally controlled switches.

In a 3 bit R – 2 R ladder DAC [Fig. 4.88 (*b*)], input is asumed as 001. Applying Thevenin's theorem at XX', YY' and ZZ' we obtain circuits of Figs. 4.89 (*a*), (*b*) and (*c*) respectively. It is immediately seen that for input 001, voltage $V_R/2^3$ is applied through 3R to the inverting terminal of the OPAMP.

Similarly for the digital input of 010 and 100, equivalent voltages are $V_R/2^2$ and $V_R/2^1$ respectively with resistance 3R in each case. Therefore, we get equivalent circuit of Fig. 4.89 (*d*) wherein voltage V_0 is given by

$$V_0 = -\left[\frac{R_F}{3R}\frac{V_R}{2^3}b_0 + \frac{R_F}{3R}\frac{V_R}{2^2}b_1 + \frac{R_F}{3R}\frac{V_R}{2^1}b_2\right]$$

$$= -\left(\frac{R_F}{3R}\right)\left(\frac{V_R}{2^3}\right)[2^2 b_2 + 2^1 b_1 + 2^0 b_0]$$

The equation shows that analog output voltage is proportional to the digital input. In general for N bit DAC.

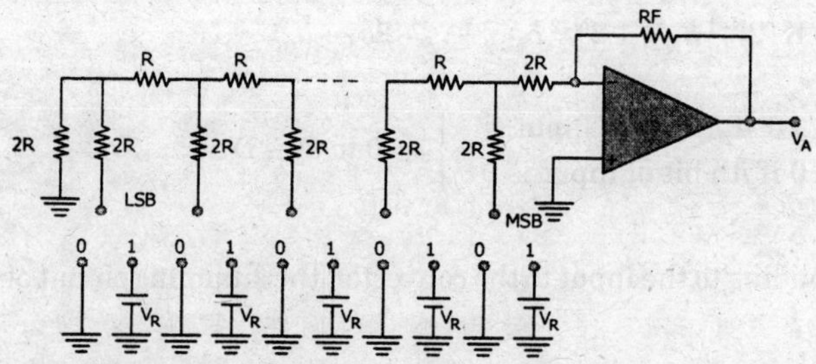

(a) R-2R ladder DAC network

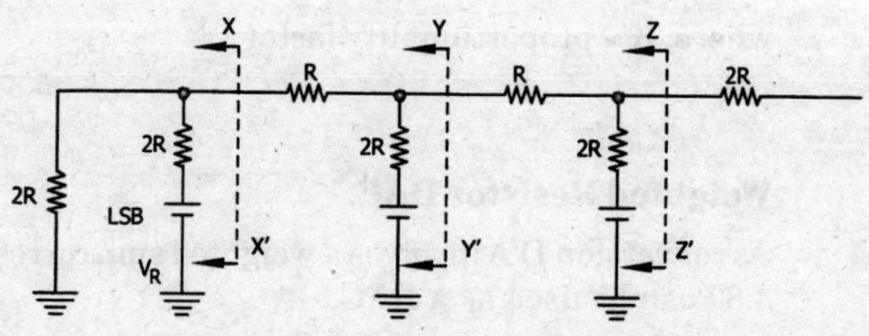

(b) 3 bit R-2R ladder DAC network

Fig. 4.88

In general for N bit NAC.

$$V_0 = V\,[2^{N-1}b_{N-1} + 2^{N-2}b_{N-2} + \ldots + 2^1 b_1 + 2^0 b_0]$$

where, $R_F = 3R$ and $V_R = -2^N V$

Number of resistors required for an N bit DAC

(*i*) In case of R–2R ladder are 2N

(*ii*) In case weighted resistor network are N

But because of wide spread in the resistance values for large N, weighted resistor DAC is not widely used.

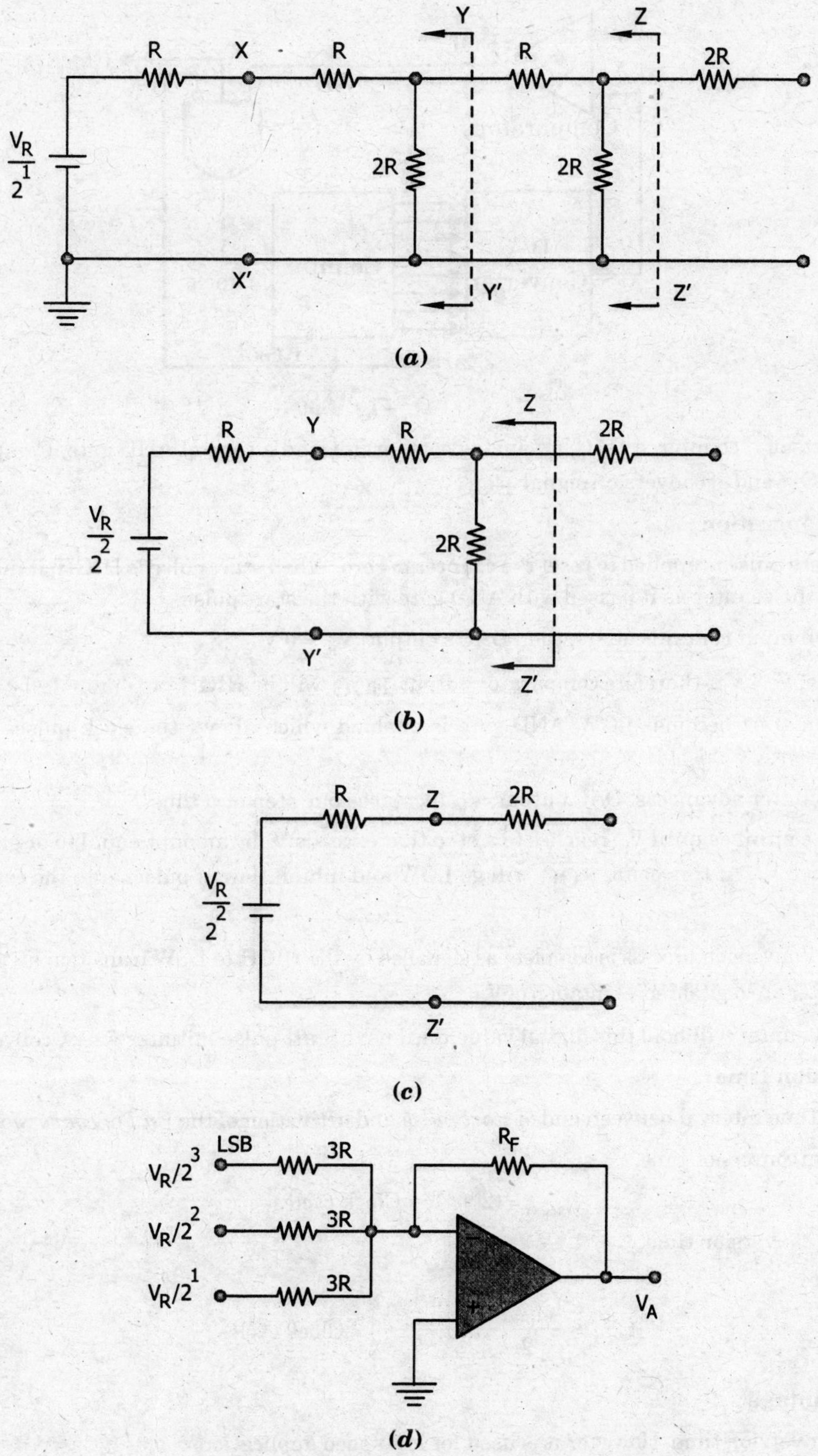

Fig. 4.89. Simplification of the circuit of

2. Analog to Digital Converter (ADC)

It takes an analog input voltage and after a certain amount of time produces a digital output code which represents analog input. A pure analog signal is more accurate than a digital system. The analog to digital conversion process is more complex and time consuming than the DAC process.

Methods of Analog to Digital Conversion.

(*i*) Digital Ramp A/D Converter.

This method is also called *stair step ramp* or *counter method,* because waveform is a step-by-step ramp (actually a staircase).

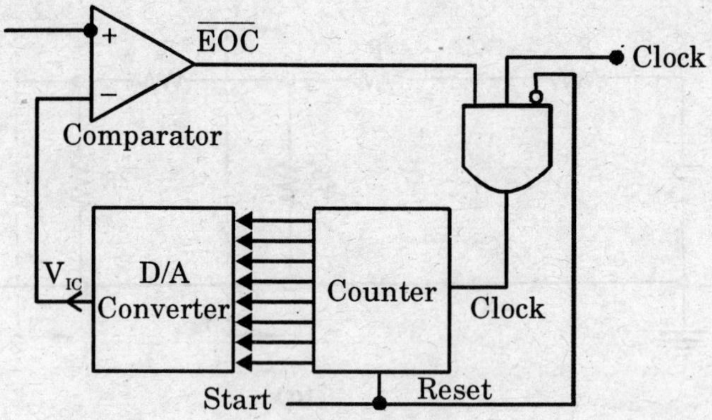

Fig. 4.90

It consists of a counter, a DAC, an analog comparator and a control AND gate. Comparator serves as the active LOW end of conversion signal $\overline{EOC}$.

Circuit operation :

(1) A state pulse is applied to reset the counter to zero. When start pulse is HIGH, it inhibit the clock to pass into the counter as it passed with AND gate with the start pulse.

(2) When input contains all 0's, then DAC's output, $V_{IC} = 0$ V.

(3) Since, $V_1 > V_{IC}$, therefore comparator output $\overline{EOC}$ will be HIGH.

(4) When start becomes LOW, AND gate is enabled which allows the clock pulses to pass through the counter.

(5) As counter advancess, DAC output, V_{IC} increases one step at a time.

This continues until V_{IC} reaches to a step that exceeds V_1 by amount equal to or greater than threshold voltage V_D. At this point, $\overline{EOC}$ will go LOW and inhibit flow of pulses into the counter and it will stop counting.

(6) Now, conversion process is complete as signalled by the HIGH to LOW transition at $\overline{EOC}$, and contents of counter are digital representation of V_1.

(7) The counter will hold this digital value until next Start pulse initiates a new conversion.

Conversion Time :

It is the time interval between end of *start pulse* and activation of the *End of conversion* output.

Maximum conversion time,

$$t_{C(max)} = (2^N - 1) \times \text{Clock cycles}$$

Average conversion time,

$$t_{C(av)} = \frac{I_{C(max)}}{2} = \left(\frac{2^N - 1}{2}\right) \times \text{Clock cycles}$$

Disadvantage :

Large conversion time. However it is used for low speed applications.

***(ii)* Successive Approximation A/D Converter.**

It is most widely used and has more complex circuitry than the digital ramp A/D converter but a much shorter conversion time. These converters have a fixed value of conversion time that is not dependent on the value of the analog input.

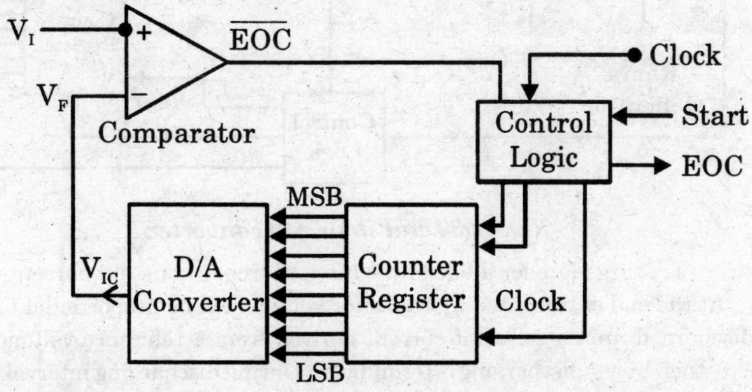

Fig. 4.91 Basic arrangement for a successive approximation A/D converter.

It is similar to the digital ramp ADC. The SAC does not use a counter to provide input to the DAC block but uses a register in place of it. The control logic modifies contents of the register bit until register data are digital equivalent of the analog input V_1 within resolution of the converter.

Advantage High speed : Total conversion time for N bit SAC is N clock. Thus an 8 bit ACD takes only periods to complete a conversion, which is a vast improvement over the ramp type method. It is used in data acquisition applications.

***(iii)* Single slope A/D Converter.**

It does not require a D/A converter. It has the advantage of relatively low cost because it does not require precision components such as a DAC or VCO. It uses linear ramp generator to produce a constant slope reference voltage.

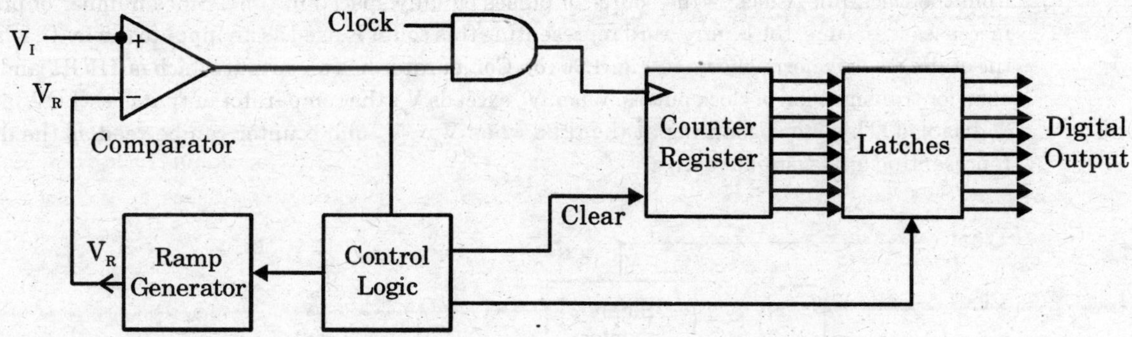

Fig. 4.92 Single slope A/D converter.

Initially, counter is reset and ramp generator output is 0, which make the input voltage greater than the reference voltage and produces a high output from the comparator. This high output of comparator enables the clock to the counter and starts the ramp generator.

Ramp output will increase until it equals the analog input V_1. At this point, ramp is reset and binary count is stored in the latches by control logic.

***(iv)* Dual slope A/D Converter.**

Operation is similar to that of single A/D converter except that here two ramp generators are used.

(*a*) variable slope ramp

(*b*) fixed slope ramp.

This possess slowest conversion time. The basic operation of this converter involves linear charging and discharging of a capacitor using constant currents.

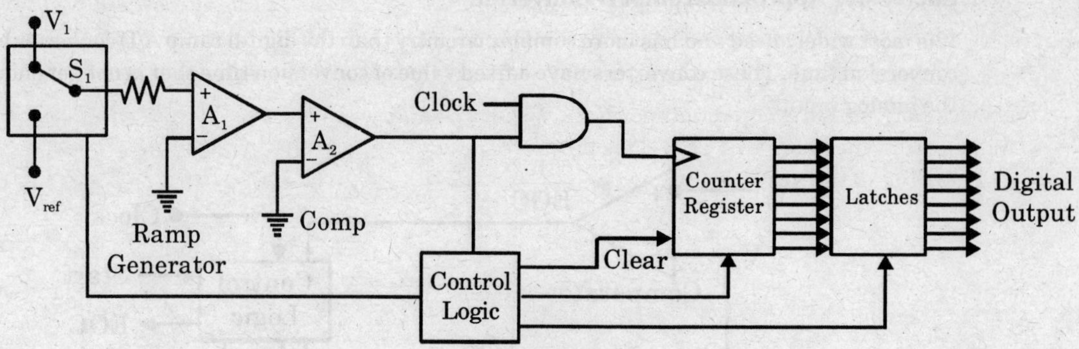

Fig. 4.93 Dual slope A/D converter.

First capacitor is charged up for a fixed time interval from a constant current derived from the analog input voltage V_1. At the end of this interval, capacitor voltage will be proportional to V_1. At this point, capacitor is linearly discharged from a constant current derived from a reference voltage V_{ref}. When capacitor voltage reaches zero, then linear discharging is terminated. During discharging interval a digital reference frequency is fed to the counter and Counted. The duration of discharge interval will be proportional to the initial capacitor voltage. Thus, at the end of the discharge interval, the counter will hold a count proportional to the initial capacitor voltage proportional to V_1. Thus binary count is latched completes one conversion cycle.

Advantages :

(*i*) Low cost

(*ii*) Low sensitivity to noise

(*iii*) Variation in its component values caused by temperature changes.

Dual ADC is not used in data acquisition applications.

Disadvantage :

Counting ADC : This system is shown in Fig. 4.94 (*a*).

The clear pulse resets the counter to the zero count. Then counter records in binary form, number of pulses from the clock line. Clock is the source of pulses equally spaced in time. Since number of pulses counted increases with time, the binary word representing this count is used as an input to the DAC, whose output is the staircase waveform shown in Fig. 4.96 (*b*). Comparator has an output which is 'HIGH' and AND gate is open for transmission of clock pulses. When V_d exceeds V_a, the comparator output goes 'LOW' and AND gate is disabled. This stops counting at the time when $V_a \approx V_d$ and counter can be read as the digital output representing analog input voltage.

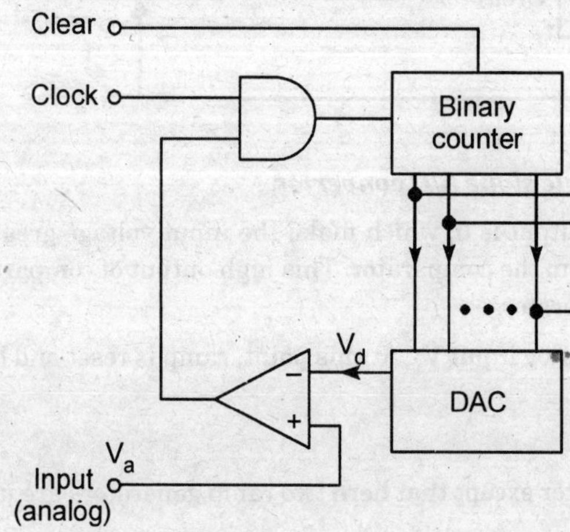

(*a*)

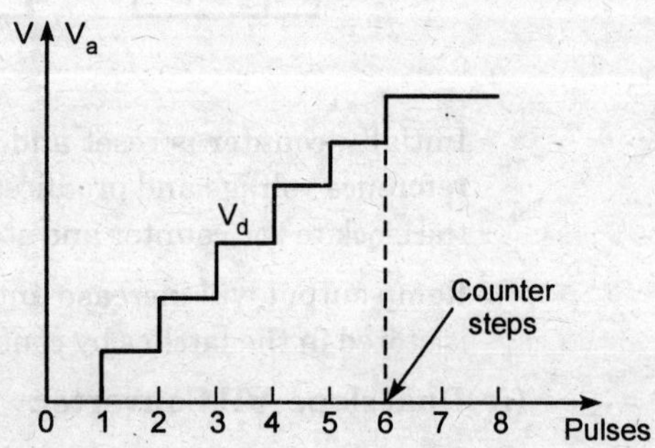

(*b*)

Fig. 4.94. Counting ADC

An improved version of the counting ADC called *tracking* or *servo converter* is shown in Fig. 4.95. To understand operation of the system, assume initially that output of the DAC is less than the analog input V_a. Then positive comparator output causes the counter to read UP. DAC output increases until it exceeds V_d. UP-$\overline{\text{DOWN}}$ control line changes state, so that it now counts down and the count decreases by one count. This causes control to change to UP and the count increases by 1 LSB. This process keeps repeating so that digital output bounces back and forth by ± 1 LSB around the correct value.

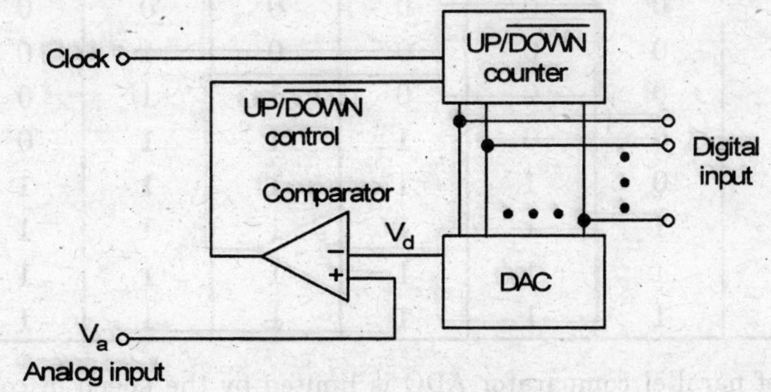

Fig. 4.95. Tracking ADC.

Parallel Comparator ADC.

This system is the fastest of all converters. Its operation is easily understood if reference is made to the 3–bit A/D converter as shown in Fig. 4.96.

Analog voltage is applied simultaneously to a bank of comparators with equally spaced thresholds (reference voltages). This type of processing is called *bin conversion*, because analog input is sorted into a given voltage range or voltage bin determined by thresholds to two adjacent comparators. For all comparators with thresholds above the input voltage, output is LOW, while for all comparators with thresholds below the input voltage, output is HIGH.

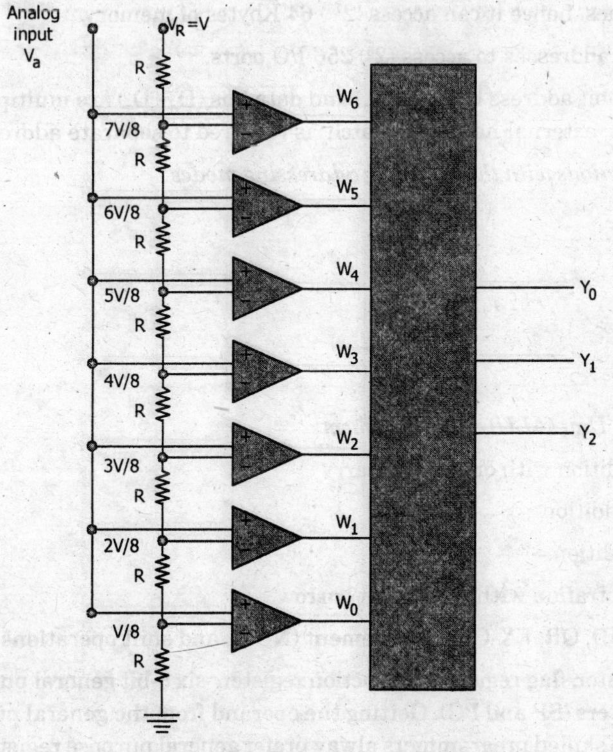

Fig. 4.96. Parallel comparator ADC.

e.g. $\left(\frac{2}{8}\right)V < V_a < \left(\frac{3}{8}\right)V$, then $W_0 = 1$ and all other W's are 0.

ROM code converter considers these inputs as addresses and gives corresponding digital 3-bit output. The truth-table with inputs W and outputs Y is given in Table 4.21.

Table 4.21. Truth-table for ADC

Inputs							Outputs		
W_6	W_5	W_4	W_3	W_2	W_1	W_0	Y_2	Y_1	Y_0
0	0	0	0	0	0	0	0	0	0
0	0	0	0	0	0	1	0	0	1
0	0	0	0	0	1	1	0	1	0
0	0	0	0	1	1	1	0	1	1
0	0	0	1	1	1	1	1	0	0
0	0	1	1	1	1	1	1	0	1
0	1	1	1	1	1	1	1	1	0
1	1	1	1	1	1	1	1	1	1

Conversion line of parallel comparator ADC is limited by the speed of comparator and ROM. Number of comparators required is $2^N - 1$, where N is number of bits. Complexity of the hardware is its major disadvantage.

4.5 FEATURES OF 8085 MICROPROCESSOR

1. It is a 8-bit microprocessor, i.e. it can accept, process, or provide 8-bit date simultaneously.
2. It operates on a single +5V power supply connected at V_{CC}; power supply ground is connected to V_{SS}.
3. It operates on clock cycle with 50% duty cycle.
4. It has on chip clock generator. This internal clock generator requires tuned circuit like LC, RC or crystal. The internal clock generator divides oscillator frequency by 2 and generates clock signal, which can be used for synchronizing external devices.
5. It can operate with a 3 MHz clock frequency. The 8085A-2 version can operate at the maximum frequency of 5 MHz.
6. It has 16 address lines, hence it can access (2^{16}) 64 Kbytes of memory.
7. It provides 8 bit I/O addresses to access (2^8) 256 I/O ports.
8. In 8085, the lower 8-bit address bus (A_0 - A_7) and data bus (D_0 - D_7) are multiplexed to reduce number of external pins. But due to this, external hardware (latch) is required to separate address lines and data lines.
9. *It supports 74 instructions with the following addressing modes :*
   (*i*) Immediate
   (*ii*) Register
   (*iii*) Direct
   (*iv*) Indirect
   (*v*) Implied
10. *The Arithmetic Logic Unit (ALU) of 8085 performs :*
    (*i*) 8 bit binary addition with or without carry
    (*ii*) 16 bit binary addition.
    (*iii*) 2 digit BCD addition.
    (*iv*) 8-bit binary subtration with or without borrow
    (*v*) 8-bit logical AND, OR, EX-OR, Complement (NOT), and shift operations.
11. It has 8-bit accumulator, flag register, instruction register, six 8-bit general purpose registers (B, C, D, E, H and L) and two 16-bit registers (SP and PC). Getting the operand from the general purpose registers is more faster than from memory. Hence skilled programmers alway prefer general purpose registers to store program variables than memory.
12. *It provide five hardware interrupts*:
    TRAP, RST 7.5, RST 6.5, RST 5.5 and INTR.

13. It has serial I/O control which allows serial communication.
14. It provides control signals (IO/ $\overline{M}$, $\overline{RD}$, $\overline{WR}$) to control the bus cycles, and hence external bus controller is not required.
15. The external hardware (another microprocessor or equivalent master) can detect which machine cycle microprocessor is executing using status signals (IO/ $\overline{M}$, S_0, S_1). This feature is very useful when more than one processors are using common system resources (memory and I/O devices).
16. It has a mechanism by which it is possible to increase its interrupt handling capacity.
17. The 8085 has an ability to share system bus with Direct Memory Access controller. This feature allows to transfer large amount of data from I/O device to memory or from memory to I/O device with high speeds.
18. It can be used to implement three chip microcomputer with supporting I/O devices like IC 8155 and IC 8355.

4.6 8085 MICROPROSESSOR FUNCTIONAL BLOCKS

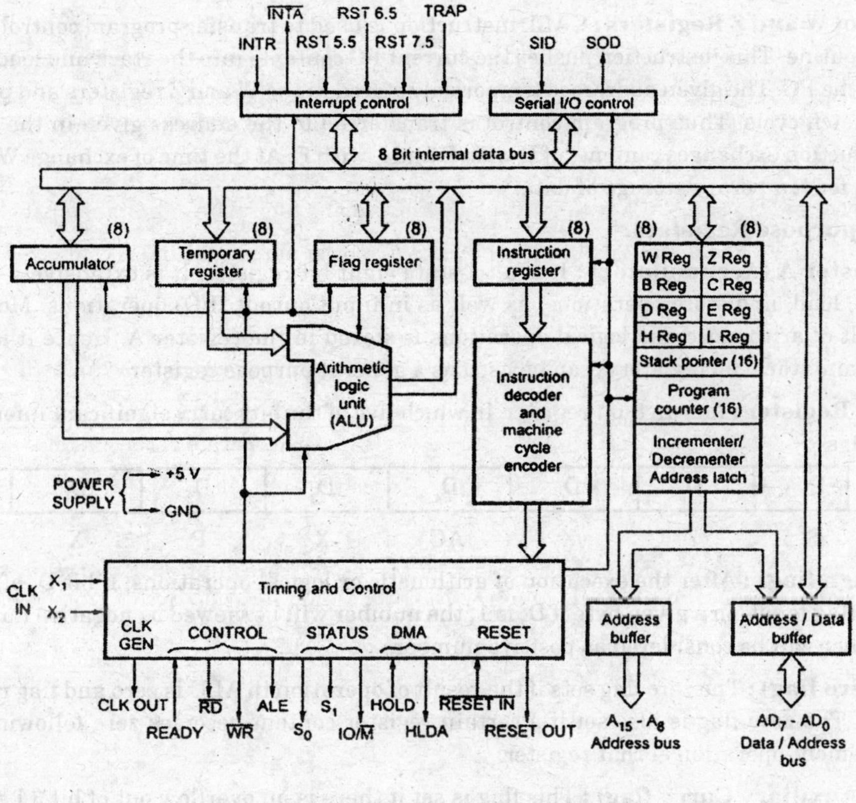

Fig. 4.97 Architecture of 8085

1. REGISTERS.

It has eight addressable 8-bit registers : A, B, C, D, E, H, L, F, and two 16-bit registers : PC and SP.

Classification

These registers can be classified as follows :

1. General purpose Registers.

B, C, D, E, H and L are 8-bit general purpose registers which can be used as a separate 8-bit registers or as 16-bit register pairs, BC, DE, and HL. When used in register pair mode, the high order byte resides in the first register (i.e. in B when BC is used as a register pair) and the low order byte in the second (i.e. in C when BC is used as a register pair).

HL pair also functions as a data pointer or memory pointer. These are also called ***scratchpad registers***, as user can store data in them. To store and read data from these registers bus access is not required, it is an internal operation. Thus it provides an efficient way to store intermediate results and use them when required. The efficient programmer prefers to use these registers to store intermediate results than the memory locations which require bus access and hence more time to perform the operation.

2. Temporary Registers.

(i) Temporary data Registers : ALU has two inputs :

(a) Input supplied by the accumulator

(b) Input from temporary data register.

The programmer can not access this temporary data register. However it is internally used from the execution of most of the arithmetic and logical instructions.

e.g. ADD B is instruction in the arithmetic group of instructions which adds contents of register A and register B and stores result in register A. Addition operation is performed by ALU. ALU takes inputs from register A and temporary data register. Contents of register B are transferred to temporary data register for applying second input to the ALU.

(ii) W and Z Registers : W and Z registers are temporary registers. These registers are used to hold 8-bit data during execution of some instructions. These registers are not available for programmer, since 8085 uses them internally.

Use of W and Z Registers : CALL instruction is used to transfer program control to a subprogram or subroutine. This instruction pushes the current PC contents into the stack and loads the given address into the PC. The given address is temporarily stored in the W and Z registers and placed on the bus for the fetch cycle. Thus program control is transferred to the address given in the instruction. XCHG instruction exchanges contents of H with D and L with E. At the time of exchange W and Z registers are used for temporary storage of data.

3. Special purpose Registers.

(i) Register A (Accumulator) : It is a tri-state eight bit register. It is extensively used in arithmetic, logic, load, and store operations, as well as in input/output (I/O) operations. Most of the times the result of arithmetic and logical operations is stored in the register A. Hence it is also identified as accumulator. The register A can be used as a general purpose register.

(ii) Flag Register : It is an 8-bit register, in which five of the bits carry significant information in the form of flags :

D_7	D_6	D_5	D_4	D_3	D_2	D_1	D_0
S	Z	X	AC	X	P	X	CY

S (Sign flag) : After the execution of arithmetic or logical operations, if bit D_7 of the result is 1, the sign flag is set. In a given byte if D_7 is 1, the number will be viewed as negative number. If D_7 is 0, the number will be considered as positive number.

Z (Zero flag) : The zero flag sets if the result of operation in ALU is zero and flag reset if result is non zero. The zero flag is also set if a certain register content becomes zero following an increment or decrement operation of that register.

AC (Auxiliary Carry flag) : This flag is set if there is an overflow out of bit 3 i.e., carry from lower nibble to higher nibble (D_3 bit to D_4 bit). This flag is used for BCD operations and it is not available for the programmer.

CY (Carry flag) : This flag is set if there is an overflow out of bit 7. The carry flag also serves as a borrow flag for subtraction. In both the examples shown below, the carry flag is set.

9B H	1001 1001	89 H	1000 1001
+ 75 H	+ 0111 0101	– AB H	– 1010 1011
Carry [1] 76 H	[1] 0000 1110	Borrow [1] DE H	[1] 1101 1110

P (Parity flag) : This flag is set when number of one's in 8 bit is odd; then flag status = 0

And if number of one's is even, then flag status = 1

(iii) Instruction Register : In a typical processor operation, the processor first fetches the opcode of instruction from memory (i.e. it places an address on the address bus and memory responds by placing the data stored at the specified address on the data bus) .The MPU stores this opcode in a register called the instruction register. This opcode is further sent to the instruction decoder to select one of the 256 alternatives.

4. **Sixteen bit Registers.**

(*i*) **Program Counter (PC) :** Program is a sequence of instructions.Microprocessor fetches these instructions from the memory and executes them sequentially. The program counter is a special purpose register which, at a given time, stores the address of the next instruction to be fetched. Program counter acts as a pointer to the next instruction. How processor increments program counter depends on the nature of the instruction; for one byte instruction it increments program counter by one, or two byte instruction it increments program counter by two and for three byte instruction it increments program counter by three such that program counter always points to the address of the next instruction.

In case of JUMP and CALL instructions, address followed by JUMP and CALL instructions is placed in the program counter. The processor then fetches the next instruction from the new address specified by JUMP or CALL instruction. In conditional JUMP and conditional CALL instructions, if the condition is not satisfied, the processor increments program counter by three so that it points the instruction followed by conditional JUMP or CALL instruction; otherwise processor fetches the next instruction from the new address specified by JUMP or CALL instruction.

(*ii*) **Stack Pointer (SP) :** The stack is a reserved area of the memory in the RAM where temporary information may be stored. A 16-bit stack pointer is used to hold the address of the most recent stack entry. Stack is normally operated as LIFO (Last Input First Output).

2. **Arithmetic Logic Unit (ALU)**

The 8085's ALU performs arithmetic and logical functions on eight bit variables. The arithmetic unit performs bitwise fundamental arithmetic operations such as addition and subtraction. The logic unit performs logical operations such as complement, AND, OR and EX-OR, as well as rotate and clear. The ALU also looks after the branching decisions.

3. **Instruction Decoder**

The processor first fetches the opcode of instruction from memory and stores this opcode in the instruction register. It is then sent to the instruction decoder. The instruction decoder decodes it and accordingly gives the timing and control signals which control the register, the data buffers, ALU and external peripheral signals (explained in later sections) depending on the nature of the instruction.

The 8085 executes seven different types of machine cycles. It gives the information about which machine cycle currently executing in the encoded form on the S_0, S_1 and IO/$\overline{M}$ lines. This task is done by machine cycle encoder.

4. **Address Buffer**

This is an 8-bit unidirectional buffer. It is used to drive external high order address bus (A_{15} -A_8). It is also used to tri-state the high order address bus under certain conditions such as reset, hold, halt, and when address lines are not in use.

5. **Address/Data Buffer**

This is an 8-bit bi-directional buffer. It is used to drive multiplexed address/data bus, i.e. low order address bus (A_7-A_0) and data bus (D_7-D_0). It is also used to tri-state the multiplexed address/data bus under certain conditions such as reset, hold, halt and when the bus is not in use. The address and data buffers are used to drive external address and data buses respectively. Due to these buffers the address and data buses can be tri-stated when they are not in use.

6. **Incrementer/Decrementer Address Latch**

This 16-bit register is used to increment or decrement the contents of program counter or stack pointer as a part of execution of instructions related to them.

7. **Interrupt Control**

The processor fetches, decodes and executes instructions in a sequence. Sometimes it is necessary to automatically execute one of a collection of special routines whenever special condition exists within a program or the microcomputer system. The most important thing is that, after execution of the special routine, the program control must be transferred to the program which processor was executing before the occurrence of the special condition. The occurrence of this special condition is referred to as interrupt.

The interrupt control block has five interrupt inputs RST 5.5, RST 6.5, RST 7.5, TRAP and INTR and one acknowlege signal $\overline{\text{INTA}}$.

8. **Serial I/O Control**

In situations like, data transmission over long distance and communication with cassette tapes or a CRT terminal, it is necessary to transmit data bit by bit to reduce the cost of cabling. In serial communication one bit is transferred at a time over a single line. The 8085' s serial I/O control provides two lines, SOD and SID for serial communication. The serial output data (SOD) line is used to send data serially and serial input data (SID) line is used to receive data serially.

9. **Timing and Control Circuitry**

The control circuitry in the processor 8085 is responsible for all the operations. The control circuitry and hence the operations in 8085 are synchronized with the help of clock signal. Along with the control of fetching and decoding operations and generating appropriate signals for instruction execution, control circuitry also generates signals required to interface external devices to the processor, 8085.

BUS STRUCTURE OF 8085.

In 8085, there are 3 types of buses:

1. **Data Bus**

It is 8 bit, bidirectional bus which is used to transfer data or instruction on memory and μp or data between input/outputdevice and μp.

In microprocessor, to reduce the number of bits, data bus is TDM with address bus.

2. **Address Bus**

It is 16 bit unidirectional bus which is out of direction of microprocessor.

16 bit address is divided in two parts:

1. Lower order ($A_0 - A_7$)
2. Higher order ($A_8 - A_{15}$)

Data bus ($D_0 - D_7$) is multiplexing with lower order address bus ($A_0 - A_7$) and commonly called *address data bus* ($AD_0 - AD_7$).

ALU signal is used to separate or demultiplex the Address Data Bus

If ALU = 1 → Address is present

If ALU = 0 → Data is present

3. **Control Bus**

It contains number of single lines, in which some are in the microprocessor and some area out of microprocessor, hence its direction is mixed direction.

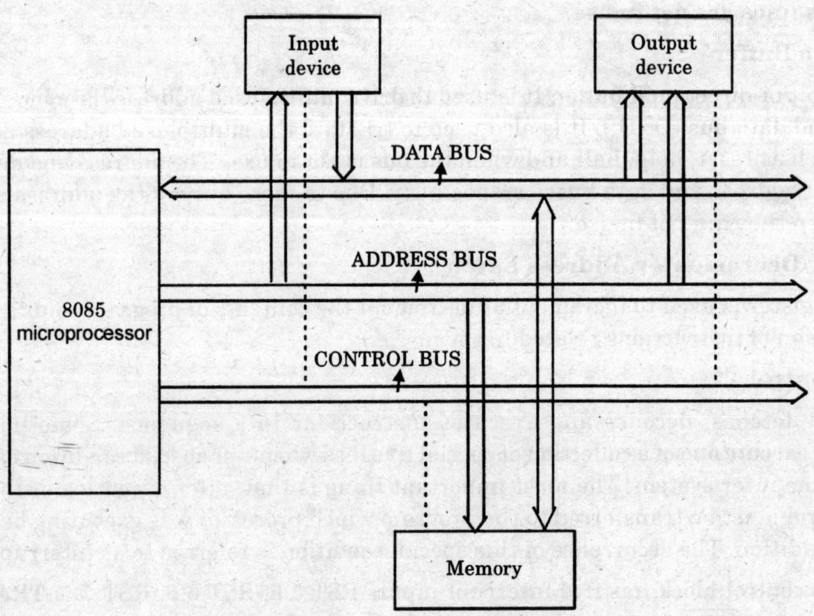

Fig. 4.98. Bus structure of 8085

4.7 PIN DEFINITIONS OF 8085

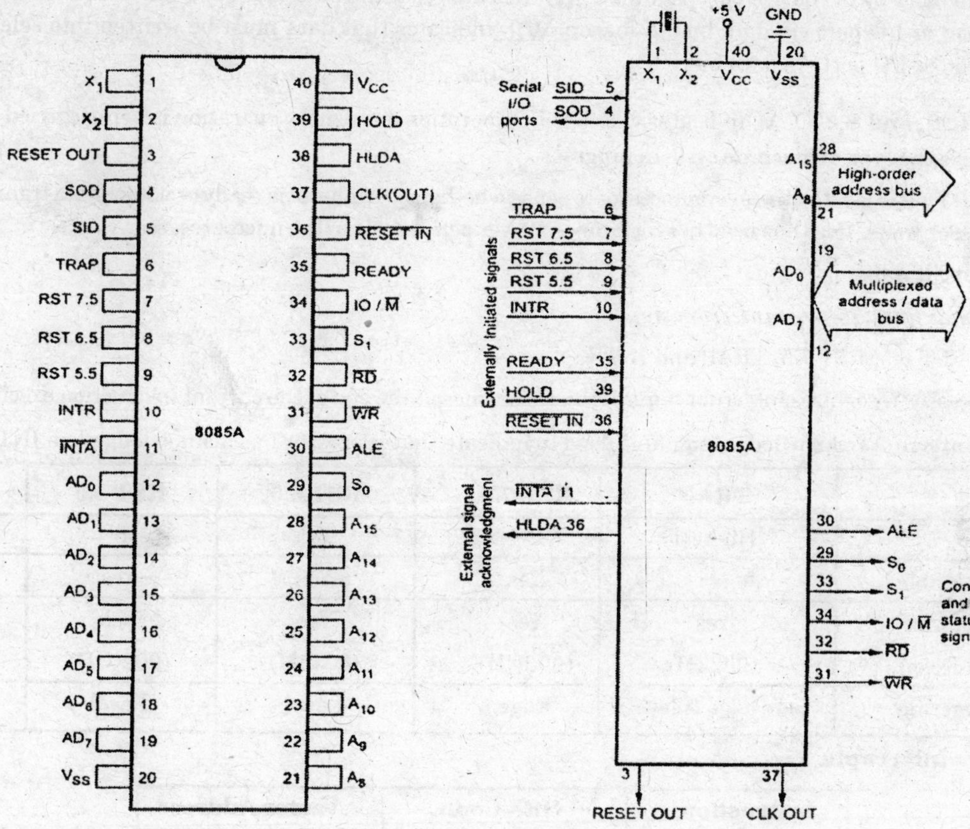

(a) Pin configuration *(b) Functional pin diagram*

Fig. 4.99. PIN Diagram

The signals of 8085 can be classified into seven groups according to their functions:

1. **Power supply and Frequency Signals**

   (i) **V_{CC}** : It requires a single +5V power supply.

   (ii) **V_{SS}** **:** Ground reference.

   (iii) **X_1 and X_2** **:** A tuned circuit like LC, RC or crystal is connected at these two pins. The internal clock generator divides oscillator frequency by 2, therefore, to operate a system at 3 MHz, the crystal of tuned circuit must have a frequency of 6 MHz.

   (iv) **CLK OUT :** This signal is used as a system clock for other devices. Its frequency is half of the oscillator frequency.

2. **Data bus and Address bus Signals**

   (i) **AD_0 to AD_7** **:** The 8 bit data bus (D_0 - D_7) is multiplexed with the lower half (A_0 - A_7) of the 16 bit address bus. During first part of the machine cycle (T_1), lower 8 bits of memory address or I/O address appear on the bus. During remaining part of the machine cycle (T_2 and T_3), these lines are used as a bi-directional data bus.

   (ii) **A_8 to A_{15}** **:** Upper half of the 16 bit address appears on the address lines A_8 to A_{15}. These lines are exclusively used for most significant 8 bits of the 16 bit address.

3. **Control and Status Signals**

   (i) **ALE (Address Latch Enable) :** AD_0 to AD_7 lines are multiplexed and lower half of address (A_0 - A_7) is available only during T_1 of the machine cycle. This lower half of address is also necessary during T_2 and T_3 of machine cycle to access specific location in memory or I/O port. This means that lower half of an address must be latched in T_1 of the machine cycle, so that it is available throughout the machine cycle. Latching of lower half of an address is done by using external latch and ALE signal from 8085.

(*ii*) $\overline{\textbf{RD}}$ **and** $\overline{\textbf{WR}}$: These signals are basically used to control the direction of the data flow between processor and memory or I/O device/port. A low on $\overline{RD}$ indicates that the data must be read from the selected memory location or I/O port via data bus. A low on $\overline{WR}$ indicates that data must be written into selected memory location or I/O port via data bus.

(*iii*) **IO/**$\overline{\textbf{M}}$ **,** S_0 **and** S_1 **:** IO/$\overline{M}$ indicates whether I/O operation or memory operation is being carried out. S_1 and S_0 indicate the type of machine cycle in progress.

(*iv*) **READY :** It is used by the microprocessor to sense whether a peripheral is ready or not for data transfer. If not, the processor waits. It is thus used to synchronize slower peripherals to the microprocessor.

4. Interrupt Signals

The 8085 has five hardware interrupt signals :

RST 5.5, RST 6.5, RST 7.5, TRAP and INTR.

Microprocessor recognizes interrupt requests on these lines at the end of the current instruction execution.

$\overline{INTA}$ (Interrupt Acknowledge) signal is used to indicate that processor has acknowledged an INTR interrupt.

	TRAP	**RST 7.5**	**RST 6.5**	**RST 5.5**	**INTR**
Priority	Highest	2nd	3rd	4th	Least
Mask able	No	Yes	Yes	Yes	Yes
Vectored	Yes	Yes	Yes	Yes	No
(Address)	(0024H)	(003CH)	(0034H)	(002 CH)	
Triggering	+ve edge & level	Edge	Level	Level	Level

Software Interrupts.

Instruction	**HEX Code**	**Vector Address**
RST 0	C7	0000H
RST 1	CF	0008H
RST 2	D7	0010 H
RST 3	DF	0018 H
RST 4	E7	0020 H
RST 5	EF	0028 H
RST 6	F7	0030 H
RST 7	FF	0038 H

5. Serial I/O Signal

(*i*) **SID (Serial I/P data) :** This input signal is used to accept serial data bit by bit from the external device.

(*ii*) **SOD (Serial O/P Data) :** This is an output signal which enables the transmission of serial data bit by bit to the external device.

6. DMA Signal

(*i*) **HOLD :** This signal indicates that another master is requesting for the uses of address bus, data bus and control bus.

(*ii*) **HLDA :** This active high signal is used to acknowledge HOLD request.

7. Reset Signals

(*i*) $\overline{\textbf{RESET IN}}$ **:** *A low on this pin*

(*a*) sets the program counter to zero (0000H).

(*b*) resets the interrupt enable and HLDA flip-flops.

(*c*) tri-states the data bus, address bus and control bus. (Note : Only during RESET is active).

(*d*) affects the contents of processor's internal registers randomly.

On reset, the PC sets to 0000H which causes the 8085 to execute the first instruction from address 0000H. For proper reset operation reset signal must be held low for at least 3 clock cycles. The power-on reset circuit can be used to ensure execution of first instruction from address 0000H.

(ii) **RESET OUT :** This active high signal indicates that processor is being reset. Signal is synchronized to the processor clock and it can be used to reset other devices connected in the system.

4.8 INSTRUCTION CLASSIFICATION

To perform a task in a particular microprocessor system, programmer has to know the instructions supported by microprocessor used in the microprocessor system.

Based on the nature of function of the instructions, instructions provided by the 8085 can be categorised into following five different groups :

1. Data transfer Operations

The data transfer instructions load given data into register, copy data from register to register, copy data from register to memory location, and vice versa. In other words, data transfer instructions copy data from source to destination. Source can be data or contents of register or contents of memory location whereas destination can be register or memory location. These instructions do not affect the flag register of the processor.

2. Arithmetic Operations

The arithmetic instructions provided by 8085 perform following operations:

(i) **Addition :** Any 8-bit number, or contents of a register, or contents of a memory location can be added to the contents of the accumulator and resulted sum is stored in the accumulator. The resulted carry bit is stored in the carry flag. In 8085, no two other registers can be added directly, i.e. contents of B and C registers cannot be added directly. To add two 16-bit numbers the 8085 provides DAD instruction. It adds the data within the register pair to the contents of the HL register pair and resulted sum is stored in the HL register pair.

(ii) **Subtraction :** Any 8-bit number, or the contents of a register, or the contents of a memory location can be subtracted from the contents of the accumulator and the result is stored in the accumulator. The resulted borrow bit is stored in the carry flag. In 8085, no two other registers can be added directly.

(iii) **Increment Decrement :** The 8085 has increment and decrement instructions to increment and decrement contents of any register, memory location or register pair by 1.

3. Logical Operations

Logical instructions provided by 8085 perform following operations :

(i) **Logical :** Using logical instructions, any 8-bit number, or contents of a register, or of a memory location can be logically ANDed, ORed, or Exclusive-ORed with contents of the accumulator and result is stored in the accumulator. The result also affects flags according to definition of flags.

e.g. zero result sets the zero flag.

(ii) **Rotate :** These instructions allow shifting of each bit in the accumulator either left or right by 1 bit position.

(iii) **Compare :** Any 8-bit number, or contents of a register, or contents of a memory location can be compared for equality, greater than, or less than, with contents of the accumulator.

(iv) **Complement :** The result of accumulator can be complemented with this instruction. It replaces all 0s by 1s and all 1s by 0s.

4. Branching Operations

These instructions allow the 8085 to change sequence of the program, either unconditionally or under certain test conditions. These instructions include branch instructions, subroutine call and return instructions and restart instructions.

5. Stack, Input/Output and Machine control Operations

These instructions control stack operations, input/output operations and machine operations.

Stack instructions allow transfer of data from register pair to stack memory and from stack memory to the register pair.

Input/output instruction allows transfer of 8-bit data to input/output port.

Machine instructions control machine operations such as interrupt, halt, or do nothing.

ELEMENTS OF INSTRUCTION.

Each instruction of the 8085 microprocessor has specific information fields. These information fields of instructions called *elements of instruction* are given below

1. Operation Code

Operation code field in the instruction specifies operation to be performed. The operation is specified by binary code, hence name operation code or simply opcode.

e.g. 8085 processor operation code for ADD B instruction is 80H.

2. Source/Destination Operand

Source/destination operand field directly specifies source/destination operand for the instruction. In 8085, instruction MOV A,B has B register contents as a source operand and A register contents as a destination operand because this instruction copies contents of register B to register A.

3. Source Operand Address

Operation specified by the instruction may require one or more operands. The source operand may be in the 8085 register or in the memory. Many times the instruction specifies address of the source operand, so that operand(s) can be accessed and operated by 8085 according to the instruction.

In 8085, source operand address for instruction ADD M is given by HL register pair.

(i) **Destination Operand Address :** Operation executed by the 8085 may produce result. Most of the times, result is stored in one of the operand. Such operand is called *destination operand*. The instruction which produce result specifies destination operand address. In 8085, the destination operand address for instruction INR M is given by HL register pair because INR M instruction increments contents of memory location specified by HL register pair and stores result in the same memory location.

(ii) **Next Instruction Address :** Next instruction address tells the 8085 from where to fetch the next instruction after completion of execution of current instruction. For BRANCH instructions, address of the next instruction is specified within the instruction. However, for other instructions, next instruction to be fetched immediately follows current instructions.

e.g. in 8085, instruction after INR B follows it. The instruction JMP 2000H specifies the next instruction address as 2000H.

INSTRUCTION FORMATS.

The 8085A instruction set consists of one, two and three byte instructions:

(i) **One byte Instruction**

The first byte is always the opcode

FORMAT :

Opcode

1 byte

Example : MOV A, B whose opcode is 78H which is one byte. The instruction copies the contents of B register in A register.

(ii) **Two byte Instruction**

In two-byte instructions, second byte is usually data

FORMAT :

Opcode	Operand

2 bytes

Example : MVI B, 02H. The opcode for this instruction is 06H and is always followed by a byte data (02H in this case). This instruction is a two byte instruction which copies immediate data into B register.

(iii) **Three byte Instruction**

In three byte instructions, the last two bytes present address or 16-bit data.

FORMAT :

Opcode	Operand	Operand

3 bytes

Example : JMP 6200H. The opcode for this instruction is C3H and is always followed by 16 bit address (6200H in this case). This instruction is a three byte instruction which loads 16 bit address into program counter.

OPCODE FORMATS.

The 8085A microprocessor has 8-bit opcodes. The opcode is unique for each instruction and contains information about operation, register to be used, memory to be used etc. The 8085A identifies all operations, register and flags with a specific code.

e.g. all internal registers are identified as shown below in the Tables 4.22 and 4.23.

Table 4.22

Registers	Code
B	0 0 0
C	0 0 1
D	0 1 0
E	0 1 1
H	1 0 0
L	1 0 1
M (Memory)	1 1 0
A	1 1 1

Table 4.23

Registers Pairs	Code
BC	0 0
DE	0 1
HL	1 0
AF or SP	1 1

Similarly, there are different codes for each operation, which are identified as follows :

Sr. No.	Function	Operation code							
		B_7	B_6	B_5	B_4	B_3	B_2	B_1	B_0
1	MVI r, data	0	0	D	D	D	1	1	0
2	LXI rp, data	0	0	D	D	0	0	0	1
3	MOV rd, rs	0	1	D	D	D	S	S	S

Note : DDD defines destination register ; SSS defines source register and DD defines register pair.

DATA FORMATS.

Operand is an another name for data.

Forms of Data Format

1. **Addresses.**

   The address is a 16-bit unsigned integer number used to refer a memory location.

2. **Numbers/Logical Data.**

   The 8085 supports following Numeric Data types :

   (i) **Signed integer :** It is either a positive number or a negative number. In 8085, 8-bits are assigned for signed integer, in which most significant bit is used for sign and remaining seven bits are used for magnitude. Sign bit 0 indicates positive number whereas sign bit 1 indicates negative number.

   (ii) **Unsigned integer :** The 8085 microprocessor supports 8-bit unsigned integer.

   (iii) **BCD number :** It stands for binary coded decimal number. It uses ten digits from 0 through 9. The 8-bit register of 8085 can store two digit BCD number.

3. Characters.

The 8085 uses ASCII code to represent characters. It is a 7-bit alphanumeric code that represent Decimal numbers, English alphabets, and other special characters.

4.9 ASSEMBLY LANGUAGE PROGRAM

Define a program statement as *write an assembly language program to add two numbers*.

Three tasks are involved in this program :

(*i*) Load two hex numbers

(*ii*) Add numbers

(*iii*) Store the result in the memory

These tasks can be symbolically presented as flow chart, as shown in Fig. 4.100

Next find the suitable 8085 assembly language instruction/s for each task.

These instructions are as follows :

Task 1 Instruction :

```
MVI A , 20H  ; Load 20H
             ; register A
MVI B, 40H   ; Load 40 H
             ; in register B
```

Task 2 Instruction :

```
ADD B  ; Add two numbers A and B and save
       ; result in register A.
```

Task 3 Instruction :

```
STA 2200H  ; Store the result in memory
           ; location 2000H
HLT        ; Stop the program execution
```

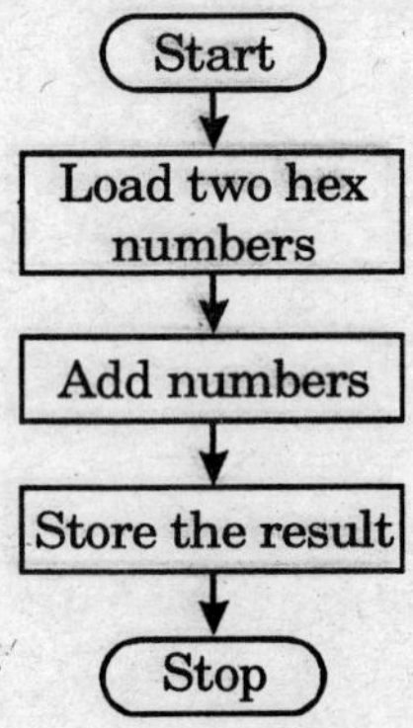

Fig. 4.100

To execute three tasks in a sequence in writng corresponding instructions in the same sequence constitutes an assembly language program.

ASSEMBLY LANGUAGE PROGRAM TO MACHINE LANGUAGE PROGRAM.

Once assembly language program is ready, it is necessary to convert it in the machine language program. This is done by referring proper hex code for each assembly instruction from the 8085 instruction set mannual. This process is called ***Hand assembly*** and resulted machine language program is also called ***Hex code***.

Hex code for Program

Memonics	**Hex code**		
MVI A, 20H	3EH	←	Opcode
	20 H	←	Operand
MVI B, 40H	06H	←	Opcode
	40H	←	Operand
ADD B	80H	←	Opcode
STA 2200H	32 H	←	Opcode
	00H	←	Operand (lower byte of address)
	22H	←	Operand (higher byte of address)
HLT	76H	←	opcode

Storing Hex Code in the Memory

Once hex code is ready, it has to be loaded in the memory of specially designed microprocessor system (Microprocessor training kit) for execution. To perform this task, one should know address range of read/write memory in the system. Assume that the read/ write memory ranges from 2000H to 22FFH. The microprocessor training kit has keypad to enter hex code in the memory. It provides a special routines (monitor program) to enter a hex code byte by byte and execute the program.

Typical Steps for storing HEX code in the memory from address 2000H :

1. Reset microprocessor system by pressing the RESET key.
2. Enter into store mode by pressing SET key.
3. Enter address of the memory 2000H, where the first hex code (starting address of the program) is to be stored using hex keys.
4. Enter hex code using hex keys.
5. Increment memory address by 1 using INC key.
6. Repeat steps 4 and 5 until the last hex code.

Executing the program

The microprocessor training kit provides a procedure to execute the program. To activate procedure we, have to enter starting address of the program (2000H in our example). To enter this address, we have to go into execute mode by pressing GO key and enter starting address using hex keys. Once starting address is entered, the program can be executed by pressing EXECUTE key. EXECUTE key procedure loads starting address of our program, 2000H into the program counter and program control is transferred from monitor program to our program.

After this, microprocessor reads one hex code at a time, and when it fetches complete instruction, it executes that instruction. Then it fetches next instruction and this process continues until last instruction in the program is executed.

4.10 ADDRESSING MODES

Part of the programming flexibility for each microprocessor is the number and different type of ways the programmer can refer to data stored in the memory. The different ways that a microprocessor can access data are called *addressing modes.*

The 8085 has following 5 Addressing Modes :

1. Immediate Addressing Mode

In this, 8 or 16 bit data can be specified as a part of instruction.

In 8085, instructions having 'I' letter fall under this category. 'I' indicates immediate addressing mode.

Example :

```
MVI A, 20H     ; Moves 8 bit immediate data (20H) into accumultor
MVI M, 30H     ; Moves 8 bit immediate data (30 H) into the memory location
               ; pointed by HL register pair
LXI SP, 2700H ; Moves 16 bit immediate data (2700H) into SP (Stack pointer)
LXI D, 10FFH  ; Moves 16 bit immediate data (10FFH) into DE register pair
               ; (D = 10H and E = FFH)
```

2. Register Addressing Mode

It specifies source operand, destination operand, or both to be contained in an 8085 registers. This results in faster execution, since it is not necessary to access memory locations for operands.

Example :

```
MOV A, B   ; Moves contents of register B into the accumulator
SPHL       ; Moves contents of HL register pair into stack pointer.
ADD C      ; Adds contents of register C into the contents of
           ; accumulator and stores result in the accumulator
```

3. Direct Addressing Mode

It specifies 16 bit address of the operand within the instruction itself. The second and third bytes of instruction contain this 16 bit address.

Example :

```
LDA 2000H  ; Loads the 8 bit contents of memory location
           ; 2000H into the accumulator
```

SHLD 3000H ; Stores the HL register pair into two consecutive memory
; locations. Lower byte i.e. the contents of L register into
; memory location 3000H and higher byte i.e. the contents
; of H register into memory location 3001 H

4. Indirect Addressing Mode

In this, memory address where operand located is specified by the contents of a register pair.

Example :

LDAX B ; Loads accumulator with the contents of memory
; location pointed by BC register pair

MOV M,A ; Stores contents of accumulator into the memory
; location pointed by HL register pair.

5. Implied Addressing Mode

In this opcode specifies address of the operands.

Example :

CMA ; Complements contents of accumulator

RAL ; Rotates contents of accumulator left through carry.

4.11. INSTRUCTION CYCLE, MACHINE CYCLE AND T–STATE

(*i*) **Instruction cycle:** Total time required by execution to execute an instruction is known as instruction cycle.

(*ii*) **T–State:**

$$T \text{ state} = \frac{1}{\text{operating freq.}} \text{ sec.}$$

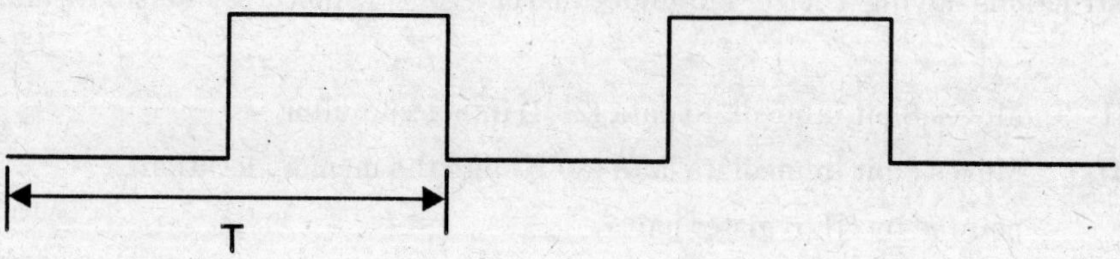

Instruction cycle is the group at one or more than one machine cycle.

(*iii*) **Machine Cycle:** Regarding different type of task during the execution of instruction, different type of machine cycle are defined.

In 8085 6 type of M-cycle is possible.

1. OP code fetch M-cycle or Machine code fetch M-cycle

   Total time required by execution to fetch (Read) Machine code regarding an instruction from memory.

$$F = 4T$$
$$S = 6T$$

   CALL & RET, RESTART, INX & DCX, SPHL & PCHL PUSH are required 6T state to read from memory all other instruction required 4T state.

   It is first and only first M-cycle of instruction.

2. Memory Read M-cycle → (R)

   Total time required by the execution to read 8 bit information from memory

$$R = 3T$$

3. Memory Write M-cycle → (W)

   Total time required by execution to store 8 bit information in memory

$$W = 3T$$

4. Input Read M-cycle → (I)

   Total time required by execution to read 8 bit data from I/P port.

$$I = 3T$$

5. Output Write M-cycle → (O)

   Total time required by execution to make available 8 bit data at O/P port.

$$O = 3T$$

6. Bus Idle M-cycle → (B)

   Duration in which buses of microprocessor in idle condition at the time of execution at some specific instruction

$$B = 3T$$

   Bus idle M-cycle required only in DAD instruction.

8085 INSTRUCTION SET

Based on the nature of functions the instruction carry out, the 8085 instruction set can be categorised into following five different groups :

1. Data Transfer Group
2. Arithmetic Group
3. Logic Group
4. Branch Group
5. Stack Input/Output and Machine Control Group

Notations used in Instructions.

Notation	Meaning
M	Memory location pointed by HL register pair
R	8-bit register
Reg.pair	16-bit register pair
Rd	Source register
addr	16-bit address/8-bit address

1. DATA TRANSFER GROUP.

These instructions load given data into register, copy data from register to register, and copy data from register to register, and copy data from register to memory location and vice versa. These instructions do not affect any flag in the flag register.

This group consists of following set of instruction :

(1) MOV: Move–Copy from Source to Destination

Opcode	Operand	Bytes	M-Cycles	T-States
MOV	Rd. Rs	1	1	4
MOV	M, Rs	2	2	7
MOV	Rd.M	1	2	7

(2) MVI: Move Immediate 8-Bit

Opcode	Operand	Bytes	M-Cycles	T-States
MVI	Reg., Data	2	2	7
	Mem., Data	2	3	10

(3) LXI: Load Register Pair Immediate

Opcode	Operand	Bytes	M-Cycles	T-States
LXI	Reg. pair, 16-bit data	3	3	10

Flags: No flags are affected.

(4) STA: Store Accumulator Direct

Opcode	Operand	Bytes	M-Cycles	T-States
STA	16-bit	3	4	13

Flags : No flags are affected.

(5) LDA: Load Accumulator Direct

Opcode	Operand	Bytes	M-Cycles	T-States
LDA	16-bit address	3	4	13

(6) LHLD : Load H and L Registers Direct

Opcode	Operand	Bytes	M-Cycles	T-States
LHLD	16-bit	3	5	16
address				

(7) SHLD: Store H and L Registers Direct.

Opcode	Operand	Bytes	M-Cycles	T-States
SHLD	16-bit	3	5	16
address				

(8) STAX: Store Accumulator Indirect

Opcode	Operand	Bytes	M-Cycles	T-States
STAX	B/D reg.	1	2	7
	Pair			

(9) LDAX: Load Accumulator Indirect

Opcode	Operand	Bytes	M-Cycles	T-States
LDAX	B/D reg.	1	2	7
Pair				

(10) XCHG: Exchange H and L with D and E

Opcode	Operand	Bytes	M-Cycles	T-States
XCHG	None	1	1	4

2. ARITHMETIC GROUP.

This group consists of following set of instructions :

(1) ADD : Add Register to Accumulator

Opcode	Operand	Bytes	M-Cycles	T-States
ADD	Reg.	1	1	4
	Mem.	1	2	7

(2) ADI : Add Immediate to Accumulator

Opcode	Operand	Bytes	M-Cycles	T-States
ADI	8-bit	2	2	7
data				

Description : 8-bit data (operand) are added to the contents of the accumulator, and result is placed in the accumulator.

Flags : All flags are modified to reflect result of the addition.

(3) ADC : Add Register to Accumulator with Carry

Opcode	Operand	Bytes	M-Cycles	T-States
ADC	Reg.	1	1	4
	Mem.	1	2	7

(4) ACI: Add Immediate to Accumulator with Carry

Opcode	Operand	Bytes	M-Cycles	T-States
ACI	8-bit	2	2	7
data				

Flags : All flags are modified to reflect result of the addition.

(5) DAD : Add Register Pair to H and L Registers

Opcode	Operand	Bytes	M-Cycles	T-States
DAD	Reg. pair	1	3	10

Flags : If result is larger than 16 bits, then CY flag is set. No other flags are affected.

SUBTRACT.

This group consists of following set of instructions :

1. SUB: Subtract Register or Memory from Accumulator

Opcode	Operand	Bytes	M-Cycles	T-States
SUB	Reg.	1	1	4
	Mem.	1	2	7

Flags : All flags are affected to reflect result of the subtraction.

2. SUI: Subtract Immediate from Accumulator

Opcode	Operand	Bytes	M-Cycles	T-States
SUI	8-bit	2	2	7
data				

Flags : All flags are modified to reflect results of the subtraction.

3. SBB: Subtract Source and Borrow from Accumulator

Opcode	Operand	Bytes	M-Cycles	T-States
SBB	Reg.	1	1	4
	Mem.	1	2	7

Flags : All flags are altered to reflect result of the subtraction.

4. SBI: Subtract Immediate with Borrow

Opcode	Operand	Bytes	M-Cycles	T-States
SBI	8-bit	2	2	7
data				

Flags : All flags are altered to reflect result of the operation.

DAA : DECIMAL ADJUST ACCUMULATOR

This instruction adjusts accumulator to packed BCD (Binary Coded Decimal) after adding two BCD numbers.

Instruction works as follows :

1. If value of the low-order four bits ($D_3 - D_0$) in the accumulator is greater than 9 or if auxiliary carry flag is set, then instruction adds 6 (06) to the low-order four bits.
2. If value of the high-order four bits ($D_7 - D_4$) in the accumulator is greater than 9 or if carry flag is set, then instruction adds 6(60) to the high-order four bits.

Number of bytes : 1 byte

Opcode : DAA

M-cycles : 1

T-states : 4

Flags : All

INCREMENT AND DECREMENT.

This group consists of the following set of instructions:

(1) **INR r :** Increment specified register

Operation : r ← r + 1

Opcode	**Operand Bytes**	**M-cycles**	**T-states**
INRr	Regi. add.	1	4

Flags : All flags except carry flag are affected

(2) **INR M** : Increment data in memory

Operation : M ← M + 1, 1 byte, M-Cycles – 3, T-states – 10.

Flags : All flags except carry flag are affected

(3) **INX :** Increment Register Pair by 1

Opcode	**Operand**	**Byes**	**M-Cycles**	**T-States**
INX	Reg. pair	1	1	6

(4) **DCR r :** Decrement specified register

Operation : r ← r – 1

Opcode	**Operand**	**Bytes**	**M-Cycles**	**T-States**
DCR	Register addressing	1	1	4

Flags : All flags except carry flag are affected

(5) **DCR M :** Decrement data in memory

Operation : M ← M – 1

Opcode	**Operand**	**Bytes**	**M-Cycles**	**T-States**
DCRM	Reg. indirect addressing	1	3	10

Flags : All flags except carry flag are affected

(6) **DCX :** Decrement Register Pair by 1

Opcode	**Operand**	**Bytes**	**M-Cycles**	**T-States**
DCX	Reg. pair	1	1	6

Flags : No flags are affected.

3. BRANCH GROUP

This instructions allow the microprocessor to change sequence of a program, either unconditionally or under certain test conditions.

This group include following instructions :

(*i*) Jump Instructions

(*ii*) Call and Return Instructions

(*iii*) Restart Instructions

JUMP

This group consists of following set of instructions :

(1) JMP addr : Jump unconditionally to the address

Operation : PC ← addr

Description : This instruction loads the PC with the address given within the instruction and resumes program execution from this location.

Number of bytes :	**3 bytes**	**M-Cycles**	**T-States**
	First byte : Opcode of JMP	3	10
	Second byte : Low order byte of the address		
	Third byte : High order byte of the address		

Addressing mode : Immediate addressing

Flags : Flags are not affected

(2) Jcondition addr : Jump conditionally to the address

Operation : If condition is true, PC ← addr, else PC ← PC + 3

Description : This instruction causes a jump to an address given in the instruction if desired condition occurs in the program before execution of the instruction.

The table below shows possible conditions for jumps :

Table 4.24 Conditional jumps

Instruction code	Description	Condition for jump
JC	Jump on carry	CY = 1
JNC	Jump on not carry	CY = 0
JP	Jump on positive	S = 0
JM	Jump on minus (Negative)	S = 1
JPE	Jump on parity even	P = 1
JPO	Jump on parity odd	P = 0
JZ	Jump on zero	Z = 1
JNZ	Jump on not zero	Z = 0

Number of bytes :	**3 bytes**	**M-Cycles**	**T-States**
	First byte : Opcode of Jcondition	2 or 3	7 or 10
	Second byte : Low order byte of the address		
	Third byte : High order byte of the address		

Addressing mode : Immediate addressing

Flags : Flags are not affected. Flags are checked

(3) PCHL : Load HL contents into program counter

Operation : PC ← HL, 1 byte, 1 M-Cycles, 6 T-States

Description : This instruction loads contents of HL register pair into the program counter. Thus program control is transferred to the location whose address is in HL register pair.

Addressing mode : Register addressing

Flags : Flags are not affected

4. LOGIC GROUP

These instructions perform logic operations such as AND, OR and XOR, compare data between registers or between register and memory, rotate and complement data in registers.

This group consists of following set of instructions:

(1) ANA : Logical AND with Accumulator

Opcode	Operand	Bytes	M-Cycles	T-States
ANA	Reg.	1	1	4
	Mem.	1	2	7

Flags: S, Z, P are modified to reflect result of the operation CY is reset.

In 8085, AC is set, and in 8080A AC is result of ORing bits D_3 of the operands.

(2) ANI: AND Immediate with Accumulator

Opcode	Operand	Bytes	M-Cycles	T-States
ANI	8-bit data	2	2	7

Flags : S, Z, P are modified to reflect results of the operation. CY is reset. In 8085, AC is set.

(3) XRA: Exclusive OR with Accumulator

Opcode	Operand	Bytes	M-Cycles	T-States
XRA	Reg.	1	1	4
	Mem.	1	2	7

Flags : Z, S, P are altered to reflect results of the operation. CY and AC are reset.

(4) XRI: Exclusive OR Immediate with Accumulator

Opcode	Operand	Bytes	M-Cycles	T-States
XRI	8-bit data	2	2	7

Flags : Z, S, P are altered to reflect results of the operation. CY and AC are reset.

(5) ORA: Logically OR with Accumulator

Opcode	Operand	Bytes	M-cycles	T-States
ORA	Reg.	1	1	4
	Mem.	1	2	7

Flags : Z, S, P are modified to reflect results of the operation. AC and CY are reset.

(6) ORI: Logically OR Immediate

Opcode	Operand	Bytes	M-Cycles	T-States
ORI	8-bit data	2	2	7

Description : Contents of the accumulator are logically ORed with 8-bit data in the operand and results are placed in the accumulator.

Flags : S, Z, P are modified to reflect results of the operation. CY and AC are reset.

(7) CMP: Compare with Accumulator

Opcode	Operand	Bytes	M-Cycles	T-States
CMP	Reg.	1	1	4
	Mem.	1	2	7

Flags : S, P, AC are also modified in addition to Z and CY to reflect results of the operation.

(8) CPI : Compare Immediate with Accumulator

Opcode	Operand	Bytes	M-Cycles	T-States
CPI	8-bit	2	2	7

Flags: S, P, AC are also modified in addition to Z and CY to reflect result of the operation.

(9) CMC: Complement Carry

Opcode	Operand	Bytes	M-Cycles	T-States
CMC	None	1	1	4

Description : Carry flag is complemented.

Flags : Carry flag is modified, no other flags are affected.

(10) CMA : Complement Accumulator

Opcode	Operand	Bytes	M-Cycles	T-States
CMA	None	1	1	4

Description : Contents of the accumulator are complemented.

Flags : No flags are affected.

ROTATE.

(1) RLC: Rotate Accumulator Left

Opcode	Operand	Bytes	M-Cycles	T-States
RLC	None	1	1	4

Description : Each binary bit of the accumulator is rotated left by one position.

Bit D_7 is placed in the position of D_0 as well as in the Carry flag.

Flags : CY is modified according to bit D7, S, Z, P, AC are not affected.

(2) RRC: Rotate Accumulator Right

Opcode	Operand	Bytes	M-Cycles	T-States
RRC	None	1	1	4

Description : Each binary bit of the accumulator is rotated right by one position. Bit D_0 is placed in the position of D_7 as well as in the Carry flag.

Flags : CY is modified according to bit D_0, A, Z, P, AC are not affected.

(3) RAL: Rotate Accumulator Left through Carry

Opcode	Operand	Bytes	M-Cycles	T-States
RAL	None	1	1	4

Flags : CY is modified according to bit D_7, S, Z, AC, P are not affected.

(4) RAR: Rotate Accumulator Right through Carry

Opcode	Operand	Bytes	M-Cycles	T-States
RAR	None	1	1	4

Flags : CY is modified according to bit D_0, S, Z, P, AC are not affected.

5. STACK OPERATIONS, INPUT/OUTPUT AND MACHINE CONTROL GROUP.

STACK OPERATIONS.

This group consists of following set of instructions :

- LXI SP, Data and SPHL
- PUSH and POP instructions
- CALL and RETURN instructions
- RESTART instructions
- XTHL

LXI SP, Data and SPHL : Initializes Stack Pointer.

Before execution of any stack related instruction, stack pointer must be initialized with a valid memory address.

Stack pointer can be initialized by two ways :

(*i*) Direct way : LXI SP, data (16) ; Loads 16-bit data into SP

(*ii*) Indirect way : LXI H, data (16) ; Load 16-bit data into HL

SPHL ; Load contents of HL into SP

Normally, stack pointer is initialized by the direct way. When a programmer wishes to set stack pointer to a value that has been computed by the program, indirect way is used. The computed value is placed in H and L and contents of HL register pair then moved into the stack pointer.

SPHL : Move data from HL to stack pointer.

Operation : SP ← HL

Description : This instruction copies contents of HL register pair into the stack pointer. Contents of H register are copied to higher order byte of stack pointer and contents of L register are copied to the lower byte of pair then moved into the stack pointer.

Opcode SPHL

Operand Reg.addressing

Bytes 1

Flags : Flags are not affected.

PUSH and POP.

When programmer realizes shortage of the registers, he stores present contents of the registers in the stack with the help of PUSH instruction and then uses registers for other function. After completion of other function, programmer loads previous contents of the register from stack with the help of POP instruction.

PUSH operation.

In PUSH operation, 16-bit data is stored on the stack. This 16-bit data is stored in two steps.

Steps involved in PUSH Operation :

In the first step, stack pointer is decremented by one and then higher byte of the 16-bit data is stored at the memory location pointed by stack pointer.

In the second step, stack pointer is again decremented by one and then lower byte of the 16-bit data is stored at the memory location pointed by stack pointer.

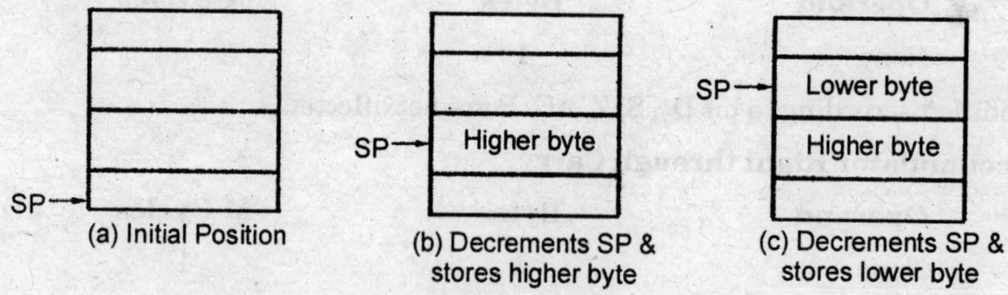

Fig. 4.101 PUSH Operation

PUSH Instructions :

(1) PUSH rp : *Stores contents specified register pair on the stack.*

Operation : SP ← SP – 1,
(SP) ← rpH,
SP ← SP – 1,
(SP) ← rpL.

Opcode PUSH rp

Operand Reg. indirect addressing

Bytes 1

M-Cycles 3

T-States 12

Flags : Flags are not affected.

2. **PUSH PSW** : Stores contents of program status word and accumulator on the stack.

Operation : SP ← SP – 1
(SP) ← A
(SP) ← SP – 1
(SP) ← Flag register

Opcode PUSH PSW

Operand Reg. indirect addressing

Bytes 1

M-Cycles 3

T-States 12

Flags : Flags arc not affected.

POP Operation.

In POP operation, 16-bit data is read from the stack. This 16-bit data is read in following two operations :

(*i*) Contents from memory location pointed by stack pointer are loaded into lower byte of register pair and then stack pointer is incremented by one.

(*ii*) Contents from memory location pointed by stack pointer are loaded into higher byte of register pair and then stack pointer is incremented by one.

Step involved in POP Operation :

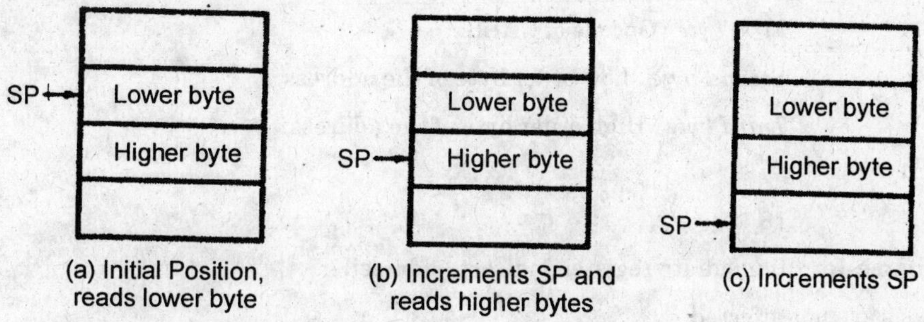

Fig. 4.102 POP Operation

POP Instructions.

(1) POP rp : Loads specified register pair with 16-bit data from the stack.

Operation : rpL ← (SP)
SP ← SP + 1
rpH ← (SP), SP ← SP + 1

Opcode POP rp

Operand Reg. indirect addressing

Bytes 1

M-Cycles 3

T-States 10

Flags : Flags are not affected.

(2) POP PSW : Loads program status word and accumulator with 16-bit from the stack.

Operation : Flag register ← (SP)
SP ← SP + 1
A ← (SP)
SP ← SP + 1

Opcode POP PSW

Operand Reg. indirect addressing

Bytes 1

M-Cycles 3

T-States 10

Flags : All flags are affected.

CALL

This group consists of following set of instructions :

1. CALL addr
2. Condition addr

(1) CALL addr

Call unconditionally a subroutine whose starting address is given within instruction

Operation : $(SP - 1) \leftarrow PC_H$

$(SP - 2) \leftarrow PC_L$

$SP \leftarrow SP - 2$

$PC \leftarrow addr$

Number of Bytes : 3 bytes

First byte : Opcode of CALL.

Second byte : Low order byte of the address.

Third byte : High order byte of the address.

M-Cycles 5

T-States 18

Addressing mode: Immediate register indirect addressing.

Flags : Flags are not affected.

RET : Return from subroutine unconditionally.

Operation : $PC_L \leftarrow (SP)$

$PC_H \leftarrow (SP + 1)$

$SP \leftarrow SP + 2$

Opcode RET

Operand Reg. indirect addressing

Bytes 1

M-Cycles 3

T-States 10

Flags : Flags are not affected.

Conditional call and Return instructions :

In addition to the unconditional CALL and RET instructions, 8085A instruction set includes eight conditional CALL instructions and eight conditional RET instructions. These conditions are checked by reading the status of respective flags.

If condition associated with the conditional CALL is not met, then instruction following CALL is executed.

If condition is met, then program counter contents are saved on the stack, and address contained in the CALL instruction is loaded into program counter.

The number of machine cycles and T-states required by a conditional CALL depends on whether or not the condition is satisfied. When condition is not satisfied, two machine cycles with a total of nine T-state are required to fetch, decode and execute instruction. When condition is satisfied, five machine cycles with 18 T-states are required.

Ccondition addr : Call subroutine conditionally at given addr.

Operation : If condition true $(SP-1) \leftarrow PC_H$

$(SP-2) \leftarrow PC_L$

$PC \leftarrow addr$

else $PC \leftarrow PC + 3$

Table 4.25. Conditional calls

Instruction code	Description	Condition for CALL
CC	Call on carry	CY = 1
CNC	Call on not carry	CY = 0
CP	Call on positive	S = 0
CM	Call on minus	S = 1
CPE	Call on parity even	P = 1
CPO	Call on parity odd	P = 0
CZ	Call on zero	Z = 1
CNZ	Call on not zero	Z = 0

Bytes: 3 bytes

First byte : Opcode at Ccondition.

Second byte : Low order byte of the address.

Third byte : High order byte of the address.

M-Cycles 2 or 5

T-States 9 or 18

Addressing mode: Immediate register indirect addressing.

Flags : Flags are not affected. Flags are checked.

Rcondition: Return from the subroutine conditionally.

Operation : If condition is true

$$PC_L \leftarrow (SP)$$

$$PC_H \leftarrow (SP + 1)$$

$$SP \leftarrow SP + 2$$

else

$$PC \leftarrow PC + 1$$

Table 4.26. Conditions for return

Instruction code	Description for RET	Condition
RC	Return on carry	CY = 1
RNC	Return on not carry	CY = 0
RP	Return on positive	S = 0
RM	Return on minus	S = 1
RPE	Return on parity even	P = 1
RPO	Return on parity odd	P = 0
RZ	Return on zero	Z = 1
RNZ	Return on not zero	Z = 0

Opcode Rcondition

Operand Reg. indirect addressing

Byte 1

M-Cycles 1 or 3

Flags : Flags are not affected.

RST : RESTART

This group consists of following set of instruction :

(1) RST: Restart

Bytes	M-Cycles	T-States
1	3	12

Opcode/Operand	Binary Code	Hex Code	Restart Address (H)
RST 0	11 000 111	C7	0000
RST 1	11 001 111	CF	0008
RST 2	11 010 111	D7	0010
RST 3	11 011 111	DF	0018
RST 4	11 100 111	E7	0020
RST 5	11 101 111	EF	0028
RST 6	11 110 111	F7	0030
RST 7	11 111 111	FF	0038

Flags : No flags are affected.

Additional 8085 Interrupts : The 8085 has four additional interrupts and these interrupts generate RST instructions internally and thus do not require any external hardware.

These instructions and their Restart address are as follows :

Interrupts	Restart Address
TRAP	24H
RST 5.5	2CH
RST 6.5	34H
RST 7.5	3CH

INPUT/ OUTPUT

This group consits of following set of instructions :

(1) IN : *Input Data to Accumulator from a Port with 8-bit Address*

Opcode	IN
	address
Operand	8-bit port
Bytes	2
M-Cycles	3
T-States	10

Flags : No flags are affected.

Comments: The operand is an 8-bit address; therefore, port addresses can range from 00H to FFH. While executing the instruction, a port address is duplicated on low-order ($A_7 - A_0$) and high-order ($A_{15} - A_8$) address buses. Any one of the sets of address lines can be decoded to enable the input port.

(2) OUT : *Output Data from Accumulator to a Port with 8-bit Address*

Opcode	OUT
	address
Operand	8-bit port
Bytes	2
M-Cycles	3
T-States	10

Flags : No flags are affected.

Comments : Operand is an 8-bit address; therefore, port addresses can range from 00H to FFH. While executing instruction, a port address is placed on the low-order address bus ($A_7 - A_0$) as well as high-order address bus ($A_{15} - A_8$). Any of the sets of address lines can be decoded to enable output port.

(3) XTHL: Exchange H and L with Top of Stack

Opcode	XTHL
Operand	None
Bytes	1
M-Cycles	5
T-States	16

Flags : No flags are affected.

MACHINE CONTROL

This group consists of following set of instructions :

(1) EI: Enable Interrupts

Opcode	EI
Operand	None
Bytes	1
M-Cycles	1
T-States	4

Flags : No flags are affected.

Comments : After a system reset or acknowledgment of an interrupt, Interrupt Enable flip-flop is reset, thus disabling interrupts. This instruction is necessary to reenable interrupts (except TRAP).

(2) DI: Disable Interrupts

Opcode	DI
Operand	None
Bytes	1
M-Cycles	1
T-States	4

Flags : No flags are affected.

Comments : This instruction is commonly used when execution of a code sequence cannot be interrupted.

(3) HLT: Halt and Enter Wait State

Opcode	HLT
Operand	None
Bytes	1
M-Cycles	2 or more
T-States	5 or more

Flags : No flags are affected.

(4) SIM: Set Interrupt Mask

Opcode	SIM
Operand	None
Bytes	1
M-Cycles	1
T-States	4

Description : This is multipurpose instruction and used to implement 8085 interrupts (RST 7.5, 6.5, and 5.5) and serial data output.

Instruction interprets accumulator contents as follows :

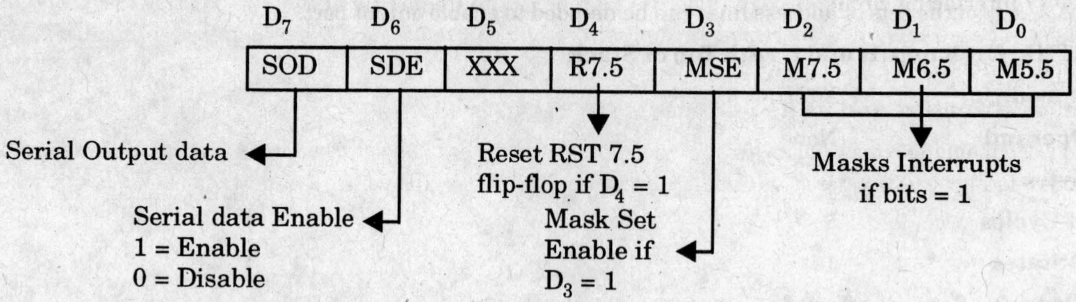

- **SOD–Output Data :** Bit D_7 of the accumulator is latched into SOD output line and made available to a serial peripheral if bit $D_6 = 1$.
- **SDE–Serial Data Enable :** If this bit = 1, it enables serial output. To implement serial output, this bit needs to be enabled.
- **XXX–Don't Care**
- **R7.5–Reset RST 7.5 :** If this bit = 1, RST 7.5 flip-flop is reset. This is additional control to reset RST 7.5.
- **MSE–Mask Set Enable :** If this bit is high, it enables functions of bis D_2, D_1, D_0. This is a master control over all interrupt masking bits. If this bit is low, bits D_2, D_1, and D_0 do not have any effect on the masks.
- M7.5–D_2 = 0, RST 7.5 is enabled
  = 1, RST 7.5 is masked or disabled
- M6.5–D1 = 0, RST 6.5 is enabled
  = 1, RST 6.5 is masked or disabled
- M5.5–D0 = 0, RST 5.5 is enabled
  = 1, RST 5.5 is masked or disabled

(5) RIM: Read Interrupt Mask

Opcode	RIM
Operand	None
Bytes	1
M-Ccyles	1
T-States	4

Description : This is a multipurpose instruction used to read status of interrupts 7.5, 7.5, 5.5 and to read serial data input bit. The instruction loads eight bits in the accumulator with following interpretations:

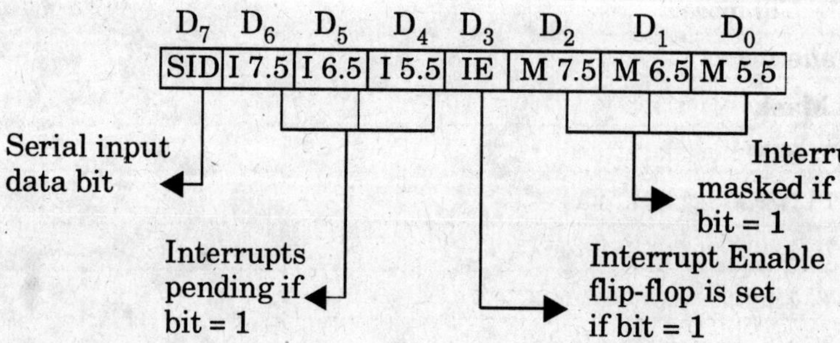

Flags : No flags are affected.

4.12 MEMORY INTERFACING

Memory interfacing circuit is used to access memory quite frequently to read instruction codes and data stored in memory. These read/write operations are monitored by control signals. The microprocessor activates these signals when it wants to read from and write into memory.

Memory Structure and its Requirements

Read/write memories consist of an array of registers, in which each register has unique address. Size of the memory is N × M as shown in Fig.(4.103), where N is number of registers and M is word length, in number of bits.

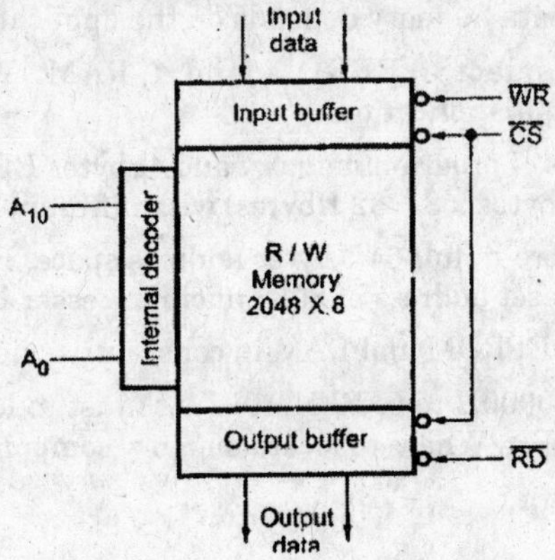

Fig. 4.103. Logic diagram for RAM

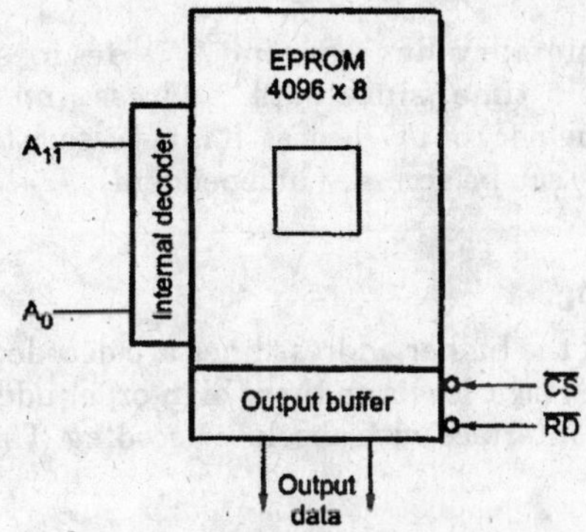

Fig. 4.104. Logic diagram for EPROM

e.g. If memory is having 12 address lines and 8 data lines, then

Number of registers/memory locations = $2^N = 2^{12} = 4096$.

Word length = M bit = 8 bit

e.g. If memory has 8192 memory locations, then it has 13 address lines.

Table 4.27 Memory capacity and Address lines required for Memory interfacing.

Memory Capacity	Address Lines Required
1K = 1024 memory locations	10
2K = 2048 memory locations	11
4K = 4096 memory locations	12
8K = 8192 memory locations	13
16K = 16384 memory locations	14
32K = 32768 memory locations	15
64K = 65536 memory locations	16

As shown in Fig. (4.103) memory chip has 11 address lines A_{10}-A_0, one chip select ($\overline{CS}$), and two control lines. Read ($\overline{RD}$) to enable output buffer and write ($\overline{WR}$) to enable the input buffer. The internal decoder is used to decode the address lines.

Fig. (4.104) shows logic diagram of a typical EPROM (Erasable Programmable Read-Only Memory) with 4096 (4K) registers. It has 12 address lines A_{11}-A_0, one chip select ($\overline{CS}$), one read control signal. Since EPROM is a read only memory, it does not require the ($\overline{WR}$) signal.

Basic concepts in Memory Interfacing .

(1) Microprocessor 8085 can access 64kbytes memory since address bus is 16-bit. But it is not always necessary to use full 64kbytes address space. Total memory size depends upon application.

(2) Generally EPROM (or EPROMs) is used as a program memory and RAM (or RAMs) as a data memory. When both, EPROM and RAM are used, then total address space 64kbytes is shared by them.

(3) Capacity of program memory and data memory depends on the application.

(4) It is not always necessary to select 1 EPROM and 1 RAM. We can have multiple EPROMs and multiple RAMs as per requirement of application.

e.g.We have to implement 32 kbytes of program memory and 4kbytes EPROMs are available. In this case, we can connect 8 EPROMs in parallel (4 Kbytes × 8 = 32 Kbytes) with different chip select for each EPROM.

(5) We can place EPROM/RAM anywhere in full 64 Kbytes address space. But program memory (EPROM) should be located from address 0000H since reset address of 8085 microprocessor is 0000H.

(6) It is not always necessary to locate EPROM and RAM in consecutive memory addresses.

e.g. If mapping of EPROM is from 0000H to 0FFFH, it is not must to locate RAM from 1000H. We can locate it anywhere between 1000H and FFFFH. Where to locate memory component totally depends on the application.

Requirements of Memory Interfacing

(1) Select chip

(2) Identify register

(3) Enable appropriate buffer.

Microprocessor system includes memory devices and I/O devices. Microprocessor can communicate (read/write) with only one device at a time, since data, address and control buses are common for all the devices. In order to communicate with memory or I/O devices, it is necessary to decode address from the microprocessor. Due to this, each device (memory or I/O) can be accessed independently.

Address Decoding Techniques

(1) Absolute Decoding/Full decoding.

In absolute decoding technique, all the higher address lines are decoded to select memory chip, and the memory chip is selected only for the specified logic levels on these high-order address lines; no other logic levels can select the chip. Fig. 4.105 shows memory interface with absolute decoding. This addressing technique is normally used in large memory systems.

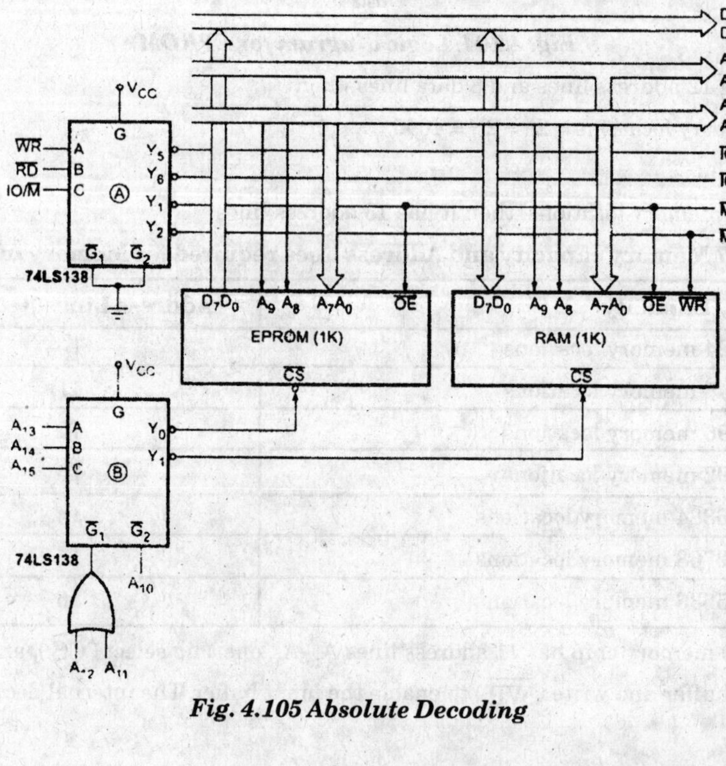

Fig. 4.105 Absolute Decoding

Memory Map :

Memory ICs	A_{15}	A_{14}	A_{13}	A_{12}	A_{11}	A_{10}	A_9	A_8	A_7	A_6	A_5	A_4	A_3	A_2	A_1	A_0	Address
Starting address of EPROM	0	0	0	0	0	0	0	0	0	0	0	0	0	0	0	0	0000H
End address of EPROM	0	0	0	0	0	0	1	1	1	1	1	1	1	1	1	1	03FFH
Starting Address of RAM	0	0	1	0	0	0	0	0	0	0	0	0	0	0	0	0	2000H
End address of RAM	0	0	1	0	0	0	1	1	1	1	1	1	1	1	1	1	23FFH

(2) Linear Decoding/Partial Decoding.

In small systems, hardware for the decoding logic can be eliminated by using individual high-order address lines to elect memory chips. This is called *linear decoding*. Fig. 4.106 shows addressing of RAM with linear decoding technique. This technique is also called *partial decoding*. It reduces cost of decoding circuit, but it has a draw-back of multiple addresses (shadow addresses).

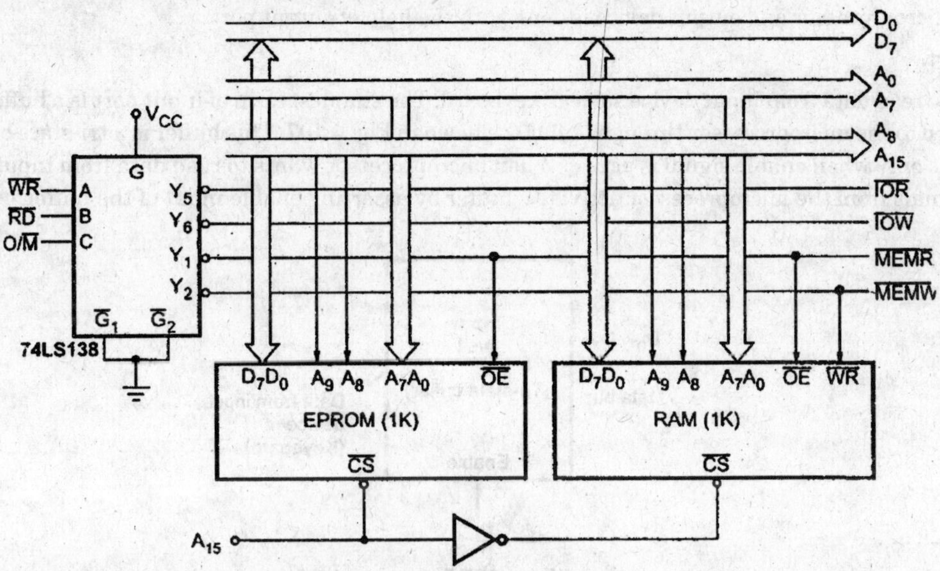

Fig. 4.106 Linear Decoding

Fig. 4.101 shows addressing of RAM with linear decoding technique. A_{15} address line, is directly connected to the chip select signal of EPROM and after inversion it is connected to the chip select signal of the RAM. Therefore, when status of A_{15} line is 'zero', EPROM gets selected and when status of A_{15} line is 'one' RAM gets selected. Ths status of the other address lines is not considered, since those address lines are not used for generation of chip select signals.

Memory Map.:

Memory ICs	A_{15}	A_{14}	A_{13}	A_{12}	A_{11}	A_{10}	A_9	A_8	A_7	A_6	A_5	A_4	A_3	A_2	A_1	A_0	Address
Starting address of EPROM	0	x	x	x	x	x	0	0	0	0	0	0	0	0	0	0	0000H
End address of EPROM	0	x	x	x	x	x	1	1	1	1	1	1	1	1	1	1	03FFH
Starting Address of RAM	1	x	x	x	x	x	0	0	0	0	0	0	0	0	0	0	8000H
End address of RAM	1	x	x	x	x	x	1	1	1	1	1	1	1	1	1	1	83FFH

Comparison between Full address decoding and Partial address decoding

Full address decoding	Partial address decoding
1. All higher address lines are decoded to select the memory or I/O device	1. Few higher address lines are decoded to select the memory or I/O device.
2. More hardware is required to design decoding logic.	2. Harware required to design decoding logic is less and sometimes itcan be eliminated.
3. Higher cost for decoding circuit.	3. Less cost for decoding circuit.
4. No multiple addresses.	4. It has a disadvantage of multiple addresses (shadow addresses).
5. Used in large systems.	5. Used in small systems.

I/O INTERFACING

The transfer of data between keyboard and microprocessor, and microprocessor and display device is called *input/output data transfer* or *I/O data transfer*.

Basic Concepts

The data transfer between microprocessor and input device is done with the help of input port. The data transfer between microprocessor and output device is done with the help of output port.

Input Port.

It is used to read data from input device such as keyboard. The simplest form of input port is a buffer. The input device is connected to the microprocessor through buffer as shown in Fig. 4.107. This buffer is a tri-state buffer and its output is available only when enable signal is active. When microprocessor wants to read data from input device (keyboard), control signals from the microprocessor activates buffer by asserting enable input of the buffer.

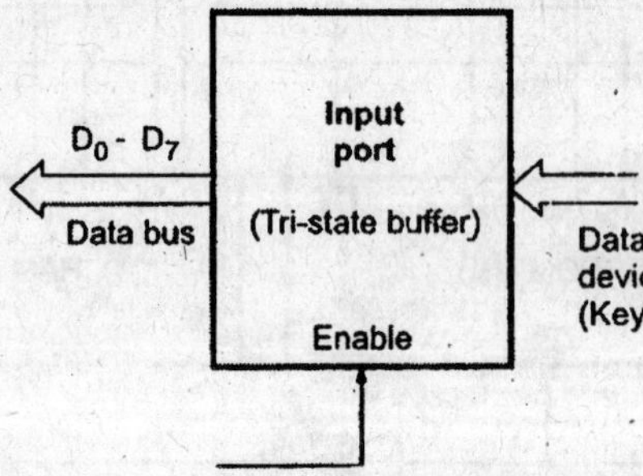

Fig. 4.107 Input port

Once buffer is enabled, data drom the input device is available on the data bus. Microprocessor reads this data by initiating read command.

Output Port.

It is used to send data to the output device such as display from the microprocessor. The simplest form of output port is a latch. The output device is connected to the microprocessor through latch, as shown in. When microprocessor wants to send data to the output divice, it puts data on the data bus and activates clock signal of the latch, latching the data from the data bus at the output of latch. Then it is available at the output of latch for the output device.

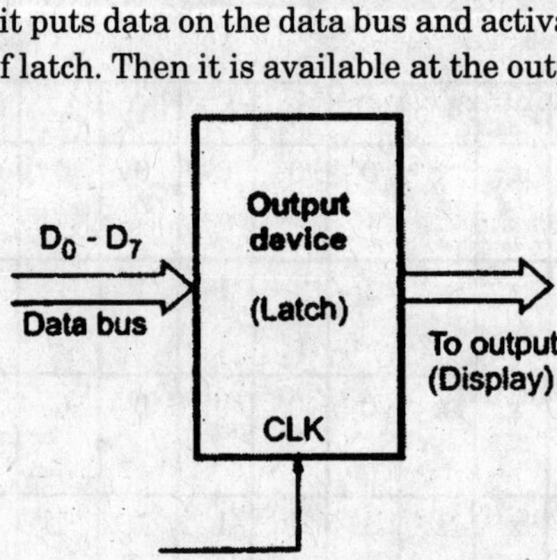

Fig. 4.108 Output port

I/O INTERFACING TECHNIQUES.

Most of the microprocessors support isolated I/O system. It partitions memory from I/O, via software, by having instructions that specifically access (address) memory, and others that specifically access I/O. When these instructions are decoded by the microprocessor, an appropriate control signal is generated to activate either memory or I/O operation. In 8085, IO/$\overline{M}$ signal is used for this purpose. The 8085 outputs a logic '1' on the IO/$\overline{M}$ line for an I/O operation and a logic '0' for memory operation. In 8085, it is possible to connect 64 Kbyte memory and 256 I/O ports in the system since 8085 sends 16 bit address for memory and 8-bit address for I/O.

I/O devices can be interfaced to an 8085A system in two ways :

1. I/O Mapped I/O
2. Memory mapped I/O

1. I/O Mapped I/O.

In this, the 8085 uses IO/$\overline{M}$ signal to distinguish between I/O read/write and memory read/write operations. The 8085 has separate instructions IN and OUT for I/O data transfer. When 8085 executes IN or OUT instruction, it places device address (port number) on the demultiplexed low order address bus as well as high order address bus, i.e., higher order address bus duplicates contents of demultiplexed low-order address bus, when 8085 microprocessor executes an IN or OUT instruction.

e.g., if device address is 60H, then contents on A_{15} to A_0 will be as follows :

A_{15}	A_{14}	A_{13}	A_{12}	A_{11}	A_{10}	A_9	A_8	A_7	A_6	A_5	A_4	A_3	A_2	A_1	A_0
0	1	1	0	0	0	0	0	0	1	1	0	0	0	0	0

Here, A_8 follows A_0, A_9 follows A_1 and so on, as shown below.

A_7	A_6	A_5	A_4	A_3	A_2	A_1	A_0	Device
A_{15}	A_{14}	A_{13}	A_{12}	A_{11}	A_{10}	A_9	A_8	Address
0	1	1	0	0	0	0	0	60H

The instruction IN inputs data from an input device (such as *keyboard*) into accumulator and instruction OUT sends contents of the accumulator to an output device such as LED display. These are two byte instructions. The second byte of the instruction specifies address or port number of an I/O device. As it is a byte, the address or port number can be any of the 256 combinations of eight bits, from 00H to FFH. Therefore, 8085 can communicate with 256 different I/O devices. When we want to interface an I/O device, it is necessary to assign a device address or a port number.

IN and OUT Instructions.

IN :

It is used to read 8-bit data from I/O device into the accumulator. This two byte instruction has, first byte as an opcode and second byte specifies device address or a port number.

IN addr : Copy data from input port into Accumulator.

Operation : A ← (addr)

Description : This instruction copies the data at the port whose address is specified in the instruction into the accumulator.

Example :

IN 80H ; This instruction will copy the data at port 80H into the

; accumulator .

Fig. 4.107 shows timing diagram of the IN instruction.

It has three machine cycles :

(i) *opcode fetch machine cycle.*

(ii) *Memory read machine cycle : Read address of port.*

(iii) *I/O read machine cycle*

The 8085 microprocessor places address of the input port on the low-order address bus AD_7-AD_0 as well as on the high-order address bus A_{15}-A_8 during T_1 of the machine cycle and asserts $\overline{RD}$ signal during T_2 and T_3 of the machine cycle. During T_2 and T_3, $\overline{RD}$ and IO/$\overline{M}$ signals are 0 and 1 respectively, which activates $\overline{IOR}$ signal. The $\overline{IOR}$ signal enables input port and the data from input port is placed on the data bus and transferred into the accumulator.

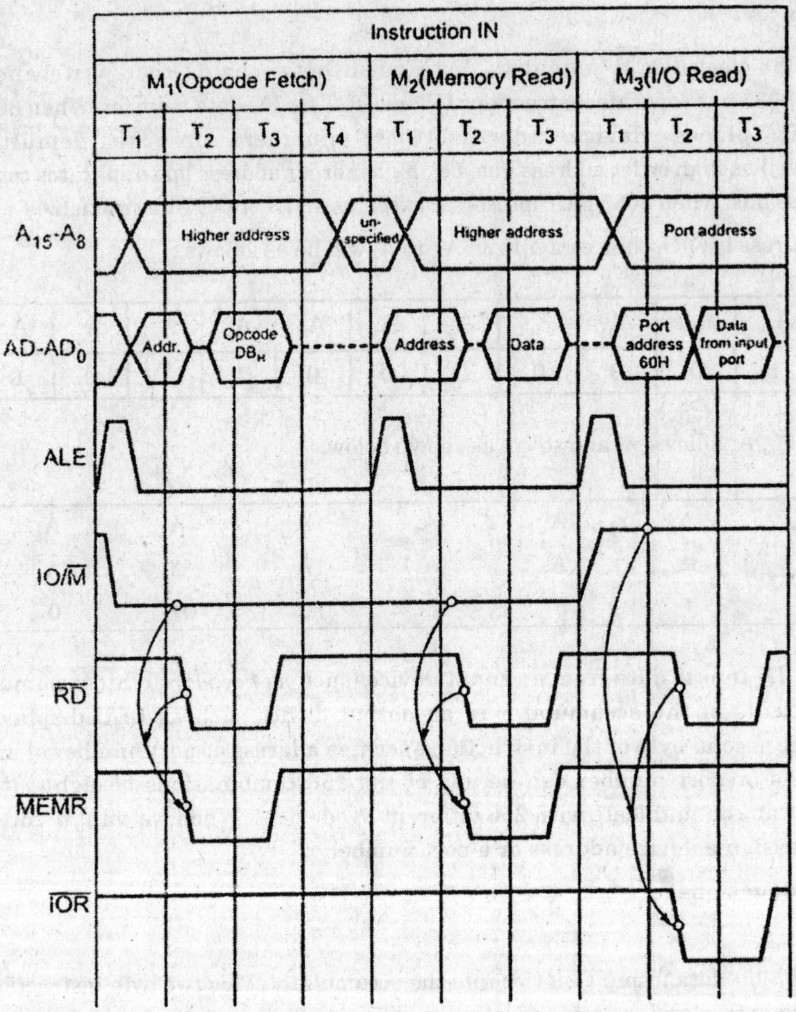

Fig. 4.109 Timing diagram for IN instruction

OUT :

It is used to send 8-bit data from accumulator to the output device.

This two byte instruction has first byte as an opcode, and

second byte specifies device address or a port number.

OUT addr : Send data to the output port.

Operation : (addr) ← A

Description : This instruction sends contents of accumulator to the output port whose address is specified within the instruction.

Example :

; A = 40H

OUT 50H ; This instruction will send the contents of accumulator

; (40H) to the output port whose address is 50H.

Fig. 4.110 shows timing diagram of OUT instruction. *It has three machine cycles.*

First machine cycle is an opcode fetch machine cycle, which reads the opcode of OUT instruction from the memory.

Second machine cycle is a memory read machine cycle. This machine cycle reads the address of the port.

Third machine cycle (I/O write), In this 8085 microprocessor places this address of the output port on the low-order address bus as well as on the high order address bus and asserts the $\overline{WR}$ signal.

During T_2 and T_3 of the I/O write machine cycle, $\overline{WR}$ and IO/$\overline{M}$ signals are 0 and 1 respectively, which activates $\overline{IOW}$ signal. The $\overline{IOW}$ signal enables output port and data from the accumulator is sent to the output port.

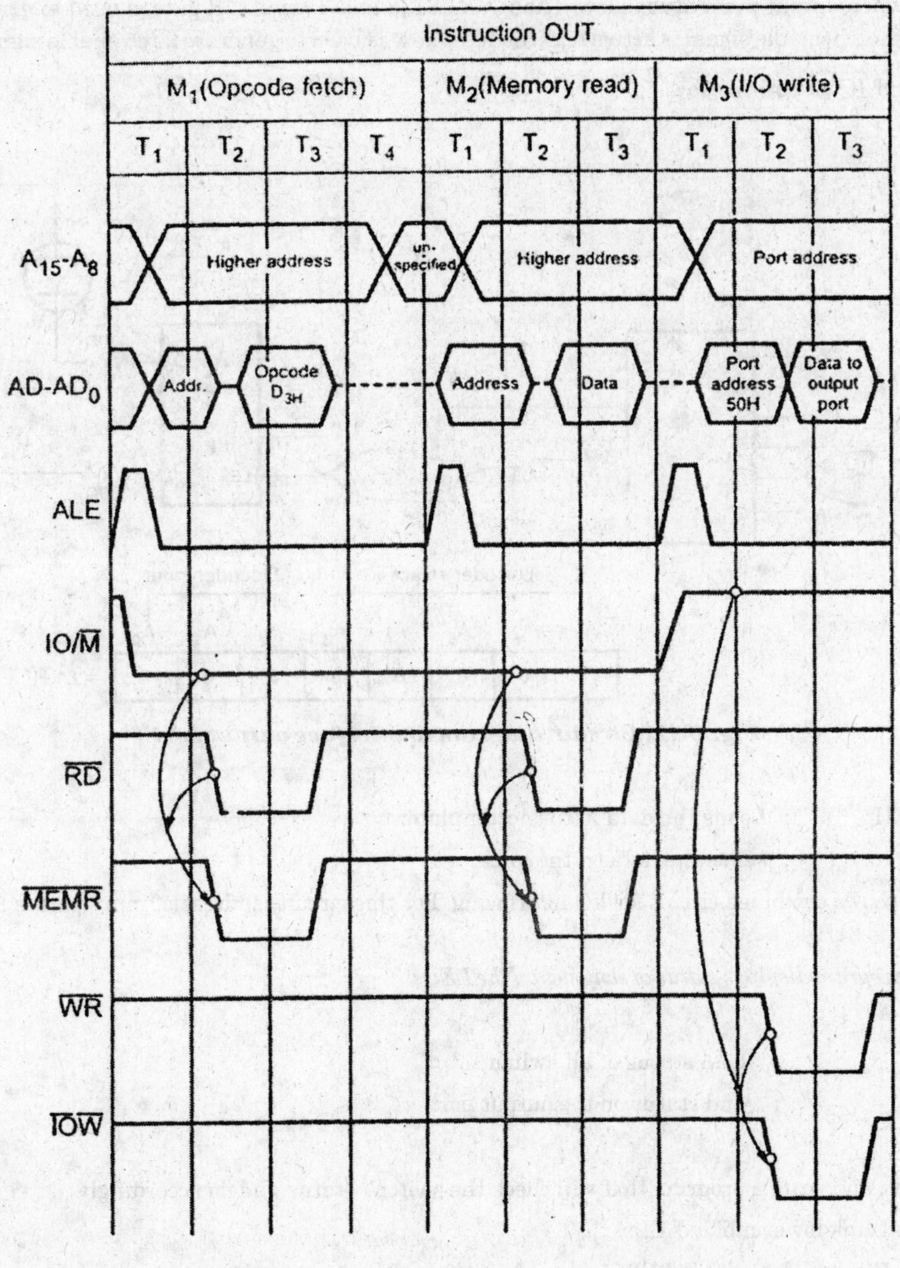

Fig. 4.110 Timing Diagram for OUT Instruction

Fig. 4.112 shows the absolute decoding circuit for the I/O device. The IC 74LS138, 3:8 decoder along with 3 input OR gate is used to generate device select signal. This signal is ORed with control signal ($\overline{IOR}$ or $\overline{IOW}$) to generate device enable signal.

To generate device select signal (Y_0) low, address on the address bus must be as given below :

$A_2\,A_1\,A_0$ = 000H ; Activates Y_0 output

$A_3\,A_4\,A_5\,A_6$ = 0000H ; Makes $\overline{G}_1$ and $\overline{G}_2$ low to enable output of decoder

A_7 = 1H ; Makes G high to enable output of decoder

Note : Decoder output is enabled only when control signals $\overline{G}_1$ and $\overline{G}_2$ are low and control signal G is high.

Interfacing Output Device.

The microprocessor 8085 sends 8 bit data to the output device such as 7 segment displays, LEDs, printer etc. Fig. 4.111 shows circuit diagram to interface output port (latch) which is used to send signal for glowing the LEDs. LED will glow when output pin status is low. The IC 74LS138 and 3 input OR gate is used to generate device select signal. The latch enable signal is active high. So NOR gate is used to generate latch enable signal, which goes high when Y_1 and $\overline{IOW}$ both are low.

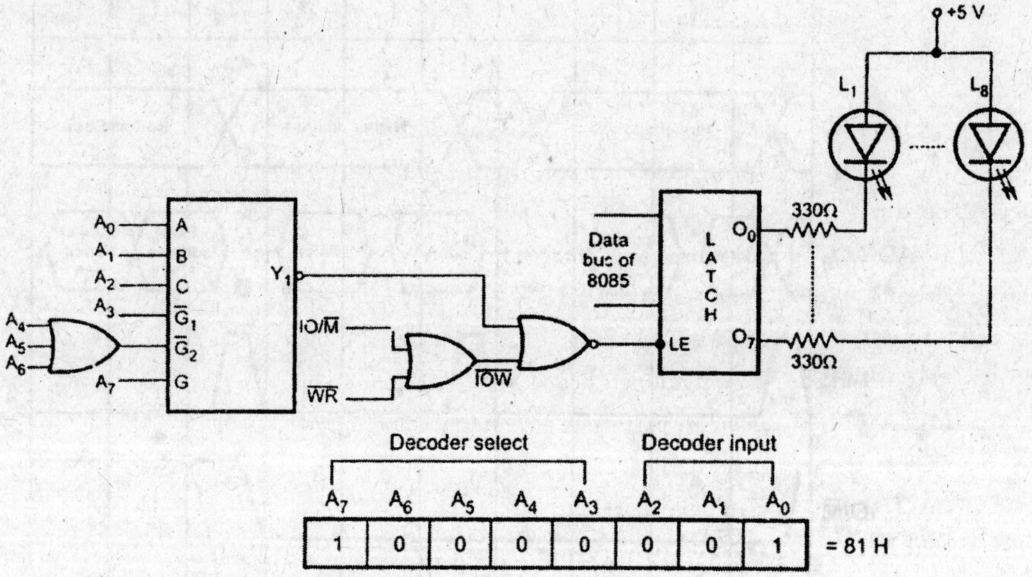

Fig. 4.111 Circuit diagram to interface output port

Program :

MVI A, DAH ; Loads the data in the accumulator.

OUT 81H ; sends the data on the latch.

Fig. 4.112 shows combined circuit for I/O interfacing. For this circuit, address of input port is 80H and address of output port is 81H.

Following program displays status of switches on the LEDs:

Program :

IN 80H ; Read status of all switches.

OUT 81H ; send status on the output port.

Example :

Fefer Figure and write a program that will check the switch1 status and do accordingly.

1. sw1 = 0 : Blink lower nibble LEDs.

2. sw1 = 1 : Blink higher nibble LEDs.

Assume delay routine is available.

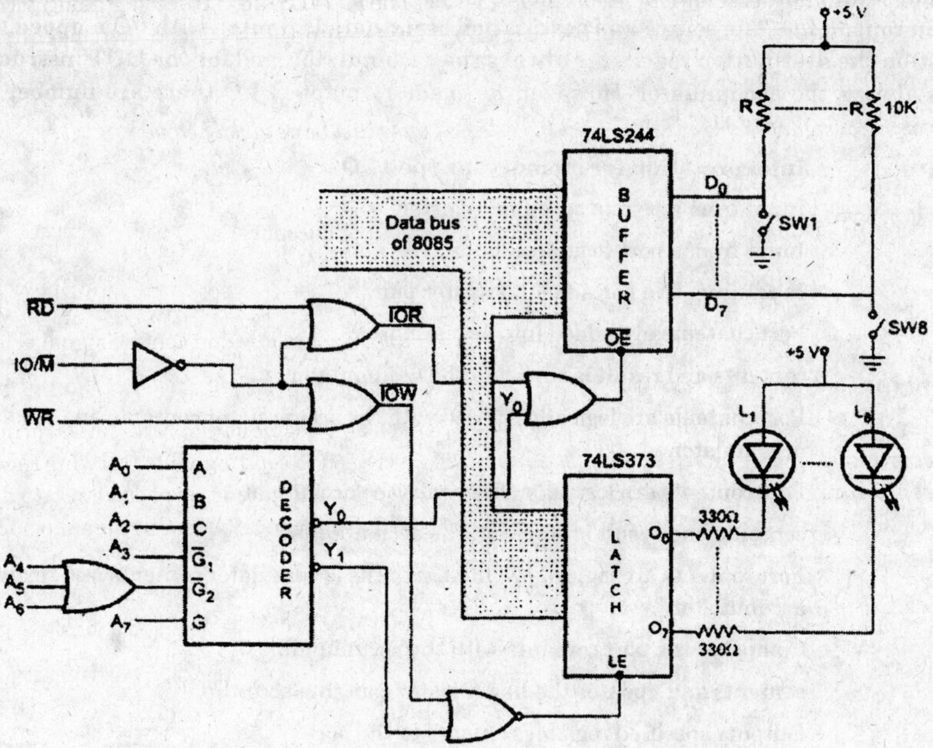

Fig. 4.112 I/O interfacing Using I/O Mapped I/O

Source Program :

```
        LXI SP, 27FFH ; Initialize stack pointer
START : IN 80H        ; Read status of switches
        ANI 01H       ; Masks Bit 1 to Bit 7
        JNZ HIGHER    ; If sw1 status is not zero go to blink higher nibble
        MVI A, F0H    ; Load bit pattern to glow lower nibble LEDs
        OUT 81H       ; Send it to output port
        CALL Delay    ; Call delay subroutine
        MVI A, FFH    ; Load bit pattern to switch off all LEDs
        OUT 81H       ; Send it to output port
        CALL Delay    ; Call delay subroutine
        JMP START     ; JUMP to START
HIGHER : MVI A, 0FH   ; Load bit pattern to glow higher nibble LEDs
        OUT 81H       ; Send it to output port
        CALL Delay    ; Call delay subroutine
        MVI A, FFH    ; Load bit pattern to switch off all LEDs
        OUT 81H       ; Send it to output port
        CALL Delay    ; Call delay subroutine
        JMP START     ; JUMP to START
```

2. Memory Mapped I/O

In memory mapped I/O, the I/O devices are assigned and identified by 16 bit addresses. The memory related instructions transfer the data between an I/O device and the microprocessor, as long as I/O port is assigned to the memory address space rather than to the I/O address space. The register associated with the I/O port is simply treated as a memory location. Thus I/O device becomes a part of the system's memory map and hence its name. In memory-mapped I/O every instruction that refers to a memory location can control I/O. The source and destination of the data is limited with I/O mapped I/O, since for an IN instruction the destination register is always the accumulator, and for the OUT instruction the source register is always the accumulator. However, for memory mapped I/O there are number of sources and destinations.

Instructions		**Interpretation for memory mapped I/O**
MOV r, M	;	Input from a port to specified register.
LDA addr	;	Input from a port to accumulator.
LHLD addr	;	Input from two ports to HL register pair.
ADD M	;	Port contents are added into accumulator
	;	contents and result is stored in the accumulator.
ANA M	;	Port contents are logically ANDed with the accumulator contents and result is stored in the accumulator.
ORA M	;	Port contents are logically ORed with the accumulator contents and result is stored in the accumulator.
XRA M	;	Port contents are logically XORed with the accumulator contents and result is stored in the accumulator.
CMP M	;	Compares the port contents with the accumulator contents and updates the flag register contents accordingly.
MOV M,r	;	Outputs specified register contents to the port.
STA addr	;	Outputs accumulator contents to the port.
SHLD addr	;	Outputs HL register contents to two ports.
MVI M, data	;	Outputs immediate data to the port.

Interfacing of I/O port with memory mapped I/O

In memory mapped I/O, $\overline{MEMR}$ (memory read) and $\overline{MEMW}$ (memory write) control signals are required to control data transfer between I/O device and microprocessor. As 8085 gives 16 bit memory address, it is necessary to decode 16 bit memory address to generate device select signal in case of memory mapped I/O.

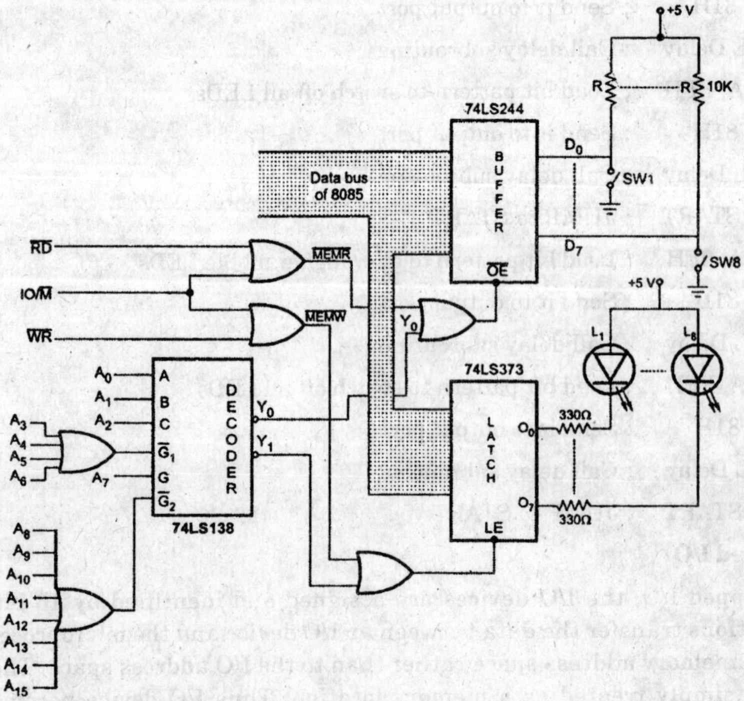

Fig. 4.113 I/O interfacing using memory mapped I/O

Comparison between Memory Mapped I/O and I/O Mapped I/O

Memory mapped I/O	I/O mapped I/O
1. In this device address is 16 bit. Thus A_0 to A_{15} lines are used to generate device address.	1. In this I/O device address is 8 bit. Thus A_0 to A_7 orA_8 to A_{15} lines are used to generate device address.
2. $\overline{MEMR}$ and $\overline{MEMW}$ control signals are used to control read and write I/O operations.	2. $\overline{IOR}$ and $\overline{IOW}$ control signals are used to control read and write I/O operations.
3. Instructions available are LDA addr, STA addr, LDAX rp, STAX rp, MOV M,R, MOV R,M ADD , M,CMP M etc.	3. Instructions available are IN and OUT.
4. Data transfer is between any register and I/O. device	4. Data transfer is between accumulator and I/O device.
5. Maximum number of I/O devices are 65536 (theoretically).	5. Maximum number of I/O devices are 256.
6. Exection speed using LDA addr, STA addr is 13 T-state & 7T-states for MOV M, r and MOV r, M instructions.	6. Execution speed is 10 T-states.
7. Decoding 16 bit address may require more hardware.	7. Decoding 8 bit address will require less hardware.

4.13. PERIPHERAL DEVICES

8255 - Programmable Peripheral Device

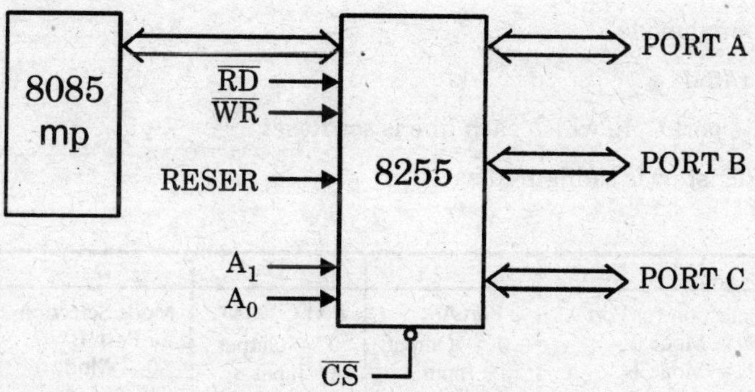

Fig. 4.114 Programmable Peripheral Device

Features of 8255

1. It is widely used, programmable, parallel I/O device.
2. It is compatible with all Intel and most other µp.
3. It is completely TTL compatible.
4. IC has 40 pin configuration.
5. *It has 3 basic ports.*
   (*a*) Port A - 8 bit
   (*b*) Port B - 8 bit
   (*c*) Port C - 8 bit
   Port C is further deviated in two parts.
   (*i*) Port C upper - 4 bit
   (*ii*) Port C lower - 4 bit

$\overline{CS}$	A_1	A_0	PORT
0	0	0	Port A
0	0	1	Port B
0	1	0	Port C
0	1	1	CWR
1	×	×	8255 is not selected.

6. Depending upon the control bit 2 basic modes will present in 8255:
   (*a*) I/O mode
   (*b*) BSR mode (Bit Set-Reset mode)
7. I/O modes have again 3 modes.
   (*a*) **Mode 0 :** Simple I/O
   - Port A, Port B, Port C upper and Port C lower can individually operated
   - Ports do not have hand shake or interrupt capability
   - Inputs are buffered, not latched
   - Output are tatchet

   (*b*) **Mode 1 :** Strobe I/O mode
   - Hand shaking modes
   - Port A and Port B are operated
   - To provide hand shaking signal, port C is used
   - Input and output data are latched
   - Interrupt logic is supported

   (*c*) **Mode 2 :** Bidirectional mode
   Only Port A is operated
8. BSR mode only operate port C, in which each line is set/Reset
9. CWR (Control Word Register) is configured as

D_7	D_6	D_5	D_4	D_3	D_2	D_1	D_0
Mode Select 0 – BSW 1 – I/O	Mode Selection for Port A 00 – Mode 0 01 – Mode 1 1X – Mode 2		Port A 0 – Output 1 – Input	Port C upper 0 – Output 1 – Input	Mode Selection for Port B 0 – Mode 0 1 – Mode 1	Port B 0 – Output 1 – Input	Port C lower 0 – Output 1 – Input

Other Peripheral Devices

8251 - Programmable Communication Interface (PCI)

8253/54 - Programmable Internal Timer (PIT)

8257/82357 - Direct Memory Access Controller (DMA controller)

8259 - Programmable Interrupt Controller (PIC)

8279 - Programmable Keyboard/Display Interface

OBJECTIVE TYPE QUESTIONS

BOOLEAN ALGEBRA AND LOGIC GATES

1. Boolean expression for the output of the logic circuit shown in the figure is

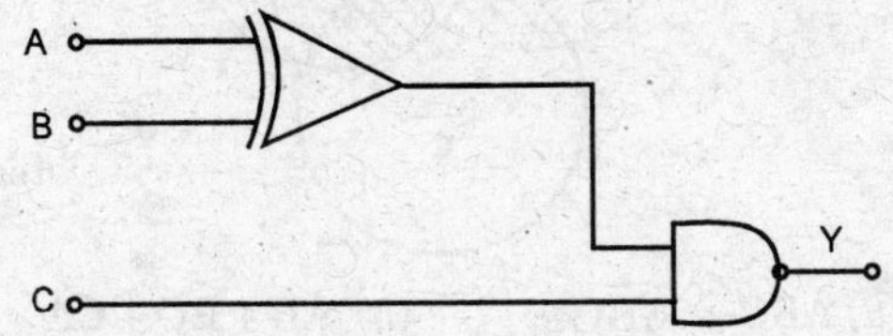

(*a*) $Y = AB + AB + C$

(*b*) $Y = \overline{A}\ \overline{B} + AB + \overline{C}$

(*c*) $Y = A\overline{B} + \overline{A}B + C$

(*d*) $Y = AB + \overline{A}B + \overline{C}$

2. A combinational circuit has inputs A, B and C and its Karnaugh Map is as shown. The output of the circuit is given by

C \ AB	00	01	11	10
0		1		1
1	1		1	

(*a*) $(\overline{A}B + A\overline{B})C$

(*b*) $(\overline{A}B + A\overline{B})\overline{C}$

(*c*) $\overline{A}\,\overline{B}\,\overline{C}$

(*d*) $A \oplus B \oplus C$

3. Assuming that only X and Y logic inputs are available and their complements $\overline{X}$ and $\overline{Y}$ are not available, then what is the minimum number of two-input nand gates require to implement $X \oplus Y$?

(*a*) 2 (*b*) 3

(*c*) 4 (*d*) 5

4. For the identity $AB + \overline{A}C + BC = AB + \overline{A}C$, the dual form is

(*a*) $(A+B)(\overline{A}+C)(B+C) = (A+B)(\overline{A}+C)$

(*b*) $(\overline{A}+\overline{B})(\overline{A}+\overline{C})(\overline{B}+\overline{C}) = (\overline{A}+\overline{B})(A+\overline{C})$

(*c*) $(A+B)(\overline{A}+C)(B+C) = (\overline{A}+\overline{B})(A+\overline{C})$

(*d*) $\overline{A}\,\overline{B} + A\overline{C} + \overline{B}\,\overline{C} = \overline{A}\,\overline{B} + A\overline{C}$

5. The logical expression $Y = A + \overline{A}B$ is equivalent to

(*a*) $Y = AB$ (*b*) $Y = A\overline{B}$

(*c*) $Y = \overline{A} + B$ (*d*) $Y = A + B$

6. Minterms coresponding to decimal number 15 is

(*a*) ABCD (*b*) $\overline{A}\,\overline{B}\,\overline{C}\,\overline{D}$

(*c*) $A + B + C + D$ (*d*) $\overline{A} + \overline{B} + \overline{C} + \overline{D}$

7. Minimized expression for the K-map shown below is

00		1		
01				
11	1	1	1	
10			1	

(*a*) $\overline{A}\,B\,\overline{C}\ \overline{D} + \overline{A}\,CD$

(*b*) $\overline{A}\,B\,\overline{C}\ \overline{D} + \overline{A}\ CD + ABC$

(*c*) $B\,\overline{C}\ \overline{D} + CD + \overline{A}\ BC$

(*d*) $B\,\overline{C}\ \overline{D} + CD + BC$

8. The dual of the Boolean theorem

A. (B + C) = A.B + A.C is

(*a*) A + (B + C) = A.B + A.C

(*b*) A. (B + C) = (A + B) (A + C)

(*c*) A + B.C = (A + B) (A + C)

(*d*) None of these

9. Boolean expression for the output of XNOR (Equivalent) logic gate with inputs A and B, is

(*a*) $A\overline{B} + \overline{A}B$ (*b*) $\overline{A}\,\overline{B} + AB$

(*c*) $(\overline{A} + B)(A + \overline{B})$ (*d*) $(\overline{A} + \overline{B})(A + B)$.

10. The output of a logic gate is '1' when all its inputs are at logic '0'. The gate is either

(*a*) NAND or EX-OR gate

(*b*) NOR or EX-NOR gate

(*c*) OR or EX-NOR gate

(*d*) AND or EX-OR gate

11. The gate shown in the figure is

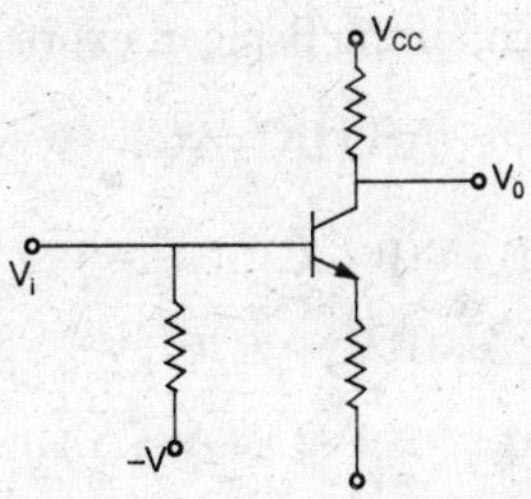

(*a*) AND gate (*b*) NAND gate

(*c*) NOT gate (*d*) OR gate

12. When signed numbers are used in binary arithmetic, then which of the following notations would have unique representation for zero ?

(*a*) Sign-magnitude

(*b*) 1's complement

(*c*) 2's complement

(*d*) 9's complement

13. The logic circuit given below converts a binary code Y_1 Y_2 Y_3 into

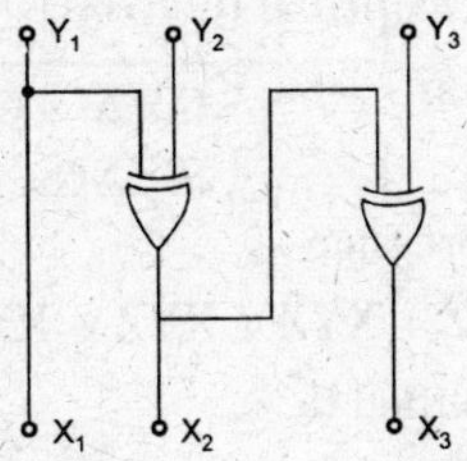

(*a*) Excess-3 code (*b*) Gray code

(*c*) BCD code (*d*) Hamming code

14. The minimum Boolean expression for the given circuit is

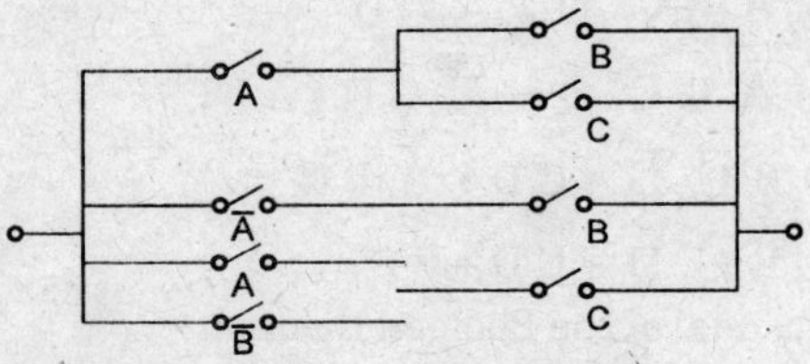

(a) AB + AC + BC (b) A + BC

(c) A + B (d) A + B + C

15. Venn diagram representing the Boolean expression $A + (\bar{A} . B)$ is

(a)

(b)

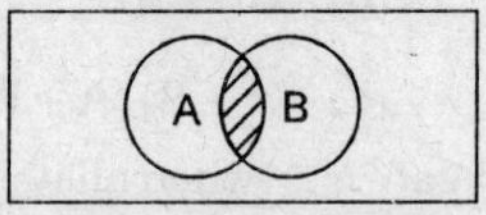

(c)

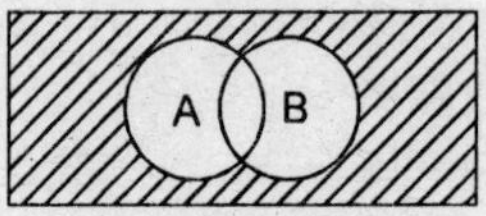

(d)

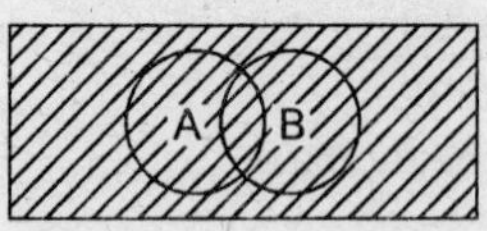

16. Complement of the Boolean expression

$$AB.(\bar{B}C+AC) \text{ is}$$

(a) $(\bar{A} + \bar{B}) + (B + \bar{C}).(\bar{A} + \bar{C})$

(b) $(\bar{A} . \bar{B}) + (B\bar{C} + \bar{A}\bar{C})$

(c) $(\bar{A} + \bar{B}).(B + \bar{C}).(\bar{A} + \bar{C})$

(d) $(A + B).(\bar{B} + C).(A + C)$

17. The logic function $f = \overline{(x . \bar{y}) + (\bar{x} . y)}$ is the same as

(a) $f = (x + y)(\bar{x} + \bar{y})$ (b) $f = \bar{x}\,\bar{y} + xy$

(c) $f = \overline{(x . y)} . (\bar{x} . \bar{y})$ (d) none of these

18. The minimal product-of-sums function described by the K-map given in the figure is, ϕ don't care

C \ AB	00	01	11	10
0	1	1	ϕ	0
1	0	0	ϕ	0

(a) A′C′ (b) A′ + C′

(c) A + C (d) AC

19. Boolean expression

$$\bar{X}Y\bar{Z} + \bar{X}\bar{Y}Z + XY\bar{Z} + X\bar{Y}Z + XYZ$$

can be simplified to

(a) $X\bar{Z} + \bar{X}Z + YZ$ (b) $XZ + \bar{Y}Z + Y\bar{Z}$

(c) $\bar{X}Y + YZ + XZ$ (d) $\bar{X}Y + Y\bar{Z} + \bar{X}Z$

20. Boolean expression for shaded area is

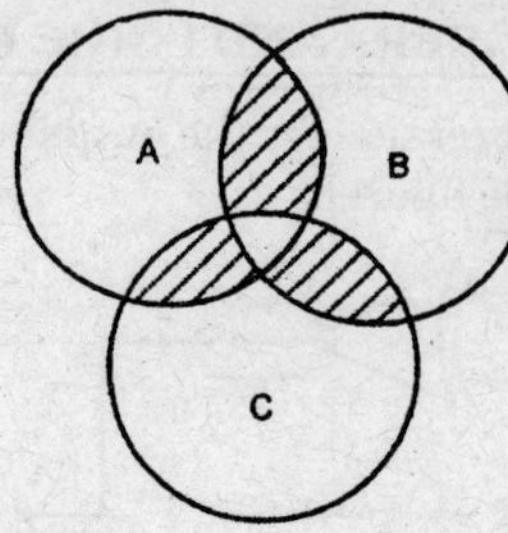

(a) $ABC + \overline{ABC}$ (b) AB + BC + CA

(c) $AB\bar{C} + A\bar{B}C + \bar{A}BC$ (d) $AB\bar{C} + \bar{A}B\bar{C} + \overline{ABC}$

21. Boolean expression for shaded area is

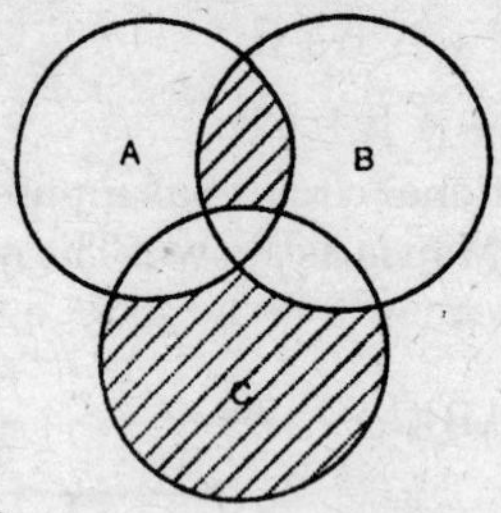

(a) $AB + \bar{B}\,\bar{C}$ (b) $ABC + A\bar{B}\,\bar{C}$

(c) $AB\bar{C} + \bar{A}BC + \bar{A}BC$ (d) $\bar{A}\,\bar{B}C + AB$

22. In the circuit shown in figure, value of input p goes from 0 → 1 and that of goes from 1 → 0. Which output forms shown in figure represents the output under a static hazard conditions ?

(a)

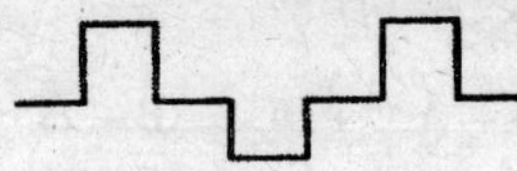

(b)

(c)

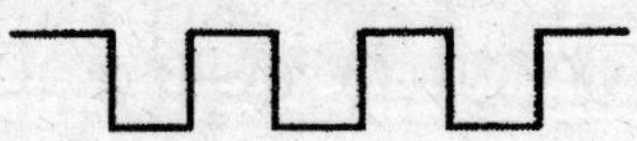

(d)

23. The maximized expression for the given K-map is (X : don't care)

CD \ AB	00	01	11	10
00		1	1	
01		1	X	
11	1	1	X	X
10	1		X	X

(a) $\bar{C}\bar{B} + BD + CD$ (b) $AB + C\bar{B} + B\bar{C}$

(c) $C\bar{B} + AC + B\bar{C}$ (d) $\bar{C}B + CD + C\bar{B}$

24. In figure shown below, $x_2 x_1 x_0$ will be 1's complement of $A_2 A_1 A_0$ if

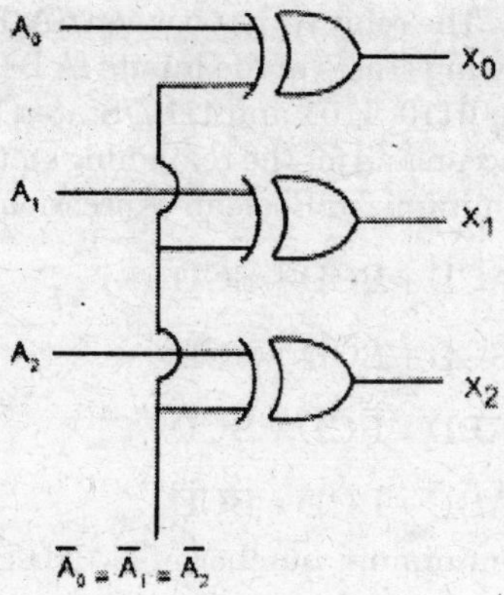

(a) Y = 0 (b) Y = 1

(c) $Y = \overline{A}_0 = \overline{A}_1 = \overline{A}_2$ (d) $Y = A_0 = A_1 = A_2$

25. The circuit of a gate in the resistor transistor logic (RTL) family shown in the given figure is a/an

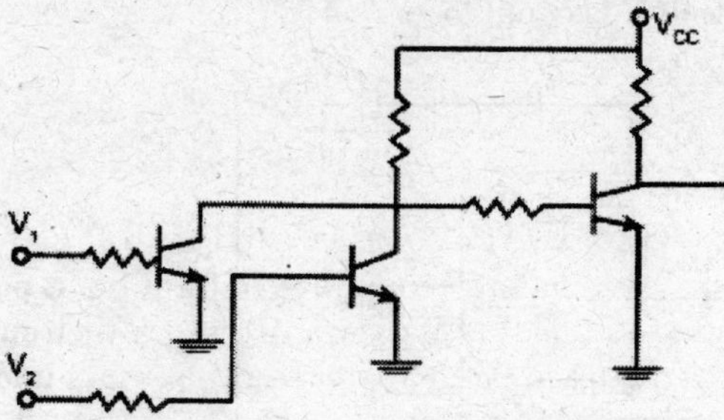

(a) AND gate (b) OR gate

(c) NAND gate (d) NOR gate

26. K-map for a Boolean function is shown in the figure. The function would be

wx \ yz	00	01	11	10
00		1	1	
01	1	1	1	1
11			1	1
10			1	

(a) $(x + \overline{z})(w + y)$ (b) $(x + z)(\overline{w} + y)$

(c) $(\overline{x} + \overline{z})(w + \overline{y})$ (d) none of these

27. For the K-map shown in figure, the minimized function in SOP form is :

WX \ YZ	00	01	11	10
00	1	1		1
01				
11			1	1
10	1		1	1

(a) $\overline{W}\,\overline{X}\,\overline{Y} + WY + \overline{X}YZ + \overline{W}\,\overline{X}\,\overline{Z}$

(b) $\overline{W}\,\overline{X}\,\overline{Y} + \overline{X}\,\overline{Z} + WY$

(c) $\overline{W}\,\overline{X}\,\overline{Y} + WY + \overline{W}\,\overline{X}Y\overline{Z} + W\overline{X}\,\overline{Y}\,\overline{Z}$

(d) $\overline{W}\,\overline{X}\,\overline{Y} + WY + \overline{W}\,\overline{X}\,\overline{Z}$

28. It is desired to generate the following three Boolean functions :

$$f_1 = a\overline{b}c + \overline{a}b\overline{c} + bc$$

$$f_2 = a\overline{b}c + ab + \overline{a}b\overline{c}$$

$$f_3 = \overline{a}\,\overline{b}\,\overline{c} + abc + \overline{a}c$$

by using an OR gate array as shown in figure, where P_1 and P_5 are product terms in one or more of the variable $a, \overline{a}, b, \overline{b}, c$ and $\overline{c}$.

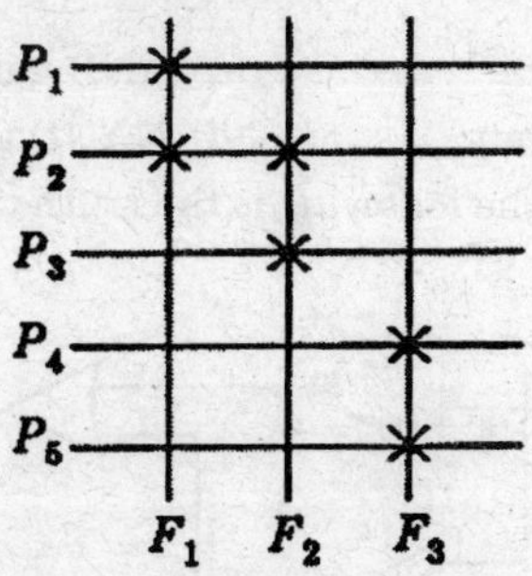

The terms P_1, P_2, P_3, P_4 and P_5 are

(a) $\overline{a}b,\ ac,\ b\overline{c},\ bc,\ \overline{a}\,\overline{b}$

(b) $a\overline{b},\ b\overline{c},\ ac,\ \overline{a}\,\overline{b}\ bc$

(c) $ac, \overline{a}b, b\overline{c},\ \overline{a}\,\overline{b},\ bc$

(d) all of these

29. The circuit shown in the figure converts

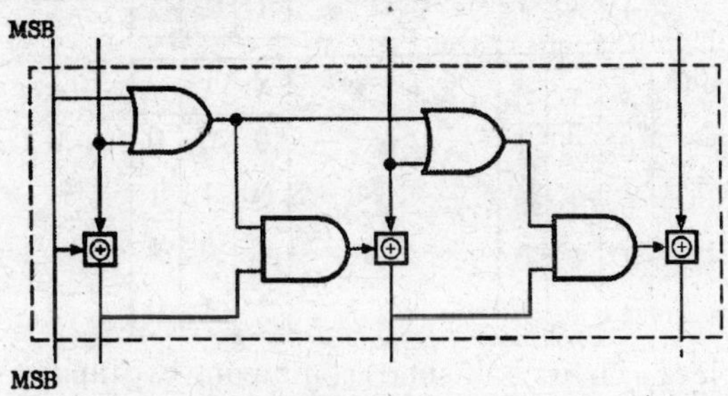

(a) BCD to binary code

(b) Binary to excess

(c) Excess-3 to Gray Code

(d) Gray to Binary code

COMBINATIONAL LOGIC CIRCUIT

30. The switching circuit given in the figure can be expressed in binary logic notation as

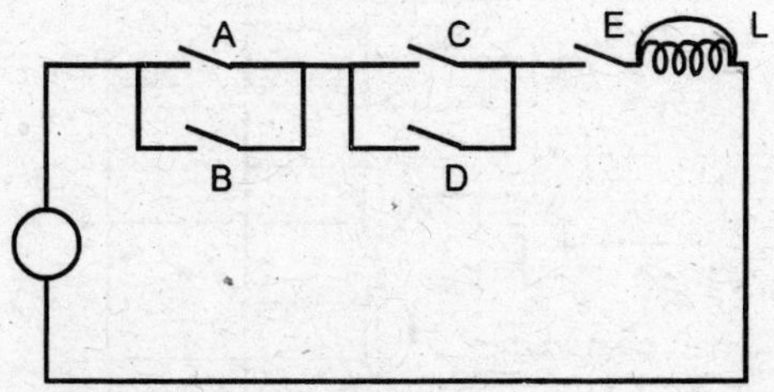

(a) L = (A + B) (C + D) E

(b) L = AB + CD + E

(c) L = E + (A + B) (C + D)

(d) L = (AB + CD) E

31. If negative logic is used, diode gate shown in the given figure will represent a/an

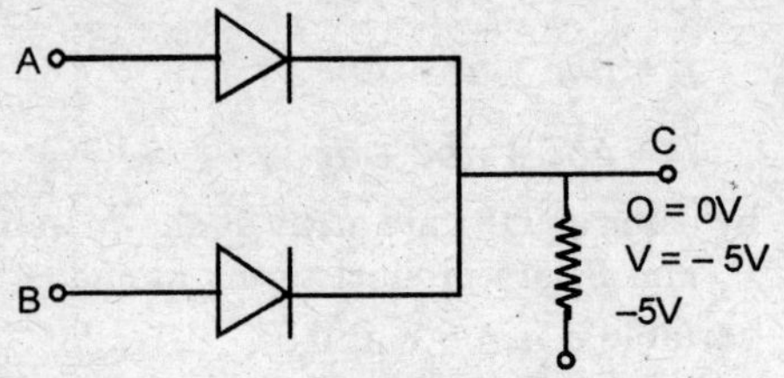

(*a*) OR gate (*b*) AND gate
(*c*) NOR gate (*d*) NAND gate

32. Which of the following is the truth table of the given logic is true ?

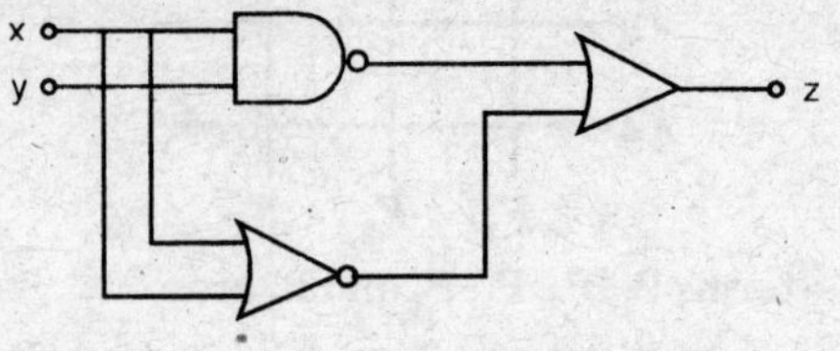

(*a*)

x	y	z
0	0	1
0	1	1
1	0	1
1	1	1

(*b*)

x	y	z
0	0	0
0	1	1
1	0	1
1	1	1

(*c*)

x	y	z
0	0	1
0	1	0
1	0	0
1	1	0

(*d*)

x	y	z
0	0	0
0	1	1
1	0	1
1	1	0

33. For a binary half-subtractor having two inputs A and B, correct set of logical expression for the outputs D (= A minimum B) and X (= borrow) are

(*a*) $D = AB + \overline{A}\,B, X = \overline{A}\,B$

(*b*) $D = \overline{A}\,B + A\overline{B}, X = A\overline{B}$

(*c*) $D = \overline{A}\,B + A\overline{B}, X = \overline{A}\,B$

(*d*) $D = AB + \overline{A}\,\overline{B}, X = A\overline{B}$

34. The circuit shown in the given figure is a/an

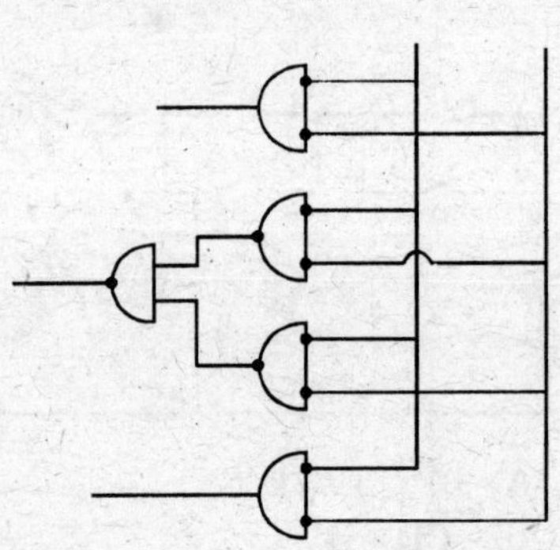

(*a*) adder (*b*) subtractor
(*c*) parity generator (*d*) comparator

35. In a certain application four inputs A, B, C, D are fed to logic circuit, producing an output which operates a relay. The relay turns on when *f*(A, B, C, D) = 1 for the following states of the inputs (A B C D) : 0000, 0010, 0101, 0110, 1101 and 1110. States 1000 and 1001 do not occur, and for the remaining states the relay is off. The minimized Boolean expression f is

(*a*) $\overline{A}C\overline{D} + BC\overline{D} + B\overline{C}D$

(*b*) $\overline{B}\overline{C}D + BC\overline{D} + \overline{A}C\overline{D}$

(*c*) $ABD + \overline{B}C\overline{D} + \overline{B}\overline{C}D$

(*d*) $\overline{A}\overline{B}\overline{D} + B\overline{C}D + BC\overline{D}$

36. The minimum number of NAND gates required to implement $A + A\overline{B} + A\overline{B}C$ is equal to

(*a*) zero (*b*) 1
(*c*) 4 (*d*) 7

37. For the logic circuit shown in the figure below, the output Y is equal to

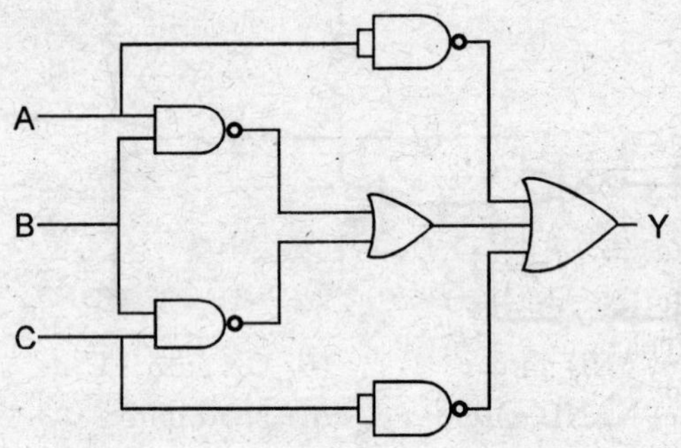

(*a*) $\overline{ABC}$ (*b*) $\overline{A} + \overline{B} + \overline{C}$

(*c*) $\overline{AB} + \overline{BC} + \overline{A} + \overline{C}$ (*d*) $\overline{AB} + \overline{BC}$

38. Output of the circuit shown in the figure is equal to

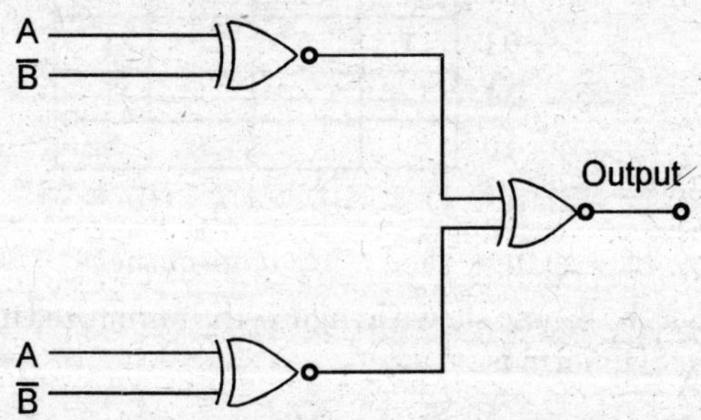

(*a*) 0

(*b*) 1

(*c*) $\overline{A}\,B + A\,\overline{B}$

(*d*) $\overline{(A*B)} * \overline{(A*B)}$

39. A carry look ahead adder is frequently used for addition because it

(*a*) is faster

(*b*) is more accurate

(*c*) uses fewer gates

(*d*) costs less

40. In the given network of AND and OR gates, f can be written as

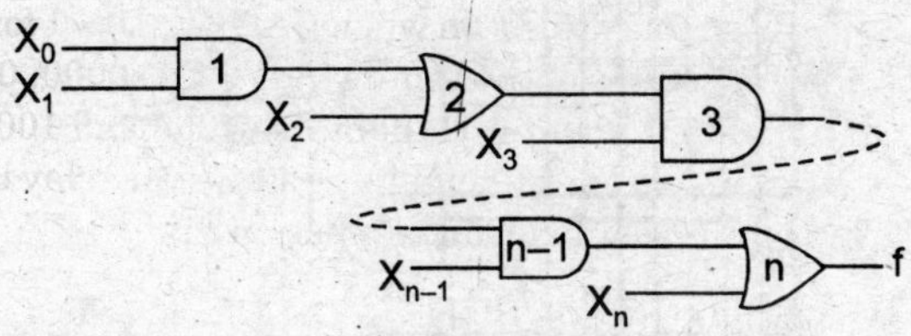

(a) $x_0 x_1 x_2 \ldots x_n + x_1 x_2 \ldots x_n + x_2 x_3 \ldots x_n \ldots . x_n$
(b) $x_0 x_1 + x_2 x_3 + \ldots + x_{n-1} . x_n$
(c) $x_0 + x_1 + x_2 + \ldots + x_n$
(d) $x_0 x_1 x_3 \ldots x_{n-1} + x_2 x_3 x_5 \ldots x_{n-1} + \ldots + x_{n-2} x_{n-1} + x_n$

41. Output Y of the circuit shown in the figure is

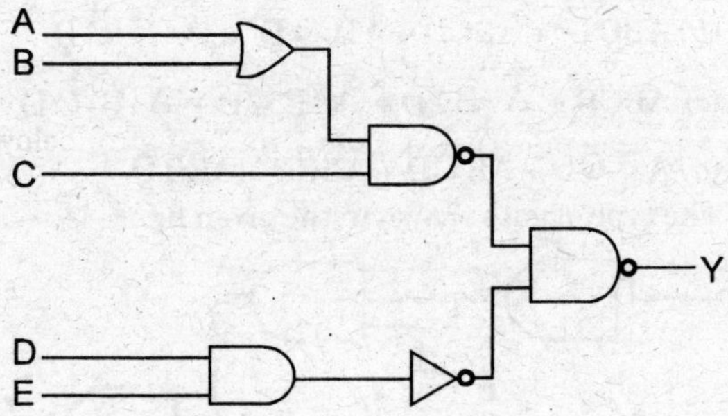

(a) (A + B) C + DE (b) AB + C (D + E)
(c) (A + B) C + D + E (d) (AB + C) . DE

42. The figure given below shows the circuit of which one of the following is

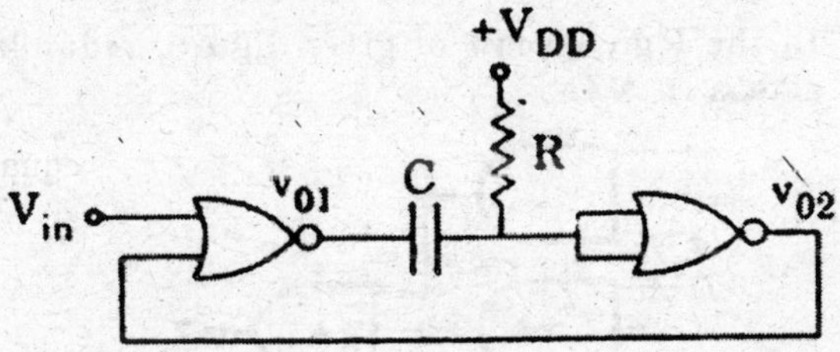

(a) Bi-stable multi-vibrator
(b) Schmitt trigger
(c) Mono-stable multi-vibrator
(d) Astable multi-vibrator

43. A full-adder can be implemented with half-adders and OR gates. A 4-bit parallel full adder without any initial carry requires
(a) 8 half-adders, 4-OR gates
(b) 8 half-adders, 3-OR gates
(c) 7 half-adders, 4-OR gates
(d) 7 half-adders, 3-OR gates

44. A four-variable switching function has minterms m_6 and m_9. If literals in these minterms are complemented, then corresponding minterm numbers are
(a) m_3 and m_0 (b) m_9 and m_6
(c) m_2 and m_0 (d) m_6 and m_9

45. For the gate network shown in the figure below, which of the following gate is redundant?

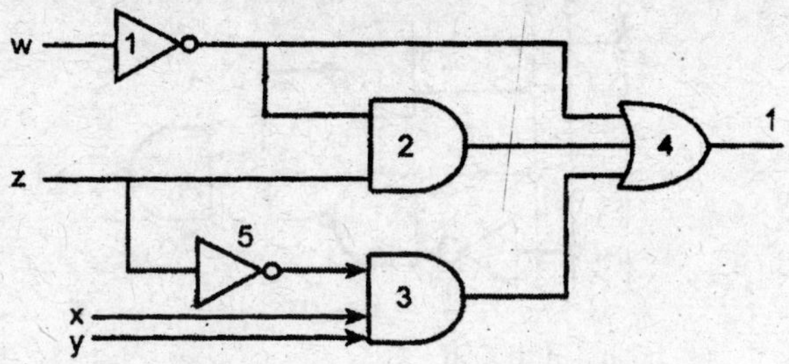

(a) Gate No-1 (b) Gate No-2
(c) Gate No-3 (d) Gate No-4

46. In the logic circuit shown in the figure, output X is

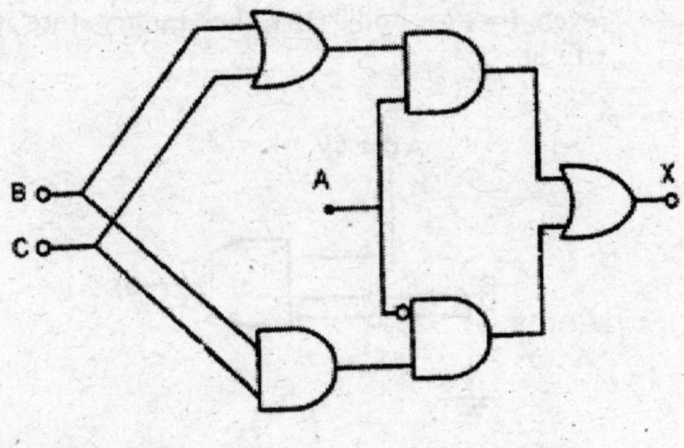

(a) $A\overline{B} + B\overline{C} + C\overline{A}$
(b) A + B + C
(c) AB + BC + CA
(d) $\overline{AB} + \overline{BC} + \overline{CA}$

47. Consider the following expressions
1. $Y = f(A, B, C, D) = \Sigma(1, 2, 4, 7, 8, 11, 13, 14)$
2. $Y = f(A, B, C, D) = \Sigma(3, 5, 7, 10, 11, 12, 13, 14)$
3. $Y = f(A, B, C, D) = \pi(0, 3, 5, 6, 9, 10, 12, 15)$
4. $Y = f(A, B, C, D) = \pi(0, 1, 2, 4, 5, 8, 9, 15)$

Which of these expressions are equivalent to the expression $Y = A \oplus B \oplus C \oplus D$?
(a) 2 and 3 (b) 1 and 4
(c) 2 and 4 (d) 1 and 3

48. For the circuit shown in figure

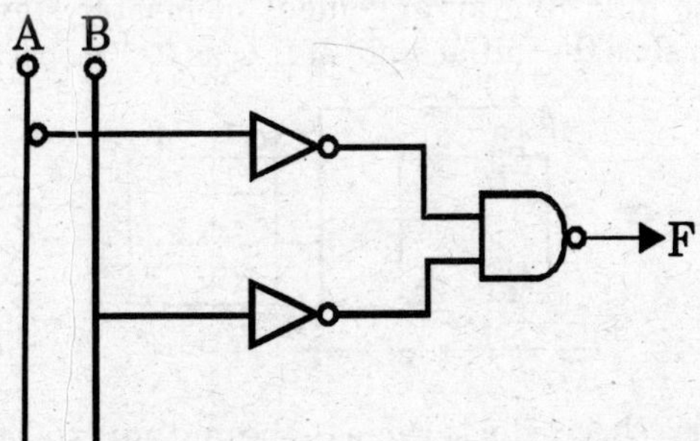

(a) F = A + B (b) F = AB
(c) $F = \overline{A} + \overline{B}$ (d) $F = \overline{AB}$

49. For the circuit shown in figure, output F = 0, when

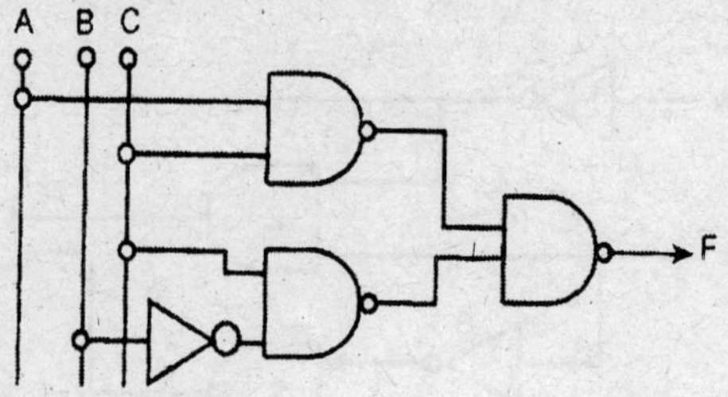

(*a*) both f_2 and f_3 are 1
(*b*) both f_2 and f_3 are 0
(*c*) f_2 is 1 and f_3 is zero
(*d*) f_2 is 1 and f_3 is one

50. A three input AND gate is shown in the figure. If circuit works off the positive voltage made logic with logic levels 1 = + 5 V and 0 = 0V, then binary state of output will be

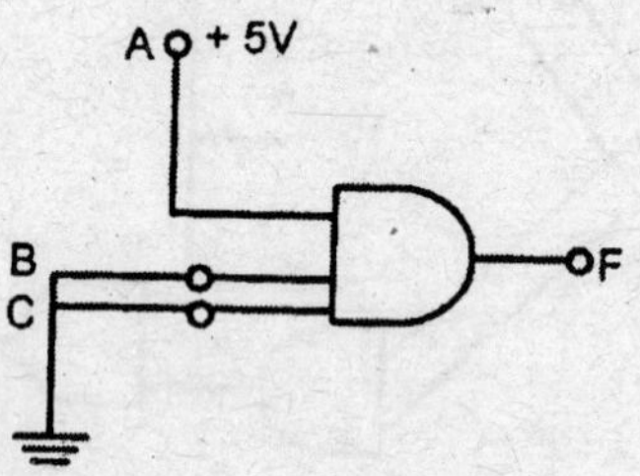

(*a*) F = 1 (*b*) F = 0
(*c*) F = 100 (*d*) F = 011

51. For the circuit shown in the figure below, what is the frequency of the output Q ?

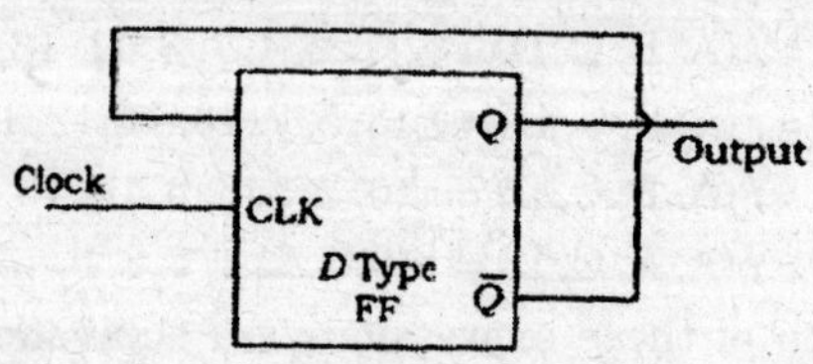

(*a*) Twice the input clock frequency
(*b*) Half the input clock frequency
(*c*) Same as the input clock frequency
(*d*) Inverse of the propagation delay of the FF

52. The following arrangement of master-slave flip flopshas the initial state of P, Q as 0, 1 respectively.

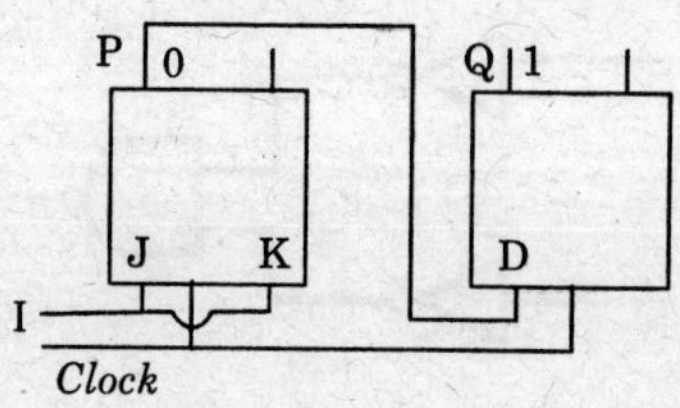

After three clock cycles, the output state P, Q respectively are
(*a*) 1,0 (*b*) 1,1
(*c*) 0,0 (*d*) 0,1

53. The output of the circuit will be

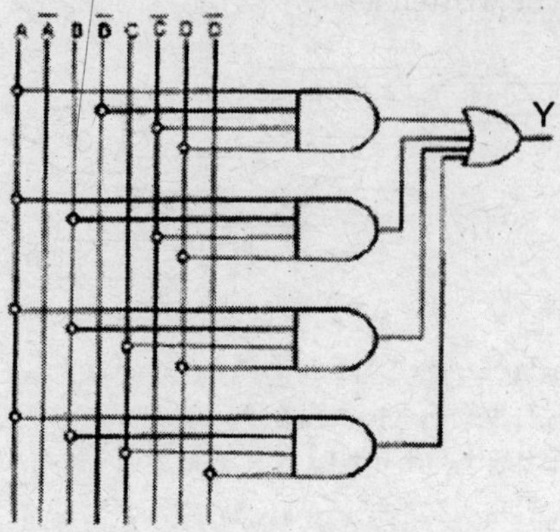

(*a*) ABC$\overline{D}$ + $\overline{A}$BC$\overline{D}$ + A$\overline{B}$C$\overline{D}$ + $\overline{A}$ $\overline{B}$ $\overline{C}$DD
(*b*) ABC$\overline{D}$ + ABCD + A$\overline{B}\,\overline{C}\,\overline{D}$ + $\overline{A}$ $\overline{B}$ $\overline{CD}$
(*c*) ABCD + $\overline{A}$ $\overline{B}$CD + $\overline{A}$ $\overline{B}$ $\overline{C}$D + $\overline{A}$ $\overline{B}$ $\overline{CD}$
(*d*) A$\overline{B}\,\overline{C}$D + AB$\overline{C}$D + ABCD + ABC$\overline{D}$

54. The type of gate shown in the given figure is

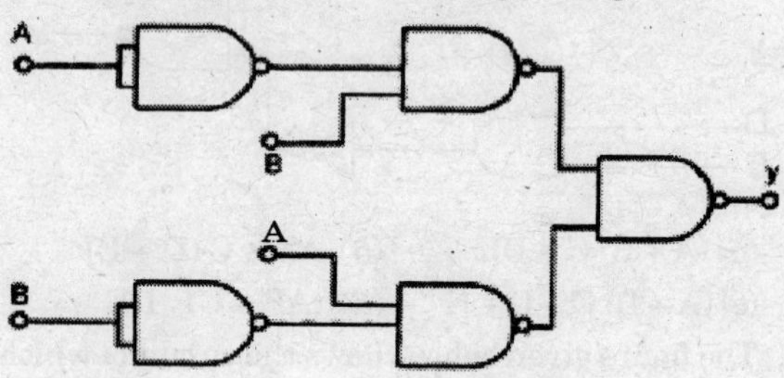

(*a*) NOR (*b*) OR
(*c*) NAND (*d*) EX-OR

55. In the logic circuit of given figure, redundant gate is

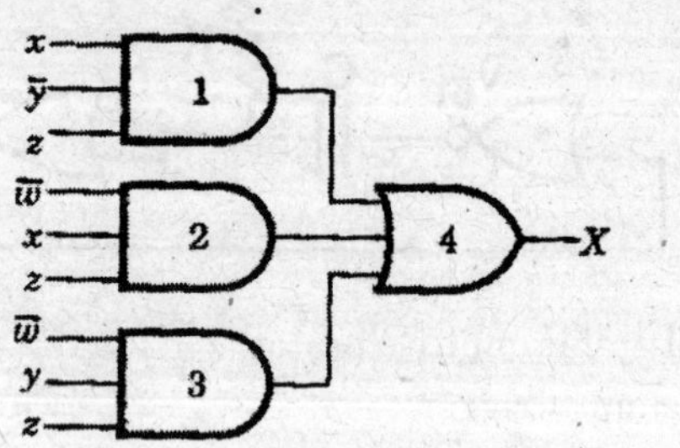

(*a*) 1 (*b*) 2
(*c*) 3 (*d*) 4

56. The input pulses to the different stages of the circuits shown in the following figure must be of

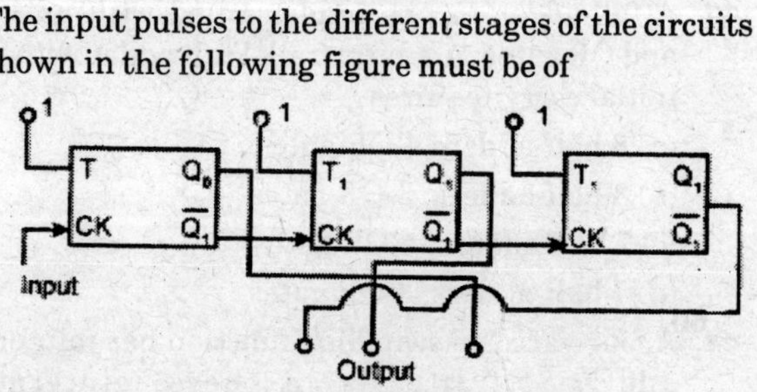

(*a*) constant frequency and constant width
(*b*) constant frequency bit variable width
(*c*) variable frequency bit constant width
(*d*) variable frequency as well as variable width

57. The output y for the logic circuit shown in the given figure is

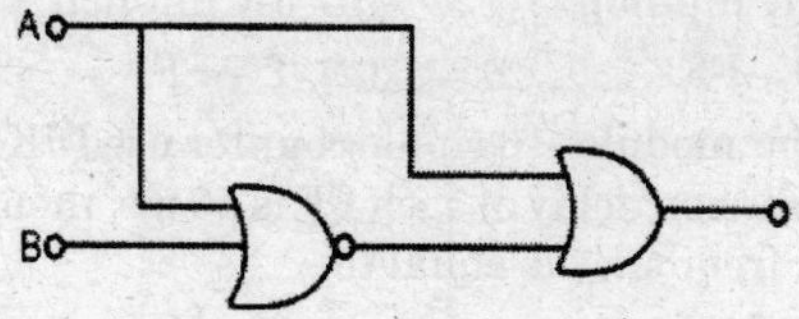

(*a*) $A\overline{B}$ (*b*) $\overline{A} + \overline{B}$

(*c*) $\overline{A} + \overline{B}$ (*d*) $A + \overline{B}$

58. The half adder circuit, in the given figure has inputs AB = 11. The logic level of P and Q outputs will be

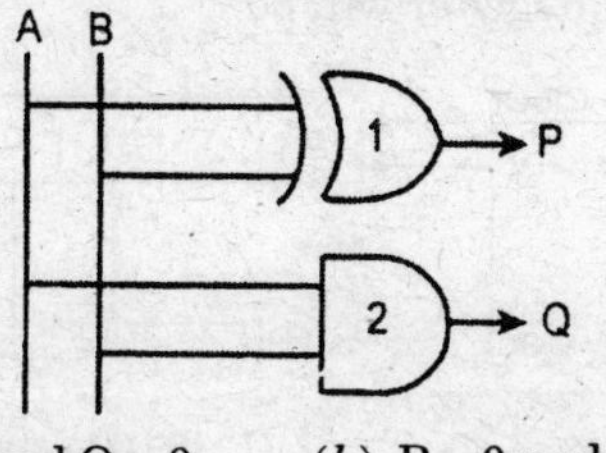

(*a*) P = 0 and Q = 0 (*b*) P = 0 and Q = 1

(*c*) P = 1 and Q = 0 (*d*) P = 1 and Q = 1

59. For the comparator circuit shown in figure forward diode voltage drop is V_y = 0.7 V and reverse Zener diode voltage is 5.6 V. If hysteresis width is 1 V, then value of R_2 is

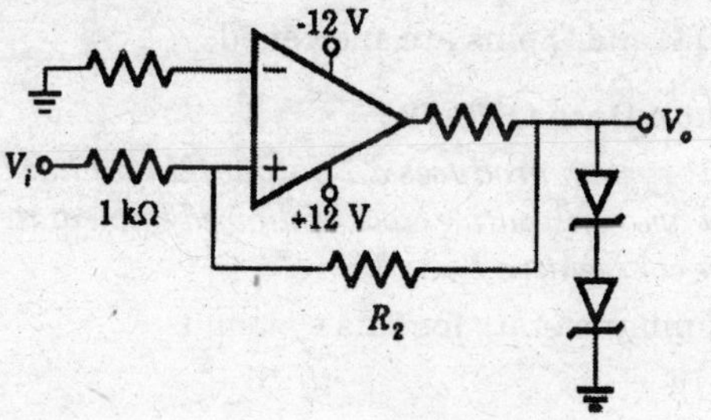

(*a*) 4 kΩ (*b*) 12.6 kΩ

(*c*) 2 kΩ (*d*) 6.3 kΩ

Statement for Q. 60–61.

Consider the regenerative comparator circuit shown in figure. Two Zener diodes are identical with $Vz_1 = Vz_2 = V_z = 4.6$ V. The voltage across conducting diode is 0.6 V.

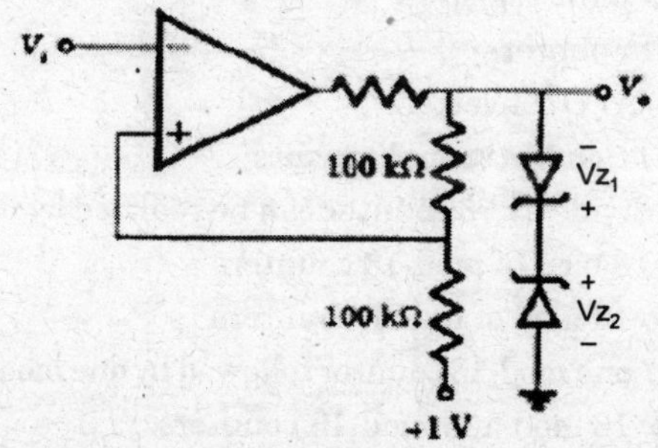

60. Upper threshold voltage is

(*a*) 0.9912 V (*b*) 1.0042 V

(*c*) 1.0094 V (*d*) 0.9938 V

61. Lower threshold voltage is

(*a*) 0.9932 V (*b*) 0.9938 V

(*c*) 1.0012 V (*d*) 1.0056 V

SEQUENTIAL LOGIC CIRCUIT

62. For the digital circuit shown in figure, the output $Q_3Q_2Q_1Q_0$ = 0001 initially. After a clock pulse appear, the output $Q_3Q_2Q_1Q_0$ will be

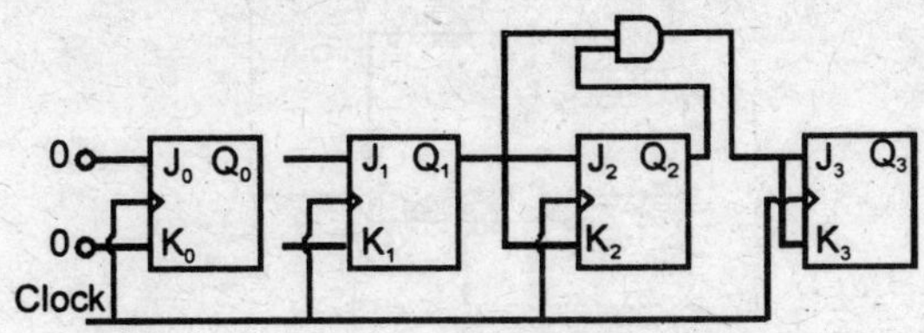

(*a*) 0001 (*b*) 0011

(*c*) 0100 (*d*) 1100

63. The output Q_n of a J-K flip-flop is zero. It change to 1 when a clock pulse is applied. The input J_n and K_n are respectively

(*a*) 1 and X (*b*) 0 and X

(*c*) X and 0 (*d*) X and 1

64. To realise the given truth table from the circuit shown in the figure, the input to J in terms of A and B would have to be

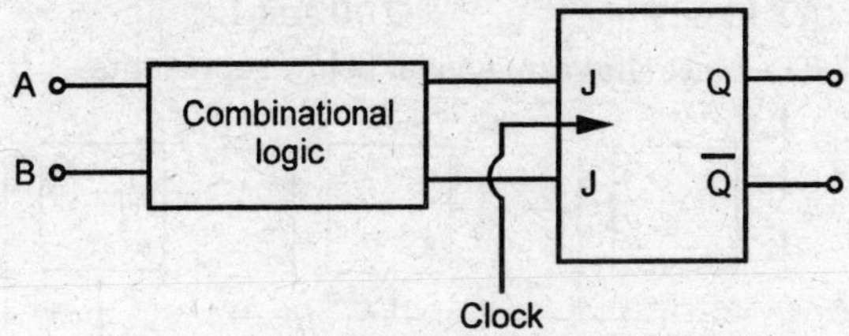

Truth Table

A	B	Q_{n+1}	J
0	0	Q_n	0
0	1	1	1
1	0	Q_n	0
1	1	0	X

(*a*) $\overline{AB}$ (*b*) $\overline{A}$

(*c*) B (*d*) AB

65. The circuit given in the figure is to be used to implement the function

$$Z = f(A, B) = \overline{A} + B.$$

what values should be selected for I and J ?

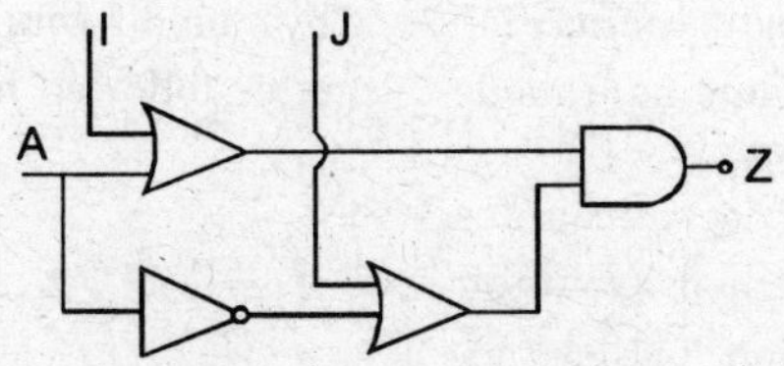

(*a*) I = 0 J = B

(*b*) I = 1 J = B

(*c*) I = B J = 1

(*d*) I = $\overline{B}$ J = 0

66. In a JK flip–flop we have $J = \overline{Q}$ and $K = 1$. Assuming the flip-flop was initially cleared and then clocked for 6 pulses, the sequence at the Q, then clock for 6 pulses, the sequence at the Q output will be

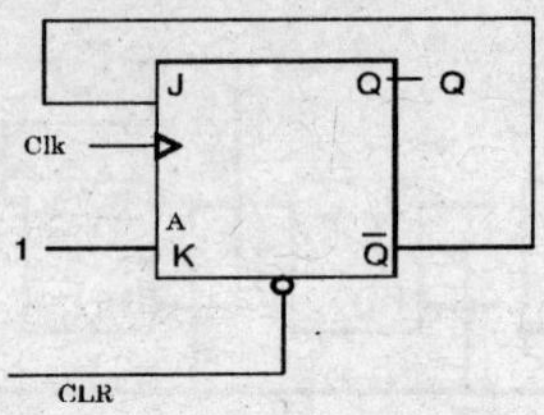

(*a*) 010000 (*b*) 011001
(*c*) 010010 (*d*) 010101

67. A memory system has a total of 8 memory chips, each with 12 address lines and 4 data lines. The total size of the memory system is

(*a*) 6 kbytes (*b*) 32 kbytes
(*c*) 48 kbytes (*d*) 64 kbytes

68. The Q output of a J–K flip-flop is '1'. The output does not change when a clock-pulse is applied.The inputs J and K will be respectively (X-denotes don't care state)

(*a*) 0 and X (*b*) X and 0
(*c*) 1 and 0 (*d*) 0 and 1.

69. The block diagram shown below represents

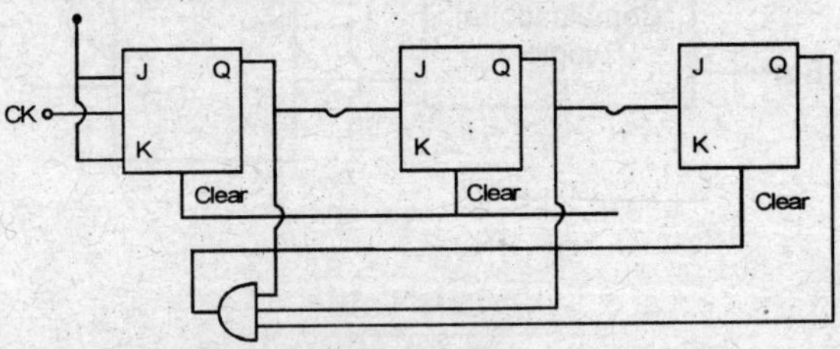

(*a*) modulo – 3 ripple counter
(*b*) modulo – 5 ripple counter
(*c*) modulo – 7 ripple counter
(*d*) modulo – 7 synchronous counter

70. The characteristic equation of the T-FF is given by

(*a*) $Q^+ = \overline{T}Q + T\overline{Q}$ (*b*) $Q^+ = T\overline{Q} + Q\overline{T}$
(*c*) $Q^+ = TQ$ (*d*) $Q^+ = T\overline{Q}$

71. A 4-bit preset table UP counter has preset input 0101. The preset operation takes place as soon as the counter becomes maximum 1111.The modulus of the counter is

(*a*) 5 (*b*) 10
(*c*) 11 (*d*) 15

72. A mod-2 counter followed by a mod-5 counter is

(*a*) same as a mode-5 counter followed by a mod-2 counter
(*b*) a decade counter
(*c*) a mod-7 counter
(*d*) none of these

73. A 4-bit-synchronous counter uses flip-flops with propagation delay time of 25 ns each. The maximum possible time required for change of state will be

(*a*) 25 ns (*b*) 50 ns
(*c*) 75 ns (*d*) 100 ns

74. A switch-tail ring counter is made by using a single D-FF. The resulting ciruit is

(*a*) SR flip-flop (*b*) JK flip-flop
(*c*) D – FF (*d*) T – FF

75. A 4–bit modulo–16 ripple counter used JK flip-flop. If progression delay of each FF is 50 ms, then maximum clock frequency is equal to

(*a*) 20 MHz (*b*) 10 MHz
(*c*) 5 MHz (*d*) 4 MHz

76. The initial contents of the 4-bit serial-in-parallel-out, right-shift. Shift Register shown in the given figure is 0110. After three clock pulses are applied, contents of the Shift Register will be

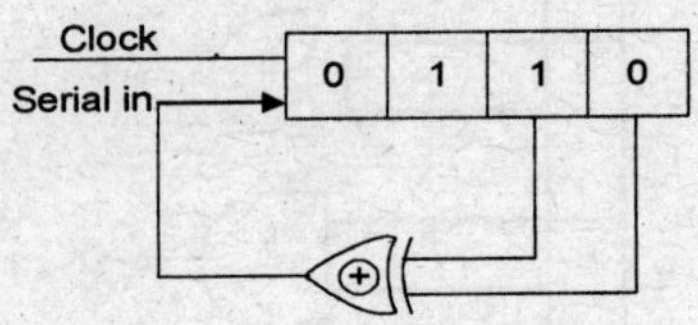

(*a*) 0000 (*b*) 0101
(*c*) 1010 (*d*) 1111

77. Metastability in D-Flip Flop occurs when

(*a*) set up time of input data is not met
(*b*) clock period is too large
(*c*) set and reset are active simultaneously
(*d*) D and Q pins are shortened.

Common Data Q.78-79 :

A Mealy system produces a 1 output if input has been 0 for at least two consecutive clocks followed immediately by two or more consecutive 1's.

78. Minimum state for this system is

(*a*) 4 (*b*) 5
(*c*) 8 (*d*) 9

79. The flip-flop required to implement this sytem are

(*a*) 2 (*b*) 3
(*c*) 4 (*d*) 5

80. Which one of the following can be used to change data from special code to temporal code ?

(*a*) Shift registers
(*b*) Counters
(*c*) A / D converters
(*d*) Combinational circuits

81. A divide by 78 counter can be realized by using

(*a*) 6 mod of mod-13 counters
(*b*) 13 mod of mod-6 counters
(*c*) one mod-13 counter followed by one mod-6 counter
(*d*) 13 mod and mod-13 counters

82. In a sequential circuit, the outputs at any instant of time depends

(*a*) only on the inputs present at that instant of time
(*b*) on past outputs as well as present inputs
(*c*) only on the past inputs
(*d*) only on the present outputs

83. How many FFs are required to build a binary counter circuit to count from 0 to 1023 ?

(*a*) 1 (*b*) 6

(*c*) 10 (*d*) 24

84. If a counter having 10 FFs is initially at 0, what count will if hold after 2060 pulses ?

(*a*) 000 000 1100 (*b*) 000 001 1100

(*c*) 000 001 1000 (*d*) 000 000 1110

85. For a flip-flop formed from two NAND gates as shown in the given figure, the unusable state corresponds to

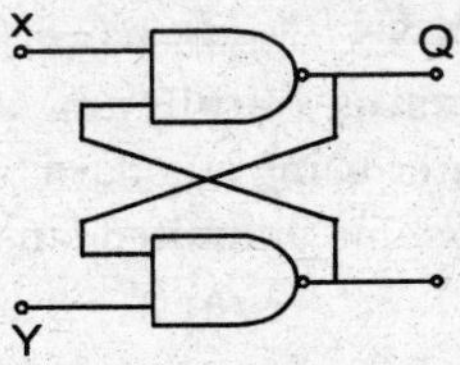

(*a*) X = 0, Y = 0 (*b*) X = 0, Y = 1

(*c*) X = 1, Y = 0 (*d*) X = 1, Y = 1

86. The shift register shown in the given figure is initially loaded with the bit pattern 1010. Subsequently the shift register is clocked, and with each clock pulse the pattern gets shifted by one bit position to the right. With each shift, the bit at the serial input is pushed to the left most position (msb). After how may clock pulses will the content of the shift register become 1010 again?

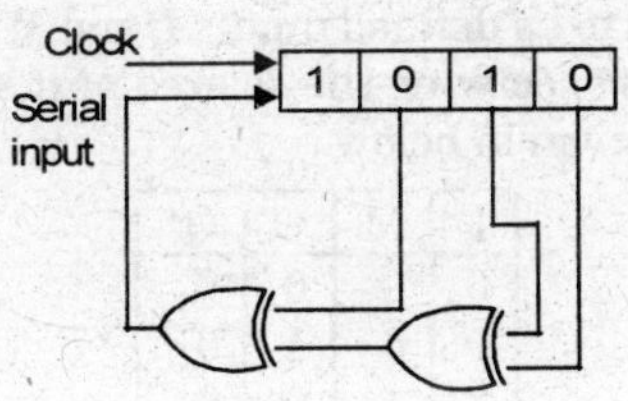

(*a*) 3 (*b*) 7

(*c*) 11 (*d*) 15

87. An X–Y flip flop, whose Characteristic Table is given below is to be implemented using a J–K flip flop.

X	Y	Q_{n+1}
0	0	1
0	1	Q_n
1	0	$\overline{Q_n}$
1	1	0

This can be done by making

(*a*) $J = X, K = \overline{Y}$ (*b*) $J = \overline{X}, K = Y$

(*c*) $J = Y, K = \overline{X}$ (*d*) $J = \overline{Y}, K = X$

88. A pulse train with a frequency of 1 MHz is counted using a modulo 1024 ripple-counter built with J-K flip-flops. For proper operation of the counter the maximum permissible propagation delay per flip-flop stage is

(*a*) 100 n sec (*b*) 50 n sec

(*c*) 20 n sec (*d*) 10 n sec

89. What is the frequency of the pulses at the points *a*, *b*, *c*, *d* in the circuit shown?

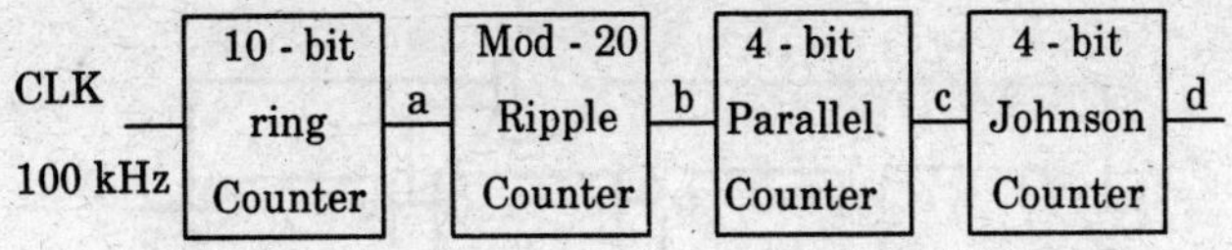

	a	b	c	d
(*a*)	10 kHz	500 Hz	31.25 Hz	3.9 Hz
(*b*)	20 kHz	510 Hz	32 Hz	4 Hz
(*c*)	15 kHz	500 Hz	30 Hz	4 Hz
(*d*)	10 kHz	520 Hz	50 Hz	5 Hz

90. In a 4 bit counter, the outputs of 3 JK FFs from MSB downward are connected to the NAND gate whose output is connected to CLR .

(*a*) It is a MOD-14 counter

(*b*) It is a MOD-13 counter

(*c*) It is a divide by-13 counter

(*d*) It is a divide by-14 counter

91. The state transition given below is realized by a clocked JK FF .

State Q_n	Transition Q_{n+1}
0	0
0	1
1	0
1	1

The JK input to realize the transition is

(*a*) J	K	(*b*) J	K	(*c*) J	K	(*d*) J	K
0	φ	φ	0	0	φ	1	φ
1	φ	φ	1	φ	0	φ	0
φ	1	1	φ	φ	1	0	φ
φ	0	0	φ	1	φ	φ	1

92. Which of the following statements are correct?

(*a*) A F/F is used to store 1-bit of information

(*b*) Race-around condition occurs in a J-K F/F when both the inputs are 1

(*c*) A transparent latch consist of a D-type F/F. Select the correct answer using the codes given below

(*d*) All of these

93. Four memory chips of 16 × 4 size have their address buses connected together. This system will be of size

(*a*) 64 × 4 (*b*) 32 × 8

(*c*) 16 × 16 (*d*) 256 × 1

94. The stable multivibrator shown in the figure has R = 300Ω and C_1 = 500 *pf*

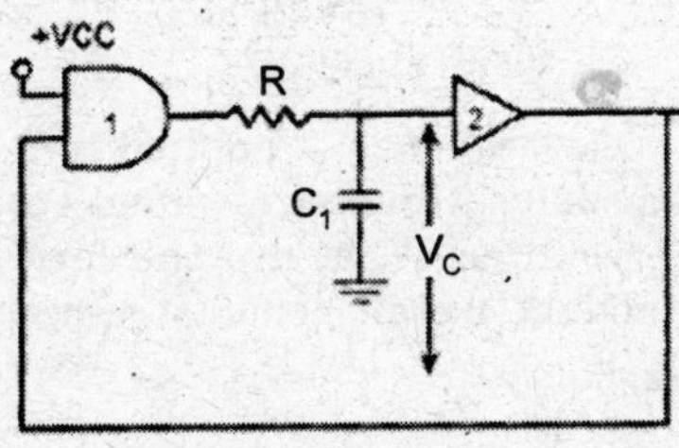

The pulse width is

(*a*) 1 nano second (*b*) 1 micro second

(*c*) 10 nano second (*d*) 1 mile second

95. Circuit in the given figure produces the output sequence

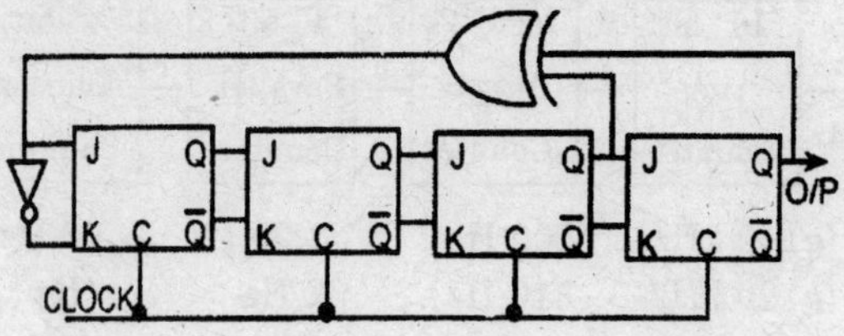

(*a*) 1111 1111 0000 0000
(*b*) 1111 0000 1111 0000
(*c*) 1111 0001 0011 0100
(*d*) 1010 1010 1010 1010

96. Which one of the circuits given below converts a JKF/F to a TF/F ?

(*a*)
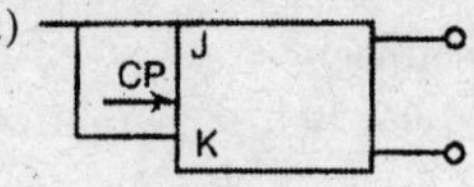

(*b*)
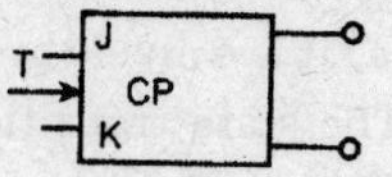

(*c*)
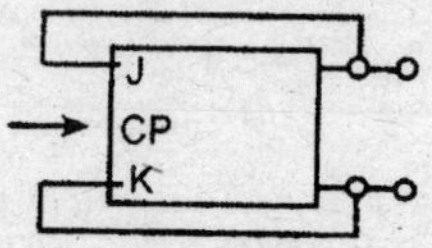

(*d*)
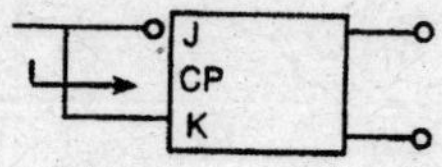

97. Figure given below shows four D type FF's connected as a shift register using an X OR gate. The initial state and 3 subsequent states for 3 clock pulses are also given.

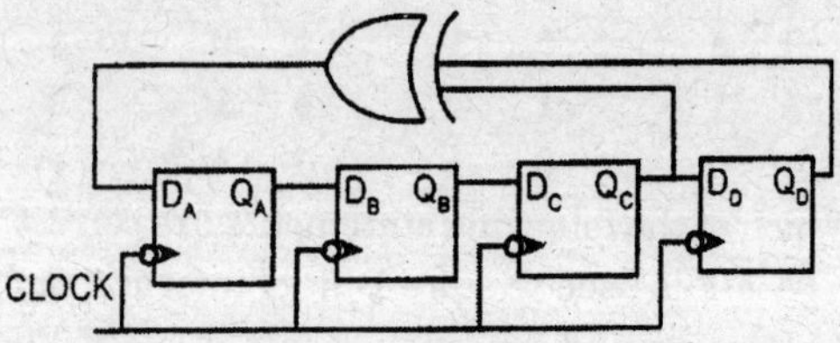

State	Q_A	Q_B	Q_C	Q_D
Initial	1	1	1	1
After the I[st] clock	0	1	1	1
After the 2nd clock	0	0	1	1
After the 3rd clock	0	0	0	1

State Q_A Q_B Q_C Q_D after fourth clock pulse is

(*a*) 0000 (*b*) 1111
(*c*) 1001 (*d*) 1000

98. The address bus width of a memory of size 1024 × 8 bits is

(*a*) 10 bits (*b*) 13 bits
(*c*) 8 bits (*d*) 18 bits

99. 12 MHz clock frequency is applied to a cascaded counter of modulus-3 counter, modulus-4 counter and modulus-5 counter. What are the lowest output frequency and the overall modulus, respectively ?

(*a*) 200 kHz, 60
(*b*) 1 MHz, 60
(*c*) 3 MHz, 12
(*d*) 4 MHz, 12

100. Consider the circuit given below with initial state $Q_0 = 1, Q_1 Q_2 = 0$. The state of the circuit is given by the value $4Q_2 + 2Q_1 + Q_0$.

The correct state sequence of the circuit is

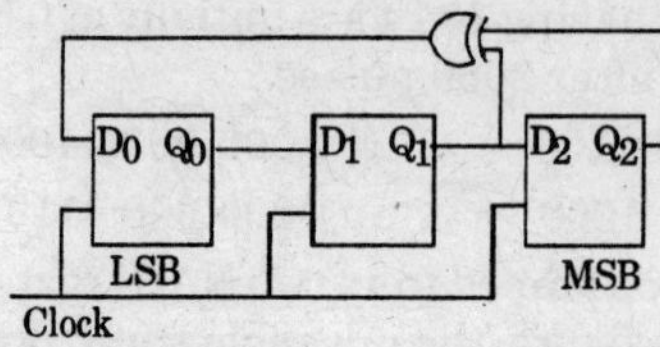

(*a*) 1, 3, 4, 6, 7, 5, 2 (*b*) 1, 2, 5, 3, 7, 6, 4
(*c*) 1, 2, 7, 3, 5, 6, 4 (*d*) 1, 6, 5, 7, 2, 3, 4

101. How many gates (minimum) are needed for a 3-bit up-counter using standard binary and using T flip-flops ? Assume unlimited fan-in.

(*a*) 4 (*b*) 3
(*c*) 2 (*d*) 1

102. The circuit shown in the figure given below

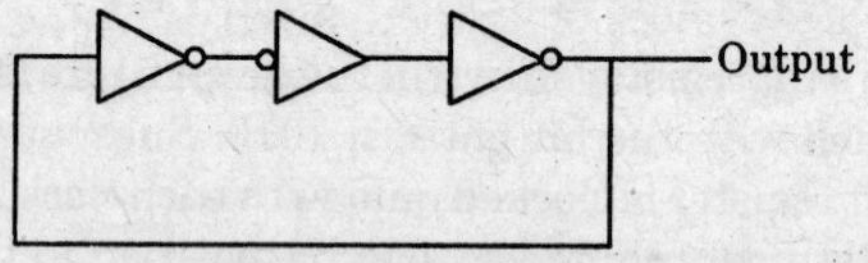

(*a*) is an oscillating circuit and its output is a square wave
(*b*) is one whose output remains stable in '1' state
(*c*) is one having output semains stable '0' state
(*d*) having a single pulse of 3 times propagation delay

103. A latch is to be defined inputs L and M (an LM latch). The table specifying the desired next state at a clock pulse is given in below.

L	M	Q	Q^+
0	0	0	0
0	0	1	0
0	1	0	0
0	1	1	0
1	0	0	1
1	0	1	1
1	1	0	1
1	1	1	0

The expression for the next state Q^+ is

(*a*) $\overline{L}M + MQ$ (*b*) $L\overline{M} + LQ$
(*c*) $\overline{L}M + M\overline{Q}$ (*d*) $L\overline{M} + L\overline{Q}$

104. The circuit shown in the figure converts

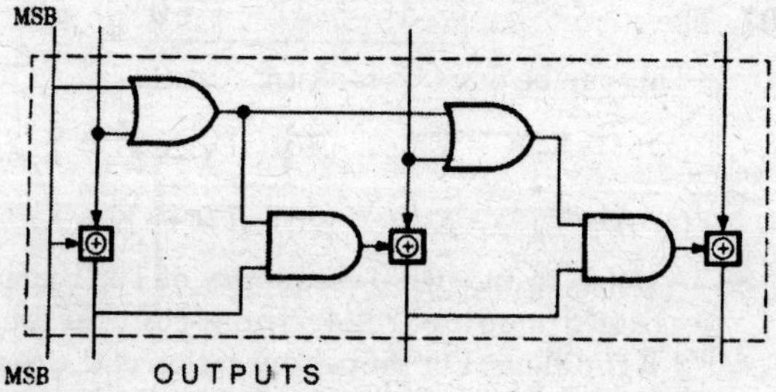

(*a*) BCD to binary code
(*b*) Binary to excess – 3 code
(*c*) Excess – 3 to Gray code
(*d*) Gray to Binary code

105. A sequential circuit using D flip-flop and logic gates is shown in the figure where X and Y are the inputs and Z is the output. The circuits is

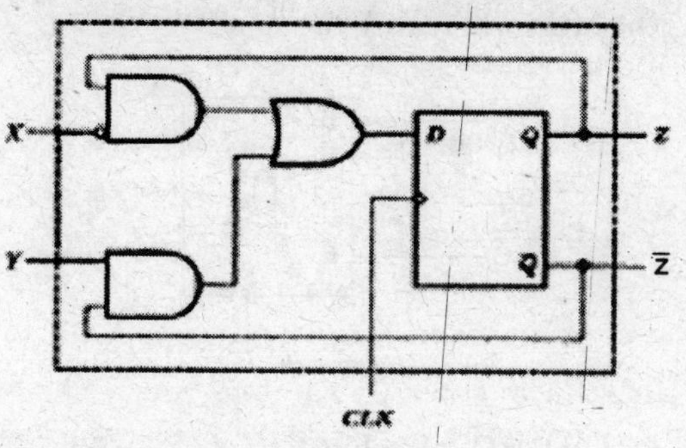

(*a*) S – R FF with inputs X = R and Y = S

(*b*) S – R FF with inputs X = S and Y = R

(*c*) J – K FF with inputs X = J and Y = K

(*d*) J – K FF with inputs X = K and Y = J

106. The digital block in figure realized using two positive edge triggered D- flip-flop. Assume that for $t < t_0$, $Q_1 = Q_2 = 0$.

The circuit in the digital block is given by

(*a*)

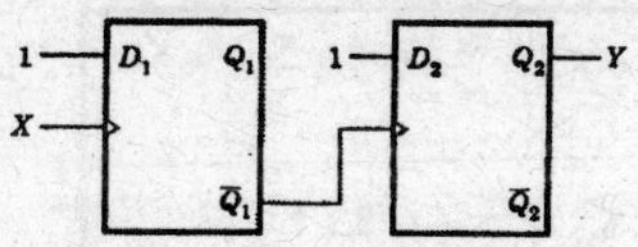

(*b*)

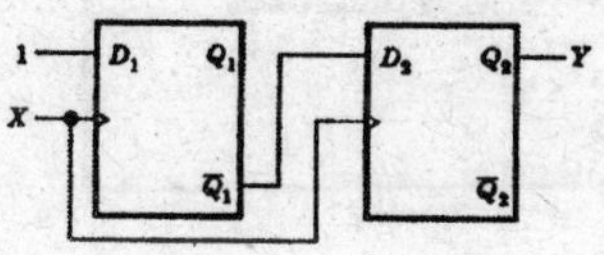

(*c*)

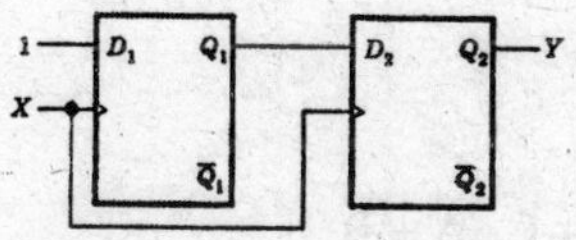

(*d*)

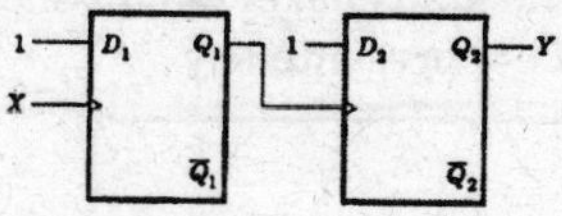

107. The circuit shown in figure

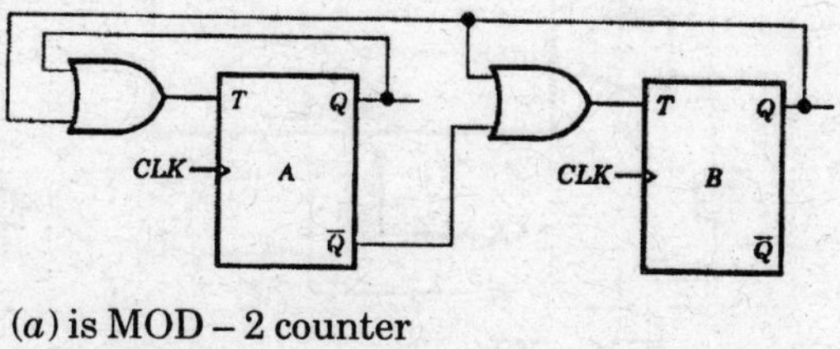

(*a*) is MOD – 2 counter

(*b*) is MOD – 3 counter

(*c*) generate sequence 00, 10, 01, 00....

(*d*) generate sequence 00, 10, 00, 10, 00.....

108. The mod-number of the asynchronous counter shown in the figure is

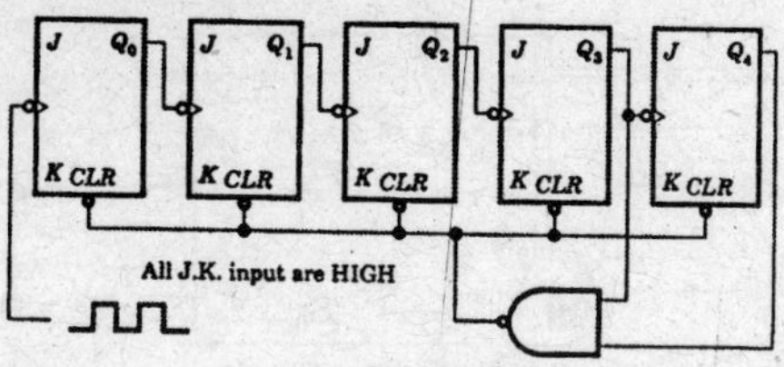

(*a*) 24 (*b*) 48

(*c*) 25 (*d*) 36

109. The three-stage Johnson counter as shown in figure is clocked at a constant frequency of f_c from the starting state of $Q_2Q_1Q_0 = 101$. The frequency of output $Q_2Q_1Q_0$ will be

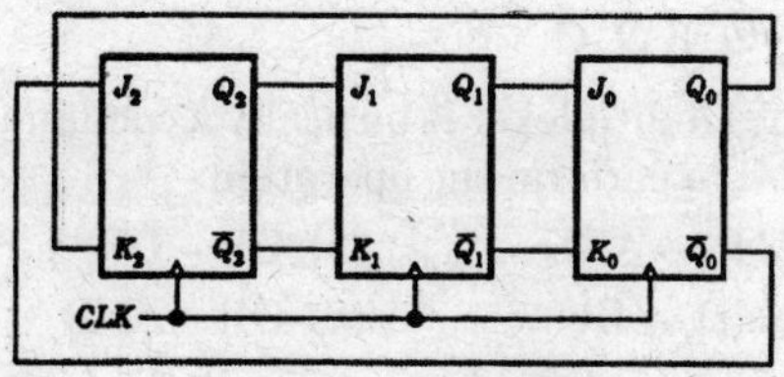

(*a*) $\frac{f_c}{8}$ (*b*) $\frac{f_c}{6}$

(*c*) $\frac{f_c}{3}$ (*d*) $\frac{f_c}{2}$

110. A 4 bit ripple counter and a 4 bit synchronous counter are made by flips flops having a propagation delay of 10 ns each. If worst case delay in the ripple counter and the synchronous counter be R and S respectively, then

(*a*) R = 10 ns, S = 40 ns

(*b*) R = 40 ns, S = 10 ns

(*c*) R = 10 ns, S = 30 ns

(*d*) R = 30 ns, S = 10 ns

111. A 4 bit modulo-6 ripple counter uses JK flip-flop. If propagation delay of each FF is 50 ns, then maximum clock frequency that can be used is equal to

(*a*) 5 MHz (*b*) 10 MHz

(*c*) 4 MHz (*d*) 20 MHz

MULTIPLEXER

112. Consider the following logic circuit consisting of 2-4 decoder for each of decoder

$f_0 = 1$ when $i_1 = 0, \quad i_2 = 0$

$f_1 = 1$ when $i_1 = 1, \quad i_2 = 0$

and so on,

which of the following gives value of $g(x, y, z)$?

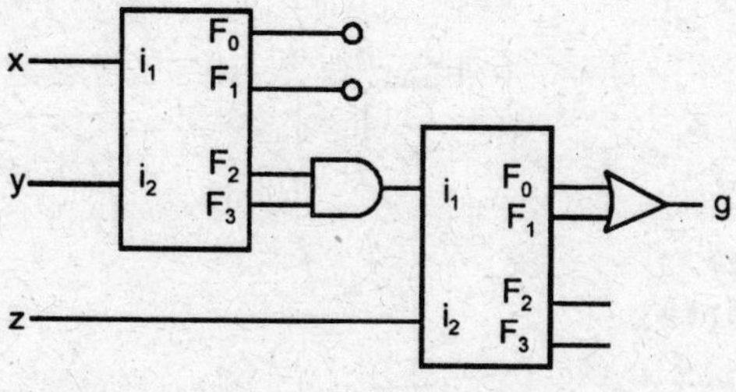

(*a*) $\bar{x}\,\bar{y} + \bar{x}\cdot\bar{y}\cdot\bar{z}$ (*b*) $x \,.\, y \,.\, z$

(*c*) $[xy + \bar{x}\,\bar{y}\,].\,z$ (*d*) 1

113. The combinational logic circuit shown in the given figure has an output Q which is

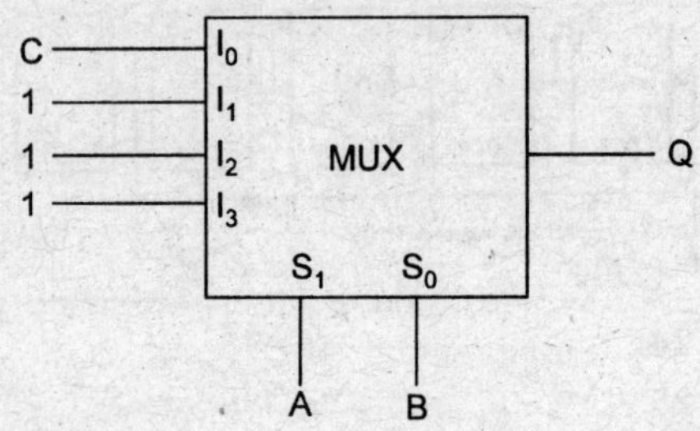

(*a*) A B C

(*b*) A + B + C

(*c*) A ⊕ B ⊕ C

(*d*) A ⊙ B ⊙ C

114. Digital multiplexer is basically a combinational logic circuit to perform the operation

(*a*) AND – AND (*b*) OR – OR

(*c*) AND – OR (*d*) OR – AND

115. The logic realized by the circuit shown in the figure below, is

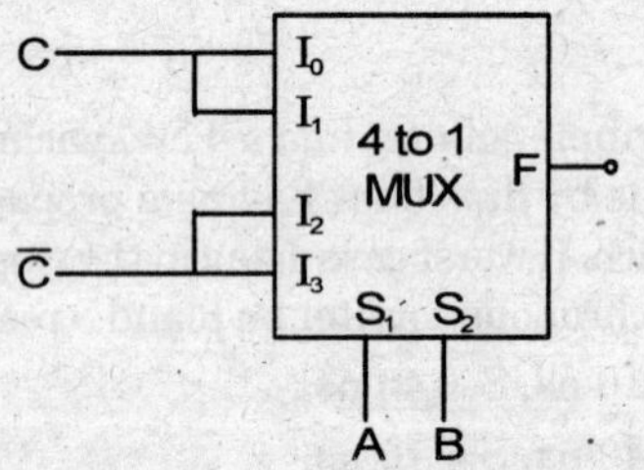

(*a*) F = A ⊙ C (*b*) F = A ⊕ C

(*c*) F = B ⊙ C (*d*) F = B ⊕ C

116. In time devision multiplexing

(*a*) time is doubled between bits of a byte

(*b*) time slicing at CPU level takes place

(*c*) total time available in the channel is divided between several users and each users is allotted a time slice

(*d*) none of these

117. The output *f* of the 4-to-1 MUX shown in the given figure is

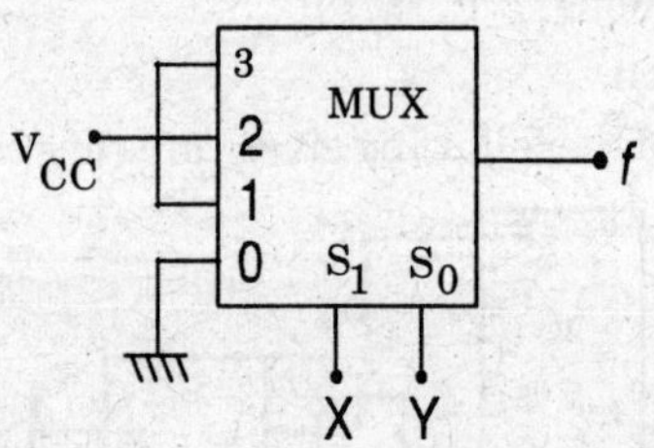

(*a*) $\overline{xy} + x$

(*b*) $x + y$

(*c*) $\overline{x} + \overline{y}$

(*d*) $xy + \overline{x}$

118. In the figure shows a 4 to 1 MUX to be used to implement the sum S of a 1-bit full adder with input bits P and Q and the carry input C_{in}. Which of the following combinations of inputs to I_0, I_1, I_2 and I_3 of the MUX will realize the sum S ?

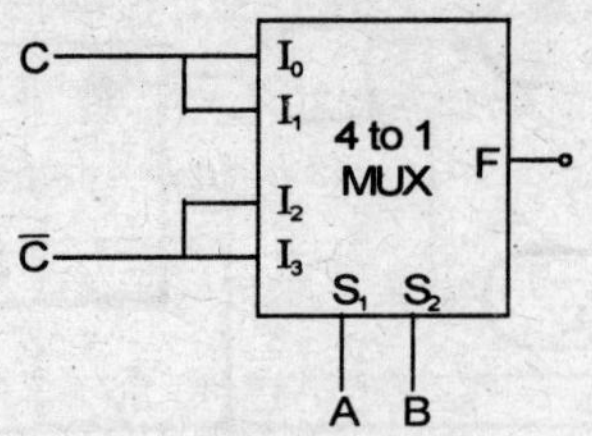

(*a*) $I_0 = I_1 = C_{in}$; $I_2 = I_3 = \overline{C}_{in}$

(*b*) $I_0 = I_1 = \overline{C}_{in}$; $I_2 = I_3 = C_{in}$

(*c*) $I_0 = I_3 = C_{in}$; $I_1 = I_2 = \overline{C}_{in}$

(*d*) $I_0 = I_3 = \overline{C}_{in}$; $I_1 = I_2 = C_{in}$

119. In TTL circuit shown in the given figure, S_2 to S_0 are select line and X_7 to X_0 are input lines S_0 and X_0 are LSB's. The outputs y is

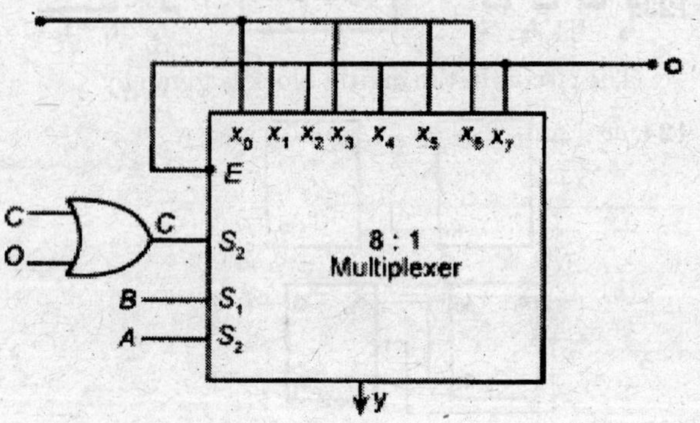

(*a*) in determine

(*b*) A ⊕ B

(*c*) $\overline{A \oplus B}$

(*d*) $\overline{C}.\ (\overline{A \oplus B}) + C.\ (A \oplus B)$

120. The output F of the multiplexer circuit shown in the given figure can be represented by

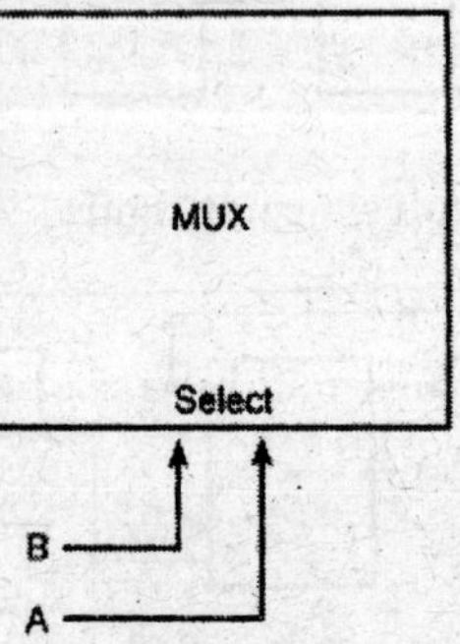

(*a*) $AB + \overline{BC} + \overline{CA} + \overline{BC}$

(*b*) A ⊕ B ⊕ C

(*c*) A ⊕ B

(*d*) $\overline{AB}C + AB\overline{C} + A\overline{BC}$

121. A sequential multiplexer is connected as shown in the figure. Each time the multiplexer receivers the clock, it switches to the next cannel (from 6 it goes to 1) if input signals are

(a) $5 \cos (2\pi) (4 \times 10^3 t)$ (b) $2 \cos 2\pi (3.8 \times 10^3 t)$

(c) $6 \cos 2\pi (2.2 \times 10^3 t)$ (d) $4 \cos 2\pi (17 \times 10^3 t)$

Statement for Q.122-123.

A MUX network is shown in the given figure

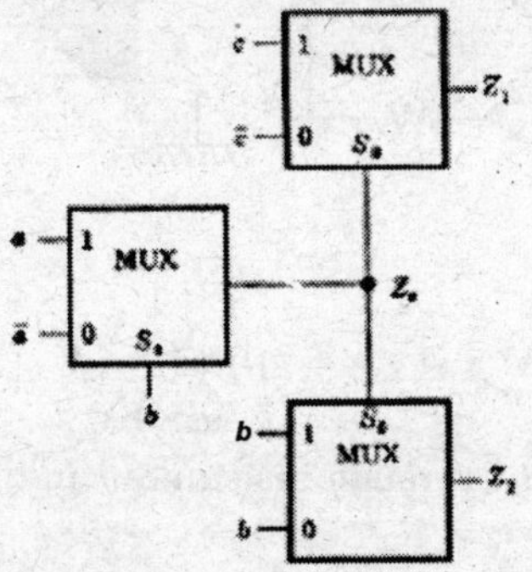

122. The value of Z_1 is

(a) $a + b + c$ (b) $ab + ac + bc$

(c) $a \odot b \odot c$ (d) $a \oplus b \oplus c$

123. The circuit act as a

(a) full adder (b) half adder

(c) full subtractor (d) half subtractor

124. The output of the 4 × 1 multiplexer shown in the figure, is

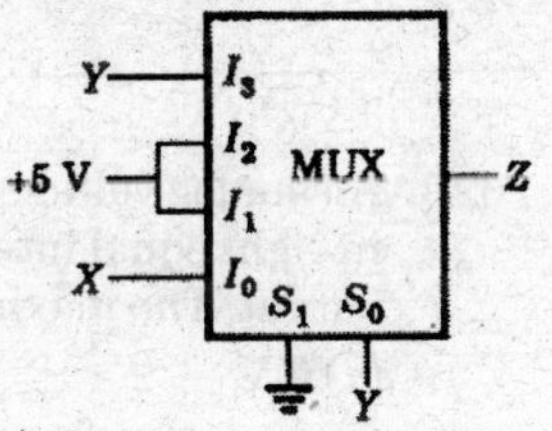

(a) $X + Y$

(b) $\overline{X} + \overline{Y}$

(c) $\overline{X}\overline{Y} + X$

(d) $X\overline{Y}$

125. For the logic circuit shown in the figure, output Y is

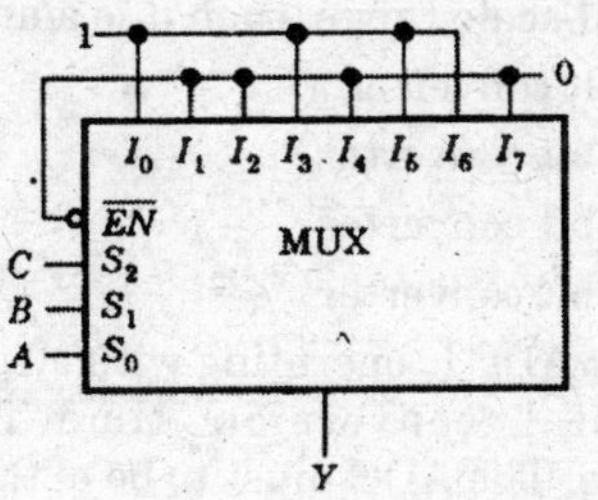

(a) $A \oplus B$ (b) $\overline{A \oplus B}$

(c) $A \oplus B \oplus C$ (d) none of these

126. The 8-to-1 multiplexer shown in the figure, realize which of the following Boolean expression?

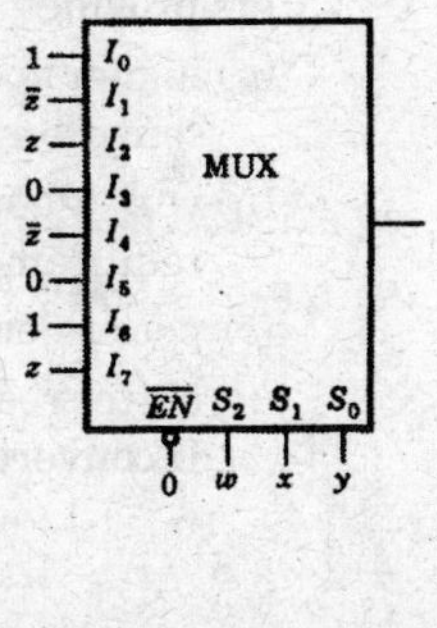

(a) $w\overline{x}z + \overline{w}\overline{x}\overline{z} + wyz + x\overline{y}\overline{z}$

(b) $wxz + \overline{w}yz + wy\overline{z} + \overline{w}\overline{x}\overline{y}$

(c) $\overline{w}\overline{x}\overline{z} + wy\overline{z} + \overline{w}\overline{y}z + wxz$

(d) MUX is not enable

SCHMITT TRIGGER

127. A retriggerable monoshot is one which

(a) can be triggered only once

(b) has two quasi-stable states

(c) cannot be triggered until full pulse has been

(d) is capable of being triggered while the output is being

128. Part of a digital phase meter is shown in the given figure. If input signals are

$V_R(t) = V_R \sin \omega t$

and $V_p(t) = -V_p \sin(\omega t + 30°)$, then reading of the meter will be

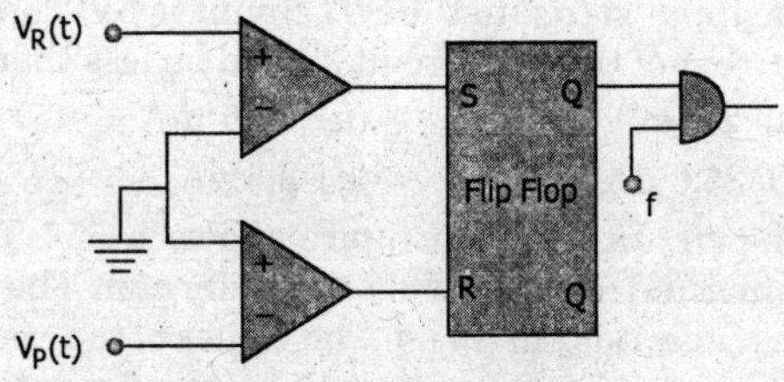

(a) 30° (b) 330°

(c) 150° (d) 210°

129. A pulse train can be delayed by a finite number periods usings of clock

(a) a serial – in – serial shift register

(b) a serial – in – parallel – out shift register

(c) a parallel – in serial – out shift register

(d) a serial – in parallel – out shift register

130. Schmitt trigger is shown in the figure. The upper and lower threshold voltage are respectively

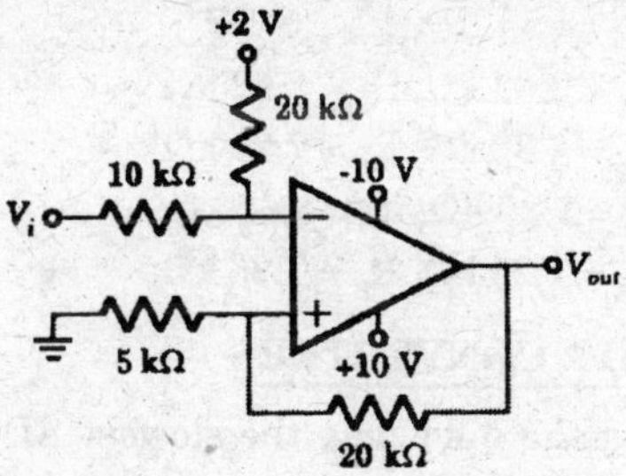

(a) 2 V, – 4 V (b) 2 V, – 2 V

(c) 4 V, – 4 V (d) 4 V, – 2 V

131. For the Schmitt trigger oscillator shown in the given figure saturation output voltage are + 10 V and – 5 V.

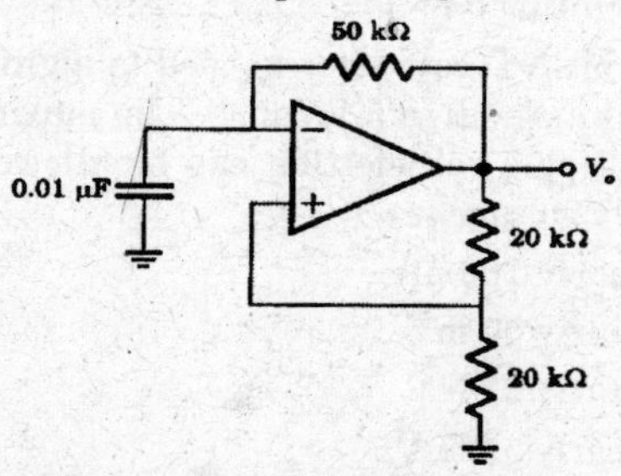

The frequency of oscillation is

(a) 2183 Hz (b) 869 Hz

(c) 1369 Hz (d) 1443 Hz

SAMPLE AND HOLD CIRCUIT

132. For a MOD-12 counter, FF has a t_{pd} = 60 ns. NAND gate has a t_{pd} of 25 ns. The clock frequency is

(a) = 3.774 MHz
(b) > 3.774 MHz
(c) < 3.774 MHz
(d) = 4.167 MHz

133. A sample-and-hold (S/H) circuit, having a holding capacitor of 0.1 nF, is used at the input of an ADC (analog-to-digital converter). The conversion time of the ADC is 1 μsec, and during this time, the capacitor should not lose more than 0.5% of the charge put across it during the sampling time. The maximum value of the input signal to the S/H circuit is 5V. The leakage current of the S/H circuit should be less than

(a) 2.5 mA (b) 0.25 mA
(c) 25.0 μA (d) 2.5 μA

134. The circuit of given figure shows a 555 Timer IC connected as an astable multivibrator. The value of the capacitor C is 10 nF. The values of the resistors R_A and R_B for a frequency of 10 kHz and a duty cycle of 0.75 for the output voltage waveform are

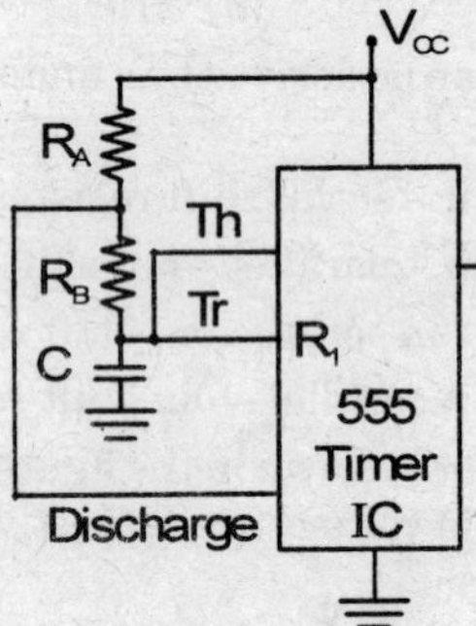

(a) R_A = 3.62 kΩ, R_B = 3.62 kΩ
(b) R_A = 3.62 kΩ, R_B = 7.25 kΩ
(c) R_A = 7.25 kΩ, R_B = 3.62 kΩ
(d) R_A = 7.25 kΩ, R_B = 7.25 kΩ

A/D AND D/A CONVERTERS

135. Among the following, the slowest ADC (Analog-to-digital converter) is

(a) parallel-comparator (i.e. flash) type
(b) successive approximation type
(c) integrating type
(d) counting type

136. A 10 bit A/D converter is used to digitise an analog signal in the 0 to 5 V range. The maximum peak to peak ripple voltage that can be allowed in the d.c. supply voltage is

(a) nearly 100 mV
(b) nearly 50 mV
(c) nearly 25 mV
(d) nearly 5.0 mV

137. The number of comparators in a parallel conversion type 8-bit A to D converter is

(a) 8 (b) 16
(c) 255 (d) 256

138. A 3-bit weighted resistor DAC shown in the figure has V_R = 2V and R_1/R = 2. For an input of 100, the output will be

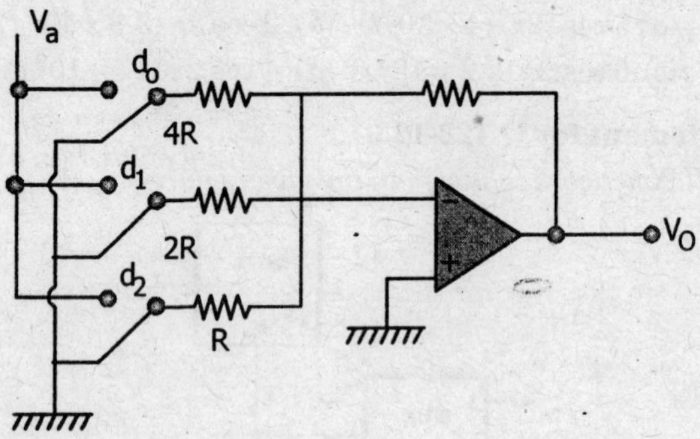

(a) – 2 V (b) – 4 V
(c) 2 V (d) 4 V

139. Current I through resistance r in the circuit shown below, is

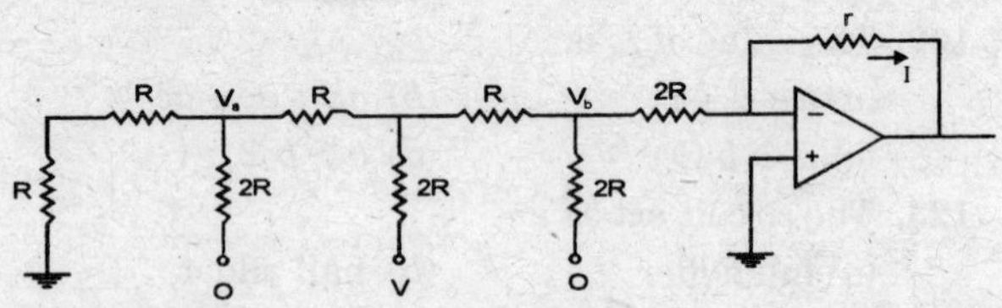

(a) $-\dfrac{V}{12R}$ (b) $\dfrac{V}{12R}$

(c) $\dfrac{V}{6R}$ (d) $\dfrac{V}{3R}$

140. An analog voltage is in the range of 0 to 8 V is divided in eight equal intervals for conversion to 3-bit digital output. The maximum quantization error is

(a) 0 V (b) 0.5 V
(c) 1 V (d) 2 V

141. If resolution of a D/A converter is approximately 0.4% of its full-scale range. then it is a/an

(a) 8 – bit converter
(b) 10 – bit converter
(c) 12 – bit converter
(d) 16 – bit converter

142. A 12–bit ADC is operating with a 1μ sec clock period and total conversion time is seen to be 14 μ secs. The ADC must to be of the

(a) flash type
(b) counting type
(c) integrating type
(d) successive approximation type

143. Dual slope integration type Analog-to-Digital converters provide

(a) higher speeds compared to all other types of A / D converters
(b) very good accuracy without putting extreme requirements on component stability
(c) poor rejection of power supply hum
(d) better resolution compared to all other types of A/D converters for the same number of bits.

144. In a 4-bit weighted resistor D/A converter, the resistor value corresponding to LSB is 32-k ohm. The resistor value corresponding to MSB will be

(*a*) 32 k-ohm (*b*) 16 k-ohm
(*c*) 8 k-ohm (*d*) 4 k-ohm

145. For a dual ADC type 3 1/2 digit DVM, reference voltage is 100 mV and first integration time is set to 300 ms. For some input voltage, "deintegration" period is 370.2 ms. The DVM will indicate

(*a*) 123.4 (*b*) 199.9 (*c*) 100.0 (*d*) 1.414

146. A dual-slope analog-to-digital converter uses an N-bit counter. When input signal V_a is being integrated, then counter is allowed to count up to a value

(*a*) equal to $2^N - 2$
(*b*) equal to $2^N - 1$
(*c*) proportional to V_a
(*d*) inversely proportional to V_a

147. The simplified block diagram of a 10-bit A/D converter of dual slope integrator type is shown in the given figure. The 10-bit counter at the output is clocked by a 1 MHz clock. Assuming negligible timing overhead for the control logic, the maximum frequency of the analog signal that can be converted using this A/D converter is approximately

(*a*) 2 kHz (*b*) 1 kHz (*c*) 500 Hz (*d*) 250 Hz

148. What overall accuracy could one reasonably expect from construction of a 10 bit A/D converter?

(*a*) 0.1% (*b*) 0.2% (*c*) 0.3% (*d*) 0.4%

149. A 5 bit D/A converter has a current output for a digital input of 10100. If an output current of 10 m A is produced, what will I_{out} be for a digital input of 11101 ?

(*a*) 12.5 mA (*b*) 13.5 mA (*c*) 14.5 mA (*d*) 15.5 mA

150. Circuit of DAC is given below. Switch are closed if input bit is 1, otherwise open.

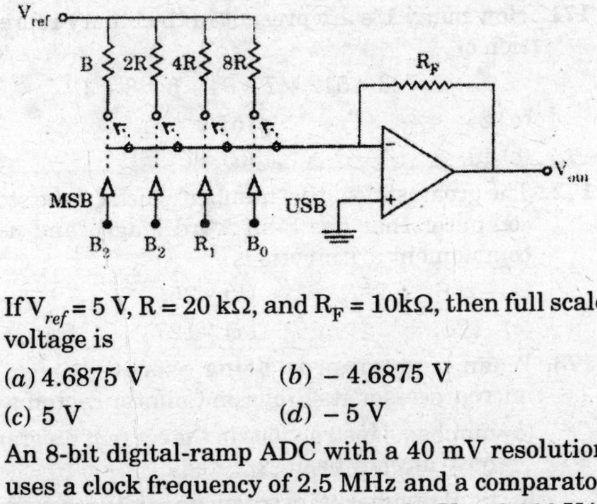

If V_{ref} = 5 V, R = 20 kΩ, and R_F = 10kΩ, then full scale voltage is

(*a*) 4.6875 V (*b*) – 4.6875 V
(*c*) 5 V (*d*) – 5 V

151. An 8-bit digital-ramp ADC with a 40 mV resolution uses a clock frequency of 2.5 MHz and a comparator with V_T = 1mV. The digital output for V_A = 6.000 V is

(*a*) 1 0 0 1 0 1 1 1
(*b*) 1 0 0 1 0 1 1 0
(*c*) 1 0 1 1 1 1 0
(*d*) 1 0 1 1 1 1 1

152. The circuit shown in figure is a 4-bit DAC. The input bits 0 and 1 are represented by 0 and 5 V respectively. The OP-AMP is ideal, but all the resistance and the 5 V inputs have a tolerance of ± 10%. The specification (rounded to the nearest multiple of 5%) for tolerance of the DAC is

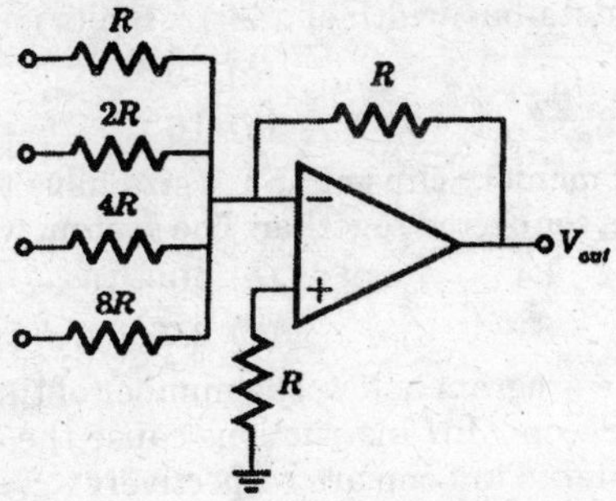

(*a*) ± 35% (*b*) ± 20%
(*c*) ± 10% (*d*) ± 5%

MICROPROCESSORS

153. PROMs are used to store

(*a*) bulk information
(*b*) sequential information
(*c*) information to be accessed rarely
(*d*) relatively permanent information

154. Each cell of a static Random Access memory contains

(*a*) 6 MOS transistors
(*b*) 4 MOS transistors and 2 capacitors
(*c*) two 2-input NORs and One X-NOR gate
(*d*) XOR gates and shift registers.

155. The decoding circuit has been used to generate the active low chip. Then signal for a microprocessor peripheral is (address line are designated as A 0 to A7 for I/O address)

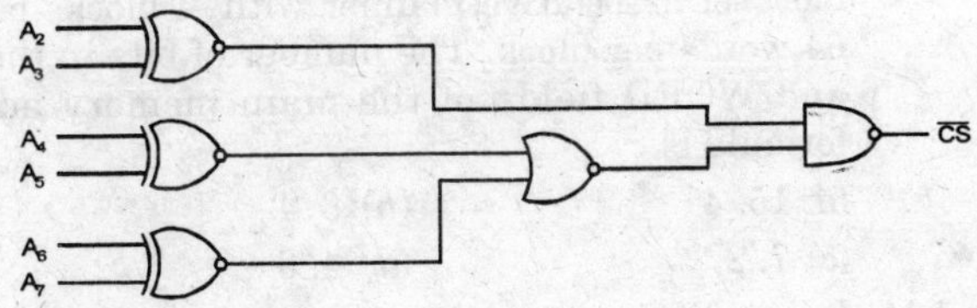

(*a*) 60H to 63 H
(*b*) A 4 to A 7 H
(*c*) 70H to 73 H
(*d*) 70 H to 73 H

156. Following sequence of instructions are executed by an 8085 microprocessor :

1000	LXI	SP, 27 FF
10003	CALL	1006
1006	POP H	

Contents of the stack pointer (SP) and HL, register pair on completion of excution of these instructions are

(*a*) SP = 27 FF, HL = 1003
(*b*) SP = 27 FD, HL = 1003
(*c*) SP = 27 FF, HL = 1006
(*d*) SP = 27 FD, HL = 1006

157. A dynamic RAM call which hold 5V has to be refreshed every 20 m secs, so that stored voltage does not fall below 0.5V. If the call has a constant discharge current of 0.1 pA, then storage capacitance of the call is

(a) 4×10^{-6} (b) 4×10^{-9}
(c) 4×10^{-12} (d) 4×10^{-15}

158. The data-bus width of a 204 × 8 bits is

(a) 8 (b) 10
(c) 12 (d) 16

159. Four memory clips of 16 × 4 size have their address bases connected together. The system will be of size

(a) 64 × 64 (b) 16 × 16
(c) 32 × 8 (d) 256 × 1

160. In the program below, the number of times the First and Second Jnz instructions cause the control to be transfared to Loop are respectively

```
                MVI    H, 02H
                MVI    L, 05H
LOOP      :     DCR    L
FIRST     :     JNZ    LOOP
                DLR    H
SECOND    :     JNZ    LOOP
```

(a) 5 and 2 (b) 4 and 1
(c) 259 and 1 (d) 260 and 1

161. A single instruction to clear the lower four bits of the accumulator in 8085 assembly language is

(a) XRI 0HF (b) ANI F0H
(c) XRI F0H (d) ANI 0FH

162. Which of the following statements is true ?

(a) ROM is a Read / Write memory
(b) PC points to the last instruction that was executed
(c) Stack works on the principle of LIFO
(d) All instructions affect the flags.

163. A computer system has a 4K word cache organised in blockset associative manner with -4 blocks per set, 64 words per block. The number of bits in the SET and WORD fields of the main memory address formula is

(a) 15, 4 (b) 6, 4
(c) 7, 2 (d) 4, 6

164. In a 8085 microprocessor system with memory mapped I / O

(a) I / O devices have 8-bit addresses
(b) I / O devices are accessed using IN and OUT instructions
(c) there can be a maximum of 256 input devices and 256 output devices
(d) arithmetic and logic operations can be directly performed with the I / O data.

165. Following programme is run on an 8085 microprocessor :

Memory address in Hex	Instruction
2000	LXI SP, 1000
2003	PUSH H
2004	PUSH D
2005	CALL 2050
2008	POP 2050
2009	HLT

As completion of execution of the program, program counter of the 8085 contains ...., and stack pointer contains ....

(a) 2050, 0FFC
(b) 2251, 0FFC
(c) 1025, 0CCF
(d) 1025, 0CCF

166. Choose correct statement(s) from the following

(a) PROM contains a programmable AND array and a fixed OR array
(b) PLA contains a fixed AND array and a programmable OR array
(c) PROM contains a fixed AND array and a programmable OR array
(d) PLA contains a programmable AND array and a programmable OR array.

167. 2's complement representation of a 16-bit number (one sign bit and 15 magnitude bits) is FFF1. It's magnitude in decimal representation is

(a) 0 (b) 1
(c) 32,767 (d) 65,767

168. In a microprocessor, the resister which holds address of the next instruction to be fetched is

(a) Accumulator
(b) Program Counter
(c) Stack Pointer
(d) Instructor Register

169. In a microcomputer, wait states are used to

(a) make the processor wait during a DMA operation
(b) make the processor wait during a power interrupt processing
(c) make the processor wait during a power shutdown
(d) interface slow peripherals to the processor

170. Decimal equivalent of the hexadecimal number E5 is

(a) 279 (b) 229
(c) 427 (d) 3000

171. How many 1 's are present in the binary representation of

$$3 \times 512 + 7 \times 64 + 5 \times 8 + 3 ?$$

(a) 8 (b) 9
(c) 10 (d) 11

172. The greatest negative number which can be stored in computer that has 8-bit word length and uses 2's complement arithmetic is

(a) –256 (b) –255
(c) –128 (d) –127

173. When a program is being executed in an 8085 microprocessor, its Program Counter contains

(a) number of instructions in the current program that have already been executed
(b) total number of instructions in the program being executed
(c) memory address of the instruction that is being currently executed
(d) memory address of the instruction that is to be executed next

174. When HLT instruction of a 8085 micro-processor is executed, the microprocessor

(a) is disconnected from the system bus till the reset is pressed

(b) halts execution of the program and returns to monitor

(c) enters into a halt state and the buses are tri-stated

(d) reloads the program form the locations 0024 and 0025 H.

175. Content of the control world register of INTEL 8252 (programmable interval timer) is given below

D_7	D_6	D_5	D_4	D_3	D_2	D_1	D_0
0	1	1	1	0	0	0	0

The control word sets

(a) counter 0 to mode 0

(b) counter 1 to mode 0

(c) counter 2 to mode 0

(d) counter 0 to mode 1

176. In an 8085 microprocessor, the instruction CMP B has been executed while the contents of accumulator is less than that of register B. As a result carry flag and zero flag will be respectively

(a) set, reset (b) reset, set

(c) reset, reset (d) set, set

177. Match correct among the following pair in the context of an 8085 microprocessor.

List I	List II
A. DAA	1. Program control instruction
B. LXI	2. Data movement instruction
C. RST	3. Interrupt instruction
D. JMP	4. Arithmetic instruction

Codes :

	A	B	C	D
(a)	1	2	3	4
(b)	4	2	3	1
(c)	3	2	1	4
(d)	2	3	4	1

178. An 8085 μP based system drives a multiplexed 5-digits 7-segment display. The digits are refreshed at a rate of 500 Hz. The ON time for each digit is

(a) 4 ms (b) 0.4 ms

(c) 10 ms (d) 25 ms

179. Serial input data of 8085 can be loaded into 7 bit to of the accumulator by.

(a) Executing a RIM instruction

(b) Execution RST 1

(c) Using TRAP

(d) None of these

180. An 8-bit μ processor has 16 bit address bus $A_0 - A_{15}$. The processor addresses a 1-k byte memory chip is as shown.

The address range for the chips.

(a) F00FH to F40EH (b) F000H to F3 FFH

(c) F100H to F4FFH (d) F700H to FAFFH

181. The contents of stack location 2109H after the call operation in the given figure will be

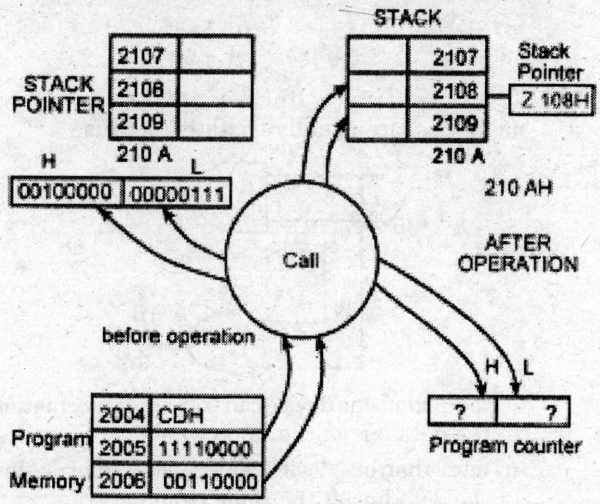

(a) 00001111 (b) 01010101

(c) 00100000 (d) 00100010

182. Which line goes low if input to the 3 to 8 decoder (74 LS 138) $(A_7 - A_0) = (110\ 1111)$?

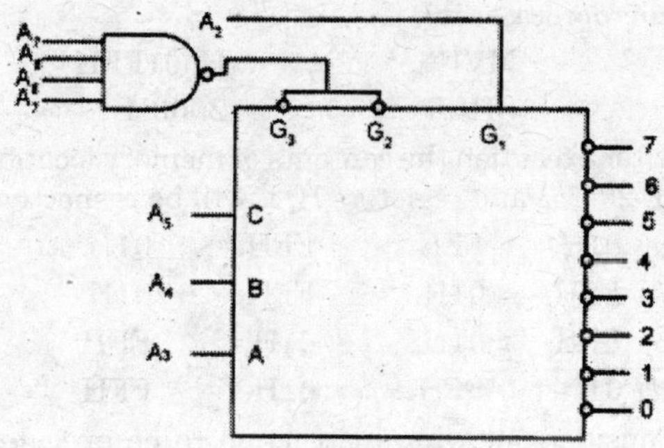

(a) 1 (b) 3

(c) 5 (d) 6

183. What is the memory map shown in the figure?

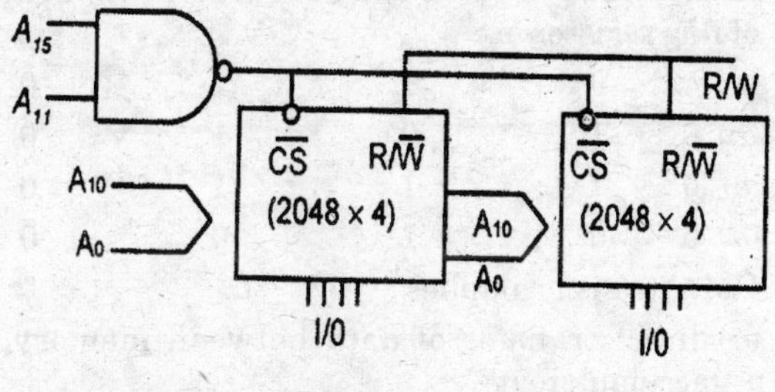

(a) 0FC00H – 0FFFFH

(b) 0FC01H – 0FFFFH

(c) 0FC18H – 0FFFFH

(d) 0FC19H – 0FFFFH

184. Which of the following interrupts are unmaskable interrupts ?

(a) RST 5.5 (b) RST 7.5

(c) TRAP (d) INTR

185. If the accumulator of 8085A μp contains 37H and the previous operation has set the carry flag, the instruction ACI 56H will result in

(*a*) 8DH (*b*) 8EH

(*c*) 17H (*d*) 18H

186. The output data lines of microprocessors and memories are usually tristated because

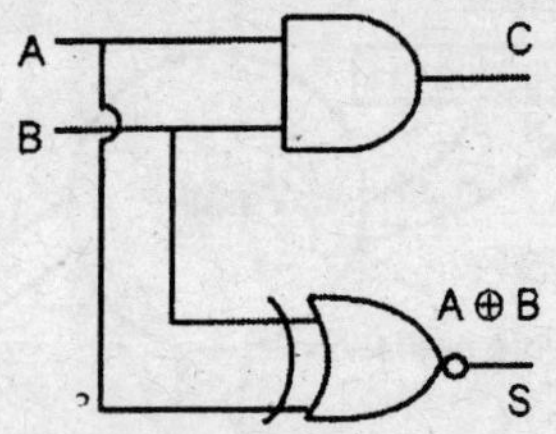

(*a*) more than one device can transmit information over the data bus at the same time

(*b*) more than one device can transmit information over the data bus at the same time.

(*c*) data lines can be multiplexed for both input and output

(*d*) it increases speed of data transfers over the data bus

187. Consider execution of the following instruction by 8085 microprocesses :

MVI	H, 01FFH
SHLD	2050H

After execution the contents of memory location 2050 H, 2051H and registers H, L will be respectively

(*a*) 01H, FFH, FFH, 01H

(*b*) FFH, 01H, FFH, 01H

(*c*) FFH, 01H, 01H, FFH

(*d*) 01H, FFH, 01H, FFH

188. Consider following instruction to be executed by a 8085 μp. The input port has an address of 01H and has a data 05H to input

IN	01H
ANI	80H

After execution of the two instructions, the contents of flag register are

(*a*) 1 0 * 1 * 1 * 0

(*b*) 0 1 * 0 * 1 * 0

(*c*) 0 1 * 1 * 1 * 0

(*d*) 0 0 * 1 * 0 * 0

189. DMA' transfer implies

(*a*) direct transfer of data between memory and accumulator

(*b*) direct transfer of data between memory and I/O devices without the use of m*p* registers

(*c*) transfer of data exclusively with input registers

(*d*) a fast transfer of data between m*p* and I/O devices

190. A memory system of size 16 K bytes is required to be designed using memory chips which have 121 address lines and 4 data lines each. Number of such chips required to design the memory system is

(*a*) 2 (*b*) 4

(*c*) 8 (*d*) 16

191. The memory address range to which RAM will respond, is

(*a*) 0000 H to 1 FFF H

(*b*) 0000 H to 5FFF H

(*c*) 4000 H to 5FFF H

(*d*) 3000 H to FFFF H

192. The address range to which I/O chip will respond, is

(*a*) 0000 H to FFFF H

(*b*) 0000 H to 5FFF H

(*c*) 4000 H to 5FFFF H

(*d*) 3000 H to FFFF H

193. Following instruction have been executed by an 8085 microprocessor :

Address (Hex)	Instruction	
6010	LXI	H,
8A 79 H		
6013	MOV	A, L
6015	ADD	H
6016	DAA	
6017	MOV	H.A
6018	PCHL	

From which address will the next instruction be fetched?

(*a*) 6019 (*b*) 0379

(*c*) 6079 (*b*) none of these

194. A stack is a/an

(*a*) 8-bit register in the microprocessor

(*b*) 16-bit register in the microprocessor

(*c*) set of memory locations in R/W memory reserved for storing information temporarily during he execution of a program

(*d*) 16-bit memory address stored in the h program counter

195. Consider following 8085 assembly program

```
        MVI     A, DATA1
        MOV     B, A
        SUI     51 H
        JC      DLT
        MOV     A, B
        SUI     82H
        JC      DSPLY
DLT :   XRA     A
        OUT PORT1
        HLT
DSPLY : MOV     A, B
        OUT PORT2
        HLT
```

This program will display

(*a*) bytes from 51H to 82H at PORT2

(*b*) 00H AT PORT1

(*c*) all byte at PORT1

(*d*) bytes from 52H to 81H at PORT2

196. It is desired to multiply the number 0AH by 0BH and store the result in the accumulator. The numbers are available in register B and C respectively. A part of the 8085 program for this purpose is given below.

```
        MVI   A,    00H
        LOOP: -------------
              -------------
              -------------
              -------------
              -------------
              HLT
              END
```

The sequence of instruction to complete the program would be

(*a*) JNZ LOOP / ADD B / DCR C
(*b*) ADD B / JNZ LOOP / DCR C
(*c*) DCR C / JNZ LOOP / ADD B
(*d*) ADD B / DCR C / JNZ LOOP

197. Consider follwing assembly language program :

```
         MVI   B, 87H
         MOV   A, B
START :  JMP   NEXT
         MVI   B, 00H
         XRA   B
         OUT   PORTI
         HLT
NEXT :   XRA   B
         JP    START
         OUT   PORT2
         HLT
```

The execution of the above program in an 8085 will result in an

(*a*) output of 87H at PORT1
(*b*) output of 87H at PORT2
(*c*) infinite looping of the program execution with accumulator data remaining at 00H
(*d*) infinite looping of the program execution with accumulator data alternating between 00H and 87H.

198. If contents of memory location 4A00H, 4A01H and 4A02H, are respectively A7H, 98H and 47H, then after execution of program contents of memory location 4A02H will be respectively

(*a*) A7H
(*b*) 98H
(*c*) 47H
(*d*) none of these

199. If input $X_3X_2X_1X_0$ to the ROM in figure, are 8-4-2-1 BCD numbers, then output $Y_3Y_2Y_1Y_0$ are

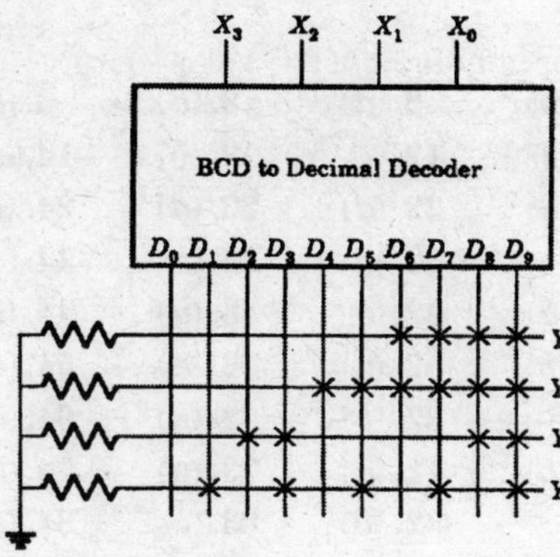

(*a*) gray code number
(*b*) 2-4-2-1 BCD number
(*c*) excess 3 code converter
(*d*) none of these

200. Consider the following loop

```
        XRA   A
        LXI   B, 0007H
LOOP :  DCX   B
        JNZ   LOOP
```

The loop will be executed

(*a*) 1 times (*b*) 8 times
(*c*) 7 times (*d*) infinite times

201. If the HLT instruction of a 8085 micro-processor is executed

(*a*) The microprocessor is disconnected form the system bus fill the reset is pressed
(*b*) The microprocessor enters into a halt state and the buses are tri-stated
(*c*) The microprocessor reloads the program from the locations 0024 and 0025H
(*d*) The microprocessor halts execution of the program and returns to monitor

202. Consider following set of instructions :

```
MVI   A, BYTE1
RLC
MOV   B, A
RLC
RLC
ADD   B
```

If BYTE1 = 07H, then content of A, after the execution of program will be

(*a*) 46H (*b*) 70H
(*c*) 38H (*d*) 68H

203. Consider following program

```
MVI   A, BYTE1
RRC
RRC
```

If BYTE1 =32H, then contents of A after execution of program will be

(*a*) 08H
(*b*) 8CH
(*c*) 12 H
(*d*) none of these

ANSWERS

1. (*b*)	**2.** (*d*)	**3.** (*d*)	**4.** (*a*)	**5.** (*d*)	**6.** (*a*)	**7.** (*d*)	**8.** (*c*)	**9.** (*c*)	**10.** (*b*)
11. (*c*)	**12.** (*c*)	**13.** (*b*)	**14.** (*a*)	**15.** (*a*)	**16.** (*a*)	**17.** (*b*)	**18.** (*a*)	**19.** (*b*)	**20.** (*c*)
21. (*d*)	**22.** (*d*)	**23.** (*d*)	**24.** (*b*)	**25.** (*c*)	**26.** (*b*)	**27.** (*b*)	**28.** (*a*)	**29.** (*d*)	**30.** (*a*)
31. (*b*)	**32.** (*a*)	**33.** (*c*)	**34.** (*d*)	**35.** (*d*)	**36.** (*a*)	**37.** (*b*)	**38.** (*a*)	**39.** (*a*)	**40.** (*d*)
41. (*a*)	**42.** (*c*)	**43.** (*d*)	**44.** (*a*)	**45.** (*b*)	**46.** (*c*)	**47.** (*d*)	**48.** (*a*)	**49.** (*a*)	**50.** (*b*)
51. (*b*)	**52.** (*a*)	**53.** (*d*)	**54.** (*d*)	**55.** (*b*)	**56.** (*d*)	**57.** (*d*)	**58.** (*b*)	**59.**(*b*)	**60.** (*b*)
61.(*b*)	**62.** (*b*)	**63.** (*a*)	**64.** (*c*)	**65.** (*b*)	**66.** (*d*)	**67.** (*b*)	**68.** (*b*)	**69.** (*c*)	**70.** (*b*)
71. (*b*)	**72.** (*a*)	**73.** (*a*)	**74.** (*d*)	**75.** (*c*)	**76.** (*c*)	**77.** (*a*)	**78.** (*a*)	**79.** (*a*)	**80.** (*a*)
81. (*c*)	**82.** (*b*)	**83.** (*c*)	**84.** (*a*)	**85.** (*a*)	**86.** (*b*)	**87.** (*d*)	**88.** (*a*)	**89.** (*a*)	**90.** (*d*)
91. (*a*)	**92.** (*d*)	**93.** (*c*)	**94.** (*b*)	**95.** (*a*)	**96.** (*a*)	**97.** (*d*)	**98.** (*a*)	**99.** (*a*)	**100.** (*b*)
101. (*c*)	**102.** (*a*)	**103.** (*d*)	**104.** (*a*)	**105.** (*d*)	**106.** (*c*)	**107.**(*b*)	**108.** (*a*)	**109.** (*d*)	**110.** (*b*)
111. (*a*)	**112.** (*d*)	**113.** (*b*)	**114.** (*c*)	**115.** (*b*)	**116.** (*c*)	**117.** (*b*)	**118.** (*c*)	**119.**(*d*)	**120.** (*d*)
121. (*d*)	**122.** (*d*)	**123.** (*a*)	**124.** (*a*)	**125.** (*d*)	**126.** (*c*)	**127.** (*d*)	**128.** (*d*)	**129.** (*a*)	**130.** (*c*)
131. (*b*)	**132.** (*a*)	**133.** (*d*)	**134.** (*c*)	**135.** (*b*)	**136.** (*d*)	**137.** (*c*)	**138.** (*b*)	**139.** (*b*)	**140.** (*c*)
141. (*a*)	**142.** (*d*)	**143.** (*b*)	**144.** (*d*)	**145.** (*a*)	**146.** (*d*)	**147.** (*b*)	**148.** (*b*)	**149.** (*c*)	**150.** (*b*)
151. (*a*)	**152.** (*a*)	**153.** (*c*)	**154.** (*a*)	**155.** (*a*)	**156.** (*d*)	**157.** (*d*)	**158.** (*a*)	**159.** (*b*)	**160.** (*c*)
161. (*b*)	**162.** (*c*)	**163.** (*d*)	**164.** (*d*)	**165.** (*a*)	**166.** (*c*)	**167.** (*c*)	**168.** (*b*)	**169.** (*d*)	**170.** (*b*)
171. (*b*)	**172.** (*c*)	**173.** (*d*)	**174.** (*c*)	**175.** (*b*)	**176.** (*a*)	**177.** (*b*)	**178.** (*b*)	**179.** (*a*)	**180.** (*b*)
181.(*c*)	**182.** (*b*)	**183.** (*a*)	**184.** (*c*)	**185.** (*b*)	**186.** (*a*)	**187.** (*c*)	**188.**(*c*)	**189.** (*b*)	**190.** (*c*)
191. (*c*)	**192.**(*b*)	**193.** (*b*)	**194.** (*c*)	**195.** (*a*)	**196.** (*d*)	**197.** (*b*)	**198.** (*a*)	**199.**(*b*)	**200.** (*a*)
201. (*b*)	**202.** (*a*)	**203.** (*b*)							

EXPLANATIONS

BOOLEAN ALGEBRA AND LOGIC GATES

1. $\overline{(A\oplus B)\cdot C} = \overline{(\bar{A}B + A\bar{B})C} = \overline{\bar{A}B + A\bar{B}} + \bar{C}$

$= \bar{A}\bar{B} + AB + \bar{C}$

2. Output $= \bar{A}\,\bar{B}\,C + \bar{A}\,B\,\bar{C} + ABC + A\bar{B}\bar{C}$

$= \bar{C}\,(\bar{A}\,B + A\,\bar{B}) + C\,(AB + \bar{A}\,\bar{B})$

$= A\oplus B\oplus C$

3.

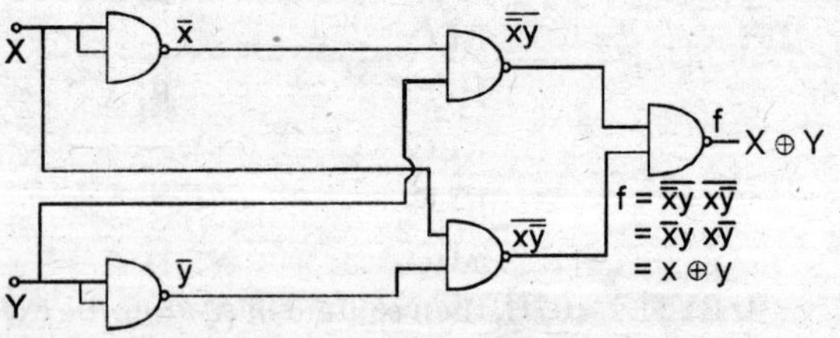

4. Changing + sign to × and vice-versa

12. In sign-magnitude, 1' s complement, + 0 and –0 represented differently but in 2's comlement there is single notation for zero.

13. In Gray code successive Code words differ by the complementation of a single bit and this logic has been complemented in the given circuit.

16. $\overline{AB(\bar{B}C+AC)} = (\bar{A} + \bar{B}) + (B + \bar{C})\,.\,(\bar{A} + \bar{C})$

17. $f = \overline{x\oplus y}$

$= x\odot y$

$= \bar{x}\,\bar{y} + xy$

19. Drawing the K-map.

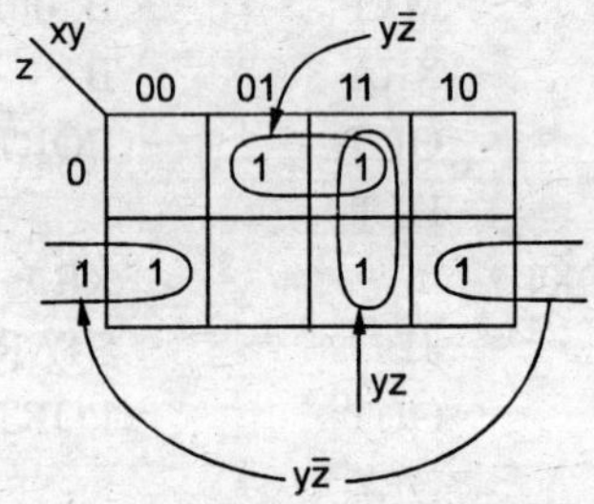

From the k-map, simplified function

$f = XZ + \bar{Y}Z + Y\bar{Z}$

26. $f = (x + z)\,(\overline{w} + y)$

WX \ YZ	00	01	11	10
00	0	1	1	0
01	1	1	1	1
11	0	0	1	1
10	0	0	1	0

27. $f = \overline{w}\,\overline{x}\,\overline{y} + \overline{x}\,\overline{z} + \overline{w}\,\overline{y}$

WX \ YZ	00	01	11	10
00	1	1		1
01				
11			1	1
10	1		1	1

28.

$f_1 =$

a \ bc	00	01	11	10
0			1	1
1		1	1	

$f_2 =$

a \ bc	00	01	11	10
0				1
1		1	1	1

$f_3 =$

a \ bc	00	01	11	10
0	1	1	1	
1			1	

$f_1 = a\bar{b}c + \bar{a}b\bar{c} + bc = ac + \bar{a}b$

$f_2 = a\bar{b}c + ab + \bar{a}b\bar{c} = ac + b\bar{c}$

$f_3 = \bar{a}\bar{b}\bar{c} + abc + \bar{a}c = \bar{a}\bar{b} + bc$

Thus,

$P_1 = \bar{a}b$, $P_2 = ac$, $P_3 = b\bar{c}$, $P_4 = \bar{b}c$, $P_5 = \bar{a}\bar{b}$

29. Let input be 1010

Output will be 1101

Let input be 0110

output will be 0100

This convert gray to Binary code

COMBINATIONAL LOGIC CIRCUIT

31. When either A or B or both are at zero potential, current flows through R, thereby bringing the potential of C to zero level, Thus logic output is zero.

When both of them are at 5V no current can flow and voltage of C stays at –5V, i.e. logic output of 1.

	Potential at		Logic input to		Potential at	Logic output
S.No.	A	B	A	B	C	C
1	0	–5	0	1	0	0
2	–5	0	1	0	0	0
3	0	0	0	0	0	0
4	–5	5	1	1	–5	1

Thus it is AND gate.

32.

x	y	x_1	x_2	z
0	0	1	0	1
0	1	1	1	1
1	0	1	1	1
1	1	0	1	1

Then

x	y	z
0	0	1
0	1	1
1	0	1
1	1	1

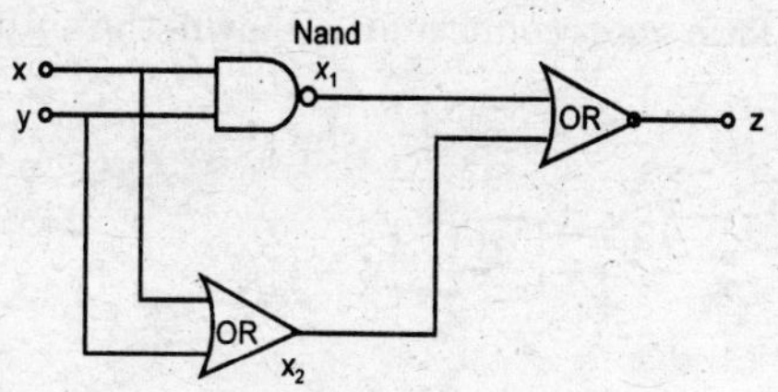

33. Truth-table for half-subtractor

A	B	X	D
0	0	0	0
0	1	1	1
1	0	0	1
1	1	0	0

Drawing K-maps,

B \ A	0	1
0	0	0
1	1	0

$X = \bar{A}B$

B \ A	0	1
0	0	1
1	1	0

$D = A\bar{B} + \bar{A}B$

35.

AB \ CD	00	01	11	10
00	1			1
01		1		1
11		1		1
10	×	×		

$\bar{A}\bar{B}\bar{D} + B\bar{C}D + BC\bar{D}$

$\overline{(A\bar{B}+\bar{A}\bar{\bar{B}})\oplus(\bar{A}B+\bar{\bar{A}}\bar{B})}$

36. $f = A + A\bar{B} + A\bar{B}C$

$= A + A\bar{B} = \mathbf{A}$

Hence, number of NAND gates required is 0.

38. The gates are XNOR

$F = \overline{(A\oplus\bar{B})\oplus(\bar{A}\oplus B)} = \overline{(A\bar{B}+\bar{A}\bar{\bar{B}})\oplus(\bar{A}B+\bar{\bar{A}}\bar{B})}$

$= \overline{(A\bar{B}+\bar{A}B)\oplus(\bar{A}B+A\bar{B})}$

$= \overline{(A\bar{B}+\bar{A}B)\oplus(\bar{A}B+A\bar{B})}$

$= \mathbf{0}$

39. Carry look ahead adder is after since the carry is generated in parallel at all stages of addition rather than sequentially as in ripple adders.

40. In terms of Boolean operations

Output of 1 is $x_0 x_1$

Output of 2 is $(x_0 x_1 + x_2)$

Output of 3 is $(x_0 x_1 + x_2) x_3 = x_0 x_1 x_3 + x_2 x_3$

Output of 4 is $x_0 x_1 x_3 + x_2 x_3 + x_4$

Output of 5 would be $x_0 x_1 x_3 x_5 + x_2 x_3 x_5 + x_4 x_5$

Output of 6 would be $x_0 x_1 x_3 x_5 + x_2 x_3 x_5 + x_4 x_5 x_6$

Thus for n gates connected as shown, the output would be

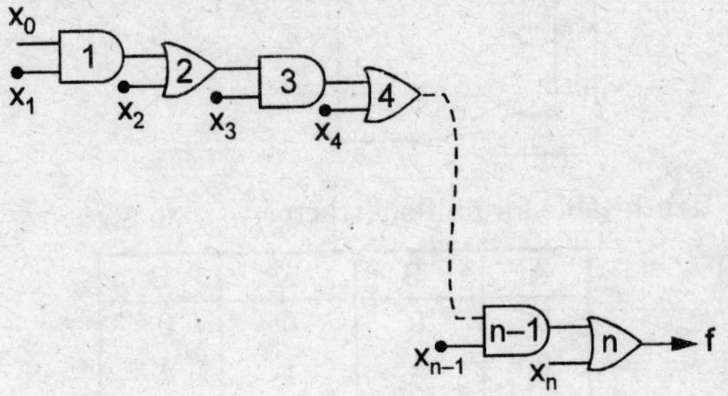

$x_0x_1x_3 .... x_{n-1}$

$+ x_2x_3x_5 .... x_{n-1}$

$+ x_4x_5x_7 .... x_{n-1}$

$+ x_{h-2}\, x_{n-1}$

$+ x_n$.

41.

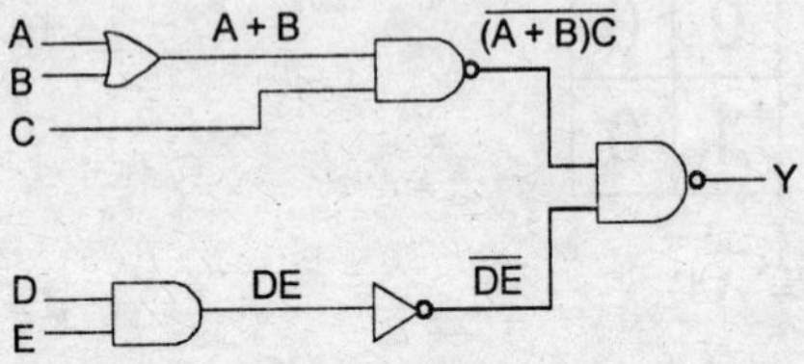

$$Y = \overline{\overline{(A + B)C}.\overline{DE}} = (A + B)\,C + DE$$

43. The circuit of a 4-bit full adder using half adders and OR gates is shown in the figure

From the figure, it is apparent that 4-bit full adder required seven half adders and 3-OR gates.

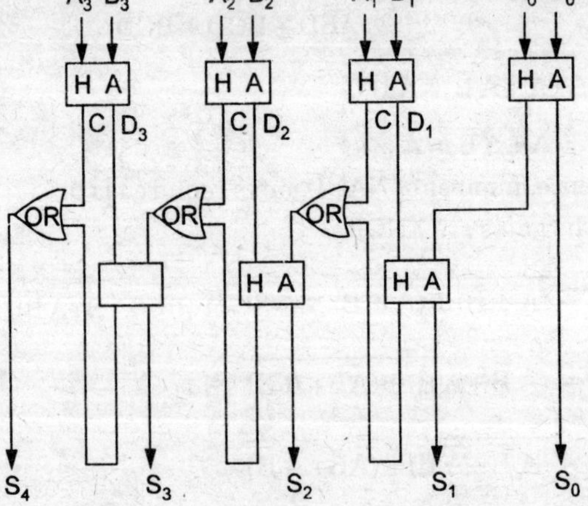

44. $m_6 = \bar{A}BC\bar{D}$, $m_9 = A\bar{B}\bar{C}D$

After complementing literal

$$m_6' = A\bar{B}\bar{C}D = m_9, \quad m_9' = \bar{A}BC\bar{D} = m_6$$

45. Before Gate No. (2) being removed

output, $F = xy\bar{z} + \bar{w}\,z + \bar{w} = xy\bar{z} + \bar{w}\,(1 + z)$

After Gate No. 2 being removed

output, $F = xy\bar{z} + \bar{w}$

46. $x = \bar{A}\,BC + AB + AC$

$= (\bar{A}\,B + A)\,C + AB$

$= (\bar{A} + A)\,(B + A)\,C + AD$

$= (A + B)\,C + AB$

$= AC + BC + AB$

55.

WX \ YZ	00	01	11	20
00			1	
01		1	1	
11		1		
10				

Using K-map,

$$f = x\bar{y}z + \bar{w}yz$$

Hence gate 2 is redundant

59. $V_H = 5.6 + 0.7 = 6.3$ V, $V_L = -5.6 - 0.7 = -6.3$ V

Let $1k\Omega = R_1$,

$$\therefore \quad V_{TH} = -\left(\frac{R_1}{R_2}\right)V_L, \text{ and } \quad V_{TL} = -\left(\frac{R_1}{R_2}\right)V_H$$

$$\therefore \quad V_{TH} - V_{TL} = 1 = -\frac{R_1}{R_2}\,(V_L - V_H)$$

$$\Rightarrow \quad 1 = \frac{1k}{R_2}\,(2)\,(-6.3)$$

$$\Rightarrow \quad R_2 = 12.6\ k\Omega$$

60.

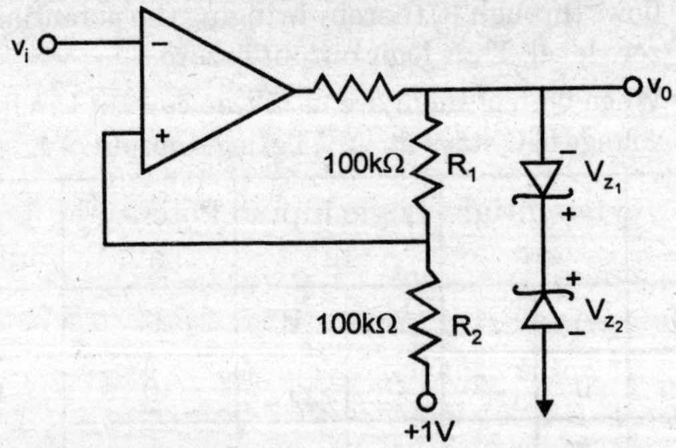

When input voltage is very low, then output voltage will be miximum positive.

It will saturate at $V_0 = V_D + V_{Z1}$.

$$\therefore \quad V_+ = \left(\frac{R_2}{R_1 + R_2}\right)(V_{z1} + V_D) + \left(\frac{R_1}{R_1 + R_2}\right)V_s$$

When the voltage at the input increases and passes through the above voltage, then voltage V_0 will change to-$(V_{z2} + V_D)$. Hence upper threshold level

$$V_{TH} = \left(\frac{0.1}{100 + 0.1}\right)(4.6 + 0.6) + \left(\frac{0.1}{100 + 0.1}\right)(1)$$

$$\approx 1.0042 \text{ V}$$

61. When $V_i > V_{TH}$, $V_0 = -(V_{z2} + V_D)$

$$V_+ = \left(\frac{-R_2}{R_1 + R_2}\right)(V_{z2} + V_D) + \left(\frac{R_1}{R_1 + R_2}\right)V_S$$

When voltage at the input decreases and passes through this value, then voltage V_0 changes to $(V_{z1} + V_D)$.

$$\therefore \quad V_{TL} = \left(\frac{-0.1}{100 + -0.1}\right)(4.6 + 0.6) + \left(\frac{100}{100 + 0.1}\right)(1)$$

$$= 0.9938V$$

SEQUENTIAL LOGIC CIRCUIT

62. When the clock pulse arrives,

$J_0 = 0$, so $Q_{n+1} = Q_n$

$K_0 = 0$ or Q_0 will remain 1

$J_1 = K = 1$ so Q_1 will become $\overline{Q}_1$ or 1

64.

A	B	Q_{n+1}	J
0	0	Q_n	0
0	1	1	1
1	0	Q_n	0
1	1	0	X

$$J = \overline{A}B + AB$$
$$= B(\overline{A} + A) = B$$

65.
$$Z = (A + I).(\overline{A} + J)$$
$$= A\overline{A} + AJ + \overline{A}I + IJ$$
$$= \overline{A}I + AJ + IJ$$

Clearly I should be 1 since A is required

$$\therefore \quad Z = \overline{A} + AJ + J$$
$$J = B, \quad Z = \overline{A} + AB + B$$
$$= \overline{A} + B(1 + A)$$
$$= \overline{A} + B$$

Here $I = 1$ $J = B$

67. Each clip has $2^{12} = 4096k$ bytes = 4 k bytes then the memory system has 8 × 4 bytes

70. Excitation table for T-FF

Q_n	Q_{n+1}	T_n
0	0	0
0	1	1
1	1	0

From the table, $Q^+ = T\overline{Q} + Q\overline{T}$

74. In a switch–tail ring counter, using D-FF, the complementary output $\overline{Q}$ is connected to D input for a single D-FF it becomes a T-FF.

75.
$$f_{max} = \frac{1}{N.T_d} = \frac{1}{4 \times 50 \times 10^{-12}}$$
$$= \mathbf{5\ MHZ.}$$

76. 4 bit SIPO

Pulse 1 XOR (1, 0) = 1 1011

2 XOR (1, 1) = 0 0101

3 XOR (0,1) = 1 1010

The contents will be 1010.

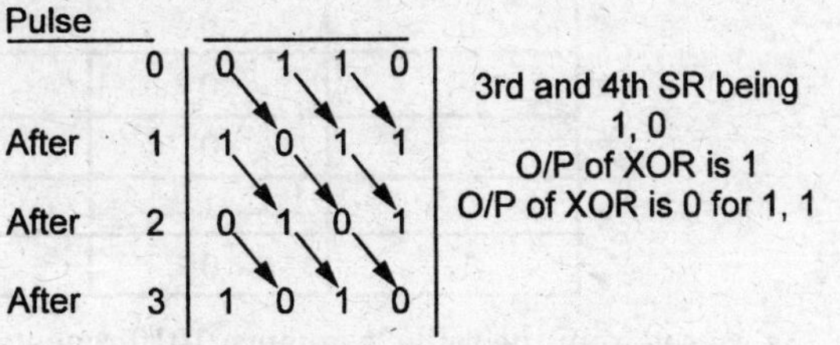

78. The state diagram is as shown below

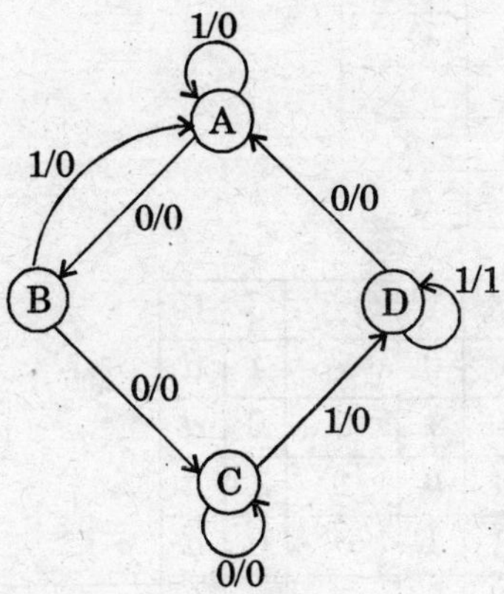

There are 4 minimum state

79. $4 = 2^2$

Thus 2 FF are required.

81. One mod-13 counters followed by the mode-6 counter will result in mod-N counter where N is divisible by both 13 and 6 *i.e.* 78.

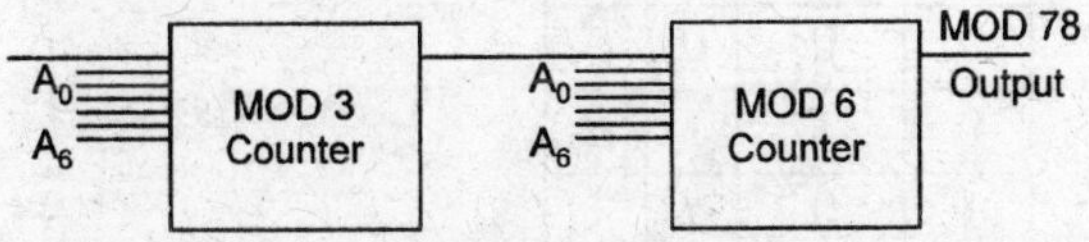

83. Number of FFS required = 2^n = 1024

$\therefore$ $n = \mathbf{10}$

84. It completes one cycle 1024 pulses

For $\frac{2060}{1024}$ = 2048 or 2cycles

Balance = 2060 – 2048 = 12 pulses

Binary 12 = 000 000 1100

86.
$$Y_2 = Q_1 \oplus Q_0$$
$$Y_1 = Q_2 \oplus Y_2$$

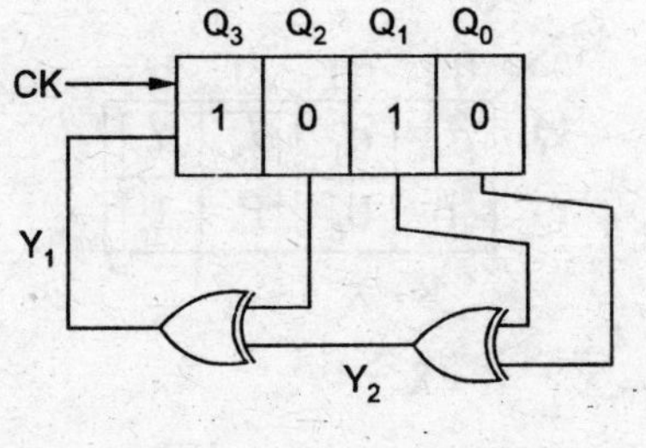

The sequences are as follows :

	Q_3 (Y_1)	Q_2	Q_1	Q_0	Y_1	Y_2
1	1	0	1	0	1	1
2	1	1	0	1	0	1
3	0	1	1	0	0	1
4	0	0	1	1	0	0
5	0	0	0	1	1	1
6	1	0	0	0	0	0
7	0	1	0	0	1	0
	1	0	1	0		

As we see from the table, sequence 1010 repeats after 7 cycles.

87.

J	K	Q_{n+1}
0	0	Q_n
0	1	0
1	0	1
1	1	$\overline{Q}_n$

Q_n	X	Y	Q_{n+1}	J	K
0	0	0	1	1	*d*
0	0	1	0	0	*d*
0	1	0	1	1	*d*
0	1	1	0	0	*d*
1	0	0	1	*d*	0
1	0	1	1	*d*	0
1	1	0	0	*d*	1
1	1	1	0	*d*	1

Q_n	Q_{n+1}	J	K
0	0	0	*d*
0	1	1	*d*
1	0	*d*	1
1	1	*d*	0

K- map For J

Q_n \ XY	00	01	11	10
Q_n	1_0	0_1	0_3	1_2
$\overline{Q}_n$	d_4	d_5	d_7	d_6

$J = \overline{y}$

K- map For K

Q_n \ XY	00	01	11	10
Q_n	d_0	d_1	d_3	d_2
$\overline{Q}_n$	0_4	0_5	1_7	1_6

K = X

$J = \overline{Y}$, K = X

88. Maximum frequency of 1 MHz corresponds to minimum time $= \dfrac{1}{1 \times 10^6}$ = 1 microsecond = **100 nanoseconds.**

89. Ring counter is a N : 1 divider

$$a = \frac{100 \times 10^3}{10} = 10\text{kHz}$$

Mod-20 is a divide by 20 counter

$$b = \frac{10 \times 10^3}{20} = 0.5 \text{ KHz} = 500 \text{ Hz}$$

A 4 bit (4 FFs) is 2^4 = 16 Mod-16 counter

$$\therefore \quad c = \frac{500}{16} = 31.25 \text{ Hz}$$

$$d = \frac{31.25}{8} = 3.9 \text{ Hz}$$

91.

	Present state	Next state
	Q_n	Q_{n+1}
$J_n = 0, k_n = 0$	0	0
	1	1
$J_n = 0, k_n = 1$	0	0
	1	0
$J_n = 1, k_n = 1$	0	1
	1	1
$J_n = 1, k_n = 1$	0	1
	1	0

93. Since all chip has same address, the capacity of word will be increased.

97. Naming the FFs as 1 to 4 from Left to Right after the 3rd clock pulse FF3 is 0 and FF4 is 1 so that X OR output is 1 which is fed to Q_A.

So Q_A to $Q_B \to 0$ Q_B to $Q_C \to 0$. $Q_C \to Q_D \to 0$

After 4th clock pulse 1000

98. There are 1024 memory locations

$\therefore \quad 1024 = 2^{10}$

Hence address bus width = 10 bits.

103. $Q^+ = L\overline{M} + LM\overline{Q} = L(\overline{M} + M\overline{Q}) = L\overline{M} + L\overline{Q}$

L	M	Q^+
0	0	0
0	1	0
1	0	1
1	1	$\overline{Q}_1$

104. All BCD combination can be convert into binary code except 1000 & 1001.
Hence best possible answer is (*a*).

105. $Z = \overline{X}Q + Y\overline{Q}$

X	Y	Z
0	0	Q
0	1	0
1	0	1
1	1	$\overline{Q}$

Comparing from the truth table of J–K FF

$Y = J, X = K$

106.

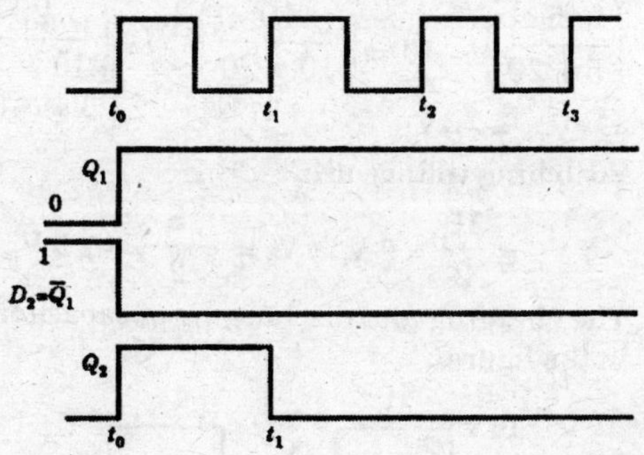

107.

Present State		FF Input		Next State	
Q_A	Q_B	T_A	T_B	Q_A^+	Q_B^+
0	0	0	1	0	1
0	1	1	1	1	0
1	0	1	0	0	0
1	1	1	1	0	0

From table it is clear that it is a MOD – 3 counter.

108. It is a 5 bit ripple counter. At 11000, output of NAND gate is LOW. This will clear all FF. So it is a Mod – 24 counter.

Note that when 11000 occur, the CLR input is activated and all FF are immediately cleared. So it is a MOD 24 counter not MOD 25.

109.

$\overline{Q}_0$	Q_0	Q_2	$\overline{Q}_2$	Q_1	$\overline{Q}_1$			
J_2	K_2	J_1	K_1	J_0	K_0	Q_2^+	Q_1^+	Q_0^+
						1	0	1
0	1	1	0	0	1	0	1	0
1	0	0	1	1	0	1	0	1
0	1	1	0	0	1	0	1	0
1	0	0	1	1	0	1	0	1

We see that 1 0 1 repeat after every two cycles, hence frequency will be $\frac{f_c}{2}$.

110. In ripple counter, delay $4T_d = 40$ ns.
If synchronous counter are clocked simultaneously then its worst delay will be equal to 10 ns.

111. 4 bit uses 4 FF
Total delay $N_{td} = 4 \times 50 \text{ ns} = 200 \times 10^{-9}$

$$f = \frac{1}{200 \times 10^{-9}} = 5 \text{ MHz}$$

MULTIPLEXER

112. $g(x \,.\, y \,.\, z) = F_0 + F_1 = \bar{i}_2 \,.\, z + z\,\bar{i}_2$

$i_2 = F_2 + F_3 = \bar{x}\, y \,.\, xy = 0$

$g(x, y, z) = \overline{z} + z = \mathbf{1}$

113. From the K-map,

$Q = A + B + C$

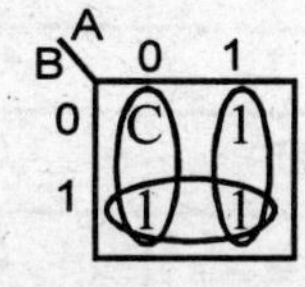

115. $F = \overline{A}\,\overline{B}C + A\overline{B}\,\overline{C} + A\overline{B}\,\overline{C}$

$= \overline{A}\,C(B + \overline{B}) + A\overline{C}\,(B + \overline{B})$

$= \overline{A}\,C + A\overline{C}$

$= \mathbf{A \oplus C}$

117.

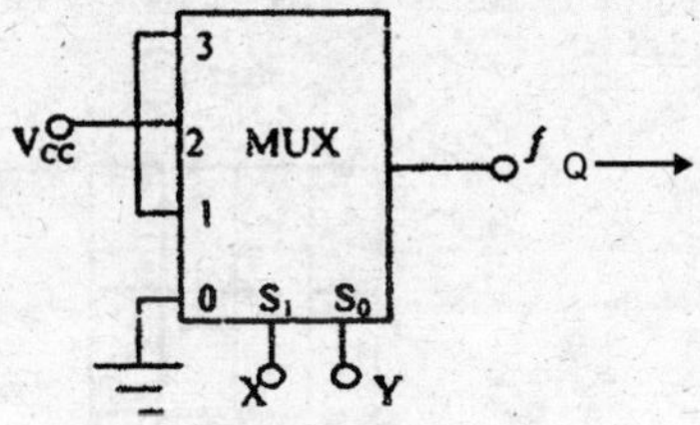

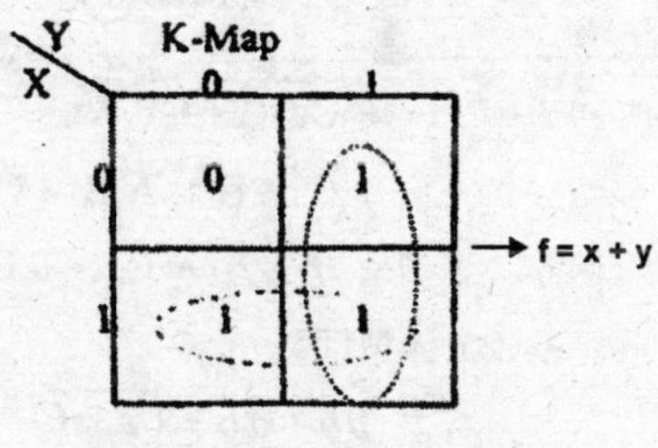

118. Logic functions generated by 4 : 1 MUX are

$F = \overline{S}_1\,\overline{S}_0\,I_0 + \overline{S}_1 S_0 I_1 + \overline{S}_1 S_0 I_2 + S_1 S_0 I_3$

Putting $I_0 = I_1 = C$

$I_2 = I_3 = \overline{C}$

$S_1 = A$

$S_0 = B$

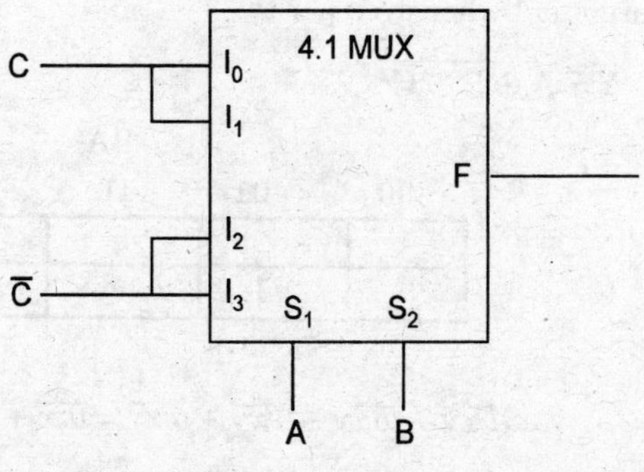

Truth-table is as shown below

S_1 (P)	S_0 (Q)	C_{in}	S
0	0	0	0
0	0	1	1
0	1	0	1
0	1	1	0
1	0	0	1
1	0	1	0
1	1	0	0
1	1	1	1

Now, Reducing the truth-table as

S_1	S_0	S	
0	0	C_{in}	I_0
0	1	$\overline{C}_{in}$	I_1
1	0	$\overline{C}_{in}$	I_2
1	1	C_{in}	I_3

Thus, $I_0 = I_3 = C_{in}$

$\overline{I}_1 = \overline{I}_2 = C_{in} \Rightarrow I_1 = I_2 = \overline{C}_{in}$

119. offset $F_1 = \overline{C}\,\overline{A}\,\overline{B} + \overline{C}\,AB = \overline{C}\,(AB + \overline{A}\,\overline{B}) = \overline{C}\,(\overline{A \otimes B})$

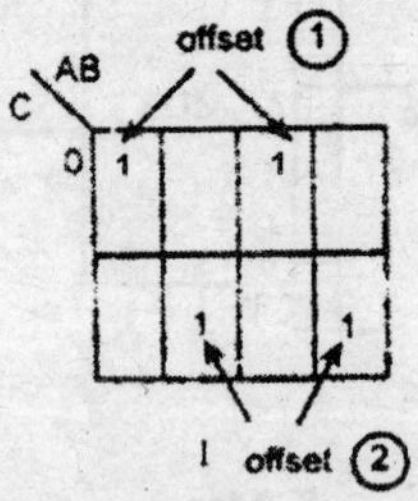

offset 2 $F_2 = C\overline{B}A + CB\overline{A}$

$= C\,(A\overline{B} + \overline{A}B) = C\,(A \oplus B)$

$F = (f_1 + f_2) = C.(A \oplus B) + \overline{C}\,(\overline{A \oplus B})$

122. Output of first MUX

$$Z_0 = ab + \overline{a}\overline{b} = (\overline{a \oplus b})$$

This is input to select S_0 of both second-level MUX

$$Z_1 = CS_0 + \overline{C}\overline{S_0} = C \oplus \overline{S_0} = a \oplus b \oplus c$$

123. The equation of Z_1 is the equation of sum of A and B with carry and equation of 2 is the resultant carry.

Thus, it is a full adder.

124. $Z = \overline{X}Y + X\overline{Y} + XY, \quad Z = X + Y$

125. Output is 1 when even parity

$\therefore\ Y = \overline{A \oplus B \oplus C}$

C \ BA	00	01	11	10
0	1		1	
1		1		1

126. Let $z = 0$

Then $f = \overline{w}\overline{x}\overline{y} + \overline{w}\overline{x}y + w\overline{x}\overline{y} + wx\overline{y} = \overline{w}\overline{x} + w\overline{y}$

If we put z = 0 in given option, then

(a) $= \overline{wx} + x\overline{y}$ (b) $= wy + \overline{wxy}$ (c) $= \overline{w}\overline{x} + w\overline{y}$

Since MUX is enable.

SCHMITT TRIGGER

130. Upper crossover voltage when $V_0 = +10$ V

At upper threshold point

$$\left(\frac{5}{5+20}\right)(10) = \left(\frac{5}{10+20}\right)(2) + \left(\frac{20}{10+20}\right)V_{TH}$$

$$\Rightarrow \frac{2}{3}V_{TH} = 2 - \frac{2}{3} \quad \Rightarrow \quad V_{Th} = 2\text{ V}$$

Lower crossover voltage when $V_0 = -10$ V

$$\left(\frac{5}{5+20}\right)(-10) = \left(\frac{10}{10+20}\right)(2) = \left(\frac{20}{10+20}\right)V_{TL}$$

$$\Rightarrow V_{TL} = -4\text{V}$$

131. Switching voltage are

$$V_+ = \frac{10}{2} = 5\text{ V}, \quad V_+ = -\frac{5}{2} = -2.5\text{ V}$$

The charging and discharging of capacitor is shown in the figure

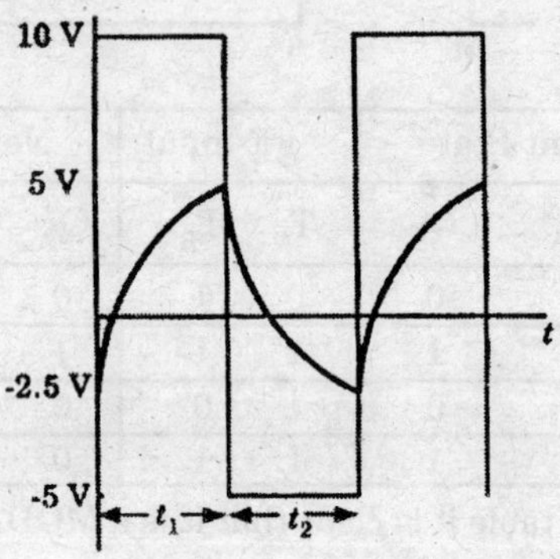

$$\therefore \quad 5 = 10 + (-2.5 - 10)\ e^{-\frac{t_1}{RC}}$$

$$\Rightarrow \quad e^{-\frac{t_1}{RC}} = \frac{2}{5} \quad \Rightarrow \quad t_1 = RC \ln 2.5$$

$$\therefore \quad -2.5 = -5 + (5 - (-5))\ e^{-\frac{t_2}{RC}}$$

$$\Rightarrow \quad e^{-\frac{t_2}{RC}} = \frac{1}{4}$$

$$\Rightarrow \quad t_2 = RC \ln 4,$$

$$T = t_1 + t_2 = RC \ln 2.5 + RC \ln 4$$

$$= RC \ln 10$$

$$R = 50\text{ k}\Omega,\ C = 0.01\ \mu\text{F}$$

$$\Rightarrow \quad T = 50k \times 0.01\ \mu \times \ln 10 = 1.15\text{ ms}$$

$$f = \frac{1}{T} = 869\text{ Hz}$$

SAMPLE AND HOLD CIRCUIT

132. For proper functioning, clock period should be equal to or greater than all the t_{pd}

MOD – 12 – 4 FFs = 4×60 = 240 ns.

t_{pd} = 25 ns.

$\therefore$ Total t_{pd} = 265 ns

f_c = **3.774 MHz**

133. $I = \frac{Q}{t} = \frac{\frac{0.5}{100} \times Q}{t}$

$= \frac{0.005 \times CV}{10^{-6}} = \frac{0.005 \times 10^{-10} \times 5}{10^{-6}}$

$= 25 \times 10^{-7} = \mathbf{2.5\ \mu A.}$

134. Duty cycle, $\alpha = \frac{T_{ON}}{T}$

$\therefore \quad T_{ON} = \alpha T = 0.75\ T$

$= 0.75 \times 10^{-4} = 75\ \mu$ sec.

As $\quad T_{ON} = 0.7C\ (R_A + R_B)$

$\therefore \quad \frac{75 \times 10^{-6}}{0.7 \times 10^{-8}} = R_A + R_B$

$\Rightarrow \quad R_A + R_B = 10.714\ k\Omega$

and $\quad T_{OFF} = 0.7C\ R_B$

$\therefore \quad R_B = \frac{25 \times 10^{-6}}{0.7 \times 10^{-8}} = 3.57\ k\Omega$

$\therefore \quad R_A = \mathbf{7.25\ k\Omega}$

A/D AND D/A CONVERTERS

136. Smallest incremental change $= \frac{1}{2^{10}} = \frac{1}{1024}$

For 5 V, $\frac{5}{1024}$ = nearly 5 mV

137. Number of comparators $= 2^N - 1 = 2^8 - 1 = \mathbf{255}$

138. $I_o = \frac{2}{R}$ and $E_o = -\left(\frac{2}{R}\right) \cdot R_f = -2 \times 2 = \mathbf{-4V}$

139. Using KVL, we have

$\frac{V_a}{2R} + \frac{V_a - V}{2R} + \frac{V_a - V_b}{R} = 0$

$\Rightarrow \quad 4V_a = 2V_b + V$

and $\quad \frac{V_b - V_a}{R} + \frac{V_a}{2R} + \frac{V_b}{2R} = 0$

$\Rightarrow \quad 2V_b = V_a$

$\therefore \quad 3V_a = V$

$\Rightarrow \quad V_b = \frac{V}{6}$ and $I = \frac{\mathbf{V}}{\mathbf{12\ R}}$

140. Quantizing error $= \frac{V}{2^N} = \frac{8}{2^3} = \mathbf{1V.}$

141. As, $\frac{1}{2^N - 1} \leq 0.004$

$\therefore \quad 2^N \geq 251 \quad \Rightarrow \quad N = 8,$

hence minimum value of N satisfying the condition.

142. For N-bit, successive A/D converter, the number of clock pulses required is N-clock pulse.

144. $2^{n-1}\ R = 32,$

where $\quad n = 4$

$\therefore \quad 2^3\ R = 32 \Rightarrow R = \mathbf{4\ k\text{-}ohm}$

147. The waveform for dual slope integrater is shown. Maximum frequency can be attained when $T_2 - T_1 = 0$ and, as $T_1 = 2^N\ T_C$ (T_C = clockperiod)

$\therefore \quad f_{max} = \frac{1}{2^N . T_C} = \frac{f_C}{2^N} = \frac{10^6}{1024} \approx \mathbf{1kHz}$

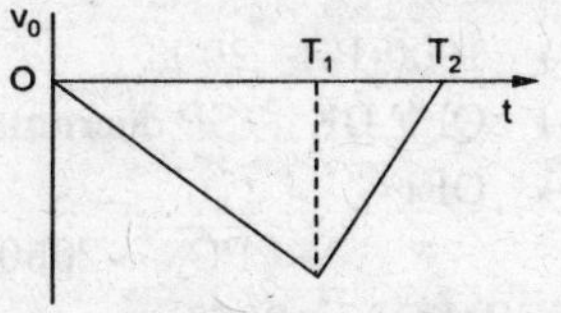

148. A 10 bit convertor has a quantization error of

$= \frac{1}{1024} = \frac{1}{2^{10}} = 0.1\%.$

If an analog portion can be constructed to an accuracy of 0.1%, it would seen reasonable to strive for an overall accuracy of 0.2 %.

149. The digital input 10100 is the binary equivalent of 20_{10}. Since, I_{out} = 10mA, for this case proportionating factor is 0.5

i.e. $\quad I_{out} = 0.5 \times$ binary value.

Thus, binary input 11101 is equivalent ot 29_{10},

$\therefore \quad I_{out} = 0.5 \times 29 = 14.5$ mA.

150. Step size $= \frac{-V_{ref}}{8R} R_F = -5 \times \frac{10k}{8} \times 20k = -0.3125V$

$1111_2 = 15_{10}$

Full scale voltage $= -0.3125 \times 15 = -4.6875$ V

151. (Digital value) × resolution $> V_A + V_T$

(Digital value) × 40 mV > 6.001 V = 6001 mV

Digital value > 150.025, $\quad 151_{10} = 10010111_2$

152. $V_{out} = -V_1 \left[\frac{R}{R} b_0 + \frac{R}{2R} b_1 + \frac{R}{4R} b_2 + \frac{R}{4R} b_3\right]$

Exact value when $V_1 = 5$, for maximum output

$V_{out} = -5\left[1 + \frac{1}{2} + \frac{1}{4} + \frac{1}{8}\right] = -9.375$

Maximum V_{out} due to tolerance

$= -5.5\left[\frac{110}{90} + \frac{110}{2 \times 90} + \frac{110}{4 \times 90} + \frac{110}{8 \times 90}\right] = -12.604$

$\therefore$ Tolerance = 34.44% = 35%

MICROPROCESSOR

156. Call decrements the top by 2.

$\therefore \quad$ SP = 27 FD.

POP H stores 06 in L register and 10 in H register

$\therefore \quad$ HL = 1006

157. $C = \frac{1\ t}{V} = \frac{0.1 \times 10^{-12} \times 20 \times 10^{-3}}{0.5} = \mathbf{4 \times 10^{-15} F}$

163. There are 64 words in a block.

Hence, 4K cache has $\frac{4 \times 1024}{64}$ = 64 blocks.

Since 1 set has 4 blocks, there are 16 sets.

16 sets need 2^4 bit representation.

In a set there are 4 blocks, so block field needs 2 bits.

Each block has 64 words, so word field has 6 bits.

164. Memory mapped I / O

1. I / O have 16 bit addresses
2. Devices are accessed like registers
3. Mass devices = 2^{16} = 256
4. Arithmetic / Logic operations can be done.

165. After instruction :

2000 SP →	1000 PC	2003
2003 SP →	OFF DE	(SP decrement by 2)
2004 SP →	OFFC	(")
2005		PC → 2050

SP has OFFC, PC has 2050

Memory address in hex	*Instruction*	*Remarks*
2000	LXI	SP 1000
2003	PUSH	H
	We do not know the contents of subroutine at 2050.	
2004	PUSH	D
2005	CALL	2025
2006	50	
2007	20	
2008	POP H	
2009	HALT	

At the completion of the execution of the program, the program counter of the 8085 contains 2050 and the stack pointer contains OFFC.

166. In this case

	OR ARRAY	AND ARRAY
PROM	Programmable	Fixed
PLA	Programmable	Programmable

167. Since one bit is used for sign, therefore

FFFF = 15 + 16 × 15 + 256 × 15 + 4096 × 7 = **32,767.**

168. The figure shows various sources of address register. The control unit maintains a special purpose or dedicated register called *Program Couter* (PC) which keeps track of which instruction is to be executed next. PC is an operational register which always holds the address of either the next instruction to be executed or the addrss of the next word of a multiword instruction that has not been completely fetched.

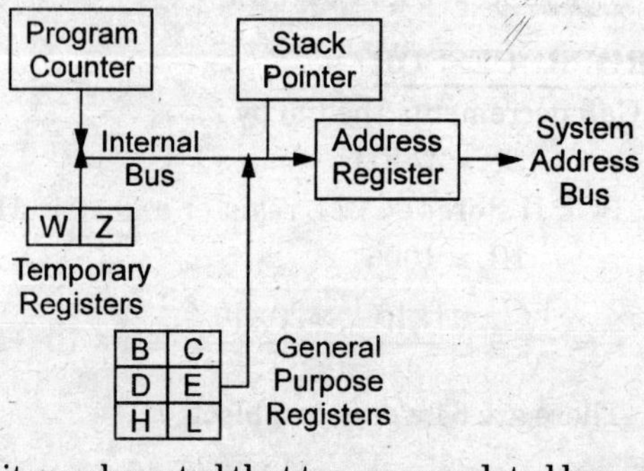

169. Here it may be noted that to accommodated long access times, the microprocessor 8085 has a state called WAIT state.

When microprocessor generates an address in state T_1 external control logic that monitors this state may ask the microprocessor to wait for a certain period of time which are integrals of check periods. To achieve this, external control logic makes the READY input t_0 state T_2 logic 0.

When input to T_2 is logic 0, then microprocessor enters state T_w (L_{WAIT}) instead of T_3.

When READY logic becomes 1, then machine cycle goes to state T_3.

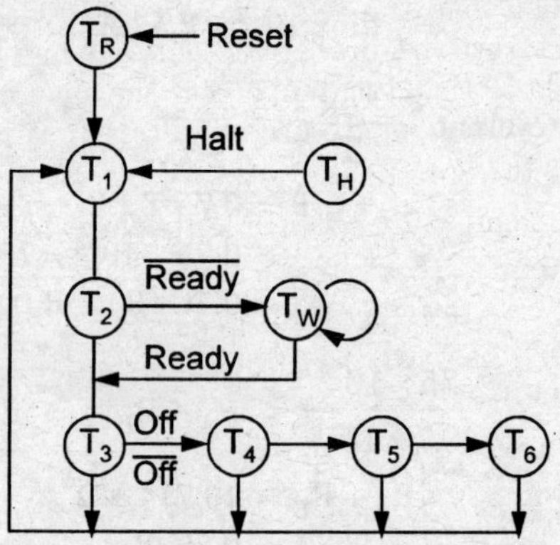

So during WAIT state, all external signals from the microprocessor are held in the same state as they were at the end of state T_2.

By this method, duration of the address is stetched and access times greater than that of microprocessor accommodated.

170. E corresponds to decimal 14 or 14_{10}

$$\therefore \quad E\,5 = 14_{10} \times 16^1 + 5_{10} \times 16^0$$
$$= 14 \times 16 + 5 \times 1$$
$$= \mathbf{229}$$

171. 512, 64, 8 and 1 an all powers of 8.

The proceeding number is translatable in second to an octal number

$$3 \times 8^3 + 7 \times 8^2 + 5 \times 8^1 + 3 \times 8^0$$
$$3753_8 = 011\ 111\ 101\ 011_2.$$

172. The greatest number which can be stored in 8 bits using 2's complement is

$$1111\ \ 1111 = \mathbf{-128}$$

175. Control word format of INTEL 8253 is :

D_7	D_6	D_5	D_4	D_3	D_2	D_1	D_0
SC_1	SCO	RW1	RWO	M2	M1	MO	BCD

SC-select number

$\overline{SC_1}$	SCO	
0	0	Select counter 0
0	1	Select counter 1
1	0	Select counter 2
1	1	Read back command

0	0	0	Mode 0
0	0	1	Mode 1
×	1	0	Mode 2
×	1	1	Mode 3
1	0	0	Mode 4
1	0	1	Mode 5

From the format, it can be inferred that control word sets counter 1 to mode 0

176. This instruction compare contents of B with the contents of accumulator.

If A < B, carry flag is set and zero flag is reset.

178. At a time 8085 can drive only a digit.
In a second each digit is refreshed 500 times.

Thus time given to each digit = $\dfrac{1}{(5\times 500)}$ = 0.4 ms.

185. ACI 56H ;A + 56H + CY → A
37H + 56H + 1 = 8EH

187. Instruction load the register pairs HL with 01FFH. SHLD instruction store the contents of L in the memory location 2050 H and content of H in the memory location 2051H. Contents of HL are not altered.

190. 12 adder + 4 data lines

bits chip = $2^{12} \times 4$ = 16 kbits/chip

Memo =16 kbytes

= 16 k × 8 bits

Number of chips = $\dfrac{16k\times 8}{16k} = 8$

195.

```
        MVI    A, DATA1   ; DATA1→ A
        MOV    B, A       ; A → B
        SUI    51H        ; A – 51H → A
        JC     DLT        ; If CY=1,
                            Jump on DLT
        MOV    A, B       ; B → A
        SUI    82H        ; A – 82H → A
        JC     DSPLY      ; If CY = 1,
                            Jump on
                          ; DSPLY
DLT:    XRA    A          ; EX-OR A
        OUT    PORT1      ; A → PORT1
DSPLY:  MOV    A, B       ; B → A
        OUT    PORT2      ; A → PORT2
        HLT
```

If DATA1 is less then 51H, SUI 51H will set the CY flag and execution will jump on DLT. After this a will be cleared and output at PORT1 will be 00. If DATA1 is greater than 51H and less than or equal to 82H, execution will jump on DSPLY and DATA1 will be displayed at PORT2.

196.

```
        MVI    A, 00H     ; Clear accumulator
LOOP:   ADD    B          ; Add the contents of
                            B to A
        DCR    C          ; Decrement C
        JNZ    LOOP       ; If C is not zero
                            jump to loop
        HLT
        END
```

This instruction set add the contents of B to accumulator to contents of C times.

197.

```
        MVI    B, 87H     ; B = 87
        MOV    A, B       ; A = B = 87
START:  JMP    NEXT       ; Jump to next
        XRA    B          ; A ⊕ B → A,
                          ; A = 00, B = 87
        JP     START      ; Since A = 00 is
                            positive
                          ; so jump to START
        JMP    NEXT       ; Jump to NEXT
                          ; unconditionally
NEXT:   XRA    B          ; A ⊕ B → A, A = 87,
                          ; B = 87H
        JP     START      ; will not jump as D7,
                            of A is 1
        OUT    PORT2      ; A = 87 → PORT2
```

198.

```
        LXI    H, 4A02H   ; Store destination
                            address
                          ; in HL pair
        LDA    4A00H      ; Load A with
                            contents of
                          ; memory location
                            A00H
        MOV    B, A       ; A → B
        LDA    4A01H      ; Load A with
                            contents of
                          ; memory location
                            4A01H
        CMA    B          ; Compare A and B
        JZ     FNSH       ; Jump to FNSH
                            if two
                          ; number are equal
        JC     GRT        ; If CY = 1, (A < B)
                            jump
                          ; to GRT
        MOV    M, A       ; Otherwise A →
                            (4A02H)
        JMP    FNSH
GRT:    MOV    M, B
FNSH:   HLT
```

This program find the larger of the two number stored in location 4A00H and 4A01H and store it in memory location 4A002.

A7H > 98H

Thus A7H will be stored at 4A02H.

199. Let $X_3X_2X_1X_0$ be 1001, then $Y_3Y_2Y_1Y_0$ will be 1111
Let $X_3X_2X_1X_0$ be 1000, then $Y_3Y_2Y_1Y_0$ will be 1110
Let $X_3X_2X_1X_0$ be 0110, then $Y_3Y_2Y_1Y_0$ will be 1100
So this converts 2-4-2-1,BCD numbers.

200. The instruction XRA will set the Z flag. LXI and DCX does not alter the flag. Hence this loop will be executed 1 times.

201.

```
        MVI    A, B7H     ; B7H → A
        ORA    A          ; Set Flags, CY = 1
        RLC               ; Rotate accumulator
                            left
```

The contents of bit D_7 are placed in bit D_0.

		Accumulator
Before	RLC	10100111
After	RLC	01001111

202. This program multiply BYTE1 by 10. Hence content of A will be 46H.

07H = 07_{10}, 7 × 10 = 70_{10} = 46H

203. Contents of Accumulator A = 0011 0010

After first RRC = 0001 1001

After second RRC = 1000 1100

PRACTICE QUESTIONS

1. The contents of some memory location of an 8085 μP based system are shown :

Address. (Hex.)	Contents (Hex.)
3000	02
3001	30
3002	00
3003	30

The program is as follows

```
LHLD   3000H
MOV    E, M
INX    H
MOV    D, M
LDAX   D
MOV    L,A
INX    D
LDAX   D
MOV    H, A
```

The contents if HL pair after the execution of the program will be

(*a*) 0030 H (*b*) 3000 H

(*c*) 3002 H (*d*) 0230 H

2. Consider following set of 8085 instruction:

```
MVI          A, DATA1
ORA          A
JP           DSPLY
XRA          A
DSPLY : OUT  PORTI
HLT
```

If DATA1= 92H, then output at PORT1 is

(*a*) 00

(*b*) FFH

(*c*) 92 H

(*d*) none of these

3. The switching speed of ECL is very high, because the transistors

(*a*) are switched between cut-off and saturation regions.

(*b*) and switched between active and saturation regions.

(*c*) and switched between active and cut-off regions.

(*d*) may operate in any of three regions.

4. In standard TTL, 'totem pole' stage refers to

(*a*) multi–emitter input stage

(*b*) phase–splitter

(*c*) output buffer

(*d*) open collector output stage

5. Data can be changed from spatial code to temporal code and vice-versa by using

(*a*) ADCs and DACs

(*b*) shift-registers

(*c*) synchronous counter

(*d*) timers

6. In the given figure, the LED.

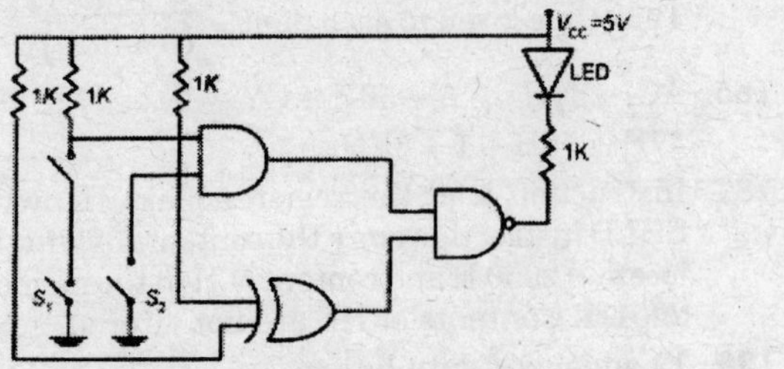

(*a*) emits light when both S_1 and S_2

(*b*) emits light when both S_1 and S_2 are open

(*c*) emits light when only one of S_1 and S_2 is closed

(*d*) does not emits light irrespective of the switch positions.

7. For the logic circuit shown in the figure, output *y* is given by

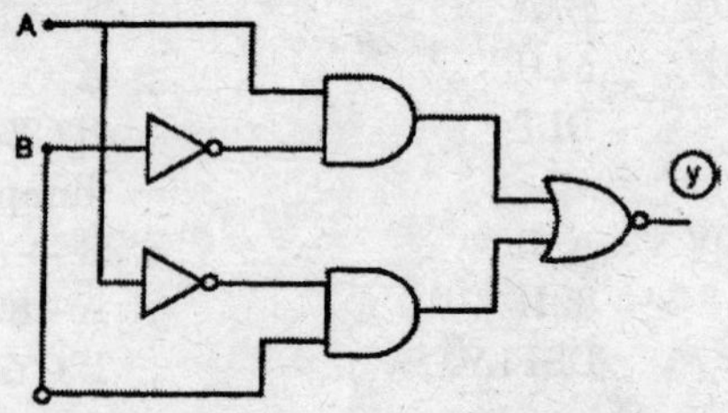

(*a*) A. B (*b*) $AB + \overline{A}\,\overline{B}$

(*c*) $A\overline{B} + \overline{A}.B$ (*d*) $A\overline{B} + \overline{A} + B$

8. To realise given truth table from the circuit shown in the figure, the input to J in terms of A and B would have to be

A	B	Q_{n+1}	J
0	0	Q_n	0
0	1	1	1
1	0	Q_n	0
1	1	0	×

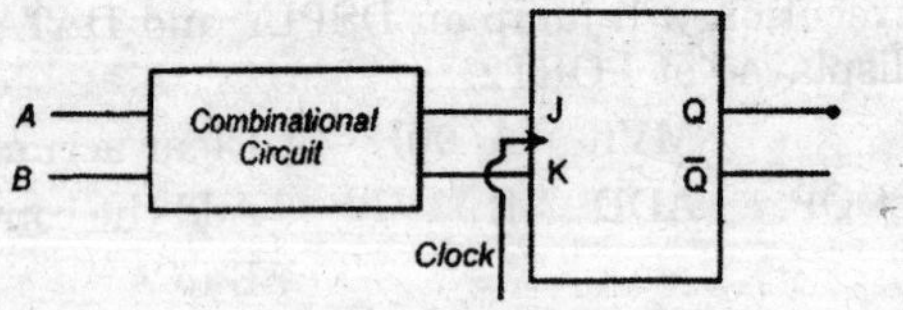

(*a*) $\overline{AB}$ (*b*) $\overline{A}$

(*c*) B (*d*) AB

9. In the circuit shown, the output will be

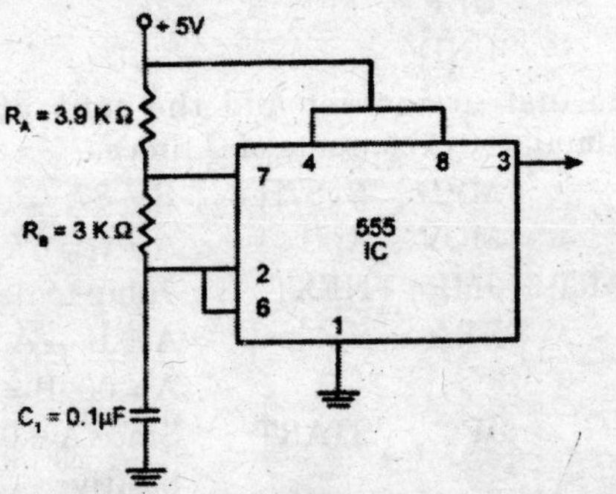

(*a*) sine wave (*b*) square wave pulse

(*c*) linear (*d*) non-linear

10. The circuit shown below is a

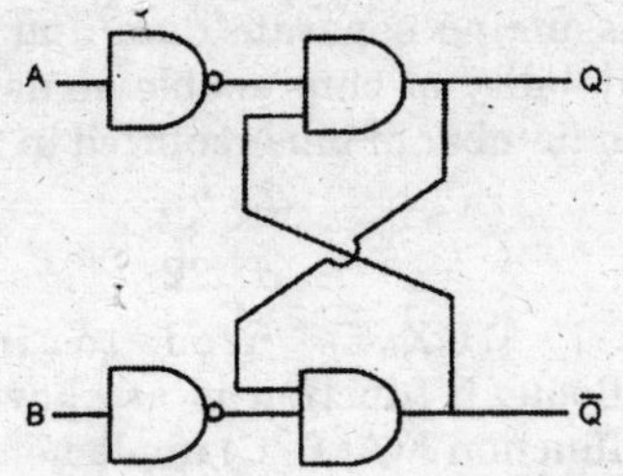

(*a*) J – K flip flop (*b*) Jhonsons counter
(*c*) R-S latch (*d*) None of these

11. The circuit shown in the figure is a

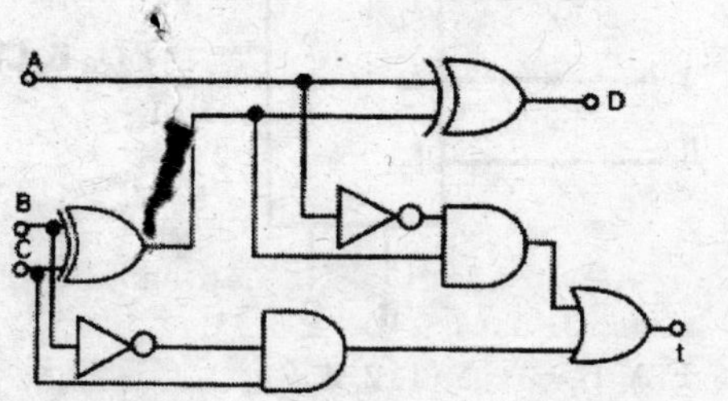

(*a*) Full adder (*b*) Full subtractor
(*c*) Shift register (*d*) Decade counter

12. In the circuit shown below, the F output is given by

(*a*) F = 1 (*b*) F = 0
(*c*) F = *x* (*d*) F = 2

13. Output voltage of a network shown in figure if digital input is 1011, is

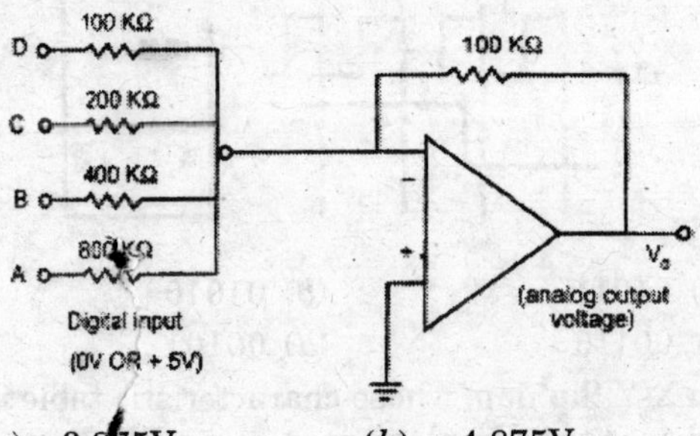

(*a*) – 3.875V (*b*) – 4.875V
(*c*) – 5.875V (*d*) – 6.875V

14. The circuit shown in the given figure is a

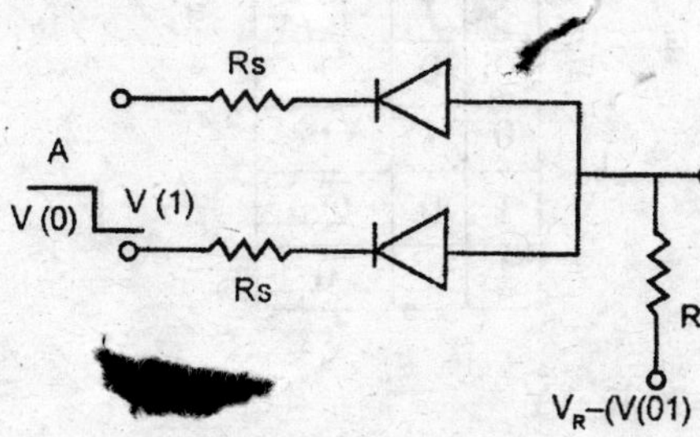

(*a*) positive logic OR circuit
(*b*) negative logic OR gate
(*c*) positive logic NAND gate
(*d*) negative logic NAND gate

15. J-K flip shown in figure is initially reset so that Q = 0. A sequence of four clock pulses is, then applied, with the J and K inputs, as given in the figure, Resulting sequence of values that the output Q will have, is given by

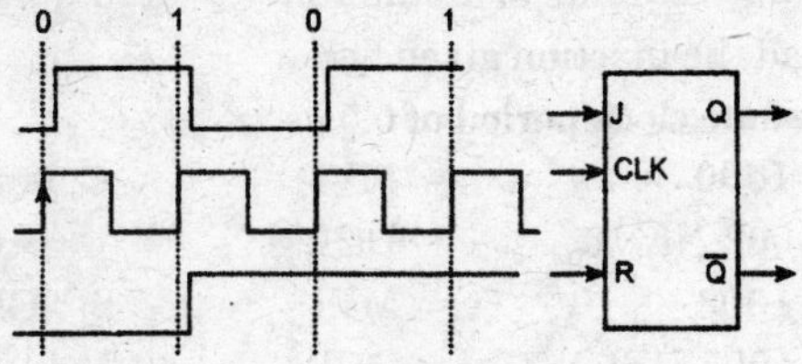

(*a*) 01011 (*b*) 01010
(*c*) 00110 (*d*) 00101

16. Which of the following statements are correct?
(*a*) A flips-flop is used to store 1 bit of information
(*b*) Race-around condition accurs in a J-k flip-flop when both the inputs are 1.
(*c*) A transparent latch consists of a D-type flip-flop
(*d*) All of these

17. Contents of accumulator after execution of following instructions will be

MVI	A, A7H
ORA	A
RLC	

(*a*) CFH (*b*) 4FH
(*c*) 4EH (*d*) CEH

18. Which of the following condition, clocked J-K flip-flop can be used as a divide-by-2 circuit when input signal is applied at clock input?
(*a*) J = K = 1 and Flip-Flop has active High Inputs
(*b*) J = K = 0 and Flip-Flop has active Low inputs
(*c*) J = K = 1 and Flip-Flop active Low inputs
(*d*) J = K = 1 and Flip-Flop should be negative edge triggerd.

19. The counter circuit shown below will reset at

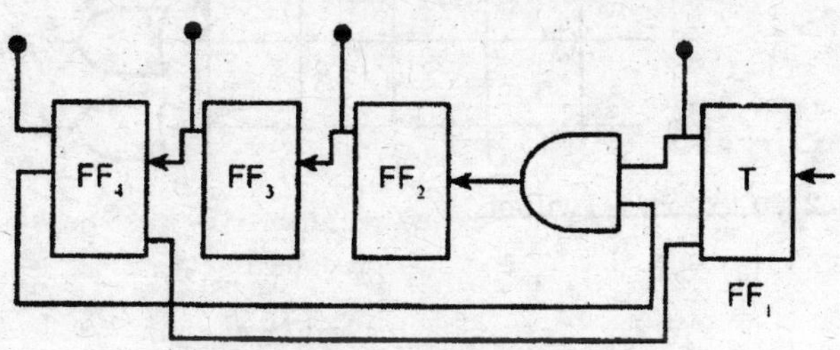

(*a*) 8th input pulse (*b*) 10th input pulse
(*c*) 12th input pulse (*d*) 16th input pulse

20. The circuit shown below is a

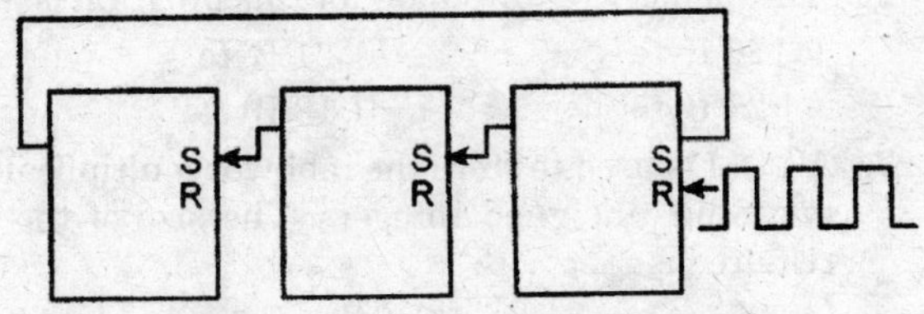

(*a*) mod-4-counter (*b*) mod-5 counter
(*c*) mod 6 counter (*d*) mod 7 counter

21. The instruction DAA

(*a*) converts binary to BCD

(*b*) converts BCD to binary

(*c*) decrements accumulator

(*d*) add contents of accumulator to accumulator.

22. Read the inaction given below

Assume clock period of 0.5 μs.

1000	MVI	C, 00H
002 NEXT	DCR	C
1003	MVI	B, 8CH
1005 DELAY	DCR	B
1006	JNZ	DELAY
1009	MOV	A, C
100 A	OUT	PORT 1
100 C	JMP	NEXT

The above program execution will display

(*a*) 8CH at port 1 (*b*) 00H at port 1

(*c*) FFH at port 1 (*d*) FFH to 00 H at port 1

23. When a subroutine is called, then address of the instruction following the CAL instruction is stored in/on the.

(*a*) Stack pointer (*b*) Accumulator

(*c*) Program counter (*d*) Stack

STATEMENT FOR Q. 24–25.

A PLA realization is shown in the figure.

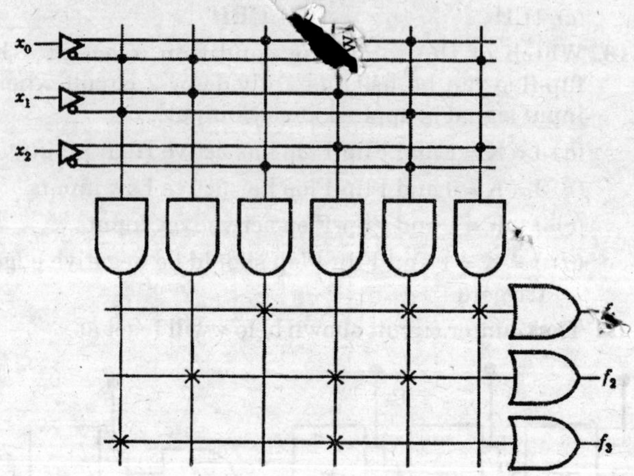

24. $f_1(x_2, x_1, x_0)$ will be

(*a*) $x_2\bar{x}_0 + \bar{x}_2x_0$ (*b*) $x_2x_0 + x_1\bar{x}_2$

(*c*) $x_2 \oplus x_0$ (*d*) $x_2 \odot x_0$

25. $f_2(x_2, x_1, x_0)$ will be

(*a*) Σm (1, 2, 5, 6) (*b*) Σm (1, 2, 6, 7)

(*c*) Σm (2, 3, 4) (*d*) none of these

26. The memory requirement for this program is

(*a*) 20 Byte (*b*) 21 Byte

(*c*) 23 Byte (*d*) 18 Byte

27. A ROM is used to store the table for multiplication of two 8-bit unsigned integers. The size of the ROM required is

(*a*) 256 × 1 (*b*) 64k × 8

(*c*) 4k × 16 (*d*) 64k × 16

28. A Read/Write memory chip has a capacity of 64 k Bytes. Assuming separate data and address lines and availability of chip enable signal, what is the minimum number of pins required in the IC chip?

(*a*) 28 (*b*) 26

(*c*) 24 (*d*) 22

29. A 4 × 1 MUX is used to implement a 3-input Boolean function is as shown below. The Boolean function F(A, B, C) implemented is

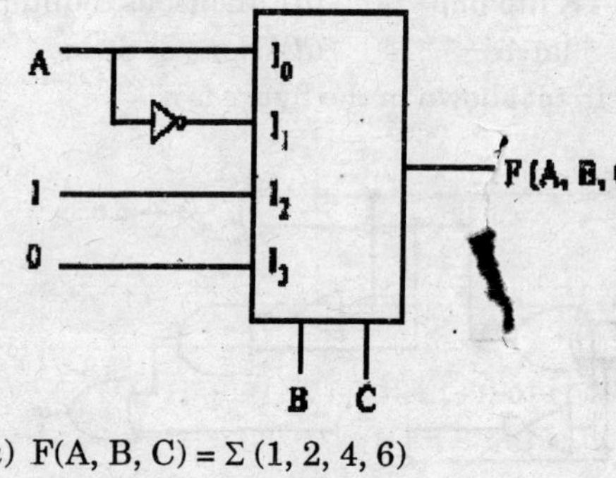

(*a*) F(A, B, C) = Σ (1, 2, 4, 6)

(*b*) F(A, B, C) = Σ (1, 2, 6)

(*c*) F(A, B, C) = Σ (2, 4, 5, 6)

(*d*) F(A, B, C) = Σ (1, 5, 6)

30. The J-K flip-flop shown below is initially reset, so that Q = 0. If a sequence of four clock pulses is then applied, with the J and K inputs as given in the figure, the resulting sequence of values that appear at the output Q starting with its initial state, is given by

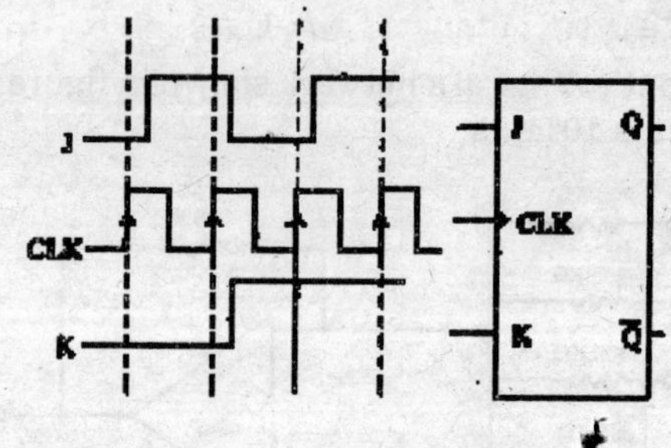

(*a*) 01011 (*b*) 01010

(*c*) 00110 (*d*) 00101

31. An X-Y flip flop, whose characteristic table is given below is to be implemented using J-K flip flop. This can be done by making

X	Y	Q_{n+1}
0	0	1
0	1	Q_n
1	0	$\bar{Q}_n$
1	1	0

(*a*) $J = X, K = \bar{Y}$

(*b*) $J = \bar{X}, K = Y$

(*c*) $J = Y, K = \bar{X}$

(*d*) $J = \bar{Y}, K = X$

10. The circuit shown below is a

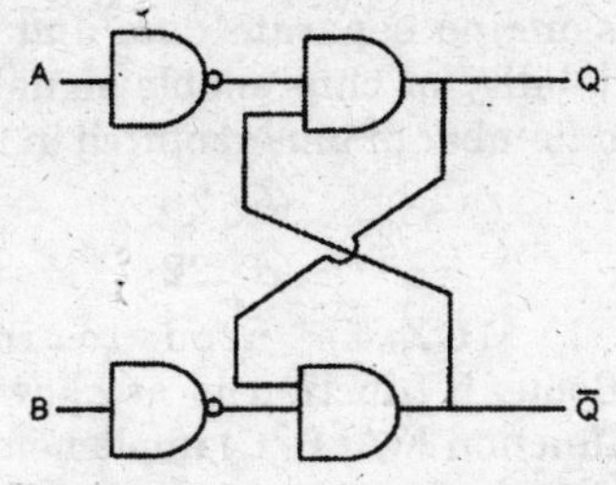

(*a*) J – K flip flop (*b*) Jhonsons counter
(*c*) R-S latch (*d*) None of these

11. The circuit shown in the figure is a

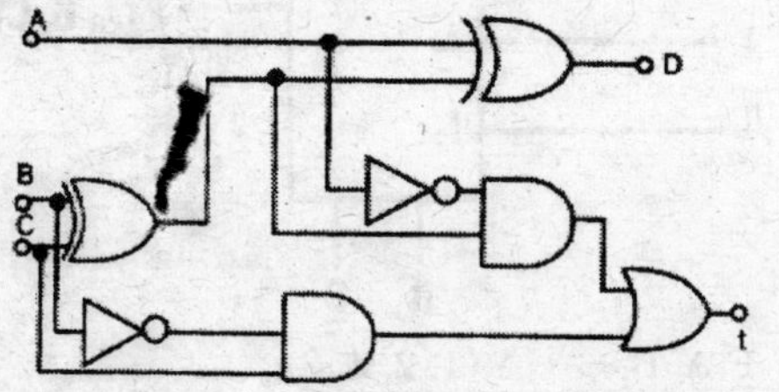

(*a*) Full adder (*b*) Full subtractor
(*c*) Shift register (*d*) Decade counter

12. In the circuit shown below, the F output is given by

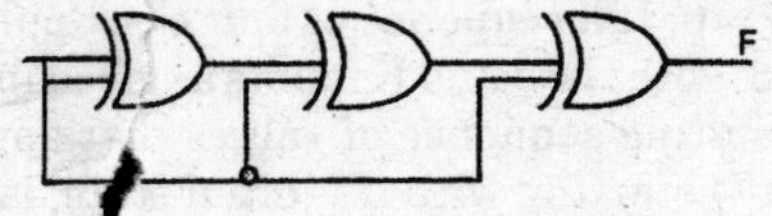

(*a*) F = 1 (*b*) F = 0
(*c*) F = *x* (*d*) F = 2

13. Output voltage of a network shown in figure if digital input is 1011, is

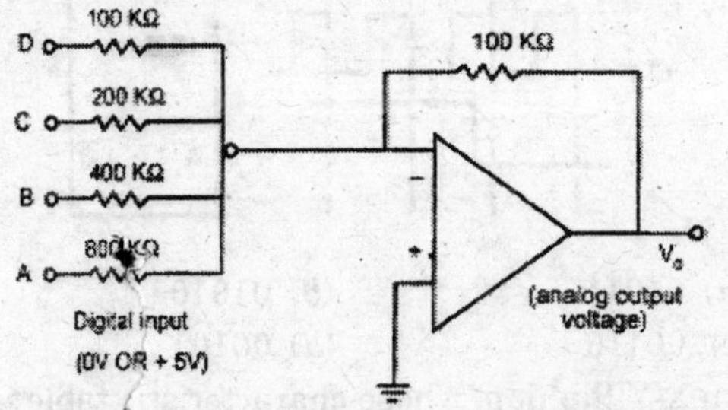

(*a*) – 3.875V (*b*) – 4.875V
(*c*) – 5.875V (*d*) – 6.875V

14. The circuit shown in the given figure is a

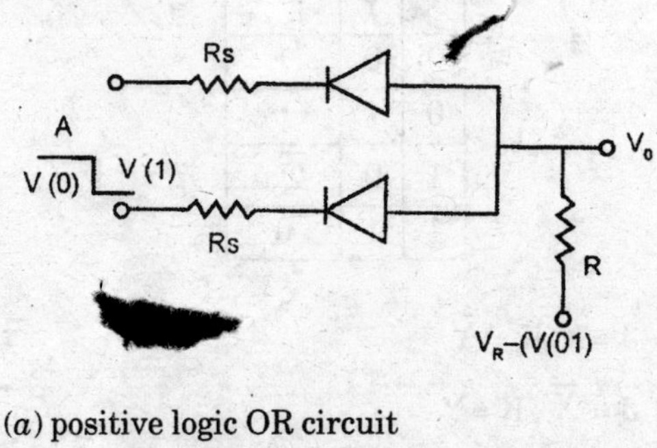

(*a*) positive logic OR circuit
(*b*) negative logic OR gate
(*c*) positive logic NAND gate
(*d*) negative logic NAND gate

15. J-K flip flop shown in figure is initially reset so that Q = 0. A sequence of four clock pulses is, then applied, with the J and K inputs, as given in the figure, Resulting sequence of values that the output Q will have, is given by

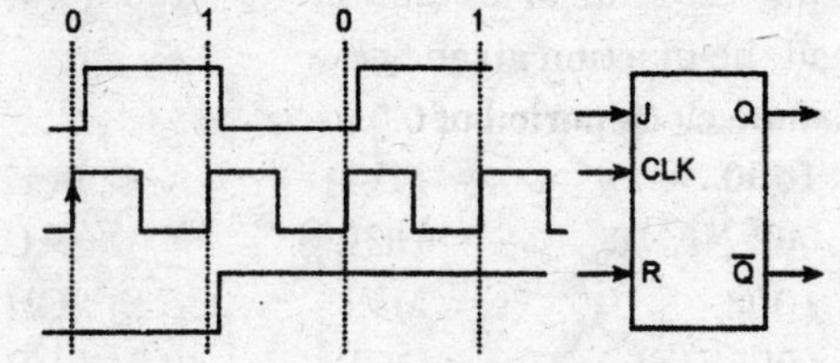

(*a*) 01011 (*b*) 01010
(*c*) 00110 (*d*) 00101

16. Which of the following statements are correct?

(*a*) A flips-flop is used to store 1 bit of information
(*b*) Race-around condition accurs in a J-k flip-flop when both the inputs are 1.
(*c*) A transparent latch consists of a D-type flip-flop
(*d*) All of these

17. Contents of accumulator after execution of following instructions will be

MVI	A, A7H
ORA	A
RLC	

(*a*) CFH (*b*) 4FH
(*c*) 4EH (*d*) CEH

18. Which of the following condition, clocked J-K flip-flop can be used as a divide-by-2 circuit when input signal is applied at clock input?

(*a*) J = K = 1 and Flip-Flop has active High Inputs
(*b*) J = K = 0 and Flip-Flop has active Low inputs
(*c*) J ⁼ K = 1 and Flip-Flop active Low inputs
(*d*) J = K = 1 and Flip-Flop should be negative edge triggerd.

19. The counter circuit shown below will reset at

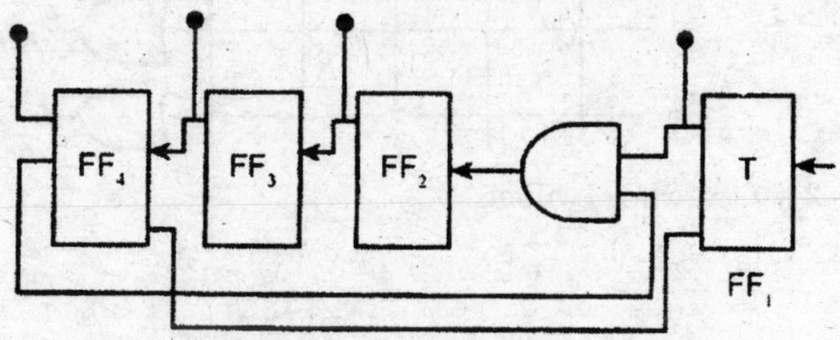

(*a*) 8th input pulse (*b*) 10th input pulse
(*c*) 12th input pulse (*d*) 16th input pulse

20⁚ The circuit shown below is a

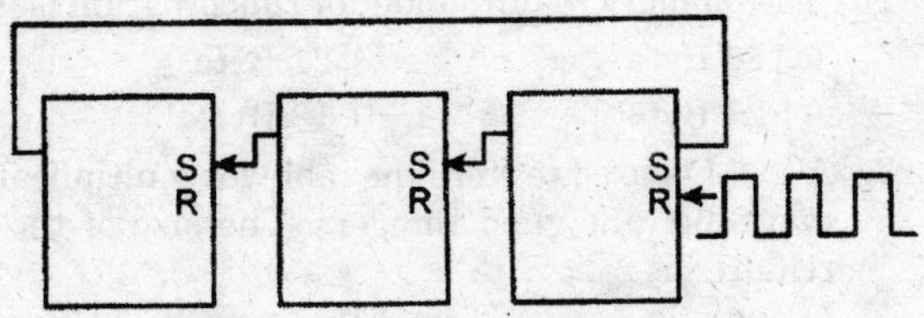

(*a*) mod-4-counter (*b*) mod-5 counter
(*c*) mod 6 counter (*d*) mod 7 counter

21. The instruction DAA

(*a*) converts binary to BCD

(*b*) converts BCD to binary

(*c*) decrements accumulator

(*d*) add contents of accumulator to accumulator.

22. Read the inaction given below

Assume clock period of 0.5 μs.

```
1000         MVI    C, 00H
002 NEXT     DCR    C
1003         MVI    B, 8CH
1005 DELAY   DCR    B
1006         JNZ    DELAY
1009         MOV    A, C
100 A        OUT    PORT 1
100 C        JMP    NEXT
```

The above program execution will display

(*a*) 8CH at port 1 (*b*) 00H at port 1

(*c*) FFH at port 1 (*d*) FFH to 00 H at port 1

23. When a subroutine is called, then address of the instruction following the CAL instruction is stored in/on the.

(*a*) Stack pointer (*b*) Accumulator

(*c*) Program counter (*d*) Stack

STATEMENT FOR Q. 24–25.

A PLA realization is shown in the figure.

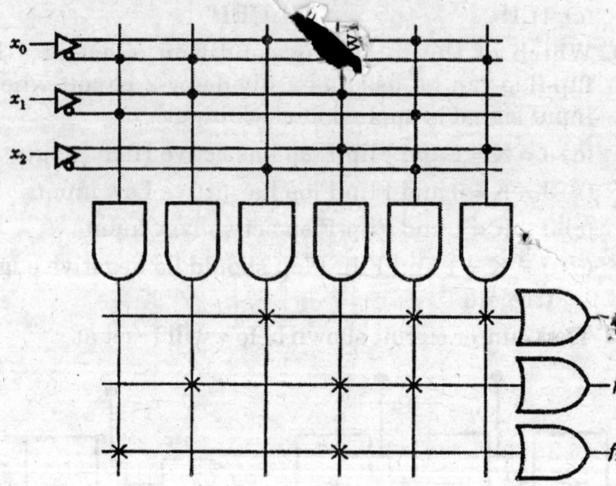

24. $f_1(x_2, x_1, x_0)$ will be

(*a*) $x_2\bar{x}_0 + \bar{x}_2x_0$ (*b*) $x_2x_0 + x_1\bar{x}_2$

(*c*) $x_2 \oplus x_0$ (*d*) $x_2 \odot x_0$

25. $f_2(x_2, x_1, x_0)$ will be

(*a*) Σm (1, 2, 5, 6) (*b*) Σm (1, 2, 6, 7)

(*c*) Σm (2, 3, 4) (*d*) none of these

26. The memory requirement for this program is

(*a*) 20 Byte (*b*) 21 Byte

(*c*) 23 Byte (*d*) 18 Byte

27. A ROM is used to store the table for multiplication of two 8-bit unsigned integers. The size of the ROM required is

(*a*) 256 × 1 (*b*) 64k × 8

(*c*) 4k × 16 (*d*) 64k × 16

28. A Read/Write memory chip has a capacity of 64 k Bytes. Assuming separate data and address lines and availability of chip enable signal, what is the minimum number of pins required in the IC chip?

(*a*) 28 (*b*) 26

(*c*) 24 (*d*) 22

29. A 4 × 1 MUX is used to implement a 3-input Boolean function is as shown below. The Boolean function F(A, B, C) implemented is

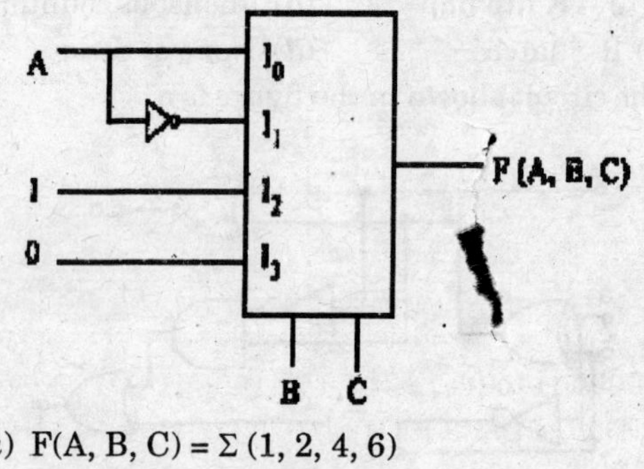

(*a*) F(A, B, C) = Σ (1, 2, 4, 6)

(*b*) F(A, B, C) = Σ (1, 2, 6)

(*c*) F(A, B, C) = Σ (2, 4, 5, 6)

(*d*) F(A, B, C) = Σ (1, 5, 6)

30. The J-K flip-flop shown below is initially reset, so that Q = 0. If a sequence of four clock pulses is then applied, with the J and K inputs as given in the figure, the resulting sequence of values that appear at the output Q starting with its initial state, is given by

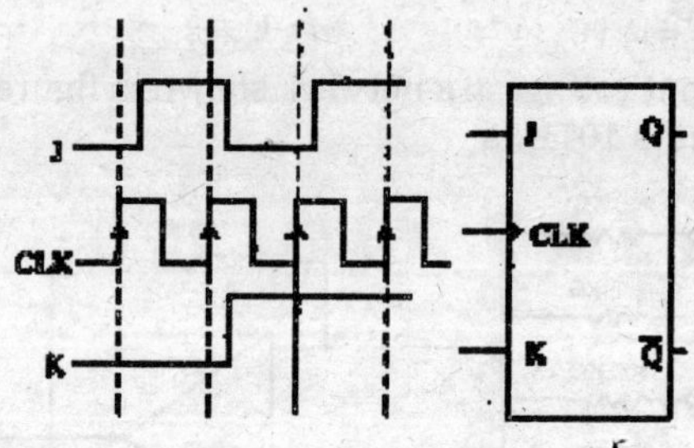

(*a*) 01011 (*b*) 01010

(*c*) 00110 (*d*) 00101

31. An X-Y flip flop, whose characteristic table is given below is to be implemented using J-K flip flop. This can be done by making

X	Y	Q_{n+1}
0	0	1
0	1	Q_n
1	0	$\bar{Q}_n$
1	1	0

(*a*) $J = X, K = \bar{Y}$

(*b*) $J = \bar{X}, K = Y$

(*c*) $J = Y, K = \bar{X}$

(*d*) $J = \bar{Y}, K = X$

32. Consider a memory chip with 1024 bytes storage connected to a 8085 chip address lines (or any microprocessor with 16 address lines) as shown below. What is the range of memory address?

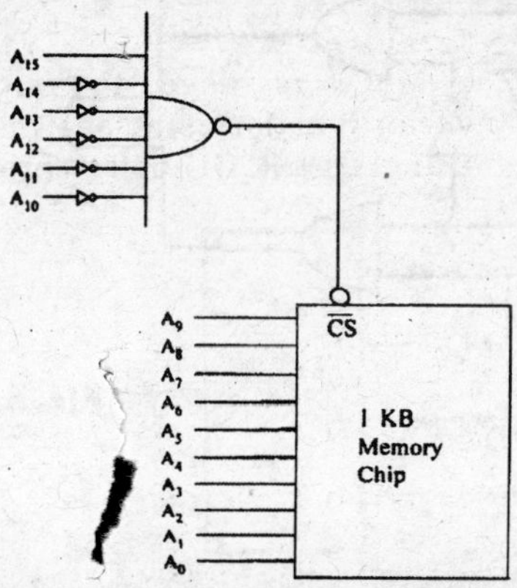

(*a*) 0000 H to 03 FFH (*b*) 1000 H to 13 FFH
(*c*) F000 H to F3 FFH (*d*) 0000 H to FFFFH

33. For the circuit shown below the counter state (Q_1 Q_0) follows the sequence

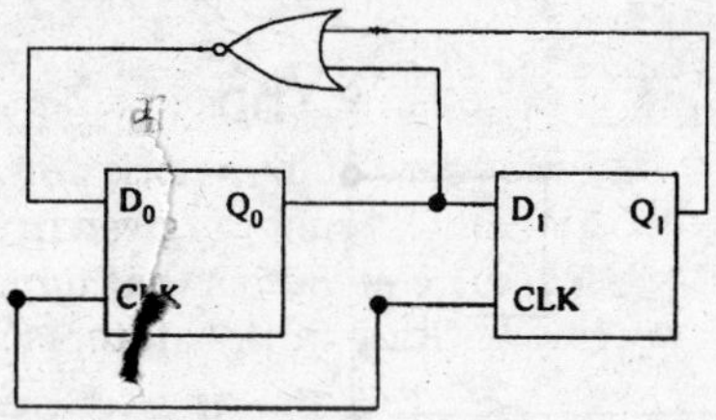

(*a*) 00, 01, 10, 11, 00 ... (*b*) 00, 01, 10, 00, 01 ...
(*c*) 00, 01, 11, 00, 01 ... (*d*) 00, 10, 11, 00, 10 ...

34.

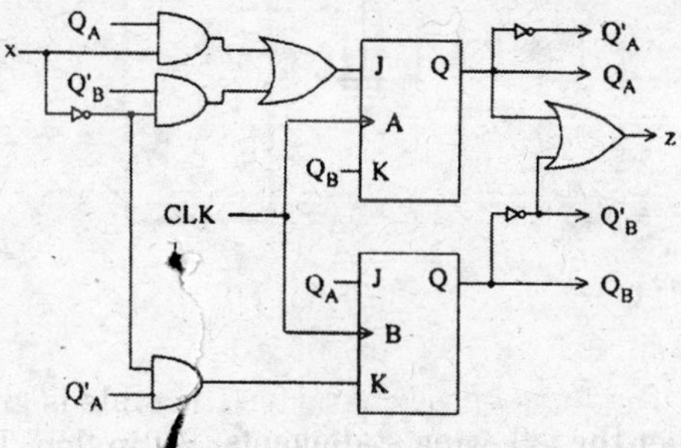

Analyze the sequential circuit shown above in figure. Assuming that initial state is 00, determine what input sequence would lead to state 11?

(*a*) 1 – 1
(*b*) 1 – 0
(*c*) 0 – 0
(*d*) State 11 is unreachable

35.

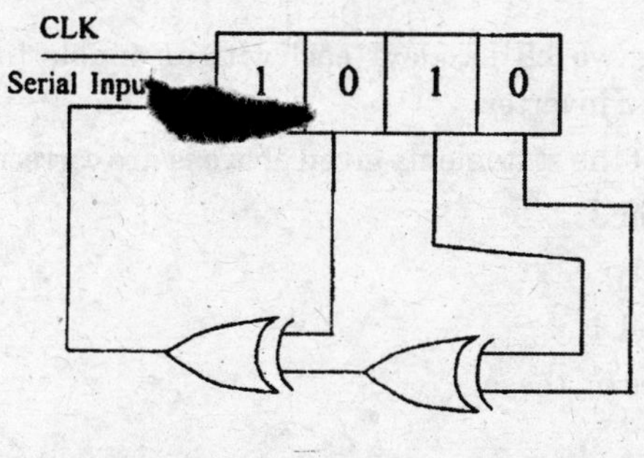

The shift register shown in the given figure is initially loaded with the bit pattern 1010. Subsequently the shift register is clocked, and with each clock pulse the pattern gets shifted by one bit position to the right. With each shift, the bit at the serial input is pushed to the msb position. After how many clock pulses will be content of the shift register become 1010 again?

(*a*) 3 (*b*) 7
(*c*) 11 (*d*) 15

36. The Boolean functions can be expressed in canonical SOP (sum of products) and POS (product of sums) form. For the function,

$Y = A + \overline{B}.\,C$, which are such two forms?

(*a*) $Y = \Sigma\,(1, 2, 6, 7)$ and $Y = \Pi\,(0, 2, 4)$
(*b*) $Y = \Sigma\,(1, 4, 5, 6, 7)$ and $Y = \Pi\,(0, 2, 3)$
(*c*) $Y = \Sigma\,(1, 2, 5, 6, 7)$ and $Y = \Pi\,(0, 1, 3)$
(*d*) $Y = \Sigma\,(1, 2, 4, 5, 6, 7)$ and $Y = \Pi\,(0, 2, 3, 4)$

37. For the logic circuit shown in the figure below, what is the required input condition (A, B, C) to make output X = 1?

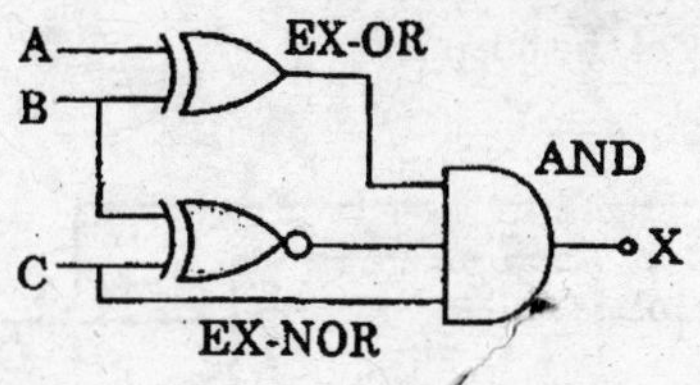

(*a*) 1, 0, 1 (*b*) 0, 0, 1
(*c*) 1, 1, 1 (*d*) 0, 1, 1

38. The circuit is given below illustrates a typical application of the JK flip-flops. What does this represent ?

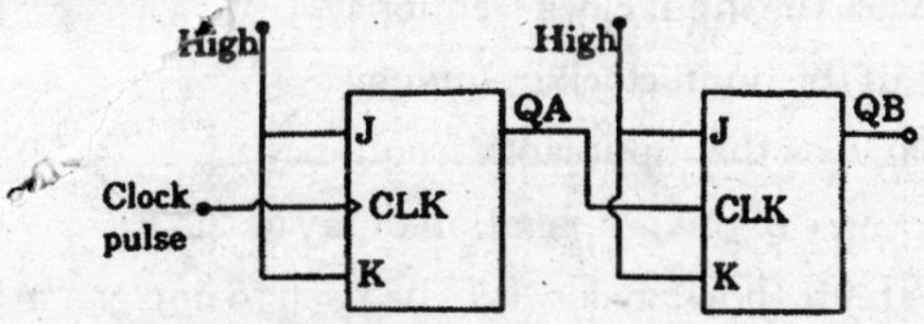

(*a*) A shift register
(*b*) A data storage device
(*c*) A frequency divider circuit
(*d*) A decoder circuit

39. The figure given below shows the circuit of which one of the following is

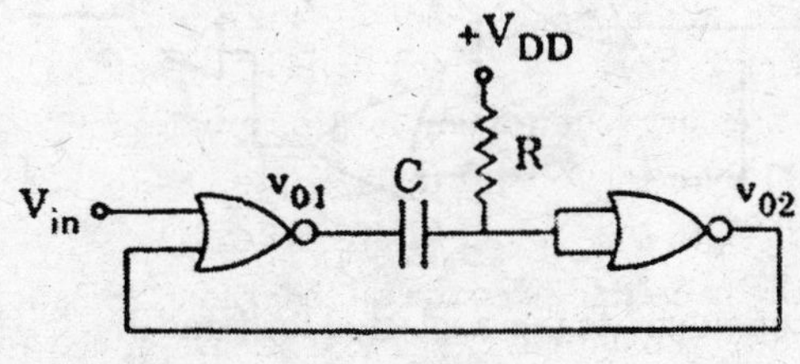

(*a*) Bi-stable multi-vibrator
(*b*) Schmitt trigger
(*c*) Mono-stable multi-vibrator
(*d*) Astable multi-vibrator

40. The black box in the figure below, consists of a minimum complexity circuit that uses only AND, OR and NOT gates.

The function $f,(x, y, z) = 1$ whenever x, y are different and 0 otherwise. In addition the 3 inputs x, y, z are never all the same value.

Which one of the following equations leads to the correct design for the minimum complexity circuit?

(*a*) $x'y + xy'$

(*b*) $x + yz'$

(*c*) $x'y'z + xy'z$

(*d*) $xy + y'z + z'$

41. For the circuit shown in the figure below, what is the frequency of the output Q ?

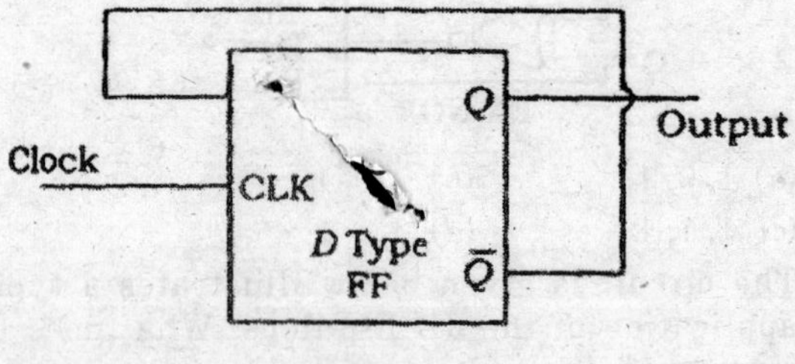

(*a*) Twice the input clock frequency

(*b*) Half the input clock frequency

(*c*) Same as the input clock frequency

(*d*) Inverse of the propagation delay of the FF

42. The circuit shown below is to be used to implement the function

$$Z = f(A, B) = \overline{A} + B.$$

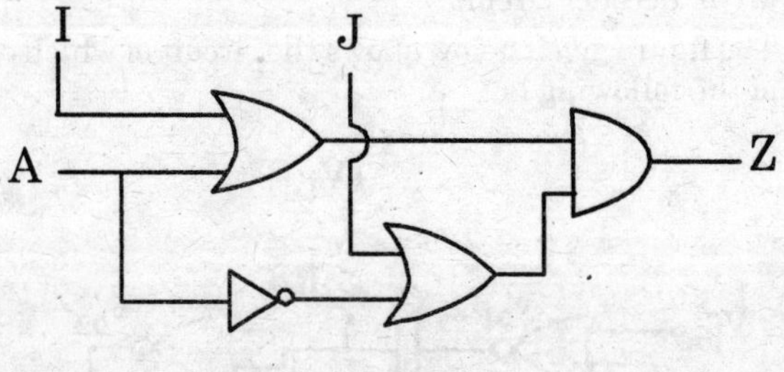

What value are to be selected for I and J?

(*a*) I = 0, J = B

(*b*) I = A, J = B

(*c*) I = B, J = 1

(*d*) I = $\overline{B}$, J = 0

43. Which one of the following logic operations is performed by the digital circuit shown below ?

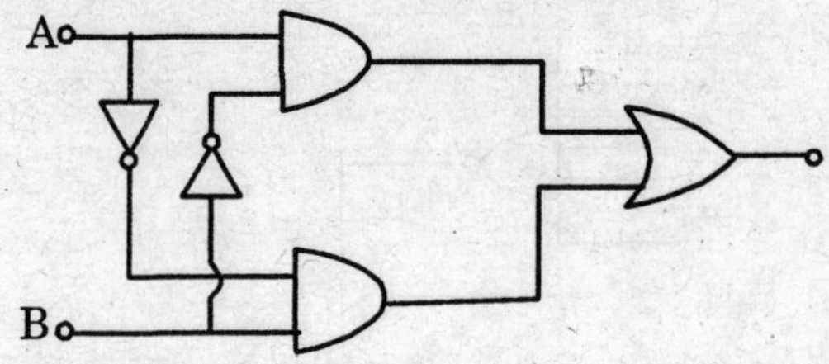

(*a*) NOR

(*b*) NAND

(*c*) X-OR

(*d*) OR

44. In the circuit given below, both transistors have the same V_T. What is the approximate value of the highest possible output voltage V_{out}, if V_{in} can range from 0 to V_{DD}? (Assume $0 < V_T < V_{DD}$)

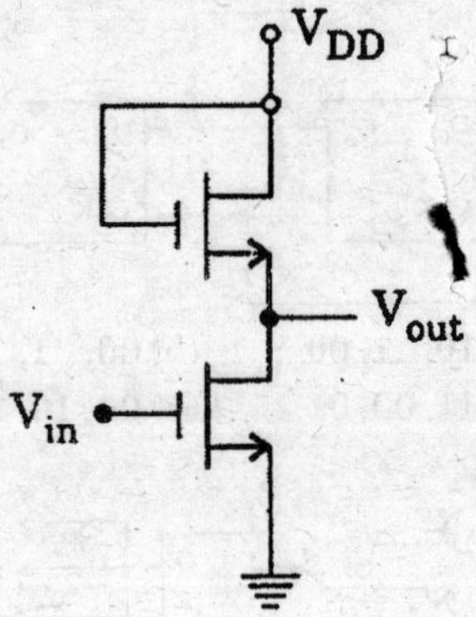

(*a*) $V_{DD} - V_T$

(*b*) V_{DD}

(*c*) V_T

(*d*) 0

45. Consider the following statements :

A 4:16,decoder can be constructed (with enable input) by

1. using four 2:4 decoders (each with an enable input) only.
2. using five 2:4 decoders (each with an enable input) only.
3. using two 3:8 decoders (each with an enable input) only.
4. using two 3:8 decoders (each with an enable input) and an inverter.

Which of the statements given above is/are correct?

(*a*) 2 and 3

(*b*) 1 only

(*c*) 2 and 4

(*d*) None of these

46. The circuit given below is that of a

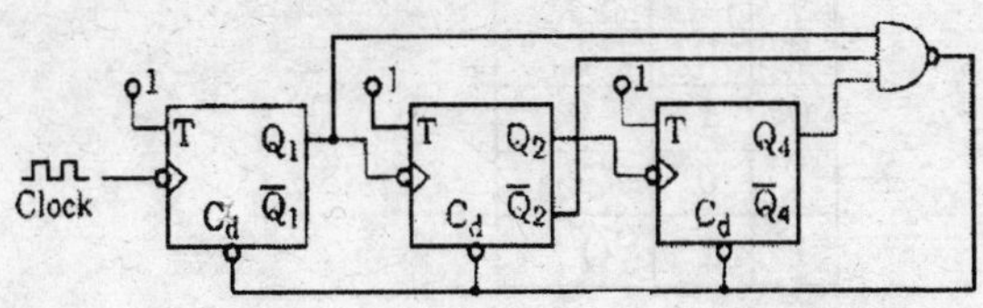

(*a*) Mod-5 counter (*b*) Mod-6 counter

(*c*) Mod-7 counter (*d*) Mod-8 counter

47. 12 MHz clock frequency is applied to a cascaded counter of modulus-3 counter, modulus-4 counter and modulus-5 counter. What are the lowest output frequency and the overall modulus, respectively ?

(*a*) 200 kHz, 60 (*b*) 1 MHz, 60

(*c*) 3 MHz, 12 (*d*) 4 MHz, 12

48. The minimized expression for the given K map (A : don't care) is

CD \ AB	00	01	11	10
00	0	0	1	1
01	0	×	×	1
11	×	×	1	×
10	1	0	1	1

(*a*) $A + \overline{B}\,C$ (*b*) $B + AC$

(*c*) $C + A\,B$ (*d*) $A\,B\,C$

49. A 10-bit ADC with full-scale output voltage of 10.24 V is designed to have a + LSB/2 accuracy. If the ADC is calibrated at 25°C and the operating temperature ranges from 0°C to 50°C, then the maximum net temperature coefficient of ADC should not exceed

(*a*) ±200 μV/°C (*b*) ±400 μV /°C

(*c*) ±600 μV/°C (*d*) ±800 μV/°C

50. Which one of the following statements is not correct?

(*a*) An 8 input MUX can be used to implement any 4 variable function

(*b*) A 3 line to 8 line DEMUX can be used to implement any 4 variable function

(*c*) A 64 input MUX can be built nine 8 input MUXs

(*d*) A 6 line to 64 line DEMUX can be built using nine 3 line to 8 line DEMUXs

51. Consider the following J-K flip-flop :

In the given J-K flip-flop,

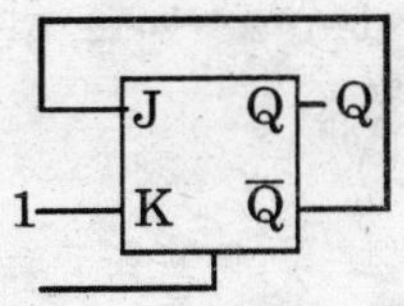

$J = \overline{Q}$ and K = 1. Assume that the flip-flop was initially cleared and then clocked for 6 pulses. What is the sequence at the Q output?

(*a*) 010000 (*b*) 011001

(*c*) 010010 (*d*) 010101

ANSWERS

1. (*c*)	**2.** (*a*)	**3.** (*c*)	**4.** (*c*)	**5.** (*a*)	**6.** (*d*)	**7.** (*b*)	**8.** (*c*)	**9.** (*b*)	**10.** (*c*)
11. (*b*)	**12.** (*b*)	**13.** (*d*)	**14.** (*b*)	**15.** (*b*)	**16.** (*d*)	**17.** (*b*)	**18.** (*a*)	**19.** (*b*)	**20.** (*a*)
21. (*a*)	**22.** (*d*)	**23.** (*c*)	**24.** (*a*)	**25.** (*b*)	**26.** (*c*)	**27.** (*c*)	**28.** (*a*)	**29.** (*a*)	**30.** (*d*)
31. (*d*)	**32.** (*b*)	**33.** (*b*)	**34.** (*c*)	**35.** (*b*)	**36.** (*b*)	**37.** (*d*)	**38.** (*c*)	**39.** (*c*)	**40.** (*a*)
41. (*b*)	**42.** (*c*)	**43.** (*c*)	**44.** (*a*)	**45.** (*c*)	**46.** (*a*)	**47.** (*a*)	**48.** (*a*)	**49.** (*a*)	**50.** (*d*)
51. (*d*)									

EXPLANATIONS

1.

```
LHLD  3000 H ; (3000 H) → HL = 3002H
MOV   E, M   ; (3002 H) → E = 2H
INX   H      ; HL + 1 → HL = 3003H
MOV   D, M   ; (M → D) = (3003H) = 30H
LDAX  D      ; (DE) A = (3000H) = 02H
MOV   L, A   ; A → L = 02H
INX   D      ; DE + 1 → DE = 3001H
LDAX  D      ; (DE) → A = (3001) = 30 H
MOV   H, A   ; A → H = 30H
```

Hence HL pair contain 3002H.

2.

```
       MVI A  DATA1  ; DATA1 → A
       ORA    A      ; Set flag
       JP     DSPLY  ; If A is positive, then
                     ; Jump to DSPLY
       XRA    A      ; Clear A
DSPLY  OUT    PORT1  ; A → PORT2
       HLT
```

If DATA1 is positive, it will be displayed at port1 otherwise 00.

8.

A	B	Q_{n+1}	J	
0	0	Q_n	0	
0	1	1	1	
1	0	Q_n	0	$J = \overline{A}B + AB$
1	1	0	×	$= B(\overline{A} + A) = B$

13. $$V_0 = -\left[V_D + \frac{1}{2}V_C + \frac{1}{4}V_B + \frac{1}{8}V_A\right]$$

As the digital is 1011, $V_D = 5V$, $V_C = 0V$

$V_B = V_A$
$= 5V$

$$V_0 = -\left[5V + 0V + \frac{1}{4}\times 5V + \frac{1}{8}\times 5V\right]$$

$= -[5 + 1.25 + 0.6250]$ V

$= -6.875$ V.

24. $f_1 = x_0\overline{x}_2 + x_0\overline{x}_1\overline{x}_2 + \overline{x}_0 x_2 = x_0\overline{x}_2(1+\overline{x}_1) + \overline{x}_0 x_2$

$= x_0\overline{x}_2 + \overline{x}_0 x_2$

25. $f_2 = \overline{x}_0 x_1 + x_1 x_2 + x_0\overline{x}_1\overline{x}_2$

$= \overline{x}_0 x_1 x_2 + \overline{x}_0 x_1 \overline{x}_2 + x_1 x_2 x_0 + x_1 x_2 \overline{x}_0 + x_0\overline{x}_1\overline{x}_2$

$= x_2 x_1 \overline{x}_0 + \overline{x}_2 x_1 \overline{x}_0 + \overline{x}_2 \overline{x}_1 x_0 + x_2 x_1 x_0$

$f_2(x_2, x_1, x_0) = \Sigma m(1, 2, 6, 7)$

27. Two 8-bit unsigned multiplication produce 16-bit integer.

To store 16-bit requires 2^{16} bit memory

2^{16} bit memory $= 2^6$ k bit $\quad (\because 1k = 2^{10})$

$= 64$ k bit

$= 4\text{ k} \times 16$ bit memory

29. $F = I_0\overline{B}\,\overline{C} + I_1\overline{B}C + I_2 B\overline{C} + I_3 BC$

$= A\overline{B}\,\overline{C} + \overline{A}\,\overline{B}C + B\overline{C} + 0.\,BC$

$= A\overline{B}\,\overline{C} + \overline{A}\,\overline{B}C + (A + \overline{A})B\overline{C}$

$= A\overline{B}\,\overline{C} + \overline{A}B\overline{C} + \overline{A}\,\overline{B}C + AB\overline{C}$

$\therefore \quad F(A, B, C) = \Sigma(1, 2, 4, 6)$

30. Truth table

	S	R	OUT
C_{IK}	J	K	Q
0	×	×	0
↑	0	0	0
↑	1	0	1
↑	0	1	0
↑	1	1	1

Output FF is 00101

31.

J	K	Q_{n+1}
0	0	Q_n
0	1	0
1	0	1
1	1	$\overline{Q}_n$

Q_n	X	Y	Q_{n+1}	J	K
0	0	0	1	1	*d*
0	0	1	0	0	*d*
0	1	0	1	1	*d*
0	1	1	0	0	*d*
1	0	0	1	*d*	0
1	0	1	1	*d*	0
1	1	0	0	*d*	1
1	1	1	0	*d*	1

Q_n	Q_{n+1}	J	K
0	0	0	*d*
0	1	1	*d*
1	0	*d*	1
1	1	*d*	0

K- map For J

Q_n \ XY	00	01	11	10
Q_n	1_0	0_1	0_3	1
$\overline{Q}_n$	d_4	d_5	d_7	d_6

$J = \overline{y}$

K- map For K

Q_n \ XY	00	01	11	10
Q_n	d_0	d_1	d_3	d_2
$\overline{Q}_n$	[illegible]$_4$	0_5	1_7	1_6

$K = X$

$J = \overline{Y}, \quad K = X$

32. Starting address

$A_{15}\,A_{14}\,A_{13}\,A_{12}\,A_{11}\,A_{10}\,A_9\,A_8\,A_7\,A_6\,A_5\,A_4\,A_3\,A_2\,A_1\,A_0$

1 0 0 0 0 0 0 0 0 0 [illegible] 0 0

Last address

1 0 0 0 0 0 1 1 1 1 1 1 1 1 1 1

Last address ⇒ 8 0 0 0 H

Starting address ⇒ 8 3 F F H

33. $D_0 = \overline{Q_0 \oplus Q_1}$

$D_1 = Q_0$

CLK	D_1	D_0	Q_1	Q_0
X	0	0	0	0
↑	0	1	0	1
↑	1	0	1	0
↑	0	0	0	0

34.

$$J_A = Q_A x + \overline{Q}s\ \overline{x}$$
$$K_A = Q_B$$
$$J_B = Q_A$$
$$K_B = \overline{Q}_A \cdot \overline{x}$$

CLK	x	J_A	K_A	J_B	K_B	Q_A	Q_B
X	0	d	d	d	d	0	0
↑	0	1	0	0	1	1	0
↑	0	1	0	1	0	1	1
↑	0	0	1	1	0	0	1
↑	0	0	1	0	1	0	0
↑	1	0	0	0	0	0	0
↑	1	[illegible]	0	0	0	0	0

For input sequence 0 – 0 would lead to state 11.

35.

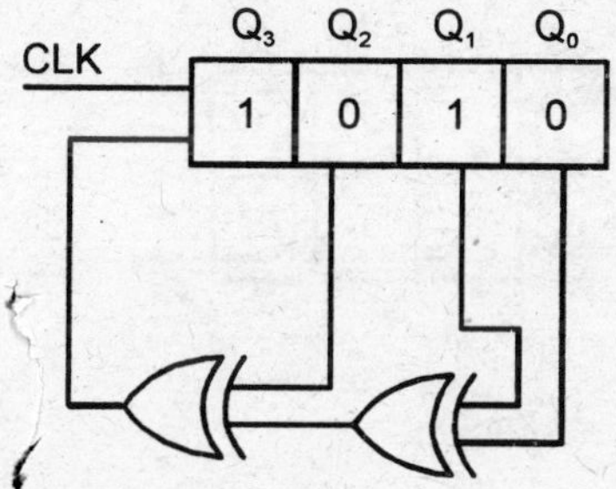

In = $Q_2 \oplus (Q_1 \oplus Q_0)$

7 pulses are required to reach again 1010.

	CLK	In	Q_3	Q_2	Q_1	Q_0
	0	d	1	0	1	0
1.	↑	1	1	1	0	1
2.	↑	0	0	1	1	0
3.	[illegible]	0	0	0	1	1
4.	[illegible]	0	0	0	0	1
5.	↑	1	1	0	0	0
6.	↑	0	0	1	0	0
7.	↑	1	1	0	1	0

36.

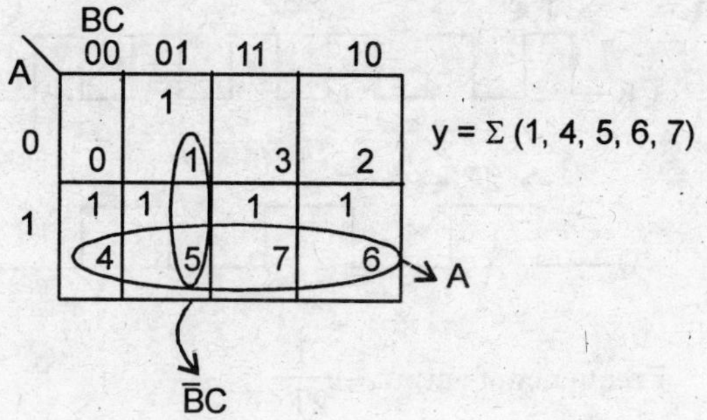

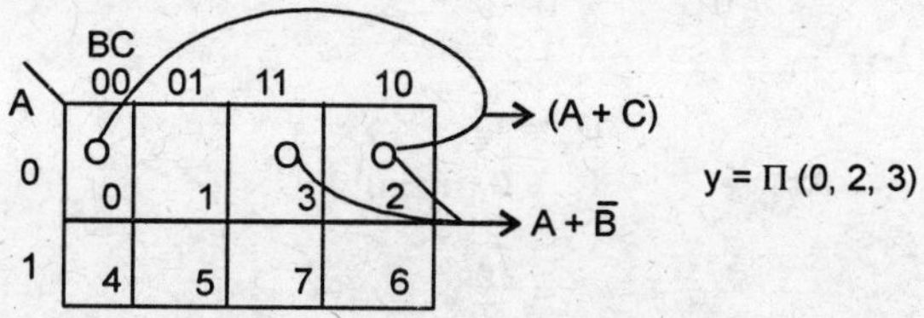

Alternate:

$$y = A + \overline{B}C$$
$$= A(B + \overline{B}) + \overline{B}C(A + \overline{A})$$
$$= AB + A\overline{B} + A\overline{B}C + \overline{A}\,\overline{B}C$$
$$= AB(C + \overline{C}) + A\overline{B}(C + \overline{C}) + A\overline{B}C + \overline{A}\,\overline{B}C$$
$$= ABC + AB\overline{C} + A\overline{B}C + A\overline{B}C + \overline{A}\,\overline{B}C$$

$\therefore\ y = \Sigma(1, 4, 5, 6, 7)$

and $y = \pi(0, 2, 3)$

37.

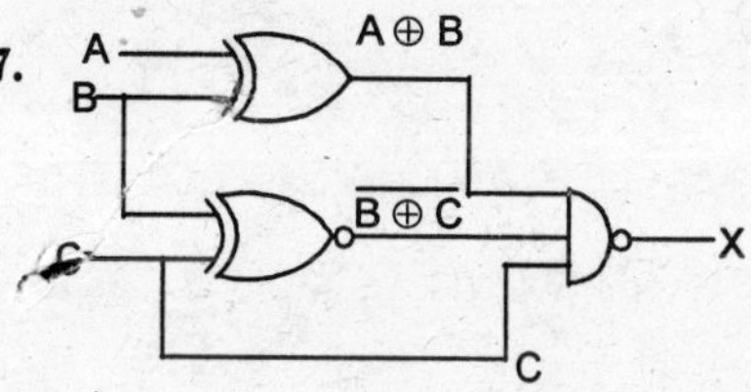

For, X = 1
A = 0
B = C = 1

$$X = A \oplus B.\ \overline{B \oplus C}.C$$
$$= (A\overline{B} + \overline{A}B).(\overline{C}\,\overline{B} + CB).C$$
$$= (A\overline{B} + \overline{A}B).BC$$
$$= \overline{A}BC$$

40.

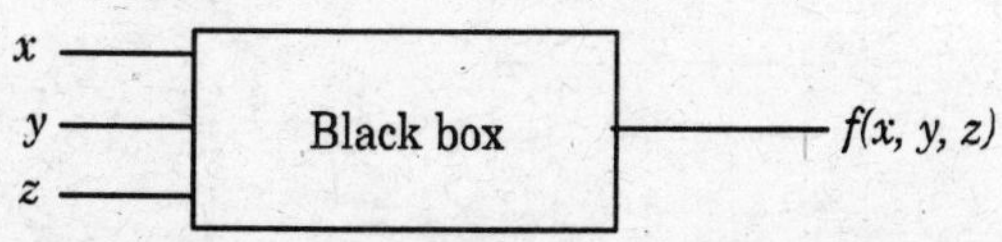

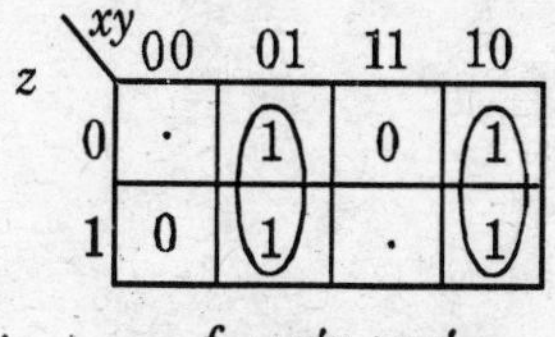

$\therefore\quad f = x'y + xy'$

41.

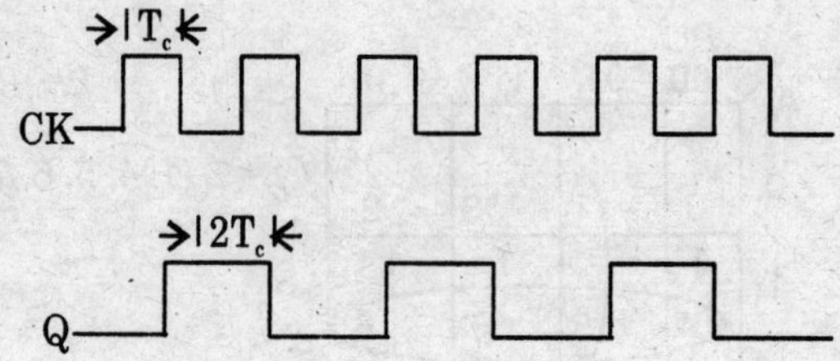

Frequency of output = $\dfrac{1}{2T_c}$

D	$Q_n + 1$
0	0
1	1

$D = \bar{Q}$

At $\quad F = 0$ (intially)

$= \dfrac{f_c}{2}$.

48.

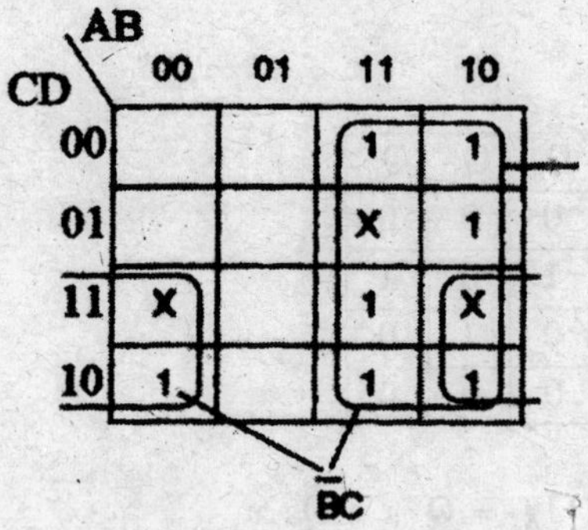

The expression is

$$Y = A + \bar{B}C$$

SIGNALS AND SYSTEMS 5

5.1 LAPLACE TRANSFORM

Laplace transform of continuous time signal $x(t)$ is denoted by X(s).

Fourier transform of continuous function $x(t)$ is given by

$$X(j\omega) = \int_{-\infty}^{\infty} x(t)e^{-j\omega t}dt \quad ...(5.1)$$

Fourier transform exists only if $x(t)$ has a finite energy. If signal is having infinite energy, then a convergence factor, $e^{-\sigma t}$ is introduced to convert $x(t)$ into finite energy signal. Then resulting transformation is denoted by X(σ + jω).

Thus equation (5.1) becomes

$$\therefore \quad X(\sigma + j\omega) = \int_{-\infty}^{\infty} x(t)e^{-j\omega t}.e^{-\sigma t}dt$$

$$X(\sigma + j\omega) = \int_{-\infty}^{\infty} x(t)e^{-(\sigma + j\omega)t}.dt \quad ...(5.2)$$

Now denoting σ + jω by letter 's'; where 's' is Laplace operator, we have

$$X(s) = \int_{-\infty}^{\infty} x(t)e^{-st}dt \quad ...(5.3)$$

Equation (5.3) represents Laplace transform of signal $x(t)$.

PROPERTIES OF LAPLACE TRANSFORM.

1. Linearity

It states that Laplace transform of Linear combination of property signals is same as linear combination of their individual Laplace transforms, while resultant ROC is intersection or overlap of individual ROC.

Consider two time domain signals $x_1(t)$ and $x_2(t)$.

If $\quad x_1(t) \xleftrightarrow{LT} X_1(s)$ and $x_2(t) \xleftrightarrow{LT} X_2(s)$

Then $\quad [a_1 x_1(t) + a_2 x_2(t)] \xleftrightarrow{LT} a_1 X_1(s) + a_2 X_2(s)$

where a_1 and a_2 are constants.

2. Time Shifting (Shifting in Time Domain)

If $x(t)$ is input – signal whose ROC is 'R', then

$$L\{x(t - t_0)\} = e^{-st_0}.X(s) \qquad ROC = R$$

Here $x(t - t_0)$ indicates that sequence $x(t)$ is shifted in time domain (delayed). Thus shifting the signal in time domain by 't_0' corresponds to multiplication by e^{-st_0} in the frequency domain, i.e. it introduces a phase shift in the frequency domain.

3. Shifting in s-Domain

If $\quad x(t) \xleftrightarrow{LT} X(s)$; ROC = R

then $\quad e^{s_0 t}\, x(t) \xleftrightarrow{LT} X(s - s_0)$ ROC : R + $R_e(s_0)$

Here X($s - s_0$) indicates frequency shift by s_0. Thus frequency shift by s_0 is equivalent to multiplying time domain signal, $x(t)$ by $e^{s_0 t}$. ROC is also shifted by $R_e(s_0)$.

4. Time Scaling

If $x(t) \xleftrightarrow{L} X(s)$; ROC = R

then $L\{x(at)\} = \frac{1}{|a|} X\left(\frac{s}{a}\right)$ with ROC $R_1 = \frac{R}{a}$

In time domain, term $x(at)$ indicates multiplication of time with some constant 'a'. Thus it is expansion of time axis.

In frequency domain, term $X\left(\frac{s}{a}\right)$ indicates compression in frequence domain. Thus expanding time axus us equivalent to compression in frequency domain. ROC is also *expanded* or *compressed* depending on value of 'a'.

5. Time Differentiation (Differentiation in Time Domain)

If $x(t) \xleftrightarrow{LT} X(s)$, ROC : R

then $\frac{d}{dt} x(t) \xleftrightarrow{LT} s\,X(s)$, ROC : R

Differentiating signal in time domain is equivalent to multiplying its Laplace transform by 's' in the frequency domain.

6. Differentiation in s-Domain

If $x(t) \xleftrightarrow{LT} X(s)$, ROC: R

then $-t\,x(t) \xleftrightarrow{LT} \frac{d}{ds} X(s)$, ROC : R

Differentiating sequence in 's' domain is equivalent to multiplying sequence in time domain by ($-t$).

7. Convolution Property

If $x(t) \xleftrightarrow{LT} X(s)$ ROC : R_1

and $h(t) \xleftrightarrow{LT} H(s)$ROC : R_2

then $x_1(t) * h(t) \xleftrightarrow{LT} X(s).\,H(s)$ ROC : intersection of R_1 and R_2

Convolution of two signals in time domain becomes a simple multiplication process in the transformed domain. Time domain response of LTI system means convolution of input signal and its impulse response. Thus to find response of LTI system, it is always better to go in Laplace domain than the time domain.

8. Time integration (Integration in Time Domain)

Integral of time domain signal corresponds to division by 's' in the Laplace domain.

If $x(t) \xleftrightarrow{LT} X(s)$, ROC : RM

then $\int_{-\infty}^{t} x(\tau)\,d\tau \xleftrightarrow{LT} \frac{X(s)}{s}$, ROC : $R \cap [\sigma > 0]$

Here symbol '$\cap$' indicates intersection.

9. Integration in s-domain (Division by t)

If $x(t) \xleftrightarrow{LT} X(s)$, ROC : R

then $\frac{X(t)}{t} \xleftrightarrow{LT} \int_{s}^{\infty} X(s)\,ds$ ROC : R

If Laplace transform of the function X(t) exists, then integral of corresponding transform with respect to 's' in the complex frequency domain will correspond to divison by 't' in the time domain.

10. Laplace Transform of Periodic Signal

If $x(t)$ is periodic function with fundamental period 'T_0',

i.e. $$x(t) = x(t + T_0)$$

then $$L\{x(t)\} = \frac{1}{1-e^{-st}} X(s)$$

If function is periodic with period T_0, then calculate Laplace transform of first term only. Total Laplace transform is obtained by multiplying Laplace transform of first term by the factor $\frac{1}{1-e^{sT_0}}$.

11. Conjugation

If $$x(t) \xleftrightarrow{LT} X(s)$$

then $$x^*(t) \xleftrightarrow{LT} X^*(s^*)$$

Here '*' indicates complex conjugate operation.

12. Initial value theorem

If $$x(t) \xleftrightarrow{LT} X(s)$$

then initial value theorem is stated as,

$$L\left\{\lim_{t\to 0} x(t)\right\} = \lim_{s\to\infty} sX(s)$$

13. Final Value Theorem

If $$x(t) \xleftrightarrow{LT} X(s)$$

then final value theorem is stated as,

$$L\left\{\lim_{t\to\infty} x(t)\right\} = \lim_{s\to 0} sX(s)$$

BASIC SYSTEM PROPERTIES.

Causality

A system is causal, if output at any time depends upon the values of the input at the present time and in the past as well. All memoryless system are causal, as the output responds only to the present value of the input.

The example of causal system is given as

$$y[n] = \sum_{k=-\infty}^{n} x[k] \qquad \text{[accumulator]}$$

and, a second example of *delay*, $y[n] = x[n-1]$

Stability

A system is said to be stable, if responses due to small inputs do not diverge.

Consider discrete-time system defined by equation as given below

$$y[n] = \frac{1}{2M+1}\sum_{k=-M}^{M} x[n-k] \qquad \text{[non-causal averaging system]}$$

If in this equation, input $x[n]$ is bounded in magnitude by some number, say C, for all values of n, then largest possible magntiude for $y[n]$ will also be C, because $y[n]$ is average of a finite set of values of the input. Therefore, $y[n]$ is bounded and the system is stable.

Next, consider a system described by the equation,

$$y[n] = \sum_{k=-\infty}^{n} x[k]$$

In this system (accumulator), output sums all the past values of the input rather than just a finite set of values, and the system is unstable, since the sum will increase indefinitely even if $x[n]$ is bounded.

e.g. if input to the accmulator is a unit step $u[n]$, then output will be

$$y[n] = \sum_{k=-\infty}^{n} x[k] = (n+1)\,k\,[n]$$

Here, $y[0] = 1$ y, $[1] = 2$, $y[2] = 3$, and $y[n]$ will increase without having limits.

Invertibility and Inverse system

A system is said to be *invertible* if distinct inputs lead to distinct outputs. For discrete time system, if a system is invertible, then an *inverse system* exists such that, when cascaded with the original system, yields an output $w[n]$ equal to input $x[n]$ to the first system.

e.g. $x[n] \longrightarrow$ $\boxed{y[n] = \sum_{k=-\infty}^{n} x[k]}$ $\xrightarrow{y[n]}$

$\boxed{w[n] = y[n] - y[n-1]} \longrightarrow w[n] = x[n]$

Also, an example of an invertible continuous time system is

$$y(t) = 2x[t]$$

For which, inverse system is, $w(t) = \dfrac{1}{2} y(t)$

$$x(t) \longrightarrow \boxed{y(t) = 2x(t)} \xrightarrow{y(t)} \boxed{w(t) = \frac{1}{2} y(t)} \longrightarrow w(t) = x(t)$$

Time invariance

A system is *time invariant,* if a time shift in the input signal results in an identical time shift in the output signal.

Consider a continuous time system defined by

$$y(t) = \sin[x(t)]$$

For an arbitrary input $x_1(t)$,

$$\text{output, } y(t) = \sin[x_1(t)] \qquad \text{...(5.4)}$$

If input $x_1(t)$ delayed by t_0, then

$$\text{new input, } x_2(t) = x_1(t - t_0)$$

and, corresponding output, $y_2(t) = \sin[x_1(t - t_0)]$

From equation (5.4), $y_1(t - t_0) = \sin[x_1(t - t_0)]$

or $y_2(t) = y_1(t - t_0)$

and, thus system is *time invariant.*

Example. *Consider a system specified by the difference equation,*

$$y[n] - \frac{1}{2} y[n-1] = x[n].$$

Determine its impulse response.

Solution:

The given equation can be rewritten as

$$y[n] = x[n] + \frac{1}{2} y[n-1]$$

Let input, $x[n] = k\,\delta[n]$

where, k = constant

Here, $\quad x[n] = 0 \quad$ for $n \leq -1$,

which implies that $\quad y[n] = 0 \quad$ for $n \leq -1$

Now,

$$y[0] = x[0] + \frac{1}{2}\, y[-1] = k$$

$$y[1] = x[1] + \frac{1}{2}\, y[0] = \frac{k}{2}$$

$$y[2] = x[2] + \frac{1}{2}\, y[1] = \left(\frac{1}{2}\right)^2 k$$

Then,

$$y[n] = \left(\frac{1}{2}\right)^n k$$

If $k = 1$, then impulse response is, $h[n] = \left(\frac{1}{2}\right)^n u[n]$

Block diagram representation of First order system

(Described by differential and difference equations).

To develop a block representation of any system, the necessary diagram of three basic operations, are shown in the Figs. 5.1 (*a*), 5.1 (*b*) and 5.1 (*c*) respectively.

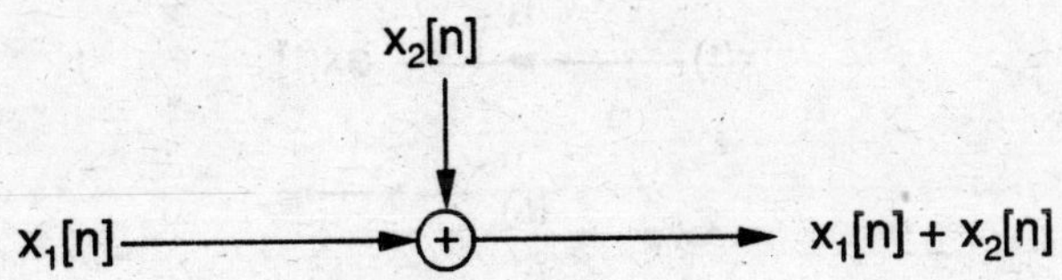

(a) An adder

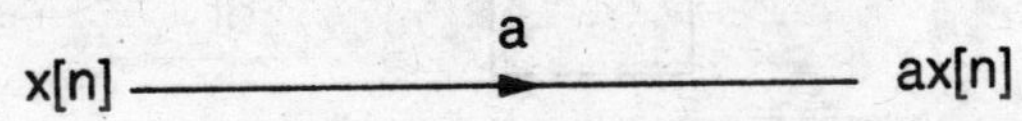

(b) Multiplication by a coefficient

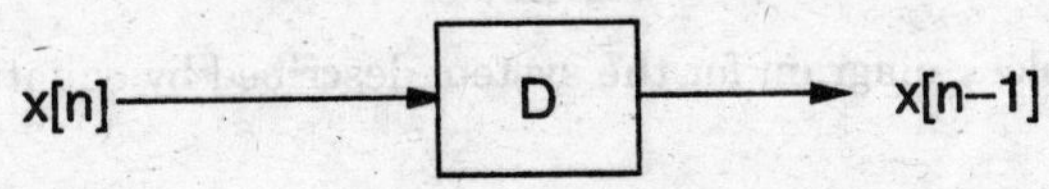

(c) A unit delay

Fig. 5.1

Now, let a causal system described by the first order differential equation

$$y[n] + a\, y[n-1] = b\, x[n]$$

Its block diagram representation is shown below using the block diagram shown in the figures above.

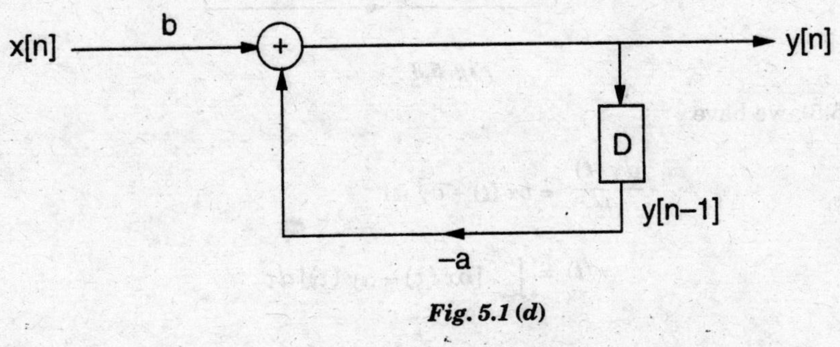

Fig. 5.1 (d)

Again consider causal continuous - time system described by a first-order differential equation

$$\frac{dy(t)}{dt} + ay(t) = bx(t)$$

or

$$y(t) = -\frac{1}{a}\frac{dy(t)}{dt} + \frac{b}{a}x(t) \quad \text{....(5.5)}$$

To defined a block diagram, it requires three basic operations :

(*i*) Addition

(*ii*) Multiplication by a coefficient

(*iii*) Differentiation.

The basic network of which is shown in Figs. 5.2 (*a*), (*b*), (*c*)

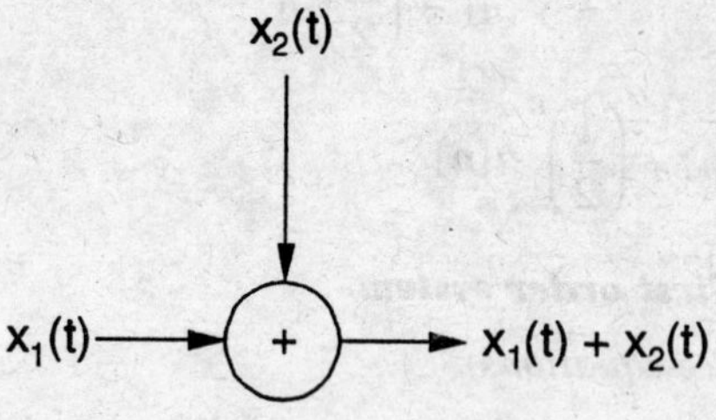

(*a*)

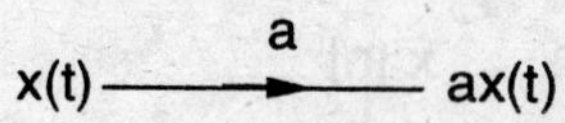

(*b*)

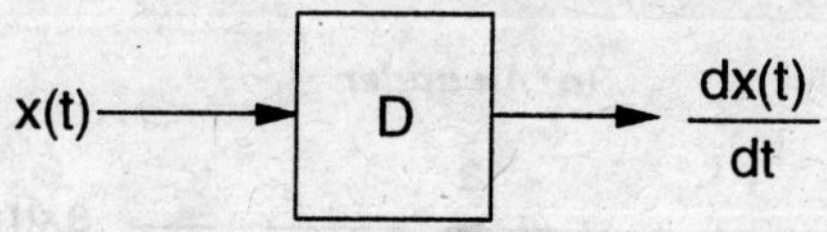

(*c*)

Fig. 5.2

On the basis of above networks, block diagram for the system described by equation (5.2) is,

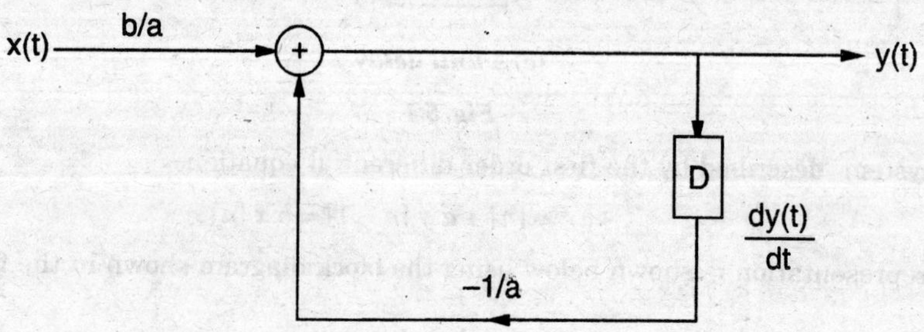

Fig. 5.3

Rewriting equation (5.5), we have

$$\frac{dy(t)}{dt} = bx(t) - ay(t)$$

or

$$y(t) = \int_{-\infty}^{t} [bx(\tau) - ay(\tau)]\, d\tau$$

Now, using integrator we can also represent the system as given below.

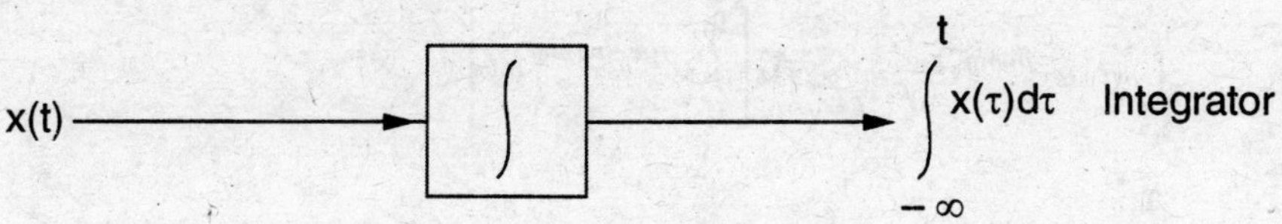

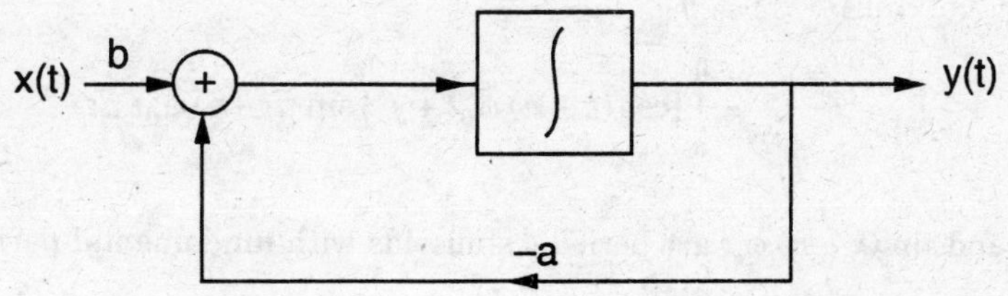

Fig .5.4

5.2 CONTINUOUS-TIME FOURIER SERIES

5.2.1. FOURIER SERIES REPRESENTATION OF CONTINUOUS-TIME PERIODIC SIGNALS.

A set of harmonically related complex exponentials associated with periodic complex exponential signal $s(t) = e^{j\omega_0 t}$ is given by

$$f_k(t) = e^{jk\omega_0 t} = e^{jk(2\pi/T_0)t},\ k = 0, \pm 1, \pm 2, \ldots$$

Each of these signals has a fundamental frequency that is a multiple of ω_0 and therefore, each is periodic with period T_0. Thus, general form of linear combination of harmonically related complex exponentials is given by

$$s(t) = \sum_{k=-\infty}^{\infty} A_k e^{jk\omega_0 t} = \sum_{k=-\infty}^{\infty} A_k e^{jk(2\pi/T_0)t} \quad \ldots(5.6)$$

This linear combination of harmonically related complex exponentials is also periodic with fundamental period T_0.

In equation (5.6),

Term $k = 0$ is a constant.

Terms for $k = 1$ and $k = -1$ both have fundamental frequency equal to ω_0 and are collectively called *fundamental components*. These are also called *first harmonic components.*

Terms for $k = 2$ and $k = -2$ both have fundamental frequency equal to $2\omega_0$ and these are called *second harmonic components*.

Generally, components $k = N$ and $k = -N$ are called *Nth harmonic components*.

Fourier series representation of continuous-time periodic signals

Any continuous time-periodic signal can be represented with the series given by

$$s(t) = \sum_{k=-\infty}^{\infty} A_k e^{jk\omega_0 t} \quad \ldots(5.7)$$

Multiplying both sides of equation (5.7) by $e^{-jn\omega_0 t}$, we get

$$s(t)\, e^{-jn\omega_0 t} = \sum_{k=-\infty}^{\infty} A_k e^{jk\omega_0 t}\, e^{-jn\omega_0 t}$$

Integrating both sides from 0 to T_0, we get

$$\int_0^{T_0} s(t)\, e^{-jn\omega_0 t} dt = \int_0^{T_0} \sum_{k=-\infty}^{\infty} A_k\, e^{jk\omega_0 t}\, e^{-jn\omega_0 t}\, dt$$

Here, T_0 = fundamental period of $s(t)$.

Interchanging order of integration and adding, we get

$$\int_0^{T_0} s(t)\, e^{-jn\omega_0 t} dt = \sum_{k=-\infty}^{\infty} A_k \left[\int_0^{T_0} e^{j(k-n)\omega_0 t} dt \right] \quad ...(5.8)$$

Now,

$$\int_0^{T_0} e^{j(k-n)\omega_0 t} dt = \int_0^{T_0} [\cos (k-n)\, \omega_0 t + j \sin (k-n)\, \omega_0 t]\, dt$$

$$= \int_0^{T_0} [\cos (k-n)\, \omega_0 t + j \int_0^{T_0} \sin (k-n)\, \omega_0 t\, dt \quad ...(5.9)$$

For $k \neq n$, $\cos (k = n)\, \omega_0 t$ and $\sin (k - n)\, \omega_0 t$ are periodic sinusoids with fundamental period $\dfrac{T_0}{|k-n|}$.

Therefore, in equation (5.9), integrate over an interval, *i.e.* fundamental period T_0 that is an integral number of periods of these signals. But the integration is equivalent to measuring total area under the functions over the interval.

Now we have

$$\int_0^{T_0} e^{j(k-n)\omega_0 t} dt = \begin{cases} T_0, & k = n \\ 0, & k \neq n \end{cases} \quad ...(5.10)$$

Substituting equation (5.10) in equation (5.11), we get

$$\int_0^{T_n} s(t)\, e^{-jn\omega_0 t} dt = \sum_{k=-\infty}^{\infty} A_k \left[\int_0^{T_0} e^{j(k-n)\omega_0 t} dt \right]$$

$$\Rightarrow \quad \int_0^{T_0} s(t)\, e^{-jn\omega_0 t} dt = A_n T_0$$

$$\Rightarrow \quad A_n = \frac{1}{T_0} \int_0^{T_0} s(t)\, e^{-jn\omega_0 t} \quad ...(5.11)$$

This equation is used for determining coefficients.

In determining equation (5.9), we use interval of integration equal to T_0 which is an integral number of periods $\cos (k - n)\, \omega_0 t$ and $\sin (k - n)\, \omega_0 t$. Therefore, if we integrate over an interval of length T_0, we get the same result.

$$\int_{T_0} e^{j(k-n)\omega_0 t} dt = \begin{cases} T_0; & k = n \\ 0; & k \neq n \end{cases}$$

Consequently, equation (5.11) can be written as

$$A_n = \frac{1}{T_0} \int_{T_0} s(t) e^{-jn\omega_0 t} dt$$

Fourier series representation of a continuous time peirodic signal and their Fourier series coefficients A_k is

$$s(t) = \sum_{k=-\infty}^{\infty} A_k e^{jk\omega_0 t}$$

$$A_k = \frac{1}{T_0} \int_{T_0} s(t) e^{-jk\omega_0 t} dt$$

where, ω_0 = fundamental frequency = $\dfrac{2\pi}{T_0}$

T_0 = fundamental period.

Example. *Determine Fourier series coefficients of a continuous-time periodic signal* $s(t) = \cos \omega_0 t$, *where* ω_0 *is fundamental frequency.*

Solution:

To determine Fourier series coefficients for the signal, $s(t) = \cos \omega_0 t$, use the equation

$$A_k = \frac{1}{T_0} \int_{T_0} s(t) e^{-jk\omega_0 t} dt$$

Expand sinusoidal signal as a linear combination of complex exponential functions and Fourier series coefficients A_k's are easily identified by inspection.

From Euler's equation $s(t) = \cos \omega_0 t = \dfrac{e^{j\omega_0 t} + e^{-j\omega_0 t}}{2}$ ...(*i*)

But equation of Fourier series representation is given as

$$s(t) = \sum_{k=-\infty}^{\infty} A_k e^{jk\omega_0 t} = \ldots + A_{-1} e^{-j\omega_0 t} + A_0 + A_1 e^{j\omega_0 t} + \ldots \quad \ldots(ii)$$

Comparing equations (*i*) and (*ii*), we get Fourier series coefficients A_k's

$$A_1 = \frac{1}{2}, \quad A_{-1} = \frac{1}{2}, \quad A_k = 0, \; k \neq +1 \text{ or } -1$$

5.2.2. PROPERTIES OF CONTINUOUS-TIME FOURIER SERIES

1. Linearity

Let $s_1(t)$ and $s_2(t)$ be two continuous time periodic signals with period T_0 and they have Fourier coefficients denoted by A_k and B_k respectively, *i.e.*

$$s_1(t) \overset{\mathfrak{I}}{\longleftrightarrow} A_k \text{ and } s_2(t) \overset{\mathfrak{I}}{\longleftrightarrow} B_k$$

Since $s_1(t)$ and $s_2(t)$ have same periods T_0, linear combination of $s_1(t)$ and $s_2(t)$ will also be periodic with period T_0. Fourier series coefficients C_k of linear combination of $s_1(t)$ and $s_2(t)$,

$$s_3(t) = \alpha\, s_1(t) + \beta\, s_2(t)$$

are given by same linear combination of the Fourier series coefficients of $s_1(t)$ and $s_2(t)$, *i.e.*

$$s_3(t) = \alpha\, s_1(t) + \beta\, s_2(t) \overset{\mathfrak{I}}{\longleftrightarrow} C_k = \alpha A_k + \beta B_k$$

2. Time shifting

By time shifting of a periodic signal, its period is preserved. Fourier series coefficients B_k of the resulting signal $s_2(t) = s_1(t - t_0)$ can be expressed as

$$B_k = \frac{1}{T_0} \int_{T_0} s(t - t_0)\, e^{-jk\omega_0 t} dt \quad \ldots(5.12)$$

Substituting $\tau = t - t_0$ in equation (5.12), we get

$$\frac{1}{T_0} \int_{T_0} s(t - t_0)\, e^{-jk\omega_0 t} = \frac{1}{T_0} s(\tau)\, e^{-jk\omega_0 (\tau + t_0)} dt$$

$$= \frac{e^{-jk\omega_0 t}}{T_0} \int_{T_0} s(\tau)\, e^{-jk\omega_0 \tau} d\tau = \frac{e^{-j\omega_0 t_0}}{T_0} A_k$$

where A_k = kth Fourier series coefficient of $s_1(t)$.

If $\quad s_1(t) \overset{\mathfrak{I}}{\longleftrightarrow} A_k$

then $\quad s(t - t_0) \overset{\mathfrak{I}}{\longleftrightarrow} e^{-jk\omega_0 t_0} A_k$

Magnitude of Fourier series coefficients remain unaltered when periodic signal is shifted in time.

3. Time reversal

Folding of a signal is called *time reversal*. The period T_0 of a periodic signal $s(t)$ also remains unaltered when the signal undergoes time reversal.

Consider a continuous time periodic signal $s_1(t)$. It's mirror image (folded) form will be given as

$$s_2(t) = s_1(-t)$$

If $$s_1(t) \stackrel{\mathfrak{I}}{\longleftrightarrow} A_k$$

then $$s_1(-t) \stackrel{\mathfrak{I}}{\longleftrightarrow} A_{-k}$$

i.e. time reversal (folding) applied to a continuous-time periodic signal results in a time reversal of the corresponding sequence of Fourier series coefficients $\{A_k\}$

If signal $s_1(t)$ is even, *i.e.*

$$s_1(-t) = s_1(t)$$

then its fourier series coefficients are also even, *i.e.* $A_{-k} = A_k$

Similarly, if signal $s_1(t)$ is odd, *i.e.* $s_1(-t) = -s_1(t)$ then its Fourier series coefficients are also odd, *i.e.*

$$A_{-k} = A_k$$

4. Time scaling

It is an operation by which period of an underlying signal changes.

If $s(t)$ is a periodic signal with period T_0, then $s(\alpha t)$ is periodic with period T_0/α, where α is a positive real number.

Since time scaling operation applies directly to each of the harmonic components of signal $s(t)$, hence Fourier series coefficients for each of these harmonic components remain the same.

If signal s(t) has Fourier series representation as

$$s(t) = \sum_{k=-\infty}^{\infty} A_k e^{jk\omega_0 t}$$

then Fourier series representation for the time scaled version of $s(t)$, *i.e.* $s(\alpha t)$ will be given by

$$s(\alpha t) = \sum_{k=-\infty}^{\infty} A_k e^{jk(\alpha\omega_0)t}$$

Hence in time scaling operation, Fourier series coefficients have not changed but Fourier series representation has changed because of the change in the fundamental frequency.

5. Multiplication

Consider two periodic signals $s_1(t)$ and $s_2(t)$ with period T_0.

$$s_1(t) \stackrel{\mathfrak{I}}{\longleftrightarrow} A_k \text{ and } s_2(t) \stackrel{\mathfrak{I}}{\longleftrightarrow} B_k$$

Since product of $s_1(t)$ and $s_2(t)$ is also periodic with T_0, hence expanding $s_1(t)\, s_2(t)$ in a Fourier series with Fourier series coefficients C_k expressed in terms of coefficients $s_1(t)$ and $s_2(t)$, we get

$$s_1(t)\, s_2(t) \stackrel{\mathfrak{I}}{\longleftrightarrow} C_k = \sum_{l=-\infty}^{\infty} A_l B_{k-1}$$

Summation on the right hand side of the above equation may be interpreted as discrete time convolution of the sequence representing Fourier series coefficients of $s_1(t)$ and the $s_2(t)$.

6. Conjugation

Taking complex conjugate of a periodic signal $s(t)$ has the effect of complex conjugation and time reversal (folding) on the corresponding Fourier series coefficients, *i.e.*

if $$s(t) \stackrel{\mathfrak{I}}{\longleftrightarrow} A_k$$

then $$s^*(t) \stackrel{\mathfrak{I}}{\longleftrightarrow} A^*_{-k}$$

Some important consequences of complex conjugation property of the signal s(t) :

- *For real signal,* if $s(t) = s^*(t)$

  then, Fourier series coefficients A_k will be conjugate symmetric, *i.e.*

$$A_{-k} = A^*_k$$

- *If s(t) is real,* then A_0 is real and $|A_k| = A_{-k}|$
- *If signal s(t) is real and even,* so are its Fourier series coefficients.
- *If s(t) is real and odd,* then its Fourier series coefficients are purely imaginary and odd. e.g. $A_0 = 0$, if $s(t)$ is real and odd.

7. Parseval's relation

For continuous time periodic signals, it is given as

$$\frac{1}{T_0}\int_{T_0} |s(t)|^2\,dt = \sum_{k=-\infty}^{\infty} |A_k|^2 \qquad ...(5.13)$$

where, A_k's = Fourier series coefficients of signal $s(t)$

T_0 = period of the signal.

Left hand side of equation (5.13) is average power in one period of the periodic signal $s(t)$.

Average power is the energy per unit time in one period of the periodic signal $s(t)$.

or $$\frac{1}{T_0}\int_{T_0} \left|A_k e^{jk\omega_0 t}\right|^2 dt = \frac{1}{T_0}\int_{T_0} |A_k|^2 dt = |A_k|^2$$

where, $|A_k|^2$ = average power in kth harmonic of the signal $s(t)$.

Thus, Parseval's relation states that, *total average power in a periodic signal is equal to sum of the average powers in all of its harmonic components.*

5.3. DISCRETE-TIME FOURIER SERIES

Let a sequence $x[n]$ periodic with fundamental period N, *i.e.*

$$x[n] = x[n + N]$$

Consider a complex exponential $e^{j\left(\frac{2\pi}{N}\right)n}$ periodic with period N, where $\frac{2\pi}{N} = \omega_0$, given as

$$\phi_k[n] = e^{jk\omega_0 n} = e^{jk\left(\frac{2\pi}{N}\right)n}, \quad k = 0, \pm 1, \pm 2 \qquad ...(5.14)$$

Now, representing equation (5.14) as a more general periodic sequence, we have

$$x[n] = \sum_k a_k \phi_k[n] = \sum_k a_k e^{jk\omega_0 n} \qquad ...(5.15)$$

where $k = 0, 1, ... N - 1$.

Equation (5.15) referred as *discrete time fourier series* and co-efficients as *fourier series coefficients.*

Now, consider Fourier series representation of equation (5.15) and multiplying by $e^{-jr\left(\frac{2\pi}{N}\right)n}$ and running over N terms, we get

$$\sum_{n=\langle N\rangle} x[n].e^{-jr\left(\frac{2\pi}{N}\right)n} = \sum_{n=\langle N\rangle}\sum_{k=\langle N\rangle} a_k.e^{j(k-r)\left(\frac{2\pi}{N}\right)n}$$

Interchanging order of summation on RHS, we get

$$\sum_{n=\langle N\rangle} x[n].e^{jr\left(\frac{2\pi}{N}\right)n} = \sum_{k=\langle N\rangle} a_k \sum_{n=\langle N\rangle} e^{j(k-r)\left(\frac{2\pi}{N}\right)n} \qquad ...(5.16)$$

Now, as $$\sum_{n=\langle N\rangle} e^{jk\left(\frac{2\pi}{N}\right)n} = \begin{cases} N, & k = 0 \pm N, \pm 2N \\ 0, & \text{otherwise} \end{cases} \quad \text{...(5.17)}$$

From equation (5.17), right hand side is zero, unless $k - r$ is zero or an integral multiple of N. Therefore, if values for r varies over the same range as that over which k varies, then

$$\sum_{n=\langle N\rangle} e^{j(k-r)\left(\frac{2\pi}{N}\right)n} = \begin{cases} N, & if\ k = r \\ 0, & if\ k \neq r \end{cases}$$

Right-hand side of equation (5.16) is

$$Na_r = \sum_{n=\langle N\rangle} x[n]\, e^{-jr\left(\frac{2\pi}{N}\right)n}$$

$$\Rightarrow \quad a_r = \sum_{n=\langle N\rangle} x[n]\,.\, e^{-jr\left(\frac{2\pi}{N}\right)n}$$

Hence, $$x[n] = \sum_{k=\langle N\rangle} a_k\, e^{j\omega_0 n} = \sum_{k=\langle N\rangle} a_k\, e^{jk\left(\frac{2\pi}{N}\right)n} \quad \text{...(5.18)}$$

$$a_k = \frac{1}{N} \sum_{n=\langle N\rangle} x[n]\,.\, e^{-jk\omega_0 n} = \frac{1}{N} \sum_{n=\langle N\rangle} x[n]\,.\, e^{-jk\left(\frac{2\pi}{N}\right)n} \quad \text{...(5.19)}$$

Here a_k is Fourier series co-efficient and equations (5.18) and (5.19) are respectively called *synthesis equation and analysis equation.*

Example. *A discrete time signal $x[n] = \sin \omega_0 n$, and $\omega_0 = \frac{2\pi}{N}$. Determine Fourier co-efficient for N = 5.*

Solution:

Here, $x[n]$ is periodic only if $\frac{2\pi}{\omega_0}$ is an integer or a ratio of integers.

When $\frac{2\pi}{\omega_0}$ is an integer, then $$\omega_0 = \frac{2\pi}{N}$$

and $$x[n] = \frac{1}{2j}\left[e^{j\left(\frac{2\pi}{N}\right)n} - e^{-j\left(\frac{2\pi}{N}\right)n}\right]$$

By synthesis equation, $$x[n] = \sum_{k=\langle N\rangle} a_k e^{jk\left(\frac{2\pi}{N}\right)n}$$

we have $$a_1 = \frac{1}{2j},\ a_{-1} = -\frac{1}{2j}$$

and remaining co-efficients are zero. These co-efficients repeat with period N

$$\therefore \quad a_{N+1} = \frac{1}{2j} \text{ and } a_{N-1} = -\frac{1}{2j}$$

Fourier series co-efficients with N = 5 are shown below,

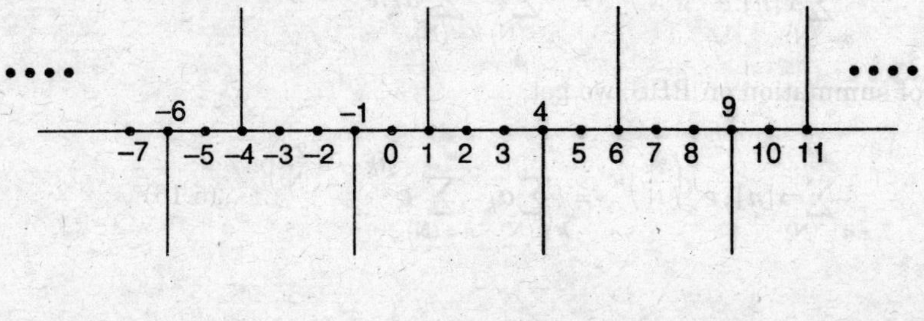

Example. *Consider a discrete time periodic signal having period N.*

$$x[N] = 1 + \sin\left(\frac{2\pi}{N}\right)n + 3\cos\left(\frac{2\pi}{N}\right)n + \cos\left(\frac{4\pi}{N}\cdot n + \frac{\pi}{2}\right)$$

Plot magnitude and phase of fourier coefficients for N = 10.

Solution:

Since, this signal is periodic with N, and

$$x[n] = 1 + \frac{1}{2j}\left[e^{j\left(\frac{2\pi}{N}\right)n} - e^{-j\left(\frac{2\pi}{N}\right)n}\right] + \frac{3}{2}\left[e^{j\left(\frac{2\pi}{N}\right)n} + e^{-j\left(\frac{2\pi}{N}\right)n}\right] + \frac{1}{2}\left[e^{j\left(\frac{4\pi n}{N}+\frac{\pi}{2}\right)} + e^{-j\left(\frac{4\pi n}{N}+\frac{\pi}{2}\right)}\right]$$

$$\Rightarrow \quad x[n] = 1 + \left(\frac{3}{2}+\frac{1}{2j}\right)e^{j\left(\frac{2\pi}{N}\right)n} + \left(\frac{3}{2}-\frac{1}{2j}\right).e^{-j2\left(\frac{2\pi}{N}\right)n}\left(\frac{1}{2}e^{j\pi/2}\right).e^{j2\left(\frac{2\pi}{N}\right)n} + \left(\frac{1}{2}e^{-j\pi/2}\right).e^{-j2\left(\frac{2\pi}{N}\right)n}$$

Hence Fourier series co-efficients are

$$a_0 = 1,\ a_1 = \frac{3}{2} - \frac{1}{2}j,\ a_{-1} = \frac{3}{2} + \frac{1}{2}j,\ a_2 = \frac{j}{2},\ a_{-2} = -\frac{j}{2}$$

and, for other values of k, $\quad a_k = 0$.

Magnitude and phase of these co-efficients are shown in Fig. (*b*) for N = 10.

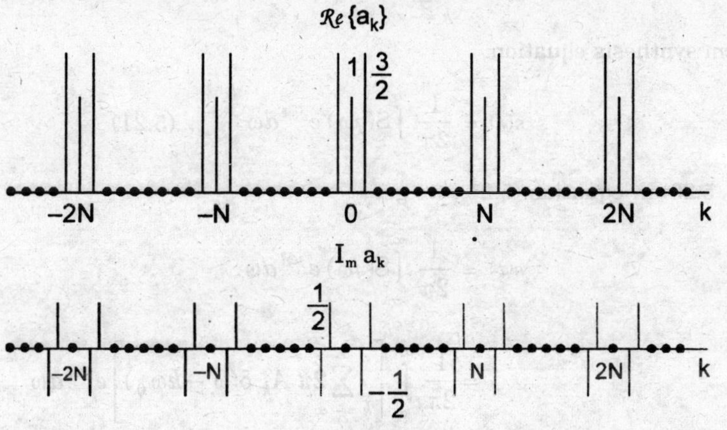

***Fig.* (*a*)**

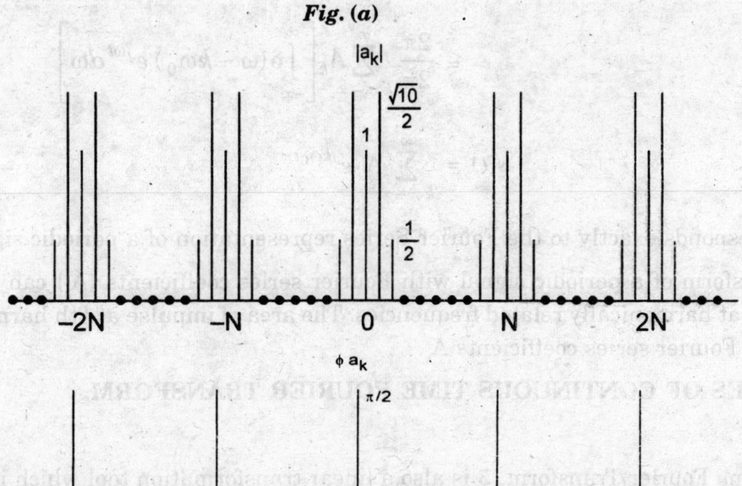

***Fig.* (*b*)**

5.4. CONTINUOUS-TIME FOURIER TRANSFORM (CTFT)

5.4.1. FOURIER TRANSFORM OF CONTI-NUOUS-TIME PERIODIC SIGNALS.

Consider a signal $s(t)$ with Fourier transform $S(j\omega)$.

Here $S(j\omega)$ is a single impulse of area 2π at $\omega = \omega_0$.

It can be written as

$$S(j\omega) = 2\pi\,\delta(\omega - \omega_0)$$

To determine signal $s(t)$ for this Fourier transform using inverse Fourier Transform relation, we have

$$s(t) = \frac{1}{2\pi}\int_{2\pi}^{\infty} S(j\omega)\,e^{j\omega t}\,d\omega$$

$$= \frac{1}{2\pi}\int_{-\infty}^{\infty} 2\pi\,\delta(\omega - \omega_0)\,e^{j\omega t}\,d\omega$$

$$= \frac{2\pi}{2\pi}\int_{-\infty}^{\infty} \delta(\omega - \omega_0)\,e^{j\omega t}\,d\omega = e^{j\omega t}$$

Generally, if $S(j\omega)$ is of the form of a linear combination of impulses equally spaced in frequency, it can be written as

$$S(j\omega) = \sum_{k=-\infty}^{\infty} 2\pi\,A_k\,\delta(\omega - k\omega_0) \qquad \text{...(5.20)}$$

From Fourier transform synthesis equation

$$s(t) = \frac{1}{2\pi}\int_{-\infty}^{\infty} S(j\omega)\,e^{j\omega t}\,d\omega \qquad \text{...(5.21)}$$

Substituting equation (5.20) in equation (5.21), we get

$$s(t) = \frac{1}{2\pi}\int_{-\infty}^{\infty} S(j\omega)\,e^{j\omega t}\,d\omega$$

$$= \frac{1}{2\pi}\int_{-\infty}^{\infty}\left[\sum_{k=-\infty}^{\infty} 2\pi\,A_k\,\delta(\omega - k\omega_0)\right] e^{j\omega t}\,d\omega$$

$$= \frac{2\pi}{2\pi}\sum_{k=-\infty}^{\infty} A_k\left[\int_{-\infty}^{\infty}\delta(\omega - k\omega_0)\,e^{j\omega t}\,d\omega\right]$$

$$\Rightarrow \qquad s(t) = \sum_{k=-\infty}^{\infty} A_k e^{jk\omega_0 t}$$

This equation corresponds exactly to the Fourier Series representation of a periodic signal.

Thus, Fourier transform of a periodic signal with Fourier series coefficients $\{A_k\}$ can be interpreted as a train of impulses occurring at harmonically related frequencies. The area of impulse at kth harmonic frequency $k\omega_0$ for $S(j\omega)$ is 2π times the kth Fourier series coefficients A_k.

5.4.2. PROPERTIES OF CONTINUOUS TIME FOURIER TRANSFORM.

1. Linearity

Continuous-Time Fourier Transform, $\Im$ is also a linear transformation tool which is used to transform a signal from time-domain to frequency domain. Fourier transform also satisfies principle of superposition.

Consider two continuous-time signals $s_1(t)$ and $s_2(t)$.

If $\qquad s_1(t) \xleftrightarrow{\Im} S_1(j\omega)$

and $\qquad s_2(t) \xleftrightarrow{\Im} S_2(j\omega)$

then from linearity of continuous time Fourier transform (CTFT), we have

$$A_1 s_1(t) + A_2 s_2(t) \overset{\Im}{\longleftrightarrow} A_1 S_1(j\omega) + A_2 S_2(j\omega)$$

where A_1 and A_2 are constants.

Also property of linearity of CTFT (Continuous-time Fourier transform) is easily extended to a linear combination of an arbitrary number of signals.

$$\therefore \quad A_1 s_1(t) + A_2 s_2(t) + A_3 s_3(t) + \ldots \overset{\Im}{\longleftrightarrow} A_1 S_1(j\omega) + A_2 S_2(j\omega) + A_3 S_3(j\omega) + \ldots.$$

2. Time shifting

It gives effect of shifting time-variable t on the CTFT of a signal $s(t)$.

If $$s(t) \overset{\Im}{\longleftrightarrow} S(j\omega)$$

then $$s(t - t_0) \overset{\Im}{\longleftrightarrow} e^{-j\omega t_0} S(j\omega)$$

To prove this property, consider CTFT synthesis equation given as

$$s(t) = \frac{1}{2\pi} \int_{-\infty}^{\infty} S(j\omega) e^{j\omega t} d\omega$$

Substituting $t = (t - t_0)$, we get

$$s(t - t_0) = \frac{1}{2\pi} \int_{-\infty}^{\infty} S(j\omega) \; e^{j\omega t - t_0} \; d\omega$$

$$= \frac{1}{2\pi} \int_{-\infty}^{\infty} S(j\omega) \; e^{j\omega t} \; e^{-j\omega t_0} \; d\omega$$

$$= \frac{1}{2\pi} \int_{-\infty}^{\infty} [S(j\omega) e^{-j\omega t_0}] e^{j\omega t} d\omega$$

$$\therefore \quad \Im\, [s(t - t_0)] = e^{-j\omega t_0}\, S(j\omega)$$

3. Conjugation and Conjugate symmetry

Complex conjugate of complex signal $s(t)$ is obtained by changing sign of imaginary part of the signal $s(t)$.

Signal $s(t)$ can be written in rectangular form as

$$s(t) = s_R(t) + j\, s_I(t)$$

where $s_R(t)$ and $s_1(t)$ are real and imaginary parts of the complex signal $s(t)$.

Complex conjugate of $s(t)$ will be expressd as

$$s^*(t) = s_R(t) - j\, s_I(t)$$

Conjugation property states that

if $$s(t) \overset{\Im}{\longleftrightarrow} S(j\omega)$$

then $$s^*(t) \overset{\Im}{\longleftrightarrow} S^*(-j\omega)$$

where $S^*(j\omega)$ = complex conjugate of CTFT of $s(t)$, *i.e.* $S(j\omega)$.

$S(j\omega)$ can be expressed in rectangular form as

$$S(j\omega) = S_R(j\omega) + j\, S_I(j\omega)$$

and its complex conjugate can be expressed as

$$S^*(j\omega) = S_R(j\omega) - j\, S_I(j\omega)$$

Therefore, $S^*(-j\omega)$ can be written as

$$S^*(-j\omega) = S_R(-j\omega) - S_I(-j\omega)$$

To prove this property, use CTFT analysis equation given as

$$S(j\omega) = \text{CTFT}\{s(t)\} = \int_{-\infty}^{\infty} s(t)\, e^{-j\omega t} dt$$

Complex conjugate of S $(j\omega)$ is determined as

$$S^*(j\omega) = \int_{-\infty}^{\infty} s^*(t)\, [e^{-j\omega t}]^* dt$$

$$= \int_{-\infty}^{\infty} s^*(t)\, e^{j\omega t} dt$$

Replacing ω by −ω, we get

$$S^*(-j\omega) = \int_{-\infty}^{\infty} s^*(t)\, e^{-j\omega t} dt \quad \text{...(5.22)}$$

Right hand side of equation (5.22) is CTFT analysis equation for $s^*(t)$.

$\therefore \quad \Im\{s^*(t)\} = S_2(-j\omega)$

Now consider a special case, i.e. when $s(t)$ is a real signal, then its CTFT, $S(j\omega)$ will have conjugate symmetry. It is given as

$$S(-j\omega) = S^*(j\omega)$$

If $s(t)$ is real, then $\quad s^*(t) = s(t)$

Hence from equation (5.22), we get

$$S^*(-j\omega) = \int_{-\infty}^{\infty} s^*(t)\, e^{-j\omega t} dt$$

$$= \int_{-\infty}^{\infty} s(t)\, e^{-j\omega t} dt = S(j\omega)$$

Replacing ω with −ω, we get

$$S(-j\omega) = S^*(j\omega)$$

Also,

$$\text{Even}\,[s(t)] \overset{\Im}{\longleftrightarrow} \text{Re}[S(j\omega)]$$

$$\text{Odd}\,[s(t)] \overset{\Im}{\longleftrightarrow} j\,\text{Im}\,[S\,(j\omega)]$$

4. **Duality**

Comparing Fourier transform and Inverse Fourier transform relations, we get

$$S(j\omega) = \int_{-\infty}^{\infty} s(t)\, e^{-j\omega t} dt$$

and

$$s(t) = \frac{1}{2\pi}\int_{-\infty}^{\infty} S\,(j\omega)\, e^{j\omega t} d\omega$$

These equations are similar but not identical in form. This symmetry leads to a property of the Fourier transform called **duality.**

Example. *Determine Fourier transform $S(j\omega)$ for the signal $s(t) = \dfrac{2}{1+t^2}$.*

Solution:

Since,

$$s(t) = e^{-2|t|} \overset{\Im}{\longleftrightarrow} S(j\omega) = \frac{2}{1+\omega^2}$$

hence, using CTFT synthesis equation

$$s(t) = \frac{1}{2\pi}\int_{-\infty}^{\infty} S\,(j\omega)\, e^{j\omega t} d\omega$$

$$e^{-2|t|} = \frac{1}{2\pi}\int_{-\infty}^{\infty} \left(\frac{2}{1+\omega^2}\right) e^{j\omega t} d\omega$$

Replacing t by $-t$, we get

$$2\pi\, e^{-2|t|} = \int_{-\infty}^{\infty}\left(\frac{2}{1+\omega^2}\right)e^{-j\omega t}\,d\omega$$

Interchanging names of variables t and ω, we get

$$2\pi\, e^{-2|\omega|} = \int_{-\infty}^{\infty}\left(\frac{2}{1+t^2}\right)e^{-j\omega t}\,dt$$

Right hand side of this equation is CTFT analysis equation for signal $s(t) = \dfrac{2}{1+t^2}$

$$\therefore \qquad \text{CTFT}\left\{\frac{2}{1+t^2}\right\} = 2\pi e^{-2|\omega|}$$

5. Parseval's relation

It says that, total energy of a signal may be determined either by computing energy per unit time and integrating over all time or by computing energy per unit frequency and integrating over all frequencies.

Parseval's relation for CTFT is given as

$$\int_{-\infty}^{\infty}|s(t)|^2 dt = \frac{1}{2\pi}\int_{-\infty}^{\infty}|S(j\omega)|^2\, d\omega$$

6. Differentiation and Integration of signal $s(t)$

By differentiation, Fourier transform synthesis equation can be given as

$$s(t) = \frac{1}{2\pi}\int_{-\infty}^{\infty} S(j\omega)e^{j\omega t}\,d\omega$$

$$\therefore \qquad \frac{d\,s(t)}{dt} = \frac{d}{dt}\left[\frac{1}{2\pi}\int_{-\infty}^{\infty} S(j\omega)\,e^{j\omega t}\,d\omega\right]$$

$$= \frac{1}{2\pi}\int_{-\infty}^{\infty} S(j\omega)\left[\frac{d}{dt}e^{j\omega t}\right]d\omega$$

$$= \frac{1}{2\pi}\int_{-\infty}^{\infty} S(j\omega)\,[j\omega e^{j\omega t}]\,d\omega$$

$$\Rightarrow \qquad \frac{d\,s(t)}{dt} = \frac{1}{2\pi}\int_{-\infty}^{\infty}[j\omega\, S(j\omega)]\,e^{j\omega t}\,d\omega$$

$$\therefore \qquad \frac{d\,s(t)}{dt} \xleftrightarrow{\Im} j\omega\, S(j\omega)$$

Precise relationship can be written as

$$\int_{-\infty}^{\infty} s(\tau)\,d\tau \xleftrightarrow{\Im} \frac{1}{j\omega}S(j\omega) + \pi\, S(0)\,\delta(\omega)$$

7. Time and Frequency scaling

Alteration of time variable t in a signal is called *time scaling*.

Similarly, alteration of frequency variable ω in a signal is called *frequency scaling*.

If
$$s(t) \xleftrightarrow{\Im} S(j\omega)$$

then
$$s(At) \xleftrightarrow{\Im} \frac{1}{|A|}S\left(\frac{j\omega}{A}\right)$$

where A is a real constant.

5.5. DISCRETE-TIME FOURIER TRANSFORM (DTFT)

Consider a sequence $x[n]$ having finite duration, and for some integers N_1, and N_2, $x[n] = 0$, outside the range $N_1 \le n \le N_2$ as shown in Fig. 5.5.

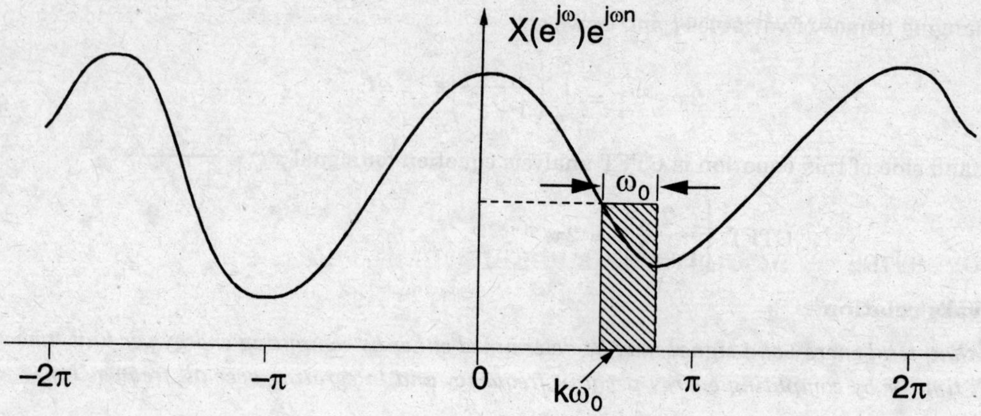

Fig. 5.5

From this aperiodic signal, a periodic sequence $\tilde{x}[n]$ can be constructed as given below.

Fourier series representation of $\tilde{x}^n[n]$ is,

$$\tilde{x}[n] = \sum_{k=\langle N\rangle} a_k e^{jk\left(\frac{2\pi}{N}\right)n} \quad \text{...(5.23)}$$

where,

$$a_k = \frac{1}{N}\sum_{n=\langle N\rangle} \tilde{x}[n]\cdot e^{-jk\left(\frac{2\pi}{N}\right)n}$$

Since $x[n] = \tilde{x}[n]$ over a period $-N_1 \le n \le N_2$

$$a_k = \frac{1}{N}\sum_{n=-N_1}^{N_2} x[n].e^{-jk\left(\frac{2\pi}{N}\right).n}$$

$$= \frac{1}{N}\sum_{n=-\infty}^{+\infty} x[n].e^{-jk\left(\frac{2\pi}{N}\right).n} \quad \text{[as, } x[n] \text{ is zero outside } -N_1 \le N \le N_2]$$

Now,

$$X(e^{j\omega}) = \sum_{n=-\infty}^{+\infty} x[n].e^{-j\omega n}$$

and

$$a_k = \frac{1}{N}X(e^{jk\omega_0}),\quad \omega_0 = \frac{2\pi}{N} \quad \text{...(5.24)}$$

is spacing of samples in the frequency domain.

From equations (5.23) and (5.24), we have

$$\tilde{x}[n] = \sum_{k=\langle N\rangle} \frac{1}{N} X(e^{jk\omega_0}).\ e^{jk\omega_0 n}$$

Using, $\omega_0 = \dfrac{2\pi}{N}$, we get

$$x^n[n] = \frac{1}{2\pi}.\sum_{K=\langle N\rangle} X(e^{jk\omega_0})\ e^{jk\omega_0 n}\,\omega_0 \quad \text{...(5.25)}$$

Now as $N \to \infty$, equation (5.25) turns into integral as drawn above.

Therefore, as $N \to \infty$, $\tilde{x}[n] = x[n]$ and equation (5.25) becomes

$$x[n] = \frac{1}{2\pi} \int_{2\pi} X(e^{j\omega})\, e^{j\omega n}\, .d\omega$$

Since $X(e^{j\omega})\, e^{j\omega n}$ is periodic with period 2π, an integral can be taken as periodic having period 2π.

Hence,
$$x[n] = \frac{1}{2\pi} \int_{2\pi} X(e^{j\omega})\, .\, e^{j\omega n}\, d\omega$$

$$X(e^{j\omega}) = \sum_{h=-\infty}^{+\infty} x[n]\, .\, e^{-j\omega n}$$

5.5.1. PROPERTIES OF DISCRETE-TIME FOURIER SERIES

1. Periodicity

DTFT of $s(n)$ is always periodic in ω with period, *i.e.*

$$s(n) \overset{\Im}{\longleftrightarrow} S(e^{j\omega})$$

$$S(e^{j(\omega+2\pi)}) = S(e^{j\omega})$$

This is in contrast of continuous-time fourier transform which in general is not a periodic function.

2. Linearity

DTFT is also a linear transformation tool as CTFT.

$$s_1(n) \overset{\Im}{\longleftrightarrow} S_1(e^{j\omega})$$

$$s_2(n) \overset{\Im}{\longleftrightarrow} S_2(e^{j\omega})$$

where $s_1(n)$ and $s_2(n)$ are discrete-time sequences whose DTFTs are $S_1(e^{j\omega})$ and $S_2(e^{j\omega})$, respectively.

From property of linearity, for above two discrete-time sequences $s_1(n)$ and $s_2(n)$

$$A_1 s_1(n) + A_2\, s_2(n) \overset{\Im}{\longleftrightarrow} A_1\, S_1(e^{j\omega}) + A_2\, S_2(e^{j\omega})$$

where, A_1 and A_2 are constants.

3. Time shifting and Frequency shifting

Consider the effect of time shifting of a discrete time sequence $s(n)$ on its DTFT $S(e^{j\omega})$ and then consider the effect of frequency shifting.

If
$$s(n) \overset{\Im}{\longleftrightarrow} S(e^{j\omega})$$

then
$$s(n-n_0) \overset{\Im}{\longleftrightarrow} e^{-j\omega n_0}\, S(e^{j\omega})$$

where, $s(n - n_0)$ = *time-shifted version of* $s(n)$.

Now we see effect of *frequency shifting.*

If
$$s(n) \overset{\Im}{\longleftrightarrow} S(e^{j\omega})$$

then
$$s^{-j\omega_0 n}\, s(n) \overset{\Im}{\longleftrightarrow} S(e^{j(\omega-\omega_0)})$$

where $S(e^{j(\omega-\omega_0)})$ = frequency shifted version of $S(e^{j\omega})$.

4. Complex conjuation and Conjugate symmetry

Let $s(n)$ be the complex discrete time signal,

$$s(n) = s_R(n) + j\, s_I(n)$$

and its DTFT is also complex, *i.e.*

$$S(e^{j\omega}) = S_R(e^{j\omega}) + j\, S_I(e^{j\omega})$$

where, $S_R(n)$ and $s_I(n)$ = real and imaginary parts of $s(n)$, respectively

$S_R(e^{j\omega})$ and $S_I(e^{j\omega})$ = real and imaginary parts of $S(e^{j\omega})$ respectively.

Now complex conjugation of $s(n)$ is given by

$$s^*(n) = s_R(n) - j\, s_I(n)$$

and complex conjugation of $S(e^{j\omega})$ is given by

$$S^*(e^{j\omega}) = S_R(e^{j\omega}) - j\, S_I(e^{j\omega})$$

If $$s(n) \xleftrightarrow{\text{DTFT}} S(e^{j\omega})$$

then $$s^*(n) \xleftrightarrow{\text{DTFT}} S^*(e^{-j\omega})$$

Also, if signal $s(n)$ is a real-valued function, then its DTFT $S(e^{j\omega})$ will be conjugate symmetric, *i.e.*

$$S(e^{j\omega}) = S^*(e^{-j\omega}) \quad \text{for } s(n) \text{ real}$$

From this equation, Re $\{S(e^{j\omega})\}$ is an even function of ω and Im $\{S(e^{j\omega})\}$ is an odd function of ω.

Similarly, magnitude of $S(e^{j\omega})$ is an even function and phase angle $\angle S(e^{j\omega})$ is an odd function.

Also, we can decomposing sequence $s(n)$ into even and odd parts.

Again, $$\text{Ev}\{s(n)\} = s_E(n) \xleftrightarrow{\text{DTFT}} \text{Re}\,\{S(e^{j\omega})\} = S_R(e^{j\omega})$$

and $$\text{Od}\,\{s(n)\} = s_0(n) \xleftrightarrow{\text{DTFT}} j\,\text{Im}\,\{S(e^{j\omega})\} = j\,S_I(e^{j\omega})$$

where Ev $\{s(n)\}$ and Od $\{s(n)\}$ are even and odd parts, respectively of $s(n)$.

Specifically, if $s(n)$ is real and even, its DTFT is also real and even.

5. Differentiating and Accmulation in time

Accumulation is discrete-time counterparts of integration. Integration is used for continuous time signals. Inverse of accumulation is called *first differencing.*

Let $s(n)$ be a discrete time signal with DTFT $S(e^{j\omega})$.

First differencing of signal $s(n)$ is given by

$$s(n) - s(n-1).$$

DTFT of first differencing of signal $s(n)$ can be determined by using properties of linearity and time shifting as

$$s(n) - s(n-1) \xleftrightarrow{\text{DTFT}} S(e^{j\omega}) - e^{-j\omega}\, S(e^{j\omega}) = (1 - e^{-j\omega})\, S(e^{j\omega})$$

Accumulation of signal $s(n)$ is given by

$$y(n) = \sum_{m=-\infty}^{n} s(m)$$

This equation can also be expressed as

$$y(n) - y(n-1) = s(n)$$

Thus, DTFT of $y(n)$ should be related to DTFT of $s(n)$ by division by $(1 - e^{j\omega})$. This is not perfectly correct but precise relation is given by

$$\sum_{m=-\infty}^{n} s(m) \xleftrightarrow{\text{DTFT}} \frac{1}{1-e^{-j\omega}}\, S(e^{j\omega}) + \pi\, S(e^{j0}) \sum_{k=-\infty}^{\infty} \delta(\omega - 2\pi k)$$

The impulse train on the RHS of this equation shows dc or average value that can result from summation.

6. Time reversal of a Discrete-time signal

Taking mirror image or folding of a discrete-time sequence is called *time reversal*.

Consider a discrete time signal or sequence $s(n)$ whose mirror image is given by $s(-n)$.

If $$s(n) \xleftrightarrow{\text{DTFT}} S(e^{j\omega})$$

then $$s(-n) \xleftrightarrow{\text{DTFT}} S(e^{-j\omega})$$

Now, $y(n) = s(-n)$

Taking DTFT of both sides of equation, we get

$$Y(e^{j\omega}) = \text{DTFT}\{y(n)\} = \sum_{n=-\infty}^{\infty} s(-n)\, e^{-j\omega n}$$

Now substituting $m = -n$, we get

$$Y(e^{j\omega}) = \sum_{m=-\infty}^{\infty} s(m)\, e^{-j\omega(-m)} = S(e^{j\omega})$$

i.e., $s(-n) \xleftrightarrow{\text{DTFT}} S(e^{-j\omega})$

7. Time expansion of a Discrete-time signal

It is equivalent to multiplication of independent variable, *i.e.* time of a signal by an integer scalar quantity A, which is greater than unity.

Time expanded signal is given by,

$$s_{(k)}(n) = \begin{cases} s(n/k), & \text{if } n \text{ is a multiple of } k \\ 0, & \text{if } n \text{ is not a multiple of } k \end{cases}$$

where, k = a positive integer

From $k = 2$, sequence $s_{(k)}(n)$ is obtained from original sequence $s(n)$ by placing $k - 1$ zeros between successive values of the original sequence. Thus $s_{(k)}(n)$ is a slowed-down version of $s(n)$.

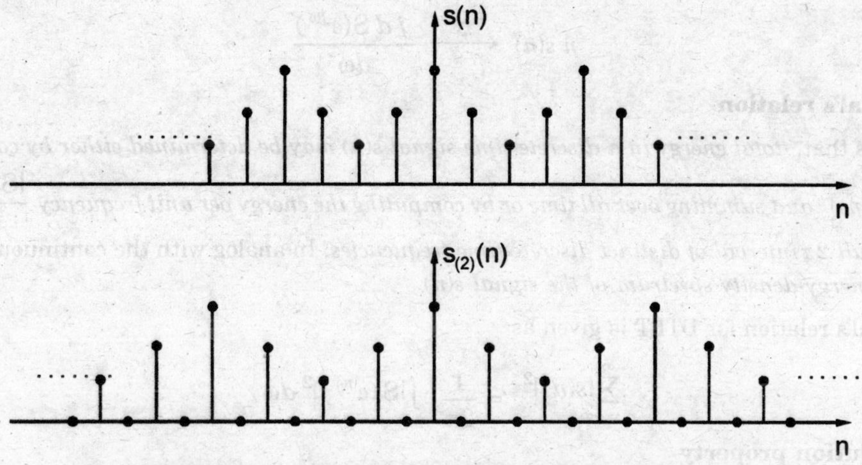

Fig. 5.6 Signal $s_{(2)}(n)$ obtained from s(n) by inserting one zero between successive values of the original signal s(n).

For $n = mk$, DTFT of $s_{(k)}(n)$ is given by

$$S_{(k)}(e^{j\omega}) = \text{DTFT}\{s_{(k)}(n)\}$$

$$= \sum_{n=-\infty}^{\infty} s_{(k)}(n) e^{-j\omega n}$$

$$= \sum_{n=-\infty}^{\infty} s_{(k)}(mk) e^{-j\omega mk}$$

Since $s_{(k)}(mk) = s(m)$, therefore

$$S_{(k)}(e^{j\omega}) = \sum_{n=-\infty}^{\infty} s(m) e^{-j(k\omega)m} = S(e^{jk\omega})$$

i.e. $s_{(k)}(n) \xleftrightarrow{\text{DTFT}} S(e^{jk\omega})$

8. Differentiation in frequency-domain

Let $$s(n) \xleftrightarrow{\text{DTFT}} S(e^{j\omega})$$

Using DTFT analysis equation,

$$S(e^{j\omega}) = \sum_{n=-\infty}^{\infty} s(n)\, e^{-j\omega n}$$

Differentiating both sides with respect to ω, we get

$$\frac{d\,S(e^{j\omega})}{d\omega} = \frac{d}{d\omega}\left[\sum_{n=-\infty}^{\infty} s(n)\, e^{-j\omega n}\right]$$

$$= \sum_{n=-\infty}^{\infty} s(n)\ [-jne^{-j\omega n}]$$

$$= -j \sum_{n=-\infty}^{\infty} n\, s(n)\ e^{-j\omega n}$$

$$= -j^2 \sum_{n=-\infty}^{\infty} n\, s(n)\ e^{-j\omega n}$$

$$= \sum_{n=-\infty}^{\infty} (n\, s(n))\ e^{-j\omega n}\ \Im\,[n\, s(n)]$$

$$\therefore \qquad n\, s(n) \xleftrightarrow{\Im} \frac{j\, d\,S(e^{j\omega})}{d\omega}$$

9. Parseval's relation

It states that, *total energy in a discrete-time signal s(n) may be determined either by computing the energy unit time* $|s(n)|^2$ *and summing over all time or by computing the energy per unit frequency* $\frac{|S(e^{j\omega})|^2}{2\pi}$ *and integrating over a full* 2π *interval of distinct discrete-time frequencies.* In analog with the continuous time signal, $|S(e^{j\omega})|$ is called *energy-density spectrum of the signal s(n).*

Parseval's relation for DTFT is given as

$$\sum_{n=-\infty}^{\infty} |s(n)|^2 = \frac{1}{2\pi} \int_{2\pi} |S(e^{j\omega})|^2\, d\omega$$

10. Convolution property

Convolution of two discrete-time signals $s_1(n)$ and $s_2(n)$ is converted into multiplication of DTFT of individual discrete time signals.

If $$s_1(n) \xleftrightarrow{\Im} S_1(e^{j\omega})$$

and $$s_2(n) \xleftrightarrow{\Im} S_2(e^{j\omega})$$

then from convolution property of DTFT,

$$s(n) = s_1(n) * s_2(n) \xleftrightarrow{\Im} S(e^{j\omega})$$

$$= S_1(e^{j\omega})\ S_2(e^{j\omega}) \qquad \text{...(5.26)}$$

Now apply DTFT for representing and analyzing discrete-time LTI systems, specifically, if $s(n)$, $h(n)$ and $y(n)$ are input, impulse response and output respectively of a discrete time LTI system.

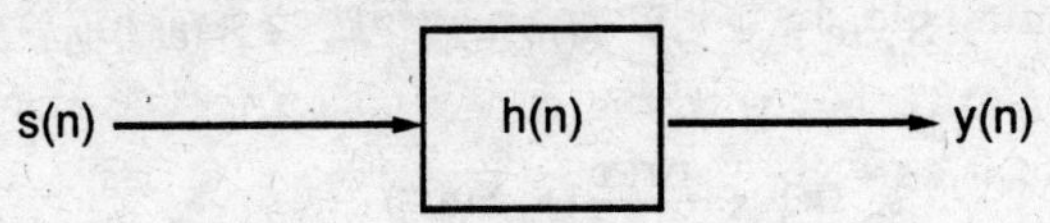

Fig. 5.7. Discrete-time LTI system

Convolving $s(n)$ and $h(n)$

$$\text{Output, } y(n) = s(n) * h(n) \quad \text{...(5.27)}$$

Using DTFT, equation (5.26) can be expressd as

$$Y(e^{j\omega}) = S(e^{j\omega})\, H(e^{j\omega}) \quad \text{...(5.28)}$$

where $S(e^{j\omega})$, $H(e^{j\omega})$ and $Y(e^{j\omega})$ are DTFTs of $s(n)$, $h(n)$ and $y(n)$ respectively.

Now, combining equations (5.27) and (5.28), we get

$$y(n) = s(n) * h(n) \overset{\mathfrak{I}}{\longleftrightarrow} Y(e^{j\omega}) = S(e^{j\omega})\, H(e^{j\omega})$$

5.6. DISCRETE FOURIER TRANSFORM (DFT)

It is also called Finite Fourier transform. It is a transform for Fourier analysis of finite-domain discrete-time signals.

It is widely used in signal processing and related fields

(*i*) to analyze frequencies contained in a sampled signal

(*ii*) to solve partial differential equations

(*iii*) to perform other operations such as convolutions

Definition

The sequence of N complex numbers $X_0, ..., X_{N-1}$ is transformed into the sequence of N complex numbers $X_0, ..., X_{N-1}$, by DFT according to the formula

$$X_k = \sum_{n=0}^{N-1} x_n e^{\frac{-2\pi j}{N} kn} \qquad k = 0,..., N-1$$

Inverse Discrete Fourier Transform (IDFT)

It is given by
$$x_n = \frac{1}{N} \sum_{k=0}^{N-1} X_k e^{\frac{j2\pi j}{N} kn} \qquad n = 0,..., N-1$$

Note :

1. Normalization factor multiplying DFT and IDFT (here 1 and 1/N) and signs of the exponents are merely conventions.
2. Normalization of $1/\sqrt{N}$ for both DFT and IDFT makes the transforms unitary, which has some theoretical advantages.
3. Convention of a negative sign in the exponent is often convenient because it means tht X_k is amplitude of *"positive frequency"* $2\pi k/N$. Equivalently, DFT is often thought of as a matched filter, when looking for a frequency of +1, one correlates incoming signal with a frequency of – 1.

Fast Fourier Transform (FFT)

It is an efficient algorithm to compute Discrete Fourier transform (DFT) and its inverse.

Let $X_0, ..., X_{N-1}$, be complex numbers. DFT is defined by the formula:

$$X_k = \sum_{k=0}^{N-1} x_n e^{\frac{-2\pi j}{N} nk} \qquad k = 0, ... N-1.$$

Evaluating these sums directly would take $O(N^2)$ arithmetical operations.

FFT is an algorithm to compute same result in only O(N log N) operations. In general, such algorithms depend opon factorization of N, but there are O(N log N) FFTs for all N, even prime N.

Many FFT algorithms only depend on the fact that $e^{\frac{-2\pi j}{N}}$ is a primitive root of unity, and thus can be applied to analogous transforms over any finite field, such as *number-theoretic transforms*.

Since inverse DFT is same as the DFT, but with the opposite sign in the exponent and a 1/N factor, any FFT algorithm can easily be adapted for it as well.

DFT can be computed efficiently in practice using a fast fourier transform (FFT) algorithm.

Comparison Between DFT and FFT

Though FFT algorithms are so commonly employed to compute DFT, there is a difference that, *"DFT" refers to a mathematical transformation, regardless of how it is computed, while "FFT" refers to any one of several efficient algorithms for the DFT.*

5.7. Z-TRANSFORM

For a discrete time linear time-invariant sysetm with impulse response $h[n]$, the response $y[n]$ of the system to a complex exponential input of the form z^n is

$$y[n] = H[z].\, z^n \quad ...(5.29)$$

where

$$H[z] = \sum_{h=-\infty}^{\infty} h[n].\, z^{-n} \quad ...(5.30)$$

For $z = e^{j\omega}$ with ω real (*i.e.* with $|z| = 1$), the sum in equation (5.30) corresponds to the discrete-time Fourier transform of $h[n]$.

Generally, when $|z|$ is not restricted to unity, then summation in equation (5.30) is referred as *z-transform of h[n].*

z-transform of a discrete time signal $x[n]$ is defined as

$$X[z] = \sum_{h=-\infty}^{+\infty} x[n].\, z^{-n}$$

where, z = a complex variable.

e.g. consider a signal $x[n]= a^n\, u[n]$, its z-transform is given by

$$X[z] = \sum_{h=-\infty}^{+\infty} a^n\, u[n].\, z^{-n} = \sum_{n=0}^{\infty} (az^{-1})^n$$

5.7.1. REGION OF CONVERGENCE (ROC).

In general, $x(z)$ converges for certain range of values of z.

For convergence of $X(z)$, $\quad \sum_{n=0}^{\infty} |az^{-1}|^n < \infty$

For which $\quad |az^{-1}| < 1$

or $\quad |z| > |a|$.

Then

$$X(z) = \sum_{n=0}^{\infty} (az^{-1})^n = \frac{1}{1-az^{-1}} = \frac{z}{z-a},\ |z| > |a| \quad ...(5.31)$$

z-transform in equation (5.31) is a rational function. Therefore z-transform can be characterized by its zeros and its poles.

Here, pole at $z = a$, and zero at $z = 0$.

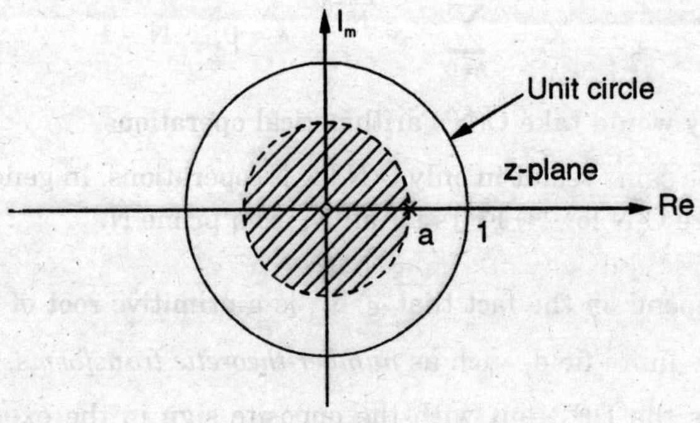

Fig. 5.8

The pole-zero plot and region of convergence shown in Fig. 5.8.

For $|a| > 1$, ROC (Region of Convergence) does not include the unit circle, Fourier transform of $a^n u[n]$ will not converge.

e.g. Let $$x[n] = -a^n u[n-1]$$

then $$X(z) = \sum_{n=-\infty}^{\infty} x[n] z^{-n} = -\sum_{n=-\infty}^{+\infty} a^n u[-n-1] z^{-n}$$

$$X(z) = -\sum_{h=-\infty}^{-1} a^n z^{-n} = 1 - \sum_{n=0}^{\infty} (a^{-1}z)^n \qquad [\because u[n-1] = 0 \text{ for } n > -1]$$

If $|a^{-1} z| < 1, \quad |z| < |a|$

and sum in equation tends to convergence

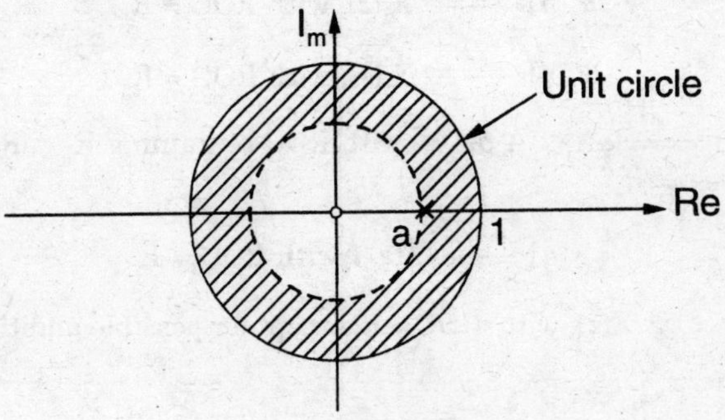

Fig. 5.9

then $$X(z) = 1 - \frac{1}{1 - a^{-1}z} = \frac{1}{1 - az^{-1}} = \frac{z}{z-a}, \quad |z| < |a|$$

The region of convergence is shown in Fig. 5.9 in the pole-zero plot.

Note : X(z) will be rational whenever $x[n]$ is a linear combination of real or complex exponentials.

Properties of ROC (Region Of Convergence).

(1) ROC of X(z) consists of a ring in the z-phase centred about the origin.

(2) ROC does not contain any poles.

(3) It $x(n)$ is of finite duration, then ROC is the entire z-plane, except possibly $z = 0$ and $z = \infty$.

(4) If $x[n]$ is a right sided sequence and if the circle $|z| = r_0$ is in the ROC, then all finite values of z for which $|z_0| > r_0$ will also be in the ROC.

(5) If $x[n]$ is two sided, and if the circle $|z_0| = r_0$ is in the ROC, then ROC will consist of a ring in the z-plane that includes the circle $|z| = r_0$.

(6) If z-transform X(z) is rational, then its ROC is bounded by poles or extends to infinity.

(7) If z-transform X(z) of $x[n]$ is rational, and if $x[n]$ is right sided, then ROC is region in the z-plane outside the outermost pole.

(8) If z-transform X(z) is rational, and if $x[n]$ is left sided, then ROC is the region in the z-plane inside the investment to non zero pole, *i.e.* inside the circle of radius equal to smallest magnitudes of the poles of X[z] other than any at $z = 0$ and extending inward to and possibly including $z = 0$.

Example. *Determine the ROC of a unit impulse signals $\delta[n]$, $\delta[n-1]$ and $\delta[n+1]$.*

Solution:

Since $$\delta[n] \Longleftrightarrow \sum_{n=-\infty}^{+\infty} \delta[n] z^{-n} = 1,$$

with an ROC includes entire z-plane, including $z = 0$ and $z = \infty$

Now, $\delta[n-1] \xrightleftharpoons{} \delta[n-1]z^{-n} = z^{-1}$

This z-transform has ROC consisting of entire z-plane, including $z = \infty$, but excluding $z = 0$.

Now, consider on the third signal

$$\delta[n+1] \rightleftharpoons \sum_{n=-\infty}^{+\infty} \delta[n+1]z^{-n} = z$$

which is well defined for all finite values of z.

Thus, ROC consists of the entire z-plane (including $z = 0$), but there is a pole at ∞.

5.7.2. PROPERTIES OF Z-TRANSFORM

1. Linearity

If $x_1[n] \xrightleftharpoons{z} X_1(z)$, with ROC = R_1

and $x_2[n] \xrightleftharpoons{z} X_2(z)$, with ROC = R_2

then $a\,x_1[n] + b\,x_2[n] \xrightleftharpoons{z} aX_1(z) + bX_2(z)$ with ROC containing $R_1 \cap R_2$.

2. Time-shifting

If $x[n] \rightleftharpoons X(z)$ with ROC = R

then $x[n-n_0] \xrightleftharpoons{z} z^{-n_0}\,X(z)$, with ROC = R, except for possible addition or deletion of origin or infinity.

3. Scaling in the z-domain

If $x[n] \xrightleftharpoons{z} X(z)$, with ROC = R

then $z_0^n\,x[n] \xrightleftharpoons{z} X\left(\dfrac{z}{z_0}\right)$, with ROC = $|z_0|R$

where $|z_0|R$ is scaled version of R, i.e. if z is a point in the ROC of $X(z)$, then point $|z_0|z$ is in the ROC of $X\left(\dfrac{z}{z_0}\right)$.

Also if $X(z)$ has a pole (or zero) at $z = a$, then $X\left(\dfrac{z}{z_0}\right)$ has a pole (or zero) at $z = z_0a$.

4. Time reversal

If $x[n] \xrightleftharpoons{z} X(z)$ with ROC = R,

then $x[-n] = X(1/z)$ with ROC = 1/R.

5. Convolution property

If $x_1[n] \xleftrightarrow{z} X_1(z)$ with ROC = R_1

and $x_2[n] \xleftrightarrow{z} X_2[z]$ with ROC = R_2

then $x_1[n] * x_2[n] \xleftrightarrow{z} X_1(z)\,X_2(z)$ with ROC containing $R_1 \cap R_2$.

6. Differentiation in z-domain

If $x[n] \xleftrightarrow{z} X(z)$ with ROC = R

then $nx[n] \xleftrightarrow{z} -z\,.\,\dfrac{dX[z]}{dz}$

7. Initial Value Theorem

If $x[n] = 0,\ n < 0,$

then $x[0] = \underset{z\to\infty}{\text{Lt}}\,X(z)$.

8. Causality

A discrete time LTI system is causal, if and only if

(*i*) ROC of the system function is extension of a circle outside the outermost pole, and

(*ii*) with H(z) expressed as a ratio of polynomials in z, the order of numerator cannot be greater than order of denominator.

Example. *Check causality of a system having transfer function given,*

$$H(z) = \frac{1}{1-\frac{z^{-1}}{z}} + \frac{1}{1-2z^{-1}},\ |z|\ z > 2$$

Solution:

$$H(z) = \frac{z - \frac{5}{2}z^{-1}}{\left(1-\frac{z^{-1}}{2}\right)(1-2z^{-1})} = \frac{2z^2 - \frac{5}{2}z}{z^2 - \frac{5}{2}z + 1}$$

Since, numerator and denominator of H(z) are both of degree two, hence system is causal.

Its impulse response, $$h[n] = \left[\left(\frac{1}{2}\right)^n + z^n\right] . u[n]$$

Since $h[n] = 0$ for $n < 0$, the system is causal.

9. Stability

An LTI system is stable if and only if ROC of its system function H(z) includes unit circle $|z| = 1$.

For a causal LTI system having rational system function H(z) to be stable, it requires that all poles of H(z) lie inside the unit circle *i.e.*, they must all have magnitude smaller than 1.

Consider a causal system having transfer function $H(z) = \frac{1}{1-az^{-1}}$ which has a pole at $z = a$.

For stability of this system it must have $|a| < 1$ as the pole must lie inside the unit circle.

Example. *If* $X(z) = \log(1 + az^{-1})$, $|z| > |a|$, *determine its inverse z-transform.*

Solution:

Using $$n\,x[n] \xrightleftharpoons{z} -z\frac{dX(z)}{dz} = \frac{az^{-1}}{1+az^{-1}},\ |z| > |a| \quad ...(i)$$

Now as $$a^n\,u[n] \xrightleftharpoons{z} \frac{z}{z-a},\ |z| > |a|$$

$$\Rightarrow \quad a^n\,u[n] \xrightleftharpoons{z} \frac{1}{1-az^{-1}},\ |z| > |a|$$

$$\Rightarrow \quad (-a)^n . u(n) \xrightleftharpoons{z} \frac{1}{1+az^{-1}},\ |z| > |a|$$

Using time-shifting property, *i.e.*

$$x[n-n_0] \xrightleftharpoons{z} z^{-n_0}\,X(z)$$

we have $$(-a)^n . u[n-1] \xrightleftharpoons{z} \frac{z^{-1}}{1+az^{-1}}$$

Using linearity property and equation (*i*), we get

$$a(-a)^n u[n-1] \overset{z}{\rightleftharpoons} \frac{az^{-1}}{1+az^{-1}}$$

$$\Rightarrow \quad a(-a)^n u[n-1] = n\, x[n]$$

$$\Rightarrow \quad x[n] = \frac{a(-a)^n}{n} \cdot u[n-1]$$

Example. *If* $X(z) = \dfrac{3 - \frac{5}{6} z^{-1}}{\left(1 - \frac{z^{-1}}{4}\right)\left(1 - \frac{z^{-1}}{6}\right)}$, *determine its corresponding discrete time signal.*

Solution:

By partial fraction, $$X(z) = \frac{1}{1-\frac{z^{-1}}{4}} + \frac{2}{1-\frac{z^{-1}}{3}}$$

Here ROC of the first term in RH-side lies outside $z = 1/4$ and that of second term outside $z = 1/3$.

Then ROC for X(z) lies outside $z = 1/3$.

Now, $$x[n] = x_1[n] + x_2[n]$$

where, $$x_1[n] \overset{z}{\rightleftharpoons} \frac{1}{1-\frac{z^{-1}}{4}}, \ |z| > \frac{1}{4}$$

$$x_2[n] \overset{z}{\rightleftharpoons} \frac{2}{1-\frac{z^{-1}}{3}}, \ |z| > \frac{1}{3}$$

Then, $$x[n] = \left(\frac{1}{4}\right)^n u[n] + 2\left(\frac{1}{3}\right)^n u[n] \ \ldots\ldots \qquad \left[\text{using } \frac{z}{z-a} \rightleftharpoons a^n u[n]\right]$$

5.8. SAMPLING THEOREM

The periodical measurement of a continuous time signal is called *periodic sampling* or *uniform sampling*. By periodic sampling, a continuous time signal $s(t)$ can be converted into a discrete-time signal $s(nT_s)$

Continuous time signal $\xleftrightarrow{\text{Periodic sampling}}$ Discrete time signal

Discrete time signal, $s(nT_s) = s(t)\big|_{t=nT_s}$

where, T_s = sampling period

The reciprocal of sampling period is called *Sampling frequency* or *Sampling rate* (F_s).

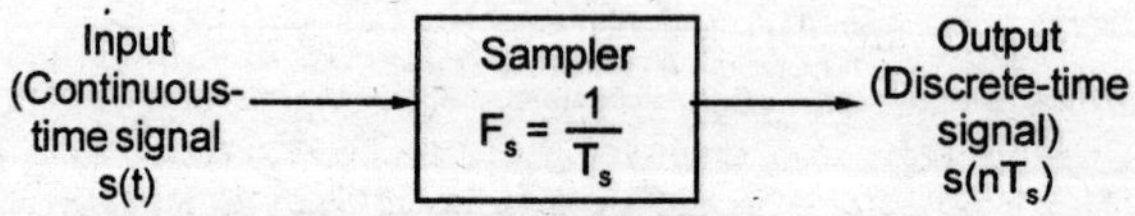

(a) Block diagram of a sampler

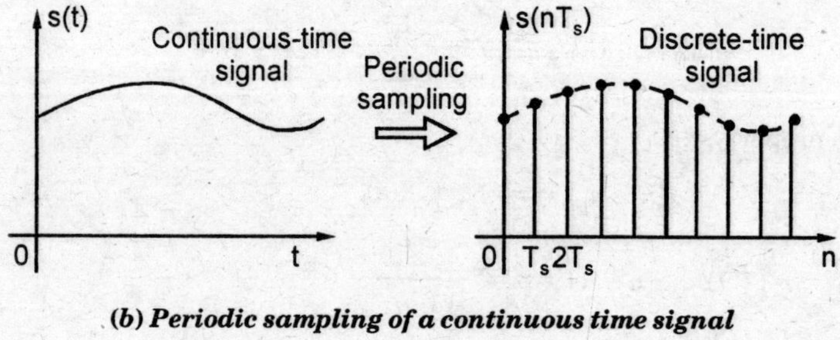

(b) Periodic sampling of a continuous time signal

Fig. 5.10

5.8.1. SAMPLING THEOREM FOR CONTI-NUOUS TIME SIGNALS.

For perfect reconstruction of a continuous time signal from its samples, sampling rate of sampling frequency should be greater than or equal to Nyquist rate of the information bearing (message signal).

According to sampling theorem,

$$\text{Sampling rate} \geq \text{Nyquist rate}$$

Nyquist rate is defined as minimum sampling rate required for perfect reconstruction of a continuous-time signal from its samples.

Nyquist rate depends upon highest frequency component of the message signal and it is expressed as

$$\text{Nyquist rate} = 2 \times \text{Highest frequency component of the message signal}$$
$$= 2 \times f_{max}$$

Periodic sampling establishes a relationship between time variables t and n of a continuous time signal and discrete time signal, respectively.

Example. *Given a continuous time signal* $s(t) = 5 \cos 200\, \pi t$.

(*i*) Minimum sampling rate, *i.e.* Nyquist rate required to avoid aliasing will be

(*a*) 50 Hz (*b*) 100 Hz (*c*) 200 Hz (*d*) 500 Hz

(*ii*) If sampling frequency F_s = 400 Hz, then discrete-time signal $s(n)$ or $s(nT_s)$ obtained after sampling will be

(*a*) $\cos \frac{\pi n}{2}$ (*b*) $2 \cos \frac{n\pi}{2}$ (*c*) $5 \cos n\pi$ (*d*) $5 \cos \frac{n\pi}{2}$

(*iii*) If sampling frequency F_s = 150 Hz, then discrete time signal $s(n)$ or $s(nTs)$ obtained after sampling, will be

(*a*) $5 \cos \frac{\pi n}{3}$ (*b*) $5 \cos \frac{2\pi n}{3}$ (*c*) $\cos \frac{\pi n}{3}$ (*d*) $\cos \frac{2 n \pi}{3}$

Ans. (*i*) c; (*ii*) d; (*iii*) *b*

Explanation.

(*i*) Highest frequency component of continuous time signal, F = 100 Hz.

Hence minimum sampling rate required to avoid aliasing

i.e. Nyquist rate = 2F = 2 × 100 = **200 Hz**

(*ii*) Continuous-time signal $s(t)$ is sampled at F_s = 400 Hz.

Frequency of discrete time signal,

$$f = \frac{\text{Frequency of continuous time signal F}}{\text{Sampling frequency, } F_s}$$

$$= \frac{100}{400} = \frac{1}{4}$$

$$\text{Discrete time signal, } s(n) = 5 \cos 2\pi f n$$

$$= 5 \cos 2\pi \times \frac{1}{4} n = \mathbf{5 \cos \frac{\pi n}{2}}$$

(*iii*) Continuous time signal $s(t)$ is sampled at F_s = 150 Hz.

$$\text{Frequency of discrete time signal, } f = \frac{F}{F_s} = \frac{100}{150} = \frac{2}{3}$$

$$\text{Discrete time signal, } s(n) = A \cos 2\pi f n$$

$$= 5 \cos 2\pi \left(\frac{2}{3}\right) n = 5 \cos \frac{4\pi}{3} n$$

$$= 5 \cos \left(2\pi - \frac{2\pi}{3}\right) n = 5 \cos \frac{2\pi n}{3}$$

Example. *Determine Nyquist rate for a continuous time signal*

$$s(t) = 5 \cos 50\,\pi t + 20 \sin 300\,\pi t - 10 \cos 100\,\pi t$$

Solution:

In a general form, any continuous time signal can be written as

$$s(t) = A_1 \cos j\omega_1 t + A_2 \cos \omega_2 t + A_3 \cos \omega_3 t$$

Comparing given signal with standard form of a signal, frequencies for the given signal are

$$F_1 = \frac{\omega_1}{2\pi} = \frac{50\,\pi}{2\pi} = 25 \text{ Hz}$$

$$F_2 = \frac{\omega_2}{2\pi} = \frac{300\,\pi}{2\pi} = 150 \text{ Hz}$$

$$F_3 = \frac{\omega_3}{2\pi} = \frac{100\,\pi}{2\pi} = 50 \text{ Hz}$$

Highest frequency component of the given message signal, $F_{max} = 150$ Hz

$\therefore$ Nyquist rate $= 2\,F_{max} = 2 \times 150 =$ **300 Hz**

5.8.2. IMPULSE TRAIN SAMPLING OF A CONTINUOUS TIME SIGNALS.

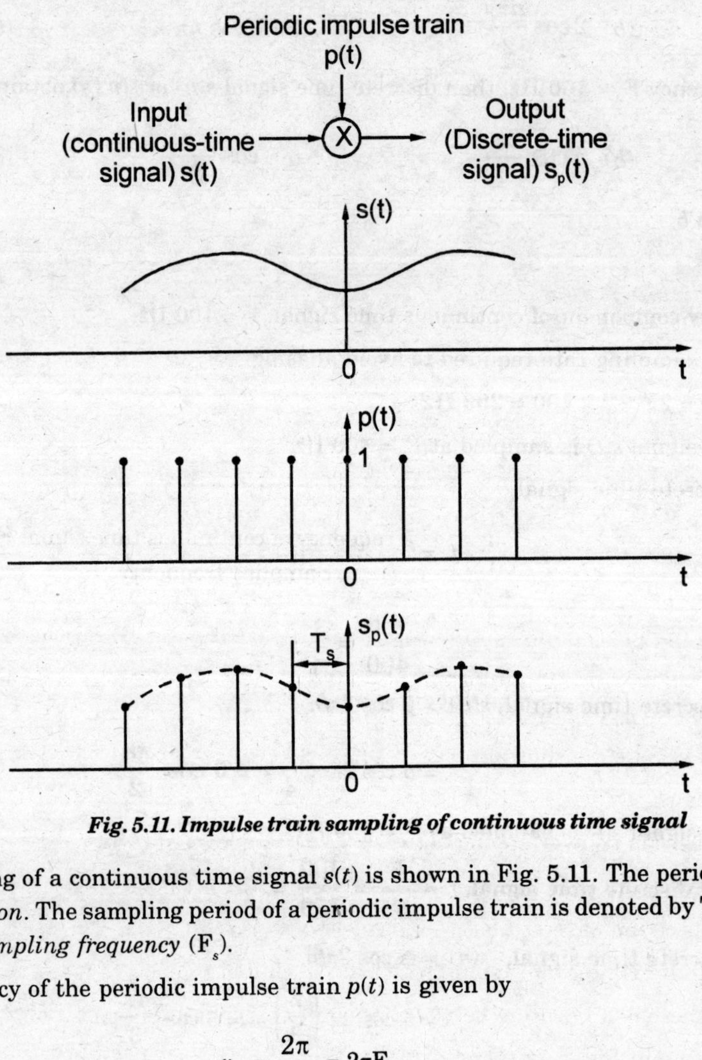

Fig. 5.11. Impulse train sampling of continuous time signal

Impulse train sampling of a continuous time signal *s(t)* is shown in Fig. 5.11. The periodic impulse train *p(t)* is also called *sampling function*. The sampling period of a periodic impulse train is denoted by T_s. The reciprocal of sampling period T_s is called *sampling frequency* (F_s).

Fundamental frequency of the periodic impulse train *p(t)* is given by

$$\omega_s = \frac{2\pi}{T_s} = 2\pi F_s.$$

It is called *angular sampling frequency.*

In time-domain, $s_p(t) = s(t)\, p(t)$ ...(5.32)

where $p(t)$ is periodic impulse train, which is given as

$$p(t) = \sum_{n=-\infty}^{\infty} \delta(t - nT_s) \qquad ...(5.33)$$

From sampling property of the unit impulse function $\delta(t)$, multiplying $s(t)$ by a unit impulse samples the value of signal at the point at which the impulse is located.

Also $s(t)\,\delta(t - t_0) = s(t_0)\,\delta(t - t_0)$ ...(5.34)

Applying property of equation (5.32) to equation (5.34), $s_p(t)$ is an impulse train with amplitude of the impulses equal to samples of $s(t)$ at intervals spaced by T_s.

$$S_p(t) = \sum_{n=-\infty}^{\infty} s(nT_s)\,\delta(t - nT_s)$$

From multiplication property of CTFT,

$$S_p(t) = s(t)\,p(t) \xleftrightarrow{\text{CTFT}} S_p(j\omega)$$

$$= \frac{1}{2\pi}[S(j\omega) * P(j\omega)]$$

$$\Rightarrow \quad S_p(j\omega) = \frac{1}{2\pi}[S(j\omega) * P(j\omega)] \qquad ...(5.35)$$

Taking CTFT of both sides of equation (5.33), we get

$$\text{CTFT}\{p(t)\} = \text{CTFT}\left\{\sum_{n=-\infty}^{\infty}\delta(t - nT_s)\right\}$$

$$\Rightarrow \quad P(j\omega) = \frac{2\pi}{T_s}\sum_{k=-\infty}^{\infty}\delta(\omega - k\omega_s) \qquad ...(5.36)$$

Substituting equation (5.36) in equation (5.35), we get

$$S_p(j\omega) = \frac{1}{2\pi}[S(j\omega) * P(j\omega)]$$

$$= \frac{1}{2\pi}\left[S(j\omega) * \frac{2\pi}{T_s}\sum_{k=-\infty}^{\infty}\delta(\omega - k\omega_s)\right]$$

$$\Rightarrow \quad S_p(j\omega) = \frac{1}{T_s}\sum_{k=-\infty}^{\infty} S(\omega - k\,\omega_s) \qquad ...(5.37)$$

[since convolution with impluse simply shifts a signal, *i.e.* $S(j\omega) * \delta(\omega - \omega_0) = S[j(\omega - \omega_0)]$]

From equation (5.37), where $S_p(j\omega)$ is a function of frequency ω consisting of a superposition of shifted version (or shifted replicas) of $S(j\omega)$ and scaled by $1/T_s$.

The spectrum of $S_p(t)$, *i.e.* $S_p(j\omega)$ is shown in Fig. 5.12.

There are three cases :

(1) If $\omega_s > 2\omega_M$, then there is no overlapping between shifted replicas of $S(j\omega)$.

In this condition, spectrum of $S_p(t)$, *i.e.* $S_p(j\omega)$ is shown in Fig. 5.12 (*c*).

(2) If $\omega_s = 2\omega_M$, then spectrum of $S_p(t)$, *i.e.*, $S_p(j\omega)$ is shown by Fig. 5.12 (*d*).

In this condition, there is no over-lapping between the shifted replicas of $S(j\omega)$.

(3) If $\omega_s < 2\omega_M$, then there is an overlap between the shifted replicas of $S(j\omega)$.

Its spectrum is shown in Fig. 5.12 (*e*).

For the cases (1) and (2), $S(j\omega)$ is faithfully reproduced at integer multiples of the sampling frequency.

Consequently, if $\omega_s \geq 2\omega_M$, continuous-time signal $s(t)$ can be recovered exactly from $s_p(t)$ by means of a low pass filter gain T_s. To perform reconstruction of the continuous-time signal $s(t)$, low pass filter will have a cutoff frequency greater than ω_M and less than $(\omega - \omega_M)$.

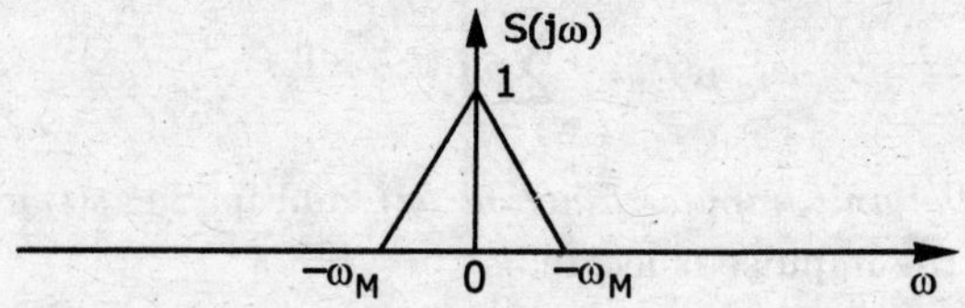

(a) Spectrum of original continuous time signal s(t).

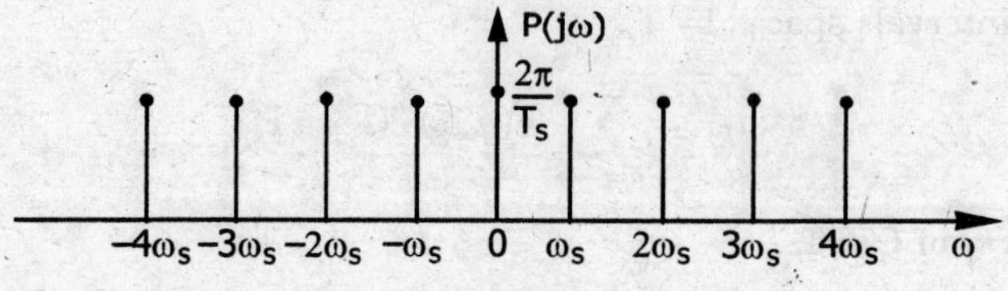

(b) Spectrum of periodic impulse train or sampling function p(t)

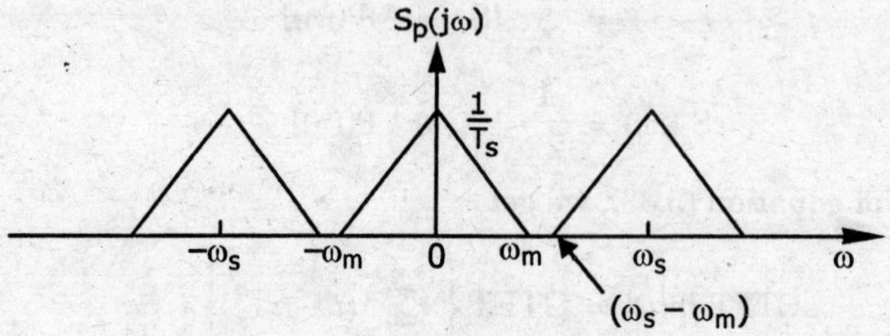

(c) Spectrum of sampled version of continuous-time signal, $s_p(t)$ with $\omega_s > 2\omega_M$

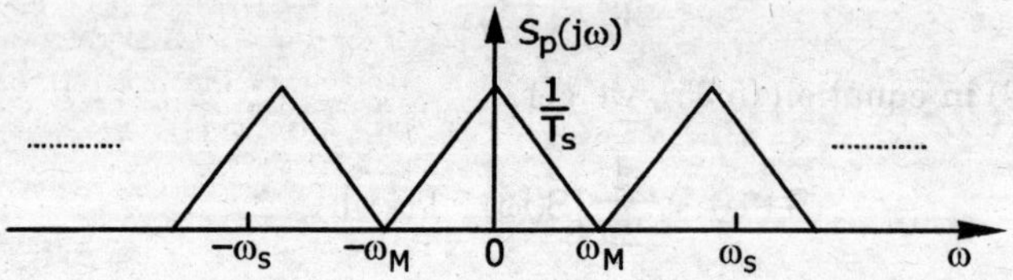

(d) Spectrum of sampled version of continuous-time signal, $s_p(t)$ with $\omega_o = 2\omega_M$

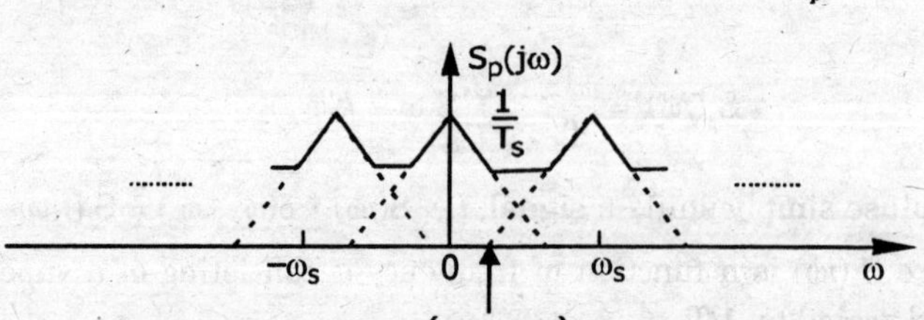

(e) Sspectrum of sampled version of continuous-time signal, $s_p(t)$ with $\omega_s < 2\omega_M$.

Fig. 5.12. Effect in the frequency domain of sampling in the time domain.

From sampling theorem,

We have a continuous time signal $s(t)$ which is a band-limited signal with $S(j\omega) = 0$ for $|\omega| > \omega_M$. Then $s(t)$ is uniquely determined by its samples

$$s(nT_s) \neq 0 \text{ for } n = 0, \pm 1, \pm 2, \ldots, \text{ if } \omega_s > 2\omega_M$$

where, $\omega_s = 2\pi F_s = \dfrac{2\pi}{T_s}$

The frequency $2\omega_M$ is called **Nyquist rate**. It is defined as, *minimum sampling rate for which continuous time signal s(t) can be reconstructed from its samples.*

Ideal filters are generally not used in practice for various reasons. In practical applications, ideal low pass filter would be replaced by a non-ideal low pass filter that approximates desired frequency characteristic accurated enough for the problem of interest.

For $|\omega| < \omega_M$, $H(j\omega) \approx 1$

For $|\omega| \geq \omega_s - \omega_M$, $H(j\omega) \approx 0$

For any such approximation in the low pass filter stage, there is some discrepancy between original signal $s(t)$ and reconstructed signal $s_r(t)$ or equivalently between $S(j\omega)$ and $S_r(j\omega)$. The particular choice of non-ideal filter depends upon the acceptable level of distortion for the application under consideration.

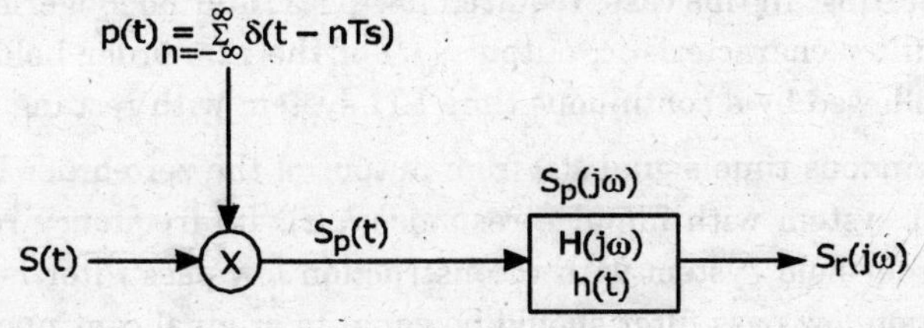

(a) System for sampling and reconstruction of a continuous time signal

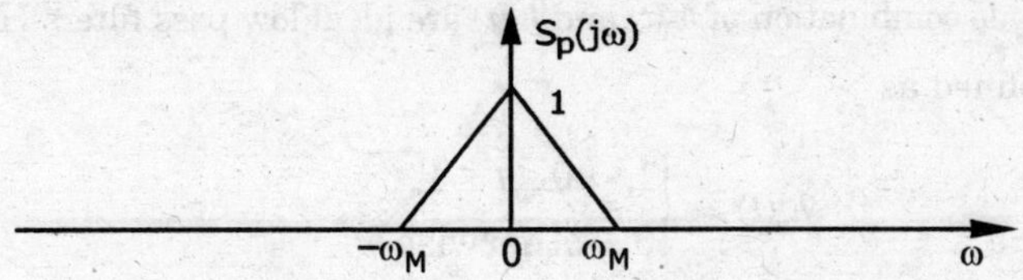

(b) Spectrum of original continuous time signal s(t).

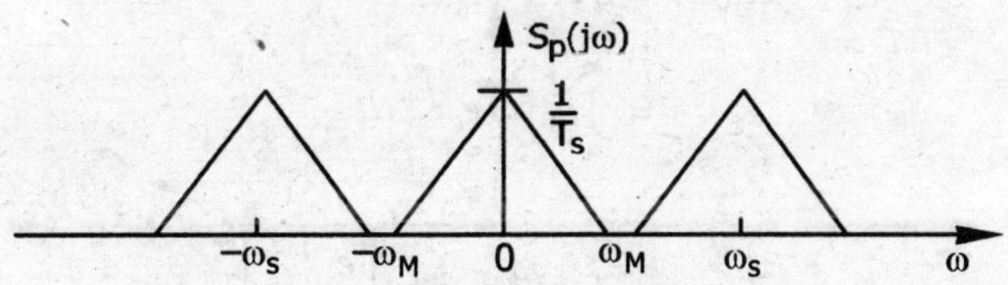

(c) Spectrum of sampled version of continuous-time signal with $\omega_0 > 2\omega_M$

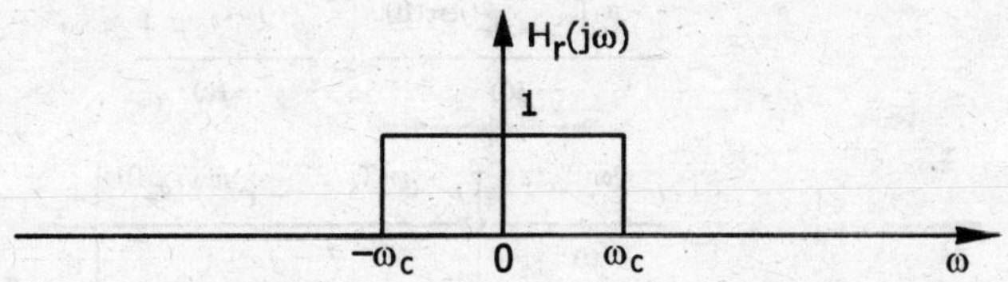

(d) Srequency response or spectrum of an ideal low pass filter that is used as a reconstruction low pass filter

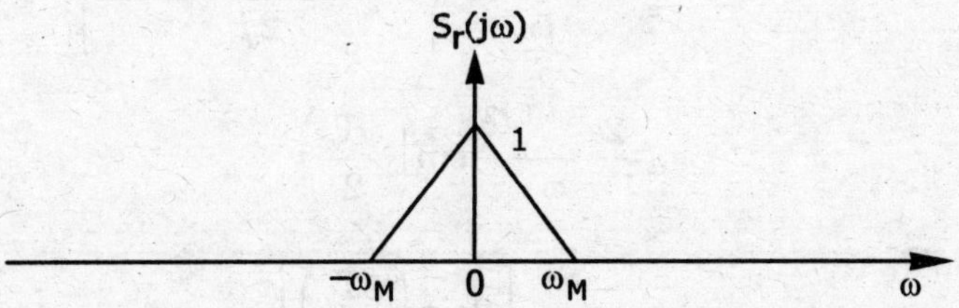

(e) Spectrum of reconstructed signal from its samples, $s_r(t)$.

Fig. 5.13. Perfect reconstruction of a continuous time signal from its samples using ideal low pass filter, i.e., reconstruction low pass filter.

5.8.3 ZERO-ORDER HOLD SAMPLING.

The zero-order hold system samples a continuous-time signal $s(t)$ at a given instant and holds that value until next instant at which another sample is taken.

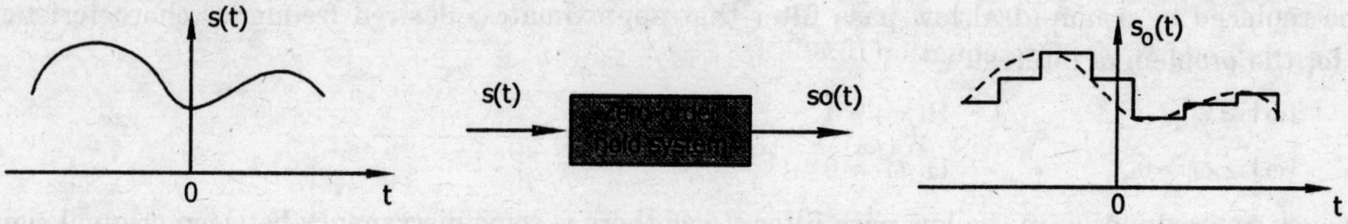

Fig. 5.14. Zero-order hold sampling

The recovery or reconstruction of a continuous time signal $s(t)$ from the output of a zero-order hold can again be carried out by low pass filtering. In this case, required low pass filter no longer has constant gain in the pass band. For developing required filter characteristic, output $s_0(t)$ of the zero-order hold can be generated in principle by impulse train sampling followed by a continuous-time LTI system with rectangular impulse response. [Fig. 5.15]

For construction of a continuous time signal $s(t)$ from output of the zero-order hold $s_0(t)$, consider processing $s_0(t)$ with continuous time LTI system with impulse response $h_r(t)$. Its frequency response is denoted by $H_r(j\omega)$. The cascade (series) of zero-order hold system with reconstruction low-pass filter is shown in Fig. 5.15. It is required that output of reconstruction low pass filter should be equal to original continuous time signal $s(t)$

i.e. $s_r(t) = s(t)$.

It is only possible when cascade combination of $h_0(t)$ and $h_r(t)$ are ideal low pass filters $H(j\omega)$ used in Fig. 5.13.

Impulse response $h_0(t)$ is defined as

$$h_0(t) = \begin{cases} 1, & 0 \le t \le T_s \\ 0, & \text{otherwise} \end{cases}$$

Fequency response $H_0(j\omega)$ can be determined by taking CTFT of the impulse response $h_0(t)$ as

$$H_0(j\omega) = \text{CTFT}\{h_0(t)\}$$

$$= \int_{-\infty}^{\infty} h_0(t)\, e^{-j\omega t}\, dt$$

$$= \int_{0}^{T_s} 1 e^{-j\omega t}\, dt = \left[\frac{e^{-j\omega t}}{-j\omega}\right]_0^{T_s}$$

$$= \frac{e^{-j\omega T_s} - e^{-j\omega x(0)}}{-j\omega} = \frac{e^{-j\omega T_s} - 1}{-j\omega}$$

$$= \frac{e^{-j\omega(T_s/2)}}{\omega}\left\{\frac{e^{-j\omega(T_s/2)} - e^{j\omega(T_s/2)}}{-j}\right\}$$

$$= \frac{2e^{-j\omega(T_s/2)}}{\omega}\left\{\frac{e^{j\omega(T_s/2)} - e^{-j\omega(T_s/2)}}{2j}\right\}$$

$$= \frac{2e^{-j\omega T_s/2}}{\omega}\sin\left(\frac{\omega T_s}{2}\right)$$

$$H_0(j\omega) = e^{-j\omega T/2}\left[\frac{2\sin\left(\frac{\omega T_s}{2}\right)}{\omega}\right] \qquad \text{...(5.38)}$$

Now, $$H(j\omega) = H_0(j\omega)\, H_r(j\omega)$$

$\Rightarrow$ Frequency response, $$H_r(j\omega) = \frac{H(j\omega)}{H_0(j\omega)}$$

Substituting value of $H_0(j\omega)$ into equation (5.38), we get

$$H_r(j\omega) = \frac{H(j\omega)}{H_0(j\omega)} = \frac{H(j\omega)}{e^{-j\omega T/2}\left[\dfrac{2\sin \omega T_s/2}{\omega}\right]}$$

$$\Rightarrow \quad H_r(j\omega) = \frac{e^{j\omega T/2} H(j\omega)}{\left(\dfrac{2\sin \dfrac{\omega T_s}{2}}{\omega}\right)}$$

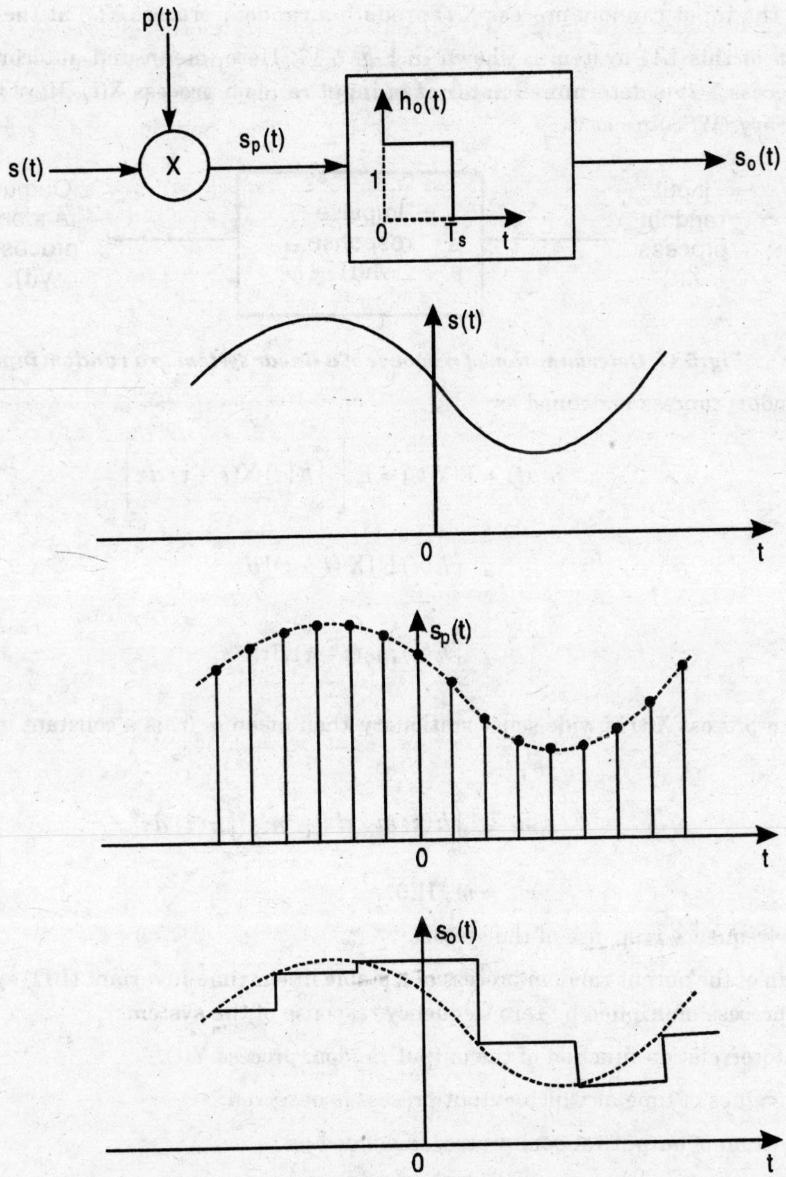

Fig. 5.15. Zero-order hold system as impulse-train sampling followed by a continuous-time LTI system with a rectangular impulse response.

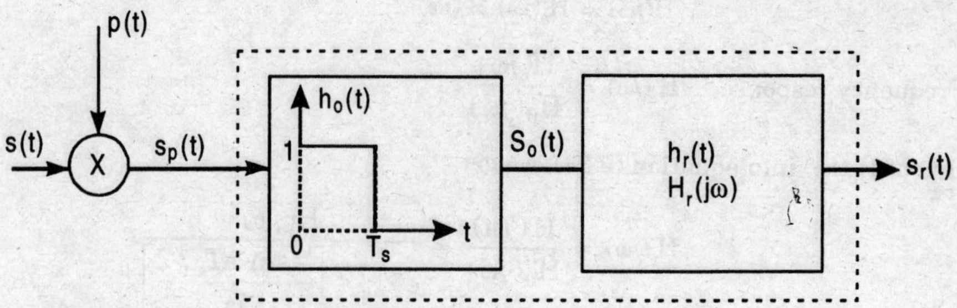

Fig. 5.16. Cascade combination of zero-order system with a reconstruction filter.

5.9. LINEAR TIME INVARIANT (LTI) SYSTEM

5.9.1. RESPONSE OF LINEAR SYSTEMS TO RANDOM INPUTS.

Let a random process $X(t)$ is applied to the input of a linear time-invariant (LTI) system having an impulse response $h(t)$. Let the input random process $X(t)$ produce a random process $Y(t)$ at the system output.

The block diagram of this LTI system is shown in Fig. 5.17. Here, mean and autocorrelation function of the output random process $Y(t)$ is determined in terms of input random process $X(t)$. Here it assumed that $X(t)$ is a wide-sense stationary (WSS) process.

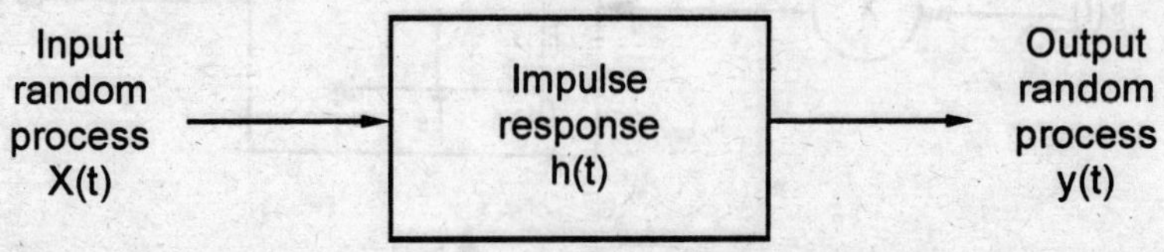

Fig. 5.17. Determination of response of a linear system to a random input.

Mean of output random process is defined as

$$m_Y(t) = E[Y(t)] = E\left[\int_{-\infty}^{\infty} h(\tau)\, X(t-\tau)\, d\tau\right]$$

$$= \int_{-\infty}^{\infty} h(\tau)\, E[X(t-\tau)]\, d\tau$$

$$= \int_{-\infty}^{\infty} h(\tau)\, m_x(t-\tau)\, d\tau \qquad ...(5.39)$$

When input random process $X(t)$ is wide sense stationary, then mean $m_x(t)$ is a constant m_X. Hence equation (5.39) can be written as

$$m_Y = \int_{-\infty}^{\infty} h(\tau)\, m_X\, d\tau = m_X \int_{-\infty}^{\infty} h(\tau)\, d\tau$$

$$\Rightarrow \qquad m_Y = m_X\, H(0) \qquad ...(5.40)$$

where, $H(0)$ = zero frequency response of the system.

It implies that mean of the output random process of a stable linear time-invariant (LTI) system is equal to mean of the input random process multiplied by zero frequency response of the system.

Now determine autocorrelation function of the output random process $Y(t)$.

Let t and u be two values of time at which output process is observed.

Autocorrelation function of output random process is defined as

$$R_Y(t, u) = E[Y(t)\, Y(u)] \qquad ...(5.41)$$

Using convolution integral, equation (5.41) can be written as

$$R_Y(t, u) = E\left[\int_{-\infty}^{\infty} h(\tau_1)\, X(t-\tau_1)\, d\tau_1 \int_{-\infty}^{\infty} h(\tau_2)\, X(u-\tau_2)\, d\tau_2\right]$$

Assuming $E[X^2(t)]$ is finite for all t and the system is stable, the order of expectation operator can be interchanged and integrate with respect to τ_1 and τ_2.

$$R_Y(t, u) = \int_{-\infty}^{\infty} h(\tau_1)\, d\tau_1 \int_{-\infty}^{\infty} h(\tau_2)\, d\tau_2\ E[X(t - \tau_1)]\ X(u - \tau_2)$$

$$= \int_{-\infty}^{\infty} h(\tau_1)\, d\tau_1 \int_{-\infty}^{\infty} h(\tau_2)\, d\tau_2\ R_X(t - \tau_1, u - \tau_2). \qquad ....(5.42)$$

When input $X(t)$ is a Wide-Sense Stationary process, the autocorrelation function of $X(t)$ is only a function of the difference between observation time $t - \tau_1$ and $u - \tau_2$.

Substituting $\tau = t - u$ in equation (5.42), we get

$$R_Y(\tau) = \int_{-\infty}^{\infty} \int_{-\infty}^{\infty} h(\tau_1)\, h(\tau_2)\, R_X(\tau - \tau_1 + \tau_2)\, d\tau_1\, d\tau_2 \qquad ...(5.43)$$

Here $R_Y(\tau)$ is function of time lag τ.

Combining the result of equations (5.40) and (5.43), if input to a stable LTI system is a WSS process, then output of the linear time invariant (LTI) system is also a WSS process.

Putting $\tau = 0$ in equation (5.43), we get

$$R_Y(0) = \int_{-\infty}^{\infty} \int_{-\infty}^{\infty} h(\tau_1)\, h(\tau_2)\, R_X(\tau_2 - \tau_1)\, d\tau_1\, d\tau_2 \qquad ...(5.44)$$

Also

$$R_Y(0) = E[Y^2(t)] \qquad ...(5.45)$$

From equations (5.44) and (5.45), we get

$$R_Y(0) = E[Y^2(t)] = \int_{-\infty}^{\infty} \int_{-\infty}^{\infty} h(\tau_1) \,.\, h(\tau_2)\ R_X(\tau_2 - \tau_1)\, d\tau_1\, d\tau_2$$

5.9.2. CONTINUOUS-TIME LINEAR TIME-INVARIANT (LTI) SYSTEMS

A system of which both input and output are continuous-time signals and possesses two properties namely linearly and time-invariance is called *continuous time linear time invariant (LTI) system.*

These systems are characterized either by their impulse response $h(t)$ or by their transfer function $H(s)$.

Continuous time signals are represented mathematically as the superposition of scaled and shifted continuous-time unit impulse functions $\delta(t)$.

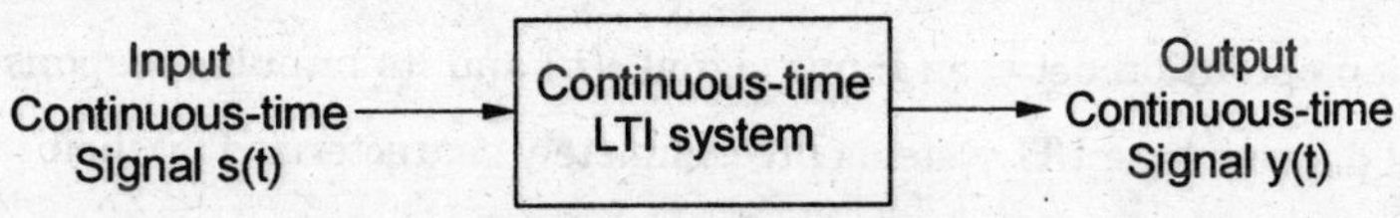

Fig. 5.18. Continuous-time LTI system

Continuous time input signal $s(t)$ is represented in terms of $\delta(t)$ as

$$s(t) = \int_{\tau=-\infty}^{\infty} s(\tau)\, \delta(t - \tau)\, d\tau$$

Continuous-time impulse response $h(t)$ is output of a continuous time system when applied input $s(t)$ is equal to unit impulse function $\delta(t)$.

Transfer function of a continuous time LTI system is the ratio of Laplace transform of output $y(n)$ and Laplace transform of input $s(n)$ of a system when the system is initially relaxed. For an initially relaxed system, all the initial conditions are zero.

Unit Impulse Response for Continuous-Time LTI Systems

Output of a continuous time LTI system is called *unit-impulse response* when an input equal to unit-impulse function $\delta(t)$ is apply

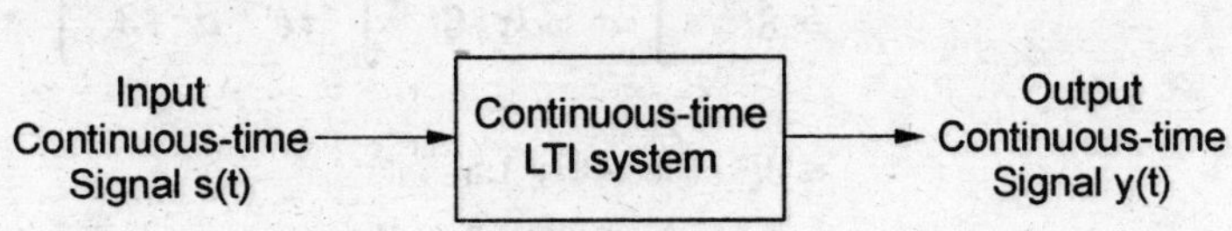

Fig. 5.19. Continuous time LTI system

If input $s(t) = \delta(t)$ is unit-impulse function, then output $y(t) = h(t)$ is unit-impulse response, where unit-impulse function $\delta(t)$ is given by

$$\delta(t) = \begin{cases} 1, & t = 0 \\ 0, & t \neq 0 \end{cases}$$

Transfer function of a continuous time LTI system is equal to Laplace transform of unit-impulse response of a continuous time LTI system.

Transfer function of continuous time LTI system,

$$H(s) = \text{Laplace transform of } h(t) = £\,[h(t)] = \int_{-\infty}^{\infty} h(t)e^{-st}\,dt$$

where s is a complex variable, and

$$s = \sigma + j\omega$$

where σ is real part and ω is imaginary part.

Convolution Integral for Continuous-Time LTI Systems

Convolution integral referred as *superposition integral* is used to compute response of a continuous time LTI system with impulse response $h(t)$ and for any arbitrary input $s(n)$. Impulse response $h(t)$ is the output of system when unit impulse function $\delta(t)$ is applied as input. Any input signal $s(t)$ can be represented in terms of unit-impulse function (Dirac-Delta function) $\delta(t)$, given by

$$s(t) = \int_{\tau=-\infty}^{\infty} s(\tau)\,\delta\,(t-\tau)\,d\tau$$

where, $\delta(t)$ = unit impulse function = $\begin{cases} 1, & t = 0 \\ 0, & t \neq 0 \end{cases}$

Convolution integral is given as

$$y\,(n) = s\,(t) * h\,(t) = \int_{\tau=-\infty}^{\infty} s(\tau)\,h(t-\tau)\,d\tau$$

$$= h(t) * s(t) = \int_{\tau=-\infty}^{\infty} h(\tau)\,s(t-\tau)\,d\tau$$

Here * denotes convolution operation between input signal $s(n)$ and its impulse response $h(t)$.

Both continuous time and discrete time LTI systems are completely characterized by their impulse response $h(t)$ or $h(n)$.

Example. *Find convolution of the two continuous time functions.*

$$s(t) = e^{-t^2}, \text{ and } h(t) = 3t^2 \text{ for all } t.$$

Solution:

Convolution integral is given by

$$y(t) = \int_{\tau=-\infty}^{\infty} s(\tau)\,h(t-\tau)\,d\tau$$

$$= \int_{\tau=-\infty}^{\infty} e^{-\tau^2}\,[3(t-\tau)^2]\,d\tau$$

$$= \int_{\tau=-\infty}^{\infty} e^{-\tau^2}\,[3t^2 - 6t\tau + 3\tau^2]\,d\tau$$

$$= 3t^2 \int_{\tau=-\infty}^{\infty} e^{-\tau^2}\,d\tau - 6t \int_{\tau=-\infty}^{\infty} \tau e^{-\tau^2}\,d\tau + 3 \int_{\tau=-\infty}^{\infty} \tau^2\, e^{-\tau^2}\,dt$$

$$= 3t^2\,\sqrt{\pi} - 0 + 1.5\,\sqrt{\pi}$$

$$= 5.31\,t^2 + 2.659, \text{ for all } t.$$

Example. *Find convolution of the two continuous-time functions*

$$s(t) = 3 \cos 2t \text{ for all } t.$$

and

$$h(t) = e^{-|t|} = \begin{cases} e^{t}, & t < 0 \\ e^{-t}, & t \geq 0 \end{cases}$$

Solution:

Convolution integral is given by

$$y(t) = s(t) * h(t) = \int_{\tau=-\infty}^{\infty} s(\tau)\, h(t-\tau)\, d\tau$$

Now

$$s(t) = 3 \cos 2\tau \quad \text{for all } t$$

and

$$y(t-\tau) = \begin{cases} e^{(t-\tau)}, & t-\tau < 0 \rightarrow \tau > t \\ e^{(\tau-t)}, & t-\tau \geq 0\ \tau \leq t \end{cases}$$

$\therefore$

$$y(t) = \int_{\tau=-\infty}^{\infty} s(\tau)\, h(t-\tau)\, d\tau$$

$$= \int_{\tau=-\infty}^{\infty} (3 \cos 2\tau)\, e^{(\tau-t)} . d\tau + \int_{\tau=t}^{\infty} (3 \cos 2\tau)\, e^{(t-\tau)}\, d\tau$$

$$= 3e^{-t} \int_{-\infty}^{t} e^{\tau} \cos 2\pi\, d\tau + 3e^{t} \int_{t}^{\infty} e^{-\tau} \cos 2\tau\, d\tau$$

$$= 3e^{-t} \left[e^{\tau} \frac{(\cos 2\tau + 2 \sin 2\tau)}{5} \right]_{-\infty}^{t} + 3e^{t} \left[(e^{-\tau} \cos 2\tau + 2 \sin 2\tau \right]_{t}^{\infty}$$

$$= \frac{6}{5} \cos 2t \quad \text{for all } t.$$

5.9.3. DISCRETE-TIME LTI SYSTEMS

Consider a discrete time signal represented as

$$x[n] = \sum_{k=-\infty}^{+\infty} x[k] . \delta[n-k] \qquad \text{...(5.46)}$$

This equation corresponds to the representation of an arbitrary sequence as a linear combination of shifted unit impulses $\delta[n-k]$, where weights are provided by $x[k]$.

Since $u[k] = 0$ for $k < 0$

and $u[k] = 1$ for $k \geq 0$,

hence equation (5.46) becomes

$$u[n] = \sum_{k=0}^{+\infty} \delta[n-k]$$

Now, consider response of a linear system to an arbitrary input $x[n]$. Equation (5.46) can be represented as a linear combination of shifted unit impulses.

Let $h_k[n]$ denotes response of linear system to the shifted unit impulse $\delta[n-k]$. Then, using superposition property for a linear system, the response $y[n]$ can be expressed as,

$$y[n] = \sum_{k=-\infty}^{+\infty} x[k]\, h_k[n] \qquad \text{...(5.47)}$$

In general, if linear system is time-*invariant*, then responses to the time-shifted unit inpulses are all time-shifted versions of each other.

Since $\delta[n-k]$ is a time-shifted version of $\delta[n]$, therefore response

$$h_k[n] = h_0[n-k]$$

Simplifying notations, we have $h[n] = h_0[n]$

Then, for an LTI system, equation (5.45) becomes

$$y[n] = \sum_{k=-\infty}^{+\infty} x[k]\, h[n-k]$$

This result is called *convolutional sum,* or *convolution of the sequence* $x[n]$ and $h[n]$.

i.e. $y[n] = x[n] * h[n]$

Properties of Discrete LTI Systems.

1. **Causality.**

Impulse response of a causal discrete-time LTI system satisfy the condition

$$h[n] = 0 \quad \text{for } n < 0$$

This condition suggests that for a causal discrete time LTI system convolutional sum

$$y[n] = \sum_{k=-\infty}^{\infty} x[k]\, h[n-k]$$

should be written as,

$$y[n] = \sum_{k=0}^{n} x[k]\, h[n-k]$$

or

$$y[n] = \sum_{k=0}^{\infty} h[k]\, x[n-k]$$

Similarly, a continuous time LTI system is causal if

$$h(t) = 0 \quad \text{for } t < 0$$

and, convolutional integral is given by

$$y(t) = \int_{-\infty}^{t} x(\tau)\,.\,h(t-\tau)\,d\tau = \int_{0}^{\infty} h(\tau)\cdot x(t-\tau)\,d\tau$$

Causality of an LTI system is equivalent to its impulse response being a causal signal.

2. **Stability.**

A system is stable if every bounded input produces a bounded output. It order to check whether, LTI systems are to be stable, let an input $x[n]$ be bounded in magntiude

$$|x[n]| < B \quad \text{for all } n$$

If this input applied to an LTI system with unit impulse response $h[n]$, then

$$|y[n]| = \left| \sum_{k=+\infty}^{+\infty} h[k]\, x[n-k] \right|$$

$$\Rightarrow \qquad |y[n]| \le \sum_{k=-\infty}^{+\infty} |h[k]|\,|x[n-k]|$$

As $|x[n-k]| < B$ for all values of k and n.

$$\therefore \qquad |y[n]| \le B\,.\sum_{k=-\infty}^{+\infty} |h[k]| \quad \text{for all } n.$$

From this equation, if impulse response is absolutely summable,

i.e. if $$\sum_{k=-\infty}^{+\infty} |h[k]| < \infty$$

then $y[n]$ is bounded in magnitude and therefore system is *stable.*

Now, in continuous time LTI system, if $|x(t)| < B$ for all t, then

$$|y(t)| = \left| \int_{-\infty}^{+\infty} h(\tau) \cdot x(t-\tau)\, d\tau \right|$$

$$\leq \int_{-\infty}^{+\infty} |h(\tau)|\,|x(t-\tau)|\, d\tau$$

$$\leq B \int_{-\infty}^{+\infty} h(\tau) \cdot d\tau$$

Hence, the system will be stable if impulse response is absolutely integrable, *i.e.* if

$$\int_{-\infty}^{+\infty} |h(\tau)|\, d\tau < \infty.$$

3. Commutative property.

Both convolution integral for continuous time LTI system and convolution sum for discrete-time systems are commutative.

For continuous time LTI system, according to commutative property

$$\text{Output, } y(t) = s(t) * h(t) = \int_{\tau=-\infty}^{\infty} s(\tau)\, h(t-\tau)\, d\tau$$

$$= h(t) * s(t) = \int_{\tau=-\infty}^{\infty} h(\tau)\, s(t-\tau)\, d\tau$$

According to commutative property, output of a continuous-time LTI system with input $s(t)$, and unit impulse response $h(t)$ is identical to the output of a continuous-time LTI system with input $h(t)$ and unit-impulse response $s(t)$.

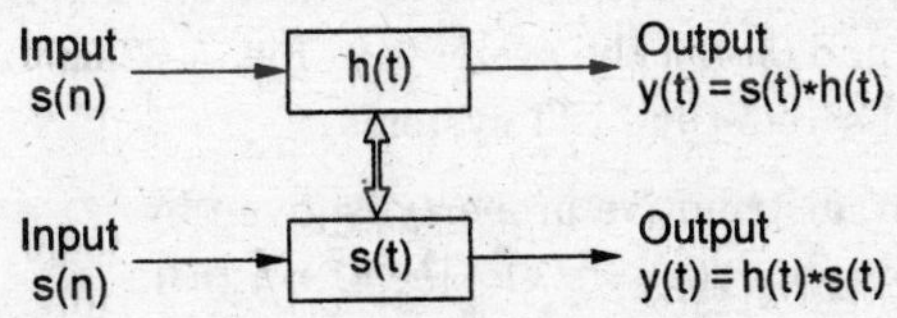

Fig. 5.20. Continuous-time LTI sytem showing commutative property

For discrete-time LTI system, according to commutative property

$$\text{output, } y(n) = s(n) * h(n) = \sum_{k=-\infty}^{\infty} s(k)\, h(n-k)$$

$$= h(n) * s(n) = \sum_{k=-\infty}^{\infty} h(k)\, s(n-k)$$

According to commutative property, output of a disc rete-time LTI system with input $s(n)$ and unit impulses response $h(n)$ is identical to the output of a discrete-time LTI system with input $h(n)$ and unit-impulse response $s(n)$.

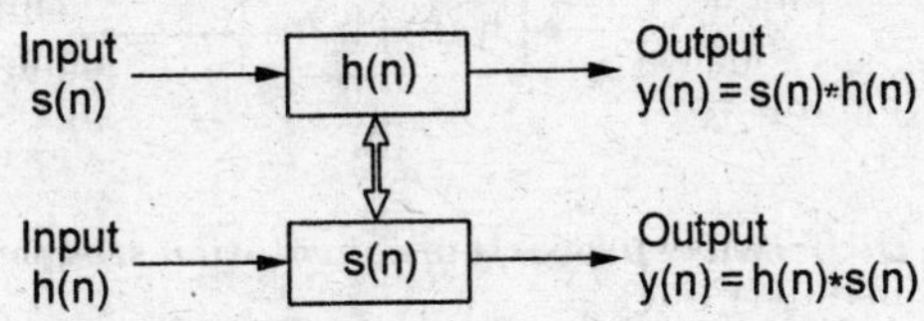

Fig. 5.21. Discrete-time LTI system showing the commutative property.

4. Distributive property.

Both convolution integral for continuous-time LTI system and convolution sum for discrete-time LTI systems are distributive.

For continous-time LTI system, distributive property is given by

$$\text{output, } y(t) = s(t) * [h_1(t) + h_2(t)]$$
$$= s(t) * h_1(t) + s(t) * h_2(t)$$

Two continuous-time LTI systems, with impulse response $h_1(t)$ and $h_2(t)$, have identical inputs, and outputs are added as

$$y_1(t) = s(t) * h_1(t) \quad \text{and} \quad y_2(t) = s(t) * h_1(t)$$

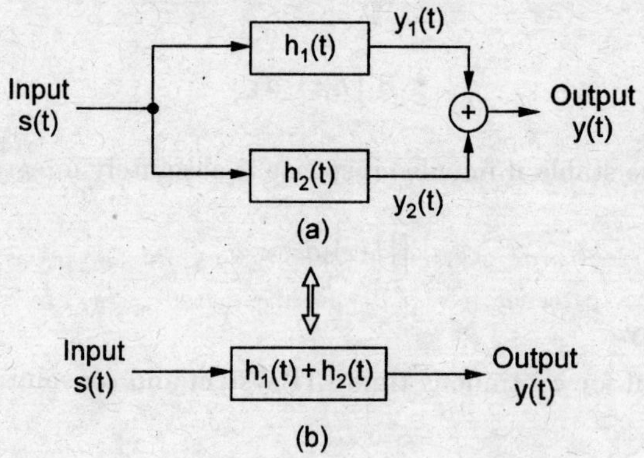

Fig. 5.22. Distributive property of convolution integral for a parallel interconnection of continuous time LTI systems

From Fig. 5.22 (*a*),

$$\text{output, } y(t) = y_1(t) + y_2(t)$$
$$= s(t) * h_1(t) + s(t) * h_2(t) \quad \text{...(5.48)}$$

From Fig. 5.22 (*b*),

$$\text{output, } y(t) = s(t) * [h_1(t) + h_2(t)] \quad \text{...(5.49)}$$

Comparing equations (5.48) and (5.49), the systems in Fig. 5.22 (*a*) and Fig. 5.22 (*b*) are identical. There is an identical interpretation for discrete-time LTI systems.

For discrete-time LTI system, distributive property is given by

$$\text{output, } y(n) = s(n) * [h_1(n) + h_2(n)]$$
$$= s(n) * h_1(n) + s(n) * h_2(n)$$

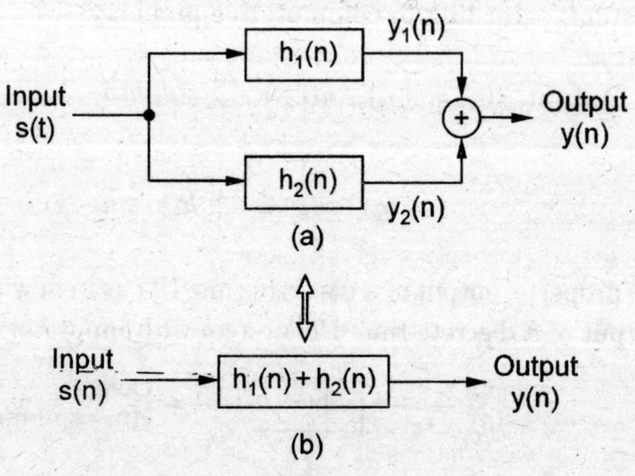

Fig. 5.23. Distributive property of convolution sum for a parallel interconnection of discrete time LTI systems

5. Associative property.

Both convolution integral for continuous time LTI systems and convolution sum for discrete time LTI systems are associative.

For continuous time LTI systems, according to associative property

$$\text{output, } y(t) = s(t) * [h_1(t) * h_2(t)]$$
$$= [s(t) * h_1(t)] * h_2(t)$$
$$\Rightarrow \quad y(t) = s(t) * h_1(t) * h_2(t)$$

An interpretation of associative property is given below.

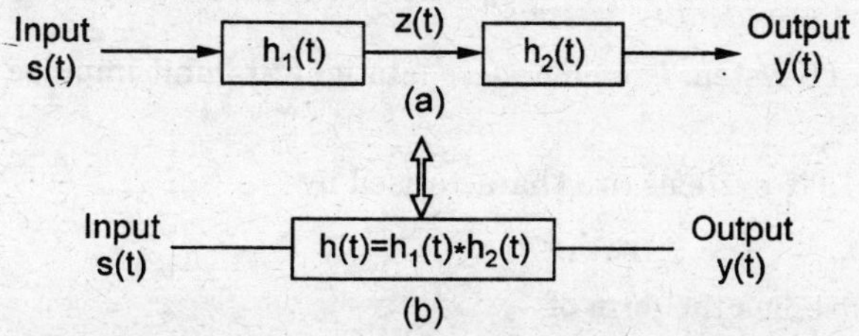

Fig. 5.24. Associative property of convolution integral for a cascade (series) interconnection of continuoustime LTI systems

In Fig. 5.24 (*a*) $\quad y(t) = z(t) * h_2(t)$

But $\quad z(t) = s(t) * h_1(t)$

$\therefore \quad y(t) = [s(t) * h_1(t)] * h_2(t)$

In Fig. 5.24 (*b*) $\quad y(t) = s(t) * h(t)$

where $\quad h(t) = h_1(t) * h_2(t)$

$\therefore \quad y(t) = s(t) * [h_1(t) * h_2(t)]$

According to associative property, cascade interconnection of two systems in Fig. 5.25. (*a*) is equivalent to the single system shown in Fig. 5.25 (*b*).

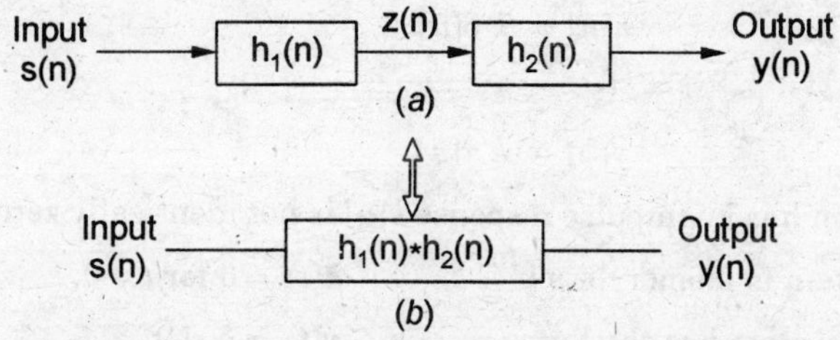

Fig. 5.25. Associative property of convolution sum for a cascade (series) interconnection of discrete time LTI sysetms

For discrete-time LTI system, according to associative property

$$\text{output, } y(n) = s(n) * [h_1(n) * h_2(n)]$$
$$= [s(n) * h_1(n)] * h_2(n)$$
$$\Rightarrow \quad y(n) = s(n) * h_1(n) * h_2(n)$$

An interpretation of associative property is given below.

In Fig. 5.24 (*a*), $\quad y(n) = z(n) * h_2(n)$

But $\quad z(n) = s(n) * h_1(n)$

$\therefore \quad y(n) = [s(n) * h_1(n)] * h_2(n)$

In Fig. 5.24 (*b*), $\quad y(n) = s(t) * h(n)$

where, $\quad h(n) = h_1(n) * h_2(n)$

$\therefore \quad y(n) = s(n) * [h_1(n) * h_2(n)]$

Hence impulse response of the cascade (series) of two LTI (either continuous-time or discrete-time) systems is convolution of their individual impulse responses.

5.9.4. STATIC AND DYNAMIC LTI SYSTEMS.

Static systems are also called *memoryless* systems. A system is called *static* if its output at any time depends only on the value of the input at the same time.

In particular, a continuous time LTI system is *memoryless* (*static*) if its unit-impulse $h(t)$ is zero for $t \neq 0$. These memoryless LTI systems are characterized by

$$y(t) = Ks(t)$$

where, K = constant.

and its impulse response, $h(t) = K\,\delta(t)$

If K = 1, then these systems are *identity systems*.

Similarly, a discrete time LTI system is memoryless (static) if its unit-impulse (unit-sample) response $h(n)$ is zero for $n \neq 0$.

Discrete time memoryless LTN systems are characterised by

$$y(n) = K\,s(n)$$

and its unit-impulse response has the form of

$$h(n) = k\,\delta\,(n)$$

If impulse response of a discrete time LTI system is not identically zero for $n \neq 0$, then system is called *dynamic system or system having memory.*

5.9.5. LTI SYSTEMS WITH AND WITHOUT MEMORY.

A memoryless system has its output at any time depends only on the value of input at that same time. For a discrete time LTI system, this is feasbile if

$$h[n] = 0 \quad \text{for } n \neq 0$$

as a equation

$$y[n] = \sum_{k=-\infty}^{+\infty} x(k)\,h[n-k] = x[n] * h[n]$$

Then, impulse response is $h[n] = k\,\delta[n]$

where $h[0]$ is a constant

then, $y[n] = k\,x[n]$

If a discrete time LTI system has an impulse response $k[n]$ is not identically zero for $n \neq 0$, then system has memory.

A continuous time LTI system is memoryless if $h(t) = 0$ for $t \neq 0$,

and such memoryless LTI system has the form, $y(t) = k\,x(t)$

For some constant k and having the impulse response $h(t) = k\,\delta(t)$

5.9.6. INVERTIBILITY OF LTI SYSTEMS.

If an LTI system in invertible, then it has an LTI inverse.

Consider, a system with impulse response $h(t)$ and inverse system having impulse response $h(t)$ interconnected as shown in Fig. 5.26 (a).

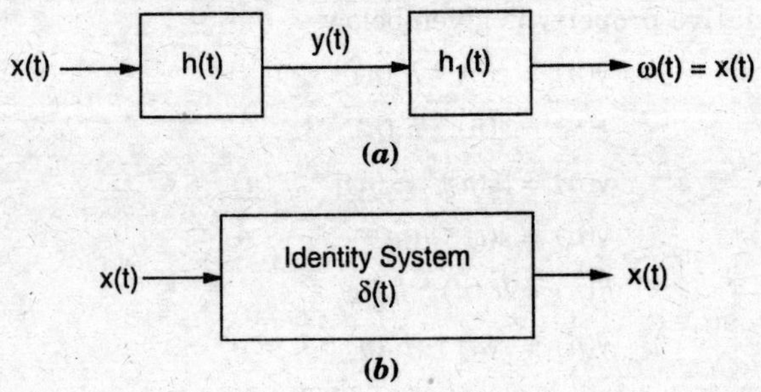

Fig. 5.26

For the system shown in Fig. 5.26 (a) to be identical to that given in Fig 5.26 (b), the overall impulse response in Fig. 5.26 (a),

$$h(t) * h_1(t) = \delta(t)$$

then the system will be *invertible.*

In discrete time, impulse response $h_1[n]$ of the inverse system for a LTI system with impulse response $h[n]$ must satisfy

$$h[n] * h_1[n] = \delta[n].$$

Now, consider LTI system consisting of a pure line shift

$$y(t) = x(t - t_0)$$

This system is

a delay if $t_0 > 0$

and an advance if $t_0 < 0$.

e.g. if $t_0 > 0$, then output at time t equals value of input at the earlier time $t - t_0$.

If $t_0 = 0$, then system is *identity system* and thus *momoryless.*

For any other value of t_0, this system has memory and responds to the value of the input at a time other than the current time.

5.9.7. UNIT-STEP RESPONSE OF AN LTI SYSTEM.

Unit-step response is output of a LTI system (either continuous time or discrete-time) for input which is equal to unit-step function or sequence.

1. **Unit-step response of continuous time LTI system.**

   It is determined by convolution integral of $u(t)$ with unit-impulse response $h(t)$ and from commutative property. It is given by

$$g(t) = u(t) * h(t) = h(t) * u(t)$$

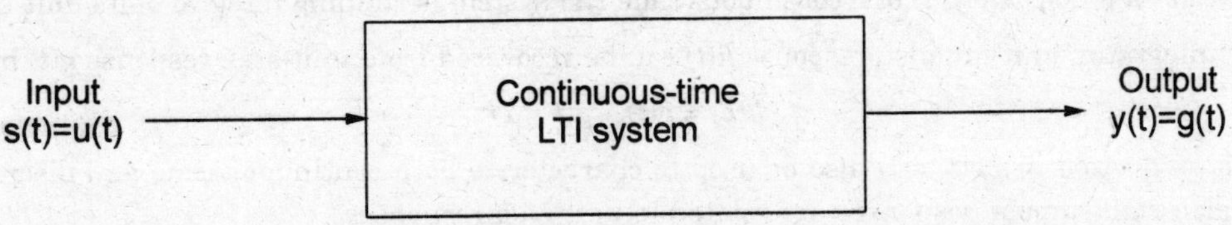

Fig. 5.27. Continuous time LTI system

   Therefore, unit-step response $g(t)$ can be viewed as response to the input $h(t)$ of a continuous time LTI system with unit-impulse response $u(t)$.

2. **Unit-step response of discrete-time LTI system.**

   It is determined by convolution sum of $u(n)$ with unit-impulse response $h(n)$ and from commutative property. It is given by

$$g(n) = u(n) * h(n) = h(n) * u(n)$$

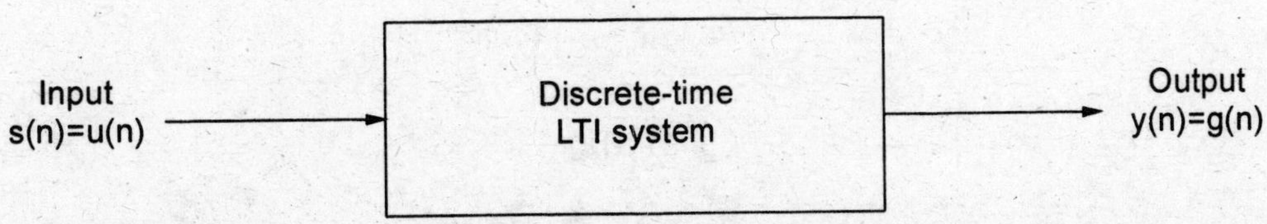

Fig. 5.28. Discrete-time LTI system

   Therefore, unit-step response $g(n)$ can be viewed as response to the input h(n) of a discrete time LTI system with multi impulse response $u(n)$.

Unit impulse response of a accumulator.

It is given by

$$h(n) = u(n)$$

Unit-step response of accumulator is determined by

$$g(n) = u(n) * h(n) = h(n) * u(n)$$

$$= \sum_{k=-\infty}^{\infty} h(k)\, u(n-k)$$

$$= \sum_{k=-\infty}^{n} h(k)$$

For accumulator, unit-impulse response $h(n)$ can be recovered from unit-step response $g(n)$ by the relation

$$h(n) = g[n] - g[n-1]$$

Unit-impulse response of an integrator.

It is given by

$$h(t) = u(t)$$

Unit-step response of integrator is determined by

$$g(t) = u(t) * h(t) = h\,(t) * u(t)$$

$$= \int_{\tau=-\infty}^{\infty} h(\tau)\, u(t-\tau)\, d\tau$$

$$= \int_{\tau=-\infty}^{t} h(\tau)\, d\tau$$

i.e. unit-step response $g(t)$ of a continuous time LTI system is running integral of its unit-impulse response $h(t)$.

For integrator, unit-impulse response $h(t)$ can be recovered from unit-step response $g(t)$ by the relation

$$h(t) = g(t) - g(t-1)$$

Unit step responses $g(t)$ can also be used to characterize both continuous time and discrete-time LTI systems because unit-impuse responses are related to unit-step responses.

Example. *Given an LTI system with impulse response $h[n] = u\,[n]$. Test its invertibility.*

Solution:

Response of this system to an arbitrary input,

$$y[n] = \sum_{k=-\infty}^{+\infty} x[k]\, u[n-k] \qquad ...(i)$$

But $\quad u\,[n-k] = 0$, if, $n-k < 0$

$\qquad = 1$, if, $n-k > 0$

$$\therefore \quad y[n] = \sum_{k=-\infty}^{n} x[k]$$

i.e. this system is a accumulator or summer which is actually invertible and its inverse is

$$y\,[n] = x\,[n] - x\,[n-1]$$

Choosing $\quad x\,[n] = \delta\,[n]$, we have

$$h_1\,[n] = \delta\,[n] - \delta\,[n-1]$$

Now,
$$\begin{aligned} h[n] * h_1[n] &= u[n] * \{\delta[n] - \delta[n-1]\} \\ &= u[n] * \delta[n] - u[n] * \delta[n-1] \\ &= u[n] - u[n-1] \\ &= \delta[n] \end{aligned}$$

Thus, as convolution of impulse response of LTI system and impulse response of inverse system is $\delta[n]$, system is *invertible.*

Impulse response for the system, $h(t) = \delta(t - t_0)$

Then $x(t - t_0) = x(t) * \delta(t - t_0)$

i.e. convolutional of a signal with a shifted impulse simply shifts the signal.

Now to invert the system, if we take $h_1(t) = \delta(t + t_0)$

then $h(t) * h_1(t) = \delta(t - t_0) * \delta(t + t_0) = \delta(t)$

Hence to invert the system, it is required to shift the output back. Then system with this compensating time shift is the inverse system.

Example. *Find convolution sum of two discrete-time signals*

$$s(n) = e^{-n^2}, \quad \textit{for all } n$$

and
$$h(n) = \begin{cases} e^{n}, & n < 0 \\ e^{-n} & n \geq 0 \end{cases}$$

Solution:

Convolution sum of $s(n)$ and $h(n)$ is given by

$$\begin{aligned} y(n) &= s(n) * h(n) \\ &= \sum_{k=-\infty}^{\infty} s(k)\, h(n-k) \end{aligned}$$

Now
$$s(k) = e^{-k^2} \quad \text{for all } k.$$

and
$$k(n-k) = \begin{cases} e^{n-k}, & n - k < 0 \rightarrow > n \\ e^{-(n-k)}, & n - k \geq 0 \rightarrow k \leq n \end{cases}$$

$\therefore$
$$\begin{aligned} y(n) &= \sum_{k=-\infty}^{\infty} s(k)\, h[n-k] \\ &= \sum_{k=-\infty}^{n} s(k)\, h(n-k) + \sum_{k=n+1}^{\infty} s(k)\, h(n-k) \\ &= \sum_{k=-\infty}^{n} e^{-k^2} e^{-(n-k)} + \sum_{k=n+1}^{\infty} e^{-k^2} e^{(n-k)} \\ &= e^{-n} \sum_{k=-\infty}^{n} e^{(k-k^2)} + e^{n} \sum_{k=n+1}^{\infty} e^{-(k+k^2)} \quad \text{for all } k. \end{aligned}$$

OBJECTIVE TYPE QUESTIONS

LAPLACE TRANSFORM

1. In Laplace transform, the variable 's' equals $(\sigma + j\omega)$. Which of the following represent the true nature of σ?

(1) σ has a damping effect.

(2) σ is responsible for convergence of intergral $\int_{\infty}^{\infty} f(t)e^{-st}\,dt$

(3) σ has a value less than zero

Select the correct answer using the codes given below :

(*a*) 1, 2 and 3 (*b*) 1 and 2

(*c*) 2 and 3 (*d*) 1 and 3

2. Which one of the following is the correct Laplace transform of the signal in the given figure ?

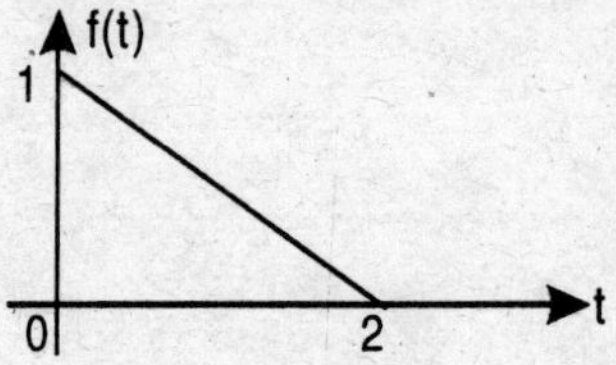

(*a*) $\frac{1}{T^2}\left[1 - e^{-Ts}(1 + Ts)\right]$

(*b*) $\frac{1}{T^2}\left[e^{-Ts}(1 + Ts)\right]$

(*c*) $\frac{1}{T^2}\left[e^{-Ts} + 1 - Ts\right]$

(*d*) $\frac{1}{T^2}\left[1 - e^{-T}s + Ts\right]$

3. Double integration of a unit step function would lead to

(*a*) an impulse (*b*) a parabola

(*c*) a ramp (*d*) a doublet

4. If $x(t)$ and its first derivative are Laplace transformable and the Laplace transform of $x(t)$ is $X(s)$, then $\lim_{t\to\infty} x(t)$ is given by

(*a*) $\lim_{s\to\infty} sX(s)$ (*b*) $\lim_{s\to 0} sX(s)$

(*c*) $\lim_{s\to\infty} \frac{X(s)}{s}$ (*c*) $\lim_{s\to 0} \frac{X(s)}{s}$

5. What is the laplace transform of a delayed unit impulse function $\delta(t-1)$?

(*a*) 1 (*b*) zero

(*c*) exp $(-s)$ (*d*) s

6. What is the Laplace transform of

$$x(t) = -e^{2t}u(t) * (tu(t))?$$

(*a*) $\frac{-1}{s^2(s+2)}$ (*b*) $\frac{-1}{s^2(s-2)}$

(*c*) $\frac{1}{s^2(s-2)}$ (*d*) $\frac{-1}{s(s-2)}$

7. The function $f(t)$ shown in the given figure will have Laplace transform as

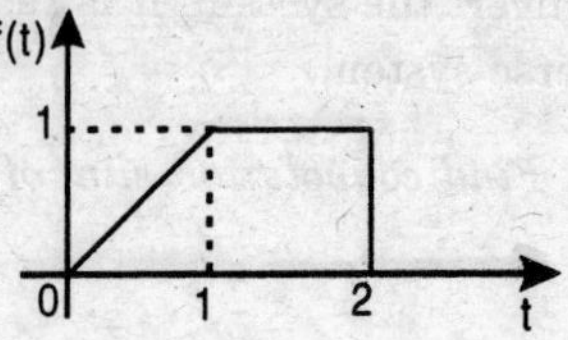

(*a*) $\frac{1}{s^2} - \frac{1}{s}e^{-s} - \frac{1}{s^2}e^{-2x}$

(*b*) $\frac{1}{s^2}\left(1 - e^{-s} - e^{-2s}\right)$

(*c*) $\frac{1}{s}\left(1 - e^{-s} - e^{-2s}\right)$

(*d*) $\frac{1}{s^2}\left(1 - e^{-s} - se^{-2s}\right)$

8. The output of a linear system to a unit step input $u(t)$ is $t^2 e^t$.

The system function H(s) is

(*a*) $\frac{2}{s^2(s+2)}$ (*b*) $\frac{2}{(s+2)^2}$

(*c*) $\frac{2}{(s+2)^3}$ (*d*) $\frac{2s}{(s+2)^3}$

9. Inverse of Laplace transform of $\frac{10}{s^2 + 5s + 4}$ is

(*a*) $10\left[e^{-t} + e^{-4t}\right]$ (*b*) $10\left[e^{-t} - e^{-4t}\right]$

(*c*) $\frac{10}{3}\left[e^{-t} + e^{-4t}\right]$ (*d*) $\frac{10}{3}\left[e^{-t} - e^{-4t}\right]$

10. Laplace transform of $e^{-at}\sin\omega t$ is

(*a*) $\frac{\omega}{(s+a)^2 + \omega^2}$ (*b*) $\frac{\omega}{(s-a)^2 + \omega^2}$

(*c*) $\frac{\omega}{(s-a)^2 - \omega^2}$ (*d*) $\frac{\omega}{(s+a)^2 - \omega^2}$

11. Laplace transform of t sin at is

(a) $\dfrac{2as}{(s^2+a^2)^2}$ (b) $\dfrac{2a}{(s^2+a^2)^2}$

(c) $\dfrac{2s}{(s^2+a^2)^2}$ (d) $\dfrac{a}{(s^2+a^2)^2}$

12. The Laplace transform of $f(t) = t$ is given by

(a) $\dfrac{1}{s^2}$ (b) $\dfrac{1}{s}$

(c) $\dfrac{2}{s^3}$ (d) s

13. If $f(t) = F(s)$, then $f(t-T)$ is equal to

(a) $e^{sT}F(s)$ (b) $e^{-sT}F(s)$

(c) $\dfrac{F(s)}{1+e^{sT}}$ (d) $\dfrac{F(s)}{1-e^{-sT}}$

14. The Laplace transform of sinh at is

(a) $\dfrac{a}{s^2-a^2}$ (b) $\dfrac{s}{s^2-a^2}$

(c) $\dfrac{s}{s^2+a^2}$ (d) $\dfrac{a}{s^2+a^2}$

15. If system is initially at rest, the response to a unit step u(t) is given by

$$\frac{1}{2}(1-e^{-2t})$$

The response to a signal $u(t) + 2\delta(t)$ is given by

(a) $\dfrac{1}{2}+\dfrac{3}{2}e^{-2t}$ (b) $1+e^{-2t}$

(c) $1+3e^{-2t}$ (d) $\dfrac{1}{2}+\dfrac{1}{2}e^{-2t}$

16.

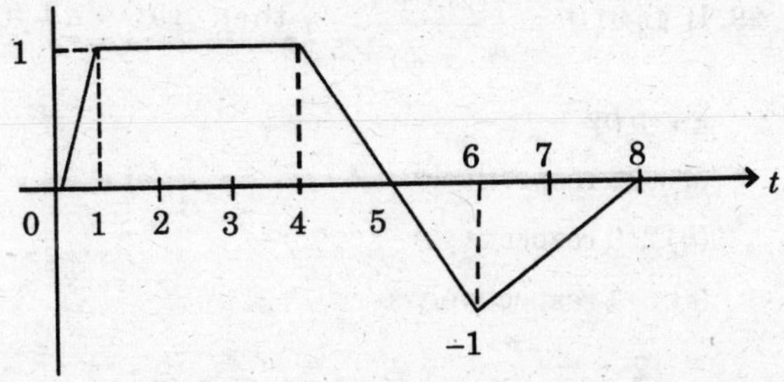

The Laplace transform of the waveform shown in the figure is

$$\frac{1}{s^2}(1 + Ae^{-s} + Be^{-4s} + Ce^{-6s} + De^{-8s}).$$

What is the value of D?

(a) – 0.5 (b) – 1.5

(c) 0.5 (d) 2.0

17. The response of an initially relaxed linear circuit to a signal V_s is $e^{-2t}u(t)$. If the signal is changed to $(V_s + 2\dfrac{dV_s}{dt})$, then response will be

(a) $-4e^{-2t}u(t)$ (b) $-3e^{-2t}u(t)$

(c) $4e^{-2t}u(t)$ (d) $5e^{-2t}4(t)$

18. The laplace transform of $(t^2 - 2t)\,u(t-1)$ is

(a) $\dfrac{2}{s^3}e^{-s}-\dfrac{2}{s^2}e^{-s}$ (b) $\dfrac{2}{s^3}e^{-2s}-\dfrac{2}{s^2}e^{-s}$

(c) $\dfrac{2}{s^3}e^{-s}-\dfrac{1}{s}e^{-s}$ (d) none of these

19. Unit impulse response of a system is given as $c(t) = -4e^{-t} + 6e^{-2t}$

The step response of the same system for $t \geq 0$ is equal to

(a) $-3e^{-2t}+4e^{-t}-2$ (b) $-3e^{-2t}+4e^{-t}+1$

(c) $-3e^{-2t}+4e^{-t}-1$ (d) $3e^{-2t}+4e^{-t}-1$

20. A system is represented by $\dfrac{dy}{dt}+2y = 4tu(t)$. The ramp constant in the forced response will be

(a) $t.u(t)$ (b) $2t\,u(t)$

(c) $3t\,u(t)$ (d) $4t\,u(t)$

21. The laplace transform of the function $i(t)$ is

$$I(s) = \frac{10s+4}{s(s+1)(s^2+4s+5)}$$

its final value will be

(a) $\dfrac{4}{5}$ (b) $\dfrac{5}{4}$

(c) 4 (d) 5

22. The impulse response of an R–L circuit is a

(a) rising exponential function

(b) decaying exponential function

(c) step function

(d) parabolic function

23. Determine final value of $x(t)$, if laplace transform of $x(t)$ is given

$$X(s) = \frac{2s^2+3}{s^2+5s+1}$$

(a) 0 (b) 2

(c) 3 (d) does not exist

24. A linear time invariatiant system has an impulse response e^{2t}, $t > 0$. If the initial conditions are zero and the input is e^{3t}, the output for $t > 0$ is

(a) $e^{3t} - e^{2t}$ (b) e^{5t}

(c) $e^{3t} + e^{2t}$ (d) None of these

25. If a plot of a signal $x(t)$ is as shown in the figure below

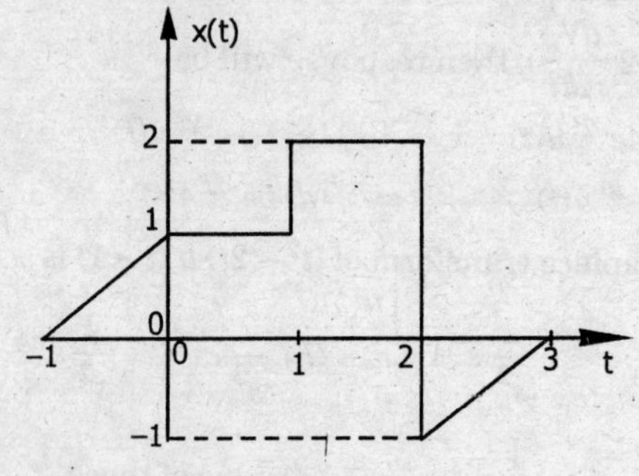

Then the plot of the signal $x(1-t)$ will be

(*a*)

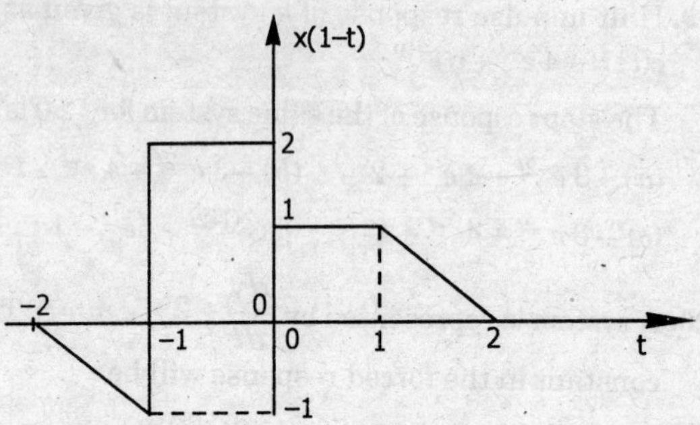

(*b*)

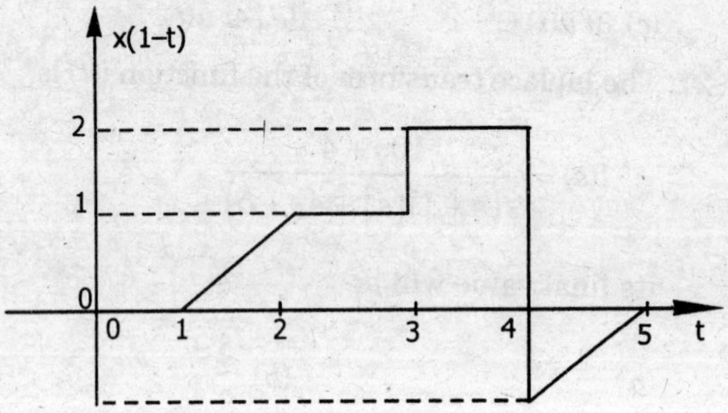

(*c*)

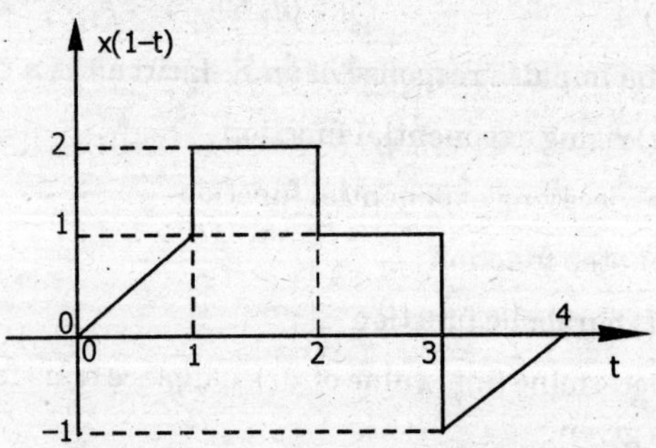

(*d*)

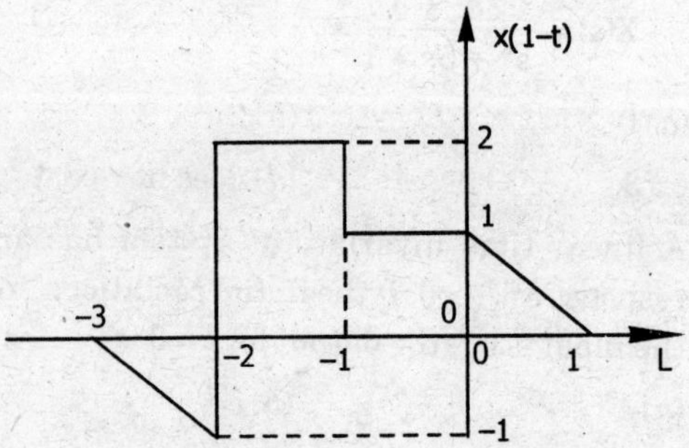

26. The Laplace transform X(*s*) of a function $x(t)$ is

$$X(s) = \left(\frac{1 - e^{-sT}}{s}\right)$$

What is the wave shape of $x(t)$?

(*a*)

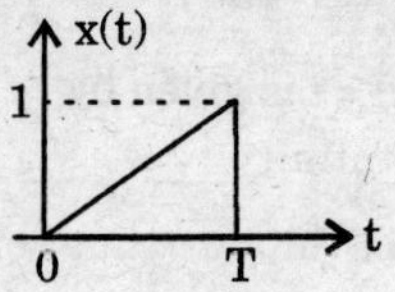

(*b*)

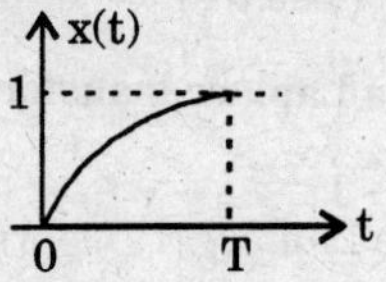

(*c*)

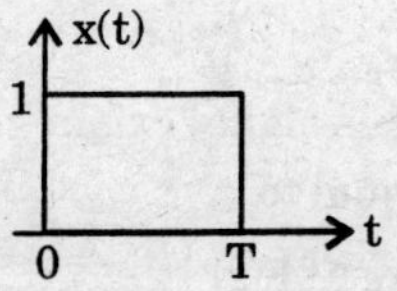

(*d*)

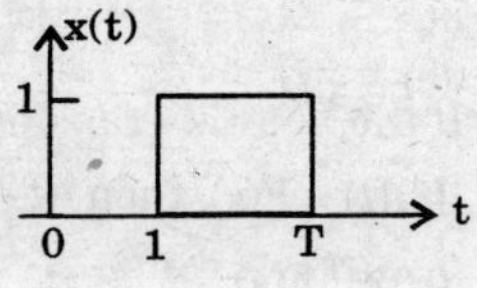

27. Given the transform pair

$$x(t)u(t) \xleftrightarrow{L} \frac{2s}{s^2 + 2}.$$

Determine the laplace transform Y(*s*) of the given time signal in question and choose correct option.

$$y(t) = x(t-2)$$

(*a*) $\dfrac{2se^{-2s}}{s^2+2}$ (*b*) $\dfrac{2se^{-2s}}{s^2+2}$

(*c*) $\dfrac{2(s-2)}{(s-2)^2+1}$ (*d*) $\dfrac{2(s+2)}{(s+2)^2+1}$

28. The unit impulse response of a linear time invariant system is unit step function $u(t)$. For $t > 0$, the response of the system to an excitation $e^{-at}\,u(t)$, $a > 0$ will be

(*a*) ae^{-at} (*b*) $\left(\dfrac{1}{a}\right)(1 - ae^{-at})$

(*c*) $a(1 - ae^{-at})$ (*d*) $1 - ae^{-at}$

29. If $L[f(t)] = \dfrac{2(s+1)}{s^2+2s+5}$, then $f(0^+)$ and $f(\infty)$ are given by

(*a*) 0, 2 respectively

(*b*) 2, 0 respectively

(*c*) 0, 1 respectively

(*d*) $\dfrac{2}{5}$, 0 respectively

30. The response of an initially relaxed linear constant parameter network to a unit impulse applied at $t = 0$ is $4e^{-2t}\,u(t)$. The response of this network to a unit step function will be

(*a*) $2[1 - e^{-2t}]\,u(t)$ (*b*) $4[e^{-t} - e^{-2t}]u(t)$

(*c*) $\sin 2t$ (*d*) $(1 - 4e^{-4t})\,u(t)$

31. The closed-loop transfer function of a control system is given by

$$\frac{C(s)}{R(s)} = \frac{2(s-1)}{(s+2)(s+1)}$$

For a unit step input the output is

(*a*) $-3e^{-2t}+4e^{-t}-1$ (*b*) $-3e^{-2t}-4e^{-t}+1$

(*c*) zero (*d*) infinity

32. The Laplace transform of a continuous-time signal $x(t)$

is, $X(s) = \dfrac{5-s}{s^2-s-2}$

If the Fourier transform of this signal exists, then $x(t)$ is

(*a*) $e^{2t}u(t)-2e^{-t}u(t)$

(*b*) $-e^{2t}u(-t)+2e^{-t}u(t)$

(*c*) $-e^{2t}u(-t)-2e^{-t}u(t)$

(*d*) none of these

33. Laplace transform of the signal

$x(t) = tu(t) * \cos 2\pi t\, u(t)$

will be

(*a*) $\dfrac{1}{s(s^2+4\pi^2)}$ (*b*) $\dfrac{2\pi}{s^2(s^2+4\pi^2)}$

(*c*) $\dfrac{1}{s^2(s^2+4\pi^2)}$ (*d*) $\dfrac{s^3}{s^2+4\pi^2}$

34. Laplace transform of the signal $x(t) = \int_0^t e^{-3\tau}\cos 2\tau d\tau$

will be

(*a*) $\dfrac{-(s+3)}{s((s+3)^2+4)}$

(*b*) $\dfrac{(s+3)}{s[(s+3)^2+4]}$

(*c*) $\dfrac{s(s+3)}{(s+3)^2+4}$

(*d*) $\dfrac{-s(s+3)}{(s+3)^2+4}$

35. The time signal $x(t)$ corresponding to

$$X(s) = \frac{s+3}{s^2+2s+2}$$

will be

(*a*) $(2e^{-2t}+e^{-t})u(t)$ (*b*) $(2e^{-t}-e^{-2t})u(t)$

(*c*) $(2e^{-2t}-e^{-t})u(t)$ (*d*) $(2e^{-t}+e^{-2t})u(t)$

36. For the transform pair below, the time signal $y(t)$ will be

$$\cos 2t\, u(t) \xleftrightarrow{L} X(s).$$

$$Y(s) = (s+1)X(s)$$

(*a*) $[\cos 2t - 2\sin 2t]\,u(t)$

(*b*) $\left(\cos 2t + \dfrac{\sin 2t}{2}\right)u(t)$

(*c*) $[\cos 2t + 2\sin 2t]\,u(t)$

(*d*) $\left(\cos 2t - \dfrac{\sin 2t}{2}\right)u(t)$

37. The bilateral Laplace transform of

$$x(t) = e^{-t}u(t+2)$$

will be

(*a*) $\dfrac{e^{2(s+1)}}{s+1}$, Re $(s) > -1$

(*b*) $\dfrac{1}{1+s}$, Re $(s) < -1$

(*c*) $\dfrac{e^{2(s+1)}}{s+1}$, Re $(s) < -1$

(*d*) $\dfrac{1}{1+s}$, Re $(s) > -1$

38. The bilateral Laplace transform of

$$x(t) = e^{-\frac{t}{2}}u(t) + e^{-t}u(t) + e^{t}u(-t)$$

will be

(*a*) $\dfrac{6s^2+2s-2}{(2s+1)(s^2-1)}$, Re $(s) < -0.5$

(*b*) $\dfrac{6s^2+2s-2}{(2s+1)(s^2-1)}$, $-1 >$ Re $(s) > 1$

(*c*) $\dfrac{1}{s+0.5}+\dfrac{1}{s+1}+\dfrac{1}{s-1}$, $-1 < \text{Re}(s) < 1$

(*d*) $\dfrac{1}{s+0.5}+\dfrac{1}{s+1}-\dfrac{1}{s-1}$, $-0.5 < \text{Re}(s) < 1$

39. the response of LTI system for

$$\frac{dy(t)}{dt} + 10y(t) = 10x(t), y(0^-) = 1, x(t) = u(t)$$

will be

(*a*) $[1-e^{-10t}]u(t)$ (*b*) $e^{-10t}u(t)$

(*c*) $u(t)$ (*d*) $[1-2e^{-10t}]u(t)$

40. $\dfrac{d^2y(t)}{dt^2} + 2\dfrac{dy(t)}{dt} + 5y(t) = \dfrac{dx(t)}{dt}$,

$y(0^-) = 2, \quad \left.\dfrac{dy(t)}{dt}\right|_{t=0} = 0, \; x(t) = u(t)$

(a) $\frac{1}{2}e^{-t}\sin t\, u(t)$

(b) $2e^{-t}\cos t\, u(t)$

(c) $2e^{-t}\cos t\, u(t) + \frac{1}{2}e^{-t}\sin t\, u(t)$

(d) $\frac{1}{2}e^{-t}\cos t\, u(t-1) + 2e^{-t}\sin t\, u(t-1)$

41. The relationship between the input $x(t)$ and output $y(t)$ of a causal system is defined as

$$\frac{d^2y(t)}{dt^2} - \frac{dy(t)}{dt} - 2y(t) = 4x(t) + 5\frac{dx(t)}{dt}$$

The impulse response of system is

(a) $3e^{-t}u(t) + 2e^{2t}u(-t)$

(b) $(3e^{-t} + 2e^{2t})\,u(t)$

(c) $3e^{-t}u(t) - 2e^{2t}u(-t)$

(d) $(3e^{-t} - 2e^{2t})\,u(-t)$

CONTINUOUS-TIME SYSTEMS

42. The raised cosine pulse $x(t)$ is defined as

$$x(t) = \begin{cases} \frac{1}{2}(\cos\omega t + 1), & -\frac{\pi}{\omega} \le t \le \frac{\pi}{\omega} \\ 0, & \text{otherwise} \end{cases}$$

The total energy of $x(t)$ is

(a) $\frac{3\pi}{4\omega}$ (b) $\frac{3\pi}{8\omega}$ (c) $\frac{3\pi}{\omega}$ (d) $\frac{3\pi}{2\omega}$

43. Sinusoidal signal $x(t) = 4\cos(200t + \pi/6)$ is passed through a square law device defined by the input output relation $y(t) = x^2(t)$. The DC component in the signal is

(a) 3.46 (b) 4 (c) 2.83 (d) 8

44. If $x(t) = \begin{cases} 1, & 0 \le t \le 1 \\ 0, & \text{elsewhere} \end{cases}$

$h(t) = x\left(\dfrac{t}{a}\right)$, where $0 < a \le 1$.

The $y(t) = x(t) * h(t)$ is

(a)
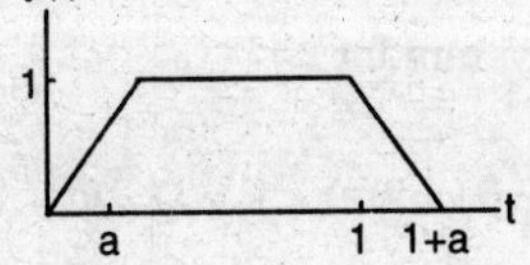

(b)
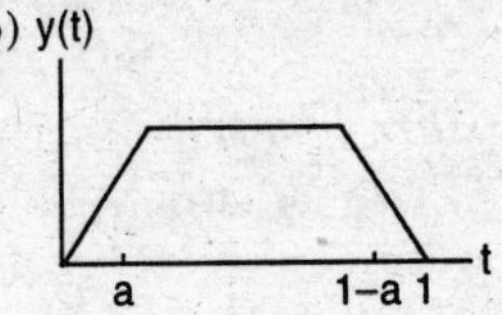

(c)
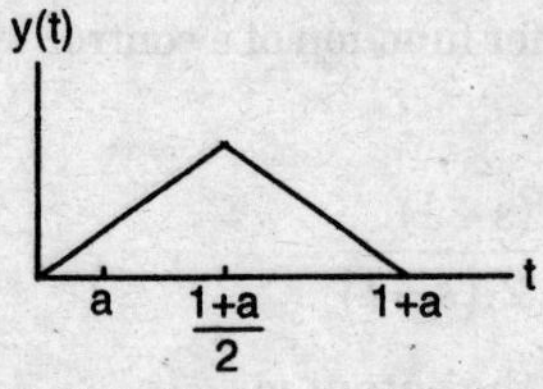

(d)
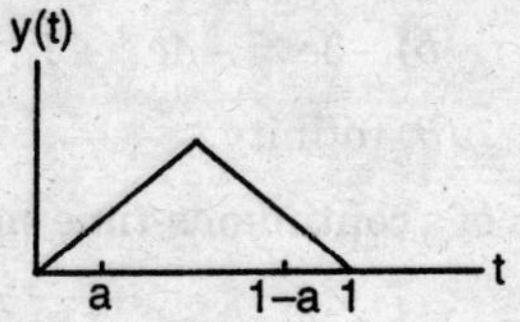

45. If the signal $x(t) = \delta(t+2) - \delta(t-2)$, then value of E_∞ for the signal

$$y(t) = \int_{\pm\infty}^{t} x(\tau)\,d\tau \quad \text{is}$$

(a) 4

(b) 2

(c) 1

(d) ∞

DISCRETE-TIME SYSTEMS

46. The even part of a function

$x[n] = u[n] - u[n-4]$ is

(a) $\frac{1}{2}\{1 + \delta[n] - u[n-4] - u[-n-4]\}$

(b) $\frac{1}{2}\{u[n+3] - u[n-4] + \delta[n]\}$

(c) $\frac{1}{2}\{u[n] + u[-n] - u[n-4] - u[-n-4]\}$

(d) all of these

47. Energy of the signal $A\delta[n]$ is

(a) A^2 (b) $\frac{A^2}{2}$

(c) $\frac{A^2}{4}$ (d) 0

48. Energy of the signal $nu[n]$ is

(a) $\dfrac{n(n+1)}{2}$

(b) $\dfrac{n(n+1)(2n+1)}{6}$

(c) $\left(\dfrac{n(n+1)}{2}\right)^2$

(d) ∞

Common data Q. 49–50 :

x[n] and y[n] are given in figure below

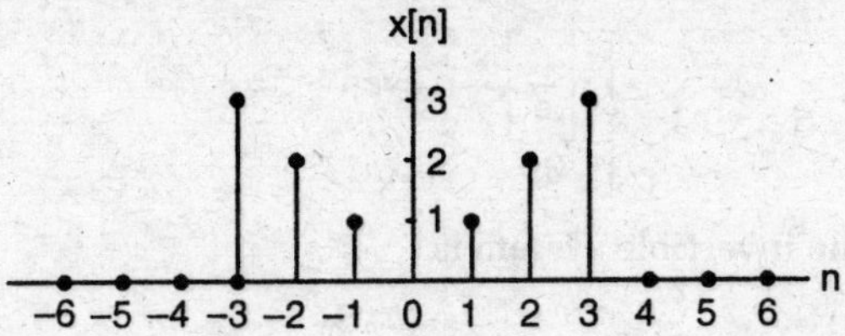

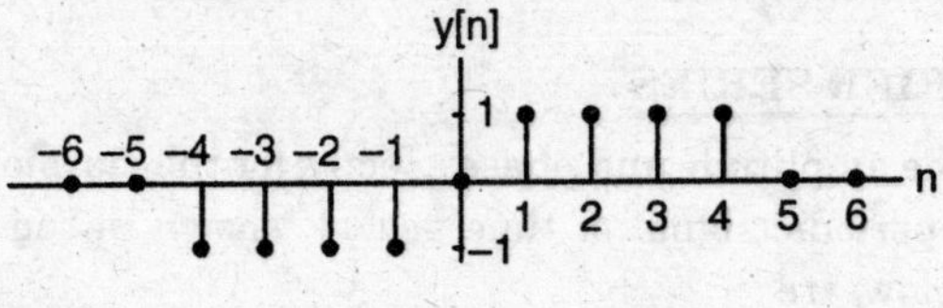

49. $x[2n]$

(*a*)

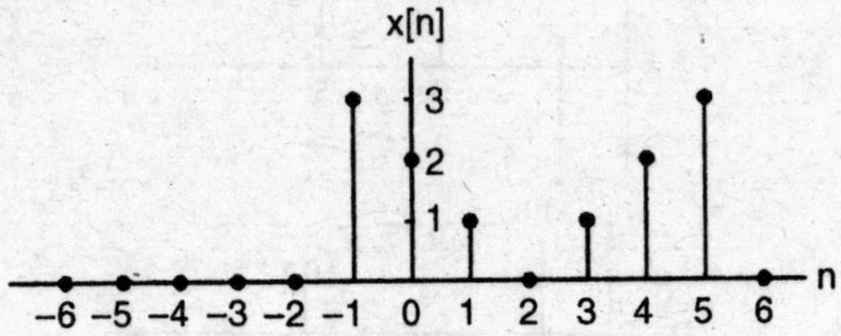

(*b*)

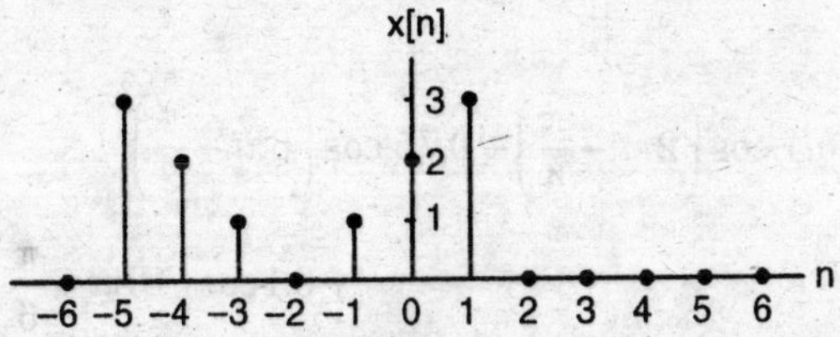

(*c*)

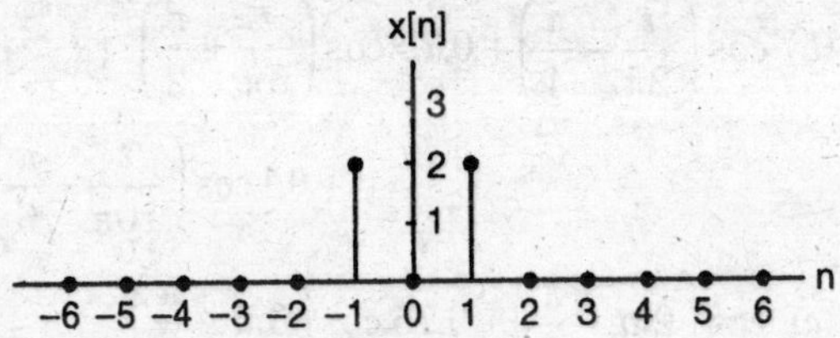

(*d*)

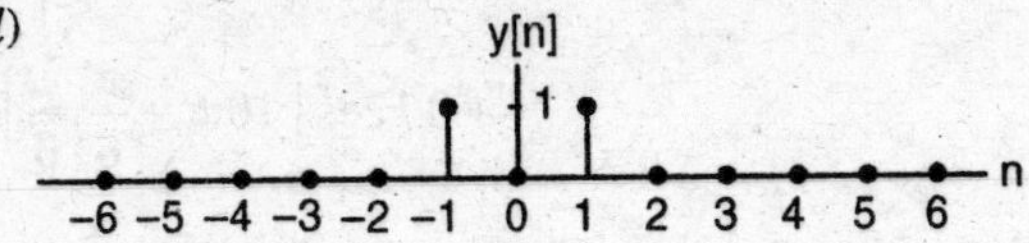

50. $x[3-n]y[-n]$

(*a*)

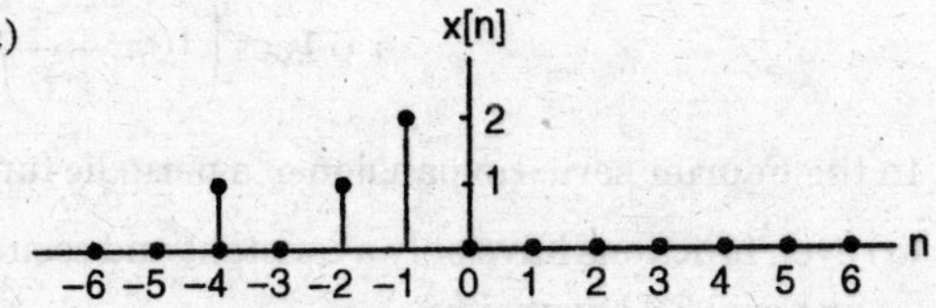

(*b*)

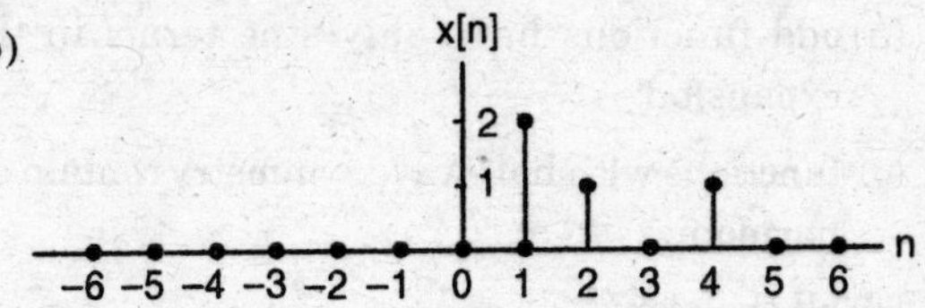

(*c*)

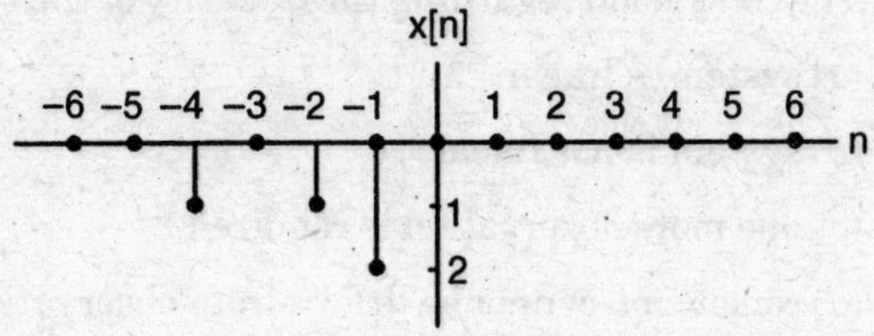

(*d*)

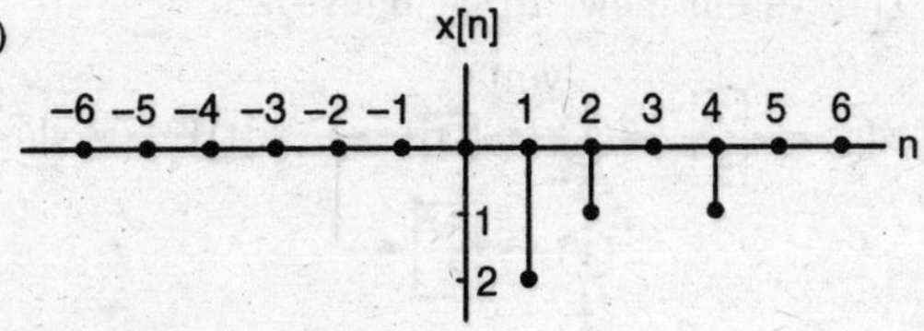

Common data Q. 51–52:

x[n] and h[n] are given in the question. Compute the convolution $y[n]=x[n]*h[n]$ and choose correct option.

51. $x[n]=\{1, 2, 4\}$, $h[n]=\{1, 1, 1, 1, 1\}$

(*a*) {1, 3, 7, 7, 7, 6, 4} (*b*) {1, 3, 3, 7, 7, 6, 4}

(*c*) {1, 2, 4} (*d*) {1, 3, 7}

52. $x[n]=\{1, 2, 3, 4, 5\}$, $h[n]=\{1\}$

(*a*) {1, 3, 6, 10, 15} (*b*) {1, 2, 3, 4, 5}

(*c*) {1, 4, 9, 16, 20} (*d*) {1, 4, 6, 8, 10}

53. Consider the following statements

(1) If S_1 and S_2 are linear, then S is linear

(2) If S_1 and S_2 are nonlinear, then S is nonlinear

(3) If S_1 and S_2 are causal, then S is causal

(4) If S_1 and S_2 are time invariant, then S is time invariant

Of these statements true statements are

(*a*) 1, 2, 3 (*b*) 2, 3, 4

(*c*) 1, 3, 4 (*d*) all of these

54. Consider the following statements:

(1) If S_1 and S_2 are linear and time invariant, then interchanging their order does not change the system.

(2) If S_1 and S_2 are linear and time varying, then interchanging their order does not change the system.

Of these statements true statements are

(*a*) Both (1) and (2) (*b*) Only (1)

(*c*) Only (2) (*d*) None of these

55. Following input output pairs have been observed during the operation of a time invariant system

$$x_1[n]=\{\underset{\uparrow}{1}, 0, 2\} \overset{S}{\longleftrightarrow} y_1[n]=\{0, \underset{\uparrow}{1}, 2\}$$

$$x_2[n]=\{0, \underset{\uparrow}{0}, 3\} \overset{S}{\longleftrightarrow} y_2[n]=\{0, 1, \underset{\uparrow}{0}, 2\}$$

$$x_3[n]=\{0, \underset{\uparrow}{0}, 0, 1\} \overset{S}{\longleftrightarrow} y_3[n]=\{1, 2, \underset{\uparrow}{1}\}$$

The conclusion regarding the linearity of the system

(*a*) system is linear

(*b*) system is not linear

(*c*) one more observation is required

(*d*) conclusion cannot be drawn from observation

56. The system shown in the figure is

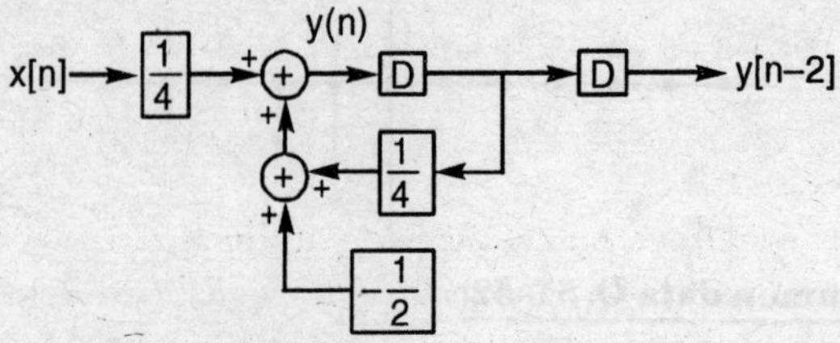

(*a*) stable and causal

(*b*) stable but not causal

(*c*) causal but unstable

(*d*) unstable and not causal

57. System shown in the figure is

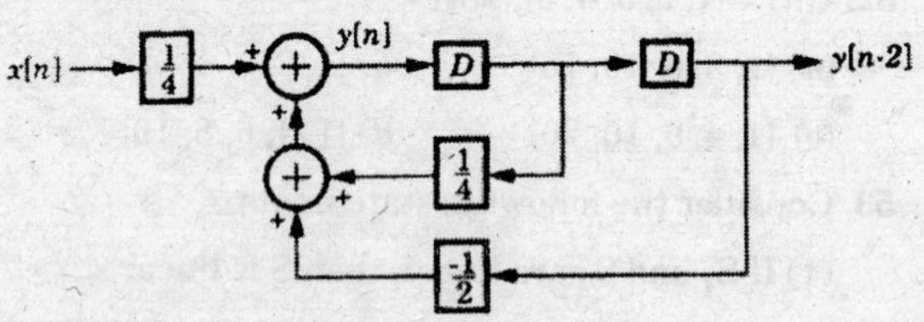

(*a*) Stable and causal

(*b*) Stable but not causal

(*c*) Causal but unstable

(*d*) unstable and not causal

58. The difference equation representation for a system is

$$y[n] - \frac{1}{2}y[n-1] = 2x[n], \quad y[-1] = 3$$

The natural response of system is

(*a*) $\frac{3}{2}\left(-\frac{1}{2}\right)^n u[n]$

(*b*) $\frac{2}{3}\left(-\frac{1}{2}\right)^n u[n]$

(*c*) $\frac{3}{2}\left(\frac{1}{2}\right)^n u[n]$

(*d*) $\frac{2}{3}\left(\frac{1}{2}\right)^n u[n]$

59. The difference equation representation for a system is

$$y[n] - 2y[n-1] + y[n-2] = x[n] - x[n-1]$$

If $y[n] = 0$ for $n < 0$ and $x[n] = \delta[n]$,

then $y[2]$ will be

(*a*) 2 (*b*) −2

(*c*) −1 (*d*) 0

60. Consider the two systems

$$S_1 : y[n] = \begin{cases} x[n+1], & n \geq 0 \\ x[n], & n \leq -1 \end{cases}$$

$$S_2 : y[n] = \begin{cases} x\left[\frac{n}{2}\right], & n \text{ even} \\ 0, & n \text{ odd} \end{cases}$$

The invertible system is

(*a*) S_1 (*b*) S_2

(*c*) Both S_1 and S_2 (*d*) None of these

FOURIER SERIES

61. The amplitude and phase spectra for the harmonics of a periodic signal of time period shown in the figure below, are

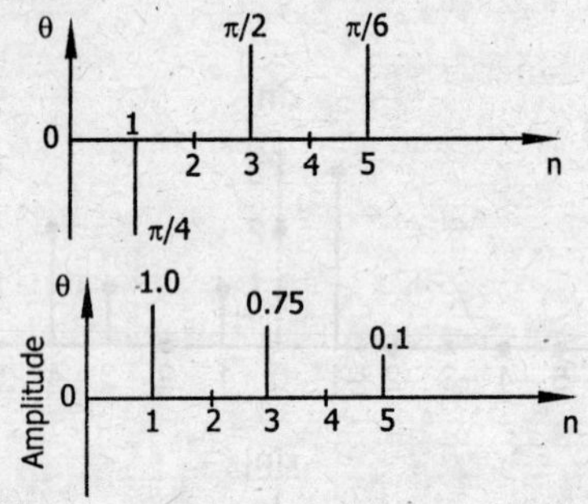

(*a*) $\cos\left(2\pi t - \frac{\pi}{4}\right) + 0.75\cos\left(6\pi t + \frac{\pi}{2}\right) + 0.1\cos\left(10\pi t + \frac{\pi}{6}\right)........$

(*b*) $\cos\left(\frac{t}{2\pi} - \frac{\pi}{4}\right) + 0.75\cos\left(\frac{t}{6\pi} + \frac{\pi}{2}\right) + 0.1\cos\left(\frac{t}{10\pi} + \frac{\pi}{6}\right)........$

(*c*) $\cos\left(2\pi t - \frac{\pi}{4}\right) + 0.75\cos\left(6\pi t + \frac{\pi}{2}\right) + 0.1\cos\left(10\pi t + \frac{\pi}{6}.\frac{1}{6}\right)........$

(*d*) $-\cos\left(2\pi t - \frac{\pi}{4}\right) + 0.75\cos\left(6\pi t + \frac{\pi}{2}\right) + 0.1\cos\left(10\pi t + \frac{\pi}{6}\right)........$

62. In the Fourier series expansion of a periodic function,

(*a*) even functions have only a constant and cosine terms in their FS expansion

(*b*) odd functions have only sine terms in their FS expansion

(*c*) functions with half-wave symmetry contain only odd harmonics

(*d*) all the above

63. The average value of the delayed full-wave rectified sine wave as shown in the given figure, is

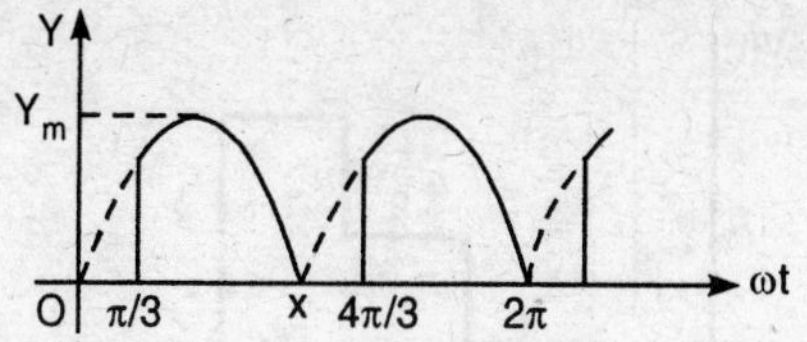

(*a*) $\frac{Y_m}{\pi}$ (*b*) $\frac{2Y_m}{\pi}$

(*c*) $\frac{3Y_m}{2\pi}$ (*d*) $\frac{Y_m}{2\pi}$

64. If $f(t) = -f(-t)$ and $f(t)$ satisfy the Dirichlet's conditions, then $f(t)$ can be expanded in a Fourier series containing

(*a*) only sine terms

(*b*) only cosine terms

(*c*) cosine terms and a constant term

(*d*) sine terms and a constant term

65. A periodic triangular wave is shown in the figure. Its Fourier components will consist only of

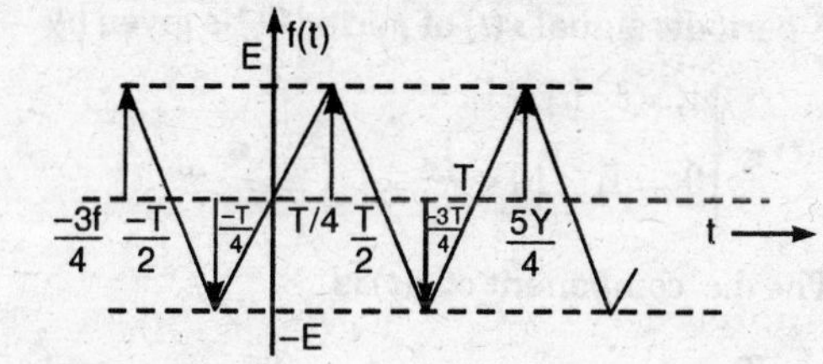

(*a*) all cosine terms

(*b*) all sine terms

(*c*) odd cosine terms

(*d*) odd sine terms

66. A linear system has the transfer function $H(j\omega) = \frac{1}{(j\omega + 1)}$. When it is subjected to an input white noise process with a constant spectral density A, the spectral density of the output will be

(*a*) $\frac{A}{(j\omega + 1)}$ (*b*) $\frac{A}{(j\omega + 1)^2}$

(*c*) $\frac{A}{(\omega^2 + 1)}$ (*d*) $\frac{A}{\sqrt{(\omega^2 + 1)}}$

67. The period of the function $\cos \frac{\pi}{4}(t-1)$ is

(*a*) $\frac{1}{8}$ s (*b*) 8 s

(*c*) 4 s (*d*) $\frac{1}{4}$ s

68. The Fourier series representation of a periodic current is

$$[2 + 6\sqrt{2}\cos \omega t + \sqrt{48}\sin 2\omega t]\text{A}.$$

The effective value of the current is

(*a*) $(2 + 6 + \sqrt{24})$A (*b*) 8A

(*c*) 6A (*d*) 2A

69. For even function, the necessary condition is

(*a*) $f(t) = -f(-t)$ (*b*) $f(t) = +f(-t)$

(*c*) $f(t) = \frac{1}{f(-t)}$ (*d*) $f(t) = -(t \pm T/2)$

70. The fourier series of the periodic function $f(t)$ shown in the figure below has coefficients a_k, b_k. The series has

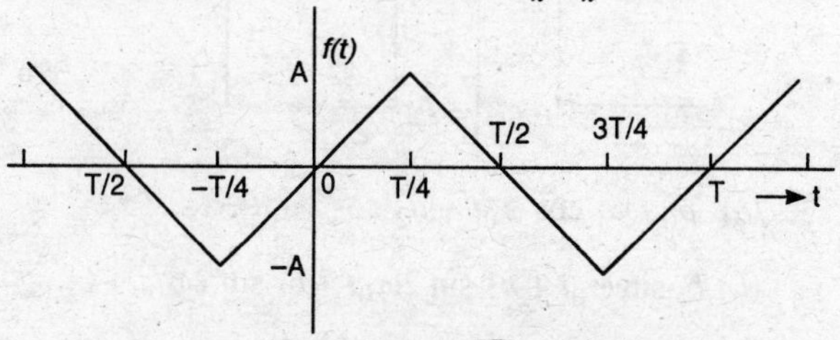

(*a*) both cosine and sine terms but only for odd values of k

(*b*) only cosine terms for odd values of k

(*c*) only sine terms for odd values of k

(*d*) a constant and sine terms for odd values of k

71. A periodic function $f(t)$ has the exponential series

$$f(t) = \frac{A}{2} + \frac{2A}{\pi^2}\left[+ \frac{e^{-j3\omega}}{(-3)^2} + \frac{e^{-j\omega}}{(-1)^2} + \frac{e^{j\omega}}{1^2} + \frac{e^{j3\omega}}{3^2} + \ldots \right]$$

The trigonometric form of the series is

(*a*) $f(t) = \frac{A}{2} + \frac{2A}{\pi}\Sigma\frac{\cos k\omega_0 t}{k^2}$ for all integers k

(*b*) $f(t) = \frac{A}{2} + \frac{2A}{\pi^2}\Sigma\frac{\cos k\omega_0 t}{k^2}$ for k odd

(*c*) $f(t) = \frac{A}{2} + \frac{4A}{\pi^2}\Sigma\frac{\cos k\omega_0 t}{k^2}$ for k odd

(*d*) $f(t) = \frac{A}{2} + \frac{4A}{\pi^2}\Sigma\frac{\cos k\omega_0 t}{k^2}$ for k odd

72. The periodic function shown in the figure below

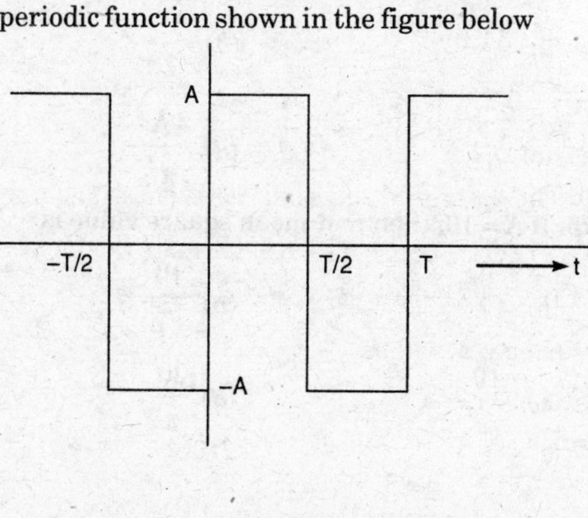

(a) is even and has no half-wave symmetry

(b) is odd and has no half-wave symmetry

(c) is even and has half-wave symmetry

(d) is odd and has half-wave symmetry

73. The Fourier series of the square wave given by the following figure where given a_k, b_k are non-zero, is

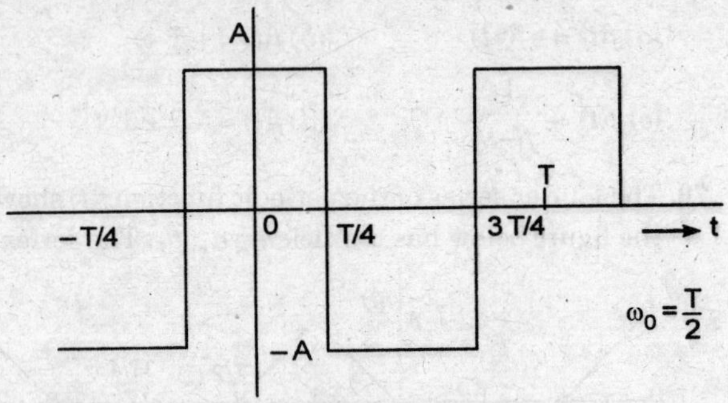

(a) $a_0 + a_1 \cos \omega_0 t + a_2 \cos 2\omega_0 t + ...$

(b) $b_1 \sin \omega_0 t + b_2 \sin 2\omega_0 t + b_3 \sin 2\omega_0 t + ...$

(c) $a_1 \cos \omega_0 t + a_3 \cos 3\omega_0 t + a_5 \cos 5\omega_0 t + ...$

(d) $b_1 \sin \omega_0 t + b_3 \sin 3\omega_0 t + b_5 \sin 5\omega_0 t + ...$

Common data Q. 74–75:

The square wave shown in the figure below is the voltage v(t) applied to a one ohm resistor. The amplitude is A and period is T. The Fourier series is given by

$$v(t) = \frac{A}{2} + \frac{2A}{p}\left(\sin\frac{2\pi t}{T} + \frac{\sin 3(2\pi t/T)}{3} + \frac{\sin 3(2\pi t/T)}{3} + \frac{\sin 5(2pt/T)}{5} + ...\right)$$

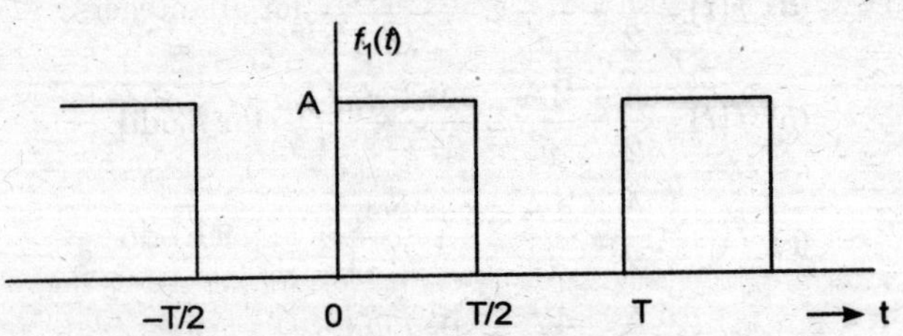

74. The power absorbed by the resistor is

(a) $\frac{A^2}{4}$ (b) $\frac{A^2}{2}$

(c) A^2 (d) $\frac{4A^2}{\pi^2}$

75. If A = 10, then root mean square value is

(a) 10 (b) $\frac{10}{\sqrt{2}}$

(c) $\frac{10}{2}$ (d) $\frac{20}{\pi}$

76. Consider the voltage waveform shown in the figure. The equation for V(t) is

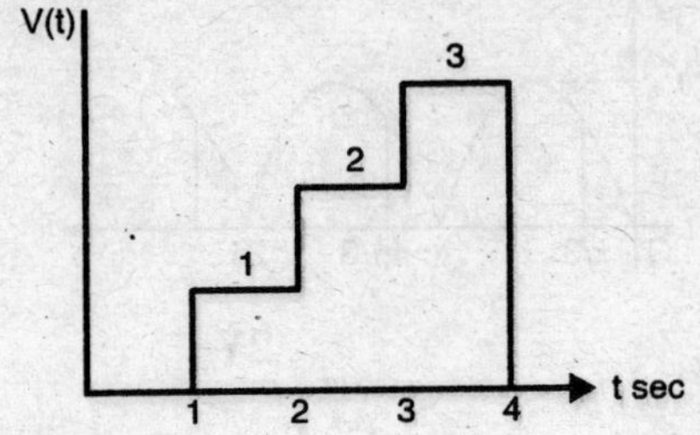

(a) $u(t-1) + u(t-2) + u(t-3)$

(b) $u(t-1) + 2u(t-2) + 3u(t-3)$

(c) $u(t) + u(t-1) + u(t-2) + u(t-4)$

(d) $u(t-1) + u(t-2) + u(t-3) - 3u(t-4)$

77. Which of the following cannot be the Fourier series expansion of a periodic signal ?

(a) $x(t) = 2\cos t + 3\cos 3t$

(b) $x(t) = 2\cos \pi t + 7\cos t$

(c) $x(t) = \cos t + 0.5$

(d) $x(t) = 2\cos 1.5\pi t + \sin 3.5\pi t$

78. A periodic signal $x(t)$ of period T_0 is given by

$$x(t) = \begin{cases} 1, & |t| < T_1 \\ 0, & T_1 < |t| < \frac{T_o}{2} \end{cases}$$

The d.c. component of $x(t)$ is

(a) $\frac{T_1}{T_0}$ (b) $\frac{T_1}{2T_0}$

(c) $\frac{2T_1}{T_0}$ (d) $\frac{T_0}{T_1}$

79. Fourier Series of an odd periodic function, contains only

(a) odd harmonics (b) even harmonics

(c) cosine terms (d) sine terms

80. The voltage across an impedance in a network is

$$V(s) = Z(s)\, I(s),$$

where V(s), Z(s) are the Laplace Transforms of the corresponding time function

$v(t)$, $z(t)$ and $i(t)$

The voltage $v(t)$ is

(a) $v(t) = z(t) \cdot v(t)$

(b) $v(t) = \int_0^t i(\tau) \cdot z(t-\tau)\, d\tau$

(c) $v(t) = \int_0^t i(\tau) \cdot z(t+\tau)\, d\tau$

(d) $v(t) = z(t) + i(t)$

81. Convolution of $x(t + 5)$ with impulse function $\delta(t - 7)$ is equal to

(*a*) $x(t - 12)$

(*b*) $x(t + 12)$

(*c*) $x(t - 2)$

(*d*) $x(t + 2)$

82. The rms value of the periodic waveform $e(t)$, shown in the figure is

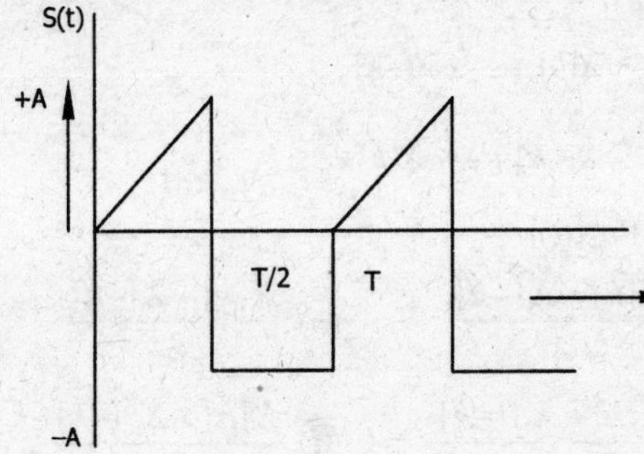

(*a*) $\sqrt{\frac{3}{2}}$ A (*b*) $\sqrt{\frac{2}{3}}$ A

(*c*) $\sqrt{\frac{1}{3}}$ A (*d*) $\sqrt{2}$ A

83. Fourier Series for the waveform, $f(t)$ shown in the given figure is

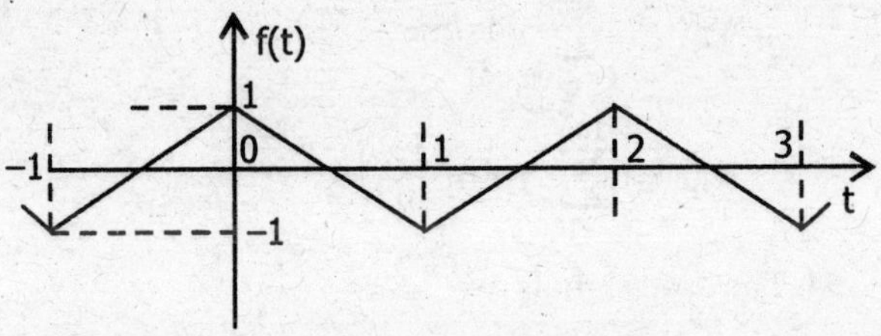

(*a*) $\frac{8}{\pi^2}$ [$\sin(\pi t) + \frac{1}{9}\sin(3\pi t) + \frac{1}{25}\sin(5\pi t) + \ldots$]

(*b*) $\frac{8}{\pi^2}$ [$\sin(\pi t) - \frac{1}{9}\cos(3\pi t) + \frac{1}{25}\sin(5\pi t) + \ldots$]

(*c*) $\frac{8}{\pi^2}$ [$\cos(\pi t) + \frac{1}{9}\cos(3\pi t) + \frac{1}{25}\cos(5\pi t) + \ldots$]

(*d*) $\frac{8}{\pi^2}$ [$\cos(\pi t) - \frac{1}{9}\sin(3\pi t) + \frac{1}{25}\cos(5\pi t) + \ldots$]

84. A linear time invariant system has an impulse response $e^{2t}, t > 0$. If the initial conditions are zero and the input is e^{3t}, the output for $t > 0$ is

(*a*) $e^{3t} - e^{2t}$

(*b*) e^{5t}

(*c*) $e^{3t} + e^{2t}$

(*d*) None of these

85. If $u(t)$ is the step function, then which of the waveforms corresponds to the convolution of $u(t) - u(t - 1)$ with $u(t) - u(t - 2)$?

(*a*)

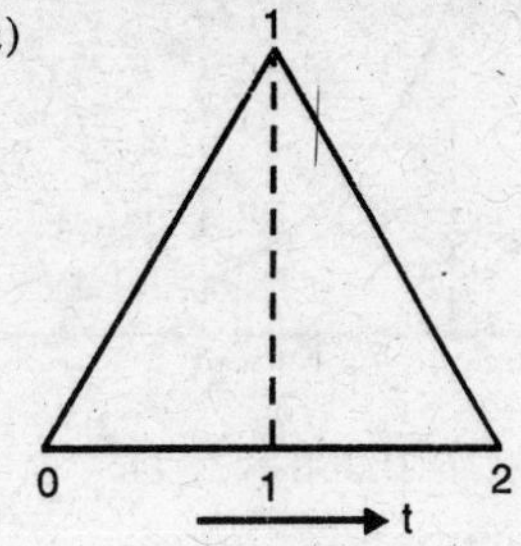

(*b*)

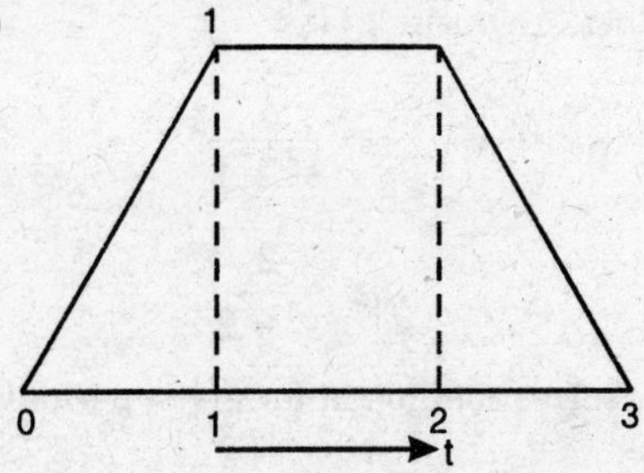

(*c*)

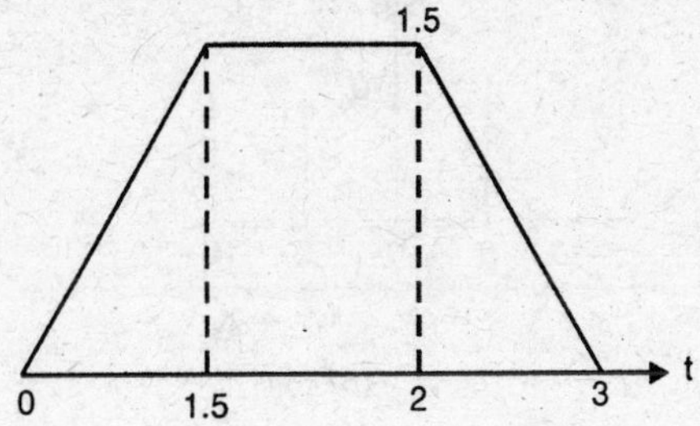

(*d*)

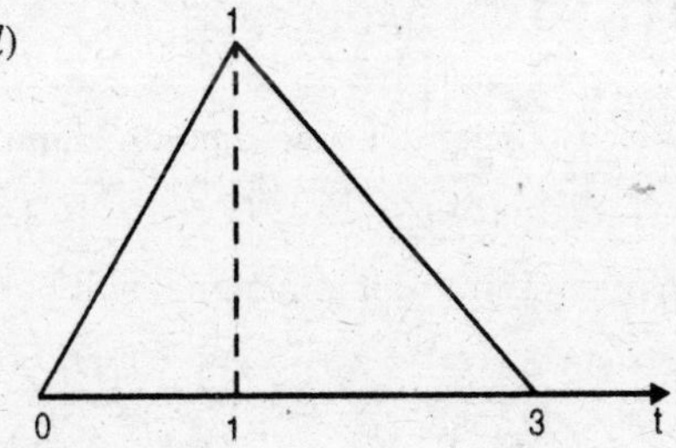

86. A periodic rectangular signal, $x(t)$ has the wave form shown in figure below. Frequency of the fifth harmonic of its spectrum is

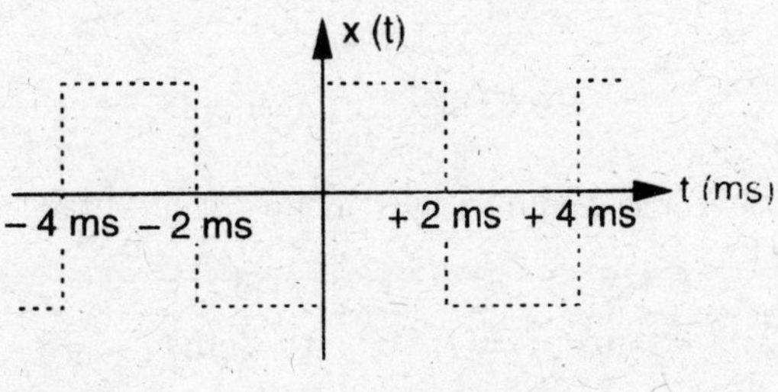

(*a*) 40 Hz (*b*) 200 Hz

(*c*) 250 Hz (*d*) 1250 Hz

87. The average value of the voltage waveform shown below is

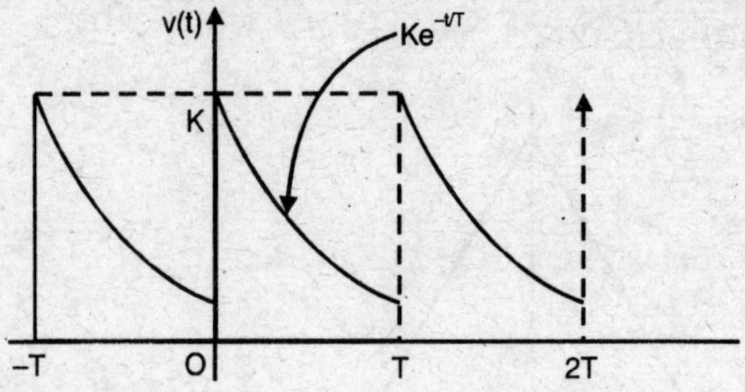

(*a*) 0.632 K (*b*) 0.368 K

(*c*) 2.71 K (*d*) None of these

88. Laplace transform of sin 2 *t* is

(*a*) $\frac{4}{s^2+2}$ (*b*) $\frac{4}{s^2+4}$

(*c*) $\frac{2}{s^2+4}$ (*d*) $\frac{2}{s^2+2}$

89. The Fourier series coefficient for given periodic signal $x(t)$ is

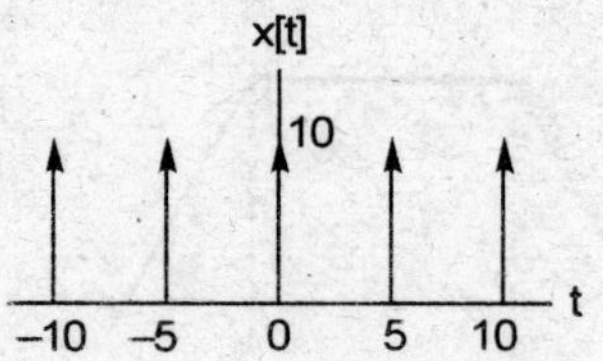

(*a*) 1 (*b*) $\cos\left(\frac{\pi}{2}k\right)$

(*c*) $\sin\left(\frac{\pi}{2}k\right)$ (*d*) 2

90. Fourier Series coefficient of time-domain signal is

$X[k] = j\delta[k-1] - j\delta[k+1] + \delta[k+3] + \delta[k-3]$, $\omega_o = 2\pi$

then corresponding time domain signal will be

(*a*) $2(\cos 3\pi t - \sin \pi t)$

(*b*) $-2(\cos 3\pi t - \sin \pi t)$

(*c*) $2(\cos 6\pi t - \sin 2\pi t)$

(*d*) $-2(\cos 6\pi t - \sin 2\pi t)$

91. Fourier Series coefficient of time-domain signal is

$$X[k] = \left(\frac{-1}{3}\right)^{|k|}, \omega_o = 1$$

then corresponding time domain signal will be

(*a*) $\frac{4}{5+3\sin t}$ (*b*) $\frac{5}{4+3\sin t}$

(*c*) $\frac{5}{4+3\cos t}$ (*d*) $\frac{4}{5+3\cos t}$

Common data Q. 92-93:

Consider a continuous time periodic signal x(t) with fundamental period T and Fourier series coefficients X[k]. Determine the Fourier series coefficient of the signal y(t).

92. $y(t) = x(t - t_o) + x(t - to)$

(*a*) $2\cos\left(\frac{2\pi}{T}kt_o\right)X[k]$

(*b*) $2\sin\left(\frac{2\pi}{T}kt_o\right)X[k]$

(*c*) $e^{-t_o}X[k] + e^{t_o}X[-k]$

(*d*) $e^{-t_o}X[-k] + e^{t_o}X[k]$

93. $y(t) = \text{Ev}\{x(t)\}$

(*a*) $\frac{X[k]+X[-k]}{2}$ (*b*) $\frac{X[k]-X[-k]}{2}$

(*c*) $\frac{X[k]+X^*[-k]}{2}$ (*d*) $\frac{X[k]+X^*[-k]}{2}$

Common data Q. 94-95:

Consider three continuous-time periodic signals whose Fourier series representation are as follows.

$$x_1(t) = \sum_{k=0}^{100}\left(\frac{1}{3}\right)^k e^{-jk\frac{2\pi}{50}t}$$

$$x_2(t) = \sum_{k=-100}^{100}\cos k\pi e^{-jk\frac{2\pi}{50}t}$$

$$x_3(t) = \sum_{k=-100}^{100} j\sin\left(\frac{k\pi}{2}\right)e^{-jk\frac{2\pi}{50}t}$$

94. The even signals are

(*a*) $x_2(t)$ only (*b*) $x_2(t)$ and $x_3(t)$

(*c*) $x_1(t)$ and $x_3(t)$ (*d*) $x_1(t)$ only

95. The real valued signals are

(*a*) $x_1(t)$ and $x_2(t)$ (*b*) $x_2(t)$ and $x_3(t)$

(*c*) $x_3(t)$ and $x_1(t)$ (*d*) $x_1(t)$ and $x_3(t)$

96. Consider a continuous-time ideal low pass filter having the frequency response

$$H(j\omega) = \begin{cases} 1, |\omega| \le 80 \\ 0, |\omega| > 80 \end{cases}$$

When the input to this filter is a signal x(t) with fundamental frequency $\omega_o = 12$ and Fourier series coefficients X[*k*], it is found that $x(t) \overset{s}{\longleftrightarrow} y(t) = x(t)$

The largest value of $|k|$, for which X[*k*] is nonzero, is

(*a*) 6 (*b*) 80

(*c*) 7 (*d*) 12

97. Find the fourier transform of

$$x(t) = \frac{20}{1+(2\pi t)^2}$$

(*a*) $x(f) = 10e^{-|f|}$

(*b*) $x(f) = 10e^{-2|f|}$

(*c*) $x(f) = 10e^{2|f|}$

(*d*) None of these

98. For the waveform for one period shown in the figure below, the trigonometric Fourier series will be

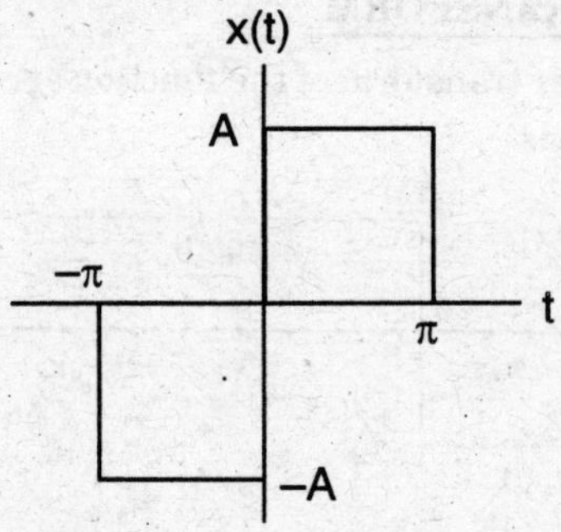

(*a*) $\frac{A}{2} + \frac{4A}{\pi}(\sin t + \frac{1}{2}\sin 2t + \frac{1}{3}\sin 3t + ...)$

(*b*) $\frac{A}{2} + \frac{4A}{\pi}(\cos t + \frac{1}{3}\cos 3t + \frac{1}{5}\cos 5t + ...)$

(*c*) $\frac{4A}{\pi}(\sin t + \frac{1}{3}\sin 3t + \frac{1}{5}\sin 5t + ...)$

(*d*) $\frac{4A}{\pi}(\cos t + \frac{1}{2}\cos 2t + \frac{1}{3}\cos 3t + ...)$

99. For the waveform for one period shown in the figure below, the trigonometric fourer series will be

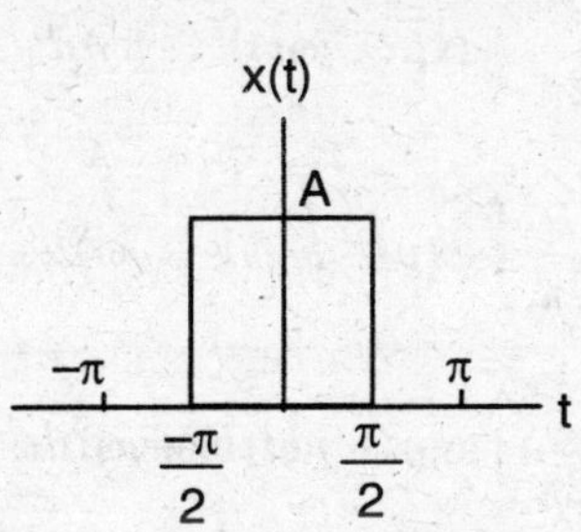

(*a*) $\frac{A}{2} + \frac{2A}{\pi}(\sin t - \frac{1}{3}\sin 3t + \frac{1}{5}\sin 5t .....)$

(*b*) $\frac{A}{2} + \frac{2A}{\pi}(\cos t - \frac{1}{2}\cos 2t + \frac{1}{3}\cos 3t ......)$

(*c*) $\frac{A}{2} + \frac{2A}{\pi}(\cos t - \frac{1}{3}\cos 3t + \frac{1}{5}\cos 5t .....)$

(*d*) $\frac{A}{2} + \frac{2A}{\pi}(\sin t + \cos t + \frac{1}{3}\sin 3t + \frac{1}{3}\cos 3t ...)$

DISCRETE-TIME FOURIER SERIES

100. The determine-time Fourier-coefficients X[*k*] for

$$x[n] = 2\sin\left(\frac{4\pi}{19}n\right) + \cos\left(\frac{4\pi}{19}n\right) + 1 \text{ will be}$$

(*a*) $-j\delta[k+2] + j\delta[k-2] + \frac{1}{2}\delta[k+5] + \frac{1}{2}\delta[k-5] + \delta[k]$

(*b*) $-j\delta[k+2] + j\delta[k-2] + \frac{1}{2}\delta[k+5] + \frac{1}{2}\delta[k-5] + 1$

(*c*) $-j\delta[k-2] + j\delta[k+2] + \frac{1}{2}\delta[k-5] + \frac{1}{2}\delta[k+5] + \delta[k]$

(*d*) None of these

101. The determine-time Fourier-coefficients X[*k*] for

$$x[n] = \sum_{m=-\infty}^{\infty} (-1)^m (\delta[n-2m] + \delta[n+3m])$$

will be

(*a*) $\frac{1}{3}(\delta[k-6] + \delta[k-4] + \delta[k+6] + \delta[k+4])$

(*b*) $\frac{1}{3}(\delta[k-6] + \delta[k-4] - \delta[k+6] - \delta[k+4])$

(*c*) $\frac{1}{6}\left(\cos\left(\frac{2\pi k}{3}\right) - \cos\left(\frac{\pi k}{2}\right) - \cos\left(\frac{\pi k}{3}\right) + 1\right)$

(*d*) $\frac{1}{6}\left(\sin\left(\frac{2\pi k}{3}\right) - \sin\left(\frac{\pi k}{2}\right) - \sin\left(\frac{\pi k}{3}\right) + 1\right)$

102. $X[k]$ is shown in the figure below

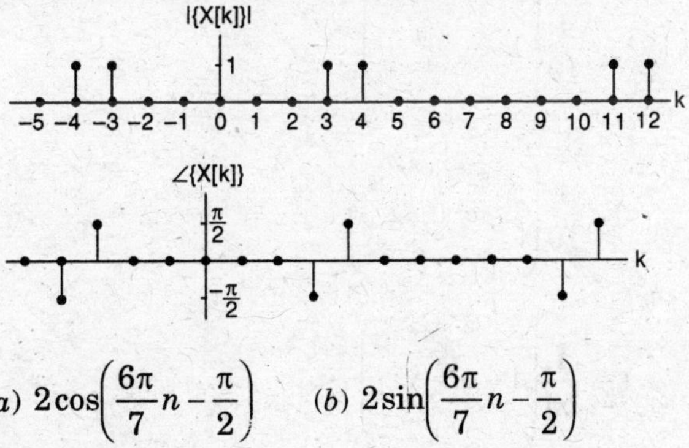

(*a*) $2\cos\left(\frac{6\pi}{7}n - \frac{\pi}{2}\right)$ (*b*) $2\sin\left(\frac{6\pi}{7}n - \frac{\pi}{2}\right)$

(*c*) $2\cos\left(\frac{6\pi}{7}n + \frac{\pi}{2}\right)$ (*d*) $2\sin\left(\frac{6\pi}{7}n + \frac{\pi}{2}\right)$

Common data Q. 103-104:

Given a periodic signal x[n] with period N and Fourier Series coefficients X[k].

103. the Fourier Series coefficients Y[k] of the signal $y[n] = x[n - n_o]$ will be

(a) $e^{j\left(\frac{2\pi}{N}\right)n_o k} X[k]$ (b) $e^{-j\left(\frac{2\pi}{N}\right)n_o k} X[k]$

(c) $kX[k]$ (d) $-kX[k]$

104. the Fourier Series coefficients Y[k] of the signal $y[n] = x[n] - x[n-2]$ will be

(a) $\sin\left(\frac{4\pi}{N}k\right)X[k]$

(b) $\cos\left(\frac{4\pi}{N}k\right)X[k]$

(c) $\left(1 - e^{-j\left(\frac{4\pi}{N}\right)k}\right)X[k]$

(d) $\left(1 - e^{j\left(\frac{4\pi}{N}\right)k}\right)X[k]$

Common data Q. 105-106:

Given a discrete-time periodic signal

$$x[n] = \begin{cases} 1, & 0 \le n \le 7 \\ 0, & 8 \le n \le 9 \end{cases}$$

with period N = 10. Also $y[n] = x[n] - x[n-1]$

105. The fundamental period of $y[n]$ are

(a) 9 (b) 10

(c) 11 (d) none of these

106. The Fourier Series coefficients of $y[n]$ are

(a) $\frac{1}{10}\left(1 - e^{j\left(\frac{8\pi}{5}\right)k}\right)$

(b) $\frac{1}{10}\left(1 - e^{-j\left(\frac{8\pi}{5}\right)k}\right)$

(c) $\frac{1}{10}\left(1 - e^{j\left(\frac{4\pi}{5}\right)k}\right)$

(d) $\frac{1}{10}\left(1 - e^{-j\left(\frac{4\pi}{5}\right)k}\right)$

107. Each of two sequence $x[n]$ and $y[n]$ has a period N = 4. The Fourier Series coefficient are

$$X[0] = X[3] = \frac{1}{2}X[1] = \frac{1}{2}X[2] = 1$$

and $Y[0], Y[1], Y[2], Y[3] = 1$

The Fourier Series coefficient Z[k] for the signal $z[n] = x[n]y[n]$ will be

(a) 6 (b) $6|k|$

(c) $6^{|k|}$ (d) $e^{j\frac{\pi}{2}k}$

FOURIER TRANSFORM

108. The fourier transform of the function sgn(t) defined in the figure is

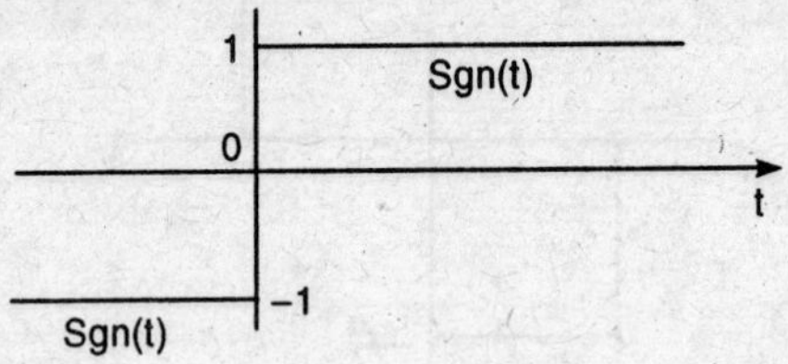

(a) $\frac{-2}{j\omega}$ (b) $\frac{4}{j\omega}$

(c) $\frac{2}{j\omega}$ (d) $\frac{1}{j\omega} + 1$

109. The inverse transform of

$$F(j\omega) = \int_{-\infty}^{\infty} \exp(-j\omega t) f(t)\, dt \text{ is}$$

(a) $f(t) = \int_{-\infty}^{\infty} \exp(+j\omega t) f(j\omega)\, d\omega$

(b) $f(t) = \frac{1}{2\pi}\int_{-\infty}^{\infty} \exp(+j\omega t) F(+j\omega)\, d\omega$

(c) $f(t) = \frac{1}{2\pi}\int_{-\infty}^{\infty} \exp(-j\omega t) F(+j\omega)\, d\omega$

(d) $f(t) = \frac{1}{2\pi}\int_{-\infty}^{\infty} \exp(-j\omega t) F(+j\omega)\, d\omega$

110. Which one of the following is the Fourier transform of the signal given in Fig. II, if the Fourier transform of the signal in Fig. I is given by $2\frac{\sin \omega T_1}{\omega}$?

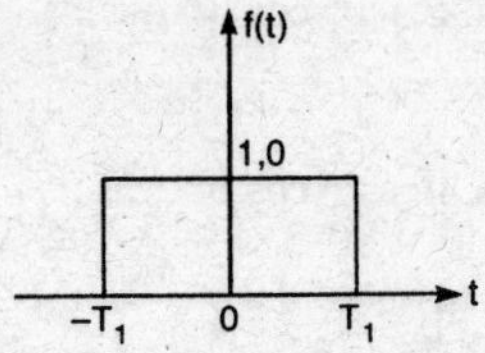

Fig. I

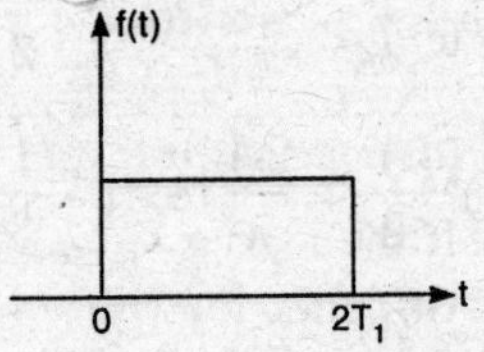

Fig. II

(a) $2\dfrac{\sin\omega T_1}{\omega}e^{+j\omega T_1}$ (b) $2\dfrac{\sin\omega T_1}{\omega}e^{-j\omega T_1}$

(c) $\dfrac{\sin\omega T_1}{\omega}e^{-j\omega T_1}$ (d) $\dfrac{\sin\omega T_1}{\omega}e^{+j\omega(T_1-2)}$

111. The two inputs to an analogue multiplier are $x(t)$ and $y(t)$ with Fourier transform $X(f)$ and $Y(f)$ respectively. The output $z(t)$ will have a transform $Z(f)$ given by

(a) $X(f).Y(f)$ (b) $X(f)+Y(f)$

(c) $X(f)/Yf$ (d) $\int_{\infty}^{\infty} X(\lambda)Y(f-\lambda)d\lambda$

112. Fourier transform of the unit step signal

$$u(t) = 1 \text{ for } t > 0$$
$$= 0 \text{ for } t < 0$$

is

(a) $\pi\delta(\omega)$ (b) $\dfrac{1}{j\omega}$

(c) $\dfrac{1}{j\omega}+\pi\delta(\omega)$ (d) $\dfrac{1}{j\omega}+2\pi\delta(\omega)$

113. Fourier transform of $v(t)\cos\omega_0 t$ is

(a) $V(f)=\dfrac{1}{2}\delta(f-f_0)$

(b) $V(f)=\dfrac{1}{2}\delta(f+f_0)$

(c) $V(f)=\dfrac{1}{2}[\delta(f-f_0)-\delta(f+f_0)]$

(d) $V(f)=\dfrac{1}{2}[\delta(f-f_0)+\delta(f+f_0)]$

114. The Fourier transform of a unit step fnction is given by

(a) $F(j\omega)=\dfrac{j}{\omega}$ (b) $F(j\omega)=j\omega$

(c) $F(j\omega)=\dfrac{1}{j\omega}$ (d) $F(j\omega)=\dfrac{1}{\omega}$

115. Fourier transform of a function $f(at)$ is given by

(a) $f(at) = a\,F(\omega)$

(b) $f(at) = \dfrac{2}{a}F(\omega)$

(c) $f(at) = \dfrac{1}{a}F\left(\dfrac{\omega}{a}\right)$

(d) none of these

116. If the fourier transform of deterministic signal $g(t)$ is $G(f)$, then the Fourier transform of $g(t-2)$ is

(a) $G(f)e^{-j4\pi f}$ (b) $G(2f)$

(c) $2G(2f)$ (d) $G(f-2)$

117. The transform of $f_1(t)=e^{-t}u(t)$ is $\dfrac{1}{(1+j\omega)}$. Then the transform of $f(t)=f_1(t)-f_1(-t)$ is

(a) $\dfrac{1}{1+\omega^2}$ (b) $\dfrac{2}{1+\omega^2}$

(c) $\dfrac{j\omega}{1+\omega^2}$ (d) $\dfrac{-2j\omega}{1+\omega^2}$

118. Given the transform pair $f_1(t)\to F_1(\omega)$ $f_1(t)e^{j\omega_0 t}\to F_1(\omega-\omega_0)$.

Given $F_1(\omega)=\dfrac{2}{1+\omega^2}$. The Fourier transform of $f_1(t)$ e^{-jat} is

(a) $\dfrac{2}{1+a^2}$ (b) $\dfrac{2}{1-a^2}$

(c) $\dfrac{2}{1+(\omega+a)^2}$ (d) $\dfrac{2}{1+(\omega-a)^2}$

119. In Figs. I and II shown below, the exponentitals decay as e^{-t}. Fourier transform of $f(t)$ in Fig. I is $F(\omega)$. The Fourier transform of the function in Fig. II will be

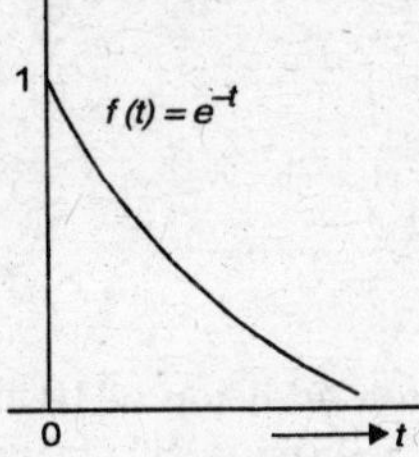

Fig. I

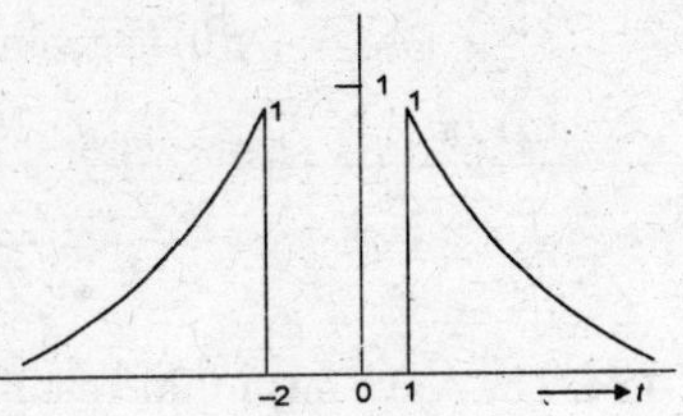

Fig. II

(a) $F(\omega)e^{-j\omega}+F(\omega)e^{2j\omega}$

(b) $F(\omega)e^{-j\omega}+F(-\omega)e^{2j\omega}$

(c) $F(\omega)e^{j\omega}+F(-\omega)e^{-2j\omega}$

(d) $F(\omega)e^{-j\omega}+F(-\omega)e^{-2j\omega}$

120. $f(t)$ is a pulse defined as

$$f(t) = 1 \text{ for } 0 < 1$$
$$= 0 \text{ otherwise.}$$

The even part of $f(t)$ is

(a) $\dfrac{1}{2}$ for $0<t<1$ and zero otherwise

(b) 1 for $-1<t<1$ and zero otherwise

(c) $\dfrac{1}{2}$ for $-1<t<1$ and zero otherwise

(d) 1 for $-\dfrac{1}{2}<t<\dfrac{1}{2}$ and zero otherwise

121. Fig. I shows $f_1(t)$ whose transform is $F_1(\omega)$. $f_2(t)$ of Fig. II has a transform (expressed in terms of $F_1(\omega)$) given by

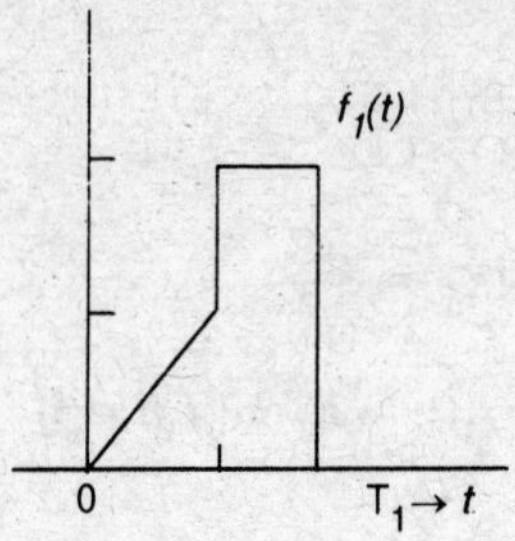

Fig. I

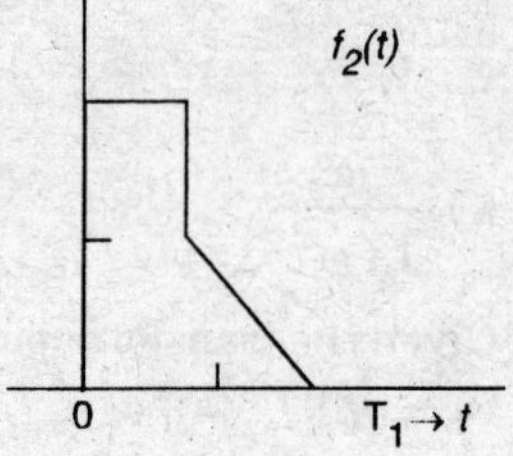

Fig. II

(a) $F_1(\omega)\, e^{j\omega T_1}$ (b) $F_1(\omega)\, e^{-j\omega T_1}$

(c) $F_1(-\omega)\, e^{-j\omega T_1}$ (d) $F_1(-\omega)\, e^{j\omega T_1}$

122. Fourier transform of $u_0(T_1 - t) + u_0(T_1 + t)$ is

(a) $\cos \omega T_1$ (b) $2 \cos \omega T_1$

(c) $2 \sin \omega T_1$ (d) $2j \sin \omega T_1$

123. $F(\omega)$ is defined as

$F(\omega) = 2$ for $0 < \omega < 2\pi$

$= 0$, otherwise. The value of $f(t)$ at $t = 0$, i.e. $f(0)$ is given by

(a) 2π (b) 4π

(c) 2 (d) $\frac{1}{2}$

124. The wave form that results from addition of $10 \sin\omega t$, $5 \sin 2\omega t$, $3.33 \sin 3\omega t$, $2.5 \sin 4\omega t$, $2 \sin 5\omega t$, $1.66 \sin 6\omega t$, $1.43 \sin 7\omega t$, $1.25 \sin 8\omega t$ and $1.11 \sin 9\omega t$ is

(a) a saw tooth waveform of a radian frequency (ω) having a finite average value.

(b) a saw tooth waveform of radian frequency (ω) with zero average value.

(c) a square waveform of radian frequency (ω)

(d) a complex waveform

125. Fourier trans form of the signal $x(t) = e^{-2t}\, u(t - 3)$ is

(a) $\dfrac{e^{-3(2-j\omega)}}{2-j\omega}$ (b) $\dfrac{e^{-3(2+j\omega)}}{2+j\omega}$

(c) $\dfrac{e^{3(2-j\omega)}}{2-j\omega}$ (d) $\dfrac{e^{3(2+j\omega)}}{2+j\omega}$

126. Fourier trans form of the signal $x(t) = e^{-4|t|}$ is

(a) $\dfrac{8}{16+\omega^2}$ (b) $\dfrac{-8}{16+\omega^2}$

(c) $\dfrac{4}{16+\omega^2}$ (d) $\dfrac{-4}{16+\omega^2}$

127. Fourier transform of the signal

$x(t) = \sin 2\pi t\, e^{-t} u(t)$ is

(a) $\dfrac{1}{2}\left[\dfrac{1}{1+j(\omega-2\pi)} - \dfrac{1}{1+j(\omega+2\pi)}\right]$

(b) $\dfrac{1}{2j}\left[\dfrac{1}{1+j(\omega-2\pi)} - \dfrac{1}{1+j(\omega+2\pi)}\right]$

(c) $\dfrac{1}{2j}\left[\dfrac{1}{1+j(\omega+2\pi)} - \dfrac{1}{1+j(\omega-2\pi)}\right]$

(d) $\dfrac{1}{2}\left[\dfrac{1}{1+j(\omega+2\pi)} - \dfrac{1}{1+j(\omega-2\pi)}\right]$

128. A Fourier transform pairs is as follows

$$x(t) \xleftrightarrow{F} X(j\omega) = \frac{2\sin\omega}{\omega}$$

where, $x(t) = \begin{cases} 1, & |t| < 1 \\ 0, & \text{otherwise} \end{cases}$

Determine the Fourier transform of the signal $y(t)$ shown in figure below

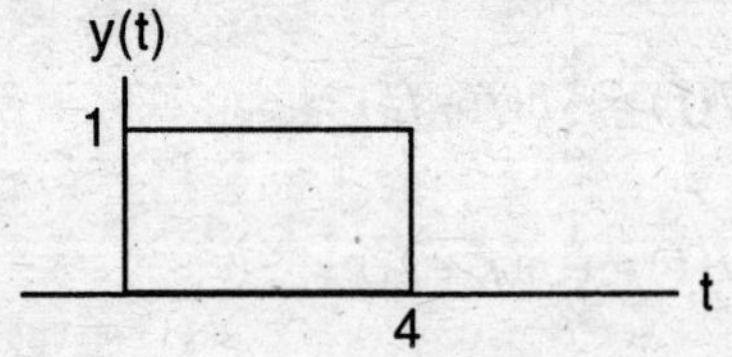

(a) $\dfrac{e^{j2\omega}\sin 2\omega}{2\omega}$ (b) $\dfrac{e^{-j2\omega}\sin 2\omega}{\omega}$

(c) $\dfrac{4e^{-j2\omega}\sin\frac{\omega}{2}}{\omega}$ (d) $\dfrac{4e^{j2\omega}\sin\frac{\omega}{2}}{\omega}$

Common data Q.129-130:

Consider the signal $X(j\omega)$ shown in figure, whose inverse Fourier transform is $x(t)$.

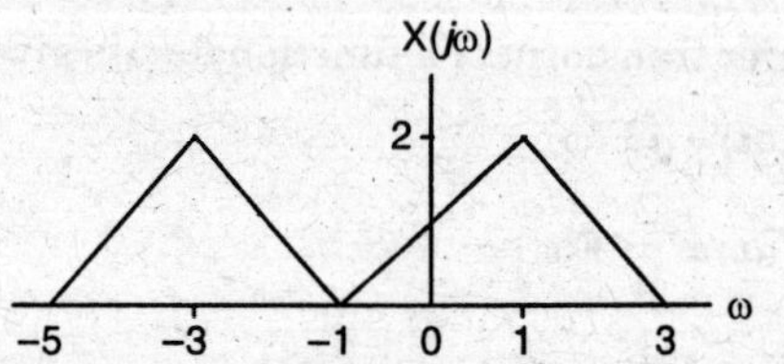

129. $\displaystyle\int_{-\infty}^{\infty} x(t)\, dt$ will be equal to

(a) 1 (b) 2π

(c) $\dfrac{1}{2\pi}$ (d) ∞

130. $\int_{-\infty}^{\infty} |x(t)|^2 \, dt$ will be equal to

(a) $\frac{16}{3}$ (b) $\frac{32}{3}$

(c) $\frac{16}{3\pi}$ (d) None of these

Common data Q.131-132:

The frequency response H(jω) of a continuous-time filter is shown in the figure below.

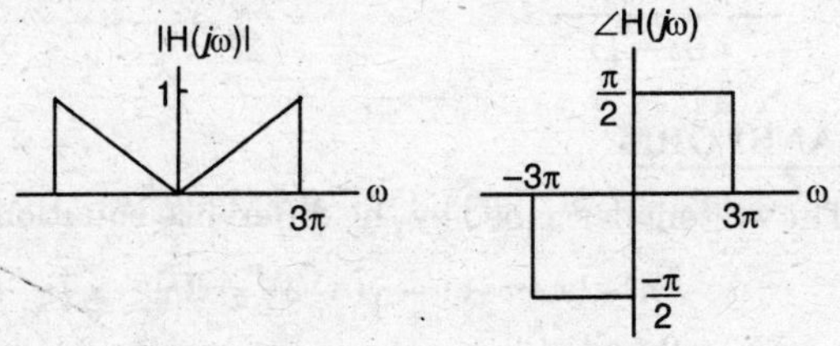

131. If the input to this system is $x(t) = \cos(2\pi t + \theta)$, then output will be

(a) $-\frac{2}{3}\sin(2\pi t + \theta)$ (b) $\frac{2}{3\pi}\sin(2\pi t + \theta)$

(c) $\frac{2\pi}{3}\sin(2\pi t + \theta)$ (d) None of these

132. If the input to this system is

$x(t) = \cos(4\pi t + \theta)$, then output will be

(a) $-\frac{4}{3}\cos(4\pi t + \theta)$ (b) $\frac{4\pi}{3}\cos(4\pi t + \theta)$

(c) $\frac{4}{3\pi}\cos(4\pi t + \theta)$ (d) 0

133. Consider a causal LTI system with frequency response

$$H(j\omega) = \frac{1}{j\omega + 3}$$

This system produces the output to input $x(t)$ as follows

$y(t) = e^{-2t}u(t) - e^{-4t}u(t)$

The input x(t) is

(a) $(2e^{-4t} - 3e^{-3t})u(t)$ (b) $e^{-4t}u(t)$

(c) $(3e^{-4t} - 2e^{-3t})u(t)$ (d) $-e^{-4t}u(t)$

134. A real and non-negative signal $x(t)$ has Fourier transform $X(j\omega)$. The following facts are given

1. $F^{-1}\{(1 + j\omega)X(j\omega)\} = Ae^{-2t}u(t)$, where A is constant

2. $\int_{\pm\infty}^{\infty} |X(j\omega)|^2 \, d\omega = 2p$

The signal $x(t)$ may be

(a) $\sqrt{12}(e^{-2t} - e^{-t})u(t)$ (b) $\sqrt{12}(e^{-t} - e^{-2t})u(t)$

(c) $\sqrt{3}(e^{-2t} - e^{-t})u(t)$ (d) $\sqrt{3}(e^{-t} - e^{-2t})u(t)$

135. Consider a continuous-time signal $x(t)$ whose magnitude and phase spectra are as follows:

$$|X(j\omega)| = 2\{u(\omega + 3) - u(\omega - 3)\},$$

$$\angle X(j\omega) = \frac{-3\omega}{2} + \pi$$

The value of t, for which $x(t) = 0$, is

(a) $\frac{k\pi}{3} + \frac{3}{2}$, for $k = 0, 1, 2, 3, ...$

(b) $\frac{k\pi}{3} + \frac{3}{2}$, for $k = 1, 2, 3, ...$

(c) $\frac{k\pi}{3} + \frac{2}{3}$, for $k = 0, 1, 2, 3, ...$

(d) $\frac{k\pi}{3} + \frac{2}{3}$, for $k = 1, 2, 3, ...$

136. The frequency response of a causal and stable LTI system is

$$H(j\omega) = \frac{1 - j\omega}{1 + j\omega}$$

The group delay of the system is

(a) $\frac{2}{1+\omega^2}$ (b) $\frac{-2}{1+\omega^2}$

(c) $2\tan^{-1}\omega$ (d) $-2\tan^{-1}\omega$

137. Determine-time Fourier Transform for the signal

$x[n] = \{-2, -1, 0, 1, 2\}$

will be

(a) $2j(2\sin 2\Omega + \sin \Omega)$ (b) $2(2\cos 2\Omega - \cos \Omega)$

(c) $-2j(2\sin 2\Omega - \sin \Omega)$ (d) $-2(2\cos 2\Omega - \cos \Omega)$

138. Determine-time Fourier Transform for the signal

$$x[n] = \sin\left(\frac{\pi}{2}n\right)$$

will be

(a) $\pi(\delta[\Omega - \pi/2] - \delta[\Omega + \pi/2])$

(b) $\frac{j}{2}(\delta[\Omega + \pi/2] - \delta[\Omega - \pi/2])$

(c) $2\pi(\delta[\Omega - \pi/2] - \delta[\Omega + \pi/2])$

(d) $j\pi(\delta[\Omega + \pi/2] - \delta[\Omega - \pi/2])$

139. The signal having the Fourier transform

$$X(e^{j\Omega}) = \begin{cases} 1, & \frac{\pi}{4} \le |\Omega| < \frac{3\pi}{4} \\ 0, & 0 \le |\Omega| < \frac{\pi}{4}, \frac{3\pi}{4} \le |\Omega| \le \pi \end{cases}$$

will be

(a) $\frac{2}{n}\left(\sin\left(\frac{2\pi n}{4}\right)-\sin\left(\frac{\pi n}{4}\right)\right)$

(b) $\frac{1}{\pi n}\left(\sin\left(\frac{3\pi n}{4}\right)-\sin\left(\frac{\pi n}{4}\right)\right)$

(c) $\frac{2}{n}\left(\cos\left(\frac{3\pi n}{4}\right)+\cos\left(\frac{\pi n}{4}\right)\right)$

(d) $\frac{1}{\pi n}\left(\cos\left(\frac{3\pi n}{4}\right)+\cos\left(\frac{\pi n}{4}\right)\right)$

140. The signal having the Fourier transform

$$X\left(e^{j\Omega}\right)=\frac{1-\frac{1}{3}e^{-j\Omega}}{1-\frac{1}{4}e^{-j\Omega}-\frac{1}{8}e^{-2j\Omega}}$$

will be

(a) $\left(\frac{2}{9}\left(\frac{1}{2}\right)^n+\frac{7}{9}\left(-\frac{1}{4}\right)^n\right)u[n]$

(b) $\left(\frac{2}{9}\left(-\frac{1}{2}\right)^n+\frac{7}{9}\left(\frac{1}{4}\right)^n\right)u[n]$

(c) $\left(\frac{2}{9}\left(-\frac{1}{2}\right)^n-\frac{7}{9}\left(\frac{1}{4}\right)^n\right)u[n]$

(d) $\left(\frac{2}{9}\left(\frac{1}{2}\right)^n-\frac{7}{9}\left(-\frac{1}{4}\right)^n\right)u[n]$

141. A real signal $x[n]$ with Fourier transform $X(e^{j\Omega})$ has following property

1. $x[n]=0$ for $n>0$
2. $x[0]>0$
3. Im $\{X(e^{j\Omega})=\sin\Omega-\sin 2\Omega\}$
4. $\frac{1}{2}\int_{-p}^{\pi}|X(e^{j\Omega})|^2\,d\Omega=3$

The signal x(n) is

(a) $2\delta[n]-\delta[n+1]-\delta[n+3]$

(b) $\delta[n]+\delta[n+1]-\delta[n+3]$

(c) $\delta[n]+\delta[n+1)-\delta[n+2]$

(d) $2\delta[n]-\delta[n+1]-\delta[n+2]$

142. A discrete-time system with input $x[n]$ and output y[n] is described by the relation

$$Y(e^{j\Omega})=e^{-j\Omega}X(e^{j\Omega})+\frac{dX(e^{j\Omega})}{d\Omega}$$

The response of the system to the input $x[n]=\delta[n]$ is

(a) $\frac{\sin\pi(n-1)}{\pi(n-1)}$

(b) $\frac{j\sin\pi(n-1)}{\pi(n-1)}$

(c) $\frac{2\pi\sin\pi(n-1)}{\pi(n-1)}$

(d) $\frac{2\sin\pi(n-1)}{\pi(n-1)}$

Z-TRANSFORM

143. The system described by the difference equation

$y(n)-2y(n-1)+y(n-2)=x(n)-x(n-1)$ has $y(n)=0$ and $n<0$.

If $x(n)=\delta(n)$, then $y(2)$ will be

(a) 2 (b) 1

(c) zero (d) –1

144. Given that F(z) and G(z) are the one-sided Z transforms of discrete time functions $f(nT)$ and $g(nT)$, the Z transform of $\Sigma f(kT)g(nT-kT)$ is given by

(a) $\Sigma f(nT)g(nT)z^{-n}$

(b) $\Sigma f(nT)z^{n}\Sigma g(nT)z^{-n}$

(c) $\Sigma f(kT)g(nT-kT)z^{-n}$

(d) $\Sigma f(nT-kT)g(nT)z^{-n}$

145. Consider the following statements regarding a linear discrete-time system

$$H(z)=\frac{z^2+1}{(z+0.5)(z-0.5)}$$

1. The system is stable.
2. The initial value $h(0)$ of the impulse response is – 4.
3. The steady-state output is zero for a sinusoidal discrete-time input of frequency equal to one-fourth the sampling frequency?

Which of these statements are correct ?

(a) 1, 2 and 3

(b) 1 and 2

(c) 1 and 3

(d) 2 and 3

146. Which one of the following is the correct state-space realization of a discrete system given by the difference equation

$c(k + 2) + \alpha\, c(k + 1) + \beta\, c(k) = u(k)$?

(a) 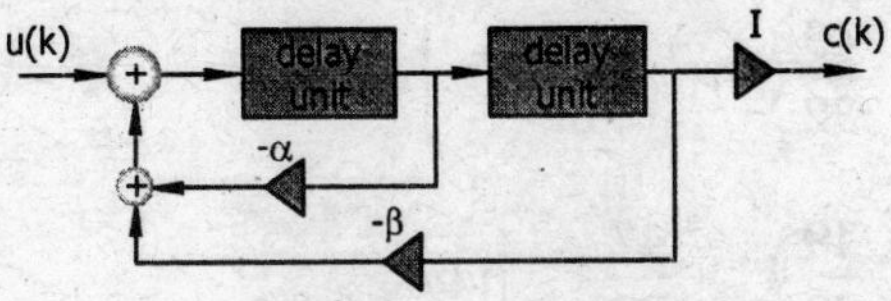

(b) 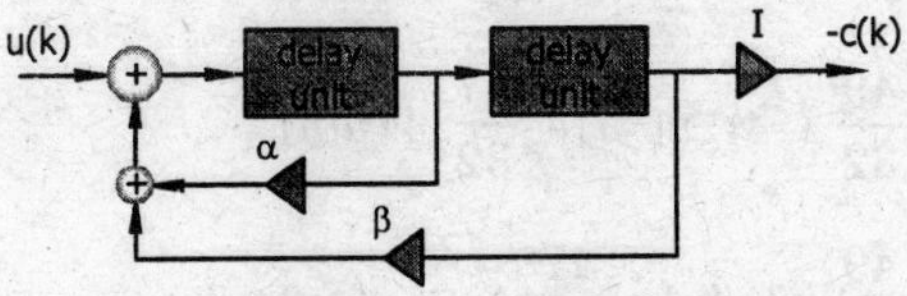

(c) 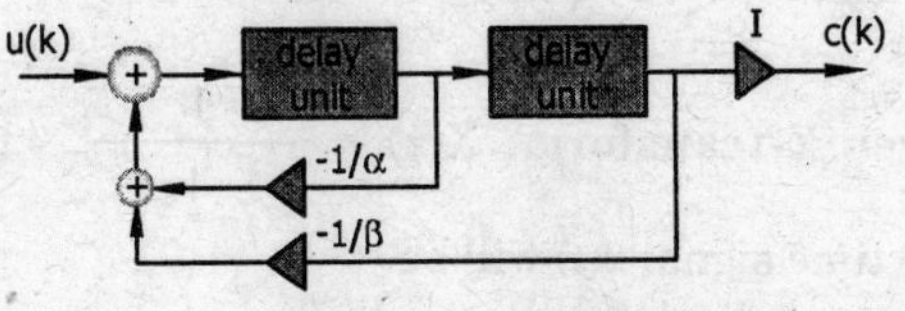

(d) 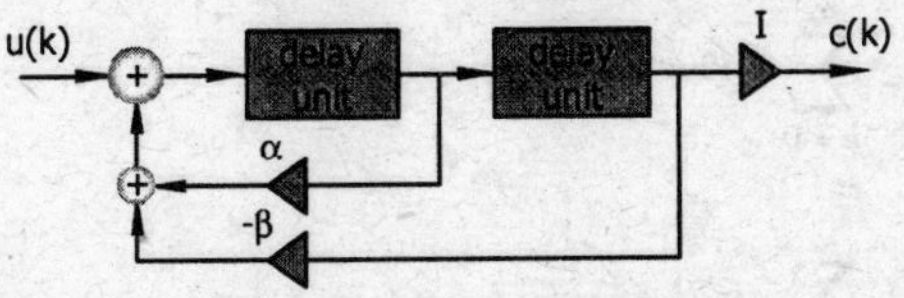

147. Consider the compound system shown in the above figure. Its output is equal to input with a delay of two units. If the transfer function of the first system is given by $H_1(z) = \dfrac{z - 0.5}{z - 0.8}$, then the transfer function of the second system would be

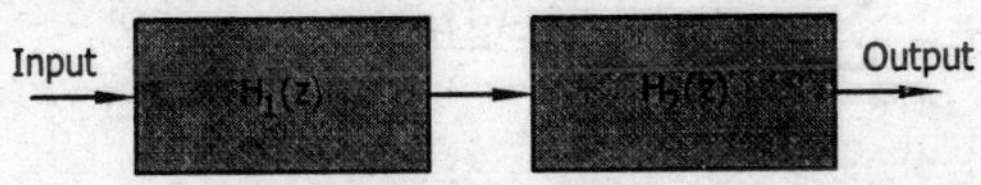

(a) $H_2(z) = \dfrac{z^2 - 0.2z^{-3}}{1 - 0.4z^{-1}}$

(b) $H_2(z) = \dfrac{z^{-2} - 0.8z^{-3}}{1 - 0.5z^{-1}}$

(c) $H_2(z) = \dfrac{z^{-1} - 0.2z^{-3}}{1 - 0.4z^{-1}}$

(d) $H_2(z) = \dfrac{z^{-2} - 0.8z^{-3}}{1 + 0.5z^{-1}}$

148. The Z-transform of the time function $\sum_{k=0}^{\infty} \delta(n - k)$ is

(a) $\dfrac{z-1}{z}$ (b) $\dfrac{z}{(z-1)^2}$

(c) $\dfrac{z}{z-1}$ (d) $\dfrac{(z-1)^2}{z}$

149. The Z-transform F(z) of $f(nT) = a^{nT}$ is

(a) $\dfrac{z}{z - a^{T}}$ (b) $\dfrac{z}{z + a^{T}}$

(c) $\dfrac{z}{z - a^{-T}}$ (d) $\dfrac{z}{z + a^{-T}}$

150. The region of convergence of the Z-transform of a unit step function is

(a) $|z| > 1$

(b) $|z| < 1$

(c) (Real part of z) > 0

(d) (Real part of z) < 0

151. If $\delta(t)$ denote the delta function, then value of the integral

$\int_{-\infty}^{\infty} \delta(t) \cos\left(\frac{3t}{2}\right) dt$ will be

(a) 1 (b) –1

(c) 0 (d) $\dfrac{\pi}{2}$

152. The Z-transform of

$x[n] = \left(\frac{1}{4}\right)^n (u[n] - u[n-5])$

will be

(a) $\dfrac{z^5 - 0.25^5}{z^4(z - 0.25)}, z > 0.25$

(b) $\dfrac{z^5 - 0.25^5}{z^4(z - 0.25)}, z > 0$

(c) $\dfrac{z^5 - 0.25^5}{z^3(z - 0.25)}, z < 0.25$

(d) $\dfrac{z^5 - 0.25^5}{z^4(z - 0.25)}$, all z

153. The Z-transform of $x[n] = \left(\frac{2}{3}\right)^{|n|}$ will be

(a) $\dfrac{-5z}{(2z-3)(3z-2)}, -\dfrac{3}{2} < z < -\dfrac{2}{3}$

(b) $\dfrac{-5z}{(2z-3)(3z-2)}, \dfrac{2}{3} < |z| < \dfrac{3}{2}$

(c) $\dfrac{5z}{(2z-3)(3z-2)}, \dfrac{2}{3} < |z| < \dfrac{3}{2}$

(d) $\dfrac{5z}{(2z-3)(3z-2)}, -\dfrac{3}{2} < z < -\dfrac{2}{3}$

154. Z-transform of $x[n] = \cos\left(\frac{\pi}{3}n\right) u[n]$ will be

(a) $\frac{z}{2} \cdot \frac{(2z-1)}{(z^2 - z + 2)}$, $0 < |z| < 1$

(b) $\frac{z}{2} \cdot \frac{(2z-1)}{(z^2 - z + 2)}$, $|z| > 1$

(c) $\frac{z}{2} \cdot \frac{(1-2z)}{(z^2 - z + 2)}$, $0 < |z| < 1$

(d) $\frac{z}{2} \cdot \frac{(1-2z)}{(z^2 - z + 2)}$, $|z| > 1$

Common data Q. 155-156:

Given the Z-transform pair

$$3n\, n^2\, u[n] \xleftrightarrow{Z} X(z)$$

155. The time signal $y(t)$ for corresponding Z-transform $Y(z) = X(2z)$ will be

(a) $n^2 3^n\, u(2n)$

(b) $\left(-\frac{3}{2}\right)^n n^2\, u[n]$

(c) $\left(\frac{3}{2}\right)^n n^2\, u[n]$

(d) $6^n\, n^2\, u[n]$

156. The time signal $y(t)$ for corresponding Z-transform $Y(z) = X(z^{-1})$

(a) $n^2\, 3^{-n}\, u[-n]$ (b) $n^2\, 3^{-n}\, u[-n]$

(c) $\frac{1}{n^2}\, 3^{\frac{1}{n}}\, u[n]$ (d) $\frac{1}{n^2}\, 3^{\frac{1}{n}}\, u[-n]$

157. Given Z-transform,

$$X(z) = \frac{z^2 - 3z}{z^2 + \frac{3}{2}z^{-1}}, \ \frac{1}{2} < |z| < 2$$

The time signal $x(t)$ will be

(a) $-\frac{1}{2^n}\, u[n] - 2^{n+1}\, u[-n-1]$

(b) $-\frac{1}{2^n} u[n] - 2^{n+1}\, u[n+1]$

(c) $\frac{1}{2^n}\, u[n] + 2^{n+1}\, u[n+1]$

(d) $\frac{1}{2^n}\, u[n] - 2^{-n-1}\, u[-n-1]$

158. Given Z-transform, $X(z) = \dfrac{3z^2 - \frac{1}{4}z}{z^2 - 16}$, $|z| > 4$ The time signal $x(t)$ will be

(a) $\left[\frac{49}{32}(-4)^n + \frac{47}{32}4^n\right] u[n]$

(b) $\left[\frac{49}{32}4^n + \frac{47}{32}4^n\right] u[n]$

(c) $\frac{49}{32}\, (-4)^n\, u[-n] + \frac{47}{32}\, 4^n\, u[n]$

(d) $\frac{49}{32}\, 4^n\, u[n] + \frac{47}{32}\, (-4)^n\, u[-n]$

159. Given Z-transform, $X(z) = \dfrac{1}{1 - 4z^{-2}}$, $|z| < \dfrac{1}{4}$

The time signal $x(t)$ will be

(a) $-\sum_{k=0}^{\infty} 2^{2(k+1)}\, \delta[-n - 2(k+1)]$

(b) $-\sum_{k=0}^{\infty} 2^{2(k+1)}\, \delta[-n + 2(k+1)]$

(c) $-\sum_{k=0}^{\infty} 2^{2(k+1)}\, \delta[n + 2(k+1)]$

(d) $-\sum_{k=0}^{\infty} 2^{2(k+1)}\, \delta[n - 2(k+1)]$

160. Given $X(z) = \dfrac{1 + \frac{7}{6}z^{-1}}{\left(1 - \frac{1}{2}z^{-1}\right)\left(1 + \frac{1}{3}z^{-1}\right)}$

For three different ROC, consider three different solution of signal $x[n]$.

1. $|z| > \frac{1}{2}$, $x[n] = \left[\frac{1}{2^{n-1}} - \left(\frac{-1}{3}\right)^n\right] u[n]$

2. $|z| < \frac{1}{3}$, $x[n] = \left[\frac{-1}{2^{n-1}} + \left(\frac{-1}{3}\right)^n\right] u[-n+1]$

3. $\frac{1}{3} < |z| < \frac{1}{2}$, $x[n] = -\frac{1}{2^{n-1}}\, u[-n-1] - \left(\frac{-1}{3}\right)^n u[n]$

Of these the correct solutions are

(a) 1 and 2 (b) 1 and 3

(c) 2 and 3 (d) 1, 2 and 3

161. The Z-transform function of a stable system is given as

$$H(z) = \frac{2 - \frac{3}{2}z^{-1}}{\left(1 - 2z^{-1}\right)\left(1 + \frac{1}{2}z^{-1}\right)}$$

The impuse response $h[n]$ is

(*a*) $2^n u[-n+1] - \left(\frac{1}{2}\right)^n u[n]$

(*b*) $2^n u[-n-1] + \left(\frac{-1}{2}\right)^n u[n]$

(*c*) $2^n u[-n-1] + \left(\frac{-1}{2}\right)^n u[n]$

(*d*) $2^n u[n] - \left(\frac{1}{2}\right)^n u[n]$

162. A system is described by the difference equation

$$y[n] = x[n] - x[n-2] + x[n-4] - x[n-6]$$

The impulse response of system is

(*a*) $\delta[n] - 2\delta[n+2] + 4\delta[n+4] - 6\delta[n+6]$

(*b*) $\delta[n] + 2\delta[n-2] - 4\delta[n-4] + 6\delta[n-6]$

(*c*) $\delta[n] - \delta[n-2] + \delta[n-4] - \delta[n-6]$

(*d*) $\delta[n] - \delta[n+2] + \delta[n+4] - \delta[n+6]$

163. The transfer function of a system is given by

$$H(z) = \frac{z(3z-2)}{z^2 - z - \frac{1}{4}}$$

The system is

(*a*) causal and stable

(*b*) causal, stable and minimum phase

(*c*) minimum phase

(*d*) none of these

164. The transfer function of a system is given as

$$H(z) = \frac{2\left(z + \frac{1}{2}\right)}{\left(z - \frac{1}{2}\right)\left(z - \frac{1}{3}\right)}$$

Consider the two statements

Statement (A) : System is causal and stable

Statement (B) : Inverse system is causal and stable

The correct option is

(*a*) (*A*) is true

(*b*) (*B*) is true

(*c*) Both are true

(*d*) Both are false

165. The Z-transform of a anti causal system is

$$X(z) = \frac{12 - 21z}{3 - 7z + 12z^2}$$

The value of $x[0]$ is

(*a*) $-\frac{7}{4}$

(*b*) 0

(*c*) 4

(*d*) none of these

166. Given the z-transforms

$$X(z) = \frac{z(8z-7)}{4z^2 - 7z + 3}$$

The final value of X(*z*) is

(*a*) 1 (*b*) 2

(*c*) ∞ (*d*) 0

LINEAR-TIME INVARIANT CIRCUITS

167. Which one of the following system is non-linear? [$y(t)$ = output; $x(t)$ = input]

(*a*) $y(t) = 2x(t-1) - 3x(t-2) + x(t-3)$

(*b*) $y(t) = 5x(t)$

(*c*) $y(t) = 2x(t-1) - 3x(t-2) - x(t-3)$

(*d*) $y(t) = 2x(t) + 3.6$

168. Which of the following transfer function of second order linear time-invariant systems, the underdamped system is represented by

(*a*) $H(s) = \frac{1}{s^2 + 4s + 4}$

(*b*) $H(s) = \frac{1}{s^2 + 5s + 4}$

(*c*) $H(s) = \frac{1}{s^2 + 4.5s + 4}$

(*d*) $H(s) = \frac{1}{s^2 + 3s + 4}$

169. If $a(n)$ is the response of a linear, time-invariant, discrete-time system to a unit step input, then the response of the same system to a unit impulse input is

(*a*) $\frac{d}{dn}\left[a(n)\right]$

(*b*) $na(n)$

(*c*) $a(n) - a(n-1)$

(*d*) $a(n+1) - 2a(n) + a(n-1)$

170. Which one of the following input-output relationship is that of a linear system ?

(a)

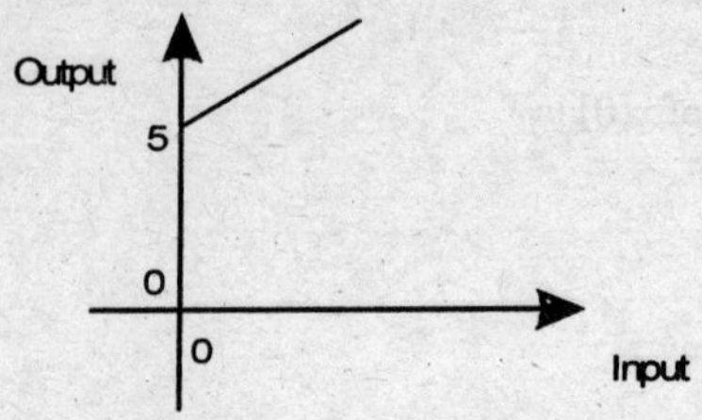

(b)

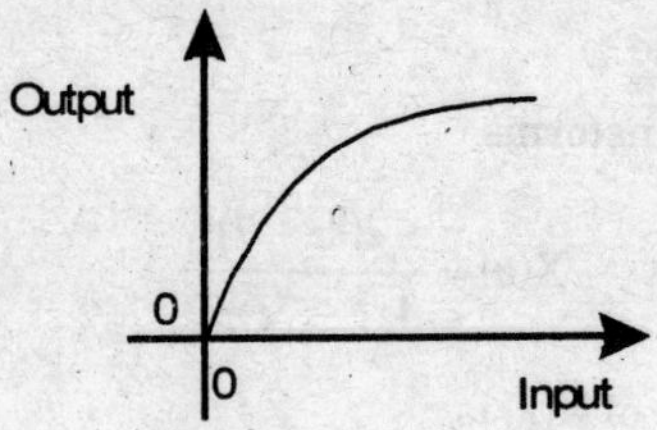

(c)

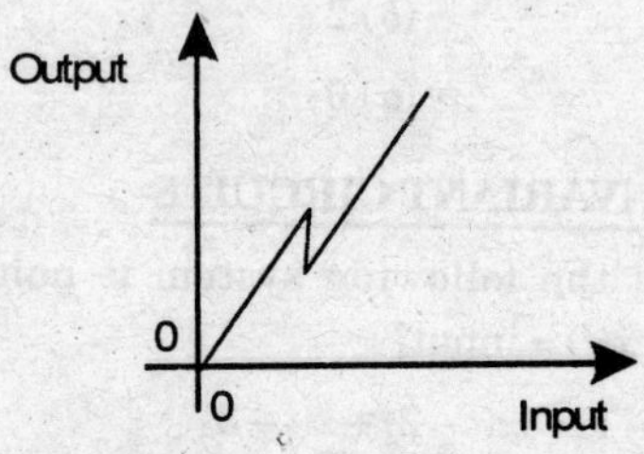

(d)

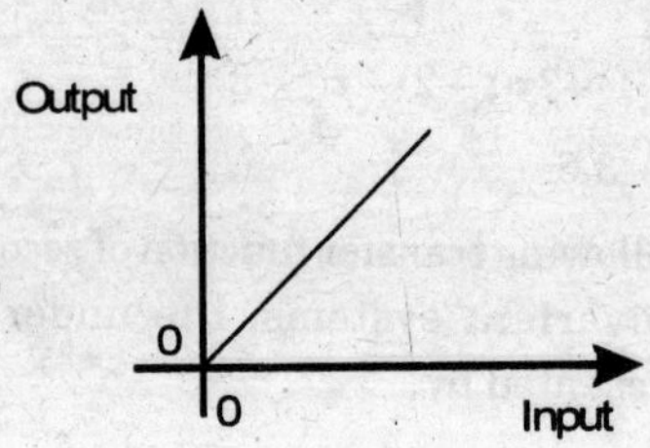

171. The discrete-time equation

$y(n+1) + 0.5n\, y(n) = 0.5x(x+1)$

is not attributable to a

(a) memoryless system

(b) time-variying system

(c) linear system

(d) causal system

172. A continuous-time system is governed by the equation $3y^2(t) + 2y^2(t) + y(t) = x^2(t) + x(t)$ {$y(t)$ and $x(t)$ respectively are output and input}. The system is

(a) linear and dynamic

(b) linear are non-dynamic

(c) non-linear and dynamic

(d) non-linear and non-dynamic

173. Which one of the following systems is a cuasual system ?

[$y(t)$ is output and $u(t)$ is a input step function].

(a) $y(t) = \sin[u(t+3)]$

(b) $y(t) = 5u(t) + 3u(t-1)$

(c) $y(t) = 5u(t) + 3u(t+1)$

(d) $y(t) = \sin[u(t-3) + \sin[u(t+3)]$

174. The discrete time system described by $y(n) = x(n^2)$ is

(a) causal, linear and time-varying

(b) causal, non-lnear and time-varying

(c) non-causal, linear and time-invariant

(d) non-causal, non-linear and time-variant

175. Given $\mathcal{L}[f(t)] = \dfrac{s+2}{s^2+1}$,

$$\mathcal{L}[g(t)] = \frac{s^2+1}{(s+3)(s+2)}$$

$$h(t) = \int_0^t f(z)\, g(t-z)\, dz.$$

Then $\mathcal{L}[h(t)]$ in

(a) $\dfrac{s^2+1}{s-3}$

(b) $\dfrac{-1}{s+3}$

(c) $\dfrac{s^2+1}{(s+3)(s+2)} + \dfrac{s+2}{s^2+1}$

(d) none of these

176. The transfer function of a system is given by

$$H(s) = \frac{1}{s^2(s-2)}$$

The impulse response of the system is

(a) $(t^2 * e^{-2t})\, u(t)$

(b) $(t * e^{2t})\, u(t)$

(c) $(t^2 e^{-2t})\, u(t)$

(d) $(t e^{-2t})\, u(t)$

ANSWERS

1. (*b*)	**2.** (*b*)	**3.** (*b*)	**4.** (*a*)	**5.** (*c*)	**6.** (*b*)	**7.** (*d*)	**8.** (*d*)	**9.** (*d*)	**10.** (*a*)
11. (*a*)	**12.** (*a*)	**13.** (*a*)	**14.** (*a*)	**15.** (*a*)	**16.** (*a*)	**17.** (*b*)	**18.** (*c*)	**19.** (*c*)	**20.** (*b*)
21. (*a*)	**22.** (*b*)	**23.** (*a*)	**24.** (*a*)	**25.** (*a*)	**26.** (*c*)	**27.** (*a*)	**28.** (*b*)	**29.** (*b*)	**30.** (*a*)
31. (*a*)	**32.** (*a*)	**33.** (*a*)	**34.** (*b*)	**35.** (*b*)	**36.** (*a*)	**37.** (*a*)	**38.** (*d*)	**39.** (*c*)	**40.** (*c*)
41. (*b*)	**42.** (*a*)	**43.** (*d*)	**44.** (*a*)	**45.** (*a*)	**46.** (*d*)	**47.** (*a*)	**48.** (*d*)	**49.** (*b*)	**50.** (*d*)
51. (*a*)	**52.** (*c*)	**53.** (*c*)	**54.** (*b*)	**55.** (*b*)	**56.** (*a*)	**57.** (*a*)	**58.** (*c*)	**59.** (*d*)	**60.** (*b*)
61. (*a*)	**62.** (*d*)	**63.** (*c*)	**64.** (*a*)	**65.** (*b*)	**66.** (*b*)	**67.** (*b*)	**68.** (*b*)	**69.** (*b*)	**70.** (*c*)
71. (*c*)	**72.** (*d*)	**73.** (*c*)	**74.** (*b*)	**75.** (*b*)	**76.** (*d*)	**77.** (*b*)	**78.** (*c*)	**79.** (*d*)	**80.** (*b*)
81. (*c*)	**82.** (*b*)	**83.** (*c*)	**84.** (*a*)	**85.** (*b*)	**86.** (*d*)	**87.** (*a*)	**88.** (*c*)	**89.** (*d*)	**90.** (*c*)
91. (*d*)	**92.** (*a*)	**93.** (*a*)	**94.** (*a*)	**95.** (*b*)	**96.** (*a*)	**97.** (*a*)	**98.** (*c*)	**99.** (*c*)	**100.** (*c*)
101. (*c*)	**102.** (*a*)	**103.** (*b*)	**104.** (*c*)	**105.** (*b*)	**106.** (*b*)	**107.** (*a*)	**108.** (*c*)	**109.** (*b*)	**110.** (*b*)
111. (*d*)	**112.** (*c*)	**113.** (*d*)	**114.** (*c*)	**115.** (*c*)	**116.** (*a*)	**117.** (*d*)	**118.** (*c*)	**119.** (*b*)	**120.** (*c*)
121. (*c*)	**122.** (*b*)	**123.** (*c*)	**124.** (*b*)	**125.** (*b*)	**126.** (*a*)	**127.** (*b*)	**128.** (*b*)	**129.** (*a*)	**130.** (*c*)
131. (*a*)	**132.** (*d*)	**133.** (*b*)	**134.** (*b*)	**135.** (*b*)	**136.** (*a*)	**137.** (*b*)	**138.** (*d*)	**139.** (*b*)	**140.** (*a*)
141. (*c*)	**142.** (*a*)	**143.** (*c*)	**144.** (*a*)	**145.** (*c*)	**146.** (*a*)	**147.** (*b*)	**148.** (*c*)	**149.** (*a*)	**150.** (*a*)
151. (*a*)	**152.** (*d*)	**153.** (*b*)	**154.** (*b*)	**155.** (*c*)	**156.** (*b*)	**157.** (*a*)	**158.** (*a*)	**159.** (*c*)	**160.** (*b*)
161. (*c*)	**162.** (*c*)	**163.** (*d*)	**164.** (*c*)	**165.** (*c*)	**166.** (*a*)	**167.** (*d*)	**168.** (*d*)	**169.** (*a*)	**170.** (*d*)
171. (*c*)	**172.** (*d*)	**173.** (*b*)	**174.** (*d*)	**175.** (*b*)	**176.** (*d*)				

EXPLANATIONS

3. $$\int_0^t u(t)dt = t$$

$$\therefore \int_0^t u(t)dt = \frac{t^2}{2}$$. This is a parabola,

6. $$X(s) = L\left[-e^{-2t}u(t)\right] . L\left[tu(t)\right]$$

Using $\mathcal{L}[x_1(t) * X_2(t)] = X_1(s) . X_2(s)$, we get

$$X(s) = \frac{-1}{(s-2)} . \frac{1}{s^2} = -\frac{1}{s^2(s-2)}$$

15. Here $C(t) = \frac{1}{2}(1-e^{-2t})$, $R(s) = \frac{1}{s}$

i.e. $$C(s) = \frac{1}{2}\left(\frac{1}{s} - \frac{1}{s+2}\right) = \frac{1}{s(s+2)}$$

$$H(s) = \frac{L(s)}{R(s)}$$

$$u(s) = \frac{1}{s+2}$$

Now for $R'(s) = \frac{1}{s} + 2$

$$\Rightarrow C'(s) = \frac{1}{(s+2)} \times \left(\frac{1}{s} + 2\right) = \frac{2s+1}{s(s+2)} = \frac{A}{s} + \frac{B}{s+2}$$

$$\therefore \quad A = \underset{s\to 0}{Lt} \frac{2s+1}{s+2} = \frac{1}{2}$$

and $$B = \underset{s\to -2}{Lt} \frac{2s+1}{s} = \frac{-4+1}{2} = +\frac{3}{2}$$

$$C'(s) = \frac{1}{2}\frac{1}{s} + \frac{3}{2} \times \frac{1}{s+2}$$

$$C'(t) = \frac{1}{2} + \frac{3}{2}e^{-2t}$$

16. $f(t) = t[U(t) - U(t-1)] + 1\,[U(t-1) - U(t-4)]$
$+ (5-t)\,[U(t-4) - U(t-6)]$
$+ \left(\frac{t}{2} - 4\right)[U(t-6) - U(t-8)]$

$$F(s) = \frac{1}{s^2}[1-e^{-s}] + \frac{1}{s}[e^{-s} - e^{-4s}] + \left(\frac{5}{s} - \frac{1}{s^2}\right)[e^{-4s} - e^{-6s}] + \left(\frac{1}{2s^2} - \frac{4}{s}\right)[e^{-6s} - e^{-8s}]$$

Comparing, we get

$$D = -0.5$$

17. When the excitation of a linear system is differential, the output also is the differentiation of previous output

$$\therefore \quad \text{Response} = e^{-2t}u(t) + 2\frac{d}{dt}\left[e^{-2t}u(t)\right] = -3e^{-2t}u(t)$$

18. $\left[(t^2-2t)u(t-1)\right]=\left[(t-1)^2u(t-1)-u(t-1)\right]$

$$=\frac{2}{s^3}e^{-s}-\frac{e^{-s}}{s}$$

19. Step response is integral of unit impulse response

$$u(t)=\int_0^t\left(-4e^{-t}+6e^{-2t}\right)dt=\left[4e^{-t}-3e^{-2t}\right]_0^t$$

$$=4e^{-t}-3e^{-2t}-1$$

20. $\frac{dy}{dt}+2y=4\,t\,u\,(t)$

Laplace transform is,

$$5y(s)+2y(s)=\frac{4}{s^2}$$

or $\quad y(s)\,[s+2]=\frac{4}{s^2}$

or $\quad y\,(s)=\frac{4}{s^2}\,[s+2]$

$$\therefore\quad y(s)=-\frac{1}{s}+\frac{2}{s^2}+\frac{1}{s+2}$$

$$=-u\,(t)+2\,tu\,(t)+e^{-2t}$$

forced response terms.

21. According to final value theorem,

$$\lim_{t\to\infty}\mathrm{I}(t)=\lim_{s\to 0}s\mathrm{I}(s)$$

$$=\lim_{s\to 0}\frac{(10s+4)}{(s+1)(s^2+4s+5)}=\frac{4}{5}$$

22. $\mathrm{I}(s)=\frac{\mathrm{V}(s)}{\mathrm{Z}(s)}$, and $\mathrm{Z}(s)=\mathrm{R}+\mathrm{L}s$

$$\mathrm{I}(s)=\frac{\mathrm{V}(s)}{\mathrm{R}+\mathrm{L}s}$$

Also, $\quad \mathrm{V}(s)=1$

$$\therefore\quad \mathrm{I}(s)=\frac{1}{\mathrm{R}+\mathrm{L}s}$$

$$i(t)=\left(\frac{1}{\mathrm{L}}\right)e^{-\frac{\mathrm{R}}{\mathrm{L}}t}$$

a decaying exponential function

23. $x(\infty)=\lim_{s\to 0}s\mathrm{X}(s)=\frac{2s^3+3s}{s^2+5s+1}=0$

24. Output $\mathrm{C}(s)=\mathrm{H}\,(s).\,\mathrm{R}\,(s)$

$$=\frac{1}{s-2}\cdot\frac{1}{s-3}$$

$$=\frac{(s-2)-(s-3)}{(s-2)\,(s-3)}$$

then $\mathrm{C}\,(t)=\mathcal{L}^{-1}\,[\mathrm{C}(s)]$

$$=\mathcal{L}^{-1}\left(\frac{1}{s-3}\right)-\mathcal{L}^{-1}\left(\frac{1}{s-2}\right)$$

$$=e^{3t}-e^{2t}$$

26. $\mathrm{L}[f(t)]=\mathrm{F}(s)$

then $\quad \mathrm{L}[f(t-\mathrm{T})]=e^{s\mathrm{T}}\,\mathrm{F}(s).$

Apply time shifting property of Laplace transform.

27. $x(t-2)\overset{L}{\longleftrightarrow}e^{-2s}\mathrm{X}(s),\ \mathrm{Y}(s)=\frac{2se^{-2s}}{s^2+2}$

28. Given : $\quad h(t)=u(t)$

$x(t)=e^{-at}u(t)$

$$\therefore\quad \mathrm{Y}(s)=\mathrm{X}(s)\,\mathrm{H}(s)=\frac{1}{s+a}\cdot\frac{1}{s}=\frac{1}{a}\left(\frac{1}{s}-\frac{1}{s+a}\right)$$

$$y(t)=\frac{1}{a}\,(1-e^{-at})\,u(t)$$

29. $\frac{2(s+1)}{(s^2+2s+5)}=\frac{2(s+1)}{(s^2+1)^2+4}=2\left[\frac{s+1}{(s+1)^2+4}\right]$

This is standard Laplace Transform for the function

$$\mathrm{L}\,|\exp\,(-\,at)\cos\omega t\,|=\frac{(s+a)}{(s+a)^2+\omega^2}$$

where $a=1,\quad \omega=2$

Hence $\quad f(t)=2e^{-t}\cos 2t$

$f(0)=f(0+)=2e^{-0}\cos 2\times 0=2$

$f(\infty)=2e^{-\infty}\,t=0$

30. $h_s(t)=4e^{-2t}\,u(t);\ \mathrm{H}(s)=\frac{4}{s+2}$

For unit step, $\mathrm{Y}(s)=\mathrm{H}(s)\,\mathrm{X}(s)$

$$\mathrm{Y}(s)=\frac{4}{s(s+2)}$$

$$=\frac{2}{5}-\frac{2}{s+2}\qquad \text{......since }[\mathrm{X}(s)=\frac{1}{s}]$$

$$y(t)=2[1-e^{-2t}]\,u(t)$$

31. $\frac{\mathrm{C}(s)}{\mathrm{R}(s)}=\frac{2(s-1)}{(s+2)\,(s+1)};\ \mathrm{R}(s)=\frac{1}{s}$

$$\therefore\quad \mathrm{C}(s)=\frac{2(s-1)}{(s+1)\,(s+2)}$$

Expanding in partial fractions

$$=\frac{k_1}{s}+\frac{k_2}{s+1}+\frac{k_3}{s+3}$$

$$\therefore\quad k_1=\frac{-2}{2}=-1$$

$$k_2 = \frac{2(s-1)}{s(s+2)}\Big|_{s=-1} = \frac{2(-2)}{-1(1)} = 4$$

$$k_3 = \frac{2(s-1)}{s(s+2)}\Big|_{s=-2} = \frac{2(-3)}{-2(-1)} = -3$$

Hence $C(s) = -\frac{1}{s} + \frac{4}{s+1} - \frac{3}{s+2}$

and output, $c(t) = [-1 + 4e^{-t} - 3e^{-2t}]\,u(t)$.

32. $X(s) = \frac{5-s}{(s+1)(s-2)} = \frac{A}{(s+1)} + \frac{B}{(s-2)}$

$$A = \frac{5-s}{s-2}\Big|_{s=-1} = -2; \text{ and } B = \frac{5-s}{s+1}\Big|_{s=2} = 1$$

then, $X(t) = \mathcal{L}^{-1}X(s) = \mathcal{L}^{-1}\left[\frac{-2}{s+1} + \frac{1}{s-2}\right]$

$= [e^{2t} - 2e^{-t}]u(t)$

33. $p(t) = tu(t) \overset{L}{\longleftrightarrow} P(s) = \frac{1}{s^2}$

$q(t) = \cos 2\pi t\, u(t) \overset{L}{\longleftrightarrow} Q(s) = \frac{s}{s^2 + 4\pi^2}$

$x(t) = p(t) * q(t) \overset{L}{\longleftrightarrow} X(s) = P(s)\,Q(s)$

$\Rightarrow X(s) = \frac{1}{s(s^2 + 4\pi^2)}$

34. $p(t) = e^{-3t}\cos 2t\, u(t) \overset{\mathcal{L}}{\longleftrightarrow} P(s) = \frac{s+3}{(s+3)^2 + 4}$

$$\int_{-\infty}^{t} p(\tau)d\tau \overset{\mathcal{L}}{\longleftrightarrow} \frac{1}{s}\int_{-\infty}^{0} p(\tau)d\tau + \frac{P(s)}{s}$$

$$X(s) = \frac{(s+3)}{s[(s+3)^2 + 4]}$$

35. $X(s) = \frac{s+3}{(s^2 + 3s + 2)} = \frac{A}{s+1} + \frac{A}{s+2}$

$$A = \frac{s+3}{s+2}\Big|_{s=-1} = 2, \quad B = \frac{s+3}{s+1}\Big|_{s=-2} = -1$$

$x(t) = [2e^{-t} - e^{-2t}]\,u(t)$

36. $sX(s) + X(s) \overset{L}{\longleftrightarrow} \frac{dx(t)}{dt} + x(t)$

$\Rightarrow y(t) = (-2\sin 2t + \cos 2t)\,u(t)$

37. $X(s) = \int_{-\infty}^{\infty} x(t)e^{-st}dt$

$$= \int_{-2}^{\infty} e^{-t}e^{-st}dt = \int_{-2}^{\infty} e^{-t(s+1)}dt$$

$$= \frac{e^{2(s+1)}}{s+1}, \text{ Re}(s) > -1$$

38. $X(s) = \int_0^{\infty} e^{-\frac{t}{2}}e^{-st} + \int_0^{\infty} e^{-t}\,e^{-st}dt + \int_{-\infty}^{0} e^{t}e^{-st}dt$

$$= \frac{1}{s+0.5} + \frac{1}{s+1} - \frac{1}{s-1}$$

Re(s) > – 0.5, Re (s) > –1, Re(s) < 1

$\Rightarrow -0.5 < \text{Re}(s) < 1$

39. Taking Laplace transform, we have

$sY(s) - y(0^-) + 10Y(s) = 10 \times (s)$

$$y(0^-) = 1, \; X(s) = \frac{1}{s}$$

$$Y(s) = \frac{10}{s(s+1)} + \frac{1}{(s+1)} = \frac{1}{s}$$

$\Rightarrow y(t) = u(t)$

40. $s^2Y(s) - 2s + 2sY(s) - 2 + 5Y(s) = 1$

$\therefore (s^2 + 2s + 5)\,Y(s) = 3 + 2s$

$$\Rightarrow Y(s) = \frac{2s+3}{s^2 + 2s + 5}$$

$$= \frac{2(s+1)}{(s+1)^2 + 2^2} + \frac{1}{(s+1)^2 + 2^2}$$

Inverse Laplace transform given,

$$\Rightarrow y(t) = 2e^{-t}\cos t\, u(t) + \frac{1}{2}e^{-t}\sin tu(t)$$

41. $Y(s)\,(s^2 - s - 2) = X(s)\,(5s - 4)$

$$H(s) = \frac{Y(s)}{X(s)} = \frac{5s-4}{s^2 - s - 2} = \frac{3}{s+1} + \frac{2}{s-2}$$

$h(t) = 3e^{-t}u(t) + 2e^{2t}u(t)$.

CONTINUOUS TIME SYSTEMS

42. $E = \int_{-\pi/\omega}^{\pi/\omega} \frac{1}{4}(\cos \omega t + 1)^2 dt$

$$= \frac{1}{2}\int_0^{\pi/\omega} (\cos^2 \omega t + 2\cos \omega t + 1)dt$$

$$= \frac{1}{2}\int_0^{\pi/\omega} (\cos^2 2\omega t + \frac{1}{2} + 2\cos \omega t + 1)dt$$

$$= \frac{1}{2}\left(\frac{3}{2}\right)\left(\frac{\pi}{\omega}\right) = \frac{3\pi}{4\omega}$$

43. $y(t) = 4^2\cos^2\left(200t + \frac{\pi}{6}\right)$

$$= 4^2\,\frac{\left(1 + \cos 2\left(200t + \frac{\pi}{6}\right)\right)}{2}$$

$$= 8 + 8\cos\left(400t + \frac{\pi}{3}\right)$$

44. For $t<0$, $y(t) = 0$

For $0 \le t \le a$, $y(t) = \int_0^t dt = t$

For $a \le t \le 1$, $y(t) = \int_0^a dt = a$

For $1 \le t \le (1+a)$, $y(t) = \int_t^{1+a} dt = 1+a-t.$

45. $$y(t) = \int_{-\infty}^{t} x(\tau)d\tau = \int_{-\infty}^{t} [\delta(\tau+2) - \delta(\tau-2)]\, d\tau$$

$$= \begin{cases} 0, & t<-2 \\ 1, & -2 \ge t \le 2 \\ 0, & t>2 \end{cases}$$

$$E_\infty = \int_{-2}^{2} dt = 4$$

DISCRETE TIME SYSTEMS

46. All describe the even part of x

47. $E = \sum_{-\infty}^{\infty} |A\delta[n]|^2 = A^2 \sum_{0}^{\infty} (1) = A^2$

48. $E = \sum_{-\infty}^{\infty} |nu[n]|^2 = \sum_{0}^{\infty} n^2 = \infty$

49. Let $v[n] = x[2n],$

$v[0] = x[0] = 0$

$v[1] = x[2] = 1,$

$v[2] = x[4] = 0$

$v[-1] = x[-2] = 1,$

$v[-2] = x[-4] = 0$

$\therefore$ $x[n] = \{3, 2, 1, 0, 1, 2, 3\}$

$x[2n] = \{2, 0, 2\} \uparrow$

$\uparrow$

50. $x[3-n] = \{3, 2, 1, 0, 1, 2, 3\}$

$\uparrow$

$y[-n] = \{1, 1, 1, 1, 0, -1, -1, -1, -1\}$

$\uparrow$

$x[3-n]y[-n] = \{0, -2, -1, 0, -1\}$

$\uparrow$

51.

	1	1	1	1	1
1	1	1	1	1	1
2	2	2	2	2	2
4	4	4	4	4	4

$y[n] = \{1, 3, 7, 7, 7, 6, 4\}$

52. $y[n] = \{1, 2, 3, 4, 5\}$

	1	2	3	4	5
1	1	2	3	4	5

53. Only statement (b) is false. For example

$S_1 : y[n] = x[n] + b$

$S_2 : y[n] = x[n] - b,$ where $b \ne 0$

$S\{x[n]\} = S_2\,\{S_1\{x[n]\}\} = S_2\,\{x\,[n] + b\} = x[n]$

Hence S is linear.

54. For example

$S_1 : y[n] = nx[n]$

$S_2 : y[n] = nx[n+1]$

If $x[n] = \delta[n]$, then

$S_2\{S_1\{\delta[n]\}\} = S_2[0] = 0,$

$S_1\{S_2\{\delta[n]\}\} = S_1\{\delta[n+1]\} = -\delta[n+1] \ne 0$

55. System is not linear. This is evident from observation of the pairs

$x_3[n] \Leftrightarrow y_3[n]$ and $x_2[n] \Leftrightarrow y_2[n]$

If the system were linear $y_2[n]$ would be of the form

$y_2[n] = \{3, 6, 3\}$ $\uparrow$

56. The difference equation is

$$y[n] = \frac{1}{4}x[n] + \frac{1}{4}y[n-1] - \frac{1}{2}\, y[n-2]$$

$$= 4y[n] - y\,[n-1] + 2y\,[n-2]$$

$$= x[n]$$

Eigen values are

$$4\alpha^2 - \alpha + 2 = 0,$$

$$\Rightarrow \qquad \alpha_{12} = 0.125 \pm j0.696$$

Its magnitude are less than 1. Thus system is stable.

$$y[n] = \frac{1}{4}(x[n] + y[n-1] + 2y\,[n-2])$$

Response at time, n, depends on the excitation at time n and the responses at previous time. It does not depend on any future values of the excitation.

57. Difference equation is

$$y[n] = \frac{1}{4}x[n] + \frac{1}{4}x[n-1] - \frac{1}{2}y[n-2]$$

$4y[n] - y[n-1] + 2y[n-2] = x[n]$

Eigen values are $4\alpha^2 - \alpha + 2 = 0,$

$\alpha_{12} = 0.125 \pm j0.696$

Its magnitude are less than 1. Thus system is stable.

$$y[n] = \frac{1}{4}(x[n] + y[n-1] + 2y[n-2])$$

Response at time, n, depends on the excitation at time n and the responses at previous time. It does not depend on any future values of the excitation

58. Characteristic equation is,

$$r - \frac{1}{2} = 0$$

$$y^{(n)}[n] = C\left(\frac{1}{2}\right)^n,$$

$$y[-1] = 3 = C\left(\frac{1}{2}\right)^{-1}, C = \frac{3}{2},$$

$$\Rightarrow \quad y^{(n)}[n] = \frac{3}{2}\left(\frac{1}{2}\right)^n u[n]$$

59. For $n = 0$,

$$y[0] = x[0] - x[-1]$$

For $n = 1$,

$$y[1] = 2y[0] + x[1] - x[0]$$

$$\Rightarrow \quad y[1] = x[0] + x[1] - 2x[-1]$$

For $n = 2$,

$$y[2] = 2y[1] - y[0] + x[2] - x[1]$$

$$y[2] = x[0] + x[1] + x[2] - 3x[-1]$$

$$y[2] = \delta[0] + \delta[1] + \delta[2] - 3\delta[-1] = 0$$

60. S_2 is invertible system

$$y[n] = x[2n],$$

S_1 is not invertible because $\delta[n]$, $2\delta[n]$ etc. result in

$$y[n] = 0.$$

FOURIER SERIES

64. Condition $f(t) = -f(-t)$ implies that it has rotational symmetry.

65. Only sine functions, as it has the odd symmetry.

67. $\frac{2\pi}{T} = \frac{\pi}{4}, \quad \Rightarrow \quad T = 8$ sec

77. $x(t) = 2\cos\pi t + 7\cos t$, does not satisfy the Dirichlet condition, therefore, it can't be expanded as Fourier series.

78. The periodic signal $X(t)$ of period T_0

$$X(t) = 1, \quad |t| < T_1$$

$$X(t) = 0, \quad T_1 < |t| < \frac{T_0}{2}$$

$$A_0 = \frac{1}{T_0}\int_{-T_1}^{T_1} x(t)dt = \frac{2T_1}{T_0}$$

80. Multiplication in frequency domain corresponds to convolution in time domain

$$z(t) = \int_0^1 u(z)\cdot z(t-z)\,dz$$

81. As, $g(t) * \delta(t - t_0) = g(t_0)$

Then, $x(t+5) * \delta(t-7) = x(t-2)$

82. $e_{rms} = \sqrt{\frac{1}{T}\int_0^T e^2(t)dt}$

$$= \sqrt{\frac{1}{T}\left[\int_0^{T/2}\left(\frac{2At}{T}\right)^2 dt + \int_{T/2}^{T} A^{2dt}dt\right]}$$

$$= \sqrt{\frac{1}{T}\left[\frac{4A^2}{T^2}\frac{1}{3}\frac{T^3}{8} + A\frac{T}{2}\right]}$$

$$= \sqrt{\frac{A^2}{6} + \frac{A^2}{2}} = \sqrt{\frac{2A^2}{3}} = \sqrt{\frac{\mathbf{2}}{\mathbf{3}}}\,\mathbf{A}$$

84. $H(s) = \frac{1}{(s-2)}, \quad R(s) = \frac{1}{(s-3)}$

$$\text{Output} = \frac{1}{(s-2)}\cdot\frac{1}{(s-3)} = \frac{1}{(s-3)} - \frac{1}{(s-2)}$$

$$C(t) = e^{3t} - e^{2t}$$

85. $\mathcal{L}[u(t) - u(t-1)] = \frac{1}{s}(1 - e^{-s}) = F_1(s)$

$$\mathcal{L}[u(t) - u(t-2)] = \frac{1}{s}(1 - e^{-2s}) = F_2(s)$$

$$F = F_1(s) \times F_2(s) = \frac{1}{s^2}(1 - e^{-s})(1 - e^{-2s})$$

$$F(t) = t - tu(t-2) - tu(t-1) + tu(t-3)$$

86. Signal shown has time period, T = 4ms.

$$\therefore \quad f = \frac{1\times 10^3}{4} = 250 \text{ Hz.}$$

This is the fundamental frequency.

Fifth harmonic frequency,

$$f_s = 250 \times 5 = 1250 \text{ Hz.}$$

87. $$<V_{av}> = \frac{\int_0^T Ke^{-\frac{t}{T}}.dt}{\int_0^T dt} = \frac{K}{T}\cdot\frac{e^{-\frac{t}{T}}}{-\frac{1}{T}}\Bigg|_0^T$$

$$= K(1 - e^{-1}) = \mathbf{0.632\,K}$$

89. $$X[k] = \frac{1}{T}\int_{-T/2}^{T/2} A\delta(t)e^{-jk\omega_o t}\,dt = \frac{A}{T}$$

Here, $A = 10, T = 5$,

$\therefore \quad X[k] = 2$

90. $$x(t) = \sum_{k=-\infty}^{\infty} X[k]e^{j2\pi kt}$$

$$= je^{j2\pi t} - je^{-j2\pi t} + e^{j6\pi t} + e^{-j6\pi t}$$

$$= -2\sin 2\pi t + 2\cos 6\pi t$$

91.
$$x(t) = \sum_{k=\infty}^{\infty} X[k]e^{jkt}$$
$$= \sum_{k=-\infty}^{-1}\left(\frac{-1}{3}\right)^{-k} e^{jkt} + \sum_{k=0}^{\infty}\left(\frac{-1}{3}\right)^{k} e^{jkt}$$
$$= \frac{\frac{-1}{3}e^{-jt}}{1+\frac{1}{3}e^{-jt}} + \frac{1}{1+\frac{1}{3}e^{jt}} = \frac{4}{5+3\cos t}$$

92. $x(t-t_o)$ is also periodic with T.

Fourier series coefficients $X_1[k]$ of $x(t-t_o)$ are
$$X_1[k] = \frac{1}{T}\int_T x(t-t_o)e^{-jk\omega_o t}\, dt$$
$$= \frac{e^{-jk\omega_o t_o}}{T}\int_T x(\tau)e^{-jk\omega_o\tau}d\tau$$
$$= e^{-jk\omega_o t_o}\, X[k]$$

Similarly, the Fourier series coefficients of $x(t+t_o)$ are
$$X_2[k] = e^{jk\omega_o t_o}\, X[k]$$

The Fourier series coefficients of

$x(t-t_o) + x(t+t_o)$ *are*

$$Y[k] = X_1[k] + X_2[k]$$
$$= e^{-jk\omega_o t_o}X[k] + e^{jk\omega_o t_o}X[k]$$
$$= 2\cos(\omega_o k t_o)\, X[k]$$

93. $\text{Ev}\{x(t)\} = \dfrac{x(t)+x(-t)}{2}$

Fourier series coefficients of $x(t)$ are
$$X_1[k] = \frac{1}{T}\int_T x(-t)e^{-jk\omega_o t}\, dt$$
$$= \frac{1}{T}\int_T x(\tau)e^{jk\omega_o\tau}\, d\tau$$
$$= X[-k]$$

Hence, Fourier series coefficient of $\text{Ev}\{x(t)\}$ are
$$Y[k] = \frac{X[k]+X[-k]}{2}$$

94. For a signal to be even, its Fourier series coefficients must be even. This is true only for $x_2(t)$.

95. If $x(t)$ is real, then $X[k]$ has to be conjugate-symmetric,

For $x_1(t)$, $X_1[k] = \begin{cases}\left(\frac{1}{2}\right)^k, & 0 \le k \le 100 \\ 0, & \text{otherwise}\end{cases}$

$X_1[k] \ne X^*[k]$, $x_1(t)$ is not real valued.

For $x_2(t)$, $X_2[k] = \begin{cases}\cos k\pi & -100 \le k \le 100 \\ 0, & \text{otherwise}\end{cases}$

$X_2[k] = X_2^*[k]$, $x_2(t)$ is real valued

For $x_3(t)$, $X_3[k] = \begin{cases} j\sin\left(\frac{k\pi}{2}\right), & -100 \le k \le 100 \\ 0, & \text{otherwise}\end{cases}$

$X_3[k] = X_3^*[-k]$, $x_3(t)$ is real valued.

96. Fourier series coefficient of $y(t)$ are
$$Y[k] = H(jk\omega_o)X[k].$$

Since $y(t)$ is identical to $x(t)$, then
$$Y[k] = X[k] \text{ for all } k,$$
$$H(j\omega) = 0 \text{ for } |\omega| \ge 80,$$
$$H(jk\omega_o) = 0 \text{ for } |k|\omega_o \ge 80$$

Therefore $X[k]$ must be zero for $|k| > 6$

98. $x(t)$ is a odd function. Thus it contain sine terms only. Average value is zero.

99. $x(t)$ is even. So it contain cosine terms only. It also have half wave symmetry if $\dfrac{A}{2}$ is subtracted. So it contains only odd harmonics.

100. $x[n] = 2\sin\left(\dfrac{4\pi}{19}n\right) + \cos\left(\dfrac{10\pi}{19}n\right) + 1$

$$= \frac{1}{j}\left(e^{j\left(\frac{4\pi}{19}\right)n} - e^{-j\left(\frac{4\pi}{19}\right)n}\right) + \frac{1}{2}\left(e^{j\left(\frac{10\pi}{19}\right)n} - e^{-j\left(\frac{10\pi}{19}\right)n}\right) + 1$$
$$= -je^{j(2)\frac{2\pi}{19}n} + je^{j(-2)\frac{2\pi}{19}n}$$
$$+\frac{1}{2}e^{j(5)\frac{2\pi}{19}n} + \frac{1}{2}e^{-j(5)\frac{2\pi}{19}n} + e^{j(0)\frac{2\pi}{19}n}$$

$$X[k] = j\delta[k-2] - j\delta[k+2] + \frac{1}{2}\delta[k-5]$$
$$+\frac{1}{2}\delta[k+5] + \delta[k]$$

101. The graph for $x[n]$ is shown in the figure.

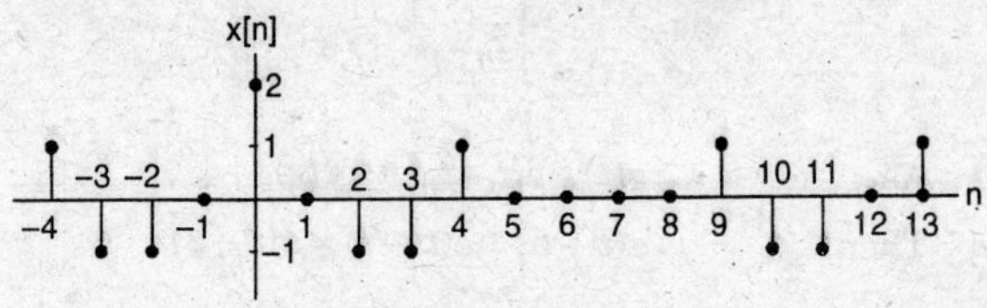

$$N = 12, \Omega_o = \frac{\pi}{6}$$

$$X[k] = \frac{1}{12}\sum_{n=-5}^{6} x[n]e^{-j\left(\frac{\pi k}{6}\right)n}$$

$$= \frac{1}{12}\left(\begin{array}{l} e^{-j(-4)\frac{\pi k}{6}} - e^{-j(-3)\frac{\pi k}{6}} - e^{-j(-2)\frac{\pi k}{6}} \\ +2 + e^{-j(2)\frac{\pi k}{6}} - e^{-j(3)\frac{\pi k}{6}} - e^{-j(4)\frac{\pi k}{6}} \end{array}\right)$$

$$= \frac{1}{6}\cos\left(\frac{2\pi k}{3}\right) - \frac{1}{6}\cos\left(\frac{\pi k}{2}\right) + \frac{1}{6}\cos\left(\frac{\pi k}{3}\right) + \frac{1}{6}$$

102. $N = 7, \Omega_o = \frac{2\pi}{7}$

$$x[n] = \sum_{n=-3}^{3} X[k]e^{j\left(\frac{2\pi}{7}\right)kn}$$

$$= e^{j\left(\frac{\pi}{2}\right)}e^{j(-3)\left(\frac{2\pi}{7}\right)n} + e^{-j\left(\frac{\pi}{2}\right)}e^{j(3)\left(\frac{2\pi}{7}\right)n}$$

$$= 2\cos\left(\frac{6\pi}{7}n - \frac{\pi}{2}\right)$$

103. $$Y[k] = \frac{1}{N}\sum_{n=0}^{N-1} x[n-n_o]e^{-j\left(\frac{2\pi}{N}\right)kn}$$

$$= \frac{1}{N}e^{-j\left(\frac{2\pi}{N}\right)kn_o}\sum_{n=0}^{N-1} x[n]e^{-j\left(\frac{2\pi}{N}\right)kn}$$

$$= e^{-j\left(\frac{2\pi}{N}\right)kn_o} X[k]$$

104. $$Y[k] = X[k] - e^{-j\left(\frac{2\pi}{N}\right)2k}X[k] = \left(1 - e^{-j\left(\frac{4\pi}{N}\right)k}\right)X[k]$$

105. *y[n]* is shown in the figure. It has fundamental period of 10.

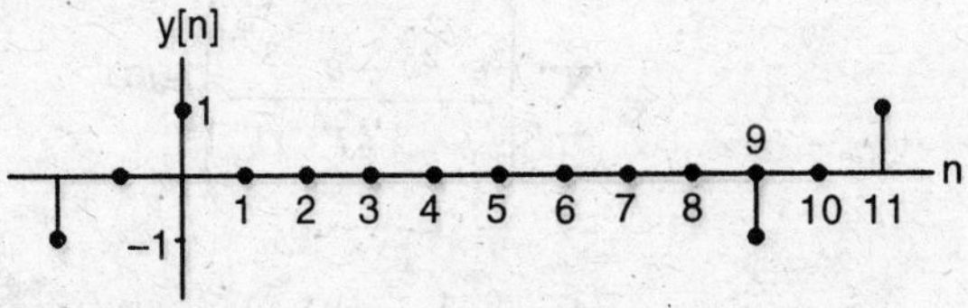

106. $$Y[k] = \frac{1}{10}\sum_{n=0}^{9} y[n]e^{-j\left(\frac{2\pi}{10}\right)kn}$$

$$= \frac{1}{10}\left(1 - e^{-j\left(\frac{2\pi}{10}\right)k8}\right) = \frac{1}{10}\left(1 - e^{-j\left(\frac{8\pi}{5}\right)k}\right)$$

107. $$z[n] = x[n]y[n] \xleftrightarrow{\text{DTFS}} \sum_{k=\langle N\rangle} X[l]Y[k-l]$$

$$\Rightarrow Z[k] = \sum_{l=0}^{3} X[l]Y[k-l]$$

$$\Rightarrow Z[k] = X[0]Y[k] + X[1]Y[k-1] + X[2]Y[k-2] + X[3]Y[k-3]$$

$$\Rightarrow Y[k] + 2Y[k-1] + 2Y[k-2] + Y[k-3]$$

Since Y[*k*] is 1 for all values of *k*.

Thus Z[*k*] = 6, for all *k*.

FOURIER TRANSFORM

111. Multiplication of two signals in frequency domain is equivalent to their convolution in time domain.

125. $$X(j\omega) = \int_{-\infty}^{\infty} x(t)e^{-j\omega t}dt$$

$$= \int_{3}^{\infty} e^{-2t}e^{-j\omega t}dt = \frac{e^{-3(2+j\omega)}}{2+j\omega}$$

126. $$X(j\omega) = \int_{-\infty}^{\infty} e^{-4|t|}e^{-j\omega t}dt$$

$$= \int_{-\infty}^{0} e^{4t}e^{-j\omega t} + \int_{0}^{\infty} e^{-4t}\cdot e^{-j\omega t}dt = \frac{8}{16+\omega^2}$$

127. $$e^{-t}u(t) \xleftrightarrow{F} \frac{1}{1+j\omega}$$

$$e^{j2\pi t}x_1(t) \xleftrightarrow{F} X_1\{j(\omega - 2\pi)\}$$

$$X(j\omega) \xleftrightarrow{F} \frac{1}{2j}\left(\frac{1}{1+j(\omega-2\pi)} - \frac{1}{1+j(\omega+2\pi)}\right)$$

128. $$y(t) = x\left(\frac{t-2}{2}\right)$$

$$\Rightarrow Y(j\omega) = e^{-j2\omega}X(j2\omega)$$

$$Y(j\omega) = \frac{e^{-j2\omega}2\sin 2\omega}{2\omega}$$

129. $$\int_{-\infty}^{\infty} x(t)dt = X(j0) = 1$$

130. $$\int_{-\infty}^{\infty}|x(t)|^2 dt = \frac{1}{2\pi}\int_{-\infty}^{\infty}|X(j\omega)|^2 d\omega$$

$$\frac{1}{2\pi}\int_{-5}^{-3}(\omega+5)^2 d\omega + \int_{-3}^{-1}(-\omega-1)^2 d\omega$$

$$+ \int_{-1}^{1}(\omega+1)^2 d\omega + \int_{-1}^{1}(-\omega-1)^2 d\omega = \frac{16}{3\pi}$$

132. $$H(j\omega) = \begin{cases} \dfrac{\omega}{2\pi}e^{\frac{j\pi}{2}} &, \quad 0 < \omega \le 3\pi \\ -\dfrac{\omega}{2\pi}e^{-\frac{j\pi}{2}} &, \quad -3\pi \le \omega \le 0 \\ 0 &, \quad \text{otherwise} \end{cases}$$

$$\Rightarrow \quad H(j\omega) = \begin{cases} \dfrac{j\omega}{3\pi}, & -3\pi \le \omega \le 3\pi \\ 0, & \text{otherwise} \end{cases}$$

$$x(t) = \cos(2\pi t + \theta)$$

$$X(j\omega) = e^{j\theta}\pi\delta(\omega - 2\pi) + e^{-j\theta}\pi\delta(\omega + 2\pi)$$

This is zero outside the region $-3\pi \le \omega \le 3\pi$

Thus $$Y(j\omega) = H(j\omega)X(j\omega) = \frac{j\omega}{3\pi}X(j\omega)$$

$$y(t) = \frac{1}{3\pi}\frac{dx(t)}{dt} = -\frac{2}{3}\sin(2\pi t + \theta)$$

133. $$x(t) = \cos(4\pi t + \theta)$$

$$X(j\omega) = e^{j\theta}\pi\delta(\omega - 2\pi) + e^{-j\theta}\pi\delta(\omega + 2\pi)$$

The non zero portion of $X(j\omega)$ lie outside the range $-3\pi \le \omega \le 3\pi$.

This implies that

$$Y(j\omega) = X(j\omega)H(j\omega) = 0$$

$$\therefore \quad Y(t) = 0.$$

134. $$Y(j\omega) = \frac{1}{3 + j\omega} - \frac{1}{4 + j\omega} = \frac{1}{(3 + j\omega)(4 + j\omega)}$$

$$X(j\omega) = \frac{Y(j\omega)}{H(j\omega)} = \frac{1}{(4 + j\omega)}$$

$$\Rightarrow \quad x(t) = e^{-4t}u(t)$$

135. $$F^{-1}\{(1 + j\omega)X(j\omega)\} = Ae^{-2t}u(t)$$

$$(1 + j\omega)X(j\omega) = \frac{A}{2 + j\omega}$$

$$\Rightarrow \quad X(j\omega) = \frac{A}{(1 + j\omega)(2 + j\omega)}$$

$$= A\left(\frac{1}{1 + j\omega} - \frac{1}{2 + j\omega}\right)$$

$$x(t) = Ae^{-t}u(t) - Ae^{-2t}u(t)$$

$$\int_{-\infty}^{\infty}|X(j\omega)|^2 d\omega = 2\pi$$

$$\Rightarrow \quad \int_{-\infty}^{\infty}|x(t)|^2 dt = 1$$

$$\int_{-\infty}^{\infty}[A^2e^{-2t} - 2A^2e^{-3t} + A^2e^{-4t}]u(t)dt = 1$$

$$\Rightarrow \quad \int_{0}^{\infty}[A^2e^{-2t} - 2A^2e^{-3t} + A^2e^{-4t}]dt = 1$$

$$\Rightarrow \quad \frac{A^2}{12} = 1, \quad \Rightarrow \quad A = \sqrt{12}.$$

We choose $\sqrt{12}$ instead $-\sqrt{12}$, because we know that $x(t)$ is non negative.

135. $$x(t) = \frac{1}{2\pi}\int_{-\infty}^{\infty}X(j\omega)e^{j\omega t}dt$$

$$= \frac{1}{2\pi}\int_{-\infty}^{\infty}2\{u(\omega + 3) - u(\omega - 3)\}e^{\left(-\frac{3}{2}\omega + \pi\right)}e^{j\omega t}d\omega$$

$$= \frac{1}{\pi}\int_{-3}^{3}e^{\left(-\frac{3}{2}\omega + \pi\right)}e^{j\omega t}d\omega = \frac{-2}{\pi\left(t - \frac{3}{2}\right)}\sin 3\left(t - \frac{3}{2}\right)$$

$x(t)$ is zero when $t = \dfrac{k\pi}{3} + \dfrac{3}{2}$ for $k \in I$, and $k \ne 0$.

136. Group delay $$\tau(\omega) = -\frac{d}{d\omega}\angle H(j\omega)$$

$$\angle H(j\omega) = \tan^{-1}(-\omega) - \tan^{-1}\omega = -2\tan^{-1}\omega$$

$$\tau(\omega) = \frac{d}{d\omega}(-2\tan^{-1}\omega) = \frac{2}{1 + \omega^2}$$

137. $$X(e^{j\Omega}) = \sum_{n=-\infty}^{\infty}x[n]e^{-j\Omega n}$$

$$= -2e^{j2\Omega} - 1e^{j\Omega} + 1e^{-j\Omega} + 2e^{-j2\Omega}$$

$$= -2(e^{j2\Omega} - e^{-j2\Omega}) - 1(e^{j\Omega} - e^{-j\Omega})$$

$$= -j2\text{2sin }2\Omega - 2j\sin\Omega$$

$$= -2j(2\sin 2\Omega - \sin\Omega)$$

138. $$X(e^{j\Omega}) = \sum_{n=-\infty}^{\infty}\sin\left(\frac{\pi}{2}n\right)e^{-j\Omega n}$$

$$= \sum_{n=-\infty}^{\infty}\left(\frac{e^{j\frac{\pi}{2}n} - e^{-j\frac{\pi}{2}n}}{2j}\right)e^{-j\Omega n}$$

$$= \frac{1}{2j}\sum_{n=-\infty}^{\infty}\left(e^{-jn(\Omega - \frac{\pi}{2})} - e^{-jn(\Omega + \frac{\pi}{2})}\right)$$

$$= \frac{1}{2j}\left(2\pi\delta\left(\Omega - \frac{\pi}{2}\right) - 2\pi\delta\left(\Omega + \frac{\pi}{2}\right)\right)$$

$$= j\pi\left(\delta(\Omega + \frac{\pi}{2}) - \delta(\Omega - \frac{\pi}{2})\right)$$

139. $$x[n] = \frac{1}{2\pi}\int_{-\pi}^{\pi} X(e^{j\Omega})e^{j\Omega n}d\Omega$$

$$= \frac{1}{2\pi}\left[\int_{-3\pi/4}^{-\pi/4} e^{j\Omega n}d\Omega + \int_{\pi/4}^{3\pi/4} e^{j\Omega n}d\Omega\right]$$

$$= \frac{1}{2\pi}\left[\frac{e^{j\Omega n}}{jn}\Bigg|_{-3\pi/4}^{-\pi/4} + \frac{e^{j\Omega n}}{jn}\Bigg|_{-\pi/4}^{3\pi/4}\right]$$

$$= \frac{1}{\pi n}\left(\sin\frac{3\pi n}{4} - \sin\frac{\pi n}{4}\right)$$

140. $$X(e^{j\Omega}) = \frac{1-\frac{1}{3}e^{-j\Omega}}{1-\frac{1}{4}e^{-j\Omega}-\frac{1}{8}e^{-2j\Omega}}$$

$$= \frac{\frac{2}{9}}{1-\frac{1}{2}e^{-j\Omega}} + \frac{\frac{7}{9}}{1+\frac{1}{4}e^{-j\Omega}}$$

$$x[n] = \frac{2}{9}\left(\frac{1}{2}\right)^n u[n] + \frac{7}{9}\left(-\frac{1}{4}\right)^n u[n]$$

141. For a real signal $x[n]$

$$\text{odd}\{x[n]\} \xleftrightarrow{\text{DTFT}} j\text{Im}\{X(e^{j\Omega})\}$$

$$j\text{Im}\{X(e^{j\Omega})\} = j\sin\Omega - j\sin 2\Omega$$

$$= \frac{1}{2}(e^{j\Omega} - e^{-j\Omega} - e^{2j\Omega} + e^{-2j\Omega})$$

$$\therefore \quad \text{odd}\{x[n]\} = F^{-1}\{jIm\{X(e^{j\Omega})\}]$$

$$= \frac{1}{2}(\delta[n+1] - \delta[n-1] - \delta[n+2] + \delta[n-2])$$

$$\text{odd}\{x[n]\} = \frac{x[n]-x[-n]}{2}$$

Since $x[n] = 0$ for $n > 0$,

$$x[n] = 2\text{odd}\{x[n]\} = \delta[n+1] - \delta[n+2] \text{ for } n < 0$$

Using Parseval's relation

$$\frac{1}{2\pi}\int_{-\infty}^{\infty}\left|X(e^{j\Omega})\right|^2 d\Omega = \sum_{n=-\infty}^{\infty}|x[n]|^2$$

$$3 = \sum_{n=-\infty}^{-1}|x[n]|^2 = (x[0])^2 + 2$$

$$x[0] = \pm 1,$$

But $x[0] = 0$,

hence $x[0] = 1$

142. For $x[n] = \delta[n]$,

$$X(e^{j\Omega}) = 1, \quad \frac{dX(e^{j\Omega})}{d\Omega} = 0$$

$$h[n] = \frac{1}{2\pi}\int_{-\pi}^{\pi} Y(e^{j\Omega})e^{j\Omega n}\, d\Omega = \frac{1}{2\pi}\int_{-\pi}^{\pi} e^{-j\Omega}e^{j\Omega n}\, d\Omega$$

$$= \frac{1}{2\pi}\int_{-\pi}^{\pi} e^{j\Omega(n-1)}\, d\Omega = \frac{\sin\pi(n-1)}{\pi(n-1)}$$

Z-TRANSFORM

143. $Y(n) - 2y(n-1) + y(n-2) = x(n) - x(n-1)$

For $n = 0$,

$$y(0) - 2y(-1) + y(-2) = x(0) - x(-1)$$

$$\therefore \quad y(0) = x(0) - x(-1)$$

$$\therefore \quad y(n) = 0 \text{ for } n < 0$$

For $n = 1$,

$$y(1) = -2y(0) + y(-1) = x(1) - x(0)$$

$$\therefore \quad y(1) = x(1) - x(0) + 2x(0) - 2x(-1)$$

$$= x(1) + x(0) - 2x(-1)$$

For $n = 2$,

$$y(2) = x(2) - x(1) + 2y(1) - y(0)$$

$$= x(2) - x(1) + 2x(1) + 2x(0) - 4x(-1) - x(0) + x(-1)$$

$$= x(2) + x(1) + x(0) - 3x(-1)$$

$$= d(2) + d(1) + d(0) - 3d(-1)$$

147. $$H_1(Z)\, H_2(Z) = Z^{-2}$$

$$\Rightarrow \quad H_2(Z) = \frac{Z^{-2}}{H_1(Z)} = \frac{Z^{-2} - 0.8Z^{-3}}{1 - 0.5Z^{-1}}$$

148. $$Z\left[\sum_{k=0}^{\infty}\delta(n-k)\right] = \sum_{-\infty}^{\infty}\sum_{k=0}^{\infty}\delta(n-k)\,z^{-k}$$

$$= \sum_{0}^{\infty}\sum_{-\infty}^{\infty}\delta(n-k)\,z^{-k}$$

Since property of delta function

$$\sum_{-\infty}^{\infty}\delta(n-k)\,f(n) = f(k)$$

$$\therefore \quad \sum_{0}^{\infty}\sum_{-\infty}^{\infty}\delta(n-k)\,z^{-k} = \sum_{-\infty}^{\infty}z^{-k}$$

$$= 1 + \frac{1}{z} + \frac{1}{z^2} + \frac{1}{z^3} + \ldots\ldots\ldots\ldots$$

150. $Z[u(t)] = \sum_{k=-\infty}^{\infty} \left(z^{-1}\right)^k$

Since $|z^{-1}| < 1 \quad \therefore |z| \,.\, 1$

151. $\int_{-\infty}^{\infty} \delta(t) f(t)\, dt = f(0)$

$\Rightarrow \int_{-\infty}^{\infty} \delta(t) \cos\left(\frac{3t}{2}\right) dt = \cos(0) = 1$

152. $X(z) = \sum_{n=0}^{4} \left(\frac{1}{4} z^{-1}\right)^4 = \dfrac{1 - \left(\frac{1}{4} z^{-1}\right)^5}{1 - \left(\frac{1}{4} z^{-1}\right)}$

$= \dfrac{z^5 - 0.25^5}{z^4 (z - 0.5)}$, all z

153. $X(z) = \sum_{-\infty}^{-1} \left(\frac{3}{2} z^{-1}\right)^n + \sum_{n=0}^{\infty} \left(\frac{2}{3} z^{-1}\right)^n$

$= \dfrac{-1}{1 - \frac{3}{2} z^{-1}} + \dfrac{1}{1 - \frac{2}{3} z^{-1}}$

$= \dfrac{-\frac{5}{6} z}{\left(z - \frac{3}{2}\right)\left(z - \frac{2}{3}\right)}, \quad \frac{2}{3} < |z| < \frac{3}{2}$

154. $x[n] = \frac{1}{2} e^{j\left(\frac{\pi}{3}\right)n} u[n] + \frac{1}{2} e^{-j\left(\frac{\pi}{3}\right)n} u[n]$

$X(z) = \frac{1}{2}\left[\dfrac{1}{1 - e^{\frac{j\pi}{3}} z^{-1}} + \dfrac{1}{1 - e^{-\frac{j\pi}{3}} z^{-1}}\right]$

$= \frac{1}{2}\left[\dfrac{2 - z^{-1}\left[e^{-\frac{j\pi}{3}} + e^{\frac{j\pi}{3}}\right]}{1 - z^{-1}\left(e^{\frac{j\pi}{3}} + e^{-\frac{j\pi}{3}}\right) + z^{-2}}\right]$

$= \frac{z}{2} \dfrac{(2z - 1)}{\left(z^2 - z + 1\right)}, \quad |z| > 1$

155. $Y(z) = X(2z) \xleftrightarrow{z} y[n] = \frac{1}{2^n} x[n]$

$\Rightarrow \quad y[n] = \frac{1}{2^n} n^2 3^n u[n]$

156. $Y(z) = X\left(\frac{1}{z}\right) \xleftrightarrow{z} y[n] = x[-n] = n^2 3^{-n} u[-n]$

157. $X(z) = \dfrac{z^2 - 3z}{z^2 + \frac{3}{2} z^{-1}} = \dfrac{1 - 3z^{-1}}{1 + \frac{3}{2} z^{-1} - z^{-2}}$

$= \dfrac{2}{1 + 2z^{-1}} - \dfrac{1}{1 - \frac{1}{2} z^{-1}}, \text{ROC}: \frac{1}{2} < |z| < 2$

$\Rightarrow \quad x[n] = -2(2)^n u[-n-1] - \frac{1}{2^n} u[n]$

158. $x[n]$ is right sided

$X(z) = \dfrac{z - \frac{1}{4} z^{-1}}{1 - 16z^{-1}} = \dfrac{\frac{49}{32}}{1 + 4z^{-1}} + \dfrac{\frac{47}{32}}{1 - 4z^{-1}}$

$\Rightarrow \quad x[n] = \left[\frac{49}{32}(-4)^n + \frac{47}{32} 4^n\right] u[n]$

159. $X(z) = -4z^2 \sum_{k=0}^{\infty} (2z)^{2k} = -\sum_{k=0}^{\infty} 2^{2(k+1)} z^{2(k+1)}$

$\Rightarrow \quad x[n] = -\sum_{k=0}^{\infty} 2^{2(k+1)} \delta[n + 2(k+1)]$

160. $X(z) = \dfrac{2}{1 - \frac{1}{2} z^{-1}} + \dfrac{-1}{1 + \frac{1}{z} z^{-1}},$

$|z| > \frac{1}{2}$ (Right-sided)

$\Rightarrow \quad x[n] = \frac{2}{2^n} u[n] - \left(\frac{-1}{3}\right)^n u[n]$

$|z| < \frac{1}{3}$ (Left-sided)

$\Rightarrow \quad x[n] = \left[\frac{-2}{2^n} + \left(\frac{-1}{3}\right)^n\right] u[-n-1]$

$\frac{1}{3} < |z| < \frac{1}{2}$ (Two-sided)

$x[n] = -\frac{2}{2^n} u[-n-1] - \left(\frac{-1}{3}\right)^n u[n]$

161. $H(z) = \dfrac{1}{1 - 2z^{-1}} + \dfrac{1}{1 + \frac{1}{2} z^{-1}}$ $h[n]$ is stable

So ROC includes $|z| = 1$

ROC : $\frac{1}{2} < |z| < 2$

$h[n] = (2)^n u[-n-1] + \left(\frac{-1}{2}\right)^n u[n]$

162. $H(z) = \frac{Y(z)}{X(z)} = (1 - z^{-2} + z^{-4} - z^{-6})$

$\Rightarrow \quad h[n] = \delta[n] - \delta[n-2] + \delta[n-4] - \delta[n-6]$

163. Zero at : $z = 0, \frac{2}{3}$, poles at $z = \frac{1 \pm \sqrt{2}}{2}$

(*i*) Not all poles are inside $|z| = 1$, the system is not causal and stable

(*ii*) Not are poles and zero are inside $|z| = 1$, the system is not minimum phase

164. Pole of system at : $z = -\frac{1}{2}, \frac{1}{3}$

Pole of inverse system at : $z = -\frac{1}{2}$

For this system and inverse system all poles are inside $|z| = 1$.

So, both system are both causal and stable.

165. Anti causal signal,

$$x[0] = \lim_{z \to \infty} X(z) = 4$$

166. The function has poles at $z = 1, \frac{3}{4}$

Thus final value theorem applies

$$\lim_{n \to \infty} x(n) = \lim_{z \to 1} (z-1) X(z) = (z-1)$$

$$\frac{z\left(2z - \frac{7}{4}\right)}{(z-1)\left(z - \frac{3}{4}\right)} = 1$$

LINEAR TIME INVARIANT

168. $\zeta = 0.75 < A$ (Under damped)

175. Here $h(t) = \int_0^t f(\zeta)\, g(t-\zeta)\, d\zeta = f(t) * g(t) = F(s) \times G(s)$

$$= \frac{s+2}{s^2+1} \times \frac{s^2+1}{(s+3)(s+2)} = \frac{1}{s+3}$$

$$\therefore \ \mathcal{L}[h(t)] = H(s) = \frac{1}{s+3}$$

176. $\mathcal{L}^{-1}[H(s)] = \mathcal{L}^{-1}\left[\frac{1}{s^2} \times \frac{1}{s-2}\right] = t * e^{-2t}$

PRACTICE QUESTIONS

1. The relationship between the input $x(t)$ and output $y(t)$ of a causal system is described by the differential equation

$$\frac{dy(t)}{dt} + 10y(t) = 10x(t)$$

The impulse response of the system is

(*a*) $-10e^{-10t}u(-t+10)$ (*b*) $10e^{-10t}u(t)$

(*c*) $10e^{-10t}u(-t+10)$ (*d*) $-10e^{-10t}u(t)$

2. The auto-correlation of the signal

$x(t) = e^{-t}u(t)$ is

(*a*) $\frac{1}{2}e^{t}u(-t) + \frac{1}{2}e^{-t}u(t)$ (*b*) $\frac{e^t}{2} + \frac{1}{2}(e^{-t} - e^{t})\, u(t)$

(*c*) $\frac{1}{2}e^{-t}u(-t) + \frac{1}{2}e^{-t}u(t)$ (*d*) $\frac{1}{2}e^{t}u(-t) - \frac{1}{2}e^{-t}u(t)$

Common data (Q. 3-4):

In question y[n] is the convolution of two signal. Choose correct option for y[n]

3. $y[n] = (-1)^n * 2^n u[2n+2]$

(*a*) $\frac{4}{6}$

(*b*) $\frac{4}{6}u[-n+2]$

(*c*) $\frac{8}{3}(-1)^n u[-n+2]$

(*d*) $\frac{8}{3}(-1)^n$

4. $y[n] = \frac{1}{4^n}u[n] * u[n+2]$

(*a*) $\left(\frac{1}{3} - \frac{1}{4^n}\right)u[n]$

(*b*) $\left(\frac{1}{3} - \frac{12}{4^n}\right)u[n+2]$

(*c*) $\left(\frac{4}{3} - \frac{1}{12}\left(\frac{1}{4}\right)^n\right)u[n+2]$

(*d*) $\left(\frac{16}{3} - \frac{1}{4^n}\right)u[n+2]$

5. A continuous-time periodic signal has a fundamental period T = 8. The non-zero Fourier series coefficients are,

$X[1] = X^*[-1] = j$, $X[5] = X[-5] = 2$

The signal will be

(*a*) $4\cos\left(\frac{\pi}{4}t\right) - 2\sin\left(\frac{\pi}{4}t\right)$

(*b*) $2\cos\left(\frac{\pi}{4}t\right) + 4\sin\left(\frac{\pi}{4}t\right)$

(*c*) $2\cos\left(\frac{\pi}{4}t\right) + 2\sin\left(\frac{\pi}{4}t\right)$

(*d*) none of these

6. $X[k]$ is shown in the figure below.

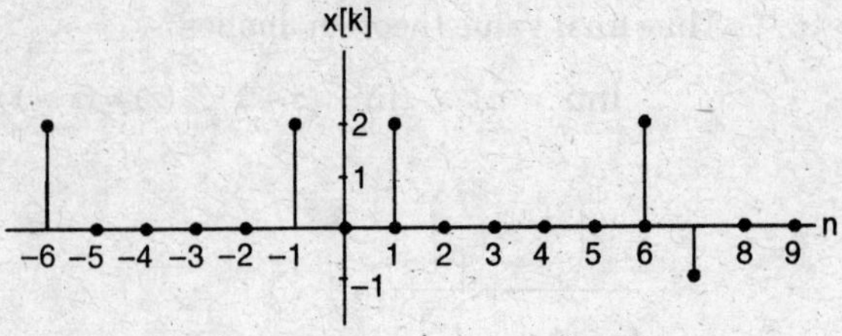

(a) $2\sin\left(\frac{\pi}{7}n\right)-1$ (b) $2\cos\left(\frac{\pi}{7}n\right)-1$

(c) $4\sin\left(\frac{2\pi}{7}n\right)-1$ (d) $4\cos\left(\frac{2\pi}{7}n\right)-1$

7. Consider a signal $x[n]$ with following facts:

1. $x[n]$ is a real and even signal
2. The period of $x[n]$ is N = 10
3. X[11] = 5
4. $\frac{1}{10}\sum_{n=0}^{9}|X[k]|^2 = 50$

The signal $x[n]$ is

(a) $5\cos\left(\frac{\pi}{10}n\right)$ (b) $5\sin\left(\frac{\pi}{10}n\right)$

(c) $10\cos\left(\frac{\pi}{5}n\right)$ (d) $10\sin\left(\frac{\pi}{5}n\right)$

8. The inverse Fourier transform of

$X(j\omega) = 2\pi\delta(\omega) + \pi\delta(\omega - 4\pi) + \pi\delta(\omega + 4\pi)$

is

(a) $2\pi(1 - \cos 4\pi t)$

(b) $\pi(1 - \cos 4\pi t)$

(c) $1 + \cos 4\pi t$

(d) $2\pi(1 + \cos 4\pi t)$

9. the inverse Fourier transform of

$X(j\omega) = e^{-2|\omega|}$

(a) $\frac{2}{\pi(4+t^2)}$ (b) $\frac{1}{2\pi(4+t^2)}$

(c) $\frac{1}{\pi(4+t^2)}$ (d) none of these

10. A causal LTI filter has the frequency response $H(j\omega)$ shown in figure for the input signal $x(t) = e^{-jt}$, output will be

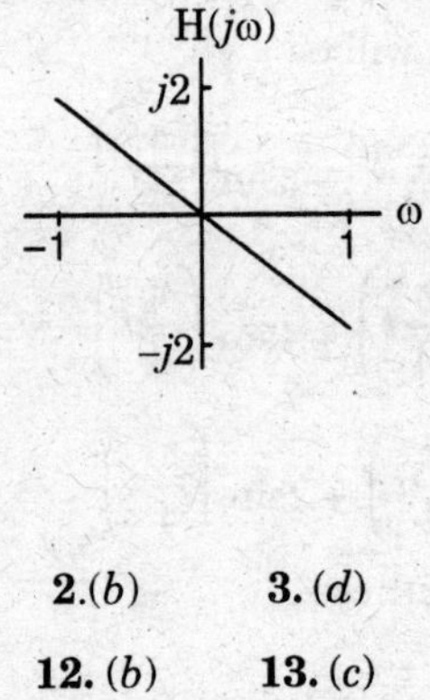

(a) $-2je^{-jt}$

(b) $2je^{-jt}$

(c) $4\pi je^{-jt}$

(d) $-4\pi je^{-jt}$

Common data (Q. 11-13):

A causal and stable LTI system has the property that

$$\left(\frac{2}{3}\right)^n u[n] \Rightarrow n\left(\frac{2}{3}\right)^n u[n]$$

11. The frequency response $H(e^{j\Omega})$ for this system is

(a) $\frac{2e^{j\Omega}}{2-3e^{j\Omega}}$

(b) $\frac{2e^{-j\Omega}}{2-3e^{-j\Omega}}$

(c) $\frac{2e^{j\Omega}}{2-3e^{j\Omega}}$

(d) $\frac{2e^{-j\Omega}}{2-3e^{-j\Omega}}$

12. The difference equation for this system relating any input $x[n]$ and the corres-ponding output $y[n]$ is

(a) $3y[n] - 2y[n-1] = 2x[n]$

(b) $3y[n] - 2y(n-1) = 2x[n-1]$

(c) $3y[n] - 2y[n+1] = 2x[n+1]$

(d) $3y[n] - 2[y+1] = 2x[n]$

13. The Z-transform of a signal is given by $\frac{z^{-1}(1-z^{-4})}{4(1-z^{-1})^2}$.

Its final value is

(a) $\frac{1}{4}$ (b) 0 (c) 1.0 (d) ∞

14. A causal system has input $x[n] = (-3)^n u[n]$ and output

$$y[n] = \left[4(2)^n - \left(\frac{1}{2}\right)^n\right] u[n]$$

The impulse response of this system is

(a) $\left[7\left(\frac{1}{2}\right)^n - 10\left(\frac{1}{2}\right)^n\right]u[n]$

(b) $\left[7(2^n) - 10\left(\frac{1}{2}\right)^n\right]u[n]$

(c) $\left[10\left(\frac{1}{2}\right)^2 - 7(2)^2\right]u[n]$

(d) $\left[10(2^n) - 7\left(\frac{1}{2}\right)^n\right]u[n]$

ANSWERS

1. (b)	**2.** (b)	**3.** (d)	**4.** (c)	**5.** (d)	**6.** (d)	**7.** (c)	**8.** (c)	**9.** (a)	**10.** (b)
11. (d)	**12.** (b)	**13.** (c)	**14.** (d)						

EXPLANATIONS

1. $sY(S) + 10Y(S) = 10X(S)$

$$H(S) = \frac{Y(s)}{X(s)} = \frac{10}{s+10}$$

$$\Rightarrow \quad h(t) = 10e^{-10t}\,u(t)$$

2. $R_{XX}(T) = X(T)^* X(T)$

For $T < 0$, $R_{XX}(T) = \int_0^{\infty} e^{t} e^{-2\tau} d\tau = \frac{1}{2}e^{t}$

For $T \geq 0$, $R_{XX}(T) = \int_0^{\infty} e^{t} e^{-2t} d\tau = \frac{1}{2}e^{-t}$

$$R_{XX}(T) = \frac{1}{2}e^{t}(1-u(t)) + \frac{1}{2}e^{-t}u(t)$$

$$= \frac{1}{2}e^{t} + \frac{1}{2}(e^{-t} - e^{t})\,u(t).$$

3. $$Y[N] = \sum_{k=n-2}^{\infty} (-1)^k\, 2^{n-k} = 2^n \sum_{k=n-2}^{\infty} \left(-\frac{1}{2}\right)^k$$

$$= \frac{2^n\left(-\frac{1}{2}\right)^{n-2}}{1+\frac{1}{2}} = \frac{8}{3}(-1)^n$$

4. For $n + 2 < 0$ or $n < -2$,

$$y[n] = 0$$

For $n + 2 \geq 0$ or $n \geq -2$,

$$y[n] = \sum_{k=0}^{n+2} \frac{1}{4}k = \frac{4}{3} - \frac{1}{12}\frac{1}{4^n}$$

$$\Rightarrow \quad y[n] = \left(\frac{4}{3} - \frac{1}{12}\left(\frac{1}{4}\right)^n\right)u[n+2]$$

5. $$x(t) = X[1]e^{j\left(\frac{2\pi}{T}\right)t} + X[-1]_e{}^{-j\left(\frac{2\pi}{T}\right)t} + X[5]e^{-j5\left(\frac{2\pi}{T}\right)t} + X[-5]e^{-j5\left(\frac{2\pi}{T}\right)t}$$

$$= je^{j\left(\frac{2\pi}{8}\right)t} - je^{-j\left(\frac{2\pi}{8}\right)t} + 2e^{j5\left(\frac{2\pi}{8}\right)t} + 2e^{-j5\left(\frac{2\pi}{8}\right)t}$$

$$= -2\sin\left(\frac{\pi}{4}t\right) + 4\cos\left(\frac{5\pi}{4}t\right)$$

6. $N = 7,\ \Omega_o = \frac{2\pi}{7}$

$$x[n] = \sum_{n=-3}^{3} X[k]e^{j\left(\frac{2\pi}{7}\right)kn} = 2e^{j(-1)\left(\frac{2\pi}{7}\right)n} - 1 + 2e^{j(1)\left(\frac{2\pi}{7}\right)n}$$

$$= 4\cos\left(\frac{2\pi}{7}n\right) - 1$$

7. Since $N = 10$, $X[11] = X[1] = 5$

Since x[n] is real and even, X[k] is also real and even.

$\therefore \quad X[1] = X[-1] = 5.$

Using Parseval's relation

$$\sum_{N} |X[k]|^2 = 50 = \sum_{k=-1}^{8} |X[k]|^2$$

$$|X[-1]|^2 + |X[1]|^2 + |X[0]|^2 + \sum_{k=2}^{8} |X[k]|^2 = 50$$

$$|X[0]|^2 + \sum_{k=2}^{8} |X[k]|^2 = 0$$

$\therefore$ X[K] = 0 for K = 0, 2, 3, ... 8.

$$x[n] = \sum_{N} X[k]e^{j\left(\frac{2\pi}{N}\right)kn} = \sum_{k=-1}^{8} X[k]e^{j\left(\frac{2\pi}{10}\right)kn}$$

$$= 5\left(e^{-j\left(\frac{2\pi}{10}\right)n} + e^{j\left(\frac{2\pi}{10}\right)n}\right) = 10\cos\left(\frac{\pi}{5}n\right)$$

8. $$x(t) = \frac{1}{2\pi}\int_{-\infty}^{\infty} [2\pi\delta(\omega) + \pi\delta(\omega - 4\pi) + \pi\delta(\omega + 4\pi)]e^{j\omega t}d\omega$$

$$= 1 + \frac{1}{2}e^{j4\pi t} + \frac{1}{2}e^{-j4\pi t}$$

$$= 1 + \cos 4\pi t$$

9. $$x(t) = \frac{1}{2\pi}\int_{-\infty}^{\infty} e^{-2|\omega|}e^{-j\omega t}d\omega$$

$$= \frac{1}{2\pi}\int_{-\infty}^{0} e^{2\omega}e^{j\omega t}d\omega + \frac{1}{2\pi}\int_{0}^{\infty} e^{-2\omega}e^{-j\omega t}d\omega$$

$$= \frac{2}{\pi(4+t^2)}$$

10. $H(j\Omega) = -2j\Omega$, $Y(j\Omega)$

$= X(j\Omega)\,H(j\Omega)$

$= -2j(\Omega)\,.\,X(j\Omega)$

$$\Rightarrow \quad y(t) = -\frac{2dx(t)}{dt} = 2je^{-jt}$$

11. $$H(e^{j\Omega}) = \frac{Y(e^{j\Omega})}{X(e^{j\Omega})},$$

$$\left(\frac{2}{3}\right)^n u[n] \xleftrightarrow{\text{DTFT}} \frac{1}{1-\frac{2}{3}e^{-j\Omega}}$$

$$n\left(\frac{2}{3}\right)^n u[n] \xleftrightarrow{\text{DTFT}} j\frac{d}{d\Omega}\left(\frac{1}{1-\frac{2}{3}e^{-j\Omega}}\right)$$

$$= \frac{\frac{2}{3}e^{-j\Omega}}{\left(1-\frac{2}{3}e^{-j\Omega}\right)^2}$$

$$H(e^{j\Omega}) = \frac{\frac{2}{3}e^{-j\Omega}}{1-\frac{2}{3}e^{-j\Omega}} = \frac{2e^{-j\Omega}}{3-2e^{-j\Omega}}$$

12. $$H(e^{j\Omega}) = \frac{Y(e^{j\Omega})}{X(e^{j\Omega})} = \frac{\frac{2}{3}e^{-j\Omega}}{1-\frac{2}{3}e^{-j\Omega}}$$

$$\Rightarrow \left(1-\frac{2}{3}e^{-j\Omega}\right) Y(e^{j\Omega}) = \frac{2}{3}e^{-j\Omega}X(e^{j\Omega})$$

$$\Rightarrow y[n]-\frac{2}{3}y[n-1] = \frac{2}{3}x[n-1]$$

$$\Rightarrow 3y[n]-2y[n-1] = 2x[n-1].$$

$$F(z) = \frac{Z^{-1}\left(\frac{z^4-1}{z^4}\right)}{4\left(\frac{z-1}{z}\right)^2} = \frac{(z^4-1)\times z^2}{z^5\times 4(z-1)^2}$$

$$= \frac{z^4-1}{4z^3(z-1)^2} = \frac{(z^2+1)(z^2-1)}{4z^3(z-1)^2}$$

$$= \frac{(z^2+1)(z+1)(z-1)}{4z^3(z-1)^2}$$

$$= \frac{(z^2+1)(z+1)}{4z^3(z-1)}$$

As per final value theoram

$$\underset{t\to\infty}{Lt}\, f(t) = \underset{z\to 1}{Lt}\, F(z)(z-1)$$

$$= \frac{(z^2+1)(z+1)(z-1)}{4z^3(z-1)} = \frac{2\times 2}{4\times 1} = 1$$

14. $$X(z) = \frac{1}{1+3z^{-1}}$$

$$Y(z) = \frac{4}{1-2z^{-1}} - \frac{1}{1-\frac{1}{2}z^{-1}}$$

$$= \frac{3}{(1-2z^{-1})\left(1-\frac{1}{2}z^{-1}\right)}$$

$$H(z) = \frac{Y(z)}{X(z)} = \frac{10}{1-2z^{-1}} + \frac{-7}{1-\frac{1}{2}z^{-1}}$$

$$\Rightarrow h[n] = \left[10(2)^n - 7\left(\frac{1}{2}\right)^n\right]u(n)$$

■■

CONTROL SYSTEMS 6

6.1. BASICS OF CONTROL SYSTEM

- **System :** It is a combination or an arrangement of different physical components which act together as an entire unit to achieve certain objective.
- **Control System :** It is an interconnection of the physical components to provide a desired function, involving some kind of controlling action in it.
- **Controller :** It is element of the system which controls the plant or the process.
- **Time Varying and Time-Invariant System**

In *time varying control systems*, parameters of the systems are varying with time. It is independent of whether input and output are functions of time or not.

In *time invariant system*, if even though the inputs and outputs are functions of time but the parameters of system are independent of time, which are not varying with time and are constants.

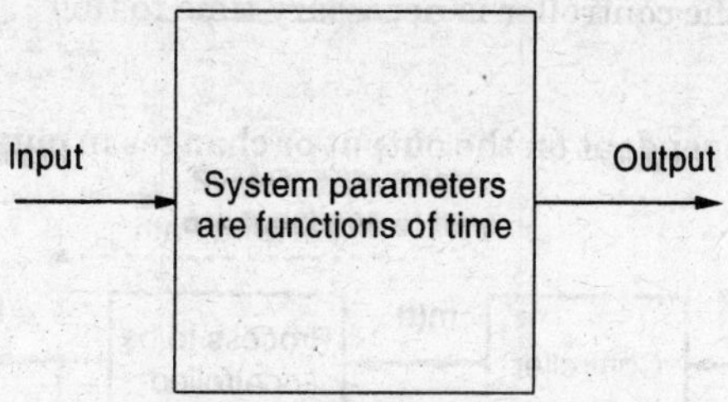

Fig. 6.1 Time variant system

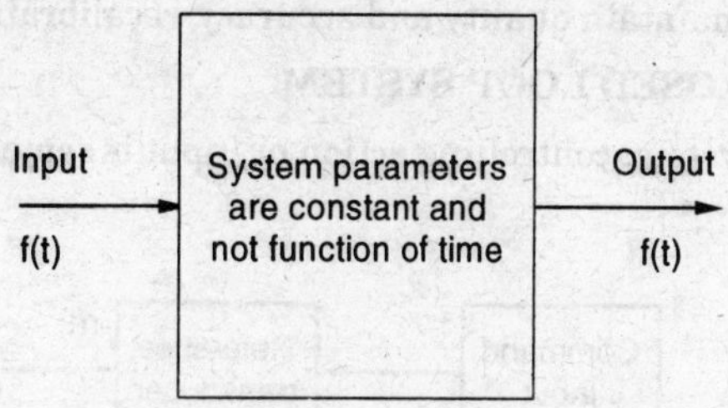

Fig. 6.2 Time invariant system

- **Linear and Non-linear Systems**

A system is said to be *linear*, if superposition principle applies to it.

Linear system must satisfies following two properties :

(i) $f(x+y) = f(x) + f(y)$

(ii) $f(\alpha x) = \alpha \cdot f(x)$

- **Continuous Time and Discrete Time Control Systems**

In *continuous time control system,* all system variables are functions of a continuous time variable '*t*'.

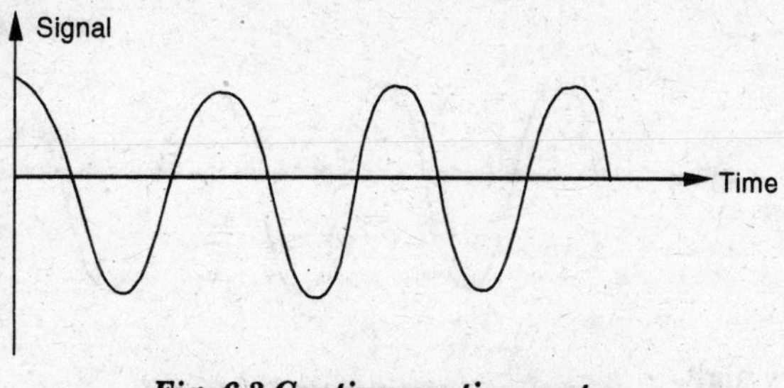

Fig. 6.3 Continuous time system

In *discrete time systems,* one or more system variables are known only at certain discrete intervals of time. They are not continuously dependent on the time.

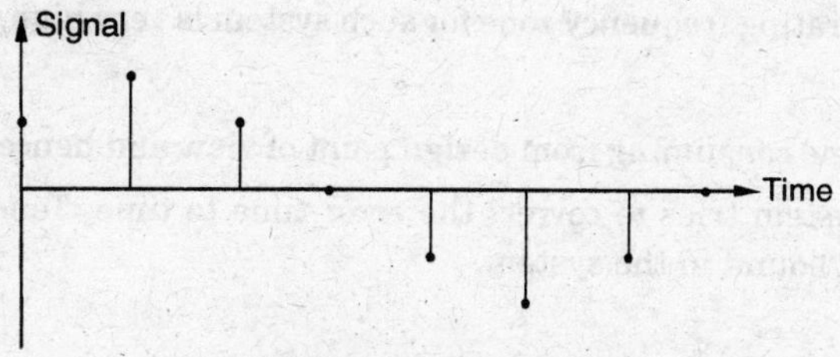

Fig. 6.4 Discrete time system

6.1.1. OPEN LOOP SYSTEM.

In this system, output is dependent on input but controlling action or input is totally independent of the output or changes in output of the system.

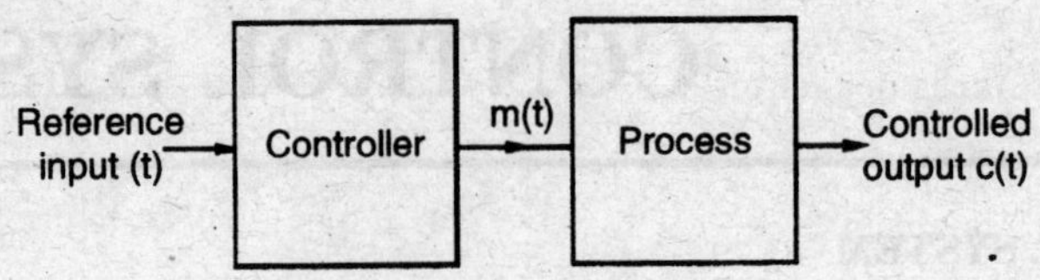

Fig.6.5. Open loop system

Advantages.

(*i*) Simple to design and hence economical.

(*ii*) Very much convenient when output is difficult to measure.

(*iii*) Easy from maintenance point of view.

(*iv*) Generally these are not troubled with the problems of stability.

Disadvantages.

(*i*) Inaccurate and unreliable.

(*ii*) Can not sense environmental changes.

(*iii*) To maintain quality and accuracy, recalibration of the controller is necessary time to time.

6.1.2. CLOSED LOOP SYSTEM.

In this system, controlling action or input is somehow dependent on the output or changes in output.

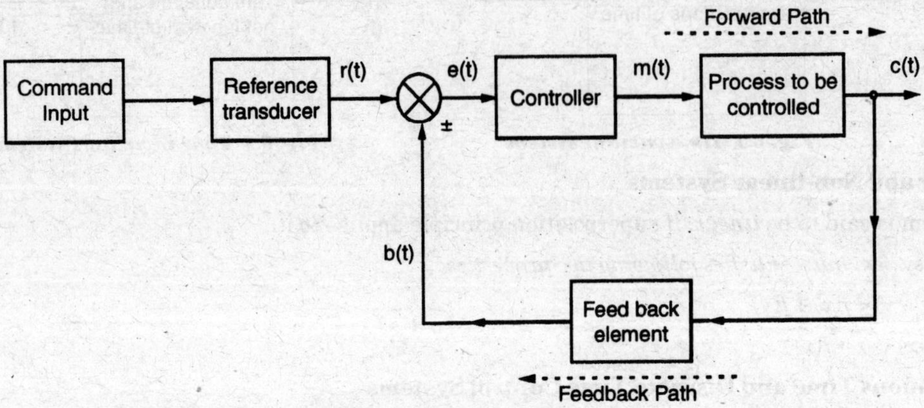

Fig. 6.6 Closed loop system

$r(t) \rightarrow$ Reference *input*

$c(t) \rightarrow$ Controlled *output*

$e(t) \rightarrow$ Error signal

$m(t) \rightarrow$ Manipulated signal

$b(t) \rightarrow$ Feedback signal

Advantages.

(*i*) Accuracy is always very high.

(*ii*) There is reduced effect of nonlinearities and distortions.

(*iii*) Senses environmental changes.

(*iv*) Band width, i.e. operating frequency zone for such system is very high.

Disadvantages.

(*i*) Complicated and time consuming from design point of view and hence costlier.

(*ii*) Due to feedback, system tries to correct the error time to time. Tendency to overcorrect the error may cause oscillations without bound in the system.

Comparison of Open loop and Closed loop control system

S.N.	Open Loop Systems	Closed Loop Systems
(*i*)	Any change in output has no effect on the input.	Changes in output, affects the input.
(*ii*)	Output measurement is not required. for operation of system.	Output measurement is necessary.
(*iii*)	Feed back element is absent.	Feedback element is present.
(*iv*)	Error detector is absent.	Error detector is necessary.
(*v*)	It is inaccurate and unreliable.	Highly accurate and reliable.
(*vi*)	Highly sensitive to the disturbances.	Less sensitive to the disturbances.
(*vii*)	Highly sensitive to the environmental changes.	Less sensitive to the environmantal changes.
(*viii*)	Bandwidth is small.	Bandwidth is large.
(*ix*)	Generally are stable in nature.	Stability is the major consideration while designing.
(*x*)	Simple to construct and cheap.	Complicated to design and hence costly.
(*xi*)	Highly affected by non-linearities.	Reduced effect of non-linearities.

6.1.3. PRINCIPAL OF FEEDBACK.

Feedback is a property of closed loop system. Feedback permits the output to be compared with the input to the system, so that appropriate control action may be formed as some function of the output and input.

Advantages and Disadvantages of feedback system.

(*i*) Increased accuracy

(*ii*) Reduced sensitivity

(*iii*) Reduced effects of non-linearities and distortion

(*iv*) Increased bandwidth

(*v*) Tendency towards oscillation or instability.

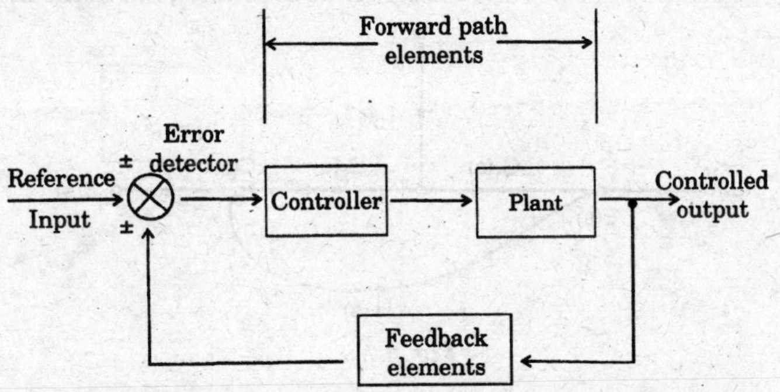

Fig. Block diagram of automatic closed-loop control system.

A basic control loop with negative feedback responds to reduce the error between command input (desired output) and the controlled input.

Controller (or a filter) is required to process the error signal such that the overall system satisfies certain criteria specifications.

Some Characteristics

(*i*) Reduction in effect of distortion signal

(*ii*) Reduction in steady state error

(*iii*) Transient response and frequency response performance

(*iv*) Sensitivity to parameter changes

Human being is a best example of a complex closed loop control system, in which
(*i*) human eyes acts as observer.
(*ii*) human brain acts as controller.
(*iii*) nervous system acts as connecting media.

Feedback characteristics.

One of the primary purpose of using feedback in control system is to reduce the sensitivity of system to parameter variations. Sensitivity is a measure of effectiveness of feedback in reducing the influence of the variations of system performance.

$$\text{Sensitivity} = \frac{\text{Percentage changes in T(s)}}{\text{Percentage changes in G(s)}}$$

$$S_G^T = \frac{\partial T}{\partial G} \times \frac{G}{T}$$

and $$S_H^T = \frac{\partial T}{\partial H} \times \frac{H}{T}$$

The sensitivity of closed loop system with respect to variation in G is reduced by a factor (1 + GH) as compared to that of open loop system.

The feedback controls the dynamics of the system by adjusting the location of its poles. The feedback introduces the possibility of instability, i.e. a closed loop system may be unstable even through the open loop system is stable.

A closed system is a low pass filter. It responds to frequency from d.c upto a certain value ω_b at which the gain drops to $\frac{1}{\sqrt{2}}$ of its dc value.

Thus closed-loop system has a bandwidth (1 + *k*) times the bandwidth of the open loop system. This implies increased response speed.

The effect of feedback is such that it reduces the effect of disturbances and noise signals in the forward path of the feedback loop.

The use of feedback shifts the position of poles and reduces time constants, but in the mean time dc gain has reduced.

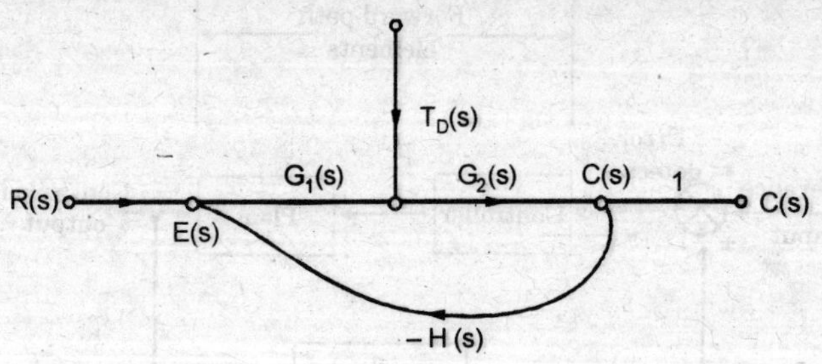

Fig. 6.7

$$\frac{C_D(s)}{T_D(s)} = \frac{G_2}{1 + G_1 G_2 H}$$

If $|G_1G_2H| >> 1$, then $$\frac{C_D(s)}{T_D(s)} = \frac{1}{G_1 H}$$

Hence it is seen that if G_1 is made sufficiently large, the effect of disturbance can be decreased by feedback. Effect of disturbance on the response of the system under consideration can be considerably reduced in closed loop system compared to that in open loop system.

The regeneration feedback sometimes used for increasing the loop gain of feedback system.

6.2. TRANSFER FUNCTION

It is defined as the ratio of Laplace transform of output (reponse) of the system to Laplace transform of input (excitation or driving function), under the assumption that all initial conditions are zero.

$$\text{Transfer Function, (T.F.)} = \frac{P(s)}{Q(s)}$$

This can be further expressed as

$$\text{T.F.} = \frac{a_o s^m + a_1 s^{m-1} + a_2 s^{m-2} + \ldots\ldots\ldots + a_m}{b_o s^n + b_1 s^{n-1} + b_2 s^{n-2} + \ldots\ldots\ldots + b_n}$$

The numerator and denominator can be factorised to get factorised form of the transfer function as

$$\text{Transfer Function} = \frac{K(s - s_a)(s - s_b)\ldots\ldots\ldots(s - s_m)}{(s - s_1)(s - s_2)\ldots\ldots\ldots(s - s_n)}$$

where, K is system gain function

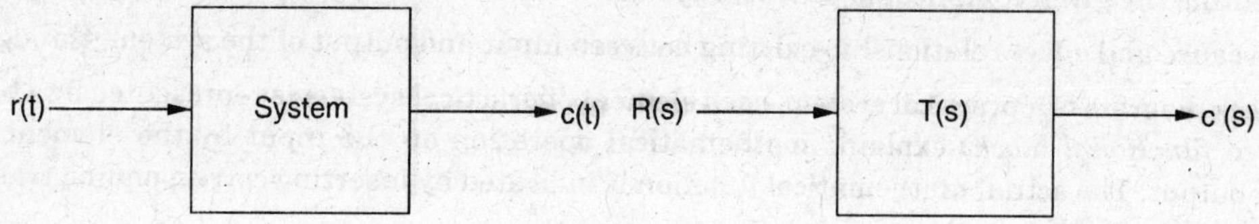

Fig. 6.8

$C(s) \rightarrow$ Laplace of $c(t)$

$R(s) \rightarrow$ Laplace of $r(t)$

If $T(s)$ is transfer function of the system, then

$$T(s) = \frac{\text{Laplace transform of output}}{\text{Laplace transform of input}}$$

$$= \frac{C(s)}{R(s)}$$

Characteristic Equation of a Transfer Function.

It is equation obtained by equating denominator of a transfer function to zero, whose roots are the poles of that transfer function.

$$F(s) = b_o s^n + b_1 s^{n-1} + b_2 s^{n-2} + \ldots + b_n = 0$$

6.2.1. PROPERTIES OF TRANSFER FUNCTION.

(*i*) The transfer function of a system is Laplace transform of its impulse response, i.e. if input to a system with transfer function $P(s)$ is an impulse and all initial values are zero, then output will be $P(s)$.

(*ii*) The system transfer function can be determined from the system differential equation by taking the Laplace transform and ignoring all terms, arising from initial values. The transfer function $P(s)$ is then given by

$$P(s) = \frac{Y(s)}{X(s)}$$

(*iii*) The system differential equation can be obtained from the transfer function by replacing the s variable with the differential operator D defined as $D = \frac{d}{dt}$.

(*iv*) The stability of a time-invarient linear system can be determined from the characteristic equation. The denominator of the system transfer function set equal to zero is the characteristic equation. Consequently if all the roots of the denominator have negative real parts, the system is stable.

(*v*) The roots of the denominator are the system poles and the roots of the numerator are the system zeros. The system transfer function can then be specified to within a constant by specifying the system poles and zeros. This constant usually denoted by 'K' is the **system gain factor.**

(*vi*) Transfer function is independent of the input, it simply gives the input-output relationship.

(*vii*) Highest power of the complex variable in the denominator of the transfer function determines order of the system.

6.2.2. POLES AND ZEROS OF TRANSFER FUNCTION.

Poles of Transfer Function.

The values of '*s*' which make the transfer function infinite after substituting in the denominator of a transfer function are called *'Poles'* of that transfer function.

So, values of $s_1, s_2, s_3 \ldots s_n$ are called *poles of the transfer function.*

Zeros of Transfer Function.

The values of 's' which make the transfer function zero after substituting in the numerator are called 'zeros' of that transfer function.

So, values of s_a, s_b ...s_m are called *zero of the transfer function.*

- Poles and zeros may be real or complex - conjugates or combination of both types.
- Poles and zeros may be located at the origin in *s*-plane.

6.3. BLOCK DIAGRAM REPRESENTATION

Black diagram is a pictorial/graphical representation of a (feedback control system) given system. It is a very simple way of representing the given complicated practical system.

It explains the cause and effect relationship existing between input and output of the system, through the blocks.

To draw the block diagram of a practical system, each element of practical system is represented by a block. Each block (which is called *functional block*) explains mathematical operation on the input by the element to produce the corresponding output. The actual mathematical function is indicated by inserting corresponding transfer function of the element inside the block.

For a closed loop systems, the function of comparing the different signals is indicated by the summing point while a point from which signal is taken for the feedback purpose is indicated by take-off point in block diagrams.

Take off point.

It is represented as a dot which signifies application of one input source to two or more systems.

Summing point.

It represents summation of two or more input signals entering in a system.

$$\textbf{Transfer function, } G(s) = \frac{C(s)}{R(s)}$$

Here, $R(s)$ = L.T. of input

$C(s)$ = L.T. of output variable

We can show above transfer function in block diagram as

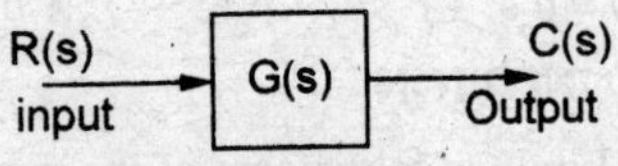

Summing or differencing point of signal is indicated as •

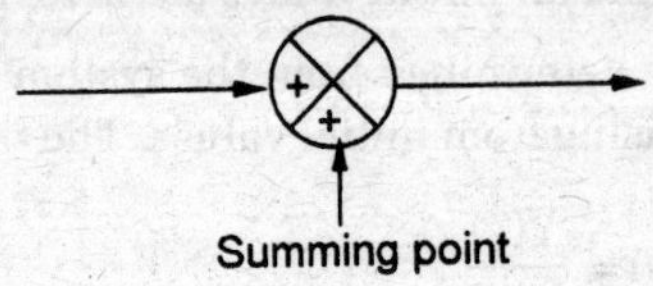

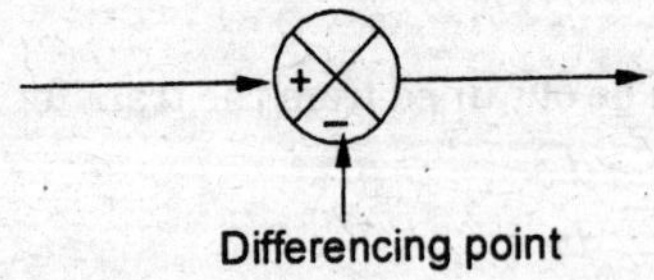

Taking off point of a signal is represented by

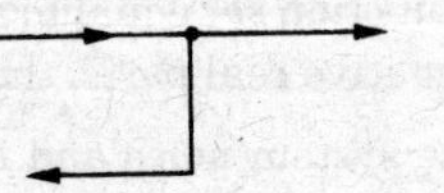

Block diagram of a Closed-Loop system.

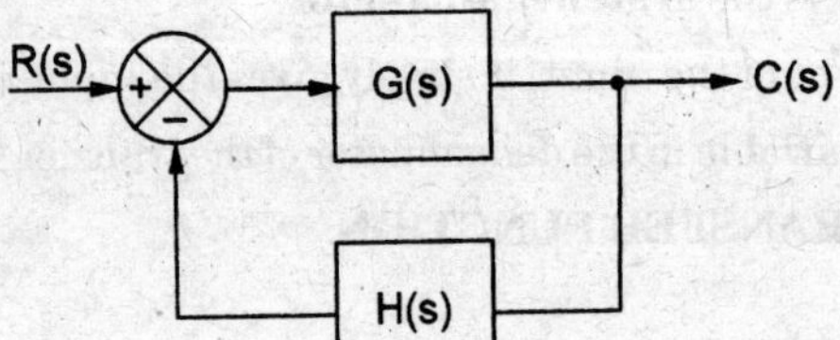

We have

$$C(s) = G(s)\,[R(s) - C(s)\,H(s)]$$

$$T(s) = \frac{C(s)}{R(s)} = \frac{G(s)}{1 + G(s)\,H(s)}$$

⇒ 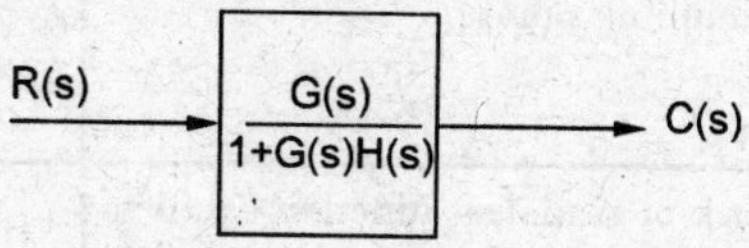

Multiple Input-Multiple Output System.

When multiple inputs are present in a linear system, each input can be treated independently of the others. Complete output of the system can be obtained by super position, i.e. output corresponding to each input alone are added together.

Two input linear system

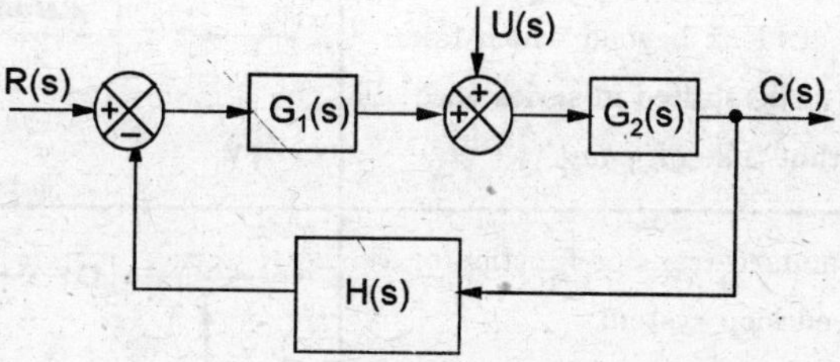

Steps :

Block Diagram Reduction Rule :

(i) Reduce series blocks

(ii) Reduce parallel blocks

(iii) Reduce minor feedback loops

(iv) Shift summing point to the left and take off point to the right as far as possible

(v) Repeat steps *(i)* to *(iv)* till canonical form is obtained

Table : Block Diagram Reduction Rules

1.	Associative Law	The two or more summing points directly connected can be interchanged.	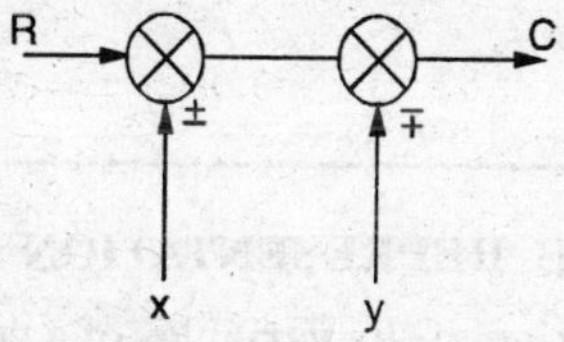	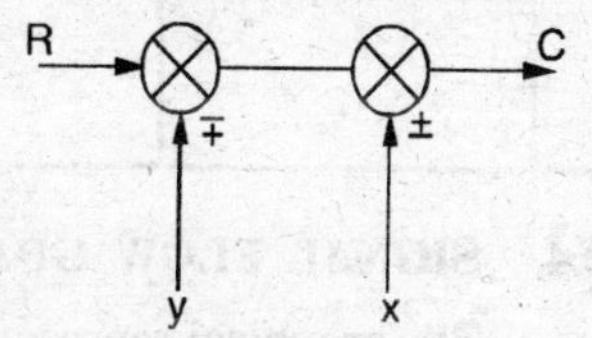
2.	Blocks in Series	Transfer function of such blocks get multiplied.	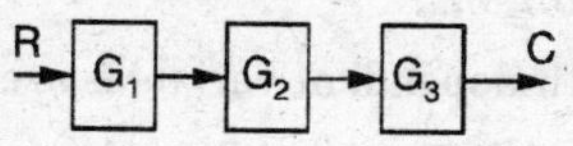	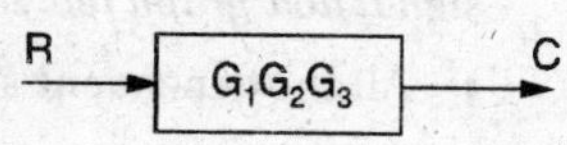
3.	Blocks in Parallel	Transfer function of such blocks get added algebrically.	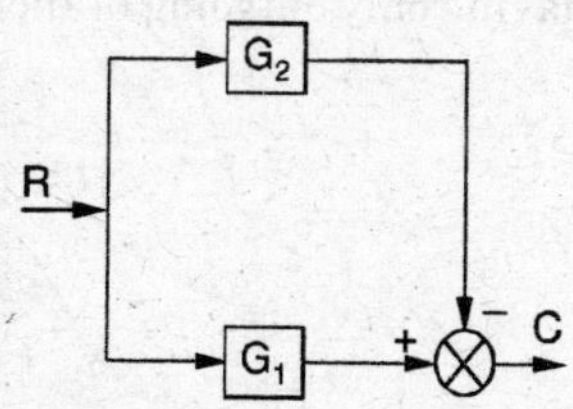	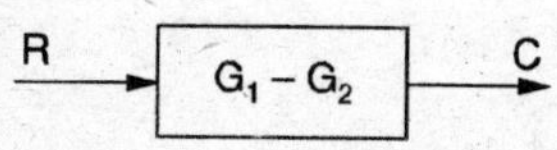
4.	Shifting summing point behind the block	Add a block of transfer function equal to recipro-cal of block behind which summing point is to be shifted in series with all signals at that summing point.	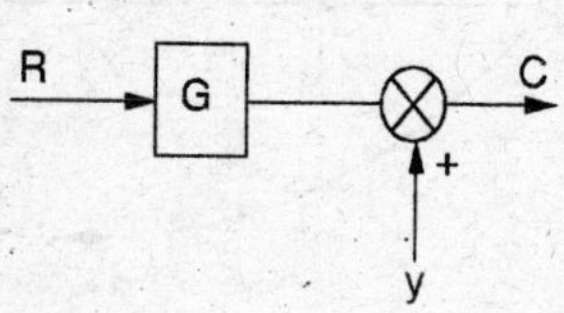	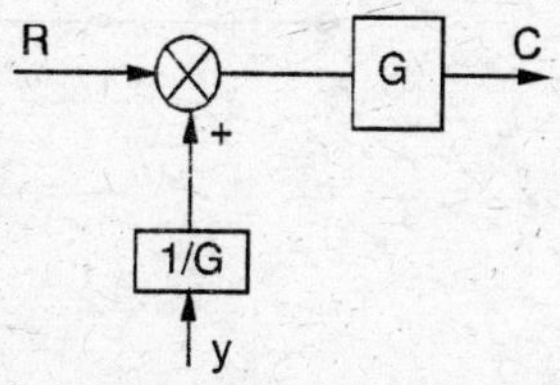

5.	**Shifting summing beyond the block**	**Add a block of transfer function same as the block beyond which summing point is to be shifted in series with all signals at that summing point.**	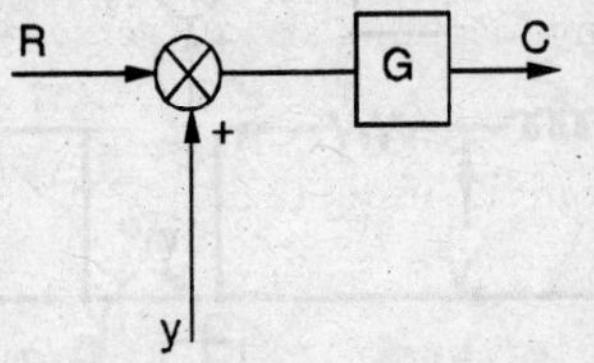	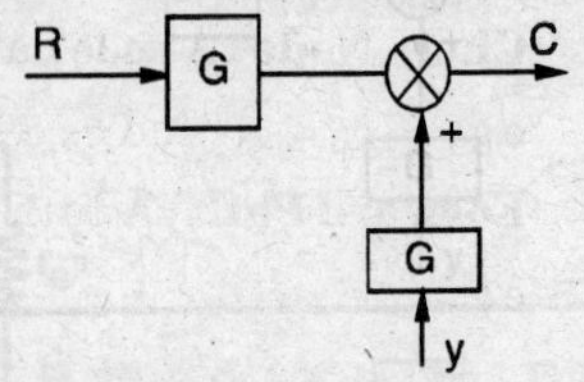
6.	**Shifting a take off behind the block**	**Add a block of transfer function equal to the block behind which take off point is to be shifted in series with all the signals at that take off point.**	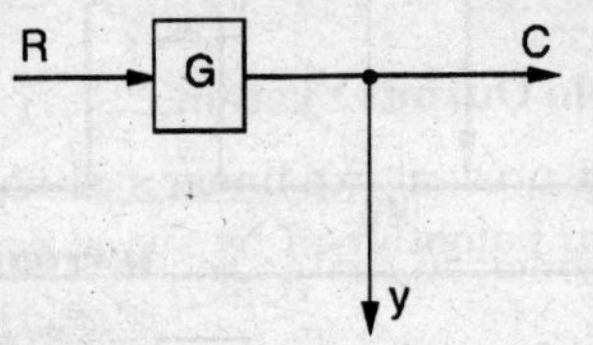	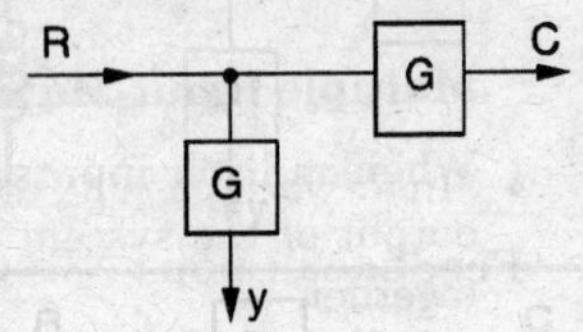
7.	**Shifting a take off beyond the block**	**Add a block of transfer function equal to recipro-cal of block beyond which take off point is to be shifted in series with all signals at that take off point.**	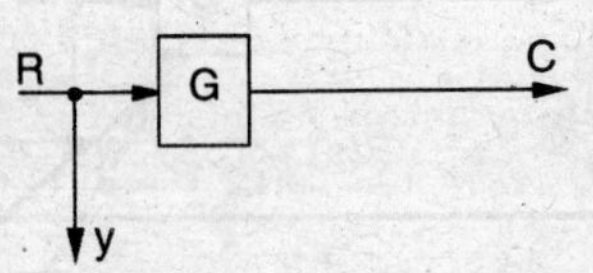	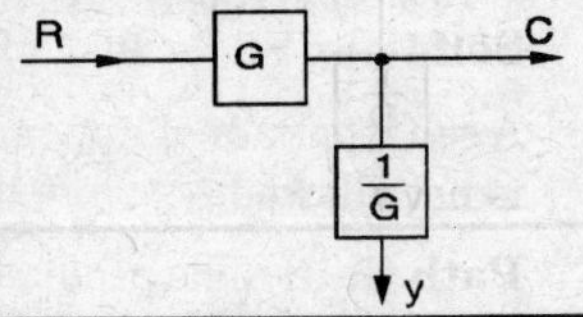
8.	**Removing minor feedback loop**	**Use the standard transfer function of a simple closed loop system.**	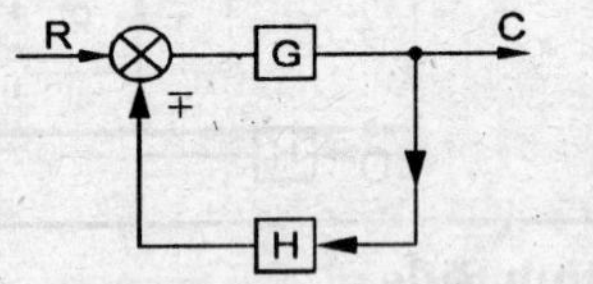	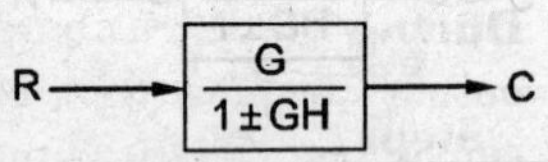
9.	**Shifting take off point after summing point**	**Add a new summing point to compensate for the shift as shown**	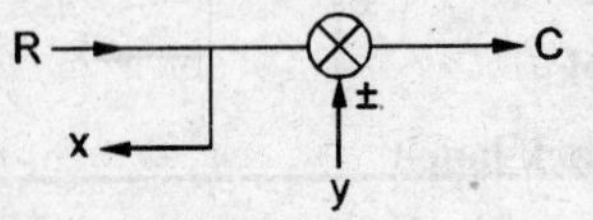	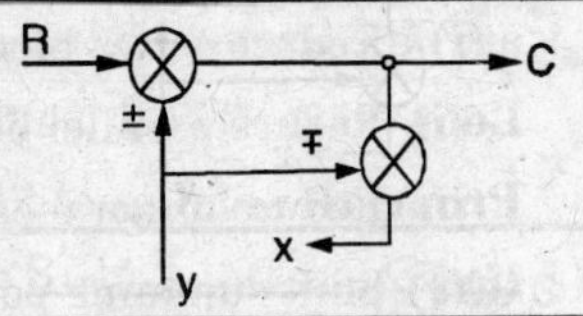
10.	**Shifting a take off point before a summing point**	**Add a summing point to compensate for a shift of take off point.**	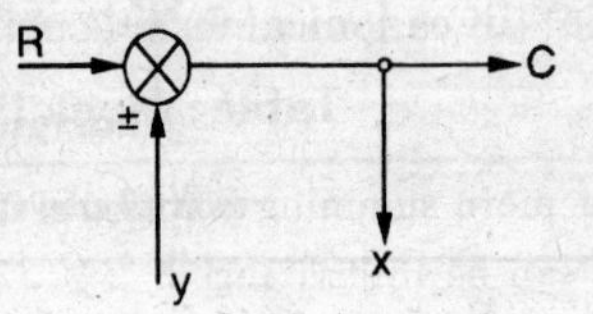	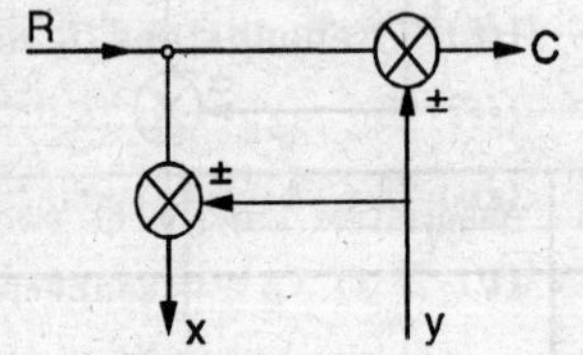

6.4. SIGNAL FLOW GRAPH REPRESENTATION

The graphical representation of the variables of a set of linear algebraic equations representing the system is called *signal flow graph representation.*

- **All the dependent and independent variables are represented by the nodes.**
- **The lines joining the nodes are called *Branches.***

Source Node : The node having only outgoing branches is known as **source or input node** e.g., x_o.

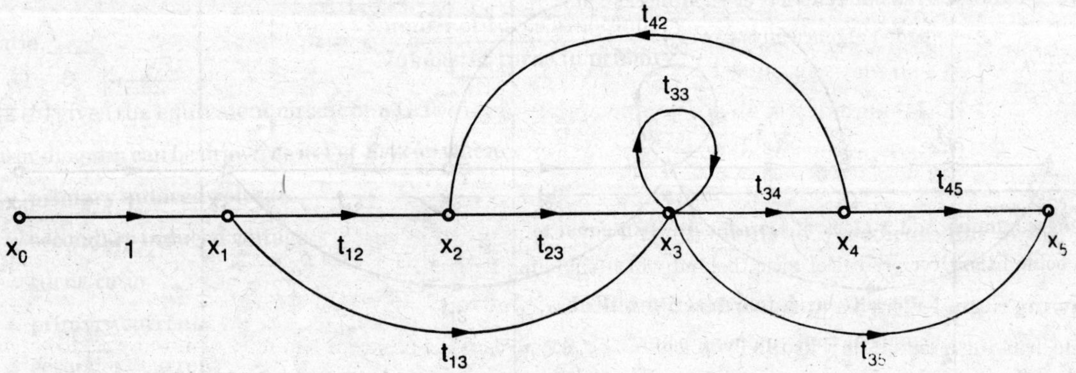

Fig. 6.9

Sink Node : The node having only incoming branches is known as **sink or output node**. e.g., x_5.

Chain Node : A node having incoming and outgoing branches is known as **chain node**.

e.g., x_1, x_2, x_3 and x_4.

Forward Path : A path from the input to output node is defined as **forward path.**

e.g., $x_o - x_1 - x_2 - x_3 - x_4 - x_5$

$x_o - x_1 - x_3 - x_5$

$x_o - x_1 - x_2 - x_3 - x_5$

$x_o - x_1 - x_3 - x_4 - x_5$

- In forward path no node is to be traced twice, or repeated.

Feedback Loop : A loop which orginates and terminates at the same node is known as **feedback path**

e.g., $x_2 - x_3 - x_4 - x_2$

Self Loop : A feedback loop consisting of only one node is called self loop. i.e., t_{33} at x_3 is self loop.

A self loop cannot appear while defining a forward path or feedback loop as node containing it gets traced twice which is not allowed.

Path Gain : The product of branch gains while going through a forward path is known as path gain.

e.g., path gain for path $x_o - x_1 - x_2 - x_3 - x_4 - x_5$ is $1 \times t_{12}\, t_{23}\, t_{34}\, t_{45}$

Dummy Node : If there exists incoming and outgoing branches both at first and last node representing input and output variables, then these cannot be called source and sink nodes. In such a case a separate input and output nodes can be created by adding branches with gain 1. Such nodes are called **dummy nodes.**

Non Touching Loops : If there is no node common and no common branch in between the two or more loops, such loops are called **non-touching loops.**

Loop Gain : The product of all the gains of the branches forming a loop is called **loop gain.**

Properties of Signal Flow Graph.

(i) Applicable only to linear time invariant systems.

(ii) The signal in the system flows along the branches and along the arrowheads associated with the branches.

(iii) The signals gets multiplied by the branch gain or branch transmittance when it travels along it.

(iv) The value of variable represented by any node is an algebraic sum of all the signals entering at the node.

(v) The value of variable represented by any node is available to all the branches leaving that node. The number of branches leaving a node does not affect the value of variable represented by that node.

Mason's Gain Formula.

The transmittance between an input node and output node is *overall transmittance*. Between these two nodes Mason's gain formula, which is applicable to the overall gain is

$$\text{Transfer Function} = \frac{\Sigma T_K \Delta_K}{\Delta}$$

where K = number of forward paths

T_K = gain of Kth forward paths

Δ = system determinant to be calculated as

Δ = 1 – [Σ all individual feedback loop gains]

+ [Σ Gain product of all possible combinations of two non-touching loops]

– [Σ Gain product of all possible combination of three non touching loops]

+ .....

Δ_K = value of above Δ by eliminating all loop gains and associated products which are touching the Kth forward path.

Drawing Signal Flow Graph from a Given Block Diagram.

While drawing a signal flow graph from a given block diagram the adjacent summing point and take off points (but not a take off point proceding a summing point in the direction of signal flow) are represented by a node and the block transfer function is represented by a line joining the respective nodes.

Rule for Drawing Signal Flow Graphs.

1. Signal travels along a branch in the direction of an arrow.
2. Input signal is multiplied by the transmittance to obtain the output signal.
3. Input signal at a node is the sum of all signals entering at that node.
4. A node transmits signal in all branches leaving that node.
5. Take off point after a summing point are represented by a single node.
6. Take off point precedes a summing point are represented by two separate nodes with a transmittance of unity between them.

The process of analysing performance and then determining transfer function of some physical systems by drawing block diagram is called mathematical modelling of control system or signal flow diagrams.

MATHEMATICAL MODELS OF PHYSICAL SYSTEMS

Mathematical models of most physical system are characterized by differential equations.

Dynamic Response.

When a mathematical model of a physical system is solved for various input conditions, the resultant represents the dynamic response of the system.

Linear System.

A mathematical model is linear if differential equations describing it has coefficients which are either function only of independent variable or are constant.

If $x_1(t)$ and $x_2(t)$ are input and $y_1(t)$ and $y_2(t)$ are responses individually, then system is linear if

$$\alpha_1 y_1(t) + \alpha_2 y_2(t) = \alpha_1 x_1(t) + \alpha_2 x_2(t)$$

If coefficient describing are function of time, then it is called *linear time varying system* and if coefficient are constant, then it is called *linear time invariant*.

- The differential equation describing a linear-time-invariant system can be reshaped into different form for the convenience of analysis.
- For transient response and frequency response analysis of single-input-single-output linear system, transfer-function representation forms a useful model.
- When a system has multiple inputs and outputs, the vector-matrix notation may be more convenient.

Consider rotational mechanical system

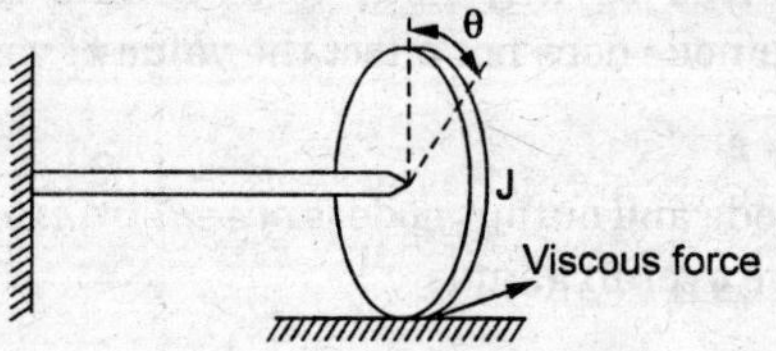

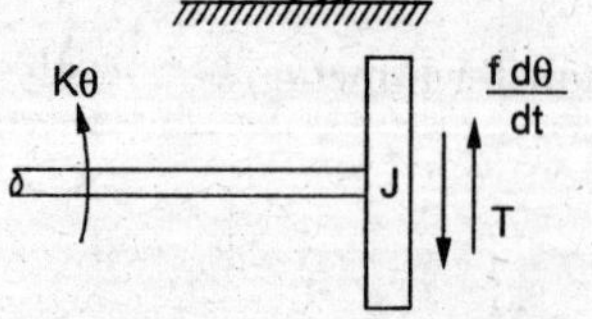

Torque equation will be,

$$T - f\frac{d\theta}{dt} \qquad - K\theta = J\frac{d\theta^2}{dt^2}$$

TRANSLATION MECHANICAL SYSTEM

Various Elements of Machine of Translation.

(i) Mass Element :

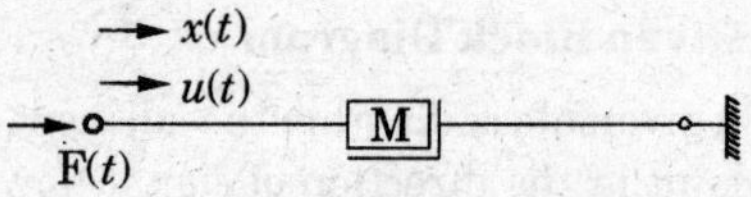

$$F(t) = M\frac{du(t)}{dt} = M\frac{d^2x(t)}{dt^2}$$

***(ii)* Spring Element :**

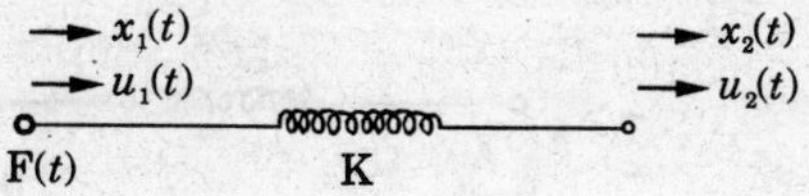

$$F(t) = K(x_1 - x_2) = Kx(t)$$

$$= K\int_{-\infty}^{t}(u_1 - u_2)\,dt = K\int_{-\infty}^{t} u\,dt$$

where, K = spring constant

***(iii)* Damper Element :**

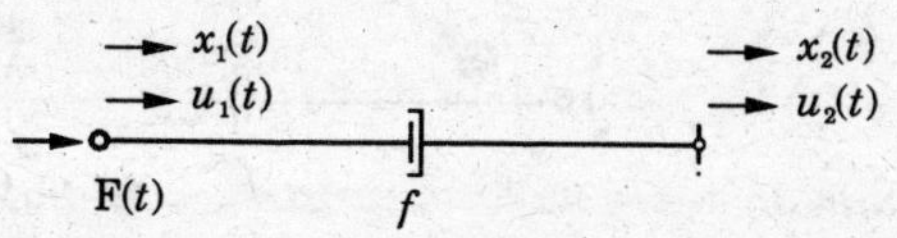

$$F(t) = f(u_1 - u_2) = fu(t) = f(\dot{x}_1 - \dot{x}_2) = f[\dot{x}(t)]$$

where f = damping constant.

Consider a translational spring-mass-damper system shown below, in which force is applied in the upward direction. Then this force is distributed on all the three element of the mass-spring damper system.

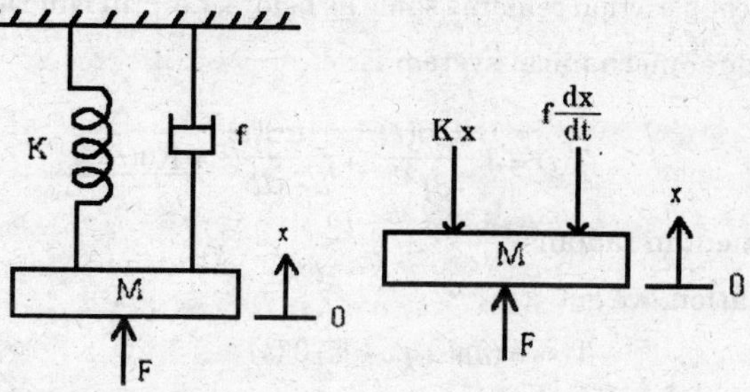

This force F is applied on mass M (unit is kg) results into displacement X. If spring deflection constant is K (Newton meter) and friction coefficient is f (Newton/rad/sec), then equation of motion for the system is obtained by applying second law of translation motion.

$$F = M\frac{d^2x(t)}{dt^2} + f\frac{dx(t)}{dt} + Kx(t) \quad ...(i)$$

This equation is a linear, constant coefficient, second order differential equation.

Taking Laplace transform of the above equation, we have

$$F(s) = M[s^2X(s) - sx(0^+) - x'(0)^+] + f[sX(s) - x(0^+)] + KX(s)$$

Now let the system starts from rest and hence initial condition is assumed zero.

Then force, $F(s) = Ms^2X(s) + fs\,X(s) + K\,X(s)$

Transfer function of the system with initial condition zero is given by

$$G(s) = \frac{X(s)}{F(s)} = \frac{1}{Ms^2 + fs + K}$$

ROTATIONAL MECHANICAL SYSTEM

***(i)* Inertia Element :**

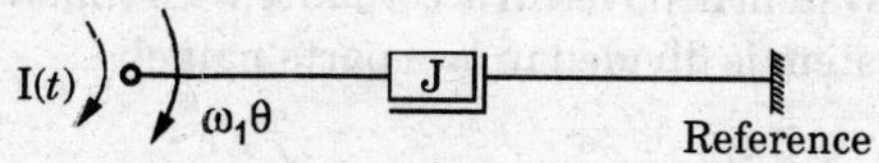

$$I(t) = J\frac{d\omega(t)}{dt} = J\frac{d_2\theta(t)}{dt^2}$$

where, J = inertia constant.

(ii) **Torsional Spring Element :**

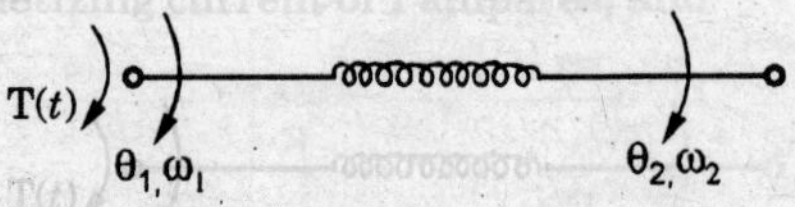

$$T(t) = K(\theta_1 - \theta_2) = K\theta(t)$$

$$= K\int_{-\infty}^{t}(\omega_1 - \omega_2)\, dt = K\int_{-\infty}^{t}\omega(t)\, dt$$

where, K = torsional spring constant.

(iii) **Damper Element :**

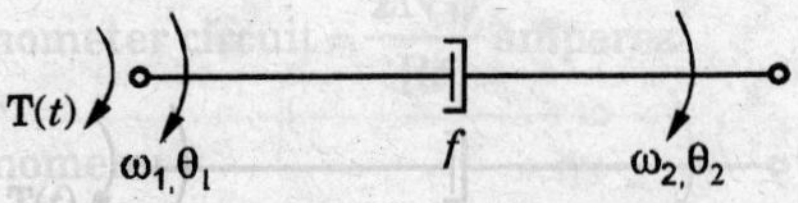

$$T(t) = f(\omega_1 - \omega_2) = f\,\omega(t)$$

$$= f(\dot{\theta}_1 - \dot{\theta}_2) = f[\dot{\theta}(t)]$$

where, f = torsional damping constant.

Apply torque T(t) (in Nm), which is analogus to force in translation system. In place of mass, take moment of inertia J (in kg-m^2). Coefficient of viscous friction remains same as before, i.e. f (in Nm/rad/sec.) K is called **torsional constant.**

Similary equation for rotational mechanical system is

$$T(t) = J\frac{d^2\theta(t)}{dt^2} + f\frac{d\theta(t)}{dt} + K\theta(t) \quad ...(ii)$$

where, θ = angular displacement in radians

Taking Laplace of above equation, we get

$$T(s) = (Js^2 + fs + K)\,\theta(s)$$

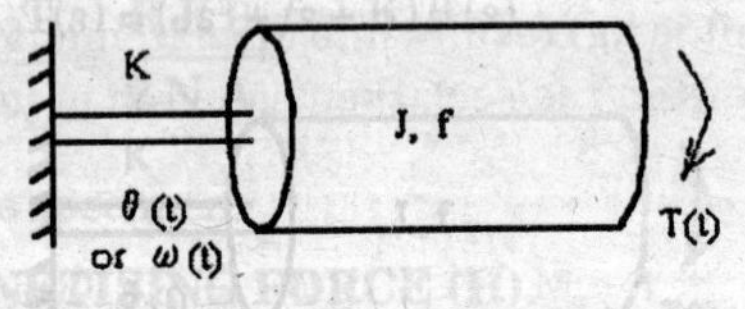

Transfer function is given by

$$\frac{\theta(s)}{T(s)} = \frac{1}{(Js^2 + fs + K)}$$

Taking output quantity in terms of angular velocity of shaft ω(t) in rad/sec, we have

$$\omega(t) = \frac{d\theta}{dt} \text{ or } \omega(s) = s\theta(s)$$

$$\therefore \quad \frac{\omega(s)}{T(s)} = \frac{s}{Js^2 + fs + K}$$

6.5. TIME RESPONSE ANALYSIS OF CONTROL SYSTEM

INTRODUCTION

Time response means how a system behaves in accordance with time when a specified input test signal is applied. The time response of a control system is divided in two parts namely :

(i) Transient response.

(ii) Steady state response.

The transient part of time response reveals the nature of response (i.e. oscillatory or overdamped) and also gives an indication about its speed.

The steady state part of time response reveals the accuracy of a control system. Steady state error is observed if the actual output does not exactly match with the input.

Comparison between Transient response and Steady state response

Transient response	Steady state response
1. The time of response up to 3T or 4T is called transient response. As time increases transient response becomes zero.	1. Response after 4 T is called steady state (T = time constant) i.e. the response which remains after the transient has died out, indicate the final accuracy of the system.
2. It does not depend on input signal.	2. It depends on the input signal applied.
3. It depends on poles and zeros of a system and reveals the nature and speed of response.	3. The steady state part reveals the accuracy of a control system.

6.5.1. Standard Test Inputs

The signals which are most commonly used as reference input are defined as **standard test inputs.**

***(i)* Step Input (Position Function) :**

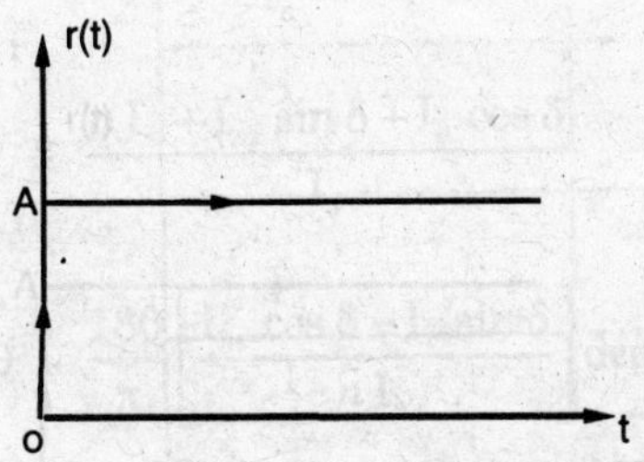

$r(t) = A$ for $t \geq 0$

$= 0$ for $t < 0$

If A = 1, then it is called **unit step,** denoted by $u(t)$

***(ii)* Ramp Input (Velocity Function) :**

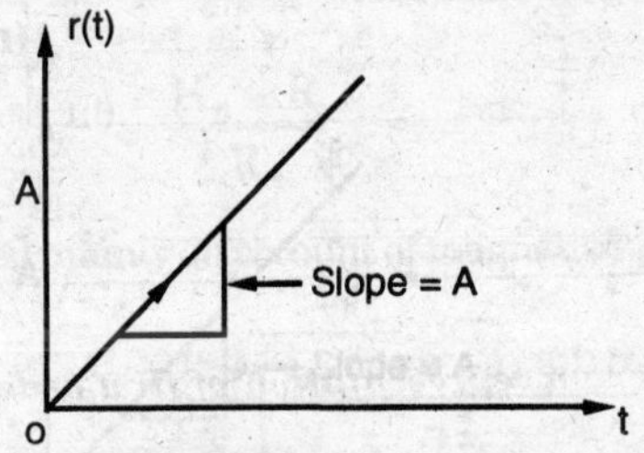

$r(t) = At$ for $t \geq 0$

$= 0$ for $t < 0$

If A = 1, it is called **unit ramp input.**

***(iii)* Parabolic Input (Acceleration Function) :**

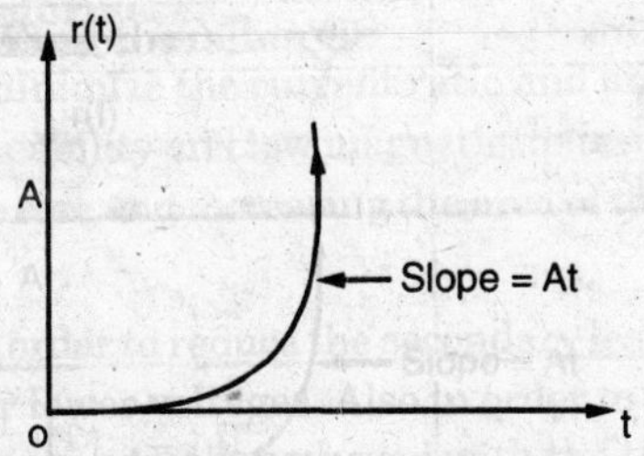

$r(t) = \frac{A}{2} t^2$ for $t \geq 0$

$= 0$ for $t < 0$

for A = 1, unit parabolic

(iv) Impulse Input :

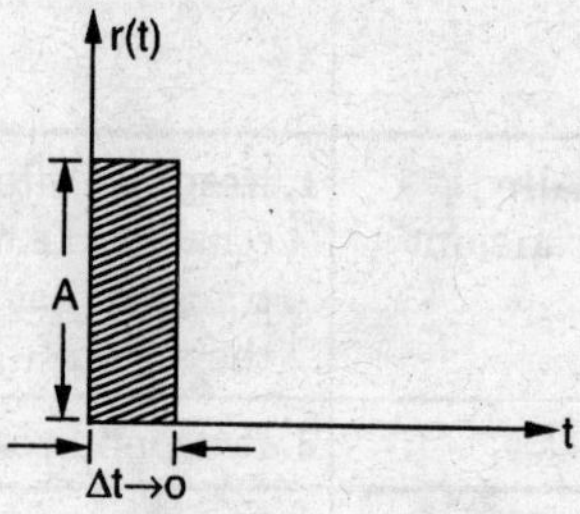

$r(t) = A$ for $t = 0$

$= 0$ for $t \neq 0$

$r(t)$	R(s)
Unit Step	$\frac{1}{s}$
Unit Ramp	$\frac{1}{s^2}$
Unit Parabolic	$\frac{1}{s^3}$
Unit Impulse	1

Time Response of a First Order Control System

For a firstorder linear control system, the highest power in donominator of its transfer function is 1. Consider the simple block diagram of a First Order unity feeback closed loop system as shown in Fig.

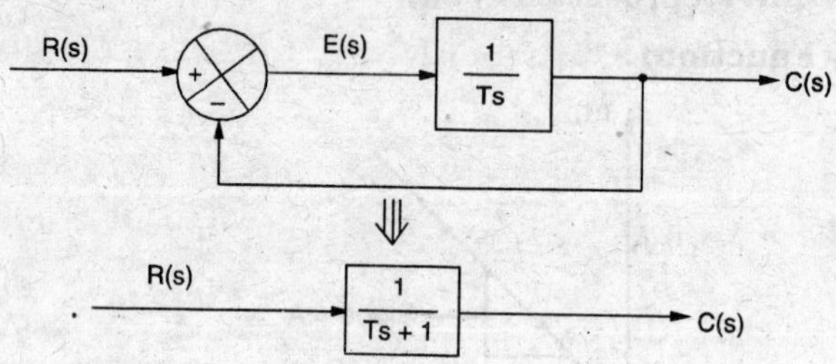

Fig. Block diagram representation of first order system.

Closed loop transfer is function given by

$$\frac{C(s)}{R(s)} = \frac{1}{Ts+1}$$

Relation between First Order system responses.

Input to the system	Response	Signal error function	Steady state Error
Unit impulse, 1	$C(t) = \frac{1}{T} e^{-t/T}$	$r(t) - c(t)$	0
Unit step, $\frac{1}{s}$	$C(t) = 1 - e^{-t/T}$	$e^{-t/T}$	0
Unit ramp, $\frac{1}{s^2}$	$C(t) = t - T + Te^{-t/T}$	$T(1 - e^{-t/T})$	T

From the above table it is clear that unit step response is the first derivative of unit ramp response and unit impulse response is the first derivative of unit step response.

Time Response of Second Order Control System

For a second order linear system, the highest power in denominator of its transfer function is 2.

Consider a simple block diagram of second order unity feedback closed loop systems as shown in Fig.

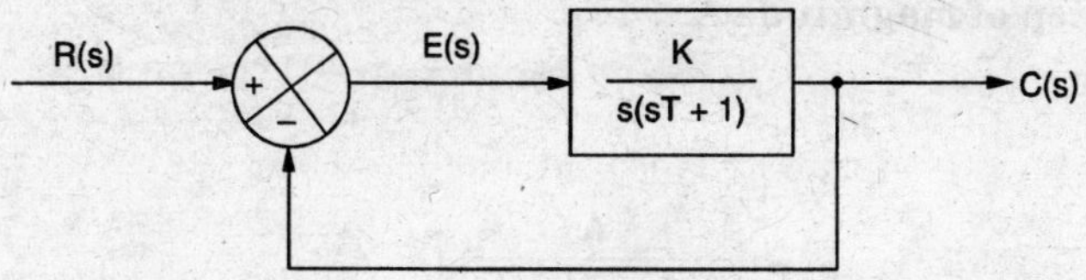

Fig. Block diagram representation of second order system

Time Response specification of Second Order System :

Steady state error

	Steady State errors		
	Type - 0	**Type - 1**	**Type - 2**
Unit step	$\frac{1}{1+k_p}$	0	0
Unit - ramp	∞	$\frac{1}{k_v}$	0
Unit - parabolic	∞	∞	$\frac{1}{k_a}$

Here, k_p = position error constant = $\lim_{S\to 0} G(s)$

k_v = velocity error constant = $\lim_{S\to 0} sG(s)$

k_a = acceleration error constant = $\lim_{S\to 0} s^2G(s)$

6.5.2. Steady State Error

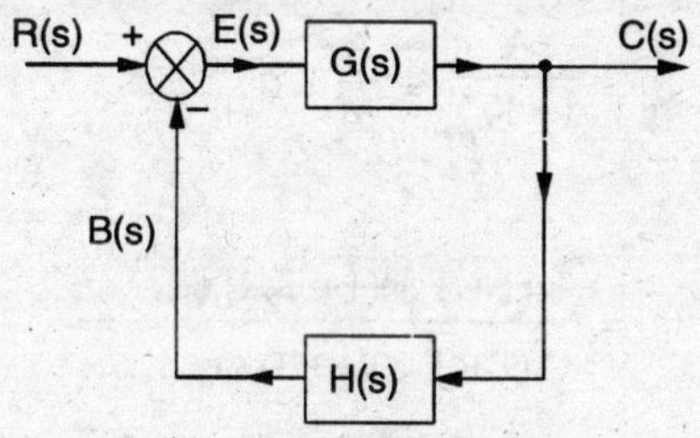

Fig. 6.10

E(s) = Error Signal B(s) = Feedback Signal

It is the difference between the actual output and the desired output.

$$E(s) = R(s) - B(s)$$

$$B(s) = C(s) \cdot H(s)$$

$$E(s) = R(s) - C(s)\,H(s)$$

$$C(s) = E(s) \cdot G(s)$$

$$E(s) = R(s) - E(s) \cdot G(s) \cdot H(s)$$

For non unity feedback $E(s) = \frac{R(s)}{1+G(s)H(s)}$

For unity feedback [H(s) = 1] $E(s) = \frac{R(s)}{1+G(s)}$

From the final value theorem, steady state error

$$e_{ss} = \underset{t\to\infty}{\text{Lt}}\, e(t) = \underset{s\to 0}{\text{Lt}}\, sE(s)$$

$$e_{ss} = \underset{s\to 0}{\text{Lt}}\left[\frac{sR(s)}{1+G(s)H(s)}\right]$$

Effect of input on Steady State Error

(*i*) Reference Input is step of magnitude A.

$$R(s) = \frac{A}{s}$$

$$e_{ss} = \frac{A}{1 + \underset{s\to 0}{\text{Lt}}\ G(s)H(s)}$$

$\lim_{s\to 0} G(s)\,H(s)$ is a constant and called **positional error coefficient**

$$e_{ss} = \frac{A}{1+K_p}$$

(*a*) *For Type '0' System :*

$$G(s)\,H(s) = \frac{K(1+T_1 s)(1+T_2 s)\ldots\ldots\ldots}{(1+T_a s)(1+T_b s)\ldots\ldots\ldots}$$

For step input, $K_p = \lim_{s\to 0} G(s)\,H(s) = K$

$$e_{ss} = \frac{A}{1+K_p} = \frac{A}{1+K}$$

(*b*) *For Type '1' system :*

$$G(s)\,H(s) = \frac{K(1+T_1 s)(1+T_2 s)\ldots\ldots\ldots}{s(1+T_a s)(1+T_b s)\ldots\ldots\ldots}$$

$$K_p = \lim_{s\to 0} G(s)\,H(s) = \infty$$

$$e_{ss} = \frac{A}{1+K_p} = \frac{A}{\infty} = 0$$

(*c*) *For Type '2' system :*

$$G(s)\,H(s) = \frac{K(1+T_1 s)(1+T_2 s)\ldots\ldots\ldots}{s^2(1+T_a s)(1+T_b s)\ldots\ldots\ldots}$$

$$K_p = \lim_{s\to 0} G(s)\,H(s) = \infty$$

$$e_{ss} = \frac{A}{1+K_p} = \frac{A}{\infty} = 0$$

(*ii*) When Reference Input is ramp of magnitude 'A'

$$R(s) = \frac{A}{s^2}$$

$$e_{ss} = \lim_{s\to 0} \frac{sR(s)}{1+G(s)H(s)} = \lim_{s\to 0} \frac{s \cdot A/s^2}{1+G(s)H(s)}$$

$$= \lim_{s\to 0} \frac{A}{s[1+G(s)H(s)]} = \lim_{s\to 0} \frac{A}{sG(s)H(s)}$$

$$K_v = \lim_{s\to 0} sG(s)\,H(s)$$

= velocity error coefficient

$$e_{ss} = \frac{A}{K_v}$$

(a) *For type '0' system :*

$$G(s)\,H(s) = \frac{K(1+T_1 s)(1+T_2 s)........}{(1+T_a s)(1+T_b s)........} = 0$$

$$K_v = \lim_{s\to 0} sG(s)\,H(s)$$

$$e_{ss} = \frac{A}{0} = \infty$$

(b) *For type '1' system subjected to ramp input :*

$$G(s)\,H(s) = \frac{K(1+T_1 s)(1+T_2 s)........}{s(1+T_a s)(1+T_b s)........}$$

$$K_v = \lim_{s\to 0} sG(s)\,H(s) = K$$

$$e_{ss} = \frac{A}{K_v} = \frac{A}{K_v} \text{ (finite)}$$

(c) *For type '2' system excited by ramp input :*

$$G(s)\,H(s) = \frac{K(1+T_1 s)(1+T_2 s)........}{s^2(1+T_a s)(1+T_b s)........}$$

$$K_v = \lim_{s\to 0} sG(s)\,H(s) = \infty$$

$$\therefore \quad e_{ss} = \frac{A}{K_v} = \frac{A}{\infty} = 0$$

(*iii*) Steady-State error due to parabolic input.

$$r(t) = \frac{A}{2} t^2$$

$$R(s) = \frac{A}{s^3}$$

$$\therefore \quad e_{ss} = \lim_{s\to 0} \frac{A}{s^2 G(s) H(s)}$$

So for a selected system, $\lim_{s\to 0} s^2\,G(s)\,H(s)$ is constant and called *acceleration error coefficient* (K_a).

$$K_a = \lim_{s\to 0} s^2\,G(s)\,H(s) = \text{acceleration error coefficient}$$

and corresponding error,
$$e_{ss} = \frac{A}{K_a}.$$

(a) *For type '0' system :*

$$G(s)\,H(s) = \frac{K(1+T_1 s)(1+T_2 s)........}{(1+T_a s)(1+T_b s)........}$$

$$K_a = \lim_{s\to 0} s^2\,G(s)\,H(s) = 0$$

$$\therefore \quad e_{ss} = \frac{A}{K_a} = \infty$$

(b) *For type '1' system :*

$$G(s)\,H(s) = \frac{K(1+T_1 s)(1+T_2 s)........}{s(1+T_a s)(1+T_b s)........}$$

$$K_a = \lim_{s\to 0} s^2\,G(s)\,H(s) = 0$$

$$\therefore \quad e_{ss} = \frac{A}{K_a} = \infty$$

(c) *For type '2' system :*

$$G(s)\,H(s) = \frac{K(1+T_1 s)(1+T_2 s)........}{s^2(1+T_a s)(1+T_b s)........}$$

$$K_a = \lim_{s\to 0} s^2\,G(s)\,H(s) = K$$

$$\therefore \quad e_{ss} = \frac{A}{K_a} = \frac{A}{K_a} \text{ (finite)}$$

Type of system	Error coefficients			Error e_{ss} for		
	K_p	K_v	K_a	Step input	Ramp input	Parabolic input
0	K	0	0	$\frac{A}{1+K}$	∞	∞
1	∞	K	0	0	$\frac{A}{K}$	∞
2	∞	∞	K	0	0	$\frac{A}{K}$

6.5.3. TRANSIENT RESPONSE (c_t).

It is defined as the output variation during the time, it takes to achieve its final value.

It may be exponential or oscillatory in nature. Symbolically it is denoted as $c_t(t)$.

For stable operating system, $\lim_{t\to\infty} c_t(t) = 0$

It can also be defined as *that part of total response which approaches zero as time approaches infinity.*

It depends only upon the system components and their arrangements and does not depend on system input.

Steady state Response (c_{ss}).

It is that part of the time response which remains after complete transient response vanishes from the system output or it can be defined as *that part of the total response which does not approach zero as time approaches infinity.*

Steady state response depends on

(*i*) system component, and

(*ii*) input to the system.

Total time response, $c(t) = c_{ss}(t) + c_t(t)$

Analysis of second order system.

In the study of control system, linear constant coefficient second-order differential equations used are of the form:

$$\frac{d^2y}{dt^2} + 2\xi\omega_n\frac{dy}{dt} + \omega_n^2 y = \omega_n^2 . u$$

Here ξ represents the damping ratio, constant ω_n is the undamped natural frequency.

Every system has tendency to oppose the oscillatory behavious of the system which is called ***damping***.

It is measured by a factor ξ, which tells, how much dominant the oppositions is to the oscillation in the output. If it will be low, then system will oscillate but slowly, i.e. with damped frequency. In some system it may be so high that system output will not oscillate at all and only it will be exponential, so slow that it will take very long time to reach the steady state.

Most of the systems are designed with damping $\xi < 1$, to acheive high speed response.

The C.L.T.F (closed loop transfer function) for a standard second order system takes the form

$$\frac{C(s)}{R(s)} = \frac{\omega_n^2}{s^2 + 2\varepsilon\omega_n s + \omega_n^2} = \frac{p(s)}{q(s)}$$

$q(s) = s^2 + 2\,\xi\omega_n s + \omega_n^2 = 0$; is called *characteristic equation.*

S.No.	Range of ξ	Type of closed loop poles	Nature of response	System classification
1.	$\xi = 0$	Purely imaginary	Oscillation with constant frequency and amplitude	Undamped or oscillatory
2.	$0 < \xi < 1$	Complex conjugates with negative real part	Damped oscillation	Under damped or damped sinusoidal
3.	$\xi = 1$	Real, equal and negative	Critical and pure exponential	Critically damped
4.	$1 < \xi < \infty$	Real, unequal and negative	Purely exponential slow and sluggish	Overdamped

Expression for $c(t)$ (underdamped case).

$$c(t) = 1 - \frac{e^{-\xi\omega_n t}}{\sqrt{1-\xi^2}} \sin(\omega_d t + \theta)$$

$$\omega_d = \omega_n \sqrt{1-\xi^2}$$

$$\theta = \tan^{-1}\left\{\frac{\sqrt{1-\xi^2}}{\xi}\right\} \text{ radians.}$$

Transient response specifications

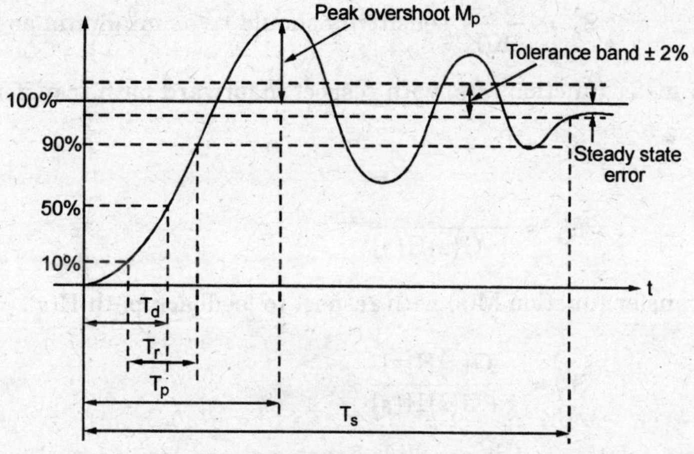

Fig. 6.11

Delay time (T_d) : It is the time required for the response to reach 50% of the final value in first attempt.

$$T_d = \frac{1 + 0.7\xi}{\omega_n}$$

Rise time (T_r) : It is the time required for the response to rise from 10% to 90% of the final value for overdamped system and 0 to 100% of the final value for underdamped systems.

$$T_r = \frac{\pi - \theta}{\omega_d} \text{ sec.} = \frac{\pi - \tan^{-1}\left\{\frac{\sqrt{1-\xi^2}}{\xi}\right\}}{\omega_n\sqrt{1-\xi^2}}$$

Peak time (T_p) : It is the time required for the response to reach its peak value. It is also defined as the time at which response undergoes the first overshoot which is always peak overshoot.

$$T_p = \frac{\pi}{\omega_d} = \frac{\pi}{\omega_n\sqrt{1-\xi^2}} \text{ sec}$$

Peak overshoot (M_p) : It is the largest error between reference input and output during the transient period.

$$\% M_p = e^{-\pi\xi/\sqrt{1-\xi^2}} \times 100$$

Settling time (T_s) : It is defined as the time required for the response to decrease and stay within specified percentage of its final value. (Generally 2% or 5% tolerance band)

$$\text{Time constant of system} = \frac{1}{\xi\omega_n} = T$$

$$T_s = 4 \times \text{Time constant}$$

$$= \frac{4}{\xi\omega_n} \text{ for a tolerance band of } \pm 2\% \text{ of steady state.}$$

$$T_s = \frac{3}{\xi\omega_n} \text{ for 5\% tolerance band.}$$

SENSITIVITY

Sensitivity gives an assessment of the system peformance as affected due to parameter variations. The use of feedback in a control system reduces the effect of parameteric variations.

Let, A is a variable in control system which changes its value and this change is considered due to parameteric variation of K, such as gain. Then sensitivity of control system is expressed as :

$$\text{Sensitivity} = \frac{\%\text{change in A}}{\%\text{change in K}}$$

$$S_K^A = \frac{\partial A/A}{\partial K/K}$$ **sensitivity should be as minimum as possible for stability**

(*a*) Sensitivity of overall transfer function M(s) with respect to forward path transfer function G(*s*).

(*i*) For Open loop. $S_G^M = 1$

(*ii*) For Close loop, $S_G^M = \dfrac{1}{1+G(s)H(s)}$

(*b*) Sensitivity of overall transfer function M(s) with respect to feedback path H(*s*).

$$S_H^M = \frac{-G(s)H(s)}{1+G(s)H(s)}$$

Comparing above sensitivity relations, it is concluded that a closed loop control system is more sensitive to variations in feedback path parameters H(*s*) than the variations in forward path parameters. Therefore feedback elements should be more rigid as compared to that of forward path elements.

6.5.4 Effect of parameter variations

(*i*) In open loop control system.

$$G(s) = \frac{C(s)}{R(s)}$$

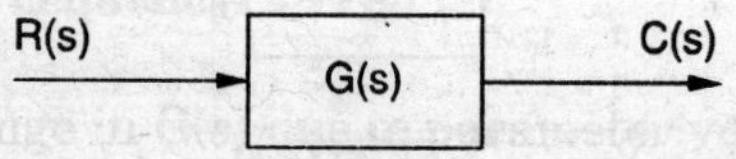

Let Δ G(*s*) be the change in G(*s*) due to parameter variations, where $|G(s)| >> |\Delta G(s)|$

The corresponding change in the output be Δ C(*s*).

$$C(s) + \Delta C(s) = [G(s) + \Delta G(s)] R(s)$$

$$\Delta C(s) = \Delta G(s) R(s)$$

(ii) Effect of Parameter Variations in an Closed Loop Control System

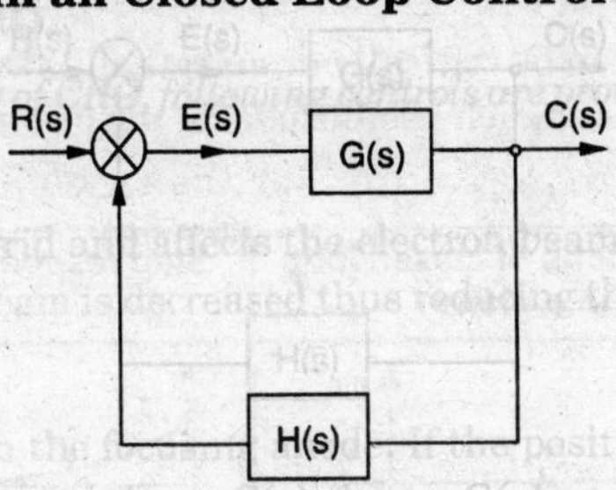

$$T(s) = \frac{C(s)}{R(s)} = \frac{G(s)}{1+G(s)H(s)}$$

Let Δ G(s) be the change in G(s) which is due to parameter variations in the system. The corresponding change in the output be Δ C(s).

$$\Delta C(s) = \frac{\Delta G(s)}{1+G(s)H(s)} \cdot R(s)$$

6.5.5. Sensitivity of a control system

It is defined as a measure of the amount by which the system transfer function differs from its nominal value when one of its parameters is varied from its nominal value.

(*i*) *Sensitivity of T(K) with respect to the parameter K*

$$S_K^{T(K)} = \frac{d \ln T(K)}{d \ln K}$$

$$= \frac{dT(K)/T(K)}{dK/K} = \frac{dT(K)}{dK}\frac{K}{T(K)}$$

(*ii*) *Sensitivity of the magnitude of T(K) with respect to the parameter K*

$$S_K^{|T(K)|} = \frac{d \ln |T(K)|}{d \ln K}$$

$$= \frac{|dT(K)|/|T(K)|}{dK/K} = \frac{d|T(K)|}{dK}\frac{K}{|T(K)|}$$

(*iii*) *Sensitivity of the phase angle ϕ_T of T(K) with respect to the parameter K*

$$S_K^{\phi_T} = \frac{d \ln \phi_T}{d \ln K} = \frac{d\phi_T/\phi_T}{dK/K} = \frac{d\phi_T}{dK}\frac{K}{\phi_T}$$

$$S_K^{T(K)} = S_K^{|T(K)|} + j\phi_T S_K^{\phi_T}$$

6.6. CONCEPT OF STABILITY

The stability of a system is determined by its response to inputs or disturbances. Intuitively, a stable system is one that will remain at rest unless excited by an external source and will return to rest if all excitations are removed. Stability can be precisely defined in terms of the impulse response of a system.

Stable system

A linear time invariant system is said to be stable if

(*i*) the system is excited by a bounded input, output is also bounded and controllable.

(*ii*) in the absence of input, output must tend to zero irrespective of the initial conditions.

Unstable system

A linear time invariant system is said to be unstable, if

(*i*) For a bounded input it produces unbounded output.

(*ii*) In absence of the input, output may not be returning to zero.

Critically or Marginally stable system

A linear time invariant system is said to be critically or marginally stable if for a bounded input its output oscillates with constant frequency and amplitude; such oscillations of output are called *undamped oscillations* or *sustained oscillations*.

S.No.	Nature of closed loop poles	Locations of closed loop poles in s-plane	Step response	Stability condition
1.	LHP real axis single pole $F(s) = \frac{1}{s+a}$	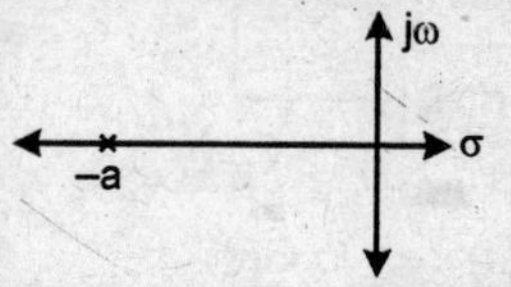	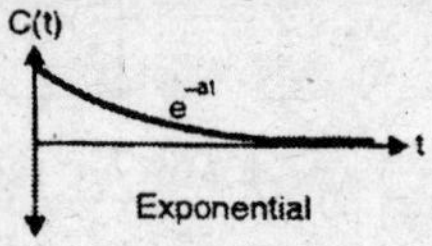 Exponential	Absolutely stable
2.	LHP real axis repeated poles $F(s) = \frac{1}{(s+a)^2}$	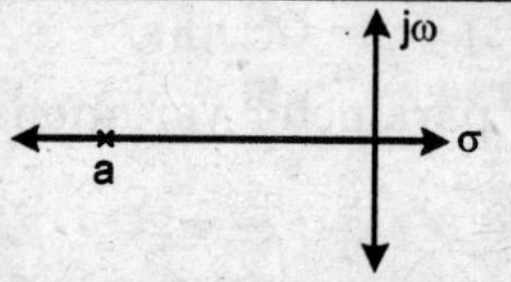	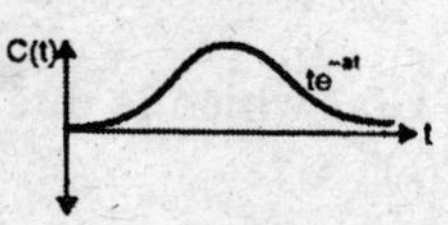	Absolutely stable
3.	LHP Complex conjugate pole $F(s) = \frac{1}{(s+a)^2 + b^2}$	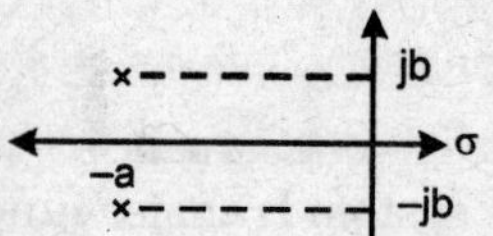	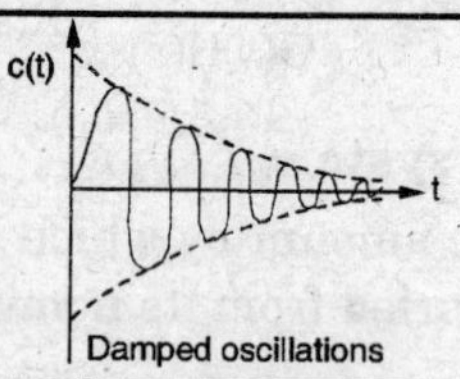 Damped oscillations	Absolutely stable
4.	jω-axis single pole $F(s) = \frac{1}{s^2 + a^2}$	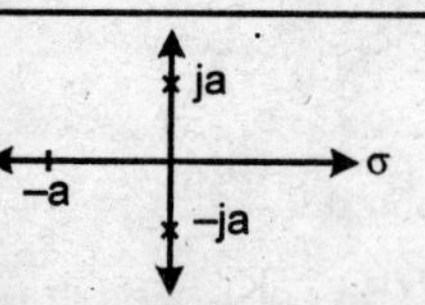	 Increasing amplitude	Marginal stable
5.	jω-axis repeated poles $F(s) = \frac{1}{(s^2 + a^2)^2}$	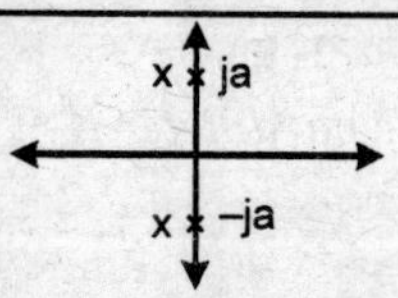	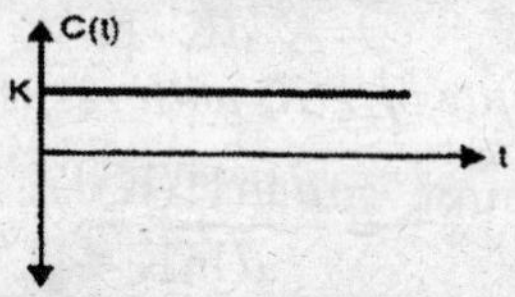	Unstable
6.	Origin single pole $F(s) = \frac{1}{s}$	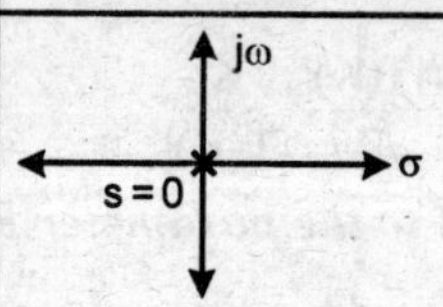	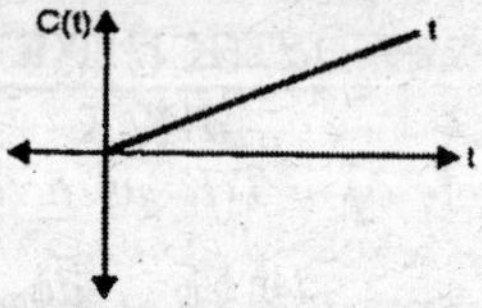	Marginal stable
7.	Origin repeated poles $F(s) = \frac{1}{s^2}$	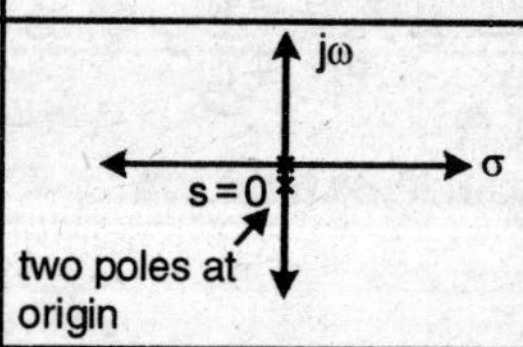	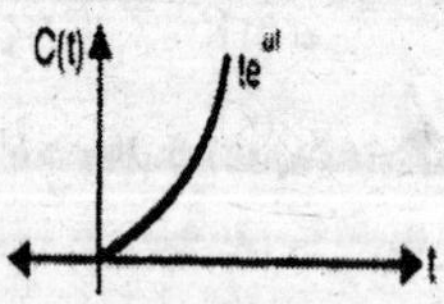	Unstable
8.	RHP real axis single pole $F(s) = \frac{1}{(s-a)}$	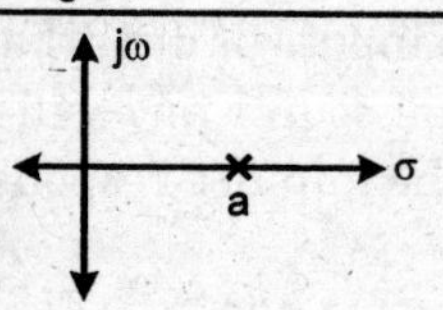	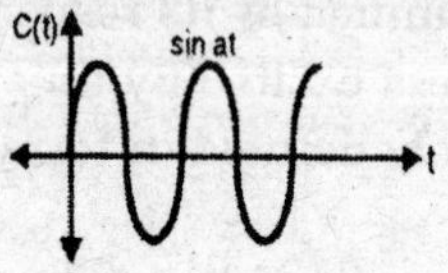 Constant amplitude oscillations	Unstable
9.	RHP real axis repeated poles $F(s) = \frac{1}{(s-a)^2}$	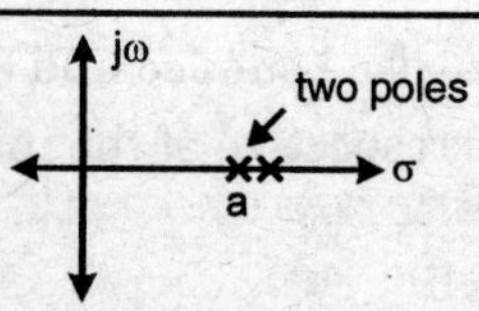	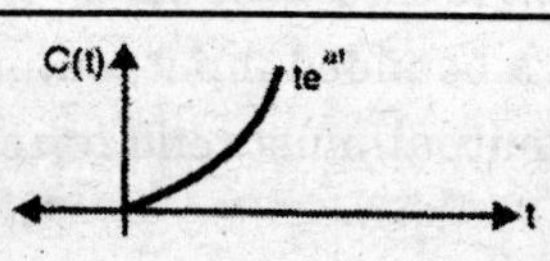	Unstable
10.	RHP complex conjugate poles $F(s) = \frac{1}{(s-a)^2 - b^2}$	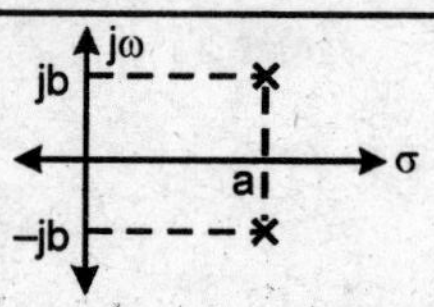	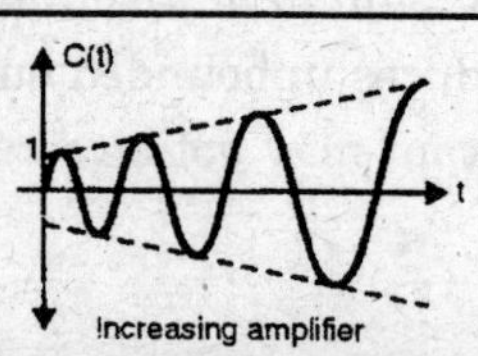 Increasing amplifier	Unstable

Conditions for Stability.

Necessary but not sufficient condition is that all the coefficient of its characteristic equation be real and have the same sign and none of the coefficient should be zero, *i.e.* for the system to be stable, all the roots should have negative real part, *i.e.* all roots are in the left half of *s*-plane.

First step in analysing the stability of the system is to examine its characteristic equation. If some coefficient are negative or zero, then it can be concluded that the system is not stable.

Stability of linear, time invariant system is defined in following ways :

(*i*) Bounded input, Bounded output stability

For a system to be stable the output should be bounded for any bounded input. If for such a system, output is unbounded, then its stability is *unpredictable*.

(*ii*) Absolute stability

A system is absolutely stable, if it remains stable for all the values of parameter variations for the bounded input.

(*iii*) Conditional stability

If a system remains stable for a particular range of parameter of any system, then it is called conditional stable system.

(*iv*) Relative stability

It gives the stability of any system in comparison to the other system. It is mainly defined in terms of gain margin, phase margin and location of poles in s-plane.

(*v*) Asymptotic stability

If input is removed from system, then output must be reduced to zero. This is called *asymptotic stability*.

Absolute stability	Relative stability
1. It is qualitative analysis of stability.	1. It is comparative analysis of stability.
2. It can be determined from location of the roots of the characteristic equation in s-plane.	2. Measures of relative stability are maximum damping ratio, gain margin, phase margin.

If order of the system is higher, it is not convenient to obtain the time solution and as such stability of such system cannot be easily determined by direct solution.

Techniques to find absolute stability.

Stability of the system is directly related to the location of poles in s-plane.

- For the system to be stable, all roots of the characteristic equation must lie on the left half of imaginary axis, i.e. in the negative part of s-plane.
- Roots of the characteristic equation must have negative real parts.
- If roots lie on the imaginary axis, then system is called *marginally stable.*
- If roots lie on the right hand side of imaginary axis, then system is called *unstable.*
- Also if there are repeated roots or poles on the imaginary axis, then the system is *unstable.*
- Greater the distance of poles from imaginary axis on negative real axis, greater will be stability of the system.

6.6.1. HURWITZ STABILITY CRITERION.

The necessary and sufficient condition to have all roots of characteristic equation in left half of *s*-plane is that, the sub-determinants, D_K, K = 1, 2 ...*n* obtained from Hurwitz's determinant 'H' must all be positive.

Method of forming Hurwitz:

Consider a nth order system having characteristic equation

$$R(s) = a_0 s^n + a_1 s^{n-1} + a_2 s^{n-2} + \ldots + a_{n-1} s + a_n = 0$$

$$H = \begin{vmatrix} a_1 & a_3 & a_5 & \cdots\cdots & a_{2n-1} \\ a_0 & a_2 & a_4 & \cdots\cdots & a_{2n-2} \\ 0 & a_1 & a_3 & \cdots\cdots & a_{2n-3} \\ 0 & a_0 & a_2 & \cdots\cdots & a_{2n-4} \\ 0 & 0 & a_1 & \cdots\cdots & a_{2n-5} \\ \ldots & \ldots & \ldots & \cdots\cdots & \ldots \\ \ldots & \ldots & \ldots & \cdots\cdots & \ldots \\ 0 & \ldots & \ldots & \cdots\cdots & a_n \end{vmatrix}$$

Hence necessary and sufficient condition for stability are :

$$D_1 = |a_1| > 0,$$

$$D_2 = \begin{vmatrix} a_1 & a_3 \\ a_0 & a_2 \end{vmatrix} > 0,$$

$$D_3 = \begin{vmatrix} a_1 & a_3 & a_5 \\ a_0 & a_2 & a_4 \\ 0 & a_1 & a_3 \end{vmatrix} > 0, \quad D_K = |H| > 0$$

6.6.2. ROUTH'S STABILITY CRITERION.

The Routh criterion is method for determining continuous system stability, for systems with an nth-order characteristic equation of the form :

$$F(s) = a_o s^n + a_1 s^{n-1} + a_2 s^{n-2} + \ldots + a_n = 0$$

Method of forming an array :

s^n	a_o	a_2	a_4	a_6 ......
s^{n-1}	a_1	a_3	a_5	a_7 ......
s^{n-2}	b_1	b_2	b_3	.....
s^{n-3}	c_1	c_2	c_3	.....
...	...	...	...	.....
...	...	...	...	.....
...	...	...	...	.....
s^0	a_n	.....		

$$b_1 = \frac{a_1 a_2 - a_o a_3}{a_1};$$

$$b_2 = \frac{a_1 a_4 - a_o a_5}{a_1};$$

$$b_3 = \frac{a_1 a_6 - a_o a_7}{a_1}$$

$$c_1 = \frac{b_1 a_3 - a_1 b_2}{b_1};$$

$$c_2 = \frac{b_1 a_5 - a_1 b_3}{b_1}$$

Routh's criterion.

The necessary and sufficient condition for system to be stable is

All the terms in the first column of Routh's array must have positive sign. There should not be any sign change in first column of Routh's array.

If there are any sign changes existing, then

(*i*) system is unstable.

(*ii*) numbers of sign changes equals the number of roots lying in the right half of the *s*-plane.

Special Cases :

(1) *First element of any of the rows of Routh's array is zero and remaining row contains at least one non-zero elements.*

e.g. $s^5 + 2s^4 + 3s^3 + 6s^2 + 2s + 1 = 0$

s^5	1	3	2
s^4	2	6	1
s^3	0	1.5	0
s^2	∞	...	...

Subsitute a small positive number 'ε' in place of a zero occurred. Complete the array with this number 'ε'. Then the examine sign change by taking $\lim_{\varepsilon \to 0}$.

s^5	1	3	2
s^4	2	6	1
s^3	ε	1.5	0
s^2	$\frac{6\varepsilon - 3}{\varepsilon}$	1	0
s^1	$\frac{\frac{1.5(6\varepsilon - 3)}{\varepsilon} - \varepsilon}{\frac{(6\varepsilon - 3)}{\varepsilon}}$	0	
s^0	1		

To examine sign change

$$\lim_{\varepsilon \to 0} = \frac{6\varepsilon - 3}{\varepsilon}$$

$$= 6 - \lim_{\varepsilon \to 0} \frac{3}{\varepsilon}$$

$$= 6 - \infty$$

$$= -\infty, \text{ sign is negative}$$

$$\lim_{\varepsilon \to 0} \frac{1.5(6\varepsilon - 3) - \varepsilon^2}{6\varepsilon - 3} = \lim_{\varepsilon \to 0} \frac{9\varepsilon - 4.5 - \varepsilon^2}{6\varepsilon - 3}$$

$= +1.5$, sign is positive.

As there are two sign changes, hence system is unstable.

The number of sign change is first column is equal to number of poles in right half s-plane.

(2) All the element of a row in a Routh's array are zero, then terms of the next row cannot be determined and Routh's test fails.

s^5	a	b	c
s^4	d	e	f
s^3	0	0	0

Procedure to eliminate this :

(*i*) Form an equation by using the coefficient of a row which is just above the zeros. Such an equation is called as *Auxillary equation denoted* as A(*s*).

$$\therefore \qquad A(s) = ds^4 + es^2 + f$$

This equation gives the *number* and *location of root pairs* of the characteristic equation which are symmetrically located in *s*-plane.

The coefficients of any row are corresponding to alternate powers of '*s*' starting from the power indicated against it.

(*ii*) Take the derivative of an auxillary equation with respect to '*s*'

$$\frac{dA(s)}{ds} = 4\,ds^3 + 2\,es$$

(*iii*) Replace row of zeros by the coefficients of $\frac{dA(s)}{ds}$

(*iv*) Complete the array in terms of these new coefficients.

Example. Show that the system whose characteristic equation is given below is stable.

$$s^4 + 6s^3 + 21s^2 + 36s + 10 = 0$$

Solution:

Form the Routh array :

s^4	1	21	10
s^3	6	36	0
s^2	$\frac{6\times21-1\times36}{6}=15$	$\frac{6\times10-1\times0}{6}=10$	
s	$\frac{15\times36-10\times6}{15}=32$	0	
s^0	$\frac{32\times10-15\times0}{32}=10$		

Since there is no sign change in first column of the Routh array, hence system is stable.

Example. How many roots of the characteristic equation :

$$s^5 + s^4 + 2s^3 + 2s^2 + 3s + 15 = 0$$

lies in the left half of the s-plane.

Solution:

Applying Routh Hurwitz criterion

s^5	1	2	3
s^4	1	2	15
s^3	ε	-12	0
s^2	$\frac{2\varepsilon-12}{\varepsilon}$	15	0
s^1	$\frac{-24\varepsilon-144-15\varepsilon^2}{2\varepsilon+12}$	0	0
s^0	15	0	0

Hence in the first column of above routh array, there are 2 sign changes. Therefore 2 roots lie in the right half of the s-plane.

6.7. ROOT LOCUS TECHNIQUE

Root locus is a graphical method in which movement of poles in the s-plane is drawn when a particular parameter of system is varied from zero to infinity. The parameter which is usually varied is the gain but any other parameters may be varied.

The roots corresponding to a particular value of the system parameter can then be located on locus or the value of parameter for a desired root location can be determined from the locus.

6.7.1. ANGLE AND MAGNITUDE CONDITION.

For a general closed loop system, the characteristic equation is

$$1 + G(s)\,H(s) = 0$$

$$G(s)\,H(s) = -1$$

As s-plane is complex, above equation can be write as

$$G(s)\,H(s) = -1 + j0$$

Angle condition :

$$G(s)\,H(s) = -1 + j0$$

Equating angles of both sides, we have

$$\angle G(s)\,H(s) = \pm(2q+1)\,180°, q = 0, 1, 2 .....$$

$\therefore$ Angle condition can be stated as,

$\angle G(s)\,H(s)\big|$ For any value of 's' $= \pm(2q+1)\,180°, q = 0, 1$ .....
is root of the equation $1 + G(s)\,H(s) = 0$

Any point in s plane which satisfies the angle condition has to be on the root locus of the corresponding system.

Magnitude condition :

If magnitudes of both sides of the equation G(*s*) H(*s*) = – 1 are equated, then a magnitude condition obtained is

$$|G(s)\,H(s)| = |-1 + j0| = 1$$

Thus magnitude condition is

$$|G(s)H(s)|_{\substack{\text{at a point in s-plane}\\ \text{which is on root locus}}} = 1$$

Magnitude condition can be used only when a point in *s*-plane is confirmed for its existence on the root locus by the use of angle condition.

6.7.2. RULES FOR CONSTRUCTION OF ROOT LOCUS.

Rule 1.

The root locus is always symmetrical about the real axis. The root of the characteristic equation are either real or complex conjugates or combination of both.

Rule 2.

Let G(*s*) H(*s*) = Open loop transfer function of the system.

P = Number of open loop poles

Z = Number of open loop zeros.

Case I. P > Z	Case II. Z > P
Number of branches equal to number of open loop poles N = P	Number of branches is equal to the number of open loop zeros N = Z
Branches will start from each of the location of open loop pole. Out of 'P' number of branches, 'Z' number of branches will terminate at the location of open zeros. The remaining 'P' – 'Z' branches will terminate to infinity.	Branches will term-inate at each of the finite location of open loop zero. But out of 'Z'numbers of branches, 'P' number of branches will start from each of the finite open loop pole locations while remaining Z – P number of branches will originate from infinity and will approach to finite zeros.

Rule 3.

A point on the real axis lies on the root locus, if the sum of the number of open loop poles and open loop zeros, on the real axis, to the right hand side of this point is odd.

Rule 4.

In root locus 'P – Z' branches will approach to infinity. The branches which are approaching to infinity, along the straight lines are called **Asymptotes of the root locus.**

Angles of asymptotes are given by

$$\theta = \frac{\pm(2q+1)\,180°}{P-Z}, \quad q = 0, 1, 2$$

Here P – Z = total number of asymptotes

Rule 5.

All the asymptotes intersect the real axis at a common point known as centroid denoted by σ. The co-ordinates of centroid can be calculated as

$$\sigma = \frac{\Sigma\text{Real parts of poles of } G(s)H(s) - \Sigma\text{Real parts of zeros of } G(s)H(s)}{P-Z}$$

Centroid is always real. It may be located on negative or positive real axis. It may or may not be the part of the root locus.

Rule 6.

Breakaway Point : It is a point on the root locus where multiple roots of the characteristic equation occurs, for a particular value of K.

(*i*) If there are adjacently placed poles on the real axis and section of real axis in between them is a part of the root locus, then there exists minimum one breakaway point in between adjacently placed poles.

(*ii*) If there are two adjacently placed zeros on real axis and section of real axis in between them is a part of the root locus, then there exist minimum one breakaway point in between adjacently placed zeros.

(*iii*) If there is a zero on real axis and to the left of that zero there is no pole or zero existing on the real axis and complete real axis to the left of this zero is a part of the root locus, then there exists minimum one breakaway point to the left of that zero.

Let $$G(s)\,H(s) = K \cdot \frac{B(s)}{A(s)}$$

Hence characteristic equation is,

$$1 + G(s)\,H(s) = 0$$

$$1 + K \cdot \frac{B(s)}{A(s)} = 0$$

Breaking points are the solution of the equation

$$A(s)\,B'(s) - A'(s)\,B(s) = 0$$

where $A'(s)$ and $B'(s)$ are derivatives of $A(s)$ and $B(s)$

Breaking points can also be obtained by $\frac{dk}{ds} = 0$

where, $K = f(s)$ {obtained from characteristic equation}

$$= \frac{-A(s)}{B(s)}$$

Rule 7.

Intersection of root locus with imaginary axis :

(*i*) Consider characteristic equation

$$1 + G(s)\,H(s) = 0.$$

(*ii*) Construct Routh's array in terms of K.

(*iii*) Determine $K_{marginal}$.

(*iv*) Construct auxillary equation $A(s) = 0$ by using coefficient of a row which is just above the row of zeros.

(*v*) Roots of auxilary equation $A(s) = 0$ for $K = K_{max}$ are the point of intersection of the root locus with imaginary axis.

Rule 8.

Angle of Departure from on open loop pole :

$$\phi_p = \pm 180° \,(2q + 1) + \phi;\; q = 0, 1, 2 \ldots.$$

where ϕ is the net angle contribution, at this pole, of all other open loop poles and zeros.

Angle of Arrival at an open loop zero :

$$\phi_z = \pm 180° \,(2q + 1) - \phi;\; q = 0, 1, 2 \ldots.$$

where ϕ is the net angle contribution at the zero under consideration of all other open loop poles and zeros.

Example. Plot the root locus for a system having open loop transfer function given by

$$G(s)\,H(s) = \frac{K}{s(s+4)\left(s^2+4s+20\right)}$$

Solution :

Step 1 : The open loop poles and zeros are,

$$s = 0, -4, -2 - 4j, -2 + 4j$$

Step 2 : Each branch of the root locus originate from open loop poles at K = 0 and terminates at open loop zero. Here zero is not there so root locus terminates at infinity.

Step 3 : The segment of root locus which is a part of root locus is between origin and – 4.

Step 4 : Angle of asymptotes, $\phi_A = \dfrac{180°(2q+1)}{(P-Z)}$;

$$q = 0, 1, 2, 3$$

Here, P = 4 and Z = 0

$\therefore$ ϕ_A = 45°, 135°, 225°, 315°

Step 5 :The point of intersection of asymptotes with the real axis:

$$\sigma_A = \frac{\left\{\sum \text{real part of open loop poles} - \sum \text{real part of open loop zeros}\right\}}{P-Z}$$

$$= \frac{\{-4-2-2-0\}}{4-0} = -2$$

Step 6 : *Breakaway point :*

$$1 + G(s)\,H(s) = 0$$

$\Rightarrow$ $s^4 + 8s^3 + 36s^2 + 80s + K = 0$

Differentiating and substituting $\dfrac{dK}{ds} = 0$, we get roots

$$s = -2, -2 + 2.55j, -2 - 2.55j$$

Step 7 :Two branches of root locus meets at a point or real axis and breaks away at an angle of

$$\pm \frac{180}{r} = \pm \frac{180}{2} = \pm 90°$$

Step 8 :**Angle of departure :** It is defined for complex poles.

Angle by which complex poles departs towards infinity,

$$\phi_d = 180° - (\phi_p - \phi_z)$$

From the root locus below, the angle made by poles ϕ_p with point $(-2 + 4j)$ is the sum of θ_1, θ_2 and θ_3.

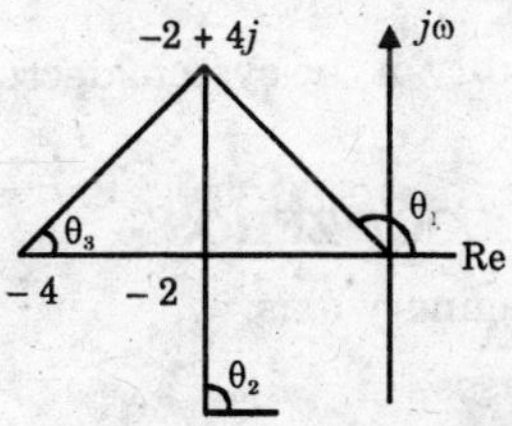

$\therefore$ $\phi_p = \theta_1 + \theta_2 + \theta_3 = 135 + 90 + 45 = 270$

and $\phi_z = 0$

$$\phi_d = 180° - (\phi_p - \phi_z)$$

$$= 180° - (270 - 0) = -90°$$

Similarly angle of departure for point (–2 –4j) is + 90°.

Step 9 :Point of intersection of root locus at imaginary axis.

$$1 + G(s)\,H(s) = s^4 + 8s^3 + 36s^2 + 80s + K = 0$$

Routh array is formed as :

s^4	1	36	K
s^3	8	80	0
s^2	26	K	0
s	$\dfrac{2080-8K}{26}$	0	
s^0	K	0	

When roots cut the imaginary axis,

$$\frac{2080 - 8K}{26} = 0$$

$$\Rightarrow \qquad K = 260$$

Auxilliary equation is

$$26s^2 + K = 0$$

$$\Rightarrow \qquad 26s^2 + 260 = 0$$

$$s = \pm \sqrt{10j}$$

or

$$\omega = \pm \sqrt{10}$$

Hence complete root locus can be drawn as

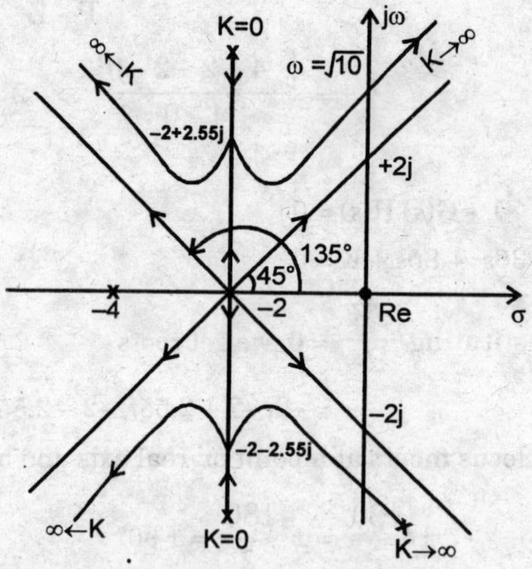

6.7.3. EFFECT OF ADDITION OF OPEN LOOP POLES AND ZEROS.

Effect of Addition of Open Loop Poles

(*i*) Root locus – shifts towards imaginary axis.

(*ii*) System stability relatively decreases.

(*iii*) System becomes more oscillatory in nature.

(*iv*) Range of operating values of 'K' for stability of the system decreases.

(*v*) Improvement in steady state accuracy.

6.7.4. EFFECT OF ADDITION OF OPEN LOOP ZEROS

(*i*) Root locus – shifts to left away from imaginary axis.

(*ii*) Relatively stability of the system increases.

(*iii*) System becomes less oscillatory.

(*iv*) Range of operating values of 'K' for stability of the system increases.

(*v*) Improvement in transient response.

6.7.5. BASICS OF FREQUENCY DOMAIN ALALYSIS.

The steady state response of a system to a purely sinusoidal input is defines as frequency response of a system. The input frequency ω is varied from 0 to ∞ and its effect on gain and phase of system transfer function is studied in frequency response analysis. The transfer function in frequency domain is obatained by replacing variables *s* by *j*ω, where ω is frequency of the input applied to the system.

There exists a corelation between time domain and frequency domain.

$$M_p = e^{\frac{-\pi\xi}{\sqrt{1-\xi^2}}}; \qquad M_r = \frac{1}{2\xi\sqrt{1-\xi^2}}$$

$$\omega_d = \omega_n \sqrt{1-\varepsilon^2}; \qquad \omega_r = \omega_n \sqrt{1-2\varepsilon^2}$$

When ε is between 0.4 to 0.707, then frequency domain and time domain specificatiion are comparable.

$$\text{Bandwidth} = \omega_n \sqrt{1 - 2\xi^2 + \sqrt{2 - 4\xi^2 + 4\xi^4}}$$

6.8. FREQUENCY RESPONSE ANALYSIS

Consider a Linear system with sinusoidal input,

$$r(t) = A \sin \omega t$$

Under steady state condition, the system output and the signals at all other points in the system are sinusoidal. The steady state output may be written as

$$C(t) = B \sin (\omega t + \phi)$$

The magnitude and phase relationship between sinusoidal input and the steady state output of a system is called *frequency response*.

In linear time invariant system, the frequency response is independent of the amplitude and phase of the input signal. Frequency response test on a system or component is normally performed by keeping the amplitude A fixed and determining B and ϕ for a suitable range of frequency.

Frequency response is evaluated from the sinusoidal transfer function ($s = j\omega$).

Frequency Response Analysis of Second order System

Consider a second-order closed loop system.

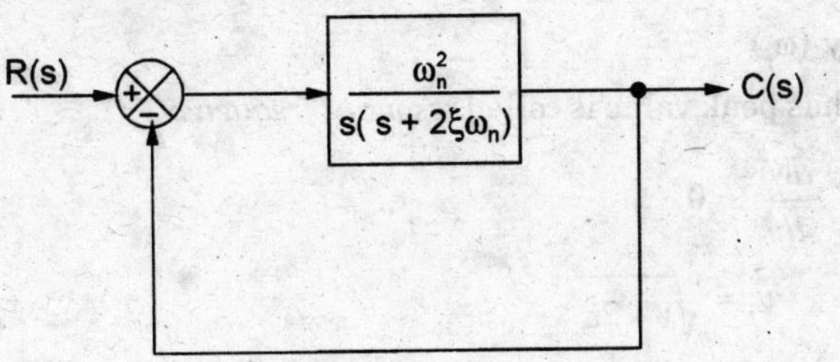

$$\frac{C(s)}{R(s)} = \frac{\omega_n^2}{s^2 + 2\xi\omega_n s + \omega_n^2}$$

The sinusoidal transfer function

$$\frac{C}{R}(j\omega) = T(j\omega) = \frac{\omega_n^2}{(j\omega)^2 + 2\xi\omega_n(j\omega) + \omega_n^2}$$

$$T(j\omega) = \frac{1}{(1-u^2) + j\,2\xi u} \;;$$

$$u = \frac{\omega}{\omega_n}$$

where, $u = \dfrac{\omega}{\omega_n}$ is *normalised driving signal frequency.*

$$|T(j\omega)| = M = \frac{1}{\sqrt{(1-u^2)^2 + (2\xi u)^2}}$$

$$\angle T(j\omega) = \phi = -\tan^{-1}\left[\frac{2\xi u}{(1-u^2)}\right]$$

The steady state output of the system for a sinusoidal input of unit magnitude and variable frequency ω is given by

$$C(u) = \frac{1}{\sqrt{(1-u^2)^2 + (2\xi u)^2}} \sin\left[\omega t - \tan^{-1}\frac{2\xi u}{(1-u^2)}\right]$$

Now, At, $u = 0$ $\quad M = 1 \quad \phi = 0$

At, $u = 1 \quad M = \dfrac{1}{2\xi} \quad \phi = -\dfrac{\pi}{2}$

At, $u \to \infty \quad M \to 0 \quad \phi \to -\pi$

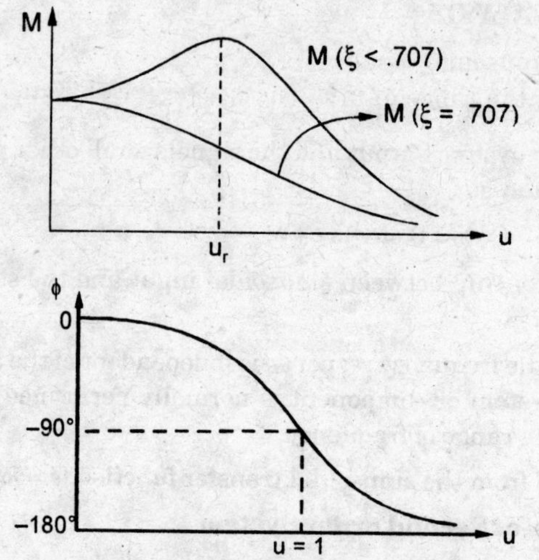

Fig. Plots of M Vs u and ϕ Vs u

1. Resonance Frequency (ω_r)

The frequency where M has peak value is called *resonant frequency*

$$\frac{dM}{du} = 0$$

$\Rightarrow$ $$u_r = \sqrt{1 - 2\xi^2}$$

or $$\omega_r = \omega_n \sqrt{1 - 2\xi^2}$$

2. Resonance Peak (M_p)

Maximum value of the magnitude called *resonant peak* (M_r) and is given by

$$M_r = \frac{1}{2\xi\sqrt{1 - \xi^2}}$$

$$\phi_r = -\tan^{-1}\left[\frac{\sqrt{1 - 2\xi^2}}{\xi}\right]$$

For $0 < \xi \leq \frac{1}{\sqrt{2}}$, the resonant frequency always has a value less than ω_n and the resonant peak has a value greater than 1, and for $\xi > \frac{1}{\sqrt{2}}$, $M_r(\text{max}) = 1$.

Hence for a second order system, resonant peak M_r of its frequency response is indicative of its damping factor ξ for $0 < \xi \leq \frac{1}{\sqrt{2}}$, and ω_r is indicative of its natural frequency ω_n for a given ξ and hence indicative of its speed of response (as $t_s = \frac{4}{\xi\,\omega_n}$).

Hence M_r and ω_r of frequency response could be used as performance indices for a second order system.

Cut- off Frequency

It is defined as the frequency at which M has a value of $\frac{1}{\sqrt{2}}$.

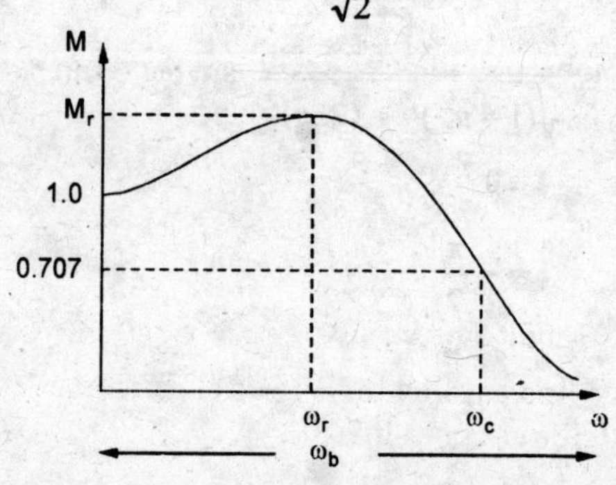

Bandwidth

For feedback control system, the range of frequencies over which M is equal to or greater than $\frac{1}{\sqrt{2}}$ is defined as bandwidth ω_b.

At, $u_b = \frac{\omega_b}{\omega_n}$, $$M = \frac{1}{\sqrt{2}} = \frac{1}{\sqrt{(1-u_b^2)^2 + (2\xi u_b)^2}}$$

$$\Rightarrow \quad u_b^4 - 2(1-2\xi^2)\,u_b^2 - 1 = 0$$

$$\Rightarrow \quad u_b = \left[1 - 2\xi^2 + \sqrt{2 - 4\xi^2 + 4\xi^4}\right]^{\frac{1}{2}}$$

$$\Rightarrow \quad \omega_b = \omega_n\left[1 - 2\xi^2 + \sqrt{2 - 4\xi^2 + 4\xi^4}\right]^{\frac{1}{2}}$$

6.8.1. BODE PLOT.

INTRODUCTION

It gives a graphical procedure for determining stability of a control system based on sinusoidal frequency response. It is an improvement of Nyquist analysis and has an advantage of being approximated by asymptotic straight lines.

Stability can be judged by seeing the plot only, without any calculations. It covers a wide range of frequency and gives relative stability of the system in terms of gain margin and phase margin.

The magnitude and phase angle of G($j\omega$) H($j\omega$) are plotted as a function of logarithmic scales of frequency ω.

Advantages of using logarithmic scales

(*i*) Plotting of low and high frequency is possible in one diagram.

(*ii*) Product terms are converted into sum terms.

In any frequency response, we plot magnitude M and angle ϕ against input frequency 'ω'.

When 'ω' is varied from 0 to ∞, there is a wide range of variations in M and ϕ and hence it becomes difficult to accommodate all such variations with linear scale, hence we use logarithmic scale.

Thus in Bode plot logarithmic, values of magnitude are to be plotted against logarithmic values of frequencies.

Bode plot consists of two plots :

(*i*) **Magnitude Plot :** Magnitude expressed in logarithmic values against logarithmic value of frequency called *Magnitude plot.*

The magnitude can be expressed in its logarithmic values by finding out the value $20 \log_{10} |G(j\omega)|$.

Hence for Bode Plot $|G(j\omega)| = 20 \log_{10} |G(j\omega)|$ *d*B

(*ii*) **Phase Angle Plot :** Phase angle in degrees against logarithmic values of frequency called *Phase angle plot.*

The angle of G($j\omega$) is to be expressed in degrees which is to be plotted against log ω.

Bode Plots of Standard factors of G($j\omega$) H($j\omega$).

(*i*) Replace '*s*' by '$j\omega$' to convert it to frequency domain.

(*ii*) Find its magnitude as a function of 'ω'.

(*iii*) Express the magnitude in '*d*B' by $20 \log |G(j\omega) H(j\omega)|$.

(*iv*) Find phase angle by using $\tan^{-1}\left[\frac{\text{Imaginary Part}}{\text{Real Part}}\right] = \phi$ in degrees.

(*v*) With required approximations, plot magnitude in *d*B and phase angle in degrees against log ω by varying ω from 0 to ∞.

Factor 1 : System gain 'K'

- Its '*d*B' value = 20 log K *d*B
- 20 log K is always constant.
- Its magnitude plot will be straight line parallel to X – axis.
- Magnitude plot for K > 1 is a line parallel to X – axis at a distance of 20 log K above 0 *d*B, while for K < 1 it is at a distance of 20 log K below 0 *d*B reference line.

Factor 2 : Poles or zeros at the origin $(j\omega)^{\pm r}$

Magnitude in $dB = -20\, r \log \omega$, where r is order of pole or zero at origin

This equation is similar to $y = mx$, i.e. 1 pole at the origin contributes to the magnitude plot according to the equation $-20\, r \log \omega$, i.e. according to the straight line of slope '-20' r dB/decade.

- The starting slope of the Bode plot for the function G(*s*) H(*s*) gets decided by number of poles or zeros at origin present in G(*s*) H(*s*).

Factor 3 : Simple poles or zeros (First order factors) $(1 + j\omega T)^{\pm 1}$

$$\text{Magnitude in } dB = -20 \log \sqrt{1+\omega^2 T^2}\ dB$$

- For low frequency range, $\omega << \dfrac{1}{T}$

Magnitude in $dB = -20 \log 1 = 0\ dB$

- For high frequency range, $\omega >> \dfrac{1}{T}$

Magnitude in $dB = 20 \log \omega T\ dB$

It is a straight line of slope $-20\ dB$/decade

The frequency at which change of slope from 0 dB to $-20\ dB$/decade occurs is called *Corner frequency*.

$$\text{Corner frequency, } \omega_c = \frac{1}{T}$$

Factor 4 : Quadratic Factors (Complex Conjugate poles)

$$G(s)\,H(s) = \frac{1}{1+\dfrac{2\varepsilon}{\omega_n}s+\dfrac{s^2}{\omega_n^2}}$$

$$\text{Magnitude in } dB = -20 \log \sqrt{\left[1-\left(\frac{\omega}{\omega_n}\right)^2\right]^2 + 4\varepsilon^2\left[\frac{\omega}{\omega_n}\right]^2}\ dB$$

Approximation :

(*i*) For low frequency, $\omega << \omega_n$

$$\therefore \quad \left(\frac{\omega}{\omega_n}\right)^2 << 1$$

Magnitude in $dB = -20 \log 1 = 0\ dB$

(*ii*) For high frequency, $\omega > \omega_n$

$$\therefore \quad 4\varepsilon^2\left(\frac{\omega}{\omega_n}\right)^2 << \left(\frac{\omega}{\omega_n}\right)^4, \text{ as } \varepsilon \text{ is very low.}$$

$$\text{Magnitude in } dB = -40 \log \omega + 40 \log \omega_n.$$

Bandwidth

It is defined as the range of frequencies over which the system will respond satisfactorily. It is also defined as range of frequencies in which the magnitude response is almost flat in nature.

Cut-off Frequency.

It is the frequency at which the magnitude of the closed loop response in 3 dB down from its zero frequency value.

Resonant Frequency (ω_r).

It is the frequency at which resonant peak M_r occurs in closed loop frequency response. It is inversely proportional to the rise time.

Gain Cross over Frequency (ω_{gc}).

It is the frequency at which magnitude of G($j\omega$) H($j\omega$) is unity, i.e. 1.

Phase Cross over Frequency (ω_{pc}).

It is the frequency at which phase angle of G(*j*ω) H(*j*ω) is – 180°.

Gain Margin (G.M.).

It is defined as the margin in gain at phase cross over frequency allowable by which gain can be increased till system reaches on the verge of instability.

Phase Margin (P.M.).

It is the amount of additional phase lag at the gain cross-voer frequency which can be introduced in the system till system reaches on the verge of instability.

$$\text{P.M} = 180° + (\text{angle of } G(j\omega)\, H(j\omega) \text{ at } \omega = \omega_{gc})$$

$$\text{G.M} = \frac{\text{Critical K}}{\text{Actual K}}$$

$$= \frac{\text{Critical } |G(j\omega)\, H(j\omega)|_{\omega=\omega_{pc}}}{\text{Actual } |G(j\omega)\, H(j\omega)|_{\omega=\omega_{pc}}}$$

$$= \frac{1}{|G(j\omega)\, H(j\omega)|_{\omega=\omega_{pc}}}$$

$$\text{G.M. in } dB = -20 \log \left[|G(j\omega)\, H(j\omega)|_{\omega=\omega_{pc}}\right]$$

If	$\lvert G(j\omega)\, H(j\omega)\rvert_{\omega=\omega_{pc}} = 1,$	system is marginally stable
If	$\lvert G(j\omega)\, H(j\omega)\rvert_{\omega=\omega_{pc}} > 1,$	system is unstable
If	$\lvert G(j\omega)\, H(j\omega)\rvert_{\omega=\omega_{pc}} < 1,$	system is stable

For G.M. and P.M. positive, i.e. stable system

$$\omega_{gc} < \omega_{pc}$$

For G.M. and P.M. negative, i.e. unstable system

$$\omega_{gc} > \omega_{pc}$$

Calculation of Transfer Function from Magnitude plot.

(*i*) *If starting slop is*

– 20 *d*B/decade→ 1 pole at origin

– 40 *d*B/decade→ 2 poles at origin

0 *d*B/decade→ No pole at origin

+ 20 *d*B/decade→ 1 zero at origin

(***ii***) Observe the shift in magnitude plot at ω = 1 which represents 20 logK from which find value of K.

(***iii***) *Identify the corner frequencies.*

The respective time constant is reciprocal of the corner frequency, i.e.

$$T = \frac{1}{\omega_c}$$

Hence determine the different factors present.

Example : *Determine the transfer function of system whose corner plot is shown in the figure below*

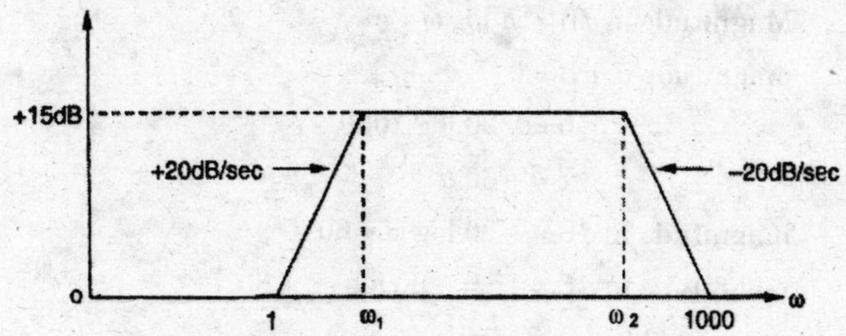

Solution :

Since starting slope is 0 dB, so no pole or zero at origin.

At each corner frequency slope changes.

First change in slope is at $\omega = 1$, $\omega_{c_1} = 1$

$$\text{Change in slope} = \text{second slope} - \text{initial slope}$$
$$= 20 - 0 = 20\ dB/sec$$

i.e. factor is simple zero with $\omega_{c_1} = 1$.

$$T_1 = \frac{1}{\omega_{c_1}} = 1$$

$\therefore$ Factor is $(1 + T_1 s)$, i.e. $(1 + s)$

Now next change in slope is at ω_1

$\therefore$
$$\omega_{c_3} = \omega_1$$
$$\text{Change in slope} = 0 - 20 = -20\ dB/sec,$$

so factor is simple pole.

Now ω_1 is not known

Now write equation for that line;

$$y = mx + c$$

i.e. magnitude in $dB = m \log \omega + c$

$$m = +20\ dB/sec$$

Now at $\omega = 1$, magnitude in $dB = 0\ dB$

$\therefore$ $0 = 20 \log 1 + c$

$\Rightarrow$ $c = 0$

Hence equation in magnitude in $dB = 20 \log \omega$

Now at $\omega = \omega_1$, Magnitude in $dB = 15\ dB$ (given)

$\therefore$ $15 = 20 \log \omega_1$

$\Rightarrow$ $\omega_1 = 5.623\ \text{rad/sec} = \omega_{c_2}$

$\therefore$
$$T_2 = \frac{1}{\omega_{c_2}} = \frac{1}{5.623} = 0.177$$

$\therefore$
$$\text{Factor} = \frac{1}{1+T_2 s} = \frac{1}{1+0.177s}$$

Next change in slope is at ω_2

$\therefore$
$$\omega_{c_3} = \omega_2$$
$$\text{Change} = -20 - 0 = -20\ dB/sec$$

Hence factor is simple pole.

To find ω_2, write equation for that line having slope $-20\ dB/sec$

$$\text{Magnitude in } dB = m \log \omega + c$$

At $\omega = 1000$, magnitude in $dB = 0$

$\therefore$ $0 = -20 \log 1000 + c$

$$c = +60\ dB$$

Hence equation is, magnitude in $dB = -20 \log \omega + 60$

At ω_2, magnitude in $dB = 15 = -20 \log \omega_2 + 60$

$\therefore$ $-20 \log \omega_2 = -45$

$$\Rightarrow \qquad \omega_2 = 177.82 = \omega_{c_3}$$

$$\therefore \qquad T_3 = \frac{1}{\omega_{c_3}} = 0.00562$$

$$\therefore \qquad \text{Factor} = \frac{1}{1+0.00562s}$$

The last change in slope is at $\omega = 1000 = \omega_{c_4}$

$$\text{Change} = 0 - (-20) = +20\ dB/\text{sec}$$

So factor is simple zero, $\omega_{c_4} = 1000$

$$\therefore \qquad T_4 = \frac{1}{\omega_{c_4}} = 0.001$$

$$\therefore \qquad \text{Factor} = (1 + T_4 s) = (1 + 0.001\ s)$$

Hence total transfer function is product of all of them

$$G(s)\,H(s) = \frac{(1+s)(1+0.001s)}{(1+0.177s)(1+0.00562s)}$$

6.8.2. NYQUIST PLOTS.

The Nyquist method handles systems with time delay without the necessity of approximations and hance yields exact results about both absolute and relative stability of the system.

Polar Plot.

It is the locus of tips of the phasors of various magnitudes plotted at the corresponding phase angles for different values of frequencies from 0 to ∞.

Determination of G.M. and P.M. from Polar plot.

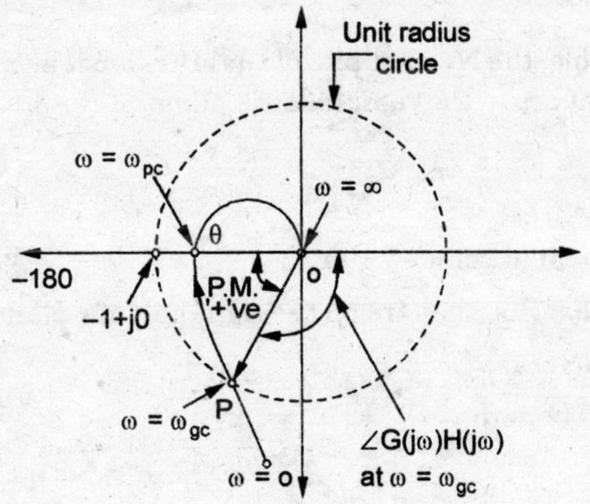

Fig. 6.14

$$\omega_{gc} < \omega_{pc}$$

Stable system

G.M. and P.M. positive

$$\text{G.M.} = \frac{1}{|G(j\omega)\,H(j\omega)|_{\omega = \omega_{pc}}}$$

$$\text{G.M.} = \frac{1}{l(OQ)}$$

In dB.
$$\text{G.M.} = 20 \log \frac{1}{|OQ|}\ dB$$

$$\text{P.M.} = 180° + \angle G(j\omega)\,H(j\omega)\,|_{\omega = \omega_{pc}}$$

Determining ω_{pc} mathematically :

(*i*) Rationalise the open loop transfer function $G(j\omega)\,H(j\omega)$.

(*ii*) Separate real and imaginary parts.

(*iii*) Equate imaginary part to zero, solve this to get value of ω which is making this imaginary part zero. i.e. value of $\omega = \omega_{pc}$.

(*iv*) Substitute this value of ω_{pc} in the real part to get the actual co-ordinates of an intersection of point of polar plot with negative real axis.

NYQUIST PLOT ANALYSIS

Pole – Zero Configuration.

Consider closed loop transfer function $\frac{C(s)}{R(s)}$ as

$$\frac{C(s)}{R(s)} = \frac{G(s)}{1+G(s)H(s)}$$

- Poles of $1 + G(s)\,H(s)$ = Open loop poles of a system
- Zeros of $1 + G(s)\,H(s)$ = Closed loop poles of a system

From Nyquist point of view, the system is absolutely stable if all the zeros of $1 + G(s)\,H(s)$, i.e. closed loop poles of the system are located in the left half of *s* plane.

Encirclement.

A point is said to be encircled by a closed path, if it is found to lie inside that closed path.

Analytic Function and Singularities.

A function is said to be analytic at a point in a plane if its value and its derivative has finite existence at that point. If at a point in a plane, the value of function or its derivative is infinite, the function is said to be non analytic at that point and such a point is called *singularity of the function*.

Mapping Theorem.

For a closed - loop system to be stable, the Nyquist plot of $G(s)\,H(s)$ must encircle the point $-1 + j0$ as many times as the number of poles of $G(s)\,H(s)$ that are in the right half of *s* plane.

Equation generally used is,

$$N = P - Z$$

where, N = number of encirclement of point $-1 + j0$

P = number of poles of $G(s)\,H(s)$ that are on the right half of *s*-plane

Z = number of zeros of $G(s)\,H(s)$

For stabiity of closed-loop, Z should be zero

i.e. $N = P$

Steps To Solve Problems.

(*i*) Count how many number of poles of $G(s)\,H(s)$ are in the right half of the *s*-plane.

(*ii*) Decide the stability criterian as N = P, *i.e.* how many times Nyquist plot should encircle $-1 + j0$ point for absolute stability.

(*iii*) Select Nyquist path as per the function $G(s)\,H(s)$.

(*iv*) Analyse the sections as starting point and terminating point.

(*v*) Mathematically find out ω_{pc} and intersection of Nyquist plot with negative real axis by rationalizing $G(j\omega)\,H(j\omega)$.

(*vi*) With the knowledge of steps (*iv*) and (*v*), sketch the Nyquist plot.

(*vii*) Count the number of encirclements N of $-1 + j0$ by Nyquist plot. If this matches with the criterion decided in step (*ii*), system is stable otherwise unstable.

Example : *Draw the Nyquist plot for a system with* $G(s)\,H(s) = \frac{10(s+3)}{s(s-1)}$. *Comment on the closed loop stability.*

Solution :

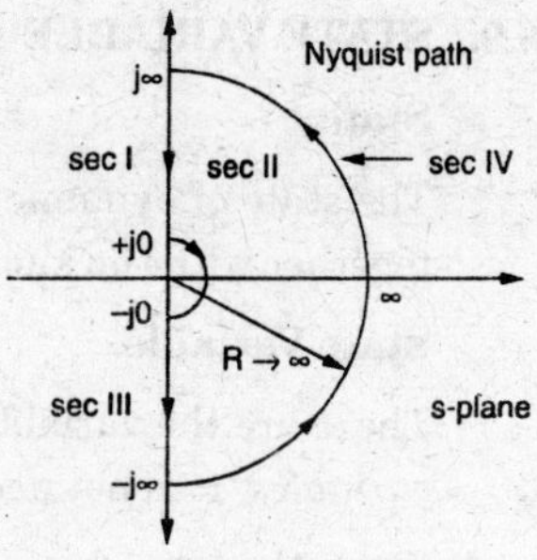

Step 1 : P = 1 as 1 pole in right half of *s*-plane.

Step 2 : N = – P = –1, i.e. Nyquist plot must encircle –1 + *j*0 point once in clockwise for stability.

Step 3 : One plot at origin, so Nyquist path is as shown in the figure

Step 4 : $$G(j\omega)\ H(j\omega) = \frac{10(3+j\omega)}{j\omega(+j\omega-1)}$$

Section I : $s = +j\infty \rightarrow s = +j0$

For, starting point $\omega \rightarrow +\infty$, we have

$$\angle G(j\omega)H(j\omega)\big|_{\omega\to\infty} = \angle -90°$$

and, $|G(j\omega)H(j\omega)|_{\omega\to\infty} = 0$

For, termination point $\omega \rightarrow +0$, we have

$$|G(j\omega)H(j\omega)|_{\omega\to 0+} = \infty\ \angle -270°$$

– 270° – (–90) = – 180° clockwise rotation

Section II : $s = +j0 \rightarrow s = -j0$

Starting point $\omega \rightarrow +0$

$\infty \angle -270°$

Termination point $\omega \rightarrow -0$

$$\infty \angle \frac{0°\cdot 0°}{-90°+180°} = \infty\ \angle -90°$$

– 90° – (–270°) = + 180° anticlockwise rotation

Section III : Mirror image of section I.

Section IV : Not required.

Step 5 : Rationalizing G(*j*ω) H(*j*ω)

$$G(j\omega)\ H(j\omega) = \frac{10\,(3+j\omega)(-j\omega)(j\omega+1)}{(j\omega)(-j\omega)(j\omega-1)(j\omega+1)} = \frac{10j\omega\,[3-\omega^2+4j\omega]}{\omega^2(1+\omega^2)}$$

$$= \frac{-40\omega^2}{D} + j\,\frac{10\omega\,(3-\omega^2)}{D} \qquad ...[D = \omega^2(1+\omega^2)]$$

Equating imaginary part to zero, we have

$$\omega(3-\omega^2) = 0$$

$\Rightarrow$ $$\omega_{pc} = \sqrt{3}$$

Substituting in real part, we get $Q = -10$

Step 6 : Nyquist plot is

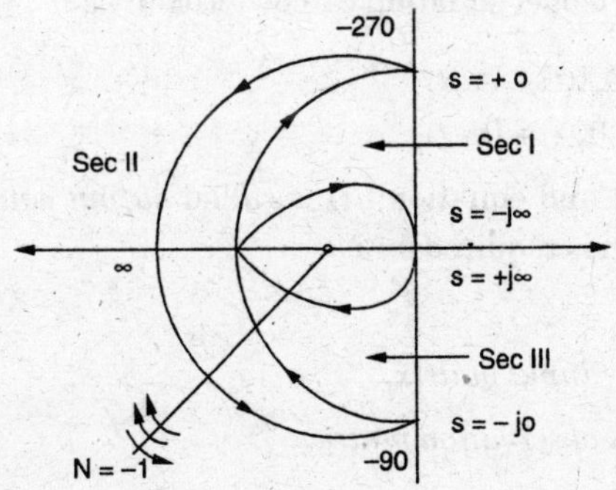

Step 7 : Net encirclement of –1 + *j*0 is N = –1

This matches with the stability criterion. Hence given system is stable in nature.

Note : This is the rare example of open loop unstable system behaves as stable closed loop system.

6.9. STATE VARIABLE ANALYSIS

State.

The state of dynamic system is defined as a minimal set of variable such that knowledge of these variable at $t = t_o$ together with the knowledge of inputs for $t \geq t_0$ completely determines the behaviour of the system for $t > t_o$.

State Variable.

These are the variables involved in determining the state of dynamic system $X(t)$, $X_1(t)$, $X_2(t) \ldots X_n(t)$ are called *state variables.* It is not neccessary that state variables be physically measurable or observable quantities.

State Vector.

The state vector $X(t)$ is the vector sum of all the state variables.

State Space.

It is the space whose coordinates axes are nothing but the 'n' state variables with time as the implicit variable.

6.9.1. STATE MODEL.

Consider the MIMO, n^{th} order system

Number of inputs = m,

Number of outputs = p

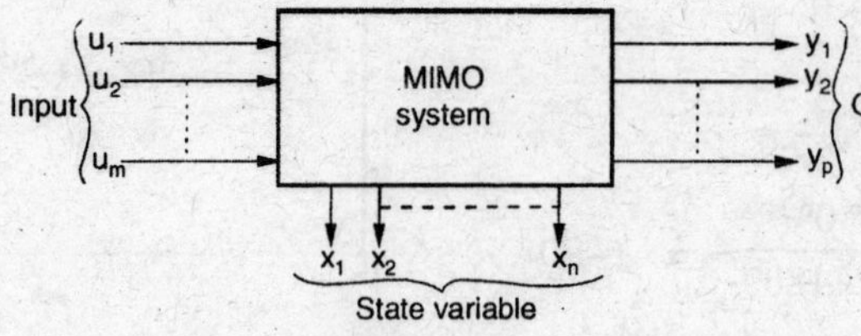

Fig. 6.15

$$u(t) = \begin{bmatrix} u_1(t) \\ u_2(t) \\ \cdots \\ \cdots \\ u_m(t) \end{bmatrix}_{m \times 1},$$

$$X(t) = \begin{bmatrix} X_1(t) \\ X_2(t) \\ \cdots \\ \cdots \\ X_n(t) \end{bmatrix}_{n\times 1} \quad \text{and} \quad Y(t) = \begin{bmatrix} Y_1(t) \\ Y_2(t) \\ \cdots \\ \cdots \\ Y_p(t) \end{bmatrix}_{p\times 1}$$

For such a system, a standard state model equation can be written as :

$$\dot{X}(t) = AX(t) + Bu(t) \quad \ldots(i)$$

$$Y(t) = CX(t) + Du(t) \quad \ldots(ii)$$

Equation (*i*) is called *state equation* and equation (*ii*) is called *output equation*. Output equation is also called as *readout function* (because no solution is required for it).

$A \rightarrow n \times n$ called *system matrix*

$B \rightarrow n \times m$ called *control matrix / input matrix*

$C \rightarrow p \times n$ called *output matrix / observation matrix*

$D \rightarrow p \times m$ called *transmission matrix.*

State Model from Differential Equation Representation.

Case I : Consider a SISO system represented by differential equation

$$y^n + a_{n-1}y^{n-1} + a_{n-2}y^{n-2} + \ldots a_1 y + a_o y = b_o u$$

where, y = output

u = input, and

$$y^n = \frac{d^n y(t)}{dt^n}$$

Select the state variable from the lowest order Y(t) term existing in equation

i.e. $\quad Y(t) = X_1(t)$

then each successive differentiation of $y(t)$ gives the required state variable.

$$\dot{Y}(t) = \dot{X}_1(t) = X_2(t)$$

$$\ddot{Y}(t) = \ddot{X}_1(t) = \dot{X}_2(t) = X_3(t)$$

$$\ldots$$

$$\ldots$$

$$Y^{n-1}(t) = X_1^{n-1}(t) = X_2^{n-2}(t) = \ldots\ldots = X_n(t)$$

$$Y^n(t) = \dot{X}_n(t)$$

As the order of system is 'n', n state variables are allowed to be selected to form minimum set of variables.

Now state equation becomes

$$\dot{X}_1(t) = X_2(t)$$

$$\dot{X}_2(t) = X_3(t)$$

$$\ldots$$

$$\ldots$$

$$\dot{X}_{n-1}(t) = X_n(t)$$

$$\dot{X}_n(t) = ?$$

$\dot{X}_n(t)$ can be obtained by actually substituting all selected variables into original equation, *i.e.*

$$Y^n(t) = \dot{X}_n(t) \quad = -a_o X_1(t) - a_1 X_2(t) \ldots - a_{n-1} X_n(t) + b_o u(t)$$

Hence in general the state model becomes

$$\begin{bmatrix} \dot{X}_1(t) \\ \dot{X}_2(t) \\ \ldots \\ \ldots \\ \dot{X}_n(t) \end{bmatrix} = \begin{bmatrix} 0 & 1 & 0 & \ldots & \ldots & 0 \\ 0 & 0 & 1 & \ldots & \ldots & 0 \\ 0 & 0 & 0 & 1 & \ldots & 0 \\ 0 & 0 & 0 & 0 & \ldots & 1 \\ -a_o & -a_1 & -a_2 & \ldots & \ldots & -a_{n-1} \end{bmatrix} \begin{bmatrix} X_1(t) \\ X_2(t) \\ \ldots \\ \ldots \\ X_n(t) \end{bmatrix} + \begin{bmatrix} 0 \\ 0 \\ 0 \\ \ldots \\ b_o \end{bmatrix} u(t)$$

$$\dot{X}(t) = AX(t) + Bu(t)$$

Now $\quad Y(t) = X_1(t)$

$$\therefore \quad Y(t) = [1\ 0\ \ldots\ldots 0] \begin{bmatrix} X_1(t) \\ X_2(t) \\ \ldots \\ \ldots \\ X_n(t) \end{bmatrix}$$

$$Y(t) = CX(t), \quad \text{where } D = 0$$

These above equations are only for pole, because there is not any involvement of derivative of input.

Case II : If pole and zero, both are involved

e.g. $$\frac{C(s)}{R(s)} = \frac{s+\alpha}{s^2 + \beta_1 s + \beta_2}$$

$$s^2\,C(s) + \beta_1 sC(s) + \beta_2 C(s) = sR(s) + \alpha R(s)$$

Taking inverse Laplace transform

$$\ddot{c}(t) + \beta_1 \dot{c}(t) + \beta_2 \dot{c}(t) = \dot{r}(t) + \alpha r$$

Now select variable

$$X_1 = c$$
$$X_2 = \dot{c} - r$$
$$\dot{X}_1 = \dot{c} = X_2 + r$$
$$\dot{X}_2 = \ddot{c} - \dot{r}$$
$$= -\beta_1(X_2 + r) - \beta_2 X_1 + \alpha r$$
$$= -\beta_2 X_1 - \beta_1 X_2 + (\alpha - \beta_1) r$$

Hence state model becomes

$$\begin{bmatrix} \dot{X}_1 \\ \dot{X}_2 \end{bmatrix} = \begin{bmatrix} 0 & 1 \\ -\beta_2 & -\beta_1 \end{bmatrix} \begin{bmatrix} X_1 \\ X_2 \end{bmatrix} + \begin{bmatrix} 1 \\ \alpha - \beta_1 \end{bmatrix} r \quad \text{...}(i)$$

$$C = [1\ 0] \begin{bmatrix} X_1 \\ X_2 \end{bmatrix} \quad \text{...}(ii)$$

Equation (*i*) is called *state equation* and equation (*ii*) is called ***output equation.***

Derivation of Transfer function from the State Model.

Consider a standard state model

$$\dot{X}(t) = AX(t) + Bu(t)$$
$$Y(t) = CX(t) + Du(t)$$

Taking Laplace transform of both sides and neglecting initial condition, we have

$$sX(s) = AX(s) + Bu(s)$$
$$Y(s) = CX(s) + Du(s)$$

Now $\quad sX(s) - AX(s) = Bu(s)$

$\therefore \quad [sI - A]\, X(s) = Bu(s)$

Premultipling by $[sI - A]^{-1}$, we get

$$X(s) = [sI - A]^{-1} Bu(s)$$

Substituting it in equation for Y(s)

$$Y(s) = C[sI - A]^{-1} Bu(s) + Du(s)$$

$$\frac{Y(s)}{u(s)} = C[sI - A]^{-1}B + D$$

where $\quad [sI - A]^{-1} = \dfrac{\text{Adj}\,[sI - A]}{|sI - A|}$

State model of a system is not unique but whatever may the state mode transfer function obtained from it has to be unique.

$$|sI - A| = 0 \text{ is called characteristic equation.}$$

6.9.2. STATE TRANSITION MATRIX.

Consider state model equation

$$\dot{X} = AX + Bu,$$
$$Y = CX + Du$$

Taking Laplace transform considering initial condition.

$$sX(s) - X(0) = AX(s) + Bu(s)$$
$$sX(s) - AX(s) = X(0) + Bu(s)$$
$$X(s)[sI - A] = X(0) + Bu(s)$$

$\therefore \quad X(s) = [sI - A]^{-1} X(0) + [sI - A]^{-1} Bu(s)$

$\because \quad \phi(s) = [sI - A]^{-1}$

$\therefore \quad \phi(t) = L^{-1}[sI - A]^{-1}$

$\phi(t)$ is called state transition matrix

For homogeneous, $u = 0$

$$\therefore \quad X(s) = \phi(s)\,X(0)$$

$$X(t) = \phi(t)\,X(0)$$

$$\text{As} \quad \dot{X} = AX$$

$$\therefore \quad X(t) = e^{At}\,X(0)$$

$$\text{Hence} \quad \phi(t) = e^{At}$$

Properties of State Transition Matrix

(*i*) $\phi(0) = e^{A \times 0} = I$ (Identity matrix)

(*ii*) $\phi^{-1}(t) = \phi(-t)$

(*iii*) $\phi(t_1 + t_2) = \phi(t_2) \cdot \phi(t_1)$

(*iv*) $e^{(A+B)t} = e^{At} \cdot e^{Bt}$

(*v*) $[\phi(t)]^n = \phi(nt)$

(*vi*) $\phi(t_1)/\phi(t_2) = \phi(t_1 - t_2)$

(*vii*) $\phi(t_2 - t_1) \cdot \phi(t_1 - t_o) = \phi(t_2 - t_o)$

6.9.3. SOLUTION OF NON HOMOGENEOUS EQUATION.

Consider equation $\quad \dot{X}(t) = AX + Bu, \quad X(0) = 0$

$$\dot{X}(t) - AX(t) = Bu(t)$$

Premultipltying both sides by e^{-At}, we get

$$e^{-At}[X(t) - AX(t)] = e^{-At}\,Bu(t)$$

$$\text{But} \quad e^{-At} \cdot \dot{X}(t) - e^{(-At)} \cdot AX(t) = \frac{d}{dt}[e^{-At}X(t)]$$

Substituting in above equation we get

$$\therefore \quad \frac{d}{dt}[e^{-At}X(t)] = e^{-At}Bu(t)$$

Assuming $t_o = 0$ and integrating both sides, we get

$$e^{-At}X(t)\Big|_0^t = \int_0^t e^{-A\tau}Bu(\tau)d\tau$$

$$\therefore \quad e^{-At}X(t) - X(0) = \int_0^t e^{-A\tau}Bu(\tau)d\tau$$

Premultiplying both sides by e^{At}, we get

$$X(t) = \underbrace{e^{At}\,X(0)}_{\text{ZIR}} + \underbrace{\int_0^t e^{-A(t-\tau)}Bu(\tau)d\tau}_{\text{ZSR}}$$

ZIR $\rightarrow$ zero input response

ZSR $\rightarrow$ zero state response

If initial time is t_o, then

$$X(t) = e^{A(t-t_o)}X(0) + \int_{t_o}^t e^{A(t-\tau)}Bu(\tau)d\tau$$

6.9.4. CONTROLLABILITY.

A system is called *completely state controllable*, if it is possible to transfer the system state from any initial state $X(t_o)$ to any other desired state $X(t_f)$ in specified finite time a control vector $u(t)$.

A general n^{th} order multi-input linear time invariant system

$$\dot{X} = AX + Bu$$

is completely controllable if and only if the rank of the composite matrix

$$Q_C = [B : AB : \dots : A^{n-1}B] \text{ is } n.$$

6.9.5. OBSERVABILITY.

A system is said to be *completely observable*, if every state $X(t_o)$ can be completely identified by measurements of the output $Y(t)$ over a finite time interval.

A general n^{th} order multi-input-multi-output time invariant system

$$\dot{X} = AX + Bu, \quad Y = CX$$

is completely observable if the rank of composite matrix $Q_o = [C^T : A^TC^T : ..... : (A^T)^{n-1} C^T]$ is n.

Example : *Consider the system with state equation*

$$\begin{bmatrix} \dot{X}_1 \\ \dot{X}_2 \\ \dot{X}_3 \end{bmatrix} = \begin{bmatrix} 0 & 1 & 0 \\ 0 & 0 & 1 \\ -6 & -11 & -6 \end{bmatrix} \begin{bmatrix} X_1 \\ X_2 \\ X_3 \end{bmatrix} + \begin{bmatrix} 0 \\ 0 \\ 1 \end{bmatrix} u$$

Check systems controllability.

Solution:

$$B = \begin{bmatrix} 0 \\ 0 \\ 1 \end{bmatrix}; \quad A = \begin{bmatrix} 0 & 1 & 0 \\ 0 & 0 & 1 \\ -6 & -11 & -6 \end{bmatrix}$$

$\therefore$
$$AB = \begin{bmatrix} 0 & 1 & 0 \\ 0 & 0 & 1 \\ -6 & -11 & -6 \end{bmatrix} \begin{bmatrix} 0 \\ 0 \\ 1 \end{bmatrix} = \begin{bmatrix} 0 \\ 1 \\ -6 \end{bmatrix}$$

and
$$A^2B = \begin{bmatrix} 0 & 1 & 0 \\ 0 & 0 & 1 \\ -6 & -11 & -6 \end{bmatrix} \begin{bmatrix} 0 \\ 1 \\ -6 \end{bmatrix} = \begin{bmatrix} 1 \\ -6 \\ 25 \end{bmatrix}$$

Now
$$Q_C = [B : AB : A^2B] = \begin{bmatrix} 0 & 0 & 1 \\ 0 & 1 & -6 \\ 1 & -6 & 25 \end{bmatrix}$$

It is easily seen that $|Q_C| \neq 0$

i.e. rank $r = n = 3$, the system is completely controllable.

Example : *Examine the observability of given system*

$$A = \begin{bmatrix} 0 & 1 & 0 \\ 0 & 0 & 1 \\ 0 & -2 & -3 \end{bmatrix}, \quad B = \begin{bmatrix} 0 \\ 0 \\ 1 \end{bmatrix}, \quad C = [3\ 4\ 1]$$

$$A^TC^T = \begin{bmatrix} 0 & 0 & 0 \\ 1 & 0 & -2 \\ 0 & 1 & -3 \end{bmatrix} \begin{bmatrix} 0 \\ 0 \\ 1 \end{bmatrix} = \begin{bmatrix} 0 \\ -2 \\ -2 \end{bmatrix}$$

Now
$$Q_o = [C^T : A^TC^T : (A^T)^2 C^T] = \begin{bmatrix} 3 & 0 & 0 \\ 4 & 1 & -2 \\ 1 & 1 & -2 \end{bmatrix}$$

Since
$$\begin{bmatrix} 3 & 0 \\ 4 & 1 \end{bmatrix} \neq 0 \quad \text{and} \quad \begin{bmatrix} 3 & 0 & 0 \\ 4 & 1 & -2 \\ 1 & 1 & -2 \end{bmatrix} = 0$$

hence rank of the matrix Q_o is $r = 2$, while $n = 3$.

Hence one of state variable is *unobservable*.

6.10. CONTROL SYSTEM COMPENSATOR

INTRODUCTION

The performance of any control system is improved by using various controllers and compensating networks in the control system. These controllers and compensating networks introduce poles and zeros for making the system response as desired.

Main performance specifications

(*i*) Time response

(*ii*) Steady state accuracy

(*iii*) Stability

Time response is improved by adjusting feedback parameter but overall gain is reduced.

INDUSTRIAL CONTROLLERS

An automatic control system is used to maintain its output within desirable limit by means of a control action. Any deviation of the output from the reference input is detected by an error detector. The error thus detected is used as an actuating signal for control action through a controller.

(*i*) Proportional Control.

In proportional control the actuating signal for the control action in a control system is proportional to the error signal.

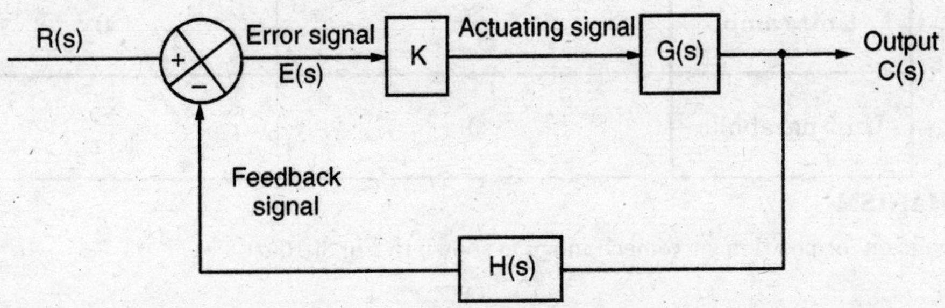

It is desirable that the control system be underdamped for the point of view of quick response. The sluggish overdamped response of a control system can be made faster by increasing forward path gain of the system.

The increase in forward path gain reduces the steady state error, but at the same time maximum overshoot is increased.

(*ii*) Derivative Control.

For the derivative control action, the actuating signal consists of proportional error signal added with derivative of the error signal.

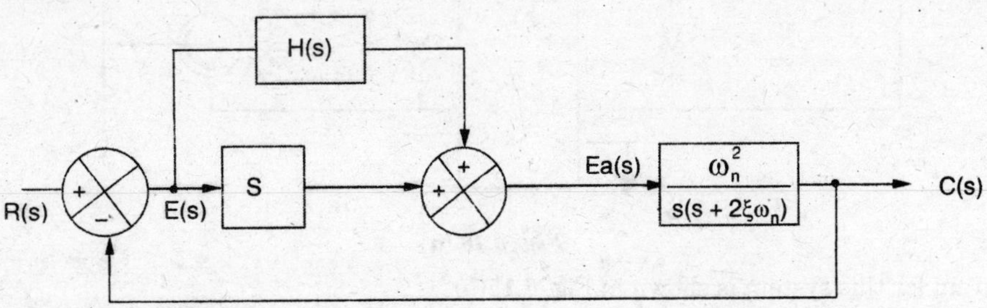

For derivative control action

$$e_a(t) = e(t) + T_d \frac{de(t)}{dt}$$

where T_d = a constant

or $$E_a(s) = E(s) + sT_d\, E(s)$$

Using derivative control the effective damping is increased and therefore the maximum overshoot is reduced. Using derivative control the natural frequency ω_n is unchanged, but the rise time is reduced.

The steady state error is not effected by derivative control action. As the derivative of the error is used in actuating signal and as such if the error varies with time then in that case the derivative control reduces the error.

***(iii)* Integral Control.**

For integral control action the actuating signal consists of proportional error signal.

For integral control action the block diagram can be shown as below :

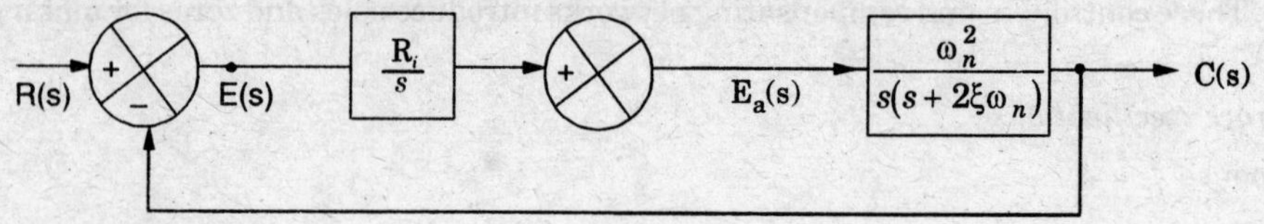

For integral control action

$$e_a(t) = e(t) + k_i \int e(t)dt$$

Taking Laplace transform

$$E_a(s) = E(s) + k_i \frac{E(s)}{s}$$

For integral control action

Input	Without integral control	With integral control
Unit ramp	$\frac{2\xi}{\omega_n}$	0
Unit parabolic	0	$\frac{2\xi}{K_i.\omega_n}$

SERVOMECHANISM

A schematic diagram for position servomechanism is shown in Fig. 6.16(*a*)

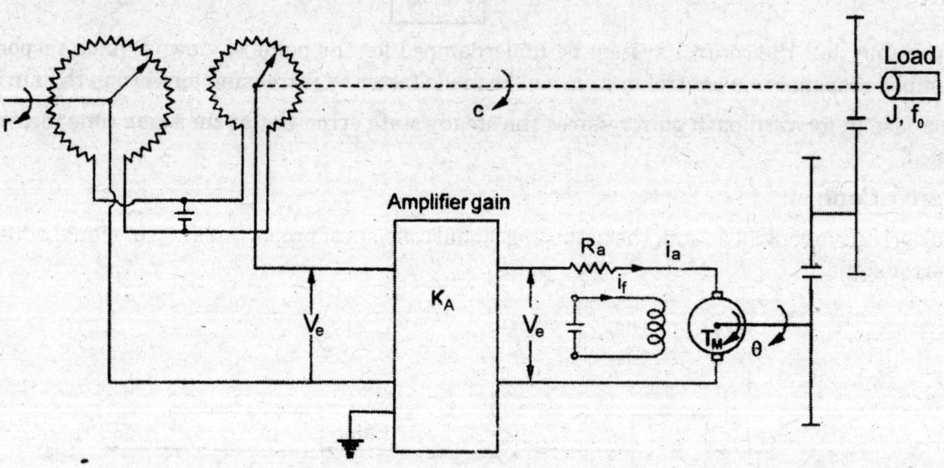

***Fig. 6.16** (a)*

The block diagram for this system is shown in Fig. 6.15(*b*)

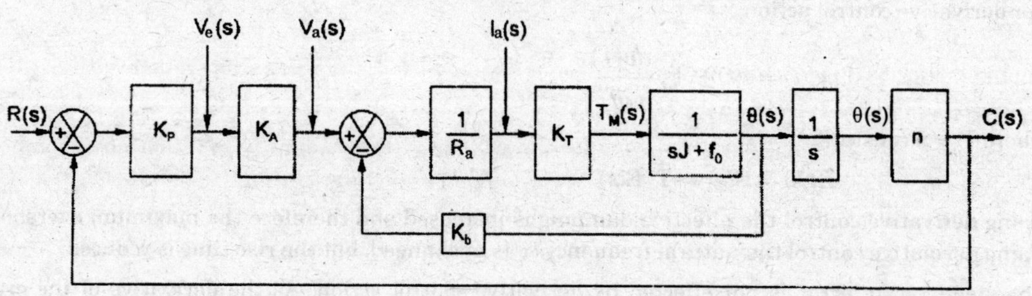

***Fig. 6.16** (b)*

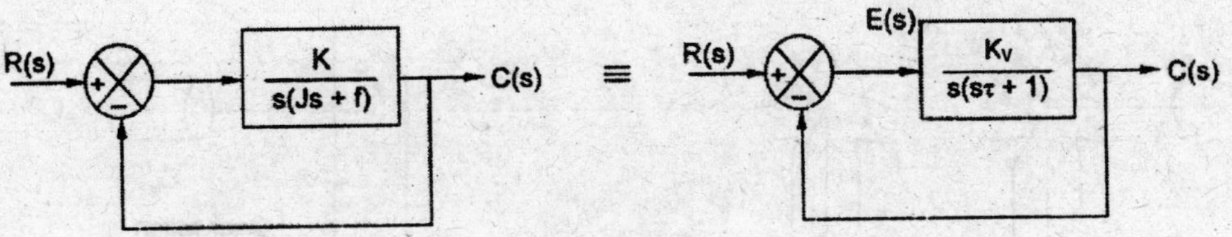

Fig. 6.16 (c)

The forward transfer function $$G(s) = \frac{K_v}{s(\tau s+1)}$$

$$K_v = \frac{K}{f}, \tau = \frac{J}{f}$$

where J and f_0 are the equivalent inertia and friction at the motor shaft.

6.10.1. DERIVATIVE ERROR COMPENSATION (PID CONTROLLER).

Introducing a PD controller into the block diagram of position servomechanism will change the block diagram as shown in Fig.6.17 (*a*). This diagram can be further reduced to Fig. 6.17 (*b*)

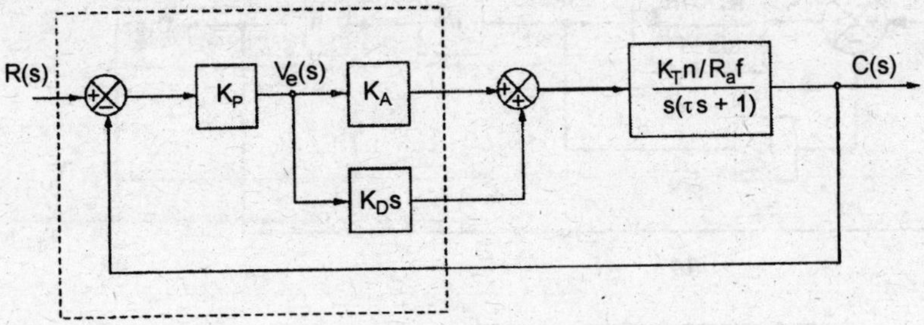

Fig. 6.17 (a)

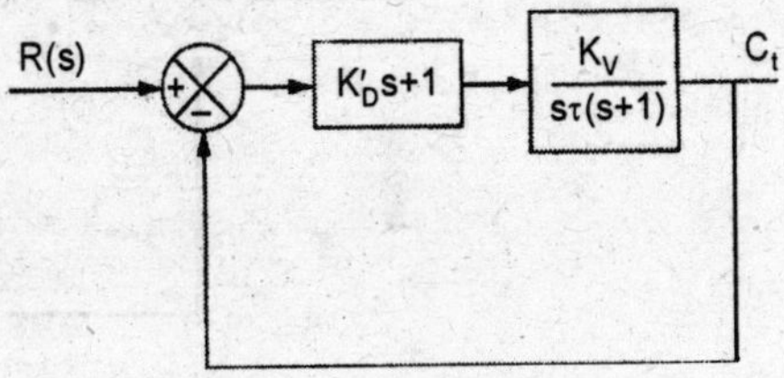

Fig. 6.17 (b)

Here, $$K_D' = \frac{K_D}{K_A}, 1\frac{J}{f},$$

$$k_v = \frac{k_P k_A . k_T n}{R_a f}$$

Now, Transfer function, $$T(s) = \frac{\frac{K_v}{\tau}(K_D' s+1)}{s^2 + \left(\frac{1+k_v k_D}{\tau}\right)s + \frac{K_v}{\tau}}$$

Then, $$\omega'_n = \sqrt{\frac{K_v}{\tau}} = \omega_n$$

$$\xi' = \frac{1+K_v K_D'}{2\sqrt{(K_v \tau)}}$$

$$= \xi \frac{K_D'}{2}\sqrt{\left(\frac{K_v}{\tau}\right)}$$

So, damping increases due to compensation with ω_n remaining fixed, thus reducing system settling time.

6.10.2. DERIVATIVE OUTPUT COMPENSATION.

A system is said to possess a derivative output compensation when the generation of its output depends upon the rate of change of output controlled variable. And for a servosystem, this compensation is obtained by using technometer feedback as shown in the Fig. 6.18.

The output voltage v_t of a d. c. technometer is feedback negatively to the amplifier input. The block diagram for Fig 6.18 (*a*) is shown in Fig. 6.18 (*b*)

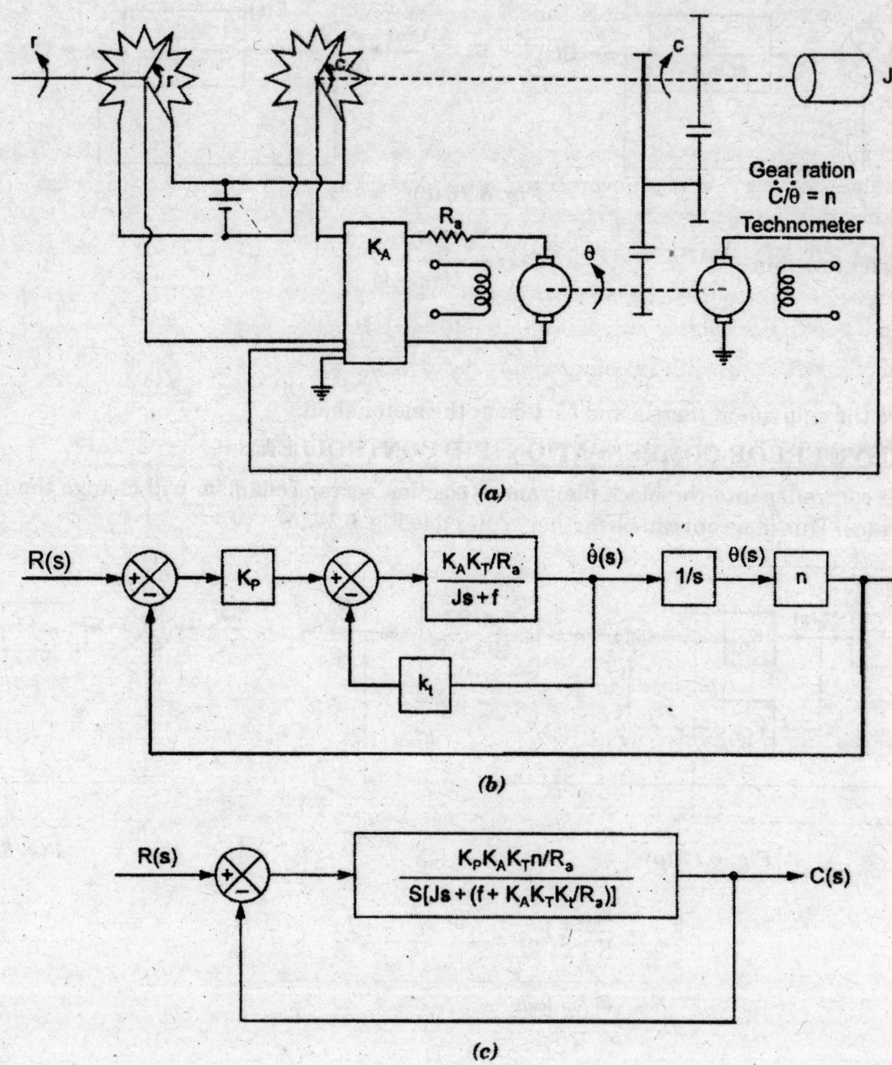

Fig. 6.18

From the block-diagram of Fig. 6.18(*c*)

$$K_v' = \frac{K_P K_A K_T n}{R_a f + K_A K_T K_t} \quad .....(i)$$

$$\tau' = \frac{J R_a}{R_a f + K_A K_T K_t}$$

The natural frequency and damping of the closed-loop is expressed as

$$\omega_n' = \sqrt{\frac{K_v'}{\tau'}} = \sqrt{\left(\frac{K_P K_A K_T n}{J R_a}\right)}$$

$$\zeta = \frac{1}{2}\sqrt{K_v'\,\tau'} = \frac{(R_a f + K_A K_T K_t)}{2\sqrt{(K_P K_A K_t n J R_a)}} \quad .....(ii)$$

From equations (*i*) and (*ii*), we have

$$\zeta' K_v' = \frac{1}{2}\sqrt{\left(\frac{K_P K_A K_T n}{J R_a}\right)}$$

$$\Rightarrow \qquad K_A = 4(\zeta' K_v')^2 \left(\frac{J R_a}{K_P K_T n}\right)$$

Using the value of K_A, technometer constant K_t can be expressed as

$$K_t = \left(\frac{K_P n}{K_v'} - \frac{R_a f}{K_A K_T}\right)$$

on account of the negative derivative feedback K_A may sometimes becomes excessively large. Hence for same value of velocity error constant, the system with compensation requires a higher value of K_A which will cause to higher damping and natural frequency thus reducing setting time.

6.10.3. INTEGRAL ERROR COMPENSATION.

This type of compensation is introduced by using a controller which produces an output signal consisting of two terms, one proportional to the actuating signal and another proportional to its integral.

The block diagram of Fig. 6.19 (*a*) with PI compensation is shown in Fig 6.19 (*b*)

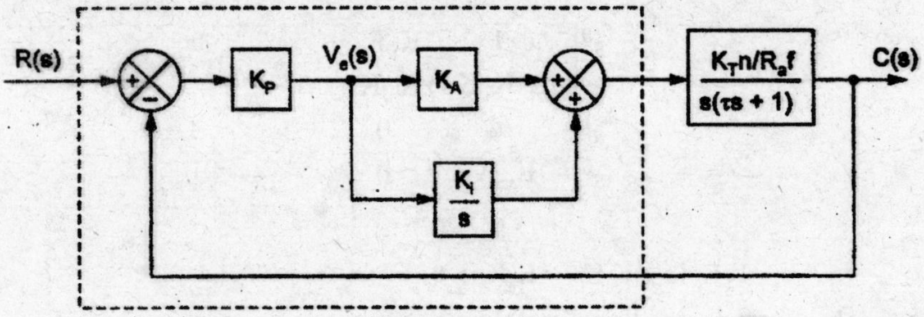

Fig. 6.19 (a)

Reduction of block-diagram of is shown in Fig.

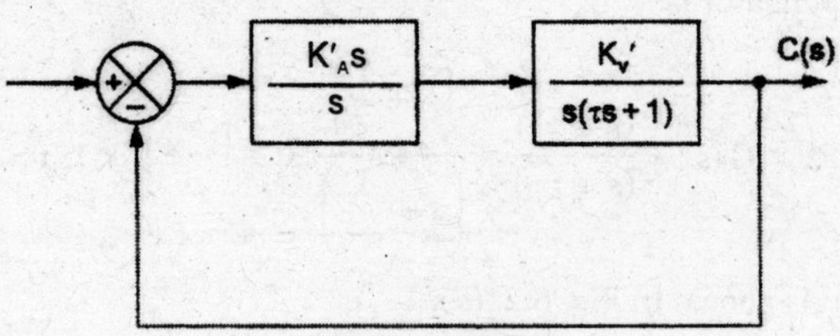

Fig. 6.19 (b)

$$K_v' = \frac{K_P K_i\ K_T n}{R_a f}$$

$$K_A' = \frac{K_A}{K_i}$$

The closed-loop transfer function,

$$T(s) = \frac{K_v'(K_A' s + 1)}{(\tau s^3 + s^2 + K_v' K_A s + K_v')}$$

Additional integration in the forward path changes the system from type-1 to type-2 system and the error of velocity input is eliminated or considerably reduced, since practical integration is not perfect. Thus, integral error compensation inproves the steady-state performance on the one side, but led to instability on the another side as there is third-order characteristic equation.

6.10.4. PROPORTIONAL PLUS INTEGRAL PLUS DERIVATIVE (PID) CONTROLLER.

To increase damping factor of the dominant poles of a PI controlled system, combine it with derivative error scheme, known as PID controller and is shown in Fig. 6.20

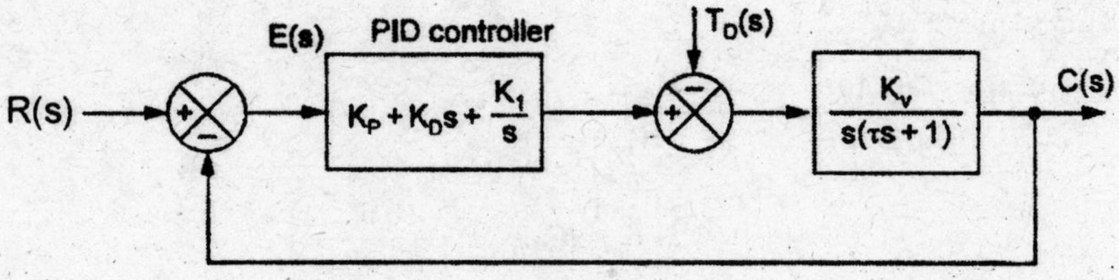

Fig. 6.20

$$\frac{C(s)}{R(s)} = \frac{K_v\left(K_D s^2 + K_P s + K_I\right)}{\tau s^3 + (1+K_v K_P)s^2 + (K_v K_P)s + K_v K_I}, \; T_D(s) = 0 \quad ...(iii)$$

$$\frac{E(s)}{R(s)} = \frac{s^2(\tau s + 1)}{\tau s^3 + (1+K_v K_D)s^2 + (K_v K_P)s + K_v K_I}, \; T_D(s) = 0 \quad ...(iv)$$

$$\frac{E(s)}{T_D(s)} = \frac{K_v s}{\tau s^3 + (1+K_v K_D)s^2 + (K_v K_P)s + K_v K_I}, \; R(s) = 0 \quad ...(v)$$

As, seen from equations (*iv*) and (*v*), e_{ss} for velocity input and step input respective zero. Inclusion of two zeroes in the numerator helps the system to acquire dynamic qualities third-order characteristic equation causes for system instability for certain combination of gains as shown by Routh-array criterion, applied to equation (*iii*)

s^3	1	$K_v K_p$
s^2	$(1 + K_v K_P)$	$K_p K_I$
s^1	b_3	0
s^0	$K_p K_I$	0

For stability, $b_3 > 0$

$\Rightarrow$ $K_v K_p(1 + K_v K_D) - K_p K_I > 0$

Thus, PID controller makes system conditionally stable.

6.11. LEAD COMPENSATOR

The general form of lead compensator is

$$G_c(s) = \frac{(s+z_c)}{(s+p_c)} = \frac{\left(s + \frac{1}{\tau}\right)}{\left(s + \frac{1}{\alpha\tau}\right)}, \; \alpha = \left(\frac{z_c}{p_c}\right) < 1, \; \tau > 0$$

and its s-plane representation is shown in Fig. 6.21(*a*),

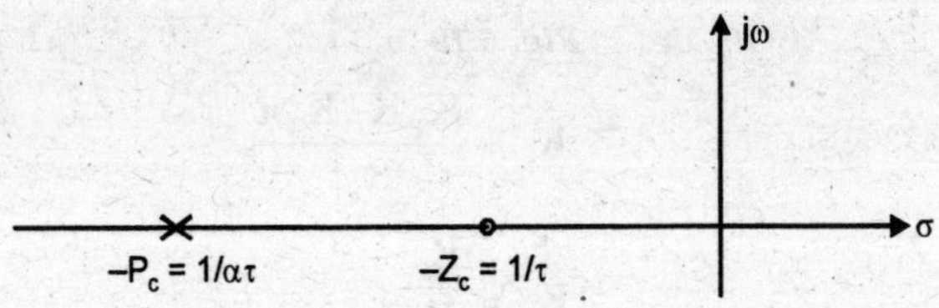

Fig. 6.21 (a)

Transfer Function.

An electric lead network and phase lead-network with amplifier is shown in Figs. 6.21 (*b*) and 6.21 (*c*) respectively.

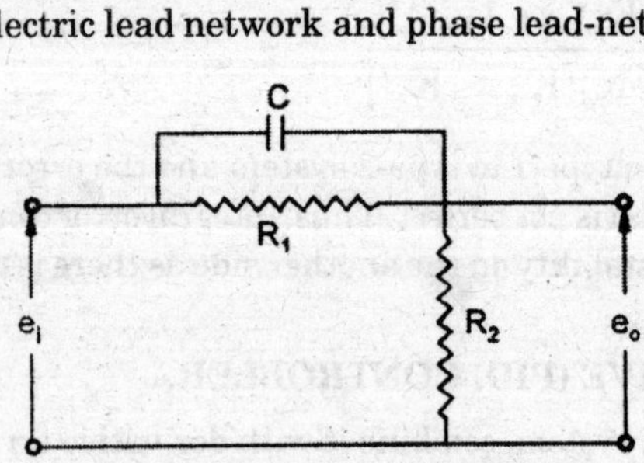

Fig. 6.21 (b)

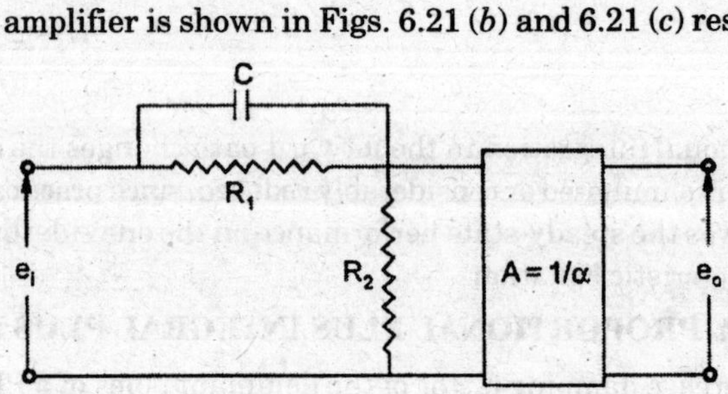

Fig. 6.21 (c)

Here, from Fig. 6.21 (*b*),

$$\frac{E_0(s)}{E_i(s)} = \frac{R_2}{R_2 + \dfrac{R_1/sC}{R_1 + 1/sC}}$$

$$= \frac{\left(s + \frac{1}{R_1C}\right)}{s + \left[\frac{R_2}{(R_1 + R_2)}\right]R_1C}$$

$$\tau = R_1C \quad \text{and} \quad \alpha = \frac{R_2}{R_1 + R_2} < 1$$

Then, sinusoidal transfer of the network;

$$G_c(j\omega) = \alpha\left(\frac{1 + j\omega\tau}{1 + j\omega\alpha\tau}\right), \alpha < 1$$

and, sinusoidal transfer function of the lead compensator is given by

$$G_c(j\omega) = \frac{1 + j\omega\tau}{1 + j\omega\alpha\tau}, \alpha < 1$$

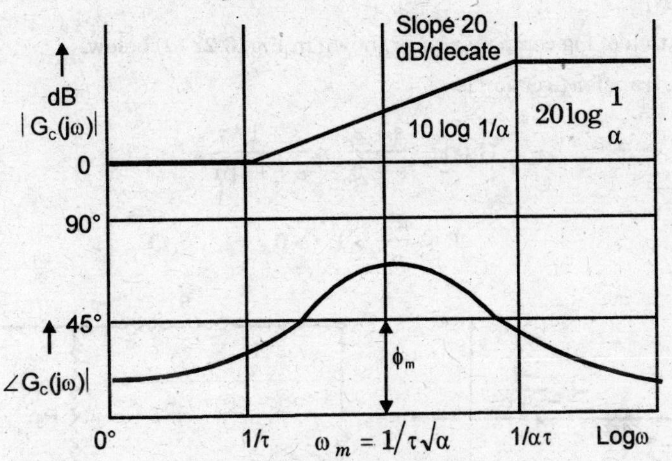

Fig. 6.21 (d)

The bode diagram of the lead compensator is given in Fig. 6.21 (*d*).

Note : Lead compensation speed up transient response and increases the margin of stability. It will increase the system error constant through a limited extent.

From equation (*i*), phase-lead of the compensator at any frequency ω is given by

$$\phi = \tan^{-1} \omega\tau - \tan^{-1} \alpha\omega\tau$$

$$\tan \phi = \frac{-\omega\tau(1 - \alpha)}{1 + \alpha\omega^2\tau^2}$$

For maximum phase-lead, $\frac{d\phi}{d\omega} = 0$

which gives $$\omega_m = \frac{1}{\tau\sqrt{\alpha}} = \sqrt{\left[\left(\frac{1}{\tau}\right)\left(\frac{1}{\alpha\tau}\right)\right]}$$

and, at $\omega = \omega_m$, $$\tan \phi_m = \frac{1 - \alpha}{2\sqrt{\alpha}}, \sin \phi_m = \frac{1 - \alpha}{1 + \alpha}$$

and $$\alpha = \frac{1 - \sin \phi_m}{1 + \sin \phi_m}$$

Magnitude of $G_c(j\omega)$ at $\omega = \omega_m$,

$$|G_C(j\omega_m)| = \left|\frac{1 + j\omega_m\tau}{1 + j\omega_m\tau}\right| = \frac{1}{\sqrt{\alpha}}$$

A plot of ϕ_m versus $\frac{1}{\alpha}$ is shown in Fig. 6.21 (*e*). As seen from the plot, to obtain phase-leads more than 60° ($\alpha \approx 0.08$), the attenuation increases rather sharply, quite out of proportion to increase in phase-lead Hence, to have a phase angle greater than 60°, two cascaded lead networks with moderate values of α rather than a single lead network with too small value of α.

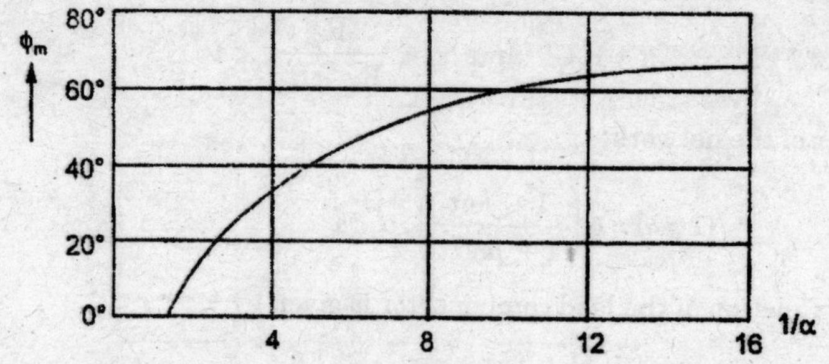

Fig. 6.21 (e)

6.12. LAG COMPENSATOR

The s-plane representation of log compensator is shown in Fig. 6.22 (*a*) below.

The general form of the transfer function is

$$G_C(s) = \frac{s + z_c}{s + p_c} = \frac{s + 1/\tau}{s + 1/\beta\tau},$$

$$\beta = \frac{z_c}{p_c} > 1, \tau > 0 \quad \text{.....}(i)$$

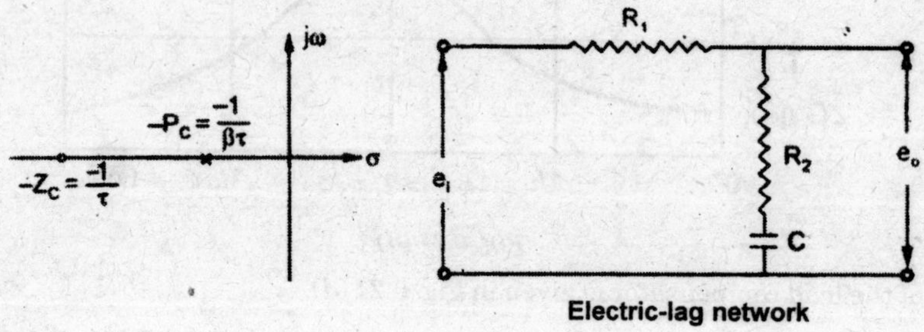

Fig. 6.22 (a)

From electric lag network,

$$\frac{E_0(s)}{E_1(s)} = \frac{R_2 + 1/sC}{R_1 + R_2 + 1/sC}$$

$$= \frac{1}{\frac{R_1 + R_2}{R_2}} \left[\frac{s + 1/R_2C}{s + \frac{1}{\left(\frac{R_1 + R_2}{R_2}\right) R_2 C}} \right] \quad \text{.....}(ii)$$

Comparing equations (*i*) and (*ii*), we have

$$\tau = R_2C, \qquad \beta = \frac{R_1 + R_2}{R_2} > 1$$

and,

$$G_C(s) = \frac{1}{\beta}\left(\frac{s + 1/\tau}{s + 1/\beta\tau}\right)$$

$$= \frac{1}{\beta}\left(\frac{s + z_c}{s + p_c}\right); \qquad \beta = \frac{z_c}{p_c} > 1$$

$$= \frac{\tau s + 1}{\beta \tau s + 1}$$

The sinusoidal transfer function of the lag network is

$$G_C(j\omega) = \frac{(1 + j\omega\tau)}{(1 + j\beta\omega\tau)}$$

Bode diagram for the $G_C(j\omega)$ is drawn in Fig. 6.22 (*b*)

Note : Lag compensator improves steady-state behaviour while persuing its transient response.

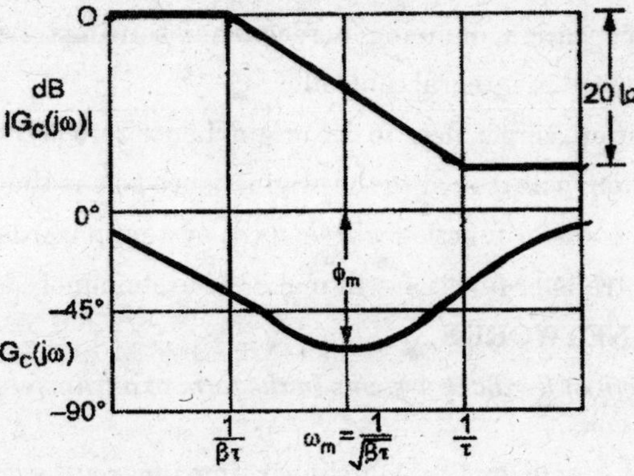

Fig. 6.22 (b)

6.13. LAG-LEAD COMPENSATOR

The general form of this compensator is

$$G_c(s) = \left(\frac{s + \frac{1}{\tau_1}}{s + \frac{1}{\beta\tau_1}}\right)\left(\frac{s + \frac{1}{\tau_2}}{s + \frac{1}{\alpha\tau_2}}\right), \beta > 1, \alpha > 1$$

The *s*-plane representation and electric lag-lead network is shown in Fig. 6.23 (*a*) and Fig. 6.23 (*b*) respectively.

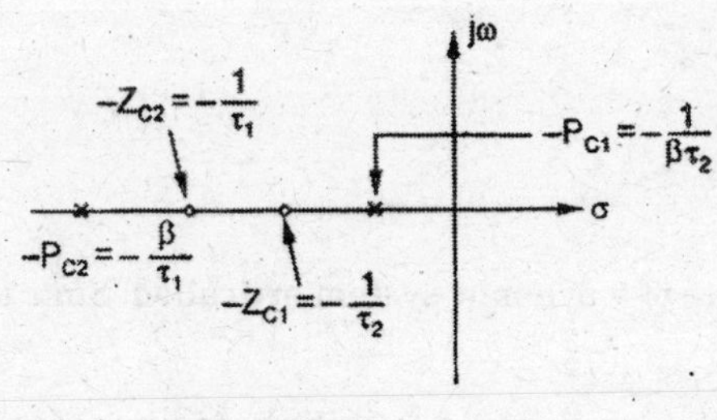

Fig. 6.23 (a)

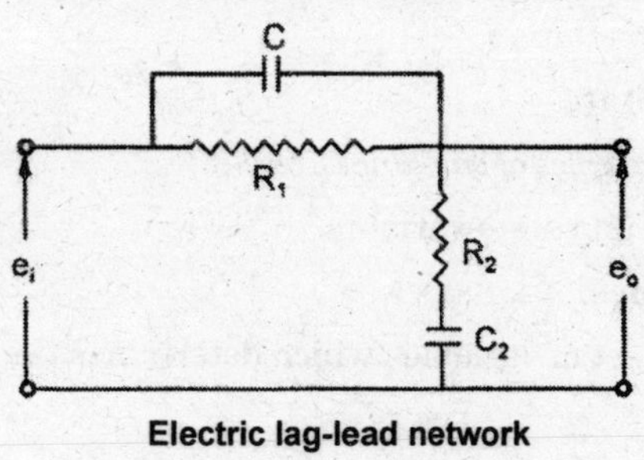

Fig. 6.23 (b)

From above figure,

$$G_c(s) = \frac{\left(s + \frac{1}{R_1C_1}\right)\left(s + \frac{1}{R_2C_2}\right)}{\left[s^2 + \left(\frac{1}{R_1C_1} + \frac{1}{R_2C_1} + \frac{1}{R_2C_2}\right)s + \frac{1}{R_1R_2C_1C_2}\right]}$$

where, $R_1C_1 = \tau_1$, $R_2C_2 = \tau_2$ and $\alpha\beta = 1$.

FEEDBACK COMPENSATION

Compensation element is introduced in the feedback path of a control system, a signal proportional to derivative of the output is feedback to improve performance of a control system. (i.e. tachogenerator feedback).

Advantages.

(*i*) Network energy transfer is from a higher to a lower energy level thereby obviating need for feedback amplification.

(*ii*) In electrical system, suitable cascade devices may not be available.

(*iii*) Provides greater stiffness against load disturbances.

(*iv*) By increasing forward path gain, speed of the response is increased.

(*v*) Derivative action improves transient response.

(*vi*) Integral action improves steady state response.

(*vii*) In derivative error compensation, damping increases and settling time decreases.

(*viii*) Steady state error is reduced in integral controller.

(*ix*) In phase lead compensation, zero is near to the origin, hence zero is the predominant factor.

(*x*) In phase lag compensation, pole is near to the origin, hence pole is the predominant factor.

(*xi*) Addition of poles to the transfer function will lead the system towards instability.

(*xii*) Addition of zeros to the transfer function will make the system more stable.

6.14. STATE EQUATIONS FOR NETWORKS

Methods of analysis and design of feedback systems in the form of a transfer function such as root locus and frequency response has following limitations.

(*i*) Transfer function model is only applicable to linear time invariant system.

(*ii*) It is for single-input single-output system.

(*iii*) It reveals only the system output for a given input and provides no information regarding internal state of the system.

Advantages of State Variable Analysis

(*i*) This method alongwith the output yields information about the state of the system variables at some predetermined points along the flow of signal.

(*ii*) It is a technique for the analysis and design of linear and non-linear time-invariant or time varying multiple-input multiple-output system.

(*iii*) The organisation of the state variable is easiely amendable to solution through digital computers.

(*iv*) The stable variable approach offers a way to look at both the continuous time and discrete time system with the same formulation.

Concept of State

There are three types of variables present :

input, output and state variable.

State Variables.

The smallest set of variables which determines the state of a dynamic system are called *State variables*.

State.

It is the smallest set of state variables, the knowledge of which at $t = t_0$ (initial condition) together with the input completely determines behaviour of the system for any time $t > t_0$.

State Vector.

If n state variables are necessary to determine behaviour of a given system, then variables can be considered as n components of a vector called *State vector*.

6.14.1. TIME-DOMAIN SOLUTION OF LTI STATE EQUATIONS.

This examines the response of linear, time-invariant models expressed in the standard state -equation form as a set of coupled, first-order differential equations.

$$\mathrm{x} = \mathrm{Ax} + \mathrm{Bu} \quad \text{...}(i)$$

$$\mathrm{y} = \mathrm{Cx} + \mathrm{Du}. \quad \text{...}(ii)$$

Solution proceeds in two steps;

(*i*) State-variable response x(t) is found by solving the set of first-order state equations, equation (*i*),

(*ii*) State response is substituted into the algebraic output equations, equation (*ii*) in order to compute y(t).

Total system state response x(t) is considered in two parts :

(*i*) Homogeneous solution $x_h(t)$ that describes the response to an arbitrary set of initial conditions x(0).

(*ii*) Particular solution $x_p(t)$ that satisfies the state equations for the given input u(*t*).

Then two components are combined to form the total response.

Note: solution methods rely heavily on matrix algebra.

6.14.2. STATE-VARIABLE RESPONSE OF LINEAR SYSTEMS.

(*i*) Homogeneous State Response:

The state-variable response of a system given by equation (*i*) with zero input, u(*t*) = 0, and an arbitrary set of initial conditions x(0) is solution of the set of *n* homogeneous first-order differential equations:

$$\dot{x} = \mathrm{Ax} \qquad ...(iii)$$

To derive homogeneous response x*h*(*t*), first consider response of a first-order (scalar) system with state equation

$$\dot{x} = ax + bu \qquad ...(iv)$$

with initial condition *x*(0).

In this case, homogeneous response $x_h(t)$ has an exponential form defined by system time constant,

$$t = -\frac{1}{a}$$

or

$$x_h(t) = e^{at}x(0) \qquad ...(v)$$

The exponential term e^{att} may be expanded as a power series, to give

$$x_h(t) = \left(1+at+\frac{a^2t^2}{2!}+\frac{a^3t^3}{3!}+.....+\frac{a^kt^k}{k!}+.....\right)x(0) \qquad ...(vi)$$

where series converges for all finite *t*>0.

Now assume that the homogeneous response $x_h(t)$ of the state vector of a higher order linear time-invariant system, given by equation (3), can also be expressed as an infinite power series, similar in form to equation (*vi*), but in terms of the square matrix A, i.e. we assume:

$$x_h(t) = \left(1+\mathrm{A}t+\frac{\mathrm{A}^2t^2}{2!}+\frac{\mathrm{A}^3t^3}{3!}+....+\frac{\mathrm{A}^kt^k}{k!}+....\right)x(0) \qquad ...(vii)$$

where *x*(0) is initial state.

Each term in this series is a matrix of size *n* × *n*, and summation of all terms yields another matrix of size *n* × *n*. To verify that the homogeneous state equation $\dot{x} = \mathrm{Ax}$ is satisfied by equation (*vii*), the series may be differentiated term by term. Matrix differentiation is defined on an element by element basis, and because each system matrix A^k contains only constant elements

$$x_h(t) = \left(0+\mathrm{A}+\mathrm{A}^2t+\frac{\mathrm{A}^2t^2}{2!}+...+\frac{\mathrm{A}^kt^{k-1}}{(k-1)!}+...\right)x(0)$$

$$= \mathrm{A}\left(1+\mathrm{A}t+\frac{\mathrm{A}^2t^2}{2!}+\frac{\mathrm{A}^3t^3}{3!}+...+\frac{\mathrm{A}^{k-1}t^{k-1}}{(k-1)!}+...\right)x(0) = \mathrm{A}x_h(t). \qquad ...(viii)$$

Equation (*viii*) shows that the assumed series form of the solution satisfies the homogeneous state equations, demonstrating that equation (*vii*) is a solution of equation (*iii*). *Thus homogeneous response to an arbitrary set of initial conditions* x(0) *can be expressed as an* infinite sum of time dependent matrix functions, involving only the system matrix A. Because of the similarity of this series to the power series defining scalar exponential, it is convenient to define *matrix exponential* of a square matrix *A* as

$$e^{\mathrm{A}t} = 1+\mathrm{A}t+\frac{\mathrm{A}^2t^2}{2!}+\frac{\mathrm{A}^3t^3}{3!}+.....+\frac{\mathrm{A}^kt^k}{k!}+.....$$

which is itself a square matrix of the same size as its defining matrix A. The matrix form of the exponential is recognized by the presence of a matrix quantity in the exponent. These system homogeneous response $x_h(t)$ may be written in terms of matrix exponential

$$x_h(t) = e^{\mathrm{A}t}\mathrm{x}(0)$$

which is similar in form to equation (6.21). The solution is often written as

$$x_h(t) = \mathrm{F}(t)\mathrm{x}(0) \qquad ...(ix)$$

where $\Phi(t)= e^{At}$ is defined to be the *state transition matrix* [1 – 5].

Equation (*ix*) gives the response at any time t to an arbitrary set of initial conditions, thus computation of e^{At} at any t yields the values of all the state variables x(t) directly.

Example. Determine matrix exponential, and hence state transition matrix, and the homogeneous response to the initial conditions $x_1(0) = 2$, $x_2(0) = 3$ of the system with state equations:

$$x_1 = -2x_1 + u; x_2 = x_1 - x_2.$$

Solution: System matrix is

$$A = \begin{bmatrix} -2 & 0 \\ 1 & -1 \end{bmatrix}$$

From Eq. (*ix*), matrix exponential (and the state transition matrix) is

$$\Phi(t) = e^{At}$$

$$= \left(1 + At + \frac{A^2t^2}{2!} + \frac{A^3t^3}{3!} + ... + \frac{A^kt^k}{k!} + ...\right)$$

$$= \begin{bmatrix} 1 & 0 \\ 0 & 1 \end{bmatrix} + \begin{bmatrix} -2 & 0 \\ 1 & -1 \end{bmatrix} t + \begin{bmatrix} 4 & 0 \\ -3 & 1 \end{bmatrix} \frac{t^2}{2!} + \begin{bmatrix} -8 & 0 \\ 7 & -1 \end{bmatrix} \frac{t^3}{3!} + ...$$

$$= \begin{bmatrix} 1 - 2t + \frac{4t^2}{2!} - \frac{8t^3}{3!} + ... & 0 \\ 0 + t - \frac{3t^2}{2!} + \frac{7t^3}{3!} + ... & 1 - t + \frac{t^2}{2!} - \frac{t^3}{3!} + ... \end{bmatrix}$$

The elements f_{11} and f_{22} are simply the series representation for e^{-2t} and e^{-t} respectively. The series for ϕ_{21} is not so easily recognized but is first four terms of the expansion of $e^{-t} - e^{-2t}$. Thus state transition matrix is

$$f(t) = \begin{bmatrix} e^{-2t} & 0 \\ e^{-1} - e^{-2t} & e^{-t} \end{bmatrix}$$

and homogeneous response to initial conditions $x_1(0)$ and $x_2(0)$ is

$$x_h(t) = \Phi(t)\mathrm{x}(0)$$

or

$$x_1(t) = x_1(0)e^{-2t}$$

$$x_2(t) = x_1(0)\,(e^{-t} - e^{-2t}) + x_2(0)e^{-t}.$$

With the given initial conditions, the response is

$$x_1(t) = 2e^{-2t} \quad .....(vi)$$

$$x_2(t) = 2\,e^{-t} - 2e^{-2t} + 3e^{-t} = 5e^{-t} - 2e^{-2}$$

In general, recognition of the exponential components from the series for each element is difficult and is not normally used for finding a closed form for the state transition matrix.

Although the sum expressed in Equation (*ix*) converges for all A, in many cases the series converges slowly, and is rarely used for the direct computation of $\Phi(t)$.

(*ii*) Forced State Response of Linear Systems :

Consider complete response of a linear system to an input $u(t)$.

Consider first a first-order system with a state equation $\dot{x} = ax + bu$

written as $\dot{x}(t) - ax(t) = bu(t)$

If both sides are multiplied by an integrating factor e^{-at}, left-hand side becomes a perfect differential

$$e^{-at}\dot{x} - e^{-at}ax = \frac{d}{dt}\left(e^{-at}x(t)\right) = e^{-at}bu$$

which may be integrated directly to give

$$\int_0^t \frac{d}{dr}\left(e^{-ar}x(r)\right)dr = e^{-at}x(t) - x(0) = \int_0^t e^{-ar}bu(r)dr$$

rearranged to give the state variable response explicitly

$$x(t) = e^{at}x(0) + \int_0^t e^{a(t-\tau)}bu(\tau)d\tau$$

Development of the expression for the response of higher order systems may be performed in a similar manner using the matrix exponential e^{-At} as an integrating factor. Matrix differentiation and integration are defined to be element by element operations, therefore if state equations $\dot{x}$ = Ax + Bu are rearranged, and all terms pre-multiplied by the square matrix e^{-At}

$$e^{-At}\dot{x}(t) - e^{-At}Ax(t) = \frac{d}{dt}(e^{-At}x(t)) = e^{-At}Bu(t).$$

Integrating $$\int_0^t \frac{d}{d\tau}\left(e^{-A\tau}x(\tau)\right)d\tau = e^{-At}x(t) - e^{-A.0}x(0)$$

$$= \int_0^t e^{-A\tau}Bu(\tau)d\tau$$

But $$e^{-A0} = I \text{ and } [e^{-At}]^{-1} = e^{At}$$

hence complete state vector response may be written in two similar forms

$$x(t) = e^{At}x(0) + e^{At}\int_0^t e^{-A\tau}Bu(\tau)d\tau \qquad ...(x)$$

$$x(t) = e^{At}x(0) + \int_0^t e^{-A\tau}Bu(\tau)d\tau \qquad ...(xi)$$

The full state response, given by Equation (x) or Equation (xi) consists of two components:

(*a*) Term similar to the system homogeneous response $x_h(t) = e^{At}x(0)$ that is dependent only on the system initial conditions x(0).

(*b*) Term in the form of a *convolution integral*, and is particular solution for the input u(*t*), with zero initial conditions.

Evaluation of the integral in Equation (*xi*) involves matrix integration. For a system of order *n* and with *r* inputs, the matrix e^{At} is $n \times n$, B is $n \times r$ and u(*t*) is an $r \times 1$ column vector. Therefore product $e^{A(t-\tau)}$ But(τ) is an $n \times 1$ column vector, and solution for each of the state equations involves a single scalar integration.

(*iii*) System Output Response:

For either homogeneous or forced responses, the system output response *y*(*t*) may be found by substitution of the state variable response into the algebraic system output equations

$$y = Cx + Du$$

But in case of homogeneous response, $u(t) = 0$

$$\therefore \qquad y_h(t) = Ce^{At}x(0),$$

But for the forced response, substitution of Equation. (*ix*) into the output equations gives

$$y(t) = Ce^{At}x(0) + C\int_0^t e^{A(t-\tau)}Bu(\tau)d\tau + Du(t)$$

(*iv*) State Transition Matrix:

Properties:

(*a*) $\Phi(0) = I$, which simply states that the state response at time $t = 0$ is identical to the initial conditions.

(*b*) $\Phi(-t) = \Phi^{-1}(t)$

Response of an unforced system before time $t = 0$ may be calculated from initial conditions $x(0)$,

$$x(-t) = \Phi(-t)x(0) = \Phi^{-1}(t)x(0)$$

and the inverse always exists.

(*c*) $\Phi(t_1)\Phi(t_2) = \Phi(t_1 + t_2)$.

With this property, state response at time *t* may be defined from the system state specified at some time other than $t = 0$

(*d*) If A is a diagonal matrix, then e^{At} is also diagonal, and each element on the diagonal is an exponential in the corresponding diagonal element of the A matrix, i.e. e^{at}.

System Eigenvalues and Eigenvectors:

The homogeneous response of linear systems is exponential in form, containing components of the form $e^{\lambda t}$, where λ is a root of the characteristic equation.

Thus it is reasonable to conjecture that for an nth order system, the homogeneous response of each of the n state variables $x_i(t)$ is a weighted sum of n exponential components

$$x_i(t) = \sum_{j=1}^{n} m_{ij} e^{\lambda_j t}$$

where m_{ij} are constant coefficients that are dependent on the system structure and initial conditions $x(0)$.

The proposed solution for the complete state vector may be written in a matrix form

$$\begin{bmatrix} x_1(t) \\ x_2(t) \\ \vdots \\ x_n(t) \end{bmatrix} = \begin{bmatrix} m_{11} & m_{12} & \cdots & m_{1n} \\ m_{21} & m_{22} & \cdots & m_{2n} \\ \vdots & \vdots & \ddots & \vdots \\ m_{n1} & m_{n2} & \cdots & m_{nn} \end{bmatrix} \begin{bmatrix} e^{\lambda_1 t} \\ e^{\lambda_2 t} \\ \vdots \\ e^{\lambda_n t} \end{bmatrix},$$

or

$$x_h(t) = \mathrm{M} \begin{bmatrix} e^{\lambda_1 t} \\ e^{\lambda_2 t} \\ \vdots \\ e^{\lambda_n t} \end{bmatrix}$$

where M is an $n \times n$ matrix of the coefficients m_{ij}.

Given a linear system of order n, described by the homogeneous equation $\dot{x} = Ax$, and where matrix A has n distinct eigen values, the homogeneous response of any state variable in the system from an arbitrary set of initial conditions $x(0)$ is a linear combination of n modal components $e^{\lambda_i t}$, where λ_i are eigen values of the matrix A.

Method for determining State Transition Matrix :

(1) Substitute numerical values into the system A matrix, and compute the system eigen values, a modal matrix M, and its inverse M^{-1}. A computer based linear algebra package provides a convenient method for doing this.

(2) Form the diagonal matrix $e^{\Lambda t}$ by placing the modal components $e^{\lambda_i t}$ on the leading diagonal.

(3) The state transition matrix $\Phi(t)$ is

$$\Phi(t) = Me^{\Lambda t}M^{-1}.$$

SAMPLED-DATA CONTROL SYSTEM

Z-Transform.

Let a series of discrete sequence is given as

$$f(k) = \{..0, 0, f(0), f(1), f(2) ..\}.$$

Z-transform of this discrete sequence is,

$$z[f(k)] = \sum_{k=0}^{\infty} f(k)\, z^{-k}$$

here z = an ordinary complex number

Let $f(k) = \{..0, 1, a, a^2 ...\}$

$= a^k$; $k > 0$

$= 0$; $k < 0$

Here a is any real number

$$Z[f(k)] = F(z) = \sum_{k=0}^{\infty} a^k z^{-k}$$

$$= \sum_{k=0}^{\infty} (az^{-1})^k = \frac{1}{1 - az^{-1}} = \frac{z}{z - a}$$

A discrete sequence can be generated from a continuous - time function $f(t)$ by mathematically sampling it at time interval T seconds apart merely by substituting $t = k\mathrm{T}$ *i.e.*

$$f_s(t) = f(k\mathrm{T})$$

Properties of Z-Transform.

(i) Linearity :

$$Z[af(k) + bg(k)] = \sum_{k=0}^{\infty}[af(k) + bg(k)]z^{-k}$$

$$= a\sum_{k=0}^{\infty} f(k)z^{-k} + b\sum_{k=0}^{\infty} g(k)z^{-k}$$

$$= aF(z) + bG(z)$$

(ii) Shifting : If

$$Z[f(k)] = F(z)$$

$$Z[f(k+1)] = ZF(z) - Zf(0)$$

$$Z[f(k+n)] = z^n F(z) - \sum_{i=0}^{n-1} f(i)\, Z^{n-i} \quad ; k > -n$$

$$= Z^n [F(z) - f(0) - f(1)z^{-1} - F(2)z^{-2} \ldots F(n-1)z^{-(k-1)}]$$

$$Z[f(k-n)] = Z^{-n} F(z)$$

(iii) Multiplication by K :

If $Z[f(k)] = F(z)$, then $\quad Z[kf(k)] = -Z\dfrac{d}{dz}F(z)$

(iv) Scale change :

If $Z[f(k)] = F(z)$, then $\quad Z[a^k f(k)] = F(z/a)$

and $\quad Z[a^{-k} f(k)] = F(az)$

Initial and Final Value Theorem.

***(i)* Initial Value Theorem :**

We have $\quad F(z) = \sum_{k=0}^{\infty} f(k)z^{-k} = f(0) + f(1)z^{-1} + F(2)z^{-2} + \ldots$

$\therefore \quad f(0) = \lim_{z\to\infty} F(z)$

***(ii)* Final Value Theorem :** Final value of series of sequence is given by

$$\lim_{k\to\infty} f(k) = \lim_{z\to 1} F(z)\cdot(z-1)$$

Z - Transform of Some Functions.

$f(k)$	$F(z)$
$\delta(k)$	1
$u(k)$ or 1	$\dfrac{z}{z-1}$
a^k	$\dfrac{z}{z-a}$
$k\,a^k$	$\dfrac{az}{(z-a)^2}$
$k^2 a^k$	$\dfrac{az(z+a)}{(z-a)^3}$
$(k+1)\,a^k$	$\dfrac{z^2}{(z-a)^2}$
$\dfrac{(k+1)(k+2)}{\underline{\lvert 2}}\,a^k$	$\dfrac{z^3}{(z-a)^3}$

$f(k)$	$F(z)$
$\dfrac{a^k}{\angle k}$	e^{az-1}
kT	$\dfrac{Tz}{(z-1)^2}$
$(kT)^2$	$\dfrac{T^2 z(z+1)}{(z-1)^3}$
e^{-akT}	$\dfrac{z}{z-e^{-aT}}$
$\sin \omega kT$	$\dfrac{z\sin\omega T}{z^2 - 2z\cos\omega T + 1}$
$\cos \omega kT$	$\dfrac{z(z-\cos\omega T)}{z^2 - 2z\cos\omega T + 1}$

OBJECTIVE TYPE QUESTIONS

TRANSFER FUNCTION

1. In the given figure, spring constant is K, viscous friction coefficient is B, mass is M and the system output motions is $x(t)$ corresponding to input force F (t).

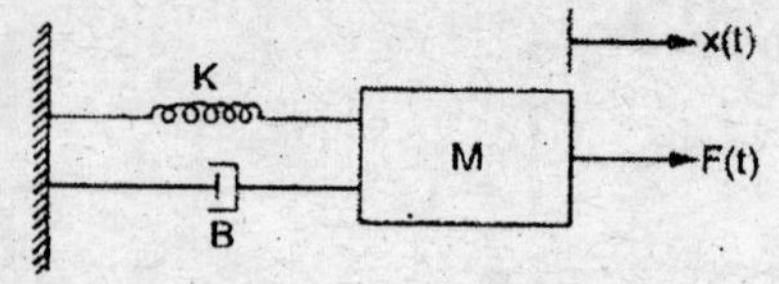

Which of the following parameters related to the above system ?

1. Time constant $= \dfrac{1}{M}$
2. Damping coefficient $= \dfrac{B}{2\sqrt{KM}}$
3. Natural frequency of oscillation $= \sqrt{\dfrac{K}{M}}$

Select the correct answer using the codes given below :

(*a*) 1, 2 and 3 (*b*) 1 and 2
(*c*) 2 and 3 (*d*) 1 and 3

2. A system is represented by the block diagram given in the figure :

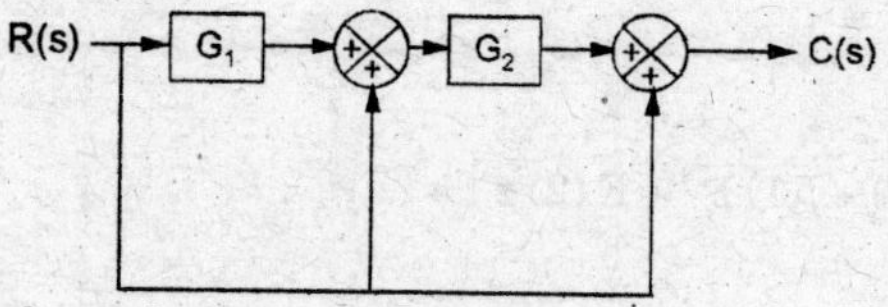

Which of the following represents the input output relationship of the above diagram ?

(*a*) R $(s) \rightarrow$ $\boxed{G_1 G_2}$ $\rightarrow$ C (s)

(*b*) R $(s) \rightarrow$ $\boxed{G_1 + G_2}$ $\rightarrow$ C (s)

(*c*) R $(s) \rightarrow$ $\boxed{1 + G_1 + G_2 G_3}$ $\rightarrow$ C (s)

(*d*) R $(s) \rightarrow$ $\boxed{1 + G_2 + G_1 G_2}$ $\rightarrow$ C (s)

3. The transfer function C/R of the system shown in the figure is

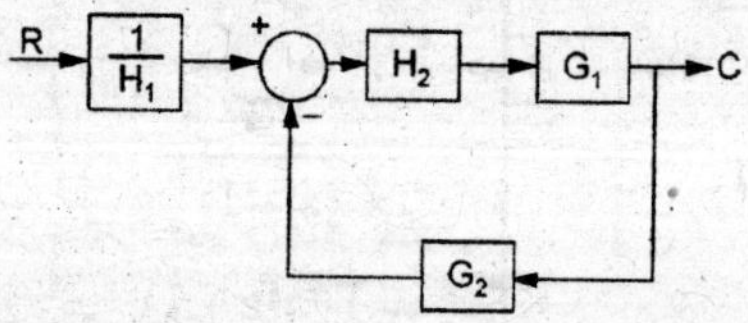

(*a*) $\dfrac{G_1 G_2 H_2}{H_1 (1 + G_1 G_2 H_2)}$ (*b*) $\dfrac{G_1 H_2}{H_1 (1 + G_1 G_2 H_2)}$

(*c*) $\dfrac{G_2 H_2}{H_1 (1 + G_1 G_2 H_1)}$ (*d*) $\dfrac{G_2 H_1}{H_2 (1 + G_1 G_2 H_2)}$

4. The transfer function of the system shown in the given figure is

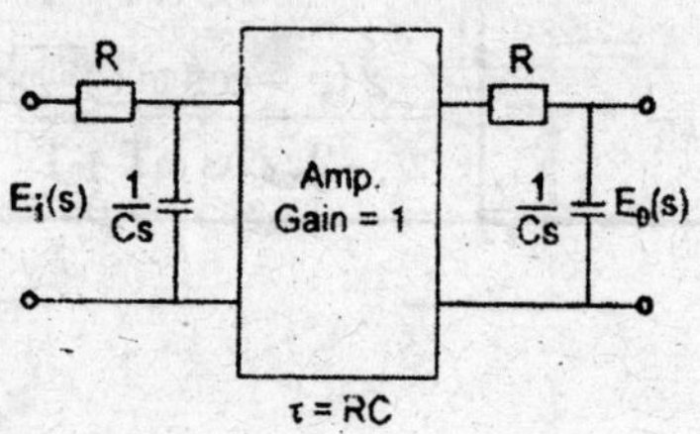

τ = RC

(*a*) $\dfrac{1}{1 + \tau s}$ (*b*) $\dfrac{1}{(1 + \tau s)^2}$

(*c*) $\dfrac{\tau s}{1 + \tau s}$ (*d*) $\dfrac{\tau s}{(1 + \tau s)^2}$

5. The closed loop system shown in the figure is subjected to a disturbance N(s). The transfer function $\dfrac{C(s)}{N(s)}$ is given by

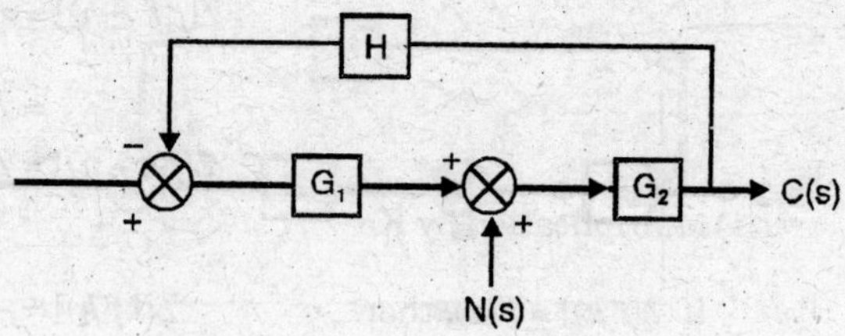

(*a*) $\dfrac{G_1 G_2}{1 + G_1 G_2 H}$ (*b*) $\dfrac{G_2}{1 + G_2 H}$

(*c*) $\dfrac{G_1}{1 + G_1 H}$ (*d*) $\dfrac{G_2}{1 + G_1 G_2 H}$

6. The transfer function C(s) / R(s) of the system, whose block diagram is given below is

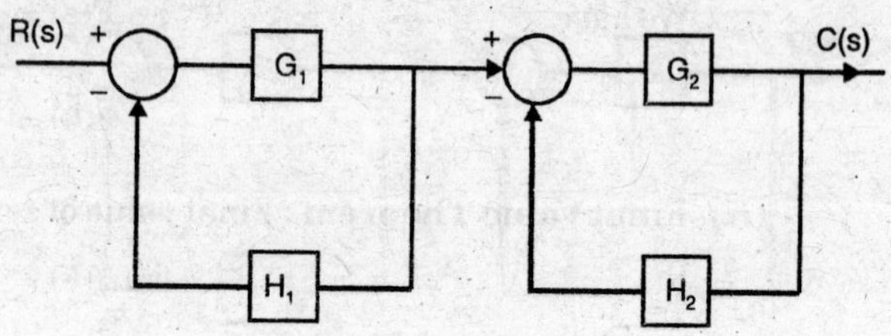

(*a*) $\dfrac{G_1 G_2}{1 + G_1 H_1 + G_2 H_2 - G_1 G_2 H_1 H_2}$

(*b*) $\dfrac{G_1 G_2}{1 + G_1 H_1 + G_2 H_2 + G_1 G_2 H_1 H_2}$

(*c*) $\dfrac{G_1 G_2}{1 + G_1 H_1 + G_2 H_2}$

(*d*) $\dfrac{G_1 (1 + G_2 H_2) + G_2 (1 + G_1 H_1)}{1 + G_1 H_1 + G_2 H_2 + G_1 G_2 H_1 H_2}$

7. Consider a simple mass-spring-friction system as given in the figure

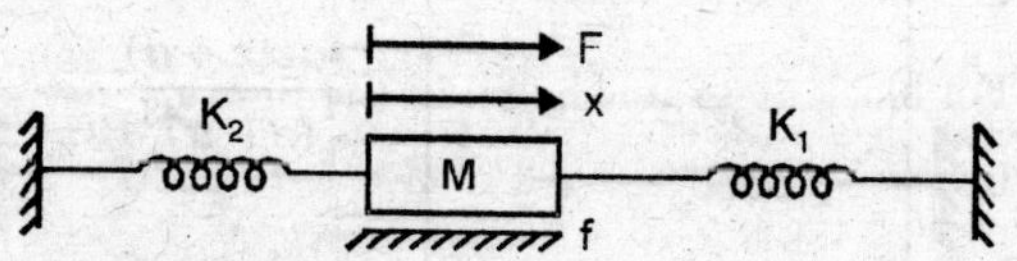

k_1 = spring constant
f = friction
M = mass
F = force
x = displacement

The transfer function $\frac{X(s)}{F(s)}$ of the given system will be

(a) $\frac{1}{Ms^2 + fs + K_1 \cdot K_2}$ (b) $\frac{1}{Ms^2 + fs + K_1 + K_2}$

(c) $\frac{1}{Ms^2 + fs + \frac{K \cdot K_2}{K_1 + K_2}}$ (d) $\frac{K_2}{Ms^2 + fs + K_1}$

8. For the system shown, the transfer function C(s) R(s) is equal to

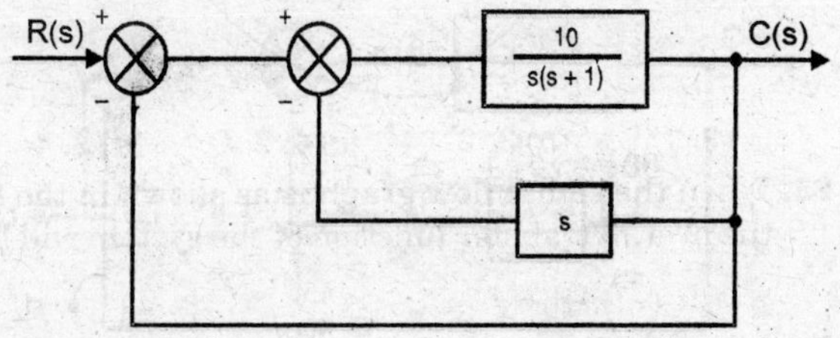

(a) $\frac{10}{s^2 + s + 10}$ (b) $\frac{10}{s^2 + 11s + 10}$

(c) $\frac{10}{s^2 + 9s + 10}$ (d) $\frac{10}{s^2 + 2s + 10}$

9. The closed loop gain of the system shown in the given figure is

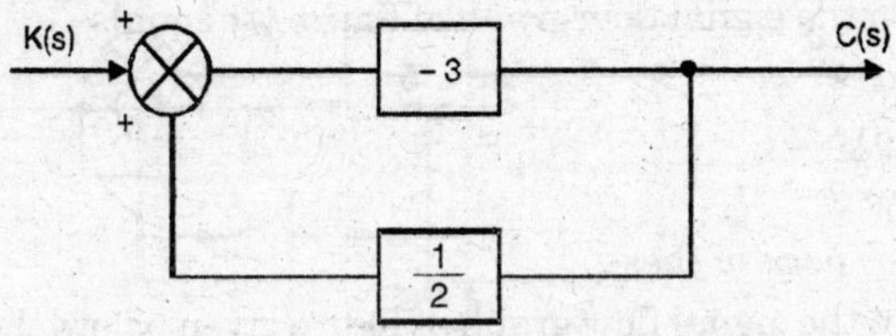

(a) $-\frac{9}{5}$ (b) $-\frac{6}{5}$

(c) $\frac{6}{5}$ (d) $\frac{9}{5}$

10. The response $c(t)$ of a system to an input r(t) is given by the following differential equation :

$$\frac{d^2c(t)}{dt^2} + 3\frac{dc(t)}{dt} + 5c(t) = 5\,r(t).$$

The transfer function of the system is given by

(a) $G(s) = \frac{5}{s^2 + 3s + 5}$ (b) $G(s) = \frac{1}{s^2 + 3s + s}$

(c) $G(s) = \frac{3s}{s^2 + 3s + 5}$ (d) $G(s) = \frac{s+3}{s^2 + 3s + 5}$

11. For block diagram shown in the figure, $\frac{C(s)}{R(s)}$ is given by

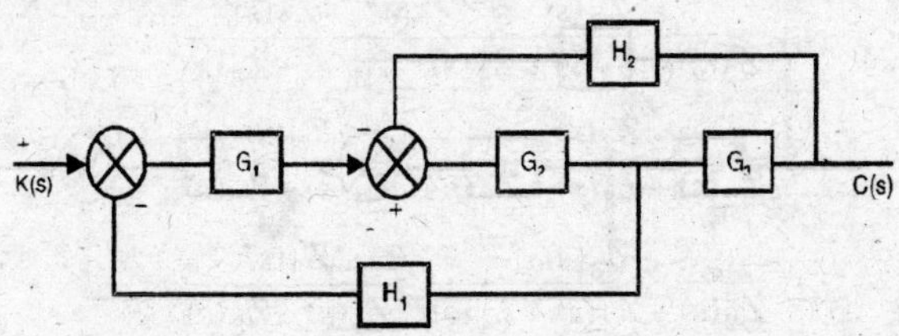

(a) $\frac{G_1G_2G_3}{1 + H_2G_2G_3 + H_1G_1G_2}$

(b) $\frac{G_1G_2G_3}{1 + G_1G_2G_3H_1H_2}$

(c) $\frac{G_1G_2G_3}{1 + G_1G_2G_3H_1 + G_1G_2G_3H_2}$

(d) $\frac{G_1G_2G_3}{1 + G_1G_2G_3H_1}$

12. In the following block diagram $G_1 = \frac{10}{s}$;

$G_2 = \frac{10}{(s+1)}$; $H_1 = s + 3$ and $H_2 = 1$.

The overall transfer function C/R isgiven by

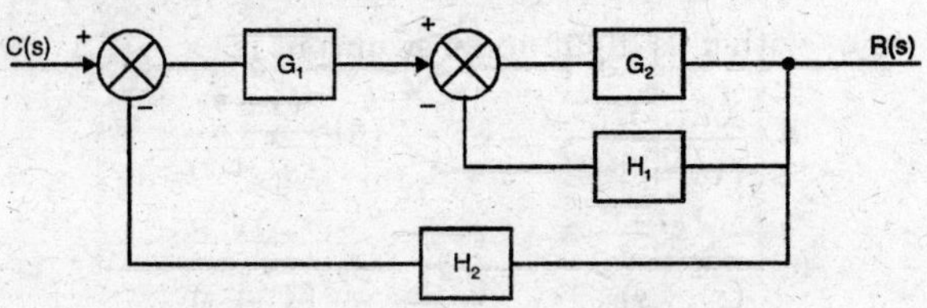

(a) $\frac{10}{11s^2 + 31s + 10}$ (b) $\frac{100}{11s^2 + 31s + 100}$

(c) $\frac{100}{11s^2 + 31s + 10}$ (d) $\frac{100}{11s^2 + 31s}$

13. A control system whose step response is

$$-0.5\,(1+e^{-2t})$$

is cascaded to another control block whose impulse response is e^{-t}. The transfer function of the cascaded combination is

(a) $\frac{1}{(s+1)(s+2)}$ (b) $\frac{1}{s(s+1)}$

(c) $\frac{1}{(s+2)}$ (d) $\frac{0.5}{(s+1)(s+2)}$

14. Equivalent of the block diagram in the figure is

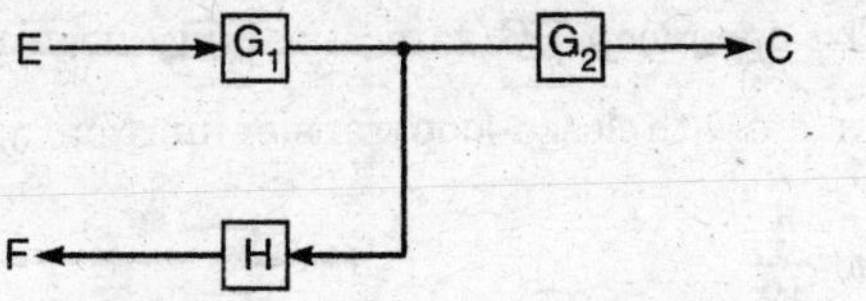

(a) 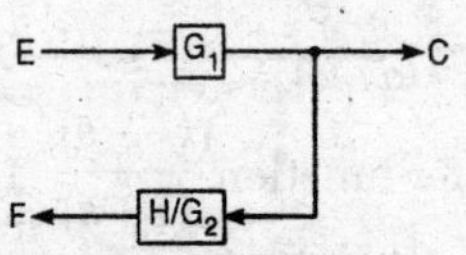

(b) 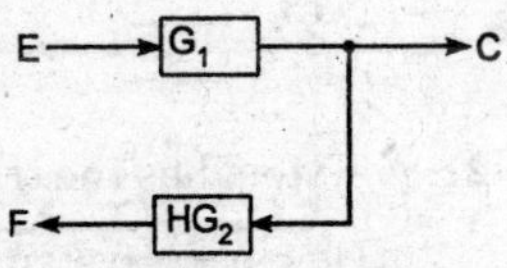

(c) 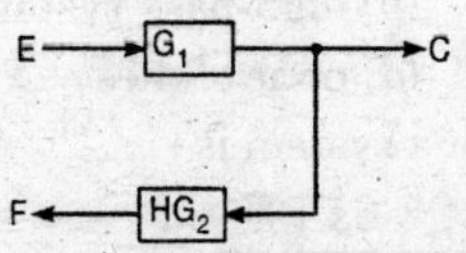

(d) 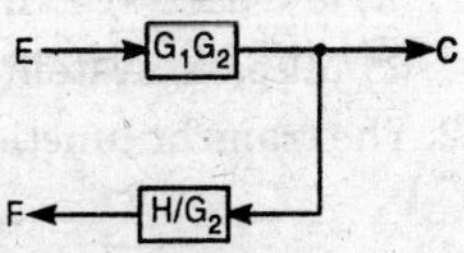

15. The transfer function of a linear system is

(a) ratio of the output, $v_o(t)$, and input $v_i(t)$

(b) ratio of the derivatives of the output and the input

(c) ratio of the Laplace transform of the output and that of the input with all initial conditions zeros

(d) none of these

16. The overall transfer function of the system in the given figure is

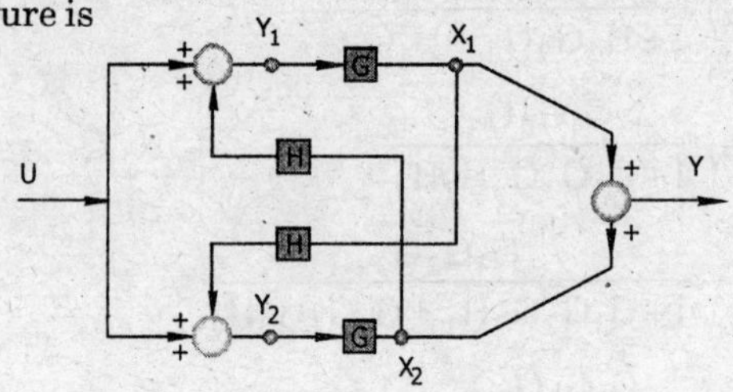

(a) $\dfrac{G}{1-GH}$ (b) $\dfrac{2G}{1-GH}$

(c) $\dfrac{GH}{1-GH}$ (d) $\dfrac{2G}{1-H}$

17. The transfer function of the system described by

$$\frac{d^2y}{dt^2}+\frac{dy}{dt}=\frac{du}{dt}+2u$$

with u as input and y as output is

(a) $\dfrac{(s+2)}{(s^2+s)}$ (b) $\dfrac{(s+1)}{(s^2+s)}$

(c) $\dfrac{s}{(s^2+s)}$ (d) $\dfrac{2s}{(s^2+s)}$

18. Consider a feedback control system with loop transfer function

$$G(s)\,H(s)=\frac{K(1+0.5s)}{s(1+s)(1+2s)}$$

The type of the closed loop system is

(a) zero (b) one (c) two (d) three

19. The unit-impulse response of a unit-feedback control system is given by

$$c(t)=-t\,e^{-t}+2\,e^{-t},\ (t\geq 0)$$

The open loop transfer function is equal to

(a) $\dfrac{s+1}{(s+2)^2}$ (b) $\dfrac{2s+1}{s^2}$

(c) $\dfrac{s+1}{(s+1)^2}$ (d) $\dfrac{s+1}{s^2}$

20. The open-loop DC gain of a unity negative feedback system with closed-loop transfer function $\dfrac{s+4}{s^2+7s+13}$ is

(a) $\dfrac{4}{13}$ (b) $\dfrac{4}{9}$

(c) 4 (d) 13

21. A system has the transfer function $\dfrac{(1-s)}{(1+s)}$. It is called

(a) low-pass system (b) high-pass system

(c) all-pass system (d) none of these

22. The transfer function of a system is

$$\frac{2s^2+6s+5}{(s+1)^2\,(s+2)}$$

The characteristic equation of the system is

(a) $2s^2+6s+5=0$

(b) $(s+1)^2\,(s+2)=0$

(c) $2s^2+6s+5+(s+1)^2\,(s+2)=0$

(d) $2s^2+6s+5-(s+1)^2\,(s+2)=0$

23. The transfer function of a tachometer is of the form

(a) Ks (b) $\dfrac{K}{s}$ (c) $\dfrac{K}{(s+1)}$ (d) $\dfrac{K}{s(s+1)}$

SIGNAL FLOW GRAPH

24. The signal flow diagram of a system is shown in the given figure. The number of forward paths and the number of pairs of non-touching loops are respectively

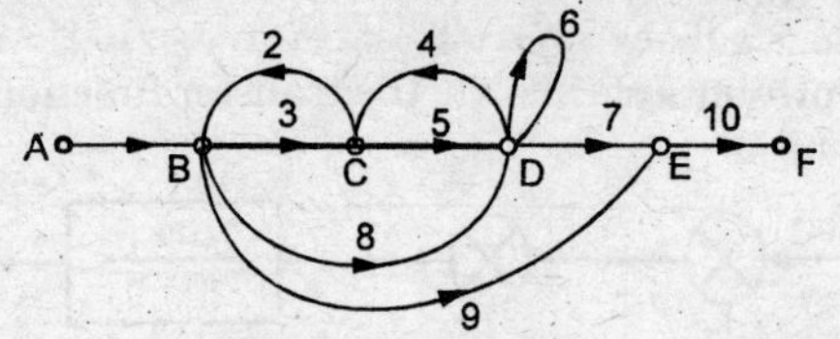

(a) 3, 1 (b) 3, 2 (c) 4, 2 (d) 2, 4

25. When the signal flow graph is as shown in the figure, the overall transfer function of the system will be

(a) $\dfrac{C}{R}=G$ (b) $\dfrac{C}{R}=\dfrac{G}{1+H_2}$

(c) $\dfrac{C}{R}=\dfrac{G}{(1+H_1)(1+H_2)}$ (d) $\dfrac{C}{R}=\dfrac{G}{1+H_1+H_2}$

26. In the signal flow graph of figure y/x equals

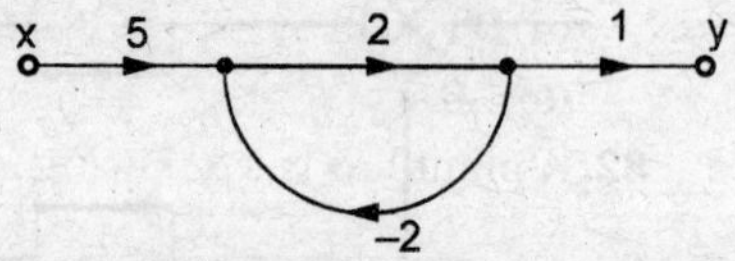

(a) 3

(b) 5/2

(c) 2

(d) none of these

27. In the signal flow graph of figure given below, the gain C/R will be

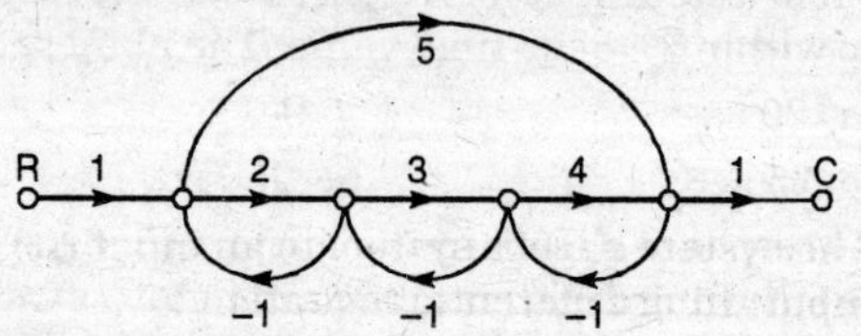

(a) 11/9 (b) 22/15 (c) 24/23 (d) 44/23

28. An electrical system and its signal-flow graph representation are shown in Fiures I and II respectively. The values of G_2 and H, respectively, are

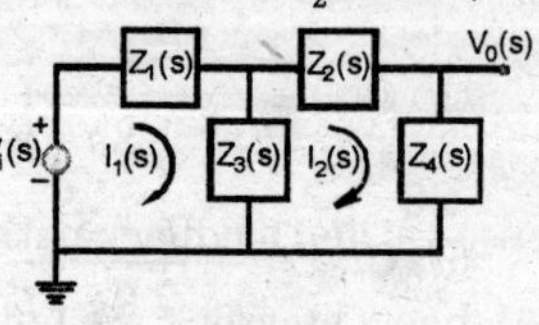

Fig. I

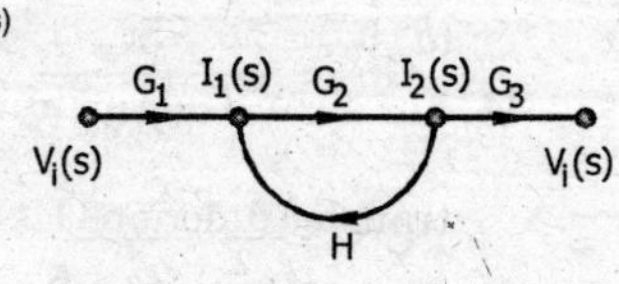

Fig. *II*

(a) $\dfrac{Z_3(s)}{Z_1(s)+Z_2(s)+Z_3(s)},\ \dfrac{-Z_3(s)}{Z_1(s)+Z_3(s)}$

(b) $\dfrac{-Z_3(s)}{Z_2(s)-Z_3(s)+Z_4(s)},\ \dfrac{-Z_3(s)}{Z_1(s)+Z_3(s)}$

(c) $\dfrac{Z_3(s)}{Z_2(s)+Z_3(s)+Z_4(s)},\ \dfrac{Z_3(s)}{Z_1(s)+Z_3(s)}$

(d) $\dfrac{-Z_3(s)}{Z_2(s)-Z_3(s)+Z_4(s)},\ \dfrac{Z_3(s)}{Z_1(s)+Z_3(s)}$

STEADY-STATE ERRORS/ RESPONSE

29. Consider a unity feedback control system with open-loop transfer function

$$G(s) = \frac{K}{s(s+1)}.$$

The steady state error of the system due to a unit step input is

(*a*) zero (*b*) K (*c*) 1 / K (*d*) ∞

30. The feedback control system shown in the given figure represents a

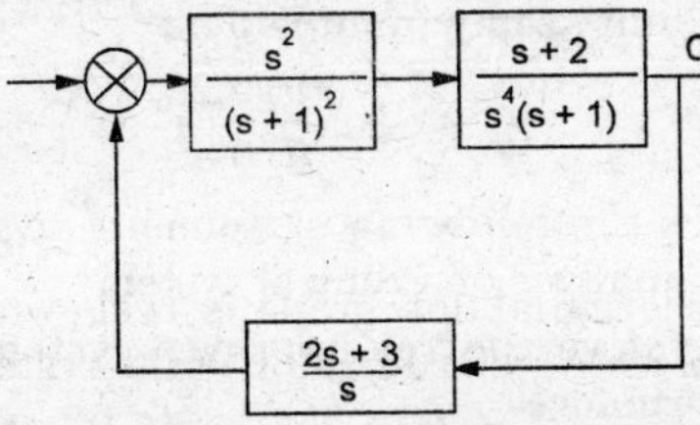

(*a*) Type 0 system (*b*) Type 1 system
(*c*) Type 2 system (*d*) Type 3 system

31. A unity feedback control system has a forward path transfer function equal to

$$\frac{42.25}{s^2(s+6.5)}$$

The unit step response of this system starting from rest, will have its maximum value at a time equal to

(*a*) 0 sec (*b*) 0.56 sec
(*c*) 5.6 sec (*d*) infinity

32. A plant has the following transfer function:

$$G(s) = \frac{1}{(s^2+0.2s+1)}$$

From a step input it is required that the response settles to within 2% of its final value. The plant setting time is

(*a*) 20 sec (*b*) 40 sec
(*c*) 35 sec (*d*) 45 sec

33. The system shown in the given figure has a unit step input. In order that the steady state error is 0.1, the value of K required is

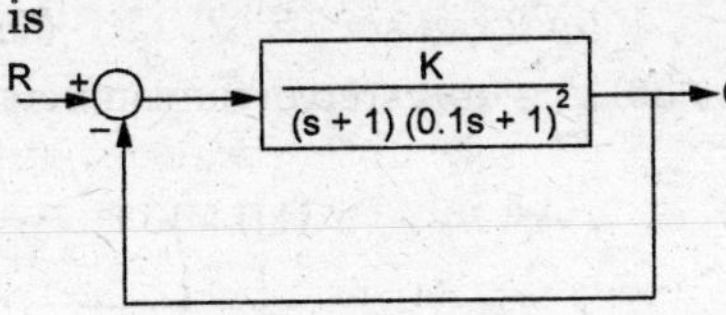

(*a*) 0.1
(*b*) 0.9
(*c*) 1.0
(*d*) 9.0

34. For a unit step input, a system with forward path transfer function $G(s) = \frac{20}{s^2}$ and feedback path transfer function $H(s) = (s+5)$, has a steady state output of

(*a*) 0 (*b*) 0.5
(*c*) 0.2 (*d*) 0.03

35. Consider a system shown in the given figure

$$U(s) \longrightarrow \frac{2}{s} \longrightarrow C(s)$$

If the system is disturbed so that C(0) = 1, then C (*t*) for a unit step input will be

(*a*) $1 + t$ (*b*) $1 - t$
(*c*) $1 + 2t$ (*d*) $1 - 2t$

36. What will be the closed loop transfer function of a unity feedback control system whose step response is given by

$$c(t) = K[1 - 1.66e^{-8t}\sin(6t + 37°)]$$

(*a*) $\frac{100K}{s^2+16s+100}$ (*b*) $\frac{10K}{s^2+16s+100}$
(*c*) $\frac{K}{s^2+16s+100}$ (*d*) $\frac{10K}{s^2+8s+10}$

37. A system is represented by

$$\frac{dy}{dt} + 2y = 4t\,u(t)$$

The ramp component in the forced response will be

(*a*) $t\,u(t)$ (*b*) $2t\,u(t)$ (*c*) $3t\,u(t)$ (*d*) $4t\,u(t)$

38. If the unit step response of a network is $(1 - e^{-\alpha t})$, then its unit impulse response will be

(*a*) $\alpha e^{-\alpha t}$ (*b*) $\alpha e^{-t/\alpha}$
(*c*) $\frac{1}{\alpha e^{-\alpha t}}$ (*d*) $(1-\alpha)e^{-\alpha t}$

39. Given : $KK_t = 99$; s = j1 rad/s

The sensitivity of the closed-loop system (shown in the figure) to variation in parameter K is approximately

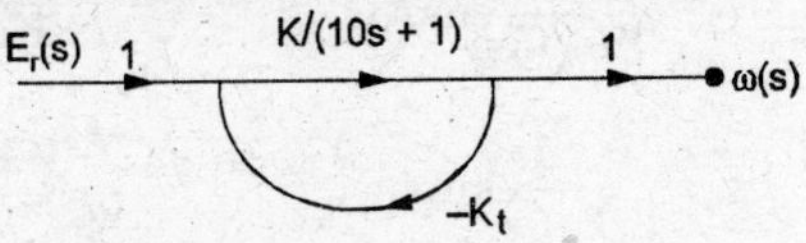

(*a*) 0.01
(*b*) 0.1
(*c*) 1.0
(*d*) 10

40. The performance specifications for a unity feedback control system having an open-loop transfer function

$$G(s) = \frac{K}{s(s+1)(s+2)}$$

are

(*i*) Velocity error coefficient $K_v > 10\ \text{sec}^{-1}$
(*ii*) Stable closed-loop operation.

The value of K, satisfying the above specifications, is

(*a*) K > 6 (*b*) 6 < K < 10
(*c*) K > 10 (*d*) none of these

41. The unit step response of a second order linear system with zero initial states is given by

$$c(t) = 1 + 1.25\exp(-6t)\ \sin(8t - \tan^{-1}1.333);\ t \geq 0$$

The damping ratio and the undamped natural frequency of oscillation of the system are respectively

(*a*) 0.6 and 10 rad/s (*b*) 0.6 and 12.5 rad/s
(*c*) 0.8 and 10 rad/s (*d*) 0.8 and 12.5 rad/s

42. For the unity feedback system shown below, the steady state error, when the input is

$$R = \frac{3}{s} - \frac{1}{s^2} + \frac{1}{2s^3},\ \text{would be}$$

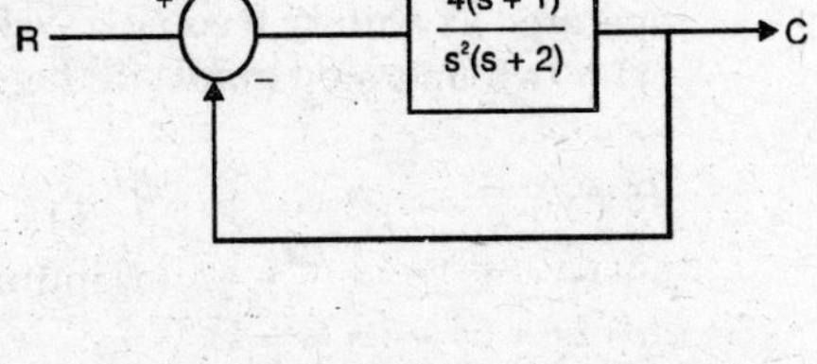

(*a*) $\frac{1}{4}$
(*b*) 0
(*c*) ∞
(*d*) $\frac{1}{2}$

43. The z-transform of a signal is given by $c(z) = \dfrac{z^{-1}(1-z^{-4})}{4(1-z^{-1})^2}$. Its final value is

(*a*) $\dfrac{1}{4}$ (*b*) zero

(*c*) 1 (*d*) infinity

44. In the derivative error compensation, damping

(*a*) decreases and settling time decreases

(*b*) increases and settling time increases

(*c*) decreases and settling time increases

(*d*) increases and settling time decreases

45. For a feedback control system of type 2, the steady state error for a ramp input is

(*a*) infinite (*b*) constant

(*c*) zero (*d*) indeterminate

46. The close-loop transfer function of a control system is given by

$$\frac{C(s)}{R(s)} = \frac{1}{1+s}.$$

For the input $r(t) = \sin t$, the steady state value of $c(t)$ is equal to

(*a*) $\dfrac{1}{\sqrt{2}}\cos t$ (*b*) 1

(*c*) $\dfrac{1}{\sqrt{2}}\sin t$ (*d*) $\dfrac{1}{\sqrt{2}}\sin\left(t-\dfrac{\pi}{4}\right)$

47. The impulse response of an initially relaxed linear system is $e^{-2t}u(t)$. To produce a response of $te^{-2t}u(t)$, the input must be equal to

(*a*) $2e^{-t}u(t)$ (*b*) $\dfrac{1}{2}e^{-2t}u(t)$

(*c*) $e^{-2t}u(t)$ (*d*) $e^{-t}u(t)$

48. The closed-loop transfer function of a control system is given by

$$\frac{C(s)}{R(s)} = \frac{2(s-1)}{(s+2)(s+1)}.$$

For a unit step input the output is

(*a*) $-3e^{-2t}+4e^{-t}-1$ (*b*) $-3e^{-2t}-4e^{-t}+1$

(*c*) zero (*d*) infinity

49. The position and velocity error coefficients for the system of transfer function

$$G(s) = \frac{50}{(1+0.1s)(1+2s)}$$

respectively are

(*a*) zero and zero (*b*) zero and infinity

(*c*) 50 and zero (*d*) 50 and infinity

50. The transfer function of a system is $\dfrac{10}{1+s}$. When operated as a unity feedback system, the steady state error to a unit step input will be

(*a*) zero (*b*) $\dfrac{1}{11}$

(*c*) 10 (*d*) infinity

51. The value of derivative feedback constant a, which will increase the damping ratio of the system to 0.7 is

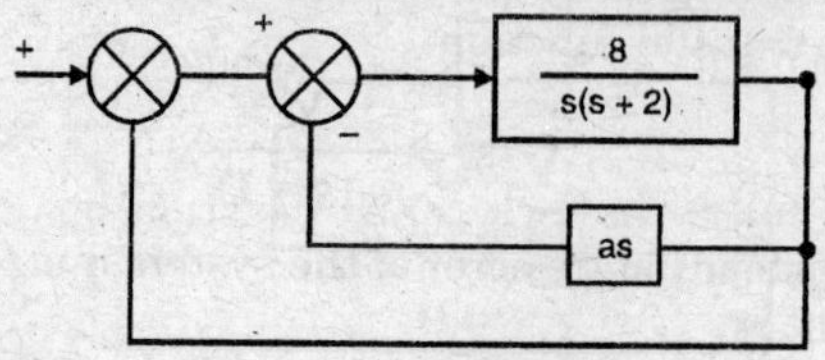

(*a*) 0.152 (*b*) 0.245

(*c*) 0.353 (*d*) 0.558

52. In the given system, (Q. 56) if $a = 0.1$, then steady state error to unity ramp input will be

(*a*) 0.16 (*b*) 0.25

(*c*) 0.35 (*d*) 0.49

53. Consider the following statements regarding time-domain analysis of a control system :

1. Derivative control improves system's transient performance
2. Integral control does not improve system's steady state performance
3. Integral control can convert a second order system into a third order system

Of these statements

(*a*) 1 and 2 are correct (*b*) 1 and 3 are correct

(*c*) 2 and 3 are correct (*d*) 1, 2 and 3 are correct

54. In the system shown in the figure,

$r(t) = \sin \omega t$

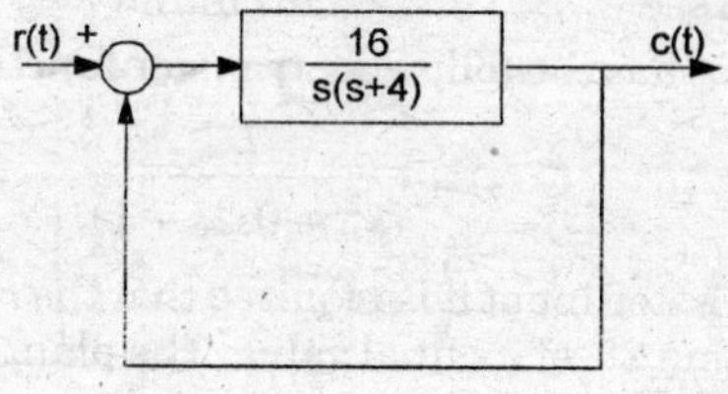

The steady-state response $c(t)$ will exhibit a resonance peak at a frequency of

(*a*) 4 rad/sec (*b*) $2\sqrt{2}$ rad/sec

(*c*) 2 rad/sec (*d*) $\sqrt{2}$ rad/sec

55. The unit step error coefficient of a system

$$G(s) = \frac{1}{(s+6)(s+1)}$$

with unity feedback is

(*a*) 1/6 (*b*) ∞

(*c*) 0 (*d*) 1

56. For the system shown in the figure, with a damping ratio ξ of 0.7. and undamped natural frequency ω_n of 4 rad / sec, the values of K and a are

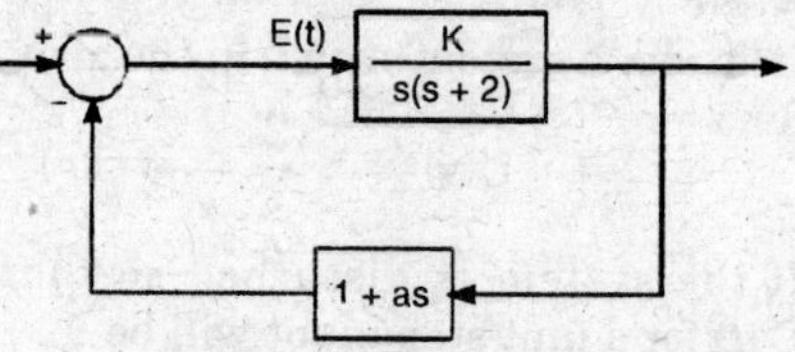

(*a*) K = 4, a = 0.35 (*b*) K = 8, a = 0.455

(*c*) K = 16, a = 0.225 (*d*) K = 64, a = 0.9

57. What is the value of k for a unity feedback system with $G(s) = \dfrac{k}{s(1+s)}$ to have a peak overshoot of 50% ?

(a) 0.53 (b) 5.3
(c) 0.6 (d) 0.047

58. A unity-feedback control system has the open-loop transfer function

$$G(s) = \frac{4(1+2s)}{s^2(s+2)}.$$

If input to the system is a unit ramp, then steady-state error will be

(a) 0 (b) 0.5 (c) 2 (d) infinity

59. The steady state error of a stable type 0 unity feedback system, for a unit step function is

(a) 0 (b) $\dfrac{1}{1+K_p}$ (c) ∞ (d) $\dfrac{1}{K_p}$

60. The output of a linear time invariant control system is $c(t)$ for a certain input $r(t)$. If $r(t)$ is modified by passing it through a block whose transfer function is e^{-s} and then applied to the system, the modified output of the system would be

(a) $\dfrac{c(t)}{1+e^{t}}$ (b) $\dfrac{c(t)}{1+e^{-t}}$
(c) $c(t-1)\,u(t-1)$ (d) $c(t)\,u(t-1)$

61. For what values of 'a' does the system shown in the figure have a zero steady state error $[\text{i.e.}, \lim_{t\to\infty} \in(t)]$ for a step input ?

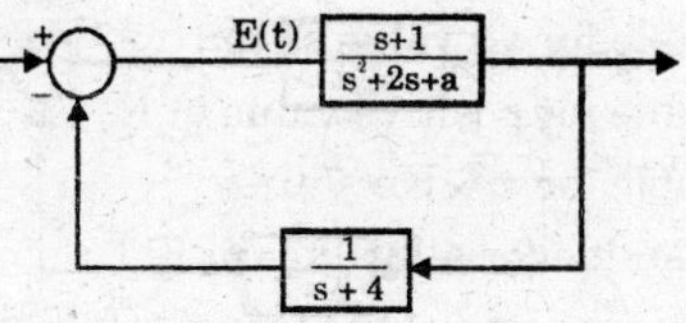

(a) $a = 0$ (b) $a = 2$
(c) $a \geq 4$ (d) for no value of 'a'

62. The transfer function of a system is

$$G(s) = \frac{100}{(s+1)(s+100)}.$$

For a unit-step input to the system, the approximate setting time for 2% criterion is

(a) 100 sec (b) 4 sec
(c) 1 sec (d) 0.01 sec

63. The characteristic polynomial of a system is,

$$q(s) = 2s^5 + s^4 + 4s^3 + 2s^2 + 2s + 1.$$

The system is

(a) stable (b) marginally stable
(c) unstable (d) oscillatory

64. A unity feedback system has open-loop transfer function $G(s) = \left\{\dfrac{25}{[s(s+6)]}\right\}.$

The peak overshoot in the step-input response of the system is approximately equal to

(a) 5 % (b) 10 %
(c) 15 % (d) 20 %

STABILITY ROUTH AND NYQUIST

65. The Nyquist plot of a loop transfer function $G(j\omega)\,H(j\omega)$ of a system encloses the $(-1, j0)$ point. The gain margin of the system is

(a) less than zero (b) zero
(c) greater than zero (d) infinity

66. By a suitable choice of the scalar parameter K, the system shown in the figure, can be made to oscillate continuously at a frequency of

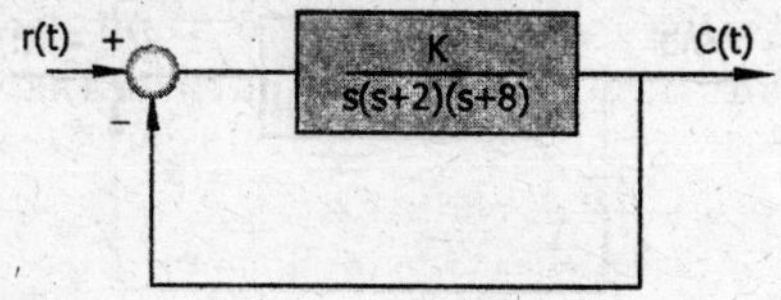

(a) 1 rad/s (b) 2 rad /s
(c) 4 rad /s (d) 8 rad /s

67. The open-loop transfer function of a unity feedback control system is

$$G(s) = \frac{K(s+2)}{(s+1)(s-7)}$$

For K > 6, the stability characteristic of the open-loop and closed-loop configurations of the system are respectively

(a) stable and unstable
(b) stable and stable
(c) unstable and stable
(d) unstable and unstable

68. The forward-path transfer function of a unity feedback system is

$$G(s) = \frac{K(s^2-4)}{s^2+3}$$

For the system to be stable the range of K is

(a) $K > -1$ (b) $K < \dfrac{3}{4}$
(c) $-1 < K < \dfrac{3}{4}$ (d) marginal stable

69. The unstable system is

(a) $G(s)H(s) = \dfrac{K}{(T_1 s+1)(T_2 s+1)}; K > 0$

(b) $G(s)H(s) = \dfrac{K(s+1)}{s^2(s+4)(s+5)}; K > 91$

(c) $G(s)H(s) = \dfrac{K(s+2)}{(s+1)(s-3)}; K > 2$

(d) $G(s)H(s) = \dfrac{K}{(Ts+1)^3}; -1 < K < 8$

70. A control system is as shown in the given figure. The maximum value of gain K for which the system is stable is

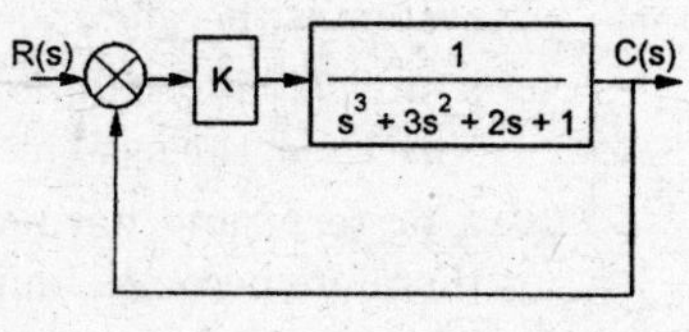

(a) $\sqrt{3}$
(b) 3
(c) 4
(d) 5

71. For the transfer function

$$G(s)\,H(s) = \frac{1}{s(s+1)\,(s+0.5)}$$

the phase cross-over frequency is

(*a*) 0.5 rad /sec

(*b*) 0.707 rad/sec

(*c*) 1.732 rad/sec

(*d*) 2 rad / sec

72. What is the unit step response of a unity feedback control system having forward path transfer function

$$G(s) = \frac{80}{s(s+18)}$$

(*a*) Overdamped

(*b*) Critically damped

(*c*) Underdamped

(*d*) Undamped oscillatory

73. The correct sequence of steps needed to improve system stability is

(*a*) insert derivative action, use negative feedback reduce gain

(*b*) reduce gain, use negative feedback, insert derivation action

(*c*) reduce gain, insert derivation action, use negative feedback

(*d*) use negative feedback, reduce gain, insert derivation action

74. Consider the following polynomials :

1. $s^4 + 7s^3 + 17s^2 + 17s + 6$.
2. $s^4 + 11s^3 + 41s^2 + 61s + 30$.
3. $s^4 + s^3 + 2s^2 + 3s + 2$.

Among these polynomials, those which are Hurwitz are

(*a*) 1 and 3 (*b*) 2 and 3

(*c*) 1 and 2 (*d*) 1, 2 and 3

75. The open-loop transfer function of a unity feedback control system is

$$G\,(s)\,H\,(s) = \frac{30}{s(s+1)\,(s+T)}$$

where T is a variable parameter.

The closed-loop system will be stable for all values of

(*a*) $T > 0$ (*b*) $0 < T < 3$

(*c*) $T > 5$ (*d*) $3 < T < 4$

76. A system has a complex conjugate root pair of multiplicity two or more in its characteristic equation. The impulse response of the system will be

(*a*) a sinusoidal oscillation which decays exponentially; the system is therefore stable.

(*b*) a sinusoidal oscillation with time multiplier; the system is therefore unstable.

(*c*) a sinusoidal oscillation which rises exponentially with time; the system is therefore unstable.

(*d*) a dc term and harmonic oscillation; the system therefore becomes limitingly stable.

77. The open loop transfer function of a system is

$$G(s)H(s) = \frac{K(1+s)^2}{s^3}$$

The Nyquist plot for this system is

(*a*)
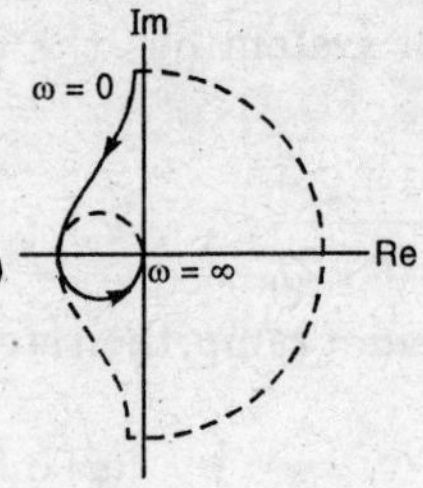

(*b*)
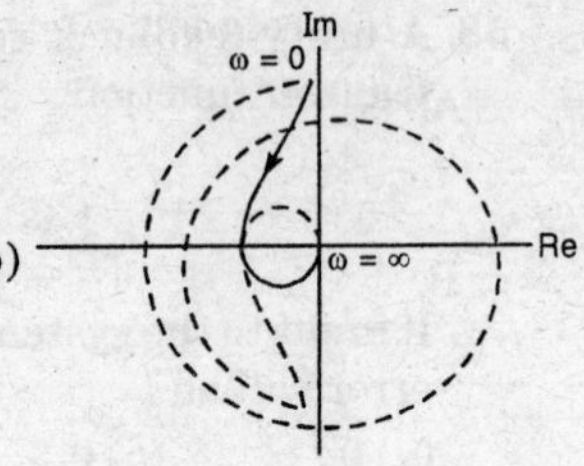

(*c*)
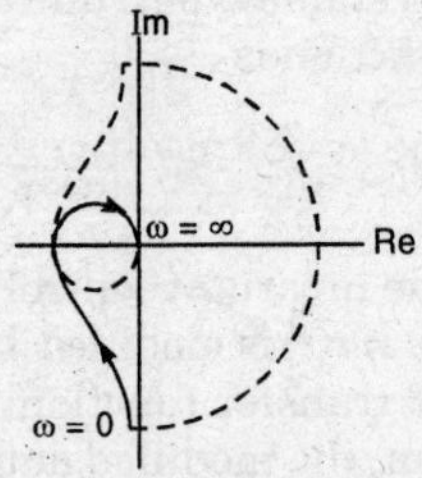

(*d*)
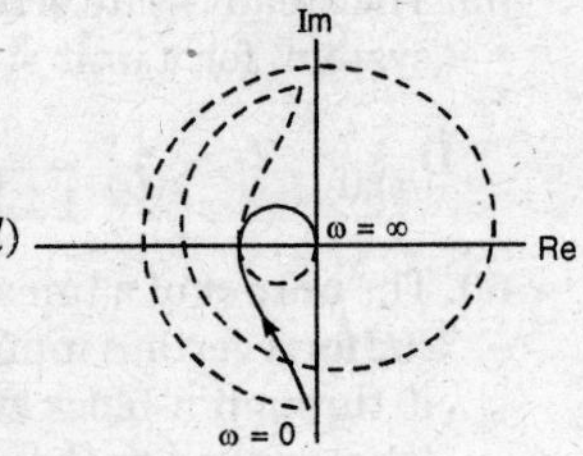

78. The number of roots of the equation

$$2s^4 + s^3 + 3s^2 + 5s + 7 = 0$$

that lie in the right half of s plane is

(*a*) zero (*b*) one

(*c*) two (*d*) three

79. The feedback system with characteristic equation

$$s^4 + 20\,Ks^3 + 5s^2 + 10s + 15 = 0 \text{ is}$$

(*a*) stable for all value of K

(*b*) stable for positive value of K

(*c*) stable for $\infty > K > 7.0$

(*d*) unstable for all values of K

80. The gain margin of the transfer function

$$G(s) = \frac{0.75}{(s+1)(s+2)}$$

will be

(*a*) 4 dB (*b*) 8 dB

(*c*) 12 dB (*d*) 16 dB

81. Consider a unity feedback system having an open-loop transfer function

$$G(j\omega) = \frac{K}{j\omega(j0.2\omega+1)(j0.05\omega+1)}$$

For K = 1, GM = 28 dB. When GM at 20 dB, K will be equal to

(*a*) 2 (*b*) 2.5

(*c*) 4 (*d*) 5

82. The characteristic equation of a feedback system is

$$s^3 + Ks^2 + 5s + 10 = 0$$

For the system to be critically stable, the value of K should be

(*a*) 1 (*b*) 2

(*c*) 3 (*d*) 4

83. Match List-I with List-II and select the correct answer using the codes given below the Lists :

List-I (Response to a unit step input)	**List-II** (Location of poles in the s-plane)
A. 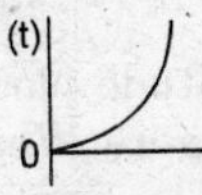	1. One at the origin
B. 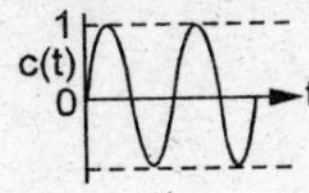	2. Two indentical roots on the negative real axis
C. 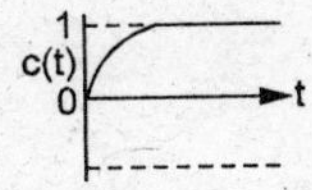	3. Two on the imaginary axis
D. 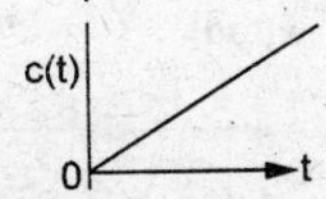	4. One on the position real axis

Codes :

	A	B	C	D
(*a*)	4	3	2	1
(*b*)	3	4	1	2
(*c*)	3	4	2	1
(*d*)	4	2	3	1

84. The characteristic equation of a closed-loop system is given by

$$s^4 + 6s^3 + 11s^2 + 6s + K = 0$$

Stable closed loop behaviour can be ensured when gain K is such that

(*a*) $0 \le K \le 10$ (*b*) $K > 10$

(*c*) $-\infty \le K < \infty$ (*d*) $0 < K \le 20$

85. A linear discrete-time system has the characteristic equation,

$$z^3 - 0.81z = 0$$

The system

(*a*) is stable

(*b*) is marginally stable

(*c*) is unstable

(*d*) stability cannot be assessed from the given information

86. The phase margin of a system with the open-loop transfer function

$$G(s)H(s) = \frac{(1-s)}{(1+s)(2+s)} \text{ is}$$

(*a*) 0° (*b*) 63.4°

(*c*) 90° (*d*) ∞

87. The Nyquist plot for the open-loop transfer fucntion G(*s*) of a unity negative feedback system is shown in the figure. If G(*s*) has no pole in the right-half of *s*-plane, the number of roots of the system characteristic equation in the right-half of *s*-plane is

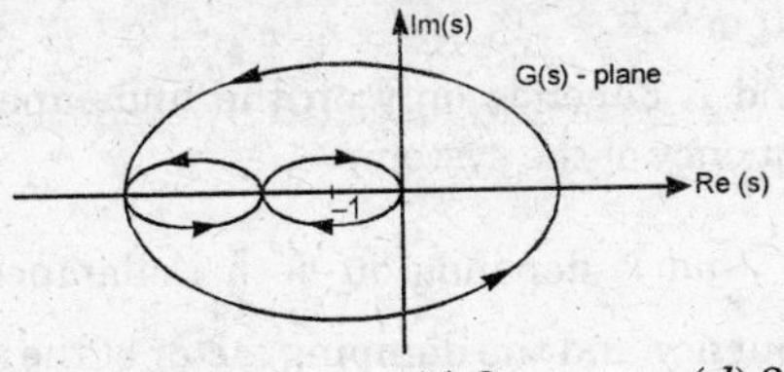

(*a*) 0 (*b*) 1 (*c*) 2 (*d*) 3

88. The number of roots of $s^3 + 5s^2 + 7s + 3 = 0$ in the right half of the s-plane is

(*a*) zero (*b*) one

(*c*) two (*d*) three

89. An electromechanical closed-loop control system has the following characteristic equation :

$$s^3 + 6Ks^2 + (K+2)s + 8 = 0$$

where K is the forward gain of the system. The condition for closed loop stability is

(*a*) K = 0.528 (*b*) K = 2

(*c*) K = 0 (*d*) K = – 2.58

90. None of the poles of a linear control system lie in the right half of s-plane. For a bounded input, the output of this system

(*a*) is always bounded (*b*) could be unbounded

(*c*) always tends to zero (*d*) none of these

91. Which of the following function is the transfer of a system having the Nyquist plot in the figure?

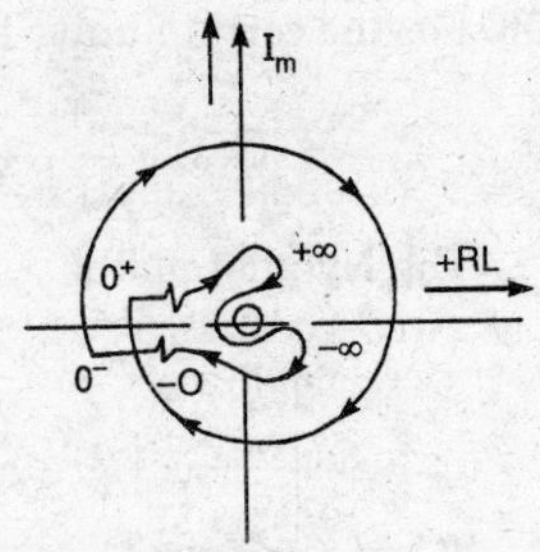

(*a*) $\dfrac{K}{s(s+2)^2(s+5)}$

(*b*) $\dfrac{K}{s^2(s+2)(s+5)}$

(*c*) $\dfrac{K(s+1)}{s^2(s+2)(s+5)}$

(*d*) $\dfrac{K(s+1)(s+3)}{s^2(s+2)(s+5)}$

92. The system shown in the figure remains stable when

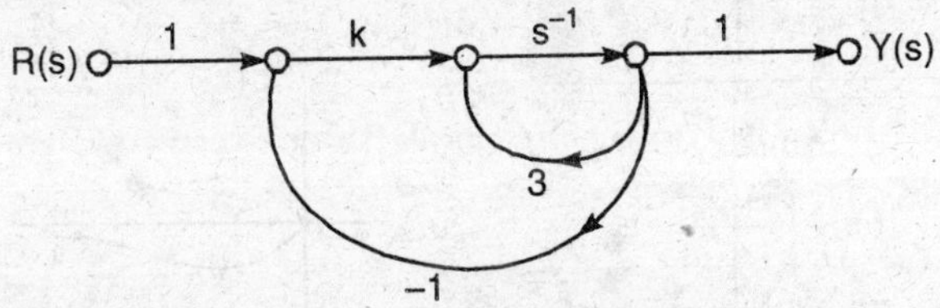

(*a*) $K < -1$ (*b*) $-1 < K < 1$

(*c*) $1 < K < 3$ (*d*) $K > 3$

93. The system with the open loop transfer function

$$G(s)H(s) = \frac{1}{s(s^2+s+1)} \text{ has a gain margin of}$$

(*a*) –6dB

(*b*) 0 dB

(*c*) 3.5 dB

(*d*) 6 dB

94. The feedback control system shown in the figure is stable

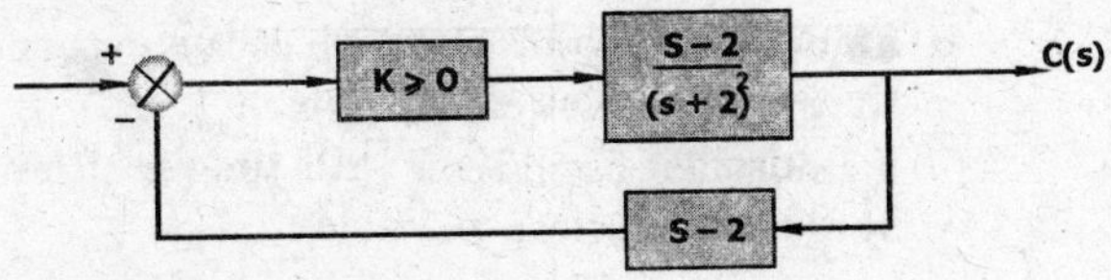

(*a*) for all $K \ge 0$

(*b*) only if $K \ge 1$

(*c*) only if $0 \le K < 1$

(*d*) only if $0 \le K \le 1$

95. Consider a unity feedback system whose open-loop transfer function is

$$G(s) = \frac{K}{s(s^2 + 2s + 2)}$$

The Nyquist plot for this system is

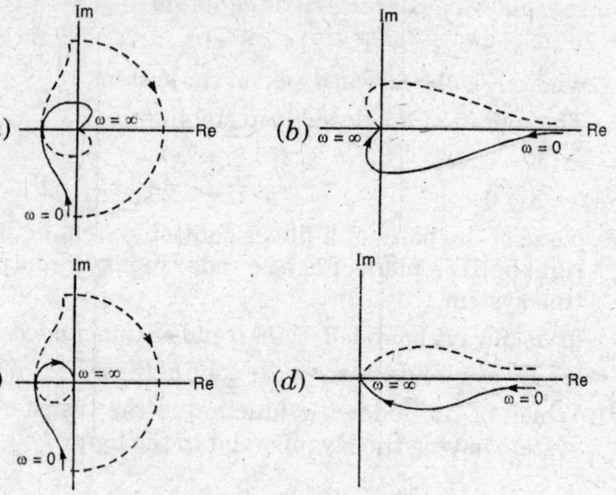

96. For the certain unity feedback system

$$G(s) = \frac{K}{s(s+1)(2s+1)(3s+1)}$$

The Nyquist plot is

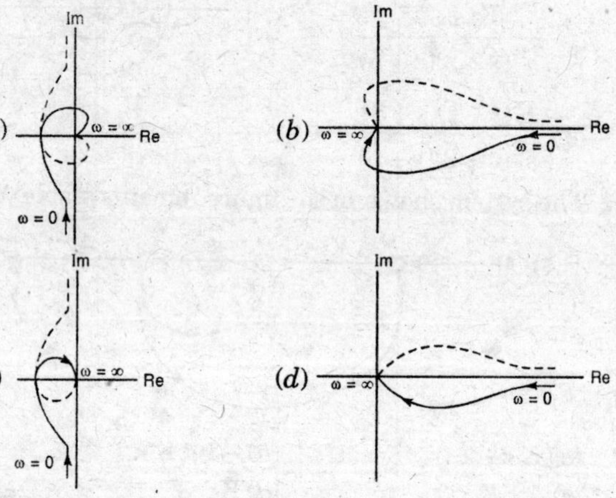

97. The Nyquist plot of a system is shown in figure. The open-loop transfer function is

$$G(s)H(s) = \frac{4s+1}{s^2(s+1)(2s+1)}$$

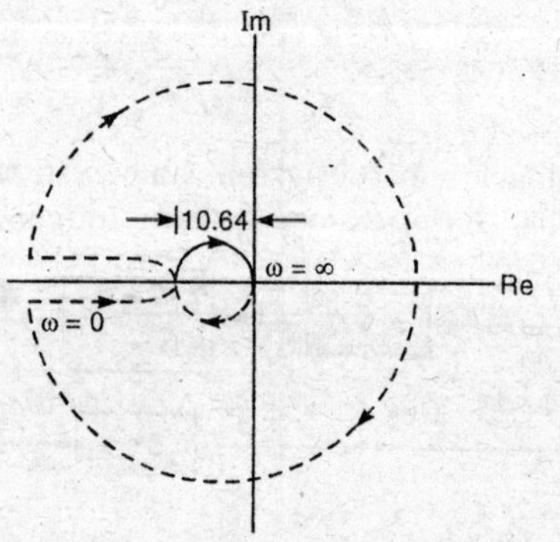

The number of poles of closed loop system in RHP are

(a) 0 (b) 1

(c) 2 (d) 4

BODE PLOTS

98. In the Bode-plot of a unity feedback control system, the value of phase of G (jω) at the gain cross over frequency is –125°. The phase margin of the system is

(a) – 125° (b) – 55°

(c) 55° (d) 125°

99. Straight line asymptotic Bode magnitude plot for a certain system is shown in the given figure. What will be its transfer function ?

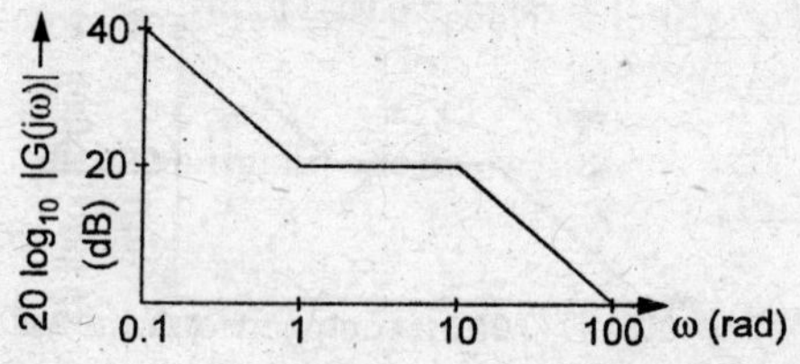

(a) $\frac{4s}{\left(1+\frac{s}{4}\right)\left(1+\frac{s}{10}\right)^2}$ (b) $\frac{4\left(1+\frac{s}{4}\right)}{\left(1+\frac{s}{10}\right)^2}$

(c) $\frac{0.25}{\left(1+\frac{s}{4}\right)\left(1+\frac{s}{10}\right)}$ (d) $\frac{0.25}{\left(1+\frac{s}{4}\right)\left(1+\frac{s}{10}\right)^2}$

100. Consider the following statements regarding the transfer function G(s) plotted in the given figure.

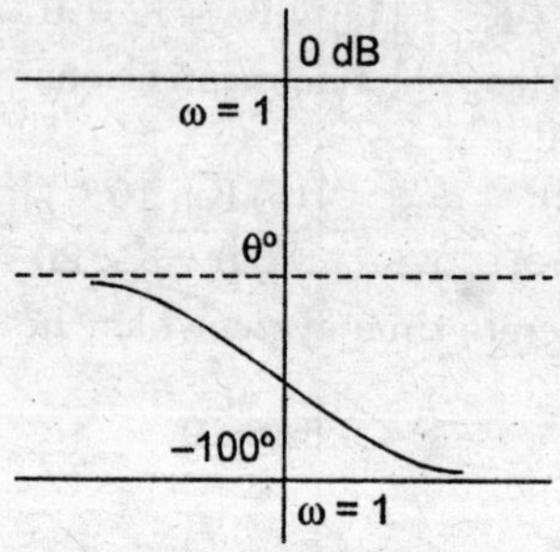

1. G(s) has corner frequencies at ω = 0.1, 1 and 10.
2. $G(s) = \frac{100(s+1)}{s(s+10)}$.
3. Magnitude of $20 \log_{10} |G(j\omega)|$ at ω = 1000 is –20 dB.

Which of these statements are correct ?

(a) 1, 2, and 3 (b) 1 and 2

(c) 2 and 3 (d) 1 and 3

101. The bandwidth of a control system is the range of frequency over which | C/R (jω) | is greater than or equal to

(a) $\frac{1}{\sqrt{2}}$ and it depends only on the undamped natural frequency of the system

(b) 1 and it depends only on the damping factor of the system

(c) 1 and it depends only on the undamped natural frequency of the system

(d) $\frac{1}{\sqrt{2}}$ and it depends on both undamped natural frequency and the damping factor of the system

102. Bode plot of a stable system is shown in the figure, the transfer function of the system is

(*a*) $G(s)=\dfrac{100}{s+10}$

(*b*) $G(s)=\dfrac{10}{s+10}$

(*c*) $G(s)=\dfrac{1}{s+10}$

(*d*) none of these

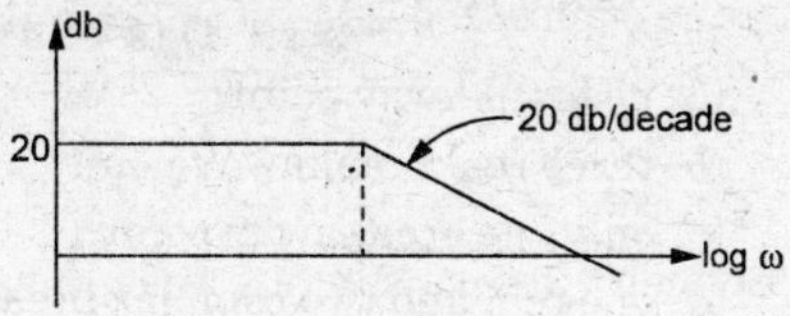

103. The 3-dB bandwidth of a typical second-order system with the transfer function

$$\frac{C(s)}{R(s)}=\frac{\omega_n^2}{s^2+2\xi\omega_n s+\omega_n^2}$$

is given by

(*a*) $\omega_n\sqrt{1-2\xi^2}$

(*b*) $\omega_n\sqrt{(1-\xi^2)+\sqrt{\xi^4-\xi^2+1}}$

(*c*) $\omega_n\sqrt{(1-2\xi^2)+\sqrt{4\xi^4-4\xi^2+2}}$

(*d*) $\omega_n\sqrt{(1-2\xi^2)+\sqrt{4\xi^4-4\xi^2+2}}$

104. In a synchro error detector, the output voltage is proportional to $[\omega(t)]^n$, where $\omega(t)$ is the rotor velocity and n equals

(*a*) –2 (*b*) –1 (*c*) 1 (*d*) 2

105. The asymptotic Bode plot of the transfer function $\dfrac{K}{1+\dfrac{s}{2}}$ is given in the figure. The error in the phase angle and dB gain at a frequency of $\omega = 0.5$ a are respectively

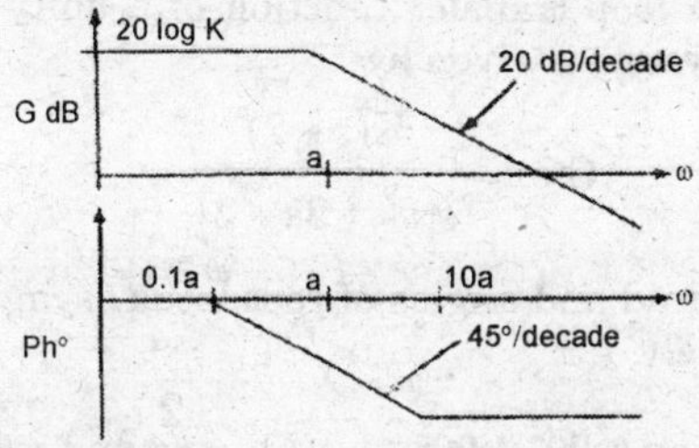

(*a*) 4.06°, 0.97 dB (*b*) 5.7°, 3 dB

(*c*) 4.9°, 3 dB (*d*) 5.7°, 0.97 dB

106. The system having the Bode magnitude plot shown in the figure has the transfer function

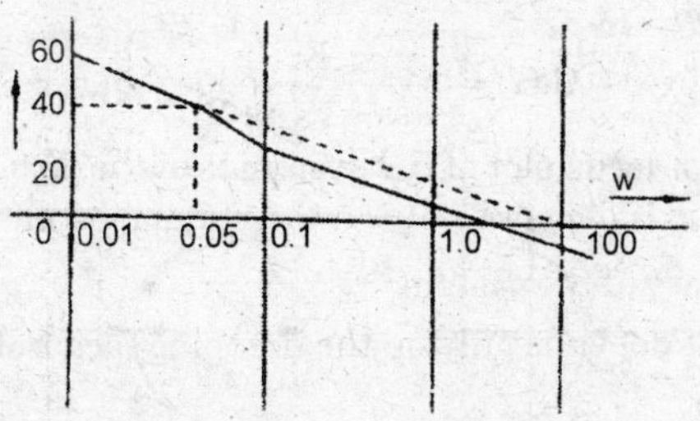

(*a*) $\dfrac{60(s+0.01)(s+0.1)}{s^2(s+0.05)^2}$ (*b*) $\dfrac{10(1+10s)}{s(1+20s)}$

(*c*) $\dfrac{3(s+0.05)}{s(s+0.1)(s+1)}$ (*d*) $\dfrac{5(s+0.1)}{s(s+0.05)}$

107. The asymptotic approximation of the log-magnitude versus frequency plot of a minimum phase system with real poles and one zero is shown in the figure. Its transfer function is

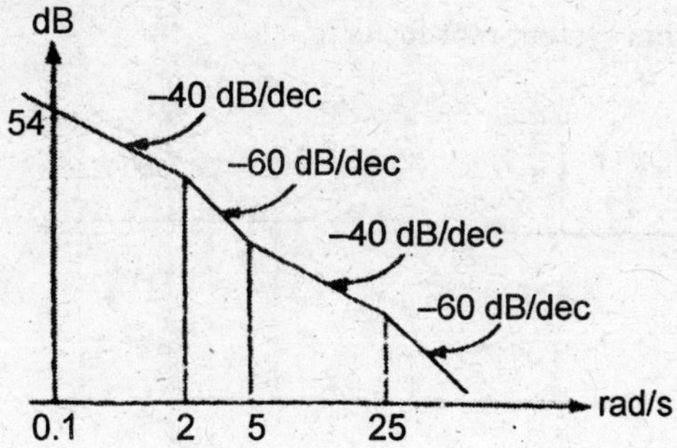

(*a*) $\dfrac{20(s+5)}{s(s+2)(s+25)}$ (*b*) $\dfrac{10(s+5)}{(s+2)s^2(s+25)}$

(*c*) $\dfrac{20(s+5)}{s^2(s+2)(s+25)}$ (*d*) $\dfrac{50(s+5)}{s^2(s+2)(s+25)}$

Statement for Q. (108-109) :

Consider the Bode plot of a unity feedback system shown in figure.

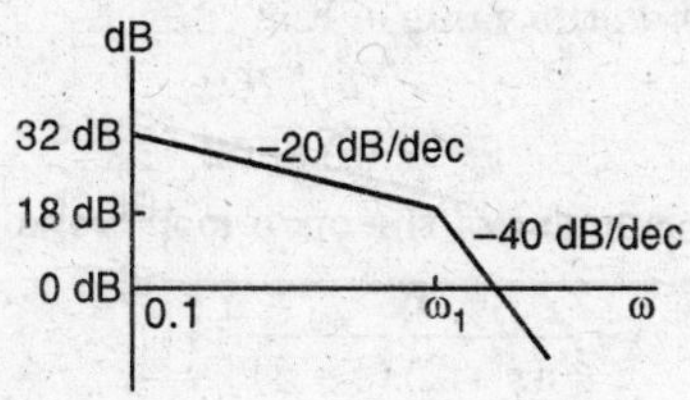

108. The steady state error corresponding to a ramp input is

(*a*) 0.25 (*b*) 0.2

(*c*) 0 (*d*) ∞

109. The damping ratio is

(*a*) 0.063 (*b*) 0.179

(*c*) 0.483 (*d*) 0.639

ROOT LOCUS

110. The open-loop transfer function of a unity feedback control system is

$$G(s)=\frac{1}{(s+2)^2}$$

The closed loop transfer function will have poles at

(*a*) – 2, – 2 (*b*) – 2, – 1

(*c*) – 2, ± *j* (*d*) – 2, 2

111. In the root-locus for open-loop transfer function

$$G(s)H(s)=\frac{K(s+6)}{(s+3)(s+5)}$$

The '*break away*' and '*break-in*', points are located respectively at

(*a*) – 2 and – 1

(*b*) – 2.47 and –3.77

(*c*) – 4.27 and – 7.23

(*d*) – 7.73 and – 4.27

112. The forward-path open-loop transfer function of a unity feedback system is

$$G(s) = \frac{K(s^2+4)}{(s^2+1)}$$

For this system root locus is

(a) 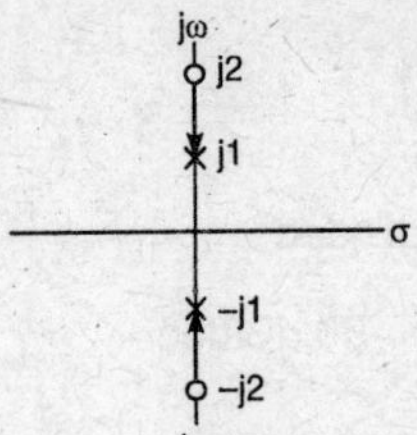

(b) 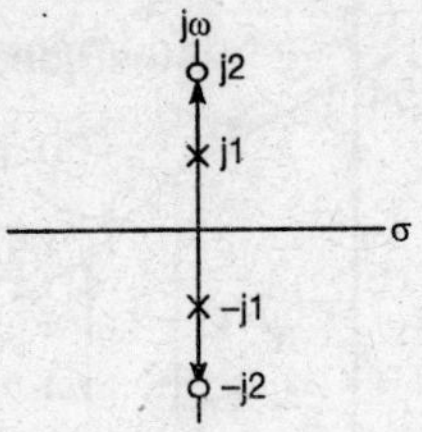

(c) 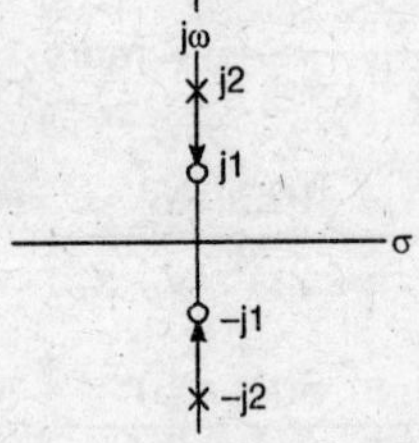

(d) 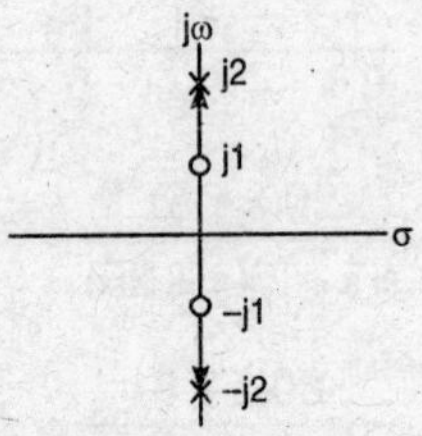

113. If open-loop transfer function of the system is

$$G(s)H(s) = \frac{K(s+10)}{s(s+8)(s+16)(s+72)}$$

then a closed loop pole will be located at s = – 12, when the value of K is

(a) 4355 (b) 5760
(c) 9600 (d) 9862

114. The root-locus plot of the open-loop transfer function

$$G(s)H(s) = \frac{K}{s(s+2)(s+4)} \text{ is}$$

(a) 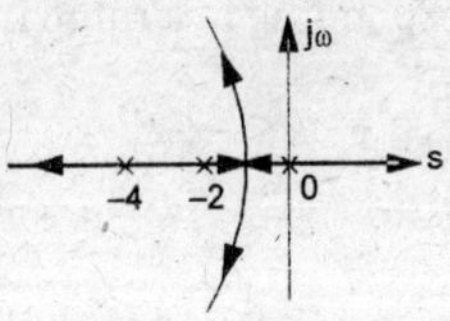

(b) 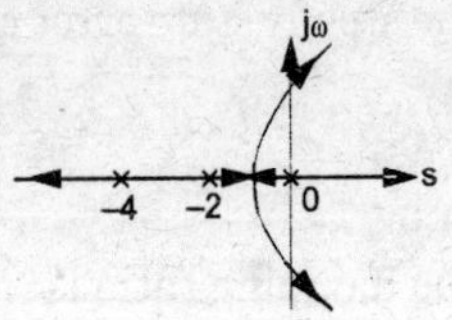

(c) 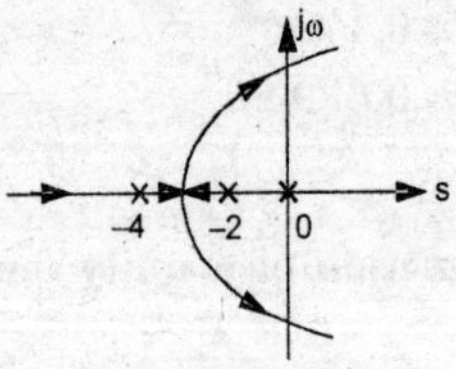

(d) 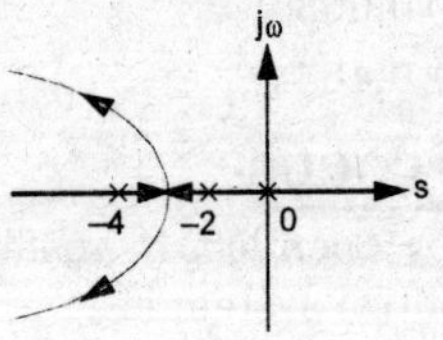

115. The root locus for K < 0 for the transfer function expressed by

$$G(s)H(s) = \frac{K}{s(s+1)(s+3)(s+4)}$$

roughly drawn as

(a) 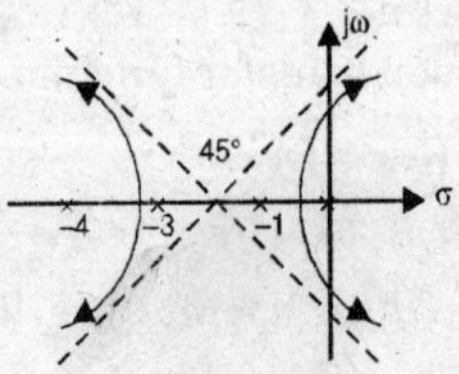

(b) 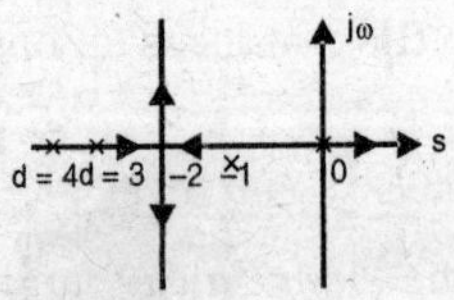

(c) 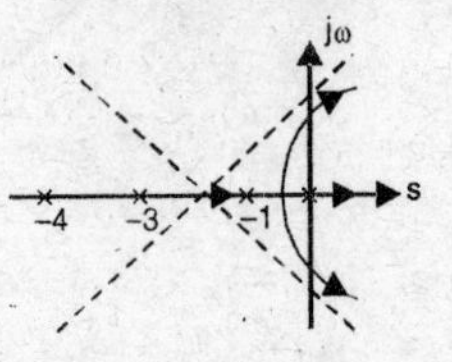

(d) none of these

116. The root locus plot of the system having the loop transfer function,

$$G(s)H(s) = \frac{K}{s(s+4)(s^2+4s+5)} \text{ has}$$

(a) no breakaway point
(b) three real breakaway point
(c) only one breakaway point
(d) one real and two complex breakaway point

117. An open loop transfer function is given by,

$$G(s)H(s) = \frac{K(s+1)}{s(s+2)(s^2+25+2)}. \text{ It has}$$

(a) one zero at infinity (b) two zeros at infinity
(c) three zeros at infinity (d) four zeros at infinity

118. The open-loop transfer function of a feedback control system is given by

$$G(s)H(s) = \frac{K(s+2)}{s(s+4)(s^2+4s+8)}.$$

In the root locus diagram of the system, the asymptotes of the root loci for large values of K meet a point in the s-plane. Which one of the following is the set of co-ordinate of that point?

(a) (–1, 0) (b) (–2, 0)
(c) $\left(\frac{-10}{3}, 0\right)$ (d) (2, 0)

119. If characteristic equation of a closed-loop system is

$$1 + \frac{K}{s(s+1)(s+2)} = 0$$

then centroid at the asymptotes in root-locus will be

(a) zero (b) 2 (c) –1 (d) –2

120. The open loop transfer function of a unity feedback control system is given by

$$G(s) = \frac{K(s+2)}{s(s^2+2s+2)}$$

The centroid and angles of root locus asymptotes are respectively

(a) zero and + 90°, –90° (b) $-\frac{2}{3}$ and + 60°, –60°
(c) zero and + 120°, –120° (d) $-\frac{2}{3}$ and –90°, + 90°

121. Given a unity feedback system with open-loop transfer function

$$G(s) = \frac{K}{s(s+1)(s+2)}$$

The root locus plot of the system is of the form

(a) 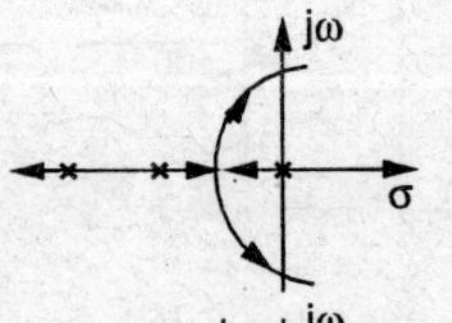

(b) 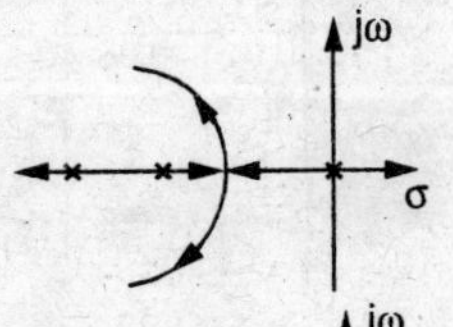

(c) 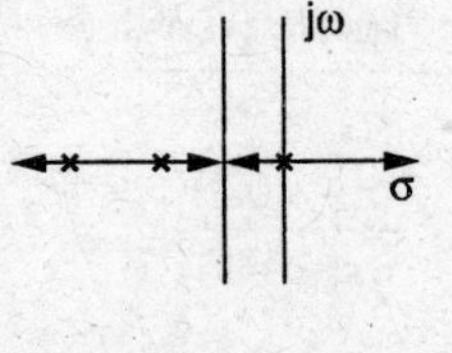

(d) 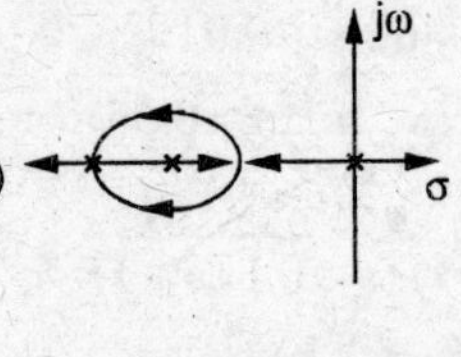

122. Which of the following points is NOT on the root locus of a system with the open-loop transfer function

$$G(s)H(s) = \frac{K}{s(s+1)(s+3)}?$$

(*a*) $s = -j\sqrt{3}$ (*b*) $s = -1.5$

(*c*) $s = -3$ (*d*) $s = -\infty$

123. The root-locus diagram for a closed-loop feedback system is shown in the figure. The system is overdamped

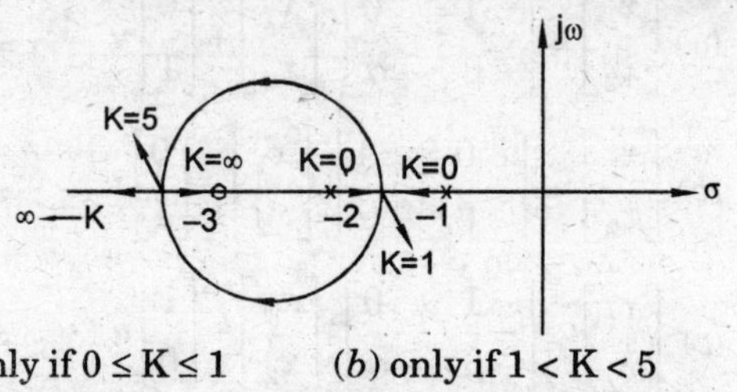

(*a*) only if $0 \le K \le 1$ (*b*) only if $1 < K < 5$

(*c*) only if $K > 5$ (*d*) if $0 \le K < 1$ or $K > 5$

124. The characteristic equation of a feedback control system is given by

$$s^3 + 5s^2 + (K+6)s + K = 0$$

where $K > 0$ is a scaler variable parameter. In the root-loci diagram of the system, the asymptotes of the root-locus for large values of K meet at a point in the s-plane, whose coordinates are

(*a*) (– 3, 0) (*b*) (– 2, 0)

(*c*) (– 1, 0) (*d*) (2, 0)

125. A unity feedback system has an open-loop transfer function of the form

$$KG(s) = \frac{K(s+a)}{s^2(s+b)};\ b > a$$

Which of the loci shown in the figure can be valid root-loci for the system ?

(*a*)

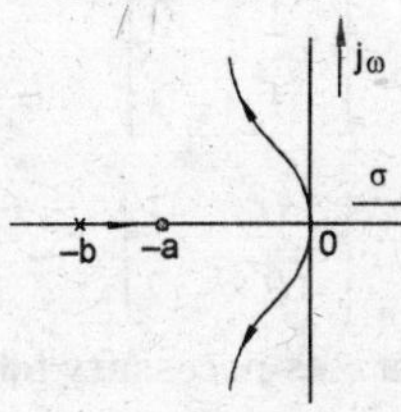

(*b*)

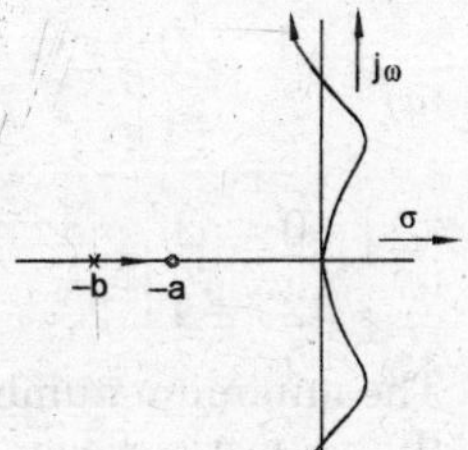

(*c*)

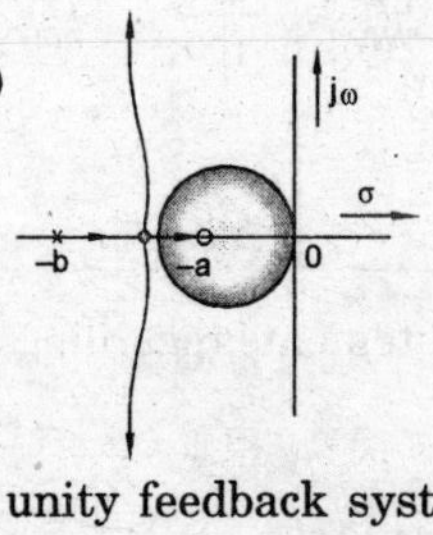

(*d*)

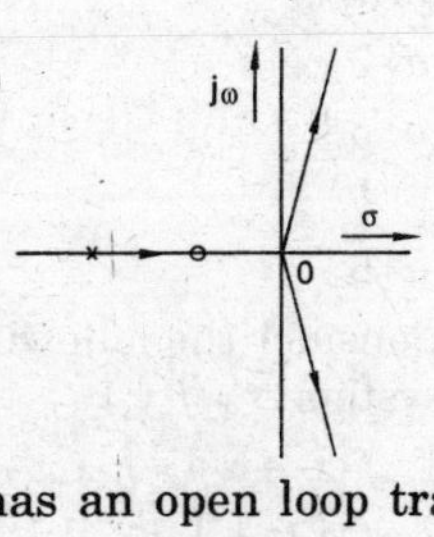

126. A unity feedback system has an open loop transfer function, $G(s) = \frac{K}{s^2}$. The root locus plot is

(*a*)

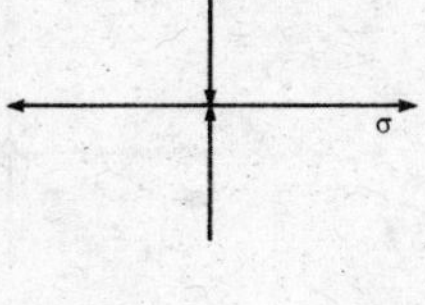

(*b*)

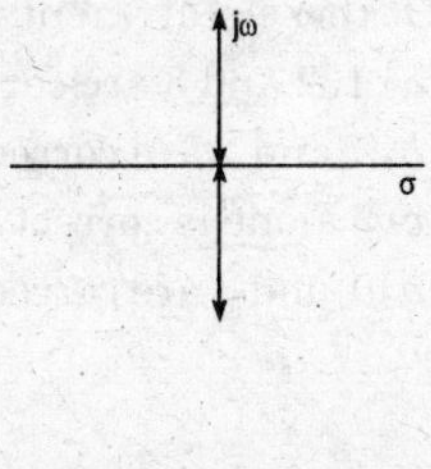

(*c*)

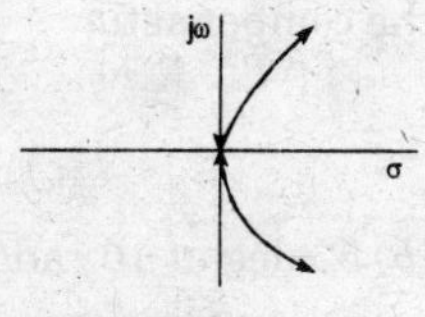

(*d*)

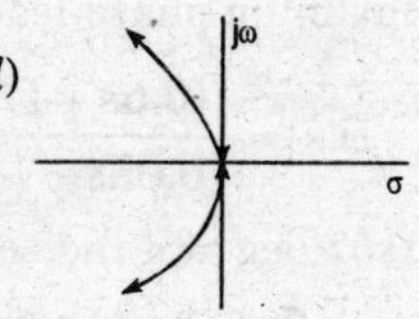

COMPENSATOR

127. For a gain constant K, the phase-lead compensator

(*a*) reduces the slope of the magnitude curve in the entire range of frequency domain

(*b*) decreases the gain cross-over frequency

(*c*) reduce the phase margin

(*d*) reduce the resonance peak M_p.

128. Consider the following statements :

Lead compensator

1. increases the margin of stability
2. speeds up transient response
3. does not affect the system error constant

Of these statements

(*a*) 2 and 3 are correct (*b*) 1 and 2 are correct

(*c*) 1 and 3 are correct (*d*) 1, 2 and 3 are correct

129. The maximum phase shift that can be provided by a lead compensator with transfer function

$$G(s) = \frac{1+6s}{1+2s} \text{ is}$$

(*a*) 15° (*b*) 30° (*c*) 45° (*d*) 60°

130. The transfer function of a compensating network is of the form $\frac{(1+\alpha Ts)}{(1+Ts)}$. If this is a phase-lag network, the value of α should be

(*a*) exactly equal to 0 (*b*) between 0 and 1

(*c*) exactly equal to 1 (*d*) greater than 1

131. A phase-lag compensation will

(*a*) improve relative stability

(*b*) increase the speed of response

(*c*) increase bandwidth

(*d*) increase overshoot

132. The maximum phase shift that can be obtained by using a lead compensator with transfer function

$$G_C(s) = \frac{4(1+0.15s)}{(1+0.05s)} \text{ is equal to}$$

(*a*) 15° (*b*) 30° (*c*) 45° (*d*) 60°

133. A phase-lead compensator has the transfer function

$$G_C(s) = \frac{10(1+.04s)}{(1+0.01s)}$$

The maximum phase angle lead provided by this compensator will occur at a frequency ω_m is equal to

(*a*) 50 rad/sec (*b*) 25 rad/sec

(*c*) 10 rad/sec (*d*) 4 rad/sec

134. The phase lead compensation is used to

(*a*) increase rise time and decrease overshoot

(*b*) decrease both rise time and overshoot

(*c*) increase both rise time and overshoot

(*d*) decrease rise time and increase overshoot

135. Maximum phase-lead of the compensator

$$D(s) = \frac{(0.5s+1)}{(0.05s+1)}, \text{ is}$$

(*a*) 52 deg at 4 rad/sec (*b*) 52 deg at 10 rad/sec
(*c*) 55 deg at 12 rad/sec (*d*) none of these

STATE VARIABLE

136. Given a system represented by equations

$$\dot{x} = \begin{bmatrix} 0 & 1 \\ -2 & -3 \end{bmatrix} x + \begin{bmatrix} 0 \\ 1 \end{bmatrix} u$$

and $y = [1\ 0]\, x$

The equivalent transfer function representation G(s) of the system is

(*a*) $G(s) = \dfrac{1}{s^2+5s+2}$ (*b*) $G(s) = \dfrac{1}{s^2+3s+2}$

(*c*) $G(s) = \dfrac{3}{s^2+3s+2}$ (*d*) $G(s) = \dfrac{3}{s^3+2s^2+2}$

137. Consider the following properties attributed to state model of a system :

1. State model is unique
2. State model can be derived from the system transfer function
3. State model can be derived from time variant systems.

Of these statements

(*a*) 1, 2 and 3 are correct (*b*) 1 and 2 are correct
(*c*) 2 and 3 are correct (*d*) 1 and 3 are correct

138. State representation of a second order system is

$$\dot{x}_1 = -x_1 + u$$
$$\dot{x}_2 = x_1 - 2x_2 + u$$

Consider the following statements regarding the above system :

1. The system is completely state controllable
2. If x_1 is the output, then the system is completely output controllable
3. If x_2 is the output, then the system is completely output controllable.

Of these statements

(*a*) 1, 2 and 3 are correct
(*b*) 1 and 2 are correct
(*c*) 2 and 3 are correct
(*d*) 1 and 3 are correct

139. The system matrix of a continuous-time system, describe in the state variable form is

$$A = \begin{bmatrix} x & 0 & 0 \\ 0 & y & -1 \\ 0 & 1 & -2 \end{bmatrix}$$

The system is stable for all values of x and y satisfying

(*a*) $x < \frac{1}{2},\ y < \frac{1}{2}$ (*b*) $x > \frac{1}{2},\ y > \frac{1}{2}$

(*c*) $x < 0, y < 2$ (*d*) $x < 0,\ y < \frac{1}{2}$

140. Consider the closed loop system shown in the give figure :

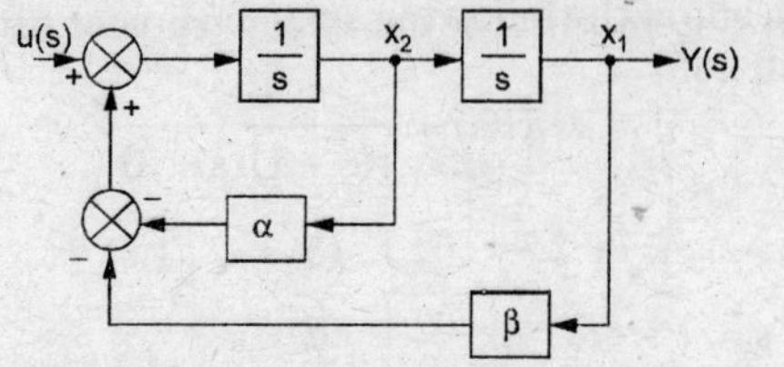

The state model of the system is

(*a*) $\begin{bmatrix} \dot{x}_1 \\ \dot{x}_2 \end{bmatrix} = \begin{bmatrix} 1 & 0 \\ -\beta & -\alpha \end{bmatrix} \begin{bmatrix} x_1 \\ x_2 \end{bmatrix} + \begin{bmatrix} 0 \\ 1 \end{bmatrix} u,\ y = [1\ 0] \begin{bmatrix} x_1 \\ x_2 \end{bmatrix}$

(*b*) $\begin{bmatrix} \dot{x}_1 \\ \dot{x}_2 \end{bmatrix} = \begin{bmatrix} 0 & 1 \\ -\beta & -\alpha \end{bmatrix} \begin{bmatrix} x_1 \\ x_2 \end{bmatrix} + \begin{bmatrix} 0 \\ 1 \end{bmatrix} u,\ y = [1\ 0] \begin{bmatrix} x_1 \\ x_2 \end{bmatrix}$

(*c*) $\begin{bmatrix} \dot{x}_1 \\ \dot{x}_2 \end{bmatrix} = \begin{bmatrix} 1 & 0 \\ -\beta & -\alpha \end{bmatrix} \begin{bmatrix} x_1 \\ x_2 \end{bmatrix} + \begin{bmatrix} 1 \\ 0 \end{bmatrix} u,\ y = [1\ 0] \begin{bmatrix} x_1 \\ x_2 \end{bmatrix}$

(*d*) none of these

141. A system is described by the state equation

$$\begin{bmatrix} \dot{x}_1 \\ \dot{x}_2 \end{bmatrix} = \begin{bmatrix} 2 & 0 \\ 0 & 2 \end{bmatrix} \begin{bmatrix} x_1 \\ x_2 \end{bmatrix} + \begin{bmatrix} 1 \\ 1 \end{bmatrix} u$$

The state transition matrix of the system is

(*a*) $\begin{bmatrix} e^{2t} & 0 \\ 0 & e^{2t} \end{bmatrix}$ (*b*) $\begin{bmatrix} e^{-2t} & 0 \\ 0 & e^{-t} \end{bmatrix}$

(*c*) $\begin{bmatrix} e^{2t} & 1 \\ 1 & e^{2t} \end{bmatrix}$ (*d*) $\begin{bmatrix} e^{-2t} & 1 \\ 1 & e^{-t} \end{bmatrix}$

142. The value of A matrix in $\dot{x} = Ax$ for the system describe by the different equation

$$\ddot{y} + 2\dot{y} + 3y = 0, \text{ is}$$

(*a*) $\begin{bmatrix} 1 & 0 \\ -2 & -1 \end{bmatrix}$ (*b*) $\begin{bmatrix} 1 & 0 \\ -1 & -2 \end{bmatrix}$

(*c*) $\begin{bmatrix} 0 & 1 \\ -2 & -1 \end{bmatrix}$ (*d*) $\begin{bmatrix} 0 & 1 \\ -3 & -2 \end{bmatrix}$

143. The minimum number of states necessary to describe the network shown in the figure in a state variable form is

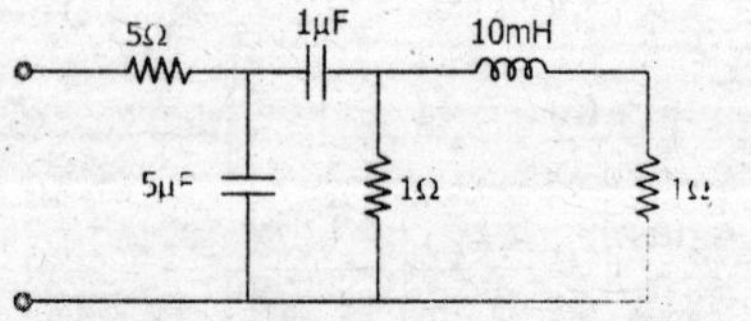

(*a*) 2
(*b*) 3
(*c*) 4
(*d*) 6

144. Consider the following statements regarding a linear system $y = f(x_1)$

1. $f(x_1 + x_2) = f(x_1) + f(x_2)$
2. $f[x(t+T)] = f[x(t)] + f[x(T)]$
3. $f(Kx) = Kf(x)$.

Of these statements

(*a*) 1, 2 and 3 are correct
(*b*) 1 and 2 are correct
(*c*) 3 alone is correct
(*d*) 1 and 3 are correct

145. Which one of the following systems is completely state controllable ?

(a) $\begin{bmatrix}\dot{x}_1\\ \dot{x}_2\end{bmatrix}=\begin{bmatrix}-1 & 0\\ 0 & -2\end{bmatrix}\begin{bmatrix}x_1\\ x_2\end{bmatrix}+\begin{bmatrix}2\\ 1\end{bmatrix}u$

(b) $\begin{bmatrix}\dot{x}_1\\ \dot{x}_2\end{bmatrix}=\begin{bmatrix}-1 & 0\\ 0 & -2\end{bmatrix}\begin{bmatrix}x_1\\ x_2\end{bmatrix}+\begin{bmatrix}2\\ 0\end{bmatrix}u$

(c) $\begin{bmatrix}\dot{x}_1\\ \dot{x}_2\end{bmatrix}=\begin{bmatrix}1 & 1\\ 0 & -1\end{bmatrix}\begin{bmatrix}x_1\\ x_2\end{bmatrix}+\begin{bmatrix}1\\ 0\end{bmatrix}u$

(d) $\begin{bmatrix}\dot{x}_1\\ \dot{x}_2\end{bmatrix}=\begin{bmatrix}0 & 0\\ 2 & -2\end{bmatrix}\begin{bmatrix}x_1\\ x_2\end{bmatrix}+\begin{bmatrix}2\\ 2\end{bmatrix}u$

146. For $\phi(s)=\begin{bmatrix}\dfrac{s+6}{s^2+6s+5} & \dfrac{1}{s^2+6s+5}\\ \dfrac{-5}{s^2+6s+5} & \dfrac{s}{s^2+6s+5}\end{bmatrix}$,

The coefficient matrix A is

(a) $\begin{bmatrix}6 & -5\\ -6 & 0\end{bmatrix}$ (b) $\begin{bmatrix}5 & -5\\ 0 & -6\end{bmatrix}$

(c) $\begin{bmatrix}6 & 0\\ -5 & -6\end{bmatrix}$ (d) $\begin{bmatrix}0 & 1\\ -5 & -6\end{bmatrix}$

147. A system is described by the state equation

$$\dot{X} = AX + BU.$$

The output is given by $Y = CX$,

where, $A=\begin{bmatrix}-4 & -1\\ 3 & -1\end{bmatrix}$, $B=\begin{bmatrix}1\\ 1\end{bmatrix}$, $C=[1\ 0]$

Transfer function G(s) of the system is

(a) $\dfrac{s}{s^2+5s+7}$ (b) $\dfrac{1}{s^2+5s+7}$

(c) $\dfrac{s}{s^2+3s+2}$ (d) $\dfrac{1}{s^2+3s+2}$

148. The matrix of any state-space equations for the transfer function C(s) / R(s) of the system shown below in the figure is

(a) $\begin{bmatrix}-1 & 0\\ 0 & -1\end{bmatrix}$ (b) $\begin{bmatrix}0 & 1\\ 0 & -1\end{bmatrix}$

(c) $[-1]$ (d) $[3]$

149. Given the homogeneous state-space equation

$$\dot{X}=\begin{bmatrix}-3 & 1\\ 0 & -2\end{bmatrix}X$$

The steady state value of $X_{ss} = \lim_{t\to\infty} X(t)$, the initial state value of $X(0) = [10\ -10]^T$, is

(a) $X_{ss}=\begin{bmatrix}0\\ 0\end{bmatrix}$ (b) $X_{ss}=\begin{bmatrix}-3\\ -2\end{bmatrix}$

(c) $X_{ss}=\begin{bmatrix}10\\ 10\end{bmatrix}$ (d) $X_{ss}=\begin{bmatrix}\infty\\ \infty\end{bmatrix}$

150. The transfer function Y(s) / U(s) of a system described by the state equations

$$\dot{x}(t) = -2x(t) + 2u(t)$$

and $y(t) = 0.5\,x(t)$, is

(a) $\dfrac{0.5}{(s-2)}$ (b) $\dfrac{1}{(s-2)}$

(c) $\dfrac{0.5}{(s+2)}$ (d) $\dfrac{1}{(s+2)}$

151. A linear time-invariant system describd by the state variable model

$$\begin{bmatrix}\dot{X}_1\\ \dot{X}_2\end{bmatrix}=\begin{bmatrix}-1 & 0\\ 0 & -2\end{bmatrix}\begin{bmatrix}X_1\\ X_2\end{bmatrix}+\begin{bmatrix}0\\ 1\end{bmatrix}u=[1\ 2]\begin{bmatrix}X_1\\ X_2\end{bmatrix}$$

(a) is completely controllable

(b) is not completely controllable

(c) is completely observable

(d) is not completely observable

152. A linear second-order single-input continuous-time system is described by the following set of differential equations :

$$\dot{X}_1(t) = -2X_1(t) + 4X_2(t)$$
$$\dot{X}_2(t) = 2X_1(t) - X_2(t) + u(t)$$

where $X_1(t)$ and $X_2(t)$ are the state variables and $u(t)$ is the control variable.

The system is

(a) controllable and stable

(b) controllable but unstable

(c) uncontrollable and unstable

(d) uncontrollable but stable

153. If vector $\begin{bmatrix}1\\ 2\\ -1\end{bmatrix}$ is an eigen vector of $A=\begin{bmatrix}-2 & 2 & -3\\ 2 & 1 & -6\\ -1 & -2 & 0\end{bmatrix}$, then one of the eigen values of A is

(a) 1 (b) 2

(c) 5 (d) – 1

154. The transfer function for the state variable representation

$$\dot{X} = AX + Bu,\quad Y = CX + Du,$$

is given by

(a) $D + C(sI - A)^{-1}B$ (b) $B(sI - A)^{-1}C + D$

(c) $D(sI - A)^{-1}B + C$ (d) $C(sI - A)^{-1}D + B$

155. The system $\dot{X}=\begin{bmatrix}2 & 3\\ 0 & 5\end{bmatrix}X+\begin{bmatrix}1\\ 0\end{bmatrix}u$ is

(a) controllable but unstable

(b) uncontrollable and unstable

(c) controllable and stable

(d) uncontrollable and stable

156. For the system $\dot{X}=\begin{bmatrix}2 & 0\\ 0 & 4\end{bmatrix}X+\begin{bmatrix}1\\ 1\end{bmatrix}u;\ y=[4\ 0]X$,

with u as unit impulse and with zero initial state, the output, y, becomes

(a) $2e^{2t}$ (b) $4e^{2t}$

(c) $2e^{4t}$ (d) $4e^{4t}$

ANSWERS

1. (*c*) **2.** (*d*) **3.** (*b*) **4.** (*b*) **5.** (*d*) **6.** (*b*) **7.** (*b*) **8.** (*b*) **9.** (*b*) **10.** (*a*)

11. (*a*) **12.** (*b*) **13.** (*c*) **14.** (*d*) **15.** (*c*) **16.** (*b*) **17.** (*a*) **18.** (*b*) **19.** (*b*) **20.** (*b*)

21. (*b*) **22.** (*b*) **23.** (*a*) **24.** (*c*) **25.** (*b*) **26.** (*c*) **27.** (*d*) **28.** (*a*) **29.** (*a*) **30.** (*d*)

31. (*d*) **32.** (*b*) **33.** (*d*) **34.** (*c*) **35.** (*c*) **36.** (*a*) **37.** (*b*) **38.** (*a*) **39.** (*b*) **40.** (*d*)

41. (*a*) **42.** (*a*) **43.** (*b*) **44.** (*d*) **45.** (*c*) **46.** (*d*) **47.** (*c*) **48.** (*a*) **49.** (*c*) **50.** (*b*)

51. (*b*) **52.** (*c*) **53.** (*b*) **54.** (*b*) **55.** (*a*) **56.** (*c*) **57.** (*a*) **58.** (*a*) **59.** (*b*) **60.** (*d*)

61. (*a*) **62.** (*b*) **63.** (*d*) **64.** (*b*) **65.** (*a*) **66.** (*c*) **67.** (*c*) **68.** (*d*) **69.** (*b*) **70.** (*d*)

71. (*b*) **72.** (*d*) **73.** (*d*) **74.** (*c*) **75.** (*c*) **76.** (*b*) **77.** (*b*) **78.** (*c*) **79.** (*d*) **80.** (*c*)

81. (*b*) **82.** (*b*) **83.** (*a*) **84.** (*a*) **85.** (*a*) **86.** (*d*) **87.** (*a*) **88.** (*a*) **89.** (*a*) **90.** (*b*)

91. (*b*) **92.** (*d*) **93.** (*b*) **94.** (*c*) **95.** (*c*) **96.** (*a*) **97.** (*c*) **98.** (*c*) **99.** (*d*) **100.** (*a*)

101. (*b*) **102.** (*a*) **103.** (*c*) **104.** (*c*) **105.** (*a*) **106.** (*d*) **107.** (*d*) **108.** (*a*) **109.** (*b*) **110.** (*c*)

111. (*d*) **112.** (*b*) **113.** (*b*) **114.** (*d*) **115.** (*b*) **116.** (*b*) **117.** (*c*) **118.** (*b*) **119.** (*c*) **120.** (*a*)

121. (*a*) **122.** (*b*) **123.** (*d*) **124.** (*b*) **125.** (*a*) **126.** (*b*) **127.** (*a*) **128.** (*b*) **129.** (*b*) **130.** (*b*)

131. (*d*) **132.** (*b*) **133.** (*a*) **134.** (*d*) **135.** (*d*) **136.** (*b*) **137.** (*c*) **138.** (*c*) **139.** (*c*) **140.** (*b*)

141. (*a*) **142.** (*d*) **143.** (*b*) **144.** (*d*) **145.** (*a*) **146.** (*d*) **147.** (*a*) **148.** (*c*) **149.** (*a*) **150.** (*d*)

151. (*b,c*) **152.** (*b*) **153.** (*c*) **154.** (*a*) **155.** (*b*) **156.** (*b*)

EXPLANATIONS

TRANSFER FUNCTION

1. $F(t) = M\dfrac{d^2x(t)}{dt^2} + B\dfrac{dx(t)}{dt} + Kx(t)$

The characteristic equation is,

$$Ms^2 + Bs + K = 0$$

or $$s^2 + 2\,\omega_n s + \omega_n^2 = 0$$

$$\therefore \quad \omega_n = \sqrt{\frac{K}{M}}; \quad \varepsilon = \frac{B}{2\sqrt{KM}}$$

Thus statements 2 and 3 are correct.

3. It is a very simple block diagram and simply by inspection we see that

$$\frac{C(s)}{R(s)} = \frac{1}{H_1}\frac{H_2G_1}{(1+H_2G_1G_2)}$$

4. $$T(s) = \frac{E_o(s)}{E_i(s)} = \frac{E_o(s)}{V(s)}\cdot\frac{V(s)}{E_i(s)}$$

$$= \frac{1}{RCs+1}\cdot\frac{1}{RCs+1} = \frac{1}{(1+\tau s)^2}$$

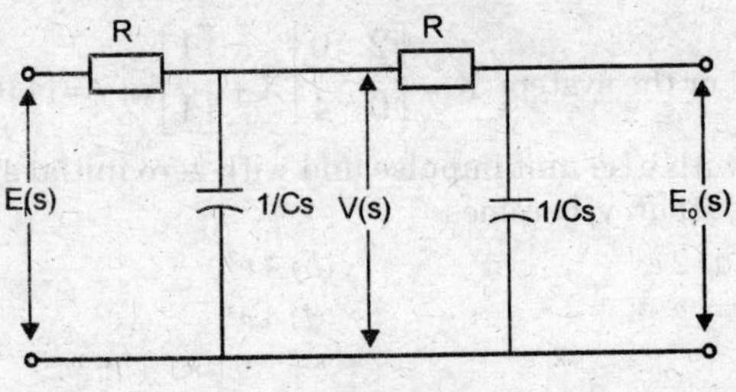

7. $$F = M\cdot\frac{d^2x}{dt} + f\frac{dx}{dt} + (K_1+K_2)x$$

$$\therefore \quad F(s) = Ms^2X(s) + f\cdot sX(s) + (K_1+K_2)X(s)$$

$$\Rightarrow \quad \frac{X(s)}{F(s)} = \frac{1}{Ms^2 + fs + (K_1+K_2)}$$

8. $$C(s) = \frac{\dfrac{10}{s(s+1)}}{1+\dfrac{10}{s(s+1)}\times s} = \frac{10}{s^2+11s}$$

$$\frac{C(s}{R(s)} = \frac{\dfrac{10}{s^2+11s}}{1+\dfrac{10}{s^2+11s}} = \frac{10}{s^2+11s+10}$$

9. For positive feedback system, the closed-loop gain of the system is given by

$$M(s) = \frac{C(s)}{R(s)} = \frac{G(s)}{1-G(s)H(s)} = \frac{-3}{1+3\times\dfrac{1}{2}} = \frac{-6}{5}$$

10. Given equation is,

$$\frac{d^2c(t)}{dt^2} + 3\frac{dc(t)}{dt} + 5c(t) = 5r(t)$$

Taking Laplace transform, we get

$$(s^2 + 3s + 5)\,C(s) = 5\,R(s)$$

$$\therefore \quad \frac{C(s)}{R(s)} = \frac{5}{s^2+3s+5}$$

11. Let output of summer is K (s). Then

$$K(s) = \frac{C(s)}{G_2G_3}$$

$$\therefore \quad \frac{C(s)}{G_2G_3} = G_1\left[R(s) - \frac{C(s)H_1}{G_3}\right] - C(s)\,H_2$$

$$\Rightarrow C(s)\,[1 + H_1 G_1 G_2 + H_2 G_2 G_3] = G_1 G_2 G_3 R(s)$$

$$\Rightarrow \frac{C(s)}{R(s)} = \frac{G_1G_2G_3}{1 + H_1G_1G_2 + H_2G_2G_3}$$

12. Successive block diagram reduction can be

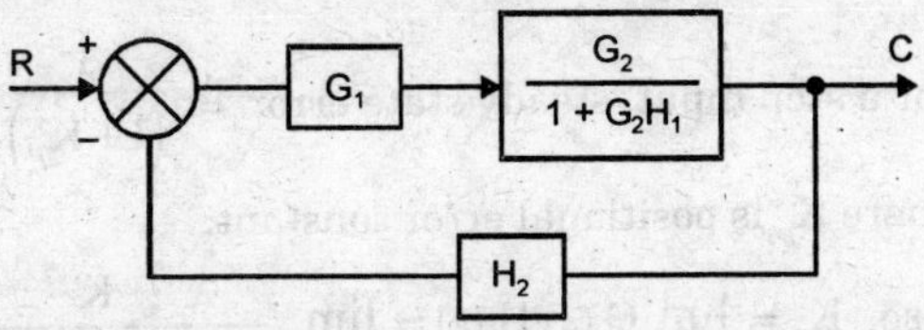

$$\frac{C(s)}{R(s)} = \frac{\dfrac{G_1G_2}{1+G_2H_1}}{1+\dfrac{G_1G_2H_2}{1+G_2H_1}}$$

$$= \frac{G_1G_2}{1+G_2H_1+G_1G_2H_2}$$

$$= \frac{\dfrac{10}{s}\cdot\dfrac{10}{(s+1)}}{1+10\dfrac{(s+3)}{s+1}+\dfrac{10}{s}\cdot\dfrac{10}{s+1}\cdot 1}$$

$$= \frac{100}{11s^2+31s+100}$$

13. $C_1(s) = 0.5\left(\dfrac{1}{s}+\dfrac{1}{s+2}\right) = \dfrac{0.5\times 2\,(s+1)}{s\,(s+2)}$

$$\therefore \quad G_1(s) = \frac{C(s)}{R(s)} = \frac{\dfrac{(s+1)}{s(s+2)}}{1/s} = \frac{(s+1)}{(s+2)}$$

$$H_2(s) = \frac{1}{s+1}$$

$$\therefore \quad H(s) = H_1(s)\,H_2(s) = \frac{1}{(s+2)}$$

16.

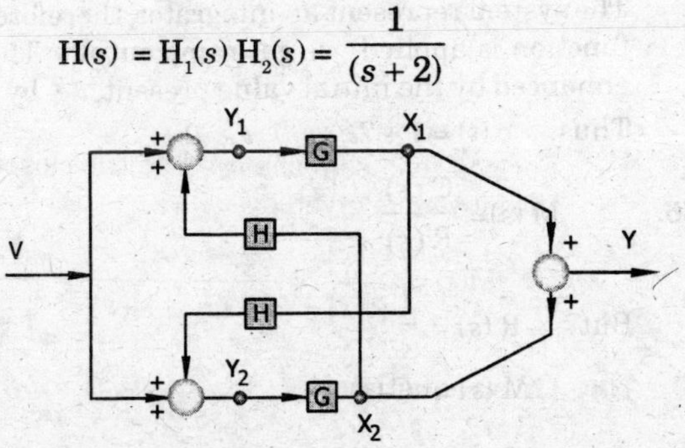

$$Y_1 = U + X_2H$$

$$Y_2 = U + X_1H$$

and $X_1 = GY_1 = GU + GX_2H$

$$X_2 = GY_2 = GU + GX_1H$$

$$\therefore \quad Y = X_1 + X_2$$

$$= 2\,GU + GH\,(X_1 + X_2)$$

$$= 2\,GU + GHY$$

$$\Rightarrow \quad Y = \frac{2GU}{1-GH}$$

$$\Rightarrow \quad \frac{Y}{U} = \frac{2G}{1-GH}$$

17. $\dfrac{d^2y}{dt^2} + \dfrac{dy}{dt} = \dfrac{du}{dt} + 2u$

$$\therefore \quad s^2y(s) + sy(s) = su(s) + 2u(s)$$

$$\Rightarrow \quad \frac{y(s)}{u(s)} = \frac{s+2}{s^2+s}$$

18. Type of closed loop system having a feedback control system as

$$G(s)\,H(s) = \frac{K(1+0.5s)}{s(1+s)(1+2s)} \text{ is one.}$$

19. $c(t) = -te^{-t} + 2e^{-t}, (t \geq 0)$

$$C(s) = -\frac{1}{(s+2)^2} + \frac{2}{(s+1)^2} = \frac{2s+1}{(s+1)^2}$$

$$C(s) = \frac{G(s)}{1+G(s)}$$

$$G(s) = \frac{C(s)}{1-C(s)} = \frac{\dfrac{2s+1}{(s+1)^2}}{1-\dfrac{2s+1}{(s+1)^2}} = \frac{2s+1}{s^2}$$

20.

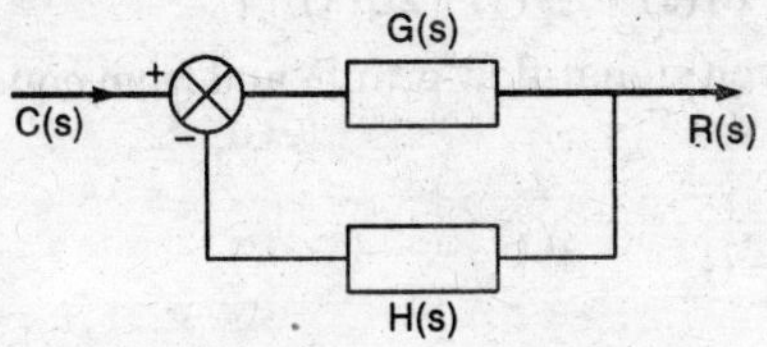

$$\frac{C(s)}{R(s)} = \frac{G(s)}{1+G(s)H(s)}$$

$$\Rightarrow \quad \frac{G(s)}{1+G(s)} = \frac{s+4}{s^2+7s+13}$$

$$\Rightarrow \quad \frac{1+G(s)}{G(s)} = \frac{s^2+7s+13}{s+4}$$

$$\Rightarrow \quad \frac{1}{G(s)} = \frac{s^2+6s+9}{s+4}$$

$$\Rightarrow \quad G(s) = \frac{s+4}{s^2+6s+9}$$

DC gain will occur at $\omega = 0$

$$|G|_{DC} = \frac{4}{9}.$$

SIGNAL FLOW GRAPH

25. $C = RG - H_2C$

$$\therefore \quad \frac{C}{R} = \frac{G}{1+H_2}$$

27. Mason gain formula, $T = \frac{1}{\Delta} \Sigma P_K \Delta_K$

Gains of loop 1 – 2
Gains of loop 2 – 3
Gains of loop 3 – 4
Gains of loop 4 – 5
loop 1 loop 3 = 8

$$\Delta = 1 + (2 + 3 + 4 + 5) + 8 = 23$$

$$\Sigma P_K \Delta_K = 5(1 + 3) + 24 = 24$$

$$\therefore \quad T = \frac{\mathbf{44}}{\mathbf{23}}$$

28. Applying loop rules to both the loops,

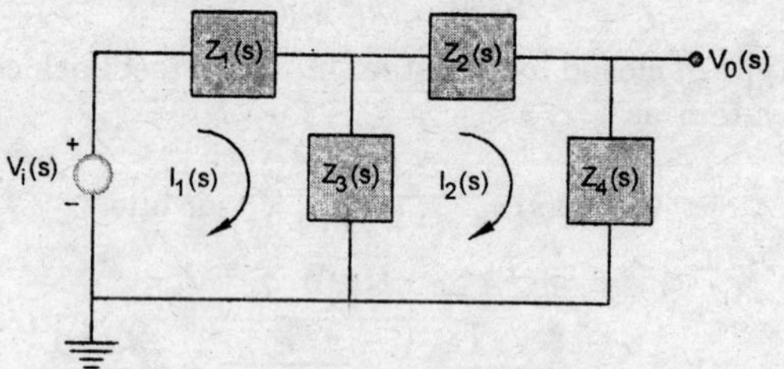

$$V_i(s) = I_1 Z_1(s) + (I_1 - I_2) Z_3(s) \qquad ...(i)$$

$$\Rightarrow \quad I_1 Z_3(s) = I_2 Z_2(s) + I_{12} Z_3(s) + I_2 Z_4(s) \qquad ...(ii)$$

From equation (*i*),

$$\frac{V_t}{Z_1(s) + Z_3(s)} = \frac{-I_2 Z_3(s)}{Z_1(s) + Z_3(s)} + I_1 \qquad ...(iii)$$

From equation (*ii*),

$$I_2 = \frac{Z_3(s) I_1(s)}{Z_1(s) + Z_2(s) + Z_3(s)} \qquad ...(iv)$$

From the given signal-flow graph, and from equation (*iv*), we get

$$\frac{I_2}{I_1} = G_2$$

$$\Rightarrow \quad G_2 = \frac{Z_3(s)}{Z_1(s) + Z_2(s) + Z_3(s)}$$

From equation (*iii*),

$$H = -\frac{Z_3(s)}{Z_1(s) + Z_3(s)}$$

STEADY STATE ERRORS/RESPONSE

29. Unity feedback control system is shown as below:

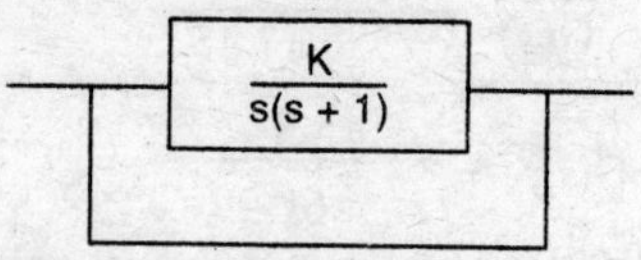

Steady state error due to unit step.

Since it is a Type 1 system, hence steady state error of system due to unit step input is zero.

$$K_p = \lim_{s \to 0} G(s)H(s) = \lim_{s \to 0} \frac{K}{s(s+1)} = \infty$$

$$\therefore \quad e_{ss} = \frac{1}{1 + K_p} = 0$$

31. Step response transform is

$$\frac{42.25}{s^2(s + 6.5)} = \frac{1}{s + 6.5} + \frac{6.5}{s^2} - \frac{1}{s}$$

$$c(t) = e^{-6.5t} + 6.5\, t\, u(t) - u(t)$$

At $t \to \infty$, $\quad c(t) \to \infty$

32. Characteristics equation $s^2 + 0.2s + 1 = 0$, when expressed in form $s^2 + 2\delta\omega_n + \omega_n^2$, then setting time is given by,

$$t_{ss} = \frac{4}{r\omega_n} = \frac{4}{0.1} = \mathbf{40\ ms.}$$

33. For a step input, steady state error $= \frac{1}{(1 + K_p)}$

where K_p is positional error constant.

Also, $K_p = \lim_{s \to 0} G(s)H(s) = \lim_{s \to 0} \frac{K}{(s+1)(0.1s+1)^2}$

$$\therefore \quad \frac{1}{1 + K_p} = \frac{1}{1 + K} = 0.1$$

$$\Rightarrow \quad K = \mathbf{9.0}$$

34. $C(s) = \frac{G(s)}{1 + G(s)H(s)} R(s)$

(Assuming negative feedback)

$$C(s) = \frac{\frac{20}{s^2}}{1 + \left(\frac{20}{s^2}\right)(s+5)} \frac{1}{s}$$

$$\lim_{t \to \infty} C(t) = \lim_{s \to 0} sC(s)$$

$$= \frac{20}{s^2 + 20(s+5)}$$

$$= \lim_{s \to 0} \frac{20}{s^2 + 20s + 100} = \mathbf{0.2}$$

35. $U(s) \longrightarrow \boxed{\frac{2}{s}} \longrightarrow C(s)$

The system represent an integrator, therefore, if a step function is applied, we get ramp output. This will be enhanced by the initial value present, *i.e.* by 1.

Thus, $\quad c(t) = 1 + 2t; \qquad t \geq 0.$

36. $M(s) = \frac{C(s)}{R(s)}$

But $\quad R(s) = \frac{1}{s}$

$$\therefore \quad M(s) = sC(s)$$

Now, $£^{-1} \frac{\omega_n^2}{s(s^2 + 2\delta\omega_n s + \omega_n^2)}$

$$= 1 + \frac{1}{\sqrt{1 - \delta^2}} e^{-\delta\omega_n t} \left(\omega_n \sqrt{1 - \delta^2}\, t - \phi\right)$$

Thus, $8 = \delta\omega_n$

and $6 = \omega_n \sqrt{1-\delta^2}$

$\Rightarrow \quad \delta = 0.8$

and since $\omega_n = 10$ satisfy these equations, therefore

$$\leq K[1 + 1.66\, e^{-8t} \sin(6t - 143°)] = \frac{100\,K}{s(s^2+16s+100)}$$

Now, $\sin(6t - 143°) = -\sin(180° + 6t - 143°)$

$= \sin(6t + 37°)$

$\therefore \quad K[1 - 66\, e^{-8t} \sin(6t + 37°)]$

$$= \frac{100\,K}{s(s^2+16s+100)}$$

$$\therefore \quad M(s) = s\,C(s) = \frac{100\,K}{s^2+16s+100}$$

37. Given : $\dfrac{dy}{dt} + 2y = 4t\,u(t)$

Laplace transofrming is

$$sY(s) + 2Y(s) = \frac{4}{s^2}$$

$$\Rightarrow \quad Y(s)[s+2] = \frac{4}{s^2}$$

$$\Rightarrow \quad Y(s) = \frac{4}{s^2(s+2)} = -\left(\frac{1}{s}\right) + \left(\frac{2}{s^2}\right) + \frac{1}{(s+2)}$$

$$y(t) = -u(t) + 2t\,u(t) + e^{-2t}$$

The ramp component in the forced response is $2t\,u(t)$

38. Unit impulse response of a linear, time invariant network is the derivative of unit step function response of the network.

Unit step response is $(1 - e^{-\alpha t})$

$\therefore$ Unit impulse response $= -(-\alpha)\,e^{-\alpha t} = \alpha e^{-\alpha t}$

39. Given : $KK_t = 99$; $s = j1$ rad/sec.

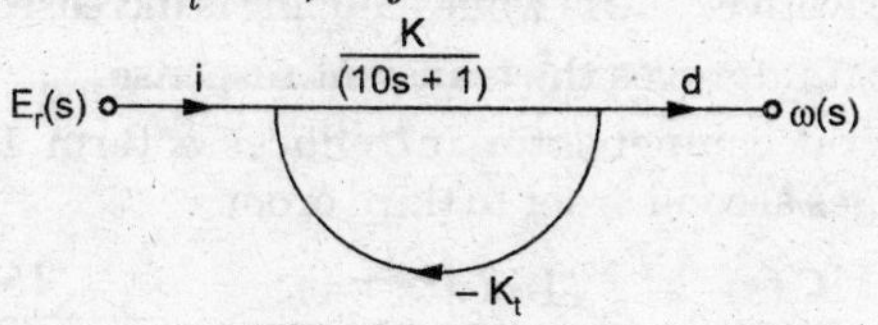

$$S_K^M = \frac{\frac{dM}{M}}{\frac{dK}{K}} = \frac{K}{M}\frac{dM}{dK}$$

$$\text{Now} \quad M = \frac{G}{1+GH} = \frac{\frac{K}{(10s+1)}}{1+\left(\frac{KK_t}{(10s+1)}\right)}$$

$$= \frac{K}{10s+1+KK_t}$$

$$\therefore \quad \frac{dM}{dK} = \frac{1\times(10s+1+KK_t) - KK_t}{(10s+1+KK_t)^2}$$

$$= \frac{10s+1}{(10s+1+KK_t)^2}$$

$$\Rightarrow \quad \frac{K}{M}\frac{dM}{dK} = \frac{K}{\frac{K}{(10s+1+KK_t)}}$$

$$= \frac{(10s+1)}{(10s+1+KK_t)^2}$$

$$= \frac{(10s+1)}{(10s+1+KK_t)}$$

$$= \frac{10s+1}{10(10+s)}$$

$$\text{With } s = j1, \quad \frac{K}{M}\frac{dM}{dK} = \frac{\sqrt{100+1}}{10\sqrt{100+1}} = \mathbf{0.1}$$

40. $K_v = \underset{s\to 0}{Lt}\ sG(s)$

$$= \underset{s\to 0}{Lt} \frac{K}{(s+1)(s+2)} = \frac{K}{2}.$$

Given : $K_v > 10$, then $K >$ **20 sec⁻¹.**

41. From the expression for c (t), we have

$$\omega_n\sqrt{1-\xi^2} = 8 \text{ and } \frac{\sqrt{1-\xi}}{\xi} = 1.33$$

$\therefore \quad \omega_n =$ **10 rad/sec.** and $\xi =$ **0.6**

42. Steady state error,

$$e(s) = \underset{s\to 0}{Lt}\ s\,E(s)$$

$$= \underset{s\to 0}{Lt} \frac{s\,R(s)}{1+G(s)H(s)}$$

$$= \underset{s\to 0}{Lt} \frac{s}{1+\frac{4(s+1)}{s^2(s+2)}} \cdot \left[\frac{3}{s} - \frac{1}{s^2} + \frac{1}{2s^3}\right] = \mathbf{\frac{1}{4}}$$

43. Final value, $f(\infty) = \underset{z\to 1}{Lt}\ (z-1)^{-1} F(z)$

$$= \underset{z\to 1}{Lt} \frac{z^{-1}(1-z^{-4})}{4(1-z^{-1})} = 0$$

46. $\dfrac{C(s)}{R(s)} = \dfrac{1}{1+s}$

$$\Rightarrow \quad \frac{C(j\omega)}{R(j\omega)} = \frac{1}{1+j\omega}$$

$$\therefore \quad \left|\frac{C(j\omega)}{R(j\omega)}\right| = \frac{1}{\sqrt{1+1}} = \frac{1}{\sqrt{2}}$$

$$\Rightarrow \quad \frac{\angle C(j\omega)}{\angle R(j\omega)} = -\tan^{-1} 1 = \frac{-\pi}{4}$$

$\therefore$ Steady state value at $c(t) = \dfrac{1}{\sqrt{2}} \sin\left(t - \dfrac{\pi}{4}\right)$

47. $H(s) = \dfrac{1}{s+2}$

$Y(s) = \dfrac{1}{(s+2)^2}$ $\quad X(s) = \dfrac{Y(s)}{H(s)} = \dfrac{1}{s+2}$

and $u(t) = e^{-2t}u(t)$

48. $\dfrac{C(s)}{R(s)} = \dfrac{2(s-1)}{(s+2)(s+1)}$; $R(s) = \dfrac{1}{s}$

Hence $\quad C(s) = \dfrac{2(s-1)}{s(s+1)(s+2)}$

$$= \frac{K_1}{s} + \frac{K_2}{s+1} + \frac{K_3}{s+2}$$

$$K_1 = \left.\frac{2(s-1)}{(s+1)(s+2)}\right|_{s=0} = -1$$

$$K_2 = \left.\frac{2(s-1)}{s(s+2)}\right|_{s=-1} = 4$$

$$K_3 = \left.\frac{2(s-1)}{s(s+1)}\right|_{s=-2} = -3$$

Hence, $\quad C(s) = \dfrac{-1}{s} + \dfrac{4}{s+1} - \dfrac{3}{s+2}$

$\Rightarrow \quad c(t) = [-1 + 4e^{-t} - 3e^{-2t}]$

49. $K_P = \lim\limits_{s\to o} G(s) = \lim\limits_{s\to o} \dfrac{50}{(1+0.1s)(1+2s)} = \mathbf{50}$

$K_V = \lim\limits_{s\to o} sG(s) = \lim\limits_{s\to 0} \dfrac{50\,s}{(1+0.1s)(1+2s)} = \mathbf{0}$

50. The given transfer function is to be taken as space open loop transfer function

$$G(s) = \frac{10}{1+s}.$$

It is type zero system.

The steady state error to a unit step input will be

$$e_{ss} = \frac{1}{1+K}$$

$$K = \lim_{s\to o} \frac{10}{1+s} = 10.$$

$\therefore \quad e_{ss} = \mathbf{\dfrac{1}{11}}$

51. Reduction of the block diagram

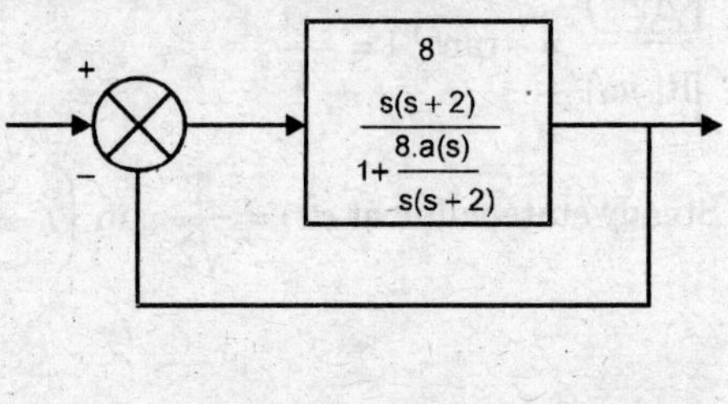

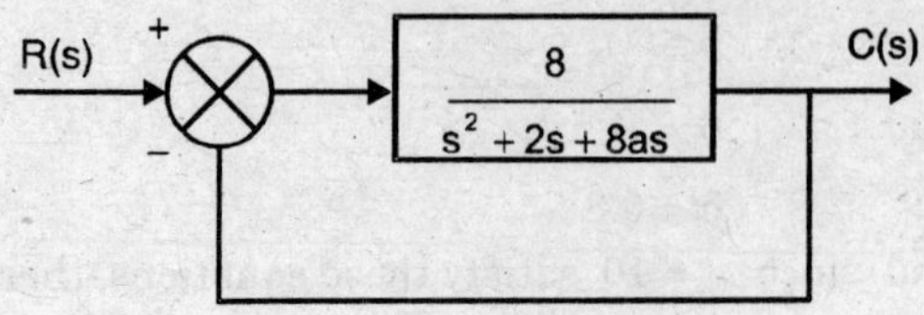

$$\therefore \quad \frac{C(s)}{R(s)} = \frac{\dfrac{8}{s^2+(2+8a)s}}{1+\dfrac{8}{s^2+(2+8a)s}}$$

$$= \frac{8}{s^2+(2+8a)s+8}$$

Characteristic equation is

$$s^2 + (2+8a) + 8 = 0$$

Equating with the equation

$s^2 + 2\xi\,\omega_n\, s + \omega_n^2$, we get

$$\omega_n = 2\sqrt{2}$$

$\therefore \quad \omega\,(2+8a) = 2\xi\omega_n = 2 \times 0.7 \times 2\sqrt{2}$

$\Rightarrow \quad a = \mathbf{0.245}$

52. Steady state error $= \dfrac{1}{\lim\limits_{s\to 0} sG(s)} = \dfrac{1}{Kv}$

$$G(s) = \frac{8}{s^2+(2+8a)s}$$

$$= \frac{8}{s^2+2.8\,s}$$

$$K_V = \lim_{s\to 0} \frac{s.8}{s^2+2.8s} = \frac{8}{2.8}$$

$\therefore \quad e_{ss} = \dfrac{1}{K_v} = \dfrac{2.8}{8} = \mathbf{0.35}$

53. For same K_v, the natural frequency ω_n remains unchanged in derivative control while damping is increased. Thus it improves the transient response.
Integral compensator introduces a term $1/s$, thus changes second order to third order.

54. $\dfrac{C(s)}{R(s)} = \dfrac{16/s(s+4)}{1+16/s(s+4)\times 1} = \dfrac{16}{16+s(s+4)}$

$$\frac{C(j\omega)}{R(j\omega)} = \frac{16}{16+j\omega(j\omega+4)} = \frac{16}{16-\omega^2+4j\omega}$$

$$= \frac{16}{\sqrt{(16-\omega)^2+(4\omega)^2}} \angle -\tan^{-1}\frac{4\omega}{(16-\omega^2)}$$

For resonance to occur

$$\frac{d}{d\omega}\sqrt{(16-\omega^2)^2+(4\omega)^2} = 0$$

$$F(\omega) = (16-\omega^2)^2 + (4\omega)^2$$

$$= \omega^4 + 256 - 32\omega^2 + 16\omega^2$$

$$= \omega^4 - 16\,\omega^2 + 256$$

$\therefore \quad \dfrac{dF(\omega)}{d\omega} = 4\omega^3 - 32\,\omega = 0$

$\Rightarrow \quad \omega = \sqrt{8} = \mathbf{2\sqrt{2}\ rad/sec}$

55. $K_p = \lim_{s\to 0} G(s)\,H(s) = \lim_{s\to 0} \dfrac{1}{(s+6)(s+1)} = \dfrac{\mathbf{1}}{\mathbf{6}}$

56. $M(s) = \dfrac{G(s)}{1+G(s)H(s)} = \dfrac{K/s(s+2)}{1+(1+as)K/s(s+2)}$

The characteristic equation is

$$s(s+2) + K(1+as) = 0$$

$$\Rightarrow \quad s^2 + s(2+aK) + K = 0$$

Compare with equation $s^2 + 2\xi\omega_n s + \omega_n^2 = 0$, we get

$$K = \omega_n^2 = 4^2 = \mathbf{16}$$

$$\therefore \quad 2\xi\omega_n = (2+aK)$$

$$\Rightarrow \quad a = \frac{2\times 0.7\times 4 - 2}{16} = \frac{3.6}{16} = \mathbf{0.225}$$

57. $T(s) = \dfrac{k}{s^2+s+k}$

$$2\xi w_n = 1,\ w_n = \sqrt{k}$$

$$\xi = \frac{0.5}{\sqrt{k}}$$

$$M_p = 0.50 = \exp\left\{\frac{-\pi\xi}{\sqrt{1-\xi^2}}\right\}$$

$$\Rightarrow \quad \frac{\xi}{\sqrt{1-\xi^2}} = 0.16$$

$$\xi = 0.15$$

$$k = \mathbf{5.3}$$

58. Open loop transfer function $= \dfrac{4(1+2s)}{s^2(s+2)}$

unit ramp

Type 2.

Steady state error = **0**

60. Linear time invariant control system is shown below.

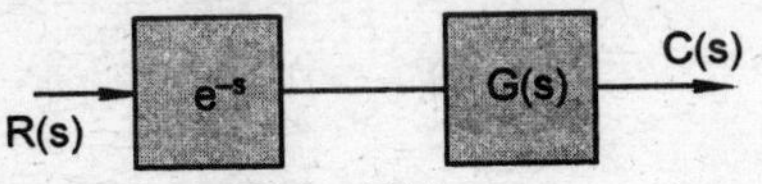

We know, $C(s) = R(s)\cdot G(s)$

After introducing e^{-s}

$$C(s) = R(s)\cdot e^{-s}\,G(s)$$

$$\Rightarrow \quad C_1(s) = e^{-s}\,C(s)$$

$$\Rightarrow \quad C_1(s) = c(t)\,u(t-1)$$

61.

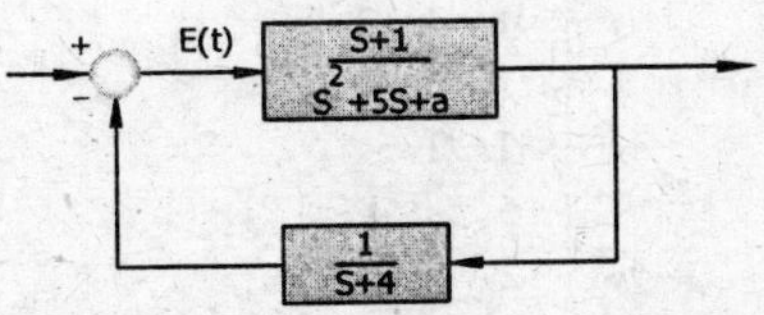

$$E(s) = X(s) - Y(s)H$$

$$= X(s) - \frac{G}{1+GH}\,H\cdot X(s) = X(s)\,\frac{G}{1+GH}$$

$$X(s) = \frac{1}{s}$$

$$\therefore \quad E(s) = \frac{1}{s(1+GH)}$$

$$= \frac{1}{s}\left[\frac{1}{1+\dfrac{s+1}{(s+4)(s^2+5s+a)}}\right]$$

Steady state error,

$$e_{ss} = \lim_{t\to\infty} \in(t) = \lim_{s\to 0} sE(s)$$

$$= \lim_{s\to 0} \frac{1}{1+\dfrac{s+1}{(s+4)(s^2+5s+a)}}$$

$$= \frac{1}{1+\dfrac{1}{4a}} = \frac{4a}{4a+1} = 0$$

or $a = \mathbf{0}$

62. Response, $C(s) = \dfrac{100}{(s+1)(s+100)}$

[For $R(s) = \dfrac{1}{s}$; unit-step input]

Then $C(t) = 1 - \dfrac{100}{99}e^{-t} + \dfrac{1}{99}e^{-100t}$

[using partial fraction]

The term $\dfrac{100}{99}e^{-t}$ will dominant on system response, then

$$\xi\omega_n = 1$$

and $t_s = \dfrac{4}{\xi\omega_n} = \dfrac{4}{1} = \mathbf{4\ sec.}$

63. The characteristics equation is

$$(2s+1)(s^4+2s^2+1) = 0$$

The roots are $s = -0.5,\ s = +j, -j$

Since, double roots are present on the imaginary axis and one root at negative real axis, therefore system response will be oscillatory.

64. Damping ratio = 0.6

and % overshoot $= e^{\frac{\pi\xi}{\sqrt{1-\xi^2}}} = \mathbf{10\%}$

65. Gain margin of the system for which Nyquist plot of a loop transfer function $G(j\omega)\,H(j\omega)$ encloses $(-1, +j0)$ point is less than zero.

STABILITY ROUTH AND NYQUIST

66. Characteristic equation is

$$1 + G(s)\,H(s) = 0$$

$$\therefore \quad s(s^2+10s+16) + K = 0$$

$$\Rightarrow \quad j\omega(-\omega^2 + 10j\omega + 16)\,K = 0$$

For this system to oscillate, j terms should be set to zero.

$$\therefore \quad -j\omega^3 + 16j\omega = 0$$

$$\Rightarrow \quad \omega = \mathbf{4\ rad/sec.}$$

Then, $-10\omega^2 + K = 0$

$$\Rightarrow \quad K = \mathbf{160.}$$

67. In open-loop system, there is a pole in RHP. So system is unstable.

In closed loop system

$$T(s) = \frac{K(s+2)}{s^2 + (K-6)s + 2K - 7}$$

For stability $K > 6$, $2K - 7 > 0$

$\Rightarrow \quad K > 6$

So for $K > 6$, system is stable.

68. Closed loop transfer function

$$T(s) = \frac{K(s^2 - 4)}{(K+1)s^2 + (3-4K)}$$

The system can be only marginally stable.

69. Characteristic equation is

$$s^4 + 9s^3 + 20s^2 + Ks + K = 0$$

Routh table is as shown below.

s^4	1	20	K
s^3	9	K	
s^2	$\frac{180-K}{9}$	K	
s^1	$\frac{K(K-99)}{K-180}$		
s^0	K		

For stability, $0 < K < 99$.

70. The characteristics equation is

$$1 + GH = 0$$

$$\therefore \quad 1 + \frac{K}{s^3 + 3s^2 + 2s + 1} = 0$$

$$\Rightarrow \quad \frac{s^3 + 3s^2 + 2s + K + 1}{s^3 + 3s^2 + 2s + 1} = 0$$

Routh-Hurwitz criterion can be applied,

s^3	1	2
s^2	3	K + 1
s^1	$\frac{6-(K+1)}{3}$	0
s^0	K + 1	0

$$\therefore \quad \frac{5-K}{3} > 0 \ \& \ K + 1 > 0$$

$\therefore \quad K < 5, K > -1$

$\Rightarrow \quad -1 < K < 5$

Hence maximum value = **5**

71. $$G(s)\,H(s) = \frac{1}{s(s+0.5)(s+1)}$$

$$G(j\omega)\,H(j\omega) = \frac{1}{j\omega(j\omega+0.5)(j\omega+1)}$$

$$\phi = \angle G(j\omega)\,H(j\omega)$$
$$= -90° - \tan^{-1} 2\omega - \tan^{-1}\omega$$

At phase cross-over point, $\phi = -180°$

$\therefore \quad \tan^{-1}\omega + \tan^{-1} 2\omega = 90°$

$$\Rightarrow \quad \tan^{-1}\frac{2\omega^2}{1-2\omega^2} = 90°$$

$$\Rightarrow \quad \frac{2\omega^2}{1-2\omega^2} = \tan 90° = \infty$$

$\therefore \quad 1 - 2\omega^2 = 0$

$$\Rightarrow \quad \omega = \frac{1}{\sqrt{2}} = \mathbf{0.707\ rad/sec.}$$

72. $$T(s) = \frac{G(s)}{1+G(s)} = \frac{80}{s^2 + 18s + 80}$$

$$\frac{C(s)}{R(s)} = \frac{80}{s^2 + 18s + 80}$$

Here, $2\xi\omega_n = 18$

and $\omega_n = \sqrt{80}$

$$\therefore \quad \xi = \frac{18}{2\sqrt{80}} = 1.006$$

Since, $\xi > 1$, the system is overdamped.

74. Since all the coefficients in all the three polynomials are positive, it is required to construct Hurwitz table for further checking.

1. $s^4 + 7s^3 + 17s^2 + 17s + 6$

This is seen to be a Hurwitz polynomial as all the terms in the first column have the same sign.

s^4	1	17	6
s^3	7	17	–
s^2	$\frac{102}{7}$	6	–
s^1	$\frac{720}{51}$	–	–
s^0	6	–	–

2. $s^4 + 11s^3 + 41s^2 + 61s + 30$

This also is a Hurwitz polynomial

s^4	1	41	30
s^3	11	61	–
s^2	$\frac{390}{13}$	30	–
s^1	$\frac{672}{31}$	–	–
s^0	30	–	–

3. $s^4 + s^3 + 2s^2 + 3s + 2$

This is not a Hurwitz polynomial

s^4	1	1	2
s^3	1	3	–
s^2	– 1	2	–
s^1	5	–	–
s^0	2	–	–

75. $$G(s)H(s) = \frac{30}{s(s+1)(s+T)}$$

The characteristics equation becomes

$$s(s+1)(s+T) + 30 = 0$$

$$\Rightarrow \quad s^3 + s^2(1+T) + sT + 30 = 0$$

Constructing Routh Tables

s^3	1	T
s^2	(1 + T)	30
s^1	$\dfrac{T^2+T-30}{(1+T)}$	0
s^0	30	–

$(1 + T) > 0$ or $T > -1$

$$\therefore \quad \frac{(T^2+T-30)}{1+T} > 0$$

$$\Rightarrow \quad \frac{(T+6)(T-5)}{(1+T)} > 0$$

$\Rightarrow \quad T > -6$, or $T > 5$

Therefore **T > 5.**

77. $$G(j\omega)H(j\omega) = \frac{K(1+j\omega)^2}{(j\omega)^3}$$

$$|G(j\omega)H(j\omega)| = \frac{K(1+\omega^2)}{\omega^3}$$

$$\angle G(j\omega)H(j\omega) = -270^\circ + 2\tan^{-1}\omega$$

For $\omega = 0$, $GH(j\omega) = \infty \angle -270^\circ$

For $\omega = 1$, $\angle GH(j\omega) = -180^\circ$

For $\omega = \infty$, $GH(j\omega) = 0 \angle -90^\circ$

As ω increases from 0 to ∞, phase goes -270° to -90°. Due to s^3 term there will be 3 infinite semicircle.

78. Routh Hurwitz criterion

s^4	2	3	7
s^3	1	5	
s^2	–7	7	
s^1	6		
s^0	7		

Since sign changes twice, therefore 2 roots in right half plane.

79. By Routh criterion

s^4	1	5	15
s^3	20K	10	
s^2	$\dfrac{10-100K}{20K}$	15	
s^1	$300K - \dfrac{10-100K}{20K}$		
s^0	15		

For this, any value at K the system is unstable.

80. $$GM = \left[\frac{K T_1 T_2}{T_1 + T_2}\right]^{-1}$$

Here, $K = 0.75$, $T_1 = 1$, $T_2 = 0.5$

$$\therefore \quad GM = \left[\frac{0.75 \times 1 \times 0.5}{1+0.5}\right]^{-1} = 2.4$$

$\therefore \quad GM = 20 \log a = \mathbf{12\ dB}$

81. For a GM of 20 db, the Nyquist plot should intersect the real axis at a,

where, $20 \log\left(\dfrac{1}{a}\right) = 20$

$\Rightarrow \quad a = 0.1$

This is achieved if the system gain is increased by a factor of $\left(\dfrac{0.1}{0.04}\right) = 2.5.$

Thus $\quad K = \mathbf{2.5}$

82. By Routh criterion

s^3	1	5
s^2	K	10
s^1	$\dfrac{10-5K}{K}$	0
s^0	10	0

For stable system,

$10 - 5K > 0$

$\Rightarrow \quad K \le \mathbf{2}$

84. $s^4 + 6s^3 + 11s^2 + 6s + K = 0$

s^4	1	11	K
s^3	6	6	–
s^2	10	K	–
s^1	6 – 0.6 K	–	–
s^0	K	–	–

For stability

$K \ge 0$ and also $6(1 - 0.1K) \ge 0$

Thus, $\mathbf{0 \le K \le 10.}$

85. Here linear discrete time system has characteristic equation

$$z^3 - 0.81z = 0$$

$$\Rightarrow \quad z(z^2 - 0.9^2) = 0$$

$$\Rightarrow \quad z(z - 0.9)(z + 0.9) = 0$$

Hence $\quad z = 0, 0.9, -0.9.$

All roots lie inside unit circle. Hence the system is **stable**.

86. $|G(j\omega)H(j\omega)| \neq 1$, for any value of ω,

Therefore phase margin ∞.

87. $P = 0$

$N = 0$, since encirclement is zero,

As, $\quad P = N + Z.$

$\therefore \quad Z = \mathbf{0}.$

88. Number of roots of $s^3 + 5s^2 + 7s + 3 = 0$ in the LHS of s-plane

s^3	1	7
s^2	5	3
s^1	$\dfrac{32}{5}$	
s^0	3	

Since no sign change, hence no root in RHS of s-plane.

89. $s^3 + 6Ks^2 + (K+2)s + 8 = 0$

s^3	1	K + 2
s^2	6 K	8
s^1	$\dfrac{(6K)(K+2)-8}{6K}$	
s^0	8	

For stablility, $\dfrac{(6K)(K+2)-8}{6} = 0$

$\Rightarrow \quad K > 0$

$\therefore \quad 3K^2 + 6K - 4 > 0$

$\Rightarrow \quad K = \dfrac{-6 \pm \sqrt{36+48}}{6}$

$= \dfrac{-6 \pm \sqrt{84}}{6} = 0.528, -2.58$

Since K > 0, hence K = **0.528**

90. For a linear control system with no poles in R.H.S. of s-plane including roots on $j\omega$ axis with bounded input, the output may be unbounded.

92. $\dfrac{Y(s)}{R(s)} = \dfrac{K}{s-3+K}$

The system will stable, when single pole lies in the RH-s plane, i.e.

$K - 3 > 0$

$\Rightarrow \quad K > 3$

93. $\angle G(j\omega)\, H(j\omega) = -180°$

$= -90° - \tan^{-1}\dfrac{\omega}{1-\omega^2}$

$\left[\text{since } G(j\omega)H(j\omega) = \dfrac{1}{j\omega(j\omega+1-\omega^2)}\right]$

$\Rightarrow \quad \tan^{-1}\dfrac{\omega}{1-\omega^2} = 90°$

$\therefore \quad \omega = 1$ rad/sec

Then, $GM = -\log|G(j\omega),\ H(j\omega)|_{\omega=1}| = 0\ dB$

94. Characteristic equation is

$(K+1)s^2 + s(4-4K) + 4 + 4K = 0$

Routh array drawn below,

s^2	K + 1	4 (1 + K)
s	4 (1 − K)	0

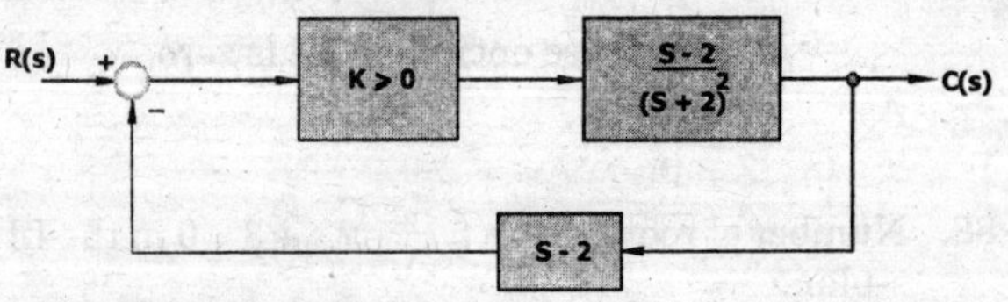

For stability, coefficient in the first column is greater then zero, i.e. +ve

$K + 1 > 0$

$1 > K$ and $K \geq 0$.

95. $GH(j\omega) = \dfrac{K}{j\omega(-\omega^2 + 2j\omega + 2)}$

$\angle GH(j\omega) = -\tan^{-1}\dfrac{2\omega}{2-\omega^2} - 90°$

$|GH(j\omega)| = \dfrac{K}{\omega\sqrt{(2-\omega^2)^2 + 4\omega^2}}$

At $\omega = 0$, $\quad GH(j\omega) = \infty\angle -90°$

At $\omega = \infty$, $\quad GH(j\omega) = 0\angle -270°$

At $\omega = 1$, $\quad GH(j\omega) = \dfrac{K}{\sqrt{5}}\angle -153.43°$

At $\omega = 2$, $\quad GH(j\omega) = \dfrac{K}{2\sqrt{18}}\angle -206.6°$.

Due to s there will be a infinite semicircle.

96. $|GH(j\omega)| = \dfrac{K}{\sqrt{1+\omega^2}\sqrt{1+4\omega^2}\sqrt{1+9\omega^2}}$

$\angle GH(j\omega) = -90° - \tan^{-1}\omega - \tan^{-1}2\omega - \tan^{-1}3\omega$,

For $\omega = 0$, $\quad GH(j\omega) = \infty\angle -90°$

For $\omega = \infty$, $\quad GH(j\omega) = 0\angle -360°$

97. The open-loop poles in RHP are P = 0.

Nyquist path enclosed 2 times the point (–1 + j0).

Taking clockwise encirclements as negative N = –2.

N = P – Z, –2 = 0 – Z, Z = 2 which implies that two poles of closed-loop system are on RHP.

BODE PLOTS

98. Given that in a Bode-plot

$|G_\phi(j\omega)|_\omega = 125°$

Phase margin of system, $\phi_M = -125 + 180 =$ **55°**

99. Initially plot has a slope of + 20 dB/decade. So there must be zero at origin.

So, at ω = 4, slope changes to 0 dB/decade, so pole at ω = 4.

Again slope at ω = 10 changes to – 40 dB/decade, so there are two poles at ω = 10.

Now, $\quad 20\log|K\omega| = 0$ at ω = 4.

$\therefore \quad K =$ **0.25.**

101. According to the definition, bandwidth of a control system is the range of frequency over which $\left|\dfrac{C}{R}(j\omega)\right|$ is greater than or equal to $1/\sqrt{2}$. Again, bandwidth depends on both – the undamped natural frequency and the damping ratio.

For instance, the characteristic equation of a second order system may be expressed as

$$s^2 + 2\xi\omega_n s + \omega_n^2 = 0$$

where ω_n is the undamped natural frequency of oscillation and δ is the damping ratio.

Also it can be shown that $2\xi\omega_n$ is the bandwidth. Thus the bandwidth is dependent on both ω_n and ξ.

102. $G(s) = \dfrac{K}{s+a}$

$G(0) = \dfrac{K}{a} = 20\ dB$

$\Rightarrow \quad \dfrac{K}{a} = 10$

$\therefore \quad a = \text{antilog } 10^1 = 10$

Hence K = 10 $a = 100$

$$\therefore \quad G(s) = \frac{100}{s+10}$$

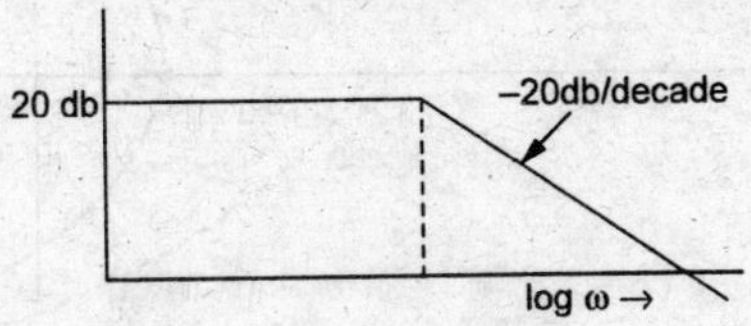

103. $$H(s) = \frac{\omega_n^2}{s^2 + 2\xi\omega_n s + \omega_n^2}$$

$$H(j\omega) = \frac{\omega_n^2}{-\omega^2 + 2\xi\omega_n j\omega + \omega_n^2}$$

$$[H(j\omega)] = \frac{\omega_n^2}{\sqrt{(\omega_n^2 - \omega^2)^2 + (\omega\xi + \omega_n\omega)^2}}$$

$$[H(j0)] = 1$$

If ω_c is the 3-dB frequency, then

$$H(j\omega_c) = \frac{\omega_n^2}{\sqrt{(\omega_n^2 - \omega_c^2)^2 + (2\xi + \omega_n\omega_c)^2}} = 0.707$$

$$\Rightarrow \omega_n^4 = 0.5[\omega_c^4 - 2\omega_c^2\omega_n^2 + 4\xi^2\omega_n^2\omega_c^2]$$

Rearranging,

$$0.5\,\omega_c^4 - \omega_c^2(\omega_n^2 - 2\xi^2\omega_n^2) - 0.5\,\omega\,\omega_n^2 = 0$$

$$\Rightarrow \omega_n^2 = \frac{(\omega_n^2 - 2\xi^2\omega_n^2) + \sqrt{(\omega_n^2 - \xi^2\omega_n^2)^2 + \omega_n^4}}{1}$$

$$= \omega_n^2[1 - 2\xi^2 \pm 2 + \sqrt{2 + 4\xi^4 - 4\xi^4 - 4\xi^2}]$$

$$\Rightarrow \omega_c = \omega_n\sqrt{(1-2\xi^2) \pm \sqrt{4\xi^4 - 4\xi^2 + 2}}$$

Since ω_c is real, hence (*c*) is correct.

105. $$\angle GH|_{\omega=0.5a} = -\tan^{-1}\frac{\omega}{a}$$

$$= -\tan^{-1} 0.5 = 26.56°$$

From the plot, at $\omega = 0$, $\angle G(s) = 22.5°$

$\therefore$ Error = – 22.50° (–26.56°) = 4.06°

At $\omega = 0$

$20 \log |GH| = 20 \log k - 20 \log |1 + j0.5|$

$= 20 \log k - 0.97$

From the plot,

$20 \log |GH| = 20 \log k$

$\therefore$ Error in dB gain = **0.97 dB**

107. Since at ω = 2 and ω = 25, slope changes from 40dB/dec to –60 dB/dec at both the value. So there are poles at ω = 2 and ω = 25.

Also at ω = 0.1, slope is – 40 dB/dec, i.e. there are two poles at origin.

Hence transfer function, should be of the form

$$T(s) = \frac{K(s+5)}{s^2(s+2)(s+25)}$$

Now, $$54 = 20 \log \frac{5K}{(0.1)^2 \times 50}$$

$\Rightarrow$ K = 50.

$$\therefore \quad T(s) = \frac{50(s+5)}{s^2(s+2)(s+25)}$$

108. The Bode plot is as shown in figure

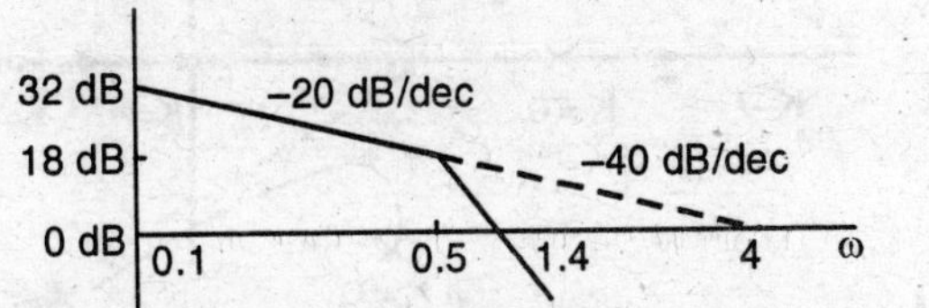

Here, $K_v = 4$,

$$\therefore \quad e_{ramp}(\infty) = \frac{1}{K_v} = \frac{1}{4} = \mathbf{0.25}$$

109. From the figure in Q.143 $\xi = \frac{\omega_2}{2\omega_3} = \frac{0.5}{2(1.4)} = \mathbf{0.179}$

ROOT LOCUS

110. $$G(s) = \frac{1}{(s+2)^2}$$

$$M(s) = \frac{G(s)}{1 + G(s)H(s)}; \quad H(s) = 1$$

$$\therefore \quad M(s) = \frac{G(s)}{1+G(s)} = \frac{1/(s+2)^2}{1 + 1/s+2)^2}$$

$$= \frac{1}{(s+2)^2 + 1}$$

The poles are at –2, ± j1.

111. Both the answers (*c*) and (*d*) are idential. The breakaway and breakin points on the root locus for which loop transfer function is G(*s*) H(*s*) are obtained as a solution of equation

$$\frac{d}{ds} G(s)H(s) = 0.$$

$$\Rightarrow \quad (s+6)(2s+8) - (s^2 + 8s + 15) = 0$$

$$\Rightarrow \quad 2s^2 + 20s + 48 - s^2 - 8s + 15 = 0$$

$$\Rightarrow \quad s^2 + 12s + 33 = 0$$

$\therefore$ s = **– 7.73** and **– 4.27**

112. In this option, locus start from poles and end on origin. In (c) and (d) poles and zero are marked incorrect.

113. $$|K| = \frac{\text{[Product of vector drawn from the poles of G(s) H(s) to the given pole]}}{\text{[Products of vectors drawn from the zeros of G(s) H(s) to the given pole]}}$$

$$= \frac{|-12 \times (-4) \times 4 \times 60|}{|-2|} = \mathbf{5760}$$

115. For $K < 0$, the asymptotes have angles of 0°, 90°. 180° and 270°. In this case, the real axis portions between ∞ and 0, between –1 and –3 and between –4 and –∞ are on the root locus. There is only one break-away point located at $K = -2$.

117. Drawing root locus of the given open loop transfer function

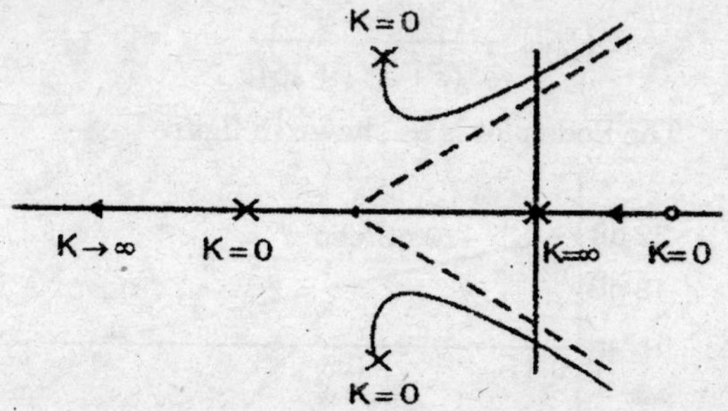

From the root locus, it can be readily seen that three asymptotes going towards infinity, this three zeros at ∞.

118. Given open-loop transfer function has one zero at $s = -2$ and four poles at $s = 0, -4, -2 + s$ and $-2-s$ respectively.

The point at which asymptates meet is called **centroid** and is given by

$$\sigma_A = \frac{\Sigma \text{real parts of pole} - \Sigma \text{real parts of zero}}{\text{number of poles} - \text{number of zero}}$$

$$= \frac{0-4-2-2+2}{4-1} = \frac{-6}{3} = -2$$

Hence co-ordinates are (– 2, 0)

119. $\sigma_A = \dfrac{\Sigma \text{ real part of poles} - \Sigma \text{ real parts of zero}}{\text{number of poles} - \text{number of zero}}$

$$= \frac{0-1-2-0}{3-1} = \mathbf{-1}$$

121. $G(s) = \dfrac{K}{s(s+1)(s+2)}$

$s^3 + 3s^2 + 2s + K = 0$

from Routh Hurwitz criterion, we have

s^3	1	2
s^2	3	K
s^1	$\dfrac{6-K}{6}$	6.K> 6
s^0	K	At the point of $j\omega$-crossing, 6–K = 0

The K = 6 point is given by,

and 3(ω)2 + K = 0

$\Rightarrow \quad \omega = \pm\sqrt{2}j$

Hence $\omega = \pm\sqrt{2}$ j. It intersects imaginary axis.

Since only plot (*a*) intersects imaginary axis, plot is the reasonable choice.

122. Root-locus is drawn below.

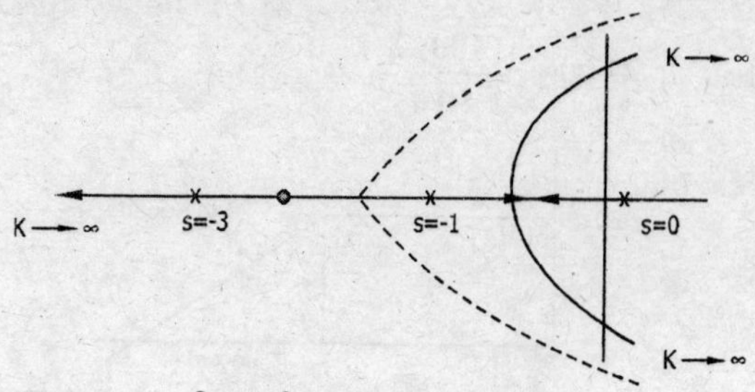

124. Given : $s^3 + 5s^2 + (K+6)s + K = 0$

Root locus-asymptotes meet at

$$s^3 + 5s^2 + 6s + K(s+1) = 0$$

$$\Rightarrow \quad 1 + \frac{K(s+1)}{s(s+2)(s+3)} = 0$$

$$\Rightarrow \quad \sigma_A = \frac{(0-2-3)+1}{3-1} = -2$$

126. $G(s) = \dfrac{K}{s^2}$

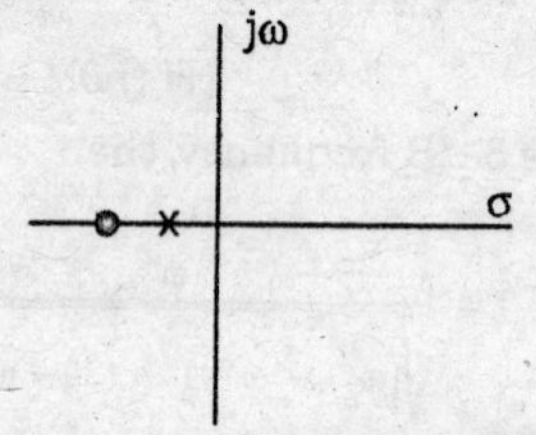

Angle of asympote, $\phi_A = \dfrac{\pm(2q+1)180}{2-0} = \pm 90$

COMPENSATOR

127. Lead compensator increases the gain-crossover frequency. It also increases the phase margin. The high frequency end of the log magnitude plot has been raised by a *d*B gain of 20 log $(\frac{1}{2})$.

128. Lead compensator speeds up the transient response and increases the margin of stability. It also helps to increase the systems error constant though to a limited extent.

129. $G(s) = \dfrac{1+6s}{1+2s}$

Phase shift, $\phi = \tan^{-1} 6\omega - \tan^{-1} 2\omega$

$$\frac{d\phi}{d\omega} = \frac{6}{1+36\omega^2} - \frac{2}{1+4\omega^2}$$

For maximum value of ϕ, $\dfrac{d\phi}{d\omega} = 0$

$\therefore \quad 3(1+4\omega^2) = 1 + 36\omega^2$

or $\quad \omega = 1/\sqrt{12}$

Thus, $\phi = \tan^{-1}\dfrac{36}{12} - \tan^{-1}\dfrac{1}{\sqrt{3}} = \mathbf{30°}$

130. The output leads the input by an angle

$$\phi = \tan^{-1} T$$

If α is > 1; ϕ is positive and if $0 < \alpha < 1$, then output will lag the input by ϕ. Since the given function is to represent a phase lag network, α should be between 0 and 1.

132. For phase-shift only $\left(\dfrac{1+0.15s}{1+0.005s}\right)$ is important.

It is identified that T = 0.05 and aT = 0.15

$\Rightarrow \quad a = 3$

Maximum phase shift is given by ϕ_m such that

$$\tan\phi_m = \frac{a-1}{2\sqrt{a}} = \frac{3-1}{2\sqrt{3}} = \frac{1}{\sqrt{3}}$$

$\therefore \quad \phi_m = \mathbf{30°}$

133. $$G(s) = \frac{10(1+0.04s)}{(1+0.01s)} = \frac{10(1+aTs)}{(1+Ts)}$$

Taking T = 0.01, "a" is seen to be equal to 4.

The maximum phase lead occurs at the frequency,

$$\omega_n = \frac{1}{\sqrt{aT}} = \frac{1}{\sqrt{4\times.01}} = \mathbf{50\ rad/sec}$$

134. System becomes fast and hence t_r is less.

135. Maximum phase lead is 55 degree at 6.32 rad/sec.

STATE VARIABLE

136. $\dot{x} = x_2$

$\dot{x}_2 = -2x_1 - 3x_2 + u$

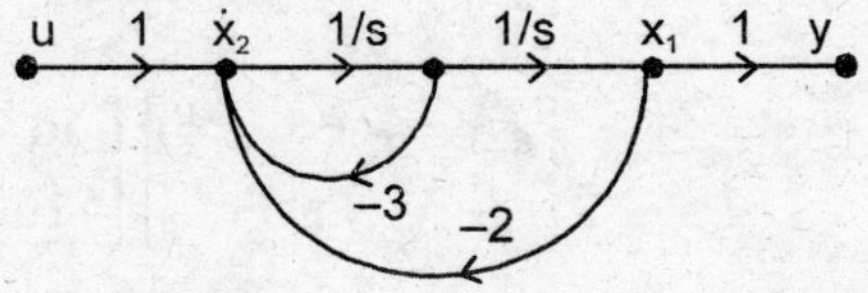

On simplifying

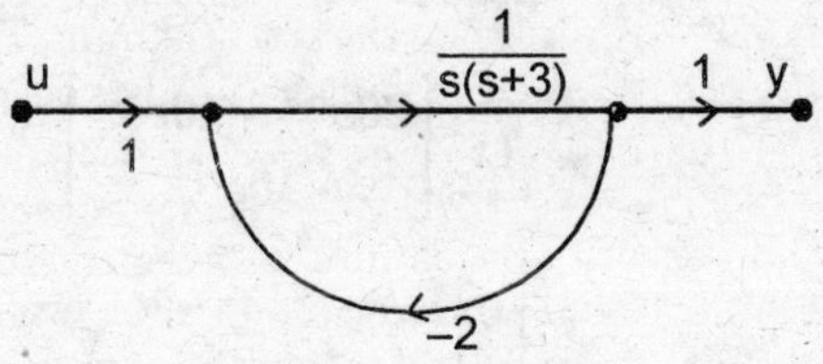

$$\frac{Y(s)}{U(s)} = \frac{\dfrac{1}{s(s+3)}}{1+\dfrac{2}{s(s+3)}} = \frac{1}{s^2+3s+2}$$

138. $\dot{x}_1 = -x_1 + u$

$\dot{x}_2 = x_1 - 2x_2 + u$

$$\therefore \quad A = \begin{bmatrix} -1 & 0 \\ 1 & -2 \end{bmatrix}; \quad B = \begin{bmatrix} 1 \\ 1 \end{bmatrix}$$

For the system to be state controllable,

$$B : AB = \begin{vmatrix} 1 & -1 \\ 1 & -1 \end{vmatrix} = 0$$

Therefore, the system is not state controllable.

Hence, all the responses containing statement 1 is incorrect.

139. $|sI - A| = 0$ should have roots in left half complex plane only.

$$|sI-A| \begin{vmatrix} s-x & 0 & 0 \\ 0 & s-y & 1 \\ 0 & -1 & (s+2) \end{vmatrix} = (s-x)[(s-y)$$

$(s+2)-(-1)] = (s-x)[s^2 + s(2-y) + 1 - 2y]$

For the roots to lie in left hand plane,

$x < 0$ and, $(2-y) > 0$ or $y < 2$

140. From given Block diagram

$Y(s) = X_1(s)$

$$\Rightarrow \quad Y = [1\ 0]\begin{bmatrix} x_1 \\ x_2 \end{bmatrix}$$

$\dot{x}_1 = x_2$

$\therefore \quad \dot{x}_2 = u - \alpha x_2 - \beta x_1$

$$\text{Thus,} \quad \begin{bmatrix} \dot{x}_1 \\ \dot{x}_2 \end{bmatrix} = \begin{bmatrix} 0 & 1 \\ -\beta & -\alpha \end{bmatrix}\begin{bmatrix} x_1 \\ x_2 \end{bmatrix} + \begin{bmatrix} 0 \\ 1 \end{bmatrix} u$$

141. Here, $A = \begin{bmatrix} 2 & 0 \\ 0 & 2 \end{bmatrix}$

The state transition matrix of the system.

$$\phi(t) = \pounds^{-1}(sI - A)^{-1}$$

$$[sI - A] = \begin{bmatrix} s & o \\ o & s \end{bmatrix} - \begin{bmatrix} 2 & 0 \\ 0 & 2 \end{bmatrix}$$

$$= \begin{bmatrix} (s-2) & 0 \\ 0 & (s-2) \end{bmatrix}$$

$$[sI - A]^{-1} = \frac{1}{(s-2)^2}\begin{bmatrix} (s-2) & 0 \\ 0 & (s-2) \end{bmatrix}$$

$$\pounds^{-1}(sI - A)^{-1} = \pounds^{-1}\begin{bmatrix} \dfrac{1}{(s-2)} & 0 \\ 0 & \dfrac{1}{(s-2)} \end{bmatrix}$$

$$= \begin{bmatrix} \dfrac{1}{(s-2)} & 0 \\ 0 & \dfrac{1}{(s-2)} \end{bmatrix}$$

$$= \begin{bmatrix} e^{2t} & 0 \\ 0 & e^{2t} \end{bmatrix}$$

142. Let $\quad x_1 = y$

and $\quad x_2 = \dot{x}_1 = \dot{y}$

$\therefore \quad \dot{x}_2 = \ddot{x}_1 = \ddot{y}$

$\ddot{y} + 2\dot{y} + 3y = 0$

$\dot{x}_2 + 2x_2 + 3x_1 = 0$

$\dot{x}_2 = -3x_1 - 2x_2$

$$\dot{x}_1 = x_2$$

$$\begin{bmatrix} \dot{x}_1 \\ x_2 \end{bmatrix} = \begin{bmatrix} 0 & 1 \\ -3 & -2 \end{bmatrix} \begin{bmatrix} x_1 \\ x_2 \end{bmatrix}$$

$$\therefore \quad A = \begin{bmatrix} 0 & 1 \\ -3 & -2 \end{bmatrix}$$

143. The minimum number of states necessary to describe a network is the number of independent energy storing elements in the network.

144. $y = f(x)$ is a linear system, then

$$f(x_1 + x_2) = f(x_1) + f(x_2)$$
$$f(Kx) = Kf(x)$$

145. $[A] = \begin{bmatrix} -1 & 0 \\ 0 & -2 \end{bmatrix}, [B] = \begin{bmatrix} 2 \\ 1 \end{bmatrix}$

Now, composite matrix, $Q_c = [B : AB] = \begin{bmatrix} 2 & -2 \\ 1 & -2 \end{bmatrix}$

then, $\det Q_c = \begin{vmatrix} 2 & -2 \\ 1 & -2 \end{vmatrix} \neq 0,$

and rank $= r = n = 2$

and system is **completely** controllable.

146. Since, $[sI - A]^{-1} = \phi(s)$

$$\therefore \quad \begin{bmatrix} s & 0 \\ 0 & s \end{bmatrix} - [A] = [\phi(s)]^{-1}$$

$$\Rightarrow \quad \begin{bmatrix} s & 0 \\ 0 & s \end{bmatrix} - [A] = \begin{bmatrix} s & -1 \\ 5 & s+6 \end{bmatrix}$$

$$\Rightarrow \quad [A] = \begin{bmatrix} 0 & 1 \\ -5 & -6 \end{bmatrix}$$

147. Transfer function G

$$G(s) = C(sI - A)^{-1} B$$

$$(sI - A) = \begin{bmatrix} s & 0 \\ 0 & s \end{bmatrix} - \begin{bmatrix} -4 & -1 \\ 3 & -1 \end{bmatrix} = \begin{bmatrix} s+4 & 1 \\ -3 & s+1 \end{bmatrix}$$

$$(sI - A)^{-1} = \frac{\begin{bmatrix} s+1 & 3 \\ -1 & s+4 \end{bmatrix}^T}{s^2 + 5s + 7} = \frac{\begin{bmatrix} s+1 & -1 \\ 3 & s+4 \end{bmatrix}}{s^2 + 5s + 7}$$

$$\text{Here, } G(s) = \frac{[1 \;\; 0]}{s^2 + 5s + 7} \begin{bmatrix} s+1 & -1 \\ +3 & s+4 \end{bmatrix} \begin{bmatrix} 1 \\ 1 \end{bmatrix} = \frac{s}{s^2 + 5s + 7}$$

148.

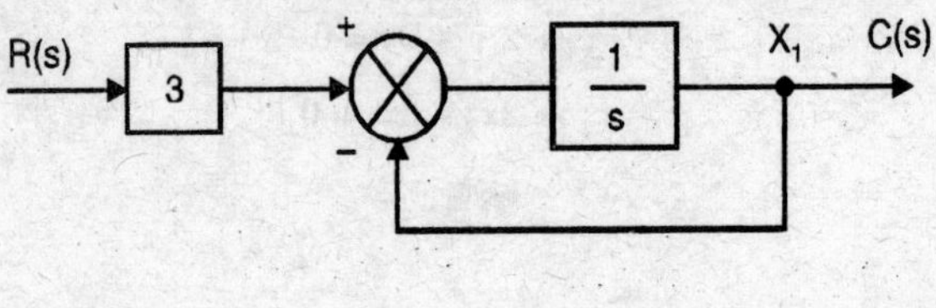

From the figure $\dot{X}_1 = -X_1 + 3r(t)$

The A matrix is [–1].

149. $\dot{X} = \begin{bmatrix} -3 & 1 \\ 0 & -2 \end{bmatrix} X = AX$

Its solution is,

$$X(t) = \left[£^{-1} [sI - A]^{-1} \right] X(0)$$

$$= £^{-1} \begin{bmatrix} s+3 & 1 \\ 0 & s+2 \end{bmatrix}^{-1} \begin{bmatrix} 10 \\ -10 \end{bmatrix}$$

$$= \left[£^{-1} \frac{\begin{bmatrix} s+2 & 1 \\ 0 & s+3 \end{bmatrix}}{(s+2)(s+3)} \right] X(0)$$

$$= \begin{bmatrix} £^{-1} \dfrac{1}{s+3} & £^{-1} \left[\dfrac{1}{s+2} \cdot \dfrac{1}{s+3} \right] \\ 0 & £^{-1} \left[\dfrac{1}{s+2} \right] \end{bmatrix} X(0)$$

$$= \begin{bmatrix} e^{-3t} & e^{-2t} - e^{-3t} \\ 0 & e^{-2t} \end{bmatrix} \begin{bmatrix} 10 \\ -10 \end{bmatrix}$$

Now, $X_{ss} = \underset{t \to \infty}{\text{Lt}} X(t)$

$$= \underset{t \to \infty}{\text{Lt}} \begin{bmatrix} 20e^{-3t} - 10e^{-2t} \\ -10e^{-2t} \end{bmatrix}$$

$$= \begin{bmatrix} 0 \\ 0 \end{bmatrix}$$

$$\dot{x}_1 = x_1 - x_2$$
$$\dot{x}_2 = x_2 + u$$
$$y = x_1 + x_2$$
$$\therefore \quad \dot{y} = \dot{x}_1 + x_2 = x_1 + u$$
$$\dot{y}|_{t=0} = 0 = 1 + 0 = 1$$

150. $s\,X(s) = -2\,X(s) + 2\,U(s)$

$$X(s)[s+2] = 2\,U(s)$$

and $Y(s) = 0.5\,X(s)$

which gives, $\dfrac{Y(s)}{U(s)} = \dfrac{1}{s+2}$

151. The linear time-invariant system :

$$\begin{bmatrix} \dot{X}_1 \\ \dot{X}_2 \end{bmatrix} = \begin{bmatrix} -1 & 0 \\ 1 & -2 \end{bmatrix} \begin{bmatrix} X_1 \\ X_2 \end{bmatrix} + \begin{bmatrix} 1 \\ 0 \end{bmatrix} u = [1 \;\; 2] \begin{bmatrix} X_1 \\ X_2 \end{bmatrix}$$

$$A = \begin{bmatrix} -1 & 0 \\ 1 & -2 \end{bmatrix}, B = \begin{bmatrix} 0 \\ 1 \end{bmatrix}, C = [1\ 2]$$

$$[B\ AB] = \begin{bmatrix} 0 & 0 \\ 1 & -2 \end{bmatrix} = |B\ AB| = 0.$$

Hence not completely controllable

$$\left[C^T\ A^TC^T\right] = \begin{bmatrix} 1 & 1 \\ 2 & -4 \end{bmatrix}$$

$$\left[C^T\ A^TC^T\right] \neq 0$$

Hence observable.

152. In matrix form

$$\begin{bmatrix} \dot{X}_1(t) \\ \dot{X}_2(t) \end{bmatrix} = \begin{bmatrix} -2 & 4 \\ 2 & -1 \end{bmatrix} \begin{bmatrix} X_1(t) \\ X_2(t) \end{bmatrix} + \begin{bmatrix} 0 \\ 1 \end{bmatrix} u(t)$$

Test for controllability

$$[B : AB] = \left[\begin{bmatrix} 0 \\ 1 \end{bmatrix} \begin{bmatrix} -2 & 4 \\ 2 & -1 \end{bmatrix} \begin{bmatrix} 0 \\ 1 \end{bmatrix}\right]$$

$$= \begin{bmatrix} 0 & 4 \\ 1 & -1 \end{bmatrix} \text{ Rank is 2, hence controllable}$$

For stability, $sI - A = 0$

$$\therefore \quad \begin{bmatrix} s+2 & 4 \\ 2 & s+1 \end{bmatrix} = 0$$

$$\Rightarrow \quad s^2 + 3s - 4 = 0$$

Routh criterion is,

s^2	1	−4
s	3	
s	−4	

Since sign changes, hence system is not stable.

153. $$A = \begin{bmatrix} -2 & 2 & -3 \\ 2 & 1 & -6 \\ -1 & -2 & 0 \end{bmatrix} X_1$$

$$= \begin{bmatrix} 1 \\ 2 \\ -1 \end{bmatrix}$$

From $(A - \lambda I) X_1 = 0$

$$\therefore \quad \begin{bmatrix} -2-\lambda & 2 & -3 \\ 2 & 1-\lambda & -6 \\ -1 & -2 & -\lambda \end{bmatrix} \begin{bmatrix} 1 \\ 2 \\ -1 \end{bmatrix} = 0$$

$$\Rightarrow \quad \begin{bmatrix} -2-\lambda+4+3 \\ 2+2\lambda+6 \\ -1-4+\lambda \end{bmatrix} = 0$$

$$\Rightarrow \quad \lambda = \mathbf{5}$$

155. $$\dot{X} = \begin{bmatrix} 2 & 3 \\ 0 & 5 \end{bmatrix} X + \begin{bmatrix} 1 \\ 0 \end{bmatrix} u$$

$$B = \begin{bmatrix} 1 \\ 0 \end{bmatrix}$$

$$A = \begin{bmatrix} 2 & 3 \\ 0 & 5 \end{bmatrix}$$

$$AB = \begin{bmatrix} 2 & 3 \\ 0 & 5 \end{bmatrix} \begin{bmatrix} 1 \\ 0 \end{bmatrix} = \begin{bmatrix} 2 \\ 0 \end{bmatrix}$$

$$\Rightarrow \quad [B : AB] = \begin{bmatrix} 1 & 2 \\ 0 & 0 \end{bmatrix}$$

This is not a 2 × 2 matrix, hence system is uncontrollable

Now $$[sI - A] = \begin{bmatrix} s & 0 \\ 0 & s \end{bmatrix} - \begin{bmatrix} 2 & 3 \\ 0 & 5 \end{bmatrix}$$

$$= \begin{bmatrix} s-2 & -3 \\ 0 & s-5 \end{bmatrix}$$

$$= (s-2)(s-5)$$

Two roots on positive half of the *y*-axis, hence the system is unstable.

156. $$\dot{X} = \begin{bmatrix} 2 & 0 \\ 0 & 4 \end{bmatrix} X + \begin{bmatrix} 1 \\ 1 \end{bmatrix} u$$

$$Y = [4\ 0]\, X$$

$$[sI - A] = \begin{bmatrix} s-2 & 0 \\ 0 & s-4 \end{bmatrix}$$

$$\phi(s) = [sI - A]^{-1} = \begin{bmatrix} \frac{1}{s-2} & 0 \\ 0 & \frac{1}{s-4} \end{bmatrix}$$

$$Y(s) = \phi(s)\, C(s) \cdot X(s)$$

$$\frac{Y(s)}{X(s)} = \begin{bmatrix} \frac{1}{s-2} & 0 \\ 0 & \frac{1}{s-4} \end{bmatrix} [4, 0]$$

$$= \frac{4}{s-2}$$

with input as $\delta(t)$, $L[\delta(t)] = 1$

$$Y(s) = \frac{4}{s-2} \cdot [1]$$

$$= \frac{4}{s-2}$$

$$Y(t) = 4e^{2t}$$

PRACTICE QUESTIONS

1. In the feedback system shown in the given figure, the noise component of output is given by (assume high loop gain at frequency of interest)

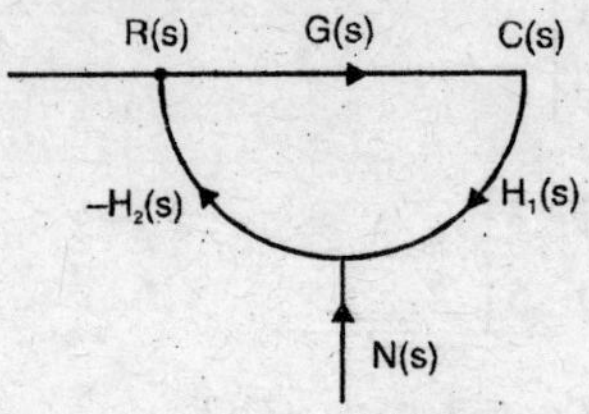

(*a*) $\frac{-N(s)}{H_1(s)}$ (*b*) $\frac{N(s)}{H_1(s)}$

(*c*) $\frac{N(s)}{H_1(s)H_2(s)}$ (*d*) $\frac{-N(s)}{H_1(s)H_2(s)}$

2. For the field-controlled dc servomotor shown in the figure, the transfer function θ (s) / E (s) contains

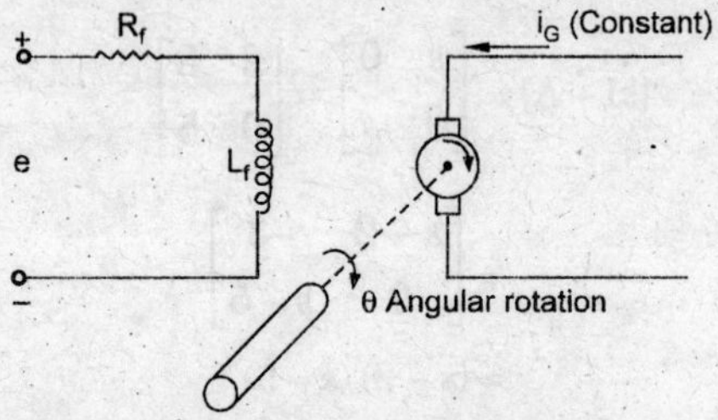

(*a*) two time constants, no integration

(*b*) two time constants, one integration

(*c*) one time constant, one integration

(*d*) one time constant, two integration

3. Consider a system shown in the given figure.

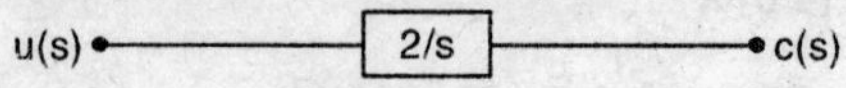

If the system is disturbed so that C(0) = 1, then c(t) for a unit step input will be

(*a*) 1 + t (*b*) 1 – t (*c*) 1 + 2t (*d*) 1 – 2t

4. The overshoot of the system $\frac{16K}{s\left(s^2+2s+16\right)}$ for a step input applied would be

(*a*) 60% (*b*) 40% (*c*) 20% (*d*) 10%

5. The position and acceleration error coefficients for the open-loop transfer function

$$G(s) = \frac{K}{s^2(s+10)(s+100)}$$

respectively are

(*a*) zero and infinity (*b*) infinity and zero

(*c*) $\frac{K}{100}$ and zero (*d*) infinity and $\frac{K}{1000}$

6. If the unit step response of a system is a unit impulse function, then transfer function of such a system will be

(*a*) 1 (*b*) $\frac{1}{s}$

(*c*) s (*d*) $\frac{1}{s^2}$

7. Consider a system with the transfer function

$$G(s) = \frac{s+6}{Ks^2+s+6}.$$

Its damping ratio will be 0.5 when the value of K is

(*a*) $\frac{2}{6}$ (*b*) 3

(*c*) $\frac{1}{6}$ (*d*) 6

8. For a second-order system with the closed-loop transfer function $T(s) = \frac{9}{s^2+4s+9}$, the settings time for 2-percent band in seconds, is

(*a*) 1.5 (*b*) 2.0

(*c*) 3.0 (*d*) 4.0

9. The transfer function of a phase lead controller is $\frac{1+3Ts}{1+Ts}$. The maximum value of phase provided by this controller is

(*a*) 90°

(*b*) 60°

(*c*) 45°

(*d*) 30°

10. Consider the following statements regarding the advantages of closed loop negative feedback control-systems over open-loop systems.

1. The overall reliability of the closed-loop system is more than that of open loop system.
2. The transient response in the closed loop system decays more quickly than in the open-loop system.
3. In the open-loop system, closing of the loop increases the overall gain of the system
4. In the closed-loop system, the effect of variation of component parameters on its performance is reduced.

Of these statements

(*a*) 1 and 3 are correct

(*b*) 1 and 2 are correct

(*c*) 2 and 4 are correct

(*d*) 3 and 4 are correct

11. Which one of the following statements is true for gain margin and phase margin of two closed-loop system having loop transfer fuction G(*s*) H (*s*) and exp (– *s*) G(*s*) H(*s*) ?

(*a*) Both gain and phase margins of the two systems will be identical

(*b*) Both gain and phase margins of G(*s*) H (*s*) will be more

(*c*) Gain margins of the two systems are the same but phase margin of G(*s*) H(*s*) will be more

(*d*) Phase margins of the two systems are the same but gain margin of G(*s*) H(*s*) will be less

12. The transfer function of system is

$$F(s) = \frac{10(1+0.2s)}{(2+0.5s)}.$$

The phase shift at $\omega = 0$ and $\omega = -\infty$ will be

(a) 90° and 0° (b) – 180° and 180°
(c) – 90° and 70° (d) none of these

13. Transfer function of transportation lag is e^{-sT}. If the lag is small as compared with the time constant of the system, it can be approximated by

(a) sT (b) $1 + sT$ (c) $1 - sT$ (d) $\frac{1}{1+sT}$

14. The gain margin (in dB) of a system having the loop transfer function

$$G(s)\,H(s) = \frac{\sqrt{2}}{s(s+1)} \text{ is}$$

(a) 0 (b) 3 (c) 6 (d) ∞

15. The transfer function of a simple RC network functioning as a controller is

$$G_c(s) = \frac{s+z_1}{s+p_1}$$

The condition for the RC network to act as a phase lead controller is

(a) $p_1 < z_1$ (b) $p_1 > 0$
(c) $p_1 = z_1$ (d) $p_1 > z_1$

16. A system described by the transfer function

$$H(s) = \frac{1}{s^3 + \alpha s^2 + Ks + 3} \text{ is stable.}$$

The constraints on α and K are

(a) $\alpha > 0$, $\alpha K < 3$ (b) $\alpha > 0$, $\alpha K > 3$
(c) $\alpha < 0$, $\alpha K > 0$ (d) $\alpha > 0$, $\alpha K < 0$

17. Non-minimum phase transfer function is defined as the transfer function, which has

(a) zeros in the right-half s-plane
(b) zeros only in the left-half s-plane
(c) poles in the right-half s-plane
(d) which has poles in the left half s-plane

18. A transfer function G (s) has the pole-zero plot as shown in the given figure. given that the steady state gain is 2, the transfer function G(s) will be given by

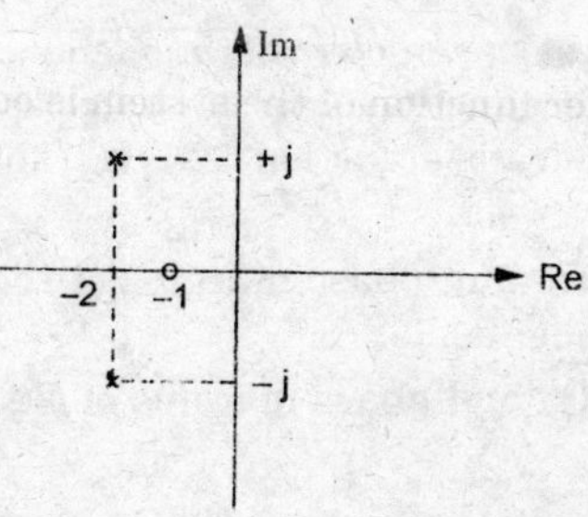

(a) $\frac{2(s+1)}{s^2+4s+5}$ (b) $\frac{5(s+1)}{s^2+4s+4}$

(c) $\frac{10(s+1)}{s^2+4s+5}$ (d) $\frac{10(s+1)}{(s+2)^2}$

19. The open-loop transfer function of a unity feedback control system is given by

$$G(s) = \frac{K}{s(s+1)}$$

If the gain is increased to infinity, then the damping ratio will tend to become

(a) $\frac{1}{\sqrt{2}}$ (b) 1
(c) 0 (d) ∞

20. A second order differential equation is given by

$$\frac{d^2x}{dt^2} + 5\frac{dx}{dt} + 7x = 7y$$

The frequency and damping ratio respectively are

(a) 1 rad/sec, 5 (b) 5 rad/sec, 7
(c) 1 rad/sec, $\sqrt{7}$ (d) $\sqrt{7}$ rad/sec, 0.94

21. If the open-loop transfer function is a ratio of a numerator polynomial of degree 'm' and a denominator polynomial of degree 'n', then the integer (n-m) represents the number of

(a) break-away points
(b) unstable poles
(c) seperate root loci
(d) asymtotes

22. Given the relationship between the input $u(t)$ and the output $y(t)$ to be

$$y(t) = \int_0^t (2 + t - \tau)e^{-3(t-\tau)}u(\tau)d\tau$$

The transfer function Y(s)/U(s) is

(a) $\frac{2e^{-2s}}{s+3}$ (b) $\frac{s+2}{(s+3)^2}$

(c) $\frac{2s+5}{s+3}$ (d) $\frac{2s+7}{(s+3)^2}$

23. The transfer function $d(s)$ to $y(s)$ is

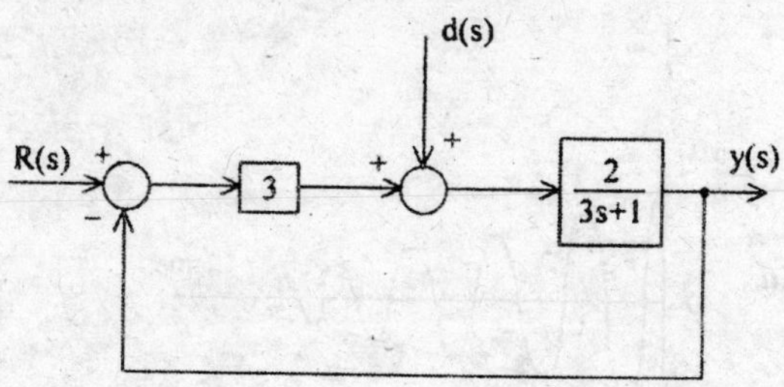

(a) $\frac{2}{3s+7}$ (b) $\frac{2}{3s+1}$

(c) $\frac{6}{3s+7}$ (d) $\frac{2}{3s+6}$

24. The addition of open loop zero pulls the root-loci towards

(a) the left and therefore system becomes more stable
(b) the right and therefore system becomes unstable
(c) imaginary axis and therefore system becomes marginally stable
(d) the left and therefore system becomes unstable

25. For the Nichols plot shown, the system is

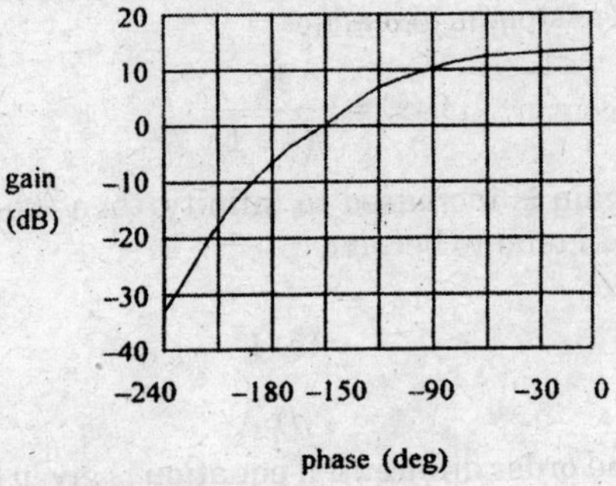

(*a*) unstable (*b*) stable

(*c*) overdamped (*d*) critically stable

26. Which of the following is the response of a spring-mass-damper with under-damping?

(*a*)

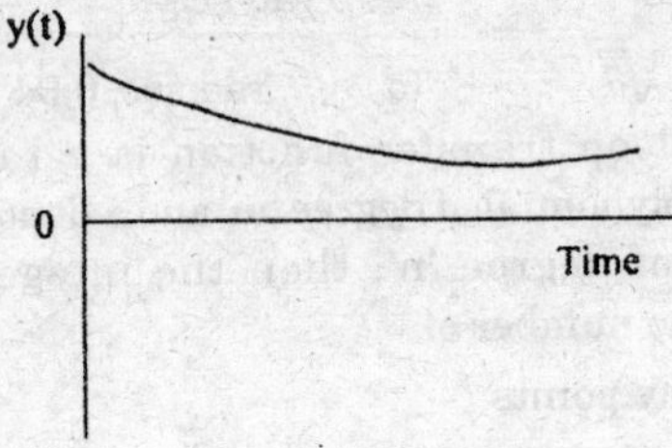

(*b*)

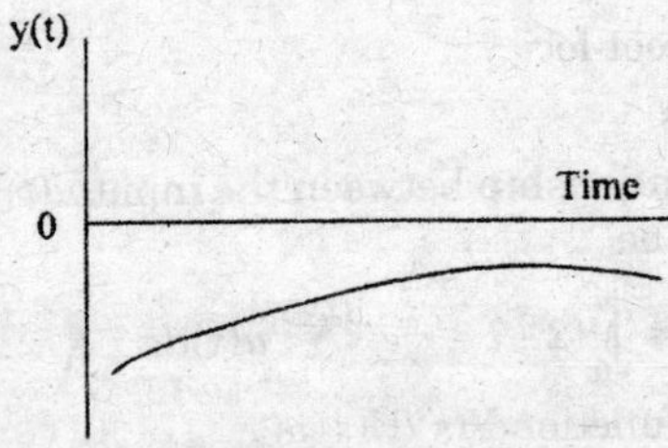

(*c*)

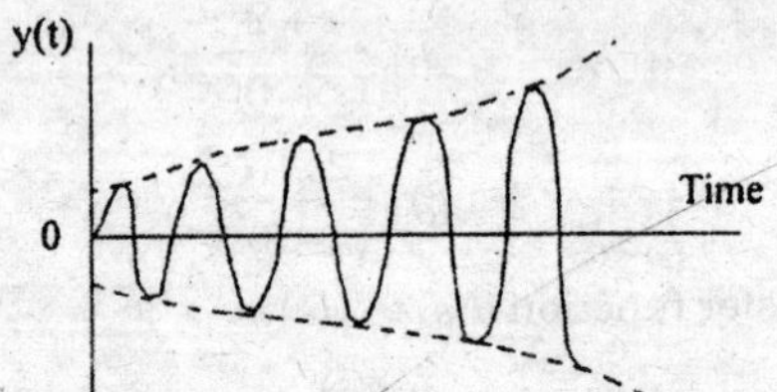

(*d*)

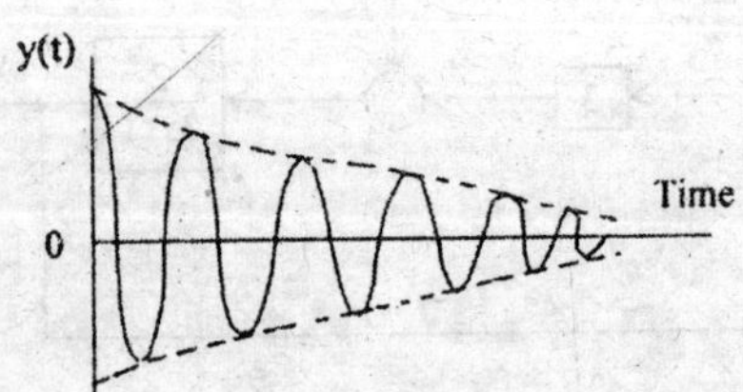

27. A linear time-invariant system initially at rest, when subjected to a unit-step input, gives a response $y|t| = te^{-t}, t > 0$. The transfer function of the system is

(*a*) $\frac{1}{(s+1)^2}$ (*b*) $\frac{1}{s(s+1)^2}$

(*c*) $\frac{s}{(s+1)^2}$ (*d*) $\frac{1}{s+1}$

28. For what positive value of K does the polynomial $s^4 + 8s^3 + 24s^2 + 32s + K$ have roots with zero real parts ?

(*a*) 10 (*b*) 20 (*c*) 40 (*d*) 80

29. The characteristic equation of a control system is given as

$$s^4 + 4s^3 + 4s^2 + 3s + K = 0.$$

What is the value of K for which this system is marginally stable ?

(*a*) $\frac{9}{16}$ (*b*) $\frac{19}{16}$

(*c*) $\frac{29}{16}$ (*d*) $\frac{39}{16}$

30. The transfer function of a controller is given as

$$K_p + K_d s + \frac{K_i}{s}$$

where K_p, K_d and K_i are constants.

What type of controller is this ?

(*a*) Proportional

(*b*) Proportional plus derivative

(*c*) Proportional plus integral

(*d*) Proportional plus integral plus derivative

31. The gain-phase plot of a linear control system is shown in the figure below:

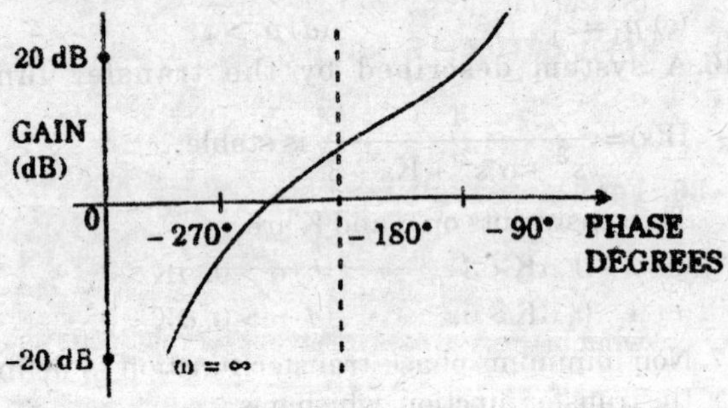

What are the gain-margin (GM) and the phase-margin(PM) of the system ?

(*a*) GM > 0 dB and PM > 0 degree

(*b*) GM > 0 dB and PM < 0 degree

(*c*) GM < 0 dB and PM > 0 degree

(*d*) GM < 0 dB and PM < 0 degree

32. The impulse response of linear time invariant system is given as

$$g(t) = e^{-t}, t > 0.$$

The transfer function of the system is equal to :

(*a*) $\frac{1}{s}$

(*b*) $\frac{1}{s(s+1)}$

(*c*) $\frac{1}{s+1}$

(*d*) $\frac{s}{s+1}$

33. The open-loop transfer function of a unity feedback control system is given by

$$G(s) = Ke^{-Ts}$$

where K and T are variables and are greater than zero. The stability of the closed-loop system depends on

(a) K only

(b) Both K and T

(c) T only

(d) Neither K nor T

34. Which one of the following polar plots corresponds to

$$G(j\omega) = \frac{1}{(j\omega)^2(1 + j\omega T)}?$$

(a) 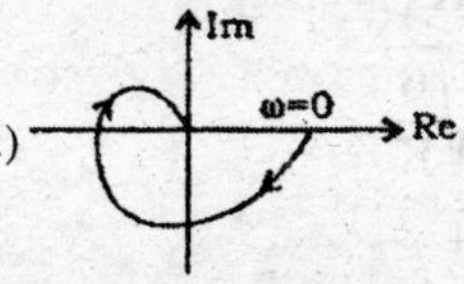

(b) 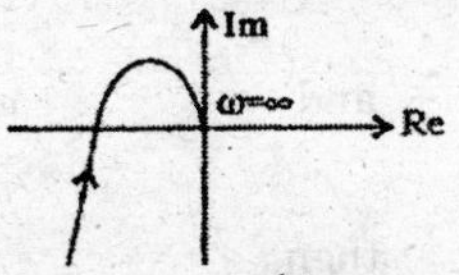

(c) 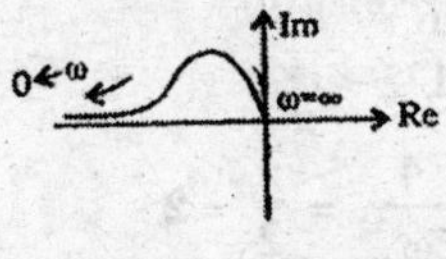

(d) 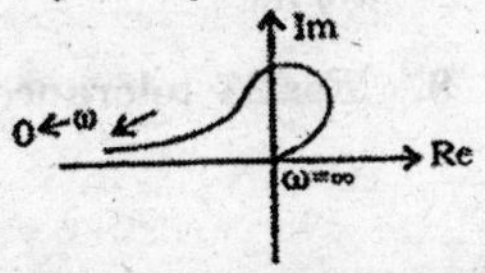

35. A phase lead compensating network consists of only capacitors and resistors. The locations of its pole and zero in s-plane are at P_c and Z_c respectively. Which of the following conditions must be satisfied?

(a) Both P_c and Z_c in LHS and $P_c < Z_c$

(b) Both P_c and Z_c in LHS and $P_c > Z_c$

(c) P_c is in LHS and Z_c can be in RHS

(d) Z_c is in LHS and P_c can be in RHS

36. For a given unity feedback system with

$$G(s) = \frac{k(s + 3)}{s(s + 1)(s + 2)(s + 5)},$$

what is the real axis intercept for root locus asymptotes?

(a) $\frac{2}{3}$ (b) $\frac{1}{4}$

(c) $-\frac{5}{3}$ (d) $-\frac{3}{2}$

37. The open loop transfer function of a unity negative feedback control system is given by

$$G(s) = \frac{k}{(s + 2)(s + 4)(s^2 + 6s + 25)}$$

What is the value of k which causes sustained oscillations in the closed loop system ?

(a) 590 (b) 666.25

(c) 990 (d) 1190

38. Which one of the following is an advantage of a PD controller in terms of damping (δ) and natural frequency (ω_n)?

(a) δ remains fixed but ω_n increases

(b) δ remains fixed but ω_n decrease

(c) ω_n remains fixed but δ increases

(d) ω_n remains fixed but δ decrease

39. An open loop system has a transfer function

$$\frac{1}{s^3 + 1.5s^2 + s - 1}.$$

It is converted into a closed loop system by providing a negative feedback having transfer function 20(s + 1). The open loop and closed loop system are, respectively

(a) stable and stable

(b) stable and unstable

(c) unstable and stable

(d) unstable and unstable

40. A closed loop system, employing lag-lead compensator $G_c(s)$ is shown in the figure given below.

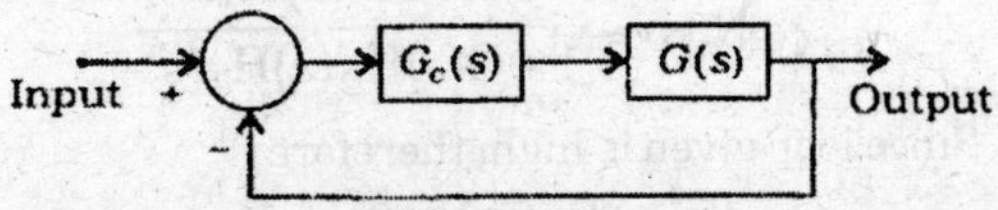

$$GC(s) = \left[\frac{1 + \tau_1 s}{1 + \left(\frac{\tau_1 s}{\beta}\right)}\right]\left[\frac{1 + \tau_2 s}{1 + \beta\tau_2 s}\right] \to \beta < 1$$

If G(s) has 3 poles in the left half of s-plane, then shape of the Bode plot for G(s) G_c(s) in the highest frequency range will be

(a) –20 dB/decade

(b) –40 dB/decade

(c) –60 dB/decade

(d) –80 dB/decade

41. The transfer function of a phase lead network, as shown in the figure given below is $\frac{K(1+0.3s)}{(1+0.17s)}$. The values of R_1 and R_2 are respectively

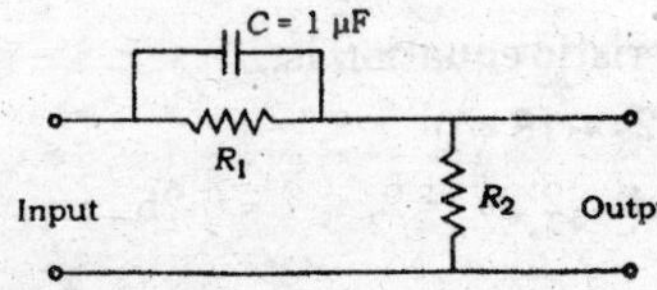

(a) 300 kΩ & 300 kΩ

(b) 300 kΩ & 400 kΩ

(c) 400 kΩ & 300 kΩ

(d) 400 kΩ & 400 kΩ

42. The Nyquist plot of

$$G(s).H(s) = \frac{10}{s^2(1+0.5s).(1+s)}$$

will start (ω = ∞) in the

(a) first quadrant and will terminate (ω = 0) in the second quadrant

(b) fourth quadrant and will terminate (ω = 0) in the second quadrant

(c) second quadrant and will terminate (ω = 0) in the third quadrant

(d) first quadrant and will terminate (ω = 0) in the fourth quadrant

ANSWERS

1. (a)	2. (b)	3. (c)	4. (b)	5. (d)	6. (c)	7. (c)	8. (b)	9. (d)	10. (c)
11. (c)	12. (d)	13. (c)	14. (d)	15. (d)	16. (b)	17. (a,c)	18. (a)	19. (c)	20. (d)
21. (d)	22. (d)	23. (a)	24. (a)	25. (b)	26. (d)	27. (c)	28. (d)	29. (d)	30. (d)
31. (b)	32. (c)	33. (b)	34. (c)	35. (b)	36. (c)	37. (b)	38. (a)	39. (c)	40. (c)
41. (b)	42. (d)								

EXPLANATIONS

1. Let noise component at the output be $N_1(s)$.

Then $N_1(s) = -G(s)\,H_2(s)\,[N(s) + N_1(s)\,H_1(s)]$

$$\therefore \quad N_1(s) = \frac{-G(s)H_2(s)N(s)}{1+G(s)H_2(s)H_1(s)}$$

Since loop given is high, therefore

$$G(s)\,H_2(s)\,H_1(s) >> 1$$

$$\therefore \quad N_1(s) = \frac{-G(s)H_2(s)}{G(s)H_2(s)H_1(s)}N(s) = -\frac{N(s)}{H_1(s)}$$

2. The transfer function is,

$$\frac{\theta(s)}{E(s)} = \frac{K}{s(1+T_1 s)(1+T_2 s)}$$

where, K, T_1 and T_2 are functions of field circuit parameters and mechanical parameters of the armature.

It contains two time constants and one integration (because of the presence of 1/*s*).

3. The system represents an integrator. Therefore if a step function is applied, we get ramp output. This will be enhanced by the initial value present *i.e.*, by I.

$$\therefore \quad c(t) = 1 + 2t$$

4. Characteristic equation is,

$$s^2 + 2s + 16 = 0$$

$$\therefore \quad \omega_n = 4, \quad 2\xi\omega_n = 2, \quad \xi = 0.25$$

$$M_p = e^{-\pi\xi/\sqrt{1-\xi^2}} = e^{-3.14\times .25/\sqrt{1-(.25)^2}} = \mathbf{40\%.}$$

5.
$$K_p = \lim_{s\to o} G(s) = \lim_{s\to o} \frac{K}{s^2(s+10)(s+100)} = \infty$$

$$K_a = \lim_{s\to o} s^2G(s) = \lim_{s\to o} \frac{K}{(s+10)(s+100)} = \frac{\mathbf{K}}{\mathbf{1000}}$$

6. Input $r(t) = u(t)$,

$$\therefore \quad R(s) = 1/s$$

Output $c(t) = \delta(t)$,

$$\therefore \quad C(s) = 1$$

$$\text{Transfer function} = \frac{C(s)}{R(s)} = \frac{1}{1/s} = s$$

7. Comparing G(*s*) with $G(s) = \dfrac{K}{s^2 + 2\xi\omega_s + \omega_n^2}$

we get, $\quad 2\xi\omega_n = \dfrac{1}{K}$

$$\Rightarrow \quad \omega_n = \frac{1}{K}$$

and $\quad \omega_n = \sqrt{\dfrac{6}{K}}$

then, $\quad K = \dfrac{1}{6}.$

8. For 2% tolerance band,

$$t_s = \frac{4}{\xi\omega_n} = \frac{4}{2} = \mathbf{2}$$

9. Given that transfer function of a phase lead controller.

$$F = \frac{1+3\,Ts}{1+Ts}$$

$$\phi = \tan^{-1} 3\,T\omega - \tan^{-1} T\omega$$

$$= \tan^{-1}\frac{2T\omega}{1+3T^2\omega^2}$$

For maximum value of ϕ,

$$\therefore \quad \frac{d\phi}{d\omega} = 1 - 3T^2\omega^2 = 0$$

$$\Rightarrow \quad 1 = 3\,T^2\omega^2$$

$$\Rightarrow \quad T\omega = \frac{1}{\sqrt{3}}$$

$$\therefore \quad \phi_{max} = \tan^{-1}\sqrt{3} - \tan^{-1}\frac{1}{\sqrt{3}}$$

$$\phi_{max} = \tan^{-1}\frac{1}{\sqrt{3}} = \mathbf{30°}$$

14.
$$G(j\omega)\,H(j\omega) = \frac{\sqrt{2}}{j\omega(j\omega+1)}$$

$$= \frac{\sqrt{2}}{\omega(j-\omega)}\cdot\frac{(j+\omega)}{(j+\omega)}$$

$$= \frac{-\sqrt{2}\omega}{\omega(1+\omega^2)} + \frac{-\sqrt{2}j}{\omega(1+\omega^2)}$$

For $\angle G(j\omega)\,H(j\omega) = -180°$, equating imaginary part of 0, we have

$$\frac{-\sqrt{2}j}{\omega(1+\omega^2)} = 0$$

$$\Rightarrow \quad \omega = \infty$$

$$\text{G.M.} = -20 \log \left| \frac{-\sqrt{2}}{\omega\sqrt{1+\omega^2}} \right|_{\omega=\infty}$$

$$= -20 \log 0$$

$$= \infty$$

15. $$G_C(s) = \frac{s+z_1}{s+p_1}$$

$$\angle G_C(s) = \tan^{-1}\frac{\omega}{z_1} - \tan^{-1}\frac{\omega}{p_1}$$

$$= \tan^{-1}\frac{\omega(p_1 - z_1)}{p_1 z_1 + \omega^2}$$

$\Rightarrow \quad p_1 > z_1$ for phase lead

16. Routh-Hurwitz Table

s^3	α	3
s^3	$\frac{(\alpha K - 3)}{\alpha}$	0
s^0	3	

i.e. $\alpha > 0, \; \alpha K > 3$

17. The transfer function can have zeros in the right half *s* -plane and poles in the right half *s*- plane.

18. $$G(s) = \frac{2(s+1)}{(s+2+j1)(s+2-j1)}$$

$$= \frac{2(s+1)}{(s+2)^2+1} = \frac{\mathbf{2(s+1)}}{\mathbf{s^2+4s+5}}$$

19. $$G(s) = \frac{K}{s(s+1)}$$

The characteristic equation corresponding to unity feedback control loop is

$$s(s+1) + K = 0$$

$$\Rightarrow \quad s^2 + s + K = 0$$

This may be written in the form

$$s^2 + 2\xi\omega_n s + \omega_n^2 = 0$$

where δ is the damping ratio

It is seen that $\omega_n = \sqrt{K} \; \xi = \frac{1}{2\sqrt{K}}$

i.e., if $K = \infty \quad \xi \to 0$

20. Characteristic equation is,

$$s^2 + 5s + 7 = 0$$

$$\therefore \quad \omega_n = \sqrt{7} \textbf{ rad/sec}$$

and $$\xi = \frac{5}{2\sqrt{7}} = \mathbf{0.94}$$

23.

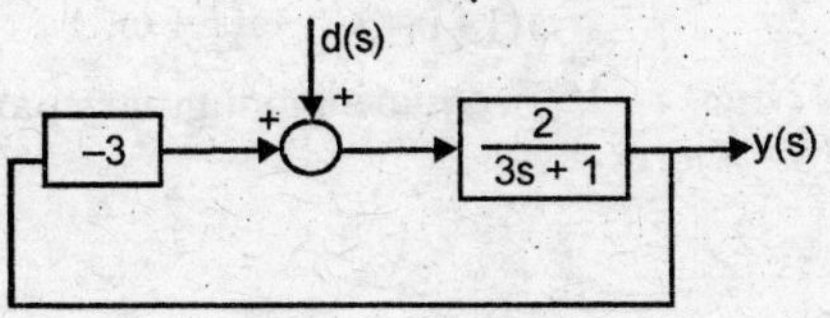

$$\left.\frac{y(s)}{d(s)}\right|_{R(s)=0} = \frac{\frac{2}{3s+1}}{1-\left(\frac{3}{2}\right)\frac{2}{3s+1}} = \frac{2}{3s+1+6} = \frac{2}{3s+7}$$

24. The addition of open loop zero pulls the root- loci towards the left and therefore system becomes more stable.

26. Spring-mass-damper is 2nd order system. 2nd order under damped circuit is

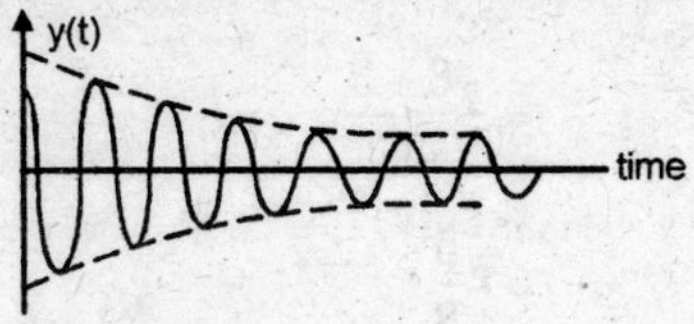

27. $$y|t| = te^{-t}$$

For $t > 0$, $\quad y(t) = te^{-t}$

By taking laplace transform

we get, $$Y(s) = \frac{1}{(s+1)^2}$$

$$R(s) = \frac{1}{s}$$

then, $$T(s) = \frac{Y(s)}{R(s)}$$

$$= \frac{s}{(s+1)^2}$$

28. Constructing Routh array

s^4	1	24	K
s^3	1	4	0
s^2	20	K	
s^1	80−K		

For roots with zero real parts, we have

$$80 - K = 0$$

$$\Rightarrow \quad K = 80$$

29.

s^4	1	4	K
s^3	4	3	0
s^2	$\frac{13}{4}$	K	
s^1	$\frac{39}{4} - 4K$	0	

For the system to be marginally stable,

$$\frac{39}{4} - 4K = 0$$

$$\Rightarrow \quad K = \frac{39}{16}$$

34. $$G(j\omega) = \frac{(-1 + j\omega T)}{\omega^2(1+(\omega T)^2)}$$

$$= \frac{-1}{\omega^2(1+(\omega T)^2)} + \frac{j\phi\, T}{\omega^2\left[1+(\omega T)^2\right]}$$

$$\angle G(j\omega) = -180° - \tan^{-1}\omega T$$

At $\omega = 0$,

$$\angle G(j\omega) = -180°$$

At $\omega = \infty$,

$$G(j\omega) = -270°$$

36. $$\sigma_A = \frac{\sum_{i=1}^{m} P_i - \sum_{j=1}^{n} Z_j}{m-n}$$

$$= \frac{-8+3}{3}$$

$$= -\frac{5}{3}$$

37. $1 + G(s) = 0$

$\Rightarrow \quad (s^2 + 6s + 25)(s^2 + 6s + 8) + k = 0$

$\Rightarrow \quad s^4 + 6s^3 + 25s^2 + 6s^3 + 36s^2 + 150s + 8s^2 + 48s + 200 + k = 0$

$\Rightarrow \quad s^4 + 12s^3 + 69s^2 + 198s + (200 + k) = 0$

Constructing Routh array, we have

s^4	1	69	$200+k$
s^3	12	198	0
s^2	52.50	$200+k$	0
s^1	$\frac{7995-12k}{52.50}$	0	
s^0	$200+k$		

For sustained oscillations,

$$7995 - 12k = 0$$

$\Rightarrow \quad k = 666.25$

39. $$G(s) = \frac{1}{s^2 + 1.5s^2 + s - 1}$$

Constructing Routh array, we have

s^3	1	1	0
s^2	1.5	−1	0
s^1	5/3	0	
s^0	−1		

Since, there is a sign change in the first column and one root in RH-s plane, therefore open loop system is unstable.

For closed loop system, the characteristic equations is,

$$1 + G(s)H(s) = 0$$

$$\therefore \quad 1 + \frac{20(s+1)}{s^3 + 1.5s^2 + s - 1} = 0$$

$\Rightarrow \quad s^3 + 1.5s^2 + 21s + 19 = 0$

s^3	1	21
s^2	1.5	19
s^1	8.33	0
s^0	19	

No change of sign in the first column, therefore system is stable.

40. Each pole will contribute a slope of 20 dB/decade; therefore in the highest frequency range, slope of Bode plot would be 60 dB/decade.

41. Transfer function,

$$T(s) = \frac{(R_1Cs + 1)\cdot\frac{R_2}{R_1 + R_2}}{\left(\frac{R_1R_2Cs}{R_1 + R_2} + 1\right)}$$

Comparing, we have

$$\frac{R_2}{R_1 + R_2} = K$$

$$R_1C = 0.3$$

$\Rightarrow \quad R_1 = 300\ k\Omega$

and $$\frac{R_1R_2C}{R_1 + R_2} = 0.17$$

$\Rightarrow \quad \frac{0.3R_2}{R_1 + R_2} = 0.17$

$\Rightarrow \quad R_2 \approx 400\ k\Omega$

42.

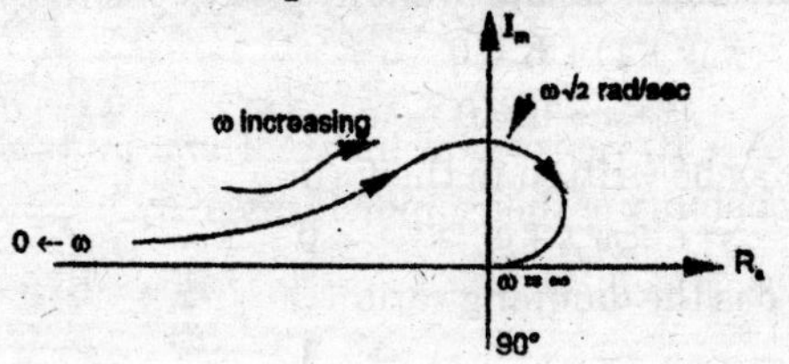

COMMUNICATIONS 7

7.1. PROBABILITY

Definition. If the number N tends to ∞, then

$$\text{Probability of event A, P (A)} = \lim_{N\to\infty} \frac{n_A}{N}$$

Every probability P (A) is a positive number and its value lies between 0 and 1.

$$\therefore \qquad 0 \le P(A)\, 1$$

Number of times event A occurs (n_A) out of the total number of trials N is given by

$$n_A \approx P(A)\,N$$

Classical Definition

Probability P(A) of event A is defined without experiment. It is given by

$$P(A) = \frac{n_A}{N}$$

where, N = number of possible outcomes

n_A = number of outcomes belonging to event A.

7.1.1. PROPERTIES OF PROBABILITY.

1. *Probability of "certain event" is 1.*

   If an event A contains all the possible outcomes of an experiment, then it is called *certain event*. It contains all the sample points in a sample space (S).

   $$\therefore \qquad P(A) = P(S) = 1$$

2. Probability of any event is always positive and less than or equal to 1, i.e.,

   $$\therefore \qquad 0 \le P(A) \le 1$$

3. If (A + B) represents union of two mutually exclusive events A and B which do not occur simultaneously, then probability of their union is given by

   $$P(A+B) = P(A) + P(B)$$

4. If $\overline{A}$ denotes the complement of event A, then

   $$P(\overline{A}) = 1 - P(A)$$

5. If events A and B are not mutually exclusive, then probability of union of A or B is given as

   $$P(A+B) = P(A) + P(B) - P(AB)$$

   Here P (AB) is called *joint probability* which is probability of simultaneous occurence of the evens A and B and is defined as

   $$P(AB) = \lim_{N\to\infty} \frac{n_{AB}}{N}$$

   For mutually exclusive events, joint probability P(AB) = 0

6. If $A_1, A_2, \ldots, A_N$ are mutually exclusive events such that

   $$A_1 + A_2 + \ldots A_N = S$$

   then $$P(A_1) + P(A_2) + \ldots + P(AN) = P(S) = 1$$

7.1.2. CONDITIONAL PROBABILITY.

P(B/A) = Probability of B given A.

P(A/B) = Probability of A given B.

Bayes' Rule

$$P(A/B) = \frac{P(A)P(B/A)}{P(B)}, \quad \text{and} \quad P(B/A) = \frac{P(B)P(A/B)}{P(A)}$$

7.1.3. STATISTICALLY INDEPENDENT EVENTS AND THEIR PROBABILITY.

Events A and B are said to be *independent events* if outcome of event B has nothing to do with the outcome of even A and vice versa. This can be expressed in terms of the conditional probability as follows :

Conditional probability of independent events

Event "B" is said to be independent of event "A", if

$$P(B/A) = P(B)$$

Similarly event "A" is said to be independent of event "B", if

$$P(A/B) = P(A)$$

Equations indicate that conditional probability is simply equal to elementary probability P(A) or P(B) if two events are statistically independent.

Joint probability of independent events

It is given by

$$P(AB) = P(A)\ P(B/A) \text{ .... Original expression}$$

Butas A and B are independent events, $P(B/A) = P(B)$

If A and B and independent events, then $P(AB) = P(A)P(B)$

Independent events A and B are also said to be *statistically independent events*, and equation tells that joint probability P(AB) of statistically independent events is equal to product of the probabilities of the individual events.

Difference between Independent and Mutually exclusive events

Equation shows that statistically independent events can occur simultaneously and probabiliy of mutually exclusive events is 0.

If A and B are mutually exclusive events, then $P(AB) = 0$

This is the difference between independent events and mutually exclusive events.

7.2. RANDOM VARIABLES

The term random variable is used to signify a rule by which a real number is assigned to each passible outcome of an experiment.

1. **Discrete Random Variable**

   A random variable can take only a finite number of values in any finite observation interval. Therefore, random variable is discrete if there exists a denumerable sequence of distinct number x_i such that

$$\sum_i P_x(x_i) = 1$$

2. **Continuous Random Variable**

   It is a random variable that can assume any value from a continuous interval. For a continuous random variable, meaningful quantity is not the probability that $x = x_i$, but the probability that

$$x < X \leq x + \Delta x$$

7.2.1. COMULATIVE DISTRIBUTION FUNCTION (CDF)

It is associated with a random variable. It is defined as probability that outcome of an experiment will be one of the outcomes for which $X \leq x$, where x is any given number. Hence, CDF $F_x(x)$ of a Random variable 'x' is the probability that 'X' takes a value less than or equal to x.

i.e., $$F_x(x) = P(X \leq x)$$

Properties of Distribution function

(*i*) Distribution function $F_x(x)$ is bounded between 0 and 1.

(*ii*) Distribution function $F_x(x)$ is a monotone non-decreasing function of x.

Properties of CDF.

(*i*) $F_x(x) \geq 0$

(*ii*) $F_x(\infty) = 1$

(*iii*) $F_x(-\infty) = 0$

(*iv*) $F_x(x)$ is a non-decreasing function, *i.e.,*

for $x_1 \leq x_2$, $$F_x(x_1) \leq F_x(x_2)$$

Proof:

$$F_x(x_2) = P(x \leq x_2)$$

$$F_x(x_2) = P[(x \leq x_1) \cup (x_1 < x \leq x_2)]$$

Since, $x \leq x_1$ and $x_1 < x \leq x_2$ are disjoint, therefore we have

$$F_x(x_2) = P(x \leq x_1) + P(x_1 < X \leq x_2)$$

$$F_x(x_2) = F_x(x_1) + P(x_1 < X \leq x_2)$$

7.2.2. PROBABILITY DENSITY FUNCTION (PDF).

It is defined in terms of CDF function F_x as

$$f_x(X) = \frac{d}{dx} F_x(X) \text{ (CDF)}$$

which is called PDF of random variable X.

Properties of PDF.

(*i*) $f_x(X) \geq 0$ for all x

This results comes from the fact that, F(x) increases monotonically.

(*ii*) $$\int_{-\infty}^{\infty} f(x)\,dx = 1$$

This result comes from the fact that,

$$\int_{-\infty}^{\infty} f(x)\,dx = F(\infty) - F(-\infty) = 1 - 0 = 1$$

(*iii*) CDF and PDF are related as, $F(x) = \int_{-\infty}^{x} f(x)\,dx$

7.3. RANDOM PROCESSES

7.3.1. STATISTICS OF RANDOM PROCESS.

Stationarity

1. **Strict-Sense stationary.**

A random process X (*t*) is called *strict-sense stationary* (SSS), if its statistics are invariant to a shift of origin. In other words, the process X (*t*) is SSS, if for any c

$$f_X(x_1, \ldots x_n; t_1 \ldots, t_n) = f_X(x_1, \ldots, x_n; t_1 + c, \ldots, t_n + c) \quad \ldots(7.1)$$

From equation (7.1) for any c $f_X(x_1; t_1) = f_X(x_1; t_1 + c)$

Hence first-order density of a stationary X (t) is independent of t

$$f_x(x_1; t) = f_x(x_1)$$

Similarly, for any c

$$f_x(x_1, x_2; t_1, t_2) = f_x(x_1, x_2; t_1 + c, t_2 + c)$$

Setting $c = -t_1$, we get

$$f_X(x_1, x_2; t_1, t_2) = f_X(x_1, x_2; t_2 - t_1)$$

which indicates that if X (t) is SSS, then joint density of the random variables X (t) and X ($t + \tau$) is independent of t and depends only on the time difference τ.

2. Wide-Sense stationary.

A random process X (t) is called *wide-sense stationary* (WSS) if its mean is constant

$$E[X(t)] = \mu x$$

and its autocorrelation depends only on the time difference τ.

$$E[X(t) X(t + \tau)] = R_{XX}(\tau) \quad \text{... (7.2)}$$

The autocovariance of a WSS process also depends only on the time difference τ.

$$C_{XX}(\tau) = R_{XX}(\tau) - \mu_x^2$$

Setting $\tau = 0$ in equation (7.2), we get

$$E[X^2(t)] = R_{XX}(0)$$

Thus average power of a WSS process is indpendent of t and equals $R_{XX}(0)$.

An SSS process is WSS but a WSS process is not necessarily SSS.

Two processes X (t) and Y (t) are called *jointly wide-sense stationary* (jointly WSS) if each is WSS and their cross-correlation depends only on the time difference τ

$$R_{XY}(t, t + \tau) = E[X(t) Y(t + \tau)] = R_{XY}(\tau) \quad \text{... (7.3)}$$

From this equation, cross-covariance of jointly WSS X (t) and Y (t) also depends only on the time difference τ.

$$C_{XY}(\tau) = R_{XY}(\tau) - \mu_X \mu_Y$$

Time averages and Ergodicity.

Time-averaged mean of a sample function $x(t)$ of a random process X (t) is defined as

$$\bar{x} = \langle x(t) \rangle = \lim_{T \to \infty} \frac{1}{T} \int_{-T/2}^{T/2} x(t)\, dt \quad \text{...(7.4)}$$

where symbol $\langle \cdot \rangle$ denotes *time-averaging*.

Similarly, time-averaged autocorrelation of the sample function $x(t)$ is defined as

$$\bar{R}_{XX}(\tau) = \langle x(t) x(t + \tau) \rangle = \lim_{T \to \infty} \frac{1}{T} \int_{-T/2}^{T/2} x(t) x(t + \tau)\, dt \quad \text{...(7.5)}$$

If X (t) is stationary, then by taking expected value on both sides of equations (7.4) and (7.5), we get

$$E[\bar{x}] = \lim_{T \to \infty} \frac{1}{T} \int_{-T/2}^{T/2} E[x(t)]\, dt = \mu_x$$

which indicates that expected value of the time-averaged mean is equal to ensemble mean, and

$$E[\bar{R}_{XX}(\tau)] = \lim_{T \to \infty} \frac{1}{T} \int_{-T/2}^{T/2} E[x(t) x(t + \tau)]\, dt = R_{XX}(\tau)$$

which also indicates that expected value of the time-averaged autocorrelation is equal to ensemble autocorrelation.

A random process X (t) is called *ergodic* if time averages are the same for all sample functions and equal to the corresponding ensemble averages. Thus, in an ergodic process, all its statistics can be obtained by observing a single sample function $x(t) = X(t, \lambda)$ (λ fixed) of the process.

A stationary process X (t) is called *ergodic in the mean* if

$$\bar{x} = \langle x(t) \rangle = E[X(t)] = \mu_X$$

Similarly, a stationary process X (t) is called *ergodic in the autocorrelation,* if

$$\bar{R}_{XX}(\tau) = \langle x(t)\, x(t+\tau) \rangle = E[X(t)\, X(t+\tau)] = R_{XX}(\tau)$$

Properties of ergodic random process.

1. $\bar{x} = \langle x(t) \rangle$ is equal to *dc* level of the signal.

2. $[\bar{x}]^2 = \langle x(t)^2 \rangle$ is equal to normalized power in the dc component.

3. $\bar{R}_{XX}(0) = \langle x^2(t) \rangle$ is equal to total average normalized power.

4. $\bar{\sigma}_X^2 = \langle x^2(t) \rangle - x\langle (t) \rangle^2$ is equal to average normalized power in time-varying or ac component of the signal.

5. $\bar{\sigma}_X$ is equal to rms value of the ac component of the signal.

7.3.2. CORRELATIONS AND POWER SPECTRAL DENSITIES.

1. Autocorrelation $R_{XX}(\tau)$

Autocorrelation of X (t) is, $R_{XX}(\tau) = E[X(t)\, X(t+\tau)]$

Properties of $R_{XX}(\tau)$.

(i) $R_{XX}(-\tau) = R_{XX}(\tau)$

(ii) $[R_{XX}(\tau)\, | \le R_{XX}(0)$

(iii) $R_{XX}(0) = E[X^2(t)]$

2. Cross-Correlation $R_{XY}(\tau)$

Cross-correlation of X (t) & Y (t) is $R_{XY}(\tau) = E[X(t)\, Y(t+\tau)]$

Properties of $R_{xy}(\tau)$.

(i) $R_{XY}(-\tau) = R_{YX}(\tau)$

(ii) $|R_{XY}(\tau)| \le \sqrt{R_{XX}(0)\, R_{YY}(0)}$

(iii) $|R_{XY}(\tau)| \le \frac{1}{2}[R_{XX}(0)) + R_{yy}(0)]$

3. Autocovariance $C_{XX}(\tau)$

Autocovariance of X (t) is,

$$C_{XX}(\tau) = E[\{X(t) - E[X(t)]\}\{X(t+\tau) - E[X(t+\tau)]\}]$$

$$= R_{XX}(\tau) - \mu_X^2$$

4. Cross-Covariance $C_{XY}(\tau)$

Cross-covariance of X (t) and Y (t) is

$$C_{XY}(\tau) = E[\{X(t) - E[X(t)]\}\{Y(t+\tau) - E[Y(t+\tau)]\}]$$

$$= R_{XY}(\tau) - \mu_X \mu_Y$$

Two processes X (t) and Y (t) are called *(mutually) orthogonal* if

$$R_{XY}(\tau) = 0$$

They are called *uncorrelated* if $C_{XY}(\tau) = 0$

5. Power spectrum density

If $R_{XX}(\tau)$ is autocorrelation of X (t), then *power spectral density* (or power spectrum) of X (t) is defined by the Fourier transform of $R_{XX}(\tau)$ as

$$S_{XX}(\omega) = \int_{-\infty}^{\infty} R_{XX}(\tau)\, e^{-j\omega\tau}\, d\tau$$

Thus $$R_{XX}(\tau) = \frac{1}{2\pi}\int_{-\infty}^{\infty} S_{XX}(\omega)\, e^{j\omega\tau}\, d\omega$$

Properties of $S_{XX}(\omega)$.

(*i*) $S_{XX}(\omega)$ is real and $S_{XX}(\omega) \leq 0$.

(*ii*) $S_{XX}(-\omega) = S_{XX}(\omega)$.

(*iii*) $\frac{1}{2\pi}\int_{-\infty}^{\infty} S_{XX}(\omega)\, d\omega = R_{XX}(0) = E[X^2(t)]$.

6. Cross spectral densities

Cross spectral densíties (or cross power spectra) $S_{XY}(\omega)$ and $S_{YX}(\omega)$ of $X(t)$ and $Y(t)$ are defined by

$$S_{XY}(\omega) = \int_{-\infty}^{\infty} R_{XY}(\tau)\, e^{-j\omega\tau}\, d\tau \qquad ...(7.6)$$

and

$$S_{YX}(\omega) = \int_{-\infty}^{\infty} R_{YX}(\tau)\, e^{-j\omega\tau}\, d\tau \qquad ...(7.7)$$

Thus, cross-correlations and cross spectral densities form Fourier transform pairs. Therefore

$$R_{XY}(\tau) = \frac{1}{2\pi}\int_{-\infty}^{\infty} S_{XY}(\omega)\, e^{j\omega\tau}\, d\omega$$

$$R_{YX}(\tau) = \frac{1}{2\pi}\int_{-\infty}^{\infty} S_{YX}(\omega)\, e^{j\omega\tau}\, d\omega$$

Using the relation $R_{XY}(\tau) = R_{YX}(-\tau)$

in equations (7.6) and (7.7), we get

$$S_{XY}(\omega) = S_{YX}(-\omega) = S^*_{YX}(\omega)$$

7.3.3. TRANSMISSION OF RANDOM PROCESSES THROUGH LINEAR SYSTEMS.

1. System response

A linear time-invariant (LTI) system is represented by

$$Y(t) = L[X(t)]$$

where $Y(t)$ is output random process of an LTI system, represented by a linear operator L with input random process $X(t)$.

Let $h(t)$ be the impulse response of an LTI system Fig. 7.1. Then

$$Y(t) = h(t) * X(t) = \int_{-\infty}^{\infty} h(\alpha)\, X(t-\alpha)\, d\alpha$$

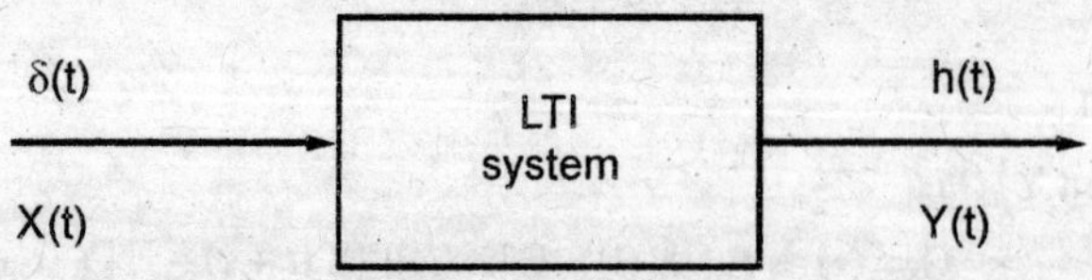

Fig. 7.1. LTI system

2. Mean and Autocorrelation of output

$$\mu_Y(t) = E[Y(t)] = E\left[\int_{-\infty}^{\infty} h(\alpha)\, X(t-\alpha)\, d\alpha\right]$$

$$= \int_{-\infty}^{\infty} h(\alpha)\, E[X(t-\alpha)]\, d\alpha$$

$$= \int_{-\infty}^{\infty} h(\alpha)\, \mu_x(t-\alpha)\, d\alpha$$

$$= h(t) * \mu_x(t) \qquad ...(7.8)$$

where * denotes convolution.

$$R_{YY}(t_1, t_2) = E[Y(t_1)Y(t_2)]$$

$$= £\left[\int_{-\infty}^{\infty}\int_{-\infty}^{\infty} h(\alpha)X(t_1-\alpha)h(\beta)X(t_2-\beta)\,d\alpha\,d\beta\right]$$

$$= \int_{-\infty}^{\infty}\int_{-\infty}^{\infty} h(\alpha)h(\beta)E[X(t_1-\alpha)X(t_2-\beta)]\,d\alpha\,d\beta$$

$$= \int_{-\infty}^{\infty}\int_{-\infty}^{\infty} h(\alpha)h(\beta)R_{XX}(t_1-\alpha, t_2-\beta)\,d\alpha\,d\beta$$

If input X (t) is WSS, then from equation (7.8) we have

$$E[Y(t)] = \int_{-\infty}^{\infty} h(\alpha)\mu_X\,d\alpha = \mu_X\int_{-\infty}^{\infty} h(\alpha)\,d\alpha = \mu_X H(0)$$

where H (0) is frequency response of the *linear system at* $\omega = 0$. Thus, *mean of the output is a constant.*

The autocorrelation of the output given in equation (7.8) becomes

$$R_{YY}(t_1, t_2) = \int_{-\infty}^{\infty}\int_{-\infty}^{\infty} h(\alpha)h(\beta)R_{XX}(t_2-t_1+\alpha-\beta)\,d\alpha\,d\beta$$

which indicates that Ryy (t_1, t_2) is a function of the time difference $\tau = t_2 - t_1$.

$$\therefore \quad R_{YY}(\tau) = \int_{-\infty}^{\infty}\int_{-\infty}^{\infty} h(\alpha)h(\beta)R_{XX}(\tau+\alpha-\beta)\,d\alpha\,d\beta \quad ...(7.9)$$

Thus, it can be concluded that if input X (t) is WSS, then output Y (t) is also WSS.

3. **Power spectral density of output**

Taking Fourier transform of both sides of equation (7.9), power spectral density of output is given as

$$S_{YY}(\omega) = \int_{-\infty}^{\infty} R_{YY}(\tau)e^{-j\omega\tau}\,d\tau$$

$$= \int_{-\infty}^{\infty}\int_{-\infty}^{\infty}\int_{-\infty}^{\infty} h(\alpha)h(\beta)R_{xx}(\tau+\alpha-\beta)e^{-j\omega\tau}\,d\tau\,d\alpha\,d\beta$$

$$= |H(\omega)|^2 S_{XX}(\omega)$$

Thus, power spectral density of the output is product of power spectral density of the input and magnitude squared of the frequency response of the system.

Autocorrelation of the output $R_{YY}(\tau)$, is expressed as

$$R_{YY}(\tau) = \frac{1}{2\pi}\int_{-\infty}^{\infty} S_{YY}(\omega)e^{j\omega\tau}\,d\omega$$

$$= \frac{1}{2\pi}\int_{-\infty}^{\infty} |H(\omega)|^2 S_{XX}(\omega)e^{j\omega\tau}\,d\omega$$

Using $E[X^2(t)] = R_{XX}(0)$, average power in the output Y (t) is given by

$$E[Y^2(t)] = R_{YY}(0) = \frac{1}{2\pi}\int_{-\infty}^{\infty} |H(\omega)|^2 S_{XX}(\omega)\,d\omega$$

7.3.4. SOME IMPORTANT RANDOM PROCESSES.

1. **White noise**

A random porcess X (t) is called *white noise*, [Fig. 7.2 (*a*)] if

$$S_{XX}(\omega) = \frac{\pi}{2}$$

Taking inverse Fourier transform, we have

$$R_{XX}(\tau) = \frac{\pi}{2}\delta(\tau)$$

which is shown in Fig. 7.2 (*b*). The mean of white noise is zero.

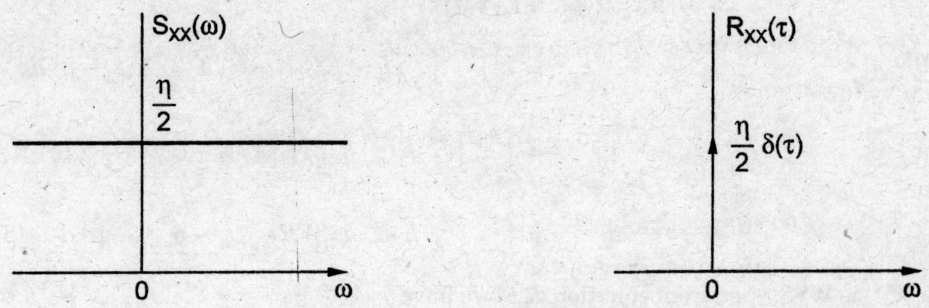

(*a*) (*b*)

Fig. 7.2. White noise

2. Band-limited White noise

A random process X (*t*) is called *band-limited white noise* if

$$S_{XX}(\omega) = \begin{cases} \dfrac{\eta}{2} & |\omega| \le \omega_B \\ 0 & |\omega| > \omega_B \end{cases}$$

Then
$$R_{XX}(\tau) = \frac{1}{2\pi}\int_{-\omega_B}^{\omega_B} \frac{\eta}{2} e^{j\omega\tau}\, d\omega = \frac{\eta\omega_B}{2\pi}\,\frac{\sin \omega_B T}{\omega_B T}$$

And $S_{XX}(\omega)$ and $R_{XX}(\tau)$ of band-limited white noise are shown in Fig. 7.3

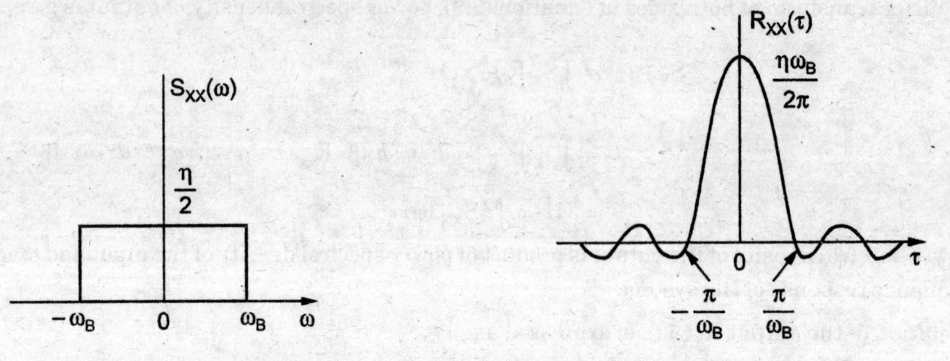

(*a*) (*b*)

Fig. 7.3. Band-limited white noise

3. Narrowband random process

Let X (*t*) is a WSS process with zero and its power spectral density $S_{XX}(\omega)$ is non-zero only in some narrow frequency band of width 2W which is very small compared to a centre frequency ω_c, as shown in Fig. 7.4. Then process X (*t*) is called *narrowband random porcess*.

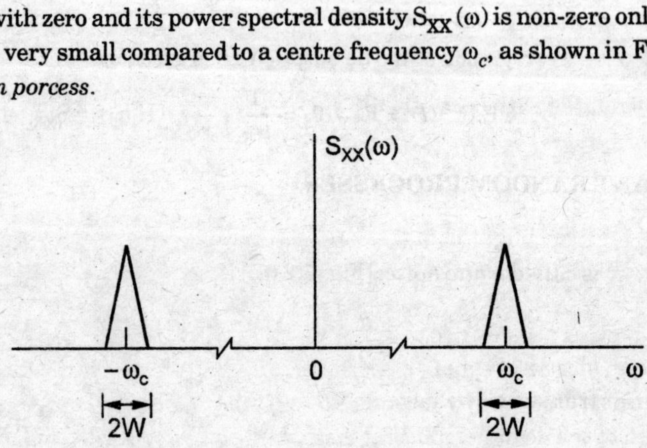

Fig. 7.4. Narrowband random process

Narrowband noise X (*t*) is expressed as,

$$X(t) = V(t)\cos[\omega_c t + \phi(t)]$$

where V(*t*) and *f*(*t*) are random processes which are called *envelope function* and *phase function*, respectively.

Equation 7.9 can be rewritten as,

$$X(t) = V(t)\cos\phi(t)\cos\omega_c t - V(t)\sin\phi(t)\sin\omega_c t$$
$$= X_c(t)\cos\omega_c t - X_s(t)\sin\omega_c t$$

where $X_c(t) = V(t)\cos\phi(t)$ (in-phase component)

$X_s(t) = V(t)\sin\phi(t)$ (quadrature component)

$$V(t) = \sqrt{X_c^2(t) + X_s^2(t)}$$

$$\phi(t) = \tan^{-1}\frac{X_s(t)}{X_c(t)}$$

This equation is called *quadrature representation* of X (*t*).

If X (*t*), its in-phase component are given, then $X_c(t)$ and quadrature component $X_c(t)$ can be obtained by using the arrangement shown in Fig. 7.5.

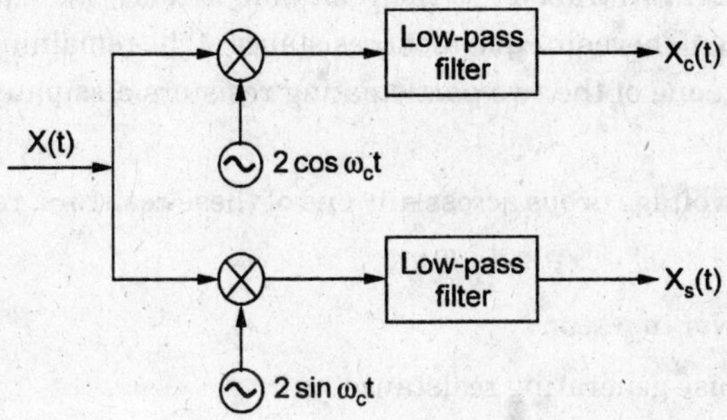

Fig. 7.5

Properties of $X_c(t)$ and $X_s(t)$.

(*i*) $X_c(t)$ and $X_s(t)$ have identical power spectral densities related to that of X (*t*) by

$$S_{X_c}(\omega) = S_{X_s}(\omega)$$
$$= \begin{cases} S_{XX}(\omega - \omega_c) + S_{XX}(\omega + \omega_c); & |\omega| \le W \\ 0 & ;\text{otherwise} \end{cases}$$

(*ii*) $X_c(t)$ and $X_s(t)$ have the same means and variances as X (*t*).

$$\mu_{X_c} = \mu_{X_s} = \mu_X = 0$$

$$\sigma^2_{X_c} = \sigma^2_{X_s} = \sigma^2_X$$

(*iii*) $X_c(t)$ and $X_s(t)$ are uncorrelated with each other.

$$E[X_c(t)X_s(t)] = 0$$

(*iv*) If X (*t*) is gaussian, then $X_c(t)$ & $X_s(t)$ are also gaussian.

(*v*) If X (*t*) is gaussian, then for fixed but arbitrary *t*, V (*t*) is a random variable with Rayleigh distribution and $\phi(t)$ is a random variable uniformly distributed over [0, 2π].

7.4. ELECTRONIC NOISE

It is a random fluctuation in an electrical signal, a characteristic of all electronic circuits. Noise generated by electronic devices varies greatly, as it can be produced by several different effects. Thermal and shot noise are unavoidable and due to laws of nature, rather than to the device exhibiting them, while other types depend mostly on manufacturing quality and semiconductor defects.

TYPES OF NOISE.

1. Thermal Noise

Johnson-Nyquist noise (sometimes *thermal, Johnson or Nyquist noise*) is unavoidable, and generated by the random thermal motion of charge carriers (usually electrons), inside an electrical conductor, which happens regardless of any applied voltage.

Thermal noise is approximately white, meaning that its power spectral density is nearly equal throughout the frequency spectrum. Amplitude of the signal has very nearly a Gaussian probability density function. A communication system affected by thermal noise is often modelled as an additive white Gaussian noise (AWGN) channel.

Root mean square (RMS) voltage due to thermal noise v_n generated in a resistance R (ohms) over bandwidth Δf (hertz) is given by

$$v_n = \sqrt{4k_B TR\Delta_f}$$

where k_B is Boltzmann's constant (joules per kelvin) and T is the resistor's absolute temperature (kelvin).

Resistor in a short circuit dissipates a noise power

$$P = \overline{v_n}^2/R = 4k_B \Delta_f$$

Noise generated at the resistor can transfer to the remaining circuit; the maximum noise power transfer happens with impedance matching when Thevenin equivalent resistance of the remaining circuit is equal to the noise generating resistance. In this case, each one of the two participating resistors dissipates noise in both itself and in the other resistor.

Since only half of the source voltage drops across any one of these resistors, resulting noise power is given by

$$P = k_B T\Delta_f$$

where, P = thermal noise power in watts.

This is independent of the noise generating resistance.

Noise current (i_n) *:*

$$i_n = \sqrt{\frac{4k_B T\Delta f}{R}}$$

2. Shot noise

It in electronic device consists of unavoidable random statistical fluctuations of the electric current in an electrical conductor. Random fluctuations are inherent when current flows, as the current is a flow of discrete charges (electrons).

3. Mode partition noise

In an optical communication link, phase jitter of the signal is caused by the combined effects of mode hopping in the optical source and intramodal distortion in the fiber.

Mode hopping causes random wavelength changes which in turn affect group velocity i.e., progagation time. Over a long length of fiber, cumulative effect is to create jitter i.e. mode partition noise. The variation of group velocity creates mode partition noise.

4. Flicker noise or Low frequency noise

It is also called *1/f noise*, is a signal or process with a frequency spectrum that falls of steadily into the higher frequencies, with a pink spectrum. It occurs in almost all electronic devices, and results from a variety of effects, though related to a direct current.

5. High Frequency Noise

If time taken by an electron to travel from emitter to collec-tor of a transistor becomes comparable to the period of the signal which is being amplified, then transit time effect takes place. This effect is observed at very high frequency.

Once this noise appears, it goes on increasing with frequency at a rate of 6 dB per octane.

7.5. ANALOG COMMUNICATION

In continuous (CW) wave modulation, a sinusoidal signal $A_c \cos(\omega_c t + \phi)$ is used to represent a carrier signal and a modulated carrier, therefore can be expressed as

$$x_c(t) = A(t) \cos[\omega_c t + \phi(t)]$$

Here ω_c is carrier frequency and A (*t*), and $\phi(t)$ are called instantaneous amplitude and phase angle of the carrier.

7.5.1. AMPLITUDE MODULATION (AM).

In AM, instantaneous amplitude *i.e.*, A(*t*) is linearly related to the message signal *m* (*t*) and, the modulated carrier is represented as

$$x_c(t) = A(t).\cos \omega_c t$$

There are many types of AM depending upon the nature of spectral relationship between A (*t*) and *m* (*t*)

7.5.2. DOUBLE-SIDEBAND MODULATION (DSB).

In DSB modulation, instantaneous amplitude, A(t) is directly proportional to the message signal *m* (*t*).

$$x_{DSB}(t) = m(t).\cos \omega_c t$$

Taking fourier transform both sides, we have

$$f[x_{DSB}(t)] = £[m(t).\cos \omega_c t]$$

$$= £\left[\frac{1}{2} m(t)\cdot\left(e^{j\omega_o t} + e^{-j\omega_o t}\right)\right]$$

$$= £\left[\frac{1}{2} m(t)\cdot e^{j\omega_o t} + \frac{1}{2} m(t)\cdot e^{-j\omega_o t}\right]$$

Using frequency-shifting theorem, we get

$$X_{DSB}(\omega) = \frac{1}{2} M(\omega - \omega_c) + \frac{1}{2} M(\omega + \omega_c)$$

Generation of DSB signals.

The DSB modulation process is shown in Fig. 7.6.

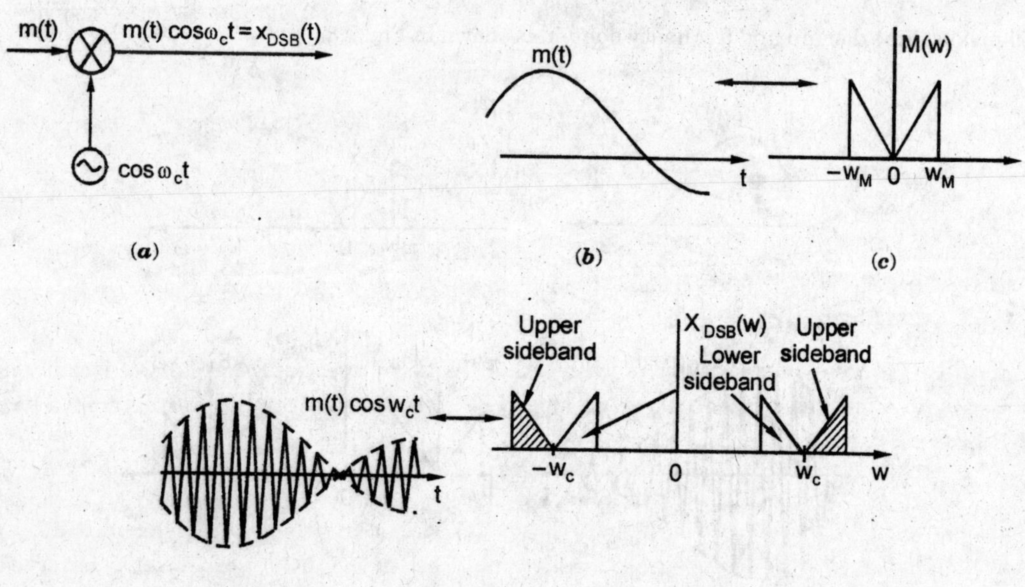

Fig. 7.6

The time domain waveforms are shown in Fig. 7.6 (*b*) and Fig. 7.6 (*c*) and their corresponding frequency-domain representation is shown in Fig. 7.6 (*d*) and Fig 7.6 (*e*). The spectral range covered by the message signal is called **baseband,** and therefore message signal is called *baseband signal*.

As seen from the spectrum, the transmission bandwidth required for DSB modulation is 2ω . Since in this type of modulation, there is no identifiable carrier contents, therefore, it is also called *Double-sideband Suppressed Carrier (DSB-SC) modulation.*

Also, carrier frequency ω_c is for greater than ω_M, *i.e.,* $\omega_c >> \omega_M$.

Demodulation of DSB Signals.

The baseband signal *m* (*t*) can be recovered from a, DSB-SC wave by first multiplying it with a locally generated sinusoidal wave and then low-pass filtering the product. Here, it is being assumed that local signal is exactly in the phase and frequency synchronism with the incoming carrier. This type of modulation is called *synchronous detection* or *coherent detection,* as shown in Fig. 7.7.

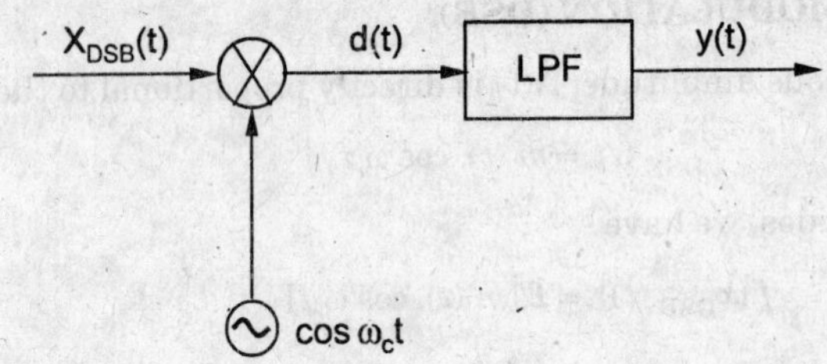

Fig. 7.7

7.5.3. ORDINARY AMPLITUDE MODULATION.

In this modulation, modulated signal is generated by adding a large carrier signal to the DSB signal, and expressed as

$$x_{AM}(t) = m(t) \cdot \cos \omega_c t + A \cos \omega_c t$$
$$= [A + m(t)] \cdot \cos \omega_c t$$

Taking fourier transform of both sides, we have

$$X_{AM}(\omega) = £[m(t) \cdot \cos \omega_c t] + £[A \cos \omega_c t]$$

$$= (\omega - \omega_c) + \frac{1}{2} M(\omega + \omega_c) + \pi A \left[\delta(\omega - \omega_c) + \delta(\omega + \omega_c) \right]$$

AM signal in both time domain and frequency domain is shown in Fig. 7.8.

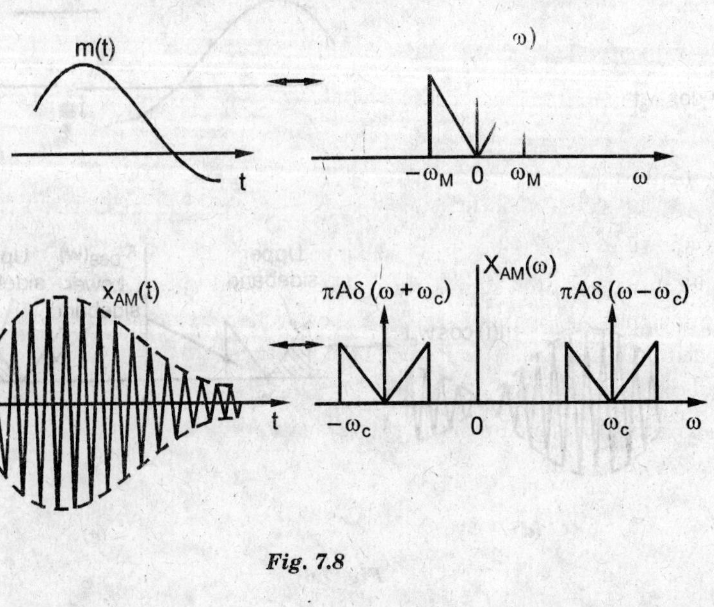

Fig. 7.8

7.5.4 DEMODULATION OF AM SIGNALS.

If amplitude of carrier wave is large enough, then envelope of the modulated waveform is directly proportional to $m(t)$ and in that case demodulation depends only upon detection of the envelope of a modulated carrier and independent of the phase or frequency of the carrier.

The condition for demodulation of AM by an envelope detector is

$$A + m(t) > 0 \quad \text{for all } t$$

or

$$A \geq |\min\{m(t)\}|$$

where $\min\{m(t)\}$ is minimum value of $m(t)$.

If A is not large enough, then envelope of $x_{AM}(t)$ is not always proportional to $m(t)$, as shown in Fig. 7.9.

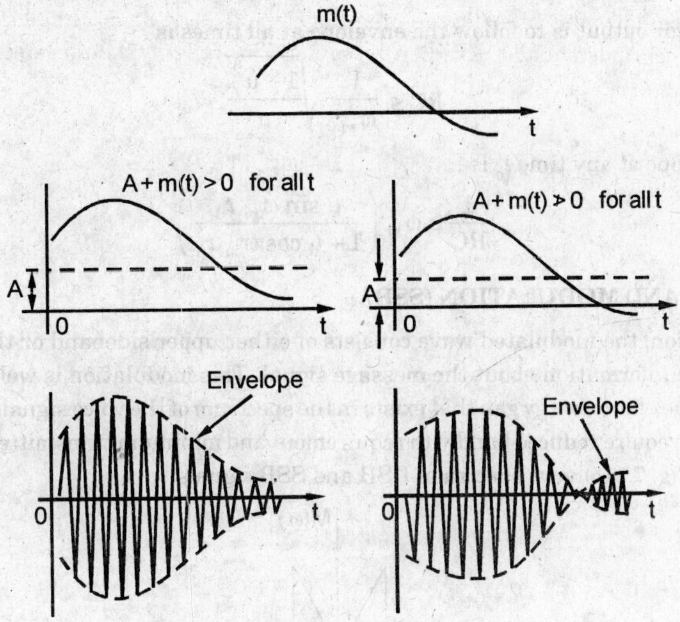

Fig. 7.9

7.5.5. MODULATION INDEX.

Modulation index for AM is defined as, $\mu = \dfrac{|\min\{m(t)\}|}{A}$

Condition for demodulation of AM by an envelope detector is $\mu \leq 1$

When $\mu > 1$, the carrier is called *overmodulated*, resulting in envelope distortion.

7.5.6. ENVELOPE DETECTOR.

The demodulation of an AM wave can be carried out by a simple and highly efficient **envelope detector** which actually consists of a diode and resistor-capacitor filter.

For proper function of envelope detector, the AM wave should be narrow-band and for this, carrier frequency should be large compared to the message bandwidth. The percentage modulation must be less than 100 percent. The operation of envelope detector as shown in Fig. 7.10.

During positive half-cycle of the input signal, the diode is forward-biased, and the capacitor C charges up rapidly to the peak value of the input signal. As the input signal falls below its maximum, the diode turns off. This is followed by a slow discharge of the capacitor through resistor R until next positive half-cycle, when input signal becomes greater than the capacitor voltage and the diode turns on again. The capacitor charges to the new peak value, and the process is repeated

For proper operation of the envelope detector, the discharge time constant RC must be chosen properly. In practice satisfactory operation requires that

$$\frac{1}{f_c} << \frac{1}{f_M}$$

where f_M is message signal bandwidth.

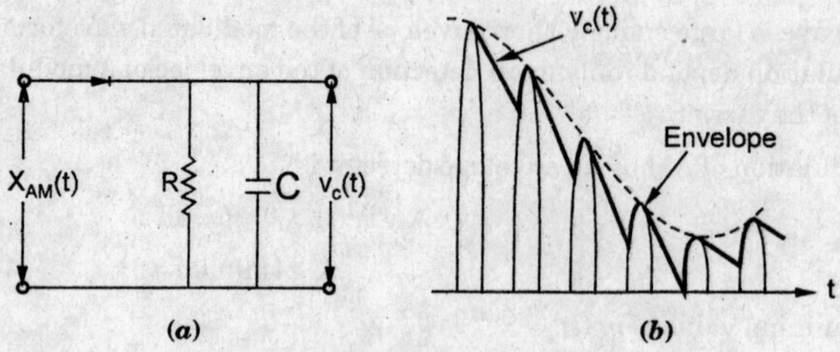

Fig. 7.10

Condition for the detector output is to follow the envelope at all times is

$$RC \le \frac{1}{\omega_m} \cdot \sqrt{\frac{1-\mu^2}{\mu}}$$

and, to follow the envelope at any time t_o is

$$\frac{1}{RC} \ge \omega_m \left(\frac{\mu \sin \omega_m t_0}{1 + \mu \cos \omega_m t_0} \right)$$

7.5.7. SINGLE-SIDEBAND MODULATION (SSB).

In this type of modulation, the modulated wave consists of either upper sideband or the lower sideband, since any of them contains complete information about the message signal. This modulation is well suited for the transmission of the voice signals by virtue of the energy gap that exists in the spectrum of the voice signals between zero and few hundred hertzs. This modulation require reduced bandwith requirement and minimum transmitted power but cost and complexity of its implementation Fig. 7.11 shows spectra of DSB and SSB signals.

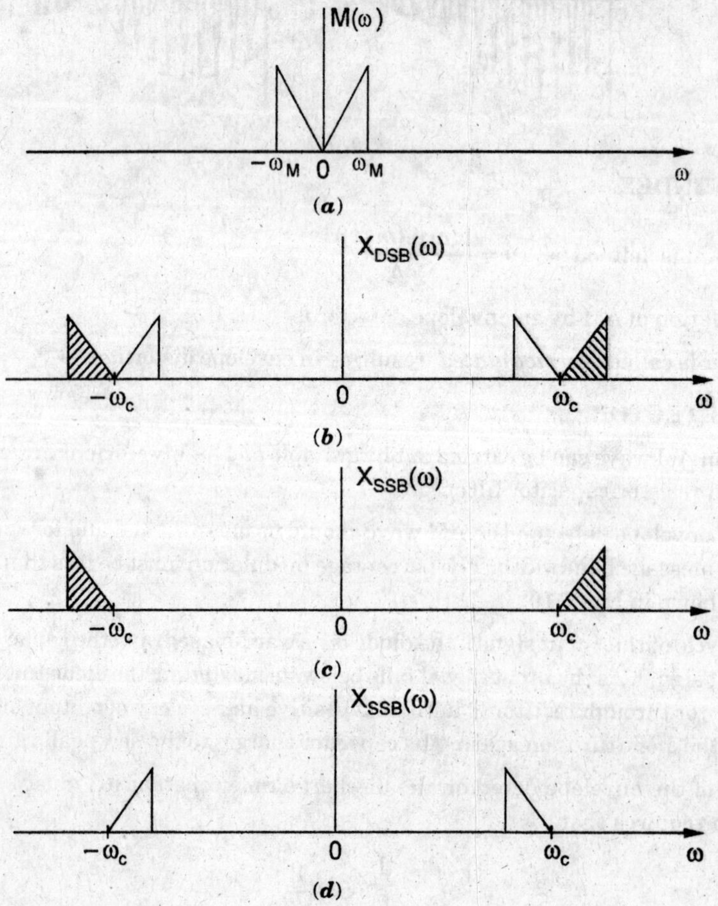

Fig. 7.11

Generation of SSB signals

1. **Frequency Discrimination method.**

To generate an SSB singal is to generate first a DSB signal and then using band-pass filter, one of the sidebands is suppressed.

In designing BPF (band-pass filter), there are three basic requirements :

(*i*) Desired sideband lies inside the passband of the filter.

(*ii*) Unwanted sideband lies inside the stopband of the filter

(*iii*) Filters transition band, separating the passband from the stopband, is twice the lowest frequency component of the message signal.

This method to generate an SSB signal is called **frequency discrimination** method, is shown in Fig. 7.12.

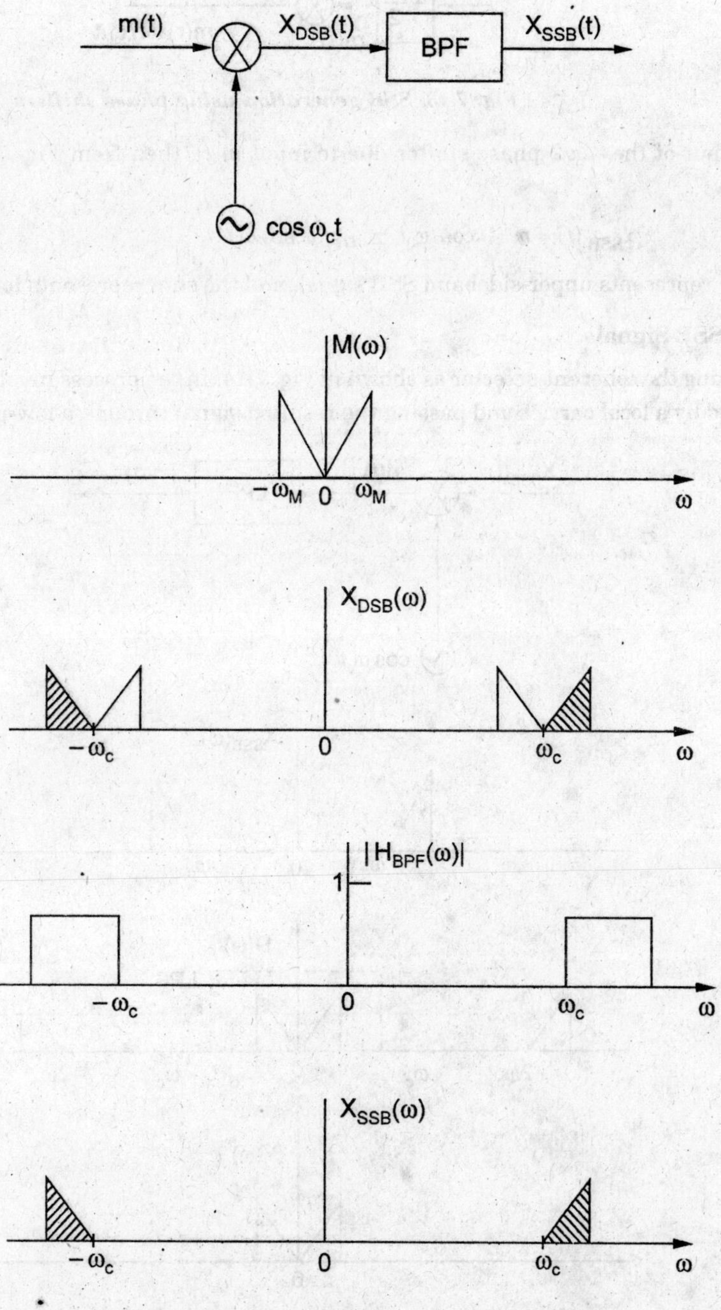

Fig. 7.12

2. Phase-shift method.

This method is employed for the generation of an SSB signal, as shown in Fig. 7.13. Two $\pi/2$ phase shifter has been incorporated to delay the phase of every frequency component by $\pi/2$.

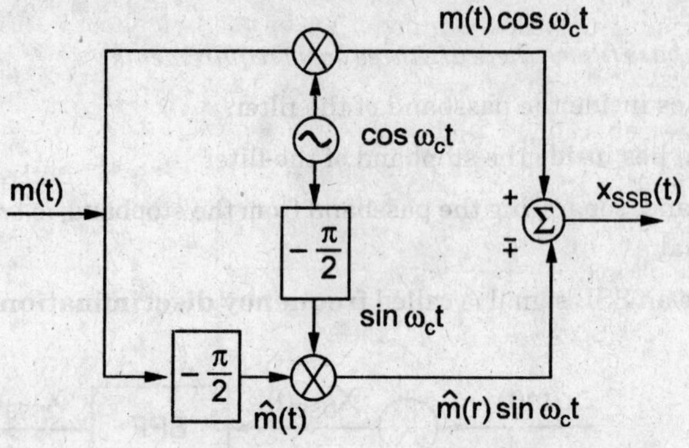

Fig. 7.13. SSB generation using phase shifters

If $\hat{m}(t)$ is output of the $-\pi/2$ phase shifter due to input $m(t)$, then from Fig. 7.13, SSB signal $x_{SSB}(t)$ can be represented by

$$x_{SSB}(t) = m(t) \cos \omega_c t \mp \hat{m}(t) \sin \omega_c t$$

The difference represents upper-sideband SSB signal, and the sum represents lower-sideband SSB signal.

Demodulation of SSB Signals.

It can be done by using the coherent detector as shown in Fig. 7.14. In the process involved, first single-sideband signal $x_{SSB}(t)$ is multiplied by a local carrier and passing the resulted signal through a low-pass filter.

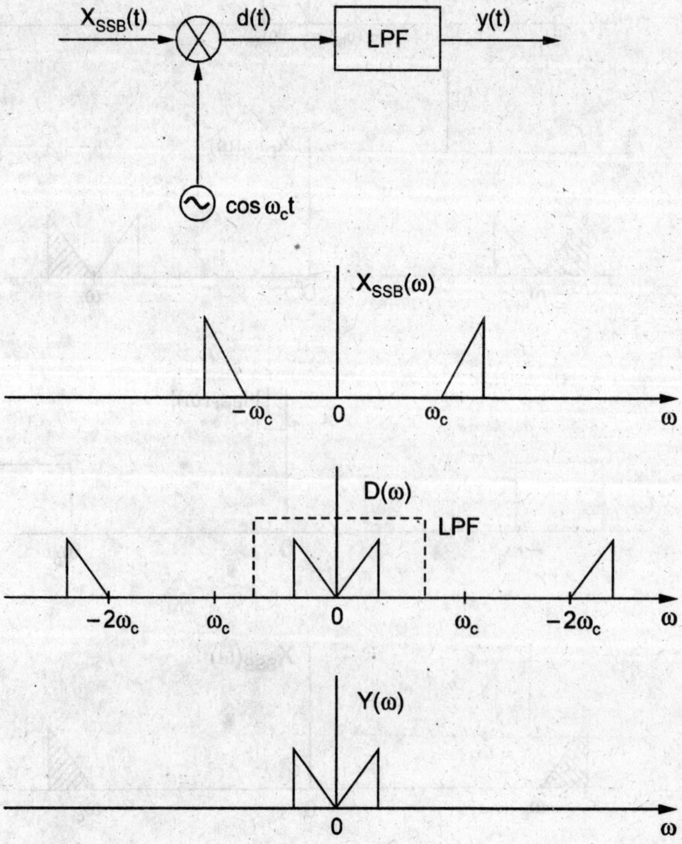

Fig. 7.14

7.5.8. VESTIGIAL-SIDEBAND MODULATION.

In this type of modulation, one sideband is passed almost completely and just a trace of other sideband is retained. Hence, the channel bandwidth required is in excess of the message bandwidth by an amount equal to the width of the vestigial sideband. This type of modulation is used in television signal transmission that contains significant components at extremely low frequencies. The typical bandwidth required to transmit a VSB signal is 1.25 times to that of SSB.

Generation of VSB signals

A VSB signal can be generated by passing a DSB signal through a sideband shaping filter as shown in Fig. 7.15 (*a*), 7.15 (*b*) and 7.15 (*c*) shows spectrum of a VSB signal in relation to that of the message signal *m* (*t*).

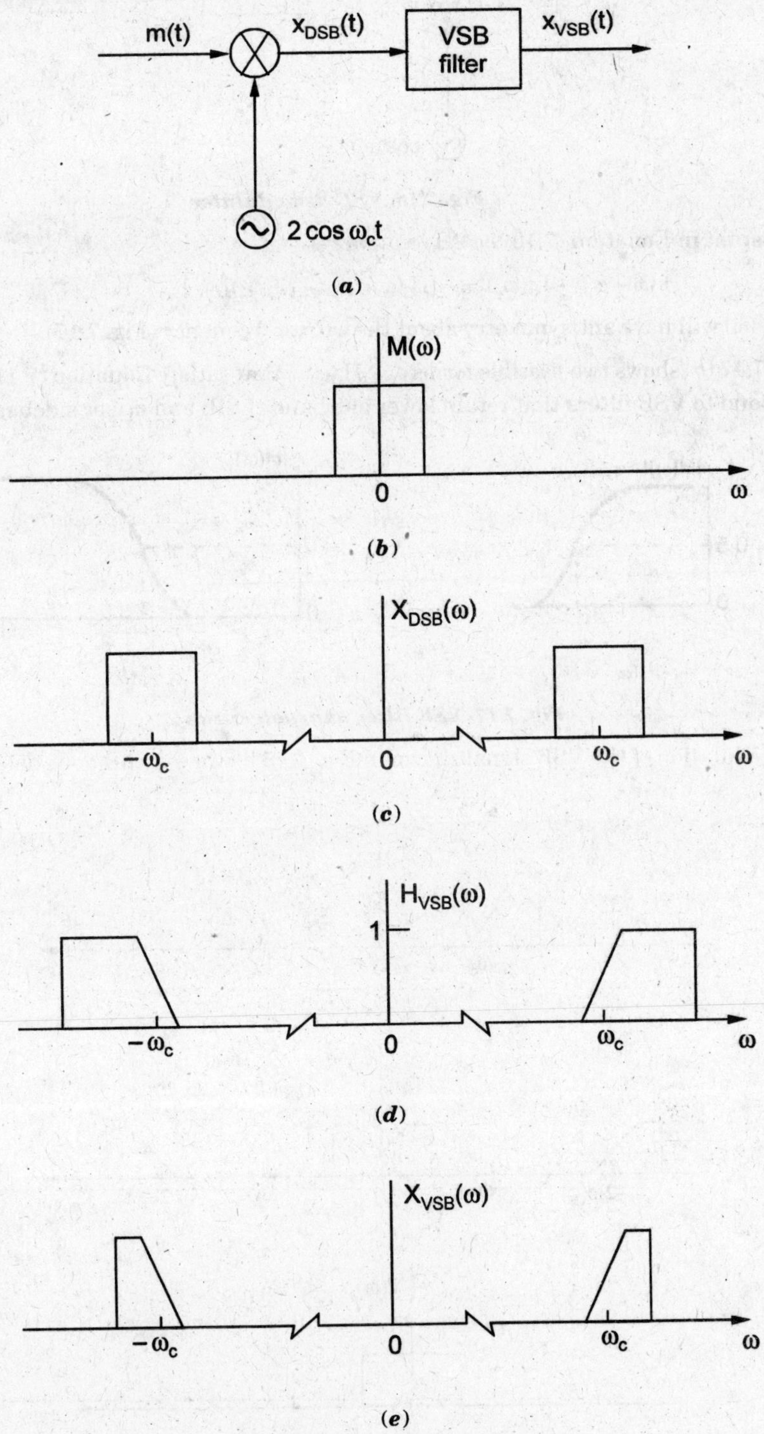

Fig. 7.15. VSB Modulation

Demodulation of VSB signals

For VSB signals, $m(t)$ can be recovered by synchronous or coherent demodulation. This determines requirements of the frequency response $H(\omega)$.

For distortionless recovery of $m(t)$

$$H(\omega + \omega_c) + H(\omega - \omega_c) = \text{constant} \quad \text{for } |\omega| \leq \omega_M \qquad \text{... (7.10)}$$

where ω_M is maximum frequency of $m(t)$.

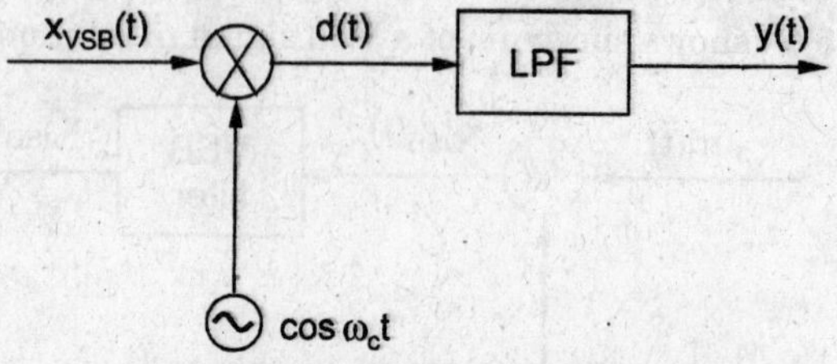

Fig. 7.16. VSB demodulator

Now letting the constant in Equation (7.10) be $2H(\omega_c)$, we get

$$H(\omega - \omega_c) - H(\omega_c) = -[H(\omega + \omega_c) - H(\omega_c)] \qquad \text{... (7.11)}$$

which shows that $H(\omega)$ will have antisymmetry about the carrier frequency (Fig. 7.17).

Figure 7.17 (*a*) and 7.17 (*b*) shows two possible forms of $|H(\omega)|$ that satisfy Equation (7.11). The filters in Fig. 7.17 (*a*) and 7.17 (*b*) correspond to VSB filters that retain lower sideband (LSB) and upper sideband (USB), respectively.

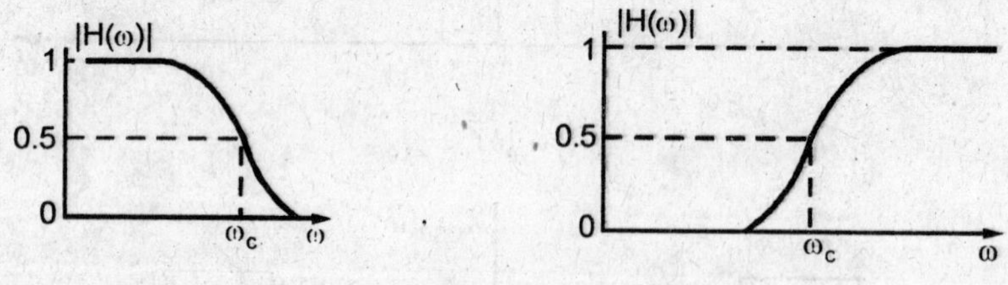

Fig. 7.17. VSB filter characteristics

Fig. 7.18 shows demodulation of the VSB signal shown in Fig. 7.15 by the synchronous detector of Fig. 7.16.

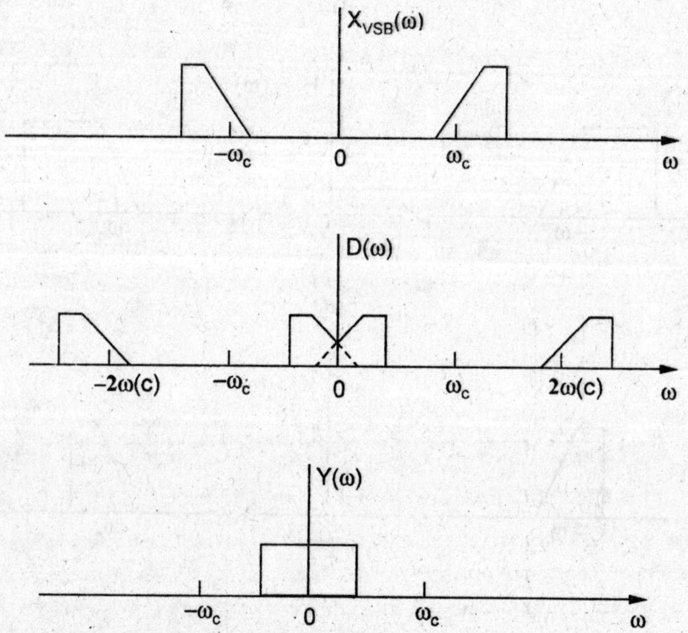

Fig. 7.18. Synchronous demodulation of VSB signals

7.5.9. FREQUENCY TRANSLATION.

During processing of signals in communication systems, it is often being desired to translate the modulated signal to a new frequency band.

This frequency translation of a modulated signal is performed by a device, called **frequency mixer.** Actually, this consists of a product modulator followed by a band-pass filter as shown in Fig. 7.19.

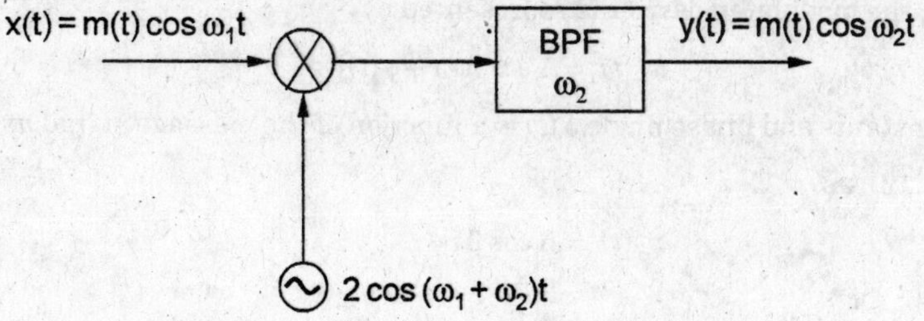

Fig. 7.19. Frequency Mixer

If carrier frequency is translated upward, then frequency of local oscillator,

$$f_l = f_2 - f_1$$

where, f_2 = frequency of modulated wave

f_1 = frequency of incoming signal.

If carrier frequency is translated downward, then corresponding frequency of the local oscillator is

$$f_l = f_1 - f_2$$

It shows that mixing is a linear operation and relation of sidebands of the incoming modulated wave to the carrier is completely preserved at the output.

7.5.10. FREQUENCY-DIVISION MULTIPLEXING.

The technique incorporating separation of signals in frequency, is called *frequency-division multiplexing (FDM)*. A block diagram depicting FDM system is shown in Fig. 7.20 with the simultaneous transmission of three message signals.

The spectra of message signals and sum of the modulated carriers are shown in Fig.7.20. DSB modulation is used in illustrating the spectra of Fig. 7.20. Any type of modulation can be used in FDM as long as the carrier spacing is sufficient to avoid spectral overlap. However, the most widely used method of modulation is SSB modulation. At the receiving end of the channel, three modulated signals are separated by bandpass filters (BPFs) and then demodulated.

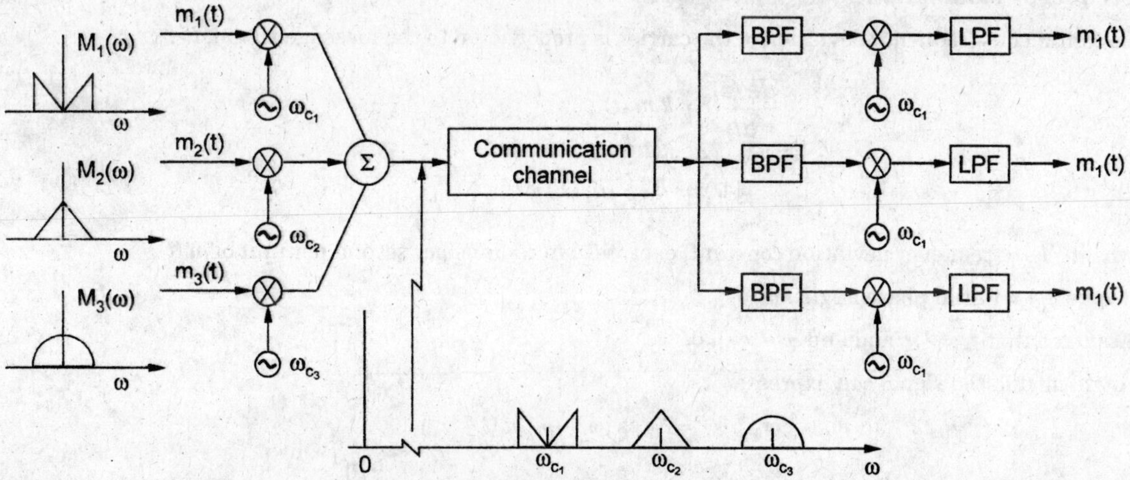

Fig. 7.20. Frequency-division multiplexing

FDM is used in telephone system, telemetry, commercial broadcast, television, and communication networks. Commercial AM broadcast stations use carrier frequency spaced 10 kHz apart in the frequency range from 540 to 1600 kHz. This separation is not sufficient to avoid spectral overlap for AM with a reasonably high-fidelity (50 Hz to 15 kHz) audio signal. Therefore, AM stations on adjacent carrier frequencies are placed geographical far apart to minimize interference.

7.5.11. ANGLE-MODULATION.

In angle modulation, spectral components of the modulated waveform are not related in any simple fashion to the message spectrum. In addition, superposition does not apply to angle-modulated signal *i.e.,* this modulation is non-linear modulation. Again, bandwidth of the angle-modulation signal is much greater than the message bandwidth.

For angle modulation, the modulated carrier is represented by

$$x_c(t) = A \cos[\omega_c t + \phi(t)] \quad \text{... (7.12)}$$

where A and ω_c are constants and phase angle $\phi(t)$ is a function of the message signal $m(t)$.

Rewriting equation (7.12), as

$$x_c(t) = A \cos \theta(t)$$

where $\theta(t) = \omega_c t + \phi(t)$

then defining instantaneous radian frequency of $x_c(t)$, denoted by ω_i, as

$$\omega_i = \frac{d\theta(t)}{dt} = \omega_c + \frac{d\phi(t)}{dt} \quad \text{... (7.13)}$$

Now, when $\phi(t)$ = constant, then $\omega_i = \omega_c$.

Functions $\phi(t)$ and $\dfrac{\phi(t)}{dt}$ are called *instantaneous phase deviation and instantaneous frequency deviation of* $x_c(t)$.

Now, $\Delta\omega = |\omega_i - \omega_c|_{max}$

This quantity is called *maximum (or peak) radian frequency deviation of the angle-modulated signal.*

7.5.12. PHASE AND FREQUENCY MODULATION.

Two basic types of angle modulation involved :

1. **Phase modulation**

   Instantaneous phase deviation of the carrier is proportional to the message signal; *i.e.*

   $$\phi(t) = k_p m(t)$$

   where k_p is phase deviation constant, expressed in radians per unit of $m(t)$.

2. **Frequency modulation**

   Instantaneous frequency deviation of the carrier is proportional to the message signal; *i.e.*

   $$\frac{d\phi(t)}{dt} = k_f m(t)$$

   $$\Rightarrow \quad \phi(t) = k_f \int_{t_0}^{t} m(\lambda)\, d\lambda + \phi(t_0)$$

   where k_f = frequency deviation constant, expressed in radians per second per unit of $m(t)$,

   $\phi(t_0)$ = initial phase angle at $t = t_0$.

   Assumed that $t_0 = -\infty$ and and $\phi(-\infty) = 0$.

   Angle-modulated signal can expressed as,

   $$x_{PM}(t) = A \cos[\omega_c t + k_p m(t)]$$

   $$x_{FM}(t) = A \cos\left[\omega_c t + k_f \int_{-\infty}^{t} m(\lambda)\, d\lambda\right]$$

   From equation 7.13, $\omega_i = \omega_c + k_p \cdot \dfrac{dm(t)}{dt}$ for PM

   and $\omega_i = \omega_c + k_f \cdot m(t)$ for FM

Hence, in PM, instantaneous frequency ω_i varies linearly with the derivative of the modulating signal and in FM, ω_i varies linearly with the modulating signal. Figure 7.21 shows AM, FM and PM waveforms produced by a sinusoidal message signal.

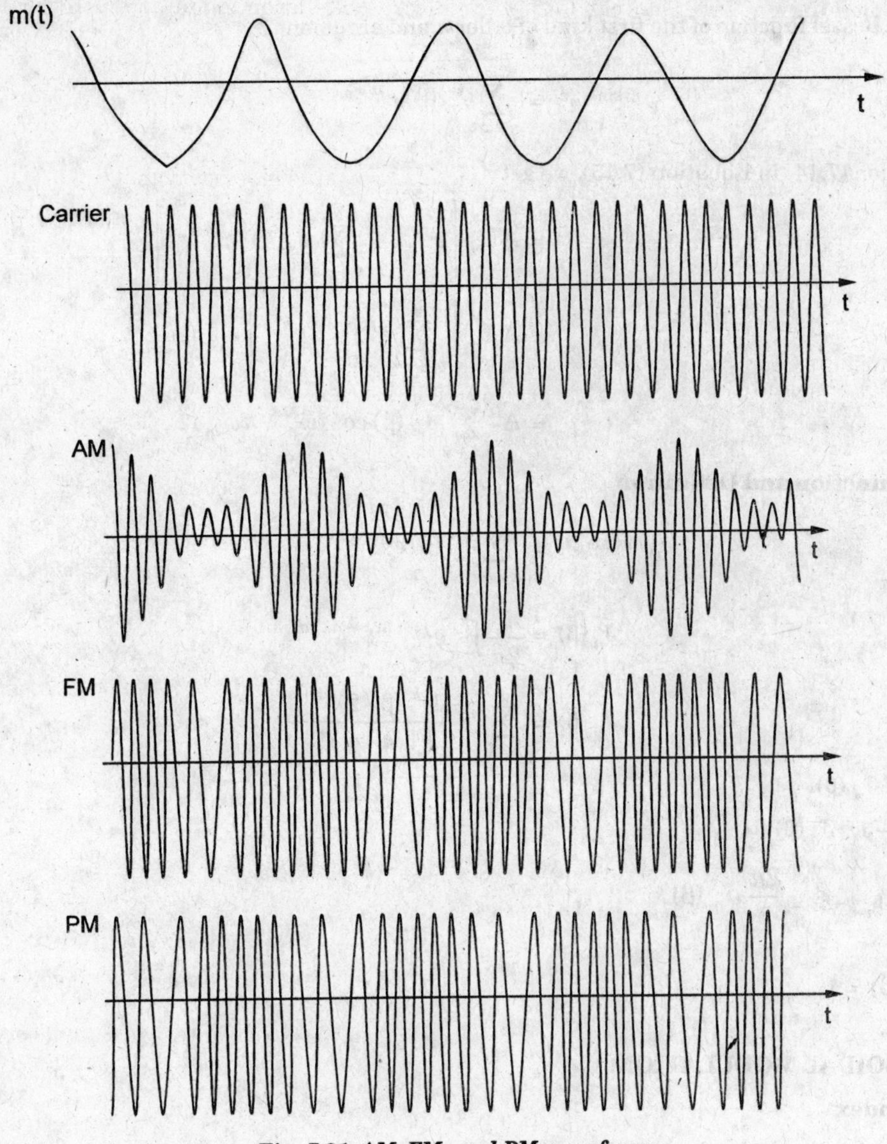

Fig. 7.21. AM, FM, and PM waveforms

7.5.13. FOURIER SPECTRUM.

As $$x_c(t) = A\cos(\omega_c t + \beta \sin \omega_m t)$$

or $$x_c(t) = A\,\mathrm{Re}\left[e^{j\omega_c t}\cdot e^{j\beta \sin \omega_m t}\right]$$

$$\omega_m = \frac{2\pi}{T_m} \qquad \text{... (7.14)}$$

Since, $e^{j\beta \sin \omega_m t}$ is periodic function, it has series representation as,

$$e^{j\beta \sin \omega_m t} = \sum_{n=-\infty}^{\infty} C_n e^{jn\omega_m t}$$

where $$C_n = \frac{\omega_m}{2\pi}\int_{-\pi/\omega_m}^{\pi/\omega_m} e^{j\beta \sin \omega_m t}\, e^{-jn\omega_m t}\, dt$$

Putting $\omega_m t = x$, we have

$$C_n = \frac{1}{2\pi}\int_{-\pi}^{\pi} e^{j(\beta \sin x - nx)}\, dx = J_n(\beta)$$

where $J_n(\beta)$ is Bessel function of the first kind of order n and argument β.

Thus
$$e^{j\beta \sin \omega_m t} = \sum_{n=-\infty}^{\infty} J_n(\beta)\, e^{jn\omega_m t} \quad \text{... (7.15)}$$

Putting Equation (7.14) in Equation (7.15), we get

$$x_c(t) = A\, R_e\left[e^{j\omega_c t} + \sum_{n=-\infty}^{\infty} J_n(\beta)\, e^{jn\omega_m t}\right]$$

$$= A\, R_e\left[\sum_{n=-\infty}^{\infty} e^{j(\omega_c + \omega_m n)t}\right]$$

$$= A \sum_{n=-\infty}^{\infty} J_n(\beta) \cos(\omega_c + n\omega_m)t$$

Generating Function and Definition

$$e^{j\beta \sin \omega_m t} = \sum_{n=-\infty}^{\infty} J_n(\beta)\, e^{jn\omega_m t}$$

$$J_n(\beta) = \frac{1}{2\pi}\int_{-\pi}^{\pi} e^{j(\beta \sin \lambda - n\lambda)}\, d\lambda$$

$$J_n(\beta) = \sum_{k=0}^{x} \frac{(-1)^k (\beta/2)^{2k+n}}{k!\,(k+n)!}$$

Properties of $J_n(\beta)$.

(*i*) $J_{-n}(\beta) = (-1)^n J_n(\beta)$

(*ii*) $J_{n-1}(\beta) + J_{n+1}(\beta) = \dfrac{2n}{\beta} J_n(\beta)$

(*iii*) $\sum_{n=-\infty}^{\infty} J_n^2(\beta) = 1$

7.5.14. SINUSOIDAL MODULATION.

Modulation index

In the message signal $m(t)$ is a pure sinusoidal, *i.e.*

$$m(t) = \begin{cases} a_m \sin \omega_m t & \text{for PM} \\ a_m \cos \omega_m t & \text{for FM} \end{cases}$$

Then, for PM, instantaneous phase deviation,

$$\phi(t) = k_p\, m(t)$$

or
$$\phi(t) = k_p\, a_m \cdot \sin \omega_m t$$

or
$$\phi(t) = \beta \sin \omega_m t$$

where
$$\beta = k_p a_m \quad \text{... (7.16)}$$

And, for FM, instantaneous phase deviation,

$$\phi(t) = k_f \int_{t_0}^{t} m(\lambda)\, d\lambda + \phi(t_0) = \frac{a_m k_f \sin \omega_m t}{\omega_m} = \beta \sin \omega_m t$$

where
$$\beta = \frac{k_f\, a_m}{\omega_m} \quad \text{... (7.17)}$$

The parameter defined in Equations (7.16) and (7.17) is called *modulation index* and is maximum value of phase deviation for both PM and FM.

β is defined only for sinusoidal modulation and expressed as

$$\beta = \frac{\Delta\omega}{\omega_m}$$

where $\Delta\omega$ = maximum frequency deviation

Table 7.1. *Selected values of Jn(s)*

η/β	0.1	0.2	0.5	1	2	5	8	10
0	0.997	0.990	0.938	0.765	0.224	−0.178	0.172	−0.246
1	0.050	0.100	0.242	0.440	0.577	−0.328	0.235	0.043
2	0.001	0.005	0.031	0.115	0.353	0.047	−0.113	0.255
3			0.003	0.020	0.129	0.365	−0.291	0.058
4				0.002	0.034	0.391	−0.105	−0.220
5					0.007	0.261	0.286	−0.234
6					0.001	0.131	0.338	−0.014
7						0.053	0.321	0.217
8						0.018	0.224	0.318
9						0.006	0.126	0.292
10						0.001	0.061	0.208
11							0.026	0.123
12							0.010	0.063
13							0.003	0.029
14							0.001	0.012
15								0.005
16								0.002

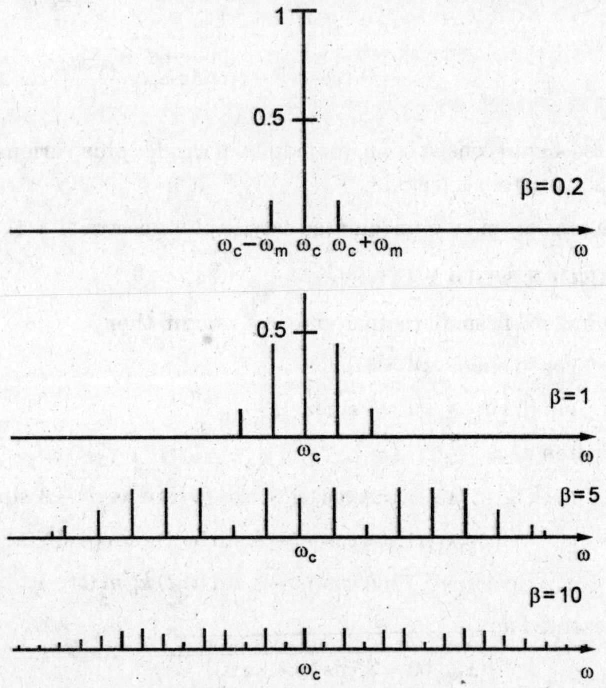

Fig. 7.22 Amplitude spectra of angle modulated signals for several values of β

7.5.15. BANDWIDTH OF ANGLE-MODULATED SIGNALS.

1. **Sinusoidal modulation**

In angle-modulated signal with sinusoidal modulation, it can be verified, that 98 percent of the normalized total signal power is contained in the bandwidth,

$$W_B \approx 2(\beta + 1)\,\omega_m$$

When $\beta << 1$, signal is an NB angle-modulated signal and its bandwidth is approximately equal to $2\omega_m$. Usually $\beta = 0.2$ is used to satisfy this criterion.

2. **Arbitrary modulation**

For an angle-modulated signal with an arbitrary modulating signal $m(t)$ band-limited to ω_M radians/sec., *deviation ratio,* D defined as

$$D = \frac{\text{maximum frequency deviation}}{\text{bandwidth of } m(t)} = \frac{\Delta\omega}{\omega_M}$$

$$W_B \text{ (bandwidth)} \approx 2(D + 1)\,\omega_M$$

For $D << 1$, $\quad W_B \approx 2\,\omega_M$

and signal is narrowband (NB) angle-modulated signal

For $D >> 1$, $\quad W_B \approx 2\,D\omega_M = 2\Delta\omega$ *i.e.,* twice the peak frequency deviation.

and signal is wideband (WB) angle-modulated signal.

7.5.16. FOURIER SPECTRA OF ANGLE-MODULATED SINGALS.

An angle-modulated carrier can be expressed in exponential form as

$$x_c(t) = \text{Re}\left[Ae^{j(\omega_c t + \phi(t))}\right] \quad \text{... (7.18)}$$

Because of this representation, the angle modulation is also called *exponential modulation*.

Now, expanding equation (7.18), we have

$$x_c(t) = \text{Re}\left\{Ae^{j\omega_c t}\left[1 + j\phi(t) - \frac{\phi^2(t)}{\underline{|2}} - \cdots + j^n \frac{\phi^n(t)}{\underline{|n}}\right]\right\}$$

$$= A\left[\cos\omega_c t - \phi(t)\sin\omega_c t - \frac{\phi^2(t)}{\underline{|2}}\cdot\cos\omega_c t + \frac{\phi^3(t)}{\underline{|3}}\cdot\sin\omega_c t + \ldots\right]$$

Here, we see angle-modulated signal consist of an unmodulated carrier plus various amplitude-modulated terms, such as $\phi(t)\sin\omega_c t$, $\phi^2(t)\cdot\cos\omega_c t$, $\phi^3(t)\sin\omega_c t$, etc.

Therefore, fourier spectrum consists of an unmodulated carrier plus spectra of $\phi(t), \phi^2(t), \phi^3(t)$ ..., etc.

7.5.17. NARROWBAND ANGLE MODULATION.

Assuming that modulation index β is small compared to one radian, then

$$\cos[\beta\sin(\omega_m t)] \approx 1$$

and

$$\sin[\beta\sin(\omega_m t)] \approx \beta\sin(\omega_m t)$$

Then PM signal can be rewritten as

$$x_c(t) = A\cos(\omega_c t)\cdot\cos[\beta\cdot\sin(\omega_m t) - A\sin(\omega_c t)\sin[B\cdot\sin B + \sin(\omega_m t)]$$

or

$$x_{NBPM}(t) \approx A\cos\omega_c t - A\sin(\omega_c t)\cdot\sin[\beta\sin(\omega_m t)]$$

$$\approx A\cos\omega_c t - A\sin(\omega_c t)\,k_p\,m(t)$$

and, FM signal can be represented as

$$x_{FM}(t) = A\cos[\omega_c t + \phi(t)]$$

$$\phi(t) = k_f\int_{-\infty}^{t} m(\lambda)\,d\lambda + \phi(t_0)$$

Here $\phi(t) = \beta \sin \omega_m t$ for FM as $m(t) = a_m \cos\omega_m t$

then $$x_{FM}(t) \approx A \cos\omega_c t - A\,\phi(t) \sin \omega_c t$$

or $$x_{NBFM}(t) \approx A \cos \omega_c t - A\left[k_f \int_{-\infty}^{t} m(\lambda)\, d\lambda\right] \sin \omega_c t \quad ...(7.19)$$

Equation 7.19 represents approximate form of a narrow-band FM signal produced by a sinusoidal modulating signal $A_m \cos(\omega_m t)$.

The block diagram showing method for generating a NBFM signal is shown below in Fig. 7.23.

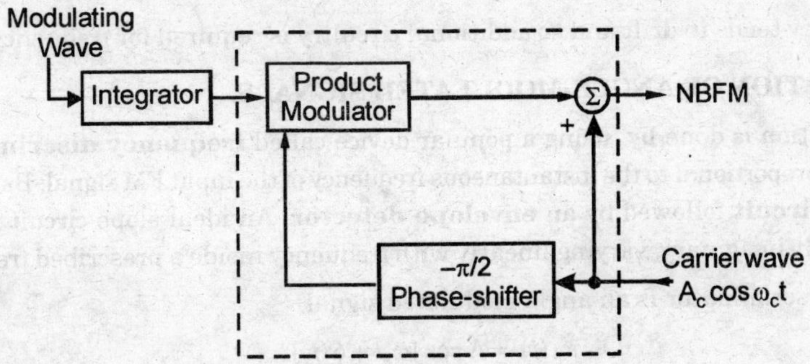

Fig. 7.23

7.5.18. WIDE-BAND ANGLE-MODULATED SIGNALS.

Generally two methods are employed to generate (WB) wide-band angle-modulated signals :

1. **Indirect method**

In this method, an narrow-band angle-modulated signal is produced first and then converted to a wide-band angle-modulated signal by using frequency multipliers. Frequency multiplier multiplies that argument of the input sinusoid by *n*.

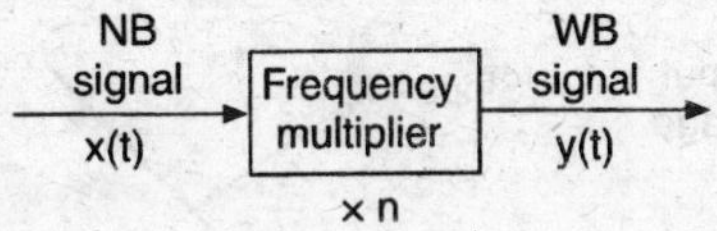

Fig. 7.24

Thus, if input of a frequency multiplier is

$$x(t) = A \cos [\omega_c t + \phi(t)]$$

then output of the frequency multiplier is

$$y(t) = A \cos [n\omega_c t + n\,\phi(t)]$$

Use of frequency multiplication normally increases carrier frequency to an impractically high value. To avoid this, a frequency conversion (using a mixer or DSB modulator) is necessary [Fig. 7.25] to shift the spectrum.

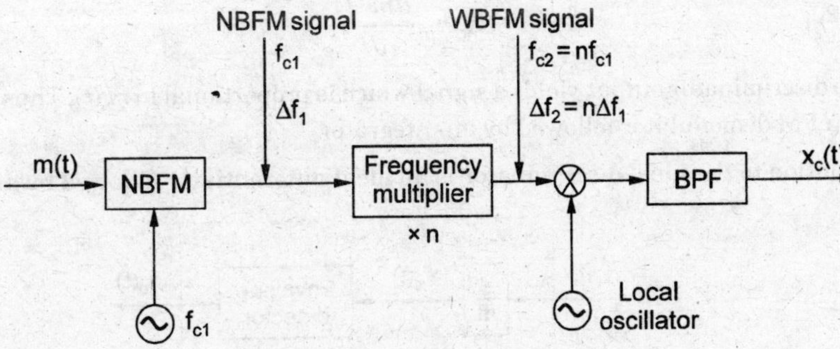

Fig. 7.25. NB-to-WB conversion

2. Direct method

In the direct method of generating an FM signal, modulating signal directly controls the carrier frequency. A common method used for generating FM directly is to vary the inductance or capacitance of a tuned electric oscillator. Any oscillator whose frequency is controlled by the modulating signal voltage is called *voltage controlled oscillator* (VCO).

Advantage of direct FM.

Large frequency deviations are possible and thus less frequency multiplication is required.

Disadvantage of direct FM

Carrier frequency tends to drift and so additional circuitry is required for frequency stablization.

7.5.19. DEMODULATION OF ANGLE-MODULATED SIGNALS.

Frequency demodulation is done by using a popular device called **frequency discriminator,** whose instantaneous amplitude is directly proportional to the instantaneous frequency of the input FM signal. Basically, frequency discriminator consists of a **slope circuit** followed by an **envelope detector**. An ideal slope circuit is characterized by a transfer function, that is purely imaginary, varying linearly with frequency inside a prescribed frequency interval.

If input to an ideal discriminator is an angle-modulated signal.

$$x_c(t) = A\cos[\omega_c t + \phi(t)]$$

then, output of the discriminator is

$$y_d(t) = k_d \cdot \frac{d\phi(t)}{dt} \qquad \text{... (7.20)}$$

where k_d = discriminator sensitivity.

For FM signal, $$\phi(t) = k_f \int_{-\infty}^{+} m(\lambda)\cdot d\lambda$$

Hence equation (7.20) becomes $y_d(t) = k_d k_f m(t)$

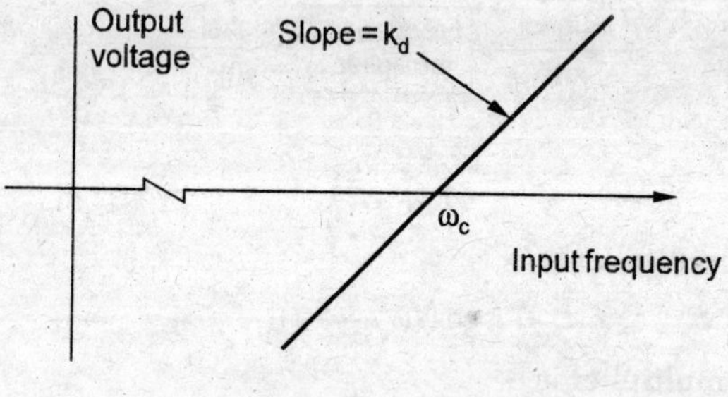

Fig. 7.26. Characteristics of an ideal frequency discriminator

The frequency discriminator can also be used to demodulate PM signals.

For PM, $$\phi(t) = k_p m(t)$$

Using equation 7.20, $$y_d(t) = k_d k_p \frac{dm(t)}{dt}$$

Integeration of the discriminator output yields a signal which is proportional to $m(t)$. Thus a demodulator for PM can be implemented as an FM demodulator followed by an integrator.

A simple approximation to the ideal discriminator is an ideal differentiator followed by an envelope detector.

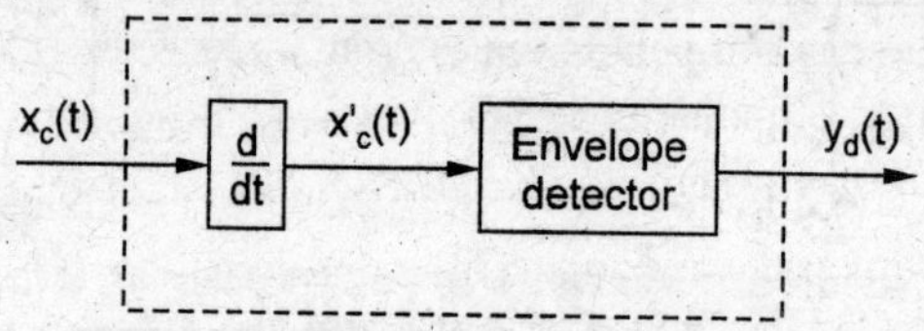

Fig. 7.27. Frequency discriminator

If input to the differentiator, $x_c(t) = A\cos[\omega_c t + \phi(t)]$

then output of the differentiator,

$$x_c'(t) = -A\left[\omega_c + \frac{d\phi(t)}{dt}\right]\sin[\omega_c t + \phi(t)]$$

The signal $x_c'(t)$ is both amplitude- and angle-modulated. The envelope of $x_c'(t)$ is

$$A\left[\omega_c + \frac{d\phi(t)}{dt}\right]$$

Output of the envelope detector, $y_d(t) = \omega_i$

which is instantaneous frequency of the $x_c(t)$.

7.6. SUPERHETERODYNE RECEIVER

The important function of a receiver is demodulation; i.e. to recover message signal from the received modulated waveform.

Other functions necessary for the proper reception of a signal

1. **Amplification :** It becomes necessary because, most often, received signal is quite weak and without sufficient amplification, it may not even be able to drive the receiver circuitry.
2. **Tuning or Selection filtering :** It becomes important especially in a broadcast situation because there is more than one station broadcasting at the same time and the receiver must pick the required station and reject inputs from the other (unwanted) stations.

Tuning also ensures that out of band noise components do not affect the receiver's performance.

Features of the receivers

(*i*) Frequency conversion (*ii*) Automatic gain control etc.

Receiver for the broadcast AM is of the superheterodyne (or superheat) variety.

Radio Frequency (RF)and Intermediate Frequency (IF)

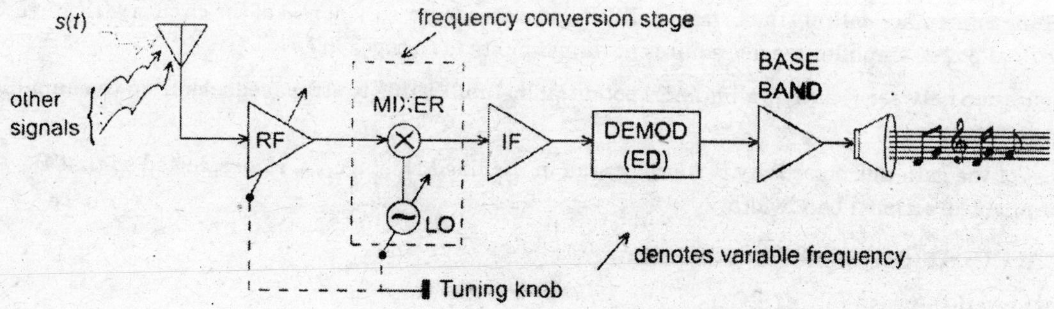

Fig. 7.28. Superheterodyne Receiver

Wanted signal $s(t)$, along with other signals and noise, is input to the Radio Frequency (RF) stage of the receiver. RF section is tuned to carrier frequency (f_c) of the desired signal $s(t)$. Bandwidth of the RF stage, B_{RF}, is relatively broad; hence along with $s(t)$, as few adjacent signals are also passed by it. Next stage in the receiver is the frequency conversion stage consisting of a mixer and local oscillator. The local oscillator frequency, f_{LO} tracks the carrier frequency f_c, and is usually $(f_c + f_{IF})$, where f_{IF} denotes intermediate frequency (IF).

The mixer output consists of frequency components at $2f_c + f_{IF}$ and f_{IF}. The following stage, called *IF stage*, is a tuned amplifier, which rejects all the other components and produces an output tht is centered at f_{IF}. The bandwidth of the IF stage, B_{IF}, is approximately equal to transmission bandwidth, B_T, of the modulation scheme under consideration.

IF stage constitutes a very important stage in a superheterodyne receiver. It is a fixed frequency amplifier and provides most of the gain of the superhet. Also, as $B_{IF} = B_T$, it also rejects adjacent channels. Next to IF, we have *detector* or *demodulation stage* which removes IF carrier and produces baseband message signal at its output. Finally, demodulator output goes through a baseband amplification stage (audio or video, depending upon type of the signal) before being applied to the final transducer (speaker, picture-tube etc.)

We should assume input to the receiver is a signal with symmetric sidebands.

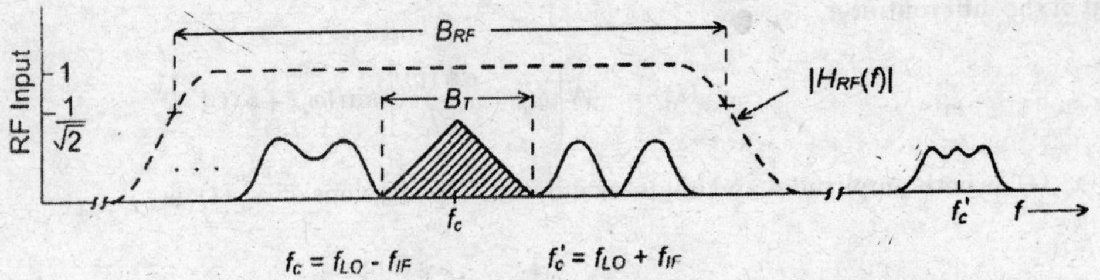

(a) Typical spectrum at the input to the RF stage of a superhet

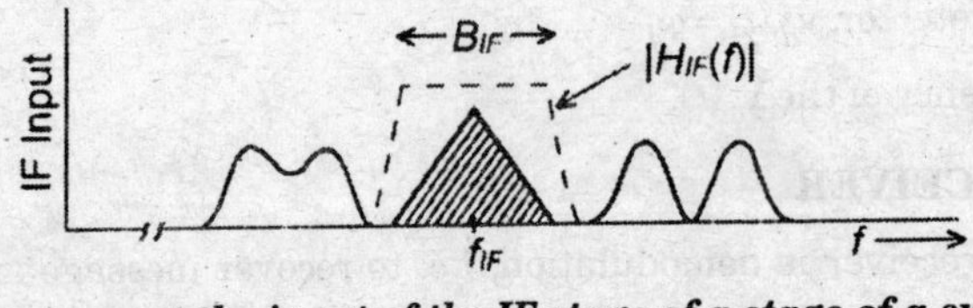

(b) Spectrum at the input of the IF stage of a stage of a superhet

Fig. 7.29

Fig. 7.29 (*a*) shows spectrum of the input signal to the RF stage. It has desired signal, plus a few adjacent channels and possibly a signal with the carrier frequency

$$f'_c = f_c + 2f_{IF} = f_{IF} + f_{IF}\ f'_c$$

is called *image frequency corresponding to* f_c.

If f'_c is allowed to pass through the RF stage, then it will also give rise to an output at the IF stage which would interfere with the wanted signal, namely the signal whose carrier frequency is f_c. Hence main task of the RF section is to pass frequency components in the range $f_c \pm \frac{B_T}{2}$ while rejecting signal with the spectrum centered at f'_c (image frequency rejection). If 3-dB bandwidth, B_{RF} is such that, $B_T < B_{RF} < 2f_{1F}$ then $H_{RF}(f)$, should be able for provide frequency response characteristic of the IF stage. IF filter takes care of adjacent channel rejection.

Advantages of Superheterodyne structure

(*i*) Tuning takes place entirely in the front end)RF and mixer tage), so that rest of the circuitry (IF stage, detector and the final power amplifier stage) requires no adjustments to changes in f_c.

(*ii*) Separation between f_c and f_{IF} eliminates potential instability due to stray feedback from the amplified output to the receiver's input.

(*iii*) Most of the gain and selectivity is concentrated in the fixed IF stage. f_{IF} is so selected so that B_{IF}/f_{IF} results in reasonable fractional bandwidth.

7.7. SNR CALCULATION (Signal-to-noise ratio)

Output signal-to-noise ratio, $(SNR)_O$

It is defined as ratio of the average of power of the demodulated message signal to the average power of the noise, both measured at the receiver output. The output signal-to-noise ratio provides an intuitive measure for describing fidelity with which demodulation process in the receiver recovers message signal from the modulated signal in the presence of additive noise.

Channel signal-to-noise ratio, $(SNR)_C$

It is defined as ratio of the average power of the modulated signal to the average power of channel noise in the message bandwidth, both measured at the receiver input.

In continuous-wave (CW) modulation systems, receiver performance is normalized by dividing output signal-to noise ratio by the channel signal-to-noise ratio.

$$\text{Figure of merit} = \frac{(SNR)_O}{(SNR)_C}$$

Higher the value of figure of merit, better will the noise, performance of the receiver be. Figure of merit may equal one, be less than one, or be greater than one, depending on type of modulation used.

7.7.1. NOISE IN LINEAR RECEIVERS.

1. Using Coherent Detection

When carrier is suppressed, then use of coherent detection is required in which case receiver is *linear*. When amplitude modulation includes transmission of the carrier, demodulation is accomplished simply by using an envelope detection, in which case receiver is *nonlinear.*

Consider the case of DSB-SC modulation. Figure 7.30 shows model of a DSB-SC of the filtered signal $x(t)$ by a locally generated sinusoidal wave $\cos(2\pi f_c t)$ and then low-pass filtering the product. To simplify the analysis, assume that amplitude of the locally generated sinusoidal wave is unity. For this demodulation scheme to operate satisfactorily, however, it is incessary that the local oscillator be synchronized both in phase and in frequency with the oscillator generating the carrier wave in the transmitter. Assume that this synchronization has been achieved. DSB-SC component of the filtered signal $x(t)$ is expressed as

$$s(t) = CA_c \cos(2\pi f_c t)\, m(t)$$

where, $A_c \cos(2\pi f_c t)$ = sinusoidal carrier wave

$m(t)$ = message signals.

In the expression for s(t) in equation we have included a *system-dependent scaling factor C*, the purpose of which is to ensure that signal component $s(t)$ is measured in the same units as the additive noise component $n(t)$.

Assume that $m(t)$ is sample function of, a stationary process of zero mean, whose power spectral density $S_M(f)$ is limited to a maximum frequency W i.e, W is message bandwidth.

Average power P of the message signal is total area under the curve of power spectral density, and is given by

$$P = \int_{-W}^{W} S_M(f)\, df$$

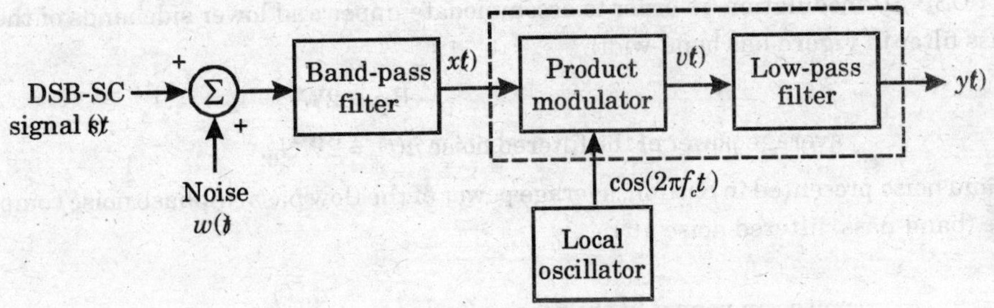

Fig. 7.30. Model of DSB-SC receiver using coherent detection.

Carrier wave is statistically independent of the message signal. To emphasize this independence, the carrier should include a random phase that is uniformly distributed over 2π radians. In the defining equation for $s(t)$, this random phase angle has been omitted for convenience of presentation. Using result of a modulated random process, we may express average power of the DSB-SC modulated signal component $s(t)$ as $C^2A_c^2\, P/2$.

With a noise spectral density of $N_0/2$, average noise power in the message bandwidth W is equal to WN_0.

Thus, channel signal-to-noise ratio of the DSB-SC modulation system is

$$(SNR)_{C,DSB} = \frac{C^2 A_c^2 P}{2WN_0}$$

where, constant C^2 in the numerator ensures that this ratio is dimensionless.

Now, output signal-to-noise ratio of the system is determined.

Using the narrowband representation of the filtered noise n(t), total signal at the coherent detector input maybe expressed as

$$\begin{aligned} x(t) &= s(t) + n(t) \\ &= CA_c \cos(2\pi f_c t) m(t) + n_1(t) \cos(2\pi f_c t) - n_Q(t) \sin(2\pi f_c t) \end{aligned}$$

where $n_1(t)$ and $n_Q(t)$ are in-phase and quadrature components of $n(t)$ with respect to the carrier.

Thus, output of the product-modulator component of the coherent detector is

$$v(t) = x(t)\cos(2\pi f_c t)$$

$$= \frac{1}{2}CA_c m(t) + \frac{1}{2}n_I(t) + \frac{1}{2}[CA_c m(t) + n_I(t)]\cos(4\pi f_c t) - \frac{1}{2}n_Q(t)\sin(4\pi f_c t)$$

Low-pass filter in the coherent detector in Figure removes high-frequency components of $v(t)$, giving

$$\text{receiver output, } y(t) = \frac{1}{2}CA_c m(t) + \frac{1}{2}n_I(t)$$

This equation indicates that

(*i*) Message signal $m(t)$ and in-phase noise component $n_I(t)$ of the filtered noise $n(t)$ appear additively at the receiver output.

(*ii*) Quadrature component $n_Q(t)$ of the noise $n(t)$ is completely rejected by the coherent detector.

These two results are independent of the input signal-to-noise ratio. Thus, coherent detection distinguishes itself from other demodulation techniques in an important property. The output message component is unmutilated and noise component always appears additively with the message, irrespective of the input signal-to-noise ratio.

$$\text{Message signal component at the receiver output} = \frac{CA_c\, m(t)}{2}$$

$$\therefore \quad \text{Average power of this component} = \frac{C^2A_c^2P}{4}$$

where, P = average power of the original message signal $m(t)$

C = system-dependent scaling factor referred to earlier.

In the case of DSB-SC modulation, in order to accommodate upper and lower sidebands of the modutated signal $s(t)$, band-pass filter in Figure has band-width

$$B_T = 2W$$

Thus, average power of the filtered noise $n(t) = 2WN_0$.

For narrowband noise presented in Section, average power of the (low pass) inphase noise component $n_I(t)$ is same as that to the (band-pass) filtered noise $n(t)$.

Since, noise component at the receiver output $= \dfrac{n_I(t)}{2}$

$$\therefore \quad \text{Average power of the noise at the receiver output} = \left(\frac{1}{2}\right)^2 2WN_0 = \frac{1}{2}WN_0$$

Thus, output signal-to-noise for a DSB-SC receiver using coherent detection

$$(SNR)_{O,\,DSB\text{-}SC} = \frac{C^2A_c^2P/4}{WN_0/2} = \frac{C^2A_c^2P}{2WN_0}$$

Using equations, we get figure of merit, $\left.\dfrac{(SNR)_O}{(SNR)_C}\right|_{DSB\text{-}SC} = 1$

2. Using Envelope Detection

In a full AM signal, both sidebands and the carrier wave are transmitted, as shown by

$$s(t) = A_c[1 + k_a m(t)]\cos(2\pi f_c t)$$

where, $A_c\cos(2\pi f_c t)$ = carrier wave

$m(t)$ = message signal

k_a = constant that determines percentage modulation.

In the expression for the amplitude-modulated signal component s(t) there, no need for the use of a scaling factor, because it is reasonable to assume that carrier amplitude A_c has same units as the additive noise component.

Average power of the carrier component in the AM signal

$$s(t) = \frac{A_c^2}{2}$$

Average power of the information-bearing component

$$A_c k_a m(t) \cos(2\pi f_c t) = \frac{A_c^2 k_a^2}{2}$$

where, P = aveage power of the message signal $m(t)$.

$$\text{Average power of the full AM signal } s(t) = \frac{A_c^2\left(1 + k_a^2 P\right)}{2}$$

As for the DSB-SC system,

$$\text{average power of noise in the message bandwidth} = WN_0.$$

∴ Channel signal-to-noise ratio for AM, $$(SNR)_{C,AM} = \frac{A_c^2(1 + k_a^2 P)}{2WN_0}$$

To evaluate output signal-to-noise ratio, first represent filtered noise n(t) in terms of its in-phase and quadrature components.

Thus define filtered signal x(t) applied to the envelope detector in the receiver model of figure as follows:

$$x(t) = s(t) + n(t)$$

$$= \{[A_c + A_c k_a m(t) + n_1(t)] - n_Q(t)\} \sin(2\pi f_c t)$$

It is informative to represent components that comprise signal $x(t)$ by means of phasors, as in Fig 7.32 (*a*). From this phasor diagram,

$$\text{receiver output, } y(t) = \text{envelope of } x(t)$$

$$= \{[A_c + A_c k_a m(t) + n_1(t)]^2 + n_Q^2(t)\}^{1/2}$$

Signal $y(t)$ defines output of an ideal envelope detector. The phase of $x(t)$ is of no interest because an ideal envelope detector is totally insensitive to variations in the phase of $x(t)$.

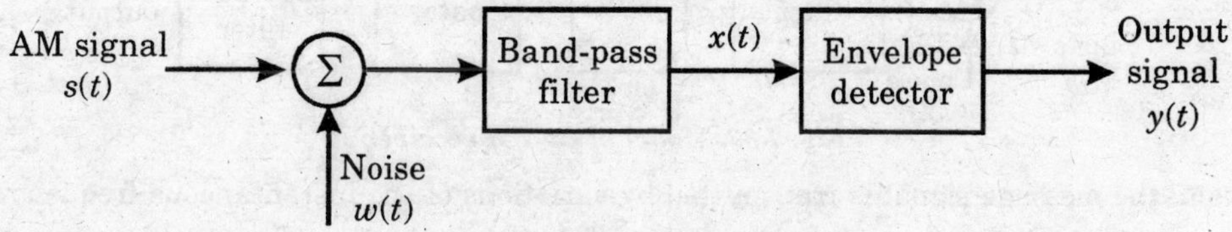

Fig. 7.31. Model of AM receiver

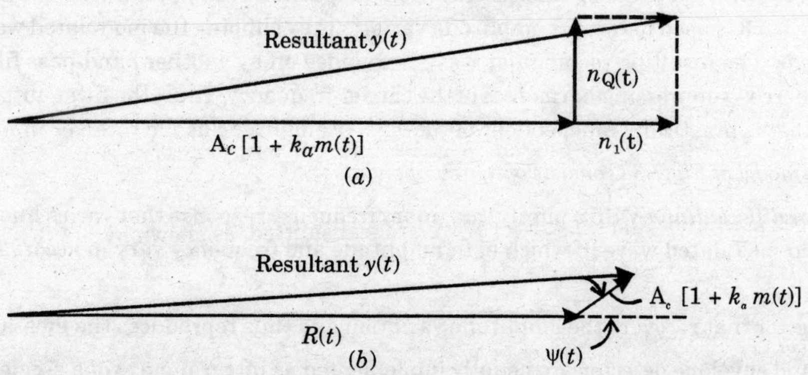

(a) Phasor diagram for AM wave plus narrowband noise for the case of high carrier-to-noise ratio

(b)Phasor diagram for AM wave plus narrowband noise for the case of low carrier-to-noise ratio.

Fig. 7.32

The expression defining $y(t)$ is complex and needs to be simplified to permit derivation of insightful results. Specifically, approximate output $y(t)$ as sum of a message term plus a term due to noise. In general, this is quite difficult to achieve. However, when average carrier power is large compared with the average noise power, so that receiver is operating satisfactorily, then signal term $A_c(1 + k_a m(t)]$ will be large compared with the noise terms $n_1(t)$ and $n_Q(t)$, at least most of the time. Then

$$\text{output, } y(t) \approx A_c + A_c k_a m(t) + n_1(t)$$

Presence of DC or constant term A_c in the envelope detector detector output $y(t)$ is due to demodulation of the transmitted carrier wave. This term may be ignored because it bears no relation whatsoever to the message signal $m(t)$. In any case, it may be removed simply by means of a blocking capacitor. Thus neglecting DC term A_c, we find that remainder has, except for scaling factors, form similar to the output of a DSB-SC receiver using coherent detection. Accordingly, output signal-to-noise ratio of an AM receiver using an envelope detector is approximately

$$(\text{SNR})_{\text{O,AM}} = \frac{A_c^2 k_a^2 P}{2WN_0}$$

Equation is valid only if following two conditions are satisfied :

(*i*) Average noise power is small compared to the average carrier power at the envelope detector input.

(*ii*) Amplitude sensitivity k_a is adjusted for a percentage modulation less than one equal to 100 percent.

Using equations, we get following figure of merit for amplitude modulation.

$$\left.\frac{(\text{SNR})_{\text{O}}}{(\text{SNR})_{\text{C}}}\right|_{\text{AM}} = \frac{k_a^2 P}{1 + k_a^2 P}$$

Thus, whereas figure of merit of a DSB-SC receiver or that of an SSB receiver using coherent detection is always unity, corresponding figure of merit of an AM receiver using envelope detection is always less than unity. In other words, *noise performance of a full AM receiver is always inferior to that of a DSB-SC receiver.*

7.7.2. NOISE IN FM RECEIVERS.

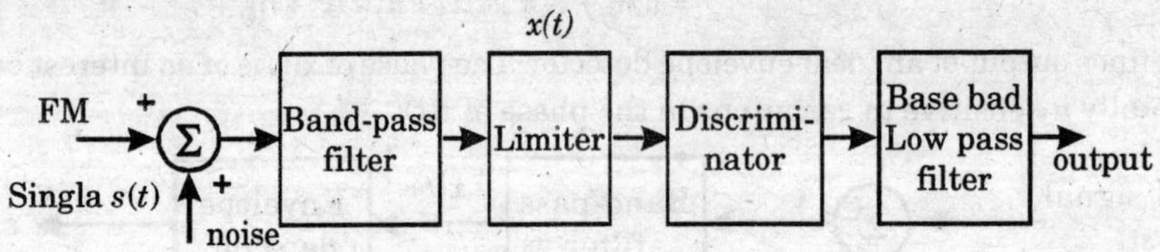

Fig. 7.33. Model of an FM receiver

In an FM system, the message signal is transmitted by variations of the instantaneous frequency of a sinusoidal carrier wave, and its amplitude is maintained constant. Therefore, any variations of the carrier amplitude at the receiver input must result from noise or interference. The amplitude limiter, following the band-pass filter in the receiver model of Fig. 7.33 is used to remove amplitude variations by clipping the modulated wave at the filter output almost to the zero axis. The resulting rectangular wave is rounded off by another band-pass filter that is an integral part of the limiter, thereby suppressing harmonics of the carrier frequency. Thus, the filter output is again sinusoidal, with an amplitude that is practically independent of the carrier amplitude at the receiver input.

Discriminator in the model of Fig. 7.33 consists of two components :

(*i*) A *slope network* or *differentiator* with a purely imaginary frequency response that varies linearly with frequency. It produces a hybrid-modulated wave in which both amplitude and frequency vary in accordance with the message signal.

(*ii*) An envelope detector that recovers the amplitude variation and thus reproduces the message signal.

The slope network and envelope detector are usually implemented as integral parts of a single physical unit.

The *postdetection filter*, labeled *"baseband low-pass filter"* in Fig. 7.33 has a bandwidth that is just large enough to accommodate the highest frequency component of the message signal. This filter removes the out-of-band components of the noise at the discriminator output and thereby keeps the effect the effect of the output noise to a minimum.

The filtered noise $n(t)$ at the band-pass filter output defined in terms of its in-phase and quadrature components by

$$n(t) = n_I(t)\cos(2\pi f_c t) - n_Q(t)\sin(2\pi f_c t)$$

Equivalently, we may express n(t) in terms of its envelope and phase as

$$n(t) = r(t)\cos[(2\pi f_c t) + \psi(t)]$$

where envelope, $r(t) = [n_I^2(t) + n_Q^2(t)]^{1/2}$

and phase, $\psi(t) = \tan^{-1}\left(\dfrac{n_Q(t)}{n_I(t)}\right)$

Envelope $r(t)$ is Rayleigh distributed, and phase $\psi(t)$ is uniformly distributed over 2π radians

$$\text{Incoming FM signal, } s(t) = A_c\cos\left[2\pi f_c t + 2\pi k_f\int_0^t m(\tau)\,d\tau\right]$$

where, A_c = carrier amplitude,

f_c = carrier frequency,

k_f = frequency sensitivity,

$m(t)$ = message signal.

As with the standard AM, in FM there is no need to introduce a scaling factor in the definition of the modulated signal $s(t)$, since it is reasonable to assume that its amplitude A_c has the same units as the additive noise component $n(t)$. To proceed, we define

$$\phi(t) = 2\pi k_f\int_0^t m(\tau)\,d\tau \qquad ...(7.21)$$

Thus in the simple form, $s(t) = A_c\cos[2\pi f_c t + \phi(t)]$

Therefore noisy signal at the band-pass filter output

$$x(t) = s(t) + n(t)$$

$$= A_c\cos[2\pi f_c t + \phi(t)] + r(t)\cos[2\pi f_c t + \psi(t)]$$

It is informative to represent $x(t)$ by means of a phasor diagram, given in Fig.7.34. In this figure the signal term are used as reference. Phase $\theta(t)$ of the resultant phasor representing $x(t)$ is obtained directly from Fig.(7.34) as

$$\theta(t) = \phi(t) + \tan^{-1}\left\{\frac{r(t)\sin[\psi(t)-\phi(t)]}{A_c + r(t)\cos[\psi(t)-\phi(t)]}\right\}$$

The envelope of $x(t)$ is of no interest because any envelope variations at the band-pass filter output are removed by the limiter.

Assume that carrier-to-noise ratio measured at the discriminator input is large compared with unity. Let R denote the random variable obtained by observing (at some fixed time) the envelope process with sample function $r(t)$ [due to the noise $n(t)$]. Then, atleast most of the time, the random variable R is small compared with the carrier amplitude A_c, and so expression for the phase $\theta(t)$ simplifies considerably as follows:

$$\theta(t) \approx \phi(t) + \frac{r(t)}{A_c}\sin[\psi(t)-\phi(t)]$$

or, using expression for $\phi(t)$ given in Equation (7.21)

$$\theta(t) \approx 2\pi k_f\int_0^t m(\tau)\,d\tau + \frac{r(t)}{A_c}\sin[\psi(t)-\phi(t)]$$

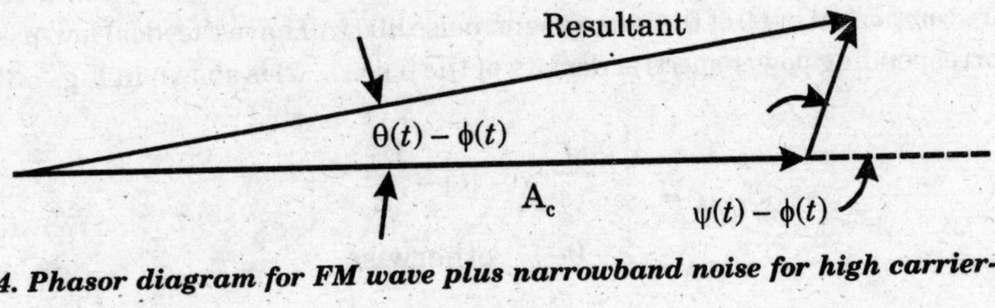

Fig.7.34. Phasor diagram for FM wave plus narrowband noise for high carrier-to-noise ratio

∴ Discriminator output,

$$v(t) = \frac{1}{2\pi}\frac{d\theta(t)}{dt} = k_f m(t) + n_d(t) \qquad ...(7.22)$$

where, noise term,

$$n_d(t) = \frac{1}{2\pi A_c}\frac{t}{dt}\{r(t)\sin[\psi(t) - \phi(t)]\} \qquad ...(7.23)$$

Thus provided carrier-to-noise ratio is high, discriminator output $v(t)$ consists of the original message signal $m(t)$ multiplied by the constant factor k_f, plus an additive noise component $n_d(t)$. Accordingly, output signal-to-noise ratio is used as previously defined to assess quality of performance of the FM receiver. Before doing this, see if expression defining noise $n_d(t)$ can be simplified.

From phasor diagram of Fig. 7.34 effect of variations in the phase $\psi(t)$ of the narrowband noise appear referred to the signal term $\phi(t)$. Phase $\psi(t)$ is uniformly distributed over 2π radians. Thus assume that phase difference $\psi(t) - \phi(t)$ is also uniformly distributed over 2π radians. If such an assumption are true, then noise $n_d(t)$ at the discriminator output would be independent of the modulating signal and would depend only on the characteristics of the carrier and narrowband noise. Theoretical considerations show that this assumption is justified provided carrier-to-noise ratio is high. Then we may simplify above Equation (7.23) as

$$n_d(t) \simeq \frac{1}{2\pi A_c}\frac{t}{dt}\{r(t)\sin[\psi(t)]\} \qquad ...(7.24)$$

However, from the defining equations for $r(t)$ and $\psi(t)$, quadrature component of the filtered noise $n(t)$,

$$n_Q(t) = r(t)\sin[\psi(t)]$$

Therefore, rewriting Equation (7.23) as

$$n_d(t) \simeq \frac{1}{2\pi A_c}\frac{dn_Q(t)}{dt} \qquad ...(7.25)$$

This means that *additive noise $n_d(t)$ appearing at the discriminator output is determined effectively by the carrier amplitude A_c and the quadrature component $n_Q(t)$ of the narrowband noise $n(t)$.*

Output signal-to-noise ratio is defined as ratio of the average output signal power to the average output noise power. From Equation (7.22) message component in the discriminator output, and therefore low-pass filter output, is $k_f m(t)$.

∴ Average output signal power = k_f^2 P

where, P = average power of the message signal $m(t)$.

To determine average output noise power, noise $n_d(t)$ at the discriminator output is proportional to time derivative of the quadrature noise component $n_Q(t)$. Since differentiation of a function with respect to time corresponds to multiplication of its Fourier transform by $j2\pi f$, it follows that the noise process $n_d(t)$ can be obtained by passing $n_Q(t)$ through a linear filter with a frequency response equal to

$$j2\pi f = if$$

i.e., power spectral density $S_{Nd}(f)$ of the noise $n_d(t)$ is related to the power spectral density $S_{NQ}(f)$ of the quadrature noise componet $n_Q(t)$ as

$$S_{Nd}(f) = \frac{f^2}{A_c^2} S_{NQ}(f)$$

With the band-pass filter in the receiver model having an ideal frequency response characterized by bandwidth B_T and midband frequency f_c, the narrowband noise $n(t)$ will have a power spectral density characteristic that is similarly shaped, i.e. quadrature component $n_Q(t)$ of the narrowband noise $n(t)$ will have the ideal low-pass characteristic shown in Fig 7.35 (*a*). The corresponding power spectral density of the noise $n_d(t)$ is shown in Fig. 7.35 (*b*)

i.e.

$$S_{Nd}(f) = \begin{cases} \dfrac{N_0 f^2}{A_c^2}, & |f| \le \dfrac{B_T}{2} \\ 0, & \text{otherwise} \end{cases}$$

In the receiver model of Fig. 7.33 discriminator output is followed by a low-pass filter with a bandwidth equal to the message bandwidth W.

For wide band FM, usually $W < B_T/2$,

where, B_T = transmission bandwidth of the FM signal.

This means that out-of-band components of noise $n_d(t)$ will be rejected. Therefore, as shown in Fig. 7.35 (*c*) power spectral density of the noise $n_o(t)$ appearing at the receiver output is defined by

$$S_{No}(f) = \begin{cases} \dfrac{N_0 f^2}{A_c^2}, & |f| \le W \\ 0, & \text{otherwise} \end{cases}$$

Average output noise power is determined by integrating power spectral density $S_{No}(f)$ from – W to W

i.e. Average power of output noise

$$= \frac{N_0}{A_c^2}\int_{-W}^{W} f^2 df = \frac{2N_0W^3}{3A_c^2}$$

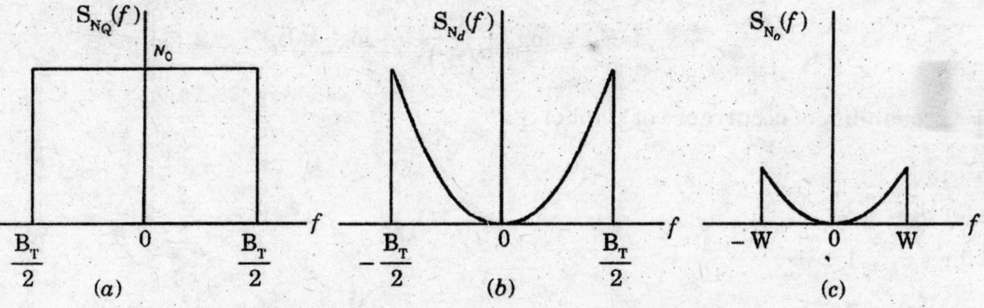

(a) Power spectral density of quadrature component $n_Q(t)$ of narrowhand noise n(t).

(b) Power spectral density of noise $n_d(t)$ at the discriminator output.

(c) Power spectral density of noise $n_o(t)$ at the receiver output.

Fig. 7.35. Noise analysis of FM receiver

$$\text{Average output noise power} \propto \frac{1}{\text{Average carrier power } A_c^2/2}.$$

Accordingly, in an FM system, increasing the carrier power has a *noise-quieting effect*.

But we know, average output signal power = k_f^2P.

Therefore, provided carrier-to-noise ratio is high, this average output signal power may be divided by the average output noise power to obtain output signal-to-noise ratio

$$(SNR)_{O,FM} = \frac{3A_c^2k_f^2P}{2N_0W^3}$$

$$\text{Average power in the modulated signal s(t)} = \frac{A_c^2}{2}$$

and average noise power in the message bandwidth = WN_0.

$$\therefore \quad \text{Channel signal-to-noise ratio, } (SNR)_{C,FM} = \frac{A_c^2}{2WN_0}$$

Dividing output signal-to-noise ratio by the channel signal-to-noise ratio, we get following figure of merit for frequency modulation:

$$\left.\frac{(SNR)_O}{(SNR)_C}\right|_{FM} = \frac{3k_f^2P}{W^2}$$

But frequency deviation, $\Delta f \propto$ frequency sensitivity k_f of the modulator.

Also, by definition,

$$\text{deviation ratio, D} = \frac{\text{frequency deviation, } \Delta f}{\text{message bandwidth, W}}$$

In other words, deviation ratio, $D \propto k_f P^{1/2}/W$.

The figure of merit of a wideband FM system is a quadratic function of the deviation ratio.

Now, in wideband FM, transmission bandwidth B_T is approximately proportional to the deviation ratio D. Accordingly, it can be stated that *when carrier to-noise ratio is high, an increase in the transmission bandwidth B_T provides a corresponding quadratic increase in the output signal-to-noise ratio or figure of merit of the FM system.*

7.8. MEASURE OF INFORMATION

7.8.1. INFORMATION CONTROL OF A SYMBOL.

Consider a discrete memoryless sources. S which takes on symbols form a fixed finite alphabet $\{s_1, s_2, s_3 ... s_m\}$.

Then information content of

$$s_p, I(S_i) = \log_2 \frac{1}{P(S_i)} = -\log_2 P(S_i)$$

where, $P(S_i)$ = probability of occurrence of symbol S_i.

Properties :

(*i*) $I(s_k) = 0$ for $p_k = 1$

(*ii*) $I(s_k) \geq 0$ for $\leq p_k \leq 1$

(*iii*) $I(s_k) > I(s_i)$ if $p_k < p_i$

(*iv*) $I(s_k\, s_l) = I(s_k) + I(s_l)$ if s_k and s_l are statistically independent.

7.8.2. ENTROPY OR AVERAGE INFORMATION.

The mean of $I(s_k)$ over the source S with k different symbols is given by

$$H(S) = E[I(s_k)] = \sum_{k=0}^{k-1} p_k \cdot I(s_k) = \sum_{k=0}^{k-1} p_k \log_2 \left(\frac{1}{p_k}\right)$$

Quantity H(S) is called *entropy of source* S and it measures average information content per source symbol.

Entropy H(S) of source S is bounded as, $0 \leq H(S) \leq \log_2 K$

where K is size of source S.

7.8.3. INFORMATION RATE (R).

It is defined as the rate at which source S emits symbols, i.e.

$$R = H(S) \text{ b/s.}$$

7.8.4. SOURCE-ENCODING THEOREM.

The process of efficient representation of data generated by a discrete source is called *source encoding* and the device which performs this representation celled *source encode.*

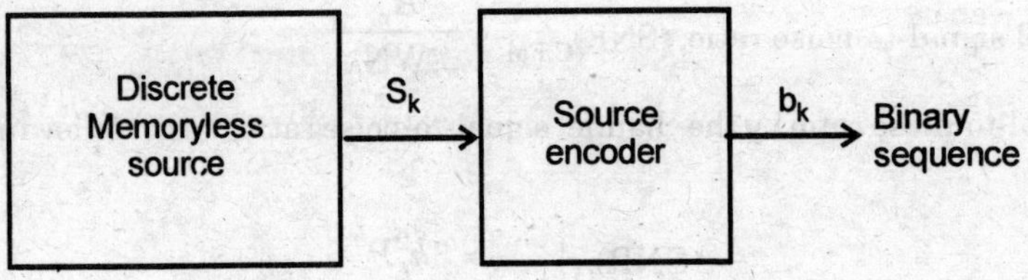

Fig.7.36. Scheme depicting source encoding

7.8.5. CODE LENGTH AND CODE EFFICIENCY.

If it is assumed that symbol S_k occurs with probability $p(S_k)$, then average code word length of the source encoder

$$I = \sum_{k=0}^{k-1} pk\, l_k$$

and

$$\text{coding efficiency, } \eta = \frac{L_{min}}{\overline{L}}$$

where, L^{mm} = minimum possible value of L.

Source encoder is called *efficient* if η approaches infinity.

Source-coding theorem

For a discrete memoryless source (DMS)S, the average code work length $\overline{L}$ per symbol is bounded as

$$\overline{L} \geq H(S)$$

where, H(S) is entropy of DMS.

Hence, with

$$L_{mi} = H(S)$$

$$\text{Code efficiency, } \eta = \frac{H(S)}{L}$$

7.8.6. DISCRETE MEMORYLESS CHANNELS (DMC).

It is a statistical model with an input X and Y, both of being random variables. During ± each signalling interval, the channel accepts an input signal for X and then generation output symbol from Y. The channel is called "*discrete*" when both the alphabet X and Y have finite sizes. It is *memoryless* when current output depends upon only input and not on nay previous inputs.

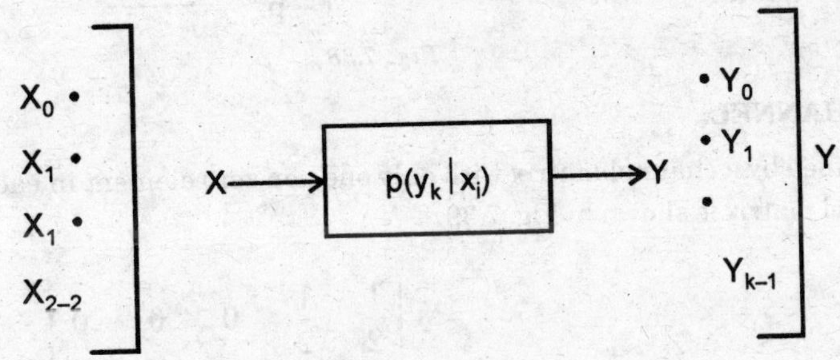

Fig.7.37. View of discrete memoryless channel

$$\text{Input, } X = \{x_0, x_1, x_2 \ldots, x_{j-1}\}$$

$$\text{Output } Y = \{y_0, y_1, y_2, \ldots, y_{k-1}\}$$

Transition probabilities,

$$p(y_k/x_j) = P(Y = y_k)(X = x_j) \text{ for all } j \text{ and } k.$$

7.8.7. CHANNEL MATRIX.

It is a complete set of transition probabilities i.e., a channel is completely specified by the channel matrix denoted as [P(Y/X)], and is given by

$$[P(Y|X)] = \begin{bmatrix} p(y_0 \mid x_0) & p(v_1 \mid x_0) & \cdots & p(y_{k-1} \mid x_0) \\ p(y_0 \mid x_1) & p(y_1 \mid x_1) & \cdots & p(y_{k-1} \mid x_1) \\ \vdots & \vdots & & \\ 0 & 0 & \cdots & p(x_{j-1}) \end{bmatrix}$$

Fundamental property of channel matrix is that, *sum of elements along any row of the matix is equal to one*

i.e.

$$\sum_{k}^{k-1} p(y_k \mid x_j) = 1 \quad \text{for all } j.$$

Now, input probabilities P(X) are expressed by the row matrix,

$$[P(X)] = [P(x_0) \quad P(x_1) \quad \ldots \quad P(x_{j-1})]$$

and

$$[P(Y)] = [P(y_0) \quad P(y_1) \quad \ldots \quad P(y_{k-1})]$$

Then,

$$[P(Y)] = [P(X)]\,[P(Y/X)]$$

Let P(X) be given as a diagonal matrix,

$$[P(X)]_d = \begin{bmatrix} p(x_1) & 0 & \ldots & 0 \\ 0 & p(x_2) & \ldots & 0 \\ \vdots & \vdots & \ldots & \vdots \\ 0 & 0 & \ldots & p(x_{j-1}) \end{bmatrix}$$

then

$$[P(X, Y)] = [P(X)]_d\,[P(Y \mid X)]$$

The matrix P(X,Y) called *joint probability matrix* and element $p(x_i, y_j)$ is point probability of transmitting x_i and receiving y_j.

7.8.8. BINARY SYMMETRIC CHANNEL.

This channel has input symbols $(x_0 = 0, x_1 = 1)$ and two output symbols $(y_0 = 1, y_1 = 1)$ and symmetric as probability of receiving *a* 1 if *a* 0 is sent is equal to the probability of receiving *a* 0 if *a* 1 sent. Transition probability diagram is shown in Fig. 7.38.

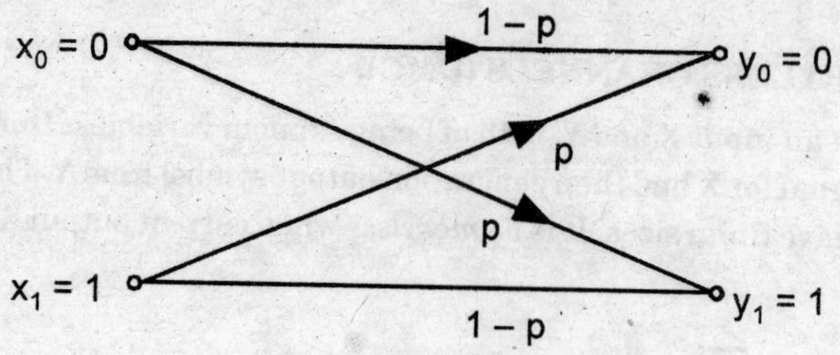

Fig. 7.38

7.8.9. LOSSLESS CHANNEL.

This channel is described by a channel matrix with only one non zero element in each column. A lossess channel and corresponding channel matrix is shown in Fig. 7.39.

$$[P(Y \mid X)] = \begin{bmatrix} \frac{1}{2} & \frac{1}{2} & 0 & 0 & 0 \\ 0 & 0 & \frac{1}{3} & \frac{1}{3} & 0 \\ 0 & 0 & 0 & 0 & 1 \end{bmatrix}$$

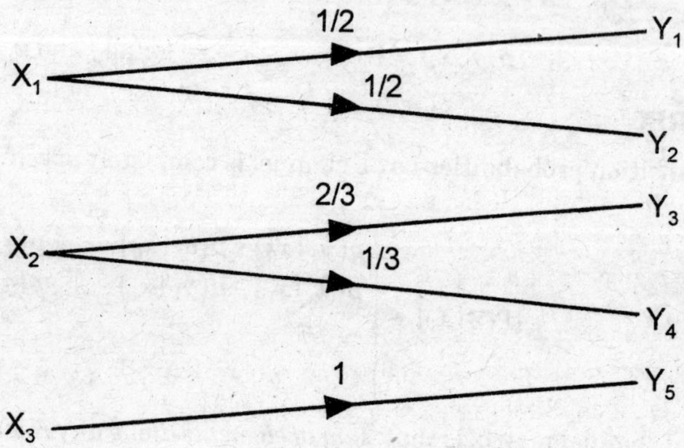

Fig. 7.39

In this channel, there is no loss of information during transmission.

7.8.10. DETERMINISTIC CHANNEL.

It is a channel having channel matrix of having only one non zero element in each row

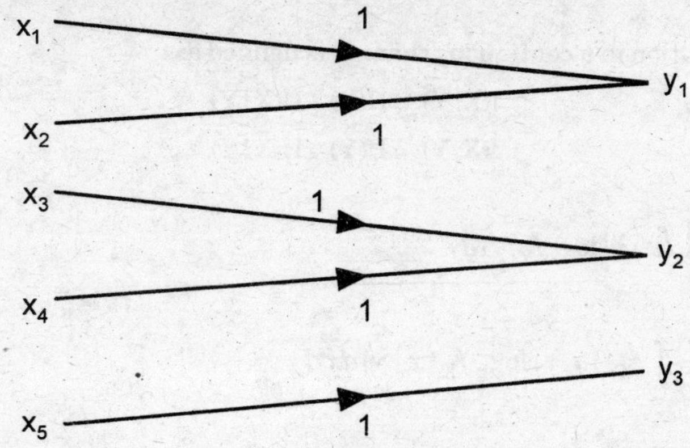

Fig. 7.40

$$P[Y \mid X] = \begin{bmatrix} 1 & 0 & 0 \\ 1 & 0 & 0 \\ 0 & 1 & 0 \\ 0 & 1 & 0 \\ 0 & 0 & 1 \end{bmatrix}$$

Since, $\sum_{k}^{k-I} P(Y_k \mid x_j) = 1$ for all j, therefore each element of the matrix in row should be 1.

7.8.11. MUTUAL INFORMATION.

Mutual information of a channel,

$$I(X; Y) = H(X) - H(X \mid Y)) \; b/\text{symbol}$$

Here, H(X) represents uncertainty about channel input before channel output is observed

H(X | Y) represents uncertainty about channel input after the channel output is observed,

Difference H(X) – H(X | Y) represent uncertainty about the channel input that is resolved by observing channel output.

Properties of Mutual Information

(*i*) Mutual information of a channel is symmetric,

i.e. $$I(X; Y) = I(Y; X)$$

(*ii*) Mutual information is always positive, i.e.

$$I(X; Y) \geq 0$$

(*iii*) Mutual information of a channel is related to the joint entropy of the channel input and channel output by

$$I(X; Y) = H(X) + H(Y) - H(X, Y)$$

where, joint entropy, $$H(X; Y) = \sum_{j=0}^{J-1} \sum_{j=0}^{k-1} p(x_j, y_k) \log_2 \left[\frac{1}{p(x_j, y_k)} \right]$$

7.8.12. CHANNEL CAPACITY.

Channel capacity of a discrete memoryless channel is defined as the maximum average mutual information I(X;Y) in any single use of the channel (*i.e.*, signaling interval), where maximization is overall possible input probability distributions $\{p(x_j)\}$ on X, i.e., if channel capacity denoted by C, then

$$C = \max_{\{p(x_j)\}} I(X; Y)$$

7.8.13. DIFFERENTIAL ENTROPY.

It is expressed as,
$$H(X) = \int_{-\infty}^{\infty} f_x(x)\, \log_2 f_X(x)\, dx \quad b/\text{sample}$$

Average mutual information in a continuous channel is defined as

$$I(X; Y) = H(X) - H(X \mid Y)$$
$$I(X; Y) = H(Y) - H(X \mid Y)$$

where,
$$H(Y) = -\int_{-\infty}^{\infty} f_Y(y) \log_2 f_Y(y)\, dy$$

$$H(X \mid Y) = -\int_{-\infty}^{\infty}\int_{-\infty}^{\infty} f_{XY}(x, y) \log_2 f_X(x \mid y)\, dx\, dy$$

$$H(Y \mid X) = -\int_{-\infty}^{\infty}\int_{-\infty}^{\infty} f_{XY}(x, y) \log_2 f_Y(y \mid x)\, dx\, dy$$

7.8.14. INFORMATION CAPACITY THEOREM.

This theorem states that, *information capacity of a continuous channel of bandwidth BHz, disturbed by additive white Gaussian noise of power spectral density $N_0/2$ and limited in Bandwidth to B is given as*

$$C = B \log_2\left(1 + \frac{P}{N_0 B}\right) \text{ bits/second}$$

where, P = average transmitted power

7.8.15. CHANNEL CODING.

It consists of mapping incoming data sequence into a channel input sequence, and inverse mapping channel output sequence into an output data sequence in a way to minimized the effect of channel noise of the system.

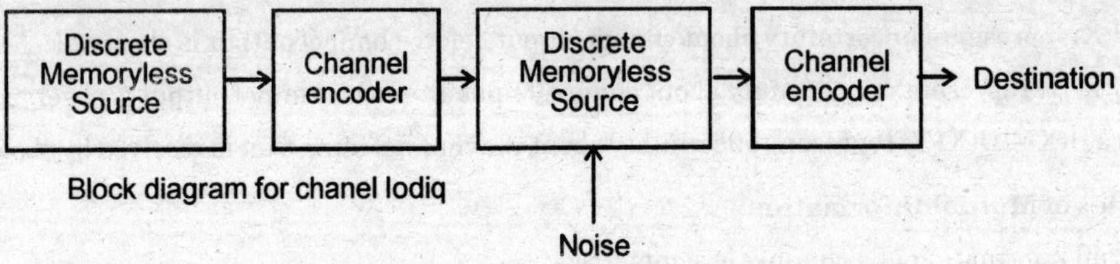

Fig.7.41. Basic block diagram for channel coding

Channel Coding theorem.

A discrete memoryless source with an alphabet S and entropy H(S) producing symbol once in every T_s seconds.

Let a discrete memoryless channel have capacity C and be used once every T_c seconds. Then, if

$$\frac{H(S)}{T_s} \le \frac{C}{T_c} \quad \text{...(7.26)}$$

then, there exists a coding scheme for which source output can be transmitted over the channel with an arbitrary small probability of error.

Conversely, if
$$\frac{H(s)}{T_s} \le \frac{C}{T_s} \quad \text{...(7.27)}$$

then it is not possible to transmit information over the channel and it with an arbitrary small probability of error. The parameter C/T_s is called *critical rate* and when equility sign holds in equation 7.26 then the system is said to be *signalling at the critical rate*.

7.9. DIGITAL COMMUNICATION SYSTEMS

7.9.1. PULSE-CODE MODULATION (PCM).

In PCM a message signal is represented by a sequence of coded pulses, which is accomplished by representing the signal in discrete form in both time and amplitude. The basic operations involved are sampling, quantizing and encoding, as shown in Fig. 7.42. The low-pass filter prior to sampling is included to prevent aliasing of the message signal. The quantizing and encoding operations are usually performed in the same circuit, which is called *analog-to-digital converter*. The basic operations in the receiver are regeneration of unpaired signals, decoding and reconstruction of the train of quantized samples as shown in Fig. 7.42 (*c*). Regeneration along the transmission path also occurs at the intermediate points as it being necessary. If time-division-multiplexing is employed, then proper synchronization between receiver and transmitter is needed.

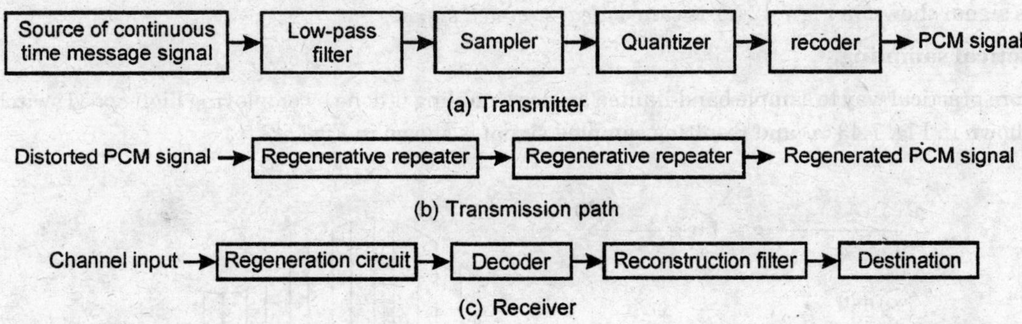

Fig. 7.42

7.9.2. SAMPLING THEOREM.

1. **Band-Limited signals**

   It is a signal *m* (*t*) for which Fourier transform of *m* (*t*) is zero above a certain frequency ω_M.

   $$m(t) \leftrightarrow M(\omega) = 0 \quad \text{for} \quad |\omega| > \omega_M = 2\pi f_M \qquad ...(7.28)$$

2. **Sampling theorem**

   If a signal *m*(*t*) is a real-valued band-limited signal fulfilling the condition given in equation (7.28), then *m* (*t*) can be uniquely determined from its values $m(nT_s)$ sampled at uniform intervals $T_s \left[\le \frac{1}{12 f_m}\right]$.

   $$\text{Then} \quad m(t) = \sum_{n=-\infty}^{\infty} m(nT_s) \frac{\sin \omega_M (t - nT_s)}{\omega_M (t - nT_s)}$$

   where, T_s is called *sampling period* and its reciprocal $f_s = 1/T_s$ is called *sampling rate*.

   Thus, sampling theorem states that, *a band-limited signal which has no frequency components higher than f_M Hz can be recovered completely from a set of samples taken at the rate of f_s ($\ge 2 f_M$) samples per second.*

   This sampling theorem is often called *uniform sampling theorem* for baseband or low-pass signals.

   The minimum sampling rate, $2f_M$ samples per second, is called *Nyquist rate*; its reciprocal $1/(2f_M)$ (measured in seconds) is called *Nyquist interval*.

7.9.3. SAMPLING.

1. **Instantaneous sampling**

   Sampling of an arbitrary signal *m* (*t*) instantaneously and at a uniform rate results in an infinite sequence of samples $\{m(nT_s)\}$, where *n* have all possible integer values. This ideal form of sampling is called *instantaneous sampling*.

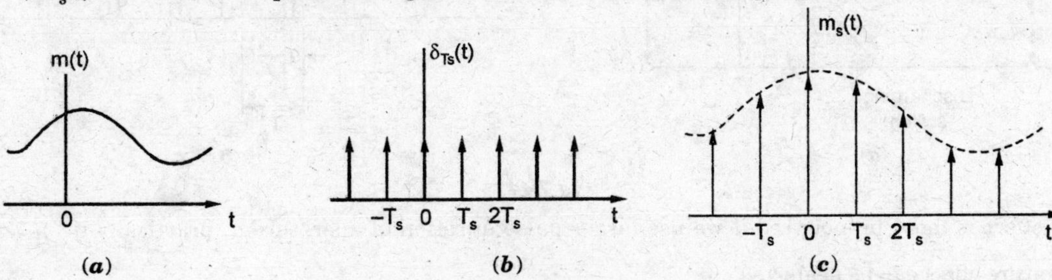

Fig. 7.43

Ideal sampled signal.

Multiplication of $m(t)$ by a unit impulse train $\delta_T(t)$ as shown in Fig. 7.43 (*b*), gives

$$m_s(t) = m(t)\,\delta T_s(t) = m(t) \sum_{n=-\infty}^{\infty} \delta(t - nT_s)$$

$$= \sum_{n=-\infty}^{\infty} m(t)\,\delta(t - nT_s)$$

Now, using the property, $x(t)\,\delta(t - t_0) = x(t_0) \cdot \delta(t - t_0)$

we have
$$m_s(t) = \sum_{n=-\infty}^{\infty} m(nT_s)\,\delta(t - nT_s)$$

This signal shown in Fig 7.42 (*c*), is called *ideal sampled signal*.

2. **Practical sampling.**

A more practical way to sample band-limited analog sampling is done by employing high-speed switching circuits, as shown in Fig. 7.43 (*a*) and resulting sampled signal is shown in Fig 7.43 (*b*).

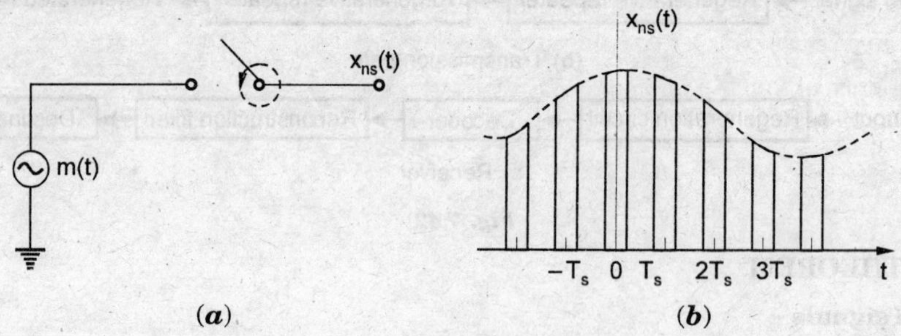

Fig. 7.43

Sampled signal, $x_{ns}(t) = m(t)\,x_p(t)$

where, $x_p(t)$ is periodic train of rectangular pulses with period T_s, and each rectangular pulse in $x_p(t)$ having width d and unit amplitude.

Since top of each pulse in $x_{nx}(t)$ retains the shape of its corresponding analog signal, it is also called *natural sampling*. The condition for the message $m(t)$ to be recovered from the natural sampled signal $x_{nx}(t)$ is that, the sampling rate is equal to or greater than twice the highest message frequency.

3. **Flat-Top sampling**

For flat-top sampling, a sample-and-hold circuit employed as shown in Fig.7.44 (*a*). This circuit produces a flat-top sampled signal. Flat-top sampling is equivalent to passing an ideal sampled signal through a filter having the frequency response

$$H(\omega) = \frac{d \sin(\omega_d / 2)}{\omega_d / 2}.$$

The high-frequency roll-off characteristic of H (ω) acts as a low-pass filter and therefore attenuates the upper portion of the message spectrum. This loss of high-frequency content is called *aperature effect*.

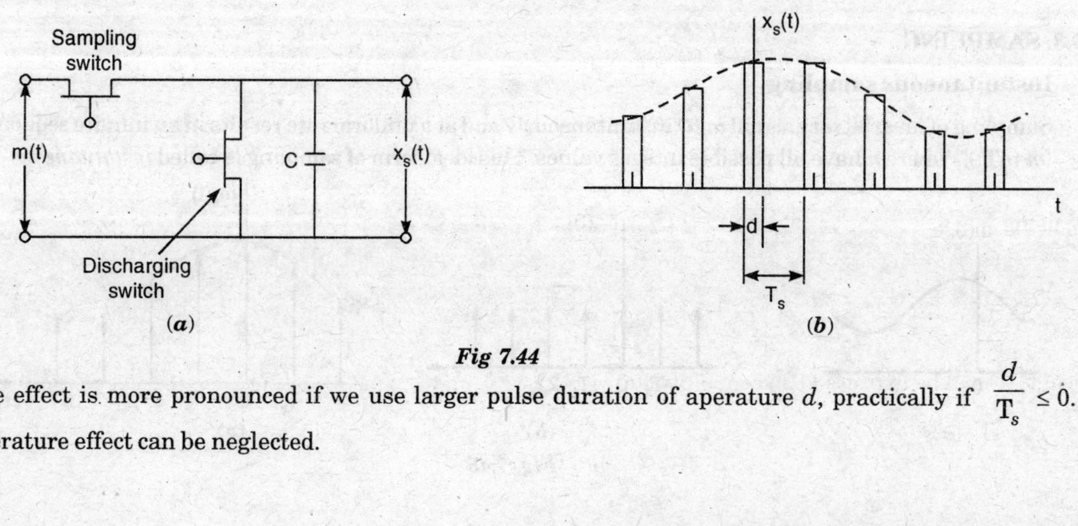

Fig 7.44

The effect is more pronounced if we use larger pulse duration of aperature d, practically if $\frac{d}{T_s} \le 0.1$, then aperature effect can be neglected.

7.9.4. PULSE AMPLITUDE MODULATION (PAM).

In PAM, amplitudes of regularly spaced pulses are varied in proportion to the corresponding sample values of a continuous message signal. This modulation is similar to natural sampling, but in natural sampling, the top of each modulated rectangular pulse varies with the message signal, whereas in PAM it is maintained flat.

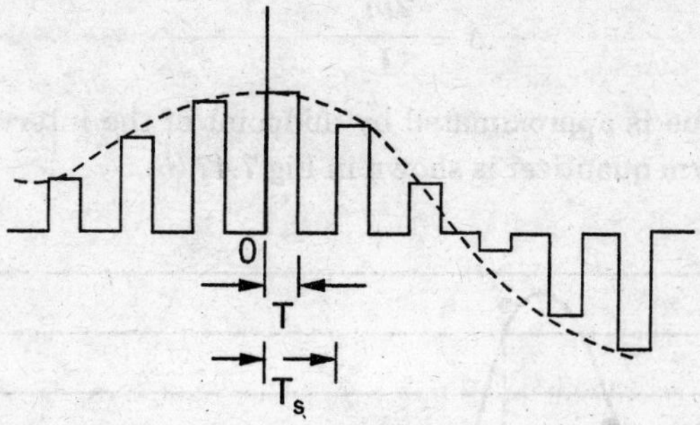

Fig 7.45

Let $x_s(t)$ denotes sequence of flat-top pulses in the way shown in Fig 7.45, then PAM signal $x_s(t)$ can be expressed as

$$x_s(t) = \sum_{n=-\infty}^{\infty} m(nT_s)\, p(t - nT_s)$$

where $p(t)$ is rectangular pulse of unit amplitude and duration d, as shown in Fig 7.46

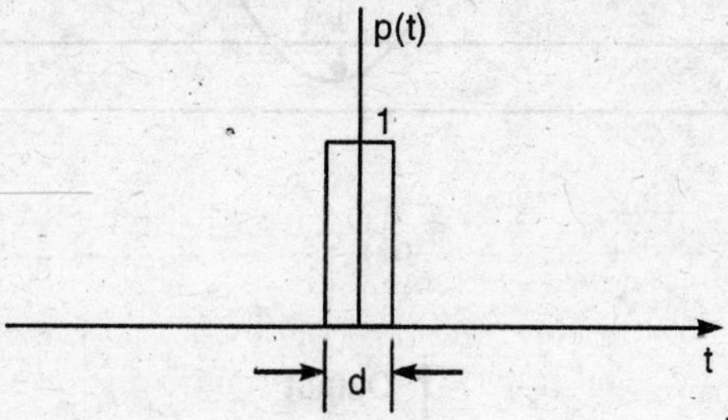

Fig 7.46

$$p(t) = \begin{cases} 1; & |t| < d/2 \\ 0; & \text{otherwise} \end{cases}$$

By definition, instantaneous sampled version of $m(t)$ is given as

$$m_s(t) = \sum_{n=-\infty}^{\infty} m(nT_s) \cdot \delta(t - nT_s)$$

Then, convolving $m_s(t)$ with $p(t)$, we have

$$m_s(t)\, p(t) = \sum_{n=-\infty}^{\infty} m(nT_s)\, \delta(t - nT_s) * p(t)$$

$$= \sum_{n=-\infty}^{\infty} m(nT_s)\, p(t) * \delta(t - nT_s)$$

Now, using $x(t) * \delta(t - t_0) = x(t - t_0)$, we get

$$m_s(t) * p(t) = \sum_{n=-\infty}^{\infty} m(nT_s)\, p(t - nT_s) = x_s(t)$$

Hence, $x_s(t)$ can be expressed as convolutional of $m_s(t)$, instan-taneously sampled signal, and the rectangular pulse $p(t)$, *i.e.*

$$x_s(t) = m_s(t) * p(t)$$

7.9.5. QUANTIZING.

1. Uniform quantizing

A quantizing operation is shown in Fig 7.47. Here, it being assumed that the amplitude of $m(t)$ is confined to the range $(-m_p, m_p)$. This range is divided in L zones, each having step size Δ is

$$\Delta = \frac{2m_p}{L} \qquad \text{... (7.29)}$$

A sample amplitude value is approximated by midpoint of the interval in which it lies. The input – output characteristics of a uniform quantizer is shown in Fig 7.47 (*b*).

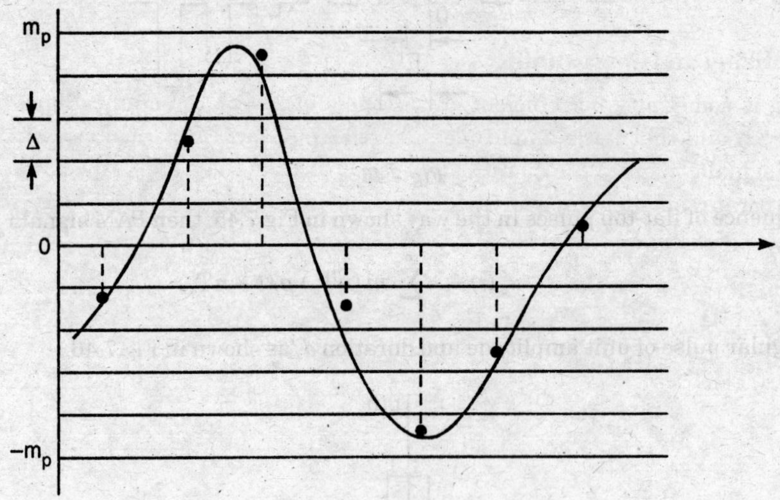

(*a*)

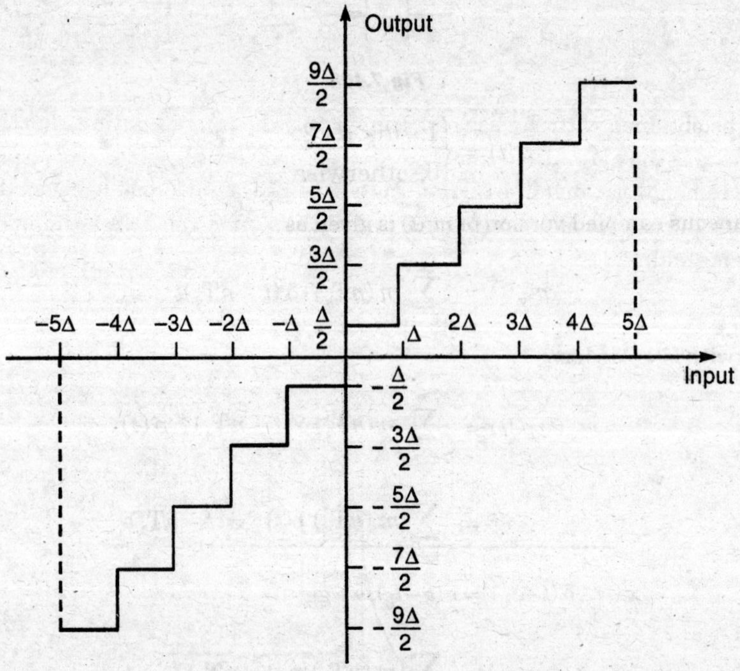

(*b*)

Fig. 7.47. Quantizing operation

2. Quantizing noise

The difference between input and output signals of the quantizer becomes the quantizing error, or quantizing noise. The quantizing error q_e varies randomly within interval,

$$\frac{-\Delta}{2} \le q_e \le \frac{\Delta}{2}$$

Assuming that error is equally likely to lie anywhere in the range $\left(-\frac{\Delta}{2}, \frac{\Delta}{2}\right)$, mean-square quantizing error,

$$<q_e^2> = \frac{1}{\Delta}\int_{-\Delta/2}^{\Delta/2} q_e^2 \, dq_e = \frac{\Delta^2}{12}$$

Using equation (7.29), we have $<q_e^2> = \dfrac{m_p^2}{3L^2}$

Nonuniform Quantizing and Companding.

Uniform quantizing is sometimes not efficient, for example in speech communication where smaller amplitudes predominate in speech and that large amplitudes are relatively rare. Thus, using uniform quantizing scheme is wasteful for speech signals, many of the quantizing levels are rarely used. Fig. 7.48 shows a nonuniform quantizing method which incorporates smaller steps for small amplitudes and larger steps for large amplitudes.

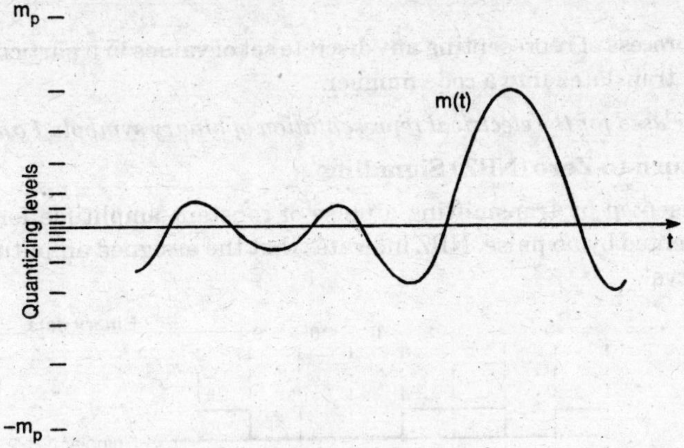

Fig. 7.48

The same result can be obtained with the use of a compressor whose input-output characteristics are shown in Fig. 7.49. The horizontal axis is the normalized input (*i.e.*, m/m_p), and vertical axis is the output signal y. The compressor maps input signal increment Δm into large increment Δy for small input signals and small increment for large input signals. Therefore, with the use of compressed signal to a uniform quantizer, a large number of steps results in a given interval Δm, when m is small.

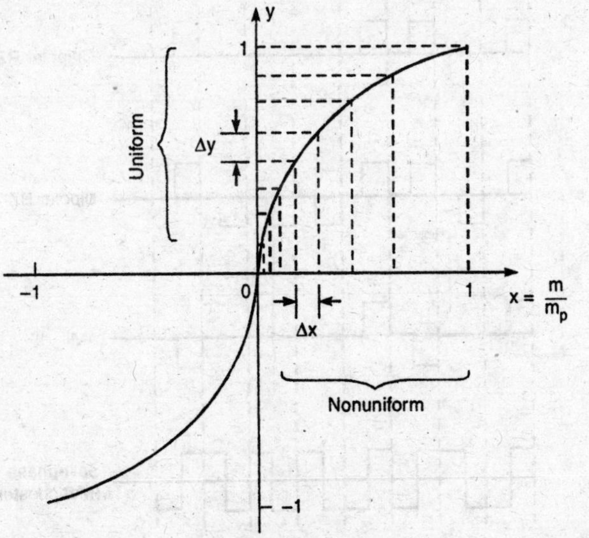

Fig. 7.49. Characteristics of a compressor

A particular form of compression law which is used in practice is called μ *law*, and is defined by

$$y = \frac{\ln\left(\left|1+\mu\frac{m}{m_p}\right|\right)}{\ln(1+\mu)}\,\text{sgn}(m); \quad \left|\frac{m}{m_p}\right| \le 1$$

where, μ = a positive constant

and
$$\text{sgn}(m) = \begin{cases} +1 & m > 0 \\ -1 & m < 0 \end{cases}$$

Another compression law that is used is *A law*, defined by

$$y = \begin{cases} \dfrac{A}{1+\ln A}\left(\dfrac{m}{m_p}\right) & \left|\dfrac{m}{m_p}\right| \le \dfrac{1}{A} \\ \dfrac{(1+\ln A\,|m/m_p|)}{1+\ln A}\,sgn(m) & \dfrac{1}{A} \le \left|\dfrac{m}{m_p}\right| \le 1 \end{cases}$$

For the μ law, μ = 255 is used in digital telephone systems in North America and for the A law A = 87.6 used in European systems. These values are selected such that to obtain a nearly constant output signal-to-quantizing ratio over an input signal power dynamic range of 40 *d*B.

7.9.6. ENCODING.

Encoding involves the process of representing any discrete set of values in a particular arrangement of discrete events *i.e.,* quantized samples translates into a code number.

Several line codes can be used for the electrical representation of binary symbols 1 and 0, as follows :

1. **Unipolar Nonreturn-to-Zero (NRZ) Signaling**

   Symbol 1 is represented by transmitting a pulse of constant amplitude for the duration of bit interval, and symbol 0 is represented by no pulse. NRZ indicates that the assigned amplitude level is maintained throughout the entire bit interval.

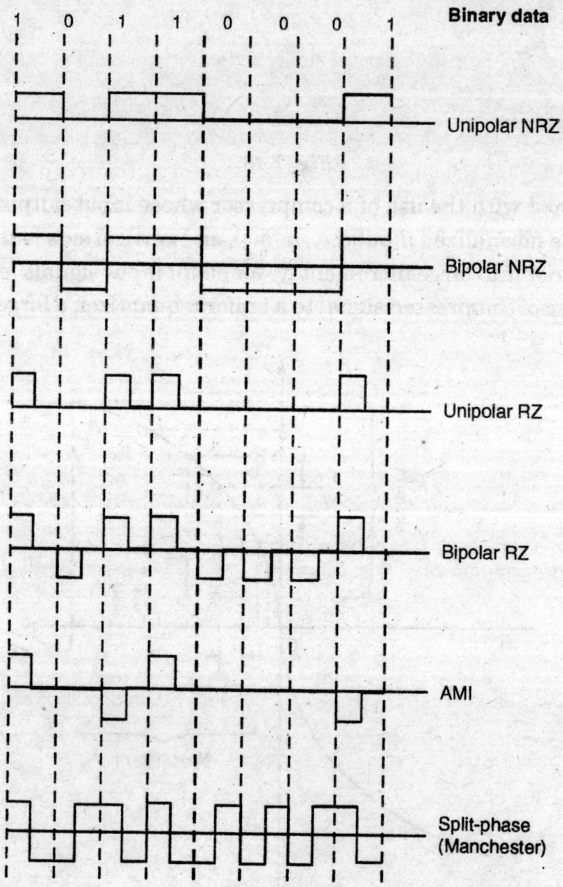

Fig. 7.50

2. **Bipolar NRZ Signaling**

   Symbols 1 and 0 are represented by pulses of equal positive and negative amplitudes. In either case, the assigned pulse amplitude level is maintained throughout the bit interval.

3. **Unipolar Return-to-Zero (RZ) Signaling**

   Symbol 1 is represented by a positive pulse that returns to zero before the end of the bit interval, and symbol 0 is represented by the absence of pulse.

4. **Bipolar RZ Signaling**

   Positive and negative pulses of equal amplitude are used for symbols 1 and 0, respectively. In either case, the pulse returns to 0 before the end of the bit interval.

5. **Alternative Mark Inversion (AMI) RZ Signaling**

   Positive and negative pulses (of equal amplitude) are used alternately for symbol 1, and no pulse is used for symbol 0. In either case the pulse returns to 0 before the end of the bit interval.

6. **Split-Phase (Manchester) Signaling**

   Symbol 1 is represented by a positive pulse followed by a negative pulse, with both pulses being of equal amplitude and half-bit duration; for symbol 0, the polarities of these pulses are reversed.

7.9.7. TIME-DIVISION MULTIPLEXING (TDM).

This multiplexing is commonly used for the transmission of several different signals through a single channel. Fig. 7.51 shows the concept of TDM. Each input signal is first restricted in bandwidth by a low-pass filter, to remove frequencies that are non-essential for adequate signal representation. Then low-pass filter outputs are applied to a commutator, which is usually implemented using electronic switching circuity. Each signal is sampled at the Nyquist rate or higher.

Commutator performs two functions :

(*i*) Take a narrow sample of each of the N input messages at a rate f_s that is slightly higher than 2W, where W is cut-off frequency of the pre-alias filter

(*ii*) Sequentially inter leave these N samples inside the sampling interval T_s.

Following the commutation process, the multiplexed signal is applied to a pulse modulator, which transform the multiplexed signal into a form suitable for transmission over the common channel. TDM introduces a bandwidth expansion factor N, since N samples are squeezed into one sampling interval. At the receiving end, the composite signal is demultiplexed by pulse demodulator. The narrow samples produced at the pulse demodulator are distributed to the appropriate low-pass filter for demodulation proper operation of this system depends upon proper synchronization between the two commutators.

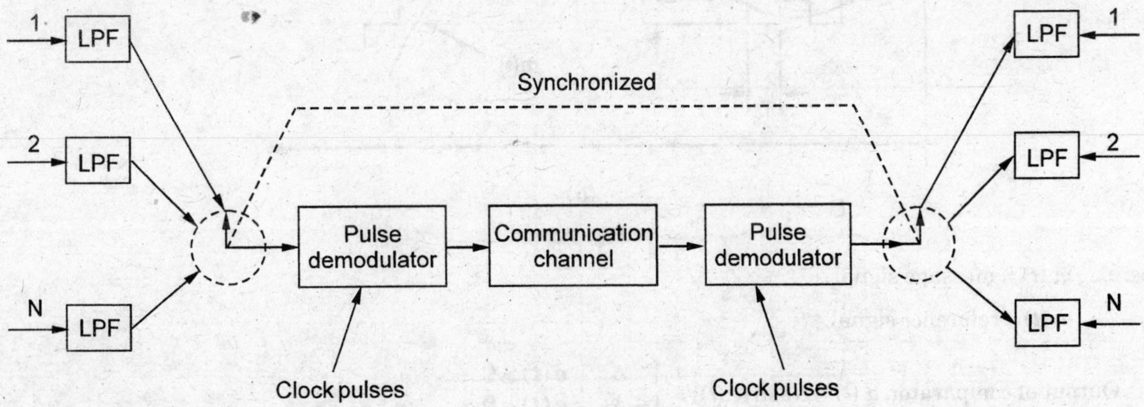

Fig. 7.51

Bandwidth requirements fo TDM

If all input signals have the same bandwidth f_m and are sampled equally, then

$$T = \frac{T_s}{n}$$

where, n = number of input signals

and $T_s = \frac{1}{f_s} \leq \frac{1}{2f_m}$ is sampling interval of each signal.

If resultant time-multipiexed signal is low-pass signal of bandwidth f_{TDM}, then

$$\text{minimum sampling rate } = 2f_{TDM}$$

Thus

$$f_{TDM} = \frac{1}{2T} = \frac{n}{2T_s} = \frac{1}{2} nf_s \geq nf_m \text{ Hz.}$$

7.9.8. DELTA MODULATION (DM).

DM, an incoming message signal is oversampled to increase the correlation between adjacent samples of the signal. This rate is much higher than the Nyquist rate.

In its basic form, DM provides a staircase approximation to the oversampled version of the message signal, as shown in Fig 7.52.

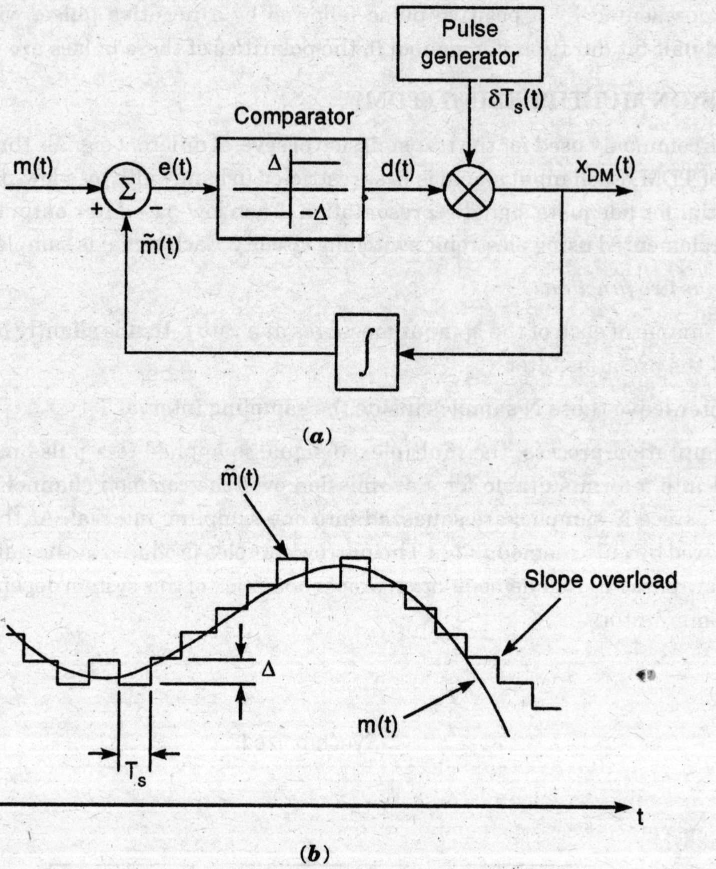

Fig. 7.52

where, $m(t)$ = message signal

$m(t)$ = reference signal.

$$\text{Output of comparator, } d(t) = \Delta \operatorname{sgn}[e(t)] = \begin{cases} \Delta & e(t) > 0 \\ -\Delta, & e(t) < 0 \end{cases}$$

Then output of delta modulator,

$$x_{DM}(t) = \Delta \operatorname{sgn}[e(t)] \sum_{n=-\infty}^{\infty} \delta(t - nT_s)$$

$$= \sum_{n=-\infty}^{\infty} \operatorname{sgn}[e(nT_s)]\, \delta(t - nT_s)$$

Thus output of the delta modulator is a series of impulses, each having positive or negative polarity depending on the sign of $e(t)$ at the sampling instants.

Integrating $x_{DM}(t)$, we get

$$m(t) = \sum_{n=-\infty}^{\infty} \Delta \, \text{sgn}[e(nT_s)]$$

which is staircase approximation of $m(t)$, as shown in Fig. 7.52 (b)

Demodulation of DM

It is accomplished by integrating $x_{DM}(t)$ to form the staircase approximation $\tilde{m}(t)$ and then passing through a low-pass filter to eliminate the discrete jumps in $\tilde{m}(t)$.

Small step size is desirable to reproduce the input waveform accurately. However, small step size must be accompanied by a fast sampling rate to avoid slope overload, as shown in Fig. 7.52 (b).

To avoid slope overload, $\dfrac{\Delta}{T_s} > \left|\dfrac{dm(t)}{dt}\right|_{\max}$

Quantizing Error

Assuming that quantizing error in DM is equally likely to lie anywhere in the interval $(-\Delta, \Delta)$, so that mean-square quantizing error is

$$\langle q_e^2 \rangle = \frac{1}{2\Delta} \int_{-\Delta}^{\Delta} q_e^2 \, dq_e = \frac{\Delta^2}{3}$$

7.9.9. DIFFERENTIAL PULSE - CODE MODULATION (DPCM).

In a PCM system, the signal $x(t)$ is sampled at a rate which is slightly higher than the Nyquist rate. The resulting sampled signal exhibits a high correlation between adjacent samples. i.e., there is a correlation between adjacent samples. Generally signal x(t) does not change rapidly from one sample to the next. Hence difference in amplitudes of adjacent samples is very small, as shown in Fig. 7.53.

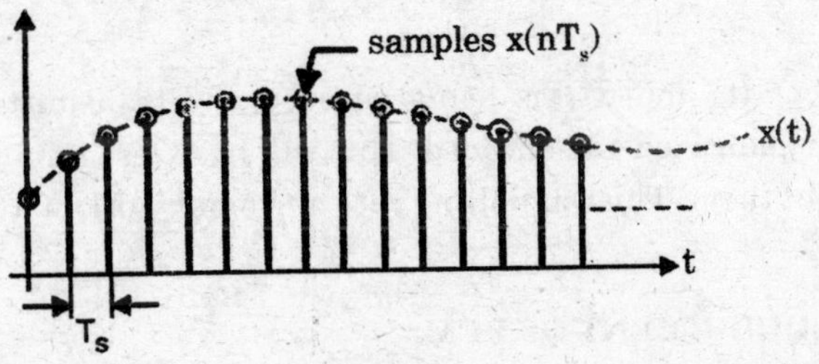

Fig. 7.53

When these highly correlated samples are encoded in a standard PCM system, resulting encoded signal contains redundant information. By removing this redundancy before encoding, a more efficiently coded signal can be obtained. DPCM system operates on this principle. In DPCM system, a special circuit called "predictor" is used, which can actually predict values of the future samples of $x(t)$. This helps in reducing the redundancy.

DPCM Transmitter

Block diagram of a DPCM transmitter and receiver is as shown in Fig. 7.54. Unlike PCM in DPCM scheme, the digital equivalent of each quantized sample is not transmitted by the transmitter. Instead digital equivalent of the "difference" between present sample value and, the previous sample value is transmitted.

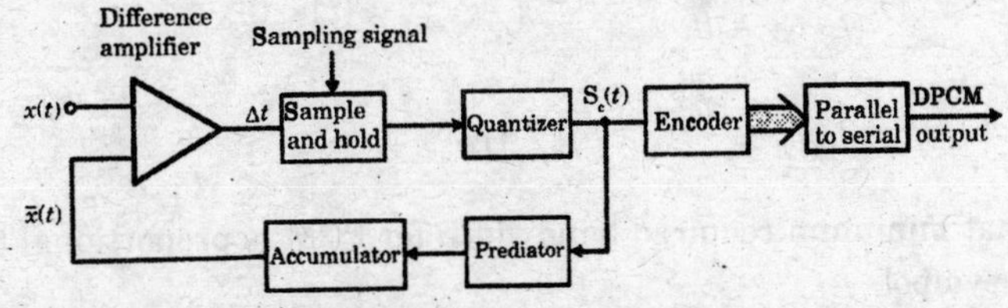

Fig. 7.54. DPCM transmitter

Operation of a DPCM transmitter :

(*i*) In block diagram of a DPCM transmitter, $x(t)$ is analog input signal and $\overline{x}(t)$ is its approximated signal. It is important to know that whether $\overline{x}(t)$ is larger or smaller than $x(t)$ and by how much.

(*ii*) At each sampling instant, difference amplifier compares x(t) and $\overline{x}(t)$ and sample and hold circuit will hold the result of this subtraction.

(*iii*) The difference signal at the output of sample and hold circuit is quantized by the quantizer. Then quantizer output $S_0(t)$ is transmitted as it is or it is encoded into a stream of bits.

(*iv*) Quantizer output is also used to produce approximated signal $\overline{x}(t)$ by passing the quantizer output through a predictor and accumulator.

Role of a predictor in DPCM

If sampling takes place at a rate which is higher than the Nyquist rate, then there is a correlation between successive samples of the signal $x(t)$. Hence a knowledge of past sample values or differences helps to predict range of next required increment or decrement at the predictor output. This reduces difference or error between x(t) and $\overline{x}(t)$. Therefore to encode this small value of error the DPCM system requires less number of bits which will ultimately reduce the bit rate.

DPCM Receiver

The received signal carriers information about the difference between x(t) and $\overline{x}(t)$ at the transmitter. From this signal "*predictor*" predict approximate value of next signal. The accumulator accuoumulator add all these differences and the filter smooth out of quantization noise. DPCM receiver block diagram is as shown in Fig. 7.55.

Fig. 7.55. DPCM receiver

Advantage of DPCM

As the difference between x(t) and $\overline{x}(t)$ is being encoded and transmitted by the PCM technique, a small difference voltage is to be quantized and encoded. This will need less number of quantization levels hence less number of bits to represent them. Thus signalling rate and bandwidth of a DPCM system will be less than that of PCM.

7.9.10. BANDWIDTH REQUIREMENT OF PCM.

Let in a binary PCM, L quantizing levels are used, satisfying

$$L = 2^n$$

$$\Rightarrow \qquad n = \log_2 L$$

where, n = integer

For this case, binary pulses must be transmitted for each sample of the message signal. If message bandwidth is f_m, sampling rate is f_s and sampling rate is f_s ($\geq 2f_m$), then nf_s binary pulses must be transmitted per second.

Assuming that PCM signal is a low-pass signal of bandwidth f_{PCM}, the required minimum sampling rate is $2f_{PCM}$. Thus

$$2\,f_{PCM} = nf_s$$

$$\Rightarrow \qquad f_{PCM} = \frac{n}{2} f_s \geq n f_m \text{ Hz}$$

This equation shows that minimum required bandwidth for PCM is proportional to the message signal bandwidth and number of bits per symbol.

7.10. DIGITAL CARRIER MODULATION SYSTEMS.

In binary modulation schemes, the modulation process corresponds to switching (or keying) the amplitude, frequency, or phase of the CW carrier between either of two values corresponding to binary symbols 0 and

7.10.1. TYPES OF DIGITAL MODULATION.

Three types of digital modulation are

1. **Amplitude-Shift Keying (ASK)**

   In ASK, modulated signal can be expressed as

$$x_c(t) = \begin{cases} A \cos \omega_c t & \text{symbol 1} \\ 0 & \text{symbol 0} \end{cases}$$

   As modulated signal is still an ON-OFF signal, thus ASK is also called *on-off keying* (OOK).

2. **Frequency-Shift Keying (FSK)**

   In FSK, modulated signal can be expressed as

$$x_c(t) = \begin{cases} A \cos \omega_1 t & \text{symbol 1} \\ A \cos \omega_2 t & \text{symbol 0} \end{cases}$$

3. **Phase-Shift Keying (PSK)**

   In PSK, modulated signal can be expressed as

$$x_c(t) = \begin{cases} A \cos \omega_c t & \text{symbol 1} \\ A \cos (\omega_c t + \pi) & \text{symbol 0} \end{cases}$$

Fig. 7.56 shows these digital modulation schemes for the case in which data bits are represented by bipolar NRZ waveform.

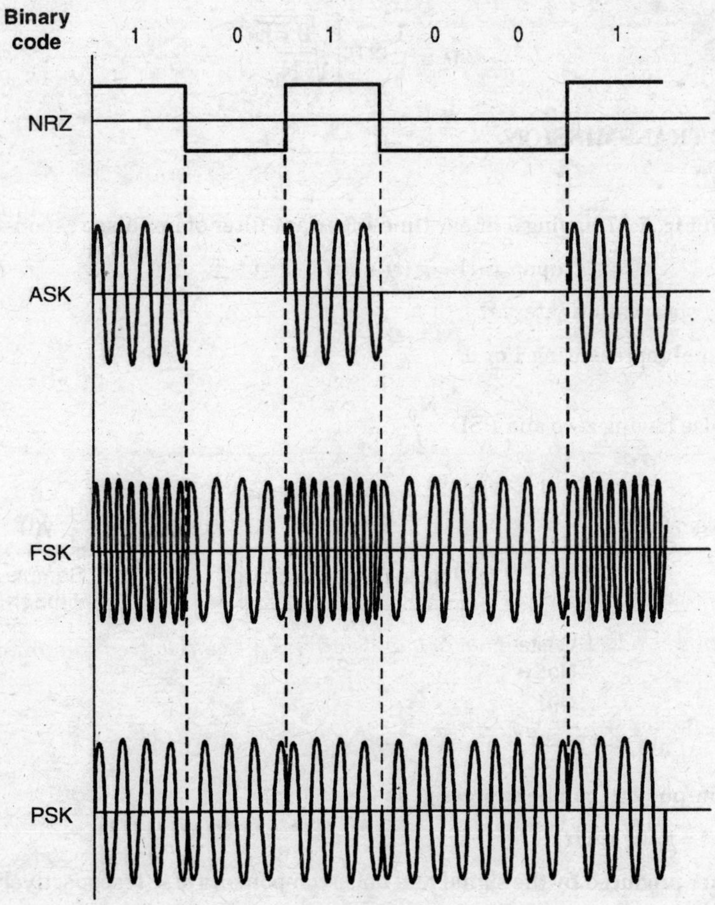

Fig. 7.56

7.10.2. COMPARISON OF DIGITAL MODULATION SYSTEMS.

Sr. No.	Parameter	Binary ASK	Binary FSK	Binary PSK
1.	Variable characteristic	Amplitude	Frequency	Phase
2.	Bandwidth (Hz)	$2f_b$	$4f_b$	$2f_b$
3.	Noise immunity	low	high	high
4.	Error probability	high	low	low
5.	Performance in presence of noise	Bad	Better than ASK	Better than FSK
6.	Complexity	Simple	Moderately complex	Very complex
7.	Bit rate	Suitable upto 100 bits/sec.	Suitable upto about 1200 bits/sec	Suitable for high bit rates
8.	Detection method	Envelope	Envelope	Coherent

7.10.3. PROBABILITIES OF VARIOUS SYSTEMS

ASK system : $P_c = \frac{1}{2}\text{erfc}[\sqrt{E/4N_0}]$

BPSK system : $P_e = \frac{1}{2}\text{erfc}[\sqrt{E/N_0}]$

BFSK system : $P_c = \frac{1}{2}\text{erfc}\left[\sqrt{\frac{0.6E}{N_0}}\right]$

7.11. BASEBAND PULSE TRANSMISSION.

7.11.1. MATCHED FILTER.

A receiver model is shown in Fig. 7.57 having a linear time-invariant filter of impulse response $h(t)$.

$$\text{Input, } x(t) = g(t) + \omega(t), \quad 0 \le t \le T$$

where, T = arbitrary observation interval

$g(t)$ = pulse signal representing 1 or 0

$\omega(t)$ = white noise having zero and PSD $\frac{N_0}{2}$.

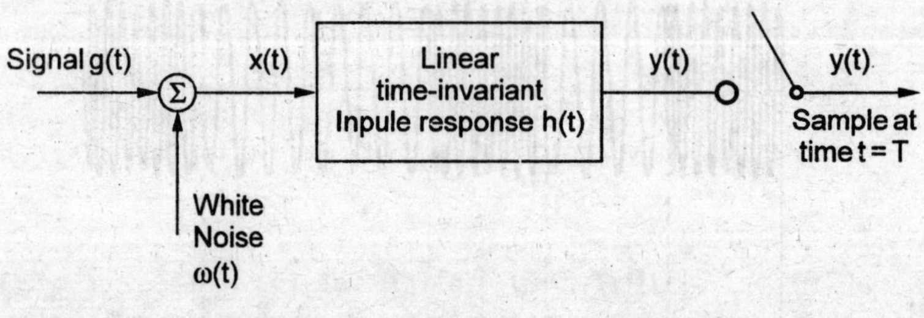

Fig. 7.57

Since filter is linear, output $y(t)$ can be expressed as

$$y(t) = g_0(t) + n(t)$$

where $g_0(t)$ and $n(t)$ are produced by the signal and noise components of $x(t)$ respectively.

Now, peak pulse signal-to-noise ratio is

$$\eta = \frac{|g_0(T)|^2}{E[n^2(t)]} \qquad \text{... (7.30)}$$

where $|g_0(T)|^2$ = instantaneous power in the output signal

$E[n^2(t)]$ = average output noise power.

The impulse response $h(t)$ of the filter should be such that η would be maximum.

Now, if $G(f)$ be the Fourier transform of the known signal $g(t)$ and $H(f)$ denote transfer function of the filter, then inverse Fourier transform of output

$$g_0(t) = \int_{-\infty}^{\infty} H(f).G(f).\exp(j2\pi ft).df$$

At $t = T$,

$$|g_0(T)|^2 = \left|\int_{-\infty}^{\infty} H(f).G(f).\exp(j2\pi fT).df\right|^2 \qquad \text{...(7.31)}$$

and, power spectral density of the output noise

$$S_N(f) = \frac{N_0}{2}|H(f)^2|$$

Average power of output noise $n(t)$ is,

$$E[n^2(t)] = \int_{-\infty}^{\infty} S_N(f).df$$

$$= \frac{N_0}{2}\int_{-\infty}^{\infty} |H(f)|^2.df \qquad \text{...(7.32)}$$

From equations (7.30), (7.31) and (7.32), we have

$$\eta = \frac{\left|\int_{-\infty}^{\infty} H(f).G(f)\exp(j2\pi T).df\right|^2}{\frac{N_0}{2}\int_{0}^{\infty}|H(f)|^2.df} \qquad \text{...(7.33)}$$

Using Schwarz's inequality for any two complex functions $\phi_1(x)$ and $\phi_2(x)$ in the real variable x, satisfying

$$\int_{-\infty}^{\infty} |\phi_1(x)|^2.dx < \infty \text{ and } \int_{-\infty}^{\infty} |\phi_2(x)|^2.dx < \infty$$

then,

$$\left|\int_{-\infty}^{\infty} \phi_1(x)\phi_2(x)dx\right|^2 \le \int_{-\infty}^{\infty} |\phi_1(x)|^2.dx \int_{-\infty}^{\infty} |\phi_2(x)|^2.dx \qquad \text{... (7.34)}$$

From equation (7.33),

$$\eta \le \frac{\int_{-\infty}^{\infty}|H(f)|^2.df \int_{-\infty}^{\infty}|G(f)|^2.df}{\frac{N_0}{2} + |H(f)|^2.df} \le \frac{2}{N_0}\cdot\int_{-\infty}^{\infty}|G(f)|^2.df$$

and

$$\eta_{max} = \frac{2}{N_0}\int_{-\infty}^{\infty}|G(f)|^2.df$$

Since equality in equation (7.34) holds if, only if,

$$\phi_1(x) = K\phi_2^*(x)$$

where K is arbitray constant.

Hence correspondingly H (*f*) assumes its optimum value

$$H_{opt}(f) = KG^*(f).\exp(-j2\pi fT)$$

and

$$h_{opt}(t) = Z^{-1}[H_{opt}(f)]$$

$$= K\int_{-\infty}^{\infty} G^*(f).\exp[-j\,2\pi f\,(T-t)]\,df$$

As for a real signal

$$G^*(f) = G(-f),$$

$$h_{opt}(f) = K\int_{-\infty}^{\infty} G(-f).\exp[-j\,2\pi f\,(T-t)].\,df$$

$$= K_g(T-t)$$

This equation tells that impulse response of the optimum filter, except for a scaling factor K, is a time reversed and delayed version of the input signal *g* (*f*). In other words, impulse response of the match filter is a delayed version of the mirror image of the signal form.

7.12. MULTIPLE ACESS SYSTEM

7.12.1. GLOBAL SYSTEM FOR MOBILE COMMUNICATIONS (GSM).

It is the most popular standard for mobile phones in the world. It is a cellular network, which means that mobile phones connect to it by searching for cells in the immediate vicinity.

GSM network operate in four different frequency ranges. Most GSM network operate in the 900 MHz or 1800 MHz bands.

Gaussian Minimum Shift Keying (GMSK)

It is modulation used in GSM. It is a kind of continuous-phase frequency shift keying.

In GMSK, the signal to be modulated onto the carrier is first smoothed with a Gaussian low-pass filter prior to being fed to a frequency modulator, which greatly reduces the interference to neighbouring channels (adjacent channel interference)

Basic structure of a GSM-network

It comprises of

(*i*) Base station subsystem (base station and their controller)

(*ii*) Network and switching subsytem

(*iii*) GRPS core Network (optional part which allows packet based Intenet connections)

Communication Domain

It communication technology, there are only three domains that can allow multiplexing to be implemented for more efficient use of the available channel bandwidth.

These domain are

(*i*) Time

(*ii*) Frequency

(*iii*) Space.

TYPES OF ACCESS.

1. Code Division Multiple Access(CDMA).

It divides the access in signal space

It describes a communication channel access principle that employs spread-spectrum technology and a special coding scheme (where each transmitter is assigned a code).

It is a form of *spread - spectrum signalling,* since modulated coded signal has a much higher bandwidth than the data being communicated.

2. Frequency Division Multiple Access(FDMA).

It divides the access by frequency.

It is an access technology that is used by radio system to share the radio spectrum. In an FDMA scheme, the given Radio Frequency (RF) bandwidth is divided into adjacent frequency segment. Each segment is provided with bandwidth to enable an associated communication signal to pass through a transmission environment with an acceptable level of interference from communication signals in adjacent frequency segments.

It is a basic technology in the analog Advanced Mobile Phone Service (AMPS), the most Widely installed cellular phone system installed in North America with FDMA, each channel can be assigned to only one user at a time. FDMA is also used in the Total Access Communication System (TACS).

3. Time Division Multiple Access(TDMA).

It divides the access by time.

It is a channel access method for shared medium (usually radio) networks. It allows several users to share the same frequency channel by dividing the signal into different **timeslots.** The users transmit in rapid succession, one after the other, each using his own timeslot. This allows multiple stations to share the same transmission medium (e.g. radio frequency channel) while using only the part of its bandwidth they require.

It is used in (GSM), IS-136, Personal Digital Cellular (PDC) and iDEN, and in the Digital Enhanced Cordless Telecommunications (DECT) standard for portable phones. It is also used extensively in satellite systems, and combat-net radio system.

It is a type of time-division multiplexing, with the special point that instead of having one transmitter connected to one receiver, there are multiple transmitters. In case of *uplink* from a mobile phone to a base station, this becomes particularly difficult because the mobile phone can move around and vary the *timing advance* required to make its transmission match the gap in transmission from its peers.

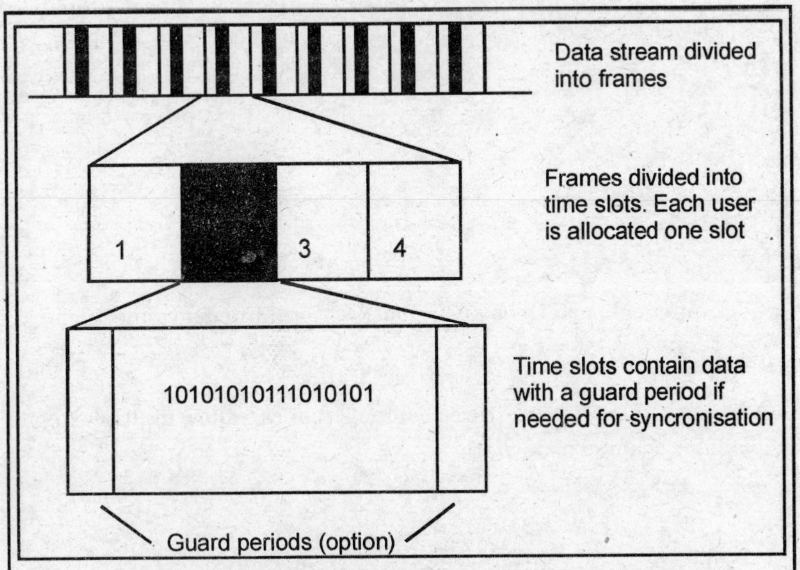

TDMA frame structure showing a data stream divided into frames and those frames divided into timeslots.

7.12.2. COMPARISON OF MULTIPLE-ACCESS SCHEMES.

In radio systems, TDMA is usually used alongside frequency-division multiple access (FDMA) and frequency division duplex (FDD). The combination is called FDMA/TDMA/FDD. This is the case in both GSM and IS-136 for example.

Advantage of TDMA

Radio part of the mobile only needs to listen and broadcast for its own timeslot. For the rest of the time, the mobile can carry out measurements on the network, detecting surrounding transmitters on different frequencies. This allows safe inter frequency handovers, something which is difficult in CDMA systems.

CDMA, by comparison, supports "*soft hand-off*" which allows a mobile phone to be in communication with up to 6 base stations simultaneously, a type of "same-frequency handover". The incoming packets are compared for quality, and the best one is selected. CDMA's "cell breathing" characteristic, where a terminal on the boundary of two congested cells will be unable to receive a clear signal, can often negate this advantage during peak periods.

Disadvantage of TDMA

These create interference at a frequency which is directly connected to the timeslot length. This is the irritating buzz which can sometimes be heard if a GSM phone is left next to a radio or speakers. Another disadvantage is that the "dead time" between timeslots limits the potential bandwidth of a TDMA channel. These are implemented in part because of the difficulty ensuring that different terminals transmit at exactly the times required. Handsets that are moving will need to constantly adjust their timings to ensure their transmission is received at precisely the right time, because as they move further from the base station, their signal will take longer to arrive. This also means that the major TDMA systems have hard limits on cell sizes in terms of range, though in practice the power levels required to receive and transmit over distances greater than the supported range would be most impractical anyway.

■■

OBJECTIVE TYPE QUESTIONS

RANDOM SIGNALS AND NOISE

1. The probability of density function of the envelope of a sinusoidal signal along with narrow band noise which of the following distribution ?

(*a*) Gaussian (*b*) Rayleigh

(*c*) Rician (*d*) Poisson

2. The mean square value of the shot noise current

(*a*) varies inversely as average current

(*b*) is independent of average current

(*c*) varies as $\sqrt{\text{average current}}$

(*d*) varies directly as average current

3. The power spectral density of white noise

(*a*) varies as square root of frequency

(*b*) varies as inverse of frequency

(*c*) varies as square of frequency

(*d*) is constant with frequency

4. Which one of the following functions qualifies to be an autocorrelation function of a real valued time signal ?

(*a*) $\sin(\omega\tau)$ (*b*) $\exp(-\tau)$

(*c*) $\delta(t)$ (*d*) $u(\tau)$

5. The autocorrelation function of white noise is

(*a*) a delta function

(*b*) a constant

(*c*) gaussian

(*d*) $\exp(-|t|)$ with usual notation

6. The spectral density of white noise is

(*a*) Exponential (*b*) Uniform

(*c*) Poisson (*d*) Gaussian

7. The power density spectrum (PSD) of noise process is given by

$$S_N(F) = \begin{cases} 10^{-8}\left(1+\dfrac{|f|-10^8}{10^8}\right) & |f| < 10^8 \\ 0 & |f| > 10^8 \end{cases}$$

The noise is passed through a unit-gain ideal band pass filter, centered at 2MHz. The output noise power will be

(*a*) $2N_B$ (*b*) N_B

(*c*) $N_B/2$ (*d*) $4N_B$

8. The pdf of a random variable x is given by

$$f_x(x) = \begin{cases} K, & 0 \le x \le 1 \\ 0, & \text{otherwise} \end{cases}$$

Than value of the k will be

(*a*) 0 (*b*) +1

(*c*) –1 (*d*) none of these

9. For a random variable x following probability density function, p(x) shown in the figure, mean and variance respectively are

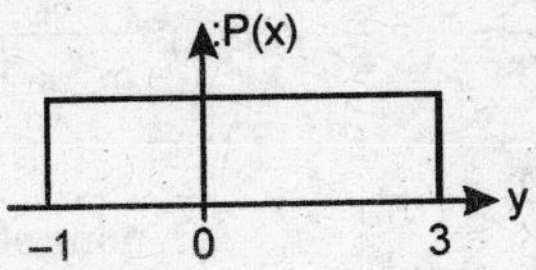

(*a*) $\frac{1}{2}$ and $\frac{2}{3}$ (*b*) 1 and $\frac{4}{3}$

(*c*) 1 and $\frac{2}{3}$ (*d*) 2 and $\frac{4}{3}$

Common Data Questions 11-12

A sonar echo system on a submarine transmits a random noise n(t) to determine the distance to another targeted submarine.

$$\text{Distance, } R = \frac{v\tau_R}{2}$$

where v =speed of the sound wave in water

τ_R = time it takes the reflected version of n(t) to return.

Assume that n(t) is a sample function of an ergodic random process N(t) and T is very large.

10. V will be

(*a*) $2R_{NN}(\tau_R - \tau_T)$ (*b*) $R_{NN}(\tau_R - 2\tau_T)$

(*c*) $R_{NN}(\tau_R - \tau_T)$ (*d*) $\frac{1}{2}R_{NN}(\tau_R - \tau_T)$

11. What value of the delay τ_T will cause v to be maximum?

(*a*) τ_T (*b*) $2\tau_T$

(*c*) $3\tau_T$ (*d*) None of these

12. Noise figure of an RF amplifier when operated at RF with noise temperature 150K will be

(*a*) 1.42 (*b*) 1.52

(*c*) 1.62 (*d*) 1.72

13. The input auto-correlation of RC-filter which is subjected to a white noise of spectral density $\frac{\eta_0}{2}$ is

(*a*) $\eta_0[\delta(\tau)]$ (*b*) $\frac{\eta_0}{2}[\delta(\tau)]$

(*c*) $-\eta_0[\delta(\tau)]$ (*d*) $-\frac{\eta_0}{2}[\delta(\tau)]$

14. Spectral density is

$$X(f) = k; |f| < f_c$$
$$= 0; \text{otherwise}$$

Auto correlation function is

(*a*) $\frac{k}{\pi j\, fe}\cos(f_e\tau)$ (*b*) $\frac{k}{\pi j}\cos(f_e\tau)$

(*c*) $\frac{k}{\pi j\, fe}\sin(f_e\tau)$ (*d*) $\frac{k}{\pi j}\cos(f_e\tau)$

15. Power spectral density of stationary noise process N(f) has auto correlation for $R_{nm}(\tau) = ke^{-3|\tau|}$

(*a*) $\frac{3k}{3+\omega^2}$ (*b*) $\frac{3k}{3-\omega^2}$

(*c*) $\frac{6k}{9+\omega^2}$ (*d*) $\frac{6k}{9-\omega^2}$

16. White noise, for which $R_{xx}(\tau) = 10^{-2}\,8(\tau)$ is applied to a network with impulse response

$$h(t) = 4(t)\,3 - te^{-41}.$$

The network's output noise power in a 1W resistor is

(*a*) 0.15 mW (*b*) 0.35 mW

(*c*) 0.55 mW (*d*) 0.95 mW

17. Output z(t) is related to input y(t) as $y = \sqrt{z}$ and probability density function of the input is

$p(y) = e^{-y};\ 0 < y < \infty$

$p(y) = 0;\ -\infty < y < 0$

Probability function will be

(a) $\frac{e^{\sqrt{z}}}{2\sqrt{z}}$ (b) $\frac{e^{-\sqrt{z}}}{2\sqrt{z}}$

(c) e^{-z} (d) e^{z}

18. What is the spectral density of random process whose auto-correlation is $e^{-2\alpha|\tau|}$?

(a) $\frac{4\alpha}{\omega^2 + 4\alpha^2}$ (b) $\frac{4\alpha}{\omega^2 - 4\alpha^2}$

(c) $\frac{\alpha}{\omega^2 + \alpha^2}$ (d) $\frac{\alpha}{\omega^2 - \alpha^2}$

19. The mean square value of a variable with probability density function

$$p(x) = 3e^{-6|x|},\ -\infty < x < \infty$$

is

(a) $\frac{1}{3}$ (b) $\frac{1}{6}$

(c) $\frac{1}{9}$ (d) $\frac{1}{18}$

20. $Y = X^2$ is a zero mean stationary Gaussain random process with auto correction for

$$R_{xx}(\tau) = \exp(-|\tau|).$$

$R_{yy}(t_1\ t_2)$ will be

(a) $1 - 2\,exp(-2|\tau|)$ (b) $1 + 2\,exp(-2|\tau|)$

(c) $1 - 4\,exp(-2|\tau|)$ (d) $1 + 4\,exp(-2|\tau|)$

21. Spectral density of

$$m(t) = \begin{cases} a\,\frac{f}{W};\ |f| < W \\ 0;\ \text{otherwise} \end{cases}$$

Output SNR at receiver will be

(a) $\frac{a A_c}{2N_0}$ (b) $\frac{a A_c}{3 N_0}$

(c) $\frac{a A_c^2}{4N_0}$ (d) $\frac{a A_c^2}{3N_0}$

22. White noise with power density $\frac{\eta_o}{2}$ is applied to a low pass network for which $|H(0)| = 2$. It has a noise bandwidth of 2 MHz. If average output noise power is 8.1 W in a 1W resistor, then η_o is

(a) 6.25×10^8 W/Hz (b) 6.25×10^{-8} W/Hz

(c) 1.25×10^8 W/Hz (d) 1.25×10^{-8} W/Hz

23. Fourier transform of a Gaussian time pulse is

(a) uniform

(b) a pair of impulses

(c) Gaussian

(d) Rayleigh

24. The autocorrelation function $R_x(\tau)$ satisfies which of the following properties?

(a) $R_x(\tau) = -R_x(-\tau)$ (b) $R_x(\tau) = R_x(-\tau)$

(c) $R_x(\tau) \geq R_x(0)$ (d) $R_x(\tau) \geq 1$

25. The autocorrelation function $R_x(\tau)$ of the signal $X(t) = V \sin \omega t$ is given by

(a) $\frac{1}{2}V^2 \cos\omega\tau$ (b) $V^2 \cos \omega\tau$

(c) $V^2 \cos^2 \omega\tau$ (d) $2V^2 \cos^2 \omega\tau$

26. If spectral density of a random signal is

$$p[\delta(\omega - \omega_0) + \delta(\omega + \omega_0)]$$

then auto-correlation function of the signal is

(a) $\cos \omega_0 \tau$ (b) $\sin \omega_0 \tau$

(c) $\cos [(\omega - \omega_0)\tau]$ (d) $\sin [(\omega - \omega_0)\tau]$

27. The probability density function of a random variable X is given as $f_X(x)$. A random variable Y is defined as $y = ax + b$, where $a < 0$.

PDF of random variable Y is

(a) $bf_X\left(\frac{y-b}{a}\right)$ (b) $af_X\left(\frac{y-b}{a}\right)$

(c) $\frac{1}{a}f_X\left(\frac{y-b}{a}\right)$ (d) $\frac{1}{b}f_X\left(\frac{y-b}{a}\right)$

Common Data Q. 28 – 29

Consider a low-pass random process with a white-noise power spectral density $S_X(\omega) = N/2$ as shown in the figure.

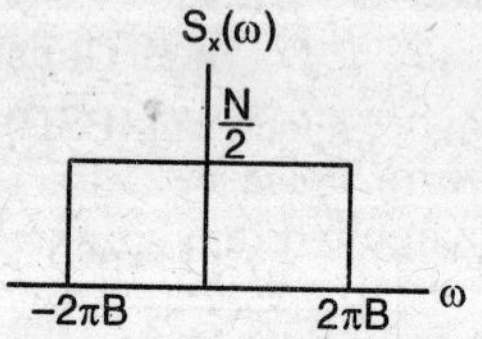

28. The auto correlation function $R_X(\tau)$ is

(a) $2NB\sin(2\pi\beta\tau)$ (b) $\pi NB\sin(2\pi\beta\tau)$

(c) $NB\sin(2\pi\beta\tau)$ (d) none of these

29. Power P_X is

(a) 2NB (b) π NB

(c) NB (d) $\frac{NB}{2\pi}$

30. A signal process m(t) is mixed with a channel noise n(t). The power spectral density are

$$S_m(\omega) = \frac{6}{9+\omega^2},\quad S_n(\omega) = 6$$

The optimum Wiener-Hoff filter is

(a) $\frac{\omega^2+9}{\omega^2+10}$ (b) $\frac{1}{\omega^2+10}$

(c) $\frac{\omega^2+10}{\omega^2+9}$ (d) none of these

31. A 1 μ F capacitor is shunted by a 1k Ω maintained at temperature 300 K. The rms noise voltage across capacitor over the entire frequency band is

(a) 6.4×10^{-8} V (b) 9.4×10^{-9} V
(c) 2.3×10^{-10} V (d) 4.3×10^{-10} V

32. An amplifier operating over the frequency range of 18 to 20 MHz has a 10 kΩ input resistance. The RMS noise voltage at the input to the amplifier at ambient temperature of 27°C is (assume Boltzman constant value as 1.38×10^{-23} J/K)

(a) 18.2 microvolts (b) 17.2 microvolts
(c) 16.2 microvolts (d) 14.2 microvolts

33. The capacity of an analog communication channel with 4 kHz bandwidth and 15 dB SNR is approximately

(a) 20,000 bps (b) 16,000 bps
(c) 10,000 bps (d) 8,000 bps

34. A system has a receiver noise resistance of 50 Ω. If it is connected to an antenna with an output resistance of 50 Ω., then noise figure of the system is

(a) 1 (b) 2
(c) 50 (d) 101

35. A 8 kHz communication channel has an SNR of 30 dB. If channel bandwidth is doubled, keeping the signal power constant, then SNR for the modified channel will be

(a) 27 dB (b) 30 dB
(c) 33 dB (d) 60 dB

36. A communication channel with additive white Gaussian noise, has a bandwidth of 4 kHz and an SNR of 15. Its channel capacity is

(a) 1.6 kbps (b) 20 kbps
(c) 32 kbps (d) 256 kbps

37. Consider a white noise of 2-sided spectral density 2×10^{-6} V^2/Hz applied to a simple RC low pass filter whose 3 dB cut-off frequency is 4 kHz. The mean squared value of the noise output will be

(a) $4\pi \times 10^{-3}$ V^2 (b) $2\pi \times 10^{-3}$ V^2
(c) $4\pi \times 10^{-5}$ V^2 (d) $\pi \times 10^{-3}$ V^2

38. A communication channel disturbed by additive white Gaussian noise has a band widh of 4 kHz and SNR of 15. The highest transmission rate that such a channel can support (in k-bits/sec) is

(a) 16 (b) 1.6
(c) 32 (d) 60

39. A binary signal S_1 (t) is + 1 or – 1V pulse during the internal (O, T). Additive white noise with PSD $n/2 = 10^{-5}$/W Hz is added to the signal. Then maximum bit rate that can be send having a bit probability of $P_e \geq 10^{-4}$, will be

[Given : $Q(x) = 10^{-4} \rightarrow x = 3.71$]

(a) 3.16 kb/sec (b) 14.52 kb/sec
(c) 7.26 kb/sec (d) none of these

40. The signal to quantizations noise ratio in a PCM system depends upon

(a) sampling rate
(b) number of quantization levels
(c) message signal bandwidth
(d) all of these

ANALOG COMMUNICATION

41. The threshold effect in demodulators is

(a) exhibited by all demodulators when input signal to noise ratio is low
(b) rapid fall on output signal to noise ratio when input signal to noise ratio falls below a particular value
(c) properly exhibited by all AM suppressed carrier coherent demodulators
(d) properly exhibited by correlation receivers

42. A 1000 kHz carrier is simultaneously modulated with 300 Hz and 2 kHz audio sine waves. The frequency which will not be present in output is

(a) 998 kHz (b) 999.7 kHz
(c) 1000.3 kHz (d) 700 kHz

43. A carrier is simultaneously modulated by two sine waves with modulation indicies of 0.3 and 0.4. If modulated power is 10 kW, then total modulated power will be

(a) 12.5 kW (b) 10 kW
(c) 10.125 kW (d) 10.5 kW

44. In a DSB-SC system with 100% modulation, the power saving is

(a) 50 % (b) 66 %
(c) 75 % (d) 100 %

45. An FM radio receiver is tuned to a 90.6 MHz broadcast station. It will receive an image frequency of

(a) 110 MHz (b) 112 MHz
(c) 114 MHz (d) 120 MHz

46. A FM signal is being broadcast in the 88.108 MHz band having a carrier swing of 125 kHz. The modulation index is

(a) 100 % (b) 83 %
(c) 67 % (d) 50 %

47. An AM voltage signal s(t), with a carrier frequency of 1.15 GHz has a complex envelope

$$g(t) = A_C[1+m(t)], \text{ where } A_C = 500 \text{ V}$$

and modulation is a 1 kHz sinusoidal test tone described by

$$m(t) = 0.8 \sin(2\pi \times 10^3 t)$$

appears across a 50Ω resistive load.

What is the actual power dissipated in the load?

(a) 165 kW (b) 82.5 kW
(c) 3.3 kW (d) 6.6 kW

48. Pre-emphasis in FM systems involves

(a) compression of the modulating signal
(b) expansion of the modulating signal
(c) amplification of lower frequency components of the modulating signal
(d) amplification of higher frequency components of the modulating signal

49. Choice of the product RC is an envelope detector using a diode and an R–C circuit is governed by

(a) both lowest and the highest modulation frequencies
(b) only depth of modulation
(c) depth of modulation and lowest modulation frequency
(d) depth of modulation and highest modulation frequency

50. The ratio $\frac{(S/N)_{WBFM}}{(S/N)_{AM}}$ for 100% amplitude modulation with identical total transmitted power (m_f is modulated index of FM) is

(a) $\frac{9}{2} m_f^2$ (b) $\frac{3}{2} m_f^2$

(c) $\frac{3}{2} m_f^3$ (d) $\frac{9}{2} m_f^3$

51. If radiated power of AM transmitter is 10 kW, then power in the carrier for modulation index of 0.6 is nearly

(a) 8.24 kW (b) 8.47 kW

(c) 9.26 kW (d) 9.6 kW

52. A signal m(t) = 5 cos 2π 100t frequency modulates a carrier. The resulting FM signal is

$$10 \cos \{(2\pi\ 10^5\ t) + 15 \sin (2\pi\ 100t)\}$$

The approximate bandwidth of the FM would be

(a) 0.1 kHz (b) 1 kHz

(c) 3.2 kHz (d) 100 kHz

53. In a superheterodyne receiver, IF is 455 kHz. If it is tuned to 1200 kHz, then image frequency will be

(a) 1655 kHz (b) 2110 kHz

(c) 745 kHz (d) 910 kHz

54. If modulation index of an AM wave is changed from 0 to 1, the transmitted power

(a) increases by 50% (b) increases by 75%

(c) increases by 100% (d) remains unaffected

55. Which one of the following statements regarding the signal :

$$x(t) = 5 \sin (2\pi \times 10^3\ t) \sin (2\pi \times 10^6\ t)$$

is correct ?

(a) Upper side band frequency is 1001000

(b) Lower side band frequency is 999000

(c) $x(t)$ is a DSB – SC signal

(d) All of these

56. For signal amplitude modulated to a depth of 100% by a sinusoidal signal, power is

(a) same as the power of unmodulated carrier

(b) twice as the power of unmodulated carrier

(c) $\frac{3}{2}$ times the power of unmodulated carrier

(d) $\frac{2}{3}$ times the power of unmodulated carrier

57. A 60 Hz carrier is amplitude modulated by speech band of 300 to 3000 Hz. The range of upper side bands will be

(a) 60.3 to 63 kHz (b) 60 to 59.7 kHz

(c) 57 to 59.7 kHz (d) 56.7 to 56.3 kHz

58. An arbitrary signal m(t) has zero average value and it is band-limited to 3·2 kHz. It is sampled at the rate of 8k samples/s. The samples are passed through an ideal band-pass filter with centre frequency of 3·2 kHz and bandwidth of 6·4 kHz. The output of the band-pass filter is

(a) AM-DSB signal with suppressed carrier

(b) AM-DSB signal with carrier

(c) AM-SSB signal with carrier

(d) a sequence of exponentially decaying sine waves

59. A 10 kW carrier is sinusoidally modulated by two carriers corresponding to a modulation index of 30% and 40% respectively. The total radiated power is

(a) 11.25 kW (b) 12.5 kW

(c) 15 kW (d) 17 kW

60. In phase modulation, frequency deviation is

(a) independent of the modulating signal frequency

(b) inversely proportional to the modulating signal frequency

(c) directly proportional to the modulating signal frequency

(d) inversely proportional to the square root of the modulating frequency

61. In an amplitude modulated system, if total power is 600 W and power in carrier is 400 W, then modulation index is

(a) 0.5 (b) 0.75

(c) 0.9 (d) 1

62. If an angle-modulated signal is given by

$$f_a(t) = \cos (2 \times 10^8\ \pi t + 75 \sin 2 \times 10^3\ \pi t)$$

then peak frequency deviation of the carrier is

(a) 1 kHz (b) 7· 5 kHz

(c) 75 kHz (d) 100 MHz

63. If radiated power of AM transmitter is 10 kW, then power in the carrier for modulation index of 0·6 is nearly

(a) 8· 24 kW (b) 8· 47 kW

(c) 9· 26 kW (d) 9· 6 kW

64. As modulation index of an FM signal with sinusoidal modulation is increased from zero to three, power in the carrier component will

(a) increase continuously

(b) decrease continuously

(c) first increase, attain a maximum and then decrease

(d) first decreases, become zero and then increase

65. A frequency-modulated voltage wave is given as

$$V = 10 \sin (2\pi \times 10^8\ t + 5 \sin 400\ \pi t).$$

The carrier frequency and maximum deviation of the signal respectively are

(a) 10 MHz and 10 kHz

(b) 100 MHz and 1 kHz

(c) 10 MHz and 10 kHz

(d) 100 MHz and 10 kHz

66. A(DSB–SC) signal is being detected synchronously. The phase error in the locally generated carrier will

(a) cause phase delay

(b) cause phase distortion only

(c) have the effect of reducing output and causing phase distrotion also

(d) reduce detected output only

67. A RF signal is amplitude modulated to a depth of 100% by a sinusoidal signal. The ratio of modulated signal power to unmodulated carrier power is

(a) 1 (b) 2

(c) $\frac{2}{3}$ (d) $\frac{3}{2}$

68. The antenna current of an AM broadcast transmitter modulated to a depth of 100 by an audio sine wave is $\sqrt{3/2}$ A, which increases to $\sqrt{2}$ A due to simultaneous modulation by another audio sine wave. The modulation index due to second sine wave is

(*a*) 0.5 (*b*) 0.707
(*c*) 1.0 (*d*) 0.866

69. The frequency deviation produced in a VHF carrier by a signal of 100 Hz is 50 kHz. The frequency modulation index is,

(*a*) 100 radians (*b*) 250 radians
(*c*) 500 radians (*d*) 750 radians

Common Data (Q. 70 – 71):

Fourier transform M(f) of a signal m(t) is shown in the figure. It is to be transmitted from a source to destination. The signal is normalized
i.e., $-1 \le m(t) \le 1$

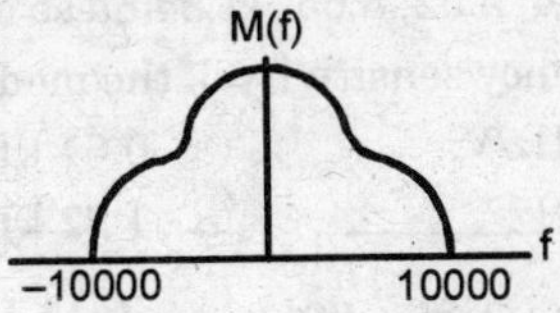

70. If USSB is employed, bandwidth of the modulated signal is

(*a*) 5 kHz
(*b*) 20 kHz, 10 kHz
(*c*) 20 kHz
(*d*) none of these

71. If DSB is employed, then bandwidth of the modulated signal is

(*a*) 5 kHz (*b*) 10 kHz
(*c*) 20 kHz (*d*) none of these

72. A 20 kW carrier is sinusoidally modulated by two carriers corresponding to a modulation index of 30% and 40% respectively. The total radiated power is

(*a*) 25 *k*W (*b*) 22.5 *k*W
(*c*) 30 *k*W (*d*) 35 *k*W

73. In a broadcast transmitter, the RF output is represented as

$$x_c(t)=100[1+0.9\cos 5000t+0.3\sin 9000t]\cos(6\times10^6 t)\text{V}.$$

The sidebands frequencies are

(*a*) 5.991, 5.995, 6.005, 6.009 MHz
(*b*) 953.5, 954.1, 955.7, 956.4 *k*Hz
(*c*) 5, 9 *k*Hz
(*d*) 795.8, 432.4 Hz

74. A diode detector has a load of 1kΩ shunted by a 10000 pF capacitor. The diode has a forward resistance of 1Ω. The maximum permissible depth of modulation, so as to avoid diagonal clipping, with modulating signal frequency of 10 kHz will be

(*a*) 0.847 (*b*) 0.628
(*c*) 0.734 (*d*) none of these

75. A non-linear device with a transfer characteristic given by

$$i = (10 \pm 2v_i \pm 0.2 v_i^2)$$

is supplied with a carrier of 1V amplitude and a sinusoidal signal of 0.5 V amplitude in series. If at the output, frequency component of AM signal is considered, then depth of modulation is

(*a*) 18 % (*b*) 10 %
(*c*) 20 % (*d*) 33.33 %

76. A message signal is periodic with period T, as shown in the figure.

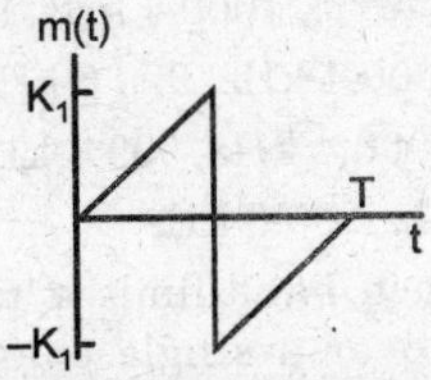

This message signals is applied to an AM modulator with modulation index $\beta=0.4$. The modulation efficiency would be

(*a*) 51 % (*b*) 11.8 %
(*c*) 5.1 % (*d*) none of these

Statement for (Q. 77 – 78) :

Figure given below shows positive portion of the envelope of the output of an AM modulator. The message signal is a waveform having zero DC value.

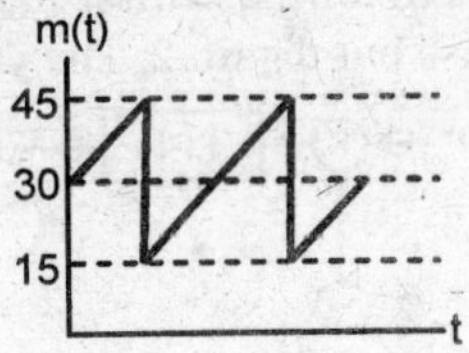

77. Modulation index is

(*a*) 0.5 (*b*) 0.6
(*c*) 0.4 (*d*) 0.8

78. Modulation efficiency is

(*a*) 8.3% (*b*) 12.3%
(*c*) 7.7% (*d*) none of these

79. The value of M, required to produce modulation index of 0.8, is

(*a*) 0.32 (*b*) 0.26
(*c*) 0.52 (*d*) 0.16

80. Let W be the BW of message signal m(t). AM signal would be recovered if

(*a*) $f_c > W$ (*b*) $f_c > 2W$
(*c*) $f_c > 3W$ (*d*) $f_c > 4W$

81. A super heterodyne receiver is designed to receive transmitted signals between 5 and 10 MHz. High-side tuning is to be used. The tuning range of the local oscillator for IF frequency 500 kHz would be

(*a*) 4.5 MHz – 9.5 MHz
(*b*) 5.5 MHz – 10.5 MHz
(*c*) 4.5 MHz – 10.5 MHz
(*d*) none of these

82. In the circuit shown in the figure between terminals 1 and 2, an a.c. voltage source of frequency 400 Hz is connected. Another a.c. voltage of 1.0 MHz is connected between 3 and 4. The output between 5 and 6 contains components at

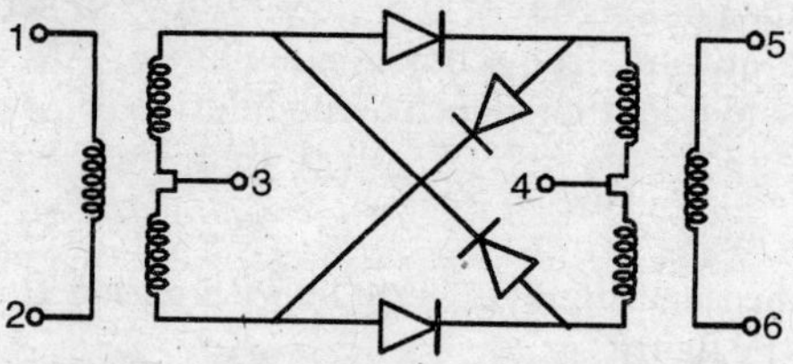

(a) 400 Hz, 1 MHz, 1000.4 kHz, 999.6 kHz

(b) 1 MHz, 1000.4 kHz, 999.6 kHz

(c) 400 Hz, 1000.4 kHz, 999.6 kHz

(d) 1000.4 kHz, 999.6 kHz

83. 12 signals each band-limited to 5 kHz are to be transmitted over a single channel by frequency division mutliplexing. If AM-SSB modulation guard band of 1 kHz is used, then band width of the multiplexed signal will be

(a) 131 kHz (b) 81 kHz

(c) 121 kHz (d) 71 kHz

84. Let x(t) be a signal band-limited to 1 kHz. Amplitude modulation is performed to produce signal

$$g(t) = x(t) \sin 2000\pi t.$$

A proposed demodulation technique is shown in the figure. The ideal low pass filter has cut-off frequency 1 kHz and pass band gain 2. The y(t) would be

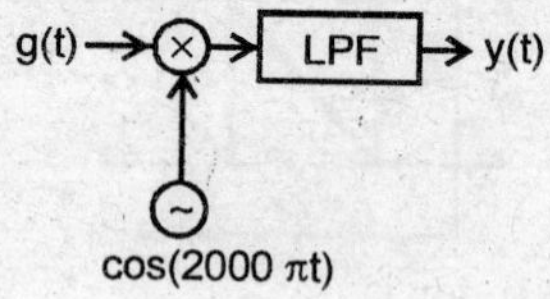

(a) $2y(t)$ (b) $y(t)$

(c) $\dfrac{y(t)}{2}$ (d) 0

85. It is required to transmit the signal

$$x(t) = \sin 200\pi t + 2\sin 400\pi t$$

using a modulation that create the signal

$$g(t) = x(t)\sin 400\pi t.$$

If product $g(t)\sin 400\pi t$ is passed through an ideal LPF with cut-off frequency 400π and pass band gain of 2, then signal obtained at the output of the LPF is

(a) $\sin 200\pi t$ (b) $\dfrac{1}{2}\sin 200\pi t$

(c) $2\sin 200\pi t$ (d) 0

86. In a AM signal, received signal power is 10^{-10} W with a maximum modulating signal of 5 kHz. The noise spectral density at the receiver input is 10^{-18} W/Hz. If noise power is restricted to the message signal bandwidth only, then signals-to-noise ratio at the input to the receiver is

(a) 43 dB (b) 66 dB

(c) 56 dB (d) 33 dB

87. A carrier wave of 1 GHz and amplitude 3V is frequency modulated by a sinusoidal modulating signal frequency of 500 Hz and of peak amplitude of 1 V. The frequency deviation is 1 kHz. The peak level of the modulating waveform is changed to 5 V and the modulating frequency is changed to 2 kHz. The expression for the new modulated wave form is

(a) $\cos[2\pi \times 10^6 t + 2.5\cos(4\pi \times 10^3 t)]$

(b) $\cos[2\pi \times 10^6 t + 5\cos(4\pi \times 10^3 t)]$

(c) $3\cos[2\pi \times 10^6 t + 2.5\cos(4\pi \times 10^3 t)]$

(d) $3\cos[2\pi \times 10^6 t + 5\cos(4\pi \times 10^3 t)]$

88. In a certain frequency-modulation experiment conducted with $f_m = 1$ kHz and increasing amplitude (starting from 0 V), it is found that carrier component of FM signal is reduced to zero for the first time when $A_m = 2$ V.

Given :Bessel function $J_0(\mathbf{x})$ is zero for

$$\mathbf{x} = 2.44, 5.52, 8.65, 11.8 \text{ and so on.}$$

The frequency sensitivity of the modulator is

(a) 1.38 kHz/V (b) 0.61 kHz/V

(c) 2.76 kHz/V (d) 1.22 kHz/V

Common Data (Q. 89 – 90) :

An FM modulation with frequency sensitivity constant, $k_f = 25$ Hz/V has the message signal shown in the figure.

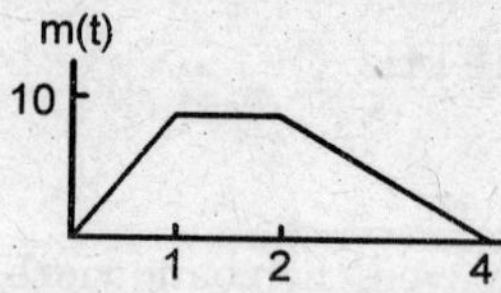

89. The plot for frequency deviation is

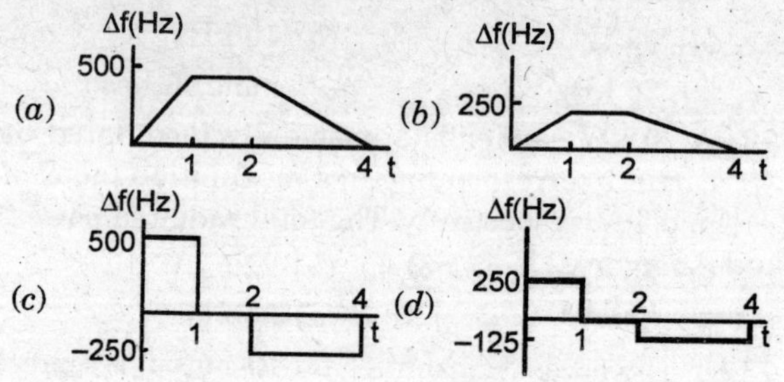

90. For $1 \le t \le 2$, the phase deviation is

(a) $500\pi t$ rad (b) $250\pi(1 + 2t)$ rad

(c) $20\pi t$ rad (d) 0

91. Let message signal, $m(t) = \cos(4\pi 10^3 t)$, and carrier signal, $c(t) = 5\cos(2\pi 10^6 t)$ are used to generate a FM signal.

If peak frequency deviation of the generated FM signal is three times the transmission bandwidth of the AM signal, then coefficient of the term $\cos(2\pi(1008 \times 10^3)t)$ in the FM signal would be

(a) $5J_4(3)$ (b) $\dfrac{5}{2}J_8(3)$

(c) $\dfrac{5}{2}J_8(4)$ (d) $5J_4(6)$

92. An audio signal has a bandwidth of 25 kHz. The maximum value of | m(t) | is 5 V. This signal frequency modulates a carrier. If frequency sensitivity constant of the modulator is 20 kHz/V, then according to Carson's rule, bandwidth of the modulator output would be

(a) 50 kHz (b) 250 kHz
(c) 200 kHz (d) 100 kHz

93. A transmitter uses a carrier frequency of 1 kHz. The transmitter output is

$$x_c(t)=\cos(2\pi 1000t+20t^2)$$

Phase and frequency deviation respectively will be

(a) $20t^2$ rad, $40t$ Hz (b) $40t$ rad, $20t^2$ Hz
(c) $20t^2$ rad, $\frac{20}{\pi}t$ Hz (d) $\frac{20}{\pi}t$ rad, $20t^2$ Hz

Common Data (Q. 94 – 95) :

A block diagram of an Armstrong FM transmitter is shown in the figure.

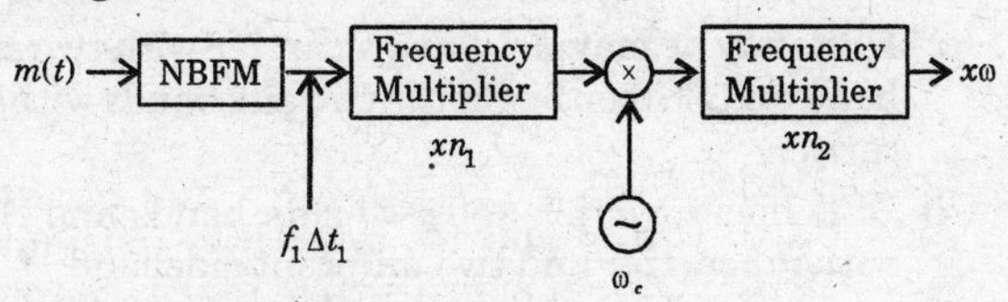

Parameter are as follows :

$$f_1=200\text{kHz},\ f_{LO}=10.8\text{MHz}$$
$$\Delta f_1=25\text{Hz},\ n_1=64,\ n_2=48$$

94. Maximum frequency deviation at the output of the FM transmitter is

(a) 100.6 kHz (b) 76.8 kHz
(c) 43.2 kHz (d) none of these

95. At output of the transmitter, carrier frequency is

(a) 96 MHz (b) 12.8 MHz
(c) 48 MHz (d) 132.4 MHz

Linked Answer (Q. 96 – 98) :

A narrowband FM signal has a carrier frequency of 100 kHz and a deviation ratio of 0.1. The modulation bandwidth is 500 Hz. This signal is used to generate a wideband FM signal with a deviation ratio of 5 and a carrier frequency of 85 MHz. The scheme used to accomplish this is shown in the figure.

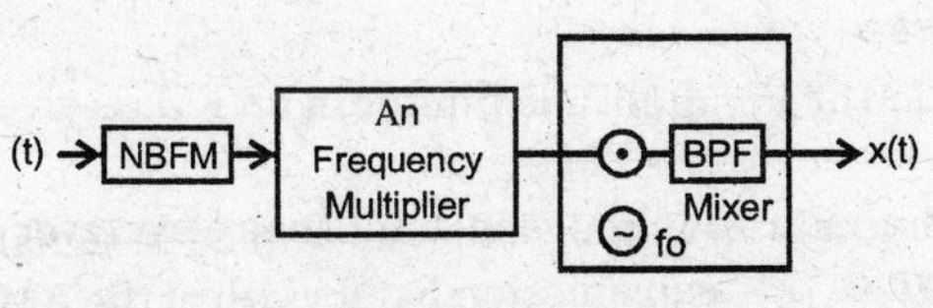

96. Required value of frequency multiplication is

(a) 50 (b) 10
(c) 20 (d) 15

97. Two possible local oscillator frequencies are

(a) 90 MHz, 80 MHz (b) 86 MHz, 84 MHz
(c) 87 MHz, 83 MHz (d) none of these

98. Bandwidth of BPF filter would be

(a) 12 kHz (b) 1 kHz
(c) 6 kHz (d) 2 kHz

99. If carrier is FM modulated with a suisoidal of 20 kHz resulting in a maximum frequency duration of 5 kHz, then bandwidth of the modulated signal will be

(a) 7 kHz (b) 10 ,kHz
(c) 14 kHz (d) 4 kHz

100. In amplitude modulation, modulation envelope has a peak value which is double the unmodulated carrier value. What is the value of the modulation index?

(a) 25% (b) 50%
(c) 75% (d) 100%

101. Given figure shows first stage of a super heterodyne receiver. The desired input signal is at a frequency of 700 MHz. The L.O. frequency is 1 GHz. The mixer is an ideal multiplier with a gain independent of frequency. A band pass filter (BPF) is used to select Intermediate frequency (IF) output at 300 MHz.

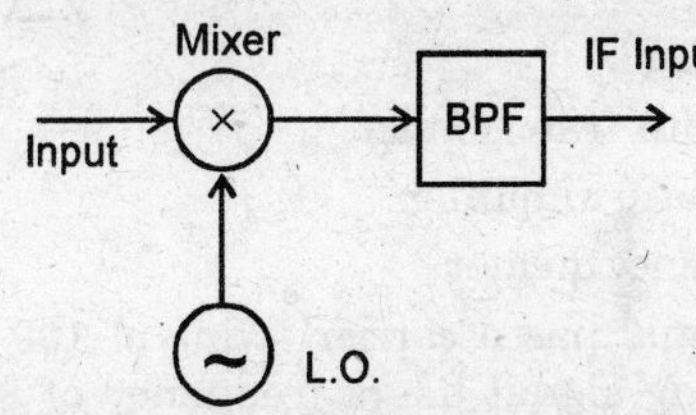

If a LPF can be used before the mixer to reject image frequency obtained, then for a perfect rejection (zero transmission) of the image desired, LPF employed with

(a) complete transmission upto 1 GHz and complete rejection of signal after 1 GHz
(b) cut-off frequency 1 MHz
(c) complete transmission upto 0.7 GHz and complete rejection of signal after 0.7 GHz
(d) none of these

Linked Answer (Q. 102 – 103):

Given :

Message signal, m(t) = sin(2000 πt)

Frequency sensitivity constant, k_f = 10 kHz/V

Phase sensitivity constant, k_p = 10 rad/V

102. Bandwidths of FM and PM respectively are

(a) 204 kHz, 44 kHz (b) 202 kHz, 22 kHz
(c) 402 kHz, 42 kHz (d) None of these

103. If message signal amplitude is doubled, then bandwidths will be respectively

(a) 200 kHz, 20 kHz (b) 402 kHz, 42 kHz
(c) 404 kHz, 44 kHz (d) 204 kHz, 24 kHz

104. An FM signal is being broadcast in the 88-108 MHz band having a carrier swing of 125 kHz. The modulation index is

(a) 100% (b) 83%
(c) 67% (d) 80%

105. A 1000 kHz carrier is simultaneously modulated with 300 Hz and 2 kHz audio sine waves. Which of the following frequencies will not be present in the output ?

(a) 998 kHz (b) 999.7 kHz
(c) 1000.3 kHz (d) 700 kHz

106. The saving in power in a DSBSC system modulated at 80% is

(*a*) Nil (*b*) 80%

(*c*) 75.76% (*d*) 50%

107. If $f_c = 25$MHz, $f_m = 400$ Hz, $E_c = 4$V, $\Delta f = 10$ kHz then equation of FM wave will be

(*a*) $4 \sin (1.57 \times 10^8 t + 25 \sin 2513 t)$

(*b*) $10 \sin (1.57 \times 10^8 t + 25 \sin 2513 t)$

(*c*) $15 \sin (1.57 \times 10^8 t + 25 \sin 2513 t)$

(*d*) $20 \sin (1.57 \times 10^8 t + 25 \sin 2513 t)$

108. The system shown in the given figure is a/an

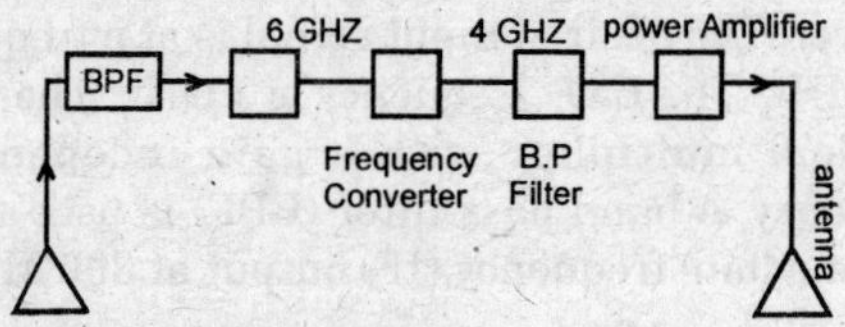

(*a*) LOS Link

(*b*) satellite transponder

(*c*) low noise amplifier

(*d*) frequency divider

109. A FM signal has a carrier swing of 100 kHz when modulating signal has a frequency of 8 kHz. The modulation index is

(*a*) 6.25 (*b*) 12.5

(*c*) 7.5 (*d*) 15

110. A modulated signal f (t) is multiplied by another signal $\cos \omega_C t$ yield $f(t) \cos^2 \omega_C t$.

If $f(t) \leftrightarrow F(\omega)$, then f (t) to yield $\cos^2 \omega_C t$ is

(*a*) $F(\omega) + F(\omega - \omega_C) + F(\omega - \omega_C)$

(*b*) $\frac{1}{2} F(\omega) + \frac{1}{2}[F(\omega + \omega_C) + F(\omega - \omega_C)]$

(*c*) $\frac{1}{2} F(t) + \frac{1}{2} f(t) \cos 2\omega_C t$

(*d*) $\frac{1}{2} F(\omega) + \frac{1}{4}[F(\omega - 2\omega_C) + F(\omega + 2\omega_C)]$

111. In AM signal, received signal power is 10^{-10} W with a maximum modulating signal of 5 kHz. The noise spectral density at the receiver input is 10^{-18} W/Hz. If noise power is restricted to the message signal bandwidth only, then signals-to-noise ratio at the input to the receiver is

(*a*) 43 dB (*b*) 66 dB

(*c*) 56 dB (*d*) 33 dB

112. Equation of the amplitude modulated wave is

(*a*) $E_k \left(1 + \frac{E_m}{E_k} \cos \omega_m t\right) \cos \omega_k t$

(*b*) $E_k \cos \omega_k t + E_k E_m \cos \omega_m t \sin \omega_k t$

(*c*) $E_k \sin \omega_k t + E_k/E_m \sin \omega_k t + \sin \omega_m t$

(*d*) $E_k \cos \omega_k t + E_k E_m \cos^2 (\omega_m + \omega_k) k$

113. A 1000 kHz carrier wave modulated 40% at 4000 Hz is applied to a resonant circuit tuned to a carrier frequency and having Q = 140. What is the degree of modulation after transmission through this circuit ?

(*a*) 40 % (*b*) 20 %

(*c*) 0.027 % (*d*) 0.54 %

114. An audio signal 15 sin 2π (1500 t) amplitude modulates a carrier 60 sin 2π (100, 00t). The frequencies shown up in a spectrum analysis of the modulated wave are

(*a*) 1.5 kHz, 100 kHz

(*b*) 1.5 kHz, 100 kHz, 103 kHz, 97 kHz

(*c*) 100 kHz, 101.500 kHz, 98.500 kHz

(*d*) 100 kHz, 103 kHz, 97 kHz

115. Number of station accommodated in a 100 kHz bandwidth with highest modulating frequency

(*a*) 5 kHz

(*b*) 10 kHz

(*c*) 15 kHz

(*d*) 20 kHz

116. The difference between a DSB and a SSB transmission is that

(*a*) DSB has two sidebands and SSB one sideband

(*b*) DSB has a carrier and two sidebands and SSB, a carrier and a sideband.

(*c*) DSB may or may not have a carrier with two side band and SSB either of the two sidebands without carrier

(*d*) DSB has a carrier and two side bands and SSB without carrier and two different sideband

117. Frequency of an local oscillator in a AM standard broadcast receiver having on IF as 455 kHz and tuned in 540kHz when local oscillator tracks above the frequency of received signal, is

(*a*) 945 kHz

(*b*) 970 kHz

(*c*) 995 kHz

(*d*) 1045 kHz

118. Minimum value of m_f for an FM system required to produce a noticeable improvement in S/N ratio over a comparable AM system with M = 1 is

(*a*) $\sqrt{3}$

(*b*) $\sqrt{2}$

(*c*) $\frac{1}{\sqrt{3}}$

(*d*) $\frac{1}{\sqrt{2}}$

119. Function of an amplitude limiter in an FM receiver is to

(*a*) eliminate any change in amplitude of receiver FM signal

(*b*) reduce the amplitude of the signal to suit IF amplifier

(*c*) amplify low frequency signals

(*d*) none of these

120. In a FM demodulator

(*a*) capacitors are charged to the amplitude of FM wave

(*b*) frequency deviations are converted into voltage

(*c*) simple diode as employed

(*d*) none of these

121. Out power (S_0) in a DSB–SC receiver shown, when channel noise PSD is $\left(\frac{\eta}{2}\right)$ with N = 10^{-7} and modulating signal m(t) as shown in the figure

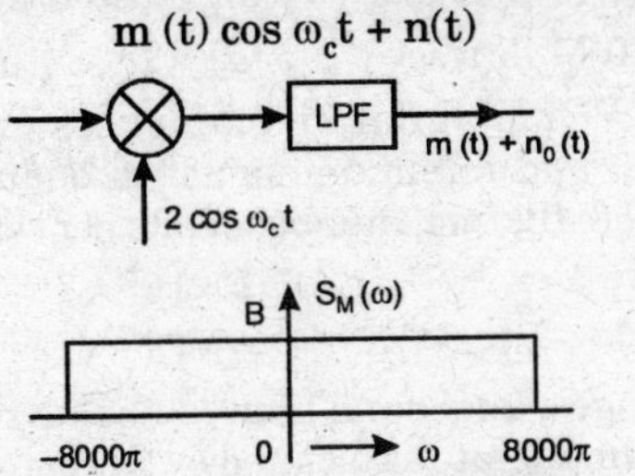

(a) 5000 β (b) 7000 β
(c) 6000 β (d) 8000 β

122. Carrier frequency at point 3 in an FM-transmitter shown below. Assuming a ring in frequency during heterodyning will be

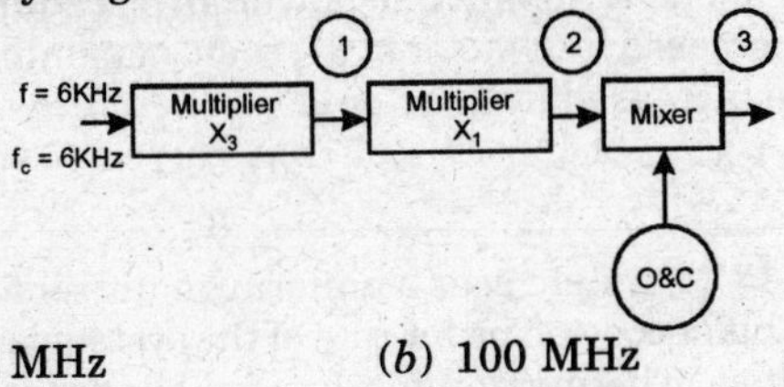

(a) 92 MHz (b) 100 MHz
(c) 96 MHz (d) 106 MHz

123. Frequency of local oscillator in a FM transmitter shown below, so as to give an IF of 50 MHz, will be

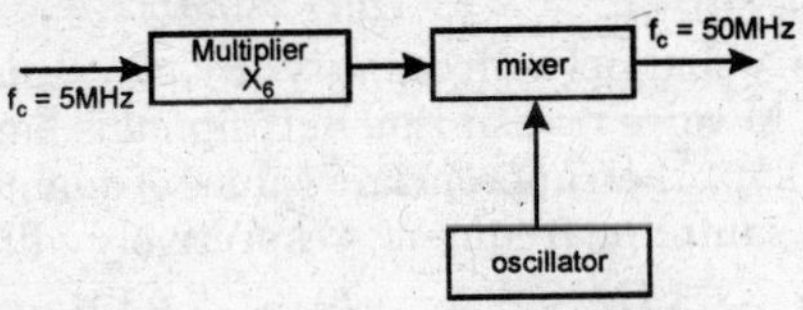

(a) 10 MHz (b) 30 MHz
(c) 20 MHz (d) 40 MHz

124. Figure of merit when a single tone modulating signal

$$f(t) = E_m \cos \omega_m t$$

phase modulates a carrier A cos ω_c t, will be

(a) $\frac{1}{4} m_f^2$ (b) $\frac{1}{2} m_f^2$
(c) $\frac{1}{3} m_f^2$ (d) $\frac{1}{5} m_f^2$

125. In an FM system with m(t) = $\cos^3$ 10000 t, k_f = 471000 carrier amplitude at receiver input $\frac{1}{3}$ and channel noise PSD, $S_n(\omega) = \frac{N}{2} = 10^{-8}$, frequency deviation is

(a) 70 kHz (b) 80 kHz
(c) 75 kHz (d) 85 kHz

126. In an FM system with white channel noise of PSD $S_n(\omega) = 10^{-9}$ and base band signal m(T) with a BW as 15 kHz, output SNR = 31 dB, output noise power (N_0) will be

[Given : $\frac{\overline{m^2(t)}}{m_p^2} = \frac{2}{9}$; β = 2;

Demodulator constant, α = 10^{-4}]

(a) 0.0325 (b) 0.0525
(c) 0.0425 (d) 0.0625

DIGITAL COMMUNICATION

127. Four signals each band–limited to 5 kHz are sampled at twice the Nyquist rate. The resulting PAM samples are transmitted over a single channel after time division multiplexing. Theoretical minimum transmissions bandwidth of the channel should be equal to

(a) 5 kHz (b) 20 kHz
(c) 40 kHz (d) 80 kHz

128. In a PCM system, each quantisation level is encoded into 8 bits. The signal to quantisation noise ratio is equal to

(a) $\frac{1}{12}\left(\frac{1}{256}\right)^2$ (b) 48 dB
(c) 64 dB (d) 256 dB

129. A band-pass signal has significant frequency components in the range of 1.5 MHz to 2 MHz. If signal is to be reconstructed from its sample, then minimum sampling frequency will be

(a) 1 MHz (b) 2 MHz
(c) 3.5 MHz (d) 4 MHz

130. A television signal is sampled at a rate of 20% above the Nyquist rate. The signal has a bandwidth of 6 MHz. The samples are quantized into 1024 levels. The minimum bandwidth required to transmit this signal would be

(a) 72 M bits/sec (b) 144 M bits/sec
(c) 72 k bits/sec (d) 144 k bits/sec

131. Four voice signals, each limited to 4 kHz and sampled at Nyquist rate, are converted into binary PCM signal using 256 quantisation levels. The bit transmission rate for the time-division multiplexed signal will be

(a) 8 kbps (b) 64 kbps
(c) 256 kbps (d) 512 kbps

132. In a carrier telephone system, a group occupies a frequency band of

(a) 36 to 48 kHz (b) 60 to 108 kHz
(c) 92 to 140 kHz (d) 140 to 172 kHz

133. In a DM (Delta modulation) system, the granular (idling) noise occurs when

(a) modulation signal increases rapidly
(b) pulse rate decreses
(c) modulating signal remains constant
(d) pulse amplitude decreases

134. PAM signals can be demodulaed by using a

(a) low pass filter (LPF) alone
(b) Schmitt trigger followed by a LPF
(c) differentiator followed by a LPF
(d) clipper circuit followed by a LPF

135. For 10–bit PCM system, the signal to quantisation noise ratio is 62 dB. If number of bits is increased by 2, then signal to quantisation noise will

(a) increase by 6 dB
(b) increase by 12 dB
(c) decrease by 6 dB
(d) decrease by 12 dB

136. In a PCM system, if number of quantization levels are 16 and maximum signal frequency is 4 kHz, then bit transmission rate is

(*a*) 64 k bits/sec (*b*) 16 k bits/sec

(*c*) 32 k bits/sec (*d*) 32 bits/sec

137. The signal to quantisation noise ratio in a PCM system depends upon

(*a*) sampling rate

(*b*) number of quantisation levels

(*c*) message signal bandwidth

(*d*) none of these

138. Bandwidth of a N bit binary coded PCM signal for modulating a signal having bandwidth of '*f*' Hz is

(*a*) $\frac{f}{N}$ Hz (*b*) $\frac{f}{N^2}$

(*c*) N*f* Hz (*d*) $N^2 f$Hz

139. In PCM system, if quantization levels are increased form 2 to 8, then relative bandwidth requirement will

(*a*) remain same (*b*) become double

(*c*) become triple (*d*) become four times

140. PCM systems require regenerative repeaters over long distances. The correct sequence of the operations which such a repeater performs, is

(*a*) timing, equalization and decision making

(*b*) equalization, timing and decision making

(*c*) timing, thresholding (decision) and equalization

(*d*) none of these

141. Four voice signals, each limited to 4 kHz and sampled at Nyquist rate, are converted into binary pcm signal using 256 quantisation levels. The bit transmission rate for the time-division multiplexed signal will be

(*a*) 8 kbps (*b*) 64 kbps

(*c*) 256 kpbs (*d*) 512 kbps

142. In a PCM, the amplitude levels are transmitted in a 7 unit code. If sampling is done at the rate of 10 Hz, then bandwidth should be

(*a*) 5 kHz (*b*) 35 kHz

(*c*) 70 kHz (*d*) 85 MHz

143. American Standard Code for Information Interchange has 128 characters, which are binary coded. If a certain computer generates 1,000,000 character per second, then minimum bandwidth required to transmit this signal will be

(*a*) 1.4 M bits/sec (*b*) 14 M bits/sec

(*c*) 7 M bits/sec (*d*) 0.7 M bits/sec

144. A binary channel with capacity 36 k bits/sec is available for PCM voic transmission. If signal is band limited to 3.2 kHz, then appropriate values of quantizing level L and sampling frequency respectively will be

(*a*) 32, 3.6 kHz (*b*) 64, 7.2 kHz

(*c*) 64, 3.6 kHz (*d*) 32, 7.2 kHz

145. Good voice reproduction via PCM requires 128 quantization levels. If bandwidth of voice channel is 4 kHz, then data rate is

(*a*) 256 kbps (*b*) 128 kbps

(*c*) 56 kbps (*d*) 28 kbps

146. A TDM link has 20 signal channels and each channel is sampled 8000 times/sec. Each sample is represented by seven binary bits and contains an additional bit for synchronization. The total bit rate for the TDM link is

(*a*) 1180 M bits/sec (*b*) 1280 K bits/sec

(*c*) 1180 M bits/sec (*d*) 1280 M bits/sec

147. For a PCM signal, if compression parameter μ is 100 and minimum signal to quantization-noise ratio is 50 dB, then number of bits per sample would be

(*a*) 8 (*b*) 10

(*c*) 12 (*d*) 14

148. A message signal band limited to 5 kHz is sampled at the minimum rate as dictated by the sampling theorem. The number of quantisation levels is 64. If samples are encoded in binary form, then transmission rate is

(*a*) 60 kbps (*b*) 50 kbps

(*c*) 32 kbps (*d*) 10 kbps

149. If peak transmitted power in a radar system is increased by a factor of 81, then maximum range will be increased by a factor of

(*a*) 3 (*b*) 9

(*c*) 27 (*d*) 81

150. A PCM system uses a uniform quantizer followed by a 8-bit encoder. The bit rate of the system is equal to 10^8 bits/s. The maximum message bandwidth for which the system operates satisfactorily is

(*a*) 25 MHz (*b*) 6.25 MHz

(*c*) 12.5 MHz (*d*) 50 MHz

151. A binary channel with capacity 36 k bits/sec is available for PCM voice transmission. If signal is band limited to 3.2 kHz, then appropriate values of quantizing level L and sampling frequency respectively will be

(*a*) 32, 3.6 kHz (*b*) 64, 7.2 kHz

(*c*) 64, 3.6 *k*Hz (*d*) 32, 7.2 *k*Hz

152. Given figure shows a PCM signals in which amplitude level of +1 volt and –1 volt are used to represent binary symbol 1 and 0 respectively. The code word used consists of three bits. The sampled version of analog signal from which this PCM signal is derived is

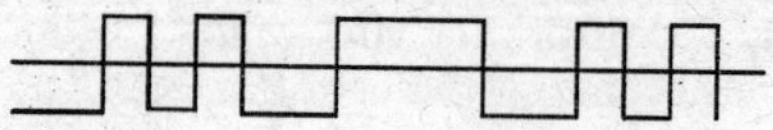

(*a*) 4 5 2 1 3 (*b*) 8 4 3 1 2

(*c*) 6 4 3 1 7 (*d*) 1 2 3 4 5

153. Twenty-four voice signals are sampled uniformly at a rate of 8 kHz and, then time-division multiplexed. The sampling process uses flat-top samples with 1 μs duration. The multiplexing operation includes provision for synchronization by adding and extra pulse of 1 μs duration. The spacing between successive pulses of the multiplexed signal is

(*a*) 4 μs (*b*) 6 μ s

(*c*) 7.2 μs (*d*) 8.4 μs

154. A linear delta modulator is designed to operate on speech signals limited to 3.4 kHz. The sampling rate is 10 time the Nyquist rate of the speech signal. The step size δ is 100 mV. The modulator is tested with a 1 kHz sinusoidal signal. The maximum amplitude of this test signal required to avoid slope overload is

(*a*) 2.04 V (*b*) 1.08 V

(*c*) 4.08 V (*d*) 2.16 V

Linked Answer (Q. 155 – 157):

Consider a linear DM system designed to accommodate analog message signals limited to bandwidth of 3.5 kHz. A sinusoidal test signals of amplitude A_{max} = 1 V and frequency f_m = 800 Hz is applied to the system. The sampling rate of the system is 64 kHz.

155. Minimum value of the step size to avoid overload is

(*a*) 240 mV (*b*) 120 mV

(*c*) 670 mV (*d*) 78.5 mV

156. Granular-noise power would be

(*a*) 1.68×10^{-3} W (*b*) 2.86×10^{-4} W

(*c*) 2.48×10^{-3} W (*d*) 1.12×10^{-4} W

157. SNR will be

(*a*) 298 (*b*) 1.75×10^3

(*c*) 4.46×10^3 (*d*) 201

158. The output signal-to-quantization-noise ratio of a 10-bit PCM was found to be 30 dB. The desired SNR is 42 dB. It can be increased by increasing the number of quantization level. In this way, fractional increase in the transmission bandwidth would be [assume $\log_2 10 = 0.3$]

(*a*) 20 % (*b*) 30 %

(*c*) 40 % (*d*) 50 %

Common Data (Q. 159 – 160):

A signal has a bandwidth of 1 MHz. It is sampled at a rate 50% higher than the Nyquist rate and quantized into 256 level using a μ-law quantizer with μ = 255.

159. The signal-to-quantization-noise ratio is

(*a*) 34.91 dB (*b*) 38.06 dB

(*c*) 42.05 dB (*d*) 48.76 dB

160. It was found that a sampling rate 20% above the rate would be adequate. So maximum SNR, that can be realized without increasing the transmission bandwidth, would be

(*a*) 60.4 dB (*b*) 70.3 dB

(*c*) 50.1 dB (*d*) none of these

161. Four signals each band limited to 5 kHz are sampled at twice the Nyquist rate. The resulting PAM samples are transmitted over a single channel after time division multiplexing. The theoretical minimum transmissions bandwidth of the channel should be equal to

(*a*) 5 kHz (*b*) 20 kHz

(*c*) 40 kHz (*d*) 80 kHz

162. Treating signal 10 sin 2π, 100 t cos² π, 300 t volt (with t in sec) to be a low signal, the Nyquist rate for this signal will be

(*a*) 1400 s/sec (*b*) 1200 s/sec

(*c*) 700 s/sec (*d*) 500 s/sec

163. Pulse rate in DM system is 56, 000 per second. Input signal is

$$5 \cos(2\pi\ 1000\ t) + 2 \cos(2\pi\ 2000\ t)\ V,$$

with t in second.

The minimum value of step size which will avoid stope overload distortion should

(*a*) be less than 0.56 V

(*b*) be equal to 0.56 V

(*c*) not be less than 0.56 V

(*d*) none of these

164. A low pass signal m(t) band limited to BHz is sampled by a periodic rectangular pulse train, $P_r(t)$ of period T_2 = 1/3B second. Assuming natural sampling and that the pulse amplitude and pulse width are A volts and 1/30B sec respectively, an expression for frequency spectrum of the sampled signal $M_2(t)$ is

(*a*) $A \sin C \left(\frac{2\pi f}{B}\right)$

(*b*) $A \sin C \left(\frac{2\pi f}{30B}\right)$

(*c*) $A \sin C \left(\frac{2\pi f}{60B}\right)$

(*d*) $A \cos C \left(\frac{2\pi f}{B}\right)$

165. A received binary NRZ signal assume the voltage level of 500 milli volts and –500 milli volts respectively for 1 and '0' transmission with a it rate or r bits/sec. The signal is corrupted by AWGN with a two-sided spectral density of 10^{-6} volt²/Hz. The received signal is processed by an integrate and Dump's circuit in every bit interval and compared with a zero threshold to take a bit decision. Assuming '1' and 0 transmission to be equally likely, maximum value of r such that the bit error probability $\leq 10^{-5}$, will be

(*a*) 12 kb/sec (*b*) 13.7 kb/sec

(*c*) 6.3 kb/sec (*d*) none of these

166. An analog signal (low pass) of 4 kHz BW is sampled at the Nyquist rate, subsequently quantized and encoded into a binary PCM wave with 128 quantization levels. The work synchronization is effected by adding a synchronizing pulse at the end of each code word. The bit rate to the resulting PCM signal will be

(*a*) 8 kHz (*b*) 32 kHz

(*c*) 16 kHz (*d*) 64 kHz

167. Band width of the input to PCM system is restricted to 4 kHz. The input varies from 3.8 V to a–3.8 V and has average power of 30 mW. The required signal to quantization noise power ratio is 20 dB. The modulator produces binary output. Assume uniform quantization. The number of bits required per sample will be

(*a*) 8 (*b*) 7

(*c*) 6 (*d*) 5

168. A speech signal occupying the bandwidth of 300 Hz to 3 kHz is converted into PCM format for use in digital communication. If sampling frequency is 8 kHz and each sample is quantized into 256 levels, then output bit the rate will be

(*a*) 3 kb/s (*b*) 8 kh/s

(*c*) 64 kb/s (*d*) 256 kb/s

169. A 7-bit hamming code (even parity checker) 0001001 for a BCD digit is known to have errors. The BCD encoded digit is

(*a*) 9 (*b*) 5

(*c*) 3 (*d*) 0

170. RMS quantization error in a 64 step binary PCM system with a reference scale from 0 to 6.4 volts, will be

(*a*) 0.01 volt (*b*) 0.03 volt

(*c*) 0.02 volt (*d*) 0.04 volt

171. What is the S/N ratio in a binary PCM system with average input noise as 50 mV, reference scale from 0 to 1.6 volts, step size as 0.1 volt and base-band signal applied to system is band limited to 8 kHz and transmission band width as 32 kHz?

(*a*) 1 (*b*) 3

(*c*) 2 (*d*) 4

172. If number of bits in a PCM system in increased from n to n + 1, then signal-to-quantization noise ratio will increase by a factor

(*a*) $\frac{(n+1)}{n}$ (*b*) $\frac{(n+1)^2}{n^2}$

(*c*) 2 (*d*) 4

173. Output S/N PCM sampling at 8000 sample/second and using 6 bits/word for transmission, is

(*a*) 12 dB (*b*) 24 dB

(*c*) 18 dB (*d*) 39 dB

174. When compression parameter, μ is 285 minimum signal to noise ratio required as 50 dB, 1024 quantizing levels, then L is

(*a*) 1002 (*b*) 1008

(*c*) 1006 (*d*) 1012

175. Probability of error for a base band PCM system with a matched filter at receiver with ± 5 volt bipolar pulses of duration 72 μ. sec and noise spectral density $= 1 \times 10^{-4}$ volts²/Hz, will be

(*a*) 0.95×10^{-5} (*b*) 1.15×10^{-5}

(*c*) 1.05×10^{-5} (*d*) 1.25×10^{-5}

176. Quantization bit rate for a an analog input signal with a bandwidth of 3.4 kHz in a delta modulator with a signal to quantization noise ratio of 25 dB, will be

(*a*) 48 kb/s (*b*) 68 kb/s

(*c*) 58 kb/s (*d*) 78 kb/s

177. What is the bit error for a non-coherent FSK system modulated by a PCM signal bit stream and operating at 10 MHz? Frequency deviation is 850 Hz, system data rate is 100 bits/sec peak to peak carrier amplitude is 2 volts and double noise spectral density is 1.0×10^{-4} volts/Hz.

(*a*) 2.74×10^{-6} (*b*) 4.74×10^{-6}

(*c*) 3.74×10^{-6} (*d*) 5.74×10^{-6}

178. What is the average probability of error in a coherent FSK (1 bit decoding) system transmitting binary data @ 2.5×10^6 bits/sec, while gaussian noise of zero mean and spectral density 10^{-20} volts/Hz added and with no noise, amplitude of required signal is 1 μV ?

(*a*) 0.55×10^{-3} (*b*) 0.75×10^{-3}

(*c*) 0.65×10^{-3} (*d*) 0.85×10^{-3}

179. If transmitted power, S_T is 200 m;

WL is 90 dB, n is 10^{-15} W/Hz and P_e is 10^{-4},

then maximum allowable bit rate using non-coherent FSK, will be

(*a*) 10 bps (*b*) 12 bps

(*c*) 11 bps (*d*) 13 bps

Common Data (Q. 180 – 182):

A single $x(t)$ is miltiplied by rectangular pulse train c(t).

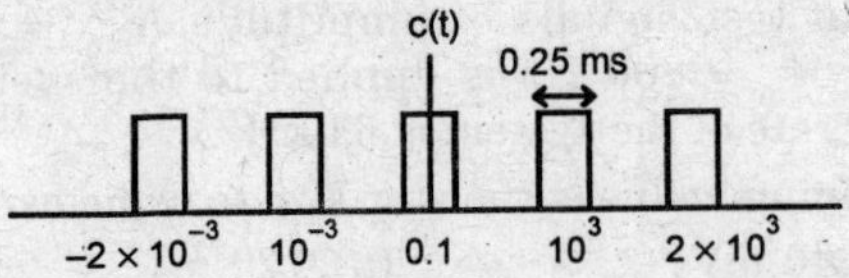

180. x(t) would be recovered from the product x(t) c(t) by using an ideal LPF if X(jω) = 0 for

(*a*) ω > 2000 π

(*b*) ω > 1000 π

(*c*) ω < 1000 π

(*d*) ω < 2000 π

181. If X(jω) satisfies the constraints required, then pass band gain A of the ideal lowpass filter needed to recover x(t) from c(t) x(t) is

(*a*) 1 (*b*) 2

(*c*) 4 (*d*) 8

182. Consider a set of 10 signals

$x_i(t)$, i = 1, 2, 3, ...10.

Each signal is band limited to 1 kHz. All 10 signals are to be time-division multiplexed after each is multiplied by a carrier c(t) shown in the figure.

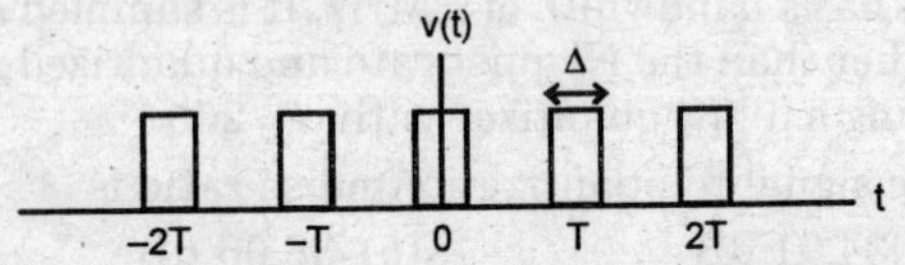

If period T of c(t) is chosen to have the maximum allowable value, then largest value of triangle would be

(*a*) 5×10^{-3} sec (*b*) 5×10^{-4} sec

(*c*) 5×10^{-5} sec (*d*) 5×10^{-6} sec

Linked Answer (Q. 183 – 184):

Ten telemetry signals, each of bandwidth 2 kHz, are to be transmitted simultaneously by binary PCM. The maximum tolerable error in sample amplitudes is 0.2% of the peak signal amplitude. The signals must be sampled at least 20% above the Nyquist rate. Framing and synchronizing requires an additional1% extra bits.

183. The minimum possible data rate must be

(*a*) 272.64 kbits/sec

(*b*) 436.32 kbits/sec

(*c*) 936.64 *k*bits/sec

(*d*) none of these

184. The minimum transmission bandwidth is

(*a*) 218.16 kHz

(*b*) 468.32 kHz

(*c*) 136.32 kHz

(*d*) none of these

185. If angle modulated signal is

$x(t) = 10 \cos [(10^8 \pi t) + 5 \sin 2\pi (10^3 t)]$,

then maximum frequency deviation will be

(*a*) 5 kHz (*b*) 1 kHz

(*c*) 2 kHz (*d*) 10 kHz

ANSWERS

1. (c)	2. (c)	3. (d)	4. (c)	5. (a)	6. (b)	7. (b)	8. (b)	9. (b)	10. (c)
11. (a)	12. (b)	13. (b)	14. (a)	15. (c)	16. (b)	17. (b)	18. (a)	19. (d)	20. (b)
21. (c)	22. (d)	23. (c)	24. (b)	25. (a)	26. (a)	27. (c)	28. (c)	29.(c)	30.(b)
31. (a)	32. (a)	33. (a)	34. (b)	35. (a)	36. (b)	37. (a)	38.(a)	39.(c)	40. (d)
41. (b)	42. (d)	43. (c)	44. (b)	45. (b)	46. (b)	47. (a)	48. (d)	49. (d)	50. (b)
51. (b)	52. (c)	53. (b)	54. (a)	55. (d)	56. (c)	57. (a)	58. (b)	59. (a)	60. (c)
61. (d)	62. (c)	63. (b)	64. (b)	65. (d)	66. (c)	67. (d)	68. (c)	69. (c)	70. (d)
71. (c)	72. (b)	73. (b)	74. (a)	75. (b)	76. (c)	77. (a)	78. (c)	79. (d)	80. (c)
81. (b)	82. (d)	83. (d)	84. (d)	85. (a)	86. (a)	87. (c)	88. (d)	89. (b)	90. (b)
91. (d)	92. (b)	93. (c)	94. (b)	95. (a)	96. (a)	97. (a)	98. (c)	99. (c)	100. (d)
101. (a)	102. (b)	103. (b)	104. (b)	105. (d)	106. (c)	107. (a)	108. (b)	109. (a)	110. (d)
111. (a)	112. (a)	113. (c)	114. (c)	115. (b)	116. (c)	117. (c)	118. (c)	119. (a)	120. (b)
121. (d)	122. (c)	123. (c)	124. (b)	125. (c)	126. (d)	127. (d)	128. (b)	129. (a)	130. (b)
131. (c)	132. (a)	133. (a)	134. (c)	135. (d)	136. (b)	137. (c)	138. (c)	139. (c)	140. (b)
141. (c)	142. (d)	143. (c)	144. (d)	145.(c)	146. (c)	147. (b)	148. (a)	149. (a)	150. (b)
151. (d)	152. (d)	153. (a)	154. (b)	155. (d)	156. (d)	157. (c)	158. (a)	159. (b)	160. (c)
161. (d)	162. (a)	163. (c)	164. (c)	165. (b)	166. (d)	167. (b)	168. (c)	169. (a)	170. (b)
171. (c)	172. (d)	173. (d)	174. (d)	175. (b)	176. (b)	177. (d)	178. (d)	179. (b)	180. (b)
181. (c)	182. (c)	183. (b)	184. (a)	185. (a)					

EXPLANATIONS

RANDOM SIGNALS AND NOISE

2. Current in FET or BTT under DC conditions is a constant at every instant. However current from emitter to the collector consists of a stream of individual electrons or holes, and it is only the time averaged flow measured as constant current.

Fluctuation observed in the number of covers is called *shot noise* and is given as

$$I_n^2 = 2q\, I_{dc}\, B$$

where, $q = 1.6 \times 10^{-19}$C

B = band width

7. PSD of noise process

$$S_N(F) = \begin{cases} 10^{-8}\left(1 + \dfrac{|f| - 10^8}{10^8}\right) & |f| < 10^8 \\ 0 & |f| > 10^8 \end{cases}$$

Noise is passed through a unity gain ideal BPF having BW of 2MHz

Here $$\frac{\pi C^2 R}{2} = (2\pi\, \Delta f)\, S_n(\omega_k)$$

$$\Rightarrow \quad C_R^2 = 4S_n(\omega_r)\, \Delta f$$

Noise signal; $n(t) = \Sigma\, C_k \cos(\omega_r t + \theta_k)$

Amplitude C_k can be calculated for noise power spectral $S_n(f)$

When filter is tuned to W_k,

$$\text{output noise power} = 2S_n(W_k)\,\Delta f = \frac{C_k^2}{2}$$

$$N_0 = 2\int_0^R S_n(\omega)\, df = 2\left(\frac{N_B}{2}\right) B = N_B$$

8. From property of *pdf*,

$$\int_{-\infty}^{\infty} f_x(x)\, dx = 1$$

$$k\int_0^1 dx = 1,\ k = 1$$

9. $$\text{Mean, } \bar{x} = \int_{-\infty}^{\infty} x\, p(x)\, dx = \int_{-1}^{3} \frac{x}{4}\, dx$$

$$= \frac{1}{4}\, \frac{x^2}{2}\Big|_{-1}^{3}$$

$$= \frac{1}{8}(9 - 1) = 1$$

$$\text{Variance, } \quad \sigma^2 = \int_{-\infty}^{\infty} x^2\, p(x)\, dx - (\bar{x})^2$$

$$= \int_{-1}^{3} x^2 . \frac{1}{4}\, dx - 1$$

$$= \frac{1}{4}\, \frac{x^3}{3}\Big|_{-1}^{3} - 1$$

$$= \frac{28}{12} - 1 = \frac{4}{3}$$

10. $$V = \frac{1}{2T}\int_{-T}^{T} n(t-\tau_T)n(t-\tau_R)dt$$

Since T is very large, therefore

$$V = \lim_{T\to\infty}\frac{1}{2T}\int_{-T}^{T} n(t-\tau_T)n(t-\tau_R)dt$$

$$= A\left[n(t-\tau_T)n(t-\tau_R)\right]$$

Since N(t) is ergodic,

$$V = R_{NN}(\tau_R - \tau_T)$$

11. Because $|R_{NN}(\tau)| \le R_{NN}(0)$ for any auto correlation function,

V will be maximum if $\tau_R = \tau_T$

12. Effective noise temperature

$$T_{eq} = (F-1)T_0$$

where, T_0 = standard temperature

$\therefore$ Noise figure, $F = \frac{T_{eq}}{T_0} + 1$

$$= \frac{150}{290} + 1 = 1.52$$

13. $T_F = H(\omega) = \frac{1}{1 + j\omega RC}$ for RC-filter

$$\Rightarrow T_F = \frac{1}{1 + \frac{j\omega}{\beta}}$$

where, $\beta = \frac{1}{RC}$

Impulse response

$$h(t) = \frac{1}{2\pi}\int_{-\infty}^{\infty}\left[\frac{1}{1+\frac{j\omega}{\beta}}\right]e^{j\omega L}d\omega$$

$$= \beta e^{-\beta t}; \quad t > 0$$

$$= 0 \quad ; \quad t > 0$$

$\therefore$ Input power spectral density,

$$S_{nn}(\omega) = \frac{\eta_0}{2}[\delta(\tau)]$$

14. $$R_{XX}(\tau) = \frac{1}{2\pi}\int_{-f_e}^{f_e} ke^{j\omega\tau}d\omega$$

$$= \frac{k}{2}\pi\left[\frac{e^{j\omega\tau}}{j\tau}\right]_{-f_e}^{f_e}$$

$$= \frac{k}{2\pi jfe}[2\cos(f_e\tau)]$$

$$= \frac{k}{\pi jfe}\cos(f_e\tau)$$

15. $$S_{nn}(\omega) = \int_{-\infty}^{\infty} R_{nm}(\tau)e^{-j\omega\tau}d\tau$$

$$= k\int_{-\infty}^{0} e^{(3-j\omega)\tau}.d\tau + k\int_{0}^{\infty} e^{-(3+j\omega)\tau}.d\tau$$

$$= \frac{k}{3-j\omega} + \frac{k}{3+j\omega}$$

$$= \frac{6k}{9+\omega^2}$$

16. $P_{YY} = R_{YY}(0)$

$$= \int_{-\infty}^{\infty}\int_{-\infty}^{\infty} 10^{-2}\delta(\varepsilon_1-\varepsilon_2)h(\varepsilon_1)h(\varepsilon_2)d\varepsilon_1 d\varepsilon_2$$

$$= -10^{-2}\int_{-\infty}^{\infty} h^2(\varepsilon_1)d\varepsilon$$

$$= -10^{-2}(9)\int_{-\infty}^{\infty}\varepsilon^2 e^{-8\varepsilon_1}d\varepsilon_1$$

$$= \frac{9}{256}(10^2)$$

$$= 0.351 \text{ mW}$$

17. $$p(y) = e^{-y} = e^{-\sqrt{z}}\frac{dy}{dx} = \frac{1}{2\sqrt{z}}$$

$$p(z) = p(y)\left|\frac{dy}{dz}\right| = \frac{e^{-\sqrt{z}}}{2\sqrt{z}}; \; 0 \le z \le \infty$$

18. $$G(f) = \int_{-\infty}^{\infty} e^{-2\alpha|\tau|}e^{-j\omega\tau}d\tau$$

$$= \int_{-\infty}^{0} e^{-2\alpha|\tau|}e^{j\omega\tau}d\tau + \int_{0}^{\infty} e^{-2\alpha t}d\tau$$

$$= \frac{4\alpha}{\omega^2 + 4\alpha^2}$$

19. $$p(x_i) = \int_{-\infty}^{x_1} 3e^{-6|x|}dx$$

$$= \frac{1}{2}\left(2 - e^{-6|x_1|}\right); \; x_1 \ge 0$$

$$= \frac{1}{2}e^{6x_1}; \quad x_1 \le 0$$

$$\Rightarrow \overline{x^2} = \int_{-\infty}^{\infty} 3x^2 e^{-6|x|}.dx = \frac{1}{18}$$

20. $$m_y(t) = E[y(t)] = E[x'(t)]$$

$$= R_{xx}(0)$$

$$= exp(0) = 1$$

$$\therefore R_{yy}(t_1 t_2) = E[y(t_1 y(t_2)]$$

$$= E[x^2(t_1)x^2(t_2)]$$

$$= [R_{xx}(0)]^2 + 2[R_{xx}(|t_1 - t_2|]^2$$

$$R_{yy}(t_1 t_2) = 1 + 2\exp(-2|\tau|)$$

21. Mean value of signal power

$$P_m = \int_{-\infty}^{\infty} S_M(f)\, df$$

$$= 2\int_{r}^{\omega} a\frac{f}{\omega}\, df$$

$$= a\omega$$

$$(SNR)_0 = \frac{A_c^{\,2} P_m}{4\,\omega\, N_0} = \frac{A_c^{\,2}\, a\omega}{4\omega N_0} = \frac{A_c^{\,2}\, a}{4N_0}$$

22. $$P_{YY} = \frac{\eta_0 |H(0)|^2 W_n}{2\pi} = 0.1$$

$$\therefore \quad \eta_0 = \frac{0.1(2\pi)}{4(2\pi)(10^6)} = \frac{10^{-7}}{8}$$

$$= 1.25\times 10^{-8}\, W/Hz$$

27. $$f_Y(y)dy = f_X(x)dx$$

$$f_Y(y) = f_X(x)\frac{dx}{dy}$$

$$y = ax + b$$

$$\Rightarrow \quad \frac{dy}{dx} = a$$

$$\Rightarrow \quad \frac{dx}{dy} = \frac{1}{a}$$

28. $$S_X(\omega) = \frac{N}{2}\,\text{rect}\left(\frac{\omega}{4\pi B}\right)$$

We know

$$R_X(\tau) \longleftrightarrow S_X(\omega)$$

$$\frac{W}{\pi}\sin(Wt) \longleftrightarrow \text{rect}\left(\frac{\omega}{2W}\right)$$

Here, $W = 2\pi B$

$$\therefore \quad R_x(\tau) = \frac{2\pi B}{\pi}\frac{N}{2}\sin(2\pi B\tau)$$

$$= NB\sin(2\pi B\tau)$$

29. $P_x = \overline{x^2} = R_x(0) = NB$ [since sin (0) = 1]

30. $$H_{op}(\omega) = \frac{S_m(\omega)}{S_m(\omega) + S_n(\omega)}$$

$$= \frac{\dfrac{6}{9+\omega^2}}{\dfrac{6}{9+\omega^2} + 6} = \frac{1}{10+\omega^2}$$

31. $$Z = \frac{R}{1 + j\omega CR};\ \text{Re}\{Z\} = \frac{R}{1+\omega^2 C^2 R^2}$$

$$\overline{v_n^2} = 4kT\int_0^{\infty} \text{Re}\{Z\}df$$

$$= 4kT\int_0^{\infty} \frac{R}{1+\omega^2C^2R^2}df$$

Substituting $\omega CR = y$, we get

$$2\pi CR df = dy$$

$$\overline{v_n^2} = 4kT\int_0^{\infty} \text{Re}\{Z\}df$$

$$= 4kT\int_0^{\infty} \frac{R}{1+\omega^2C^2R^2}df$$

$$= \frac{1.38\times 10^{-23}\times 300}{10^{-6}} = 4.14\times 10^{-15}V^2$$

$$V_{nrms} = 6.4\times 10^{-8}\,V$$

32. $$V_n = \sqrt{4kT\delta f R}$$

$$= \sqrt{4\times 1.38\times 10^{-23}\times(273+27)\times 2\times 10^6\times 10\times 10^3}$$

$$= \sqrt{33120\times 10^{-14}}$$

$= 181.989 \times 10^{-7}$

= 18.2 microvolts

33. $$C = \delta f \log_2(1 + S/N)$$

where, $S/N = \text{antilog}\,\frac{15}{10} = 31.62$

$$\therefore \quad C = 4000\log_2 31.62$$

$$= \frac{4000\log_{10}31.62}{\log_{10}2}$$

$$= 19931.56$$

$\approx$ ***20000 bps***

34. $$F = 1 + \frac{R_{eq}}{R_a} = 1 + \frac{50}{50} = 2.$$

35. $$\left(\frac{S}{N}\right)_0 = \frac{S_i}{\eta B}$$

where, B = bandwidth of the channel

For white noise, $S_{nn}(\omega) = \eta B$

Now, $10\log\left(\frac{S}{N}\right)_{01} - 10\log\left(\frac{S}{N}\right)_{02}$

$$= 10\log\frac{S_i}{\eta B_2} - 10\log\frac{S_i}{\eta B_2}$$

$$\Rightarrow \quad 30 - 10\log\left(\frac{S}{N}\right)_{02} = 10\log\frac{B_2}{B_1} = 3\text{ dB}$$

$$\Rightarrow \quad 10\log\left(\frac{S}{N}\right)_{02} = (30-3)\text{ dB}$$

= 27 dB

36. $$C = 400\log_2(1 + S/N)$$

where, $S/N = \text{antilog}\,\frac{15}{10} = 31.623$

$\therefore$ Channel capacity, $C = 4000\log_2(1 + 31.623)$

$$= \frac{4000\log_{10}32.623}{\log_{10}2}$$

= 20.11 kbps

37. White noise of 2 sided spectral density 2×10^{-6} V²/Hz RC LPF 3 dB cut-off 4 kHz to find mean squared noised out-put

$$G_y(f) = |H(f)|^2 G_x(f)$$

$$R_y(\tau) = f^{-1}[|H(f)|^2 G_x(f)]$$

$$y^{-2} = R_y(0) = \int_{-\infty}^{\infty} H(f)^2 G_x(f)\,df$$

$$y_n^2 = \eta \int_0^{\infty} \frac{1}{1+\frac{f^2}{16}}\,df \left[H(s) = \frac{1}{\frac{s}{4}+1} \right]$$

$$= (2 \times 10^{-6}) \times \frac{\pi}{2} \times 4 \times 10^{-13}$$

$$= 4\pi \times 10^{-3}\ V^2$$

39. $$P_e = Q\left[\sqrt{\frac{2A\ 2T}{n}}\right] \le 10^{-4}$$

$$\Rightarrow \quad \sqrt{\frac{2A^2T}{n}} = 3.71\ T = (3.71)^2 \times 10^{-5}$$

$$\Rightarrow \quad T = 13.76 \times 10^{-5}\ \text{sec}$$

$$\text{Transmission rate}, R = \frac{1}{T} = 7.26\ \text{kb/sec}$$

40. Quantization noise can be reduced by increasing number of standard levels. But more levels require more bits to send them. Obviously, it needs more bandwidth required which is proportional to the number of bits sent per second.

A block diagram for a super receiver for AM signal is shown below.

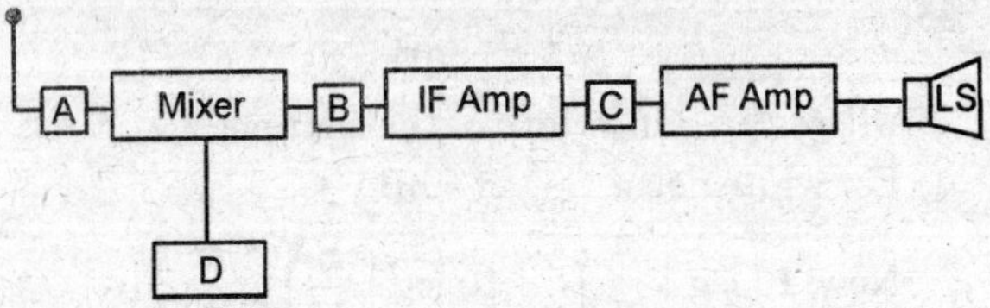

42. f_c = 1000 k Hz

Following frequencies will be present in the modulated wave

1000 ± 0.3 Hz, 1000 Hz, 1000 ± 2

Hence 700 kHz will not be present in the modulated waves.

13. $$m_t = \sqrt{m_1^2 + m_2^2}$$

$$= \sqrt{(0.3)^2 + (0.4)^2} = \sqrt{0.25}$$

∴ Total modulated power,

$$P_t = P_c\left(1+\frac{m^2}{2}\right)$$

$$= 10\left(1+\frac{(0.5)^2}{2}\right) = \mathbf{10.125\ kW}$$

44. $P_c = \frac{2}{3}P$.

If carrier is suppressed, then $\frac{2}{3}P$ or 66% power will be saved.

47. Given : Modulation index, $\alpha = 1$.

$$\therefore \quad P_t = \frac{A_c^2}{2}\left[1+\frac{\alpha^2|m(t)^2|}{2}\right]$$

$$= \frac{500^2}{2}\left[1+\frac{0.8^2}{2}\right]$$

$$= 165\ \text{KW}$$

51. $$P_t = P_c\left(1+\frac{m^2}{2}\right)$$

$$\Rightarrow \quad 10 = P_c\left(1+\frac{0.6^2}{2}\right)$$

$$\therefore \quad \mathbf{P_c = 8.4746\ kW}$$

52. We know, $m = \frac{\delta}{f_m} = 15$

where, $f_m = \frac{2\pi \times 100}{2\pi} = 100$ Hz

∴ $\delta = 15 \times 1000 = 1500$ Hz

∴ Approximate bandwidth

$= 2(f_m + \Delta f)$

$= 2(100 + 1500)$

$= 3200$ Hz

= 3.2 kHz

53. Given: $f_i = 455$ kHz; and $f_s = 1200$ kHz

∴ Image frequency $= f_s + 2f_i$

$= 1200 + 2 \times 455$

= 2110 kHz

54. If modulation index α is 0, then

$$P_{t1} = \frac{A_c^2}{2}\left(1+\frac{0^2}{2}\right) = \frac{A_c^2}{2}$$

If modulation index is 1 then

$$P_{t2} = \frac{A_c^2}{2}\left(1+\frac{1^2}{2}\right) = \frac{3}{4}A_c^2$$

$$\therefore \quad \frac{P_{t2}}{P_{t1}} = \frac{3}{2}$$

57. Upper side band = 60 + 0.3 to 60 + 3

= 60.3 to 63 kHz

59. Given: $$P_c = \frac{A_c^2}{2} = 10\ \text{kW}$$

$$\mu = \sqrt{\mu_1^2 + \mu_2^2}$$

$$= \sqrt{0.30^2 + 0.40^2} = 0.50$$

$$\therefore \quad P_t = \frac{A_c^2}{2} + \frac{A_c^2}{4}\mu^2$$

$$= \frac{A_c^2}{4}(\mu^2 + 2) = \mathbf{11.25\ kW}$$

60. PM signal, $x_{PM}(t) = A\cos[\omega_c(t) + \phi(t)]$
$= A\cos\theta(t)$

where, $\phi(t) = k_p m(t)$
$= k_p a_m \sin\omega_m t$

Instaneous radian frequency,

$$\omega_i = \frac{d\theta(t)}{dt} = \omega_c + \frac{d\phi(t)}{dt}$$

$\Rightarrow$ $|\omega_i - \omega_c| = k_p a_m \omega_m$
$\propto \omega_m$ (frequency deviation)

Hence, frequency deviation is proportional to modulating frequency.

61. Total power, $P_t = P_c + P_s$

$$= \frac{A_c^2}{2} + \frac{A_c^2}{4}\mu^2$$

$$= \frac{A_c^2}{2}\left(1+\frac{\mu^2}{2}\right) = 600 \text{ W}$$

and $P_c = \frac{A_c^2}{2} = 400$ W

$\therefore$ $\frac{600}{400} = 1 + \frac{\mu^2}{2}$

$\Rightarrow$ $\frac{\mu^2}{2} = \frac{1}{2}$

$\therefore$ Modulation index, $\mu = 1$.

62. $f_a(t) = \cos(2\times10^8\pi t + 75\sin 2\times10^3\pi t)$

and $\theta(t) = 2\times10^8\pi t + 75\sin 2\times10^3\pi t$

$\Rightarrow$ $\omega_i = \frac{d\theta(t)}{dt}$
$= 2\times10^8\pi + 75\times2\times10^3\pi\cos 2\times10^3\pi t$

$\Rightarrow$ $|\omega_i - 2\times10^8\pi|_{max} = \Delta\omega$
$= 75\times2\pi\times10^3$ rad/sec

$\Rightarrow$ $\Delta f = 75\times10^3$ Hz = **75 kHz.**

63. $\Rightarrow$ $P_c\left(1+\frac{\mu^2}{2}\right) = 10$ kW

$\Rightarrow$ $P_c = \frac{10\text{ kW}}{1+\frac{\mu^2}{2}} = \frac{10\text{ kW}}{1+18} =$ **8.47 kW**

67. $P_t = P_c\left(1+\frac{m^2}{2}\right)$

$\Rightarrow$ $\frac{P_t}{P_c} = 1 + \frac{m^2}{2}$

$$= 1 + \frac{1^2}{2} = \frac{3}{2}$$

68. $I_t = I_c\sqrt{1+\frac{m^2}{2}}$

$$= I_c\sqrt{1+\frac{1^2}{2}} = I_c\sqrt{\frac{3}{2}}$$

Given: $I_t = \sqrt{\frac{3}{2}} = I_c\sqrt{\frac{3}{2}}$

$\Rightarrow$ $I_c = 1$ amp.

Now with simultaneous modulation by another sine wave

$$\sqrt{2} = I_c\sqrt{1+\frac{m^2}{2}} = 1\sqrt{1+\frac{m^2}{2}}$$

$\therefore$ $2 = 1 + \frac{m^2}{2}$

$\Rightarrow$ $m = \sqrt{2} = 1.41$

Now, $m = \sqrt{m_1 + m_2^{\,2}}$

$\Rightarrow$ $m_2 = \sqrt{m^2 - m_1^{\,2}}$
$= \sqrt{2-1} = 1.0$

69. Modulation index $= \frac{\delta}{f_m} = \frac{50000}{100} =$ **500 radians**

70. When USSB is employed, bandwidth of the modulated signal is same as bandwidth of the message signal.

$\therefore$ $W_{USSB} = W = 10^4$ Hz

71. When DSB is used, then bandwidth of the transmitted signal is twice the bandwidth of the message signal.

$\therefore$ $W_{DSB} = 2W = 2\times10^4$ Hz

72. $P_t = P_c\left(1+\frac{\beta_1^2}{2}+\frac{\beta_2^2}{2}\right)$,

Here, $\beta_1 = 0.3$, $\beta_2 = 0.4$

$\therefore$ $P_t = 20\left(1+\frac{0.09}{2}+\frac{0.16}{2}\right) = 22.5k$W

73. Side band frequencies are,

$(6\times10^6 \pm 5000)$ rad and $(6\times10^6 \pm 9000)$ rad

$\omega_{sb} = 5.995, 6.005, 5.991$ and 6.009MHz

$f_{sb} = \frac{\omega_{sb}}{2\pi} = 953.5, 955.7, 954.1, 956.4\,k$Hz

74. Given: $f_m = 10k$Hz, $R = 1000\Omega$, $C = 10000pF$

$\therefore$ $2\pi f_m RC = 2\pi\times10^4\times10^3\times10^{-8} = 0.628$

$\therefore$ $\beta_{max} = (1+(0.628)^2)^{-\frac{1}{2}} = 0.847$

75. $v_i(t) = \cos\omega_c t + 0.5\cos\omega_m t$

$i = 10 + 2(\cos\omega_c t + 0.5\cos\omega_m t)os\omega_m t)^2$
$+ 0.2(\cos\omega_c t + 0.5c$

AM signal $= 2\cos\omega_c t + 0.2\cos\omega_c t\cos\omega_m ts\omega_c t$
$= (2 + 0.2\cos\omega_m t)\cos$ s

$\therefore$ $\beta = \frac{0.2}{2} = \frac{1}{10} = 10\%$

76. Normalized message signal is

$$m(t) = \frac{2}{T}t,\ 0 < t \le \frac{T}{2}$$

$$\overline{m^2(t)} = \frac{2}{T}\int_0^{T/2}\left(\frac{2}{T}t\right)^2 dt = \frac{1}{3}$$

$$E_{eff} = \frac{\beta^2\overline{m^2(t)}}{1+\beta^2\overline{m^2(t)}} = \frac{(0.4)^2\frac{1}{3}}{1+(0.4)^2\frac{1}{3}} = 5.1\%$$

77. $A_c(1+\mu) = 45$ and $A_c(1-\mu) = 15$

$\therefore \quad \frac{1+\mu}{1-\mu} = 3$

$\Rightarrow \quad \mu = 0.5$

78. Normalized message signal is

$$m(t) = \frac{2}{T}t,\ 0 < t \le \frac{T}{2}$$

$$\overline{m^2(t)} = \frac{2}{T}\int_0^{T/2}\left(\frac{2}{T}t\right)^2 dt = \frac{1}{3}$$

$$\therefore \quad E_{eff} = \frac{(0.5)^2\frac{1}{3}}{1+(0.5)^2\frac{1}{3}} = 0.0769 \text{ or } 7.69\%$$

79.

$$y(t) = 4(m(t)+\cos\omega_c t) + 10(m(t)+\cos\omega_c t)^2$$

$$= 4m(t) + 4\cos\omega_c t + 10m^2(t)_c t + 20m(t)\cos\omega_c t + 5 + 5\cos 2\omega$$

$$y(t) = 5 + 4m(t) + 10m^2(t) + 4(1+5m(t))\cos\omega_c t + 5\cos 2\omega_c t$$

AM signal is

But $x_c(t) = 4[1+5m(t)]\cos\omega_c t$

$m(t) = Mm_n(t)$

$\therefore \quad x_c(t) = 4[1+5Mm_n(t)]\cos\omega_c t$

$\Rightarrow \quad 5M = 0.8,\ M = 0.16$

80. Filter characteristic is shown in the figure.

$f_c - W > 2W$

$\Rightarrow f_c > 3W,$

$f_c + W < 2f_c$

$\Rightarrow f_c > W$

$f > 3W$

81. Since High-side tuning is used, therefore

$$f_{LO} = f_m + f_{IF}$$

$$f_{IF} = 500 kHz$$

Here, $f_{LOL} = 5 + 0.5 = 5.5\,\text{MHz}$,

$$f_{LOU} = 10 + 0.5 = 10.5\,\text{MHz}$$

82. Given circuit is a ring modulator.

Since output is DSB-SC signal, so it will contain $m(t)\cos(n\omega_c t)$, where $n = 1, 2, 3....$

Hence there will be only $(1\text{MHz} \pm 400\text{Hz})$ frequency component.

83. Total signal bandwidth = 5 × 12 = 60 *k*Hz.

There would be 11 guard band between 12 signals.

$\therefore$ Guard band width = 11 *k*Hz.

Total band width = 60 + 11 = 71 *k*Hz

84. $x_1(t) = g(t)\cos(2000\pi t)$

$$= x(t)\sin(2000\pi t)\cos(2000\pi t)$$

$$= \frac{1}{2}x(t)\sin(4000\pi t)$$

$$X_1(j\omega) = \frac{1}{4j}X(j(\omega - 4000\pi)) - X(j(\omega + 4000\pi))$$

This implies that $X_1(j\omega)$ is zero for $|\omega| \le 2000\pi$ because $\omega < 2\pi f_m = 2\pi 1000$.

When $x_1(t)$ is passed through a LPF with cut-off frequency 2000π, the output will be zero.

85. $y(t) = g(t)\sin(400\pi t) = x(t)\sin^2(400\pi t)$

$$= (\sin(200\pi t) + 2\sin(400\pi t))\frac{(1-\cos(800\pi t))}{2}$$

$$= \frac{1}{2}[\sin(200\pi t) - \sin(200\pi t)\cos(800\pi t) + 2\sin(400\pi t) - \sin(400\pi t)\cos(800\pi t)]$$

$$= \frac{1}{2}\sin(200\pi t) - \frac{1}{4}[\sin(1000\pi t) - \sin(600\pi t)] + \sin(400\pi t) - \frac{1}{4}[\sin(1200\pi t) - \sin(400\pi t)]$$

If this signal is passed through LPF with frequency 400π and gain 2, the output will be $\sin(200\pi t)$

86. Message signal BW, $f_m = 5\,kHz$

Noise power density = 10^{-18} W/Hz.

Total noise power = $10^{-18} \times 5k = 5 \times 10^{-15}$ W

Input signal-to-noise ratio

$$(\text{SNR})_i = 10\log_{10} 2\times 10^4 = 43\,dB$$

87. Frequency sensitivity constant

$$k_f = \frac{\Delta f}{A_m} = \frac{1\times 10^3}{1} = 1\text{kHz/V}$$

Now for the second case,

$A_m = 5$ V and $f_m = 2$ kHz.

Frequency deviation,

$$\Delta f = k_f \times A_m = 5\,kHz$$

Modulation index $= \frac{\Delta f}{f_m} = \frac{5k}{2k} = 2.5$

FM signal is,

$$3\cos[2\pi\times 10^6 t + 2.5\sin(4\pi\times 10^3 t)]$$

88. Modulation index

$$\beta = \frac{\Delta f}{f_m} = \frac{k_f A_m}{f_m} = \frac{\beta f_m}{A_m}$$

Since $J_0(\beta) = 0$ for the first time when $\beta = 2.44$

$$\therefore \quad k_f = \frac{2.44\times 10^3}{2} = 1.22\times 10^3 \text{ Hz/V}$$

89. $\omega_i = \omega_c + k_f m(t)$

So frequency deviation will be $m(t)$ multiplied by k_f

90. Phase deviation $\Delta\phi(t) = 2\pi k_f \int_0^t m(\tau)d\tau$

For $0 \le t \le 1$,

$$\Delta\phi(t) = 2\pi(25)\int_0^t 10\tau d\tau = 250\pi t^2$$

$$\Delta\phi(1) = 250\pi$$

For $1 \le t \le 2$

$$\Delta\phi(t) = \phi(1) + 2\pi(25)\int_0^t 10\,dt$$

$$= 250\pi + 500\pi t$$

$$= 250\pi(1+2t) \text{ rad}$$

91. AM band width = $2f_m$

Peak frequency deviation = $3(2f_m) = 6f_m$

Modulation index $\beta = \frac{6f_m}{f_m} = 6$

FM signal is represented in terms of Bessel function as

$$x_{FM}(t) = A_c \sum_{n=-\infty}^{\infty} J_n(\beta)\cos(\omega_c + n\omega_m)t$$

$\Rightarrow \quad \omega_c + n\omega_m = 2\pi(1008 \times 10^3)$

$\Rightarrow \quad 2\pi \times 10^6 + n \times 4\pi \times 10^3 = 2\pi(1008 \times 10^3)$

$\Rightarrow \quad n = 4$

$\therefore \quad$ Coefficient = $5J_4(6)$

92. Deviation ratio, $D = \frac{5 \times 20k}{25k} = 4$

Bandwidth of output = 2(4 + 1)25k = 250 kHz

93. Phase deviation $\Delta\phi(t) = 20t^2$ rad

Frequency deviation, $\frac{d\phi(t)}{dt} = 40t$ rad/s

$$\frac{1}{2\pi}\frac{d\phi(t)}{dt} = \frac{20t}{\pi} \text{ Hz}$$

94. $\Delta f = (\Delta f_1)n_1 n_2 = (25)(64)(48) = 76.8\,\text{kHz}$

95. $f_2 = n_1 f_1 = (64)(200)(10^3) = 12.8\,\text{MHz}$

$f_3 = f_2 \pm f_{LO} = (12.8 \pm 10.8) = 23.6\,\text{MHz},\ 2.0\,\text{MHz}$

When $f_3 = 23.6$ MHz, then

$$f_c = n_2 f_3 = (48)(23.6) = 1132.8\,\text{MHz}$$

When $f_3 = 2$ MHz, then

$$f_c = n_2 f_3 = (48)(2) = 96\,\text{MHz}$$

96. Deviation ratio at narrow band output = 0.1
Deviation ratio at wide band output = 5

$$\therefore \quad n = \frac{5}{0.1} = 50$$

97. Carrier frequency at the output of multiplier = nf_{c_1}

= 50(100,000) = 5 MHz

Two permissible frequencies for local oscillator are

85 – 5 = 80 MHz, 85 + 5 = 90 MHz

98. According to Carson's rule

BW = 2(D + 1)W

= 2(5 + 1)500

= 6000 Hz

99. $B = \frac{k_f a_m}{\omega_m} = \frac{\Delta f}{f_m} = \frac{5 \times 10^3}{2 \times 10^3} = 2.5$

$f_\beta = 2\,(B + 1)f_m$

= 2(2.5 + 1)2

= 14 kHz

100. $x(t) = A_c(1 + \mu\cos 2\pi f_m t)\cos 2\pi f_c t$

Here, $A_c(1 + \mu) = 2A_c$

$\therefore \quad \mu = 1$

Hence modulation index is 1 or 100% modulation

101.

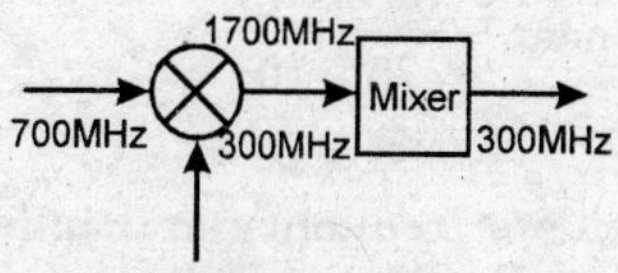

First stage of receiver is given with

f_{in} = 700 MHz = 0.7 GHz

f_{osc} = 1 GHz

Mixer is ideal multiplier and BPF → if output at 300 MHz

Image frequency = 700 + 2(300) = 1300 MHz

$$f_i = f_s + 2f_{if} = f_0 + f_{if}$$

where, f_i = image frequency

f_s = signal frequency

f_{if} = IF frequency

f_0 = oscillator frequency

$\therefore$ Image frequency > f_0, *i.e.* 1 GHz

Hence LPF employed should allow complete transmission upto 1 GHz and complete rejection of signal after 1 GHz

102. *For FM*

instantaneous frequency, $f_i = f_c + k_f m(t)$

where k_f = a constant in Hz/V

Peak frequency deviation

$$\Delta f = k_f |m(t)|_{\max}$$

$$= 100k \times 1 = 100 \text{ kHz}$$

Base band signal bandwidth

$$B_m = \frac{2000\pi}{2\pi} = 1 \text{ kHz}$$

$$B_{FM} = 2(\Delta f + B_m) = 2(200 + 1) \text{ kHz}$$

For PM

Instantaneous angle, $\theta(t) = \omega t + k_p m(t)$

Frequency, $\frac{d\theta(t)}{dt} = \omega_c + k_p \frac{dm(t)}{dt}$

$m(t) = \sin 2000\pi t$

Frequency deviation

$$\Delta f = \frac{k_p \times 2000\pi \times 1}{2\pi} = 10 \text{ kHz}$$

$$\therefore \quad B_{PM} = 2(\Delta f + B_m)$$

$$= 2(10 + 1) = 22 \text{ kHz}$$

103. *For FM*

$$\Delta f = 2 \times 100 = 200 \text{ kHz}$$

$$\therefore \quad B_{FM} = (200 + 1) = 402 \text{ kHz}$$

For PM

$$\Delta f = 2 \times 10 = 20 \text{ kHz}$$

$$B_{PM} = 2(20 + 1) = 42 \text{ kHz}$$

104. $$\Delta f = \frac{\text{Carrier swing}}{2}$$

$$= \frac{125 \times 10^3}{2} = 62.5 \text{ kHz}$$

Since maximum frequency deviation for the FM broadcast band is 15 kHz

$$\therefore \quad \text{Modulation index} = \frac{62.5 \times 10^3}{75 \times 10^3}$$

$$= 0.83 \text{ or } 83\ \%$$

Figure below shows frequency multiplier and heterodyne portion of a FM transmitter.

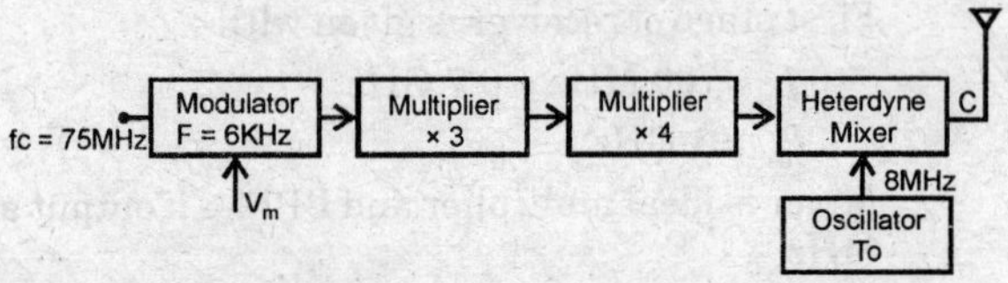

105. Following frequencies will be present in the output:

1000 ± 0.3 =1000.3 kHz and 999.7 kHz

Also, 1000 ± 2 =1002 kHz and 998 kHz

106. $$P_T = P_0\left(1 + \frac{m^2}{2}\right) = P_0\left(1 + \frac{0.8^2}{2}\right) = P_0\,(1.32)$$

Since in DSBSC, saving in power is P_0,

$$\therefore \quad \text{saving} = \frac{P_0}{P_0 \times 1.32} \times 100\%$$

$$= \frac{1}{1.32} \times 100 = \mathbf{75.76\ \%}$$

107. $$\omega_c = 2\pi \times 25 \times 10^6$$

$$= 1.57 \times 10^8 \text{ rad/sec}$$

$$\omega_m = 2\pi \times f_m$$

$$= 2\pi \times 400 = 2513 \text{ rad/sec}$$

$$m = \frac{\delta}{f_m} = \frac{10,000}{400} = 25$$

108. Carrier swing = $2\Delta f$ = 100 kHz

Frequency deviation, Δf = 50 kHz

Here, f_m = 8 kHz

$$\therefore \quad \text{Modulation index} = \frac{\Delta f}{f_m} = \frac{50}{8} = \mathbf{6.25}$$

111. Message signal BW, f_m = 5 kHz

Noise power density = 10^{-18} W/Hz

Total noise power = $10^{-18} \times 5 \times 10^3 = 5 \times 10^{-15}$ W

Input signal-to-noise ratio

$$\text{SNR} = \frac{10^{-10}}{5 \times 10^{-15}} = \mathbf{2 \times 10^4 \text{ or } 43 \text{ dB}}$$

113. Resulting depth of modulation

$$m_0 = M(1 + 4Q^2\delta^2)^{-1/2}$$

where, $$\delta = \frac{(f_C + f_m) - f_C}{f_C} = \frac{f_m}{f_C}$$

Here, $f_C = 1000 \times 10^8$ Hz, $f_m = 4 \times 10^3$ Hz

$$\therefore \quad \delta = \frac{1004 - 1000}{1000} = \frac{4}{1000}$$

$$m_0 = \frac{0.4}{\sqrt{1 + 4 \times 140^2 \times \left(4 \times 10^{-3}\right)^2}}$$

$$= \frac{0.4}{\sqrt{2.2544}} = \mathbf{0.27}$$

114. Frequency spectrum of an amplitude modulated wave consists of $f_C, f_C + f_m, f_C - f_m$

$$f_C = 100 \text{ kHz}, f_M = 1500 \text{ Hz}$$

$$f_C + f_m = 100 \text{ kHz} + 1500 \text{ Hz}$$

$$= 101.500 \text{ kHz}$$

$$f_C - f_m = 100 \text{ kHz} - 1.500 \text{ kHz}$$

$$= 98.500 \text{ kHz}$$

115. Any station being modulated by a 5kHz signal will produce an upper side frequency 5kHz above its carrier and a lower side frequency 5 kHz below its carrier. Thereby requiring bandwidth of 10 kHz per station.

117. $$f_{LO} = f_{IF} + f_C$$

$$= 455 \times 10^3 + 540 \times 10^3 = \mathbf{995 \text{ kHz}}$$

118. $$\left(\frac{S_0}{N_0}\right)_{FM} = 3\, m_f^2 \left(\frac{S_0}{N_0}\right)_{AM}$$

For improvement to be noticeable

$$3\, m_f^2 = 1$$

$$\Rightarrow \quad m_f = \frac{1}{\sqrt{3}}$$

130. Nyquist rate = 2 × 6 MHz = 12 MHz

Actual sampling rate = 1.2 × 12 = 14.4 MHz

$1024 = 2^{10}$, so that 10 bits or binary pulses are needed to encode each sample,

Minimum bandwidth = 144.4 M × 10

= 144 M bits/sec.

135. $$\left(\frac{S}{N}\right)_{0\,dB} = 1.76 + 6.02n = 62 \text{ dB}$$

If number of bits is increased by 2, then

$$\left(\frac{S}{N}\right)'_{0\,dB} = 1.76 + 6.02 \times (n + 2)$$

$$= 62 + 12.04 \text{ dB (increase by 12 dB)}$$

$$= 1.76 + 6.02 \times \left(\frac{62 - 1.76}{6.02} + 2\right)$$

$$= 195.12$$

136. Given: N = 16, and δf = 4000

Now, C = 4000 $\log_2 16$ = 4000 × 4

= 16000 *kbps* = **16 *bps***

138. Bandwidth for PCM,

$$f_{PCM} = \frac{\eta}{2} f_s \geq n f_m \text{ Hz}$$

139. If $L = 2$, then $2 = 2^n$

$\Rightarrow n = 1$ ND

If $L = 8$, then $8 = 2^n$

$\Rightarrow n = 3.$

Hence relative bandwidth will be tripled.

140. Block diagram of a regenerative repeater is shown below:

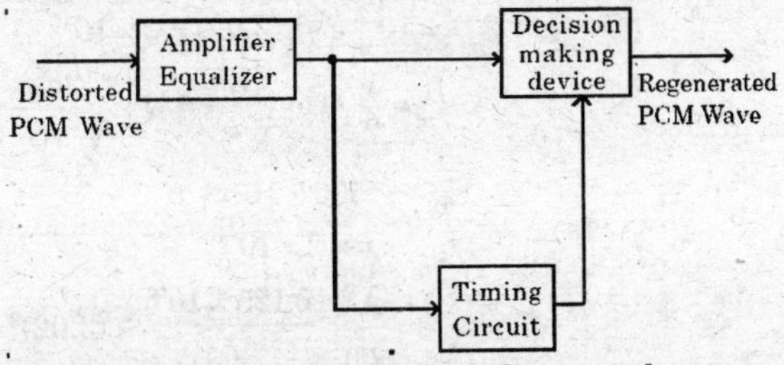

It can be inferred from the block diagram that, correct sequence is *(b)*.

141. Sampling rate for each signal = $2 f_M = 8$ kHz

Since there are four voice signals it requires

= 4 × 8 kHz

= 32 kHz = 32k samples/sec.

and each sample is encoded by ($\log_2 256 = 8$) bits

Hence resultant bit transmission rate

= 8 × 32 kbps = 256 kbps (kilo bits/sec)

142. $f_{PCM} = \frac{n}{2} f_s = \frac{7}{2} \times 10 = 35$ kHz.

143. $128 = 2^7$.

We need 7 bits/character.

For 1,000,000 character, we need 7 Mbits/second.

∴ Minimum bandwidth = 7 Mbits/sec.

144. $fs > 2fm = 6400$ Hz, $nfs \leq 63000$

$$n \leq \frac{36000}{6400} = 5.63$$

Take $n = 5$

$L = 2n = 32$

$$f_s = \frac{36000}{5} = 7.2 \text{ kHz}$$

145. Data rate = $2\,\delta f \log_2 N$

$= 2 \times 4 \log_2 128 =$ **56** kbps

147. $$\frac{S_o}{N_o} = \frac{3L^2}{[\ln(\mu+1)]^2} \geq 50\ dB$$

Here, $\mu = 100$

$$\therefore \frac{3L^2}{[\ln 101]^2} = 1000000$$

$\Rightarrow$ L = 842.6

Because L is power of 2, we select

$L = 1024 = 2^{10}$

Thus 10 bits are required.

149. As $R_{max} \propto (P_t)^{1/4}$

$\therefore R'_{max} \propto (81P_t)^{1/4} = 3\,R_{max}.$

150. Message bandwidth = W,

Nyquist rate = 2 W

Bandwidth = 2W × 8 = 16 bit/s

∴ $16W = 10^8$

$$\Rightarrow W = \frac{10^8}{16} = 6.25\ MHz$$

151. $f_s > 2f_m = 6400$ Hz

Now $nf_3 \leq 36000$

$$n \leq \frac{36000}{6400} = 5.63$$

For $n = 5$, $L = 2^n = 2^5 = 32$

$$\therefore f_s = \frac{36000}{5} = 7.2\,k\text{Hz}$$

152. Transmitted code word are

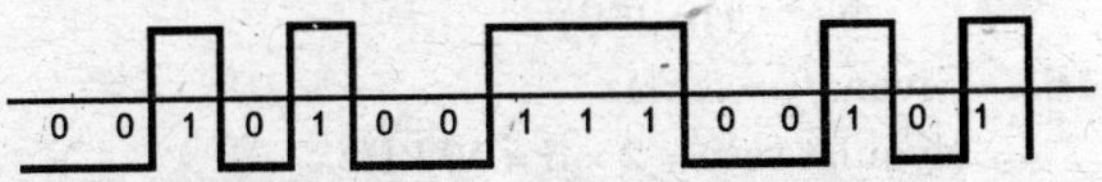

In 1st word 001(1) In 2nd word 010(2)

In 3rd word 011(3) In 4th word 100(4)

In 5th word 101(5)

153. Sampling interval $T_s = \frac{1}{8k} = 125\,\mu s$

Since there are 24 channels and 1 sync pulse

∴ Time alloted to each channel, $T_c = \frac{T_s}{25} = 5\,\mu s$

Since pulse duration is $1\,\mu s$, thus time between pulse is $4\,\mu s$.

154. $$A_{max.} = \frac{\delta f_s}{\omega_m} = \frac{0.1 \times 68k}{2\pi \times 10^3} = 1.08\,V$$

155. $$A_{max.} = \frac{\delta f_s}{\omega_m}$$

$$\Rightarrow \delta = \frac{A_{max.}\omega_m}{f_s} = \frac{1 \times 2\pi \times 800}{50 \times 10^3} = 78.5\,mV$$

156. $$N_o = \frac{\delta^2 B}{3f_s} = \frac{(0.0785)^2 \times 3500}{3 \times 64000} = 1.12 \times 10^{-4}\,W$$

157. $$S_o = \frac{A^2_{max.}}{2} = 0.5$$

$$\therefore \frac{S_o}{N_o} = \frac{0.5}{1.12 \times 10^{-4}} = 4.46 \times 10^3$$

158. $\frac{S_o}{N_o} \propto L^2$,

$$L = 2^n \left(\frac{S_o}{N_o}\right)_{dB}$$

$= 10 \log (C2^{2n})$

$= \log C + 20n \log 2$

$= \alpha + 6n\ dB$

This equation shows that increasing n by one bits increase the by 6 dB. Hence an increase in the SNR by 12 dB can be accomplished by increasing is from 10 to 12. If n is increased from 10 to 12, then transmission bandwidth would be increased by 20%.

159. $\frac{S_o}{N_o} = \frac{3L^2}{[\ln(\mu+1)]^2} = \frac{3(256)^2}{(\ln 256)^2} = 6394 = 38.06\,dB$

160. Nyquist rate = 2MHz

$\therefore$ 50% higher rat = 3 MHz

L = 256 = 2^8

$\therefore$ Transmission bandwidth = 3 MHz × 8 = 24 Mbits/sec.

Since new sampling rate is at 20% above the Nyquist rate, therefore

Sampling rate = 1.2 × 2

= 2.4 MHz bits per second

$= \frac{24\text{ Mbits/sec}}{2.4\text{ MHz}} = 10\text{ bits}$

Level= 2^{10} = 1024

$\therefore \frac{S_o}{N_o} = \frac{3(1024)^2}{(\ln 256)^2} = 102300 = 50.1\,dB$

161. Given: f_m = 5 kHz

Nyquist rate = 2 × 5 = 10 kHz

Since signal are sampled at twice the Nyquist rate

$\therefore$ Sampling rate = 2 × 10 = 20 kHz

Total transmission bandwidth = 4 × 20 = 80 kHz

162. High frequency component = 100 + 2 × 300 = 700 Hz

Nyquist sampling rate = 2 × 700 = 1400 s/sec

163. Given: Pulse rate = 56,000 per sec.

$V_{in} = 5\cos.(2\pi\, 1000\, t) + 2\cos(2\pi\, 2000\, t)$

Minimum step size is given by

$Sf_s \geq 2\pi f A$

$S \geq 2\pi \frac{f}{f_s} A$

$S \geq 2\pi \left[\frac{1000}{56000}\right] 5$

$\Rightarrow S \geq 2\pi \left[\frac{2000}{56000}\right] 2$

$\Rightarrow S \geq \frac{10\pi}{56} = 0.56\text{ V}$

$\Rightarrow S \geq \frac{8\pi}{56} = 0.45\text{ V}$

Hence, S should not be less than 0.56 V

164. Output sampled signal is given by

$$M_s(t) = \sum_k m(kT_s)\, p(t - kT_s)$$

where, $p(t)$ = rectangular pulse train.

Spectrum of $m_s(t)$ is given by

$$M_s(f) = P(f)\,[f_s\, M(f - kf_s)]$$

where, $f_s = \frac{1}{T_s} = 3B$

and $P(f) = \frac{1}{1/30\,B} - \int_{-1/60\,B}^{1/60\,B} dt$

$= 30\,BA \frac{e^{-j2\pi ft}}{-j2\pi f} \int_{-1/60B}^{-1/60B} Ae^{-j2\pi ft}.dt$

$= A \sin C\left(\frac{2\pi f}{60\,B}\right)$

165. Given: $x = \frac{1}{\sqrt{2\pi}} \int_x^{\infty} e^{-z^{2/z}}\, dz = 10^{-5}$ at $x = 4.27$

$erfc\, x = \frac{1}{\sqrt{\pi}} \int_x^{\infty} e^{-z^{2/2z}}\, dz = 2 \times 10^{-5}$ at $x = 3.02$

Binary NRZ bit rate = r bits/sec

Signal + noise $\frac{\eta}{2} = 10^{-6}$ volts²/Hz

Integrator and Dump

$P_e \leq 10^{-5}$

$Q(4.27) = 10^{-5}\, erfc(3.02) = 2 \times 10^{-5}$

$P_e = \frac{1}{2}\text{ erfc}\sqrt{\frac{E_B}{\eta}} = Q\left[\sqrt{\frac{2E_B}{\eta}}\right]$

$\frac{E_B}{\eta} = \frac{500 \times 10^{-3}}{r \times 2 \times 10^{-6}}$

$= \frac{A^2}{r\eta}\ \frac{0.125 \times 10^6}{r} \geq (3.02)^2$

$r_{max} = \frac{0.125 \times 10^6}{(3.02)^2} = 13.7\text{ kb/sec}$

166. Analog low pass signal BW = 4 kHz

Nyquist rate encode to binary PCM with 128 levels.

Word synchronization pulse is added at each code.

By sampling theorem,

$f_{s\,min}$ = 2 BW = 8 kHz

For 128 levels :

Number of bits anti $\log_2 128 = 7$

Total bits = 7 + 1 (work synch) = 8

Bit rate = 8 kHz × 8 = 64 kHz

167. B = 4kHz

Input-input = –3.8 to 3.8 ($-m_p$ to m_p)

Average power = 30 mW

$\frac{S}{N}$ = 20 dB

$\frac{S_0}{N_0} = 3\,(2^{2n})\left(\frac{m_z}{m_p{}^2}\right)$

$\Rightarrow 100 = 3 \times 2^{2n} \times \frac{(30 \times 10^{-3})^2}{(3.8)^2}$

$\Rightarrow 2n = \frac{100\,(3.8)^2}{3 \times (3 \times 10^{-2})^2} = 126.7$

$\Rightarrow n = 7$

168. f_s = 8 kHz

$2^n = 256$

$\Rightarrow n = 8$

$\therefore$ Bit rate = 8 × 8k = **64 kHz/sec.**

169. Given : code is 0001001

Even parity at positions 1, 3, 5, 7 fails, $C_1 = 1$

Even parity at positions 2, 3, 6, 7 fails, $C_2 = 1$

Even parity at positions 4, 5, 6, 7 passes; $C_4 = C$

$\therefore$ Error is at position 011 = 3

Hence correct code is 0011001

and corresponding BCD digit is 1001 = 9

170. Mean square quantizing error,

$$\sqrt{e^2(t)} = \frac{(\Delta V)^2}{12}$$

where, ΔV = step size

$$= \frac{A}{S} = \frac{6.4}{64} = 0.1$$

$$\therefore \quad \sqrt{e^2(t)} = \frac{\Delta V}{\sqrt{12}} = \frac{0.1}{\sqrt{12}} = \mathbf{0.03\ volts}$$

171. Constant, $K = \frac{A}{\Delta n}$

$$= \frac{\text{Maximum reference on scale}}{\text{Average input noise}}$$

$$= \frac{1.6}{50 \times 10^{-3}} = 32$$

$$\therefore \quad \frac{S_0/N_0}{S_i/N_i} = \frac{8}{K^2} \times 2^{\left(\frac{2B}{f_m}\right)} = \frac{8}{32^2} 2^{\left(\frac{64}{8}\right)}$$

$$= \frac{8}{1024} \times 2^8 = 2$$

172. $\frac{S_o}{N_o} \propto 2^{2n}$

If PCM is increased form n to $n + 1$, then ratio will increase by a factor 4, which is independent of n.

173. Bit rate $= nf_s = 6 \times 8000 = 48$ kHz

N. Q. BW $= \frac{1}{2}$ bit rate = 24 kHz

$$\frac{S}{N} = 2Q^2 = 2(2^n)^2 = 2 \times 2^{2n}$$

$$B = \frac{nf_s}{2}$$

$$\therefore \quad \frac{S}{N} = 2 \times 2^{4B/f_s} = 39 \text{ dB}$$

174. 50dB $= 10^5$

$$\frac{S_0}{N_0} = 10^5 = \frac{3L^2}{[\ln(1+\mu)]^2}$$

$$= \frac{3L^2}{(\ln 256)^2} = \frac{3L^2}{30.75}$$

$$\therefore \quad L = \sqrt{\frac{105 \times 30.75}{3}} = 1012$$

175. $E_b = V^2 T_b$

$= 5^2 (72 \times 10^{-6})$

$= 1.8 \times 10^{-3}$

$$\frac{N_0}{2} = 1.0 \times 10^{-4}$$

$$\Rightarrow \quad N_0 = 2 \times 10^{-4}$$

$$\frac{P_e}{2} = \frac{1}{2} \frac{\text{erfc}}{\sqrt{\left(\frac{E_b}{N_0}\right)}}$$

$$= \frac{1}{2} \text{erfc} \sqrt{\left(\frac{1.8 \times 10^{-3}}{2 \times 10^{-4}}\right)}$$

$$= \frac{1}{2} \text{erfc}(3)$$

$$= \frac{2.3 \times 10^{-5}}{2}$$

$$= 1.15 \times 10^{-5}$$

176. Here, $\frac{P_{so}}{P_{qn}} = 25$ dB, $f_c = 3.4$ kHz

Now $P_{so} = 0.04 \left(\frac{f_b}{f_c}\right)^3$

$$\therefore \quad 25 = 10 \log \left[0.04 \left(\frac{f_b}{f_c}\right)^3\right]$$

$$\Rightarrow 0.04 \left(\frac{f_b}{f_c}\right)^3 = \text{antilog}(2.5) = 316.2$$

$$\Rightarrow \quad \frac{f_b}{f_c} = 20$$

$$\therefore \quad f_b = 68 \text{ kb/sec}$$

177. Peak carrier amplitude,

$$A = \frac{V_{pp}}{2} = \frac{2}{2} = 1 \text{ volt}$$

Bit period, $T = \frac{1}{f_b} = \frac{1}{\text{system data rate}} = \frac{1}{110}$

Average bit energy,

$$E_b = \frac{A^2 T}{2}$$

$$= \frac{1 \times (1/110)}{2}$$

$$= 4.55 \times 10^{-3} \text{ joule}$$

Noise spectral density $= \frac{N_0}{2} = 1 \times 10^{-4}$

$\therefore$ $N_0 = 2 \times 10^{-4}$ volts²/Hz

$\therefore$ Bit error rate = Probability of error

$$\Rightarrow \quad P_e = \frac{1}{2} e^{E_b/N_0} = \frac{1}{2} \left(e^{\frac{4.55 \times 10^{-3}}{2 \times 2 \times 10^{-4}}}\right)$$

$$= \frac{1}{2} e^{-11.38} = 5.7 \times 10^{-6}$$

178. Bit duration $= \frac{1}{2.5 \times 10^{-6}} = 0.4$ μs

Signal energy 1 bit $= \frac{1}{2} A_c^2 T_b$

$$= \frac{1}{2} (10^{-6})^2 \, 0.4 \times 10^{-6} = 2 \times 10^{-19} \text{J}$$

Now $P_e = \frac{1}{2} \text{erfc} \left(\sqrt{\frac{E_b}{2N_0}}\right)$

$$= \frac{1}{2} \text{erfc}\left(\sqrt{5}\right) = 0.85 \times 10^{-3}$$

179. $\frac{S_T}{L} = S_R = E_b r_b = \eta V_b r_b$

$$r_b = \frac{S_T}{\eta L V_b} = \frac{2 \times 10^5}{V_b}$$

Also, $\frac{1}{2}\, e^{-V_b/2} \le 10^{-4}$

$\Rightarrow \quad V_b \ge 2 \log \frac{1}{2 \times 10^{-4}} = 17$

$\therefore \quad$ Bit rate $\le \frac{2 \times 10^5}{17} = 11.8$ kbps

180. In order to avoid aliasing,

$$\frac{2\pi}{T} > 2\omega_m$$

where ω_m = maximum frequency in x(t)

T = period of $c(t)$

Here, $T = 10^{-3}$, $\omega_m < 1000\,\pi$

$X(j\omega) = 0$ for $\omega > 1000\,\pi$

181. Fourier transform of $Y(j\omega)$ of the signal $y(t) = x(t)\,c(t)$ consists of shifted replica of $X(j\omega)$. The replica of $X(j\omega)$ centered around $\omega = 0$ is scaled by $\frac{\Delta}{T}$, where Δ is width of each pulse c(t).

LPF needs to have a pass band gain of

$$\frac{T}{\Delta} = \frac{10^{-3}}{0.25 \times 10^{-4}} = 4$$

182. T should be chosen such that

$$\frac{2\pi}{T} > 2\omega_m$$

In this case $\omega_m = 2000\,\pi$

$\therefore \quad T \le 0.5$ ms

There will be 10 different pulse within a duration of T. Therefore each pulse can be at most 0.5×10^{-4} sec wide.

183. If m_p is peak sample amplitude, then

$$\text{error} \le \frac{(0.2)m_p}{100} = \frac{m_p}{500}$$

If L level are used, then each sample is separated by

$$\delta = \frac{2m_p}{L}$$

Maximum quantization error

$$= \frac{\delta}{2} = \frac{2m_p}{2L} = \frac{m_p}{L} = \frac{m_p}{500}$$

$\therefore \quad L = 500.$

We choose $\quad L = 512 = 2^9$

This require 9 bits binary code per sample.

Nyquist rate = 2 *k*Hz × 2 = 4 *k*Hz

Actual sampling rate = 4 *k*Hz × 1.20 = 4.8 *k*Hz.

Thus each signal has 4800 samples/sec, and each sample is coded by 9 bits.

Hence each signal uses

9 × 4800 = 43.2 *k*bits/sec.

The signal are multiplex. Hence we need 432 × 10 432 *k*bits/sec.

Framing and synchronization bits

$$= \frac{432k \times 1}{100}$$

= 4320 additional bits

Total = 432 *k* + 4320

= 436.32 *k* bits/sec.

184. Since each Hz has two bits

$\therefore$ Minimum transmission width

$$= \frac{436.32k}{2} \text{ bits/sec} = 218.16\ k\text{Hz}$$

185. Here, $\theta(t) = \omega_c t + \phi(t)$

$\phi(t) = 5 \sin(2\pi - 10^3 t)$

$|\phi'(t)|_{max} = 5 \times 2\pi \times 10^3$

$|\Delta\omega|_{max} = 5$ kHz

PRACTICE QUESTIONS

1. A 8 kHz communication channel has an SNR of 30 dB. If channel bandwidth is doubled, keeping signal power constant, then SNR for the modified channel will be

(*a*) 27 dB (*b*) 30 dB (*c*) 33 db (*d*) 60 dB

2. The information capacity (bits/sec) of a channel with bandwidth W and transmission time T is given by

(*a*) $C \propto WT$ (*b*) $C = \frac{W}{T}$ (*c*) $C = \frac{T}{W}$ (*d*) $C = \frac{W^2}{T}$

3. For distortionless transmission through a channel, the channel should be such that

(*a*) its attenuation response is an even function and phase response is an odd function of frequency

(*b*) its attenuation response is flat and phase response is linear with frequency

(*c*) ratio of line inductance to line capacitance is constant

(*d*) its termination is by a matched impedance

4. The channel capacity under the Gaussian noise environment for a discrete memory less channel with a bandwidth of 4 MHz and SNR of 31 is

(*a*) 20 Mbps (*b*) 4 Mbps (*c*) 8 kbps (*d*) 4 kbps

5. An image uses 512 × 512 picture elements. Each of the picture elements can take any of the s distinguishable intensity levels. The maximum entropy in the above image will be

(*a*) 2097152 bits (*b*) 786432 bits

(*c*) 648 bits (*d*) 144 bits

6. An AWGN channel with 4 kHz BW and noise power spectral density $\eta/2 = 10^{-12}$ W/Hz. If signal power required at receiver is 0.1 mW, then capacity of the channel will be

(*a*) 54.44 kb/sec (*b*) 8 kb/sec

(*c*) 64.44 kb/sec (*d*) 34.32 kb/sec

7. In a noisy binary channel with bit error probability $p_e = 5 \times 10^{-5}$, assume 10000 bits are being transmitted over such a channel. The probability that there will be 2 or less number of bits in error is

(*a*) 10^{-4} (*b*) ~ 0.5 (*c*) ~1 (*d*) 10^4

8. An FM signal with a deviation δ is passed through a mixer and has its frequency reduced fivefold. The deviation in the output of the mixer is

(*a*) 5δ (*b*) intermediate

(*c*) $\frac{\delta}{5}$ (*d*) δ

9. As modulation index of an FM signal with sinusoidal modulation is increased from zero to three, then power in the carrier component will

(*a*) increase continuously

(*b*) decrease continuously

(*c*) first increase, attain a maximum and then decrease

(*d*) first decrease, become zero and then increase

10. The phase shift method for generation of SSB signal is most suitable for

(*a*) data signals

(*b*) weak modulating signals

(*c*) larger bandwidth modulating signals

(*d*) smaller bandwidth modulating singnals

11. A superheterodyne FM receiver operates in the frequence range of 88-108 MHz. The IF and local oscillator frequency are chosen such that $f_{IF} < f_{LO}$. The image frequency must fall outside of the 88-108 MHz region. The range of variation in f_{LO} is

(*a*) [98, 128] (*b*) [78, 128] MHz

(*c*) [98, 118] MHz (*d*) [78, 98] MHz

12. A super heterodyne receiver is to operate in the frequency range of 550 kHz – 1650 kHz, with the intermediate frequency of 450 kHz. The receiver is tuned to 700 kHz. The capacitance ratio $R = C_{max.}/C_{min.}$ of the local oscillator would be

(*a*) 4.41 (*b*) 2.1 (*c*) 3 (*d*) 9

13. A base band signal m(t) modulates a carrier to produce the angle modulated signal,

$$A_c \cos(2\pi \times 10^8 t + k_p m(t))$$

where m(t) is shown in the figure below.

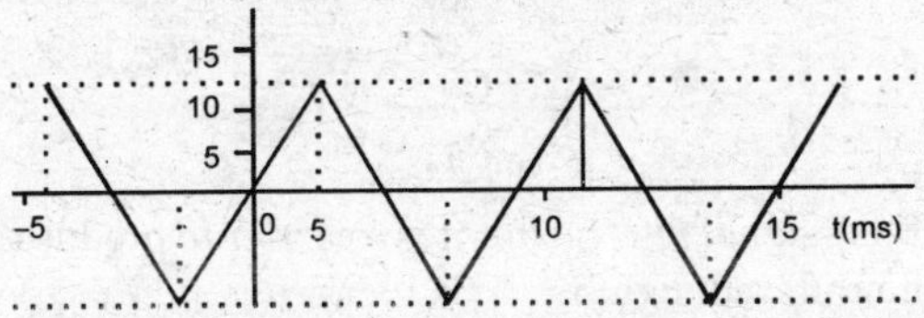

What is the value of k_p so that peak to peak frequency deviation of the carrier is 100 kHz?

(*a*) $\Delta f = k_p m'p$ (*b*) $\dfrac{k_p m' p}{4\pi}$

(*c*) $\Delta f = \dfrac{1}{2\pi} k_p m'p$ (*d*) $\dfrac{k_p m' p}{\pi}$

14. If an amplitude modulated signal occupies a frequency range from 395 kHz to 405 kHz, then it can be demodulated by

(*a*) using an enveloped detector and filter

(*b*) multiplying with a 395 kHz local signal

(*c*) multiplying with a 405 kHz local signal

(*d*) low pass filtering with cut off at 400 kHz

15. If a carrier signal at frequency 100 MHz is frequency modulated with modulation index 2 by a signal at 2 kHz, then sidebands produced at frequencies

(*a*) 102 MHz and 98 MHz

(*b*) 100 MHz + 2 kHz and 100 MHz – 2 kHz

(*c*) 100 MHz $\pm \Delta f_d$,
where, f_d is frequency deviation

(*d*) 100 MHz $\pm n2$ kHz,
where, n is 1, 2,...., 5 integer

16. If in a modulator, the amplitude spectrum consists of a component at f_c, the carrier frequency and one component each at $f_c - f_s$ and $f_c + f_s$, where f_s is modulating signal frequency, then modulator used is

(*a*) AM

(*b*) AM and/or Narrow band FM with depth ≤ 0.5

(*c*) FM

(*d*) PAM

17. A comparison of frequency division and time division multiplexing systems shows that

(*a*) FDM requires a lower bandwidth, but TDM has greater noise immunity

(*b*) FDM has greater noise immunity and requires lower bandwidth than TDM

(*c*) FDM requires channel synchronisation, while TDM has greater noise immunity

(*d*) FDM requires more multiplexing while TDM requires band pass filter.

18. The use of non–uniform quantisation leads to

(*a*) reduction in transmission bandwidth

(*b*) increase in maximum SNR

(*c*) increase in SNR for low level signals

(*d*) simplification of quantisation process

19. The spectral range of a band pass signal extends from 10 MHz to 10.4 MHz. What is the minimum sampling frequency required for reconstruction ?

(*a*) 20 MHz (*b*) 20.8 MHz

(*c*) 20.4 MHz (*d*) 0.8 MHz

20. The constellation diagram of a modem has four states as shown in the figure given below. What is the bit rate of this modem?

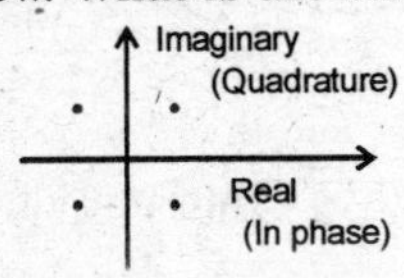

(*a*) Two times its band rate

(*b*) Four times its band rate

(*c*) Same as band rate

(*d*) Sufficient information is not given to give the answer

21. The constellation diagram of a modem is shown in the figure given below. What does the modem use?

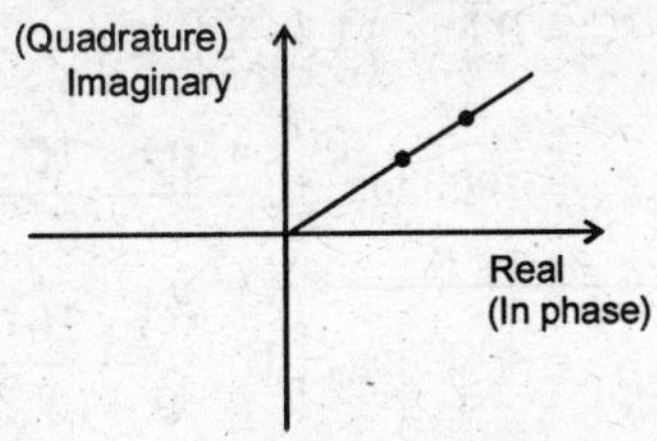

(*a*) QAM (*b*) PSK

(*c*) Both QAM and PSK (*d*) ASK

22. Quantization process used in analog to digital conversion process is a

(*a*) one-to-many mapping which causes loss of information

(*b*) many-to-one mapping. It causes a loss of information at the transmitter which can be recovered at the receiver

(*c*) one-to-one mapping

(*d*) many-to-one mapping. The loss of information at the transmitter cannot be recovered at the receiver

23. Equalisation is

(*a*) required in telephone lines but not in wireless communication

(*b*) required both in telephone lines and wireless communication

(*c*) required in wireless communication whereas this is not required in telephone lines.

(*d*) not required in wireless communication since phase equalisation is required only when lines are used

24. If in a BPSK signal detector, local oscillator has a fixed phase error of 20°, then this phase error deteriorate the SNR at the output at the rate

(*a*) $\cos^2 20°$ (*b*) $\cos 20°$ (*c*) $\cos 40°$ (*d*) $\cos 70°$

25. Minimum Shift Keying (MSK) also called FSK with frequency spacing $2 f_d$ between state frequencies r_b is the data rate, then

(*a*) $f_d = \frac{r_b}{4}$ (*b*) $f_d = \frac{r_b}{2}$

(*c*) $f_d = \frac{3r_b}{4}$ (*d*) $f_d = r_b$

ANSWERS

1. (*a*)	**2.** (*d*)	**3.** (*b*)	**4.** (*a*)	**5.** (*b*)	**6.** (*a*)	**7.** (*b*)	**8.** (*d*)	**9.** (*b*)	**10.** (*d*)
11. (*c*)	**12.** (*a*)	**13.** (*c*)	**14.** (*d*)	**15.** (*d*)	**16.** (*b*)	**17.** (*c*)	**18.** (*c*)	**19.** (*d*)	**20.** (*a*)
21. (*a*)	**22.** (*d*)	**23.** (*a*)	**24.** (*b*)	**25.** (*a*)					

EXPLANATIONS

1. *Given :* df = 8000 Hz, SNR = 30 d B

$\therefore$ SNR for modified channel = $\text{antilog}_{10} \frac{30}{10}$

$= \mathbf{27\ dB}$

4. Capacity, $C = B \log_2\left(1+\frac{S}{N}\right)$

$= (4\ \text{MHz}) \cdot \log_2 32$

$= \mathbf{20\ Mbps}$

5. Picture elements (pixel) = 512 × 512 = 262144

Information per picture element

$N = \log_2 M$

$\Rightarrow$ $M = 2^N$

$\therefore$ $8 = 2^N$

$\Rightarrow$ $N = 3$

Information for 262144 pixels

$= 262144 \times 3$

$= 786432$ bits

Entropy is same as average information per message.

6. $C = B \log_2\left(1+\frac{S}{N}\right)$

$= 4000 \log_2\left(1+\frac{0.1\times 10^{-3}}{\eta B}\right)$

$= 4000 \log_2\left(1+\frac{0.1\times 10^{-3}}{8\times 10^{-9}}\right)$

$= \mathbf{54.44\ kb/sec}$

11. Since $88\ \text{MHz} < f_c < 108\ \text{MHz}$

and $|f_c - f_c'| = 2f_{IF}$ if $f_{IF} < f_{LO}$

hence in order for the image frequency f_c' to fall outside the interval [88, 108] MHz, the minimum frequency f_{IF} is such that

$2 f_{IF} = 108 - 88$

$\Rightarrow$ $f_{IF} = 10$ MHz

If $f_{IF} = 10$ MHz, then

range of f_{LO} = [88+10, 108 + 101]

= [98, 118] MHz

12. $f_{max.} = 1650 + 450 = 2100\,k\text{Hz}$

$f_{min.} = 550 + 450 = 1000\,k\text{Hz}$

$$f = \frac{1}{2\pi\sqrt{LC}}$$

Thus when frequency is minimum, capacitance will be maximum

$\therefore$ $R = \frac{C_{max.}}{C_{min.}} = \frac{f^2_{max.}}{f^2_{min.}} = (2.1)^2$

$\Rightarrow$ $R = 4.41$

13. Base signal $m(t)$ modulates a carrier to produce angle modulated signal

$A_c \cos [2\pi + 10^8 t + k_p m(t)]$

Given : Peak-peak frequency duration of the carrier is 100Hz.

$f_i = f_c + \frac{k_p}{2\pi} m(t)$

$f_i(\min) = 10^8 - 100\text{Hz}$ .... as $f_c = 10^8$

$f_i(\max) = 10^8 + 100$ Hz

$\phi_{pm}(t) = A \cos [\omega_c t + k_p m(t)]$

$= A \cos [\omega_c t + \frac{\pi}{2} m(t)]$

When $m(t) = -1$,

$\phi_{pm}(t) = A \sin \omega_c t$

When $m(t) = 1$,

$\phi_{pm}(t) = -A \sin \omega_c t$

$\Delta f = \frac{1}{2\pi} k_p m'p$

■■

ELECTRICAL AND ELECTRONICS MEASUREMENTS 8

8.1. ERRORS ANALYSIS

Error is defined as the deviation of the true value from the desired value. It is expressed either as absolute or as a percentage of error.

Absolute error is defined as the difference between the true value of the variable and the measured value of the variable, or

$$\varepsilon_0 = Y_n - X_n$$

where ε_0 = absolute error, Y_n = true value, and X_n = measured value

Hence
$$\% \text{ Error} = \frac{\text{Absolute value}}{\text{True value}} \times 100$$

$$= \frac{\varepsilon_o}{Y_n} \times 100$$

$$\% \text{ Error} = \left(\frac{Y_n - X_n}{Y_n}\right) \times 100$$

8.1.1. Accuracy and Precision

Accuracy. It is the closeness with which an instrument reading approaches the true value of the quantity being measured. It is specified in terms of limits of errors and is expressed as either percentage of scale or range of percentage of true value.

Precision. It is a measure of the reproducibility of the measurements, i.e. for a fixed value of a quantity, precision is a measure of the degree of agreement within a group of measurements. An indication of the precision of the measurement is obtained from the number of significant figures in which it is expressed. The more the significant figures, the greater the precision of measurement.

8.1.2. Types of Errors

Static Error. It is the numerical difference between the true value of a quantity and its value as obtained by measurement. These are sub-divided into

1. Gross Errors
2. Systematic Errors
3. Random Errors

1. **Gross Errors.** These errors are due to human mistakes in reading or in using instruments or errors in recording observations.

2. **Systematic Errors.** These errors occur due to shortcomings of the instrument such as defective or worn parts or ageing or effects of the environment on the instrument.

   (*i*) *Instrumental Errors.* These are inherent in measuring instruments, because of their mechanical structure. These can be avoided by selecting a suitable instrument for the particular measurement application or by applying correction factors after determining the amount of instrumental error of calibrating the instrument against a standard.

   (*ii*) *Environment Errors.* These are due to conditions external to the measuring device including conditions in the area surrounding the instrument such as effects of changes in temperature, humidity, barometric pressure or effect of magnetic or electrostatic fields.

   (*iii*) *Observational Errors.* These are errors introduced by the observer. The most common is the parallax error introduced in reading a meter scale and the error of estimation.

3. **Random Errors.** These are due to unknown causes and are normally small and follow the law of probability. These are treated mathematically.

8.1.3 Sources of Errors

(*i*) Insufficient knowledge of process parameters and design conditions.

(*ii*) Poor maintenance.

(*iii*) Change in process parameters irregularities, upsets etc.

(*iv*) Poor design.

(*v*) Design limitations

(*vi*) Due to person operating the instrument.

When two or more quantities, each of which is subjected to error, are combined, following rules will σ.

(1) Sum of two or more quantities

Suppose the final result Y is sum of measured quantities u, v and z, each of which is subjected to possible systematic error $\pm \delta u, \pm \delta v, \pm \delta z$

Nominal result is $y = u + v + z$

$$\frac{dy}{y} = \frac{d(u+v+z)}{y} = \frac{du}{y} + \frac{dv}{y} + \frac{dz}{y}$$

Expressing in terms of relative increments

$$\frac{dy}{y} = \frac{u}{y}\frac{du}{u} + \frac{v}{y}\frac{dv}{v} + \frac{z}{y}\frac{dz}{z}$$

or $$\frac{\delta y}{y} = \pm\left(\frac{u}{y}.\frac{\delta u}{u} + \frac{v}{y}.\frac{\delta v}{v} + \frac{z}{y}.\frac{\delta z}{z}\right)$$

Hence the resultant systematic error is equal to the sum of the products formed by multiplying the individual systematic errors by the ratio of each terms to the function.

(2) Difference of two quantities

Let $$y = u - v$$

$$\frac{dy}{y} = \frac{du}{y} - \frac{dv}{y}$$

$$\frac{dy}{y} = \frac{u}{y}.\frac{du}{u} - \frac{v}{y}.\frac{dv}{v}$$

Relative limiting error δy in y is

$$\frac{\delta y}{y} = \pm\left(\frac{u}{y}.\frac{\delta u}{u} + \frac{v}{y}.\frac{\delta v}{v}\right)$$

(3) Product of two or more quantities

Let $$y = u\,v\,z$$

Taking logarithm of both the sides, we get

$$\log_e y = \log_e u + \log_e v + \log_e z$$

Differentiating with respect to y, we get

$$\frac{1}{y} = \frac{1}{y}.\frac{du}{dy} + \frac{1}{v}.\frac{dv}{dy} + \frac{1}{z}.\frac{dz}{dy}$$

or $$\frac{dy}{y} = \frac{du}{u} + \frac{dv}{v} + \frac{dz}{z}$$

$\therefore$ Relative limiting error is, $\dfrac{\delta y}{y} = \pm\left(\dfrac{\delta u}{u} + \dfrac{\delta v}{v} + \dfrac{\delta z}{z}\right)$

Relative limiting error of the product of the terms is equal to the sum of the relative errors of the terms.

(4) Quotient of two quantities

Let $$y = \frac{u}{v}$$

Taking logarithm of both the sides,

$$\log_e y = \log_e u - \log_e v$$

Differentiating with respect to y, we get

$$\frac{1}{y} = \frac{1}{u}\frac{du}{dy} - \frac{1}{v}\frac{dv}{dy}$$

or $$\frac{dy}{y} = \frac{du}{u} - \frac{dv}{v}$$

$\therefore$ Relative limiting error, $$\frac{\delta y}{y} = \pm\frac{\delta u}{u} \mp \frac{\delta v}{v}$$

The maximum possible error occurs when $\dfrac{\delta u}{u}$ is positive and $\dfrac{\delta v}{v}$ is negative or vice versa.

$$\frac{\delta y}{y} = \pm\left(\frac{\delta u}{u} + \frac{\delta v}{v}\right)$$

(5) Power of a Factor

Let $y = u^n$

where n may be positive or negative, integral or fractional

Taking logarithm of both side, we get

$$\log_e y = n \log_e u$$

Differentiating with respect to y, we get

$$\frac{1}{y} = n\frac{1}{u}\frac{du}{dy}$$

or $$\frac{dy}{y} = n\frac{du}{u}$$

$\therefore$ Relative limiting error is, $\dfrac{\delta y}{y} = \pm\, n\dfrac{\delta u}{u}$

(6) Composite Factors

Let $y = u^n u^m$

Taking logarithm of both the side, we get

$$\log_e y = n \log_e u + m \log_e v$$

Differentiating with respect to y, we get

$$\frac{1}{y} = \frac{n}{u}\frac{du}{dy} + \frac{m}{v}\frac{du}{dy}$$

or $$\frac{dy}{y} = n\frac{du}{u} + m\frac{dv}{v}$$

$\therefore$ Relative limiting error of y is,

$$\frac{\delta y}{y} = \pm\left(n\frac{\delta u}{u} + m\frac{\delta v}{v}\right)$$

8.1.4. Statistical Analysis

(1) Arithmetic Mean

$$\overline{X} = \frac{X_1 + X_2 + X_3 + \dots + X_n}{n} = \frac{\Sigma X}{n}$$

where $\overline{X}$ = Arithmetic mean, $X_1, X_2, X_3 \dots X_n$ are the readings taken

and n = number of readings taken.

(2) Deviation from means

Deviation of $X_1 = d_1 = X_1 - \overline{X}$

Deviation of $X_2 = d_2 = X_2 - \overline{X}$

(3) Average deviation

$$D = \frac{|d_1| + |d_2| + |d_3| + \dots + |d_n|}{n} = \frac{\Sigma|d|}{n}$$

(4) Standard deviation

$$\sigma = \frac{\sqrt{d_1^2 + d_2^2 + d_3^3 + \dots + d_n^2}}{n} = \frac{\sqrt{\Sigma d^2}}{n}$$

(5) Variance

Variance = Mean square deviation = σ^2

(6) Probable error of one reading

$$r_1 = 0.6745 \frac{\sqrt{\Sigma|d|^2}}{n-1}$$

(7) Probable error of mean

$$r_m = \frac{r_1}{\sqrt{n-1}}$$

8.2. ELECTRICAL. MEASURING INSTRUMENTS

These are broadly divided into two classes:

(1) Absolute instruments are those which give the value of the quantity to be measured in terms of the constants of the instrument and their deflection only. No previous calibration or comparison is necessary in their case. The example of such an instrument is tangent galvanometer which gives the value of current in terms of the tangent of defection produced by the current, the radius and number of turns of wire used and the horizontal component of earth's field.

(2) Secondary instruments are those in which the value of electrical quantity to be measured can be determined from the deflection of the instruments only when they have been pre-calibrated by comparison with an absolute instrument.

Another way to classify secondary instruments is divided them into

(*i*) indicating instruments

(*ii*) recording instruments, and

(*iii*) integrating instruments.

(*i*) Indicating Instruments.

These instruments indicate the instantaneous value of the electrical quantity being measured at the time at which it is being measured. Their indications are given by pointers moving over calibrated dials. Ordinary ammeters, voltmeters and wattmeters belong to this class.

(*ii*) Recording Instruments.

These instruments give a continuous record of the variations of a quantity over a selected period of time. The moving system of the instrument carries an inked pen which rests lightly on a chart or graph that is moved at a uniform and low speed, in a direction perpendicular to that of the deflection of the pen. The path traced out by the pen presents a continuous record of the variations in the deflection of the instrument.

***(iii)* Integrating Instruments.**

These instruments measure and register by a set of dials and pointers, either the total quantity of electricity (in amp-hours) or the total amount of electrical energy (in watt-hours or kWh) supplied to a circuit in a given time. This summation gives the product of time and the electrical quantity but gives no direct indication as to the rate at which the quantity or energy is being supplied because their registrations are independent of this rate provided the current flowing through the instrument is sufficient to operate it. Ampere-hour and watt-hours meters fall in this class.

Electrical Principles of Operation

All electrical measuring instruments depend for their action on one of the many physical effects of an electric current or potential and are generally classified according to which of these effects is utilized in their operation. The effects generally utilized are

1. Magnetic effect - for ammeters and voltmeters usually.
2. Electrodynamic effect - for ammeters, voltmeters and wattmeters.
3. Electromagnetic effect - for ammeters, voltmeters, wattmeters and watt hour meters.
4. Thermal effect - for ammeters and voltmeters.
5. Chemical effect - for d.c. ampere-hour meters.
6. Electrostatic effect - for voltmeters only

8.3. INDICATING INSTRUMENTS

All such instruments essentially consist of a pointer moving over a calibrated scale and attached to the moving system pivoted in jewel bearings. In order to ensure the proper operation of indicating instruments, the following three torques are needed.'

(i) Deflecting torque

(ii) Controlling torque

(iii) Damping torque

***(i)* Deflecting Torque (T_d).**

One important requirement in a indicating instruments is the arrangement for producing deflecting or operating torque when the instrument is connected in the electrical circuit to measure the given electrical quantity. The deflecting torque causes the moving system (and hence, the pointer attached to it) to move from zero position when the instrument is connected in the circuit to measure the given electrical quantity.

***(ii)* Controlling Torque (T_c).**

Under the action of deflecting torque, the pointer will continue to move indefinitely and shall be independent of the value of electrical quantity to be measured. This necessitates that the controlling torque must be provided. This controlling torque should oppose the deflecting torque and should increase with the deflection of the moving system so that the pointer is brought to rest at a position when the two opposing torques are equal.

The controlling torque performs the following two functions.

(a) It oppose the deflecting torque and increases with the deflection of the moving system. It thus, limits the movement of the pointer so that the magnitude of deflection is always the same for the given value of electrical quantity to be measured.

(b) If brings the pointer back to zero position when the deflecting torque is removed. If it were not provided, the pointer once deflected would not return to zero position on removing the deflecting torque.

The controlling or restoring or balancing torque is provided either by a spring or by gravity. A hair spring usually of phosphor-bronze is attached to the moving system of the instrument. With the movement of pointer, the spring is twisted in opposite direction. This twist in spring produces restoring torque. Gravity control is obtained by attaching a small adjustable weight to the moving system. Such that the two exert torques in opposite directions.

***(iii)* Damping Torque.**

If the moving system is acted upon by deflecting and controlling torque alone, then the pointer due to its inertia will oscillate about final position before coming to rest. These oscillations are undesirable and must be prevented. In order to avoid these oscillations of the pointer and to bring it quickly to its deflected position, damping torque is provided which opposes the movement (backward or forward) of the pointer and operates only when the system is moving.

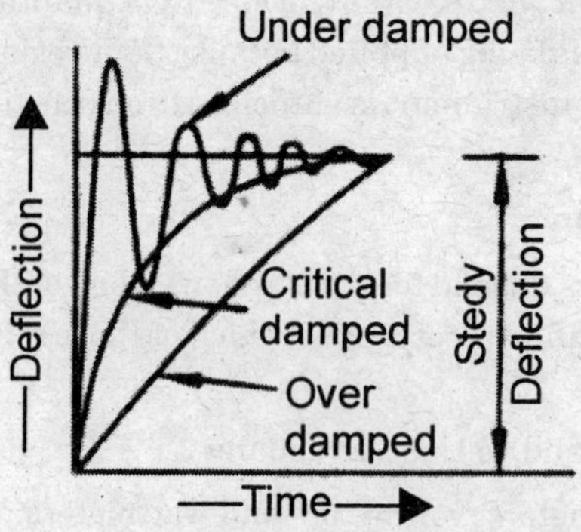

Fig. 6.1

It is worthwhile to mention here that damping torque acts only when the pointer is in motion.

The degree of damping decides the behaviour of the moving system. If the instrument is under damped, the pointer will oscillate about the final position and take some time to come to rest. On the other hand, if the instrument is overdamped, the pointer will become slow and lithargic. However, if the degree of damping is adjusted to such a value that the pointer moves and quickly comes to its final position, the instrument is said to be dead beat. Fig. 8.1 shows the graph for under damping, over damping and critical damping (dead beat).

Damping force can be produced by *air friction, eddy currents and fluid friction.*

In air-friction damping an aluminium piston attached to the moving system is arranged to travel in a fixed air chamber closed at one end. The necessary damping effect is produced by movement of piston in the chamber. Fluid friction is similar in action to the air friction. Damping is produced by movement of piston in oil.

The most efficient type of damping is obtained by eddy-current damping. A non-magnetic metallic disc, attached to the moving system, cuts the magnetic flux. Hence, eddy currents are produced in the disc which produce a damping force in such a direction to oppose the cause producing them, i.e. the motion of moving system.

Indicating instruments are of the following types:

(*i*) Moving iron instruments

(*ii*) Moving coil instruments

(*iii*) Dynamometer type instruments

(*iv*) Hot wire instruments

(*v*) Electrostatic instruments

(*vi*) Induction type instrument

8.3.1. Moving Iron Instruments.

Moving iron instruments are of two types :

1. Attraction type
2. Repulsion type

1. Attraction Type Moving Iron Instruments

Principle. These instruments are based on the principle that when an unmagnetised soft iron piece is placed in the magnetic field of a coil, then the piece is attracted towards the coil. The moving system of the instrument is attached to the soft iron piece and the operating current is passed through a coil placed near it. The operating current sets up magnetic field which attracts the iron piece and thus moves the pointer over the scale.

Construction. It consists of a hollow cylindrical coil or solenoid which is kept fixed as shown in the Fig. 8.2. An oval shaped soft iron pieces is attached to the spindle in such a way that it can move in or out of the coil. The pointer is attached to the spindle so that it is deflected with the motion of the soft iron piece. The controlling torque on the moving system is provided by spring control method while damping is provided by air friction.

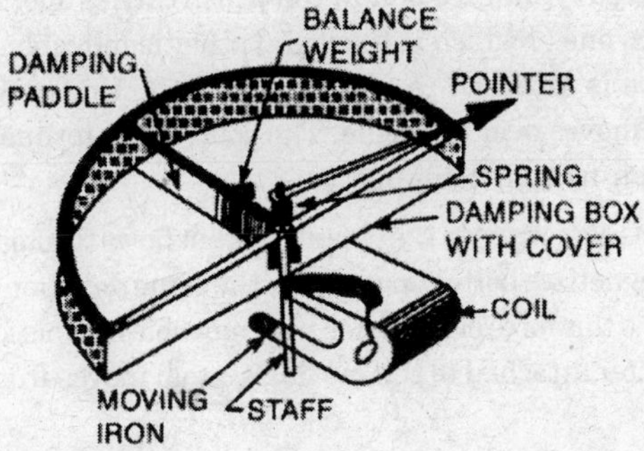

(a)

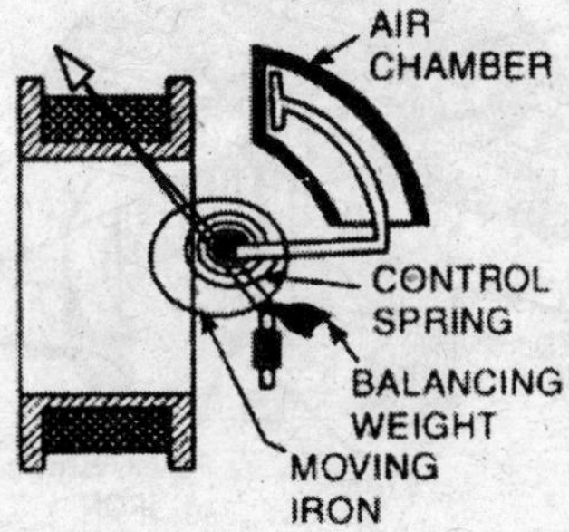

(b)

Fig. 8.2.Attraction type Moving Iron Instruments

Working. When the instrument is connected in the circuit, the operating current flows through the coil. The current sets up magnetic field in the coil. In other words, the coil behaves like a magnet and, therefore, it attracts the soft iron piece towards it. The result is that the pointer attached to the moving system moves from zero position.

If current in the coil is reversed, the direction of magnetic field also reverses and so does the magnetism produced in soft iron piece. Therefore, the direction of deflecting torque remains unchanged. It follows, therefore, that such instruments can be used for both D.C. as well as A.C. work.

Deflecting torque. The force F pulling the soft iron piece towards the coil depends upon:

(*i*) Field strength H produced by the coil.

(*ii*) Pole strength m developed by the piece

$$F \propto mH$$

$$F \propto H^2 \qquad ...(\because m \propto H)$$

$$\therefore \quad \text{Deflecting torque, } T_d \propto F \propto H^2$$

If permeability of iron is assumed constant, then

$$H \propto I$$

$$\therefore \quad T_d \propto I^2$$

If the controlling torque is provided by the springs,

$$T_c \propto \theta \text{ (deflection)}$$

In the steady position of deflection,

$$T_d = T_c$$

$$\theta \propto I^2 \qquad ...(\text{for d.c.})$$

$$\propto I_{rms} \qquad ...(\text{for a.c.})$$

Since deflection $\theta \propto I^2$, therefore, scale of such instruments is non-uniform, being crowded in the beginning. In order to make the scale of such instruments uniform, suitably shaped (tongue shaped) iron piece is used.

2. Repulsion type Moving Iron Instruments

Principle. These instruments are based on the principle of repulsion between the two iron pieces similarly magnetized.

Construction. It consists of a fixed cylindrical hollow coil which carries operating current (Fig. 8.3.) Inside the coil, there are two soft iron pieces or vanes, one of which is fixed and other is movable. The fixed iron piece is attached to the coil whereas the movable iron piece is attached to the pointer shaft. Under the action of deflecting torque, the pointer attached to the moving system moves over the scale. The controlling torque is produced by spring control method and damping torque is provided by air friction damping.

Working. When the instrument is connected in the circuit, current flows through the coil. This current sets up magnetic field in the coil. The magnetic field magnetizes both iron pieces in the same direction i.e. both pieces become similar magnets and hence they repel each other. Due to this force of repulsion only movable iron piece moves as the other piece is fixed and cannot move. The result is that the pointer attached to the moving system moves from zero position.

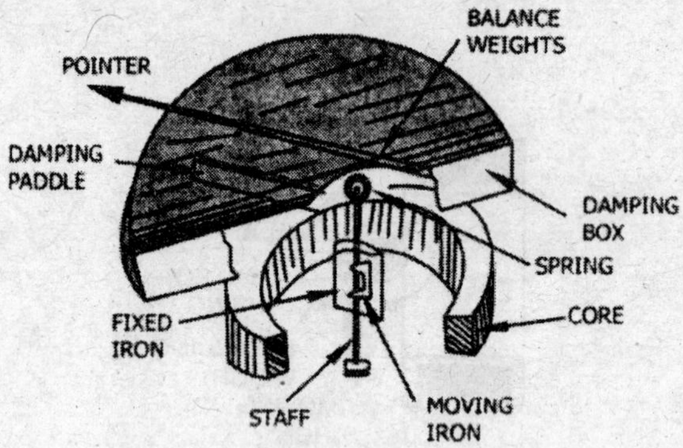

(a)

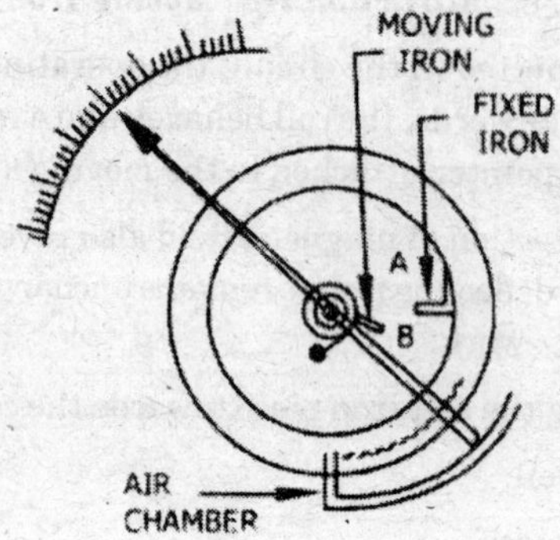

(b)

Fig. 8.3. Repulsion type Moving Iron Instruments

Deflecting Torque. The deflecting torque results due to the repulsion between the similarly magnetized iron pieces. If two pieces develop pole strengths m_1 and m_2 respectively, then,

Instantaneous deflecting torque $\propto$ repulsive force

$$\propto m_1 m_2$$

Since pole strengths developed are proportional to H, therefore

Instantaneous deflecting torque,

$$T_d \propto H^2$$

Assuming constant permeability,

$$H \propto \text{current } i \text{ through the coil}$$

$\therefore$ Deflecting torque, $T_d \propto i^2$

Controlling torque provided by springs, $T_c \propto \theta$

In the steady position of deflection, $T_d = T_c$

$$\therefore \quad \theta \propto i^2$$

$$\propto I^2 \quad \text{...(for d.c.)}$$

$$\propto I_{r.m.s} \quad \text{...(for a.c.)}$$

Since deflection θ is proportional to square of current through the coil, therefore, scale of such instruments is non-uniform being crowed in the beginning. However, scale of such instruments can be made uniform by using tongue shaped iron pieces.

Advantages and Disadvantages of Moving Iron Instruments

Advantages.

(*i*) These are cheap, robust and simple in construction.

(*ii*) The instruments can be used for both A.C. as well as D.C. circuits.

(*iii*) These instruments have high operating torque.

(*iv*) These instruments are reasonably accurate.

Disadvantages.

(*i*) Such instruments have non-uniform scale.

(*ii*) These instruments are not very sensitive.

(*iii*) Errors are introduced due to changes in frequency in case of a.c. measurements.

(*iv*) Higher power consumption.

8.3.2. Moving Coil Instruments

Moving coil instruments are of two types:

1. Permanent magnet type (for d.c. work only) : Direct current indicating Instrument.
2. Dynamo meter type (for both a.c. and d.c. works)

1. Permanent Magnet Moving Coil Instruments

These instruments are employed either as ammeters or voltmeters and can be used for d.c. work only.

Principle. This type of instrument is based on the principle, (PMMC) : (permanent-magnet moving coil mechanism) i.e. when a current carrying conductor is placed in a magnetic field, mechanical force acts on the conductor. The coil placed in magnetic field and carrying operating current is attached to the moving system. With the movement of the coil the pointer moves over the scale.

Construction. It consists of a powerful permanent magnet with soft iron pieces and light rectangular coil of many turns of fine wire wound on aluminium former inside which is an iron core as shown in Fig. 8.4. The purpose of coil is to make the field uniform. The coil is mounted on the spindle and acts as the moving element. The current is led into and out of the coil by means of the two control hair springs, one above and the other below the coil. The springs also provides the controlling torque. Eddy current damping is provided by aluminium former.

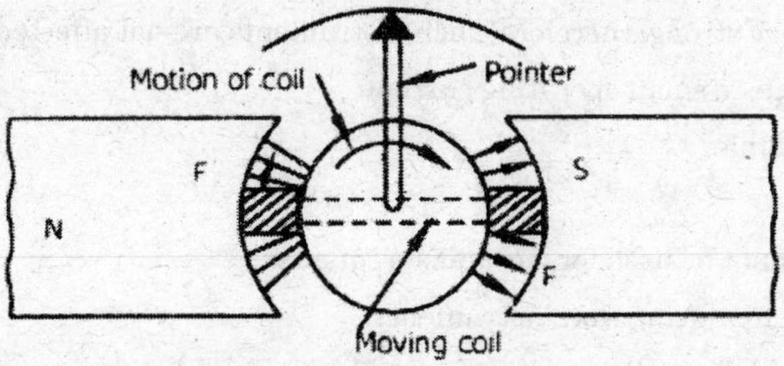

Fig. 8.4. Moving coil instrument

Working. When the instrument is connected in the circuit, operating current flows through the coil. This current carrying coil is placed in the magnetic field produced by the permanent magnet and therefore, mechanical force acts on the coil. As the coil attached to the moving system, the pointer moves over the scale.

It may be noted here that if current direction is reversed, the torque will also be reversed since the direction of the field of permanent magnet is same. Hence, the pointer will move in the opposite direction, i.e. it will go on the wrong side of zero (below zero). In other words, these instruments work only when current in the circuit is passed in a definite direction i.e., for d.c. circuit only.

Deflecting Torque. When current is passed through the coil, a deflection torque is produced due to the reaction between permanent magnet field and the magnetic field of the coil as shown in Fig. 8.4.

Let B = flux density in wb/m² in the air gap between the magnetic poles and iron core

l = active length of the coil side in meters

N = number of turns of coil

If a current of I amperes flows in the coil in the direction shown, then force F acting on each coil side is given by

$$F = BIlN \text{ newtons}$$

∴ Deflecting torque,

$$T_d\,\omega = \text{Force} \times \text{perpendicular distance}$$

$$= F \times 2\,r \text{ newton-meters}$$

where, r = distance of coil side from the axis of rotation in meters

$$T_d = NB\,Il \times 2\,r \text{ newton-meters}$$

If A ($= l\,.\,2\,r$) is the surface area of the coil, then

$$T_d = NBIA \text{ newton-meters}$$

i.e. Deflection torque = Ampere turns on coil (NI) × Area of coil (A) × flux density B

Since N, B and A are constant, therefore,

$$T_d \propto I \qquad \text{... }(i)$$

Since the control is by springs, therefore controlling torque is proportional to the angle of deflection, i.e.

$$T_c \propto I \qquad \text{... }(ii)$$

The pointer will come to rest at a position when,

$$T_d = T_c$$

From equation (*i*) and (*ii*), we get

$$\theta \propto I$$

Thus, the deflection θ is directly proportional to the operating current. Therefore, such instruments have uniform scale.

Advantages.

(*i*) Uniform scale.

(*ii*) Very effective eddy current damping.

(*iii*) Power consumption is low.

(*iv*) No hysteresis loss.

(*v*) As working field is very strong, therefore, such instruments are not affected stray fields.

(*vi*) Such instruments require small operating current.

(*vii*) Very accurate and reliable.

Disadvantages.

(*i*) Such instruments cannot be used for a.c. measurements.

(*ii*) Costlier as compared to moving iron instruments.

(*iii*) Some errors are caused due to the ageing of control springs and the permanent magnet.

2. Dynamometer Type Instruments.

These instruments are the modified form of permanent magnet type. Here operating field is produced not by a permanent but by another fixed coil. The moving system and the control system are similar to those of permanent magnet type. Such instruments can be used for both a.c. and d.c. circuits. They can be used as ammeters and voltmeters but are generally used as wattmeters.

Principle. These instruments are based on that principle the mechanical force exists between the current carrying conductors.

Construction. A dynamometer type instrument as shown in Fig. 8.5 essentially consists of a fixed coil and a moving coil. The fixed coil is split into two equal parts which are placed close together and parallel to each other. The moving coil is pivoted in between the two fixed coils. The fixed and moving coils may be excited separately or they may be connected in series depending upon the use to which the measurement is put. The moving coil is attached to the moving system so that under the action of deflecting torque, the pointer moves over the scale.

The controlling torque is provided by two springs which also serve the additional purpose of leading the current into and out of the moving coil. Air friction damping is provided in such instruments

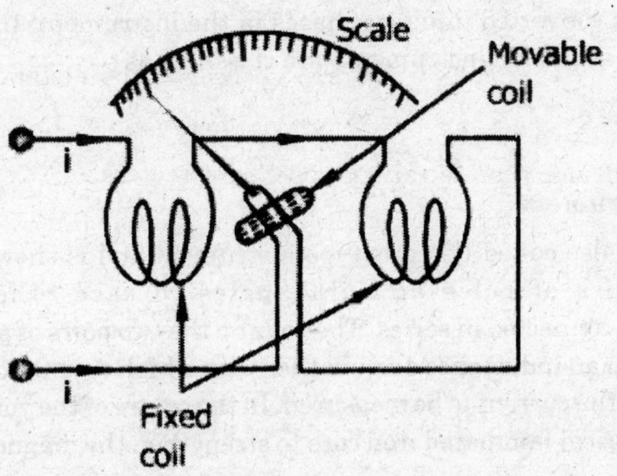

Fig. 8.5.

Working. When instrument is connected in the circuit, operating currents flow through the coils. Due to this, mechanical force exists between the coils. The result is that the moving coil (which is capable of moving) moves the pointer over the scale. The pointer comes to rest at a position where deflecting torque is equal to the controlling torque.

By reversing the current, the field due to fixed coils is reversed as well as the current in the moving coil, so that direction of deflecting torque remains unchanged. Therefore, such instruments can be used for both d.c. and a.c. measurements.

Deflecting Torque

Let I_f is current through fixed coil and I_m is current through moving coil

$$\therefore \quad T_d \propto I_f I_m$$

Since, $I_f = I_m$ because the fixed and coils are in series,

$$\therefore \quad T_d \propto I^2 \qquad \text{... } (i)$$

Since the control is by springs, therefore, controlling torque is proportional to the angle of deflection θ, i.e.

$$T_c \propto \theta \qquad \text{... } (ii)$$

The pointer will come to rest at a position when $T_d = T_c$.

From equations (*i*) and (*ii*), we get

$$\theta \propto I^2$$

It is clear that deflection of the pointer is directly proportional to the square of the operating current.

Hence, the scales of these instruments is non-uniform being crowded in their lower parts and spread out at the top.

Advantages.

(*i*) These instruments can be used for both a.c. and d.c. measurements.

(*ii*) Such instruments are free from hysteresis and eddy current errors.

Disadvantages.

(*i*) Since torque/weight ratio is small, therefore, such instruments have frictional errors which reduce sensitivity.

(*ii*) Scale is not uniform (in case of ammeters and voltmeters).

(*iii*) A good amount of screening of the instruments is required to avoid the effect of stray fields.

(*iv*) These instruments are costlier and, so they are rarely used.

8.3.4. Induction Type Instruments.

These instruments are based on the principle of induction motor.

Principle. When a drum or disc of a non-magnetic conducting material is placed in a rotating magnetic field, eddy currents are induced in it. The reaction between the rotating flux and the eddy current produced by it creates a torque which rotates the disc or drum. The rotating flux is produced by the current or voltage to be measured. The eddy current again is proportional to the flux.

$$\therefore \qquad T \propto \phi i \propto i^2$$

The single phase supply is converted into two phases in the instrument, this is done by split phase or shaded pole arrangement. Accordingly induction instruments are classified as

(1) Split phase type

(2) Shaded pole type

1. Split Phase Type Instrument

Construction. This is also called Ferraris type instrument and is shown in Fig. 8.6. It consists of a laminated magnet with the pairs of poles at right angles to each other. Coils are wound on the poles, the opposite poles being connected in series. The coils on the two pairs of poles are connected in parallel. One set of coil is connected through an inductance and another with a high resistance to create a phase difference of 90°. The input to both the coils is the current to be measured. In the centre of the yoke and coil is an aluminium drum. Inside the drum there is cylindrical laminated iron core to strengthen the magnetic field.

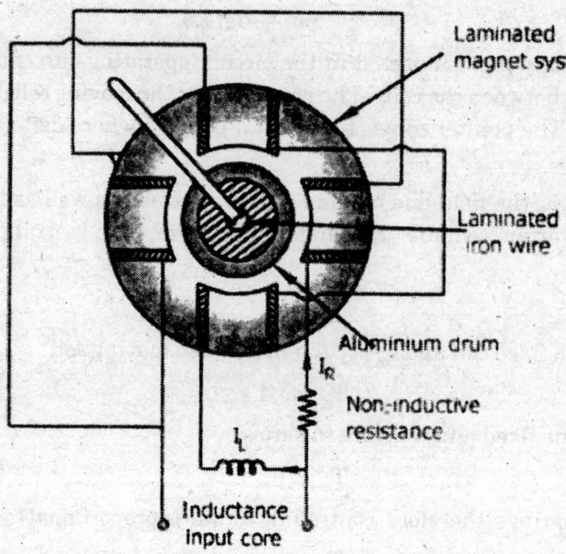

Fig. 8.6. Split phase type induction instrument

Working. When the instrument is connected in the circuit current flows through the coils. A rotating magnetic field is produced. This field induces eddy currents in the drum and a torque is produced by the reaction of magnetic field and current. This torque deflects the pointer attached to the drum. Controlling torque is produced by spring.

Deflecting torque. Deflecting torque produced, is given by

$$T \propto \frac{I_R I_L f}{Z} \cos\theta \sin\alpha$$

For an ammeter, $T \propto \frac{I_2}{Z} \cos\theta \sin\alpha$

For a voltmeter, $T \propto \frac{V^2}{Z} \cos\theta \sin\alpha$

where, I_R = current through resistor

I_L = current through inductor

f = supply frequency

Z = impedance of eddy current path

θ = phase angle between voltage and current in resistor

α = phase angle between currents in resistor and inductor

θ is almost zero and R is very much larger than reactive part of eddy paths. Hence

$$T \propto \frac{I^2}{R} \sin \alpha$$

Obviously α should be as high as possible for high torque.

2. Shaded Pole Type Instrument

Construction. Shaded pole type instrument is shown in Fig. 8.7. A band of copper is placed in pole faces, this makes the two fluxes of shaded and unshaded portions of differ in phase by 90°. A metallic disc rotates between the pole faces.

The damping is provided by another magnet as shown in Fig. 8.7.

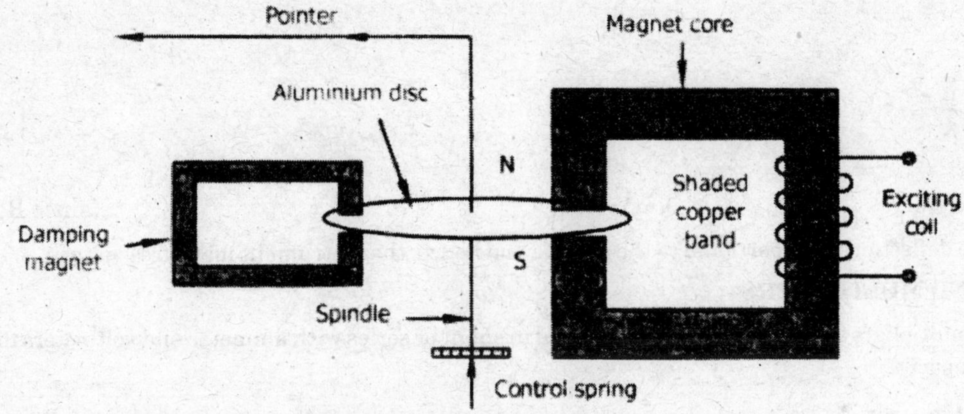

Fig. 8.7. Shaded pole type Induction Instrument

Working. The current flowing through the exciting coil sets up flux. Eddy currents are induced in the Cu band. Flux of the eddy current opposes the flux in the magnetic core and a two phase flux same as Ferraris type instrument.

8.4. MEASUREMENT OF ELECTRIC VOLTAGE AND CURRENT

Moving iron instruments are used as ammeters and voltmeters only. They work on both a.c. and d.c. systems.

1. Ammeter.

An instrument which is used to measure electric current in a circuit is called an *ammeter*. It is always connected in series with the circuit and carries the current to be measured. This current flowing through the operating coil produce the desired deflecting torque (Fig. 8.8). Since it is to be connected in series, therefore, it should have a low resistance. Hence, when a moving iron instrument is used as ammeter, the operating coil is provided with a few turns of thick wire so that it has low resistance.

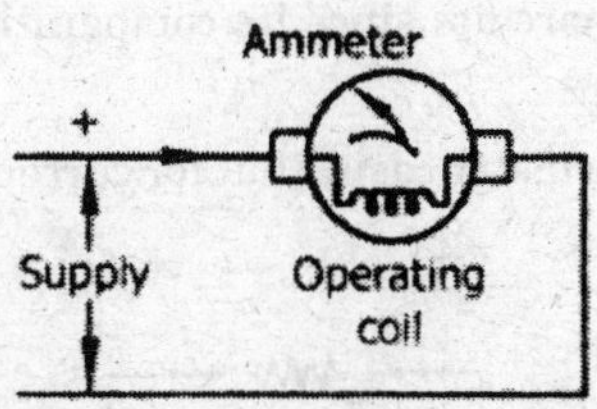

Fig. 6.8.

2. Voltmeter.

An instrument which is used to measure voltage between two points in a circuit is called a *voltmeter.* A voltmeter is always connected in parallel with the portion whose voltage is to be measured. This current flowing through the operating coil of the meter produces the deflecting torque. Since voltmeter is connected in parallel and in order that its connection does not disturb the circuit conditions, therefore, the resistance of the voltmeter should be very high. To do so, a high resistance (of the order of kilo ohms) is connected in series with the coil of the instrument as shown.

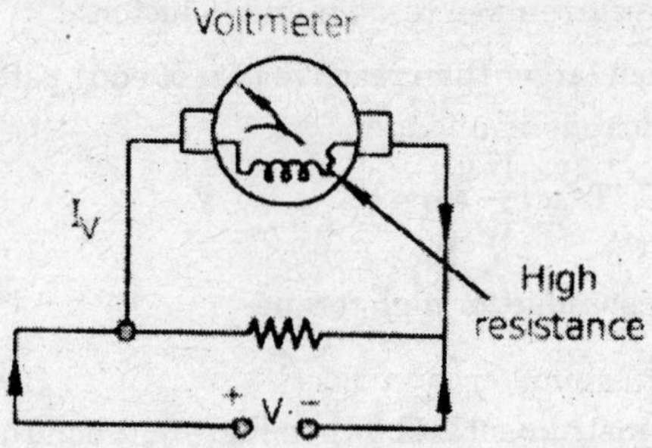

Let R_v be the total resistance (resistance of operating coil + high series resistance) of the instrument.

The small current I_v flowing through the instrument is given by

$$I_v = \frac{V}{R_v}$$

Clearly,

$$\text{deflection, } \theta \propto I_v \propto \frac{V}{R_v} \qquad \ldots\left[\text{since } I_v = \frac{V}{R_v}\right]$$

$$\therefore \qquad \theta \propto V \qquad \ldots[\text{since } R_v \text{ is constant}]$$

Therefore deflection is proportional to the voltage and hence, the instrument measures voltage.

8.5. SHUNTS AND MULTIPLIERS

Shunts and multipliers are the resistances connected in shunt or series with ammeter and voltmeters to enhance their measuring capacity.

8.5.1 SHUNTS.

A resistance placed in parallel with an instrument (or galvanometer) to control the current passing through it, when placed in a circuit carrying a fairly large current is called a *shunt*.

The shunt resistance used with a basic instrument may consists of a length of constant temperature resistance wire within the box of the instrument. Alternatively, there may be an external (manganin or constantan) shunt having very low resistance.

General requirements of a shunt :

(*i*) The temperature coefficient of the shunt and instrument should be low and nearly identical.

(*ii*) The resistance of the shunt should not vary with time.

(*iii*) It should carry the current without excessive temperature rise.

(*iv*) It should have a low thermal emf.

Manganin is usually used as a shunt for d.c. instruments since it gives a low value of thermal emf with copper. Constantan is a useful material for a.c. circuits since its comparatively high thermal emf being unidirectional, is ineffective on these circuits.

Shunts for low current are enclosed in the meter casing but for currents above 200A, they are mounted separately.

Shunt with ammeter.

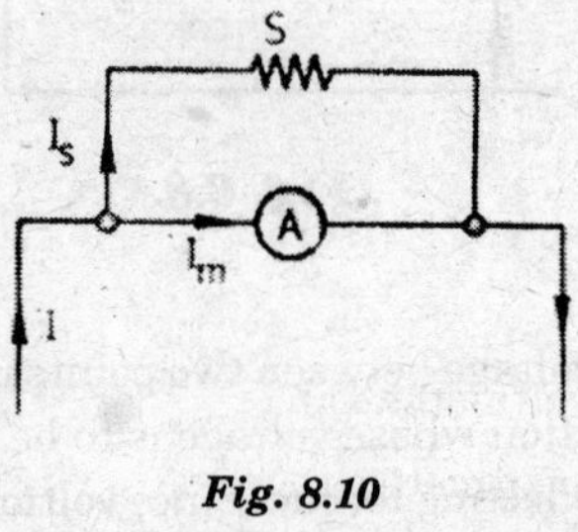

Fig. 8.10

Low resistance shunt is connected across the coil of ammeter.

Let I be the circuit current to be measured.

R_m = Ammeter resistance

S = Shunt resistance

I_m = Full scale deflection current of ammeter

I_s = Shunt current

Then $$I = I_s + I_m$$

or $$I_s = I - I_m$$

Since the voltage across shunt and ammeter is same,

$$\therefore \quad I_m R_m = (I - I_m) R_s \qquad ...[\because I_s = I - I_A]$$

$$\Rightarrow \quad I_m (R_m + R_s) = IR_s$$

$$\Rightarrow \quad \frac{I}{I_m} = \frac{R_m + R_s}{R_s}$$

$$\Rightarrow \quad I = I_m \frac{R_m + R_s}{R_s}$$

i.e. Circuit current = f.s.d. current × $\frac{R_m + R_s}{R_s}$

Instrument constant.

It is the ratio of current to be measured to full scale deflection current.

Instrument constant, $m = \frac{I}{I_m} = \frac{R_m + R_s}{R_s}$

It is clear that with different shunts, the same instruments will have different instrument constants.

8.5.2 MULTIPLIERS.

A high resistance in series with a galvanometer is connected, to limit the current flowing through the meter, so that it does not exceed the value for full scale deflection and thus prevents the instrument from being damaged. Such a resistance is called *multiplier.*

Multiplier with Voltmeter.

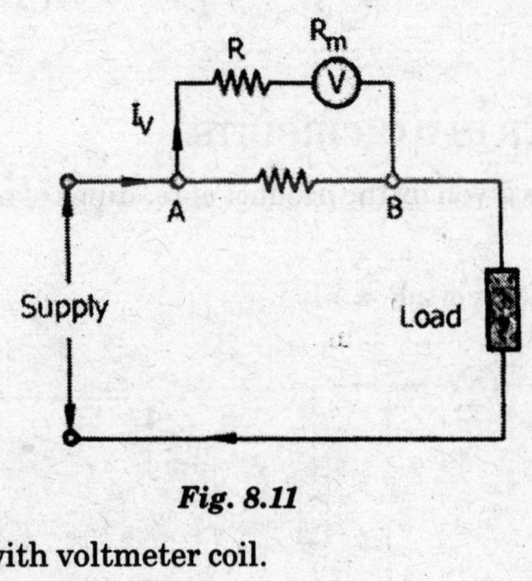

Fig. 8.11

High resistance is connected in series with voltmeter coil.

Let R_m = voltmeter resistance

R = high resistance in series with voltmeter coil

I_m = full scale deflection current for voltmeter.

Since voltmeter is connected in parallel with circuit AB,

∴ Voltage across AB = Voltage across voltmeter

$$\Rightarrow \quad V = I_m (R + R_m)$$

$$\Rightarrow \quad R + R_m = \frac{V}{I_m}$$

$$\Rightarrow \quad R = \frac{V}{I_m} - R_m$$

$$\text{Multiplier constant, } m = \frac{V}{v} = \frac{I_m (R_m + R_s)}{I_m R_m} = 1 + \frac{R}{R_m}$$

$$\textit{i.e. } \text{Required high resistance, } R = \frac{\text{Maximum voltage to be measured}}{\text{R.s.d. voltmeter current}} - \text{voltmeter resistance}$$

Shunt for a.c. instruments.

In order to maintain the current division between the shunt and instrument, constant for all frequencies, the ratio of impedances of the instrument and leads to that of the shunt must remain constant.

If L_m and L_s are inductances of the instrument and shunt respectively, then the ratio $\frac{\sqrt{R_m^2 + \omega^2 L_m^2}}{\sqrt{R_s^2 + \omega^2 L_s^2}}$ should remain constant for all frequencies, which is possible only when time constants of the shunt and instrument are same.

i.e.

$$\frac{L_m}{R_m} = \frac{L_s}{R_s} = k$$

$$\text{Multiplying factor, } N = \frac{I}{I_m} = \frac{I_s + I_m}{I_m} = \frac{I_s}{I_m} + 1$$

$$= \frac{\sqrt{R_m^2 + \omega^2 L_m^2}}{\sqrt{R_s^2 + \omega^2 L_s^2}} + 1$$

$$= \frac{R_m \sqrt{1 + \omega^2 (L_m / R_m)^2}}{R_s \sqrt{1 + \omega^2 (L_s / R_s)^2}} + 1$$

$$= \frac{R_m \sqrt{1 + \omega^2 k^2}}{R_s \sqrt{1 + \omega^2 k^2}} + 1 = \frac{R_m}{R_s} + 1$$

8.6. MEASUREMENT OF POWER

8.6.1 MEASUREMENT OF POWER IN D.C. CIRCUITS.

The power taken from a d.c. supply is given by the product of readings of an ammeter and voltmeter when connected as shown in Fig. 8.12.

Power in d.c. circuit, P = VI.

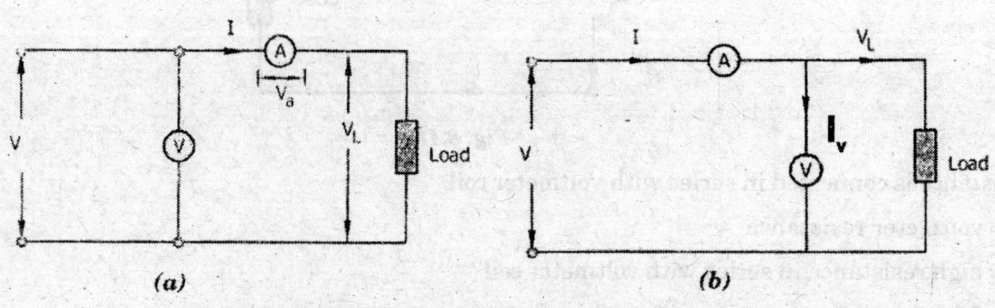

Fig. 8.12 Measurement of power in D.C. Circuits

From Fig. 8.12 (*a*),

Power consumed by load $= V_L I$

$= (V - V_a) I$

$= VI - V_a I = VI - I^2 R_a$

∴ Power indicated by instruments = Power consumed in load + Power loss in ammeter

From Fig. 8.12 *(b)*,

Power consumed by load $= VI_L = V(I - I_v)$

$$= V\left(I - \frac{V}{R_v}\right) = VI - \frac{V^2}{R_v}$$

∴ Power indicated by instruments = Power consumed in load + Power loss in voltmeter

Thus in both the cases, power indicated by the instruments is equal to the power consumed by the load plus the power consumed by the instrument nearer to the load terminals. In order to obtain the true power, corrections must be applied for power loss in instruments.

8.6.2 MEASUREMENT OF POWER IN A.C. CIRCUITS.

In a.c. circuits, power is given by $P = VI \cos \phi$

where V and I are voltage across the load and current through the load respectively and cos ϕ is the power factor of the load.

So Voltmeter-Ammeter method is not applicable in A.C. circuits, because of involvement of power factor. Wattmeters are used to take into account the power factor.

Wattmeters.

There are two types of wattmeters :

1. Induction type wattmeter
2. Electrodynamometer type wattmeter.

1. Induction Type Wattmeter.

The induction type wattmeter is used to measure a.c. power only.

Principle : The principle of operation of an induction wattmeter is the same as that of induction ammeters and voltmeters, *i.e.* induction principle. However, it differs from induction ammeter or voltmeter in so far that separate two coils are used to produced the rotating flux in place of one coil with phase split arrangement.

Construction : Fig. 8.13 shows the principle parts of an induction wattmeter. It consists of two laminated electromagnets. One electromagnet, called shunt magnet is connected across supply and carries current proportional to the applied voltage. The coil of this magnet is made highly inductive so that the current (and hence the flux) in it lags behind the supply voltage by 90°. The other electromagnet, called series magnet is connected in series with supply and carries the load current. The coil of this magnet is made highly non-inductive so that the angle of lag or lead in determined wholly by the load.

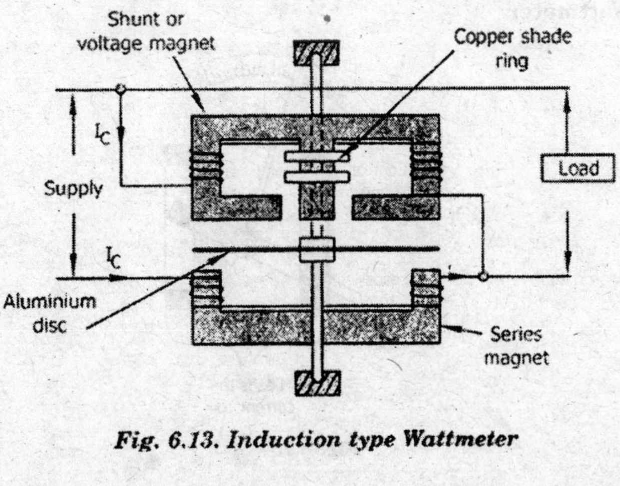

Fig. 6.13. Induction type Wattmeter

A thin aluminium disc mounted on the spindle is placed in between the two magnets so that it cuts the fluxes of both the magnets. The controlling torque is provided by spiral springs. The damping is electromagnetic and is usually provided by a permanent magnet embracing the aluminium disc. Two or more closed copper rings, called shading rings are provided on the central limb of the shunt magnet. By adjusting the position of these rings, the shunt magnet flux can be made to lag behind supply voltage by exactly 90°.

Working : When the wattmeter is connected in the circuit to measure a.c. power, the shunt magnet carries current proportional to the supply voltage and the series magnet carries the load current. The two fluxes produced by the magnets induce eddy currents in the aluminium disc. The interaction between the fluxes and eddy currents produce the deflecting torque on the disc, causing the pointer connected to the moving system to move over the scale.

Deflecting Torque :

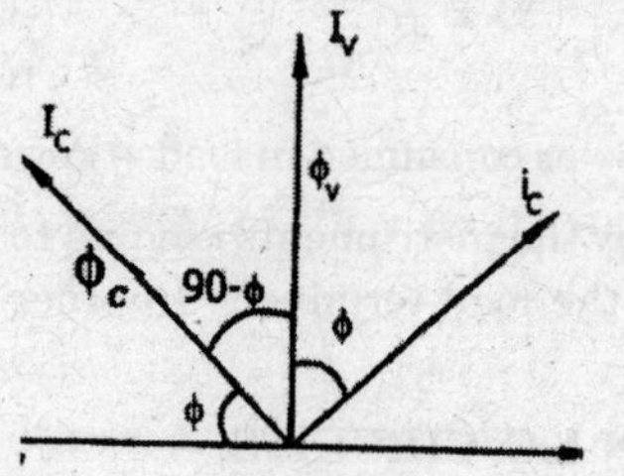

Fig. 8.14

Let V = applied voltage

I_c = load current carried by the series magnet

I_v = current carries by the shunt magnet

cos ϕ = lagging power factor of the load

The current I_v in the shunt magnet lags the applied voltage V by 90° and so does the flux ϕ_v produced by it. The current I_c in the series magnet is the load current and hence lags behind the applied voltage by ϕ. The flux ϕ_c produced by this current (*i.e.* I_c) is in phase with it.

Therefore, two currents I_c in the current coil and I_v in the voltage coil and also the corresponding fluxes ϕ_v and ϕ_c are $(90 - \phi°)$ apart.

The flux ϕ_v induces eddy currents i_v in the aluminium disc which lags behind ϕ_v by 90°. Similarly, ϕ_c induces eddy currents i_c which again lags behind ϕ_c by 90°.

$\therefore$ Mean deflecting torque, $T_d \propto \phi_c \sin(90° - \phi)$

$\Rightarrow$ $T_d \propto VI\cos\phi$ ...[$\because \phi_v \propto V$ and $\phi_c \propto I$]

$\Rightarrow$ $T_d \propto$ a.c. power

Since control is by springs, therefore $T_c \propto \theta$

For steady deflected position, $T_d = T_c$

$\theta \propto$ power

Hence, such instruments have uniform scale.

2. Dynamometer Type Wattmeter.

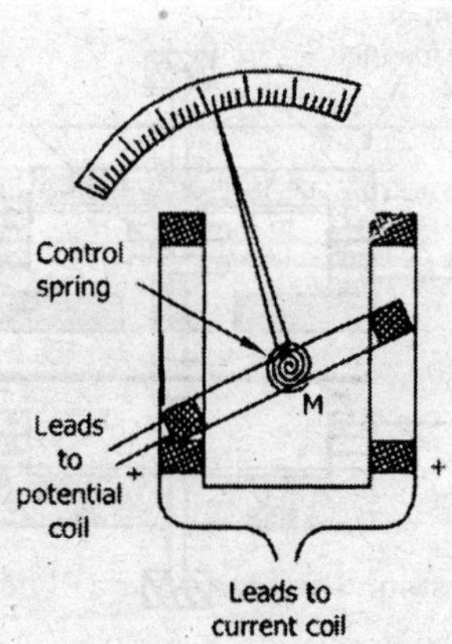

Fig. 8.15

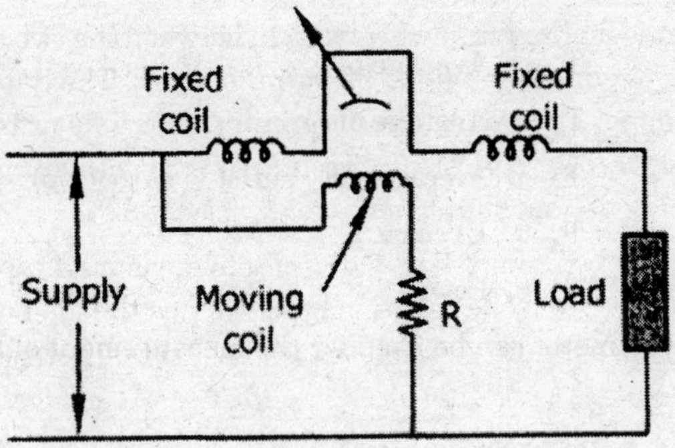

Fig. 8.16

A dynamometer type wattmeter is most commonly employed for measurement of power in a.c. as well as d.c. circuits.

Principle : It is based on the principle that mechanical force exists between two current carrying conductors.

Construction : It essentially consists of two coils, namely fixed coil and moving coil. The fixed coil is split into two equal parts which are placed close together and parallel to each other. The moving coil is pivoted between the two fixed coils and is placed on the spindle to which the pointer is attached.

The fixed coils are connected in series with the load and carry the circuit current. It is, therefore, called current coil. The moving coil is connected across the load and carries current proportional to the voltage. It therefore, called potential coil. Generally, a high resistance is connected in series with potential coil to limit the current through it.

The controlling torque is provided by springs which also serve the additional purpose of leading current into and out of the moving coil. Air friction damping is employed in such instruments.

Working : When power is to be measured in a circuit, the instrument is suitably connected in the circuit. The current coil is connected in series with load so that it carries the circuit current. The potential coil is connected across the load so that it carries current proportional to the voltage.

Due to the current in the coils, mechanical force exists between them. The result is that the moving coil (which is capable of moving), moves the pointer over the scale. The pointer comes to rest at a position where deflecting torque is equal to the controlling torque.

Reversing the current, reverses the field due to fixed coil as well as the current in the moving coil so that the direction of the deflection torque remains unchanged. Therefore, such instruments can be used for the measurement of a.c. as well as d.c. power.

Deflecting Torque :

It can be easily proved that deflecting torque is proportional to the power in the circuit.

Operation on D.C.

Let in a d.c. circuit, V is voltage across load, and I is current through load.

∴ Current through fixed coil, $I_f \propto I$

Current through moving coil, $I_m \propto V$

Deflecting torque T_d is due to the current I_f and I_m

∴ $$T_d \propto I_m\, I_f \propto VI \propto \text{power}$$

Operation on A.C.

Let in an a.c. circuit, e is instantaneous voltage across load, and i is instantaneous current through load.

If the load has a lagging power factor of cos ϕ, then equations become

$$e = E_m \sin \omega t$$

$$i = I_m \sin (\omega t - \phi)$$

Current through fixed coil, $i_f \propto i$

Current through moving coil, $i_m \propto e$

Due to large inertia of the moving system, the deflection will be proportional to the average torque.

Mean deflecting torque,

$$T_d \propto \text{Average of } i_m i_f$$

$$\Rightarrow \quad T_d \propto \text{Average of } e_i$$

$$\Rightarrow \quad T_d \propto \text{Average of } E_m \sin \omega t \, I_m \sin(\omega t - \phi)$$

$$\Rightarrow \quad T_d \propto EI \cos \phi$$

$$\Rightarrow \quad T_d \propto \text{Power}$$

Hence, dynamometer type wattmeter can be used for the measurement of a.c. as well as d.c. power.

Scale.

We have seen that, $T_d \propto$ power

and $T_c \propto \theta$ (spring controlled)

$\therefore$ $\theta \propto$ power

Hence such instruments have uniform scale.

8.6.3 ERRORS IN ELECTRODYNAMOMETER WATTMETER.

1. Potential coil inductance.

In an idealized wattmeter, potential coil is assumed to be purely resistive. In practice, the potential coil has inductance also, because of which current through the coil lags the voltage by an angle say β and is not in phase with it.

$$\beta = \tan^{-1} \frac{\omega L}{R_p} = \tan^{-1} \frac{\omega L}{(r_p + R)}$$

where, r_p = resistance of potential coil

R = resistance in series with potential coil

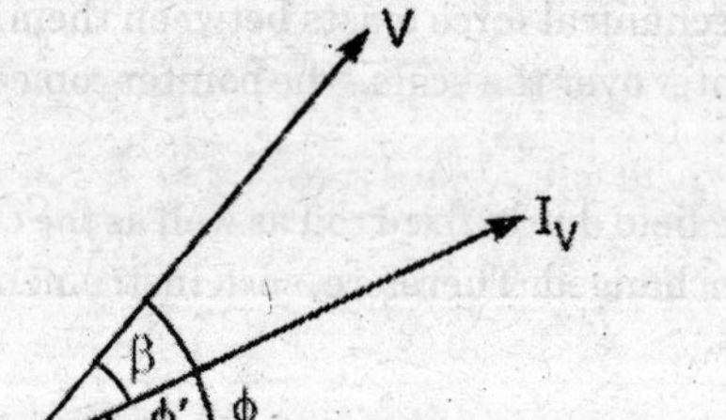

Fig. 8.17

As shown in Fig. 8.17, for a lagging power factor, the angle between current in current coil and current in potential coil is less than ϕ and is equal to ϕ = (ϕ – B)

Actual wattmeter reading ∝ VI cos (ϕ – β) cos β

But true power = VI cos ϕ

$$\therefore \quad \text{Correction factor} = \frac{\text{True power}}{\text{Actual wattmeter reading}}$$

$$= \frac{\cos \phi}{\cos \beta \cos(\phi - \beta)}$$

$$\text{For leading, } p.f. = \frac{\cos \phi}{[\cos \beta . \cos(\phi + \beta)]}$$

$$\approx \frac{1}{1 + \tan \phi \tan \beta}$$

Compensation for this error can be provided by connecting a capacitor across a portion of the external resistance R.

2. **Potential coil capacitance.**

The potential coil may possess capacitance in addition to inductance. This capacitance is mainly due to in turn capacitance of the series resistance. The effect of capacitance opposite to that produced by inductance, the wattmeter reads high on lagging power factors of load.

3. **Mutual inductance of coils.**

Errors are caused due to mutual inductance between current and potential coils of the wattmeter. These errors are quite low at power frequencies but they increase and become important as frequency is increased. The effect of mutual inductance is to increase the phase angle for the connection at which potential coil is connected on the load side and to decrease the phase angle when the current coil is connected on the load side. This change in phase angle is $\tan^{-1} \dfrac{\omega M}{R_p}$.

4. **Errors because of connections.**

The wattmeter can be connected in either of the two ways shown in Fig. 8.18. Errors are introduced in the measurement owing to the power loss in current and potential coils.

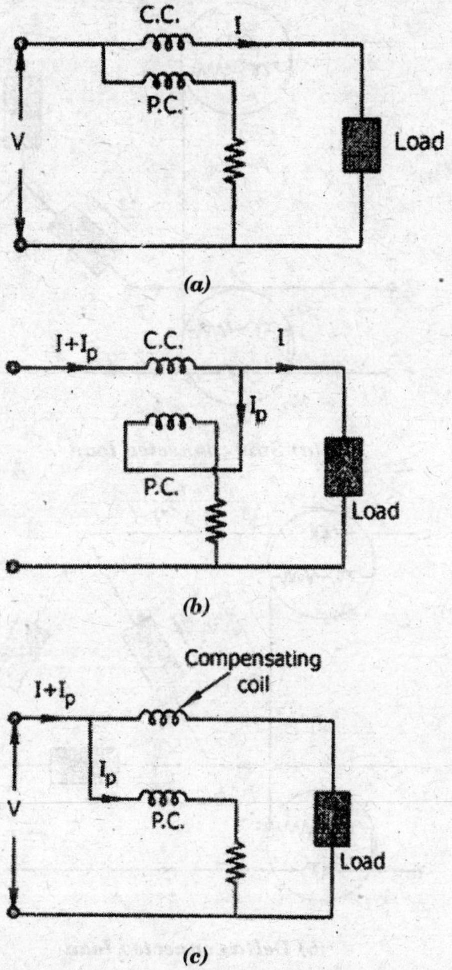

Fig. 8.18 Wattmeter connections

In Fig. 8.18(a), the potential coil is connected on the supply side and the voltage across it is equal to the sum of voltages across the current coil and load. The wattmeter measures power consumed by load and power loss in current coil. In connection of Fig. 8.18 (b), the current coil is on supply side and it carries the load current plus the potential coil current. The wattmeter reads power loss in potential coil plus the power consumed by the load. The use of the above connection holds good only if the power loss in the instrument is low. The connection of Fig. 8.18 is used for small load currents and that of Fig. 8.18 used for large load currents.

The power taken by the potential coil is constant if the voltage is constant and becomes a smaller percentage of the total power as a larger amount of power is measured. However, in cases where the load current is large and the power factor is small, connection *(b)* results in larger error since the total power measured is small. In such cases a compensating coil is used in the instrument to compensate for the error caused by power loss in potential coil circuit as shown in Fig. 8.18 (*c*).

The compensating coil is connected in series with the potential coil and is identical and coincident with current coil. It opposes the field of the current coil. The current coil carries current equal to $I + I_p$ and potential coil carries current equal to I_p. The resultant field is due to current I only. Hence the error is neutralized.

5. Eddy current errors.

Eddy currents are induced in the solid metal parts and within the thickness of the conductors by alternating magnetic field of the current coil. These currents produce a field of their own and alter the magnitude and phase of the current coil field thus cause errors.

8.6.4 MEASUREMENT OF POWER IN THREE-PHASE CIRCUITS.

Two wattmeter method is used to measure power in 3-ϕ circuits. The current coils of two wattmeters are inserted in any two lines and potential coil is connected from its own current coil to the line without a current coil. The power supplied is sum of the two wattmeter readings. The circuit arrangements for star and delta connected loads are shown in Fig. 8.19.

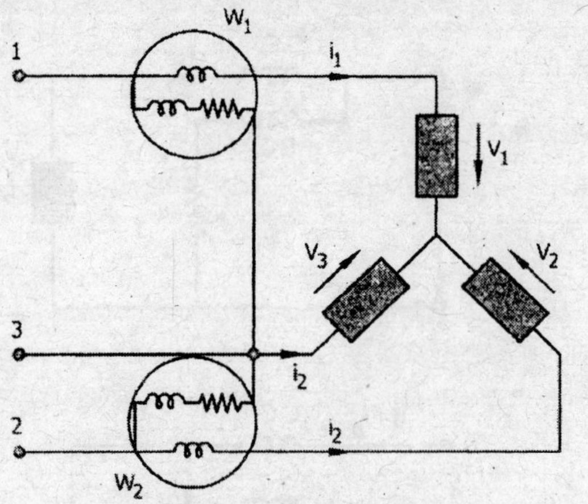

(a) Star connected load

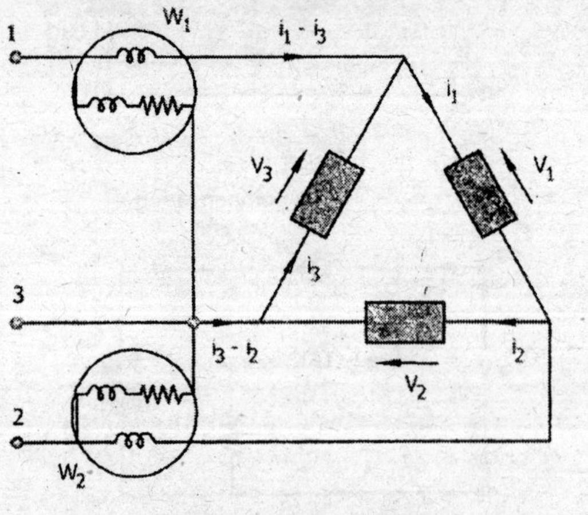

(b) Delta connected load

Fig. 8.19 Two wattmeter method of measurement of Power

For both the connections,

Power consumed by load, $P = W_1 + W_2$

Here $W_1 = VI \cos (30° - \phi)$

and $W_2 = VI \cos (30° + \phi)$

$$\text{Power factor angle of the load} = \phi = \tan^{-1}\left[\frac{\sqrt{3}\,(W_1 - W_2)}{W_1 + W_2}\right]$$

- When both wattmeter readings are equal, *i.e.* $W_1 = W_2$, $\tan\phi = 0°$, $\cos\phi = 1$.
  The load purely resistive.
- When only one wattmeter reads, $W_1 = 0$, $\tan\phi = \sqrt{3}$, $\cos\phi = 0.5$, $\phi = 60°$ lagging
- When wattmeter readings are equal and opposite $W_1 = -W_2$, $\tan\phi = \infty$, $\phi = 90°$, $\cos\phi = 0$.
  The load is purely reactive.
- When $60° < \theta < 90°$, $0.5 > \cos\phi > 0$,
  one wattmeter reading is positive and another negative. As one wattmeter cannot indicate negative reading, coil has to be reversed preferably the pressure coil
  $$W_T = W_2 - W_1.$$
- When the power factor is leading by ϕ,
  $$W_1 = VI\cos(30° - \phi)$$
  and
  $$W_2 = VI\cos(30° - \phi)$$
  i.e. readings of the two wattmeters are only interchanged.

8.7. MEASUREMENT OF ENERGY

INDUCTION TYPE SINGLE PHASE ENERGY METER.

Single phase induction type energy meter is extensively used to measure energy supplied to a single phase circuit.

Operating Principle.

The operation of induction type enevgy meter depends on the passage of alternating current through two suitably located coils (current coil and pressure coil) producing rotating magnetic field which interacts with a metallic disc suspended near to the coils and cause the disc to rotate.

The current coil carries the line current and produces field in phase with the line current. The pressure coil is made highly inductive so that the current through it lags behind the supply voltage by 90°. Thus, a phase difference of 90° exists between the fluxes produced by the two coils. This sets up rotating field which interacts with the disc to cause it to rotate.

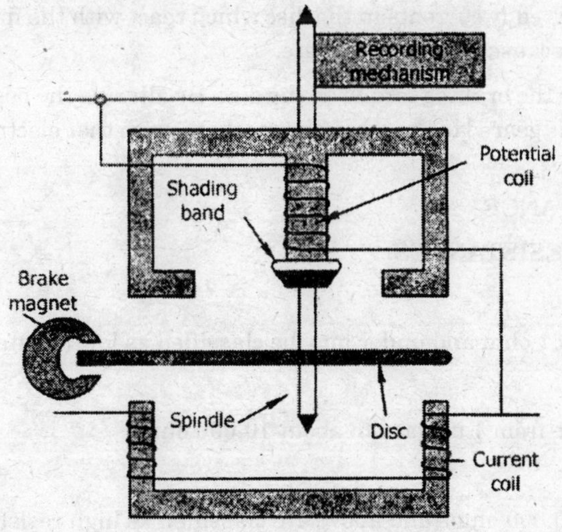

Fig. 8.20 Energy meter

Construction.

A single phase induction type energy meter generally has following systems :

1. **Moving System :**

   It consists of a light aluminium disc mounted on a vertical spindle. The spindle is supported by a cup-shaped jewelled bearings at the bottom end and has a spring journal bearing at the top end.

   There is no pointer and control spring so that the disc makes continuous rotation under the action of deflecting torque.

2. **Operating Mechanism:**

It consists of following magnets :

(*i*) **Series magnet :** It consists of a number of U-shaped laminations assembled together to form a core. A thick wire of few turns is wound on both legs of the U-shaped laminated core. The wound coil is known as current coil and is connected in series with the load so that it carries the load current. The series magnet is placed underside the aluminium disc and produces magnetic field proportional to and in phase with the current.

(*ii*) **Shunt magnet :** It consists of a number of M-shaped laminations assembled together to form a core. A fine wire of large turns is wound on the central limb of this magnet. The wound coil is known as pressure coil and is connected across the load so that it carries current proportional to supply voltage. The shunt magnet is placed above the aluminium disc as shown.

In order to obtain deflecting torque, current in the pressure coil must lag behind the supply voltage by 90°. This necessary phase shift is obtained by placing a copper ring (also known as compensating loop) over central limb of shunt magnet. This copper ring acts as a short circuited transformer secondary. As its inductance is high as compared with its resistance, the current circulating in the ring will lag by nearly 90° behind the voltage producing it.

(*iii*) **Braking magnet :** The speed of aluminium disc is controlled to the required value by the C-shaped permanent breaking magnet. The magnet is mounted so that the disc revolves in the air gap between the polar extremities. As the disc rotates, currents are induced in the disc because it cuts the flux produced by the braking magnet. The direction of the current in the disc is such that it opposes the rotation of the disc (Lenz's Law.) Since the induced currents in the disc are proportional to the speed of the disc, therefore, braking torque is proportional to the disc speed,

i.e. $$T_B \propto N$$

3. **Recording Mechanism :**

The number of revolutions of the disc is a measure of the electrical energy passing through the meter and is recorded on dials which are geared to the shaft.

Working : When the energy meter is connected in the circuit to measure electrical energy, the current coil carries the load current whereas the pressure coil carries current proportional to the supply voltage. The magnetic field due to current coil is in phase with line current whereas the magnetic field produced due to pressure coil lags approximately 90° behind the supply voltage.

The current coil field produces eddy currents in the disc which react with the field due to the pressure coil. Thus, a driving force is created which causes the disc to rotate.

The braking magnet provides the braking torque on the disc. By altering the position of this magnet, desired speed can be obtained. The spindle is geared to the recording mechanism so that electrical energy consumed in the circuit is directly registered in kWh.

8.8. MEASUREMENT OF RESISTANCE

8.8.1 CLASSIFICATION OF RESISTANCES.

1. **Low resistance.**

All resistances of the order of 1 ohm and under may be classified as low resistance.

2. **Medium resistance.**

This class includes resistance from 1 upward to about 10,000 ohms.

3. **High resistance.**

Resistance of the order of 100,000 ohms and above are classified as high resistance.

8.8.2 MEASUREMENT OF LOW RESISTANCE.

Following methods are used for the measurement of low resistances.

1. **Ammeter-Voltmeter Method.**

Circuit diagram is shown in Fig. 8.21 Voltmeter can be connected in two ways as shown by dotted lines.

Current through ammeter = Current through unknown resistance + Current through voltmeter

i.e. $$I = I_x + I_v$$

$\Rightarrow$ $$I_x = I - I_v$$

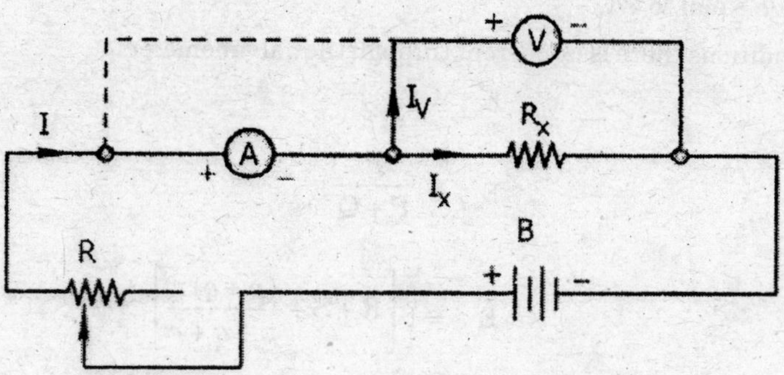

Fig. 8.21 Ammeter-voltmeter Method of measuring low resistance

∴ True value of unknown resistance,

$$R_x = \frac{V}{I_x} = \frac{V}{I - I_v}$$

$$= \frac{V}{1 - \frac{V}{R_v}} = \frac{V/I}{\left(1 - \frac{V}{I R_v}\right)} = \frac{R'}{\left(1 - \frac{R'}{R_v}\right)}$$

where, V = voltage reading

R_v = resistance of voltmeter

I = current read by ammeter

R′ = circuit resistance = $\frac{V}{I}$

Accuracy of this method is limited by the accuracies of voltmeter and ammeter.

2. Kelvin's Double Bridge Method.

It is modification of the Wheatstone bridge and provides increased accuracy. It incorporates the idea of second set of ratio arms, hence the name double bridge and the use of four terminal resistances for the low resistance arms.

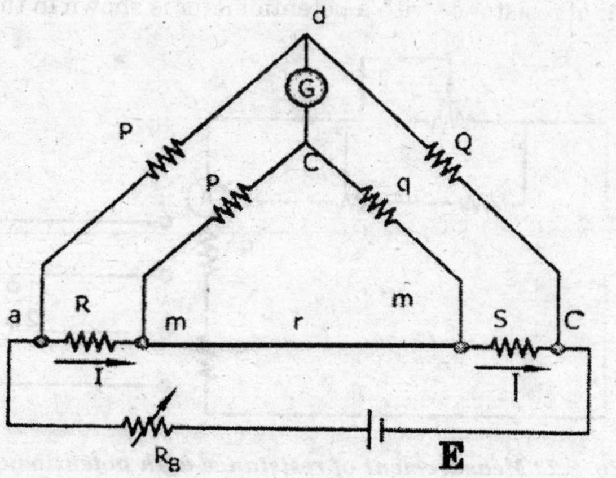

Fig. 8.22.

The circuit diagram is shown in the Fig. 8.22.

Here, R= Unknown resistance

S= Standard resistance of the order of magnitude as R

r= Connecting link of low resistance

P, Q and *p*, *q* are two pairs of known non-inductive resistances and one pair P, *p* or Q, *q* is variable.

The ratio p/q is made equal to P/Q.

Under balanced conditions there is no current through the galvanometer.

i.e. $$E_{ad} = E_{amc}$$

Since $$E_{ad} = \frac{P}{P+Q}E_{ab}$$

and $$E_{ab} = I\left[R + S + \frac{(p+q)r}{p+q+r}\right]$$

and $$E_{amc} = I\left[R + \frac{p}{p+q}\left\{\frac{(p+q)r}{p+q+r}\right\}\right]$$

$$= I\left[R + \frac{pr}{p+q+r}\right]$$

For balanced conditions $$E_{ad} = E_{amc}$$

$$\Rightarrow \quad \frac{P}{P+Q} I\left[R + S + \frac{(p+q)r}{p+q+r}\right] = I\left[R + \frac{pr}{p+q+r}\right]$$

$$\Rightarrow \quad R = \frac{P}{Q}.S + \frac{qr}{p+q+r}\left[\frac{P}{Q} - \frac{p}{q}\right]$$

Now if $$\frac{P}{Q} = \frac{p}{q}$$

then, $$R = \frac{P}{Q}S.$$

3. Potentiometer Method.

The circuit for measurement of resistance with a potentiometer is shown in the Fig. 8.23.

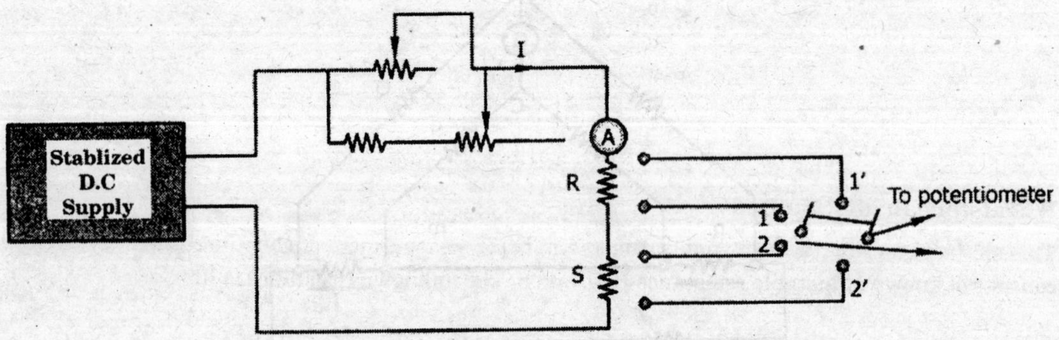

Fig. 8.23 Measurement of resistance with potentiometer

It is based on comparison of one resistance against another. The unknown resistance R, an ammeter A and a variable resistance for limiting current and a standard resistance S are connected in series with a low voltage, high current supply. The current flowing through the circuit is adjusted so that the potential difference across each of the resistor is about 1V. The voltage drop across both the unknown resistor R and standard resistor S are measured by a d.c. potentiometer.

$$\frac{R}{S} = \frac{\text{Potentiometer reading across R}}{\text{Potentiometer reading across S}} = \frac{V_R}{V_S}$$

8.8.3 MEASUREMENT OF MEDIUM RESISTANCE.

1. Ammeter-Voltmeter Method

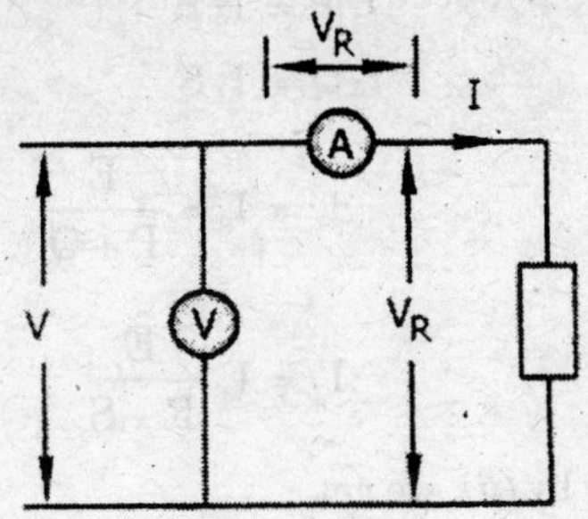

(a)

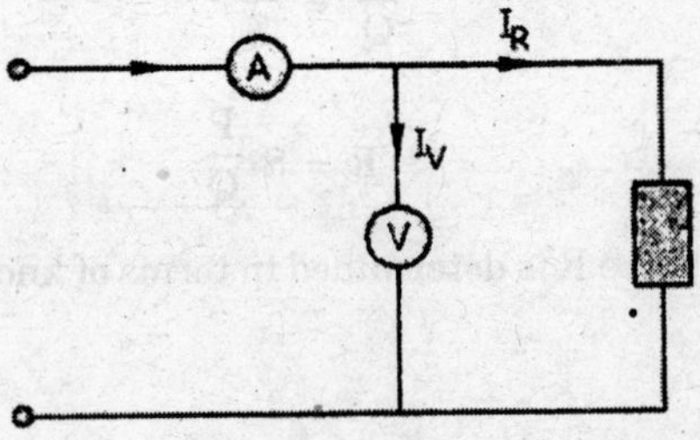

(b)

Fig. 8.24 Ammeter-Voltmeter method

This method is similar to that described for measurement of low resistance.

2. Substitution Method

The circuit diagram is shown in Fig. 8.25. R is the unknown resistance, S is standard variable resistance and *r* is regulating resistance. The switch is put at position 1 and resistance R is connected in the circuit, *r* is adjusted till the ammeter points to the chosen reading.

Now the switch is thrown to position 2 putting the standard variable resistance S in the circuit. The value of S is varied till the same deflection as that for R is obtained in the ammeter. For same value of current, the value of unknown resistance R is equal to the dial settings of resistance S.

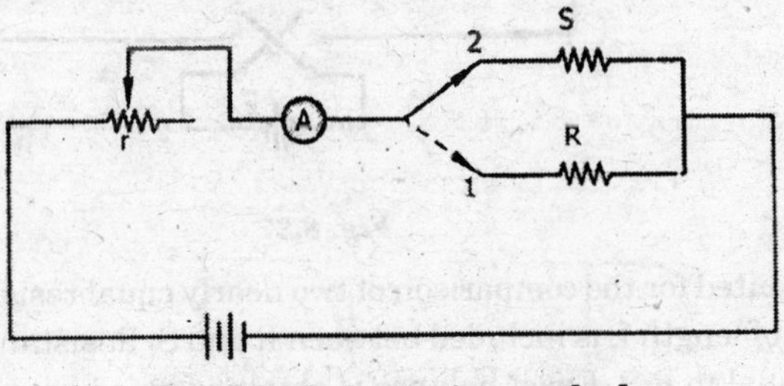

Fig. 8.25 Substitution method

3. Wheatstone Bridge Method

This method is one of the most widely used methods for measurement of medium resistance. As shown in Fig. 8.26, it consists of known adjustable resistance P, Q, and S. The unknown resistance is R.

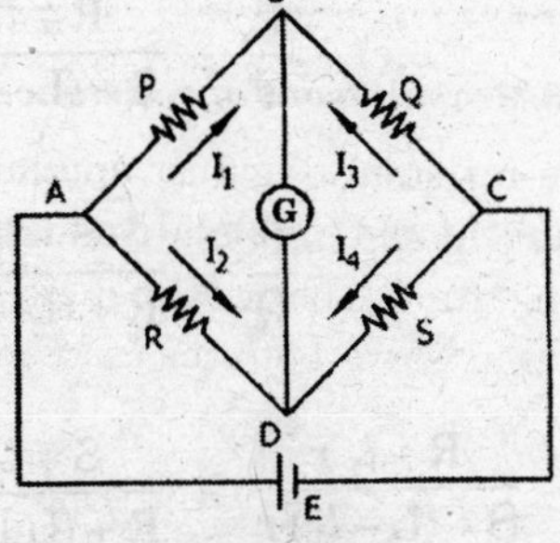

Fig. 8.26

The resistances are arranged to form two parallel circuits. A sensitive galvanometer is bridged across the two circuits between B and D. While balancing the bridge, the values of resistance P, Q and S are so adjusted that

At balance, $$I_1 P = I_2 R \quad \text{... (i)}$$

and $$I_3 Q = I_4 S \quad \text{... (ii)}$$

But $$I_1 = I_3 = \frac{E}{P+Q}$$

$\therefore$ $$I_2 = I_4 \frac{E}{R+S}$$

Dividing equation *(i)* by *(ii)*, we get

$$\frac{P}{Q} = \frac{R}{S}$$

$\Rightarrow$ $$R = S\frac{P}{Q}$$

Thus the value of unknown resistance R is determined in terms of known resistances.

4. Carey-Foster Bridge Method

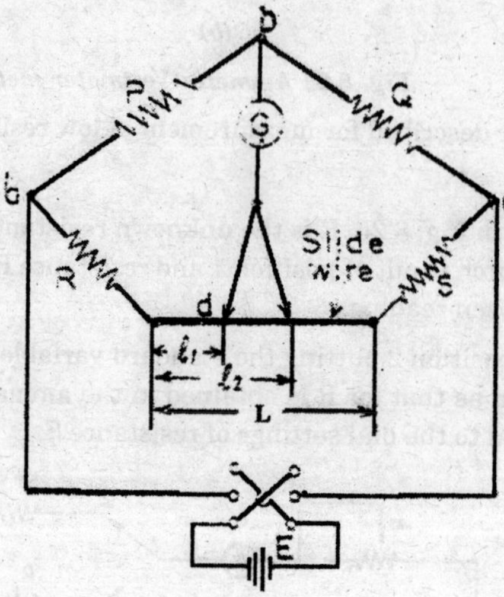

Fig. 8.27

This bridge is specially suited for the comparison of two nearly equal resistances. The circuit arrangement is shown in Fig. 8.27, a slide wire of length L is included between R and S. Resistances P and Q are adjusted so that the ratio P/Q is approximately equal to R/S. Exact balance is obtained by adjustment of the sliding contact on slide-wire.

Let l_1 be the distance of the sliding contact from the left hand end of the slide-wire. The resistance R and S are interchanged and balance is again obtained. Let the distance now is l_2.

Let r = resistance/unit length of slide wire

For first balance, $$\frac{P}{Q} = \frac{R + l_1 r}{S + (L - l_1) r}$$

For second balance, $$\frac{P}{Q} = \frac{S + l_2 r}{R + (L - l_2) r}$$

Comparing, $$\frac{R + l_1 r}{S + (L - l_1) r} = \frac{S + l_2 r}{R + (L - l_2) r}$$

$$\Rightarrow \quad \frac{R + l_1 r}{S + (L - l_1) r} + 1 = \frac{S + l_2 r}{R + (L - l_2) r} + 1$$

$$\Rightarrow \quad \frac{R + l_1 r + S + Lr - l_1 r}{S + (L - l_1) r} = \frac{S + l_2 r + R + Lr - l_2 r}{R + (L - l_2) r}$$

$$\Rightarrow \quad \frac{R + S + L r}{S + (L - l_1) r} = \frac{S + R + L r}{R + (L - l_2) r}$$

$$\Rightarrow \quad S + (L - l_1) r = R + (L - l_2) r$$

$$\Rightarrow \quad S - R = (l_1 - l_2) r$$

$$\therefore \quad R = \frac{S (l_1' - l_2') - S' (l_1 - l_2)}{l_1' - l_2' - l_1 + l_2}$$

where l_1 and l_2 are balanced points when slide wire is calibrated by shunting S with a known resistance and S' is value of S when it is shunted by a known resistance.

8.8.4 MEASUREMENT OF HIGH RESISTANCE.

1. Direct Deflection Method

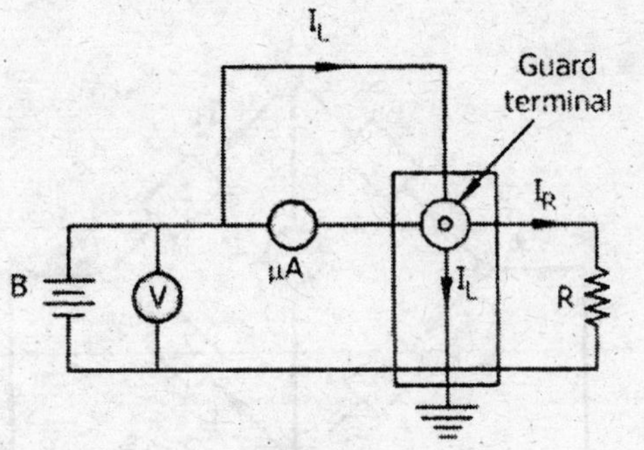

Fig. 8.28

Circuit arrangement is shown in Fig 8.28. A guard terminal surrounding resistance terminal is connected to the battery side and a micro-ammeter. The guard terminal and resistance terminal are almost at the same potential and hence there is no flow of current between them. The leakage current I_L which would otherwise flow through the μ-ammeter, bypasses the μ-ammeter. The μ-ammeter indicates the current I_R only.

The resistance value is determined by the readings of voltmeter and ammeter as,

$$R = \frac{V}{I_R} \Omega$$

2. Megger Method

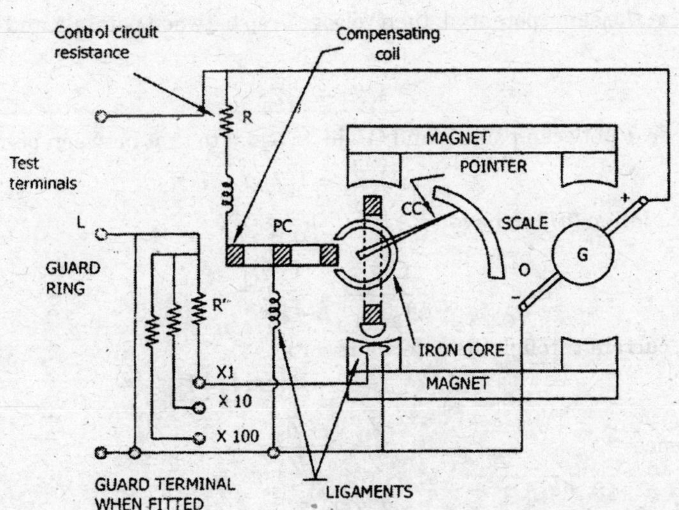

Fig. 8.29

This the most commonly used method for measurement of high resistance. The essential parts of a megger are shown in Fig. 8.29.

It consists of a hand driven d.c. generator and a direct reading ohmmeter. Permanent magnets provided field for both. The moving element consists of three coils, one current coil, potential or pressure coil and compensating coil. The coils are mounted over a rigid shaft and are free to rotate over a C-shaped stationary iron-core. The coils are connected to the circuit by means of flexible leads or ligaments. E and L are the test terminals. The current coil is connected in series with the terminal L. The series resistance R' protects the current coil in case the test terminals are short-circuited and controls the range of the instrument. The pressure coil, in series with a compensating coil and protection resistance R is connected across the generator terminals. Compensating coil is provided for better scale proportions and to make the instrument astatic.

When the current from the generator flows through pressure coil, the coil tends to align itself at right angles to the permanent magnet field. For infinite resistance (*i.e.* test terminals open) no current flows through the current coil and pressure coil governs the motion of the moving element causing it to move its extreme counter-clockwise position, the point under this condition is marked infinite resistance. Current coil produces clockwise torque on moving element. When the terminals L and E are short-circuited, the current flowing through current coil (corresponding to zero external resistance) is large enough to move the pointer to its extreme clockwise position, marked zero. For any resistance connected between L and E, the opposing torque of the coils balance each other so that pointer comes to rest at some intermediate point on the scale.

8.9. BRIDGES

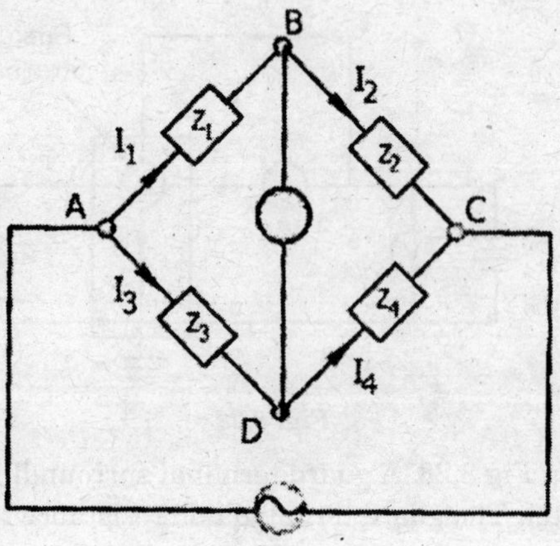

Fig. 8.30

Measurement of inductance and capacitance may be made conveniently and accurately by employing a.c. bridge networks. The a.c. bridge is modified Wheatstone brides. In its basic form, it consists of four arms, a source of excitation and a balance detector. Fig. 8.30 shows an a.c. bridge in its basic form. Each of the four arms is an impedances and the detector is sensitive to small alternating potential differences. The detector could be head-phone, vibration galvanometer or tunable amplifier detector. Let Z_1, Z_2, Z_3 and Z_4 are the four arm impedances.

When points B and D are at the same potential, then voltage drop between points A and B will be equal to voltage drop between points A and D.

So
$$I_1 Z_1 = I_3 Z_3 \qquad \text{... (i)}$$

In this condition voltage drop between point B and C will be equal to that between points D and C also

i.e.
$$I_2 Z_2 = I_4 Z_4 \qquad \text{... (ii)}$$

Dividing equation *(i)* by equation *(ii)*, we have

$$\frac{I_1 Z_1}{I_2 Z_2} = \frac{I_3 Z_3}{I_4 Z_4} \qquad \text{... (iii)}$$

But in balance condition, current through the detector is zero

∴
$$I_1 = I_2 \text{ and } I_3 = I_4$$

Hence equation *(iii)* becomes
$$\frac{Z_1}{Z_2} = \frac{Z_3}{Z_4}$$

⇒
$$Z_1 Z_4 = Z_2 Z_3 \qquad \text{... (iv)}$$

In polar form
$$(Z_1 \angle \theta_1)(Z_4 \angle \theta_4) = (Z_2 \angle \theta_2)(Z_3 \angle \theta_3)$$
$$\Rightarrow \quad Z_1 Z_4 \angle \theta_1 + \theta_4 = Z_2 Z_3 \angle \theta_1 + \theta_3$$

Hence two condition must be satisfied for balancing the bridges :

(*i*) Magnitude of the impedances must satisfy the relationship
$$Z_1 Z_4 = Z_2 Z_3$$

(*ii*) Phase angles of the impedances must satisfy the relationship
$$\angle \theta_1 + \angle \theta_4 = \angle \theta_2 + \angle \theta_3$$

8.9.1 MEASUREMENT OF INDUCTANCE.

1. Maxwell's Bridge

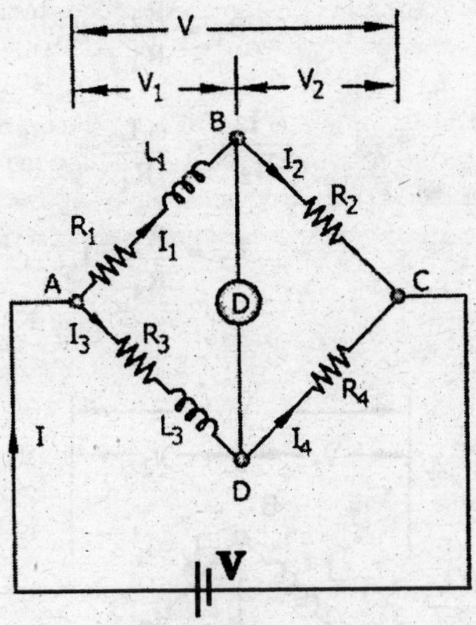

(a) Circuit diagram

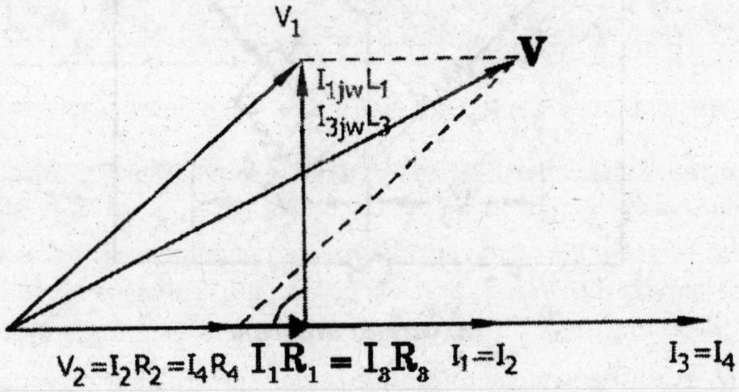

(b) Vector diagram

Fig. 8.31 Maxwell's bridge

When the bridge is balanced, the current flowing through detector D is zero and hence
$$I_1 = I_2$$
and
$$I_3 = I_4$$

p.d. across arm AB= *p.d.* across arm AD = V_1

i.e.
$$I_1 Z_1 = I_3 Z_3 = V_1$$
$$\Rightarrow \quad I_1 (R_1 + j\omega L_1) = I_3 (R_3 + j\omega L_3) = V_1 \qquad \text{... (i)}$$

and *p.d.* across arm BC = *p.d.* across arm CD = V_2
$$I_2 R_2 = I_4 R_4 = V_2$$
$$\Rightarrow \quad I_1 R_2 = I_3 R_4 \qquad \text{... (ii)}$$

Dividing equation (*i*) by (*ii*), we have

$$\frac{R_1 + j\omega L_1}{R_2} = \frac{R_3 + j\omega L_3}{R_4}$$

$$\Rightarrow \quad \frac{R_1}{R_2} + \frac{j\omega L_1}{R_2} = \frac{R_3}{R_4} + \frac{j\omega L_3}{R_4}$$

Equating the real and imaginary parts of both sides, we have

$$\frac{R_1}{R_2} = \frac{R_3}{R_4}$$

$$\Rightarrow \quad R_1 = \frac{R_2}{R_4} \times R_3$$

and

$$\frac{\omega L_1}{R_2} = \frac{\omega L_3}{R_4}$$

$$\Rightarrow \quad L_1 = \frac{R_2}{R_4} \times L_3$$

2. Maxwell-Wein Bridge

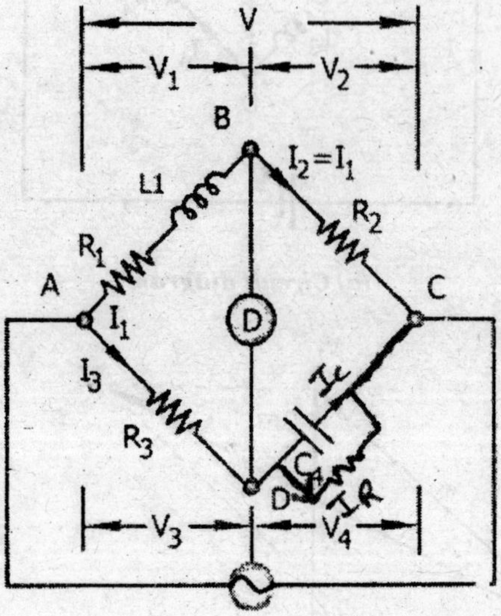

(a) Circuit diagram

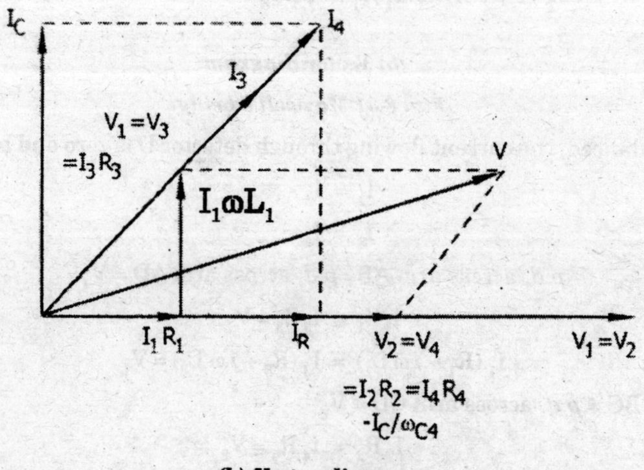

(b) Vector diagram

Fig. 8.32 Maxwell Wein bridge

Here,
$$Z_1 = R_1 + j\omega L_1$$
$$Z_2 = R_2$$
$$Z_3 = R_3$$
$$Z_4 = \frac{1}{\frac{1}{R_4}+\frac{1}{jX_c}} = \frac{1}{\frac{1}{R_4}+j\omega C_4} = \frac{R_4}{1+j\omega C_4 R_4}$$

At balance,
$$Z_1 Z_4 = Z_2 Z_3$$

$$\therefore \quad \frac{(R_1 + j\omega L_1) R_4}{1+j\omega C_4 R_4} = R_2 R_3$$

$$\Rightarrow \quad R_1 R_4 + j\omega L_1 R_4 = R_2 R_3 + j\omega C_4 R_2 R_3 R_4$$

Equating real and imaginary quantities separately, we have
$$R_1 R_4 = R_2 R_3$$
$$\Rightarrow \quad \mathbf{R_1 = \frac{R_2 R_3}{R_4}}$$

and
$$j\omega L_1 R_4 = j\omega C_4 R_4 R_2 R_3$$
$$\Rightarrow \quad \mathbf{L_1 = C_4 R_2 R_3}$$

3. Hay's Bridge

It is a modification of Maxwell's bridge.

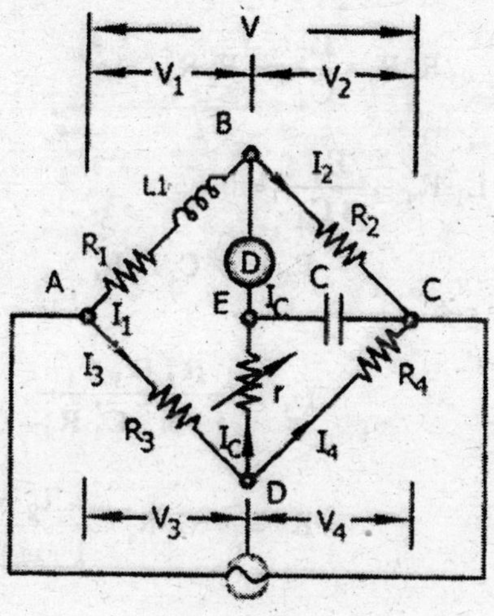

(a) Circuit diagram

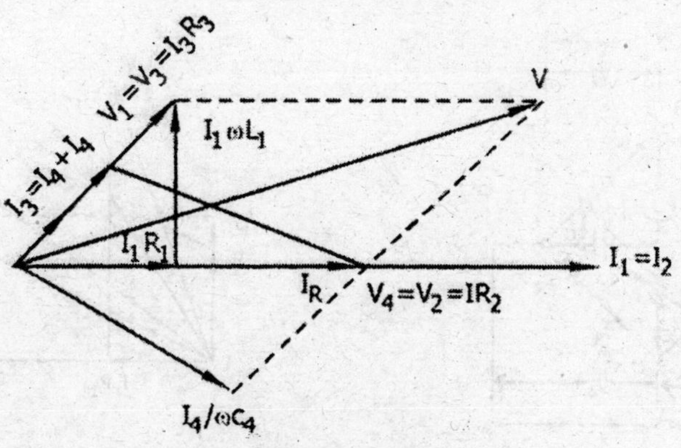

(b) Vector diagram

Fig. 8.33. Hay's bridge

At balance $I_2 = I_1$, and $I_4 = I_3$

$V_1 = V_3$; and $V_2 = V_4$

Since $V_1 = I_1 Z_1 = I_1 (R_1 + j\omega L_1)$

But $V_1 = V_3$

$$\therefore \quad I_1(R_1 + j\omega L_1) = I_3 R_3 \quad ...(i)$$

and since $V_2 = I_2 R_2 = I_1 R_2$

$$V_4 = I_4 Z_4 = I_3 \left(R_4 - \frac{j}{\omega C_4}\right)$$

But $V_2 = V_4$

$$\therefore \quad I_1 R_2 = I_3 \left(R_4 - \frac{j}{\omega C_4}\right) \quad ...(ii)$$

Dividing equation *(i)* by *(ii)*, we have

$$\frac{R_1 + j\omega L_1}{R_2} = \frac{R_3}{\left(R_4 - \frac{j}{\omega C_4}\right)}$$

$$\Rightarrow \quad R_1 R_4 + \frac{L_1}{C_4} + j\left(\omega L_1 R_4 - \frac{R_1}{\omega C_4}\right) = R_2 R_3$$

Separating real and imaginary parts, we have

$$R_1 R_4 + \frac{L_1}{C_4} = R_2 R_3 \quad ...(iii)$$

and $$\omega L_1 R_4 - \frac{R_1}{\omega C_4} = 0$$

$$\Rightarrow \quad R_1 = \omega^2 C_4 L_1 R_4 \quad ...(iv)$$

Solving equations *(iii)* and *(iv)*, we get

$$L_1 = \frac{R_2 R_3 C_4}{1 + \omega^2 C_4^2 R_4^2}$$

and $$R_1 = \omega^2 C_4 R_4 \times \frac{R_2 R_3 C_4}{1 + \omega^2 C_4^2 R_4^2} = \frac{R_2 R_3 R_4 C_4^2 \omega^2}{1 + \omega^2 C_4^2 R_4^2}$$

4. Anderson's Bridge

In this method inductance is measured in terms of a standard capacitor.

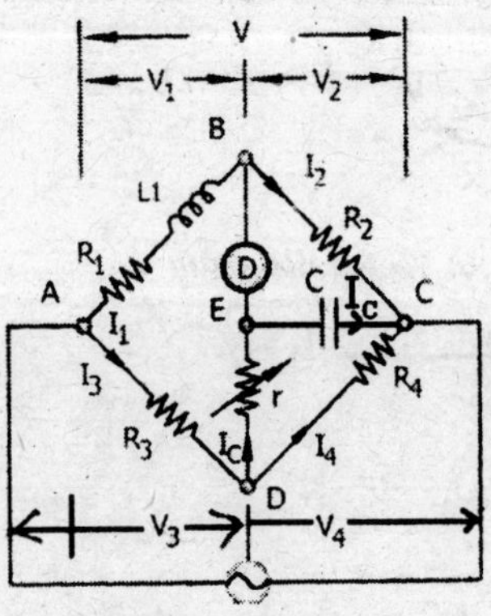

(a) Circuit diagram

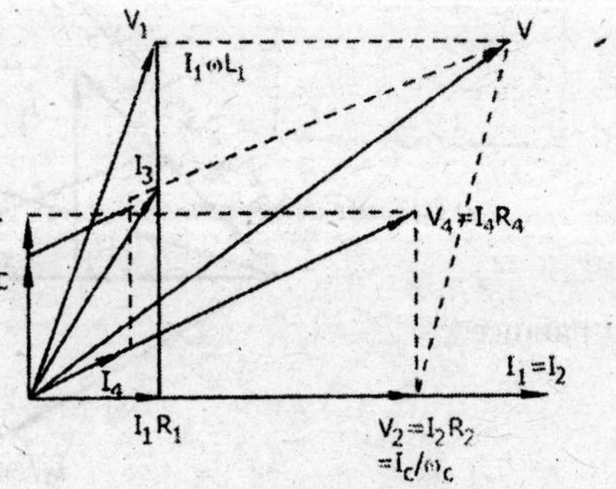

(b) Vector diagram

Fig. 8.34 Anderson's bridge

At balance, $I_1 = I_2$ and $I_3 = I_c + I_4$

Now, $$I_1 Rz_2 = I_c \cdot \frac{1}{j\omega C}$$

$\therefore$ $$I_c = I_1 j\omega C R_2$$

Also, $$I_1 (R_1 + j\omega L_1) = I_3 R_3 + I_c r$$

and $$I_c\left(r + \frac{1}{j\omega C}\right) = (I_3 - I_c) R_4$$

Substituting value of I_c in above equations, we have

$$I_1 (R_1 + j\omega L_1) = I_3 R_3 + jI_1 \omega CR_2 r$$

$\Rightarrow$ $$I_1 (R_1 + j\omega L_1 - j\omega CR_2 r) = I_3 R_3 \quad \ldots (i)$$

And $$j\omega CR_2 I_1\left(r + \frac{1}{j\omega C}\right) = (I_3 - I_1 j\omega CR_2) R_4$$

$\Rightarrow$ $$I_1 (j\omega CR_2 r + R_2 + j\omega CR_2 R_4) = I_3 R_4 \quad \ldots (ii)$$

From equations *(i)* and *(ii)*, we get

$$I_1 (R_1 + j\omega L_1 - j\omega CR_2 r) = I_1\left(\frac{R_2 R_3}{R_4} + \frac{j\omega C R_2 R_3 r}{R_4} + j\omega C R_2 R_3\right)$$

Equating real and imaginary parts, we get

$$\mathbf{R_1 = \frac{R_2 R_3}{R_4};}$$

and $$\mathbf{L_1 = C \frac{R_2}{R_4} [r (R_3 + R_4) + R_3 R_4]}$$

5. Owen's Bridge

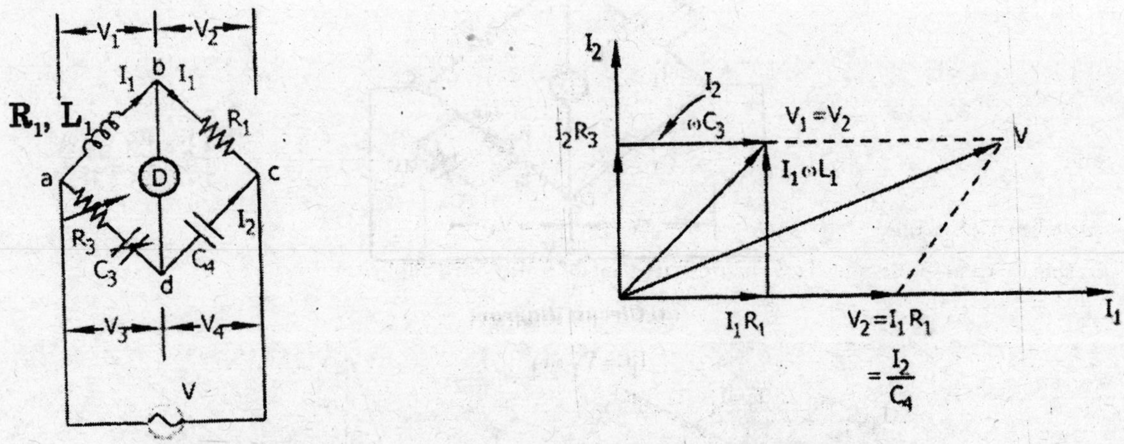

(a) Circuit diagram ***(b) Vector diagram***

Fig. 8.35 Owen's Bridge

At balance,

$$(R_1 + j\omega L_1)\left(\frac{1}{j\omega C_4}\right) = \left(R_3 + \frac{1}{j\omega C_3}\right) R_2$$

Separating real and imaginary parts, we get

$$\mathbf{L_1 = R_2 R_3 C_4;\ \text{and}\ \ R_1 = R_2 \frac{C_4}{C_3}}$$

8.9.2 MEASUREMENT OF CAPACITANCE.

1. De Sauty's Bridge

The bridge is the simplest method of comparing two capacitances.

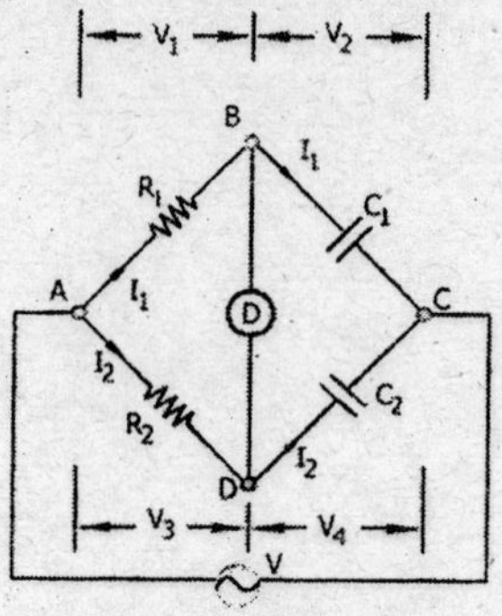

(a) Circuit diagram

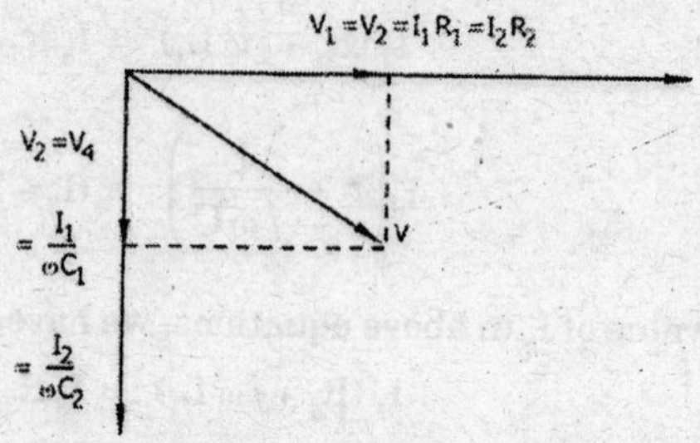

(b) Vector diagram

Fig. 8.36 De Sauty's Bridge

At balance, $$I_1 R_1 = I_2 R_2 \quad \text{... (i)}$$

and $$\frac{-j}{\omega C_1} I_1 = \frac{-j}{\omega C_2} I_2 \quad \text{...... (ii)}$$

Dividing equation *(i)* by *(ii)*, we have

$$\frac{-R_1}{-j/\omega C_1} = \frac{R_2}{-j/\omega C_2}$$

$$\Rightarrow \quad C_1 = C_2 \frac{R_2}{R_1}$$

2. Schering Bridge

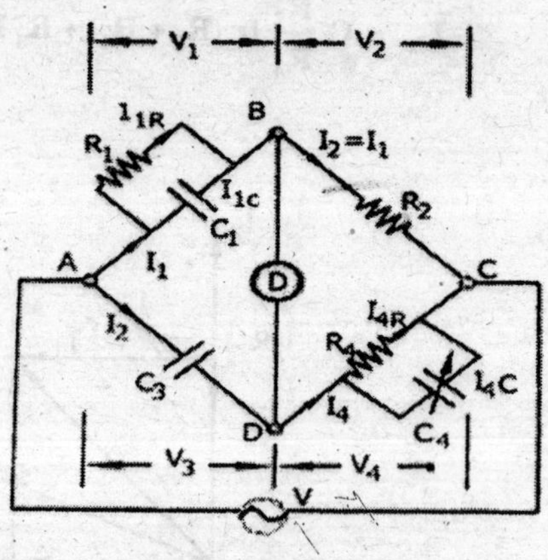

(a) Circuit diagram

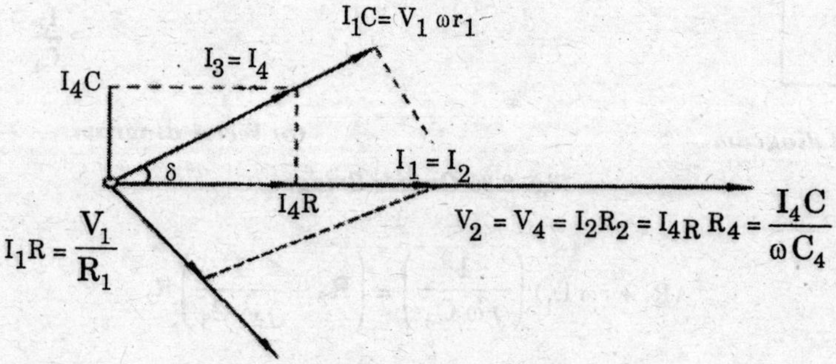

(b) Vector diagram

Fig. 8.37 Schering Bridge

Here,
$$Z_1 = \frac{1}{\frac{1}{R_1} + \frac{1}{-j/\omega C_1}} = \frac{R_1}{1 + j\omega C_1 R_1}$$
$$Z_2 = R_2$$
$$Z_3 = -\frac{j}{\omega C_3}$$
$$Z_4 = \frac{R_4}{1 + j\omega C_4 R_4}$$

At balance,
$$Z_1 Z_4 = Z_2 Z_3$$

Solving, we get
$$\frac{R_1 R_4}{1 + \omega^2 C_1^2 R_1^2} = \frac{C_4 R_4 R_2}{C_3}$$
$$\Rightarrow \quad \frac{R_1}{1 + \omega^2 C_1^2 R_1^2} = \frac{C_4 R_2}{C_3} \quad \text{... (i)}$$

From vector diagram shown in Fig. 8.37 *(b)* for the capacitor C_1 and R_1 to be in parallel
$$\cos\delta = \frac{I_{1C}}{I_1} = \frac{I_{1C}}{\sqrt{(I_{1C})^2 + (I_{1R})^2}} = \frac{V_1 \omega C_1}{\sqrt{V_1^2 \omega^2 C_1^2 + \frac{V_1^2}{R_1^2}}}$$
$$\Rightarrow \quad \cos\delta = \frac{\omega C_1 R_1}{\sqrt{1 + \omega^2 C_1^2 R_1^2}}$$
$$\Rightarrow \quad \cos^2\delta = \frac{\omega^2 C_1^2 R_1^2}{1 + \omega^2 C_1^2 R_1^2}$$

Substituting value of $\cos^2\delta$ in equation *(i)*, we have
$$\frac{\cos^2\delta}{\omega^2 C_1^2 R_1} = \frac{C_4 R_2}{C_3}$$
$$\Rightarrow \quad C_1 = \frac{C_3 \cos^2\delta}{\omega^2 C_1 C_4 R_1 R_2} \quad \text{... (ii)}$$

Again from vector diagram shown in Fig. 8.37 (*b*), for the bridge network under balance conditions
$$\tan\delta = \frac{I_{4C}}{I_{4R}} = \frac{V_4 \omega C_4}{V_4 / R_4} = \omega C_4 R_4$$

and alsotan
$$\delta = \frac{I_{1R}}{I_{1C}} = \frac{V_1 / R_1}{V_1 \omega C_1} = \frac{1}{\omega C_1 R_1}$$
$$\therefore \quad \omega C_4 R_4 = \frac{1}{\omega C_1 R_1}$$
$$\Rightarrow \quad R_4 = \frac{1}{\omega^2 C_1 C_4 R_1} \quad \text{... (iv)}$$

Substituting value of R_1 in equation *(ii)*, we get
$$C_1 = \frac{C_3 R_4 \cos^2\delta}{R_2}$$

where δ is called *loss angle of capacitor* and $\sin\delta$ is called *power factor* of the capacitor.

3. Wein's Bridge

The Wein's bridge is primarily used for measurement of frequency. It's balance equation involves frequency even the performance of individual bridge elements is independent of frequency. It may be employed in harmonic distortion analyzer and audio and HF oscillators.

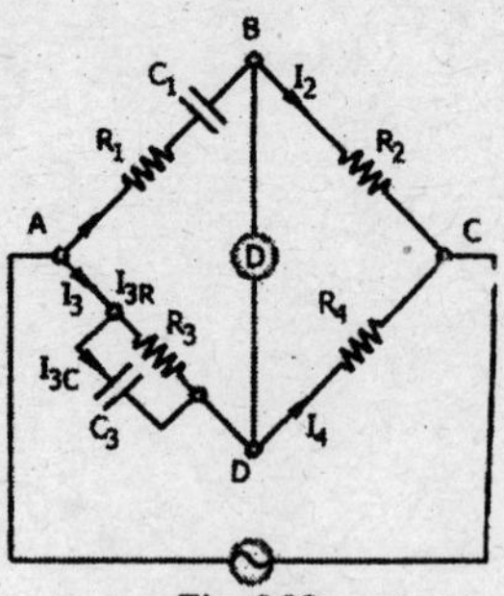

Fig. 8.38

Here,

$$Z_1 = R_1 - \frac{j}{\omega C_1}$$

$$Z_2 = R_2$$

$$Z_3 = \frac{R_3}{1 + j\omega C_3 R_3} \text{ S}$$

$$Z_4 = R_4$$

Under balance conditions of bridge

$$Z_1 Z_4 = Z_2 Z_3$$

$$\left(R_1 - \frac{j}{\omega C_1}\right) R_4 = R_2 \frac{R_3}{1 + j\omega C_3 R_3}$$

$$R_4 \left(R_1 - \frac{j}{\omega C_1}\right) (1 + j\omega C_3 R_3) = R_2 R_3$$

Separating real and imaginary terms we have

$$R_1 R_4 + R_3 R_4 \frac{C_3}{C_1} = R_2 R_3$$

$$\Rightarrow \qquad \frac{C_3}{C_1} = \frac{R_2}{R_4} - \frac{R_1}{R_3}$$

and

$$\frac{-R_4}{\omega C_1} + \omega C_3 R_1 R_3 R_4 = 0$$

$$\Rightarrow \qquad \omega^2 = \frac{1}{R_1 R_3 C_1 C_3}$$

$$\Rightarrow \qquad C_1 = \frac{1}{\omega^2 R_1 R_3 C_3}$$

For measurement of frequency, we can write

$$\omega = \frac{1}{\sqrt{R_1 R_3 C_1 C_3}},$$

and

$$f = \frac{1}{2\pi\sqrt{R_1 R_3 C_1 C_3}} \text{ Hz}$$

8.9.3 MEASUREMENT OF MUTUAL INDUCTANCE.

1. Heaviside's Bridge

This bridge measures mutual inductance in terms of a known self inductance.

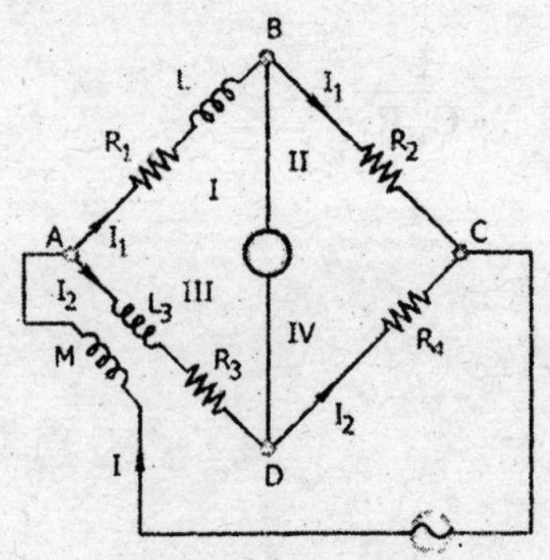

(a) Connection diagram

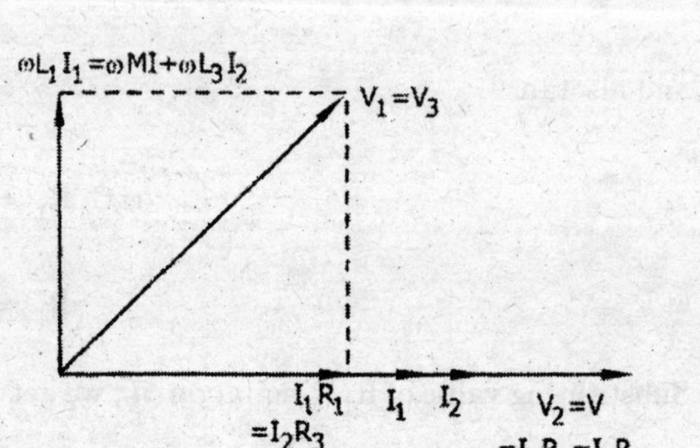

(b) Vector diagram

Fig. 8.39 Heaviside's bridge

At balance, $I_1 R_2 = I_2 R_4$ ... (i)

$$I_1 (R_1 + j\omega L_1) = I_2 (R_3 + j\omega L_3) + j\omega MI$$

But $I = I_1 + I_2$

$$\therefore \quad I_1 (R_1 + j\omega L_1) = I_2 (R_3 + j\omega L_3) + j\omega M (I_1 + I_2)$$

$$\Rightarrow \quad I_1 [R_1 + j\omega (L_1 - M)] = I_2 [R_3 + j\omega (L_3 + M)] \quad \text{... (ii)}$$

Dividing equation *(ii)* by equation *(i)*, we get

$$\frac{R_1 + j\omega (L_1 - M)}{R_2} = \frac{R_3 + j\omega (L_3 + M)}{R_4}$$

Separating real and imaginary quantities, we have

$$R_1 R_4 = R_2 R_3 \quad \text{... (iii)}$$

and

$$\frac{L_1 - M}{R_2} = \frac{L_3 + M}{R_4} \quad \text{... (iv)}$$

$$\Rightarrow \quad L_1 = \frac{(L_3 + M) R_2}{R_4} + M$$

$$\Rightarrow \quad L_1 = \frac{M (R_2 + R_4) + L_3 R_2}{R_4} \quad \text{... (v)}$$

If resistance R_2 and R_4 are equal, then

$$L_1 = L_3 + 2M$$

Thus with a calibrated standard of mutual inductance, the value of a self inductance can be determined by this bridge.

From equation *(iii)*, we get $R_1 = \dfrac{R_2 R_3}{R_4}$

The same bridge can be used for measurement of mutual inductance in terms of a known self inductance. From equation *(v)*, we have

$$(L_1 - M) R_4 = (L_3 + M) R_2$$

$$\Rightarrow \quad L_1 R_4 - MR_4 = L_3 R_2 + MR_2$$

$$\Rightarrow \quad MR_2 + MR_4 = L_1 R_4 - L_3 R_2$$

$$\Rightarrow \quad M = \frac{L_1 R_4 - L_3 R_2}{R_2 + R_4}$$

2. Campbell's Bridge

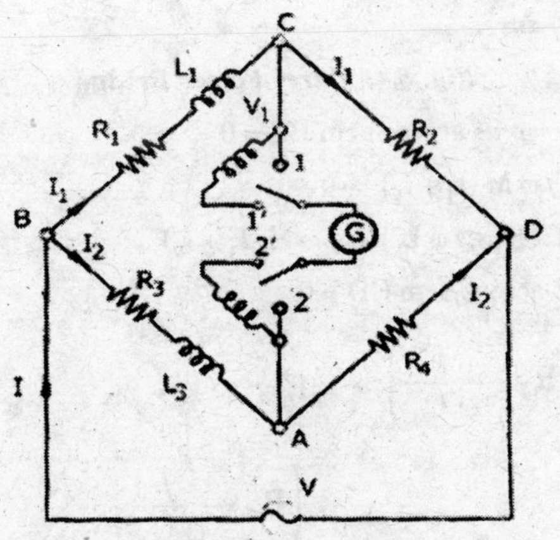

Fig. 8.40 Campbell's bridge

The bridge measures an unknown mutual inductance in terms of a standard mutual inductance.

Here, M_1 = unknown mutual inductance

L_1 = self inductance of secondary of mutual inductance.

M_3 = variable standard mutual inductance

L_3 = self inductance of secondary of mutual inductance

R_1, R_2, R_3, R_4 = non-inductive resistance

There are two steps required in the balancing process:

(i) Detector is connected between 1 and 2. The circuit becomes self-inductance comparison bridge.

At balance,
$$\frac{L_1}{L_3} = \frac{R_1}{R_3} = \frac{R_2}{R_4}$$

Balance is obtained by adjusting R_2 (or R_4) and R_1 (or R_3).

(ii) Detector is connected between 1 and 2.

To get balance mutual inductance M_3 is varied, then
$$\frac{M_1}{M_3} = \frac{R_2}{R_4}$$

$$\Rightarrow \quad M_1 = M_3 \frac{R_2}{R_4}$$

3. Carey-Foster Bridge

The bridge is used for measurement of mutual inductance in terms of a standard capacitance and also for measurement of capacitance in terms of standard mutual inductance.

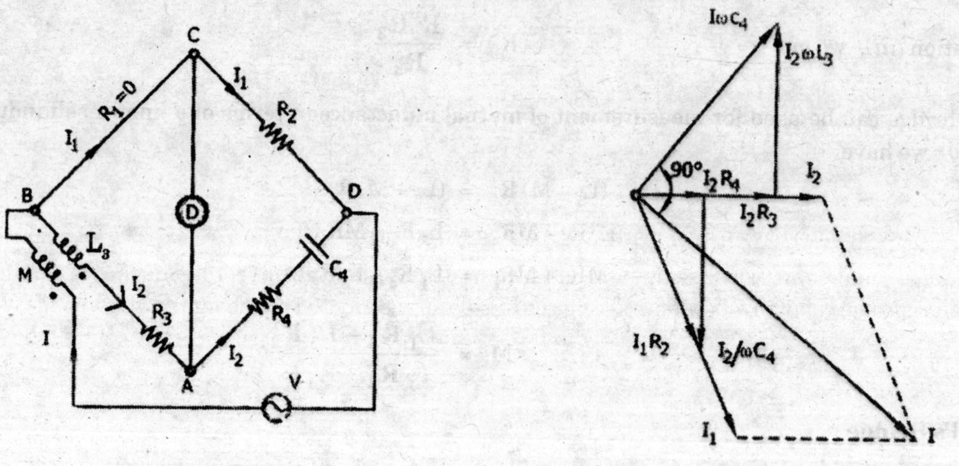

(a) Circuit diagram *(b) Vector diagram*

Fig. 8.41 Carey-Foster Bridge

At balance, *p.d.* across arm AB = *p.d.* across arm BC = 0

$$\therefore \quad I_2[R_3 + j\omega L_3] - j\omega M(I_1 + I_2) = 0$$

$$\Rightarrow \quad I_2[R_3 + j\omega L_3] = j\omega M(I_1 + I_2) \quad \text{...(i)}$$

Also, *p.d.* across arm AD = *p.d.* across arm CD = 0

$$\therefore \quad I_2\left(R_4 - \frac{j}{\omega C_4}\right) = I_1 R_2$$

$$\Rightarrow \quad I_1 = I_2 \frac{\left(R_4 - \frac{j}{\omega C_4}\right)}{R_2}$$

Substituting value of I_1 in equation *(i)* we have

$$I_2 [R_3 + j\omega L_3] = j\omega M \left(I_2 \frac{R_4 - j/\omega C_4}{R_2} + I_2 \right)$$

$$R_3 + j\omega L_3 = j\omega M \left(\frac{R_4 - j/\omega C_4}{R_2} + 1 \right)$$

Separating real and imaginary terms, we have

$$R_3 = \frac{M}{C_4 R_2} \quad \text{or} \quad C_4 = \frac{M}{R_2 R_3}$$

and

$$L_3 = M\left(\frac{R_4}{R_2} + 1\right) \quad \text{or} \quad M = \frac{L_3}{(1 + R_4/R_2)}$$

8.10 INSTRUMENT TRANSFORMERS

These are used in a.c. systems for the measurement of current, voltage, power and energy. These also have a wide application in protection circuits of power system for the operation of various relays.

Advantages of instrument transformers.

(*i*) These enable single range instruments to cover a large current or voltage range.

(*ii*) Power loss is small.

(*iii*) Measuring instruments can be located far from the high voltage circuit by using long loads connecting the instrument transformer to the instrument. Hence the instruments is isolated from high voltages and stray fields providing safety in use to both instrument and the observer.

(*iv*) By using current transformer with a suitably split and hinged core, upon which the secondary windings is wound, the current in a heavy current bus bar is measured without breaking the circuit.

(*v*) Due to inductance of instrument winding being in parallel with the non-inductive shunt, shunt on a.c. does not give a straight line relation between instrument current and by-passed current. On the other hand, in case of C.T., the whole current passes through the primary, a proportional voltage is induced in the secondary which sends a current in direction proportion around the secondary circuit.

Disadvantage of instrument transformers.

These transformers cannot be used for dc measurements.

8.10.1 TYPES OF INSTRUMENT TRANSFORMERS.

These are of two types :

(1) Current (Series) transformer

(2) Potential (Parallel) transformer

1. Current Transformers (C.T.)

As it is seen from Fig. 8.42, the primary winding of a current transformer is connected in series with the load and carries the load current to be measured. It consists of very few turns. The secondary winding consists of more turns and instrument is connected directly across it. The amount of power which the C.T. handles is small. The product of voltage and current on the secondary side of C.T. when it is supplying the instrument with its maximum rated value of current is called *rated burden* and is measured in volt amperes. Its secondary is kept short-circuited always.

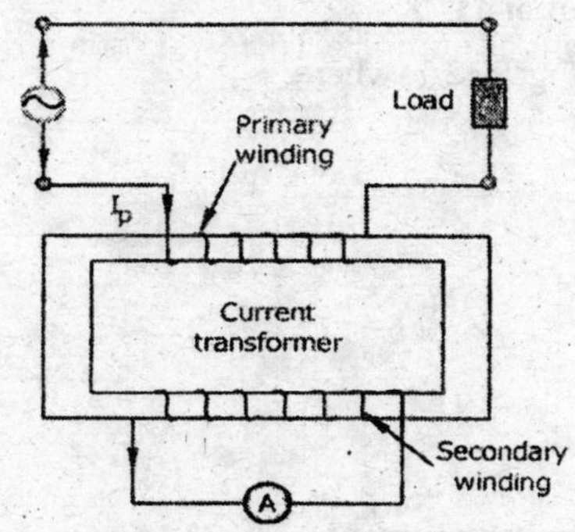

(a) Connection

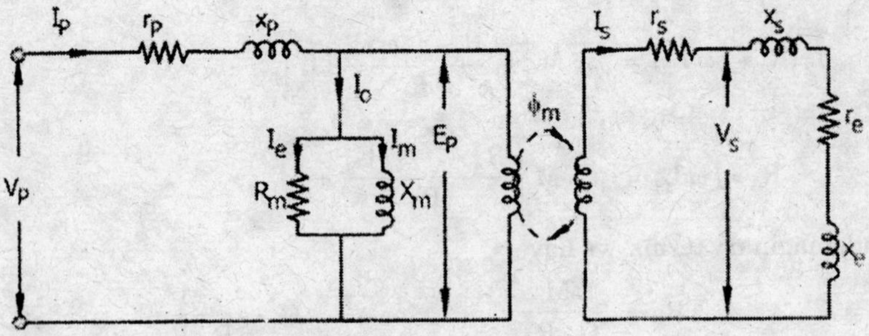

(b) Equivalent circuit

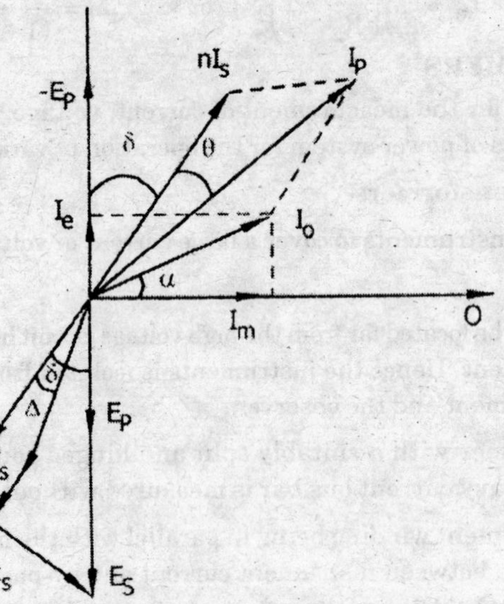

(c) Phasor diagram

Fig. 8.42 Current transformer

Ratios of Current transformers.

Transformation ratio,

$$R = \frac{\text{Primary winding current}}{\text{Secondary winding current}}$$

Nominal ratio,

$$K_n = \frac{\text{Rated primary current}}{\text{Rated secondary current}}$$

Turns ratio, $$n = \frac{\text{Number of turns in secondary}}{\text{Number of turns in primary}}$$

Fig. 8.42 (*b*) gives the equivalent circuit of a C.T.

The phasor diagram can be drawn as in Fig. 8.42 (*c*) where,

E_p = primary induced voltage

E_s = secondary induced voltage

n = turns ratio

I_p = primary current

I_s = secondary current

I_o = exciting current

I_m = magnetising component of exciting current

I_e = loss component of exciting current

ϕ = working flux of C.T.

α = angle between I_0 and ϕ

$$\delta = \tan^{-1}\left(\frac{x_s + x_e}{r_s + r_e}\right) = \text{angle between } E_s \text{ and } I_s$$

$$\Delta = \tan^{-1}\left(\frac{x_e}{r_e}\right) = \text{phase angle of secondary burden}$$

θ = phase angle of transformer

Transformation ratio from the phasor diagram is

$$R \approx \frac{n I_s + I_o \sin(\delta + \alpha)}{I_s}$$

$$\approx \frac{n I_s + I_m \sin\delta + I_e \cos\delta}{I_s} \qquad ...[\because I_o \cos\alpha = I_m \text{ and } I_o \sin\alpha = I_e]$$

Phase angle,

$$\theta \approx \frac{180}{\pi}\left[\frac{I_m \cos\delta - I_e \sin\delta}{n I_s}\right] \text{degree}$$

Types of errors in Current transformer.

***(i)* Ratio error.** It is mainly due to energy component of excitation current.

$$\text{Ratio error} = \frac{\text{Nominal ratio} - \text{Actual ratio}}{\text{Actual ratio}}$$

$$= \frac{K_n - R}{R}$$

***(ii)* Phase angle error.** It is introduced mainly on account of magnetizing component of excitation current.

$$\theta = \frac{180}{\pi}\left(\frac{I_m \cos\delta - I_e \sin\delta}{n I_s}\right) \text{degree}$$

$$\theta = \frac{180}{\pi}\left(\frac{I_m}{I_p}\right) \text{degree } (approx.)$$

Design Features of Current Transformers.

The C.T. is designed with a view to minimize the current ratio and phase angle errors as far as possible. I_m and I_e are kept small by using core of high permeability and low magnetic materials. The core reluctance is reduced by shortening the length of the magnetic path in the core and increasing the area of the magnetic path in the core. The transformer has rectangular or ring shaped core.

The coils are wound close together in order to reduce the secondary leakage reactance. These are separately wound and are insulated by tape and varnish for lower voltages. Also in order to reduce the ratio and phase angle errors we keep the number of exciting ampere turns very small compared with the total primary ampere turns.

2. Potential Transformers

These are used for measurement of high voltages by means of low range voltmeters or for energising the potential coils of wattmeters, energy meters. The primary winding of the transformer is connected across the line carrying the voltage to be measured that the voltage circuit is connected across the secondary winding. Connections of a potential transformer are shown in Fig. 8.43.

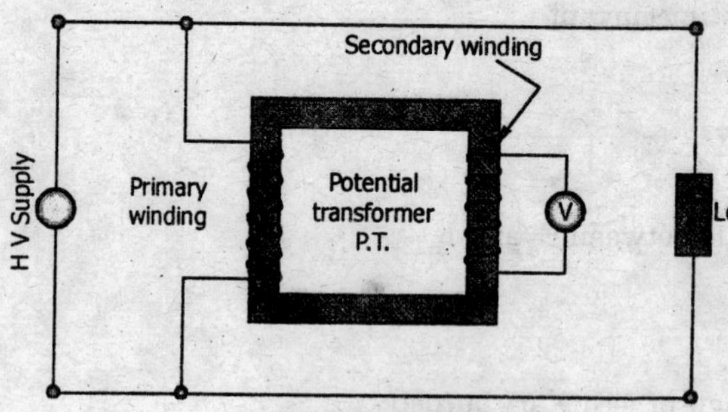

(a) Connection

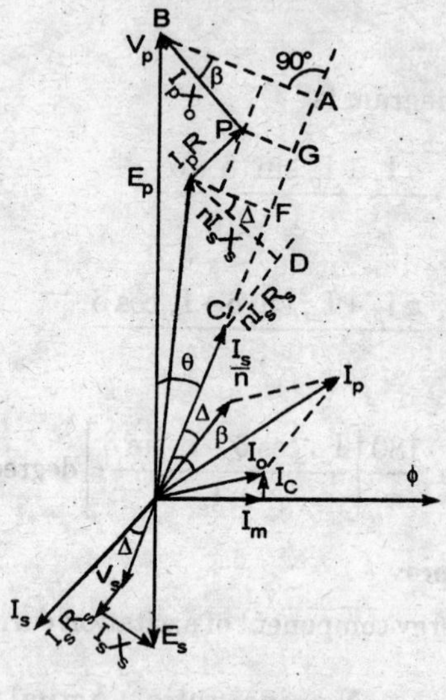

(b) Vector diagram

Fig. 8.43 Potential transformer

Here, θ = angle between V_p and V_s reversed

= phase angle of transformer

β = phase angle between I_p and V_s reversed.

Δ = phase angle of secondary load circuit.

Ratios of Potential transformer.

$$\text{Transformation ratio, } R = \frac{\text{Primary winding voltage}}{\text{Secondary winding voltage}}$$

$$\text{Nominal Ratio, } K_n = \frac{\text{Rated primary voltage}}{\text{Rated secondary voltage}}$$

$$\text{Turns ratio, } n = \frac{\text{Number of turns of primary winding}}{\text{Number of turns of secondary winding}}$$

Transformation ratio from the phasor diagrams,

$$R = \frac{V_p}{V_s} = n + \frac{n\, I_s (R_s \cos\Delta + X_s \sin\Delta) + I_s\, r_p + I_m\, x_p}{V_s}$$

$$\text{Phase angle, } \theta = \frac{I_s}{V_s}(X_s \cos\Delta - R_s \sin\Delta) + \frac{I_e\, x_p - I_m\, r_p}{n\, V_s} \text{ rad}$$

Types of Errors in Potential transformers are

(i) **Ratio error** $= \frac{K_n - R}{R} \cdot 100$

(ii) **Phase angle error,** $\theta = \frac{I_s}{V_s}(X_s \cos\Delta - R_s \sin\Delta) + \frac{I_e\, x_p - I_m\, r_p}{n\, V_s}$

Design Features of Potential Transformers.

The errors introduced by Pontential Transformers are less pronouned than those introduced by current transformers. The ratio error is compensated by increasing the turn on the secondary winding by appropriate small amount. The increased secondary turns compensate the voltage drop in the potential transformers.

Errors of potential transformers are controlled to a large extent by reducing the no load current. The reluctance of the potential transformers core is made small and flux density in the core is kept low. To reduce the core losses, core material of high quality is used. The windings are wound one over the other to reduce leakage to the minimum.

8.11 MAGNETIC MEASUREMENTS

Magnetic measurements are performed to get the knowledge of characteristics of various magnetic materials.

Tests performed on Magnetic materials

1. **Ballistic test.**

   To measure flux, permeability, field strength, plotting of B.H curves and Hysteresis loops.

2. **A.C. test.**

   To know power loss in magnetic materials under the influence of alternating currents.

   Main difficulties in these measurements

   (i) Magnetic flux can not be measured directly.

   (ii) Flux does not confine itself to a definite path.

   (iii) Magnetic materials are not homogenous.

   (iv) Non-uniformity in magnetic properties between different batches of material. When ferro-magnetic materials are subjected to an alternating magnetic field, power loss due to hysteresis effects and eddy currents is present. The hysteresis loss depends upon frequency, maximum flux density of the magnetic field to which the specimen is subjected.

$$P_h = K_h f B_{max}^{1.6}$$

where, P_h = hysteresis loss in watts/cubic meter volume of material

f = frequency of alternating flux in Hz

B_{max} = maximum flux density (wb/m^2)

K_h = hysteresis loss constant for given material

Eddy current loss depends upon wave shape of the variation of flux with time, frequency and maximum flux density of the magnetic field to which the specimen is subjected.

Eddy current loss is given by the expression

$$P_e = K_e K_f^2 f^2 B_{max}^2$$

where P_e = eddy current loss in watts/cubic meter volume of material

K_f = form factor of the alternating flux

K_e = eddy current loss constant for the given material

8.11.1 MEASUREMENT OF MAGNETIC FLUX.

The circuit arrangement for measurement of magnetic flux is shown in Fig. 8.44.

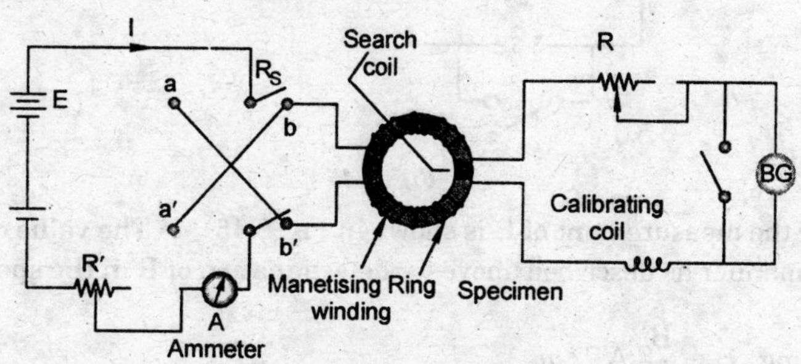

Fig. 8.44 Measurement of flux

A current I is flowing through the magnetizing winding uniformly wound on the ring specimen.

Let ϕ = flux in webers produced by magnetizing current of I amperes, and

t = time of reversal of flux

then rate of change of flux = $\frac{2\phi}{t}$ wb/s

Average emf induced in search coil, $e = \frac{2N\phi}{t}$ volts

where, N = number of turns in search coil

Current through the ballistic galvanometer circuit = $\frac{2N\phi}{Rt}$ amperes

where R = total resistance of galvanometer

Quantity of electricity discharged through galvanometer

$$Q = \frac{2N\phi}{Rt} \times t = \frac{2N\phi}{R} \text{ Coulombs}$$

Also, quantity of electricity discharged through galvanometer, $Q = K\theta_1$

where K = Ballistic galvanometer constant

θ_1 = first deflection of galvanometer

When primary current is reversed, then $\frac{2N\phi}{R} = K\theta_1$

$$\therefore \quad \phi = \frac{RK\theta_1}{2N} \text{ webers}$$

Also, Magnetic flux density, $B = \frac{\phi}{A_s} = \frac{RK\theta_1}{2NA_s}$

where, A_s = cross-sectional area of the specimen.

8.11.2 MEASUREMENT OF MAGNETISING FORCE (H).

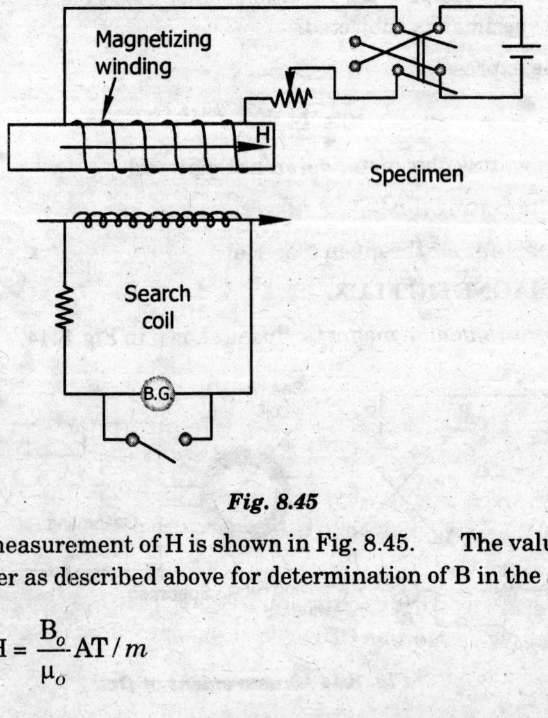

Fig. 8.45

The circuit diagram for the measurement of H is shown in Fig. 8.45. The value of flux density B_o in search coil is measured in a similar manner as described above for determination of B in the specimen.

Now H is calculated using, $H = \frac{B_o}{\mu_o}$ AT/m

8.11.3 DETERMINATION OF B-H CURVE.

B-H curve is obtained by step-by-step method in which there is no reversal of magnetising current.

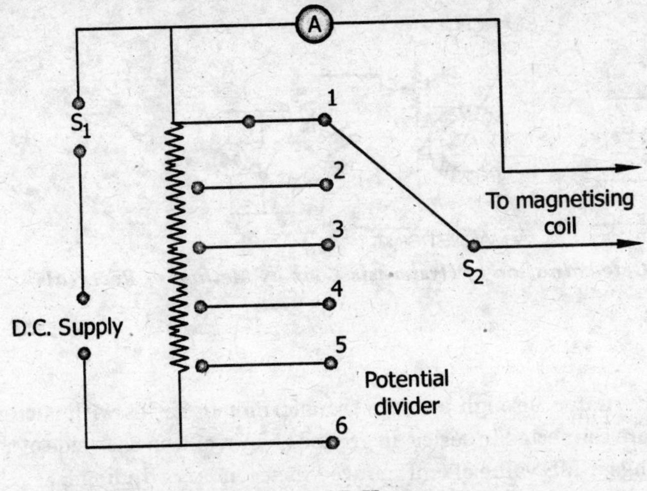

Fig. 8.46 Determination of B-H curve

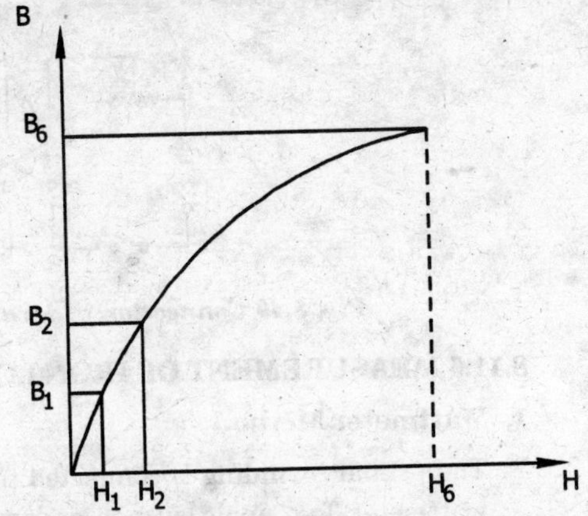

Fig. 8.47 B-H curve

The circuit arrangement for the method is shown in Fig. 8.46. The direct current is supplied to the magnetising coil through a potential divider having a number of tapings which are so arranged that the value of magnetising current I and so magnetising force H is increased to desired maximum value in number of steps. Ring specimen with search coil and magnetising winding is first subjected to demagnetisation and the potential divider is set on position 1 and switch S_1 is closed. The galvanometer throw is observed. The value of flux density B_1 and magnetising force H_1 corresponding to position 1 of potential divider is found. Similarly the magnetising force is then increased to H_2 by suddenly changing the position of switch S_2 from position 1 to 2 and corresponding increase in flux density is determined from the galvanometer throw. Process is repeated for other values of H to maximum point and complete. B-H curve is obtained as shown in Fig. 8.47.

8.11.4 DETERMINATION OF HYSTERESIS LOOP.

The galvanometer is connected to the circuit by the key K and reversing switch RS_2 is placed on contacts aa'. Value of B_{max} is found corresponding to magnetising force H_{max} from the deflection of the galvanometer observed on reversing switch RS_2 and point A on the hysteresis loop is found. The switch S_2 is put to contact 2 in order to connect a resistance R_4 across the magnetising winding and to reduce the magnetising force to H_K. The corresponding reduction in flux density is obtained from the galvanometer throw and point K is found.

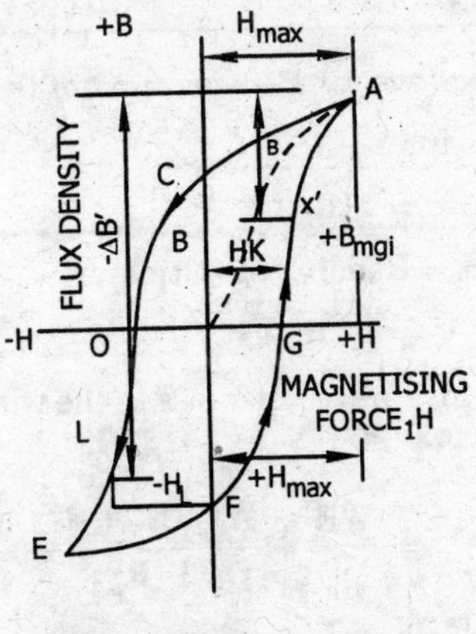

Fig. 8.48 Hysteresis Loop

The galvanometer is then short-circuited by closing key K and reversing switch RS_2 is put to contacts bb'. Switch S_2 is moved to off position and the reversing switch RS_2 is moved back to contacts aa'. The specimen is brought back to point A gain.

Section AC of loop is obtained by adjusting the shunting resistance R_4 to give different reduced value of H and finding corresponding reduction in B. For section CDE of loop, galvanometer is short circuited, S_2 is put in off position and RS_2

to contacts aa'. Again the switch S_2 is put on to contacts 1, key K is opened and RS_2 to bb'. Corresponding galvanometer throw is noted. Specimen magnetisation is brought back to A by key K opening switch S_2 and RS_2 to aa'.

Rest of the portion of loop is obtained as two halves of the loops are identical.

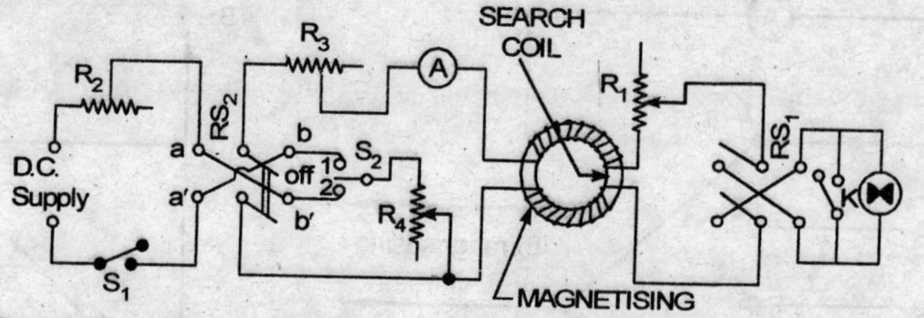

Fig. 8.49 Connection diagram for Determination of Hysteresis Loop by Method of Reversals

8.11.5 MEASUREMENT OF IRON LOSSES.

1. Wattmeter Method

The primary winding is connected to an alternator through an auto transformer in series with current coil of wattmeter. Two single layer secondary coils are connected in series, in groups of four, one on each side of the core to give two exactly similar and separate windings. RMS value of emf induced in secondary winding S_2

$$E = 4\,K_f B_{max}\,A f N_2 \text{ volts}$$

where K_f = maximum flux density in wb/m^2

A = cross sectional area in m^2

f = supply frequency in Hz

N_2 = number of turns on secondary winding

Hence $$B_{max} = \frac{E}{4\,K_f\,A\,f\,N_2}\;wb/m^2$$

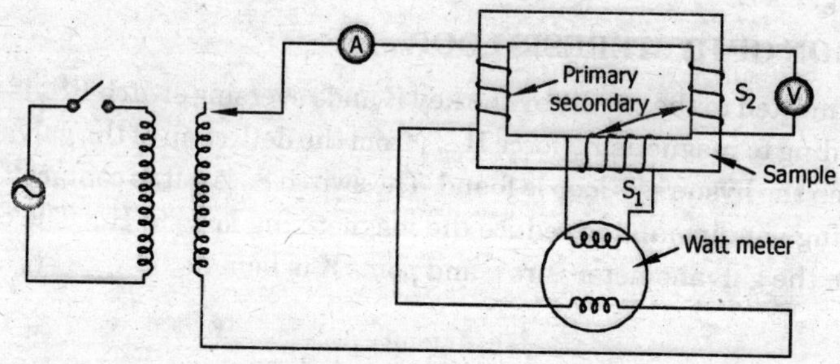

Fig. 8.50 Connections for Measurement of Iron Loss (Wattmeter Method)

Voltage applied to the pressure coil circuit,

$$V = I_p R_p$$

Induced emf in secondary winding S_2 = Reading of voltmeter

$$V = I_p (R_p + R_s)$$

Total power loss in the iron, i.e. iron loss and copper loss in the winding of the secondary as well as in the pressure coil

$$= \frac{WE}{V} = \frac{WI_p (R_p + R_s)}{I_p R_p} = \frac{W (R_p + R_s)}{R_p} = W\left(1 + \frac{R_p}{R_s}\right)$$

Total copper loss in both R_p and R_s

$$= I_p^2 (R_p + R_s) = \frac{E^2}{R_p + R_s}$$

$$\therefore \quad \text{Iron loss, } P_i = W\left(1 + \frac{R_s}{R_p}\right) - \frac{E^2}{R_p + R_s}$$

This method is not sufficient sensitive for testing laminated core material at low flux densities.

2. A.C. Potentiometer Method

The primary winding (N_1 turns) on the specimen is supplied from sinusoidal voltages alternator. A standard resistance SR is connected in series with the primary winding.

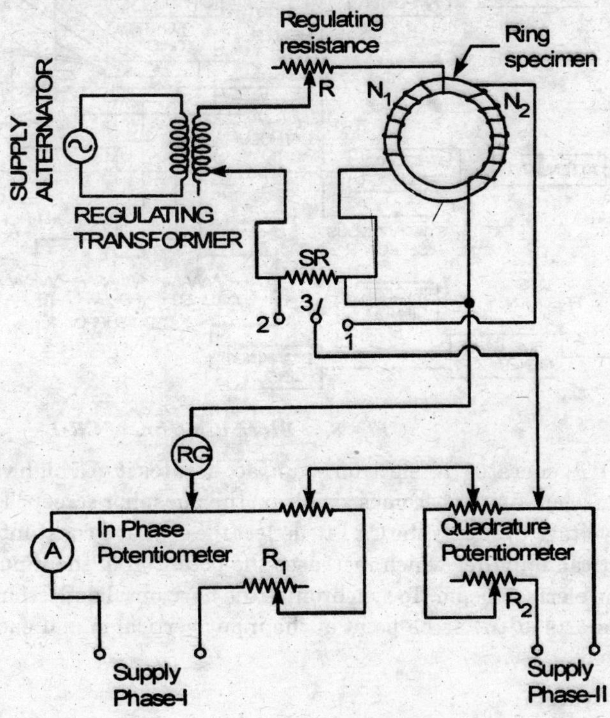

Fig. 8.51 AC Potentiometer Method of Measurement of Iron Loss

$$B_{max} = \frac{E}{4 K_f A f N_2} = \frac{E}{4.44 A f N_2} \quad \text{...(since } K_f = 1.11\text{)}$$

where E = rms value of emf induced in the secondary winding

A = area of cross section of specimen

f = supply frequency

K_f = form factor

The switch S is kept to position 1. The quadrature potentiometer is set at zero in-phase potentiometer is adjusted for zero deflection in vibration galvanometer. The setting of in-phase potentiometer gives E directly. Switch is now put to position 2 and both potentiometers are adjusted for zero deflection.

Value of $I_e R_s$ is given by in-phase potentiometer and $I_m R_s$ by quadrature potentiometer.

8.12 CATHODE RAY OSCILLOSCOPE (CRO)

It is a very useful and versatile laboratory instrument used for display, measurement analysis of waveforms and other phenomena in electrical and electronic circuits. It displays an input signal versus another signal or time.

Various parts of a CRO are shown in the block diagram in Fig. 8.52

1. Cathode Ray Tube (CRT)
2. Vertical Amplifier
3. Time base
4. Horizontal Amplifier
5. Trigger circuit
6. Power supplies

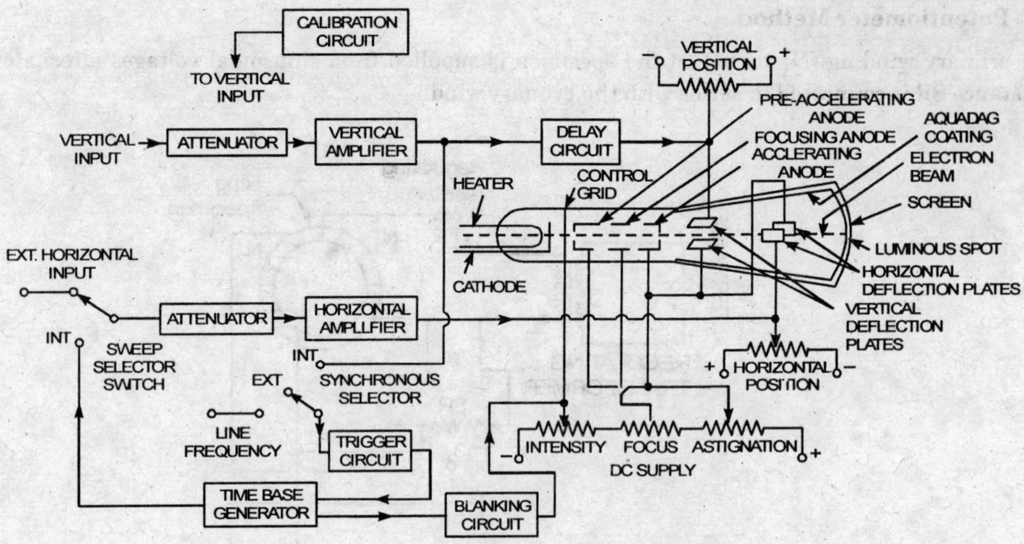

Fig. 8.52 Block diagram of CRO

In an oscilloscope, a CRT generates the electron beam, accelerates it to a high velocity, deflects the beam to create the image and the electron beam finally becomes visible on the phosphor screen. The oscilloscope has a time base which generates the correct voltage to supply the CRT to deflect the spot at a constant time dependent rate. The signal to be viewed is fed to a vertical amplifier which increases the potential of the input signal to a level that will provide a usable deflection of the electron beam. To synchronize the horizontal deflection with the vertical input such that the horizontal deflection starts at the same point of the input vertical signal each time it sweeps, a synchronizing or triggering circuit is used.

Vertical Deflection System

It provides an amplified signal of the proper level to drive the vertical deflection plates without introducing any appreciable distortion into the system. The attenuater sets the sensitivity of the oscilloscope.

Horizontal Deflection System

It consists of a time base generator, a trigger circuit and a horizontal amplifier. The time base generator controls the rate at which the beam is scanned across the face of the CRT and is adjusted from the front panel. The trigger circuit ensures that the horizontal sweep starts at the same point of the vertical input signal. The horizontal amplifier is similar to the vertical amplifier to increase the amplitude to the signal generated in the sweep generator to the level required by the horizontal deflection plates of the CRT.

Vertical Delay Line.

All electronic circuitry in the oscilloscope (attenuators, amplifiers, pulse shapers, generators etc.) causes a certain amount of time delay in the transmission of signal voltages to the deflection plates. The horizontal signal is initiated by the portion of the output signal applied to the vertical CRT plates. Signal processing in the horizontal channel consists of generating and shaping a trigger pulse that starts the sweep generator, whose output is fed to horizontal amplifier and then to the horizontal deflection plates. This whole process takes time of the order of 80 ns or so. Hence to allow the operator to observe the leading edge of the signal wave form, the signal drive for the vertical CRT plates must be delayed by atleast the same amount of time. The signal voltage to the CRT plates is delayed by some time and horizontal sweep is started prior to the vertical deflection.

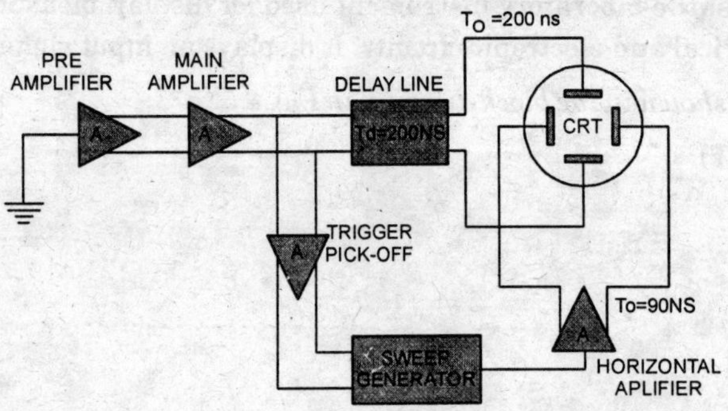

Fig. 8.53 Delay of Vertical Signal allows the horizontal sweep to start prior to vertical deflection

8.12.1 VARIOUS CONTROLS OF CRO.

In order to facilitate the proper functioning of CRO, following controls are provided on the front panel of CRO.

1. **Intensity Control**

   It regulates the bias on the control grid and affects the electron beam intensity. If the negative bias on the grid is increased, the intensity of electron beam is decreased thus reducing the brightness of the spot.

2. **Focus Control**

   It regulates the positive potential on the focusing anode. If the positive potential on this anode is increased, the electron beam becomes quite narrow and the spot on the screen is a pin point.

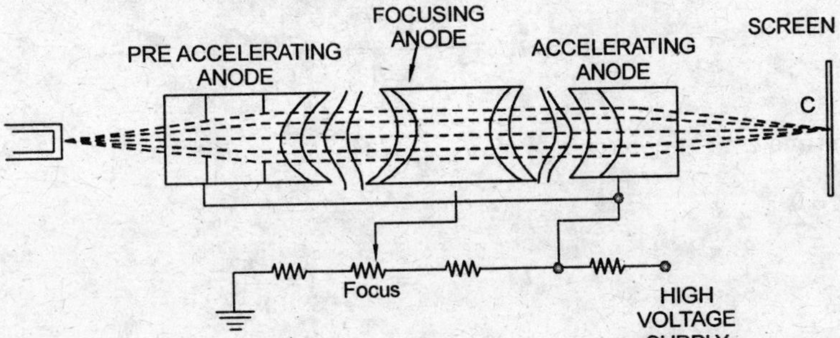

Fig 8.54 Electrostatic Focusing System of a CRT

3. **Horizontal Position Control**

   It regulates the amplitude of d.c. potential which is applied to the horizontal deflection plates, in addition to the usual saw tooth wave. By adjusting this control, the spot can be moved to right or left as required.

4. **Vertical Position Control**

   It regulates the amplitude of d.c. potential which is applied to the vertical deflection plates addition to the signal. By adjusting this control, the image can be moved up or down as required.

8.12.2 DEFLECTION OF MOVING ELECTRONS IN CRO TUBE.

Force on the electron in a uniform electric field of intensity E is

$$F = QE = -eE = ma$$

Hence

$$a = \frac{F}{m} = -\frac{eE}{m}\, m/s^2$$

where a = acceleration of electron, in m/s^2

F = force on electron in Newtons

m = mass of electron in Kg

As shown in the Fig. 8.55, an electron entering the field in the positive X direction with an initial velocity v_{ox} will experience a force. As the field acts along the Y axis only, there will be no force along Z or X axis. The acceleration of the electron along these axes will be zero. Zero acceleration means constant velocity and since the electron enters the field in the positive X direction, with an initial velocity V_{ox}, it will continue to travel along X axis at this velocity.

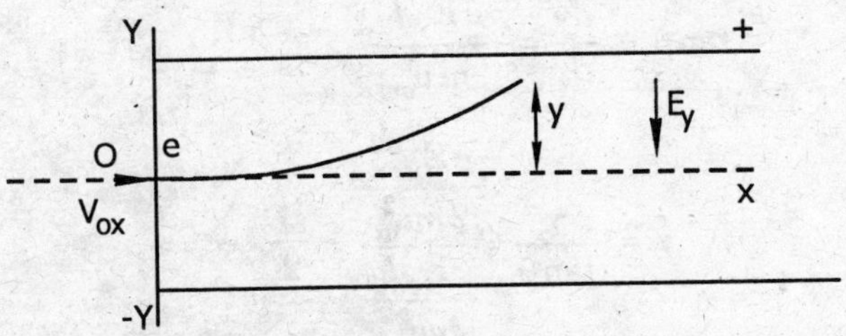

Fig. 8.55 Path of moving electron in a uniform electric field

Hence in y direction, $F = m\,a_y$

$$\Rightarrow \quad a_y = \frac{F}{m} = -\frac{eE_y}{m}$$

Since $v = v_0 + at$

and $$x = x_0 + v_0 t + \frac{1}{2}at^2$$

Putting initial conditions, $$v_y = a_y\,t = -\frac{e\,E_y\,t}{m}$$

$$\therefore \quad y = \frac{1}{2}a_y t = -\frac{e\,E_y\,t^2}{2\,m}$$

Distance travelled in time t, $$x = x_o + v_{ox}\,t + \frac{1}{2}a_x\,t^2$$

Since $x_0 = 0$ and $a_x = 0$

$$\therefore \quad x = v_{ox}\,t \quad \Rightarrow \quad t = \frac{x}{v_{ox}}$$

Hence vertical deflection as a function of horizontal distance travelled by electron

$$y = \left[\frac{-e\,E_y}{2\,v_{ox}^2\,m}\right]x^2 \text{ meters}$$

Hence path of an electron, travelling through an electric field of constant intensity and entering the field at right angles to the lines of force is parabola.

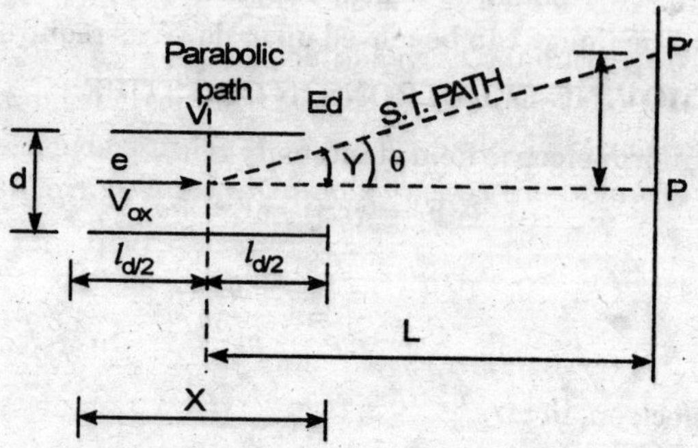

Fig. 8.56 Deflection of Cathode Ray Beam

Now we consider two parallel deflection plates at a distance d and connected to a source of potential difference V_d. Hence

$$E = \frac{V_d}{d}\ \text{V/m}$$

Slope of the parabola at a distance $X = l_d$ is defined as

$$\tan\theta = \frac{dy}{dx} = -\frac{e\,E_y\,l_d}{m\,v_{ox}^2}$$

$$x = \frac{y}{\tan\theta} = \frac{\dfrac{e\,E_y\,l_d^2}{2\,mv_{ox}^2}}{\dfrac{e\,E_y\,l_d}{mv_{ox}^2}} = \frac{l_d}{2}$$

Deflection on the screen, $D = L\tan\theta = L\dfrac{e\,E_y\,l_d}{m\,v_{ox}^2}$

Kinetic energy of electron entering the deflection plates is

$$\frac{1}{2} m v_{ox}^2 = e V_a$$

$$\Rightarrow \quad v_{0x}^2 = \frac{2 e V_a}{m}$$

$$\therefore \quad D = \frac{L e E_y l_d}{m v_{ox}^2} = \frac{L l_d}{2 V_a} \cdot \frac{V_d}{d}$$

where, V_d = deflection voltage in volts

V_a = accelerating voltages in volts

Deflection sensitivity S is defined as the deflection on the screen (in meters) per volt of deflection voltage.

$$S = \frac{D}{V_d} = \frac{L l_d}{2 d V_a} \quad (m/V)$$

$$\text{Deflection factor, } G = \frac{1}{S} = \frac{2 d V_a}{L l_d} \text{ V/m}$$

8.12.3 APPLICATION OF CRO.

1. Examination of Waveforms

(*i*) Spot deflection for a Sinusoidal Voltage applied to the Horizontal Deflection Plates

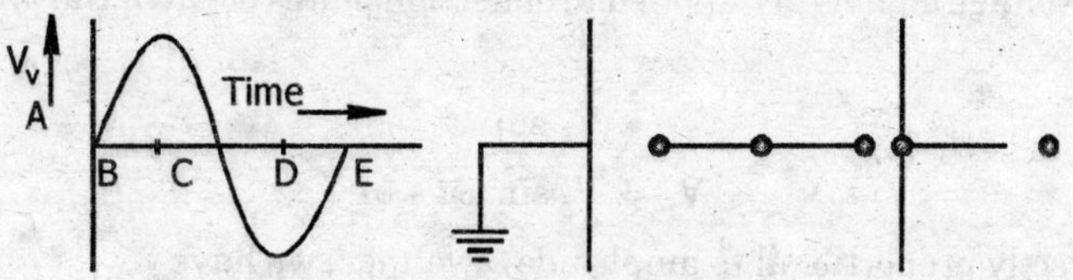

Fig. 8.57

(*ii*) Spot deflection for a Sinusoidal Voltage applied to the Vertical Deflection Plates

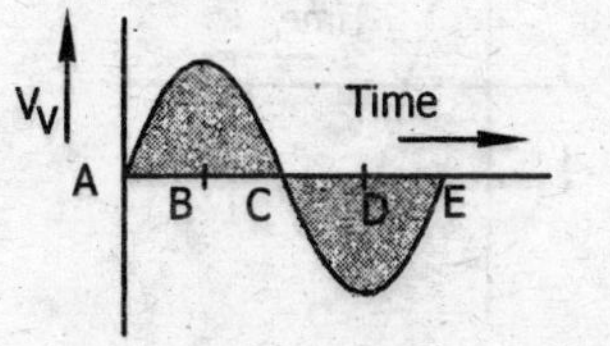

Fig. 8.58

(*iii*) Two sinusoidal voltage signals equal in magnitude and frequency and in phase applied to both horizontal and vertical deflection plates.

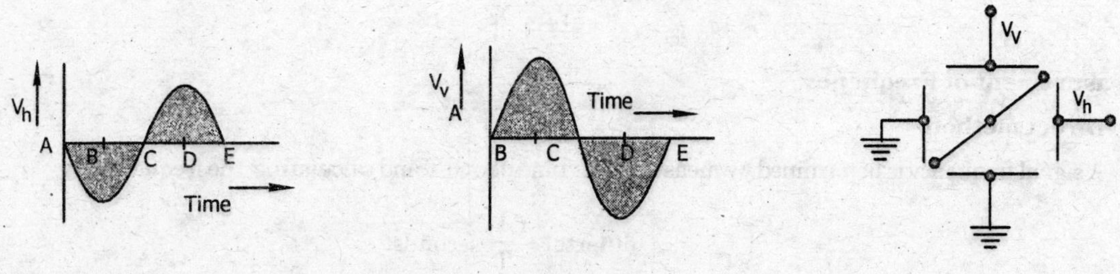

Fig. 8.59 Deflection of Sinusoidal Voltages 180° out of phase

(*iv*) Two sinusoidal signals equal in magnitude and frequency but opposite in phase applied to both horizontal and vertical deflection plates.

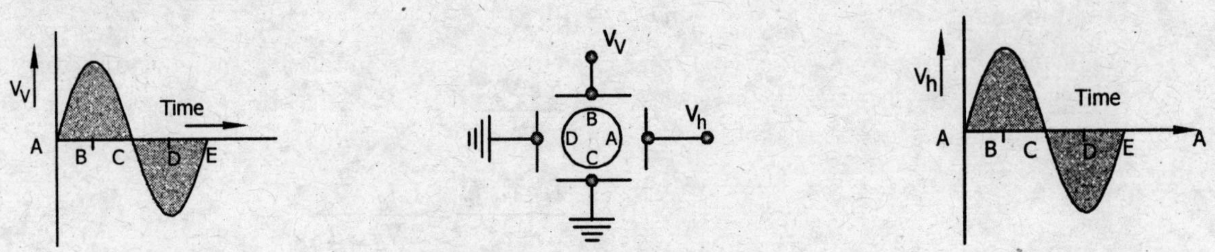

Fig. 8.60 Deflection for Sinusoidal Voltages in phase

(*v*) Two sinusoidal signals of equal amplitude and frequency but 90° out of phase are applied to both horizontal and vertical deflection plates.

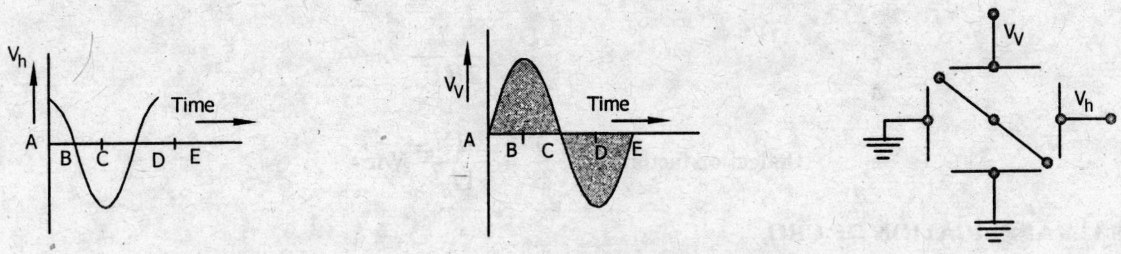

Fig. 8.61 Deflection for Sinusoidal Voltages having 90° phase difference

2. Measurement of Phase Difference

When two sinusoidal voltage signals are applied to deflection plates of CRO, the phase difference (ϕ) is determined as follows.

$$V_h = V_h \sin \omega t$$
$$V_v = V_v \sin(\omega t + \phi)$$

Since deflection is directly proportional to amplitude of voltage, we have

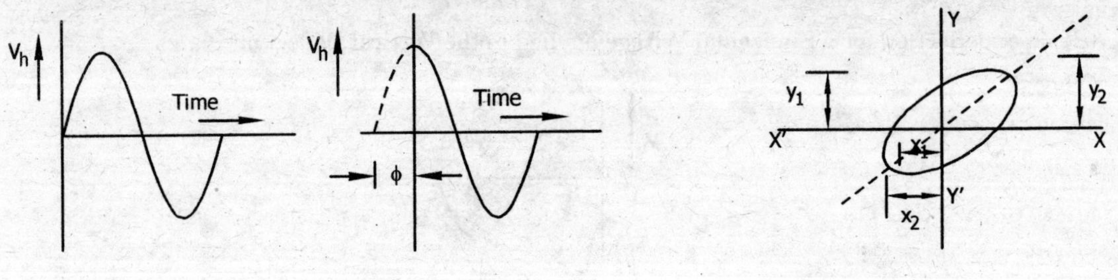

(a) Input waveforms *(b) Output on CRO (Lissajous Pattern)*

Fig. 8.62

$$\sin \phi = \frac{Y_1}{Y_2} = \frac{X_1}{X_2}$$

3. Measurement of Frequency

(*i*) Direct method.

A signal frequency is determined by measuring its time period T and calculating the frequency by

$$f\,(\text{hertz}) = \frac{1}{T} \text{ seconds.}$$

The input waveform is fed into the vertical input, with vertical sensitivity sweep speed and triggering controls are adjusted for at least one complete stable cycle of waveform.

The number of horizontal divisions for a complete cycle is determined and the time period is found by

T = (number of horizontal division of one cycle) × (sweep speed in s/division)

(*ii*) Lissajous method.

Frequency of a signal can be accurately measured by Lissajous patterns. The signal of unknown frequency is applied to Y-plates. The signal of known frequency is applied to X-plates. Depending on the frequency ratio, patterns (circle or ellipses) are obtained.

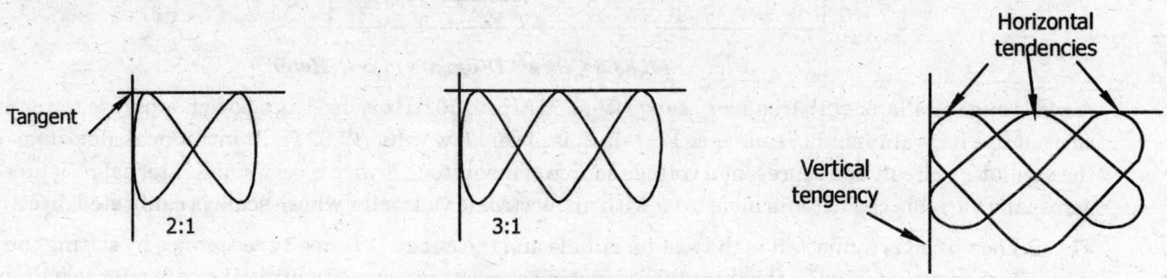

Fig. 8.63 Some Lissajous patterns

For all the cases of patterns obtained, the ratios of the two frequencies is

$$\frac{f_y}{f_x} = \frac{\text{Number of horizontal tangencies}}{\text{Number of vertical tangencies}}$$

where, f_y = frequency of signal applied to Y-plates

and f_x = frequency of signal applied to X-plates

For open Lissajous patterns, free end is treated as 1/2 tangency.

4. Measurement of Voltage/Current of any Electrical Signal

It is done, since the electrostatic beam is directly proportional to the deflection plate voltage. The spot is centred on the screen without applying any voltage signal to the deflection plates. The voltage is applied between a pair of deflection plates and deflection of the spot is observed on the screen. The magnitude of the deflection multiplied by the deflection factor gives the value of voltage applied. In case of an alternating voltage of sinusoidal waveform, the length of straight line is measured. Knowing the deflection sensitivity, peak to peak value of applied a.c. voltage can he found. The rms value of a.c. voltage applied will be equal to this peak to peak divided by $2\sqrt{2}$ for sinusoidal waveform.

The current is measured by passing through a non-inductive resistance and the voltage drop is measured by CRO.

8.13 Q-METER

It is used to measure the Q-factor of the coil and some electrical properties of coil and capacitors. The principal of the Q meter is based on series resonance.

At resonance, $X_L = X_C$; $E_C = IX_C$; $E_L = IX_L$; $E = IR$

where E = applied voltage

I = circuit current

E_C = voltage across capacitor

X_C = capacitive reactance

X_L = inductive reactance

R = coil resistance

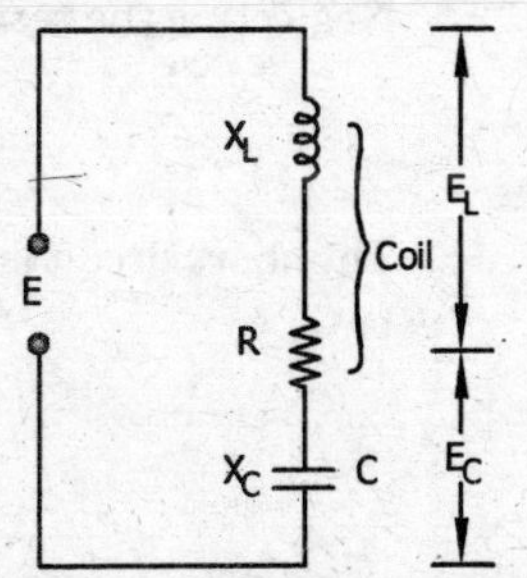

Fig. 8.64

Hence $Q = \frac{X_L}{R} = \frac{X_C}{R} = \frac{E_C}{E}$

Hence if a fixed voltage is applied to a circuit, a voltmeter across a capacitor can be calibrated to read Q directly. If E is kept constant, the voltage across the capacitor can be measured by voltmeter calibrated to read directly in terms of Q.

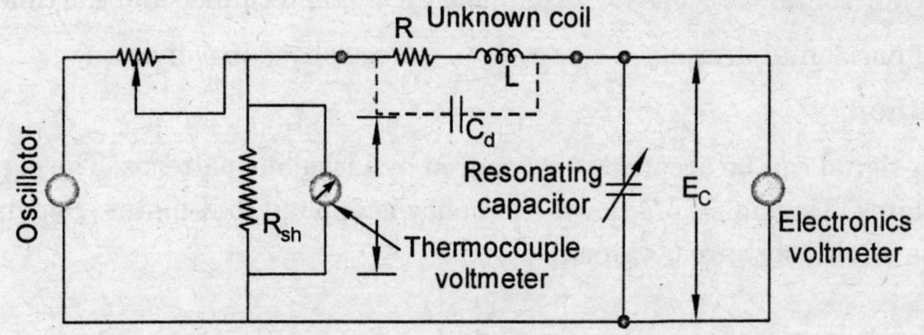

Fig. 8.65 Circuit Diagram of a Q-Meter

A wide range oscillator with frequency range from 50 kHz to 50MHz is used as a power supply to the circuit. It delivers current to a low value shunt resistance R_{sh} which is of very low value. (0.02 Ω). It introduces almost no resistance into the oscillatory circuit and represent a voltage source of magnitude E with a very small internal resistance. The voltage across the variable capacitor is measured with an electronic voltmeter whose scale is calibrated directly in Q values.

The unknown coil is connected to the test terminals and the circuit is tuned to resonance by setting the oscillator to a given frequency and varying the internal resonating capacitor or by presenting the capacitor to a desired value and adjusting the frequency of the oscillator.

The resonance output voltage E corresponding to $E_C = Q \cdot E$.

Since E is known, electronic voltmeter is calibrated to read Q directly.

The inductance of coil is calculated from the known values of frequency (f) resonating capacitance C.

Since, $X_L = X_C$, therefore $L = \dfrac{1}{(2\pi f)^2 C}$ Henry

Measurement of Low impedance components

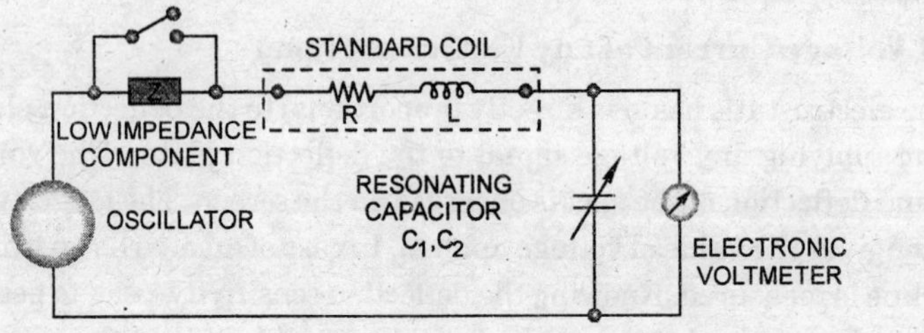

Fig. 8.66 Measurement of Q-factor of low impedance component

The circuit arrangement for the measurement is shown Fig. 8.66. Z is the low impedance component to be measured. Firstly the unknown impedance is short circuited and circuit is resonated which is the reference condition.

$$X_{C_1} = X_L$$

or

$$\frac{1}{\omega C_1} = \omega L$$

Neglecting the resistance of measuring circuit

$$Q_1 = \frac{\omega L}{R} = \frac{1}{\omega C_1 R}$$

The short circuit is now removed and circuit is now returned giving a new value of C_2 and a change in Q value from Q_1 to Q_2.

$$X_s = X_{C_1} - X_L, \; X_s = \frac{1}{\omega C_2} - \frac{1}{\omega C_1}$$

$$\Rightarrow \quad X_s = \frac{C_1 - C_2}{\omega C_1 C_2}$$

If $C_1 > C_2$, X_s is inductive and if $C_1 < C_2$, X_s is capacitive.

Also

$$R_s = \frac{C_1 Q_1 - C_2 Q_2}{\omega C_1 C_2 Q_1 Q_2}$$

If Z is purely resistive, $C_1 = C_2$

$$R_s = \frac{Q_1 - Q_2}{\omega C_1 Q_1 Q_2}$$

If Z is a small inductor,

$$L_s = \frac{C_1 - C_2}{\omega^2 C_1 C_2}$$

$$Q_s = \frac{X_s}{R_s} = \frac{(C_1 - C_2) Q_1 Q_2}{C_1 Q_1 - C_2 Q_2}$$

If Z is a large capacitor,

$$C_s = \frac{C_1 C_2}{C_2 - C_1}$$

Measurement of High Impedance Component

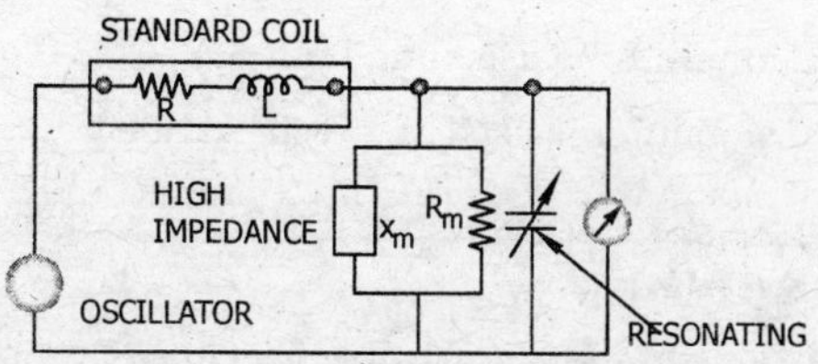

Fig. 8.67 Measurement of Q-factor of high impedance component

These are measured by connecting them in parallel with the measuring circuit. At initial resonance condition, when unknown impedance is not yet connected into the circuit, the standard coil is tuned by the capacitor C_1.

Hence $\omega L = \frac{1}{\omega C_1}$, and $Q_1 = \frac{\omega L}{R} = \frac{1}{\omega C_1 R}$.

Now the unknown impedance is connected into the circuit and capacitor tuned for resonance

$$X_L = \frac{X_{C_2} X_P}{X_{C_2} + X_P}, \quad X_P = \frac{1}{\omega (C_1 - C_2)}$$

If unknown impedance is inductor, $X_P = \omega L_P$

$$\therefore \quad L_P = \frac{1}{\omega^2 (C_1 - C_2)}$$

If unknown impedance is capacitor, $X_P = \frac{1}{\omega C_P}$

$$\therefore \quad C_P = C_1 - C_2$$

Total resistance of the circuit,

$$R_T = Q_2 X_L = Q_2 X_{C_1} = \frac{Q_2}{\omega C_1}$$

8.14 ANALOG AND DIGITAL VOLTMETERS

8.14.1 ANALOG ELECTRONIC VOLTMETER.

These voltmeters use a moving coil meter in which the torque acting on the movement is proportional to the average current flowing through it.

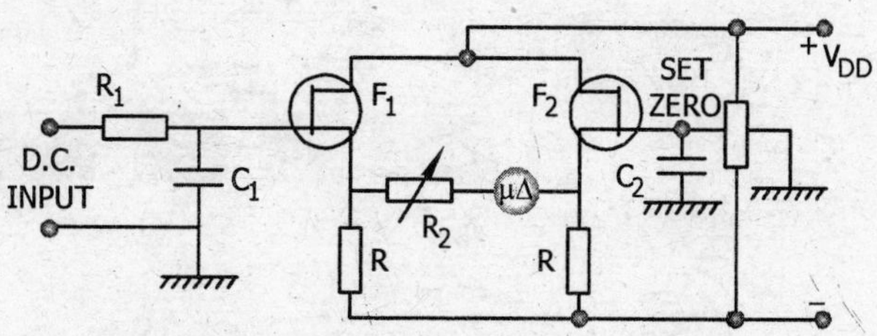

Fig. 8.68 Diagram of d.c. electronic voltmeter

A circuit of d.c. electronic voltmeter using FETs is shown in Fig. 8.68. It is bridge circuit with the two FET's forming one half of the bridge and source resistor R forming the other half. The moving coil meter is coupled between the two source resistor R. The circuit R_1 C_1 acts as an attenuator to a.c. signal if any, superimposed on d.c. voltage. The bridge is balanced by set zero control which changes the bias applied to F_2. The capacitor C_2 decouples the gate of F_2 to earth.

If the gate of F_1 is raised to a positive potential, the potential of the source is raised by a similar amount and current flows through the meter from F_1 to F_2. A variable resistor R_2 in series with meter is used for calibration.

Sensitivity of this instrument = $\frac{g_m}{2}$

where, g_m = mutual conductance of FET

For example, if g_m is 4 mA/V, then sensitivity of the instrument is 2 m A/V.

For measuring a.c. quantities the instruments are rectifier amplifier or amplifier rectifier type.

Note:

- *In rectifier amplifier type*, a d.c. amplifier is used and both A.C. or D.C quantities can be measured.
- *In amplifier rectifier type*, an a.c. amplifier is used and rectification takes place at the output. Only A.C. quantities are measured.

8.14.2 DIGITAL VOLTMETERS (DVM).

These display the value of a.c. or d.c. voltages being measured directly as discrete numerals in the decimal number system. Here analog to digital conversion is used. The voltage is changed to a proportional time interval and it starts and stops a clock oscillator. The oscillator output is applied to an electronic counter.

Types of DVMs

1. Continuous Balance Type DVM.

Initially, the counter is set to zero at the beginning

of the measuring process. Afterwards the counter holds a succession of numbers. These are converted into a analog signal V_2 by the digital to analog converter. The output is compared with input signal

in an electronic comparator.

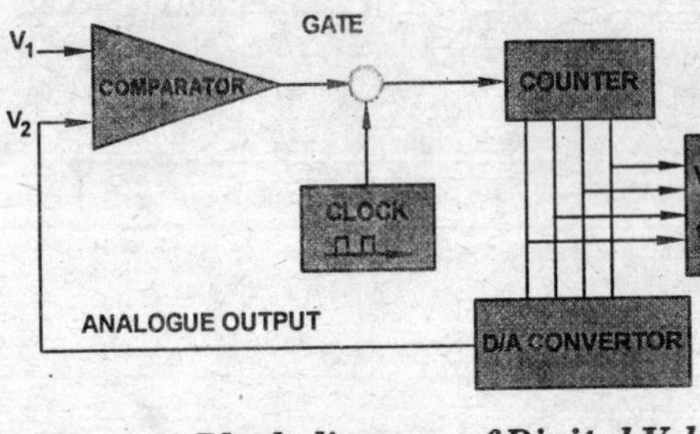

Fig. 8.69 Block diagram of Digital Voltmeter

If $V_1 > V_2$, output from comparator is highest. The electronic gate is open and clock pulses are allowed to be fed into the counter. The number stored in the counter increases as it counts clock pulses.

If $V_2 = V_1$, output comparator suddenly falls to zero, closing circuit.

2. Ramp Type DVM.

The operating principle of a ramp type DVM is to measure the time that a linear ramp voltage takes to change from level of input voltage to zero voltage (or vice versa). This interval is measured with an electronic time interval counter and the count is displayed as a number of digits on electronic indicating tubes of the output read out of the voltmeter.

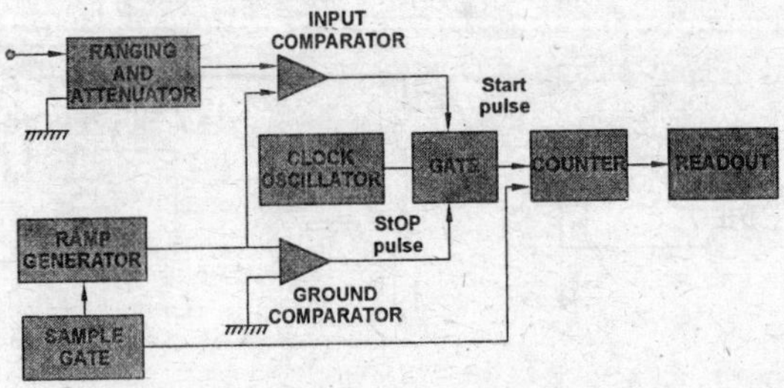

Fig. 8.70 Block diagram of a Ramp DVM

At the start of measurement a ramp voltage is initiated. The ramp voltage value is continuously compared with the unknown voltage. At the instant, the value of ramp voltage is equal to that of unknown voltage, a coincidence circuit called an input comparator, generates a pulse which opens a gate. The ramp voltage continues to decrease till it reaches ground level. At this instant another comparator called ground comparator generates a pulse and close the gate. During this time interval the pulses passing through the gate are counted and displayed.

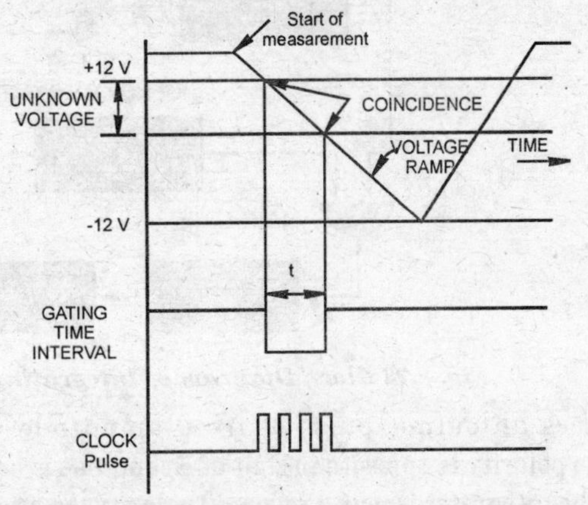

Fig. 8.71 Timing diagram showing voltage to time conversion

3. Successive Approximation Type DVM.

The essential difference between the continuous balance DVM and the successive approximation DVM lies in the sequence of test voltages used to balance the voltmeter.

Let we were to try the sequence 8, 4, 2, 1. The first clock pulse in the successive approximation type sets the counter to 8. This is compared with V_1, and since $V_1 > V_2$, the comparator allows the count to continue in the 'up' direction. The next clock pulse adds another 4 to the count, which now becomes 12, this is compared with V_1, and the count continues is the 'up' direction. The next clock pulse adds 2 to the count stored in the counter, making it 14. The comparator must then instruct the counter to count 'down' by the previous count, reducing the number in the counter to 12 again. The comparator now recognized that $V_2 > V_1$, and the counter then counts 'up' by the next sample number which is unity, making the stored number equal to 13. At this point, after five steps, the DVM balances. Clearly, the successive-approximation DVM is potentially far more rapid in operation than the more simple continuous balance DVM, but only at an increase in complexity and capital cost.

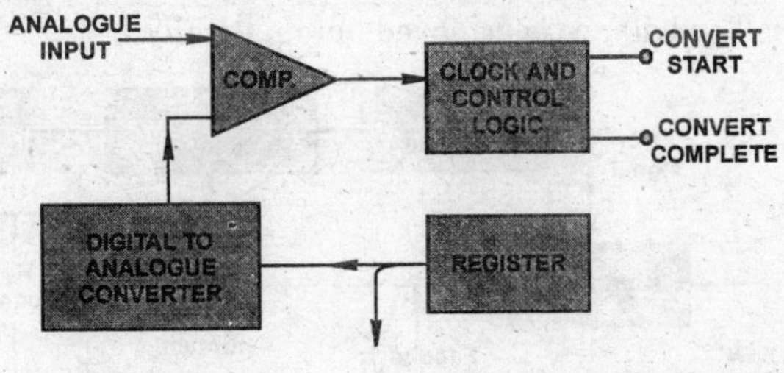

Fig. 8.72 Successive approximation type DVM

4. Integrating Type DVM.

It measure the true average value of the input voltage over a fixed measuring period. Here voltage to frequency conversion is used. The voltage-frequency conversion function as a feed back control system which controls the rate of pulse generation in proportion to the magnitude of the input pulse.

A train of pulse whose frequency depends upon the unknown voltage is generated. The number of pulses appearing in a definite time interval is counted. Since the frequency of these pulses is a function of the unknown voltage, then number of pulses counted in that period of time is an indication of the unknown voltage.

The unknown voltage E_i is applied to the input of the integrator, and the output voltage E_o starts to rise. The slope of the output voltage E_o is determined by value of E_i. This voltage is fed to a level detector and when E_o reaches a certain reference level, the detector sends a pulse to the pulse generator gate. The output voltage from integrator is compared with the fixed voltage of an internal reference source and when E_o reaches that level, the detector produces an output pulse. Greater the value of input voltage E_i, the sharper will be slope of output voltage E_o and quicker the output voltage will reach its reference level. The output pulse of the level detector opens the pulse level gate, permitting pulses from a clock oscillator to pass through pulse generator.

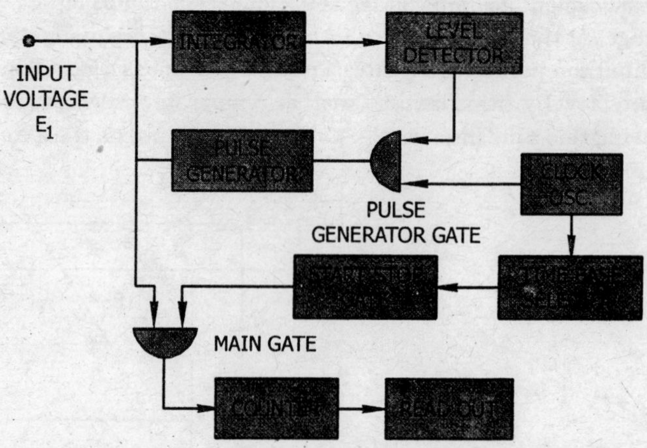

Fig. 8.73 Block Diagram of Integrating type DVM

This generator produces an output pulse of fixed amplitude and width for every pulse it receives. This output pulse, whose polarity is opposite to that of E_i and has greater amplitude is fed back to the integrator. Hence the net input to the integrator is now a reversed polarity. As a result of this reversed input, E_o drops back to its original level, and there is no output from the detector to the pulse generator and the gate gets closed. When the output voltage pulse from the pulse generator has passed, E_i is restored to its original value and E_o starts to rise again. Once again when it reaches the level of reference voltage, the gate is opened, the cycle is repeated. Thus the waveform of E_o is a sawtooth wave, whose rise time depends upon E_i and fall time on the width of the output pulse from the pulse generator.

The frequency of sawtooth is measured by coupling the number of pulses in a given interval of time. Pulses from the clock oscillator are applied to a time base selector. The first pulse passes through start/stop gate, producing an output which is applied to the main gate. The same output from the pulse generator also pass through the main gate. The next pulse from time base closes the start/stop and main gate. The counter thus counts the number of pulses that have passed during a known interval of time.

5. Potentiometric Type DVM.

In this DVM the unknown voltage is compared with a reference voltage whose value is fixed by the setting of the calibrated potentiometer. Under the balanced conditions the value of the unknown voltage is indicated by the dial setting of the potentiometer. The balance is achieved automatically.

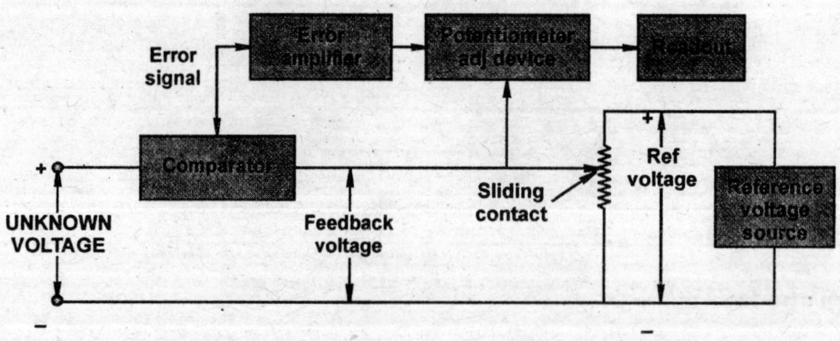

Fig. 8.74 Block diagram of Potentiometer DVM

The unknown voltage is filtered and attenuated to a suitable level. This is applied to a comparator. Reference voltage obtained from a fixed voltage source is applied to potentiometer R. The feedback voltage depends upon the position of the sliding contact. This feedback voltage and the unknown voltage are compared in the comparator. The error signal so obtained is amplified and is fed to potentiometer adjustment device which moves sliding contact of the potentiometer is proportion to the error signal. The sliding contact moves to such a place where the feedback signal equals the unknown voltage. In such a case there is no error signal and movement of sliding contact is stopped. The position of potentiometer adjustment device at this point is indicated in numerical form on the digital readout and it is the unknown voltage.

8.15 TRANSDUCERS

The input quantity for most instrumentation system is non-electric, in order to use electrical methods and technique for measurement , the non electric quantity are converted into an electric signal by a device called transducers.

8.15.1 MEASUREMENT OF STRAIN.

Strain Gauge.

The strain gauges are used for measurement of strain and associated stress. These are based on the principle that, "if a mėtal conductor is stretched or compressed, its resistance changes on account of change in length and diameter of conductor, also there is change in resistivity of conductor, due to strain.

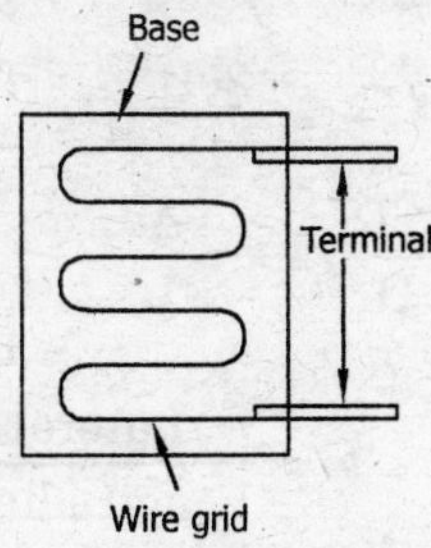

Fig. 8.75 Resistance wire strain gauge

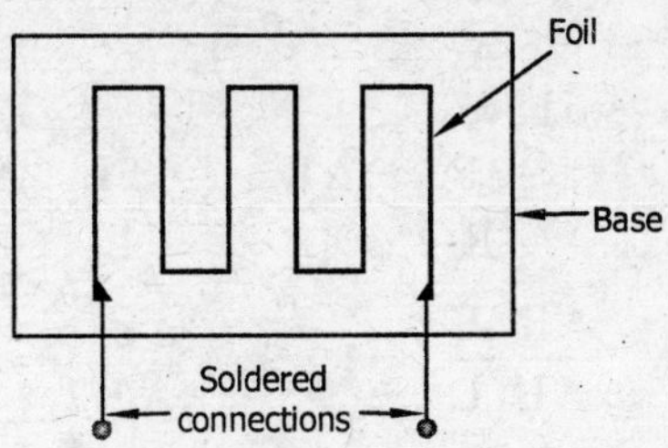

Fig. 8.76 Bonded metal foil gauge

Theory of Strain Gauge

Consider a strain gauge made of circuit wire.

The wire has dimensions :

length = L, area = A, diameter = D before being strained.

The material of wire has resistivity.

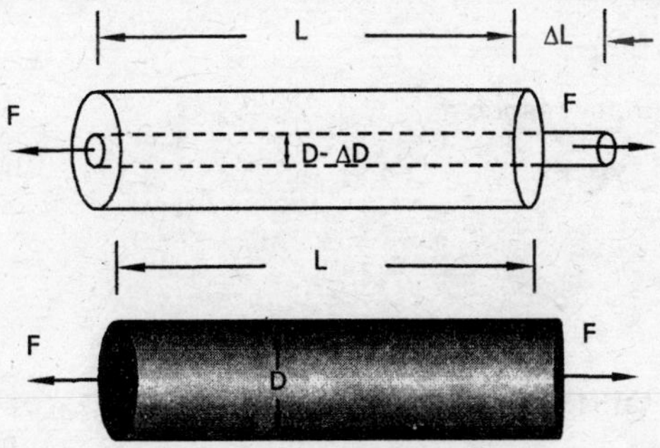

Fig. 8.77 Change in dimensions of strain gauge element when subjected to a tensile force

Resistance of unstrained conductor, $R = \rho \frac{L}{A}$

On the application of stress, resistance changes by ΔR due to change in length ΔL and change in cross-section by ΔA.

$$\frac{dR}{ds} = \frac{d}{ds}\left(\rho \frac{L}{A}\right) = \frac{\rho}{A} \cdot \frac{dL}{ds} - \frac{\rho L}{A^2} \frac{dA}{ds} + \frac{L}{A} \frac{d\rho}{ds}$$

Dividing this equation by resistance $R = \frac{PL}{A}$, we get

$$\frac{1}{R} \frac{dR}{ds} = \frac{1}{L} \frac{dL}{ds} - \frac{1}{A} \frac{dA}{ds} + \frac{1}{\rho} \frac{d\rho}{ds}$$

$$\Rightarrow \quad \frac{\Delta R}{R} = \frac{\Delta L}{L} - \frac{\Delta A}{A} + \frac{\Delta \rho}{\rho} \quad \text{... (i)}$$

Under strained conditions, Area, $A = \frac{\pi}{4} D^2$

$$\Rightarrow \quad \frac{\partial A}{\partial s} = 2 \times \frac{\pi}{4} D \frac{\partial D}{\partial s}$$

$$\Rightarrow \quad \frac{\partial A}{A} = \frac{2 \partial D}{D}$$

$\therefore$ Change in diameters, $\frac{\Delta D}{D} = v \frac{-\Delta L}{L}$

(change in length)

where, $v = \frac{\text{Lateral strain}}{\text{Longitudinal strain}} = \frac{-\partial D / D}{\partial L / L}$

= Poissons's ratio

$$\frac{\Delta A}{A} = -2v \frac{\Delta L}{L} \quad \text{... (ii)}$$

Substituting equation *(ii)* in equation *(i)*, we have

$$\frac{\Delta R}{R} = \frac{\Delta L}{L} + 2v \frac{\Delta L}{L} + \frac{\Delta \rho}{\rho}$$

$$\Rightarrow \quad \frac{\Delta R / R}{\Delta L / L} = 1 + 2v + \frac{\Delta \rho / \rho}{\Delta l / l} = G$$

The gauge factor G indicates the strain sensitivity of the gauge in resistance per unit strain. Neglecting change in resistivity of the material under strained condition, the gauge factor will be

$$G = 1 + 2v$$

Characteristics of Strain Gauges.

(i) Element should be of low resistance temperature coefficient.

(ii) Should have high value of gauge factor.

(iii) Should have linear characteristics.

(iv) Should have very high resistance.

(v) Should have very good frequency response.

Strain gauges are mainly of 3 types:

(i) Wire Strain gauge

(ii) Foil Strain gauge

(iii) Semiconductor gauge

8.15.2 MEASUREMENT OF DISPLACEMENT.

Here an inductive transducer for translating the linear motion into an electrical signal is used. A plate is placed at right angles to the axis of the coil. The displacement of the plate causes a change in the inductance of the coil.

Linear Variable Differential Transformer (LVDT)

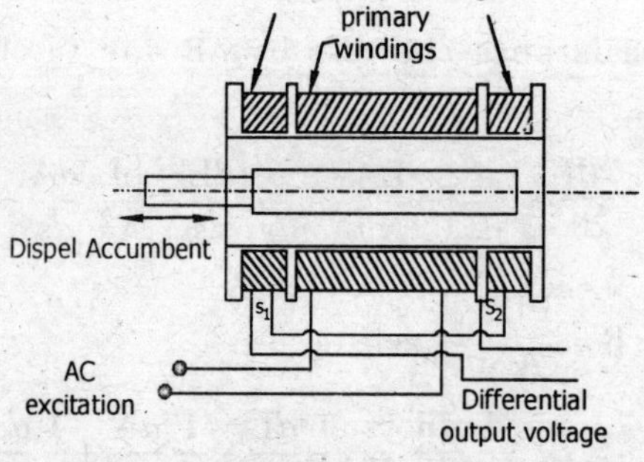

Fig. 8.78 Linear Variable Differential Transformer

It is most widely used inductive transducer.

It consists of single primary winding P and two secondary winding S_1 and S_2 wound on a cylindrical former. Primary winding is connected to an a.c. source. A movable soft iron core is placed inside former. The displacement to be measured is applied to an arm attached to the soft iron core. When the core is in null position, equal voltages are in the two secondary winding. When the core is moved to right of left, difference of the two voltages is produced.

In null position, $E_{s1} = E_{s2}$

$\therefore$ $E_o = 0$

When the core is moved to left $E_{s1} > E_{s2}$

$\therefore$ $E_o = E_{s1} - E_{s1}$

When the core is moved to right, $E_o = E_{s2} - E_{s1}$

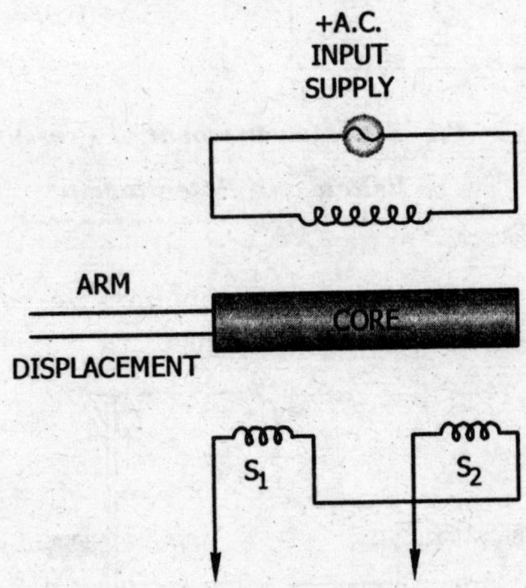

Fig. 8.79 Circuit of LVDT

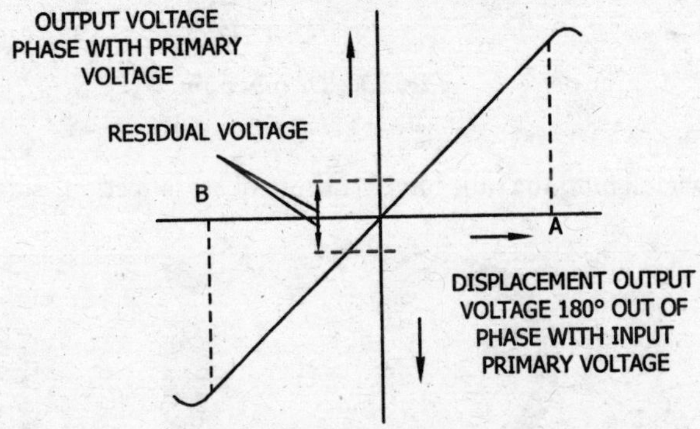

Fig. 8.80 Variation of Differential Output Voltage With Displacement of LVDT

Hence, the difference of output voltages of secondary windings gives the amount of displacement.

Advantages:

(i) Almost linear characteristics.

(ii) Infinite resolution.

(iii) Low power consumption.

(iv) Output impedance is constant.

Disadvantages :

(i) Affected by vibrations.

(ii) Sensitive to stray magnetic fields.

(iii) Performance affected by temperature.

(iv) Larger displacements necessary for appreciable differential output.

8.15.3. MEASUREMENT OF FORCE OR PRESSURE.

The measurement of force or pressure is done by changing the applied force/pressure into displacement.

Following Sensors are used for measurements of pressure / force

1. Bellows.

These are corrugated shaped having thin walled tube. These provide high force and wide pressure range.

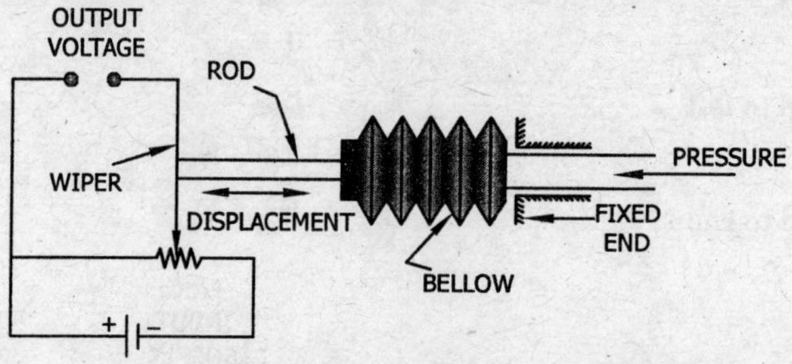

Fig. 8.81 Measurement of Pressure using Bellow and Potentiometer

2. Diaphragms.

These are made of metal alloys such as bronze, phosphor bronze, beryllium, copper, stainless steel, ferrous nickel alloy etc. These have a high accuracy and good response.

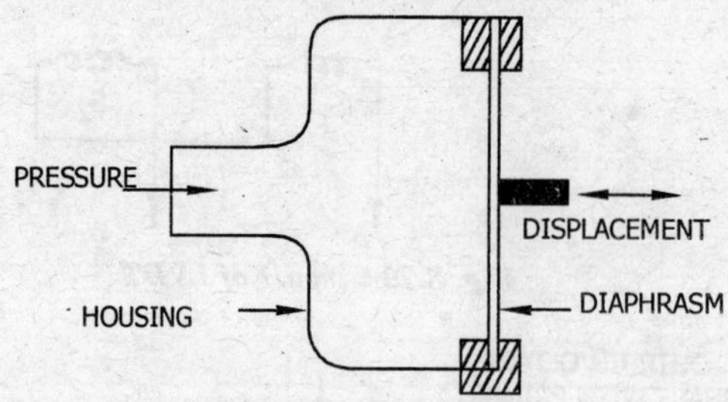

Fig. 8.82 Diaphragm

3. Bourden Tube.

These are curved or twisted metallic tube having elliptical cross section and is made of a long thin walled cylinder.

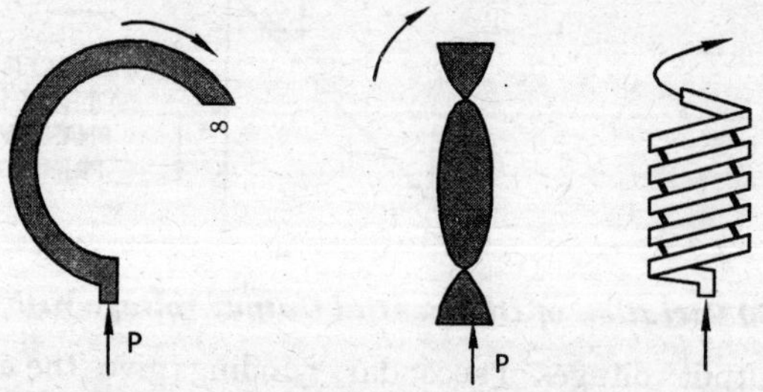

(a) C-Shaped Bourden (b) Twisted Bourden (c) Helical Bourden

Fig. 8.83

8.15.4 MEASUREMENT OF VELOCITY.

1. Moving coil velocity pick-up

EMF induced in a coil is given by, $E = Blv \sin\theta$ volts

where B = flux density of the magnetic field in Tesla

l = length of moving conductor in meters

v = velocity of conductor in the magnetic field in m/s

θ = angle of conductor with the direction of field

Since B, l and θ are constant, induced emf is a function of its velocity.

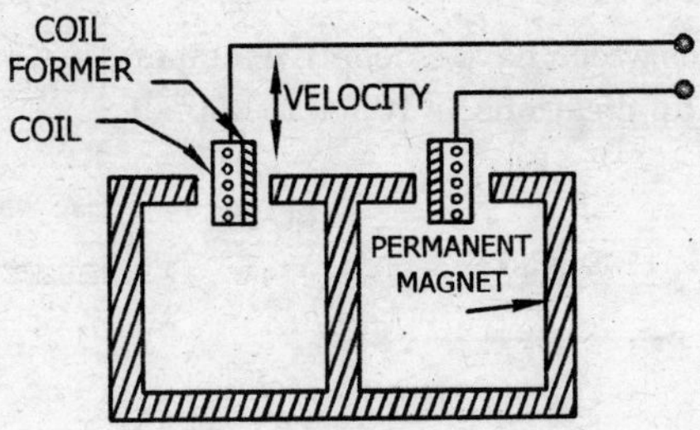

Fig. 8.84 Moving coil velocity Pick-up

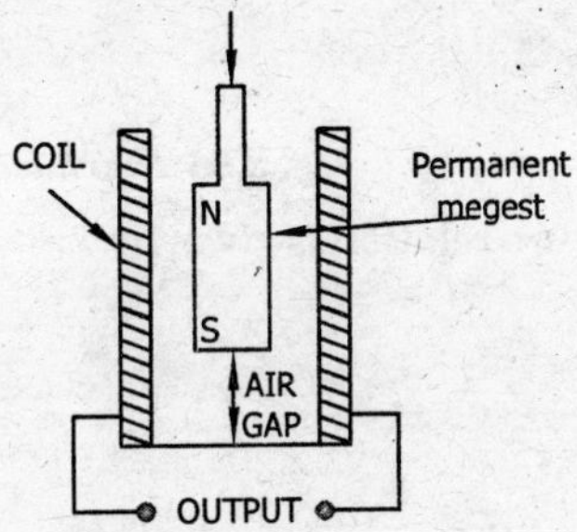

Fig. 8.85 Moving magnet velocity Pick-up

2. Moving magnet velocity pick-up.

Here coil is kept fixed and a permanent magnet moves inside the coil which induces an emf in the coil proportional to the velocity of the magnet. It allows more number of turns on the coil which ensures a sufficient high output voltage.

8.15.5 MEASUREMENT OF TEMPERATURE.

Following devices are used of temperature measurement.

1. Resistance Thermometers

For a change in temperature, change in electrical resistance is constant for a given conductor. Since electrical resistance can be determined accurately, hence the temperature. Platinum is mostly used for measurement of temperature.

$$R_t = R_0\,(1 + \alpha\, t - \beta\, t^2)$$

where R_t = resistance of resistor at t°C

R_0 = resistance of resistor at 0°C α and β are constants

For Platinum $\alpha = 0.0037$ and $\beta = 0.00000057$

For small changes in temperature, $R_t = R_0\,(1 + kt)$

where k = fundamental constant = $\dfrac{R_{100} - R_0}{100\,R_0}$

$$\therefore \quad R_t = R_0\left[1 + \frac{R_{100} - R_0}{100\,R_0}\,t\right] = R_0 + \frac{R_{100} - R_0}{100}\,t$$

Advantages :

(i) Wide temperature range.

(ii) Good stability accuracy.

(iii) Fast response.

Disadvantages :

(i) Expensive.

(ii) Large in size.

(iii) Required power supply and bridge circuit sets.

2. Thermistors

These are semiconductor devices which have a negative temperature coefficient of resistance. These are widely used in the low temperature range applications (– 100°C to 300°C).

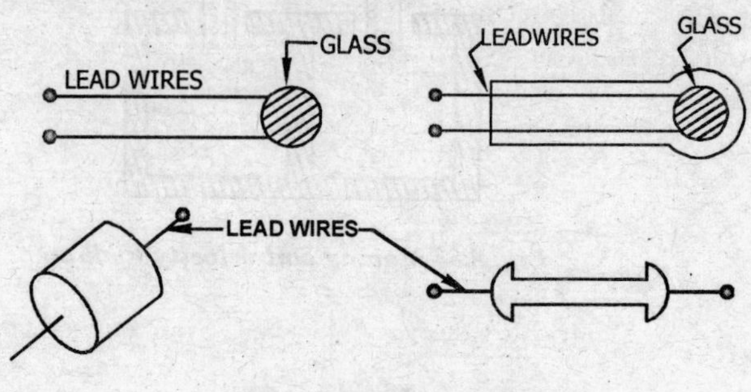

Fig. 8.86 Thermistors

The non-linear resistance temperature relation is given by

$$R_1 = R_0 \left[\beta\left(\frac{1}{T_1} - \frac{1}{T_0}\right)\right]$$

where R_1 = Resistance at temperature T_1

R_0 = Resistance at temperature T_0

β = characteristic constant of material

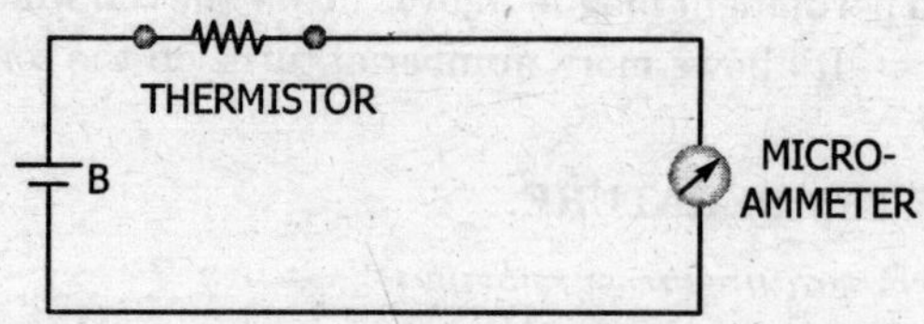

Fig. 8.87

Temperature in measured by connecting a thermistor in series with a battery and a micro ammeter. The micro-ammeter is calibrated to read temperature directly in case of using constant emf battery and limited current.

3. Pyrometers.

These are used for measurement of high temperatures of the order of thousand.

(*i*) Radiation Pyrometers.

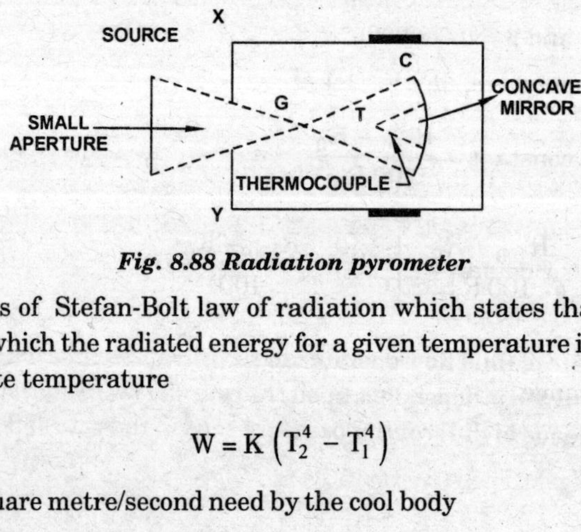

Fig. 8.88 Radiation pyrometer

These operate on the basis of Stefan-Bolt law of radiation which states that the energy radiated by a noted black body (*i.e.* a body for which the radiated energy for a given temperature is maximum) is proportional to the fourth power of its absolute temperature

$$W = K\left(T_2^4 - T_1^4\right)$$

where W = energy per square metre/second need by the cool body

K = constant = 1.279 . 10^{-8} *gm* calories/second/sq meter

T_1 = absolute temperature of a colder body near it

T_2 = absolute temperature of a hot body near it

(*ii*) Optical Pyrometers.

It consists of a standard lamp fed from source of variable voltage, galvanometer calibrated to read temperature directly by measurement of current flowing through the lamp and lens which is used to focus the light radiated from the hot body upon the plane containing the lamp filament. The light from the hot body and that from the lamp are viewed though an eye piece. A red glass is used to made the light monochromatic, which is very helpful in comparing brightness.

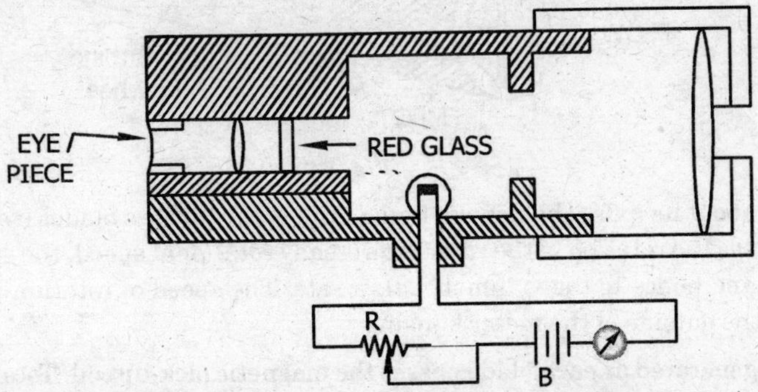

Fig. 8.89 Disappearing type Optical pyrometer

The current flowing through the standard lamp is adjusted till the brightness of the lamp filament is equal to that of the hot body viewed through red glass by means of the eye piece. When the two brightness are equal, the filament disappears into the surrounding field of light from the hot body. The current producing the equality of brightness indicates the actual temperature of the hot body, which is given directly by the indicating instrument.

4. Thermo Couples

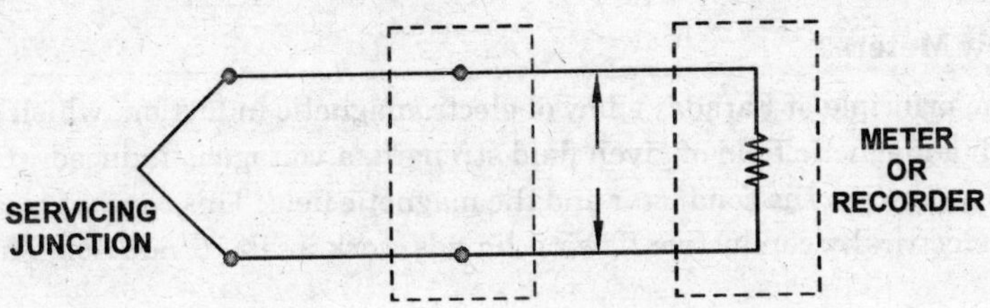

Fig. 8.90 Basic Thermocouple circuit

These consist of a pair of dissimilar metal wires joined together at one end and terminated at the other end which is maintained at a known constant temperature. When a temperature difference exists between the sensing junction and the reference junction, an emf is produced that causes a current in the circuit

$$e = \alpha(T - T_0) + \beta\left(T^2 - T_0^2\right)$$

where e = thermo-electric emf in volts

T = absolute temperature of hot junction

T_0 = absolute temperature of cold junction

α and β are constants

8.15.6 MEASUREMENT OF FLOW.

Devices used for sensing rate of fluid flow operate on the principle of placing an obstruction in the path of fluid causing a change in fluid pressure which is dependent upon the rate of flow. By measuring the difference in pressure before and after the obstruction by means of differential pressure sensor, the rate of flow may be determined.

Flow meters used for measuring the fluid flow

1. Turbine Flow Meter

It is used for the measurement of liquid gas and gases of very low flow rate. It consists of a multibladed rotor (called turbine wheel) which is mounted 90° to the axis of the flowing liquid.

The rotor is supported by the ball or sleeve bearing on a shaft.

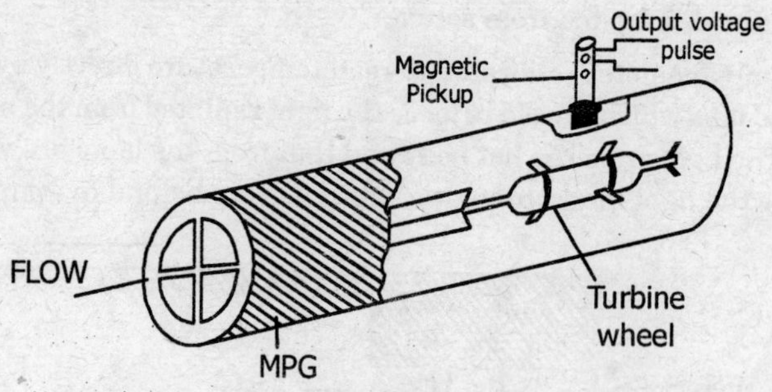

Fig. 8.91.

It is free to rotate about its axis. The flowing liquid strikes the turbine blades (rotor) imparting a force to the blade surface which causes the rotation of the rotor. At a steady rotational speed, the speed of the rotor is proportional to the fluid velocity and hence to the volumetric flow rate. The speed of rotation is monitored by magnetic pick-up which is fitted to the outside of the meter housing.

A voltage pulse is generated as each blade passes the magnetic pick-up coil. Total number of pluses give a measure of the flow. The K factor is given as number of pulses generated per gallon flow.

$$K = \frac{T_k\, f}{Q}$$

where K = pulses per unit volume

T_k = time constant in minutes

f = frequency in Hz.

Q = volumetric flow rate in gmp

2. Magnetic flow Meters

It works on the principle of Faraday's law of electromagnetic induction, which states that whenever a conductor moves through a magnetic field of given field strength, a voltage is induced in the conductor proportional to the relative velocity between the conductor and the magnetic field. This concept is used in electric generators. In case of flowmeter, electrically conductive flowing liquids work as the conductor. The induced voltage is given by the equation.

$$E = C \cdot B \cdot L \cdot V$$

where E = induced voltage in volts

C = dimensional constants

B = magnetic flux in Wb/m^2

L = length of the conductor (fluid) in m

V = velocity of the conductor (fluid) in m/s

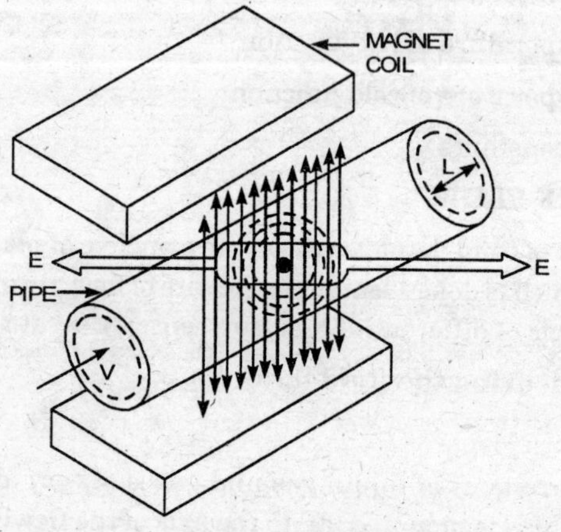

Fig. 8.92 Working principle of Magnetic Flowmeter

The equation to convert a velocity measurement to volumetric flow rate is

$$Q = V \cdot A$$

where Q = volumetric flow rate

V = fluid velocity

A = cross-sectional area of the flowmeter

Since $$V = \frac{E}{CBL}$$

$$\therefore \quad Q = \frac{EA}{CBL}$$

For a given flowmeter, A, C, B, L are constants, therefore

$$Q = K \cdot E$$

where, $$K = \frac{A}{CBL}$$

Therefore the induced voltage is linear and directly proportional to the volumetric flow rate.

The basic principle of a magnetic flowmeter in which the flowing liquid acts as a conductor is shown in Fig. 8.91.

The length L is the distance between the electrodes and equals the pipe diameter. As liquid passes through the pipe section, it also passes through the magnetic field set up by the magnet coils thus inducing a voltage in the liquid, which is detected by a pair of electrodes mounted on the pipe wall. The amplitude of the induced voltage is proportional to the velocity of the flowing liquid.

Advantages :

(i) It can handle slurries and greasy materials.

(ii) It can handle corrosive fluids.

(iii) It has very low pressure drop.

(iv) It is totally obstructionless.

(v) It is available in large pipe sizes and capacity as well as in several construction materials.

(vi) It is capable of handling low volume flows (with minimum size, less than 3.175 mm inside diameter) and very high volume flow rate (with sizes as large as 3.04m).

(vii) It can be used as bi-directional meter.

Disadvantages :

(i) It is relatively expensive.

(ii) It is relatively heavy, especially in large sizes.

(iii) It must be full at all times.

(iv) It must be explosion proof when installed in hazardous electrical areas.

8.15.7 PIEZO-ELECTRIC TRANSDUCER.

These are used for measurement of force and pressure. Materials used are quartz, crystal, rochelle salt etc. When mechanical force is applied on to it, then due to dimensional changes, a potential difference appears across the opposite faces of the materials.

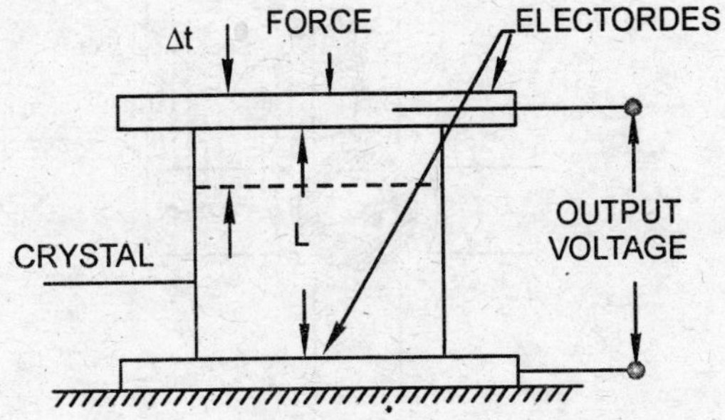

Fig. 8.93. Piezo-electric transducer

Equivalent circuit.

In Fig. 8.94 (*a*), charge Q is generated by the crystal across leakage resistance R_C and capacitance C_C. This is equivalent to a voltage source of voltage, $V = \frac{Q}{C_C}$, since R_C is very high it is omitted in Fig. 8.94 (*c*).

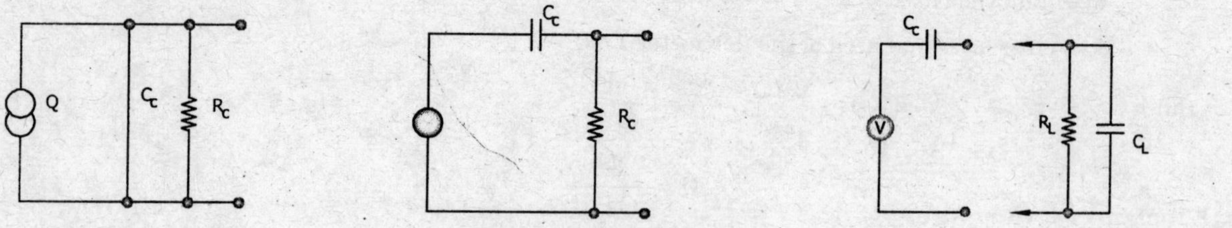

(a) Equivalent circuit *(b) Simplified equivalent circuit* *(c) Transducer with Electrical load*

Fig. 8.94 Equivalent circuits

Total impedance offered to voltage source

$$Z_s = \frac{1}{j\omega C_C} + \frac{R_L}{1 + j\omega C_L R_L}$$

$$= \frac{1 + j\omega R_L (C_C + C_L)}{j\omega C_C (1 + j\omega C_L R_L)}$$

$$V_{out} = \frac{Z_L}{Z_s} V$$

$$= \left[\frac{R_L}{1 + j\omega C_L R_L} \cdot \frac{j\omega C_C (1 + j\omega C_L R_L)}{1 + j\omega R_L (C_C + C_L)}\right] V$$

$$= \frac{j\omega C_C R_L}{1 + j\omega R_L (C_C + C_L)} V$$

and

$$V = \frac{Q}{C_C} = \frac{dF}{C_C}$$

Putting this value of voltage V in above expression

$$V_{out} = \left[\frac{j\omega R_L C_C}{1 + j\omega R_L (C_C + C_L)}\right] \frac{dF}{C_C}$$

$$= \left[\frac{j\omega R_L}{1 + j\omega R_L (C_C + C_L)}\right] dF$$

This relates the output voltage, V_{out} of transducer with applied force F.

8.15.8. MEASUREMENT OF SPEED OF ROTATION BY TACHOMETER.

1. Inductive Tachometer

It works on the principle of variable coupling. The object whose angular velocity is to be measured is coupled to shaft S of the rotor shown in Fig.8.95

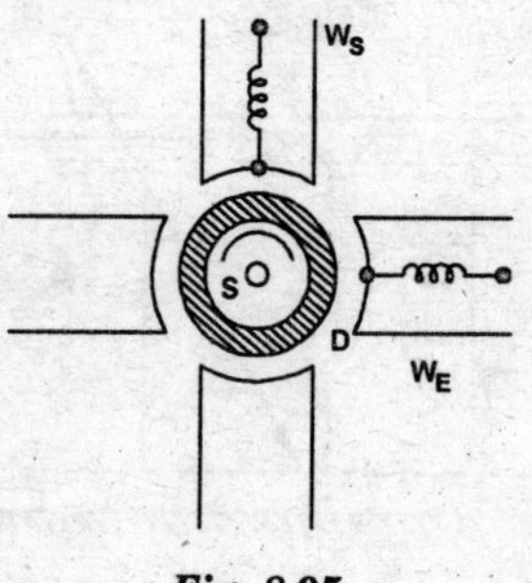

Fig. 8.95

2. D.C. Tachometer Generator

It consists of a small armature which is coupled to a machine whose angular velocity is to be measured as shown in Fig. 8.96. The e.m.f. is measured using moving coil voltmeter

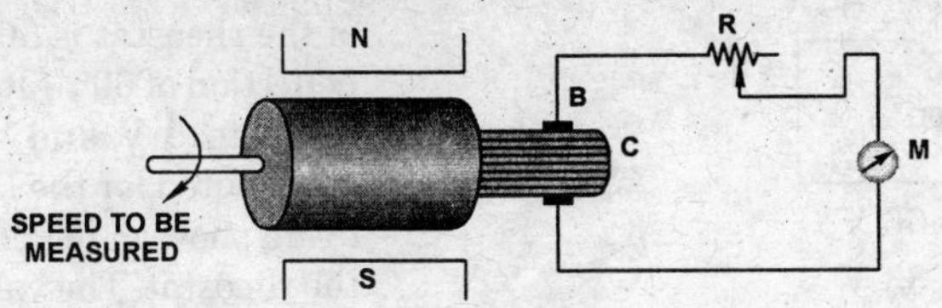

Fig. 8.96 D.C. Tachometer Generator

3. A. C. Tachometer Generator

It is shown in Fig.8.97. The rotation of magnet causes on e.m.f. to be induced whose amplitude and frequency are proportional to speed of rotation.

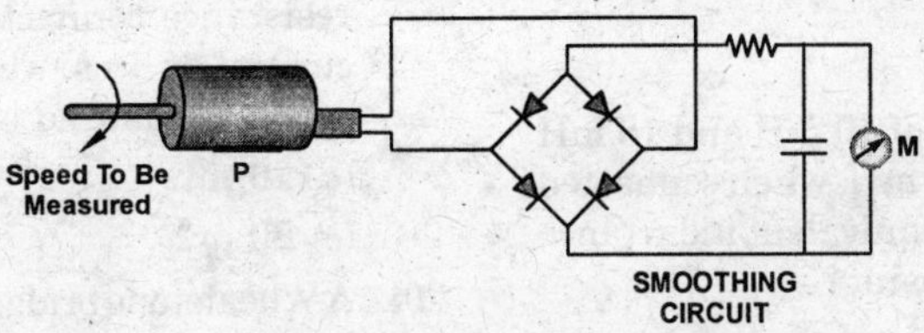

Fig. 8.97 A.C. Tachometer Generator

OBJECTIVE TYPE QUESTIONS

BRIDGES AND POTENTIOMETERS

1. The given figure shows wein bridge connection for frequency measurement. C and R are variables and ganged together. For balanced condition the expression for frequency is $f = \dfrac{1}{2\pi CR}$ when

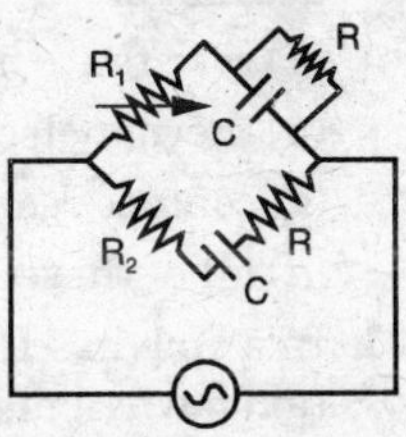

(*a*) $R_1 = R_2$
(*b*) $R_1 = 2R_2$
(*c*) $R_1 = \dfrac{R_2}{2}$
(*d*) $R_1 = 3R_2$

2. Piezoelectric accelerometers
(*a*) should not be used for high frequencies above 100 Hz
(*b*) should be used for low frequencies
(*c*) should use a monitoring source of low input impedance
(*d*) have a low natural frequency

3. Which of the following conditions are to be satisfied in the figure shown, so that the common variable shaft of resistance R_1 and R_2 can be graduated in frequency to measure the frequency of E under balanced condition?

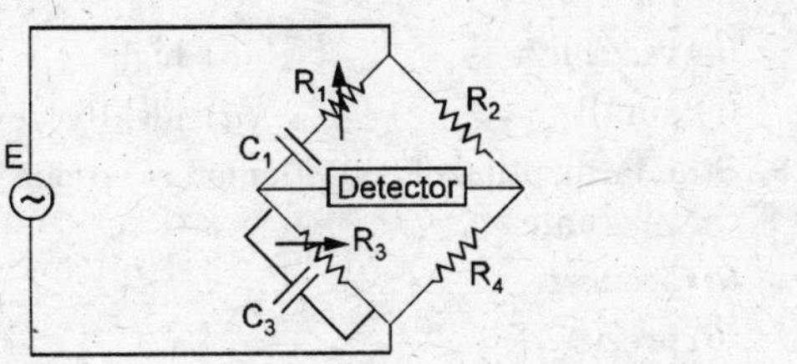

1. $R_1 = R_3$ 2. $C_1 = C_3$
3. $R_2 = 2R_4$ 4. $R_2 = R_4$

Select the correct answer using the codes given below:
(*a*) 1 and 4 (*b*) 1 and 2
(*c*) 2 and 4 (*d*) 1, 2 and 3

4. The meter constant of a single-phase 240 V induction watthour meter is 400 revolutions per kWh. The speed of the meter disc for a current of 10 amperes of 0.8 p.f. lagging will be
(*a*) 12.8 rpm (*b*) 16.02 rpm
(*c*) 18.2 rpm (*d*) 21. 1 rpm

5. Dummy strain gauges are used for
(*a*) compensation of temperature changes
(*b*) increasing the sensitivity of bridge in which they are included
(*c*) compensating for different expansion
(*d*) calibration of strain gauges

6. In the Maxwell bridge as shown in the figure below, the values of resistance R_x and inductance L_x of a coil are to be calculated after balancing the bridge. The component values are shown in the figure at balance. The values of R_x and L_x will respectively be

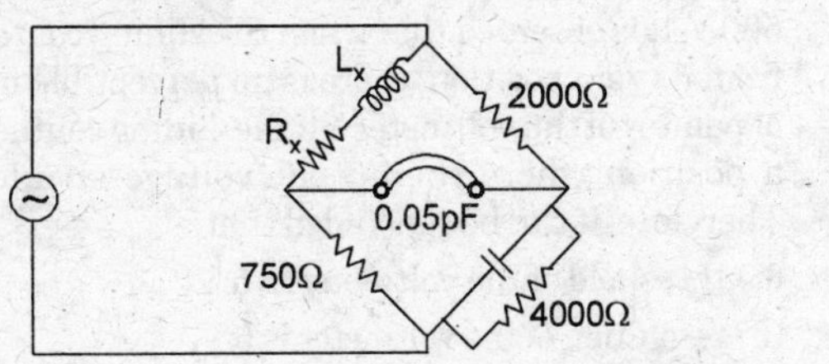

(*a*) 375 ohm. 75 mH (*b*) 75 ohm, 150 mH
(*c*) 37.5 ohm, 75 mH (*d*) 75 ohm, 75 mH

7. In the bridge given in the figure, the reading of the high impedance voltmeter is

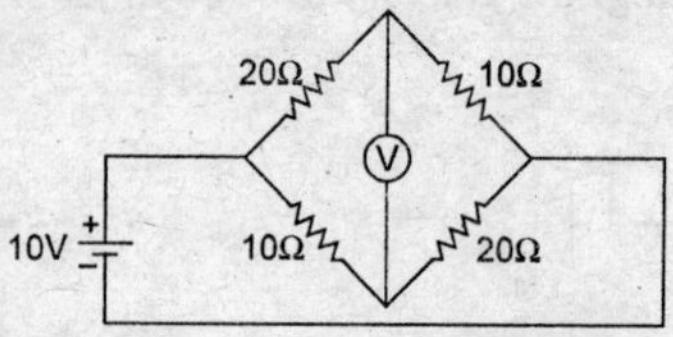

(*a*) zero (*b*) 6.66 V
(*c*) 4.20 V (*d*) 3.33 V

8. The Wheatstone bridge method of resistance measurement is idealy suitable for the measurement of resistance values in the range of

(*a*) 0.001 ohm to 1 ohm
(*b*) 0.1 ohm to 100 ohm
(*c*) 100 ohm to 10 k-ohm
(*d*) 100 k-ohm to 10 M-ohm

9. The coils having self-inductance of 10 mH and 15 mH have an effective inductance of 40 mH, when connected in series aiding. What will be the equivalent inductance if we connect them in series-opposing?

(*a*) 20 mH (*b*) 10 mH
(*c*) 5 mH (*d*) zero

10. For the ac bridge circuit shown in the figure at balance, the value of R_d, L_d and Q_d will be respectively

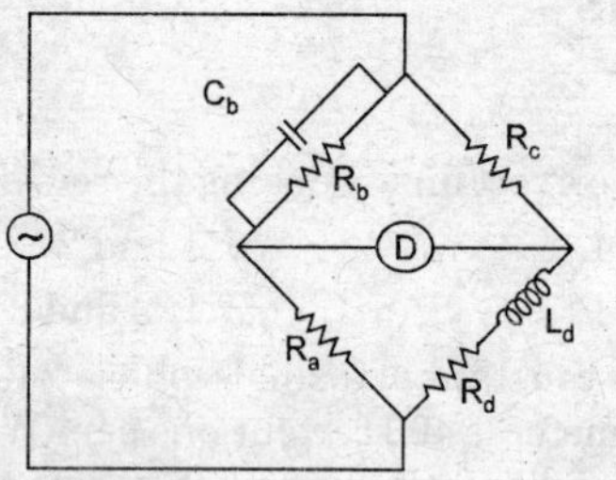

(*a*) $\frac{R_a}{R_c} R_b ; \frac{R_a R_c}{C_b} ; \omega C_b R_b$
(*b*) $\frac{R_b}{R_a} R_c ; \frac{R_a R_c}{C_b} ; \omega C_b R_b$
(*c*) $\frac{R_b}{R_a} R_c ; R_a R_c C_b ; \omega C_b R_c$
(*d*) $\frac{R_a}{R_b} R_c ; R_a R_c C_b ; \omega C_b R_b$

11. The scale of a 0-500 V voltmeter is divided into ten large divisions representing 50 V each and each large division a further subdivided into 10 small divisions, each representing 5 V. It is used for measurement of output voltage of a potentiometer which can be varied from 0 to 500 V. It is observed that when the sliding contact moved from its zero position, there is no perceptible movement of pointer of the voltmeter till the sliding contact reaches a position where the output voltage should be 5 V. Therefore, it can be concluded that

(*a*) threshold of the voltmeter is 5 V
(*b*) resolution of the voltmeter is 5 V
(*c*) sensitivity of the voltmeter is 5V
(*d*) none of these

12. A unknown resistance is measured by substitution method. First a standard known resistance of 100Ω is connected in series with a circuit having a rheostat and a galvanometer. The battery voltage is 10 V and the setting of the rheostat is 500 Ω and the galvanometer shows a deflection of 60°. After this test, the battery voltage goes down to 9 V and when the unknown resistance is substituted for the known resistance, the galvanometer again shows a deflection of 60° with the same setting of the rheostat. The value of unknown resistance is

(*a*) 100 Ω (*b*) 54 Ω
(*c*) 90 Ω (*d*) none of these

13. Equal resistances of 100 Ω each are connected in each arm of a Wheatstone bridge which is supplied by a 2 V battery source. The galvanometer of negligible resistance connected to the bridge can sense as low current as 1 μs. The smallest value of resistance that can be measured is

(*a*) 20 mΩ (*b*) 2 μΩ
(*c*) 20 μΩ (*d*) none of these

14. A Wheatstone bridge has ratio arms of 1000 W and 100 W resistance, the standard resistance arms consists 4 decade resistance boxes of 1000, 100, 10, 1 W steps. The maximum and minimum values of unknown resistance which can be determined with this set up is

(*a*) 111100 Ω, 1Ω
(*b*) 111100 Ω, 10 Ω
(*c*) 111100 Ω, 10 Ω
(*d*) none of these

15. A Wheatstone bridge cannot be used for precision measurements because errors are introduced into on account of

(*a*) resistance of connecting leads
(*b*) thermo-electric emfs
(*c*) contact resistances
(*d*) all of these

16. In a Kelvin's Double Bridge, two sets of readings are taken when measuring a low resistance, one with the current in one direction and the other with direction of current reversed. This is done to eliminate the effect of

(*a*) contact resistance
(*b*) resistance of leads
(*c*) changes in battery voltage
(*d*) thermo-electric emfs

17. When a potentiometer is used for measurement of voltage of an unknown source, the power consume in the circuit of the unknown source under null conditions is

(*a*) very high (*b*) high
(*c*) small (*d*) ideally zero

18. Standardization of potentiometers is done in order that, they become

(*a*) accurate
(*b*) precise
(*c*) accurate and direct reading
(*d*) accurate and precise

19. A volt-ratio box is designed with a resistance 100 Ω/V. It has input terminals of 300 V, 150 V and 75 V, and an output terminal of 1.5 V which is connected to the potentiometer. Supposing a voltage of 270 V is connected to 300 V terminal, what is voltage indicated by the potentiometer and what is the power consumption under null condition?

(*a*) 1.5 V, 3 W (*b*) 1.35 V, 3 W
(*c*) 1.5 V, 2.43 W (*d*) 1.35 V, 2.34 W

20. The equations under balance condition for a bridge are

$$R_1 = R_2 \frac{R_2 R_3}{R_4} \text{ and } L_1 = R_2 R_3 C_4$$

where R_1 and L_1 are respectively unknown resistance and inductance.

In order to achieve converging balance

(*a*) R_2 and R_3 should be chosen as variables
(*b*) R_2 and C_4 should be chosen as variables
(*c*) R_4 and C_4 should be chosen as variables
(*d*) R_3 and C_4 should be chosen as variables

21. Sensitivity of a potentiometer can be increased by

(*a*) decreasing the length of potentiometer wire
(*b*) increasing the length of potentiometer wire
(*c*) decreasing the current in potentiometer wire
(*d*) decreasing the resistance in the rheostat in series with the battery.

22. A bridge type rectifier meter and a thermo couple meter employ moving-coil movement for indication. Both are calibrated on a 100 Hz sinusoidal waveform. If a 100 Hz rectangular waveform is applied to each, the ratio of their readings will be

(*a*) 2 : 1 (*b*) 1.11 : 1
(*c*) 1.41 : 1 (*d*) 1.21 : 1

23. A slide wire potentiometer has 10 wires at 1 m each. With the help of a standard voltage source of 1.018 V it is standardised by keeping the jockey at 101.8 cm. If the resistance of the potentiometer wires is 1000 ohm, then the value of the working current will be

(*a*) 0.1 mA (*b*) 0.5 mA
(*c*) 1 mA (*d*) 10 mA

24. In d.c. potentiometer measure-ments, a second reading is often taken after reversing the polarities of the d.c. supply and the unknown voltage and the average of the two reading is taken. This is with a view of eliminate the effects of

(*a*) ripples in the d.c. supply
(*b*) stray magnetic fields
(*c*) stray thermal emf's
(*d*) erroneous standardisation

25. For full wave rectification, a four diode bridge rectifier is claimed to have the following advantages over a two diode circuit :

1. less expensive transformer
2. smaller size transformer, and
3. suitability for higher voltage application.

Of these

(*a*) only (1) and (2) are true (*b*) only (1) and (3) are true
(*c*) only (2) and (3) are true (*d*) all (1), (2) and (3) are true

MEASURING INSTRUMENTS

26. Law of intermediate temperature in thermocouples allows them to

(*a*) reference junction compensation
(*b*) meters for measurement without disturbing the circuit conditions
(*c*) extension wires of materials other than one used for making thermocouples
(*d*) both (*b*) and (*c*)

27. A d.c voltmeter has a sensitivity of 1000 Ω / volt. When it measures half full scale in 100 V range, the current through the voltmeter will be

(*a*) 100 mA (*b*) 1 mA
(*c*) 0.5 mA (*d*) 50 mA

28. A capacitive transducer working on the principle of change of capacitances with change of displacement, exhibits non linear characteristic. The repose of these transducers can be made linear by using

(*a*) different arrangement
(*b*) use of an OPAMP
(*c*) working then over a small displacement range
(*d*) all of these

29. The dynamic characteristics of capacitive transducer are similar to those of

(*a*) low pass filters
(*b*) high pass filters
(*c*) notch filters
(*d*) band stop filters

30. Capacitive transducers are normally used for

(*a*) static measurements
(*b*) dynamic measurements
(*c*) both static and dynamic measurements
(*d*) transient measurements

31. An L.V.D.T.

(*a*) exhibits linear characteristics up to a displacement of ± 5 mm
(*b*) has a linearity of 0.05%
(*c*) has an infinite resolution and a high sensitivity which is of the order of 40 V/mm
(*d*) all of these

32. In an L.V.D.T. the two secondary windings are connected in differential to obtain

(*a*) higher output
(*b*) an output voltage which is phase sensitive i.e. the output voltage has a phase which can lead us to a conclusion whether the displacement of the core took place from right to left or from left to right
(*c*) in order to establish the null or the reference point for the displacement of the core
(*d*) both (*b*) and (*c*)

33. Two inductive transducers working on the principle of change of self inductance L, are connected in push pull arrangement. If the change of inductance of transducers is 6L, the change of inductance exhibited at the output terminals is

(*a*) 6L (*b*) 2 ΔL
(*c*) ± 2 ΔL (*d*) zero

34. Thermocouples are
(*a*) passive transducers
(*b*) active transducers
(*c*) both (*a*) and (*b*)
(*d*) output transducers

35. Three types of temperature transducers are compared as regards their sensitivity. The order in which they exhibit their sensitivities (highest to lowest) is
(*a*) thermistors, RTDs, thermocouples
(*b*) thermocouples, RTDs, thermistors
(*c*) RTDs, thermistors, thermocouples
(*d*) RTDs, thermocouples, thermistors

36. The temperature transducers exhibit no–linear behaviour. The order in which they exhibit no linearity (highest to lowest) is
(*a*) thermocouples, RTD, thermistors
(*b*) thermistors, thermocouples, RTDs
(*c*) RTDs, thermocouples, thermistors
(*d*) Thermistors, RTDs, thermocouples

37. The resistance value of a thermistor is 5000 Ω at 25° C and its resistance temperature coefficient is 0.04/° C. A measurement with a lead resistance of 10 Ω will cause an error of
(*a*) 0.02°C (*b*) 0.05°C
(*c*) 0.1°C (*d*) none of these

38. Some wire-wound resistors have bifilar winding. This type of winding is used to
(*a*) increase the thermal stability
(*b*) reduce the tolerance
(*c*) reduce the inductance of winding
(*d*) double the power rating of the resistance

39. A metal strain gauge factor of two. Its nominal resistance is 120 ohms. If it undergoes a strain of 10^{-5}, the value of change of resistance in response to the strain is
(*a*) 240 ohms
(*b*) 2×10^5 ohm
(*c*) 2.4×10^{-3} ohm
(*d*) 1.2×10^{-3} ohm

40. A wattmeter is reading back-wards in an experiment. Upscale reading can be obtained by reversing
(*a*) pressure coil connection only
(*b*) current coil connection only
(*c*) both pressure and current coil connection only.
(*d*) either pressure or current connection

41. A thermistor exhibits
(*a*) only a negative change of resistance with increase in temperature
(*b*) only a positive change of resistance with increases in temperature
(*c*) can exhibit either a negative or positive change of resistance with increase of temperature depending upon the type of material
(*d*) none of these

42. A 35 V d.c. supply is connected across a combined resistance of 600 ohms and an unknown resistance of R ohms in series. A voltmeter having a resistance of 1.2 kW is connected across 600 ohm resistor and reads 5 V. The resistance R will be

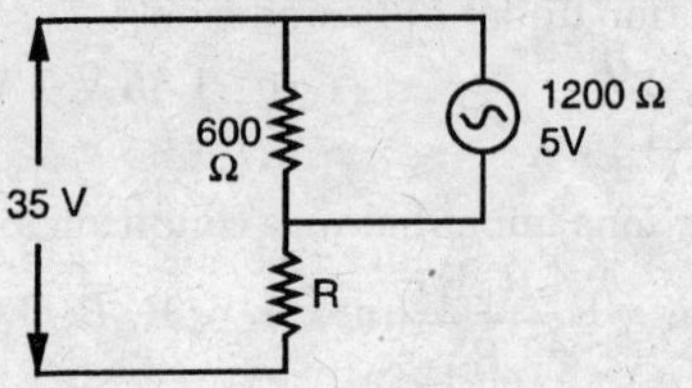

(*a*) 120 ohms (*b*) 500 ohms
(*c*) 1.7 k ohms (*d*) 2.4 k ohms

43. If the practical units of voltage and current wave each made 20 times as large as they are at present, what would be the consequent alteration in the size of the unit of capacitance?
(*a*) 200 times (*b*) 60 times
(*c*) 20 times (*d*) Nil

44. A thermo-couple ammeter gives full-scale deflection of 10A. when it reads one fifth of the scale, the current will be
(*a*) 2 A (*b*) 4 A
(*c*) 4.47 A (*d*) 5.78 A

45. Ratio of the readings of two watt meters connected to measure power in a balanced 3-phase load is 5 : 3 and the load is inductive. The power factor at load is
(*a*) 0.917 lead (*b*) 0.917 lag
(*c*) 0.6 lead (*d*) 0.6 lag

46. A basic d'Arsonval movement with internal resistance 100 Ω and full scale current 1 mA is to be converted into a multirange dc voltmeter with voltage ranges 0 – 10V, 0–30 V, 0 – 100 V and 0 – 300 V. The circuit arrangement is shown in the figure. The value of R_1 will be

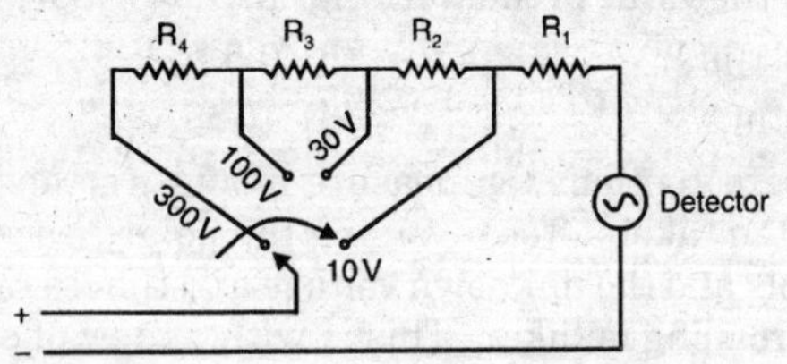

(*a*) 0.0 Ω (*b*) 100 Ω
(*c*) 9.9 kΩ (*d*) 10 kΩ

47. Rectifier moving coil instruments respond to
(*a*) peak value, irrespective of the nature of the wave form
(*b*) average value for all wave forms
(*c*) rms value for all wave forms
(*d*) rms value for symmetrical square wave form

48. A meter has a full-scale deflection of 90° at a current of 1 A. The response of the meter is square law. Assuming spring control, the current for a deflection at 45° will be
(*a*) 0.25 A (*b*) 0.50 A
(*c*) 0.67 A (*d*) 0.707 A

49. A permanent magnet moving coil type ammeter and a moving iron type ammeter are connected in series in a resistive circuit fed from output of a half wave rectifier voltage source. If the moving iron type instrument reach 5 A, the permanent magnet moving coil type instrument is likely to read

(*a*) zero (*b*) 2.5 A

(*c*) 3.18 A (*d*) 5 A

50. The sensitivity of thermostats as compared with sensitivity of platinum resistance temperature detector over a temperature range of–100° to 400°C to change in temperature is

(*a*) 100 times

(*b*) 10^6 times

(*c*) 10^7 times

(*d*) 10^3 times

51. Which one of the following methods is used to measure power output of a radio transmitter while it is radiating?

(*a*) Electrostatic meter

(*b*) Three-wattmeter method

(*c*) Three-ammeter method

(*d*) Two-wattmeter method

52. The resistance of a thermometer is 5 Ω at 30°C and 6.5 Ω at 60°C. Using linear approximation, the value of resistance temperature co-efficient at 45° is

(*a*) 0.009/°C (*b*) 0.0087/°C

(*c*) 0.0085/°C (*d*) 0.01/°C

53. A zero to 300 V voltmeter has an error of 12% of the full-scale deflection. If the true voltage is 30V, then the range of readings on this voltmeter would be

(*a*) 20 V to 40 V

(*b*) 24 V to 36 V

(*c*) 29.4 V to 30.6 V

(*d*) 29.94 to 30.06 V

54. A single-phase energymeter is operating on 230 V, 50 Hz supply with a load of 20 A for two hours at upf. The meter makes 1380 revolutions in that period. The meter constant is

(*a*) 695 rev/kWh

(*b*) 150 rev/kWh

(*c*) 0.15 rev/kWh

(*d*) 1/150 rev/kWh

55. What will happen if a voltmeter is connected like an ammeter in series to the load?

(*a*) The meter will burn out

(*b*) The measurement will be too high

(*c*) An inadmissably high current will flow

(*d*) There will be almost no current in the circuit

56. Which one of the following types of indicating instruments is an electrometer?

(*a*) Electrodynamometer

(*b*) PMMC

(*c*) Electrostatic

(*d*) Moving iron

57. For the voltmeter circuit shown in the given figure, the basic D'Arsonval meter used has full-scale current of 1 mA and meter resistance (R_m) of 100 ohms. The values of the series resistance R_1 and R_2 required for 10 V range and 50 V range will be respectively

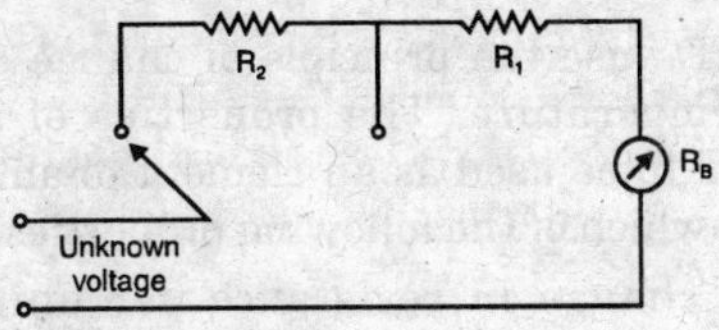

(*a*) 9.9 kΩ and 40 kΩ

(*b*) 10 kΩ and 50 kΩ

(*c*) 20 kΩ and 30 kΩ

(*d*) 200 kΩ and 250 kΩ

58. In the case of power measurement by two wattmeter method in a balanced 3-phase system with a pure inductive load

(*a*) both the wattmeters will indicates the same value but with opposite signs

(*b*) both the wattmeter will indicate zero

(*c*) both the wattmeter will indicate the same value with same sign

(*d*) one wattmeter will indicate zero and the other will indicate some non-zero value

59. A 230 V, 10 A, single-phase energymeter makes 90 revolutions in 3 minutes at half load rated voltage and unity pf. If the meter constant is 1800 revolutions / kWh, then its error at half load will be

(*a*) 13.04 % slow

(*b*) 13.04 % fast

(*c*) 15 % slow

(*d*) 15 % fast

60. A certain meter has a sensitivity of 50,000 Ω/V. The current required to deflect the meter movement to full-scale will be

(*a*) 5 μ A

(*b*) 10 μ A

(*c*) 20 μ A

(*d*) 50 μ A

61. A 1000 ohms/V meter is used to measure a resistance on 150 V scale. The meter resistance is

(*a*) 150 kΩ (*b*) 1 kΩ

(*c*) 6.67 ohms (*d*) 0.001 ohm

62. One single-phase wattmeter operating on 230 V and 5 A for 5 hours makes 1940 revolutions. Meter constant in revolutions is 400. The power factor of the load will be

(*a*) 1 (*b*) 0.8

(*c*) 0.7 (*d*) 0.6

63. An unfinished moving iron voltmeter is used to measure the voltage in an a.c. circuit. If a stray d.c. magnetic field having a component along the axis of the meter coil appears, the meter reading would be

(*a*) unaffected

(*b*) decreased

(*c*) increased

(*d*) either decreased or increased depending on the direction of the d.c. field.

64. A 0-10 mA PMMC ammeter reads 4 mA in a circuit. Its bottom control spring snaps suddenly. The meter will now read nearly

(*a*) 10 mA (*b*) 8 mA

(*c*) 2 mA (*d*) Zero

65. The RTDs use the principle of change of resistance with temperature. The properties of a conductor material to be used as an element of an RTD should possess which of the following properties?

(*a*) The change in resistance per unit change in temperature should be as small as possible

(*b*) The resistance of the materials should not have a continuous and stable relationship with temperature

(*c*) The change of resistance with temperature should not be a linear function

(*d*) All of these

66. Hysteresis in an instrument means

(*a*) repeatability of the instrument

(*b*) reliability of the instrument

(*c*) change in same reading when input is first increased and then decreased

(*d*) the inaccuracy due to change in temperature

67. A resistance strain gauge with a gauge factor of 3 is fastened to a steel member subjected to a stress of 100 N/mm². The modulus of elasticity of steel is approximately 2×10^5 N/mm². The percentage change in resistance is

(*a*) 1.5 (*b*) 1

(*c*) 0.15 (*d*) 0.1

68. A periodic signal shown is applied to the ideal diode circuit below. Find the RMS value for the output voltage $v_0(t)$?

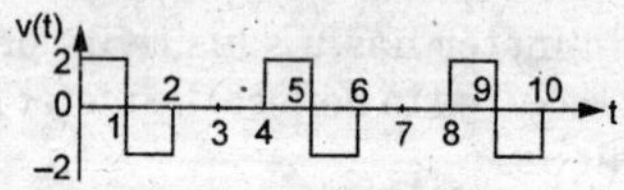

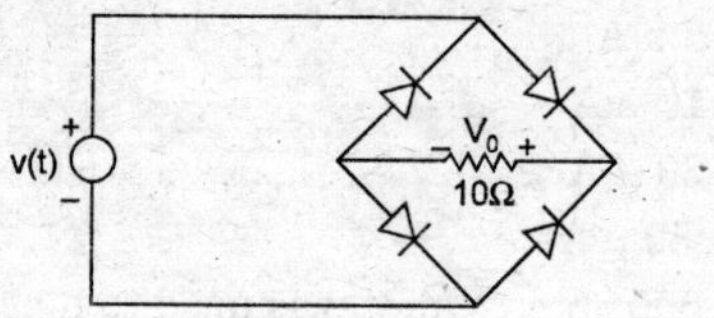

(*a*) 10 (*b*) 2

(*c*) $\frac{1}{\sqrt{2}}$ (*d*) $\sqrt{2}$

69. Strain sensing transducers are mode of various materials in various sizes and shapes. The sensitivity of a strain gauge is expressed in terms of a gauge factor. For a certain application, a gauge factor of 100 is desired. The proper strain gauge to be used in this case would be

(*a*) constantan strain gauge

(*b*) nichroma-V strain gauge

(*c*) semiconductor strain gauge

(*d*) platinum-tungsten alloy strain gauge.

70. It is required to measure temperature in the range of 1300° C to 1500° C. The most suitable thermocouple to be used as a transducer would be

(*a*) Chromel-constantan (*b*) Iron-constantan

(*c*) Chromel-alumel (*d*) Platinum-rhodium

71. An LVDT is used to measure displacement. The output of the LVDT is connected to a voltmeter of range 0 to 5 V through an amplifier having a gain of 250. For a displacement of 0.5 mm, the output of the LVDT is $\frac{1}{2}$ mV. The sensitivity of the instrument would be

(*a*) 0.1 V/ mm (*b*) 0.5 V / mm

(*c*) 1 V / mm (*d*) 5 V / mm

72. Consider the following statements about LVDT as a transducer:

1. The relationship between input displacement and output voltage is almost linear.
2. The range of displacement that can be measured is wide.
3. It does not form a loading on the mechanical system.

Of these statements

(*a*) 1, 2 and 3 are correct

(*b*) 2 and 3 are correct

(*c*) 1 and 2 are correct

(*d*) 1 and 3 are correct

73. A shunt type ohmmeter is shown in the figure below. With R_x disconnected, the meter reads full scale. S represents the meter current as a fraction of full scale current with R_x connected such that

$$S = \frac{R_x}{R_x + R_p}$$

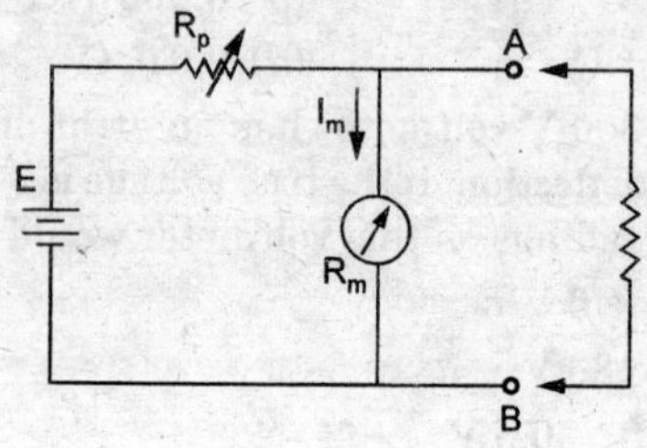

The value of R_p is given by

(*a*) R_m (*b*) $R_1 + R_m$

(*c*) $\frac{R_1 R_x}{(R_1 + R_m)}$ (*d*) $\frac{R_1 R_m}{(R_1 + R_m)}$

74. The power in a resistor R is estimated by measuring the voltage and current using the voltmeter-ammeter method. Two different arrangements can be used as shown in circuits I and II. Less erroneous results are obtained by adopting

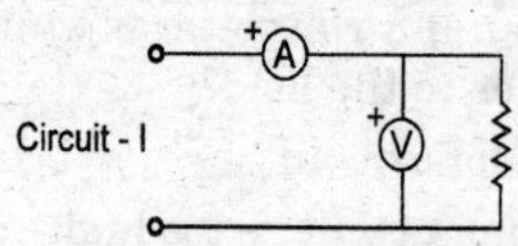

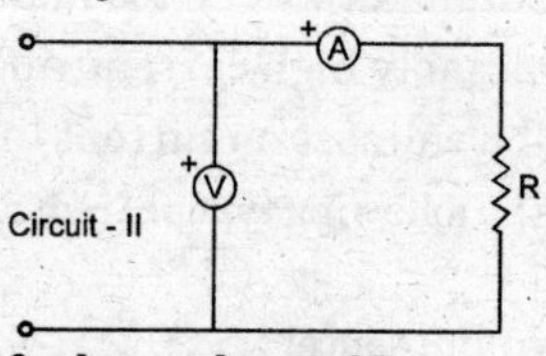

(*a*) circuit I for low values of R

(*b*) circuit II for values of R

(*c*) circuit I for values of R

(*d*) circuit II for low and high values of R

75. A simple d.c. potentiometer is to be standardised by keeping the sidewire setting at 1. 0813 V. If by mistake, the setting is at 1.0138 V and the standardisation is made to obtain a source voltage of 1.0318 V, then the reading of the potentiometer will be

(*a*) 1.0138 V

(*b*) 1.0183 V

(*c*) $(1.0138)^2$ / 1.0183 V

(*d*) $(1.0138)^2$ V

76. A galvanometer is tested shown in figure, in the circuit, where E = 1.5 V, R_1 = 1.0 ohm, R_2 = 2500 ohm and R_3 is variable. With R_3 set at 450 ohm, the galvanometer deflection is 140 mm and with R_3 set at 950 ohm, the galvanometer deflection is 70 mm. The resistance of the galvanometer is

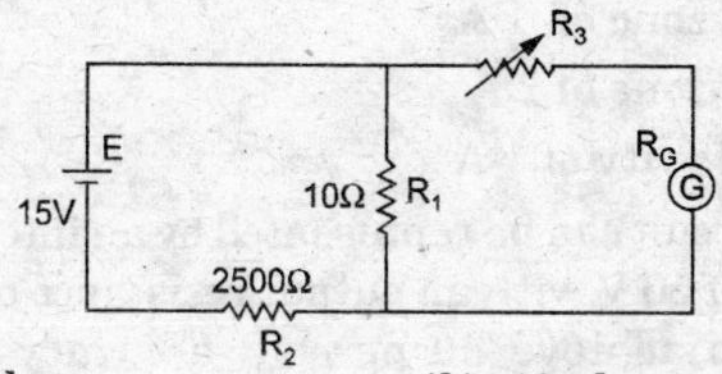

(*a*) 99 ohm (*b*) 49 ohm

(*c*) 25 ohm (*d*) 10 ohm

77. A closed coil spring has a stiffness of 20 × 10^{-6} N/m. If diameter of the wire is doubled, its outer diameter is made two times and its number of turns are made two times, the stiffness of then new spring will be

(*a*) 20 × 10^{-6} N/m

(*b*) 80 × 10^{-6} N/m

(*c*) 10 × 10^{-6} N/m

(*d*) 160 × 10^{-6} N/m

78. The effective reactance of an inductive coil

(*a*) increases because of stray capacitance as the frequency increases

(*b*) decreases because of stray capacitances as the frequency increases

(*c*) remain the same irrespective of the increase in frequency even if stray series capacitances are present

(*d*) none of these

79. A compensated wattmeter has its reading corrected for error due to the

(*a*) frequency

(*b*) friction

(*c*) power consumed in current coil

(*d*) power consumed in potential coil

80. While measuring power in three phase load by two wattmeter method, the reading of the two wattmeters will be equal and opposite when

(*a*) power factor is unity

(*b*) load is balanced

(*c*) phase angle is between 60° and 90°

(*d*) the load is purely inductive

81. The sensitivity of a voltmeter using 0 to 5 mA meter movement is

(*a*) 50 ohm / volt

(*b*) 100 ohm / volt

(*c*) 200 ohm / volt

(*d*) 500 ohm / volt

82. If a dynamometer type wattmeter is connected in an ac circuit, the power indicated by the wattmeter will be

(*a*) volt-ampere product (*b*) average power

(*c*) peak power (*d*) instantaneous power

83. DC voltage of the order of a few mV can be measured accurately using a / an

(*a*) moving coil voltmeter

(*b*) null-balancing potentiometer.

(*c*) moving iron voltmeter

(*d*) electrostatic voltmeter

84. The "accuracy" of a measuring instrument is determined by

(*a*) closeness of the value indicated by it to the correct value of the measurand

(*b*) repeatability of the measured value

(*c*) speed with which the instruments's reading approaches the final value

(*d*) least change in the value of the measurand that could be detected by the instrument

85. In the two-wattmeter method of measuring power in a balanced three-phase circuit, one wattmeter shows zero and the other positive maximum. The load power factor is

(*a*) zero (*b*) 0.5 (*c*) 0.866 (*d*) 1.0

86. A 35 V dc supply is connected across a resistance of 600 ohm in series with an unknown resistance R_x. A voltmeter having a resistance of 1.2 k-ohm is connected across 600 ohm resistance and reads 5V. The value of resistance R_x will be

(*a*) 120 ohm (*b*) 400 ohm

(*c*) 1.8 ohm (*d*) 2.4 k-ohm

87. 'Creep' is energy meters can be prevented by

(*a*) using extra turns on the voltage coil

(*b*) having two holes on opposite sides of the disc

(*c*) using a stronger brake magnet

(*d*) using steel laminations of high permeability

88. The sensitivity of an instrument is the

(*a*) smallest increment in the input that can be detected with certainty

(*b*) largest input change to which the instrument fails to respond

(*c*) ratio of the change in the magnitude of the output to the corresponding change in the magnitude of the input

(*d*) closeness of the output values for repeated applications of a constant input

89. The internal resistance of a Weston standard cell is of the order of

(*a*) 1 ohm (*b*) 10 ohm

(*c*) 100 ohm (*d*) 1000 ohm

90. A 50 Hz voltage is measured with a moving iron voltmeter and a rectifier type ac voltmeter connected in parallel. If the meter readings are V_1 and V_2 respectively and the meters are free from calibration errors, then the form factor of the ac voltage may be estimated as

(*a*) $\frac{V_1}{V_2}$ (*b*) $\frac{1.11V_1}{V_2}$

(*c*) $\frac{\sqrt{2}V_1}{V_2}$ (*d*) $\frac{\pi V_1}{V_2}$

91. If a dc voltmeter is made from an ammeter having a full-scale deflection of 100 micro amperes, then its sensitivity (in k-ohm / V) will be

(*a*) 1 (*b*) 10
(*c*) 100 (*d*) 1000

92. When damping of an instrument is adjusted to enable the pointer to rise quickly to its deflected position without overshooting, in that case the instrument is said to be

(*a*) dead-beat
(*b*) off-beat
(*c*) over-damped
(*d*) under-damped

93. The resistance of two coils of a wattmeter are 0-0.1 ohm and 1000 ohms respectively and both are non-inductive. The load current is 20 A and the voltage across the load is 30 V. In one of the two ways of connecting the voltage coil, the error in the reading would be

(*a*) 0.1 % too high
(*b*) 0.2% too high
(*c*) 0.15% too high
(*d*) zero

94. The measurement of a quantity

(*a*) is an act of comparison of an unknown quantity with another quantity
(*b*) is a act of comparison of an unknown quantity with a known quantity whose accuracy may be known or may not be known
(*c*) is an act of comparison of an unknown quantity with a predefined acceptable standard which is accurately known
(*d*) none of these

95. A piezo electric transducer has the following parameter values :

Crystal capacitance = 10^{-9} F
Cable capacitance = 2×10^{-10} F
Charge sensitivity = 4×10^{-6} coulomb/cm

If the oscilloscope used for read-out has an input resistance of 1 MW in parallel with $C = 4 \times 10^{-10}$ F, then the voltage sensitivity constant will be

(*a*) 2500 V/cm (*b*) 3334 V/cm
(*c*) 4000 V/cm (*d*) 4500 V/cm

96. The power factor in a single phase circuit is $\cos\phi = \dfrac{P}{VI}$ where P power read by an wattmeter,

V = voltage read by a voltmeter and
I = current read by an ammeter.

All the three instruments have a limiting error of ± 1%. The power factor of the circuits can be known if only one meter i.e. an electrodynamometers type power factor having an limiting error ± 1% used. The preferred method is to use a single instrument like a power factor meter rather than using 3 instruments because the error with using wattmeter, voltmeter and ammeter is

(*a*) ± 2% (*b*) ± 3%
(*c*) ± 1% (*d*) –1%

97. The voltage of a circuit is measured by a voltmeter having an input impedance comparable with the output impedance of the circuit thereby causing error in voltage measurement. This error may be called

(*a*) Gross error
(*b*) Random error
(*c*) Error caused by misuse of instrument
(*d*) Error caused by loading effect

98. In the center zero analog ammeter having a range of – 10 A to + 10 A, there is a detectable change of the pointer from its zero position on either side of the scale only if the current reaches a value of 1 A (on either side). The ammeter has a

(*a*) resolution of 1 A
(*b*) dead zone of 1 A
(*c*) dead zone of 2 A
(*d*) sensitivity of 1 A

99. A d.c. circuit can be represented by an internal voltage source of 50 V with an output resistance of 100 kΩ. In order to achieve 99 percent accuracy for voltage measurement across its terminals, the voltage measuring device should have a resistance of

(*a*) atleast 10 MΩ
(*b*) 100 kΩ
(*c*) at least 10 Ω
(*d*) none of these

100. The power in a circuit is measured by measuring a current through a resistor. The current is measured with an accuracy of ± 1.5% and the tolerance band of the resistor of ± 0.5%. The errors are limiting or guarantee errors. The accuracy with which power is measured is

(*a*) ± 1.125% (*b*) ± 3.5%
(*c*) ± 2% (*d*) ± 2.5%

101. The maximum current that can be drawn from a saturated Weston cell without damaging it, is

(*a*) 100 mA momentarily
(*b*) 100 μA continuously
(*c*) 100 μA momentarily
(*d*) 1 mA momentarily

102. The internal resistance of a saturated Weston cell is of the order of a

(*a*) few ohm (*b*) few kilo ohm
(*c*) few hundreds of ohm (*d*) fraction of ohm

103. A 1 mA ammeter has a resistance of 100 Ω. It is to be converted to a 1 A ammeter. The value of shunt resistance is

(*a*) 0.001 Ω (*b*) 0.1001 Ω
(*c*) 100000 Ω (*d*) 100 Ω

104. The decrease in the value of emf of an unsaturated Weston cell is about

(*a*) 1 μV per year
(*b*) 1 mV per year
(*c*) 5 – 10 μV per year
(*d*) 30 – 50 μV per year

105. If an analog PMMC, 0 – 10 A ammeter is provided with no controlling mechanision and the moving parts are free to rotate, what will be the reading of the instrument if a current of 1 A (d.c.) passed through the moving coil (torque produced is sufficient to overcome the frictional losses)?

(*a*) 1 A
(*b*) 10 A
(*c*) The pointer will continuously rotate
(*d*) The pointer will remain stationary

106. A voltage of 200 V produces a deflection of 90° in PMMC spring controlled instrument. If the same instruments provided with gravity control, what would be the deflection?

(*a*) 90°
(*b*) 45°
(*c*) 64.2°
(*d*) Cannot be known from the data given

107. A spring producers a controlling torque of 16×10^{-6} Nm for a deflection of 120°. Suppose its width and length are made two times their original value and the thickness is halved, then value of controlling torque for the same deflection will be

(*a*) 16×10^{-6} Nm (*b*) 8×10^{-6} Nm
(*c*) 32×10^{-6} Nm (*d*) 2×10^{-6} Nm

108. Air friction damping should not be used where the deflecting torque in the instrument is produced due to

(*a*) magnetic field
(*b*) electrostatic field
(*c*) thermo-electric emf
(*d*) none of these

109. Fluid friction damping can be used in

(*a*) horizontally mounted instru-ment
(*b*) vertically mounted instrument
(*c*) both in horizontally and vertically mounted instrument
(*d*) none of these

110. Power in a d.c. circuit is measured by measuring the voltage across and current through the circuit. The voltage and current measurement are made to an accuracy of ± 2% and ± 3% respectively. The errors are limiting errors. The error in measurement of power is

(*a*) ± 2% (*b*) ± 3%
(*c*) ± 6% (*d*) ± 5 %

111. A wattmeter has a full scale range of 2500 W. It has an error ± 1 % of true value. If true power is 1250 W, range of reading will be

(*a*) 1225 W – 1275 W
(*b*) 1245 W – 1255 W
(*c*) 1200 W – 1300 W
(*d*) 1237.5 W – 1262.5 W

112. A d'Arsonval galvanometer uses a light and scale arrangement. The light source is placed 1 m away from the moving system of galvanometer. The arrangement uses a circular scale calibrated in mm. The deflection indicated by the scale is

(*a*) 1000 mm (*b*) 2000 mm
(*c*) 500 mm (*d*) none of these

113. A 0 – 300 V voltmeter has an error of ± 2 % of full scale deflection. If true voltage is 30 V, the range of readings will be

(*a*) 24 V – 36 V
(*b*) 29.4 V – 30.6 V
(*c*) 20 V to 40 V
(*d*) none of these

114. An 0 – 10 A ammeter has guaranteed accuracy of 1 percent of full scale deflection. The limiting error while reading 2.5 is

(*a*) 1 % (*b*) 2 %
(*c*) 4 % (*d*) none of these

115. The power in a 3-phase, 3-wire load is measured using two 100W full-scale wattmeters W_1 and W_2. W_1 is of a accuracy class ± 1% and reads 100 W. W_2 is of accuracy class ± 0.5% and reads –50 W. Then the uncertainty in the computation to total power is

(*a*) ± 1.5% (*b*) ± 0.5 %
(*c*) ± 4% (*d*) ± 3%

116. A voltmeter has a resistance of 2000 Ω. When it is connected across a d.c. circuit, its power consumption is 2 mW. The circuit condition remain undisturbed. If this voltmeter is replaced by a voltmeter of 4000 Ω resistance, then power consumption will be

(*a*) 4 mW (*b*) 1 mW
(*c*) 2 mW (*d*) none of these

117. A milliammeter of resistance 100 Ω is connected in series with a circuit. Its power consumption is 0.1 mW. Supposing it is replaced with a milliammeter of 200Ω resistance the power consumption will be

(*a*) 0.2 mW (*b*) 0.05 mW
(*c*) 0.1 mW (*d*) none of these

118. The high torque to weight ratio in an analog indicating instrument indicates

(*a*) high friction loss
(*b*) low friction loss
(*c*) nothing as regards friction loss
(*d*) none of these

119. A PMMC instrument produces a deflection of 90° when a current 2 mA passes through its moving coil. The instrument is spring controlled. Supposing the instrument is redesigned with its spring constant as before, and its permanent magnet is replaced with a new permanent magnet which reduces twice the flux density as before, what would be the deflection if a current of 1 mA is passed through the coil ? The other features of the PMMC instrument remain the same.

(*a*) 180° (*b*) 90°
(*c*) 45° (*d*) 135°

120. A 1 mA ammeter has a resistance of 100Ω. It is to be converted to a 1 A ammeter. The value of shunt resistance is

(*a*) 0.001 Ω (*b*) 0.1001 Ω
(*c*) 100000 Ω (*d*) 100 Ω

121. A zero to 300 V voltmeter has guaranteed accuracy of 1% full scale reading. The voltage measured by the instrument is 83V. The percent limiting error is

(*a*) 0.95 (*b*) 1.81
(*c*) 3.62 (*d*) 4.85

122. In order to reduce errors on account of temperature, instruments are provided with shunts use series connected swamping resistance. In order that errors on account temperature changes be low, the swamping resistance

(*a*) should be made of a material giving a high resistance temperature co-efficient

(*b*) should be made of a material having a low resistance temperature co-efficient with the value of swamping resistance equal to meter resistance

(*c*) should be made of a material having low resistance temperature co-efficient and should have a value of about 20-30 times that of meter resistance

(*d*) should have an infinite value

123. A 4-range milliammeter having ranges of 0 – 10 mA, 0 – 50 mA, 0 – 100 mA and 0 – 500 mA. It is used for measurement of current whose magnitude is not known. In order to prevent damage to the instrument the selector switch of the ammeter should be first placed at

(*a*) 0 – 50 mA range

(*b*) 0 – 100 mA range

(*c*) 0 – 10 mA range

(*d*) 0 – 500 mA range

124. A 1 mA d'Arsonval movement has resistance of 100 Ω. It is to be converted to a 10 V voltmeter. The value of multiplier resistance is

(*a*) 999 Ω (*b*) 9999 Ω

(*c*) 9900 Ω (*d*) 990 Ω

125. A d'Arsonval movement is rated at 50 μA. Its sensitivity is

(*a*) 20000 Ω / V

(*b*) 200000 Ω / V

(*c*) 200 Ω / V

(*d*) cannot be determined

126. The power consumption PMMC instruments is typically about

(*a*) 0.25 W to 2 W

(*b*) 0.25 mW to 2 mW

(*c*) 25 μW to 200 μW

(*d*) none of these

127. Series type ohmmeter

(*a*) 0 marking is on the left hand side of side while ∞ marking is on the right hand side

(*b*) marking is on the right hand side of scale and ∞ infinity marking on the left hand side

(*c*) any of the above two marking can be on left or right side of the scale

(*d*) 0 marking is in the middle of scale

128. Which of the following are disadvantages of shunts for use at high currents?

(*a*) It is difficult to achieve good accuracy with shunts

(*b*) Power consumption of the shunts is large

(*c*) The metering circuit is not electrically isolated from the power circuit

(*d*) All of these

129. In electrodynamometer type of wattmeters, the inductance of pressure coil circuit produces error, which is

(*a*) constant irrespective of the power factor of the load

(*b*) higher at low power factors

(*c*) lower at low power factors

(*d*) none of these

130. When measuring power with an electrodynamometer wattmeter in a circuit where the load current is small

(*a*) the current coil should be connected on the load side

(*b*) the pressure coil should be connected on the load side

(*c*) it is immaterial whether current coil or pressure coil is connect on the load side

(*d*) none of these

131. Which of the following meter is most suitable for measuring radio frequency currents?

(*a*) Moving-coil meter

(*b*) Moving-iron meter

(*c*) Thermocouple meter

(*d*) VTVM

132. When measuring power with an electrodynamometer wattmeter in a circuit having a low power factor

(*a*) the current coil should be connected on the load side

(*b*) the current coil should be connected on the supply side

(*c*) the pressure coil should be connected on the load side

(*d*) a compensated wattmeter with pressure coil connected on the load side should be used

133. The power in a 3 phase circuit is measured with the help of 2 wattmeters. The readings of one of wattmeters is positive and that of the others is negative. The magnitude of readings is different. It can be concluded that the power factor of the circuit is

(*a*) unity (*b*) zero (lagging)

(*c*) 0.5 (lagging) (*d*) less than 0.5 (lagging)

134. The breaking torque provided by a permanent magnet in a single phase energy meter is proportional to the

(*a*) square of the flux of the permanent magnet

(*b*) speed of the meter

(*c*) distance of the permanent magnet from the center of the revolving disc

(*d*) all of these

135. In the single phase induction meter, in order to obtain true value of energy, the shunt magnet flux should lag behind the applied voltage by

(*a*) 90° (*b*) 0°

(*c*) 45° (*d*) none of these

136. In an induction type of meter, maximum torque is produced when the phase angle, between the two fluxes is

(*a*) 0° (*b*) 45° (*c*) 60° (*d*) 90°

137. In a single phase induction type energy, the lag adjustment is done

(*a*) to make the current coil flux to lag 90° behind the applied voltage

(*b*) to make the pressure coil flux to lag 90° behind the applied voltage

(*c*) to bring the pressure coil flux in phase with the applied voltage

(*d*) none of these

138. In a circuit of a single phase induction energy meter, the pressure coil lags the voltage 88° the errors while measuring power in two circuits having power factors of unity and 0.5 lagging are respectively are

(*a*) – 0.061%, + 6.1%

(*b*) + 0.061%, – 6.1%

(*c*) – 0.061%, – 6.1%

(*d*) – 6.1%, – 6.1%

139. Phantom loading for testing of energy meters is used

(*a*) to isolate the current and potential circuits

(*b*) to reduce power loss during testing

(*c*) for meters having low current ratings

(*d*) to test meters having a large current rating for which loads may not be available

140. In an induction type energy meter, compensation for static fraction is provided by

(*a*) shading bands which are actuated by to provide a constant torque irrespective of load

(*b*) lag circuits

(*c*) drilling holes in the disc

(*d*) none of these

141. If an induction type energy meter runs fast it can be slowed down by

(*a*) lag adjustment

(*b*) light load adjustment

(*c*) adjusting the position of braking magnet and making it come closer to the center of the disc

(*d*) adjusting the position of braking magnet and making it move away for the center of the disc.

142. Creeping in a single phase induction type energy meter may be due to

(*a*) overcompensation for friction

(*b*) over voltage

(*c*) vibrations

(*d*) all of these

143. Light load adjustments for induction type energy meters are usually done at

(*a*) 10% of full load current

(*b*) 5% of full load current

(*c*) 50% of full load current

(*d*) 1% of full load current

144. The controlling torque I single phase-power factor meters is provided by

(*a*) spring control

(*b*) gravity control

(*c*) stiffness of suspension

(*d*) none of these

145. There will be serious errors, if power factor of non-sinusoidal waveforms is measured by electrodynamometer power factor meters. This is true of

(*a*) only single phase meters

(*b*) only 3 phase meters

(*c*) both single and three phase meters

(*d*) none of these

146. A resistance of value 10 Ω approximately is to be measured-voltmeter method with resistance of ammeter is 0.02 Ω and that of voltmeter is 5000 Ω. The resistance should be measured by

(*a*) connecting the ammeter on the side of unknown resistance as this connection

(*b*) connection the voltmeter on the side of unknown resistance as this connection gives batter accuracy

(*c*) any of the two connection, as both of them give equal accuracy

(*d*) none of these

147. The power consumption of a d.c. voltmeter using a direct coupled amplifier when measuring a voltage 0.5 V is of the order of a few

(*a*) watt (*b*) milliwatt

(*c*) microwatt (*d*) nanowatt

148. A true rms reading voltmeter uses two thermocouples in order

(*a*) to increase sensitivity

(*b*) that the second thermocouple cancels out the no-linear effects of the first thermocouple

(*c*) to prevent drift in the d.c. amplifier

(*d*) all of these

INSTRUMENT TRANSFORMER

149. A current transformer has a rating of 100/5 A. Its magnetizing and loss component of exciting current are 10 A and 0.6 A respectively and secondary winding burden is purely resistive, its transformation ratio at rated current is

(*a*) 20.12 (*b*) 20.2

(*c*) 200.2 (*d*) none of these

150. A current transformer has a rating of 1000/5 A. Its magnetizing current and loss component of exciting current are 10 A and 6 A respectively. The phase angle between secondary winding induced voltage and current is 30°. The phase angle error of the transformer at rated current is

(*a*) 0.65°

(*b*) 0.305°

(*c*) 0.496°

(*d*) none of these

151. The errors in current transformers can be reduced by designing them with

(*a*) high permeability and low loss core materials, avoiding any joints in the core and also keeping the flux density to a low value

(*b*) using primary and secondary windings as close to each other as possible

(*c*) using large cross-sections for both primary and secondary winding conductors

(*d*) all of these

152. Turns compensation is used in current transformers primarily for reduction of

(*a*) phase angle error

(*b*) both ratio and phase angle errors

(*c*) ratio error reduction in phase error is incidental

(*d*) none of these

153. The ratio and phase angle errors in potential transformers may be reduced by

(*a*) increasing the exciting current

(*b*) increasing the resistance and leakage reactance in the transformer

(*c*) by not employing turns compensation

(*d*) none of these

154. Capacitive potential transformers are used

(*a*) for primary winding phase voltages above 100 kV

(*b*) for keeping the value of transformation ratio constant irrespective of the burden by making certain adjustment

(*c*) because they are cheaper than the electromagnetic trans-formers above a certain voltage range

(*d*) all of these

155. The size of potential transformers is

(*a*) the same as that of power trans- formers of the same VA rating

(*b*) much greater than that of power transformers of the same VA rating because they are designed for low ratio and phase angle errors which require large sized cores and winding conductors

(*c*) smaller than that of power transformers of the same VA rating

(*d*) none of these

ELECTRONIC INSTRUMENT

156. Electronic voltmeter provides more accurate readings in high resistance circuit as compared to a non-electronic voltmeter because of its

(*a*) high V/ohm ratings

(*b*) high ohm/V ratings

(*c*) low meter resistance

(*d*) high resolution

157. Modern electronic multimeters measure resistance by

(*a*) using a bridge circuit

(*b*) using an electronic bridge compensator for nulling

(*c*) forcing a constant current and measuring the voltage across the unknown resistance

(*d*) none of these

158. In digit voltmeter, over-ranging implies that

(*a*) next 4 digits are switched on

(*b*) $\frac{1}{2}$ digit is switched off

(*c*) $\frac{1}{2}$ digit is switched on

(*d*) an indicator short growing

159. The number of comparators needed in a parallel conversion type 8-bit A to D convertor is

(*a*) 8 (*b*) 16

(*c*) 255 (*d*) 256

160. In a dual stop integrating type digital voltmeter, the first integration is carried out for 10 periods of the supply frequency of 50 Hz. If the reference voltage used is 2 V, the total conversion time for an input of 1 V is

(*a*) 0.01 sec (*b*) 0.05 sec

(*c*) 0.1 sec (*d*) 1 sec.

161. A 10 bit A/D converter is used to digitise an analog signal in the 0 to 5 V range. The maximum peak to ripple voltage that can be allowed in the D.C. supply voltage is

(*a*) nearly 100 mV (*b*) nearly 50 mV

(*c*) nearly 25 mV (*d*) nearly 5.0 mV

162. A digital voltmeter measures

(*a*) peak value

(*b*) peak-to-peak value

(*c*) rms value

(*d*) average value

163. Sensitivity inaccuracy of a recording instrument means

(*a*) the amount of input required to produce unit pen deflection

(*b*) the smallest signal required to produce detectable output

(*c*) the maximum error in sensitivity displayed by a pen

(*d*) degree to which instrument in not sensitive enough to repeat readings

164. In the multimeter circuit shown in the figure for ac voltage measurement, the function of diode D_1 is to

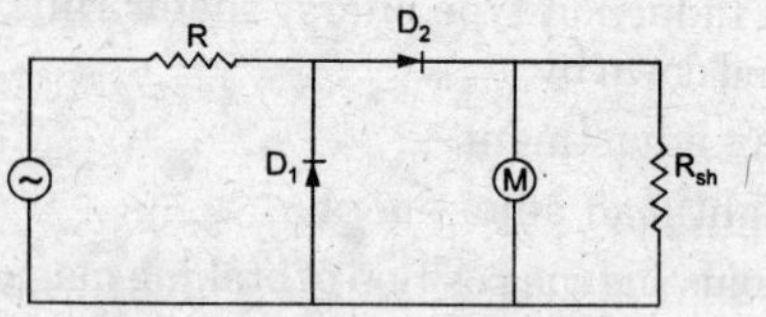

(*a*) provide half wave rectification

(*b*) make the recitifier D_2 perform full-wave rectification

(*c*) by-pass revers leakage current of D_2 in the negative cycle of the input

(*d*) short circuit-over range voltages

165. The main advantage in using a three OP-AMP instrumentation amplifier over a single OP-AMP differential amplifier lies in

(*a*) higher value of CMRR

(*b*) lower noise figure

(*c*) elimination of the need for accurate matching of resistors

(*d*) simplicity of gain adjustment

166. The measurement of very low and very high frequencies is invariably done using a frequency counter / timer in the

(*a*) frequency measurement mode only

(*b*) period measurement mode only

(*c*) frequency and period measurement modes respectively

(*d*) period and frequency measurement modes respectively

167. In the particular form of frequency meter, 1μ F capacitor is connected across a symmetrical square wave signal of 1V peak value. If average value of the current taken by the capacitor, after full wave rectification is measured as 2 mA, then the frequency of signal will be

(*a*) 1000 / π Hz (*b*) 500 Hz

(*c*) 1000 Hz (*d*) 1000 π Hz.

168. A digital voltmeter uses a 10 MHz clock and has a voltage controlled generator which provides a width of 10 μ sec per volt of unit signal. 10 volts of input signal would correspond to a pulse count of

(*a*) 500 (*b*) 750
(*c*) 1000 (*d*) 1500

169. An analog voltage signal whose highest significant is 1 kHz is to be digitally coded with a resolution of 0.01 % covering the voltage range of 0 to 10 volts. To avoid loss of information, the MINIMUM number of bits in the digital code should be

(*a*) 4 (*b*) 8
(*c*) 10 (*d*) 14

170. Which one of the following terms is NOT associated with a sample-and-hold circuit?

(*a*) Conversion time
(*b*) Acquisition time
(*c*) Aperture time
(*d*) Sample mode

171. Two resistance 100 Ω ± 5 Ω and 150 Ω are connected in series. If the errors are specified as standard deviations, the resultant error will be

(*a*) ± 10 Ω (*b*) ± 10.6 Ω
(*c*) ± 15.8 Ω (*d*) ± 20 Ω

172. Consider the following state-ments:

DC potentiometer is the best means available for measurement of dc voltages because

1. The precision in measurement is independent of the type of detector used.
2. It is based on null-balance technique.
3. It is possible to standardize before a measurement is undertaken.
4. It is possible to measure dc voltages ranging in value from millivolts to hundreds of volts.

Of these statements

(*a*) 2 and 3 are correct
(*b*) 1 and 4 are correct
(*c*) 2 and 4 are correct
(*d*) 3 and 4 are correct

173. An average response rectifier type electronic ac voltmeter has dc voltage of 10 V applied to it. The meter reading will be

(*a*) 7.1 V (*b*) 10.0 V
(*c*) 11.1 V (*d*) 22.2 V

174. Consider the following statements regarding the sources of error in a Q-meter.

1. If a coil with a resistance R is connected in the direct measurement mode and if the residual resistance of the Q-meter is 0.1 R, then the measured Q of the coil would be 1.1 times the actual Q.
2. If the inductance to be measured is less than 0.1 μ H, the error due to the presence of residual inductance cannot be neglected.
3. The presence of distributed capacitance in a coil modifies the effective Q of the coil.

Of these statements

(*a*) 1, 2 and 3 are correct (*b*) 1 and 2 are correct
(*c*) 2 and 3 are correct (*d*) 1 and 3 are correct

175. An advantage with a VTVM has over a nonelectronic voltmeter is

(*a*) lower power consumption
(*b*) lower input impedance
(*c*) the ability to measure wider ranges of voltage and resistance
(*d*) greater portability

176. Which of the following are the advantages of a balanced bridge vacuum tube voltmeter in comparison with a conventional VTVM?

1. Higher input impedance.
2. Meter zero has less tendency to shift.
3. Effects to changes due to variation of valve characteristics are minimised.
4. Power supply fluctuations have a smaller effect on the measuring circuit.

Select the correct answer using the codes given below :

Codes :

(*a*) 3 and 4 (*b*) 1 and 2
(*c*) 1, 2 and 3 (*d*) 1, 2, 3 and 4

177. In a digital voltmeter, the oscillator frequency is 400 kHz and ramp voltage falls from 8V to 0 V is 20 m sec. The number of pulses counted by the counter is

(*a*) 800 (*b*) 2000 (*c*) 4000 (*d*) 8000

178. The maximum percentage quantization error for a 12-bit analog to digital converter is

(*a*) ± 0.00076% (*b*) ± 0.012207%
(*c*) ± 3.125% (*d*) ± 4.17%

179. A 3-bit weighted resistor DAC shown in the figure has $V_R = 2V$ and $R_1/R = 2$. For an input of 100, the output will be

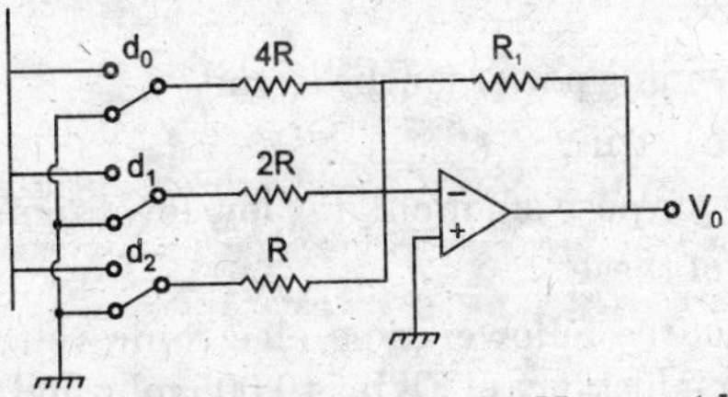

(*a*) –2 V (*b*) –4 V (*c*) 2 V (*d*) 4 V

180. Which one of the following instruments should be used at M in the given figure for the measurement of magnitude as well as direction of the displacement?

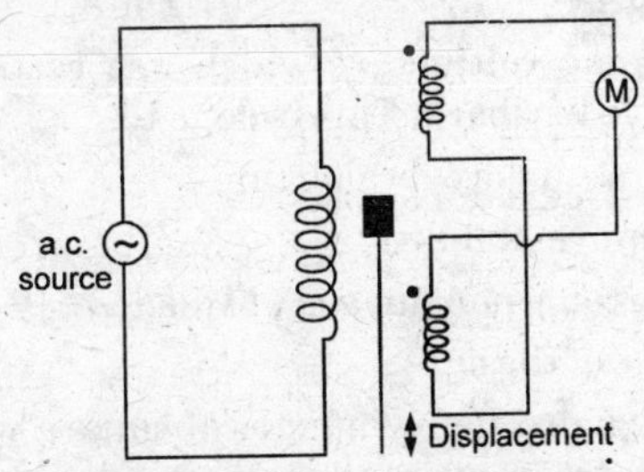

(*a*) Permanent magnet moving coil voltmeter
(*b*) Vacuum Tube voltmeter (VTVM)
(*c*) Transistor voltmeter (TVM)
(*d*) Phase Sensitive Detector (PSD).

181. An integrating digital voltmeter measures
(*a*) true average value
(*b*) rms value
(*c*) peak value
(*d*) peak to peak value

182. A 10 V full-scale voltmeter having 100 k-ohm / V sensitivity is used to measure the output of a photovoltaic cell having an internal resistance of 1 M-ohm. The voltmeter reads 5V. The voltage generated by the photovoltaic cell is
(*a*) 5 V
(*b*) 10 V
(*c*) greater than 5 V but less than 10 V
(*d*) greater than 10 V

183. In a reed type frequency meters all the reeds
(*a*) have the same natural frequency
(*b*) have different natural frequency
(*c*) have different natural frequencies but the difference in natural frequency adjacent reeds is ± 0.5 Hz
(*d*) none of these

184. A 53 Hz reed type frequency meter is polarized with d.c. The new range frequency meter is
(*a*) 106 Hz (*b*) 26.5 Hz
(*c*) 53 Hz (*d*) none of these

185. An average reading VTVM use one diode connected in series with an external resistance. A high value of series resistance is used so that the instrument should have
(*a*) a high input impedance
(*b*) a linear $v - i$ characteristics
(*c*) low power consumption
(*d*) all of these

186. In a compensated shunt type peak reading VTVM a bucking battery with a series adjustable resistance is used for
(*a*) providing power for the circuit
(*b*) zero setting
(*c*) the purpose of amplifying low level signal
(*d*) all of these

187. In a source follower type electronic voltmeter, the transconductance of FETs is 0.005 mho and resistance of the meter is 100 Ω. The approximated value of current through the meter, when the input voltages is 1 V, is
(*a*) 2.5 mA (*b*) 5 mA
(*c*) 2 mA (*d*) 1 mA

188. Electronic voltmeters which use rectifiers employ negative feedback. This is done to
(*a*) increase the overall gain
(*b*) improve stability
(*c*) overcome non linearity of diodes
(*d*) none of these

189. A voltage having symmetrical square wave shape is applied to an average reading voltmeter with scale calibrated in terms of rms value of a sinusoidal wave has an error of
(*a*) – 3.9% (*b*) + 3.9%
(*c*) – 11% (*d*) + 11%

190. In an electronic ohmmeter, an OP-AMP is used as a
(*a*) summer
(*b*) multiplier
(*c*) buffer amplifier
(*d*) integrator

191. A voltmeter with a broad band width has
(*a*) low noise level and high sensitivity
(*b*) high noise level and high sensitivity
(*c*) high noise level and low sensitivity
(*d*) low noise level and low sensitivity

192. The deflection of an electron beam on a CRT screen is 10 mm. If the pre-accelerating anode voltage is halved and the potential between deflecting plates is doubled, the deflection of then electron beam will be
(*a*) 80 mm (*b*) 40 mm
(*c*) 20 mm (*d*) 10 mm

193. If the distance of screen from a CRT to center of deflection plates is 15 cm. Length of deflection plates is 2 cm, distance between plates is 1 cm and the accelerating voltage is 500 V, then deflection sensitivity is
(*a*) 33.2 V/cm
(*b*) 0.03 cm/V
(*c*) 66.4 V/cm
(*d*) 0.015 cm/V

194. In modern electronic multimeter, a FET or MOS FET is preferred over BJT because
(*a*) its input resistance is high
(*b*) its input resistance is high and does not change with range switch
(*c*) its input resistance is low
(*d*) it is cheaper

195. If the Q factor of a coil which is $\frac{\omega_0 L}{R}$ is measured by varying the frequency, the
(*a*) plot between Q and frequency is linear
(*b*) value of Q initially decreases with increase of frequency and afterwards increases with increases frequency
(*c*) value of Q initially decreases with increase of frequency and afterwards increases with increases frequency
(*d*) Q factor remains constant irrespective of the value of frequency

196. The Q factor or of a coil at the resonant frequency 1.5 MHz of an RLC series circuit is 150. The bandwidth will be
(*a*) 225 MHz (*b*) 1.06 MHz
(*c*) 10 kHz (*d*) none of these

197. The resonant frequency of an RLC series circuit is 1.5 MHz with the tuning capacitor set at 150 pF. The bandwidth is 10 kHz. The effective resistance of the circuit is
(*a*) 29.5 Ω (*b*) 14.75 Ω
(*c*) 9.4 Ω (*d*) 4.7 Ω

198. In a Q meter, distributed capacitance of coil is measured by changing the capacitance of the tuning capacitor. The values of tuning capacitor are C_1 and C_2 for resonant frequencies f_1 and $2f_1$ respectively. The value of distributed capacitance is

(*a*) $\frac{C_1 - C_2}{2}$ (*b*) $\frac{C_1 - 2C_2}{3}$

(*c*) $\frac{C_1 - 4C_2}{3}$ (*d*) $\frac{C_1 - 3C_2}{2}$

199. The true value of Q of a coil is 245 and the measured value of 244.5. The ratio of distributed capacitance to self capacitance of the coil is

(*a*) 2.04×10^{-3}

(*b*) 1.002

(*c*) 0.997

(*d*) none of these

200. A photo voltaic cell is connected across a very large value of resistance, its sensitivity at higher illumination levels is typical

(*a*) infinity

(*b*) zero

(*c*) some finite value which is very large

(*d*) some finite value which is very small and nears zero

201. Which of the following photo-electric devices is most suitable for digital applications?

(*a*) Photo-emissive cell (*b*) Photo diode

(*c*) Photo transistor (*d*) Photo voltaic cell

202. If an information is required to be stored over a short interval of time

(*a*) a single number devices should be used

(*b*) a storage type oscilloscope should be used

(*c*) a CRO with photographic equipment should be used

(*d*) a direct writing recorder or a magnetic tape recorder should be used

203. Digital instruments have input impedance of the order of

(*a*) 1 Ω (*b*) kΩ

(*c*) MΩ (*d*) mΩ

CRO

204. A vertical amplifier for a CRO can be designed for

(*a*) only a high gain

(*b*) only a broad bandwidth

(*c*) a constant gain times band-width product

(*d*) all of these

205. On an oscilloscope, the Lissajous pattern of eight keeps on changing the shape when the ratio of frequencies is

(*a*) not exactly 1 : 1

(*b*) not exactly 2 : 1

(*c*) exactly 3 : 1

(*d*) exactly 4 : 1

206. The source of emission of electrons in a CRT is

(*a*) PN function diode

(*b*) a barium and strontium oxide coated cathode

(*c*) accelerating anodes

(*d*) post-accelerating anodes

207. In a CRT, the focusing anode is located

(*a*) between pre-accelerating and accelerating anodes

(*b*) after accelerating anode

(*c*) before pre-accelerating anode

(*d*) none of these

208. A CRO screen has ten divisions on the horizontal scale. If a voltage signal 5 sin (314*t* + 45°) is examined with a line base setting of 5 msec/div, the number of cycle of signal displayed on the screen will be

(*a*) 0.5 cycle (*b*) 2.5 cycles

(*c*) 5 cycles (*d*) 10 cycles

209. A certain oscilloscope with 4 cm by 4 cm screen has its own speed output fed to its input at the *x* and *y* sensitivities are same. the oscilloscope will display a

(*a*) triangular wave (*b*) diagonal line

(*c*) sine wave (*d*) circle

210. In CRT aquadag carries

(*a*) aqueous solution of araphite

(*b*) sweep voltage

(*c*) secondary emission electrons

(*d*) none of these

211. If the transients during switching of a power supply are to be studied, which of the following oscilloscope will be preferred?

(*a*) An ordinary oscilloscope with high frequency sweep generator

(*b*) Dual beam oscilloscope

(*c*) Dual trace oscilloscope

(*d*) Storage oscilloscope

212. A signal of 10 mV at 75 MHz is to be measured with which of the following instruments?

(*a*) VTVM

(*b*) Cathode ray oscilloscope

(*c*) Moving iron voltmeter

(*d*) Digital multimeter

213. How many times base circuits does a dual trace CRO can have?

(*a*) 1 (*b*) 2

(*c*) 3 (*d*) 4

214. A Lissajous pattern on an oscilloscope has 5 horizontal tangencies and 2 vertical tangencies. The frequency of the horizontal input is 100 Hz. The frequency of the vertical input will be

(*a*) 400 Hz (*b*) 2500 Hz

(*c*) 4000 Hz (*d*) 5000 Hz

215. In measurements made using a Q-meter, high impedance elements should preferably be connected in

(*a*) star (*b*) delta

(*c*) series (*d*) parallel

216. Which meter is suitable for the measurement of 10 m V at 50 MHz?

(*a*) Moving-iron voltmeter

(*b*) VTVM

(*c*) Electrostatic voltmeter

(*d*) C.R.O.

217. The Lissajous pattern obtained on a CRO screen is shown in the given figure. The frequency ratio of the vertical signal to the horizontal signal is

(*a*) 3 : 2 (*b*) 5 : 1
(*c*) 1 : 5 (*d*) 2 : 3

218. To the *y*-input of a CRO a signal defined by 10 sin 100*t* is applied. To the *x*-input the signal 10 cos 100*t* is fed. The gain for both *x*-channel and *y*-channel is the same. The screen shows

(*a*) sinusoidal
(*b*) a straight line
(*c*) an ellipse
(*d*) a circle

219. A CRO screen has ten divisions on the horizontal scale. If a voltage signal 5 sin (314 *t* + 45°) is examined with a line base setting of 5 m sec/div, the number of cycles of signal displayed on the screen will be

(*a*) 0.5 cycles (*b*) 2.5 cycles
(*c*) 5 cycles (*d*) 10 cycles

220. A Lissajous pattern, as shown in the figure is observed on the screen of a CRO when voltage of frequencies f_x and f_y are applied to the X and Y plates respectively. Then $f_x : f_y$ is then equal to

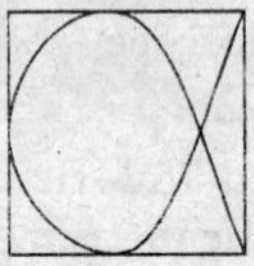

(*a*) 3 : 2 (*b*) 1 : 2
(*c*) 2 : 3 (*d*) 2 : 1

221. Two sine waves of same frequency are impressed of the *x* and *y* plates of a CRO and the Lissajous figure seen is shown in the given figure. The phase difference between the signals is

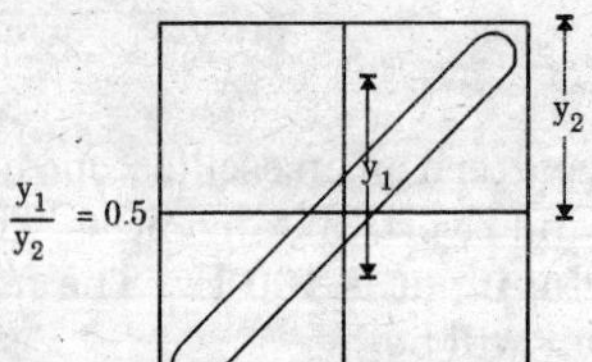

(*a*) 30° or 330° or 150° or 210°
(*b*) 30° or 330° or 150°
(*c*) 30° or 330°
(*d*) 30°

222. When the horizontal deflecting plates of a CRO are kept at the ground potential and 30 V dc is applied to the vertical deflecting plates, then the picture observed on the screen would be

(*a*) a spot approximately 3 cm away from the centre
(*b*) a vertical line 2 cm long
(*c*) a vertical line approximately 3 cm long
(*d*) two spots 2 cm vertical above each other

223. To minimize the loading of the circuit under test, the input impedance of a CRO should

(*a*) be low
(*b*) be high
(*c*) be capacitive
(*d*) match with the output impedance of the circuit

224. Two sinusoidal signals having the same amplitude and frequency are applied to the X and Y inputs of a CRO. The observed Lissajous' figure is a straight line.The phase shift between the two signals would be

(*a*) zero
(*b*) 90 degrees
(*c*) either zero or 180 degrees
(*d*) either 90 degrees or 270 degrees

225. A sinusoidal waveform, when observed on an oscilloscope, has a peak to peak amplitude of 6 cm. If the vertical sensitivity setting is 5V/ cm, then rms value of the voltage will be

(*a*) 10.6 V (*b*) 11.1 V
(*c*) 12.6 V (*d*) 15 V.

226. In the cirucuit given in the figure, the limiting error in the power dissipation I2R in the resistor R is

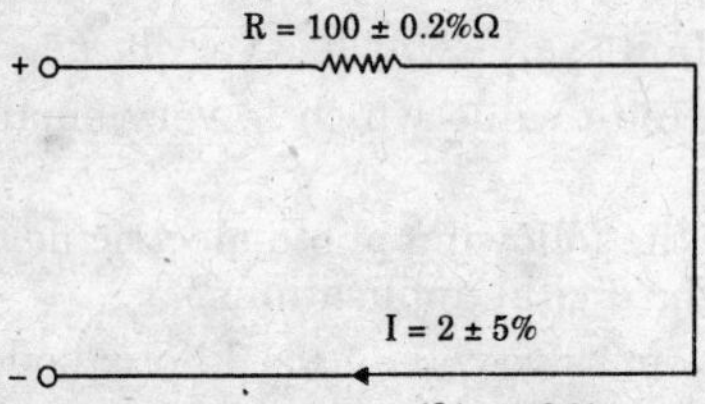

(*a*) 1.2% (*b*) 5.2%
(*c*) 10.2% (*d*) 25.2%

227. A 150 V moving iron voltmeter of accuracy class 1-0 reads 75 V when used in a circuit under standard conditions. The maximum possible percentage error in the reading is

(*a*) 0.5 (*b*) 1.0
(*c*) 2.0 (*d*) 4.0

228. A distorted sinusoid has the amplitudes $A_1, A_2, A_3, ...$ of the fundamental second harmonic third harmonic, ... respectively. The total harmonic distortion is

(*a*) $\sqrt{\dfrac{A_1^2 + A_2^2 + A_3^2 + ----}{A_1}}$

(*b*) $\sqrt{\dfrac{A_2^2 + A_3^2 + ----}{A_1}}$

(*c*) $\sqrt{\dfrac{A_2^2 + A_3^2 + ----}{A_1^2 + A_2^2 + A_3^2 + ---}}$

(*d*) $1 - \sqrt{\dfrac{A_2^2 + A_3^2 + ----}{A_1}}$

229. A resistance is measured by the voltmeterammeter method employing d.c. excitation and a voltmeter of very high resistance connected directly across the unknown resistance. If the voltmeter and ammeter readings are subject to maximum possible errors of ± 2.4% and ± 1.0 % respectively, then the magnitude of maximum possible percentage error in the value of resistance deduced from the measurement is nearly

(*a*) 1.4% (*b*) 1.7%
(*c*) 2.4% (*d*) 3.4%

ERROR ANALYSIS

230. Four ammeter M_1, M_2, M_3 and M_4 with the following specifications are available :

Instrument	Type	Full scale value (A)	Accuracy % of FS
M_1	3½ digit dual scope	20	± 0.10
M_2	PMMC	10	± .20
M_3	Electrodynamic	5	± 0.50
M_4	Moving iron	1	± 1.00

A current of 1 A is to be measured. To obtain minimum error in the reading, one should select meter

(*a*) M_1 (*b*) M_2
(*c*) M_3 (*d*) M_4

231. Which one of the following statement is not correct?

(*a*) It is not possible to have precise measurement which are not accurate

(*b*) Correctness in measurement requires both accuracy and precision

(*c*) Reproducibility and consistency are expressions that best describe precision in measurements

(*d*) An instrument with 2% accuracy is better than another with 5% accuracy

232. The limiting error of measurement of power consumed by and the current passing through a resistance are ± 1.5% and ±1% respectively. Then the limiting error of measurement of resistance will be

(*a*) ± 0.5 % (*b*) ± 1.0%
(*c*) ± 2.5% (*d*) ± 3.5%

ANSWERS

1. (*c*)	**2.** (*b*)	**3.** (*d*)	**4.** (*a*)	**5.** (*a*)	**6.** (*a*)	**7.** (*d*)	**8.** (*b*)	**9.** (*b*)	**10.** (*d*)
11. (*a*)	**12.** (*b*)	**13.** (*a*)	**14.** (*c*)	**15.** (*d*)	**16.** (*d*)	**17.** (*d*)	**18.** (*c*)	**19.** (*d*)	**20.** (*c*)
21. (*c*)	**22.** (*b*)	**23.** (*c*)	**24.** (*c*)	**25.** (*d*)	**26.** (*d*)	**27.** (*d*)	**28.** (*d*)	**29.** (*b*)	**30.** (*b*)
31. (*d*)	**32.** (*a*)	**33.** (*d*)	**34.** (*b*)	**35.** (*a*)	**36.** (*b*)	**37.** (*b*)	**38.** (*c*)	**39.** (*c*)	**40.** (*d*)
41. (*c*)	**42.** (*d*)	**43.** (*d*)	**44.** (*c*)	**45.** (*b*)	**46.** (*c*)	**47.** (*b*)	**48.** (*d*)	**49.** (*c*)	**50.** (*b*)
51. (*c*)	**52.** (*b*)	**53.** (*c*)	**54.** (*b*)	**55.** (*d*)	**56.** (*c*)	**57.** (*a*)	**58.** (*a*)	**59.** (*c*)	**60.** (*c*)
61. (*c*)	**62.** (*b*)	**63.** (*d*)	**64.** (*d*)	**65.** (*d*)	**66.** (*c*)	**67.** (*c*)	**68.** (*d*)	**69.** (*c*)	**70.** (*d*)
71. (*c*)	**72.** (*d*)	**73.** (*d*)	**74.** (*a*)	**75.** (*c*)	**76.** (*b*)	**77.** (*a*)	**78.** (*b*)	**79.** (*d*)	**80.** (*d*)
81. (*c*)	**82.** (*b*)	**83.** (*b*)	**84.** (*a*)	**85.** (*b*)	**86.** (*d*)	**87.** (*b*)	**88.** (*c*)	**89.** (*a*)	**90.** (*b*)
91. (*b*)	**92.** (*a*)	**93.** (*c*)	**94.** (*c*)	**95.** (*a*)	**96.** (*b*)	**97.** (*b*)	**98.** (*c*)	**99.** (*a*)	**100.** (*b*)
101. (*c*)	**102.** (*c*)	**103.** (*b*)	**104.** (*b*)	**105.** (*c*)	**106.** (*b*)	**107.** (*d*)	**108.** (*d*)	**109.** (*b*)	**110.** (*d*)
111. (*d*)	**112.** (*b*)	**113.** (*a*)	**114.** (*c*)	**115.** (*d*)	**116.** (*b*)	**117.** (*a*)	**118.** (*b*)	**119.** (*b*)	**120.** (*b*)
121. (*c*)	**122.** (*c*)	**123.** (*d*)	**124.** (*c*)	**125.** (*a*)	**126.** (*c*)	**127.** (*b*)	**128.** (*d*)	**129.** (*b*)	**130.** (*a*)
131. (*c*)	**132.** (*d*)	**133.** (*d*)	**134.** (*d*)	**135.** (*a*)	**136.** (*d*)	**137.** (*b*)	**138.** (*c*)	**139.** (*d*)	**140.** (*a*)
141. (*b*)	**142.** (*d*)	**143.** (*d*)	**144.** (*d*)	**145.** (*a*)	**146.** (*a*)	**147.** (*d*)	**148.** (*b*)	**149.** (*a*)	**150.** (*d*)
151. (*a*)	**152.** (*c*)	**153.** (*d*)	**154.** (*b*)	**155.** (*d*)	**156.** (*b*)	**157.** (*c*)	**158.** (*c*)	**159.** (*c*)	**160.** (*c*)
161. (*d*)	**162.** (*d*)	**163.** (*c*)	**164.** (*c*)	**165.** (*c*)	**166.** (*d*)	**167.** (*a*)	**168.** (*c*)	**169.** (*b*)	**170.** (*a*)
171. (*c*)	**172.** (*a*)	**173.** (*c*)	**174.** (*c*)	**175.** (*a*)	**176.** (*d*)	**177.** (*d*)	**178.** (*b*)	**179.** (*d*)	**180.** (*d*)
181. (*a*)	**182.** (*b*)	**183.** (*c*)	**184.** (*a*)	**185.** (*d*)	**186.** (*d*)	**187.** (*c*)	**188.** (*c*)	**189.** (*d*)	**190.** (*c*)
191. (*c*)	**192.** (*d*)	**193.** (*d*)	**194.** (*b*)	**195.** (*c*)	**196.** (*c*)	**197.** (*d*)	**198.** (*c*)	**199.** (*a*)	**200.** (*d*)
201. (*d*)	**202.** (*d*)	**203.** (*c*)	**204.** (*c*)	**205.** (*b*)	**206.** (*d*)	**207.** (*a*)	**208.** (*b*)	**209.** (*b*)	**210.** (*a*)
211. (*d*)	**212.** (*b*)	**213.** (*c*)	**214.** (*b*)	**215.** (*d*)	**216.** (*d*)	**217.** (*b*)	**218.** (*d*)	**219.** (*b*)	**220.** (*b*)
221. (*c*)	**222.** (*c*)	**223.** (*a*)	**224.** (*a*)	**225.** (*a*)	**226.** (*c*)	**227.** (*c*)	**228.** (*b*)	**229.** (*d*)	**230.** (*c*)
231. (*b*)	**232.** (*d*)								

EXPLANATIONS

BRIDGES AND POTENTIOMETERS

1. From the balance equation,

$$R_1\left(R+\frac{1}{j\omega C}\right)=R_2\,\frac{R\cdot\frac{1}{j\omega C}}{R+\frac{1}{j\omega C}}$$

or $$\frac{R_1(j\omega CR+1)}{j\omega C}=\frac{R_2R}{(j\omega CR+1)}$$

or $$R_1(-C^2\omega^2R^2+1+2j\omega CR)=jR_2C\omega R$$

or $$2C\omega RR_1=C\omega RR_2$$

$\therefore$ $$R_1=\frac{R_2}{2}\quad\text{and}\quad -C^2\omega^2R^2+1=0,$$

or $$\omega=\frac{1}{RC}$$

or $$f=\frac{1}{2\pi RC}$$

3. Writing the bridge balance equations :

$$\left[R_1+\frac{1}{jC_1\omega}\right]R_4=R_2\left[\frac{R_3(1/jC_3\omega)}{R_3+(1/jC_3\omega)}\right]$$

$$\Rightarrow\quad\left[R_1+\frac{1}{j\omega C_1}\right]R_4=R_2\cdot\frac{R_3}{jR_3C_3\omega+1}$$

or $$\left(R_1+\frac{1}{jC_1\omega}\right)(1+jR_3C_3\omega)=\frac{R_2R_3}{R_4}$$

It gives, $$R_1+R_3\,\frac{C_3}{C_1}=\frac{R_2R_3}{R_4},$$

and $$R_1R_3C_3\omega=\frac{1}{C_1\omega}$$

or $$\omega=\frac{1}{\sqrt{R_1R_3C_1C_3}}$$

If $C_1=C_3$, then first equation becomes

$$R_1+R_3=\frac{R_2R_3}{R_4}.$$

Again if $R_1=R_3$ and the common variable short of resistance R_1 and R_2 can be graduated in frequency to measure the frequency ω. Thus conditions to be satisfied are

$$C_1=C_3,\ R_2=2R_4,\ \text{and}\ R_1=R_3$$

4. $n=k\times$ power $\times$ time in hour

$$=\frac{400\times240\times10\times0.8}{100}\times\frac{1}{3600}\,rph=\mathbf{12.8\ rpm}$$

6. Applying the usual balance condition relation,

$$Z_1Z_4=Z_2Z_3.$$

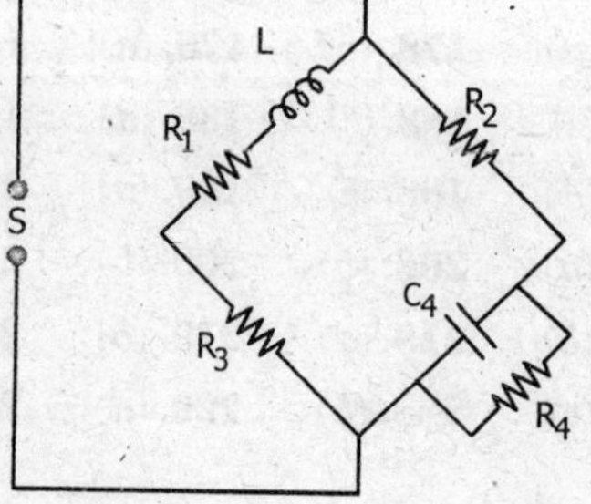

we have $$(R_1+jL_1\omega)\frac{1/R_4jC_4\omega}{R_4+1/jC_4\omega}=R_2R_3$$

or $$(R_1+jL_1\omega)\frac{R_4/jC_4\omega}{R_4+1/jC_4\omega}=R_2R_3$$

or $$R_1R_4+jL_1\omega R_4=R_2R_3+jR_2R_3R_4C_4\omega$$

$\therefore$ $$R_1=R_2\frac{R_3}{R_4},\quad L_1=R_2R_3C_4$$

$$R_1=2000\times\frac{750}{4000}=\mathbf{375\ ohm.}$$

$\therefore$ $$L_1=2000\times750\times0.05\times10^{-6}=\mathbf{75\ mH.}$$

7. Current in either branch is

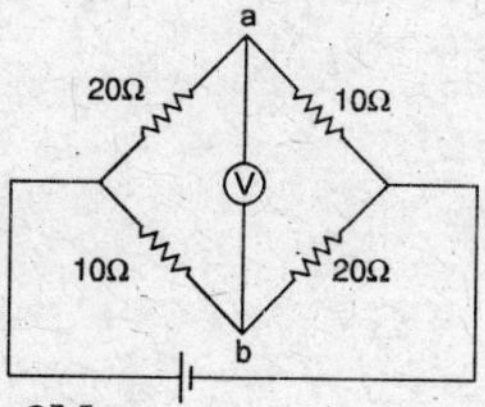

$$I=\frac{10}{30}=\frac{1}{3}\ \text{A.}$$

$$V_{ab}=20\times\frac{1}{3}+10\times\frac{1}{3}=\mathbf{3.33\ V}$$

9. $L=L_1+L_2\pm2M.$

When ordinary, $L=L_1+L_2+2M$

$\therefore$ $40=10+15+2M.$

$\therefore$ $2M=15$ mH

When opposing, $L=L_1+L_2-2M$

$=10+15-15=\mathbf{10\ mH}$

10. From balance condition

$$R_aR_c=(R_d+j\omega L_d)\frac{R_b}{1+j\omega_{cb}R_b}$$

or $$(1+j\omega_{cb}R_b)R_aR_c=R_b(R_d+j\omega L_d)$$

or $$R_bR_d=R_aR_c\qquad\therefore\quad R_d=\frac{R_aR_c}{R_b}$$

and $$\omega C_bR_bR_aR_c=\omega R_bL_d$$

or $$L_d=R_aR_cC_b$$

23. Total length of the slide wire = 1000 cm

Total resistance of the slide wire = 1000 ohm

$\therefore$ Resistance per cm = 1 ohm

Resistance of 101.8 cm segment of the wire = 101.8 ohm

This corresponds to a voltage of 1.018 V.

$\therefore$ $$\text{Current}=\frac{1.018}{101.8}=\mathbf{1\ mA}$$

24. Error in the potentiometer is due to thermo electric emfs set up at junctions of dissimilar metals and also by the heat from the operator's hand during adjustment of the working parts of the potentiometer. Reversing of polarity and taking reading will give error in the negative direction. Suppose the reading with error due to one direction is $\Delta+\Delta R$ and in the other direction is $\Delta-\Delta R$, then

$$\text{mean value}=\frac{\Delta+\Delta R+\Delta-\Delta R}{2}$$

which is the actual value.

MEASURING INSTRUMENTS

27. Sensitivity of d.c. voltmeter = 1000 Ω/volt

For half scale in 100 V range, *i.e.* 50 V current through the voltmeter,

$$I=\frac{50}{1000}=\mathbf{50\ mA}$$

39. Gauge factor $= \dfrac{dR/R}{\xi_a}$

$\therefore \quad \dfrac{dR}{R} = 2 \times 10^{-5}$

or $\quad dR = 2 \times 120 \times 10^{-5} = \mathbf{2.4 \times 10^{-3}}$

42. Parallel sum of 600 ohm and 1200 ohm

$$= \frac{600 \times 1200}{1800} = 400 \text{ ohm}$$

$\therefore \quad \dfrac{R}{35.5} = \dfrac{400}{5}$

or $\quad R = \mathbf{2400\ ohms = 2.4\ k\ ohms}$

43. Capacitance, $C = \dfrac{\text{Charge, Q}}{\text{Voltage, V}} = \dfrac{It}{V}$

Since I and V units are both charged by the same factor and time unit is not changed, hence capacitance unit is not affected.

44. $\dfrac{Q_1}{Q_2} = \dfrac{I_1^2}{I_2^2} \qquad \therefore \quad \dfrac{5}{1} = \dfrac{10^2}{I_2^2}$

or $\quad I_2 = \mathbf{4.47\ A}$

45. $\tan\phi = \sqrt{3}\,\dfrac{W_1 - W_2}{W_1 + W_2} = \sqrt{3}\,\dfrac{5-3}{5+3} = \dfrac{\sqrt{3}}{4}$

$\therefore \quad \cos\phi = \dfrac{1}{\sqrt{19}} = 0.917 \text{ (lag)}$

46. $\dfrac{10}{R_1 + 100} = 10^{-3}$

or $\quad R_1 + 100 = 10.000$

or $\quad R_1 = \mathbf{9900\ ohm = 9.9\ k\Omega}$

48. We know, $\quad T_D = C\theta \quad$ ....(*i*)

Also $\quad T_D = KI^2 \quad$ ....(*ii*)

From equations (*i*) and (*ii*),

$$I^2 = \frac{C}{K}\theta = C'.\theta$$

$$\therefore \quad \frac{I^2}{1} = \frac{C'.\frac{\pi}{1}}{C'.\frac{\pi}{2}} = \frac{1}{2}$$

or $\quad I = \mathbf{0.707\ A}$

49. For half wave rectifier output,

$$I_{dc} = \frac{I_m}{\pi} \text{ and } I_{rms} = \frac{I_m}{2}$$

Hence PMMC reading will be,

$$I_{dc} = \frac{2 \times 5}{\pi} = \mathbf{3.18\ amp}$$

53. Maximum possible error that can be present on any reading

$$= 30 \times \frac{2}{100} = 0.6 \text{ V}$$

Thus the voltmeter reading can be within 29.4 V to 30.6 V

54. Energy consumed $= \dfrac{230 \times 20 \times 1 \times 2}{1000} = 9.2 \text{ kWh}$

Revolution made = 1380

$\therefore$ Meter constant $= \dfrac{1380}{9.2} = 150$ rev/kWh

57. Full scale meter current = 1 mA

For $\quad$ 10 V range, $10^{-3} = \dfrac{10}{(100 + R_1)}$

or $\quad R_1 = 9.9 \times 10^3\ \Omega$

For $\quad$ 50 V range, $10^{-3} = \dfrac{50}{(100 + R_1 + R_2)}$

or $\quad R_1 + R_2 = 49.9 \times 10^3$

$\therefore \quad R_2 = \mathbf{40\ k\Omega}$

58. Two wattmeter readings are,

$W_1 = V_L I_L \cos(30 - \phi)$
$= V_L I_L \cos(30 - 90°) = V_L I_L \cos 60°$
$W_2 = V_L I_L \cos(30 + \phi)$
$= V_L I_L \cos 120° = -V_L I_L \cos 60°$

59. Energy consumed as indicate by energy meter

$$= \frac{90}{1800} = 0.05 \text{ kWh}$$

Actual energy consumed

$$= 230 \times \left(\frac{10}{2}\right) \times 1 \times \left(\frac{3}{60}\right) \times 10^{-3} = 0.0575 \text{ kWh}$$

$\therefore$ Error = 0.0500 – 0.0575 = – 0.0075 kWh

Hence meter is slow by $\dfrac{0.0075}{0.0500} \times 100 = \mathbf{15\%}$

60. Current $= \dfrac{\text{Voltage}}{\text{resistance}} = \dfrac{1}{50{,}000\Omega/V} = 20\ \mu A$

61. Resistance = Sensitivity at ohm × Voltage in volts

$$= \frac{1000}{150} = \mathbf{6.67\ ohms}$$

62. Energy consumed = 230 × 5 × 5 = 5750 Wh = 5.57 kWh

Revolution constant = 400 rev/kWh

$\therefore \quad \text{kWh} = \dfrac{1940}{400} = 4.8$

Power factor $= \dfrac{4.8}{5.75} = 0.8$

63. The meter reading will either decrease or increase depending upon the direction of flux.

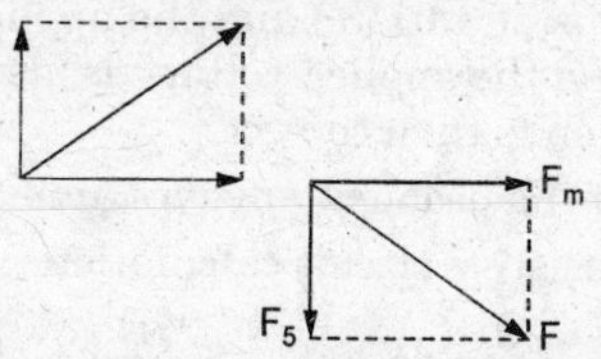

As shown in figure let FM be the flux due to meter coil and F, is due to stray magnetic field, then resultant will be F. Similarly when F is in opposite direction. Thus the reading will either increase or decrease.

64. The spring gives the controlling torque and is connected in series with the coil. If the spring is snapped, there will be no deflection.

67. Gauge factor $= \dfrac{\nabla R/R}{\Delta L/L}$

But $\quad \dfrac{\nabla L}{L} = \dfrac{100}{2 \times 10^5} \qquad \therefore \quad \dfrac{\nabla R}{R} = \dfrac{3 \times 100}{2 \times 10^5}$

$\therefore$ Percentage change $= \dfrac{\nabla R}{R} \times 100 = \mathbf{0.15}$

68. RMS or root mean square value is defined as

$$(V_o)_{RMS} = \sqrt{\frac{1}{T}\int_0^T V_0^{\,2}(t)dt}$$

The diode circuit provides full wave rectification.

$$\therefore \quad (V_o)_{RMS} = \sqrt{\frac{1}{4}\int_0^T 4dt} = \sqrt{2}$$

71. Sensitivity of LVDT $= \dfrac{\text{output voltage}}{\text{displacement}}$

$$= \frac{1/2 \times 10^{-3}}{0.5} = 1\text{V/mm}$$

73. $$I_{fs} = \frac{E}{R_1 + R_m}$$

With R_x connected,

$$I_m = \frac{R_x}{R_x + R_m} \quad \frac{E}{R_1 + (R_m R_x)/(R_m + R_x)}$$

$$= \frac{R_2R_3}{R} = \frac{ER_x}{R_x(R_1 + R_m) + R_1R_m}$$

$$= \frac{E}{(R_1 + R_x)} \quad \frac{R_x}{R_x + (R_1R_m)/(R_1 + R_m)}$$

$$= I_{fs} \frac{R_x}{R_m + R_p}$$

where, $R_P = \dfrac{R_1R_m}{(R_1 + R_m)}$

74. For low resistance measurements, if circuit II is used, the ammeter resistance which may be comparable with the low resistance being measured gets added to the unknown and thereby causing larger error.

75. The setting of the potentiometer is at 1.0138 instead of 1.0813. Therefore, working current in the slide wise is more than what it would have been if the setting was at 1.0813,

i.e. correct value for applied voltage of 1.0813V,

$I = 1.0813, \quad I_c = 1.0138$

It the setting is at 1.01138 and the applied voltage is also 1.0138 and the applied voltage is also 1.0138, the standardisation is then correct.

(Statement of the problem appears ambiguous).

76. It is simple resistive circuit calculation.

$$I_c = \frac{1}{1 + R_3 + R_G} \quad \frac{E}{2500 + \dfrac{1(R_3 + R_G)}{1(R_3 + R_G)}}$$

From the given data,

$$\frac{1}{1 + 450 + R_G} \quad \frac{1}{2500 + \dfrac{450 + R_G}{1 + 450 + R_G}}$$

$$= \frac{1}{1 + 950 + R_G} \quad \frac{2E}{2500 + \dfrac{950 + R_G}{1 + 950 + R_G}}$$

or $2500\,(451 + R_G) + 450 + R_G = 2500\,(951 + R_G) + 50$

or $2501\,R_G = 2500\,(951 - 902) + 50$

or R_G = **49 ohms.**

79. A compensated wattmeter has its reading corrected for error due to power consumed in potential coil.

80. The wattmeter readings are proportional to cos (30 + θ). When θ = 90°, the two quantities are equal and opposite. Therefore, when the load is purely inductive or capacitive, the given situation will occur.

81. Sensitivity $= \dfrac{I}{I_B} = \dfrac{1}{5}$ mA = 200 ohm/V

84. The "accuracy" of measuring instrument is determined by the closeness of the value indicated by it to the correct value of the measurand.

85. The wattmeters reading is proportional to cos (30 + ϕ)

Then other is proportional cos (30 – ϕ)

Thus whenever load p.f. angle ϕ becomes 60°, one of the wattmeters would read zero.

Hence for the given condition load

load p.f = cos 60° = **0.5**

86. Voltage across R_1, $V_1 = 35 - 5 = 30$ V

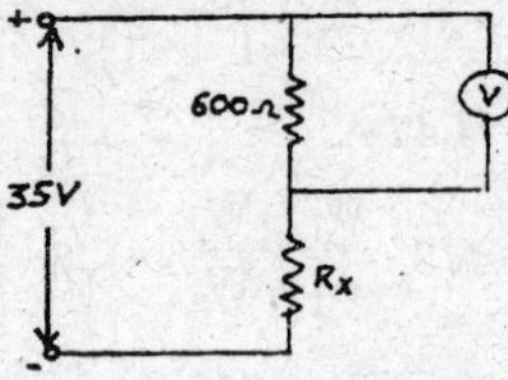

Current in the circuit, $I = \dfrac{5}{\dfrac{600 \times 1200}{600 + 1200}} = \dfrac{5}{400}$ A

$$\therefore \quad R_x = \frac{30 \times 400}{5} = 2.4\text{k}\,\Omega$$

88. Sensitivity of an instrument is ratio of the change in the magnitude of the output to the corresponding change in the magnitude of the input.

90. Form factor of the wave $= \dfrac{\text{rms Value}}{\text{Mean Value}}$

Moving iron Instrument will show rms value. Rectifier voltmeter is calibrate to read rms value of sinusoidal voltage, *i.e.* with form factor of 1.11.

$\therefore$ Mean value of the applied voltage $= \dfrac{V_2}{1.11}$.

$$\therefore \text{ Form factor} = \frac{V_1}{V_2/1.11} = \frac{1.11V_1}{V_2}$$

91. Sensitivity

$$= \frac{\text{Total of resistance of the instrument}}{\text{Full scale current figure}} \text{ ohm/V}$$

$$= \frac{1}{10 \times 10^{-6}} = 10 \text{ k-ohm/V}$$

93. $r_{cc} = 0.01$ ohm, $r_{vc} = 1000$ ohm.

There are two ways in which the current coil and voltage coil can be connected. The wattmeter reads high by an amount equal to power loss in current coil in one case and in voltage coil in the other.

The two possible power losses are

(i) $I_C^{\,2}\, r_{cc} = 20^2 \times 0.01 = 4$W

(ii) $\dfrac{V^2}{r_{vc}} = \dfrac{30^2}{1000} = 0.9$ W

The two percentage errors are

(i) $\frac{4 \times 100}{600} = \frac{2}{3}$

(ii) $\frac{0.9 \times 100}{600} = 0.15$

95. Total capacitance

= Crystal capacitance + Cable capacitance + Oscilloscope capacitance

$= (10 + 2 + 4) \times 10^{-10}$ F

Change sensitivity = 4×10^6 C/cm

$$\text{Voltage sensitivity} = \frac{\text{Change sensitivity}}{\text{Total capacitance}}$$

$$= \frac{4 \times 10^{-6}}{16 \times 10^{-10}} = \mathbf{2500\ V/cm}$$

115. $W_1 = 100W + 1W;$

$W_2 = -50 + 0.5W$

$\therefore \quad W_1 + W_2 = \left(50 \pm \frac{1.5}{50}\right) \times 100 = \pm 3\%$

121. 1% accuracy means that a maximum possible error of

$\frac{300 \times 1}{100} = 3$ may be present in any reading.

Since the deflection is 83V, therefore

$$\text{percent limiting error} = \frac{3}{83} \times 100 = \mathbf{3.62.}$$

ELECTRONIC INSTRUMENT

159. For parallel conversion type A to D converter,

number of comparators required = $2^N - 1$,

where, N is the number of bits = $2^8 - 1$ = **255**

160. In a dual slope integrating type digital voltmeter,

$$\left(\frac{t_2}{t_1}\right) V_{in} = V_{ref}$$

where, t_1 = first integration time = $10 \times \frac{1}{50} = 0.2$s

But $V_{in} = 1V_1$, and $V_{ref} = 2$

$\therefore \quad t_2 = \frac{V_{in} t_1}{V_{ref}} = \frac{1 \times 0.2}{2} = \mathbf{0.1\ sec.}$

161. Smallest incremental change = $\frac{1}{2^{10}} = \frac{1}{1024}$

For 5 V, Incremental change = $\frac{5}{1024}$ = nearly 5 mV

164. If D_1 were not there in the negative half cycle of the applied voltage, there would be some small reverse current through D_2 (in the reverse direction) and the meter, there by giving erroneous mean value and hence of the applied voltage. With D_1 as in circuit, the current in the negative half cycle flows through R_{sh} and D_1 and there is no voltage across D_2 and hence no current through D_2.

165. There is no need for accurate matching of resistor's.

167. $f = \frac{2}{2\pi\sqrt{10^{-6}}} = \frac{1000}{\pi}$ Hz.

171. Given $R_1 = 100$ ohm $\pm$ 5 ohm.

$R_2 = 150$ ohm $\pm$ 15 ohm.

Now $R = R_1 + R_2$

The errors are specified at standard deviations The probable errors in this case.

$$R = \pm\sqrt{R_1^2 + R_2^2} = \pm\sqrt{5^2 + 15^2} = \mathbf{\pm 15.8\ ohms.}$$

173. A rectifier type instrument is calibrated to read rms values for sinusoidal waveforms Thus it shows 1.11 time and average value.

Therefore, reading should be $10 \times 1.11 = 11.1$V.

174. Q = Lω/R.

With Q-meter resistance considered, the measured or indicated Q is 1/1.11 times the actual Q. Thus statement 1 is not correct.

Hence statements 2 and 3 are correct.

175. A VTVM draws a very small fraction of power from the circuit on which measurement is made, It thus offers very high input impedance and has low power consumption.

177. Assuming that gate opens when the ramp is 8V and closes when the ramp reached zero.

∴ Number of pulses counted by counter

$= 400 \times 10^3 \times 20 \times 10^{-3} = 8000.$

179. $I_0 = \frac{2}{R}$ and $E_0 = (\frac{2}{R}) \times R_1 = 2 \times 2 = \mathbf{4V}$

180. M should be able to detect phase reversal if not strictly phase sensitive. Phase sensitive detector can well serve the purpose.

182. Voltmeter resistance = $100 \times 10 = 1000\ k\Omega = 1\ M\Omega$

Photovoltaic cell internal resistance= 1 M-ohm.

The voltmeter reads 5V.

Therefore, the internal voltage is 10 V

CRO

208. Lines base setting = 5 msec/div

Input frequency = $\frac{1}{5 \times 10^{-3}} = 200$ Hz

Frequency input signal = 314 = ω = 2π*f*

or $f = \frac{314}{2\pi} = 50$ Hz

Number of cycles at signal displayed = $\frac{50}{200} \times 10 = \mathbf{2.5}$

213. Dual trace ocsilloscope uses a single electron gun and produces multiple traces by switching the *y*-deflection plates from one input signal to another.

214. $\frac{f_v}{f_h} = \frac{T_h}{T_v} \Rightarrow f_v = \frac{5}{2} \times 1000 = \mathbf{2500\ Hz}$

217. $\frac{f_v}{f_h} = \frac{\text{No. of intersection of Lissajous fig. on a horizontal line}}{\text{No. of intersection of Lissaious fig. on a vertical line}}$

$= \frac{10}{2} = 5:1$

218. $x^2 + y^2 = 10^2\ |\ \sin^2(100\,t) + \cos^2(100\,t)\,|$

= 100, which is constant

Hence the circle.

219. The lines base setting = 5 msec/div

Input frequency = $\frac{1}{5 \times 10^{-3}} = 200$ Hz

Now, Frequency of input signal = 314 = ω.

or $2\pi f = 314$ or $f = 314/2\pi = 50$ Hz

Number of cycles of signal displayed = $\frac{50 \times 10}{200} = 2.5$

220. $\frac{f_x}{f_y} = \frac{\text{points of tangency to vertical line}}{\text{points of tangency to horizontal line}} = \frac{1}{2}$

or $f_x : f_y = 1 : 2$

221. When major area of the Lissajous figure lies in the 1st and 3rd quadrant, then the angle is within 0 and ± 90°. If the loop lies in 2nd and 4th quadrant, then the angle is 180° – θ, where θ is within 0 and + 90°.

In the present case the angle is given by

$$\theta = \sin^{-1}(Y_1/Y_2) = \sin^{-1} 0.5 = 30^\circ$$

Hence, the phase difference is 30° or –30°, *i.e.* 30° or 300°.

Y_1 is the deflection on the Y-plates when X-plates deflection is zero, *i.e.* when $V_x(t) = 0$ and $V_y(t) = V_{my} \sin \phi$ and Y_2 is the deflection due to V_{my}.

222. Total length observed will be proportional to $2V_m$

$$= 2\sqrt{2} \times 30.$$

30 V dc causes 1 cm deflection from the centre point.

Length observed = $2\sqrt{2}$ cm = 3 cm.

225. Amplitude of the signal $= \frac{6 \times 5}{2} = 15\text{V}$

$\therefore$ rms value $= \frac{15}{\sqrt{2}} = 10.6$ V

226. $P = I^2R$

$$\therefore \quad \frac{dP}{P} = \frac{2dI}{1} + \frac{dR}{R}$$

Therefore, limiting error in the power $= 2 \times 0.05 + 0.002$

$= 0.102 = \mathbf{10.2\%}$

227. The error specified is always with respect to full scale reading and this is the maximum error that may be present at any deflection

$$\therefore \quad \% \text{ error} = \frac{1.0}{100} \times 150 \times \frac{1}{75} \times 1000 = \mathbf{2.0}$$

229. Ammeter error, Δ I = ± 2.4%

Voltmeter error, Δ V = ± 2.4%

Resistance to be measured, $R = \frac{V}{I}$

In case error in resistance measurement is ± ΔR, then the maximum possible error will be

$$R + \Delta R = V + \frac{V + \Delta V}{I - \Delta I}$$

or $RI + I\Delta R - R - \Delta I\Delta R = V + \Delta V$

Neglecting ΔIΔR being small and substituting V = RI, we have

$$V + I\Delta R - R\Delta I\Delta R = V + \Delta V$$

or $I\Delta R - R\Delta I = \Delta V$

Dividing by IR, we get

$$\frac{\Delta R}{R} - \frac{\Delta I}{I} = \frac{\Delta V}{IR} - \frac{\Delta V}{I} = \frac{\Delta V}{V}$$

or $\frac{\Delta R}{R} = \frac{\Delta V}{V} + \frac{\Delta I}{I}$

Therefore maximum percentage error

= 2.4 % + 1% = 3.4%

ERROR ANALYSIS

230. $M_1 = 20 \times 0.001 = 0.02,$

$\therefore$ Relative error at 1 A $= \frac{0.02}{1} = 2\%$

$M_2 = 10 \times 0.002 = 0.02,$

$\therefore$ Relative error $= \frac{0.02}{1} = 2\%$

$M_3 = 5 \times 0.005 = 0.025,$

$\therefore$ Relative error $= \frac{0.025}{1} = 2.5\%$

$M_4 = 1 \times 0.01 = 0.01,$

$\therefore$ Relative error $= \frac{0.01}{1} = 1\%$

232. If $W = U^a/V^b$, then

Limiting error (in W)

= *a* × limiting error in U + *b* × limiting error in V

$$R = \frac{P}{I^2}$$

$\therefore$ Limiting error in measurement of resistance R = limiting error in the measurement of power + 2 × limiting error in the measurement of current = ± (1.5 + 2 × 1) = **± 3.5%**

PRACTICE QUESTIONS

1. A thermocouple
   (*a*) has a low time constant when it is bare
   (*b*) has a low time constant if is provided with a sheath
   (*c*) has the same time constant whether it is bare or is provided with sheath
   (*d*) none of these
2. Two strain gauges are used to measure strain in a cantilever. One gauge is mounted on top of the cantilever and the other is placed at the bottom. The two strain gauges form two arms of a voltage sensitive wheat stone bridge. This bridge configuration is called
   (*a*) a guarter bridge (*b*) a half bridge
   (*c*) a full bridge (*d*) a null bridge
3. A null type of instrument as compared to a deflection type instrument has
   (*a*) a higher accuracy (*b*) a lower sensitivity
   (*c*) a faster response (*d*) all of these
4. When measuring insulation resistance of cables using d.c. source, the galvanometer used should be initial short circuited because
   (*a*) cables have a low value of initial resistance
   (*b*) cables have a high value of capacitance which draws a high value of charging current
   (*c*) cables have a low value of capacitance which draws a high value of charging current
   (*d*) none of these
5. The value of resistance of an earthing electrode depends upon
   (*a*) shape and material of electrode
   (*b*) depth to which electrode is driven into earth
   (*c*) specific resistance of soil
   (*d*) all of these

6. Which of the photoelectric transducers is used for production of electric energy by converting solar energy?

(*a*) Photo emissive cell

(*b*) Photo diode

(*c*) Photo transistor

(*d*) Photo voltaic cell

7. If two 300 V full-scale voltmeters V_1 and V_2 having sensitivities of 100 kΩ/V and 150 kΩ/V are connected in series to measure 500 V. Then

(*a*) V_1 and V_2 will read 250 V each

(*b*) V_1 will read 200 V and V_2 will read 300 V

(*c*) V_1 will read 300 V and V_2 will read 200 V

(*d*) V_1 and V_2 will read 0

8. Two-wattmeter method is employed to measure power in a 3-phase balanced system with the current coils connected in the A and C lines. The phase sequence is ABC. If the wattmeter with its current coil in A-phase line reads zero, then power factor of the 3-phase load will be

(*a*) zero lagging (*b*) zero leading

(*c*) 0.5 lagging (*d*) 0.5 leading

9. The shunt type ohmmeter is NOT suitable for high resistance measurements because

(*a*) a very low resistance of the meter would short the high unknown resistance

(*b*) scale is highly cramped for high resistance values

(*c*) full-scale value of the meter may be exceeded

(*d*) battery cannot supply the necessary current for proper meter detection

10. The major cause of creeping in an energy meter is

(*a*) over-compensation for friction

(*b*) mechanical vibrations

(*c*) excessive voltage across the potential coil

(*d*) stray magnetic fields

11. In moving-coil meters, damping is provided by

(*a*) eddy current disk

(*b*) the aluminium frame of the coil

(*c*) damping vane in the airtight chamber

(*d*) the coil spring attached to the moving

12. In the statement "the wattmeter commonly used for power measurement at commercial frequencies is of the X type. This meter consists of two coil systems, the fixed system being the Y coil and moving system being Z coil". X, Y and Z stand respectively for

(*a*) dynamometer, voltage and current

(*b*) dynamometer, current and voltage

(*c*) induction, voltage and current

(*d*) induction, current and voltage

13. A spring controlled instrument uses phosphor bronze springs to produce controlling torque. If the ratio of length of spring to thickness of spring is 3000 for a deflection 90°, what should be this ratio if the scale is to be extended to 120° ?

(*a*) 4000 (*b*) 2250

(*c*) 2000 (*d*) none of these

14. A d.c. circuit can be represented by a voltage source of 10 V in series with an output resistance of 1 kΩ. An ammeter of 50 Ω resistance is connected to the source terminals for measurement of current. The accuracy of measurement is nearly

(*a*) – 4.8 % (*b*) + 4.8 %

(*c*) 99 % (*d*) 95.2 %

15. Which of the following are disadvantages of using multipliers with voltmeters at high voltages?

(*a*) The power consumption of multipliers becomes large average voltages.

(*b*) The multipliers at high voltages have to be shielded in order to prevent capacitive currents.

(*c*) The metering circuit is not electrically from the power circuit.

(*d*) All of these.

16. At high frequency the accuracy of all the measuring meters

(*a*) increases

(*b*) decreases

(*c*) remains the same

(*d*) depends upon the type of meter

17. The braking torque provided by a permanent magnet in a single phase energy meter can be changed by

(*a*) providing a magnetic shunt and changing its position

(*b*) changing the distance of the permanent magnet from the center of the revolving disc

(*c*) both (*a*) and (*b*)

(*d*) none of these

18. The power in d.c. circuit is measured with the help of ammeter and a voltmeter. The voltmeter is connected on the load side. The power indicated by the product of reading of two instruments (VI) is

(*a*) the power consumed in the load

(*b*) the sum of power consumed by load and the voltmeter

(*c*) the sum of power consumed by load and the ammeter

(*d*) none of these

19. When testing a coil having a resistance of 10 ohms, resonance occured when the oscillator frequency was 10 MHz and the rotating capacitor was set at $500/2\pi$ pF. The effective value of the Q of the coil is

(*a*) 200 (*b*) 254 (*c*) 314 (*d*) 542

20. Pulses of a frequency of 1 MHz are applied to the time base selector of a digital frequency meter which consists of 6 frequency dividers, each dividing the incoming frequency by a factor of 4th frequency divider starting from the input is

(*a*) 1 ms (*b*) 10 ms

(*c*) 100 ms (*d*) 1 s

21. A series RLC circuit is used for measurement of inductance of a coil using resonant method. Reasonable conditions are produced by varying the capacitance of a thermo electric type ammeter guised in series with the circuit. Also an electronic voltmeter is connected across the tuning capacitor?

(*a*) The condition of resonance are more reliably indicated when the ammeter reads maximum

(*b*) The conditions of resonance are more reliably indicated when the voltmeter connected across the capacitor reads maximum

(*c*) The condition of resonance are the same when both ammeter and voltmeter read maximum

(*d*) The conditions of resonance are indicated when both ammeter and voltmeter read minimum

22. A resistor of 10k-ohm with 5% tolerance is connected in series with a 5 k-ohms resistor at 10% tolerance. The tolerance limit of the series network will be

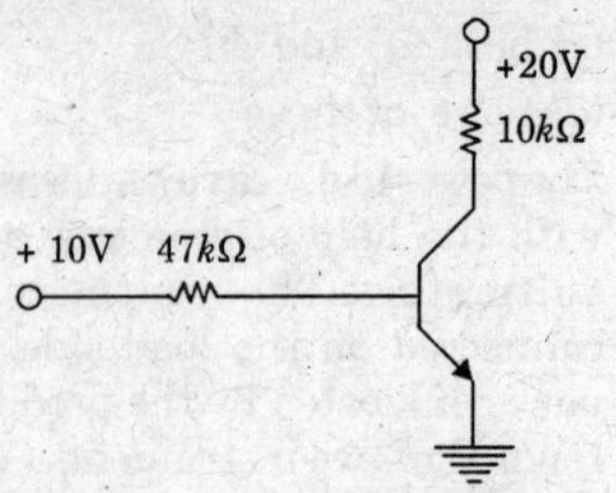

(*a*) 5% (*b*) 6.67%
(*c*) 10% (*d*) 8.38%

23. If the Q-factor of a coil is measured by varying the frequency, then
(*a*) the plot between Q and frequency is linear
(*b*) the value of Q initially decreases with increase of frequency and afterwards it will increase with increase of frequency
(*c*) the value of Q initially increases with increase of frequency and afterwards it will decrease with increase of frequency
(*d*) the Q-factor remains constants irrespective of value of frequency

24. A dc circuit can be represented by an internal voltage source of 50 V with an output resistance of 100 kΩ.In order to achieve accuracy better than 99% for voltage measurement across its terminals, the voltage measuring device should have a resistance of atleast
(*a*) 10 MΩ (*b*) 1 MΩ
(*c*) 10 kΩ (*d*) 1 kΩ

25. An analogue voltage signal whose highest significant frequency is 1 kHz is to be coded with a resolution of 0.01 percent for a voltage range of 0 – 10 V. The minimum sampling frequency and the minimum number of bits should respectively be
(*a*) 1 kHz and 12
(*b*) 1 kHz and 14
(*c*) 2 kHz and 12
(*d*) 2 kHz and 14

26. An ac voltmeter using full-wave rectification and having a sinusoidal input has an ac sensitivity equal to
(*a*) 1.414 times dc sensitivity
(*b*) dc sensitivity
(*c*) 0.90 times dc sensitivity
(*d*) 0.707 times dc sensitivity

27. A 1 cm piezoelectric transducer having a g-coefficient of 58 V/kg/m^2 is subjected to a constant pressure of 10 kg/m^2 for about 15 minutes. The piezo voltage developed by the transducer will be
(*a*) 116 mV (*b*) 58 mV
(*c*) 29 mV (*d*) 0 mV

28. In an oscilloscope, two Lissajous figure (X) and (Y) are observed. This indicates that ratio of vertical input signal frequency to that of horizontal input frequency are

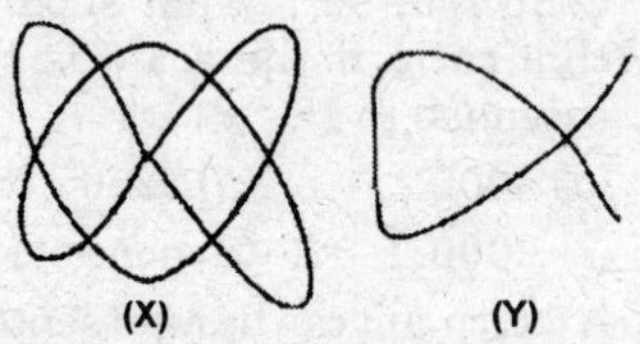

(X) (Y)

(*a*) $\frac{5}{3}$ for X and $\frac{3}{2}$ for V
(*b*) $\frac{3}{2}$ for X and $\frac{5}{3}$ for Y
(*c*) $\frac{5}{3}$ for X and $\frac{5}{3}$ for Y
(*d*) $\frac{3}{2}$ for X and $\frac{3}{2}$ for Y

29. A C.R.O. is operated with X and Y settings of 0,5 mV/cm and 100 mV/cm. The screen of the C.R.O. is 10 cm × 8 cm (X and Y). A sine wave of frequency 200 Hz and r.m.s. amplitude of 300 mV is applied to the Y-input. The screen will show
(*a*) one cycle of the undistorted sine wave
(*b*) two cycles of the undistorted sine wave
(*c*) one cycle of the sine wave with clipped amplitude
(*d*) two cycles of the sine wave with clipped amplitude

30. A Wien-bridge is used to measure the frequency of the input signal. However, the input signal has 10% third harmonic distortion. Specifically the signal is 2 sin 400 πt + 0.2 sin 1200 πt (with t in sec). With this input the balance will
(*a*) lead to a null indication and setting will correspond to a frequency of 200 Hz
(*b*) lead to a null indication and setting will correspond to 260 Hz
(*c*) lead to a null indication and setting will correspond to 400Hz
(*d*) not lead to null indication

31. Three d.c. voltmeters are connected in series across a 120 V d.c. supply. The voltmeters are specified as follows:
Voltmeter A : 100 V, 5 mA
Voltmeter B : 100 V, 250 ohms/V
Voltmeter C : 10 mA, 15,000 ohms
The voltages read by the meters A, B and C are, respectively
(*a*) 40, 50 and 30 V
(*b*) 40, 40 and 40 V
(*c*) 60, 30 and 30 V
(*d*) 30, 60 and 30 V

32. A 0 to 200 V voltmeter has a guaranteed accuracy of 1% of full scale reading. The voltage measured by this instrument is 50 V. What is the limiting error?
(*a*) 4% (*b*) 2%
(*c*) 1% (*d*) 0.25%

33. Which one of the following methods decreases the error due to connections in a dynamometer type wattmeter?
(*a*) Using bifilar compensating winding in place of current coil
(*b*) Using non-inductive pressure coil circuit
(*c*) Using a capacitor across a part of high resistance of pressure coil circuit
(*d*) Using a swamping resistance

34. An electronic voltmeter is more reliable as compared to multimeter for measuring voltage across low impedance because
(*a*) its sensitivity is high
(*b*) it offers high input impedance
(*c*) it does not alter the measured voltage
(*d*) its sensitivity, and input impedance are high and do not alter the measured value

35. Which one of the following decides the time of response of an indicating instrument?
(*a*) Deflecting system
(*b*) Controlling system
(*c*) Damping system
(*d*) Pivot and Jewel bearing

36. Consider the signal
$V_m \sin 100t + 2V_m \sin 200t$
to be sampled and stored in a data acquisition system. The same is to be extracted off-line later on. In order to extract the signal effectively, the original sampling frequency has to be
(*a*) 100 rad/s
(*b*) 200 rad/s
(*c*) 210 rad/s
(*d*) $\sqrt{100^2 + 200^2}$ rad/s

37. What is the effect of inductance in the pressure coil on performance of a dynamometer type wattmeter ?
(*a*) It reads low on lagging power factor and high on leading power factor
(*b*) It reads high on lagging power factor and low on leading power factor
(*c*) Its reading is not affected at all
(*d*) It always reads low

38. The maximum temperature rise of a transformer is 50°C. It attains a temperature of 31.6° $\frac{1}{2}$ hour. What is its thermal time constant ?
(*a*) 2 hours (*b*) $\frac{1}{2}$ hour
(*c*) 1 hour (*d*) $\frac{1}{4}$ hour

39. A moving-coil instrument gives full-scale deflection for 1 mA and has a resistance of 5 Ω. If a resistance of 0.55 Ω is connected in parallel to the instrument, what is the maximum value of current it can measure?
(*a*) 5 mA (*b*) 10 mA
(*c*) 50 mA (*d*) 100 mA

40. A single slide wire is used for the measurement of current in a circuit. The voltage drop across a standard resistance of 1.0 Ω is balanced at 70 cm. What is the magnitude of the current, if the standard cell having an e.m.f. of 1.45 volts is balanced at 50 cm?
(*a*) 3.09 A (*b*) 2.65 A
(*c*) 2.03 A (*d*) 1.45 A

41. A sinusoidal voltage of 1 V r.m.s. value at 10 Hz is applied across the two terminals of a PMMC type of voltmeter. What is the deflection of the pointer?
(*a*) Zero volt
(*b*) 1 volt
(*c*) $\sqrt{2}$ volts
(*d*) The pointer oscillates around zero volt

42. Which one of the following is the correct statement ?
Due to inductance in the pressure coil the dynamometer wattmeter
(*a*) reads low on lagging p.f. and high on leading p.f.
(*b*) reads high on lagging p.f. and low on leading p.f.
(*c*) reading is not affected at all
(*d*) always reads low

43. A waveform shown in the figure, is fed to a.d.c. ammeter. What is the reading shown by the meter?

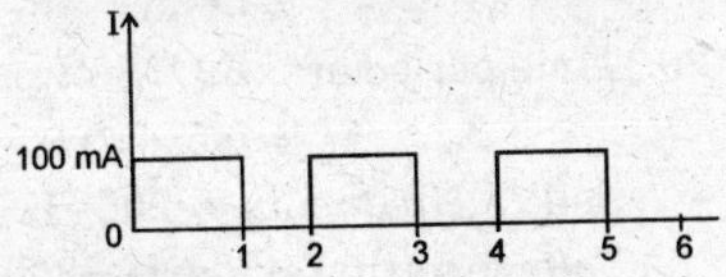

(*a*) Zero (*b*) 50 mA
(*c*) 75 mA (*d*) 100 mA

44. The oscilloscope has an input capacitance of 50 pF and a resistance of 2 MΩ and the voltage divider ratio (*k*) of 10. What are the parameters of a high-impedance probe ?
(*a*) C_1 = 5.55 pF and R_1 = 9 MΩ
(*b*) C_1 = 5.55 pF and R_1 = 18 MΩ
(*c*) C_1 = 3.33 pF and R_1 = 9 MΩ
(*d*) C_1 = 1.11 pF and R_1 = 18 MΩ

45. A strain gauge having a resistance of 500 ohm and a gauge factor 3.0 is bonded on a member of structure undergoing tensile stress. If the change in resistance of the gauge is accurately measured as 1.5 ohm, what is the value of strain suffered by the member ?
(*a*) 0.01 (*b*) 0.001
(*c*) 0.1 (*d*) 0.003

46. In a digital voltmeter, the oscillator frequency is 400 kHz. The ramp voltage falls from 8 V to 0 V in 20 ms. What is the number of pulses counted by the counter ?
(*a*) 8000 (*b*) 4000
(*c*) 3200 (*d*) 1600

47. A (0 – 25) Amp ammeter has a guaranteed accuracy of 1 per cent of full scale reading. The current measured by this ammeter is 10 Amp. The limiting error in percentage for this instrument is
(*a*) 2.5% (*b*) 0.5%
(*c*) 0.25% (*d*) 0.025%

48. A moving coil ammeter having a resistance of 1 ohm gives full scale deflection when a current of 10 mA is passed through it. The instrument can be used for the measurement of voltage up to 10 V by
(*a*) connecting a resistance of 999 ohm in series with the instrument
(*b*) connecting a resistance of 999 ohm parallel to the ammeter
(*c*) connecting a resistance of 999 ohm parallel to the load
(*d*) connecting a resistance of 1000 ohm in series with the load

49. A resistance strain gauge with gauge factor (S_f) of 2 is bonded to a steel member, which is subjected to a strain of 1×10^{-6}. The original resistance value of this strain gauge is 120 Ω. The change in resistance due to the applied strain is
(*a*) 60 Ω (*b*) 240×10^{-6} Ω
(*c*) 240 Ω (*d*) 60×10^{-6} Ω

50. The measurement of Hall coefficient of a semiconductor with one type of charge carrier gives the information about
(*a*) sign of charge carrier
(*b*) density of charge carrier
(*c*) both sign and density of charge carrier
(*d*) mass of the charge carrier

51. A piezoelectric crystal has a thickness of 2.5 mm and a voltage sensitivity of 0.05 Vm/N. The piezoelectric crystal is subjected to an external pressure of 1.6×10^6 N/m², then the corresponding output voltage is
(*a*) 200 volts
(*b*) 3.2×10^9 volts/m of thickness
(*c*) 0.07×10^{-9} V/(m³/New)
(*d*) 200 m volts

52. A 4-digit DVM (digital voltmeter) with a 100-mV lowest full-scale range would have a sensitivity of how much value while resolution of this DVM is 0.0001?
(*a*) 0.1 mV (*b*) 0.01 mV
(*c*) 1.0 mV (*d*) 10 mV

ANSWERS

1. (a)	2. (b)	3. (a)	4. (b)	5. (d)	6. (d)	7. (b)	8. (c)	9. (b)	10. (c)
11. (b)	12. (b)	13. (a)	14. (d)	15. (d)	16. (b)	17. (c)	18. (d)	19. (a)	20. (b)
21. (b)	22. (c)	23. (a)	24. (a)	25. (d)	26. (c)	27. (b)	28. (d)	29. (a)	30. (d)
31. (a)	32. (a)	33. (a)	34. (d)	35. (c)	36. (b)	37. (b)	38. (b)	39. (b)	40. (c)
41. (a)	42. (b)	43. (b)	44. (b)	45. (b)	46. (a)	47. (a)	48. (a)	49. (b)	50. (c)
51. (a)	52. (b)								

EXPLANATIONS

7. $\frac{V_1}{V_2} = \frac{100 \times 10^3 \times 300}{150 \times 10^3 \times 300} = \frac{1}{1.5}$

and $V_1 + V_2 = 500$ V

$\therefore$ $V_1 = 200$ V and $V_2 = 300$ V

8. For the phase sequence and connections specified, the reading in the wattmeter of line A is proportional to $(30° + \theta)$, where θ is the lagging load power factor angle.

Since it reads zero, $\theta = 60°$

or load p.f. is $\cos 60° = 0.5$ lagging.

9. Meter current, $I_m = I_{fs} \frac{R_x}{R_x + R_p}$

where, R_x is unknown

and $R_p = \frac{R_1 R_m}{R_1 + R_m}$

(quite a low value)

Variation in the value of R_x when R_x is in the high value range, cause hardly any variation in I_m and thus the scale is highly cramped for high resistance values.

10. The correction friction compensation is done at normal voltage. If the voltage is above the normal voltage, the friction compensating torque is in excess and will cause the meter to creep.

11. The movement induces emf and hence current in the aluminium frame of the coil. The torque developed due to this current is the damping torque.

12. In the induction type of instrument there is no moving coil. Therefore, the wattmeter in question is of dynamometer type. The fixed coil is the current coil and moving coil the pressure or voltage coil.

19. $Q = \frac{L\omega_0}{R} = \frac{1}{C\omega_0 R}$

$= \frac{1}{(500/2) \times 10^{-12} \times 2\pi \times 10^7 \times 10}$

$= \frac{10^4}{500} = \mathbf{200}$

20. $f = \frac{1 \times 10^6}{1 \times 10^4} = 100$

$\therefore$ $T = \frac{1}{100} = \mathbf{10\ ms.}$

27. Voltage developed,

$V = g.p.$

$= 58 \times 10^{-3}$

$= 58$ mV

29. Time period of C.R.O. Setting

$= 0.5 \times 10 = 5$ mV

and frequency $= 200$ Hz

Voltage setting at Y-axis $= 800$ mV

Therefore, as voltage setting is greater than amplitude of sine wave, the wave will go undisturbed.

31. $R_1 = \frac{100}{5 \times 10^{-3}} = 20000\ \Omega$

$R_2 = 250 \times 100 = 25000\ \Omega$

$R_3 = 15000\ \Omega$

Voltage developed across voltmeter will be in proportional to their resistance.

32. Magnitude of the limiting error of instrument

$\delta A = e_r A_s$

$= 0.01 \times 200$

$= 2$V

Hence limiting error at the 50 V voltage

$e_r = \frac{\delta A}{A}$

$= \frac{2}{50} \times 100 = 4\%$

36. $f_s = 400$ rad/sec

For reconstruction in SH circuit for signal we keep frequency $f_s/2$ to have a linear phase response.

$\therefore$ Sampling rate of signal

$= \frac{400}{2} = 200$ rad/s

38. $31.6 = 50\left(1 - e^{t/T}\right)$

$\Rightarrow$ $1 - e^{t/T} = 0.632$

$\therefore$ $T = 1/2$ hrs

39.

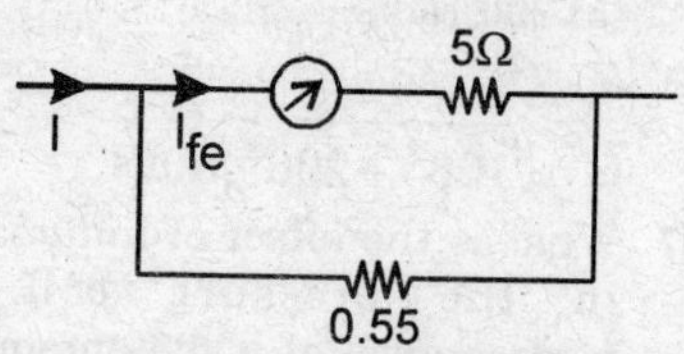

$I_{fe} = I \times \frac{0.55}{5 + 0.55}$

$\Rightarrow$ $1 = I \times \frac{1}{10}$

$\Rightarrow$ $I = 10$ mA

47. $\delta_x = \pm \delta_l \cdot \frac{X_{FS}}{\chi}$

$= \pm \frac{1 \times 25}{10} = \pm 2.5\%$

48.

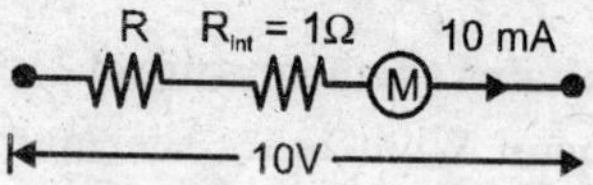

From figure

$10 \times 10^{-3} = \frac{10}{R + 1}$

$\Rightarrow$ $R + 1 = 1000$

$\Rightarrow$ $R = 999$ ohm (in series with first resistance)

49. We know, $\frac{\Delta R}{R} = G_f t$

Here, ΔR = change in resistance

R = original resistance

t = strain hange

G_f = Gauge factor

$\therefore$ $\Delta R = RG_f t$

$= 120 \times 2 \times 1 \times 10^{-6}$

$= 240 \times 10^{-6}\ \Omega$

50. Hall coefficient, $R_H = \frac{-1}{ne}$

Here, n = charge carrier density

e = electronic charge

51. Corresponding output voltage,

$E_0 = gtp$

where, g = voltage sensitivity

t = thickness of crystal

p = external pressure

$\therefore$ $E_0 = 0.05 \times 2.5 \times 10^{-3} \times 1.6 \times 10^6$

$= 200$ volts

ANALYTICAL, OPTICAL AND BIOMEDICAL INSTRUMENTATION 9

9.1. SPECTROSCOPY

It is separation, detection and recording of energy changes involving nuclei, atoms, ions or molecules. These changes are due to emission, absortion or scattering of electromagnetic radiation or particles.

S.No.	Spectroscopic methods	Energy states of matter
1.	Nuclear magnetic resonance	Nuclear spin with an applied magnetic field
2.	Microwave spectroscopy	Rotation of molecules
3.	Electron spin resonance	Spin coupling of unpaired electrons with an applied magnetic field.
4.	Infrared and Raman spectroscopy	Rotation of molecules, vibration of molecules, rotation/vibration of molecules, electronic transitions (some large molecules only)
5.	Ultraviolet-visible spectroscopy	Electronic energy changes, impinging monoenergetic electrons causing valence-electron excitations
6.	X-ray spectroscopy	Inner-shell electronic transitions, diffraction and reflection of X-ray radiation from atomic layers.

MASS SPECTROSCOPY.

It is used to measure relative abundance, masses of isotopes and relative masses of ions.

***(i)* Aston's mass spectrograph.**

This system consists of static electric and magnetic fields is used to determine $\frac{e}{m}$ ratio. S is source and S_1, S_2, S_3 are slits.

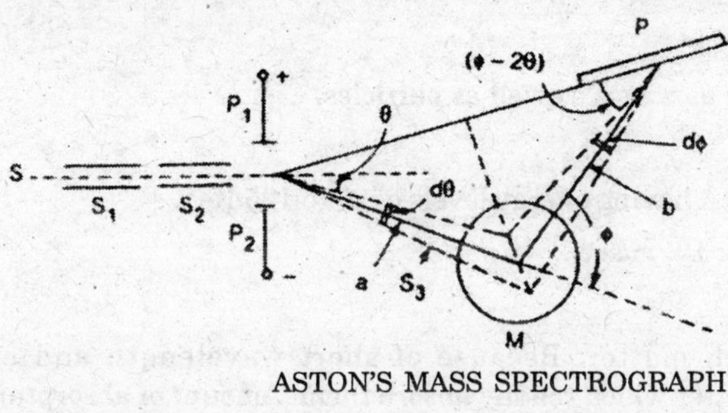

ASTON'S MASS SPECTROGRAPH

Electric field is applied between plates P_1 and P_2 and M is an electromagnetic.

θ is angle of deviation in electric field, and ϕ is angle of deviation in magnetic field

***(ii)* Bainbridge mass spectrograph.**

In this relative abundance is measured from densities of photographic image.

Radius of circular path of a changed particle in magnetic field,

$$R = \frac{mv}{qB}$$

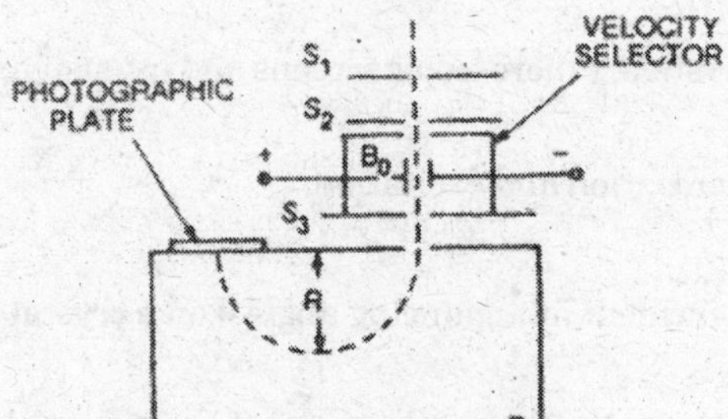

BAINBRIDGE MASS SPECTROGRAPH

9.2. X-RAY METHODS

Soft X-ray.

Voltage used is 20 kV.

Hard X-ray.

10^{-9} to 10^{-13} m. Voltage used is 100 kV.

- Short wavelength limit, $\lambda_{min} = \frac{12400}{V}$ Å
- Intensity of X-ray beam depend on number of electrons striking target/sec.

Frequency of X-rays.

$$\frac{1}{2}mv^2 = eV = hf$$

Frequency f of X-rays emitted where electrons are accelerated to a velocity v by a potential difference V and then allowed to collide with a metal target

or $$f = \frac{eV}{h}$$

Absorption of X-rays.

If I_0 is intensity of an X-ray beam of original intensity and I is intensity of X-ray beam after passing a distance x through the material, then

$$I = I_0 e^{-\mu x}.$$

where, μ = absorption co–efficient of material

= fractional decrease in intensity of X-rays per unit thickness of absorber material.

$$= \frac{0.693}{T}$$

Properties of X-rays.

- Electromagnetic rays which behave as waves as well as particles.
- Electrically neutral.
- Wavelength ranges from 0.1Å – 0.5 Å having energy levels of 25 to 125 KeV.
- Travel at the speed of light, i.e., 3×10^8 m/sec.
- They travel in a straight line.
- Absorbed while passing through matter. Because of short wavelength and extremely high energy, X-rays are able to penetrate the matter which readily absorb them. Amount of absorption depends on the density of the material. This forms the basis of radiography.
- Liberate minute amounts of heat on passing through matter.
- Produce secondary radiation in all the matter through which they pass. These secondary or scattered radiations are used in diagnostic radiology.
- Produce ionisation in gases and influence electrical properties of liquids and solids. Ionising property is useful in the construction of radiation measuring instruments.
- Affect photographic film, i.e. produce photographic effect on silver halide crystals in the same way as ordinary visible light.
- Cause fluorescence of certain crystals. Fluoroscopic screens and intensifying screens have been constructed on this property.
- Produce biological changes by ionisation and excitation.

X-ray diffraction-Bragg's law.

A beam of X-rays of wavelength is incident at a glancing angle θ on a crystal where atomic planes are separated by a distance d.

Path difference between waves reflected at the top plane and those reflected at second plane ABC

$$= 2d \sin \theta.$$

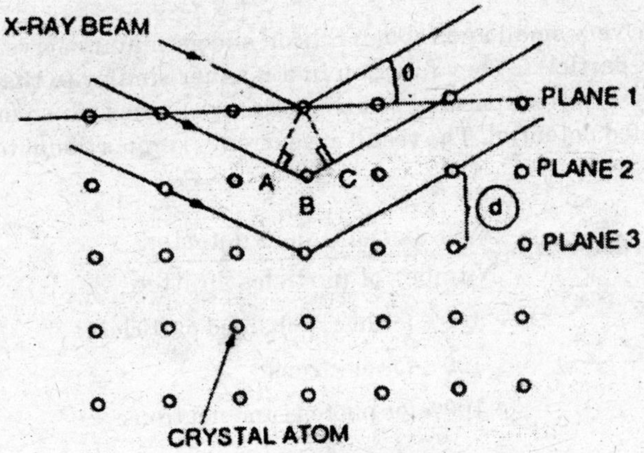

Crystal Atom

Constructive interference occurs when this path difference is equal to a whole number of wavelengths.

$$2d \sin \theta = m\lambda \qquad \text{Bragg's Law}$$

where, m is a whole numbers.

Compton scattering.

Due to Compton scattering, change in wavelength of scattered X-rays is given as

$$\Delta\lambda = 0.024(1 - \cos \theta) \text{ Å}.$$

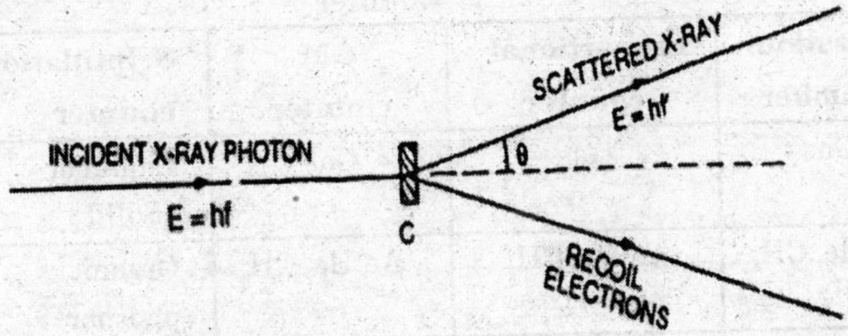

X-ray spectrum.

If initial absorption of energy results in the ejection of one or two electrons from K-shell level, X-rays produced are called *K-series X-rays.*

L-series X-rays are produced when vacancy is created in the L-shell.

Wavelength of K-series X-rays are smaller than L-series X-rays. The characteristic X-rays from substances of high atomic weight are of shorter wavelength than those from substances of low atomic weight and hence, are more penetrating.

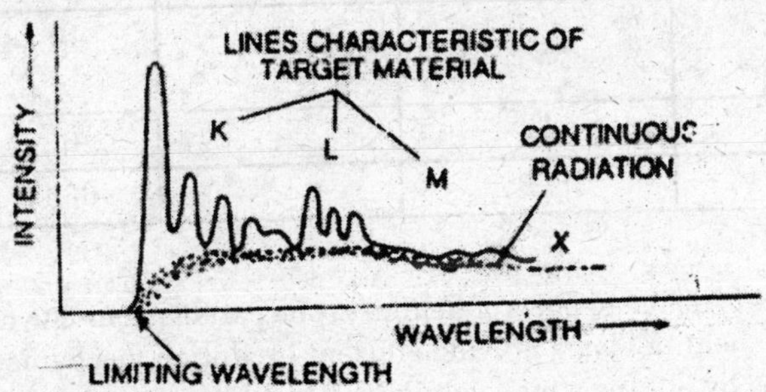

9.3. NUCLEAR RADIATION MEASUREMENTS

Ionization detectors.

These detectors are devices in which electric charge of the ion-pairs formed through radiation interactions is collected and electronically amplified.

Scintillation detectors.

The passage of radiation through certain inorganic materials produces excited atomic states, whereas in certain organic materials molecular vibrational states get excited. In both cases, the light that is emitted during de-excitation is converted into electric pulses and fed to measuring system. The detectors based on this principle are called *scintillation detectors.*

Semi-conductor detectors.

These detectors can be made very small and robust. Silicon and germanium crystals have been employed mainly for counting alpha and beta particles. They function in a manner similar to that of gas ionisation chamber. On absorption of radiation in crystal, electrons and positive holes are formed which move towards opposite electrodes under the influences of applied potential. The resulting current is proportional to energies of ionising radiation.

Counting efficiency.

$$\text{Intrinsic efficiency of a detector} = \frac{\text{Number of pulses detected}}{\text{Number of particles emitted}}$$

= 100% for heavy charged particles

≤ 100% for electrons

< 100% for photons and neutrons

$$\text{Absolute efficiency} = \frac{\text{Number of pulses detected}}{\text{Number of particles emitted}}$$

$$= E_{int} \frac{d\Omega}{4\pi} T$$

where, $d\Omega$ = solid angle substended by detector

T = transmission co-efficient in the medium between source and detector.

Radiation detector and measuring systems.

	Counter				
	Ionization chamber	**Proportional counter**	**GM counter**	**Scintillation counter**	**Solid state counter**
Normal detection state	Gas	Gas	Gas	Liquid or Solid	Solid
Detection Medium	Ar, He, CH_4	Ar, He, CH_4	Ar, He, CH_4	Organic phospor	Si
Radiation	α, β	α, β	α, β, γ	α, β, γ	α, β, γ
Multiplication of primary change	1	10^4	10^8	10^8	10
Energy dispersive	Yes	Yes	No	Yes	Yes
Resolution at KeV		0.7		40	12
%		12		6	0.25
E_0		5.9		660	4860

He–Ne laser.

The active medium is a mixture of about 10 parts of helium to one part of neon. The neon provides the energy levels for the laser transitions while the helium atoms provide efficient excitation mechanism for the neon atoms. Excitation occurs in a dc discharge created by placing a high voltage (≈ 2 to 4 kV) across the gas contained in a narrow diameter glass tube at a pressure of 10 T_{orr}.

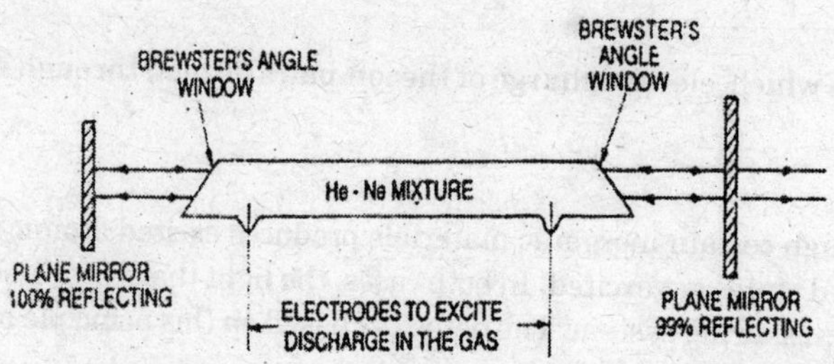

Ends of the glass tube containing the gas are inclined at Brewster's angle [tan (θ) = n]. The wave with the polarisation vector in the place of incidence is then transmitted through ends of the tube without partial reflection and output beam is consequently polarised in this plane.

Excited energy states of the helium and the neon atoms are almost the same. As the electrons are released from the dc power supply, they are drawn through the active region by the power supply's positive pole. The electrons collide with the gaseous helium atoms. The helium atoms are raised to an excited energy state. Those excited helium atoms in turn collide with neon atoms, transfer all their energy to the neon atoms. The collisions occur more often at high pressure. This process is called resonant excitations. When this transfer happens often enough and at a fast enough rate to be larger than the decay rate to ground energy state, then population inversion can take place. In the figure, stimulated emission occurs between the excited energy state and an intermediate state. This stimulated emission is occurring at a wavelength of 0.6328 micron. Stimulated emission can occur in neon at several wavelengths. Others are 1.152 and 3.390 microns.

Semi-conductor (PN-junction diode) lasers.

These consists of 2-layers of semi-conductor material sandwiched together. The end faces which are perpendicular to the p–n junction are polished serving as mirrors and thus forming a resonat optical cavity. Forward current *pumps* a large population of the molecules to an excited energy level. *Population inversion* occurs due to movement of electrons from n-side and holes from p-side due to applied electric field. Simulated emission is produced by feedback from the mirrors.

The most common diode laser is gallium arsenide laser with a central emission of 840 nm.

LASERS IN MEDICINE.

Clinical use of lasers.

Dermatology	Pulsed dye laser, Ar, CO_2, Nd : YAG, ruby
ENT	CO_2, Nd : YAG
Opthalmology	Ar, kV, Nd : YAG (Pulsed), Excimer, dye
Urology	Na : YAG, Sapphire
Plastic surgery	CO_2
Stone fragmentation	Pulsed dye, pulsed Nd : YAG etc.

(*i*) **In medicine,** the lasers are used primarily to deliver energy to tissue, the laser wavelength used should be strongly absorbed by tissue. The laser energy directed at human tissue; causes a rapid rise in temperature and can destroy the tissue. The amount of damage to living tissue depends on how long the tissue is at the increased temperature. Lasers are used in opthalmology and treating certain types of cancer.

(*ii*) **In opthalmology**, lasers are primarily used for photo coagulation of the retina, i.e. heating a blood visual to the point where the blood coagulates and blocks the vessel. The amount of laser energy needed for photo coagulation depends on the spot size used.

A complications of diabetes that affects the retina called *diabetic retinopathy* is also treated with photo coagulation. Because of the small spot size available (~50 μm), it is possible to use the laser even in the small region where our detail vision takes place.

(*iii*) **In neurosurgery,** large tumors of brain stem and spinal chord are vaporized using CO_2, argon and Nd : YAG lasers.

(*iv*) **In urology,** treatment of tumors of bladder and contractures or structures of urethra is done through YAG lasers. The fiber is inserted through a urethroscope.

(*v*) **In orthopedics,** argon laser is used for photocoagulation of bleeding vessels near spinal chord. Injuries to cartilages of the knee are repaired using arthroscopes and YAG lasers.

(*vi*) **In dermatology- phastic surgery,** laser is used in the treatment of Portwine strains (PWS), Removing tattoos, and Removing Telangiectasis (small red spots on skin).

(*vii*) **In obstetrics-gynecology,** in traepithelial cancers of vulva or skin of genitalia and premalignant and malignant conditions of Cervix and Vagina are treated by using CO_2 lasers coupled with a calposcope which is magnifying microscope designed, so that pre-malignant area can be visualized and observed during coagulative vaporisation procedure.

MICHELSON INTERFEROMETER.

Michelson Interferometer is used to measure the wavelength of light by utilizing interference between two light waves.

Transducers for Biomedical applications.

Biomedical parameter	Transducer type
1. Blood pressure	(*i*) Strain gauge bonded/unbonded silicon (*ii*) Variable capacitance type (*iii*) Differential transformer (LVDT) (*iv*) Low frequency microphone (*v*) Catheter tip pressure
2. Blood flow	Electromagnetic, Ultrasonic doppler
3. Cardiac output	Electromagnetic flowmeter and integrator
4. Heart rate	Photoelectric plethysmograph or phonocardiogram
5. Heart sounds/Korot koffs sound	Crystal/Moving microphone
6. Respiration rate	Thermistor, Strain gauge, doppler shift
7. Gases in expired air	Infrared sensor Mass spectroscopy
8. Body temperature	Thermocouples, Electric resistance thermometers, Thermistor, Silicon diode, Optical fibre
9. Uterine constructions during labour	Strain gauge
10. Dissolved gases and pH	Glass and Calomel electrodes.

RECORDING TERMS.

Electroncephalography. Recording of electric currents developed in the brain via scalp electrodes.

Electro-oculography. Detection of a standing potential between the front and back of the eyeball via electrodes placed on the skin surface near the eye socket.

Electro-cardiography. Recording of electric currents from heart muscles.

Electromyography. Recording of changes in the electrical potential of muscles.

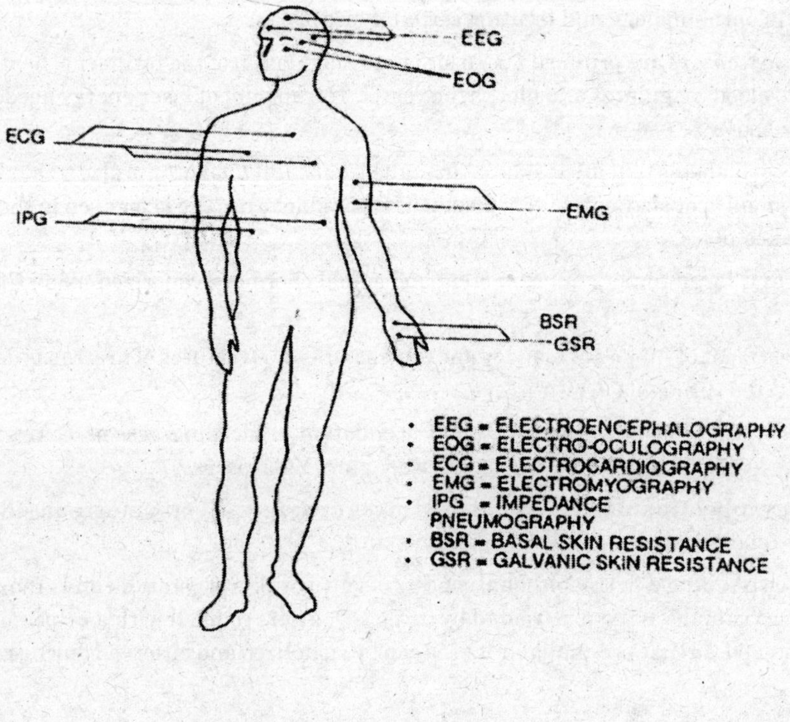

SOME COMMON PHYSIOLOGICAL SIGNALS.

	Typical signal range	Frequency range
Heart potential (ECG)	50 microvolts to 5 millivolts EKG in German)	0.05 Hz to 100 Hz (3 dB points prescribed by the American Heart Association)
Brain potential (EEG)	2 Microvolts to 10 microvolts (Scalp)	1 Hz to 100 Hz (Scalp)
Muscle potential (EMG)	20 microvolts to 10 millivolts electrode)	10 Hz to 2 kHz (needle 10 Hz to kHz (gross electrode)
Electro-oculogram (EOG)	10 microvolts to 4 millivolts	0.1 Hz to 100 Hz
Blood pressure pulse	5 to 15 meters/sec.	
Blood pressure (indirect measurement)	0 to 300 mm Hg	0.1 Hz to 500 Hz
Blood pressure (direct measurement)	0 to 40 mm Hg (venous) 0 to 300 mm Hg (arterial)	
Blood flow	1 to 30 cc/sec	
Heart sounds Phonocardiogram (PCG)		5 Hz to 4 kHz
Respiration rate	500 cc/ air ; 10-20 times per minute	

OBJECTIVE TYPE QUESTIONS

1. Korotkoff sounds are used in
(*a*) in blood flow measurements
(*b*) in blood pressure measurements
(*c*) in heart valve functioning
(*d*) as a reference for sound level measurement

2. CMRR in an ECG amplifier when input impedance is 2 MΩ and difference of electrode skin contact as 1 kΩ, is
(*a*) 1000 (*b*) 2000
(*c*) 3000 (*d*) 5000

3. A graphic record of heart sounds is
(*a*) Electrocardiogram (*b*) Phonocardiogram
(*c*) Vectorcardiogram (*d*) Electroencephatogram

4. Instrument measuring volume changes in any part of the body due to pulsations of blood occurring with each heart beat is
(*a*) Plethysmograph (*b*) Arithmetic unit
(*c*) Ventilator (*d*) Cardiac pacemaker

5. The triangle whose sides represent the line along which 3 projections of ECG are measured is
(*a*) Galvani triangle (*b*) Einthoven triangle
(*c*) Abbott triangle (*d*) Korotkoff triangle

6. Non-invasive device that measures impulses from eyes and ears to record blood flow between heart and brain
(*a*) Doppler flowmeter
(*b*) Echoencephalograph
(*c*) Oculoplethysmograph
(*d*) Electrode contact analyser

7. Disadvantage of silicon diode as a temperature sensor is
(*a*) produces an output and to temperature
(*b*) requirement of a stable calibration source
(*c*) noisy
(*d*) none of these

8. To produce a magnified image atleast distance of distinct vision with the help of a simple microscope, the object should be placed at
(*a*) focus
(*b*) a point far away from focus
(*c*) a point between focus and optical centre
(*d*) none of these

9. To increase the magnifying power of a telescope, which of the following should be increased ?
(*a*) Focal length of the objective
(*b*) Focal length of eye piece
(*c*) Aperture of the objective
(*d*) Aperture of the eye piece

10. If an observer looks at a tree of height 15 m with a telecope of magnifying power 10, then to him, tree appears
(*a*) 10 times taller (*b*) 15 times taller
(*c*) 10 times nearer (*d*) 15 times nearer

11. A fly is siting on the objective of a telescope pointed to the moon. What effect is expected in the photograph of the moon taken through the telescope?
(*a*) Entire yield of vision is blocked
(*b*) There is an image of the fly on the photograph
(*c*) There is no effect at all
(*d*) Image of the moon is of lesser intensity

12. For observing a cricket match, binocular is preferred to terrestrial telescope because the binocular
(*a*) is very easy to handle
(*b*) provides three dimensional vision
(*c*) produces image free of chromatic aberration
(*d*) produces erect image.

13. In nuclear instrumentation, heaviest and flow moving particles are
(*a*) Beta particles (*b*) Alpha particles
(*c*) Gamma rays (*d*) Protons

14. Synchro is a transducer
(*a*) variable reluctance (*b*) parabolic
(*c*) angular position (*d*) synchronisation

15. If a transducer has an output impedance of 1 kΩ and the load resistance is 1 MΩ, then transducer behaves as a constant
(*a*) current source (*b*) voltage source
(*c*) power source (*d*) none of these

16. A differential transformer is a
(*a*) variable inductance transducer
(*b*) variable pressure transducer
(*c*) constant displacement transducer
(*d*) constant pressure transformer

17. When measuring strain, ballast circuits use a capacitor to act as high pass filter. This is done when
(*a*) static strains are being measured
(*b*) dynamic strains are being measured
(*c*) both static and dynamic strains are being measured
(*d*) none of these

18. Match the following and select the correct answer from the codes given below.

Transducer	**Information change**
A. Thermocouple	1. Resistance
B. Photoconductive cell	2. Strain
C. Strain gauge	3. Displacement
D. LVDT	4. emf
E. Venturi gauge	5. Pressure difference

Codes :

	A	B	C	D	E
(*a*)	4	1	2	3	5
(*b*)	5	3	2	1	4
(*c*)	5	2	3	4	1
(*d*)	5	3	1	4	2

19. In semi-conductor strain gauges, the change in resistance on application of strain

(*a*) is much higher than that in the case of metal strain gauges and this is mainly due to change in dimension

(*b*) is much higher than that in the case of metal strain gauges and this is mainly due to change in resistivity

(*c*) is lower than that in the case of metal strain gauges

(*d*) none of these

20. Dummy strain gauges are used for

(*a*) compensation of temperature changes

(*b*) increasing the sensitivity of bridge in which they are included

(*c*) compensating for different expansion

(*d*) calibration of strain gauges.

21. The main reason for insertion of two strain gauges in the adjacent arms of a bridge circuit is

(*a*) achievement of higher sensitivity

(*b*) elimination of radio frequency interference

(*c*) elimination of effect of environmental temperature

(*d*) to facilitate quick balancing of the bridge

22. A ray is incident at an angle of incidence i on one surface of a prism of small angle A and emerges normally from the opposite surface. If refractive index of the material of the prism is μ, then angle of incidence i is nearly equal to

(*a*) $\frac{A}{\mu}$ (*b*) $\frac{A}{2\mu}$

(*c*) μA (*d*) $\frac{\mu A}{2}$

23. Given figure shows the view through the eye piece of a prism spectrometer with its slit illuminated by the source of light emitting three wavelengths corresponding to yellow (Y), green (G) and unknown colour (X). The colour X may be

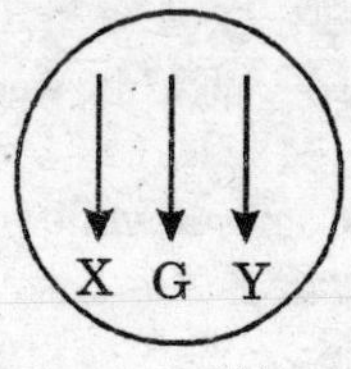

(*a*) red (*b*) orange

(*c*) pink (*d*) none of these

24. Light appears to travel in straight lines, since

(*a*) it is not absorbed by the atmosphere

(*b*) it is reflected by the atmosphere

(*c*) its wavelength is very small

(*d*) its velocity is very large

25. One cannot see through fog, because

(*a*) for absorbs light

(*b*) the refractive index of fog is infinity

(*c*) light suffers total internal reflection at the droplet in a fog

(*d*) light is scattered by the droplets in fog

26. Strain gauge, LVDT and thermocouple may be classified as

(*a*) active transducers (*b*) analog transducers

(*c*) primary transducers (*d*) none of these

27. Platinum is the commonly used metal for TRDs. This is because

(*a*) platinum has a constant value of resistance temperature co-efficient of 0.004/°C for a temperature range between 0 to 100°C

(*b*) the resistivity of platinum tends to increase less rapidly at higher temperatures

(*c*) platinum is available in pure form for commercial applications and has a stability over higher ranges of temperature

(*d*) all of these

28. For measurement of temperature which of the following type of transducer can be used ?

(*a*) Intrinsic type fibre optic transducers

(*b*) Interferometric type fibre optic transducers

(*c*) Both (*a*) and (*b*)

(*d*) none of these

29. The best method for the measurement of temperatures of hot bodies radiating energy in the visible spectrum is

(*a*) bolometer (*b*) optical pyrometers

(*c*) thermocouples (*d*) thermopile

30. Thermocouples are

(*a*) passive transducers (*b*) active transducers

(*c*) both (*a*) and (*b*) (*d*) output transducers

31. A thermocouple ammeter is used to measure a 10 MHz sine wave and it indicates a current of 2 A in a pure resistance. Peak current in the wave from is

(*a*) 1 A (*b*) 2.83 A

(*c*) 5 A (*d*) 10 A

32. A thermocouple instrument can be used on

(*a*) ac circuits

(*b*) dc circuits

(*c*) polyphase circuits

(*d*) ac as well as on dc circuits

33. A diaphragm has a natural frequency of 30 kHz. If both its diameter and thickness are halved, then natural frequency is

(*a*) 15 kHz (*b*) 240 kHz

(*c*) 60 kHz (*d*) 120 kHz

34. Pirani gauge is

(*a*) used for gas pressure measurement in the range 1 to 10 atmospheres

(*b*) used for gas pressure measurement in the range 1 nm to 10^{-3} mm of Hg

(*c*) used as an ionization gauge

(*d*) dependent on variation of thermal conductivity of gases with pressure

35. The principle of Pirani gauge is based on

(*a*) humidity of the medium

(*b*) thermal conductivity of the medium

(*c*) combustibility of the medium

(*d*) none of these

36. Which of the following devices can measure pressure directly ?

(*a*) LVDT (*b*) Strain gauge

(*c*) Rotameter (*d*) Bourdon tube

37. A spectrum analyser displays

(*a*) different frequency amplitude with respect to time

(*b*) p-p amplitude of modulating signal

(*c*) different signal amplitude with respect to frequency

(*d*) lissajous figures

38. A double convex lens of refractive index μ_1 is immersed in a liquidof refractive index μ_2. The lens will act as

(*a*) diverging lens, if $\mu_1 > \mu_2$

(*b*) diverging lens, if $\mu_1 < \mu_2$

(*c*) converging lens, if $\mu_1 > \mu_2$

(*d*) converging lens, if $\mu_1 < \mu_2$

39. Two lenses having powers + 6D and – 4D are placed in contact.The power of the combination is

(*a*) – 2D (*b*) – 4D

(*c*) + 4D (*d*) + 2D

40. Static fluid pressure measurement is done using

(*a*) Bourdon tubes

(*b*) Pitot tubes

(*c*) Piezoelectric transducers

(*d*) Diaphragms

41. An L.V.D.T

(*a*) has very good frequency response as the mass of the core to which the input signal is applied, is fairly large

(*b*) is immune to stray magnetic fields

(*c*) has a zero voltage at the null point even if the supply voltage contains and harmonics and even if the two secondary windings are not exactly similar and even asymmetrically placed with respect to primary winding

(*d*) none of these

42. A piezoelectric pick-up is an

(*a*) active transducer

(*b*) passive transducer

(*c*) temperature transducer

(*d*) flow transducer

43. Piezo-electric crystal can be used to measure

(*a*) temperature (*b*) velocity

(*c*) acceleration (*d*) flow

44. Piezoelectric transducer works under the variation of

(*a*) intensity of light (*b*) pressure intensity

(*c*) temperature variation (*d*) all of these

45. A pieze-electrical transducer has an output voltage of 3 V at no load conditions. It has a capacitance 250 pF. It is connected to load capacitance of 125 pF. Then voltage across the load at high frequencies will be

(*a*) 1 V

(*b*) 2 V

(*c*) 9 V

(*d*) cannot be determined with the data given

46. Output of a piezoelectric crystal has

(*a*) low amplitude and low impedance

(*b*) high amplitude and high impedance

(*c*) low amplitude and high impedance

(*d*) high amplitude and low impedance

47. A photo conductive cell is useful for

(*a*) high frequency applications

(*b*) medium frequency applications

(*c*) low frequency applications

(*d*) all of these

48. Quartz and Rochelle salt belong to

(*a*) natural group of piezoelectric materials

(*b*) synthetic group of piezolelectric materials

(*c*) can belong to natural or synthetic group of piezoelectric materials provided properly polarized

(*d*) all of these

49. Ceramic materials are used for piezoelectric transducers because

(*a*) they are polycrystalline in nature

(*b*) they are basically made of barium titanate

(*c*) they do not have piezoelectric properties in their original state but these properties are produced by special polarizing treatment

(*d*) all of these

50. A photo diode functions as

(*a*) photo conductive device while working with reverse voltage

(*b*) photo voltaic device while working without a reverse voltage

(*c*) photo voltaic devices while working with or without reverse voltage

(*d*) none of these

51. Moire Fringes are used for measurement of rotary displacement alongwith

(*a*) contact type encoders (*b*) optical encoders

(*c*) both (*a*) and (*b*) (*d*) none of these

52. Normal action potential in the heat originates from the

(*a*) atrioventricular node (*b*) sinoatrial node

(*c*) purkinje fibre (*d*) vosomotor centre

53. When ECG is recorded by connecting 2-electrodes, one is left arm and other in left leg, recording is made in

(*a*) Lead I configurations

(*b*) Lead II configurations

(*c*) Both Lead I and II configurations

(*d*) Lead II configuration

54. The lung volume expired during maximal forced expiration following a maximal inspiration is

(*a*) vital capacity

(*b*) total functional residual capacity

(*c*) total lung capacity

(*d*) total ventillatory capacity

55. In diagnostic applications, ultrasound is both generated and detected by the piezoelectric effect in the

(*a*) MF and HF ranges (*b*) LF range

(*c*) VLF range (*d*) EHF range

56. Which of the following materials may be used to produce polaroids ?

(*a*) Tourmaline

(*b*) Calcite

(*c*) Quartz

(*d*) Crystals of quining iodosulphate

57. In double slit experiment affected, if a source of blue light is used in place of yellow light producing the same intensity, then in interference pattern

(*a*) fringe width will decrease

(*b*) fringes will increase

(*c*) fringes will become fainter

(*d*) fringes will become brighter

58. In Youngs double slit experiment the fringe width is

(*a*) directly proportional to distance between the sources

(*b*) inversely proportional to distance between the sources

(*c*) inversely proportional to distance of screen from the sources

(*d*) inversely proportional to wavelength of light used

59. The photo diode as compared to a photo transistor has

(*a*) faster switching time

(*b*) lower sensitivity

(*c*) higher size for the same value of output current

(*d*) all of these

60. Spectrophotometer uses

(*a*) selection filter (*b*) silver wire

(*c*) monochrometer (*d*) chloridimeter

61. Haemoglobin is contained in

(*a*) WBC'S (*b*) RBC'S

(*c*) Platelets (*d*) Protein

62. One gram haemoglobin when fully saturated carries of gas

(*a*) 0.34 ml (*b*) 0.68 ml

(*c*) 1.02 ml (*d*) 1.34 ml

63. X-ray electromagnetic radiation lie in the range

(*a*) 2.5 μm to 25 μm (*b*) 400 mm to 700 mm

(*c*) 0.1 mm to 1 mm (*d*) 10 nm to 100 nm

64. A laser beam is used to measure very large distances because

(*a*) unidirectional (*b*) coherent

(*c*) monochromatic (*d*) not absorbed

65. Interferometer is used for

(*a*) wavelength dispersion

(*b*) magnifying power

(*c*) flatness measurement

(*d*) none of these

66. In Young's double slit experiment, no fringe will be observed if

(*a*) width of one of the slits is doubled

(*b*) source is replaced by a source emitting more than one wavelength

(*c*) slits are illuminated by 2 identical sources of monochromatic light

(*d*) none of these

67. Newton's rings are formed when an air film is enclosed between

(*a*) two convex surfaces

(*b*) plane and concave surfaces

(*c*) two concave surfaces

(*d*) plane and convex surfaces.

68. *Which of the following statements regarding X-rays are correct?*

1. X-ray are electromagnetic radiation.
2. The characteristic X-ray spectrum depends on the atomic number of the element.
3. X-rays do not obey the wave particle duality.
4. X-ray are identified with cathode rays codes all given as

(*a*) 1 and 2 (*b*) 2 and 3

(*c*) 1, 2 and 4 (*d*) 1, 3 and 4

69. If the voltage across and X-ray tube is doubled, then energy of the characteristic X-rays emitted by this tube will

(*a*) become double (*b*) become quadrupled

(*c*) become half (*d*) remain the same

70. X-rays of different wavelengths 3 Å, 4 Å, 5 Å, and 6 Å are incident on a block of a metal. X-rays which penetrate the most will be

(*a*) 3 Å (*b*) 4 Å

(*c*) 5 Å (*d*) 6 Å

71. If potential difference applied to an X-ray tube is increased, then in the emitted radiation

(*a*) intensity increases

(*b*) minimum wavelength increases

(*c*) intensity decreases

(*d*) minimum wavelength decreaseds

72. If half life of the radio active radon is 3.8 days, then time at the end of which $\frac{1}{20}$ th of the radon sample will remain undecayed is

(*a*) 3.8 days (*b*) 16.5 days

(*c*) 33 days (*d*) 76 days

73. Reciprocal of decay constant of a radioactive substance is known as

(*a*) mean life (*b*) half life

(*c*) total life (*d*) none of these

74. Lasers are put to many uses due to

(*a*) small angular spread

(*b*) small wavelength spread

(*c*) small angular and small wavelength spread

(*d*) large angular and large wavelength spread

75. He-Ne laser has wavelength

(*a*) 514.5 nm (*b*) 632.8 nm

(*c*) 1.06 μm (*d*) 10.6 μm

76. Sphygmomanometer is used for

(*a*) respiratory volume measurement

(*b*) blood pressure measurement

(*c*) electrical activity in heart

(*d*) none of these

77. Disintegration constant of a radio active substance with a half life of 50 days is

(*a*) 0.01186 per day (*b*) 0.01286 per day

(*c*) 0.01386 per day (*d*) none of these

78. Average life of a radio active substance with half life as 50 days is

(*a*) 42.15 days (*b*) 52.15 days

(*c*) 62.15 days (*d*) 72.15 days

79. Percentage of blood volume in platelets when diameter of platelet si about 2 μm is

(*a*) 0.1% (*b*) 0.7%

(*c*) 0.5% (*d*) none of these

80. When one leg of a Michelson interferometer is lengthened slightly, 150 dark fringes sweep through the field of view. If the light used has $\lambda = 480$ nm, how far was the mirror in that leg moved ?

(*a*) 0.016 mm (*b*) 0.026 mm

(*c*) 0.036 mm (*d*) 0.046 mm

81. What is the separation on photographic plate in the velocity selector of Bain bridge mass spectro-cope with E = 200 V/cm and H = 0.2 Tesla, H in main chamber as 0.3 Tesla? Mixture of signgly charged ions of carbon isotopes C^{12} and C^{13} is analysed.

(*a*) 0.69 cm (*b*) 0.59 cm

(*c*) 0.49 cm (*d*) 0.39 cm

82. What is the thickness of a thin glass plate ($\mu = 1.5$) introduced in one of the arms of a Michelson interferometer using 5890 Å with a shift of 10 fringes?

(*a*) 4.89 μm (*b*) 5.89 μm

(*c*) 6.89 μm (*d*) 7.89 μm

83. A person looks into a swimming pool at the 5-ft-deep level. How deep does it look to the person ?

(*a*) 2.75 ft (*b*) 3.72 ft

(*c*) 4.75 ft (*d*) 5.75 ft

84. Cardiac output Q (lit/minute) from the dilution curve when 10 mg of indicator injected and average concentration 5 mg/lit for a curve duration of 20 ns will be

(*a*) 2 lit/min (*b*) 4 lit/min

(*c*) 6 lit/min (*d*) 8 lit/min

85. What is the shortest λ of X-rays produced in a X-ray tube with accelerating potential as 70 kV ?

(*a*) 0.017 (*b*) 0.018

(*c*) 0.019 (*d*) 0.015

86. The optical fibre is 2 m long and has a diameter of 20 μm. If a ray of light is incident on one end of the fibre at an angle $\theta_1 = 40°$, how many reflections does it make before emerging from the other end ? (index of refraction of the fibre is 1.30).

(*a*) 27000 (*b*) 37000

(*c*) 47000 (*d*) 57000

87. In practice, optical fibres have a coating of glass ($n_3 = 1.512$) to protect the optical surface of the fibre. If the fibre itself has an index of refraction $n_2 = 1.700$, what is the critical angle for total reflection of a ray inside the fibre ?

(*a*) 42.7° (*b*) 52.7°

(*c*) 62.7° (*d*) 72.7°

88. What is the reduction in divergence of a laser beam which is collimated by passing it through a telescope with an objective lens to eyepiece lense focal length ratio of 30 : 1 in a He-Ne laser with a plasma tube diameter of 3 mm ?

(*a*) 1.2″ (*b*) 1.3″

(*c*) 1.4″ (*d*) 1.5″

89. What is the pulse separation in a mode locked Nd : YAG laser when the fluoresecent line width is 1.1×10^{11} Hz and laser rod is 0.1 m long?

(*a*) 0.5 ns (*b*) 0.6 ns

(*c*) 0.7 ns (*d*) 0.8 ns

90. Light is incident at angle θ_1 on an isosceles triangular prism of apex angle α and refractive index n > 1. The expression for the minimum angular deviation, δ_{min}, produced by the prism is

(*a*) $\dfrac{\sin \alpha + \delta_{min}}{2} = n \sin \dfrac{\alpha}{2}$

(*b*) $\dfrac{\sin \alpha - \delta_{min}}{2} = n \sin \dfrac{\alpha}{2}$

(*c*) $\dfrac{\cos \alpha + \delta_{min}}{2} = n \cos \dfrac{\alpha}{2}$

(*d*) $\dfrac{\cos \alpha - \delta_{min}}{2} = n \cos \dfrac{\alpha}{2}$

91. What is the deflection at centre for a pressure of 150 kN/m when pressure is 300 kN/m²?

(*a*) 0.0105 (*b*) 0.0205

(*c*) 0.0305 (*d*) 0.0405

92. What is the speed in rpm of a variable reluctance type tachometer having 60 rotar teeth when counter records 3600 counts/minute ?

(*a*) 400 rps (*b*) 50 rps

(*c*) 60 rps (*d*) 70 rps

93. What is transit time of beam through deflecting plates of a CRO : axial lengths 2 cm potential difference 1000 V, separation of plates = 5 mm potential difference between plates = 20 V ?

Distance of CRT screen from centre of deflecting plates 25 cm.

(*a*) 1×10^{-3} s (*b*) 1×10^{-5} s

(*c*) 1×10^{-7} s (*d*) 1×10^{-9} s

94. What is deflection sensitivity of CRO when anode voltage is 2 kV, 15 mm long deflecting plates and 5 mm apart when screen is 500 mm for centre of deflecting plates ?

(*a*) 0.175 mm/V (*b*) 0.275 mm/V

(*c*) 0.375 mm/V (*d*) 0.475 mm/V

95. What is the cardiac output when heart rate is 75 beats/min and stroke volume is 50 mL/beat ?

(*a*) 2.75 Lit/min (*b*) 3.75 Lit/min

(*c*) 4.75 Lit/min (*d*) 5.75 Lit/min

96. What is loss in an optical fiber when an optical signal after traversing a distance of 400 meters in fibre has lost 75% of its input power ?

(*a*) 5 db/km (*b*) 10 db/km

(*c*) 15 db/km (*d*) 20 db/km

97. What is minimum speed of striking the target in a X-ray tube when it passes 5 mA at a potential difference of 100 kV ?

(*a*) 1.38×10^3 m/sec (*b*) 1.38×10^4 m/sec

(*c*) 1.38×10^5 m/sec (*d*) 1.38×10^6 m/sec

98. What is the mean corpuscular volume (MCV) in blood with PCV = 45% and RBC count = 5.0 millions/mm^3?

(*a*) 40 cubic microns (*b*) 60 cubic microns

(*c*) 80 cubic microns (*d*) 90 cubic microns

99. What is the mean corpuscular haemoglobin in blood with Hb concentration as 15.0 g (%) and RBC count as 5.0 millions/mm^3?

(*a*) 10 pg

(*b*) 20 pg

(*c*) 30 pg

(*d*) 40 pg

100. What is the mean corpuscular haemoglobin concentration (MCHC) in blood with Hb as 15 g percent and PCV as 45 percent ?

(*a*) 11.1%

(*b*) 22.2%

(*c*) 33.3%

(*d*) 55.5%

101. What is the cardiac output when 5 mg indicator is injected and average concentration of indicates is 1.6 mg/L is

(*a*) 1.1 (*b*) 2.1

(*c*) 3.1 (*d*) 4.1

102. Transmittance of light in a blood when light absorbed is half to initial light is

(*a*) 30% (*b*) 50%

(*c*) 70% (*d*) 100%

103. Half life of radium is 1600 years. After how many years, it would integrate to one fourth of its present value ?

(*a*) 1600 years (*b*) 2400 years

(*c*) 3200 years (*d*) 4000 years

104. What is the half life period of a radio active material, if its activity drops to $\frac{1}{16}$th of its initial value in 20 years ?

(*a*) 1 year (*b*) 3 years

(*c*) 5 years (*d*) 7 years

105. In a spectrophotometer, the monochromator must be able to resolve two wavelengths 599.9 nm and 600.1 nm. The required resolution is

(*a*) 100 (*b*) 500

(*c*) 1000 (*d*) 3000

106. What is the power into the target when a fluoroscope operate continuously at a potential of 80 kV and a current of 3 mA ?

(*a*) 140 W

(*b*) 180 W

(*c*) 240 W

(*d*) none of these

107. Find linear attenuation coefficient of beam, if half-value layer of an X-ray beam is at 3 mm

(*a*) 0.131/mm

(*b*) 0.231/mm

(*c*) 0.331/mm

(*d*) none of these

108. What is the radiation intensity 0.35 m from an unshielded 7.5 GBq source of 198 Av?

(*a*) 0.2 R/hr

(*b*) 0.3 R/hr

(*c*) 0.4 R/hr

(*d*) none of these

109. Find exposure rate 0.3 m from a syringe containing 500 MBq of 99 mTc for a brain scan ?

(*a*) 5 mR/hr

(*b*) 10 mR/hr

(*c*) 15 mR/hr

(*d*) none of these

110. Volume of blood the heat pumps to systemic circulation each day is

(*a*) 4.3×10^3 cm^3

(*b*) 4.3×10^5 cm^3

(*c*) 8.3×10^3 cm^3

(*d*) 8.3×10^6 cm^3

111. Given : Oxygen uptake= 250 ml/min

Oxygen content of venous (pulmonary arterial blood) = 14 ml/100 ml.

Oxygen content of arterial (brachial arterial blood) = 19 ml/100 ml

What is the cardiac output (Co) in litres/min?

(*a*) 4 L/min

(*b*) 5 L/min

(*c*) 7 L/min

(*d*) none of these

112. What is the cardiac output when 10 mg of indicator was injected and average concentration as calculated from curve was 5 mg/l for a duration of 20 sec ?

(*a*) 4 L/min

(*b*) 5 L/min

(*c*) 6 L/min

(*d*) none of these

113. What is the amount of oxygen (ml/minute) delivered to tissues when 100 ml of blood gives it 5 ml of O_2 to the tissues ? Normal cardiac output as 5 l/min/

(*a*) 100 ml/min

(*b*) 150 ml/min

(*c*) 200 ml/min

(*d*) 250 ml/min

ANSWERS

1. (*b*)	**2.** (*a*)	**3.** (*b*)	**4.** (*a*)	**5.** (*b*)	**6.** (*c*)	**7.** (*b*)	**8.** (*c*)	**9.** (*a*)	**10.** (*c*)
11. (*d*)	**12.** (*b*)	**13.** (*b*)	**14.** (*c*)	**15.** (*b*)	**16.** (*a*)	**17.** (*b*)	**18.** (*a*)	**19.** (*b*)	**20.** (*a*)
21. (*a*)	**22.** (*c*)	**23.** (*d*)	**24.** (*c*)	**25.** (*d*)	**26.** (*b*)	**27.** (*d*)	**28.** (*c*)	**29.** (*b*)	**30.** (*b*)
31. (*b*)	**32.** (*d*)	**33.** (*c*)	**34.** (*b*)	**35.** (*b*)	**36.** (*d*)	**37.** (*c*)	**38.** (*c*)	**39.** (*d*)	**40.** (*d*)
41. (*d*)	**42.** (*a*)	**43.** (*c*)	**44.** (*b*)	**45.** (*b*)	**46.** (*c*)	**47.** (*c*)	**48.** (*a*)	**49.** (*d*)	**50.** (*a*)
51. (*b*)	**52.** (*b*)	**53.** (*d*)	**54.** (*c*)	**55.** (*a*)	**56.** (*d*)	**57.** (*a*)	**58.** (*b*)	**59.** (*d*)	**60.** (*c*)
61. (*b*)	**62.** (*d*)	**63.** (*c*)	**64.** (*a*)	**65.** (*c*)	**66.** (*c*)	**67.** (*d*)	**68.** (*a*)	**69.** (*d*)	**70.** (*a*)
71. (*d*)	**72.** (*b*)	**73.** (*a*)	**74.** (*c*)	**75.** (*b*)	**76.** (*b*)	**77.** (*c*)	**78.** (*d*)	**79.** (*a*)	**80.** (*c*)
81. (*a*)	**82.** (*b*)	**83.** (*b*)	**84.** (*c*)	**85.** (*a*)	**86.** (*c*)	**87.** (*c*)	**88.** (*c*)	**89.** (*c*)	**90.** (*a*)
91. (*b*)	**92.** (*c*)	**93.** (*d*)	**94.** (*c*)	**95.** (*b*)	**96.** (*c*)	**97.** (*d*)	**98.** (*d*)	**99.** (*c*)	**100.** (*c*)
101. (*c*)	**102.** (*b*)	**103.** (*c*)	**104.** (*c*)	**105.** (*d*)	**106.** (*c*)	**107.** (*c*)	**108.** (*c*)	**109.** (*b*)	**110.** (*d*)
111. (*b*)	**112.** (*c*)	**113.** (*d*)							

EXPLANATIONS

80. Darkness is observed when the light beams from the two legs are 180° out of phase. As length of one leg is increased by $\frac{\lambda}{2}$, the path length (down and back) increases by λ and the field of view changes from dark to bright to dark.

When 150 fringes pass, the leg is lengthened by

$$150\left(\frac{1}{2}\lambda\right) = (150)\,(240\text{ nm})$$
$$= 36000\text{ nm}$$
$$= 0.036\text{ mm}.$$

81. $$v = \frac{E}{B} = \frac{200\times10^2}{0.2} = 10^5$$

$$\text{Separation} = 2(R_1 - R_2) = \frac{2V(m_2 - m_1)}{qB}$$
$$= \frac{(2\times10^5)(13-12)(1.67\times10^{-27})}{1.6\times10^{-19}\times0.3}$$
$$= 0.69\text{ cm}.$$

82. We know $2(\mu - 1)\,t = N\lambda$

or $$t = \frac{N\lambda}{2(\mu - 1)}$$

Here, N = 10, $\lambda = 5890\times10^{-10}$ m, $\mu = 1.5$

$$\therefore \quad t = \frac{10\times5890\times10^{-10}}{2\times0.50}$$
$$= 5.89\ \mu\text{m}.$$

83. We know, $$n = \frac{\text{actual depth}}{\text{apparent depth}}$$

$$\therefore \quad 1.333 = \frac{5}{y}ft$$

or apparent depth, y = 3.75 ft

84. Let M is quantity of injected indicator (mg), then Cardiac output,

$$Q = \frac{M}{\text{Av. concentration of indicator per litre of blood for duration of curve}}\ \text{lit/sec}$$
$$= \frac{M\times60}{\text{Area under curve}}\ \text{lit/sec}$$
$$= \frac{10\times10^{-3}\times60}{5\times10^{-3}\times20}\ \text{lit/min} = 6\text{ lit/min}.$$

85. $$\lambda_{min} = \frac{hC}{eV} = \frac{6.626\times10^{-34}\times3\times10^8}{1.6\times10^{-19}\times70\times10^3}$$
$$= 0.017\text{ nm}.$$

86. Since codition for total internal reflection is fulfilled, therefore

$$\sin\theta_2 = \frac{n_1}{n_2}\sin\theta_1 = \frac{\sin 40°}{1.3} = 0.495$$

or $\theta_2 = 29.7°$.

Length along fibre to the first reflection,

$$l = \frac{d}{\sin\theta_2}$$
$$= \frac{2\times10^{-5}\text{ m}}{0.495}$$
$$= 4.04\times10^{-5}\text{ m}$$

Hence by the law of reflection, l also represents the length along the fibre between successive reflections,

$$\therefore \quad \text{Number of reflections} = \frac{L}{l} = \frac{2\text{m}}{4.04\times10^{-5}\text{ m}}$$
$$= 49504 \approx 47000.$$

87. The critical angle is determined by the interface between fibre and coating.

$$\therefore \quad \sin\theta_c = \frac{n_3}{n_2} = \frac{1.512}{1.700} = 0.889$$

or $\theta_c = 62.7°$

88. Since divergence θ of the beam from the laser $= \frac{\lambda}{D}$

$$\therefore \quad \theta_1 = \frac{633\times10^{-9}}{3\times10^{-3}} = 2.1\times10^{-4}\text{ rad }(0.7')$$

After collimation angle of divergence will be reduced by a factor of 30 to

$$\theta_2 = 7\times10^{-6}\text{ rad (or 1.4}'')\text{.}$$

89. $$\text{Mode separation} = \frac{C}{2L} = 1.5\times10^9\text{ Hz}$$

$$\therefore \quad \text{Number of modes oscillating} = \frac{1.1\times10^{11}}{1.5\times10^9} = 73$$

$$\therefore \quad \text{Pulse separation} = \frac{2L}{C} = 0.7\text{ ns}.$$

90. Because prism is symmetrical and light paths are reversible, it is easy to see that the deviation δ will be a minimum when $\theta_1 = \theta_3 = K$.

Under this condition, Snell's law gives at the two interfaces

$$\sin K = n\sin\theta_2$$

and $$n\sin(\alpha - \theta_2) = \sin K$$

$$\therefore \quad n\sin\theta_2 = n\sin(\alpha - \theta_2)$$

or $$\theta_2 = \alpha - \theta_2$$

or $$\theta_2 = \frac{\alpha}{2}$$

$$\therefore \quad \sin K = n\sin\frac{\alpha}{2}$$

But $\delta_{min} = \theta_1 + \theta_3 - \alpha = 2K - \alpha$

or $K = \dfrac{\alpha + \delta_{min}}{2}$

$\therefore \sin\dfrac{\alpha + \delta_{min}}{2} = n \sin\dfrac{\alpha}{2}.$

91. For deflection, putting the values, we get

$$D = \frac{3(1-0.028^2)(15\times10^{-3})^4 \times 150\times10^3}{256\times200\times9\times(0.205\times10^{-3})^3}$$

$= 20.5 \times 10^{-6}$ m

$= 0.0205$ mm.

92. $\text{Speed} = \dfrac{\text{Pulses per second}}{\text{Number of teeth}} = \dfrac{3600}{60} = 60 \text{ rps.}$

94. $S = \dfrac{lL}{2d\,V_d} = \dfrac{500\times10^{-3}\times15\times10^{-3}}{2\times5\times10^{-3}\times2000} = 0.375 \text{ mm/V}$

95. Cardiac output CO in lit/min = Heart rate (beats/min) × Stroke volume (L/beat)

$= 75 \times 50 \times \dfrac{1L}{1000ml}$

$= 3.75$ lit/min.

96. Let P = power at input

and p′ = power at output

then $\dfrac{P'}{P} = 0.25$

$\text{Loss} = \dfrac{10}{L}\log\left(\dfrac{P}{P'}\right) = \dfrac{10}{L}\log\left(\dfrac{P}{0.25\,P}\right)$

$= \dfrac{10}{0.4}\log\left(\dfrac{1}{0.25}\right) = 15$ db/km.

97. Required speed, $v = 5.93 \times 10^5 \sqrt{V} = 5.93 \times 10^5 \sqrt{100000} = 1.38 \times 10^6$ m/sec.

98. $\text{MCV} = \dfrac{\text{PCV}\times10}{\text{RBC count in millions / mm}^3}$

$= \dfrac{0.45\times10^{-6}}{5} = 90$ Cubic microns.

99. $\text{MCH} = \dfrac{\text{Hb in g percent} \times 10}{\text{RBC count in millions / mm}^3}$

$= \dfrac{15\times10^{-3}\times10^{-9}}{5} = 30$ picogms.

100. $\text{MCHC} = \dfrac{\text{Hb in 9 per 100 ml blood}}{\text{Volume of packed RBC / 100 ml blood}} \times 100$

$= \dfrac{15}{45} \times 100 = 33.3\%$

101. $\text{Cardiac output} = \dfrac{\text{Amount of indicator injected}}{\text{Average concentration}}$

$= \dfrac{5 \text{ mg}}{1.6 \text{ mg / L}} = 3.1$ L.

102. Transmission, $T = \dfrac{I_1}{I_0} \times 100\% = \dfrac{1}{2}\dfrac{I_0}{I_0} \times 100\% = 50\%$

103. $\dfrac{N_0}{4} = No\left(\dfrac{1}{2}\right)^n$

$\therefore \dfrac{1}{4} = \left(\dfrac{1}{2}\right)^n$

or $\dfrac{1}{2^2} = \dfrac{1}{2^n}$

or $n = 2$

$\therefore$ Time $= n \times T = 2 \times 1600 = 3200$ years.

104. We know $\dfrac{N_0}{16} = N_0\left[\dfrac{1}{2}\right]^n$

$\therefore n = 4$

$\therefore$ Half life period $= n \times \lambda = 4 \times \lambda = 20$ years

$\therefore \lambda = 5$ years.

105. $\text{Resolution} = \dfrac{1}{2}\left(\dfrac{600.1+599.9}{600.1-599.9}\right) = 3000.$

106. $P = VI = 80 \times 10^3 \times 3 \times 10^{-3} = 240$ W.

107. $\mu = \dfrac{0.693}{3 \text{ mm}} = 0.231$/mm.

108. $T(198\ A_v) = 6.2 \times 10^{-6}$ R m²/MBq hr.

$\therefore I = \dfrac{6.2\times10^{-6}\times75\times10^3}{(0.35)^2} = 0.4$ R/hr.

109. $I = T\dfrac{N}{D^2} = \dfrac{1.9\times10^{-6} \text{ R m}^2\text{/ MBq hr.} \times 500 \text{ MBq}}{(0.3 \text{ m})^2}$

$= 0.01$ R/hv $= 10$ mR/hr.

110. 1 day $= 24 \times 60 = 1440$ min

$\therefore$ Volume of blood $=$ (80 cm³/beat) (72 beats/min) (1440 min/day)

$= 8.3 \times 10^6$ cm³/day.

111. $\text{Cardiac output (Co)} = \dfrac{O_2 \text{ consumption (uptake) / min}}{PVO_2 - PAO_2}$

$= \dfrac{250\times100}{(19-14)\times1000} = 5$ L/min.

112. $\text{Cardiac output} = \dfrac{M\times60}{\text{Area under curve}}$ L/min

$= \dfrac{10\times60}{20\times5} = 6$ litre/min.

113. Given : Normal cardiac output = 5 lit/min

$\therefore$ Total amount of O_2 delivered to tissues

$= \dfrac{5}{100} \times 5000$

$= 250$ ml of O_2 per minute.

PRACTICE PAPER

IN : INSTRUMENTATION ENGINEERING

Duration : Three Hours | **Maximum Marks : 100**

Read the following instructions carefully.

1. All questions in this paper are of objective type.
2. There are a total of 65 questions carrying 100 marks.
3. Questions 1 through 25 are 1-mark questions, question 26 through 55 are 2-mark questions.
4. Questions 48 and 51 (2 pairs) common data questions and question pairs (Q. 52 and Q.53) and (Q. 54 and Q.55)are linked answer questions. The answer to the second question of the above pair depends on the answer to the first question of the pair. If the first question in the linked pair is wrongly answered or is un-attempted, then the answer to the second question in the pair will not be evaluated.
5. Questions 56 - 65 belong to general aptitude (GA). Questions 56 - 60 will carry 1-mark each, and questions 61-65 will carry 2-marks each. The GA questions will begin on a fresh page.
6. Un-attempted questions will carry zero marks.
7. Wrong answers will carry NEGATIVE marks. For Q.1 to Q.25 and Q.56 - Q.60, 1/3 mark will be deducated for each worng answer. For Q. 26 to Q. 51, and Q.61 - Q.65, 2/3 mark will be deducated for each wrong answer. The question pairs (Q. 52, Q. 53) and (Q. 54, Q. 55) are questions with linked answers. There will be negative marks only for wrong answer to the first question of the linked answer question pair i.e. for Q. 52 and Q.54, 2/3 mark will be deducated for each worng answer. There is no negative marking for Q. 53 and Q.55..
8. Calculator (without data connectivity) is allowed.
9. Charts, graph sheets or tables are NOT allowed.

Q. 1-25 carry one mark each

1. If $\begin{vmatrix} a & a^2 & a^3 & -1 \\ b & b^2 & b^3 & -1 \\ c & c^2 & c^3 & -1 \end{vmatrix} = 0$ in which a, b, c are different, then abc is

(a) 0 (b) 1

(c) 2 (d) 3

2. The directional derivative of $f(x, y, z) = xy^2 + yz^3$ at the point (2, –1, 1) in the direction of vector $\hat{i} + 2\hat{j} + 2\hat{k}$ is

(a) $-1\frac{2}{3}$ (b) $-2\frac{2}{3}$

(c) $-3\frac{2}{3}$ (d) $-4\frac{2}{3}$

3. For the differential equation $\frac{dy}{dt} + 5y = 0$, with $y(0) = 1$, the general solution is

(a) $5e^{5t}$ (b) e^{-5t}

(c) e^{5t} (d) $5e^{-5t}$

4. The order of error in the Simpson's rule for numerical integration with a step size is

(a) h (b) h^2

(c) h^3 (d) h^4

5. The unit circle of the Nyquist plot transforms into 0 dB line of the amplitude plot the Bode diagram at

(a) zero frequency (b) low frequency

(c) high frequency (d) any frequency

6. The spectral density of pink nosie varies as

(a) $\frac{1}{f^2}$ (b) f^2

(c) $\frac{1}{f}$ (d) f

7. The bandwith of an RF tuned amplifier is dependent on

(a) Q- factor of the tuned output circuit

(b) Q-factor of the tuned input circuit

(c) Quiescent operating point

(d) Q-factors of the output and input circuits as well as the quiescent operating point.

8. The laplace transform of the following voltage waveform is

(a) $\frac{V_0}{T_s^2} + \frac{V_0}{T_s^2} e^{-sT}$ (b) $\frac{V_0}{T_s^2} - \frac{V_0}{T_s^2} e^{-sT}$

(c) $\frac{V_0}{T_s^2} - \frac{V_0}{T_s} e^{-sT}$ (d) $\frac{V_0}{T_s^2} - \frac{V_0}{T_s^2} e^{-sT(1+sT)}$

9. The decimal number 85 in encoded as 1100-0101 in

(a) 8421 code (b) 4421 code

(c) 2421 code (d) 2221 code

10. The binary fraction 0.0111 in decimal form is equal to

(a) 0.4375 (b) 0.6225

(c) 0.8325 (d) 0.1105

11. In order to add 1111 + 1101, we require

(a) One FA, one HA

(b) Three FA

(c) Three FA and one HA

(d) None of these

12. A 250 μH inductance uses as a choke 10 MHz. At 12 MHz the choke

(a) does not have enough inductance

(b) has more reactance

(c) has less reactance

(d) needs more turns

13. A system function $H(s) = \frac{V(s)}{I(s)} = \frac{s+2}{2s+1}$

The system is at rest for $t < 0$, $i(t) = 0$ = unit step. The value of $v(t)$ at $t = 0$ and $t = \infty$ respectively are

(a) 2 and $\frac{1}{2}$ (b) $\frac{1}{2}$ and 2

(c) 0 and indeterminate (d) 2 and indeterminate

14. The current i_1 and i_2 in the given circuit is given by

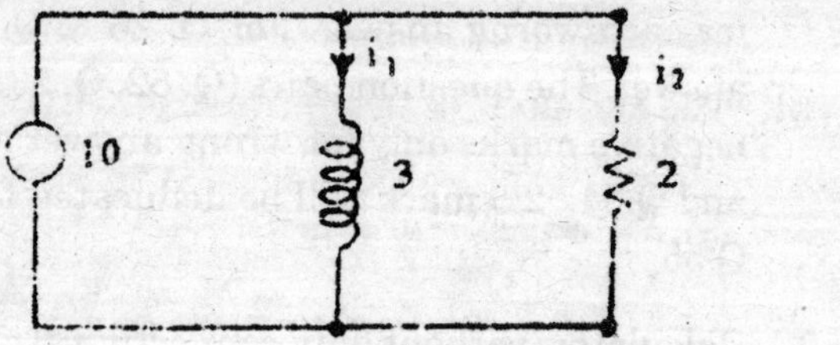

(a) 4, 4 amp (b) 6, 6 amp

(c) 4, 6 amp (d) 6, 4 amp

15. If the drift velocity of holes under a field gradient of amf of 100 V/m is 5 m/s their mobility (in the same SI units) is

(a) 0.05 (b) 0.5

(c) 50 (d) 500

16. The Geiger Counter has high quantum efficiency in the wavelength (Å) range

(a) 0.2 to 0.3

(b) 0.4 to 0.5

(c) 1.5 to 2.1

(d) 6 to 7

17. The Duane-Hunt law represents the minimum wavelength λ(Å) of X-rays generated for an applied voltage V (volts) and given by

(*a*) $V = \dfrac{12400}{\lambda}$ (*b*) $V = 12400\lambda$

(*c*) $V = \dfrac{12400}{\lambda^2}$ (*d*) $V = 12400\lambda$

18. The equations under balance conditions for a bridge are $R_1 = \dfrac{R_2R_3}{R_4}$ and $L_1 = R_2R_3C_4$, where R and L are respectively unknown resistance and inductance. In order to achieve faster balance which of the following variables are chosen

(*a*) R_2 and R_3 (*b*) R_2 and C_4

(*c*) R_4 and C_4 (*d*) R_3 and C_4

19. Assuming uniform pressure over the supported area, the friction moment in an exial bearing of a shaft of diameter *d* for an exial load of F (with co-efficient of friction μ) is given by

(*a*) $\dfrac{4}{3}F\mu d$ (*b*) $\dfrac{1}{3}F\mu d$

(*c*) $\dfrac{2}{3}F\mu d$ (*d*) $F\mu d$

20. The ideal linear characteristics for transmitting angular motion between two misaligned shafts is achieved by

(*a*) Dog coupling

(*b*) Universal coupling

(*c*) Flexible spring coupling

(*d*) Oldham's coupling

21. The output 'F' of the multiplexer circuit shown in the given figure will be

(*a*) $AB + B\bar{C} + \bar{C}A + \bar{B}\bar{C}$

(*b*) $A \oplus B \oplus C$

(*c*) $A \oplus B$

(*d*) $\bar{A}\bar{B}C + \bar{A}B\bar{C} + A\bar{B}\bar{C} + ABC$

22. The schematic shown in the figure represents a

(*a*) divide by seven counter

(*b*) divide by five counter

(*c*) binary coded decimal counter

(*d*) divide by twelve counter

23. A magnetic flux of 25,000 lines through an area of 5 cm^2 results in

(*a*) 5 lines flux

(*b*) 5000 Mx. of flux

(*c*) flux density of 5000 G

(*d*) none of these

24. A parallel LC resonant circuit resonates at 1000 kHz and has Q of 100. Its 3dB bandwith is

(*a*) 5 kHz (*b*) 10 kHz

(*c*) $\dfrac{10}{2\pi}$ kHz (*d*) $\dfrac{50}{2\pi}$ kHz

25. A passive network has

(*a*) no voltage source but current sources

(*b*) no current source but voltage sources

(*c*) no voltage or current sources

(*d*) none of these

Q.26-55 carry two marks each

26. $H(s) = \dfrac{V(s)}{I(s)} = \dfrac{4s+6}{s+2}$, $i(t)$ is unit step. $v(t)$ as $t \to \infty$ is given by

(*a*) 0 (*b*) 3

(*c*) 4 (*d*) ∞

27. A driving point impedance $Z_d(s) = \dfrac{v(s)}{I(s)} = \dfrac{s+1}{s+2}$. The system is initially at rest. For a voltage signal at unit step, the current $i(t)$ through Z_d is given by

(*a*) $1 - e^{-t}$ (*b*) $2 - e^{-t}$

(*c*) $2 - 2e^{-t}$ (*d*) $\dfrac{1}{2}\left(1-e^{-2t}\right)$

28. The number of different Boolean functions of 4 variables is

(*a*) 2^{16} (*b*) 16^2

(*c*) 4^2 (*d*) 16^4

29. Expression for *y*(A, B, C) in figure A, B and C are Boolean variables is

(*a*) $\overline{AB} + \bar{A}BC$ (*b*) $A + BC$

(*c*) $\overline{AB} + BC$ (*d*) $\left(AB + A\bar{B}\right)C$

30. The open loop transfer functions of a system is given by $\dfrac{k}{s(s+2)(s+3)}$ for drawing root locus, the point of intersection of the a symptotes with the real axis is

(*a*) – 1/3 (*b*) –2/3

(*c*) –5/3 (*d*) 0

31. In feedback control system with $G(s) = \dfrac{16}{s(s+4)}$ and $H(s) = 1 + ks$, the damping ratio of 0.6 will be achieved for *k* equal to

(*a*) 0.1 (*b*) 0.02

(*c*) 0.025 (*d*) 0.05

32. Hilbert transform of A sin $(2\pi f_0 t)$ is

(*a*) –A sin $(2\pi f_0 t)$ (*b*) A cos $(2\pi f_0 t)$

(c) –A cos $(2\pi f_0 t)$ (*d*) A sin $(2\pi f_0 t)$

33. An amplifier has an input power of 2 microwatts. The power gain of the amplifier is 60 dB. The output power will be

(*a*) 6 μw (*b*) 120μw

(c) .2*mw* (*d*) 2 watt

34. RLC tuned circuit has maximum impedance Z_{max} = 70 k ohm at f = 1000 kHz. Given Q = 100, the impedance becomes 50 k ohms at frequency f is given by

(*a*) 1000 ± 200 kHz (*b*) 1000 ± 100 kHz

(c) 1000 ± 10 kHz (*d*) 1000 ± 5 kHz

35. For the resonant circuit the shown $w_0 = 10^5$, Q = 50, R = 400. The value of CM given by

(*a*) 250 *pf* (*b*) 1000 *pf*

(c) 500 *pf* (*d*) 1.25 μf

36. Initial voltage on capacitor V_0 as marked $|V_0|$ = 4.6 volts. $V_s = 7.5\,u(t)$ where $u(t)$ is a unit step. The voltage marked v at $t = 0^+$ given by

(*a*) 0

(*b*) $\frac{1}{2}$

(c) 1

(*d*) 2

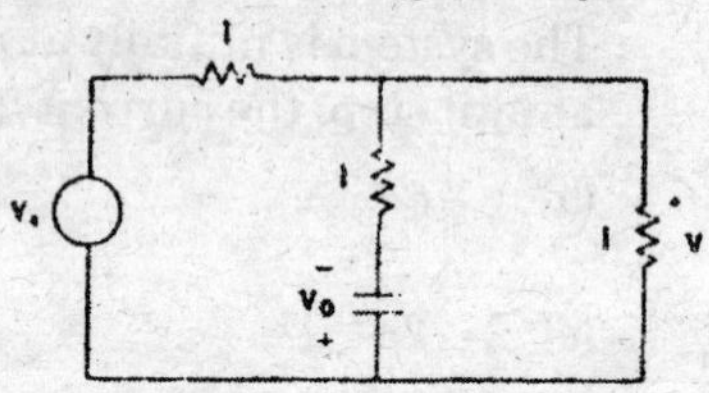

37. In order to separate channels in a time division multiplex receiver, it is necessary to use

(*a*) AND gates (*b*) band pass filters

(*c*) differentiation (*d*) integration

38. 1000 kHz carrier wave modulated 40% at 4000 Hz is applied to a resonant circuit tuned to a carrier frequency and having Q = 140. What is the degree of modulation after transmission through this circuit?

(*a*) 60% (*b*) 30%

(c) 27% (*d*) 54%

39. The algebraic sum of the angles of the vectors from all poles and zeros to the point on any root locus segment is

(*a*) 45° (*b*) 90°

(c) 180° (*d*) 110° or its odd multiple

40. A.C. systems are usually preferred to the D.C. systems in control applications because

(*a*) A.C. systems are cheaper

(*b*) A.C. systems are more stable

(c) A.C. systems have better performance characteristics and are smaller in size

(*d*) All of these

41. The maximum efficiency of a full-wave reactifier is

(*a*) 81.2% (*b*) 25%

(c) 40% (*d*) 75%

42. Three-phase half-wave rectification, if the input frequency is 50 Hz, then output frequency is

(*a*) 100 Hz (*b*) 150 Hz

(c) 75 Hz (*d*) 25 Hz

43. An op. amp has an offset voltage of 1 mV and is ideal in all other respects. If this op. amp is used in the circuit shown in the figure, the output voltage will be (select the nearest value)

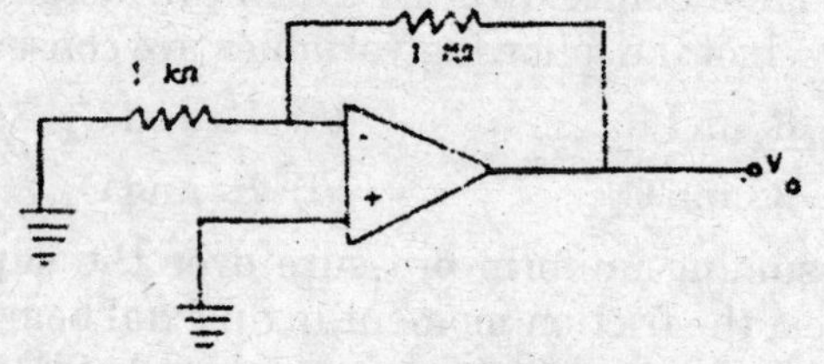

(*a*) 1 mV (*b*) 1 V

(c) ± 1 V (*d*) 0 V

44. The circuit of the figure uses an ideal op. amp. For small positive values of V_m, the circuit works as

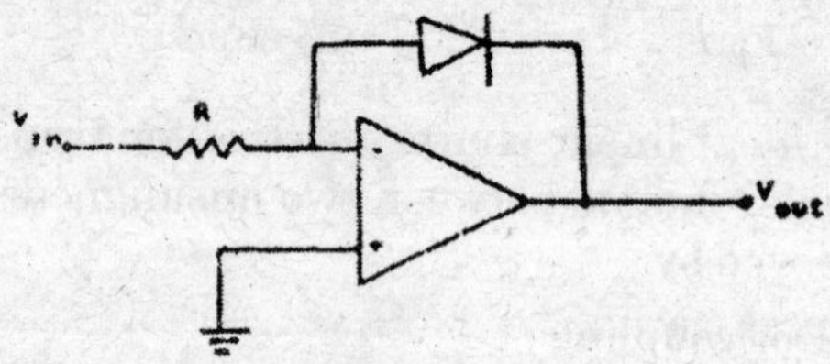

(*a*) a halfwave rectifier

(*b*) a differentiator

(*c*) a logarithmic amplifier

(*d*) an exponential amplifier

45. Assume that the operational amplifier in the figure is ideal. The current, I, though the 1 k ohm resistor is

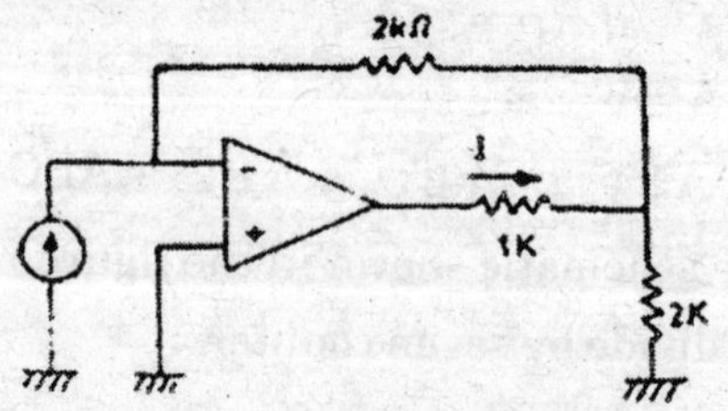

(*a*) 2 mA (*b*) 4 mA

(c) –4 mA (*d*) 0

46. If R_s is the source resistance, the output resistance of an emitter-follower using the simplified hybrid model would be

(*a*) $\dfrac{h_{ie}+R_s}{1+h_{fe}}$ (*b*) $\dfrac{h_{ie}+R_s}{h_{fe}}$

(c) $R_s\dfrac{1}{h_{fe}}$ (*d*) $\dfrac{1}{h_{fe}}$

47. The power in a series RLC circuit will be half of that at resonance and magnitude of current will be

(a) $\frac{V}{2R}$ (b) $\frac{V}{\sqrt{3}R}$

(c) $\frac{V}{\sqrt{2}R}$ (d) $\frac{\sqrt{2}V}{R}$

Common Data Q. 48 and 49

The root locus plot for a system, with transfer function $\frac{2}{s(s+1)(s+2)}$, is shown in a unity feedback proportional control system is built using this system.

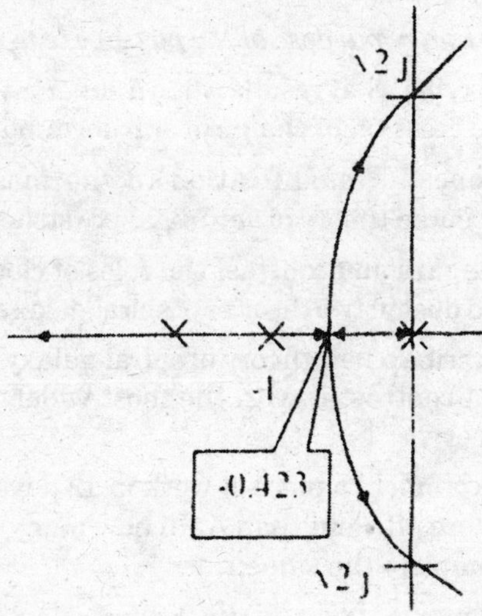

48. The maximum possible controller gain, for which the unity feed back system is stable, is approximately

(a) 6.0 (b) 3.0

(c) 0.4 (d) 0.2

49. The maximum possible controller gain, for which the unity feedback system exhibits a non-oscillatory response to a unit step input, is

(a) 0.6 (b) 3.0

(c) 0.4 (d) 0.2

Common Data Q. 50 and 51

A bonded metal strain gauge has the following specifications:

Guauge factor = 2.0

Unstrained resistance = 120 Ω at 0 °C

Maximum operating temperature = 150 °C

Temperature coefficient of resistance = (2×10^{-5}) °C^{-1}

Maximum tensile and compressive strain = 2×10^{-2}

50. The temperature-induced resistance error at the maximum operating temperature expressed as the percentage of resistance change due to maximum tensile strain only, assuming self-heating effects to be negligible, is

(a) 0.0625 (b) 0.625

(c) 6.26 (d) 7.5

51. Two strain gauges, with the specifications given above are mounted on a structural member in a push-pull configuration, connected in a bridge along with two standard resistances, whose output is fed to an amplifier as shown in the figure. The output voltage V_0 per unit battery voltage, under maximum loading, is

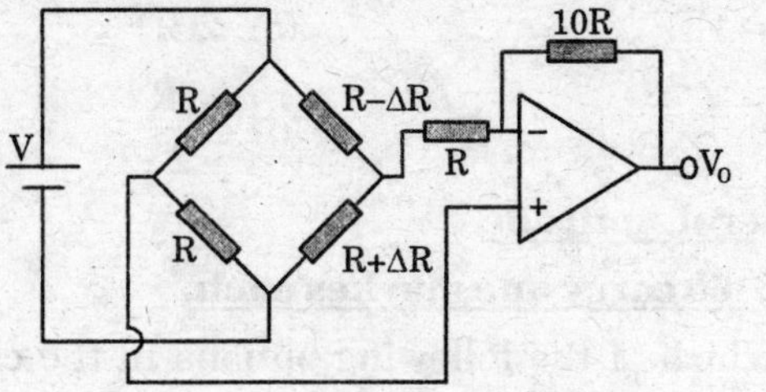

(a) –0.4 V (b) – 0.37 V

(c) 0.37 V (d) 0.4 V

Linked Answer Q. 52 and 53

For the circuit shown in figure, I_E = 1 mA, β = 99 and V_{BR} = 0.7 V.

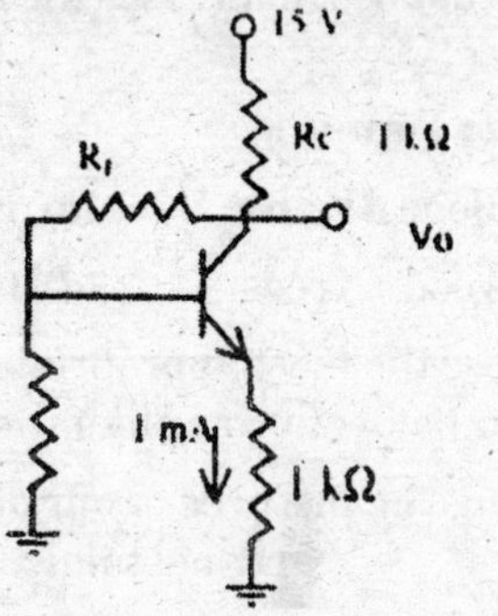

52. The current through R_1 is

(a) 0.1 mA (b) 0.35 mA

(c) 0.2 mA (d) none of the above

53. The value of R_F is

(a) 150.3 kΩ (b) 110.9 kΩ

(c) 171.5 kΩ (d) none of these

Linked Answer Q. 54 and 55

Assuming ideal op-amps, and the circuit shown in the figure below, simulates an inductor,

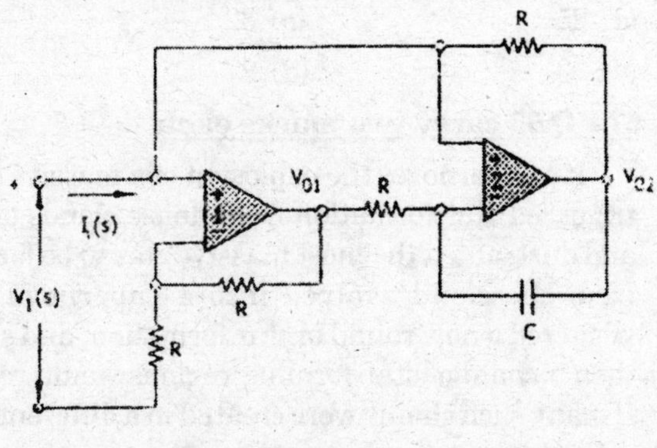

54. The $\frac{V_i(s)}{I_i(s)}$ will be equal to

(*a*) sL (*b*) $\frac{s}{L}$

(*c*) $\frac{L}{s}$ (*d*) none of these

55. The effective inductance L_{eff} will be equal to

(*a*) CR^2 (*b*) $2CD^2$

(*c*) $\frac{CR^2}{2}$ (*d*) $\frac{CR}{2}$

General Aptitude

Q.56 -60 carry one markes each.

56. Which of the following options in the closest in meaning to the word below:

Gist

(*a*) contribution (*b*) substance

(*c*) prestige (*d*) accessory

57. The question below consists of a pair of related words followed by four pairs of words. Select the pair that best expresses the relation in the original pair.

Fuel : Pipes

(*a*) Blood : Veins (*b*) Food Stomach

(*c*) Wood : Trees (*d*) Cars : Expressway

58. Choose the most appropriate word from the option given below to complete the following sentence:

Seeing the pictures of our old home made me feel __________ and nostalgic.

(*a*) fastidious (*b*) conciliatory

(*c*) indignant (*d*) wistful

59. Choose the most appropriate word from the option given below to complete the following sentence:

The fans were __________ when their team lost its seventyh game in a row.

(*a*) irascible (*b*) despondent

(*c*) lucid (*d*) didactic

60. What least number must be added to 8961 to make it exactly divisible by 84?

(*a*) 25 (*b*) 32

(*c*) 33 (*d*) 27

Q. 61 – Q.65 carry two marks each

61. If a supernova (the explosion of a massive star) triggered star formation from dense clouds of gas and dust, and if the most massive star to be formed from the cloud evolved into a supernova and triggered a new round of star formation, and so on, then a chain of star-forming regions would result. If many such chains were created in a differentially rotating galaxy, the distribution of stars would resemble the observed distribute in a spiral galaxy. This line of reasoning underlies an exciting new theory of spiral-galaxy structure. A computer simulation based on this theory has reproduced the appearance of many spiral galaxies without assuming an underlying density wave, the hallmark of the most widely accepted theory of the large-scale structure of spiral galaxies. That theory maintains that a density wave of spiral form sweeps through the central plane of a galaxy, compressing clouds of gas and dust, which collapse into stars that form a spiral pattern.

The primary purpose of the passage is to

(*a*) describe what results when a supernova triggers the creation of chains of star-forming regions

(*b*) propose a modification in the most widely accepted theory of spiral-galaxy structure

(*c*) compare and contrast the roles of clouds of gas and dust in two theories of spiral-galaxy structure

(*d*) describe a new theory of spiral-galaxy structure and contrast it with the most widely accepted theory

62. A can complete a piece of work in 12 days and B is 60% more efficient than A. In how many days B will complete the same work ?

(*a*) 4 days (*b*) 5 days

(*c*) 7.5 days (*d*) 9 days

63. A group of labourers promise to do a piece of work in 12 days, but 5 of them do not turn up. If the rest of the group do the work in 18 days, find the original number of men.

(*a*) 15 (*b*) 25

(*c*) 35 (*d*) 45

Directions for Q. 64 to 65

Answer these questions based on the information given below

A boy is asked to put in a basket one mango when ordered 'One', one orange when ordered 'Two', one apple when ordered 'Three' and is asked to take out from the basket one mango and an orange when ordered 'Four'. A sequence of orders is given as

1 2 3 3 2 1 4 2 3 1 4 2 2 3 3 1 4 1 1 3 2 3 4

64. How many total organges were in the basket at the end of the above sequence ?

(*a*) 1 (*c*) 4

(*b*) 3 (*d*) 2

65. How many total fruits will be in the basket at the end of the above order sequence ?

(*a*) 9 (*b*) 8

(*c*) 11 (*d*) 10

ANSWERS

1. (*b*)	**2.** (*c*)	**3.** (*b*)	**4.** (*b*)	**5.** (*d*)	**6.** (*a*)	**7.** (*a*)	**8.** (*d*)	**9.** (*b*)	**10.** (*a*)
11. (*c*)	**12.** (*b*)	**13.** (*b*)	**14.** (*c*)	**15.** (*a*)	**16.** (*d*)	**17.** (*b*)	**18.** (*c*)	**19.** (*d*)	**20.** (*a*)
21. (*d*)	**22.** (*a*)	**23.** (*c*)	**24.** (*b*)	**25.** (*c*)	**26.** (*b*)	**27.** (*b*)	**28.** (*c*)	**29.** (*c*)	**30.** (*c*)
31. (*d*)	**32.** (*b*)	**33.** (*d*)	**34.** (*d*)	**35.** (*c*)	**36.** (*c*)	**37.** (*a*)	**38.** (*c*)	**39.** (*d*)	**40.** (*d*)
41. (*a*)	**42.** (*b*)	**43.** (*c*)	**44.** (*c*)	**45.** (*c*)	**46.** (*a*)	**47.** (*b*)	**48.** (*b*)	**49.** (*d*)	**50.** (*b*)
51. (*b*)	**52.** (*a*)	**53.** (*b*)	**54.** (*a*)	**55.** (*c*)	**56.** (*b*)	**57.** (*a*)	**58.** (*d*)	**59.** (*b*)	**60.** (*d*
61. (*d*)	**62.** (*c*)	**63.** (*a*)	**64.** (*d*)	**65.** (*c*)					

EXPLANATIONS

26. $\dfrac{v(s)}{I(s)} = \dfrac{4s+6}{s+2}$, $v(t)$ as $f \to \infty$

$$\underset{s\to 0}{v(s)} = \underset{s\to 0}{\text{Lt}} \frac{(4s+6)}{s+2} = \underset{s\to 0}{\text{Lt}} \frac{4s+6}{s+2} = \frac{6}{2} = 3$$

27. Then $\quad I(s) = \dfrac{(s+2)}{s(s+1)} = \dfrac{A}{s} + \dfrac{B}{s+1}$

$\therefore \quad A = 2, \quad B = \dfrac{-1+2}{-1} - 1$

$\therefore \quad I(t) = L^{-1}[I(s)] = L^{-1}\left[\dfrac{A}{s} + \dfrac{B}{s+1}\right] = 2 - e^{-t}$

28. Number of difference Boolean functions

$$= 2^4 = 16 = 4^2$$

29.

$$\bar{y} = \bar{A}\bar{B}I_0 + \bar{A}BI_1 + A\bar{B}I_2 + ABI_3$$
$$= \bar{A}\bar{B} \times 1 + \bar{A}BC + A\bar{B} \times 0 + ABC$$
$$= \bar{A}\bar{B} + \bar{A}BC + ABC$$
$$= \bar{A}\bar{B} + BC\left(A + \bar{A}\right)$$
$$= \overline{AB} + BC$$

30. Poles at $s = 0, -2, -3$

$$\sigma = \frac{\Sigma p - \Sigma z}{p-n} = \frac{-2-3-0}{3} = \frac{-5}{3}$$

31. Given: $g = 0.6$

Characteristic equation is,

$1 + H(s)\,G(s) = 0$

$\Rightarrow \quad 1 + \dfrac{(1+sk)16}{(s+4)s} = 0$

i.e. $\quad s^2 + 4s + 16ks + 16 = 0$

i.e. $\quad s^2 + (16k+4)s + 16 = 0$

$\omega_n = 4,$

$2\Sigma\omega_n = 16k + 4$

$\Rightarrow \quad 2 \times 0.6 \times 4 = 16k + 4$

i.e. $\quad 0.8 = 16k$

i.e. $\quad k = \dfrac{0.8}{16} = \dfrac{1}{20} = 0.05$

32. $f(t) = A\sin(2\pi f_0 t)$, $H[f(t)]$

$$= A\sin\left(2\pi f_0 t + \frac{\pi}{2}\right)$$
$$= A\cos(2\pi f_0 t)$$

33. $10 \log \dfrac{p_o}{p_i} = 60$

i.e. $\quad \dfrac{p_o}{p_i} = 10^6$

$p_o = 10^6 \times 2 \times 10^{-6} = 2$ watt

34. $\dfrac{z_{max}}{\sqrt{2}} = \dfrac{70}{\sqrt{2}} = 50$

$BW = \dfrac{f_0}{Q} = \dfrac{1000 \times 10^3}{100} = 10k$

$f_{12} = \pm 5$ kHz

$f = 1000 \pm 5$ kHz

35. $\dfrac{\omega L}{R} = Q$

$\therefore \quad \dfrac{10^5 \times L}{400} = 50$

$\therefore \quad L = \dfrac{400 \times 50}{10^5}$

$= \dfrac{20}{100} = 0.2$

and $\quad C = \dfrac{1}{\omega_0^2 L}$

$= \dfrac{1}{10^{10} \times 0.2}$

$= 5 \times 10^{-10} = 500\ pf$

48. At $s = 0 \pm \sqrt{2}j$, the system will have maximum controller gain and

$$k = \left|\frac{s(s+1)(s+2)}{2}\right|_{s=\sqrt{2}j}$$

$$= \left|\frac{(\sqrt{2}j)(1+\sqrt{2}j)(2+\sqrt{2}j)}{2}\right| = 3$$

49. At $s = -0.425$, the system have maximum non-oscillatory response, because after that the system will become oscillatory since roots will be become complex.

then,

$$k = \left|\frac{s(s+1)(s+2)}{2}\right|_{s=-0.425} = 0.2$$

52.

$$I_E = 1 \text{ mA}$$

$$\beta = 99$$

$$V_{BE} = 0.7 \text{ V}$$

$$\alpha = \frac{\beta}{\beta+1} = \frac{99}{99+1} = 0.99$$

$$\frac{I_C}{I_E} = \alpha = 0.99$$

$$I_C = 0.99\, I_E = 0.99 \text{ mA}$$

$$\frac{I_C}{I_\beta} = \beta$$

$$I_\beta = \frac{I_C}{I_\beta} = \frac{0.99}{99} = 0.01 \text{ mA}$$

Current through

$$R_1 = \frac{V_{EE}+1\times 1}{17} = \frac{0.7+1}{17} = 0.1 \text{ mA}$$

Current through

$$R_F = I_B + 0.1 = 0.01 + 0.1 = 0.11$$

Current through

$$R_C = I_C + 0.11 = 0.99 + 0.11 = 1.1 \text{ mA}$$

53.

$$R_F = \frac{V_0 - V_{EE} - 1\times 1}{0.11}$$

$$= \frac{13.9 - 0.7 - 1}{0.11} = 110.9 \text{ k}\Omega$$

54. $V_{02} = V_{01} \times \frac{1}{sCR}$

and $V_{01} = V_i(s)\left(1+\frac{R}{R}\right)$

$$= 2V_i(s)$$

$$\Rightarrow \quad V_{02} = -\frac{2V_i(10)}{sCR}$$

$$\Rightarrow \quad V_{02} = -I_i(s)\,R$$

Equating, we get $\frac{-2V_i(s)}{sCR} = -I_i(s)\,R$

$$\Rightarrow \quad \frac{V_i(s)}{I_i(s)} = \frac{sCR^2}{2} = sL$$

55. $L_{eff} = \frac{CR^2}{2}$

62. A's efficiency or A's one day work $= \frac{1}{12}$

B's efficiency is 60% more than A

$$\Rightarrow \quad \frac{160}{100} \times \frac{1}{12} = \frac{2}{15}$$

$$\Rightarrow \quad \frac{15}{2}\text{ days} = 7.5 \text{ days}$$

64. (1) (2) 3 3 2 1 4 (2) 3 (1) 4 2 (2) 3 3 (1) 4 1 (1) (3) (2) 3 4

Total number of oranges were in the basket = 2

65. Total fruits in the basket = 11

Mock Tests and Solved Paper

MOCK TEST - 1

INSTRUCTIONS

1. Total of 65 questions carrying 100 marks, out of which 10 questions carrying a total of 15 marks are in General Aptitude (GA)
2. The Engineering Mathematics will carry around **15% of the total marks,** the General Aptitude section will carry **15% of the total marks** and the **remaining 70% of the total marks.**
3. **Types of Questions**
   (a) Multiple Choice Questions (MCQ) carrying 1 or 2 marks each in all papers and sections. These questions are objective in nature, and each will have a choice of four options, out of which the candidate has to mark the correct answer(s).
   (b) Numerical Answer Questions of 1 or 2 marks each in all papers and sections. For these questions the answer is a real number, to be entered by the candidate using the virtual keypad. No choices will be shown for these type of questions.
4. For **1-mark** multiple-choice questions, **1/3 marks** will be deducted for a wrong answer. Likewise, for **2-marks** multiple-choice questions, **2/3** marks will be deducted for a wrong answer. There is no negative marking for numerical answer type questions.

GENERAL APTITUDE (GA)

(Q.1 – 5) : Carry One Mark Each

1. Complete the sentence: Universalism is to particularism as diffuseness is to ____

(a) specific (b) neutrality
(c) generality (d) adapt

2. Which of the following option is closest in meaning of word below GRAVID ?

(a) Convert (b) Covet
(c) Pregnant (d) Cornivorous

3. Select the choice pair that has the same relation as the pair given below

dilate : expand

(a) can : discharge (b) idyllic : carefree
(c) exit : missionary (d) fear : profile

4. Find the odd man out from the group of four words

(a) Progression (b) Headway
(c) Forge ahead (d) Deviant

5. What is the sum of all odd numbers from 1 to 100.?

(Q.6 –10) : Carry Two Marks Each

6. A person starts his journey from his house towards north-east and travel for 4 km, then the turn to his right and travel for 5 km. Then he turn to his left to travel another 4 km and turn his right and travel 1 km. Which direction is he facing when he complete his journey and how far is the place from his house ?

(a) North-west, 8 km (b) North-east, 10 km
(c) South-west, 8 km (d) South-east, 10 km

7. An article costing ₹ 9000 is sold at a discount which is equal to the simple interest on ₹ 3000 for N months. Find N if the rate of discount is same as the rate of interest.

8. If 137 + 276 = 435, how much is 371 + 726 ?

9. If GO = 32 and SHE = 49, then what is SOME?

10. Though one eye is kept firmly on the ______, the company now also promotes ___ contemporary art.

(a) Present, Experimental
(b) Present, Popular
(c) Future, Popular
(d) Market, Popular

TECHNICAL SECTION

(Q.1 – 25) : Carry One Mark Each

1. The order of error in the Simpson's rule for numerical integration with a step size is

(a) h (b) h^2
(c) h^3 (d) h^4

2. The unit circle of the Nyquist plot transforms into 0 dB line of the amplitude plot the Bode diagram at

(a) zero frequency (b) low frequency
(c) high frequency (d) any frequency

3. The spectral density of pink nosie varies as

(a) $\frac{1}{f^2}$ (b) f^2
(c) $\frac{1}{f}$ (d) f

4. The bandwith of an RF tuned amplifier is dependent on

(*a*) Q- factor of the tuned output circuit

(*b*) Q-factor of the tuned input circuit

(*c*) Quiescent operating point

(*d*) Q-factors of the output and input circuits as well as the quiescent operating point.

5. The laplace transform of the following voltage waveform is

(*a*) $\frac{V_0}{T_s^2}+\frac{V_0}{T_s^2}e^{-sT}$

(*b*) $\frac{V_0}{T_s^2}-\frac{V_0}{T_s^2}e^{-sT}$

(*c*) $\frac{V_0}{T_s^2}-\frac{V_0}{T_s}e^{-sT}$

(*d*) $\frac{V_0}{T_s^2}-\frac{V_0}{T_s^2}e^{-sT(1+sT)}$

6. A 250 μH inductance uses as a choke 10 MHz. At 12 MHz the choke

(*a*) does not have enough inductance

(*b*) has more reactance

(*c*) has less reactance

(*d*) needs more turns

7. A system function $H(s)=\frac{V(s)}{I(s)}=\frac{s+2}{2s+1}$

The system is at rest for $t<0$, $i(t)=0=$ unit step. The value of $v(t)$ at $t=0$ and $t=\infty$ respectively are

(*a*) 2 and $\frac{1}{2}$

(*b*) $\frac{1}{2}$ and 2

(*c*) 0 and indeterminate

(*d*) 2 and indeterminate

8. The current i_1 and i_2 in the given circuit is given by

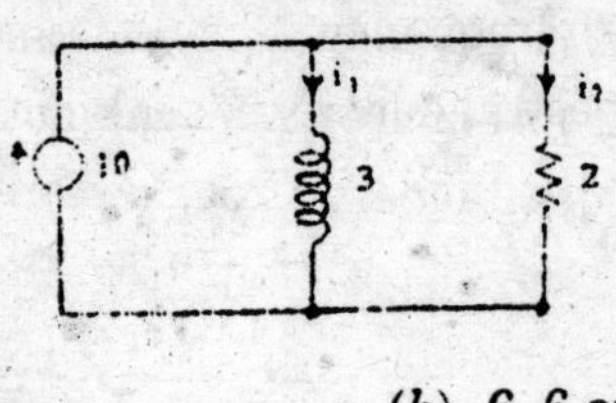

(*a*) 4, 4 amp (*b*) 6, 6 amp

(*c*) 4, 6 amp (*d*) 6, 4 amp

9. $V_1 = 10 \sin \omega t$

$V_2 = 10 \cos (\omega t + \pi/4)$

If V_1 and V_2 are applied to x and y plates of CRO then the pattern observed is

(*a*) Straight line

(*b*) Multiple folded pattern

(*c*) Circle

(*d*) Ellipse

10. If A modulate signal $S(t) = m(t) \cos 40000\pi t$ is given and $m(t)$ does not contain frequency component mere then 5 kHz. The minimum sampling frequency in kHz for proper reconstruction of signal is ________

11. Newton Raphson algorithm for finding K[th] root of a number is ______.

(*a*) $x_{i+1}=\frac{x_i}{K}\left[K+1+\frac{\text{Number}}{x_i^K}\right]$

(*b*) $x_{i+1}=\frac{x_i}{K}\left[K-1+\frac{\text{Number}}{x_i^K}\right]$

(*c*) $x_{i+1}=\frac{x_i}{K}\left[K-1-\frac{\text{Number}}{x_i^K}\right]$

(*d*) $x_{i+1}=-\frac{x_i}{K}\left[K-1+\frac{\text{Number}}{x_i^K}\right]$

12. Semiconductor strain gauges have better gauges factor than a normal strain gauge because

(*a*) –Ve temp. coefficient of semiconductors

(*b*) Large piezo-resistive coefficient

(*c*) Piezo electric effect

(*d*) None of these

13. The initial contents of the 4-bit serial-in-parallel-out right-shift, shift, register shown in the given figure is 0110. After three clock pulses are applied, the contents of the shift register will be

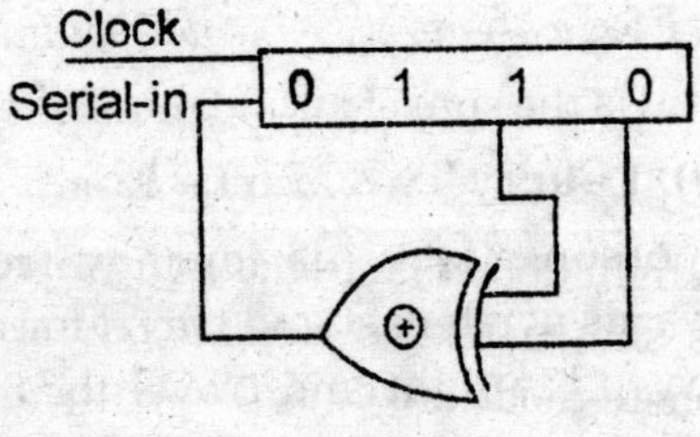

(*a*) 0000

(*b*) 0101

(*c*) 1010

(*d*) 1111

14. Find R_{eq}

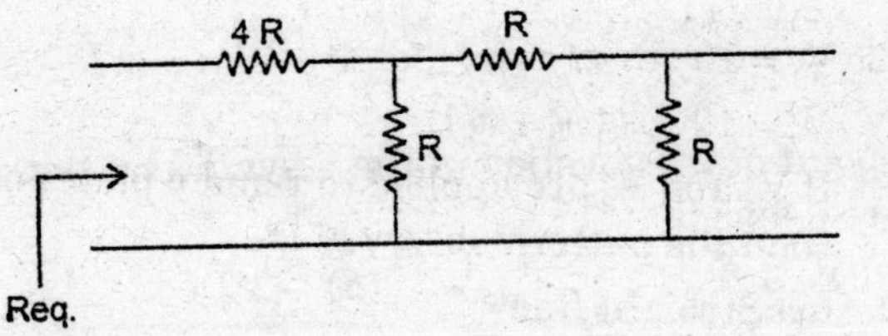

15. The Bode plot of a transfer function G(s) is shown in the figure below.

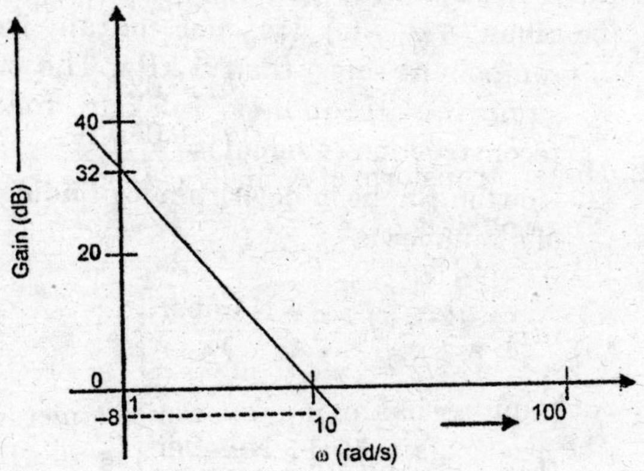

The gain (20 log|G(s)|) is 32 dB and –8 dB at 1 rad/s and 10 rad/s respectively. The phase is negative for all ω. Then G (s) is

(a) $\frac{39.8}{s}$ (b) $\frac{39.8}{s}$

(c) $\frac{32}{s}$ (d) $\frac{32}{s^2}$

16. CMRR in an ECG amplifier when input impedance is 2 MΩ and difference of electrode skin contact as 1 kΩ, is

(a) 1000 (b) 2000

(c) 3000 (d) 5000

17. The voltage (E_0) developed across a glass electrode for pH measurement is related to the temperature (T) by the relation

(a) $E_o \propto \frac{1}{T^2}$ (b) $E_o \propto \frac{1}{T}$

(c) $E_o \propto T$ (d) $E_o \propto T^2$

18. A light detector circuit using an ideal photo-diode is shown in the figure. The sensitivity of the photo-diode is 0.5 μA/μW. With V_r = 6V, the output voltage V_o = – 1.0 for 10 μW of incident light. If V_r is changed to 3V, keeping all other parameters the same, the value of V_o in volts is _______ V.

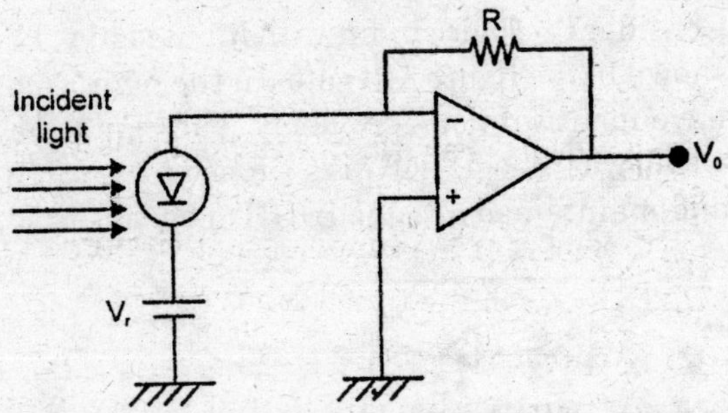

19. The logic evaluated by the circuit at the output is

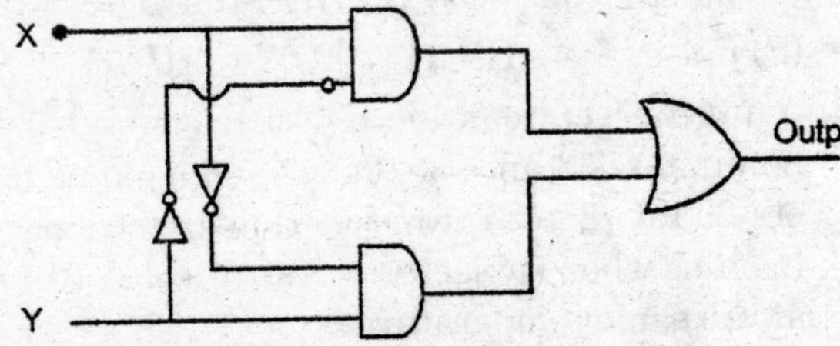

(a) $X\bar{Y}+Y\bar{X}$ (b) $(\overline{X+Y})XY$

(c) $\overline{XY}+XY$ (d) $\bar{X}Y+X\bar{Y}+X+Y$

20. The highest frequency present in the signal $x(t)$ is f_{max}. The highest frequency present in the signal $y(t) = x^2(t)$ is

(a) $\frac{1}{2}f_{max}$ (b) f_{max}

(c) $2f_{max}$ (d) $4f_{max}$

21. The double integral $\int_0^a\int_0^y f(x,y)dx\,dy$ is equivalent to

(a) $\int_0^x\int_0^y f(x,y)dx\,dy$ (b) $\int_0^a\int_x^y f(x,y)dx\,dy$

(c) $\int_0^a\int_x^a f(x,y)dx\,dy$ (d) $\int_0^a\int_0^a f(x,y)dx\,dy$

22. In the circuit shown, the switch is momentarily closed and then opened. Assuming the logic gates to have non-zero delay, at steady state, the logic states of X and Y are

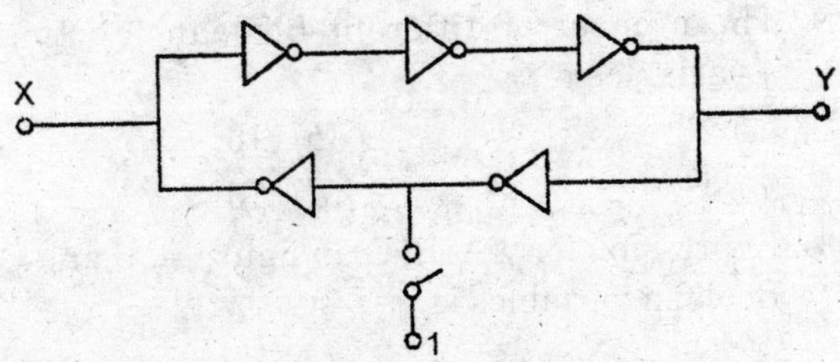

(a) X is latched, Y toggles continuously

(b) X and Y are both latched

(c) Y is latched, X toggles continuously

(d) X and Y both toggle continuously

23. Consider the logic circuit with input signal TEST shown in the figure. All gates in the figure shown have identical non-zero delay. The signal TEST which was at logic LOW is switched to logic HIGH and maintained at logic HIGH. The output

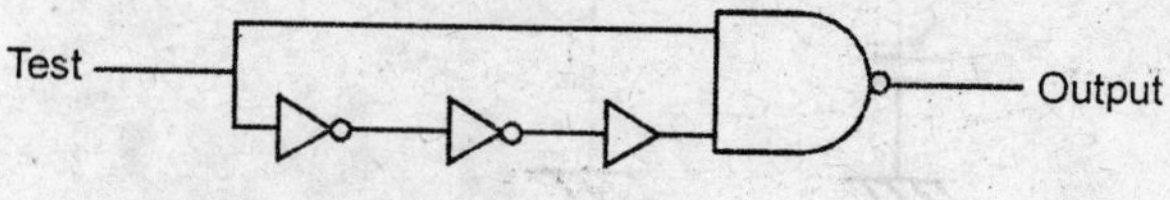

(*a*) stays HIGH throughout
(*b*) stays LOW throughout
(*c*) pulses from LOW to HIGH to LOW
(*d*) pulses from HIGH to LOW to HIGH

24. A p-type semiconductor strain gauge has a nominal resistance of 1000 Ω and a gauge factor of + 200 at o 25°C. The resistance of the strain gauge in ohms when subjected to a strain of $+ 10^{-4}$ m/m at the same temperature is _______ Ω.

25. Liquid flow rate is measured using

(*a*) a Pirani gauge (*b*) a pyrometer
(*c*) an orifice plate (*d*) a Bourdon tube

(Q. 26 – 55) : Carry Two Marks Each

26. $H(s) = \dfrac{V(s)}{I(s)} = \dfrac{4s+6}{s+2}$, $i(t)$ is unit step. $v(t)$ as $t \to \infty$ is given by

(*a*) 0 (*b*) 3
(*c*) 4 (*d*) ∞

27. A driving point impedance $Z_d(s) = \dfrac{v(s)}{I(s)} = \dfrac{s+1}{s+2}$.

The system is initially at rest. For a voltage signal at unit step, the current $i(t)$ through Z_d is given by

(*a*) $1 - e^{-f}$
(*b*) $2 - e^{-f}$
(*c*) $2 - 2e^{-f}$
(*d*) $\frac{1}{2}\left(1 - e^{-2f}\right)$

28. The number of different Boolean functions of 4 variables is

(*a*) 2^{16} (*b*) 16^2
(*c*) 4^2 (*d*) 16^4

29. Expression for *y*(A, B, C) in figure A, B and C are Boolean variables is

(*a*) $\overline{AB} + \overline{A}BC$
(*b*) A + BC
(*c*) $\overline{AB} + BC$
(*d*) $\left(AB + A\overline{B}\right)C$

30. The open loop transfer functions of a system is given by $\dfrac{k}{s(s+2)(s+3)}$ for drawing root locus, the point of intersection of the a symptotes with the real axis is.

(*a*) – 1/3 (*b*) –2/3
(*c*) –5/3 (*d*) 0

31. In feedback control system with $G(s) = \dfrac{16}{s(s+4)}$ and H(*s*) = 1 + *ks*, the damping ratio of 0.6 will be achieved for *k* equal to

(*a*) 0.1 (*b*) 0.02
(*c*) 0.025 (*d*) 0.05

32. Hilbert transform of A sin $(2\pi f_0 t)$ is

(*a*) –A sin $(2\pi f_0 t)$
(*b*) A cos $(2\pi f_0 t)$
(*c*) –A cos $(2\pi f_0 t)$
(*d*) A sin $(2\pi f_0 t)$

33. An amplifier has an input power of 2 microwatts. The power gain of the amplifier is 60 dB. The output power will be

(*a*) 6 μ*w* (*b*) 120μ*w*
(*c*) .2*mw* (*d*) 2 watt

34. RLC tuned circuit has maximum impedance Z_{max} = 70 k ohm at *f* = 1000 kHz. Given Q = 100, the impedance becomes 50 k ohms at frequency *f* is given by

(*a*) 1000 ± 200 kHz (*b*) 1000 ± 100 kHz
(*c*) 1000 ± 10 kHz (*d*) 1000 ± 5 kHz

35. For the resonant circuit the shown $w_0 = 10^5$, Q = 50, R = 400. The value of CM given by

(*a*) 250 *pf* (*b*) 1000 *pf*
(*c*) 500 *pf* (*d*) 1.25 μ*f*

36. $A\begin{bmatrix}1 & 2 & 3\\7 & 8 & 9\\4 & 5 & 6\end{bmatrix} = \begin{bmatrix}1 & 2 & 3\\4 & 5 & 6\\7 & 8 & 9\end{bmatrix}$

Then Eigen values of A =

(*a*) 1, 1, 0 (*b*) 1, 1, 1
(*c*) +1, +1, – 1 (*d*) 1, j, – j

37. Consider the signals:

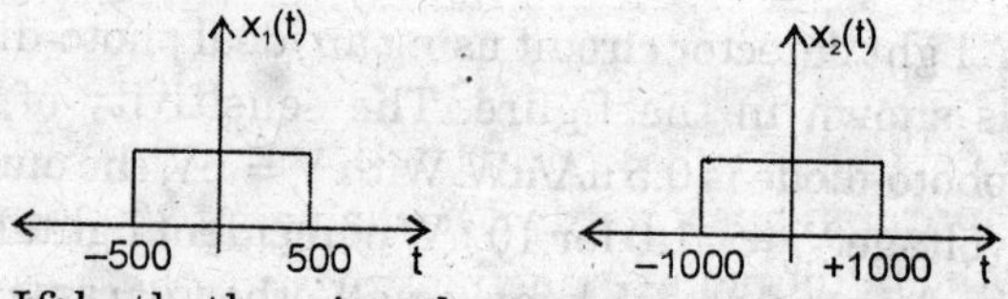

If both the signals are multiplied, then the Nyquist rate is _______ Hz.

38. The amplifier shown in figure. The BJT parameters are, V_{BE} = 0.7 V, β = 200 V, V_T = 250 mV. Find the gain $\frac{V_0}{V_i}$ = _______.

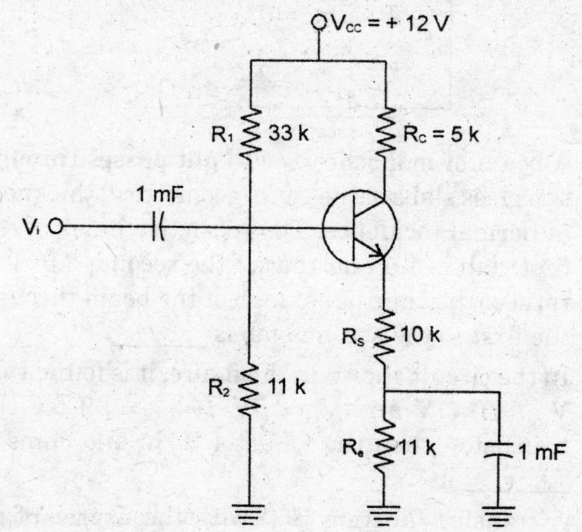

39. Find R_{AB} = ?

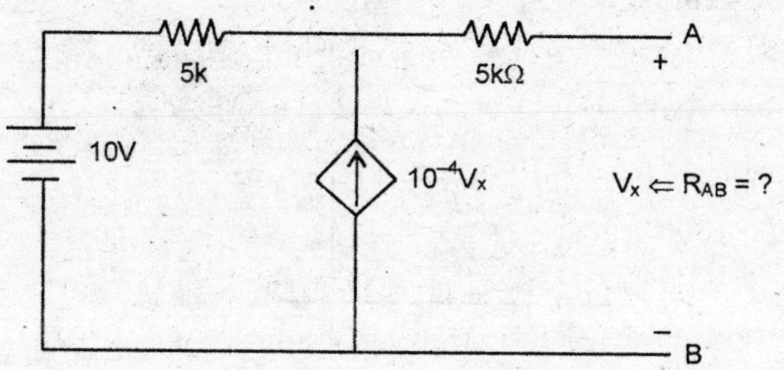

40. A white noise process X(*t*) with two-sided power spectral density 1×10^{-10} W/Hz is input to a filter whose magnitude squared response is shown below.

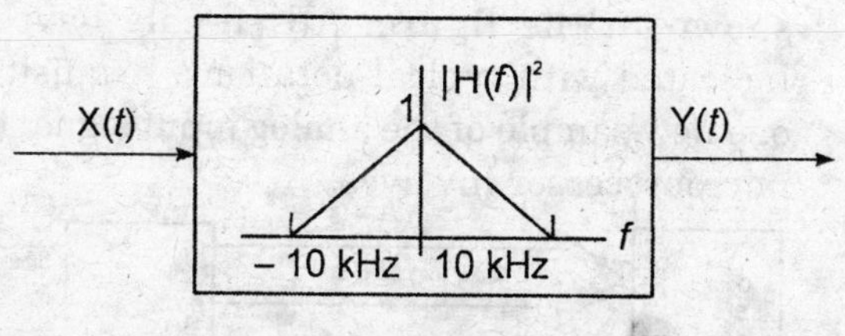

The power of the output process Y(t) is given by

(*a*) 5×10^{-7} W (*b*) 1×10^{-6} W

(*c*) 2×10^{-6} W (*d*) 1×10^{-5} W

41. A diaphragm has a natural frequency of 30 kHz. If both its diameter and thickness are halved, then natural frequency is

(*a*) 15 kHz (*b*) 240 kHz

(*c*) 60 kHz (*d*) 120 kHz

42. For the given 8 1 multiplex, the output (*y*) will be

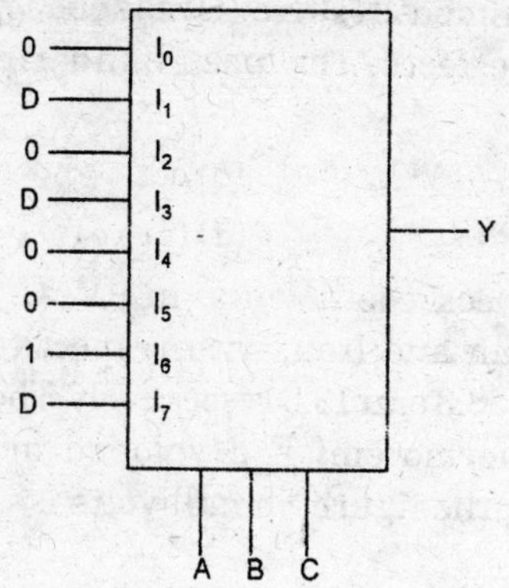

(*a*) $y = AB\bar{C} + \bar{A}CD$

(*b*) $y = \bar{A}BC + A\bar{B}D$

(*c*) $y = A\bar{\bar{B}}C + \bar{A}CD$

(*d*) $y = \bar{A}\bar{B}D + A\bar{B}C$

43. A potentiometer circuit is shown in the figure. The jockey of the potentiometer is kept exactly at the mid-point and the ammeter reads the current, I, as 0.2 mA. When V_x is reversed the ammeter reads 3.8 mA. The internal resistance of the ammeter and the unknown potential V_x are respectively

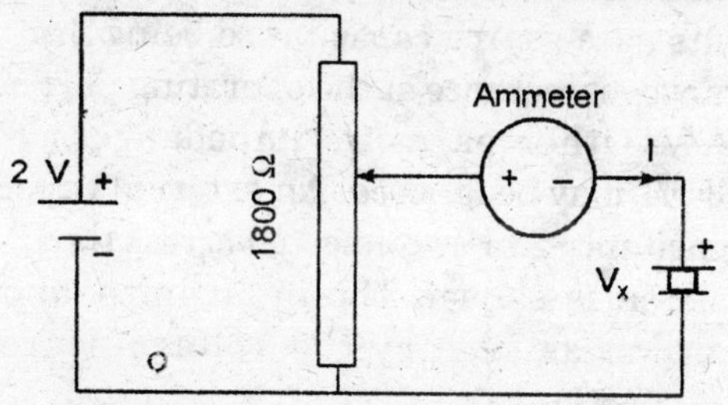

(*a*) 500 Ω, 1.1 V (*b*) 50Ω, 1.1V

(*c*) 500 Ω, 0.9 V (*d*) 50 Ω, 0.9 V

44. What is the speed in rpm of a variable reluctance type tachometer having 60 rotar teeth when counter records 3600 counts/minute ?

(*a*) 400 rps (*b*) 50 rps

(*c*) 60 rps (*d*) 70 rps

45. Find $\frac{v_0}{i_{in}}$ = ?

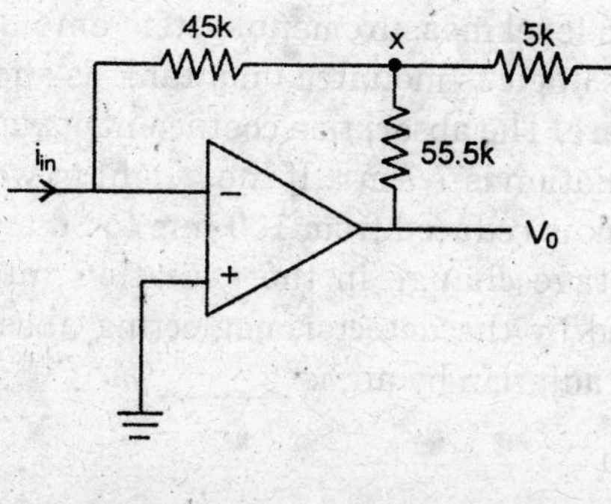

46. Consider a low-pass filter module with a pass-band ripple of δ in the gain magnitude. If M such identical modules are cascaded, ignoring the loading effects, the pass-band ripple of the cascade is

(*a*) $1-(1-\delta)^M$ (*b*) δ^M

(*c*) $(1-\delta^M)$ (*d*) $(1-\delta)^M$

47. The Seebeck coefficients, in μV/°C, for copper, constantan and iron, with respect to platinum, are 1.9, – 38.3 and 13.3 respectively. The magnitude of the thermo emf E developed in the circuit shown in the figure, in millivolts is ______ mV.

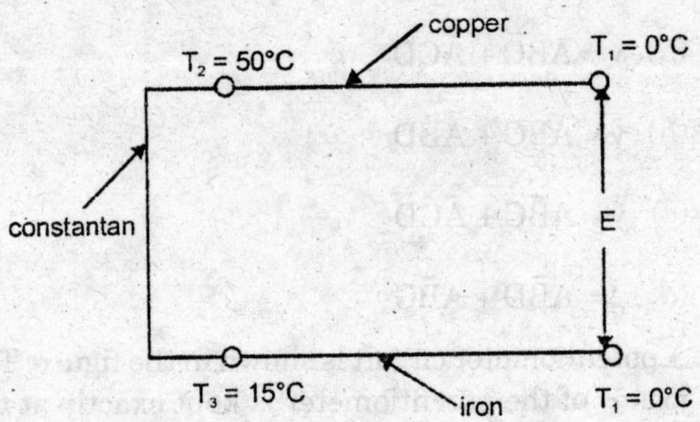

48. In the circuit shown, the voltage source $V(t) = 15 + 0.1 \sin(100t)$ volts. The PMOS transistor is biased such that it is in saturation with its gate-source capacitance being $4nF$ and its transcon ductance at the operating part being 1 mA/V. Other parasitic impedances of the MOSFET may be ignored. An external capacitor of capacitance $2\,nF$ is connected across the PMOS transistor as shown. The input impedance in mega ohm as seen by the voltage source is ______ MΩ.

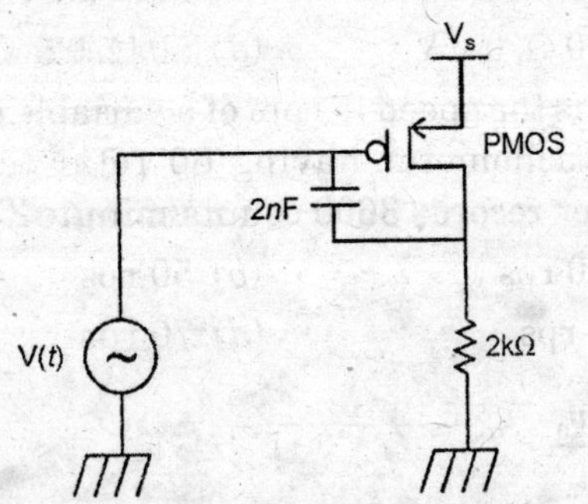

49. A liquid level measurement system employing a radio-isotopic is mounted on a tank as shown in the figure. The absorption coefficient of water for the radiation is 7.7 m^{-1}. If the height of water in the tank is reduced from 100 mm to 90 mm, the percentage change in the radiation intensity received by the detector, neglecting absorption of the radiation by air, is ______ %.

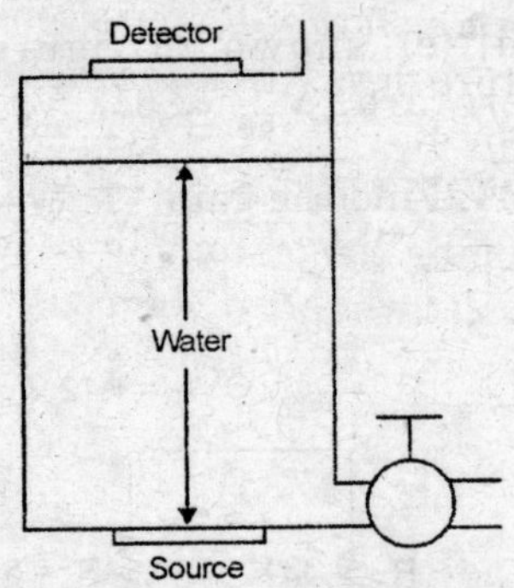

50. A beam of monochromatic light passes through two glass slabs of the same geometrical thickness at normal incidence. The refractive index of the first slab is 1.5 and that of the second, 2.0. The ratio of the time of passage of the beam through the first to the second slab is ______.

51. In the circuit shown in the figure, it is found that $V_{BE} = 0.7$ V and $V_E = 0$V. If $\beta_{dc} = 99$ for the transistor, then the value of R_B in kilo ohms is ______ kΩ.

52. A transfer function G(*s*) with the degree of its numerator polynomial zero and the degree of its denominator polynomial two has a Nyquist plot shown in the figure. The transfer function represents

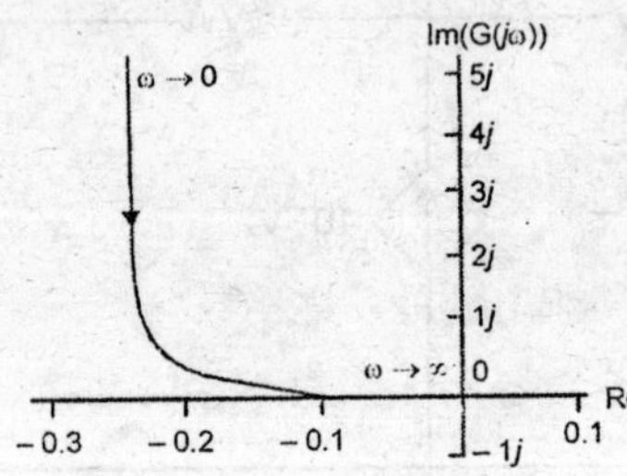

(*a*) a stable, type-0 system

(*b*) a stable, type-1 system

(*c*) an unstable, type-0 system

(*d*) an unstable, type-1 system

53. An ADC is interfaced with a microprocessor as shown in the figure. All signals have been indicated with typical notations. Acquisition of one new sample of the analog input signal by the microprocessor involves

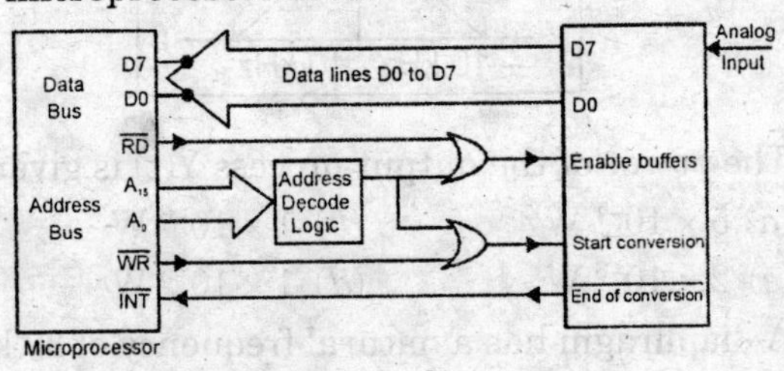

(*a*) One READ cycle only

(*b*) One WRITE cycle only

(*c*) One WRITE cycle followed by one READ cycle

(*d*) One READ cycle followed by one WRITE cycle

54. In the figure shown, R_T represents a resistance temperature device (RTD), whose characteristic is given by $R_T = R_0\,(1 + \alpha T)$, where $R_0 = 100\Omega$, $\alpha = 0.0039°C^{-1}$ and T denotes the temperature in °C. Assuming the op-amp to be ideal, the value of V_0 in volts when T = 100°C, is ______ V.

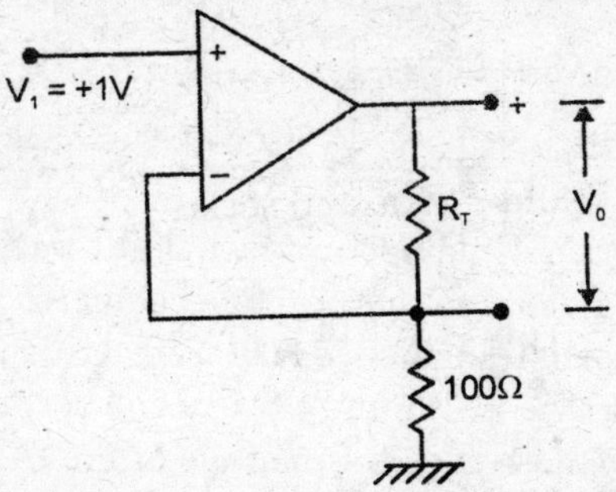

55. A signal is band-limited to 0 to 12 kHz. The signal spectrum is corrupted by additive noise which is band-limited to 10 to 12 kHz. Theoretically, the minimum rate in kilohertz at which the noisy signal must be sampled so that the **UNCORRUPTED PART** of the signal spectrum can be recovered, is ______ kHz.

ANSWERS

General Aptitude (GA)

1. (*a*)	**2.** (*c*)	**3.** (*a*)	**4.** (*d*)	**5.** (2500)	**6.** (*d*)	**7.** (36)	**8.** (11119)
9. (76)	**10.** (*d*)						

Technical Section

1. (*b*)	**2.** (*d*)	**3.** (*a*)	**4.** (*a*)	**5.** (*d*)	**6.** (*b*)	**7.** (*b*)	**8.** (*c*)
9. (*d*)	**10.** (25)	**11.** (*b*)	**12.** (*b*)	**13.** (10)	**14.** (14R/3)	**15.** (*b*)	**16.** (*a*)
17. (*c*)	**18.** (– 1)	**19.** (*a*)	**20.** (*c*)	**21.** (*c*)	**22.** (*d*)	**23.** (*d*)	**24.** (1020)
25. (*c*)	**26.** (*b*)	**27.** (*b*)	**28.** (*c*)	**29.** (*c*)	**30.** (*c*)	**31.** (*d*)	**32.** (*b*)
33. (*d*)	**34.** (*d*)	**35.** (*c*)	**36.** (1/3)	**37.** (3000)	**38.** (– 0.48)	**39.** (600 k)	**40.** (*b*)
41. (*c*)	**42.** (*a*)	**43.** (*c*)	**44.** (*c*)	**45.** (600 k)	**46.** (*)	**47.** (– 1.236)	**48.** (1)
49. (8.5)	**50.** (0.75)	**51.** (93)	**52.** (*d*)	**53.** (*c*)	**54.** (1.39)	**55.** (20)	

EXPLANATIONS

9. When V_1 = 10 sinwt and $V_2 = 10\cos\left(\omega t + \dfrac{\pi}{4}\right)$ are applied to x and y plates of CRO, the pattern of ellipse is formed.

10. $x(t) \longleftrightarrow X(F)$

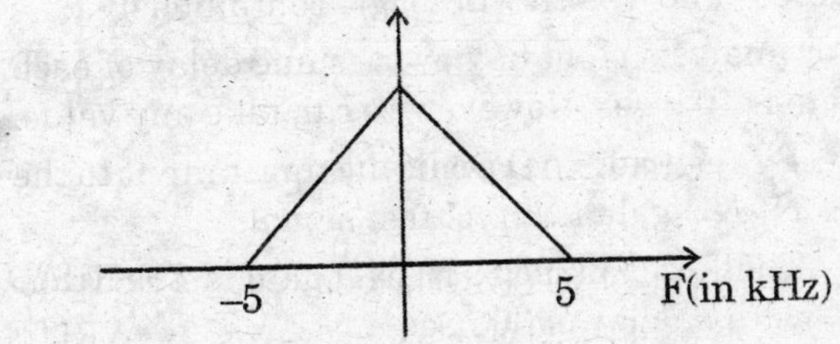

After modulation

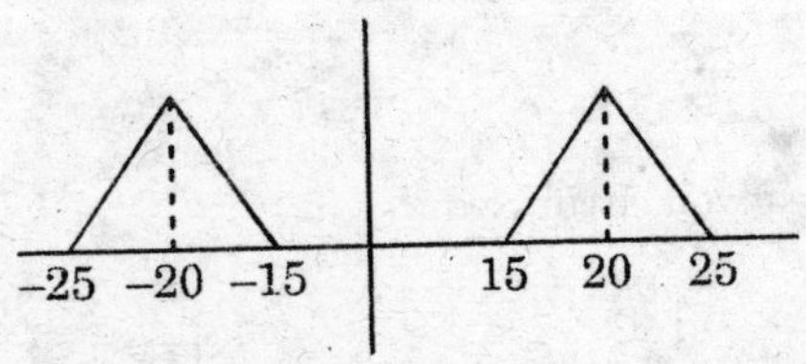

In order to find minimum sampling frequency for proper reconstruction of signal, we can use band pass sampling.

$$F_{s(min)} = \frac{2F_H}{K}$$

where K = Integral part of $\left(\frac{F_H}{F_H - F_Z}\right)$

F_H = 25 KHz ;

F_2 = 15 KHz

$\therefore$ K = Integral part of $\left(\frac{25}{10}\right) = 2$

$\therefore$ $F_{s(min)} = \frac{2 \times 25K}{2} = 25$ KHz

11. Newton Raphson algorithm for finding k^{th} root of a number is given by

$$x_{i+1} = \frac{x_i}{K}\left[K - 1 + \frac{\text{Number}}{x_i^K}\right]$$

12. Due to large piezo-resistive coefficient the semiconductor strain gauges have better gauges factor than a normal strain gauge.

13.

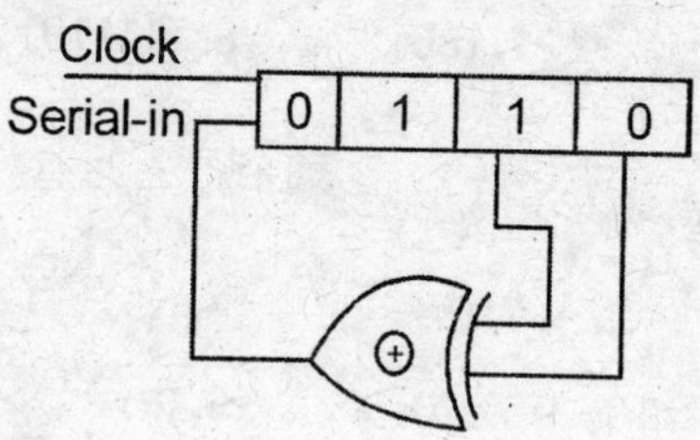

The initial content of 4- bit SIPO shift register is 0110

After 1st clock pulse content of 4-bit SIPO shift register will be 1 0 1 1 $[\because 1 \oplus 0 = 1]$

After 2nd clock pulse content of 4 bit SIPO shift register wil be 0 1 0 1 $[\because 1 \oplus 1 = 0]$

After 3rd clock pulse content of 4 bit SIPO shift register will be 1 0 1 0 $[\because 0 \oplus 1 = 1]$

14.

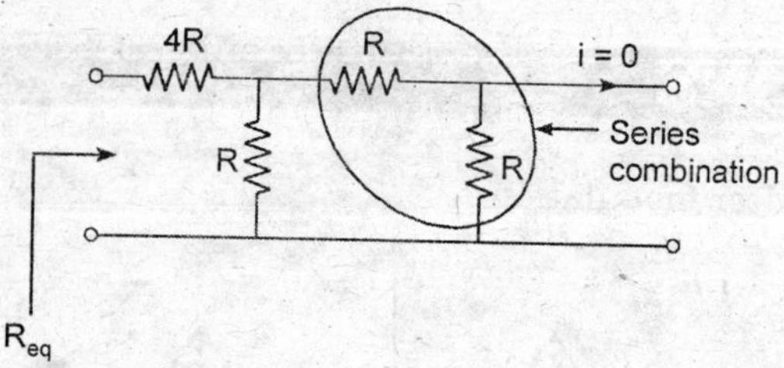

the given circuit reduces to

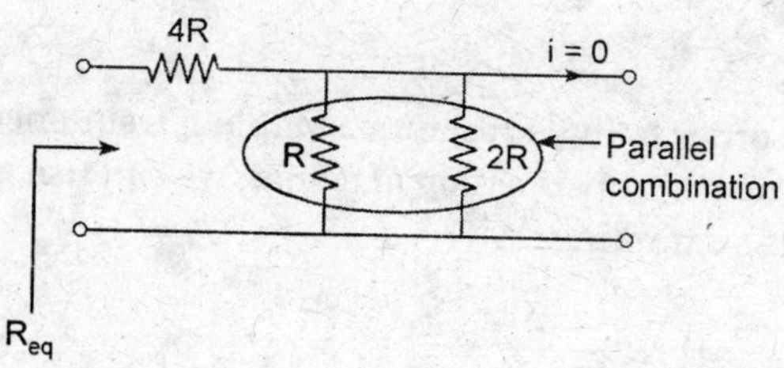

Again the circuit reduces to

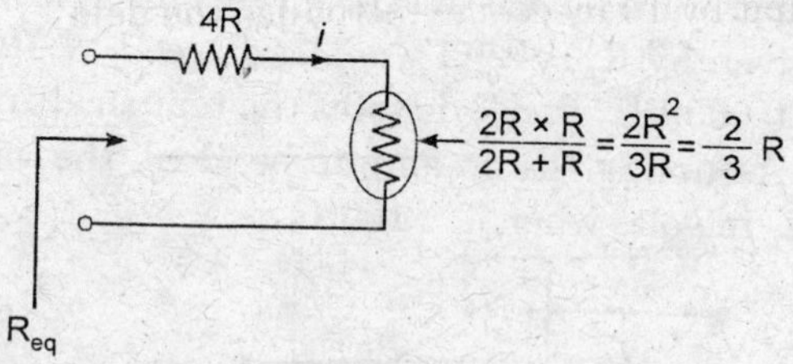

Now 4R and $\frac{2}{3}$R are in series

$\therefore$ $R_{eq} = 4R + \frac{2}{3}R = \frac{14}{3}R$

15. $20 \log k = 32$

$k = 10^{1.6}$

$= 39.8$

$$T(s) = \frac{39.8}{s^2}$$

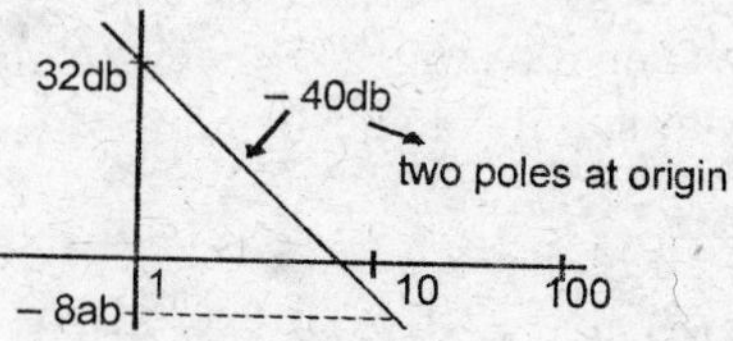

19. The function of AND gate is to multiply and OR gate is to add

Hence, output of upper AND gate is $X\bar{Y}$

Output of lower AND gate is $\bar{X}Y$.

Output of OR gate is $X\bar{Y} + \bar{X}Y$

$\therefore$ option (*a*) is correct.

20. Multiplication in time domain corresponds to convolution in frequency domain

$\therefore$ $x(t) \cdot x(t) \rightarrow x(f) * x(f)$

From limit property of convolution

$x^2(t)$ have maximum frequency $2f_m$.

22. The given circuit is a stable multivibrator, where odd numbers of inverter are there in the loop. For such a circuit, irrespective of the position of output, it always toggles.

→ Latching means X and Y will be fixed to same value.

Here X and Y both will toggle continuously

23. For analysis point of view, assume delay of each gate is 10 msec. However we can take any value.

→ By referring the circuit the upper input to the NAND gate is direct test signal.

The lower input to NAND gate is TEST but with a delay of 30 nsec.

→ Assuming the delay of NAND gate is 0. First draw output waveform (ideal case) then shift that by 10 msec. i.e. introduce the delay.

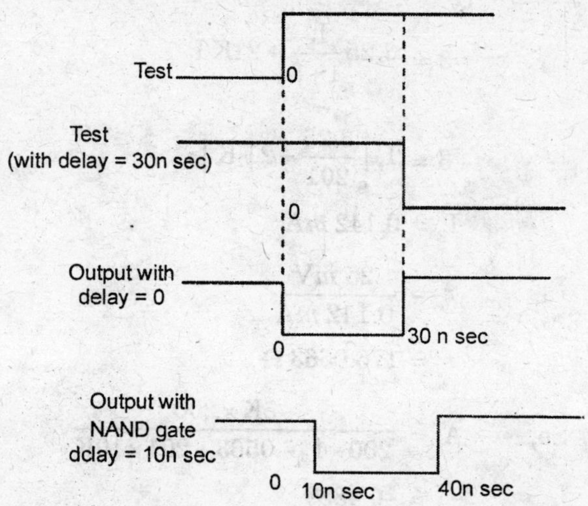

So we can clearly say that initial output change from high to low, then it changes from low to high and then finally at steady state output is 1.

26. $\frac{v(s)}{I(s)} = \frac{4s+6}{s+2}$, $v(t)$ as $f \to \infty$

$$s \xrightarrow{v(s)} 0 = \underset{s+0}{\text{Lt}} \frac{(4s+6)}{s+2} = \underset{s+0}{\text{Lt}} \frac{4s+6}{s+2} = \frac{6}{2} = 3$$

27. Then $I(s) = \frac{(s+2)}{s(s+1)} = \frac{A}{s} + \frac{B}{s+1}$

$$\therefore \quad A = 2, \quad B = \frac{-1+2}{-1} - 1$$

$$\therefore \quad I(t) = L^{-1}[I(s)] = L^{-1}\left[\frac{A}{s} + \frac{B}{s+1}\right] = 2 - e^{-t}$$

28. Number of difference Boolean functions

$$= 2^4 = 16 = 4^2$$

29.

$$\bar{y} = \bar{A}\bar{B}I_0 + \bar{A}BI_1 + A\bar{B}I_2 + ABI_3$$

$$= \bar{A}\bar{B} \times 1 + \bar{A}BC + A\bar{B} \times 0 + ABC$$

$$= \bar{A}\bar{B} + \bar{A}BC + ABC$$

$$= \bar{A}\bar{B} + BC(A + \bar{A})$$

$$= \overline{AB} + BC$$

30. Poles at $s = 0, -2, -3$

$$\sigma = \frac{\Sigma p - \Sigma z}{p-n} = \frac{-2-3-0}{3} = \frac{-5}{3}$$

31. Given: $g = 0.6$

Characteristic equation is,

$1 + H(s)\,G(s) = 0$

$$\Rightarrow \quad 1 + \frac{(1+sk)16}{(s+4)s} = 0$$

i.e. $s^2 + 4s + 16ks + 16 = 0$

i.e. $s^2 + (16k + 4)s + 16 = 0$

$\omega_n = 4,$

$2\Sigma\omega_n = 16k + 4$

$\Rightarrow \quad 2 \times 0.6 \times 4 = 16k + 4$

i.e. $0.8 = 16k$

i.e. $k = \frac{0.8}{16} = \frac{1}{20} = 0.05$

32. $f(t) = A \sin(2\pi f_0 t)$, $H[f(t)]$

$$= A \sin\left(2\pi f_0 t + \frac{\pi}{2}\right)$$

$$= A \cos(2\pi f_0 t)$$

33. $10 \log \frac{p_o}{p_i} = 60$

i.e. $\frac{p_o}{p_i} = 10^6$

$p_o = 10^6 \times 2 \times 10^{-6} = 2$ **watt**

34. $\frac{z_{max}}{\sqrt{2}} = \frac{70}{\sqrt{2}} = 50$

$$BW = \frac{f_0}{Q}$$

$$= \frac{1000 \times 10^3}{100} = 10k$$

$f_{12} = \pm 5$ kHz

$f = 1000 \pm 5$ kHz

35. $\frac{\omega L}{R} = Q$

$$\therefore \quad \frac{10^5 \times L}{400} = 50$$

$$\therefore \quad L = \frac{400 \times 50}{10^5}$$

$$= \frac{20}{100} = 0.2$$

and $C = \dfrac{1}{\omega_0^2 L}$

$= \dfrac{1}{10^{10} \times 0.2}$

$= 5 \times 10^{-10} = 500\ pf$

37. Multiplication in time domain = convolution in frequency domain.

$x_1(t) \cdot x_2(t) = X_1(j\omega)\, X_2(j\omega)$

$\therefore$ Fundamental frequencies

$= f_1, f_1 \pm f_2, f_1 \pm 2f_2 \ldots$

$= 500, 1500 \ldots$

Nyquist rate = 2 1500 = 3000 Hz

38.

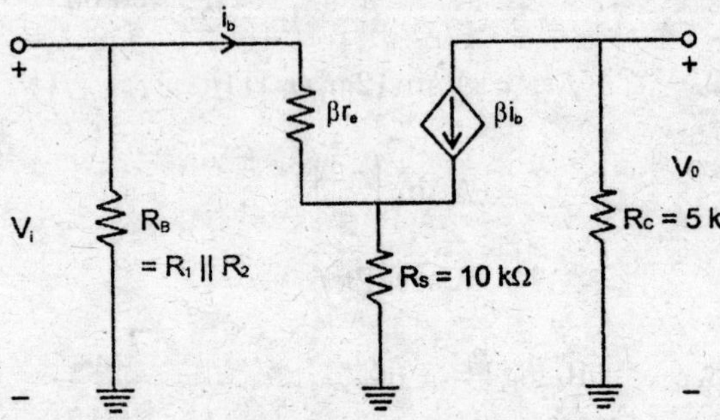

$V_i = \beta i_b r_e + (i_b + \beta i_b)\, R_s$

$V_i = \beta i_b r_e + i_b(1+\beta)\, R_s$

$V_i = i_b[\beta r_e + (1+\beta)\, R_s]$ ...(*i*)

$V_0 = -R_c \beta i_b$ ...(*ii*)

$\therefore \quad \dfrac{V_0}{V_i} = \dfrac{-R_c \times \beta \times i_b}{i_b\left[\beta r_e + (1+\beta) R_s\right]}$

$A_V = \dfrac{-R_c \times \beta}{\beta r_e + (1+\beta) R_s}$ ...(*iii*)

where r_e is given by $r_e = \dfrac{V_T}{I_E}$

from *dc* analysis

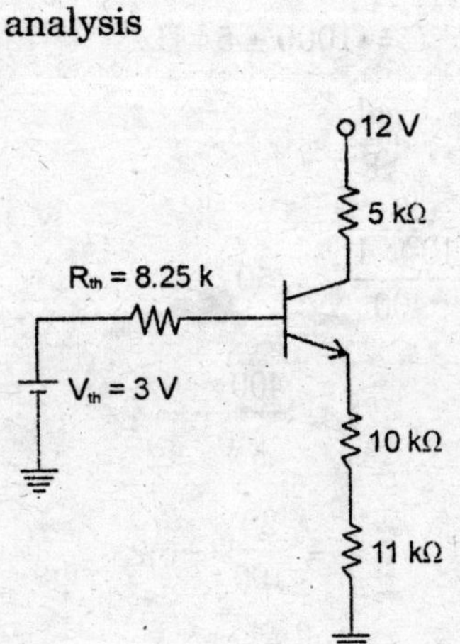

$R_{th} = 33K \,\|\, 11K = 8.25K$

$V_{th} = \dfrac{11 \times 12}{44} = 3V$

$3 = 8.25K\, I_B + 21K\, I_E$

$3 = 8.25 \dfrac{I_E}{1+\beta} + 21K\, I_E$

$3 = I_E\left[\dfrac{8.25}{201} + 21\ K\right]$

$I_E = 0.142\ mA$

$r_e = \dfrac{25\ mV}{0.142\ mA}$

$r_e = 176.0563\ \Omega$

So, $A_v = \dfrac{-5K \times 200}{200 \times 176.0563 + 201 \times 10K}$

$= -0.4889$

40. Power output = Area under $|H(f)|^2$

$Y(t) = X(t) \times 10\ kHz$

$= 10^{-10} \times 10^4$

$= 1 \times 10^{-6}$ W

(Frequency in negative side is just replica of positive frequency.)

42. $y = \bar{A}\bar{B}C \cdot I_1 + \bar{A}BCI_3 + AB\bar{C}I_6$

$\therefore\ y = \bar{A}\bar{B}C \cdot D + \bar{A}BCD + AB\bar{C} \cdot (1)$

$\therefore\ y = \bar{A}CD(B + \bar{B}) + AB\bar{C}$

$= AB\bar{C} + \bar{A}CD$

43. $V_{AB} = V_{BC} = 1$ volt.

$R_{BC} = R_{AB} = 900\Omega$

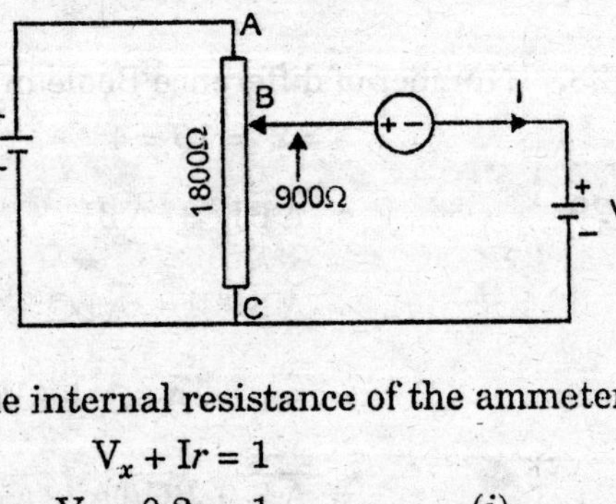

Let r be the internal resistance of the ammeter.

$V_x + Ir = 1$

or $V_x + 0.2r = 1$ ...(*i*)

Also $-V_x + Ir = 1$

or $-V_x + 3.8r = 1$ ...(*ii*)

From equations (*i*) and (*ii*)

$r = 500\ \Omega,\ V_x = 0.9$ V

44. Speed $= \dfrac{\text{Pulses per second}}{\text{Number of teeth}} = \dfrac{3600}{60} = 60$ rps.

45.

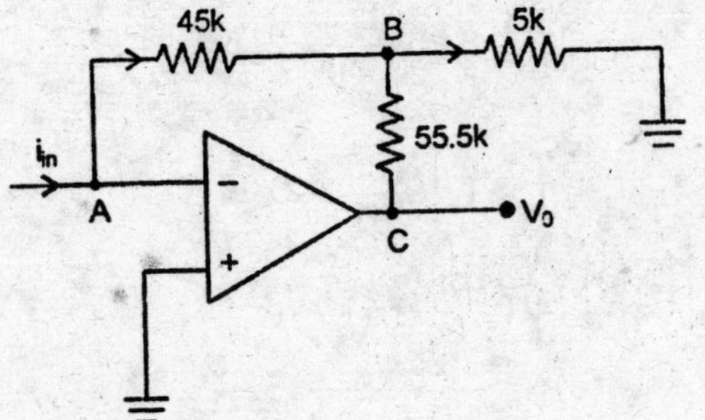

Applying KCL

At node A

$$I_{in} = \frac{0 - V_B}{45k} \quad \text{... (i)}$$

At node B

$$\frac{0 - V_B}{45k} = \frac{V_B - 0}{5k} + \frac{V_B - V_O}{55.5k} \quad \text{....}(ii)$$

Putting value of V_B from equation (*i*) in (*ii*) we get

$$\frac{0-(-45kI_n)}{45k} = \frac{-45kI_n}{5k} + \frac{(-45kI_n) - V_O}{55.5k}$$

$$I_n = -9\,I_n + \left(\frac{-45k\,I_n - V_O}{55.5k}\right)$$

$$10\,I_n = -\left(\frac{45k\,I_n + V_O}{55.5k}\right)$$

$$555k\,I_n = -45\,k\,I_n + V_o$$

$$600\,k\,I_n = V_O$$

$$\therefore \quad \frac{V_O}{I_n} = 600\text{ k}$$

54. Using the given equation

$$R_T = R_0[1 + \alpha T]$$

$$= 100[1 + 0.0039 \times 100] = 139\Omega$$

By virtual ground concept

$$\left(1 + \frac{R_f}{R_1}\right)V_1 = \left(1 + \frac{139}{100}\right) = 2.39\text{V}$$

→ But here V_0 is not w.r.t. ground, it is across R_T

So $\quad V_0 = (2.39 - 1)\text{V} = 1.39\text{ V}$

55.

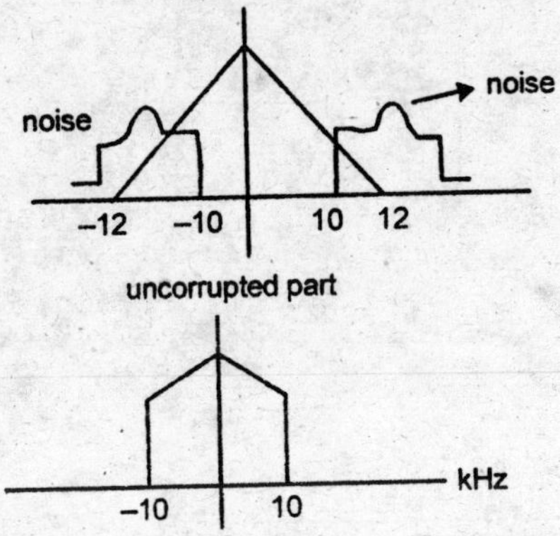

■■

MOCK TEST - 2

INSTRUCTIONS

1. Total of 65 questions carrying 100 marks, out of which 10 questions carrying a total of 15 marks are in General Aptitude (GA)
2. The Engineering Mathematics will carry around **15% of the total marks,** the General Aptitude section will carry **15% of the total marks** and the **remaining 70% of the total marks.**
3. **Types of Questions**
   (*a*) **Multiple Choice Questions (MCQ)** carrying 1 or 2 marks each in all papers and sections. These questions are objective in nature, and each will have a choice of four options, out of which the candidate has to mark the correct answer(s).
   (*b*) **Numerical Answer Questions** of 1 or 2 marks each in all papers and sections. For these questions the answer is a real number, to be entered by the candidate using the virtual keypad. No choices will be shown for these type of questions.
4. For **1-mark** multiple-choice questions, **1/3 marks** will be deducted for a wrong answer. Likewise, for **2-marks** multiple-choice questions, **2/3** marks will be deducted for a wrong answer. There is no negative marking for numerical answer type questions.

GENERAL APTITUDE (GA)

(Q. 1 – 5) : Carry One Mark Each

1. Which of the following options is the closest in meaning to the word below:

Gist

(*a*) contribution (*b*) substance
(*c*) prestige (*d*) accessory

2. The question below consists of a pair of related words followed by four pairs of words. Select the pair that best expresses the relation in the original pair.

Fuel : Pipes

(*a*) Blood : Veins (*b*) Food : Stomach
(*c*) Wood : Trees (*d*) Cars : Expressway

3. Choose the most appropriate word from the option given below to complete the following sentence:

Seeing the pictures of our old home made me feel __________ and nostalgic.

(*a*) fastidious (*b*) conciliatory
(*c*) indignant (*d*) wistful

4. Choose the most appropriate word from the option given below to complete the following sentence:

The fans were ________ when their team lost its seventieth game in a row.

(*a*) irascible
(*b*) despondent
(*c*) lucid
(*d*) didactic

5. What least number must be added to 8961 to make it exactly divisible by 84 ?

(*a*) 25 (*b*) 32
(*c*) 33 (*d*) 27

Q. (6 – 10) : Carry Two Marks Each

6. If a supernova (the explosion of a massive star) triggered star formation from dense clouds of gas and dust, and if the most massive star to be formed from the cloud evolved into a supernova and triggered a new round of star formation, and so on, then a chain of star-forming regions would result. If many such chains were created in a differentially rotating galaxy, the distribution of stars would resemble the observed distribute in a spiral galaxy. This line of reasoning underlies an exciting new theory of spiral-galaxy structure. A computer simulation based on this theory has reproduced the appearance of many spiral galaxies without assuming an underlying density wave, the hallmark of the most widely accepted theory of the large-scale structure of spiral galaxies. That theory maintains that a density wave of spiral form sweeps through the central plane of a galaxy, compressing clouds of gas and dust, which collapse into stars that form a spiral pattern.

The primary purpose of the passage is to

(*a*) describe what results when a supernova triggers the creation of chains of star-forming regions

(*b*) propose a modification in the most widely accepted theory of spiral-galaxy structure (*c*) compare and contrast the roles of clouds of gas and dust in two theories of spiral-galaxy structure

(*d*) describe a new theory of spiral-galaxy structure and contrast it with the most widely accepted theory

7. A can complete a piece of work in 12 days and B is 60% more efficient than A. B will complete the same work in ....

8. A group of labourers promise to do a piece of work in 12 days, but 5 of them do not turn up. If the rest of the group do the work in 18 days, find the original number of men.

(*a*) 15 (*b*) 25

(*c*) 35 (*d*) 45

Directions (Q. 9 – 10) : *Answer these questions based on the information given below*

A boy is asked to put in a basket one mango when ordered 'One', one orange when ordered 'Two', one apple when ordered 'Three' and is asked to take out from the basket one mango and an orange when ordered 'Four'. A sequence of orders is given as

1 2 3 3 2 1 4 2 3 1 4 2 2 3 3 1 4 1 1 3 2 3 4

9. How many total oranges were in the basket at the end of the above sequence ?

(*a*) 1 (*b*) 3

(*c*) 4 (*d*) 2

10. How many total fruits will be in the basket at the end of the above order sequence ?

(*a*) 9 (*b*) 8

(*c*) 11 (*d*) 10

TECHNICAL SECTION

(Q.1 – 25) : Carry One Mark Each

1. If $\begin{vmatrix} a & a^2 & a^3 & -1 \\ b & b^2 & b^3 & -1 \\ c & c^2 & c^3 & -1 \end{vmatrix} = 0$ in which a, b, c are different, then abc is

(*a*) 0 (*b*) 1

(*c*) 2 (*d*) 3

2. The directional derivative of $f(x, y, z) = xy^2 + yz^3$ at the point (2, –1, 1) in the direction of vector $\hat{i} + 2\hat{j} + 2\hat{k}$ is

(*a*) $-1\frac{2}{3}$ (*b*) $-2\frac{2}{3}$

(*c*) $-3\frac{2}{3}$ (*d*) $-4\frac{2}{3}$

3. For the differential equation $\frac{dy}{dt} + 5y = 0$, with $y(0) = 1$, the general solution is

(*a*) $5e^{5t}$ (*b*) e^{-5t}

(*c*) e^{5t} (*d*) $5e^{-5t}$

4. If the drift velocity of holes under a field gradient of amf of 100 V/m is 5 m/s their mobility (in the same SI units) is

(*a*) 0.05 (*b*) 0.5

(*c*) 50 (*d*) 500

5. The Geiger Counter has high quantum efficiency in the wavelength (Å) range

(*a*) 0.2 to 0.3

(*b*) 0.4 to 0.5

(*c*) 1.5 to 2.1

(*d*) 6 to 7

6. Assuming uniform pressure over the supported area, the friction moment in an exial bearing of a shaft of diameter *d* for an exial load of F (with co-efficient of friction μ) is given by

(*a*) $\frac{4}{3}F\mu d$ (*b*) $\frac{1}{3}F\mu d$

(*c*) $\frac{2}{3}F\mu d$ (*d*) $F\mu d$

7. A passive network has

(*a*) no voltage source but current sources

(*b*) no current source but voltage sources

(*c*) no voltage or current sources

(*d*) none of these

8.

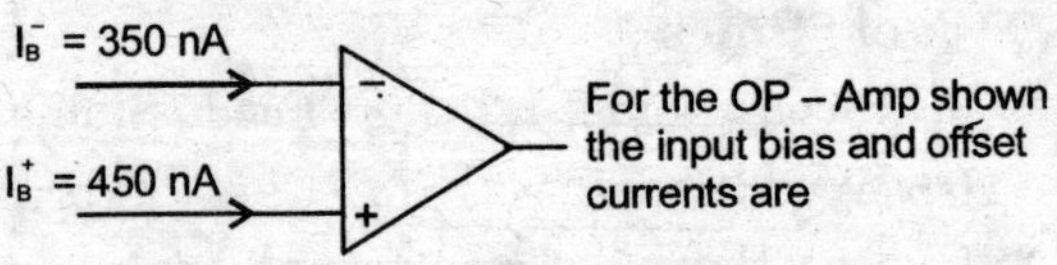

(*a*) 800 nA 100 nA (*b*) 400 nA 50 nA

(*c*) 400 nA 100 nA (*d*) 800 nA 50 nA

9. The given circuit represents ______

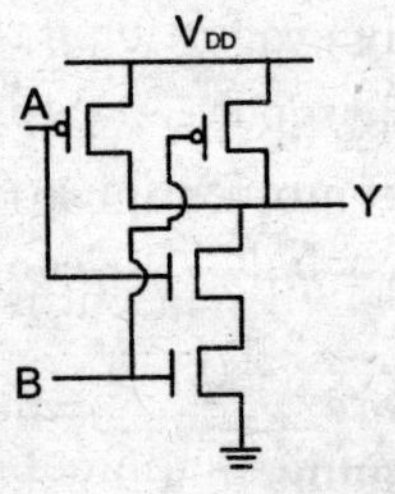

(*a*) NAND (*b*) NOR

(*c*) AND (*d*) OR

10. The given graph is solution of differential equation

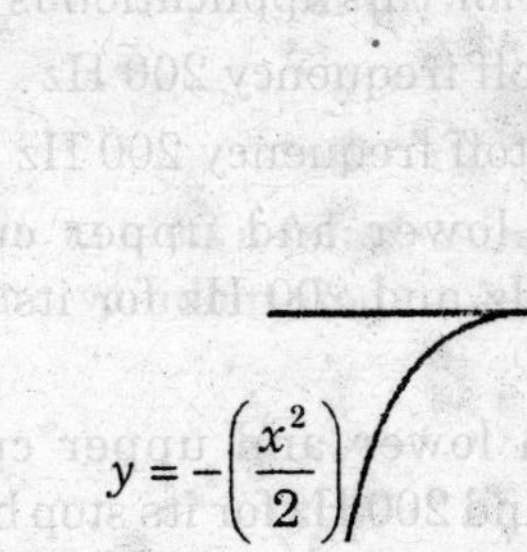

(a) $\frac{dy}{dx} = x$ (b) $\frac{d^2y}{dx^2} = 1$

(c) $\frac{dy}{dx} = 1$ (d) $\frac{dy}{dx} = |x|$

11. Consider LTI system with T.F. $H(s) = \frac{1}{s(s+4)}$ if the input to all system is $\cos(3t)$ and steady state output is $A\sin(3t + \alpha)$, then value of A is

(a) $\frac{1}{30}$ (b) $\frac{1}{15}$

(c) $\frac{3}{4}$ (d) $\frac{4}{5}$

12.

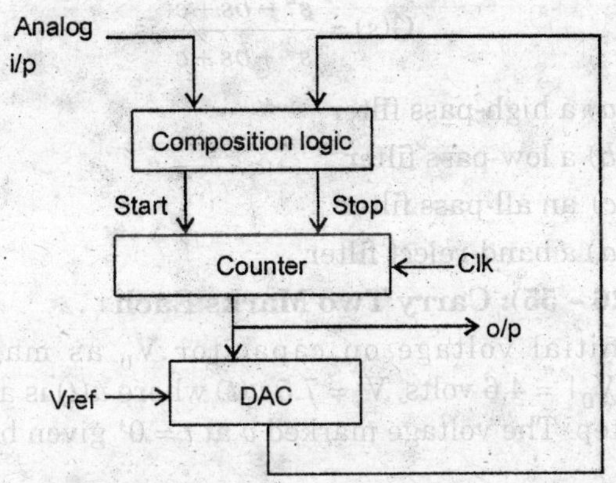

In the shown above ADC ERROR of convertion is related to

(a) Directly proportional to V_{ref}

(b) Inversely proportional to V_{ref}

(c) Directly proportional to f_{clk}

(d) Inversely proportional to f_{clk}

13. If $f(x) = \frac{1}{k}[e^{-x/2}]$ is a pdf is $(0, \infty)$ then value of K = ?

14. If the CE–configuration of the BJT transistor is not provided with by-pass capacitor, it will have

(a) Ri↑Av↑ (b) Ri↑Av↓

(c) Ri↓Av↓ (d) Ri↓Av↑

15. Consider minterm expansion of the function F

$$F(P, Q, R, S) = \Sigma(0, 2, 5, 7, 8, 10, 13, 15)$$

When minterms 2, 7, 8, 13 are "do not care" terms. The minimal Sum of Product from of F is

(a) $Q\bar{S} + \bar{Q}S$

(b) $\bar{Q}\bar{S} + QS$

(c) $\bar{Q}\bar{R}\bar{S} + \bar{Q}R\bar{S} + Q\bar{R}S + QRS$

(d) $\bar{P}\bar{Q}\bar{S} + \bar{P}QS + PQS + P\bar{Q}\bar{S}$

16. Transconductance characteristics depends on

(a) high input resistance and high output resistance

(b) high input resistance and low output resistance

(c) Low input resistance and high output resistance

(d) Low input and low input resistance

17. A mass-spring-damper system with force as input and displacement of the mass as output has a transfer function $G(s) = \frac{1}{(s^2 + 24s + 900)}$. A force input $F(t) = 10\sin(70t)$ Newtons is applied at time $t = 0$s. A beam from an optical stroboscope is focused on the mass. In steady state, the strobe frequency in hertz at which the mass appears to be stationary is

(a) $\frac{5}{\pi}$ (b) $\frac{15}{\pi}$

(c) $\frac{35}{\pi}$ (d) $\frac{50}{\pi}$

18. Consider the ammeter-voltmeter method of determining the value of the resistance R using the circuit shown in the figure. The maximum possible errors of the voltmeter and ammeter are known to be 1% and 2% of their readings, respectively. Neglecting the effects of meter resistances, the maximum possible percentage error in the value of R determined from the measurements, is ______ %.

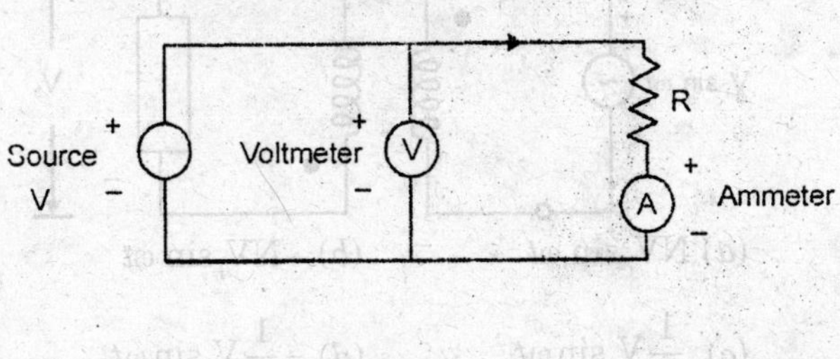

19. The magnitude of the directional derivative of the function $f(x, y) = x^2 + 3y^2$ in a direction normal to the circle $x^2 + y^2 = 2$, at the point (1, 1), is

(*a*) $4\sqrt{2}$ (*b*) $5\sqrt{2}$

(*c*) $7\sqrt{2}$ (*d*) $9\sqrt{2}$

20. A power line is coupled capacitively through various parasitic capacitances to a shielded signal line as shown in the figure. The conductive shield is grounded solidly at one end. Assume that the length of the signal wire extending beyond the shield, and the shield resistance are negligible. The magnitude of the noise voltage coupled to the signal line is

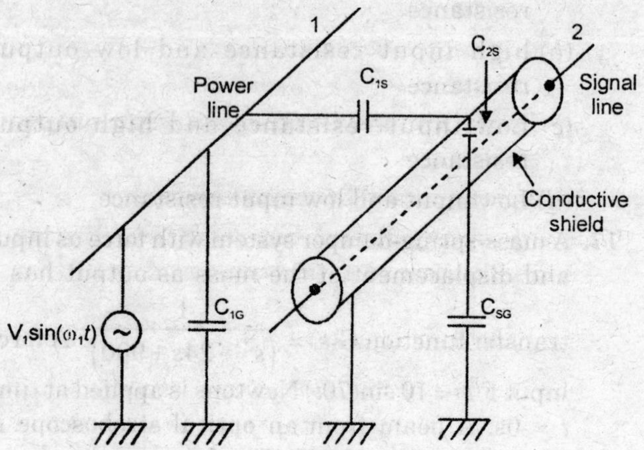

(*a*) directly proportional to C_{1G}

(*b*) inversely proportional to the power line frequency

(*c*) inversely proportional to C_{15}

(*d*) Zero

21. The torque transmitted by a cylindrical shaft is to be measured by using two strain gauges. The angles for mounting the strain gauges relative to the axis of the shaft for maximum sensitivity are

(*a*) ± 45° (*b*) ± 60°

(*c*) ± 90° (*d*) ± 180°

22. The output voltage of the ideal transformer with the polarities and dots shown in the figure is given by

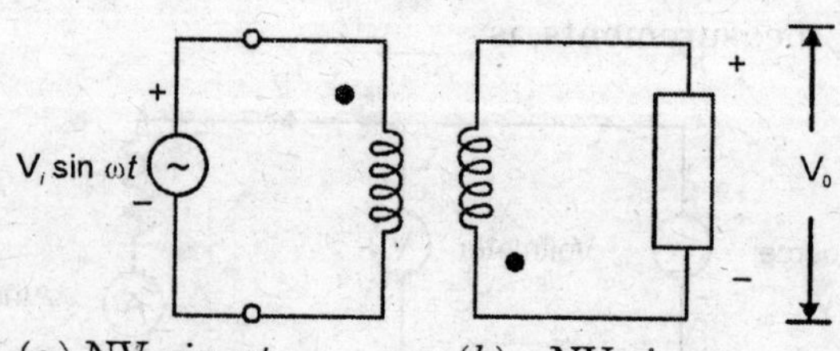

(*a*) $NV_i \sin \omega t$ (*b*) $-NV_i \sin \omega t$

(*c*) $\frac{1}{N}V_i \sin \omega t$ (*d*) $-\frac{1}{N}V_i \sin \omega t$

23. An apparatus to capture ECG signals has a filter followed by a data acquisition system.

The filter best suited for this application is

(*a*) low pass with cutoff frequency 200 Hz

(*b*) high pass with cutoff frequency 200 Hz

(*c*) band pass with lower and upper cutoff frequencies 100 Hz and 200 Hz for its pass band

(*d*) band reject with lower and upper cutoff frequencies 1 Hz and 200 Hz for its stop band.

24. The figure shows a half-wave rectifier circuit with input voltage $V(t) = 10 \sin(100\,\pi t)$ volts. Assuming ideal diode characteristics with zero forward voltage drop and zero reverse current, the average power consumed in watts by the load resistance R_L is ____ W.

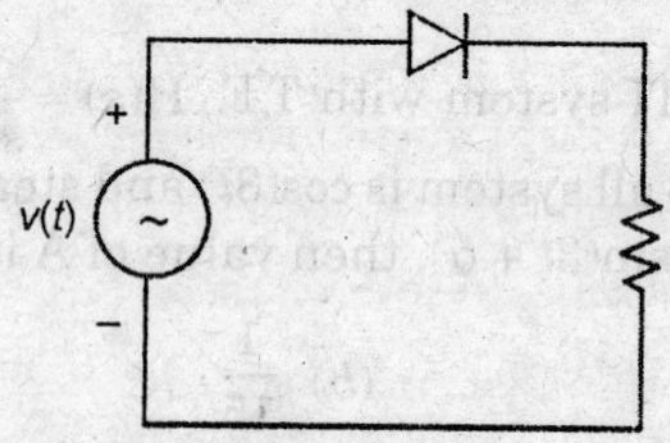

25. The filter whose transfer function is of the form

$$G(s) = \frac{s^2 - bs + c}{s^2 + bs + c} \text{ is}$$

(*a*) a high-pass filter

(*b*) a low-pass filter

(*c*) an all-pass filter

(*d*) a band-reject filter

(Q. 26 – 55): Carry Two Marks Each

26. Initial voltage on capacitor V_0 as marked $|V_0| = 4.6$ volts. $V_s = 7.5\,u(t)$ where $u(t)$ is a unit step. The voltage marked v at $t = 0^+$ given by

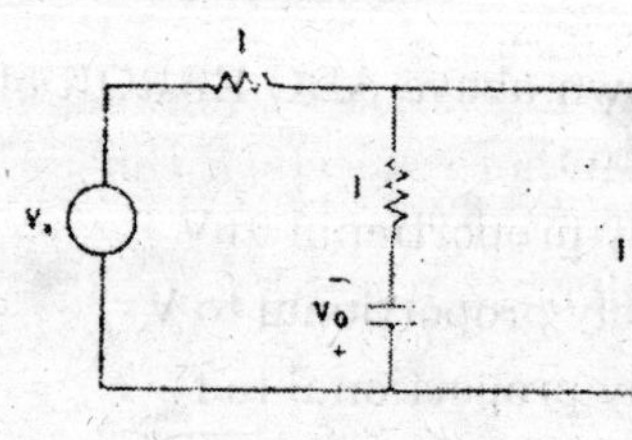

(*a*) 0 (*b*) $\frac{1}{2}$

(*c*) 1 (*d*) 2

27. In order to separate channels in a time division multiplex receiver, it is necessary to use

(*a*) AND gates (*b*) band pass filters

(*c*) differentiation (*d*) integration

28. 1000 kHz carrier wave modulated 40% at 4000 Hz is applied to a resonant circuit tuned to a carrier frequency and having Q = 140. What is the degree of modulation after transmission through this circuit?

(*a*) 60%

(*b*) 30%

(*c*) 27%

(*d*) 54%

29. The algebraic sum of the angles of the vectors from all poles and zeros to the point on any root locus segment is

(*a*) 45°

(*b*) 90°

(*c*) 180°

(*d*) 110° or its odd multiple

30. A.C. systems are usually preferred to the D.C. systems in control applications because

(*a*) A.C. systems are cheaper

(*b*) A.C. systems are more stable

(*c*) A.C. systems have better performance characteristics and are smaller in size

(*d*) All of these

31. The maximum efficiency of a full-wave reactifier is

(*a*) 81.2%

(*b*) 25%

(*c*) 40%

(*d*) 75%

32. Three-phase half-wave rectification, if the input frequency is 50 Hz, then output frequency is

(*a*) 100 Hz

(*b*) 150 Hz

(*c*) 75 Hz

(*d*) 25 Hz

33. An op. amp has an offset voltage of 1 mV and is ideal in all other respects. If this op. amp is used in the circuit shown in the figure, the output voltage will be (select the nearest value)

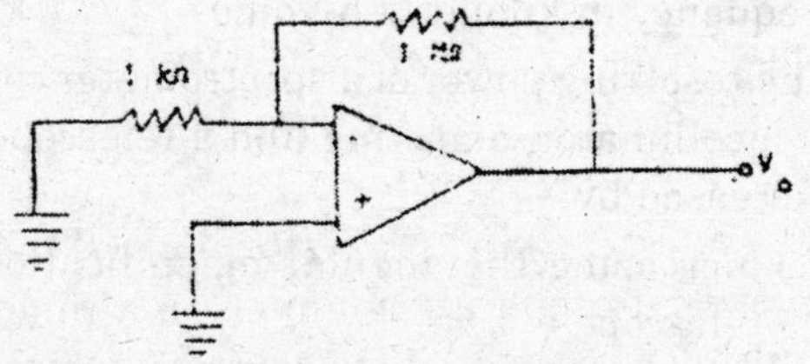

(*a*) 1 mV (*b*) 1 V

(*c*) ± 1 V (*d*) 0 V

34. The circuit of the figure uses an ideal op. amp. For small positive values of V_m, the circuit works as

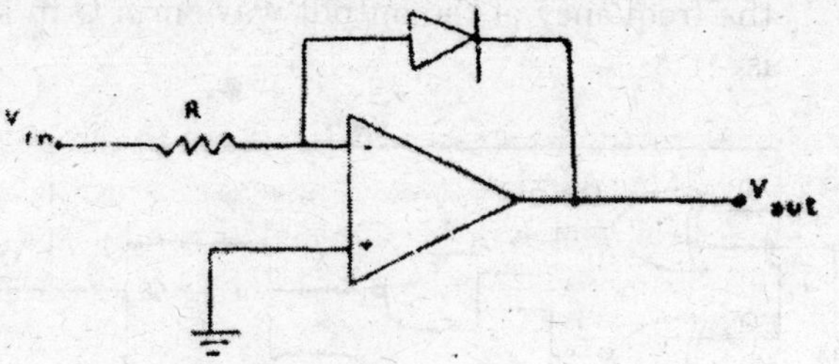

(*a*) a halfwave rectifier

(*b*) a differentiator

(*c*) a logarithmic amplifier

(*d*) an exponential amplifier

35. Assume that the operational amplifier in the figure is ideal. The current, I, though the 1 k ohm resistor is

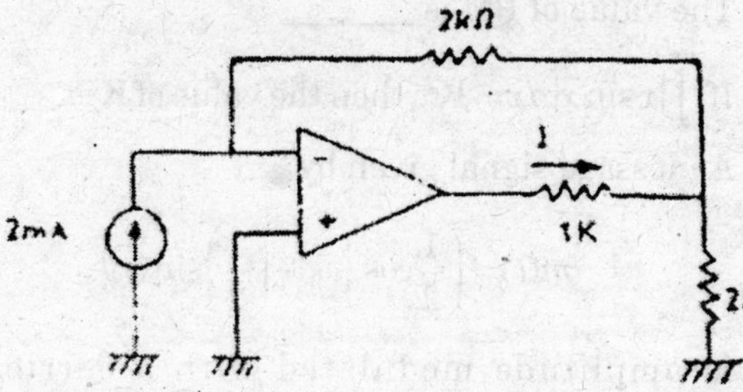

(*a*) 2 mA (*b*) 4 mA

(*c*) –4 mA (*d*) 0

36. If for the given system

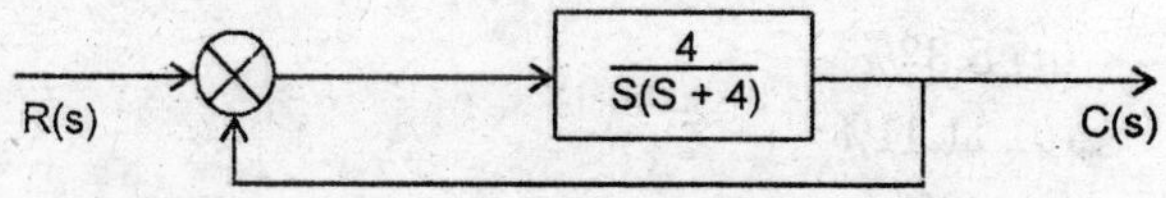

Then natural frequency of the system is

(*a*) 2

(*b*) 4

(*c*) 5

(*d*) 6

37. In the figure there is a low pass filter with a cut-off frequency of 5 kHz. The value of R_2 in (KΩ) ______.

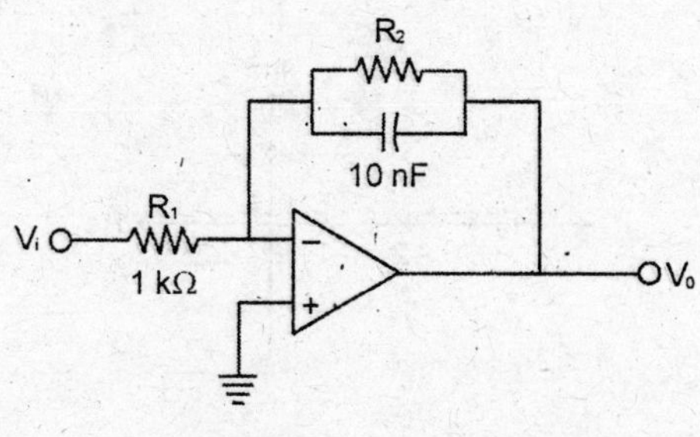

38. The clock frequency applied to the digital circuit shown in the figure below is 1 kHz. If the initial state of the output Q of the flip-flop is '0', then the frequency of the output wave orm Q in kHz is

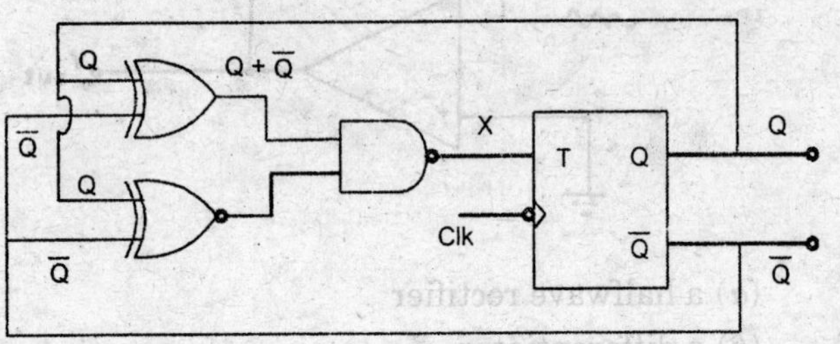

(*a*) 0.25 (*b*) 0.5

(*c*) 1 (*d*) 2

39. Given $G(s) = \dfrac{10}{(s+1)(s+0.1)(s+10)}$

The value of PM is ______.

40. If $\int_0^{2\pi} |x \sin x| dx = K\pi$, then the value of K is ______

41. A message signal given by

$$m(t) = \left(\frac{1}{2}\cos\right)\omega_1 - \left(\frac{1}{2}\right)\sin\omega_2 t$$

is amplitude modulated with a carrier of frequency ω_c to generate

$$s(t) = [1 + m(t)]\cos\omega_c t\,.$$

What is the power efficiency achieved by this modulation scheme ?

(*a*) 8.33%

(*b*) 11.11%

(*c*) 20%

(*d*) 25%

42. Let X be random variable with p.d.f

$f(x) = 0.2 \quad |x| \le 1$

$0.1 \quad 1 \le |x| \le 4$

$0 \quad$ else where

$P[0.5 < x < 5] =$ ______

43. Root locus of unity feedback system is shown in figure.

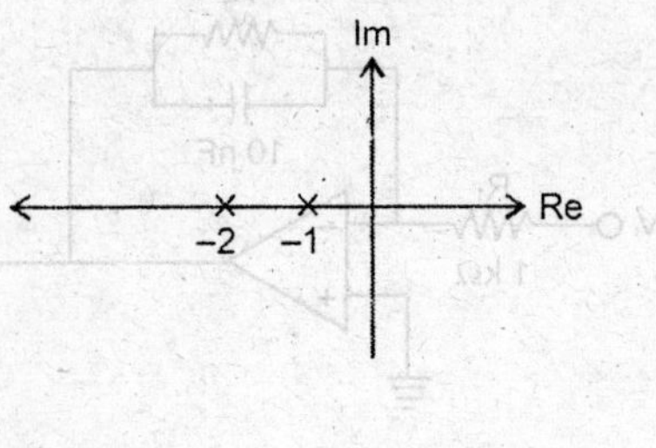

Find closed loop transfer function.

(*a*) $\dfrac{K}{(s+1)(s+2)}$

(*b*) $\dfrac{-K}{(s+1)(s+2)+K}$

(*c*) $\dfrac{-K}{(s+1)(s+2)-K}$

(*d*) $\dfrac{K}{(s+1)(s+2)+K}$

44. A piezoelectirc transducer has a capacitance of 1000 pF and a charge sensitivity of 40×10^{-3} C/m. The capacitance of connecting cable is 300 pF and that if oscilloscope for readout is 50 pF parallel with a resistance of 1 MΩ. The sensitivity of transducer alone is

(*a*) 10×10^6 V/m

(*b*) 20×10^6 V/m

(*c*) 30×10^6 V/m

(*d*) 40×10^6 V/m

45. What is loss in an optical fiber when an optical signal after traversing a distance of 400 meters in fibre has lost 75% of its input power ?

(*a*) 5 db/km

(*b*) 10 db/km

(*c*) 15 db/km

(*d*) 20 db/km

46. The probability that a thermistor randomly picked up from a production unit is defective is 0.1. The probability that out of 10 thermistors randomly picked up, 3 are defective is

(*a*) 0.001

(*b*) 0.057

(*c*) 0.0107

(*d*) 0.3

47. The output frequency of an LC tank oscillator employing a capacitive sensor acting as the capacitor of the tank is 100 kHz. If the sensor capacitance increases by 10%, the output frequency in kilohertz becomes ______ kHz.

48. The resolving power of a spectrometer consisting of a collimator, a grating and a telescope can be increased by

(*a*) increasing the angular magnification of the telescope

(*b*) increasing the period of the grating

(*c*) decreasing the period of the grating

(*d*) decreasing the slit-width of the collimator

49. For the circuit shown in the figure, the rising edge triggered D-flip flop with asynchronous reset has a clock frequency of 1 Hz. The NMOS transistor has an ON resistance of 1000Ω and an OFF resistance of infinity. The nature of the output waveform is

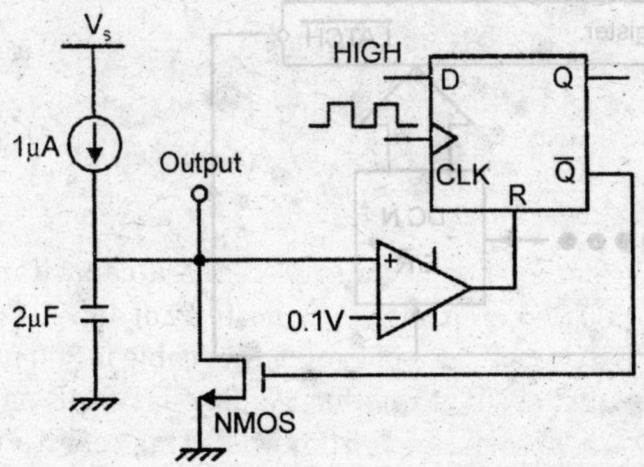

(*a*) 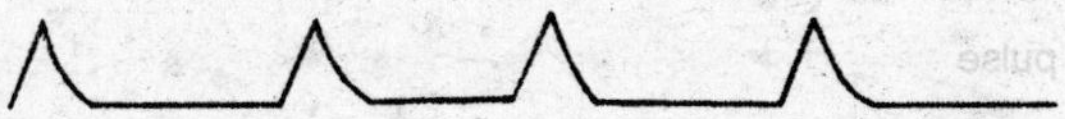

(*b*) 

(*c*) 

(*d*) 

50. Consider the circuits shown in the figure. The magnitude of the ratio of the currents, i.e., $|I_1/I_2|$, is ________.

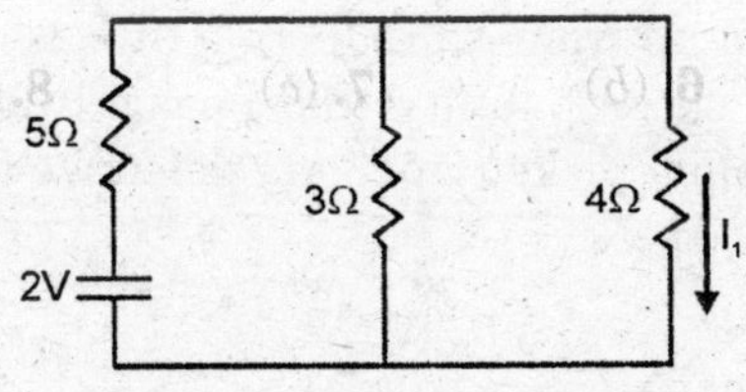

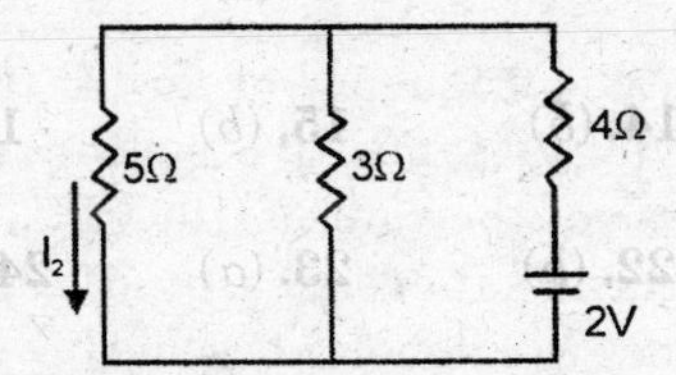

51. The figure shows a spot of light of uniform intensity 50 W/m² and size 10mm × 10 mm incident at the exact centre of a photo-detector, comprising two identical photo-diodes D_1 and D_2. Each diode has a sensitivity of 0.4 A/W and is operated in the photoconductive mode. If the spot of light is displaced upwards by 100μm, the resulting difference between the photocurrents generated by D_1 and D_2 in micro amperes, is ________ μA.

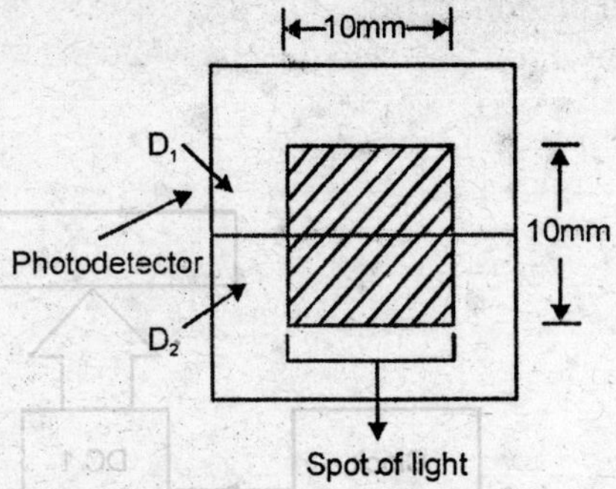

52. The signal $x[n] = \sin(\pi n/6)/(\pi n)$ is processed through a linear filter with the impulse response $h[n] = \sin(\omega_c n)/(\pi n)$ where $\omega_c > \pi/6$. The output of the filter is

(*a*) $\sin(2\omega_c n)/(\pi n)$

(*b*) $\sin(\pi n/3)/(\pi n)$

(*c*) $[\sin(\pi n/6)/(\pi n)]^2$

(*d*) $[\sin(\pi n/6)/(\pi n)]$

53. In the circuit shown in the figure, both the NMOS transistors are identical with their threshold voltages being 5V. Ignoring channel length modulation, the output voltage V_{out} in volt is ________ V.

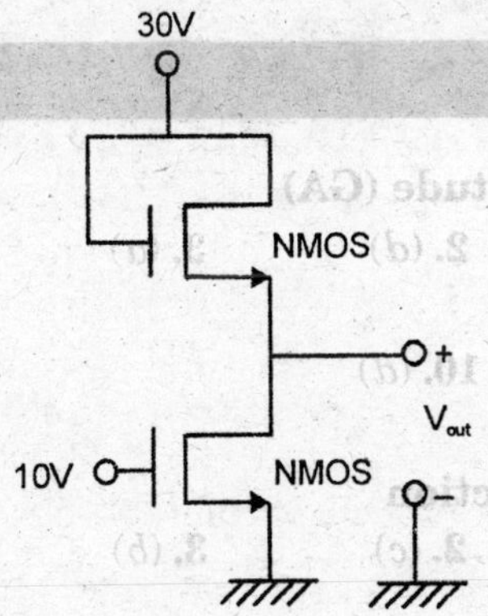

54. The open loop transfer function of a system is

$$G(s) = \frac{s^2 + 6s + 10}{s^2 + 2s + 2}.$$

The angles of arrival of its root loci are

(*a*) $\pm\frac{\pi}{4}$

(*b*) $\pm\frac{\pi}{3}$

(*c*) $\pm\frac{\pi}{2}$

(*d*) $\pm\frac{5\pi}{6}$

55. The number of clock cycles for the duration of an input pulse is counted using a cascade of N decade counters (DC 1 to DC N) as shown in the figure. If the clock frequency in mega hertz is f, the resolution and range of measurement of input width, both in μs, are respectively

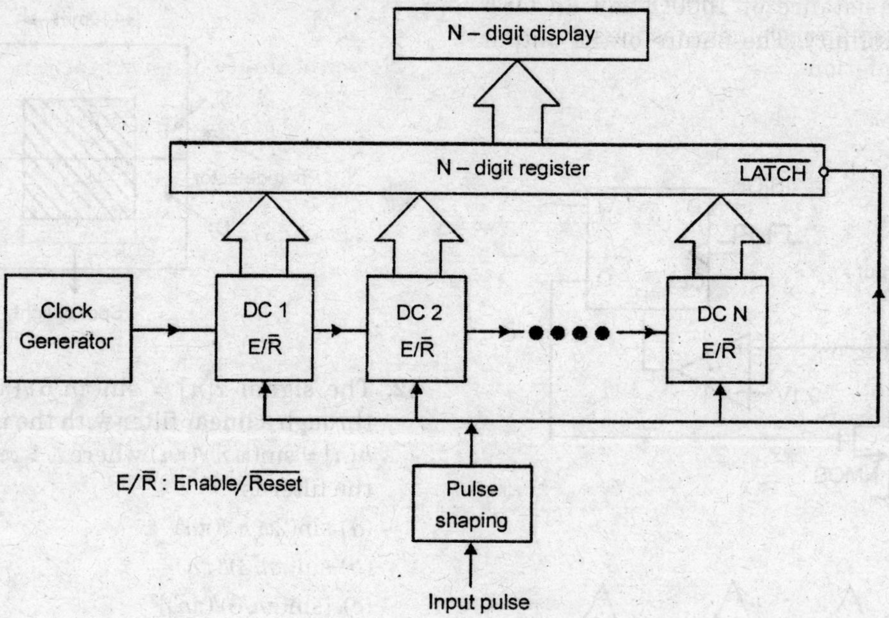

(a) $\frac{1}{f}$ and $\frac{(2^N - 1)}{f}$

(b) $\frac{1}{f}$ and $\frac{(10^N - 1)}{f}$

(c) $\frac{10^N}{f}$ and $\frac{(10^N - 1)}{f}$.

(d) $\frac{2^N}{f}$ and $\frac{(2^N - 1)}{f}$

ANSWERS

General Aptitude (GA)

1. (c)	**2.** (d)	**3.** (a)	**4.** (c)	**5.** (c)	**6.** (b)	**7.** (c)	**8.** (c)
9. (d)	**10.** (d)						

Technical Section

1. (b)	**2.** (c)	**3.** (b)	**4.** (a)	**5.** (d)	**6.** (d)	**7.** (c)	**8.** (d)
9. (a)	**10.** (d)	**11.** (b)	**12.** (b)	**13.** (2)	**14.** (b)	**15.** (b)	**16.** (a)
17. (c)	**18.** (3)	**19.** (a)	**20.** (d)	**21.** (a)	**22.** (b)	**23.** (a)	**24.** (0.25)
25. (d)	**26.** (c)	**27.** (a)	**28.** (c)	**29.** (d)	**30.** (d)	**31.** (a)	**32.** (b)
33. (c)	**34.** (c)	**35.** (c)	**36.** (a)	**37.** (3.184)	**38.** (b)	**39.** (55.57.)	**40.** (4)
41. (c)	**42.** (0.4)	**43.** (c)	**44.** (d)	**45.** (c)	**46.** (b)	**47.** (95.34)	**48.** (c)
49. (a)	**50.** (1)	**51.** (40)	**52.** (d)	**53.** (20)	**54.** (a)	**55.** (b)	

EXPLANATIONS

9. The given circuit represents NAND gate.

10. By looking the graph, which indicates the solution of differential equation

For option (*d*)

$$\frac{dy}{dx} = |x|$$

For $x > 0$

$$\therefore \quad \frac{dy}{dx} = x$$

∴ Now integrating both side

$$\int \frac{dy}{dx}.dx = \int x dx$$

$$y = \frac{x^2}{2} + c$$

and for $x < 0$

$$\frac{dy}{dx} = -x$$

Now integrating on both side

$$\int \frac{dy}{dx} dx = \int -x\, dx$$

$$y = -\frac{x^2}{2} + c$$

Now while plotting the graph of the solution of differential equation $\frac{dy}{dx} = |x|$

we get

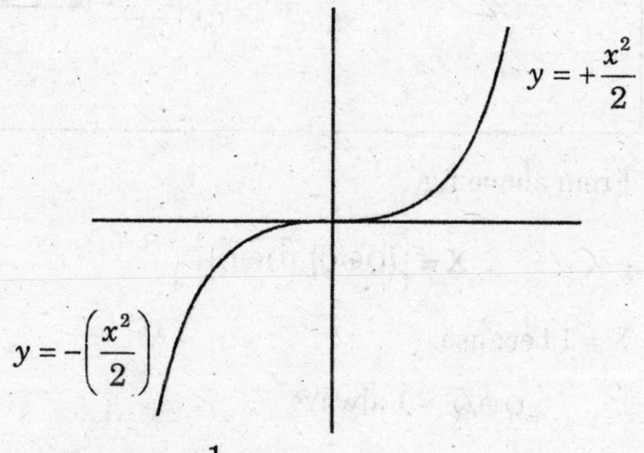

11. $$H(s) = \frac{1}{s(s+4)}$$

Input = cos(3*t*)

Steady state output = A sin(3*t* + α)

$$|H(s)| = \left|\frac{1}{j\omega(j\omega+4)}\right| = \frac{1}{3\times\sqrt{9+16}} = \frac{1}{15}$$

$$A = \frac{1}{15}$$

13. $F(x) = \frac{1}{k}e^{-x/2}$

Now probability density function

$$\int_0^\infty f(x)dx = 1$$

$$\therefore \quad \int_0^\infty \frac{1}{K}e^{-x/2}dx = 1$$

$$\left[\frac{1}{K}\frac{e^{-x/2}}{-\frac{1}{2}}\right]_0^\infty = 1$$

$$\frac{-2}{K}\left[e^{-x/2}\right]_0^\infty = 1$$

$$\frac{-2}{K}\left[e^{-\infty} - 1\right] = 1$$

$$\frac{-2}{K}[0-1] = 1 \qquad [\because e^{-\infty} = 0]$$

$$\frac{2}{K} = 1$$

$$\therefore \quad K = 2$$

15.

PQ \ RS	00	01	11	10
00	1			X
01		1	X	
11		X	1	
10	X			1

Minimal SOP form = $QS + \overline{Q}\overline{S}$

18.

$$R_x = \frac{V_x}{I_x}$$

$$= \frac{V_x 12\%}{I_x \pm 1\%}$$

$$= R_x \pm 3\%$$

22.

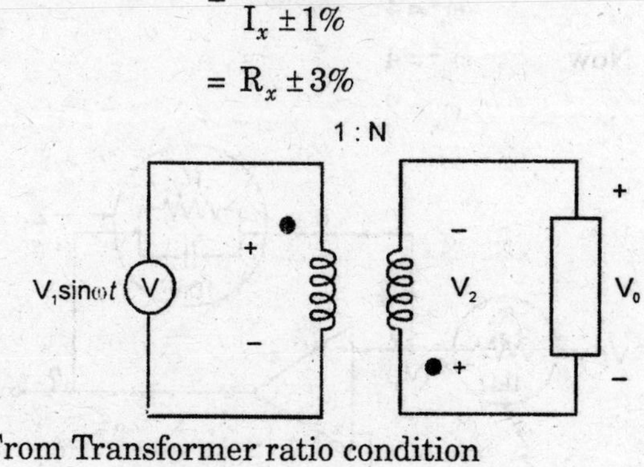

From Transformer ratio condition

$$\frac{V_2}{V_1} = \frac{N_2}{N_1}$$

$$\Rightarrow \quad V_2 = V_i\left(\frac{N_2}{N_1}\right)$$

$$= V_i\left(\frac{N}{1}\right)\sin \omega t$$

$$= NV_1 \sin \omega t$$

$$\therefore \quad V_0 = -V_2 = -NV_i \sin \omega t \qquad (\because V_2 = V_0)$$

24. The voltage waveform at R = 100Ω is as shown below.

$$P_{avg} = \frac{V_{rms}^2}{R}$$

$$= \frac{\left(10/2\right)^2}{100}$$

$$= 0.25 \text{ Watt}$$

36.

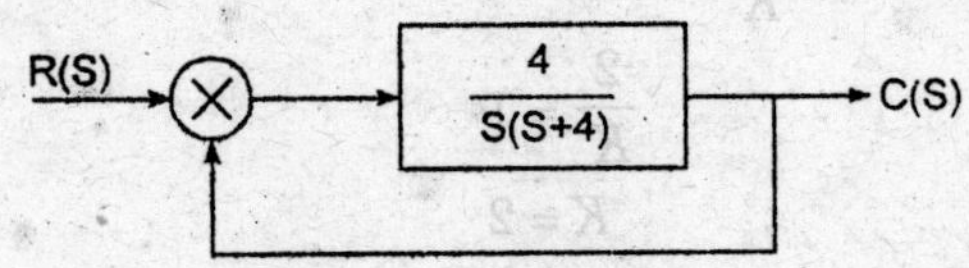

$$\frac{C(S)}{R(S)} = \frac{G(S)}{1+G(S)H(S)}$$

$$= \frac{\frac{4}{S(S+4)}}{1+\frac{4}{S(S+4)}} \qquad [\because H(s) = 1]$$

$$= \frac{4}{S(S+4)+4}$$

$$= \frac{4}{S^2+4S+4}$$

$\therefore$ Comparing $S^2 + 4S + 4$ with original equation $s^2 + 2\xi\omega_n s + \omega_n^2$

$$\therefore \quad \omega_n^2 = 4$$

Now $\quad \omega_n^2 = 4$

$$\therefore \quad \omega_n = 2$$

37.

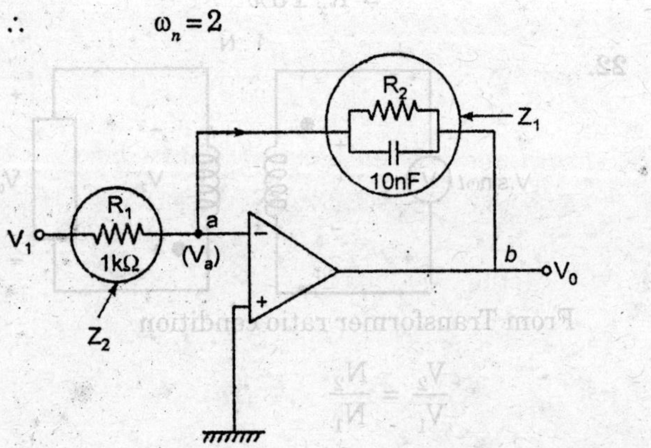

$V_a = 0V$ [reference voltage]

$$\therefore \quad \frac{V_i - O}{Z_2} = \frac{O - V_0}{Z_1}$$

$$\frac{V_i}{Z_2} = \frac{-VO}{Z_1}$$

$$\therefore \quad \frac{V_o}{V_i} = \frac{-Z_1}{Z_2}$$

$$= \frac{-\left(\dfrac{R_2 \times \frac{1}{CS}}{R_2 + \frac{1}{CS}}\right)}{1K}$$

$$\frac{V_o}{V_i} = \frac{-R_2}{1000(R_2\, CS+1)}$$

Now $|R_2CS + 1| = 0$ (at resonance)

$$\therefore \quad R_2CS = -1$$

$$\therefore \quad R_2 = \frac{1}{CS}$$

$$= \frac{1}{C2\pi F} \qquad (\because s = j\omega j2\pi F)$$

$$= \frac{1}{2\pi \times 5000 \times 10 \times 10^{-9}}$$

$$= 3.18 \text{ k}\Omega.$$

38.

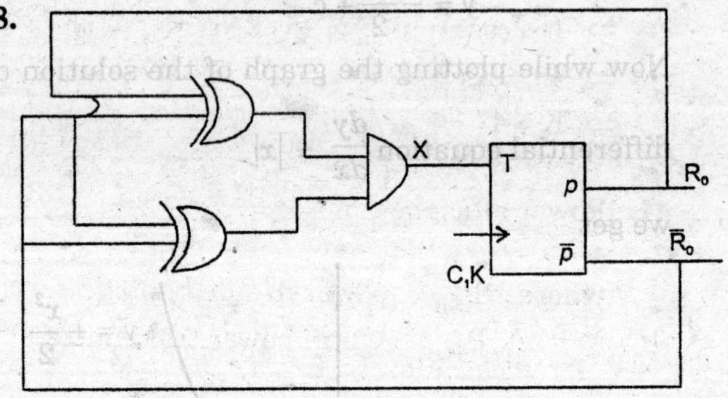

From above fig.

$$X = \left[(Q\oplus\bar{Q})\cdot\left(\overline{Q\oplus\bar{Q}}\right)\right]$$

X = 1 because

$$Q\oplus\bar{Q} = 1 \text{ always}$$

$$\Rightarrow \quad \overline{Q\oplus\bar{Q}} = 0 \text{ always}$$

$$\therefore \quad \overline{(Q\oplus\bar{Q})\cdot\left(\overline{Q\oplus\bar{Q}}\right)} = \left(\overline{1\cdot 0}\right) = \bar{0} = 1$$

$\therefore$ 'T' input = 1 always

for 'τ' flip flop of input = 1 then O/P will be implemented at the time of triggering.

$$\therefore \quad f_1 = 0.5(f) = 0.5(1) = 0.5\text{kHz}$$

39. Finding $\omega_{gc} = \dfrac{10}{\sqrt{\omega^2+1}\sqrt{\omega^2+0.01}\sqrt{\omega^2+100}} = 1$

$$= \frac{100}{(\omega^2+1)(\omega^2+0.01)(\omega^2+100)} = 1$$

$$100 = (\omega^4 + 1)[\omega^4 + 0.01\omega^2 + 100\omega^2 + 1]$$

$$= \omega^6 + 100.01\omega^4 + 101.01\omega^2 - 99 = 0$$

or $\omega^2 = 0.6, -1.6, -99.99.989$

$\therefore$ $\omega_{gc} = \sqrt{0.6} = 0.774$ rad/sec

$$PM = 180° + \angle G(\omega)|_{\omega=\omega_{gc}}$$

$$= 180° - \tan^{-1}\left(\frac{\omega_{gc}}{1}\right) - \tan^{-1}\left(\frac{\omega_{gc}}{0.1}\right) - \tan^{-1}\left(\frac{\omega_{gc}}{10}\right)$$

$$= 180° - 37.74° - 82.638° - 4.426°$$

$$= 55.57°$$

40. $\int_0^{2\pi} |x\sin x|dx = K\pi$

$$\Rightarrow \int_0^{\pi}|x\sin x|dx + \int_{\pi}^{2\pi}|x\sin x|dx = K\pi$$

$$\Rightarrow \int_0^{\pi} x\sin x dx + \int_{\pi}^{2\pi} -(x\sin x)dx = K\pi$$

$$\Rightarrow (-x\cos x + \sin x)|_0^{\pi} - (-x\cos x + \sin x)|_{\pi}^{2\pi} = K\pi$$

$$\Rightarrow 4\pi = K\pi$$

$$\Rightarrow K = 4$$

41. Power efficiency, $\eta = \dfrac{P_{SB}}{P_{TOT}}$

where, P_{SB} = power in side bands

P_{TOT} = total power transmitted

$$s(t) = \left[1 + \frac{1}{2}\cos\omega_1 t - \frac{1}{2}\sin\omega_2 t\right]\cos\omega_c t$$

$$= \cos\omega_c t + \frac{1}{4}\cos[(\omega_1+\omega_c)t] + \frac{1}{4}\cos[(\omega_1-\omega_c)t]$$

$$+\left\{\frac{1}{4}\sin[(\omega_2+\omega_c)t] + \frac{1}{4}\sin[(\omega_2+\omega_c)t]\right\}$$

Power in side bands,

$$P_{SB} = \frac{1}{2}\left[\frac{1}{16}+\frac{1}{16}+\frac{1}{16}+\frac{1}{16}\right] = \frac{1}{8}$$

$$P_{TOT} = \frac{1}{2} + \frac{1}{8} = \frac{5}{8}$$

$\therefore$ $\eta = \dfrac{1/8}{5/8} = \dfrac{1}{5} = 0.20 = 20\%$

Alternately

$$m_1 = \frac{1}{2}$$

$$m_2 = \frac{1}{2}$$

$$m = \sqrt{m_1^2 + m_2^2} = \frac{1}{\sqrt{2}}$$

Power efficiency, $\eta = \dfrac{m^2}{2+m^2}$

$$= \frac{\frac{1}{2}}{2+\frac{1}{2}}$$

$$= \frac{1}{5} = 20\%$$

42. Here $f(x) = 0.2, |x| \le 1$

$= 0.2, -1 \le x \le 1$

and $f(x) = 0.1, 1 \le x \le 4$

Now $\int_{-\infty}^{\infty} f(x)dx = 1$

For $P[0.5 < x < 5]$

$$= \int_{0.5}^{1} f(x)\,dx + \int_1^4 f(x)\,dx + \int_4^5 f(x)\,dx$$

$$= \int_{0.5}^{1} 0.2\,dx + \int_1^4 0.1\,dx + 0$$

$$= 0.2[x]_{0.5}^{1} + 0.1[x]_1^4$$

$$= 0.2\,(1 - 0.5) + 0.1\,(4 - 1)$$

$$= 0.2\,(0.5) + 0.1\,(3)$$

$$= 0.1 + 0.3$$

$$= 0.4$$

44. $K = \dfrac{K_q}{C_p} = \dfrac{40\times10^{-3}}{1000\times10^{-12}} = 40 \times 10^6$ V/m.

45. Let P = power at input

and p′ = power at output

then $\dfrac{P'}{P} = 0.25$

$$\text{Loss} = \frac{10}{L}\log\left(\frac{P}{P'}\right)$$

$$= \frac{10}{L}\log\left(\frac{P}{0.25\,P}\right)$$

$$= \frac{10}{0.4}\log\left(\frac{1}{0.25}\right) = 15 \text{ db/km.}$$

50. From the given circuit diagram,

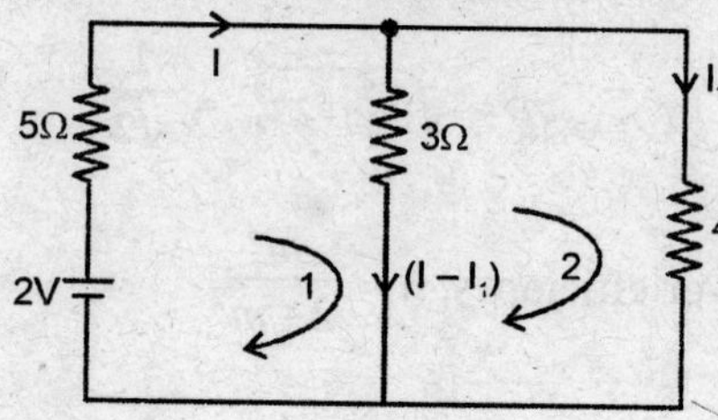

From loop 1

$$-2 + 5I + 3I - 3I_1 = 0$$

$$\therefore \quad 8I - 3I_1 = 2 \quad ...(i)$$

From loop 2

$$-3(I - I_1) + 4I_1 = 0$$

$$-3I + 3I_1 + 4I_1 = 0 \qquad \therefore \left|\frac{I_1}{I_2}\right| = 1$$

$$\therefore \quad -3I + 7I_1 = 0 \quad ...(ii)$$

Solving equation (*i*) and (*ii*) we get

$$I_1 = \frac{6}{47}$$

For circuit

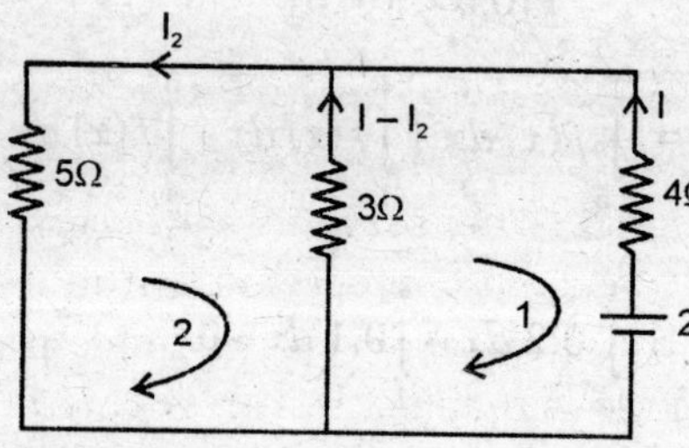

From loop 1

$$-3I + 3I_2 - 4I + 2 = 0$$

$$\therefore \quad -7I + 3I_2 = -2 \quad (iii)$$

From loop 2

$$-5I_2 + 3I - 3I_2 = 0$$

$$3I - 8I_2 = 0 \quad ...(iv)$$

Solving equation (*iii*) and (*iv*) we get

$$I_2 = \frac{6}{47}$$

52. $$\left[\frac{\sin \alpha n}{\pi n}\right] \times \left[\frac{\sin \beta n}{\pi n}\right] = \left[\frac{\sin \gamma n}{\pi n}\right]$$

where $\gamma = \min(\alpha, \beta)$

Output $g(n) = x(n) * h(n)$

In frequency domain they will be multiplied.

54. Angle of arrival is calculated on a complex zero and it is given by,

$$\phi_a = 180 - \underline{|GH}$$

(at a + ve imaginary zero)

$$G(s) = \frac{(s+3+i)(s+3-i)}{(s+1+i)(s+1-i)}$$

$$G(-3+i) = \frac{[-3+i+3][-3+i+3-i]}{[-3-i+1+i][-3+i+1-i]}$$

$$= \frac{[2i]}{[-2+2i][-2]}$$

$$\underline{|G(-3+i)} = 90° - \left[180° - \tan^{-1}\frac{2}{2}\right] - [180°]$$

$$= 90° - 180° + 45 - 180° = 135°$$

$$\phi_a = 180° - 135° = 45° = \frac{\pi}{4}$$

Other angle will be same with opposite sign $\pm\frac{\pi}{4}$

■■

MOCK TEST - 3

INSTRUCTIONS

1. Total of 65 questions carrying 100 marks, out of which 10 questions carrying a total of 15 marks are in General Aptitude (GA)
2. The Engineering Mathematics will carry around **15% of the total marks,** the General Aptitude section will carry **15% of the total marks** and the **remaining 70% of the total marks.**
3. **Types of Questions**

   (a) Multiple Choice Questions (MCQ) carrying 1 or 2 marks each in all papers and sections. These questions are objective in nature, and each will have a choice of four options, out of which the candidate has to mark the correct answer(s).

   (b) Numerical Answer Questions of 1 or 2 marks each in all papers and sections. For these questions the answer is a real number, to be entered by the candidate using the virtual keypad. No choices will be shown for these type of questions.
4. For **1-mark** multiple-choice questions, **1/3 marks** will be deducted for a wrong answer. Likewise, for **2-marks** multiple-choice questions, **2/3** marks will be deducted for a wrong answer. There is no negative marking for numerical answer type questions.

GENERAL APTITUDE (GA)

(Q. 1 - 5) : Carry One Mark Each

1. Which of the following options is the closest in meaning to the word below:

Often

(*a*) never (*b*) always

(*c*) quickly (*d*) frequently

2. The question below consists of a pair of related words followed by four pairs of words. Select the pair that best expresses the relation in the original pair.

Harm: Damage

(*a*) sweet : Sour

(*b*) Stour : weak

(*c*) injure : incapacitate

(*d*) hook : crook

3. Choose the most appropriate word from the option given below to complete the following sentence:

You must attend ___________ the lecture

(*a*) on (*b*) with

(*c*) in (*d*) to

4. Choose the most appropriate word from the option given below to complete the following sentence:

He deals ___________vegetables these days.

(*a*) out (*b*) to

(*c*) for (*d*) in

5. In an A.P., 2,5,8,.... upto 60 terms, and 3,5,7,9,... up to 50 terms, the terms identical in both are

(*a*) 15

(*b*) 17

(*c*) 25

(*d*) 30

(Q.6 – 10) : Carry Two Marks Each

6. Because of its accuracy in outlining the Earth's subsurface, the seismic-reflection method remains the most important tool in the search for petroleum reserves. In field practice, a subsurface is mapped by arranging a series of wave-train sources, such as small dynamite explosions, in a grid pattern. As each source is activated, it generates a wave train that moves downward at a speed determined uniquely by the rock's elastic characteristics. As rock interfaces are crossed, the elastic characteristics encountered generally change abruptly, which causes part of the energy to be reflected back to the surface, where it is recorded by seismic instruments. The seismic records must be processed to correct for positional differences between the source and the receiver, for unrelated wave trains, and for multiple reflections from the rock interfaces. Then the data acquired at each of the specific source locations are combined to generate a physical profile of the subsurface, which can eventually be used to select targets for drilling.

The passage is primarily concerned with

(*a*) describing an important technique

(*b*) discussing a new method

(*c*) investigating a controversial procedure

(*d*) announcing a significant discovery

7. A certain basketball team that has played 2/3 of its games has a record of 17 wins and 3 losses. What is the greatest number of the remaining games that the team can lose and still win at least 3/4 of the total games played?

(*a*) 4 (*b*) 7

(*c*) 5 (*b*) 6

8. A group of labourers promise to do a piece of work in 12 days, but 5 of them do not turn up. If the rest of the group do the work in 18 days, find the original number of men.

(*a*) 15 (*b*) 25

(*c*) 35 (*d*) 45

9. A and B can complete a piece of work in 12 days while B and C in 15 days. A did the work for 3 days, B for 8 days and C for 10 days to complete the work. In how many days C alone can complete the work?

(*a*) 6 days (*b*) 9 days

(*c*) 10 days (*d*) 12 days

10. A group of labourers promise to do a piece of work in 12 days, but 5 of them do not turn up. If the rest of the group do the work in 18 days, find the original number of men.

(*a*) 15 (*b*) 25

(*c*) 35 (*d*) 45

TECHNICAL SECTION

(Q.1 – 25) : Carry One Mark Each

1. The decimal number 85 in encoded as 1100-0101 in

(*a*) 8421 code

(*b*) 4421 code

(*c*) 2421 code

(*d*) 2221 code

2. The binary fraction 0.0111 in decimal form is equal to

(*a*) 0.4375

(*b*) 0.6225

(*c*) 0.8325

(*d*) 0.1105

3. In order to add 1111 + 1101, we require

(*a*) One FA, one HA

(*b*) Three FA

(*c*) Three FA and one HA

(*d*) None of these

4. The Duane-Hunt law represents the minimum wavelength λ(Å) of X-rays generated for an applied voltage V (volts) and given by

(*a*) $V = \dfrac{12400}{\lambda}$ (*b*) $V = 12400\lambda$

(*c*) $V = \dfrac{12400}{\lambda^2}$ (*d*) $V = 12400\lambda$

5. The equations under balance conditions for a bridge are $R_1 = \dfrac{R_2R_3}{R_4}$ and $L_1 = R_2R_3C_4$, where R and L are respectively unknown resistance and inductance. In order to achieve faster balance which of the following variables are chosen

(*a*) R_2 and R_3 (*b*) R_2 and C_4

(*c*) R_4 and C_4 (*d*) R_3 and C_4

6. The ideal linear characteristics for transmitting angular motion between two misaligned shafts is achieved by

(*a*) Dog coupling

(*b*) Universal coupling

(*c*) Flexible spring coupling

(*d*) Oldham's coupling

7. The output 'F' of the multiplexer circuit shown in the given figure will be

(*a*) $AB + B\overline{C} + \overline{C}A + \overline{BC}$

(*b*) $A \oplus B \oplus C$

(*c*) $A \oplus B$

(*d*) $\overline{A}\,\overline{B}C + \overline{A}B\overline{C} + A\overline{B}\,\overline{C} + ABC$

8. The schematic shown in the figure represents a

(*a*) divide by seven counter

(*b*) divide by five counter

(*c*) binary coded decimal counter

(*d*) divide by twelve counter

9. A magnetic flux of 25,000 lines through an area of 5 cm^2 results in

(*a*) 5 lines flux

(*b*) 5000 Mx. of flux

(*c*) flux density of 5000 G

(*d*) none of these

10. A parallel LC resonant circuit resonates at 1000 kHz and has Q of 100. Its 3dB bandwith is

(*a*) 5 kHz (*b*) 10 kHz

(*c*) $\frac{10}{2\pi}$ kHz (*d*) $\frac{50}{2\pi}$ kHz

11. Compared to the upstream to the throat of a venturi meter, which of the following is true

(*a*) Pressure, velocity both increases

(*b*) Pressure, velocity both decreases

(*c*) Pressure increases and velocity decreases

(*d*) Pressure decreases and velocity increases

12. Address and data are busses int and int A are 1 bit signal. Interrupt controller is a vectored interrupt controller which collected multiple interrupts (Ext_int 0 to Ext_int n) from outside and send a single interrupt to processor; then which of the following sequence is correct ?

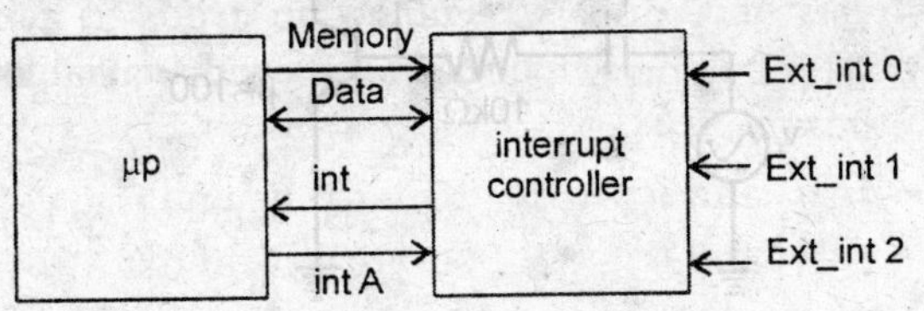

(*a*) Ext_int→int→int_A→Data

(*b*) Ext_int→Data→int→int_A

(*c*) Ext_int→int_A→int→Data

(*d*) Ext_int→int_A→Data→int

13. For the circuit given below. The largest value of arm when it is converted into delta form is____.

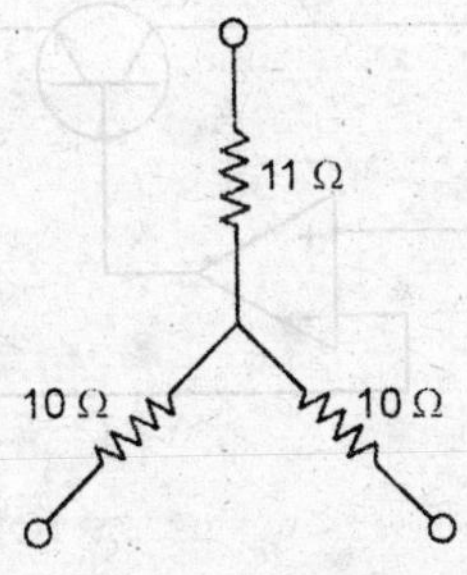

14. Mechanical measurements are classified into

(*a*) Mechanics type (*b*) Power type

(*c*) Both (*a*) and (*b*) (*d*) None of these

15. The following Boolean expression is $f(w,x,y,z) = \overline{w}\overline{x}\,\overline{z} + w\overline{x}\,\overline{z} + xz + xy + \overline{w}y + wy$. Then all the essential prime implicants of the expression

(*a*) $y, \overline{w}\overline{x}\,\overline{z}, xy$ (*b*) $xz, wy, w\overline{x}\,\overline{z}$

(*c*) y, xz, xy (*d*) $y, \overline{x}\,\overline{z}, xz$

16. $G(s) = \dfrac{20}{(s+0.1)(s+2)(s+100)}$ then by dominant pole compensation the transfer function will look like

(*a*) $\dfrac{20}{s+0.1}$ (*b*) $\dfrac{0.1}{s+0.1}$

(*c*) $\dfrac{2}{s+0.1}$ (*d*) $\dfrac{10}{s+0.1}$

17. To achieve balance in the above bridge z_3 must be

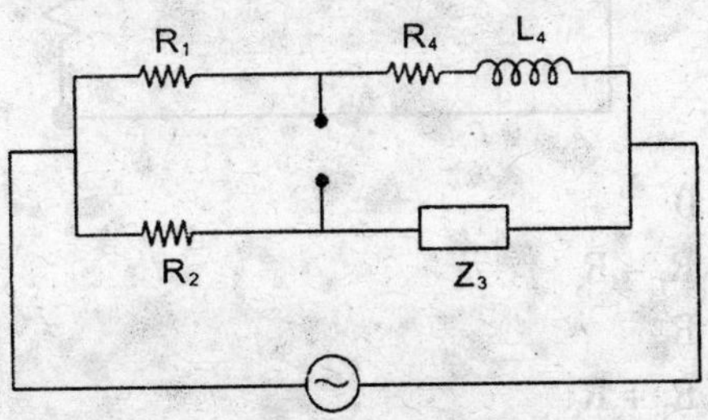

(*a*) R only (*b*) R and L

(*c*) R and C (*d*) L and C

18. If $f(x) = xe^{-x}$, the maximum value of the function in the interval $(0, \infty)$ is,

(*a*) e^{-1} (*b*) e

(*c*) $1 - e^{-1}$ (*d*) $1 + e^{-1}$

19. The capacitor shown in the figure is initially charged to +10 V. The switch closes at time $t = 0$. Then the value of $V_c(t)$ in volts at time $t = 10$ ms is _____ V.

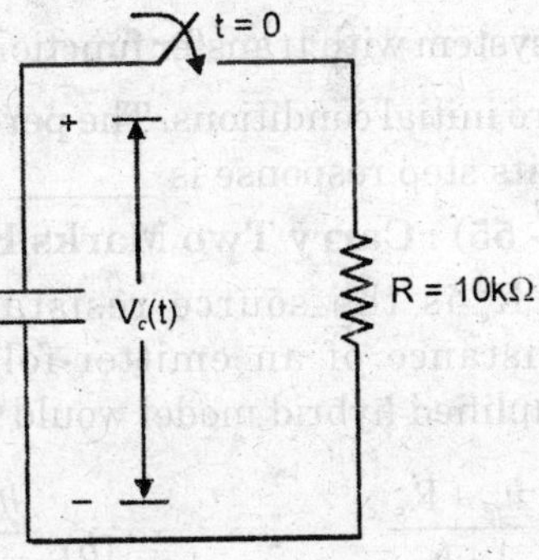

20. Let $3 + 4j$ be a zero of a fourth order linear — phase FIR filter. The complex number which is NOT a zero of this filter is

(*a*) $3 - 4j$ (*b*) $\frac{3}{25} + \frac{4}{25}j$

(*c*) $\frac{3}{25} - \frac{4}{25}j$ (*d*) $\frac{1}{3} - \frac{1}{4}j$

21. The bridge most suited for measurement of a four-terminal resistance in the range of 0.001 Ω to 0.1 Ω is

(*a*) Wien's bridge (*b*) Kelvin double bridge

(*c*) Maxwell's bridge (*d*) Schering bridge

22. A load resistor R_L is connected to a battery of voltage E with internal resistance R_i through a resistance R_s as shown in the figure. For fixed values of R_L and R_i, the value of R_S (≥ 0) for maximum power transfer to R_L is

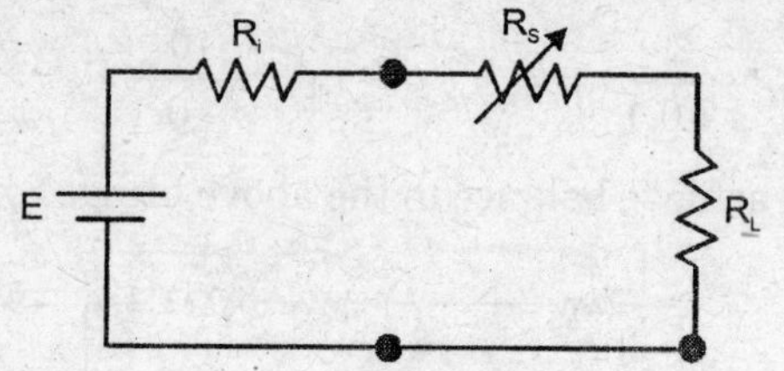

(*a*) 0
(*b*) $R_L - R_i$
(*c*) R_L
(*d*) $R_L + R_i$

23. The value of $\oint \frac{1}{z^2} dz$, where the contour is the unit circle traversed clockwise, is

(*a*) $-2\pi i$ (*b*) 0
(*c*) $2\pi i$ (*d*) $4\pi i$

24. Let A be an $n \times n$ matrix with the rank r $(0 < r < n)$. Then $Ax = 0$ has p independent solutions, where p is

(*a*) r (*b*) n
(*c*) $n - r$ (*d*) $n + r$

25. A system with transfer function $G(s) = \frac{1}{s^2 + 1}$ has zero initial conditions. The percentage overshoot in its step response is ______ %.

(Q. 26 – 55) : Carry Two Marks Each

26. If R_s is the source resistance, the output resistance of an emitter-follower using the simplified hybrid model would be

(*a*) $\frac{h_{ie} + R_S}{1 + h_{fe}}$ (*b*) $\frac{h_{ie} + R_S}{h_{fe}}$

(*c*) $R_S \frac{1}{h_{fe}}$ (*d*) $\frac{1}{h_{fe}}$

27. The power in a series RLC circuit will be half of that at resonance and magnitude of current will be

(*a*) $\frac{V}{2R}$ (*b*) $\frac{V}{\sqrt{3}R}$

(*c*) $\frac{V}{\sqrt{2}R}$ (*d*) $\frac{\sqrt{2}V}{R}$

28. $G(s) \cdot H(s) = \frac{k}{s(s+1)(9s+1)}$ the phase cross over frequency is ______.

29. The pressure at a remote point is measured by an instrumentation system comprising a transmitter [specified accuracy (SA) within ± 0.3%], a relay (SA within ± 1.1%) and a receiver element (SA with ± 0.6%). The maximum possible error of the measurement system will be

(*a*) ± 1.1% (*b*) ± 1.4%
(*c*) ± 2.0% (*d*) ± 2.2%

30. The voltage gain A_e of the circuit shown below is

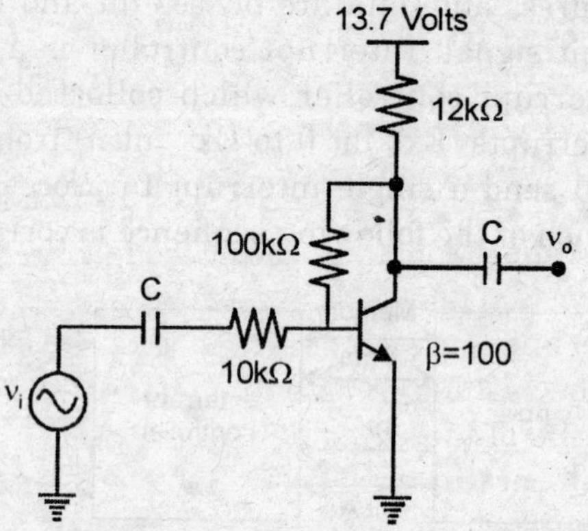

(*a*) $|A_v| = 200$ (*b*) $|A_v| = 100$
(*c*) $|A_v| = 20$ (*d*) $|A_v| = 10$

31. In the voltage regulator shown in figure op-amp is ideal. The BJT has V_{BE} = 0.7 V and β = 100 and Zener voltage V_z is 4.7 V for a regulated output of 9 V the value of R in Ω is______.

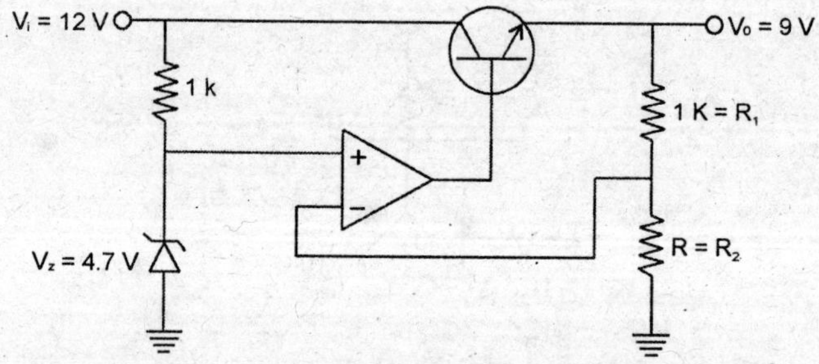

32. Consider the circuit shown below. Given $V_c(0) = -2V$. The value of voltage (V_s) across the current source in the circuit is

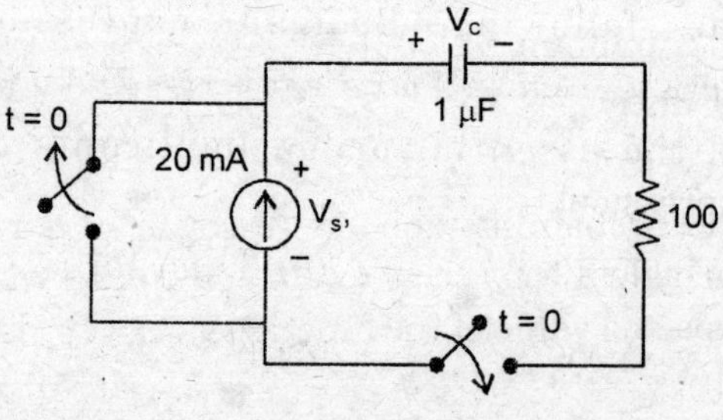

33. In a town, 10% of population have disease the test used to detect the disease has 95% accuracy on affected patients and 90% accuracy on un-affected patient. If a patient is detected positive in the test. What is the probability of disease?

34. Find Z – parameter (Z_{11}, Z_{12}, Z_{21}, Z_{22})

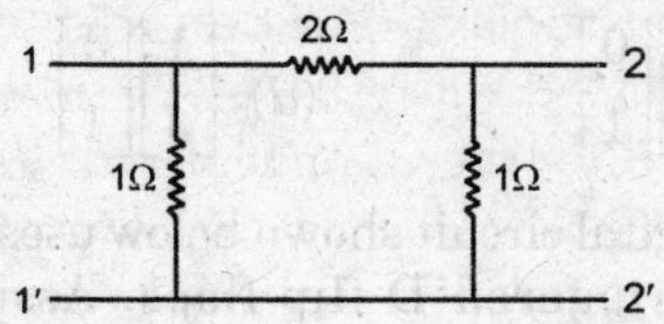

(*a*) $\begin{bmatrix} 3/4\Omega & 1/4\Omega \\ 1/4\Omega & 3/4\Omega \end{bmatrix}$ (*b*) $\begin{bmatrix} 1/4\Omega & 3/4\Omega \\ 3/4\Omega & 1/4\Omega \end{bmatrix}$

(*c*) $\begin{bmatrix} 1/2\Omega & 3/4\Omega \\ 3/4\Omega & 1/2\Omega \end{bmatrix}$ (*d*) $\begin{bmatrix} 3/4\Omega & 1/2\Omega \\ 1/2\Omega & 3/4\Omega \end{bmatrix}$

35. A copper constant, thermocouple with reference junction temperature of 20°C is used to measure an unknown temperature. ($E_2 - E_0$) = 0.7936 mV. The reading of potentiometer is 2.877 mV. The slope of the curve is 0.04 mV/°C. The unknown temperature will be

(*a*) 46°C (*b*) 70.7°C

(*c*) 86.6°C (*d*) 92°C

36. In the circuit shown below, capacitors C_1 and C_2 are very large and are shorts at the input frequency, v_i is a small signal input. The gain magnitude $|v_a / v_i|$ at 10 Mrad/s is

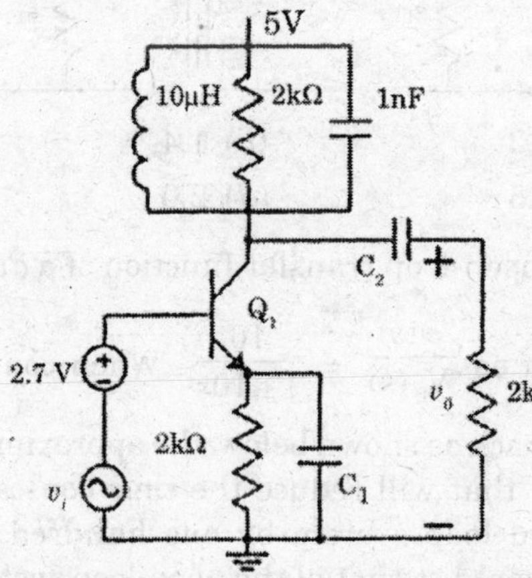

(*a*) maximum

(*b*) minimum

(*c*) unity

(*d*) zero

37. The probability density function of a random variable X is $p_x(x) = e^{-x}\ x \geq 0$ and 0 otherwise. The expected value of the function $g_x(x) = e^{3x/4}$ is ______.

38. A system is represented in state-space as $\dot{X}$ = AX + Bu, where $A = \begin{bmatrix} 1 & 2 \\ \alpha & 6 \end{bmatrix}$ and $B = \begin{bmatrix} 1 \\ 1 \end{bmatrix}$

The value of α for which the system is not controllable is ________.

39. The current in amperes through the resistor R in the circuit shown in the figure is ________.

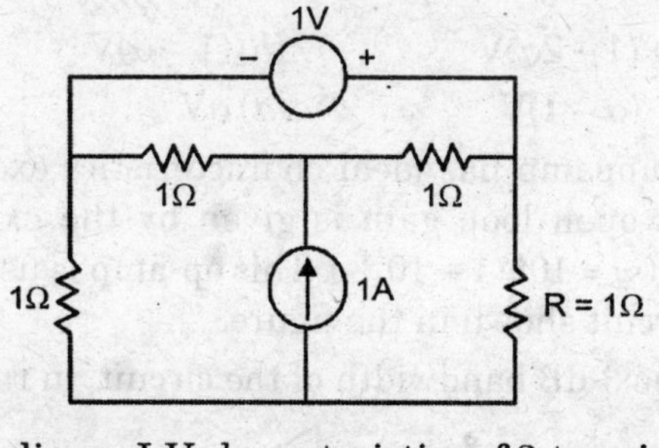

40. The linear I-V characteristics of 2-terminal non-ideal dc sources X and Y are shown in the figure. If the sources are connected to a 1Ω resistor as shown, the current through the resistor in amperes is ______ A.

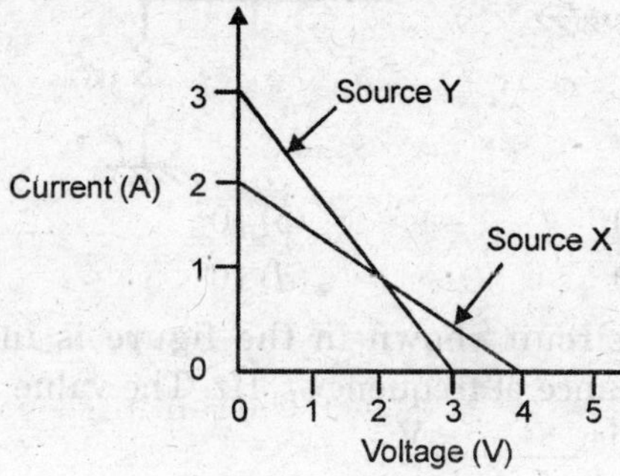

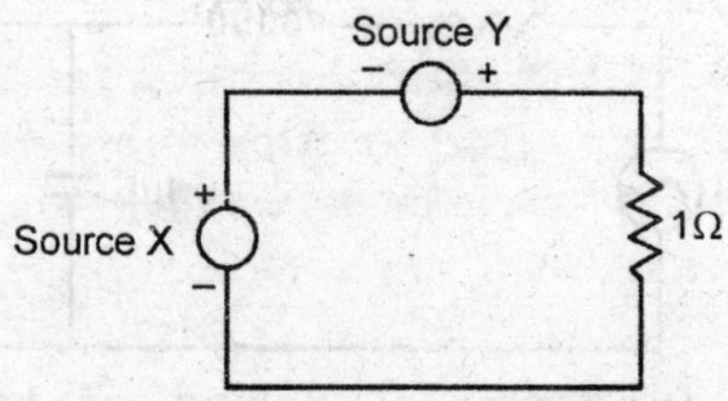

41. If the deflection of the galvanometer in the bridge circuit shown in the figure is zero, then the value of R_x in ohms is ______ Ω.

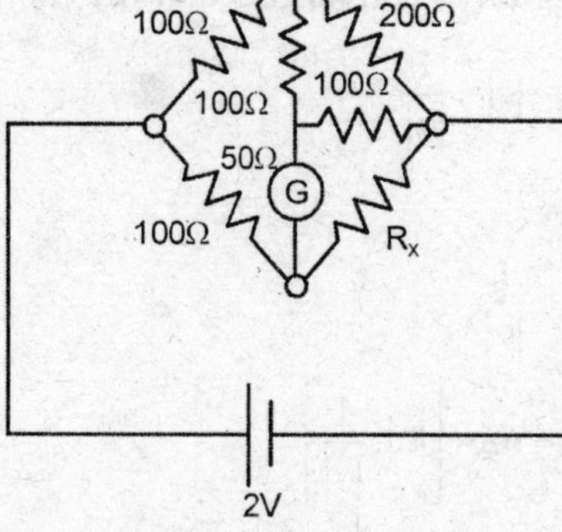

42. In the potentiometer circuit shown in the figure, the expression for V_x is

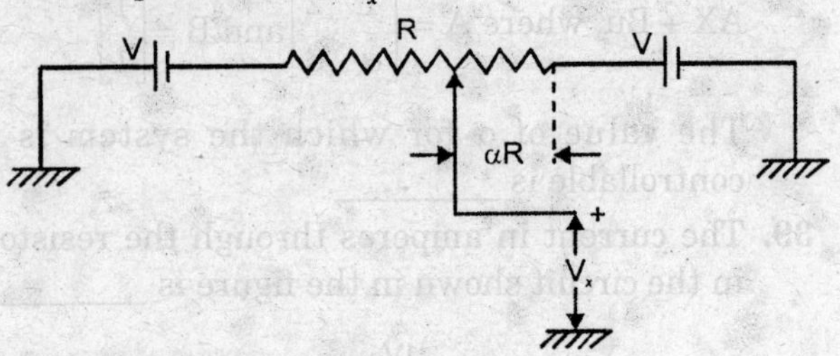

(a) $(1-2\alpha)V$ (b) $(1-\alpha)V$

(c) $(\alpha-1)V$ (d) αV

43. An opamp has ideal characteristics except that its open loop gain is given by the expression $A_V(s) = 10^4/(1 + 10^{-3}s)$. This op-amp is used in the circuit shown in the figure.

The 3-dB bandwidth of the circuit, in rad/s, is

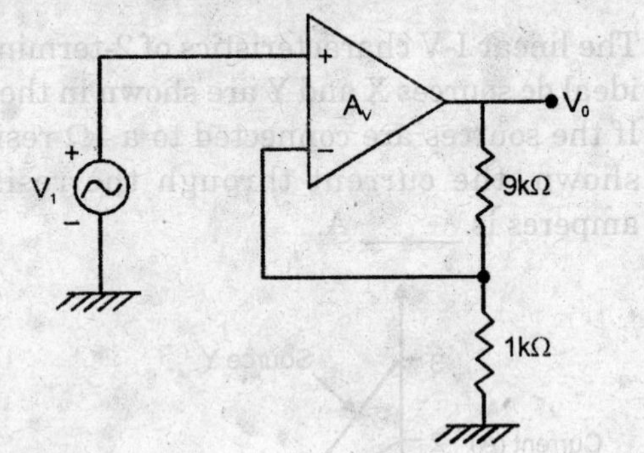

(a) 10^2 (b) 10^3

(c) 10^4 (d) 10^6

44. The circuit shown in the figure is in series resonance of frequency f_c Hz. The value of V_c in volts is ______ V.

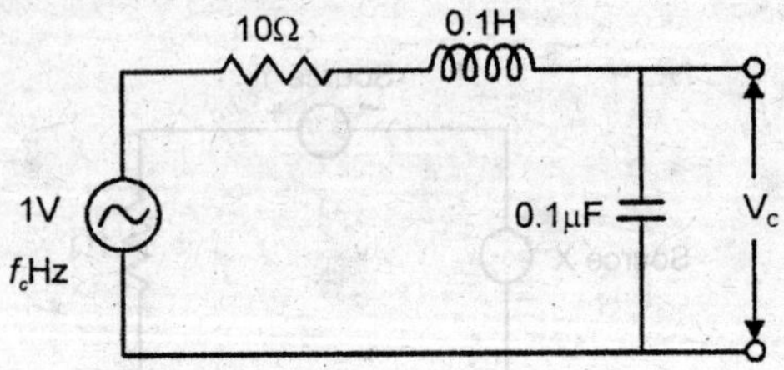

45. The fundamental period of the signal $x(t) = 2\cos\left(\frac{2\pi t}{3}\right) + \cos(\pi t)$, in seconds, is ______ s.

46. The z-transform of $x[n] = a^{|n|}$, $0 < |\alpha| < 1$, is X(z). The region of convergence of X(z) is

(a) $|\alpha| < |z| < \frac{1}{|\alpha|}$

(b) $|z| > a$

(c) $|z| > \frac{1}{|\alpha|}$

(d) $|z| < \min\left[|\alpha|, \frac{1}{|\alpha|}\right]$

47. One part of eigenvectors corresponding to the two eigenvalues of the matrix $\begin{bmatrix} 0 & -1 \\ 1 & 0 \end{bmatrix}$ is

(a) $\begin{bmatrix} 1 \\ -J \end{bmatrix}\begin{bmatrix} J \\ -1 \end{bmatrix}$ (b) $\begin{bmatrix} 0 \\ 1 \end{bmatrix}\begin{bmatrix} -1 \\ 0 \end{bmatrix}$

(c) $\begin{bmatrix} 1 \\ J \end{bmatrix}\begin{bmatrix} 0 \\ 1 \end{bmatrix}$ (d) $\begin{bmatrix} 1 \\ J \end{bmatrix}\begin{bmatrix} J \\ 1 \end{bmatrix}$

48. The digital circuit shown below uses two negative edge-triggered D-flip-flops. Assuming intial condition of Q1 and Q0 as zero, the output Q1Q0 of this circuit is

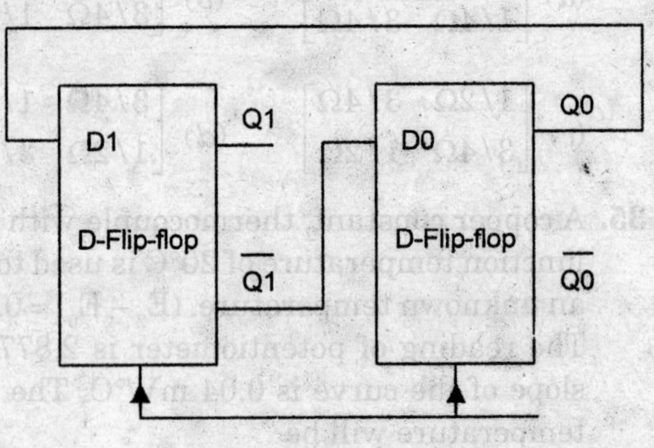

(a) 00,01, 10, 11,00 (b) 00,01,11,10,00

(c) 00,11,10,01,00 (d) 00,01,11,11,00

49. Considering the transformer to be ideal, the transmission parameter 'A' of the 2-port network

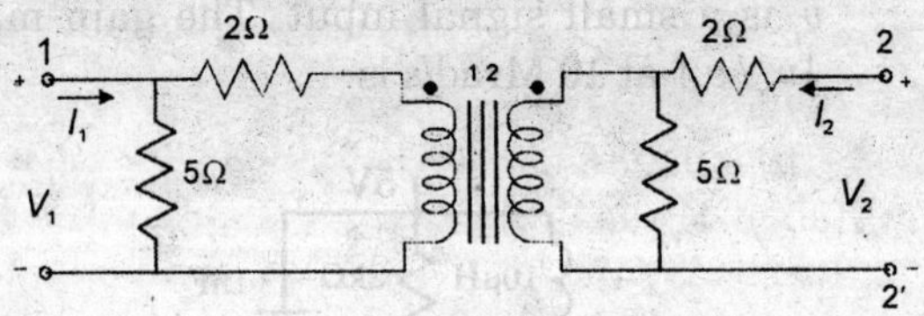

(a) 1.3 (b) 1.4

(c) 0.5 (d) 2.0

50. The open-loop transfer function of a *dc* motor is given as $\frac{\omega(s)}{V_a(s)} = \frac{10}{1+10s}$. When connected in feedback as shown below, the approximate value of K_a that will reduce the time constant of the closed loop system by one hundred times as compared to that of the open-loop system is

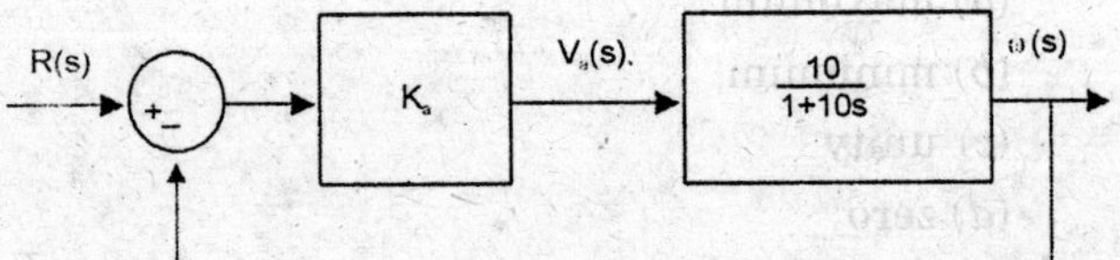

(a) 1 (b) 5

(c) 10 (d) 100

51. For the circuit shown below, the knee current of the ideal Zener diode is 10 mA. To maintain 5 V across R_L, the minimum value of the load resistor R_L in Ω and the minimum power rating of the Zener diode in mW respectively are

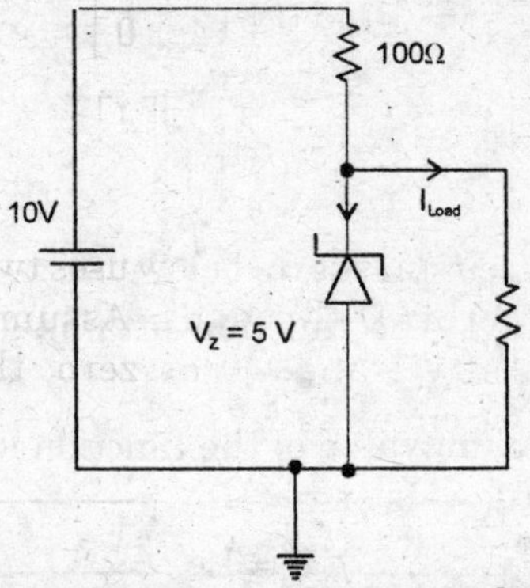

(*a*) 125 and 125 (*b*) 125 and 250
(*c*) 250 and 125 (*d*) 250 and 250

52. In the circuit shown below, if the source voltage $V_s = 100\angle 53 : 13°$ volts then the Thevenin's equivalent voltage in volts as seen by the load resistance R_L is

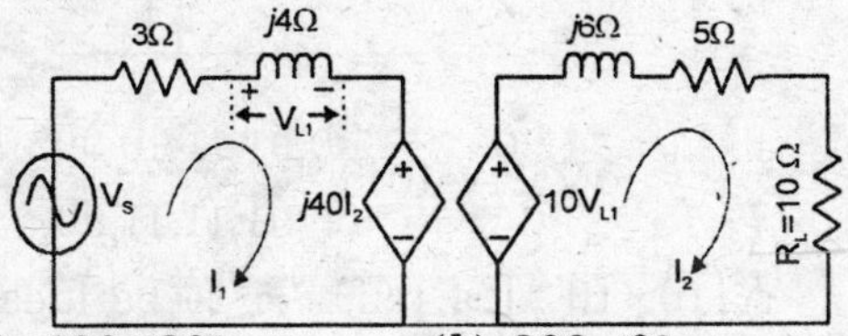

(*a*) $100\angle 90°$ (*b*) $800\angle 0°$
(*c*) $800\angle 90°$ (*d*) $100\angle 60°$

53. A signal $V_1(t) = 10 + 10\sin 100\pi t + 10\sin 4000\pi t + 10\sin 100000\pi t$ is supplied to a filter circuit (shown below) made up of ideal op-amps. The least attenuated frequency component in the output will be

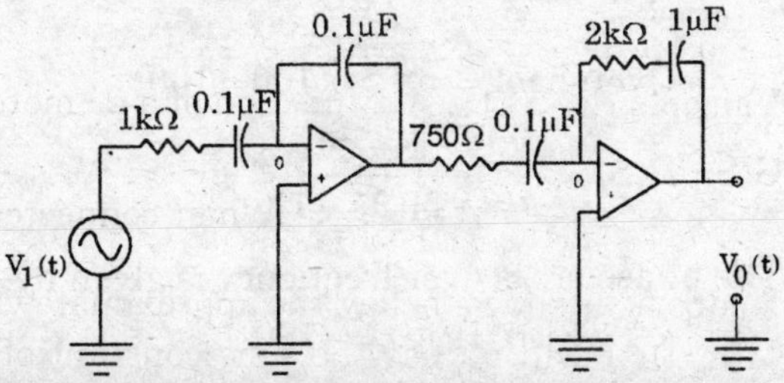

(*a*) 0 Hz (*b*) 50 Hz
(*c*) 2 k Hz (*d*) 50 kHz

54. The signal flow graph for a system is given below. The transfer function $\frac{Y(s)}{U(s)}$ for this system is

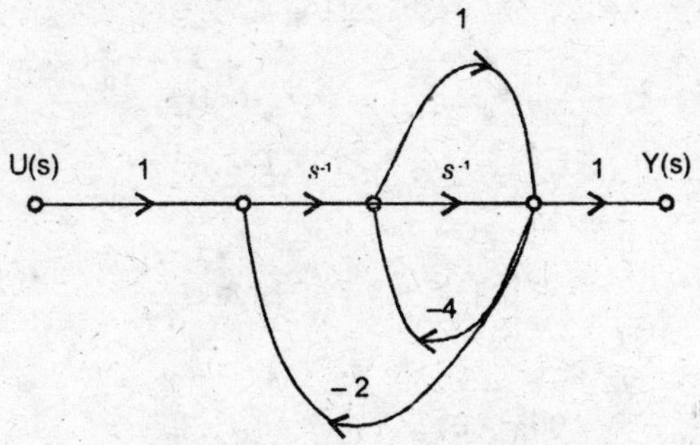

(*a*) $\frac{s+1}{5s^2+6s+2}$ (*b*) $\frac{s+1}{s^2+6s+2}$

(*c*) $\frac{s+1}{s^2+4s+2}$ (*d*) $\frac{1}{5s^2+6s+2}$

55. In the circuit shown below, Q_1 has negligible collector-to-emitter saturation voltage and the diode drops negligible voltage across it under forward bias. If V_{cc}, is + 5 V, X and Y are digital signals with 0 V as logic 0 and V_{cc} as logic 1, then the Boolean expression for Z is

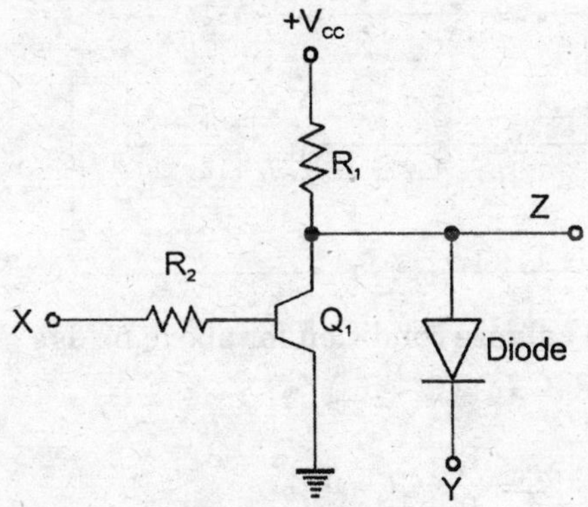

(*a*) X Y (*b*) $\overline{X}Y$
(*c*) $X\overline{Y}$ (*d*) $\overline{XY}$

ANSWERS

General Aptitude (GA)

1. (*d*) 2. (*c*) 3. (*d*) 4. (*d*) 5. (*b*) 6. (*d*) 7. (*a*) 8. (*a*) 9. (*d*) 10. (*a*)

Technical Section

1. (*b*) 2. (*a*) 3. (*c*) 4. (*b*) 5. (*c*) 6. (*a*) 7. (*d*) 8. (*a*) 9. (*c*) 10. (*b*)
11. (*d*) 12. (*a*) 13. (32) 14. (*c*) 15. (*d*) 16. (*b*) 17. (*b*) 18. (*a*) 19. (3.67) 20. (*d*)
21. (*c*) 22. (*a*) 23. (*b*) 24. (*c*) 25. (100) 26. (*a*) 27. (*b*) 28. (1/3) 29. (*c*) 30. (*d*)
31. (1093.023) 32. ($2 \times 10^4 t$) 33. (0.185) 34. (*a*) 35. (*d*) 36. (*a*) 37. (4) 38. (– 3)
39. (1) 40. (1.75) 41. (33.33) 42. (*a*) 43. (*d*) 44. (100) 45. (6) 46. (*a*) 47. (*a*) 48. (*b*)
49. (*a*) 50. (*c*) 51. (*b*) 52. (*c*) 53. (*a*) 54. (*a*) 55. (*b*)

EXPLANATIONS

11. Comparing the upstream to the throat of a venturi meter, the pressure decreases and velocity increases.

13.

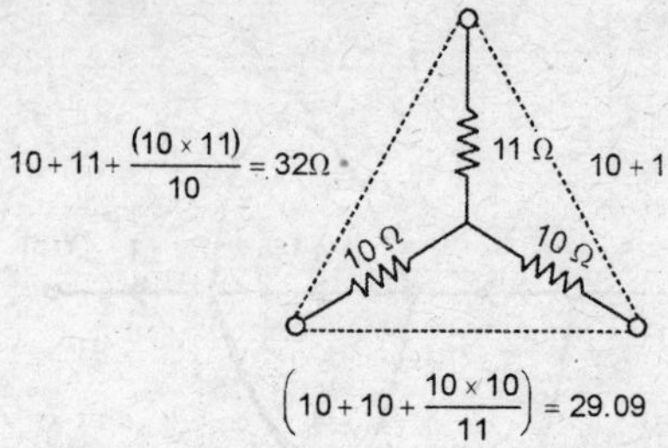

15.

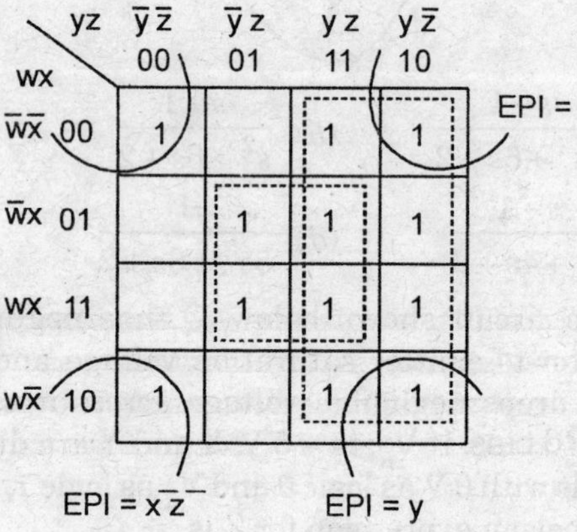

17.

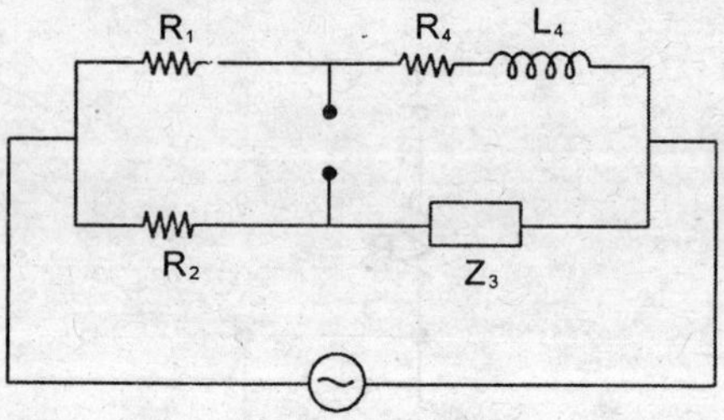

The balance condition for above bridge is

$$R_1Z_3 = R_2(R_4 + L_4)$$

$$\therefore \quad Z_3 = \frac{R_2}{R_1}(R_4 + L_4)$$

Hence to achieve balance in the bridge Z_3 should be replaced by combination of resistor and inductor *i.e* R and L.

18. The given function is $f(x) = x.e^{-x}$

Now differentiating the given function w.r.t. to x.

$$\frac{d}{dx}f(x) = \frac{d}{dx}x.e^{-x}$$

$$f'(x) = x\frac{d}{dx}e^{-x} + e^{-x}\frac{d}{dx}x$$

$$= -x\,e^{-x} + e^{-x}$$

$$= e^{-x}(1-x)$$

Now let $f'(x) = 0$

$\therefore \quad e^{-x}(1-x) = 0$

For $x = 1$ and ∞, $f'(x) = 0$

Now $f''(x) = e^{-x}\dfrac{d}{dx}(1-x) + (1-x)\dfrac{d}{dx}e^{-x}$

$$= e^{-x}(-1) - (1-x)\,e^{-x}$$

$$= -e^{-x}(1-(1-x))$$

$$= -e^{-x}(x)$$

$$= -x\,e^{-x}$$

For $x = 1$, $f''(x) = -1.e^{-1} < 0$

$\therefore$ At $x = 1$, the function attains a maximum value

$\therefore$ Maximum value of the function $f(x) = x\,e^{-x}$ in interval $(0, \infty)$ is at $x = 1$

$$\therefore \quad f(1) = 1.e^{-1} = e^{-1}$$

19. It is a source free network where capacitor voltage is given by

$$V_c(t) = V_0e^{-t/\tau}; t > 0$$

$$= 10e^{-t/r} \quad (\because V_0 = 10\text{ V})$$

Now $V = R_c$

$$= \frac{1}{1000}$$

$$\therefore \quad V_c(t) = 10e^{-1000t}$$

$$\therefore \quad V_c\left(10\times10^{-3}\right) = 10e^{-\left[100\times10\times10^{-3}\right]}$$

$$= 3.67\text{ V}$$

23. Residue at $z = 0$ is 0

$$\therefore \text{ By C.J.T} \oint\frac{dz}{z^2} = 2\pi i\times 0 = 0$$

25. Comparing $s^2 + 1$ with $s^2 + 2\xi\omega_n s + 2\omega_n^2$

we get $\xi = 0$

$$\therefore \ \%\text{ Overshoot} = e^{\frac{-\pi\xi}{\sqrt{1-\xi^2}}}\times 100 = 100$$

28. $$G(S).\,H(S) = \frac{K}{s(s+1)(9s+1)}$$

The phase cross over frequency is given by

$$\angle G(j\omega).\,H(j\omega) = -180$$

Now $$G(j\omega)\,H(j\omega) = \frac{K}{j\omega(j\omega+1)(9j\omega+1)}$$

Now $\angle G(j\omega)\,H(j\omega)$

$$= -90 - \tan^{-1}(\omega) - \tan^{-1}(9\omega)$$

Phase cross over frequency

$$\angle G(j\omega)\,H(j\omega) = -180°$$

$$\therefore \quad -90 - \tan^{-1}(\omega) - \tan^{-1}(9\omega) = -180$$

$$\therefore \quad -\tan^{-1}(\omega) - \tan^{-1}(9\omega) = -180 + 90$$

$$\therefore \quad -(\tan^{-1}\omega + \tan^{-1}(9\omega)) = -90$$

$\therefore \quad \tan^{-1}\omega + \tan^{-1} 9\omega = 90$

$\therefore \quad \tan^{-1}\left(\frac{\omega+9\omega}{1-9\omega^2}\right) = 90$

$\therefore \quad \frac{10\omega}{1-9\omega^2} = \tan 90$

$\therefore \quad \frac{10\omega}{1-9\omega^2} = \frac{1}{0}$

$\therefore \quad 1-9\omega^2 = 0$

$\therefore \quad 9\omega^2 = 1$

$\therefore \quad \omega = \pm\frac{1}{3}$

$\therefore \quad \omega = \frac{1}{3}$

29. $\pm(\alpha_1 + \alpha_2 + \alpha_3 +) = \pm 2\%. \pm (1.1 + 0.3 + 0.6) = \pm 2\%$

30.

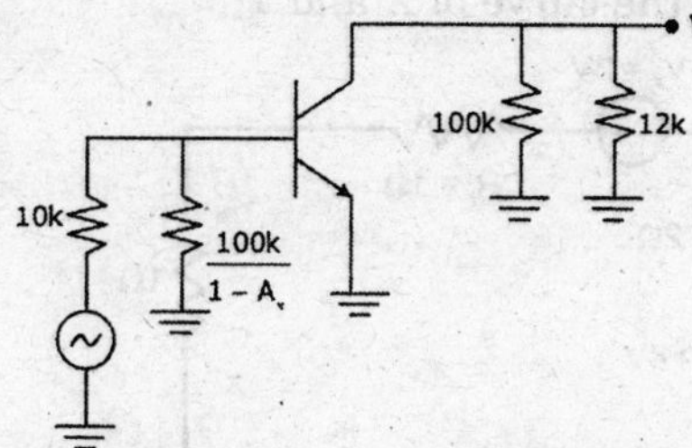

KVL in put loop, $13.7-(I_C+I_B)12k-100k(I_B)-0.7=0$

$\Rightarrow \quad I_B = 9.9\mu A;$

$I_C = \beta I_B = 0.99 mA;$

$I_E = 1 \text{ mA}$

$\therefore \quad r_e = \frac{26mA}{I_E} = 26\Omega;$

$z_i = \beta r_e = 2.6 \text{ k}\Omega;$

$\therefore \quad A_V = \frac{(100k\,||\,12k)}{26} = 412$

$z_i' = z_i\,||\left(\frac{100k}{1+412}\right) = 221\Omega;$

$A_{vs} = A_v\frac{z_i'}{z_i'+R_s}$

$= (412)\left(\frac{221}{221+10k}\right)$

$|A_{vs}| \approx 10$

31. The circuit shown in the figure is op-amp series Regulator

$\therefore \quad \frac{V_0}{V_z} = 1+\frac{R_1}{R_2}$

$\therefore \quad \frac{9}{4.7} = 1+\frac{1000}{R_2}$

$\therefore \quad \frac{9}{4.7} = \frac{R_2+1000}{R_2}$

$\therefore \quad 9R_2 = 4.7R_2 + 4700$

$4.3R_2 = 4700$

$\therefore \quad R_2 = 1093.023\ \Omega$

32. At $t = 0^-$

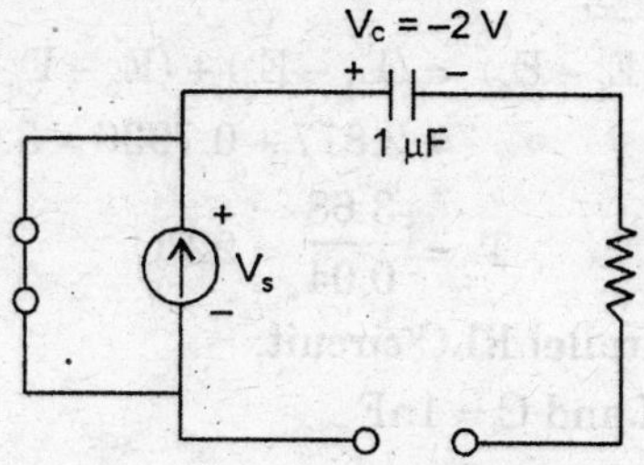

$\therefore \quad V_s = 0V|_{t=0^-}$

At $t = 0^+$

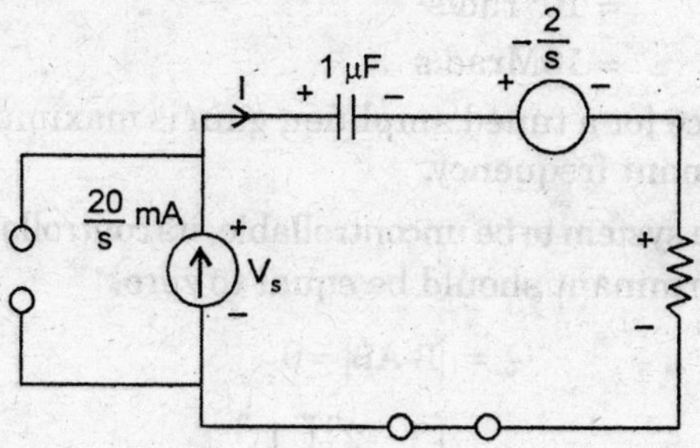

By KVL

$\left(\frac{-2}{s}\right)+\frac{1}{sC}+100I = V_s$

$\Rightarrow \quad \frac{-2}{s}+\frac{20\times10^{-3}}{s}\times\frac{1}{s\times10^{-6}}+100\times\frac{20\times10^{-3}}{s} = V_s$

$\Rightarrow \quad V_s = -\frac{2}{s}+\frac{20\times10^3}{s^2}+\frac{2}{s}$

$V_s(s) = \frac{2}{s^2}\times10^4$

$\therefore \quad V_s(t) = 2\ \ 10^4 t$

$\therefore$

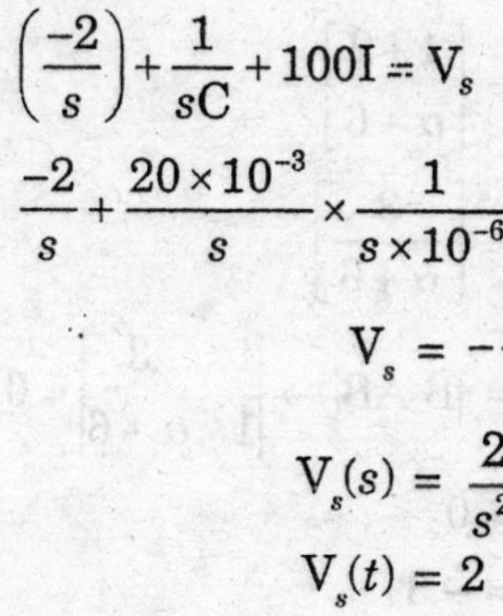

33. The Probability of Disease

$= \frac{1}{10}\times\frac{9}{10}+\frac{1}{10}\times\frac{95}{100}$

$= \frac{9}{100}+\frac{1}{10}\times\frac{19}{20}$

$= \frac{18+19}{200} = \frac{37}{200} = 0.185$

34. $\begin{bmatrix} \frac{3}{4}\Omega & \frac{1}{4}\Omega \\ \frac{1}{4}\Omega & \frac{3}{4}\Omega \end{bmatrix}$

35.
$$(E_i - E_0) = (E_1 - E_2) + (E_2 - E_0)$$
$$= 2.877 + 0.7936 = 3.68 \text{ mV}$$
$$\therefore \quad T = \frac{3.68}{0.04} = 92°C.$$

36. In the parallel RLC circuit,

L = 10μH and C = 1nF

$$\therefore \quad \omega_g = \frac{1}{\sqrt{LC}} = \frac{1}{\sqrt{10\times10^{-6}\times10^{-9}}}$$
$$= 10^7 \text{ rad/s}$$
$$= 10\text{Mrad/s}$$

Hence for a tuned amplifier, gain is maximum at resonant frequency.

38. For a system to be uncontrollable, its controllability determinant should be equal to zero.

$$\therefore \quad Q_c = |B \; AB| = 0$$

Now
$$AB = \begin{bmatrix} 1 & 2 \\ \alpha & 6 \end{bmatrix}\begin{bmatrix} 1 \\ +1 \end{bmatrix}$$
$$= \begin{bmatrix} 1+2 \\ \alpha+6 \end{bmatrix}$$
$$= \begin{bmatrix} 3 \\ \alpha+6 \end{bmatrix}$$
$$\therefore \quad Q_c = |B \; AB| \rightarrow \begin{vmatrix} 1 & 3 \\ 1 & \alpha+6 \end{vmatrix} = 0$$
$$\therefore \quad \alpha + 6 - 3 = 0$$
$$\therefore \quad \alpha = -3$$

For α = – 3, system will be uncontrolable.

39.

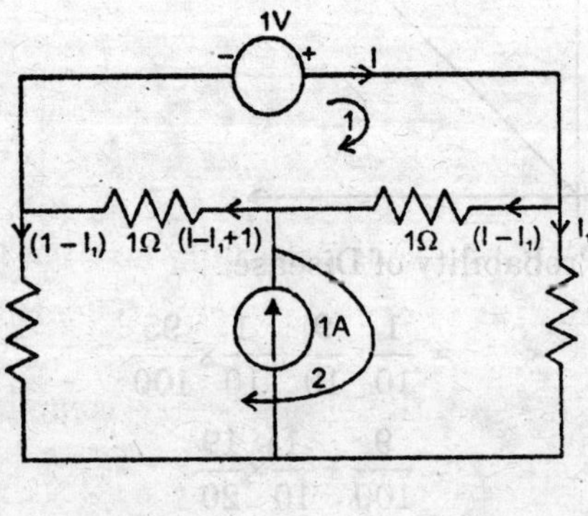

From loop 1
$$-1 + (I - I_1) + (I - I_1 + 1) = 0$$
$$2I - 2I_1 = 0$$
$$2I = 2I_1$$
$$\therefore \quad I = I_1$$

From loop 2
$$-(1 - I_1) - (I - I_1 + 1) - I + I_1 + I_1 = 0$$
$$-1 + I_1 - I + I_1 - 1 - I + I_1 + I_1 = 0$$
$$4I_1 - 2I - 2 = 0$$
$$2I_1 = 2 \qquad (\because I_1 = I)$$
$$\therefore \quad I_1 = 1A$$

40. The transfer characteristic curve and the circuit of a non ideal source is given below.

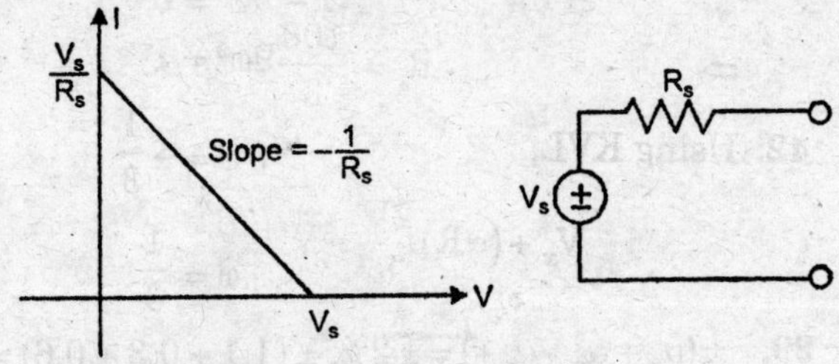

Comparing the curve of X and Y

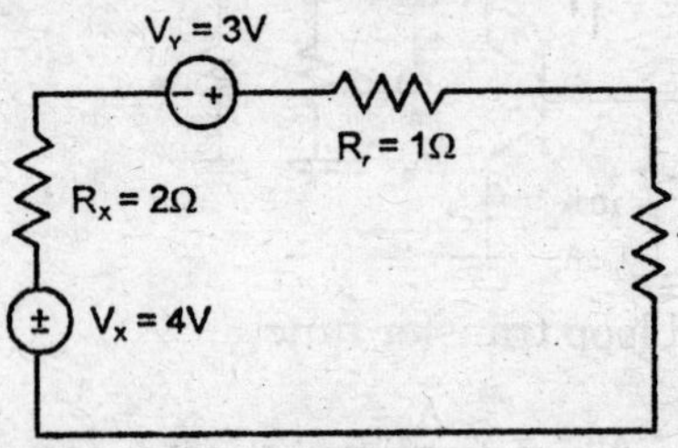

we can conclude that

X : $V_x = 4V, R_8 = 2W$

Y : $V_y = 3V, Ry = 1W$

When we connect these the circuit becomes,

$$I_{1\Omega} = \frac{4+3}{2+1+1} = 1.75 \text{ A}$$

41. When the current through galvanometer is 0 then its 2 end voltage are same or we can say the open circuit voltage across galvanometer is 0.

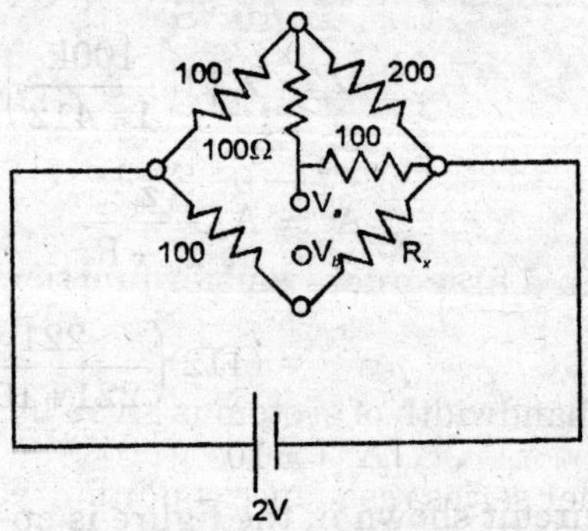

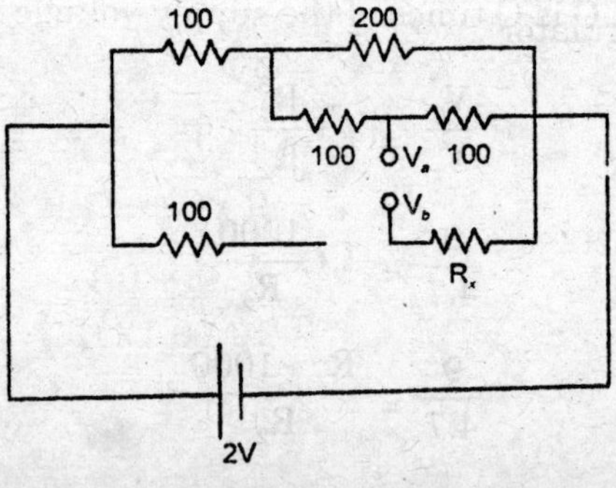

By voltage division rule

$$V_a = 0.5\ V$$

$$V_b = \left(\frac{2}{100 + R_x}\right) R_x$$

$$V_a = V_b$$

$$\frac{1}{2} = \frac{2R_x}{100 + R_x}$$

$$\Rightarrow \quad 100 + R_x = 4R_x$$

$$\Rightarrow \quad R_x = \frac{100}{3} = 33.33\ \Omega$$

42. Using KVL,

$$V_x + (\alpha R)\frac{2V}{R} - V = 0$$

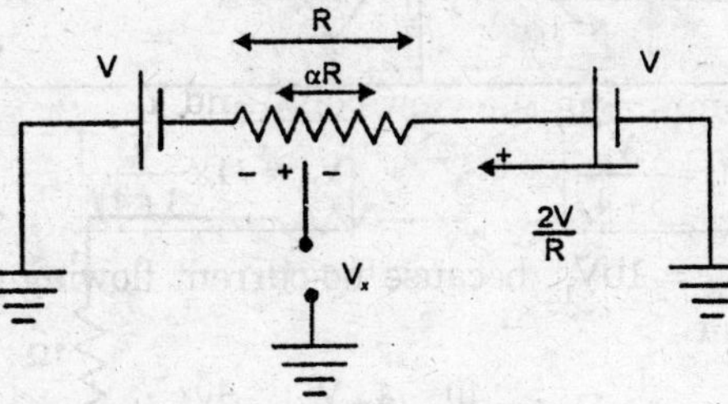

43. Closed loop transfer function A_{CL}

$$A_{CL} = \frac{A_{OL}}{1 + A_{OL}\beta}$$

Here $\quad A_{OL} = \dfrac{10^4}{1 + 10^{-3}S}$,

$$\beta = \frac{R_i}{R_i + R_f} = \frac{1}{9+1} = 0.1$$

$$A_{OL} = \frac{\dfrac{10^4}{1+10^{-3}S}}{1 + \dfrac{10^4 \times 0.1}{1+10^{-3}S}} = \frac{10^4}{1 + 10^{-3}S + 10^3}$$

$$= \frac{10}{10^{-3} + 10^{-6}S + 1} \approx \frac{10}{1 + \dfrac{S}{10^6}}$$

→ In a first order transfer function $\dfrac{k}{1 + S\tau}$

the bandwidth of system is given by $\dfrac{1}{\tau}$ B.W = 10^6

44. Under series resonance condition, voltage across L, C is Q times of the supply voltage.

$$V_C = QV$$

$$Q = \frac{1}{R}\sqrt{\frac{L}{C}}$$

$$= \frac{1}{10}\sqrt{\frac{0.1}{0.1 \times 10^{-6}}} = 100$$

$$V_c = QV$$

$$= (100)(1)$$

$$= 100V$$

45. $\quad \omega_0 = \dfrac{\text{H.C.F}(2\pi, \pi)}{\text{L.C.M}(3,1)} = \dfrac{\pi}{3}$

$$\frac{2\pi}{T} = \frac{\pi}{3}$$

$$\Rightarrow \quad T = 6\ \text{sec}$$

46. $\quad x(n) = \alpha^{|n|}$

$$= \alpha^n u(n) + \left(\frac{1}{\alpha}\right)^n u(-n-1)$$

$$|z| > \alpha\ ;\ |z| < \frac{1}{\alpha}$$

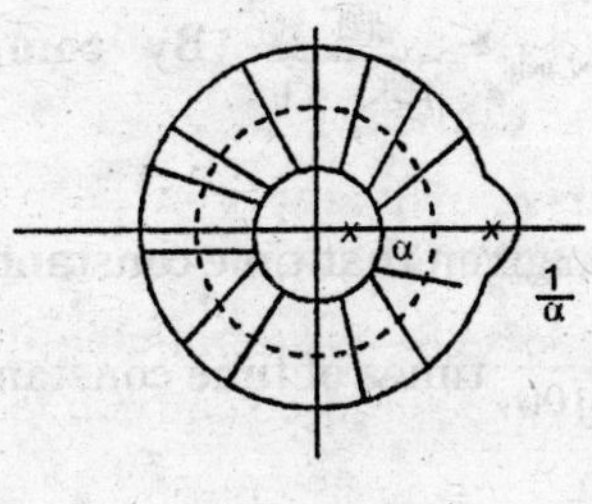

47. $\quad \lambda = j, -j$ are eigen values

$$(A - jI)x = 0 \Rightarrow \begin{bmatrix} -j & -1 \\ 1 & -j \end{bmatrix}\begin{bmatrix} x \\ y \end{bmatrix} = \begin{bmatrix} 0 \\ 0 \end{bmatrix}$$

$\therefore$ Eigen vector for $j = \begin{bmatrix} j \\ 1 \end{bmatrix}$

and $(A + jI)x = 0 \Rightarrow \begin{bmatrix} i & -1 \\ 1 & j \end{bmatrix}\begin{bmatrix} x \\ y \end{bmatrix} = \begin{bmatrix} 0 \\ 0 \end{bmatrix}$

$\therefore$ Eigen vector for $-j$ is $\begin{bmatrix} 1 \\ j \end{bmatrix}$

50. Given:

Open loop transfer function of a dc motor as

$$\frac{w(s)}{V_a(s)} = \frac{10}{1 + 10s}$$

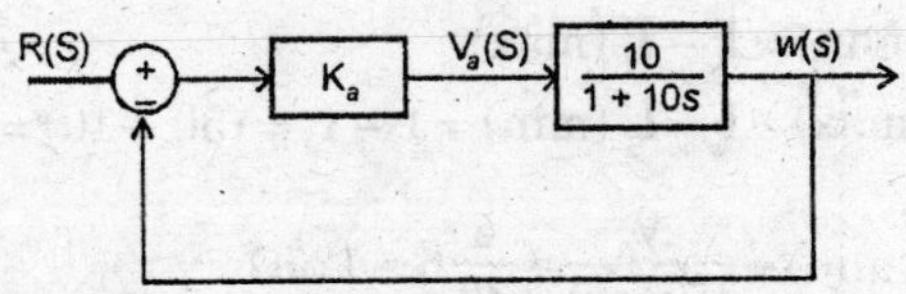

Topic : P controller with unity feed back

Formula: For first order system loop transfer function is $\dfrac{C(s)}{R(s)} = \dfrac{K}{1 + sT}$ comparing with

$$\frac{w(s)}{V_a(s)} = \frac{10}{1 + 10s} \quad T_{\text{open loop}} = 10$$

Now for closed loop overall transfer function is given by

$$\frac{w(s)}{R(s)} = \frac{K_a\left(\frac{10}{1+10s}\right)}{1+K_a\left(\frac{10}{1+10s}\right)}$$

$$= \frac{K_a 10}{1+10s+K_a 10} = \frac{10K_a}{10s+(10K_a+1)}$$

Dividing numerator and denominator by $10K_a + 1$

Now $$\frac{w(s)}{R(s)} = \frac{\frac{10K_a}{10K_a+1}}{1+\left(\frac{10}{10K_a+1}\right)s}$$

So $T_{closed\ loop} = \frac{10}{10K_a+1}$ (By comparing from formula)

In Question given that time constant of closed loop system is $\frac{1}{100}$ times of time constant of open loop system

so $\frac{10}{10K_a+1} = \frac{1}{100} 10 \left(T_{closed\ loop} = \frac{1}{100} T_{openloop}\right)$

$10\ K_a + 1 = 100$

$10\ K_a = 99$

$K_a = 9.9 \simeq 10$

$\therefore$ $\boxed{K_a = 10}$ approximate value

51. $I_s = I_z + I_L$

$I_s - I_z = I_L$

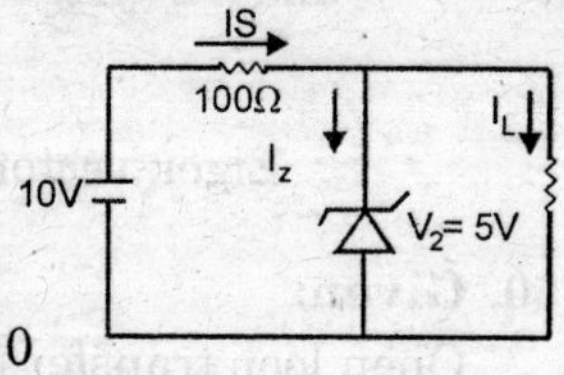

Two extreme condition:

If I_z(min), then I_L (max)

If I_z (max) then I_L (min) = 0

$I_z(\text{max}) = I_s = \frac{10-5}{10} = 50\text{ mA}$

$I_z(\text{min}) = I_s - I_L(\text{max})$

$I_L(\text{max}) = I_s - I_z(\text{min}) = I_s - I_z = (50 - 10) = 40\text{mA}$

$R_L(\text{min}) = \frac{V}{I_L(\text{max})} = \frac{5}{40}K = 125\Omega$

$P_z = V_z \times I_z(\text{max}) = 5 \times 50\text{ mA} = 250\text{ mw}$

52. Given: $V_s = 100\angle 53.13°V$

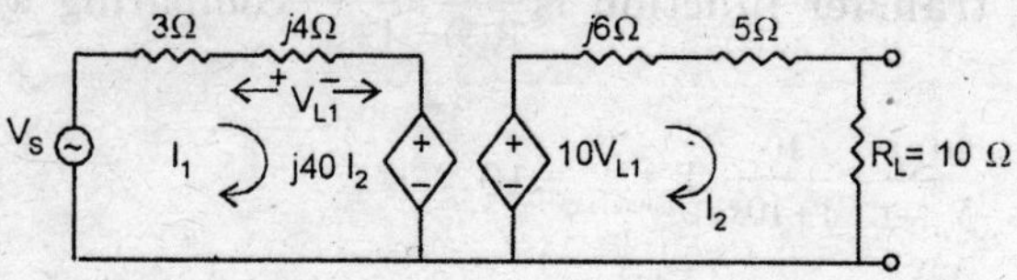

To find: Thevenin's voltage across Load resistonce

Solution

* For V_{th}' open it.

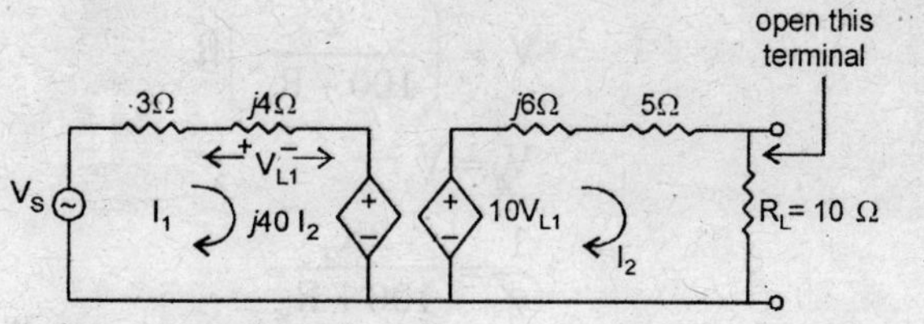

* Opening, then $I_2 = 0$
* When $I_2 = 0$, then $j40I_2 = 0$ {voltage source will short circuit)

$\therefore$ Circuit became

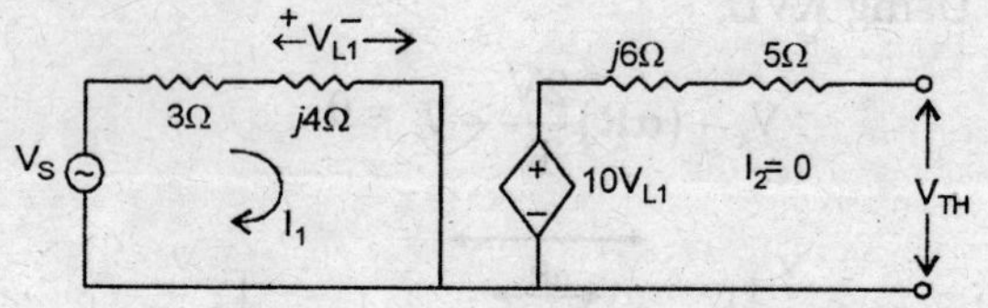

$\therefore$ $\boxed{I_1 = \frac{V_s}{3+4j}}$ $\therefore$ $\boxed{V_{L1} = j4 \times \frac{V_s}{3+4j}}$

* $V_{TH} = 10V_{L1}$ because no-current flowing through circuit.

$$V_{TH} = \frac{10 \times j4 \times V_s}{3+4j} = \frac{40j\ V_s}{3+4j}$$

From rectangular domain to polar domain.

$$= \frac{40\underline{|90°}}{5\underline{|53\cdot13}} \times 100\underline{|53\cdot13°}$$

$$\boxed{V_{TH} = 800\underline{|90°}}$$

54.

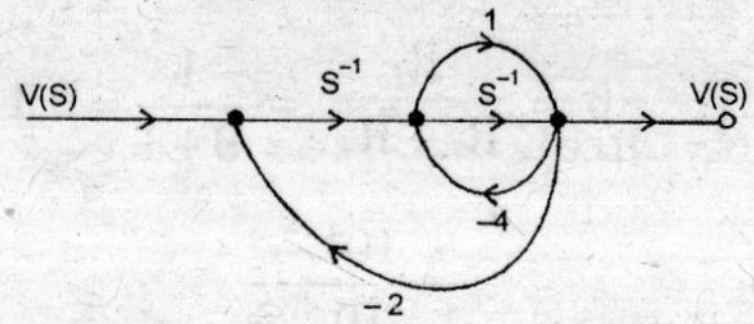

Forward path =

$P_1 = S^{-1}, S^{-1} = S^{-2}$ | $\Delta_1 = 1$

$P_2 = S^{-1}$ | $\Delta_2 = 1$

Loop =

$L_1 = -4S^{-1}$

$L_2 = -2S^{-1}S^{-1} = -2S^{-2}$

$L_3 = -2S^{-1}$

$L_4 = -4$

$$T(S) = \frac{S^{-2}+S^{-1}}{1+4+2S^{-1}+2S^{-2}+4S^{-1}}$$

$$= \frac{S^{-1}+S^{-2}}{S+6S^{-1}+2S^{-2}} = \frac{S+1}{5S^2+6S+2}$$

55.

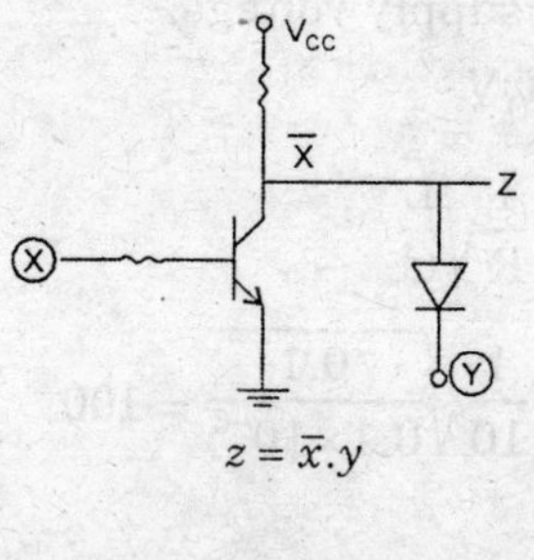

$z = \bar{x}.y$

SOLVED PAPER - 2018

INSTRUCTIONS

1. Total of 65 questions carrying 100 marks, out of which 10 questions carrying a total of 15 marks are in General Aptitude (GA)
2. The Engineering Mathematics will carry around **15% of the total marks,** the General Aptitude section will carry **15% of the total marks** and the **remaining 70% of the total marks.**
3. **Types of Questions**
   (*a*) **Multiple Choice Questions (MCQ)** carrying 1 or 2 marks each in all papers and sections. These questions are objective in nature, and each will have a choice of four options, out of which the candidate has to mark the correct answer(s).
   (*b*) **Numerical Answer Questions** of 1 or 2 marks each in all papers and sections. For these questions the answer is a real number, to be entered by the candidate using the virtual keypad. No choices will be shown for these type of questions.
4. For **1-mark** multiple-choice questions, **1/3 marks** will be deducted for a wrong answer. Likewise, for **2-marks** multiple-choice questions, **2/3** marks will be deducted for a wrong answer. There is no negative marking for numerical answer type questions.

Chapter-Wise Analysis

#	Chapters	Marks		
		1	2	Total
1	General Aptitude	5	5	15
2	Electrical Circuits	3	4	11
3	Signals and Systems	3	5	13
4	Control Systems	1	2	5
5	Analog Electronics	2	4	10

#	Chapters	Marks		
		1	2	Total
6	Digital Electronics	2	3	8
7	Measurements	2	3	8
8	Sensors and Industrial Instrumentation	1	3	7
9	Communications	2	2	6
10	Optical Instrumentation	1	2	5

GENERAL APTITUDE

1. "When she fell down the ______. She received many ______ but little help." The words that best fill the blanks in the above sentence are

(*a*) stairs, stares

(*b*) stairs, stairs

(*c*) stares, stairs

(*d*) stares, stares

2. "In spite of being warned repeatedly, he failed to correct his ______ behaviour." The word that best fills that blank in the above sentence is

(*a*) rational (*b*) reasonable

(*c*) errant (*d*) good

3. For $0 \le x \le 2\pi$, sinx and cosx are both decreasing functions in the interval ______.

(*a*) $\left\{0, \frac{\pi}{2}\right\}$ (*b*) $\left\{\frac{\pi}{2}, \pi\right\}$

(*c*) $\left\{\pi, \frac{\pi}{2}\right\}$ (*d*) $\left\{\frac{3\pi}{2}, 2\pi\right\}$

4. The area of an equilateral triangle is $\sqrt{3}$. What is the perimeter of the triangle?

(*a*) 2

(*b*) 4

(*c*) 6

(*d*) 8

5. Arrange the following three-dimensional objects in the descending order of their volumes:

(i) A cuboid with dimensions 10 cm, 8 cm and 6 cm

(ii) A cube of side 8 cm

(iii) A cylinder with base radius 7 cm and height 7 cm

(iv) A sphere of radius 7 cm

(*a*) (i), (ii), (iii), (iv)

(*b*) (ii), (i), (iv), (iii)

(*c*) (iii), (ii), (i), (iv)

(*d*) (iv), (iii), (ii), (i)

6. An automobile travels from city A to city B and returns to city A by the same route. The speed of the vehicle during the onward and return journeys were constant at 60 km/h and 90 km/h, respectively. What is the average speed in km/h for the entire journey?

(*a*) 72 (*b*) 73

(*c*) 74 (*d*) 75

7. A set of 4 parallel lines intersect with another set of 5 parallel lines. How many parallelograms are formed?

(*a*) 20 (*b*) 48

(*c*) 60 (*d*) 72

8. To pass a test, a candidate needs or answer at least 2 out of 3 questions correctly. A total of 6,30,000 candidates appeared for the test. Question A was correctly answered by 3,30,000 candidates. Question B was answered correctly by 2,50,000 candidates. Question C was answered correctly by 2,60,000 candidates. Both questions A and B were answered correctly by 1,00,000 candidates. Both questions B and C were answered correctly by 90,000 candidates. Both questions A and C were answered correctly by 80,000 candidates. If the number of students answering all questions correctly is the same as the number answering none, how many candidates failed to clear the test?

(*a*) 30,000 (*b*) 2,70,000

(*c*) 3,90,000 (*d*) 4,20,000

9. If $x^2 + x - 1 = 0$ what is the value of $x^4 + \frac{1}{x^4}$?

(*a*) 1 (*b*) 5

(*c*) 7 (*d*) 9

10. In a detailed study of annual crow births in India, it was found that there was relatively no growth during the period 2002 to 2004 and a sudden spike from 2004 to 2005. In another unrelated study, it was found that the revenue from cracker sales in India which remained fairly flat from 2002 to 2004, saw a sudden spike in 2005 before declining again in 2006. The solid line in the graph below refers to annual sale of crackers and the dashed line refers to the annual crow births in India. Choose the most appropriate inference from the above data.

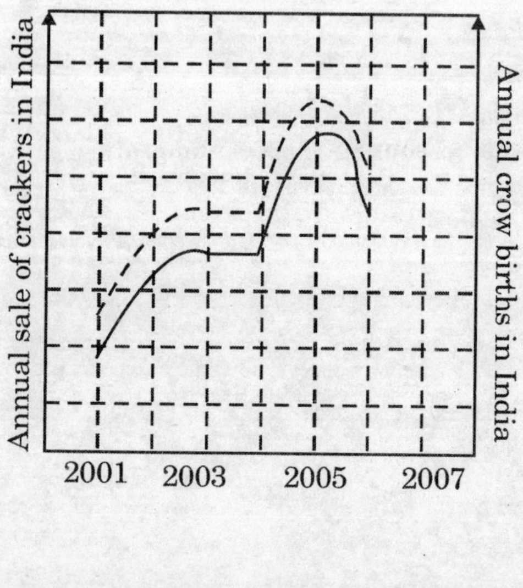

(*a*) There is a strong correlation between crow birth and cracker sales.

(*b*) Cracker usage increases crow birth rate.

(*c*) If cracker sale declines, crow birth will decline.

(*d*) Increased birth rate of crows will cause an increase in the sale of crackers.

TECHNICAL SECTION

1. Let N be a 3 by 3 matrix with real number entries. The matrix N is such that $N^2 = 0$. The eigen values of N are

(*a*) 0, 0, 0 (*b*) 0, 0, 1

(*c*) 0, 1, 1 (*d*) 1, 1, 1

2. Let $f_1(z) = z^2$ and $f_2(z) = \bar{Z}$ be two complex variable function. Here $\bar{Z}$ is the complex conjugate of z. Choose the correct answer.

(*a*) Both $f_1(z)$ and $f_2(z)$ are analytic

(*b*) Only $f_1(z)$ is analytic

(*c*) Only $f_2(z)$ is analytic

(*d*) Both $f_1(z)$ and $f_2(z)$ are not analytic

3. X and Y are two independent random variables with variances 1 and 2, respectively. Let Z = X – Y. The variance of Z is

(*a*) 0 (*b*) 1

(*c*) 2 (*d*) 3

4. Consider two functions $f(x) = (x - 2)^2$ and $g(x) = 2x - 1$, where x is real. The smallest value of x for which f(x) = g (x) is ________.

5. Considers a sequence of tossing of a fair coin where the outcomes of tosses are independent. The probability of getting the head for the third time in the fifth toss is

(*a*) $\frac{5}{16}$ (*b*) $\frac{3}{16}$

(*c*) $\frac{3}{5}$ (*d*) $\frac{9}{16}$

6. A series R-C circuit is excited by a $1\angle 0$ V sinusodial ac voltage source. The locus diagram of the phasor current I = (x + jy) A. When C is varied, while keeping R fixed, is

(*a*)

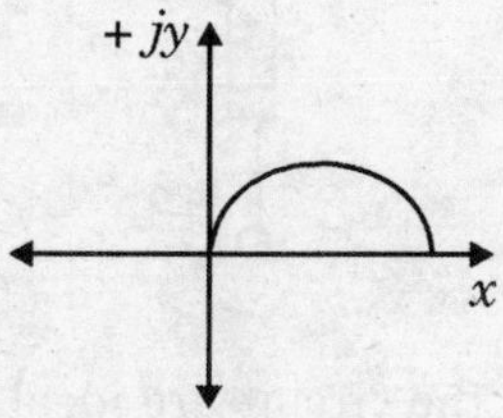

(*b*)

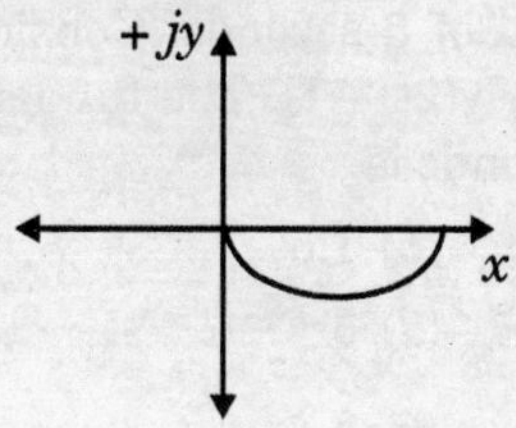

(*c*)

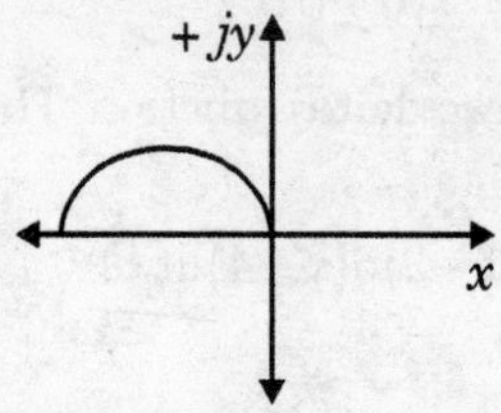

(*d*)

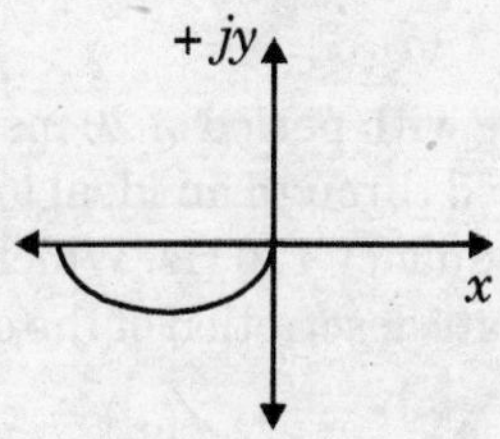

7. The Thevenin equivalent circuit representation across terminals p-q of the circuit shown in the figure is a

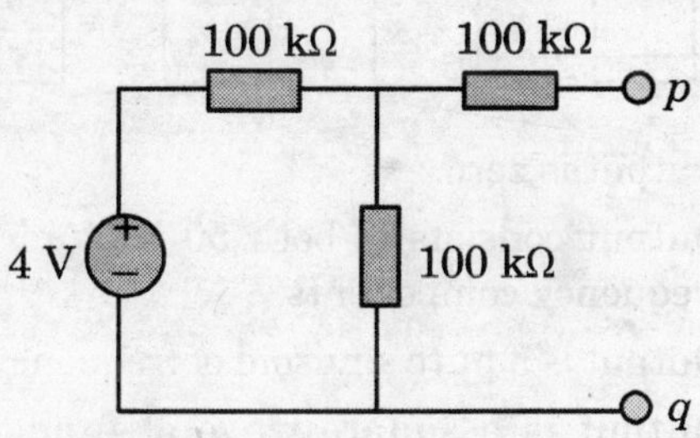

(*a*) 1 V source in series with 150 kΩ

(*b*) 1 V source in parallel with 100 kΩ

(*c*) 2 V source in series with 150 kΩ

(*d*) 2 V source in parallel with 200 kΩ

8. A coil having an impedance of (10 + j100) Ω is connected in parallel to a variable capacitor as shown in figure. Keeping the excitation frequency unchanged, the value of the capacitor is changed so that parallel resonance occurs. The impedance across terminals p - q at resonance (in Ω) is

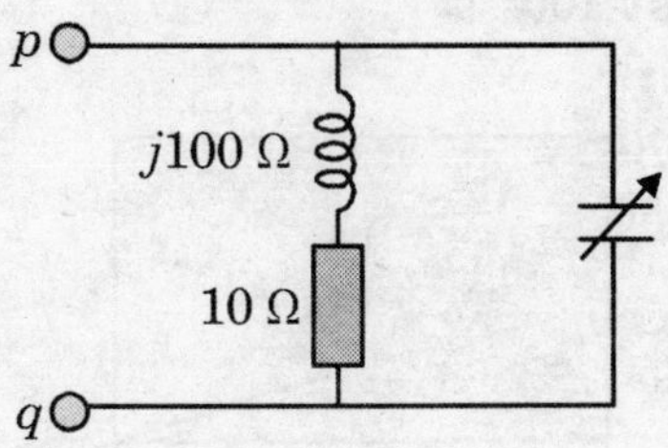

9. Two periodic signals x(t) and y(t) have the same fundamental period of 3 seconds. Consider the signal z(t) = x(–t) + y(2t + 1). The fundamental period of z(t) in seconds is

(*a*) 1 (*b*) 1.5

(*c*) 2 (*d*) 3

10. Consider signal $x(t)=\begin{cases}1, & |t|\le 2\\ 0, & |t|>2\end{cases}$. Let δ(t) denote the unit impulse (Dirac-delta) function. The value of the integral $\int_0^5 2x(t-3)\delta(\tau-4)dt$ is

(*a*) 2 (*b*) 1

(*c*) 0 (*d*) 3

11. An ideal square wave with period of 20 ms shown in the figure, is passed through an ideal low pass filter with cut-off frequency 120 Hz. Which of the following is an accurate description of the output?

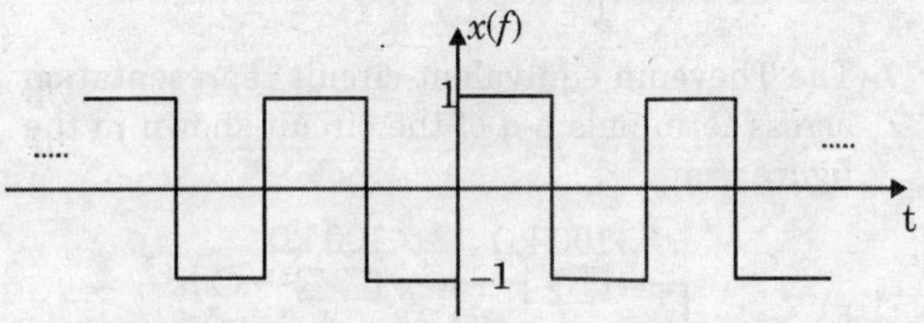

(*a*) Output is zero.

(*b*) Output consists of both 50 Hz and 100 Hz frequency components.

(*c*) Output is a pure sinusoid of frequency 50 Hz.

(*d*) Output is a square wave of fundamental frequency 50 Hz.

12. An input p(t) = sin(t) is applied to the system $G(s)=\frac{s-1}{s+1}$. The corresponding steady state output is y(t) = sin(t + ϕ), where the phase f (in degrees). When restricted to 0° ≤ f ≤ 360°, is ________.

13. The approximate phase response of $\frac{100^2 e^{-0.01s}}{s^2+0.2s+100^2}$ is

(*a*)

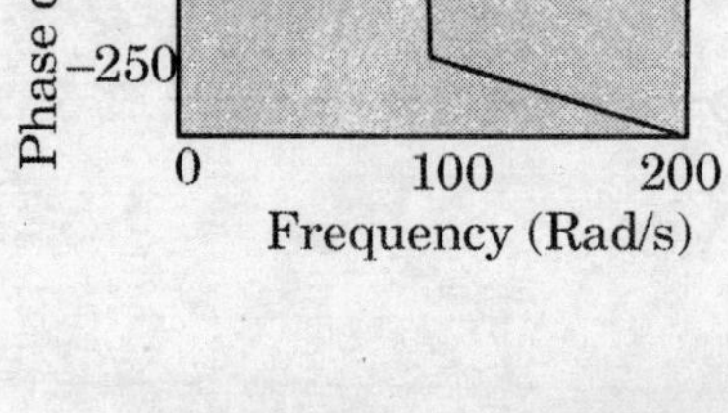

(*b*)

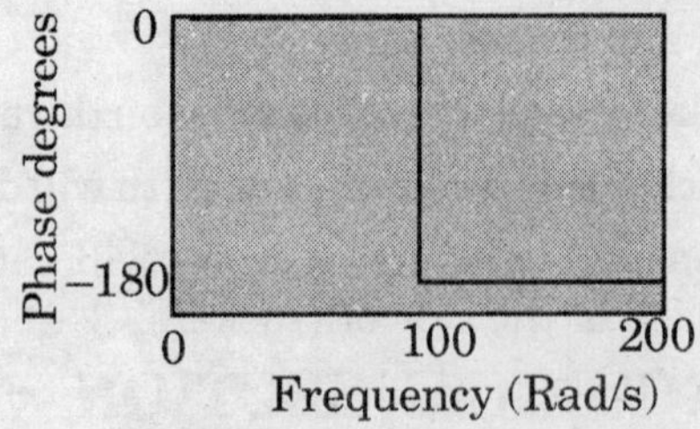

(*c*)

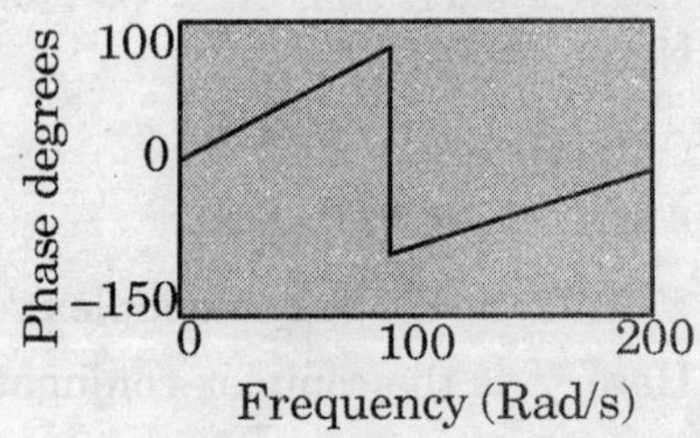

(*d*)

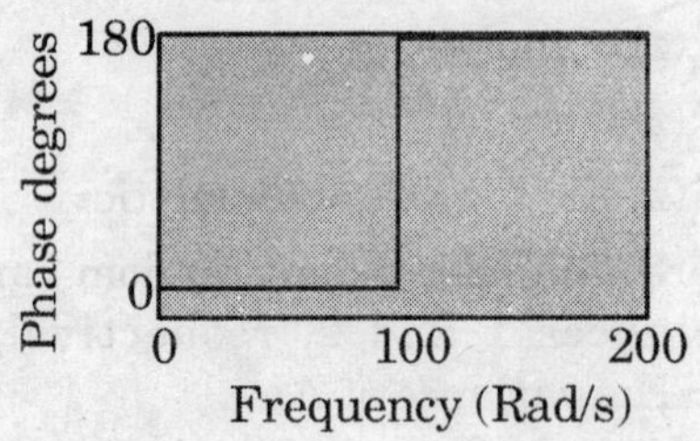

14. Consider the transfer function

$G(s)=\frac{2}{(s+1)(s+2)}$. The phase margin of G(s) in degrees is ________.

15. In the given circuit, assume that the opamp is ideal and the transistor has a β of 20. The current I_0 (in μA) following through, the load Z_L is

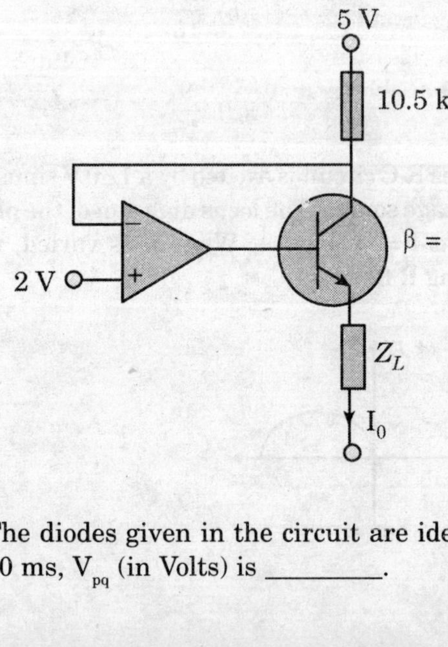

16. The diodes given in the circuit are ideal. At t = 60 ms, V_{pq} (in Volts) is ________.

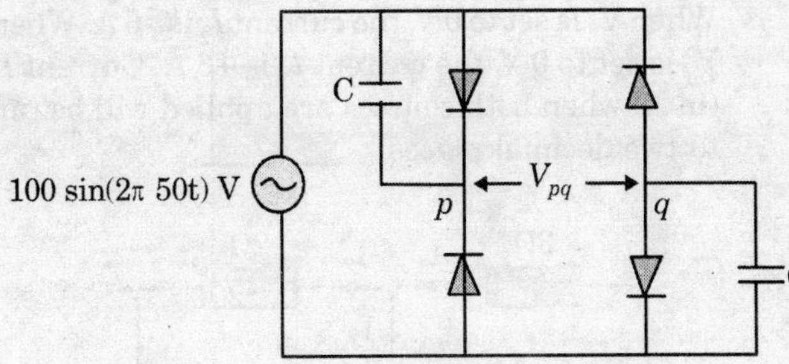

17. For the 3-bit binary counter shown in the figure, the output increments at every positive transition in the clock (CLK). Assume ideal diodes and the starting state of the counter as 000. If output high is 1 V and output low is 0 V, the current I (in mA) flowing through the 50 Ω resistor during the 5th clock cycle is (up to one decimal place) ________.

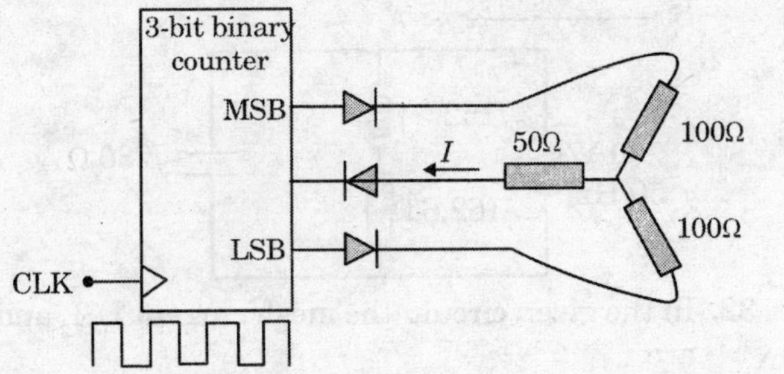

18. The representation of the decimal number $(27.625)_{10}$ in base-2 number system is

(*a*) 11011.110 (*b*) 11101.101

(*c*) 11011.101 (*d*) 10111.110

19. The number of comparators required for implementing an 8-bit flash analog-to-digital converter is

(*a*) 8 (*b*) 128

(*c*) 255 (*d*) 256

20. A voltage of 6cos(100πt) V is fed as y-input to a CRO. The waveform seen on the screen of the CRO is shown in the figure. The Y and X axes settings for the CRO are respectively

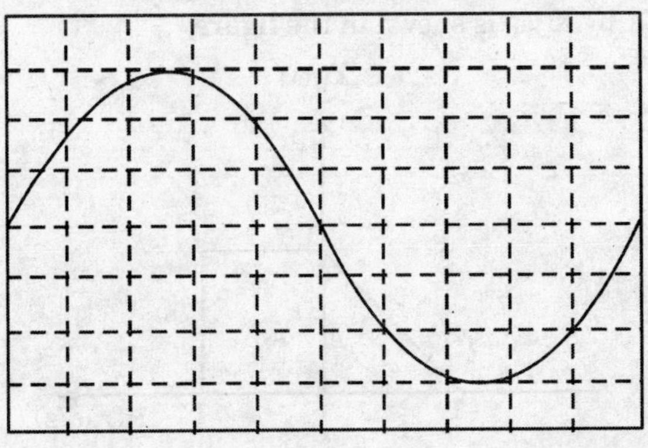

(*a*) 1 V/div and 1 ms/div

(*b*) 1 V/div and 2 ms/div

(*c*) 2 V/div and 1 ms/div

(*d*) 2 V/div and 2 ms/div

21. A 300 V, 5 A, 0.2 pf low power factor wattmeter is used to measure the power consumed by a load. The wattmeter scale has 150 divisions and the pointer is on the 100th division. The power consumed by the load (in Watts) is ________.

22. As shown in the figure, temperature θ is measured using a K type thermocouple. It has a sensitivity of 40 μV/°C. The gain (G) of the ideal instrumentation amplifier is 25. If the output V_0 is 96 mV, then the value of θ (in °C) is ________.

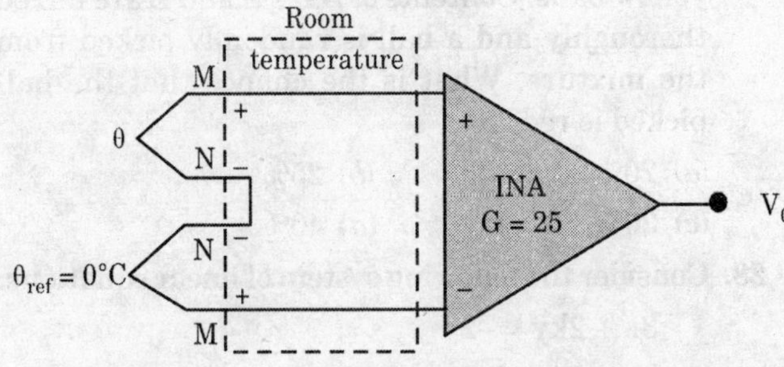

23. A piezoelectric pressure sensor has a bandpass characteristic with cut-off frequencies of 0.1 Hz and 1 MHz and a senstivity of 100 mV/kPa. The sensor is subjected to a static constant pressure of 100 kPa. Its steady-state output will be

(*a*) 0 V (*b*) 0.1 V

(*c*) 1 V (*d*) 10 V

24. An amplitude modulated signal is shown in the figure. The modulation index is (up to one decimal place) ________.

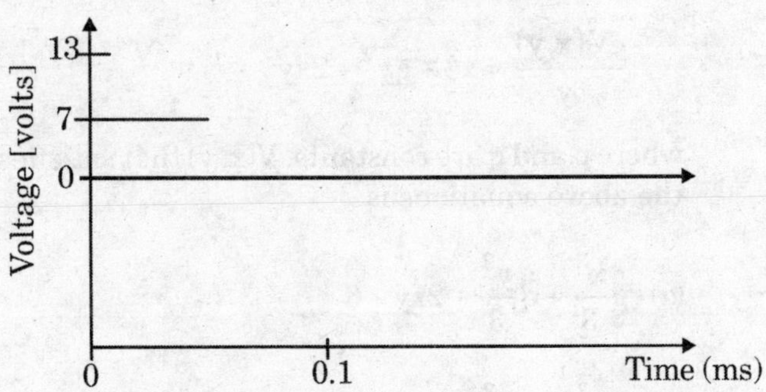

25. An optical pulse containing 6 × 10^6 photons is incident on a photodiode and 4.5 × 10^6 electron-hole pairs are created. The maximum possible quantum efficiency (in %) of the photodiode is ________.

26. Given $\vec{F} = \left(x^2 - 2y\right)\vec{i} - 4yz\vec{j} + 4xz^2\vec{k}$, the value of the line integral $\int_c \vec{F}\cdot dl$ along the straight line c from (0, 0, 0) to (1, 1, 1) is

(*a*) $\frac{3}{16}$ (*b*) 0

(*c*) $\frac{-5}{12}$ (*d*) –1

27. Two bags A and B have equal number of balls. Bag A has 20% red balls and 80% green balls. Bag B has 30% red balls. 60% green balls and 10% yellow balls. Contents of Bags A and B are mixed thoroughly and a ball is randomly picked from the mixture. What is the chance that the ball picked is red?

(*a*) 20% (*b*) 25%

(*c*) 30% (*d*) 40%

28. Consider the following system of linear equations:

$3x + 2ky = -2$

$kx + 6y = 2$

Here, x and y are the unknown and k is a real constant. The value of k for which there are infinite number of solutions is

(*a*) 3 (*b*) 1

(*c*) –3 (*d*) –6

29. Consider the following equations

$$\frac{\partial V(x,y)}{\partial x} = px^2 + y^2 + 2xy$$

$$\frac{\partial V(x,y)}{\partial y} = x^2 + qy^2 + 2xy$$

where p and q are constants. V(x, y) that satisfies the above equations is

(*a*) $p\frac{x^3}{3} + q\frac{y^3}{3} + 2xy + 6$

(*b*) $p\frac{x^3}{3} + q\frac{y^3}{3} + 5$

(*c*) $p\frac{x^3}{3} + q\frac{y^3}{3} + x^2y + xy^2 + xy$

(*d*) $p\frac{x^3}{3} + q\frac{y^3}{3} + x^2y + xy^2$

30. In the given circuit, superposition is applied. When V_2 is set to 0 V, the current I_2 is –6 A. When V_1 is set to 0 V, the current I_1 is +6 A. Current I_3 (in A) when both sources are applied will be (up to two decimal places) ________.

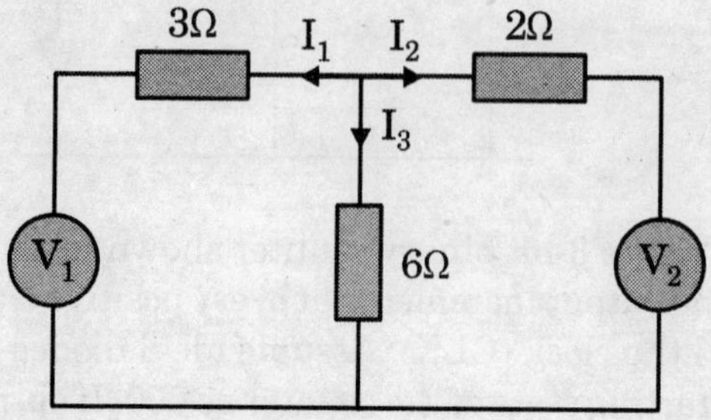

31. In the figure, an RLC load is supplied by a 230 V, 50 Hz single phase source. The magnitude of the reactive power (in VAr) supplied by the source is ________.

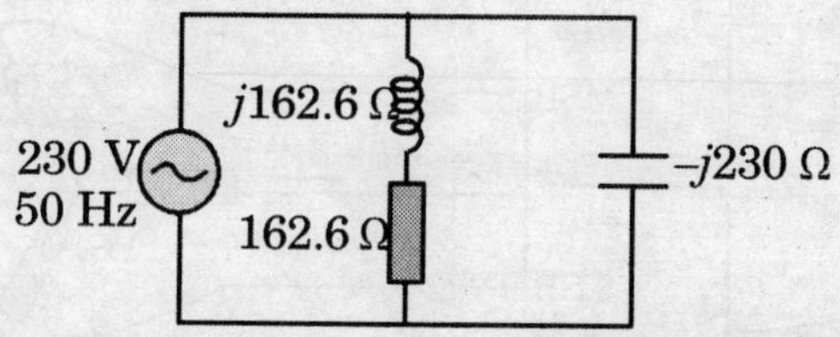

32. In the given circuit the mesh current I_1, I_2 and I_3 are

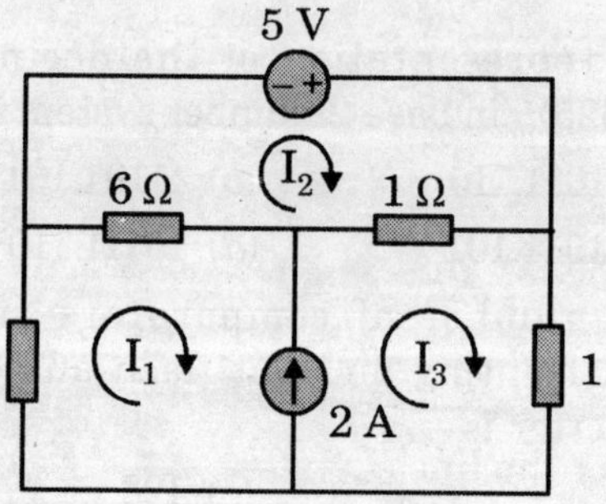

(*a*) I_1 = 1 A, I_2 = 2 A and I_3 = 3 A

(*b*) I_1 = 2 A, I_2 = 3 A and I_3 = 4 A

(*c*) I_1 = 3 A, I_2 = 4 A and I_3 = 5 A

(*d*) I_1 = 4 A, I_2 = 5 A and I_3 = 6 A7

33. The Fourier Transform of a signal x(t), denoted by X(jω) is shown in the figure.

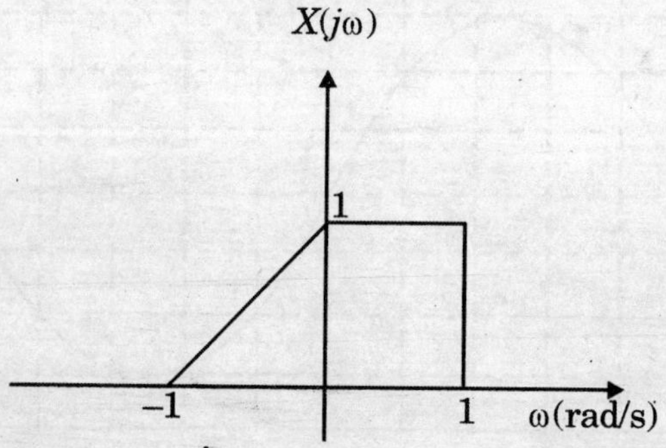

Let $y(t) = x(t) + e^{jt}x(t)$. The value of Fourier transform of y(t) evaluated at the angular frequency $\omega = 0.5$ rad/s is

(a) 0.5 (b) 1

(c) 1.5 (d) 2.5

34. Let $y[n] = x[n] * h[n]$, where * denotes convolution and x[n] and h[n] are two discrete time sequence. Given that the z-transform of y[n] is $Y(z) = 2 + 3z^{-1} + z^2$, the z-transform of $p[n] = x[n] * h[n-2]$ is

(a) $2 + 3z + z^{-2}$

(b) $3z + z^{-2}$

(c) $2z^2 + 3z + 1$

(d) $2z^{-2} + 3z^3 + z^{-4}$

35. For the sequence $x[n] = \{1, -1, 1, -1\}$, with n = 0, 1, 2, 3 the DFT is computed as

$$X(k) = \sum_{n=0}^{3} x[n]e^{-j\frac{2\pi}{4}nk}$$, for k = 0, 1, 2, 3. The value of k for which X(k) is not zero is

(a) 0 (b) 1

(c) 2 (d) 3

36. Consider the standard negative feedback configuration with $G(s) = \frac{s^2 + 0.2s + 100}{s^2 - 0.2s + 100}$ and

$H(s) = \frac{1}{2}$. The number of clockwise encirclements of (–1, 0) in the Nyquist plot of the Loop transfer-function G(s) H(s) is ________.

37. Consider the linear system $\dot{x} = \begin{bmatrix} -1 & 0 \\ 0 & -2 \end{bmatrix}x$, with

initial condition $x(0) = \begin{bmatrix} 1 \\ 1 \end{bmatrix}$. The solution x(t) for

this system is

(a) $x(t) = \begin{bmatrix} e^{-t} & te^{-2t} \\ 0 & e^{-2t} \end{bmatrix}\begin{bmatrix} 1 \\ 1 \end{bmatrix}$

(b) $x(t) = \begin{bmatrix} e^{-t} & 0 \\ 0 & e^{-2t} \end{bmatrix}\begin{bmatrix} 1 \\ 1 \end{bmatrix}$

(c) $x(t) = \begin{bmatrix} e^{-t} & -t^2e^{-2t} \\ 0 & e^{-2t} \end{bmatrix}\begin{bmatrix} 1 \\ 1 \end{bmatrix}$

(d) $x(t) = \begin{bmatrix} e^{-t} & 0 \\ 0 & e^{-2t} \end{bmatrix}\begin{bmatrix} 1 \\ 1 \end{bmatrix}$

38. Consider a standard negative feedback configuration with $G(s) = \frac{1}{(s+1)(s+2)}$ and

$H(s) = \frac{s+\alpha}{s}$. For the closed loop system to have poles on the imaginary axis, the value of α should be equal to (up to one decimal place) ________.

39. Unit step response of a linear time invariant (LTI) system is given by $y(t) = (1 - e^{-2t})\,u(t)$. Assuming zero initial condition, the transfer function of the system is

(a) $\frac{1}{s+1}$ (b) $\frac{2}{(s+1)(s+2)}$

(c) $\frac{1}{s+2}$ (d) $\frac{2}{s+2}$

40. In the given relaxation oscillator, the opamps and the zener diodes are ideal. The frequency (in kHz) of the square wave output v_0 is ________.

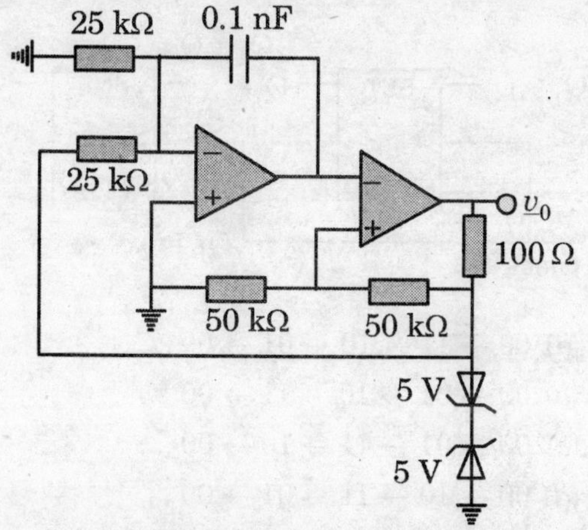

41. An opamp that is powered from a ± 5 V supply is used to build a non-inverting amplifier having a gain of 15. The slew rate of the opamp is 0.5×10^6 V/s. For a sinusoidal input with amplitude of 0.3 V, the maximum frequency (in kHz) up to which it can be operated without any distortion is (up to one decimal place) ________.

42. The circuit given use ideal opamps. The current *I* (in μA) drawn from the source v_s is (up to two decimal places) ________.

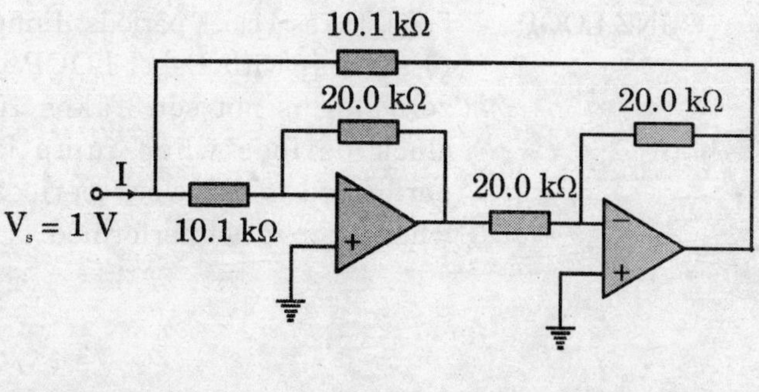

43. The product of sum expression of a Boolean function F(A, B, C) of three variables is given by

$$F(A+B+C) = (A+B+\bar{C}).(A+\bar{B}+\bar{C})$$
$$.(\bar{A}+B+C).(\bar{A}+\bar{B}+\bar{C})$$

The canonical sum of product expression of F(A, B, C) is given by

(*a*) $\bar{A}\bar{B}C + \bar{A}BC + A\bar{B}\bar{C} + ABC$

(*b*) $\bar{A}\bar{B}\bar{C} + \bar{A}B\bar{C} + A\bar{B}C + AB\bar{C}$

(*c*) $AB\bar{C} + A\bar{B}\bar{C} + \bar{A}BC + \bar{A}\bar{B}\bar{C}$

(*d*) $\bar{A}\bar{B}\bar{C} + \bar{A}BC + AB\bar{C} + ABC$

44. A 2-bit synchronous counter using two J-K flip flops is shown. The expressions for the inputs to the J-K flip flops are also shown in the figure. The output sequence of the counter starting from $Q_1Q_2 = 00$ is

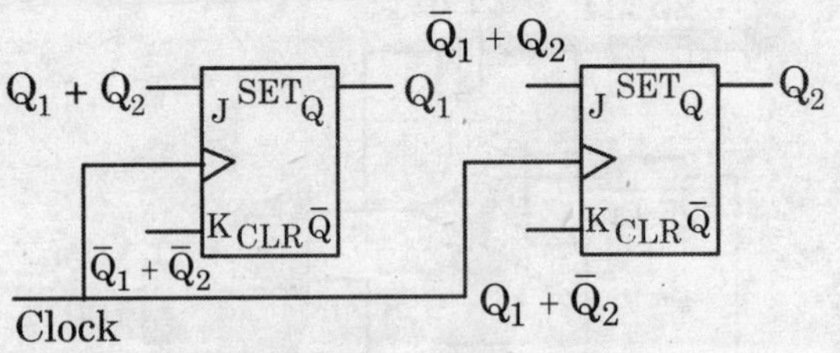

(*a*) 00 → 11 → 10 → 01 → 00 ....

(*b*) 00 → 01 → 10 → 11 → 00 ....

(*c*) 00 → 01 → 11 → 10 → 00 ....

(*d*) 00 → 10 → 11 → 01 → 00 ....

45. A portion of an assembly language program written for an 8-bit microprocessor is given below along with explanations. The code is intended to introduce a software time delay. The processor is driven by a 5 MHz clock. The time delay (in μs) introduced by the program is ________.

MVI B, 64 H : Move immediate the given byte into register B. Takes 7 clock periods.

LOOP : DCRB JNZ LOOP Decrement register B. Affects flags. Takes 4 clock periods. Jump to address with Label LOOP if zero flag is not set. Takes 10 clock periods when jump is performed and 7 clock periods when jump is not performed.

46. The Boolean function F(X, Y) realized by the given circuit is

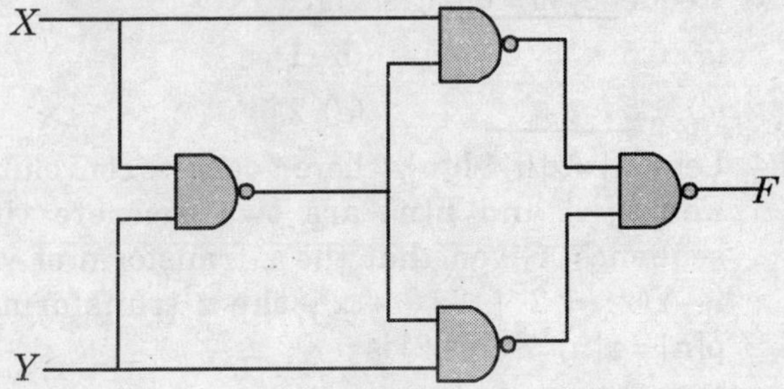

(*a*) $\bar{X}Y + X\bar{Y}$ (*b*) $\bar{X}\bar{Y} + XY$

(*c*) $\bar{X} + Y$ (*d*) $\bar{X} . \bar{Y}$

47. The voltage and current drawn by a resistive load are measured with a 300 V voltmeter of accuracy ± 1% of full scale and a 5 A ammeter of accuracy ± 0.5% of full scale. The readings obtained are 200 V and 2.5 A. The limiting error (in %) in computing the load resistance is (up to two decimal places) ________.

48. A high Q coil having distributed (self) capacitance is tested with Q-meter. First resonance at $\omega_1 = 10^6$ rad/s is obtained with a capacitance of 990 pF. The second resonance at $\omega_2 = 2 \times 10^6$ rad/s is obtained with a 240 pF capacitance. The value of the inductance (in mH) of the coil is (up to one decimal place) ________.

49. The inductance of a coil is measured using the bridge shown in the figure. Balance (D = 0) is obtained with C_1 = 1 nF, R_1 = 2.2 MΩ, R_2 = 22.2 kΩ, R_4 = 10 kΩ.

The value of the inductance L_x (in MH) is______.

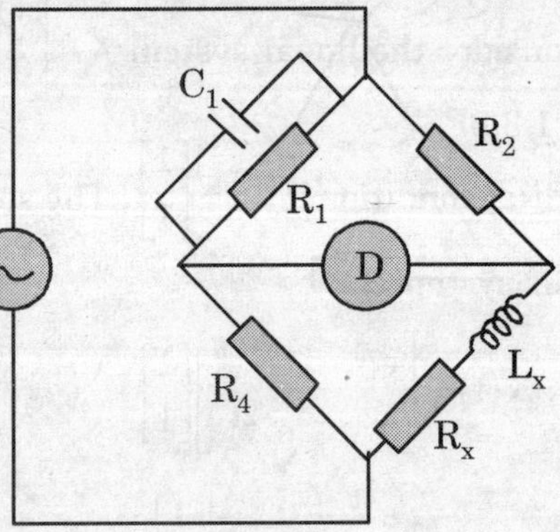

50. The average velocity v of flow of clear water in a 100 cm (inner) diameter tube is measured using the ultrasonic flow meter as shown in the figure. The angle θ is 45°. The measured transit times are t_1 = 0.9950 ms and t_2 = 1.0000 ms. The velocity v (in m/s) in the pipe is (up to one decimal place) ________.

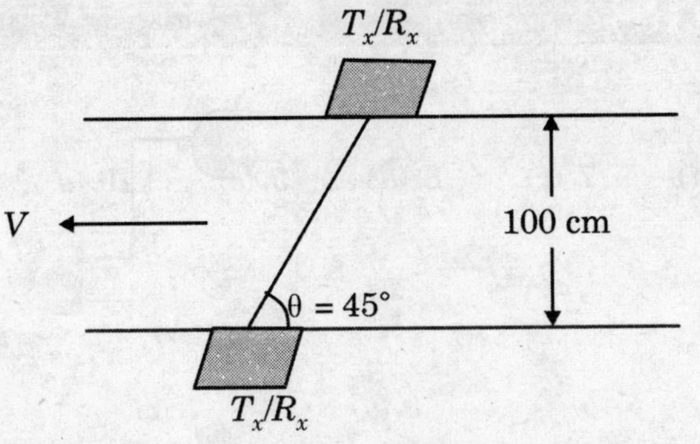

51. A 1000 Ω strain gauge (R_g) has a gauge factor of 2.5. It is connected in the bridge as shown in figure. The strain gauge is subjected with a positive strain of 400 μm/m. The output V_0 (in mV) of the bridge is (up to two decimal places) ________.

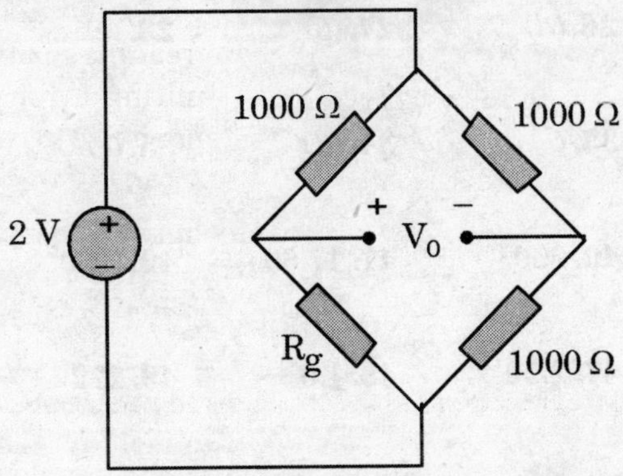

52. Assuming ideal opamp, the RMS voltage (in mV) in the output V_0 only due to the 230 V, 50 Hz interference is (up to one decimal place) ________.

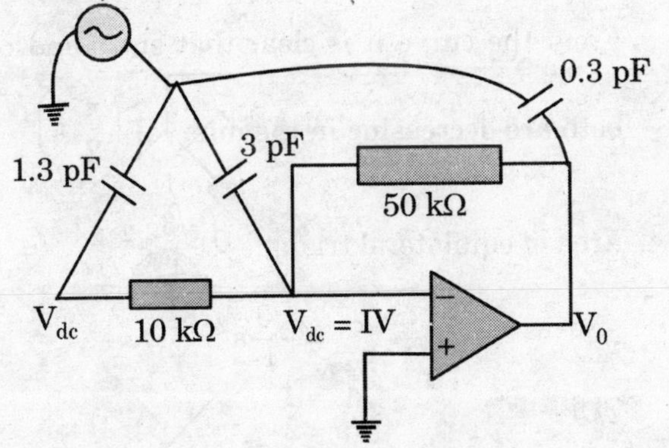

53. The sampling rate for Compact Discs (CDs) is 44,000 samples/s. If the samples are quantized to 256 levels and binary coded, the corresponding bit rate (in bits per second) is ________.

54. A Michelson Interferometer using a laser source of wavelength λ_0 = 500 nm with both the mirrors (M_1 and M_2) fixed and positioned equidistant from the splitter/combiner is shown in the figure. When a dielectric plate of refractive index n = 1.5, of thickness t, is placed in front of the mirror M_2, a dark fringe is observed on the detector. When the dielectric plate is removed without changing the position of the mirrors M_1 & M_2, a bright fringe is observed on the detector. The minimum thickness t (in nm) of the dielectric is ________.

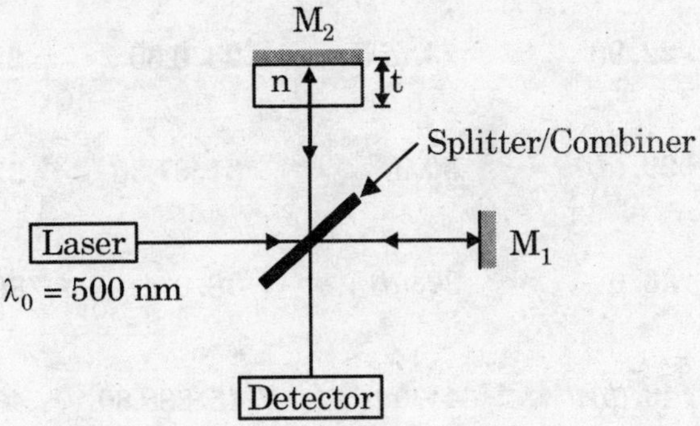

55. A multi-mode optical fiber with a large core diameter has a core refractive index n_1 = 1.5 and cladding refractive index n_2 = 1.4142. The maximum value of θ_A (in degrees) for which the incident light from air will be guided in the optical fiber is ± ________.

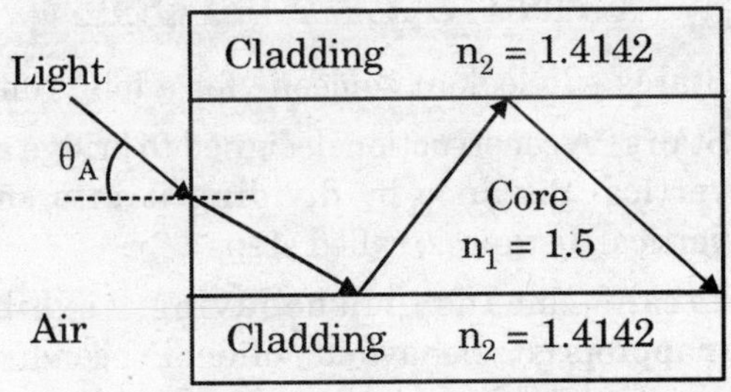

ANSWERS

General Aptitude (GA)

1. (*a*)	**2.** (*c*)	**3.** (*b*)	**4.** (*c*)	**5.** (*d*)	**6.** (*a*)	**7.** (*c*)	**8.** (*d*)	**9.** (*c*)	**10.** (*a*)

Technical Section

1. (*a*)	**2.** (*b*)	**3.** (*d*)	**4.** 1	**5.** (*b*)	**6.** (*a*)	**7.** (*c*)
8. 1010	**9.** (*d*)	**10.** (*a*)	**11.** (*c*)	**12.** 90	**13.** (*a*)	**14.** 180
15. 300	**16.** 200	**17.** 10	**18.** (*c*)	**19.** (*c*)	**20.** (*d*)	**21.** 200
22. 96	**23.** (*a*)	**24.** 0.30	**25.** 75	**26.** (*d*)	**27.** (*b*)	**28.** (*c*)
29. (*d*)	**30.** 1	**31.** 67.36	**32.** (*a*)	**33.** (*c*)	**34.** (*d*)	**35.** (*c*)
36. 0	**37.** (*d*)	**38.** 9	**39.** (*d*)	**40.** 200	**41.** 17.69	**42.** 0.99
43. (*b*)	**44.** (*c*)	**45.** 280.80	**46.** (*a*)	**47.** 2.50	**48.** 1.0	**49.** 222
50. 5.02	**51.** 0.5	**52.** 10.84	**53.** 352000	**54.** 250	**55.** 30	

EXPLANATIONS

GENERAL APTITUDE

1. Stares - To look at someone for a long time

Stairs - A construction designed to bridge a large vertical distance by dividing it into smaller vertical distances, called steps

2. Errant means misbehaving, exhibiting inappropriate behaviour / offending conduct.

3.

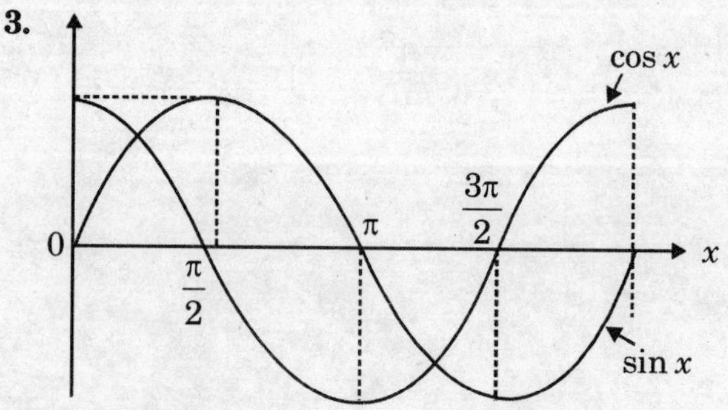

From the curve it is clear that sin x and cos x both are decreasing in the interval $\left(\frac{\pi}{2}, \pi\right)$

4. Area of equilateral triangle = $\frac{\sqrt{3}}{4}a^2$

$\therefore \quad \sqrt{3} = \frac{\sqrt{3}}{4}a^2$

$\therefore \quad a^2 = 4$

$\therefore \quad a = 2$

Now perimeter of equilateral triangle

$= 3a = 3 \times 2 = 6$

5. (i) Volume of cuboid = $(8 \times 10 \times 6)$ cm^3 = 480 cm^3

(ii) Volume of cube = $(8 \times 8 \times 8)$ cm^3 = 512 cm^3

(iii) Volume of cylinder = $\pi r^2 h$

$\left(\frac{22}{7} \times 7 \times 7 \times 7\right)$ cm^3 = 1078 cm^3

(iv) Volume of Sphere $= \frac{4}{3}\pi r^3 = \left(\frac{4}{3}\pi \times (7)^2\right) cm^3$

$= 1436.75\ cm^3$

Hence, the descending order of their volumes is (iv), (iii), (ii), (i).

6. Average speed $= \frac{2(S_1 \times S_2)}{S_1 + S_2}$

$= \frac{2(60 \times 90)}{(60+90)}$ km/h

$= \frac{2 \times 60 \times 90}{150} = 72$ km/h

7. Number of parallelogram $= {}^4C_2 \times {}^5C_2$

$= \frac{4!}{2! \times 2!} \times \frac{5!}{3! \times 2!}$

$= 6 \times \frac{5 \times 4}{2}$

$= 60$

8.

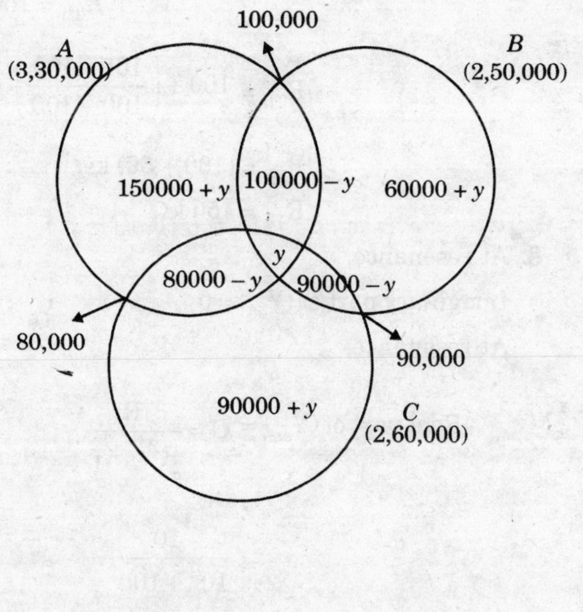

From above diagram,

$\therefore$ 6,30,000 = 2y + 1,50,000 + 100000 + 80000 + 60000 + 90000 + 90000

$\therefore$ 63000 = 2y + 57000

$\therefore$ 6,30,000 – 5,70,000 = 2y

$\therefore$ 60000 = 2y

$\therefore$ y = 30000

Students who failed to clear the test

= 150000 + 60000 + 90000 + 4y

= 300000 + 4 × 30000 ($\because$ y = 30000)

= 420000

Students who failed to clear the test = 420000

9. $x^2 - 1 = -x$

$x - \frac{1}{x} = -1$

$x^2 + \frac{1}{x^2} = 0.2$

Now, $x^4 + \frac{1}{x^4} = \left(x^2 + \frac{1}{x^2}\right)^2 - 2$

$= (3)^2 - 2$

$= 9 - 2$

$= 7$

TECHNICAL SECTION

1. $N^2 = 0$

Let the eigen values of N are $\lambda^1, \lambda^2, \lambda^3$:

Now eigen values of N^2 will be $\lambda^2{}_1, \lambda^2{}_2, \lambda^2{}_3$

But $N^2 = 0$

$\Rightarrow \lambda_1^2 = 0, \lambda_2^2 = 0, \lambda_3^2 = 0$

$\therefore$ Eigen values of N are 0, 0, 0

2. Only $f_1(z) = z^2$ is analytic

$f_2(z) = \bar{Z}$ is not analytic

3. $Var(aY) = a^2 Var(Y)$

So, $Var(-Y) = (-1)^2 Var(Y)$

$= var(Y)$ ($\because a = -1$)

Since X and Y are independent random variables,

$\therefore Var(Z) = Var(X) + Var(-Y)$

$= Var(X) + Var(Y)$

$= 1 + 2 = 3$

4. $(x-2)^2 = 2x-1$

$x^2 - 6x + 5 = 0$

$x = 1, 5$

$\therefore$ Smallest value of 'x' is 1

5. Probability of getting head in a toss $= p = \frac{1}{2}$

Probability of getting tail in a toss $= q = 1 - p = \frac{1}{2}$

$$\text{Required probability} = \begin{pmatrix}\text{Probability of getting}\\ \text{2 heads in first 4 tosses}\end{pmatrix} \times \begin{pmatrix}\text{Probability of getting}\\ \text{head in } 5^{th} \text{ toss}\end{pmatrix}$$

$$= \left({}^4C_2p^2q^2\right) \times \left(\frac{1}{2}\right)$$

$$= \frac{4!}{(4-2)!\,2!} \times \frac{p^2+q^2}{2}$$

$$= \frac{4!}{2! \times 2!} \times \frac{p^2q^2}{2}$$

$$= 6 \times \frac{1}{4} \times \frac{1}{4} \times \frac{1}{2}$$

$$= \frac{6}{32} = \frac{3}{16}$$

6.

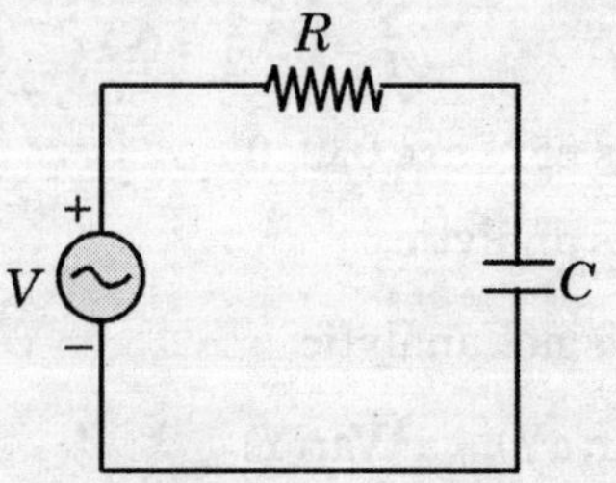

$C = \infty$	$C \downarrow$	
$X_C = 0$	$X_C \uparrow$	$C = 0$
$Z = R$	$Z \uparrow$	$X_C = \infty$
$I = V/R$	$I \downarrow$	$Z = \infty$
$\theta = 0$	$\theta = \tan^{-1}\left(\frac{-X_C}{R}\right) \uparrow$	$I = 0$

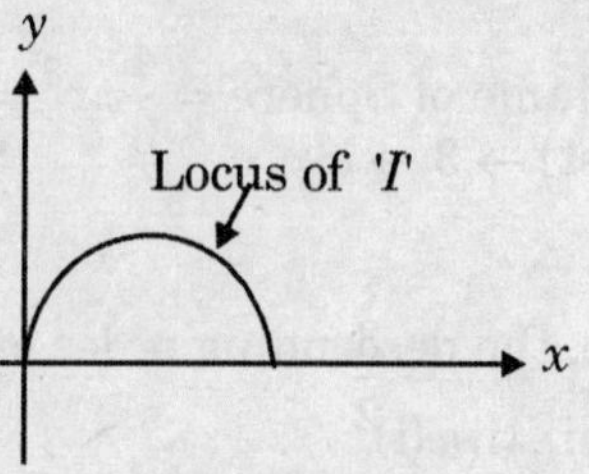

7. Case I: (V_{OC}) (short circuited)

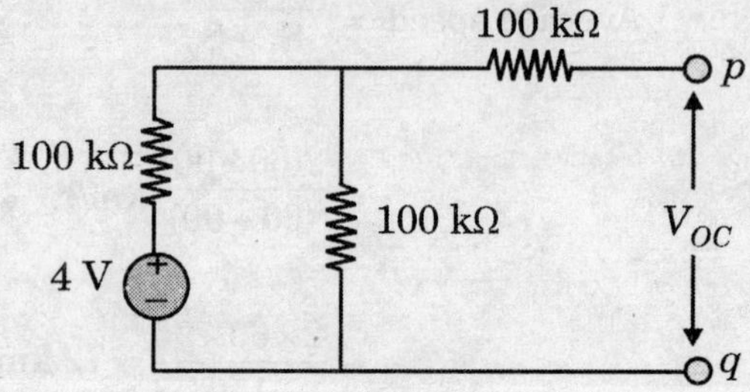

$$V_{OC} = 4 \times \frac{100}{100+100} = 2V$$

Case II: (R_{Th}) (Open circuited)

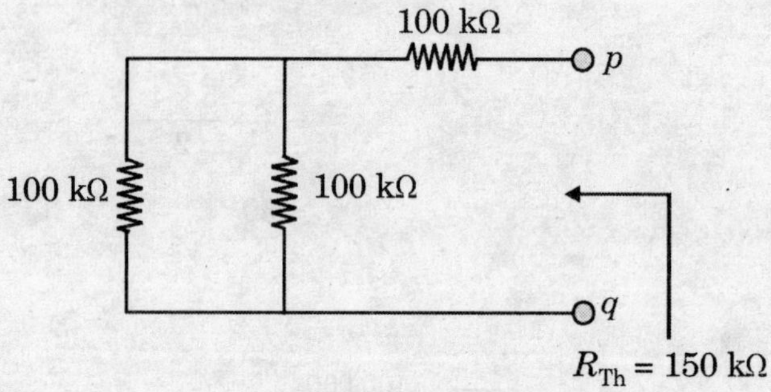

$$R_{Th} = 100 + \left(\frac{100 \times 100}{100+100}\right)$$

$$R_{Th} = (100 + 50)\ k\Omega$$

$$R_{Th} = 150\ k\Omega$$

8. At resonance,

Imaginary part of $(Y_{eq}) = 0$

At resonance,

$$\text{Real part of } (Y_{eq}) = G = \frac{R}{R^2 \times X_L^2}$$

$$= \frac{10}{10^2 + 100^2}$$

Now $$Z = \frac{1}{G} = \frac{100 + 10000}{10}$$

$$= \frac{10100}{10} = 1010\Omega$$

9. $x(-t) \rightarrow 3 \rightarrow \omega_{01} = \frac{2\pi}{3}$

$y(2t+1) \rightarrow \frac{3}{2} \rightarrow \omega_{02} = \frac{2\pi}{3/2} = \frac{4\pi}{3}$

Now, $\omega_0 = \text{GCD}\left\{\frac{2\pi}{3}, \frac{4\pi}{3}\right\}$

Now, $\omega_0 = \frac{2\pi}{T}$

$T = \frac{2\pi}{2\pi/3} = 3\,\text{sec}$

10. $\int_0^5 2x(t-3)\cdot\delta(t-4)dt$

$= 2\int_0^5 x(t-3)\cdot\delta(t-4)dt = 2x(1) = 2$

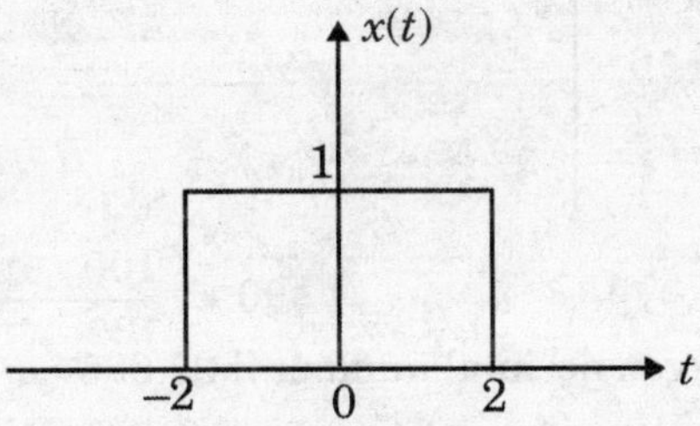

11. $T = 20$ msec

Fundamental frequency,

$(f_0) = \frac{1}{20\,\text{m sec}} \frac{1000}{20} = 50$ Hz

The given signal is an odd signal and it also has half wave symmetry. So, it will have spectral components only for odd harmonics. So, the spectrum of the signal will have component of 50 Hz, 150 Hz, 250 Hz, 350 Hz, ...

When passed through an LPF of cut-off frequency 120 Hz, the output of filter has only 50 Hz component. So, option (c) is correct.

12. $G(s) = \frac{s-1}{s+1}$

$p(t) = \sin t$

$y(t) = \sin(t + \phi)$

$\therefore \quad \phi = \angle p(t) + \angle G(j\omega)$ at $\omega = 1$

$= 0° + 180° - 90°$

$= 90°$

13. $\text{TF} = \frac{100^2 e^{-0.01s}}{s^2 + 0.2s + 100^2}$

Here, phase of $\frac{100^2}{s^2 + 0.2s + 100^2}$ varies from 0° to –180° as $\omega : 0 \rightarrow \infty$, therefore $e^{-0.01s}$ causes further phase lag, hence the correct answer is (a).

14. $G(s) = \frac{2}{(s+1)(s+2)}$

Phase margin (PM) = $180° + \angle G(j\omega)\big|_{\omega=\omega_{gc}}$

Now at, $\omega = \omega_{gc}$, $|G(j\omega)|_{\omega=\omega_{gc}} = 1$

$\therefore \quad \frac{2}{\sqrt{\omega_{gc}^2 + 1}\sqrt{\omega_{gc}^2 + 4}} = 1$

$\therefore \quad \omega_{gc} = 0$

And PM = (180° + 0) =180°

15. $V_C = 2V$

Now $I_C = \frac{5V - 2V}{10.5k\Omega} = \frac{3}{10.5}$ mA

Now $I_0 = I_E = \frac{(1+\beta)I_C}{\beta}$

$= \frac{21 \times 3}{20 \times 10.5}$ mA

$= 0.3$ mA

$= 300\ \mu$A

16.

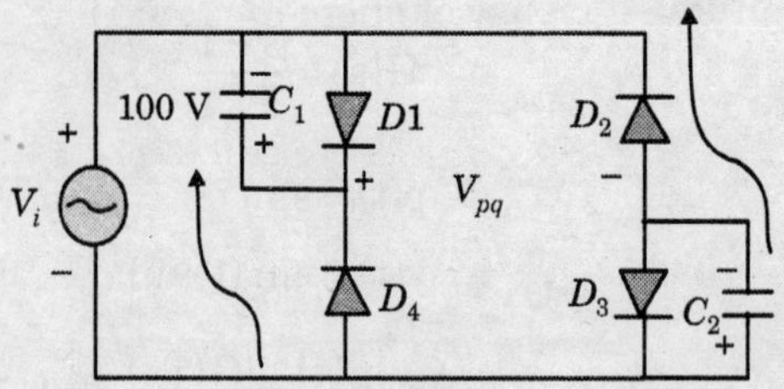

During +ve cycle: D_2 and D_4 are OFF ⇒ no current flows.

During –ve cycle:

C_1 charges through D_4 upto 100 V

and C_2 charges through D_2 upto 100 V

Now applying KVL, we get

$$-V_i - 100 + V_{pq} - 100 = 0$$

$$\therefore \quad V_{pq} = 200 + V_i$$

At t = 60 msec, $V_i = 0$

$$V_{pq} = 200 \text{ V}$$

17. Equivalent circuit,

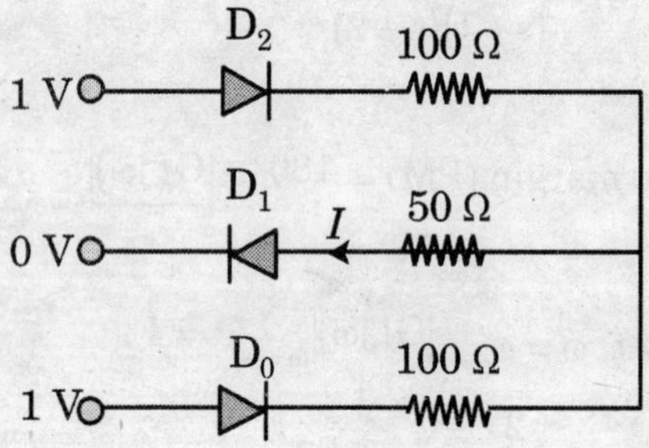

Let us assume all the three diodes are in ON state. Hence equivalent circuit will be:

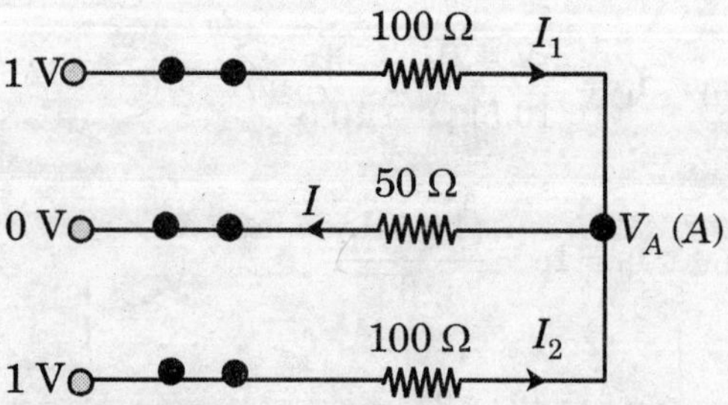

Now applying KCL at node A, we get,

$$\frac{1-V_A}{100} + \frac{1-V_A}{100} = \frac{V_A - 0}{50}$$

$$\therefore \quad \frac{1-V_A}{50} = \frac{V_A}{50}$$

$$\therefore \quad V_A = 1 - V_A$$

$$\therefore \quad V_A = \frac{1}{2} V$$

Now $\quad I_1 = \frac{1-V_A}{100} = \frac{1}{200} A = 5mA$

and $\quad I_2 = \frac{1-V_A}{100} = \frac{1}{200} A = 5mA$

$$\therefore \quad I = \frac{V_A}{50} = \frac{1}{100} A = 10mA$$

$I_1 > 0, I_2 > 0, I > 0.$ ∴ our assumption is correct and the correct answer is,

$$\therefore \quad I = 10 \text{ mA}$$

18.

2	27		↑
2	13	1	
2	6	1	
2	3	0	
2	1	1	
	0	1	

The given decimal number if 27.625

Conversion of decimal part, into binary

$$(27)_{10} = (11011)_2$$

Conversion of fractional part, into binary

$$0.625 \times 2 = 1.250 \Rightarrow 1$$

$$0.250 \times 2 = 0.500 \Rightarrow 0$$

$$0.500 \times 2 = 1.000 \Rightarrow 1$$

$$(0.625)_{10} = (0.101)_2$$

$$\therefore \quad (27.625)_{10} = (11011.101)_2$$

19. In general, in n-bit flash type ADC, the number of comparators needed is equal to, $2^n - 1$. Hence, for 8-bit ADC, the number of comparators needed = $2^8 - 1 = (256 - 1) = 255$.

20. By observing the waveform, 3 divisions on the Y axis means that the Y setting is 2 V/div.

An angular frequency of 100πt would corresponds to frequency of 50 Hz.

$$\Rightarrow \quad \text{Time period} = \frac{1}{50} = 20 \text{ msec}$$

$\therefore$ 10 correspond to a X setting of

$$\frac{20}{10} = 20 \text{ m sec/ div}$$

$\therefore$ option (d) is correct.

21. At full scale the wattmeter will indicate

$$300 \times 5 \times 0.2 = \frac{300 \times 5 \times 2}{10} = 300 \text{ Watts}$$

As the scale of the wattmeter is uniform.

150 divisions in 300 W

$$100 \text{ divisions} = \frac{300 \times 100}{150} = 200 \text{ Watts}$$

22. From the given figure,

Output of thermocouple,

$$V_{OT} = e_{M/N}(\theta - \theta_{Ref})$$

where, $e_{M/N}$ is sensitivity of thermocouple.

Total output voltage

$$V_0 = A_1 \times V_{OT}$$

where, A_I is gain of instrumentation amplifier

$$\therefore \quad 96 \times 10^{-3} = 25 \times e_{M/N}(\theta - 0)$$

$$\therefore \quad e_{M/N}\,\theta = \frac{96 \times 10^{-3}}{25}$$

$$\therefore \quad \theta = \frac{96 \times 10^{-3}}{25 \times e_{M/N}}$$

$$\therefore \quad \theta = \frac{96 \times 10^{-3}}{25 \times 40 \times 10^{-6}} = 96°C$$

24. Modulation index,

$$(\mu) = \frac{A_{max} - A_{min}}{A_{max} + A_{min}} = \frac{13-7}{13+7} = \frac{6}{20} = 0.3$$

25. Number of incident photons 'N' = 6×10^6

Number of electron-hole pairs generated 'n' = 4.5 × 106

Quantum efficiency of photo-diode

$$= \left[\frac{n}{N} \times 100\right] = \frac{4.5 \times 10^6}{6 \times 10^6} = 75$$

26. $x = y = z \Rightarrow dx = dy = dz$

$$\int_C \vec{F} \cdot \overline{dl} = \int_0^1 \left(x^2 - 2x - 4x^2 + 4x^3\right)dx$$

$$= -3\left[\frac{x^3}{3}\right]_0^1 - 2\left[\frac{x^2}{2}\right]_0^1 + 4\left[\frac{x^2}{4}\right]_0^1$$

$$= -1 - 1 + 1 = -1$$

27.

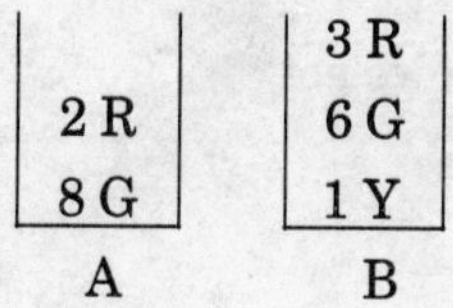

$$\text{Required probability} = \left[\frac{5}{20} \times 100\right]\% \text{ or } 25\%$$

28. Now from option (c),

Putting k = –3 in options,

$$3x + 2ky = -2 \Rightarrow 3x - 6y = -2$$

$$Kx + 6y = 2 \Rightarrow 3x - 6y = -2$$

Both the equations are reducing in the same form, thus the system will have infinite number of solutions. $\left(\because \frac{d_1}{d_2} = \frac{b_1}{b_2} = \frac{c_1}{c_2}\right)$

30. Case I:

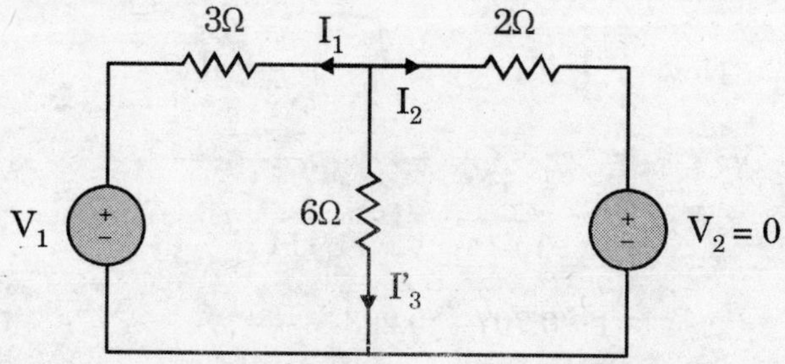

$I_2 = -6\text{ A}$

Apply current division and KCL we get

$I_3' = -2\text{ A}$

Case II:

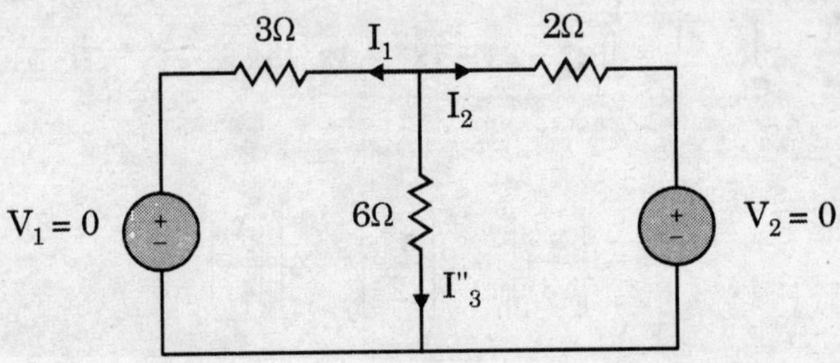

$I_1 = 6\text{ A}$

Apply current division we get

$I_3'' = 3\text{ A}$

$$I_3 = I_3' + I_3'' = -2 + 3 = 1\text{ A}$$

31.

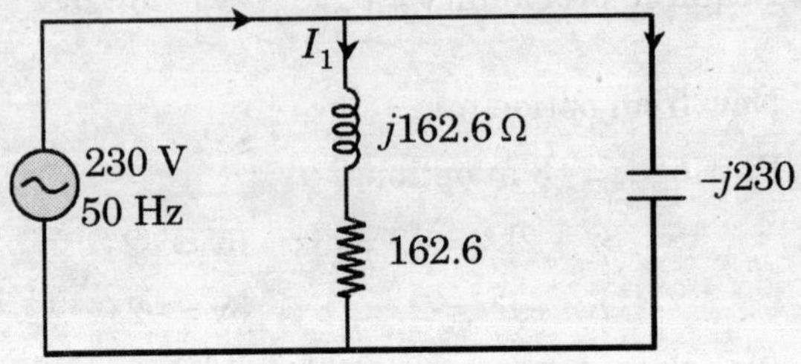

$$I_1 = \frac{230}{162.6 + j162.6} = 1\underline{|-45}$$

and $$I_2 = \frac{230}{230\underline{|-90}} = 11\underline{|+90}$$

Now $$I = I_1 + I_2 = \frac{1}{\sqrt{2}} - j\frac{1}{\sqrt{2}} + j1$$

$$\therefore \quad I = \frac{1}{1.414} + \left(1 - \frac{1}{1.414}\right)j$$

$$\therefore \quad I = 0.707 + j0.293$$

$$\therefore \quad I = 0.765\underline{|22.51}$$

Now $Q = VI \sin\theta$

$= 230(0.765)\sin(22.51)$

$= 67.36\text{ VAR}$

32.

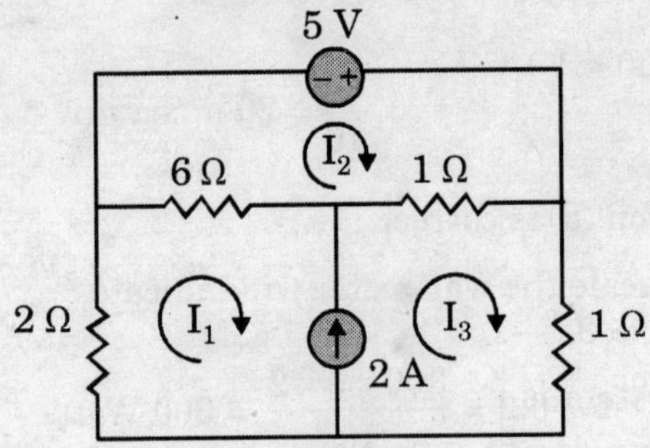

$8I_1 - 6I_2 + 2I_3 - I_2 = 0$ ....(i)

$I_3 - I_1 = 2A$ ....(ii)

$-6I_1 + 7I_2 - I_3 = 5$ ....(iii)

By solving above equations,

$I_1 = 1\text{ A}, I_2 = 2\text{ A}$ and $I_3 = 3\text{ A}$

33. $y(t) = x(t) + e^{jt}\,x(t)$

Taking laplare transform

$Y(\omega) = X(\omega) + X(\omega - 1)$

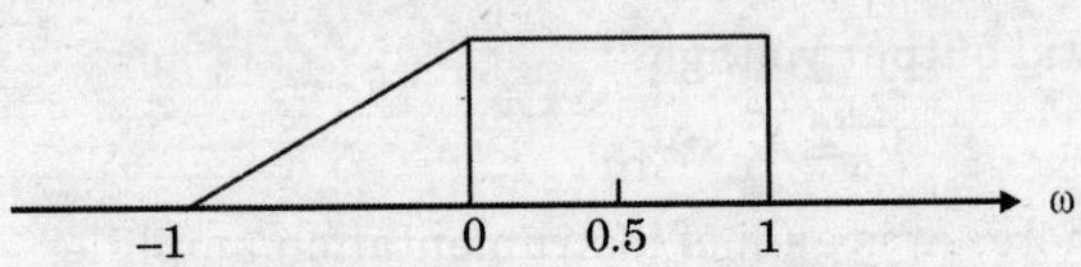

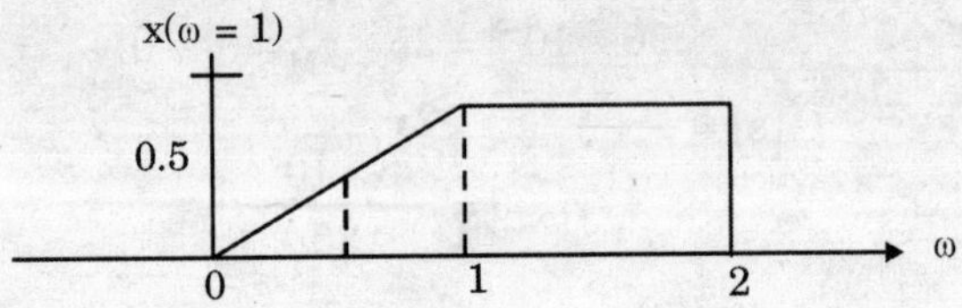

$$Y(\omega)\big|_{\omega=0.5} = 1.5$$

34. $y[n] = x[n] * h[n]$

$Y(z) = 2 + 3z^{-1} + z^{-2} = Z(z) \times H(z)$

$P(z) = z^{-2}\,[X(z) \times H(z)] = 2z^{-2} + 3z^{-3} + z^{-4}$

35. $$X[k] = \begin{bmatrix} 1 & 1 & 1 & 1 \\ 1 & -j & -1 & j \\ 1 & -1 & 1 & -1 \\ 1 & j & -1 & -j \end{bmatrix} \begin{bmatrix} 1 \\ -1 \\ 1 \\ -1 \end{bmatrix}$$

$X[k] = 0$

$X[1] = 1 + j - 1 - j = 0$

$X[2] = 1 + 1 + 1 + 1 = 4$

X[2] is non-zero.

36. Given,

$$G(s) = \frac{s^2 + 0.2s + 100}{s^2 - 0.2s + 100}, H(s) = \frac{1}{2}$$

Now $q(s) = 1 + G(s)\,H(s) = 0$

$$\therefore\ q(s) = 1 + \left(\frac{s^2 + 0.25 + 100}{s^2 + 0.25 + 100}\right)\frac{1}{2} = 0$$

$$= 3s^2 - 0.2s + 300 = 0$$

This system is unstable with two roots in right side of s-plane.

$$\therefore\quad P - N = 2$$

$$\therefore\quad N = 0$$

37. $\dot{X} = \begin{bmatrix} -1 & 0 \\ 0 & -2 \end{bmatrix}; x(0) = \begin{bmatrix} 1 \\ 1 \end{bmatrix}$

Now $X(t) = \phi(t) \,.\, x(0)$

$$\therefore\ \phi(t) = L^{-1}\left[(sI - A)^{-1}\right] = \begin{bmatrix} e^{-1} & 0 \\ 0 & e^{-2t} \end{bmatrix}$$

$$\therefore\quad X[t] = \begin{bmatrix} e^{-t} & 0 \\ 0 & e^{-2t} \end{bmatrix}\begin{bmatrix} 1 \\ 1 \end{bmatrix}$$

38. $G(s) = \dfrac{1}{(s+1)(s+2)}; H(s) = \dfrac{s+\alpha}{s}$

$$q(s) = s^3 + 3s^2 + 3s + \alpha = 0$$

For marginal stability, $\alpha = 3 \times 3 = 9$

39. $x(t) = u(t) \xrightarrow{\ 7\ } y(t) = \left(1 - e^{-2t}\right)u(t)$

$$\frac{1}{s} \rightarrow Y(s) = \frac{1}{s} - \frac{1}{s+2} \qquad \frac{s+2-s}{s(s+2)} = \frac{2}{s(s+2)}$$

$$\therefore\quad H(s) = \frac{2}{s+2}$$

40.

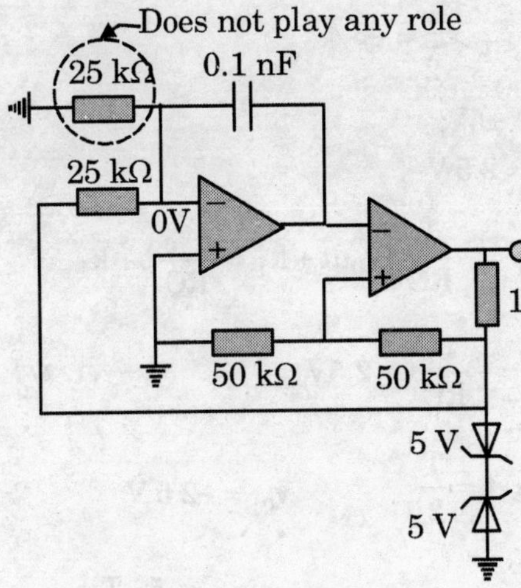

Re drawing above circuit :

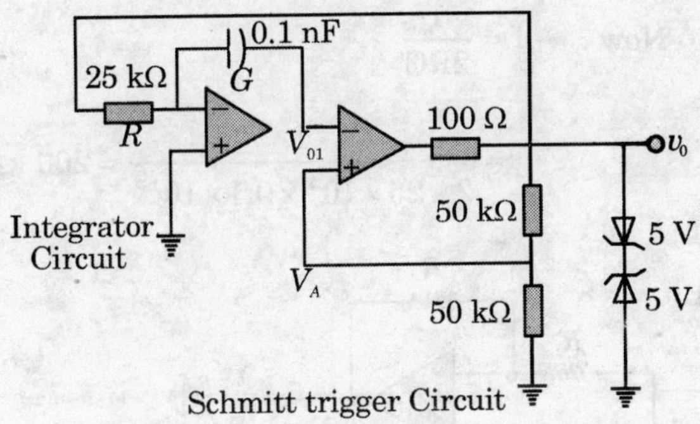

Here, $\quad V_0 = \pm 5V, \quad \Rightarrow \quad V_A = \dfrac{V_0}{2} = \pm 2.5V$

$$V_{01} = -\frac{1}{RC}\int v_0\,dt + k$$

when v_{01} exceed 2.5 V, v_0 falls from 5V to –5V

when v_{01} falls below –2.5V, v_0 falls **from** –5V to 5V

Therefore,

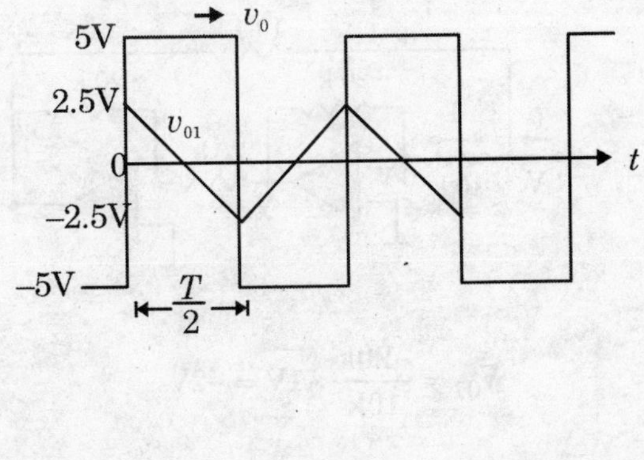

For, $0 < t < \frac{T}{2}$:

$v_0 = \pm 5V;$

$V_A = 2.5\text{ V}$

$$V_{01} = -\frac{1}{RC}\int v_0 dt + k_1 = \frac{-v_0}{RC}t + k_1$$

$$= -\frac{5}{RC}t + 2.5V \qquad (\because V_0 = 5V)$$

Now, at $t = \frac{T}{2}$, $\quad v_{01} = -2.5\text{ V}$

$$-2.5 = \frac{-5}{RC}\cdot\frac{T}{2} + 2.5$$

Now $\quad T = 2RC$

Now $\quad f = \frac{1}{2RC}$

$$= \frac{1}{2 \times 25 \times 10^3 \times 0.1 \times 10^{-9}} = 200\text{ kHz}$$

41.

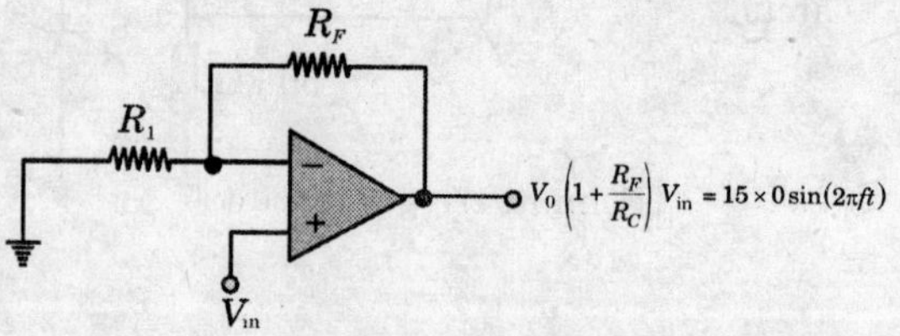

Slew rate, $\quad SR = \left|\frac{\partial V_0}{\partial t}\right|_{max} = A \cdot V_m \cdot 2\pi f$

$$0.5 \times 10^6 = 15 \times 0.3 \times 2\pi f$$

$$f = \frac{0.5 \times 10^6}{2\pi \times 15 \times 0.3}$$

$$\therefore \quad f_{max} = \frac{0.5 \times 10^6}{9\pi} = 17.69\text{ kHz}$$

42.

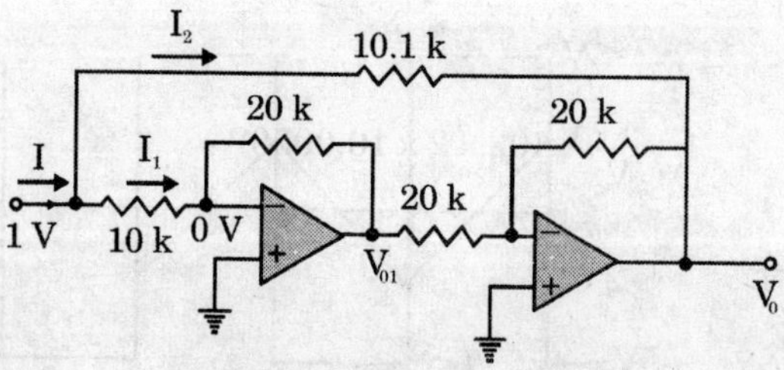

$$V_{01} = \frac{-20k}{10k} \times 1V = -2V$$

Now $\quad V_0 = \frac{-20k}{20k} \times V_{01} = 2V$

Now $\quad I_1 = \frac{1-0}{10k} = 0.1\text{mA}$

and $\quad I_2 = \frac{1-2}{10.1k} = -0.099\text{mA}$

$\therefore \quad I = I_1 + I_2 = 0.1\text{ mA} - 0.099\text{ mA} = 0.99\ \mu A$

43. The function is given in POS form as,

$$F = (A + B + \bar{C})(A + \bar{B} + \bar{C})(\bar{A} + B + C)(\bar{A} + \bar{B} + \bar{C})$$

the above function can also be expressed as,

$$F(A, B, C) = \Pi M(1, 3, 4, 7)$$

and the function can be expressed in SOP form as,

$$F(A, B, C) = \Sigma m(0, 2, 5, 6)$$

$$= \bar{A}\bar{B}\bar{C} + \bar{A}B\bar{C} + A\bar{B}C + AB\bar{C}$$

44. The state table of the counter circuit can be drawn as follows,

Present state		Flip-Flop Inputs				Next state	
Q_1	Q_2	J_1 $(Q_1 + Q_2)$	K_1 $(\bar{Q}_1 + \bar{Q}_2)$	J_2 $(\bar{Q}_1 + Q_2)$	K_2 $(Q_1 + \bar{Q}_2)$	Q_1	Q_2
0	0	0	1	1	1	0	1
0	1	1	1	1	0	1	1
1	1	1	0	1	1	1	0
1	0	1	1	0	1	0	0

Hence, the sequence of states followed by the counter is,

00, 01, 11, 10, 00, 01 ....

45. $\quad 64H = (6 \times 16 + 4)_{10} = (100)_{10}$

Instruction	Number of times executed	Clock cycles required for one time execution
MVI B, 64H	1	7
DCR B	100	4
JNZ Loop	99 (jump performed) + 1(jump not performed)	10 (jumped performed) and 7 (jump not performed)

Total number of clock cycles

$= 7 + 400 + (99 \times 10 + 1 \times 7)$

$= 407 + 990 + 7 = 1404$

$$T_{clock} = \frac{1}{f_{clock}} = \frac{1}{5MHz} = \frac{1}{5}\mu sec$$

$$\text{Time delay introduced} = \frac{1404}{5}\mu sec = 280.80\ \mu sec$$

46. The given circuit is the standard circuit. It is the implementation of EX-OR gate using NAND gates.

Hence, $F = X \oplus Y = \bar{X}Y + X\bar{Y}$

47. 1% of 300 V = 3v

$\therefore$ 0.5% of 5 A = $\frac{1}{40}$A

Now $V_L = 200\text{ V} \pm 3\text{ V} = 200\text{ V} \pm 1.5\%$

and $I_L = 2.5\text{ A} \pm \frac{1}{40}\text{A} = 2.5\text{ A} \pm 1\%$

$$\therefore \quad R_L = \frac{V_L}{I_L} = \frac{200}{2.5} \pm (2.5\%) = 80 \pm 2.5\%\Omega$$

48. Given, $\omega_1 = 10^6$ rad/sec $\quad C_1 = 990$ pF

$\omega_2 = 2 \times 10^6$ rad/sec $\quad C_2 = 240$ pF

Here, $\omega_2 = 2\omega_1$

$$\therefore \quad C_d = \frac{C_1 - 4C_2}{3} = \frac{990 - 40 \times 240}{3} = 10\text{pF}$$

At resonance

$$f = \frac{1}{2\pi\sqrt{L(C + C_d)}}$$

or

$$L = \frac{1}{4\pi^2 f^2 (C + C_d)}$$

Now total C = C_1 = 990 pF

$$\therefore \quad L = \frac{1}{\omega_1^2 (C + C_d)}$$

$$= \frac{1}{10^6 \times 10^6 \times (990 + 10) \times 10^{-12}}$$

$$= 1.0 \text{ mH}$$

49. In the given bridge CKT.

$$Z_1 = \frac{R_1}{1 + j\omega C_1 R_1}$$

and $Z_2 = R_2$

and $Z_3 = R_x + j\omega L_x$

and $Z_4 = R_4$

Now balanced bridge condition,

$$Z_1 Z_3 = Z_2 Z_4$$

$$\therefore \quad \frac{R_1}{1 + j\omega C_1 R_1}(R_x + j\omega L_x) = R_2 R_4$$

$$\therefore \quad R_1 R_x + j\omega R_1 L_x = R_2 R_4 + j\omega C_1 R_1 R_2 R_4$$

Equality the imaginary parts, we get

$$L_x = C_1 R_2 R_4$$

Substituting the values we have

$$\therefore \quad L_x = 1 \times 10^{-9} \times 22.2 \times 10^3 \times 10 \times 10^3$$

$$= 222 \text{ mH}$$

50. From the given figure and Information

$$\text{Transit time, } t_1 = 0.995 \times 10^{-3} = \frac{L}{C + v\cos\theta}$$

$$\text{Transit time, } t_2 = 1 \times 10^{-3} = \frac{L}{C + v\cos\theta}$$

Where 'L' is the length of the line joining both the transducers.

'C' is velocity of ultra sound in water.

'v' is velocity of fluid in pipe.

'θ' is the given angle 45°.

From the given figure,

$$\sin\theta = \frac{D}{L}$$

$$L = \frac{D}{\sin\theta}$$

$$\text{So,} \quad C + v\cos\theta = \frac{L}{0.995 \times 10^{-3}} \quad \text{....(i)}$$

$$C - vos\theta = \frac{L}{1 \times 10^{-3}} \quad \text{....(ii)}$$

Now solving eq. (i) and (ii) we get

$$\therefore \quad 2v\cos\theta = 1000 \cdot L\left[\frac{1}{0.995} - 1\right]$$

$$\therefore 2 \times v \times \cos 45 = 1000 \times \frac{100 \times 10^{-2}}{\sin 45}\left[\frac{1}{0.995} - 1\right]$$

$$\left(\because L = \frac{D}{\sin\theta}\right)$$

$$\therefore \quad 2 \times v \times \frac{1}{\sqrt{2}} = 10^3 \times \sqrt{2} \times (0.00502)$$

$$\therefore \quad V = \frac{103 \times 2 \times 10.00502}{2}$$

$$v = 5.02 \text{ m/sec}$$

51. From the given "Quarter Bridge"

Output voltage of the bridge is

$$V_0 = \frac{V_s}{4R_b} \cdot \Delta R \quad [\text{where } V_s = 2\text{ V}]$$

$$V_0 = \frac{2}{4R_b} \cdot R_0 G_f \cdot \in \quad [\because \Delta R = R \cdot Gf \in]$$

$$\therefore \quad V_0 = \frac{2}{4} \times \frac{1000}{1000} \times 2.5 \times 400 \times 10^{-6}$$

$\therefore \quad V_0 = 0.5$ mV

52. When voltage at the output due to only 230 V, 50 Hz supply is to be calculated, the DC supply should be short circuited as shown below.

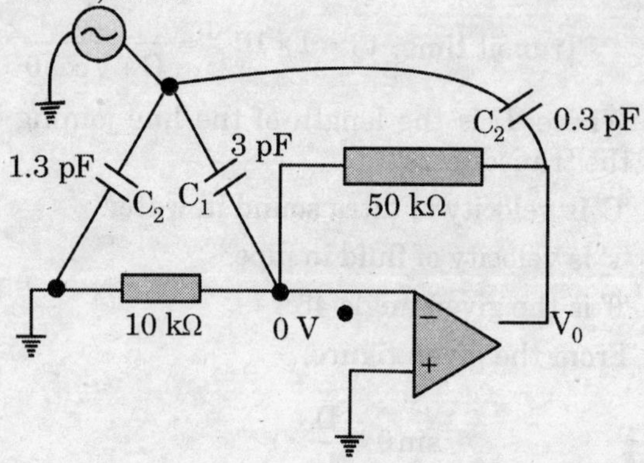

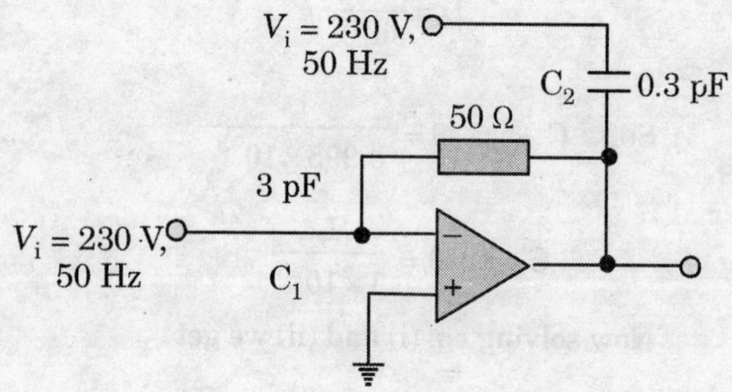

[equivalent circuit]

$$V_0 = -\frac{50k\Omega}{1/j\omega C_1} V_i = -j\omega C_1 (50k) V_i$$

$$\therefore V_{0(rms)} = (2\pi \times 50) \times 3 \times 10^{-12} \times 50 \times 10^3 \times V_{i(rms)}$$

$$= 2\pi \times 75 \times 10^{-7} \times 230 \text{ V}$$

$$= \frac{345\pi}{100} \text{mV} = 10.84 \text{mV}$$

53. Given, $f_s = 44000$ samples/sec

Number of quantization levels, L = 256

Number of bits per sample, $n = \log_2 L = 8$

$\therefore \quad R_b = nf_s = 8 \times 44000$

$= 352000$ bits/sec

54. From the given explanation, we can understand that, "when a tissue of thickness 't' of refractive index 'N', is placed then a dark fringe is observed"

So, $\quad$ Path difference $= \dfrac{\lambda_0}{2}$ ..(*i*)

Path difference = 2(N – 1)t ...(*ii*)

Now equating (i) and (ii) we get

$$2(N-1)t = \frac{\lambda_0}{2}$$

$$\therefore \quad 2(1.5-1)t = \frac{500\text{nm}}{2}$$

$$\therefore \quad t = 250 \text{ nm}$$

55. From the given figure

$$\text{N.A.} = n_0 \sin\theta_A = \sqrt{n_1^2 - n_2^2}$$

where,

n_0 is Refractive index of air [$n_0 = 1$]

n_1 is Refractive index of core [$n_1 = 1.5$]

n_2 is Refractive index of cladding [$n_2 = 1.4142$]

θ_A is Maximum acceptance angle

$$\text{Now } \theta_A = \sin^{-1}\left[\sqrt{n_1^2 - n_2^2}\right]$$

$$\therefore \quad \theta_A = \sin^{-1}\left[\sqrt{(1.5)^2 - (1.4142)^2}\right]$$

$$\therefore \quad \theta_A = \sin^{-1}\left(\frac{1}{2}\right)$$

$$\therefore \quad \theta_A = 30°$$

SOLVED PAPER - 2019

GENERAL APTITUDE

1. Some students were not involved in the strike. If the above statement is true, which of the following conclusions is/are logically necessary?

1. Some who were involved in the strike were students.
2. No students was involved in the strike.
3. At least one student was involved in the strike.
4. Some who were not involved in the strike were students.

(*a*) 1 and 2 (*b*) 3
(*c*) 4 (*d*) 2 and 3

2. Until Iran came along, India had never been _______ in kabaddi.

(*a*) defeated (*b*) defeating
(*c*) defeat (*d*) defeatist

3. Five numbers 10, 7, 5, 4 and 2 are to be arranged in a sequence from left to right following the directions given below:

1. No two odd or even numbers are next to each other.
2. The second number from the left is exactly half of the left-most number.
3. The middle number is exactly twice the right-most number.

Which is the second number from the right?

(*a*) 2 (*b*) 4
(*c*) 7 (*d*) 10

4. The radius as well as the height of a circular cone increases by 10%. The percentage increase in its volume is ________.

(*a*) 17.1 (*b*) 21.0
(*c*) 33.1 (*d*) 72.8

5. The fishermen, _________ the flood victims owed their lives, were rewarded by the government.

(*a*) whom (*b*) to which
(*c*) to whom (*d*) that

6. Two trains started at 7AM from the same point. The first train travelled north at a speed of 80k/h and the second train travelled south at a speed of 100km/h. The time at which they were 540km apart is _______ AM.

(*a*) 9 (*b*) 10
(*c*) 11 (*d*) 11.30

7. The nomenclature of Hindustani music has changed over the centuries. Since the medieval period dhrupad styles were identified as baanis. Terms like gayaki and baaj were used to refer to vocal and instrumental styles, respectively. With the institutionalization of music education the term gharana became acceptable. Gharana originally referred to hereditary musicians from a particular lineage, including disciples and grand disciples.

Which one of the following pairings is NOT correct?

(*a*) dhrupad, baani (*b*) gayaki, vocal
(*c*) baaj, institution (*d*) gharana, lineage

8. "I read somewhere that in ancient times the prestige of a kingdom upon the number of taxes that it was able to levy on its people. It was very much like the prestige of a head-hunter in his own community."

Based on the paragraph above, the prestige of a head-hunter depended upon_____

(*a*) the prestige of the kingdom
(*b*) the prestige of the heads
(*c*) the number of taxes he could levy
(*d*) the number of heads he could gather

9. In a country of 1400 million population, 70% own mobile phones. Among the mobile phone owners, only 294 million access the internet. Among these users, only half buy goods from e-commerce portals. What is the percentage of these buyers in the country?

(*a*) 10.50 (*b*) 14.70
(*c*) 15.00 (*d*) 50.00

10. Since the last one year, after a 125 basis point reduction in repo rate by the Reserve Bank of India, banking institutions have been making a demand to reduce interest rates on small saving schemes. Finally, the government announced yesterday a reduction in interest rates on small schemes to bring them on par with fixed deposit interest rates.

Which of the following statements can be inferred from the given passage?

(*a*) Whenever the Reserve Bank of India reduces the repo rate, the interest rates on small saving schemes are also reduced.

(*b*) Interest rates on small saving schemes are always maintained on par with fixed deposit interest rates.

(*c*) The government sometime takes into consideration the demands of banking institutions before reducing the interest rates on small saving schemes.

(*d*) A reduction in interest rates on small saving schemes follow only after a reduction in repo by the Reserve Bank of India.

INSTRUMENTATION ENGINEERING

1. The circuit shown in the figure below uses ideal positive edge-triggered synchronous j-K flip flops with outputs X and Y. If the initial state of the outputs is X = 0and Y = 0 just before the arrival of the first clock pulse, the state of the output just before the arrival of the second clock pulse is

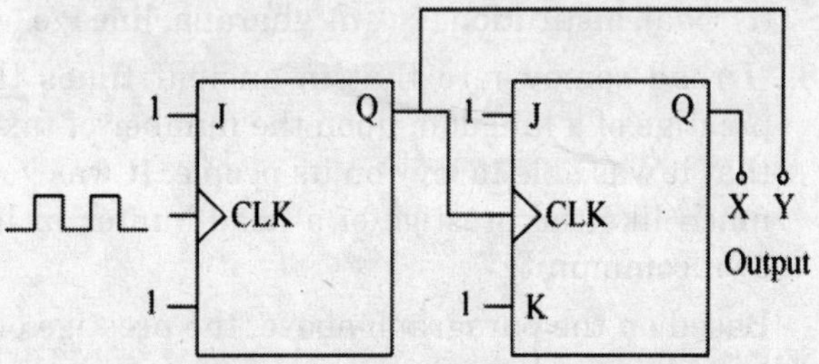

(*a*) X = 0, Y = 0 (*b*) X = 0, Y = 1

(*c*) X = 1, Y = 0 (*d*) X = 1, Y = 1

2. In the Figures (*a*) and (*b*) shown below, the transformers are identical and ideal, except that the transformer in Figure (*b*) is centre-tapped. Assuming ideal diodes, the ratio of the root-meansquare (RMS) voltage across the resistor R in Figure (*a*) to that in Figure (*b*) is

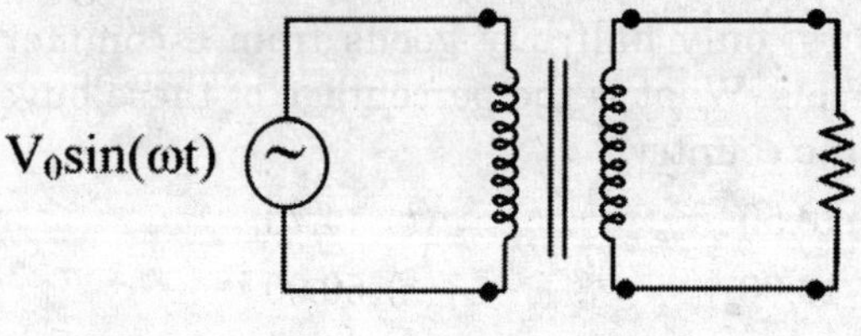

Figure (a)

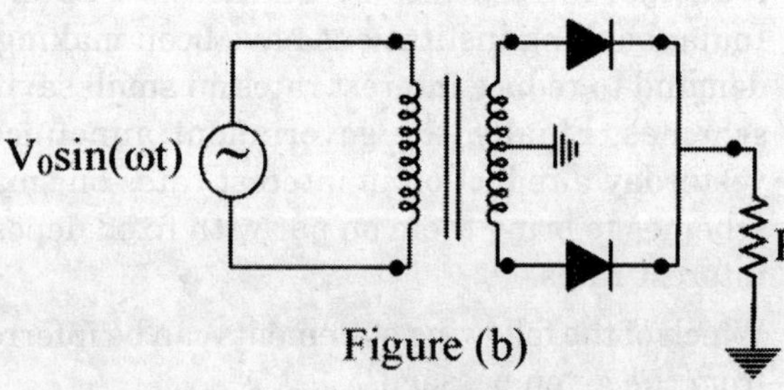

Figure (b)

(*a*) $\sqrt{2}:1$ (*b*) $2:1$

(*c*) $2\sqrt{2}:1$ (*d*) $4:1$

3. The correct biasing conditions for typical operation of light emitting diodes, photodiodes, Zener diodes are, respectively

(*a*) forward bias, reverse bias, reverse bias

(*b*) reverse bias, reverse bias, forward bias

(*c*) forward bias, forward bias, reverse bias

(*d*) reverse bias, forward bias, reverse bias

4. The output y(t) of a system is related to its input x(t) as $y(t) = \int_0^1 x(\tau - 2)d\tau$, where, x(t) = 0 and y(t) = 0 for $t \le 0$. The transfer function of the system is

(*a*) $\frac{1}{s}$ (*b*) $\frac{(1-e^{-2s})}{s}$

(*c*) $\frac{e^{-2s}}{s}$ (*d*) $\frac{1}{s} - e^{-2s}$

5. A signal $\cos(2\pi f_m t)$modulates a carrier $\cos(2\pi f_c t)$ using the double-sideband-with-carrier (DSBWC) scheme to yield a modulated signal $\cos(2\pi f_c t) + 0.3\cos(2\pi f_m t)\cos(2\pi f_c t)$.

The modulation index is ________. (Answer should be rounded off to one decimal place)

6. If each of the values of inductance and resistance of a series LCR circuit are doubled, the Q factor of the circuit would

(*a*) reduce by a factor $\sqrt{2}$

(*b*) reduce by a factor 2

(*c*) increase by a factor $\sqrt{2}$

(*d*) increase by a factor 2

7. The input x[n] and output y[n] of a discrete-time system are related as $y[n] = \alpha y[n-1] + x[n]$. The condition on α for which the system is Bounded-Input Bounded-Output (BIBO) stable is

(*a*) $|\alpha| < 1$

(*b*) $|\alpha| = 1$

(*c*) $|\alpha| > 1$

(*d*) $|\alpha| < 3/2$

8. In a single-mode optical fiber, the zero-dispersion wavelength refers to the wavelength at which the

(*a*) material dispersion is zero.

(*b*) waveguide dispersion is zero.

(*c*) sum of material dispersion and waveguide dispersion is zero.

(*d*) material dispersion and waveguide dispersion are simultaneously zero.

9. The resistance of a resistor is measured using a voltmeter and an ammeter. The voltage measurements have a mean value of 1V and standard deviation of 0.12V while current measurements have a mean value of 1mA with standard deviation of 0.05mA. Assuming that the errors in voltage and current measurements are independent, the standard deviation of the calculated resistance value is _____ Ω.

10. The figure below shows that i^{th} full-adder block of a binary adder circuit. C_i is the input carry and $C_i + 1$ is the output carry of the circuit. Assuming that each logic gate has a delay of 2 nanosecond, with no additional time delay due to the interconnecting wires. If the inputs Ai, Bi are available and stable throughout the carry propagation, the maximum time taken for an input C_i to produce a steady-state output C_{i+1} is _____ nanosecond.

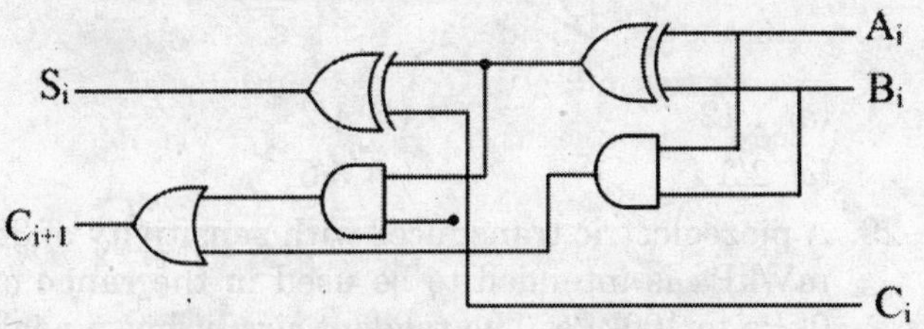

11. A pitot-static tube is used to estimate the velocity of an incompressible fluid of density $1 kg/m^3$. If the pressure difference measured by the tube is $200 N/m^2$, the velocity of the fluid assuming the pitot-tube coefficient to be 1.0, is _____ m/s

12. $\vec{a}, \vec{b}, \vec{c}$ are three orthogonal vectors, Given that $\vec{a} = \hat{i} + 2\hat{j} + 5\hat{k}$ and $\vec{b} = \hat{i} + 2\hat{j} - \hat{k}$, the vector $\vec{c}$ is parallel to

(*a*) $\hat{i} + 2\hat{j} + 3\hat{k}$ (*b*) $2\hat{i} + \hat{j}$

(*c*) $2\hat{i} - \hat{j}$ (*d*) $4\hat{k}$

13. Consider a circuit comprising only resistors with constant resistance and ideal independent DC voltage sources. If all the resistances are scaled down by a factor 10, and all source voltages are scaled up by a factor 10, the power dissipated in the circuit scales up by a factor of _____.

14. The total number of Boolean function with distinct truth-tables that can be defined over 3 Boolean variables is _____.

15. Four strain gauges in a Wheatstone bridge configuration are connected to an instrumentation amplifier as shown in the figure. From the choices given below, the preferred value for the common mode rejection ratio (CMRR) of the amplifier, in dB, would be

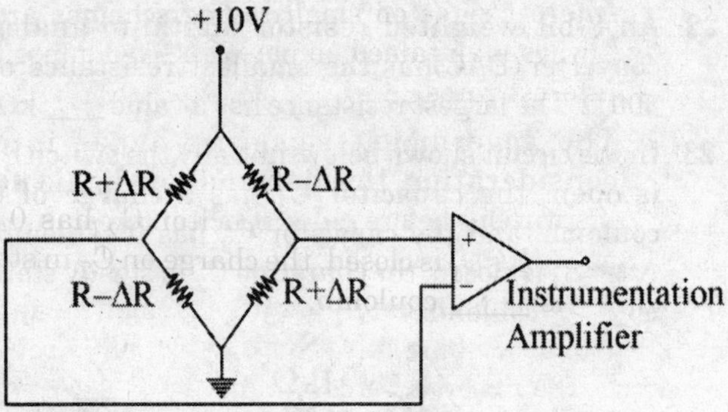

(*a*) – 20 (*b*) 0

(*c*) 3 (*d*) 100

16. The vector function $\vec{A}$ is given by $\vec{A} = \vec{\nabla} u$, where u(x, y) is a scalar function. Then $|\vec{\nabla} \times A|$ is

(*a*) – 1 (*b*) 0

(*c*) 1 (*d*) ∞

17. In a cascade control system, the loop transfer function of the inner loop may be assumed to have a single time-constant τ_1. Similarly, the closed loop transfer function of the outer loop may be assumed to have a single time-constant τ_2. The desired relationship between τ_1 and τ_2 in a well-designed control system is

(*a*) τ_1 is much less than τ_1

(*b*) τ_1 is equal to τ_2

(*c*) τ_1 is much greater than τ_2

(*d*) τ_1 is independent of τ_2

18. A 3 – 3 matrix has eigen values 1, 2 and 5. The determinant of the matrix is _____.

19. The loop-gain function L(s) of a control system with unity feedback is given to be

$L(s) = \dfrac{k}{(s+1)(s+2)(s+3)}$ where k > 0. If the gain cross-over frequency of the loop-gain function is less than its phase cross-over frequency, the closed-loop system is

(*a*) unstable (*b*) marginally stable

(*c*) conditionally stable (*d*) stable

20. A box has 8 red balls and 8 green balls. Two balls are drawn randomly in succession from the box without replacement. The probability that the first ball drawn is red and the second ball drawn is green is

(*a*) 4/15 (*b*) 7/16

(*c*) 1/2 (*d*) 8/15

21. Thermocouple measure temperature based on

(*a*) Photoelectric effect (*b*) Seebeck effect

(*c*) Hall effect (*d*) Thermal expansion

22. An 8-bit weighted resistor digital-to-analog converter (DAC)has the smallest resistance of 500 Ω. The largest resistance has a value ____ kΩ.

23. In the circuit shown below, initially the switch S_1 is open, the capacitor C_1 has a charge of 6 coulomb, and the capacitor C_2 has 0 coulomb. After S_1 is closed, the charge on C_2 in steady state is ______ coulomb.

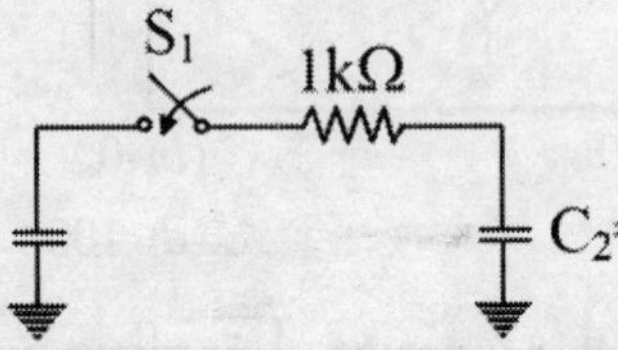

24. In the circuit shown below, maximum power is transferred to the load resistance RL, when

R_L = ________ Ω.

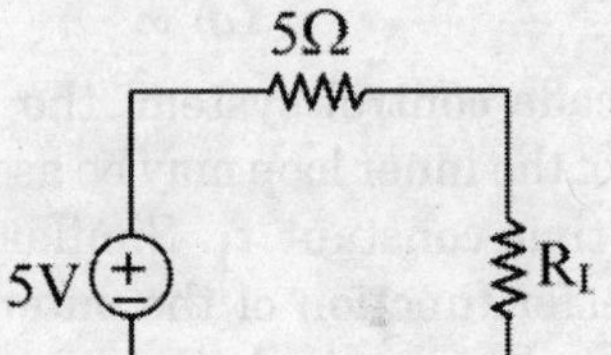

25. In the circuit shown below, the input voltage V_{in} is positive. The current (I)- voltage (V) characteristics of the diode can be assumed to be $I = I_0 e^{V/V_T}$ under the forward bias condition, where V_T is the thermal voltage and I_0 is the reverse saturation current. Assuming an ideal op-amp, the output voltage V_{out} of the circuit is proportional to

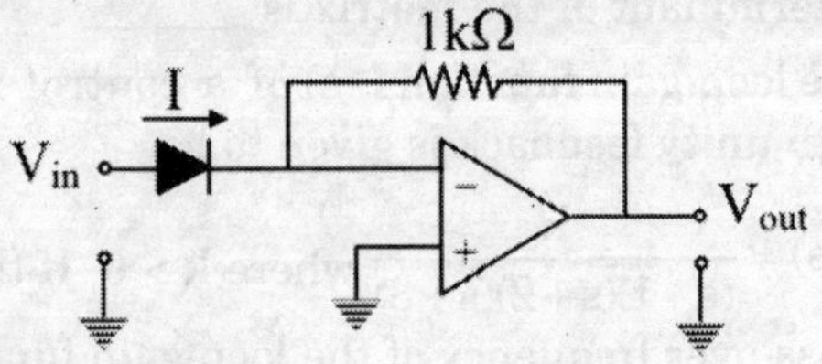

(*a*) $\log_e (V_{in}/V_T)$ (*b*) $2V_{in}$

(*c*) e^{V_{in}/V_T} (*d*) V_{in}^2

26. A differential capacitive sensor with a distance between the extreme plates 100mm is shown in figure below. The difference voltage $\Delta V = V_1 - V_2$, where V_1 and V_2, are the rms values, for a downward displacement of 10mm of the intermediate plate from the central position, in volts, is

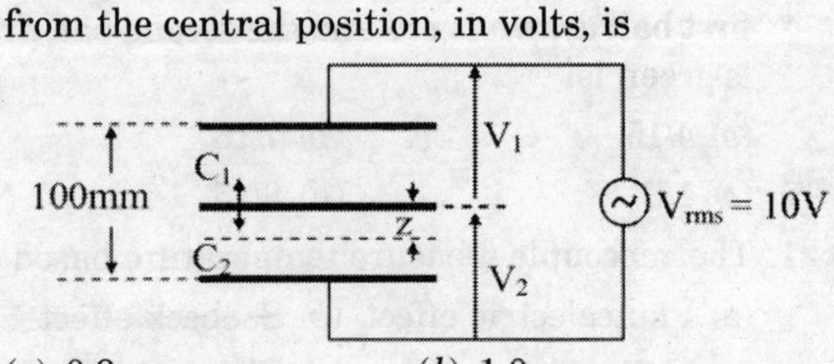

(*a*) 0.9 (*b*) 1.0

(*c*) 1.1 (*d*) 2

27. In a microprocessor with a 16 bit address buss, the most significant address lines A15 to A12 are used to select a 4096 word memory unit, while lines A0 to A11 are used to address a particular word in the memory unit. If the 3 least significant lines of the address bus A0 to A2 are shortcircuited to ground, the addressable number of words in the memory unit is ______ .

28. In the circuit shown below, assume that the comparators are ideal and all components have zero propagation delay. In one period of the input signal $V_{in} = 6\sin(\omega t)$, the fraction of the time for which the output OUT is in logic state HIGH is

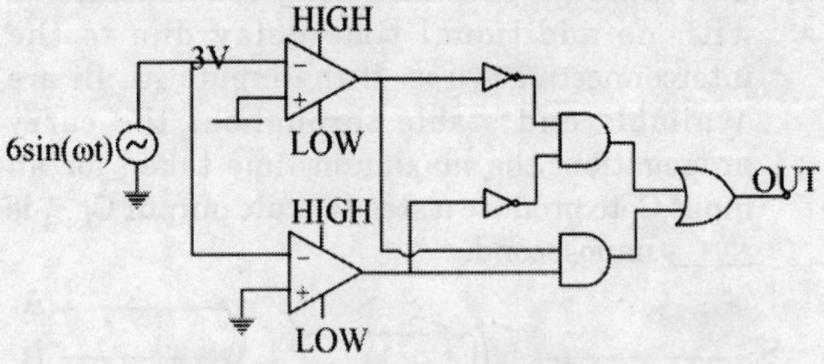

(*a*) 1/12 (*b*) 1/2

(*c*) 2/3 (*d*) 5/6

29. A piezoelectric transducer with sensitivity of 30 mV/kPa is intended to be used in the range of 0kPa to 100kPa. The readout circuit has a peak noise amplitude of 0.3mV and measured signals over the full pressure range are encoded with 10 bits. The smallest pressure that produce a nonzero output, in units of Pa, is approximately.

(*a*) 10 (*b*) 100

(*c*) 240 (*d*) 300

30. A voltage amplifier is constructed using enhancement mode MOSFETs labelled M1, M2, M3 and M4 in the figure below. M1, M2 and M4 are n-channel MOSFETs and M3 is a p-channel MOSFET. All MOSFETs operate in saturation mode and channel length modulation can be ignored. The low frequency, small signal input and output voltage are V_{in} and V_{out} respectively and the dc power supply voltage is VDD. All n-channel MOSFETs have identical transconductance g_{mn} while the p-channel MOSFET has transconductance g_{mp}. The expressions for the low frequency small signal voltage gain V_{out}/V_{in} is

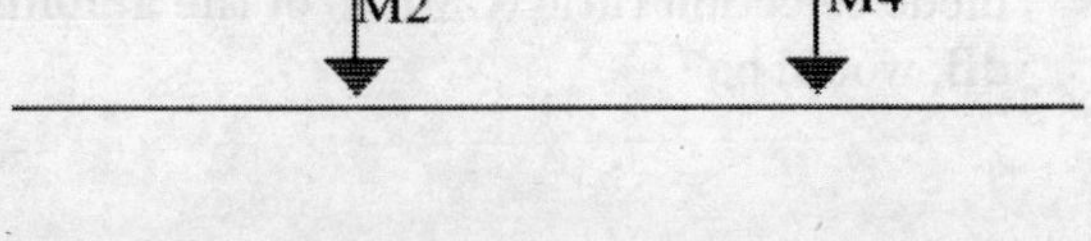

(*a*) $-g_{mn} / g_{mp}$

(*b*) $-g_{mn}\,(g_{mn} + g_{mp})^{-1}$

(*c*) $+g_{mn} / g_{mp}$

(*d*) $g_{mn}\,(g_{mn} + g_{mp}) - 1$

31. In the circuit shown below, all OPAMPS are ideal. The current I = 0 A when the resistance R = ______ kΩ.

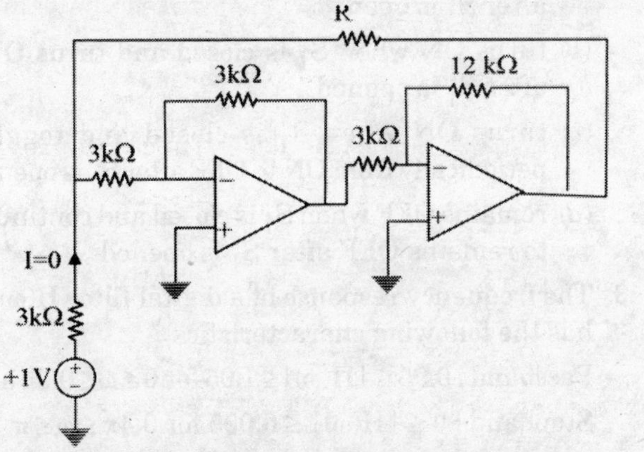

32. The transfer function relating the input x(t) to the output y(t)of a system is given by G(s) = 1/(s+3). A unit-step input is applied to the system at time t = 0. Assuming that y(0) = 3, the value of y(t)at time t = 1 is ______ (Answer should be rounded off to two decimal places)

33. $X = X_1X_0$ and $Y = Y_1Y_0$ are 2 – bit binary numbers. The Boolean function S that satisfies the condition "If X > Y, then S = 1", in its minimized form, is

(*a*) $X_1Y_1 + X_0Y_0$

(*b*) $X_1\overline{Y}_1 + X_0\overline{Y}_0\overline{Y}_1 + X_0\overline{Y}_0X_0$

(*c*) $X_1\overline{Y}_1X_0\overline{Y}_0$

(*d*) $X_1Y_1 + X_0\overline{Y}_0Y_1 + X_0\overline{Y}_0\overline{X}_1$

34. Consider a Michelson interferometer as shown in the figure below. When the wavelength of the laser light source is switched from 400 nanometer ti 500 nanometer, it is observed that the intensity measured at the output port P goes from a minimum to a maximum. This observation is possible when the smallest path difference between the two arms of the interferometer is ______ nanometer.

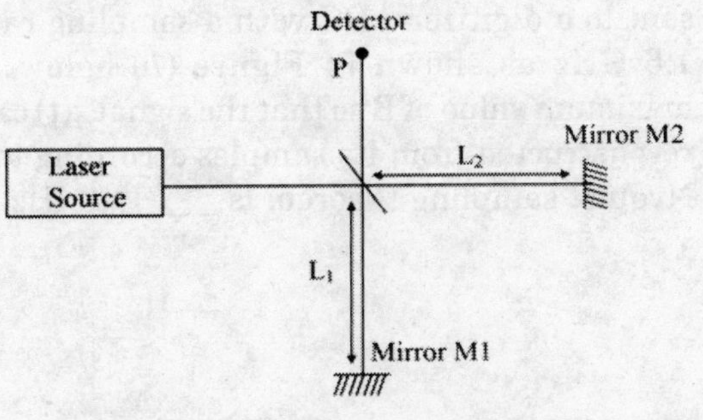

35. In the circuit shown below, all transistors are n-channel enhancement mode MOSFETs. They are identical and are biased to operate in saturation mode. Ignoring channel length modulation, the output voltage Vout is ______ V.

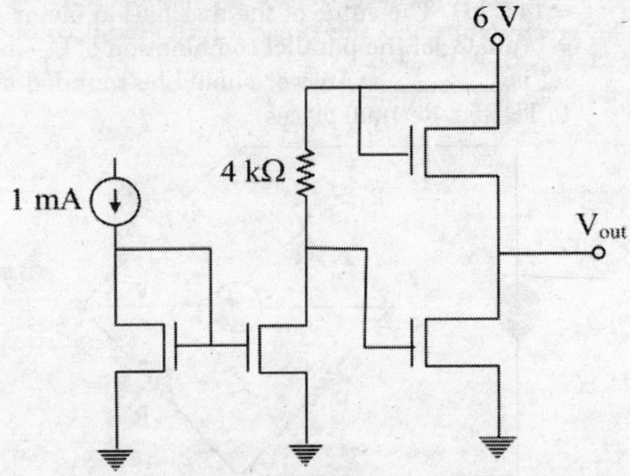

36. A complex function f(z) = u(x,y) + I v(x,y) and its complex conjugate f*(z) = u(x,y) – I v(x,y) are both analytic in the entire complex plane, where z = x + i y and $i = \sqrt{-1}$. The function f is then given by

(*a*) f (z) = x + i y

(*b*) $f(z) = x^2 - y^2 + i\,2xy$

(*c*) f(z) = constant

(*d*) $f(z) = x^2 + y^2$

37. The dynamics of the state $\begin{bmatrix} x_1 \\ x_2 \end{bmatrix}$ of a system is governed by the differential equation

$$\begin{bmatrix} \dot{x}_1 \\ \dot{x}_2 \end{bmatrix} = \begin{bmatrix} 1 & 2 \\ -3 & -4 \end{bmatrix}\begin{bmatrix} x_1 \\ x_2 \end{bmatrix} + \begin{bmatrix} 20 \\ 10 \end{bmatrix}$$

Given that the initial state is $\begin{bmatrix} 0 \\ 0 \end{bmatrix}$, the steady state value of $\begin{bmatrix} x_1 \\ x_2 \end{bmatrix}$ is

(*a*) $\begin{bmatrix} -30 \\ -40 \end{bmatrix}$ (*b*) $\begin{bmatrix} -20 \\ -10 \end{bmatrix}$

(*c*) $\begin{bmatrix} 5 \\ -15 \end{bmatrix}$ (*d*) $\begin{bmatrix} 50 \\ -35 \end{bmatrix}$

38. The output of a continuous-time system y(t) is related to its input x(t)as $y(t) = x(t) + \frac{1}{2}x(t-1)$.

If the Fourier transforms of x(t) and y(t) are X(ω) and Y(ω) respectively and $|X(0)|^2 = 4$, the value of $|Y(0)|^2$ is ______.

39. The parallel resistance-capacitance bridge shown below has a standard capacitance value of $C_1 = 0.1\ \mu F$ and a resistance value of $R_3 = 10\ k\Omega$. The bridge is balanced at a supply frequency of 100 Hz for $R_1 = 375\ k\Omega$, $R_3 = 10\ k\Omega$ and $R_4 = 14.7\ k\Omega$. The value of the dissipation factor D $= 1/(\mu R_p C_p)$of the parallel combination of C_p and R_p is ________. (Answer should be rounded off to THREE decimal places)

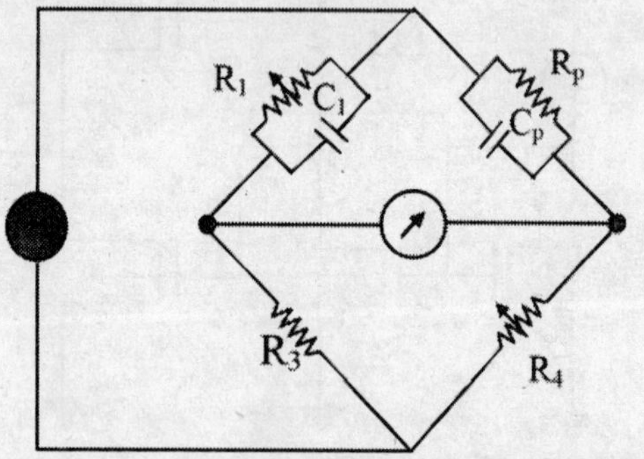

40. In the control system shown in the figure below, a reference signal r(t)= t^2 is applied at time t = 0. The control system employs a PID controller C(s) $= K_p + K_I/s + KDs$ and the plant has a transfer function P(s)= 3/s. If $K_p = 10$, $K_I = 1$ and $K_D = 2$, the steady state value of e is

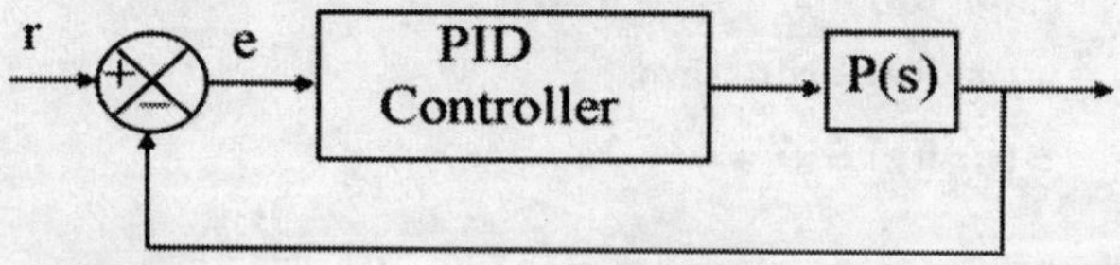

(*a*) 0 (*b*) 2/3

(*c*) 1 (*d*) ∞

41. In the circuit shown below, a step input voltage of magnitude 5 V is applied at node A at time t = 0. If the capacitor has no charge for t ≤ 0, the voltage at node P at t = 6 μs is ______ V.

(Answer should be rounded off to two decimal places)

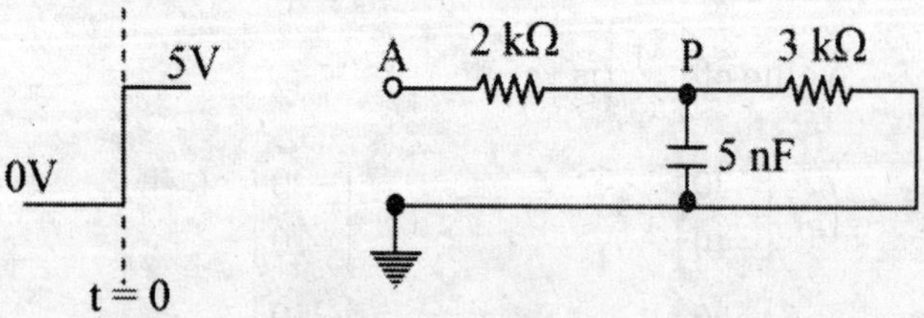

42. In the circuit below, the light dependent resistor (LDR)receives light from the LED. The LDR has resistances of 5 kΩ and 500Ω under dark and illuminated conditions, respectively. The LED is OFF at time t < 0. At time t = 0s, the switch S_1 is closed for 1 ms and then kept open thereafter. Assuming zero propagation delay in the devices, the LED

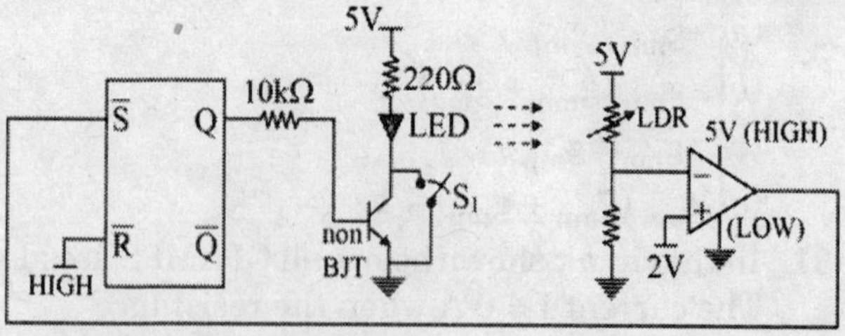

(*a*) turns ON when S_1 is closed and remains ON after S_1 is opened

(*b*) turns ON when S_1 is closed and turns OFF after S_1 is opened

(*c*) turns ON when S_1 is closed and toggles periodically from ON to OFF after S_1 is opened

(*d*) remains OFF when S_1 is closed and continues to remains OFF after S_1 is opened

43. The frequency response of a digital filter H(ω) has the following characteristics

Passband : $0.95 \le |H(\omega)| \le 1.05$ for $0 \le \omega \le 0.3\pi$ and

Stopband : $0 \le |H(\omega)| \le 0.005$ for $0.4\pi \le \omega \le \pi$,

Where ω is the normalized angular frequency in rad/sample. If the analog upper cut off frequency for the passband of the above digital filter is to be 1.2 kHz, then the sampling frequency should be ________ kHz.

44. A 100 W light source emits uniformly in all directions. A photodetector having a circular active area whose diameter is 2 cm is placed 1 m away from the source, normal to the incident light. If the responsivity of the photodetector is 0.4 A/W, the photo-current generated in the detector, in units of mA, is

(*a*) 1

(*b*) 4

(*c*) 100

(*d*) 400

45. A signal x(t)has a bandwidth 2B about a carrier frequency of $f_c = 2$ GHz as shown in Figure (*a*) below. In order to demodulate this signal, it is first mixed (multiplied)with a local oscillator of frequency $f_{LO} = 1.5$ GHz and then passed through an ideal low-pass filter (LPF) with a cut-off frequency of 2.8 GHz. The output of the LPF is sent to a digitizer ADC with a sampling rate of 1.6 GHz as shown in Figure (*b*) below. The maximum value of B so that the signal x(t) can be reconstructed from its samples according to the Nyquist sampling theorem is ______ MHz.

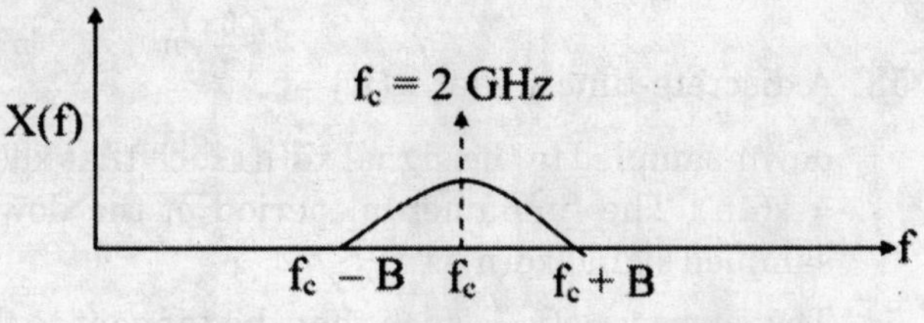

Figure (a)

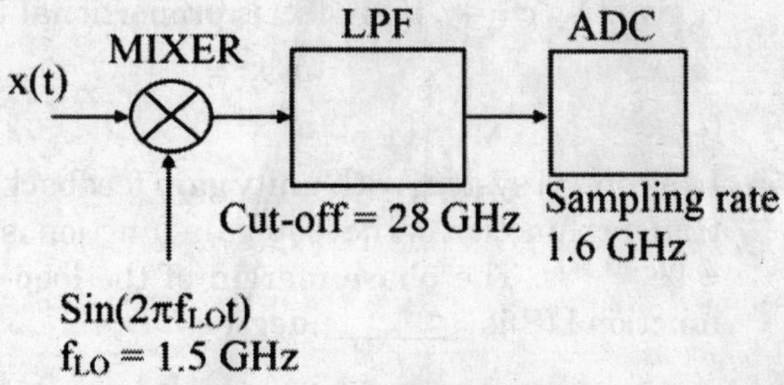

Figure (b)

46. The forward path transfer function L(s) of the control system shown in Figure (*a*) has the asymptotic Bode plot shown in figure (*b*). If the disturbance d(t) is given by $d(t) = 0.1 \sin(\omega t)$ where ω = 5 rad/s, the steady-state amplitude of the output y(t) is

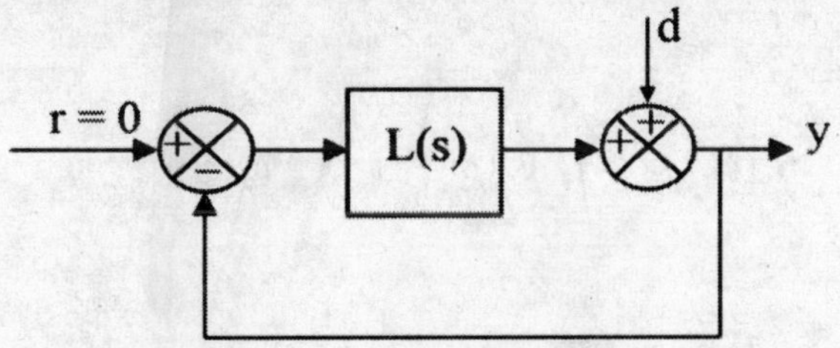

Figure (a)

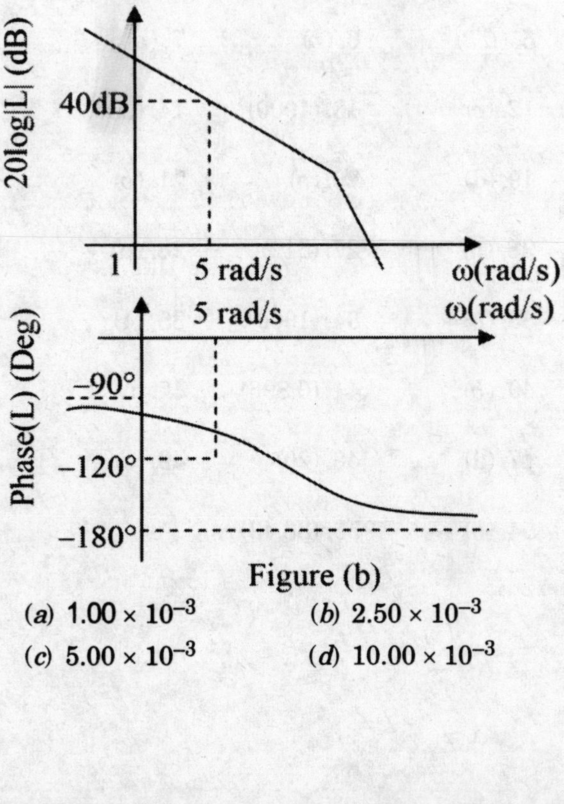

Figure (b)

(*a*) 1.00×10^{-3} (*b*) 2.50×10^{-3}

(*c*) 5.00×10^{-3} (*d*) 10.00×10^{-3}

47. A pulsed laser emits rectangular pulses of width 1 nanosecond at a repetition of 1kHz. If the average power output is 1 mW, the average power over a single pulse duration, in watts, is

(*a*) 1 (*b*) 10

(*c*) 100 (*d*) 1000

48. In the circuit shown below, the angular frequency ω at which the current is in phase with the voltage is ______ rad/s.

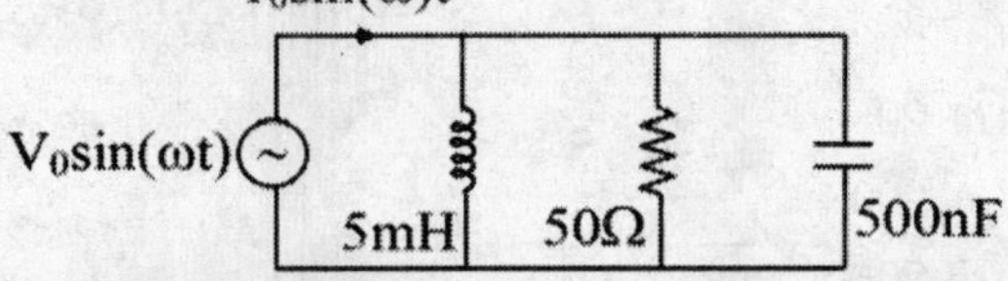

49. In a control system with unity gain feedback, the plant has the transfer function p(s) = 3/x.

Assuming that a controller of the form C(s) = K. (s + p) is used, where k is a positive constant, the value of p for which the root-locus of the closed-loop system passes through the points

$-3 \pm j3\sqrt{3}$ where $j = \sqrt{-1}$, is

(*a*) 3 (*b*) $3\sqrt{3}$

(*c*) 6 (*d*) 9

50. The function p(x) is given by $p(x) = A/x^{\mu}$ where A and μ are constants with $\mu > 1$ and $1 \le x < \infty$ and $p(x) = 0$ for $-\infty < x < 1$. For p(x) to be a probability density function, the value of A should be equal to

(*a*) $\mu - 1$ (*b*) $\mu + 1$

(*c*) $1/(\mu - 1)$ (*d*) $1/(\mu + 1)$

51. Four identical resistive strain gauges with gauge factor of 2.0 are used in a Wheatstone bridge as shown in the figure below. Only one of the strain gauges R_{SENSE} changes its resistance due to strain. If the output voltage V_{out} is measured to be 1 mV, the magnitude of strain, in units of microstrain, is

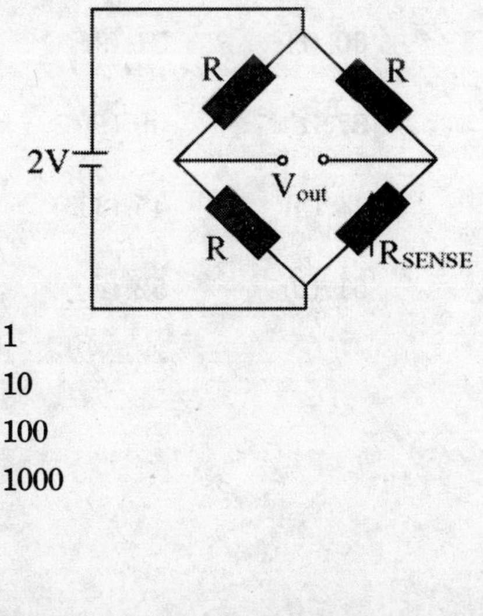

(*a*) 1

(*b*) 10

(*c*) 100

(*d*) 1000

52. A resistance-meter has five measurement range-settings between 200 Ω and 2 MΩ in multiples of 10. The meter measures resistance of a device by measuring resistance of a device by measuring a full-range voltage of 2V across the device by passing an appropriate constant current for each range-setting. If a device having a resistance value in the range 8 kΩ to 12kΩ and a maximum power rating of 100μW is to be measure safely with this meter, the choice for range-setting on the meter for best resolution in measurement, in kΩ, is

(*a*) 2

(*b*) 20

(*c*) 200

(*d*) 2000

53. A discrete-time signal $x(n) = e^{j\left(\frac{5\pi}{3}\right)n} + e^{j\left(\frac{\pi}{4}\right)n}$ is down-sampled to the signal xd(n) such that xd(n) = x(4n). The fundamental period of the down-sampled signal xd(n) is

54. The curve y = f(x) is such that the tangent to the curve at every point (x, y) has a Y-axis intercept c, given by c = –y. then, f(x) is proportional to

(*a*) x^{-1} (*b*) x^2

(*c*) x^3 (*d*) x^4

55. In a control system with unity gain feedback, the transfer function of the loop-gain function is L(s) = $9e^{-0.1s}/s$. The phase margin of the loop-gain function L(S)is ______ degree.

ANSWERS

General Aptitude

1. (*c*)	2. (*a*)	3. (*c*)	4. (*c*)	5. (*c*)	6. (*b*)	7. (*c*)
8. (*d*)	9. (*a*)	10. (*d*)				

Instrumentation Engineering

1. (*d*)	2. (*b*)	3. (*a*)	4. (*c*)	5. (*0.3*)	6. (*b*)	7. (*a*)
8. (*c*)	9. (0.13)	10. (4)	11. (20m/sec)	12. (*c*)	13. (1000)	14. (256)
15. (*d*)	16. (b)	17. (a)	18. (10)	19. (d)	20. (*a*)	21. (*b*)
22. (64)	23. (4)	24. (5)	25. (*c*)	26. (*d*)	27. (512)	28. (*d*)
29. (*b*)	30. (*c*)	31. (9)	32. (0.466)	33. (*b*)	34. (1000)	35. (4)
36. (c)	37. (*d*)	38. (*9*)	39. (0.042)	40. (*b*)	41. (0.896)	42. (a)
43. (8)	44. (*a*)	45. (300)	46. (a)	47. (d)	48. (20)	49. (*c*)
50. (*a*)	51. (*d*)	52. (*c*)	53. (6)	54. (*b*)	55. (38.43)	

EXPLANATIONS

GENERAL APTITUDE

1. From the given statement, the following venn-diagram can be formed

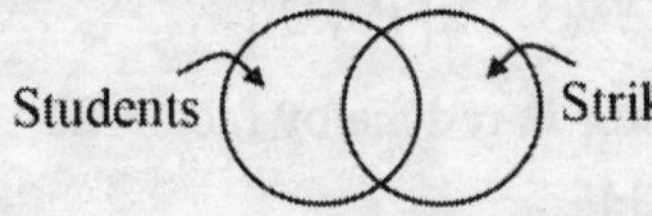

Some who were not involved in the strike were also students so, 4th statement will be true logically.

∴ Hence, option (c) is correct.

2. It is in the passive voice so had + been $+V_3$ form.
3. As no two odd or even numbers are next to each other and second number from left is exactly half of the left most number, the only possibility is

Left most 10 5 _ _ _ _

Now, middle number is twice the right most number, thus —

Left most 10 5 4 __ 2 Right most

Therefore, 7 must be the 2nd number from the right

Left most 10 5 4 7 2 Right most

4. Volume of cone is given by $\frac{1}{3}\pi r^2 h$

Now according to question, radius and height both increase by 10%

We know that, change in volume = Successive change of increase in radius and height.

∴ Successive change of 10%, 10% and 10% = successive of 21% and 10% i.e. 33.1%

Thus, percentage change in volume = 33.1%

5. The fishermen, to whom the flood victims owed their lives, were rewarded by the government.
6. Relative speed of both trains (80 + 100) = 180 km/hr

Initially they are separated by distance of 540 km

$$\therefore \text{ Time taken to meet } \frac{\text{Sum of distance}}{\text{Sum of speeds}} = \frac{540}{180} = 3\text{hrs}$$

Thus, they meet 3hrs after 7AM i.e., 10AM.

7. As per the data given

→ "baaj" is associated with "instrumental"

→ "gharana" is associated with "lineage"

→ "dhrupad" is associated with "baani"

→ "gayaki" is associated with "vocal"

Thus, baaj, institution is not correct

Hence option (c) is correct.

8. Head-hunter refers to the number of heads he could gather.
9. Population: 1400 million

Population with mobile phones

$$= \frac{70}{100} \times 1400 = 980$$

Population with mobile phones who can access internet = 294 million (given)

Population with mobile phones who access internet and buy goods from e-commerce portals

$$= \frac{50}{100} \times 294 = 147 \text{ million}$$

∴ Percentage of buyers in country

$$= \left[\frac{147}{1400} \times 100\right] = 10.5\%$$

10. The word 'some times' is not possible as you find indications like 'since the last one year' and the word 'finally' means almost coming to the conclusion. In addition to that the government comes in after RBI reduces repo rate.

INSTRUMENTATION ENGINEERING

1. It is a 2-bit asynchronous down counter, which counts XY = 00, 11, 10, 01, 11,

After one clerk pulse

2. For fig-(a)

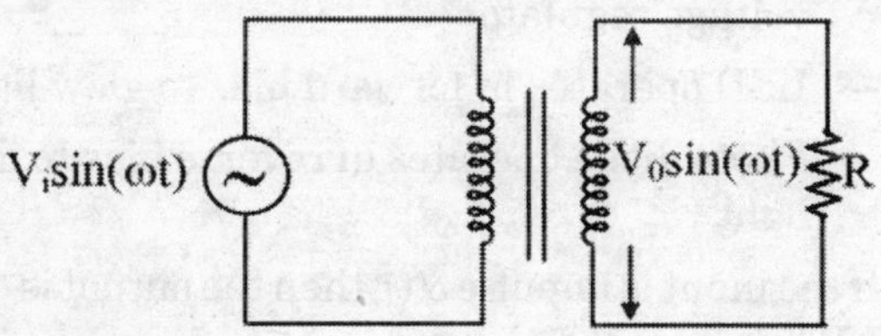

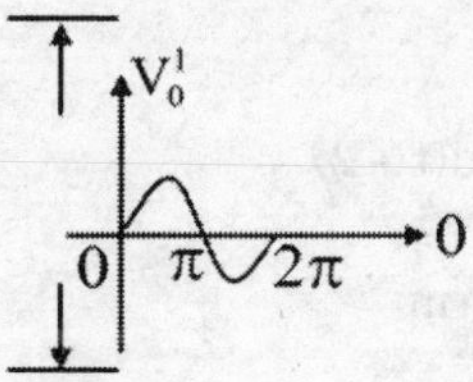

Here

$$V_{01} = V_0 \sin \omega t (\text{or}) V_{01} = V_0 \sin\theta (0 < \theta < 2\pi)$$

$$\therefore (V_{rms})_{o/p} = \sqrt{\frac{1}{2\pi}\int_0^{2\pi} V_0^2 d\theta}$$

$$= \sqrt{\frac{1}{2\pi}\int_0^{2\pi} V_0^2 \sin^2\theta d\theta}$$

$$= \sqrt{\frac{V_0^2}{2\pi}\int_0^{2\pi}\frac{1-\cos 2\theta}{\theta}d\theta} = \frac{V_0}{\sqrt{2}}$$

For fig-b

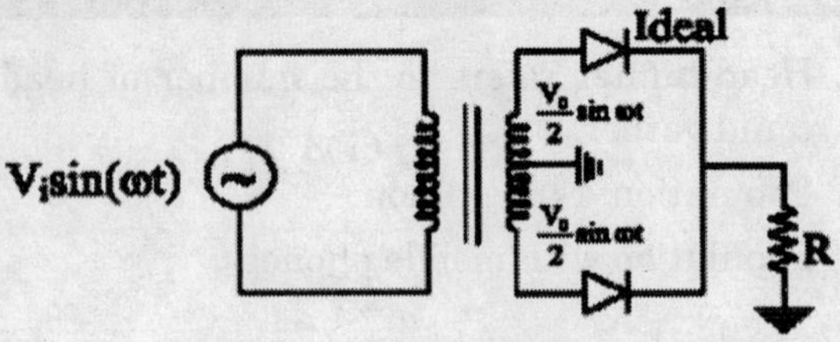

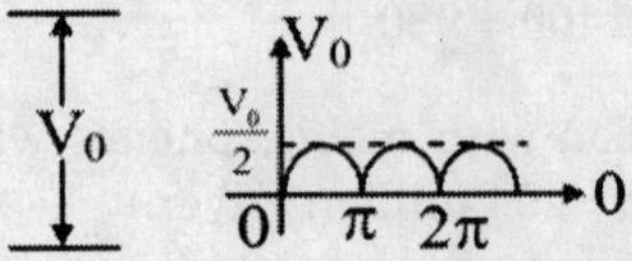

$$\therefore (V_{rms})_{0/p} = \sqrt{\frac{1}{2\pi}\int_0^{2\pi}\left(\frac{V_0}{2}\right)^2 \sin^2\theta d\theta}$$

$$= \frac{V_0}{2\sqrt{2}}$$

$$\therefore (V_{rms})_{0/p} = \frac{V_0}{2\sqrt{2}}$$

or

$$\therefore V_0 = V_0 \sin\omega t (\text{for} + \text{Ve half})$$

∴ The ratio of r.m.s of voltage fig-a to fig-b is

$$\frac{(V_{rms})_{fig-a}}{(V_{rms})_{fig-b}} = \frac{\frac{V_0}{\sqrt{2}}}{\frac{V_0}{2\sqrt{2}}} = \frac{2}{1} = 2:1$$

∴ option 'b' is correct one

3. → zener diode operates in reverse bias to act as voltage regulator
→ LED operates in forward bias to glow light
→ Photo diode operates in reverse bias to detect light

4. If the input is impulse $\delta(t)$, then the output is called I.R $h(t)$

$$\therefore \quad h(t) = \int_0^t \delta(t-2)d\tau = u(t-2)$$

Taking Lapalce transform

$$H(s) = \frac{e^{-2s}}{s}$$

5. Given modulated signal is

$$s(t) = \cos(2\pi f_c t) + 0.3\cos(2\pi f_m t)\cos(2\pi f_c t)$$
$$= \cos(2\pi f_c t)[1 + 0.3\cos(2\pi f_m t)]$$

$$\therefore \ s(t) = \cos(2\pi f_c t)[1 + 0.3\cos(2\pi f_m t)]$$

$$s_{Am}(t) = A_c\,[1 + \mu Ý\cos(2\pi f_m t)]\cos(2\pi f_c t)$$

$$\mu = 0.3$$

6. $Q_s = \frac{1}{R}\sqrt{\frac{L}{C}}$

Each is doubled

$$Q_s = \frac{1}{2R}\sqrt{\frac{2L}{2C}} = \frac{1}{2}\left[\frac{1}{R}\sqrt{\frac{L}{C}}\right]$$

So, Q-factor is reduce by factor '2'.

7. BIBO stable

$\therefore \ y(n) = \alpha y(n-1) + x(n)$

$\therefore \ |\alpha| < 1$

8. Zero dispersion wavelength or zero dispersion point the measured wavelength in a optical fiber where material dispersion and wavelength dispersion cancel each other.

9. $d_1 = 0.12V$, $d_2 = 0.05mA$

$$R = \sqrt{d_1^2 + d_2^2} = \sqrt{(0.12)^2 + (0.05)^2}$$
$$= \sqrt{0.0144 + 0.0025} = \sqrt{0.0169} = 0.13$$

10. A and B inputs are available at t = 0 and state throughout process.

The max time taken for input 'C_i' to produce C_{i+1} output is $= t_{AND} + t_{OR} = 2 + 2 = 4$

11. $S_{fluid} = 1kg/m^3$

$\Delta p = 200N/m^2$

$C_V = 1.0$

$$V_f = C_V\sqrt{2\frac{\Delta p}{\rho}} = 1\sqrt{\frac{2\times 200}{1}} = 20\,m/s$$

12. Given $\vec{a} = i + 2j + 5k$

$$\vec{b} = i + 2j - k$$

The vectors $\vec{a}, \vec{b}, \vec{c}$ are orthogonal

$\therefore \ \vec{a}.\,\vec{b} = 0,\ \vec{b}.\,\vec{c} = 0,\ \vec{a}.\,\vec{c} = 0$

∴ Option (c) satisfies

$\therefore \ \vec{c} = 2i - j$

Clearly $\vec{a}.\,\vec{c} = (i + 2j + 5k).(2i - j) = 2 - 2 = 0$

$\vec{b}.\,\vec{c} = (i + 2j - k).(2i - j) = 2 - 2 = 0$

13.

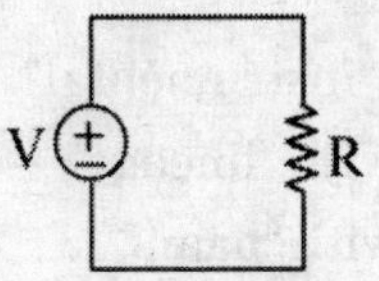

$$P_{abs} = \frac{V^2}{R}$$

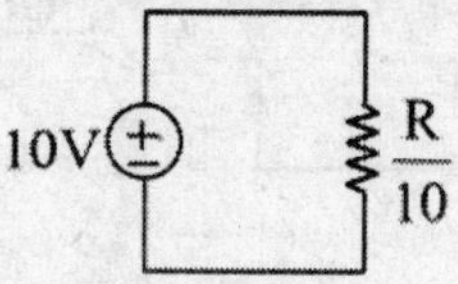

$$P_{abs} = \frac{(10V)^2}{R/10} = 1000\left[\frac{V^2}{R}\right]$$

14. Total No of Boolean functions formed by 3 Boolean variables is $= 2^{2^3} = 2^8 = 256$

15. CMRR for an ideal instrumentation Amplifier is infinite, $= \left|\frac{A_d}{A_{CM}}\right|$

$$CMRR_{dB} = 20\log\left|\frac{A_d}{A_{CM}}\right|$$

Option (a) will not be answer because of negative dB

Option (b) will not be answer as $A_d \neq A_{CM}$

Option (c) will not be answer $A_d \neq 1.5\,A_{CM}$

Option (d) could be the answer.

16. Given $\vec{A} = \nabla u$

$\therefore$ curl $(\vec{A}) = \text{curl}(\nabla u) = 0.$

For any scalar function

17. In a cascade (or) master-slave control system, the slave loop (inner loop) must be faster than the master loop (outer loop)

For proper control, slave loop should be atleast 3 times faster than the master loop (outer loop)

$\tau_{\text{outer Loop}} \geq 3\tau_{\text{inner Loop}}$

$\tau_2 \geq 3\tau_1$

Hence we can say inner loop time constant is much lower than the outer loop time constant

18. Given that eigen values of 3 × 3 matrix are 1, 2, 5

We know that det = product of eigen values

$= 1 \times 2 \times 5 = 10$

19. $L(s) = \frac{k}{(s+1)(s+2)(s+3)}$

Gain crossover frequency < Phase crossover frequency

$\omega_{gc} < \omega_{pc}$

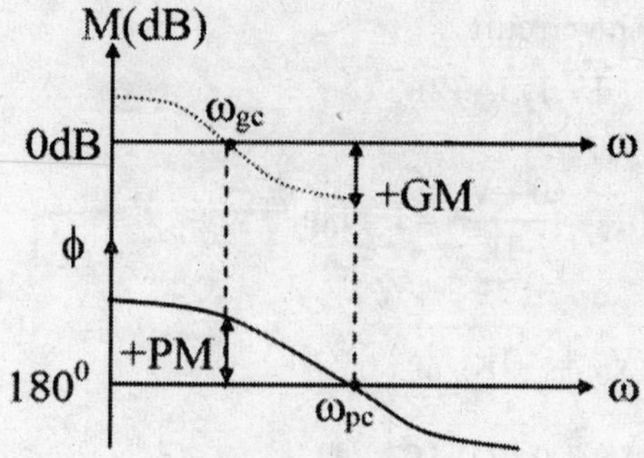

$\omega_{pc} > \omega_{gc}$ system is stable because, in this case GM and PM is positive.

20. Given that Box contains 8 Red Balls and 8 Green Balls and two Balls are drawn successively without replacement.

Required Probablity $= \frac{8}{16} \times \frac{8}{15} = \frac{4}{15}$

21. Thermocouple is an active transducer works on the principle of seebeck effect

22. In a N-Bit Binary weighted resistor Digital to Analog converter, the largest value of resistance

$= 2^{N-1}R = 2^{(8-1)}, (500)$

$= 128 \times 0.5 = 64k\Omega$

23.

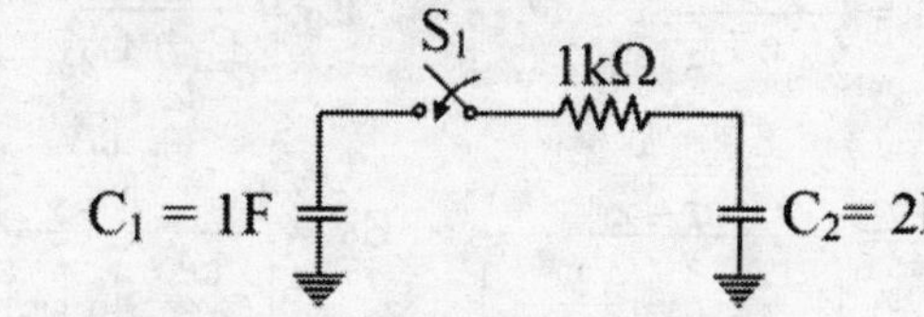

By law of conservation of charge

$q_T = q_1 + q_2$

$C_T V_T = C_1 V_1 + C_2 V_2$

Where $C_1 = 1F, V_1 = 6V$ and $q_1 = 6C$

$C_2 = 2F, V_2 = 0V$ and $q_2 = 0$

Parallel, $[1 + 2]\, V_T = (1)\,(6) + (2)\,(0)$

$V_T = 2$ volts

So, $q_2 = C_2 V_T = (2)\,(2) = 4C$

24. P_{max} occurs if $R_L = R_S$

So, $R_L = 5\Omega$

25.

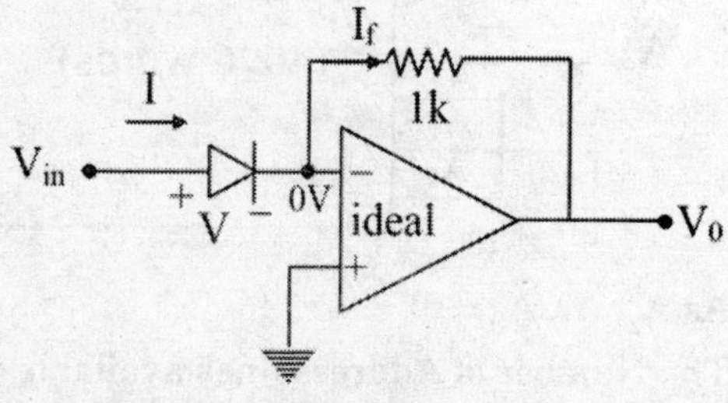

given that $I = I_0 e^{\frac{V}{V_T}} \rightarrow (1)$

from the circuit

$$I = I_f \rightarrow (2)$$

$$I_f = \frac{0 - V_0}{1k} = I = I_0 e^{\frac{V}{V_T}}$$

$$\therefore \quad V_0 = (-1k) I_0 e^{\frac{V}{V_T}}$$

$$\therefore \quad V_0 = 0 - (1k) I_0 e \frac{V_{in}}{V_T}$$

Hence $V_0 \alpha\, e^{\frac{V_{in}}{V_T}}$

$\therefore$ option 'c' is correct one

26. $\Delta V = V_1 - V_2$

$$\Delta V = \frac{x}{d} E$$

$$= \frac{10mm}{50mm} \times 10 = 2V$$

Detailed solution

$$C_1 = \frac{\varepsilon A}{d + x}, \qquad C_2 = \frac{\varepsilon A}{d - x}$$

$$E_1 = \frac{C_2}{C_1 + C_2}.E \qquad E_2 = \frac{C_1.E}{C_1 + C_2}$$

$$E_1 = \frac{\frac{\varepsilon A}{d-x}}{\left(\frac{\varepsilon A}{d-x}\right) + \left(\frac{\varepsilon A}{d+x}\right)} \qquad E_2 = \frac{\frac{\varepsilon A}{d+x}}{\left(\frac{\varepsilon A}{d-x}\right) + \left(\frac{\varepsilon A}{d+x}\right)}$$

$$E_1 = \frac{d+x}{2d}.E \qquad E_2 = \frac{d-x}{2d}$$

$$\Delta V = E_1 - E_2 = E\frac{x}{d} = 2V$$

27.

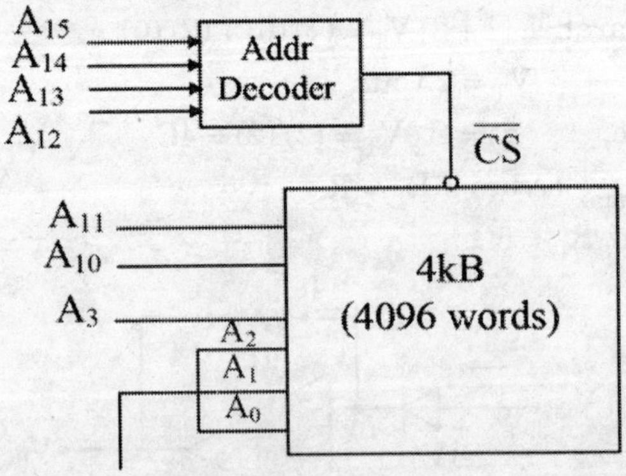

As $A_2, A_1, A_0 = 0$

The Number of Address lines available for main internal Access is = 12 – 3 = 9 the number of words addressable = $2^9 = 512$

28.

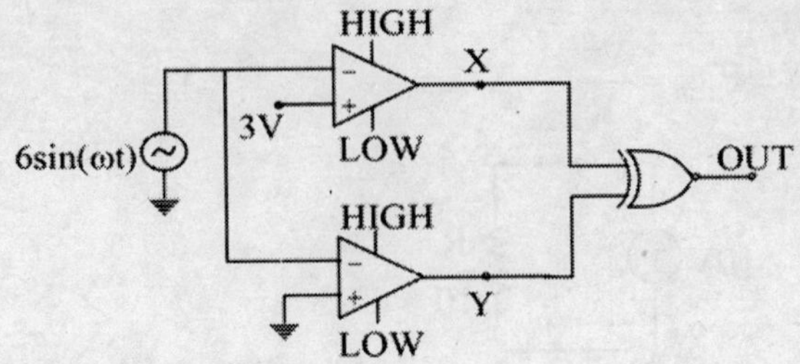

$V_{in} \geq 3 \Rightarrow X = 0$

$V_{in} < 3 \Rightarrow X = 1$

$V_{in} < 0 \Rightarrow \pm Y = 0$

$V_{in} < 0 \Rightarrow Y = 1$

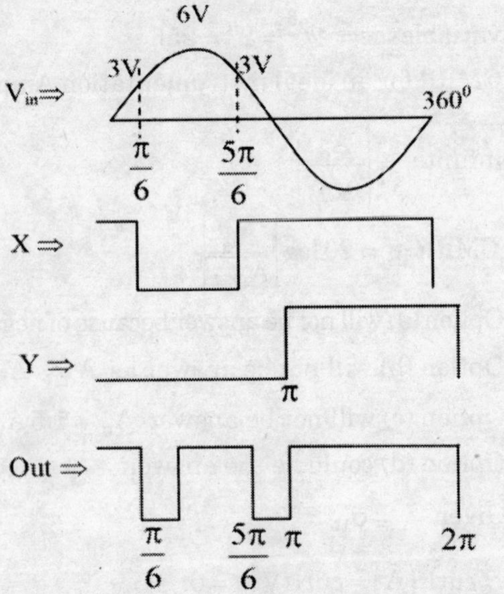

The output is high for $\left(\frac{\pi}{6} \text{to} \frac{5\pi}{6}\right)$ and $(\pi \text{ to} 2\pi)$

$$= \left(\frac{5\pi}{6} - \frac{\pi}{6}\right) + (2\pi - \pi) = \frac{10\pi}{6}$$

$$\text{Ratio} \Rightarrow \frac{10\frac{\pi}{6}}{2\pi} = \frac{5}{6}$$

29. Resolution of encoder $= \frac{V_{ref}}{2^n - 1}$

1kPa ⇒ 30mV

100kPa ⇒ 3000 mV = 3V

Noise of readout circuit = 3V + 0.3mV

$V_{ref} = 3.0003V$

$$\text{Resolution} = \frac{3.0003}{2^{10} - 1} = \frac{3.0003}{1023} = 0.00293V$$

1kPa → 30mV

$$0.00293V \times \frac{1kPa}{30mV} \leftarrow 0.00293V$$

Resolution from i/p side = 97.666Pa ≈ 100Pa

30.

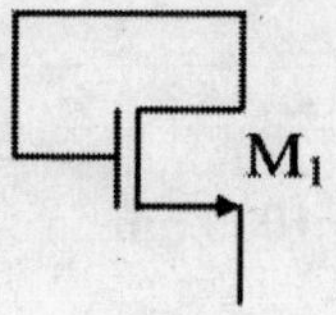

$$\frac{1}{g_{mn}} \parallel r_{on} \approx \frac{1}{g_{mn}}$$

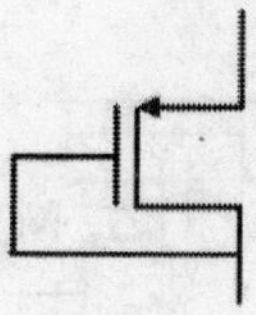

$$\frac{1}{g_{mp}} \parallel r_{op} \approx \frac{1}{g_{mp}}$$

AC Equivalent

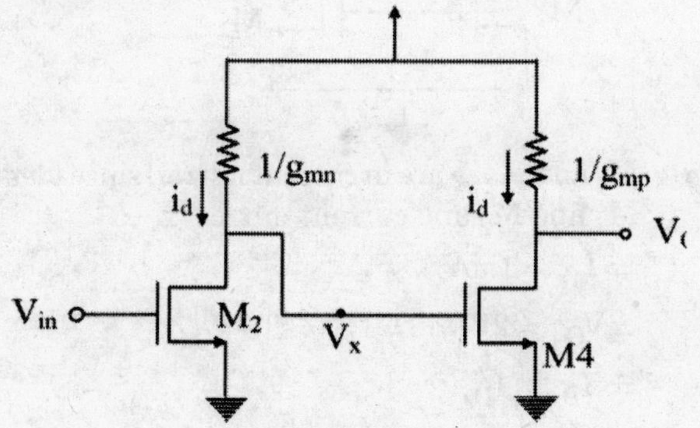

$$\frac{V_0}{V_{in}} = \frac{V_0 V_x}{V_x V_{in}} = \frac{-i_d\left[\frac{1}{g_{mp}}\right]}{V_g S_2} \cdot \frac{-i_d\left[\frac{1}{g_{mn}}\right]}{V_g S_2}$$

$$= \frac{-\frac{1}{g_{mn}}}{\frac{1}{g_{mp}}} \cdot \frac{-\frac{1}{g_{mp}}}{\frac{1}{g_{mn}}} = \frac{g_{mn}}{g_{mp}}$$

31.

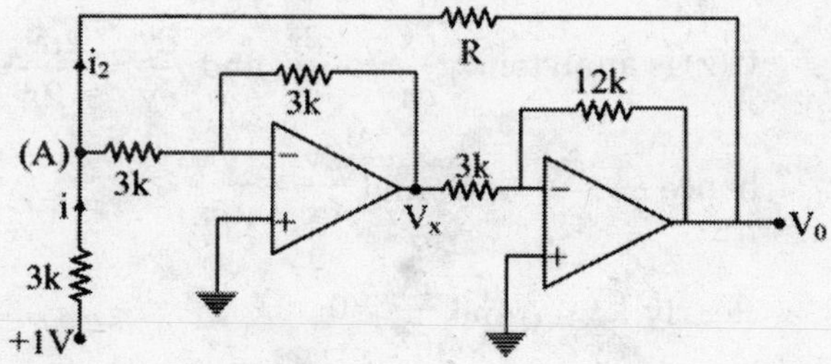

At Node (A), KCL →

$$i = i_1 + i_2 \Rightarrow \frac{1-V_A}{3k} = \frac{V_A - 0}{3k} + \frac{V_A - V_0}{R}$$

Given i = 0

$$\Rightarrow \frac{1-V_A}{3k} = 0 \Rightarrow V_A = 1 \to 0$$

$$\Rightarrow \frac{1-0}{3k} + \frac{1-V_0}{R} = 0$$

$$\Rightarrow 1 - V_0 = \frac{-R}{3k} \Rightarrow R = 3k(V_0 - 1)$$

if we find V_0, we get the answer from Op-Amp (1),

$$V_x = \frac{-3k}{3k}(V_A) = -1V$$

Also from op-Amp(2),

$$V_0 = \frac{-12k}{3k}(V_x) = -4(-1) = 4V$$

$\therefore$ R = 3k (4 − 1) = 9kW

(OR)

Ideal op-amp; I = 0

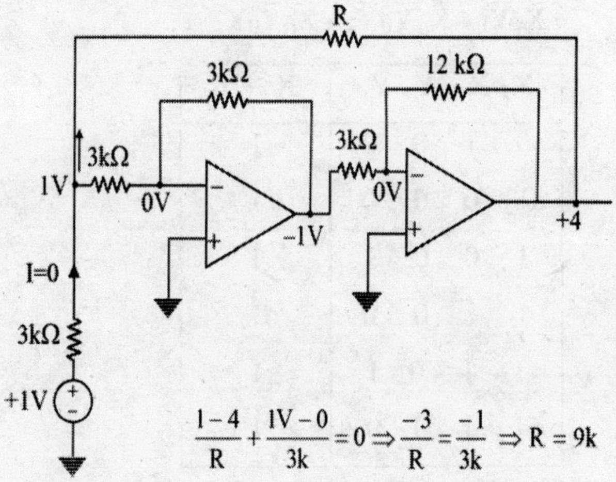

$$\frac{1-4}{R} + \frac{1V-0}{3k} = 0 \Rightarrow \frac{-3}{R} = \frac{-1}{3k} \Rightarrow R = 9k$$

32. $\frac{Y(s)}{X(s)} = \frac{1}{s+3}$

Convert into differential equation

(s + 3) Y(s) = X (s)

$$\frac{dy}{dt} + 3y = x(t) \qquad \frac{dy}{dt} + 3y = u(t)$$

Apply Laplace Transform

$$sY(s) - Y(0) + 3Y(s) = X(s)$$

$$Y(s)(s+3) = \frac{1}{s} + 3$$

$$Y(s)(s+3) = \frac{3s+1}{s} = \frac{3\left(s+\frac{1}{3}\right)}{s}$$

$$Y(s)(s+3) = \frac{3\left(s+\frac{1}{3}\right)}{s(s+3)} = \frac{A}{s} + \frac{B}{s+3}$$

$$A = \frac{3\times\frac{1}{3}}{3} = \frac{1}{3}$$

$$B = \frac{3\left(-3+\frac{1}{3}\right)}{3} = \frac{-1(-9+1)}{3} = \frac{-1(-8)}{3} = \frac{8}{3}$$

$$y(t) = \frac{1}{3} + \frac{8}{3}e^{-3t}$$

$$y(1) = \frac{1}{3} + \frac{8}{3}e^{-3} = 0.466$$

33. Method : 1

X > Y if $X_1 > Y_1$ and $X_0 > Y_0$

i.e X > Y if $X_1\overline{Y}_1 + (X_1 \odot Y_1)X_0\overline{Y}_0$

$= X_1\overline{Y}_1 + \left[\overline{X}_1\overline{Y}_1 + X_1X_1\right]X_0\overline{Y}_0$

$= X_1\overline{Y}_1 + X_1\overline{Y}_1X_0\overline{Y}_0 + X_1Y_1X_0\overline{Y}_0$

$= X_1\overline{Y}_1 + \overline{Y}_1X_0\overline{Y}_0 + X_1Y_1X_1\overline{Y}_0$

$= X_1\overline{Y}_1 + \overline{Y}_1X_0\overline{Y}_0 + X_1X_0\overline{Y}_0$

$= X_1\overline{Y}_1 + X_0\overline{Y}_0\overline{Y}_1 + X_0\overline{Y}_0X_1$

X_1 X_0 Y_1 Y_0	X > Y
0 1 0 0	1
1 0 0 0	1
1 0 0 1	1
1 1 0 0	1
1 1 0 1	1
1 1 1 0	1

⇒ X > Y expression is

S = Σm (4, 8, 9, 12, 13, 14)

Y_1Y_0 1/0 X_1X_0	Y_1Y_0 00	Y_1Y 01	Y_1Y_0 11	Y_1Y_0 10
$\overline{X}_1\overline{X}_0$ 00				
$\overline{X}_1X_0$ 01	1			
X_1X_0 11	1	1		1
$X_1\overline{X}_0$ 10	1	1		

$S = X_1\overline{Y}_1 + X_1X_0\overline{Y}_0 + X_0\overline{Y}_1\overline{Y}_0$

34. For bright spot OPD = $n\lambda_1$

$2x = n\lambda_1$

For dark spot $2x = (2m + 1)\dfrac{\lambda_2}{2}$

$$n\lambda_1 = (2m+1)\frac{\lambda_2}{2}$$

$$n(500) = (2m+1)\frac{400}{2}$$

5n = 4m + 2

For m = 2 conditions satisfied

and for n = 2

So, $2x = n\lambda$

2x = (2) (500 nm)

2x = 1000nm

Optical path difference = 2x = 1000 nm

35. $(6 - V_0 - V_{TH})_2 = (2 - V_{TH})^2$

$6 - V_0 - V_{TH} = 2 - V_{TH}$

$V_0 = 4V$

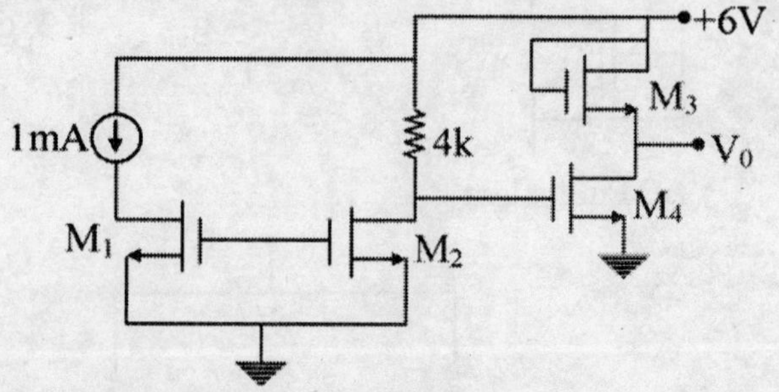

M_1 and M_2 → are in current mirror, since identical M_1 and M_2 and current mirror

$\Rightarrow I_{4k} = 1mA$

$\therefore V_{G4} = 2V\,(\because 6 = I_{4k}(4k) + V_{G4}).$

$\Rightarrow I_{D_3} = I_{D_4}$

$\therefore (6 - V_0 - V_{th})^2 = (2 - 0 - V_{th})^2$

$6 - V_0 = 2 \Rightarrow V_0 = 4V.$

36. Given f(z) = u (x,y) + i v(x,y) is analytic

And conjugate f*(z) = u(x,y) – i v(x,y) also analytic in entire complex plane.

f(z) is analytic ⇒ C R equations holds

$\dfrac{\partial x}{\partial x} = \dfrac{\partial v}{\partial y}$ ad $\dfrac{\partial y}{\partial y} = -\dfrac{\partial v}{\partial x}$

f*(z) is analytic ⇒ $\dfrac{\partial x}{\partial x} = -\dfrac{\partial v}{\partial y}$ and $\dfrac{\partial y}{\partial y} = -\dfrac{\partial v}{2x}$

hence ⇒ $\dfrac{\partial v}{\partial y} = -\dfrac{\partial v}{\partial y}$ and $\dfrac{\partial v}{\partial x} = -\dfrac{\partial v}{\partial x}$

clearly $\dfrac{\partial v}{\partial y} = 0$ and $\dfrac{\partial v}{\partial x} = 0$

∴ v = constant

∴ u = constant

∴ f(z) = u + i v = constant

37. $\begin{bmatrix}\dot{x}_1\\ \dot{x}_2\end{bmatrix} = \begin{bmatrix}1 & 2\\ -3 & -4\end{bmatrix}\begin{bmatrix}x_1\\ x_2\end{bmatrix} + \begin{bmatrix}20\\ 10\end{bmatrix}$

$\dot{x} = AX + K$

Where $A = \begin{bmatrix}1 & 2\\ -3 & -4\end{bmatrix}$

$K = \begin{bmatrix}20\\ 10\end{bmatrix}$

$$\dot{x}(t) = Ax(t) + K$$

$$sX(s) - X(0) = AX(s) + \frac{K}{s}$$

$$(sI - A)\,X(s) = X(0) + \frac{K}{s}$$

$$X(s) = (sI - A)^{-1}\,X(0) + (sI - A)^{-1}\,\frac{K}{s}$$

$$x(t) = L^{-1}\,(sI - A)^{-1}\,x(0) + L^{-1}\,(sI - A)^{-1}\,\frac{K}{s}$$

Now, $x(\infty) = \underset{s\to 0}{Lt}\ sX(s)$

$$= \underset{s\to 0}{Lt}\left[(sI - A)^{-1}x(0) + (sI - A)^{-1}\frac{K}{s}\right]$$

$$= (sI - A)^{-1}x(0) + \underset{s\to 0}{Lt}\,(sI - A)^{-1}\frac{K}{s}$$

$$= 0 + \underset{s\to 0}{Lt}\,(sI - A)^{-1}K$$

$$(sI - A)^{-1} = \left[s\begin{bmatrix}1 & 0\\ 0 & 1\end{bmatrix} - \begin{bmatrix}1 & 2\\ -3 & -4\end{bmatrix}\right]^{-1}$$

$$= \begin{bmatrix}s-1 & -2\\ 3 & s+4\end{bmatrix}^{-1}$$

$$= \frac{1}{(s+4)(s-1)+6}\begin{bmatrix}s-4 & -2\\ -3 & s-1\end{bmatrix}$$

$$x(\infty) = \underset{s\to 0^s}{Lt} = \frac{\begin{bmatrix}s-4 & 2\\ -3 & s-1\end{bmatrix}}{(s+4)(s-1)+6}\frac{\begin{bmatrix}20\\ 10\end{bmatrix}}{s}$$

$$= \frac{\begin{bmatrix}4 & 2\\ -3 & -1\end{bmatrix}\begin{bmatrix}20\\ 10\end{bmatrix}}{-4+6} = \frac{\begin{bmatrix}80+20\\ -16-10\end{bmatrix}}{2}$$

$$x(\infty) = \frac{\begin{bmatrix}100\\ -70\end{bmatrix}}{2} = \begin{bmatrix}50\\ -35\end{bmatrix}$$

38. $y(t) = x(t) + \frac{1}{2}x(t-1)$

$$Y(\omega) = X(\omega) + \frac{1}{2}e^{-j\omega}X(\omega)$$

$$Y(\omega) = \left(1 + \frac{1}{2}e^{-j\omega}\right)X(\omega)$$

$$\therefore\ H(\omega) = 1 + \frac{1}{2}e^{-j\omega}$$

$$Y(\omega) = X(\omega).H(\omega)$$

$$|Y(\omega)|^2 = |X(\omega)|^2\,.\,|H(\omega)|$$

$$\therefore\ |Y(0)|^2 = |X(0)|^2\,.\,|H(0)|^2 = 4\frac{9}{4} = 9$$

$$H(0) = 1 + \frac{1}{2} = \frac{3}{2}$$

$$\therefore\ |Y(0)|^2 = 9$$

39. $z_1 z_2 = z_2 z_3$

$$\left(R_1 \,//\, \frac{1}{j\omega C_1}\right)(R_4) = \left(R_2 \,//\, \frac{1}{j\omega C_2}\right)(R_3)$$

$$\left(\frac{R_1}{1 + j\omega C_1 R_1}\right)(R_4) = \left(\frac{R_2}{1 + j\omega C_2 R_2}\right)(R_3)$$

$$\frac{R_1 R_4}{1 + j\omega C_1 R_1} = \frac{R_2 R_3}{1 + j\omega C_2 R_2}$$

$$R_1 R_4 + j\omega R_1 R_4 R_2 C_2 = R_2 R_3 + j\omega R_1 R_2 R_3 C_1$$

$$R_1 R_4 = R_2 R_3$$

$$R_2 = \frac{R_1 R_4}{R_3} = \frac{375k \times 14.7k}{10k} = 551.25k\Omega$$

$$R_1 R_4 R_2 C_2 = R_1 R_2 R_3 C_1$$

$$C_2 = \frac{R_1 R_2 R_3 C_1}{R_1 R_4 R_2} = \frac{R_3 C_1}{R_4} = \frac{0.1\mu F \times 10k}{14.7k}$$

$$D = \frac{1}{2\pi \times 100 \times 551.25k0.068\mu F} = 0.04248$$

40.

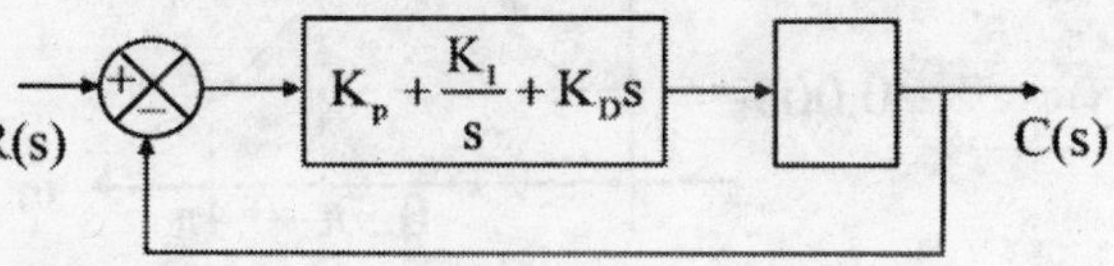

$$G(s) = \left(10 + \frac{1}{s} + 2s\right)\left(\frac{3}{s}\right)$$

$$G(s) = \frac{3\left(2s^2 + 10s + 1\right)}{s^2}$$

$r(t) = t^2$

Steady state error, $e_{ss}\left(t^2\right) = \left(\frac{2}{K_a}\right)$

$$K_a = \underset{s\to 0}{Lt}\ s^2 G(s) = \underset{s\to 0}{Lt}\ s^2\left[\frac{3(2s^2 + 10s + 1)}{s^2}\right]$$

$$e_{ss} = \frac{2}{K_a} = \frac{2}{3}$$

41. $V(t) = V(\infty) + [V(0) - V(\infty)]e^{-t/\tau}$

$V(0) = 0V$

$$V(\infty) = 5\left[\frac{3k}{5k}\right] = 3V$$

$$\tau = R_{eq}.C$$

$$R_{eq} = 2k // 3k = \frac{6}{5}k$$

$$T = \frac{6}{5}k \times 5nF = 6\mu sec$$

$$V(t) = 3[1 - e^{-t/6\mu}]$$

$$V(t = 6\mu)$$

$$V(t) = 3\left[1 - e^{-1}\right] = 3[1 - 0.367] = 1.896 \text{ Volts}$$

42. Step (ii) :

At t = 0 sec

⇒ ± switch S1 is closed

⇒ LED is ON ⇒ ± LDR resistance becomes 500Ω

⇒ ± $V_{1k\Omega}$ = 2V ⇒ $\bar{S}$ = 0 and $\bar{R}$ = 1

i.e S = 1 and R = 0 ⇒ Q = 1

⇒ ± As Q = 1 ⇒ BJT is ON

Step (ii) :

At t = 1msec ⇒ Switch S_1 is open, but BJT is still ON as Q =1

Thus LED is permanently ON once the switch is closed.

43.

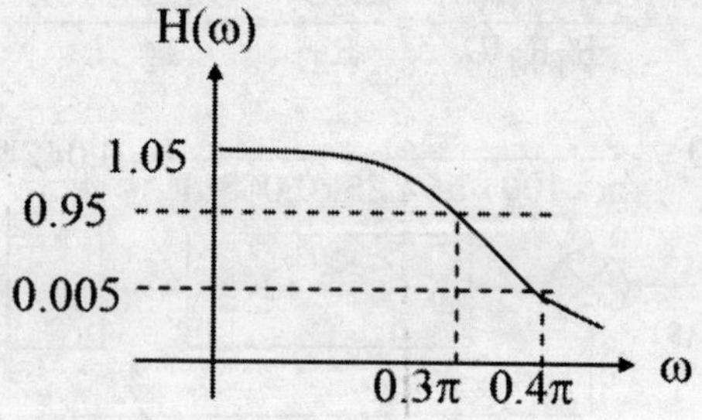

$$\therefore \Omega = \frac{\omega}{f_s}$$

$$\Rightarrow f_s = \frac{\omega}{\Omega} = \frac{1.2k(2\pi)}{0.3\pi} = \frac{2.4}{0.3} = 8kHz$$

44. P_{inc} = 100 W

Light intensity $I = \frac{P_{inc}}{4\pi r^2} = \frac{100}{4\pi \times 1^2} = 7.96 \, W/m^2$

Detector diameter = d = 2 cm = 0.02 m,

r = d/2 = 0.01 m

Power incident on photo detector

= 7.96 W/m^2 × π × 0.01^2 m^2

= 25 × 0.01^{2}W

Photo current generated in detector

= I = RP

= 0.4A/W × 25 × 0.01^2 W

= 1 mA

45. $V_1(t) = x(t)\sin(2\pi f_0 t)$

$$V_1(f) = \frac{1}{2j}[X(f - f_0) - X(f + f_0)]$$

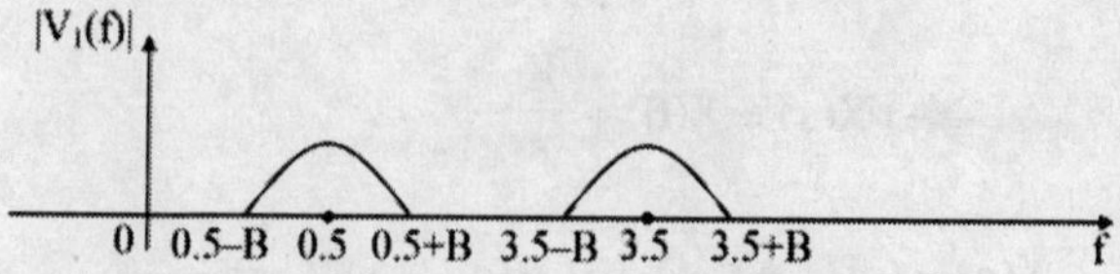

$V_1(f)$ passed through LPF with cut-off frequency 2.8GHz

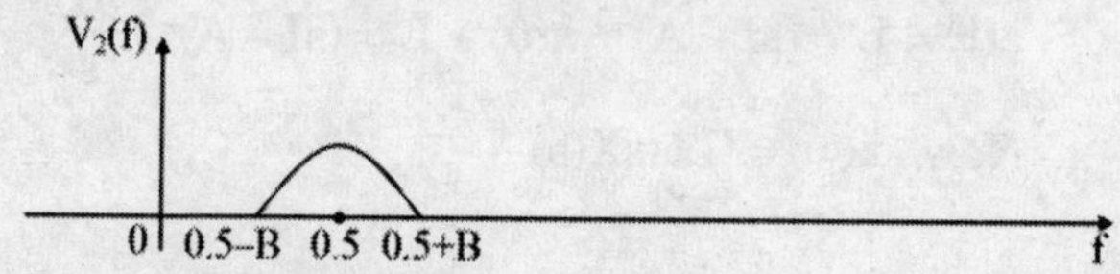

Sampled at 1.6 GHz ≥ 2fm

1.6 ≥ 2[0.5 + B]

1.6 ≥ 1+ 2B

2B ≤ 0.6

B ≤ 0.3 GHz

B ≤ 300 MHz

46.

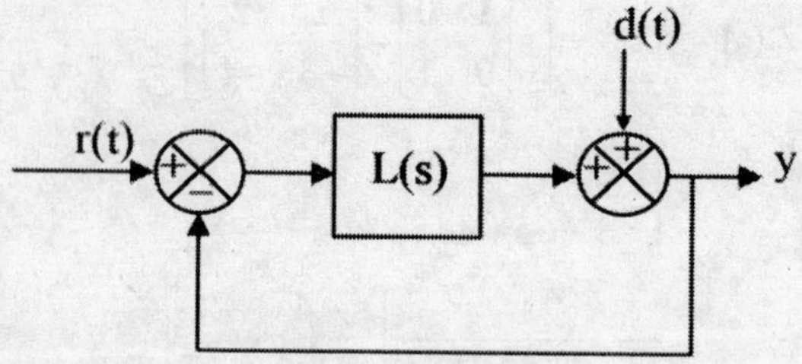

$$y = \frac{rL + d}{1 + L}$$

$$\frac{y}{d} = \frac{1}{1 + L}$$

$$\Rightarrow y = \frac{d}{1 + L} = \frac{0.1}{1 + 1.00} \approx 0.1 \times 10^{-2} = 10^{-3}$$

47. P_{width} = 1 nanosec

Pulsed laser f = 1kHz → T = $\frac{1}{f}$ =1msec

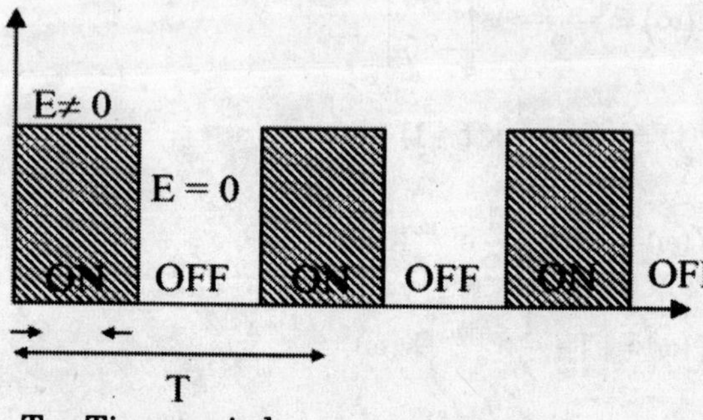

T = Time period

Energy of laser pulse width = $\frac{E}{T}$

$$P_{peak} = \frac{E}{\Delta t} = P_{single\ pulse}$$

E will be same for both cases

$P_{avg} \times T = E$

$P_{peak} \times \Delta t = E$

By equating E

$P_{avg} \times T = P_{peak} \times \Delta t$

$$\frac{P_{avg} \times T}{\Delta t} = P_{peak}$$

$$\frac{1mW \times 1m\sec}{1n\sec} = \frac{10^{-3} \times 10^{-3}}{10^{-9}} = 1000W$$

48. At resonance

$$\omega_0 = \frac{1}{\sqrt{LC}} = \frac{1}{\sqrt{5 \times 10^{-3} \times 500 \times 10^{-9}}}$$

$$= \frac{1}{\sqrt{25 \times 10^{-10}}} = \frac{1}{5 \times 10^{-5}} = \frac{10^5}{5}$$

= 20000rad / sec = 20 krad/sec

49.

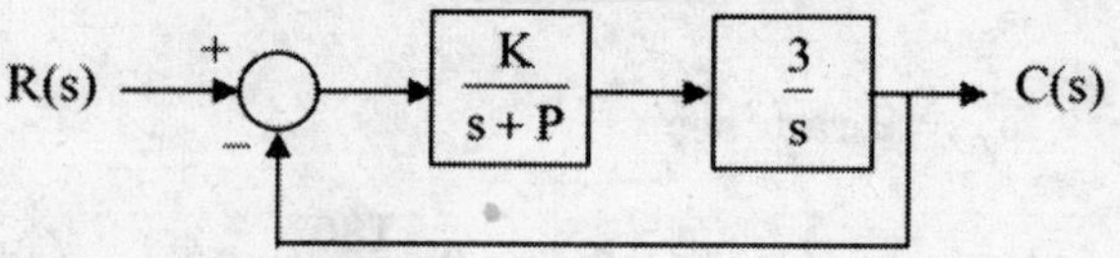

$$G(s) = \frac{3k}{s(s+P)}$$

$s = 3 + j3\sqrt{3}$

Now,

$$\phi\angle G(-3+j3\sqrt{3}) = \frac{\angle(3k)}{\angle -3 + j3\sqrt{3}\angle -3 + j3\sqrt{3} + P}$$

$$= \frac{\angle 0°}{\left(\pi - \tan^{-1}(\sqrt{3})\right)\left(\tan^{-1}\left(\frac{3\sqrt{3}}{P-3}\right)\right)}$$

$$-\left(120° + \tan^{-1}\left(\frac{3\sqrt{3}}{P-3}\right)\right) = -180°$$

$$\tan^{-1}\left(\frac{3\sqrt{3}}{P-3}\right) = 60°$$

$$\frac{3\sqrt{3}}{P-3} = \sqrt{3}$$

$P - 3 = 3$

$\therefore \; P = 6$

50. Given $P(x) = \frac{A}{x^u} 1 \le x < \infty$

For a valid probability density function

$$\int_1^\infty P(x)dx = 1$$

$$\Rightarrow \int_1^\infty \frac{A}{X^u}dx = 1 \Rightarrow A - \left.\frac{X^{-u+1}}{-u+1}\right|_1^\infty = 1$$

$$\frac{A}{1-u}[0-1] = 1$$

$$\Rightarrow \frac{A}{u-1} = 1$$

$\therefore \; A = u - 1$

51. $V_{Bri} = \frac{V_s}{4}\frac{\Delta R}{R}$

$$V_{Bri} = \frac{V_s}{4}G_f \times \text{strain}$$

$$1 \times 10^{-3} = \frac{2}{4} \times 2 \times \text{strain}$$

$$\text{Strain} = 1 \times 10^{-3} = 1000\mu$$

52. Full range voltage : 2 volts

Maximum full scale current rating in individual range are:

$200\ \Omega$ range $\Rightarrow \pm \frac{2}{200} = 10mA$

$2\ k\Omega$ range $\Rightarrow \pm \frac{2}{200} = 1mA$

$20\ k\Omega$ range $\Rightarrow$ 0.1 mA = 100 nA

$200\ k\Omega$ range $\Rightarrow$ 0.01 mA = 10 nA

$2000\ k\Omega$ range $\Rightarrow$ 1 nA

Specifications of given device : 100μ W, $8\ k\Omega - 12\ k\Omega$

Current rating corresponding to $8\ k\Omega$

$$\Rightarrow I_1 = \sqrt{\frac{100 \times 10^{-6}}{8 \times 10^3}}$$

$$= \sqrt{12.5 \times 10^{-9}} = \sqrt{1.25 \times 10^{-8}}$$

$I_1 = 0.118$ mA

Current rating corresponding to $12\ k\Omega$

$$\Rightarrow I_2 = \sqrt{\frac{100 \times 10^{-6}}{12 \times 10^3}}$$

$$= \sqrt{8.33 \times 10^{-9}} = \sqrt{0.833 \times 10^{-8}}$$

$= 0.0912$ mA

If $20k\Omega$ range selected then maximum current flow would be 0.1mA and it is more than current rating of device (0.0912 mA) if resistance of device is $12\ k\Omega$. Hence device would be damaged.

The next best range for measurement is $200k\Omega$ where maximum current rating of range is 0.01 mA which is less than current rating of device and it is safe. The best resolution is possible for lower safe range for given specifications.

53. $x(n) = e^{j\left(\frac{5\pi}{3}\right)n} + e^{j\left(\frac{\pi}{4}\right)n}$

$$x_d(n) = x(4n) = e^{j\left(\frac{20\pi}{3}\right)n} + e^{j\pi n}$$

$$\omega_0 = \text{GCD}\left(\frac{20\pi}{3}, \pi\right) = \text{GCD}\left(\frac{20\pi}{3}, \frac{3\pi}{3}\right) = \frac{\pi}{3}$$

$$\text{Fundamental period} = N = \frac{2\pi}{\frac{\pi}{3}} = 6$$

54. For the curve $y = x^2$, every point (x, y) on the curve, if we draw the tangent at (x, y) the tangent intersects y-axis with negative intercept.

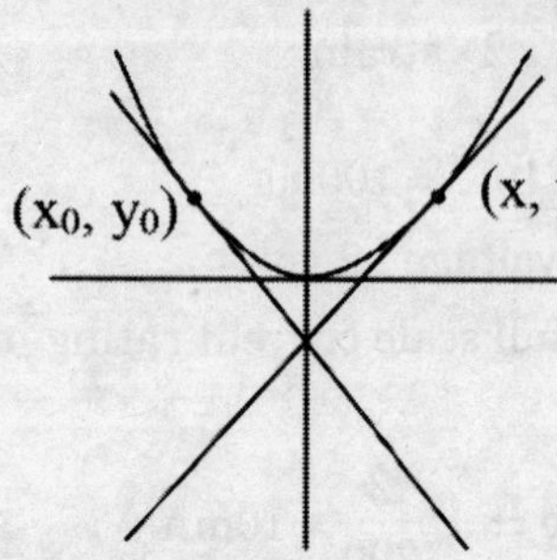

From the option (b) if we take the curve $y = x^2$. Let (x_0, y_0) is a point on the curve. Then tangent at (x_0, y_0) is $y - y_0 = m(x - x_0)$

$$\Rightarrow \pm y - y_0 = 2x_0(x - x_0) \qquad \frac{d}{dx}(x^2) = 2x$$

$$\Rightarrow \pm y - y_0 = 2x_0(0 - x_0)$$

(Since it has y intercept only)

$$\Rightarrow \pm y = y_0 - 2x_0^2$$

$$\Rightarrow \pm y = y_0 - 2y_0 \qquad (\because y_0 = x_0^2)$$

$$\Rightarrow \pm y = -y_0$$

55. $L(s) = \dfrac{9e^{-0.1s}}{s}$

$$s = j\omega$$

$$L(j\omega) = \frac{9e^{-j0.1\omega}}{j\omega}$$

$$M = \frac{9}{\omega}$$

$$\phi = -0.1\omega \times \frac{180°}{\pi} - 90°$$

$$\omega_{gc} M = 1$$

$$\frac{9}{\omega_{gc}} = 1$$

$$\omega_{gc} = 9 \text{ rad/sec}$$

Now, $\phi_{sys}(\omega_{gc}) = -0.1\omega \times 9 \times \dfrac{180°}{\pi} - 90° = -141.5°$

Phase margin $\Rightarrow PM = 180° + \phi_{sys}(\omega_{gc}) = 38.43°$